FINANCIAL TIMES

WORLD DESK REFERENCE

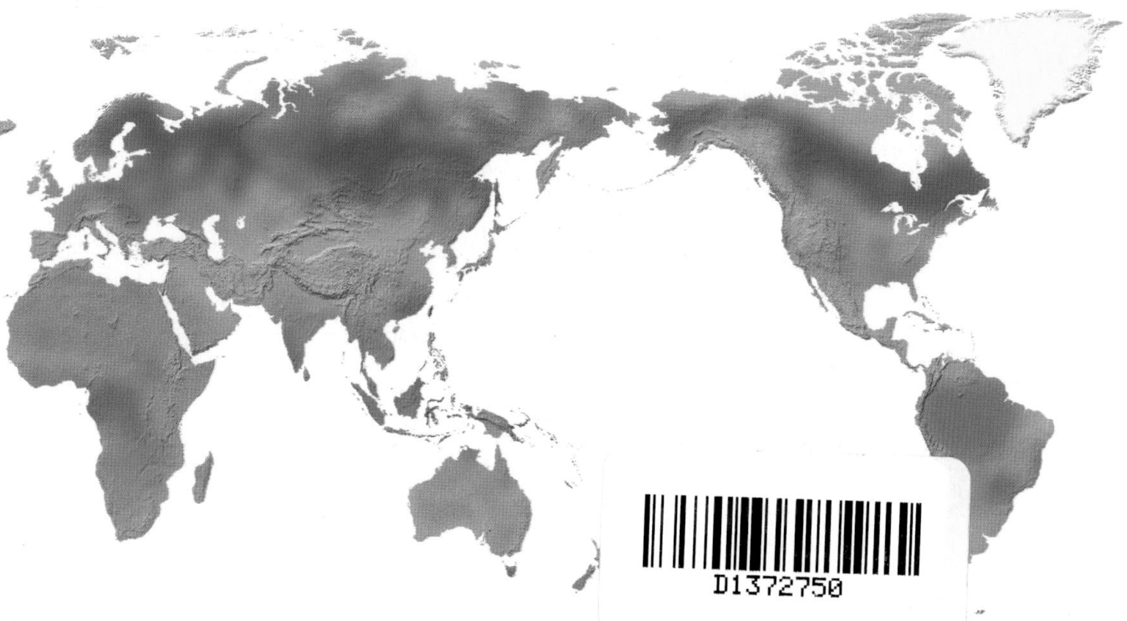

DORLING KINDERSLEY PUBLISHING, INC.
LONDON • NEW YORK • MUNICH • MELBOURNE • DELHI

For the very latest information, visit:
www.dk.com and click on the Maps & Atlases icon

A DORLING KINDERSLEY BOOK
www.dk.com

FOR THE SIXTH EDITION

EDITOR-IN-CHIEF
Andrew Heritage

SENIOR CARTOGRAPHIC MANAGER
David Roberts

SENIOR CARTOGRAPHIC EDITOR
Simon Mumford

SYSTEMS COORDINATOR
Phil Rowles

SIXTH EDITION UPDATED AND EDITED BY
Cambridge International Reference on Current Affairs (CIRCA)

PROJECT MANAGER
Catherine Jagger

EDITORIAL SUPERVISION
Roger East

EDITORS
Richard J. Thomas, Philippa Youngman, Matthew Cann

DATABASE
Carolyn Postgate, Kate Yedigaroff

GRAPHICS
Jenny Durham, Alex Yedigaroff

EDITORIAL AND RESEARCH
John Coggins, Alan Day, Ian Gorvin, Helen Hawkins Lawrence Joffe,
Frances Nicholson, Farzana Shaikh, Jo Skelt, Paul Sutton

DIGITAL CONTENT MANAGEMENT
Nina Blackett, Nishi Bhasin, Pooja Huria

PICTURE RESEARCH
Louise Thomas

DORLING KINDERSLEY CARTOGRAPHY

EDITORIAL DIRECTION
Andrew Heritage

MANAGING EDITORS
Ian Castello-Cortes, Wim Jenkins

PROJECT EDITORS
Debra Clapson, Catherine Day,
Jo Edwards, Jane Oliver

EDITORS
Alastair Dougall, Ailsa Heritage,
Nicholas Kynaston, Lisa Thomas,
Susan Turner, Chris Whitwell, Elizabeth Wyse

ADDITIONAL EDITORIAL ASSISTANCE
Sam Atkinson, Louise Keane, Zoë Ellinson,
Caroline Lucas, Sophie Park, Laura Porter,
Jo Russ, Crispian Martin St. Valery,
Sally Wood, Ulrike Fritz-Weltz

READERS
Jane Bruton, Reg Grant, Ann Kramer, Lesley Riley

ART DIRECTION
Chez Picthall, Philip Lord

PROJECT DESIGNERS
Martin Biddulph, Scott David,
Carol Ann Davis, David Douglas,
Yahya El-Droubie, Karen Gregory

DESIGNERS
Tony Cutting, Rhonda Fisher,
Nicola Liddiard, Katy Wall

ADDITIONAL DESIGN ASSISTANCE
Paul Bayliss, Carol Ann Davis,
Adam Dobney, Kenny Laurenson,
Paul Williams

DIGITAL CONTENT MANAGER
Nina Blackett

PRODUCTION
Wendy Penn

PROJECT CARTOGRAPHERS
Caroline Bowie, Ruth Duxbury,
James Mills-Hicks, John Plumer, Julie Turner

CARTOGRAPHERS
James Anderson, Dale Buckton,
Roger Bullen, Tony Chambers,
Jan Clark, Tom Coulson, Martin Darlison,
Claire Ellam, Julia Lunn, Michael Martin,
Alka Ranger, Peter Winfield, Claudine Zante

PICTURE RESEARCH
Alison McKittrick, Sarah Moule,
Christine Rista, Louise Thomas

DATABASE MANAGER
Simon Lewis

INDEX GAZETTEER
Margaret Hynes, Julia Lynch,
Barbara Nash, Jayne Parsons, Janet Smy

Printed and bound in Italy by Graphicom

Published in the United States
by Dorling Kindersley Publishing Inc.
375 Hudson Street, New York, New York 10014
A Penguin Company

Previously published as the DK World Reference Atlas

First American Edition 1994
10 9 8 7 6

Second Edition 1996. Revised 1998. Third Edition (revised) 2000. Fourth Edition (revised) 2002.
Fifth Edition (revised) 2003. Sixth Edition (revised) 2004.

A catalog record for this book is available from the Library of Congress.

ISBN: 0-7566-0343-9

FOREWORD

THIS DESK REFERENCE is presented to the public in the full knowledge that the world is in a state of continual flux. Political fashions and personalities come and go, while the ebb and flow of peoples and ideas across the face of the planet creates constant shifts in the cultural landscape. All the material assembled for this book has been researched from the most up-to-date and authoritative sources; our team of consultants and contributors, designers, editors, and cartographers have endeavored not only to explain the meaning of this material, to place it in a useful and clear context, but also to present it in a way that has a lasting value and relevance, regardless of the turmoil of daily events. This new edition, bearing the imprimatur of the *Financial Times*, has been completely revised and updated, to reflect the global changes of the past few years. It includes the latest statistical data, and over 60 new photographs.

The publishers would like to thank the many consultants and contributors whose diligence, perseverance, and attention to detail made this book possible.

GENERAL CONSULTANTS

Anthony Goldstone, Senior Editor Asia-Pacific, *The Economist* Intelligence Unit, London
Professor Jack Spence, Director of Studies, The Royal Institute of International Affairs, London

REGIONAL CONSULTANTS

ASIA
Anthony Goldstone, London

AFRICA
James Hammill, Lecturer in African Politics, University of Leicester
Kaye Whiteman, Editor-in-Chief, *West Africa Magazine*, London

RUSSIA AND CIS
Martin McCauley, Senior Lecturer, School of Slavonic and East European Studies, University of London

CENTRAL AND SOUTH AMERICA
Nick Caistor, Producer, Latin American Section, BBC World Service

USA
Michael Elliot, Diplomatic Editor, *Newsweek*, Washington DC

EUROPE
John Ardagh, London
Rory Clarke, Senior Editor Europe, *The Economist* Intelligence Unit, London
Charles Powell, Centre for European Studies, St Antony's College, Oxford

MIDDLE EAST
John Whelan, Ex Editor-in-Chief, *Middle East Economic Digest*

PACIFIC
Jim Boutilier, Professor in History, Royal Roads Military College, Victoria, Canada

CARIBBEAN
Canute James, *Financial Times*, Kingston, Jamaica

CONTRIBUTORS

Janice Bell, School of Slavonic and East European Studies, University of London
Gerry Bourke, Asia Correspondent, *The Guardian*, Islamabad
Vincent Cable, Director, International Economics Programme
P K Clark, MA, Former Chief Map Research Officer, Ministry of Defence
Ken Davies, Senior Editor, *The Economist* Intelligence Unit, London
Roger Dunn, Analyst, Control Risks Group, London
Aidan Foster-Carter, Senior Lecturer in Sociology, University of Leeds
Professor Murray Forsyth, Centre for Federal Studies, University of Leicester
Natasha Franklin, School of Slavonic and East European Studies, London
Adam Hannestad, *Blomberg Business News*, Copenhagen
Peter Holden, *The Economist* Research Department, London
Tim Jones, Knight Ritter, Brussels
Angella Johnstone, Home Affairs Correspondent, *The Guardian*, London
Oliver Keserü, International Chamber of Commerce, Paris
Robert Macdonald, *The Economist* Intelligence Unit
William Mader, Former Europe Bureau Chief, *Time Magazine*, Washington DC
Professor Brian Matthews, Institute of Commonwealth Studies, London
Nick Middleton, Oriel College, Oxford
Professor Mya Maung, Department of Finance, Boston College, Massachusetts
Judith Nordby, Leeds University
Simon Orme, London
Professor Richard Overy, Department of History, King's College, London
Steve Percy, East Asia Service, BBC World Service
Douglas Rimmer, Honorary Senior Research Fellow, Centre for West African Studies, University of Birmingham
Donna Rispoli, Linacre College, Oxford
Ian Rodger, *The Financial Times*, Zürich
The Royal Institute of International Affairs, London
Struan Simpson, St. James Research, London
Julie Smith, Brasenose College, Oxford
Elizabeth Spencer, London
Michiel Van Kuyen, Erasmus University, Rotterdam
Steven Whitefield, Pembroke College, Oxford
Georgina Wilde, Regional Director, Asia-Pacific, *The Economist* Intelligence Unit, London
H P Willmott, Visiting Professor, Dept. of Military Strategy & Operations, The National War College, Washington DC
Andrew Wilson, Sydney Sussex College, Cambridge
Tom Wingfield, *Reuters*, Bangkok
The World Conservation Monitoring Centre, Cambridge
Cambridge International Reference on Current Affairs (CIRCA)

CONTENTS

1
WORLD FACTFILE

2
THE NATIONS OF THE WORLD

OVERSEAS TERRITORIES & DEPENDENCIES

3
GLOSSARIES

COVER FLAPS

Key to Charts and Icons

ICONS AND TREND INDICATORS vary. Not all variations are shown in the key below, but where they do occur the symbols have been "stacked."

COUNTRY PROFILES

1952 — Date of country's independence, or formation.

1847 — Date when the country's current borders were established.

Aug 2 — National Day

GB — Vehicle country identifying code

+3 — Time zone(s) of country (hours plus or minus from GMT)

+44 — International telephone dialling code

.de — Internet country identifying code

CLIMATE

Indication of the climatic types and zones found in each country.

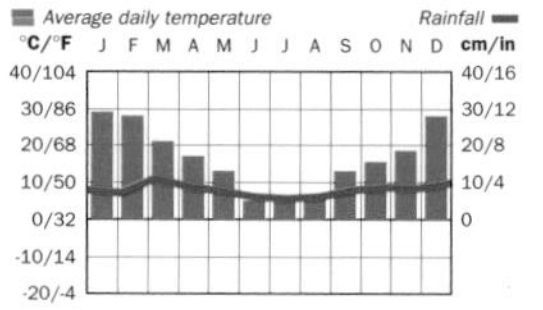

Average daily temperature
Rainfall
°C/°F
J F M A M J J A S O N D
cm/in
40/104
30/86
20/68
10/50
0/32
-10/14
-20/4
40/16
30/12
20/8
10/4
0

Statistics are given for the national capital. They represent maximum summer and minimum winter averages.

TRANSPORTATION

Indicates on which side of the road vehicles are driven in each country.

The country's principal international airport with annual passenger numbers.

Total size of national merchant or cargo fleet.

THE TRANSPORTATION NETWORK

National communications infrastructure given in kilometers and miles.

Extent of national paved road network

Extent of expressways, freeways, or major highways

Extent of commercial rail network

Extent of inland waterways navigable by commercial craft

TOURISM

The ratio of foreign visitors to population.

Number of visitors per year, including business travelers.

Indicators showing trend in recent visitor numbers (up/level/down).

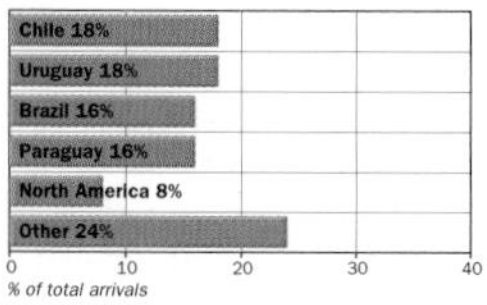

Chile 18%
Uruguay 18%
Brazil 16%
Paraguay 16%
North America 8%
Other 24%
0
10
20
30
40
% of total arrivals

The state of each nation's tourism is explained, with reasons given when there is no significant tourist industry. The chart shows the percentage of total visitors by country of origin.

PEOPLE

An easy indication of the population density in each country (high/medium/low).

Main languages spoken, including official languages.

Population density. This is an average over the whole country.

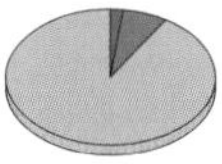

The pie chart proportions show the religious affiliations of those who profess a belief.

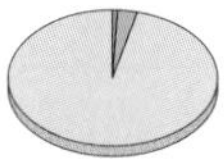

This pie chart illustrates the ethnic origin of the country's population.

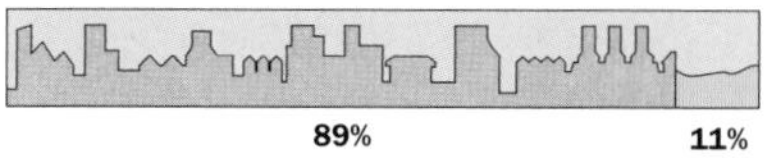

89%
11%

This graph represents the proportion of the population living in urban areas (gray) and rural areas (green).

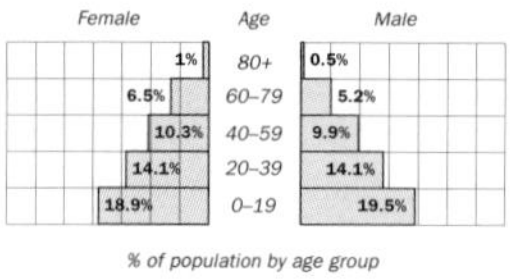

Female
Age
Male
1%
80+
0.5%
6.5%
60–79
5.2%
10.3%
40–59
9.9%
14.1%
20–39
14.1%
18.9%
0–19
19.5%
% of population by age group

This chart shows the breakdown of the population by age groupings, providing an interesting insight into the country's demography.

POLITICS

Indicates the type of elections held within each country.

Dates of last and next legislative elections for Lower (L.) and Upper (U.) Houses.

Name of head of state. In many cases this is a nominal position and does not indicate that this is the country's most powerful person.

A graphic representation of the political makeup of the country's government, based on each party's showing at the last election. Where there are two houses, the more important elected body is shown first.

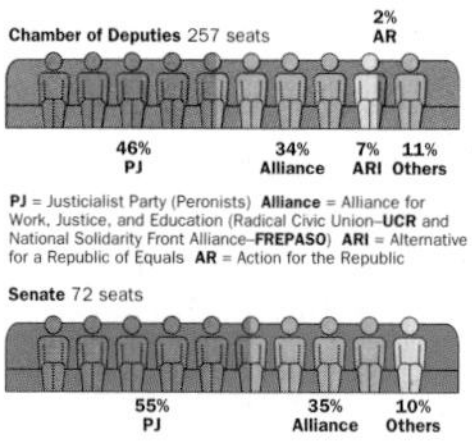

Chamber of Deputies 257 seats
2% AR
46% PJ
34% Alliance
7% ARI
11% Others
PJ = Justicialist Party (Peronists) Alliance = Alliance for Work, Justice, and Education (Radical Civic Union–UCR and National Solidarity Front Alliance–FREPASO) ARI = Alternative for a Republic of Equals AR = Action for the Republic
Senate 72 seats
55% PJ
35% Alliance
10% Others

WORLD AFFAIRS

Indication of membership of the UN (United Nations), and date of entry.

Comm — Abbreviations indicate membership of international organizations.

Nonmembership of additional international organizations.

AID

Indication as to which countries are aid givers (donors) or aid recipients.

The amount of net international aid given or received is shown in US$. Undisclosed military aid is not included.

Symbols indicate whether aid payments or receipts are rising, level, or declining.

DEFENSE

An indication of the status of conscription and mandatory military service.

The defense budget, the country's annual expenditure (in US$) on arms and military personnel.

Symbols indicate if the trend in defense spending is rising, level, or declining.

THE ARMED FORCES

Icons represent the main branches of the national armed forces.

Army: equipment and personnel

Navy: equipment and personnel

Air force: equipment and personnel

Nuclear capability: armaments

ECONOMICS

An indication of the average rate of inflation per annum, over the period indicated.

Gross National Product (GNP) – the total value (in US$) of goods and services produced by a country.

Latest midyear exchange rate against the US$, with previous year's rate for comparison.

❑ World GNP Ranking	24th
❑ GNP per Capita	$24,388
❑ Balance of Payments	$2.2bn
❑ Inflation	5.6%
❑ Unemployment	10.6%

The score cards are intended to give a broad picture of the country's economy. Gross National Product (GNP), unlike GDP, includes income from investments and businesses held abroad. Balance of payments is the difference between a country's payments to and receipts from abroad.

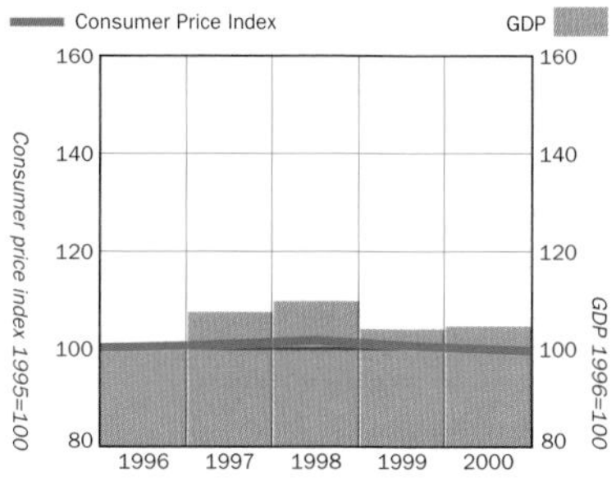

Consumer Price Index
GDP
160
140
120
100
80
1996
1997
1998
1999
2000
Consumer price index 1995=100
GDP 1996=100

This graph shows year-on-year variations in GDP and consumer prices.

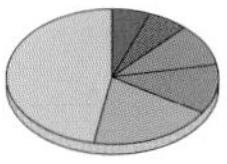

This pie chart gives a broad picture of the country's principal export trading partners.

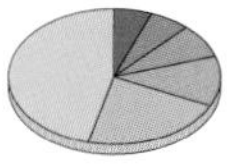

This pie chart gives a broad picture of the country's principal import trading partners.

RESOURCES

▷ Indicates the capacity of the combined national electricity generating sources (in kilowatts).

Fish catch per year (where fishing is a major industry).

Oil produced in barrels per day (b/d). Refining output and oil reserves are given where applicable.

Estimated livestock resources.

Main mineral reserves are listed in descending order of economic importance.

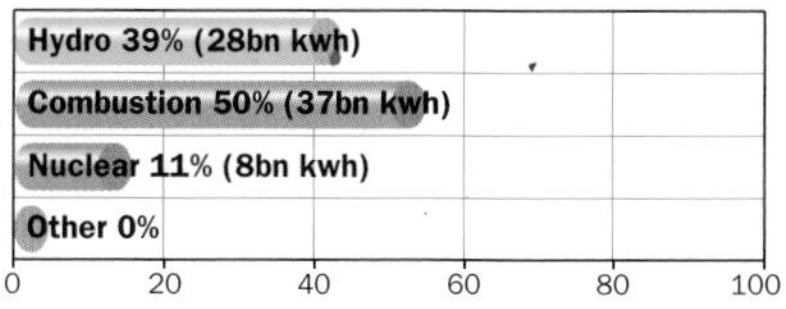

Hydro 39% (28bn kwh)
Combustion 50% (37bn kwh)
Nuclear 11% (8bn kwh)
Other 0%
0
20
40
60
80
100

% of total generation by type

Percentages of the different energy sources used for the generation of electricity are represented graphically ("Combustion" indicates the burning of fossil fuels, wood etc.). An account of the country's resource base is given in the text.

ENVIRONMENT

▷ The 2002 Index of progress toward environmental sustainability, based on 22 core indicators. Compiled by the World Economic Forum taskforce.

Protected area (including marine areas) as a percentage of total land area. Protection is often theoretical.

Trend in total CO_2 emissions since 1990 (up/level/down) and current emissions per capita.

ENVIRONMENTAL TREATIES

National parties to international environmental treaties.

Ramsar: (wetlands)

Basel: (hazardous wastes)

CITES: (endangered species)

Montreal Protocol: (CFC emissions)

CBD: (biological diversity)

Kyoto: (greenhouse gases)

MEDIA

▷ Indicates the average rates of television ownership across the country.

Media free to express critical views.

Partial controls or constraints on media freedom.

Severe restrictions on media freedom.

PUBLISHING AND BROADCAST MEDIA

National broadcast and print media, by size and ownership.

Main national newspapers

Television services: state-owned/independent

Radio services: state-owned/independent

CRIME

▷ An indication of the status of capital punishment and the death penalty.

Prison population statistics

Symbols show general trend in crime figures.

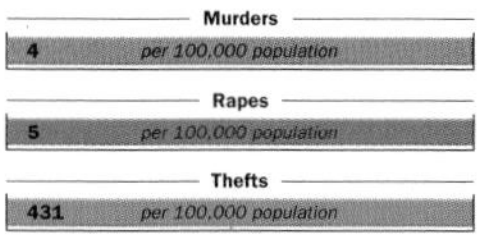

Murders
4
per 100,000 population
Rapes
5
per 100,000 population
Thefts
431
per 100,000 population

This section records official crime figures only. Reported statistics are normally lower than the actual figures.

CHRONOLOGY

Beginning at a significant date in the recent history of the country, the outline chronology continues through to the present day, and highlights key dates and turning points.

EDUCATION

▷ Displays the age until which children are legally required to attend school.

Literacy rate. UNESCO defines as literate anyone who can read and write a short statement.

The number of students in all forms of tertiary education within that country.

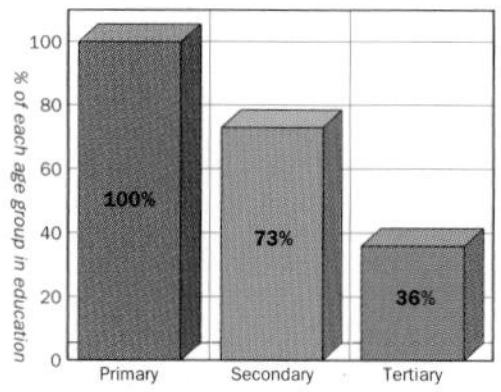

100
80
60
40
20
0
% of each age group in education
100%
73%
36%
Primary
Secondary
Tertiary

This graph shows, for each level of education, the total enrollment, regardless of age, as a percentage of the population of the age group that officially corresponds to that level.

HEALTH

▷ An indication of the existence of health benefits provided by the state.

Ratio of the number of people per doctor is given as a national average.

Major causes of death are listed.

SPENDING

▷ Indicates the trend in GDP per capita since 1990.

Levels of car ownership (per 1000 head of population)

Rates of telephone landline connectivity (per 1000 head of population)

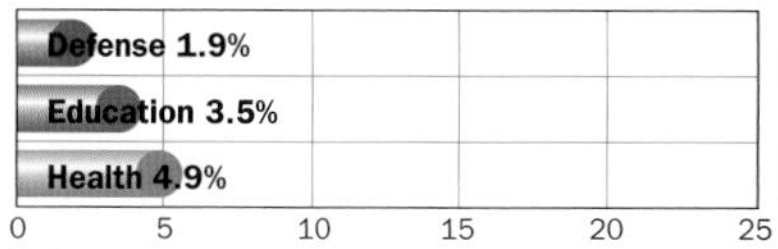

Defense 1.9%
Education 3.5%
Health 4.9%
0
5
10
15
20
25

Defense, Health, Education spending as % of GDP

Percentage of the country's GDP that is spent by the government on defense, education, and health.

WORLD RANKING

Each country is ranked in the world by four key indicators and by the UN Human Development Index, which reflects all-around attainment in health, education, and wealth (covering 174 countries and Hong Kong).

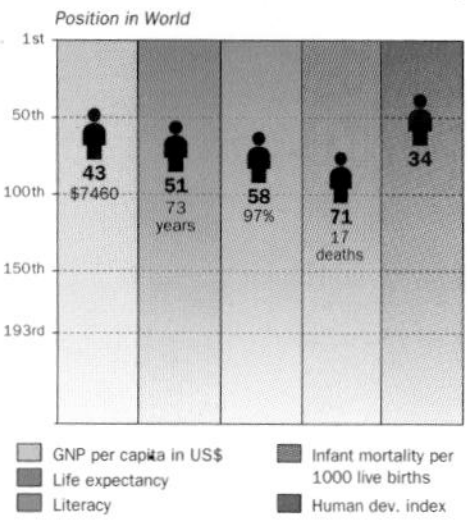

Position in World
1st
50th
100th
150th
193rd
43
$7460
51
73 years
58
97%
71
17 deaths
34
GNP per capita in US$
Life expectancy
Literacy
Infant mortality per 1000 live births
Human dev. index

Sources of Statistical Data Used in This Book

Airports Council International

Amnesty International

Automobile Association (AA)

British Petroleum (BP):
World Energy Data

Cambridge International Reference on Current Affairs (CIRCA)

Canadian International Development Agency

Commonwealth Secretariat:
Small States Economic Review and Basic Statistics

Dorling Kindersley

Europa World Yearbook

European Bank for Reconstruction and Development (EBRD)

Financial Times

Fischer Weltalmanach

Food and Agriculture Organization (FAO)

International Atomic Energy Agency (IAEA)

International Institute for Strategic Studies (IISS):
The Military Balance

International Labor Organization (ILO):
World Labor Report

International Monetary Fund (IMF):
Balance of Payments Statistics Yearbook,
Direction of Trade Statistics Yearbook,
Government Financial Statistics Yearbook,
International Financial Statistics,
World Economic Outlook

International Road Federation

International Union for Conservation of Nature (IUCN)

International Union of Railways

INTERPOL International Crime Statistics

Lloyd's Register of Shipping

Organization for Economic Cooperation Development (OECD):
Economic surveys

OECD Development Assistance Committee (DAC):
Development Cooperation Report

Organization of Petroleum Exporting Countries (OPEC)

Ramsar Convention Bureau

Reporters without Borders

Royal Automobile Club (RAC)

United Nations (UN)
Department of Economic and Social Affairs Statistics Division:
United Nations Demographic Yearbook,
United Nations Energy Statistics Yearbook,
United Nations Industrial Commodity Statistics Yearbook,
United Nations International Trade Statistics Yearbook,
United Nations Statistical Yearbook

United Nations Children's Fund (UNICEF)

United Nations Development Program (UNDP):
Human Development Report

United Nations Economic and Social Commission for
Asia and the Pacific (UNESCAP):
United Nations Statistical Yearbook of Asia and the Pacific

United Nations Educational, Scientific, and
Cultural Organization (UNESCO):
Statistical Yearbook

United Nations Environment Program (UNEP):
Ozone Secretariat
Secretariat of the Basel Convention
Secretariat of the Convention on Biological Diversity (CBD)
Secretariat of the Convention on International Trade in Endangered
Species (CITES)

United Nations Framework Convention on Climate Change

United Nations Population Fund (UNFPA):
The State of World Population

United States Central Intelligence Agency (CIA)

World Bank (IBRD):
World Development Indicators,
World Development Report,
World Bank Atlas

World Conservation Monitoring Center (WCMC):
Biodiversity Data Sourcebook

World Economic Forum

World Health Organization (WHO)

World Prison Population List (Research, Development, and Statistics
Directorate, UK Home Office)

World Tourist Organization (WTO)

Worldwide Fund for Nature (WWF)

1

WORLD FACTFILE

THE PHYSICAL WORLD

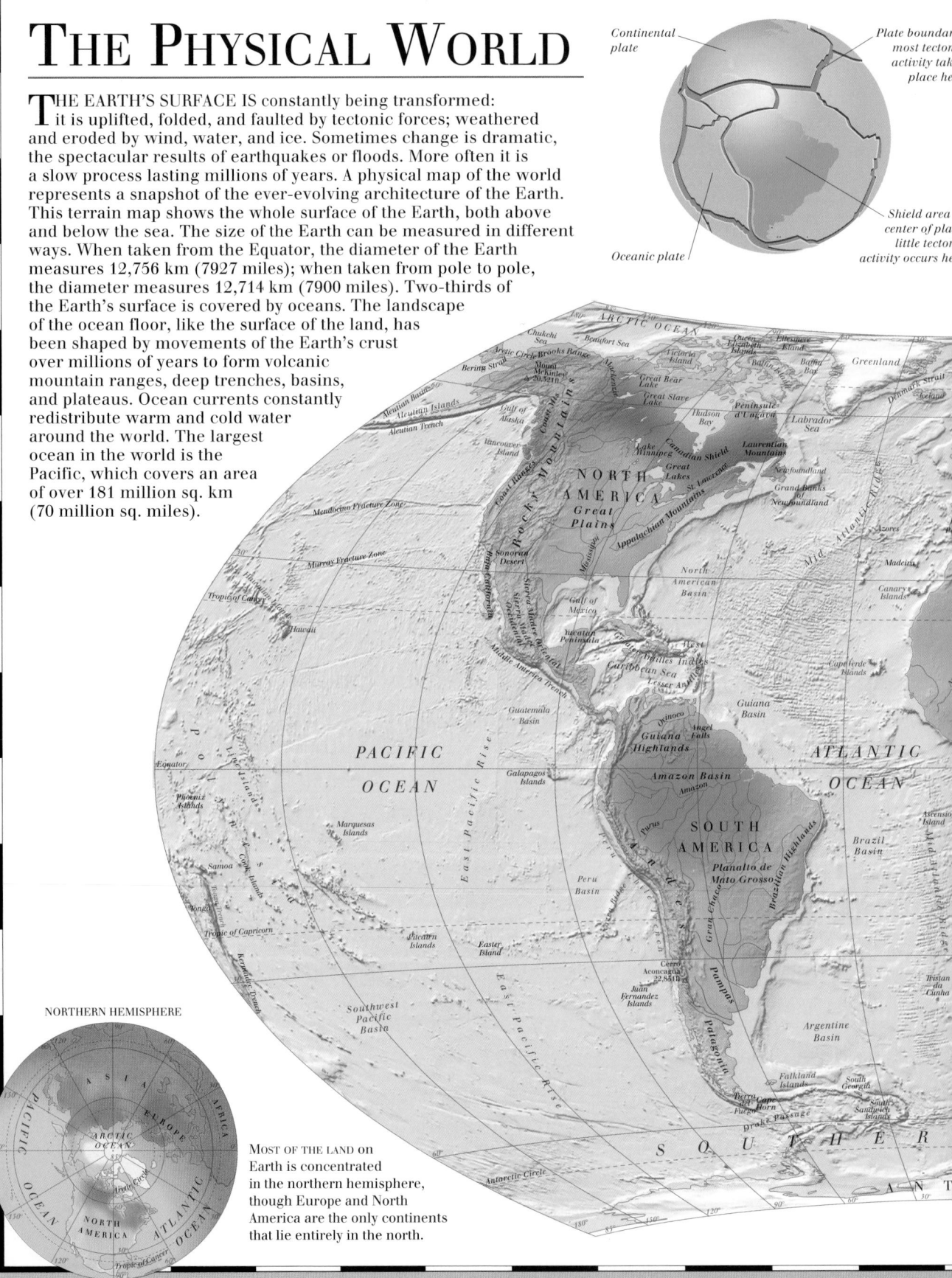

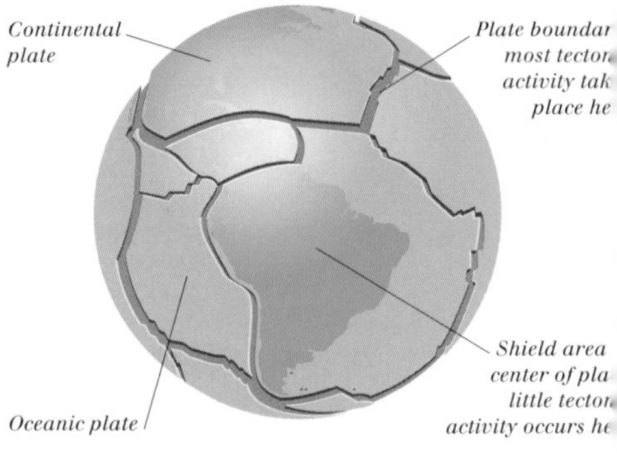
Continental plate
Plate boundar
most tecto
activity tak
place he
Shield area
center of pla
little tecto
activity occurs he
Oceanic plate

THE EARTH'S SURFACE IS constantly being transformed: it is uplifted, folded, and faulted by tectonic forces; weathered and eroded by wind, water, and ice. Sometimes change is dramatic, the spectacular results of earthquakes or floods. More often it is a slow process lasting millions of years. A physical map of the world represents a snapshot of the ever-evolving architecture of the Earth. This terrain map shows the whole surface of the Earth, both above and below the sea. The size of the Earth can be measured in different ways. When taken from the Equator, the diameter of the Earth measures 12,756 km (7927 miles); when taken from pole to pole, the diameter measures 12,714 km (7900 miles). Two-thirds of the Earth's surface is covered by oceans. The landscape of the ocean floor, like the surface of the land, has been shaped by movements of the Earth's crust over millions of years to form volcanic mountain ranges, deep trenches, basins, and plateaus. Ocean currents constantly redistribute warm and cold water around the world. The largest ocean in the world is the Pacific, which covers an area of over 181 million sq. km (70 million sq. miles).

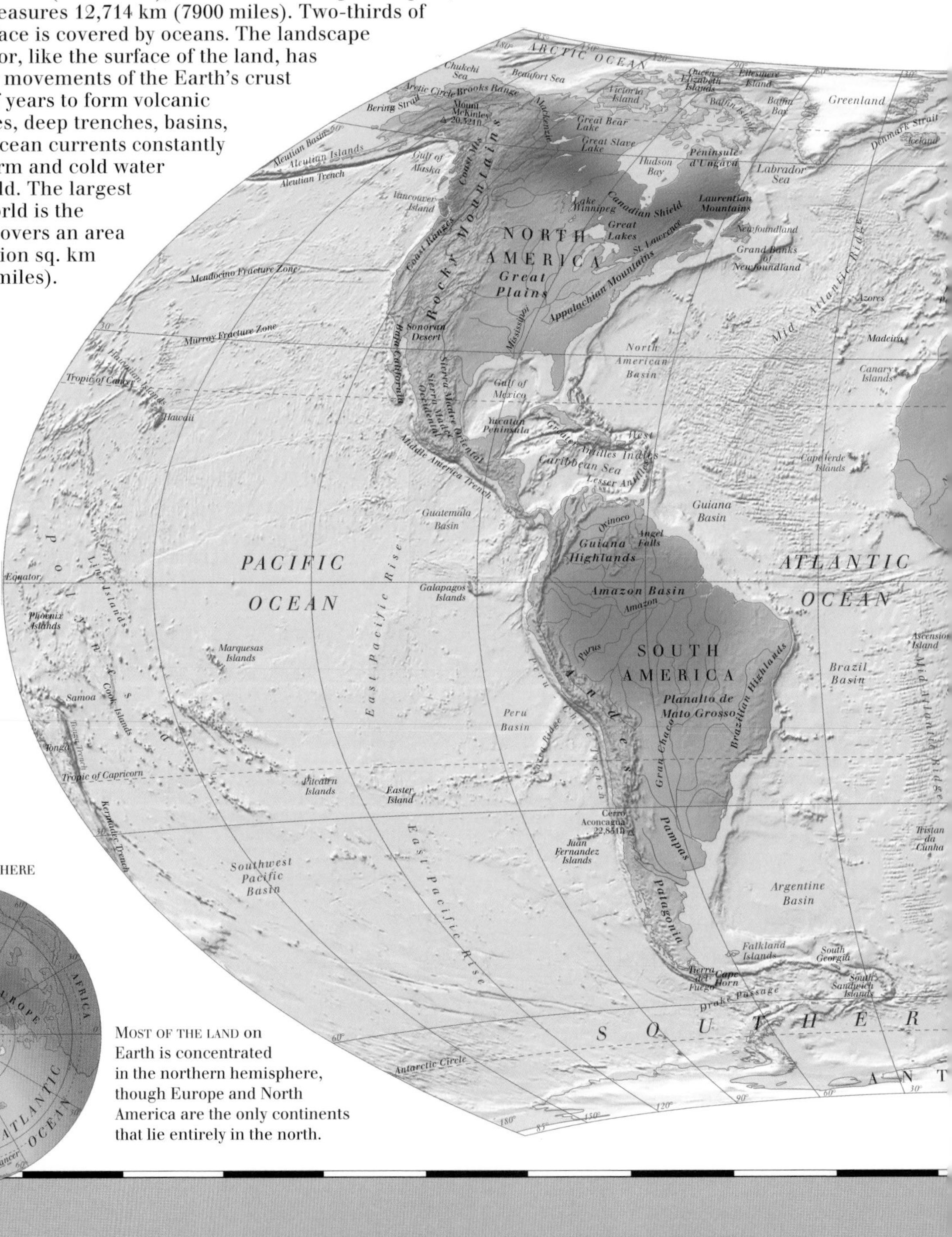
ARCTIC OCEAN
Chukchi Sea
Beaufort Sea
Brooks Range
Arctic Circle
Bering Strait
Mount McKinley 20,321ft
Victoria Island
Queen Elizabeth Islands
Ellesmere Island
Baffin Island
Baffin Bay
Greenland
Denmark Strait
Iceland
Great Bear Lake
Great Slave Lake
Mackenzie
Aleutian Basin
Aleutian Islands
Aleutian Trench
Gulf of Alaska
Coast Mountains
Hudson Bay
Peninsule d'Ungava
Labrador Sea
Vancouver Island
Lake Winnipeg
Canadian Shield
Laurentian Mountains
Coast Ranges
Rocky Mountains
NORTH AMERICA
Great Lakes
St. Lawrence
Newfoundland
Grand Banks of Newfoundland
Great Plains
Appalachian Mountains
Mendocino Fracture Zone
Mid-Atlantic Ridge
Azores
Murray Fracture Zone
Sonoran Desert
Baja California
Mississippi
Madeira
North American Basin
Canary Islands
Hawaiian Islands
Tropic of Cancer
Hawaii
Sierra Madre Occidental
Sierra Madre Oriental
Gulf of Mexico
Yucatan Peninsula
West Indies
Greater Antilles
Caribbean Sea
Lesser Antilles
Middle America Trench
Cape Verde Islands
Guatemala Basin
Guiana Basin
Orinoco
Angel Falls
Guiana Highlands
PACIFIC OCEAN
ATLANTIC OCEAN
Equator
Galapagos Islands
Amazon Basin
Amazon
Line Islands
Phoenix Islands
Polynesia
Marquesas Islands
East Pacific Rise
Purus
SOUTH AMERICA
Peru
Andes
Brazilian Highlands
Planalto de Mato Grosso
Brazil Basin
Ascension Island
Samoa
Cook Islands
Peru Basin
Tonga
Tonga Trench
Gran Chaco
Tropic of Capricorn
Pitcairn Islands
Easter Island
Kermadec Trench
Cerro Aconcagua 22,831ft
Juan Fernandez Islands
Pampas
Tristan da Cunha
Southwest Pacific Basin
Patagonia
Argentine Basin
Falkland Islands
South Georgia
Tierra del Fuego
Cape Horn
South Sandwich Islands
Drake Passage
Antarctic Circle
S O U T H E R

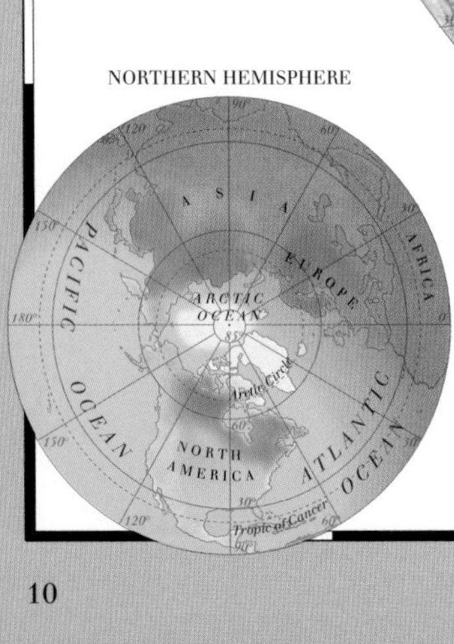
NORTHERN HEMISPHERE
ASIA
EUROPE
AFRICA
PACIFIC OCEAN
ARCTIC OCEAN
Arctic Circle
NORTH AMERICA
ATLANTIC OCEAN
Tropic of Cancer

MOST OF THE LAND on Earth is concentrated in the northern hemisphere, though Europe and North America are the only continents that lie entirely in the north.

THE DYNAMIC EARTH

THE EARTH'S CRUST is made up of eight major (and several minor) rigid continental and oceanic tectonic plates, which constantly move relative to one another. It is this movement which causes volcanic eruptions, earthquakes, and sometimes tsunamis along the plate boundaries. The largest volcanoes formed by this process are Aconcagua in Argentina at 6959 m (22,831 ft) and Kilimanjaro in Tanzania at 5895 m (19,340 ft), both of which are now extinct. Plate tectonics are responsible for the formation of the Himalayas – which were created by two colliding plates – and the Hawaiian Islands, created by the Pacific plate's movement over a "hot spot" of magma.

GEOGRAPHICAL REGIONS

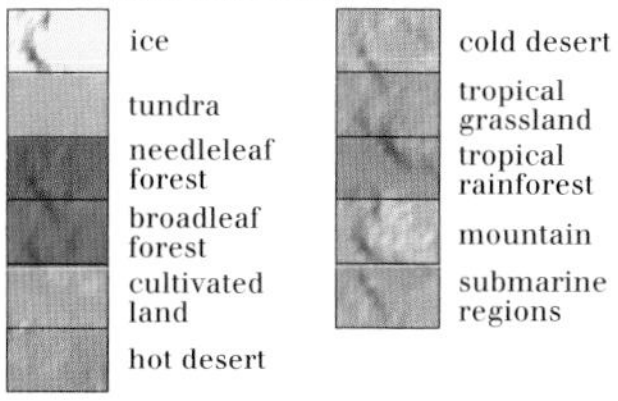
ice
tundra
needleleaf forest
broadleaf forest
cultivated land
hot desert
cold desert
tropical grassland
tropical rainforest
mountain
submarine regions

PHYSICAL WORLD FACTFILE

HIGHEST MOUNTAINS

1 **Everest**	8850 m	(29,035 ft)
2 **K2**	8611 m	(28,251 ft)
3 **Kangchenjunga I**	8590 m	(28,169 ft)
4 **Makalu I**	8463 m	(27,766 ft)
5 **Cho Oyu**	8201 m	(26,906 ft)

LONGEST RIVERS

1 **Nile**	6695 km	(4160 mi.)
2 **Amazon**	6516 km	(4048 mi.)
3 **Chang Jiang**	6380 km	(3964 mi.)
4 **Mississippi /Missouri**	6019 km	(3740 mi.)
5 **Ob'-Irtysh**	5570 km	(3461 mi.)

LARGEST DESERTS

1 **Sahara**	9,065,000 km²	(3,263,400 mi²)
2 **Australian**	3,750,000 km²	(1,350,000 mi²)
3 **Gobi**	1,295,000 km²	(466,200 mi²)
4 **Arabian**	750,000 km²	(270,000 mi²)
5 **Sonoran**	311,000 km²	(111,960 mi²)

ARCTIC OCEAN
EUROPE
ASIA
Siberia
West Siberian Plain
Central Siberian Plateau
Ural Mountains
North European Plain
Gobi
Manchurian Plain
Altai Mountains
Tien Shan
Pamirs
Hindu Kush
Himalayas
Plateau of Tibet
Kunlun Mountains
Great Plain of China
Mount Everest 29,035ft
Thar Desert
Deccan
Arabian Peninsula
Arabian Sea
Bay of Bengal
AFRICA
Congo Basin
Kilimanjaro 19,340ft
Ethiopian Highlands
Kalahari Desert
Madagascar
INDIAN OCEAN
PACIFIC OCEAN
AUSTRALIA
Great Sandy Desert
Great Victoria Desert
Nullarbor Plain
Great Dividing Range
Tasmania
New Zealand
Mount Cook 12,283ft
Borneo
Sumatra
Philippine Sea
South China Sea
Sea of Japan
Sea of Okhotsk
Tropic of Cancer
Equator
Tropic of Capricorn
Antarctic Circle
South Indian Basin

SOUTHERN HEMISPHERE

INDIAN OCEAN
SOUTHERN OCEAN
ANTARCTICA
ATLANTIC OCEAN
PACIFIC OCEAN
AFRICA
AUSTRALIA
SOUTH AMERICA
Antarctic Circle
Tropic of Capricorn

OCEANS DOMINATE the southern hemisphere. Australia and Antarctica are the only continental landmasses that lie entirely in the south.

The Political World

IN 2002, EAST TIMOR joined the international community, becoming the world's 193rd recognized independent state. In 1950 there were only 82. With the exception of Antarctica, where territorial claims have been deferred by international treaty, every land area of the Earth's surface either belongs to, or is claimed by, one country or another. Some 60 overseas dependent territories remain, administered variously by Australia, Denmark, France, the Netherlands, New Zealand, Norway, the UK, and the US. Over the last half-century, national self-determination has been a driving force for many states with a history of colonialism or oppression. While some new states on gaining independence moved peacefully to establish a democracy, many others have been torn by religious or ethnic conflicts or became submerged in power struggles resulting in dictatorship by a military regime or an individual despot.

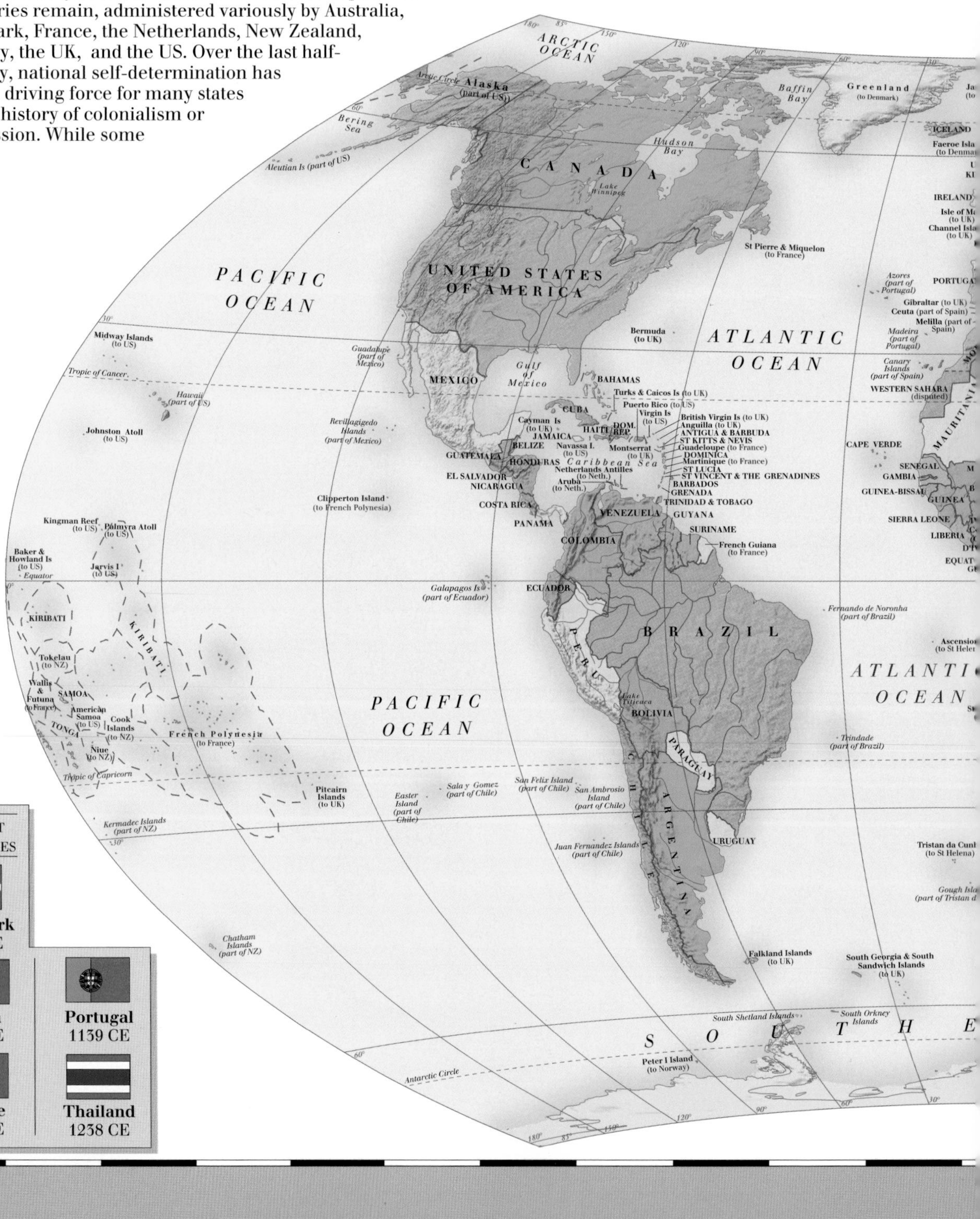

ARCTIC OCEAN
Alaska (part of US)
Bering Sea
Aleutian Is (part of US)
Baffin Bay
Greenland (to Denmark)
ICELAND
Faeroe Isla (to Denma
Hudson Bay
CANADA
Lake Winnipeg
IRELAND
Isle of M (to UK)
Channel Isla (to UK)
St Pierre & Miquelon (to France)
PACIFIC OCEAN
UNITED STATES OF AMERICA
Azores (part of Portugal)
PORTUGA
Gibraltar (to UK)
Ceuta (part of Spain)
Melilla (part of Spain)
Madeira (part of Portugal)
Midway Islands (to US)
Bermuda (to UK)
ATLANTIC OCEAN
Canary Islands (part of Spain)
Guadalupe (part of Mexico)
Tropic of Cancer
Gulf of Mexico
MEXICO
BAHAMAS
WESTERN SAHARA (disputed)
Hawaii (part of US)
Turks & Caicos Is (to UK)
Puerto Rico (to US)
Virgin Is (to US)
CUBA
British Virgin Is (to UK)
Anguilla (to UK)
ANTIGUA & BARBUDA
ST KITTS & NEVIS
Guadeloupe (to France)
DOMINICA
Martinique (to France)
ST LUCIA
ST VINCENT & THE GRENADINES
BARBADOS
GRENADA
TRINIDAD & TOBAGO
Johnston Atoll (to US)
Revillagigedo Islands (part of Mexico)
Cayman Is (to UK)
JAMAICA
HAITI
DOM. REP.
BELIZE
Navassa I. (to US)
Montserrat (to UK)
GUATEMALA
HONDURAS
Caribbean Sea
Netherlands Antilles (to Neth.)
Aruba (to Neth.)
EL SALVADOR
NICARAGUA
COSTA RICA
PANAMA
CAPE VERDE
SENEGAL
GAMBIA
GUINEA-BISSAU
GUINEA
SIERRA LEONE
LIBERIA
MAURITANIA
Clipperton Island (to French Polynesia)
VENEZUELA
GUYANA
SURINAME
French Guiana (to France)
COLOMBIA
Kingman Reef (to US)
Palmyra Atoll (to US)
Baker & Howland Is (to US)
Jarvis I (to US)
Equator
Galapagos Is (part of Ecuador)
ECUADOR
Fernando de Noronha (part of Brazil)
KIRIBATI
BRAZIL
PERU
Ascension (to St Helen
Tokelau (to NZ)
Wallis & Futuna (to France)
SAMOA
American Samoa (to US)
Cook Islands (to NZ)
TONGA
Niue (to NZ)
French Polynesia (to France)
PACIFIC OCEAN
Lake Titicaca
BOLIVIA
ATLANTIC OCEAN
Trindade (part of Brazil)
PARAGUAY
Tropic of Capricorn
Pitcairn Islands (to UK)
Easter Island (part of Chile)
Sala y Gomez (part of Chile)
San Felix Island (part of Chile)
San Ambrosio Island (part of Chile)
Kermadec Islands (part of NZ)
CHILE
ARGENTINA
URUGUAY
Juan Fernandez Islands (part of Chile)
Tristan da Cun (to St Helena)
Gough Isla (part of Tristan d
Chatham Islands (part of NZ)
Falkland Islands (to UK)
South Georgia & South Sandwich Islands (to UK)
South Shetland Islands
South Orkney Islands
SOUTHE
Peter I Island (to Norway)
Antarctic Circle

Oldest Countries

Denmark
950 CE

China
960 CE

Portugal
1139 CE

France
987 CE

Thailand
1238 CE

KEY

———	Full borders
· · · · · · · · ·	Disputed borders
- - - - - -	Undefined borders
– – – –	Extent of dependent island territories
— — —	Extent of country boundaries for island territories
Tristan da Cunha (to St Helena)	Dependent territory with self-government
Gough Island (part of Tristan da Cunha)	Territory without self-government (the state it belongs to is given in brackets)

International Borders

BOUNDARIES BETWEEN states fall into three categories. Full borders are internationally recognized territorial boundaries. Undefined borders exist where no fixed boundary has been demarcated. A disputed border is where a de facto boundary exists which is not agreed upon or is subject to arbitration. Disputed borders exist throughout the world, such as the land borders between India and China and between Ethiopia and Eritrea, and the maritime border between Samoa and American Samoa.

Countries with the Most Land Borders

1 **China:** *14* (Afghanistan, Bhutan, Burma, India, Kazakhstan, North Korea, Kyrgyzstan, Laos, Mongolia, Nepal, Pakistan, Russian Federation, Tajikistan, Vietnam)

Russian Federation: *14* (Azerbaijan, Belarus, China, Estonia, Finland, Georgia, Kazakhstan, North Korea, Latvia, Lithuania, Mongolia, Norway, Poland, Ukraine)

2 **Brazil:** *10* (Argentina, Bolivia, Colombia, French Guiana, Guyana, Paraguay, Peru, Suriname, Uruguay, Venezuela)

ARCTIC OCEAN
Barents Sea
Arctic Circle
RUSSIAN FEDERATION
FINLAND
EST.
LAT.
LITH.
RUSS. FED.
POLAND
BELARUS
GERMANY
SLOVAKIA
UKRAINE
MOLDOVA
HUNGARY
ROMANIA
CROATIA
B.H.
BULGARIA
MACEDONIA
ALBANIA
GREECE
TURKEY
GEORGIA
ARMENIA
AZERBAIJAN
Black Sea
Caspian Sea
KAZAKHSTAN
Aral Sea
Lake Balkhash
Lake Baikal
MONGOLIA
UZBEKISTAN
TURKMENISTAN
KYRGYZSTAN
TAJIKISTAN
MALTA
Mediterranean Sea
CYPRUS
LEBANON
ISRAEL
SYRIA
IRAQ
JORDAN
IRAN
AFGHANISTAN
PAKISTAN
CHINA
NEPAL
BHUTAN
BANGLADESH
INDIA
LIBYA
EGYPT
KUWAIT
BAHRAIN
QATAR
UAE
The Gulf
Red Sea
SAUDI ARABIA
OMAN
YEMEN
Arabian Sea
Socotra (part of Yemen)
NIGER
CHAD
SUDAN
ERITREA
DJIBOUTI
ETHIOPIA
SOMALIA
CENTRAL AFRICAN REPUBLIC
CAMEROON
GABON
CONGO
DEM. REP. CONGO
UGANDA
KENYA
RWANDA
BURUNDI
TANZANIA
ANGOLA
ZAMBIA
MALAWI
MOZAMBIQUE
ZIMBABWE
NAMIBIA
BOTSWANA
SWAZILAND
LESOTHO
SOUTH AFRICA
MADAGASCAR
COMOROS
Mayotte (to France)
SEYCHELLES
Agalega Islands (part of
Tromelin (part of Réunion)
Réunion (to France)
MAURITIUS
Rodrigues (part of Mauritius)
INDIAN OCEAN
Laccadive Is (part of India)
MALDIVES
SRI LANKA
Bay of Bengal
Andaman Is (part of India)
Nicobar Is (part of India)
British Indian Ocean Territory (to UK)
Cocos (Keeling) Islands (to Australia)
Christmas Island (to Australia)
BURMA (MYANMAR)
LAOS
THAILAND
VIETNAM
CAMBODIA
Paracel Is (disputed)
South China Sea
Spratly Is (disputed)
PHILIPPINES
BRUNEI
MALAYSIA
SINGAPORE
INDONESIA
Java Sea
EAST TIMOR
Ashmore & Cartier Islands (to Australia)
PAPUA NEW GUINEA
AUSTRALIA
Coral Sea Islands (to Australia)
New Caledonia (to France)
VANUATU
FIJI
SOLOMON ISLANDS
TUVALU
NAURU
KIRIBATI
Equator
MICRONESIA
PALAU
MARSHALL ISLANDS
Guam (to US)
Northern Mariana Is (to US)
Wake Island (to US)
TAIWAN
Ryukyu Is (part of Japan)
Tropic of Cancer
Tropic of Capricorn
PACIFIC OCEAN
NORTH KOREA
SOUTH KOREA
Sea of Japan
JAPAN
Sea of Okhotsk
Kurile Is (to Russ. Fed.)
Aleutian Is. (part of US)
Norfolk Island (to Australia)
Lord Howe Island (part of Australia)
NEW ZEALAND
Bounty Islands (part of NZ)
Antipodes Islands (part of NZ)
Auckland Islands (part of NZ)
Campbell Island (part of NZ)
Macquarie Island (part of Australia)
Amsterdam Island
St Paul Island
Prince Edward Islands (part of South Africa)
Crozet Islands
French Southern & Antarctic Territories (to France)
Kerguelen
Heard & McDonald Islands
SOUTHERN OCEAN
ANTARCTICA
Antarctic Circle

Youngest Countries

East Timor
2002

Slovakia
1993

Palau
1994

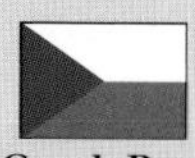

Czech Rep.
1993

Eritrea
1993

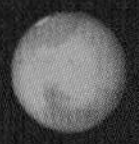

MARS

- **Diameter:** *6786 km*
- **Mass:** *642 billion billion tons*
- **Temperature:** *–137 to 37°C*
- **Distance from Sun:** *228 million km*
- **Length of year:** *1.88 years*
- **Surface gravity:** *1 kg = 0.38 kg*

EARTH

- **Diameter:** *12,756 km*
- **Mass:** *5976 billion billion tons*
- **Temperature:** *–70 to 55°C*
- **Distance from Sun:** *150 million km*
- **Length of year:** *365.25 days*
- **Surface gravity:** *1kg = 1 kg*

THE EARTH

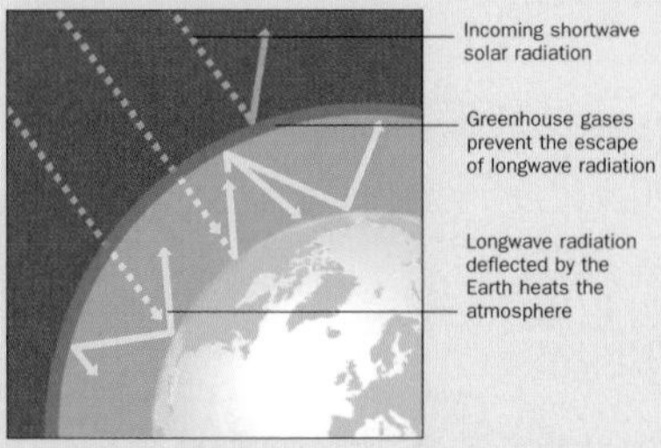
Incoming shortwave solar radiation
Greenhouse gases prevent the escape of longwave radiation
Longwave radiation deflected by the Earth heats the atmosphere

GASES SUCH AS CARBON dioxide are known as "greenhouse gases" because they prevent shortwave solar radiation from entering the Earth's atmosphere, but help to stop longwave radiation from escaping. This traps heat, raising the Earth's temperature. An excess of these gases traps more heat and can lead to global warming.

VENUS

- **Diameter:** *12,102 km*
- **Mass:** *4870 billion billion tons*
- **Temperature:** *457°C*
- **Distance from Sun:** *108 million km*
- **Length of year:** *224.7 days*
- **Surface gravity:** *1 kg = 0.88 kg*

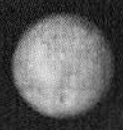

MERCURY

- **Diameter:** *4878 km*
- **Mass:** *330 billion billion tons*
- **Temperature:** *–173 to 427°C*
- **Distance from Sun:** *58 million km*
- **Length of year:** *87.97 days*
- **Surface gravity:** *1 kg = 0.38 kg*

THE SOLAR SYSTEM

THE SOLAR SYSTEM CONSISTS of the nine major planets, their moons, the asteroids, and the comets that orbit around the Sun. The Sun itself is composed of 70% hydrogen and 30% helium, and at its core nuclear fusion reactions turning hydrogen into helium produce the heat and light which make life possible on Earth. Of the planets, the inner four (Mercury, Venus, Earth, and Mars) are termed terrestrial, while the next four (Jupiter, Saturn, Uranus, and Neptune) are termed gas giants. Pluto, at the edge of the solar system, is much smaller, and made of rock. The largest natural satellite in the Solar System is Ganymede (5262 km – 3270 miles – in diameter), which orbits around Jupiter, the largest planet. Halley's comet is the brightest comet when seen from Earth, and orbits the Sun once every 76 years. The largest asteroid is named Ceres (940 km – 584 miles – in diameter), which is found in the asteroid belt between Mars and Jupiter. The planet Earth is unique within the solar system (and possibly the universe), being the only planet capable of sustaining life.

JUPITER

- **Diameter:** *142,984 km*
- **Mass:** *1,900,000,000 billion billion tons*
- **Temperature:** *–153°C*
- **Distance from Sun:** *778 million km*
- **Length of year:** *11.86 years*
- **Surface gravity:** *1 kg = 2.53 kg*

SATURN

- *Diameter:* *120,660 km*
- *Mass:* *570,000 billion billion tons*
- *Temperature:* *–185°C*
- *Distance from Sun:* *1427 million km*
- *Length of year:* *29.46 years*
- *Surface gravity:* *1 kg = 1.07 kg*

URANUS

- *Diameter:* *51,118 km*
- *Mass:* *102,000 billion billion tons*
- *Temperature:* *–214°C*
- *Distance from Sun:* *2870 million km*
- *Length of year:* *84.01 years*
- *Surface gravity:* *1 kg = 0.92 kg*

MOON AND TIDES

TIDES ARE CREATED by the pull of the Sun's and the Moon's gravity on the surface of the oceans. Waves are formed by wind blowing over the surface of the oceans. The highest tides occur when the Earth, the Moon, and the Sun are aligned (*below left*). The lowest tides are experienced when the Sun and Moon align at right angles to one another (*below right*).

NEAR SIDE OF THE MOON

FAR SIDE OF THE MOON

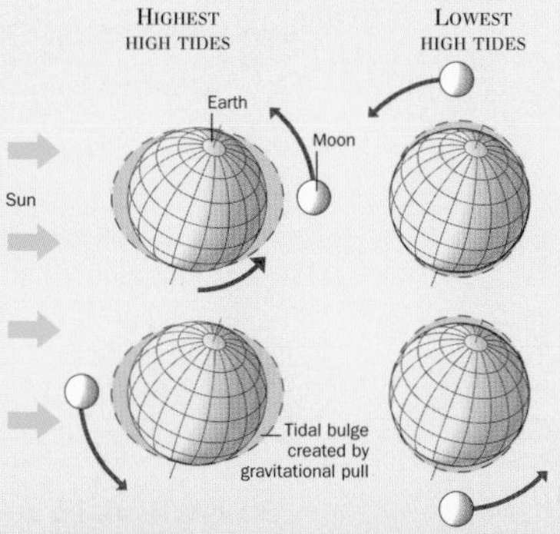
HIGHEST HIGH TIDES
LOWEST HIGH TIDES
Earth
Moon
Sun
Tidal bulge created by gravitational pull

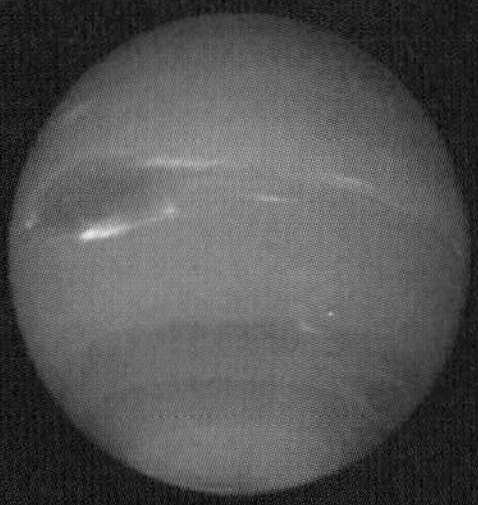

NEPTUNE

- *Diameter:* *49,528 km*
- *Mass:* *13 billion billion tons*
- *Temperature:* *–225°C*
- *Distance from Sun:* *4497 million km*
- *Length of year:* *164.79 years*
- *Surface gravity:* *1 kg = 1.18 kg*

PLUTO

- *Diameter:* *2300 km*
- *Mass:* *13 billion billion tons*
- *Temperature:* *–236°C*
- *Distance from Sun:* *5900 million km*
- *Length of year:* *248.54 years*
- *Surface gravity:* *1 kg = 0.30 kg*

Timeline of Space Exploration

1957: USSR launches Sputnik I - first artificial satellite

Oct 10, 1959: Luna 3 sends back first pictures of dark side of the Moon

Apr 12, 1961: Yuri Gagarin (USSR) first person in space

Jul 10, 1962: Launch of Telstar I, first commercial communications satellite

Feb 13, 1966: Luna 9 first probe to land on Moon

Jul 21, 1969: Neil Armstrong and Buzz Aldrin first people to land on Moon

1976: Missions of Viking 1 and 2 analyze surface of Mars

Jan 28, 1986: Challenger shuttle explodes; all seven crew members killed

Feb 20, 1986: Launch of space station Mir

Aug 25, 1989: Voyager 2 probe passes Neptune on way out of Solar System

Apr 24, 1990: Launch of Hubble Space Telescope

1998: Launch of first part of International Space Station

2001: *Near* probe lands on Eros asteroid. *Mir* brought to earth. Dennis Tito is first space tourist. 100th shuttle mission completed

2003: Columbia space shuttle explodes. Three separate missions head for Mars: ESA's Beagle 2, NASA's Rovers, and Japan's Nozomi. First Chinese manned space flight planned

2004: Provisional date for a probe landing on Titan (Saturn's largest moon)

1955 1960 1970 1980 1990 2000 2010

THE CLIMATE

THE EARTH'S CLIMATIC REGIONS consist of stable patterns of weather conditions averaged out over a long period of time. Different climates are categorized according to particular combinations of temperature and humidity. By contrast, weather consists of short-term fluctuations in wind, temperature, and humidity conditions. Different climates are determined by latitude, altitude, the prevailing wind, and circulation of ocean currents. Longer-term changes in climate, such as global warming or the onset of ice ages, are punctuated by shorter-term events which comprise the day-to-day weather of a region, such as frontal depressions, hurricanes, and blizzards.

CLIMATE ZONES

- Ice cap
- Tundra
- Subarctic
- Cool continental
- Warm humid
- Mediterranean
- Semi-arid
- Arid
- Tropical
- Humid equatorial

OCEAN CURRENTS
- Warm
- Cold

PREVAILING WINDS
- Warm
- Cold

LOCAL WINDS
- Warm
- Cold
- June Seasonal*

* (seasonal winds which can either be warm or cold)

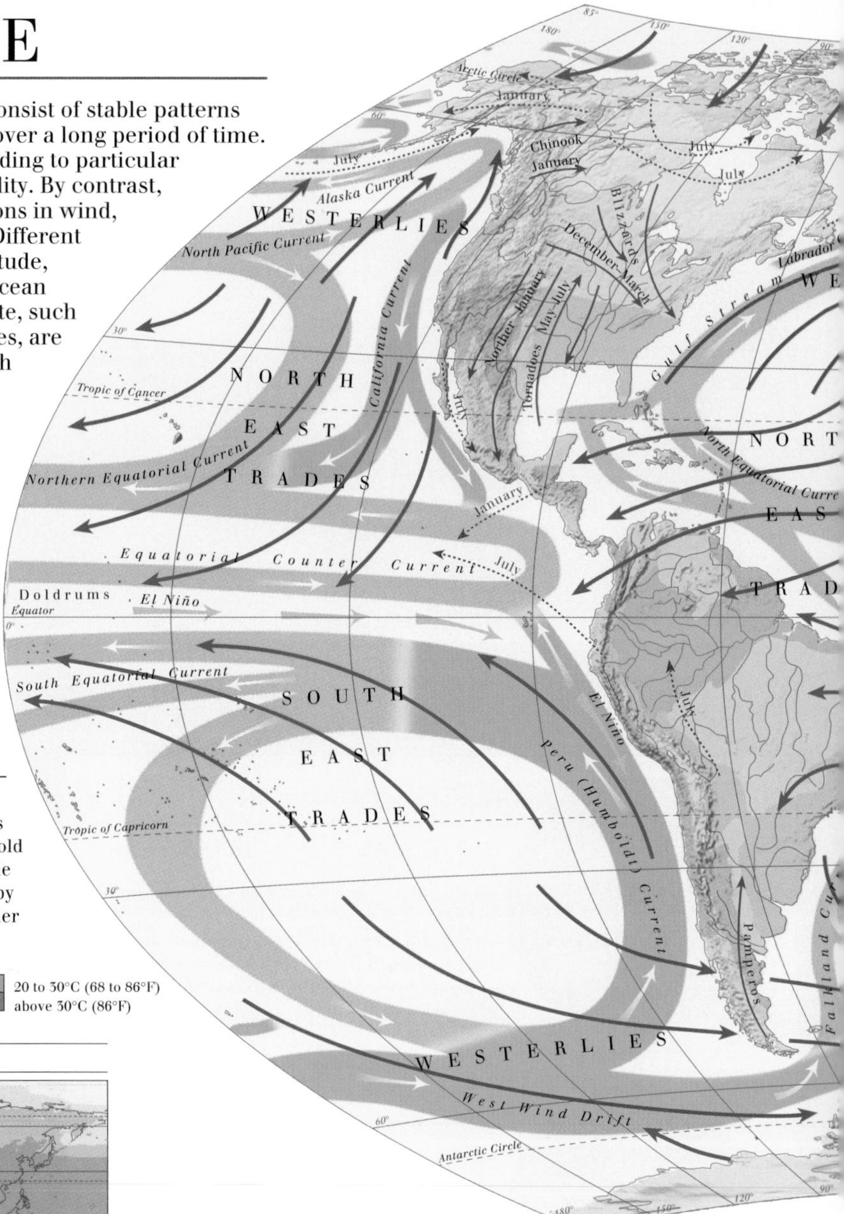

Arctic Circle
January
July
Chinook
January
Alaska Current
WESTERLIES
North Pacific Current
Blizzards
December-March
Norther January
Tornadoes May-July
California Current
Labrador Current
Gulf Stream
Tropic of Cancer
NORTH
EAST
TRADES
Northern Equatorial Current
North Equatorial Current
January
July
Equatorial Counter Current
Doldrums
El Niño
Equator
South Equatorial Current
SOUTH
EAST
TRADES
El Niño
Peru (Humboldt) Current
Tropic of Capricorn
Pamperos
Falkland Current
WESTERLIES
West Wind Drift
Antarctic Circle

TEMPERATURE

THE WORLD CAN BE DIVIDED into three major climatic zones, stretching like large belts across the latitudes: the tropics which are warm, the cold polar regions, and the temperate zones which lie between them. Temperature is also controlled by altitude: mountainous regions are typically colder than those at sea level.

- below - 30°C (-22°F)
- -30 to - 20°C (-22 to -4°F)
- -20 to - 10°C (-4 to 14°F)
- -10 to 0°C (14 to 32°F)
- 0 to 10°C (32 to 50°F)
- 10 to 20°C (50 to 68°F)
- 20 to 30°C (68 to 86°F)
- above 30°C (86°F)

AVERAGE JULY TEMPERATURE

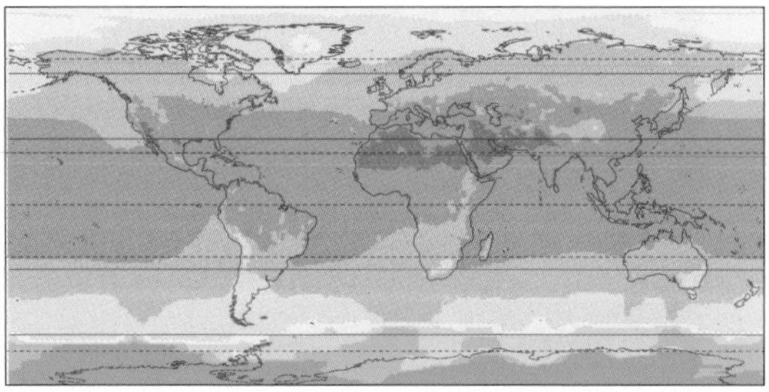

AVERAGE JANUARY TEMPERATURE

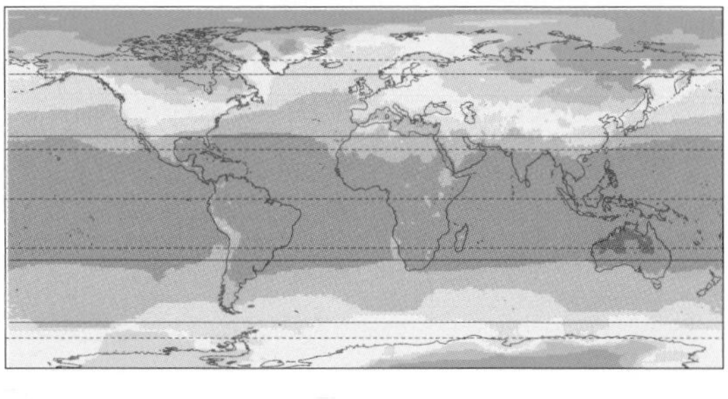

AVERAGE JULY RAINFALL

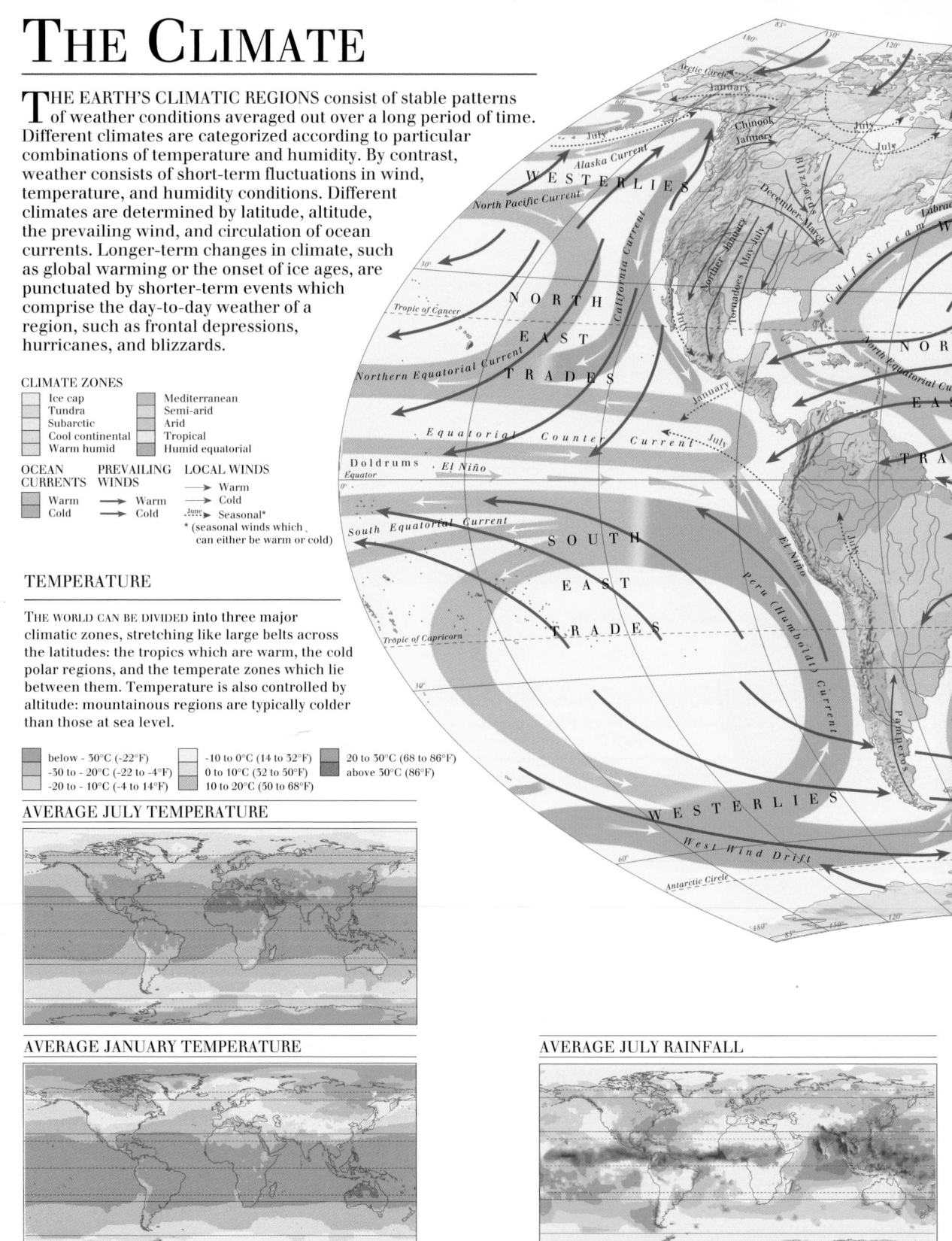

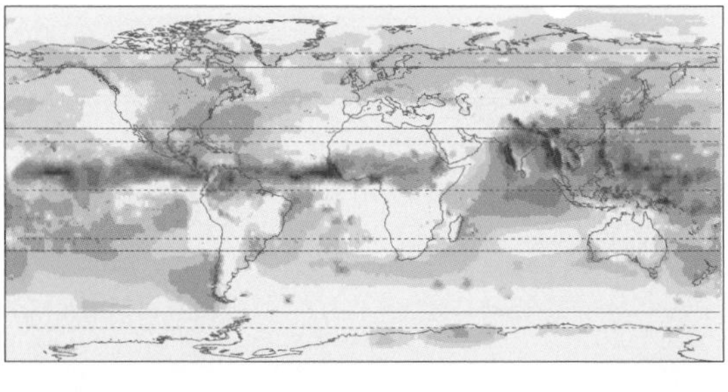

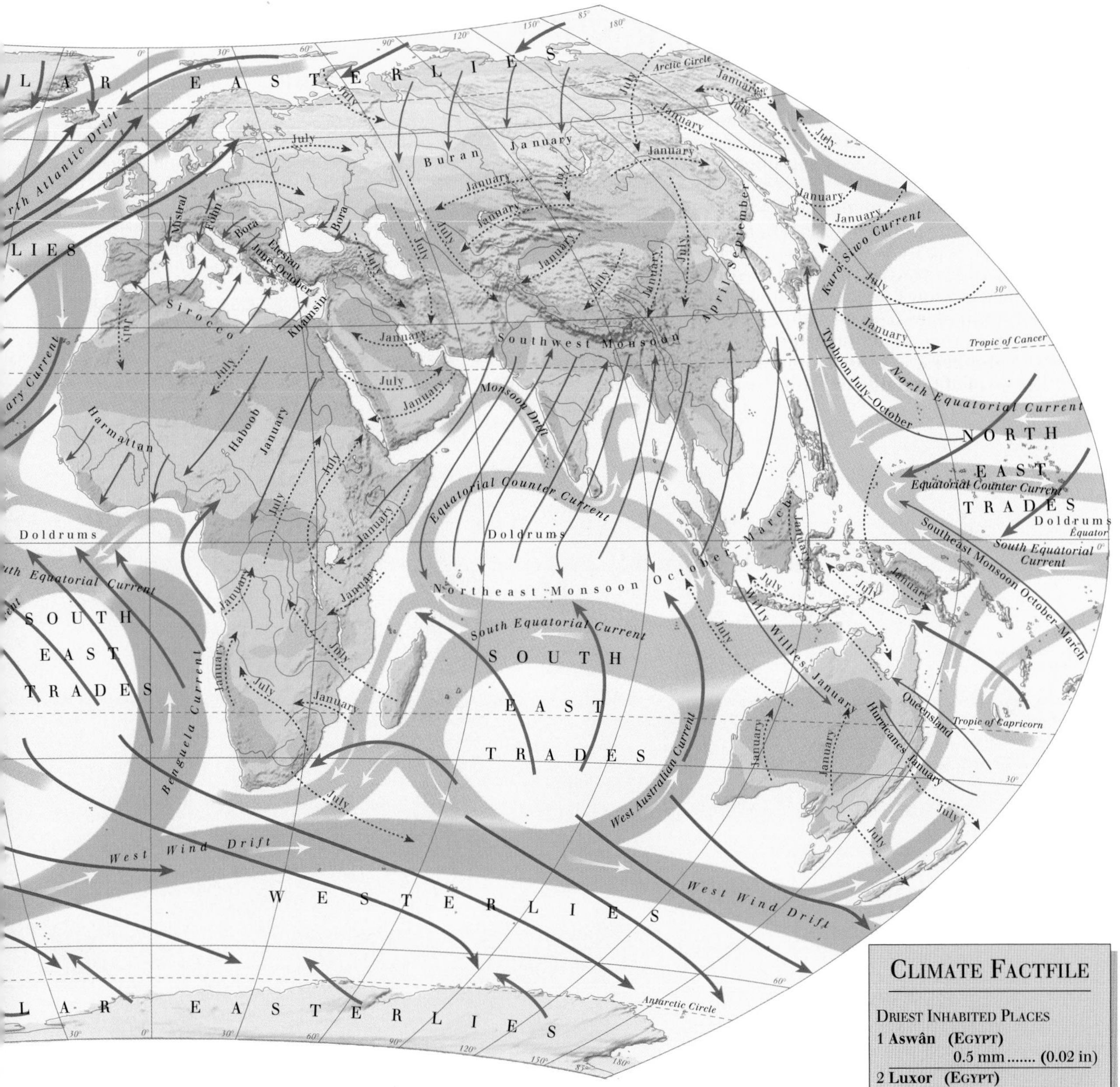

L A R E A S T E R L I E S
North Atlantic Drift
Arctic Circle
July
January
Buran
Mistral
Föhn
Bora
Etesian June-October
LIES
Sirocco
Khamsin
Southwest Monsoon
April-September
Kuro Siwo Current
Typhoon July-October
Tropic of Cancer
North Equatorial Current
NORTH EAST TRADES
Equatorial Counter Current
Doldrums
Equator
South Equatorial Current
Southeast Monsoon October-March
Harmattan
Haboob
Monsoon Drift
Equatorial Counter Current
Doldrums
Northeast Monsoon October-March
South Equatorial Current
SOUTH EAST TRADES
Benguela Current
West Australian Current
Willy Willies
Queensland
Hurricanes
Tropic of Capricorn
West Wind Drift
WESTERLIES
Antarctic Circle
L A R E A S T E R L I E S

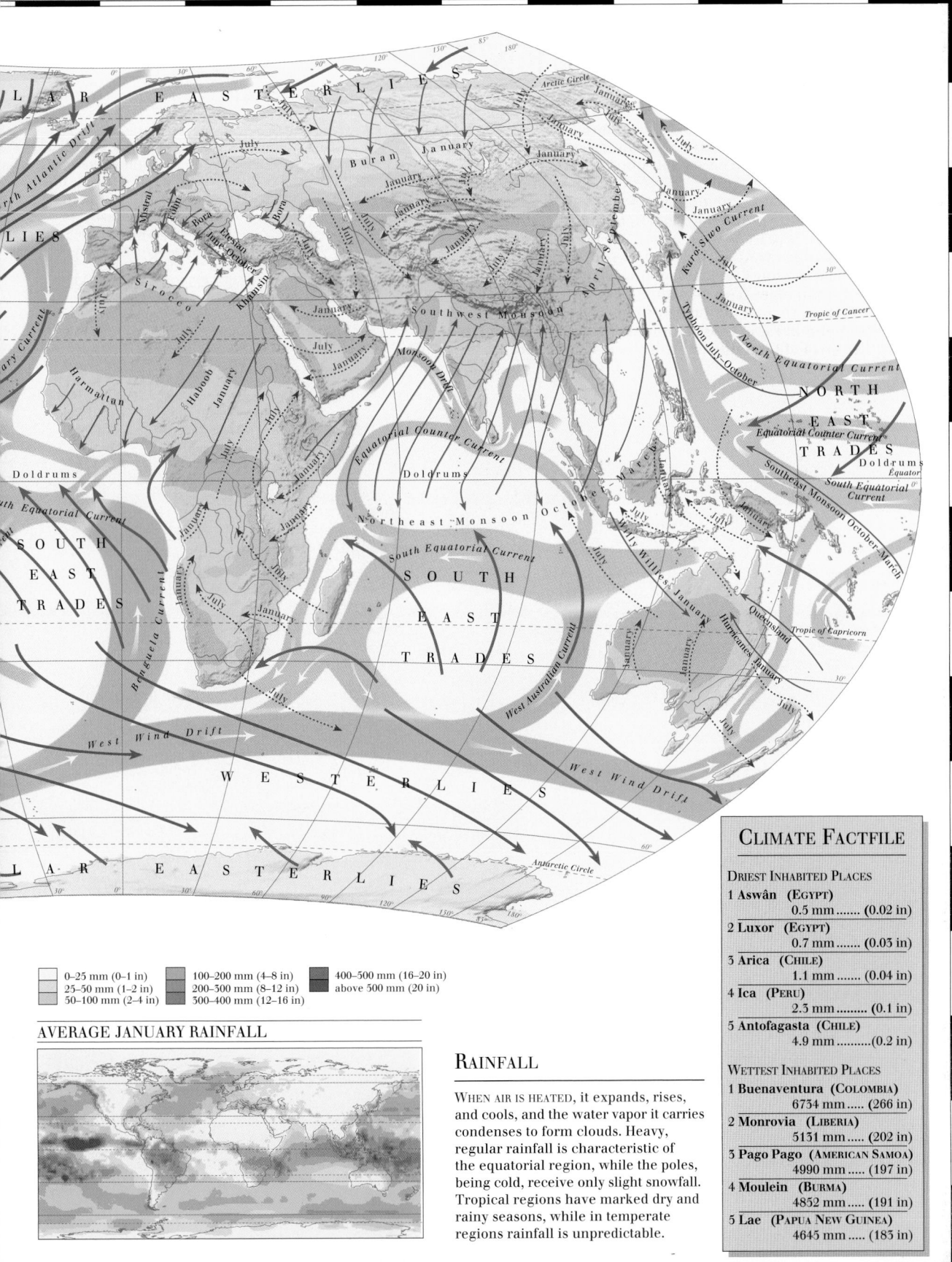

0–25 mm (0–1 in)
25–50 mm (1–2 in)
50–100 mm (2–4 in)
100–200 mm (4–8 in)
200–300 mm (8–12 in)
300–400 mm (12–16 in)
400–500 mm (16–20 in)
above 500 mm (20 in)

AVERAGE JANUARY RAINFALL

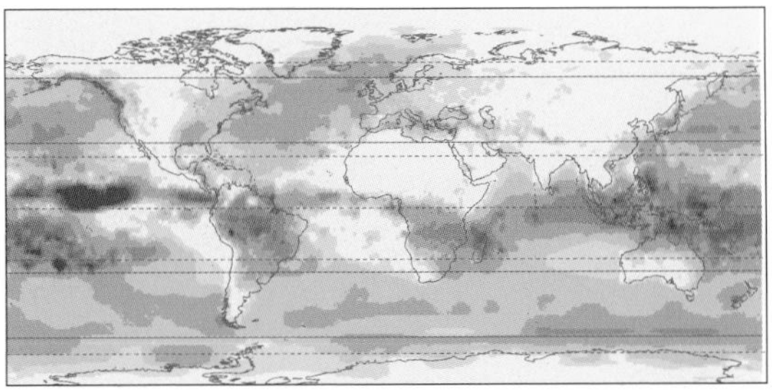

RAINFALL

WHEN AIR IS HEATED, it expands, rises, and cools, and the water vapor it carries condenses to form clouds. Heavy, regular rainfall is characteristic of the equatorial region, while the poles, being cold, receive only slight snowfall. Tropical regions have marked dry and rainy seasons, while in temperate regions rainfall is unpredictable.

CLIMATE FACTFILE

DRIEST INHABITED PLACES

1 **Aswân** (EGYPT) 0.5 mm .... (0.02 in)
2 **Luxor** (EGYPT) 0.7 mm .... (0.03 in)
3 **Arica** (CHILE) 1.1 mm .... (0.04 in)
4 **Ica** (PERU) 2.3 mm .... (0.1 in)
5 **Antofagasta** (CHILE) 4.9 mm ....(0.2 in)

WETTEST INHABITED PLACES

1 **Buenaventura** (COLOMBIA) 6734 mm ..... (266 in)
2 **Monrovia** (LIBERIA) 5131 mm ..... (202 in)
3 **Pago Pago** (AMERICAN SAMOA) 4990 mm ..... (197 in)
4 **Moulein** (BURMA) 4852 mm ..... (191 in)
5 **Lae** (PAPUA NEW GUINEA) 4645 mm ..... (183 in)

The Environment

THE EARTH CAN BE DIVIDED into a series of biogeographic regions, or biomes – ecological communities where certain species of plant and animal coexist within particular climatic conditions. Within these broad classifications, other factors affect the local distribution of species in each biome, including soil richness, altitude, and human activities such as urbanization, intensive agriculture, and deforestation. Apart from the polar ice caps, there are few areas which have not been colonized by animals or plants over the course of the Earth's history. Because of all animals' reliance on plants for survival, plants are known as primary producers. The availability of nutrients and the temperature of an area define its primary productivity, which affects the number and type of animals which are able to live there; the level of humidity or aridity is also a determining factor.

Biodiversity

THE NUMBER OF PLANT AND ANIMAL SPECIES, and the range of genetic diversity within the populations of each species, make up the Earth's biodiversity. The plants and animals which are endemic to a region – that is, those which are found nowhere else in the world – are also important in determining levels of biodiversity. Human settlement and intervention have encroached on many areas of the world once rich in endemic plant and animal species. Increasing international efforts are being made to monitor and conserve the biodiversity of the Earth's remaining wild places.

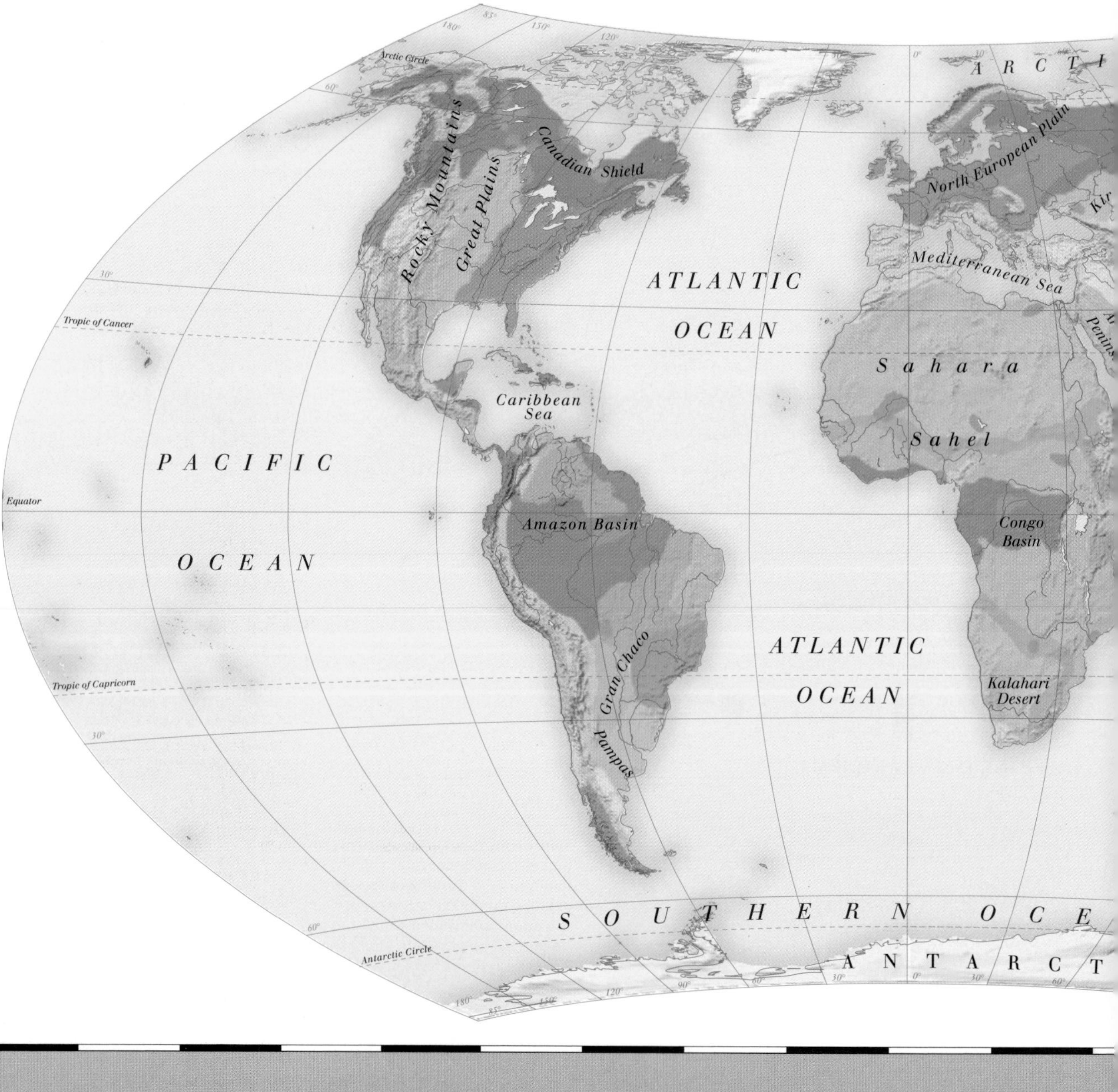
Arctic Circle
Tropic of Cancer
Equator
Tropic of Capricorn
Antarctic Circle
Rocky Mountains
Great Plains
Canadian Shield
ATLANTIC OCEAN
Caribbean Sea
PACIFIC OCEAN
Amazon Basin
Gran Chaco
Pampas
ATLANTIC OCEAN
North European Plain
Mediterranean Sea
Sahara
Sahel
Congo Basin
Kalahari Desert
SOUTHERN OCE
ANTARCT
ARCTI

ANIMALS

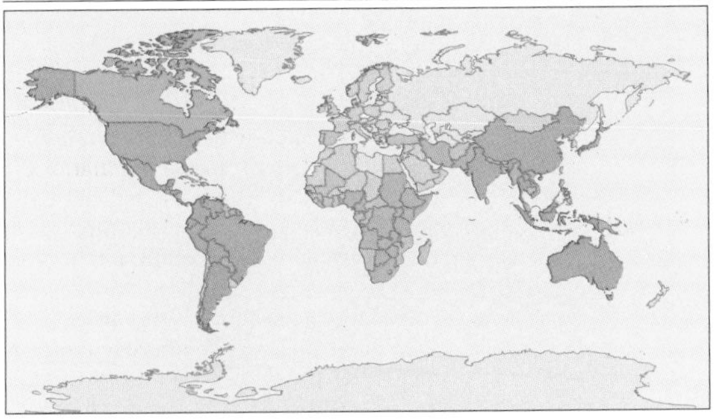

Number of animal species per country

- More than 2000
- 1000–1999
- 700–999
- 400–699
- 200–399
- 100–199
- 0–99
- Data not available

ANIMAL ADAPTATION

THE DEGREE OF AN ANIMAL'S ADAPTABILITY to different climates and conditions is extremely important in ensuring its success as a species. Many animals, particularly the largest mammals, are becoming restricted to ever-smaller regions as human development and agricultural practices reduce their natural habitats. In contrast, humans have been responsible – deliberately and accidentally – for the spread of some of the world's most successful species, many of which now outnumber the indigenous animal populations.

PLANTS

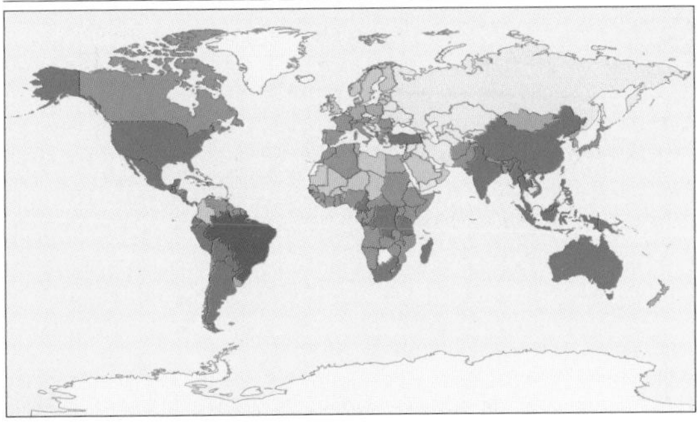

Number of plant species per country

- More than 50,000
- 7000–49,999
- 3000–6999
- 2000–2999
- 1000–1999
- 600–999
- 0–599
- Data not available

PLANT ADAPTATION

ENVIRONMENTAL CONDITIONS, such as climate, soil type, and competition with other organisms, influence the development of plants into distinctive forms. Similar conditions in different parts of the world create similar adaptations in the plants, which may then be modified by other, local, factors specific to the region.

C E A N
Arctic Circle
i b e r i a
G o b i
Himalayas
Thar Desert
Deccan
Tropic of Cancer
PACIFIC
OCEAN
Equator
INDIAN
OCEAN
Great Victoria Desert
Tropic of Capricorn
Antarctic Circle
A

BIOME TYPES

- Mountains
- Polar regions
- Tundra
- Tropical rainforests
- Dry woodlands
- Savanna
- Temperate grasslands
- Mediterranean
- Coniferous forests
- Temperate rainforests
- Broadleaf forests
- Cold deserts
- Hot deserts
- Wetlands

ENVIRONMENT FACTFILE

LARGEST PROTECTED AREAS

(Land and marine, as percentage of land area)

Dominican Republic 174%
Tuvalu 132%
Seychelles 111%
Slovakia 76%
Venezuela 64%

HIGHEST ANNUAL DEFORESTATION

Brazil	25,476 km²	(9859 mi²)
China	18,060 km²	(6989 mi²)
Indonesia	13,120 km²	(5077 mi²)
Sudan	9590 km²	(3711 mi²)
Zambia	8510 km²	(3293 mi²)

IDENTIFIED SPECIES

Microorganisms 5800
Invertebrates 1,021,000
Plants 322,500
Fish 19,100
Reptiles & amphibians ..12,000
Mammals 4000

ENDANGERED SPECIES

Mammals 484
Birds 403
Reptiles 100
Amphibians 49
Fish 291
Invertebrates 763

POPULATION
over 5 000 000
over 1 000 000
over 500 000
over 100 000
over 50 000
under 50 000
LAND HEIGHT
4000m/13 124ft
3000m/9845ft
2000m/6562ft
1000m/3281ft
200m/656ft
Sea Level
Line of cross-section
A R C T I C
O C E A N
North Pole
GREENLAND
(to Denmark)
NUUK
ICELAND
Denmark Strait
Arctic Circle
Davis Strait
Baffin Bay
Baffin Island
Iqaluit
Ellesmere I.
Queen Elizabeth Islands
Devon I.
Somerset I.
Cornwallis I.
Bathurst I.
Prince of Wales I.
Melville I.
Victoria I.
Banks I.
Beaufort Sea
Southampton I.
Hudson Strait
Péninsule d'ungava
Hudson Bay
James Bay
C A N A D A
N U N A V U T
NORTHWEST TERRITORIES
YUKON TERRITORY
Inuvik
Great Bear Lake
Great Slave Lake
Yellowknife
Dawson
Mackenzie Mts
R o c k y M o u n t a i n s
Coast Mountains
ALBERTA
Edmonton
Calgary
Athabasca
Medicine Hat
SASKATCHEWAN
Saskatoon
Regina
MANITOBA
Lake Winnipeg
Winnipeg
Churchill
O N T A R I O
Thunder Bay
Sault Saint Marie
Toronto
OTTAWA
Q U E B E C
Québec
Montréal
Sept Iles
Labrador City
NEWFOUNDLAND & LABRADOR
Labrador
Newfoundland
St. John's
ST PIERRE & MIQUELON (to France)
PRINCE EDWARD I.
NEW BRUNSWICK
NOVA SCOTIA
Halifax
St Lawrence
BRITISH COLUMBIA
Vancouver
Vancouver I.
Queen Charlotte Is
Alexander Archipelago
Juneau
ALASKA (to US)
Brooks Range
Fairbanks
Alaska Range
Mt McKinley (Denali) 6194m
Anchorage
Yukon
Gulf of Alaska
Kodiak I.
Alaska Peninsula
Aleutian Islands
Unimak
Unalaska
Umnak
Atka
Attu
Bering Sea
Bering Strait
St Lawrence I.
Arctic Circle
RUSSIAN FEDERATION
G r e a t P l a i n s
Prairies
Great Lakes
L. Superior
L. Michigan
L. Huron
L. Erie
L. Ontario
Missouri
Mississippi
Snake
Hudson
U N I T E D S T A T E S
WASHINGTON
Seattle
Spokane
OREGON
Portland
IDAHO
Boise
MONTANA
WYOMING
NORTH DAKOTA
SOUTH DAKOTA
MINNESOTA
Minneapolis
St Paul
WISCONSIN
Milwaukee
MICHIGAN
Detroit
IOWA
NEBRASKA
Omaha
KANSAS
Kansas City
MISSOURI
St Louis
ILLINOIS
Chicago
INDIANA
OHIO
Cleveland
Cincinnati
PENNSYLVANIA
Pittsburgh
Philadelphia
NEW YORK
Buffalo
New York
NEW JERSEY
DELAWARE
Baltimore
VERMONT
NEW HAMPSHIRE
MAINE
MASSACHUSETTS
Boston
RHODE ISLAND
CONNECTICUT
COLORADO
Denver
UTAH
Salt Lake City
NEVADA
Reno
Las Vegas
Death Valley
Great Basin
Cascade Range
Sierra Nevada
Coast Ranges
CALIFORNIA
Sacramento
San Francisco
Los Angeles
San Diego
ARIZONA
Colorado
P A C I F I C

NORTH AMERICA

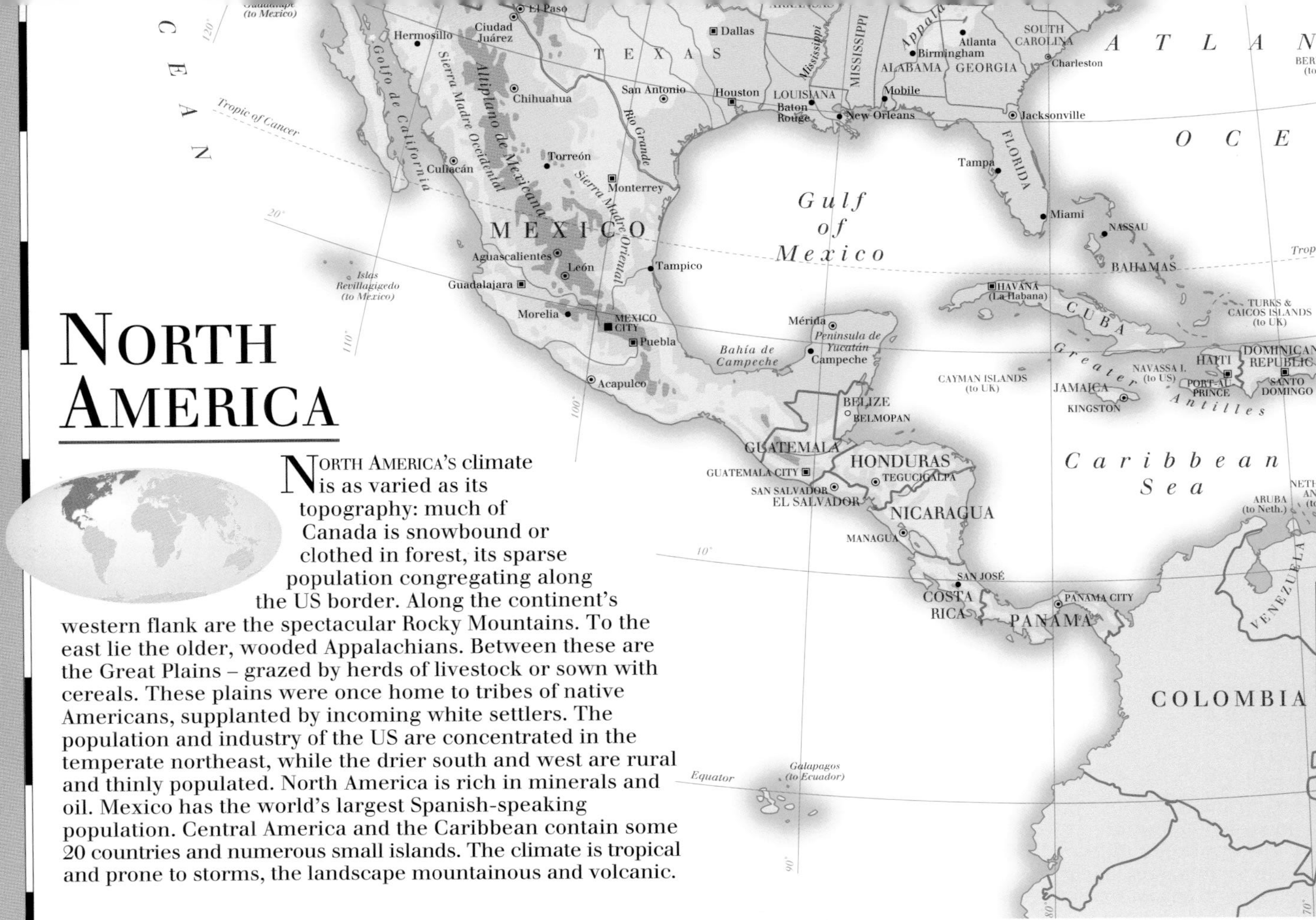

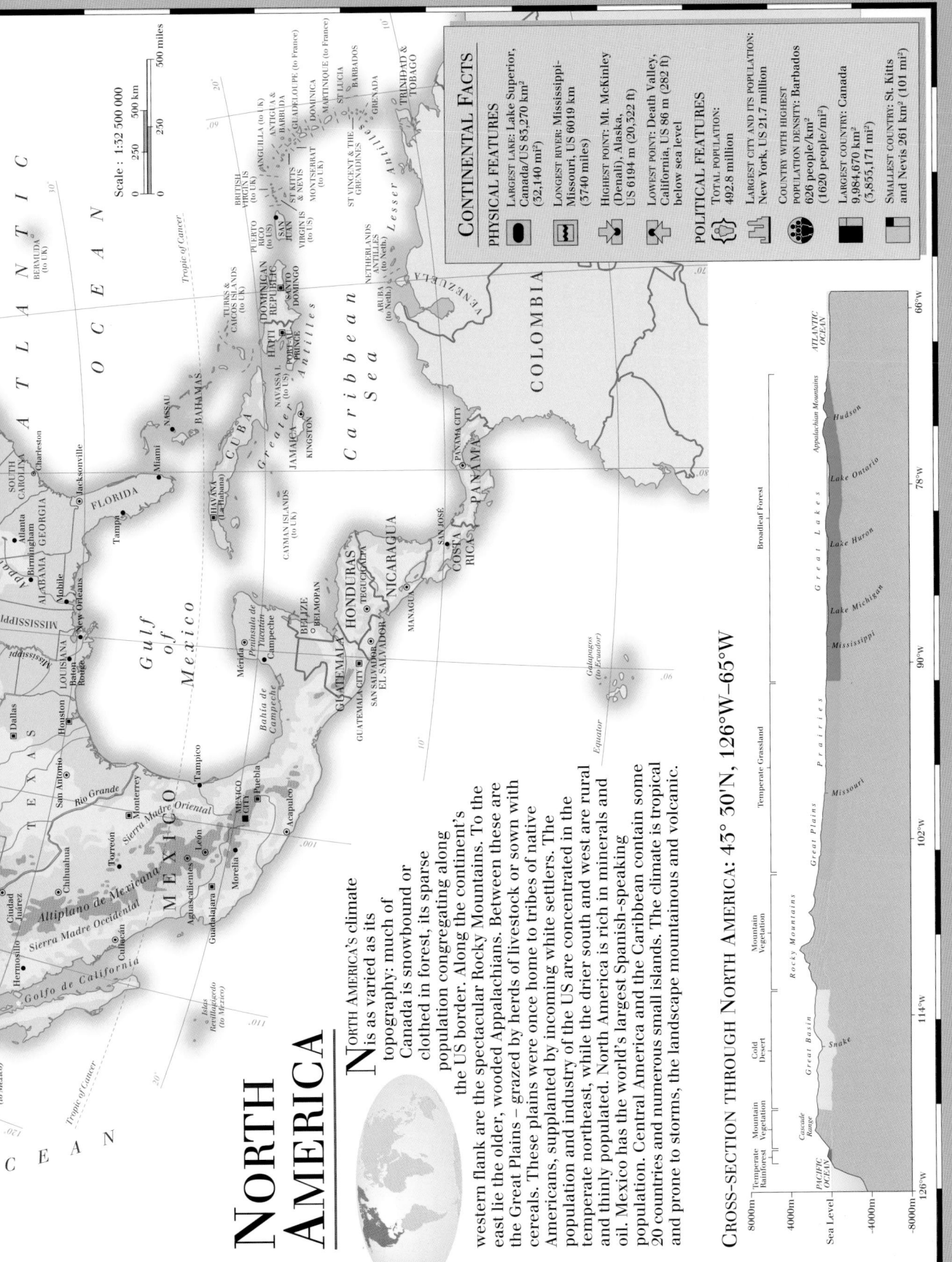

C E A N
Tropic of Cancer
Hermosillo
Ciudad Juárez
El Paso
Chihuahua
Culiacán
Golfo de California
Sierra Madre Occidental
Altiplano de Mexicano
Torreón
Monterrey
Sierra Madre Oriental
MEXICO
Aguascalientes
León
Guadalajara
Morelia
MEXICO CITY
Puebla
Tampico
Acapulco
Islas Revillagigedo (to Mexico)
TEXAS
Dallas
San Antonio
Rio Grande
Houston
LOUISIANA
Baton Rouge
New Orleans
Mississippi
MISSISSIPPI
ALABAMA
Birmingham
Mobile
Atlanta
GEORGIA
SOUTH CAROLINA
Charleston
Jacksonville
FLORIDA
Tampa
Miami
ATLANTIC OCEAN
BERMUDA (to UK)
Gulf of Mexico
Bahía de Campeche
Mérida
Península de Yucatán
Campeche
BELIZE
BELMOPAN
GUATEMALA
GUATEMALA CITY
SAN SALVADOR
EL SALVADOR
HONDURAS
TEGUCIGALPA
NICARAGUA
MANAGUA
SAN JOSÉ
COSTA RICA
PANAMA
PANAMA CITY
COLOMBIA
VENEZUELA
NASSAU
BAHAMAS
HAVANA (La Habana)
CUBA
CAYMAN ISLANDS (to UK)
JAMAICA
KINGSTON
Greater Antilles
NAVASSA I. (to US)
HAITI
PORT-AU-PRINCE
DOMINICAN REPUBLIC
SANTO DOMINGO
TURKS & CAICOS ISLANDS (to UK)
PUERTO RICO (to US)
SAN JUAN
VIRGIN IS (to US)
BRITISH VIRGIN IS (to UK)
ANGUILLA (to UK)
ANTIGUA & BARBUDA
ST KITTS & NEVIS
MONTSERRAT (to UK)
GUADELOUPE (to France)
DOMINICA
MARTINIQUE (to France)
ST LUCIA
BARBADOS
ST VINCENT & THE GRENADINES
GRENADA
TRINIDAD & TOBAGO
ARUBA (to Neth.)
NETHERLANDS ANTILLES (to Neth.)
Lesser Antilles
Caribbean Sea
Galapagos (to Ecuador)
Equator
Scale : 1:32 500 000
0 250 500 km
0 250 500 miles

NORTH AMERICA'S climate is as varied as its topography: much of Canada is snowbound or clothed in forest, its sparse population congregating along the US border. Along the continent's western flank are the spectacular Rocky Mountains. To the east lie the older, wooded Appalachians. Between these are the Great Plains – grazed by herds of livestock or sown with cereals. These plains were once home to tribes of native Americans, supplanted by incoming white settlers. The population and industry of the US are concentrated in the temperate northeast, while the drier south and west are rural and thinly populated. North America is rich in minerals and oil. Mexico has the world's largest Spanish-speaking population. Central America and the Caribbean contain some 20 countries and numerous small islands. The climate is tropical and prone to storms, the landscape mountainous and volcanic.

CROSS-SECTION THROUGH NORTH AMERICA: 43° 30'N, 126°W–65°W

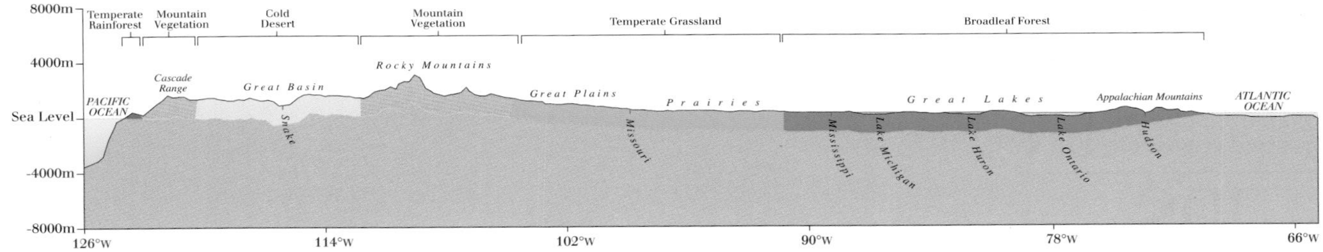

8000m
4000m
Sea Level
-4000m
-8000m
Temperate Rainforest
Mountain Vegetation
Cold Desert
Mountain Vegetation
Temperate Grassland
Broadleaf Forest
PACIFIC OCEAN
Cascade Range
Great Basin
Snake
Rocky Mountains
Great Plains
Missouri
Prairies
Mississippi
Great Lakes
Lake Michigan
Lake Huron
Lake Ontario
Appalachian Mountains
Hudson
ATLANTIC OCEAN
126°W
114°W
102°W
90°W
78°W
66°W

CONTINENTAL FACTS

PHYSICAL FEATURES

- LARGEST LAKE: Lake Superior, Canada/US 83,270 km² (32,140 mi²)
- LONGEST RIVER: Mississippi-Missouri, US 6019 km (3740 miles)
- HIGHEST POINT: Mt. McKinley (Denali), Alaska, US 6194 m (20,322 ft)
- LOWEST POINT: Death Valley, California, US 86 m (282 ft) below sea level

POLITICAL FEATURES

- TOTAL POPULATION: 492.8 million
- LARGEST CITY AND ITS POPULATION: New York, US 21.7 million
- COUNTRY WITH HIGHEST POPULATION DENSITY: Barbados 626 people/km² (1620 people/mi²)
- LARGEST COUNTRY: Canada 9,984,670 km² (3,855,171 mi²)
- SMALLEST COUNTRY: St. Kitts and Nevis 261 km² (101 mi²)

SOUTH AMERICA

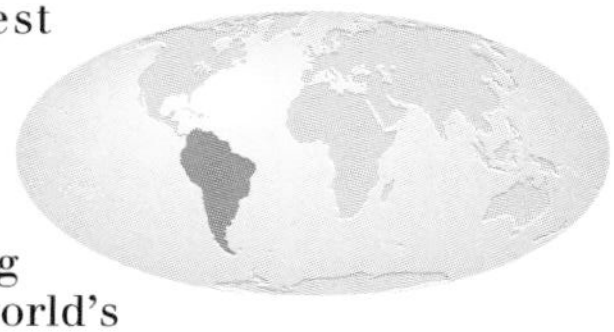

THE WORLD'S fourth-largest continent includes one of its most important resources – the Amazonian rainforest. It is a major source of oxygen and includes half of all known living species, while the Amazon – the world's second-longest river – contains one-fifth of the world's fresh water. The Andes mountain chain reaches down South America's western flank, sheltering the prairies of the Gran Chaco, the Pampas, and the wastes of the far south. Most South Americans are *mestizo* – of mixed European and Amerindian descent – and live in the coastal regions. Spanish is the most widely spoken language, and over 90% of South Americans are Roman Catholic. South America has massive mineral resources, many exploited by US and European multinationals.

Caribbean Sea
Lesser Antilles
ARUBA (to Neth.)
NETHERLANDS ANTILLES (to Neth.)
TRINIDAD & TOBAGO
PANAMA
Barranquilla
Montería
Maracaibo
Lago de Maracaibo
Valencia
Maracay
CARACAS
Cucuta
Medellín
BOGOTÁ
Cali
COLOMBIA
VENEZUELA
Llanos
Orinoco
Apure
Arauca
Meta
Magdalena
Cauca
Caroní
Salto del Angel
Guiana Highlands
Morawhanna
Charity
GEORGETOWN
New Amsterdam
Bartica
Linden
GUYANA
Essequibo
Totness
Brokopondo
PARAMARIBO
Nieuw Amsterdam
St-Laurent-du-Maroni
CAYENNE
SURINAME
FRENCH GUIANA (to France)
Equator
QUITO
ECUADOR
Guayaquil
Gulf of Guayaquil
Caquetá
Putumayo
Napo
Japurá
Negro
Branco
Amazon Basin
Amazon
Manaus
Marañon
Juruá
Purus
Madeira
Tapajós
Ucayali
PERU
Trujillo
LIMA
Andes
PACIFIC
Belém
São Luis
Imperatriz
Teresina
Fortaleza
ATLANTIC OCEAN
Cabo de São Roque (to Brazil)
Fernando de Noronha (to Brazil)
João Pessoa
Olinda
Recifé
Maceio
Aracaju
Salvador
Represa de Sobradinho
São Francisco
Araguaia
Tocantins
Xingu
BRAZIL
Planalto de Mato Grosso
Brazilian Highlands
BRASÍLIA
Goiânia
Guaporé
Mamoré
BOLIVIA
Lake Titicaca
Arequipa
LA PAZ
Oruro
Santa Cruz
SUCRE
80°
70°
60°
50°
40°
10°
20°

PARAGUAY
ASUNCIÓN
Fernando de la Mora
Lambaré
Campinas
São Paulo
Santos
Sorocaba
Juiz de Fora
Nova Iguaçu
Rio de Janeiro
Curitiba
Tropic of Capricorn
Porto Alegre
Salto
Paysandú
URUGUAY
Las Piedras
MONTEVIDEO
Río de la Plata
BUENOS AIRES
La Plata
Rosario
Córdoba
L. Mar Chiquita
Salado
Paraná
Uruguay
Cerro Aconcagua 6959m
SANTIAGO
Valparaíso
Concepción
Puerto Montt
Isla de Chiloé
Isla Wellington
Islas de los Desventurados (to Chile)
Islas Juan Fernández (to Chile)
Colorado
Negro
Bahía Blanca
Golfo San Matías
Península Valdés
Chubut
Deseado
Golfo San Jorge
Bahía Grande
Tierra del Fuego
Beagle Channel
Cape Horn
FALKLAND ISLANDS (to UK)
ATLANTIC OCEAN
OCEAN
ARGENTINA
CHILE
Pampas
Patagonia
Andes
Atacama
30°
40°
50°
60°
70°
80°
20°

POPULATION

- over 5 000 000
- over 1 000 000
- over 500 000
- over 100 000
- over 50 000
- under 50 000

LAND HEIGHT

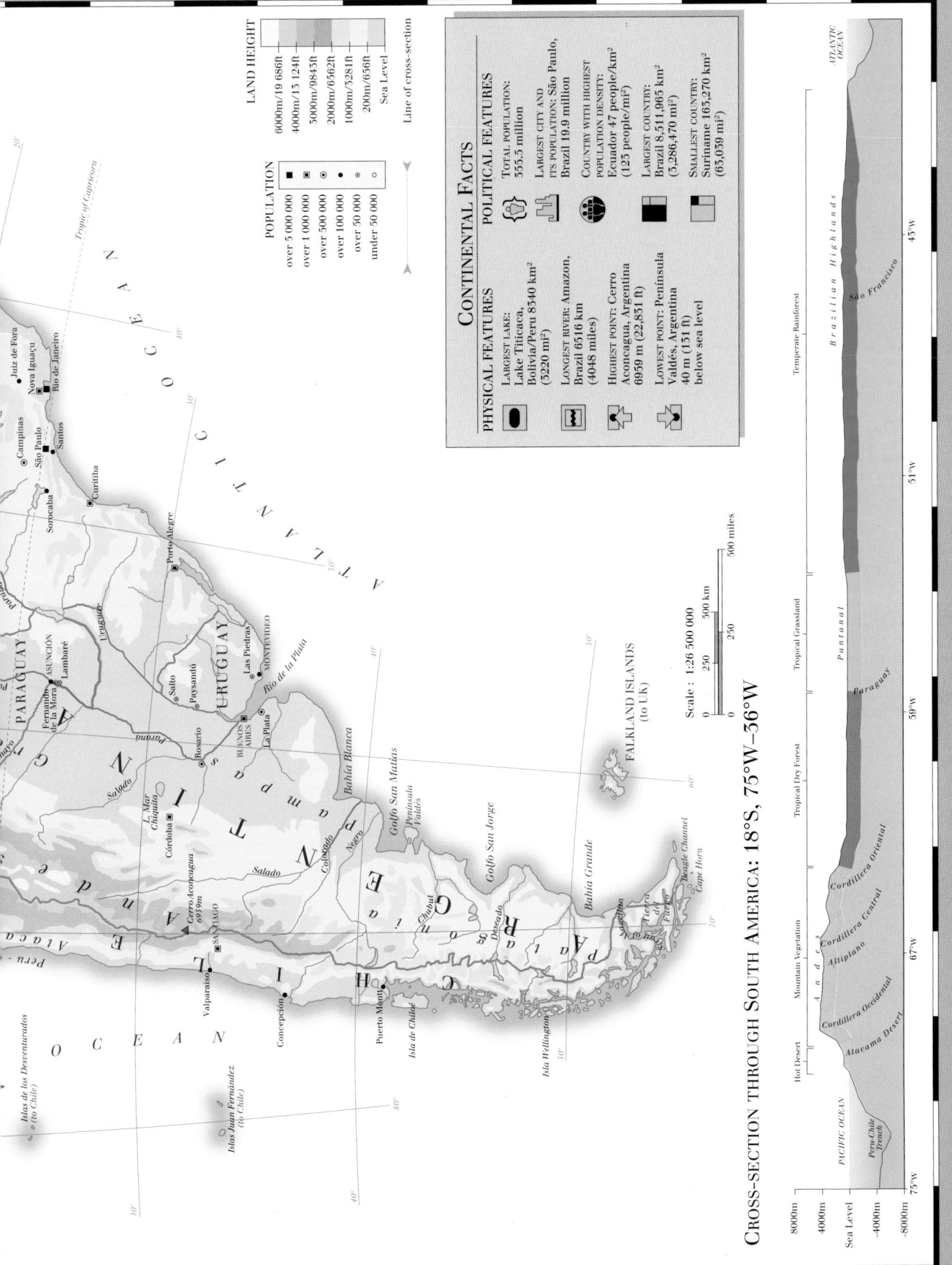

- 6000m/19 686ft
- 4000m/13 124ft
- 3000m/9843ft
- 2000m/6562ft
- 1000m/3281ft
- 200m/656ft
- Sea Level

Line of cross-section

Scale : 1:26 500 000

0 250 500 km

0 250 500 miles

CONTINENTAL FACTS

PHYSICAL FEATURES

LARGEST LAKE: Lake Titicaca, Bolivia/Peru 8340 km² (3220 mi²)

LONGEST RIVER: Amazon, Brazil 6516 km (4048 miles)

HIGHEST POINT: Cerro Aconcagua, Argentina 6959 m (22,831 ft)

LOWEST POINT: Península Valdés, Argentina 40 m (131 ft) below sea level

POLITICAL FEATURES

TOTAL POPULATION: 355.5 million

LARGEST CITY AND ITS POPULATION: São Paulo, Brazil 19.9 million

COUNTRY WITH HIGHEST POPULATION DENSITY: Ecuador 47 people/km² (123 people/mi²)

LARGEST COUNTRY: Brazil 8,511,965 km² (3,286,470 mi²)

SMALLEST COUNTRY: Suriname 163,270 km² (63,039 mi²)

CROSS-SECTION THROUGH SOUTH AMERICA: 18°S, 75°W–36°W

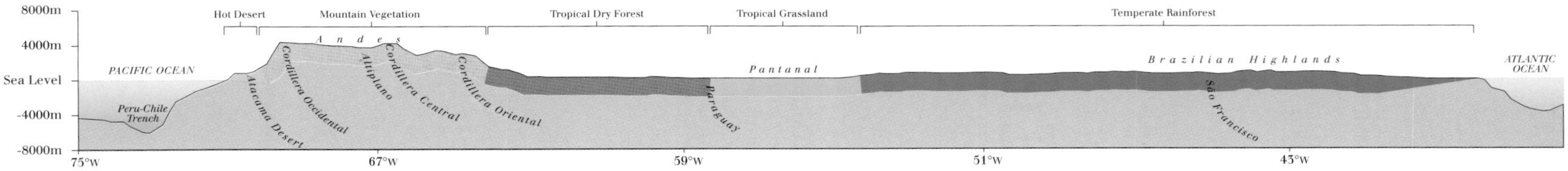
8000m
4000m
Sea Level
-4000m
-8000m
Hot Desert
Mountain Vegetation
Tropical Dry Forest
Tropical Grassland
Temperate Rainforest
PACIFIC OCEAN
Peru-Chile Trench
Atacama Desert
Cordillera Occidental
Altiplano
Cordillera Central
Cordillera Oriental
Andes
Pantanal
Paraguay
Brazilian Highlands
São Francisco
ATLANTIC OCEAN
75°W
67°W
59°W
51°W
43°W

Europe

THE SMALLEST CONTINENT AFTER AUSTRALIA, Europe has a wide variety of climates and landscapes. The tundra of the far north gives way to a cool, wet, heavily forested region. The North European Plain is well-drained, fertile, and rich in oil, coal, and natural gas. The shores of the Mediterranean are generally warm, dry, and hilly, ideal for cultivating olives, citrus fruit, and grapes. A great curve of mountain ranges, including the Pyrenees, Alps, and Carpathians, divides north from south. To the east, the rolling plains of European Russia and Ukraine, clad in coniferous forests or cultivated for wheat, run up to the Ural Mountains. Europeans are mainly Christian – Catholic, Orthodox, or Protestant – and speak a variety of languages, most of which spring from Latin (Romance), Germanic, or Slavic roots.

GREENLAND
(to Denmark)
Arctic Circle
JAN MAYEN
(to Norway)
Denmark Strait
REYKJAVÍK
Akureyri
ICELAND
Norwegian Sea
FAEROE IS
(to Denmark)
Shetland Is
Orkney Is
Outer Hebrides
Edinburgh
Belfast
IRELAND
ISLE OF MAN
(to UK)
DUBLIN
UNITED KINGDOM
Manchester
Cork
Birmingham
Cardiff
LONDON
English Channel
CHANNEL ISLANDS
(to UK)
Seine
PARIS
Nantes
Loire
FRANCE
Bay of Biscay
Bordeaux
Massif Central
Toulouse
Pyrenees
ANDORRA
A Coruña
Porto
Zaragoza
SPAIN
Barcelona
Ebro
MADRID
PORTUGAL
Tagus
LISBON
Valencia
Mallorca
Palma
Eivissa
Balearic Is
Sevilla
Málaga
GIBRALTAR
(to UK)
Ceuta (to Spain)
Melilla (to Spain)
MOROCCO
ALGER
ATLANTIC OCEAN
Azores
(to Portugal)
POPULATION
over 5 000 000
over 1 000 000
over 500 000
over 100 000
over 50 000
under 50 000
LAND HEIGHT
3000m/9843ft
2000m/6562ft
1000m/3281ft
200m/656ft
Sea Level
Line of cross-section
Scale : 1:22 500 000
0
250
500 km
0
250
500 miles

Cross-section through Europe: 46°N, 5°W–48°E

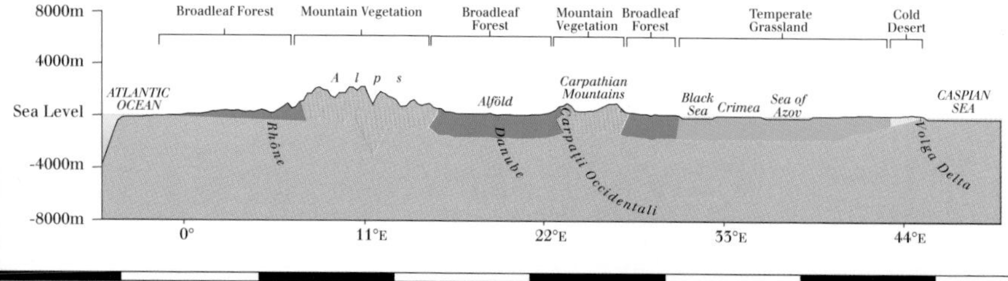
8000m
4000m
Sea Level
-4000m
-8000m
Broadleaf Forest
Mountain Vegetation
Broadleaf Forest
Mountain Vegetation
Broadleaf Forest
Temperate Grassland
Cold Desert
ATLANTIC OCEAN
Alps
Rhône
Alföld
Danube
Carpathian Mountains
Carpatii Occidentali
Black Sea
Crimea
Sea of Azov
CASPIAN SEA
Volga Delta
0°
11°E
22°E
33°E
44°E

CONTINENTAL FACTS

PHYSICAL FEATURES

LARGEST LAKE: Ladoga, European Russia 18,390 km² (7100 mi²)

LONGEST RIVER: Volga, European Russia 3688 km (2290 miles)

HIGHEST POINT: El' brus, Caucasus, European Russia 5642 m (18,510 ft)

LOWEST POINT: Volga Delta, Caspian Sea, European Russia 28 m (92 ft) below sea level

POLITICAL FEATURES

TOTAL POPULATION: 768.6 million

COUNTRY WITH HIGHEST POPULATION DENSITY: Monaco 16,404 people/km² (42,649 people/mi²)

LARGEST CITY AND ITS POPULATION: Moscow, European Russia 13.2 million

LARGEST COUNTRY: European Russia 3,955,818 km² (1,527,341 mi²)

SMALLEST COUNTRY: Vatican City, Italy 0.44 km² (0.17 mi²)

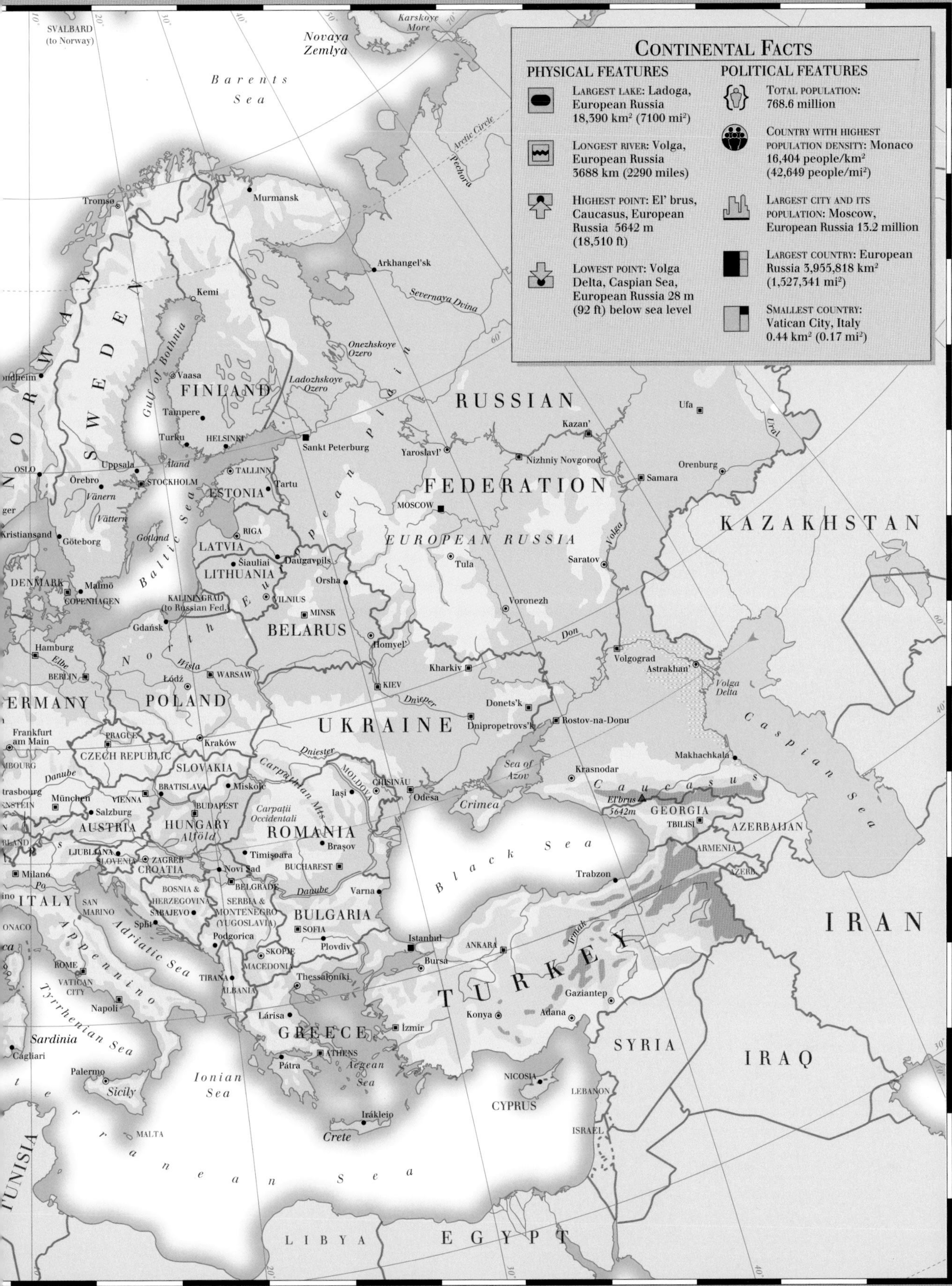
SVALBARD (to Norway)
Novaya Zemlya
Karskoye More
Barents Sea
Arctic Circle
Pechora
Murmansk
Tromsø
Arkhangel'sk
Severnaya Dvina
Kemi
Gulf of Bothnia
Onezhskoye Ozero
Ladozhskoye Ozero
Vaasa
FINLAND
NORWAY
SWEDEN
Tampere
Turku
HELSINKI
Åland
Uppsala
OSLO
Örebro
STOCKHOLM
TALLINN
ESTONIA
Tartu
Vänern
Vättern
Gotland
Kristiansand
Göteborg
RIGA
LATVIA
Baltic Sea
Šiauliai
Daugavpils
LITHUANIA
DENMARK
Malmö
COPENHAGEN
KALININGRAD (to Russian Fed.)
VILNIUS
MINSK
BELARUS
Orsha
North European Plain
Gdańsk
Hamburg
Elbe
BERLIN
GERMANY
Wisła
WARSAW
Łódź
POLAND
Homyel'
Frankfurt am Main
PRAGUE
CZECH REPUBLIC
Kraków
SLOVAKIA
Danube
Strasbourg
München
VIENNA
BRATISLAVA
Miskolc
Salzburg
AUSTRIA
BUDAPEST
HUNGARY
Alföld
LJUBLJANA
SLOVENIA
ZAGREB
CROATIA
Novi Sad
Milano
Po
ITALY
SAN MARINO
BOSNIA & HERZEGOVINA
SARAJEVO
BELGRADE
SERBIA & MONTENEGRO (YUGOSLAVIA)
Split
Podgorica
Adriatic Sea
Appennino
ROME
VATICAN CITY
Napoli
Tyrrhenian Sea
Sardinia
Cagliari
Palermo
Sicily
MALTA
TUNISIA
Mediterranean Sea
RUSSIAN FEDERATION
EUROPEAN RUSSIA
Yaroslavl'
Nizhniy Novgorod
Kazan'
Ufa
Ural
Orenburg
Samara
MOSCOW
Sankt Peterburg
Tula
Voronezh
Saratov
Volga
KAZAKHSTAN
Don
Volgograd
Astrakhan'
Volga Delta
Caspian Sea
Kharkiv
KIEV
Dnieper
Donets'k
Dnipropetrovs'k
Rostov-na-Donu
UKRAINE
Dniester
MOLDOVA
CHIȘINĂU
Odesa
Iași
Carpathian Mts
Carpații Occidentali
ROMANIA
Timișoara
Brașov
BUCHAREST
Danube
Varna
BULGARIA
SOFIA
Plovdiv
SKOPJE
MACEDONIA
TIRANA
ALBANIA
Thessaloníki
Sea of Azov
Crimea
Krasnodar
Caucasus
El'brus 5642m
GEORGIA
TBILISI
AZERBAIJAN
ARMENIA
AZERB.
Makhachkala
Black Sea
Trabzon
Istanbul
ANKARA
Bursa
Irmak
TURKEY
Gaziantep
Konya
Adana
İzmir
Lárisa
GREECE
ATHENS
Pátra
Aegean Sea
Ionian Sea
NICOSIA
CYPRUS
LEBANON
ISRAEL
SYRIA
IRAQ
IRAN
Iráklejo
Crete
LIBYA
EGYPT

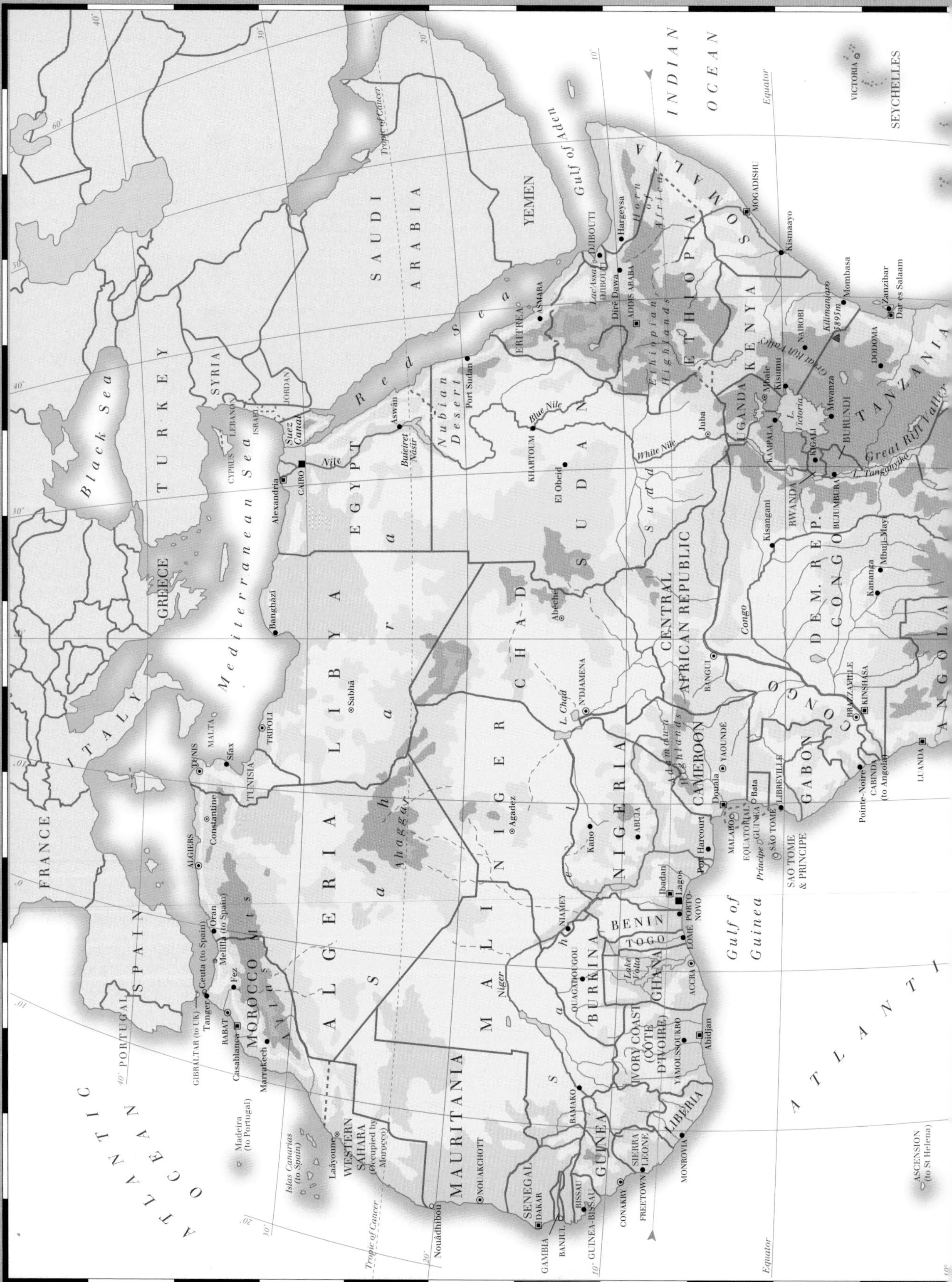
ATLANTIC OCEAN
INDIAN OCEAN
ATLANTIC
Mediterranean Sea
Black Sea
Red Sea
Gulf of Aden
Gulf of Guinea
Tropic of Cancer
Equator
FRANCE
SPAIN
PORTUGAL
ITALY
GREECE
TURKEY
SYRIA
LEBANON
ISRAEL
JORDAN
CYPRUS
MALTA
SAUDI ARABIA
YEMEN
MOROCCO
ALGERIA
TUNISIA
LIBYA
EGYPT
SUDAN
ERITREA
DJIBOUTI
ETHIOPIA
SOMALIA
KENYA
UGANDA
RWANDA
BURUNDI
TANZANIA
DEM. REP. CONGO
CONGO
GABON
CAMEROON
CENTRAL AFRICAN REPUBLIC
CHAD
NIGER
NIGERIA
BENIN
TOGO
GHANA
BURKINA
MALI
MAURITANIA
WESTERN SAHARA (Occupied by Morocco)
SENEGAL
GAMBIA
GUINEA-BISSAU
GUINEA
SIERRA LEONE
LIBERIA
IVORY COAST (COTE D'IVOIRE)
EQUATORIAL GUINEA
SAO TOME & PRINCIPE
ANGOLA
SEYCHELLES
Sahara
Atlas Mts
Ahaggar
Nubian Desert
Ethiopian Highlands
Horn of Africa
Great Rift Valley
Adamawa Highlands
Sudd
Nile
Blue Nile
White Nile
Niger
Congo
L. Chad
L. Victoria
L. Tanganyika
Lake Volta
Lac Assal
Kilimanjaro 5895m
Suez Canal
Bueiret Nasir
Madeira (to Portugal)
Islas Canarias (to Spain)
ASCENSION (to St Helena)
CABINDA (to Angola)
GIBRALTAR (to UK)
Ceuta (to Spain)
Melilla (to Spain)
Tanger
RABAT
Casablanca
Marrakech
Fez
Oran
ALGIERS
Constantine
TUNIS
Sfax
TRIPOLI
Banghāzī
Sabhā
Alexandria
CAIRO
Aswān
Port Sudan
KHARTOUM
El Obeid
ASMARA
DJIBOUTI
Hargeysa
Dire Dawa
ADDIS ABABA
MOGADISHU
Kismaayo
Mombasa
Zanzibar
Dar es Salaam
DODOMA
NAIROBI
Kisumu
Mbale
KAMPALA
Mwanza
KIGALI
BUJUMBURA
Juba
Kisangani
Mbuji-Mayi
Kananga
KINSHASA
BRAZZAVILLE
Pointe-Noire
LUANDA
LIBREVILLE
Bata
MALABO
SÃO TOMÉ
Príncipe
YAOUNDÉ
Douala
BANGUI
N'DJAMENA
Abéché
Agadez
NIAMEY
Kano
ABUJA
Port Harcourt
Ibadan
Lagos
PORTO-NOVO
LOMÉ
ACCRA
OUAGADOUGOU
Abidjan
YAMOUSSOUKRO
MONROVIA
FREETOWN
CONAKRY
BISSAU
BANJUL
DAKAR
NOUAKCHOTT
Nouâdhibou
Laâyoune
BAMAKO
VICTORIA

ST HELENA (to UK)
C E A N
Namibe
Walvis Bay
WINDHOEK
NAMIBIA
BOTSWANA
Kalahari Desert
GABORONE
Francistown
ZIMBABWE
HARARE
Bulawayo
LUSAKA
Zambezi
Blantyre
Quelimane
Beira
MOZAMBIQUE
Limpopo
PRETORIA
Johannesburg
MAPUTO
MBABANE
SWAZILAND
BLOEMFONTEIN
MASERU
LESOTHO
Orange
SOUTH AFRICA
Drakensberg
Durban
East London
Port Elizabeth
CAPE TOWN
Cape of Good Hope
Mozambique Channel
MADAGASCAR
Mahajanga
ANTANANARIVO
Fianarantsoa
Farafangana
MAURITIUS
PORT LOUIS
RÉUNION (to France)
Tropic of Capricorn
Scale : 1:36 000 000
0 500 1000 km
0 500 1000 miles
POPULATION
over 5 000 000
over 1 000 000
over 500 000
over 100 000
over 50 000
under 50 000
LAND HEIGHT
4000m/13 124ft
3000m/9843ft
2000m/6562ft
1000m/3281ft
200m/656ft
Sea Level
Line of cross-section

AFRICA

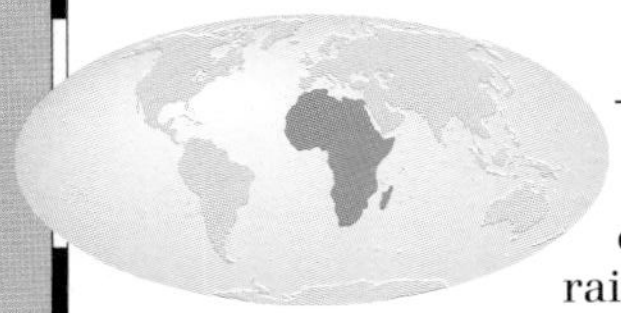

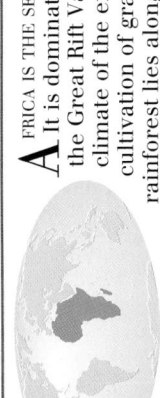

Africa is the second-largest continent after Asia. It is dominated by the Sahara in the north and the Great Rift Valley in the east. The Mediterranean climate of the extreme north and south enables cultivation of grapes and other fruit. A belt of tropical rainforest lies along the Equator, while Africa's great tropical grasslands provide grazing for herds of wild animals and domestic livestock. A narrow strip of Egypt is watered by the world's longest river, the Nile, which has sustained communities from prehistoric times. The center and south of the continent are rich in minerals. Just over one-tenth of the world's population lives in Africa – a wide variety of peoples with their own distinctive languages and cultures. Though Islam and Christianity are widespread, many Africans adhere to their own local customs and religious beliefs.

Continental Facts

Physical Features

- Largest lake: Lake Victoria, Kenya/Tanzania/Uganda 68,880 km² (26,560 mi²)
- Longest river: Nile, Uganda/Sudan/Egypt 6695 km (4160 miles)
- Highest point: Kilimanjaro, Tanzania 5895 m (19,340 ft)
- Lowest point: Lac' Assal, Djibouti 156 m (512 ft) below sea level

Political Features

- Total population: 831.6 million
- Largest city and its population: Cairo, Egypt 15.3 million
- Country with highest population density: Mauritius 645 people/km² (1671 people/mi²)
- Largest country: Sudan 2,505,810 km² (967,493 mi²)
- Smallest country: Seychelles 455 km² (176 mi²)

Cross-section through Africa 7°N, 15°W–55°E

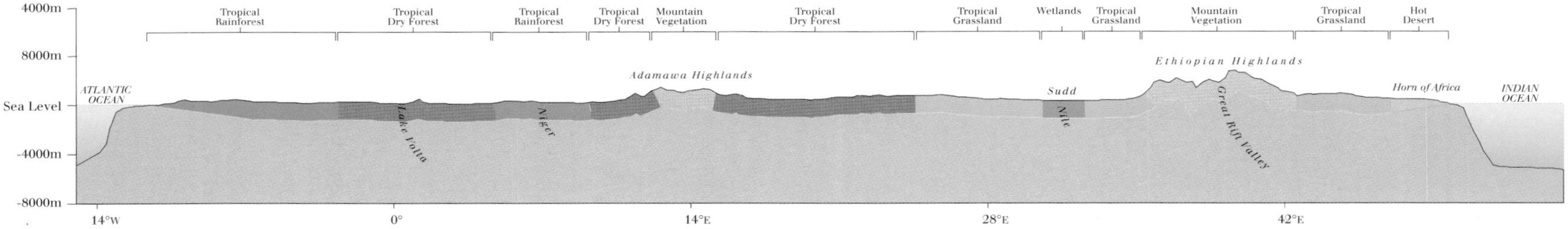
4000m
8000m
Sea Level
-4000m
-8000m
Tropical Rainforest
Tropical Dry Forest
Tropical Rainforest
Tropical Dry Forest
Mountain Vegetation
Tropical Dry Forest
Tropical Grassland
Wetlands
Tropical Grassland
Mountain Vegetation
Tropical Grassland
Hot Desert
ATLANTIC OCEAN
Lake Volta
Niger
Adamawa Highlands
Sudd
Nile
Ethiopian Highlands
Great Rift Valley
Horn of Africa
INDIAN OCEAN
14°W
0°
14°E
28°E
42°E

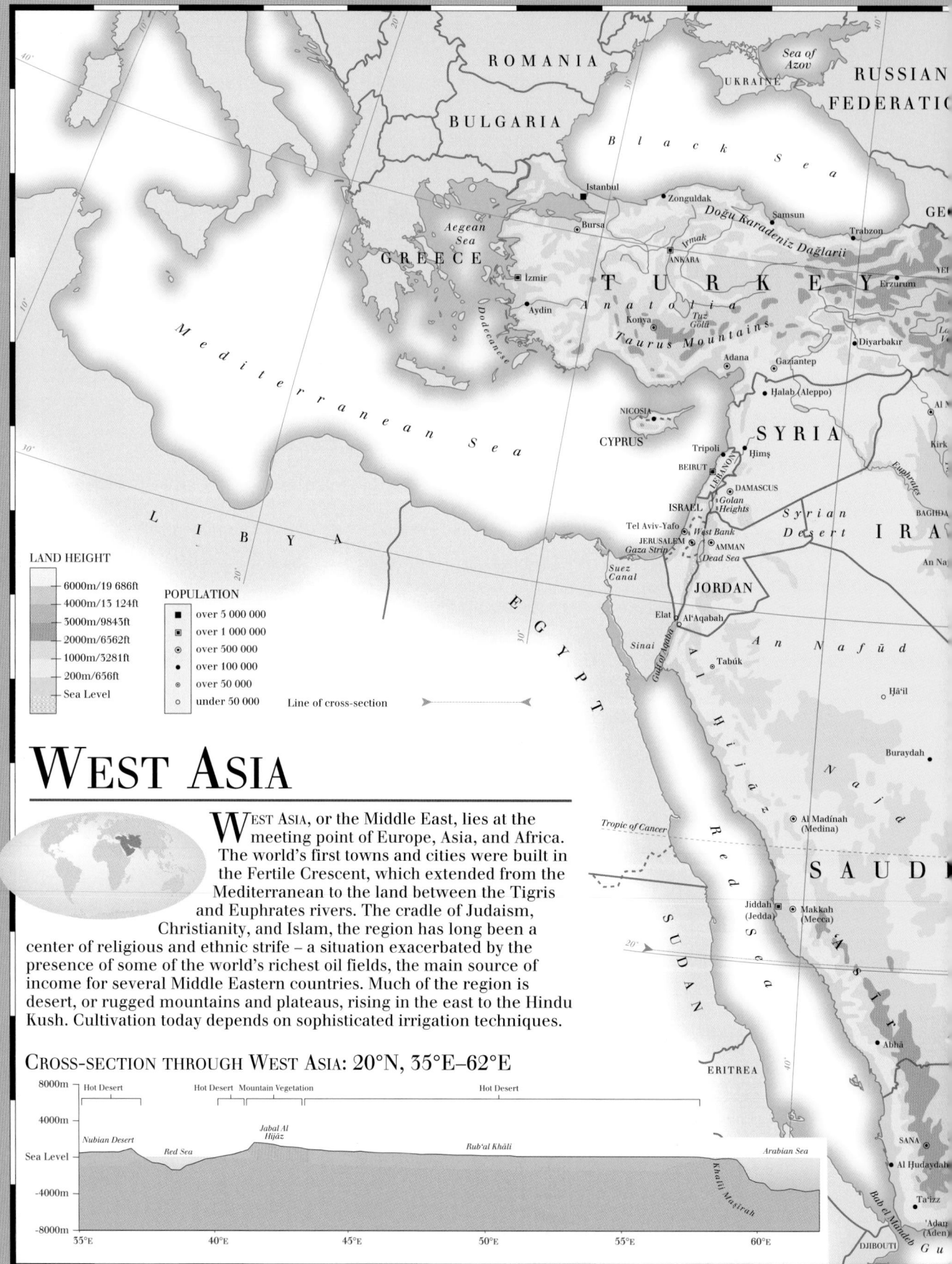

ROMANIA
BULGARIA
GREECE
TURKEY
UKRAINE
RUSSIAN FEDERATIO
Sea of Azov
Black Sea
Istanbul
Zonguldak
Samsun
Trabzon
Doğu Karadeniz Dağlarii
Bursa
Irmak
ANKARA
Izmir
Aydin
Erzurum
Aegean Sea
Dodecanese
Anatolia
Konya
Tuz Gölü
Taurus Mountains
Diyarbakır
Adana
Gaziantep
Halab (Aleppo)
Mediterranean Sea
NICOSIA
CYPRUS
SYRIA
Tripoli
Hims
BEIRUT
LEBANON
DAMASCUS
ISRAEL
Golan Heights
Syrian Desert
Tel Aviv-Yafo
West Bank
JERUSALEM
AMMAN
Gaza Strip
Dead Sea
LIBYA
Suez Canal
JORDAN
EGYPT
Elat
Al'Aqabah
Sinai
Gulf of Aqaba
An Nafūd
Tabūk
Ḩā'il
Buraydah
Al Ḩijāz
Najd
Euphrates
BAGHDA
IRA
Kirk
An Na
LAND HEIGHT
6000m/19 686ft
4000m/13 124ft
3000m/9843ft
2000m/6562ft
1000m/3281ft
200m/656ft
Sea Level
POPULATION
over 5 000 000
over 1 000 000
over 500 000
over 100 000
over 50 000
under 50 000
Line of cross-section

West Asia

West Asia, or the Middle East, lies at the meeting point of Europe, Asia, and Africa. The world's first towns and cities were built in the Fertile Crescent, which extended from the Mediterranean to the land between the Tigris and Euphrates rivers. The cradle of Judaism, Christianity, and Islam, the region has long been a center of religious and ethnic strife – a situation exacerbated by the presence of some of the world's richest oil fields, the main source of income for several Middle Eastern countries. Much of the region is desert, or rugged mountains and plateaus, rising in the east to the Hindu Kush. Cultivation today depends on sophisticated irrigation techniques.

Tropic of Cancer
Al Madīnah (Medina)
SAUDI
Red Sea
Jiddah (Jedda)
Makkah (Mecca)
SUDAN
'Asīr
Abhā
ERITREA
SANA
Al Hudaydah
Ta'izz
'Adan (Aden)
Bab el Mandeb
DJIBOUTI

Cross-section through West Asia: 20°N, 35°E–62°E

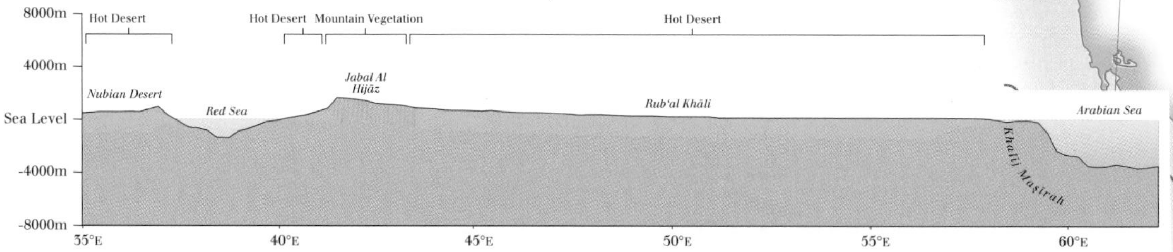
8000m
4000m
Sea Level
-4000m
-8000m
Hot Desert
Hot Desert
Mountain Vegetation
Hot Desert
Nubian Desert
Red Sea
Jabal Al Hijāz
Rub'al Khāli
Arabian Sea
Khalīj Maşīrah
35°E
40°E
45°E
50°E
55°E
60°E

KAZAKHSTAN
Aral Sea
UZBEKISTAN
Qizilqum
KYRGYZSTAN
BISHKEK
Karakol
Ozero Issyk-Kul'
Kirghiz Range
Naryn
Tien Shan
TASHKENT
Namangan
Osh
Aydarko'l Ko'li
Daşoguz
Urganch
Khŭjand
CHINA
Caspian Sea
AZERBAIJAN
BAKU
Garagum
Samarqand
TAJIKISTAN
DUSHANBE
Pamirs
Türkmenbaçy
Balkanabat
Qarshi
Türkmenabat
TURKMENISTAN
Amyderya
Kŭlob
Khorugh
Länkäran
Köpetdag Gershi
AŞGABAT
Kurgan-Tyube
K2 8611m
Karakoram Range
Indus
Mary
Mazār-e-Sharīf
Rasht
Gorgān
Baghlān
Hindu Kush
Reshteh-ye Kuhhā-ye Alborz
Mashhad
TEHRĀN
Jalālābād
Peshāwar
ISLĀMĀBĀD
KĀBUL
Rāwalpindi
Hamadān
Qom
Herāt
Dasht-e-Kavīr
AFGHANISTAN
Gujrānwāla
Bākhtarān
Lahore
IRAN
Chenāb
Faisalābād
Eşfahān
Iranian Plateau
Kandahār
Hāmūn-e Şāberī
Helmand
Multān
Ahvāz
Quetta
Zagros Mountains
Ābādān
Kermān
Zāhedān
Thar Desert
Shīrāz
KUWAIT CITY
Sukkur
PAKISTAN
INDIA
The Gulf
Bandar-e 'Abbās
BAHRAIN
Strait of Hormuz
Hyderābād
MANAMA
Karāchi
Tropic of Cancer
DOHA
Sharjah
Al Hufūf
QATAR
Dubai
Gulf of Oman
ABU DHABI
Şuḩār
Arabian Sea
Harad
MUSCAT
UNITED ARAB EMIRATES
Ar Rustāq
ARABIA
Nizwa
Şūr
Scale : 1:17 000 000
0 200 400 km
0 200 400 miles
Khalīj Maşīrah
OMAN
INDIAN OCEAN
Şalālah
YEMEN
Hadhramaut
Al Mukallā
Socotra (to Yemen)
Aden

Continental Facts

Physical Features

Largest lake: Caspian Sea 371,000 km² (143,205 mi²)

Longest river: Euphrates, Turkey/Syria/Iraq 2815 km (1750 miles)

Highest point: K2, Kashmir, India/Pakistan 8611m (28,251 ft)

Lowest point: Dead Sea, Israel/Jordan 392 m (1286 ft) below sea level

Political Features

Total population: 473.4 million

Largest city and its population: Karachi, Pakistan 12.6 million

Country with highest population density: Bahrain 939 people/km² (2429 people/mi²)

Largest country: Saudi Arabia 1,960,582 km² (756,981 mi²)

Smallest country: Bahrain 620 km² (239 mi²)

UKRAINE
EUROPEAN RUSSIA
Karskoye More
Ostrov Komsomolets
Ostrov Oktyabr'skoy Revolyutsii
Ostrov Bol'shevik
Severnaya Zemlya
Poluostrov Taymyr
Ozero Taymyr
Severo-Sibirskaya Nizmennost
Poluostrov Yamal
Gydanskiy Poluostrov
Salekhard
Nadym
Noril'sk
Ob'
Arctic Circle
Ural Mountains
Serov
Ural'sk
Ural
Yekaterinburg
Chelyabinsk
Tyumen'
Khanty-Mansiysk
Zapadno-Sibirskaya Ravnina
Nizhnevartovsk
RUSSIA
ASIATIC RUSSIA
Yenisey
Nizhnyaya Tunguska
Podkamennaya Tunguska
Sredne-Sibirskoye Ploskogorye
Atyrau
Aktobe
Aktau
Caspian Sea
Kostanay
Irtysh
Ishim
KAZAKHSTAN
Ustyurt Plateau
Omsk
Aral Sea
Aral'sk
Syr Darya
ASTANA
Tomsk
Novosibirsk
Zhezkazgan
Karaganda
Barnaul
Krasnoyarsk
Bratsk
Lena
TURKMENISTAN
UZBEKISTAN
Kyzylorda
Rubtsovsk
Semipalatinsk
Abakan
Ozero Balkhash
Ozero Baykal
Shymkent
Taraz
Ili
Ozero Zaysan
Uvs Nuur
Kyzyl
Irkutsk
Ulan-Ude
Chita
Yablonovyy
Taldykorgan
Almaty
Ölgiy
Hovd
Hyargas Nuur
Hövsgöl Nuur
AFGHANISTAN
TAJIKISTAN
KYRGYZSTAN
Yining
Altai Mountains
Erdenet
Darhan
ULAN BATOR
Choybalsan
Kerulen
Kashi
Tien Shan
Ürümqi
Altay
MONGOLIA
Tarim He
Turpan Hami
Hami
Bayanhongor
PAKISTAN
Hotan
Taklimakan Shamo
Saynshand
Gobi
Aksai Chin
Kunlun Shan
Altun Shan
Yumen
Qaidam Pendi
Qilian Shan
Baotou
Datong
BEIJING (PEKING)
Tianjin
Huang He
Qingzang Gaoyuan (Plateau of Tibet)
Golmud
Qinghai Hu
Xining
INDIA
Himalayas
TIBET
Lanzhou
Taiyuan
Shijiazhuang
CHINA
Xi'an
Huang He (Yellow R.)
Zhengzhou
NEPAL
Brahmaputra
Xixabangma Feng 8012m
Lhasa
Salween
Mekong
Tropic of Cancer
BHUTAN
Chengdu
Chang Jiang (Yangtze)
Chongqing
Wuhan
Dongting Hu
Changsha
Guiyang
Kunming
Xi Jiang
BURMA (MYANMAR)
LAOS
VIETNAM
Nanning
Guangzhou
Shantou
Hong Kong (Xianggang)
Macao (Aomen)
Gulf of Tongking
Haikou
Hainan Dao
South China Sea

Continental Facts

Physical Features

Largest lake: Aral Sea, Kazakhstan/Uzbekistan 66,500 km² (25,700 mi²)

Longest river: Chang Jiang (Yangtze), China 6380 km (3964 miles)

Highest point: Xixabangma Feng, China 8012 m (26,286 ft)

Lowest point: Turpan Hami (Turfan Basin), China 154 m (505 ft) below sea level

Political Features

Total population: 1562 million

Largest city and its population: Tokyo, Japan 35.1 million

Country with highest population density: Taiwan 699 people/km² (1810 people/mi²)

Largest country: Asiatic Russia 13,119,382 km² (5,065,394 mi²)

Smallest country: Taiwan 35,980 km² (13,892 mi²)

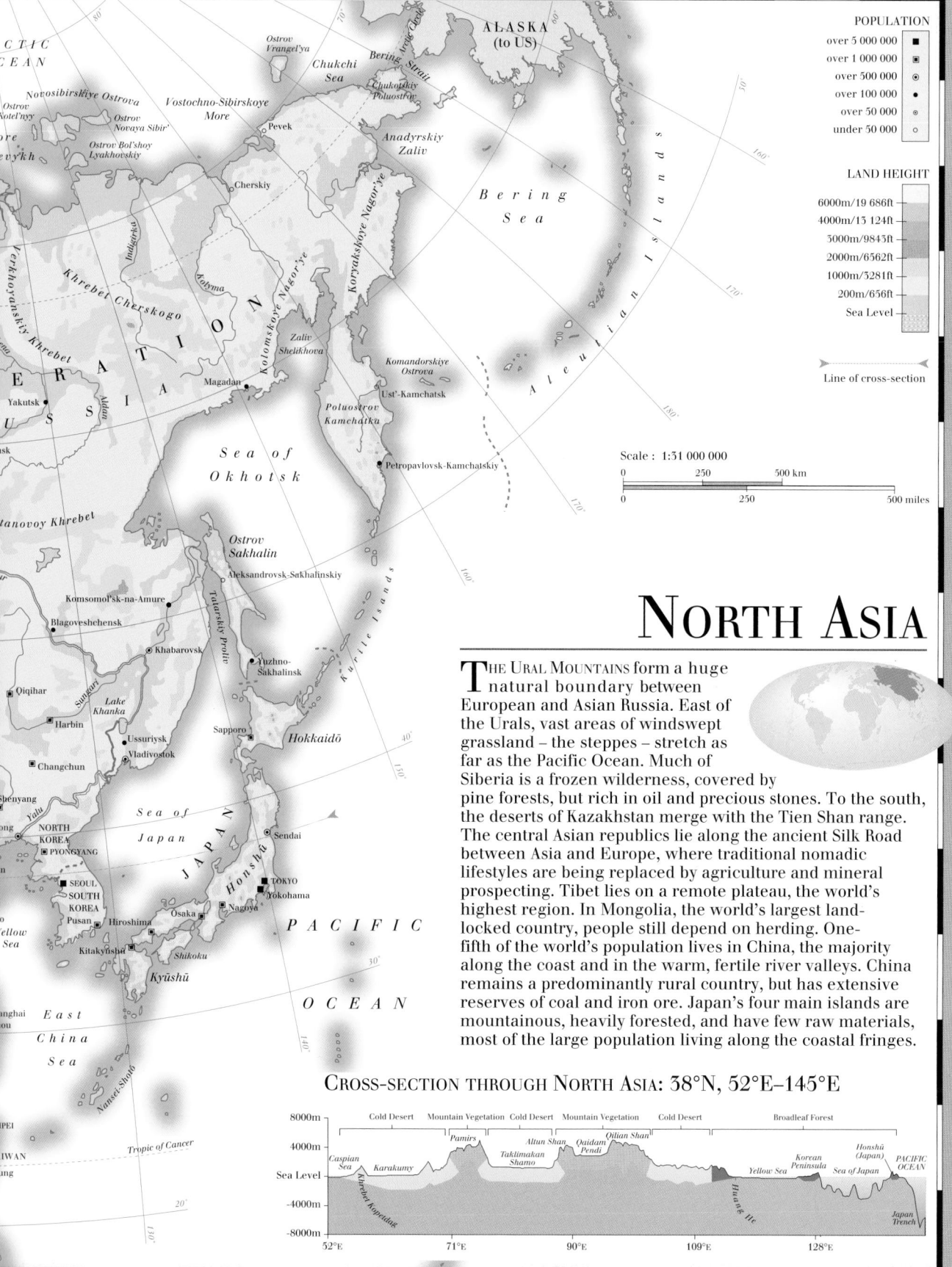

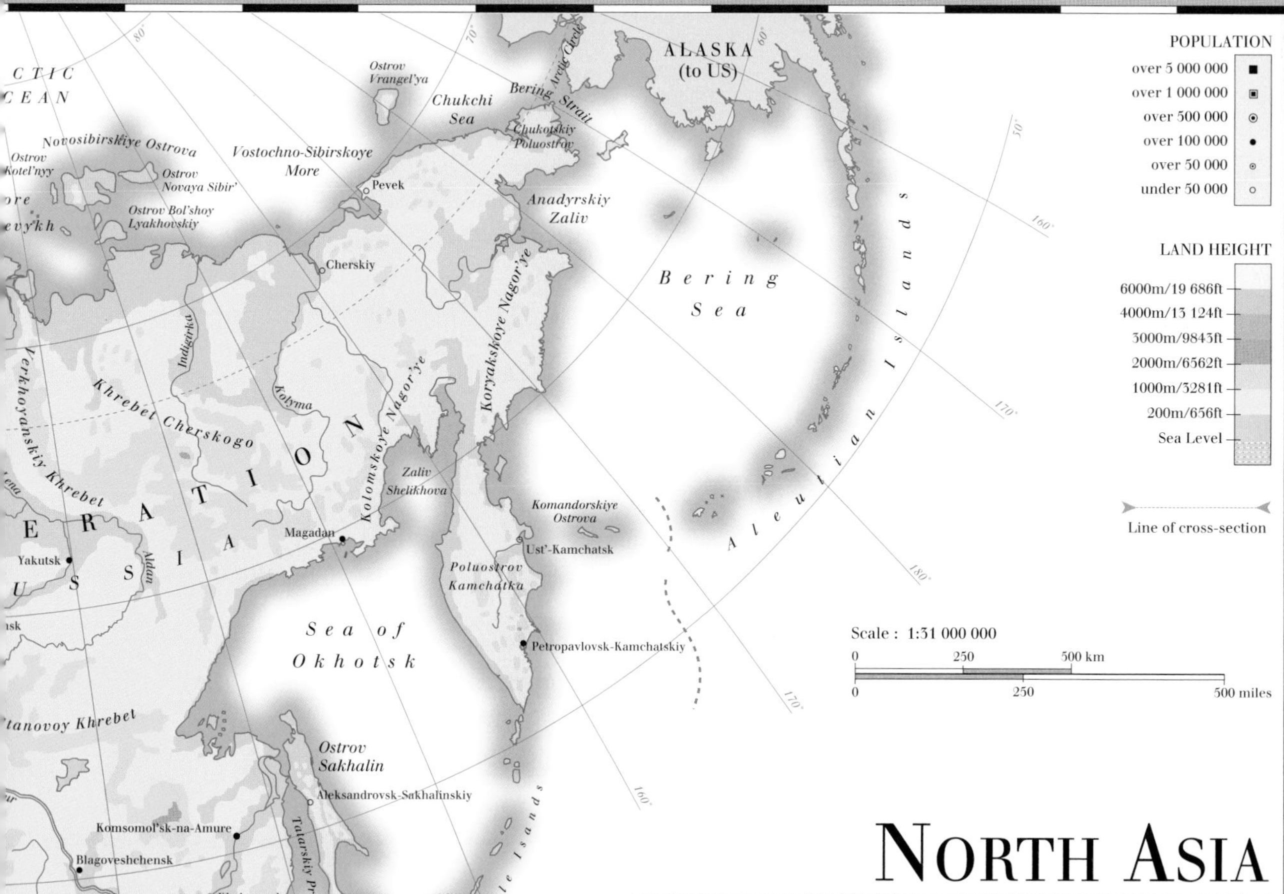

POPULATION
over 5 000 000
over 1 000 000
over 500 000
over 100 000
over 50 000
under 50 000
LAND HEIGHT
6000m/19 686ft
4000m/13 124ft
3000m/9843ft
2000m/6562ft
1000m/3281ft
200m/656ft
Sea Level
Line of cross-section
Scale : 1:31 000 000
0
250
500 km
0
250
500 miles
ALASKA (to US)
Ostrov Vrangel'ya
Chukchi Sea
Bering Strait
Arctic Circle
Chukotskiy Poluostrov
Novosibirskiye Ostrova
Ostrov Kotel'nyy
Ostrov Novaya Sibir'
Ostrov Bol'shoy Lyakhovskiy
Vostochno-Sibirskoye More
Pevek
Anadyrskiy Zaliv
Cherskiy
Bering Sea
Aleutian Islands
Koryakskoye Nagor'ye
Kolomskoye Nagor'ye
Indigirka
Kolyma
Khrebet Cherskogo
Verkhoyanskiy Khrebet
RUSSIAN FEDERATION
Zaliv Shelikhova
Komandorskiye Ostrova
Ust'-Kamchatsk
Magadan
Yakutsk
Aldan
Poluostrov Kamchatka
Sea of Okhotsk
Petropavlovsk-Kamchatskiy
Stanovoy Khrebet
Ostrov Sakhalin
Aleksandrovsk-Sakhalinskiy
Komsomol'sk-na-Amure
Blagoveshchensk
Tatarskiy Proliv
Khabarovsk
Yuzhno-Sakhalinsk
Kurile Islands
Qiqihar
Sungari
Lake Khanka
Harbin
Ussuriysk
Vladivostok
Sapporo
Hokkaidō
Changchun
Shenyang
Yalu
NORTH KOREA
PYONGYANG
Sea of Japan
JAPAN
Sendai
Honshū
SEOUL
SOUTH KOREA
TOKYO
Yokohama
Nagoya
Pusan
Hiroshima
Ōsaka
Kitakyūshū
Shikoku
Kyūshū
PACIFIC OCEAN
Yellow Sea
East China Sea
Nansei-shotō
Tropic of Cancer

NORTH ASIA

THE URAL MOUNTAINS form a huge natural boundary between European and Asian Russia. East of the Urals, vast areas of windswept grassland – the steppes – stretch as far as the Pacific Ocean. Much of Siberia is a frozen wilderness, covered by pine forests, but rich in oil and precious stones. To the south, the deserts of Kazakhstan merge with the Tien Shan range. The central Asian republics lie along the ancient Silk Road between Asia and Europe, where traditional nomadic lifestyles are being replaced by agriculture and mineral prospecting. Tibet lies on a remote plateau, the world's highest region. In Mongolia, the world's largest land-locked country, people still depend on herding. One-fifth of the world's population lives in China, the majority along the coast and in the warm, fertile river valleys. China remains a predominantly rural country, but has extensive reserves of coal and iron ore. Japan's four main islands are mountainous, heavily forested, and have few raw materials, most of the large population living along the coastal fringes.

CROSS-SECTION THROUGH NORTH ASIA: 38°N, 52°E–145°E

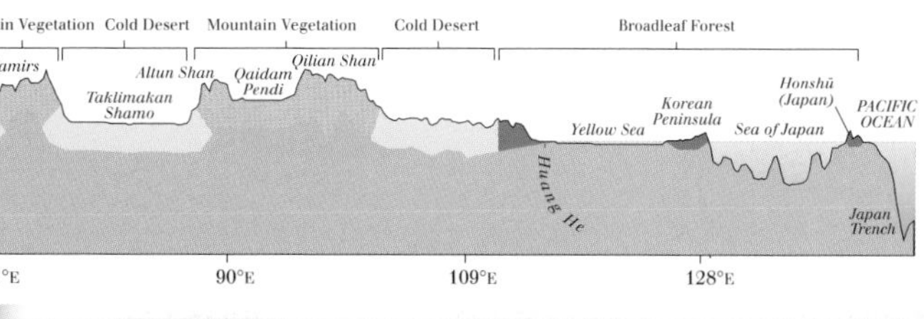
8000m
4000m
Sea Level
-4000m
-8000m
Cold Desert
Mountain Vegetation
Cold Desert
Mountain Vegetation
Cold Desert
Broadleaf Forest
Caspian Sea
Karakumy
Khrebet Kopetdag
Pamirs
Taklimakan Shamo
Altun Shan
Qaidam Pendi
Qilian Shan
Huang He
Yellow Sea
Korean Peninsula
Sea of Japan
Honshū (Japan)
PACIFIC OCEAN
Japan Trench
52°E
71°E
90°E
109°E
128°E

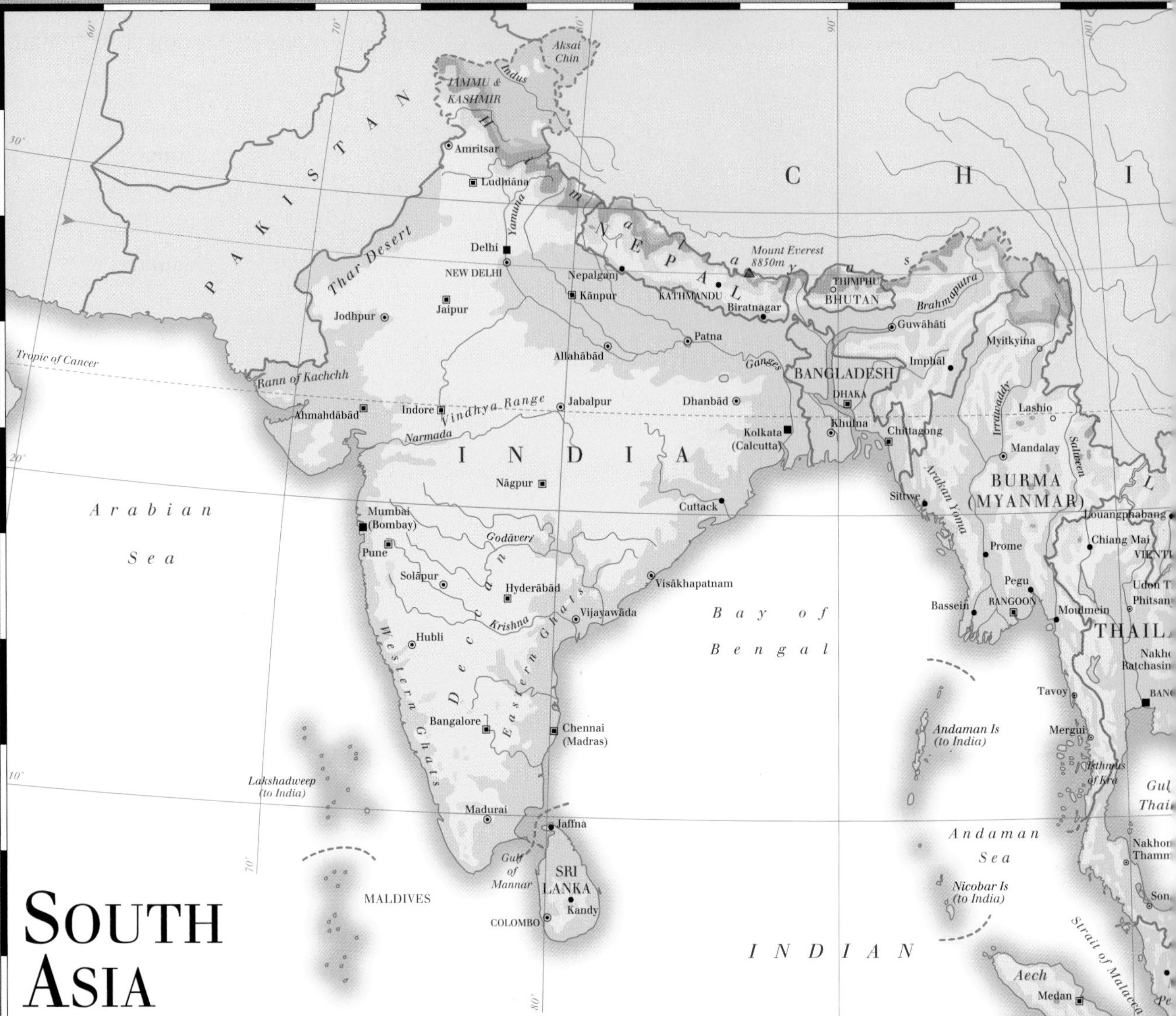
Aksai Chin
JAMMU & KASHMIR
Indus
P A K I S T A N
Amritsar
Ludhiāna
Thar Desert
Yamuna
Delhi
NEW DELHI
Jodhpur
Jaipur
Tropic of Cancer
Rann of Kachchh
Ahmadābād
Indore
Vindhya Range
Narmada
Jabalpur
Allahābād
Kānpur
Nepalganj
N E P A L
KATHMANDU
Biratnagar
Mount Everest 8850m
THIMPHU
BHUTAN
Brahmaputra
Guwāhāti
Patna
Ganges
BANGLADESH
DHAKA
Khulna
Dhanbād
Kolkata (Calcutta)
Chittagong
Imphāl
Myitkyina
Lashio
Irrawaddy
Mandalay
Salween
BURMA (MYANMAR)
Sittwe
Arakan Yoma
C H I
I N D I A
Nāgpur
Cuttack
Arabian Sea
Mumbai (Bombay)
Pune
Godāveri
Solāpur
Hyderābād
Deccan
Krishna
Vijayawāda
Visākhapatnam
Eastern Ghats
Western Ghats
Hubli
Bangalore
Chennai (Madras)
Bay of Bengal
Lakshadweep (to India)
Madurai
Jaffna
Gulf of Mannar
SRI LANKA
Kandy
COLOMBO
MALDIVES
Andaman Is (to India)
Andaman Sea
Nicobar Is (to India)
I N D I A N O C E A N
Equator
Prome
Pegu
RANGOON
Bassein
Moulmein
Tavoy
Mergui
Isthmus of Kra
Louangphabang
Chiang Mai
VIENTI
Udon T
Phitsan
THAIL
Nakho Ratchasin
BANG
Gul Thai
Nakhon Thamm
Son
Strait of Malacca
Aech
Medan
Pematangsiantar
Danau Toba
KUAL LUMPU
Pekanbaru
Sum
Pa

SOUTH ASIA

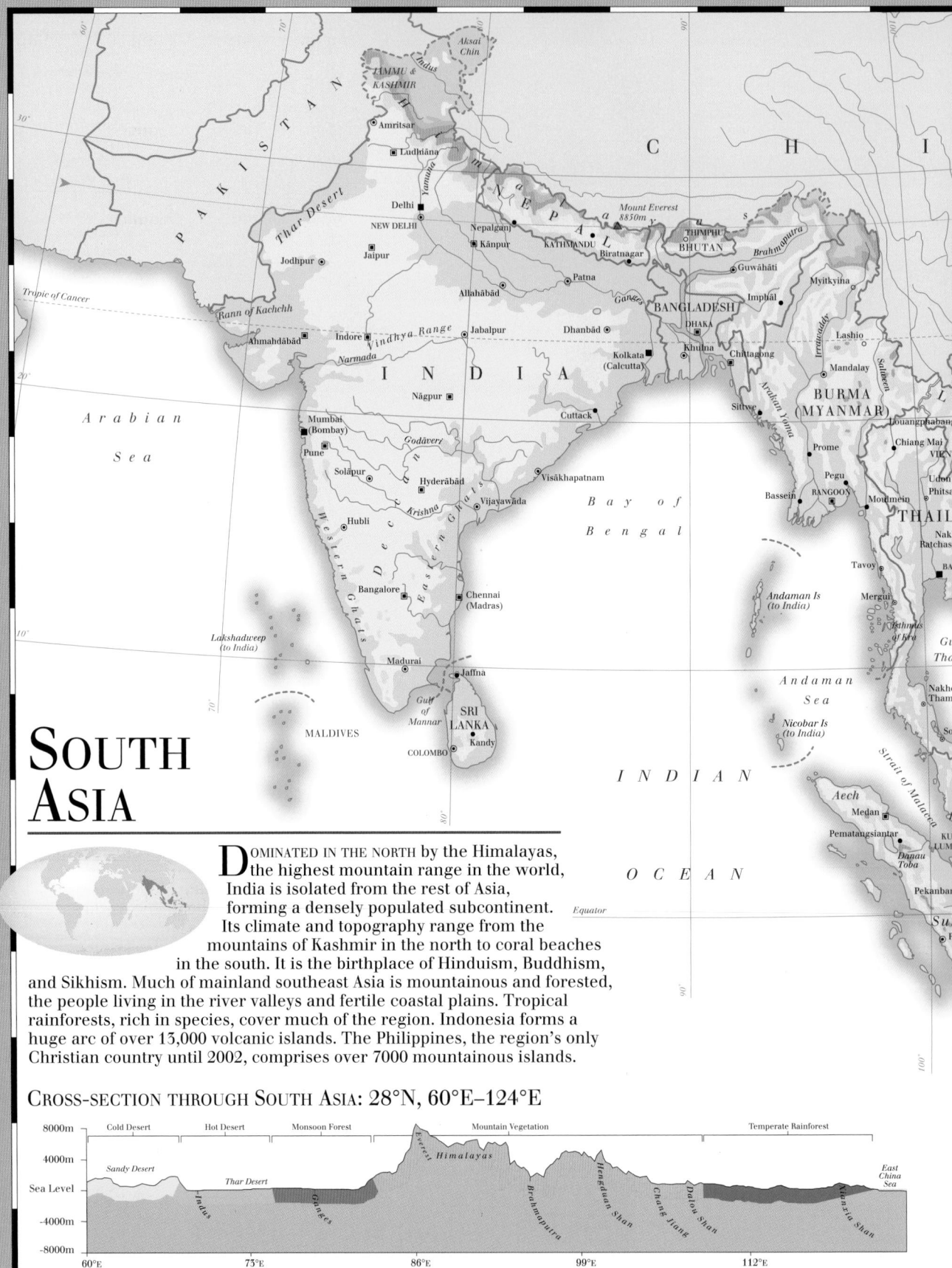

DOMINATED IN THE NORTH by the Himalayas, the highest mountain range in the world, India is isolated from the rest of Asia, forming a densely populated subcontinent. Its climate and topography range from the mountains of Kashmir in the north to coral beaches in the south. It is the birthplace of Hinduism, Buddhism, and Sikhism. Much of mainland southeast Asia is mountainous and forested, the people living in the river valleys and fertile coastal plains. Tropical rainforests, rich in species, cover much of the region. Indonesia forms a huge arc of over 13,000 volcanic islands. The Philippines, the region's only Christian country until 2002, comprises over 7000 mountainous islands.

CROSS-SECTION THROUGH SOUTH ASIA: 28°N, 60°E–124°E

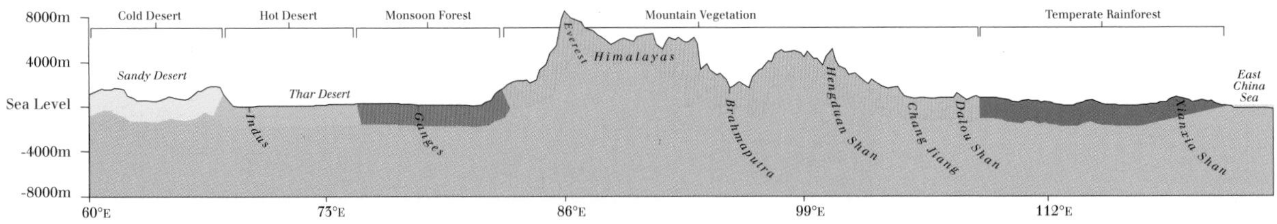
8000m
4000m
Sea Level
-4000m
-8000m
Cold Desert
Hot Desert
Monsoon Forest
Mountain Vegetation
Temperate Rainforest
Sandy Desert
Thar Desert
Indus
Ganges
Everest
Himalayas
Brahmaputra
Hengduan Shan
Chang Jiang
Dalou Shan
Nianxia Shan
East China Sea
60°E
73°E
86°E
99°E
112°E

CONTINENTAL FACTS

PHYSICAL FEATURES

LARGEST LAKE: Tônlé Sap, Cambodia 2850 km² (1000 mi²)

LONGEST RIVER: Mekong, China/Burma/Laos/Thailand/Cambodia/Vietnam 4425 km (2750 miles)

HIGHEST POINT: Mount Everest, Nepal 8850 m (29,035 ft)

LOWEST POINT: About half of Bangladesh lies between sea level and 8 m (25 ft)

POLITICAL FEATURES

TOTAL POPULATION: 1768 million

LARGEST CITY AND ITS POPULATION: Mumbai, India 18.4 million

COUNTRY WITH HIGHEST POPULATION DENSITY: Singapore 6885 people/km² (17,797 people/mi²)

LARGEST COUNTRY: India 3,287,590 km² (1,269,338 mi²)

SMALLEST COUNTRY: Maldives 300 km² (116 mi²)

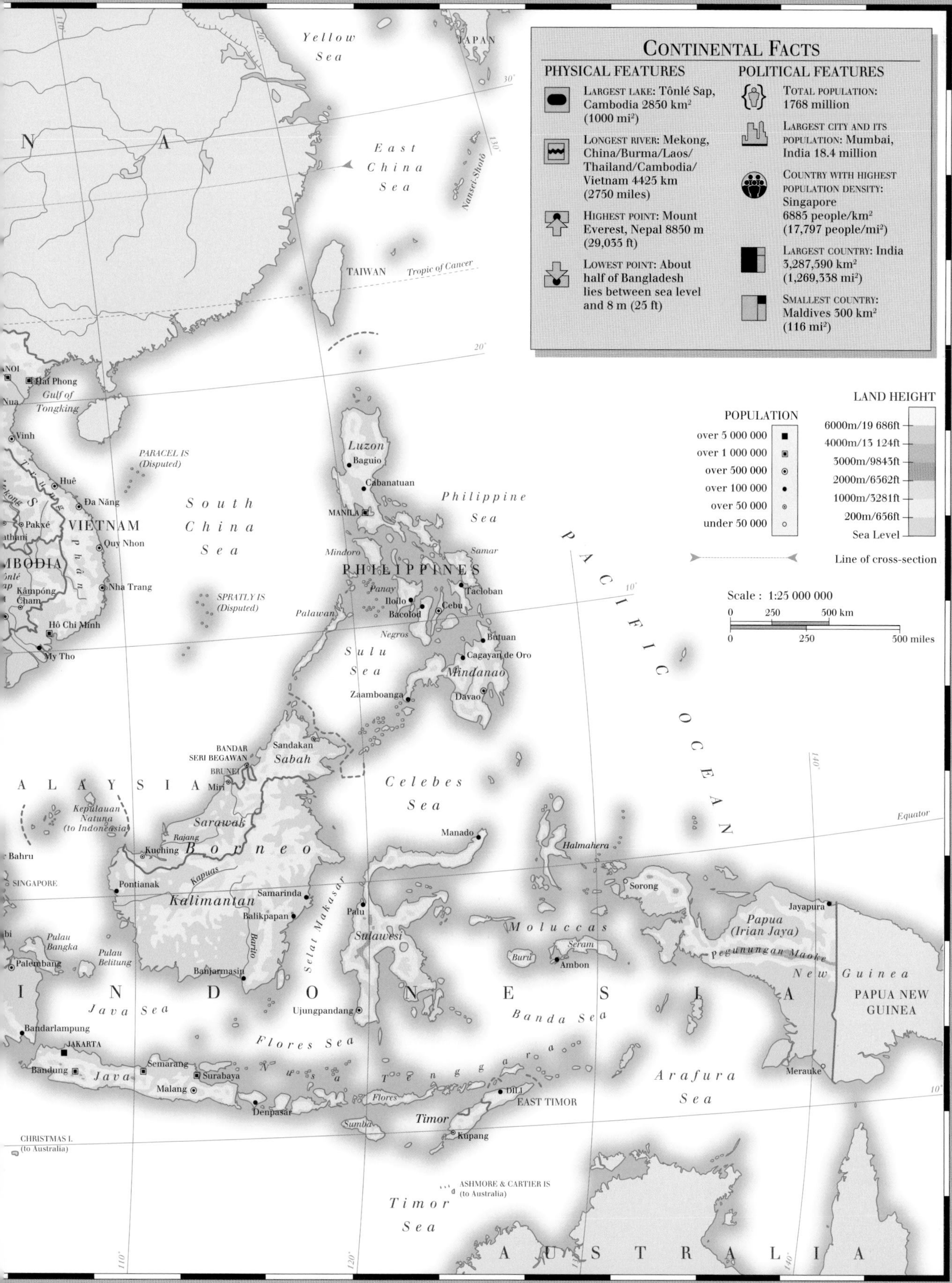
POPULATION
over 5 000 000
over 1 000 000
over 500 000
over 100 000
over 50 000
under 50 000
LAND HEIGHT
6000m/19 686ft
4000m/13 124ft
3000m/9843ft
2000m/6562ft
1000m/3281ft
200m/656ft
Sea Level
Line of cross-section
Scale : 1:25 000 000
0 250 500 km
0 250 500 miles
Yellow Sea
JAPAN
East China Sea
Nansei-Shotō
TAIWAN
Tropic of Cancer
Hai Phong
Gulf of Tongking
Vinh
PARACEL IS (Disputed)
Huê
Đa Năng
Pakxé
VIETNAM
Quy Nhon
Nha Trang
Kâmpóng Cham
Hô Chi Minh
My Tho
South China Sea
SPRATLY IS (Disputed)
Luzon
Baguio
Cabanatuan
MANILA
Philippine Sea
Mindoro
Samar
PHILIPPINES
Panay
Iloilo
Bacolod
Cebu
Tacloban
Palawan
Negros
Butuan
Sulu Sea
Cagayan de Oro
Mindanao
Zaamboanga
Davao
PACIFIC OCEAN
BANDAR SERI BEGAWAN
BRUNEI
Sandakan
Sabah
Miri
Celebes Sea
Kepulauan Natuna (to Indonesia)
Sarawak
Rajang
Kuching
Borneo
Manado
Halmahera
Equator
SINGAPORE
Pontianak
Kapuas
Kalimantan
Samarinda
Balikpapan
Selat Makasar
Palu
Sorong
Jayapura
Papua (Irian Jaya)
Pulau Bangka
Pulau Belitung
Barito
Sulawesi
Moluccas
Buru
Seram
Ambon
Pegunungan Maoke
Palembang
Banjarmasin
New Guinea
PAPUA NEW GUINEA
INDONESIA
Java Sea
Ujungpandang
Banda Sea
Bandarlampung
JAKARTA
Flores Sea
Semarang
Surabaya
Bandung
Java
Malang
Nusa Tenggara
Merauke
Arafura Sea
DILI
EAST TIMOR
Flores
Denpasar
Sumba
Timor
Kupang
CHRISTMAS I. (to Australia)
ASHMORE & CARTIER IS (to Australia)
Timor Sea
AUSTRALIA

Tropic of Cancer
TAIWAN
South China Sea
Philippine Sea
PHILIPPINES
Sulu Sea
MALAYSIA
BRUNEI
Celebes Sea
NORTHERN MARIANA ISLANDS (to US)
Saipan
GUAM (to US)
WAKE I. (to US)
PACIFIC
MARSHALL ISLANDS
Ratak Chain
Ralik Chain
Majuro
MICRONESIA
Pohnpei
PALIKIR
Kosrae
Chuuk Is
Yap
KOROR
Babeldaob
PALAU
BAIRIKI
Tarawa
NAURU
KIRIBATI
Equator
INDONESIA
Bismarck Archipelago
Bismarck Sea
Rabaul
New Britain
Bougainville
Mt Wilhelm 4509m
PAPUA NEW GUINEA
New Guinea
Solomon Sea
SOLOMON ISLANDS
Santa Isabel
Malaita
Guadalcanal
HONIARA
San Cristobal
Rennell
Santa Cruz Is
PORT MORESBY
Banda Sea
Arafura Sea
Torres Strait
EAST TIMOR
Timor Sea
ASHMORE & CARTIER ISLANDS (to Australia)
Darwin
Gulf of Carpentaria
Cairns
Coral Sea
CORAL SEA ISLANDS (to Australia)
Great Barrier Reef
Espiritu Santo
Malekula
PORT-VILA
Efate
VANUATU
NEW CALEDONIA (to France)
Iles Loyauté
New Caledonia
NOUMÉA
INDIAN OCEAN
Townsville
MacKay
Rockhampton
Broome
Great Sandy Desert
NORTHERN TERRITORY
QUEENSLAND
AUSTRALIA
Alice Springs
Simpson Desert
Gibson Desert
Musgrave Ranges
Lake Eyre
Great Dividing Range
Brisbane
Gold Coast
Toowoomba
NORFOLK ISLAND (to Australia)
Lord Howe I. (to Australia)
Ball's Pyramid (to Australia)
WESTERN AUSTRALIA
Great Victoria Desert
SOUTH AUSTRALIA
Lake Torrens
Grey Range
Darling
NEW SOUTH WALES
Newcastle
Sydney
Wollongong
CANBERRA
Murray
Tropic of Capricorn
Geraldton
Kalgoorlie
Great Australian Bight
Port Lincoln
Adelaide
VICTORIA
Bendigo
Melbourne
Geelong
AUSTRALIAN CAPITAL TERRITORY
Perth
Esperance
Bunbury
Albany
Bass Strait
Launceston
TASMANIA
Hobart
Tasman Sea
North Island
Auckland
Hamilton
NEW ZEALAND
WELLINGTON
South Island
Christchurch
Dunedin
Bounty Islands (to NZ)
Antipodes Islands (to NZ)
Auckland Islands (to NZ)
LAND HEIGHT
3000m/9843ft
2000m/6562ft
1000m/3281ft
200m/656ft
Sea Level
POPULATION
over 5 000 000
over 1 000 000
over 500 000
over 100 000
over 50 000
under 50 000
Scale : 1:40 000 000
0
500
1000 km
0
500
1000 miles

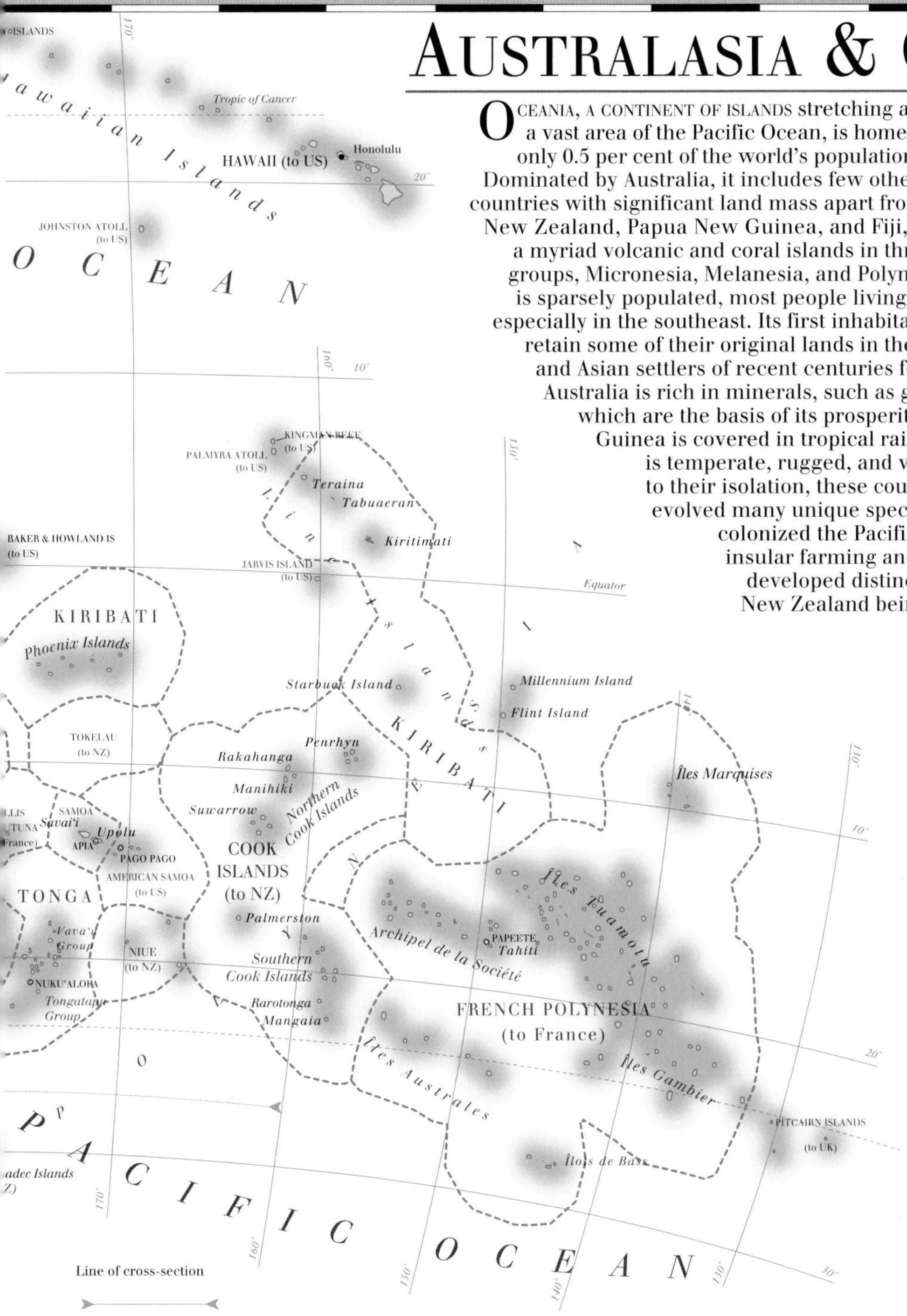
ISLANDS
Hawaiian Islands
Tropic of Cancer
HAWAII (to US)
Honolulu
JOHNSTON ATOLL (to US)
OCEAN
KINGMAN REEF (to US)
PALMYRA ATOLL (to US)
Line Islands
Teraina
Tabuaeran
Kiritimati
BAKER & HOWLAND IS (to US)
JARVIS ISLAND (to US)
Equator
KIRIBATI
Phoenix Islands
Starbuck Island
Millennium Island
Flint Island
TOKELAU (to NZ)
Rakahanga
Penrhyn
Manihiki
Northern Cook Islands
Suwarrow
SAMOA
Savai'i
Upolu
APIA
PAGO PAGO
AMERICAN SAMOA (to US)
COOK ISLANDS (to NZ)
Îles Marquises
TONGA
Vava'u Group
NIUE (to NZ)
Palmerston
Southern Cook Islands
NUKU'ALOFA
Tongatapu Group
Rarotonga
Mangaia
Archipel de la Société
PAPEETE
Tahiti
Îles Tuamotu
FRENCH POLYNESIA (to France)
Îles Australes
Îles Gambier
PITCAIRN ISLANDS (to UK)
Îlots de Bass
adec Islands
PACIFIC OCEAN
Line of cross-section

Australasia & Oceania

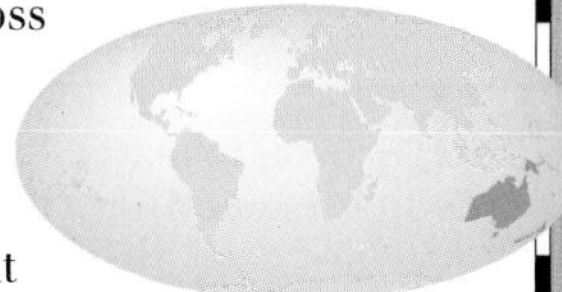

Oceania, a continent of islands stretching across a vast area of the Pacific Ocean, is home to only 0.5 per cent of the world's population. Dominated by Australia, it includes few other countries with significant land mass apart from New Zealand, Papua New Guinea, and Fiji, but a myriad volcanic and coral islands in three main groups, Micronesia, Melanesia, and Polynesia. Australia, flat and dry, is sparsely populated, most people living along the coastal lowlands, especially in the southeast. Its first inhabitants, the Aboriginal peoples, retain some of their original lands in the interior, but the European and Asian settlers of recent centuries form most of the population. Australia is rich in minerals, such as gold, uranium, and iron ore, which are the basis of its prosperity. Mountainous Papua New Guinea is covered in tropical rainforest, while New Zealand is temperate, rugged, and volcanic in the north. Owing to their isolation, these countries' flora and fauna have evolved many unique species. The peoples of Oceania colonized the Pacific by 1100 CE, and the many insular farming and fishing communities have developed distinctive cultures, the Maoris of New Zealand being among the most notable.

Continental Facts

Physical Features

Largest lake: Lake Eyre, Australia 9583 km^2 (3700 mi^2)

Longest river: Murray-Darling, Australia 3750 km (2330 miles)

Highest point: Mt. Wilhelm, Papua New Guinea 4509 m (14,794 ft)

Lowest point: Lake Eyre, Australia 16 m (52 ft) below sea level

Political Features

Total population: 30.6 million

Largest city and its population: Sydney, Australia 4.2 million

Country with highest population density: Nauru 587 people/km^2 (1522 people/mi^2)

Largest country: Australia 7,686,850 km^2 (2,967,893 mi^2)

Smallest country: Nauru 21 km^2 (8.1 mi^2)

Cross-section through Australia: 27°S, 112°E–160°W

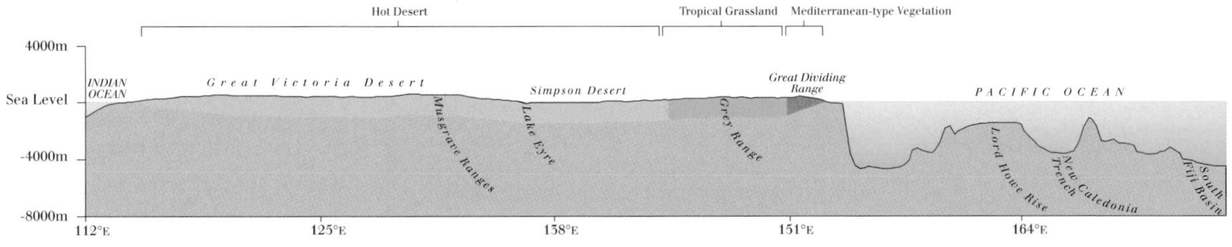
Hot Desert
Tropical Grassland
Mediterranean-type Vegetation
4000m
Sea Level
-4000m
-8000m
INDIAN OCEAN
Great Victoria Desert
Simpson Desert
Great Dividing Range
PACIFIC OCEAN
Musgrave Ranges
Lake Eyre
Grey Range
Lord Howe Rise
New Caledonia Trench
South Fiji Basin
112°E
125°E
138°E
151°E
164°E

CHRONOLOGY OF WORLD HISTORY

THIS TABLE PRESENTS A SUMMARY of the world's crucial historical events, from the first evidence of settlement and agriculture until 2001 CE. Each of the six columns is shaded a different color, with each color representing a particular continent. Reading across the columns, one can follow the development of cultures across the major landmasses of the world. By reading downwards, each continent's particular cultural history can be seen, from its first steps toward civilization, through periods of migration, empire, and revolution, to its involvement in the global wars and political diplomacy of the 20th and 21st centuries.

NORTH AMERICA

- **15,000 BCE** Evidence of human settlement in North America
- **4000 BCE** Earliest cultivation of corn in Central America
- **100 CE** Teotihuacan becomes capital of largest state in Mesoamerica
- **c.300 CE** Start of classic Mayan civilization in Yucatan
- **900** Toltecs rise to power after Teotihuacan and Mayan states collapse
- **c.1000** Vikings colonize Greenland and discover America (Vinland)
- **1200** Aztecs enter Valley of Mexico
- **1325** Tenochtitlan founded by Aztecs
- **1492** Columbus reaches Caribbean
- **c.1500** Inuit peoples found throughout Arctic region
- **1502** Introduction of African slaves to Caribbean
- **1519** Cortes begins conquest of Aztec empire
- **1565** First African slaves arrive on mainland North America
- **1607** First permanent English settlement in North America (Jamestown, Virginia)
- **1608** French colonists found Québec
- **1620** Puritans on *Mayflower* land in New England
- **1759** British capture Québec
- **1776** American Declaration of Independence
- **1789** George Washington becomes first president of US
- **1791** Revolution in Haiti
- **1803** Louisiana Purchase nearly doubles size of US
- **1810** Revolution in Mexico
- **1819** US buys Florida from Spain
- **1821** Mexico gains independence
- **1828** Federalist–Centralist wars in Mexico (to 1859)
- **1845** Texas annexed by US
- **1846** US–Mexican War (to 1848)
- **1848** Californian Gold Rush

SOUTH AMERICA

- **c.20,000 BCE** First settlers arrive
- **c.11,000 BCE** Evidence of settlement at Monte Verde in present-day Chile
- **c.4500 BCE** Evidence of agriculture and herding in central Andes
- **c.2500 BCE** Masonry building and temple architecture on Pacific coast
- **c.1800 BCE** Ceremonial center of La Florida built in Peru
- **c.450 CE** Nazca culture flourishing; lines and giant figures drawn in desert
- **c.900 CE** Wari and Tiwanaku flourish as capitals of first competing empires
- **1100** Emergence of Chimu state on north coast of Peru
- **1380** Beginning of Inca empire in central highlands
- **1475** Chimu conquered by Incas
- **1494** Treaty of Tordesillas divides western hemisphere between Spain and Portugal
- **1500** Cabral sights Brazilian coast
- **1502** First expedition sent from Portugal to exploit coast of Brazil
- **c.1510** First African slaves brought to South America
- **1525** Civil war in Inca empire
- **1532** Pizarro begins defeat of Incas (to 1540)
- **1562** War and disease kill much of Amerindian population of Brazil (to 1563)
- **1630** Dutch establish New Holland, covering much of northern Brazil
- **1654** Portuguese regain control of Brazil
- **1663** Brazil becomes viceroyalty
- **1695** Gold discovered in Brazil
- **1739** Viceroyalty of New Granada established to defend Spanish interests on Caribbean coast
- **1750** Treaty of Madrid defines boundary between Spanish colonies and Brazil

EUROPE

- **c.6500 BCE** Farming spreads rapidly into central Europe
- **c.2800 BCE** Building of Stonehenge begins
- **c.1600 BCE** Minoan Palace civilization on Crete
- **c.750 BCE** Beginnings of Greek city-states
- **510 BCE** Roman Republic founded
- **431 BCE** Outbreak of Peloponnesian War between Sparta and Athens
- **218 BCE** Carthaginians invade Italy under command of Hannibal
- **49 BCE** Julius Caesar conquers Gaul
- **43 CE** Roman invasion of Britain
- **238 CE** Goths begin to invade borders of Roman Empire
- **330** Constantinople becomes new capital of Roman Empire
- **410** Invasion and pillage of Rome by Visigoths
- **711** Spain invaded by Muslims
- **793** Viking raids across Europe
- **800** Charlemagne becomes first Holy Roman Emperor
- **950** Harold Bluetooth consolidates the unification of Denmark
- **987** Feudal lords elect first Capetian king of France
- **1066** Norman conquest of England
- **1236** Russia invaded by Mongols
- **1337** Onset of Hundred Years War
- **1453** Byzantine Empire collapses as Ottoman Turks capture Constantinople
- **1478** Ivan III first czar of Russia
- **c.1500** Italian Renaissance
- **1521** Beginning of Protestant Reformation
- **1534** Henry VIII of England breaks with Rome
- **1588** Spanish Armada defeated by English
- **1618** Onset of Thirty Years War
- **1642** English Civil War (to 1649)
- **1756** Onset of Seven Years War
- **1789** French Revolution

AFRICA

❑ **c.400,000** BCE First evidence of *Homo sapiens* (modern humans) in Rift Valley

❑ **3100** BCE King Narmer unifies Upper and Lower Egypt and becomes first pharaoh

❑ **c.2650** BCE Start of great pyramid building in Egypt

❑ **2040** BCE Beginning of Middle Kingdom in Egypt

❑ **1352** BCE Pharaoh Akhenaten promotes Aten (sun) worship in Egypt

❑ **814** BCE Foundation of Phoenician colony of Carthage

❑ **146** BCE Rome conquers Carthage

❑ **31** BCE Cleopatra's death marks end of Ptolemaic dynasty in Egypt

❑ **c.600** CE Kingdom of Ghana founded

❑ **641** CE Muslims conquer Egypt

❑ **c.900** CE Emergence of Great Zimbabwean state

❑ **1067** Almoravids destroy kingdom of Ghana

❑ **c.1300** Emergence of empire of Benin (Nigeria)

❑ **1390** Formation of kingdom of Kongo

❑ **1443** Portuguese begin mass export of slaves from Atlantic coast to Europe

❑ **1498** Vasco da Gama rounds Cape of Good Hope

❑ **1502** First slaves taken to New World

❑ **1570** Establishment of Portuguese colony of Angola

❑ **1652** Dutch establish colony at Cape of Good Hope

❑ **1787** British establish Sierra Leone for freed slaves

❑ **1795** British capture Cape of Good Hope from the Dutch

❑ **1798** Occupation of Egypt by Napoléon Bonaparte

❑ **1816** Shaka leads expansion of Zulu

❑ **1822** Freed black slaves found colony of Liberia

❑ **1830** French invasion of Algeria

❑ **1836** Start of Boer Great Trek

❑ **1848** Boers found Orange Free State

❑ **1853** Livingstone finds Victoria Falls (Musi-o-Tunya)

❑ **1869** Opening of Suez Canal

❑ **1875** Stanley establishes source of Nile

ASIA AND THE MIDDLE EAST

❑ **c.12,000** BCE Beginnings of farming in Palestine

❑ **c.4800** BCE 'Ubaid culture builds towns in Mesopotamia

❑ **c.3500** BCE Fortified towns built throughout northern China

❑ **c.2800** BCE Emergence of city-states in Indus Valley
❑ Wheel used in Mesopotamia

❑ **c.1750** BCE Foundation of Old Babylonian Empire under Hammurabi

❑ **c.1200** BCE Traditional date for exodus of the Jews from Egypt

❑ **c.1100** BCE Phoenician civilization spreads throughout Mediterranean

❑ **c.660** BCE Japanese empire founded

❑ **550** BCE Persian Empire founded

❑ **c.480** BCE Death – or *parinibbana* – of Gautama Buddha

❑ **334** BCE Alexander the Great invades Asia Minor

❑ **332** BCE Foundation of Mauryan empire in India

❑ **202** BCE Han dynasty begins in China

❑ **c.112** BCE "Silk Road" links China to West

❑ **c.30** CE Crucifixion of Jesus of Nazareth, founder of Christianity

❑ **c.350** CE Huns invade Persia and India

❑ **622** Mohammed, founder of Islam, flees Mecca; start of Muslim calendar

❑ **960** China united under Sung dynasty

❑ **1044** Foundation of Burma

❑ **1099** Jerusalem sacked in First Crusade

❑ **1185** Minamoto shoguns rule Japan

❑ **1206** Mongols begin to conquer Asia under Genghis Khan

❑ **1238** Foundation of first Thai kingdom

❑ **1258** Baghdad sacked by Mongols

❑ **1264** Yuan dynasty founded in China by Kublai Khan

❑ **1275** Marco Polo arrives in China

❑ **1333** Civil war in Japan

❑ **1368** Ming dynasty begins in China

❑ **1392** Korea proclaims independence

❑ **1498** Vasco da Gama completes first European voyage to India

❑ **1526** Foundation of Mughal empire in India

❑ **1600** Charter granted to East India Company

❑ **1609** Beginning of Tokugawa shogunate in Japan

❑ **1619** Dutch found Batavia (Jakarta)

❑ **1644** Manchus seize Peking

AUSTRALASIA AND OCEANIA

❑ **c.60,000** BCE First people arrive in Australia

❑ **c.30,000** BCE Aboriginal rock art begins to appear

❑ **c.8000-6000** BCE Rising sea level covers New Guinea land bridge

❑ **c.6000** BCE Migrations from southeast Asia give rise to Austronesian culture

❑ **c.4000** BCE Austronesians reach southwestern Pacific islands

❑ **c.1000** BCE Emergence of archaic Polynesian society in Fiji, Tonga, and Samoa

❑ **c.300** CE Easter Island settled

❑ **c.600** CE Polynesians arrive in Hawaii

❑ **1520** Magellan enters Pacific

❑ **1526** Jorge de Meneses first European to sight New Guinea

❑ **1606** Torres sails through strait that now bears his name; proves New Guinea is an island

❑ **1642** Tasman, searching for a southern continent, finds Tasmania and New Zealand

❑ **1688** Dampier first Englishman to visit Australia

❑ **1768** Cook's first voyage

❑ **1773** Cook crosses Antarctic Circle and explores Southern Ocean (to 1775)

❑ **1779** Cook killed in Hawaii on third voyage

❑ **1788** First penal settlement established at Port Jackson (Sydney)

❑ **1802** Flinders circumnavigates Australia (to 1803)

❑ **1818** Start of Maori "Musket Wars" in New Zealand

❑ **1819** Bellingshausen's expedition sights Antarctica

❑ **1829** Britain annexes western and final third of Australian continent

❑ **1830** A mere 200 foreigners, mostly British, permanently resident in New Zealand

❑ **1840** Treaty of Waitangi grants sovereignty over New Zealand to British

❑ **1841** New Zealand becomes a separate Crown colony

❑ **1845** Northern War in New Zealand (to 1846)

see pages 68–69 for CHRONOLOGY 2002–2003

North America (continued)

❑ **1861** US Civil War (to 1865)

❑ **1863** Emancipation Proclamation

❑ **1865** Lee surrenders to Grant at Appomattox
❑ Assassination of President Lincoln
❑ Slavery abolished in US

❑ **1867** US buys Alaska from Russia
❑ Dominion of Canada established

❑ **1869** 15th Amendment gives vote to freed slaves in US

❑ **1871** Start of Apache Wars

❑ **1876** Battle of Little Big Horn: Sioux warriors kill 250 US soldiers

❑ **1890** Massacre of Sioux warriors at Wounded Knee ends Amerindian wars

❑ **1896** Klondike Gold Rush, Alaska

❑ **1898** Spanish–American War

❑ **1899** Spain cedes Cuba and Puerto Rico to US

❑ **1910** Mexican Revolution begins

❑ **1921** US restricts immigration

❑ **1929** Wall Street Crash

❑ **1933** President Roosevelt introduces New Deal

❑ **1940s** Race riots in Harlem, Los Angeles, Detroit, and Chicago

❑ **1941** US enters war against Germany and Japan

❑ **1945** End of World War II

❑ **1949** Formation of NATO
❑ Cold War begins

❑ **1950** US supports south in Korean War (to 1953)

❑ **1959** Cuban Revolution

❑ **1962** Cuban missile crisis

❑ **1963** Martin Luther King leads march on Washington D.C.
❑ Assassination of President Kennedy

❑ **1964** US Congress approves sending first troops to Vietnam

❑ **1968** Assassination of Martin Luther King sparks riots in 124 US cities

❑ **1969** Neil Armstrong becomes first person on moon

❑ **1973** US withdraws from Vietnam

❑ **1974** President Nixon resigns over Watergate scandal

❑ **1979** Civil war in Nicaragua (to 1990)
❑ Civil war in El Salvador (to 1992)

❑ **1994** North American Free Trade Agreement (NAFTA) established

❑ **1999** President Clinton survives impeachment

❑ **2000** George W. Bush wins presidential elections without receiving majority of popular vote

❑ **2001** World's worst ever terrorist attack kills thousands in New York and Washington D.C.

South America (continued)

❑ **1811** Bolívar starts fight to liberate Venezuela
❑ Paraguay independent

❑ **1817** San Martin wins decisive victory over Spanish and liberates Chile

❑ **1821** Peru independent

❑ **1822** Brazil independent

❑ **1823** Slavery abolished in Chile

❑ **1825** Bolivia independent

❑ **1828** Uruguay independent

❑ **1830** Ecuador, Colombia, and Venezuela (formerly Gran Colombia) become separate states

❑ **1851** Slavery abolished in Colombia

❑ **1853** Slavery abolished in Ecuador, Argentina, and Uruguay

❑ **1854** Slavery abolished in Bolivia and Venezuela

❑ **1864** Paraguayan War: Brazil, Argentina, and Uruguay defeat Paraguay

❑ **1870** Slavery abolished in Paraguay

❑ **1888** Slavery abolished in Brazil

❑ **1900** Major Italian migration to Argentina

❑ **1914** Panama Canal opens

❑ **1930** Military revolution in Brazil

❑ **1932** Chaco War between Bolivia and Paraguay (to 1935); Paraguay defeats Bolivia

❑ **1937** "New State" in Brazil launched by Vargas

❑ **1946** Peron comes to power in Argentina

❑ **1955** Peron ousted by military coup; returns to power in 1973

❑ **1968** Tupamaros urban guerrilla group founded in Uruguay
❑ Military junta takes over Peru

❑ **1970** Allende elected president of Chile

❑ **1973** US backs Pinochet coup against elected government in Chile; Allende assassinated

❑ **1976** "Dirty War" of right-wing death squads in Argentina

❑ **1982** Falklands War between Argentina and UK

❑ **1983** Democracy restored in Argentina

❑ **1985** Democracy restored in Brazil and Uruguay

❑ **1989** Democracy restored in Chile

❑ **1999** Panama takes control of Panama Canal

❑ **2001** Earthquakes devastate El Salvador

Europe (continued)

❑ **1804** Napoléon becomes emperor of France

❑ **1815** Napoléon defeated
❑ Treaty of Vienna

❑ **1845** Beginning of Irish potato famine

❑ **1854** Crimean War (to 1856)

❑ **1861** Italy unified
❑ Emancipation of serfs in Russia

❑ **1870** Franco-Prussian War

❑ **1871** Germany unified

❑ **1914** World War I (to 1918)

❑ **1917** Russian Revolution

❑ **1922** Mussolini comes to power in Italy after Fascist "March on Rome"

❑ **1933** Nazis take power in Germany; Hitler is elected chancellor

❑ **1936** Spanish Civil War (to 1939)

❑ **1939** Germany invades Poland precipitating World War II

❑ **1941** German forces invade Russia

❑ **1944** British and US troops land in Normandy; Russians advance into eastern Europe

❑ **1945** Defeat of Germany

❑ **1949** Formation of NATO
❑ Cold War begins

❑ **1957** Treaties of Rome establish European Economic Community

❑ **1961** Building of the Berlin Wall
❑ Yuri Gagarin first person in space

❑ **1968** Troubles in Northern Ireland

❑ **1973** UK and Ireland join European Communities

❑ **1975** End of dictatorship in Spain with death of Gen. Franco

❑ **1986** Explosion at Chernobyl nuclear power reactor
❑ Soviet launch of *Mir* space station

❑ **1989** Democratic revolutions in eastern Europe
❑ Berlin Wall demolished

❑ **1990** Reunification of Germany

❑ **1991** The Soviet Union splits into its component countries
❑ Slovenia and Croatia claim their independence

❑ **1992** Civil war in Bosnia & Herzegovina (to 1995)

❑ **1993** Velvet Divorce: separation of Czech Republic and Slovakia

❑ **1994** Outbreak of war in Chechnya

❑ **1995** EU expands to 15 members

❑ **1999** "Ethnic cleansing" of Albanians in Kosovo leads to NATO air strikes against Yugoslavia

❑ **2000** President Milosevic is ousted in Yugoslavia (Serbia & Montenegro) in popular revolution

❑ **2001** Netherlands legalizes euthanasia

AFRICA (CONTINUED)

❏ **1879** British defeat Zulus

❏ **1881** French occupy Tunisia

❏ **1882** Britain occupies Egypt

❏ **1883** France begins conquest of Madagascar

❏ **1889** Colonization of "Rhodesia"

❏ **1890** Land connection between Angola and Mozambique ended

❏ **1894** Britain occupies Uganda

❏ **1896** Ethiopian emperor Menelik II defeats Italians at Adawa

❏ **1899** Boer War (to 1902)

❏ **1910** Formation of Union of South Africa

❏ **1911** Italian conquest of Libya

❏ **1935** Second Italian invasion of Ethiopia

❏ **1942** British halt German advance at El Alamein

❏ **1948** Pro-apartheid National Party wins power in South Africa

❏ **1956** UK fails to block Egypt's nationalization of Suez Canal

❏ **1960** Outbreak of civil war in Belgian Congo
❏ Fifteen countries gain independence

❏ **1962** Algeria gains independence

❏ **1963** Zambia and Malawi granted independence
❏ Organization of African Unity (OAU) founded

❏ **1964** Nelson Mandela sentenced to life imprisonment

❏ **1974** Emperor Haile Selassie of Ethiopia deposed

❏ **1975** Angola and Mozambique gain independence; civil wars ensue

❏ **1980** Black majority rule established in Zimbabwe

❏ **1981** President Sadat of Egypt assassinated

❏ **1984** Worst recent famine in Ethiopia

❏ **1990** Mandela released: apartheid begins to be dismantled
❏ Namibia becomes independent

❏ **1994** South Africa holds first multiracial election; Mandela wins presidency
❏ Attempted genocide of Tutsis by Hutu in Rwanda

❏ **1997** Overthrow of Mobutu in Zaire (Democratic Republic of the Congo – DRC)

❏ **1998** Start of civil war in DRC

❏ **1999** Nigeria returns to democracy

❏ **2000** Ethiopia–Eritrea conflict ends

❏ **2001** Civil war ends in Sierra Leone after ten years

ASIA AND THE MIDDLE EAST (CONTINUED)

❏ **1757** East India Company defeats Nawab of Bengal's forces at Plassey

❏ **1842** Opium Wars (to 1854), Britain compels China to open Treaty Ports and annexes Hong Kong

❏ **1851** Taiping rebellion in China, 20 million killed (to 1864)

❏ **1868** Meiji Restoration in Japan

❏ **1877** Queen Victoria proclaimed empress of India

❏ **1911** Manchu dynasty overthrown in China, republic declared

❏ **1922** The last Ottoman sultan is deposed; Turkey proclaimed a republic

❏ **1932** Kingdom of Saudi Arabia founded

❏ **1937** Japanese forces invade China

❏ **1941** Pearl Harbor attacked by Japan

❏ **1945** Atom bombs dropped on Hiroshima and Nagasaki; c.210,000 killed, Japan surrenders

❏ **1947** Partition of India: Pakistan and India independent

❏ **1948** Burma and Ceylon (Sri Lanka) proclaim their independence
❏ Establishment of Israel

❏ **1949** People's Republic of China proclaimed
❏ Indonesia independent

❏ **1950** Korean War (until 1953)

❏ **1954** Laos, Cambodia, and Vietnam proclaim their independence

❏ **1959** China occupies Tibet

❏ **1965** US combat troops in Vietnam

❏ **1966** Cultural Revolution in China

❏ **1971** East Pakistan (Bangladesh) claims independence

❏ **1975** Fall of Saigon ends Vietnam War
❏ Civil war in Lebanon (to 1989)

❏ **1979** Overthrow of shah in Iran, Islamic Republic founded
❏ Vietnam pushes Khmer Rouge from Cambodia

❏ **1980** Iran–Iraq War (to 1988)

❏ **1982** Israeli invasion of Lebanon

❏ **1986** Marcos deposed in Philippines

❏ **1989** Massacre in Tiananmen Square

❏ **1990** Invasion of Kuwait by Iraq

❏ **1991** Gulf War

❏ **1996** *Taliban* take over in Afghanistan

❏ **1997** Hong Kong is returned to China
❏ Asian financial crisis

❏ **1998** Suharto regime collapses in Indonesia
❏ India and Pakistan test nuclear weapons

❏ **2000** Palestinians begin new *intifada*

❏ **2001** US-led war ousts *taliban* regime in Afghanistan

AUSTRALASIA AND OCEANIA (CONTINUED)

❏ **c.1850** Migrant workers from China, Japan, and Philippines start arriving in Hawaii

❏ **1851** Gold discovered in New South Wales

❏ **1858** King Movement demands Maori state and opposes further land sales

❏ **1860** European settlers outnumber Maoris in New Zealand

❏ **1862** Second Maori War

❏ **1864** First French convict settlers in New Caledonia

❏ **1865** 1000 Chinese brought to Tahiti to work cotton plantation (to 1866)

❏ **1869** Last convict ship arrives in Australia

❏ **1870** Maori resistance crushed
❏ Germans start to buy up large tracts of Western Samoa

❏ **1874** Indian sugarcane workers arrive in Fiji

❏ **1888** Chile starts colonization of Easter Island

❏ **1890** Gold discovered in Western Australia

❏ **1898** US annexes Hawaii and seizes Guam from Spain

❏ **1901** Australia is self-governing federation within British Empire

❏ **1912** Amundsen's expedition reaches South Pole

❏ **1914** Over 60,000 Australian troops and more than 15,000 New Zealanders lose their lives in World War I (to 1918)

❏ **1930s** Australia hit hard by global Depression

❏ **1942** Australia under threat of invasion as Japanese bomb Darwin

❏ **1946** US begins nuclear tests at Eniwetok and Bikini atolls in Micronesia

❏ **1952** UK begins nuclear tests (to 1991) on mainland Australia

❏ **1966** France begins nuclear tests in Tuamotu Islands (to 1996)

❏ **1975** Restrictions imposed on immigrants to Australia

❏ **1985** South Pacific Forum declares nuclear-free Pacific

❏ **1988** Bicentennial celebrations in Australia occasion Aboriginal protests

❏ **1998** Ethnic conflict in Solomon Islands (to 2000)

❏ **1999** Australian referendum rejects proposal on becoming republic

❏ **2000** Coup in Fiji ousts first ethnic Indian government

❏ **2001** Peace accord signed in Bougainville, Papua New Guinea, ending 13 years of conflict

see pages 68–69 for CHRONOLOGY 2002–2003

The Formation of The Modern World

THE WORLD AS WE KNOW IT today, like all of the species that inhabit it, is the product of many thousands of years of evolution. The political and cultural map of the globe bears the hallmark of many varied courses of human development the world over. Nevertheless, much of the modern human geography of the planet can be traced to developments in the relatively recent past. The following pages chart the rise and fall of the various states and empires of the early modern and modern ages. Beginning with the first great achievement of European exploration, the "discovery" of the Americas in 1492, the maps show the way in which various European and Asian powers expanded their cultural and political influence and control down to the present day. This process left indelible cultural imprints in the form of language, religion, education, and systems of government on every part of the planet.

Major Migrations Since 1500

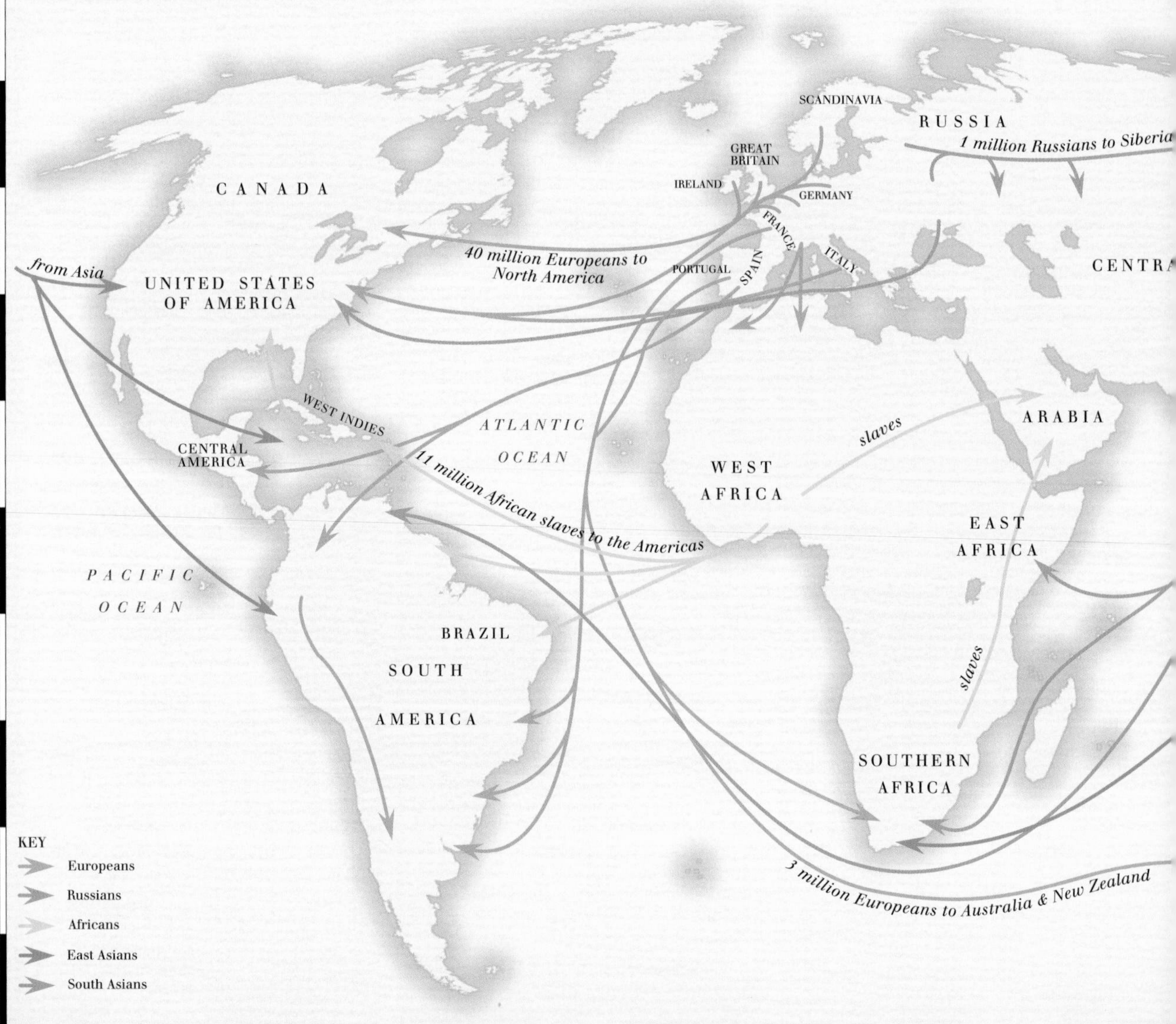

SCANDINAVIA
RUSSIA
1 million Russians to Siberia
GREAT BRITAIN
IRELAND
GERMANY
CANADA
FRANCE
ITALY
PORTUGAL
SPAIN
40 million Europeans to North America
from Asia
UNITED STATES OF AMERICA
CENTRA
WEST INDIES
ATLANTIC OCEAN
slaves
ARABIA
CENTRAL AMERICA
WEST AFRICA
11 million African slaves to the Americas
EAST AFRICA
PACIFIC OCEAN
BRAZIL
SOUTH AMERICA
slaves
SOUTHERN AFRICA
3 million Europeans to Australia & New Zealand
KEY
Europeans
Russians
Africans
East Asians
South Asians

LANGUAGES OF THE WORLD
KEY
Arabic
Chinese
English
French
Portuguese
Russian
Spanish
Hindi
Others
NAHUATL
MAYA
QUECHUA
AYMARA
ATLANTIC OCEAN
GERMANIC
SLAVIC
TURKIC
BERBER
AMHARIC
BANTU
AFRIKAANS
PERSIAN
MONGOL
UIGHUR
MONGOL
TIBETAN
KOREAN
JAPANESE
AUSTRO-ASIATIC
FILIPINO, CEBUANO
AUSTRONESIAN
INDIAN OCEAN
PACIFIC OCEAN

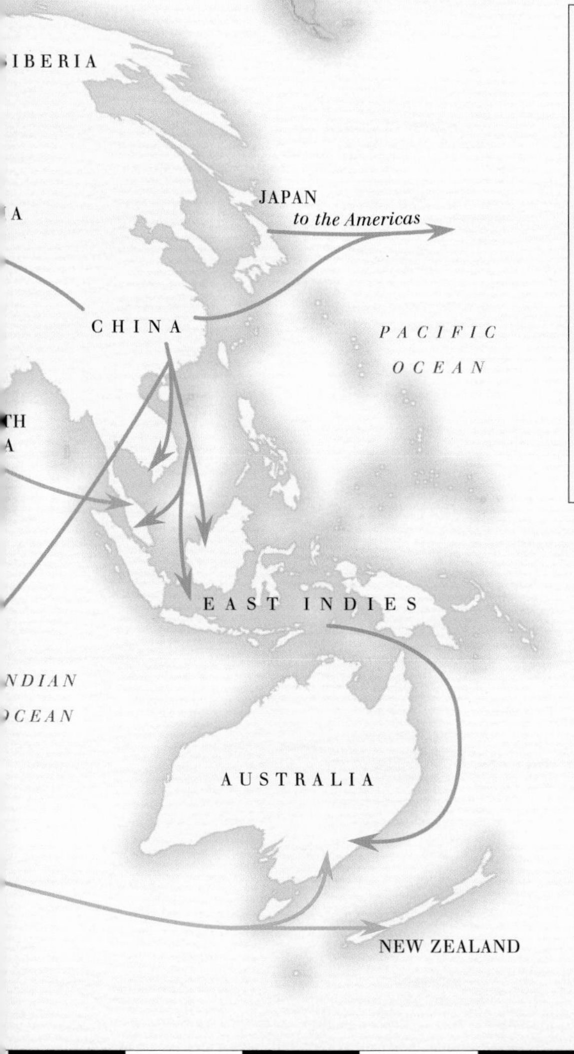
SIBERIA
JAPAN
to the Americas
CHINA
PACIFIC OCEAN
EAST INDIES
INDIAN OCEAN
AUSTRALIA
NEW ZEALAND

LANGUAGES OF THE WORLD

THERE ARE OVER 3000 LANGUAGES or "speech communities" in the world today; some are spoken by many millions, some by only dozens. Many people speak more than one language. The diffusion of the major languages throughout the world during the modern era has seen the emergence of a few dominant languages (shown on the map). In many areas, the language of a colonial power has been maintained either as an official language or has become the *lingua franca* of the region. The largest single language, encompassing many dialects, is Chinese, with over one billion speakers; Hindi (400 million) and Arabic (200 million), are the next largest first languages. The most successful colonial languages are English (estimated at up to 1500 million, including those using English as a second language), French (200 million), and Spanish (270 million). While the last is now estimated to be the world's fastest-growing language, owing to Latin America's burgeoning population growth, both English and French are spoken in a wide variety of patois, pidgins, and creoles, thus achieving unique levels of cultural penetration.

MAJOR MIGRATIONS SINCE 1500

THE LAST FIVE HUNDRED YEARS have witnessed a dramatic redistribution of the world's population, which occurred in a series of waves. The first of these involved, in the 16th–18th centuries, the mass transshipment of captive peoples from sub-Saharan Africa to supply the slave markets of West Asia and to work newly founded European plantations in the Americas. The rapidly growing populations of Europe and Asia encouraged a heavy flow of migration. The Cantonese from southern China spread throughout southeast Asia, while from the 16th century millions of Europeans emigrated to the "New Worlds" of the Americas and, later, Australasia. This European diaspora reached a peak at the end of the 19th century. Then, as the colonial empires coalesced in the early years of the 20th century, there was a final wave of global movement within them, when south and east Asians migrated to fill labor markets and exploit opportunities in Africa and the Americas. While homogeneous societies have developed in North America and Australia, many diverse ethnic communities remain scattered across the world.

The World in 1492

When Christopher Columbus sailed west from Europe, seeking a quicker route to Asia, he launched a process of discovery that was eventually to bring the disparate regions of the world into closer contact, to form the global map we know today. The largest political entity in the world at that time was the Chinese Ming empire. Culturally, the Islamic faith had forged a bond of religious unity which extended in a broad swathe from southeast Asia to the Atlantic coast of north Africa. Europe was a mêlée of rival monarchies; sub-Saharan Africa a patchwork of trading kingdoms; the Americas, a separate world of rich tribal cultures, with empires established only in Central America and the central Andes.

Global States and Territories

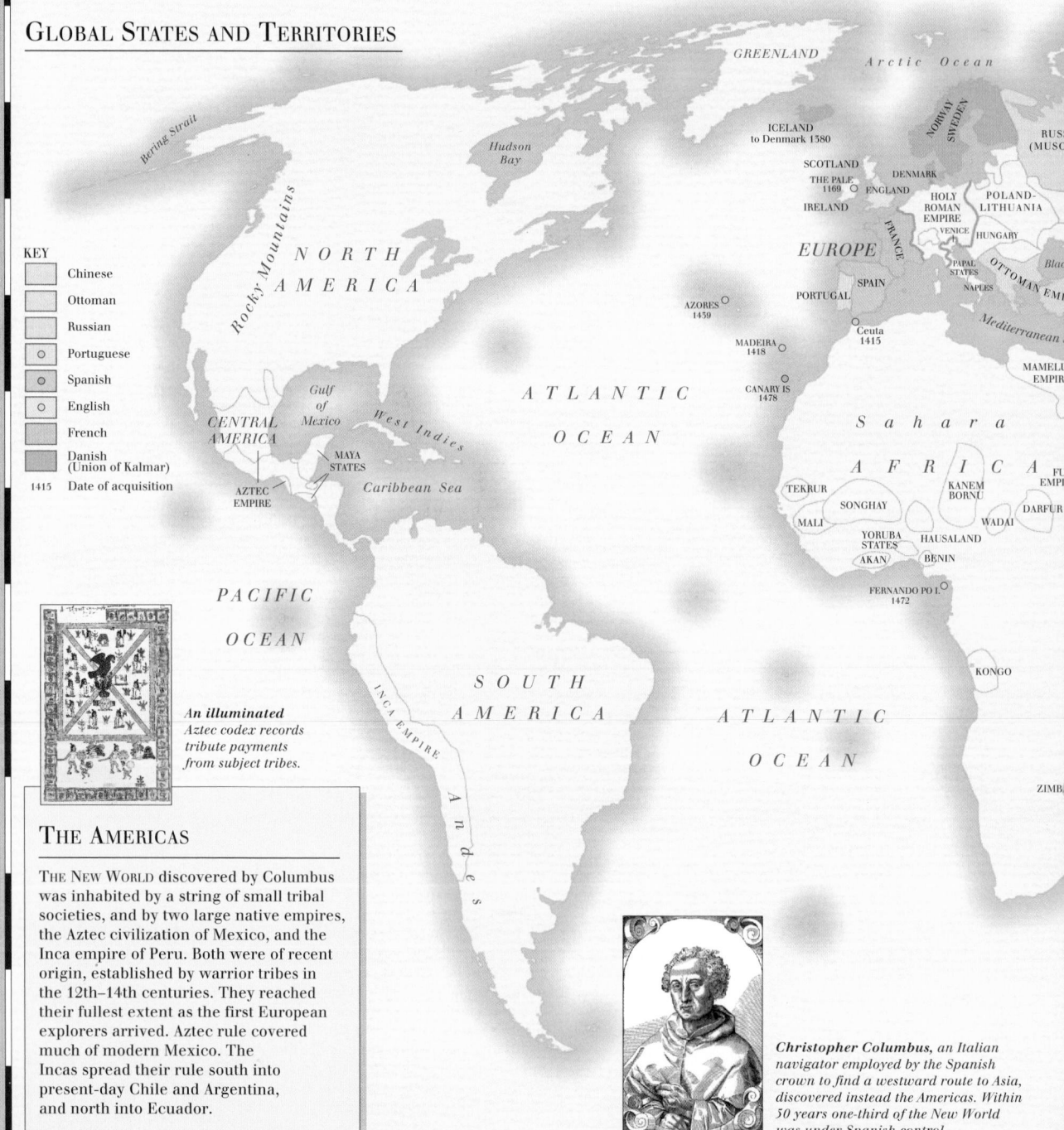

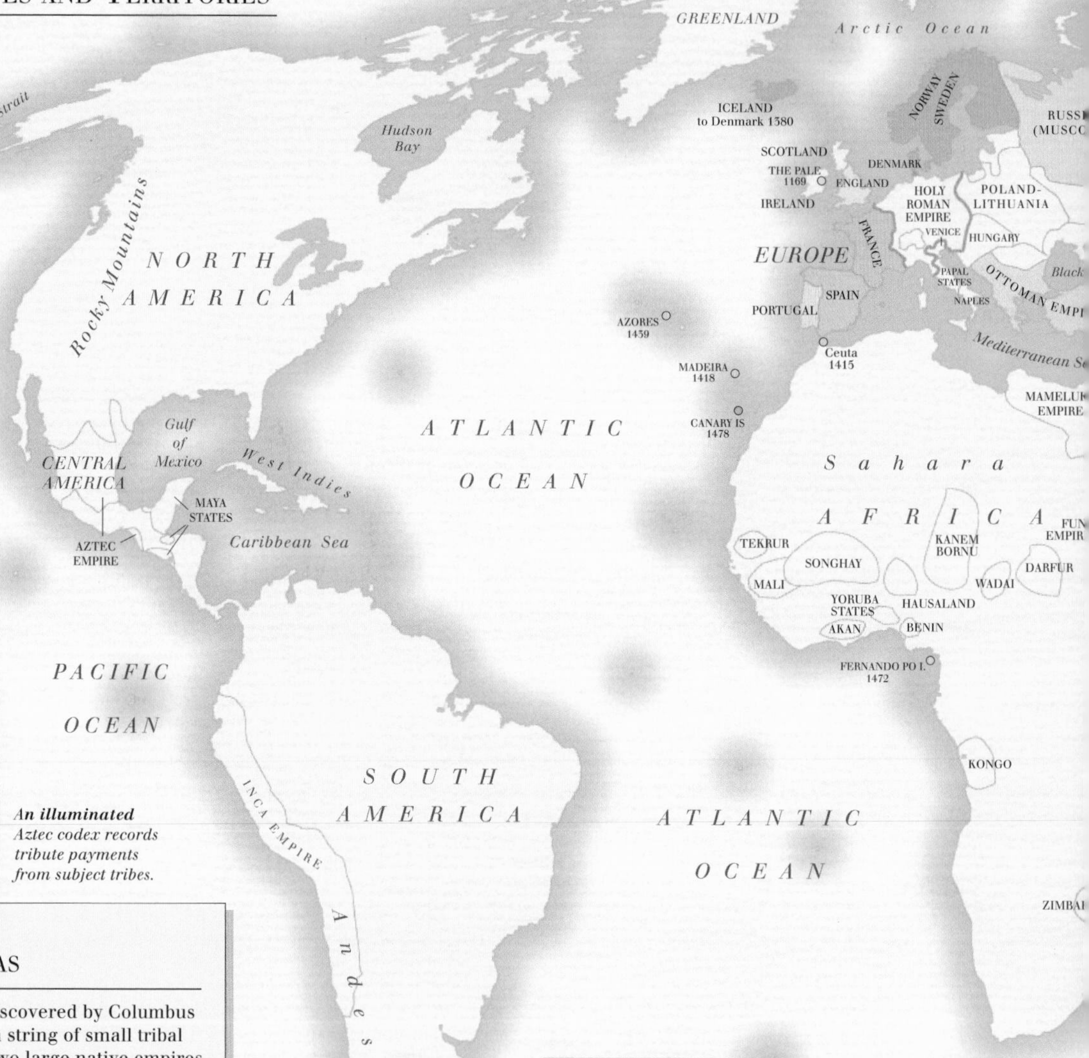
KEY
Chinese
Ottoman
Russian
Portuguese
Spanish
English
French
Danish (Union of Kalmar)
1415 Date of acquisition
GREENLAND
Arctic Ocean
Bering Strait
Hudson Bay
ICELAND to Denmark 1380
NORWAY
SWEDEN
RUSSI (MUSCO
SCOTLAND
THE PALE 1169
ENGLAND
DENMARK
IRELAND
HOLY ROMAN EMPIRE
POLAND-LITHUANIA
VENICE
HUNGARY
FRANCE
EUROPE
PAPAL STATES
NAPLES
OTTOMAN EMPI
Black
SPAIN
PORTUGAL
Rocky Mountains
NORTH AMERICA
AZORES 1439
MADEIRA 1418
Ceuta 1415
Mediterranean Se
MAMELUK EMPIRE
CANARY IS 1478
Gulf of Mexico
West Indies
ATLANTIC OCEAN
CENTRAL AMERICA
MAYA STATES
AZTEC EMPIRE
Caribbean Sea
Sahara
AFRICA
FUN EMPIR
TEKRUR
SONGHAY
KANEM BORNU
DARFUR
WADAI
MALI
YORUBA STATES
HAUSALAND
AKAN
BENIN
FERNANDO PO I. 1472
PACIFIC OCEAN
KONGO
SOUTH AMERICA
INCA EMPIRE
ATLANTIC OCEAN
ZIMBAI
Andes

***An illuminated** Aztec codex records tribute payments from subject tribes.*

The Americas

The New World discovered by Columbus was inhabited by a string of small tribal societies, and by two large native empires, the Aztec civilization of Mexico, and the Inca empire of Peru. Both were of recent origin, established by warrior tribes in the 12th–14th centuries. They reached their fullest extent as the first European explorers arrived. Aztec rule covered much of modern Mexico. The Incas spread their rule south into present-day Chile and Argentina, and north into Ecuador.

***Christopher Columbus,** an Italian navigator employed by the Spanish crown to find a westward route to Asia, discovered instead the Americas. Within 50 years one-third of the New World was under Spanish control.*

The Portuguese caravel, buoyant, sturdy, and lateen-rigged, was an ideal ocean-going vessel.

EUROPE

THOUGH CHRISTIAN EUROPE later transformed the exploration and settlement of the world, the Europe from which Columbus sailed was an unstable, violent continent, threatened by invaders from Asia to the east, and from the Ottoman Empire to the south. Civil wars and dynastic conflict resulted in shifting frontiers and small, militarily weak states. Only France, united by the late 15th century, Spain, a single monarchy from the 1490s, Portugal, and England were close to their modern forms.

EAST ASIA

THE MOST POWERFUL STATE in the world in 1492 was Ming China. Set up in 1386 after the collapse of Mongol power, the Ming dynasty ruled an area from Manchuria in the north to the borders of Vietnam in the south. Based on a traditional structure of bureaucratic control, the Ming emperors controlled their vast empire from Peking (Beijing), from where they launched punitive wars against the Mongols and Japanese pirates along the coast. Chinese culture and trade spread throughout east and southeast Asia, and Chinese navigators reached the Red Sea and the east African coast.

***Chinese junks** plied the China seas, and traded as far as the East Indies, Ceylon (Sri Lanka), and east Africa.*

Bering Strait
Siberia
ASIA
Aral Sea
UZBEKH KHANATE
TIMURID PERSIA
Gobi
Sea of Japan
JAPAN
KOREA
MING EMPIRE
Himalayas
NEPAL
TIBET
SULTANATE OF DELHI
The Gulf
Arabian Sea
YEMEN
Bay of Bengal
AVA
PEGU
LAOS
ANNAM
SIAM
CAMBODIA
South China Sea
VIJAYANAGAR
Ceylon
PACIFIC OCEAN
Micronesia
Melanesia
SRIVIJAYAN EMPIRE
East Indies
INDIAN OCEAN

SOUTH ASIA AND OCEANIA

THE ETHNIC, POLITICAL, and religious map of southeast Asia was largely in place by the late 15th century. However, the largest state was the vast Srivijayan Hindu–Buddhist empire, which spanned the East Indies archipelago. Muslim traders were in the process of incorporating this rich region into an Indian Ocean trading empire. Further east, the scattered island groups of the Pacific were being successively colonized by waves of Melanesians.

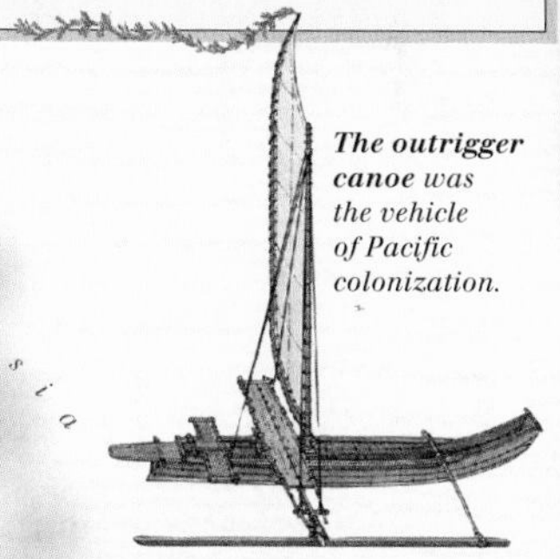

***The outrigger canoe** was the vehicle of Pacific colonization.*

***Arab dhows** built a trading network around the Indian Ocean.*

1878·25

***The magnetic compass,** in use since the 13th century, was a primary navigational tool for the first ocean-going explorers, although early compasses were not always reliable, and ships often went astray. Accurate navigation only came later with the invention of the chronometer.*

MIDDLE EAST AND AFRICA

AFTER CENTURIES OF INVASION from the Christian West and Asian nomadic empires, the Middle Eastern world stabilized around a revival of the Ottoman Empire. Vassal states extended across north Africa to Morocco, which linked the trading kingdoms of sub-Saharan Africa with the markets of Asia. The great cities of the Middle East surpassed those of Europe in wealth and learning.

The Age of Discovery: 1492–1648

THE FIRST STATE to take advantage of the new age of exploration was Spain. By the middle of the 16th century, under the Emperor Charles V, Spain was established as the foremost European colonial power, and one of the richest and most powerful kingdoms in Europe. Spanish rule was extended over the whole of Central America, much of South America, Florida, and the Caribbean; in Asia, Spanish rule was established in the Philippines. Spain led the way in establishing European settler colonies overseas. By the middle of the 17th century, British, Dutch, and French colonists began to challenge Spanish dominance in the Americas and east Asia, while pirates around the world plundered Spain's wealthy merchant convoys.

Global States and Territories

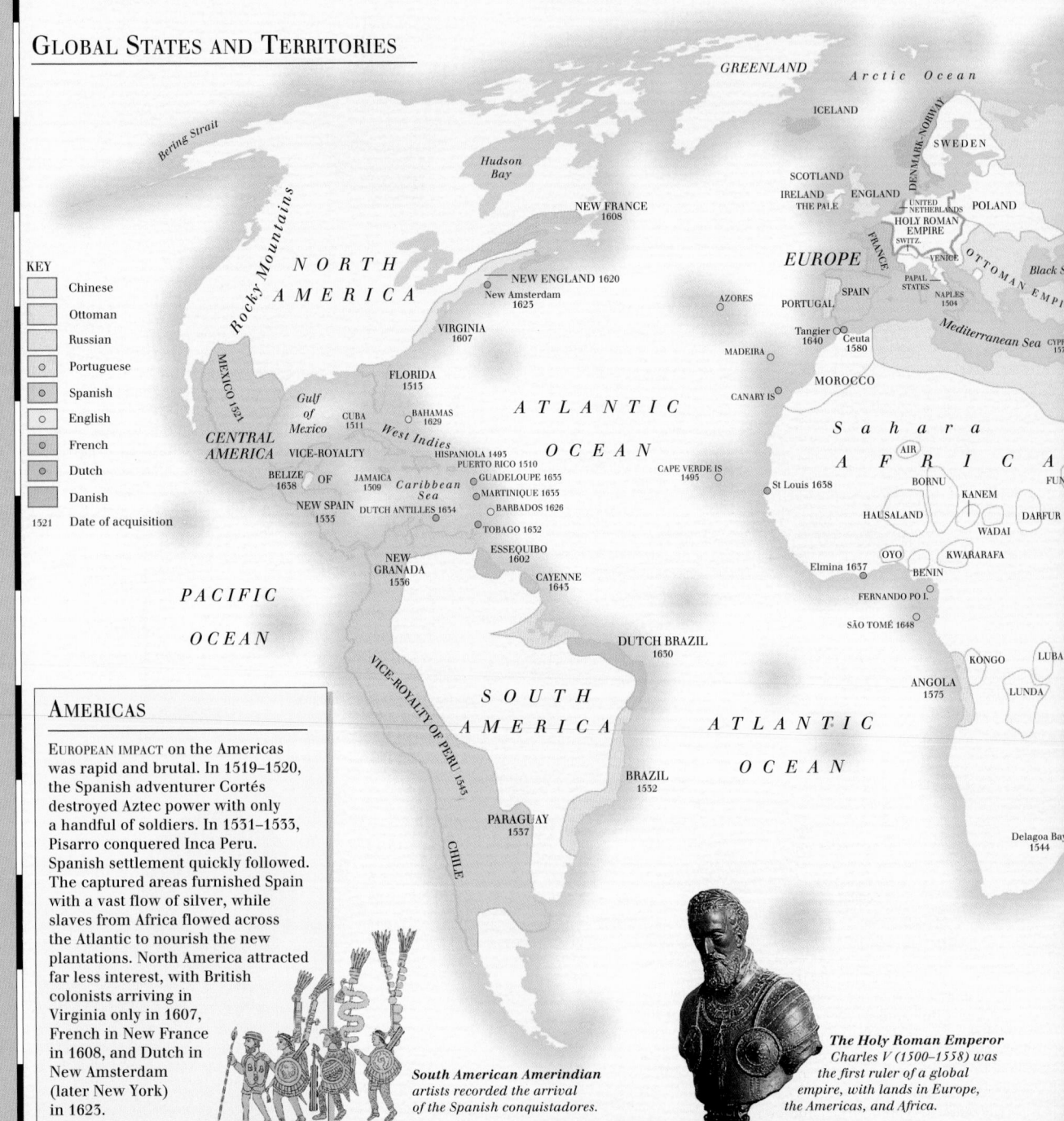

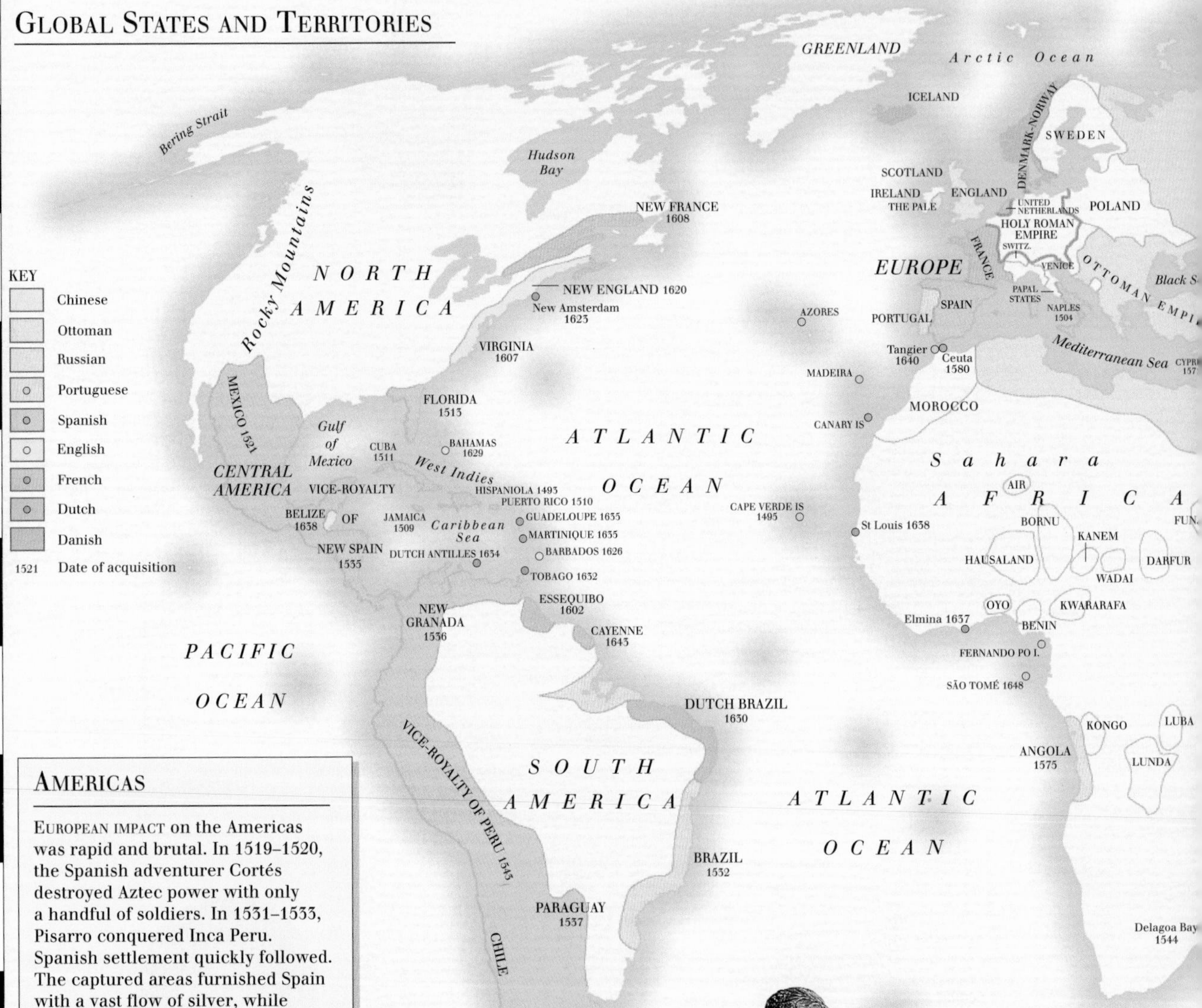
KEY
Chinese
Ottoman
Russian
Portuguese
Spanish
English
French
Dutch
Danish
1521 Date of acquisition
GREENLAND
Arctic Ocean
ICELAND
DENMARK-NORWAY
SWEDEN
Bering Strait
Hudson Bay
SCOTLAND
IRELAND
THE PALE
ENGLAND
UNITED NETHERLANDS
POLAND
NEW FRANCE 1608
HOLY ROMAN EMPIRE
SWITZ.
FRANCE
VENICE
OTTOMAN EMPIRE
Black Sea
Rocky Mountains
NORTH AMERICA
EUROPE
NEW ENGLAND 1620
New Amsterdam 1623
AZORES
PORTUGAL
SPAIN
PAPAL STATES
NAPLES 1504
VIRGINIA 1607
Tangier 1640
Ceuta 1580
Mediterranean Sea
MADEIRA
MEXICO 1521
FLORIDA 1513
MOROCCO
CANARY IS
Gulf of Mexico
CUBA 1511
BAHAMAS 1629
ATLANTIC
CENTRAL AMERICA
West Indies
Sahara
VICE-ROYALTY
HISPANIOLA 1493
OCEAN
AIR
AFRICA
PUERTO RICO 1510
CAPE VERDE IS 1495
BELIZE 1638
OF
JAMAICA 1509
Caribbean Sea
GUADELOUPE 1635
MARTINIQUE 1635
St Louis 1638
BORNU
KANEM
NEW SPAIN 1535
DUTCH ANTILLES 1634
BARBADOS 1626
HAUSALAND
DARFUR
TOBAGO 1632
WADAI
ESSEQUIBO 1602
OYO
KWARARAFA
NEW GRANADA 1536
Elmina 1637
BENIN
CAYENNE 1643
PACIFIC
FERNANDO PO I.
SÃO TOMÉ 1648
OCEAN
DUTCH BRAZIL 1630
KONGO
LUBA
VICE-ROYALTY OF PERU 1545
ANGOLA 1575
SOUTH AMERICA
LUNDA
ATLANTIC
OCEAN
BRAZIL 1532
PARAGUAY 1537
CHILE
Delagoa Bay 1544

Americas

European impact on the Americas was rapid and brutal. In 1519–1520, the Spanish adventurer Cortés destroyed Aztec power with only a handful of soldiers. In 1531–1533, Pisarro conquered Inca Peru. Spanish settlement quickly followed. The captured areas furnished Spain with a vast flow of silver, while slaves from Africa flowed across the Atlantic to nourish the new plantations. North America attracted far less interest, with British colonists arriving in Virginia only in 1607, French in New France in 1608, and Dutch in New Amsterdam (later New York) in 1623.

***South American Amerindian** artists recorded the arrival of the Spanish conquistadores.*

***The Holy Roman Emperor** Charles V (1500–1558) was the first ruler of a global empire, with lands in Europe, the Americas, and Africa.*

EUROPE

FOR MORE THAN A CENTURY after Martin Luther inspired the Protestant Reformation in the 1520s, Europe was torn by religious wars. Scandinavia, England, and Scotland adopted the new beliefs, but elsewhere bitter civil conflicts led to the prolonged warfare and persecution known as the Thirty Years War. This ended in 1648; it destroyed wide areas of central Europe and decimated the German population, but resulted in a religious settlement which continues to the present. The Dutch Republic and northern Germany became Protestant while southern Germany, Poland, and southwest Europe remained Roman Catholic.

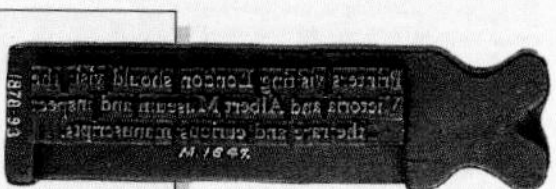

***Printing**, using movable type, was a key development in the dissemination of ideas, knowledge, and commerce in early modern Europe.*

ASIA

IN 1480, THE SMALL PRINCIPALITY OF MUSCOVY (Moscow) threw off Mongol control, and proceeded to expand Muscovite power over the whole of the area from the Arctic Ocean to the Caspian Sea. In the 1550s, the conquest of Kazan brought Russian power to the Urals, and over the next century it spread across Siberia, reaching the Pacific coast by 1649. Much of the area remained uninhabited, but to the south this new empire jostled uneasily with a string of central Asian Muslim khanates, and with the newly established Manchurian Ch'ing dynasty, which wrested control of China from the Ming in 1644.

***European navigators** and surveyors produced accurate maps and charts of their voyages.*

***The Indian Mughal** ruler Shahjahan (1592–1648), builder of the Taj Mahal.*

SOUTH ASIA AND OCEANIA

THE PORTUGUESE and the Spanish were the first European powers to open trade with the powerful Asian states of Mughal India and Ch'ing China. The Spanish opened trans-Pacific routes between Central America, the Philippines, and China. But the establishment of the Dutch and British East India companies in the early 17th century announced the advent of two new maritime powers.

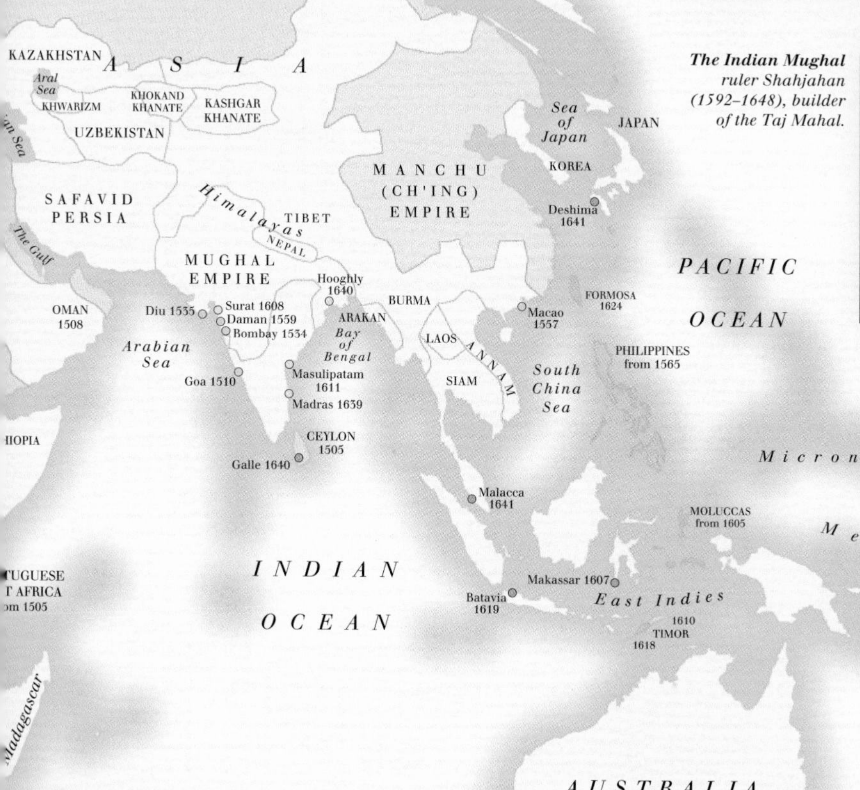

USSIAN EMPIRE
Siberia
Bering Strait
KAZAKHSTAN
ASIA
Aral Sea
KHWARIZM
KHOKAND KHANATE
KASHGAR KHANATE
UZBEKISTAN
Sea of Japan
JAPAN
KOREA
SAFAVID PERSIA
Himalayas
TIBET
NEPAL
MANCHU (CH'ING) EMPIRE
Deshima 1641
The Gulf
MUGHAL EMPIRE
Hooghly 1640
PACIFIC OCEAN
OMAN 1508
Diu 1535
Surat 1608
Daman 1559
Bombay 1534
ARAKAN
BURMA
FORMOSA 1624
Macao 1557
Arabian Sea
Bay of Bengal
LAOS
ANNAM
PHILIPPINES from 1565
Goa 1510
Masulipatam 1611
Madras 1639
SIAM
South China Sea
CEYLON 1505
Galle 1640
Micronesia
Malacca 1641
MOLUCCAS from 1605
Melanesia
INDIAN OCEAN
Makassar 1607
Batavia 1619
East Indies
1610 TIMOR 1618
AUSTRALIA
NEW ZEALAND
Madagascar

***West African** trading kingdoms produced artifacts such as this bronze Portuguese soldier from Benin.*

AFRICA AND THE MIDDLE EAST

WHILE EUROPE WAS DIVIDED by the Reformation, Islam experienced a remarkable resurgence in the 16th century. The revival of the Ottoman Empire brought Islamic rule over much of southeast Europe. Islam spread along trade routes to sub-Saharan Africa. In east Africa, it spread south along the coast. Further east, Muslim rulers established new imperial states in Persia (Iran) and India.

***The sextant** allowed navigators to take accurate measurements of heavenly bodies in relation to the horizon, thus allowing latitude to be calculated correctly. Early sextants had to be hand-held and were often used on shore rather than on board ship.*

THE AGE OF EXPANSION: 1648–1789

THE YEARS FROM the middle of the 17th century to the end of the 18th century saw a massive consolidation of European discovery and exploration, which took the form of colonial settlement and political expansion. This period also witnessed the beginning of a sharp rise in European population and in its economic strength, accompanied by rapid developments in the arts and sciences. All these factors powered European expansion – a process that would bring European culture to every part of the globe, gradually filling in the world map, and bringing it into often fatal contact with less robust indigenous cultures. By the last quarter of the 18th century, with Europe poised on the brink of political turmoil, only Africa and Australasia remained largely unmolested by European attentions.

GLOBAL STATES AND TERRITORIES

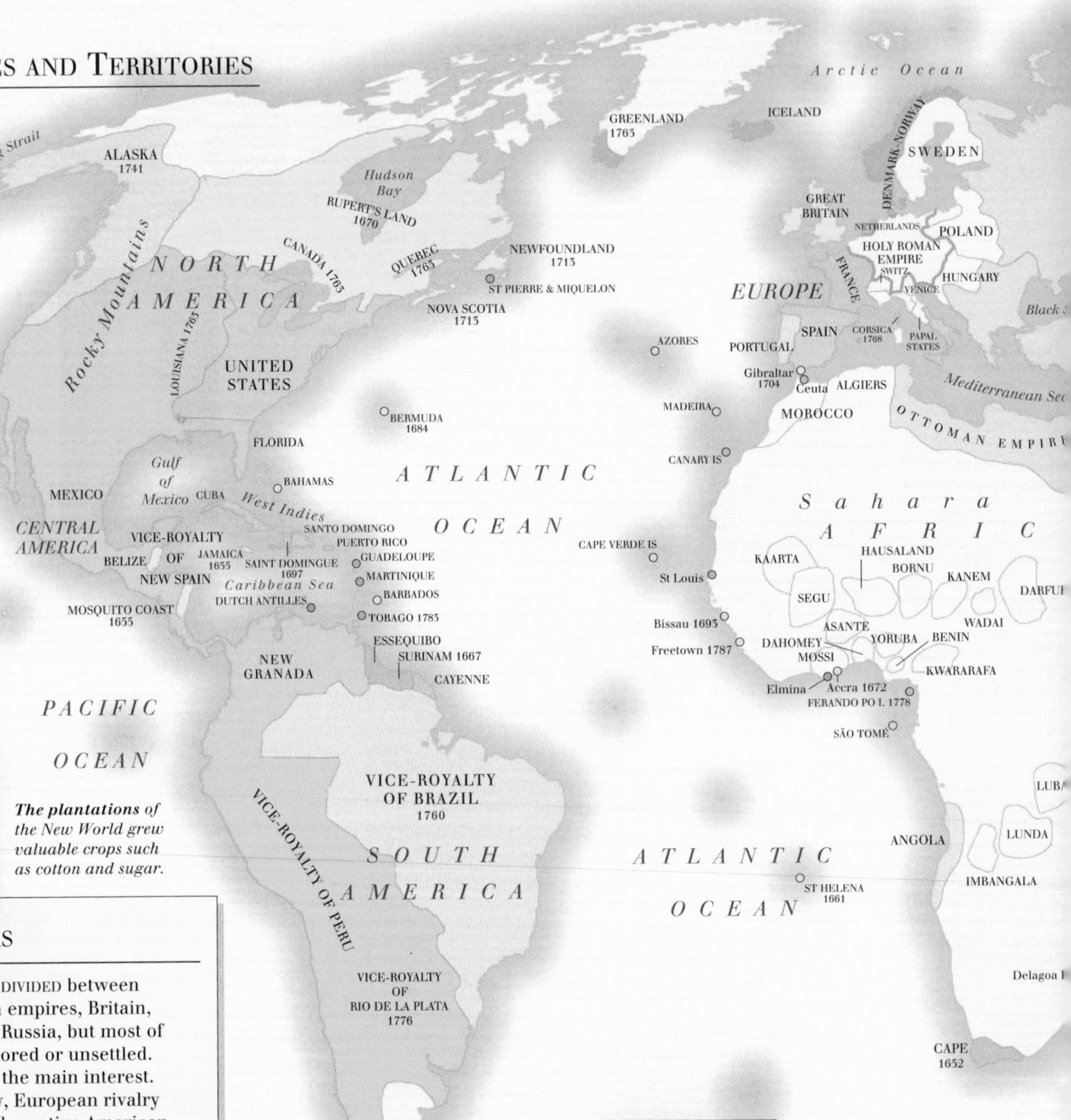

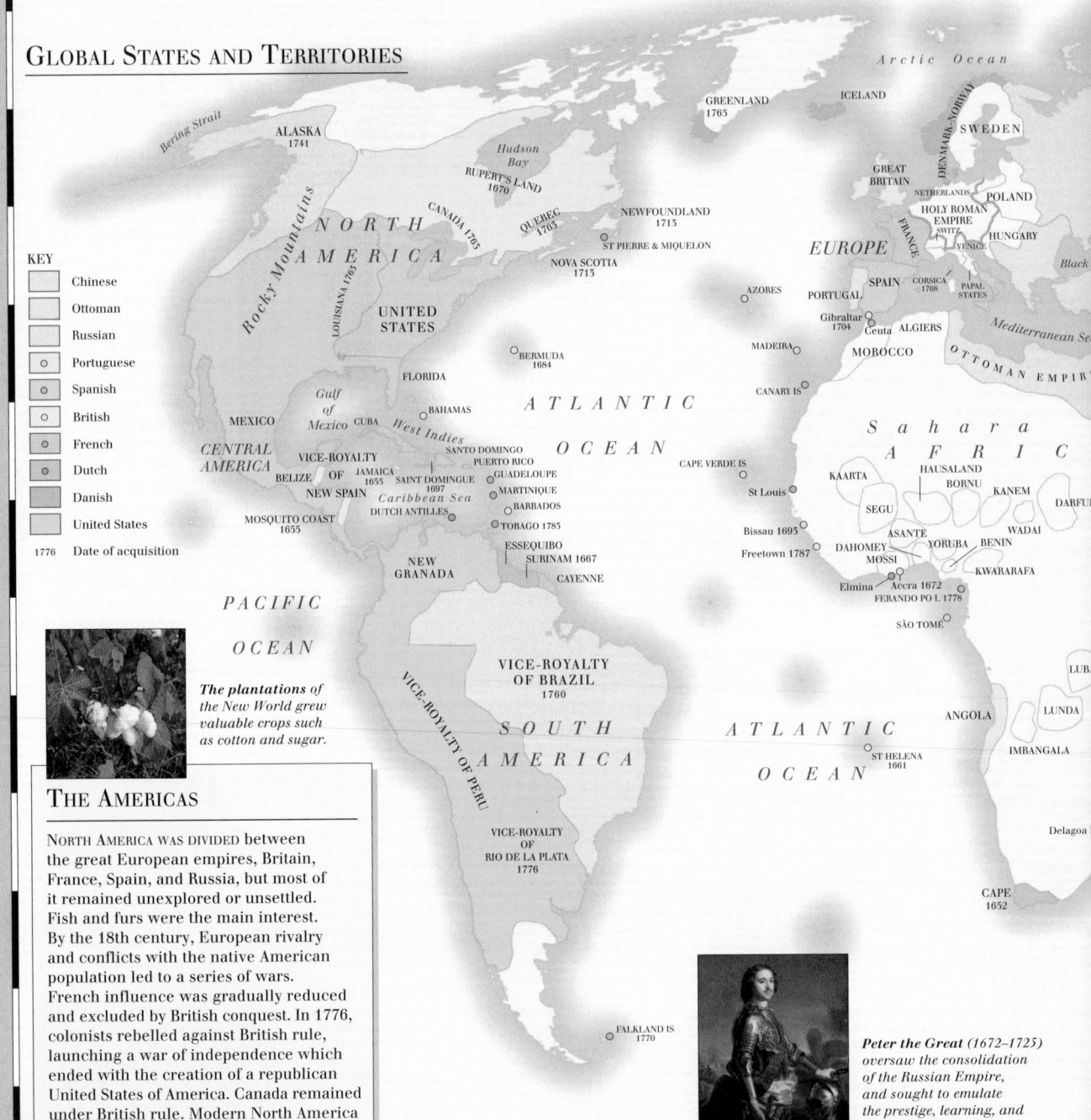

KEY
Chinese
Ottoman
Russian
Portuguese
Spanish
British
French
Dutch
Danish
United States
1776 Date of acquisition
Arctic Ocean
Bering Strait
ALASKA 1741
Hudson Bay
RUPERT'S LAND 1670
GREENLAND 1763
ICELAND
DENMARK-NORWAY
SWEDEN
GREAT BRITAIN
NETHERLANDS
POLAND
HOLY ROMAN EMPIRE
SWITZ.
HUNGARY
VENICE
FRANCE
EUROPE
Black
Rocky Mountains
NORTH AMERICA
CANADA 1763
QUEBEC 1763
NEWFOUNDLAND 1713
ST PIERRE & MIQUELON
NOVA SCOTIA 1713
LOUISIANA 1763
UNITED STATES
AZORES
PORTUGAL
SPAIN
CORSICA 1768
PAPAL STATES
Gibraltar 1704
Ceuta
ALGIERS
Mediterranean Sea
MADEIRA
MOROCCO
OTTOMAN EMPIRE
BERMUDA 1684
FLORIDA
Gulf of Mexico
BAHAMAS
CANARY IS
ATLANTIC OCEAN
MEXICO
CUBA
West Indies
Sahara
AFRICA
CENTRAL AMERICA
VICE-ROYALTY OF NEW SPAIN
SANTO DOMINGO
PUERTO RICO
JAMAICA 1655
SAINT DOMINGUE 1697
GUADELOUPE
MARTINIQUE
BARBADOS
BELIZE
Caribbean Sea
DUTCH ANTILLES
TOBAGO 1783
MOSQUITO COAST 1655
CAPE VERDE IS
St Louis
KAARTA
HAUSALAND
BORNU
KANEM
DARFUR
SEGU
Bissau 1693
ASANTE
WADAI
DAHOMEY
YORUBA
BENIN
MOSSI
Freetown 1787
KWARARAFA
ESSEQUIBO
SURINAM 1667
CAYENNE
NEW GRANADA
Elmina
Accra 1672
FERANDO PO I. 1778
SÃO TOMÉ
PACIFIC OCEAN
VICE-ROYALTY OF BRAZIL 1760
VICE-ROYALTY OF PERU
SOUTH AMERICA
ATLANTIC OCEAN
ST HELENA 1661
ANGOLA
LUNDA
IMBANGALA
VICE-ROYALTY OF RIO DE LA PLATA 1776
Delagoa
CAPE 1652
FALKLAND IS 1770

The plantations of the New World grew valuable crops such as cotton and sugar.

THE AMERICAS

NORTH AMERICA WAS DIVIDED between the great European empires, Britain, France, Spain, and Russia, but most of it remained unexplored or unsettled. Fish and furs were the main interest. By the 18th century, European rivalry and conflicts with the native American population led to a series of wars. French influence was gradually reduced and excluded by British conquest. In 1776, colonists rebelled against British rule, launching a war of independence which ended with the creation of a republican United States of America. Canada remained under British rule. Modern North America was gradually taking shape.

***Peter the Great** (1672–1725) oversaw the consolidation of the Russian Empire, and sought to emulate the prestige, learning, and sophistication of the western European monarchies.*

EUROPE

AFTER THE CRISIS of the Thirty Years War, Europe began to develop a more settled state system as successful dynastic houses imposed more centralized rule. The Habsburgs acquired control over Hungary and much of central Europe. Russia's frontiers pushed into Poland and the Ukraine. The French Bourbon monarchy became the most powerful in Europe. Its material wealth and culture made it a rival to the older empires of Asia. French became the common language of educated Europeans, and French philosophy led to the intellectual "Enlightenment."

Isaac Newton *(1642–1727), the leading scientist of Europe's Age of Reason.*

ASIA

THE CH'ING DYNASTY forged the shape of modern China. By 1658 the whole of southern China was under Manchu control. Formosa (Taiwan) was occupied in 1683, outer Mongolia in 1697. A protectorate was established over Tibet in 1751. Over the course of this expansion, the population of China tripled and the economy boomed through trade in tea, porcelain, and silk with Russia and the West. Manchu China was powerful enough to resist incursions by the European empires, avoiding the fate of the crumbling Mughal empire in India, where Britain and France competed for trade and territory.

Dutch and British *East Indiamen carried the vast European trade with Asia.*

RUSSIAN EMPIRE
Bering Strait
KAZAKHSTAN
A S I A
Aral Sea
Caspian Sea
MONGOLIA 1697
KHOKAND
SINKIANG 1760
TURKESTAN
MANCHU (CH'ING) EMPIRE
Sea of Japan
JAPAN
KOREA
PERSIA
AFGHANISTAN
Himalayas
TIBET 1751
Deshima
PACIFIC OCEAN
The Gulf
BALUCHISTAN
NEPAL
BENGAL 1757
MARATHA CONFEDERACY
Surat
Diu
Daman
Bombay 1661
Chandernagore
BURMA 1688
Bay of Bengal
Macao
FORMOSA 1683
Arabian Sea
Goa
NORTHERN CIRCARS 1756
SIAM
ANNAM
PHILIPPINES
South China Sea
MARIANAS 1668
Mahé 1725
MADRAS
Pondicherry 1674
Karikal 1738
ANDAMAN IS 1789
CAROLINE IS 1686
ETHIOPIA
Galle
CEYLON 1658
Penang 1786
MALAYA
Micronesia
INDIAN OCEAN
MOLUCCAS
Melanesia
CHAGOS IS 1784
DUTCH EAST INDIES
PORTUGUESE AFRICA
TIMOR
Madagascar
RÉUNION 1662
Fort Dauphin 1766
AUSTRALIA
LORD HOWE I. 1788
NEW SOUTH WALES 1788
NEW ZEALAND

Maori New Zealand *was one of the few indigenous cultures to remain untouched by European contact until the 19th century.*

OCEANIA

SOUTHEAST ASIA AND OCEANIA were areas of small, warring kingdoms, increasingly prey to the ambitions of European traders, first Spanish and Portuguese, then Dutch and British. Yet, by the late 18th century, there was still little formal colonization. Officially discovered by Europeans in the early 17th century, most of Australasia was still unexplored and unsettled, except for a number of small penal colonies set up by the British in New South Wales (1788) and Tasmania (1804).

African slavers *marched their human cargo from the interior to the coast for transshipment.*

AFRICA

DURING THE 17TH AND 18TH CENTURIES Africa was regarded by the rest of the world as a source of two things: gold and slaves. Some 13.5 million slaves were shipped in the 1700s, from the west coast and from Portuguese Angola. African dealers sold to European middlemen, who in turn sold on the surviving slaves. In northern and northeastern Africa, Arab slavers traded with the Ottoman Empire. But the rest of Africa remained isolated from the outside world.

Harrison's chronometer, *invented in 1762, allowed navigators to measure time accurately, and thus calculate longitude correctly. This greatly reduced the risk of shipwreck and heralded the beginning of accurate mapping of the world.*

The Age of Revolution: 1789–1830

In 1789 royal power was shattered by the French Revolution. The collapse of the most powerful monarchy in Europe reverberated worldwide. The revolutions in France and America ushered in the idea of the modern nation state, and of popular representative government. Revolutionary outbreaks occurred elsewhere in Europe, and overseas colonies in Latin America won their independence. At the same time, an industrial revolution was taking place in Europe, transforming the old trading economy into a manufacturing base which would require a global supply of raw materials and a global market to fuel it. The revolutionary years thus marked the beginning of the modern political and economic world order.

Global States and Territories

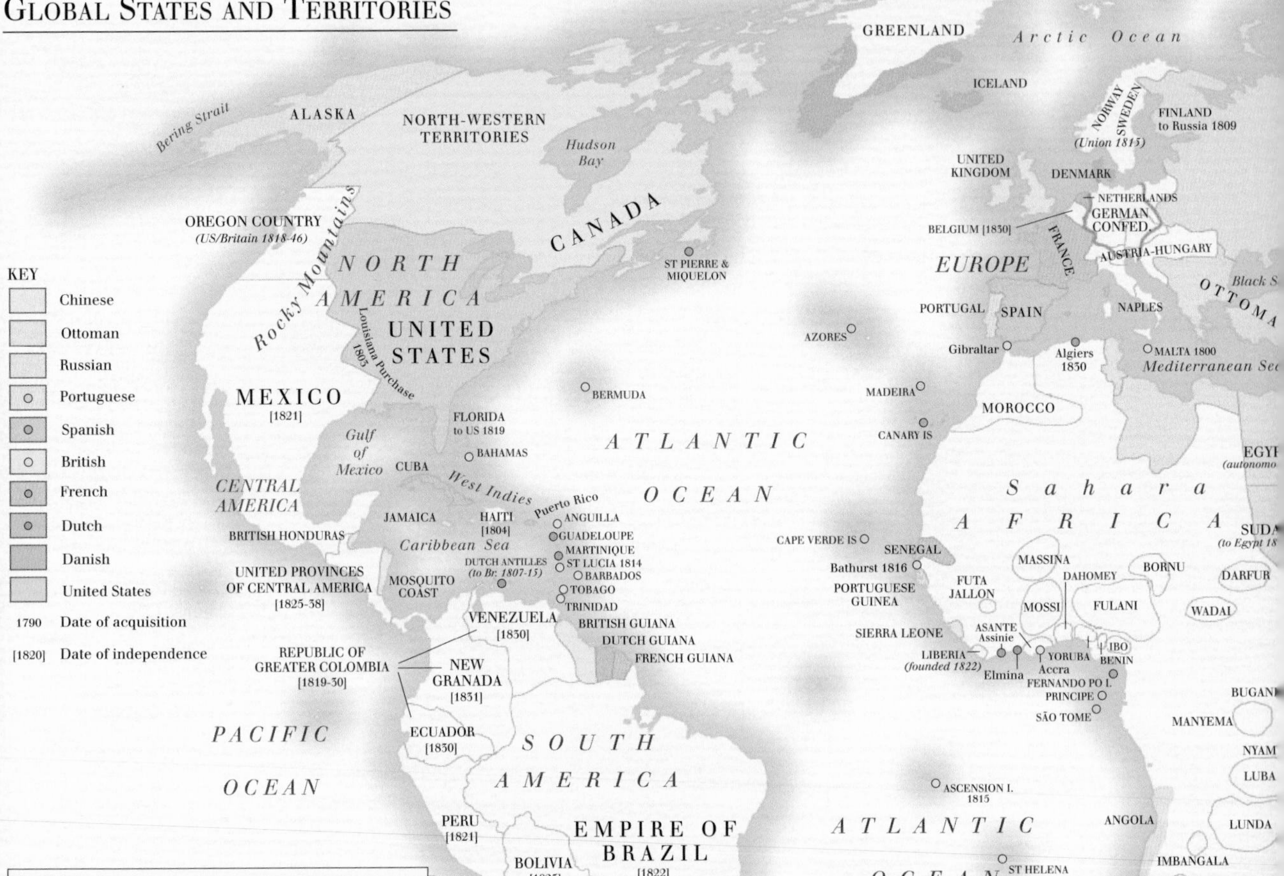

KEY
Chinese
Ottoman
Russian
Portuguese
Spanish
British
French
Dutch
Danish
United States
1790 Date of acquisition
[1820] Date of independence
GREENLAND
Arctic Ocean
ICELAND
NORWAY
SWEDEN
(Union 1815)
FINLAND to Russia 1809
Bering Strait
ALASKA
NORTH-WESTERN TERRITORIES
Hudson Bay
UNITED KINGDOM
DENMARK
NETHERLANDS
GERMAN CONFED.
BELGIUM [1830]
FRANCE
AUSTRIA-HUNGARY
OREGON COUNTRY (US/Britain 1818-46)
Rocky Mountains
CANADA
NORTH AMERICA
Louisiana Purchase 1803
UNITED STATES
ST PIERRE & MIQUELON
EUROPE
Black S
OTTOMA
PORTUGAL
SPAIN
NAPLES
AZORES
Gibraltar
Algiers 1830
MALTA 1800
Mediterranean Se
MEXICO [1821]
BERMUDA
MADEIRA
MOROCCO
FLORIDA to US 1819
Gulf of Mexico
BAHAMAS
ATLANTIC OCEAN
CANARY IS
EGYP (autonomo
CUBA
West Indies
CENTRAL AMERICA
Puerto Rico
ANGUILLA
JAMAICA
HAITI [1804]
GUADELOUPE
MARTINIQUE
Caribbean Sea
ST LUCIA 1814
BARBADOS
DUTCH ANTILLES (to Br. 1807-15)
TOBAGO
TRINIDAD
BRITISH HONDURAS
UNITED PROVINCES OF CENTRAL AMERICA [1825-38]
MOSQUITO COAST
Sahara
AFRICA
SUDA (to Egypt 18
CAPE VERDE IS
SENEGAL
Bathurst 1816
MASSINA
BORNU
DAHOMEY
DARFUR
PORTUGUESE GUINEA
FUTA JALLON
MOSSI
FULANI
WADAI
VENEZUELA [1830]
BRITISH GUIANA
DUTCH GUIANA
FRENCH GUIANA
SIERRA LEONE
ASANTE
Assinie
IBO
LIBERIA (founded 1822)
Elmina
Accra
YORUBA
BENIN
FERNANDO PO I.
PRINCIPE
SÃO TOMÉ
REPUBLIC OF GREATER COLOMBIA [1819-30]
NEW GRANADA [1831]
PACIFIC OCEAN
ECUADOR [1830]
SOUTH AMERICA
BUGAN
MANYEMA
NYAM
LUBA
ASCENSION I. 1815
PERU [1821]
EMPIRE OF BRAZIL [1822]
ATLANTIC OCEAN
ANGOLA
LUNDA
BOLIVIA [1825]
ST HELENA
IMBANGALA
OVIMBUNDU
PARAGUAY [1811]
MATABELELAN
Delagoa B
SWAZI
SOTHO
ZULU
ARGENTINA [1816]
CAPE COLONY
CHILE [1818]
URUGUAY [1828]
TRISTAN DA CUNHA 1815
Patagonia
FALKLAND IS (to Argentina 1820-33)

The Americas

The fledgling United States of America began to expand rapidly, purchasing the Midwest territories from France in 1803, and Florida from Spain in 1819. Revolutionary fervor both here and in Europe weakened the control of France, Spain, and Portugal throughout Latin America. From 1810 there followed 20 years of violent revolt, with native armies fighting their European masters and each other. The new states were prey to political violence and instability, but they never again came under European rule.

Simón Bolívar (1783–1830) led armies of liberation in Peru, Bolivia, and Venezuela.

Napoléon Bonaparte (1769–1821) began his career as a commander in the French Revolutionary wars. By 1804 he had become emperor of France, which dominated much of western Europe.

EUROPE

UNDER NAPOLÉON BONAPARTE, France subordinated a large part of Europe and destroyed the old feudal order. Napoléon helped to shape the new nation states that emerged in 19th-century Europe – Belgium, Italy, and Germany. He gave much of Europe its modern legal code and systems of measurement, education, and local government.

Steam-powered engines *transformed the European industrial economy.*

ASIA

THE PRINCIPAL COLONIAL POWER in Asia was Russia, whose consolidation of its empire in northern and central Asia continued throughout the 19th century. But now the Dutch began to extend their control of the East Indies, while a bitter struggle between the British and the French was conducted in and around the Indian Ocean. France was gradually forced to concede many of its footholds in India, where the British East India Company rapidly extended its interests by a mixture of diplomacy and military force. But the elusive key to Asia's largest markets remained the slumbering giant of Ch'ing China, whose Manchu rulers, like the shoguns of Japan, remained unimpressed by European overtures.

The spices of the East Indies, *such as pepper, were among the most highly valued trade commodities from Asia.*

RUSSIAN EMPIRE
Bering Strait
A S I A
Aral Sea
Caspian Sea
MONGOLIA
MANCHU (CH'ING) CHINA
Sea of Japan
JAPAN
KOREA
PERSIA
AFGHAN-ISTAN
TIBET (Chinese protectorate from 1750)
Himalayas
NEPAL
BHUTAN
The Gulf
ARABIA
OMAN
Diu
Daman
INDIA
Bay of Bengal
BURMA
ANNAM
SIAM
Macao
FORMOSA
PACIFIC OCEAN
MARIANAS
Arabian Sea
Goa
TENASSERIM 1826
South China Sea
PHILIPPINES
Mahé
Pondicherry
LACCADIVE IS 1791
Karikal
ANDAMAN IS
THIOPIA
CAROLINE IS
Micronesia
Ceylon
MALAYA
Malacca 1824
MALDIVE IS 1887
SINGAPORE 1819
Melanesia
ANZIBAR
SEYCHELLES 1794
CHAGOS IS
DUTCH EAST INDIES
New Guinea
Timor
ORTUGUESE AST FRICA
INDIAN OCEAN
Madagascar
HOVA KINGDOM
MAURITIUS 1810
RÉUNION
WESTERN AUSTRALIA 1829
NEW SOUTH WALES
AUSTRALIA
LORD HOWE I.
NEW ZEALAND
CHATHAM IS 1791
TASMANIA (Van Diemen's Land)
AUCKLAND IS 1806
MACQUARIE IS 1811

James Cook *(1728–1779) charted much of the Pacific.*

OCEANIA

THOUGH PORTUGUESE and Dutch explorers had confirmed the existence of Australasia in the 17th century, it was not until the voyages of Captain Cook in the 1770s that the geography of the Pacific was established, and the fertile eastern coast of Australia was explored and charted. Over the next 30 years, small settlements were established around the coast; by 1829, Britain had brought the whole of Australia under the British flag.

The first European *migrants to Africa settled in Cape Colony.*

AFRICA

THE NORTHERN REGIONS OF AFRICA were part of the vast Islamic Ottoman Empire; from here Islam spread south to west Africa and the Horn of Africa. Holy wars (or *jihads*) in the late 18th and early 19th centuries completed the conversion to Islam of much of Saharan and sub-Saharan Africa. Large tribal kingdoms flourished in the Congo basin and southern Africa.

The development *during the European industrial revolution of mechanized manufacturing plant and machinery, such as power looms, gave Europe effective control of a booming global trade in raw materials and mass-manufactured commodities.*

The Age of Empire: 1830–1914

THE 19TH CENTURY was dominated by the spread of modern industry and transportation, and the expansion of European trade and influence worldwide. Industry made Europe rich and powerful; its capital cities were monuments to the self-confidence of the new European age. Railroads and steamships revolutionized communications, bringing a stream of industrial goods, technical know-how, and European settlers across America, Africa, and Asia. Modern industry and weapons brought Europe to the summit of global influence. In these developments lay the origins of the division of the world into rich and poor regions; a developed, prosperous north and an underdeveloped, dependent south.

Global States and Territories

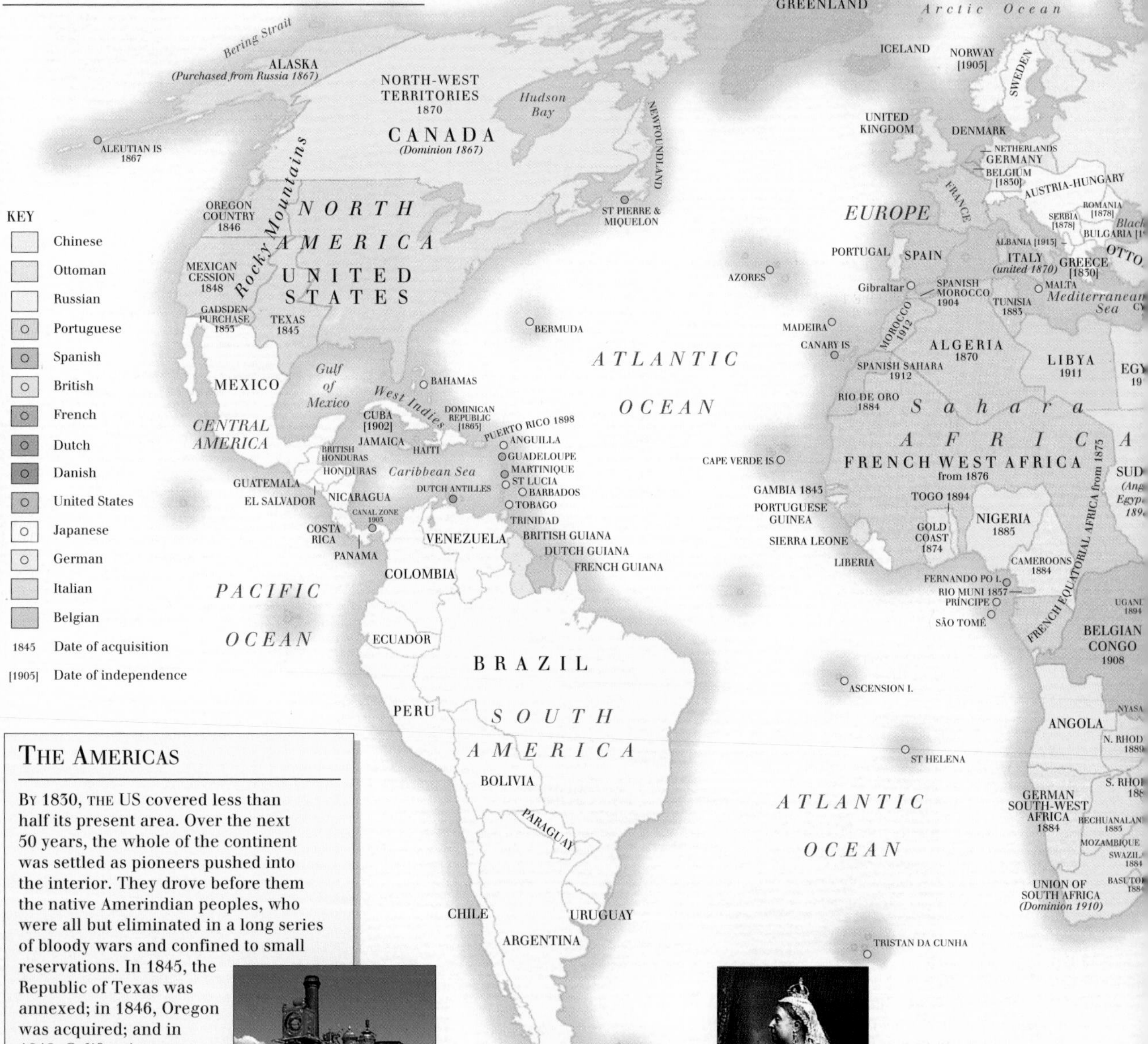

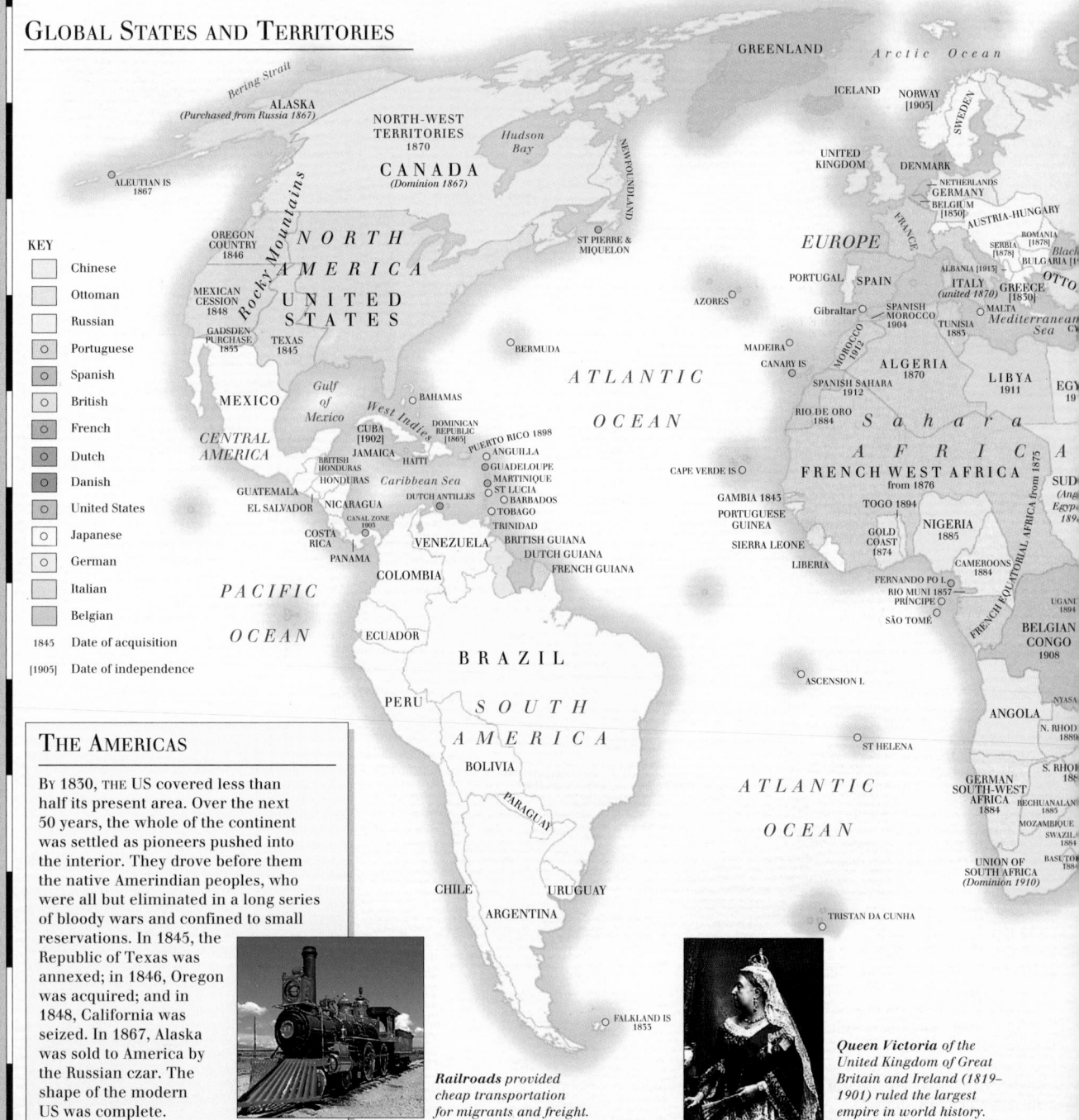

KEY
Chinese
Ottoman
Russian
Portuguese
Spanish
British
French
Dutch
Danish
United States
Japanese
German
Italian
Belgian
1845 Date of acquisition
[1905] Date of independence
Bering Strait
ALASKA (Purchased from Russia 1867)
ALEUTIAN IS 1867
NORTH-WEST TERRITORIES 1870
CANADA (Dominion 1867)
Hudson Bay
NEWFOUNDLAND
ST PIERRE & MIQUELON
Rocky Mountains
OREGON COUNTRY 1846
NORTH AMERICA
MEXICAN CESSION 1848
UNITED STATES
GADSDEN PURCHASE 1853
TEXAS 1845
MEXICO
Gulf of Mexico
BERMUDA
BAHAMAS
West Indies
CUBA [1902]
DOMINICAN REPUBLIC [1865]
PUERTO RICO 1898
JAMAICA
HAITI
ANGUILLA
GUADELOUPE
MARTINIQUE
ST LUCIA
BARBADOS
TOBAGO
TRINIDAD
CENTRAL AMERICA
BRITISH HONDURAS
HONDURAS
Caribbean Sea
GUATEMALA
EL SALVADOR
NICARAGUA
DUTCH ANTILLES
CANAL ZONE 1903
COSTA RICA
PANAMA
VENEZUELA
BRITISH GUIANA
DUTCH GUIANA
FRENCH GUIANA
COLOMBIA
PACIFIC OCEAN
ECUADOR
BRAZIL
PERU
SOUTH AMERICA
BOLIVIA
PARAGUAY
CHILE
URUGUAY
ARGENTINA
FALKLAND IS 1833
ATLANTIC OCEAN
AZORES
MADEIRA
CANARY IS
CAPE VERDE IS
ASCENSION I.
ST HELENA
TRISTAN DA CUNHA
ATLANTIC OCEAN
GREENLAND
Arctic Ocean
ICELAND
NORWAY [1905]
SWEDEN
UNITED KINGDOM
DENMARK
NETHERLANDS
GERMANY
BELGIUM [1830]
AUSTRIA-HUNGARY
FRANCE
EUROPE
ROMANIA [1878]
SERBIA [1878]
BULGARIA
PORTUGAL
SPAIN
ALBANIA [1913]
ITALY (united 1870)
GREECE [1830]
OTTO
Gibraltar
SPANISH MOROCCO 1904
MALTA
Mediterranean Sea
TUNISIA 1883
MOROCCO 1912
ALGERIA 1870
LIBYA 1911
SPANISH SAHARA 1912
RIO DE ORO 1884
Sahara
AFRICA
FRENCH WEST AFRICA from 1876
GAMBIA 1843
PORTUGUESE GUINEA
TOGO 1894
SIERRA LEONE
GOLD COAST 1874
NIGERIA 1885
LIBERIA
CAMEROONS 1884
FERNANDO PO I.
RIO MUNI 1857
PRÍNCIPE
SÃO TOMÉ
FRENCH EQUATORIAL AFRICA from 1875
BELGIAN CONGO 1908
ANGOLA
N. RHOD
GERMAN SOUTH-WEST AFRICA 1884
BECHUANALAND 1885
MOZAMBIQUE
SWAZIL 1884
UNION OF SOUTH AFRICA (Dominion 1910)

The Americas

By 1830, the US covered less than half its present area. Over the next 50 years, the whole of the continent was settled as pioneers pushed into the interior. They drove before them the native Amerindian peoples, who were all but eliminated in a long series of bloody wars and confined to small reservations. In 1845, the Republic of Texas was annexed; in 1846, Oregon was acquired; and in 1848, California was seized. In 1867, Alaska was sold to America by the Russian czar. The shape of the modern US was complete.

***Railroads** provided cheap transportation for migrants and freight.*

***Queen Victoria** of the United Kingdom of Great Britain and Ireland (1819–1901) ruled the largest empire in world history.*

EUROPE

IN THE 19TH CENTURY, Europe was transformed into an industrial economy. In the new industrial cities, pressure developed for liberal reforms and parliamentary politics. Nationalists created new states in Germany, Italy, Greece, Serbia, and Belgium. While the modern map of Europe gradually began to take shape, European imperialists brought still more areas of the world under their control.

***Sailing ships** carried most oceanic trade until 1900.*

ASIA

BUILDING ON COLONIAL INTERESTS that stretched back into the 18th century, Britain and France transformed the political world of south Asia. Britain extended its rule in India and, in 1885, Burma was brought under British control. The Vietnamese and Chinese Empires were pressured by Europeans anxious to trade and to spread Christianity: the Ch'ing empire conceded areas of influence; the Vietnamese empire resisted and was brought under French domination by force. By the 1890s the whole of southern Asia except for Siam was dominated by Europe, which created the modern state structure of the region.

***The Japanese emperor Meiji** (1852–1912) opened Japan to Western trade and influence.*

***The colonization** of Australia and New Zealand was based on sheep farming.*

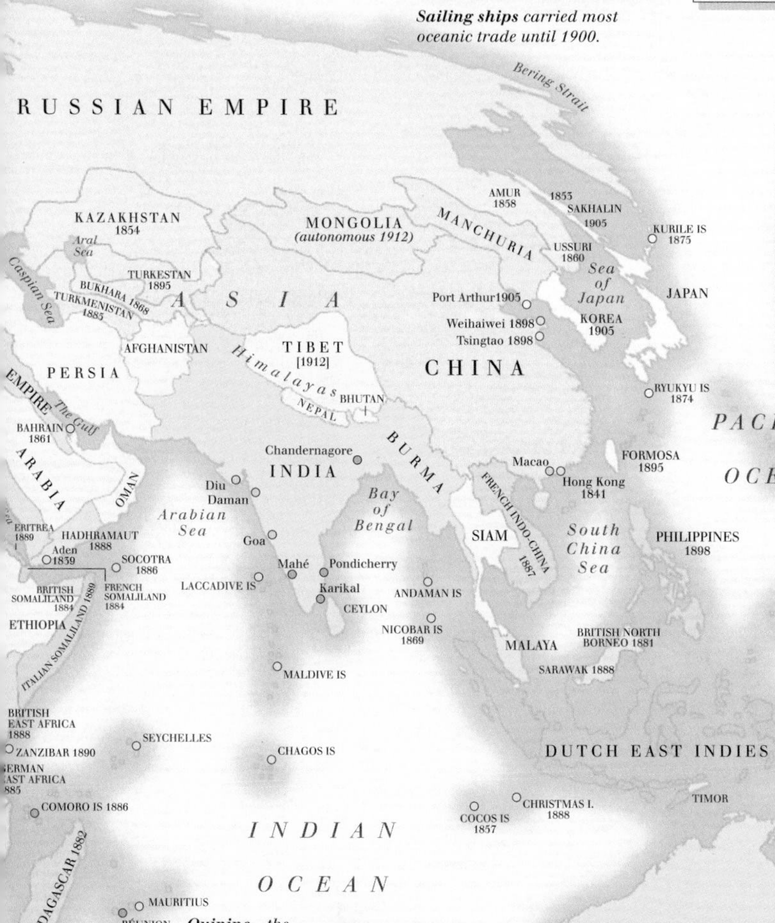
RUSSIAN EMPIRE
Bering Strait
KAZAKHSTAN 1854
Aral Sea
Caspian Sea
MONGOLIA (autonomous 1912)
MANCHURIA
AMUR 1858
1855
SAKHALIN 1905
KURILE IS 1875
USSURI 1860
Sea of Japan
JAPAN
TURKESTAN 1895
BUKHARA 1868
TURKMENISTAN 1885
ASIA
Port Arthur 1905
Weihaiwei 1898
Tsingtao 1898
KOREA 1905
AFGHANISTAN
TIBET [1912]
Himalayas
BHUTAN
NEPAL
CHINA
PERSIA
EMPIRE
The Gulf
BAHRAIN 1861
RYUKYU IS 1874
PACIFIC OCEAN
ARABIA
OMAN
Chandernagore
INDIA
BURMA
Macao
Hong Kong 1841
FORMOSA 1895
Diu
Daman
Arabian Sea
Bay of Bengal
FRENCH INDO-CHINA 1887
ERITREA 1889
HADHRAMAUT 1888
Aden 1839
SOCOTRA 1886
Goa
SIAM
South China Sea
PHILIPPINES 1898
MARIANAS 1899
Mahé
Pondicherry
Karikal
GUAM 1898
BRITISH SOMALILAND 1884
FRENCH SOMALILAND 1884
LACCADIVE IS
ANDAMAN IS
CEYLON
CAROLINE IS 1899
Micronesia
ETHIOPIA
ITALIAN SOMALILAND 1889
NICOBAR IS 1869
MALAYA
BRITISH NORTH BORNEO 1881
SARAWAK 1888
MALDIVE IS
BRITISH EAST AFRICA 1888
BISMARCK ARCHIPELAGO 1884
NAURU 1888
Melanesia
SEYCHELLES
ZANZIBAR 1890
CHAGOS IS
DUTCH EAST INDIES
NEW GUINEA
PAPUA 1906
SOLOMON IS 1893
GERMAN EAST AFRICA 1885
COMORO IS 1886
CHRISTMAS I. 1888
COCOS IS 1857
TIMOR
INDIAN OCEAN
MADAGASCAR 1882
MAURITIUS
RÉUNION
NEW CALEDONIA 1853
AUSTRALIA (Commonwealth 1901)
NORFOLK ISLAND
NEW ZEALAND 1840 (Dominion 1907)
CHATHAM IS.
TASMANIA
AUCKLAND IS
MACQUARIE IS

OCEANIA

DURING THE 19TH century, Australia and New Zealand remained closely tied to the British homeland. British settlers came to farm and later to prospect for gold and other valuable minerals. In 1840, New Zealand came under British rule and the native Maoris were forced off the land. Not until 1872 was the continent of Australia traversed, and not until 1901 was a single state, the Commonwealth of Australia, proclaimed.

***Quinine** – the cure for malaria.*

***New medicines** made the colonization of Africa possible.*

AFRICA

THE POLITICAL STRUCTURE of independent Africa was torn up by encroaching European empires. As native societies reacted violently to European intrusion, so European military and political power was increased to secure European interests. In 1884, in Berlin, the European powers divided Africa between them. The "Partition of Africa" established the modern frontiers of many states.

***The Gatling gun,** the most successful of the hand-crank-operated machine guns of the 19th century.*

***The European** imperial powers maintained control of their often far-flung colonies by military superiority. Native forces were rarely a match for the large, highly trained armies, powerful navies, and technically advanced weaponry which the Europeans had at their disposal.*

The Age of Global War: 1914–1945

In 1914, imperial and military rivalry in Europe provoked the first of two world wars, the largest and most destructive wars in human history. At the end of the first war, in 1918, the old international order was dead. The Russian Empire collapsed in revolution and was transformed by a communist minority into the Soviet Union. The German, Habsburg, and Ottoman empires were dismembered. A fragile peace ensued but the old equilibrium was gone. The rise of strident nationalism in Germany, Japan, and Italy destroyed the peace once again in 1939. The second war cost the lives of 50 million people and ravaged Europe and Asia. At its end, in 1945, the US and the Soviet Union had emerged as the new superpowers.

Global States and Territories

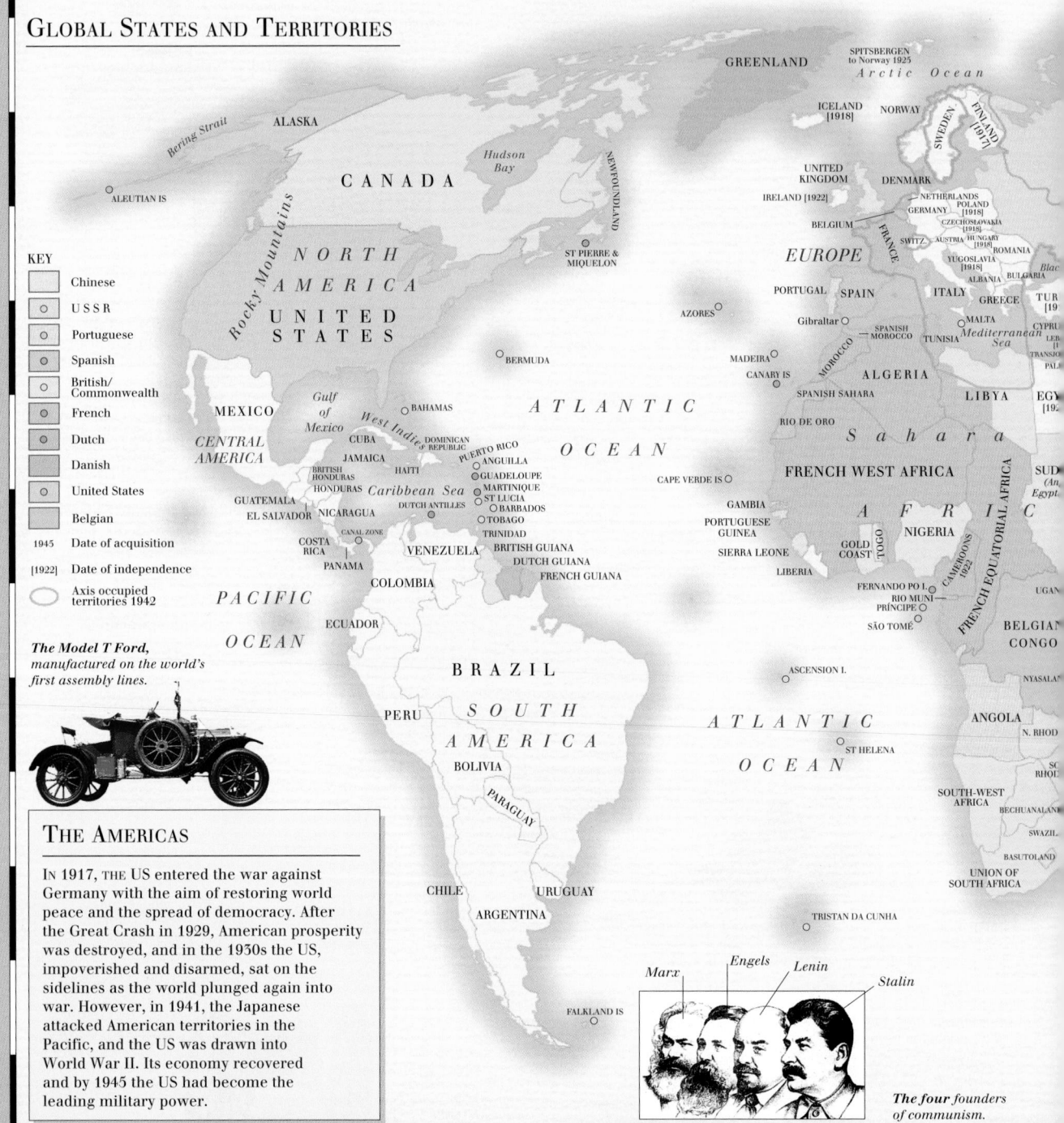

KEY
Chinese
USSR
Portuguese
Spanish
British/ Commonwealth
French
Dutch
Danish
United States
Belgian
1945 Date of acquisition
[1922] Date of independence
Axis occupied territories 1942
GREENLAND
SPITSBERGEN to Norway 1925
Arctic Ocean
ICELAND [1918]
NORWAY
SWEDEN
FINLAND [1917]
ALASKA
Bering Strait
ALEUTIAN IS
Hudson Bay
CANADA
NEWFOUNDLAND
Rocky Mountains
NORTH AMERICA
UNITED STATES
ST PIERRE & MIQUELON
UNITED KINGDOM
DENMARK
IRELAND [1922]
NETHERLANDS
POLAND [1918]
GERMANY
CZECHOSLOVAKIA [1918]
BELGIUM
FRANCE
SWITZ.
AUSTRIA
HUNGARY [1918]
ROMANIA
EUROPE
YUGOSLAVIA [1918]
ALBANIA
BULGARIA
PORTUGAL
SPAIN
ITALY
GREECE
AZORES
Gibraltar
SPANISH MOROCCO
MALTA
TUNISIA
Mediterranean Sea
BERMUDA
MADEIRA
MOROCCO
CANARY IS
ALGERIA
SPANISH SAHARA
LIBYA
MEXICO
Gulf of Mexico
BAHAMAS
West Indies
ATLANTIC OCEAN
RIO DE ORO
Sahara
CENTRAL AMERICA
CUBA
DOMINICAN REPUBLIC
PUERTO RICO
JAMAICA
HAITI
ANGUILLA
BRITISH HONDURAS
GUADELOUPE
HONDURAS
Caribbean Sea
MARTINIQUE
ST LUCIA
DUTCH ANTILLES
BARBADOS
GUATEMALA
EL SALVADOR
NICARAGUA
TOBAGO
CANAL ZONE
TRINIDAD
COSTA RICA
PANAMA
VENEZUELA
BRITISH GUIANA
DUTCH GUIANA
FRENCH GUIANA
COLOMBIA
CAPE VERDE IS
FRENCH WEST AFRICA
GAMBIA
PORTUGUESE GUINEA
SIERRA LEONE
LIBERIA
GOLD COAST
TOGO
NIGERIA
AFRICA
CAMEROONS 1922
FRENCH EQUATORIAL AFRICA
FERNANDO PO I.
RIO MUNI
PRÍNCIPE
SÃO TOMÉ
BELGIAN CONGO
PACIFIC OCEAN
ECUADOR
BRAZIL
ASCENSION I.
PERU
SOUTH AMERICA
ATLANTIC OCEAN
ST HELENA
ANGOLA
N. RHOD
BOLIVIA
PARAGUAY
SOUTH-WEST AFRICA
BECHUANALAND
SWAZIL.
BASUTOLAND
UNION OF SOUTH AFRICA
CHILE
URUGUAY
ARGENTINA
TRISTAN DA CUNHA
FALKLAND IS

The Model T Ford, manufactured on the world's first assembly lines.

The Americas

In 1917, the US entered the war against Germany with the aim of restoring world peace and the spread of democracy. After the Great Crash in 1929, American prosperity was destroyed, and in the 1930s the US, impoverished and disarmed, sat on the sidelines as the world plunged again into war. However, in 1941, the Japanese attacked American territories in the Pacific, and the US was drawn into World War II. Its economy recovered and by 1945 the US had become the leading military power.

Marx
Engels
Lenin
Stalin

The four founders of communism.

EUROPE

BOTH WORLD WARS had their origins in Europe. In 1914, Germany invaded Belgium; Britain, France, and Russia combined to defeat it, with US help. In 1918 new nation states were established in eastern Europe. But, by 1939, revived German nationalism started a second world war; much of western Europe came under a German "New Order" until the Soviet Union, Britain, and the US developed sufficient military strength to reconquer Europe and defeat Germany.

World War II *was decided by mechanical and industrial superiority.*

ASIA

THE COLLAPSE OF THE CHINESE EMPIRE in 1911, followed in 1917 by the disappearance of the Russian Empire, produced instability across Asia. Full-scale war broke out between Japan and China in 1937, with Japan trying to conquer China. The Soviet Union was the victim of German aggression from 1941. Both Japan and Germany were held at bay by communist forces which eventually succeeded in imposing stable politics on Asia. By 1945, the Soviet Union had reconquered its lost territories and dominated eastern Europe. In China, communist armies filled the vacuum left by the Japanese defeat.

Mahatma Gandhi *(1868–1948) led India to independence through peaceful noncooperation and protest.*

U S S R
Bering Strait
SAKHALIN 1945
MONGOLIA [1924]
Aral Sea
Caspian Sea
A S I A
KURILE IS 1945
Sea of Japan
JAPAN
KOREA [1945]
C H I N A
IRAQ [1932]
IRAN (Persia)
AFGHANISTAN
Himalayas
TIBET
NEPAL
BHUTAN
The Gulf
BAHRAIN
RYUKYU IS 1945
PACIFIC OCEAN
Chandernagore
INDIA
SAUDI ARABIA [1932]
YEMEN [1918]
OMAN
Red Sea
ERITREA 1941
HADHRAMAUT
Aden
Diu
Daman
Arabian Sea
Goa
Bay of Bengal
BURMA
Macao
Hong Kong
TAIWAN (Formosa) 1945
FRENCH INDO-CHINA
THAILAND (Siam)
South China Sea
PHILIPPINES
MARIANAS 1945
SOCOTRA
Mahé
Pondicherry
Karikal
LACCADIVE IS
ANDAMAN IS
CEYLON
NICOBAR IS
BRITISH SOMALILAND
FRENCH SOMALILAND
ITALIAN SOMALILAND 1941
ETHIOPIA
GUAM
CAROLINE IS 1945
Micronesia
BRITISH NORTH BORNEO
MALAYA
SARAWAK
MALDIVE IS
KENYA
BISMARCK ARCHIPELAGO 1945
NAURU 1945
ZANZIBAR
SEYCHELLES
CHAGOS IS
DUTCH EAST INDIES
NEW GUINEA
Melanesia
PAPUA
SOLOMON IS
TANGANYIKA
MOZAMBIQUE
COMORO IS
INDIAN OCEAN
CHRISTMAS I. 1888
COCOS IS
TIMOR
MADAGASCAR
MAURITIUS
RÉUNION
NEW CALEDONIA
AUSTRALIA (Dominion 1926)
LORD HOWE I.
NEW ZEALAND
CHATHAM IS
TASMANIA
AUCKLAND IS
MACQUARIE IS

OCEANIA

FOR THE ONLY TIME in its history, Australia was faced with the very real prospect of invasion. In World War II, Japanese armies reached the island of New Guinea, and bombed towns in northern Australia. Japanese submarines attacked Sydney harbor. The Battle of the Coral Sea, in May 1942, saved Australia, but it took almost three years to clear Japanese forces from the South Pacific, where they hung on grimly to the rich oil and mineral resources they had captured.

RISE OF ASIA

Japan promoted *itself as the liberator of Asia from the chains of European colonialism.*

Haile Selassie *(1892–1975), ruler of Ethiopia, the only independent empire in Africa.*

MIDDLE EAST

IN 1918, THE OTTOMAN EMPIRE disappeared after being in existence for 400 years. The modern map of north Africa and the Middle East was carved out of its ruins by the victors of World War I. The genocide of Europe's Jews by Nazi Germany during World War II accelerated the foundation of a new state of Israel in 1948, leading inexorably to conflict between displaced native Arabs and Jewish migrants.

A German Zeppelin *airship of the 1930s.*

The conquest *of the air was the most important technological achievement of the period. It added a devastating dimension to warfare, in the form of aerial bombing, while transforming civil transportation.*

THE MODERN AGE: 1945–PRESENT DAY

TWO NUCLEAR EXPLOSIONS in Japan finally ended World War II and ushered in a new era of global rivalry. Total destruction by nuclear weapons was a real possibility as the two superpowers, the Soviet Union and the US, became locked with their allies in a fearful Cold War. Various side conflicts were staged in the ruins of the old empires where new nation states, with old colonial borders, were emerging.

By 1991, communist power in the Soviet Union and Eastern Europe had crumbled, while the capitalism of the West had gained in strength.

The US is now the sole global superpower and has used its status to push Western goods and ideals to every corner of the globe, provoking often violent reactions among proud, conservative cultures. The age of globalization has begun.

GLOBAL STATES AND TERRITORIES

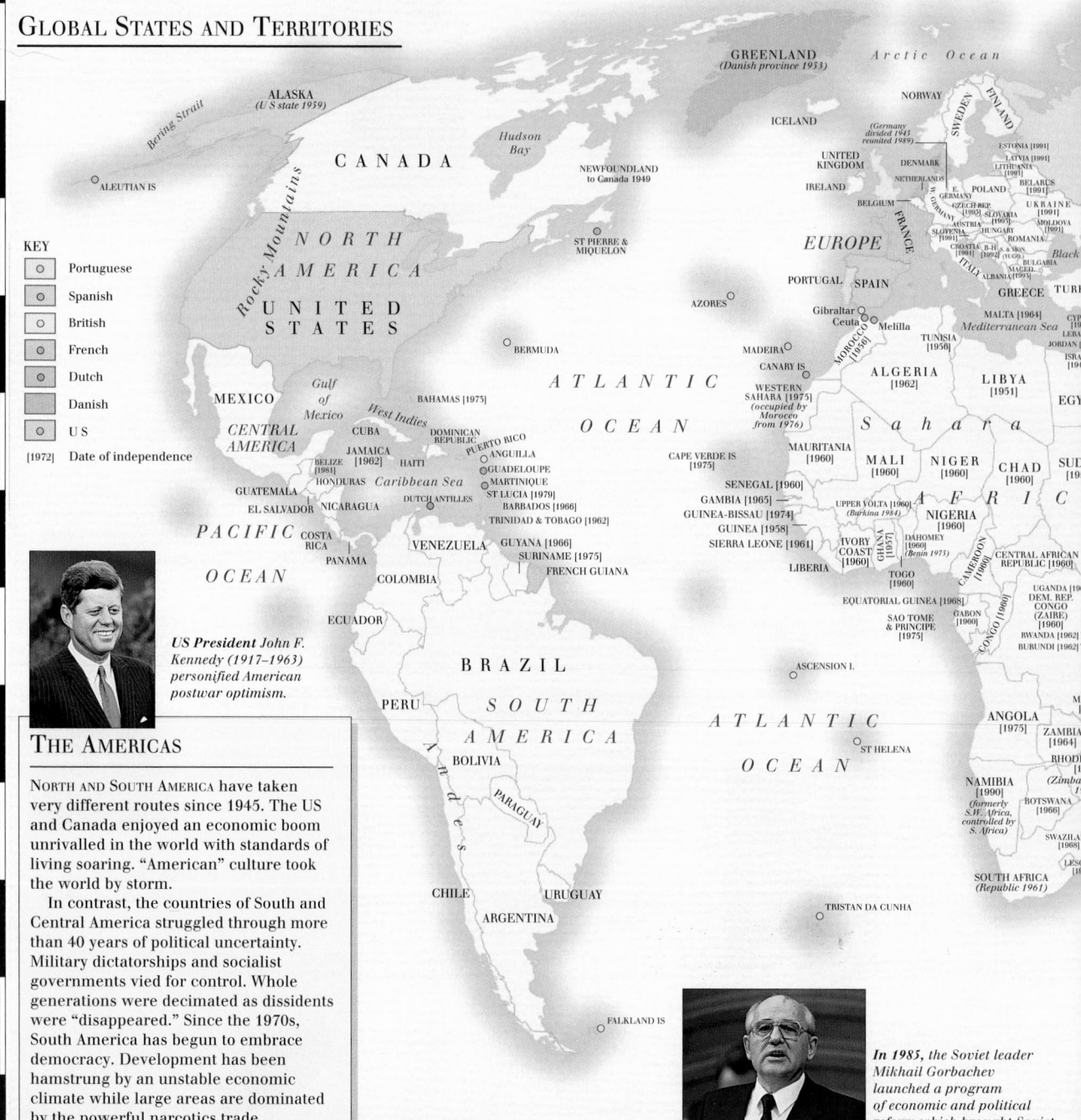

KEY
Portuguese
Spanish
British
French
Dutch
Danish
US
[1972] Date of independence
GREENLAND (Danish province 1953)
Arctic Ocean
ALASKA (U S state 1959)
Bering Strait
ALEUTIAN IS
Hudson Bay
CANADA
NEWFOUNDLAND to Canada 1949
ST PIERRE & MIQUELON
Rocky Mountains
NORTH AMERICA
UNITED STATES
MEXICO
Gulf of Mexico
CENTRAL AMERICA
West Indies
CUBA
BAHAMAS [1975]
DOMINICAN REPUBLIC
PUERTO RICO
JAMAICA [1962]
HAITI
BELIZE [1981]
HONDURAS
Caribbean Sea
ANGUILLA
GUADELOUPE
MARTINIQUE
ST LUCIA [1979]
BARBADOS [1966]
TRINIDAD & TOBAGO [1962]
DUTCH ANTILLES
GUATEMALA
EL SALVADOR
NICARAGUA
COSTA RICA
PANAMA
PACIFIC OCEAN
VENEZUELA
GUYANA [1966]
SURINAME [1975]
FRENCH GUIANA
COLOMBIA
ECUADOR
BRAZIL
PERU
SOUTH AMERICA
BOLIVIA
PARAGUAY
Andes
CHILE
URUGUAY
ARGENTINA
FALKLAND IS
BERMUDA
AZORES
ATLANTIC OCEAN
ICELAND
NORWAY
SWEDEN
FINLAND
(Germany divided 1945 reunited 1989)
UNITED KINGDOM
IRELAND
DENMARK
NETHERLANDS
BELGIUM
W. GERMANY
E. GERMANY
POLAND
ESTONIA [1991]
LATVIA [1991]
LITHUANIA [1991]
BELARUS [1991]
UKRAINE [1991]
MOLDOVA [1991]
CZECH REP. [1993]
SLOVAKIA [1993]
AUSTRIA
HUNGARY
SLOVENIA [1991]
CROATIA [1991]
ROMANIA
BULGARIA
FRANCE
EUROPE
ITALY
ALBANIA
GREECE
PORTUGAL
SPAIN
Gibraltar
Ceuta
Melilla
MOROCCO [1956]
MADEIRA
CANARY IS
TUNISIA [1956]
MALTA [1964]
Mediterranean Sea
ALGERIA [1962]
LIBYA [1951]
WESTERN SAHARA [1975] (occupied by Morocco from 1976)
Sahara
MAURITANIA [1960]
MALI [1960]
NIGER [1960]
CHAD [1960]
CAPE VERDE IS [1975]
SENEGAL [1960]
GAMBIA [1965]
GUINEA-BISSAU [1974]
GUINEA [1958]
SIERRA LEONE [1961]
UPPER VOLTA [1960] (Burkina 1984)
AFRICA
NIGERIA [1960]
IVORY COAST [1960]
GHANA [1957]
DAHOMEY [1960] (Benin 1975)
LIBERIA
TOGO [1960]
CAMEROON [1960]
CENTRAL AFRICAN REPUBLIC [1960]
EQUATORIAL GUINEA [1968]
SAO TOME & PRINCIPE [1975]
GABON [1960]
CONGO [1960]
DEM. REP. CONGO (ZAIRE) [1960]
RWANDA [1962]
BURUNDI [1962]
ASCENSION I.
ST HELENA
ANGOLA [1975]
ZAMBIA [1964]
NAMIBIA [1990] (formerly S.W. Africa, controlled by S. Africa)
BOTSWANA [1966]
SWAZILAND [1968]
SOUTH AFRICA (Republic 1961)
TRISTAN DA CUNHA

US President John F. Kennedy (1917–1963) *personified American postwar optimism.*

THE AMERICAS

NORTH AND SOUTH AMERICA have taken very different routes since 1945. The US and Canada enjoyed an economic boom unrivalled in the world with standards of living soaring. "American" culture took the world by storm.

In contrast, the countries of South and Central America struggled through more than 40 years of political uncertainty. Military dictatorships and socialist governments vied for control. Whole generations were decimated as dissidents were "disappeared." Since the 1970s, South America has begun to embrace democracy. Development has been hamstrung by an unstable economic climate while large areas are dominated by the powerful narcotics trade.

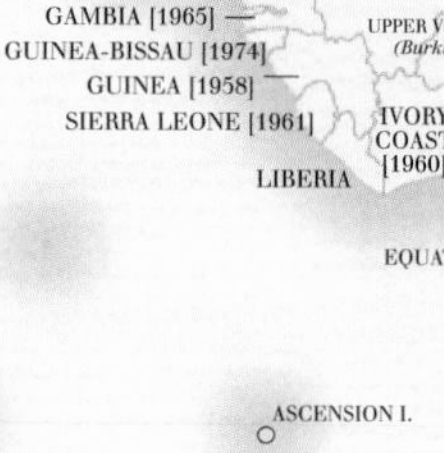

In 1985, the Soviet leader Mikhail Gorbachev launched a program of economic and political reform which brought Soviet communism to an end.

The Berlin Wall, symbol of the Cold War division of Europe, was demolished in 1989.

EUROPE

IN 1945, EUROPE LAY IN RUINS. The iron curtain descended to divide capitalist West from communist East. The West underwent an economic boom which restored widespread prosperity and political stability. It progressed toward economic and political unity under the EU. The East, meanwhile, labored under planned economies and quickly sought to catch up with the West after 1989, with most countries now aspiring to join the EU.

ASIA

IN SOUTHERN ASIA, popular nationalist movements came to power in India, Burma, Malaya, and Indonesia; in China and Indo-China, power passed to native communist movements whose roots went back to the 1920s. After 1949, China under Mao Zedong became, with its vast population and large military forces, a second communist superpower. Japan, meanwhile, was Asia's capitalist "miracle." Its economy and cities laid waste by bombing in 1945, it rebuilt with US aid so successfully that by the 1980s, it was the world's second-largest economy. China's potential economic growth, however, could put Japan's past achievements in the shade.

兵民是胜利之本

***Chinese communism,** based on the mobilization of peasants and workers, has nevertheless recognized the need for economic reforms.*

RUSSIAN FEDERATION
Bering Strait
KAZAKHSTAN [1991]
Aral Sea
ASIA
MONGOLIA
UZBEKISTAN [1991]
KYRGYZSTAN [1991]
TURKMENISTAN [1991]
TAJIKISTAN [1991]
CHINA
Sea of Japan
JAPAN
S. KOREA [1948]
IRAN
AFGHANISTAN
Himalayas
PAKISTAN [1947]
BHUTAN
NEPAL
The Gulf
QATAR [1971]
BANGLADESH [1971] (formerly E. Pakistan)
AUDI ARABIA
OMAN
INDIA [1947]
Arabian Sea
Bay of Bengal
(Vietnam united 1976)
THAILAND
South China Sea
PACIFIC OCEAN
MARIANAS
GUAM
(Yemen united 1990)
DJIBOUTI [1977]
HIOPIA
BRUNEI [1984]
PALAU [1995]
MICRONESIA [1991]
INDONESIA [1949]
SEYCHELLES [1976]
CHAGOS IS
Melanesia
SOLOMON IS [1978]
E. TIMOR (2002)
INDIAN OCEAN
MADAGASCAR [1960]
RÉUNION
NEW CALEDONIA
AUSTRALIA
NEW ZEALAND
AUCKLAND IS (to N Z)
MACQUARIE IS (to Australia)

***A treaty** banning the testing of nuclear bombs in the Pacific was signed in 1986.*

OCEANIA

THE POSTWAR economies of Japan, the US, and Australia had by the 1990s created a new industrial and trading network around the Pacific Rim. Cheap labor and low overheads drew younger states – South Korea, Taiwan, Singapore, Malaysia, Indonesia – into the system and much of the world's manufacturing is now concentrated there, creating a consequent shift in the balance of the global economy.

***Gamal Abd al-Nasser** (1918–1970) of Egypt, galvanized the Arab states to resist the West.*

AFRICA AND THE MIDDLE EAST

THE COLONIAL POWERS, weakened by war, faced an irresistible wave of demands for self-determination. Between 1958 and 1975, 41 African countries gained independence. In north Africa and throughout the Middle East a new form of anti-imperialism emerged in the 1970s in the form of Islamic fundamentalism. In South Africa, white rule and the apartheid system ended in 1994.

***From the 1950s** to the 1970s, superpower rivalry focused on space exploration. The Soviets put the first man in space in 1961, and the Americans landed on the moon in 1969. Since then, both manned and unmanned missions have become almost everyday events.*

POPULATION

THE WORLD'S POPULATION – 6.2 billion in 2002 – is likely to reach nearly ten billion by 2050. Better nutrition, health care, and sanitation mean fewer infant deaths and longer life expectancy, though around 800 million people in the developing world are malnourished and over one billion live in extreme poverty. In much of Africa in particular, the AIDS epidemic is so severe that the population is set to fall significantly. Elsewhere it is lower birthrates, already familiar in most industrialized countries, that have slowed the rate of growth. The result is a rapidly aging population: it is thought that by 2050 there will be around two billion people over the age of 60. The distribution of population is very uneven, dependent on climate, terrain, natural resources, and economic factors. The great majority of people live in coastal zones and along river valleys. Urbanization is on the increase, and by 2003 just under half of the world's population lived in cities – most of them in Asia. The mass migration of people from rural areas in search of work has resulted in the growth of huge sprawling squatter camps on the edge of many Third World cities.

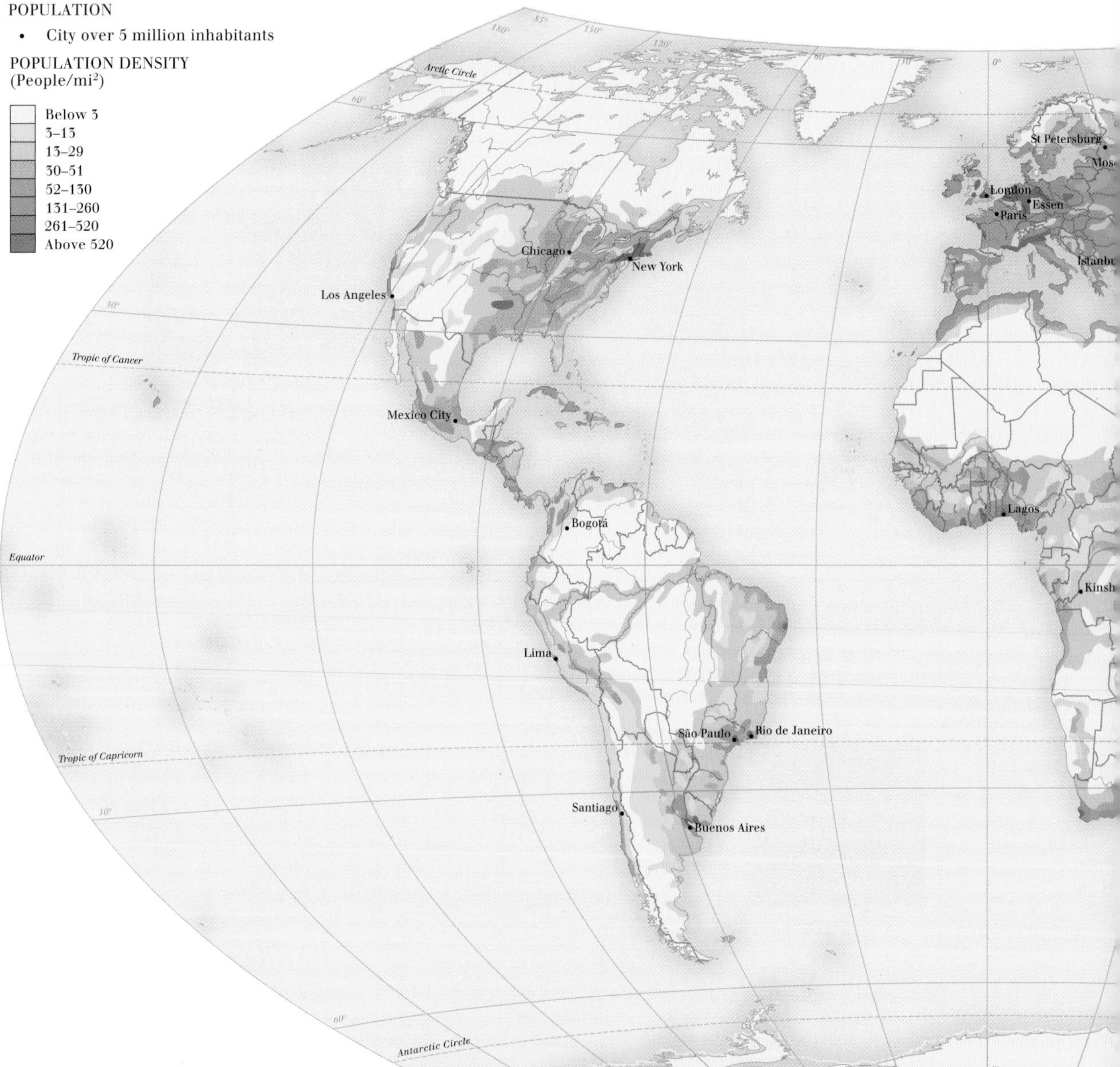

POPULATION
• City over 5 million inhabitants
POPULATION DENSITY
(People/mi²)
Below 3
3–13
13–29
30–51
52–130
131–260
261–520
Above 520
Arctic Circle
Tropic of Cancer
Equator
Tropic of Capricorn
Antarctic Circle
Chicago
New York
Los Angeles
Mexico City
Bogotá
Lima
São Paulo
Rio de Janeiro
Santiago
Buenos Aires
St Petersburg
London
Essen
Paris
Lagos

INFANT MORTALITY

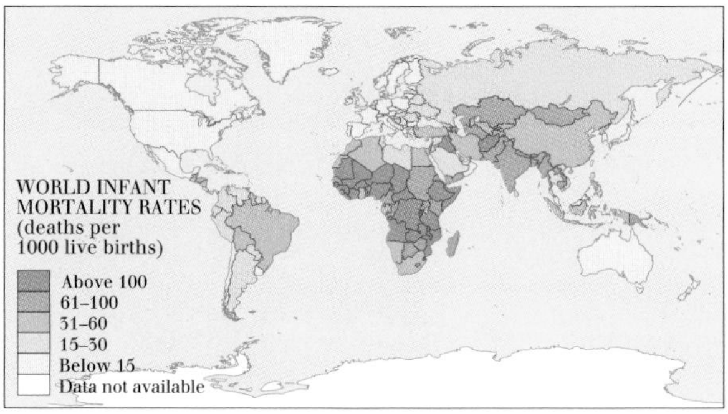
WORLD INFANT MORTALITY RATES (deaths per 1000 live births)
Above 100
61–100
31–60
15–30
Below 15
Data not available

Infant Mortality

INFANT MORTALITY RATES are highest in Africa, South America, and south Asia, where poverty and disease are rife, and where average standards of health care are not as good as in North America or Europe. The country with the highest infant mortality rate is Sierra Leone, where years of conflict have devastated communities.

LIFE EXPECTANCY

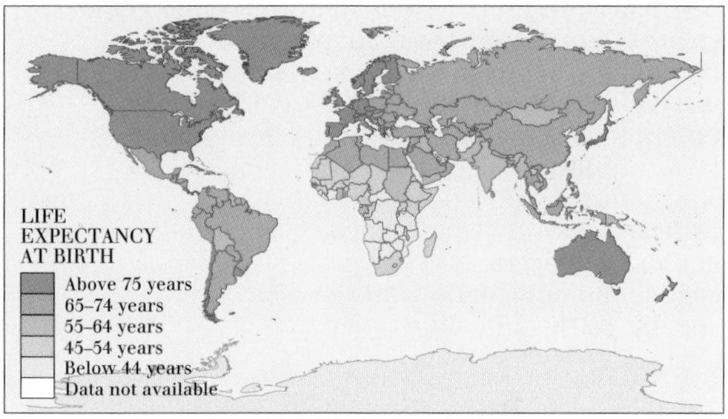
LIFE EXPECTANCY AT BIRTH
Above 75 years
65–74 years
55–64 years
45–54 years
Below 44 years
Data not available

Arctic Circle
Tropic of Cancer
Equator
Tropic of Capricorn
Antarctic Circle
Tehran
Lahore
Delhi
Karachi
Dhaka
Calcutta (Kolkata)
Mumbai (Bombay)
Hyderabad
Bangalore
Chennai (Madras)
Beijing
Tianjin
Seoul
Tokyo
Osaka
Wuhan
Shanghai
Chongqing
Hong Kong
Bangkok
Manilla
Jakarta

Life Expectancy

LIFE EXPECTANCY IS poorest in Africa, for reasons similar to those noted above. In western Europe and North America, life expectancy is increasing at such a rate that each successive generation may expect to live longer than the last. In the developed world, people can now expect to live twice as long as they did a century ago.

Population Factfile

LARGEST POPULATIONS	
1 China	1294 million people
2 India	1041 million people
3 USA	289 million people
LARGEST COUNTRIES BY AREA	
1 Russian Federation	17,075,200 km^2 (6,592,735 mi^2)
2 Canada	9,984,670 km^2 (3,855,171 mi^2)
3 US	9,626,091 km^2 (3,717,792 mi^2)
MOST DENSELY POPULATED COUNTRIES	
1 Monaco	16,404 people/km^2 (42,649 people/mi^2)
2 Singapore	6885 people/km^2 (17,797 people/mi^2)
3 Vatican City	2045 people/km^2 (5294 people/mi^2)
MOST SPARSELY POPULATED COUNTRIES	
1 Mongolia	2 people/km^2 (4 people/mi^2)
2 Namibia	2 people/km^2 (6 people/mi^2)
3 Australia	3 people/km^2 (7 people/mi^2)

World Economy

THE WEALTHY COUNTRIES of the developed world, with their aggressive, market-led economies and their access to productive new technologies and international markets, dominate the world economic system. At the other extreme, many of the countries of the developing world are locked in a cycle of unrepayable debt, rising populations, and unemployment. State-managed systems in the former communist bloc were dismantled in the 1990s, and China has emerged as a major 21st century economic power following decades of isolation. Technological advances mean that transactions between financial centers can occur at even greater speed, and new markets have sprung up throughout the world.

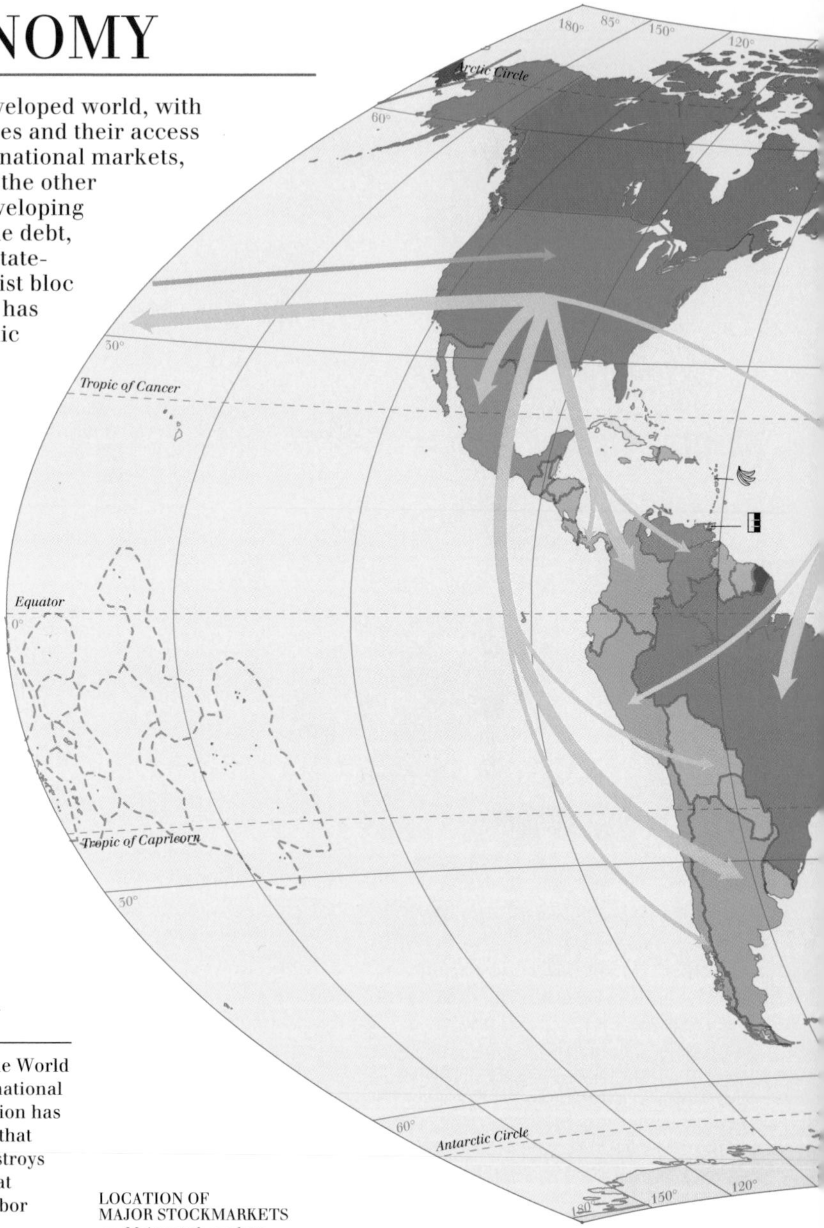

Arctic Circle
Tropic of Cancer
Equator
Tropic of Capricorn
Antarctic Circle

BALANCE OF TRADE (MILLIONS US $)

Surplus:
- over 20,000
- 10,000–19,999
- 1000–9999
- 0–999

Deficit:
- 0–999
- 1000–9999
- 10,000–19,999
- below 20,000

- data unavailable

DIRECT INVESTMENT
- from US
- from Europe
- from Japan

COUNTRIES RELIANT ON A SINGLE EXPORT
- bananas
- coffee
- oil/petroleum
- copper

World Trade and Globalization

A basic tenet of liberal economics, embodied in the World Trade Organization, is that free trade stimulates national economies and encourages growth. Global recession has not shaken this faith, but its vocal critics contend that "globalization" undermines local cultures and destroys local economies. It is multinational companies that benefit, they say, by producing goods wherever labor costs and environmental standards are lowest.

LOCATION OF MAJOR STOCKMARKETS
- Major stock markets

INTERNATIONAL TRADE

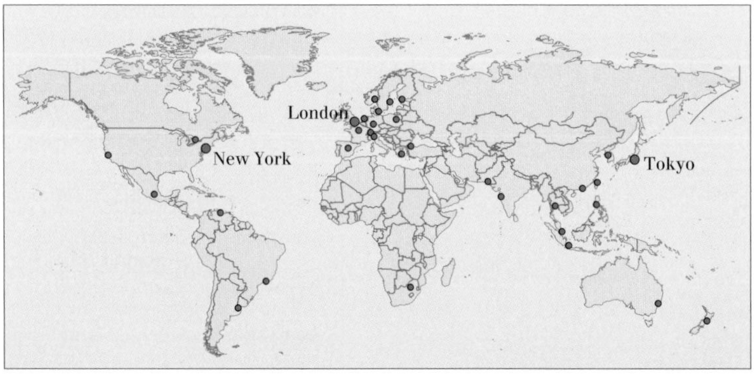

London
New York
Tokyo

World Economies

HIGHEST GNP PER CAPITA

1 **Liechtenstein**	$50,000
2 **Luxembourg**	$39,840
3 **Switzerland**	$38,330
4 **Norway**	$35,630
5 **Japan**	$35,610

LOWEST GNP PER CAPITA

1 **Congo, Dem. Rep.**	$80
2= **Ethiopia**	$100
2= **Burundi**	$100
4 **Somalia**	$120
5= **Sierra Leone, Liberia**	$140

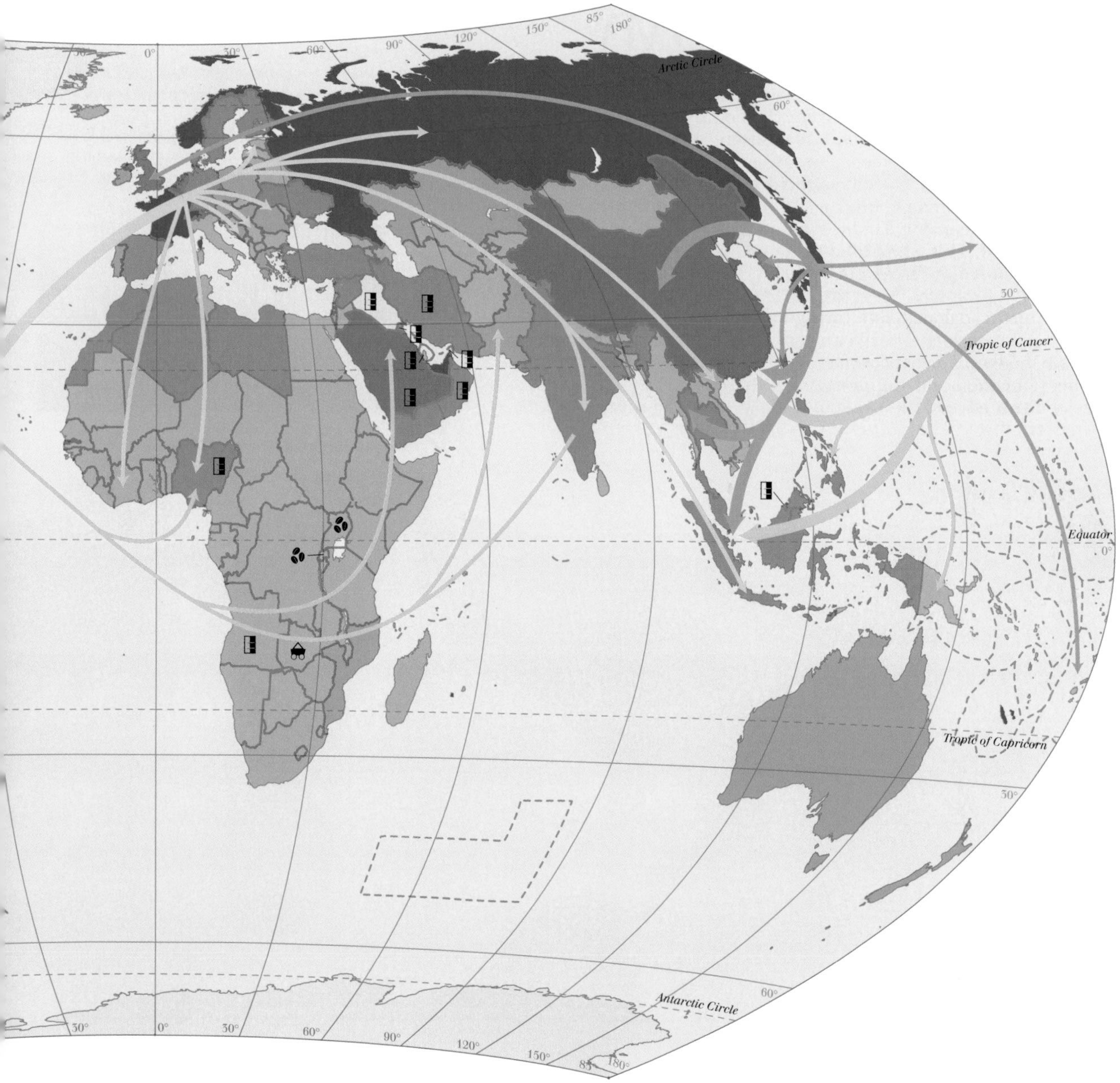
Arctic Circle
Tropic of Cancer
Equator
Tropic of Capricorn
Antarctic Circle
0°
30°
60°
90°
120°
150°
180°
85°

TRADE BLOCS

INTERNATIONAL TRADE BLOCS are formed when groups of countries, often already enjoying close military and political ties, join together to offer mutually preferential terms of trade for both imports and exports. Global trade is dominated by three main blocs: the expanding EU, NAFTA, and ASEAN. They are supplanting older trade blocs such as the Commonwealth, a legacy of colonialism.

TRADE BLOCS

- EU
- ASEAN
- NAFTA
- SADC
- MERCOSUR
- ECOWAS

TRADE BLOCS

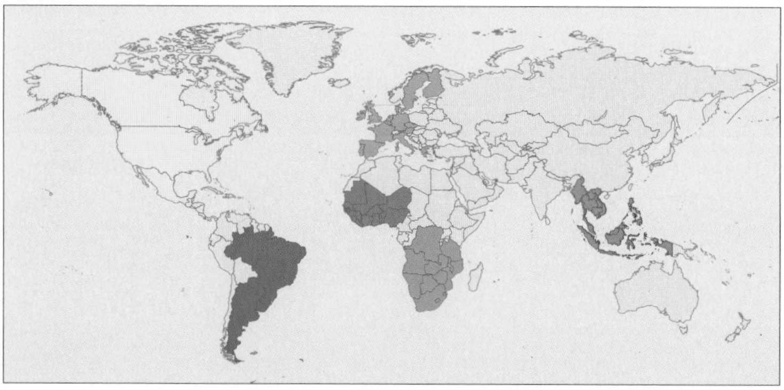

WORLD ECONOMY

THE SIZE OF A COUNTRY'S economy does not relate directly to its population or even its resources. Japan, for example, has a much "bigger" economy than China, India, Russia, or Latin America as a whole. Such imbalances usually occur because countries differ enormously in their living standards, the education and skills of their workforces, the productivity of their agriculture, and the value of their markets. A country's economic performance can be evaluated by calculating its gross national product (GNP). This is the total value of both the goods and the services (including so-called "invisible exports" – financial services, tourism, and so on) that it produces. Most trade (62% of the global total by value) is in manufactured goods, but during the last three decades the most rapidly growing sector has been services – banking, insurance, tourism, consultancy, accountancy, films, music and other cultural services, airlines, and shipping. Accounting for 20% of the total, services now exceed the value of trade in food and raw materials.

COMPARATIVE WORLD WEALTH

A global assessment of GNP by country reveals great disparities. The developed world, with only a quarter of the world's population, has 80% of the world's manufacturing income. This imbalance is maintained as war and political instability undermine poor countries' prospects.

***Mass-market tourism** is now an all-important source of revenue in many countries.*

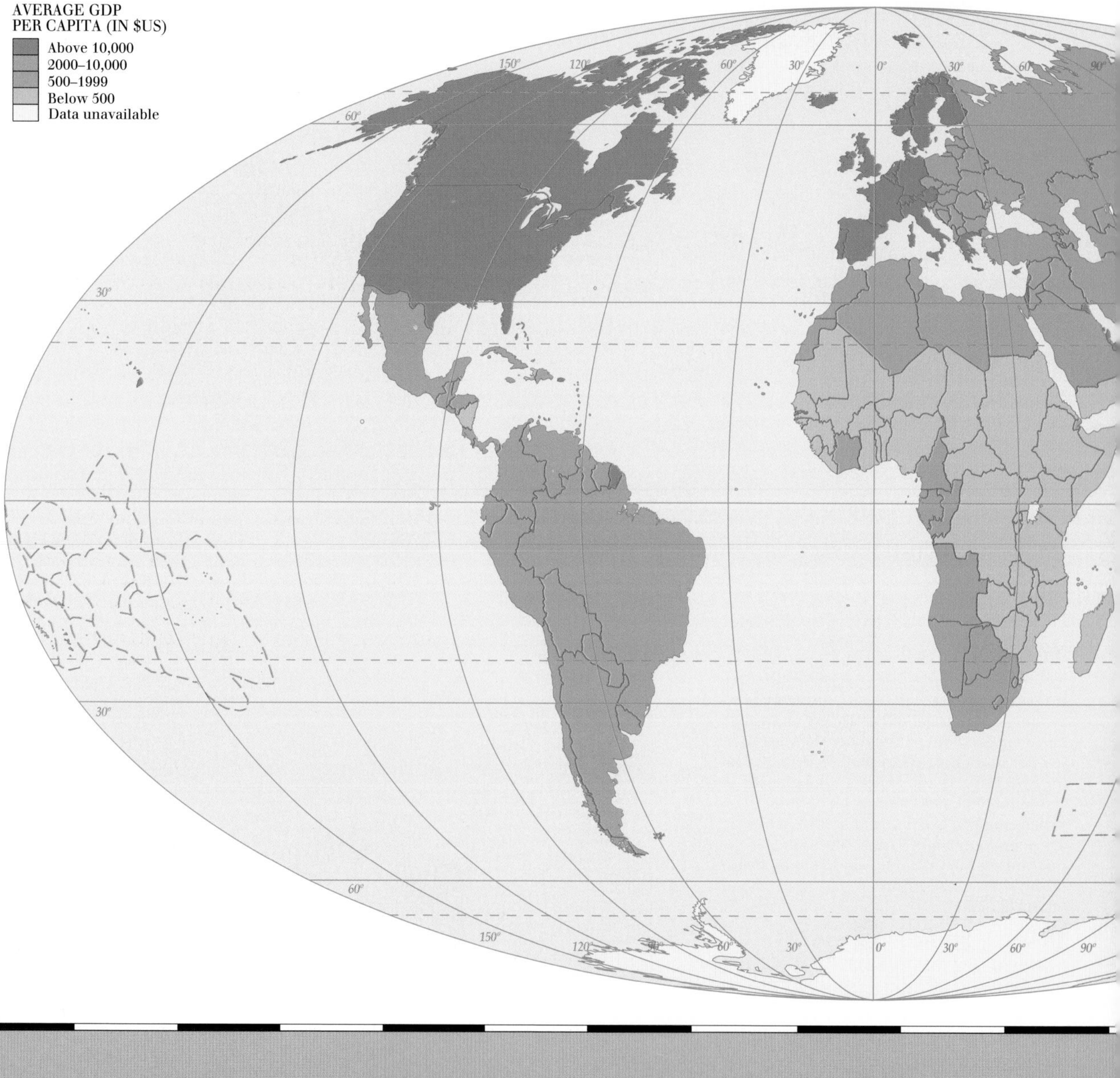
AVERAGE GDP
PER CAPITA (IN $US)
Above 10,000
2000–10,000
500–1999
Below 500
Data unavailable
150°
120°
60°
30°
0°
30°
60°
90°
60°
30°
30°
60°
150°
120°
90°
60°
30°
0°
30°
60°
90°

DEBT OF POOR AND MIDDLE-INCOME COUNTRIES

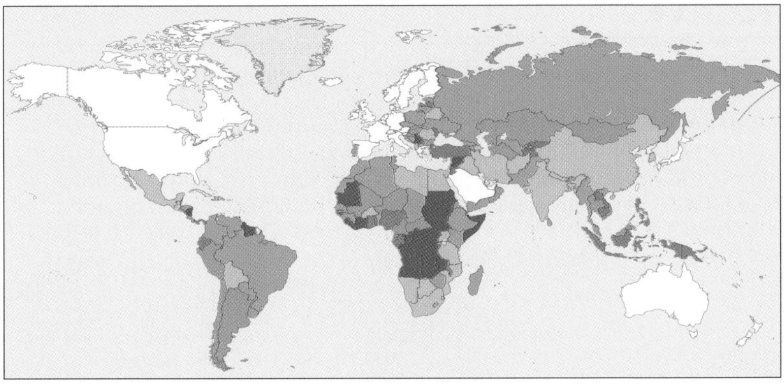

INTERNATIONAL DEBT (AS PERCENTAGE OF GNP)

over 100% | 70–100% | 50–69% | 30–49% | below 30 | negligible | not applicable | data unavailable

INTERNATIONAL DEBT

In response to unsustainable levels of debt in the developing world, the IMF and World Bank have introduced a program to help heavily indebted poor countries (HIPCs) manage their repayments. The Jubilee 2000 campaign, advocating debt cancellation, won some qualified support among creditor countries.

WORLD'S 20 LARGEST CORPORATIONS

		2002, $ millions
1	**Wal-Mart Stores (US)**	**$246,525**
2	**General Motors (US)**	**$186,763**
3	**Exxon Mobil (US)**	**$182,466**
4	**Royal Dutch/Shell Group (UK/Neth.)**	**$179,431**
5	**British Petroleum (UK)**	**$178,721**
6	**Ford Motor Company (US)**	**$163,630**
7	**DaimlerChrysler (US/Germany)**	**$141,421**
8	**Toyota Motor Company (Japan)**	**$131,754**
9	**General Electric (US)**	**$131,698**
10	**Mitsubishi (Japan)**	**$109,386**
11	**Mitsui (Japan)**	**$108,631**
12	**Allianz (Germany)**	**$101,930**
13	**ChevronTexaco (US)**	**$99,049**
14	**Total Fina Elf (France)**	**$96,945**
15	**Citigroup (US)**	**$92,556**
16	**Nippon Telegraph and Telephone (Japan)**	**$89,644**
17	**ING Group (Neth.)**	**$88,102**
18	**Itochu (Japan)**	**$85,856**
19	**Intl. Business Machines (US)**	**$83,132**
20	**Volkswagen (Germany)**	**$82,204**

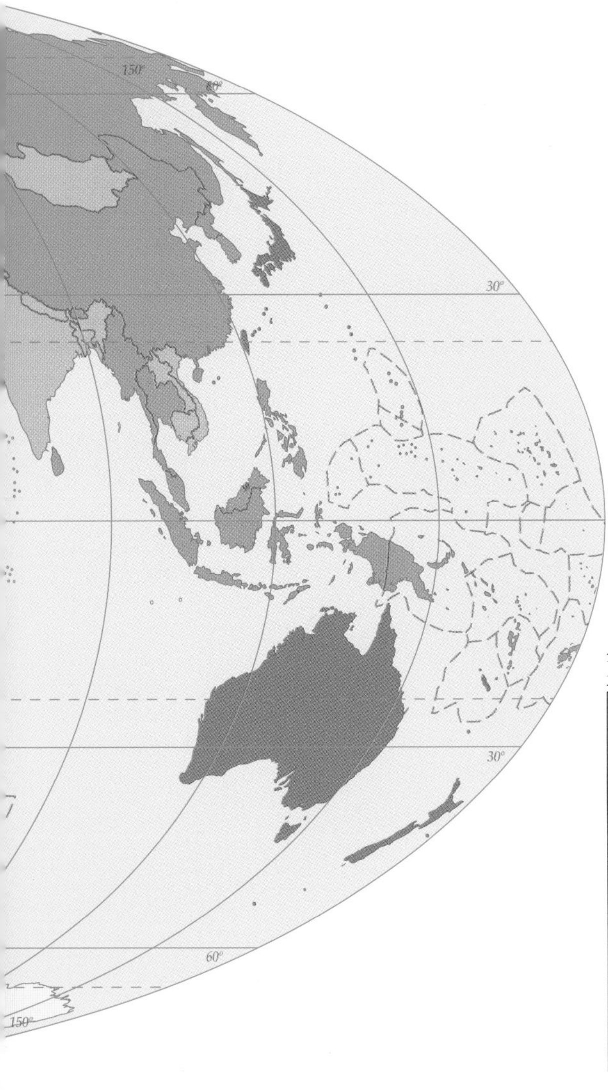
150°
60°
30°
30°
60°
150°

NEWLY INDUSTRIALIZED COUNTRIES

In the 1990s, the fast-growing export-oriented "Asian tiger" economies, such as Singapore, South Korea, and Taiwan, offered exciting prospects for foreign investors. The 1997–1998 Asian financial crisis came as a severe shock. Some countries quickly returned to growth, but investors became more cautious about their exposure in NICs around the world.

NEWLY INDUSTRIALIZED AND INDUSTRIALIZING COUNTRIES

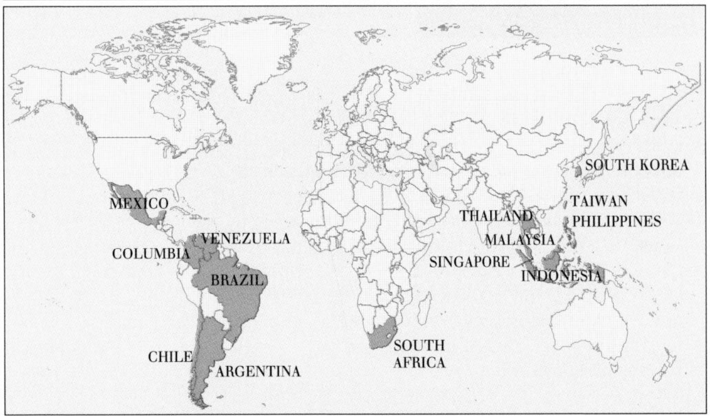
MEXICO
VENEZUELA
COLUMBIA
BRAZIL
CHILE
ARGENTINA
SOUTH AFRICA
SOUTH KOREA
TAIWAN
PHILIPPINES
THAILAND
MALAYSIA
SINGAPORE
INDONESIA

Global Tourism

Tourism is the world's biggest industry. In 2002 there were a record 715 million tourists worldwide, a number expected to rise to over one billion by 2010. The industry had bounced back quickly from the global downturn in 2001. France is the world's most popular destination country, with 77 million visitors annually, but with cheaper flights, improved transportation, and increased leisure time, many of the countries of the developing world are rapidly becoming tourist meccas. Since the 1960s, mass tourism has become increasingly specialized, encompassing sporting and adventure holidays as well as ecological tours. Tourism employs 200 million people worldwide – 8% of the working population. However, the benefits of tourism are not always felt at a local level, where jobs are often low-paid and menial.

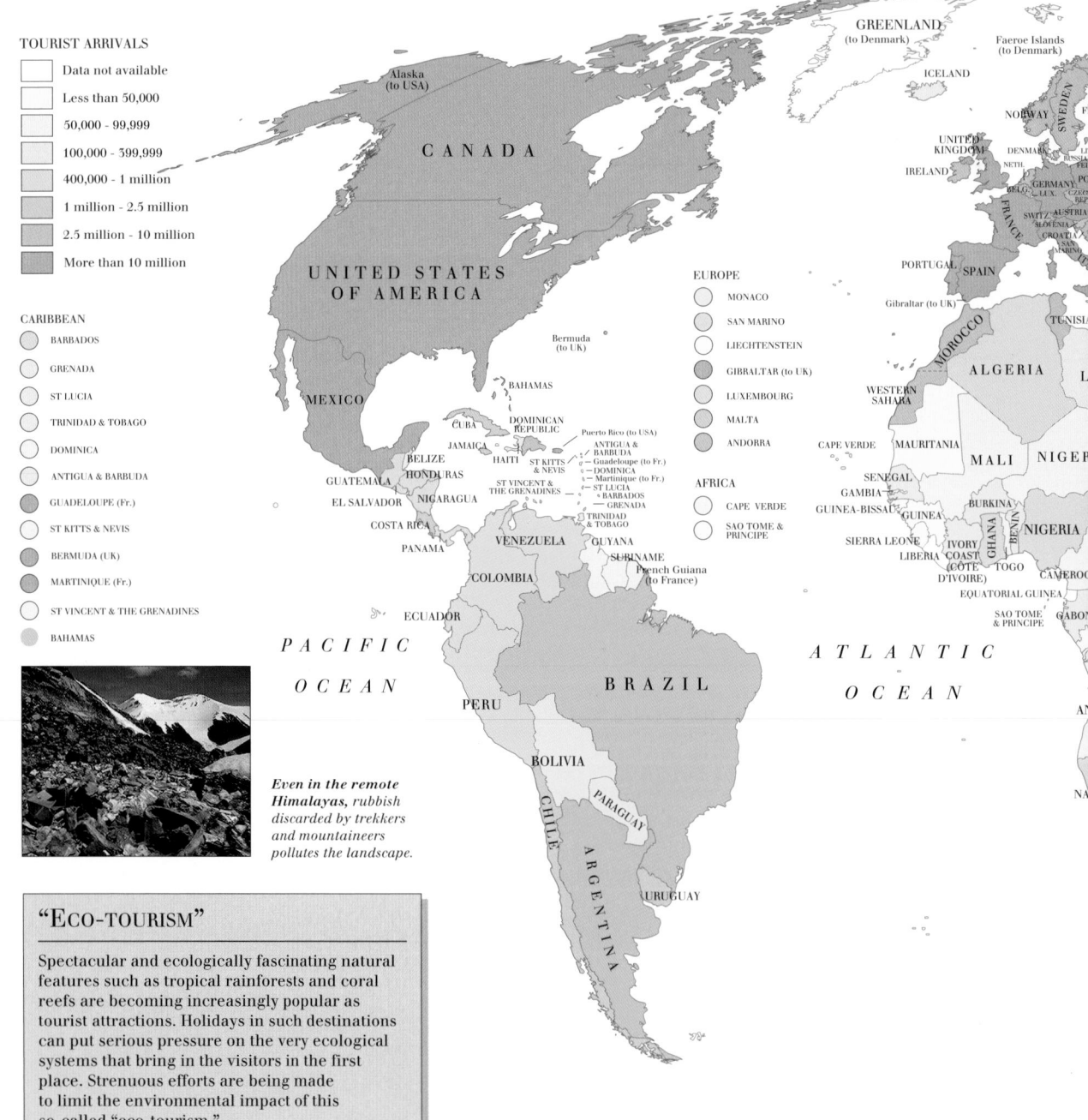

TOURIST ARRIVALS
Data not available
Less than 50,000
50,000 - 99,999
100,000 - 399,999
400,000 - 1 million
1 million - 2.5 million
2.5 million - 10 million
More than 10 million
CARIBBEAN
BARBADOS
GRENADA
ST LUCIA
TRINIDAD & TOBAGO
DOMINICA
ANTIGUA & BARBUDA
GUADELOUPE (Fr.)
ST KITTS & NEVIS
BERMUDA (UK)
MARTINIQUE (Fr.)
ST VINCENT & THE GRENADINES
BAHAMAS
EUROPE
MONACO
SAN MARINO
LIECHTENSTEIN
GIBRALTAR (to UK)
LUXEMBOURG
MALTA
ANDORRA
AFRICA
CAPE VERDE
SAO TOME & PRINCIPE
GREENLAND (to Denmark)
Faeroe Islands (to Denmark)
ICELAND
Alaska (to USA)
CANADA
UNITED STATES OF AMERICA
MEXICO
Bermuda (to UK)
BAHAMAS
CUBA
DOMINICAN REPUBLIC
JAMAICA
HAITI
Puerto Rico (to USA)
ANTIGUA & BARBUDA
Guadeloupe (to Fr.)
DOMINICA
Martinique (to Fr.)
ST LUCIA
BARBADOS
GRENADA
ST KITTS & NEVIS
ST VINCENT & THE GRENADINES
TRINIDAD & TOBAGO
BELIZE
HONDURAS
GUATEMALA
EL SALVADOR
NICARAGUA
COSTA RICA
PANAMA
VENEZUELA
GUYANA
SURINAME
French Guiana (to France)
COLOMBIA
ECUADOR
PERU
BRAZIL
BOLIVIA
PARAGUAY
CHILE
ARGENTINA
URUGUAY
PACIFIC OCEAN
ATLANTIC OCEAN
NORWAY
SWEDEN
UNITED KINGDOM
IRELAND
DENMARK
NETH.
BELG.
LUX.
GERMANY
POL
CZECH REP.
FRANCE
SWITZ.
AUSTRIA
SLOVENIA
CROATIA
SAN MARINO
PORTUGAL
SPAIN
Gibraltar (to UK)
MOROCCO
TUNISIA
ALGERIA
WESTERN SAHARA
CAPE VERDE
MAURITANIA
MALI
NIGER
SENEGAL
GAMBIA
GUINEA-BISSAU
GUINEA
SIERRA LEONE
LIBERIA
BURKINA
IVORY COAST (CÔTE D'IVOIRE)
GHANA
TOGO
BENIN
NIGERIA
CAMEROON
EQUATORIAL GUINEA
SAO TOME & PRINCIPE
GABON

Even in the remote ***Himalayas,*** *rubbish discarded by trekkers and mountaineers pollutes the landscape.*

"Eco-tourism"

Spectacular and ecologically fascinating natural features such as tropical rainforests and coral reefs are becoming increasingly popular as tourist attractions. Holidays in such destinations can put serious pressure on the very ecological systems that bring in the visitors in the first place. Strenuous efforts are being made to limit the environmental impact of this so-called "eco-tourism."

***The beautiful island** of Phuket, Thailand, has been taken over by tourist developments.*

A TOURIST PARADISE?

THE MOST REMOTE CORNERS of the world are now being penetrated by tourists in their quest for the exotic. In many parts of the developing world, tourism can be described as a form of "neocolonialism"; hotels and beaches are owned by multinational companies, and most of the profits are taken outside the country. Tourism frequently alienates local people from their own land, and has a negative impact on the local culture and environment.

RUSSIAN FEDERATION
KAZAKHSTAN
MONGOLIA
GEORGIA
ARM.
AZERB.
UZBEKISTAN
KYRGYZSTAN
TURKMENISTAN
TAJIKISTAN
NORTH KOREA
SOUTH KOREA
JAPAN
SYRIA
IRAQ
IRAN
AFGHANISTAN
CHINA
PACIFIC OCEAN
JORDAN
KUWAIT
PAKISTAN
NEPAL
BHUTAN
BAHRAIN
QATAR
UAE
BANGLADESH
TAIWAN
SAUDI ARABIA
OMAN
INDIA
BURMA (MYANMAR)
LAOS
ERITREA
YEMEN
THAILAND
VIETNAM
PHILIPPINES
Guam (to USA)
DJIBOUTI
CAMBODIA
ETHIOPIA
SOMALIA
MALDIVES
SRI LANKA
UGANDA
KENYA
MALAYSIA
SINGAPORE
TANZANIA
SEYCHELLES
INDONESIA
PAPUA NEW GUINEA
EAST TIMOR
COMOROS
MALAWI
INDIAN OCEAN
MOZAMBIQUE
MADAGASCAR
MAURITIUS
SWAZILAND
LESOTHO
AUSTRALIA
NEW ZEALAND
PACIFIC OCEAN
FIJI
MICRONESIA
NAURU
SOLOMON ISLANDS
VANUATU
SAMOA
TONGA
KIRIBATI
MIDDLE EAST
BAHRAIN
INDIAN OCEAN
COMOROS
MALDIVES
MAURITIUS
SEYCHELLES
ASIA
SINGAPORE

***"Eco-tourists"** travel to the distant Antarctic, where they observe its rich wildlife.*

Global Security

THE ENDING OF THE COLD WAR in 1989 greatly reduced the risk of another global (and possibly nuclear) war, but did little to resolve localized tensions and conflicts. Since then territorial disputes, and particularly ethnic and religious tensions, have undermined peace and security around the world. In its efforts to bring together the international community the UN has become the accepted arbiter of world peace. It prefers to use economic sanctions, but will support military action as a last resort. However, slow decision-making processes and internal politicking have often left it unable to react quickly or effectively, as in the failure to halt the 1994 genocide in Rwanda. Perhaps its greatest contribution to global security has been the organization of peacekeeping missions which are frequently called into conflict situations to oversee peace treaties and aid postwar reconstruction. The September 11, 2001, attacks on the US prompted a shift in that country's foreign policy and it has now chosen to flex its muscles as the sole remaining superpower. Identifying terrorism as the greatest challenge to world security, and sidelining the UN if necessary, it has drawn on ad hoc coalitions of willing partners in its global "war on terrorism." It advocates the use of preemptive strikes to ensure future security.

UNITED STATES OF AMERICA
ICELA
Rockall
Northern Ireland
Gibraltar
Ceuta
MOROCCO
WESTERN SAHARA
MAURITANIA
SENEGAL
SIERRA LEONE
LIBERIA
IVORY COAST (CÔTE D'IVORY)
CUBA
Guantánamo Bay
HAITI
BELIZE
GUATEMALA
EL SALVADOR
NICARAGUA
VENEZUELA
GUYANA
SURINAME
French Guiana
COLOMBIA
Falkland Islands

Iraq

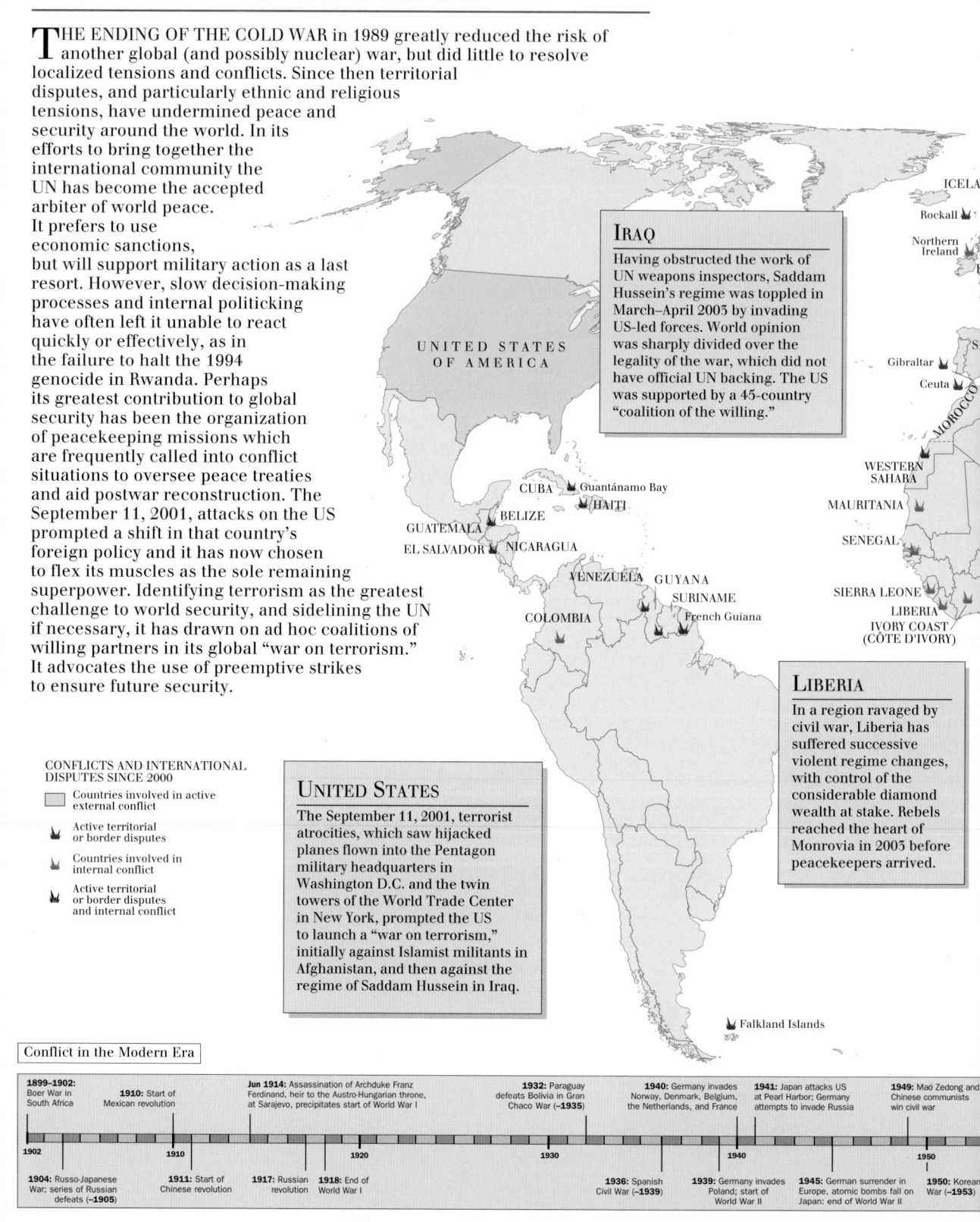

Having obstructed the work of UN weapons inspectors, Saddam Hussein's regime was toppled in March–April 2003 by invading US-led forces. World opinion was sharply divided over the legality of the war, which did not have official UN backing. The US was supported by a 45-country "coalition of the willing."

Liberia

In a region ravaged by civil war, Liberia has suffered successive violent regime changes, with control of the considerable diamond wealth at stake. Rebels reached the heart of Monrovia in 2003 before peacekeepers arrived.

CONFLICTS AND INTERNATIONAL DISPUTES SINCE 2000

- Countries involved in active external conflict
- Active territorial or border disputes
- Countries involved in internal conflict
- Active territorial or border disputes and internal conflict

United States

The September 11, 2001, terrorist atrocities, which saw hijacked planes flown into the Pentagon military headquarters in Washington D.C. and the twin towers of the World Trade Center in New York, prompted the US to launch a "war on terrorism," initially against Islamist militants in Afghanistan, and then against the regime of Saddam Hussein in Iraq.

Conflict in the Modern Era

- **1899–1902:** Boer War in South Africa
- **1904:** Russo-Japanese War; series of Russian defeats (**–1905**)
- **1910:** Start of Mexican revolution
- **1911:** Start of Chinese revolution
- **Jun 1914:** Assassination of Archduke Franz Ferdinand, heir to the Austro-Hungarian throne, at Sarajevo, precipitates start of World War I
- **1917:** Russian revolution
- **1918:** End of World War I
- **1932:** Paraguay defeats Bolivia in Gran Chaco War (**–1935**)
- **1936:** Spanish Civil War (**–1939**)
- **1939:** Germany invades Poland; start of World War II
- **1940:** Germany invades Norway, Denmark, Belgium, the Netherlands, and France
- **1941:** Japan attacks US at Pearl Harbor; Germany attempts to invade Russia
- **1945:** German surrender in Europe, atomic bombs fall on Japan: end of World War II
- **1949:** Mao Zedong and Chinese communists win civil war
- **1950:** Korean War (**–1953**)

1902 · 1910 · 1920 · 1930 · 1940 · 1950

Nepal

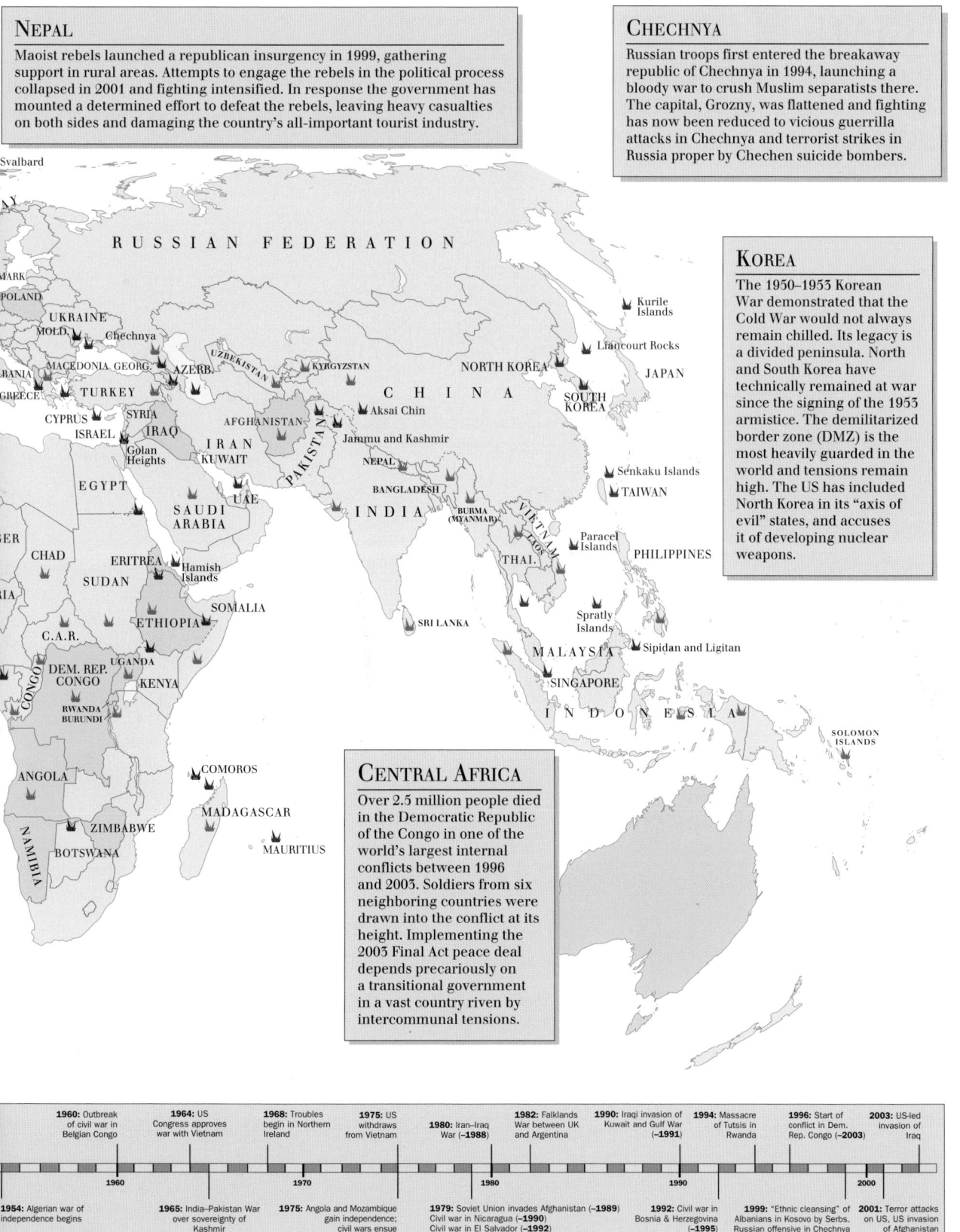

Maoist rebels launched a republican insurgency in 1999, gathering support in rural areas. Attempts to engage the rebels in the political process collapsed in 2001 and fighting intensified. In response the government has mounted a determined effort to defeat the rebels, leaving heavy casualties on both sides and damaging the country's all-important tourist industry.

Chechnya

Russian troops first entered the breakaway republic of Chechnya in 1994, launching a bloody war to crush Muslim separatists there. The capital, Grozny, was flattened and fighting has now been reduced to vicious guerrilla attacks in Chechnya and terrorist strikes in Russia proper by Chechen suicide bombers.

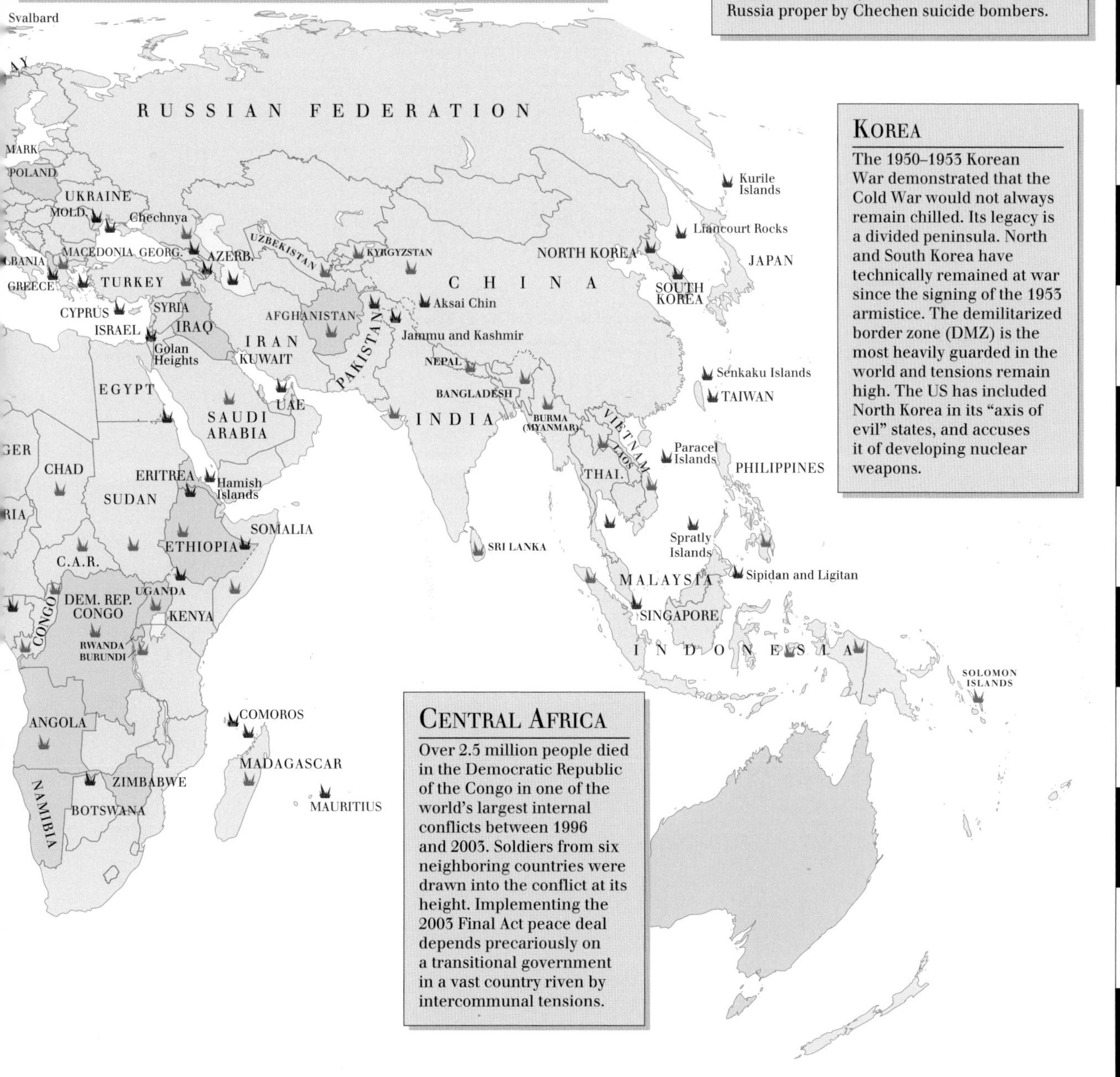
Svalbard
RUSSIAN FEDERATION
MARK
POLAND
UKRAINE
MOLD.
Chechnya
BANIA
MACEDONIA
GEORG.
AZERB.
GREECE
TURKEY
CYPRUS
SYRIA
ISRAEL
IRAQ
Golan Heights
IRAN
KUWAIT
AFGHANISTAN
UZBEKISTAN
KYRGYZSTAN
PAKISTAN
Aksai Chin
Jammu and Kashmir
NEPAL
BANGLADESH
INDIA
BURMA (MYANMAR)
CHINA
NORTH KOREA
SOUTH KOREA
JAPAN
Kurile Islands
Liancourt Rocks
Senkaku Islands
TAIWAN
Paracel Islands
PHILIPPINES
VIETNAM
LAOS
THAI.
Spratly Islands
Sipidan and Ligitan
MALAYSIA
SINGAPORE
INDONESIA
SOLOMON ISLANDS
SRI LANKA
EGYPT
UAE
SAUDI ARABIA
GER
CHAD
ERITREA
Hamish Islands
SUDAN
RIA
SOMALIA
ETHIOPIA
C.A.R.
UGANDA
DEM. REP. CONGO
CONGO
KENYA
RWANDA
BURUNDI
ANGOLA
COMOROS
MADAGASCAR
MAURITIUS
ZIMBABWE
NAMIBIA
BOTSWANA

Korea

The 1950–1953 Korean War demonstrated that the Cold War would not always remain chilled. Its legacy is a divided peninsula. North and South Korea have technically remained at war since the signing of the 1953 armistice. The demilitarized border zone (DMZ) is the most heavily guarded in the world and tensions remain high. The US has included North Korea in its "axis of evil" states, and accuses it of developing nuclear weapons.

Central Africa

Over 2.5 million people died in the Democratic Republic of the Congo in one of the world's largest internal conflicts between 1996 and 2003. Soldiers from six neighboring countries were drawn into the conflict at its height. Implementing the 2003 Final Act peace deal depends precariously on a transitional government in a vast country riven by intercommunal tensions.

- **1954:** Algerian war of independence begins
- **1960:** Outbreak of civil war in Belgian Congo
- **1964:** US Congress approves war with Vietnam
- **1965:** India–Pakistan War over sovereignty of Kashmir
- **1968:** Troubles begin in Northern Ireland
- **1975:** US withdraws from Vietnam
- **1975:** Angola and Mozambique gain independence; civil wars ensue
- **1979:** Soviet Union invades Afghanistan (**–1989**) Civil war in Nicaragua (**–1990**) Civil war in El Salvador (**–1992**)
- **1980:** Iran–Iraq War (**–1988**)
- **1982:** Falklands War between UK and Argentina
- **1990:** Iraqi invasion of Kuwait and Gulf War (**–1991**)
- **1992:** Civil war in Bosnia & Herzegovina (**–1995**)
- **1994:** Massacre of Tutsis in Rwanda
- **1996:** Start of conflict in Dem. Rep. Congo (**–2003**)
- **1999:** "Ethnic cleansing" of Albanians in Kosovo by Serbs. Russian offensive in Chechnya
- **2001:** Terror attacks on US, US invasion of Afghanistan
- **2003:** US-led invasion of Iraq

1960 1970 1980 1990 2000

TIME ZONES

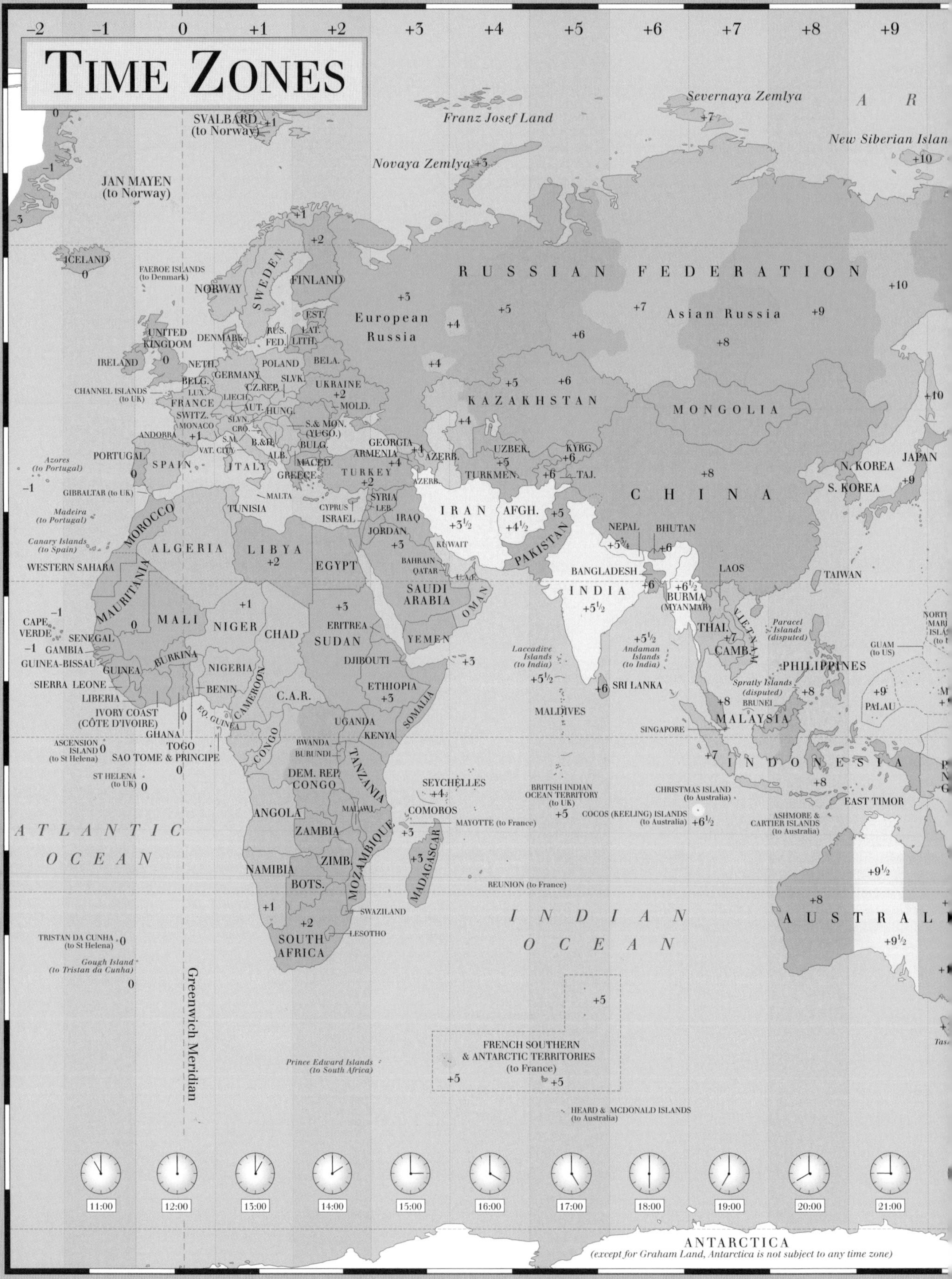

–2
–1
0
+1
+2
+3
+4
+5
+6
+7
+8
+9
SVALBARD (to Norway) +1
Franz Josef Land
Severnaya Zemlya
+7
New Siberian Islan
+10
Novaya Zemlya +3
JAN MAYEN (to Norway)
–1
–3
ICELAND 0
FAEROE ISLANDS (to Denmark)
NORWAY
SWEDEN
FINLAND
+1
+2
RUSSIAN FEDERATION
European Russia
+3
+4
+5
+6
+7
Asian Russia
+8
+9
+10
UNITED KINGDOM
0
IRELAND
DENMARK
EST.
LAT.
LITH.
RUS. FED.
POLAND
BELA.
NETH.
BELG.
LUX.
GERMANY
CZ.REP.
SLVK.
UKRAINE +2
CHANNEL ISLANDS (to UK)
FRANCE
LIECH.
SWITZ.
MONACO
AUT.
HUNG.
MOLD.
SLVN.
CRO.
B.&H.
S.& MON. (YUGO.)
ANDORRA
+1
S.M.
VAT. CITY
BULG.
ALB.
MACED.
GREECE
ITALY
SPAIN
PORTUGAL
0
Azores (to Portugal)
–1
GIBRALTAR (to UK)
MALTA
TURKEY +2
GEORGIA
ARMENIA +4
AZERB. +4
KAZAKHSTAN
+5
+6
+4
MONGOLIA
UZBEK. +5
KYRG. +6
TURKMEN.
+6
TAJ.
N. KOREA
S. KOREA
JAPAN
+9
+10
CHINA
+8
Madeira (to Portugal)
MOROCCO
TUNISIA
CYPRUS
SYRIA
LEB.
ISRAEL
IRAQ
IRAN +3½
AFGH. +4½
+5
JORDAN
+3
KUWAIT
PAKISTAN
NEPAL +5¾
BHUTAN +6
Canary Islands (to Spain)
ALGERIA
LIBYA +2
EGYPT
BAHRAIN
QATAR
U.A.E.
WESTERN SAHARA
SAUDI ARABIA
OMAN
BANGLADESH +6
INDIA +5½
BURMA (MYANMAR) +6½
LAOS
TAIWAN
MAURITANIA
MALI
0
NIGER
+1
CHAD
+3
ERITREA
SUDAN
YEMEN
CAPE VERDE –1
SENEGAL
–1 GAMBIA
GUINEA-BISSAU
GUINEA
BURKINA
NIGERIA
DJIBOUTI
+3
THAI.
+7
VIETNAM
CAMB.
Paracel Islands (disputed)
GUAM (to US)
PHILIPPINES
Laccadive Islands (to India)
+5½
Andaman Islands (to India)
+5½
SIERRA LEONE
LIBERIA
BENIN
CAMEROON
C.A.R.
ETHIOPIA +3
+6 SRI LANKA
Spratly Islands (disputed)
BRUNEI
+8
+9
PALAU
IVORY COAST (CÔTE D'IVOIRE)
GHANA
0
TOGO
EQ. GUINEA
UGANDA
SOMALIA
KENYA
MALDIVES
+8
MALAYSIA
SINGAPORE
ASCENSION ISLAND (to St Helena) 0
SAO TOME & PRINCIPE 0
CONGO
RWANDA
BURUNDI
TANZANIA
DEM. REP. CONGO
+7
INDONESIA
+8
ST HELENA (to UK) 0
SEYCHELLES +4
BRITISH INDIAN OCEAN TERRITORY (to UK) +5
CHRISTMAS ISLAND (to Australia)
EAST TIMOR
ATLANTIC OCEAN
ANGOLA
MALAWI
COMOROS
MAYOTTE (to France)
+3
COCOS (KEELING) ISLANDS (to Australia) +6½
ASHMORE & CARTIER ISLANDS (to Australia)
ZAMBIA
MOZAMBIQUE
MADAGASCAR
+3
ZIMB.
NAMIBIA
BOTS.
+9½
REUNION (to France)
+1
SWAZILAND
+8
AUSTRAL
+2
SOUTH AFRICA
LESOTHO
INDIAN OCEAN
+9½
TRISTAN DA CUNHA (to St Helena) 0
Gough Island (to Tristan da Cunha) 0
Greenwich Meridian
+5
FRENCH SOUTHERN & ANTARCTIC TERRITORIES (to France)
+5
+5
Prince Edward Islands (to South Africa)
HEARD & MCDONALD ISLANDS (to Australia)
11:00
12:00
13:00
14:00
15:00
16:00
17:00
18:00
19:00
20:00
21:00
ANTARCTICA
(except for Graham Land, Antarctica is not subject to any time zone)

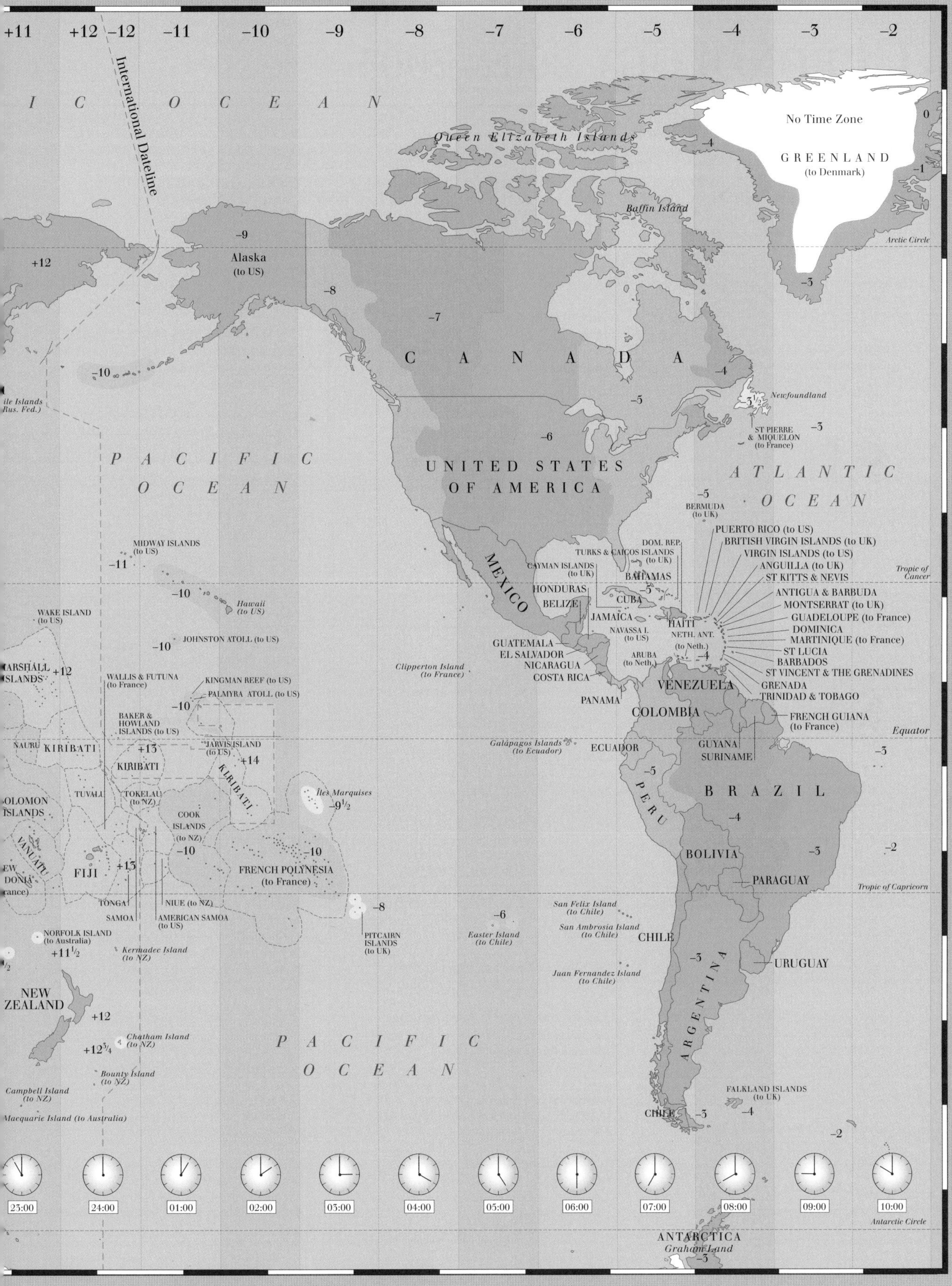
+11
+12
-12
-11
-10
-9
-8
-7
-6
-5
-4
-3
-2
International Dateline
P A C I F I C O C E A N
Queen Elizabeth Islands
No Time Zone
GREENLAND
(to Denmark)
Baffin Island
Arctic Circle
Alaska
(to US)
CANADA
Newfoundland
-3½
ST PIERRE & MIQUELON
(to France)
UNITED STATES OF AMERICA
ATLANTIC OCEAN
BERMUDA
(to UK)
PACIFIC OCEAN
MIDWAY ISLANDS
(to US)
Hawaii
(to US)
WAKE ISLAND
(to US)
JOHNSTON ATOLL (to US)
MARSHALL ISLANDS
WALLIS & FUTUNA
(to France)
KINGMAN REEF (to US)
PALMYRA ATOLL (to US)
BAKER & HOWLAND ISLANDS (to US)
JARVIS ISLAND
(to US)
NAURU
KIRIBATI
+13
+14
SOLOMON ISLANDS
TUVALU
TOKELAU
(to NZ)
COOK ISLANDS
(to NZ)
Îles Marquises
-9½
VANUATU
FIJI
NEW CALEDONIA
(to France)
FRENCH POLYNESIA
(to France)
TONGA
SAMOA
NIUE (to NZ)
AMERICAN SAMOA
(to US)
PITCAIRN ISLANDS
(to UK)
NORFOLK ISLAND
(to Australia)
+11½
Kermadec Island
(to NZ)
NEW ZEALAND
Chatham Island
(to NZ)
+12¾
Bounty Island
(to NZ)
Campbell Island
(to NZ)
Macquarie Island (to Australia)
MEXICO
DOM. REP.
TURKS & CAICOS ISLANDS
(to UK)
CAYMAN ISLANDS
(to UK)
BAHAMAS
HONDURAS
BELIZE
CUBA
JAMAICA
HAITI
NAVASSA I.
(to US)
NETH. ANT.
(to Neth.)
ARUBA
(to Neth.)
GUATEMALA
EL SALVADOR
NICARAGUA
COSTA RICA
PANAMA
PUERTO RICO (to US)
BRITISH VIRGIN ISLANDS (to UK)
VIRGIN ISLANDS (to US)
ANGUILLA (to UK)
ST KITTS & NEVIS
ANTIGUA & BARBUDA
MONTSERRAT (to UK)
GUADELOUPE (to France)
DOMINICA
MARTINIQUE (to France)
ST LUCIA
BARBADOS
ST VINCENT & THE GRENADINES
GRENADA
TRINIDAD & TOBAGO
Tropic of Cancer
Clipperton Island
(to France)
VENEZUELA
COLOMBIA
FRENCH GUIANA
(to France)
Equator
Galápagos Islands
(to Ecuador)
ECUADOR
GUYANA
SURINAME
PERU
BRAZIL
BOLIVIA
PARAGUAY
Tropic of Capricorn
San Felix Island
(to Chile)
San Ambrosia Island
(to Chile)
Easter Island
(to Chile)
CHILE
Juan Fernandez Island
(to Chile)
URUGUAY
ARGENTINA
FALKLAND ISLANDS
(to UK)
23:00
24:00
01:00
02:00
03:00
04:00
05:00
06:00
07:00
08:00
09:00
10:00
Antarctic Circle
ANTARCTICA
Graham Land

Chronology 2002–2003

THE ARRIVAL OF East Timor as the world's newest country in May 2002 and the departure of Yugoslavia in February 2003 encapsulate the extremes taking place in the world in 2002–2003. Long-running conflicts in Angola and Sri Lanka were ended after more than 20 years of fighting, and calm was brought to the DRC. Hopeful plans for peace, such as the Middle East "roadmap" and peacekeeping missions in Africa, achieved only limited results, while a US-led Coalition disregarded popular opinion to invade Iraq in March 2003, killing thousands but toppling the dictator Saddam Hussein.

North America

❑ **February 1, 2002** US president George W. Bush labels Iran, Iraq, and North Korea an "axis of evil."

❑ **June 17, 2002** Asteroid 2002MN whistles past the earth but is only detected by US astronomers three days later.

❑ **July 21, 2002** Just seven months after the collapse of the Enron corporation, telecommunications firm WorldCom files the largest corporate bankruptcy in US history amid revelations of false accounting.

❑ **October 24, 2002** John Allen Muhammed and John Lee Boyd, the Washington snipers, are apprehended after a 22-day killing spree which left ten people dead.

❑ **February 1, 2003** Seven astronauts are killed when the US space shuttle *Columbia* crashes before landing.

❑ **April 7, 2003** Statistics show that the US prison population exceeds two million.

❑ **April 13, 2003** The human genome is mapped, two years ahead of schedule, by international researchers.

❑ **April 15, 2003** After nine years in power, the separatist Partí Québécois is ousted from the Québec government.

❑ **August 14, 2003** Biggest power cut in US history blacks out New York City.

Central and South America

❑ **January 1, 2002** Eduard Duhalde is sworn in as Argentina's fifth president in 12 days. The country continues to suffer economic chaos.

❑ **February 20, 2002** Peace talks in Colombia are abandoned: the country returns to full-scale civil war.

❑ **April 14, 2002** President Hugo Chávez is returned to power in Venezuela after a 48-hour coup.

❑ **June 30, 2002** Brazil wins the soccer World Cup for a record fifth time.

❑ **January 1, 2003** The veteran left-wing leader "Lula" da Silva is inaugurated as president of Brazil.

❑ **February 2, 2003** A two-month strike in Venezuela ends, having failed to bring down the government of President Chávez.

❑ **March 18, 2003** A crackdown on prodemocracy activists begins in Cuba: 75 people are arrested.

Europe

❑ **January 1, 2002** The euro is introduced at midnight in 12 EU countries. Six months later the franc, deutsche mark, drachma, and other old currencies are consigned to history.

❑ **February 12, 2002** The trial begins in The Hague of former Serbian ruler Slobodan Milosevic.

❑ **April 21, 2002** Far-right leader Jean-Marie Le Pen shocks the world by coming second in the first round of the French presidential elections.

❑ **May 28, 2002** A Russia–NATO council is established giving Russia more input into NATO policy.

❑ **July 14, 2002** French president Jacques Chirac survives an assassination attempt by right-wing activist Maxime Brunerie.

❑ **September 10, 2002** Switzerland officially becomes the 190th member of the UN.

❑ **October 16, 2002** The shortest-lived Dutch government in history collapses after just 87 days. It had included the party of anti-immigrant populist Pim Fortuyn who had been assassinated in May.

❑ **October 26, 2002** A hostage crisis in a Moscow theater ends with the death of 128 hostages and their 41 Chechen captors.

❑ **November 16, 2002** The *Prestige* tanker sinks, spilling thousands of tonnes of oil along the Galician coast of Spain.

❑ **December 13, 2002** Ten east European and Mediterranean countries are formally invited to join the EU in May 2004.

❑ **February 2, 2003** Playwright and veteran dissident Vaclav Havel steps down as president of the Czech Republic after ten years in office.

❑ **February 4, 2003** The rump "Yugoslavia" ceases to exist and is replaced by Serbia & Montenegro.

❑ **February 14, 2003** Around five million people demonstrate in Europe's capitals against the impending war on Iraq.

❑ **March 12, 2003** Serbian prime minister Zoran Djindjic is assassinated by members of the former Serbian secret service.

❑ **April 23, 2003** The Green Line which divides Cyprus is opened for the first time in 29 years.

❑ **July 7, 2003** The UK government is formally cleared of misleading Parliament in its efforts to go to war with Iraq.

Africa

❑ **January 28, 2002** Over 1000 people die trying to escape a fire at a munitions dump in Lagos, Nigeria.

❑ **February 22, 2002** After elections, Marc Ravalomanana declares himself president of Madagascar, prompting a violent four-month standoff with incumbent, Didier Ratsiraka. Ravalomanana is recognized by the international community in June.

❑ **April 4, 2002** A cease-fire, prompted by the death of UNITA leader Joseph Savimbi, ends 27 years of civil war in Angola.

❑ **September 26, 2002** Over 1800 people die when the *Joola* ferry capsizes off the coast of Senegal.

❑ **December 27, 2002** Veteran politician, lately opposition leader, Mwai Kibaki is elected president of Kenya, ending KANU's 40-year rule.

❑ **March 16, 2003** Veteran rebel Gen. François Bozizé leads a military coup in the Central African Republic.

❑ **April 2, 2003** The Final Act is signed outlining a definitive peace plan for the DRC. Rebel leaders are sworn in as vice presidents in July.

❑ **May 21, 2003** Over 2100 people die in a powerful earthquake in Algiers.

❑ **June 10, 2003** The skull of "Herto" is unveiled in Ethiopia. At 160,000 years of age he is the oldest human being ever found.

❑ **July 4, 2003** The civil war in Ivory Coast is declared over after almost ten months.

❑ **July 23, 2003** President Fradique de Menezes returns to São Tomé & Príncipe, a week after a military coup.

❑ **August 4, 2003** Nigerian peacekeepers arrive in Liberia in an effort to end the civil war.

West Asia/Middle East

❑ **February 14, 2002** Bahrain is declared a constitutional monarchy.

❑ **March 19, 2002** US forces complete Operation Anaconda in Afghanistan, leaving more than 500 al-Qaida and *taliban* fighters dead.

❑ **May 10, 2002** The five-week siege in Bethlehem of the Church of the Nativity is finally lifted; 39 Palestinian militants involved go into exile.

❑ **June 19, 2002** Israeli forces begin the construction of a fence between Israel proper and the Palestinian West Bank.

❑ **November 4, 2002** The neo-Islamist Justice and Development Party wins elections in Turkey.

❑ **March 20, 2003** The invasion of Iraq by US, UK, and other "Coalition" forces begins. The regime of Saddam Hussein is toppled by April 9.

❑ **May 1, 2003** The US publishes its "roadmap" to peace in the Middle East. The plan is accepted by both Israel and the Palestinians, but is violated almost immediately.

❑ **June 2, 2003** Islamic *sharia* law is imposed in Pakistan's Northwest Frontier Province.

❑ **July 22, 2003** Uday and Qusay Hussein, the sons of the ousted Iraqi dictator, are killed in a six-hour siege.

North and East Asia

❑ **April 11, 2002** The Chinese government admits that there are around 850,000 people in China who are HIV-positive. The UN estimates that the figure is already likely to be more than one million.

❑ **June 7, 2002** Figures indicate that a six-month recession has come to an end in Japan.

❑ **September 17, 2002** The first ever meeting between the leaders of Japan and North Korea takes place; Japanese prime minister Junichiro Koizumi travels to Pyonyang.

❑ **December 31, 2002** The world's first commercial maglev train begins operating in Shanghai, China.

❑ **February 18, 2003** 133 people die in an arson attack on the Seoul subway in South Korea.

❑ **May 15, 2003** Hu Jintao becomes president of China at the head of a new generation of Communist leaders.

❑ **June 1, 2003** The controversial Three Gorges Dam in China is flooded with the waters of the Yangtze River.

❑ **June 26, 2003** Beijing is declared free of Severe Acute Repiratory Syndrome (SARS): 191 people had died in the Chinese capital alone.

❑ **July 8, 2003** The House of Representatives votes to allow Japanese troops to serve abroad for the first time since World War II.

South Asia

❑ **February 21, 2002** A cease-fire in Sri Lanka promises peace after 19 years of civil war.

❑ **February 28, 2002** The murder of 58 Hindus in Gujarat, India, sparks sectarian violence across the state, leaving over 500 people – mostly Muslims – dead.

❑ **May 14, 2002** Kashmiri separatists kill 34 people in a terrorist attack, raising tensions between India and Pakistan and bringing them to the brink of possible nuclear war.

❑ **October 4, 2002** King Gyanendra of Nepal dismisses the government, sparking prolonged protests.

❑ **January 13, 2003** Leaders of the Naga independence movement declare their decades-long war with the Indian government over. Peace talks begin.

❑ **May 30. 2003** Burmese opposition leader Aung San Suu Kyi is rearrested once again following an attack on her motorcade. Her detention prompts widespread international condemnation.

Southeast Asia

❑ **May 20, 2002** East Timor becomes an independent country.

❑ **June 22, 2002** Prime Minister Mahathir Mohamed of Malaysia announces that he will resign in 2003, after 22 years in power.

❑ **October 12, 2002** A terrorist bomb kills more than 200 people in Bali, Indonesia. Most of the victims are Australian tourists.

❑ **January 19, 2003** Anti-Thai riots force 511 ethnic Thais to flee the Cambodian capital Phnom Penh.

❑ **May 19, 2003** The Indonesian government launches a major offensive against separatist rebels in Aceh district.

❑ **May 25, 2003** It is announced that over 2000 people have died during the Thai government's crackdown on the illegal narcotics trade.

Australia and Oceania

❑ **May 14, 2002** AusAid predicts that 40% of Papua New Guinea's adults could die of AIDS by 2020.

❑ **July 2, 2002** US adventurer Steve Fosset lands in Australia after completing the first solo circumnavigation of the Earth in a hot air balloon.

❑ **December 29, 2002** Vanuatu experiences its first ever hailstorm.

❑ **March 10, 2003** Bernard Dowiyogo, the veteran president of Nauru, dies in office.

❑ **May 25, 2003** Archbishop Peter Hollingworth, the governor-general of Australia, resigns amid scandal over child abuse in the Australian Church.

❑ **May 26, 2003** Campbell Island, south of New Zealand, is declared rat-free two years after the biggest extermination project ever.

❑ **July 18, 2003** The Fijian Supreme Court rules the government illegal, since it includes no members of the main, ethnic-Indian, opposition.

❑ **July 24, 2003** Peacekeepers arrive in the Solomon Islands to restore law and order, on invitation of the government.

International Organizations

THIS LISTING GIVES the full names of all international organizations referred to, often by acronym, in the World Desk Reference (political parties are to be found under the Politics heading within each country entry). The full names are followed by the date of the establishment or foundation, an indication of membership, where appropriate, and a summary of the organization's aims and functions.

ACC
Arab Cooperation Council
established 1989
members – Egypt, Iraq, Jordan, Yemen
Promotes Arab economic cooperation

ACP
African, Caribbean, and Pacific Countries
established 1976
members – 78 developing countries and territories
Preferential economic and aid relationship with the EU under the Lomé Convention

ACS
Association of Caribbean States
established 1994
members – 25 countries in the Caribbean region
Promotes economic, scientific, and cultural cooperation in the region

ADB
Asian Development Bank
established 1966
members – 44 Asia–Pacific countries and territories, 17 nonregional countries
Encourages regional development

AfDB
African Development Bank
established 1964
members – 53 African countries, 24 non-African countries
Encourages African economic and social development

AFESD
Arab Fund for Economic and Social Development
established 1968
members – 21 Arab countries (including Palestine)
Promotes social and economic development in Arab states

AL
League of Arab States (Arab League)
established 1945
members – 22 Arab countries (including Palestine)
Forum to promote Arab cooperation on social, political, and military issues

ALADI
Latin American Integration Association
established 1960
members – 12 Central and South American countries
Promotes trade and regional integration

AmCC
Amazonian Cooperation Council
established 1978
members – Bolivia, Brazil, Colombia, Ecuador, Guyana, Peru, Suriname, Venezuela
Promotes the harmonious development of the Amazon region

AMF
Arab Monetary Fund
established 1977
members – 22 Arab countries (including Palestine)
Promotes monetary and economic cooperation

AMU
Arab Maghreb Union
established 1989
members – Algeria, Libya, Mauritania, Morocco, Tunisia
Promotes integration and economic cooperation among north African Arab states

ANZUS
Australia–New Zealand–United States Security Treaty
established 1951
members – Australia, New Zealand, US
Trilateral security agreement. Security relations between the US and New Zealand were suspended in 1984 over the issue of US nuclear-powered or potentially nuclear-armed naval vessels visiting New Zealand ports. High-level contacts between the USA and New Zealand were resumed in 1994

AP
Andean Pact (Acuerdo de Cartegena), also known as Andean Community
established 1969
members – Bolivia, Colombia, Ecuador, Peru, Venezuela
Promotes development through integration

APEC
Asia–Pacific Economic Cooperation
established 1989
members – 21 Pacific Rim countries and Hong Kong
Promotes regional economic cooperation

ASEAN
Association of Southeast Asian Nations
established 1967
members – Brunei, Burma, Cambodia, Indonesia, Laos, Malaysia, Philippines, Singapore, Thailand, Vietnam
Promotes economic, social, and cultural cooperation

AU
African Union
established 2002
members – 52 African countries and Western Sahara
Promotes unity and cooperation in Africa (successor to the Organization of African Unity (OAU), established in 1963)

BADEA
Arab Bank for Economic Development in Africa
established 1973
members – 18 Arab countries (including Palestine)
Established as an agency of the Arab League to promote economic development in Africa

BDEAC
Central African States Development Bank
established 1975
members – Cameroon, Central African Republic, Chad, Congo, Equatorial Guinea, France, Gabon, Germany, Kuwait
Furthers economic development

Benelux
Benelux Economic Union
established 1960
members – Belgium, Luxembourg, Netherlands
Develops economic ties between member countries

BOAD
West African Development Bank
established 1973
members – Benin, Burkina, Guinea-Bissau, Ivory Coast, Mali, Niger, Senegal, Togo
Promotes economic development and integration in West Africa

BSEC
Organization of the Black Sea Economic Cooperation
established 1992
members – Albania, Armenia, Azerbaijan, Bulgaria, Georgia, Greece, Moldova, Romania, Russia, Turkey, Ukraine
Furthers regional stability through economic cooperation

CAEU
Council of Arab Economic Unity
established 1957
members – 12 Arab countries (including Palestine)
Encourages economic integration

Caricom
Caribbean Community and Common Market
established 1973
members – 14 Caribbean countries and Montserrat
Fosters economic ties in the Caribbean

CBSS
Council of the Baltic Sea States
established 1992
members – 11 Baltic Sea states and the European Commission
Promotes cooperation among Baltic Sea states

CDB
Caribbean Development Bank
established 1969
members – 17 Caribbean countries/dependencies, 8 non-Caribbean countries
Promotes regional development

CE
Council of Europe
established 1949
members – 45 European countries
Promotes unity and quality of life in Europe

CEFTA
Central European Free Trade Agreement
established 1992
members – Bulgaria, Czech Republic, Hungary, Poland, Romania, Slovakia, Slovenia
Promotes trade and cooperation

CEI
Central European Initiative
established 1989
members – 17 east and central European countries
Evolved from the Hexagonal Group; promotes economic and political cooperation, within the OSCE

CEMAC
Central African Economic and Monetary Community
established 1994
members – Cameroon, Central African Republic, Chad, Congo, Equatorial Guinea, Gabon
Aims to promote subregional integration, by economic and monetary union (replaced UDEAC)

CEPGL
Economic Community of the Great Lakes Countries
established 1976
members – Burundi, Democratic Republic of the Congo, Rwanda
Promotes regional economic cooperation

CERN
European Organization for Nuclear Research
established 1954
members – 20 European countries
Provides for collaboration in nuclear research for peaceful purposes

CILSS
Permanent Interstate Committee for Drought Control in the Sahel
established 1973
members – 9 African countries in the Sahel region
Promotes prevention of drought and crop failure in the region

CIS
Commonwealth of Independent States
established 1991
members – Armenia, Azerbaijan, Belarus, Georgia, Kazakhstan, Kyrgyzstan, Moldova, Russia, Tajikistan, Turkmenistan, Ukraine, Uzbekistan
Promotes interstate relationships among former republics of the Soviet Union

CMCA
Central American Monetary Council
established 1960
members – Costa Rica, El Salvador, Guatemala, Honduras, Nicaragua
Now a subsystem of SICA. Furthers economic ties between members; one of its institutions is the BCIE – Central American Bank for Economic Integration

COI
Indian Ocean Commission
established 1982
members – Comoros, France (representing Réunion), Madagascar, Mauritius, Seychelles
Promotes regional cooperation

COMESA
Common Market for Eastern and Southern Africa
established 1993
members – 20 African countries
Promotes economic development and cooperation (replaced PTA)

Comm
Commonwealth
established 1931
members – 54 countries (though Pakistan and Zimbabwe are currently suspended). Members are chiefly former members of the British Empire
Develops relationships and contacts between members

CP
Colombo Plan
established 1950
members – Four donor countries: Australia, Japan, New Zealand, US; and 21 Asia–Pacific countries
Encourages economic and social development in Asia–Pacific region

CPLP
Community of Portuguese-speaking Countries
established 1996
members – Portugal, Brazil, and five Portuguese-speaking African countries – Angola, Cape Verde, Guinea-Bissau, Mozambique, São Tomé and Príncipe
To promote political and diplomatic links between member states, and cooperation on economic, social, cultural, judicial, and scientific development among Portuguese-speaking countries

Damasc
Damascus Declaration
established 1991
members – Bahrain, Egypt, Kuwait, Oman, Qatar, Saudi Arabia, Syria, United Arab Emirates
A loose association, formed after the 1991 Gulf War, which aims to secure the stability of the region

EAC
East African Community
established 2001
members – Kenya, Tanzania, Uganda
Promotes economic cooperation

EAPC
Euro-Atlantic Partnership Council
established 1991
members – The 19 members of NATO plus 27 other European countries
Forum for cooperation on political and security issues (successor to the North Atlantic Cooperation Council, NACC)

EBRD
European Bank for Reconstruction and Development
established 1991
members – 60 countries
Helps transition of former communist European states to market economies

ECO
Economic Cooperation Organization
established 1985
members – Afghanistan, Azerbaijan, Iran, Kazakhstan, Kyrgyzstan, Pakistan, Tajikistan, Turkey, Turkmenistan, Uzbekistan
Aims at cooperation in economic, social, and cultural affairs

ECOWAS
Economic Community of West African States
established 1975
members – 15 west African countries
Promotes regional economic cooperation

EEA
European Economic Area
established 1994
members – The 15 members of the EU, and Iceland, Liechtenstein, and Norway
Aims to include EFTA members in the EU single market

EEC
Eurasian Economic Community
established 2001
members – Belarus, Kazakhstan, Kyrgyzstan, Russia, Tajikistan
Coordinates regional trade

EFTA
European Free Trade Association
established 1960
members – Iceland, Liechtenstein, Norway, Switzerland
Promotes economic cooperation

ESA
European Space Agency
established 1973
members – 15 European countries
Promotes cooperation in space research for peaceful purposes

EU
European Union
established 1992
members – 15 European countries; 10 other European countries have been invited to join in 2004
Aims to integrate the economies of member states and promote cooperation and coordination of policies (successor to the European Communities (EC), established in 1957 by the Treaties of Rome)

FZ
Franc zone
established Not applicable
members – France (including overseas departments and territories) and 15 African countries
Aims to form monetary union among countries whose currencies are linked to that of France

G3
Group of 3
established 1987
members – Colombia, Mexico, Venezuela
Aims to ease trade restrictions

G7
Group of 7
established 1975
members – The seven major industrialized countries: Canada, France, Germany, Italy, Japan, UK, US
Summit meetings of the seven major industrialized countries, originally for economic purposes. For political purposes summit meetings are now held as the G8, including Russia

G8
Group of 8
established 1994
members – Canada, France, Germany, Italy, Japan, Russia, UK, US
Global forum of world's major powers, which holds regular summit meetings

G10
Group of 10
established 1962
members – 11 members: G7 members, plus Belgium, Netherlands, Sweden, and Switzerland
Ministers meet to discuss monetary issues

G15
Group of 15
established 1989
members – 19 developing countries
Meets annually to further cooperation among developing countries

G24
Group of 24
established Not applicable
members – 24 developing countries within the IMF
Promotes the interests of developing countries on monetary and development issues

GCC
Gulf Cooperation Council
established 1981
members – Bahrain, Kuwait, Oman, Qatar, Saudi Arabia, United Arab Emirates
Promotes cooperation in social, economic, and political affairs

Geplacea
Latin American and Caribbean Sugar Exporting Countries
established 1974
members – 23 countries
A forum for consultation on the production and sale of sugar

GGC
Gulf of Guinea Commission
established 2001
members – Angola, Cameroon, Congo, Democratic Republic of the Congo, Equatorial Guinea, Gabon, Nigeria, São Tomé and Príncipe
Promotes regional cooperation

IAEA
International Atomic Energy Agency
established 1957
members – 136 countries
Promotes and monitors peaceful use of atomic energy

IBRD
International Bank for Reconstruction and Development (also known as the World Bank)
established 1945
members – 184 countries
UN agency providing economic development loans

ICRC
International Committee of the Red Cross
established 1863
members – Up to 25 Swiss nationals form the international committee. Red Cross or Red Crescent societies exist in 176 countries
Coordinates all international humanitarian activities of the International Red Cross and Red Crescent Movement, giving legal and practical assistance to the victims of wars and disasters. It works through national committees of Red Cross or Red Crescent societies

IDB
Inter-American Development Bank
established 1959
members – 28 American countries and 18 nonregional countries
Promotes development in Latin America and the Caribbean through the financing of economic and social development projects and the provision of technical assistance

IGAD
Intergovernmental Authority on Development
established 1996
members – Djibouti, Eritrea, Ethiopia, Kenya, Somalia, Sudan, Uganda
Promotes cooperation on food security, infrastructure, and other development issues (supersedes IGADD, founded 1986, to promote cooperation on drought-related matters)

IMF
International Monetary Fund
established 1945
members – 184 countries. The voting rights of Liberia are currently suspended.
Promotes international monetary cooperation, the balanced growth of trade, and exchange-rate stability; provides credit resources to members experiencing balance-of-trade difficulties

IsDB
Islamic Development Bank
established 1975
members – 54 countries (including Palestine)
Promotes economic development on Islamic principles among Muslim communities (agency of the OIC)

IWC
International Whaling Commission
established 1946
members – 49 countries
Reviews conduct of whaling throughout world; coordinates and funds whale research

LCBC
Lake Chad Basin Commission
established 1964
members – Cameroon, Central African Republic, Chad, Niger, Nigeria
Encourages economic and environmental development in Lake Chad region

Mekong River
Mekong River Commission
established 1995
members – Cambodia, Laos, Thailand, Vietnam
Accord on the sustainable development of the Mekong River basin (replacing the 1958 interim Mekong Secretariat)

Mercosur
Southern Common Market
established 1991
members – Argentina, Brazil, Paraguay, Uruguay
Promotes economic integration, free trade, and common external tariffs

MRU
Mano River Union
established 1973
members – Guinea, Liberia, Sierra Leone
Aims to create customs and economic union in order to promote development

NAFTA
North American Free Trade Agreement
established 1994
members – Canada, Mexico, US
Free trade zone

NAM
Non-Aligned Movement
established 1961
members – 114 countries (including Palestine). Serbia and Montenegro was suspended in 1992, and is now an observer
Fosters political and military cooperation away from traditional Eastern or Western blocs

NATO
North Atlantic Treaty Organization
established 1949
members – 19 countries
Promotes mutual defense cooperation. Since January 1994, NATO's Partnership for Peace program has provided a loose framework for cooperation with former members of the Warsaw Pact and the ex-Soviet republics. A historic Founding Act signed between Russia and NATO in May 1997 allowed for the organization's eastward expansion, under which the Czech Republic, Hungary, and Poland were the first three countries to join

NC
Nordic Council
established 1952
members – Denmark, Finland, Iceland, Norway, Sweden
Promotes cultural and environmental cooperation in Scandinavia

OAPEC
Organization of Arab Petroleum Exporting Countries
established 1968
members – Algeria, Bahrain, Egypt, Iraq, Kuwait, Libya, Qatar, Saudi Arabia, Syria, United Arab Emirates
Aims to promote the interests of member countries and increase cooperation in the petroleum industry

OAS
Organization of American States
established 1948
members – 35 American countries (though Cuba has been suspended since 1962)
Promotes security and economic and social development in the Americas

OAU
Organization of African Unity
Predecessor of the AU

OECD
Organization for Economic Cooperation and Development
established 1961
members – 30 industrialized democracies
Forum for coordinating economic policies among industrialized countries

OECS
Organization of Eastern Caribbean States
established 1981
members – Antigua and Barbuda, Dominica, Grenada, Montserrat, St. Kitts and Nevis, St. Lucia, St. Vincent and the Grenadines
Promotes political, economic, and defense cooperation

OIC
Organization of the Islamic Conference
established 1971
members – 57 countries (including Palestine)
Furthers Islamic solidarity and cooperation

OIF
International Organization of Francophony
established 1970
members – 47 countries and the governments of Québec, New Brunswick, and the French Community of Belgium
To promote cooperation and cultural and technical links among French-speaking countries and communities

OMVG
Gambia River Development Organization
established 1978
members – Gambia, Guinea, Guinea-Bissau, Senegal
Promotes integrated development of the Gambia River basin

Opanal
Agency for the Prohibition of Nuclear Weapons in Latin America and the Caribbean
established 1969
members – 33 countries
Aims to ensure compliance with the Treaty of Tlatelolco (banning nuclear weapons from South America and the Caribbean)

OPEC
Organization of the Petroleum Exporting Countries
established 1960
members – Algeria, Indonesia, Iran, Iraq, Kuwait, Libya, Nigeria, Qatar, Saudi Arabia, United Arab Emirates, Venezuela
Aims to coordinate oil policies to ensure fair and stable prices

OSCE
Organization for Security and Cooperation in Europe
established 1972
members – 55 countries
Aims to strengthen democracy and human rights, and settle disputes peacefully (formerly CSCE)

PC
Pacific Community
established 1948
members – 27 countries and territories
A forum for dialogue between Pacific countries and powers administering Pacific territories (formerly South Pacific Commission)

PfP
Partnership for Peace
see NATO
established Not applicable
members – 27 members: eastern European and former Soviet countries, Sweden, Finland, Malta, Austria, and Switzerland

PIF
Pacific Islands Forum
established 1971
members – 16 countries and self-governing territories
Develops regional political cooperation (formerly South Pacific Forum)

RG
Rio Group
established 1987
members – 19 Latin American and Caribbean countries
Forum for Latin American and Caribbean issues (evolved from Contadora Group, established 1948)

SAARC
South Asian Association for Regional Cooperation
established 1985
members – Bangladesh, Bhutan, India, Maldives, Nepal, Pakistan, Sri Lanka
Encourages economic, social, and cultural cooperation

SACU
Southern African Customs Union
established 1969
members – Botswana, Lesotho, Namibia, South Africa, Swaziland
Promotes cooperation in trade and customs matters among southern African states

SADC
Southern African Development Community
established 1992
members – 14 southern African countries
Promotes economic integration

San José
San José Group
established 1988
members – Costa Rica, El Salvador, Guatemala, Honduras, Nicaragua, Panama
A "complementary, voluntary, and gradual" economic union

SCO
Shanghai Cooperation Organization
established 1996
members – China, Kazakhstan, Kyrgyzstan, Russia, Tajikistan, Uzbekistan
Promotes regional security and cooperation (formerly Shanghai Five)

SELA
Latin American Economic System
established 1975
members – 28 countries
Promotes economic and social development through regional cooperation

SICA
Central American Integration System
established 1991
members – Costa Rica, El Salvador, Guatemala, Honduras, Nicaragua, Panama
Coordinates the political, economic, social, and environmental integration of the region

UEMOA
West African Economic and Monetary Union
established 1994
members – 8 west African countries
Aims for convergence of monetary policies and economic union

UN
United Nations
established 1945
members – 191 countries
Taiwan and the Vatican City do not belong to the UN
permanent members of the Security Council – China, France, Russia, UK, US
Aims to maintain international peace and security and to promote cooperation over economic, social, cultural, and humanitarian problems

Agencies include the regional commissions of the UN's Economic and Social Council:
ECA (Economic Commission for Africa – established 1958);
ECE (Economic Commission for Europe – established 1947);
ECLAC (Economic Commission for Latin America and the Caribbean – established 1948);
ESCAP (Economic and Social Commission for Asia and the Pacific – established 1947);
ESCWA (Economic and Social Commission for Western Asia – established 1973).

Other bodies of the UN, in which most members participate, include
IDA(the International Development Association);
UNCTAD (the UN Conference on Trade and Development);
UNDP (the UN Development Program);
UNFPA (the UN Population Fund);
UNHCR (the UN High Commissioner for Refugees);
UNICEF (the UN Children's Fund).

WEU
Western European Union
established 1955
members – 10 countries
A forum for European military cooperation

World Bank
see IBRD

WTO
World Trade Organization
established 1995
members – 143 countries and Hong Kong, Macao, and the EU
Aims to liberalize trade through multilateral trade agreements (successor to the General Agreement on Tariffs and Trade, GATT)

2

THE NATIONS OF THE WORLD

THE NATIONS OF THE WORLD

• AFGHANISTAN ~ ZIMBABWE

OVERSEAS TERRITORIES & DEPENDENCIES

ASIA
Turkmenistan
Uzb.
Tajikistan
China
AFGHANISTAN
Iran
Pakistan
Asia

AFGHANISTAN

OFFICIAL NAME: Islamic State of Afghanistan **CAPITAL:** Kabul
POPULATION: 23.3 million **CURRENCY:** New afghani **OFFICIAL LANGUAGES:** Pashtu and Dari

1919 | 1919 | Aug 19 | AFG | +4.5 | +93 | .af

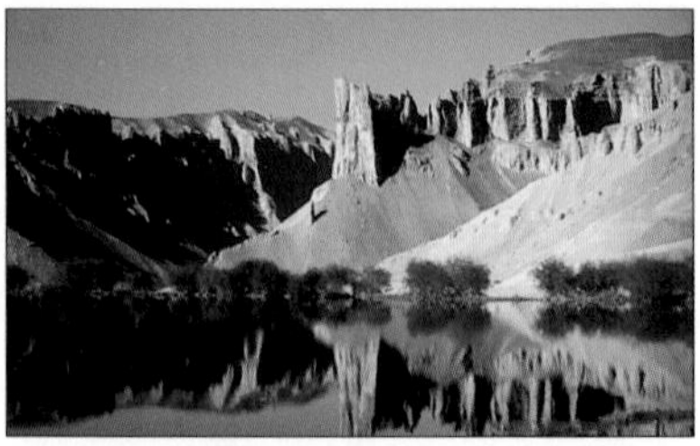

The Band-i-Amir River, in the Hindu Kush. Afghanistan is mountainous and arid. Many Afghans are nomadic sheep farmers.

AFGHANISTAN LIES LANDLOCKED in central Asia, three-quarters of its territory inaccessible terrain. Its political system, economy, and infrastructure have been devastated by decades of armed conflict. In the 1980s Islamic *mujahideen* factions defeated the Soviet-backed communist regime, but rivalries undermined their fragile power-sharing agreement and the hard-line *taliban* militia swept to power in 1996. Islamic dress codes and behavior were vigorously enforced and women left with few rights or opportunities. The *taliban* regime crumbled in the face of the US-led "war on terrorism" launched in late 2001.

CLIMATE

Mountain/cold desert

WEATHER CHART FOR KABUL

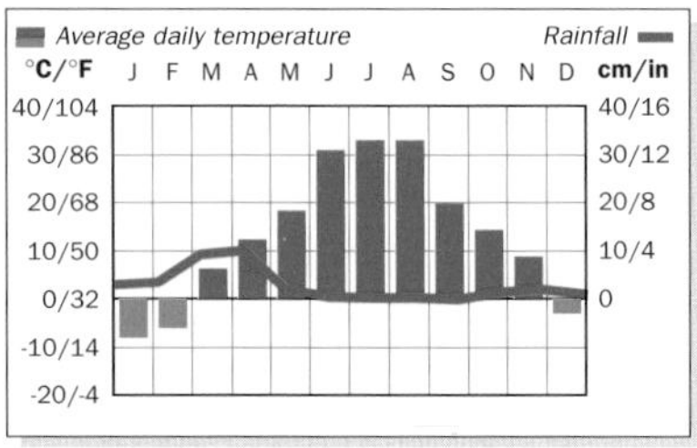
Average daily temperature
Rainfall
°C/°F
J F M A M J J A S O N D
cm/in
40/104
30/86
20/68
10/50
0/32
-10/14
-20/-4
40/16
30/12
20/8
10/4
0

Afghanistan has the world's widest temperature range, with lows of –50°C (–58°F) and highs of 53°C (127°F). Severe drought, a frequent problem, affected half the population in 2000.

TRANSPORTATION

Drive on right

Kabul International

Has no fleet

THE TRANSPORTATION NETWORK

2793 km (1735 miles)	None
25 km (16 miles)	1200 km (746 miles)

The repair and reconstruction of the roads, severely damaged by war, and the modernization of the air traffic control system are the most urgent priorities. The rebuilding of roads is usually carried out by local communities. However, neighboring Pakistan has undertaken to rebuild a number of key routes, including the Kabul–Peshawar link, which will benefit its own trade with central Asia.

Securing key supply routes was a crucial factor in intra-*mujahideen* feuding and in the *taliban*'s efforts to gain control over the whole country. Anti-*taliban* forces relied heavily on supplies from the north. Much of Afghanistan's outlying territory is sown with land mines.

TOURISM

Visitors : Population 1:5825

4000 visitors

No change in 1995–1998

MAIN TOURIST ARRIVALS

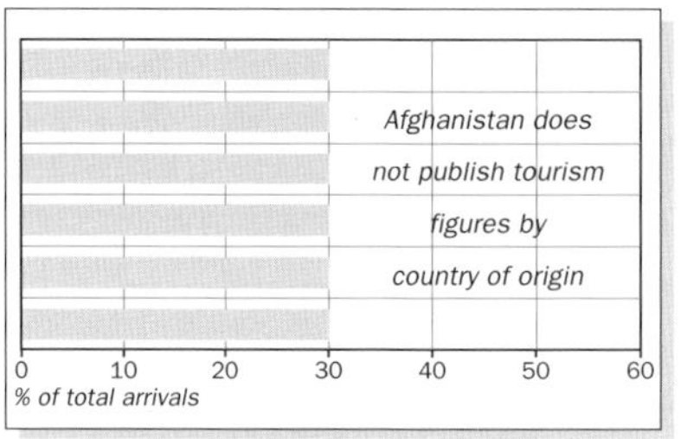
Afghanistan does not publish tourism figures by country of origin
0
10
20
30
40
50
60
% of total arrivals

Afghanistan has yet to recover from decades of war. Few hotels are open in Kabul, and travel in the land-mine-strewn and lawless interior is dangerous. The lack of a formal economy means that there are few visits from businessmen, and most expatriates left Kabul during the *taliban* period. Most major cultural treasures, such as the famous carvings of Buddha at Bamian, have been destroyed or looted, while Air Ariana, the national airline, lost six of its eight aircraft in the 2001 US bombing.

PEOPLE

Pop. density low

Pashtu, Tajik, Dari, Farsi, Uzbek, Turkmen

36/km² (93/mi²)

THE URBAN/RURAL POPULATION SPLIT

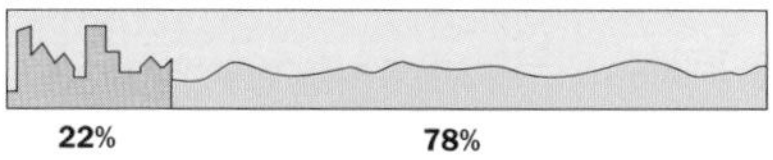
22%
78%

RELIGIOUS PERSUASION

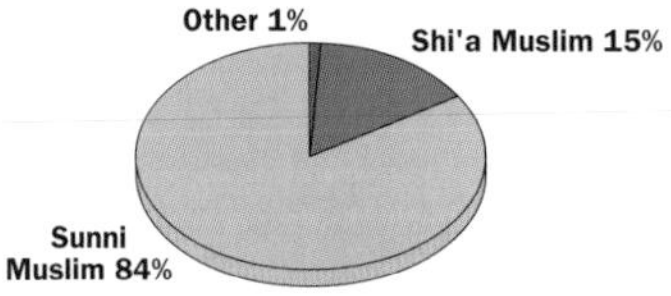
Other 1%
Shi'a Muslim 15%
Sunni Muslim 84%

ETHNIC MAKEUP

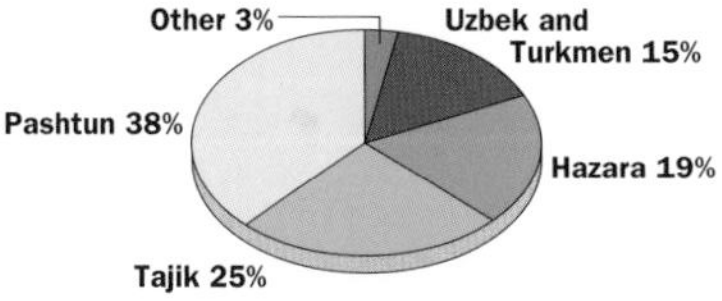
Other 3%
Uzbek and Turkmen 15%
Pashtun 38%
Hazara 19%
Tajik 25%

Ethnicity largely determined intra-*mujahideen* feuding after 1992. Pashtuns have traditionally been the rulers of Afghanistan, and dominated the *taliban*. The fall of that regime in 2001 provided the opportunity for the Tajik–Uzbek alliance to enforce a power-sharing agreement. Pashtuns have since faced reprisal attacks, particularly in the north, where they are a minority. Religious differences between Sunnis and Shi'as became acute under the Sunni taliban regime.

Some two million people were killed in the ten-year conflict which followed the invasion by Soviet Union forces in 1979 and in the post-1992 civil war. As many people again were maimed. A further six million people were forced to flee to Pakistan and Iran; many returned, but the US attacks in 2001 which ousted the *taliban* created a fresh wave of refugees and left hundreds of thousands more people internally displaced.

Women had few rights under the rigid Islamic regime of the *taliban*. The interim government has lifted the ban on women in employment and allowed girls to resume schooling, but social restrictions still exist.

POPULATION AGE BREAKDOWN

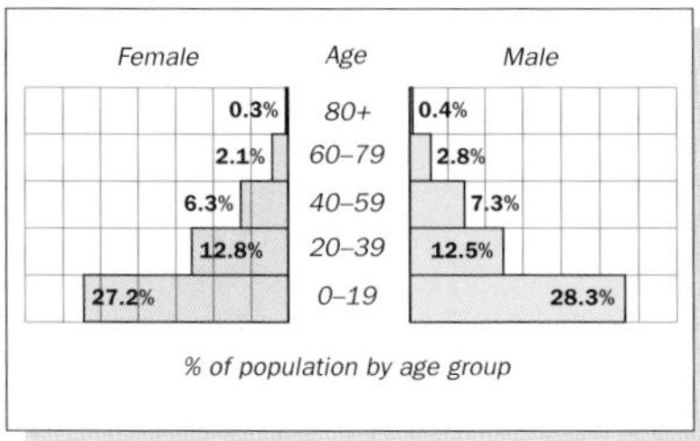
Female
Age
Male
0.3%
80+
0.4%
2.1%
60–79
2.8%
6.3%
40–59
7.3%
12.8%
20–39
12.5%
27.2%
0–19
28.3%
% of population by age group

POLITICS

In transition

1988/2004

President Hamid Karzai

AT THE LAST ELECTION

House of Representatives (dissolved)

Following the downfall of Najibullah's regime in April 1992, both houses were dissolved and an interim *mujahideen* legislature formed.

Senate (dissolved)

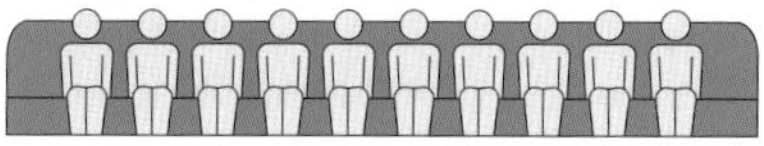

Emerging from almost 30 years of constant war, in 2002 Afghanistan chose a transitional government through its Loya Jirga (grand council) as the foundation of a democratic, presidential system. Elections are due in 2004.

PROFILE

Civil war was fueled from outside by Cold War rivalries. *Mujahideen* factions fought first against Soviet invaders, and then against each other, before a potent new force, the Islamist *taliban*, arose in 1995. After capturing Kabul in 1996 the *taliban* declared Afghanistan to be a "complete" Islamic state, and imposed a strict Islamic code.

After September 11, 2001, the US targeted Afghanistan on the basis that it harbored international Islamist terrorists. A full-scale bombing campaign tipped the balance in favor of the opposition Northern Alliance, and the *taliban* were swiftly removed from power. In their place the US sponsored the formation of an interim government around the Pashtun leader Hamid Karzai, who was duly elected president in 2002.

MAIN POLITICAL ISSUE
Political stability and central control

The control of the Kabul government is precarious, its formation having been based upon the ad hoc unity of the Northern Alliance and the military might of the US. Promised aid has been slow to arrive. Instability has increased, with political assassinations and terrorist attacks against government and Western forces blamed on the reemergence of Islamist groups – particularly along the border with Pakistan – and the ambitions of regional warlords. Karzai has been forced to threaten to resign in order to rein in wayward regional governors.

Hamid Karzai was confirmed as head of state in 2002 by the traditional Loya Jirga council.

WORLD AFFAIRS

Joined UN in 1946

CP | ECO | IBRD | NAM | OIC

The nature of the Islamist *taliban* regime made Afghanistan a pariah state and the first target of the US-led "war on terrorism" in 2001. The new interim government is consequently heavily dependent on the countries which effectively installed it, making good relations with them essential for future aid. Pakistan was the last country to break off links with the *taliban* and remains Afghanistan's most delicately placed partner, with a history of religious as well as ethnic sympathies with the ousted, Pashtun-dominated, Islamist regime. Plans for a gas pipeline, carrying Turkmen gas to south Asia, have been revived, and it is now a crucial economic issue.

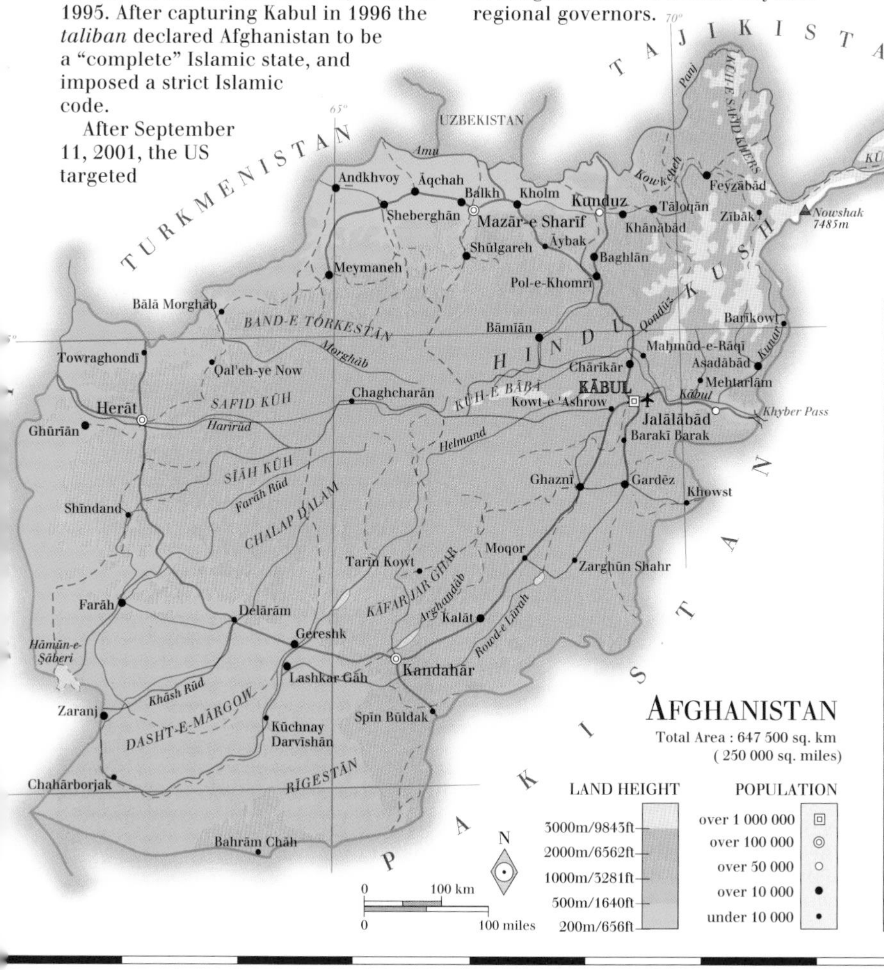
AFGHANISTAN
Total Area : 647 500 sq. km
(250 000 sq. miles)
LAND HEIGHT
3000m/9843ft
2000m/6562ft
1000m/3281ft
500m/1640ft
200m/656ft
POPULATION
over 1 000 000
over 100 000
over 50 000
over 10 000
under 10 000
0 100 km
0 100 miles
TAJIKISTAN
UZBEKISTAN
TURKMENISTAN
CHINA
PAKISTAN
KĀBUL
Herāt
Kandahār
Mazār-e Sharīf
Kunduz
Jalālābād
HINDU KUSH
Khyber Pass
Nowshak 7485m

CHRONOLOGY

The foundations of an Afghan state of Pashtun peoples were laid in the mid-18th century, when Durrani Ahmad Shah became paramount chief of the Abdali Pashtun peoples.

- **1838–1842** First Anglo-Afghan war.
- **1878** Second British invasion of Afghan territory.
- **1879** Under Treaty of Gandmak signed with Amir Yaqub Ali Khan, various Afghan areas annexed by Britain. Yaqub Ali Khan later exiled. New treaty signed with Amir Abdul Rahman, establishing the Durand line, a contentious boundary between Afghanistan and Pakistan.
- **1919** Independence declared.
- **1933** Mohammed Zahir Shah ascends throne.
- **1953–1963** Mohammed Daud Khan prime minister; resigns after king rejects proposals for democratic reforms.

CHRONOLOGY *continued*

- **1965** Elections held, but monarchy retains power. Marxist Party of Afghanistan (PDPA) formed and banned. PDPA splits into the Parcham and Khalq factions.
- **1973** Daud mounts a coup, abolishes monarchy, and declares republic. *Mujahideen* rebellion begins. Refugees flee to Pakistan.
- **1978** Opposition to Daud from PDPA culminates in Saur revolution. Revolutionary Council under Mohammad Taraki takes power. Daud assassinated.
- **1979** Taraki ousted. Hafizullah Amin takes power. Amin killed in December coup backed by USSR. 80,000 Soviet troops invade Afghanistan. *Mujahideen* rebellion stepped up into full-scale guerrilla war, with US backing.
- **1980** Babrak Karmal, leader of Parcham PDPA, installed as head of Marxist regime.
- **1986** Najibullah replaces Karmal as head of government.
- **1989** Soviet Army withdraws. Najibullah remains in office.
- **1992** Najibullah hands over power to *mujahideen* factions.
- **1993** *Mujahideen* agree on formation of government.
- **1994** Power struggle between Burhanuddin Rabbani and Gulbuddin Hekmatyar.
- **1996** *Taliban* take power and impose strict Islamic regime.
- **1998** Earthquake in northern regions kills thousands.
- **1999** Power-sharing agreement between *taliban* and Northern Alliance breaks down.
- **2000** Worst drought in 30 years. UN imposes sanctions in response to *taliban* support for Osama bin Laden.
- **2001** *Taliban* government falls after intense US-led air strikes from October – first campaign in "war on terrorism." Interim government formed under Hamid Karzai; peacekeepers deployed in Kabul.
- **2002** Earthquakes kill thousands. Ex-king Zahir Shah returns from exile. Loya Jirga convenes, elects Karzai head of state.

AID

Recipient

$402m (receipts) — Up 185% in 2001

The fall of the *taliban* opened the way for massive inflows of aid. However, pledges by the US and its allies not to "forget" Afghanistan have been tested greatly as international priorities have shifted; only a fraction of the promised aid has arrived. Working conditions for aid personnel are extremely hazardous.

DEFENSE

Compulsory military service

$245m — Down 2% in 2001

AFGHAN ARMED FORCES

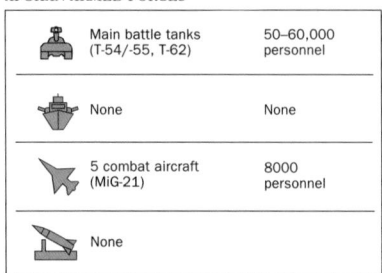

Main battle tanks (T-54/-55, T-62)	50–60,000 personnel
None	None
5 combat aircraft (MiG-21)	8000 personnel
None	

The new regime is establishing a national army. Private armies have been banned. An international peacekeeping force maintains security in Kabul, while effective control elsewhere is maintained by local warlords. The US continues to launch major offensives against the remaining al-Qaida and *taliban* forces.

Regional factions are heavily armed thanks to decades of military assistance from the US and the USSR during the Cold War. Although direct involvement by these superpowers came to an end in 1991, the arms supplied to rival groups remain prevalent. The US is concerned in particular about the presence of hundreds of Stinger surface-to-air missiles. Worried that they might be used against civilian airliners, the US government has frequently launched drives to buy them back.

Foreign Islamic militants have also helped to flood the country with arms. The bulk of these weapons originate in eastern Europe and the former Soviet Union. The movement of Islamist militants and weapons between Tajikistan and Afghanistan is now tackled by CIS troops.

ECONOMICS

Not available

$5.68bn — 43 new afghanis (4750)

SCORE CARD

- World GNP Ranking 109th
- GNP per Capita $250
- Balance of Payments .... –$143m
- Inflation 56.7%
- Unemployment 8%

EXPORTS

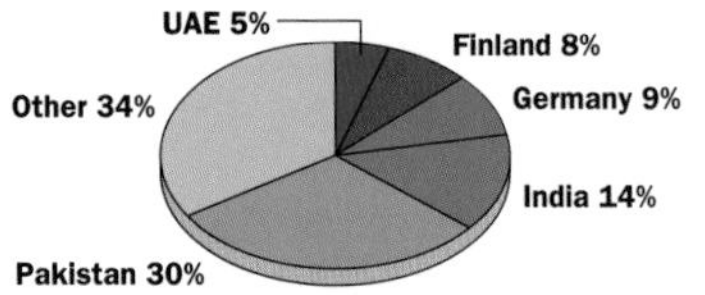
UAE 5%
Finland 8%
Germany 9%
India 14%
Pakistan 30%
Other 34%

IMPORTS

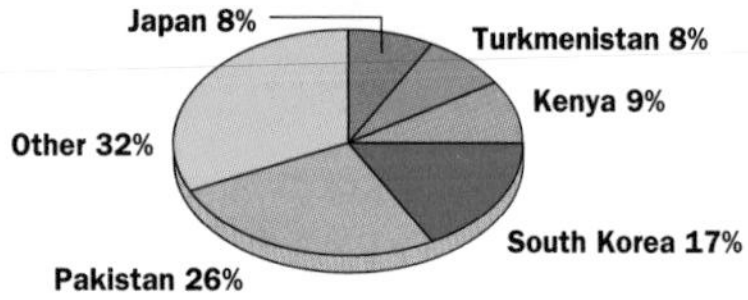
Japan 8%
Turkmenistan 8%
Kenya 9%
South Korea 17%
Pakistan 26%
Other 32%

Strengths

Very few, apart from illicit opium trade. Revalued currency issued in 2002. Overseas assets unfrozen from 2002.

Weaknesses

Decades of fighting: infrastructure, agriculture, and industry in ruins. Communication links damaged by earthquakes and devastated by bombing. Aid slow to materialize.

Profile

The protracted fighting has left Afghanistan one of the poorest and least developed countries in the world. It is estimated that some $15 billion is needed to rebuild the country and that over 80% of infrastructure has been destroyed. Agricultural activity has fallen back from pre-1979 levels; the Soviet "scorched earth" policy laid waste large areas, and much of the rural population fled to the cities. Many farmers turned back to growing poppies for opium production, but saw little profit, despite Afghanistan being one of the world's largest sources of opium. Although prohibited, poppy cultivation has increased under the new, less intimidating, regime.

ECONOMIC PERFORMANCE INDICATOR

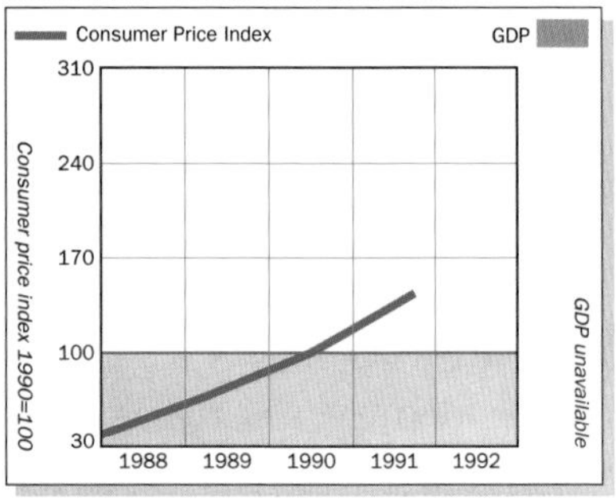
Consumer Price Index
GDP
310
240
170
100
30
Consumer price index 1990=100
GDP unavailable
1988
1989
1990
1991
1992

Much of Afghanistan's infrastructure, already damaged by decades of civil war, was reduced to ruins by heavy US bombardment in 2001.

RESOURCES

Electric power 499,000 kW

1000 tonnes

Not an oil producer and has no refineries

11m sheep, 5m goats, 2m cattle, 6.5m chickens

Natural gas, salt, coal, copper, lapis lazuli, barytes, talc

ELECTRICITY GENERATION

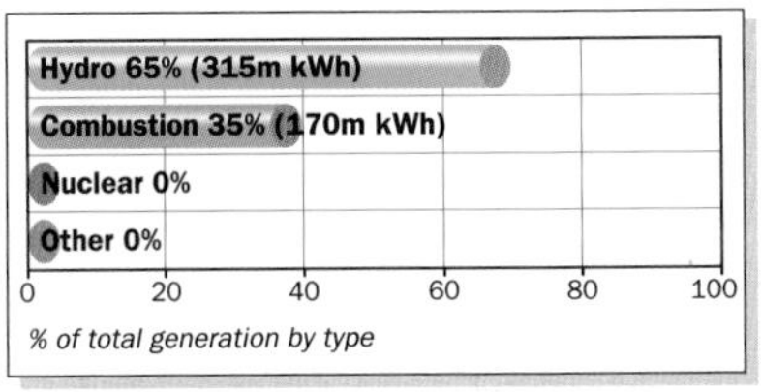
Hydro 65% (315m kWh)
Combustion 35% (170m kWh)
Nuclear 0%
Other 0%
0
20
40
60
80
100
% of total generation by type

Natural gas and coal are the most important strategic resources. In 2002 Afghanistan signed a gas agreement with Pakistan and Turkmenistan, which could generate revenue estimated at $300 million. Restoring the power generation system is a government priority. The construction of dams on the Kunar and Laghman rivers is being considered. Coal production has fallen from prewar levels and mines are in urgent need of rehabilitation.

AFGHANISTAN : LAND USE

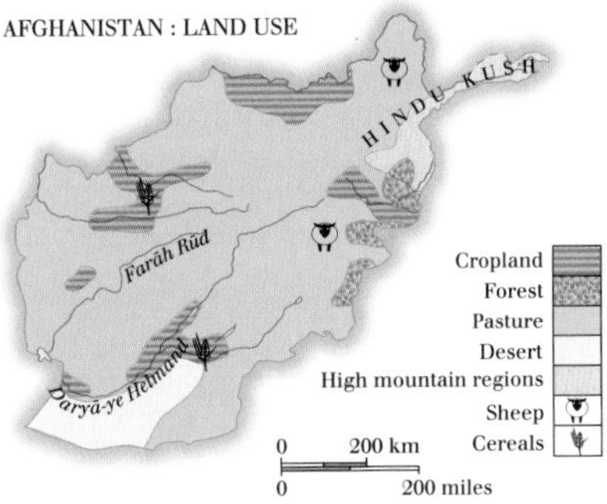
HINDU KUSH
Farāh Rūd
Daryā-ye Helmand
Cropland
Forest
Pasture
Desert
High mountain regions
Sheep
Cereals
0
200 km
0
200 miles

HEALTH

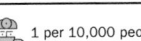

No welfare state health benefits

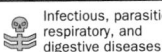

1 per 10,000 people

Infectious, parasitic, respiratory, and digestive diseases

The health service has collapsed completely and almost all medical professionals have left the country. Infant and maternal mortality rates are among the highest in the world, and life expectancy is very low.

Parasitic diseases and infections are a particular problem. The UN organized a program for the chlorination of well water, following an outbreak of cholera in Kabul, and launched a mass measles vaccination program in January 2002.

Under the *taliban* regime most women in Afghanistan had very little access to health care: their admission to hospital was strongly discouraged, as was the employment of female medical staff.

ENVIRONMENT

Not available

0.3% (0.2% partially protected)

0.05 tonnes per capita

ENVIRONMENTAL TREATIES

No	Yes	Yes
No	No	No

Environmental priorities are low. However, the country's lack of industry, even in Kabul, means that industrial pollution is minimal. The biggest problem facing Afghanistan is land mines: over ten million have been laid, and the UN estimates that it will take 100 years to make the country safe for civilians. Half the country's forests have been lost since 1977.

CRIME

Death penalty in use

Afghanistan does not publish prison figures

Levels of all crimes remain very high

CRIME RATES

Afghanistan does not publish statistics for murders, rapes, or thefts

Gun law operates widely. Journeys in rural areas are vulnerable to armed robbery. Cities vary according to which faction is dominant and the level of disruption caused by war. A new national police force is being trained.

SPENDING

GDP/cap. decrease

CONSUMPTION AND SPENDING

0.2 per 1000 population

1 per 1000 population

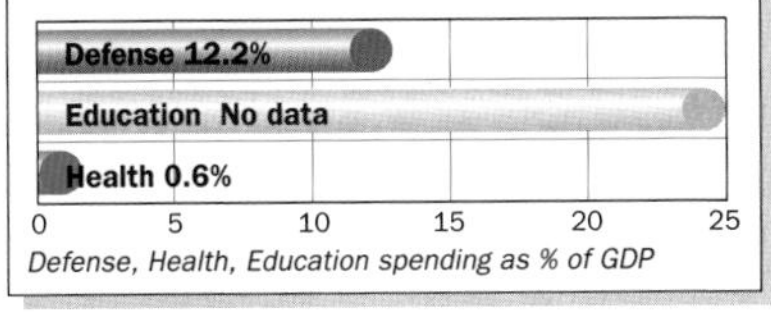
Defense 12.2%
Education No data
Health 0.6%
0
5
10
15
20
25
Defense, Health, Education spending as % of GDP

The vast majority of Afghans live in conditions of extreme poverty. The country does not have the resources to feed its people at present – a situation exacerbated by the severe drought of 2000, the 2001 fighting, and the 2002 earthquakes. The return of refugees from neighboring Pakistan and Iran makes Afghanistan even more dependent on outside assistance for its rehabilitation.

A number of *mujahideen* leaders accumulated personal fortunes during the civil war. These derive in part from the substantial foreign aid that was once available and, in some cases, from the trafficking of opium.

MEDIA

TV ownership low

Daily newspaper circulation 5 per 1000 people

PUBLISHING AND BROADCAST MEDIA

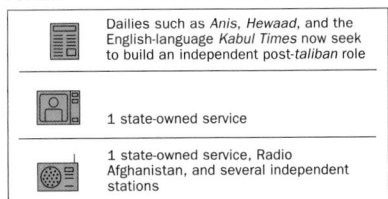

Dailies such as *Anis*, *Hewaad*, and the English-language *Kabul Times* now seek to build an independent post-*taliban* role

1 state-owned service

1 state-owned service, Radio Afghanistan, and several independent stations

Various factions run newspapers and radio stations. The *taliban* banned television and the Internet, and though television broadcasts restarted in Kabul in 2001, the new Supreme Court in 2003 banned cable TV as un-Islamic.

The BBC, which produces radio programs in Pashtu and Persian (Dari), is popular, especially for its soap operas, which inform on welfare issues.

EDUCATION

School leaving age: 12

36%

12,800 students

THE EDUCATION SYSTEM

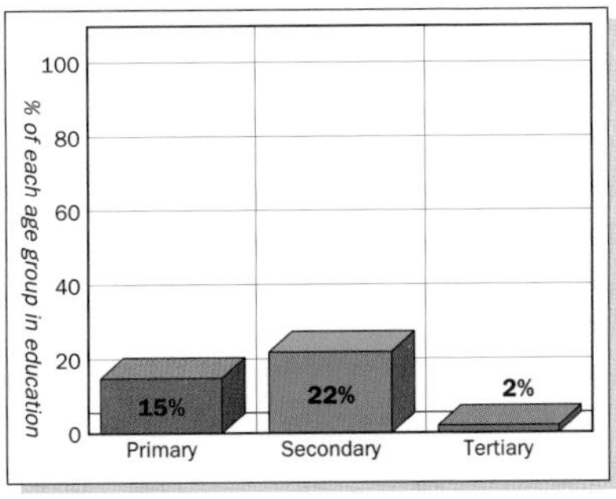
100
80
60
40
20
0
% of each age group in education
15%
22%
2%
Primary
Secondary
Tertiary

Under the *taliban* regime, education for women was extremely limited and segregation rigidly enforced; the literacy rate for women is the lowest in the world. The Northern Alliance announced the lifting of restrictions on female education in November 2001.

Kabul University, which had been closed in 1992, has now been partially reopened.

WORLD RANKING

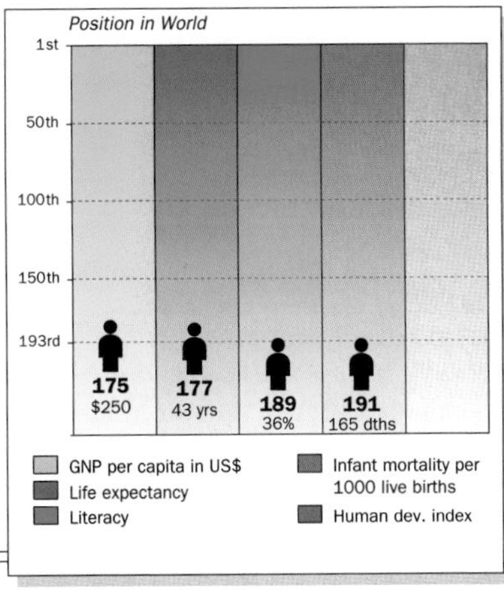
Position in World
1st
50th
100th
150th
193rd
175
$250
177
43 yrs
189
36%
191
165 dths
GNP per capita in US$
Life expectancy
Literacy
Infant mortality per 1000 live births
Human dev. index

A

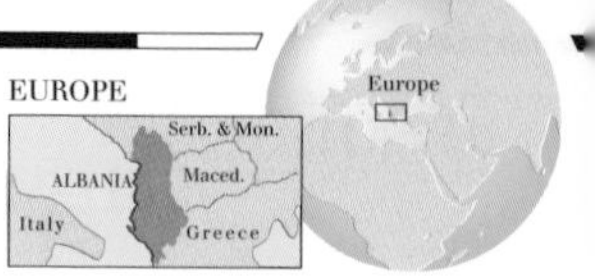
EUROPE
Europe
Serb. & Mon.
ALBANIA
Maced.
Italy
Greece

ALBANIA

OFFICIAL NAME: Republic of Albania **CAPITAL:** Tirana
POPULATION: 3.2 million **CURRENCY:** Lek **OFFICIAL LANGUAGE:** Albanian

1912 | 1921 | Nov 28 | AL | +1 | +355 | .al

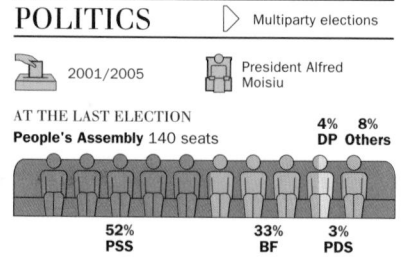

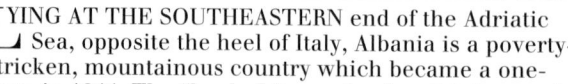

LYING AT THE SOUTHEASTERN end of the Adriatic Sea, opposite the heel of Italy, Albania is a poverty-stricken, mountainous country which became a one-party communist state in 1944. The "land of the eagles," as it is known by its people, became a multiparty democracy in 1991. It has struggled to progress from the economic collapse and regional strife which characterized the 1990s, and remains one of the poorest countries in Europe.

CLIMATE

Mediterranean/continental

WEATHER CHART FOR TIRANA

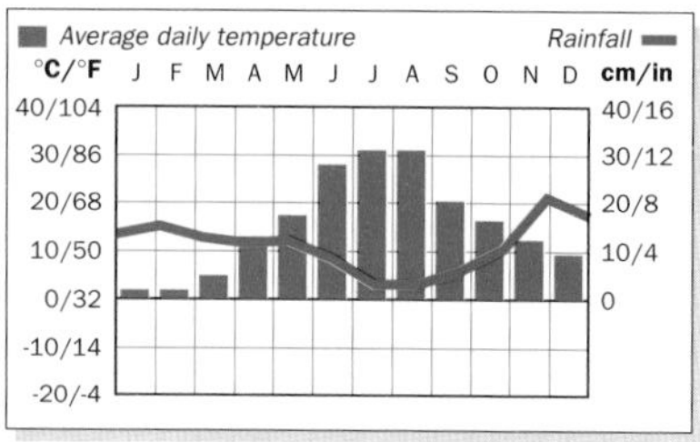
Average daily temperature
Rainfall
°C/°F J F M A M J J A S O N D cm/in
40/104
30/86
20/68
10/50
0/32
-10/14
-20/-4
40/16
30/12
20/8
10/4
0

The coastal climate is Mediterranean, but rather wet in winter. Heavy rain or snow falls in winter in the mountains.

TRANSPORTATION

Drive on right

Tirana (Rinas)

33 ships 25,200 grt

THE TRANSPORTATION NETWORK

5400 km (3355 miles)

None

440 km (273 miles)

43 km (27 miles)

The transportation infrastructure is poor: the rail network is limited and roads are in disrepair. Private cars were first allowed in 1991. Buses and private vans are the main means of transportation.

TOURISM

Visitors : Population 1:94

34,000 visitors

Down 13% in 2000–2001

MAIN TOURIST ARRIVALS

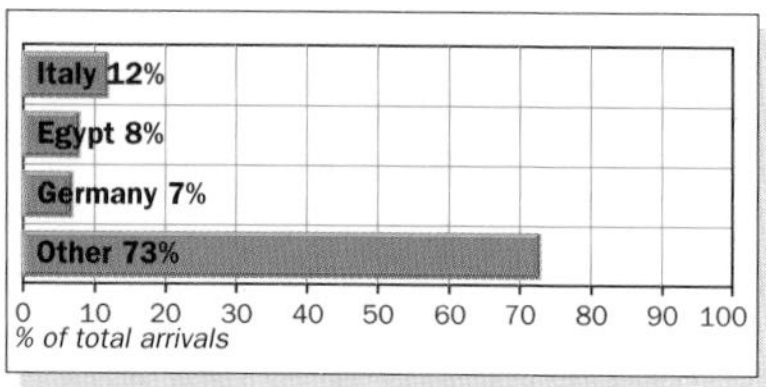
Italy 12%
Egypt 8%
Germany 7%
Other 73%
0 10 20 30 40 50 60 70 80 90 100
% of total arrivals

Instability and then the war in Kosovo upset plans to exploit Albania's scenic beauty. Facilities remain very limited, especially outside Tirana.

PEOPLE

Pop. density medium

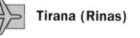

Albanian, Greek

117/km² (302/mi²)

THE URBAN/RURAL POPULATION SPLIT

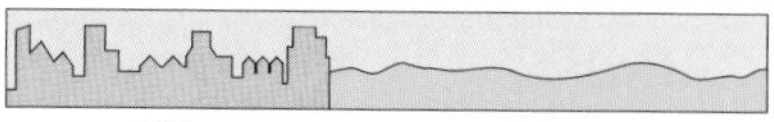
43%
57%

RELIGIOUS PERSUASION

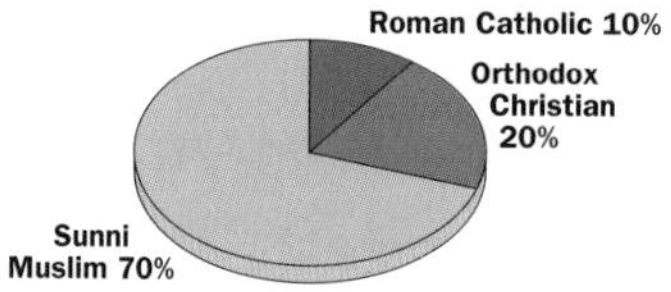
Roman Catholic 10%
Orthodox Christian 20%
Sunni Muslim 70%

The existence of ethnic minorities was only officially acknowledged in 1989. The Greek minority strongly contests official statistics, which state that 95% of the population are Albanian. Located mainly in the south, the Greeks claim to make up over 10% of the population. They suffer considerable discrimination.

Most Albanians converted to Islam under Ottoman suzerainty. Under communism, Albania was the only officially atheist state in the world. Religious practice has been permitted since 1991.

Society is traditional and male-dominated. Men are expected to be providers, and unemployment levels have decreased the chances of women finding work. Many women pay to be smuggled to the West, only to end up as prostitutes. Albania is a major transit point for human trafficking.

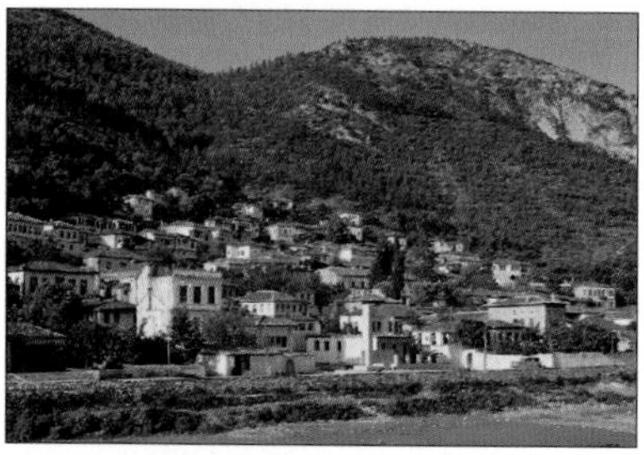

City of a thousand windows. *Berat was preserved as a museum while a new town was built further down the valley.*

POLITICS

Multiparty elections

2001/2005

President Alfred Moisiu

AT THE LAST ELECTION

People's Assembly 140 seats

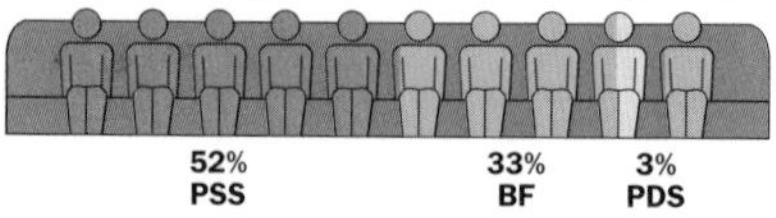
4% DP
8% Others
52% PSS
33% BF
3% PDS

PSS = Socialist Party of Albania **BF** = Union for Victory (led by the Democratic Party – **PD**) **DP** = Democrat Party (splinter from PD) **PDS** = Social Democratic Party

Albania was dominated for more than 40 years by communist ruler Enver Hoxha, who died in 1985. An exodus of Albanians in 1991 finally persuaded the regime to call multiparty elections. The resulting center-right coalition failed, however, to create a Western-style liberal state.

Many people were ruined by investing in "pyramid" savings schemes which collapsed in 1997, prompting rebellion in the south and forcing the resignation of the government. A new coalition led by the PSS was elected later that year, and won a further term in 2001, as Prime Minister Ilir Meta claimed credit for restoring a measure of security and hope. Following its reelection the PSS became divided by internal disputes. Veteran party leader Fatos Nano emerged victorious, and has since concentrated power in his own hands, becoming prime minister in July 2002.

WORLD AFFAIRS

Joined UN in 1955

WTO | CE | OSCE | OIC | PfP

Foreign policy in the late 1990s was dominated by the fate of Kosovo, the predominantly ethnic Albanian province in neighboring Serbia. Ethnic Albanian separatism also erupted in Macedonia in 2001, although Albania was not directly involved. Membership of NATO and the EU is a long-term goal. In 2001 an interim EU "stabilization and association agreement" was offered.

AID

Recipient

$269m (receipts)

Down 16% in 2001

Since 1991 the West has provided aid. Food aid was stepped up in 1997, when anarchy swept the country, and again in 1999 to help cope with the hundreds of thousands of refugees arriving from Kosovo, part of neighboring Serbia. EU aid now focuses on helping structural reforms.

DEFENSE

Compulsory military service

$106m

Down 6% in 2001

Officer ranks were reestablished in 1991, and in 2000 a ten-year reconstruction program was launched. There is no civilian alternative to military service. Seventy commandos were sent to Iraq to help the US-led Coalition in 2003.

ECONOMICS

Inflation 34% p.a. (1990–2001)

$4.24bn

118.5 lekë (140)

SCORE CARD

- ❑ WORLD GNP RANKING........................118th
- ❑ GNP PER CAPITA.............................$1340
- ❑ BALANCE OF PAYMENTS....................–$218m
- ❑ INFLATION...3.1%
- ❑ UNEMPLOYMENT..................................16%

STRENGTHS

Oil and gas reserves. Remittances from expatriate Albanians. Progress with privatization.

WEAKNESSES

Rudimentary public services and energy, transportation, and water networks: failings deter foreign investors.

EXPORTS

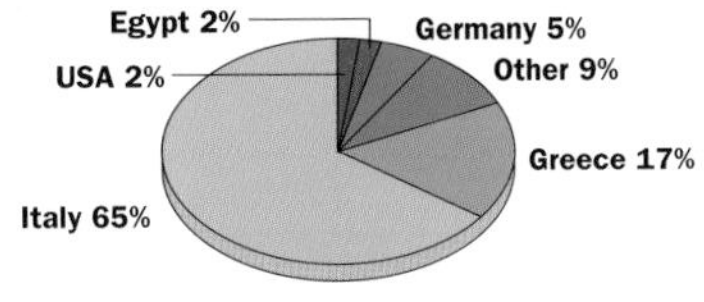
Egypt 2%
Germany 5%
USA 2%
Other 9%
Greece 17%
Italy 65%

IMPORTS

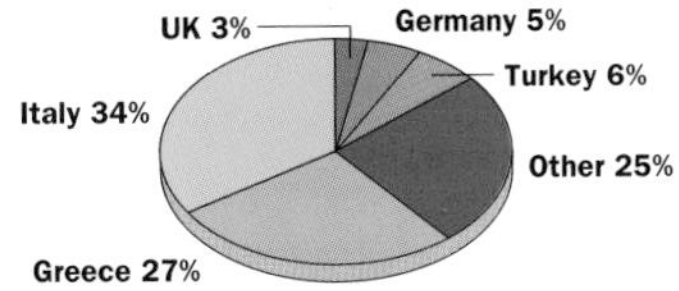
UK 3%
Germany 5%
Turkey 6%
Italy 34%
Other 25%
Greece 27%

ALBANIA

Total Area : 28 748 sq. km (11 100 sq. miles)

POPULATION

- over 100 000
- over 50 000
- over 10 000
- under 10 000

LAND HEIGHT

- 2000m/6562ft
- 1000m/3281ft
- 500m/1640ft
- 200m/656ft
- Sea Level

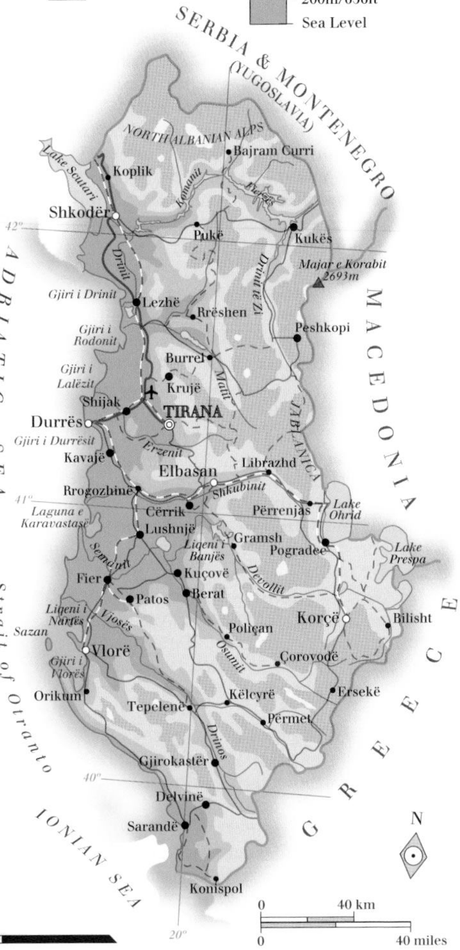
SERBIA & MONTENEGRO (YUGOSLAVIA)
MACEDONIA
GREECE
ADRIATIC SEA
Strait of Otranto
IONIAN SEA
NORTH ALBANIAN ALPS
Lake Scutari
Koplik
Shkodër
Bajram Curri
Pukë
Kukës
Majae e Korabit 2693m
Gjiri i Drinit
Lezhë
Rrëshen
Peshkopi
Gjiri i Rodonit
Burrel
Gjiri i Lalëzit
Krujë
Shijak
TIRANA
Durrës
Gjiri i Durrësit
Kavajë
Elbasan
Librazhd
Rrogozhinë
Laguna e Karavastasë
Cërrik
Lushnjë
Përrenjas
Lake Ohrid
Gramsh
Pogradec
Lake Prespa
Fier
Kuçovë
Berat
Patos
Liqeni i Nartës
Sazan
Vlorë
Gjiri i Vlorës
Orikum
Poliçan
Korçë
Bilisht
Çorovodë
Ersekë
Tepelenë
Këlcyrë
Përmet
Gjirokastër
Delvinë
Sarandë
Konispol
Drini
Drinit të Zi
Mati
Erzenit
Shkumbinit
Semanit
Devollit
Osumit
Vjosës
Drinos
42°
41°
40°
20°
N
0 40 km
0 40 miles

RESOURCES

Electric power 1.9m kW

3627 tonnes

6476 b/d (reserves 182m barrels)

1.84m sheep, 929,000 goats, 4.45m chickens

Chromium, oil, coal, natural gas, copper, nickel

Albania needs huge capital investment to develop its minerals and to create a modern electricity supply system.

ENVIRONMENT

Sustainability rank: 24th

4% (2% partially protected)

0.5 tonnes per capita

Toxic waste pollution from communist-era heavy industry is among the worst in Europe. Years of shortages mean that most materials are recycled.

MEDIA

TV ownership medium

Daily newspaper circulation 35 per 1000 people

PUBLISHING AND BROADCAST MEDIA

There are 4 daily newspapers, including *Rilindja Demokratike*, *Zëri i Popullit*, and *Koha Jonë*, the best-selling newspaper

1 state-run service, 75 private stations

1 state-run service, 30 private stations

Although media freedom has generally improved, overly critical papers face harassment. A 1998 law banned political or religious control of TV stations.

CRIME

Death penalty not used in practice

3053 prisoners

Down 11% in 2000–2002

Lawlessness is widespread; guns are easily available after the anarchy of 1997. Cannabis is widely grown.

CHRONOLOGY

Albania gained independence in 1912 for the first time in its history.

- ❑ **1924–1939** Ahmet Zogu in power; crowned King Zog in 1928.
- ❑ **1939–1943** Occupied by Italy.
- ❑ **1944** Communist state; led by Enver Hoxha until 1985.
- ❑ **1991** First multiparty elections.
- ❑ **1997** Economic chaos as failure of pyramid schemes causes revolt.
- ❑ **1999** Refugee influx from Kosovo.
- ❑ **2001** PSS wins second term.

EDUCATION

School leaving age: 13

85%

40,859 students

The communist-derived system is being reformed to European standards. Albania has eight universities.

HEALTH

Welfare state health benefits

1 per 752 people

Heart and respiratory diseases, cancers

The health service is rudimentary, and dependent on Western aid for most drugs and medical supplies.

SPENDING

GDP/cap. increase

CONSUMPTION AND SPENDING

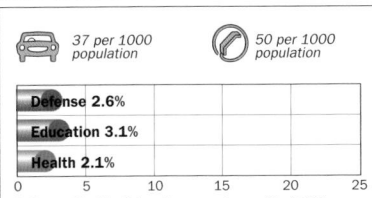

37 per 1000 population

50 per 1000 population

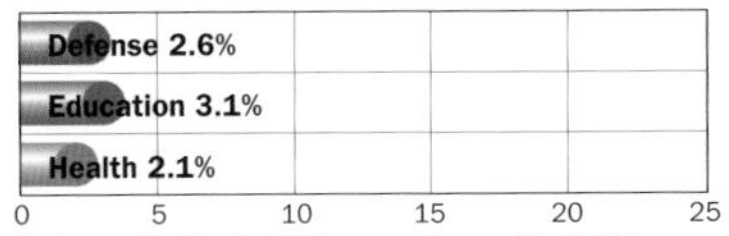
Defense 2.6%
Education 3.1%
Health 2.1%
0
5
10
15
20
25

Defense, Health, Education spending as % of GDP

Wealth is limited to a few private-sector entrepreneurs. Poverty is worst in northern rural areas but also acute in slum settlements around Tirana and other cities.

WORLD RANKING

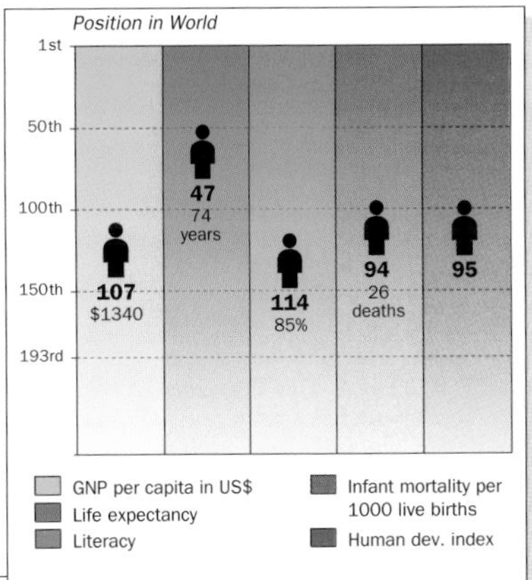
Position in World
1st
50th
100th
150th
193rd
107
$1340
47
74 years
114
85%
94
26 deaths
95
GNP per capita in US$
Life expectancy
Literacy
Infant mortality per 1000 live births
Human dev. index

A

ALGERIA

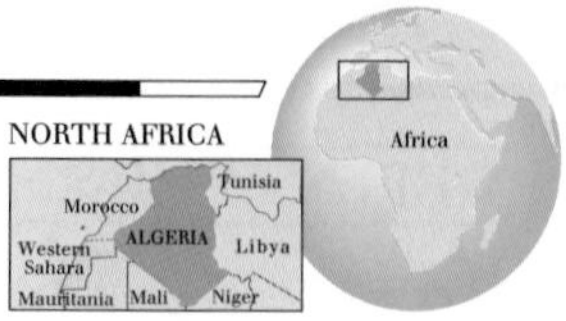
NORTH AFRICA
Africa
Morocco
Tunisia
Western Sahara
ALGERIA
Libya
Mauritania
Mali
Niger

OFFICIAL NAME: People's Democratic Republic of Algeria **CAPITAL:** Algiers
POPULATION: 31.4 million **CURRENCY:** Algerian dinar **OFFICIAL LANGUAGE:** Arabic

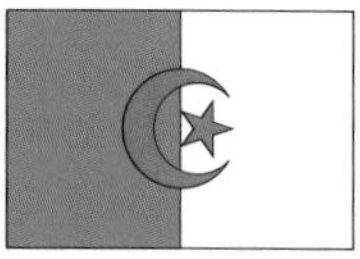

1962 | 1962 | Nov 1 | DZ | +1 | +213 | .dz

AFRICA'S SECOND-LARGEST country, which extends from a densely populated Mediterranean coast to the empty northern Sahara, Algeria won independence from France in 1962. The military blocked radical Islamists from taking power after winning elections in 1991, setting up a new civilian regime and fighting a bloody terrorist conflict ever since. Algeria has one of the youngest populations in the north African region.

CLIMATE

Hot desert/ Mediterranean

WEATHER CHART FOR ALGIERS

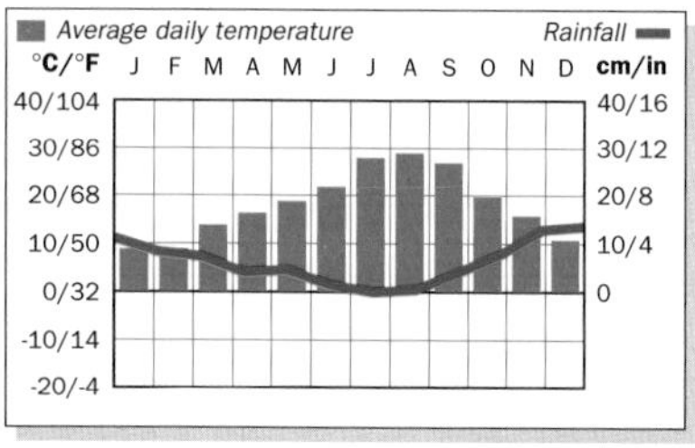
Average daily temperature
Rainfall
°C/°F
J F M A M J J A S O N D
cm/in
40/104
30/86
20/68
10/50
0/32
-10/14
-20/-4
40/16
30/12
20/8
10/4
0

Coastal areas have a warm, temperate climate. The whole area to the south of the Atlas Mountains is hot desert.

TRANSPORTATION

Drive on right

Houari Boumedienne, Algiers
4.29m passengers

143 ships
96,300 grt

THE TRANSPORTATION NETWORK

71,656 km (44,525 miles)

640 km (398 miles)

3973 km (2469 miles)

None

There are four international airports. Rail is the quickest way to travel between the main urban centers.

TOURISM

Visitors : Population 1:35

901,000 visitors

Up 4% in 2001

MAIN TOURIST ARRIVALS

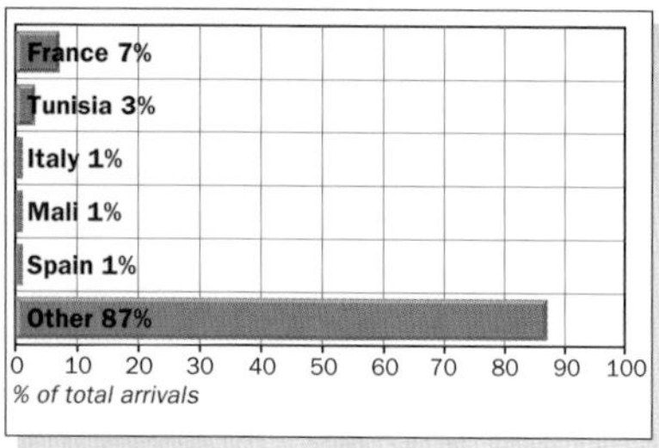
France 7%
Tunisia 3%
Italy 1%
Mali 1%
Spain 1%
Other 87%
0 10 20 30 40 50 60 70 80 90 100
% of total arrivals

The once-popular desert safaris are now rare. Tourists are a target for militant Islamist groups.

PEOPLE

Pop. density low

Arabic, Tamazight (Kabyle, Shawia, Tamashek), French

13/km² (34/mi²)

THE URBAN/RURAL POPULATION SPLIT

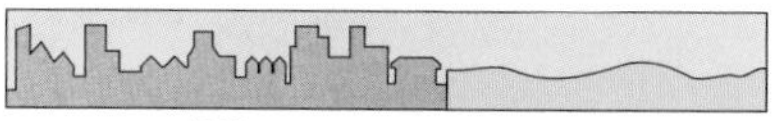
58%
42%

RELIGIOUS PERSUASION

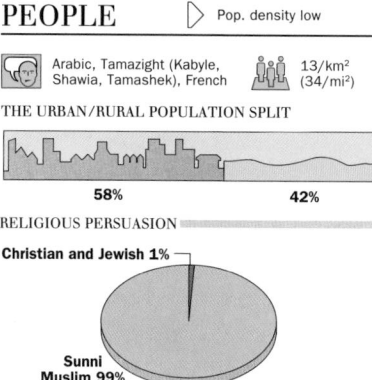

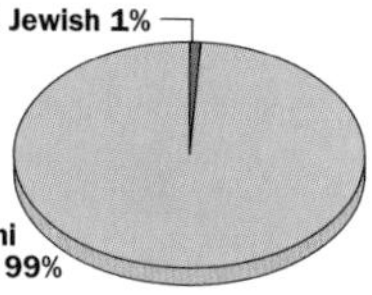
Christian and Jewish 1%
Sunni Muslim 99%

ETHNIC MAKEUP

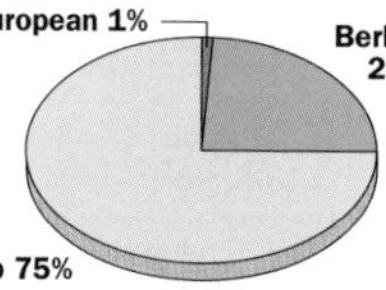
European 1%
Berber 24%
Arab 75%

Algeria's population is predominantly Arab, under 30 years of age, and urban; around a quarter are Berber. More than 85% speak Arabic and 99% are Sunni Muslim. Mosques also provide social and medical services. Of the million or so French who settled in Algeria before independence, only about 6000 remain. Most Berbers consider the mountainous Kabylia region their homeland. Demonstrations there have met with violent police crackdowns, particularly in the Berber Spring of 1980, and since its anniversary in 2001. The Berber language, Tamazight, was recognized as a "national" language in 2002.

POPULATION AGE BREAKDOWN

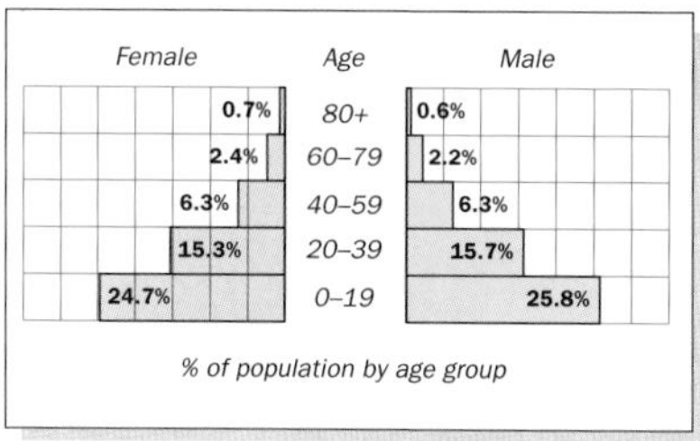
Female
Age
Male
0.7%
80+
0.6%
2.4%
60–79
2.2%
6.3%
40–59
6.3%
15.3%
20–39
15.7%
24.7%
0–19
25.8%
% of population by age group

POLITICS

Multiparty elections

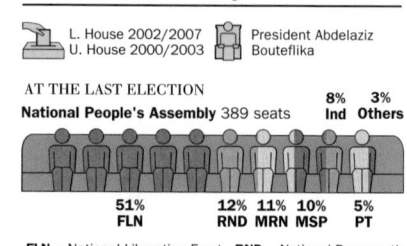

L. House 2002/2007
U. House 2000/2003

President Abdelaziz Bouteflika

AT THE LAST ELECTION

National People's Assembly 389 seats

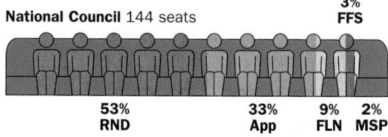

8% Ind
3% Others
51% FLN
12% RND
11% MRN
10% MSP
5% PT

FLN = National Liberation Front **RND** = National Democratic Rally **MRN** = Movement for National Reform **MSP** = Movement for a Peaceful Society **Ind** = Independents **PT** = Workers' Party **App** = Appointed **FFS** = Front of Socialist Forces

National Council 144 seats

3% FFS
53% RND
33% App
9% FLN
2% MSP

96 seats are elected, 48 are appointed by the president

Algeria is a multiparty democracy.

PROFILE

Until 1988, Algeria was a single-party socialist-style regime. The subsequent adoption of privatization policies was strongly opposed by Islamist militants. The Islamic Salvation Front (FIS) won the first round of elections in 1991, but the second round was canceled by the military-dominated High Security Council. Since then there has been appalling violence between Islamists and the state, and tens of thousands of people have been killed. The election of President Abdelaziz Bouteflika in 1999 raised hopes for peace, despite an opposition boycott. Legislative elections in 2002, won by the FLN, also suffered from a low turnout and a partial boycott.

An earthquake in May 2003 killed over 2000 people in the Algiers region; a key priority is rebuilding infrastructure.

MAIN POLITICAL ISSUES

Islamic fundamentalism

Islamist militants want Algeria to become a theocracy. The steps taken in 1992 to prevent the FIS taking office unleashed violence spearheaded by the extremist Armed Islamic Group (GIA) and more recently the Salafist Group for Preaching and Combat. The annual death toll exceeds 1500.

Human rights and democracy

Agitation among Islamists and Berbers is fueled by poor living conditions and the lack of adequate representation. An official state of emergency has been in place since 1992; security forces have been accused of meeting insurrection with repression and violence.

WORLD AFFAIRS

Joined UN in 1962

AL | AMU | OIC | NAM | OPEC

Algeria's struggle for independence from France lasted from 1954 until 1962. Throughout the 1960s and 1970s, its success in rejecting a colonial power made it a champion for the developing world. It had a leading voice within the UN, the Arab League, and the Organization of African Unity. At the same time, relations with the West remained essentially stable. In the 1980s, Algeria was increasingly seen by the diplomatic community as a useful bridge between the West and Iran. In 1981, Algerian diplomats helped to secure the release of US hostages being held in Tehran. Algeria also attempted to adopt a mediating role during the 1980–1988 Iran–Iraq War.

Algeria's influence overseas has diminished as its political stability has declined. Support for the fundamentalist FIS has raised concerns across the region over the spread of Islamist militancy. The US has been keen to forge an alliance with the Algerian authorities as part of its "war on terrorism." France also fears the spillover of terrorism and has been shocked by the ongoing levels of violence.

European governments are anxious to help stabilize the regime to avoid the entry of refugees into France, Spain, and Italy. The EU has been calling for improvements in human rights and good governance.

AID

Recipient

$182m (receipts) | Up 12% in 2001

As a major oil producer, Algeria receives relatively little aid. The collapse in the 1990s of the trade of eastern European manufactures in return for oil led Algeria to turn to the West for loans. The growing weight of Western economic involvement in turn fortified the regime against criticism of its hard-line methods against Islamist opponents. The EU and France are now the largest donors, the bulk of funding going toward improving education facilities. After the 2003 earthquakes, aid for reconstruction became a priority.

Saharan town, showing the wide range of Algeria's scenery, from lush, irrigated gardens near water sources to barren dunes beyond. 80% of Algeria is desert.

ALGERIA

Total Area:
2 381 740 sq. km
(919 590 sq. miles)

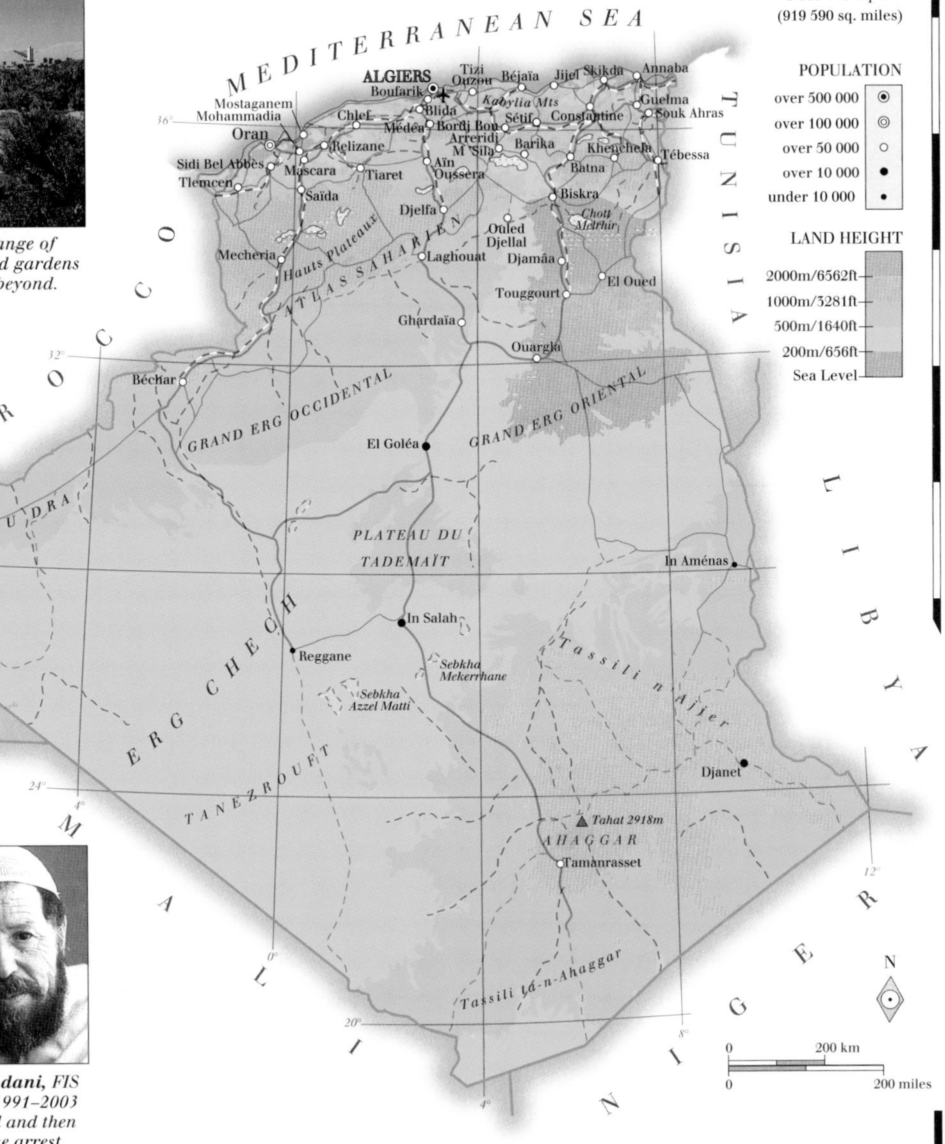
MEDITERRANEAN SEA
ALGIERS
Boufarik
Tizi Ouzou
Béjaïa
Jijel
Skikda
Annaba
Mostaganem
Mohammadia
Oran
Chlef
Blida
Médéa
Bordj Bou Arreridj
Sétif
Constantine
Guelma
Souk Ahras
Kabylia Mts
Relizane
M'Sila
Barika
Khenchela
Tébessa
Sidi Bel Abbès
Mascara
Tiaret
Aïn Oussera
Batna
Tlemcen
Saïda
Biskra
Djelfa
Chott Melrhir
Ouled Djellal
Mecheria
Hauts Plateaux
ATLAS SAHARIEN
Laghouat
Djamâa
El Oued
Touggourt
Ghardaïa
Ouargla
Béchar
GRAND ERG OCCIDENTAL
GRAND ERG ORIENTAL
El Goléa
MOROCCO
TUNISIA
LIBYA
HAMADA DU DRA
PLATEAU DU TADEMAÏT
Tindouf
WESTERN SAHARA
MAURITANIA
In Aménas
In Salah
ERG CHECH
Reggane
Sebkha Mekerrhane
Sebkha Azzel Matti
Tassili n'Ajjer
TANEZROUFT
Djanet
Tahat 2918m
AHAGGAR
Tamanrasset
MALI
NIGER
Tassili Ta-n-Ahaggar
POPULATION
over 500 000
over 100 000
over 50 000
over 10 000
under 10 000
LAND HEIGHT
2000m/6562ft
1000m/3281ft
500m/1640ft
200m/656ft
Sea Level
N
0
200 km
200 miles

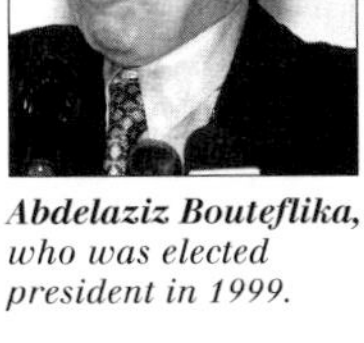

Abdelaziz Bouteflika, *who was elected president in 1999.*

Abassi Madani, *FIS leader, in 1991–2003 imprisoned and then under house arrest.*

A

CHRONOLOGY

The conquest of Algeria by France began in 1830. By 1900, French settlers occupied most of the best land. In 1954, war was declared on the colonial administration by the National Liberation Front (FLN).

- ❑ **1962** Cease-fire agreed, followed by independence of Algerian republic.
- ❑ **1965** Military junta topples government of Ahmed Ben Bella. Revolutionary council set up.
- ❑ **1966** Judiciary "Algerianized." Tribunals try "economic crimes."
- ❑ **1971** Oil industry nationalized. President Boumedienne continues with land reform, a national health service, and "socialist" management.
- ❑ **1976** Socialist state established.
- ❑ **1980** Ben Bella released after 15 years' detention. Agreement with France whereby latter gives incentives for return home of 800,000 Algerian immigrants.
- ❑ **1981** Algeria helps to negotiate release of hostages from US embassy in Tehran, Iran.
- ❑ **1985** Two most popular Kabyle (Berber) singers given three-year jail sentences for opposing regime.
- ❑ **1987** Limited economic liberalization. Cooperation agreement with Soviet Union.
- ❑ **1988** Anti-FLN violence; state of emergency. Algeria negotiates release of Kuwaiti hostages from aircraft; Shi'a hijackers escape.
- ❑ **1989** Constitutional reforms diminish power of FLN. New political parties founded, including FIS. AMU established.
- ❑ **1990** Political exiles able to return. FIS victorious in municipal elections.
- ❑ **1991** FIS leaders Abassi Madani and Ali Belhadj arrested, jailed for 12 years. FIS wins most seats in first round of legislative elections; second round canceled.
- ❑ **1992** President Chadli overthrown by military. President Boudiaf assassinated.
- ❑ **1994** Political violence led by GIA.
- ❑ **1995** Democratic presidential elections won by Liamine Zéroual.
- ❑ **1996** Murders continue, notably of Catholic clergy and GIA leader.
- ❑ **1997** Madani released, subsequently under house arrest.
- ❑ **1999** Abdelaziz Bouteflika elected president in poll boycotted by opposition candidates.
- ❑ **2001** Fresh investment in oil and gas benefits economy. Resurgence of Berber protests.
- ❑ **2002** Berber language Tamazight recognized as national language. FLN election victory.
- ❑ **2003** Over 2000 die in earthquakes. Madani and Belhadj released.

DEFENSE

Compulsory military service

$3.15bn

Up 5% in 2001

The National Liberation Army (NLA), equipped mainly with Russian weapons, is the dominant power in politics. There have been fears that parts of the army would forge an alliance with Muslim militants; the extreme rebel Armed Islamic Group, which has split from the FIS, is led by former army officers. However, the military are also suspected of taking part in reprisal killings of large numbers of Islamists.

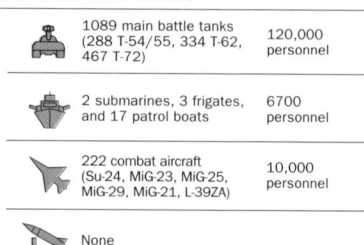

ALGERIAN ARMED FORCES

1089 main battle tanks (288 T-54/55, 334 T-62, 467 T-72)	120,000 personnel
2 submarines, 3 frigates, and 17 patrol boats	6700 personnel
222 combat aircraft (Su-24, MiG-23, MiG-25, MiG-29, MiG-21, L-39ZA)	10,000 personnel
None	

ECONOMICS

Inflation 17% p.a. (1990–2001)

$51bn

78.38 Algerian dinars (80.04)

SCORE CARD

❑ World GNP Ranking	47th
❑ GNP per Capita	$1650
❑ Balance of Payments	$8.9bn
❑ Inflation	3%
❑ Unemployment	30%

ECONOMIC PERFORMANCE INDICATOR

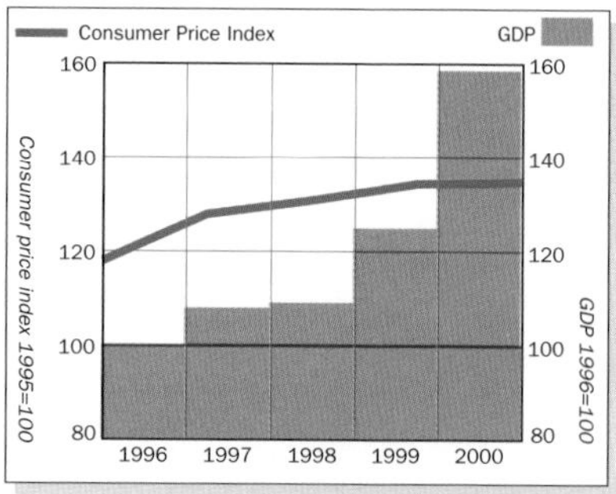

Consumer Price Index
GDP
160
140
120
100
80
1996
1997
1998
1999
2000
Consumer price index 1995=100
GDP 1996=100

EXPORTS

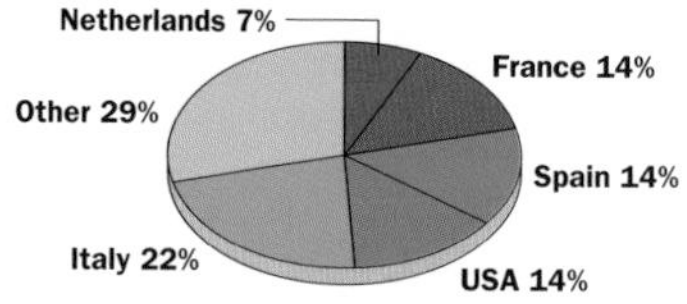

Netherlands 7%
France 14%
Other 29%
Spain 14%
Italy 22%
USA 14%

IMPORTS

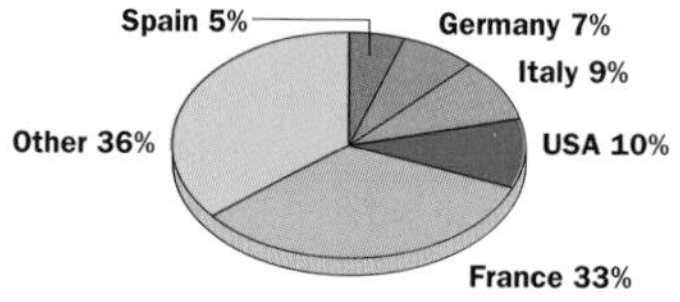

Spain 5%
Germany 7%
Italy 9%
Other 36%
USA 10%
France 33%

Strengths

Oil and gas. Recent collaboration with Western oil companies should see improvements in productivity. Natural gas is supplied to Europe, with plans in hand for the construction of a third undersea pipeline.

Weaknesses

Political turmoil, leading to exodus of European and other important expatriate workers. Cost of earthquake reconstruction. Lack of skilled labor coupled with high unemployment. Limited agriculture. Shortages of basic foodstuffs. Thriving black market.

Profile

Under the pro-Soviet National Liberation Front, centralized socialist planning dominated the Algerian economy. In the late 1980s, the economic collapse of the Soviet Union led to a change in policy, and Algeria began moving toward a market economy. These reforms were frozen following the military takeover in 1992, though many have since been resumed under pressure from the IMF and the World Bank. The majority of the economy's most productive sectors remain under state control, although private investment is encouraged in the oil industry and, since early 2001, in telecommunications. A number of Western oil companies have signed exploration contracts with Algeria since it has accepted more competitive production-sharing agreements. Investment levels are likely to remain small, however, as long as the political situation is unstable. The government pledged $1.8 billion in 2003 for post-earthquake reconstruction.

ALGERIA : MAJOR BUSINESSES

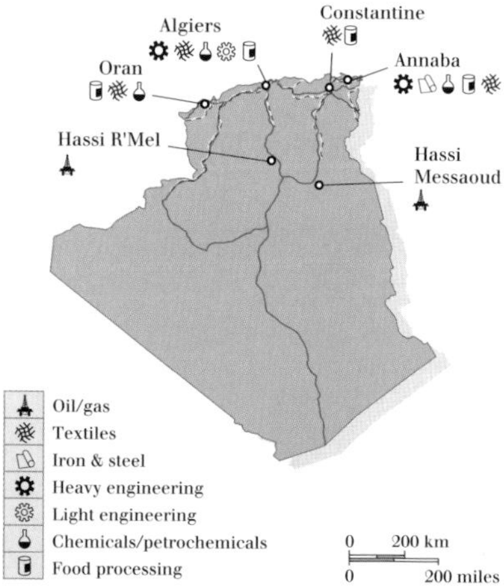

Algiers
Constantine
Oran
Annaba
Hassi R'Mel
Hassi Messaoud
Oil/gas
Textiles
Iron & steel
Heavy engineering
Light engineering
Chemicals/petrochemicals
Food processing
0 200 km
0 200 miles

A

RESOURCES

Electric power 6m kW

100,275 tonnes

1.66m b/d (reserves 9.2bn barrels)

17.3m sheep, 3.2m goats, 1.6m cattle, 110m chickens

Oil, natural gas, iron, phosphates, lead, zinc, silver, copper, gold

ELECTRICITY GENERATION

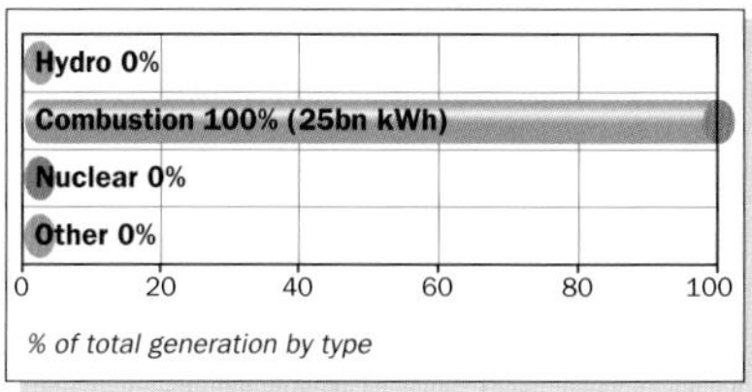

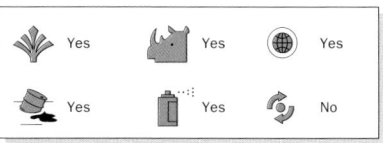

Hydro 0%
Combustion 100% (25bn kWh)
Nuclear 0%
Other 0%
0 20 40 60 80 100
% of total generation by type

Crude oil and natural gas, Algeria's main resources, have been produced since the 1950s. Algeria also has diverse minerals, including iron ore, zinc, silver, copper ore, lead, gold, and phosphates. In the 1960s and 1970s, Algeria sought to become a major manufacturer, with investments in building materials, refined products, and steel; none of these sectors are competitive on world markets. Agriculture employs one-quarter of Algeria's workforce, but its importance to the economy is diminishing. Forests cover less than 1% of the land. Most are brushwood, but some areas include cork oak trees, Aleppo pine, evergreen oak, and cedar. Algeria has a large fishing fleet. Sardines, anchovies, tuna, and shellfish are the major commercial catches.

ALGERIA : LAND USE

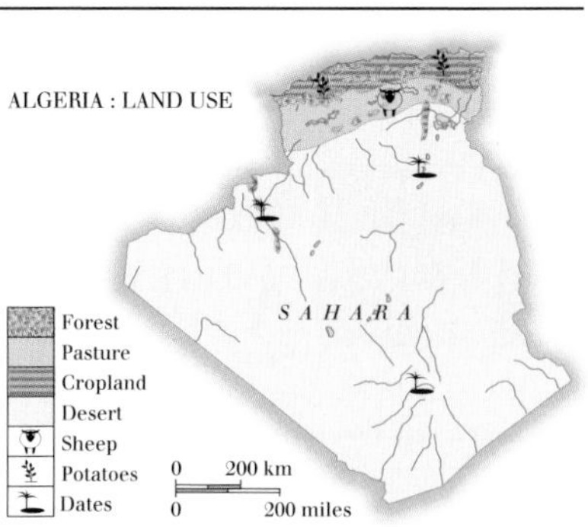

SAHARA
Forest
Pasture
Cropland
Desert
Sheep
Potatoes
Dates
0 200 km
0 200 miles

ENVIRONMENT

Sustainability rank: 70th

5% (0.1% partially protected)

3.1 tonnes per capita

ENVIRONMENTAL TREATIES

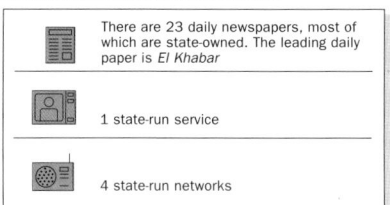

Yes Yes Yes

Yes Yes No

Since most of Algeria is desert or semidesert, over 90% of the population are forced to live on what remains – some 20% of the land. The desert is moving northward. Vegetation has been stripped for use as firewood and animal fodder, leaving fragile soils exposed which then require expensive specialist care to conserve them. Techniques for water purification are substandard, and rivers are being increasingly contaminated by untreated sewage, industrial effluent, and wastes from petroleum refining.

MEDIA

TV ownership medium

Daily newspaper circulation 27 per 1000 people

PUBLISHING AND BROADCAST MEDIA

There are 23 daily newspapers, most of which are state-owned. The leading daily paper is *El Khabar*

1 state-run service

4 state-run networks

Newspapers, TV, and radio are mainly state-controlled and are cautious in reporting violence, but there is no overt censorship. TV is broadcast in Arabic, French, and Tamazight. The three main daily newspapers have a combined circulation of over one million. However, distribution is limited outside the major cities.

CRIME

Death penalty in use

34,243 prisoners

Up 71% in 2000–2001

CRIME RATES

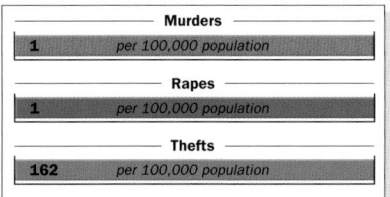

Murders
1 per 100,000 population

Rapes
1 per 100,000 population

Thefts
162 per 100,000 population

Thousands of people have been killed by radical Islamists since 1992, while human rights groups have accused progovernment death squads of brutal reprisal killings and of persecuting suspected Islamist militants.

EDUCATION

School leaving age: 15

68%

456,358 students

THE EDUCATION SYSTEM

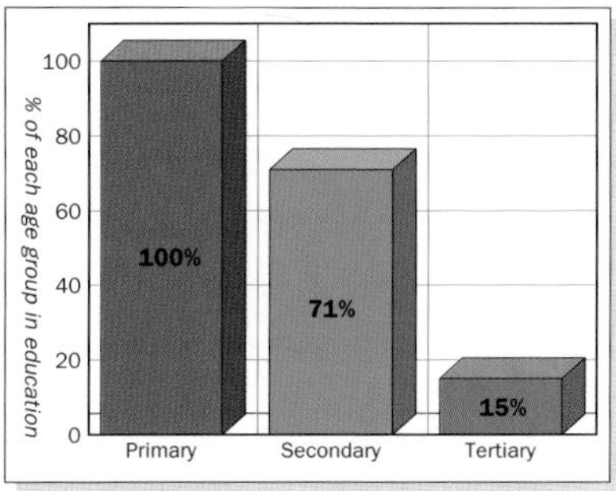

% of each age group in education
100
80
60
40
20
0
100%
71%
15%
Primary
Secondary
Tertiary

Over three-quarters of the school-age population receive a formal education, and the literacy rate is rising.

Since 1973, the curriculum has been Arabicized and the teaching of French restricted. Though the use of Arabic is enforced in public life, Tamazight was allowed in schools from 2003.

Ten main universities, and several polytechnics and technical colleges provide higher education.

HEALTH

Welfare state health benefits

1 per 1176 people

Respiratory, heart, and cerebrovascular diseases, malaria

Since 1974 all Algerians have had the right to free health care. Primary health care is rudimentary outside main cities. Because the formal health care system is overburdened, many people turn to alternative forms of medicine. The infant mortality rate has risen recently and is now higher than in the other coastal states of north Africa.

SPENDING

GDP/cap. increase

CONSUMPTION AND SPENDING

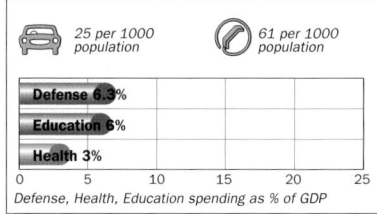

25 per 1000 population

61 per 1000 population

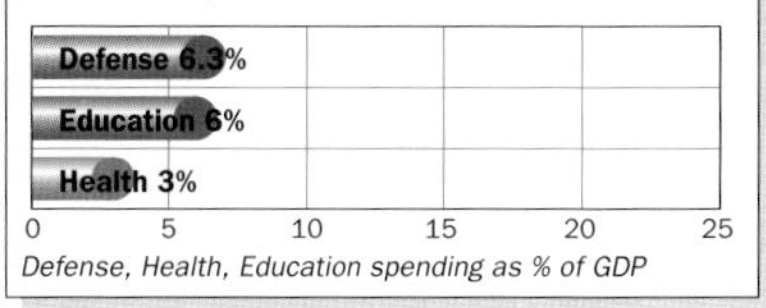

Defense 6.3%
Education 6%
Health 3%
0 5 10 15 20 25
Defense, Health, Education spending as % of GDP

There is great disparity in wealth between the political elite and the rest of the population. Those with connections in the military are the wealthiest group. Most Algerians have had to contend with soaring prices for basic necessities.

WORLD RANKING

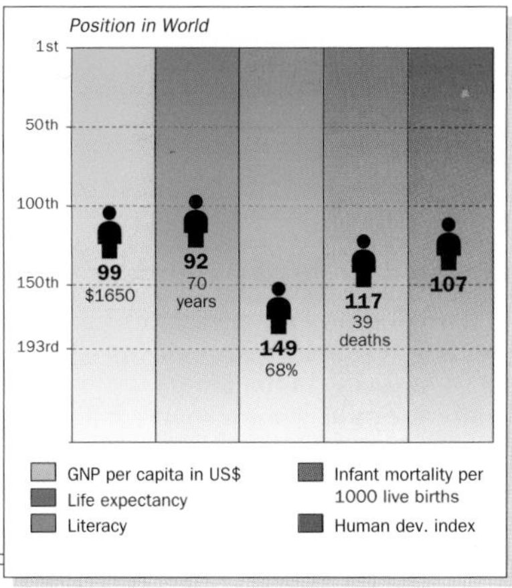

Position in World
1st
50th
100th
150th
193rd
99
$1650
92
70 years
149
68%
117
39 deaths
107
GNP per capita in US$
Life expectancy
Literacy
Infant mortality per 1000 live births
Human dev. index

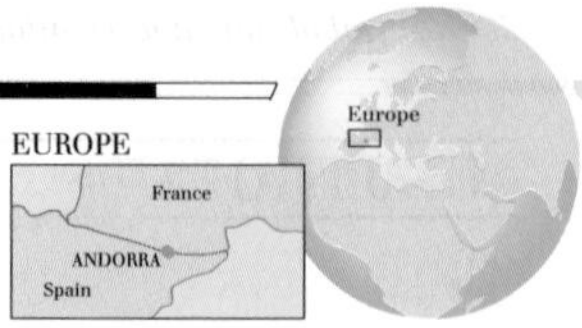
EUROPE
France
ANDORRA
Spain
Europe

ANDORRA

OFFICIAL NAME: Principality of Andorra **CAPITAL:** Andorra la Vella
POPULATION: 68,243 **CURRENCY:** Euro **OFFICIAL LANGUAGE:** Catalan

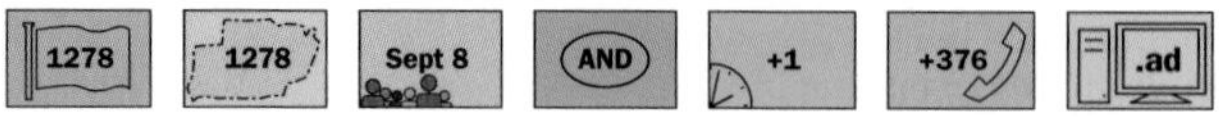
1278
1278
Sept 8
AND
+1
+376
.ad

A TINY, LANDLOCKED principality between France and Spain, Andorra lies high in the eastern Pyrenees. From the 13th century, French and Spanish coprinces (today the President of France and the Bishop of Urgell) have ruled Andorra. In December 1993, the principality held its first full elections. Andorra's spectacular scenery, alpine climate, and duty-free shopping have made tourism, especially skiing, its main source of income.

Andorra's outstanding mountain scenery *attracts skiers in winter, walkers in summer.*

CLIMATE

Mountain

WEATHER CHART FOR ANDORRA LA VELLA

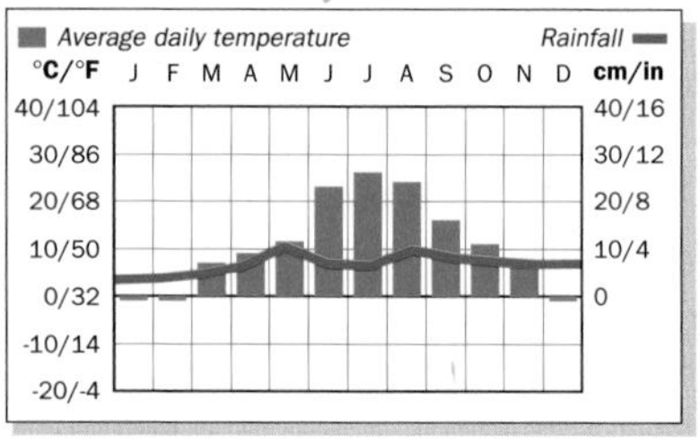
Average daily temperature
Rainfall
°C/°F J F M A M J J A S O N D cm/in
40/104
30/86
20/68
10/50
0/32
-10/14
-20/-4
40/16
30/12
20/8
10/4
0

Springs are cool and wettest in May; summers are relatively dry and warm. Snowfalls in December and January provide snow for good skiing up to March. Andorra's climate supports an abundance of wild flowers.

TRANSPORTATION

Drive on right

None

Has no fleet

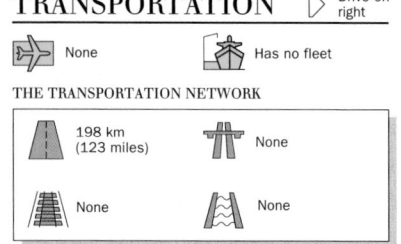

THE TRANSPORTATION NETWORK

198 km (123 miles)

None

None

None

The road from France to Spain climbs to 2704 m (8875 ft) through one of the most dramatic mountain passes in Europe. Traffic congestion is a major problem in Andorra la Vella, especially in the summer. In 2001 plans for an overhead rail system were announced.

TOURISM

Visitors : Population 50:1

3.39m visitors

Down 4% in 2002

MAIN TOURIST ARRIVALS

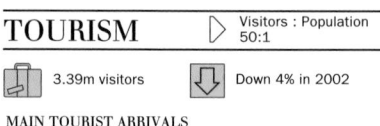

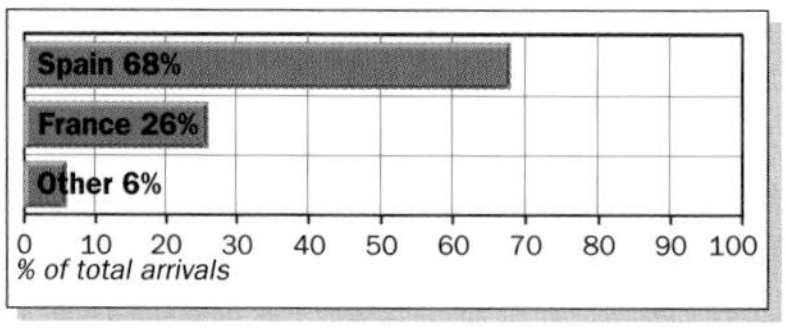
Spain 68%
France 26%
Other 6%
0 10 20 30 40 50 60 70 80 90 100
% of total arrivals

Most tourists visit Andorra to ski or shop. Traditionally there are a great many day-trippers from France and Spain, drawn by the many tax-free designer-label boutiques.

Five resorts offer Alpine skiing facilities, and specialize in Nordic skiing. In summer they cater instead for mountain hikers; Andorra's wild flowers attract many visitors, but there is also much for birdwatchers and entomologists to see.

Though not strongly promoted, hunting wild boar is popular, and the goat-like chamois can be hunted under special license.

PEOPLE

Pop. density medium

Spanish, Catalan, French, Portuguese

147/km² (379/mi²)

THE URBAN/RURAL POPULATION SPLIT

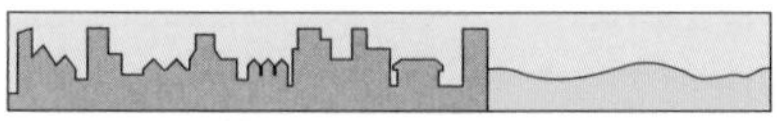
63%
37%

RELIGIOUS PERSUASION

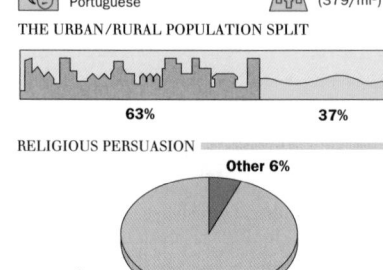

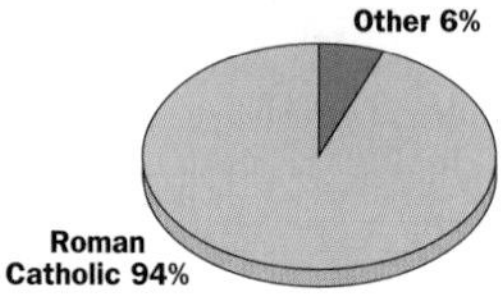
Other 6%
Roman Catholic 94%

Immigration is restricted to French and Spanish nationals intending to work in Andorra. Divorce is not allowed and the marriage rate is low.

POLITICS

Multiparty elections

2001/2005

Coprinces Jacques Chirac and Joan Enric Vives Sicília

AT THE LAST ELECTION

General Council of the Valleys 28 seats

54% PLA
21% PSD
18% PD
7% UL

PLA = Liberal Party of Andorra **PSD** = Social Democratic Party **PD** = Democratic Party **UL** = Unió Laurediana

14 members are elected on a national list and 14 are elected in seven dual-member parishes.

Andorra was a semifeudal state until 1993, when a referendum approved measures which legalized political parties and the right to strike, and altered relations with the coprinces. The ruling PLA, led by Marc Forné, has twice been returned to power.

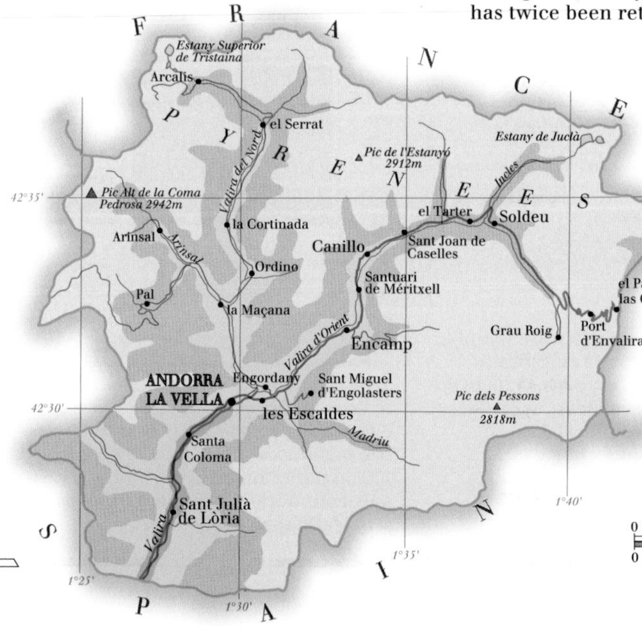
FRANCE
SPAIN
PYRENEES
Estany Superior de Tristaina
Arcalis
el Serrat
Valira del Nord
Pic de l'Estanyó 2912m
Estany de Juclà
Incles
Pic Alt de la Coma Pedrosa 2942m
la Cortinada
el Tarter
Soldeu
Arinsal
Arinsal
Canillo
Sant Joan de Caselles
Ordino
Santuari de Meritxell
Pal
la Maçana
Grau Roig
el Pas de las Casa
Port d'Envalira
Valira d'Orient
Encamp
ANDORRA LA VELLA
Engordany
Sant Miquel d'Engolasters
les Escaldes
Pic dels Pessons 2818m
Madriu
Santa Coloma
Sant Julià de Lòria
Valira
42°35'
42°30'
1°25'
1°30'
1°35'
1°40'

ANDORRA

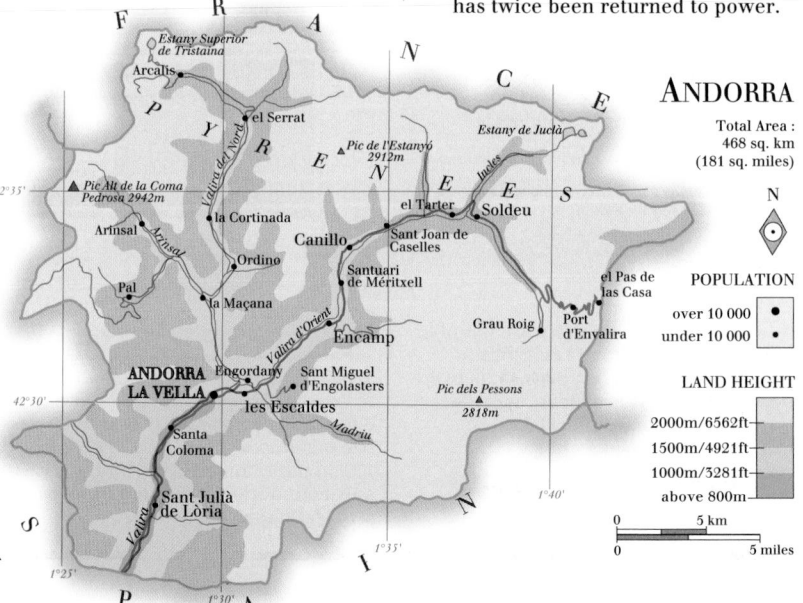

Total Area : 468 sq. km (181 sq. miles)

N

POPULATION

over 10 000

under 10 000

LAND HEIGHT

2000m/6562ft

1500m/4921ft

1000m/3281ft

above 800m

0 5 km

0 5 miles

WORLD AFFAIRS

Joined UN in 1993

CE | OSCE

In 1991 Andorra became a member of the EU customs union and adopted the euro as its official currency in 2002. It joined the UN in 1993. Andorra's status as a tax haven has prompted criticism from the OECD.

AID

Not applicable

Andorra has no aid receipts or donations

Not applicable

The principality of Andorra neither receives nor provides aid, and has no plans to do so.

DEFENSE

No compulsory military service

Andorra has no defense budget

Not applicable

Andorra has no defense budget; France and Spain provide protection. The last military action was intervention by French *gendarmes* to restore order after a royalist coup in 1933.

ECONOMICS

Not available

$1.28bn

0.871 euros (1.013)

SCORE CARD

- ❑ WORLD GNP RANKING........................150th
- ❑ GNP PER CAPITA $19,368
- ❑ BALANCE OF PAYMENTS ..Included in Spanish total
- ❑ INFLATION 4.3%
- ❑ UNEMPLOYMENT ....Low unemployment

STRENGTHS

Tourism underpins the economy. Strict banking secrecy laws make Andorra an important tax haven. Healthy luxury retail sector. Farming: cereals, potatoes, and tobacco are the major products.

WEAKNESSES

France and Spain effectively decide economic policy. Dependence on imported food and raw materials.

EXPORTS

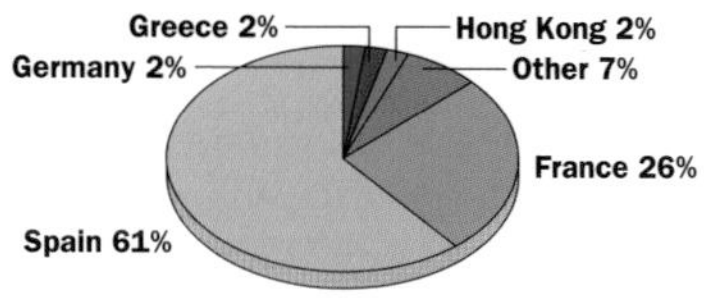
Greece 2%
Hong Kong 2%
Germany 2%
Other 7%
France 26%
Spain 61%

IMPORTS

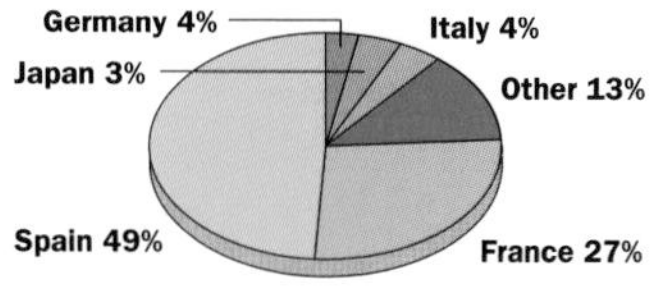
Germany 4%
Italy 4%
Japan 3%
Other 13%
Spain 49%
France 27%

RESOURCES

Not available

None

Not an oil producer and has no refineries

1586 sheep, 1181 cattle, 1037 horses, 854 goats

None

Water is a major resource, hydropower providing most energy needs. However, Andorra has to import twice as much electricity as it produces, and plans to develop wind power. A third of the country is designated forest.

ENVIRONMENT

Not available

None

Not available

The impact of millions of visitors each year on Andorra's alpine ecology is of great concern. The development of hotels, ski resorts, and transportation links threaten to despoil the country's picturesque mountain landscape. It is also endangering the remarkable flora, and creates pressure to clear forested areas.

Hunting is no longer promoted but remains a popular attraction; the wild boar and the Pyrenean chamois are particularly targeted. Some restrictions have been introduced to preserve rarer animal species.

MEDIA

TV ownership high

Daily newspaper circulation 60 per 1000 people

PUBLISHING AND BROADCAST MEDIA

There are 2 daily newspapers, *Diari d'Andorra* and *El Periódic d'Andorra*

1 independent commercial channel

6 independent commercial stations

Andorra has one domestic broadcaster, Radio i Televisio d'Andorra, and receives French and Spanish television channels. A Spanish TV company broadcasts one hour a day of programs for Andorra.

CRIME

No death penalty

48 prisoners

Up 20% in 2000

Tourists are natural targets for thieves, most of whom are not Andorran. Thefts of expensive cars for resale in France and Spain are on the increase.

Andorra's two criminal courts are known as the *Tribunals de Corts*.

EDUCATION

School leaving age: 14

99%

3186 students

There are around 30 schools in Andorra, with instruction in Catalan, French, and Spanish. The University of Andorra specializes in distance learning using the Internet.

CHRONOLOGY

Since 1278, Andorra has been autonomous, ruled by French and Spanish coprinces.

- ❑ **1970** Women get the vote.
- ❑ **1982** First constitution enshrines popular sovereignty.
- ❑ **1983** General Council votes in favor of income tax.
- ❑ **1984** Government resigns over attempt to introduce indirect taxes.
- ❑ **1991** EU customs union comes into effect.
- ❑ **1992** Political demonstrations demanding constitutional reform. Government resigns.
- ❑ **1993** Referendum approves new constitution.
- ❑ **1994** Government falls; replaced by center-right Liberal cabinet, which is reelected in 1997 and 2001.

HEALTH

Welfare state health benefits

1 per 395 people

Heart and cerebrovascular diseases

Andorra has one public hospital. Health spas are popular, and the hot springs at les Escaldes attract rheumatism sufferers.

SPENDING

GDP/cap. increase

CONSUMPTION AND SPENDING

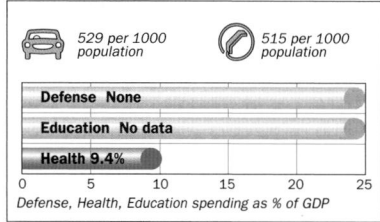

529 per 1000 population

515 per 1000 population

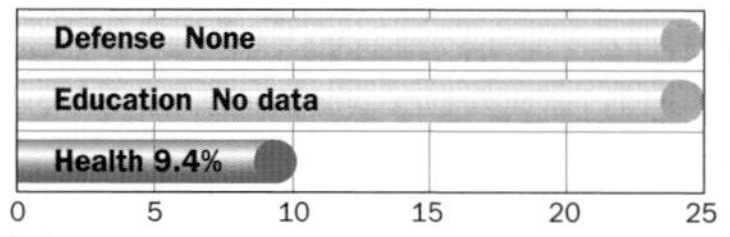
Defense None
Education No data
Health 9.4%
0
5
10
15
20
25

Defense, Health, Education spending as % of GDP

Hotel owners form the wealthiest group of citizens in Andorran society; many of them choose to live across the border in neighboring Spain.

WORLD RANKING

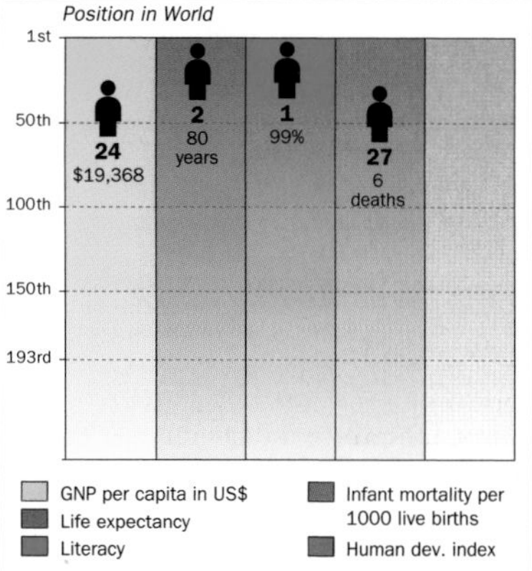
Position in World
1st
50th
100th
150th
193rd
24
$19,368
2
80
years
1
99%
27
6
deaths
GNP per capita in US$
Life expectancy
Literacy
Infant mortality per 1000 live births
Human dev. index

A

ANGOLA

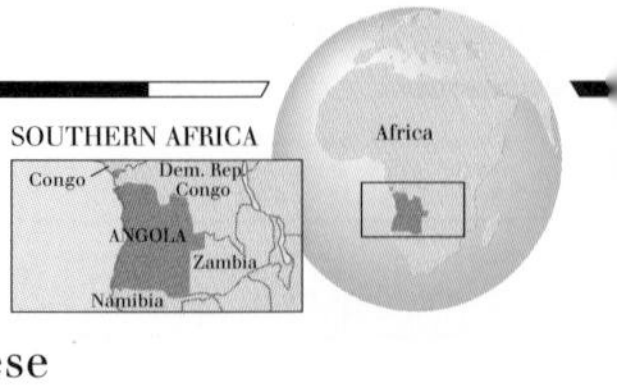
SOUTHERN AFRICA
Congo
Dem. Rep. Congo
ANGOLA
Zambia
Namibia
Africa

OFFICIAL NAME: Republic of Angola **CAPITAL:** Luanda
POPULATION: 13.9 million **CURRENCY:** Readjusted kwanza **OFFICIAL LANGUAGE:** Portuguese

1975 | 1975 | Nov 11 | ANG | +1 | +244 | .ao

Angola's capital, Luanda. Founded in 1575 by the Portuguese, it became a transshipment point for slaves en route to Brazil.

AN OIL- AND DIAMOND-RICH country in southwest Africa, Angola has suffered almost continuous civil war since independence from Portugal in 1975. During the Cold War the West supported UNITA rebels against the Soviet-backed MPLA government. After many failed peace initiatives, the latest, in 2002, has raised hopes yet again of a more permanent end to the violence.

CLIMATE

Tropical/steppe

WEATHER CHART FOR LUANDA

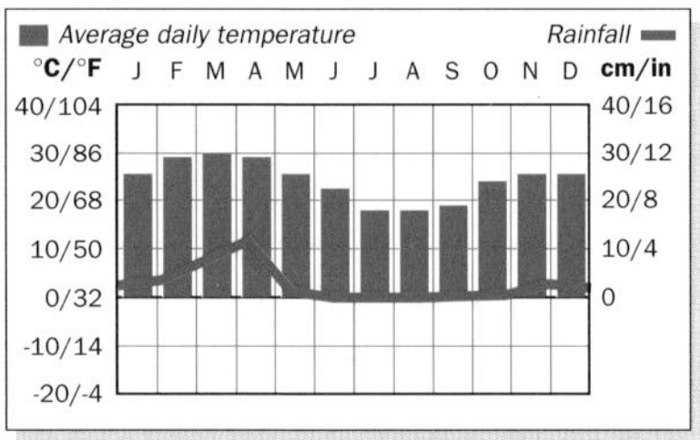
Average daily temperature
Rainfall
°C/°F
J F M A M J J A S O N D
cm/in
40/104
30/86
20/68
10/50
0/32
-10/14
-20/-4
40/16
30/12
20/8
10/4
0

The climate varies from temperate to tropical. Rainfall decreases from north to south. The Benguela Current makes the coast unusually cool and dry.

TRANSPORTATION

Drive on right

Luanda International 766,077 passengers

123 ships 63,141 grt

THE TRANSPORTATION NETWORK

19,156 km (11,903 miles)

Much of this infrastructure has been destroyed by civil war.

2771 km (1722 miles)

1295 km (805 miles)

War has destroyed infrastructure, restricted movement of people and goods, and devastated port traffic. UN peacekeepers have tried to clear mines and repair roads, bridges, and railroads.

TOURISM

Visitors : Population 1:207

67,000 visitors

Up 31% in 2001

MAIN TOURIST ARRIVALS

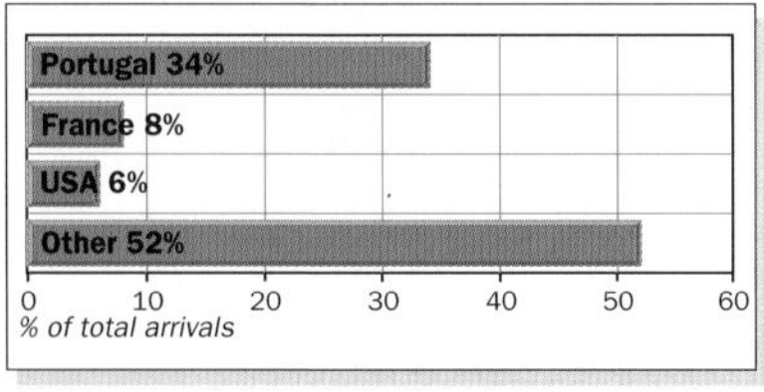
Portugal 34%
France 8%
USA 6%
Other 52%
0 10 20 30 40 50 60
% of total arrivals

A war zone since independence, Angola does not attract tourists. Most visitors are journalists or employees of the oil multinationals in Cabinda.

PEOPLE

Pop. density low

Portuguese, Umbundu, Kimbundu, Kikongo

11/km² (29/mi²)

THE URBAN/RURAL POPULATION SPLIT

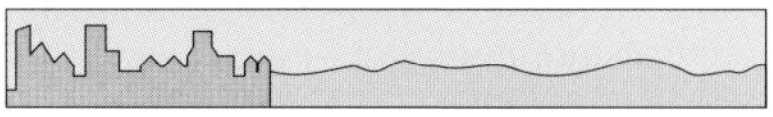
35%
65%

ETHNIC MAKEUP

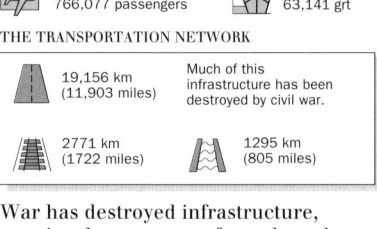

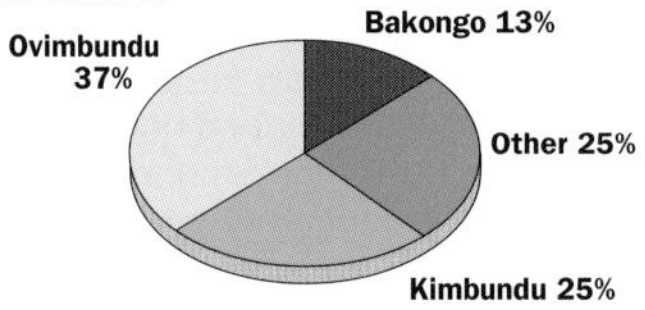
Ovimbundu 37%
Bakongo 13%
Other 25%
Kimbundu 25%

The predominantly rural-dwelling Ovimbundu and the mainly urban-based Kimbundu are the main ethnic groups and generally supported UNITA or the MPLA respectively. The small mixed race (Portuguese–African) community enjoys the highest standard of living. Christianity (mostly Roman Catholicism) is practiced alongside indigenous beliefs.

POLITICS

In transition

1992/1998 (postponed)

President José Eduardo dos Santos

AT THE LAST ELECTION

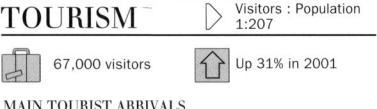

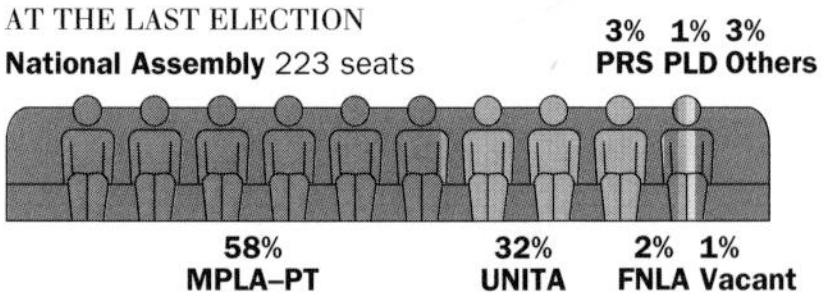
National Assembly 223 seats
3% PRS
1% PLD
3% Others
58% MPLA–PT
32% UNITA
2% FNLA
1% Vacant

MPLA–PT = Popular Movement for the Liberation of Angola –Workers' Party **UNITA** = National Union for the Total Independence of Angola **PRS** = Social Renewal Party **FNLA** = Angolan National Liberation Front **PLD** = Liberal Democratic Party
The seats allotted to members from abroad remained vacant

In power since 1975, the MPLA abandoned one-party rule in 1991 and, under President José Eduardo dos Santos, won the first multiparty elections in 1992. Jonas Savimbi's defeated UNITA responded by restarting the civil war. Although a 1994 peace accord signed in Lusaka (Zambia) resulted in UNITA's joining a government of national unity in 1997, peace was shortlived. UNITA left the government as fighting escalated once more in 1998. Savimbi's death in early 2002 led to a renewed peace initiative, a "definitive cease-fire," and UNITA's disarmament.

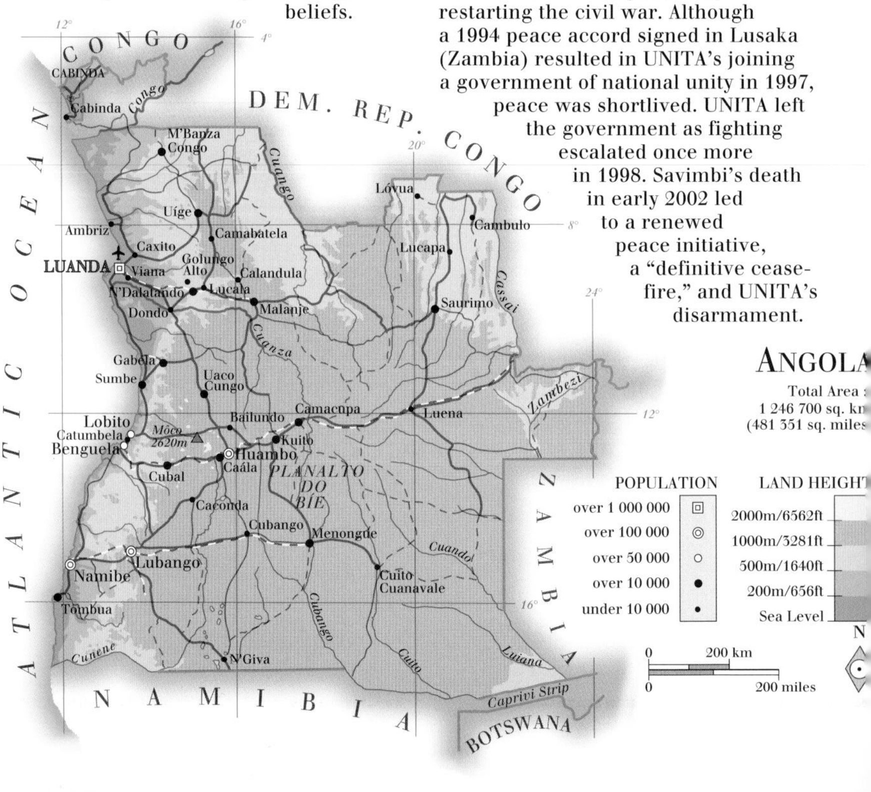
CONGO
CABINDA
Cabinda
Congo
DEM. REP. CONGO
ATLANTIC OCEAN
M'Banza Congo
Cuango
Uíge
Lóvua
Cambulo
Ambriz
Caxito
Camabatela
Lucapa
LUANDA
Viana
Golungo Alto
Calandula
N'Dalatando
Lucala
Dondo
Malanje
Saurimo
Cassai
Cuanza
Gabela
Sumbe
Uaco Cungo
Lobito
Catumbela
Benguela
Môco 2620m
Bailundo
Camacupa
Kuito
Luena
Zambezi
Huambo
Caála
PLANALTO DO BIÉ
Cubal
Caconda
Cubango
Menongue
Cuando
Namibe
Lubango
Cuito Cuanavale
Tômbua
Cunene
N'Giva
Cuito
Luiana
ZAMBIA
NAMIBIA
Caprivi Strip
BOTSWANA
ANGOLA
Total Area : 1 246 700 sq. km (481 351 sq. miles)
POPULATION
over 1 000 000
over 100 000
over 50 000
over 10 000
under 10 000
LAND HEIGHT
2000m/6562ft
1000m/3281ft
500m/1640ft
200m/656ft
Sea Level
0 200 km
0 200 miles

WORLD AFFAIRS

Joined UN in 1976

COMESA IBRD NAM AU SADC

Angola was a key Cold War frontier in the 1980s, but after 1992 UNITA lost Western support. Postapartheid South Africa joined the US, Russia, and Portugal as guarantors of Angola's peace process after 1994. Relations with Zambia suffered when fighting spilled across the border. In 2000 controls were tightened on the international diamond trade in support of UN sanctions then in place on UNITA-held regions. UNITA tried to secure territory and influence in the DRC during its civil war.

AID

Recipient

$268m (receipts) — Down 13% in 2001

The return of peace in 2002 greatly improved the ability of aid agencies and international donors to provide assistance to Angola. The immediate focus was on the massive humanitarian crisis left by decades of war. The government hopes to turn soon to more constructive development projects.

DEFENSE

No compulsory military service

$1.47bn — Down 26% in 2001

By 2002 superior government forces had asserted control over more than 90% of the country. Under the cease-fire, some 5000 UNITA troops were integrated into the regular army. The remaining 80,000 were demobilized. Since then the army's main priority has been to tackle the separatist rebellion in the Cabinda exclave.

ECONOMICS

Inflation 659% p.a. (1990–2001)

$6.71bn — 78.25 readjusted kwanza (43.35)

SCORE CARD

- WORLD GNP RANKING........................102nd
- GNP PER CAPITA..............................$500
- BALANCE OF PAYMENTS....................–$355m
- INFLATION..153%
- UNEMPLOYMENT..................................50%

STRENGTHS

Oil. Rich mineral deposits. Large private sector. Lifting of wartime sanctions on UNITA territory.

WEAKNESSES

Damaged infrastructure. Subsistence agriculture. Drought. Land mines maim civilians, disrupt farming. Corruption. Continuing conflict in Cabinda.

EXPORTS

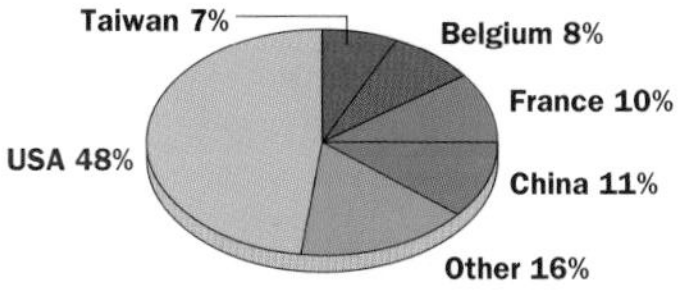
Taiwan 7%
Belgium 8%
France 10%
USA 48%
China 11%
Other 16%

IMPORTS

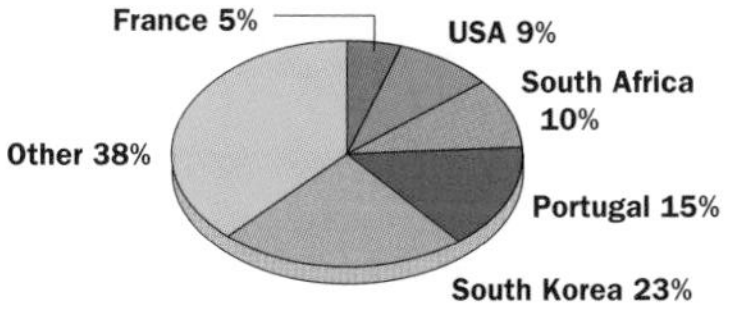
France 5%
USA 9%
South Africa 10%
Other 38%
Portugal 15%
South Korea 23%

RESOURCES

Electric power 462,000 kW

238,351 tonnes

905,000 b/d (reserves 5.4bn barrels)

4.15m cattle, 2.05m goats, 780,000 pigs, 6.8m chickens

Oil, diamonds, iron, copper, lead, zinc, gold, manganese

Deepwater oil fields have been found. The rich alluvial diamond deposits were controlled by UNITA during the civil war.

ENVIRONMENT

Sustainability rank: 111th

7% (2% partially protected) — 0.9 tonnes per capita

War has damaged the water supply. UNITA has been accused of widescale ivory poaching.

MEDIA

TV ownership low

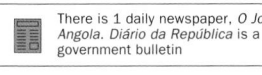

Daily newspaper circulation 11 per 1000 people.

PUBLISHING AND BROADCAST MEDIA

There is 1 daily newspaper, *O Jornal de Angola. Diário da República* is a daily government bulletin

1 state-controlled service

3 services: 1 state-owned, 2 independent

The news agency and *O Jornal de Angola* are state-owned. Independent media are critical but can face harassment.

CRIME

No death penalty

4975 prisoners — Down 50% in 2000

Murder, theft, corruption, and diamond smuggling are commonplace. Rural areas are effectively controlled by gangs. Both the MPLA and UNITA have poor human rights records. Global companies assisted UNITA in sanctions-busting.

EDUCATION

School leaving age: 9

40% — 7845 students

A government-backed initiative, Adra, is making progress in reviving schooling in cities.

CHRONOLOGY

The Portuguese first established coastal forts in 1482.

- **1975** Independence. Civil war between MPLA and UNITA.
- **1979** José Eduardo dos Santos (MPLA) becomes president.
- **1991** UN-brokered peace.
- **1992** MPLA election victory provokes UNITA to resume fighting.
- **1994** Lusaka peace agreement.
- **1998** Civil war reerupts.
- **2000** Fighting spreads as UNITA increases guerrilla activity.
- **2002** UNITA leader Jonas Savimbi killed. April, cease-fire signed.

HEALTH

No welfare state health benefits

1 per 20,000 people

Malaria, diarrheal and respiratory diseases, severe malnutrition

Angola's health system is barely able to cope with casualties of war and the threat of epidemics. Angola has the greatest number of amputees (caused by land mines) in the world.

Immunization of three million children against polio began in 2002.

SPENDING

GDP/cap. increase

CONSUMPTION AND SPENDING

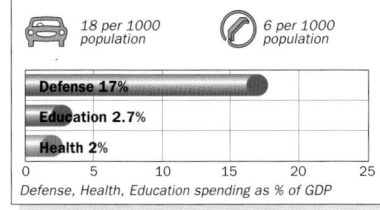

18 per 1000 population — *6 per 1000 population*

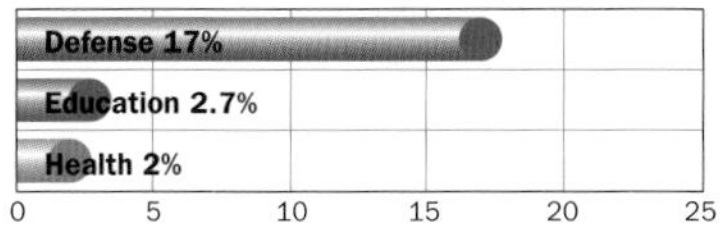
Defense 17%
Education 2.7%
Health 2%
0
5
10
15
20
25

Defense, Health, Education spending as % of GDP

State officials enjoy various luxuries, such as access to cars and other consumer goods, while the majority struggles to survive. The MPLA accuses its own generals of illicit diamond mining.

WORLD RANKING

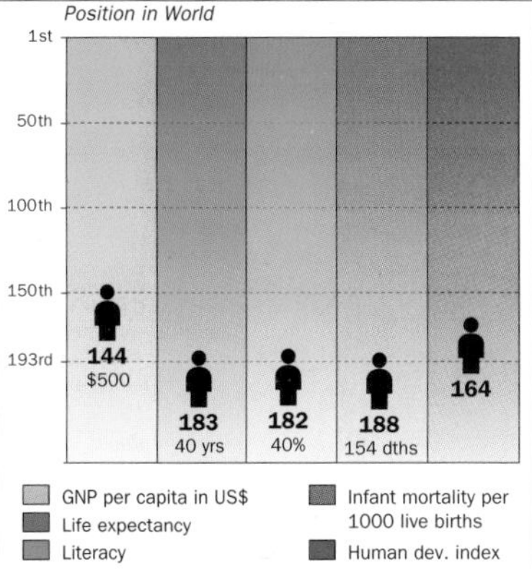
Position in World
1st
50th
100th
150th
193rd
144
$500
183
40 yrs
182
40%
188
154 dths
164
GNP per capita in US$
Life expectancy
Literacy
Infant mortality per 1000 live births
Human dev. index

A

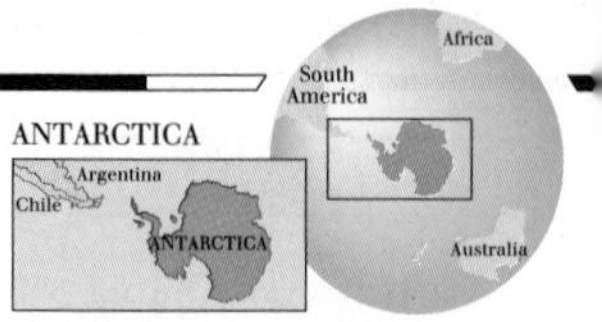
Africa
South America
ANTARCTICA
Argentina
Chile
ANTARCTICA
Australia

ANTARCTICA

OFFICIAL NAME: Antarctica **CAPITAL:** None
POPULATION: None **CURRENCY:** None **OFFICIAL LANGUAGE:** None

1961 | 1961 | n/a | n/a | n/a | n/a | .aq

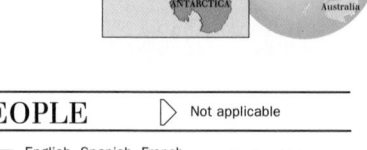

THE WORLD'S fifth-largest continent, Antarctica is almost entirely covered by ice over 2000 m (6560 ft) thick. The area sustains a varied wildlife, including seals, whales, and penguins. The Antarctic Treaty, signed in 1959 and in force since 1961, provides for international governance of Antarctica. To gain Consultative Status, countries have to set up a program of scientific research into the continent. Following a 1994 international agreement, a whale sanctuary was established around Antarctica.

CLIMATE

Freezing

WEATHER CHART

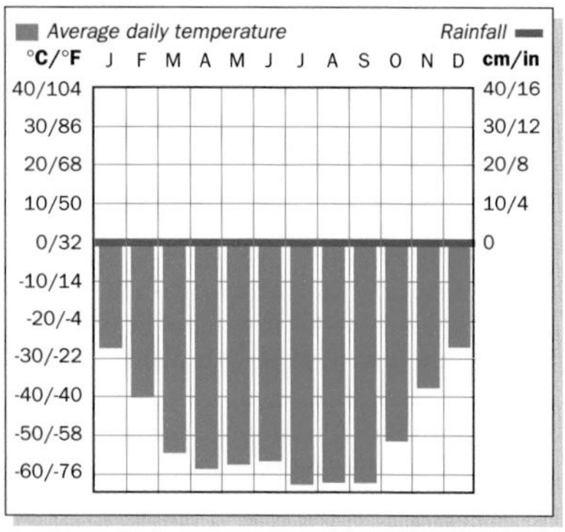
Average daily temperature
Rainfall
°C/°F
J F M A M J J A S O N D
cm/in
40/104
30/86
20/68
10/50
0/32
-10/14
-20/-4
-30/-22
-40/-40
-50/-58
-60/-76
40/16
30/12
20/8
10/4
0

Antarctica is the windiest as well as the coldest continent. Powerful winds create a narrow storm belt around the continent, which brings cloud, fog, and severe blizzards. Icebergs barricade more than 90% of the coastline, and climate change has seen an increase in their number and size in recent years. Antarctica contains over 80% of the world's fresh water.

TRANSPORTATION

Not applicable

Airstrips to some stations

Has no fleet

Ships are the main mode of transportation to Antarctica. They are also used for marine research projects. Air traffic from Chile is growing, and France and the UK are building new airstrips. Most planes have to be equipped with skis for landing.

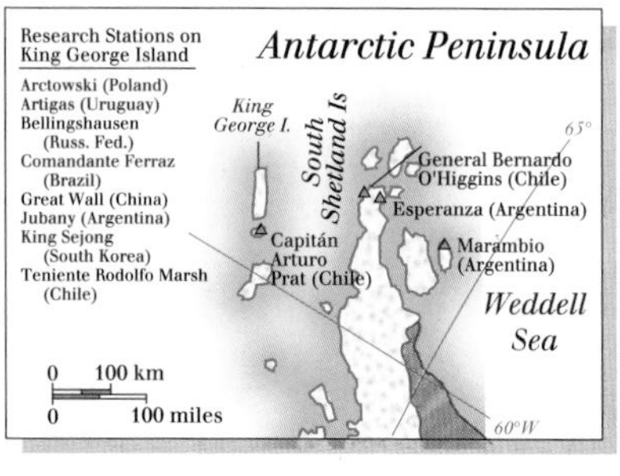
Research Stations on King George Island
Arctowski (Poland)
Artigas (Uruguay)
Bellingshausen (Russ. Fed.)
Comandante Ferraz (Brazil)
Great Wall (China)
Jubany (Argentina)
King Sejong (South Korea)
Teniente Rodolfo Marsh (Chile)
Antarctic Peninsula
King George I.
South Shetland Is
General Bernardo O'Higgins (Chile)
Esperanza (Argentina)
Capitán Arturo Prat (Chile)
Marambio (Argentina)
Weddell Sea
65°
60°W
0 100 km
0 100 miles

TOURISM

Not applicable

17,000 visitors

Up 81% in 2000–2002

Tourism is mainly by cruise ship to the Antarctic Peninsula, the Ross Sea, and the sub-Antarctic islands. In 1983, Chile began flights to King George Island, where there is a government-run hotel. Main attractions are the wildlife, skiing, and visits to scientific stations and historic huts. The rapid growth of tourism since the late 1990s has disrupted scientific programs, and official regulation of tourism is now essential.

PEOPLE

Not applicable

English, Spanish, French, Norwegian, Chinese, Polish, Russian, German, Japanese

Not applicable

ETHNIC MAKEUP

Antarctica has a transient population of Americans, British, French, Norwegians, Argentinians, Chileans, Chinese, Russians, Poles, and Japanese. Most are involved in research. Few stay more than two years.

Antarctica has no indigenous population. Around 80 Chilean settlers live at any one time in the continent's only permanent community on King George Island. The rest of the population are scientists and logistical staff working at the 40 permanent, and as many as 100 temporary, research stations. Most stations are too far apart for direct contact between different nationalities.

ANTARCTICA

Total Area : 14 000 000 sq. km (5 405 000 sq. miles)

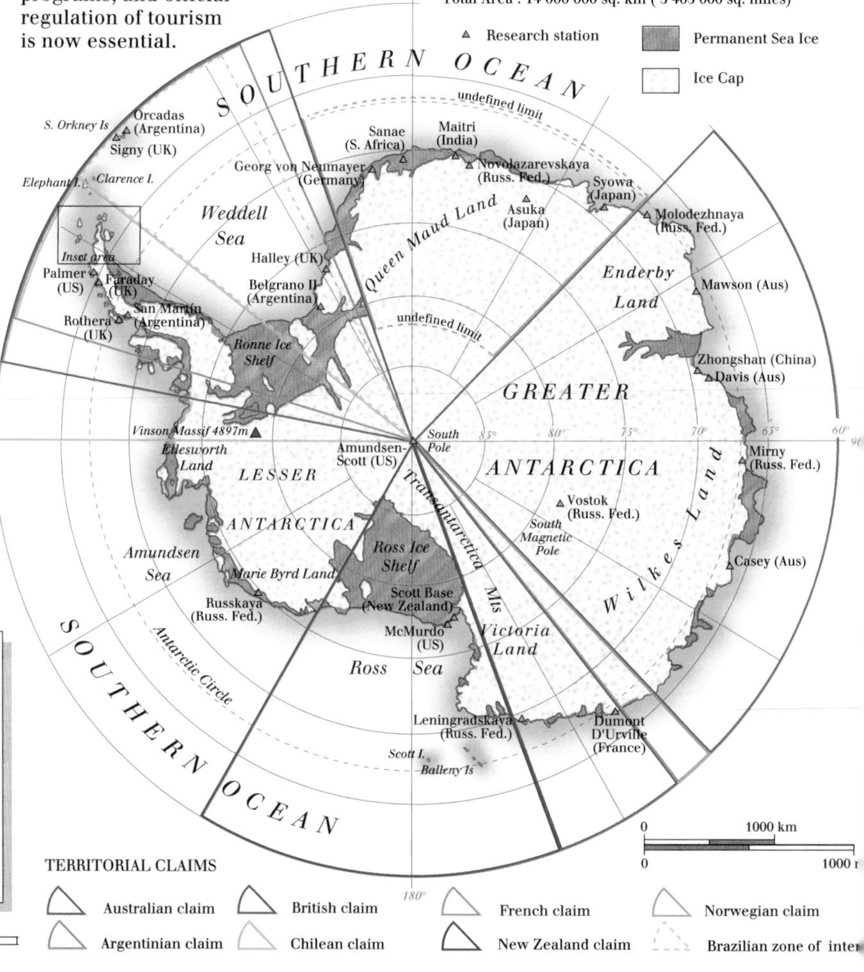
Research station
Permanent Sea Ice
Ice Cap
SOUTHERN OCEAN
undefined limit
S. Orkney Is
Orcadas (Argentina)
Signy (UK)
Elephant I.
Clarence I.
Sanae (S. Africa)
Maitri (India)
Georg von Neumayer (Germany)
Novolazarevskaya (Russ. Fed.)
Syowa (Japan)
Asuka (Japan)
Molodezhnaya (Russ. Fed.)
Queen Maud Land
Weddell Sea
Inset area
Halley (UK)
Palmer (US)
Faraday (UK)
Belgrano II (Argentina)
San Martin (Argentina)
Rothera (UK)
Ronne Ice Shelf
Enderby Land
Mawson (Aus)
Zhongshan (China)
Davis (Aus)
GREATER ANTARCTICA
Vinson Massif 4897m
Ellesworth Land
LESSER ANTARCTICA
Amundsen-Scott (US)
South Pole
Transantarctic Mts
Mirny (Russ. Fed.)
Vostok (Russ. Fed.)
South Magnetic Pole
Amundsen Sea
Ross Ice Shelf
Marie Byrd Land
Casey (Aus)
Wilkes Land
Russkaya (Russ. Fed.)
Scott Base (New Zealand)
McMurdo (US)
Victoria Land
Antarctic Circle
Ross Sea
Leningradskaya (Russ. Fed.)
Dumont D'Urville (France)
Scott I.
Balleny Is
0°
90°W
180°
85° 80° 75° 70° 65° 60°
0 1000 km
TERRITORIAL CLAIMS
Australian claim
British claim
French claim
Norwegian claim
Argentinian claim
Chilean claim
New Zealand claim
Brazilian zone of interest

***Neumayer Channel, Antarctica.** Many states are pressing for the whole of Antarctica to be protected as an international park.*

POLITICS

Not applicable

Not applicable

Consultative Parties to Antarctic Treaty

NO LEGISLATIVE OR ADVISORY BODIES

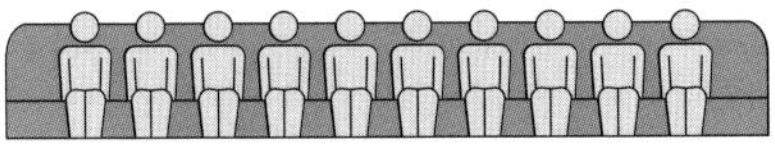

The Antarctic Treaty of 1959 was signed by 12 countries. Consultative meetings are held most years to discuss scientific, environmental, and political matters.

There are 27 parties to the Antarctic Treaty and 18 nations with observer status. There are territorial claims by Australia, France, New Zealand, and Norway, and overlapping claims in the Antarctic Peninsula by Argentina, Chile, and the UK. Other states do not recognize these claims.

Of main concern is the adoption of a wide range of environmental protection measures. Proposals include the monitoring of all scientific activities and also the prosecution of any country if it were demonstrated that its research would lead to detrimental global change.

WORLD AFFAIRS

Not a UN member

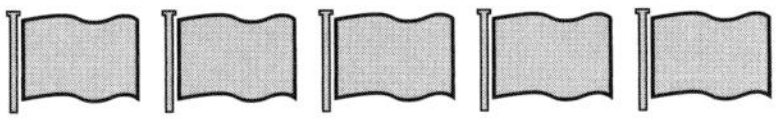

Rivalries exist between nations wishing to preserve Antarctica as a world park and those pursuing territorial claims.

AID

Recipient

Research is funded by governments

Subject to individual government budgets

Scientific programs in the Antarctic are almost entirely funded by government agencies in the home countries. Funding is occasionally provided by scientific institutions and universities.

DEFENSE

Not applicable

No defense force

Not applicable

Under the Antarctic Treaty, Antarctica can be used only for peaceful purposes. Any military personnel present perform purely scientific or logistic roles.

ECONOMICS

Not applicable

Not applicable

Antarctica has no currency

Research is government-funded and is therefore subject to reductions. The exploitation of marine stocks provides no income for Antarctica.

RESOURCES

Not applicable

Included in national fish catch totals

Not an oil producer and has no refineries

None

Mineral extraction is banned

Antarctica's main resources are its marine stocks, including fin fish, seals, and whales. A campaign by environmental groups, supported by Australia and France, to ban mining and declare Antarctica a world park was rewarded with an agreement in 1991 to impose a 50-year ban on mining, and in 1994 by the approval of a whale sanctuary. Prospects for energy sources alternative to fossil fuels, such as solar power and wind generators, are being explored.

ENVIRONMENT

Not applicable

Most of Antarctica is protected

Not applicable

Antarctica is one of the Earth's last great wildernesses. Its layer of ice, 4000 m (13,120 ft) thick in places, has formed over thousands of years. Its ecosystem is such that a "footprint" will leave its mark for many years. Several species are unique to the continent, including king penguins. The blood of polar fish contains antifreeze agents. Ecological concerns include overfishing, particularly of krill, cod, and squid; the disintegration of ice shelves; the depletion of the ozone layer over Antarctica; and the various knock-on effects of global warming. In 1994 the IWC agreed to a French proposal to create an Antarctic whale sanctuary which, together with the Indian Ocean sanctuary, protects the feeding grounds of 90% of the world's whales.

MEDIA

Not applicable

There are no daily newspapers produced in Antarctica

A few bases publish newssheets for local consumption. Local radio stations are found at some of the larger bases.

CRIME

Not applicable

There are no prisons in Antarctica

Crime is negligible

Each person in Antarctica is subject to their national laws. Occasional petty theft from stations is linked to visits from tourists.

CHRONOLOGY

The Russian explorer, Thaddeus von Bellingshausen, was the first to sight Antarctica, in 1820. The South Pole was first reached by the Norwegian, Roald Amundsen, in December 1911.

- ❑ **1957–1958** International Geophysical Year launches scientific exploration of Antarctica.
- ❑ **1959** Antarctic Treaty signed by 12 countries. Territorial claims frozen.
- ❑ **1978** Convention limiting seal hunting comes into force.
- ❑ **1985** Ozone depletion disclosed.
- ❑ **1994** Establishment of Antarctic whale sanctuary.
- ❑ **1998** Agreement on 50-year ban on mineral extraction comes into force.

EDUCATION

Not applicable

Not applicable

None

Schoolhouses exist on the Chilean base, Villa Las Estrellas, and the Argentinian base, Esperanza. Teaching is geared to the relevant national system. Some researchers' studies contribute to higher degrees.

Antarctic-based research has resulted in a number of scientific breakthroughs, including the discovery of the depletion of the ozone layer.

HEALTH

Not applicable

1 medical officer per station

Deaths are extremely rare in Antarctica

Each station has its own medical officer. The problems usually associated with polar conditions, such as frostbite and snow blindness, are very rare. All personnel are medically screened before arrival. If serious illnesses develop, patients have to be evacuated by air, including in recent years an acute case of gallstones and a doctor who self-diagnosed breast cancer.

SPENDING

Not applicable

US bases are the best-funded, while the budgets of other bases are subject to domestic politics. Most stations have TVs and video recorders. Telephone systems operate only within stations. Computers are supplied for scientific research. A 1670-km (1040-mile) fiber optic cable is set to provide Internet access to the South Pole by 2009.

WORLD RANKING

The UN Human Development Index conditions are not applicable to Antarctica.

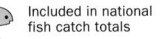

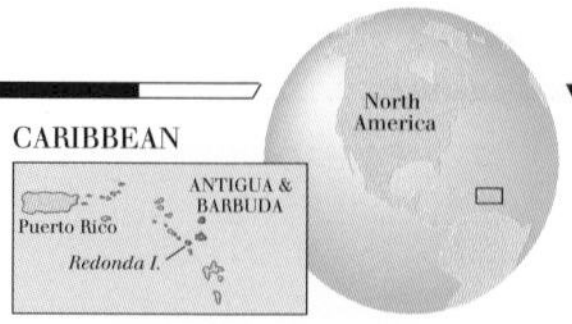
North America
CARIBBEAN
ANTIGUA & BARBUDA
Puerto Rico
Redonda I.

ANTIGUA & BARBUDA

OFFICIAL NAME: Antigua and Barbuda **CAPITAL:** St. John's
POPULATION: 67,448 **CURRENCY:** Eastern Caribbean dollar **OFFICIAL LANGUAGE:** English

1981 | 1981 | Nov 1 | AG | -4.5 | +1268 | .ag

PART OF THE Leeward Islands chain, Antigua was in turn a Spanish, French, and British colony. British influence is still strong and most clearly revealed in the Antiguans' passion for cricket. Antigua has two dependencies: Barbuda, 50 km (30 miles) to the north, sporting a magnificent beach, and Redonda, 40 km (25 miles) west, an uninhabited rock with its own king.

CLIMATE

Tropical oceanic

WEATHER CHART FOR ST. JOHN'S

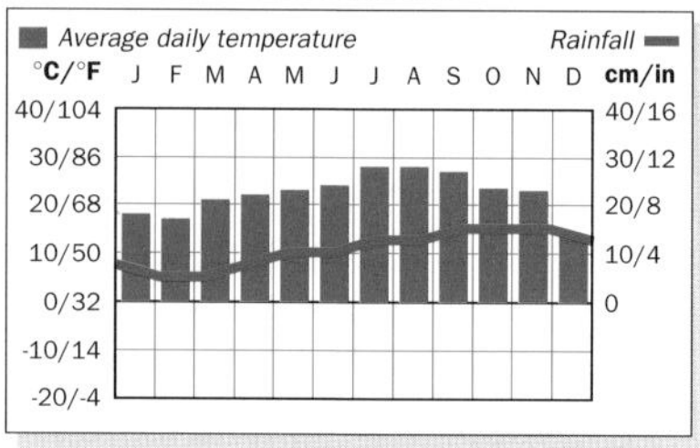
Average daily temperature
Rainfall
°C/°F J F M A M J J A S O N D cm/in
40/104 30/86 20/68 10/50 0/32 -10/14 -20/-4
40/16 30/12 20/8 10/4 0

Antigua is less humid than other Caribbean islands. Year-round trade winds moderate the heat.

TRANSPORTATION

Drive on left

V. C. Bird International, St. John's 727,292 passengers

840 ships 4.67m grt

THE TRANSPORTATION NETWORK

250 km (155 miles)	None
77 km (48 miles)	None

Recent multimillion EC$ projects have expanded the international airport and provided 140 km (90 miles) of roads with all-weather surfaces.

TOURISM

Visitors : Population 3.1:1

207,000 visitors

Down 11% in 2000

MAIN TOURIST ARRIVALS

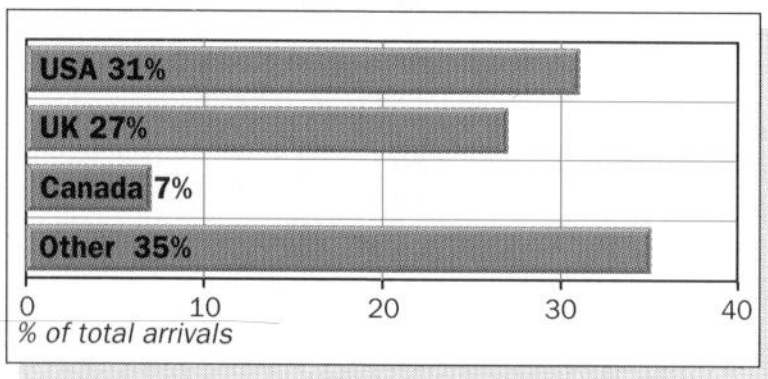
USA 31%
UK 27%
Canada 7%
Other 35%
0 10 20 30 40
% of total arrivals

Antigua is especially popular with US cruise ship tourists. Among other draws are the annual international tennis championship, the islands' three golf courses, and the attraction of large duty-free shopping malls.

PEOPLE

Pop. density medium

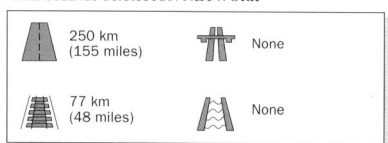

English, English patois

153/km² (397/mi²)

THE URBAN/RURAL POPULATION SPLIT

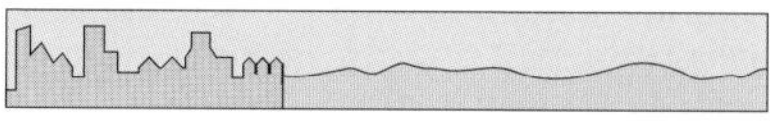
37%
63%

RELIGIOUS PERSUASION

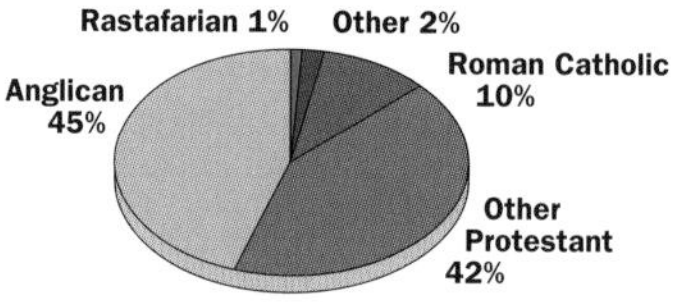
Rastafarian 1%
Other 2%
Roman Catholic 10%
Anglican 45%
Other Protestant 42%

Most of the population are descended from Africans, brought over between the 16th and 19th centuries. There are, in addition, a few Europeans and South Asians. Racial tension is rare. Some 4000–5000 Montserratians have been given shelter since the volcanic eruptions on Montserrat in the 1990s. Around 10% of the population are of Hispanic origin, mainly coming from the Dominican Republic. By Caribbean standards, wealth disparities are small.

POLITICS

Multiparty elections

L. House 1999/2004
U. House 1999/2004

H.M. Queen Elizabeth II

AT THE LAST ELECTION

House of Representatives 17 seats

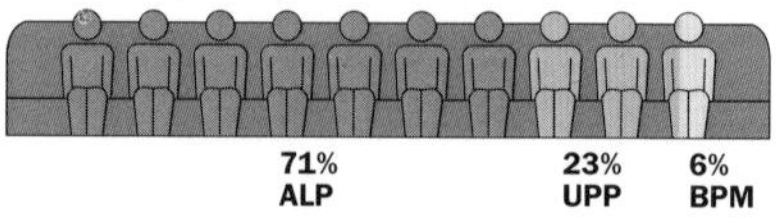
71% ALP
23% UPP
6% BPM

ALP = Antigua Labour Party **UPP** = United Progressive Party
BPM = Barbuda People's Movement

Senate 17 seats

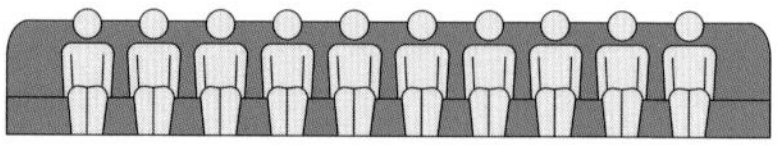

The members of the Senate are appointed. Eleven are chosen by the prime minister, four by the leader of the opposition, one by the governor-general, and one by the Barbuda Council

Antigua has been dominated for four decades by the Bird family. Vere Bird Sr., premier since 1960, retired in 1994 and was succeeded by his younger son Lester, who led the ALP into its sixth consecutive term in 1999. The family has been dogged by allegations of corruption. Vere Jr. was removed from public office in 1990 after accusations of gun-running, while Lester Bird himself has been forced to deny a sex and narcotics scandal.

ANTIGUA & BARBUDA

Total Area : 442 sq. km (170 sq. miles)

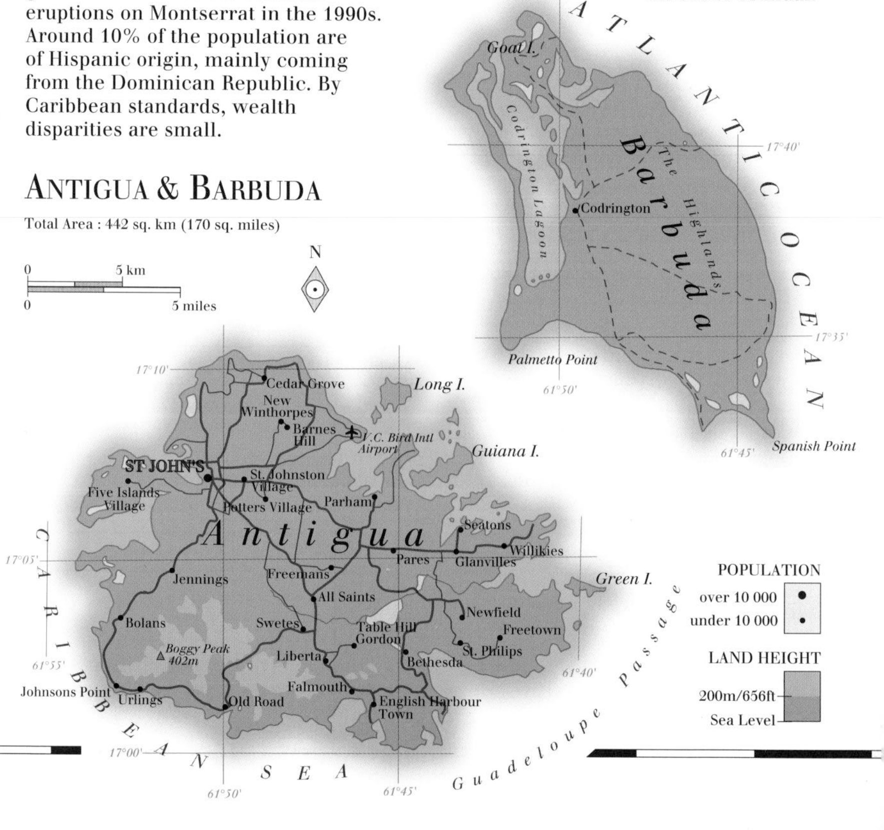
0 5 km
0 5 miles
N
ATLANTIC OCEAN
Goat I.
Codrington Lagoon
Barbuda
The Highlands
Codrington
Palmetto Point
Spanish Point
Long I.
Guiana I.
Cedar Grove
New Winthorpes
Barnes Hill
V.C. Bird Intl Airport
ST JOHN'S
St. Johnston Village
Five Islands Village
Potters Village
Parham
Antigua
Seatons
Pares
Glanvilles
Willikies
Green I.
Jennings
Freemans
All Saints
Bolans
Swetes
Table Hill Gordon
Newfield
Freetown
St. Philips
Boggy Peak 402m
Liberta
Bethesda
Falmouth
Johnsons Point
Urlings
Old Road
English Harbour Town
CARIBBEAN SEA
Guadeloupe Passage
POPULATION
over 10 000
under 10 000
LAND HEIGHT
200m/656ft
Sea Level

WORLD AFFAIRS

Joined UN in 1981

ACS | Caricom | Comm | OECS | OAS

While rejecting attempts by the OECD to regulate tax havens, Antigua has been internationally praised for its own efforts to combat money laundering.

AID

Recipient

US$9m (receipts) | Down 10% in 2001

Major recent donors are the UK, Japan, the EU, and the US. In 1998, the opposition accused the Bird regime of manipulating the distribution of hurricane relief for electoral gain.

DEFENSE

No compulsory military service

US$4m | No change in 2001

There is a 170-strong defense force. Reports that the government had privately imported weaponry from the US in 1998 were denied. Two military bases are leased to the US.

ECONOMICS

Inflation 2.2% p.a. (1990–2001)

US$627m | 2.67 Eastern Caribbean dollars (2.7)

SCORE CARD

❑ WORLD GNP RANKING	164th
❑ GNP PER CAPITA	US$9150
❑ BALANCE OF PAYMENTS	–US$79m
❑ INFLATION	3.2%
❑ UNEMPLOYMENT	7%

STRENGTHS

Tourism and construction of tourist hotels and infrastructure. Financial and communications services linked to offshore financial sector.

WEAKNESSES

High levels of debt, exceeding 80% of GDP. Overdependence on tourism, made more vulnerable by Antigua's promotion as an expensive destination. Lack of natural resources.

EXPORTS

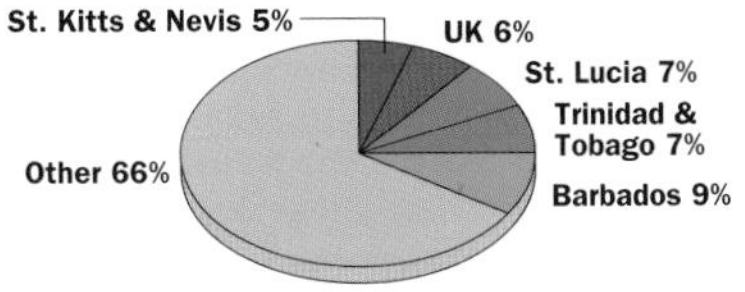
St. Kitts & Nevis 5%
UK 6%
St. Lucia 7%
Trinidad & Tobago 7%
Barbados 9%
Other 66%

IMPORTS

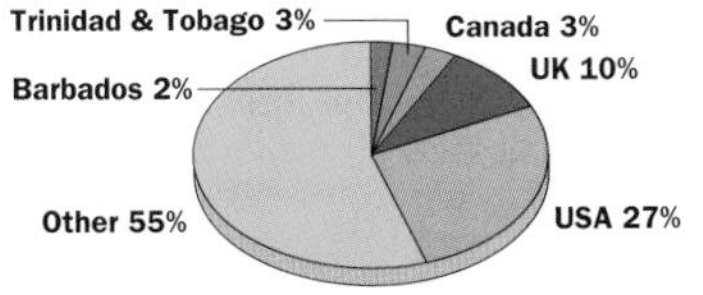
Trinidad & Tobago 3%
Canada 3%
Barbados 2%
UK 10%
Other 55%
USA 27%

Nelson's Dockyard. Luxury yachts fitted with state-of-the-art gadgetry contrast with the 18th-century St. John's harbor.

RESOURCES

Electric power 27,000 kW

1481 tonnes | Not an oil producer

35,000 goats, 18,500 sheep, 98,000 chickens | None

Antigua has no strategic or commodity resources and has to import almost all its energy requirements.

ENVIRONMENT

Not available

15% | 4.9 tonnes per capita

Sewage from hotels causes major problems. Untreated effluent pollutes the sea, while uncontrolled disposal has killed valuable inshore fish stocks in the mangrove swamps; the whole swamp ecosystem is under threat from poorly planned hotel development.

MEDIA

TV ownership hgh

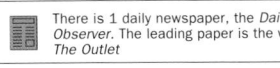

Daily newspaper circulation 91 per 1000 people

PUBLISHING AND BROADCAST MEDIA

There is 1 daily newspaper, the *Daily Observer*. The leading paper is the weekly *The Outlet*

2 services: 1 state-owned, 1 independent | 5 services: 1 state-owned, 4 independent

Arson was alleged when the printing equipment of opposition weekly *The Outlet* was destroyed in 1998. Of the privately owned broadcasting services, one is affiliated to the opposition.

CRIME

Death penalty in use

186 prisoners | Little change from year to year

Murder is rare. Rape, armed robbery, and burglary are main concerns, as is offshore money laundering.

EDUCATION

School leaving age: 16

87% | 631 students

Education is based on the former British selective system. Students go on to the University of the West Indies, or to study in the UK or the US.

CHRONOLOGY

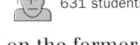

In 1667, Antigua became a British colony. Barbuda, formerly owned privately by the Codrington family, was annexed in 1860.

- ❑ **1951** Universal adult suffrage introduced.
- ❑ **1981** Independence from UK; opposed by Barbudan secessionist movement.
- ❑ **1983** Supports US invasion of Grenada.
- ❑ **1994** Lester Bird elected prime minister.
- ❑ **1995** New taxes provoke protests.
- ❑ **1999** ALP wins sixth consecutive elections; Lester Bird remains prime minister.

HEALTH

Welfare state health benefits

1 per 5882 people | Heart and respiratory diseases, cancers

By Caribbean standards, the health system is efficient, with easy access to the state-run clinics and hospitals. A new hospital has been built in the capital, St. John's.

SPENDING

GDP/cap. increase

CONSUMPTION AND SPENDING

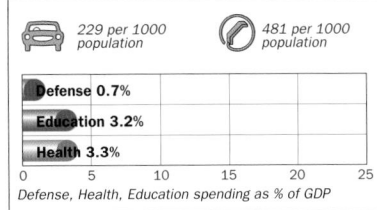

229 per 1000 population | *481 per 1000 population*

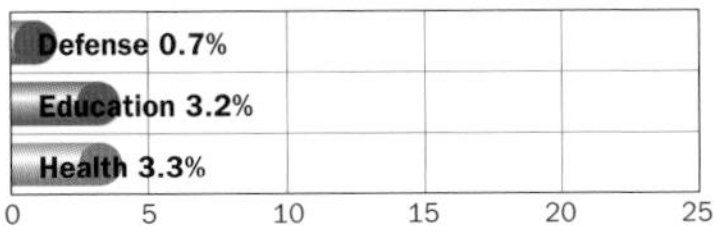
Defense 0.7%
Education 3.2%
Health 3.3%
0
5
10
15
20
25

Defense, Health, Education spending as % of GDP

Wealthy Antiguans are active in running the thriving tourist industry; some are allegedly also involved in money laundering. Unemployment is relatively low and the average per capita income is among the highest in the Caribbean.

WORLD RANKING

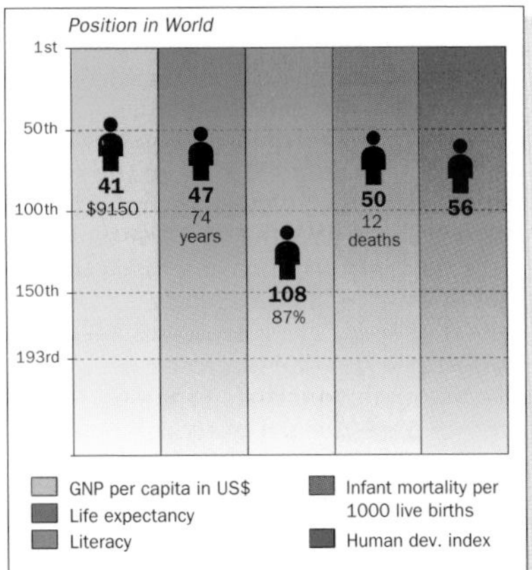
Position in World
1st
50th
100th
150th
193rd
41
$9150
47
74 years
108
87%
50
12 deaths
56
GNP per capita in US$
Life expectancy
Literacy
Infant mortality per 1000 live births
Human dev. index

A

ARGENTINA

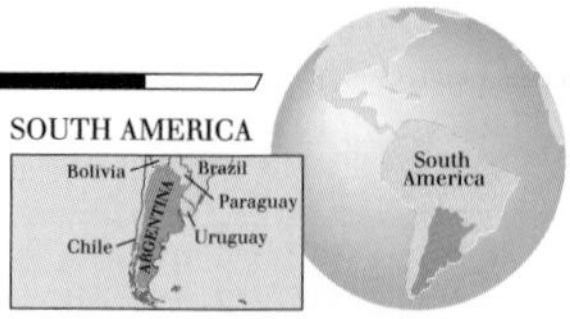
SOUTH AMERICA
Bolivia
Brazil
Paraguay
Uruguay
Chile
ARGENTINA
South America

OFFICIAL NAME: Republic of Argentina **CAPITAL:** Buenos Aires
POPULATION: 37.9 million **CURRENCY:** Argentine peso **OFFICIAL LANGUAGE:** Spanish

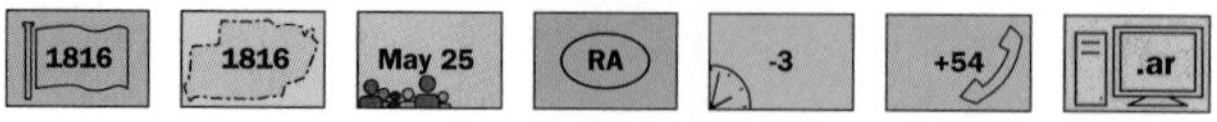
1816
1816
May 25
RA
-3
+54
.ar

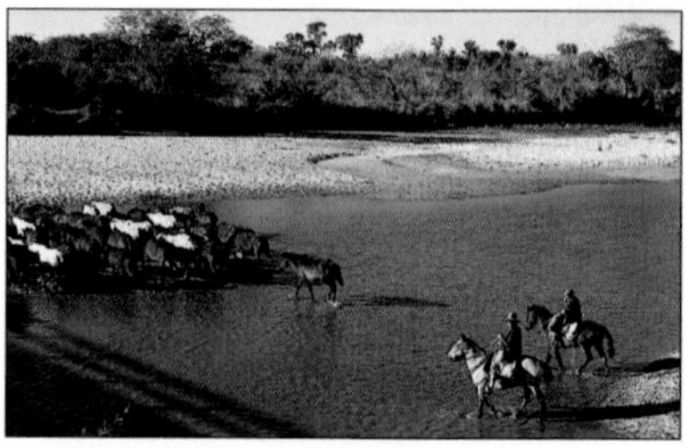

Herding cattle in the northeast, near Corrientes. Beef, Argentina's initial source of wealth, remains a major export.

OCCUPYING MOST OF THE southern portion of South America, Argentina extends 3460 km (2150 miles) from the Gran Chaco to Tierra del Fuego. The Andes mountains in the west run north–south, forming a natural border with Chile. To the east they slope down to the fertile central pampas, the region known as Entre Ríos. Agriculture, especially beef, wheat, and fruit, and energy resources are Argentina's main sources of wealth. Politics in Argentina was characterized in the past by periods of military rule, but in 1983 Argentina returned to a system of multiparty democracy.

CLIMATE

Mountain/steppe/subtropical

WEATHER CHART FOR BUENOS AIRES

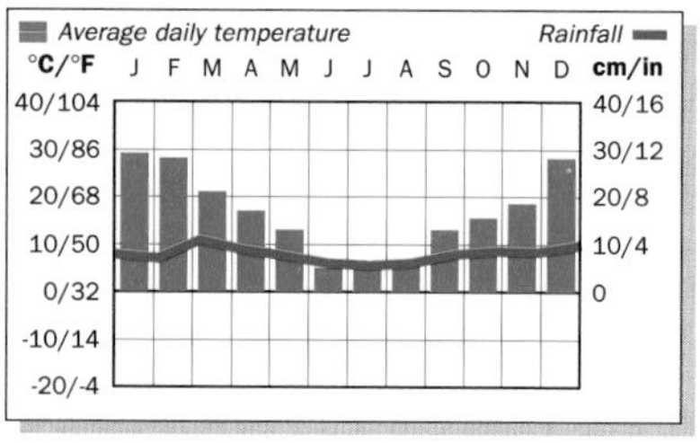
Average daily temperature
Rainfall
°C/°F
J F M A M J J A S O N D
cm/in
40/104
30/86
20/68
10/50
0/32
-10/14
-20/-4
40/16
30/12
20/8
10/4
0

The northeast of Argentina is near-tropical. The Andes are semiarid in the north and snowy in the south. The western lowlands are desert, while the pampas have a mild climate with heavy summer rains.

TRANSPORTATION

Drive on right

Jorge Newberry, Buenos Aires
4.52m passengers

478 ships
421,600 grt

THE TRANSPORTATION NETWORK

63,553 km (39,490 miles)

734 km (456 miles)

33,744 km (20,968 miles)

10,950 km (6804 miles)

Air travel is expensive, and inadequate connections between provinces frustrate business and tourism. The national airline, Aerolineas Argentinas, was privatized in 1990 but in 2000 was the object of a rescue plan; airports are privately operated. The privatized railroad, one of the largest in the world, is primarily used for freight, but Buenos Aires' subway and commuter lines have attracted strong investment and heavy use. Some 9500 km (6000 miles) of roads are privatized, and tolls are among the highest worldwide. The six main terminals in the port of Buenos Aires are privately run. A $20 billion national infrastructure program announced in 2001 has been stalled due to the economic crisis.

TOURISM

Visitors : Population 1:13

3.02m visitors

Up 15% in 2002

MAIN TOURIST ARRIVALS

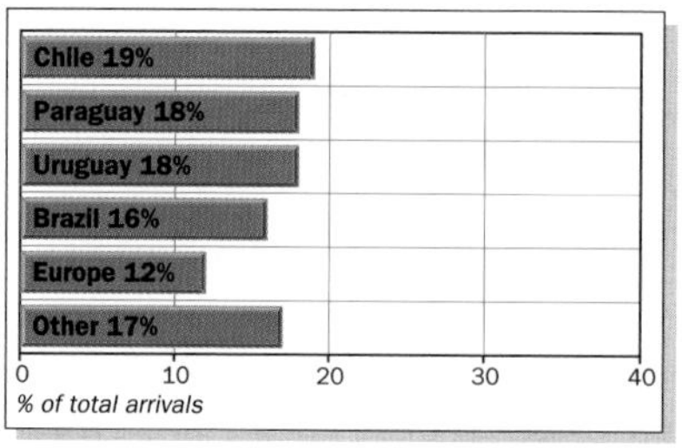
Chile 19%
Paraguay 18%
Uruguay 18%
Brazil 16%
Europe 12%
Other 17%
0
10
20
30
40
% of total arrivals

Tourism has been undersold, and the government, working with business, has launched a huge international marketing campaign. Visitors, still mostly from neighboring countries, are attracted by Buenos Aires' rich city life, the Atlantic coastal resort of Mar del Plata, ski stations such as Bariloche and Las Leñas in the Andes, and wineries around Mendoza; the fashion for tango is also a draw. Other major attractions are Antarctic cruises, the Iguazú National Park, and whale-watching off Peninsula Valdés, northeast of Trelew.

PEOPLE

Pop. density low

Spanish, Italian, Amerindian languages

14/km² (36/mi²)

THE URBAN/RURAL POPULATION SPLIT

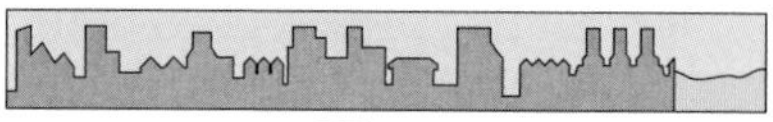
88%
12%

RELIGIOUS PERSUASION

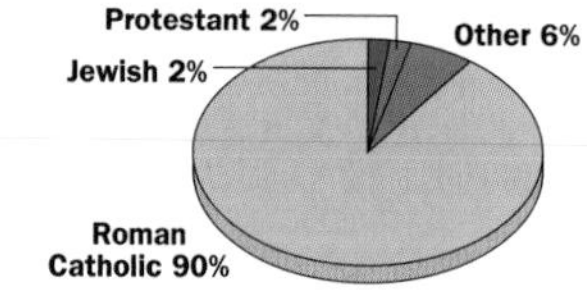
Protestant 2%
Other 6%
Jewish 2%
Roman Catholic 90%

ETHNIC MAKEUP

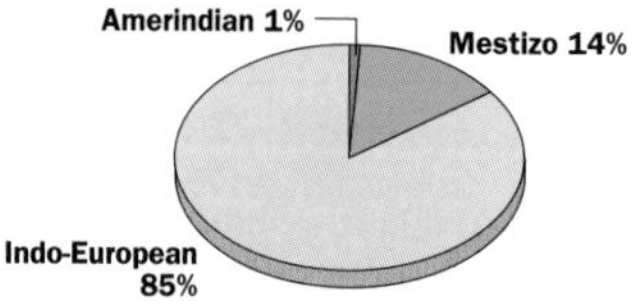
Amerindian 1%
Mestizo 14%
Indo-European 85%

Most Argentinians of European descent are from recent 20th-century migrations: over one-third are of Italian origin. Indigenous peoples now form a tiny minority, living mainly in Andean regions or in the Gran Chaco. Argentina also has communities of Welsh, Lebanese, Syrians, Armenians, Japanese, and Koreans.

POPULATION AGE BREAKDOWN

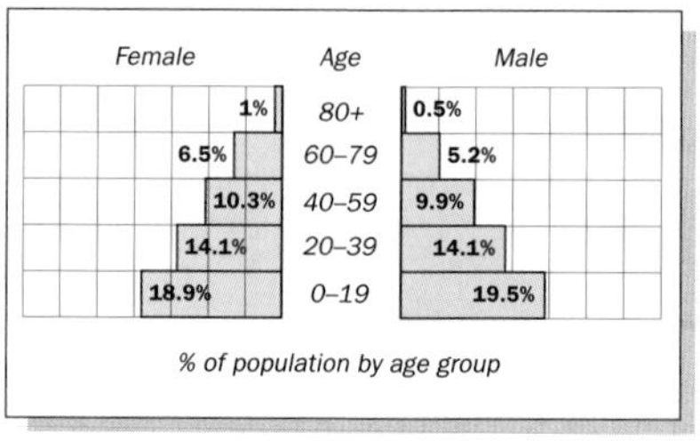
Female
Age
Male
1%
80+
0.5%
6.5%
60–79
5.2%
10.3%
40–59
9.9%
14.1%
20–39
14.1%
18.9%
0–19
19.5%
% of population by age group

The vast majority of Argentinians are urban dwellers, with some 40% of the population living in Buenos Aires, one of the largest cities in Latin America.

Catholicism and the extended family remain strong in Argentina. In addition, the family forms the basis of many successful businesses.

Women have a higher profile than in most Latin American states, and were enfranchised in 1947. Today, many enter the professions and rise to positions of influence in service businesses such as the media, but are less prominent in party politics. Eva Perón, who inspired the musical *Evita*, helped to push women into a more active political role in the 1940s and 1950s, but this trend was reversed under military rule.

POLITICS

Multiparty elections

L. House 1999/2003
U. House 2001/2003

President Néstor Kirchner

Argentina is a multiparty democracy; the president is head of government.

PROFILE

The Peronists dominated politics from the 1940s. The party, founded on mass working-class and left-wing intellectual support, was inimical to the military; coups were staged in 1955, 1966, and 1976. Carlos Menem, president from 1989 to 1999, steered the Peronists toward a right-wing agenda, conquering hyperinflation but reaping strong public disapproval for his free-market policies.

The UCR, having only come to power in 1983 on the back of a protest vote, won the presidency again in 1999 as part of a shaky center-left alliance with FREPASO. President Fernando de la Rúa was brought down by the economic crisis of 2001; there were early elections in 2003 after four stopgap presidents. The much-vilified Menem won the first round, but then withdrew, knowing that he was unlikely to generate enough support to defeat fellow Peronist Néstor Kirchner, who consequently won the contest by default.

AT THE LAST ELECTION

Chamber of Deputies 257 seats

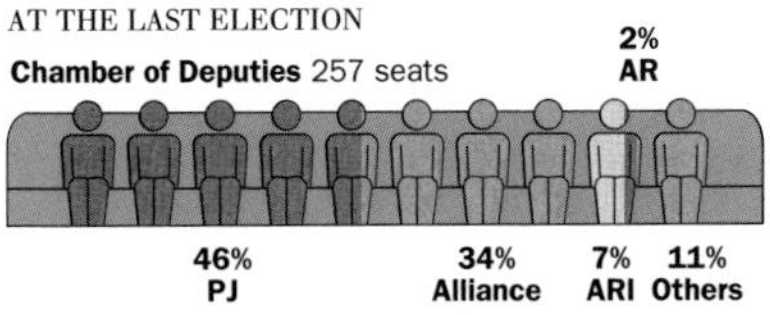
2%
AR
46%
PJ
34%
Alliance
7%
ARI
11%
Others

PJ = Justicialist Party (Peronists) **Alliance** = Alliance for Work, Justice, and Education (Radical Civic Union–**UCR** and National Solidarity Front Alliance–**FREPASO**) **ARI** = Alternative for a Republic of Equals **AR** = Action for the Republic

Senate 72 seats

55%
PJ
35%
Alliance
10%
Others

MAIN POLITICAL ISSUES

Durability of government

The nature of Kirchner's electoral victory in 2003 raised the prospect of struggles within a Peronist party divided by rival loyalties, jeopardizing the passage of serious reforms. In the absence of a trusted opposition, the public remains deeply cynical of traditional party politics. Principal concerns are corruption, governmental transparency, and an end to the socially divisive free-market macroeconomics of the 1990s.

Recovery from economic collapse

A near cashless population was reduced to bartering in 2001–2002 by industrial collapse, fiscal austerity, and restrictions on bank withdrawals. Fragile signs of recovery emerged in early 2003. A long-awaited IMF agreement gave a temporary breathing space on debt repayments. Businesses responded well to a period of exchange-rate stability coupled with strong export earnings and the gradual recuperation of the crisis-ridden banking sector.

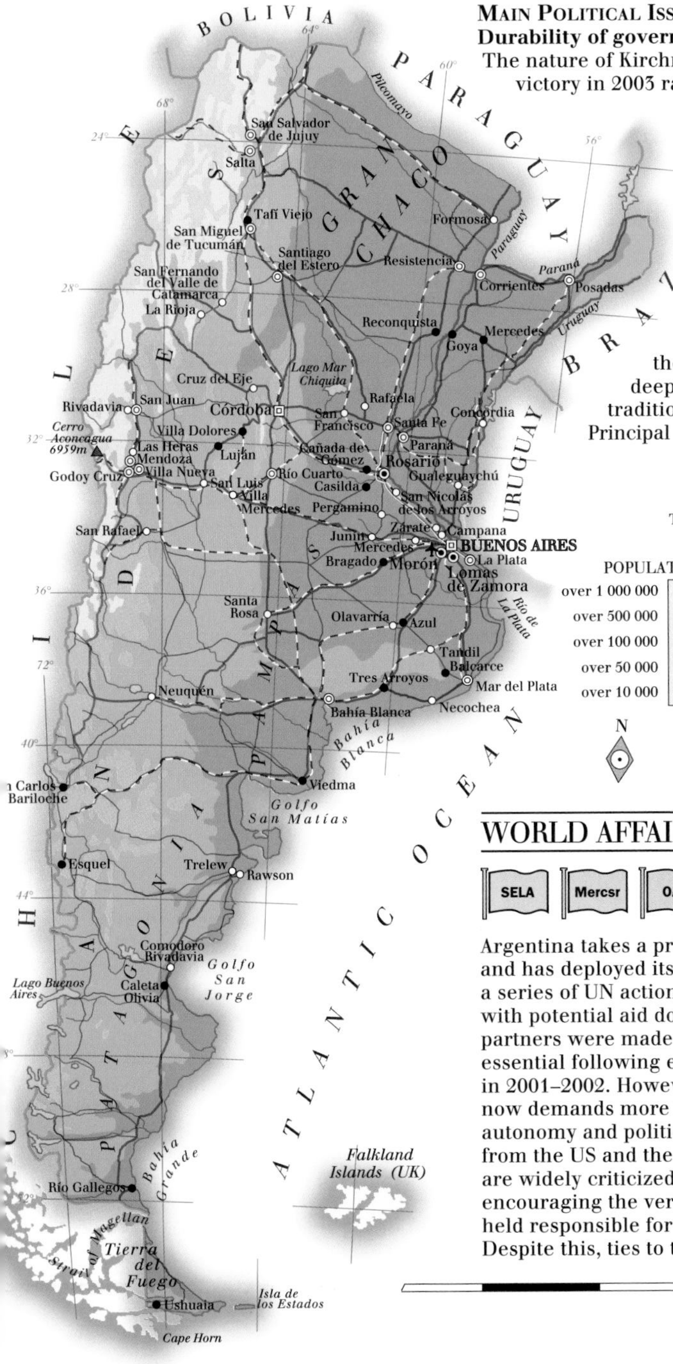
BOLIVIA
PARAGUAY
BRAZIL
URUGUAY
CHILE
ATLANTIC OCEAN
GRAN CHACO
PAMPAS
PATAGONIA
BUENOS AIRES
Córdoba
Rosario
Mendoza
San Miguel de Tucumán
Salta
San Salvador de Jujuy
Santiago del Estero
Resistencia
Corrientes
Formosa
Posadas
Santa Fe
Paraná
Mar del Plata
Bahía Blanca
La Plata
Lomas de Zamora
Morón
Neuquén
Viedma
Rawson
Trelew
Comodoro Rivadavia
Río Gallegos
Ushuaia
Tierra del Fuego
Falkland Islands (UK)
Cerro Aconcagua 6959m
Cape Horn
Isla de los Estados
Strait of Magellan

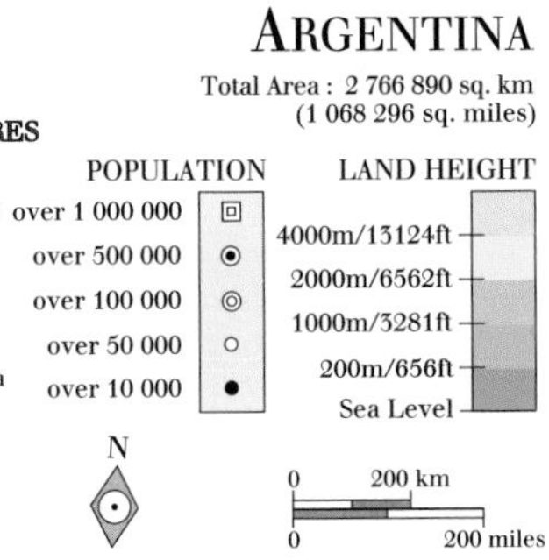
ARGENTINA
Total Area : 2 766 890 sq. km
(1 068 296 sq. miles)
POPULATION
over 1 000 000
over 500 000
over 100 000
over 50 000
over 10 000
LAND HEIGHT
4000m/13124ft
2000m/6562ft
1000m/3281ft
200m/656ft
Sea Level
N
0
200 km
0
200 miles

Carlos Menem: authoritarian rule overshadowed free-market reforms.

Néstor Kirchner defeated Menem in the 2003 presidential elections.

WORLD AFFAIRS

Joined UN in 1945

SELA | Mercsr | OAS | RG | G15

Argentina takes a pro-Western stance and has deployed its armed forces in a series of UN actions. Solid relations with potential aid donors and trade partners were made all the more essential following economic crisis in 2001–2002. However, public opinion now demands more regional economic autonomy and political independence from the US and the IMF, both of which are widely criticized by the public for encouraging the very economic policies held responsible for the recession. Despite this, ties to the US remain strong, although US pressure for an open-skies agreement and issues of royalty payments on patented drugs have created tensions.

Friction with Brazil over trade rules complicates Argentina's membership of Mercosur. It wants Mercosur to be strengthened, and widened to include Chile as a full member.

The normalizing of relations with the UK in 1998 sidelined Argentina's claim to sovereignty over the Falkland Islands (known locally as Las Islas Malvinas), the focus of the 1982 war between the two countries. Direct flights between the islands and the mainland have been permitted since 2001.

A

AID

Recipient

$151m (receipts) | Up 99% in 2001

Though one massive "financial shield" was agreed in 2001, the IMF's refusal of a further rescue package precipitated the crash in December that year.

CHRONOLOGY

The Spanish first established settlements in the Andean foothills in 1543. The indigenous Amerindians, who had stopped any Inca advance into their territory, also prevented the Spaniards from settling in the east until the 1590s.

- 1816 United Provinces of Río de la Plata declare independence; 70 years of civil war follow.
- 1835–1852 Dictatorship of Juan Manuel Rosas.
- 1853 Federal system set up.
- 1857 Europeans start settling the Pampas; six million by 1930.
- 1877 First refrigerated ship starts frozen beef trade to Europe.
- 1878–1883 War against Pampas Amerindians (almost exterminated).
- 1916 Hipólito Yrigoyen wins first democratic presidential elections.
- 1930 Military coup.
- 1943 New military coup. Gen. Juan Perón organizes trade unions.
- 1946 Perón elected president, with military and labor backing.
- 1952 Eva Perón, charismatic wife of Juan Perón, dies of leukemia.
- 1955 Military coup ousts Perón. Inflation, strikes, unemployment.
- 1973 Perón reelected president.
- 1974 Perón dies; succeeded by his third wife "Isabelita," who is unable to exercise control.
- 1976 Military junta seizes power. Political parties are banned. Brutal repression during "dirty war" sees "disappearance" of over 15,000 "left-wing suspects."
- 1981 Gen. Galtieri president.
- 1982 Galtieri orders invasion of Falkland Islands. UK retakes them.
- 1983 Pro-human rights candidate Raúl Alfonsín (UCR) elected president. Hyperinflation.
- 1989 Carlos Menem (Peronist) president.
- 1992 Inflation down to 25%.
- 1995 Economy enters recession.
- 1998–1999 Argentina weathers financial crisis in Brazil.
- 1999 Fernando de la Rúa of UCR–FREPASO alliance elected president.
- 2001 December, government is brought down by economic crisis.
- 2002 Eduardo Duhalde becomes fifth president in 12 days.
- 2003 Néstor Kirchner president by default after Menem pulls out of poll.

DEFENSE

No compulsory military service

$4.41bn | Down 8% in 2001

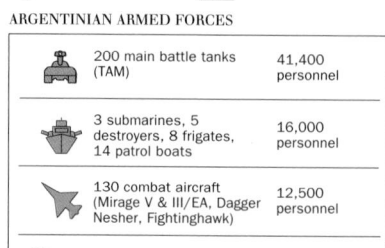

ARGENTINIAN ARMED FORCES

200 main battle tanks (TAM)	41,400 personnel
3 submarines, 5 destroyers, 8 frigates, 14 patrol boats	16,000 personnel
130 combat aircraft (Mirage V & III/EA, Dagger Nesher, Fightinghawk)	12,500 personnel
None	

The end of dictatorship led to trials and prison for the top brass, but subsequent immunity laws were meant to placate the military and close the chapter on the "dirty war" (1976–1983), during which some 15,000 to 30,000 were killed or "disappeared." The military made public admissions of guilt in 1995. A 2001 ruling, however, said that such immunity was unconstitutional, clearing the way for further trials of military personnel. Former junta leader Gen. Leopoldo Galtieri was arrested in 2002, but died the following year before his trial was completed. The armed forces now participate in international peacekeeping and see themselves as modernized. Nonetheless, President Kirchner felt the need to initiate an overhaul of the military leadership in early 2003.

ECONOMICS

Inflation 4.3% p.a. (1990–2001)

$260bn | 2.82 Argentine pesos (3.87)

SCORE CARD

World GNP Ranking	18th
GNP per Capita	$6940
Balance of Payments	–$4.55bn
Inflation	–1.1%
Unemployment	16%

EXPORTS

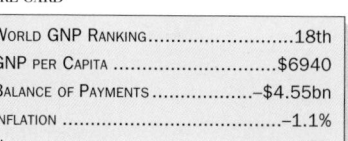

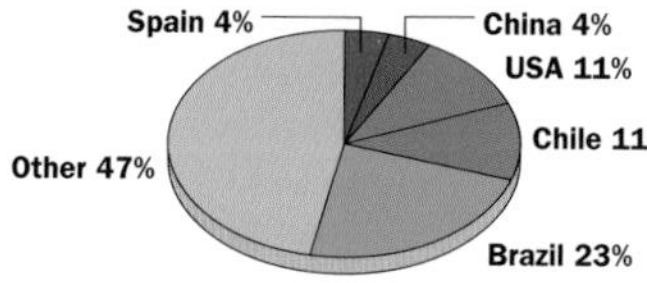
Spain 4%
China 4%
USA 11%
Chile 11%
Brazil 23%
Other 47%

IMPORTS

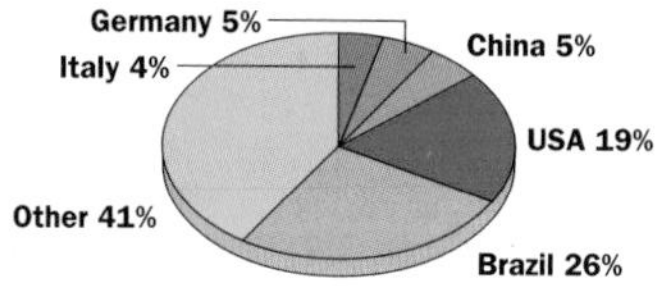
Germany 5%
Italy 4%
China 5%
USA 19%
Brazil 26%
Other 41%

Strengths

Rich and varied agricultural base. Powerful agribusiness (mainly beef, soybean, wheat, fruit, and wine) and wealth of energy resources. Net exporter of oil. Weakened peso boosted exports.

Weaknesses

Vulnerability to external shocks and downturns in Brazil (largest single export market). Investors scared by changes in assessment of country risk in emerging markets. Heavy debts, public and private, to refinance. Weak banking sector. Global fluctuations in prices of vital non-oil commodities. High unemployment and risk of unrest. Endemic tax evasion. Subsidies and trade barriers bar agricultural produce from US and EU.

ECONOMIC PERFORMANCE INDICATOR

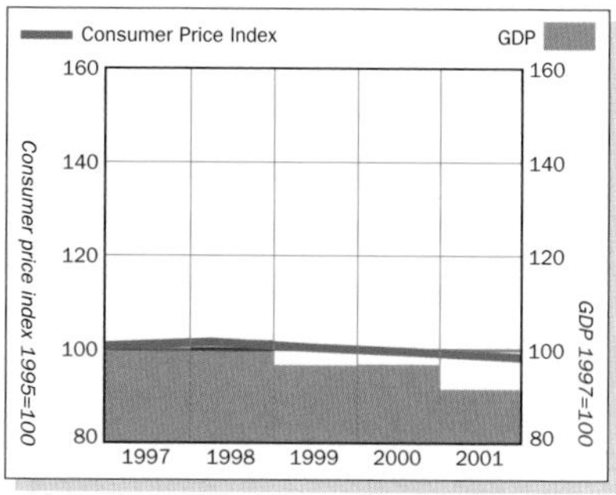
Consumer Price Index
GDP
160
140
120
100
80
Consumer price index 1995=100
GDP 1997=100
1997
1998
1999
2000
2001

Profile

The "miracle" recovery of the 1990s was based on stabilizing the peso (by pegging it to the US dollar) and on a combination of neoliberal reforms accompanied by privatization. Argentina rode out the Mexican crisis of 1995, but was hit by damage to foreign investor confidence and a shrinking Brazilian market in 1998–1999. Regional recession in 2001 brought economic crisis, and the world's largest default on international debt.

ARGENTINA : MAJOR BUSINESSES

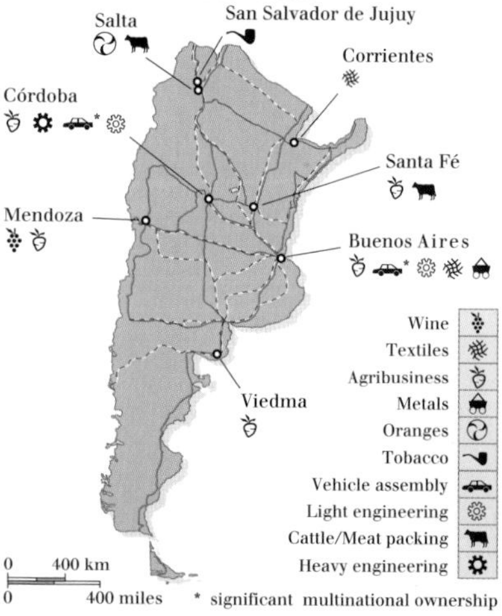
Salta
San Salvador de Jujuy
Corrientes
Córdoba
Santa Fé
Mendoza
Buenos Aires
Viedma
Wine
Textiles
Agribusiness
Metals
Oranges
Tobacco
Vehicle assembly
Light engineering
Cattle/Meat packing
Heavy engineering
0 400 km
0 400 miles
* significant multinational ownership

RESOURCES

▷ Electric power 23.7m kW

919,509 tonnes

800,000 b/d (reserves 2.9bn barrels)

50.7m cattle, 14m sheep, 4.25m pigs, 110m chickens

Oil, natural gas, coal, iron, zinc, lead, uranium, tin, silver, copper, gold

ELECTRICITY GENERATION

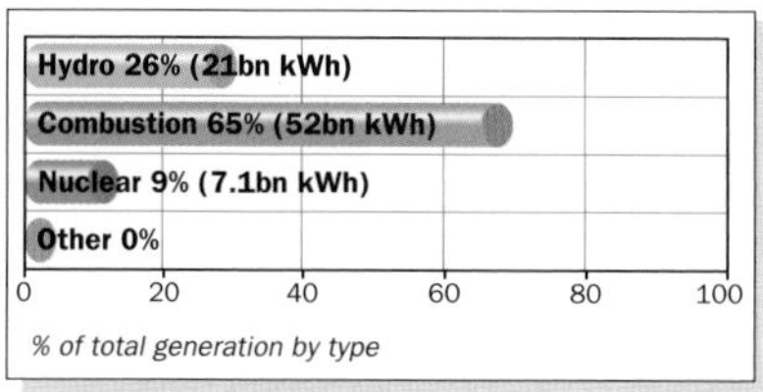
Hydro 26% (21bn kWh)
Combustion 65% (52bn kWh)
Nuclear 9% (7.1bn kWh)
Other 0%
0
20
40
60
80
100
% of total generation by type

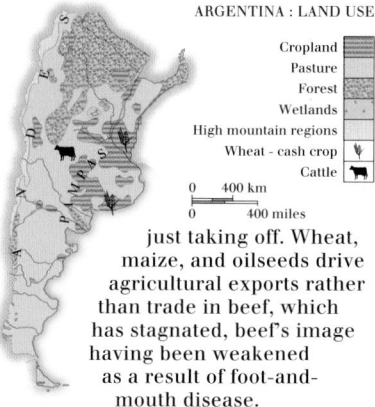

ARGENTINA : LAND USE

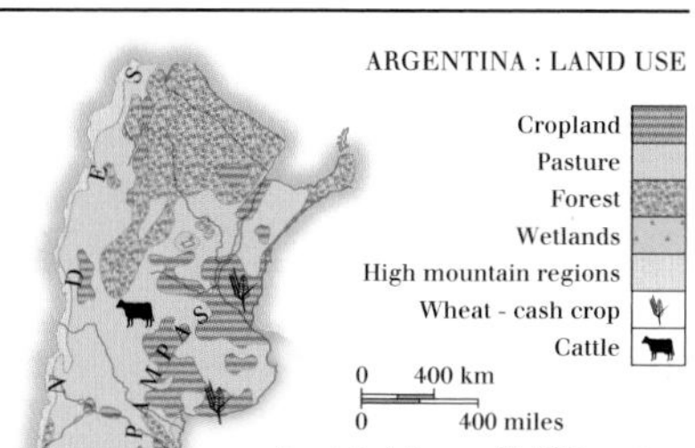
Cropland
Pasture
Forest
Wetlands
High mountain regions
Wheat - cash crop
Cattle
0 400 km
0 400 miles
PAMPAS

Oil and gas are now major exports; reserves are becoming increasingly exploited. Copper and gold mining are just taking off. Wheat, maize, and oilseeds drive agricultural exports rather than trade in beef, which has stagnated, beef's image having been weakened as a result of foot-and-mouth disease.

ENVIRONMENT

▷ Sustainability rank: 15th

7% (2% partially protected)

3.8 tonnes per capita

ENVIRONMENTAL TREATIES

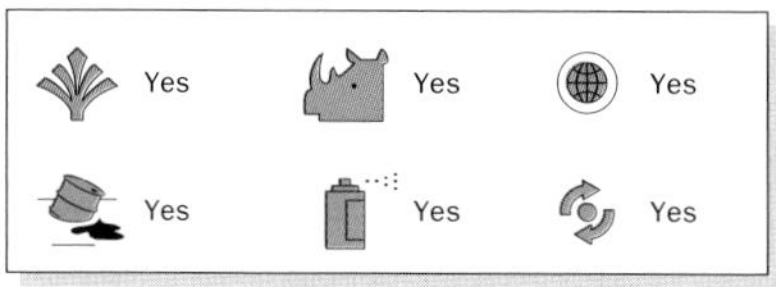
Yes
Yes
Yes
Yes
Yes
Yes

Environmental protection has low governmental priority. Legislation is weak and largely ignored by states, which retain a good deal of autonomy. Political parties typically shy away from the level of public spending needed to tackle major environmental problems, and a corrupt judiciary has meant poor enforcement of existing laws. Key problems are hazardous waste, poor urban water and air quality, inadequate sewers, pesticide contamination due to agribusiness, deforestation, and illegal hunting.

MEDIA

▷ TV ownership high

Daily newspaper circulation 56 per 1000 people

PUBLISHING AND BROADCAST MEDIA

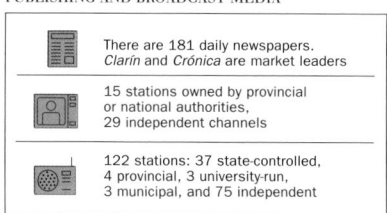

There are 181 daily newspapers. *Clarín* and *Crónica* are market leaders

15 stations owned by provincial or national authorities, 29 independent channels

122 stations: 37 state-controlled, 4 provincial, 3 university-run, 3 municipal, and 75 independent

Many journalists were murdered by the military in the 1970s, but the press was liberated under the UCR (1983–1989) and harries governments, especially on corruption. Investigative journalists, however, still face intimidation.

The Internet had reached over 10% of the population by 2001.

CRIME

▷ Death penalty not used in practice

38,604 prisoners

Up 61% in 2000–2001

CRIME RATES

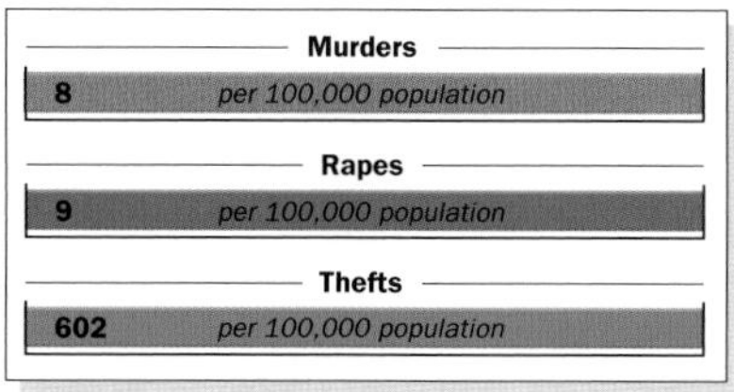
Murders
8 per 100,000 population
Rapes
9 per 100,000 population
Thefts
602 per 100,000 population

Economic collapse has led to increased levels of violent crime. Ordinary people have responded by buying more guns. The judiciary and the police command little respect. Overcrowded prisons lead to frequent riots, and criminal cases can take over a year to reach court.

EDUCATION

▷ School leaving age: 14

97%

1.6m students

THE EDUCATION SYSTEM

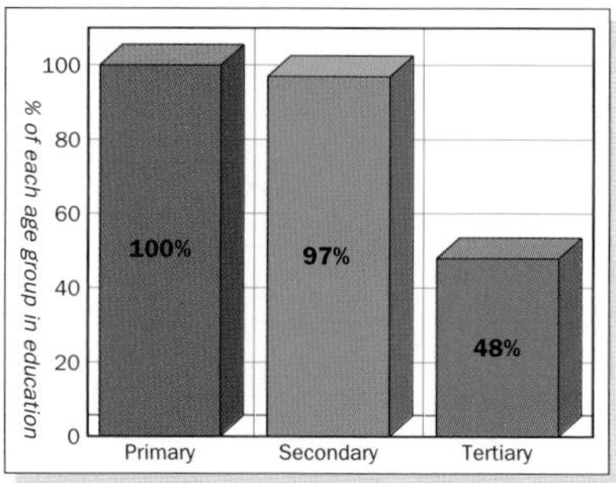
100
80
60
40
20
0
% of each age group in education
100%
97%
48%
Primary
Secondary
Tertiary

Public schooling is free and compulsory to the age of 14. Huge numbers of poor students drop out of the system near or after this age. Middle-class students began to enter the public system en masse as the economy faltered, forcing thousands of private schools to close. There are more private universities than state-run institutions.

HEALTH

▷ Welfare state health benefits

1 per 340 people

Cancers, heart diseases, accidents

There are more than 1000 state-run hospitals, but free state provision suffers from underfunding, poorly paid staff, and long queues. Government-sponsored vaccination programs, mother-and-child schemes, feeding programs, and rural health projects barely tackle such problems as malnutrition, lack of decent sanitation, and threadbare medical cover in the poorest provinces. A health care deregulation bill was decreed in 2001 to dismantle the trade unions' monopoly of health insurance schemes.

SPENDING

▷ GDP/cap. increase

CONSUMPTION AND SPENDING

140 per 1000 population

224 per 1000 population

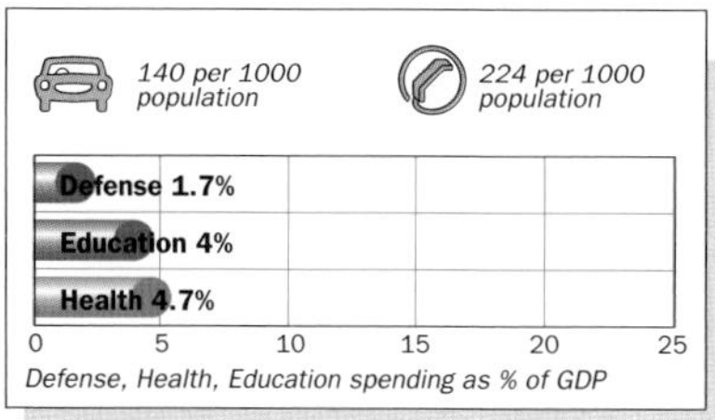
Defense 1.7%
Education 4%
Health 4.7%
0
5
10
15
20
25
Defense, Health, Education spending as % of GDP

Members of the wealthy elite, who travel in private jets to *estancias* (country estates), vacation in Europe and the US, and hold dollar accounts offshore to avoid tax, escaped the worst of the economic collapse in 2001–2002. Middle-income groups, squeezed after years of free-market reforms, lost out in the crisis which forced some 15 million below the poverty line, with four million in extreme poverty. Emergency government aid offered in 2002 to one million unemployed people with children under 18 was at a level below half the legal minimum salary. The precrisis figure of some 40% of workers in the low-wage black economy was set to balloon. Millions of cashless and poor people resorted to exchanging goods at barter clubs.

WORLD RANKING

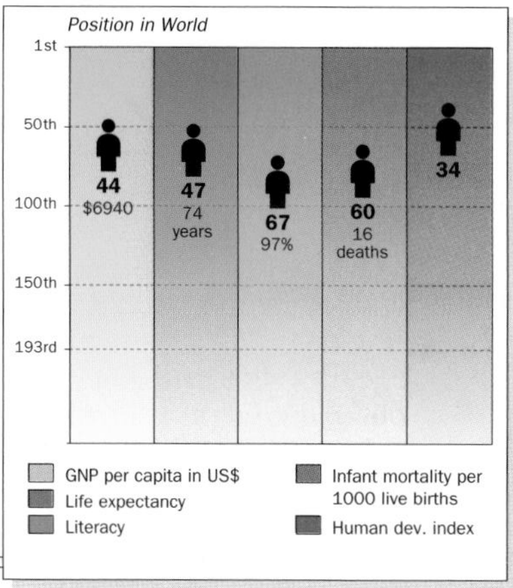
Position in World
1st
50th
100th
150th
193rd
44
$6940
47
74 years
67
97%
60
16 deaths
34
GNP per capita in US$
Life expectancy
Literacy
Infant mortality per 1000 live births
Human dev. index

A

ARMENIA

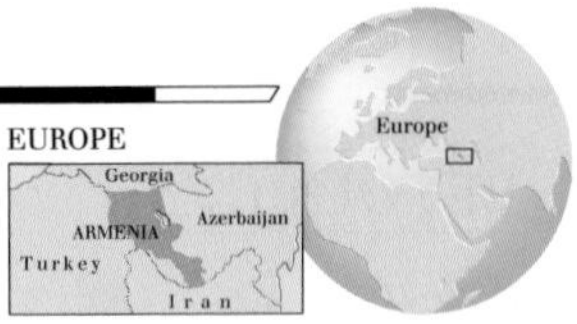
EUROPE
Europe
Georgia
ARMENIA
Azerbaijan
Turkey
Iran

OFFICIAL NAME: Republic of Armenia **CAPITAL:** Yerevan
POPULATION: 3.8 million **CURRENCY:** Dram **OFFICIAL LANGUAGE:** Armenian

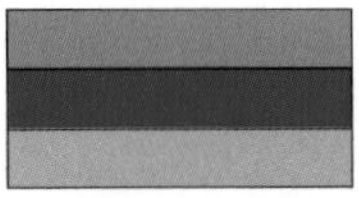

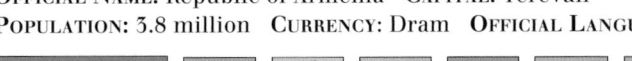

1991 | 1991 | Sept 21 | ARM | +4 | +374 | .am

LANDLOCKED IN THE Lesser Caucasus mountains, Armenia is the smallest of the former Soviet republics. It was the first country to adopt Christianity as its state religion, early in the 4th century. Keen to deepen links with the rest of the CIS, Armenia has kept to a path of radical economic reform, including privatization. The confrontation with Azerbaijan over the exclave of Nagornyy Karabakh has dominated national life since 1988.

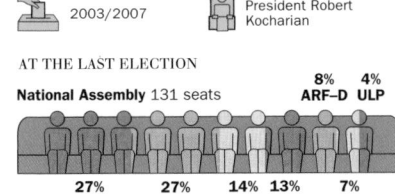

Landscape near Yerevan. *Armenia's very dry climate results in expanses of semidesert. Its famous vineyards flourish in sheltered areas.*

CLIMATE

Mountain

WEATHER CHART FOR YEREVAN

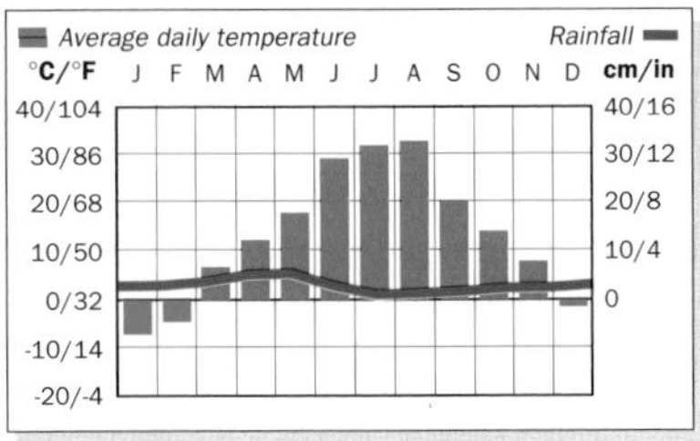
Average daily temperature
Rainfall
°C/°F
J F M A M J J A S O N D
cm/in
40/104
30/86
20/68
10/50
0/32
-10/14
-20/-4
40/16
30/12
20/8
10/4
0

Armenia has a continental climate, with little rainfall in the lowlands. Winters can be very cold.

TRANSPORTATION

Drive on right

Yerevan International

Has no fleet

THE TRANSPORTATION NETWORK

15,998 km (9941 miles)

7567 km (4702 miles)

842 km (523 miles)

None

Fuel prices are high due to a blockade imposed by neighboring Azerbaijan. Road and rail links with Georgia, connecting with the main east–west corridor, need upgrading.

TOURISM

Visitors : Population 1:127

30,000 visitors

Down 27% in 2000

MAIN TOURIST ARRIVALS

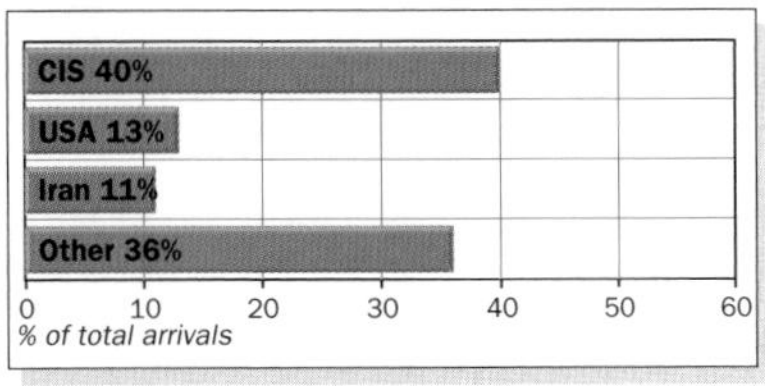
CIS 40%
USA 13%
Iran 11%
Other 36%
0
10
20
30
40
50
60
% of total arrivals

The 1700th anniversary of Armenian Christianity in 2001 boosted the war-damaged tourist industry. Most visitors are diaspora Armenians.

PEOPLE

Pop. density medium

Armenian, Russian

128/km² (330/mi²)

THE URBAN/RURAL POPULATION SPLIT

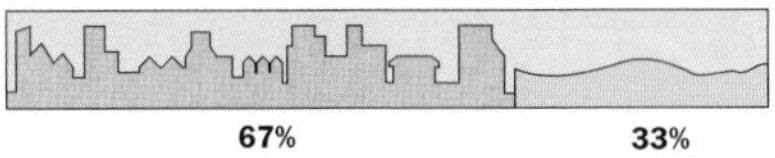
67%
33%

ETHNIC MAKEUP

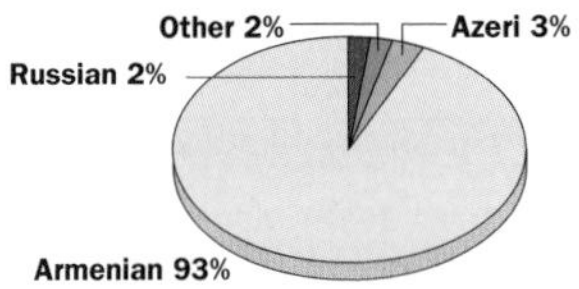
Other 2%
Azeri 3%
Russian 2%
Armenian 93%

Minority nationalities are well integrated in Armenia. There are strong contacts with the many Armenian emigrants, numbering over seven million, principally in the US, France, and Syria.

Conflict with Azerbaijan forced the repatriation of 350,000 Armenians and 190,000 Azeris. The small Russian population is centered in Yerevan.

POLITICS

Multiparty elections

2003/2007

President Robert Kocharian

AT THE LAST ELECTION

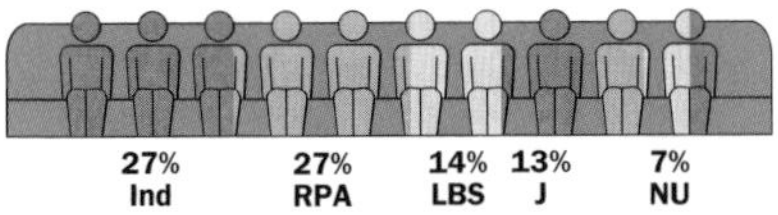
National Assembly 131 seats
8% ARF–D
4% ULP
27% Ind
27% RPA
14% LBS
13% J
7% NU

Ind = Independents **RPA** = Republican Party of Armenia
LBS = Law-based State **J** = Justice Bloc
ARF–D = Armenian Revolutionary Federation–Dashnaktsutyun
NU = National Unity **ULP** = United Labor Party

A multiparty democracy since 1991, Armenia held its first legislative elections in 1995. The war with Azerbaijan, over the separatist ambitions of the Armenian exclave of Nagorno Karabakh (inside Azerbaijan), has simmered since a 1994 cease-fire. Levon Ter-Petrossian, the country's first president, resigned in 1998 after parliament opposed his softer line in search of peace. He was succeeded by Robert Kocharian, a former premier and ex-governor of Nagorno Karabakh. In 1999, RPA prime minister Vazgen Sarkissian was shot dead in a dramatic attack in parliament. He was succeeded first by his brother Aram, then in 2000 by Andranik Markarian. Kocharian was reelected in a disputed ballot in early 2003. His authoritarian rule has provoked large-scale protests.

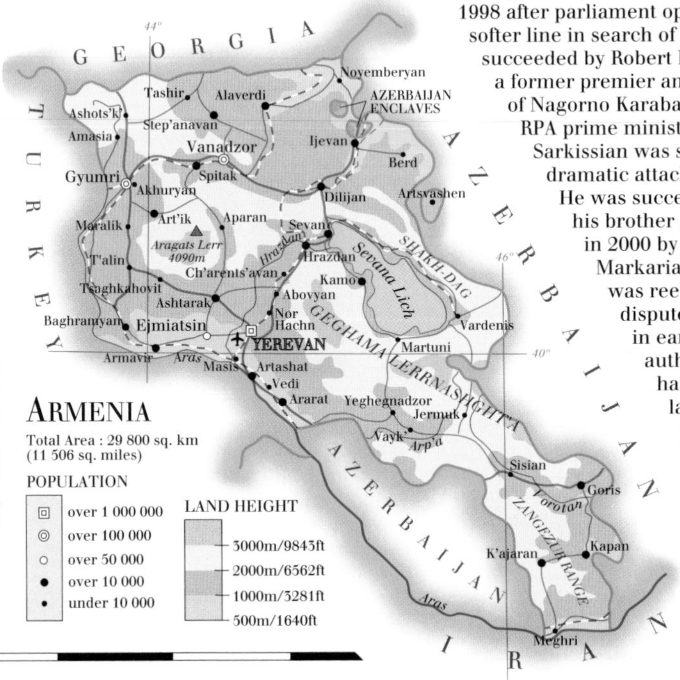
GEORGIA
TURKEY
AZERBAIJAN
IRAN
Noyemberyan
AZERBAIJAN ENCLAVES
Tashir
Alaverdi
Ashots'k'
Step'anavan
Amasia
Vanadzor
Ijevan
Berd
Gyumri
Spitak
Akhuryan
Dilijan
Artsvashen
Maralik
Art'ik
Aparan
Sevan
Aragats Lerr 4090m
Hrazdan
T'alin
Ch'arents'avan
Sevana Lich
SHAKH-DAG
Kamo
Tsaghkahovit
Ashtarak
Abovyan
Nor Hachn
GEGHAMA
Baghramyan
Ejmiatsin
Vardenis
YEREVAN
Martuni
Armavir
Aras
Masis
Artashat
Vedi
Ararat
Yeghegnadzor
Jermuk
VARDENIS LERRNASHGHTA
Vayk'
Arp'a
Sisian
Goris
Vorotan
ZANGEZUR RANGE
K'ajaran
Kapan
Meghri
ARMENIA
Total Area : 29 800 sq. km (11 506 sq. miles)
POPULATION
over 1 000 000
over 100 000
over 50 000
over 10 000
under 10 000
LAND HEIGHT
3000m/9843ft
2000m/6562ft
1000m/3281ft
500m/1640ft
N
0
50 km

WORLD AFFAIRS

Joined UN in 1992

BSEC | CIS | CE | EAPC | OSCE

Continuing tension with Azerbaijan is diplomatically damaging. A Turkish trade embargo has been in place since 1988. Russia has been less pro-Armenian since Azerbaijan rejoined the CIS. A Council of Europe member since 2001, Armenia faces criticism for imprisoning Jehovah's Witnesses who refuse military service on religious grounds.

AID

Recipient

$212m (receipts) — Down 2% in 2001

Expatriates such as US billionaire Kirk Kerkorian are a major source of funds. Control of utilities has passed to Russia in lieu of debt payments.

DEFENSE

Compulsory military service

$637m — Down 8% in 2001

Successes in the fighting over the Nagorno Karabakh exclave in Azerbaijan increased the profile and autonomy of the army, which includes conscripts on 24-month national service. A cease-fire has broadly held since 1994, but fresh peace talks, held in 1999–2000, proved to be inconclusive.

ECONOMICS

Inflation 172% p.a. (1990–2001)

$2.17bn — 558.1 drams (582.4)

SCORE CARD

❑ World GNP Ranking	136th
❑ GNP per Capita	$570
❑ Balance of Payments	–$201m
❑ Inflation	2.9%
❑ Unemployment	12%

Strengths

Strong ties with Armenian emigrants. Deposits of rare metals, currently unexploited. Machine building and manufacturing – includes textiles and bottling mineral water. Development of private sector.

Weaknesses

Dependent on imported energy, raw materials, and semifinished goods. High unemployment. Corruption.

EXPORTS

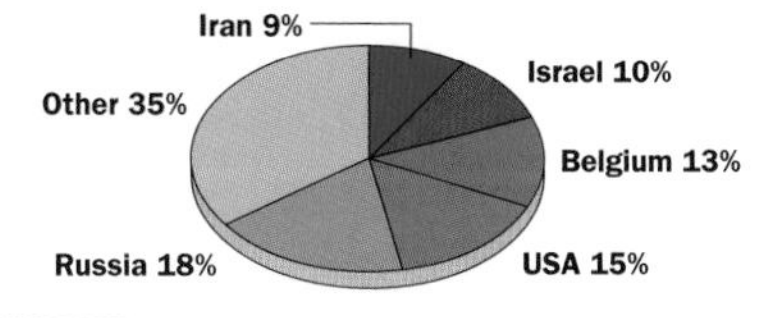
Iran 9%
Israel 10%
Other 35%
Belgium 13%
Russia 18%
USA 15%

IMPORTS

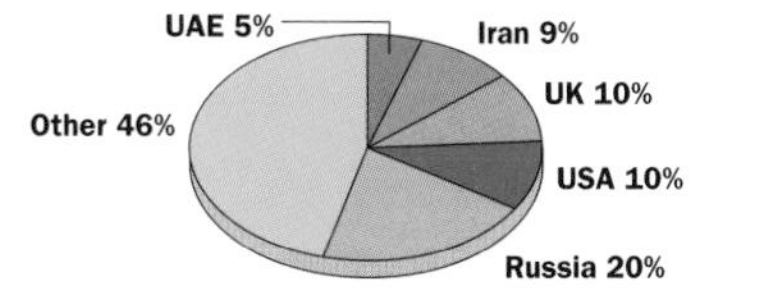
UAE 5%
Iran 9%
UK 10%
Other 46%
USA 10%
Russia 20%

RESOURCES

Electric power 3m kW

2007 tonnes — Minimal oil production

555,000 sheep, 520,000 cattle, 4.5m chickens — Coal, oil, natural gas, rare metals

Energy resources are negligible, and mismanagement of the energy industry was deemed to have cost the country $200 million in the 1990s. Vegetables and fruit are grown in fertile lowlands, and grains in the hills; agriculture accounts for over a fifth of GDP.

ENVIRONMENT

Sustainability rank: 38th

8% — 1 tonne per capita

Environmental groups, backed by the EU, demand the closure of the Medzamor nuclear power station, declared unsafe after the 1988 earthquake, but reopened in 1995 owing to the energy crisis. HEP generation near Lake Sevan has seriously lowered its water level.

MEDIA

TV ownership medium

Daily newspaper circulation 5 per 1000 people

PUBLISHING AND BROADCAST MEDIA

There are 11 daily newspapers, including *Azg, Haiastan*, and *Ankakhutiun*

1 state-controlled service, several independent stations — 1 state-controlled service, several independent stations

Numerous TV and broadcasting stations assist media freedom. Independent journals and newspapers depend on the government-controlled paper industry.

CRIME

Death penalty not used in practice

7428 prisoners — Up 42% in 2000–2002

Reforms to the legal system introduced in 1999 included the replacement of the Supreme Court by an appeals court. Assassinations of political figures are common.

EDUCATION

School leaving age: 17

99% — 68,704 students

The education system, previously conforming to that of the USSR, now emphasizes Armenian history and culture. One in eight adults have received higher education.

CHRONOLOGY

Armenia lost its autonomy in the 14th century. In 1639, Turkey took the west and Persia the east; Persia ceded its part to Russia in 1828.

- ❑ **1877–1878** Massacre of Armenians during Russo-Turkish war.
- ❑ **1915** Ottomans exile 1.75 million Turkish Armenians; most die.
- ❑ **1920** Independence.
- ❑ **1922** Becomes a Soviet republic.
- ❑ **1988** Earthquake kills 25,000. Conflict with Azerbaijan over Nagorno Karabakh begins.
- ❑ **1991** Independence from USSR.
- ❑ **1994** Cease-fire with Azerbaijan.
- ❑ **1995** First parliamentary elections.
- ❑ **1998** Kocharian elected president.
- ❑ **1999** Prime minister assassinated.
- ❑ **2003** Kocharian reelected.

HEALTH

No welfare state health benefits

1 per 328 people — Cerebrovascular and heart diseases, cancers

Hospitals suffer from the erratic electricity supply. Poor sewerage and other services have led to a rise in hepatitis, tuberculosis, and cholera.

SPENDING

GDP/cap. decrease

CONSUMPTION AND SPENDING

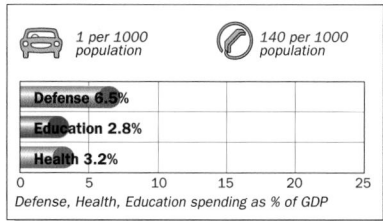

1 per 1000 population — *140 per 1000 population*

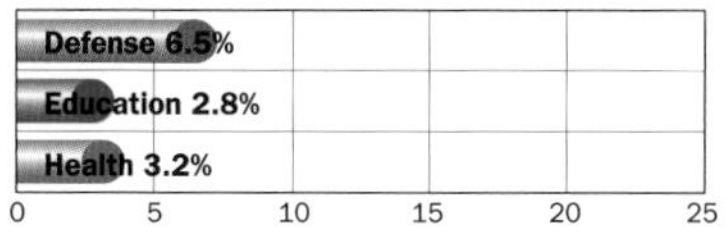
Defense 6.5%
Education 2.8%
Health 3.2%
0
5
10
15
20
25

Defense, Health, Education spending as % of GDP

The richest Armenian people are those living away from Armenia itself, particularly in the US and France. The many refugees from Baku, Azerbaijan, are the poorest.

WORLD RANKING

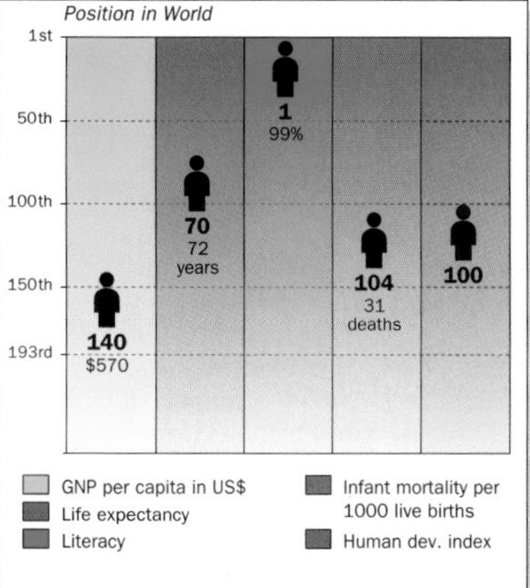
Position in World
1st
50th
100th
150th
193rd
140
$570
70
72
years
1
99%
104
31
deaths
100
GNP per capita in US$
Life expectancy
Literacy
Infant mortality per 1000 live births
Human dev. index

A

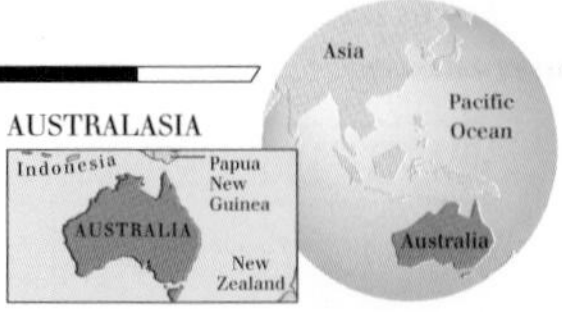
AUSTRALASIA
Indonesia
Papua New Guinea
AUSTRALIA
New Zealand
Asia
Pacific Ocean
Australia

AUSTRALIA

OFFICIAL NAME: Commonwealth of Australia **CAPITAL:** Canberra
POPULATION: 19.5 million **CURRENCY:** Australian dollar **OFFICIAL LANGUAGE:** English

1901
1901
Jan 26
AUS
+8 to +11
+61
.au

THE WORLD'S SIXTH-LARGEST country, Australia is an island continent located between the Indian and Pacific Oceans. Its varied landscapes include tropical rainforests, the deserts of the arid "red center," snowcapped mountains, rolling tracts of pastoral land, and magnificent beaches. Famous natural features include Uluru (Ayers Rock) and the Great Barrier Reef. Most Australians live on the coast, and all the state capitals, including Sydney, host of the 2000 Olympics, are coastal cities. Only Canberra, the national capital, lies inland. The vast interior is dotted with large reserves, sparsely inhabited by communities from the small Aboriginal population.

Uluru (Ayers Rock), Northern Territory. *The renaming of Ayers Rock reflects growing Aboriginal influence on Australian culture.*

CLIMATE

Hot desert/steppe/tropical/Mediterranean

WEATHER CHART FOR CANBERRA

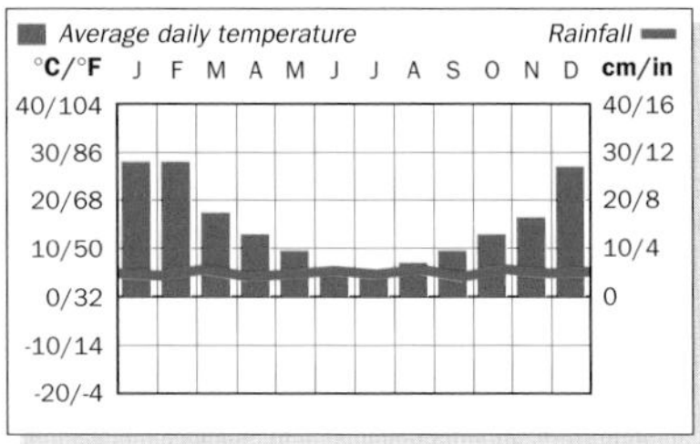
Average daily temperature
Rainfall
°C/°F J F M A M J J A S O N D cm/in
40/104
30/86
20/68
10/50
0/32
-10/14
-20/4
40/16
30/12
20/8
10/4
0

The interior, west, and south are arid or semiarid and very hot in summer; central desert temperatures can reach 50°C (122°F). The north, around Darwin and Cape York Peninsula, is hot all year and humid during the summer monsoon. Only the east and southeast, within 400 km (250 miles) of the coast, and the southwest, around Perth, are temperate: most Australians live in these areas.

TRANSPORTATION

Drive on left

Kingsford Smith, Sydney 23.9m passengers

622 ships 1.89m grt

THE TRANSPORTATION NETWORK

353,331 km (219,549 miles)

1363 km (847 miles)

39,848 km (24,760 miles)

8368 km (5200 miles)

Air transportation is well developed and vital to Australia's sparsely populated center and west. Sydney suffers from air congestion, but proposals for a new West Sydney airport remain controversial. A proposed high-speed train network on the east coast has been shelved due to cost. Most long-distance freight in Australia travels in massive trucks known as "road trains." Improvements in urban transportation are a priority and gained impetus in Sydney from the 2000 Olympic Games.

TOURISM

Visitors : Population 1:4

4.84m visitors

Little change in 2002

MAIN TOURIST ARRIVALS

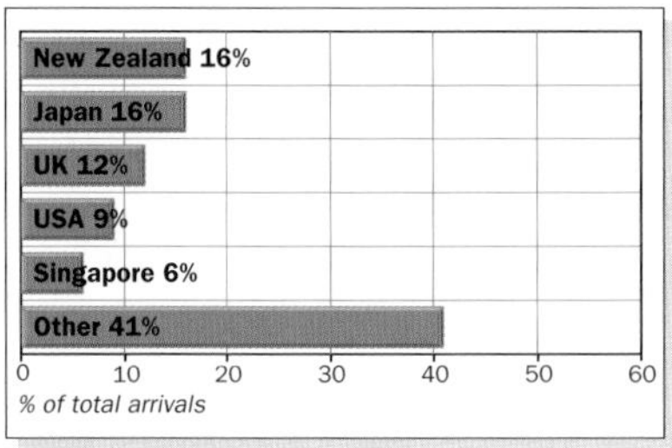
New Zealand 16%
Japan 16%
UK 12%
USA 9%
Singapore 6%
Other 41%
0 10 20 30 40 50 60
% of total arrivals

Tourism is now one of Australia's largest single foreign exchange earners. Faster, cheaper air travel and highly successful government marketing campaigns, both on a national and a state level, attract tourists in increasing numbers. The focus during the 1990s on drawing tourists from nearby Asian countries left the Australian tourist industry vulnerable after the Asian financial crisis of 1997. In recent years New Zealanders have equaled the Japanese as the largest category of visitors to Australia. However, tourists from southeast Asia continue to arrive in significant numbers.

The country's many attractions include wildlife, swimming and surfing off Pacific and Indian Ocean beaches, skin diving along the Great Barrier Reef, and skiing in the Australian Alps. Uluru, Aboriginal culture, and the town of Alice Springs are among the outback's attractions. The far north has tropical resorts, the northwest, pearl fishing. The vineyards of the south and southeast attract many visitors, as do the cultural life of Melbourne and Sydney and the arts festivals held in state capitals. Sydney's famous landmarks and cosmopolitan feel, as well as the world-renowned Bondi Beach, make it a favorite.

The mid-1980s saw a phenomenal boom; tourist arrivals almost tripled in five years to reach two million in 1990. Even though growth slowed during the early 1990s, by 2000 the number of visitors had reached almost five million, boosted greatly by the celebrated Sydney Olympic Games.

INDIAN OCEAN
Bonaparte Archipelago
Derby
Broome
Port Hedland
GREAT SA
DESERT
Onslow
Hamersley Range
Newman
Paraburdoo
Lake Disappo
WESTERN AUSTRALIA
Lake Macleod
Carnarvon
Shark Bay
Dirk Hartog Island
Lake Carnegie
Meekatharra
Mount Magnet
Geraldton
Kalgoorlie
Moora
Perth
Fremantle
Northam
Merredin
Norseman
Rockingham
Bunbury
Wagin
Collie
Bridgetown
Esperance
Ravensthorpe
Cape Leeuwin
Manjimup
Albany

AUSTRALIA

Total Area : 7 686 850 sq. km (2 967 893 sq. miles)

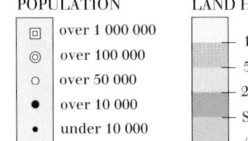

POPULATION	LAND HEIGHT
over 1 000 000	1000m/3281ft
over 100 000	500m/1640ft
over 50 000	200m/656ft
over 10 000	Sea Level
under 10 000	-200m/-656ft

PEOPLE

Pop. density low

English, Italian, Cantonese, Greek, Arabic, Vietnamese, Aboriginal languages

3/km² (7/mi²)

THE URBAN/RURAL POPULATION SPLIT

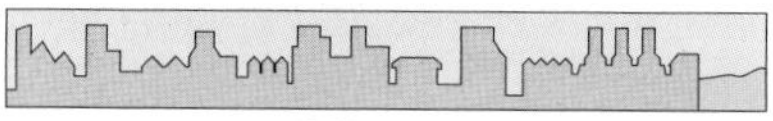
91%
9%

The first settlers arrived in Australia at least 100,000 years ago. Their modern descendants, the Aborigines, today make up less than 3% of the population. European settlement began in 1788 and was dominated by British and Irish immigrants – some of whom were convicts – until the gold rushes of the 1850s. Immigrants of other nationalities – including many Chinese – arrived to prospect for gold, then settled in the cities, especially Melbourne and Sydney. When the new federal government was installed in 1901, one of its first acts was to prevent further Chinese immigration. The act set out the "White Australia" policy, which conditioned attitudes to immigration for almost 70 years.

A massive immigration drive after World War II brought many more British settlers to Australia in the 1950s. Further government initiatives to "populate or perish" saw the arrival of large numbers of Italians and Greeks. From the late 1960s, the "White Australia" policy was progressively wound down. It was officially ended during the 1972–1975 Whitlam administration. Ever since, up to 50% of immigrants each year have come from Asia, transforming Australia from an almost exclusively European enclave into a multicultural society in which immigrant groups are encouraged to maintain connections with their own cultures and languages.

Aborigines, the exception in an otherwise integrated society, number around 410,000. Economically and socially marginalized, they face considerable discrimination. Until the mid-1960s, they were denied the vote and full social benefits. Their land had been occupied as *terra nullius* – belonging to no one. Since the 1970s, Aborigines have made a more organized stand on land and civil rights. Native title to land was recognized in 1993, though controversies continue over the extent of its application. Civil rights campaigns have moved on from the initial phase of antiracist protests to demand greater equality in areas such as health, housing, and education. Average life expectancy is still 20 years lower than the rest of the population. Alcoholism is a pervasive problem both in towns and rural areas. Aborigines in urban areas may be relatively better housed but face particular problems in asserting their cultural identity.

During the 1950s and 1960s, Catholic–Protestant differences were sufficient to cause a rift in the ALP. However, a subsequent policy encouraging mixed denomination schooling, coupled with a decline in religious observance, has largely neutralized the issue.

PAPUA NEW GUINEA
ARAFURA SEA
Torres Strait
GREAT BARRIER REEF
CORAL SEA
Gulf of Carpentaria
Darwin
Katherine
Arnham Land
Cooktown
Cairns
Karumba
Townsville
Mount Isa
Cloncurry
Hughenden
Mackay
Winton
Longreach
Rockhampton
Emerald
NORTHERN TERRITORY
QUEENSLAND
Alice Springs
Tennant Creek
TANAMI DESERT
Great Artesian Basin
SIMPSON DESERT
Birdsville
Charleville
Bundaberg
Maryborough
Gympie
Brisbane
Gold Coast
Surfers Paradise
Toowoomba
Ipswich
Cunnamulla
Lismore
SOUTH AUSTRALIA
Lake Eyre
Uluru (Ayers Rock)
Moree
Grafton
Armidale
Coffs Harbour
Bourke
Tamworth
Port Macquarie
Taree
Broken Hill
NEW SOUTH WALES
Dubbo
Maitland
Newcastle
Gosford
Port Augusta
Whyalla
Port Pirie
Orange
Bathurst
Lithgow
Sydney
Wollongong
Goulburn
Queanbeyan
CANBERRA
AUST. CAPITAL TERRITORY
Adelaide
Mildura
Griffith
Wagga Wagga
Albury
Port Lincoln
Kangaroo I.
VICTORIA
Shepparton
Bendigo
Horsham
Ballarat
Melbourne
Mount Gambier
Warrnambool
Geelong
Traralgon
Sale
Morwell
Bass Strait
TASMAN SEA
SOUTH PACIFIC OCEAN
Great Australian Bight
Flinders I.
King I.
Burnie
Devonport
Launceston
TASMANIA
Hobart
0 400 km
0 400 miles

RELIGIOUS PERSUASION

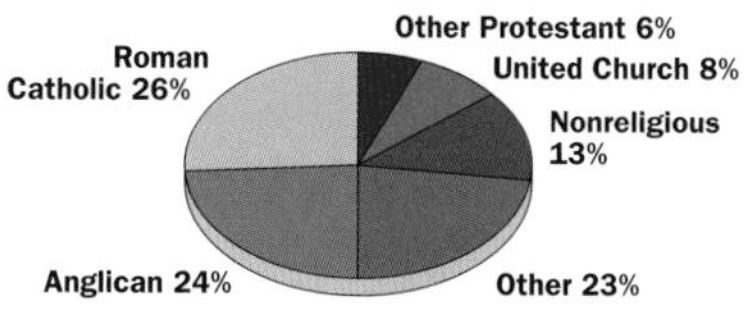
Other Protestant 6%
Roman Catholic 26%
United Church 8%
Nonreligious 13%
Anglican 24%
Other 23%

ETHNIC MAKEUP

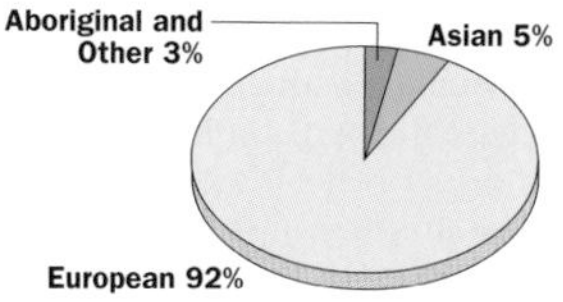
Aboriginal and Other 3%
Asian 5%
European 92%

POPULATION AGE BREAKDOWN

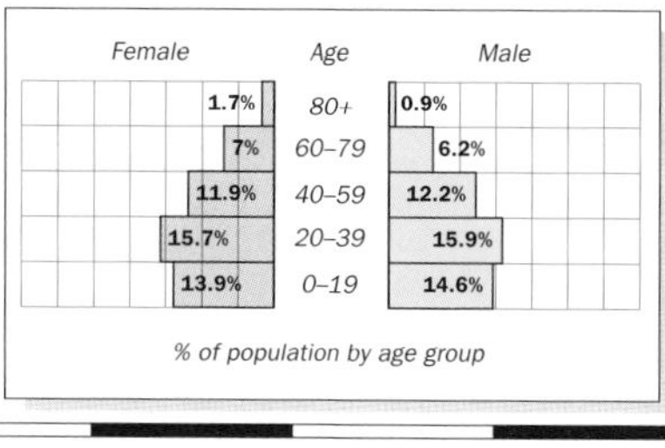
Female
Age
Male
1.7%
80+
0.9%
7%
60–79
6.2%
11.9%
40–59
12.2%
15.7%
20–39
15.9%
13.9%
0–19
14.6%
% of population by age group

A

CHRONOLOGY

Dutch, Portuguese, French, and – decisively – British incursions throughout the 17th and 18th centuries signaled the end of millennia of Aboriginal isolation. Governor Arthur Philip raised the British Union Flag at Sydney Cove on January 26, 1788.

- ❑ **1901** Inauguration of Commonwealth of Australia.
- ❑ **1915** Australian troops suffer heavy casualties at Gallipoli.
- ❑ **1939** Prime Minister Robert Menzies announces Australia will follow UK into war with Germany.
- ❑ **1942** Fall of Singapore to Japanese army. Japanese invasion of Australia seems imminent. Government turns to US for help.
- ❑ **1950** Australian troops committed to UN/US Korean War against North Korean communists.
- ❑ **1962** Menzies government commits Australian aid to war in Vietnam.
- ❑ **1966** Adopts decimal currency.
- ❑ **1972** Whitlam government elected. Aid to South Vietnam ceases.
- ❑ **1975** Whitlam government dismissed by Governor-General Sir John Kerr. Malcolm Fraser forms coalition government.
- ❑ **1983** Bob Hawke becomes prime minister of ALP administration.
- ❑ **1985** Corporate boom followed by deepening recession.
- ❑ **1992** Paul Keating defeats Hawke in leadership vote, becomes prime minister; announces "Turning toward Asia" policy. High Court's "Mabo Judgment" recognizes Aboriginal land rights.
- ❑ **1993** Against most predictions, Keating's ALP government reelected. Native Title Act provides compensation for Aboriginal rights extinguished by existing land title.
- ❑ **1996** Liberal John Howard prime minister. Shooting of 35 people in Tasmania prompts tightening of gun control laws. First death under Northern Territory's controversial euthanasia legislation; legislation later overruled at federal level.
- ❑ **1998** Elections: Howard's Liberal and National coalition retains power with reduced majority; fears of right-wing One Nation party breakthrough prove unfounded.
- ❑ **1999** Referendum rejects proposals to replace Queen as head of state by indirectly elected president.
- ❑ **2000** Olympic Games in Sydney.
- ❑ **2001** Surprise reelection of Liberal–National coalition.
- ❑ **2002** Bali bomb kills 88 Australians.
- ❑ **2003** Governor-general resigns amid church child abuse scandal.

POLITICS

Multiparty elections

L. House 2001/2004
U. House 2001/2004

H.M. Queen Elizabeth II

AT THE LAST ELECTION

House of Representatives 150 seats

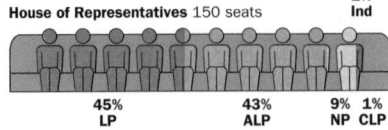

2%
Ind
45%
LP
43%
ALP
9%
NP
1%
CLP

LP = Liberal Party **ALP** = Australian Labor Party **NP** = National Party **Ind** = Independents **CLP** = County–Liberal Party **AD** = Australian Democrats **G** = Greens

Senate 76 seats

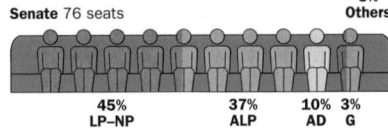

5%
Others
45%
LP–NP
37%
ALP
10%
AD
3%
G

12 seats in the Senate are apportioned to each of the country's constituent states and two each to the Northern Territory and the Australian Capital Territory

Australia is a parliamentary democracy on the British model. There are six state governments, all but one (Queensland) bicameral. The Northern Territory became self-governing in 1978.

Profile

The ALP and the Liberal and National parties have dominated Australian politics since 1945. The last two, politically to the right, work together in coalition and broadly represent big business and agricultural interests. The ALP gained some of this support in the 1980s, adopting free-market policies and blurring the differences between parties, but 13 years of ALP rule ended in 1996, when a Liberal–National coalition took office under John Howard. It retained power with a much reduced majority in the 1998 poll, and again in 2001.

Main Political Issues

Political leadership

The election success of Prime Minister Howard in the 2001 polls took analysts by surprise. It had been expected that the state of the economy and Howard's own unpopularity would be enough to guarantee victory for the ALP. Howard was saved in part by a successful campaign which capitalized on the two greatest fears of late 2001 – the apparent increase in the number of illegal immigrants and the specter of international terrorism – but also by the even lower rating of his main adversary, the ALP's Kim Beazley. Despite clear grass-roots support for the ALP – as attested in early 2002 when it took control of all regional governments – it has been unable to build on deep opposition to Howard's conservative policies, notably its commitment to the war on Iraq in 2003. Instead it is mired in factional infighting; Beazley, who had stepped down as party leader in 2001, launched an unsuccessful leadership challenge in 2003 against his successor, the equally unpopular Simon Crean. For his part, Howard glossed over previous hints that he would retire in 2003, having reached 64 years of age, and pledged to remain at the Liberal helm.

Vineyards in South Australia. *Wine-making has been one of Australia's greatest agricultural success stories in recent years.*

Immigration

There is considerable concern at images of boatloads of would-be immigrants entering Australian waters and the dramatic attempts by asylum seekers to protest over the conditions in which they are housed. The Howard government has actively courted mistrust of refugees, focusing on "unacceptable" behavior. Its allegations that immigrants had thrown children overboard in an effort to secure asylum were proved groundless in 2002, and its notorious "Pacific solution" – using tiny Pacific states to house asylum applicants in exchange for aid – has been roundly criticized by the international community.

Rightward drift

The acceptance of right-wing policies in the political mainstream has been aided by the local success of the far-right xenophobic One Nation party. Even the ALP has conspicuously toned down its support for immigration and embraced market economics.

Governor-General Michael Jeffrey. *His predecessor resigned amid scandal in 2003.*

John Howard, *leader of the LP, was elected prime minister in 1996.*

Aden Ridgeway, *Aboriginal senator and former deputy leader of the AD.*

WORLD AFFAIRS

Joined UN in 1945

APEC | PC | Comm | OECD | PIF

Geopolitically Australia is in an ambiguous position. Isolated from its historic cultural and economic relatives in Europe and North America, it is seen as a Western outsider by the Asian states with which it has sought closer links. It sees the US and EU as its main rivals in the lucrative Asian marketplace.

As membership of the EU eroded the UK's trade links with Australia, there was a determined effort in the 1990s to "turn toward Asia." Trade and aid ties were developed, though market liberalization slowed after the 1997 Asian financial crisis.

Building on its role as the leading power in the south Pacific, Australia has championed the development of APEC (from 1989) as a regional trading bloc. In order to boost stability, it has also made regional security a priority concern. In 1999 it led peacekeeping efforts in East Timor, and it played a pivotal role in securing peace in the Solomon Islands in 2000. In 2003 it pushed the concept of "cooperative intervention," particularly in relation to the Solomons, where it now leads a regional policing mission in an effort to restore law and order.

A major concern since 2001 has been the perceived threat to Australian nationals from Islamist terrorists, highlighted by the Bali bombing in October 2002. To this end it has sought close cooperation from its neighbors and has strengthened ties with the US. In February 2003 it expressed interest in the US national missile defense project, and later, in a deeply unpopular move, supplied troops for the invasion of Iraq – though Australian soldiers are not involved in the reconstruction effort there. Prime Minister Howard has even backed the idea of preemptive strikes against terrorists and their supporters.

Australia has been strongly criticized for its treatment of the Aboriginal population and asylum seekers. The "Pacific Solution" to the immigration problem, adopted in late 2001, prompted international condemnation.

AID

Donor

US$873m (donations) | Down 12% in 2001

Australia spends only 0.25% of its GNP on aid programs. Most is spent in the Asia–Pacific region. Particular areas of focus are HIV/AIDS programs and nongovernmental organizations. The recipient of by far the greatest amount is Papua New Guinea, where Australian companies have major mining operations. Trade barriers were dropped for 50 developing countries in 2002.

DEFENSE

No compulsory military service

US$6.75bn | Up in 2002

Strategic ties with the US remain key: Australia committed 2000 troops to the Iraq invasion in 2003, its largest deployment since the Vietnam War. Defense arrangements exist with the Philippines, Brunei, and Thailand, and Australia sees itself as a major regional power. Spending increased dramatically in 2002. Combating terrorism has become a major priority, with a special elite unit created in 2002.

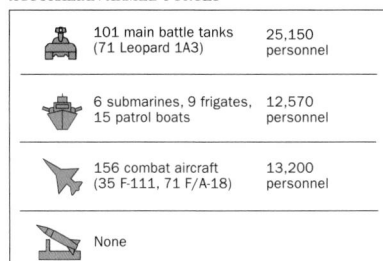

AUSTRALIAN ARMED FORCES

101 main battle tanks (71 Leopard 1A3)	25,150 personnel
6 submarines, 9 frigates, 15 patrol boats	12,570 personnel
156 combat aircraft (35 F-111, 71 F/A-18)	13,200 personnel
None	

ECONOMICS

Inflation 1.7% p.a. (1990–2001)

US$386bn | 1.491 Australian dollars (1.781)

SCORE CARD

❑ WORLD GNP RANKING	15th
❑ GNP PER CAPITA	US$19,900
❑ BALANCE OF PAYMENTS	-US$9.19bn
❑ INFLATION	4.4%
❑ UNEMPLOYMENT	7%

ECONOMIC PERFORMANCE INDICATOR

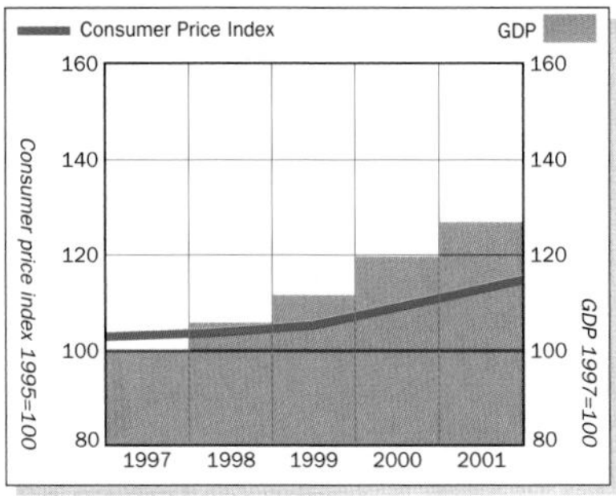
Consumer Price Index
GDP
160
140
120
100
80
Consumer price index 1995=100
GDP 1997=100
1997
1998
1999
2000
2001

EXPORTS

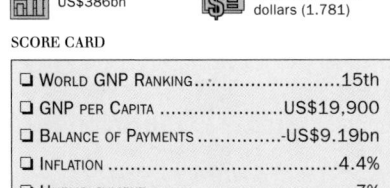

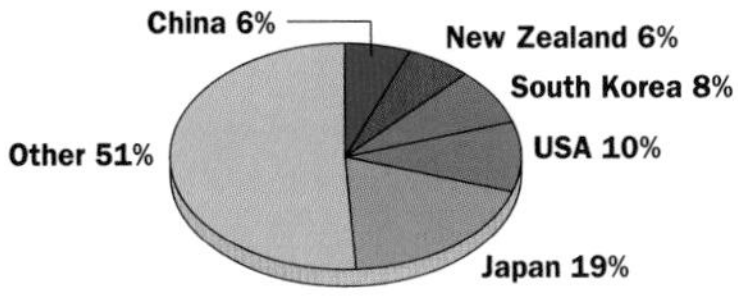
China 6%
New Zealand 6%
South Korea 8%
USA 10%
Japan 19%
Other 51%

IMPORTS

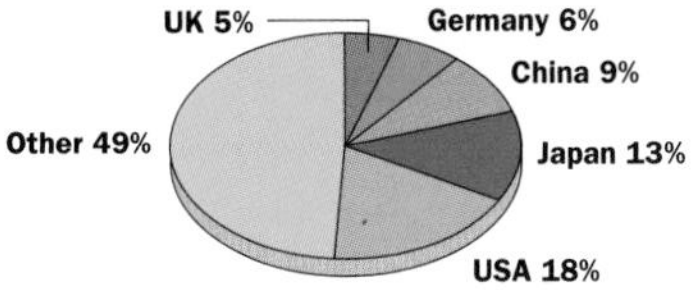
UK 5%
Germany 6%
China 9%
Japan 13%
USA 18%
Other 49%

STRENGTHS

Efficient agricultural and mining industries. Viticulture. Vast mineral deposits. Highly profitable tourist industry with record of dramatic growth. Good history regarding both economic growth and inflation.

WEAKNESSES

May suffer from EU and NAFTA protectionist policies. Political and financial instability in export markets in southeast Asia. Competition from Asian economies with lower wage rates and poorer working conditions. Unemployment likely to remain high. Balance-of-payments deficit.

PROFILE

Australian companies concentrated during the 1990s on the Asian market, which grew to take 60% of Australia's trade. They were hit hard when the 1997 Asian financial crisis tipped the region into recession. Japan remains the key trading partner. In order to compete in Asia, the economy has been undergoing massive structural adjustment. The Howard government, like its ALP predecessor, has been dismantling the tariffs that had made Australia one of the OECD's most protected economies. Unemployment and the collapse of many businesses have resulted. However, recovery has been quick, with positive growth and lower unemployment in 2002, though progress was hampered in 2003 by serious drought and the global SARS epidemic.

AUSTRALIA : MAJOR BUSINESSES

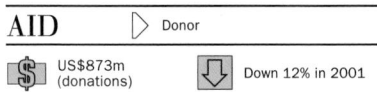

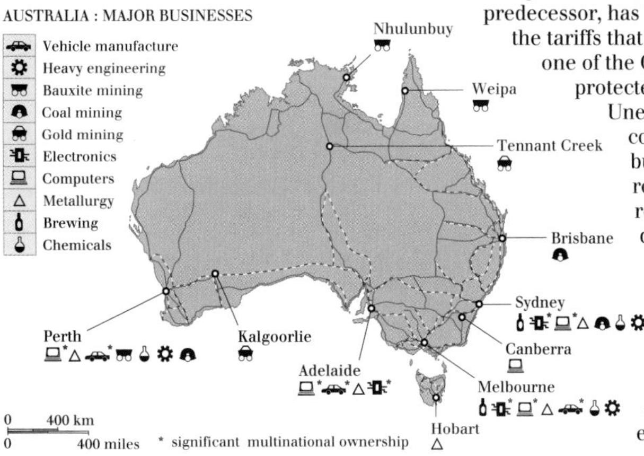
Vehicle manufacture
Heavy engineering
Bauxite mining
Coal mining
Gold mining
Electronics
Computers
Metallurgy
Brewing
Chemicals
Nhulunbuy
Weipa
Tennant Creek
Brisbane
Sydney
Canberra
Melbourne
Hobart
Adelaide
Kalgoorlie
Perth
0 400 km
0 400 miles
* significant multinational ownership

A

RESOURCES

Electric power 44.2m kW

251,300 tonnes

730,000 b/d (reserves 3.5bn barrels)

113m sheep, 30.5m cattle, 93m chickens

Coal, iron, bauxite, zinc, lead, copper, nickel, oil, opals, gold, uranium

ELECTRICITY GENERATION

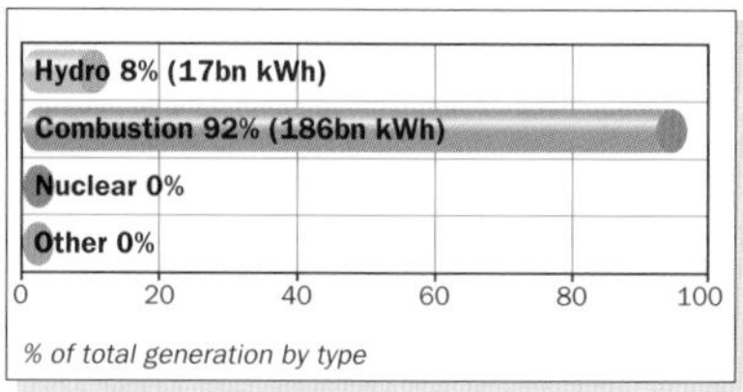

Hydro 8% (17bn kWh)
Combustion 92% (186bn kWh)
Nuclear 0%
Other 0%
0
20
40
60
80
100
% of total generation by type

Australia has one of the world's most important mining industries. It is a major exporter of coal, iron ore, gold, bauxite, and copper, and is self-sufficient in all minerals bar petroleum.

Since the first discoveries of coal in 1798, mineral production has risen every year; in the decade to 1992 it doubled. The share of minerals in the total economy is expected to continue growing, but, having benefited from Australia's location close to the markets of southeast Asia, it was left vulnerable following the regional crisis of 1997.

While minerals underpin much of Australia's wealth, there is growing concern at the environmental cost of extraction. There is also ongoing uncertainty over the possibility of Aboriginal claims to land holding valuable minerals. The 1992 "Mabo Judgment" recognized Aboriginal land rights predating European settlement, and was backed by later judgements, but legislation passed by the government in 1998, in deference to powerful mining interests, cut back Aborigines' rights to make such claims, and in 2002 the High Court ruled that land rights did not apply to the minerals beneath the ground.

Viticulture is increasingly important and Australia is now the world's fourth-largest wine exporter, principally to the UK.

AUSTRALIA : LAND USE

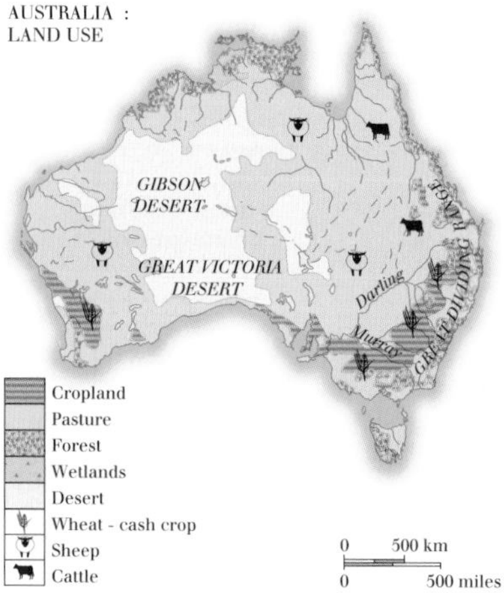

GIBSON DESERT
GREAT VICTORIA DESERT
Darling
Murray
GREAT DIVIDING RANGE
Cropland
Pasture
Forest
Wetlands
Desert
Wheat - cash crop
Sheep
Cattle
0 500 km
0 500 miles

Green Island in the far north of Queensland. It is part of the Great Barrier Reef which stretches 1995 km (1240 miles) down the coast.

ENVIRONMENT

Sustainability rank: 16th

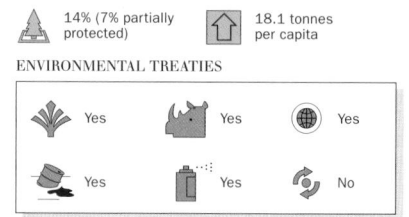

14% (7% partially protected)

18.1 tonnes per capita

ENVIRONMENTAL TREATIES

Yes Yes Yes

Yes Yes No

Australia boasts a number of unique wildlife species, including the egg-laying duck-billed platypus and the iconic koala and kangaroo. Many native species have been adversely affected by the arrival of introduced species such as the dingo and the rabbit. The world famous Great Barrier Reef is at risk from rising sea temperatures. The world's largest marine reserve was created in Australian waters in the southern Indian Ocean in 2002.

Despite a high degree of public awareness, green issues are dominated by NGOs such as Greenpeace, while the government has been criticized for favoring business and industry.

MEDIA

TV ownership high

Daily newspaper circulation 293 per 1000 people

PUBLISHING AND BROADCAST MEDIA

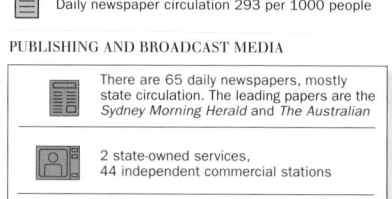

There are 65 daily newspapers, mostly state circulation. The leading papers are the *Sydney Morning Herald* and *The Australian*

2 state-owned services, 44 independent commercial stations

6 state-owned networks, 166 independent commercial stations

The printed press is firmly in the grip of "barons" such as Rupert Murdoch and Kerry Packer: four companies own 80% of papers. Private stations overshadow the state-funded Australian Broadcasting Corporation (ABC) and the multicultural Special Broadcasting Service (SBS). A 2002 High Court ruling enables Australians to sue foreign-based websites for defamation, on the basis that they can be read in Australia.

CRIME

No death penalty

22,458 prisoners

Up 7% in 2000

CRIME RATES

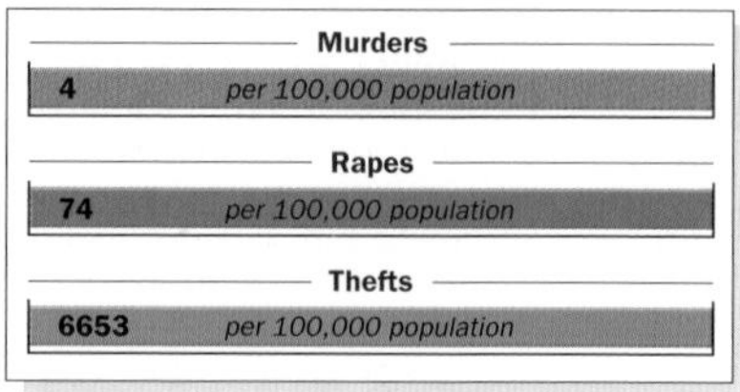

Murders
4 per 100,000 population
Rapes
74 per 100,000 population
Thefts
6653 per 100,000 population

Each state has its own police force and court system. The High Court and Family Court both have national jurisdiction. Since the 1970s, the legal system has been placing greater emphasis on individual rights. The disproportionate number of Aboriginal deaths in custody is of concern, as are rising narcotics-related offenses. Australia is active in narcotics control throughout southeast Asia. Gun control laws were strengthened following the 1996 Port Arthur shooting, when a lone gunman killed 35 people. In 1997 the Wood inquiry uncovered widespread police corruption in New South Wales and led to major reforms.

EDUCATION

School leaving age: 15

99%

845,132 students

THE EDUCATION SYSTEM

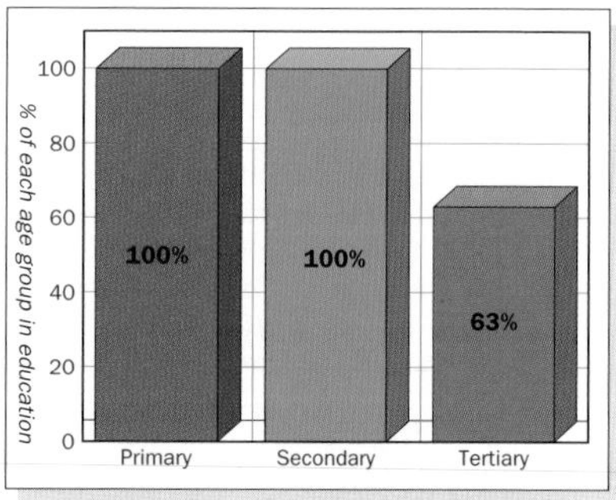

100
80
60
40
20
0
% of each age group in education
100%
100%
63%
Primary
Secondary
Tertiary

Education in Australia is a state responsibility, except in Canberra (where it is funded by the federal government). State education departments run the government schools and set the policies for educational practice and standards for all schools. Nongovernment schools, run by religious and other groups, exist in all states. Special provision is made for inaccessible outback areas, with recent moves to bring new technologies to the bush.

Schooling is compulsory from age 5–6 to age 15–16 in all states. After their final year at school, students sit for the Higher School Certificate. Universities are independent of state control and are funded by the federal government.

ABORIGINAL RIGHTS

CENTRAL TO ABORIGINAL culture and beliefs is the relationship with tribal lands. The Aborigines' land rights campaign, like their civil rights campaign, began gathering momentum in the 1960s, when they were first included in the census and won the right to vote. Now a key political issue, it has far-reaching implications for national identity, for the country's most disadvantaged people, and for powerful mining and farming interests.

***An Aboriginal elder** surveys his native land in Western Australia.*

BACKGROUND

In the millennia before the arrival of Europeans, Aboriginal peoples ranged widely over their land. Their number was then greatly reduced by exposure to disease and by conflict. Settlers acquired land without reference to any preexisting rights of tribal peoples, based on the legal doctrine that before 1788 the land was *terra nullius* – belonging to no one. Those Aborigines still living a traditional lifestyle were largely confined to reserves.

Land rights campaigns won an initial breakthrough when land councils were set up, first in the Northern Territory in 1976, then in other states. These provided a structure for holding freehold title to land in trust for its tribal inhabitants. However, in the absence of a uniform national land rights policy conservative states such as Queensland – with the largest Aboriginal population – resisted moves to consolidate Aborigine ownership. Particular flashpoints arose when mining companies were granted concessions to exploit sacred sites.

NATIVE TITLE LEGISLATION

The first nationwide Native Title Act was introduced in 1993, in the new situation created by a crucial 1992 court ruling. The so-called "Mabo Judgment" had established that rights to land ownership based on native title did indeed exist in common law. This effectively reversed the concept of *terra nullius* and recognized the pre-1788 Aboriginal occupancy.

the 10

***Native dancers from Kuranda,** northern Queensland, perform a traditional dance in front of protesters marching for increased Aboriginal land rights.*

The 1993 law specified that native title existed for all Crown land held by federal or by state government, unless it had specifically been extinguished. Native title met powerful resistance from mining companies, especially in Western Australia. A court case brought by the Wik people of the Cape York Peninsula in Queensland took the matter further. The 1996 Wik ruling said that native title still coexisted with the rights of farmers who had long leases from the Crown on huge tracts of grazing land, granted earlier in the century. Changes of use on such land (to allow mining, cash crops, and tourist developments) would therefore require consultation with Aborigines.

The Liberal–National government responded with a plan to protect leaseholders. Its own Native Title Amendment Bill, tightly restricting Aborigine claims, split the country but was eventually passed in 1998.

As the indigenous population (410,000 and rising) develops a sense of pride and assertiveness, court battles continue over mining developments on sensitive tribal sites. Meanwhile, Liberal prime minister John Howard has resisted making a formal government apology for white settlers' mistreatment of Aboriginal people. Campaigners for such an apology see it as central to a national reconciliation agreement. Another dimension of Australia's struggle to come to terms with the past is the recent controversy over the "stolen generation" – Aboriginal children forcibly removed from their families and brought up by whites under an assimilation policy which continued until the late 1960s.

HEALTH

Welfare state health benefits

1 per 385 people

Cancers, heart diseases, accidents

Australia's extensive public health service has among the highest standards in the world, though hospital waiting lists are lengthening. Outback areas are serviced by the efficient Royal Flying Doctor Service. Vigilance continues in the areas of hygiene, nutrition, and general living standards; current priorities are heart disease, injury prevention, personal fitness, Aboriginal health, and the prevention of cancers. Despite the popular image of Australians as athletic, 21% of over-25-year-olds are obese. Government encouragement of private health insurance has raised concerns over public health funding and quality.

SPENDING

GDP/cap. increase

CONSUMPTION AND SPENDING

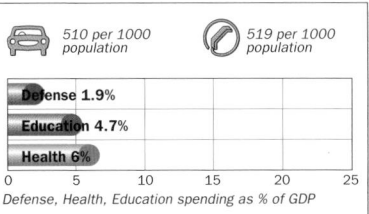

510 per 1000 population

519 per 1000 population

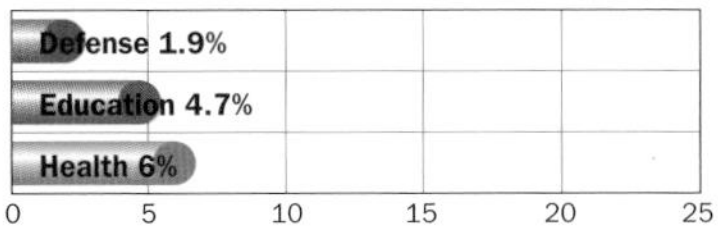
Defense 1.9%
Education 4.7%
Health 6%
0
5
10
15
20
25

Defense, Health, Education spending as % of GDP

Australians traditionally enjoyed reasonable equality of wealth distribution. A large proportion of families own two cars and have relatively high disposable incomes, and a benign climate helps most people to live comfortably. However, high unemployment during the 1990s recession widened the gap between rich and poor, and Australia slipped down the world's standard of living list for a few years. The incidence of homelessness, critical poverty, and child neglect due to poverty have increased in recent years.

WORLD RANKING

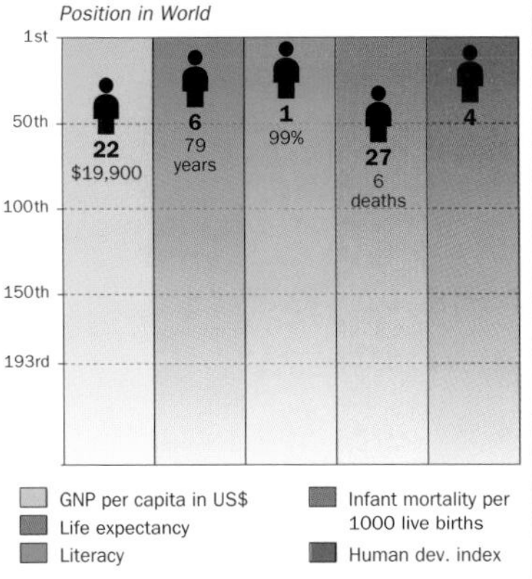
Position in World
1st
50th
100th
150th
193rd
22
$19,900
6
79 years
1
99%
27
6 deaths
4
GNP per capita in US$
Life expectancy
Literacy
Infant mortality per 1000 live births
Human dev. index

A

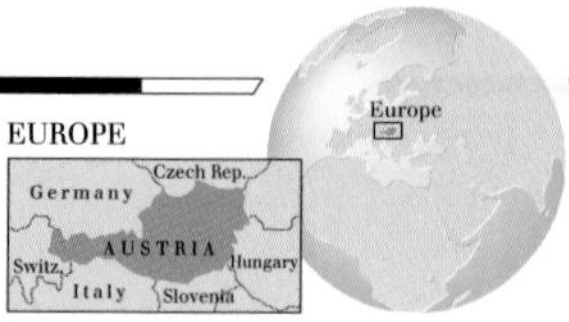
Europe
EUROPE
Germany
Czech Rep.
AUSTRIA
Hungary
Switz.
Italy
Slovenia

AUSTRIA

OFFICIAL NAME: Republic of Austria **CAPITAL:** Vienna
POPULATION: 8.1 million **CURRENCY:** Euro **OFFICIAL LANGUAGE:** German

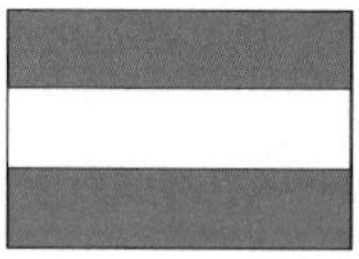

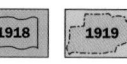

1918 | 1919 | Oct 26 | A | +1 | +43 | .at

LYING IN THE HEART OF EUROPE, Austria is dominated by the Alps in the west, while fertile plains make up the east and north. A separate republic after the collapse of the Austro-Hungarian Empire, Austria was absorbed into Hitler's Germany in 1938. It regained independence in 1955 after the departure of the last Soviet troops from the Allied Occupation Force. Its economy encompasses successful high-tech sectors, a tourist industry which attracts wealthier visitors, and a strong agricultural base. Having joined the EU in 1995, in 2002 it was one of 12 EU states to adopt the euro.

CLIMATE

Mountain/continental

WEATHER CHART FOR VIENNA

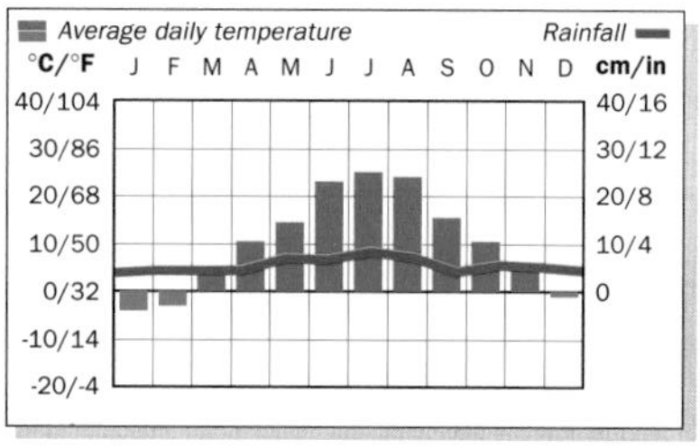
Average daily temperature
Rainfall
°C/°F
J F M A M J J A S O N D
cm/in
40/104
30/86
20/68
10/50
0/32
-10/14
-20/-4
40/16
30/12
20/8
10/4
0

Austria has a temperate continental climate. Alpine areas experience colder temperatures and higher precipitation.

TRANSPORTATION

Drive on right

Schwechat, Vienna
12m passengers

8 ships
35,300 grt

THE TRANSPORTATION NETWORK

200,000 km (124,000 miles)

1634 km (1015 miles)

5665 km (3520 miles)

358 km (222 miles)

Austria's central location in Europe has encouraged the development of a sophisticated communications and transportation network.

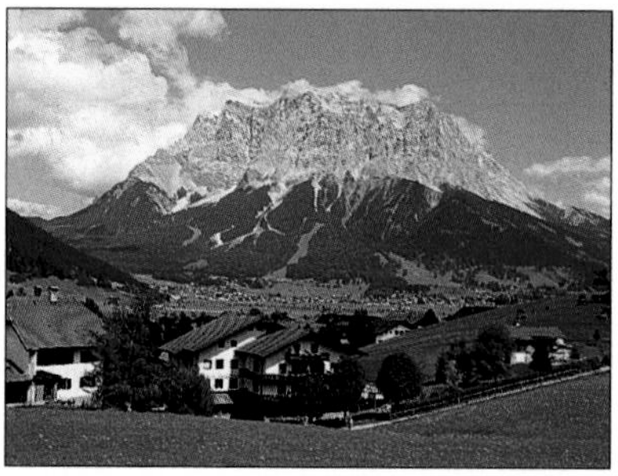

***The Tirol** is situated in the heart of Austria's Alps. It is the most mountainous region of all and attracts both winter and summer visitors.*

TOURISM

Visitors : Population
2.3:1

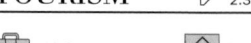

18.6m visitors

Up 2% in 2002

MAIN TOURIST ARRIVALS

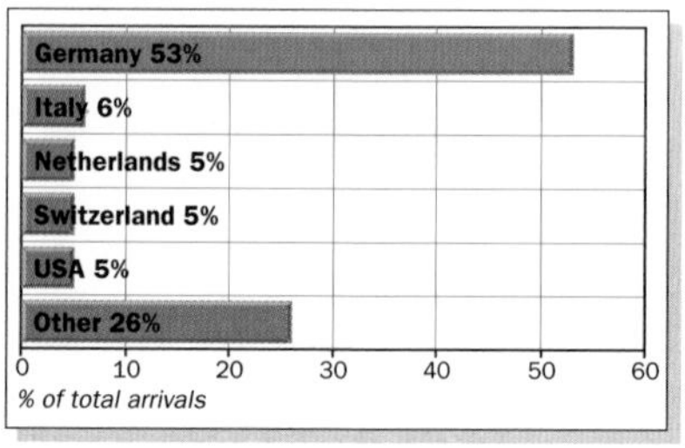
Germany 53%
Italy 6%
Netherlands 5%
Switzerland 5%
USA 5%
Other 26%
0 10 20 30 40 50 60
% of total arrivals

Well-developed Alpine skiing and winter sports resorts account for almost one-third of the country's total tourist earnings. Many resorts, such as St. Anton and Kitzbühel, cater for the top end of the market. In the summer season, which peaks in July and August, tourists visit the scenic Tirol and the lakes around Bad Ischl. Year-round major attractions are Vienna, with its coffee houses and the Prater park (whose Ferris wheel was immortalized in *The Third Man*), and Salzburg, Austria's second city. The latter is internationally famous for its summer music festival and as the birthplace of Mozart.

AUSTRIA

Total Area : 83 858 sq. km (32 378 sq. miles)

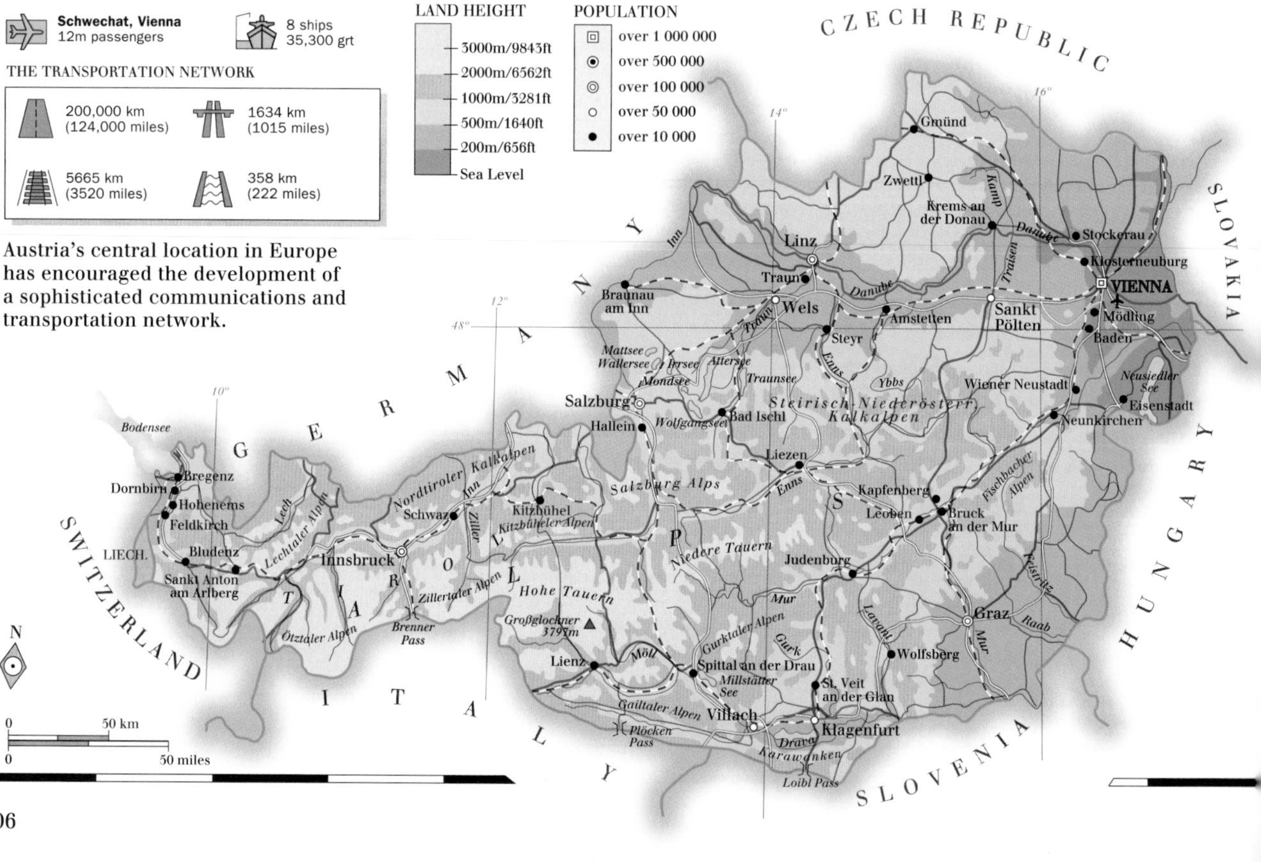
LAND HEIGHT
3000m/9843ft
2000m/6562ft
1000m/3281ft
500m/1640ft
200m/656ft
Sea Level
POPULATION
over 1 000 000
over 500 000
over 100 000
over 50 000
over 10 000
CZECH REPUBLIC
SLOVAKIA
HUNGARY
SLOVENIA
ITALY
SWITZERLAND
GERMANY
LIECH.
Gmünd
Zwettl
Krems an der Donau
Kamp
Danube
Stockerau
Klosterneuburg
VIENNA
Mödling
Baden
Linz
Traun
Wels
Braunau am Inn
Inn
Steyr
Amstetten
Sankt Pölten
Traisen
Enns
Ybbs
Wiener Neustadt
Neusiedler See
Eisenstadt
Neunkirchen
Mattsee
Wallersee
Irrsee
Attersee
Mondsee
Traunsee
Salzburg
Hallein
Wolfgangsee
Bad Ischl
Steirisch-Niederösterr. Kalkalpen
Liezen
Salzburg Alps
Kapfenberg
Leoben
Bruck an der Mur
Fischbacher Alpen
Bodensee
Bregenz
Dornbirn
Hohenems
Feldkirch
Bludenz
Sankt Anton am Arlberg
Lech
Lechtaler Alpen
Nordtiroler Kalkalpen
Schwaz
Ziller
Kitzbühel
Kitzbüheler Alpen
Innsbruck
Zillertaler Alpen
Hohe Tauern
Niedere Tauern
Judenburg
Ötztaler Alpen
Brenner Pass
Großglockner 3797m
Mur
Lavant
Raab
Feistritz
Graz
Wolfsberg
Lienz
Möll
Gurktaler Alpen
Gurk
Spittal an der Drau
Millstätter See
St. Veit an der Glan
Gailtaler Alpen
Villach
Plöcken Pass
Drava
Klagenfurt
Karawanken
Loibl Pass
N
0 50 km
0 50 miles

PEOPLE

Pop. density medium

German, Croatian, Slovenian

98/km² (254/mi²)

THE URBAN/RURAL POPULATION SPLIT

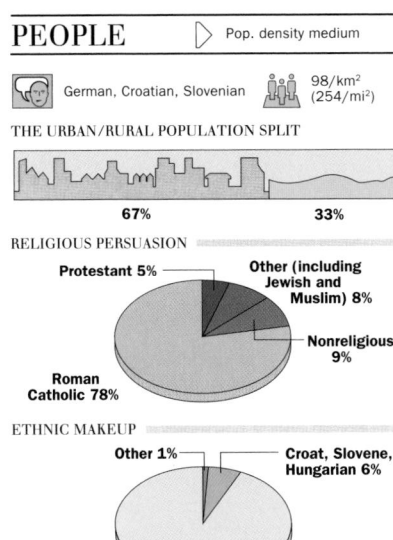

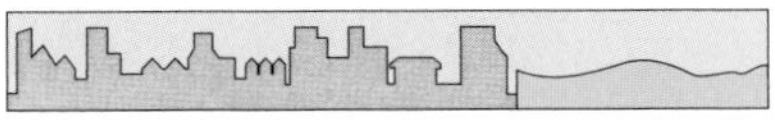
67%
33%

RELIGIOUS PERSUASION

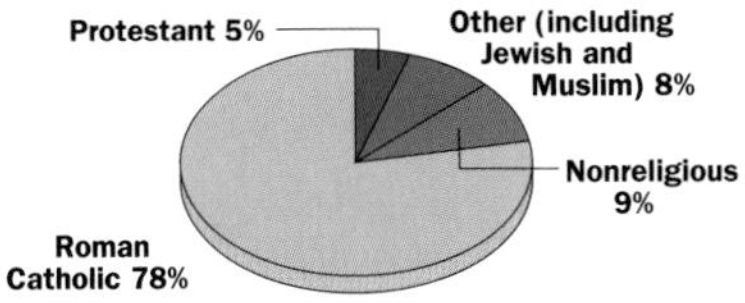
Protestant 5%
Other (including Jewish and Muslim) 8%
Nonreligious 9%
Roman Catholic 78%

ETHNIC MAKEUP

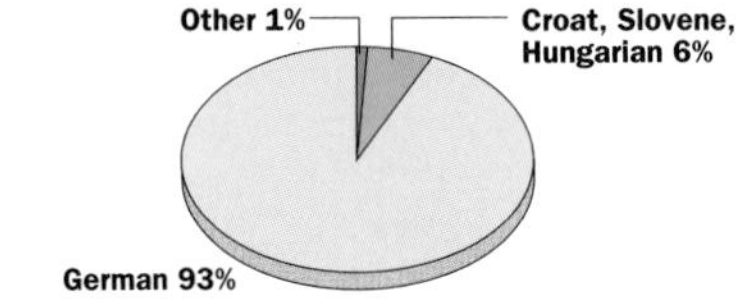
Other 1%
Croat, Slovene, Hungarian 6%
German 93%

Austrian society is homogeneous. Almost all Austrians are German-speakers, though Austrians like to stress their distinctive identity in relation to Germany. Minorities are few; there are some ethnic Slovenes, Croats, and Hungarians in the south and east, as well as some Roma communities. These minorities have been augmented by large numbers of immigrants from eastern Europe and one-time refugees from the former Yugoslavia. The result has been a perceptible increase in ethnic tension, particularly as the far right claims that migrants are taking jobs from the local population.

The nuclear family is the norm, and it is common for both parents to work. While gender equality is enshrined in the constitution, in practice society is still strongly patriarchal.

Young Austrians tend to live in the parental home until they complete their higher education. This reflects the relatively long time taken to complete university degrees and the lack of maintenance grants from the state for students. The average age for marriage is in line with the EU, but in 2002, 44 per 100 initial marriages ended in divorce. Nominally a Roman Catholic country, Austria is socially less conservative than the Catholic *Länder* in Germany.

POPULATION AGE BREAKDOWN

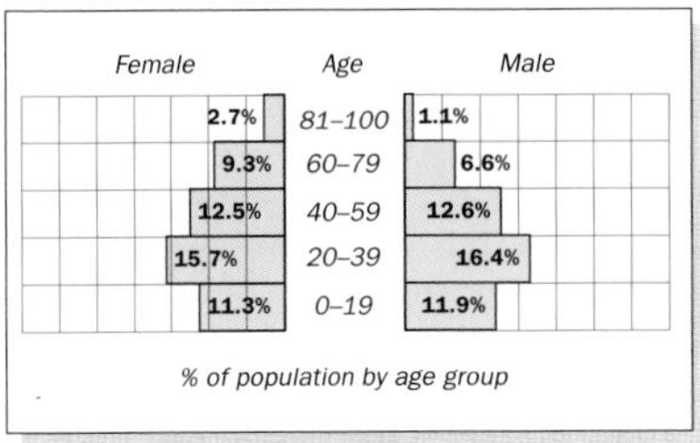
Female
Age
Male
2.7%
81–100
1.1%
9.3%
60–79
6.6%
12.5%
40–59
12.6%
15.7%
20–39
16.4%
11.3%
0–19
11.9%
% of population by age group

POLITICS

Multiparty elections

L. House 2002/2006
U. House varies by province

President Thomas Klestil

AT THE LAST ELECTION

National Council 183 seats

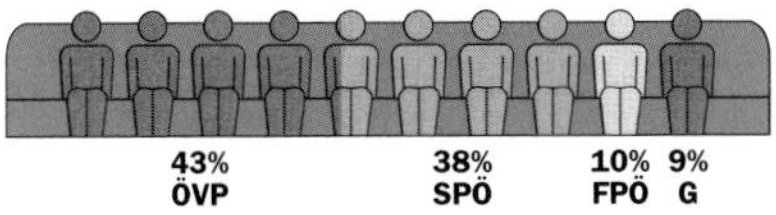
43% ÖVP
38% SPÖ
10% FPÖ
9% G

ÖVP = Austrian People's Party
SPÖ = Social Democratic Party of Austria
FPÖ = Freedom Party of Austria **G** = Greens

Federal Council 64 seats

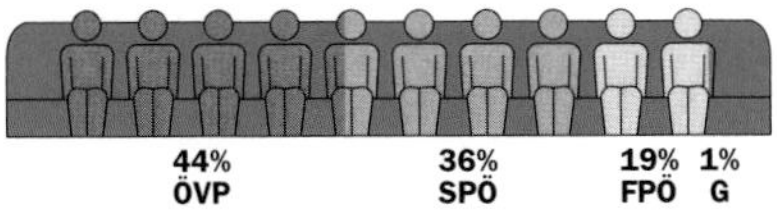
44% ÖVP
36% SPÖ
19% FPÖ
1% G

Austria is a federal, multiparty democracy. The chancellor (premier) holds real executive power.

PROFILE

The socialist SPÖ and the conservative ÖVP have dominated postwar politics. They governed Austria in coalition for 20 years until 1966, and then in 1987, after a period when the SPÖ had dominated, formed the "grand coalition" in power until 1999. Their hold on power, with no real alternative, reached into all areas of public life. The far-right FPÖ achieved a breakthrough in elections in October 1999, when it came equal second with the ÖVP. A new right-wing coalition of the ÖVP and the FPÖ, headed by ÖVP leader Wolfgang Schüssel, was met with regional and international criticism. FPÖ leader Jörg Haider drew strong condemnation, having openly expressed admiration for some of Hitler's policies. He remained a driving force behind the party, despite resigning formal leadership in 2000. In September 2002 the ruling coalition collapsed over FPÖ opposition to flood damage taxes, prompting fresh elections. Though the ÖVP's popularity reached a 40-year high, and support for the FPÖ dwindled, the coalition was re-formed in February 2003 when the ÖVP could find no other partner.

The nine provincial assemblies and governments have considerable powers. Vienna, with provincial status, has long been dominated by the SPÖ.

MAIN POLITICAL ISSUE
Relations with EU partners

Austria's population is divided over the merits of EU membership. While the farming lobby remains apprehensive of EU agricultural policies, the country as a whole has benefited from lower food prices and greater consumer choice. Fears that membership is eroding national identity, as well as encouraging an influx of cheap east European labor, provided an electoral basis for the nationalist FPÖ. In turn, EU states responded to the FPÖ's inclusion in the ruling coalition in 2000 by imposing diplomatic sanctions for seven months.

Dr. Thomas Klestil, the ÖVP candidate, was elected president in 1992.

Wolfgang Schüssel, ÖVP chancellor since 2000.

WORLD AFFAIRS

Joined UN in 1955

EU CE PfP OECD OSCE

Despite the importance of relations with Germany, Austria's powerful northern neighbor and main trading partner, there has been a conscious policy of stressing Austria's independence and creating some diplomatic distance. Austria is keen to maintain its relationship with the US, which is reinforced by Austria's role as supplier of small arms to the US Army. The inclusion of the far right in the Austrian government in 2000 provoked the imposition of diplomatic sanctions by EU states for seven months.

Austria's status as a neutral state has begun to be questioned since it joined the EU and NATO's Partnership for Peace program. Austria is part of the Schengen Convention ending border controls between participating EU members. Its geopolitical position gives it considerable influence in eastern Europe, and exports to the region trebled in the 1990s. The ÖVP has strongly supported the eastward enlargement of the EU, but the FPÖ is more hostile.

AID

Donor

$533m (donations)

Up 26% in 2001

New projects are now assessed for their impact on the environment and on gender issues. Austria targets funds to its east European neighbors and the poorest developing countries. A major exporter to the former Yugoslavia before the wars there in the 1990s, Austria has since held a key role in regional reconstruction.

CHRONOLOGY

Austria came under the control of the Habsburgs in 1273. In 1867, the Dual Monarchy of Austria-Hungary was formed under Habsburg rule. Defeat in World War I in 1918 led to the breakup of the Habsburg empire and the formation of the Republic of Austria.

- **1934** Chancellor Dollfuss dismisses parliament and starts imprisoning social democrats, communists, and National Socialist (Nazi) Party members. Nazis attempt coup.
- **1938** The Anschluss – Austria incorporated into Germany by Hitler.
- **1945** Austria occupied by Soviet, British, US, and French forces. Elections result in ÖVP–SPÖ coalition.
- **1950** Attempted coup by Communist Party fails. Marshall Aid helps economic recovery.
- **1955** Occupying troops withdrawn. Austria recognized as a neutral sovereign state.
- **1971** SPÖ government formed under Chancellor Bruno Kreisky who dominates Austrian politics for 12 years.
- **1983** Socialists and FPÖ form coalition government under Fred Sinowatz.
- **1986** Kurt Waldheim, former UN secretary-general, elected president, despite war crimes allegations. Franz Vranitzky replaces Sinowatz as federal chancellor. Nationalist Jörg Haider becomes FPÖ leader, prompting SPÖ to pull out of government. Elections produce stalemate: "grand coalition" of SPÖ–ÖVP.
- **1990** ÖVP loses support in elections.
- **1992** Thomas Klestil (ÖVP) elected president. Elections confirm some traditional ÖVP supporters defecting to FPÖ.
- **1995** Austria joins EU. Early elections; SPÖ and ÖVP increase representation; "grand coalition" re-forms in early 1996.
- **1997** Vranitzky resigns; replaced by Viktor Klima.
- **1998** Klestil reelected president.
- **1999** Haider's FPÖ wins 40% of votes in Carinthia regional poll, is equal second with ÖVP in general election in October; SPÖ remains as largest party.
- **2000** ÖVP accepts FPÖ into coalition: political crisis. EU imposes diplomatic sanctions, lifted after seven months.
- **2002** Euro fully adopted. September, FPÖ quits coalition. November, ÖVP wins elections.
- **2003** ÖVP–FPÖ coalition re-formed.

DEFENSE

Compulsory military service

$1.47bn

Down 9% in 2001

The 1955 State Treaty, which restored Austria's independence, enshrined the country's neutrality. However, it has participated in NATO's Partnership for Peace program since 1995.

Despite the small size of Austria's armed forces, its arms industry is strong. It not only meets most of the hardware needs of its own army, but also exports arms to the US and other countries.

AUSTRIAN ARMED FORCES

274 main battle tanks (160 M-60A3, 114 Leopard 2A4)	27,750 personnel
None	
52 combat aircraft (23 Saab J-350e, 29 Saab 1050e)	6850 personnel
None	

ECONOMICS

Inflation 1.8% p.a. (1990–2001)

$195bn

0.871 euros (1.013)

SCORE CARD

World GNP Ranking	22nd
GNP per Capita	$23,940
Balance of Payments	–$4.1bn
Inflation	2.7%
Unemployment	5%

EXPORTS

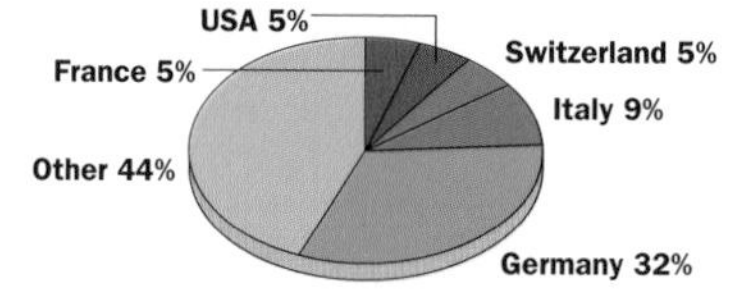
USA 5%
Switzerland 5%
France 5%
Italy 9%
Other 44%
Germany 32%

IMPORTS

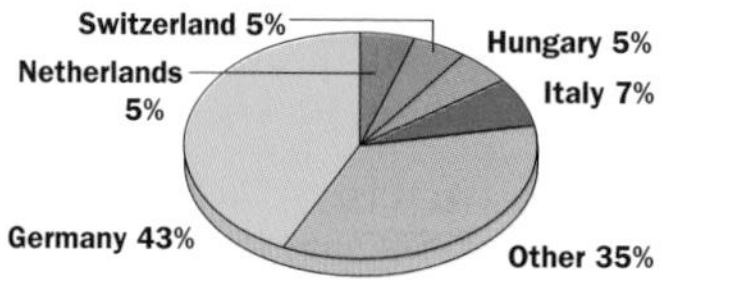
Switzerland 5%
Hungary 5%
Netherlands 5%
Italy 7%
Germany 43%
Other 35%

Strengths

Large manufacturing base. Strong chemical and petrochemical industries. Electrical engineering sector, textiles, and wood processing industries. Highly skilled labor force. Tourism is an important foreign currency earner.

Weaknesses

Lacks natural resources. Reliant on imported raw materials, particularly oil and gas. Process of introducing greater competition and deregulation has been slow.

Profile

Austria's industrial and high-tech sector is well developed and contributes over a quarter of GDP. Some services, notably tourism, are highly sophisticated and profitable, though tourism receipts have been down in recent years.

A recession in the early 1990s was reversed by a rapid increase in exports to eastern Europe and Germany and by increased domestic demand.

ECONOMIC PERFORMANCE INDICATOR

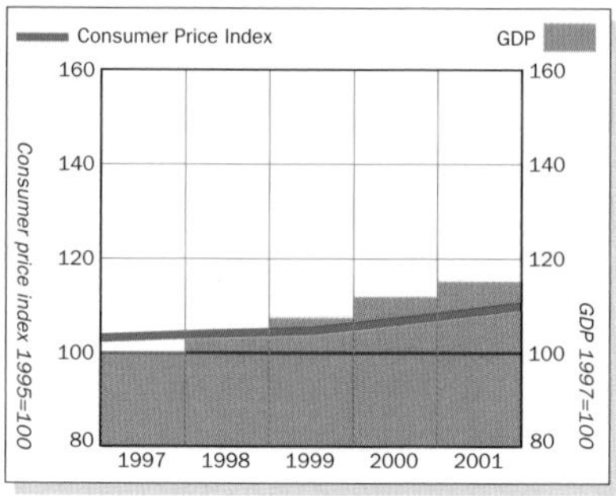
Consumer Price Index
GDP
160
140
120
100
80
Consumer price index 1995=100
GDP 1997=100
1997
1998
1999
2000
2001

The impact of EU membership has been largely positive. Foreign investment has increased, as more multinationals locate their headquarters for east European operations in Austria. A far-reaching fiscal stabilization program enabled Austria to meet the economic convergence criteria necessary for it fully to adopt the euro in 2002. The labor market has seen an influx of migrant laborers more willing to accept flexible working arrangements and lower wages. As in other countries in western Europe, the increasing age of the population has obliged the government to reform the pension system, reducing payments and postponing retirement.

AUSTRIA : MAJOR BUSINESSES

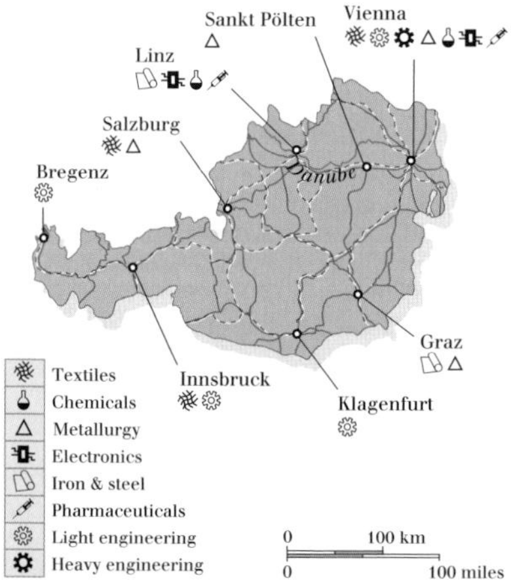
Sankt Pölten
Vienna
Linz
Salzburg
Bregenz
Danube
Innsbruck
Graz
Klagenfurt
Textiles
Chemicals
Metallurgy
Electronics
Iron & steel
Pharmaceuticals
Light engineering
Heavy engineering
0
100 km
0
100 miles

RESOURCES

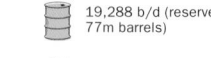

Electric power 18.4m kW

3706 tonnes

19,288 b/d (reserves 77m barrels)

3.44m pigs, 2.12m cattle, 11m chickens

Iron, coal, magnesite, zinc, lead

ELECTRICITY GENERATION

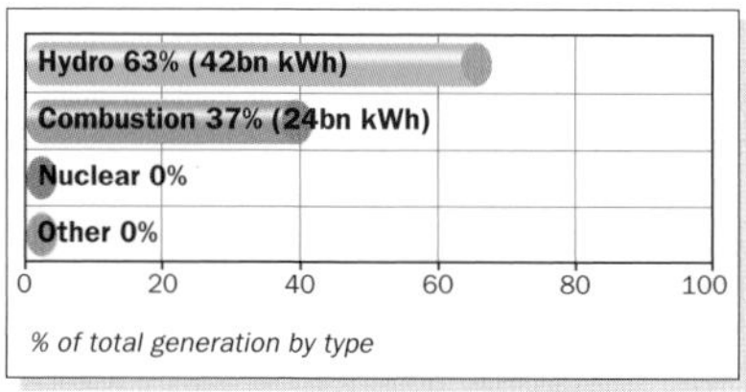
Hydro 63% (42bn kWh)
Combustion 37% (24bn kWh)
Nuclear 0%
Other 0%
0
20
40
60
80
100
% of total generation by type

AUSTRIA : LAND USE

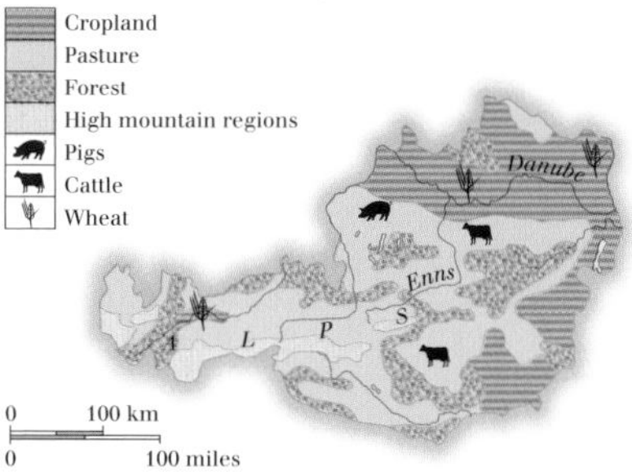
Cropland
Pasture
Forest
High mountain regions
Pigs
Cattle
Wheat
Danube
Enns
L
P
S
0
100 km
0
100 miles

Austria has few resources. It lacks significant oil, coal, and gas deposits and has to import a large amount of its energy. Russia is a key energy supplier, and gas is provided via pipelines running through the Czech Republic and Slovakia. Oil is imported up the Danube. Iron ore and raw steel for Austria's industry have traditionally come from Russia and Germany.

ENVIRONMENT

Sustainability rank: 7th

34% (29% partially protected)

8.2 tonnes per capita

ENVIRONMENTAL TREATIES

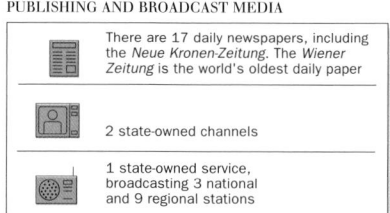

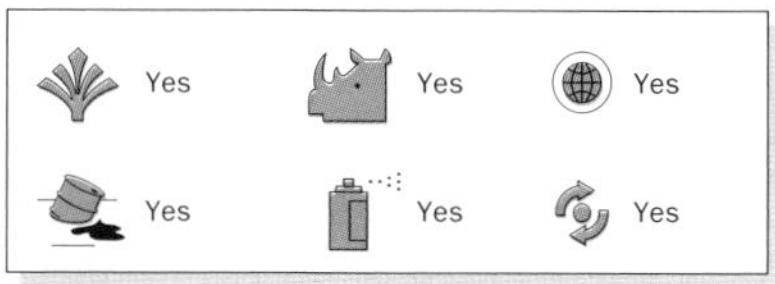
Yes
Yes
Yes
Yes
Yes
Yes

Environmental awareness is high and the government invests nearly 3% of GDP in environmental protection. Roughly half of all domestic waste is separated for recycling, with heavy fines for failing to observe regulations. The safety of nuclear reactors in the neighboring Czech Republic, Slovakia, and Slovenia is a major concern.

MEDIA

TV ownership high

Daily newspaper circulation 296 per 1000 people

PUBLISHING AND BROADCAST MEDIA

There are 17 daily newspapers, including the *Neue Kronen-Zeitung*. The *Wiener Zeitung* is the world's oldest daily paper

2 state-owned channels

1 state-owned service, broadcasting 3 national and 9 regional stations

TV and radio are controlled by the Austrian Broadcasting Company (ÖRF), which has a politically appointed general director. Private radio stations are restricted to regional broadcasting. Cable TV is licensed by ÖRF to prevent it taking viewers from existing stations. A German-language satellite channel is run jointly with German and Swiss TV.

CRIME

No death penalty

6915 prisoners

Up 6% in 2000–2001

CRIME RATES

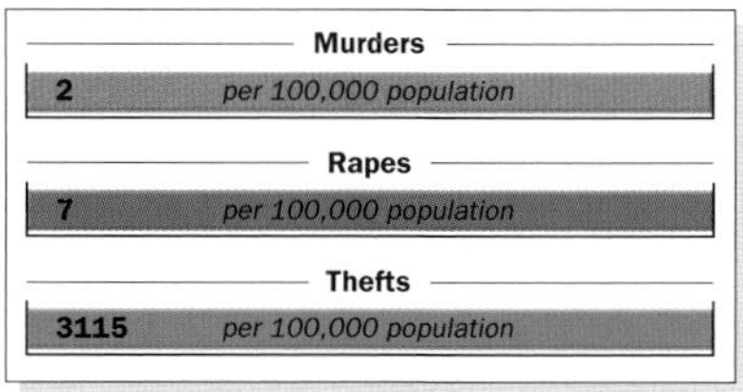
Murders
2 per 100,000 population
Rapes
7 per 100,000 population
Thefts
3115 per 100,000 population

Austria's crime rate is steadily climbing, with the number of burglaries rising in particular. The arrival of the Russian mafia in Vienna has led to an increase in money laundering.

EDUCATION

School leaving age: 15

99%

264,669 students

THE EDUCATION SYSTEM

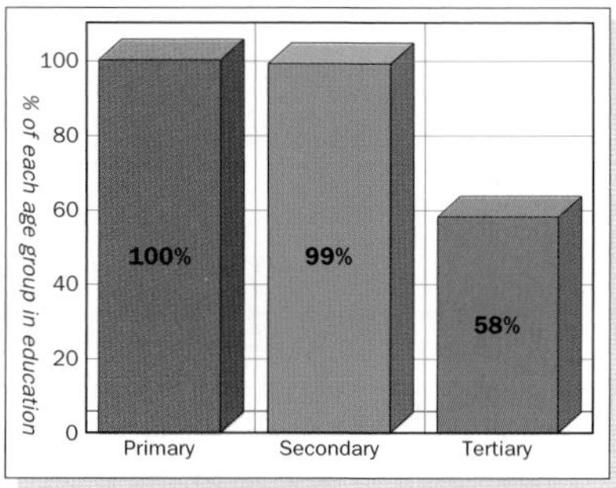
100
80
60
40
20
0
% of each age group in education
100%
99%
58%
Primary
Secondary
Tertiary

Of total government expenditure some 6% is on education. Secondary education is divided between lower schools (11–15) and higher schools (15–18). Children showing early academic aptitude can attend a *Gymnasium* from age 11. Students hoping to study at university must pass the *Reifeprüfung* or *Matura*. An alternative vocational qualification, the *Berufsreifeprüfung*, was introduced for 18-year-olds in 1997.

HEALTH

Welfare state health benefits

1 per 331 people

Heart and cerebrovascular diseases, cancers

Funding for health has shifted to a more streamlined government budget. Private spending is becoming more important and accounts for over one-quarter of the total, as patients increasingly choose to use the private health sector to avoid waiting lists for operations. Control of hospitals and other facilities is being decentralized to the regional *Länder*.

SPENDING

GDP/cap. increase

CONSUMPTION AND SPENDING

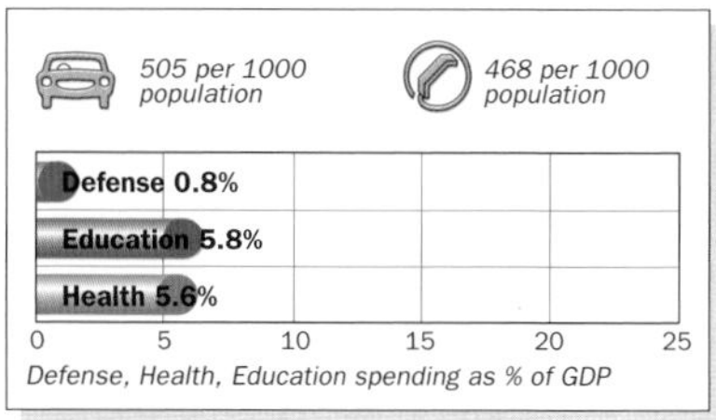
505 per 1000 population
468 per 1000 population
Defense 0.8%
Education 5.8%
Health 5.6%
0
5
10
15
20
25
Defense, Health, Education spending as % of GDP

Austria has retained many of its traditional social divisions. Inherited wealth is still respected above earned wealth, and there is less social mobility than in neighboring Germany.

Austrians have become less cautious with their money, and a previously high savings rate has fallen dramatically. Relatively few Austrians own stocks and shares, and most companies are dominated by a single shareholder. Legislation in 2000 banned anonymous savings accounts, a system unique in the EU to Austria which, it had been argued, encouraged money laundering and insider dealing. Government bonds offer low rates of interest and the property market is weak; many people, particularly in Vienna, tend to rent rather than buy their apartments. Refugees from the conflicts in the former Yugoslavia form the poorest group in Austrian society.

WORLD RANKING

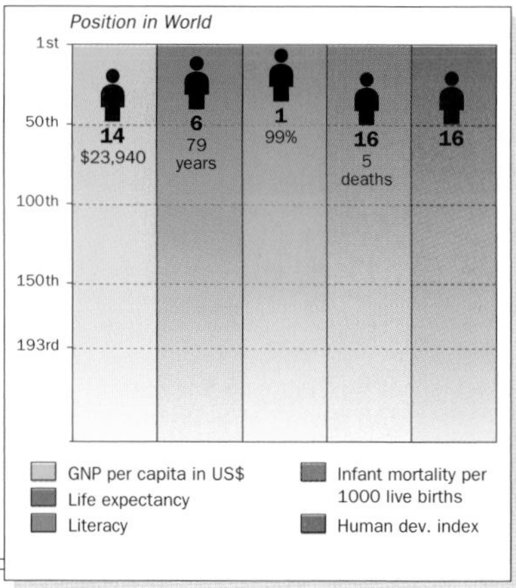
Position in World
1st
50th
100th
150th
193rd
14
$23,940
6
79
years
1
99%
16
5
deaths
16
GNP per capita in US$
Life expectancy
Literacy
Infant mortality per 1000 live births
Human dev. index

A

AZERBAIJAN

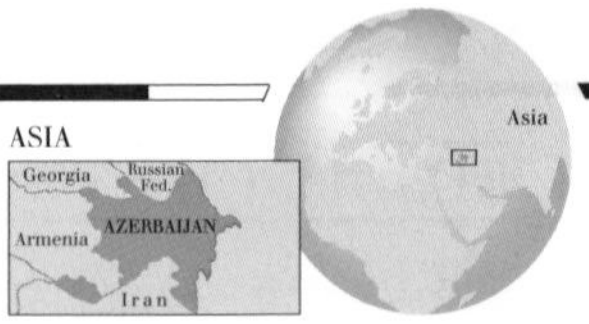
ASIA
Georgia
Russian Fed.
Armenia
AZERBAIJAN
Iran
Asia

OFFICIAL NAME: Republic of Azerbaijan **CAPITAL:** Baku
POPULATION: 8.1 million **CURRENCY:** Manat **OFFICIAL LANGUAGE:** Azeri

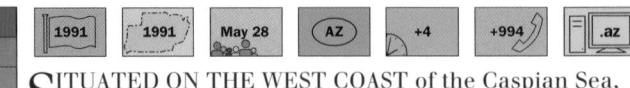

1991 | 1991 | May 28 | AZ | +4 | +994 | .az

SITUATED ON THE WEST COAST of the Caspian Sea, Azerbaijan was the first Soviet republic to declare independence. The issue of the disputed enclave of Nagorno Karabakh, whose Armenian population seeks secession, led to full-scale war (1988–1994) and is still a dominant concern. Over 200,000 refugees, and more than twice as many internally displaced, added to the problems of the troubled economy. Azerbaijan's oil wealth, however, gives it long-term potential.

Landscape typical of the Lesser Caucasus mountains near Qazax in the extreme northwest of Azerbaijan.

CLIMATE

Mountain/steppe

WEATHER CHART FOR BAKU

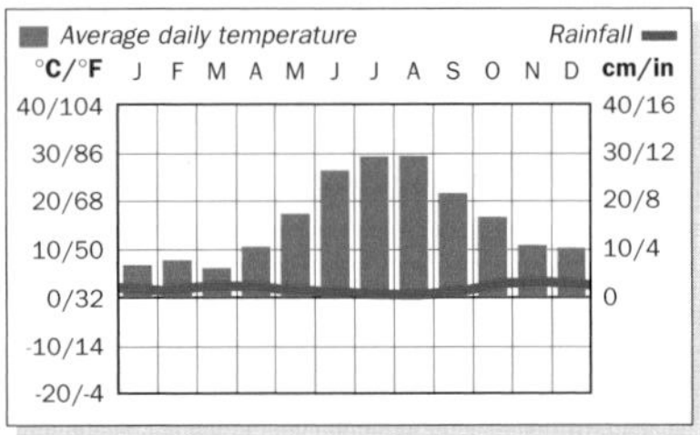
Average daily temperature
Rainfall
°C/°F
J F M A M J J A S O N D
cm/in
40/104
30/86
20/68
10/50
0/32
-10/14
-20/-4
40/16
30/12
20/8
10/4
0

Coastal areas are subtropical, but bitter winters inland have become a life-or-death issue for thousands of refugees.

TRANSPORTATION

Drive on right

Baku

283 ships 641,200 grt

THE TRANSPORTATION NETWORK

23,057 km (14,327 miles)

None

2116 km (1315 miles)

None

Buses provide the most efficient public transportation. Access to the Naxçivan enclave is by air or via Iran.

TOURISM

Visitors : Population 1:11

766,000 visitors

Up 13% in 2001

MAIN TOURIST ARRIVALS

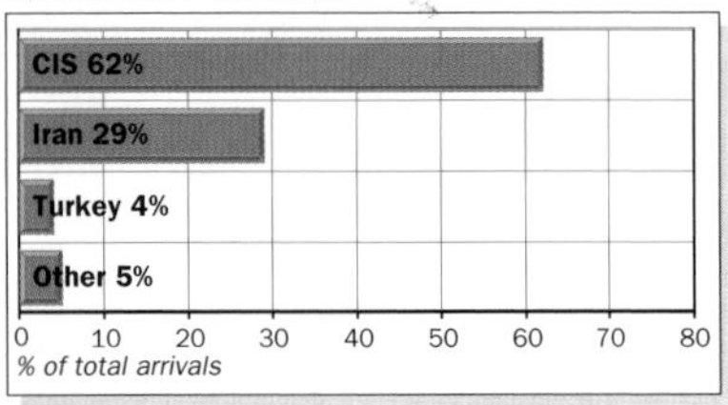
CIS 62%
Iran 29%
Turkey 4%
Other 5%
0 10 20 30 40 50 60 70 80
% of total arrivals

Because of the Nagorno Karabakh conflict, and strong anti-Western feelings (Azerbaijan perceives the West as taking the Armenian side), there are few visitors, most of them on business.

PEOPLE

Pop. density medium

Azeri, Russian

94/km² (242/mi²)

THE URBAN/RURAL POPULATION SPLIT

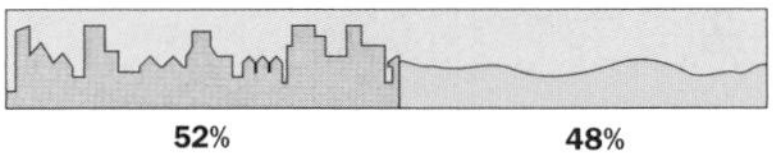
52%
48%

ETHNIC MAKEUP

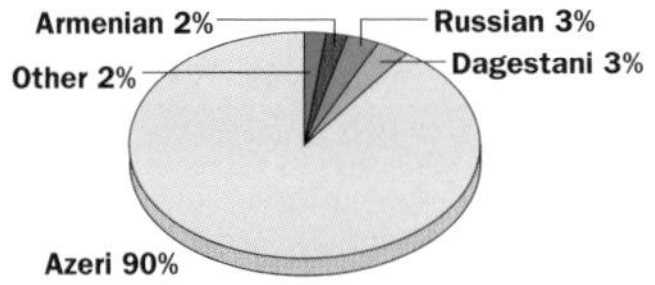
Armenian 2%
Russian 3%
Other 2%
Dagestani 3%
Azeri 90%

The Azeris are a Shi'a Muslim people with close ethnic links to the Turks. Before the collapse of the Soviet Union, and the violence of 1990s, Orthodox Christian Armenians and Russians accounted for 11% of the population. Now ethnic Armenians are concentrated in the Nagorno Karabakh enclave and operate de facto independence.

Women, who were once prominent in the ruling party, have lost their political status and their general status is declining.

POLITICS

Multiparty elections

2000/2005

President Heydar Aliyev

AT THE LAST ELECTION

National Assembly 125 seats

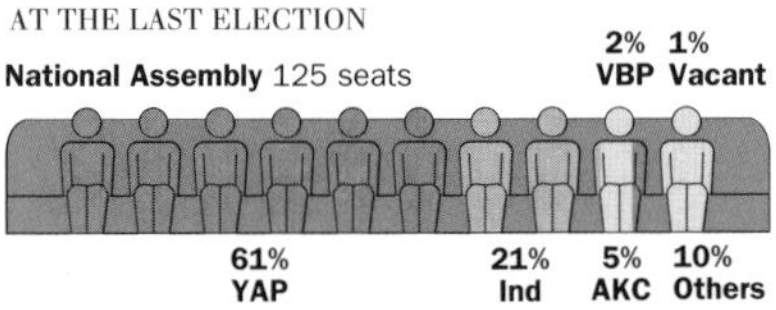
2% VBP
1% Vacant
61% YAP
21% Ind
5% AKC
10% Others

YAP = New Azerbaijan Party **Ind** = Independents
AKC = Azerbaijan Popular Front **VBP** = Civic Solidarity Party
Vacant = Seat reserved for member from Nagorno Karabakh

Azerbaijan became an independent democracy amid war with Armenian forces in the early 1990s. A lasting solution to tensions is elusive. The YAP, in power since 1995, was controversially reelected in 2000. It supports the aging, and visibly ailing, President Heydar Aliyev, who won his second term in office in 1998, aged 75. His autocratic style, and overt efforts to install his son Ilham as his successor, regularly provoke large protests in Baku.

AZERBAIJAN

Total Area : 86 600 sq. km (33 436 sq. miles)

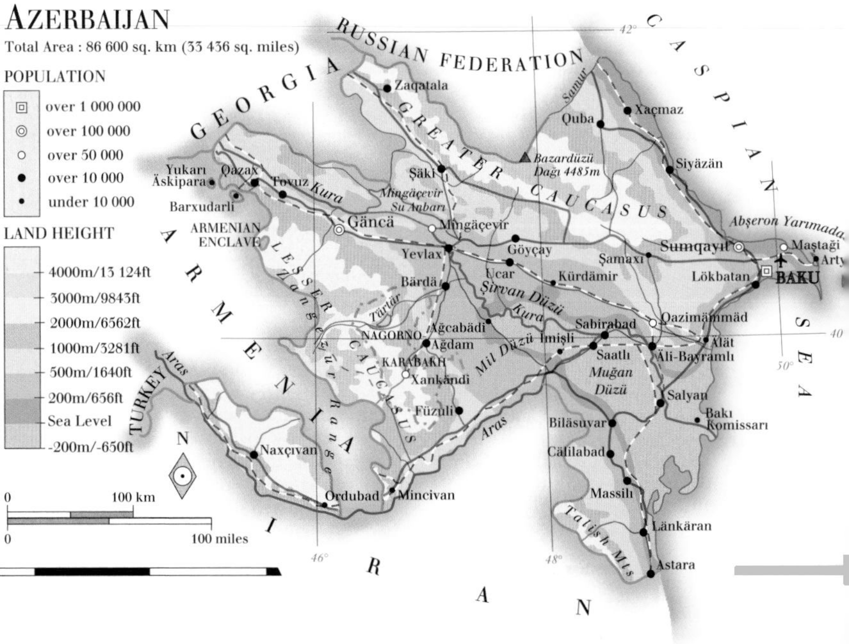
POPULATION
over 1 000 000
over 100 000
over 50 000
over 10 000
under 10 000
LAND HEIGHT
4000m/13 124ft
3000m/9843ft
2000m/6562ft
1000m/3281ft
500m/1640ft
200m/656ft
Sea Level
-200m/-650ft
0 100 km
0 100 miles
RUSSIAN FEDERATION
GEORGIA
ARMENIA
TURKEY
IRAN
CASPIAN SEA
GREATER CAUCASUS
LESSER CAUCASUS
Zaqatala
Xaçmaz
Quba
Bazardüzü Dağı 4485m
Siyäzän
Şäki
Yukarı Äskipara
Qazax
Tovuz
Barxudarli
ARMENIAN ENCLAVE
Gäncä
Mingäçevir
Mingäçevir Su Anbarı
Kura
Abşeron Yarımadası
Sumqayıt
Maştağı
Artyom
BAKU
Lökbatan
Şamaxı
Göyçay
Yevlax
Ucar
Kürdämir
Bärdä
Şirvan Düzü
Tärtär
NAGORNO KARABAKH
Ağcabädi
Ağdam
Xankändi
Füzuli
Imişli
Sabirabad
Qazimämmäd
Älät
Äli-Bayramlı
Saatlı
Muğan Düzü
Salyan
Bakı Komissarı
Biläsuvar
Cälilabad
Massılı
Länkäran
Astara
Talış Mts
Mil Düzü
Aras
Naxçıvan
Ordubad
Mincivan
Samur
N
42°
40°
46°
48°
50°

WORLD AFFAIRS

Joined UN in 1992

CIS | CE | EAPC | OIC | OSCE

Relations with Armenia remain the central issue. Turkey – with its common religion and culture – is a natural ally. The West, as well as neighboring Iran (with a large, ethnically related Azari population) and Russia, are interested in Caspian oil fields. Azerbaijan has stated its intention to join NATO.

AID

Recipient

$226m (receipts)

Up 63% in 2001

Japan is the biggest donor. A pro-Armenia US Congress allowed only limited humanitarian aid in 1992–2002.

DEFENSE

Compulsory military service

$833m

No change in 2001

Part of NATO's Partnership for Peace program since 1994, Azerbaijan hopes to become a full NATO member. Its naval forces operate under CIS control.

ECONOMICS

Inflation 97% p.a. (1990–2000)

$5.27bn

4921 manats (4857)

SCORE CARD

- ❑ World GNP Ranking........111th
- ❑ GNP per Capita........$650
- ❑ Balance of Payments........–$52m
- ❑ Inflation........1.5%
- ❑ Unemployment........1%

Strengths

Extensive oil and natural gas reserves starting to come on stream. Oil pipeline to Turkey under construction. Iron, copper, lead, and salt deposits. Cotton and silk.

Weaknesses

Antiquated Soviet-era industry. Poor infrastructure; corruption. Fallout from Nagorno Karabakh conflict still drains state resources.

EXPORTS

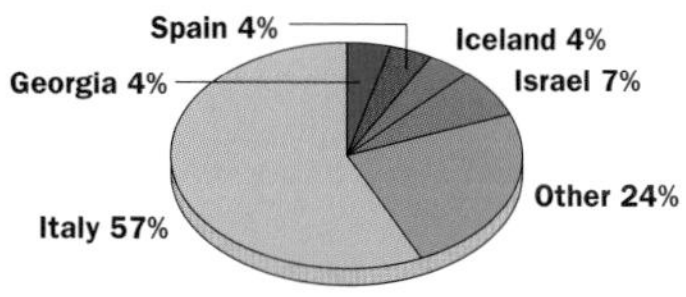
Spain 4%
Iceland 4%
Georgia 4%
Israel 7%
Other 24%
Italy 57%

IMPORTS

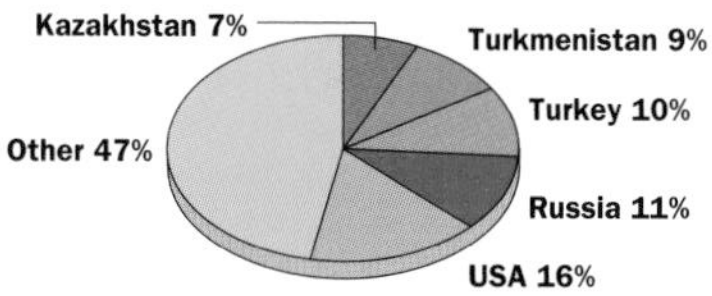
Kazakhstan 7%
Turkmenistan 9%
Turkey 10%
Other 47%
Russia 11%
USA 16%

RESOURCES

Electric power 5.2m kW

18,917 tonnes

308,000 b/d (reserves 7bn barrels)

6m sheep, 2.1m cattle, 15.4m chickens

Iron, bauxite, copper, lead, zinc, limestone, salt, oil, gas

Relatively neglected in the Soviet period, Azerbaijan's Caspian Sea oil fields have attracted international interest. The shallow-water Guneshli field alone has over four million barrels of reserves. Offshore natural gas is also plentiful.

ENVIRONMENT

Sustainability rank: 114th

6% (3% partially protected)

4.2 tonnes per capita

Under the Soviet regime oil pollution devastated the Caspian Sea, and pesticides were massively overused in agriculture. Major rivers suffer heavy pollution from Georgia and Armenia. Lack of funds restricts action.

MEDIA

TV ownership high

Daily newspaper circulation 10 per 1000 people

PUBLISHING AND BROADCAST MEDIA

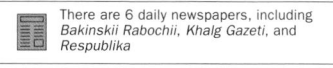

There are 6 daily newspapers, including *Bakinskii Rabochii*, *Khalg Gazeti*, and *Respublika*

1 state-controlled service, 1 independent station

1 state-controlled service

A 1998 decree abolished censorship, but freedom is limited by newsprint controls, license restrictions, and intimidation.

CRIME

No death penalty

23,504 prisoners

Up 7% in 2000–2002

The judicial system returned to political control in 1993. Criminality is a particular problem in camps for those displaced in the Nagorno Karabakh conflict. Elsewhere, there is a low rate of violent crime, but assaults in the street have become less rare.

EDUCATION

School leaving age: 16

97%

156,832 students

When it came to power in the mid-1990s, the YAP began reversing communist control over education policy, which had been particularly noticeable in the teaching of history. Baku State is the largest of an increasing number of universities.

HEALTH

Welfare state health benefits

1 per 280 people

Circulatory and heart diseases, cancers

The already poor health care system effectively collapsed as a result of war and the transition to a market economy.

CHRONOLOGY

Under consecutive Persian, Ottoman, and Russian influences, Azerbaijan, one of the world's major oil producers in 1900, attained independence in 1918.

- ❑ **1920** Red Army invades. Soviet republic established.
- ❑ **1922** Incorporated in Transcaucasian Soviet Federative Socialist Republic (TSFSR).
- ❑ **1930** Forced collectivization of agriculture.
- ❑ **1936** TSFSR disbanded; Azerbaijan a full union republic (ASSR).
- ❑ **1945** Attempted annexation of Azari region of Iran.
- ❑ **1985** Gorbachev tackles corruption in Communist Party of Azerbaijan.
- ❑ **1988** Nagorno Karabakh seeks unification with Armenia.
- ❑ **1990** Nagorno Karabakh attempts secession. Soviet troops move in.
- ❑ **1991** Independence.
- ❑ **1993** Heydar Aliyev president; reelected in 1998.
- ❑ **1994** Cease-fire in war with Armenia over Nagorno Karabakh.
- ❑ **1995, 2000** General elections. Noncommunist YAP in power.

SPENDING

GDP/cap. decrease

CONSUMPTION AND SPENDING

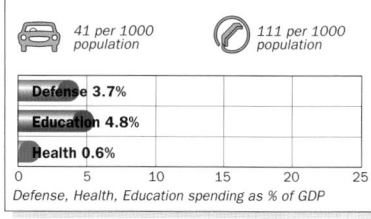

41 per 1000 population

111 per 1000 population

Defense 3.7%
Education 4.8%
Health 0.6%
0
5
10
15
20
25

Defense, Health, Education spending as % of GDP

New oil revenues are threatening to create a nouveau riche elite without reaching the 60% of Azerbaijan's population currently living in poverty.

WORLD RANKING

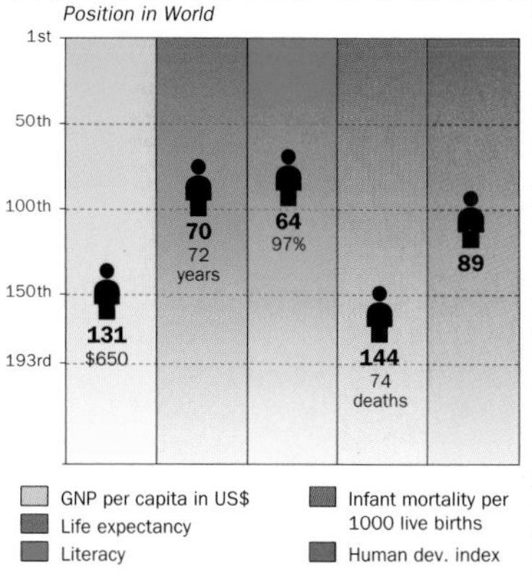
Position in World
1st
50th
100th
150th
193rd
131
$650
70
72
years
64
97%
144
74
deaths
89
GNP per capita in US$
Life expectancy
Literacy
Infant mortality per 1000 live births
Human dev. index

BAHAMAS

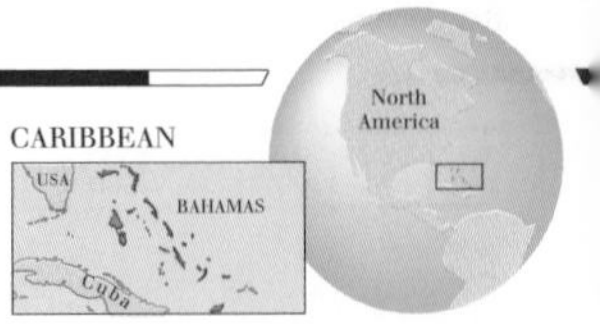

North America
CARIBBEAN
USA
BAHAMAS
Cuba

OFFICIAL NAME: Commonwealth of the Bahamas **CAPITAL:** Nassau
POPULATION: 312,000 **CURRENCY:** Bahamian dollar **OFFICIAL LANGUAGE:** English

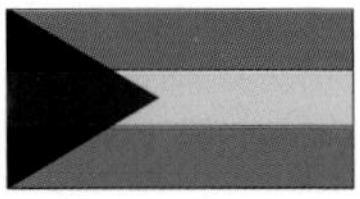

1973 | 1973 | July 10 | BS | -5 | +1242 | .bs

THE BAHAMAS, THOUGH OFTEN bracketed with Caribbean countries, actually lies northeast of Cuba in the western Atlantic. The archipelago has 700 islands and 2400 cays: just 30 are inhabited. Long established as a tourist resort, the Bahamas today is also a major offshore financial center. It has one of the world's largest open-registry fleets; only a tiny fraction is owned by Bahamian nationals.

CLIMATE

Tropical oceanic

WEATHER CHART FOR NASSAU

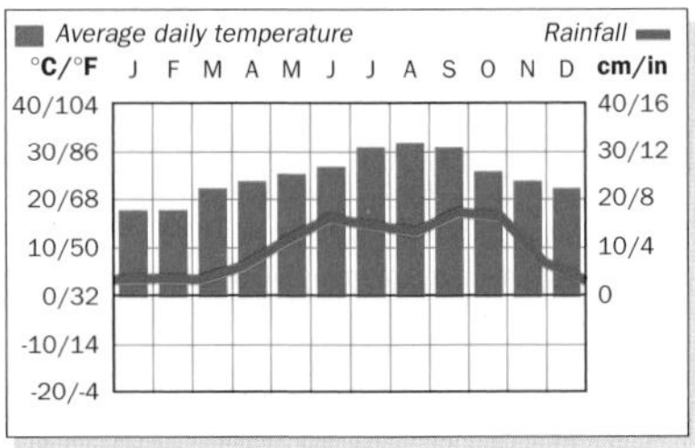

Average daily temperature
Rainfall
°C/°F
J F M A M J J A S O N D
cm/in
40/104
30/86
20/68
10/50
0/32
-10/14
-20/-4
40/16
30/12
20/8
10/4
0

The whole of the Bahamas chain has a typically subtropical climate with consistently mild winters. Hurricanes may occur from July to December.

TRANSPORTATION

Drive on left

Freeport International 1.23m passengers

3.34m grt

THE TRANSPORTATION NETWORK

1546 km (961 miles)

None

None

None

While traveling around and between the major islands is relatively easy, transportation links for the many "Out Islands" are greatly restricted.

TOURISM

Visitors : Population 4.5:1

1.4m visitors

Down 9% in 2002

MAIN TOURIST ARRIVALS

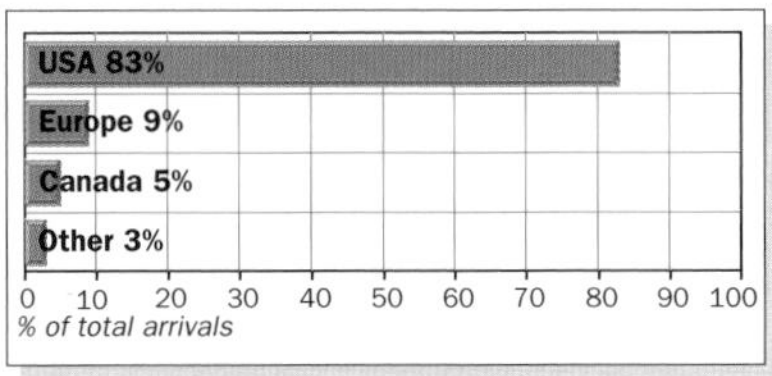

USA 83%
Europe 9%
Canada 5%
Other 3%
0 10 20 30 40 50 60 70 80 90 100
% of total arrivals

The tourist industry, built around beaches, casinos, and cruise ships, employs over 40% of the population. Larger hotel complexes on the main islands compete with small, family-run guesthouses in the outlying destinations.

PEOPLE

Pop. density low

English, English Creole, French Creole

31/km² (81/mi²)

THE URBAN/RURAL POPULATION SPLIT

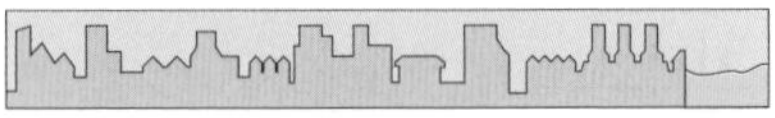

89%
11%

RELIGIOUS PERSUASION

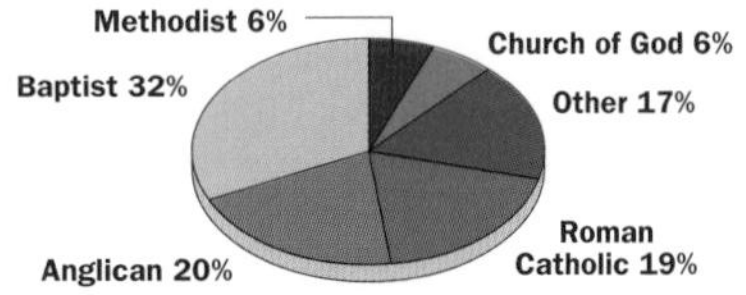

Methodist 6%
Church of God 6%
Baptist 32%
Other 17%
Roman Catholic 19%
Anglican 20%

Africans first arrived as slaves in the 16th century; their descendants constitute most of the population, alongside a rich white minority. About two-thirds of the population live on New Providence Island, and most of them in Nassau. More women are now entering the professions.

POLITICS

Multiparty elections

L. House 2002/2007
U. House 2002/2007

H.M. Queen Elizabeth II

AT THE LAST ELECTION

House of Assembly 40 seats

73% PLP
17% FNM
10% Ind

PLP = Progressive Liberal Party
FNM = Free National Movement
Ind = Independents

Senate 16 seats

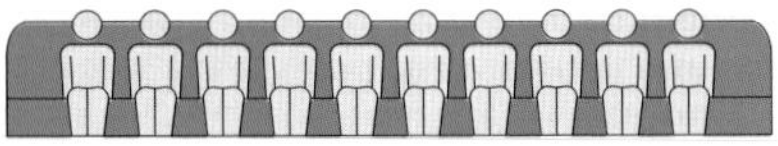

The members of the Senate are appointed by the governor-general on the recommendation of the prime minister and the leader of the opposition

Twenty-five years of unbroken rule by the PLP under Prime Minister Lynden Pindling were brought to an end by the 1992 elections. His legacy of steering the Bahamas to independence and ending white political domination was undermined by allegations of narcotics-related corruption. There followed a decade of FNM government under Hubert Ingraham, who emphasized tightening up ministerial accountability, introduced legislation to counter money laundering, and achieved relative economic success. However, his privatization drive proved deeply unpopular and the FNM was roundly defeated in 2002 by a resurgent PLP now led by Perry Christie.

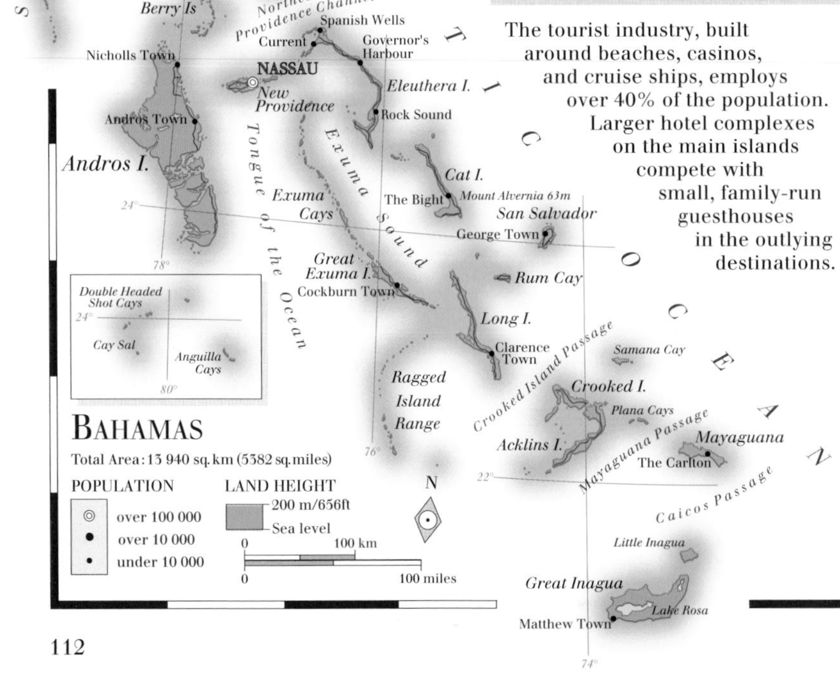

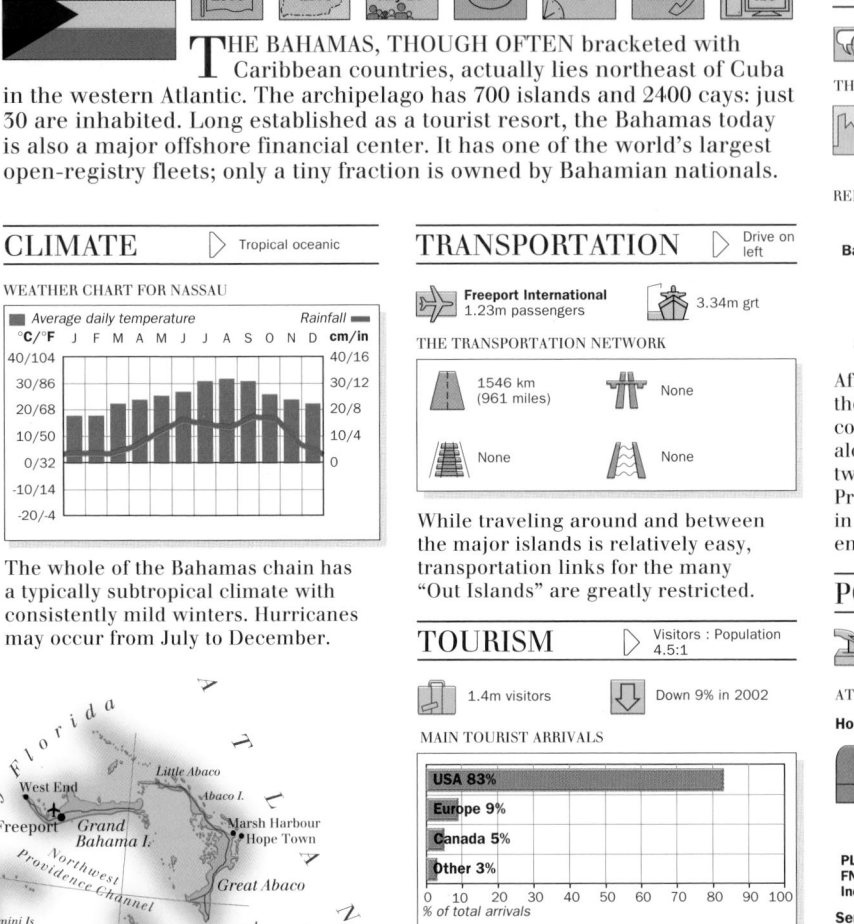

Straits of Florida
ATLANTIC OCEAN
West End
Freeport
Grand Bahama I.
Little Abaco
Abaco I.
Marsh Harbour
Hope Town
Great Abaco
Northwest Providence Channel
Bimini Is
Berry Is
Northeast Providence Channel
Spanish Wells
Current
Governor's Harbour
Nicholls Town
NASSAU
New Providence
Eleuthera I.
Rock Sound
Andros Town
Andros I.
Tongue of the Ocean
Exuma Sound
Exuma Cays
Cat I.
The Bight
Mount Alvernia 63m
San Salvador
George Town
Great Exuma I.
Cockburn Town
Rum Cay
Long I.
Clarence Town
Samana Cay
Crooked Island Passage
Crooked I.
Plana Cays
Ragged Island Range
Acklins I.
Mayaguana Passage
Mayaguana
The Carlton
Caicos Passage
Little Inagua
Great Inagua
Lake Rosa
Matthew Town
Double Headed Shot Cays
Cay Sal
Anguilla Cays
BAHAMAS
Total Area: 13 940 sq. km (5382 sq. miles)
POPULATION
over 100 000
over 10 000
under 10 000
LAND HEIGHT
200 m/656ft
Sea level
0 100 km
0 100 miles
N

B

WORLD AFFAIRS

Joined UN in 1973

ACS | Caricom | Comm | NAM | OAS

A reputation as a center for money laundering and narcotics transshipment remains, though the government has taken vigorous action to combat both. Unauthorized immigrants from Haiti and Cuba dominate regional relations.

AID

Recipient

US$8m (receipts) — Up 33% in 2001

Aid is modest. The IDB and the US offer interest-free development loans. China in 1998 loaned Nassau US$17 million for a convention and theater complex.

DEFENSE

No compulsory military service

US$29m — Down 3% in 2001

The UK is the main trainer of and supplier for the small naval defense force. The interception of narcotics and illegal immigrants is the force's main activity. There is no land army.

ECONOMICS

Inflation 2.7% p.a. (1990–2000)

US$4.53bn — 1 Bahamian dollar (1)

SCORE CARD

❑ World GNP Ranking	117th
❑ GNP per Capita	US$14,860
❑ Balance of Payments	–US$402m
❑ Inflation	2%
❑ Unemployment	9%

Strengths

Major international financial services sector, including banking, insurance, and business trade center. Major tourism and cruise ship destination. Growing container port. International ship registration.

Weaknesses

Growing competition in financial services and tourism from neighboring states. Overdependence on US visitors.

EXPORTS

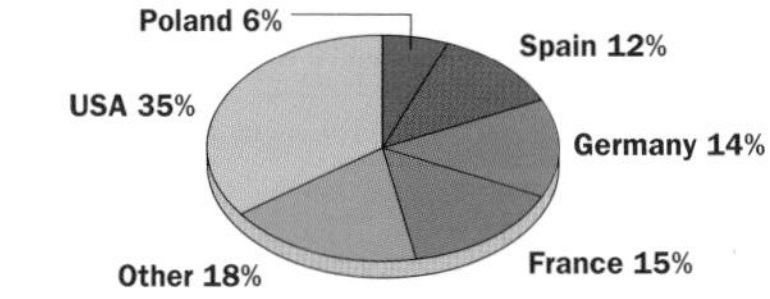
Poland 6%
Spain 12%
USA 35%
Germany 14%
Other 18%
France 15%

IMPORTS

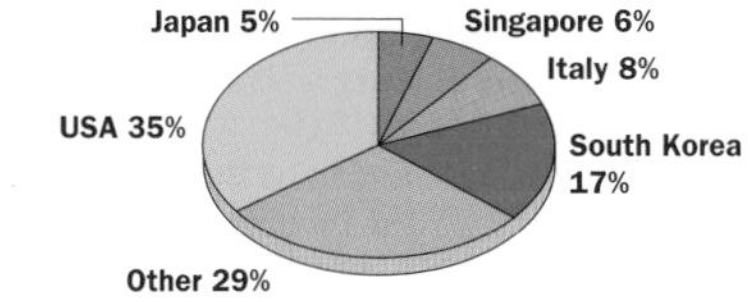
Japan 5%
Singapore 6%
Italy 8%
USA 35%
South Korea 17%
Other 29%

Archetypal island paradise. Its natural beauty attracts more than four tourists per inhabitant to the Bahamas every year.

RESOURCES

Electric power 401,000 kW

10,502 tonnes — Not an oil producer

13,852 goats, 6418 sheep, 4900 pigs, 4.1m chickens — Salt, aragonite

The Bahamas has no strategic resources. A 13.5 MW electricity generating plant was opened in 1998.

ENVIRONMENT

Not available

11% (0.1% partially protected) — 6 tonnes per capita

As on many Caribbean islands, hotel overdevelopment is a major cause for concern. Environmental groups have also pointed out the potential for accidents posed by the Bahamas' enormous oil storage depots.

MEDIA

TV ownership medium

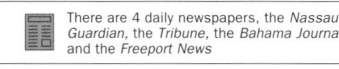

Daily newspaper circulation 99 per 1000 people

PUBLISHING AND BROADCAST MEDIA

There are 4 daily newspapers, the *Nassau Guardian*, the *Tribune*, the *Bahama Journal*, and the *Freeport News*

1 state-owned service — 5 services: 1 state-owned, 4 independent

The state-owned TV channel faces very stiff competition from Florida-based US broadcasters.

CRIME

Death penalty in use

1280 prisoners — Down 29% in 1999

The death penalty remains in force. Violent crime, ranging from narcotics-related murders to serious vandalism, is on the increase. Tourists can be targets for petty thefts. Illegal weapons are readily available.

EDUCATION

School leaving age: 16

96% — 5305 students

Schooling follows the former British selective system. Tertiary students attend the University of the West Indies or colleges in the US.

CHRONOLOGY

Once an English pirate base, the Bahamas, whose first parliament sat in 1729, formally became a British colony in 1783.

- ❑ **1920–1933** US prohibition laws turn Bahamas into prosperous bootlegging center.
- ❑ **1959–1962** Introduction of full male suffrage; women gain the vote.
- ❑ **1973** Independence.
- ❑ **1983** Narcotics-smuggling scandals involving the government.
- ❑ **1992** FNM wins elections, ending 25 years of PLP rule.
- ❑ **2002** PLP returned to power.

HEALTH

Welfare state health benefits

1 per 943 people — Obstetric causes, heart diseases, cancers, murders, accidents

The health service combines state and private systems. In the outlying islands access to care relies on the Flying Doctor Service and around 50 local health centers. Three of the country's four hospitals are on New Providence.

SPENDING

GDP/cap. increase

CONSUMPTION AND SPENDING

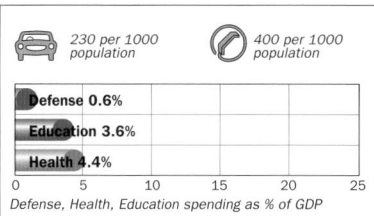

230 per 1000 population — *400 per 1000 population*

Defense 0.6%
Education 3.6%
Health 4.4%
0
5
10
15
20
25

Defense, Health, Education spending as % of GDP

There are marked wealth disparities: urban professionals who work in the financial sector are at one end of the scale, and the poor fishermen from the outlying islands are near the other. Cuban and Haitian refugees, who have no legal status, are the poorest group of all.

WORLD RANKING

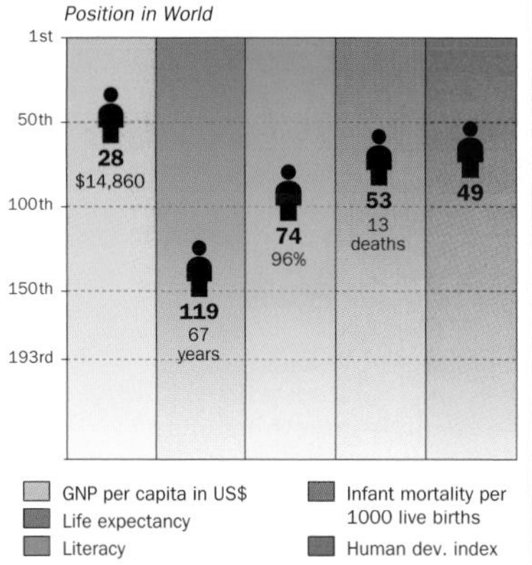
Position in World
1st
50th
100th
150th
193rd
28
$14,860
119
67
years
74
96%
53
13
deaths
49
GNP per capita in US$
Life expectancy
Literacy
Infant mortality per 1000 live births
Human dev. index

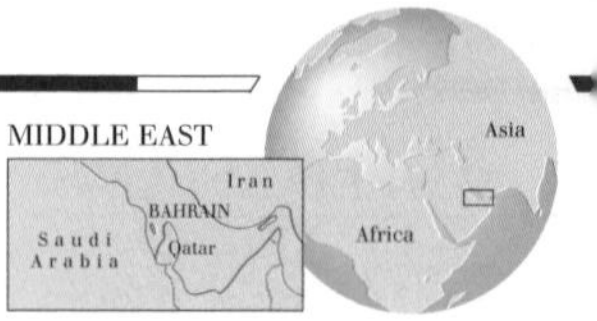
MIDDLE EAST
Iran
BAHRAIN
Saudi Arabia
Qatar
Asia
Africa

BAHRAIN

OFFICIAL NAME: Kingdom of Bahrain **CAPITAL:** Manama
POPULATION: 663,000 **CURRENCY:** Bahraini dinar **OFFICIAL LANGUAGE:** Arabic

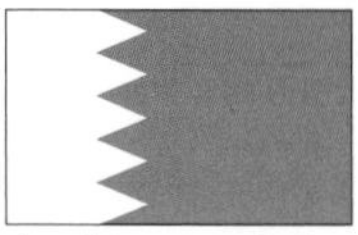

1971 | 1971 | Dec 16 | BRN | +3 | +973 | .bh

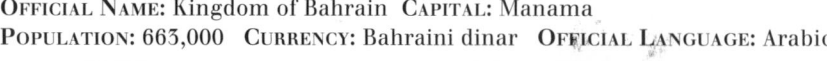

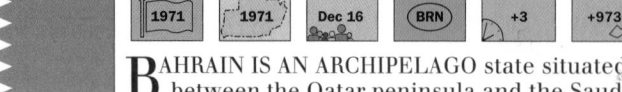

BAHRAIN IS AN ARCHIPELAGO state situated between the Qatar peninsula and the Saudi Arabian mainland. Only three of its islands are inhabited. Bahrain Island is connected to Saudi Arabia's Eastern Province by a causeway opened in 1986. Bahrain was the first Gulf emirate to export oil; its reserves are now almost depleted. Services such as offshore banking, insurance, and tourism are major employment sectors for skilled Bahrainis.

POLITICS

Nonparty elections

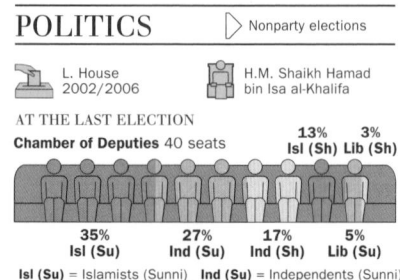

L. House 2002/2006

H.M. Shaikh Hamad bin Isa al-Khalifa

AT THE LAST ELECTION

Chamber of Deputies 40 seats

13% Isl (Sh)
3% Lib (Sh)
35% Isl (Su)
27% Ind (Su)
17% Ind (Sh)
5% Lib (Su)

Isl (Su) = Islamists (Sunni) **Ind (Su)** = Independents (Sunni)
Ind (Sh) = Independents (Shi'a) **Isl (Sh)** = Islamists (Shi'a)
Lib (Su) = Liberals (Sunni) **Lib (Sh)** = Liberals (Shi'a)

Consultative Council 40 seats

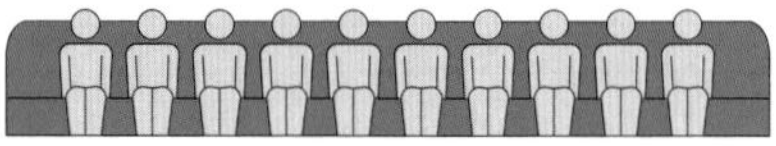

The Consultative Council is appointed by the king

The al-Khalifa family has dominated politics since 1783, but the amir was advised from 1993 by an appointed Consultative Council, and in 2002, following a referendum, Bahrain became a constitutional monarchy. Its first legislative elections were held that year: moderate Islamists gained the most seats, while radical candidates boycotted the poll. Shaikh Hamad bin Isa al-Khalifa, who has ruled since 1999, supports the economic liberalization initiated by his father. Repeal in 2001 of the State Security Law promised an end to the detention of political dissidents.

CLIMATE

Hot desert

WEATHER CHART FOR MANAMA

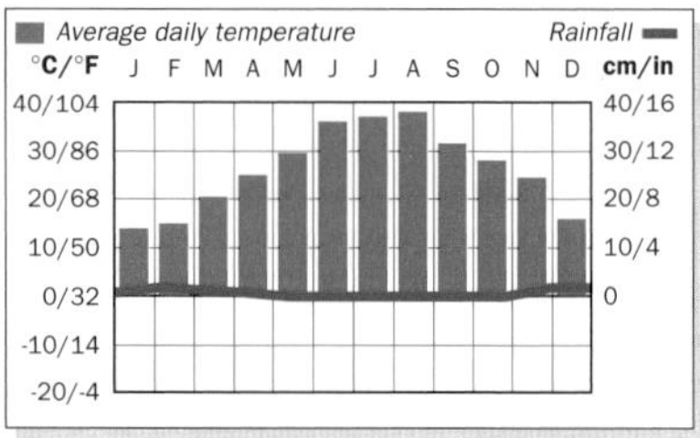
Average daily temperature
Rainfall
°C/°F
J F M A M J J A S O N D
cm/in
40/104
30/86
20/68
10/50
0/32
-10/14
-20/-4
40/16
30/12
20/8
10/4
0

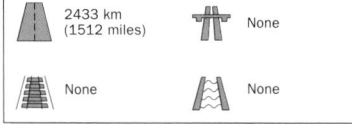

Temperatures soar toward 40°C (104°F) in June–August. In December– March the weather is pleasantly warm.

TRANSPORTATION

Drive on right

Bahrain International, Manama 4.15m passengers

121 ships 338,091 grt

THE TRANSPORTATION NETWORK

2433 km (1512 miles)		None	
None		None	

The King Fahd Causeway connects Bahrain to Saudi Arabia, and ferries travel regularly to Iran. Buses are the main form of public transportation.

TOURISM

Visitors : Population 3.7:1

2.42m visitors

Up 20% in 2000

MAIN TOURIST ARRIVALS

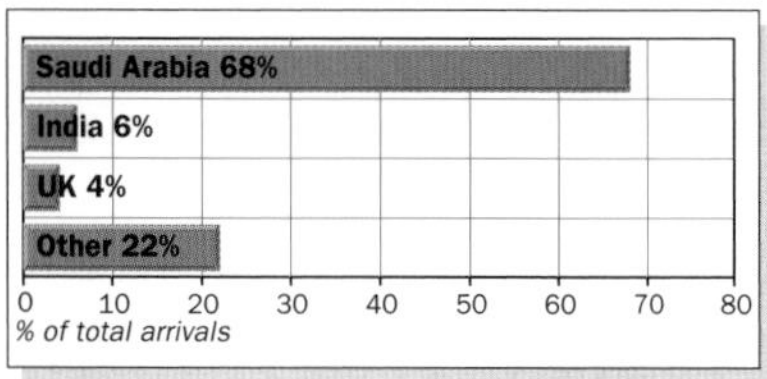
Saudi Arabia 68%
India 6%
UK 4%
Other 22%
0 10 20 30 40 50 60 70 80
% of total arrivals

Bahrain's relatively liberal lifestyle has made it something of a magnet for visitors from neighboring Gulf states. Bahrain has a modern airport and is a center for business conventions.

PEOPLE

Pop. density high

Arabic

939/km² (2429/mi²)

THE URBAN/RURAL POPULATION SPLIT

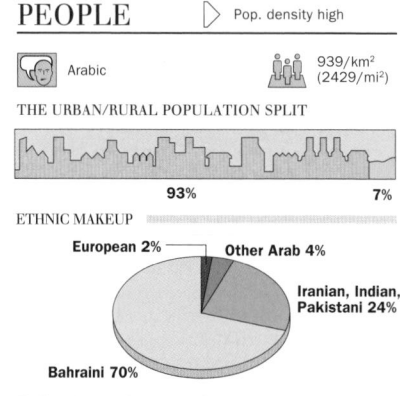

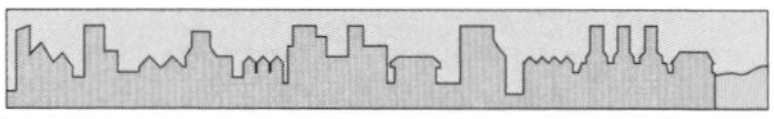
93%
7%

ETHNIC MAKEUP

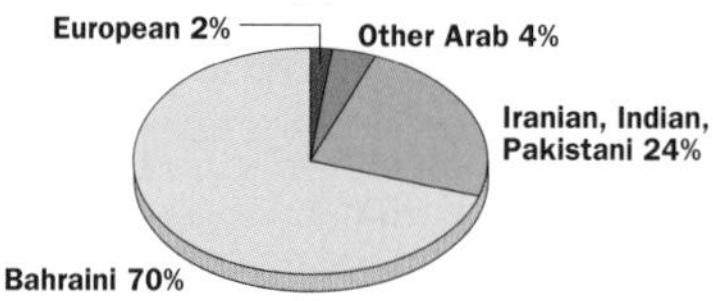
European 2%
Other Arab 4%
Iranian, Indian, Pakistani 24%
Bahraini 70%

Bahrain is the smallest and most densely populated Arab state. The key division is between Sunni and Shi'a Muslims, about 30% and 70% of the population respectively. Sunnis hold the best jobs in business and government. Shi'a Muslims tend to do menial work and have a lower standard of living. The most impoverished Shi'a Muslims tend to be of Iranian descent.

Bahrain has a smaller expatriate population than many other Arab countries. The ruling al-Khalifa family has responded to declining oil reserves by diversifying the economy to provide service industry jobs for Bahrainis.

Bahrain is the most liberal of the Gulf states. Alcohol is freely available. Women have access to education and are not obliged to wear the veil. Since 2000 they have been entitled to participate in politics.

***The Grand Mosque, Manama.** The largest building in Bahrain, it can accommodate 7000 people.*

WORLD AFFAIRS

Joined UN in 1971

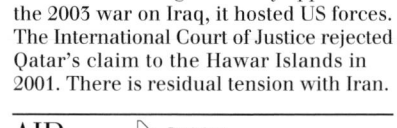

AL | Damasc | GCC | OIC | OAPEC

Bahrain has good relations with the UK and the US. Though formally opposed to the 2003 war on Iraq, it hosted US forces. The International Court of Justice rejected Qatar's claim to the Hawar Islands in 2001. There is residual tension with Iran.

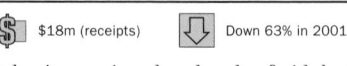

AID

Recipient

$18m (receipts)

Down 63% in 2001

Bahrain receives low levels of aid, but takes the lion's share from the offshore oil field shared with Saudi Arabia, effectively a subsidy from the latter.

DEFENSE

No compulsory military service

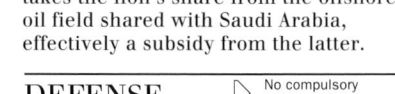

$364m

Up 13% in 2001

The defense force includes a small but well-equipped air force. The navy is hard-pressed to patrol the 49-island archipelago. Bahrain is home to the US 5th Fleet, and US air bases there have been used in recent conflicts.

ECONOMICS

Inflation 0.8% p.a. (1990–2001)

$7.25bn

0.377 Bahraini dinars (0.377)

SCORE CARD

❑ World GNP Ranking	101st
❑ GNP per Capita	$11,130
❑ Balance of Payments	$113m
❑ Inflation	1.5%
❑ Unemployment	15%

STRENGTHS

Oil and gas: production and refining. Major offshore banking sector. Inward investment. Tourism. Aluminum production. Near self-sufficiency in food.

WEAKNESSES

Depleted oil reserves and insufficient diversification. High unemployment. High levels of government borrowing.

EXPORTS

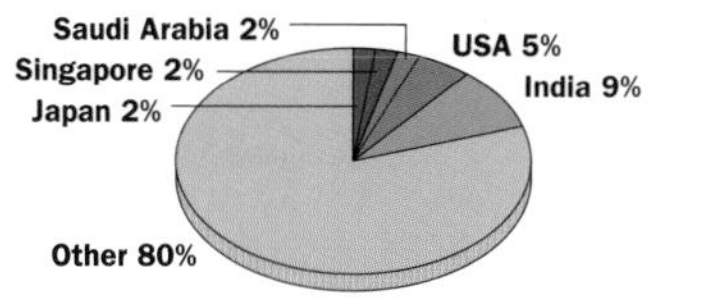
Saudi Arabia 2%
Singapore 2%
Japan 2%
USA 5%
India 9%
Other 80%

IMPORTS

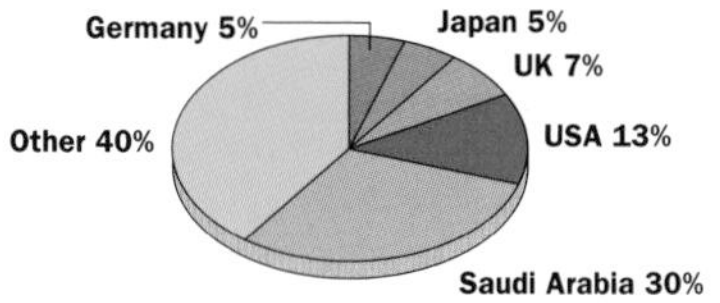
Germany 5%
Japan 5%
UK 7%
USA 13%
Other 40%
Saudi Arabia 30%

BAHRAIN

Total Area : 655 sq. km (253 sq. miles)

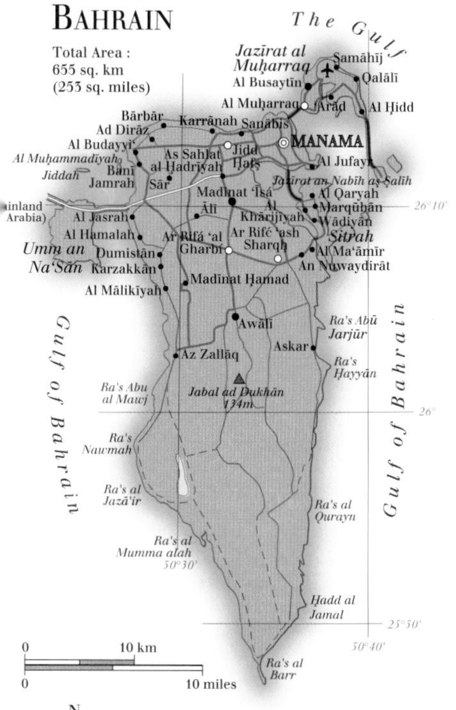
The Gulf
Jazīrat al Muḩarraq
Samāhīj
Qalālī
Al Busaytīn
Al Muḩarraq
'Arād
Al Ḩidd
Bārbār
Karrānah
Sanābis
Ad Dirāz
Al Budayyi'
MANAMA
As Sahlat
Jidd Ḩafs
Al Muḩammadīyah
Bānī Jamrah
al Ḩadrīyah
Al Jufayr
Jiddah
Sār
Jazīrat an Nabīh as Şāliḩ
Madīnat 'Īsā
Al Qaryah
'Ālī
Marqūbān
Al Jasrah
Khārijīyah
Wādiyān
Al Ḩamalah
Ar Rifā 'al Gharbī
Ar Rifā 'ash Sharqī
Sitrah
Umm an Na'Sān
Dumistān
Al Ma'āmīr
Karzakkān
An Nuwaydirāt
Madīnat Ḩamad
Al Mālikīyah
'Awālī
Ra's Abū Jarjūr
Askar
Az Zallāq
Ra's Ḩayyān
Gulf of Bahrain
Ra's Abu al Mawj
Jabal ad Dukhān 134m
Ra's Nawmah
Ra's al Jazā'ir
Ra's al Qurayn
Ra's al Mumma alah
Ḩadd al Jamal
Ra's al Barr
0 10 km
0 10 miles
N

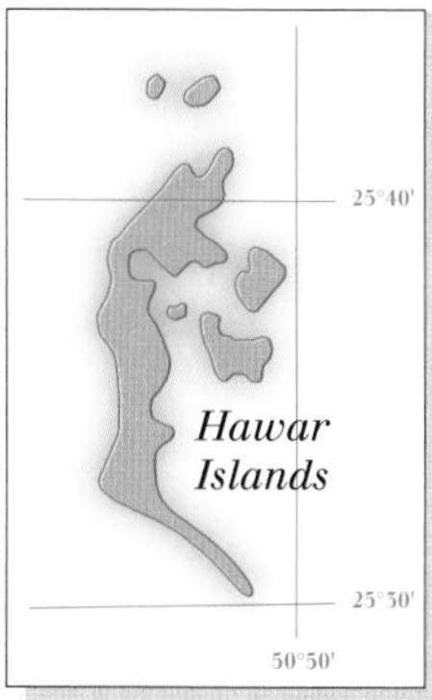
Hawar Islands

POPULATION

- ◎ over 100 000
- ○ over 50 000
- ● over 10 000
- • under 10 000

LAND HEIGHT

100m/328ft

Sea Level

RESOURCES

Electric power 1.4m kW

11,730 tonnes

37,413 b/d (reserves 219m barrels)

17,500 sheep, 16,300 goats, 465,000 chickens

Oil, natural gas

Bahrain remains dependent on its oil and gas industry. Production of crude oil has declined sharply since the 1970s, and there are fears that reserves may run out by 2010. As oil has declined, so gas has assumed greater importance. Most is used to supply local industries, particularly the aluminum plant, which was established in 1972.

ENVIRONMENT

Not available

1% partially protected

28.8 tonnes per capita

Local marine life, particularly the dugong, is vulnerable to upstream oil pollution from the Gulf. Bahrain and Abu Dhabi (UAE) signed an agreement in 2000 on environmental concerns.

MEDIA

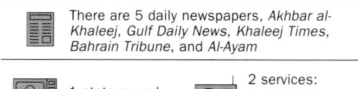

TV ownership high

Daily newspaper circulation 117 per 1000 people

PUBLISHING AND BROADCAST MEDIA

There are 5 daily newspapers, *Akhbar al-Khaleej*, *Gulf Daily News*, *Khaleej Times*, *Bahrain Tribune*, and *Al-Ayam*

1 state-owned service

2 services: 1 state-owned, 1 independent

Bahrain has a less authoritarian media regime than most of the Gulf, though government critics have been prosecuted. CNN and BBC satellite TV are freely available.

CRIME

Death penalty in use

911 prisoners

Down 62% in 1996–1998

Crime is minimal, and theft and muggings are rare. Suspected political dissidents are monitored by the police.

CHRONOLOGY

Bahrain became a British Protected State in the 19th century.

- ❑ **1971** Independence from Britain.
- ❑ **1981** Founder member of GCC.
- ❑ **1991** Supports US-led action expelling Iraq from Kuwait.
- ❑ **1999** Accession of Shaikh Hamad.
- ❑ **2001** Referendum approves transition to democracy.
- ❑ **2002** Becomes a constitutional monarchy. Islamists win elections.

B

EDUCATION

School leaving age: 15

88%

11,048 students

Female literacy rates are among the highest in the Gulf. The University of Bahrain opened in 1986.

HEALTH

Welfare state health benefits

1 per 592 people

Circulatory diseases, perinatal deaths, injury, poisonings

The high-quality health service is free to Bahraini nationals. Some go abroad for advanced care. The Muharraq Health Center was upgraded in 2001.

SPENDING

GDP/cap. increase

CONSUMPTION AND SPENDING

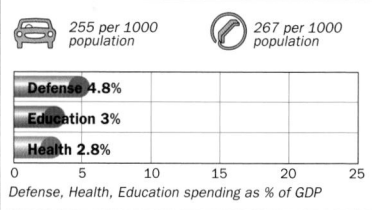

255 per 1000 population

267 per 1000 population

Defense 4.8%
Education 3%
Health 2.8%
0
5
10
15
20
25

Defense, Health, Education spending as % of GDP

Beneficiaries of the king's extensive patronage form the wealthiest group in society. Bahrain's largest religious community, the Shi'a Muslims, is also the poorest.

WORLD RANKING

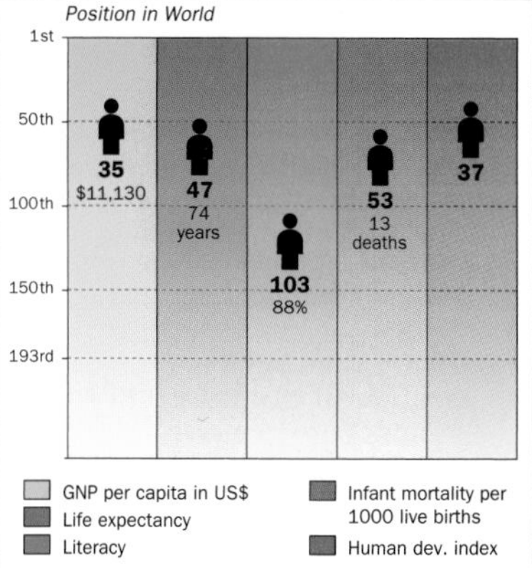
Position in World
1st
50th
100th
150th
193rd
35
$11,130
47
74 years
103
88%
53
13 deaths
37
GNP per capita in US$
Life expectancy
Literacy
Infant mortality per 1000 live births
Human dev. index

B

BANGLADESH

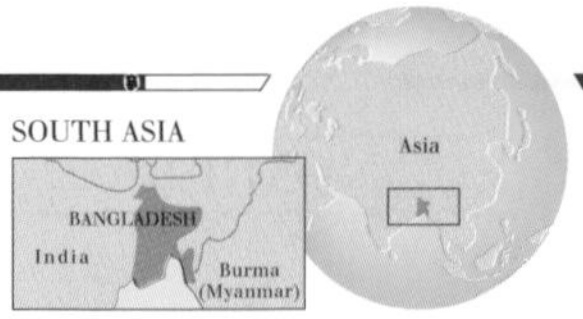
SOUTH ASIA
Asia
BANGLADESH
India
Burma (Myanmar)

OFFICIAL NAME: People's Republic of Bangladesh **CAPITAL:** Dhaka
POPULATION: 143 million **CURRENCY:** Taka **OFFICIAL LANGUAGE:** Bengali

1971 | 1971 | March 26 | BD | +6 | +880 | .bd

LOCATED AROUND the confluence of the mighty Ganges and Jamuna rivers, Bangladesh is the eastern half of historic Bengal. Most of the country is composed of fertile alluvial plains; the north and northeast are mountainous, as is the Chittagong region in the southeast. After seceding from Pakistan in 1971, Bangladesh had a troubled history of political instability, with periods of emergency rule. Effective democracy was restored in 1991. Bangladesh's major economic sectors are jute production, textiles, and agriculture. Its climate can wreak havoc – in 1991 a massive cyclone killed more than 140,000 people.

CLIMATE

Tropical/subtropical

WEATHER CHART FOR DHAKA

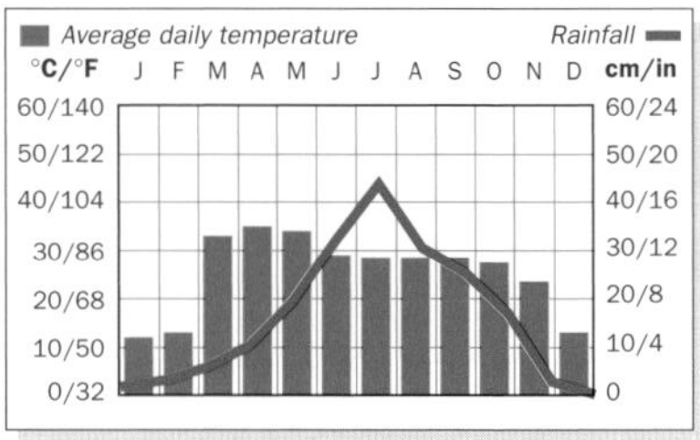
Average daily temperature
Rainfall
°C/°F
J F M A M J J A S O N D
cm/in
60/140
50/122
40/104
30/86
20/68
10/50
0/32
60/24
50/20
40/16
30/12
20/8
10/4
0

During the monsoon, the water level generally rises 6 m (20 ft) above normal, flooding up to two-thirds of the country. The floods are made much worse when the Ganges, Jamuna, and Meghna rivers, which converge in a huge delta in Bangladesh, are swollen by the melting of the Himalayan snows and heavy rain in India. Cyclones build up regularly in the Bay of Bengal, with sometimes devastating effects on the flat coastal region.

TRANSPORTATION

Drive on left

Zia International, Dhaka 2.87m passengers

317 ships 387,600 grt

THE TRANSPORTATION NETWORK

19,112 km (11,876 miles)	None
2745 km (1706 miles)	8046 km (5000 miles)

Most transportation in Bangladesh is by water, although government policy is now concentrating on developing road and rail links, including the reopening in mid-2000 of a passenger rail service into India. The 4.8-km (3-mile) Bangabandhu road and rail bridge across the Jamuna River at Sirajganj was finally inaugurated in 1998 and is now a major artery. Bangladesh's two major ports, Mungla and Chittagong, are being upgraded to take advanced container ships.

Begum Khaleda Zia, reelected as prime minister in 2001.

Sheikh Hasina Wajed, AL leader and former prime minister.

TOURISM

Visitors : Population 1:693

207,000 visitors

Up 4% in 2001

MAIN TOURIST ARRIVALS

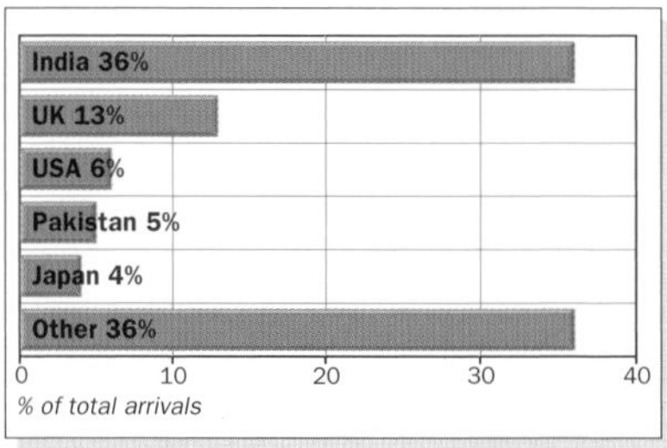
India 36%
UK 13%
USA 6%
Pakistan 5%
Japan 4%
Other 36%
0
10
20
30
40
% of total arrivals

The Mughal architecture in Dhaka and the Pala dynasty (7th–10th centuries) city of Sonargaon, just to the southeast, are major attractions, but tourists may be deterred by social and political unrest. Most visitors are Indian businessmen or Bangladeshis living overseas who return to visit relatives.

Traders on the Meghna River. Life is governed by the vast network of rivers. The floodplains are among the most fertile in the world.

PEOPLE

Pop. density high

Bengali, Urdu, Chakma, Marma (Magh), Garo, Khasi, Santhali, Tripuri, Mro

1071/km² (2774/mi²)

THE URBAN/RURAL POPULATION SPLIT

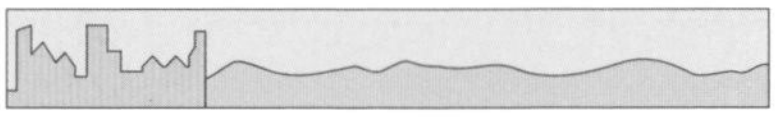
26%
74%

RELIGIOUS PERSUASION

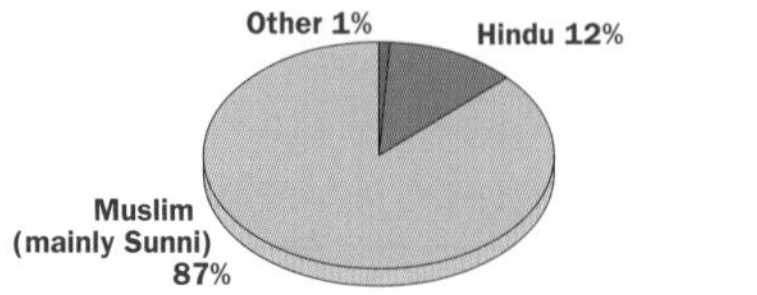
Other 1%
Hindu 12%
Muslim (mainly Sunni) 87%

ETHNIC MAKEUP

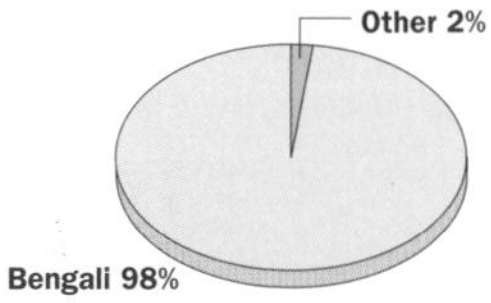
Other 2%
Bengali 98%

Bangladesh is one of the most densely populated countries in the world, despite the fact that three-quarters of the population is rural. As in India, there is considerable Muslim–Hindu tension; in 2001, thousands of Hindus and members of other religious minorities claimed persecution by the new nationalist government.

Though more than half of Bangladeshis, rural and urban, still live below the poverty line, there has been an improvement in living standards over the past decade.

The textile trade has been one factor in the growing emancipation of Bangladeshi women, many of whom now enjoy an independent income. Women are now included in official employment statistics and are the main customers of the Grameen Bank, the most successful rural bank. They have led both the government and the opposition. However, Bangladesh was criticized by Amnesty International in 2000 for insufficiently protecting women's rights, and a UN report later that year revealed that nearly half of Bangladeshi women are victims of domestic violence.

POPULATION AGE BREAKDOWN

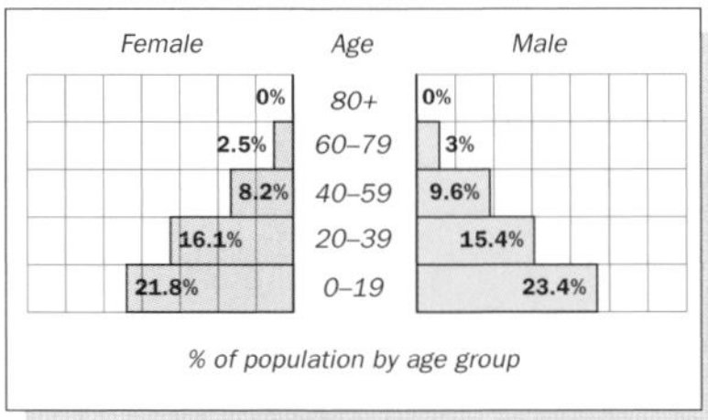
Female
Age
Male
0%
80+
0%
2.5%
60–79
3%
8.2%
40–59
9.6%
16.1%
20–39
15.4%
21.8%
0–19
23.4%
% of population by age group

POLITICS

Multiparty elections

2001/2006

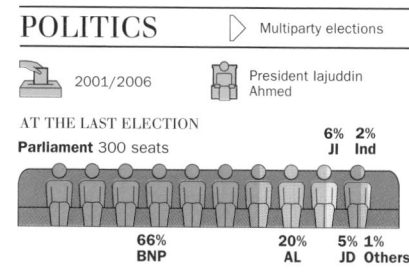

President Iajuddin Ahmed

AT THE LAST ELECTION

Parliament 300 seats

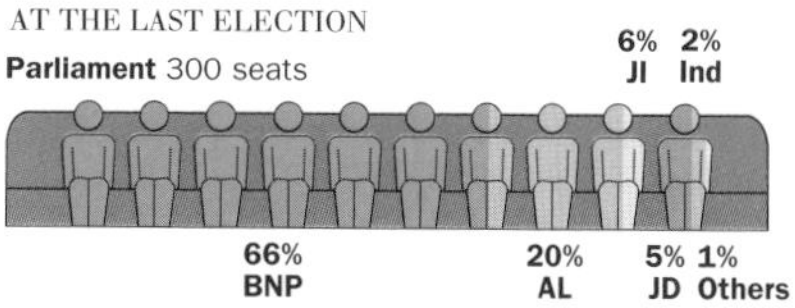
6% JI
2% Ind
66% BNP
20% AL
5% JD
1% Others

BNP = Bangladesh Nationalist Party and allies
AL = Awami League **JI** = Jamaat-e-Islami
JD = Jatiya Dal (Ershad) **Ind** = Independents

Bangladesh returned to multiparty democracy in 1991, following a period of military rule.

PROFILE

Between 1975 and 1990 the military was in power in Bangladesh. The overthrow of President Ershad in 1990 saw a return to multiparty politics; the army remains poised, however, to intervene in the event of a breakdown in internal order.

Bangladesh's first woman prime minister, Begum Khaleda Zia, head of the BNP, was elected in 1991.

BANGLADESH

Total Area : 144 000 sq. km (55 598 sq. miles)

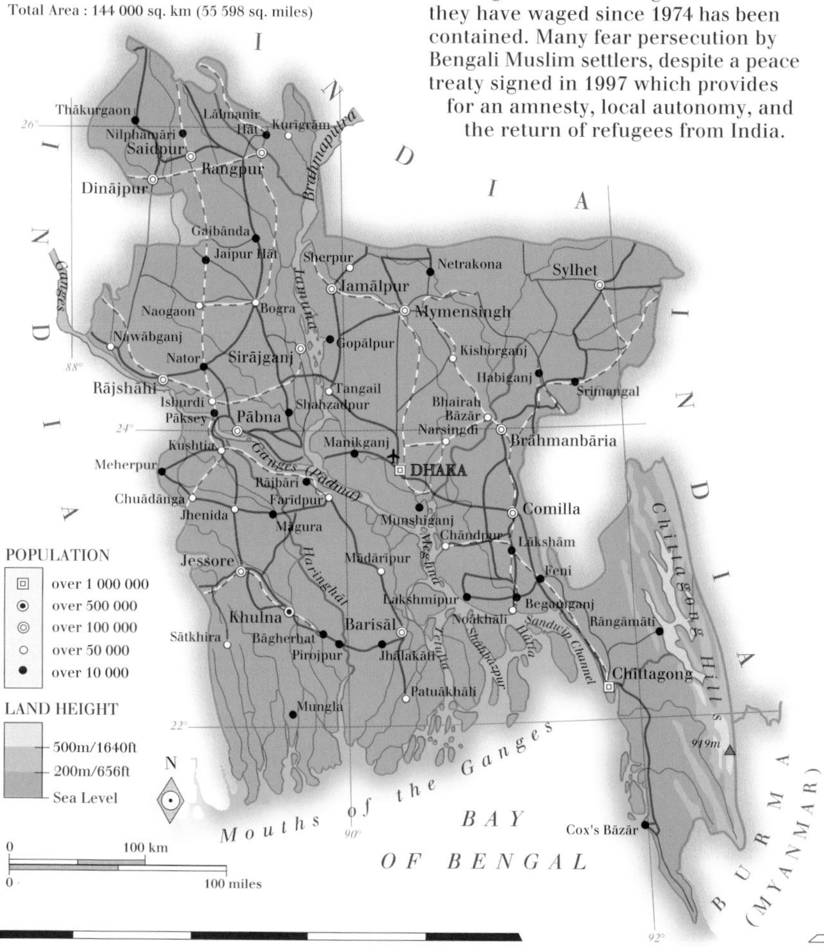
INDIA
Thākurgaon
Lālmanir Hāt
Kurigrām
Nilphāmāri
Saidpur
Rangpur
Dinājpur
Brahmaputra
Gaibānda
Jaipur Hāt
Sherpur
Netrakona
Sylhet
Jamālpur
Mymensingh
Ganges
Naogaon
Bogra
Jamuna
Nawābganj
Gopālpur
Kishorganj
Nator
Sirājganj
Habiganj
Rājshāhi
Tangail
Srimangal
Ishurdi
Pāksey
Pābna
Shahzadpur
Bhairab Bāzār
Narsingdi
Brāhmanbāria
Kushtia
Mānikganj
Meherpur
Ganges (Padma)
DHAKA
Rājbāri
Faridpur
Chuādānga
Comilla
Jhenida
Munshiganj
Māgura
Chāndpur
Lākshām
Meghna
Jessore
Mādāripur
Feni
Haringhāta
Lakshmipur
Begamganj
Noākhāli
Rāngāmāti
Khulna
Sandwip Channel
Sātkhira
Bāgherhat
Barisāl
Pirojpur
Jhālakāti
Tetulia
Chittagong
Chittagong Hills
Patuākhāli
Mungla
919m
Mouths of the Ganges
BAY OF BENGAL
Cox's Bāzār
BURMA (MYANMAR)
POPULATION
over 1 000 000
over 500 000
over 100 000
over 50 000
over 10 000
LAND HEIGHT
500m/1640ft
200m/656ft
Sea Level
N
0
100 km
100 miles
26°
24°
22°
88°
90°
92°

Constitutional changes soon replaced a presidential with a parliamentary system of government.

The AL, which had steered Bangladesh to independence in 1971, mounted a sustained campaign against Khaleda Zia's regime, in 1996 forcing a rerun of elections. It won the largest number of seats and its leader, Sheikh Hasina Wajed, went on to become the first prime minister to complete a full term. The revived BNP returned to power in the October 2001 poll, amid much electoral violence, and formed a coalition with the Islamist JI.

MAIN POLITICAL ISSUES

The state sector
Bangladesh is coming under mounting pressure from multilateral lending institutions, which account for the vast majority of the country's capital inflows, to cut costs in the state sector. Simultaneously, state-sector workers are demanding wage increases in line with inflation.

Autonomy for Chittagong Hill Tracts
Buddhist Mongol groups – the Chakma – continue to demand greater autonomy, although the low-level guerrilla war they have waged since 1974 has been contained. Many fear persecution by Bengali Muslim settlers, despite a peace treaty signed in 1997 which provides for an amnesty, local autonomy, and the return of refugees from India.

WORLD AFFAIRS

Joined UN in 1974

Comm | NAM | OIC | SAARC | WTO

Good relations with the West, the main source of essential aid, are a priority. Relations with Pakistan have slowly improved since Pakistan's agreement in 1991 to accept the 250,000 pro-Pakistan Bihari Muslims who have been in Bangladeshi refugee camps since 1971. Relations with India are improving. The damaging effects of the construction of the Farakka Dam on the Ganges, which deprived Bangladesh of irrigation water, have been alleviated by a 30-year agreement signed in 1996 guaranteeing the right of both parties to share the Ganges water. Tensions persist over the illegal migration of Bangladeshis into neighboring Indian states.

AID

Recipient

$1.02bn (receipts)

Down 13% in 2001

Aid disbursements to Bangladesh each year are substantially greater than the annual value of foreign investment in the country. Aid also finances the bulk of state capital spending. The Bangladesh Development Aid Consortium meets annually to discuss aid spending under the auspices of the World Bank. One result of the level of aid is that Bangladesh has fallen into one of the traps of an aid-dependent economy: the large middle class has a vested interest in perpetuating a system which provides its members with lucrative contracts and access to external resources.

CHRONOLOGY

Bengal was the first part of the Indian subcontinent to come under British rule when the East India Company was made the *diwani* (tax collector) by the Mughal emperor in 1765.

- **1905** Muslims persuade British rulers to partition state of Bengal, to create a Muslim-dominated East Bengal.
- **1906** Muslim League established in Dhaka.
- **1912** Partition of 1905 reversed.
- **1947** British withdrawal from India. Partition plans establish a largely Muslim state of East (present-day Bangladesh) and West Pakistan, separated by 1600 km (1000 miles) of Indian, and largely Hindu, territory.
- **1949** AL founded to campaign for autonomy from West Pakistan.
- **1968** Gen. Yahya Khan heads government in Islamabad.

B

B

CHRONOLOGY *continued*

- **1970** Elections give AL, under Sheikh Mujibur Rahman, clear majority. Rioting and guerrilla warfare following Yahya Khan's refusal to convene assembly. Year ends with worst recorded storms in Bangladesh's history – between 200,000 and 500,000 dead.
- **1971** Civil war, as Sheikh Mujib and AL declare unilateral independence. Ten million Bangladeshis flee to India. Pakistani troops defeated in 12 days by Mukhti Bahini – the Bengal Liberation Army.
- **1972** Sheikh Mujib elected prime minister. Nationalization of key industries, including jute and textiles. Bangladesh achieves international recognition and joins Commonwealth. Pakistan withdraws in protest.
- **1974** Severe floods damage rice crop.
- **1975** Sheikh Mujib assassinated. Military coups end with Gen. Ziaur Rahman taking power. Institution of single-party state.
- **1976** Banning of trade union federations.
- **1977** Zia assumes presidency. Islam adopted as first principle of constitution.
- **1981** Zia assassinated.
- **1982** Gen. Ershad takes over.
- **1983** Democratic elections restored by Ershad. Ershad assumes presidency.
- **1986** Elections. AL and BNP fail to unseat Ershad.
- **1987** Ershad announces state of emergency.
- **1988** Islam becomes constitutional state religion.
- **1990** Ershad resigns following demonstrations.
- **1991** Elections won by BNP. Khaleda Zia (widow of Zia) becomes prime minister. Ershad imprisoned. Role of the president reduced to ceremonial functions. Floods following cyclone kill 140,000 people.
- **1994** Author Taslima Nasreen, who is accused of blasphemy, escapes to Sweden.
- **1996** Election returns BNP to power. Results are rejected by opposition parties, which force fresh elections. Sheikh Hasina Wajed of AL then takes power.
- **2001** Supreme Court declares issuing of religious decrees (*fatawa*) to be a criminal offense. BNP returned to power following violence-marred elections.
- **2002** Privatization program begins.

DEFENSE

No compulsory military service

$639m

Down 8% in 2001

The military, which dominated politics between 1975 and 1990, still wields considerable influence, despite the restoration of civilian government. The army was mobilized to fight rising crime from 2002. Defense spending is high and controversial. Some of the air force's Russian-built MiG-29 fighters were cut from the fleet in 2002, just two years after their purchase by the previous government.

BANGLADESHI ARMED FORCES

200 main battle tanks (100 PRC Type-59/69, 100 T-54/55)	120,000 personnel
5 frigates and 33 patrol boats	10,500 personnel
83 combat aircraft (18 A-5C Fantan, 16 F-6, 23 F-7M/FT-7B, 8 MiG-29)	6500 personnel
None	

ECONOMICS

Inflation 3.9% p.a. (1990–2001)

$48.6bn

58.41 taka (57.45)

SCORE CARD

- World GNP Ranking 51st
- GNP per Capita $360
- Balance of Payments .... –$816m
- Inflation 1.4%
- Unemployment 3%

EXPORTS

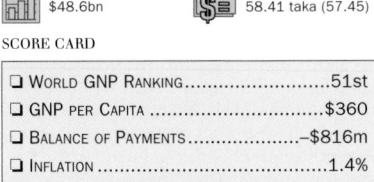

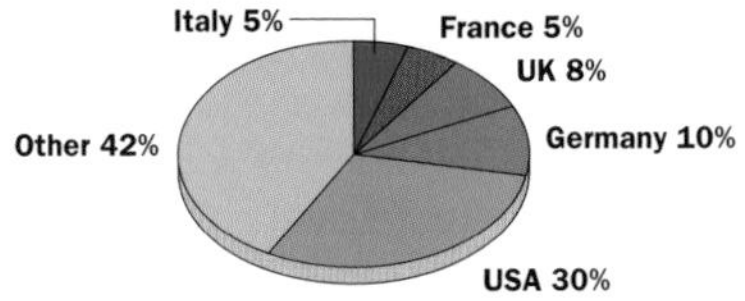
Italy 5%
France 5%
UK 8%
Germany 10%
USA 30%
Other 42%

IMPORTS

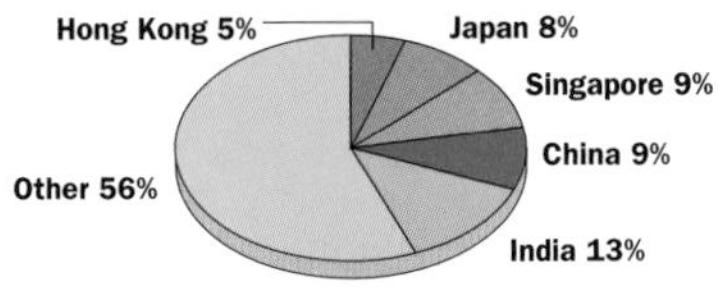
Hong Kong 5%
Japan 8%
Singapore 9%
China 9%
India 13%
Other 56%

Strengths

80% of the world's jute fiber exports come from Bangladesh. Low wages ensure a competitive and expanding textile industry, which provides over three-quarters of manufacturing export earnings.

Weaknesses

The agricultural sector, employing the majority of Bangladeshis, is vulnerable to the violent and unpredictable climate. Poor infrastructure deters investment. Large and inefficient state sector.

Profile

Government ministers like to portray Bangladesh as an emerging NIC, but its economy is still overwhelmingly dependent on agriculture and large aid inflows. Agriculture, which provides jute and tobacco, is productive; Bangladesh's soils, fed by the Ganges, Jamuna, and Meghna rivers, are highly fertile. However, severe weather frequently destroys a whole year's crop. Agricultural wages are among the lowest in the world.

The state sector, which owns large, inefficient, and massively loss-making companies, is in difficulty. The World Bank, the source of most aid, wishes to see loss-making concerns cut their workforces or close down. In 2002 a privatization program was announced.

Textiles and garments are currently the healthiest sectors. Economic zones (export processing zones) with special concessions have attracted foreign investment, as well as helping to promote a small indigenous electronics industry. Bangladesh receives generous textile import quotas from the EU and NAFTA.

ECONOMIC PERFORMANCE INDICATOR

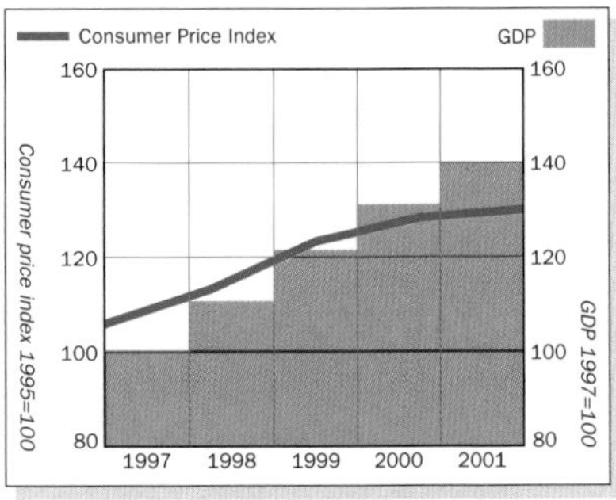
Consumer Price Index
GDP
160
140
120
100
80
1997
1998
1999
2000
2001
Consumer price index 1995=100
GDP 1997=100

BANGLADESH : MAJOR BUSINESSES

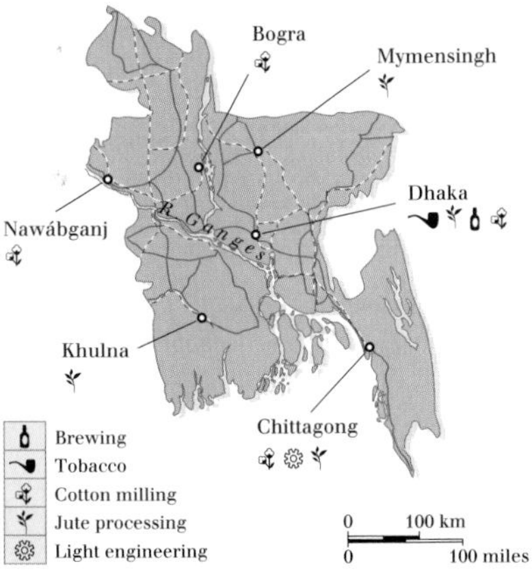
Bogra
Mymensingh
Dhaka
Nawábganj
R. Ganges
Khulna
Chittagong
Brewing
Tobacco
Cotton milling
Jute processing
Light engineering
0
100 km
0
100 miles

B

RESOURCES

Electric power 3.5m kW

1.66m tonnes

20 b/d (reserves 70,000 barrels)

34.4m goats, 24m cattle, 13m ducks, 140m chickens

Salt, oil, natural gas, limestone

Bangladesh is the world's major jute producer, accounting for 80% of world jute fiber exports and about 50% of world jute manufactures exports.

Bangladesh holds world-class gas reserves, estimated to last as long as 200 years at the present extraction rate. Natural gas from the Bay of Bengal, exploited by the state-owned Bangladesh Oil, Gas, and Minerals Corporation, came on stream in 1988.

ELECTRICITY GENERATION

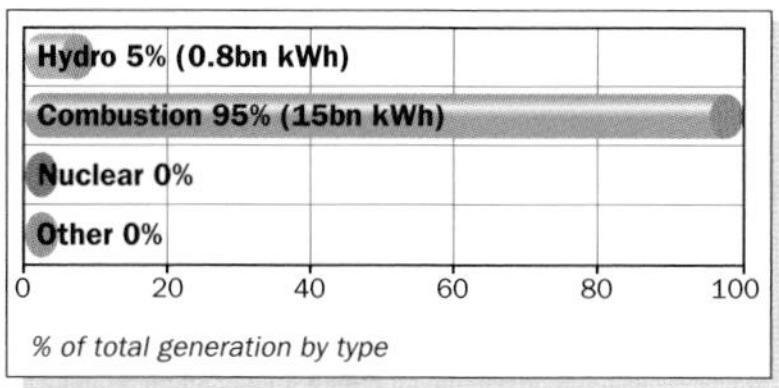
Hydro 5% (0.8bn kWh)
Combustion 95% (15bn kWh)
Nuclear 0%
Other 0%
0
20
40
60
80
100
% of total generation by type

BANGLADESH : LAND USE

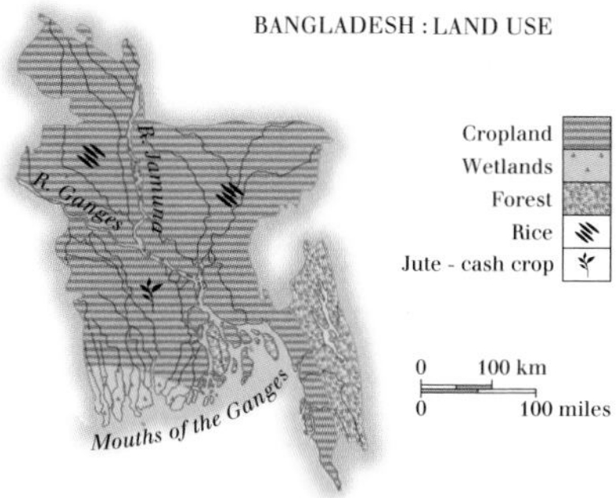
R. Ganges
R. Jamuna
Mouths of the Ganges
Cropland
Wetlands
Forest
Rice
Jute - cash crop
0 100 km
0 100 miles

ENVIRONMENT

Sustainability rank: 86th

0.8% (0.7% partially protected)

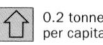

0.2 tonnes per capita

Bangladesh's climate gives rise to devastating floods and cyclones, with consequent huge death tolls and substantial damage to crops. The country is too poor to finance environmental initiatives.

ENVIRONMENTAL TREATIES

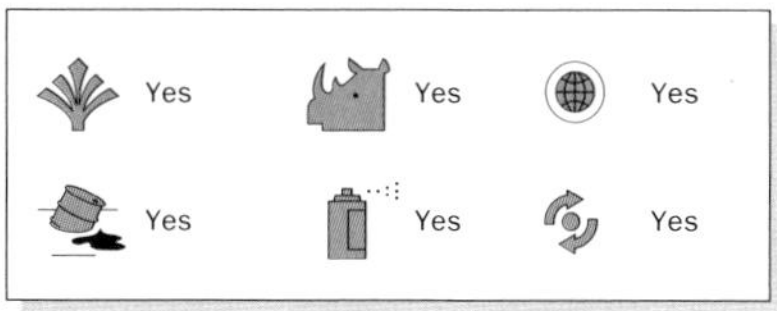
Yes
Yes
Yes
Yes
Yes
Yes

HEALTH

Welfare state health benefits

1 per 5000 people

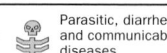

Parasitic, diarrheal, and communicable diseases

Although primary health care in rural areas improved in the 1990s, problems remain severe and are exacerbated by a shortage of medical staff and facilities. Sanitation is a major problem; drinking water is contaminated with disease and high levels of arsenic. Simple cloth filters could cut cholera infections by half. Priority for birth control programs has reduced the population growth rate dramatically in the last 20 years.

MEDIA

TV ownership low

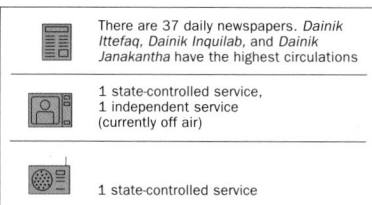

Daily newspaper circulation 53 per 1000 people

PUBLISHING AND BROADCAST MEDIA

There are 37 daily newspapers. *Dainik Ittefaq, Dainik Inquilab,* and *Dainik Janakantha* have the highest circulations

1 state-controlled service, 1 independent service (currently off air)

1 state-controlled service

With fewer than half of the population able to read, newspaper circulation is limited. English-language dailies appeal to the urban elite. Over 70% of TV programs are produced locally by the state-run service. The only independent service was taken off air in 2002. Foreign satellite channels are increasingly available but are subject to government bans. Press freedoms, which emerged briefly after the fall of President Ershad in 1990, have since been eroded.

SPENDING

GDP/cap. increase

CONSUMPTION AND SPENDING

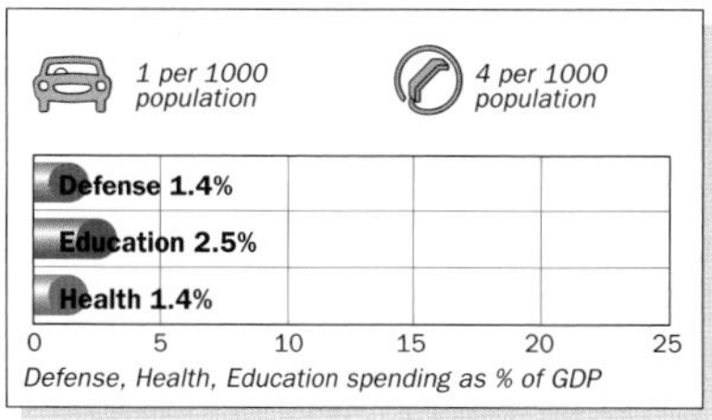
1 per 1000 population
4 per 1000 population
Defense 1.4%
Education 2.5%
Health 1.4%
0
5
10
15
20
25
Defense, Health, Education spending as % of GDP

Average incomes in Bangladesh remain very low, but wealth disparities are not quite as marked as in India. State officials tend to be among the better-off members of society.

CRIME

Death penalty in use

70,000 prisoners

Up 17% in 1996–1998

CRIME RATES

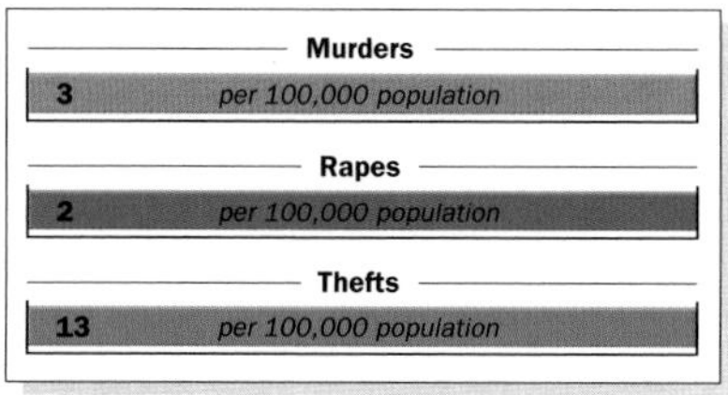
Murders
3 per 100,000 population
Rapes
2 per 100,000 population
Thefts
13 per 100,000 population

Rising levels of sectarian violence have led to the introduction of antiterrorism laws allowing summary justice and heavy penalties, including death. Deaths in prisons are common, and the human rights record of the security forces, especially the paramilitary Bangladesh Rifles, is questionable. From 2002, soldiers have been deployed to support police. Opposition activists have been targeted in crackdowns. Women are increasingly the victims of murder, rape, abduction, and acid attacks.

EDUCATION

School leaving age: 10

41%

878,537 students

THE EDUCATION SYSTEM

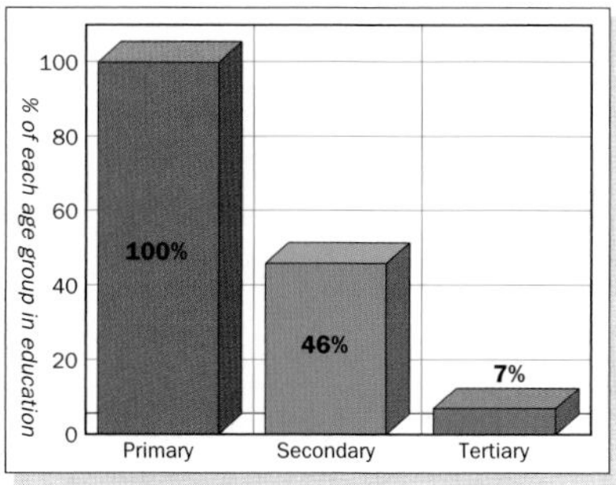
100
80
60
40
20
0
% of each age group in education
100%
46%
7%
Primary
Secondary
Tertiary

A dramatic reduction in the 1990s in the number of child workers meant an accompanying rise in school attendance. Islamic *madaris* are run parallel to the state system. There was an outcry from urban schools in 2002 when goat husbandry was put on the national curriculum. Exam cheating is a serious problem. Universities are frequently beset by political violence.

WORLD RANKING

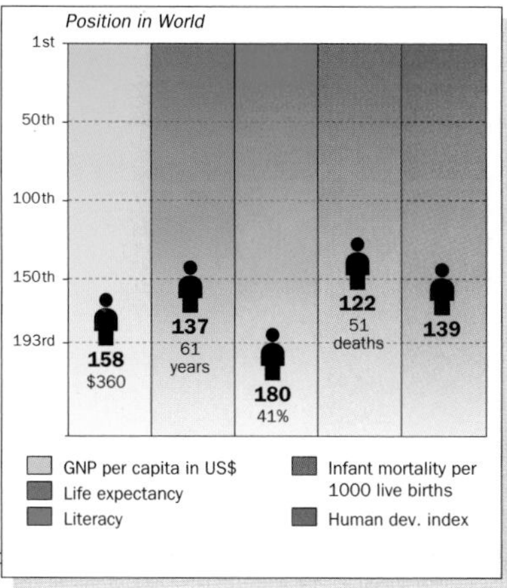
Position in World
1st
50th
100th
150th
193rd
158
$360
137
61
years
180
41%
122
51
deaths
139
GNP per capita in US$
Life expectancy
Literacy
Infant mortality per 1000 live births
Human dev. index

BARBADOS

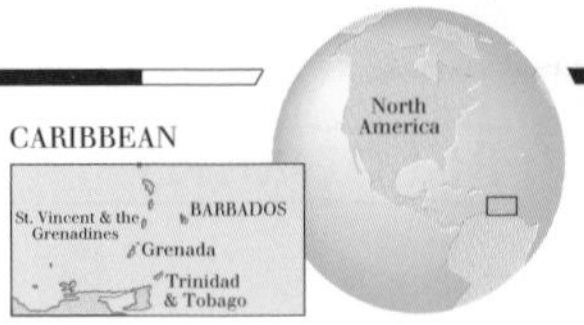
CARIBBEAN
North America
St. Vincent & the Grenadines
BARBADOS
Grenada
Trinidad & Tobago

OFFICIAL NAME: Barbados **CAPITAL:** Bridgetown
POPULATION: 269,000 **CURRENCY:** Barbados dollar **OFFICIAL LANGUAGE:** English

1966 | 1966 | Nov 30 | BDS | -4 | +1246 | .bb

SITUATED TO THE NORTHEAST of Trinidad, Barbados is the most easterly of the West Indian Windward Islands. In the 16th century, the Portuguese were the first Europeans to reach the island, then inhabited by Arawak Indians. However, Barbados was not colonized until the 1620s, when British settlers arrived. Popularly referred to by its neighbors as "little England," Barbados now seeks to forge a new national identity for itself.

CLIMATE

Tropical oceanic

WEATHER CHART FOR BRIDGETOWN

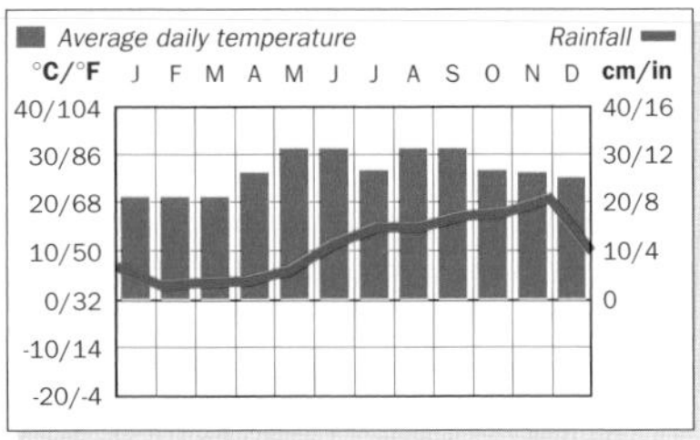
Average daily temperature
Rainfall
°C/°F
J F M A M J J A S O N D
cm/in
40/104
30/86
20/68
10/50
0/32
-10/14
-20/-4
40/16
30/12
20/8
10/4
0

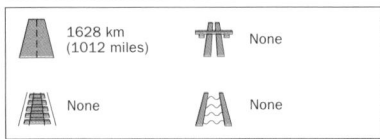

Barbados has a moderate tropical climate and is sunnier and drier than its more mountainous Caribbean neighbors. Hurricanes may occur in the rainy season.

TRANSPORTATION

Drive on left

Grantley Adams International, Bridgetown
2m passengers

68 ships
687,331 grt

THE TRANSPORTATION NETWORK

1628 km (1012 miles)	None
None	None

A multimillion dollar expansion program has upgraded facilities at the international airport. Piers at Bridgetown's port have been improved with foreign aid, as have the island's paved roads. There are bus routes over most of the island.

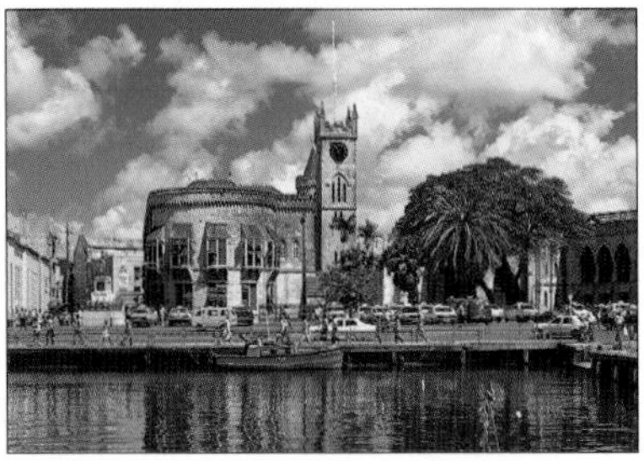

House of Assembly, Trafalgar Square, Bridgetown. Barbados's parliament, the third oldest in the Commonwealth, dates from 1639.

TOURISM

Visitors : Population 1.9:1

498,000 visitors

Down 2% in 2002

MAIN TOURIST ARRIVALS

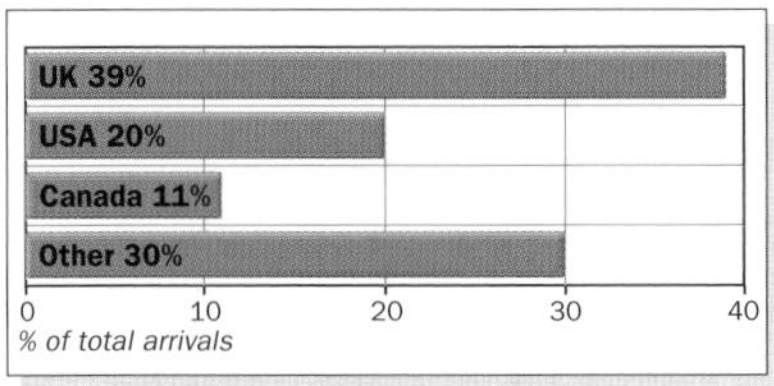
UK 39%
USA 20%
Canada 11%
Other 30%
0
10
20
30
40
% of total arrivals

Tourists, essential to the Barbadian economy, are attracted by the white sandy beaches and sporting activities, as well as the post-colonial ambience and the generally laid-back culture.

PEOPLE

Pop. density high

Bajan (Barbadian English), English

626/km² (1620/mi²)

THE URBAN/RURAL POPULATION SPLIT

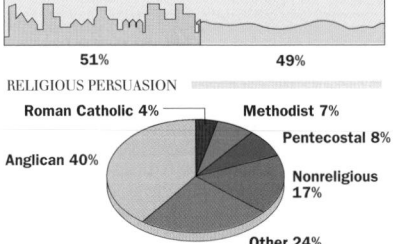

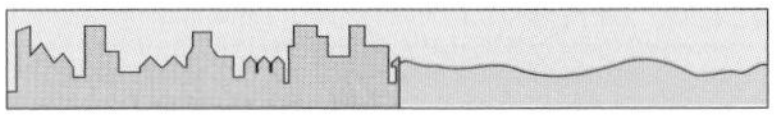
51%
49%

RELIGIOUS PERSUASION

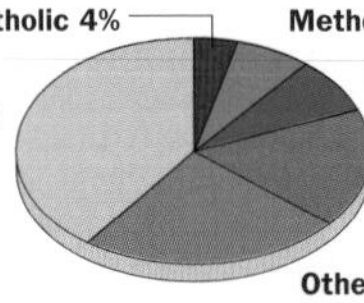
Roman Catholic 4%
Methodist 7%
Pentecostal 8%
Nonreligious 17%
Other 24%
Anglican 40%

Most Barbadians are descended from Africans brought to the island between the 16th and 19th centuries; there are also small groups of south Asians and Europeans, mainly expatriates from the UK, many of whom take up residence on retirement. There is some latent tension between the white community, which controls most of the economy, and the majority black population, though this rarely spills over into violence. Increasing social mobility has allowed many black Barbadians to move into the professions and the civil service. Barbados enjoys a higher standard of living than most Caribbean countries.

POLITICS

Multiparty elections

L. House 2003/2008
U. House 2003/2008

H.M. Queen Elizabeth II

AT THE LAST ELECTION

House of Assembly 30 seats

77% BLP
23% DLP

BLP = Barbados Labour Party
DLP = Democratic Labour Party

Senate 21 seats

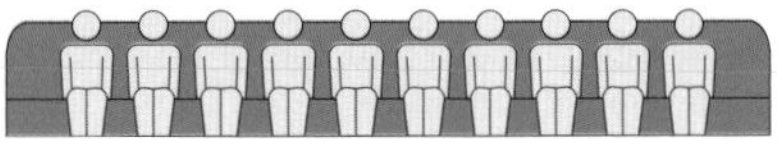

The members of the Senate are appointed. Twelve are chosen by the prime minister, two by the leader of the opposition, and seven independents by the governor-general

Barbados is a multiparty democracy. Owen Arthur, BLP leader and prime minister, prioritizes economic growth and international competitiveness. His party was swept to power in 1994 and won further victories in 1999 and 2003. However, the opposition DLP made significant gains in the 2003 poll as the government began to encounter economic difficulties. Arthur has previously pledged to transform Barbados into a republic.

WORLD AFFAIRS

Joined UN in 1966

ACS | Comm | Caricom | NAM | OAS

Prime Minister Arthur has promoted closer regional integration and has championed small states internationally.

AID

Recipient

No net receipts

Loan repayments exceeded aid received in 2001

Most aid comes from the EU, the US, and the UN, mainly in the form of development project loans and balance-of-payments support.

DEFENSE

No compulsory military service

US$13m

No change in 2001

The small Barbadian army and the constabulary benefit from financial support and training from the US and UK governments, which also supply equipment. Barbados is the headquarters of the Regional Security System, established in 1982 by the Windward and Leeward Islands, a body which acts as a multinational security force for its members.

B

ECONOMICS

Inflation 2.9% p.a. (1990–2001)

US$2.61bn

1.99 Barbados dollars (1.99)

SCORE CARD

- ❑ WORLD GNP RANKING.......................132nd
- ❑ GNP PER CAPITA.........................US$9750
- ❑ BALANCE OF PAYMENTS................–US$146m
- ❑ INFLATION.......................................2.6%
- ❑ UNEMPLOYMENT.................................10%

STRENGTHS

Well-developed tourism based on climate and accessibility. Information processing and financial services are important new growth sectors.

WEAKNESSES

Narrow economic base and an ailing sugar industry. Tourism is vulnerable to global downturns, especially as Barbados is promoted as a luxury destination. Relatively high manufacturing costs.

EXPORTS

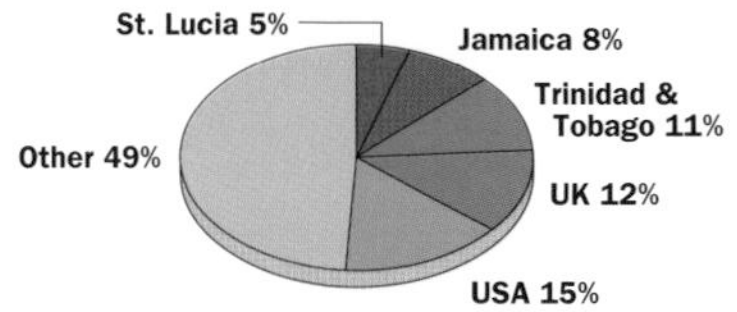
St. Lucia 5%
Jamaica 8%
Trinidad & Tobago 11%
UK 12%
USA 15%
Other 49%

IMPORTS

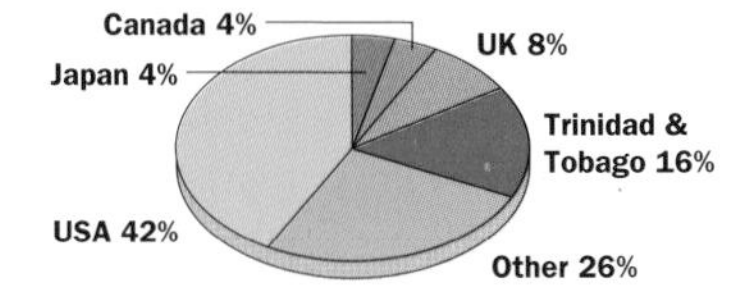
Canada 4%
Japan 4%
UK 8%
Trinidad & Tobago 16%
Other 26%
USA 42%

BARBADOS

Total Area : 430 sq. km (166 sq. miles)

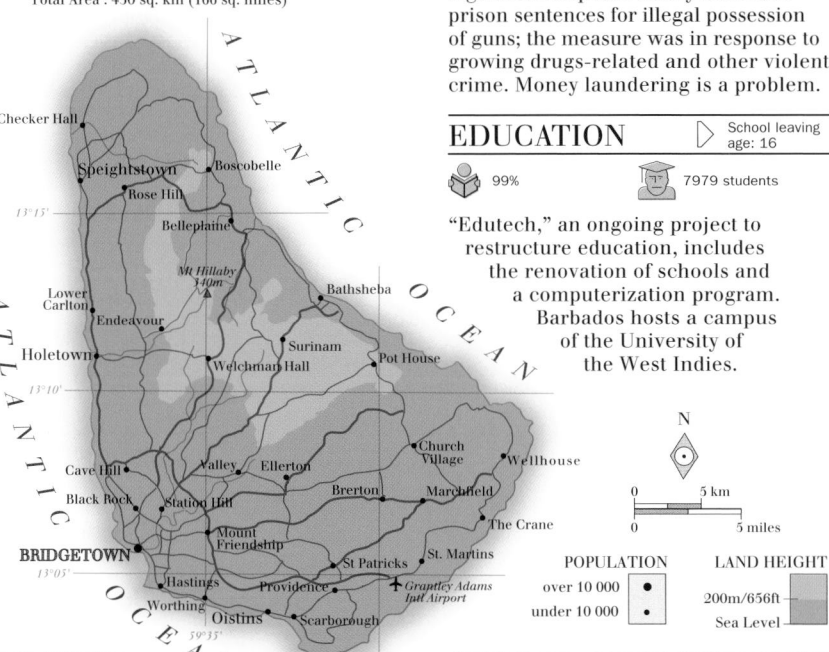

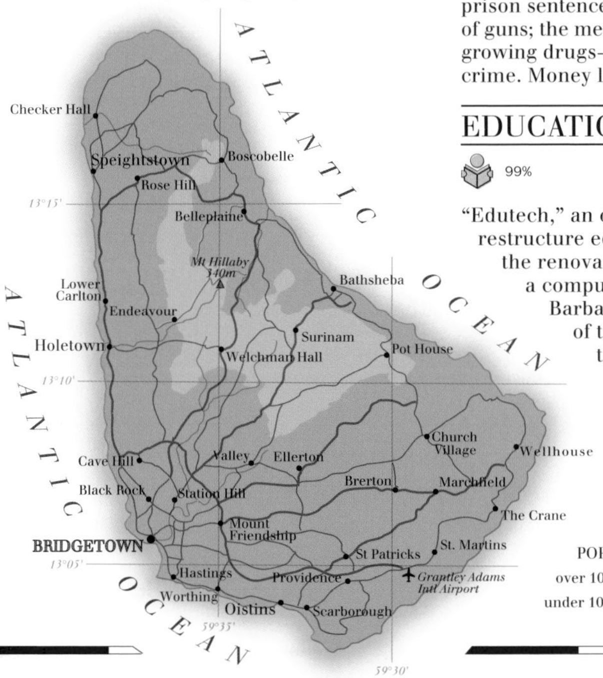
ATLANTIC OCEAN
ATLANTIC OCEAN
Checker Hall
Speightstown
Boscobelle
Rose Hill
Belleplaine
Mt Hillaby 340m
Bathsheba
Lower Carlton
Endeavour
Holetown
Surinam
Welchman Hall
Pot House
Church Village
Wellhouse
Cave Hill
Valley
Ellerton
Black Rock
Station Hill
Brerton
Marchfield
The Crane
Mount Friendship
BRIDGETOWN
St Patricks
St. Martins
Hastings
Providence
Grantley Adams Intl Airport
Worthing
Oistins
Scarborough
13°15'
13°10'
13°05'
59°35'
59°30'
N
0 5 km
0 5 miles
POPULATION
over 10 000
under 10 000
LAND HEIGHT
200m/656ft
Sea Level

RESOURCES

Electric power 161,000 kW

3100 tonnes

1945 b/d (reserves 7.1m barrels)

41,300 sheep, 35,000 pigs, 3.43m chickens

Oil, natural gas

Barbados has few strategic resources. Oil extracted by Barbados is refined in Trinidad and Tobago and then returned for domestic use.

ENVIRONMENT

Not available

0.5%

7.6 tonnes per capita

Oil slicks created by waste dumped from passing ships are polluting the encircling reef and adversely affecting the life cycle of the flying fish, Barbados's main fish stock.

MEDIA

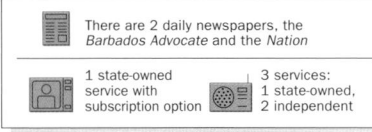

TV ownership high

Daily newspaper circulation 199 per 1000 people

PUBLISHING AND BROADCAST MEDIA

There are 2 daily newspapers, the *Barbados Advocate* and the *Nation*

1 state-owned service with subscription option

3 services: 1 state-owned, 2 independent

There is no political interference in the media. The two daily newspapers are privately owned. Multichannel TV is available on subscription.

CRIME

Death penalty in use

850 prisoners

Up 7% in 2000

An update in 2000 to firearms legislation imposed heavy fines and prison sentences for illegal possession of guns; the measure was in response to growing drugs-related and other violent crime. Money laundering is a problem.

EDUCATION

School leaving age: 16

99%

7979 students

"Edutech," an ongoing project to restructure education, includes the renovation of schools and a computerization program. Barbados hosts a campus of the University of the West Indies.

CHRONOLOGY

Colonized by the British in 1627, Barbados grew rich in the 18th century from sugar produced using slave labor.

- ❑ **1951** Universal adult suffrage introduced.
- ❑ **1961** Full internal self-government.
- ❑ **1966** Independence from the UK.
- ❑ **1983** Barbados supports and provides a base for the US invasion of Grenada.
- ❑ **1994–2003** The BLP wins three successive general elections.

HEALTH

Welfare state health benefits

1 per 826 people

Heart and cerebrovascular diseases, cancers

The health system is based on subsidized government-run clinics and hospitals, supplemented by more expensive private clinics and private doctors. Facilities are within easy reach of all Barbadians.

SPENDING

GDP/cap. increase

CONSUMPTION AND SPENDING

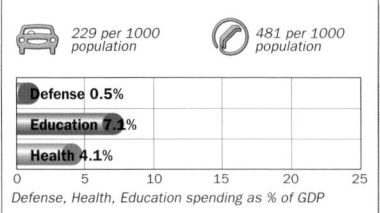

229 per 1000 population

481 per 1000 population

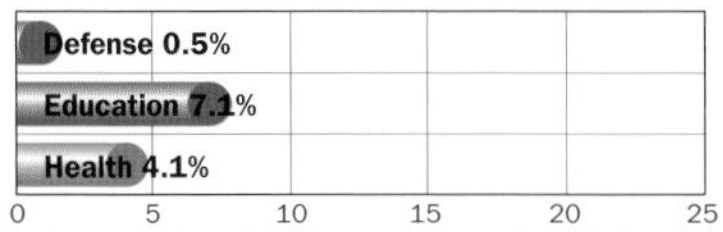
Defense 0.5%
Education 7.1%
Health 4.1%
0
5
10
15
20
25

Defense, Health, Education spending as % of GDP

A significant disparity exists between most Barbadians and a small affluent group, usually of European origin, which owns and controls business and industry, and parades status symbols such as yachts. Prime Minister Arthur stated in 1998 that "abject poverty" existed in the country.

WORLD RANKING

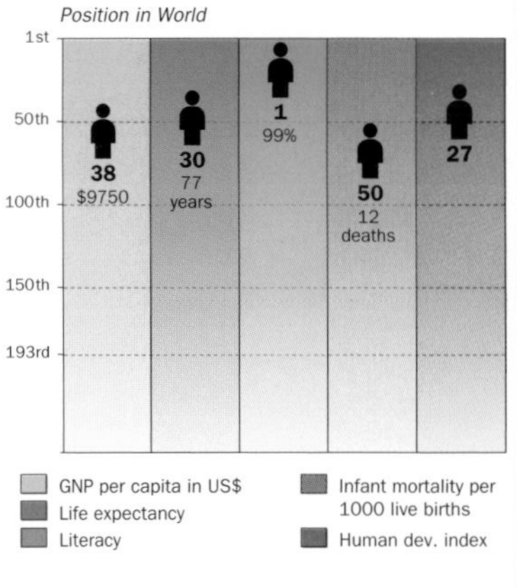
Position in World
1st
50th
100th
150th
193rd
38
$9750
30
77 years
1
99%
50
12 deaths
27
GNP per capita in US$
Life expectancy
Literacy
Infant mortality per 1000 live births
Human dev. index

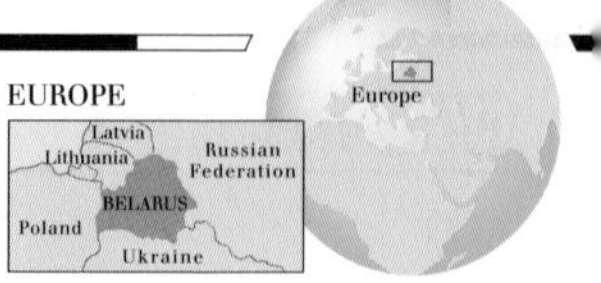
EUROPE
Europe
Latvia
Lithuania
Russian Federation
BELARUS
Poland
Ukraine

Belarus

B

Official Name: Republic of Belarus **Capital:** Minsk **Population:** 10.1 million
Currency: Belarussian rouble **Official Languages:** Belarussian and Russian

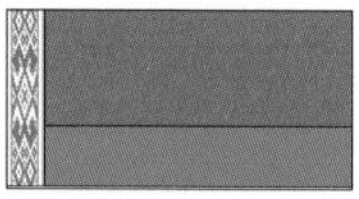

1991 | 1991 | July 3 | BY | +2 | +375 | .by

BELARUS LITERALLY MEANS "white Russia," a color associated in Slavic culture with freedom, and a reference to the fact that the country was never conquered by the Mongol Golden Horde. Devastated in World War II, and with few resources other than agriculture, Belarus only reluctantly became independent of Moscow in 1991, and President Aleksandr Lukashenka has maintained close links with Russia. The Chernobyl nuclear disaster in Ukraine in 1986 has had lasting effects on the environment and on the health of Belarussians.

TRANSPORTATION

Drive on right

Minsk International 395,050 passengers

Has no fleet

THE TRANSPORTATION NETWORK

60,567 km (37,635 miles)	None
5512 km (3425 miles)	Extensive canal and river systems

Belarus has no direct access to the sea, but is close to the Baltic ports. Railroad communications are good.

CLIMATE

Continental

WEATHER CHART FOR MINSK

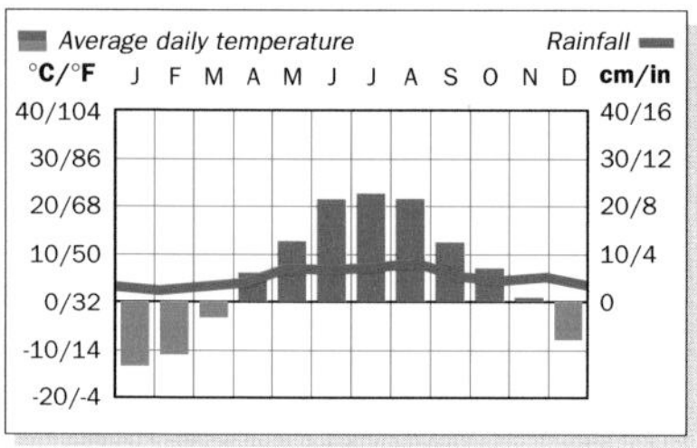
Average daily temperature
Rainfall
°C/°F
J F M A M J J A S O N D
cm/in
40/104
30/86
20/68
10/50
0/32
-10/14
-20/-4
40/16
30/12
20/8
10/4
0

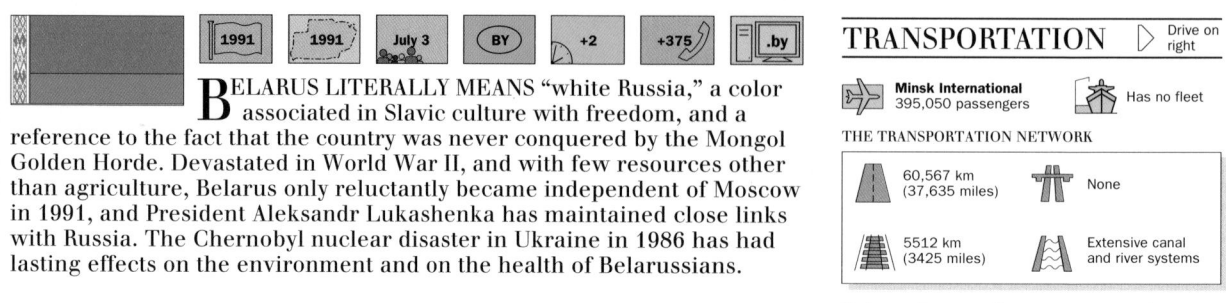

Much of southern Belarus *is marshy and sparsely populated. It includes the vast Pripet Marshes and the Dnieper lowlands.*

Belarus has a continental climate somewhat moderated by the influence of the nearby Baltic Sea. Temperatures in winter drop well below freezing, however, while summers can be hot and humid. Summer is also the main season for rainfall.

TOURISM

Visitors : Population 1:28

355,000 visitors

Up 42% in 1998

MAIN OVERSEAS ARRIVALS

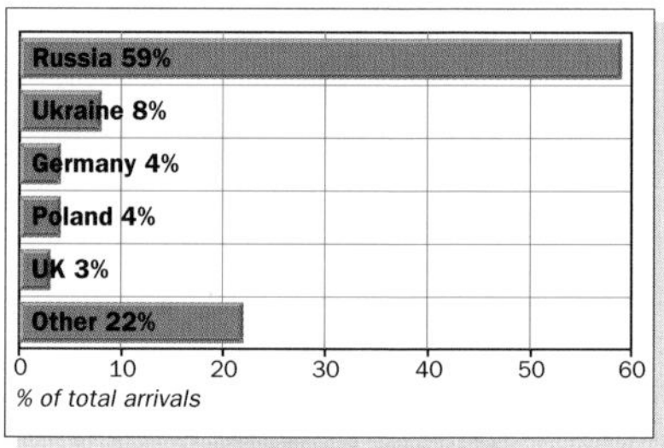
Russia 59%
Ukraine 8%
Germany 4%
Poland 4%
UK 3%
Other 22%
0
10
20
30
40
50
60
% of total arrivals

Belarus has fewer tourists than its neighbors. Many of its historic buildings were destroyed during World War II. Minsk was totally flattened, and is now characterized by Stalinist and other high-rise buildings. There is little of mass appeal on which to build a tourist industry.

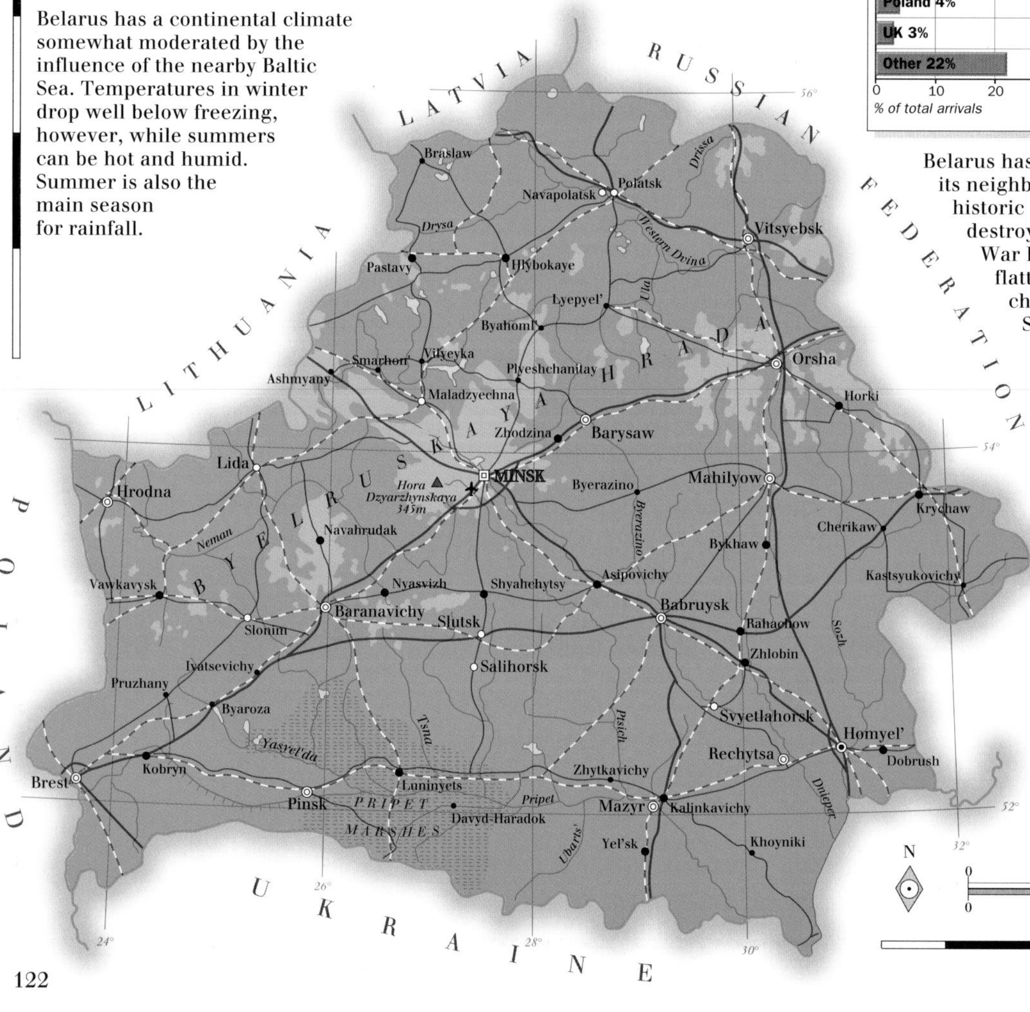
LATVIA
RUSSIAN FEDERATION
LITHUANIA
POLAND
UKRAINE
BYELARUSKAYA HRADA
Braslaw
Navapolatsk
Polatsk
Drysa
Drissa
Western Dvina
Vitsyebsk
Pastavy
Hlybokaye
Lyepyel'
Ula
Byahoml'
Orsha
Smarhon'
Vilyeyka
Ashmyany
Plyeshchanitsy
Maladzyechna
Horki
Zhodzina
Barysaw
Lida
MINSK
Hora Dzyarzhynskaya 345m
Byerazino
Mahilyow
Hrodna
Navahrudak
Berezino
Krychaw
Cherikaw
Neman
Bykhaw
Vawkavysk
Nyasvizh
Shyahehytsy
Asipovichy
Kastsyukovichy
Baranavichy
Babruysk
Slonim
Slutsk
Rahachow
Sozh
Ivatsevichy
Salihorsk
Zhlobin
Pruzhany
Byaroza
Tsna
Ptsich
Svyetlahorsk
Yasyel'da
Homyel'
Dobrush
Rechytsa
Zhytkavichy
Brest
Kobryn
Luninyets
Dnieper
Pinsk
PRIPET MARSHES
Pripet
Davyd-Haradok
Mazyr
Kalinkavichy
Ubarts'
Yel'sk
Khoyniki
24°
26°
28°
30°
32°
52°
54°
56°

Belarus

Total Area : 207 600 sq. km (80 154 sq. miles)

POPULATION

- over 1 000 000
- over 500 000
- over 100 000
- over 50 000
- over 10 000
- under 10 000

LAND HEIGHT

200m/656ft
100m/328ft

N

0 — 100 km
0 — 100 miles

B

PEOPLE

Pop. density low

Belarussian, Russian

49/km²
(126/mi²)

THE URBAN/RURAL POPULATION SPLIT

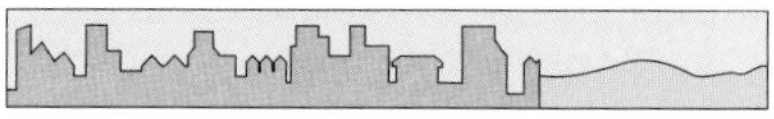
70%
30%

RELIGIOUS PERSUASION

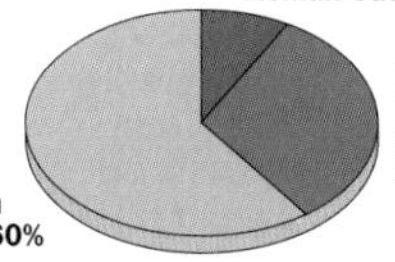
Roman Catholic 8%
Other (including Muslim, Jews, and Protestant) 32%
Russian Orthodox 60%

ETHNIC MAKEUP

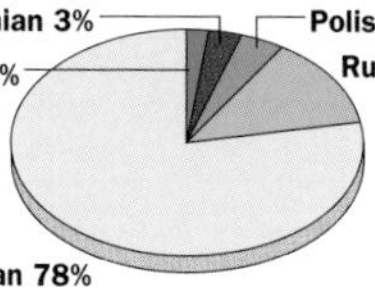
Ukrainian 3%
Other 2%
Polish 4%
Russian 13%
Belarussian 78%

Only 2% of the population are non-Slav and there is little ethnic tension. Most people speak Russian, and only 11% of the population are fluent in Belarussian, which is used mainly in rural areas; both languages have equal status. The social position of the Orthodox Church has increased since 1991 and was officially strengthened in 2002 at the expense of the growing number of Protestant churches.

POPULATION AGE BREAKDOWN

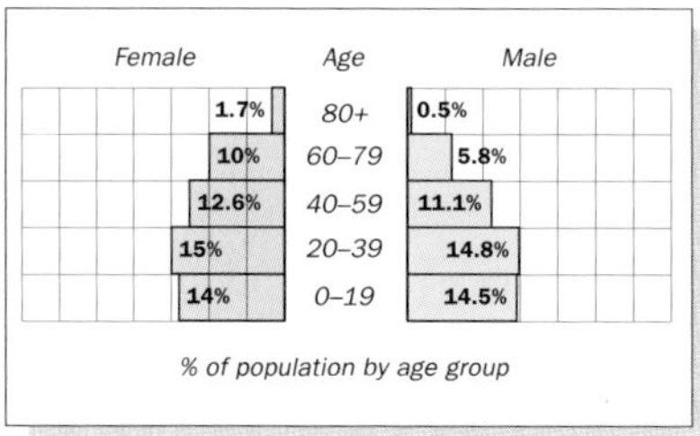
Female
Age
Male
1.7%
80+
0.5%
10%
60–79
5.8%
12.6%
40–59
11.1%
15%
20–39
14.8%
14%
0–19
14.5%
% of population by age group

POLITICS

Multiparty elections

L. House 2000/2004
U. House 2000/2004

President Aleksandr Lukashenka

AT THE LAST ELECTION

House of Representatives 110 seats

97%
PKB
2%
Opp
1%
Ind

PKB = Party of Communists of Belarus and government supporters **Opp** = Minor opposition parties
Ind = Independents

Council of the Republic 64 seats

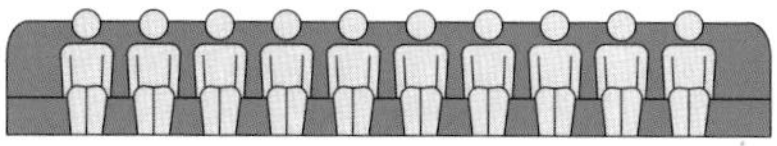

The Council of the Republic is indirectly elected

Belarus has a directly elected executive president, and a bicameral parliament.

PROFILE

Belarus, by far the slowest of the former Soviet states to implement political reform, has struggled to find an identity since 1991. A post-Soviet constitution was not adopted until 1994, and only in 1995 was the first fully fledged post-Soviet parliament elected, dominated by the PKB and its Agrarian Party ally. Aleksandr Lukashenka was unexpectedly elected Belarus's first president in 1994. He has since concentrated power in his own hands, drawing fierce criticism. However, a strong pluralist culture has yet to be established, with opposition parties hamstrung by internal divisions and easily outmaneuvered by the powerful presidency. A clampdown on political opponents effectively invalidated parliamentary elections in late 2000/early 2001. Lukashenka's reelection in late 2001 was immediately condemned by observers.

MAIN POLITICAL ISSUES

The relationship with Russia

In 1994 an accord (reinforced in 1999 and 2000) was signed on future monetary union with Russia. Lukashenka has sought ever closer relations, with the ultimate goal of a joint presidency. A union treaty was signed in late 1999, but it is more symbolic than practical. With Russian reticence prevailing over Belarus's enthusiasm for the union, the treaty has produced no significant developments toward joint state institutions or economic programs.

Powers of the presidency

The role of the president was strengthened in 1996 in a revised constitution and a new House of Representatives has since been easily dominated by the pro-Lukashenka PKB. Described as a dictator by his detractors, Lukashenka has an authoritarian style which has put him into conflict with his own government, let alone the international community, the domestic political opposition, and the public.

***President Aleksandr Lukashenka** seeks closer ties with the Russian Federation.*

***Vladimir Goncharik**, Lukashenka's main rival in presidential elections in 2001.*

WORLD AFFAIRS

Joined UN in 1945

EAPC | CIS | IAEA | CEI | OSCE

Relations with Russia are paramount. Numerous bilateral agreements were signed after independence in 1991. Ties have been strengthened further by the pro-Russian stance of Lukashenka, though many in Russia fear that closer links will drain Moscow's resources for little strategic gain.

Concerns over human rights and authoritarianism damage relations with many other countries. A move to relax EU sanctions was scuppered by a clampdown on political opponents in March 2001, and Lukashenka and members of his government were banned altogether from entering any EU country in November 2002.

AID

Recipient

$39m (receipts)

Down 2% in 2001

Although both the World Bank and the IMF provided loans for Belarus in the early 1990s, the lack of structural reforms since Lukashenka's administration came to power in 1994 has meant that further aid has been stalled. Some US bilateral aid continued, but the EU in particular has made it clear that support will depend on human rights improvements and the reversal of authoritarian threats to democracy.

Both the US and the EU extended credits to Belarus to assist in the conversion of the defense industry to nonmilitary production. Belarus also still requires aid to combat the effects of radiation pollution in the wake of the Chernobyl nuclear accident of 1986.

CHRONOLOGY

After forming part of medieval Kievan Rus, Belarus was ruled by three of its neighbors – Lithuania, Poland, and Russia – before incorporation into the USSR.

- **1918** Belarussian Bolsheviks stage coup. Independence as Belorussian Soviet Socialist Republic (BSSR).
- **1919** Invaded by Poland.
- **1920** Minsk retaken by Red Army. Eastern Belorussia reestablished as Soviet Socialist Republic.
- **1921** Treaty of Riga – Western Belorussia incorporated into Poland.
- **1922** BSSR merges with Soviet Russia and Ukraine to form USSR.
- **1929** Stalin implements collectivization of agriculture.
- **1939** Western Belorussia reincorporated into USSR when Soviet Red Army invades Poland. ⇨

B

CHRONOLOGY *continued*

- **1941–1944** Occupied by Germany during World War II.
- **1945** Founding member of UN.
- **1965** K. T. Mazurau, Communist Party of Belorussia (PKB) leader, becomes first deputy chair of Soviet government.
- **1986** Radioactive fallout after Chernobyl accident affects 70% of country.
- **1988** Evidence revealed of mass executions (over 300,000) by Soviet military between 1937 and 1941 near Minsk. Popular outrage fuels formation of nationalist Belorussian Popular Front (BPF), with Zyanon Paznyak as president. PKB authorities crush demonstration.
- **1989** Belarussian adopted as republic's official language.
- **1990** PKB prevents BPF from participating in elections to Supreme Soviet. BPF members join other opposition groups in Belorussian Democratic Bloc (BDB). BDB wins 25% of seats. PKB bows to opposition pressure and issues Declaration of the State Sovereignty of BSSR.
- **1991** March, 83% vote in referendum to preserve union with USSR. April, strikes against PKB and its economic policies. August, independence declared. Republic of Belarus adopted as official name. Stanislau Shushkevich elected chair of Supreme Soviet. December, Belarus, Russia, and Ukraine establish CIS.
- **1992** Supreme Soviet announces that Soviet nuclear weapons must be cleared from Belarus by 1999. Help promised from US.
- **1993** Belarussian parliament ratifies START-I and nuclear nonproliferation treaties.
- **1994** New presidential constitution approved; Aleksandr Lukashenka defeats conservative prime minister Vyacheslav Kebich in elections. Monetary union (reentry into rouble zone) agreed with Russia.
- **1995** First fully fledged post-Soviet parliament elected.
- **1996** Referendum approves changes to constitution strengthening Lukashenka's powers.
- **1997** Belarus and Russia ratify union treaty and Charter.
- **1998** Eviction from embassies sparks withdrawal of Western ambassadors.
- **1999** Union treaty with Russia.
- **2000–2001** Disputed parliamentary elections; clampdown on PKB's political opponents.
- **2001** Lukashenka reelected; observers label election seriously flawed.

DEFENSE

Compulsory military service

$1.96bn — Down 7% in 2001

BELARUSSIAN ARMED FORCES

Army	1608 main battle tanks (1484 T-72, 29 T-55, 95 T-80)	29,300 personnel
Navy	None	
Air force	212 combat aircraft (35 Su-24, 76 Su-25, 23 Su-27, 35 MiG-23, 43 MiG-29)	22,000 personnel
Missiles	None	

After the breakup of the Soviet Union in 1991, Belarus briefly adopted a policy of neutrality. It also committed itself to disposing of its inherited nuclear capability. Tactical nuclear weapons were removed by 1993 and strategic nuclear weapons by 1996.

Despite joining the CIS collective security agreement in 1993, Belarus joined NATO's Partnership for Peace program in 1995. Lukashenka has not developed NATO ties further, preferring to establish stronger military links with Moscow. Under the Belarus–Russia union treaty defense policies in Belarus and Russia are to be harmonized. From 2002 Belarussian troops have been allowed to serve abroad, despite there theoretically being constitutional barriers.

ECONOMICS

Inflation 318% p.a. (1990–2001)

$12.9bn — 2066 Belarussian roubles (1804)

SCORE CARD

World GNP Ranking	81st
GNP per capita	$1290
Balance of Payments	–$270m
Inflation	61.1%
Unemployment	2%

EXPORTS

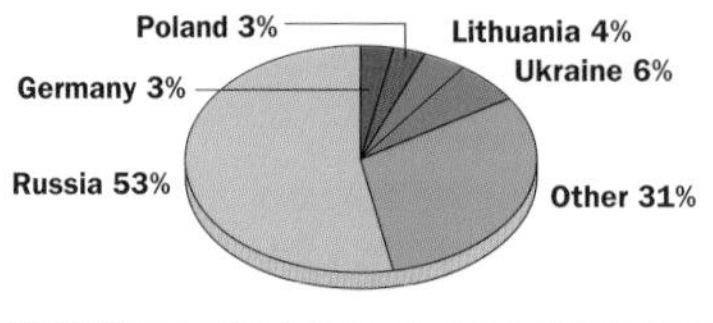

Poland 3%
Lithuania 4%
Ukraine 6%
Germany 3%
Russia 53%
Other 31%

IMPORTS

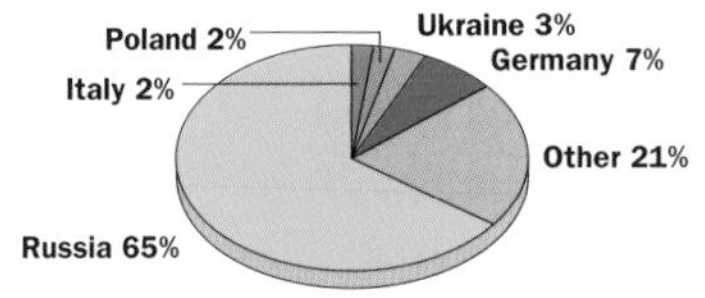

Poland 2%
Ukraine 3%
Germany 7%
Italy 2%
Other 21%
Russia 65%

Strengths

Low unemployment combined with relative social stability. Potential of forestry and agriculture.

Weaknesses

Lack of economic restructuring; support for outmoded businesses. Few natural resources. Dependence on Russia for energy and raw materials. Cleanup costs of Chernobyl. High inflation.

Profile

After 1991, Belarus adopted economic reform at a slower pace than other former Soviet states. Attempts to move more quickly to a market economy were thwarted by the largely Communist parliament. Upon election in 1994, Lukashenka suspended privatization moves, resuming them only halfheartedly in 1995, under a policy of "market socialism." Traditional industries continued to receive big subsidies, as the government printed money to increase production.

A currency crisis in 1998, and rampant inflation, coincided with two successive bad harvests in 1998–1999. Inflation receded in 2000–2001, but the rate of economic growth has slowed.

ECONOMIC PERFORMANCE INDICATOR

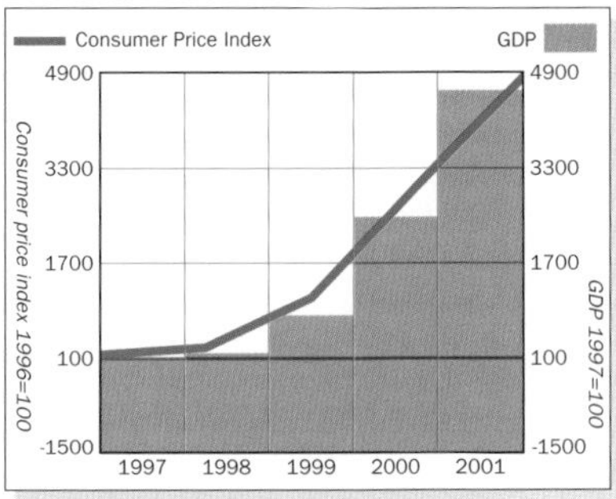

Consumer Price Index
GDP
4900
3300
1700
100
-1500
Consumer price index 1996=100
GDP 1997=100
1997
1998
1999
2000
2001

BELARUS : MAJOR BUSINESSES

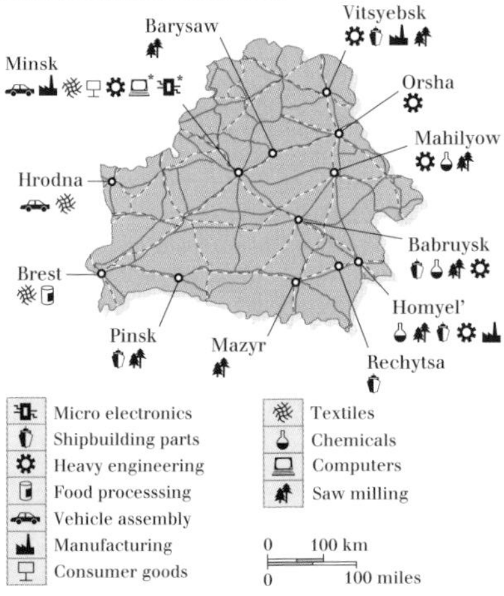

Barysaw
Vitsyebsk
Minsk
Orsha
Mahilyow
Hrodna
Babruysk
Brest
Homyel'
Pinsk
Mazyr
Rechytsa
Micro electronics
Shipbuilding parts
Heavy engineering
Food processsing
Vehicle assembly
Manufacturing
Consumer goods
Textiles
Chemicals
Computers
Saw milling
0 100 km
0 100 miles

* significant multinational ownership

B

RESOURCES

Electric power 7.8m kW

7269 tonnes

36,892 b/d (reserves 202m barrels)

4.08m cattle, 3.37m pigs, 33m chickens

Potash, oil, natural gas, coal, rock salt

ELECTRICITY GENERATION

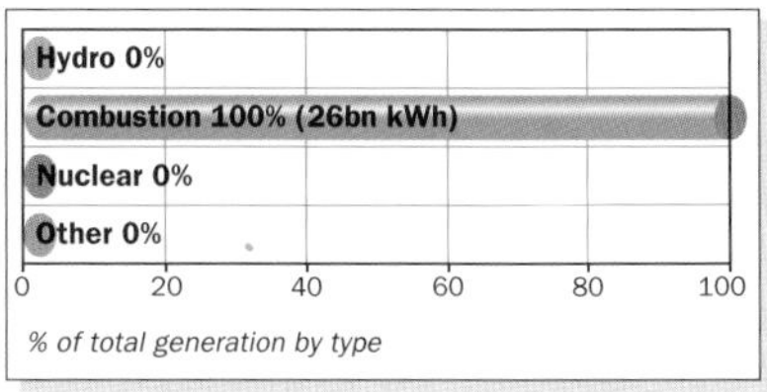
Hydro 0%
Combustion 100% (26bn kWh)
Nuclear 0%
Other 0%
0
20
40
60
80
100
% of total generation by type

Belarus is the world's third-largest producer of potash. Apart from this, there are no other significant strategic resources and the country is heavily dependent on Russia for fuel and energy supplies.

BELARUS : LAND USE

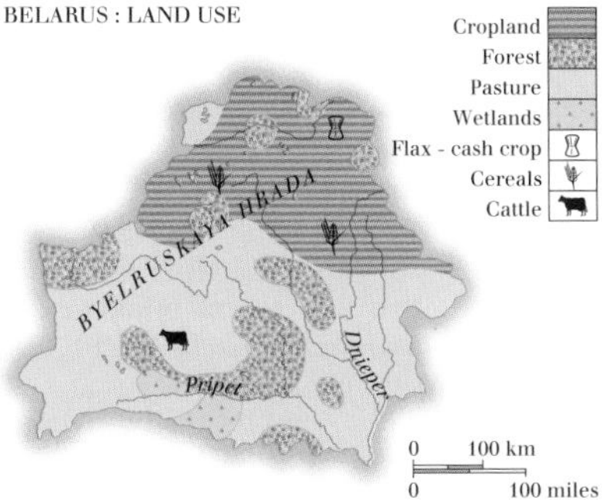
Cropland
Forest
Pasture
Wetlands
Flax - cash crop
Cereals
Cattle
BYELRUSKAYA HRADA
Pripet
Dnieper
0
100 km
0
100 miles

ENVIRONMENT

Sustainability rank: 49th

6% (3% partially protected)

5.7 tonnes per capita

ENVIRONMENTAL TREATIES

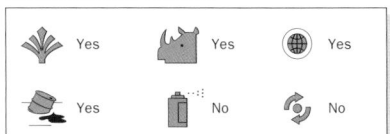

Yes · Yes · Yes

Yes · No · No

The massive leak from Ukraine's Chernobyl nuclear plant in 1986 released a huge cloud of radiation. Some 70% of the fallout fell on Belarus; 2.3 million people were immediately affected, and cases of leukemia and cancer continue to emerge. Farmland, forests, and water were all contaminated, including underwater streams feeding rivers in eastern Poland. Some areas in the fallout zone are still being farmed. The cleanup program swallows 20% of government finances, despite substantial Western aid, but the threat of further leaks has been removed by the closure in 2000 of Chernobyl's last reactor.

The Belavezhskaya Pushcha primeval forest, on the border with Poland, is one of Europe's largest nature reserves. It is now a habitat for the rare European bison or wisent.

MEDIA

TV ownership high

Daily newspaper circulation 152 per 1000 people

PUBLISHING AND BROADCAST MEDIA

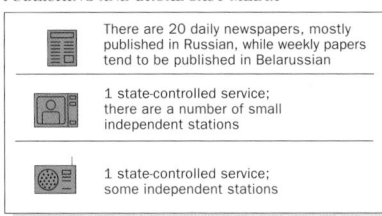

There are 20 daily newspapers, mostly published in Russian, while weekly papers tend to be published in Belarussian

1 state-controlled service; there are a number of small independent stations

1 state-controlled service; some independent stations

There are some independent media outlets, but government critics face harassment. Press freedom is curbed; state-backed publications predominate.

CRIME

Death penalty in use

56,000 prisoners

Up 4% in 2000–2002

CRIME RATES

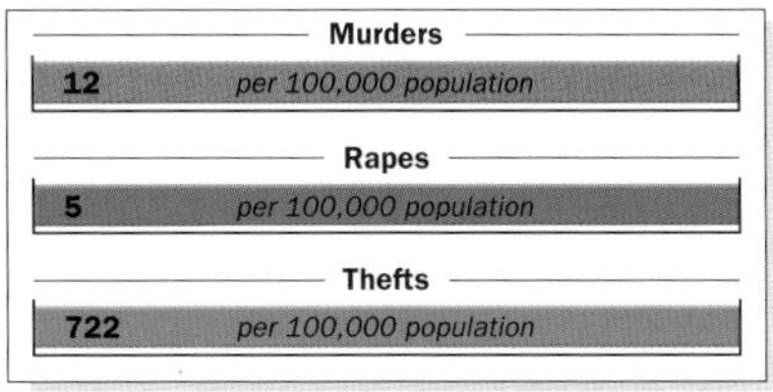
Murders
12
per 100,000 population
Rapes
5
per 100,000 population
Thefts
722
per 100,000 population

As elsewhere in the former Soviet Union, economic hardship and a general breakdown in law and order have resulted in a significant rise in crime. The prison population exceeds the intended capacity of 40,000. Belarus has become a transshipment point for illegal narcotics destined for western Europe, while locally produced opium supplies the internal market.

EDUCATION

School leaving age: 14

99%

437,995 students

THE EDUCATION SYSTEM

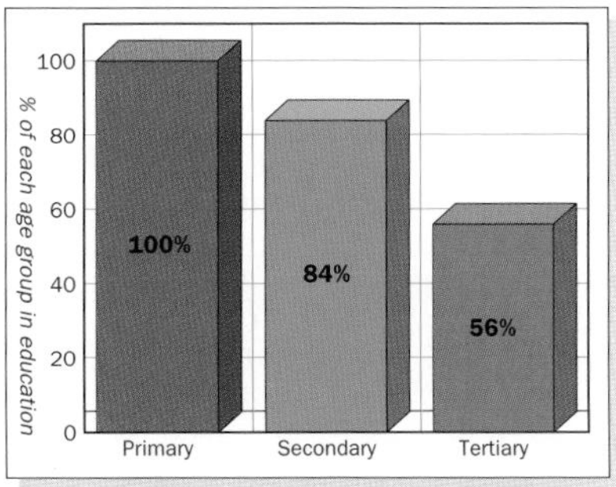
100
80
60
40
20
0
% of each age group in education
100%
84%
56%
Primary
Secondary
Tertiary

Education is officially compulsory for nine years, and teaching is mainly in Russian. Activists complain that because of political bias there is inadequate provision for the teaching of Belarussian. University education – taught in Russian – is of a fairly high standard.

HEALTH

Welfare state health benefits

1 per 219 people

Cerebrovascular and heart diseases, cancers, violence

Belarus's health service, which hitherto had been adequate, has been under enormous strain since the Chernobyl nuclear disaster in neighboring Ukraine in 1986. A Chernobyl tax funds assistance for victims of the accident. The number of cancer and leukemia cases has soared, and extra wards and specialist units have had to be built. Many Belarussian doctors are being trained in the latest bone-marrow techniques in Europe and the US.

HIV/AIDS is a growing problem; most infections are via intravenous drug use.

SPENDING

GDP/cap. decrease

CONSUMPTION AND SPENDING

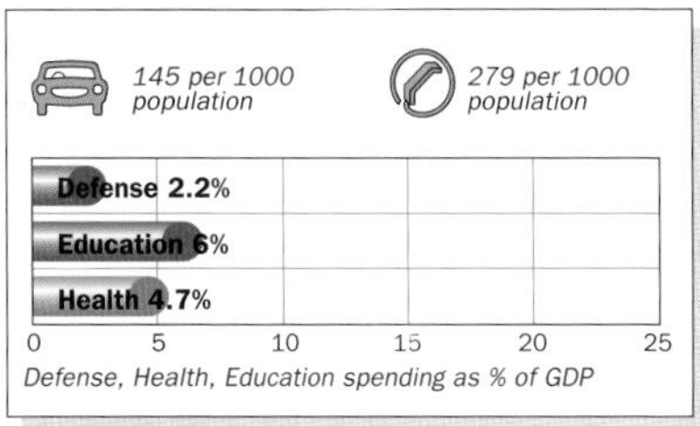
145 per 1000 population
279 per 1000 population
Defense 2.2%
Education 6%
Health 4.7%
0
5
10
15
20
25
Defense, Health, Education spending as % of GDP

The deteriorating economic situation has resulted in an overall drop in living standards. Wealth is concentrated among a small, communist elite which is opposed to market mechanisms. Since it has had the upper hand, its members have strengthened their grip on the state's resources. Thus far Belarus has not seen the expansion of entrepreneurial activity found in other former Soviet bloc countries such as Poland or Russia.

Wage increases in 2001 – an election year – brought salaries to levels which were unaffordable, so that enterprise profitability and investment were severely affected.

WORLD RANKING

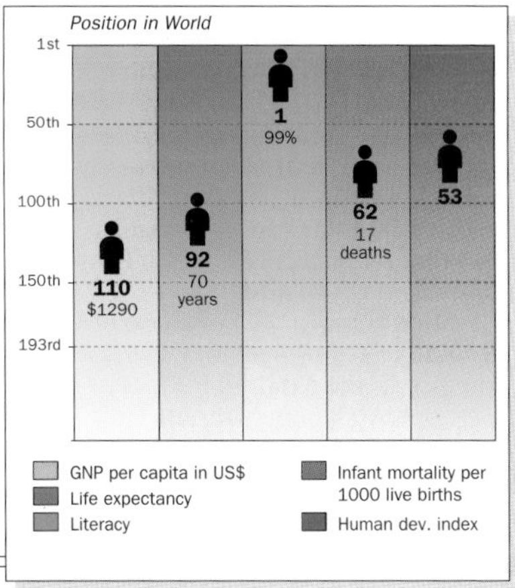
Position in World
1st
50th
100th
150th
193rd
110
$1290
92
70
years
1
99%
62
17
deaths
53
GNP per capita in US$
Life expectancy
Literacy
Infant mortality per 1000 live births
Human dev. index

B

BELGIUM

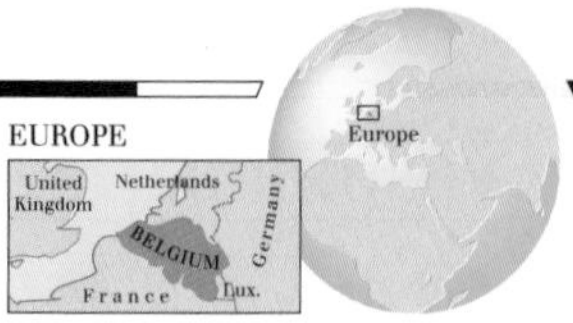
EUROPE
Europe
United Kingdom
Netherlands
Germany
BELGIUM
France
Lux.

OFFICIAL NAME: Kingdom of Belgium **CAPITAL:** Brussels **POPULATION:** 10.3 million
CURRENCY: Euro **OFFICIAL LANGUAGES:** Dutch, French, and German

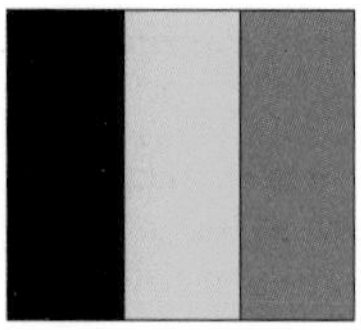

1830 | 1919 | July 21 | B | +1 | +32 | .be

LOCATED BETWEEN GERMANY, France, and the Netherlands, Belgium has a short coastline on the North Sea. The south includes the forested Ardennes region, while the north is crisscrossed by canals. Belgium has been fought over many times in its history; it was occupied by Germany in both world wars. Tensions have existed between the Dutch-speaking Flemings and French-speaking Walloons since the 1830s. These have been somewhat defused by Belgium's move to a federal political structure and the national consensus on the benefits of EU membership.

CLIMATE

Maritime

WEATHER CHART FOR BRUSSELS

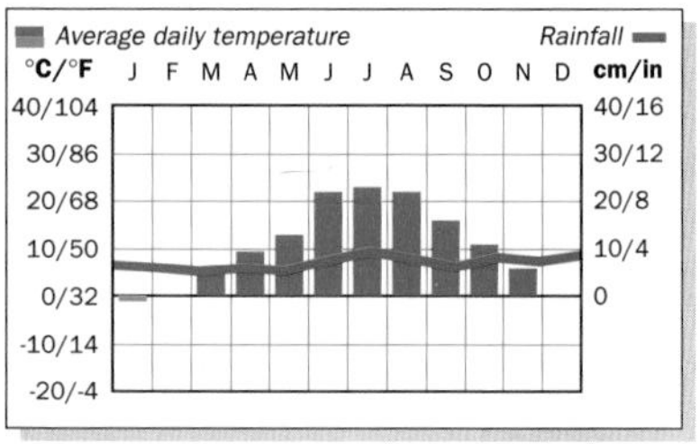
Average daily temperature
Rainfall
°C/°F
J F M A M J J A S O N D
cm/in
40/104
30/86
20/68
10/50
0/32
-10/14
-20/-4
40/16
30/12
20/8
10/4
0

Belgium has a typical maritime climate and is influenced by the Gulf Stream. Temperatures are mild, accompanied by heavy cloud cover and much rain. Widely fluctuating weather conditions, caused by cyclonic disturbances, can disrupt the climate on the coast. Summers tend to be short.

TRANSPORTATION

Drive on right

Brussels International 14.4m passengers

185 ships 151,000 grt

THE TRANSPORTATION NETWORK

116,182 km (72,192 miles)

1702 km (1058 miles)

3471 km (2157 miles)

1570 km (976 miles)

Belgium can be crossed within four hours by car or train. The expressway network is extensive, and although the railroad system has been reduced since 1970, it still constitutes one of the world's densest networks. Using high-speed TGV lines, Paris is just 80 minutes from Brussels, and London via the Channel Tunnel takes 2 hours 40 minutes.

National airline Sabena collapsed dramatically in November 2001, amid a slump in the aviation industry. A section of Sabena subsequently formed the basis for a new private airline, SN Brussels Airlines.

Antwerp is Europe's second-largest port.

TOURISM

Visitors : Population 1:1.5

6.72m visitors

Up 4% in 2002

MAIN TOURIST ARRIVALS

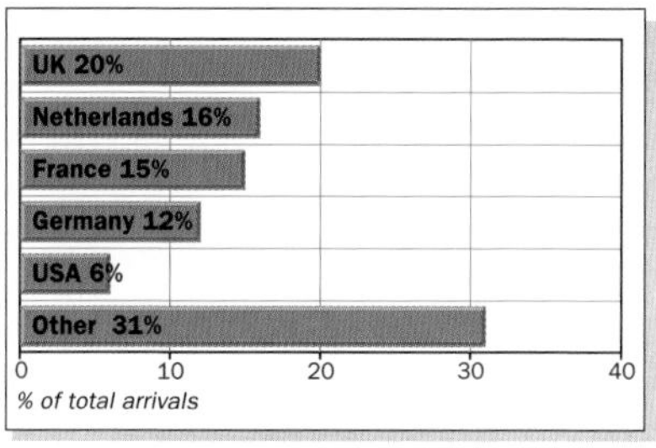
UK 20%
Netherlands 16%
France 15%
Germany 12%
USA 6%
Other 31%
0
10
20
30
40
% of total arrivals

Belgium's main attractions are its historic cities and the museums of Flemish art. Bruges, the capital of West Flanders, is often referred to as the "Venice of the North." With Gothic and Renaissance architecture and a complex canal system, it has become a favored destination for British weekend trippers and Japanese honeymooners. In Brussels, the famous "Grande Place," a cluster of Gothic, Renaissance, and Baroque buildings in a cobbled square, survived bombing during World War II. Much of the rest of the old city center, however, was destroyed. Belgium has 15 resorts on its 62-km (38-mile) coastline, with a single tramline running its entire length. Forests in the Ardennes to the south attract hikers.

The Ardennes plateau, *in the southeast, is famous for its scenery and cuisine. It is dissected by rivers, such as the Meuse and Semois.*

PEOPLE

Pop. density high

Dutch, French, German

314/km² (813/mi²)

THE URBAN/RURAL POPULATION SPLIT

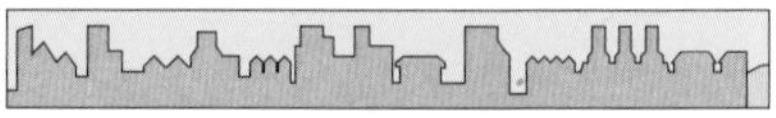
97%
3%

RELIGIOUS PERSUASION

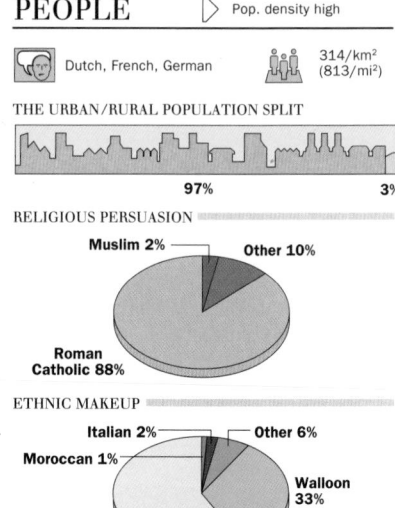

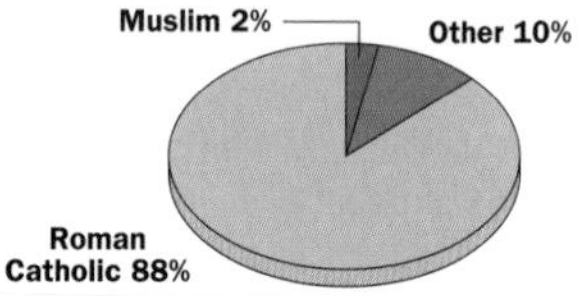
Muslim 2%
Other 10%
Roman Catholic 88%

ETHNIC MAKEUP

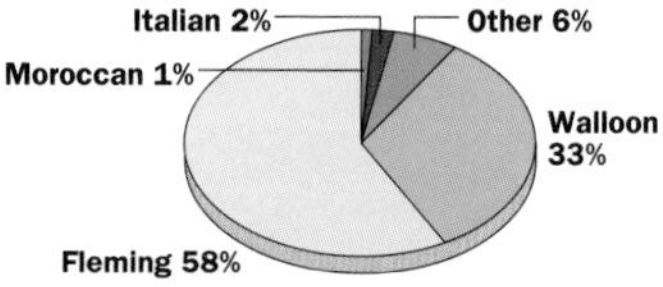
Italian 2%
Other 6%
Moroccan 1%
Walloon 33%
Fleming 58%

Belgium has been marked by the divisions between its Flemish and Walloon communities. The majority Dutch-speaking Flemings are concentrated in Flanders. Wallonia is French-speaking and Brussels is 85% francophone. French-speakers were in the ascendancy for many years, their greater economic wealth reinforced by a constitution giving them political control; tensions between Walloons and Flemings occasionally erupted into violence. In the past three decades, however, the situation has been reversed: Wallonia's industries have declined and Flanders is now the wealthier region. To defuse tensions, Belgium began in 1980 to change from being the most centralist to the most federal state in Europe; each community now controls most of its affairs and has its own government. A small German-speaking community in the east has extensive autonomy in educational and cultural matters.

Belgium has a sizable immigrant population. Women account for 40% of the workforce but only 19% of administrators and managers.

POPULATION AGE BREAKDOWN

Female
Age
Male
2.7%
80+
1.1%
9.7%
60–79
7.9%
12.4%
40–59
12.5%
14.6%
20–39
15.1%
11.7%
0–19
12.3%
% of population by age group

BELGIUM

Total Area : 30 510 sq. km (11 780 sq. miles)

POPULATION

- over 1 000 000
- over 100 000
- over 50 000
- over 10 000

LAND HEIGHT

- 500m/1640ft
- 200m/656ft
- Sea Level

0 40 km

0 40 miles

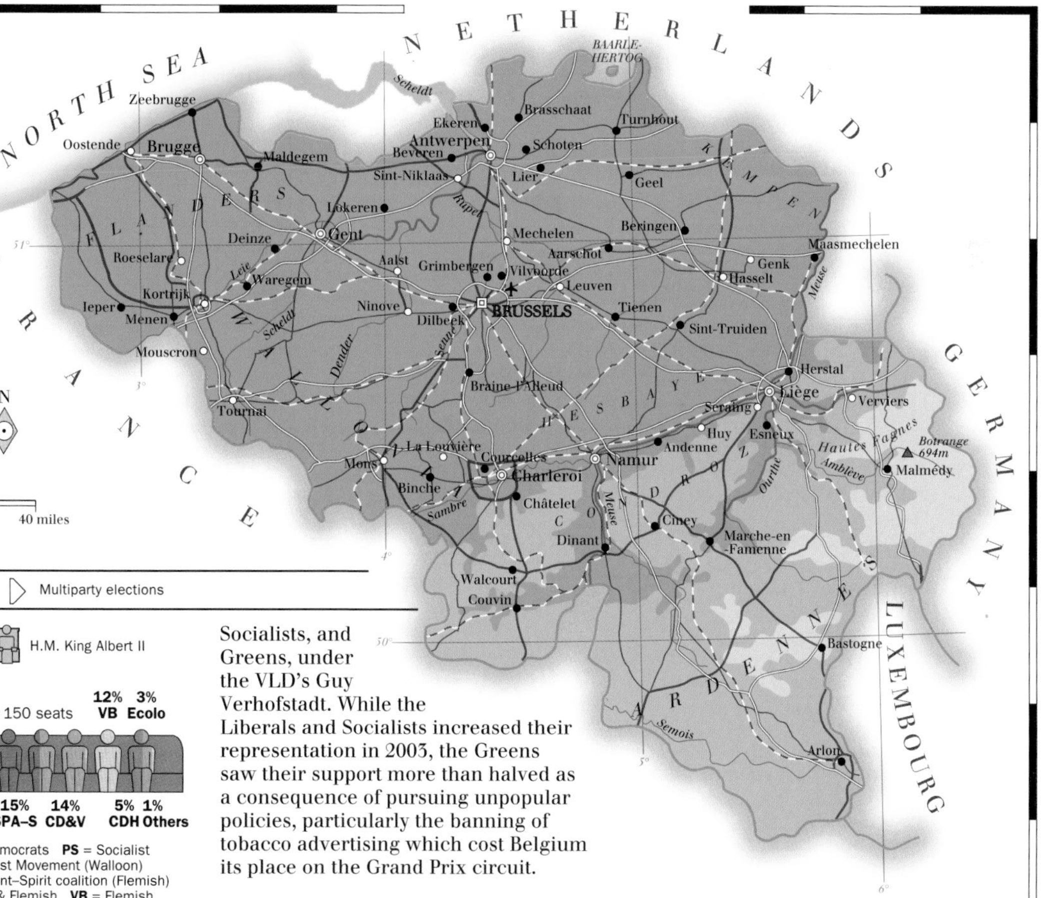
NORTH SEA
NETHERLANDS
FRANCE
GERMANY
LUXEMBOURG
FLANDERS
WALLONIA
KEMPEN
HESBAYE
CONDROZ
ARDENNES
Hautes Fagnes
Botrange 694m
BAARLE-HERTOG
Zeebrugge
Oostende
Brugge
Maldegem
Eekeren
Antwerpen
Beveren
Brasschaat
Schoten
Turnhout
Sint-Niklaas
Lier
Geel
Lokeren
Gent
Deinze
Roeselare
Mechelen
Beringen
Maasmechelen
Aarschot
Genk
Hasselt
Aalst
Grimbergen
Vilvoorde
Leuven
Waregem
Kortrijk
Ieper
Menen
Ninove
Dilbeek
BRUSSELS
Tienen
Sint-Truiden
Mouscron
Herstal
Liège
Verviers
Seraing
Braine-l'Alleud
Tournai
Huy
Esneux
Andenne
La Louvière
Mons
Courcelles
Charleroi
Namur
Malmédy
Binche
Châtelet
Ciney
Marche-en-Famenne
Dinant
Walcourt
Couvin
Bastogne
Arlon
Scheldt
Rupel
Leie
Dender
Senne
Sambre
Meuse
Ourthe
Amblève
Semois
N

POLITICS

Multiparty elections

L. House 2003/2007
U. House 2003/2007

H.M. King Albert II

AT THE LAST ELECTION

Chamber of Representatives 150 seats

12% VB
3% Ecolo
17% VLD
17% PS
16% MR
15% SPA–S
14% CD&V
5% CDH
1% Others

VLD = Flemish Liberals and Democrats **PS** = Socialist Party (Walloon) **MR** = Reformist Movement (Walloon) **SPA–S** = Socialist Party Different–Spirit coalition (Flemish) **CD&V** = Christian Democratic & Flemish **VB** = Flemish Block **CDH** = Humanist Democratic Center (Walloon) **Ecolo** = Greens (Walloon) **Co-op** = Co-opted members

Senate 71 seats

10% SPA–S
8% PS
7% VB
3% CDH
44% Co-op
10% VLD
8% CD&V
7% MR
3% Others

The Senate has 40 directly elected members and 31 co-opted members

Since 1993, Belgium has been a federal monarchy. Tensions between language groups had led to successive federalist reforms in the 1980s, culminating in agreement in 1992 on constitutional reform and the 1993 St. Michel Accords.

PROFILE

Belgian politics is defined along lines of language. Apart from this, a high degree of consensus exists over the benefits of membership of the EU and monetary union.

The St. Michel Accords gave the regional governments – Flanders, Wallonia, and Brussels – significant powers under a federal government. A centrist coalition of the Socialist and Christian Democrat parties had difficulty in securing the necessary majority for the constitutional reforms enacted in the accords and was defeated in the 1999 elections. It was replaced by a "rainbow" coalition composed of the Liberals, Socialists, and Greens, under the VLD's Guy Verhofstadt. While the Liberals and Socialists increased their representation in 2003, the Greens saw their support more than halved as a consequence of pursuing unpopular policies, particularly the banning of tobacco advertising which cost Belgium its place on the Grand Prix circuit.

MAIN POLITICAL ISSUES

Language

Tensions between the two language groups have been mitigated by progressive decentralization. Each community has a version of each political party.

The far right

In recent years, support has increased for Belgium's far-right parties, the VB in Flanders and the smaller National Front in Wallonia. Insisting on the "assimilation" of the growing number of immigrants, the VB won 18% of the vote in Flanders in the 2003 election, its best ever result. The party has risen in the face of social liberalization undertaken by the current government, including the legalization of euthanasia and the decriminalization of cannabis.

King Albert II, *succeeded his brother King Baudouin, who died in 1993.*

Guy Verhofstadt, *youthful leader of the VLD and prime minister since 1999.*

WORLD AFFAIRS

Joined UN in 1945

Benelux | CE | EU | OECD | NATO

Belgium's key concern is its role in the EU. It is a keen supporter of economic and monetary union. As a historic victim of wars between France and Germany, Belgium sees the EU as a guarantor of western European peace. It is also perceived as an important foundation for Belgium's own federalist structure, without which many fear that Belgium could split into two.

Belgium has little in the way of an independent foreign policy, but frequently contributes troops to the UN's operations. Belgian soldiers have served in the Democratic Republic of the Congo (DRC) and the Middle East in recent years, and a number were killed in Rwanda in 1994.

AID

Donor

$867m (donations)

Up 6% in 2001

Some 0.37% of GNP goes in overseas development aid. Belgian aid focuses on education and agricultural projects in Africa; the major beneficiaries are the former Belgian colonies of Burundi, Rwanda, and the DRC.

B

CHRONOLOGY

Previously ruled by the French dukes of Burgundy, Belgium became a Habsburg possession in 1477. It passed to the Austrian Habsburgs in 1713. Belgium was incorporated into France in 1797.

- ❑ **1814–1815** Congress of Vienna; European powers decide to merge Belgium with the Netherlands under King William I of Orange.
- ❑ **1830** Revolt against Dutch; declaration of independence.
- ❑ **1831** European powers install Leopold Saxe Coburg as king.
- ❑ **1865** Leopold II crowned king.
- ❑ **1885** Berlin Conference gives Congo basin to Leopold as colony.
- ❑ **1914** German armies invade. Belgium occupied until 1918.
- ❑ **1921** Belgo-Luxembourg Economic Union formed. Belgian and Luxembourg currencies locked.
- ❑ **1932** Dutch language accorded equal official status with French.
- ❑ **1936** Belgium declares neutrality.
- ❑ **1940** Leopold III capitulates to Hitler. Belgium occupied till 1944.
- ❑ **1948** Customs union with Netherlands and Luxembourg (Benelux) formed.
- ❑ **1950** King abdicates in favor of son, Baudouin.
- ❑ **1957** Becomes one of six original signatories of Treaty of Rome, the principal foundation of what develops into the EU.
- ❑ **1992** Christian Democrat and Socialist government led by Jean-Luc Dehaene takes over federal government.
- ❑ **1993** Culmination of reforms creating federal state. Greater powers for regions and city governments. Death of Baudouin. Succeeded by Albert II.
- ❑ **1995** Allegations of corruption and murder involving French-speaking PS force resignations of Walloon premier, federal deputy premier, and Willy Claes, NATO secretary-general.
- ❑ **1996** Murder and disappearance of young girls arouse fears of international kidnapping and pedophile ring.
- ❑ **1999** Claes found guilty of bribery in connection with defense contract to buy helicopters. Liberals win general election. New coalition formed, including Greens for first time.
- ❑ **2001** Collapse of national airline Sabena.
- ❑ **2002** January, euro fully adopted – withdrawal of Belgian franc. May, legalization of euthanasia.
- ❑ **2003** Government reelected; Greens lose seats, VB makes gains.

DEFENSE

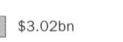

No compulsory military service

$3.02bn — Down 6% in 2001

BELGIAN ARMED FORCES

132 main battle tanks (Leopard 1A5)	26,400 personnel
3 frigates	2400 personnel
135 combat aircraft (F-16A, F-16B, Mirage 5)	8600 personnel
None	

Belgium spends less on defense than the NATO average of 2.2% of GDP. In 1994, the government abolished conscription and undertook to cut troop levels. It also targeted all three military services for cuts as part of a program to reduce government debt. The defense budget was frozen for five years.

However, spending on paratroops and transport planes has increased. The aim is to allow Belgian forces to fulfill their role in NATO's new rapid reaction forces. It will also make Belgian forces more useful to the UN's worldwide operations. In 1996, the Belgian and Netherlands navies came under a joint operational command. In 2003, the government agreed in principle to the creation of a European Security and Defense Union.

ECONOMICS

Inflation 1.9% p.a. (1990–2001)

$245bn — 0.871 euros (1.013)

SCORE CARD

❑ World GNP Ranking	20th
❑ GNP per Capita	$23,850
❑ Balance of Payments	$13bn
❑ Inflation	2.5%
❑ Unemployment	7%

EXPORTS

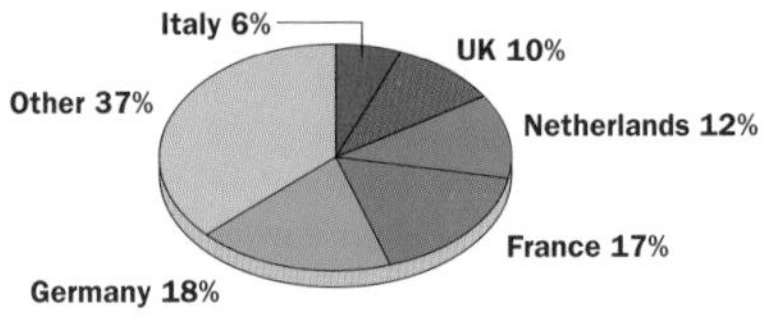
Italy 6%
UK 10%
Netherlands 12%
France 17%
Germany 18%
Other 37%

IMPORTS

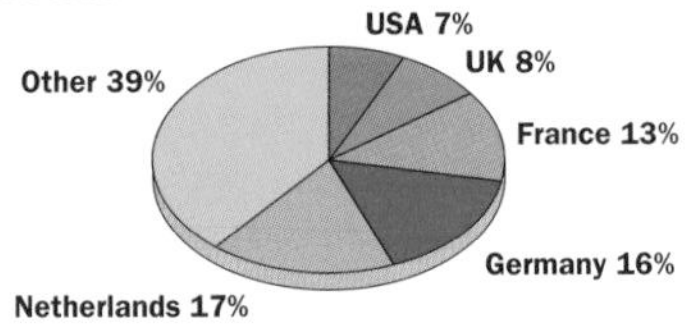
USA 7%
UK 8%
France 13%
Germany 16%
Netherlands 17%
Other 39%

ECONOMIC PERFORMANCE INDICATOR

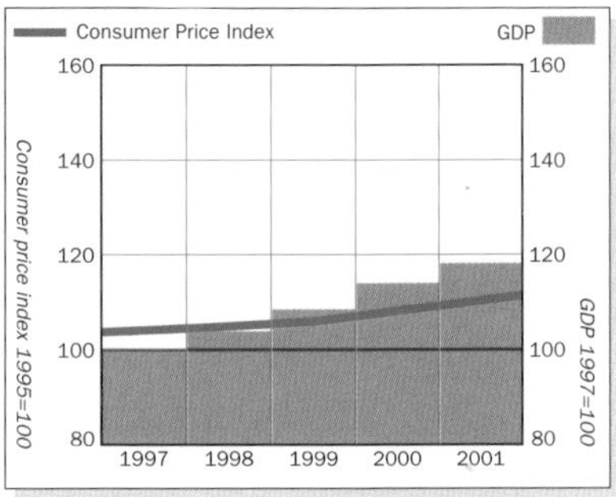
Consumer Price Index
GDP
160
140
120
100
80
1997
1998
1999
2000
2001
Consumer price index 1995=100
GDP 1997=100

Profile

Recession and rising unemployment in the early 1990s prompted the introduction of work-sharing schemes and benefit reforms. Unemployment and the massive public debt are declining gradually. Against a background of a downturn in the world economy, the government is committed to both greater fiscal stringency, in pursuit of a budget surplus, and reduction in taxation over 2002–2005.

Strengths

One of world's most efficient producers of metal products and textiles. Flanders is a world leader in new high-tech industries. Successful chemicals industry. Highly educated and motivated multilingual workforce: estimates suggest productivity is 20% above that of Germany. Location attractive for US multinationals. Good sea outlets and access to Rhine inland waterway from Antwerp and Ghent.

Weaknesses

Public debt of around 100% of GDP, well over EU target of 60%. High long-term and low-skill joblessness with sharp local variations. Early retirement of large numbers of workers results in high state pension bill. Bureaucracy larger than European average.

BELGIUM : MAJOR BUSINESSES

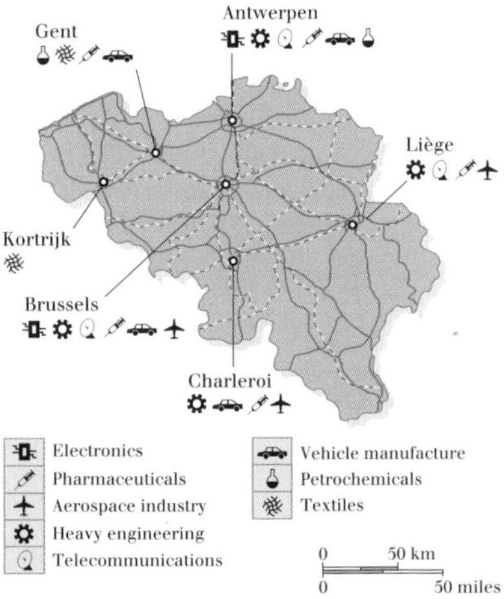
Gent
Antwerpen
Liège
Kortrijk
Brussels
Charleroi
Electronics
Pharmaceuticals
Aerospace industry
Heavy engineering
Telecommunications
Vehicle manufacture
Petrochemicals
Textiles
0
50 km
0
50 miles

RESOURCES

Electric power 15.6m kW

31,441 tonnes

Not an oil producer; refines 717,000 b/d

6.85m pigs, 3.11m cattle, 56m chickens

Coal, natural gas, shale, marble, sandstone, dolomite

ELECTRICITY GENERATION

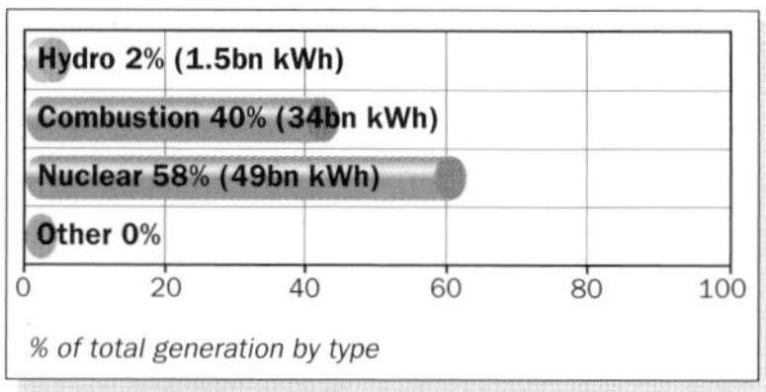
Hydro 2% (1.5bn kWh)
Combustion 40% (34bn kWh)
Nuclear 58% (49bn kWh)
Other 0%
0
20
40
60
80
100
% of total generation by type

Belgium has few natural resources and depends largely on the export of goods and services. The once-rich coal mines of Wallonia closed for good in 1992. There is some deciduous and conifer forestry in the Ardennes region.

BELGIUM : LAND USE

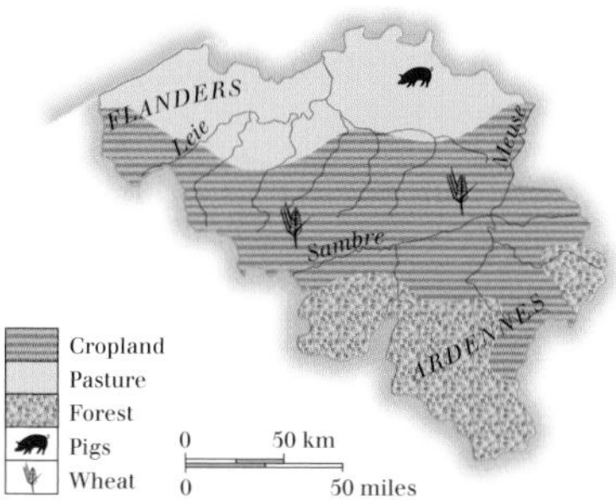
FLANDERS
Leie
Meuse
Sambre
ARDENNES
Cropland
Pasture
Forest
Pigs
Wheat
0
50 km
0
50 miles

ENVIRONMENT

Sustainability rank: 125th

3% partially protected

12.4 tonnes per capita

ENVIRONMENTAL TREATIES

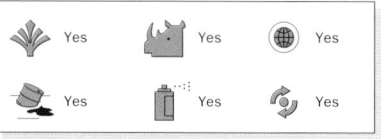

Yes	Yes	Yes
Yes	Yes	Yes

Flanders is concerned about the pollution of groundwater supplies through acid rain, heavy metals, fertilizers, and pesticides. Its government operates an environmental management plan to raise standards. Wallonia has strict laws against illegal tipping of waste, and regulations on air quality and emissions. Awareness of environmental issues is reflected in the rise of the two green parties, which entered government for the first time in the coalition formed in 1999.

MEDIA

TV ownership high

Daily newspaper circulation 160 per 1000 people

PUBLISHING AND BROADCAST MEDIA

There are 30 daily newspapers, published in Dutch, French, and German, including *Het Nieuwsblad, Le Soir,* and *De Standaard*
3 state-owned services, broadcasting in Dutch, French, and German, and 5 independent commercial services
3 state-owned services, broadcasting in Dutch, French, and German, and numerous private stations

Newspapers tend to be regional and divided by language. Individual circulations are low: that of the most widely read paper is only 370,000. Control of broadcasting is divided along linguistic lines between two major corporations. Over 95% of Belgians have cable TV, receiving channels from all over Europe. Commercial TV only began in 1989, with the Flemish station VTM.

CRIME

No death penalty

8764 prisoners

Up 1% in 1999–2001

CRIME RATES

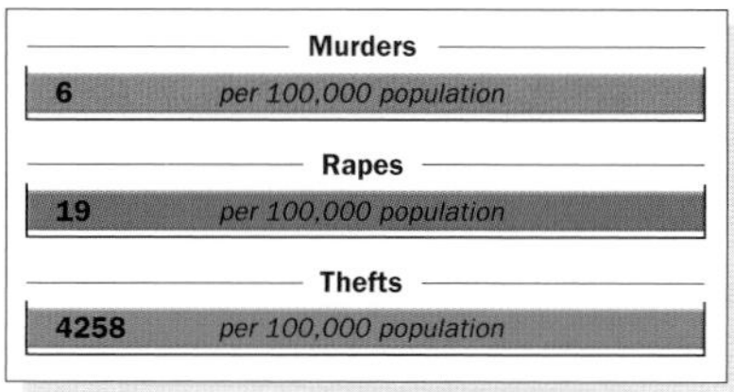
Murders
6
per 100,000 population
Rapes
19
per 100,000 population
Thefts
4258
per 100,000 population

Penalties for illegal drug use are strict. The "universal competence law," which had allowed the trial of non-Belgians for crimes against humanity, was watered down beyond use in 2003.

EDUCATION

School leaving age: 18

99%

355,748 students

THE EDUCATION SYSTEM

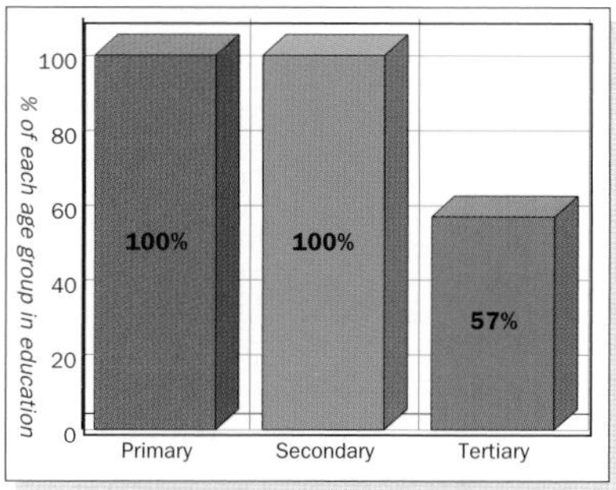
100
80
60
40
20
0
% of each age group in education
100%
100%
57%
Primary
Secondary
Tertiary

In Belgium, parents can choose between schooling provided by the two main language communities, by public authorities, or by private interests. Roman Catholic schools constitute the greatest number of "free" (privately organized) establishments. Since 1989 the system has been administered by the governments of the two main language groups. All universities are run along language lines.

HEALTH

Welfare state health benefits

1 per 253 people

Heart and respiratory diseases, cancers, accidents

The quality of health care is among the best in the world, and government spending is high. Belgium is a world leader in fertility treatment and heart and lung transplants. Treatment is not free, but Belgians are able to claim up to 75% of their costs.

Accidents rate unusually high in Belgium as a cause of death. In 2001 there were around 8500 people living with HIV/AIDS.

In 2002 Belgium became the second country (after the Netherlands) to legalize euthanasia.

SPENDING

GDP/cap. increase

CONSUMPTION AND SPENDING

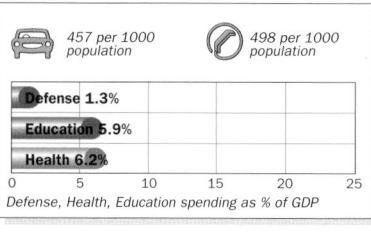

457 per 1000 population

498 per 1000 population

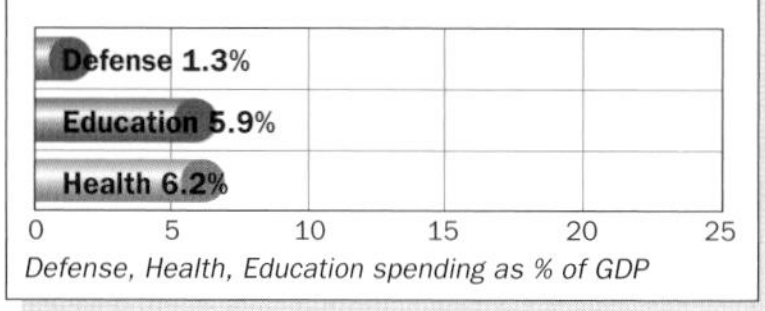
Defense 1.3%
Education 5.9%
Health 6.2%
0
5
10
15
20
25
Defense, Health, Education spending as % of GDP

Despite high levels of state debt and failing traditional industries, Belgium is one of Europe's richest countries. GNP per capita is lower than for the Netherlands, the UK or Austria, but higher than for France or Germany. There are considerable regional differences, however: in Flanders the level of unemployment is only half that in Wallonia. The recession of the early 1990s prompted Belgians to save a higher proportion of their income, but the level of savings has fallen since then as consumer confidence has recovered.

The presence of highly paid EU officials and international company employees and bankers has made Brussels a distinctly wealthy, and expensive, city.

WORLD RANKING

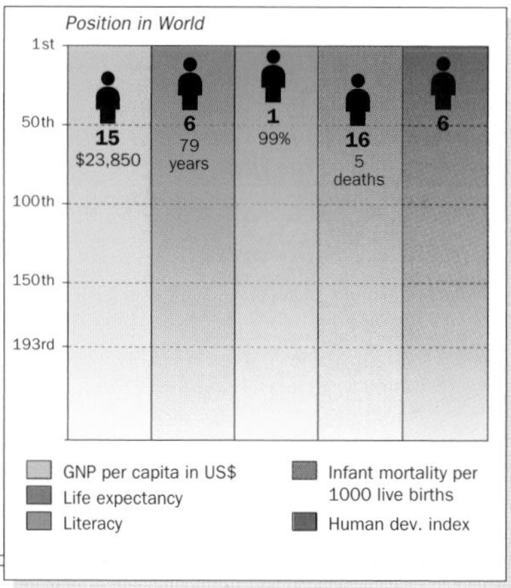
Position in World
1st
50th
100th
150th
193rd
15
$23,850
6
79
years
1
99%
16
5
deaths
6
GNP per capita in US$
Life expectancy
Literacy
Infant mortality per 1000 live births
Human dev. index

B

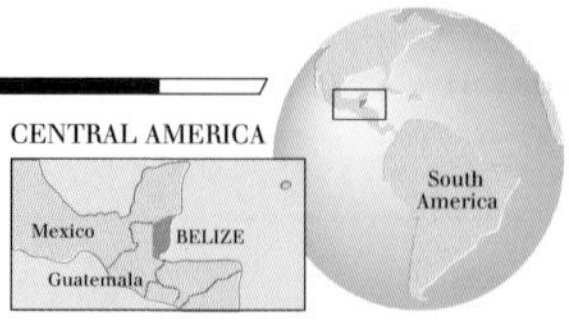
CENTRAL AMERICA
Mexico
BELIZE
Guatemala
South America

BELIZE

OFFICIAL NAME: Belize **CAPITAL:** Belmopan
POPULATION: 236,000 **CURRENCY:** Belizean dollar **OFFICIAL LANGUAGE:** English

1981 | 1981 | Sept 21 | BZ | -6 | +501 | .bz

FORMERLY BRITISH HONDURAS, Belize was the last Central American country to gain its independence, in 1981. It lies on the southeastern shore of the Yucatan peninsula and shares a border with Mexico along the River Hondo. Belize is Central America's least populous country, and almost half of its land area is still forested. Its swampy coastal plains are protected from flooding by the world's second-largest barrier reef.

***Small fishing village near Belize City.** About 500 tonnes of Caribbean spiny lobster, the main inshore species, are caught every year.*

CLIMATE

Tropical equatorial

WEATHER CHART FOR BELMOPAN

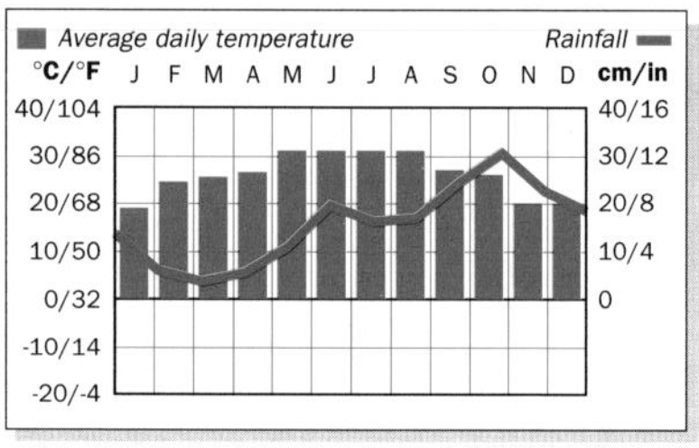
Average daily temperature
Rainfall
°C/°F
J F M A M J J A S O N D
cm/in
40/104
30/86
20/68
10/50
0/32
-10/14
-20/-4
40/16
30/12
20/8
10/4
0

Conditions are hot and humid. Coastal regions are affected by hurricanes, notably Hurricane Iris in late 2001.

TRANSPORTATION

Drive on right

Phillip S. W. Goldson, Belize City 272,000 passengers

1516 ships 1.83m grt

THE TRANSPORTATION NETWORK

Roads	488 km (303 miles)	Motorways	None
Railways	None	Waterways	825 km (513 miles)

A US$16 million IDB loan in 1998 helped improve the country's road network and its feeder roads. A terminal and a runway extension have been completed at the international airport near Belize City.

TOURISM

Visitors : Population 1:1.2

200,000 visitors

Up 2% in 2002

MAIN TOURIST ARRIVALS

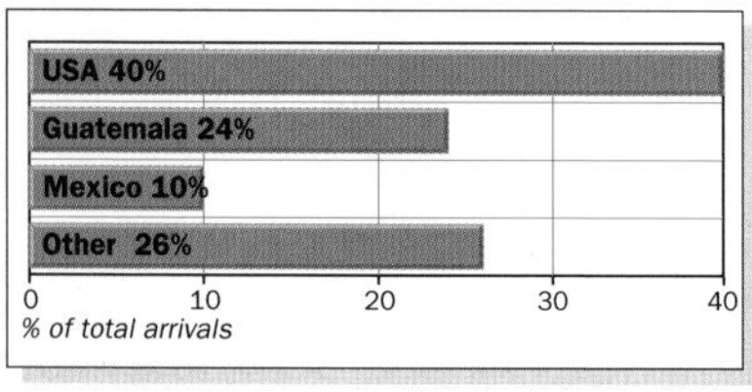
USA 40%
Guatemala 24%
Mexico 10%
Other 26%
0
10
20
30
40
% of total arrivals

The barrier reef, good beaches, and Mayan ruins draw visitors. "Eco" attractions need conservation.

PEOPLE

Pop. density low

English Creole, Spanish, English, Mayan, Garifuna (Carib)

10/km² (27/mi²)

THE URBAN/RURAL POPULATION SPLIT

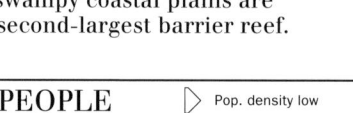

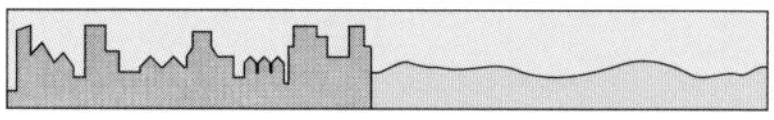
48%
52%

ETHNIC MAKEUP

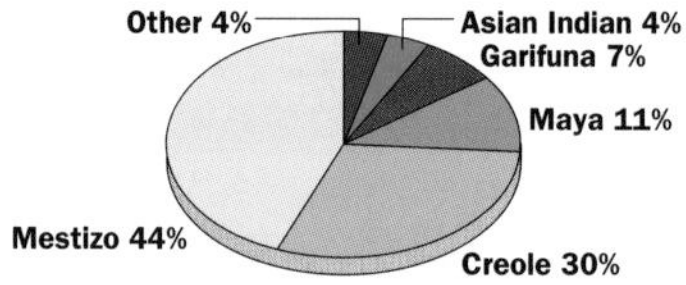
Other 4%
Asian Indian 4%
Garifuna 7%
Maya 11%
Mestizo 44%
Creole 30%

Along with the Spanish-speaking *mestizo* and English-speaking Creole there are the Afro-Carib *garifuna*, who have their own language. Around half the population are Roman Catholic. The number of Spanish speakers is rising, mostly through immigration from neighboring countries.

POLITICS

Multiparty elections

L. House 2003/2008
U. House 2003/2008

H.M. Queen Elizabeth II

AT THE LAST ELECTION

House of Representatives 29 seats

76% PUP
24% UDP

PUP = People's United Party
UDP = United Democratic Party

Senate 13 seats

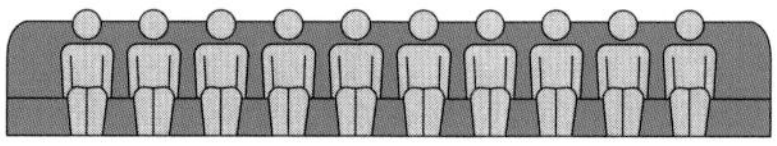

The members of the Senate are appointed by the governor-general

The PUP negotiated Belize's independence from the UK in 1981. Since then, control of the government has swung between the PUP and the UDP, in the absence of any major ideological or policy distinctions. The PUP, under Said Musa, won a crushing victory in 1998 and gained a historic second term in 2003, with a slightly reduced majority. Major political issues include a rise in narcotics-related crimes and political corruption. The controversial practice of selling Belizean passports under the "economic citizenship" program was finally suspended in 2002.

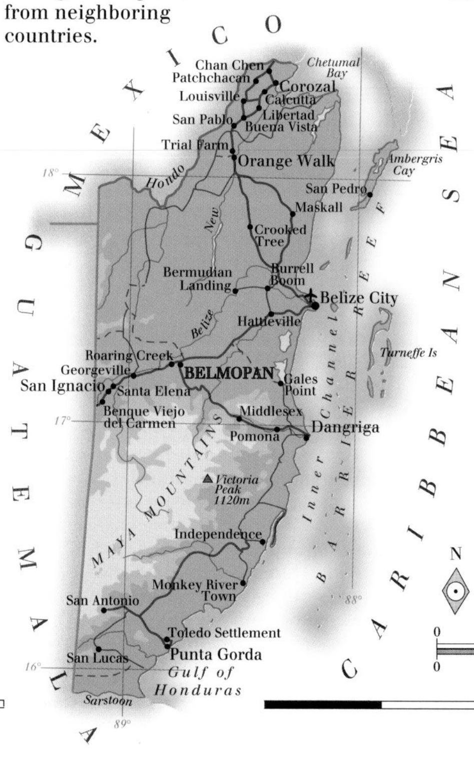
MEXICO
GUATEMALA
CARIBBEAN SEA
Chan Chen
Patchchacan
Louisville
Corozal
Calcutta
San Pablo
Libertad
Buena Vista
Chetumal Bay
Trial Farm
Orange Walk
Ambergris Cay
Hondo
San Pedro
Maskall
New
Crooked Tree
Bermudian Landing
Burrell Boom
Belize City
Hattieville
Belize
Turneffe Is
Roaring Creek
Georgeville
BELMOPAN
Gales Point
San Ignacio
Santa Elena
Benque Viejo del Carmen
Middlesex
Pomona
Dangriga
Victoria Peak 1120m
MAYA MOUNTAINS
Inner Channel
BARRIER REEF
Independence
Monkey River Town
San Antonio
Toledo Settlement
San Lucas
Punta Gorda
Gulf of Honduras
Sarstoon
18°
17°
16°
88°
89°

BELIZE

Total Area : 22 966 sq. km (8867 sq. miles)

POPULATION
- over 10 000
- under 10 000

0 50 km
0 50 miles

LAND HEIGHT
- 1000m/3281ft
- 500m/1640ft
- 200m/656ft
- Sea Level

WORLD AFFAIRS

Joined UN in 1981

ACS | Comm | Caricom | NAM | OAS

Ties, traditionally to the Caribbean, are refocusing on Central America. The major concern is Guatemala's periodically restated claim to over half of Belize.

AID

Recipient

US$21m (receipts) — Up 40% in 2001

In 1999 the IDB, the Commonwealth Development Corporation, the European Investment Bank, and the CDB invested in citrus farms. Belize is one of the highest per capita recipients of US aid.

DEFENSE

No compulsory military service

US$18m — No change in 2001

The small Belize Defense Force took over full responsibility from the UK in 1994 for the country's defense. The UK withdrew its garrison in the same year, but continues to maintain a jungle training school.

ECONOMICS

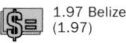

Inflation 1.8% p.a. (1990–2001)

US$727m — 1.97 Belizean dollars (1.97)

SCORE CARD

- World GNP Ranking....................159th
- GNP per Capita....................US$2940
- Balance of Payments...............–US$139m
- Inflation....................1.2%
- Unemployment....................13%

STRENGTHS

Sugar, textile manufacture, agriculture, fishing, and considerable tourist potential. Sustainable public debt; fair access to concessionary foreign finance. Free trade zones and offshore banking.

WEAKNESSES

Narrow export base dependent on preferential market access; reliance on imports of processed foods. Hurricane damage.

EXPORTS

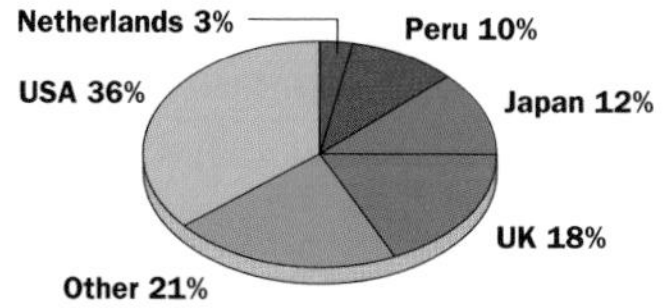
Netherlands 3%
Peru 10%
USA 36%
Japan 12%
UK 18%
Other 21%

IMPORTS

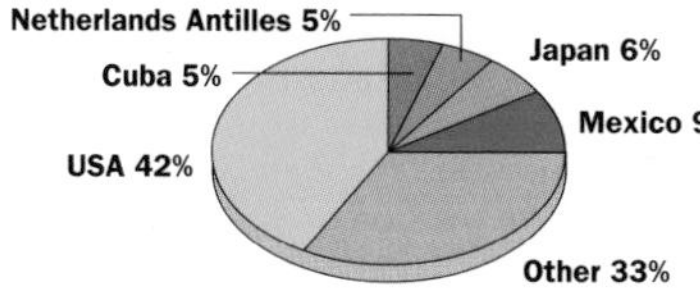
Netherlands Antilles 5%
Japan 6%
Cuba 5%
Mexico 9%
USA 42%
Other 33%

RESOURCES

Electric power 43,000 kW

63,707 tonnes — Not an oil producer

56,949 cattle, 36,000 turkeys, 1.4m chickens — None

Hopes of finding significant oil and gas deposits in the north of the country have so far proved fruitless.

ENVIRONMENT

Not available

40% (31% partially protected) — 2.6 tonnes per capita

Tourist developments and logging have depleted the dense tropical forests. Mahogany is endangered, and all exports and transshipments now require a certificate of origin. Global warming poses a major threat to the corals of the barrier reef.

MEDIA

TV ownership medium

There are no daily newspapers

PUBLISHING AND BROADCAST MEDIA

There are no daily newspapers. The leading papers are the weekly *Belize Times, Amandala,* and *Reporter*

9 services: 1 state-owned, 8 independent — 6 independent services

Belize has not suffered the degree of press interference experienced in neighboring states, but successive governments have remained sensitive to even minor criticisms. The two radio stations of the public Broadcasting Corporation of Belize were sold in 1998 to two local stations, but the government has retained ownership of the transmitters. Two official newspapers compete with party-political and independent publications.

CRIME

Death penalty in use

1097 prisoners — Increase in drugs- and gun-related crime

Belize is a major transit point to the US for cocaine, despite being decertified in 1997 for its antinarcotics efforts. Drugs-related crime is high. Armed robberies by criminal gangs based in neighboring Guatemala are also a major concern. A government ombudsman was appointed in 2000 to investigate police brutality and corruption.

EDUCATION

School leaving age: 14

93% — 2853 students

Although most schools are run by the different churches, a handful are funded by the government, particularly those catering for special needs. The University College of Belize provides for higher education.

CHRONOLOGY

The Mayan heartland included what is now Belize. Between 1798 and 1981 it was effectively a British colony.

- **1919** Demands for more political rights by black Belizeans returning from World War I.
- **1936** New constitution.
- **1950** PUP formed. Voting age limit for women reduced from 30 to 21.
- **1954** Full adult suffrage.
- **1972** Guatemala threatens invasion. Britain sends troops.
- **1981** Full independence.
- **2000** Guatemala revives claim to half of Belize.
- **2001** Hurricane Iris hits Belize.
- **2003** PUP wins second term.

HEALTH

Welfare state health benefits

1 per 1818 people — Cancers, heart diseases, accidents, violence

The health service provided by the government includes seven hospitals, more than 30 regional health centers, and numerous mobile clinics. Water supplies and sanitation have been improved; most homes in Belmopan now have both.

SPENDING

GDP/cap. increase

CONSUMPTION AND SPENDING

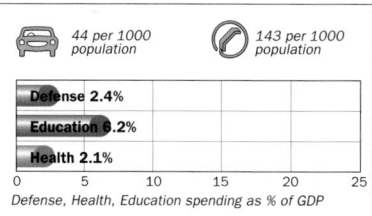

44 per 1000 population — *143 per 1000 population*

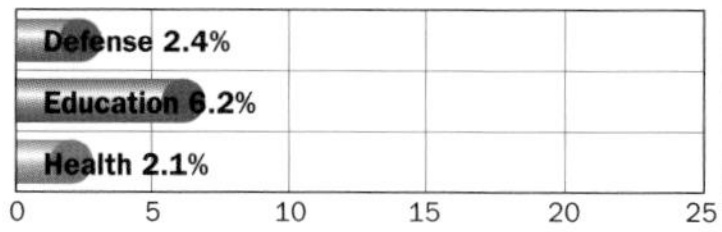
Defense 2.4%
Education 6.2%
Health 2.1%
0
5
10
15
20
25

Defense, Health, Education spending as % of GDP

The European Development Fund in 1999 granted 3.5 million Belizean dollars toward the reduction of rural poverty. Narcotics trading remains a source of wealth.

WORLD RANKING

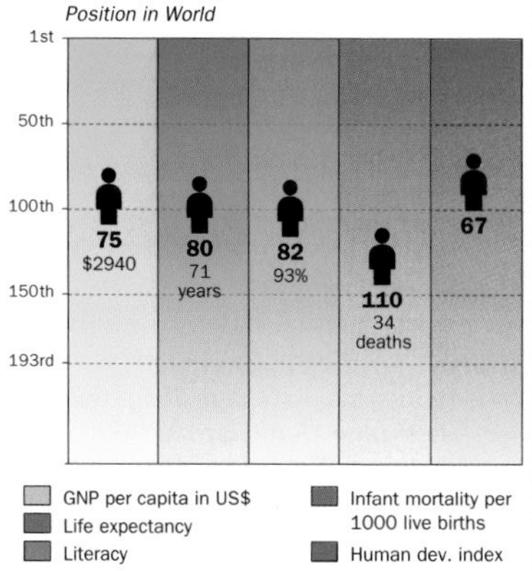
Position in World
1st
50th
100th
150th
193rd
75
$2940
80
71 years
82
93%
110
34 deaths
67
GNP per capita in US$
Life expectancy
Literacy
Infant mortality per 1000 live births
Human dev. index

B

BENIN

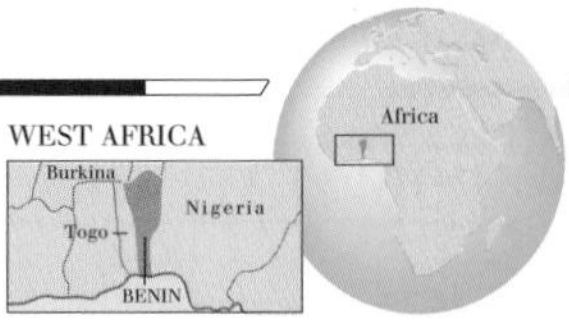
WEST AFRICA
Burkina
Togo
Nigeria
BENIN
Africa

OFFICIAL NAME: Republic of Benin **CAPITAL:** Porto-Novo
POPULATION: 6.6 million **CURRENCY:** CFA franc **OFFICIAL LANGUAGE:** French

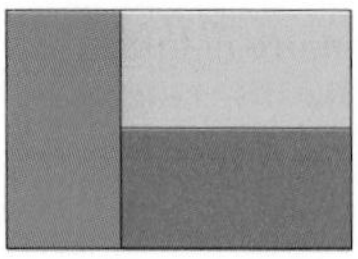

1960 | 1960 | Aug 8 | DY | +1 | +229 | .bj

BENIN STRETCHES NORTH from the west African coast, with a 100-km (60-mile) shoreline on the Bight of Benin. Formerly the kingdom of Dahomey, Benin was under French colonial rule, becoming part of French West Africa, until independence in 1960. In 1990 Benin was a pioneer of multipartyism in Africa, ending 17 years of one-party Marxist-Leninist rule. Benin's economy is based on well-diversified agriculture.

CLIMATE

Tropical wet and dry

WEATHER CHART FOR PORTO-NOVO

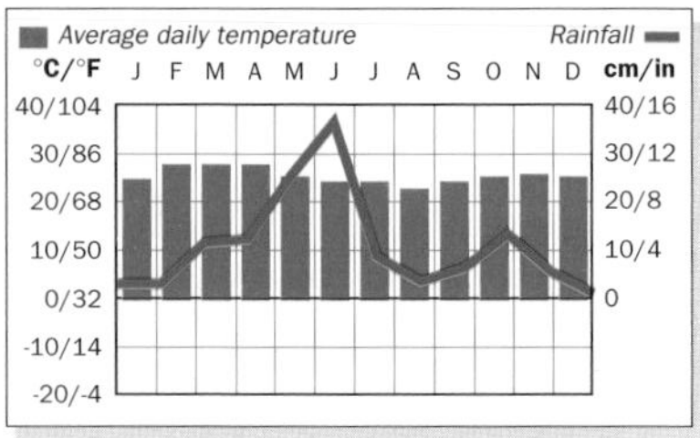
Average daily temperature
Rainfall
°C/°F J F M A M J J A S O N D cm/in
40/104
30/86
20/68
10/50
0/32
-10/14
-20/-4
40/16
30/12
20/8
10/4
0

There are two rainy seasons. The hot, dusty *harmattan* wind characterizes the December to February dry season.

TRANSPORTATION

Drive on right

Cotonou 264,922 passengers

6 ships 1000 grt

THE TRANSPORTATION NETWORK

1357 km (843 miles)

10 km (6 miles)

458 km (285 miles)

Sections of streams are navigable

The cofunded Benin–Niger railroad stops short at Parakou. The Cotonou–Porto-Novo line reopened in 1999.

TOURISM

Visitors : Population 1:43

152,000 visitors

Up 1% in 1998

MAIN TOURIST ARRIVALS

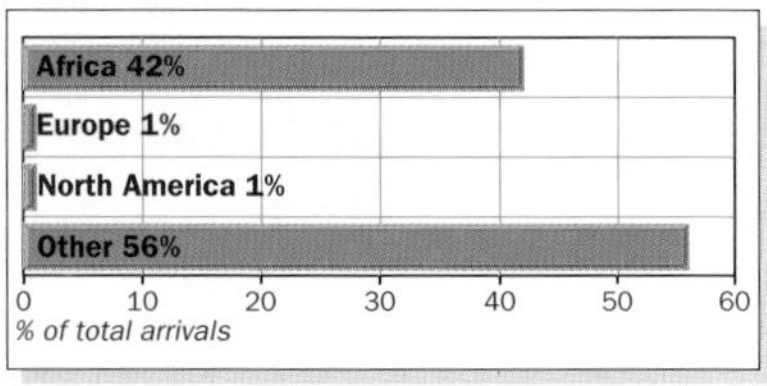
Africa 42%
Europe 1%
North America 1%
Other 56%
0 10 20 30 40 50 60
% of total arrivals

Tourism is not well developed; there are plans to increase package vacations. There is some safari tourism in the north, particularly in the Atakora Mountains. Benin can be included as a short break for vacationers in Nigeria.

PEOPLE

Pop. density medium

Fon, Bariba, Yoruba, Adja, Houeda, Somba, French

60/km² (155/mi²)

THE URBAN/RURAL POPULATION SPLIT

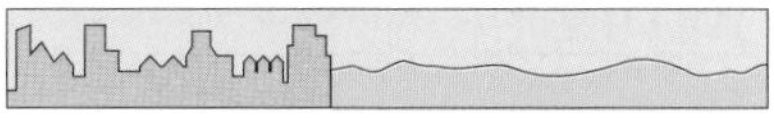
43%
57%

RELIGIOUS PERSUASION

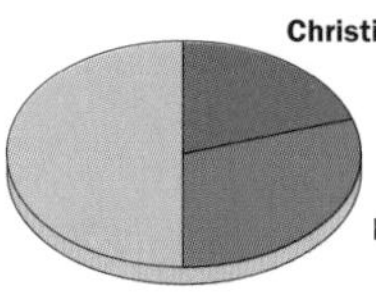
Christian 20%
Voodoo 50%
Muslim 30%

There are 42 different ethnic groups: the southern Fon have tended to dominate politically. North–south tension is mainly due to the south being better developed. Voodoo is thought to have originated in Benin. French culture is highly prized in Porto-Novo.

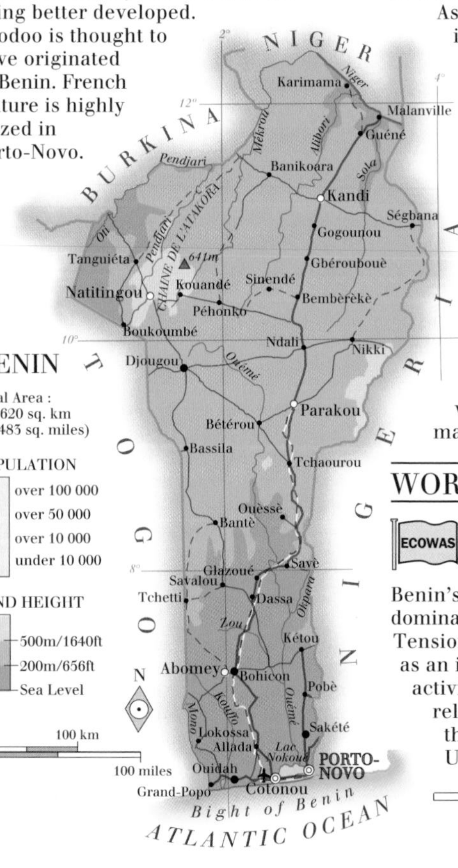
NIGER
BURKINA
TOGO
NIGERIA
Niger
Karimama
Malanville
Guéné
Mékrou
Alibori
Sota
Pendjari
Banikoara
Kandi
Ségbana
Gogounou
Tanguiéta
Oti
CHAÎNE DE L'ATAKORA
641m
Gbéroubouè
Natitingou
Kouandé
Sinendé
Bembèrèkè
Péhonko
Boukoumbé
Ndali
Nikki
Djougou
Ouémé
Parakou
Bétérou
Bassila
Tchaourou
Ouèssè
Banté
Savè
Glazoué
Savalou
Tchetti
Dassa
Okpara
Zou
Kétou
Abomey
Bohicon
Pobè
Kouffo
Mono
Ouémé
Lokossa
Sakété
Allada
Lac Nokoué
PORTO-NOVO
Ouidah
Cotonou
Grand-Popo
Bight of Benin
ATLANTIC OCEAN
12°
10°
8°
2°
4°
N

BENIN

Total Area : 112 620 sq. km (43 483 sq. miles)

POPULATION
- over 100 000
- over 50 000
- over 10 000
- under 10 000

LAND HEIGHT
- 500m/1640ft
- 200m/656ft
- Sea Level

0 100 km
0 100 miles

POLITICS

Multiparty elections

2003/2007

President Mathieu Kérékou

AT THE LAST ELECTION

National Assembly 83 seats

13% PRD
63% MP
18% PRB
6% Other Opp

MP = Presidential Rally **PRB** = Benin Renaissance Party
PRD = Party of Democratic Renewal
Other Opp = Other opposition supporters

Benin's image as a leader in African democratization was tarnished by allegations of fraud over the 2001 presidential election.

Democratization had begun at the National Conference of 1990, when Mathieu Kérékou agreed to hold multiparty elections after years of Marxist-Leninist one-party military rule. The main political parties in Benin tend to be regionally based and depend on the leadership of individuals influential in local communities.

Kérékou became the first of the African one-party leaders to hand over power peacefully, to Nicéphore Soglo, a former World Bank official, after elections in 1991. Soglo did not have an automatic majority in the National Assembly, and was forced to include members of the opposition parties in his government. The main political issue became his World Bank-style deregulation of the economy. He was defeated in a controversial election in 1996 which brought Kérékou back to power as president. Kérékou dismissed claims of vote rigging in the 2001 presidential election, saying that democracy was "alive and kicking." The MP, which supports Kérékou, won an outright legislative majority in 2003.

WORLD AFFAIRS

Joined UN in 1960

ECOWAS | AU | OIC | FZ | UEMOA

Benin's foreign relations are largely dominated by its huge neighbor, Nigeria. Tensions exist over the use of Benin as an illegal transit point for Nigerian activists. The continuation of good relations with France (currently the main aid source) and the US is considered to be critical.

AID

Recipient

$273m (receipts)

Up 14% in 2001

Benin's poverty is such that the maintenance of aid is at the top of the political agenda. France, the main protector of Benin since independence in 1960, is the major aid donor. Other donors include the World Bank, the US, the EU, Germany, Denmark, and the African Development Bank. Almost all development finance comes from aid, and some has been used to finance debt servicing. There is the usual problem of finding suitable projects, although Benin has a large, well-educated (if top heavy) civil service, making implementation easier than in many parts of Africa.

DEFENSE

Compulsory military service

$41m

Up 11% in 2001

The 4300-strong army is actively involved in the attempt to curb smuggling on the Nigerian border. In 1989 the army was employed internally against rioters.

ECONOMICS

Inflation 8.2% p.a. (1990–2001)

$2.42bn

571.2 CFA francs (664.2)

SCORE CARD

❑ World GNP Ranking	135th
❑ GNP per Capita	$380
❑ Balance of Payments	–$74m
❑ Inflation	4%
❑ Unemployment	2%

Strengths

Agriculture. Small, but well-diversified manufacturing sector. Regional agreements support cotton trade. Exports competitive with weak CFA franc. Growing services sector.

Weaknesses

Large-scale smuggling. Transportation and commerce greatly affected by fluctuations in Nigeria. Reliance on electricity imports from Ghana.

EXPORTS

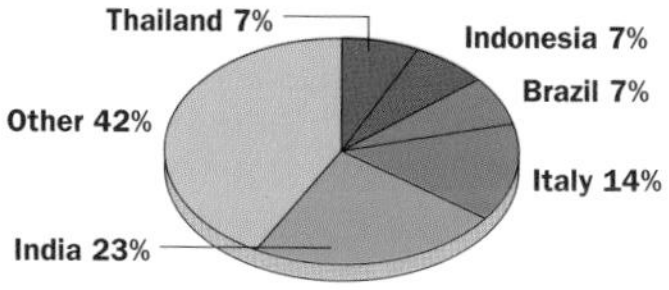
Thailand 7%
Indonesia 7%
Brazil 7%
Other 42%
Italy 14%
India 23%

IMPORTS

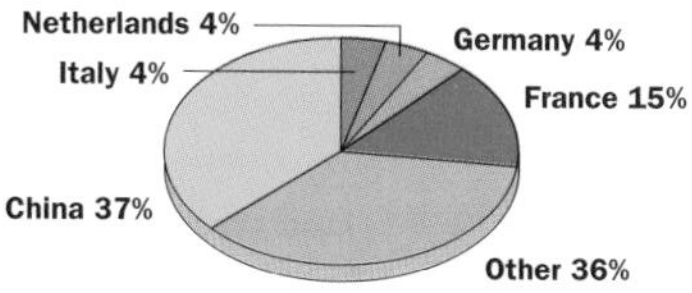
Netherlands 4%
Germany 4%
Italy 4%
France 15%
China 37%
Other 36%

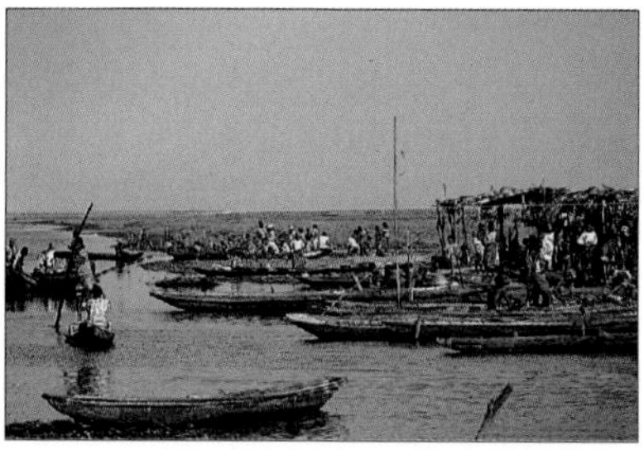

Flat landscape near Cotonou, *characteristic of Benin's coastal region. Numerous lagoons lie behind its short coastline.*

RESOURCES

Electric power 49,000 kW

32,324 tonnes

882 b/d (reserves 29m barrels)

1.55m cattle, 1.27m goats, 10m chickens

Oil, limestone, marble, gold

Most of Benin's electricity is derived from dams in neighboring countries. Since a drought in Ghana in 1994 it has attempted to diversify its sources.

ENVIRONMENT

Sustainability rank: 95th

11% (4% partially protected)

0.2 tonnes per capita

Desertification in the north is the major problem. Benin has been used in the past as a dumping ground for toxic waste.

MEDIA

TV ownership low

Daily newspaper circulation 5 per 1000 people

PUBLISHING AND BROADCAST MEDIA

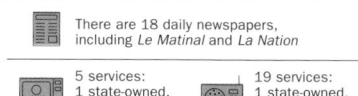

There are 18 daily newspapers, including *Le Matinal* and *La Nation*

5 services: 1 state-owned, 4 independent

19 services: 1 state-owned, 18 independent

Benin publishes over 50 newspapers and periodicals. The press has considerable freedom, and a media code of practice was introduced in 1999.

CRIME

Death penalty in use

4961 prisoners

Up sharply in 1996–1998

Armed crime has risen sharply since 1995, despite the reintroduction of the death penalty. Smuggling, including child trafficking, is a major problem.

EDUCATION

School leaving age: 11

39%

18,753 students

More is spent on education than on defense, and this is reinforced by Benin's active intellectual community, the "Latin Quarter of Africa." The university at Abomey-Calavi is rated highly in medicine and law.

CHRONOLOGY

In 1625 the Fon, indigenous slave traders, founded the kingdom of Dahomey. Dahomey in turn conquered the neighboring kingdoms of Dan, Allada, and the coast around Porto-Novo.

- ❑ **1857** French establish trading post at Grand-Popo.
- ❑ **1889** French defeat King Behanzin.
- ❑ **1892** French protectorate.
- ❑ **1904** Part of French West Africa.
- ❑ **1960** Full independence.
- ❑ **1975** Renamed Benin.
- ❑ **1989** Marxism-Leninism abandoned as official ideology.
- ❑ **1996** Former ruler Kérékou defeats Soglo in controversial election.
- ❑ **2001** Kérékou reelected to presidency amid claims of electoral fraud.

HEALTH

No welfare state health benefits

1 per 10,000 people

Communicable and diarrheal diseases, malaria

Outside the major towns, health services and doctors are scarce. It is forecast that by 2030 one million Beninese will have died from AIDS.

SPENDING

GDP/cap. increase

CONSUMPTION AND SPENDING

7 per 1000 population

9 per 1000 population

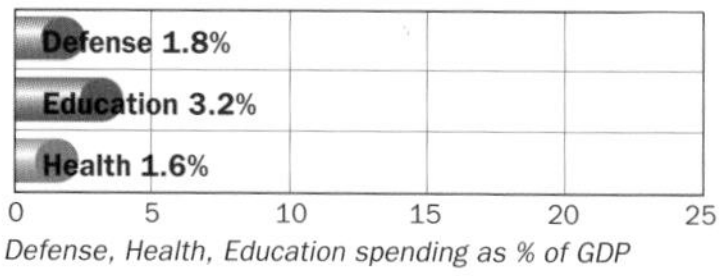
Defense 1.8%
Education 3.2%
Health 1.6%
0
5
10
15
20
25
Defense, Health, Education spending as % of GDP

Substantial differences in wealth reflect the strongly hierarchical nature of society, especially in the south. French cars are considered to be status symbols.

WORLD RANKING

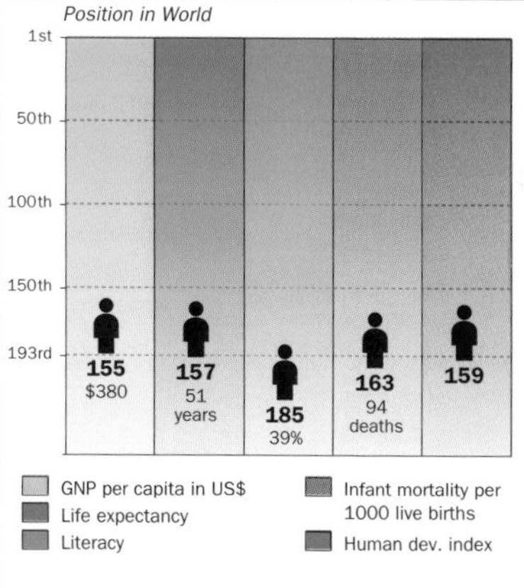
Position in World
1st
50th
100th
150th
193rd
155
$380
157
51 years
185
39%
163
94 deaths
159
GNP per capita in US$
Life expectancy
Literacy
Infant mortality per 1000 live births
Human dev. index

B

BHUTAN

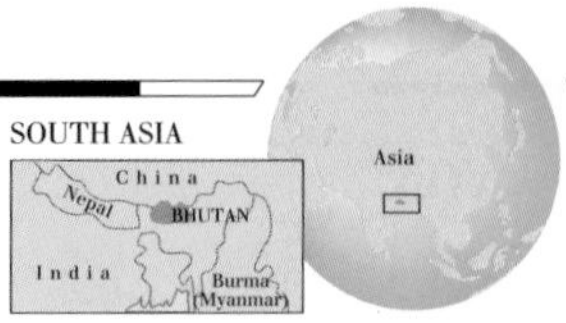
SOUTH ASIA
China
Nepal
BHUTAN
India
Burma (Myanmar)
Asia

OFFICIAL NAME: Kingdom of Bhutan **CAPITAL:** Thimphu
POPULATION: 2.2 million **CURRENCY:** Ngultrum **OFFICIAL LANGUAGE:** Dzongkha

1656 | 1865 | Dec 17 | BT | +6 | +975 | .bt

PERCHED IN THE HIMALAYAS between India and China, Bhutan is 70% forested. The land rises from the low, tropical southern strip through the fertile central valleys to the high Himalayas, inhabited by seminomadic yak herders. Formally a Buddhist state where power is shared by the king and the government, Bhutan began modernizing in the 1960s, but has chosen to do so gradually, and remains largely closed to the outside world.

CLIMATE

Mountain

WEATHER CHART FOR THIMPHU

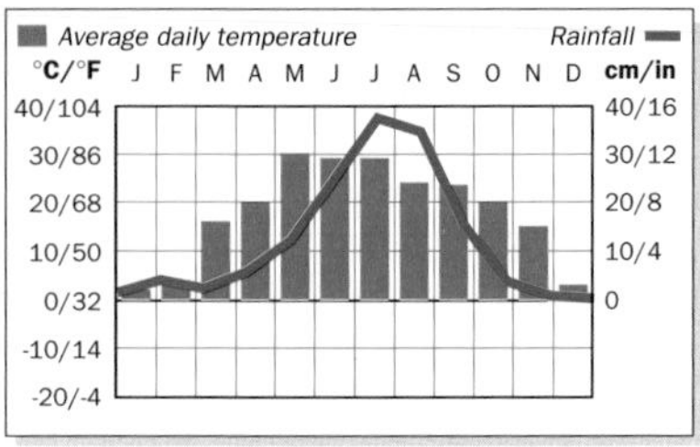
Average daily temperature
Rainfall
°C/°F J F M A M J J A S O N D cm/in
40/104
30/86
20/68
10/50
0/32
-10/14
-20/-4
40/16
30/12
20/8
10/4
0

The south is tropical, the north alpine, cold, and harsh. The central valleys are warmer in the east than in the west. The summer monsoon affects all parts.

TRANSPORTATION

Drive on left

Paro International 19,939 passengers

Has no fleet

THE TRANSPORTATION NETWORK

1994 km (1239 miles)

None

None

None

The main surfaced road runs east–west across central Bhutan. Two others run south into India. Only the national airline, Druk Air, flies into Bhutan.

TOURISM

Visitors : Population 1:355

6200 visitors

Up 4% in 1999

MAIN TOURIST ARRIVALS

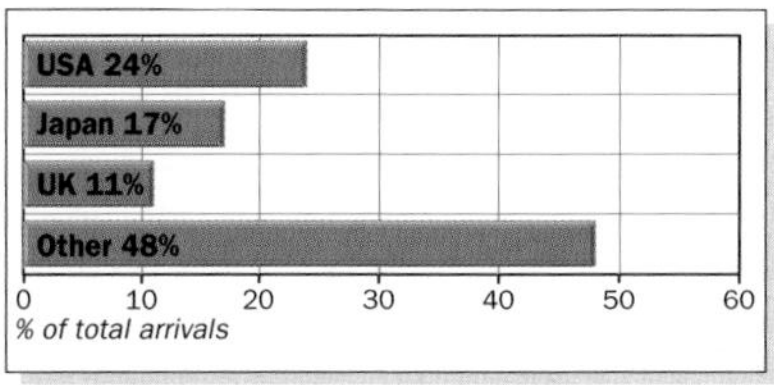
USA 24%
Japan 17%
UK 11%
Other 48%
0 10 20 30 40 50 60
% of total arrivals

Tourism is restricted to protect Bhutan's culture and natural environment; entry has been easier since the industry was privatized in 1991. Most monasteries are closed to tourists. In 1998, fire damaged the famous Taktsang monastery.

***Less than 10% of Bhutan is arable,** but its fertility allows almost any crop to grow. The diversity of wild plant species inspired its old name: Southern Valleys of the Medicinal Herbs.*

PEOPLE

Pop. density low

Dzongkha, Nepali, Assamese

47/km² (121/mi²)

THE URBAN/RURAL POPULATION SPLIT

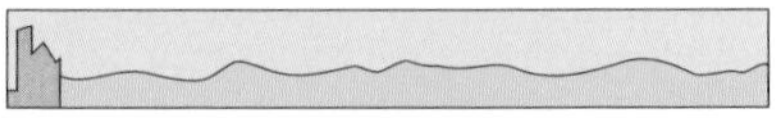
7%
93%

RELIGIOUS PERSUASION

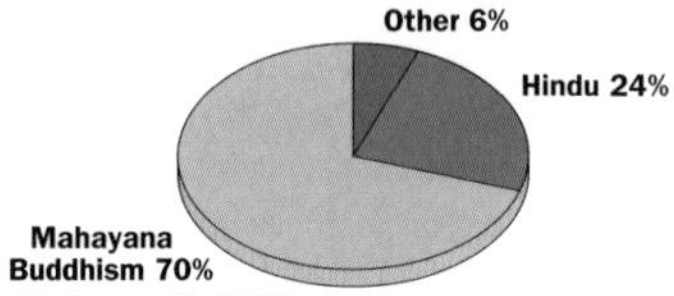
Other 6%
Hindu 24%
Mahayana Buddhism 70%

The majority of the population, the Drukpa peoples, originated from Tibet and are devoutly Buddhist. The Hindu minority is made up of Nepalese who settled in the south from 1910 to 1950. Bhutan has 20 languages. Dzongkha, the language of western Bhutan, native to less than a quarter of the population, was made the official language in 1988. The Nepalese community has reacted strongly, regarding this as "cultural imperialism."

POLITICS

Nonparty elections

Not applicable

H.M. Druk Gyalpo (Dragon King) Jigme Singye Wangchuk

LEGISLATIVE OR ADVISORY BODIES

National Assembly 150 seats

There are no legal political parties; members are elected individually to the National Assembly, to advise the king, who rules as an absolute monarch

The modernization of Bhutan's absolute monarchy began in 1961. Under further changes proposed in 1998, the king relinquished his right to appoint the government in favor of a cabinet elected by the National Assembly. The National Assembly was also empowered to pass a vote of no confidence against the king. These proposals came as a response to a prodemocracy movement fueled by ethnic Nepalese opposed to the Drukpa-dominated political system.

BHUTAN

Total Area : 47 000 sq. km (18 147 sq. miles)

LAND HEIGHT

6000m/19686ft
4000m/13124ft
2000m/6562ft
1000m/3281ft
500m/1640ft
200m/656ft
160m/252ft

POPULATION

- over 10 000
- under 10 000

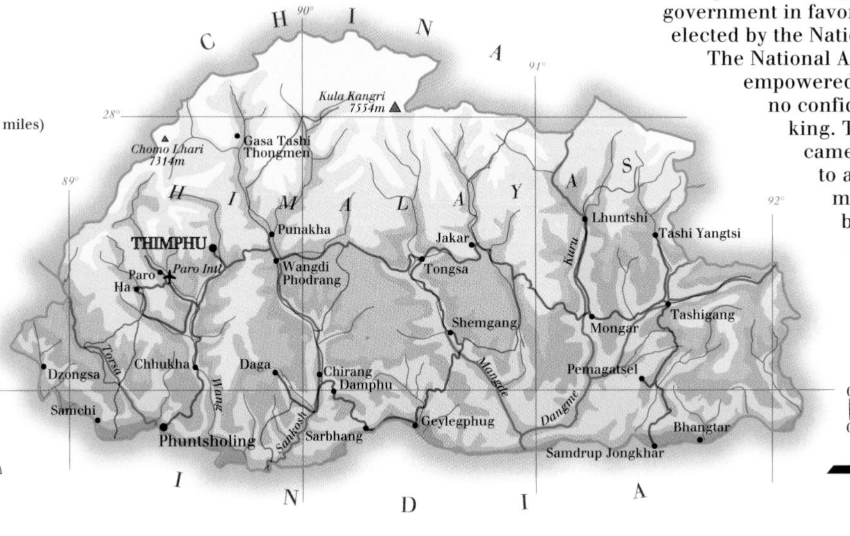
CHINA
INDIA
HIMALAYAS
Kula Kangri 7554m
Chomo Lhari 7314m
Gasa Tashi Thongmen
THIMPHU
Paro
Paro Intl
Ha
Punakha
Wangdi Phodrang
Jakar
Tongsa
Lhuntshi
Tashi Yangtsi
Kuru
Mongar
Tashigang
Shemgang
Pemagatsel
Dzongsa
Torsa
Chhukha
Daga
Chirang Damphu
Wang
Samchi
Phuntsholing
Sankosh
Sarbhang
Geylegphug
Mangde
Dangme
Bhangtar
Samdrup Jongkhar
N
0 50 km
0 50 miles

WORLD AFFAIRS

Joined UN in 1971

CP | IBRD | NAM | SAARC | ADB

Bhutan's closest links are with India. Relations with China are cordial, and negotiations to settle the China–Bhutan border have progressed smoothly since 1984. There is tension with Nepal over Bhutan's treatment of its ethnic Nepalese minority and the influx of Bhutanese refugees into Nepal.

AID

Recipient

$59m (receipts)

Up 11% in 2001

Bhutan relies on foreign aid for half of its annual budget. The largest donors are Denmark and Japan.

DEFENSE

No compulsory military service

$19m

Down 10% in 2001

The army is under the command of the king, and is trained by Indian military instructors. India provides de facto military protection and is obliged to defend Bhutan against attack.

ECONOMICS

Inflation 9.3% p.a. (1990–2001)

$529m

46.47 ngultrum (48.86)

SCORE CARD

❑ WORLD GNP RANKING	170th
❑ GNP PER CAPITA	$640
❑ BALANCE OF PAYMENTS	–$87m
❑ INFLATION	7.5%
❑ UNEMPLOYMENT	Low rate

STRENGTHS

New development of cash crops for Asian markets (cardamoms, apples, oranges, apricots). Hardwoods in south, especially teak, but exploitation currently tightly controlled. Large hydroelectric potential.

WEAKNESSES

Dependence on Indian workers for many public-sector jobs from road building to teaching. The majority of the population are dependent on agriculture. Cultivated land is extremely restricted because of steep mountain slopes. Very little industry. Few mineral resources.

EXPORTS

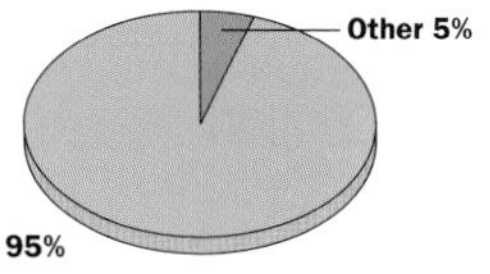
Other 5%
India 95%

IMPORTS

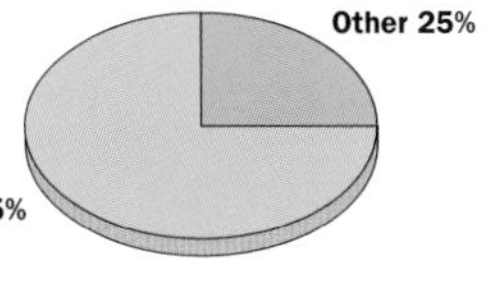
Other 25%
India 75%

RESOURCES

Electric power 356,000 kW

330 tonnes

Not an oil producer and has no refineries

355,400 cattle, 41,400 pigs, 231,000 chickens

Talc, gypsum, coal, limestone, slate, dolomite

Bhutan's forests remain largely intact, and logging is very strictly controlled. Hydroelectric potential is considerable, but few dams have been built. Power is sold to India from the Chhukha Dam, bringing in substantial foreign earnings.

ENVIRONMENT

Sustainability rank: 30th

21% (5% partially protected)

0.2 tonnes per capita

Bhutan's forests stabilize the steep mountainsides and supply the bulk of its fuel needs. Road building, begun in the 1960s, is the biggest cause of deforestation, which has led to topsoil erosion. The high northern pastures are at risk from overgrazing by yaks. Traditional Buddhist values instilling respect for nature and forbidding the killing of animals are still observed.

MEDIA

TV ownership low

There are no daily newspapers

PUBLISHING AND BROADCAST MEDIA

There are no daily newspapers. *Kuensel* is published weekly by the government in Dzongkha, English, and Nepali

1 state-owned service

1 state-owned service

Until 1999 TV was banned, in order to protect cultural values. An Internet café opened in Thimphu in 2000.

CRIME

Death penalty not used in practice

Bhutan does not publish prison figures

Little variation from year to year

Levels of violent crime and theft are low. In 1991, *driglam namzha*, an ancient code of conduct including the requirement to wear traditional dress, was revived, with imprisonment or fines for those not in compliance.

EDUCATION

School leaving age: 16

47%

1837 students

Education is free. A small minority of children attend secondary school. Teaching is in English and Dzongkha. There are no universities.

CHRONOLOGY

The Drukpa, originally from Tibet, united Bhutan in 1656. In 1865 the Drukpa lost the Duars Strip to British India.

- ❑ **1907** Monarchy established.
- ❑ **1949** Indo-Bhutan Treaty of Friendship.
- ❑ **1953** National Assembly set up.
- ❑ **1968** King forms first cabinet.
- ❑ **1971** Bhutan joins UN.
- ❑ **1990** Ethnic Nepalese launch campaign for minority rights.
- ❑ **1998** King proposes to reform government.
- ❑ **1999** First TV service inaugurated.

HEALTH

Welfare state health benefits

1 per 6250 people

Diarrheal, respiratory diseases, tuberculosis, malaria, infant deaths

Free clinics, along with Thimphu's hospital, provide basic health care. Progress is being made in child immunization, and monks have been persuaded to teach hygiene. Infant mortality is high. Bhutanese, Tibetan, and Chinese traditional medicines are widely practiced.

SPENDING

GDP/cap. increase

CONSUMPTION AND SPENDING

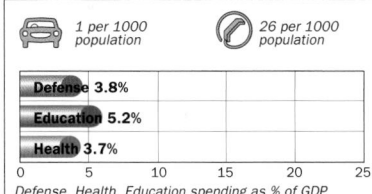

1 per 1000 population

26 per 1000 population

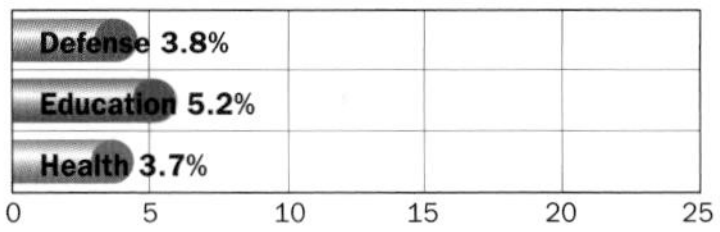
Defense 3.8%
Education 5.2%
Health 3.7%
0
5
10
15
20
25

Defense, Health, Education spending as % of GDP

Most of Bhutan's people are chronically poor, although starvation is virtually unknown. There is a small middle class, consisting of public employees and storekeepers.

WORLD RANKING

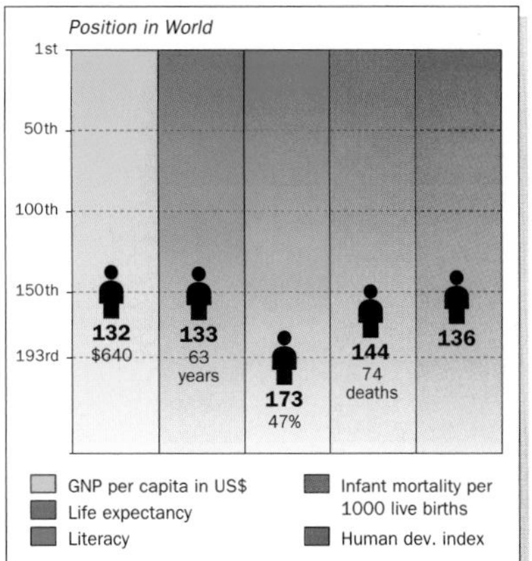
Position in World
1st
50th
100th
150th
193rd
132
$640
133
63 years
173
47%
144
74 deaths
136
GNP per capita in US$
Life expectancy
Literacy
Infant mortality per 1000 live births
Human dev. index

Bolivia

SOUTH AMERICA
Peru
Brazil
BOLIVIA
Chile
Paraguay
South America

Official Name: Republic of Bolivia **Capitals:** La Paz (administrative); Sucre (judicial)
Population: 8.7 million **Currency:** Boliviano **Official Languages:** Spanish, Quechua, and Aymara

1825 | 1938 | Aug 6 | BOL | -4 | +591 | .bo

BOLIVIA LIES LANDLOCKED high in central South America, and is one of the continent's poorest nations. Over half of the population lives on the *altiplano*, the windswept plateau between two ranges of the Andes, 3500 m (11,500 ft) above sea level. La Paz, the highest capital in the world, has spawned a neighboring large twin, El Alto. Bolivia has the world's highest golf course, ski run, and soccer stadium. The eastern lowland regions are tropical and underdeveloped but are rapidly being colonized.

TOURISM

Visitors : Population 1:29

300,000 visitors

Down 12% in 2000–2001

MAIN TOURIST ARRIVALS

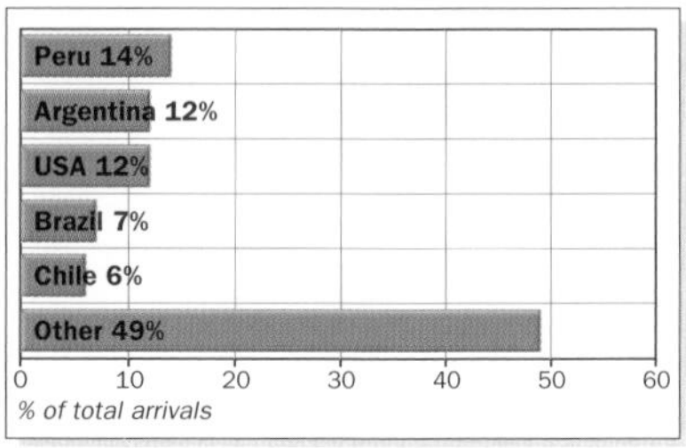
Peru 14%
Argentina 12%
USA 12%
Brazil 7%
Chile 6%
Other 49%
0 10 20 30 40 50 60
% of total arrivals

Foreign tourists are drawn by the traditional festivals, especially carnivals in February or March, the variety of Bolivia's scenery, and its Spanish colonial architecture. Major attractions include the Silver Mountain at Potosí, and Lake Titicaca, the highest navigable lake in the world, covering an area of 8970 sq. km (3463 sq. miles). Recent political stability encouraged some growth in tourism in the 1990s, but potential is limited by Bolivia's isolation, the rugged, inaccessible terrain, and the limited infrastructure.

CLIMATE

Tropical/mountain

WEATHER CHART FOR LA PAZ

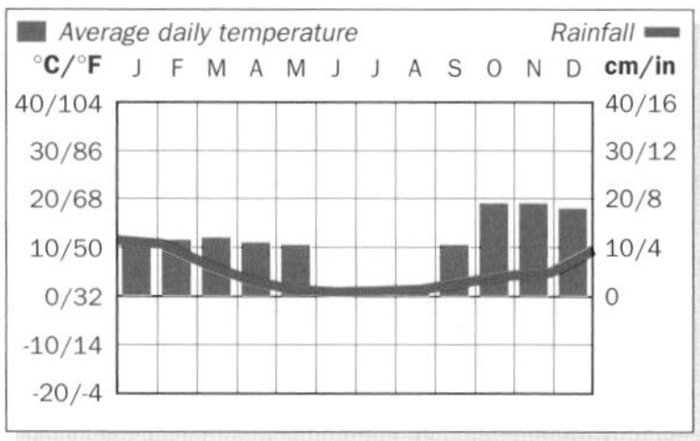
Average daily temperature
Rainfall
°C/°F J F M A M J J A S O N D cm/in
40/104
30/86
20/68
10/50
0/32
-10/14
-20/-4
40/16
30/12
20/8
10/4
0

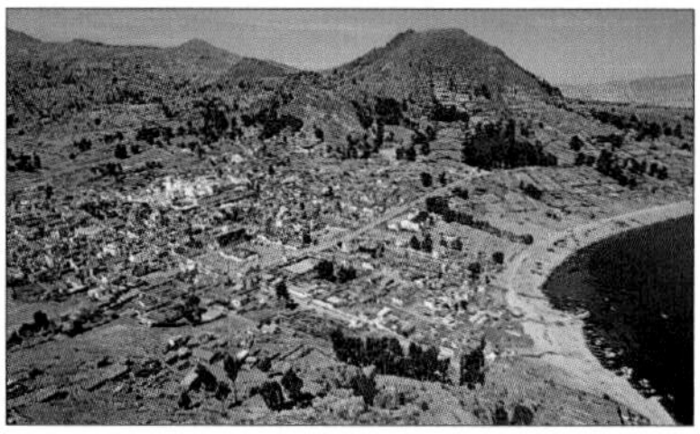

***Copacabana** on the shores of Lake Titicaca. It lies on a large headland owned by Bolivia on the Peruvian side of the lake.*

The Andean *altiplano* has an extreme tropical highland climate with winter night frosts. Annual rainfall in the west is only 25 cm (10 in). The hot eastern lowlands receive most rain in summer.

TRANSPORTATION

Drive on right

El Alto, La Paz

1 ship 15,800 dwt

THE TRANSPORTATION NETWORK

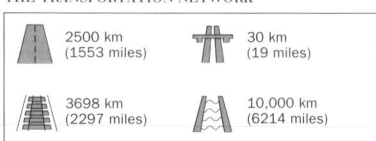

2500 km (1553 miles)	30 km (19 miles)
3698 km (2297 miles)	10,000 km (6214 miles)

Obtaining port access to the Pacific coast for landlocked Bolivia is important. Only 5% of roads are paved. The national railroad was privatized in 1996. Domestic airlines are generally reliable.

***Potato harvest** on the* altiplano. *Migration to the more fertile lands in the east has been encouraged.*

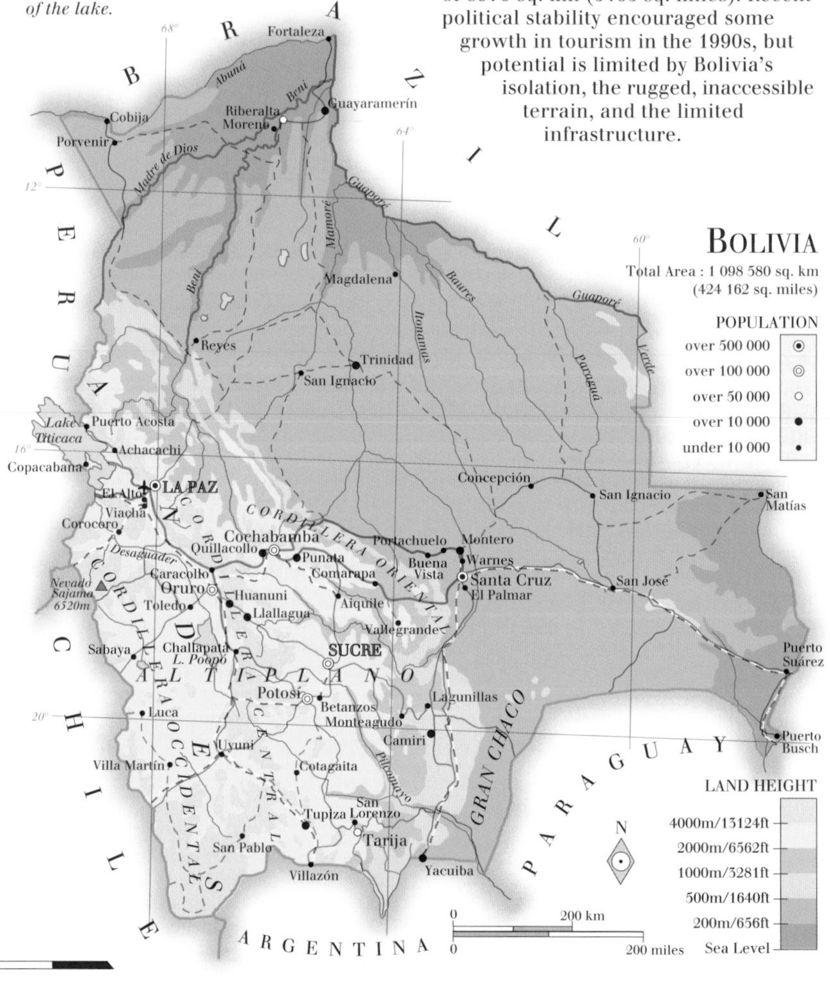
BRAZIL
PERU
CHILE
ARGENTINA
PARAGUAY
Fortaleza
Cobija
Porvenir
Riberalta
Moreno
Guayaramerín
Magdalena
Reyes
Trinidad
San Ignacio
Puerto Acosta
Lake Titicaca
Achacachi
Copacabana
El Alto
LA PAZ
Viacha
Corocoro
Cochabamba
Quillacollo
Punata
Portachuelo
Montero
Warnes
Buena Vista
Santa Cruz
El Palmar
Concepción
San Ignacio
San Matías
San José
Puerto Suárez
Puerto Busch
Caracollo
Oruro
Huanuni
Llallagua
Toledo
Nevado Sajama 6520m
Sabaya
Challapata
L. Poopó
SUCRE
Aiquile
Comarapa
Vallegrande
Potosí
Betanzos
Monteagudo
Lagunillas
Camiri
Luca
Uyuni
Villa Martín
Cotagaita
Tupiza
San Lorenzo
Tarija
San Pablo
Villazón
Yacuiba
CORDILLERA ORIENTAL
CORDILLERA OCCIDENTAL
CORDILLERA CENTRAL
ALTIPLANO
GRAN CHACO
Abuná
Beni
Madre de Dios
Mamoré
Guaporé
Baures
Itonamas
Paraguá
Verde
Desaguadero
Pilcomayo
68°
64°
60°
12°
16°
20°
BOLIVIA
Total Area : 1 098 580 sq. km (424 162 sq. miles)
POPULATION
over 500 000
over 100 000
over 50 000
over 10 000
under 10 000
LAND HEIGHT
4000m/13124ft
2000m/6562ft
1000m/3281ft
500m/1640ft
200m/656ft
Sea Level
0 200 km
0 200 miles
N

B

PEOPLE

Pop. density low

Aymara, Quechua, Spanish

8/km² (21/mi²)

THE URBAN/RURAL POPULATION SPLIT

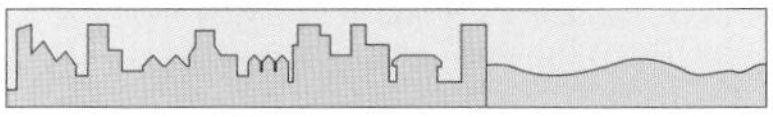
63%
37%

RELIGIOUS PERSUASION

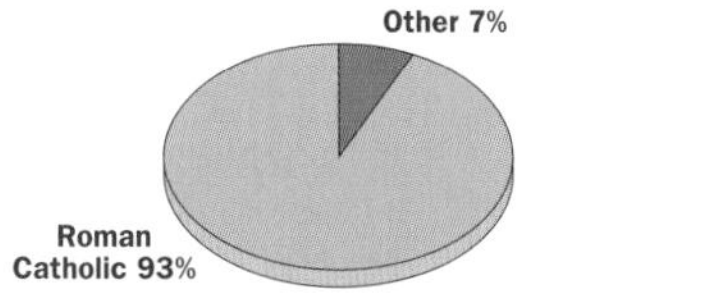
Other 7%
Roman Catholic 93%

ETHNIC MAKEUP

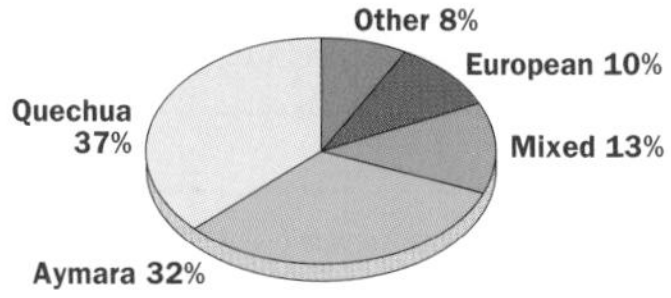
Other 8%
European 10%
Mixed 13%
Quechua 37%
Aymara 32%

Two-thirds of Bolivians are Quechua and Aymara Amerindians who historically have been marginalized. In recent years, however, they have played a more active role in politics by supporting new populist parties.

Wealthy city elites, dating back to Spanish colonial rule, retain great influence, but new entrepreneurs with political ambitions have appeared. Most Bolivians are subsistence farmers, miners, small traders, or artisans earning low incomes. Government schemes, spontaneous colonization, and the collapse of tin mining have led in the last few decades to large-scale migration from the Andes to lowland eastern regions. Some 130,000 lowland Amerindians live in highland cities in the western regions.

Family life tends to be close-knit; Amerindians practice Roman Catholicism mixed with their own traditions and culture. Women have low status.

POPULATION AGE BREAKDOWN

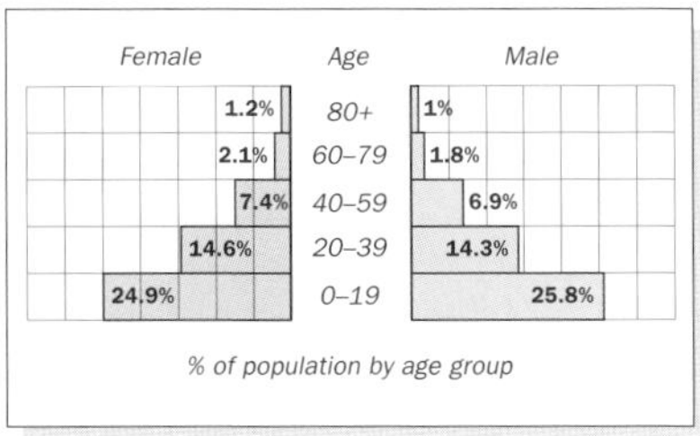
Female
Age
Male
1.2% 80+ 1%
2.1% 60–79 1.8%
7.4% 40–59 6.9%
14.6% 20–39 14.3%
24.9% 0–19 25.8%
% of population by age group

WORLD AFFAIRS

Joined UN in 1945

AP | AmCC | NAM | OAS | RG

Bolivia's overriding foreign policy concern has always been to gain improved access to the Pacific via Peru and Chile. Historic grievances have fueled public opposition to a gas pipeline through Chile – the investors' choice – favoring instead a Peruvian route. Current gas export projects, coupled with the opening of the telecoms sector, and the extension of the Andean Trade Preference Act with the US are essential for growth. Current US aid is conditional on the Bolivian government taking measures to destroy the cocaine-producing and trafficking industry, involving military and police attacks on impoverished coca growers.

Bolivia is an associate member, along with Chile, of Mercosur. This southern grouping, under the leadership of Brazil, will act as a strong negotiating bloc in upcoming talks for a Free Trade Area of the Americas (FTAA), due in 2005.

***Hugo Banzer Suárez**, former dictator, who was elected president (1997–2001).*

***Gonzalo Sánchez de Lozada**, president in 1993–1997, was reelected in 2002.*

POLITICS

Multiparty elections

L. House 2002/2007
U. House 2002/2007

President Gonzalo Sánchez de Lozada

AT THE LAST ELECTION

Chamber of Deputies 130 seats

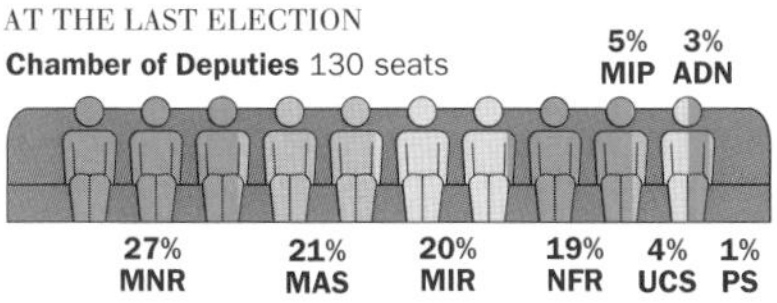
5% MIP
3% ADN
27% MNR
21% MAS
20% MIR
19% NFR
4% UCS
1% PS

MNR = Nationalist Revolutionary Movement **MAS** = Movement for Socialism **MIR** = Movement of the Revolutionary Left **NFR** = New Republican Force **MIP** = Pachakuti Indigenous Movement **UCS** = Union for Civic Solidarity **ADN** = Nationalist Democratic Action **PS** = Socialist Party

Chamber of Senators 27 seats

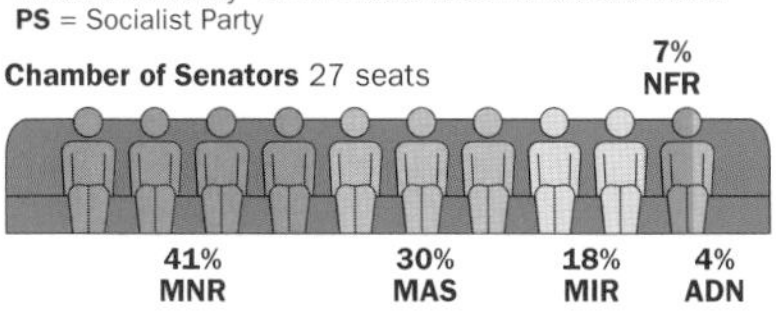
7% NFR
41% MNR
30% MAS
18% MIR
4% ADN

Bolivia is a multiparty democracy.

Profile

From 1825 to the early 1980s, Bolivia experienced, on average, more than one armed coup a year, punctuated by a national revolution in 1952 which delivered important reforms. The fragmented and drug-tainted military finally stepped down in 1982, but full elections were delayed until 1985.

New populist parties have emerged to challenge traditional politics and even the drift to free-market economics. Coalitions are unstable, nepotism is still rife, and the narcotics trade, the profits of which underpin the economy, is frequently implicated in political corruption scandals. The main trade union federation COB was traditionally the focus of opposition, but coca growers and other popular groups have now assumed this role; peasant leader Evo Morales was even a close second in presidential elections in 2002.

The austerity policies of the MNR were continued after its defeat in 1997 by former dictator Hugo Banzer. Ill health forced his resignation in 2001, and the MNR was returned to power in 2002 with Gonzalo Sánchez de Lozada resuming the presidency.

Main Political Issues

Economic austerity

Public opposition to economic reforms demanded by the IMF is vocal and increasingly violent. Widespread opposition on the streets in 2003 forced President Sánchez to drop a controversial new income tax.

Coca growers

Poor farmers oppose the government's forced eradication of coca crops in an anticocaine drive to ensure more US aid. Serious clashes between farmers and government security forces have erupted sporadically since 2000. The *cocaleros* complain that modest government subsidies to switch crops take no account of the low prices of other potential cash crops, such as bananas, pineapples, and palm hearts.

CHRONOLOGY

The Aymara civilization was conquered by the Incas in the late 1400s. Fifty years later, the Incas were defeated by the *conquistadores*, and Upper Peru, as it became, was governed by Spain from Lima.

- **1545** Cerro Rico, the Silver Mountain, discovered at Potosí. Provides Spain with vast wealth.
- **1776** Upper Peru becomes part of Viceroyalty of Río de la Plata centered on Buenos Aires.
- **1809** Simón Bolívar inspires first revolutionary uprisings in Latin America at Chuquisaca (Sucre), La Paz, and Cochabamba, but they fail.
- **1824** Spaniards suffer final defeat by Bolívar's general, José de Sucre.
- **1825** Independence.
- **1836–1839** Union with Peru fails. Internal disorder.
- **1864–1871** Ruthless rule of Mariano Melgarejo. Three Amerindian revolts over seizure of ancestral lands.

B

CHRONOLOGY *continued*

- **1879–1883** War of the Pacific, won by Chile. Bolivia left landlocked.
- **1880–1930** Period of stable governments. Exports from revived mining industry bring prosperity.
- **1903** Acre province ceded to Brazil.
- **1914** Republican Party founded.
- **1920** Amerindian rebellion.
- **1923** Miners bloodily suppressed.
- **1932–1935** Chaco War with Paraguay; in 1938 treaty Bolivia loses three-quarters of Chaco. Rise of radicalism and labor movement.
- **1951** Víctor Paz Estenssoro of MNR elected president. Military coup.
- **1952** Revolution. Paz Estenssoro and MNR brought back. Land reforms improve Amerindians' status. Education reforms, universal suffrage, tin mines nationalized.
- **1964** Military takes over in coup.
- **1967** Che Guevara killed while trying to mobilize Bolivian workers.
- **1969–1979** Military regimes rule with increasing severity. 1979 coup fails. Interim civilian rule.
- **1980** Military takes over again.
- **1982** President-elect Siles Zuazo finally heads leftist civilian MIR government. Inflation 24,000%.
- **1985** MNR wins elections. Austerity measures bring down inflation.
- **1986** Tin market collapses. 21,000 miners sacked.
- **1989** MIR takes power after close-run elections. President Paz Zamora makes pact with 1970s dictator Gen. Hugo Banzer, leader of ADN.
- **1990** 1.6 million hectares (4 million acres) of rainforest recognized as Amerindian territory.
- **1993** MNR back in power. Gonzalo Sánchez de Lozada president.
- **1997** Banzer wins presidency.
- **1999** Opposition demands inquiry into Banzer's role in regional military repression in 1970s.
- **2001** Banzer resigns due to ill health.
- **2001–2002** Government program of coca eradication and bans on coca trading and marketing provoke clashes with peasant farmers.
- **2002** MNR wins elections. Sánchez returns as president.

AID

Recipient

$729m (receipts) — Up 53% in 2001

Most aid comes from the US and depends on progress in coca crop eradication. Smaller amounts come from western European countries. Poor rural areas get project aid from Western religious organizations, NGOs, and charities. The IDB provided emergency aid after flash floods destroyed infrastructure and badly damaged the historic center of La Paz in 2002.

DEFENSE

Compulsory military service

$135m — Up 5% in 2001

BOLIVIAN ARMED FORCES

36 light tanks (SK-105 Kuerassier)	25,000 personnel
60 riverine craft	3500 personnel
37 combat aircraft (18 AT-33AN)	3000 personnel
None	

Although the military has not actively interfered in politics for more than two decades, it is frequently used to quell internal dissent. The army is the major focus of defense spending, weaponry being bought mainly from the US. The Bolivian navy consists chiefly of gunboats on Lake Titicaca, which borders Peru, and on the Pilcomayo River. The army has worked with US forces against the cocaine business, although its integrity is questioned due to its past associations with narcotics trafficking. The main ambition of the military, apart from protecting its own interests and privileges, is the unrealizable aim of recapturing territory that would allow Bolivia access to the Pacific.

Military service lasts for one year.

ECONOMICS

Inflation 8% p.a. (1990–2001)

$8.07bn — 7.659 bolivianos (7.17)

SCORE CARD

World GNP Ranking	95th
GNP per Capita	$950
Balance of Payments	–$293m
Inflation	1.6%
Unemployment	4%

EXPORTS

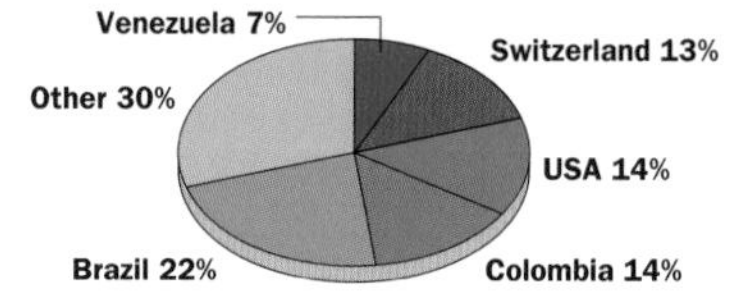
Venezuela 7%
Switzerland 13%
Other 30%
USA 14%
Brazil 22%
Colombia 14%

IMPORTS

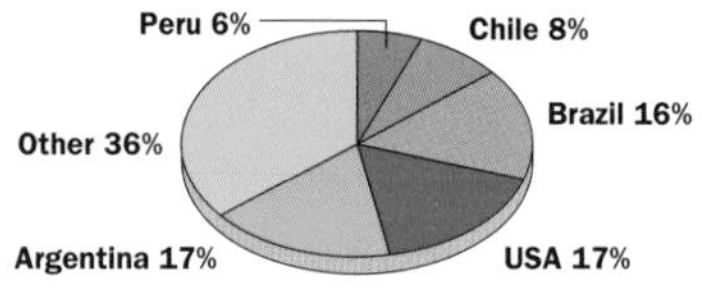
Peru 6%
Chile 8%
Brazil 16%
Other 36%
Argentina 17%
USA 17%

Strengths

Mineral riches: gold, silver, zinc, lead, tin. Newly discovered oil and natural gas deposits attracting foreign investment.

Weaknesses

Raw materials vulnerable to fluctuating world prices. Lack of processed or manufactured exports with higher added value. Lack of integration between economic sectors and regions. Poor infrastructure.

Profile

Traditionally, the state used earnings from the publicly owned state mining sector to control the economy. Years of deep recession in the 1980s, accompanied by accelerating inflation and a collapsing currency, saw the introduction of severe, IMF-approved, austerity policies. These, along with the introduction of a new currency and tax reform, succeeded in curbing inflation, reducing public spending, and restoring international loans, but at the price of great social unrest. Growth was restored in the 1990s and stakes in state companies were offered to investors. A plan to reactivate the economy through public works has been financed by multilateral funding in return for austerity. Growth in oil and gas is needed for a sustained upturn.

ECONOMIC PERFORMANCE INDICATOR

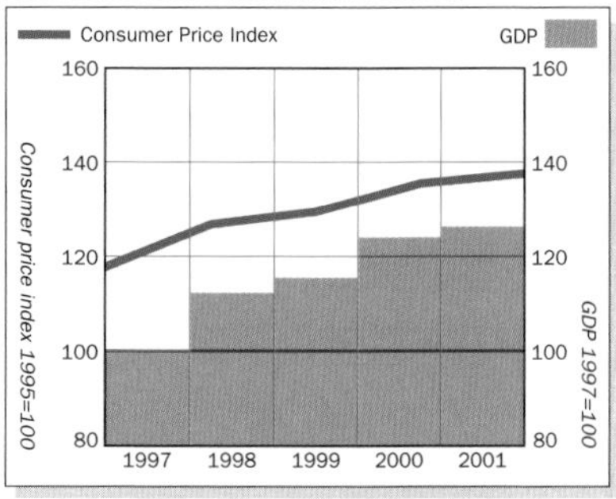
Consumer Price Index
GDP
160
140
120
100
80
Consumer price index 1995=100
GDP 1997=100
1997
1998
1999
2000
2001

BOLIVIA : MAJOR BUSINESSES

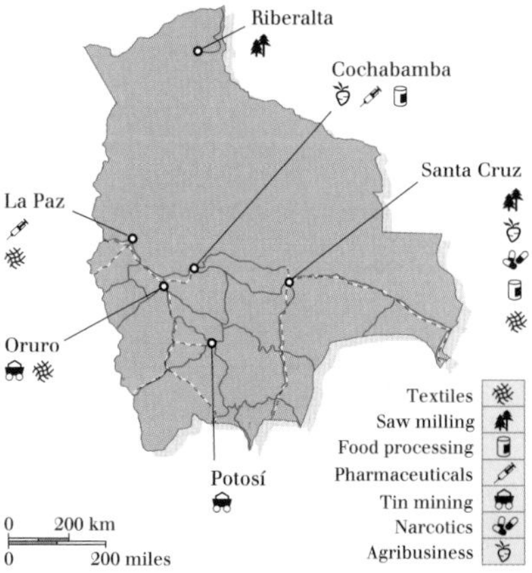
Riberalta
Cochabamba
Santa Cruz
La Paz
Oruro
Potosí
Textiles
Saw milling
Food processing
Pharmaceuticals
Tin mining
Narcotics
Agribusiness
0 200 km
0 200 miles

B

RESOURCES

Electric power 1.2m kW

6511 tonnes

30,195 b/d (reserves 110m barrels)

8.9m sheep, 6.58m cattle, 2.85m pigs, 74.5m chickens

Tin, natural gas, oil, zinc, tungsten, gold, antimony, silver, lead

ELECTRICITY GENERATION

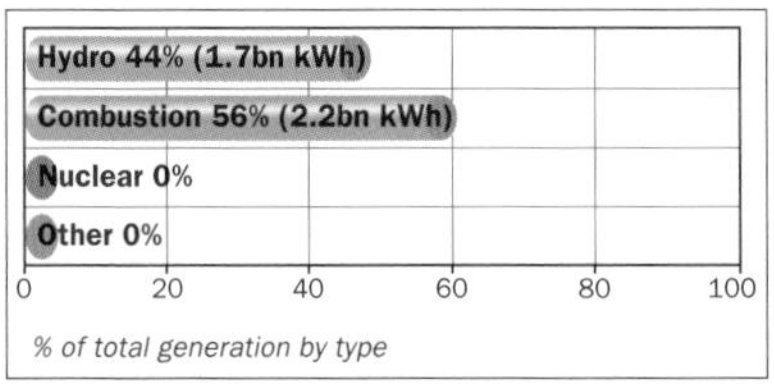
Hydro 44% (1.7bn kWh)
Combustion 56% (2.2bn kWh)
Nuclear 0%
Other 0%
0
20
40
60
80
100
% of total generation by type

Bolivia is the world's fifth-largest tin producer. The government is allowing foreign companies to prospect for more oil, and to increase sales of natural gas to Brazil and Argentina.

BOLIVIA : LAND USE

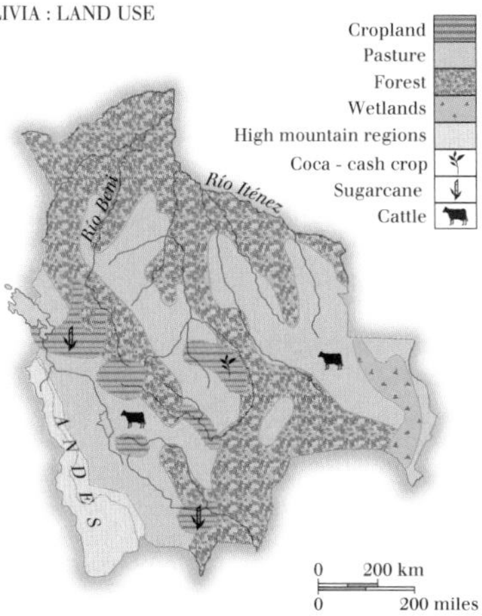
Cropland
Pasture
Forest
Wetlands
High mountain regions
Coca - cash crop
Sugarcane
Cattle
Río Beni
Río Iténez
ANDES
0
200 km
0
200 miles

ENVIRONMENT

Sustainability rank: 21st

16% (7% partially protected)

1.4 tonnes per capita

ENVIRONMENTAL TREATIES

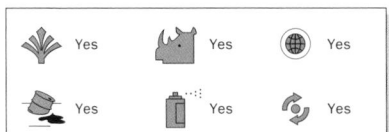

Yes | Yes | Yes

Yes | Yes | Yes

Deforestation is Bolivia's major ecological problem, as throughout the Amazon region. Land clearances are running at 161,100 hectares (398,000 acres) a year. Much of the cleared land is turned over to cattle ranching or the growing of coca. Pesticide and fertilizer overuse in the coca business is a concern. The industry is effectively uncontrolled and rivers in Amazonia have high pollution levels.

Pollution problems are compounded by waste chemicals used in minerals industries. Mercury, used in the extraction of silver, has been found in dangerous quantities in river systems.

MEDIA

TV ownership medium

Daily newspaper circulation 55 per 1000 people

PUBLISHING AND BROADCAST MEDIA

There are 18 daily newspapers, including *Presencia*, *El Diario*, and *La Razón*

1 state-owned service with 9 stations, 36 independent stations

1 state-owned service, 145 independent stations

Bolivia has strict defamation laws and considerable self-censorship. One of the TV stations is university-run, broadcasting mainly educational programs.

CRIME

Death penalty not used in practice

8315 prisoners

Down 18% in 1999–2000

CRIME RATES

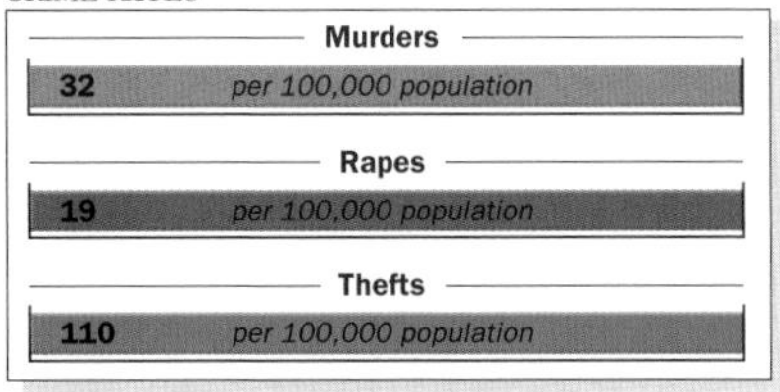
Murders
32
per 100,000 population
Rapes
19
per 100,000 population
Thefts
110
per 100,000 population

Violent crime is centered on narcotics-trafficking towns in the eastern lowlands, particularly Santa Cruz. Main cities are much safer for tourists, and have lower crime rates than cities in neighboring Peru. The police and army have a history of mistreating poor farmers and miners.

EDUCATION

School leaving age: 13

86%

278,763 students

THE EDUCATION SYSTEM

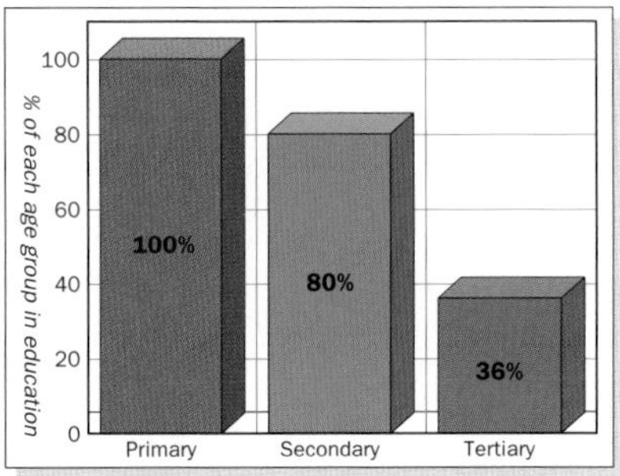
% of each age group in education
100
80
60
40
20
0
100%
80%
36%
Primary
Secondary
Tertiary

IMF targets for increased school attendance are being met, but education, based on a combination of the French and US systems, is seriously underfunded.

Although the majority of people speak indigenous languages, most teaching is in Spanish. Bolivia has one of the lowest literacy rates in South America. Reform and multilateral aid have led to some improvements.

HEALTH

No welfare state health benefits

1 per 769 people

Influenza, tuberculosis, other communicable diseases, malaria

Great disparities exist between rural and urban populations. Around 30% of children under three years of age in rural areas suffer from chronic malnutrition, compared with about 20% in urban centers. Overall Bolivia has one of the worst rates of infant mortality in the Western hemisphere. Conditions are particularly acute among the Quechua Amerindians living in the highland areas. In 1994 the government decentralized the health system in an effort to redress the imbalance. Immunization drives have now reached most of the population. Traditional medicine and its practitioners are still widely used, especially midwives. Care for the elderly is still lacking.

SPENDING

GDP/cap. increase

CONSUMPTION AND SPENDING

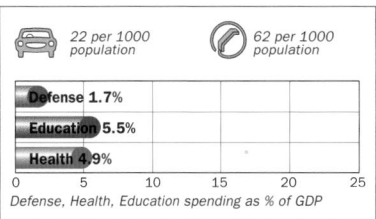

22 per 1000 population

62 per 1000 population

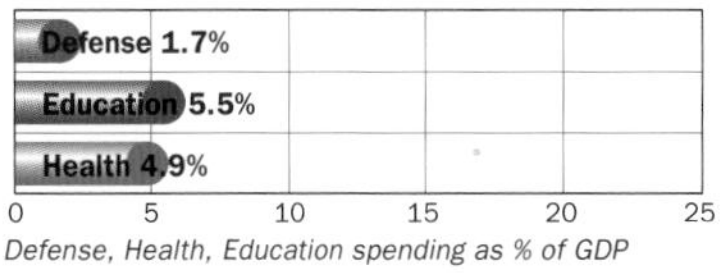
Defense 1.7%
Education 5.5%
Health 4.9%
0
5
10
15
20
25
Defense, Health, Education spending as % of GDP

Havoc created by economic reforms has widened the already huge gap between rich and poor. Generally, the indigenous population who form the rural poor are the worst off. The Andean highlands suffer from grinding poverty that has hardly changed in generations. Migrants to more prosperous eastern regions have faired better, but skewed land ownership remains a big problem. Poor housing, and the lack of utilities and a regular income are common to urban poverty.

WORLD RANKING

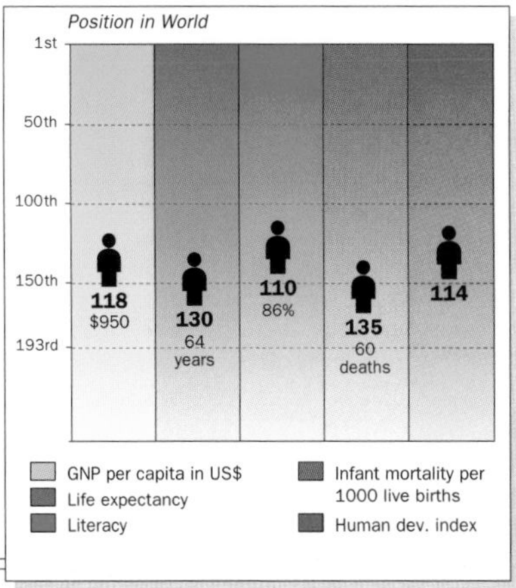
Position in World
1st
50th
100th
150th
193rd
118
$950
130
64
years
110
86%
135
60
deaths
114
GNP per capita in US$
Life expectancy
Literacy
Infant mortality per 1000 live births
Human dev. index

Bosnia & Herzegovina

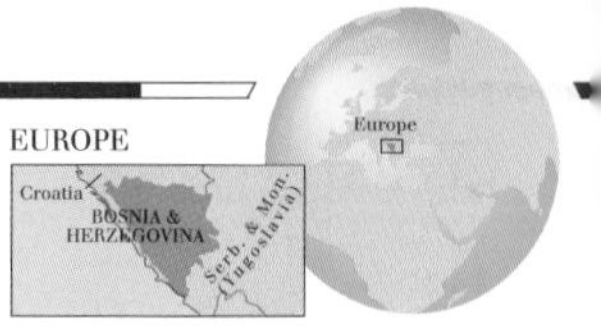
EUROPE
Europe
Croatia
BOSNIA & HERZEGOVINA
Serb. & Mon. (Yugoslavia)

Official Name: Bosnia and Herzegovina **Capital:** Sarajevo
Population: 4.1 million **Currency:** Marka **Official language:** Serbo-Croat

1992 | 1992 | March 1 | BIH | +1 | +387 | .ba

A MOUNTAINOUS COUNTRY in southeast Europe, Bosnia and Herzegovina has access to the Adriatic Sea via a corridor south of Mostar. The collapse of the Socialist Federal Republic of Yugoslavia gave rise to fierce ethnic rivalries between the country's Bosniaks, Serbs, and Croats. Around 250,000 people died and more than two million were displaced before the 1995 Dayton peace accord ended three years of war. The country is now effectively an international protectorate.

CLIMATE

Continental

WEATHER CHART FOR SARAJEVO

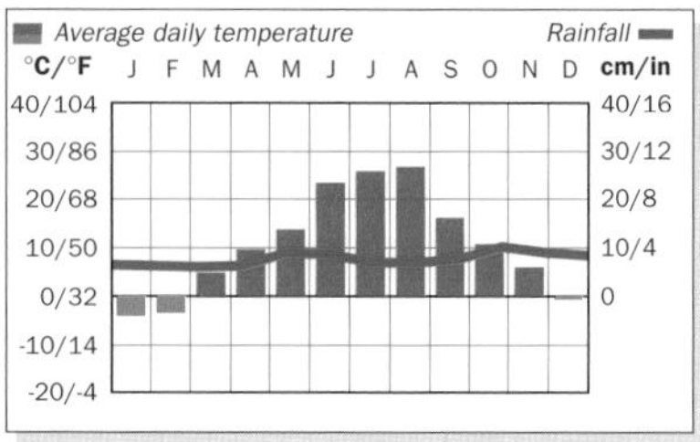
Average daily temperature
Rainfall
°C/°F
J F M A M J J A S O N D
cm/in
40/104
30/86
20/68
10/50
0/32
-10/14
-20/-4
40/16
30/12
20/8
10/4
0

Bosnia has a continental climate with warm summers and bitterly cold winters, often with heavy snow.

TRANSPORTATION

Drive on right

Sarajevo International
310,121 passengers

Has no fleet

THE TRANSPORTATION NETWORK

14,020 km (8712 miles)	None
943 km (586 miles)	Debris and silt block the Sava River

Although bridges, roads, and railroads were wrecked in the war, reconstruction and mine removal have enabled most main routes to be reopened. Sarajevo remains the hub of the communications network.

TOURISM

Visitors : Population 1:37

110,000 visitors

Up 24% in 2000

MAIN TOURIST ARRIVALS

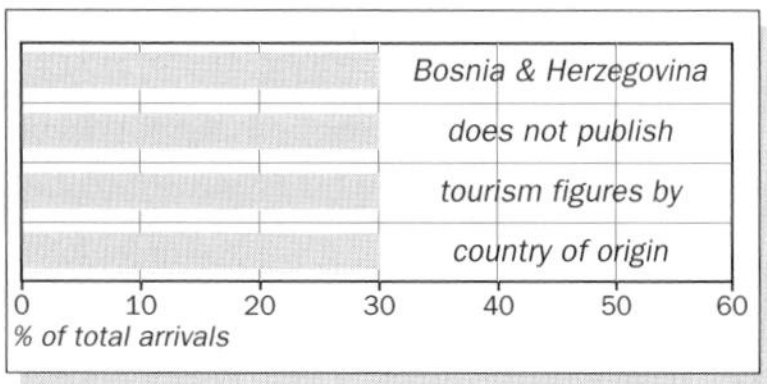
Bosnia & Herzegovina
does not publish
tourism figures by
country of origin
0 10 20 30 40 50 60
% of total arrivals

Even before the war, Bosnia did not have much tourism infrastructure; only the adventurous have begun to visit.

PEOPLE

Pop. density medium

Serbo-Croat

80/km² (208/mi²)

THE URBAN/RURAL POPULATION SPLIT

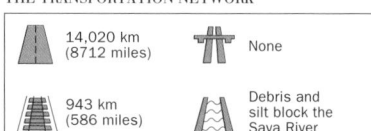

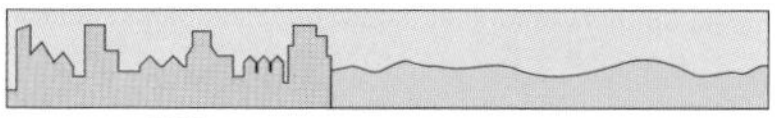
43%
57%

ETHNIC MAKEUP

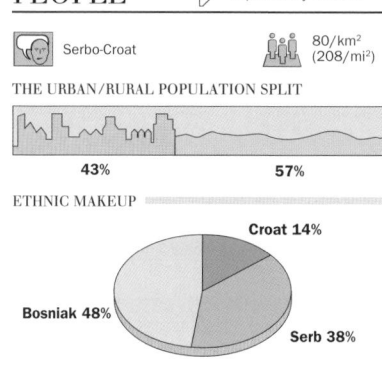

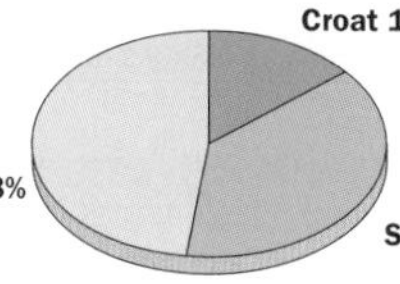
Croat 14%
Bosniak 48%
Serb 38%

Despite sharing the same origin and spoken language, Bosnia's population has been divided by history between Muslim Bosniaks, Orthodox Christian Serbs, and Roman Catholic Croats. Ethnic cleansing, practiced by all sides in the 1992–1995 civil war, left the once integrated communities sharply polarized and geographically redistributed. The process of returning refugees to their old homes has been slow.

POLITICS

Multiparty elections

L. House 2002/2004
U. House 2002/2004

Chair of the Presidency
Dragan Covic

AT THE LAST ELECTION

House of Representatives 42 seats

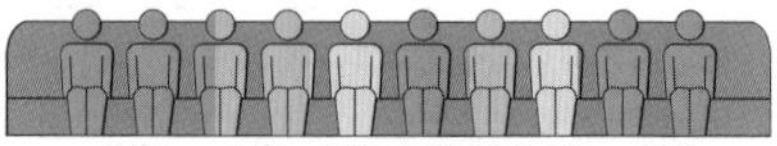
24% SDA
14% SBiH
12% SDS
12% HDZ
10% SDP
7% SNS
21% Others

SDA = Party of Democratic Action **SBiH** = Party for Bosnia & Herzegovina **SDS** = Serb Democratic Party **HDZ** = Croatian Democratic Union **SDP** = Social Democratic Party **SNS** = Independent Social Democrats

28 members are elected from the Federation of Bosnia-Herzegovina and 14 from the Republika Srpska

House of Peoples 15 seats

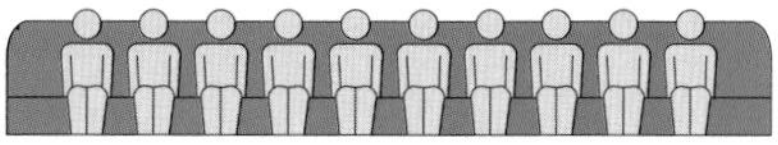

Ten members are appointed from the Federation of Bosnia-Herzegovina and five from the Republika Srpska

Bosnia is subdivided into the Muslim–Croat Federation and the Serb Republika Srpska (RS), plus the multiethnic district of Brčko. There are two levels of government: the overall Republic – with a rotating three-member collective presidency – and the constituent entities, with their own presidents, governments, and parliaments. A UN High Representative retains ultimate control. Nationalist parties have substantial support, though moderate policies are favored in government. Bosniaks have led the way in supporting nonethnic parties. Croats in the Federation have agitated for greater autonomy.

CROATIA
Bosanska Gradiška
Bosanski Brod
Bosanski Šamac
Kozara
Vrbas
Sava
Modriča
Derventa
Prijedor
Cazin
Brčko
Gradačac
Sava
Bihać
Banja Luka
Bijeljina
Grmeč
Sana
REPUBLIKA SRPSKA
Doboj
Gračanica
Tuzla
Teslić
Maglaj
Bosna
Ključ
Una
DINARIC ALPS
Zvornik
Jajce
Travnik
Zenica
Vlasenica
FEDERACIJA BOSNA I HERCEGOVINA
Bugojno
Srebrenica
Vranica
Livno
SARAJEVO
Treskavica
Konjic
Foča
Drina
Neretva
Mostar
Maglić 2387m
Trebinje
SERBIA & MONTENEGRO (YUGOSLAVIA)
ADRIATIC SEA
CROATIA
44°
16°
18°
BOSNIA & HERZEGOVINA
Total Area : 51 129 sq. km (19 741 sq. miles)
POPULATION
over 100 000
over 50 000
over 10 000
under 10 000
LAND HEIGHT
2000m/6562ft
1000m/3281ft
500m/1640ft
200m/656ft
Sea Level
N
0 50 km
0 50 miles

WORLD AFFAIRS

Joined UN in 1992

CEI | EBRD | OSCE | IBRD | IAEA

International agencies maintain security. The Stabilization Force (SFOR) is NATO-led; its 35 participant countries include Russia. Policing came under the EU's mandate from 2003.

AID

Recipient

$639m (receipts) — Down 13% in 2001

Aid for reconstruction and refugee return, totaling several billion dollars, has come mainly from the EU and the US. Major objectives have included developing a market economy and job creation, housing, and infrastructure.

DEFENSE

Compulsory military service

$141m — Down 14% in 2001

Both political entities maintain their own armed forces, creating a huge drain on resources. Attempts to create a single national army are fiercely resisted. Overall security is provided by SFOR.

ECONOMICS

Inflation 2.7% p.a. (1992–2001)

$5.04bn — 1.71 maraka (2.264)

SCORE CARD

- ❏ WORLD GNP RANKING.......................114th
- ❏ GNP PER CAPITA $1240
- ❏ BALANCE OF PAYMENTS.................–$1.38bn
- ❏ INFLATION 5%
- ❏ UNEMPLOYMENT.................................40%

STRENGTHS

Potential to revive prewar industries and become a thriving market economy, with solid manufacturing base. Growth in 2000 of 10%. End of cross-border tariffs with Slovenia from 2002.

WEAKNESSES

War damage of $20–40 billion. Lowest foreign investment in entire region. Corruption. High unemployment.

EXPORTS

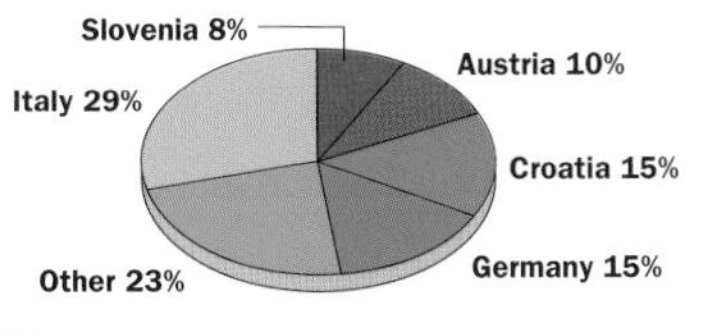
Slovenia 8%
Italy 29%
Austria 10%
Croatia 15%
Germany 15%
Other 23%

IMPORTS

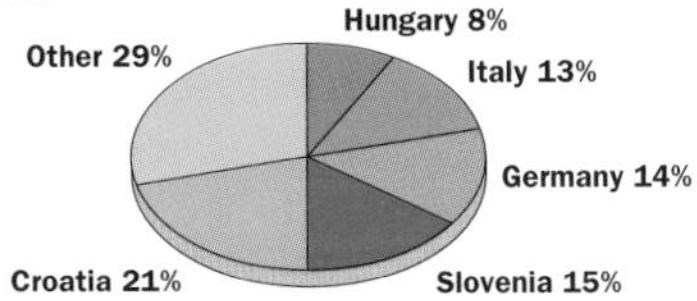
Hungary 8%
Other 29%
Italy 13%
Germany 14%
Croatia 21%
Slovenia 15%

RESOURCES

Electric power 2.7m kW

- 2500 tonnes
- Not an oil producer
- 670,000 sheep, 440,000 cattle, 4.7m chickens
- Coal, lignite, iron, bauxite, cement

Bosnia's land is not well suited to agriculture, but has mineral deposits, forests, and hydroelectric potential.

ENVIRONMENT

Sustainability rank: 57th

0.5% (0.2% partially protected) — 1.3 tonnes per capita

Apart from war damage, Bosnia faces the effects of industrial pollution incurred during the communist regime.

MEDIA

TV ownership medium

Daily newspaper circulation 152 per 1000 people

PUBLISHING AND BROADCAST MEDIA

There are 6 daily newspapers. *Oslobodjenje* (*Liberation*) was published daily throughout the war

8 independent services — 10 independent services

Constitutionally free, media outlets remain under pressure from government bodies and the danger of violence against journalists, and most are still highly partisan along ethnic lines.

CRIME

Death penalty not used in practice

2248 prisoners — Crime is rising

All sides in the war, but especially the Serbs, have been accused of war crimes. The International Criminal Tribunal for the former Yugoslavia (ICTY) in The Hague indicted over 60 suspects in relation to crimes committed in Bosnia. Serb leader Radovan Karadzic and around 20 others have evaded arrest. The RS finally passed laws on cooperating with the tribunal in 2001.

EDUCATION

School leaving age: 15

93% — 40,000 students

Ethnic bias and educational segregation are being combated by the development of a new coordinated curriculum.

The Muslim town of Mostar. *Its 16th-century bridge at a strategic river crossing and much of the old town were destroyed in the war.*

CHRONOLOGY

In 1945, Bosnia and Herzegovina became one of Yugoslavia's six constituent republics.

- ❏ **1990** Nationalists defeat communists in multiparty elections.
- ❏ **1991** Parliament announces republican sovereignty.
- ❏ **1992** EU and US recognize Bosnia. Serbs declare "Serbian Republic." Civil war begins.
- ❏ **1995** NATO air strikes on Serbs; US-brokered Dayton peace accord.
- ❏ **1996** First international war crimes trial since 1945 opens in The Hague. Elections held under Dayton accord.
- ❏ **2001** Ethnic Croats briefly establish autonomy in Herzegovina (in south).
- ❏ **2002** Elections: renewed support for nationalist parties.

B

HEALTH

No welfare state health benefits

1 per 714 people — Cholera and diphtheria epidemics, violence, deaths from war-stress

War strained health services severely and many died for lack of basic care. Reconstruction includes reform of the primary health care system.

SPENDING

GDP/cap. increase

CONSUMPTION AND SPENDING

27 per 1000 population — *111 per 1000 population*

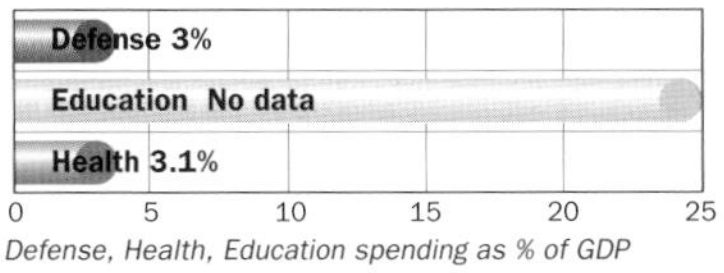
Defense 3%
Education No data
Health 3.1%
0
5
10
15
20
25
Defense, Health, Education spending as % of GDP

The war displaced 60% of the population. Housing, jobs, and reintegration are key challenges, while a lack of significant investment means that postwar poverty remains.

WORLD RANKING

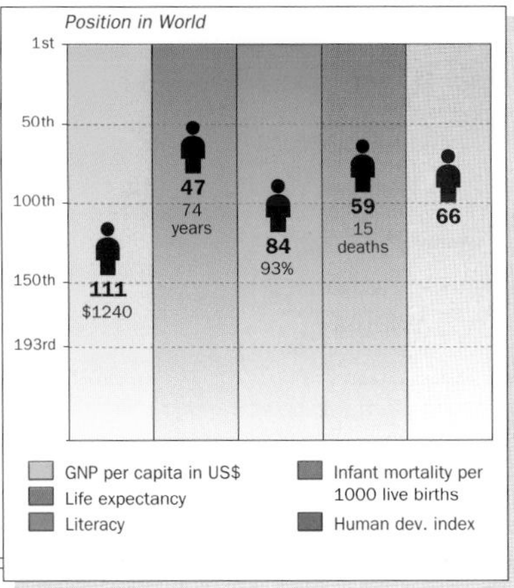
Position in World
1st
50th
100th
150th
193rd
111
$1240
47
74 years
84
93%
59
15 deaths
66
GNP per capita in US$
Life expectancy
Literacy
Infant mortality per 1000 live births
Human dev. index

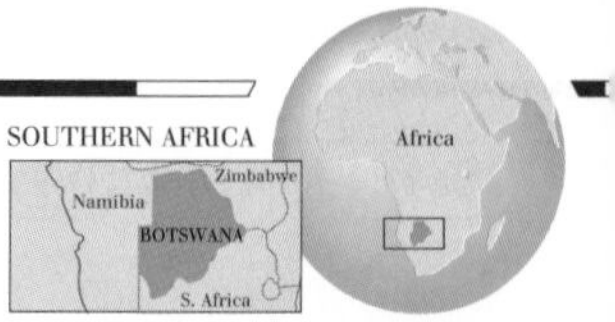
SOUTHERN AFRICA
Africa
Namibia
Zimbabwe
BOTSWANA
S. Africa

BOTSWANA

OFFICIAL NAME: Republic of Botswana **CAPITAL:** Gaborone
POPULATION: 1.6 million **CURRENCY:** Pula **OFFICIAL LANGUAGE:** English

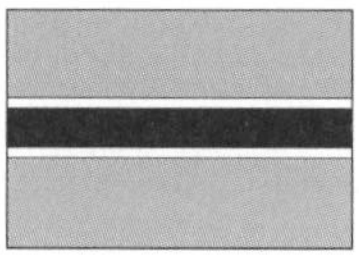

1966 | 1966 | Sept 30 | RB | +2 | +267 | .bw

BOTSWANA IS ARID and landlocked, its central plateau separating the populous eastern grasslands from the Kalahari Desert and the swamps of the Okavango Delta in the west. Diamonds provide Botswana with a prosperous economy, but rain is an even more precious resource, honored in the name of the currency, the pula. Botswana has the world's highest rate of HIV infection among adults: a staggering 38.8% at end-2001.

The Okavango Delta, "jewel of the Kalahari," is the largest inland river delta in the world and home to a rich variety of wildlife.

CLIMATE

Steppe/hot desert

WEATHER CHART FOR GABORONE

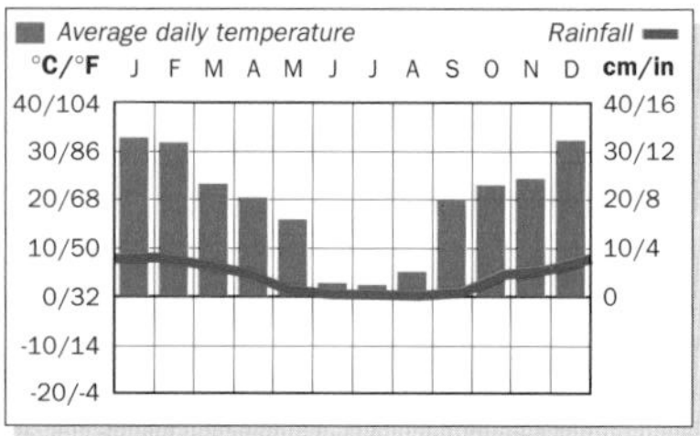
Average daily temperature
Rainfall
°C/°F
J F M A M J J A S O N D
cm/in
40/104
30/86
20/68
10/50
0/32
-10/14
-20/-4
40/16
30/12
20/8
10/4
0

The subtropical climate is dry and prone to drought. Rainfall declines from 64 cm (25 in) in the north to under 10 cm (4 in) in the Kalahari Desert in the west.

TRANSPORTATION

Drive on left

Sir Seretse Khama International, Gaborone
240,526 passengers

Has no fleet

THE TRANSPORTATION NETWORK

5620 km (3492 miles)	None
888 km (552 miles)	None

The opening of the trans-Kalahari road to Namibia in 1998 has reduced Botswana's dependence on South African ports. Upgrading existing rail and road networks is a priority.

TOURISM

Visitors : Population 1:1.6

995,000 visitors

Up 18% in 2000

MAIN TOURIST ARRIVALS

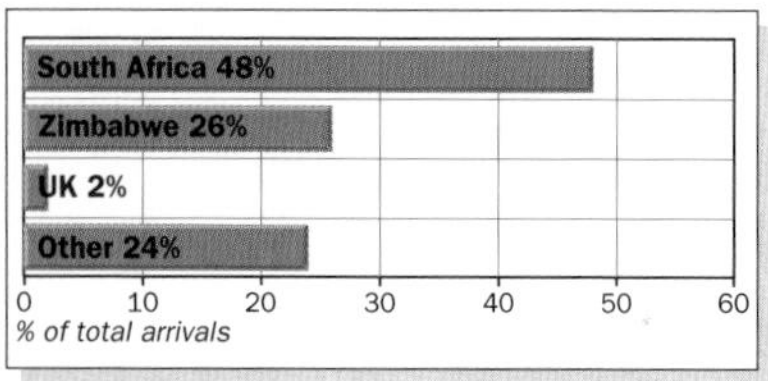
South Africa 48%
Zimbabwe 26%
UK 2%
Other 24%
0
10
20
30
40
50
60
% of total arrivals

Tourism is aimed at wealthy wildlife enthusiasts and focuses on safaris, especially to the Okavango Delta.

PEOPLE

Pop. density low

Setswana, English, Shona, San, Khoikhoi, isiNdebele

3/km² (7/mi)²

THE URBAN/RURAL POPULATION SPLIT

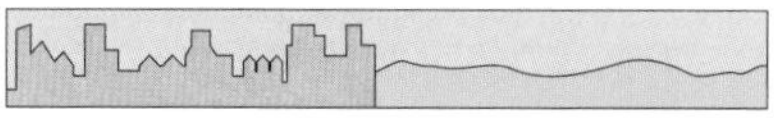
49%
51%

ETHNIC MAKEUP

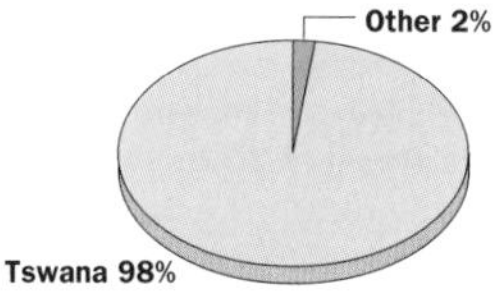
Other 2%
Tswana 98%

Botswana's stability reflects its ethnic homogeneity (98% Tswana) and the power of traditional authorities. The Bangwato form the largest clan. The indigenous San (once known as Bushmen) of the Kalahari were ordered to abandon their nomadic way of life in 2002. A small white community still dominates the professions. Some 80% of people are Christian, but traditional beliefs are also widely practiced.

POLITICS

Multiparty elections

1999/2004

President Festus Mogae

AT THE LAST ELECTION

National Assembly 46 seats

13%
App
72%
BDP
13%
BNF
2%
BCP

BDP = Botswana Democratic Party **BNF** = Botswana National Front **App** = Appointed **BCP** = Botswana Congress Party

In addition to 40 elected members, four are co-opted and the president and the attorney general are ex-officio members

Though Botswana is formally a multiparty democracy, it has been ruled by the BDP since independence. In 1994, however, economic problems, corruption scandals, and increasing urbanization led to the mainly town-based BNF gaining seats at the expense of the BDP, which nevertheless retained its absolute parliamentary majority.

Power was transferred smoothly from President Ketumile Masire to Festus Mogae in 1998. The opposition BNF split in two, and the 1999 elections confirmed the BDP's hold on power.

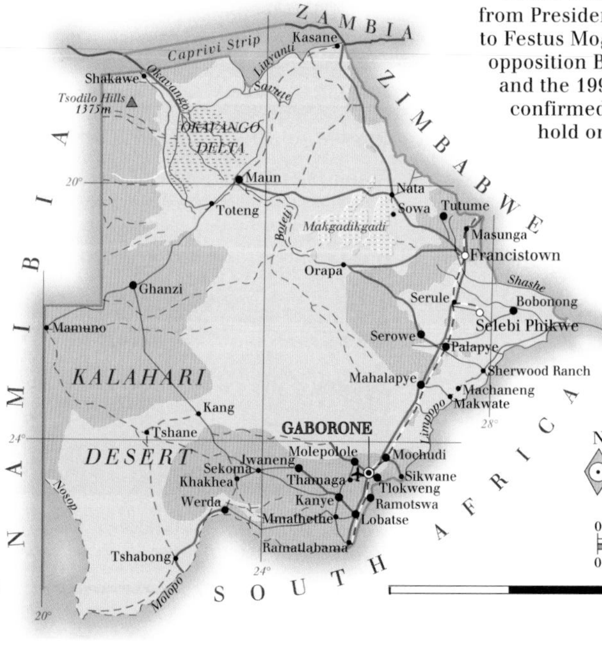
ZAMBIA
ZIMBABWE
NAMIBIA
SOUTH AFRICA
Caprivi Strip
Kasane
Linyanti
Shakawe
Okavango
Tsodilo Hills
1375m
Savute
OKAVANGO DELTA
Maun
Nata
Sowa
Tutume
Toteng
Boteti
Makgadikgadi
Masunga
Francistown
Orapa
Shashe
Ghanzi
Serule
Bobonong
Mamuno
Selebi Phikwe
Serowe
Palapye
KALAHARI
Mahalapye
Sherwood Ranch
Machaneng
Makwate
Limpopo
Kang
Tshane
GABORONE
DESERT
Molepolole
Mochudi
Jwaneng
Sekoma
Thamaga
Sikwane
Khakhea
Tlokweng
Kanye
Ramotswa
Werda
Mmathethe
Lobatse
Nossop
Ramatlabama
Tshabong
Molopo
20°
24°

BOTSWANA

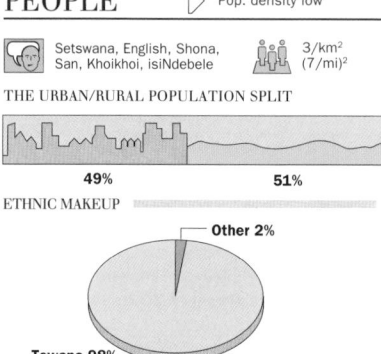

Total Area : 600 370 sq. km (231 803 sq. miles)

POPULATION
over 100 000
over 50 000
over 10 000
under 10 000

LAND HEIGHT
1000m/3281ft
500m/1640ft

0 200 km
0 200 miles

B

WORLD AFFAIRS

Joined UN in 1966

Comm | NAM | AU | SADC | WTO

Botswana has strongly backed a politically and economically stable postapartheid South Africa, and in 1994 appointed its first ambassador to Pretoria since 1966. Potential South African domination of the SADC is a concern. Traditionally pro-Western in orientation, Botswana cherishes its relations with the UK and the US.

AID

Recipient

$29m (receipts) | Down 6% in 2001

Botswana's political and economic record has made it a favored aid recipient, notably from Japan, Germany, the EU, the UK, and Norway. Some 90% of EU aid goes to projects which try to balance wildlife needs with rural development. Aid also targets transportation projects.

DEFENSE

No compulsory military service

$203m | Down 26% in 2001

Reforms of the armed forces in mid-2000 aimed at improving morale included the raising of the compulsory retirement age and the enlistment of women.

ECONOMICS

Inflation 9% p.a. (1990–2001)

$5.25bn | 4.926 pula (6.179)

SCORE CARD

- World GNP Ranking........................112th
- GNP per Capita.............................$3100
- Balance of Payments......................$438m
- Inflation...6.6%
- Unemployment.................................40%

STRENGTHS

Diamonds. Recent economic growth among highest in world. Prudent management, large financial reserves, and exchange control liberalization. Lucrative exports of assembly-produced vehicles, copper, nickel, beef. Transportation links. Tourism potential. Relatively low corruption levels.

WEAKNESSES

Spread of AIDS. Overdependence on diamonds. Agriculture and industry weak. Small population, water shortages, and drought. Impact of beef industry on environment. High transportation costs to coast. Widespread unemployment.

EXPORTS

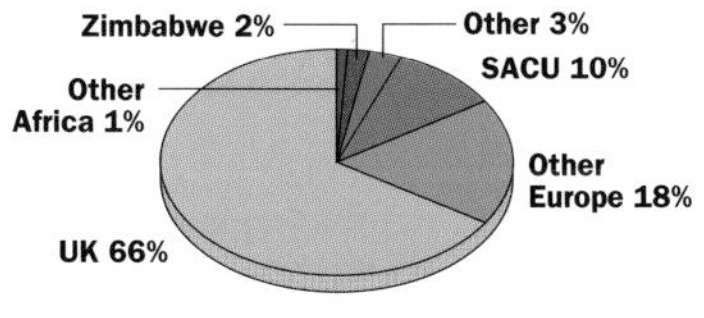
Zimbabwe 2%
Other 3%
SACU 10%
Other Africa 1%
Other Europe 18%
UK 66%

IMPORTS

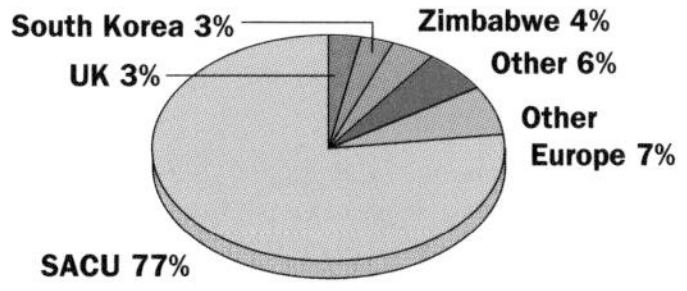
South Korea 3%
Zimbabwe 4%
UK 3%
Other 6%
Other Europe 7%
SACU 77%

RESOURCES

Electric power: Included in South African total

166 tonnes | Included in South African total

2.25m goats, 1.7m cattle, 370,000 sheep, 4m chickens | Diamonds, copper, coal, nickel, soda ash, gold

Botswana is one of the world's top diamond producers. Large coal deposits are the basis of power grid expansion. Water is Botswana's scarcest resource.

ENVIRONMENT

Sustainability rank: 13th

19% (10% partially protected) | 2.3 tonnes per capita

Botswana is trying to help communities to earn a living from wildlife protection. A campaign has been launched to curb the use of agrochemicals.

MEDIA

TV ownership low

Daily newspaper circulation 27 per 1000 people

PUBLISHING AND BROADCAST MEDIA

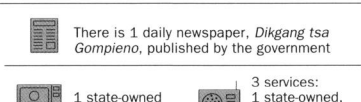

There is 1 daily newspaper, *Dikgang tsa Gompieno*, published by the government

1 state-owned service | 3 services: 1 state-owned, 2 independent

A government-funded TV service began broadcasting in 2000. The government bias of radio and the one daily paper is offset in the many journals.

CRIME

Death penalty in use

6102 prisoners | Crime is rising

President Mogae warned of a "crime wave" in 1999. Diamond smuggling remains a major concern. Human rights are generally respected.

EDUCATION

School leaving age: 15

78% | 7651 students

Revenues from the diamond industry have helped to fund educational programs which have improved the country's literacy rate.

CHRONOLOGY

From 1600, Tswana migrations slowly displaced San people. In 1895, at local request, the UK set up the Bechuanaland Protectorate to preempt annexation by South Africa.

- **1965** BDP, led by Sir Seretse Khama, wins first general election and all subsequent general elections.
- **1966** Independence declared.
- **1980** Death of Khama; succeeded by Vice President Quett (later Sir Ketumile) Masire.
- **1985–1986** South African raids.
- **1992–1993** Strikes and corruption scandals prompt resignations of senior BDP figures.
- **1994** BDP support eroded in general election.
- **1998** Masire retires; succeeded by Vice President Festus Mogae.

HEALTH

Welfare state health benefits

1 per 3846 people | AIDS, tuberculosis, heart diseases, pneumonia

With the world's highest rate of HIV-positive adults (38.8%), Botswana in 2001 became the first sub-Saharan country to provide antiretroviral drugs through its public health service.

SPENDING

GDP/cap. increase

CONSUMPTION AND SPENDING

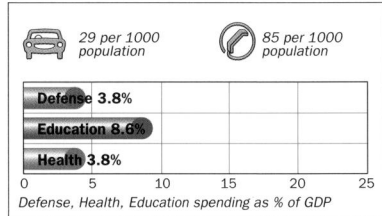

29 per 1000 population | *85 per 1000 population*

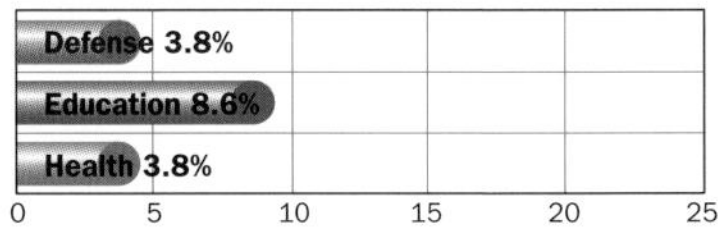
Defense 3.8%
Education 8.6%
Health 3.8%
0
5
10
15
20
25

Defense, Health, Education spending as % of GDP

GNP per capita is among Africa's highest, but about half the population live below the poverty line. Economic growth has exacerbated wealth inequalities.

WORLD RANKING

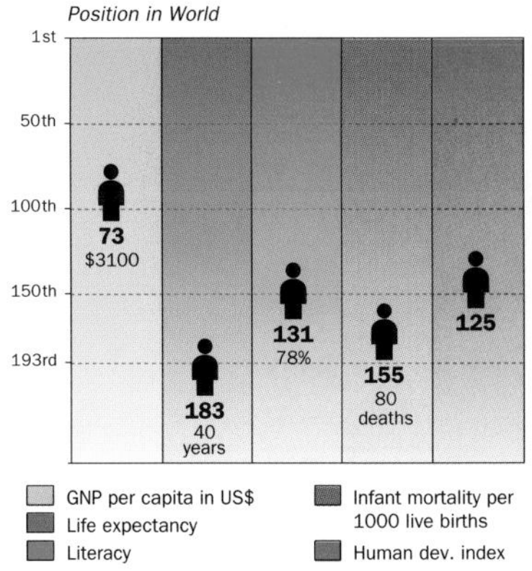
Position in World
1st
50th
100th
150th
193rd
73
$3100
183
40 years
131
78%
155
80 deaths
125
GNP per capita in US$
Life expectancy
Literacy
Infant mortality per 1000 live births
Human dev. index

B

BRAZIL

SOUTH AMERICA
Venezuela
Colombia
Peru
Bolivia
BRAZIL
Paraguay
South America

OFFICIAL NAME: Federative Republic of Brazil **CAPITAL:** Brasília
POPULATION: 175 million **CURRENCY:** Real **OFFICIAL LANGUAGE:** Portuguese

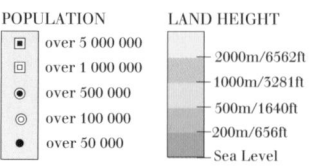

1822
1828
Sept 7
BR
-3
+55
.br

THE LARGEST COUNTRY in South America, Brazil became independent of Portugal in 1822. Today, it is renowned as the site of the world's largest tropical rainforest, the threat to which led to the UN's first international environment conference, held in Rio de Janeiro in 1992. Covering one-third of Brazil's total land area, the rainforest grows around the massive Amazon River and its delta. Apart from the basin of the River Plate in the south, the rest of the country consists of highlands. The mountainous northeast is part forested and part desert. Brazil is the world's leading coffee producer and also has rich reserves of gold, diamonds, oil, and iron ore. Cattle ranching is an expanding industry. The city of São Paulo is the world's fifth-biggest conurbation, with some 20 million inhabitants.

BRAZIL

Total Area : 8 511 965 sq. km
(3 286 470 sq. miles)

POPULATION
- over 5 000 000
- over 1 000 000
- over 500 000
- over 100 000
- over 50 000

LAND HEIGHT
- 2000m/6562ft
- 1000m/3281ft
- 500m/1640ft
- 200m/656ft
- Sea Level

VENEZUELA
COLOMBIA
SERRA PACARAIMA
Serra Parima
Boa Vista
RORAIMA
Branco
G U I A N A
Pico da Neblina 3014m
Negro
Japurá
Içá
Solimões(Amazon)
A M A Z O N A S
Amazon Basin
Javari
Juruá
Purus
Madeira
ACRE
Porto Velho
Rio Branco
RONDÔNIA
Chapada dos Parecis
Guaporé
PERU
BOLIVIA
N
0
500 km
500 miles
70°
60°

CLIMATE

Tropical equatorial/hot and dry/subtropical/steppe

WEATHER CHART FOR BRASÍLIA

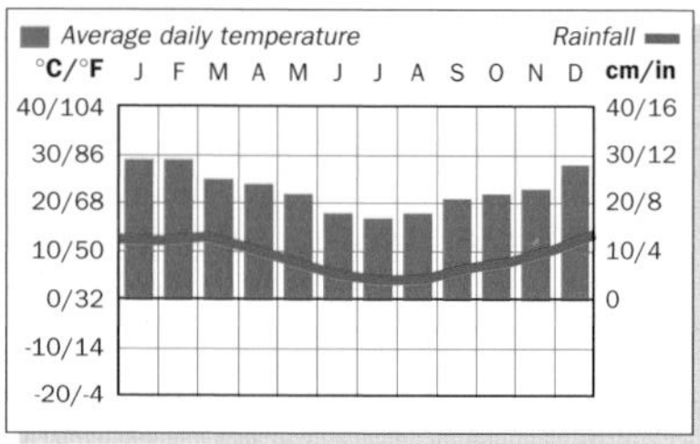
Average daily temperature
Rainfall
°C/°F
J F M A M J J A S O N D
cm/in
40/104
30/86
20/68
10/50
0/32
-10/14
-20/-4
40/16
30/12
20/8
10/4
0

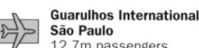

Brazil's share of the Amazon basin, occupying half of the country, has a model equatorial climate. Its 150–200 cm (59–79 in) of rain are spread throughout the year. Temperatures are high, with almost no seasonal variation, but scarcely ever rise above 38°C (100°F).

The Brazilian plateau, occupying most of the rest of the country, has far greater temperature ranges. Rain falls mainly between October and April. The northeast, the least productive region of Brazil, is very dry and is frequently prone to severe drought. However, periodic bouts of torrential rain can devastate coastal regions, leading to severe flooding in recent years.

The southern states have hot summers and cool winters, when frost may occur.

TRANSPORTATION

Drive on right

Guarulhos International, São Paulo
12.7m passengers

475 ships
3.69m grt

THE TRANSPORTATION NETWORK

184,140 km (114,419 miles)

5000 km (3107 miles)

31,125 km (19,340 miles)

50,000 km (31,069 miles)

Brazil's size means that internal air travel is often essential. However, flights are expensive. Many Brazilians make use of the extensive if arduous bus routes. Urban roads are congested. Rail services have been cut back.

Parati, in Rio state, *was one of Brazil's major gold-exporting ports in the 17th century. Its colonial architecture is well preserved.*

TOURISM

Visitors : Population
1:37

4.77m visitors

Down 10% in 2001

MAIN TOURIST ARRIVALS

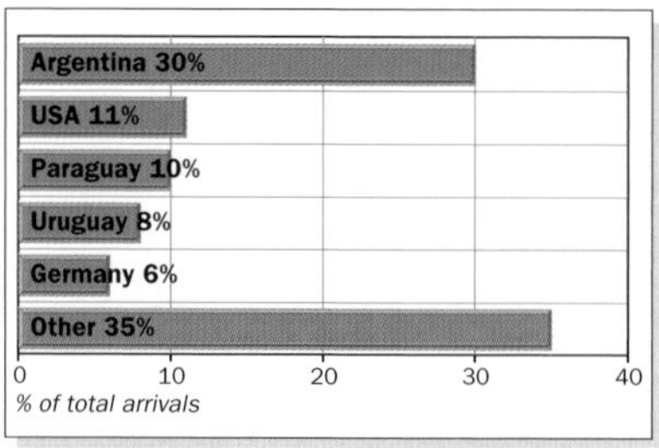
Argentina 30%
USA 11%
Paraguay 10%
Uruguay 8%
Germany 6%
Other 35%
0
10
20
30
40
% of total arrivals

Brazil is underperforming in tourism, with revenues falling to just over 0.5% of GDP in 2000, compared with a world average of over 10%.

Attractions are the celebrated beaches and world famous carnival of Rio de Janeiro – the center of the tourist trade – Brasília, the modern capital, Atlantic beaches stretching 2000 km (1250 miles), the Amazon River basin, the spectacular Iguaçu Falls, the Pantanal – the vast wetland region in the west – and the Afro-Brazilian culture of Salvador. They are offset by the limited availability of medium- to low-cost travel and budget hotels, which deter both domestic and foreign travelers.

In the virtual absence of low-cost charter flights, domestic air travel is expensive. This is blamed on high airport charges and inertia in Brazil's aviation department, which is controlled by the air force.

Average overnight hotel rates are higher than in Europe and the US, and the quality of service is generally poor. Basic infrastructure, such as sanitation and water supply, is also deficient.

***Rio de Janeiro** and Sugar Loaf Mountain seen from Corcovado (Hunchback) Peak. With a population of over 12 million, the Rio conurbation is Brazil's largest after São Paulo.*

PEOPLE

Pop. density low

Portuguese, German, Italian, Spanish, Polish, Japanese, Amerindian languages

21/km² (54/mi²)

THE URBAN/RURAL POPULATION SPLIT

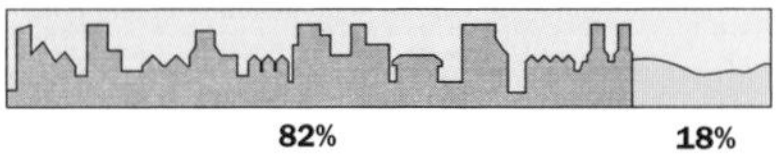
82%
18%

RELIGIOUS PERSUASION

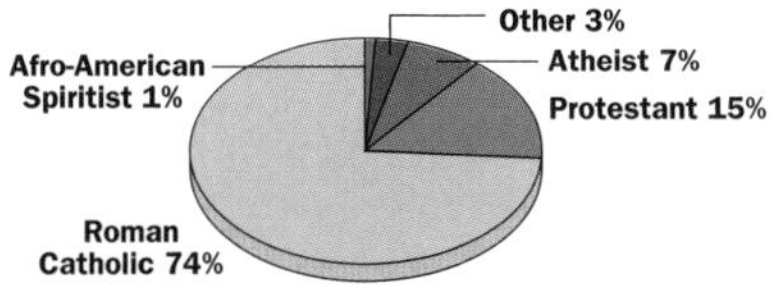
Other 3%
Atheist 7%
Protestant 15%
Afro-American Spiritist 1%
Roman Catholic 74%

ETHNIC MAKEUP

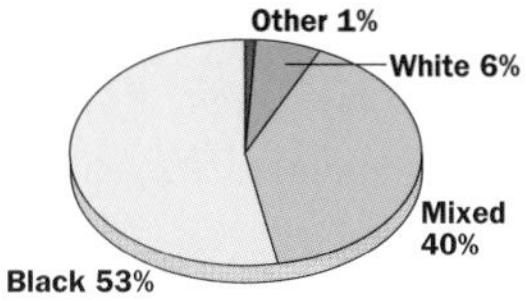
Other 1%
White 6%
Mixed 40%
Black 53%

POPULATION AGE BREAKDOWN

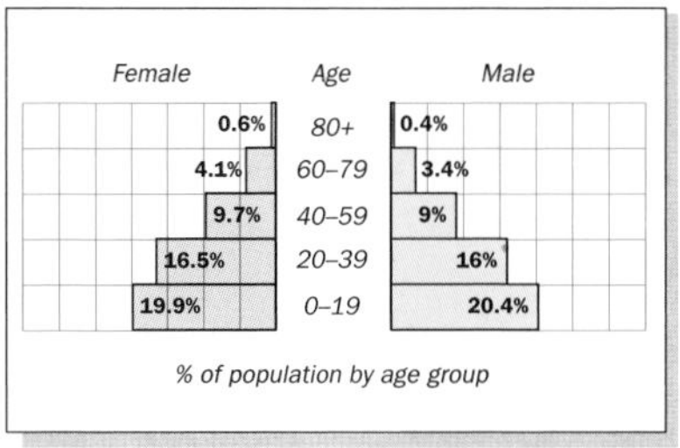
Female
Age
Male
0.6%
80+
0.4%
4.1%
60–79
3.4%
9.7%
40–59
9%
16.5%
20–39
16%
19.9%
0–19
20.4%
% of population by age group

ATLANTIC OCEAN
FRENCH GUIANA
AMAPÁ
Macapá
Ilha Caviana de Fora
Ilha Mexiana
Baía de Marajó
Equator
Ilha Grande de Gurupá
Ilha de Marajó
Belém
Amazon
Santarém
Baía de São Marcos
São Luís
Fortaleza
TERRITÓRIO DE FERNANDO DE NORONHA
Atol das Rochas
Fernando de Noronha
PARÁ
Marabá
Imperatriz
Teresina
MARANHÃO
CEARÁ
Mossoró
RIO GRANDE DO NORTE
Natal
Juazeiro do Norte
PARAÍBA
Campina Grande
João Pessoa
Olinda
Recife
Jaboatão
PERNAMBUCO
PIAUÍ
TOCANTINS
Maceió
ALAGOAS
Aracaju
SERGIPE
Feira de Santana
Taguatinga
BAHIA
GOIÁS
Salvador
Baía de Todos os Santos
DISTRITO FEDERAL
BRASÍLIA
Itabuna
Vitória da Conquista
Anápolis
Goiânia
Montes Claros
MINAS GERAIS
Uberlândia
Governador Valadares
Uberaba
Contagem
Belo Horizonte
ESPÍRITO SANTO
Vitória
São José do Rio Preto
Divinópolis
SÃO PAULO
Marília
Ribeirão Preto
Juiz de Fora
Presidente Prudente
Bauru
Campos
Volta Redonda
Petrópolis
RIO DE JANEIRO
Londrina
Maringá
Campinas
Taubaté
Duque de Caxias
Sorocaba
Niterói
São Paulo
Rio de Janeiro
PARANÁ
Nova Iguaçu
São Vicente
São José dos Campos
Ponta Grossa
Santo André
Santos
Curitiba
São Bernardo do Campo
SANTA CATARINA
Joinville
Blumenau
Passo Fundo
Lages
Florianópolis
Caxias do Sul
Canoas
Porto Alegre
Lagoa dos Patos
Rio Grande
Lake Mirim
ATLANTIC

Brazil's population is highly diverse. It includes indigenous Amerindian groups, as well as the descendants of its Portuguese colonizers and the Africans brought to work the sugar plantations in the 17th century. More recent immigrant groups include both Italians and Japanese. Extremes of social disadvantage challenge the widely held notion that Brazil is a "racial democracy." Poor, mixed-race migrants are treated as outcasts in cities. Afro-Brazilians suffer higher infant mortality and poverty and more racial and job discrimination than other groups – a program of "positive discrimination" was launched in 2002.

Amerindians also experience widespread prejudice, and of the estimated 1000 groups present at the time of the arrival of the first Portuguese, about 200 remain – a total population of about 220,000, who struggle to secure land rights.

Brazil is strongly Catholic, but other religions also flourish. The traditional emphasis on the family is under pressure in urban areas: migrants in search of work often have to leave their families behind.

Women gained the vote in 1934, but are still discriminated against in jobs and politics.

CHRONOLOGY

The first Portuguese, Pedro Alvares Cabral, arrived in Brazil in 1500. By the time Portugal took control of the region, in 1580, it was a thriving community drawing its wealth from sugar plantations in the northeast, worked by imported Africans or Amerindians captured from farther inland.

- **1637–1654** Dutch control sugar-growing areas.
- **1763** Rio becomes capital.
- **1788** *Inconfidência* rebellion, led by Tiradentes, fails.
- **1807** French invade Portugal. King João VI flees to Brazil with British naval escort. In return, Brazil's ports opened to foreign trade.
- **1821** King returns to Portugal; his son Pedro made regent of Brazil.
- **1822** Pedro I declares independence and is made emperor of Brazil.
- **1828** Brazil loses Uruguay.
- **1831** Military revolt after war with Argentina (1825–1828). Emperor abdicates; his five-year-old son succeeds him as Pedro II.
- **1835–1845** Rio Grande secedes.
- **1865–1870** Brazil with Argentina and Uruguay wins war of Triple Alliance against Paraguay.
- **1888** Pedro II abolishes slavery; landowners and military turn against him.
- **1889** First Republic established. Emperor goes into exile in Paris. Increasing prosperity as result of international demand for coffee.
- **1891** Federal constitution established.
- **1914–1918** World War I causes coffee exports to slump.
- **1920s** Working-class and intellectual movements call for end to oligarchic rule.
- **1930** Coffee prices collapse. Revolt led by Dr. Getúlio Vargas, the "Father of the Poor," who becomes president. Fast industrial growth.
- **1937** Vargas's position as benevolent dictator formalized in "New State," based on fascist model.
- **1942** Declares war on Germany. ➩

B

CHRONOLOGY *continued*

- ❑ **1945** Vargas forced out by military.
- ❑ **1950** Vargas reelected president.
- ❑ **1954** US opposes Vargas's socialist policies. The right, backed by the military, demands his resignation. Commits suicide.
- ❑ **1956–1960** President Juscelino Kubitschek, backed by Brazilian Labor Party (PTB), attracts foreign investment for new industries, especially from US.
- ❑ **1960–1961** Conservative Jânio da Silva Quadros president. Tries to break dependence on US trade.
- ❑ **1961** Brasília, built in three years, becomes new capital. PTB leader, João Goulart, elected president.
- ❑ **1961–1964** President's powers briefly curtailed as right wing reacts to presidential policies.
- ❑ **1964** Bloodless military coup under army chief Gen. Castelo Branco.
- ❑ **1965** Branco assumes dictatorship; bans existing political parties, but creates two official new ones. He is followed by a succession of military rulers. Fast-track economic development, the Brazilian Miracle, is counterbalanced by ruthless suppression of left-wing activists.
- ❑ **1974** World oil crisis marks end of economic boom. Brazil's foreign debt now largest in world.
- ❑ **1979** More political parties allowed.
- ❑ **1980** Huge migrations into Rondônia state begin.
- ❑ **1985** Civilian senator Tancredo Neves wins presidential elections as candidate of new liberal alliance, but dies before taking office. Illiterate adults granted the vote.
- ❑ **1987** Gold found on Yanomami lands in Roraima state; illegal diggers rush in by the thousand.
- ❑ **1988** New constitution promises massive social spending but fails to address land reform. Chico Mendes, rubber-tappers' union leader and environmentalist, murdered.
- ❑ **1989** First environmental protection plan. Yearly inflation reaches 1000%. Fernando Collor de Mello wins first presidential election held under completely free conditions.
- ❑ **1992** Earth Summit in Rio. Collor de Mello resigns and is impeached.
- ❑ **1994–1995** Plan Real ends hyperinflation. Congress resists constitutional reforms, but passes key privatizations of state monopolies.
- ❑ **1998–1999** Fernando Henrique Cardoso, in power since 1995, reelected president. Real devalued in economic crisis.
- ❑ **2001–2002** Recovery of economy threatened by crisis in Argentina.
- ❑ **2003** Lula da Silva becomes president.

POLITICS

Multiparty elections

L. House 2002/2006
U. House 2002/2006

President Luiz Inácio da Silva

AT THE LAST ELECTION

Chamber of Deputies 513 seats

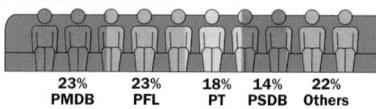

5% PTB
18% Others
18% PT
16% PFL
14% PMDB
14% PSDB
10% PPB
5% PL

PT = Workers' Party **PFL** = Liberal Front Party
PMDB = Brazilian Democratic Movement Party
PSDB = Brazilian Social Democracy Party
PPB = Brazilian Progressive Party
PTB = Brazilian Labor Party **PL** = Liberal Party

Federal Senate 81 seats

23% PMDB
23% PFL
18% PT
14% PSDB
22% Others

Brazil is a democratic federal republic with 27 regional parliaments and a national Congress. In 1993, Brazilians voted to retain the direct election of their president.

Profile

Military rule between 1964 and 1985 led to gross human rights abuses, against Amazon Amerindians in particular, and to economic mismanagement, which left Brazil with a legacy of huge debts and inefficient state industries.

Brazil's weak party system is centered on personalities. Parties do not have set ideological programs, but form shaky coalitions and engage in horse-trading to get legislation through the Congress. The preponderance of small parties and corruption adds to the problems. Former president Collor de Mello was impeached in 1992 on fraud charges.

Despite popular dissatisfaction with the center right in the 1990s, the left-wing PT, led by the charismatic Luiz Inácio "Lula" da Silva, was hindered by a lack of fresh ideas. Conservative Fernando Cardoso held on to the presidency from 1995. He kept a shaky coalition together, designing an anti-inflation plan for the real and emergency fiscal adjustments which saved Brazil from a return to persistent economic crisis. By 2002, the economic outlook had become less secure in the face of chaos in neighboring Argentina. With Cardoso constitutionally barred from seeking a third term, Lula, who had sufficiently toned down his socialism, was elected president in October – his fourth successive attempt.

Main Political Issues

Political stability

President Lula was elected on a social platform, notably prioritizing the fight against hunger, and his government came to power with unprecedented public support. Nonetheless, he was not eager to stray too far from the successful policy mix promoted by his predecessor, President Cardoso, which had provided stability and boosted consumer and investor confidence. Thus maintaining fiscal discipline while fulfilling his election promises is likely to prove difficult. Early signs of frustration with his commitment to the existing center-right policies materialized in early 2003 from the left wing of his own PT party, trade unions, and the landless peasant movement.

Fernando Cardoso, *president from 1995 to 2002.*

Luiz Inácio "Lula" da Silva, *left-wing leader, elected president in 2002.*

Economic management

Rapid recovery from the 1999 currency crisis relied on a tight monetary and fiscal regime backed by a sound macroeconomic policy. This permitted modest growth in 2001 and 2002, despite the global downturn and energy rationing at home. Plaudits from the IMF separated Brazil in investors' minds from the economic turmoil in Argentina. Efforts to manipulate the constitution in order to secure further reforms will require delicate consensus politics in a Congress eager to review the state-funding arrangements established under Cardoso.

Land redistribution

The Landless Workers' Movement (MST) has spearheaded an active campaign to redistribute vast tracts of private and often fallow land through a series of illegal invasions. These have led on occasion to violent confrontations with the security forces. The movement stepped up its campaign in 2003, despite the inauguration of the left-leaning President Lula.

Coffee plantation, *São Paulo state. Coffee was introduced into Brazil in the early 18th century. It is declining in importance and now accounts for less than 4% of export revenues.*

B

WORLD AFFAIRS

Joined UN in 1945

AmCC | G24 | Mercosr | OAS | RG

Brazil has ambitions to act as main broker in future talks with the US on the Free Trade Area of the Americas (FTAA), which is due to be signed in 2005. It hosted a conference in 2002 of the FTAA candidate countries and has strengthened ties with Mexico, its chief rival for regional leadership. Free trade talks with the EU and Mercosur have raised the prospect of compromise by Europe on agriculture, long the main bone of contention between the two regions. Though pragmatic in his relations with the US, President Lula has supported left-wing president Hugo Chávez in Venezuela's domestic crisis and has offered to mediate in Colombia, despite protests about supposed support in Brazil for left-wing Colombian guerrillas.

AID

Recipient

$349m (receipts) | Up 8% in 2001

Aid, mainly from Japan and EU states, funds environmental, basic sanitation, road-building, and antipoverty projects. As a consequence of the Argentine economic crisis, the IMF loaned Brazil $10 billion in 2002, and promised $30 billion more in the following years.

DEFENSE

Compulsory military service

$10.5bn | Down 27% in 2001

BRAZILIAN ARMED FORCES

178 main battle tanks (87 Leopard 1, 91 M-60A3)	189,000 personnel
4 submarines, 1 carrier, 14 frigates, 4 corvettes, 50 patrol boats	48,600 personnel
264 combat aircraft (53 AT-26, 47 F-5E/B/F, 33 AMX, 18 Mirage F-103E/D)	50,000 personnel
None	

The military still has an important internal security role, particularly in the north. The arms industry is large, but Brazil states that it has no intention of using its nuclear energy for military purposes: the Comprehensive Test Ban and Nuclear Non-Proliferation treaties were signed in 1998.

Membership of the Mercosur trade bloc has led to increased regional cooperation. Brazilian troops have participated in UN peacekeeping, most recently in East Timor. A $750 million order for US fighter aircraft was suspended in 2003, preference being given to social initiatives.

ECONOMICS

Inflation 168% p.a. (1990–2001)

$529bn | 2.869 reals (2.851)

SCORE CARD

World GNP Ranking	11th
GNP per Capita	$3070
Balance of Payments	–$23.2bn
Inflation	6.9%
Unemployment	7%

EXPORTS

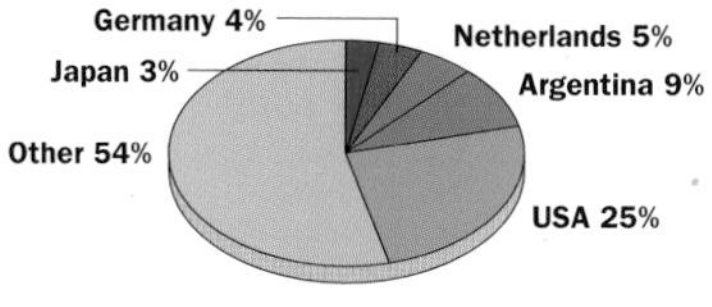
Germany 4%
Japan 3%
Netherlands 5%
Argentina 9%
Other 54%
USA 25%

IMPORTS

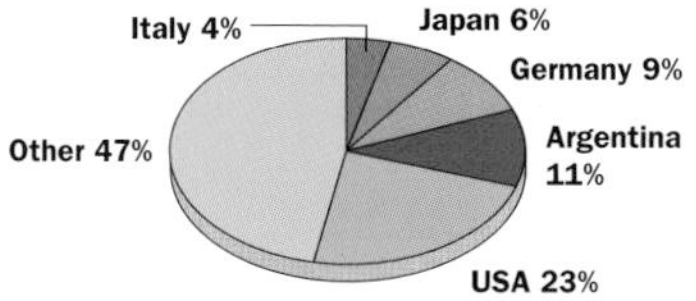
Italy 4%
Japan 6%
Germany 9%
Argentina 11%
Other 47%
USA 23%

Strengths

Dominant economy in region. Strong foreign direct investment flows. Huge growth potential: immense natural resources; major producer of coffee, soybeans, sugar, oranges; large deposits of gold, silver, and iron; major steel producer; expanding oil industry. Development aided by cross-border infrastructural projects and modernization of telecoms.

Weaknesses

Expensive domestic borrowing. Weak local capital markets. Vulnerability to external shocks and commodity price fluctuations. Modest productivity. Heavy debt burden. Social inequalities threaten unrest. High cost of crime. Electricity blackouts caused by badly maintained transmission network or failure of hydropower supply due to drought.

Profile

Brazil is the world's 11th-largest economy. Average growth from the start of the 20th century to the early 1970s was over 5%, second only to Japan over a comparable period. Diversification and industrialization transformed Brazil into a producer of cars, computers, and aircraft, but profligate spending produced heavy debts in the 1980s. International lenders demanded belt tightening in return for rescheduling, and a steep recession followed in 1990–1992.

The launching of the new currency, the real, in 1994, was the fifth attempt at monetary stabilization since 1986; it contributed to a dramatic fall in inflation. Economic growth in 1994 boosted regional confidence and facilitated the launch of Mercosur. In 1995 a fractious Congress blocked reforms of the tax and social security systems, but finally agreed to end state monopolies in such sectors as telecommunications and oil, thus reviving the privatization program.

The economy grew strongly through 1996 and 1997, but was seriously threatened in 1998 by an international financial crisis. A $41.5 billion rescue package was arranged by the IMF, but foreign currency reserves were heavily depleted in a bid to support the real, which was devalued in 1999 due to speculative pressures. A deep recession was avoided, however, by the successful application over 18 months of tight fiscal and monetary policies, restoring domestic and international confidence.

Modest growth was posted in 2001, but the economic meltdown in Argentina and the effects of global downturn brought the value of the real down in 2002. The IMF calmed market jitters when it approved a billion-dollar credit line. It expressed confidence that President Lula's administration would keep macroeconomic discipline, even though the economy remains sluggish, notwithstanding an increase in exports.

ECONOMIC PERFORMANCE INDICATOR

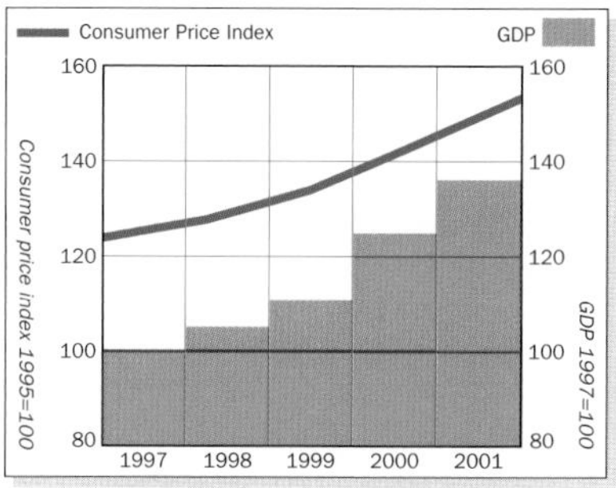
Consumer Price Index
GDP
160
140
120
100
80
Consumer price index 1995=100
GDP 1997=100
1997
1998
1999
2000
2001

BRAZIL : MAJOR BUSINESSES

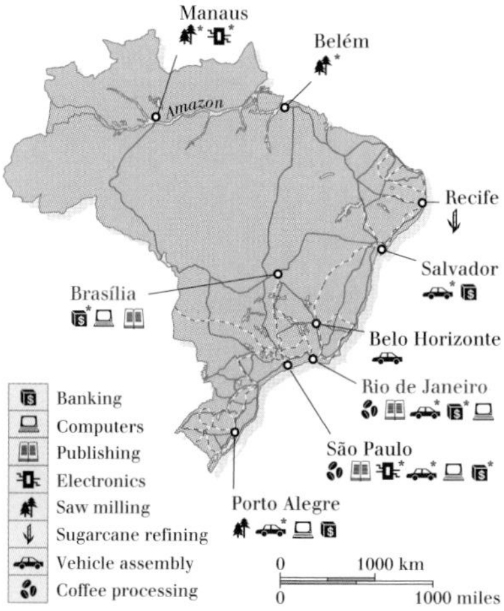
Manaus
Belém
Amazon
Recife
Salvador
Brasília
Belo Horizonte
Rio de Janeiro
São Paulo
Porto Alegre
Banking
Computers
Publishing
Electronics
Saw milling
Sugarcane refining
Vehicle assembly
Coffee processing
0 1000 km
0 1000 miles

* significant multinational ownership

B

RESOURCES

Electric power 68.2m kW

847,268 tonnes

1.5m b/d (reserves 8.3bn barrels)

176m cattle, 30m pigs, 15m sheep, 1.05bn chickens

Iron, manganese, coal, bauxite, nickel, oil, tin, silver, diamonds, gold, natural gas

ELECTRICITY GENERATION

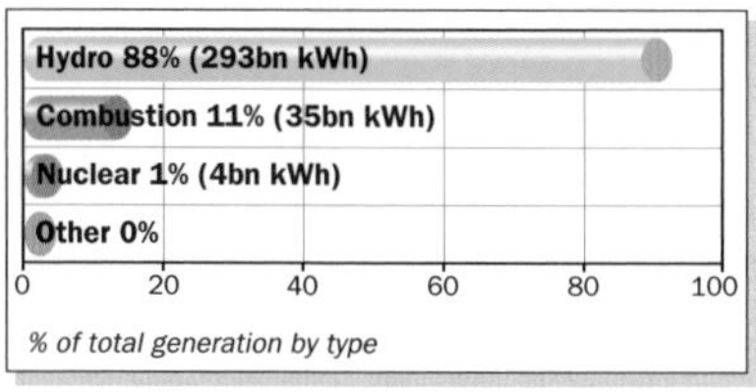
Hydro 88% (293bn kWh)
Combustion 11% (35bn kWh)
Nuclear 1% (4bn kWh)
Other 0%
0
20
40
60
80
100
% of total generation by type

Brazil pumps in gas from Argentina and Bolivia, and has similar plans with Venezuela and Uruguay. Nuclear power has been dogged by controversy and high costs. Hydropower, which accounts for almost 90% of electricity generation, is extremely vulnerable to drought, which forced energy rationing in 2001–2002. Producing ethanol from sugar represents an attempt to reduce gasoline imports, and the welcoming of foreign companies in areas of exploration and production is set to increase known oil and natural gas reserves. Exploration of the Amazon's biodiversity was brought under government control in mid-2000, with all new ventures involving any living thing requiring official approval.

Amazon
AMAZON BASIN
BRAZIL : LAND USE
Cropland
Forest
Pasture
Cattle
Coffee – cash crop
Oranges
0
1000 km
0
1000 miles

Equatorial vegetation near Manaus in the center of Amazonas state. The brown waters of the Rio Solimões and the black waters of the Rio Negro meet near Manaus.

ENVIRONMENT

Sustainability rank: 20th

7% (4% partially protected)

1.8 tonnes per capita

ENVIRONMENTAL TREATIES

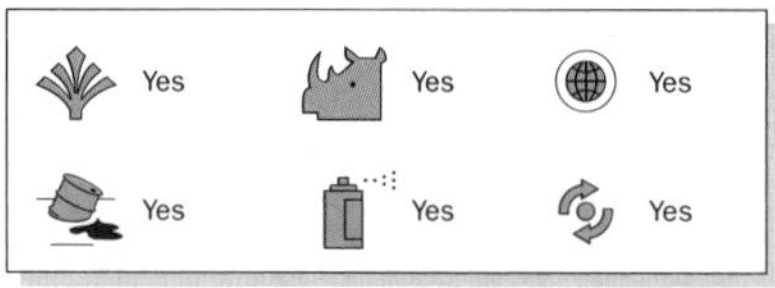
Yes
Yes
Yes
Yes
Yes
Yes

Federal agencies charged with protecting the Amazon Rainforest are underfunded, understaffed, and accused of corruption.

The forest contains an estimated 90% of all the world's plant and animal species. However, 38 million animals a year are smuggled out of the region, and irreplaceable genetic diversity is being lost year by year with the forest's continuing destruction for the sake of cattle pasture, logging, and soybean farming. In 2002 the world's largest tropical forest reserve was created in northern Brazil.

Opencast bauxite mines pollute rivers and threaten indigenous Amerindians, while in 2000 the worst oil spill in 25 years devastated the Iguaçu River. Urban industrial pollution and untreated sewage are also major problems.

MEDIA

TV ownership high

Daily newspaper circulation 46 per 1000 people

PUBLISHING AND BROADCAST MEDIA

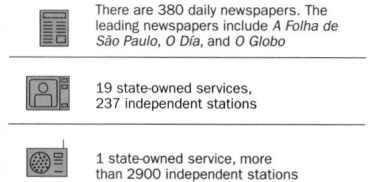

There are 380 daily newspapers. The leading newspapers include *A Folha de São Paulo*, *O Dia*, and *O Globo*

19 state-owned services, 237 independent stations

1 state-owned service, more than 2900 independent stations

TV and radio licenses have been notoriously awarded as political favors. The huge Globo group dominates the home market, with radio, press, and online interests: its TV network is one of the largest in the world. However, it is being challenged by the Internet and the growth of new media companies, involving foreign multinationals. A constitutional amendment in 2002 allows foreign groups to take 30% stakes in TV, radio, and the press.

CRIME

Death penalty not used in practice

233,859 prisoners

Up 19% in 2000–2001

CRIME RATES

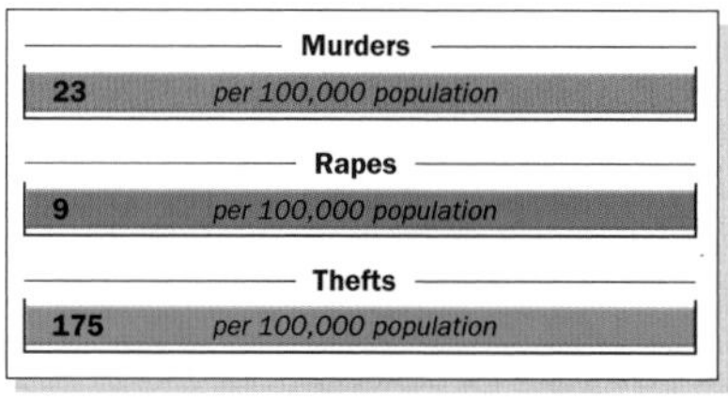
Murders
23 per 100,000 population
Rapes
9 per 100,000 population
Thefts
175 per 100,000 population

In cities, crime levels are among the world's highest, with armed robbery and narcotics-related organized crime uppermost. Badly paid police are frequently accused of extortion, violence, and murder. Death squads, thought to be linked to the police, have targeted street children in major cities. A combination of atrocious conditions and overcrowding means that violent disturbances in prisons are common. An explosion in muggings and kidnappings was a key issue in the 2002 elections.

In the countryside, landless squatters and indigenous peoples have been wounded and murdered in the process of being driven off land by gunmen funded by large landowners. In Roraima state, the discovery of large gold deposits has led to the homelands of Brazil's largest tribe, the Yanomami, being invaded by thousands of gun-toting prospectors, *garimpeiros*.

EDUCATION

School leaving age: 14

87%

2.78m students

THE EDUCATION SYSTEM

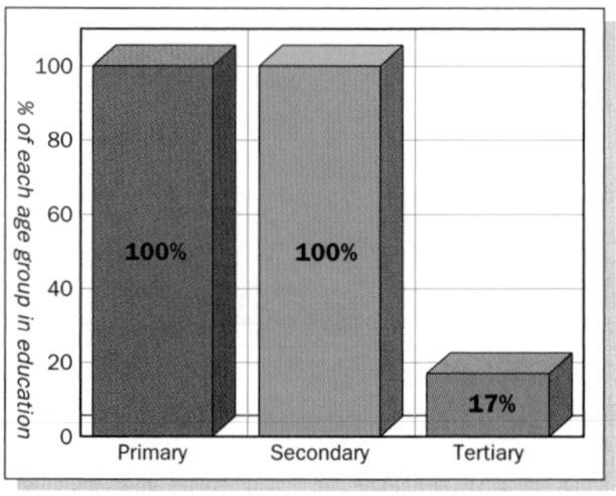
100
80
60
40
20
0
% of each age group in education
100%
100%
17%
Primary
Secondary
Tertiary

The average time spent at school is less than that in other Latin American countries. The portion of GDP spent on education is comparable to that of European countries, but it is misapplied, so that basic primary education remains weak, while many children of wealthy families receive excellent tuition at free public universities. Of Brazil's 150 universities, 77 are administered by the state. Children living in remote communities in Amazonia and the slums around major cities, and urban street children, have limited access to mainstream education. Classes frequently include children older than the expected age range. Despite an anti-illiteracy campaign, begun in 1971, the adult illiteracy rate is 13%.

— EXPLOITATION VERSUS PROTECTION IN AMAZONIA —

In the vast Amazon River basin lies one of the world's last great virgin rainforests. Major road-building projects mean that it no longer enjoys the protection of inaccessibility. Researchers have warned that the massive "Advance Brazil" road- and dam-building project will leave at best 28% of the forest untouched by 2020.

Damage is done by mining, especially for gold, with associated pollution of soil and water. Land clearance for ranching occurs wherever access roads are built. Logging is an ongoing threat: a score of foreign-owned multinationals dominate the timber export business, and some 2500

***Deforestation** continues inexorably.*

logging companies and sawmills operate in the Brazilian Amazon. While Brazilian mahogany is now protected by a moratorium on exploitation, the government estimates that 80% of all timber from the Amazon is removed illegally.

Since 1970, when it was still 99% intact, 650,000 sq. km (over 250,000 sq. miles) of Amazonia, between 15% and 20% of the total, have been lost. The rate of destruction was thought to have slowed down until a shocking revelation that over 25,000 sq. km (almost 10,000 sq. miles) had been lost in the year to August 2002, mainly because of land demand for soybean farming. In June 2003 Environment Minister Marina Silva, herself a former rubber tapper from the Amazon, promised emergency action.

Environmental consequences

The rainforest typically has poor and shallow soil. Its ecology depends on the recycling of minerals in the leaf litter on the forest floor. In a damp environment, this is broken down rapidly by soil organisms. Once exposed by the loss of tree cover, however, it dries out quickly and can easily be washed away by the next rain. The forest cannot regenerate growth where substantial areas have been cleared. The deforestation has far-reaching implications. Forests act as "carbon sinks," fixing carbon dioxide produced by the burning of fuel, and thus helping to counteract the buildup of the "greenhouse gases" linked with global warming.

Amazonia is immensely rich in native plant and animal species. Its resource value, taking account of the potential significance of its gene pool, for example in medicine or agriculture, was estimated by a government research project in 2001 at $2000 billion. This biodiversity, including much as yet undiscovered by the international scientific community, is dependent on proper protection of rainforest habitat.

Indigenous peoples

Exploitation has brought violence and devastating epidemics to the forest's indigenous peoples, along with the loss of their lands, forced removal, confinement to reservations, and the destruction of their lifestyle and culture. Many of them suffered extinction in the last half century. There remain about 200 distinct known forest-dwelling indigenous peoples. One-fifth of the Amazon is Amerindian land and under the 1988 constitution, forest peoples have the right to inhabit their ancestral lands, but they do not have legal title. Of 580 identified Amerindian territories, only two-thirds are demarcated, offering legal protection from logging, mining, and other industrial activities. The National Indian Foundation (FUNAI), a government agency responsible for demarcation, has been heavily criticized internationally for failing to provide adequate protection.

***Some 200 indigenous groups** remain in the rainforest.*

HEALTH

Welfare state health benefits

1 per 633 people

Heart diseases, cancers, accidents, violence

Federal health is underfunded. Fewer than 20% of hospitals are state-run, and they need modernization, while private care is beyond the means of the majority. On average only 15% of the health budget goes to child health, immunization, and other preventive programs. However, infant mortality, at 95 per 1000 children in 1970, had dropped to one-third of that level by 2000; access to potable water increased from 74% of the population in 1992 to 87% in 2000. In 2001 international drug companies and the US dropped patent infringement claims against Brazil for distributing anti-AIDS drugs free to more than 100,000 HIV patients.

SPENDING

GDP/cap. increase

CONSUMPTION AND SPENDING

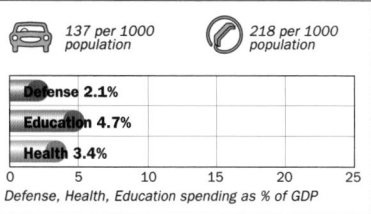

137 per 1000 population

218 per 1000 population

Defense 2.1%
Education 4.7%
Health 3.4%
0
5
10
15
20
25

Defense, Health, Education spending as % of GDP

Brazil's income distribution is among the most skewed in the world. The richest 10% of the population take 50% of the income and the poorest 50% only 10%. Up to five million families remain landless, while nearly 66% of arable land is owned by just 3% of the population. Vast tracts of disputed land are marked for redistribution, but invasions by landless workers continue. In 2003 President Lula launched a Zero Hunger campaign to provide benefits to the poorest families, and pledged to end economic slavery, by which 25,000 people are forced to work in order to pay largely invented debts.

WORLD RANKING

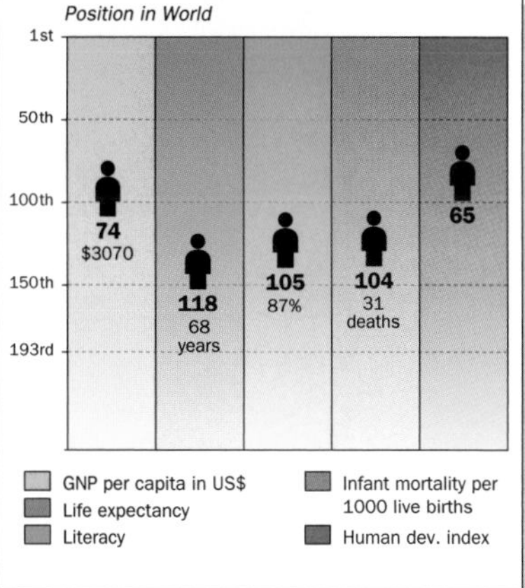
Position in World
1st
50th
100th
150th
193rd
74
$3070
118
68
years
105
87%
104
31
deaths
65
GNP per capita in US$
Life expectancy
Literacy
Infant mortality per 1000 live births
Human dev. index

B

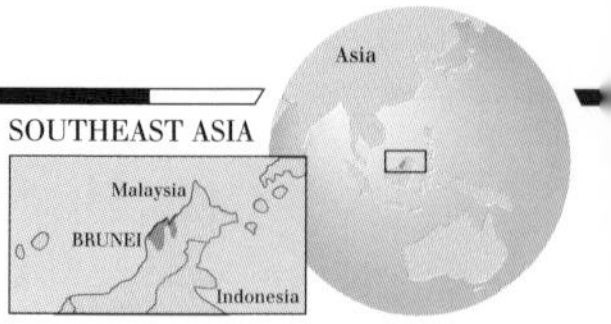
Asia
SOUTHEAST ASIA
Malaysia
BRUNEI
Indonesia

BRUNEI

OFFICIAL NAME: Sultanate of Brunei **CAPITAL:** Bandar Seri Begawan
POPULATION: 341,000 **CURRENCY:** Brunei dollar **OFFICIAL LANGUAGE:** Malay

1984 | 1984 | Feb 23 | BRU | +8 | +673 | .bn

LYING ON THE NORTHWESTERN coast of the island of Borneo, Brunei is divided in two by a strip of the surrounding Malaysian state of Sarawak. The interior is mostly rainforest. Independent from the UK since 1984, Brunei is ruled by decree of the sultan. It is undergoing increasing Islamicization. Oil and gas reserves have brought one of the world's highest standards of living.

CLIMATE

Tropical equatorial

WEATHER CHART FOR BANDAR SERI BEGAWAN

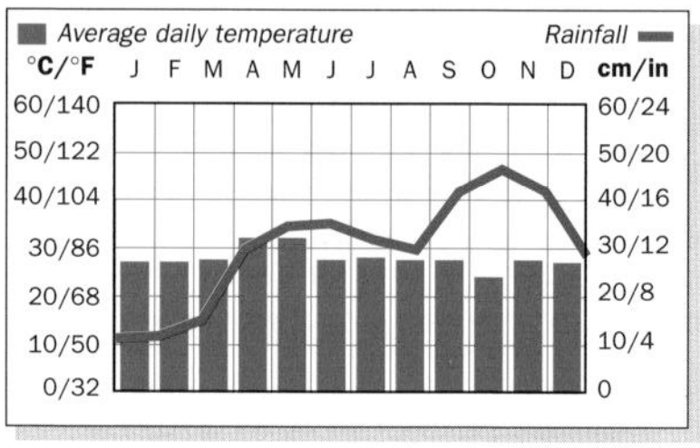
Average daily temperature
Rainfall
°C/°F J F M A M J J A S O N D cm/in
60/140
50/122
40/104
30/86
20/68
10/50
0/32
60/24
50/20
40/16
30/12
20/8
10/4
0

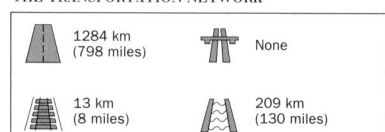

Just 480 km (300 miles) north of the equator, Brunei has a long rainy season with extremely high humidity.

TRANSPORTATION

Drive on left

Brunei International, Bandar Seri Begawan 1.06m passengers

97 ships 362,700 grt

THE TRANSPORTATION NETWORK

1284 km (798 miles)	None
13 km (8 miles)	209 km (130 miles)

Interest-free loans for civil servants, subsidized gasoline, and limited public transportation account for the high rates of car ownership.

TOURISM

Visitors : Population 2.8:1

964,000 visitors

Up 13% in 1998

MAIN TOURIST ARRIVALS

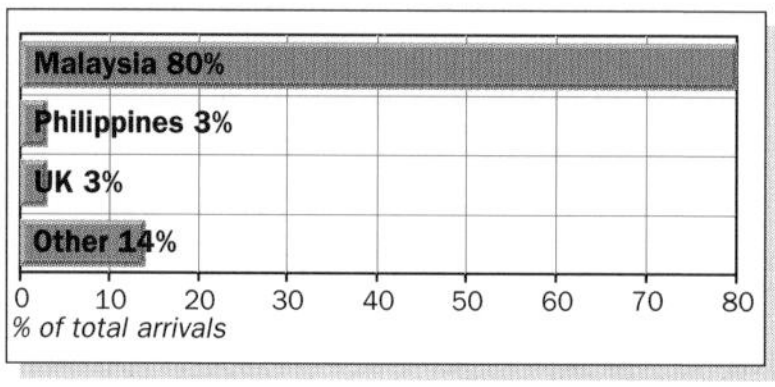
Malaysia 80%
Philippines 3%
UK 3%
Other 14%
0 10 20 30 40 50 60 70 80
% of total arrivals

Though the government is keen to protect Bruneians from Western influence, it wants to encourage quality tourism as part of its diversification program. Promoted as the "Gateway to Borneo," Brunei's rainforests could be developed for tourism. The Winston Churchill Museum, founded by the late Sultan Omar Ali Saifuddin, has now been superseded by the Museum of Royal Regalia.

PEOPLE

Pop. density medium

Malay, English, Chinese

65/km² (168/mi²)

THE URBAN/RURAL POPULATION SPLIT

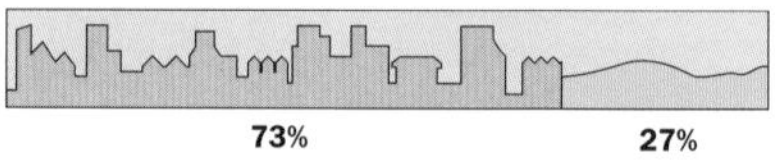
73%
27%

ETHNIC MAKEUP

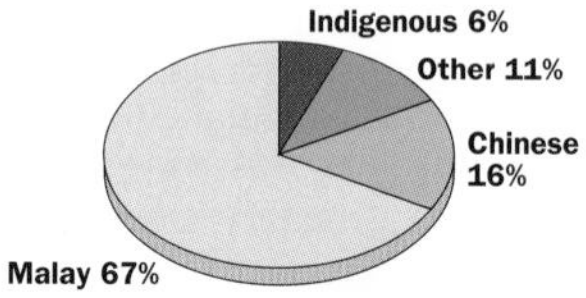
Indigenous 6%
Other 11%
Chinese 16%
Malay 67%

Malays are the beneficiaries of positive discrimination; many in the Chinese community are either stateless or hold British protected person passports. Among indigenous groups, the Murut and Dusuns are favored over the Ibans. Women, less restricted than in some Muslim states, are obliged to wear headscarves but not the veil. Many hold influential posts in the civil service.

POLITICS

No legislative elections

Not applicable

H.M. Sultan Haji Sir Hassanal Bolkiah Mu'izzadin Waddaulah

LEGISLATIVE OR ADVISORY BODIES

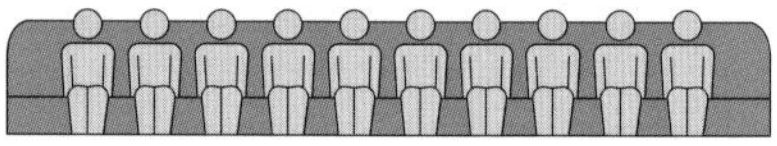

Brunei is an absolute monarchy; the sultan consults four advisory councils: Religious Council, Privy Council, Council of Cabinet Ministers, and Council of Succession, which he appoints. Political parties have been banned since 1988.

Since a failed rebellion in 1962, a state of emergency has been in force and the sultan has ruled by decree. Hopes for democracy were dashed when political parties were banned in 1988. In 1990, "Malay Muslim Monarchy" was introduced, promoting Islamic values as the state ideology. This further alienated the large Chinese and expatriate communities. Power is closely tied to the royal family. One of the sultan's brothers holds the foreign affairs portfolio and the sultan himself looks after defense and finance.

WORLD AFFAIRS

Joined UN in 1984

APEC | ASEAN | Comm | OIC | WTO

Brunei leads calls for a regional free trade area. Political exiles opposed to the government and based in Malaysia are a main concern. Relations with the UK, the ex-colonial power, are good.

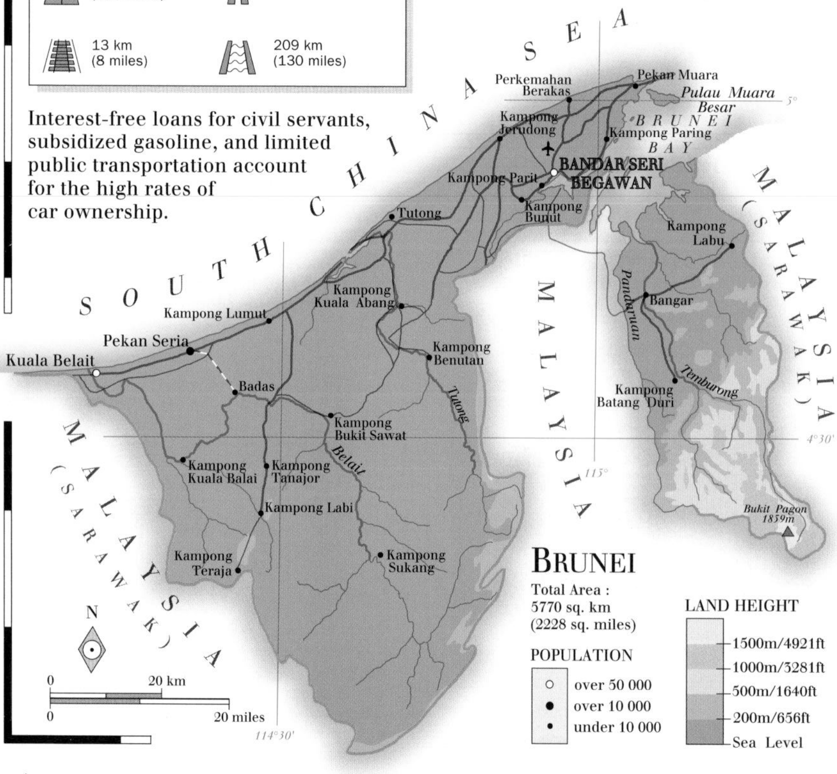
SOUTH CHINA SEA
Perkemahan Berakas
Pekan Muara
Pulau Muara Besar
Kampong Jerudong
Kampong Paring
BRUNEI BAY
Kampong Parit
BANDAR SERI BEGAWAN
Kampong Bunut
Tutong
Kampong Labu
MALAYSIA (SARAWAK)
Pandaruan
Bangar
Kampong Kuala Abang
Kampong Lumut
Pekan Seria
Kuala Belait
Kampong Benutan
Badas
Temburong
Kampong Batang Duri
MALAYSIA
Tutong
Kampong Bukit Sawat
Belait
Kampong Kuala Balai
Kampong Tanajor
Kampong Labi
Bukit Pagon 1859m
Kampong Teraja
Kampong Sukang
5°
4°30'
115°
114°30'
N
0 20 km
0 20 miles
BRUNEI
Total Area : 5770 sq. km (2228 sq. miles)
POPULATION
over 50 000
over 10 000
under 10 000
LAND HEIGHT
1500m/4921ft
1000m/3281ft
500m/1640ft
200m/656ft
Sea Level

B

The magnificent Omar Ali Saifuddin Mosque *is surrounded by an artificial lagoon.*

AID

Donor

Ad hoc handouts from the sultan

Not applicable

Aid spending is largely ad hoc. It has included donations to the Contras in Nicaragua, the Bosnian Muslims, and the homeless of New York.

DEFENSE

No compulsory military service

US$279m

Down 21% in 2001

As well as being head of the 5900-strong armed forces, the sultan has a personal bodyguard of 2000 UK-trained Gurkhas. The UK and Singapore are close defense allies.

ECONOMICS

Inflation 1.1% p.a. (1990–1999)

US$7.75bn

1.761 Brunei dollars (1.767)

SCORE CARD

- World GNP Ranking 97th
- GNP per Capita .... US$24,100
- Balance of Payments .... US$2.09bn
- Inflation 1%
- Unemployment 5%

Strengths

Nearly 20 years of known oil reserves; over 30 years of gas. Earnings from massive overseas investments, mainly in the US and Europe, now exceed oil and gas revenues.

Weaknesses

Single-product economy. Failure of diversification programs could lead to problems in the future.

EXPORTS

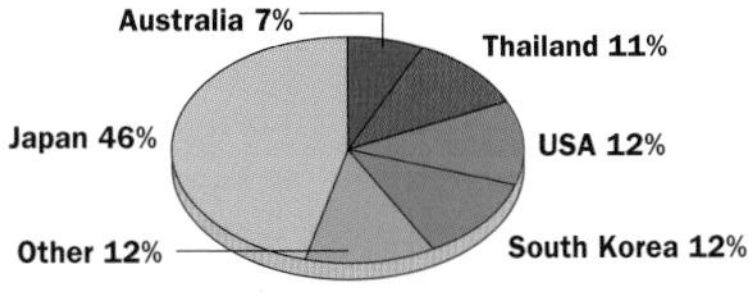
Australia 7%
Thailand 11%
Japan 46%
USA 12%
Other 12%
South Korea 12%

IMPORTS

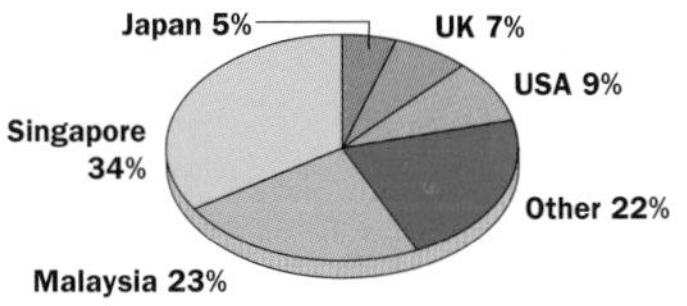
Japan 5%
UK 7%
USA 9%
Singapore 34%
Other 22%
Malaysia 23%

RESOURCES

Electric power 481,000 kW

2594 tonnes

210,000 b/d (reserves 1.4bn barrels)

7000 buffaloes, 12.5m chickens, 60,000 ducks

Oil, natural gas

Oil and gas are the major resources. Energy policy is now focused on regulating output in order to conserve stocks, since reserves are of limited duration. Almost all food is imported.

ENVIRONMENT

Not available

21% (0.2% partially protected)

14.3 tonnes per capita

The Forestry Strategic Plan aims to protect Brunei's forests (which take up 80% of its land area). It has allocated 64% of their area for protection and recreation and the prevention of soil erosion. However, Brunei's mangrove swamps, the largest on the island of Borneo, remain unprotected.

MEDIA

TV ownership high

Daily newspaper circulation 69 per 1000 people

PUBLISHING AND BROADCAST MEDIA

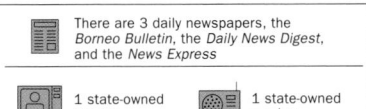

There are 3 daily newspapers, the *Borneo Bulletin*, the *Daily News Digest*, and the *News Express*

1 state-owned service

1 state-owned service

State controls were relaxed somewhat in 2000, but self-censorship on political and religious content continues.

CRIME

Death penalty not used in practice

401 prisoners

Down 21% in 2000–2001

Crime levels are low. Most crime involves petty theft or is linked to alcohol and narcotics (both banned). A stolen car often makes TV news headlines. The state of emergency enables the government to detain without charge or trial for indefinitely renewable two-year periods.

EDUCATION

School leaving age: 16

92%

3984 students

Free schooling is available to the entire population, with the exception of the stateless Chinese, who do not qualify. The University of Brunei Darussalam was opened in 1985.

HEALTH

Welfare state health benefits

1 per 1176 people

Heart diseases, cancers

The health service is free, though if major surgery is required Bruneians tend to travel to Singapore.

CHRONOLOGY

Under British control since 1841, Brunei became a formal British Protectorate in 1888.

- **1929** Oil extraction begins.
- **1959** First constitution enshrines Islam as state religion. Internal self-government.
- **1962** Prodemocracy rebellion. State of emergency; sultan rules by decree.
- **1984** Independence from Britain. Brunei joins ASEAN.
- **1990** Ideology of "Malay Muslim Monarchy" introduced.
- **1991** Imports of alcohol banned.
- **1992** Joins Non-Aligned Movement.
- **1998** Sultan's son, Prince Al-Muhtadee Billah, made crown prince.

SPENDING

GDP/cap. decrease

CONSUMPTION AND SPENDING

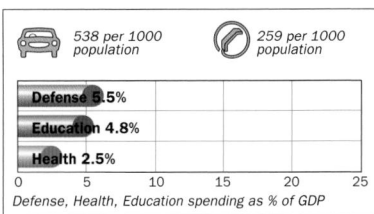

538 per 1000 population

259 per 1000 population

Defense 5.5%
Education 4.8%
Health 2.5%
0
5
10
15
20
25

Defense, Health, Education spending as % of GDP

The wealthiest people in Brunei are those close to the sultan, one of the world's richest men. A generally high standard of living, along with a degree of social mobility among Malays, keeps discontent to a minimum. Bruneians are major consumers of high-tech hi-fi and video equipment, designer-label watches, and Western designer clothes. The sultan's younger brother, Prince Jefri, in 2001 auctioned his possessions, ranging from fire engines to marble baths, after the failure of his business left him with debts of US$3 billion.

WORLD RANKING

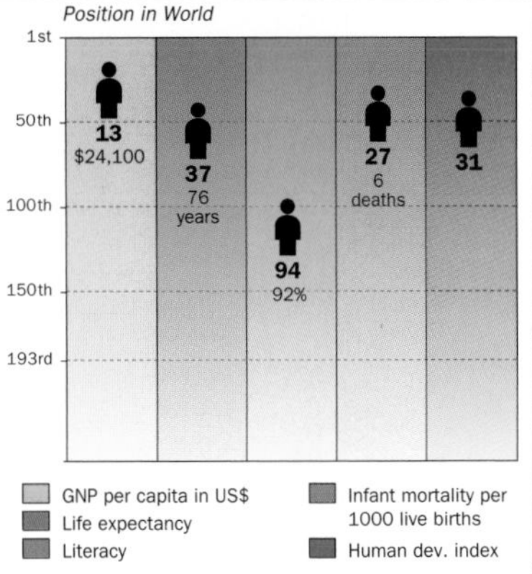
Position in World
1st
50th
100th
150th
193rd
13
$24,100
37
76
years
94
92%
27
6
deaths
31
GNP per capita in US$
Life expectancy
Literacy
Infant mortality per 1000 live births
Human dev. index

BULGARIA

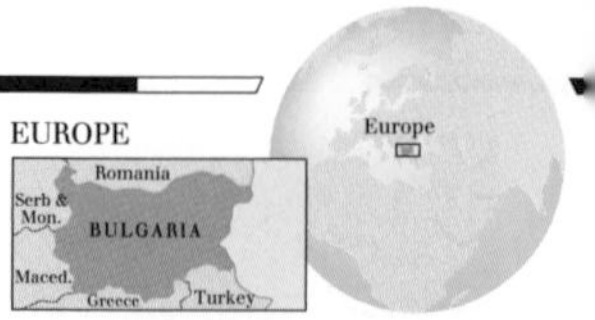
EUROPE
Romania
Serb & Mon.
BULGARIA
Maced.
Greece
Turkey
Europe

OFFICIAL NAME: Republic of Bulgaria **CAPITAL:** Sofia
POPULATION: 7.8 million **CURRENCY:** Lev **OFFICIAL LANGUAGE:** Bulgarian

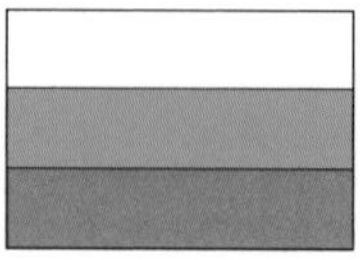

1908 | 1947 | March 3 | BG | +2 | +359 | .bg

EXTENDING SOUTH FROM the River Danube, Bulgaria has a mountainous interior, with the popular resorts of the Black Sea to the east. The most populated areas are around Sofia in the west, Plovdiv in the south, and along the Danube plain. Bulgaria was directly ruled by the Ottomans until 1878; Communists overthrew the monarchy in 1946 and, under General Secretary Todor Zhivkov from 1954, Bulgaria was one of the Soviet Union's most loyal allies. Economic and political reform after 1989 was slow, but Bulgaria now hopes to build its future as an integral part of Europe.

***Rila Monastery** in the Rila Mountains. It is famous for its 1200 National Revival period frescoes dating from the mid-19th century.*

CLIMATE

Mediterranean/ continental

WEATHER CHART FOR SOFIA

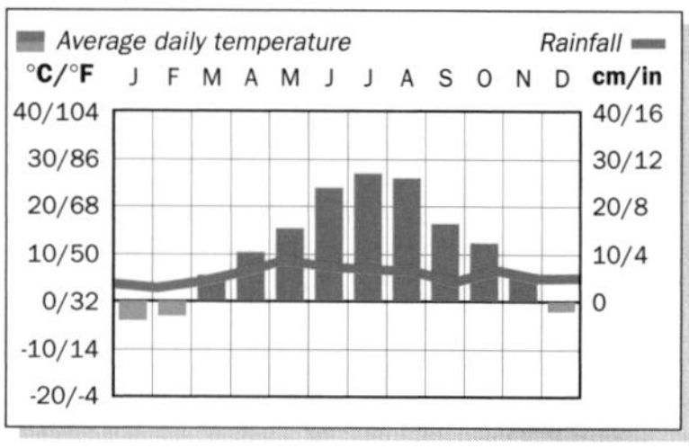
Average daily temperature
Rainfall
°C/°F
J F M A M J J A S O N D
cm/in
40/104
30/86
20/68
10/50
0/32
-10/14
-20/-4
40/16
30/12
20/8
10/4
0

The central valley and the lowlands have warm summers and cold, snowy winters, but hot or cold winds from Russia can bring spells of more extreme weather. The hotter summers on the Black Sea coast have encouraged the growth of tourist resorts. Snow may lie on the high mountain peaks until June.

TRANSPORTATION

Drive on right

Sofia International 1.21m passengers

172 ships 955,300 grt

THE TRANSPORTATION NETWORK

33,786 km (20,994 miles)

324 km (201 miles)

4320 km (2684 miles)

470 km (292 miles)

At the crossroads between Europe and Asia, Bulgarian railroads and expressways were underfunded under Zhivkov (when north–south routes were left undeveloped) and in the economically uncertain 1990s. Funding for modernizing key routes is now in place. Ferries are used for most cross-Danube traffic. In 2000 agreement was reached with Romania on building a second bridge across the river, scheduled to open in 2005.

TOURISM

Visitors : Population 1:2.4

3.19m visitors

Up 14% in 2001

MAIN TOURIST ARRIVALS

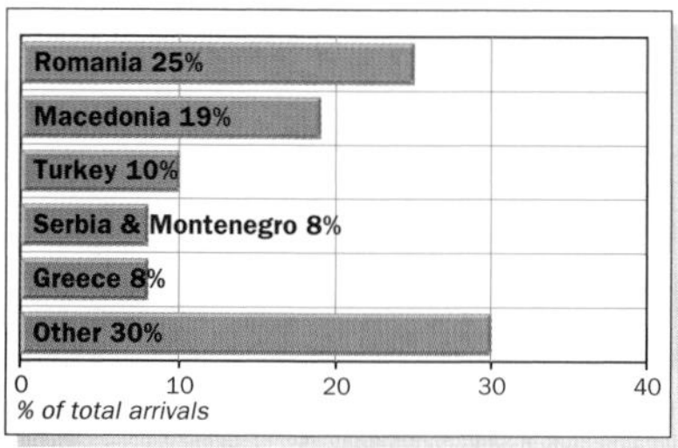
Romania 25%
Macedonia 19%
Turkey 10%
Serbia & Montenegro 8%
Greece 8%
Other 30%
0
10
20
30
40
% of total arrivals

The tourist industry formerly catered for the east European mass market. Western tourists are attracted by low prices for skiing and beach vacations. Bulgaria is now privatizing the industry and seeks to move it upmarket by stressing its heritage. Since the mid-1990s a slump in earnings has been reversed: Russians are returning in larger numbers and there are more tours from western Europe, especially from Germany.

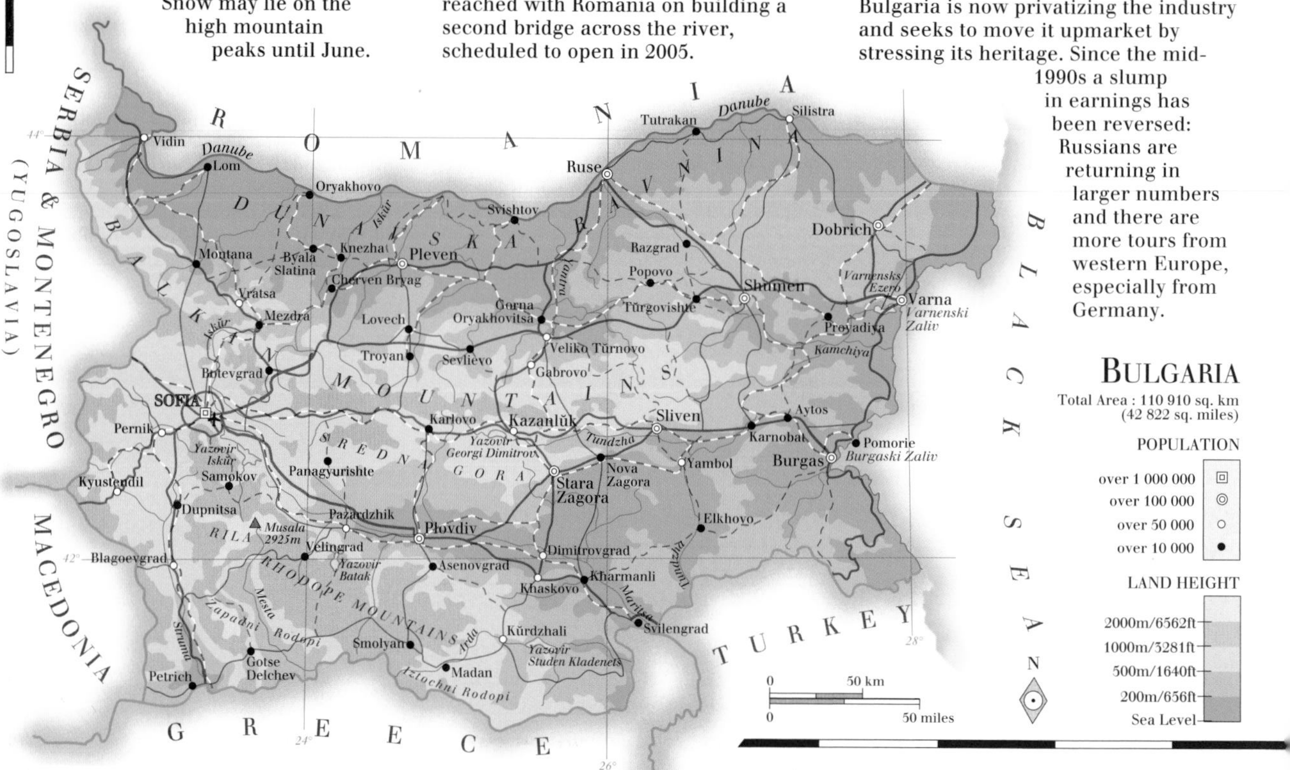
ROMANIA
SERBIA & MONTENEGRO (YUGOSLAVIA)
MACEDONIA
GREECE
TURKEY
BLACK SEA
Danube
Vidin
Lom
Oryakhovo
Iskur
Svishtov
Ruse
Tutrakan
Silistra
DUNAVSKA RAVNINA
BALKAN MOUNTAINS
Montana
Byala Slatina
Knezha
Pleven
Cherven Bryag
Vratsa
Mezdra
Lovech
Troyan
Gorna Oryakhovitsa
Veliko Turnovo
Sevlievo
Gabrovo
Razgrad
Popovo
Turgovishte
Shumen
Dobrich
Varnensko Ezero
Varna
Varnenski Zaliv
Provadiya
Kamchiya
Botevgrad
SOFIA
Pernik
Kyustendil
Samokov
Yazovir Iskur
Panagyurishte
SREDNA GORA
Karlovo
Kazanluk
Yazovir Georgi Dimitrov
Tundzha
Sliven
Stara Zagora
Nova Zagora
Yambol
Karnobat
Aytos
Burgas
Pomorie
Burgaski Zaliv
Elkhovo
Dupnitsa
RILA
Musala 2925m
Pazardzhik
Plovdiv
Velingrad
Yazovir Batak
Asenovgrad
Dimitrovgrad
Khaskovo
Kharmanli
Maritsa
Svilengrad
Blagoevgrad
RHODOPE MOUNTAINS
Zapadni Rodopi
Mesta
Struma
Arda
Kurdzhali
Yazovir Studen Kladenets
Smolyan
Madan
Iztochni Rodopi
Gotse Delchev
Petrich
0
50 km
50 miles
N
BULGARIA
Total Area : 110 910 sq. km (42 822 sq. miles)
POPULATION
over 1 000 000
over 100 000
over 50 000
over 10 000
LAND HEIGHT
2000m/6562ft
1000m/3281ft
500m/1640ft
200m/656ft
Sea Level

PEOPLE

Pop. density medium

Bulgarian, Turkish, Romany

71/km² (183/mi²)

THE URBAN/RURAL POPULATION SPLIT

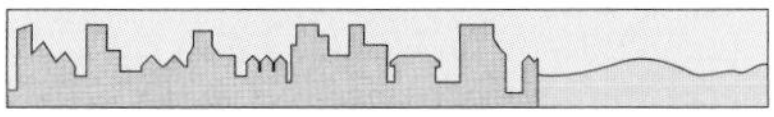
70%
30%

RELIGIOUS PERSUASION

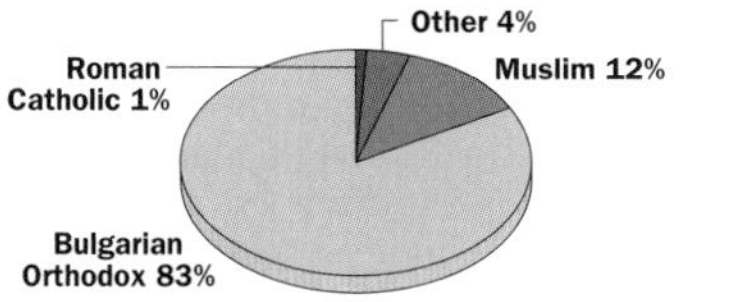
Other 4%
Muslim 12%
Roman Catholic 1%
Bulgarian Orthodox 83%

ETHNIC MAKEUP

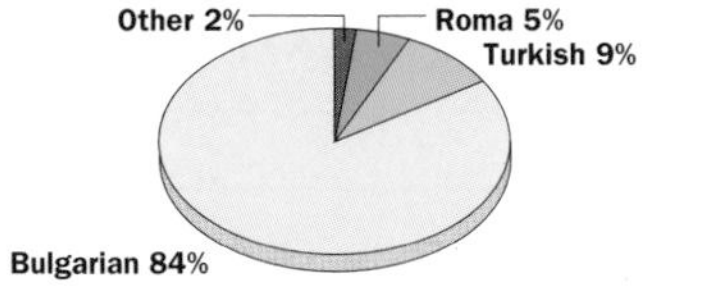
Other 2%
Roma 5%
Turkish 9%
Bulgarian 84%

The Communist era was marked by the active suppression of minority cultural identities. In the 1970s, Bulgarian Muslims, or Pomaks, were forced to change Muslim names to Bulgarian ones. Bulgarian Turks were particularly targeted in the 1980s. Linguistic and religious freedom was granted in 1989, but 300,000 Turks, or 40%, still left for Turkey – an option denied to Pomaks. The farming skills of the Turkish community have traditionally been important, but many Turks have been left landless by recent privatizations, causing new waves of emigration.

Roma suffer discrimination at all levels. It is thought that the number of Roma is much higher than officially recognized, since many disguise their ethnicity in an effort to avoid persecution. Other minorities include Russians, Armenians, and Vlachs.

Women have equal rights in theory, but society remains patriarchal, especially among Turks.

POPULATION AGE BREAKDOWN

Female
Age
Male
1.4%
80+
0.9%
10.5%
60–79
8.6%
13.5%
40–59
12.9%
13.7%
20–39
14%
11.9%
0–19
12.6%
% of population by age group

WORLD AFFAIRS

Joined UN in 1955

BSEC | CE | EAPC | CEFTA | OSCE

Although Bulgaria is not to be included in the 2004 expansion of the EU, it has been told that membership is likely in 2007. It has also applied to join NATO.

Bulgaria conscientiously adhered to UN sanctions against Yugoslavia, despite the costs of lost trade. Relations with Russia are no longer close, but are maintained carefully because of dependence on Russia for oil and gas. Relations with Turkey have greatly improved since the tensions of the final years of communist rule.

AID

Recipient

$346m (receipts)

Up 11% in 2001

IMF, World Bank, and EBRD loans are mainly intended for infrastructure improvements. Large-scale EU assistance toward reforms, in preparation for Bulgaria's eventual EU membership, is estimated at 2% of GDP. Humanitarian aid focuses mainly on medical provision and children's homes.

POLITICS

Multiparty elections

2001/2005

President Georgi Purvanov

AT THE LAST ELECTION

National Assembly 240 seats

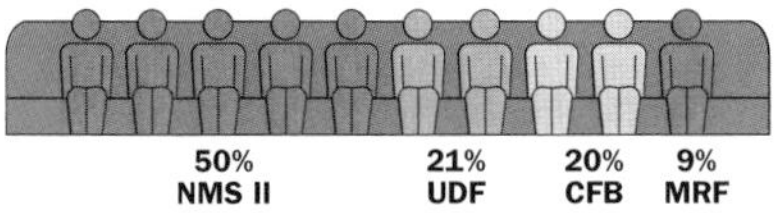
50% NMS II
21% UDF
20% CFB
9% MRF

NMS II = National Movement Simeon II
UDF = United Democratic Forces (led by the Union of Democratic Forces–**UDF**) **CFB** = Coalition for Bulgaria (led by the Bulgarian Socialist Party–**BSP**)
MRF = Movement for Rights and Freedoms

Bulgaria is a multiparty democracy.

PROFILE

Having moved falteringly to a pluralist democratic system after the fall of the communist Zhivkov regime in 1989, Bulgaria suffered during the 1990s from successive weak governments, each brought down by no-confidence votes.

The UDF, a broad anticommunist alliance, fell from office in 1992, and by the time of the 1994 general election the former communist BSP appeared to be firmly in the ascendant, winning an overall majority. The BSP government resisted political and economic change; the result was one of the slowest privatization programs in eastern Europe, with the old communist web of patronage still intact.

A new UDF government in 1997 launched free-market reforms backed by the IMF. Its considerable success, and reorientation of policy toward the goals of EU and NATO membership, allowed the UDF to approach the June 2001 elections with some confidence, despite a surge in support for a monarchist party launched by ex-king Simeon II (who had left Bulgaria as a small child in 1946). The poll, however, left the UDF with fewer than a quarter of the National Assembly seats, exactly half of which went to the NMS II.

Bulgarianizing his family name, Prime Minister Simeon Saxecoburggotski formed a coalition with the MRF (which traditionally represents the ethnic Turkish minority) and in 2002 secured cooperation from the BSP and the UDF. However, the government's popularity has declined as its promised "spiritual and economic revival" has been slow to unfold. Divisions within the ideologically vague NMS II and revitalized opposition from the BSP and UDF threaten the government's survival.

Ex-king Simeon II *(Saxecoburggotski) returned as prime minister in 2001.*

Georgi Purvanov, *of the BSP, elected president against expectations in 2001.*

CHRONOLOGY

Part of the Ottoman Empire from 1396, Bulgaria gained autonomy in 1878 and independence in 1908. Under King Ferdinand, it sided with Germany during World War I, and subsequently lost valuable territory to Greece and Serbia. Under King Boris, Bulgaria once again sided with Germany in World War II.

- **1943** Child king Simeon II accedes.
- **1944** Allies firebomb Sofia. Soviet army invades. Antifascist Fatherland Front coalition, including Agrarian Party and Bulgarian Communist Party (BCP), takes power in bloodless coup. Kimon Georgiev prime minister.
- **1946** September, referendum abolishes monarchy. Republic proclaimed. October, general election results in BCP majority.
- **1947** Prime Minister Georgi Dmitrov discredits Agrarian Party leader Nikola Petkov. Petkov arrested and sentenced to death. International recognition of Dmitrov government. Soviet-style constitution adopted; one-party state established. Country renamed People's Republic of Bulgaria. Nationalization of economy begins.
- **1949** Dmitrov dies, succeeded as prime minister by Vasil Kolarov.
- **1950** Kolarov dies. "Little Stalin" Vulko Chervenkov replaces him

B

CHRONOLOGY *continued*

and begins BCP purge and collectivization.

- **1953** Stalin dies; Chervenkov's power begins to wane.
- **1954** Chervenkov yields power to Todor Zhivkov. Zhivkov sets out to make Bulgaria an inseparable part of the Soviet system.
- **1955–1960** Zhivkov exonerates victims of Chervenkov's purges.
- **1965** Plot to overthrow Zhivkov discovered by Soviet agents.
- **1968** Bulgarian troops aid Soviet army in invasion of Czechoslovakia.
- **1971** New constitution. Zhivkov becomes president of State Council and resigns as premier.
- **1978** Purge of BCP: 30,000 members expelled.
- **1984** Turkish minority forced to take Slavic names.
- **1989** June–August, exodus of 300,000 Bulgarian Turks. November, Zhivkov ousted as BCP leader and head of state. Replaced by Petur Mladenov. Mass protest in Sofia for democratic reform. December, Union of Democratic Forces (UDF) formed.
- **1990** Economic collapse. Zhivkov arrested. BCP loses constitutional role as leading political party, changes name to Bulgarian Socialist Party (BSP). Elections: BSP victory. Parliament chooses Zhelyu Zhelev, UDF leader, as president. Country renamed Republic of Bulgaria; communist symbols removed from national flag.
- **1991** February, price controls abolished; steep price rises. July, new constitution adopted. October, UDF wins elections.
- **1992** Continued political and social unrest. October, UDF resigns after losing vote of confidence. December, Movement for Rights and Freedoms (MRF) forms government. Zhivkov convicted of corruption and human rights abuses.
- **1993** Ambitious privatization program begins.
- **1994** General elections return BSP to power.
- **1995** BSP leader, Zhan Videnov, heads coalition government.
- **1996** Financial crisis and collapse of lev. Presidential elections won by opposition UDF candidate, Peter Stoyanov.
- **1997** General election won by UDF, whose leader Ivan Kostov becomes prime minister.
- **2001** Despite economic upturn, voters turn to new party headed by ex-king, who, as Simeon Saxecoburggotski, becomes prime minister. November, BSP leader Georgi Purvanov elected president.

DEFENSE

Compulsory military service

$365m

Up 6% in 2001

BULGARIAN ARMED FORCES

1475 main battle tanks (1042 T-55, 433 T-72)	31,050 personnel
1 submarine, 1 frigate, and 23 patrol boats	4370 personnel
232 combat aircraft (Su-22, Su-25, MiG-21, MiG-23, MiG-29)	17,780 personnel
None	

Defense spending fell from 14% of GDP in 1985 to 2.8% in 2000. Plans to join NATO, announced in 1997 with the hope of joining in 2004, involved a major reorientation in defense thinking.

In late 1999 the government adopted "Plan 2004," which embodies a radical acceleration of its previous plans to restructure the armed forces. The new plan envisages downsizing from 75,000 to 45,000 personnel by 2004, and moving to an emphasis on rapid reaction capabilities. It was considered that this smaller but combat-ready force would be less costly to maintain in the long run than a larger force.

In 1999 the crisis in Kosovo prompted Bulgaria to make its airspace available to NATO.

ECONOMICS

Inflation 93% p.a. (1990–2001)

$13.2bn

1.695 leva (1.976)

SCORE CARD

World GNP Ranking	79th
GNP per Capita	$1650
Balance of Payments	-$889m
Inflation	7.4%
Unemployment	18%

EXPORTS

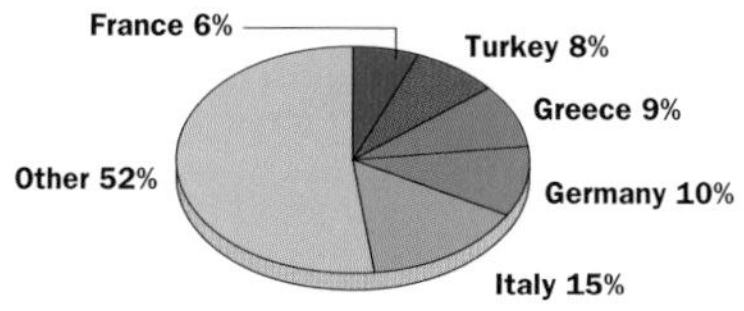
France 6%
Turkey 8%
Greece 9%
Germany 10%
Italy 15%
Other 52%

IMPORTS

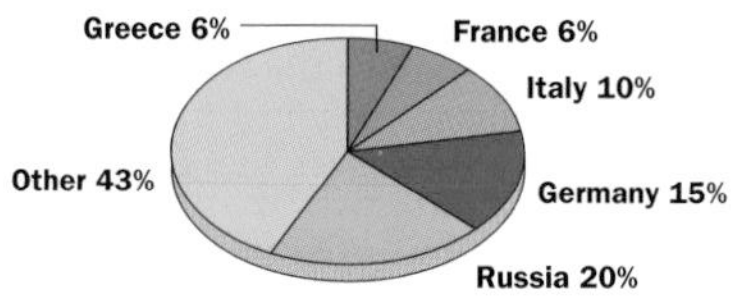
Greece 6%
France 6%
Italy 10%
Germany 15%
Russia 20%
Other 43%

ECONOMIC PERFORMANCE INDICATOR

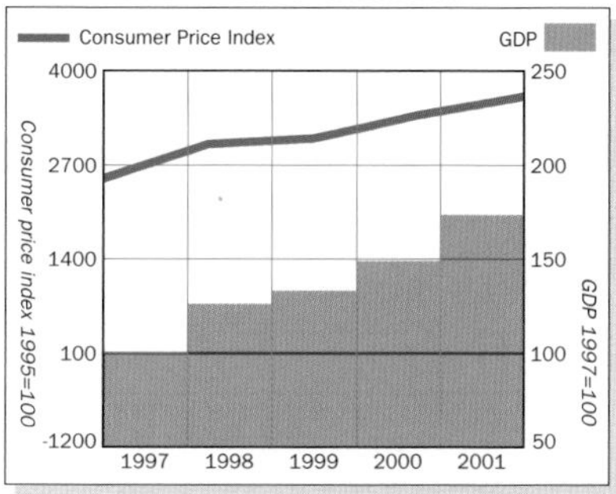
Consumer Price Index
GDP
4000
2700
1400
100
-1200
250
200
150
100
50
Consumer price index 1995=100
GDP 1997=100
1997
1998
1999
2000
2001

Strengths

Coal and natural gas. Good agricultural production, especially grapes for well-developed wine industry, and tobacco. Increased ties with EU. Strong expertise in computer software.

Weaknesses

Outdated infrastructure and equipment, and outstanding debt throughout industry.

Profile

Restructuring the economy is linked to privatization – a process delayed for political and technical reasons until the late 1990s. A financial crisis in 1996 triggered the collapse of the national currency, the lev. Foreign investment is still low, despite laws that since 1992 have allowed foreign firms to own companies outright. Trade has shifted toward the EU, while that with the former Soviet Union has fallen sharply. The UDF government which was returned in 1997 followed IMF advice and made free-market reforms, backed by foreign loans, successfully bringing inflation under control. These policies have been continued under Saxecoburggotski, with the stated aim of joining the EU, which confirmed Bulgaria as a market economy in 2002. Growth has been steady.

BULGARIA : MAJOR BUSINESSES

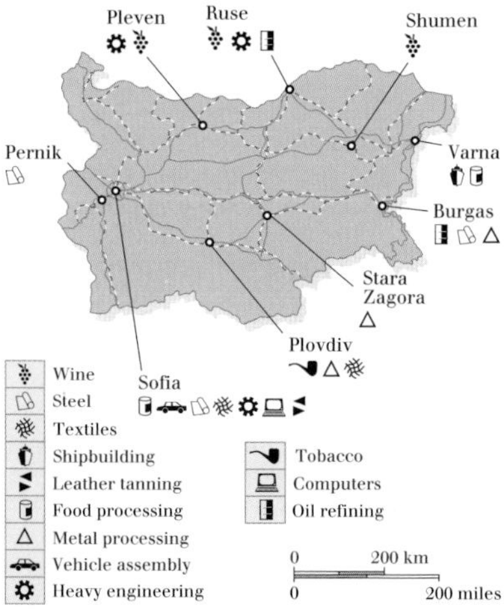
Pleven
Ruse
Shumen
Pernik
Varna
Burgas
Stara Zagora
Plovdiv
Sofia
Wine
Steel
Textiles
Shipbuilding
Leather tanning
Food processing
Metal processing
Vehicle assembly
Heavy engineering
Tobacco
Computers
Oil refining
0
200 km
0
200 miles

RESOURCES

Electric power 12.1m kW

10,652 tonnes

802 b/d (reserves 15m barrels)

2.42m sheep, 1.01m pigs, 18m chickens

Coal, iron, copper, lead, zinc, natural gas, oil, manganese

ELECTRICITY GENERATION

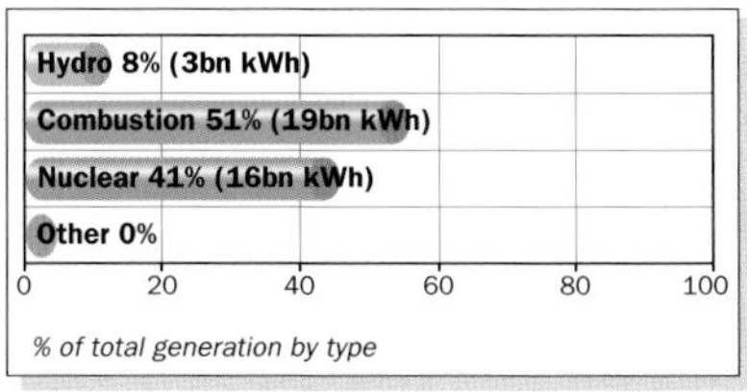
Hydro 8% (3bn kWh)
Combustion 51% (19bn kWh)
Nuclear 41% (16bn kWh)
Other 0%
0
20
40
60
80
100
% of total generation by type

Rising production of coal – Bulgaria's chief fossil fuel – and the increasing efficiency of the Kozloduy nuclear power plant have made Bulgaria a major regional energy exporter.

The EU is providing aid to upgrade two nuclear reactors at Kozloduy, in return for the closure of old reactors there which pose particular safety risks. A new plant north of Pleven is planned to open in 2008. Bulgaria's strategic position between the rest of Europe and oil-producing countries of the Middle East and Russia has raised the possibility of lucrative deals for oil and gas transit, particularly as it can offer routes which avoid the relatively precarious Bosphorus. Almost 10% of energy is provided by HEP, produced primarily by the Belmekan–Sestrimo facility in the Rila mountains.

BULGARIA : LAND USE

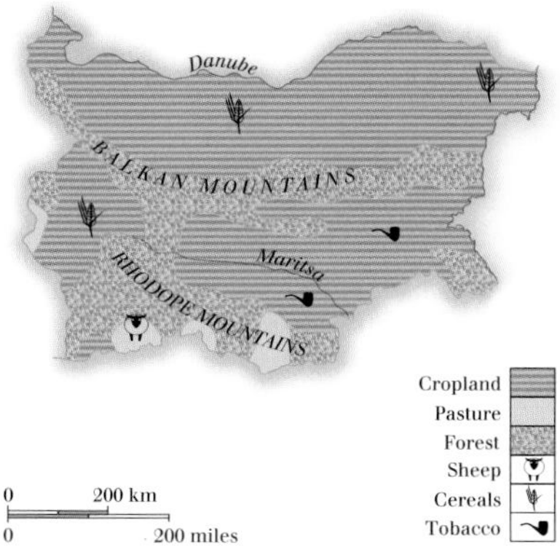
Danube
BALKAN MOUNTAINS
Maritsa
RHODOPE MOUNTAINS
Cropland
Pasture
Forest
Sheep
Cereals
Tobacco
0
200 km
0
200 miles

ENVIRONMENT

Sustainability rank: 71st

5% (2% partially protected)

5.9 tonnes per capita

ENVIRONMENTAL TREATIES

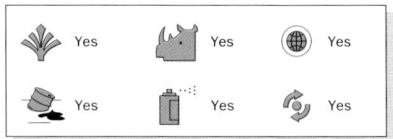

Yes Yes Yes

Yes Yes Yes

Environmental degradation led to the foundation in 1989 of the Ecoglasnost party. It circulated information on pollution and nuclear waste dump locations, and brought polluters to court. The Kozloduy nuclear complex, east of Lom, was restarted in 1995 despite safety concerns. It is in the process of closing its oldest reactors. Air pollution has diminished, but problems remain. NATO bombing of Serbian chemical and oil refineries on the Danube in 1999 led to downriver pollution in Bulgaria.

MEDIA

TV ownership high

Daily newspaper circulation 116 per 1000 people

PUBLISHING AND BROADCAST MEDIA

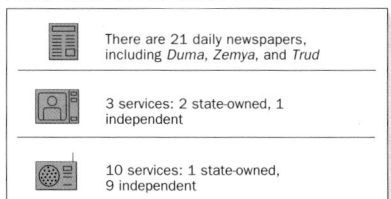

There are 21 daily newspapers, including *Duma*, *Zemya*, and *Trud*

3 services: 2 state-owned, 1 independent

10 services: 1 state-owned, 9 independent

State-run broadcasters retained an effective monopoly until the 2000 launch of a national commercial channel, bTV, owned by the international giant News Corporation. One group dominates the newspaper market, while political parties own much of the remainder. Internet providers are regulated. Journalists complain of the tough libel laws.

CRIME

No death penalty

9283 prisoners

Up 5% in 2000–2002

CRIME RATES

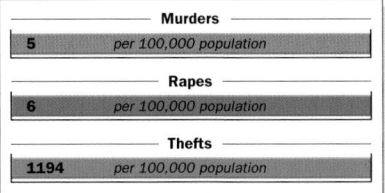

Murders
5 per 100,000 population

Rapes
6 per 100,000 population

Thefts
1194 per 100,000 population

In the 1990s Bulgaria became a key narcotics trafficking route to western Europe. Former security agents, party officials, and prestigious ex-athletes moved into protection rackets, counterfeiting, and similar activities. Violations of minority rights are a sensitive political issue.

EDUCATION

School leaving age: 15

99%

247,006 students

THE EDUCATION SYSTEM

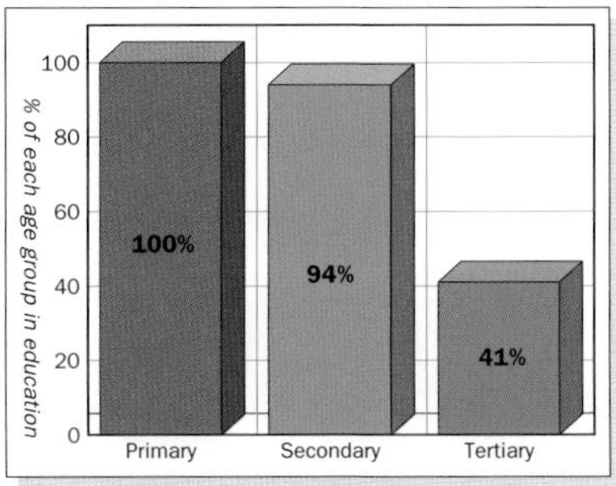
100
80
60
40
20
0
% of each age group in education
100%
94%
41%
Primary
Secondary
Tertiary

Education is free and compulsory between the ages of seven and 15. The system has been changed from a Soviet-inspired to a west European-style model. Over 10,000 teachers were dismissed in 2002 as part of a restructuring of the sector. Standards continue to be lowest in the rural and Turkish communities.

HEALTH

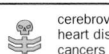

Welfare state health benefits

1 per 291 people

cerebrovascular and heart diseases, cancers

Hospital facilities have kept pace with population growth, but the 1997 economic crisis brought the health service to the brink of collapse. A new health policy was formulated in 1999. The plan of action emphasizes primary care. The Bulgarian Red Cross assists in health administration.

SPENDING

GDP/cap. decrease

CONSUMPTION AND SPENDING

234 per 1000 population

359 per 1000 population

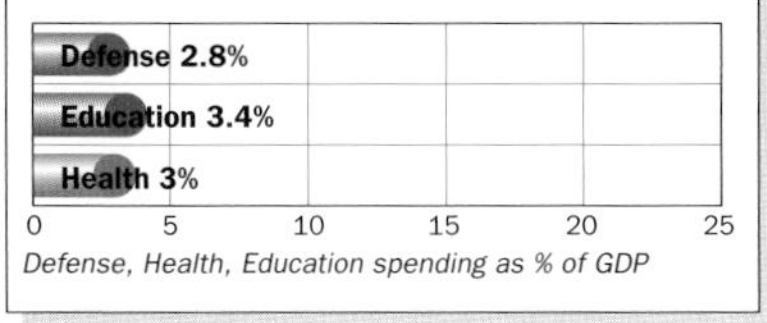
Defense 2.8%
Education 3.4%
Health 3%
0
5
10
15
20
25
Defense, Health, Education spending as % of GDP

Conquering the hyperinflation of 1995–1997 has remedied the most acute crisis, and associated hardship has been reduced. Turks and Roma remain the poorest people.

WORLD RANKING

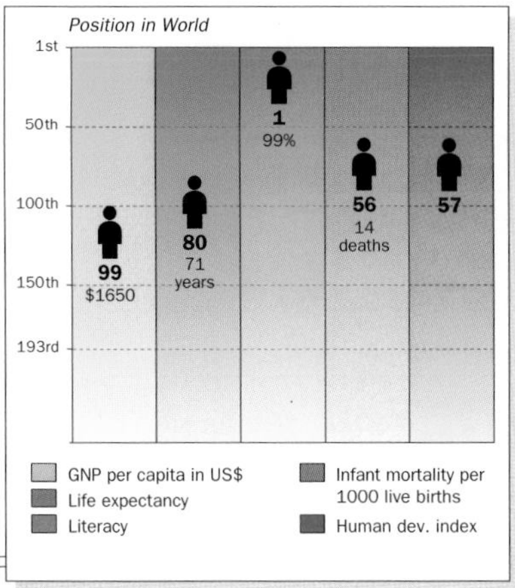
Position in World
1st
50th
100th
150th
193rd
99
$1650
80
71 years
1
99%
56
14 deaths
57
GNP per capita in US$
Life expectancy
Literacy
Infant mortality per 1000 live births
Human dev. index

B

BURKINA

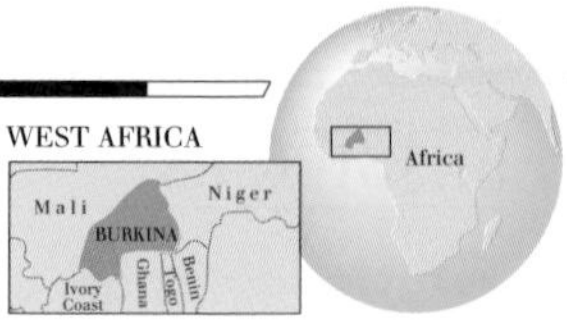
WEST AFRICA
Africa
Mali
Niger
BURKINA
Benin
Togo
Ghana
Ivory Coast

OFFICIAL NAME: Burkina Faso **CAPITAL:** Ouagadougou
POPULATION: 12.2 million **CURRENCY:** CFA franc **OFFICIAL LANGUAGE:** French

1960 | 1960 | Dec 11 | BF | 0 | +226 | .bf

LANDLOCKED IN WEST AFRICA, Burkina (formerly Upper Volta) gained independence from France in 1960. The majority of Burkina lies in the arid fringe of the Sahara known as the Sahel. Ruled by military dictators for much of its postindependence history, Burkina became a multiparty state in 1991. However, much power still rests with President Blaise Compaoré. Burkina's economy remains largely based on agriculture.

CLIMATE

Tropical/steppe

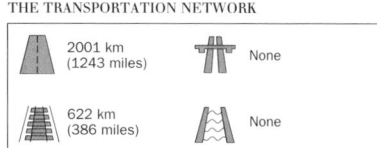

WEATHER CHART FOR OUAGADOUGOU

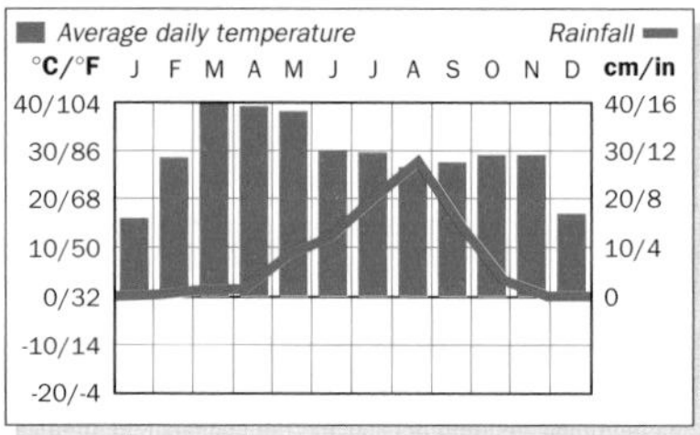
Average daily temperature
Rainfall
°C/°F J F M A M J J A S O N D cm/in
40/104
30/86
20/68
10/50
0/32
-10/14
-20/-4
40/16
30/12
20/8
10/4
0

The tropical climate comprises two seasons – unreliable rains from June to October, and a long dry season.

TRANSPORTATION

Drive on right

Ouagadougou International 208,055 passengers

Has no fleet

THE TRANSPORTATION NETWORK

2001 km (1243 miles)	None
622 km (386 miles)	None

The railroad to the port of Abidjan in Ivory Coast provides the main commercial route to the sea. Roads through Benin, Togo, and Ghana provide alternative access.

TOURISM

Visitors : Population 1:97

126,000 visitors

Down 42% in 2000

MAIN TOURIST ARRIVALS

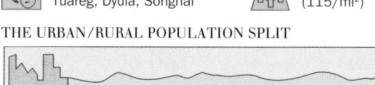

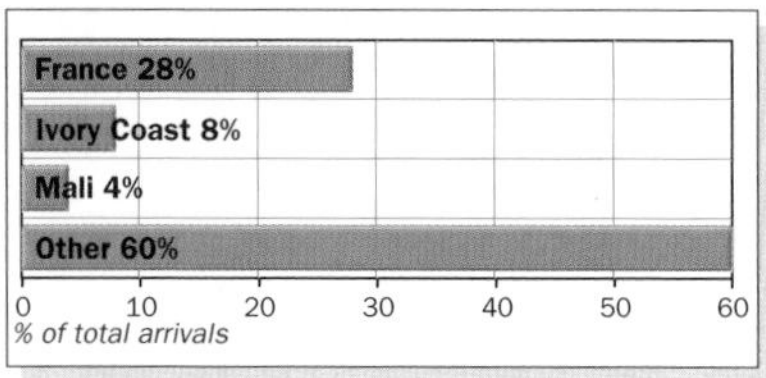
France 28%
Ivory Coast 8%
Mali 4%
Other 60%
0 10 20 30 40 50 60
% of total arrivals

Some potential exists for safari tourism, and the cities offer an attractive mix of colonial and African architecture. Big game hunting is allowed in some areas.

PEOPLE

Pop. density low

Mossi, Fulani, French, Tuareg, Dyula, Songhai

45/km² (115/mi²)

THE URBAN/RURAL POPULATION SPLIT

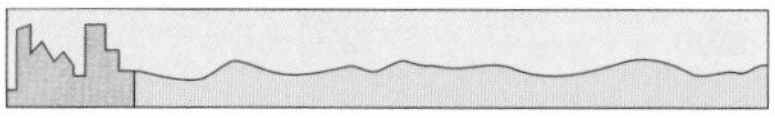
17%
83%

RELIGIOUS PERSUASION

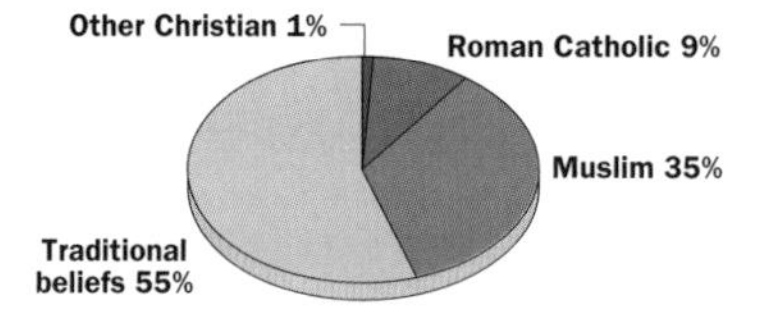
Other Christian 1%
Roman Catholic 9%
Muslim 35%
Traditional beliefs 55%

No ethnic group is dominant, although the Mossi people who live in the area of their old empire around Ouagadougou are the most numerous, making up over 40% of the population, and have always played an important political role. The first president, Maurice Yameogo, and the incumbent Blaise Compaoré are both Mossi. The communities in the west are the most ethnically mixed. Extreme poverty has led to a strong sense of egalitarianism within society, but has, along with population pressure, prompted mass emigration, mostly to Ghana and Ivory Coast. The 200,000 or so Burkinabes in Ivory Coast were caught up in the recent conflict there.

The extended family is important. The absence of women in public life belies their real power and social influence. However, most women are still denied access to education and the professions.

Camel plowing. Burkina's poor soils and frequent droughts lead many young men to emigrate seasonally in search of work.

POLITICS

Multiparty elections

L. House 2002/2007
U. House varies

President Blaise Compaoré

AT THE LAST ELECTION

National Assembly 111 seats

9% PDP
51% CDP
15% ADF–RDA
4% PAREN
21% Others

CDP = Congress for Democracy and Progress
ADF–RDA = Alliance for Democracy and Federation–African Democratic Rally **PDP** = Party for Democracy and Progress
PAREN = Party for National Renewal

House of Representatives 178 seats

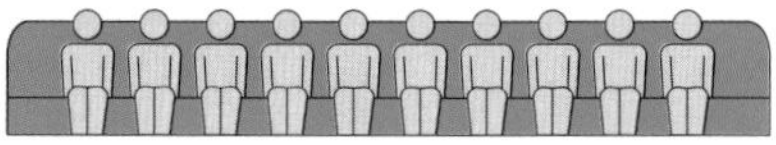

Members of the House of Representatives are appointed or indirectly elected on a nonparty basis by provincial councils and various communities

A multiparty democracy in theory, Burkina is dominated by former military dictator Blaise Compaoré, and the army remains influential behind the scenes. Compaoré has been in power since the assassination in 1987 of Capt. Thomas Sankara, his former superior. Several of Compaoré's close military colleagues have been murdered. His grip on power in Burkina appears to be solid, and he was reelected president in 1998 with almost 90% of the vote.

The CDP and the government came under unexpected pressure in 1998 and 1999 after the assassination of a popular newspaper editor, Norbert Zongo, in which leading establishment figures were implicated. Most opposition leaders are still living in exile, but opposition parties made unexpected gains in the 2002 polls.

WORLD AFFAIRS

Joined UN in 1960

CILSS | ECOWAS | AU | OIC | FZ

Burkina's landlocked position means that good relations with countries to the south are a major concern. The illegal trade in diamonds from war-torn Sierra Leone continued in 2000–2003, despite the threat of US sanctions.

AID

Recipient

$389m (receipts)

Up 16% in 2001

External aid, mostly from the World Bank and France, is important to the economy. The large number of NGOs has caused organizational problems; there is often difficulty in finding suitable projects for all the prospective donors.

BURKINA

Total Area : 274 200 sq. km
(105 869 sq. miles)

POPULATION

- over 100 000
- over 50 000
- over 10 000
- under 10 000

LAND HEIGHT

- 500m/1640ft
- 200m/656ft
- Sea Level

N

0 100 km
0 100 miles

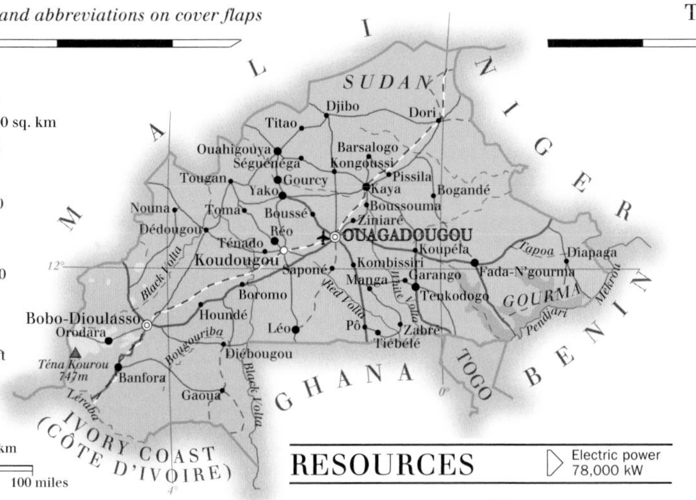
MALI
NIGER
SUDAN
Djibo
Dori
Titao
Ouahigouya
Séguénéga
Barsalogo
Kongoussi
Tougan
Gourcy
Yako
Pissila
Bogandé
Kaya
Boussouma
Ziniaré
Nouna
Dédougou
Toma
Boussé
Réo
Fénado
OUAGADOUGOU
Koupéla
Koudougou
Saponé
Kombissiri
Manga
Garango
Tenkodogo
Fada-N'gourma
Diapaga
Tapoa
GOURMA
Boromo
Houndé
Léo
Pô
Zabré
Tiébélé
Bobo-Dioulasso
Orodara
Téna Kourou 747m
Banfora
Gaoua
Diébougou
Black Volta
Red Volta
White Volta
Bougouriba
Pendjari
Mékrou
Léraba
GHANA
TOGO
BENIN
IVORY COAST (CÔTE D'IVOIRE)
12°
4°
0°

DEFENSE

No compulsory military service

$36m

No change in 2001

The main role of the 5800-strong army has been maintaining internal security. Burkina is reliant on France for most equipment and training.

ECONOMICS

Inflation 4.5% p.a. (1990–2001)

$2.53bn

571.2 CFA francs (664.2)

SCORE CARD

- ❑ WORLD GNP RANKING.........................133rd
- ❑ GNP PER CAPITA $220
- ❑ BALANCE OF PAYMENTS......................–$338m
- ❑ INFLATION 4.9%
- ❑ UNEMPLOYMENT.....................................1%

STRENGTHS

Remittances from plantation workers in Ghana and the Ivory Coast. Strongly improved economic management. Low debt burden. Ability to attract foreign aid. Cotton. Potential for exploitation of mineral resources

WEAKNESSES

Landlocked. Poor soil quality. Food crop fluctuations. Overseas remittances have dropped. Access to Abidjan port affected by instability in Ivory Coast. Drought and desertification in the Sahel.

EXPORTS

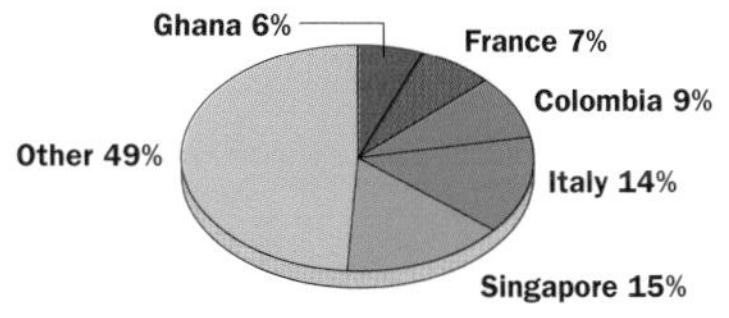
Ghana 6%
France 7%
Colombia 9%
Other 49%
Italy 14%
Singapore 15%

IMPORTS

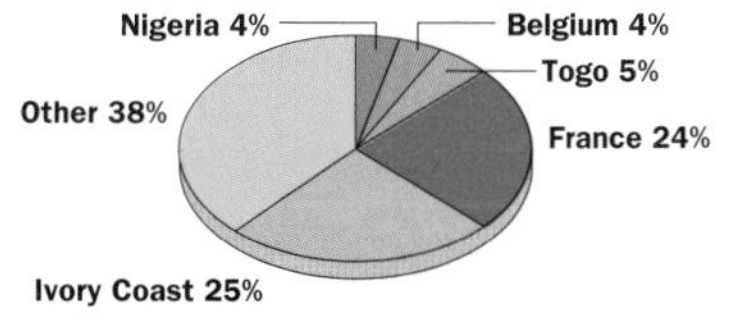
Nigeria 4%
Belgium 4%
Togo 5%
Other 38%
France 24%
Ivory Coast 25%

RESOURCES

Electric power 78,000 kW

8505 tonnes

Not an oil producer and has no refineries

8.7m goats, 6.8m sheep, 4.8m cattle, 23m chickens

Gold, antimony, marble, manganese, silver, zinc

Burkina has considerable mineral wealth. Falling world prices led to the closure in 1999 of the largest gold mine. It is hoped that the construction of large hydroelectric dams will reduce dependence on energy from combustion.

ENVIRONMENT

Sustainability rank: 101st

10% (8% partially protected)

0.09 tonnes per capita

Like other countries on the southern rim of the Sahara, desertification is the major ecological issue. The rate of tree cutting for fuel is on the increase.

MEDIA

TV ownership medium

Daily newspaper circulation 1 per 1000 people

PUBLISHING AND BROADCAST MEDIA

There are 6 daily newspapers, including *Sidwaya, Le Pays, Le Journal de Soir*, and *L'Observateur Paalga*

4 services: 1 state-owned, 3 independent

1 state-owned service, 46 independent stations

There are a number of small independent newspapers funded by opposition groups. A code of practice was introduced in 1999.

CRIME

Death penalty not used in practice

2800 prisoners

Crime is rising

Crime levels have traditionally been low. However, the urbanization of society and the increase in political violence have seen levels increase.

EDUCATION

School leaving age: 16

25%

8911 students

Education is based on the French system. Recently, practical subjects have received more emphasis.

CHRONOLOGY

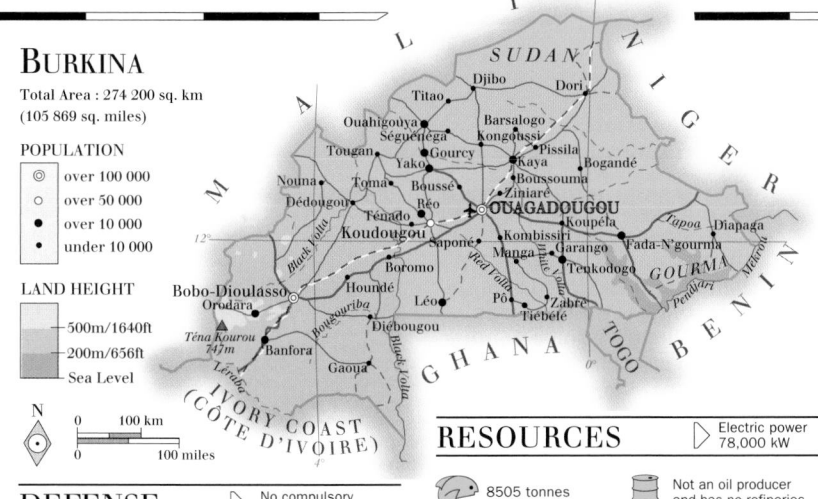

Ruled by Mossi kings from the 16th century, Upper Volta, a province of French West Africa in the late 19th century, gained independence in 1960.

- ❑ **1980** Ousting of military ruler; Col. Saye Zerbo becomes president.
- ❑ **1982** Capt. Thomas Sankara takes power. People's Salvation Council (PSC) begins radical reforms.
- ❑ **1984** Renamed Burkina.
- ❑ **1987** Sankara assassinated, Capt. Blaise Compaoré takes power.
- ❑ **1991** New constitution. Compaoré elected president.
- ❑ **1999** Biggest gold mine closed. General strike.
- ❑ **2001** HIV infection rate second-highest in west Africa.
- ❑ **2001–2003** Meningitis kills thousands.
- ❑ **2002 CDP narrow election victory.**

HEALTH

No welfare state health benefits

1 per 33,333 people

Malaria, diarrheal and respiratory diseases

Health spending focuses on primary health care and vaccination. More than 6% of adults were HIV positive in 2001.

SPENDING

GDP/cap. increase

CONSUMPTION AND SPENDING

4 per 1000 population

5 per 1000 population

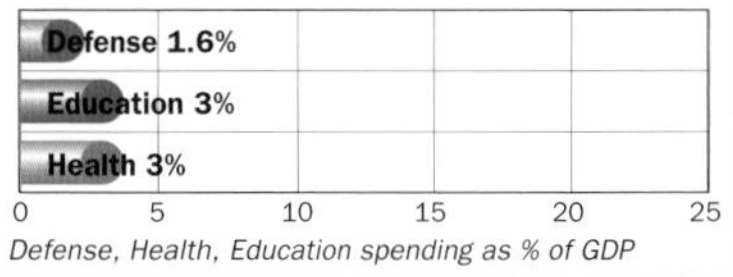
Defense 1.6%
Education 3%
Health 3%
0
5
10
15
20
25

Defense, Health, Education spending as % of GDP

Burkina is a country of extreme, almost universal, poverty. Displays of wealth are rare and ownership of high-tech items is limited to a small elite.

WORLD RANKING

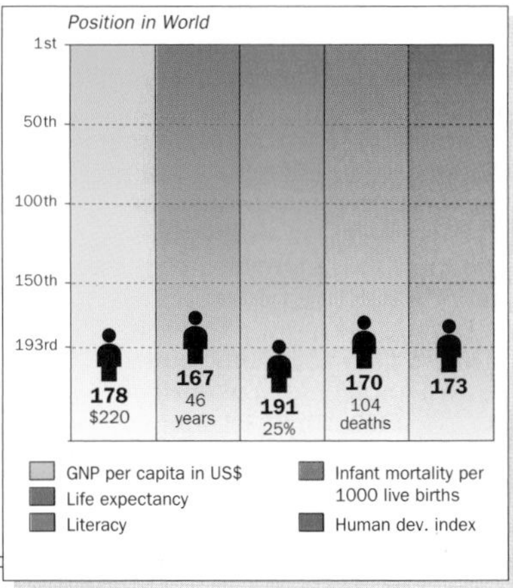
Position in World
1st
50th
100th
150th
193rd
178
$220
167
46 years
191
25%
170
104 deaths
173
GNP per capita in US$
Life expectancy
Literacy
Infant mortality per 1000 live births
Human dev. index

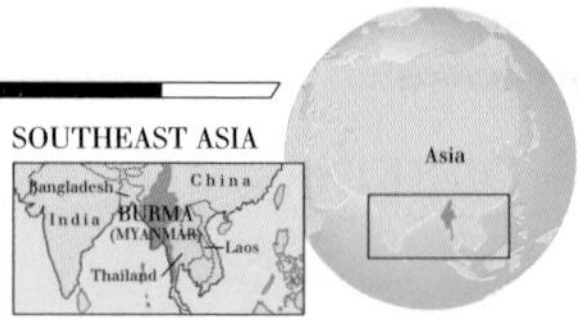
SOUTHEAST ASIA
Bangladesh
China
India
BURMA (MYANMAR)
Laos
Thailand
Asia

BURMA (MYANMAR)

OFFICIAL NAME: Union of Myanmar **CAPITAL:** Rangoon (Yangon)
POPULATION: 49 million **CURRENCY:** Kyat **OFFICIAL LANGUAGE:** Burmese (Myanmar)

1948 | 1948 | Jan 4 | BUR | +6.5 | +95 | .mm

A PREDOMINANTLY BUDDHIST country on the northeastern shores of the Indian Ocean, Burma is mountainous in the north and east, while the fertile Irrawaddy basin occupies most of the country. Rocked by ethnic conflict ever since gaining independence from the UK in 1948, Burma has been ruled by repressive military regimes since 1962. The National League for Democracy (NLD) gained a majority in free elections in 1990, but has been prevented from taking power by the military. Rich in natural resources, which include fisheries and teak forests, Burma remains a mostly agricultural economy.

***Transporting timber** on the Irrawaddy River near Mandalay. Burma once had the world's largest reserves of teak.*

CLIMATE

Tropical/mountain

WEATHER CHART FOR RANGOON

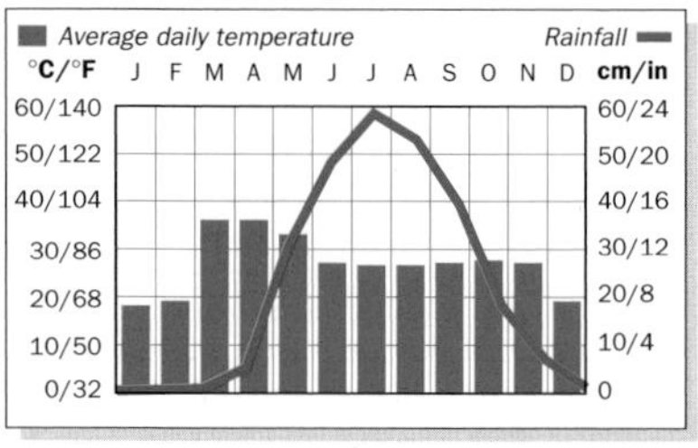
Average daily temperature
Rainfall
°C/°F J F M A M J J A S O N D cm/in
60/140 50/122 40/104 30/86 20/68 10/50 0/32
60/24 50/20 40/16 30/12 20/8 10/4 0

There are three seasons: the wet season, when rainfall in the far south Tenasserim region and Irrawaddy delta can reach 500 cm (197 in); summer, when northern Burma experiences 50°C (122°F) and 100% humidity; and winter, when it is rarely cooler than 15°C (59°F) except in the northern mountains.

TRANSPORTATION

Drive on right

Mingaladon, Rangoon 580,000 passengers

124 ships 379,819 grt

THE TRANSPORTATION NETWORK

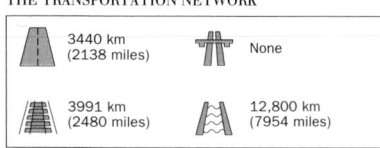

3440 km (2138 miles)

None

3991 km (2480 miles)

12,800 km (7954 miles)

Burma's main transportation corridors run north–south. Most traffic is concentrated between Rangoon and Mandalay. A daily express train runs between these two cities, though visitors are urged to take internal flights on the state-owned carriers. The Irrawaddy River and its tributaries also provide an important artery for travel.

Beyond the Irrawaddy basin transportation is limited and hazardous. The vast majority of roads remain unpaved, and access to neighboring countries is restricted. At certain points on the Chinese border, access is one-way only: out of China.

TOURISM

Visitors : Population 1:239

205,000 visitors

Down 1% in 2001

MAIN TOURIST ARRIVALS

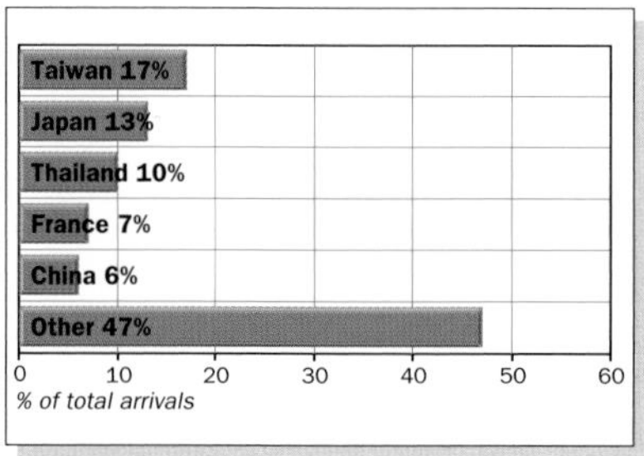
Taiwan 17%
Japan 13%
Thailand 10%
France 7%
China 6%
Other 47%
0 10 20 30 40 50 60
% of total arrivals

Since 1988 the military authorities have courted tourists for their economic value. The previous one-week restriction for visitors arriving to marvel at Burma's stunning Buddhist heritage was increased to 28 days. The state-run tourist agency is heavily promoted, while independent travelers are required to spend a minimum of $200 during their stay. However, whole provinces remain entirely off-limits, and elsewhere official guides are often required. Opposition groups wish to discourage people from traveling to Burma at all.

PEOPLE

Pop. density medium

Burmese, Karen, Shan, Chin, Kachin, Mon, Palaung, Wa

75/km² (193/mi²)

THE URBAN/RURAL POPULATION SPLIT

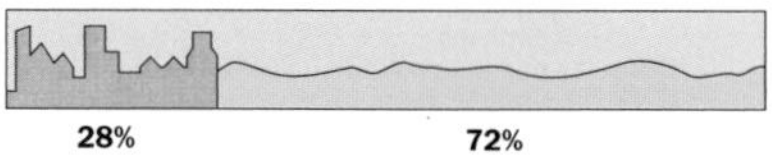
28%
72%

RELIGIOUS PERSUASION

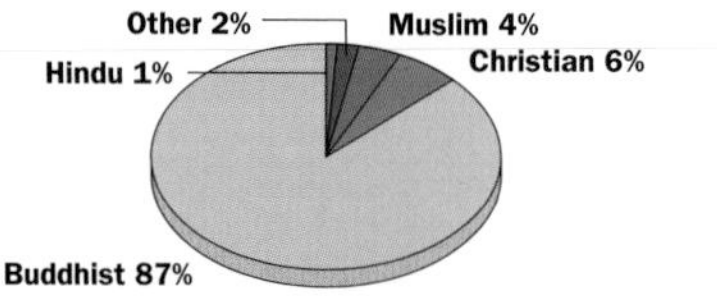
Other 2%
Muslim 4%
Hindu 1%
Christian 6%
Buddhist 87%

ETHNIC MAKEUP

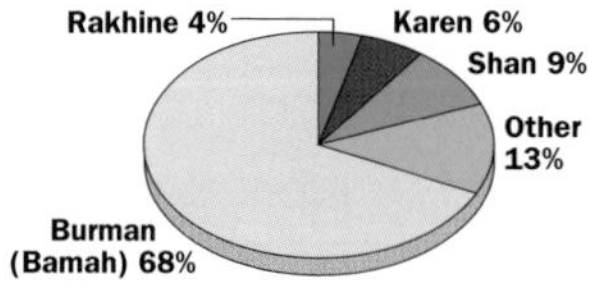
Rakhine 4%
Karen 6%
Shan 9%
Other 13%
Burman (Bamah) 68%

A savage history of ethnic repression at the hands of the Burman majority still plays a large part in the mistrust felt by the smaller minority communities. Each group maintains a distinct cultural identity. At independence the Chin, Kachin, Karen, Karenni, Mon, and Shan all unsuccessfully demanded their own state within a federation. Despite uniting against the military dictatorship in 1988, most factions had by 1996 signed peace agreements. Only the Shan and Karen remain militarily active to any significant degree, the former agreeing to a short-lived cease-fire in 2000. While the Burman claim racial purity, many of them are in fact of mixed blood or ethnically Chinese.

Accusations of forced labor lie at the heart of international criticism of the military regime, with ethnic minorities apparently at highest risk.

Domestic life in Burma is still based around the extended family. Women have a prominent role, and access to education. Many run or own businesses in their own right. However, top jobs in government are still held almost exclusively by men.

POPULATION AGE BREAKDOWN

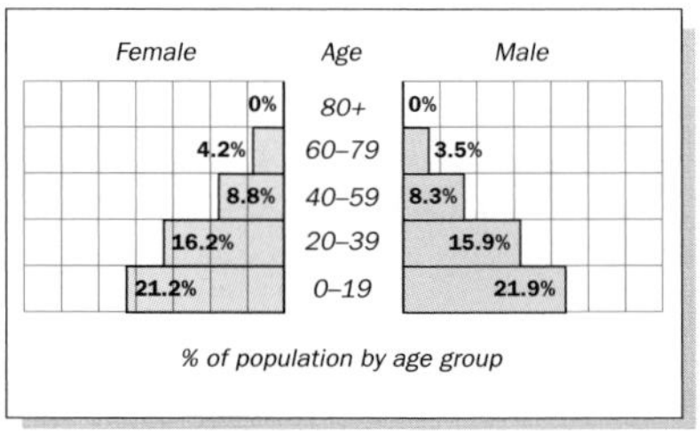
Female
Age
Male
0% 80+ 0%
4.2% 60–79 3.5%
8.8% 40–59 8.3%
16.2% 20–39 15.9%
21.2% 0–19 21.9%
% of population by age group

POLITICS

No legislative elections

1990/suspended

Chairman Than Shwe

AT THE LAST ELECTION

Constituent Assembly 485 seats

2% RDL
1% MNDF
1% NDP
81% NLD
5% SNLD
2% NUP
8% Others

NLD = National League for Democracy
SNLD = Shan National League for Democracy
RDL = Rakhine Democracy League
NUP = National Unity Party
MNDF = Mon National Democratic Front
NDP = National Democratic Party for Human Rights

A Constituent Assembly, responsible for the drafting of a new constitution and with no legislative power, was elected in 1990, but prevented from convening by the regime

Burma is ruled by the military-backed State Peace and Development Council (SPDC), under Gen. Than Shwe.

PROFILE

The military has ruled since 1962. Gen. Saw Maung seized power amid mass prodemocracy protests in 1988.

The regime has never recognized the NLD's 1990 electoral victory and has suppressed all democratic opposition. Recent moves toward negotiation have produced few tangible results.

Ethnic rebellion in outer regions degenerated into cross-border guerrilla activity after a concerted government offensive in 1996.

MAIN POLITICAL ISSUES

Restoring democracy

In a nod to international pressure and the popularity of the prodemocracy movement, the junta has talked openly of steering Burma toward "disciplined democracy." In reality there has been little progress toward ending the dictatorship. The opposition NLD is led by the charismatic Aung San Suu Kyi who has been intermittently under house arrest since 1990. Her latest detention, in 2003, followed violence in the north.

Aung San Suu Kyi, leader of the pro-democracy movement.

Gen. Than Shwe, leader of the military junta since 1992.

BURMA

Total Area : 678 500 sq. km (261 969 sq. miles)

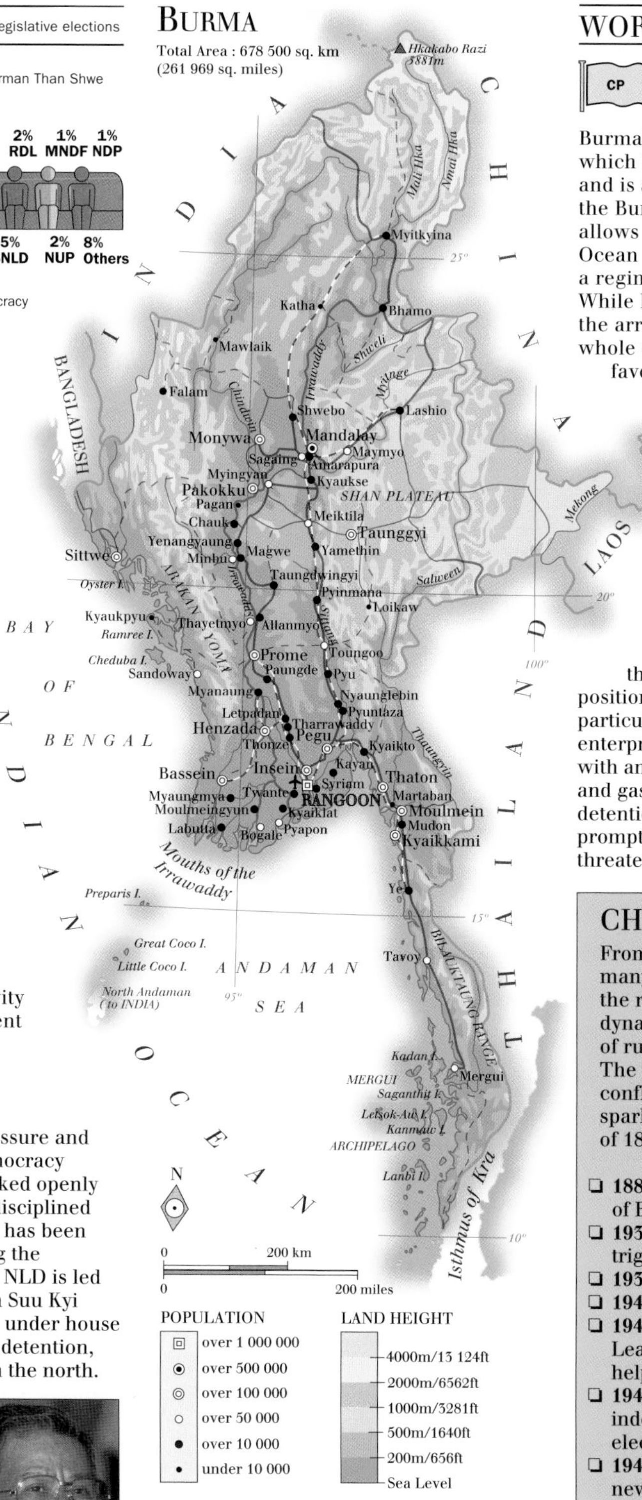
Hkakabo Razi 5881m
INDIA
CHINA
BANGLADESH
LAOS
THAILAND
BAY OF BENGAL
INDIAN OCEAN
ANDAMAN SEA
Myitkyina
Bhamo
Katha
Mawlaik
Falam
Shwebo
Lashio
Monywa
Mandalay
Sagaing
Maymyo
Amarapura
Kyaukse
Myingyan
Pakokku
Pagan
Chauk
SHAN PLATEAU
Meiktila
Taunggyi
Yenangyaung
Magwe
Minbu
Yamethin
Sittwe
Oyster I.
Taungdwingyi
Pyinmana
Loikaw
Kyaukpyu
Ramree I.
Thayetmyo
Allanmyo
Cheduba I.
Sandoway
Prome
Paungde
Toungoo
Pyu
Myanaung
Nyaunglebin
Pyuntaza
Letpadan
Henzada
Tharrawaddy
Pegu
Thonze
Kyaikto
Bassein
Insein
Kayan
Thaton
Myaungmya
Twante
Syriam
RANGOON
Martaban
Moulmeingyun
Kyaiklat
Moulmein
Mudon
Labutta
Bogale
Pyapon
Kyaikkami
Mouths of the Irrawaddy
Preparis I.
Ye
Great Coco I.
Little Coco I.
North Andaman (to INDIA)
Tavoy
Kadan I.
MERGUI ARCHIPELAGO
Mergui
Saganthit I.
Letsok-Aw I.
Kanmaw I.
Lanbi I.
Isthmus of Kra
BILAUKTAUNG RANGE
ARAKAN YOMA
Irrawaddy
Chindwin
Shweli
Myitnge
Mali Hka
Nmai Hka
Mekong
Salween
Thaungyin
Sittang
25°
20°
15°
10°
95°
100°
N
0 200 km
0 200 miles
POPULATION
over 1 000 000
over 500 000
over 100 000
over 50 000
over 10 000
under 10 000
LAND HEIGHT
4000m/13 124ft
2000m/6562ft
1000m/3281ft
500m/1640ft
200m/656ft
Sea Level

Forced labor

The practice of using slave labor in rural areas was officially banned in 2000. However, many groups, including the International Labor Organization, insist that the military authorities still regularly make use of slave laborers.

WORLD AFFAIRS

Joined UN in 1948

CP | IAEA | ASEAN | NAM | WTO

B

Burma's key relationship is with China, which backs the SPDC military regime and is a major supplier of weapons to the Burmese army. The relationship allows China access to the Indian Ocean and gives it influence over a regime dependent on its support. While Burma's neighbors fear that the arrangement could destabilize the whole of the Asia–Pacific region, many favor a policy of "constructive engagement" with the SPDC. In 1997, Burma was admitted to ASEAN, despite continuing concerns about its human rights record.

The EU and Western members of the UN have strongly condemned the human rights violations in Burma. In practice, however, the West has held an ambivalent position. Economic ties have expanded, particularly between SPDC-owned state enterprises and Western multinationals with an interest in Burmese offshore oil and gas drilling sectors. However, the detention of Aung San Suu Kyi in 2003 prompted most Western countries to threaten economic sanctions.

CHRONOLOGY

From the 11th century, Burma's many ethnic groups came under the rule of three Tibeto-Burman dynasties, interspersed with periods of rule by the Mongols and the Mon. The Third Dynasty came into conflict with the British in India, sparking the Anglo-Burmese wars of 1824, 1852, and 1885.

- **1886** Burma becomes a province of British India.
- **1930–1931** Economic depression triggers unrest.
- **1937** Separation from India.
- **1942** Japan invades.
- **1945** Antifascist People's Freedom League (AFPFL), led by Aung San, helps Allies reoccupy country.
- **1947** UK agrees to Burmese independence. Aung San wins elections, but is assassinated.
- **1948** Independence under new prime minister, U Nu, who initiates socialist policies. Revolts by ethnic separatists, notably Karen liberation struggle.
- **1958** Ruling AFPFL splits into two. Shan liberation struggle begins.
- **1960** U Nu's faction wins elections.
- **1961** Kachin rebellion begins.

B

CHRONOLOGY *continued*

- **1962** Gen. Ne Win stages military coup. "New Order" policy of "Buddhist Socialism" deepens international isolation. Mining and other industries nationalized. Free trade prohibited.
- **1964** Socialist Program Party declared sole legal party.
- **1976** Social unrest. Attempted military coup. Ethnic liberation groups gain control of 40% of country.
- **1982** Nonindigenous people barred from public office.
- **1988** Thousands die in student riots. Ne Win resigns. Martial law. Aung San Suu Kyi, daughter of Aung San, and others form NLD. Gen. Saw Maung leads military coup. State Law and Order Restoration Council (SLORC) takes power. Ethnic resistance groups form Democratic Alliance of Burma.
- **1989** Army arrests NLD leaders and steps up antirebel activity. Officially renamed Union of Myanmar.
- **1990** Elections permitted. NLD wins landslide. SLORC remains in power, however. More NLD leaders arrested.
- **1991** Aung San Suu Kyi awarded Nobel Peace Prize.
- **1992** Gen. Than Shwe takes over as SLORC leader.
- **1996** Student agitation over renewed repression of NLD.
- **1997** Ruling SLORC renamed State Peace and Development Council (SPDC). Burma joins ASEAN. US imposes sanctions and bans further investment.
- **1998** NLD sets deadline for convening parliament; junta refuses.
- **1999** Aung San Suu Kyi rejects conditions set by SPDC for visiting the UK to see her husband, Michael Aris, who dies of cancer.
- **2000** Negotiations between junta and NLD begin.
- **2003** Aung San Suu Kyi detained once more, after a year's freedom.

AID

Recipient

$127m (receipts) — Up 19% in 2001

Moves in 2000 to begin talks with the democratic opposition were welcomed by the UN, but were not enough to lift the sanctions on aid imposed in 1988. Some humanitarian assistance is provided through agencies such as WHO. Japan led the way in rewarding Burma's conciliatory gestures and became the largest single donor, but in 2003 joined countries suspending aid when Aung San Suu Kyi was rearrested.

DEFENSE

No compulsory military service

$1.09bn — Up 7% in 2001

BURMESE ARMED FORCES

100 main battle tanks (PRC Type-69II)	325,000 personnel
73 patrol boats	10,000 personnel
113 combat aircraft (50 F-7, 10 FT-7, 22 A-5M)	9000 personnel
None	

The military authorities have steadily increased the country's military power, doubling the size of the army and obtaining modern weapons and military technology from around the world, primarily from China, which since 1989 has delivered arms worth over $1 billion to Burma, including tanks and jet fighters.

Burma's growing military capability is used mainly to control internal dissent, and the army has suppressed most ethnic insurgent campaigns by utilizing its military superiority and cutting numerous deals with rebel leaders. The remaining militant groups are now combated in cooperation with neighboring states. The army is accused of human rights abuses and of forcibly recruiting underage soldiers.

ECONOMICS

Inflation 25% p.a. (1990–2001)

$46bn — 6.201 kyats (6.514)

SCORE CARD

World GNP Ranking	52nd
GNP per Capita	$1000
Balance of Payments	–$218m
Inflation	21.1%
Unemployment	7%

EXPORTS

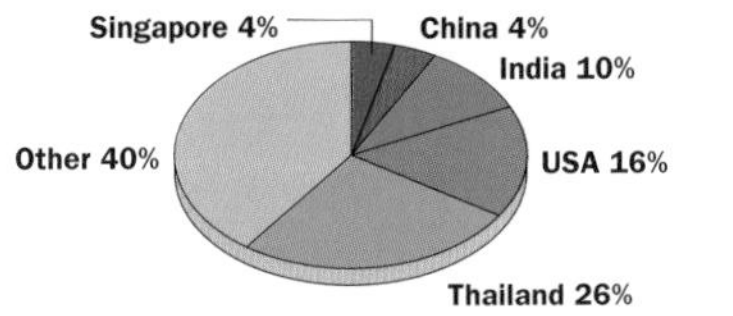
Singapore 4%
China 4%
India 10%
Other 40%
USA 16%
Thailand 26%

IMPORTS

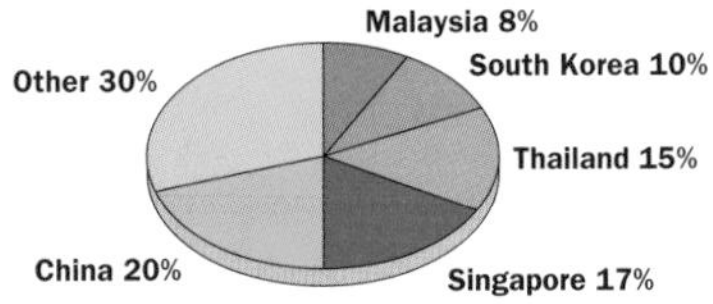
Malaysia 8%
Other 30%
South Korea 10%
Thailand 15%
China 20%
Singapore 17%

ECONOMIC PERFORMANCE INDICATOR

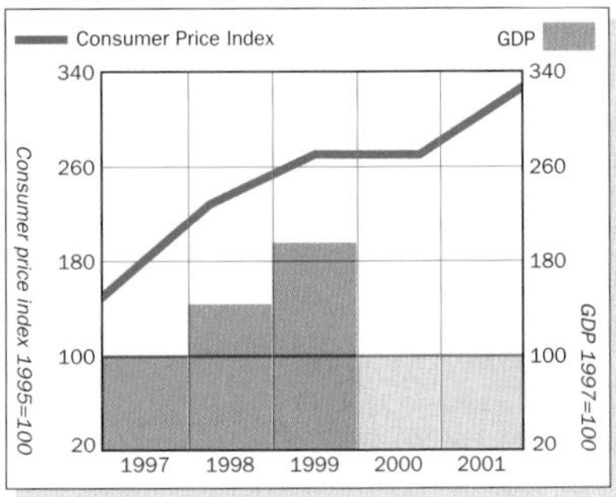
Consumer Price Index
GDP
340
260
180
100
20
1997
1998
1999
2000
2001
Consumer price index 1995=100
GDP 1997=100

Since 1989, the SPDC's open-door market-economy policy has brought a flood of foreign investment in oil and gas (by Western companies), and in forestry, tourism, and mining (by Asian companies). The resulting boom in trade with China has turned less developed Upper Burma into a thriving business center. A narcotics-eradication program has been initiated in the northeastern border states, which account for about 60% of the world's heroin, by encouraging farmers to grow food crops instead of poppies. Few plans exist for the manufacturing sector, however, and dependence on imports continues.

Strengths

Very rich in natural resources: fertile soil, rich fisheries, timber including diminishing teak reserves, gems, offshore natural gas, and oil.

Weaknesses

Shortage of skilled workforce. Huge external debt. Rudimentary financial systems and institutions. Nationwide black market. Dependence on imported manufactures. Economic sanctions.

Profile

Burma's economy is agriculture-based and functions mainly on a cash and barter system. Its key industries are controlled by military-run state enterprises. Every aspect of economic life is permeated by a black market, where prices are rocketing – a reaction to official price controls.

BURMA : MAJOR BUSINESSES

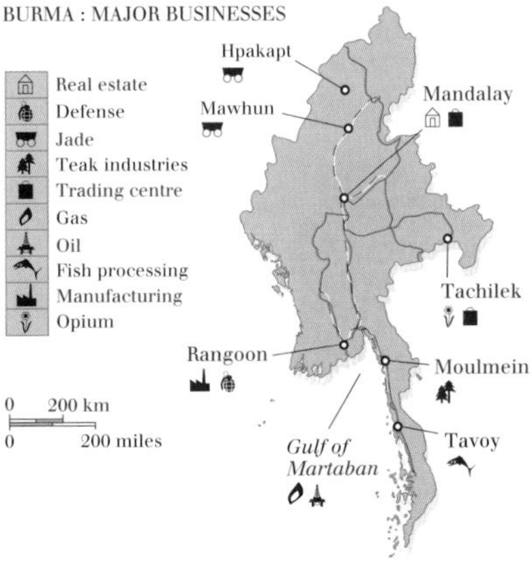
Real estate
Defense
Jade
Teak industries
Trading centre
Gas
Oil
Fish processing
Manufacturing
Opium
Hpakapt
Mawhun
Mandalay
Tachilek
Rangoon
Moulmein
Tavoy
Gulf of Martaban
0 200 km
0 200 miles

RESOURCES

Electric power 1.5m kW

1.17m tonnes

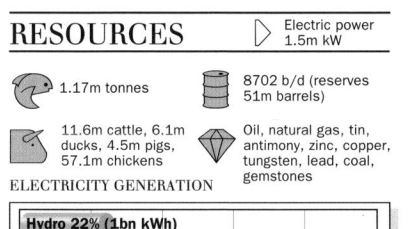

8702 b/d (reserves 51m barrels)

11.6m cattle, 6.1m ducks, 4.5m pigs, 57.1m chickens

Oil, natural gas, tin, antimony, zinc, copper, tungsten, lead, coal, gemstones

ELECTRICITY GENERATION

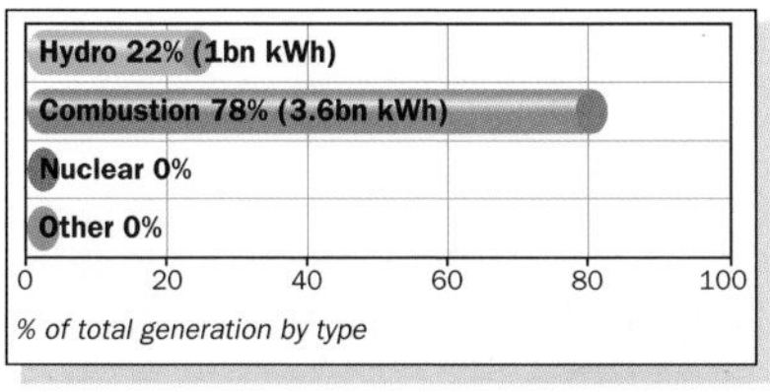
Hydro 22% (1bn kWh)
Combustion 78% (3.6bn kWh)
Nuclear 0%
Other 0%
0
20
40
60
80
100
% of total generation by type

Burma is one of the world's largest teak exporters. It is also a producer of pearls, rubies, and other gems. Crude oil is produced from onshore wells while natural gas is mainly found offshore. Extraction is mostly funded by foreign investors.

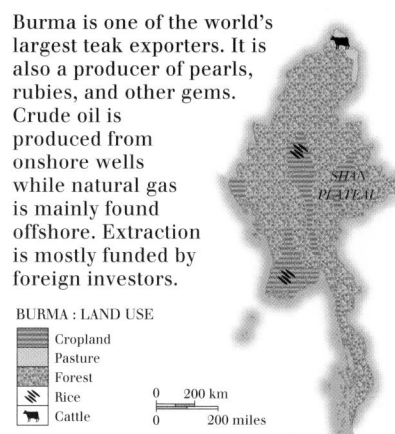

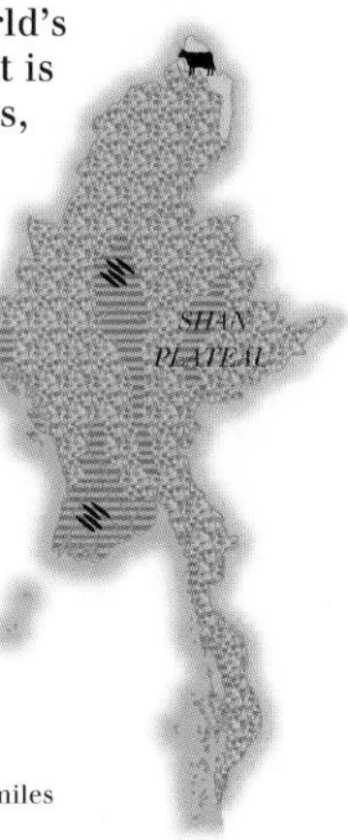
SHAN PLATEAU
BURMA : LAND USE
Cropland
Pasture
Forest
Rice
Cattle
0
200 km
0
200 miles

ENVIRONMENT

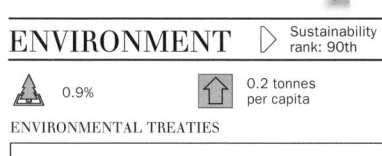

Sustainability rank: 90th

0.9%

0.2 tonnes per capita

ENVIRONMENTAL TREATIES

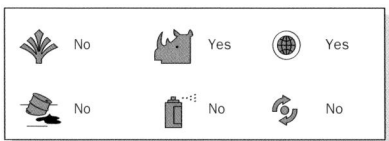

No Yes Yes

No No No

Deforestation is a major problem, and it has increased since the 1988 coup. Chinese companies have been given unrestricted logging concessions.

MEDIA

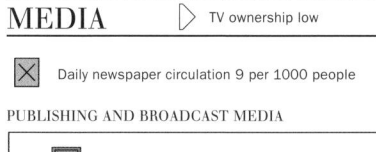

TV ownership low

Daily newspaper circulation 9 per 1000 people

PUBLISHING AND BROADCAST MEDIA

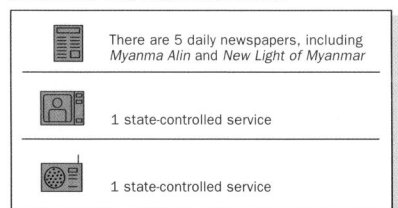

There are 5 daily newspapers, including *Myanma Alin* and *New Light of Myanmar*

1 state-controlled service

1 state-controlled service

Political dissent of any kind is a criminal offense. An underground prodemocracy press produces antigovernment material.

CRIME

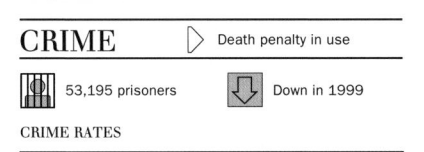

Death penalty in use

53,195 prisoners

Down in 1999

CRIME RATES

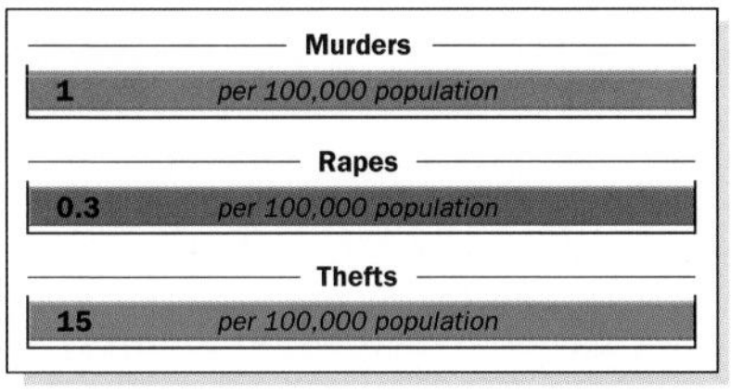
Murders
1 per 100,000 population
Rapes
0.3 per 100,000 population
Thefts
15 per 100,000 population

Even compared with similar totalitarian regimes, levels of bribery, corruption, embezzlement, and black marketeering are high. The state is guilty of illegal activity. The UN reports regularly on human rights abuses against civilians, and the murder of innocent civilians including children, women, Buddhist monks, students, minorities, and political dissidents.

There is a nominal civilian judicial system in Burma, but in practice all judges and lawyers are appointed by the junta and all legal functions are executed by the SPDC. The most common charge is that of sedition against the state or the army under the 1975 "Law to Protect the State from Destructionists." Among the SPDC's frequent arbitrary "notices" is Order 2/88, prohibiting assemblies of more than five persons. Most detainees have no legal rights of representation and are either jailed, used as forced labor, or put under house arrest without public trial. Amnesty International is banned.

EDUCATION

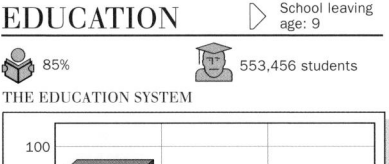

School leaving age: 9

85%

553,456 students

THE EDUCATION SYSTEM

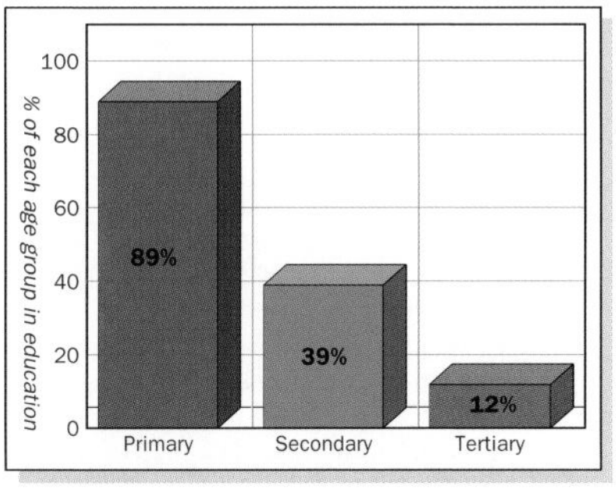
100
80
60
40
20
0
% of each age group in education
89%
39%
12%
Primary
Secondary
Tertiary

The education system offers 11 years of schooling; the first five are compulsory. A shortage of teachers, many of whom have left or are in jail, has disrupted education. Ethnic-language schools are discouraged. All but two universities were closed in the late 1990s by the regime, but quietly reopened in 2000. The NLD has criticized the shortened and "sanitized" courses on offer.

HEALTH

Welfare state health benefits

1 per 3333 people

Malaria, fevers, heart and diarrheal diseases

Health services are well developed and staff well trained, but provision is not comprehensive. Leprosy has a high prevalence in Burma, though programs to target the disease have helped bring the rate down dramatically since the 1970s. It still has the third-highest rate of infection in Asia. The growing number of AIDS cases is largely due to migrant prostitution across the Thai–Burmese border, putting an additional strain on health facilities.

SPENDING

GDP/cap. increase

CONSUMPTION AND SPENDING

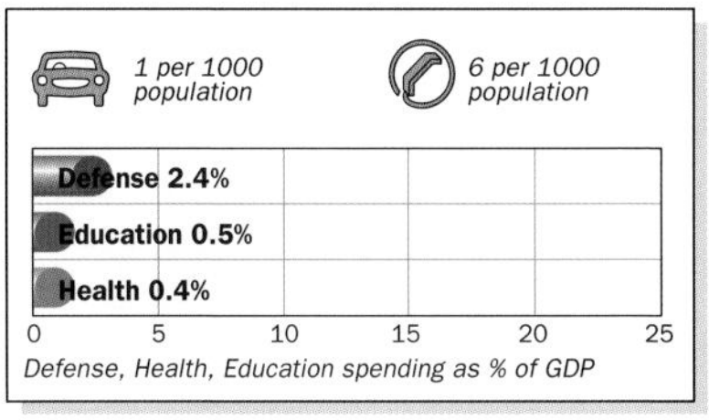
1 per 1000 population
6 per 1000 population
Defense 2.4%
Education 0.5%
Health 0.4%
0
5
10
15
20
25
Defense, Health, Education spending as % of GDP

The state monopoly of the production and distribution of goods by rationing under Gen. Ne Win's administration led to an increase in corruption and the rise of a nationwide black market, with huge disparities between official and unofficial prices. Only the military elite and their supporters could afford to live well. The situation has not changed significantly since 1988. Giant military enterprises grouped under a Defense Services holding company now reap wealth and distribute privileges for a minority. Nevertheless, traditional social and economic mobility still exists. Climbing the socioeconomic ladder is mainly a matter of loyalty to the military. Dissidents forced out of their jobs and hill tribes form the poorest groups. Officially, 23% of the population live in poverty.

WORLD RANKING

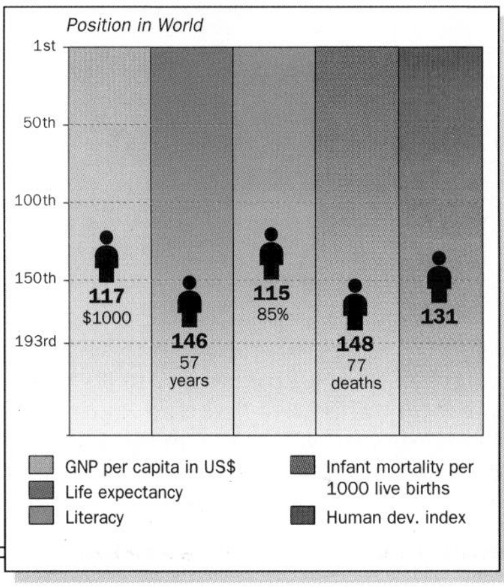
Position in World
1st
50th
100th
150th
193rd
117
$1000
146
57
years
115
85%
148
77
deaths
131
GNP per capita in US$
Life expectancy
Literacy
Infant mortality per 1000 live births
Human dev. index

B

B

BURUNDI

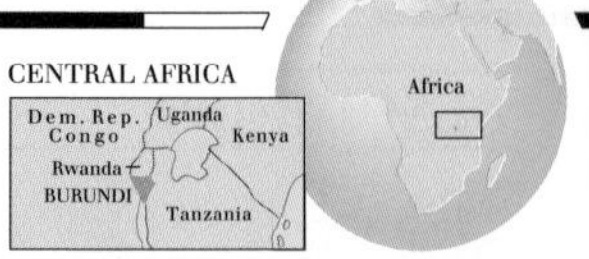
CENTRAL AFRICA
Africa
Dem. Rep. Congo
Uganda
Kenya
Rwanda
BURUNDI
Tanzania

OFFICIAL NAME: Republic of Burundi **CAPITAL:** Bujumbura
POPULATION: 6.7 million **CURRENCY:** Burundi franc **OFFICIAL LANGUAGES:** French and Kirundi

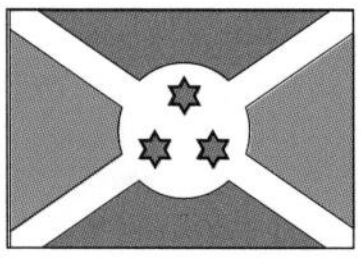

1962 | 1962 | July 1 | RU | +2 | +257 | .bi

LANDLOCKED BURUNDI lies just south of the equator on the Nile–Congo watershed. Lake Tanganyika forms part of its border with the Democratic Republic of the Congo (DRC). Tension between the Hutu majority and the dominant Tutsi minority remains the main factor in politics. The current political unrest dates from October 1993, when the assassination of the first Hutu president in a coup by the Tutsi-dominated army sparked terrible violence.

***Pig farming and fish ponds.** Much of the population depends on subsistence farming.*

CLIMATE

Tropical wet and dry

WEATHER CHART FOR BUJUMBURA

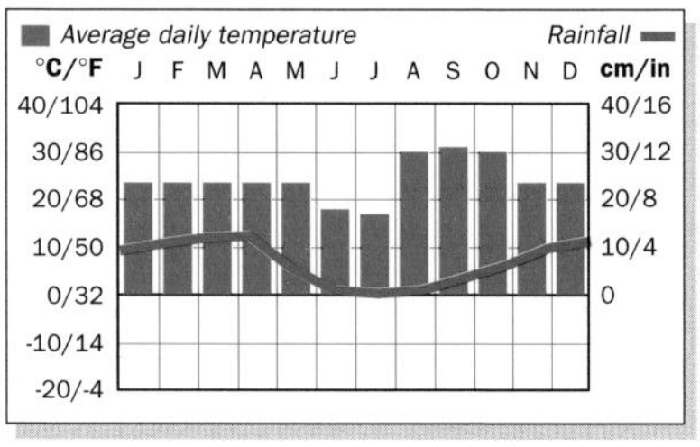
Average daily temperature
Rainfall
°C/°F
J F M A M J J A S O N D
cm/in
40/104
30/86
20/68
10/50
0/32
-10/14
-20/-4
40/16
30/12
20/8
10/4
0

Burundi is temperate with high humidity, much cloud, and frequent heavy rain. The highlands have frost.

TRANSPORTATION

Drive on right

Bujumbura International 71,394 passengers

Has no fleet

THE TRANSPORTATION NETWORK

1028 km (639 miles)

None

None

Lake Tanganyika is navigable

The dense road network has been rehabilitated. There are plans for a railroad to link Burundi with Rwanda, Uganda, and Tanzania.

TOURISM

Visitors : Population 1:223

30,000 visitors

Up 15% in 2000

MAIN TOURIST ARRIVALS

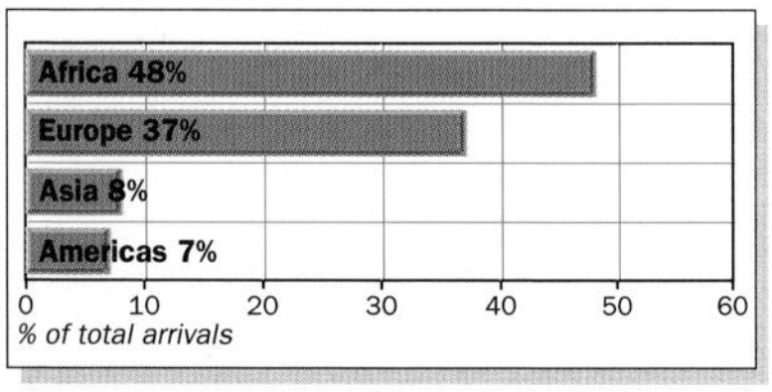
Africa 48%
Europe 37%
Asia 8%
Americas 7%
0 10 20 30 40 50 60
% of total arrivals

A lack of basic infrastructure and violent political strife have deterred tourists. The industry has limited potential, since Burundi lacks its neighbors' spectacular scenery and game parks.

PEOPLE

Pop. density high

Kirundi, French, Kiswahili

261/km² (677/mi²)

THE URBAN/RURAL POPULATION SPLIT

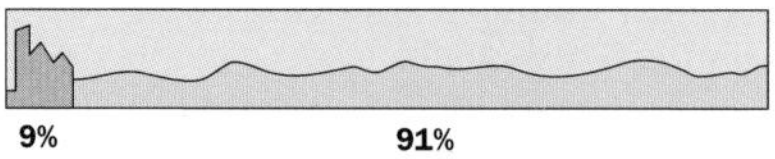
9%
91%

ETHNIC MAKEUP

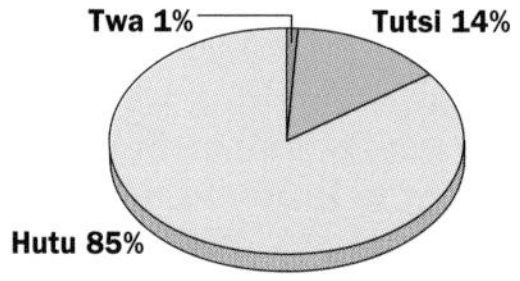
Twa 1%
Tutsi 14%
Hutu 85%

Burundi's history has been marked by violent conflict between the majority Hutu and the Tutsi, formerly the political elite, who still control the army. Large-scale massacres have occurred repeatedly over the past two decades. Hundreds of thousands of people, mostly Hutu, have been killed in political and ethnic conflict since 1993. The Twa pygmy minority, however, has not been greatly affected.

Most Burundians are subsistence farmers. The vast majority of the population are Roman Catholic.

POLITICS

In transition

L. House 2002/2003
U. House 2002/2003

President Domitien Ndayizeye

AT THE LAST ELECTION

Transitional National Assembly 170 seats

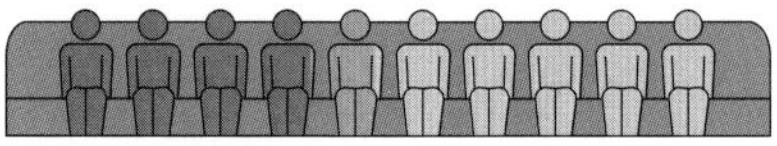

38% Frodebu **10% Uprona** **52% Others**

Frodebu = Front for Democracy in Burundi
Uprona = Union for National Progress

The Transitional National Assembly consists of members of all parties that signed the Arusha peace accord, and members of "civil society."

Transitional Senate 51 seats

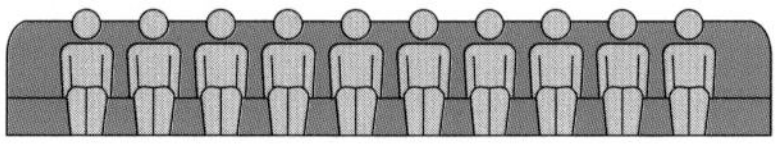

The indirectly elected Transitional Senate comprises 24 Hutus, 24 Tutsis, and three Twas, as formulated under the 2000 Arusha peace accord.

After a series of coups, the imposition of a one-party state in 1981, and widespread ethnic violence, Burundi adopted a multiparty system in 1992 under Tutsi coup leader Pierre Buyoya. The first Hutu president, Melchior Ndadaye of Frodebu, was assassinated in 1993 within months of his election, provoking further ethnic massacres. In 1994 Burundi plunged into a vicious civil war between the Tutsi-dominated army and Hutu militias. Buyoya staged another coup in 1996, agreeing to a transitional constitution in 1998. In 2001 a joint Hutu–Tutsi transitional government was installed amid ongoing conflict. Buyoya handed over to his Hutu deputy Domitien Ndayizeye in April 2003, but by July fighting had reached Bujumbura.

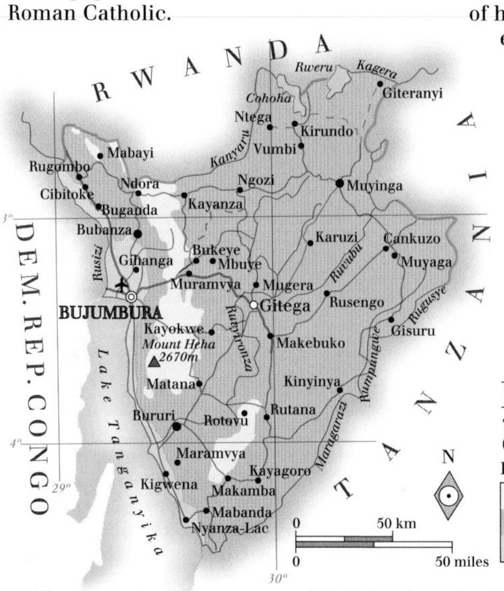
RWANDA
TANZANIA
DEM. REP. CONGO
Rweru
Kagera
Giteranyi
Cohoha
Ntega
Kirundo
Vumbi
Kanyaru
Mabayi
Rugombo
Cibitoke
Ndora
Ngozi
Muyinga
Buganda
Kayanza
Bubanza
Karuzi
Cankuzo
Muyaga
Bukeye
Mbuye
Gihanga
Muramvya
Mugera
Rusizi
Ruvubu
BUJUMBURA
Gitega
Rusengo
Kayokwe
Mount Heha 2670m
Ruvironza
Makebuko
Gisuru
Rugusye
Lake Tanganyika
Kinyinya
Matana
Rumpungwe
Rutana
Bururi
Rotovu
Maragarazi
Maramvya
Kayagoro
Kigwena
Makamba
Mabanda
Nyanza-Lac
3°
4°
29°
30°
N
0 50 km
0 50 miles

BURUNDI

Total Area : 27 830 sq. km (10 745 sq. miles)

LAND HEIGHT
2000m/6562ft
1000m/3281ft
500m/1640ft

POPULATION
over 100 000
over 50 000
over 10 000
under 10 000

WORLD AFFAIRS

Joined UN in 1962

ACP | CEPGL | COMESA | OIF | AU

In 2003 the warring factions agreed to the formation of an African peacekeeping force for Burundi.

AID

Recipient

$131m (receipts) — Up 41% in 2001

The flight of hundreds of thousands of people since 1993 has disrupted agriculture, and many people remain dependent on UN food aid.

DEFENSE

No compulsory military service

$35m — Down 17% in 2001

The 40,000-strong army is run by Tutsi. The attempt to bring Hutu into officer ranks was a cause of the 1993 coup. A state of virtual civil war now exists between the army and rebel Hutu militias. A UNICEF program to remove over 14,000 child soldiers from these militias was announced in 2001.

ECONOMICS

Inflation 13% p.a. (1990–2001)

$692m — 1075 Burundi francs (866.4)

SCORE CARD

- ❑ WORLD GNP RANKING........................161st
- ❑ GNP PER CAPITA $100
- ❑ BALANCE OF PAYMENTS......................–$24m
- ❑ INFLATION 9.2%
- ❑ UNEMPLOYMENT.......Widespread underemployment

STRENGTHS

Small quantities of gold and tungsten. Potential of massive nickel reserves and oil in Lake Tanganyika.

WEAKNESSES

Harsh regional sanctions since 1996 coup. Agricultural economy under pressure from high birthrate, war damage, and displacement. Little prospect of lasting political stability.

EXPORTS

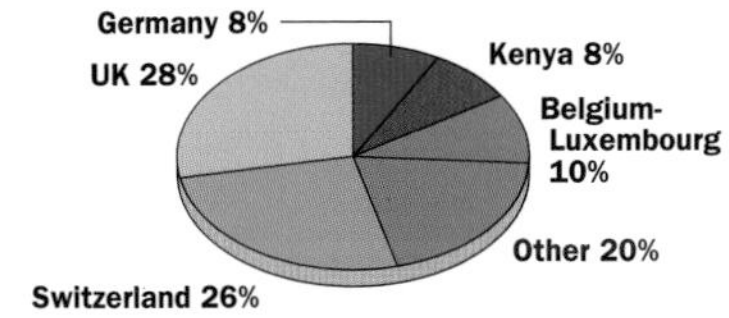
Germany 8%
UK 28%
Kenya 8%
Belgium-Luxembourg 10%
Other 20%
Switzerland 26%

IMPORTS

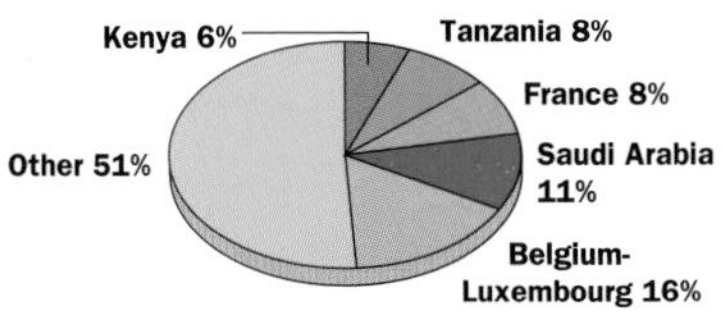
Kenya 6%
Tanzania 8%
France 8%
Saudi Arabia 11%
Other 51%
Belgium-Luxembourg 16%

RESOURCES

Electric power 43,000 kW

10,055 tonnes — Not an oil producer and has no refineries

750,000 goats, 315,000 cattle, 4.3m chickens — Gold, tungsten, nickel, vanadium, uranium, oil

Burundi has around 5% of the world's nickel reserves. Extraction, however, is not economically viable. There are also deposits of gold and vanadium. Surveys in the 1980s detected oil reserves below Lake Tanganyika, but production has yet to begin. Burundi used to import gasoline from Iran and electricity from the DRC. New HEP plants at Mugera and Rwegura, in the north, are intended to meet most domestic electricity requirements.

ENVIRONMENT

Sustainability rank: 115th

6% (5% partially protected) — 0.04 tonnes per capita

Only 2% of Burundi is forest, and even this is under pressure from one of Africa's highest birthrates. Burundi suffers from the problems associated with deforestation, particularly soil erosion. Some soils are also being exhausted from overuse. Several tree-planting programs have been introduced. UNESCO is also running ecological education initiatives at village level, aimed at women farmers.

MEDIA

TV ownership low

Daily newspaper circulation 2 per 1000 people

PUBLISHING AND BROADCAST MEDIA

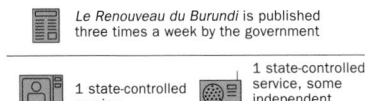

Le Renouveau du Burundi is published three times a week by the government

1 state-controlled service — 1 state-controlled service, some independent stations

Pro-Hutu/anti-Tutsi radio stations have been broadcasting since 1994. Radio Umwizero, an EU-funded station promoting peace, was launched in 1996.

CRIME

Death penalty in use

8647 prisoners — Crime is rising

Burundi has an appalling human rights record. There have been frequent massacres of Hutu by the army. The worst pogroms occurred in 1972, 1988, 1993, and 1994.

EDUCATION

School leaving age: 12

49% — 6289 students

Elementary schooling begins at six, and is compulsory to age 12. Civil war has prevented thousands of children from attending school. There is one state-run university.

CHRONOLOGY

From the 16th century, Burundi (formerly Urundi) was ruled by the minority Tutsi with the majority Hutu as their serfs. Merged with Rwanda, Burundi was controlled by Germany from 1884 and by Belgium from 1919.

- ❑ **1959** Split from Rwanda.
- ❑ **1962** Independence.
- ❑ **1966** Army overthrows monarchy.
- ❑ **1972** 150,000 Hutu massacred.
- ❑ **1993** Ndadaye wins first free elections; killed four months later.
- ❑ **1996** Pierre Buyoya retakes power.
- ❑ **2000** Renewed violence. Arusha peace accord signed by most groups.
- ❑ **2001** Multiethnic transitional government appointed.
- ❑ **2003** Domitien Ndayizeye becomes president in peaceful transfer.

B

HEALTH

No welfare state health benefits

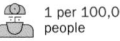

1 per 100,000 people — Communicable infections, parasitic diseases

Over half of the population of Burundi are underfed, and over 30% do not have access to health services. By 2001 9% were living with HIV/AIDS.

SPENDING

GDP/cap. decrease

CONSUMPTION AND SPENDING

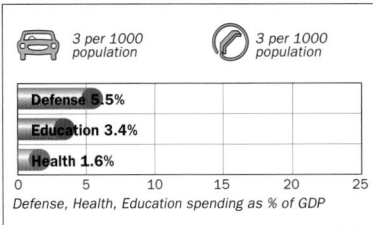

3 per 1000 population — *3 per 1000 population*

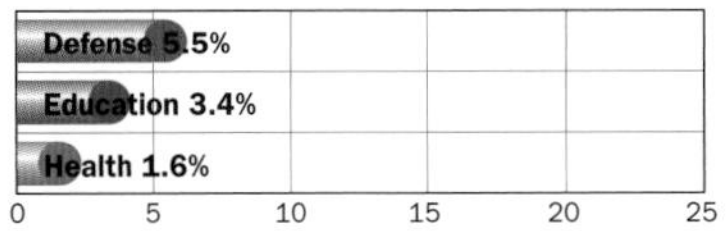
Defense 5.5%
Education 3.4%
Health 1.6%
0
5
10
15
20
25

Defense, Health, Education spending as % of GDP

Wealth is concentrated within the Tutsi political and business elite. Most of Burundi's people live at the level of subsistence farming.

WORLD RANKING

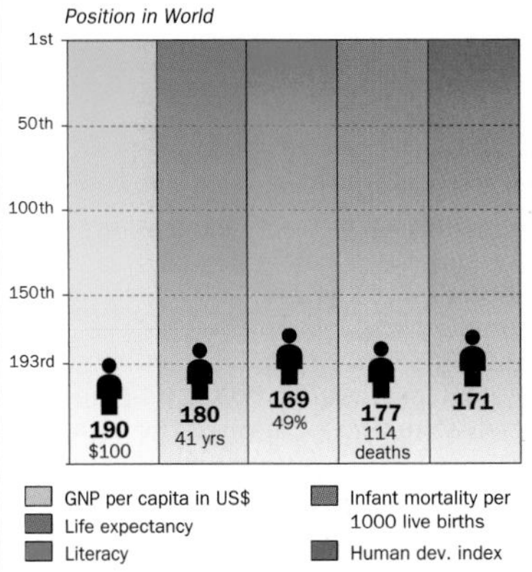
Position in World
1st
50th
100th
150th
193rd
190
$100
180
41 yrs
169
49%
177
114
deaths
171
GNP per capita in US$
Life expectancy
Literacy
Infant mortality per 1000 live births
Human dev. index

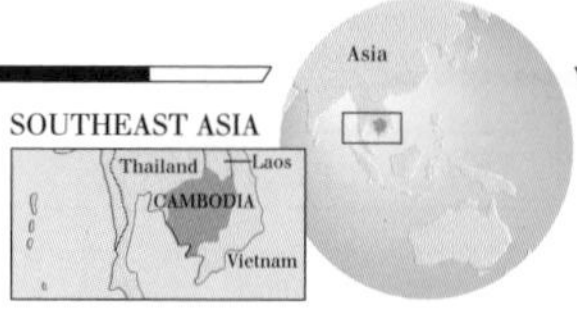
Asia
SOUTHEAST ASIA
Thailand
Laos
CAMBODIA
Vietnam

CAMBODIA

OFFICIAL NAME: Kingdom of Cambodia **CAPITAL:** Phnom Penh
POPULATION: 13.8 million **CURRENCY:** Riel **OFFICIAL LANGUAGE:** Khmer

1953 | 1953 | Nov 11 | K | +7 | +855 | .kh

THE ANCIENT KINGDOM of Cambodia emerged from French colonial rule in 1953, only to be plunged into violent civil conflict. Under the extremist Khmer Rouge, headed by the infamous Pol Pot, the country endured one of the world's most brutal totalitarian regimes. Since the withdrawal of Vietnamese troops in 1989 the country has gradually returned to relative stability. The dominating geographic feature is the Tônlé Sap, or Great Lake, which drains into the Mekong River. Over three-quarters of Cambodia is forested, with mangroves lining the coast.

CLIMATE

Tropical monsoon

WEATHER CHART FOR PHNOM PENH

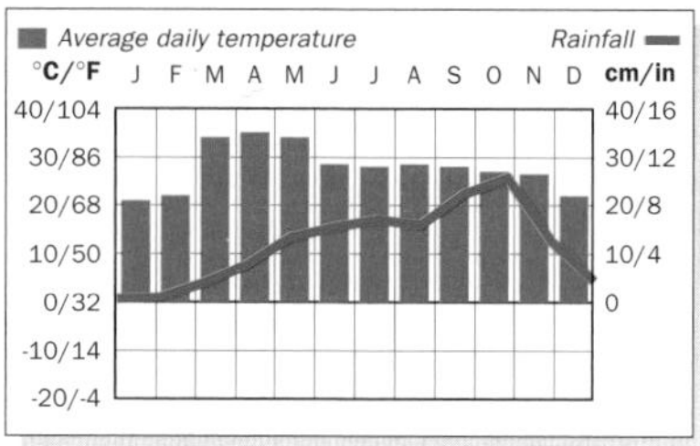
Average daily temperature
Rainfall
°C/°F J F M A M J J A S O N D cm/in
40/104
30/86
20/68
10/50
0/32
-10/14
-20/-4
40/16
30/12
20/8
10/4
0

Cambodia has a varied climate. Low-lying regions have moderate rainfall and the most consistent year-round temperatures. The dry season from December to April is characterized by high temperatures and an average of eight hours of sunshine a day. From May to September, winds are southeasterly, while from October to April they are north or northeasterly. During the rainy season, Cambodia is sultry and humid. The monsoons in 2000 caused severe flooding of the Mekong River, which inundated Phnom Penh.

TRANSPORTATION

Drive on right

Pochentong, Phnom Penh 948,614 passengers

564 ships 2m grt

THE TRANSPORTATION NETWORK

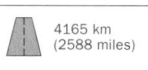

4165 km (2588 miles)

None

601 km (373 miles)

3700 km (2299 miles)

Years of war led to a near-collapse of Cambodia's rail and road systems. Though international aid has helped fund key projects, the state of the country's roads remains appalling. The government has pledged to make reconstruction a priority. The Mekong River is vital for accessing the interior. Taxi-mopeds, bicycles, and rickshaws dominate urban transportation.

***Angkor Wat** stands in the ruins of the ancient city of Angkor, once the capital of the Khmer empire. It is now one of Cambodia's leading tourist attractions.*

TOURISM

Visitors : Population 1:52

265,000 visitors

Up 1% in 2000

MAIN TOURIST ARRIVALS

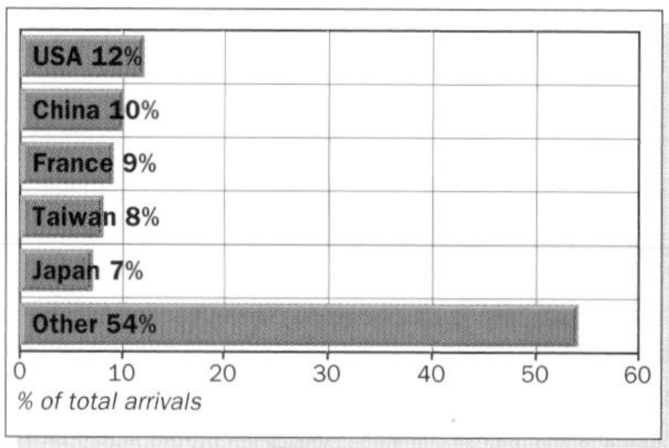
USA 12%
China 10%
France 9%
Taiwan 8%
Japan 7%
Other 54%
0 10 20 30 40 50 60
% of total arrivals

Cambodia, the center of the Khmer empire between 800 and 1400 CE, has some of the most impressive temples in southeast Asia. The most famous is Angkor Wat, near Siem Reap (Siemreab), which is now largely safe for tourists after the Khmer Rouge relinquished control of the area in 1998. Kidnappings and murders of tourists by the Khmer Rouge kept Cambodia off the backpacker circuit in the mid-1990s. Once the political situation is fully stabilized and land mines have been cleared, there is considerable potential, not just for adventurous independent travelers.

PEOPLE

Pop. density medium

Khmer, French, Chinese, Vietnamese, Cham

78/km² (202/mi²)

THE URBAN/RURAL POPULATION SPLIT

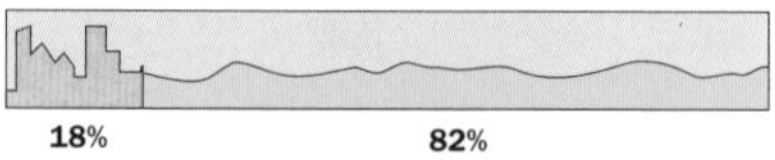
18%
82%

RELIGIOUS PERSUASION

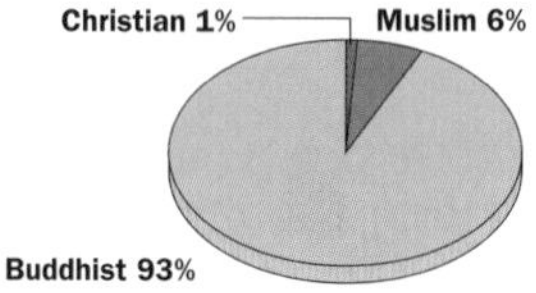
Christian 1%
Muslim 6%
Buddhist 93%

ETHNIC MAKEUP

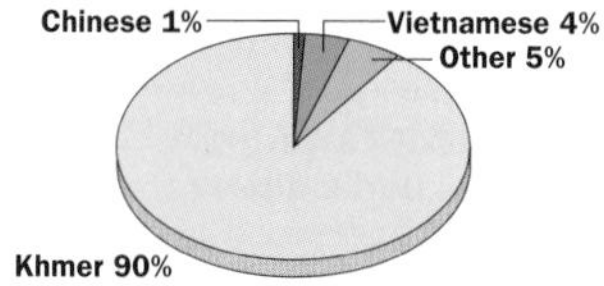
Chinese 1%
Vietnamese 4%
Other 5%
Khmer 90%

Cambodia underwent one of the 20th century's most horrific experiments in social transformation between 1975 and 1979 under Pol Pot's Khmer Rouge regime. Warfare, starvation, exhaustion, or execution killed one in eight of the population. Half a million more fled to Thailand. The Pol Pot regime's extreme radical beliefs led to the scrapping of money, possessions, and hierarchy. "Bourgeois" learning was despised, whereas peasants, soldiers of the revolution, and some industrial workers were officially given higher status. Boys and girls of 13 and 14 were taken from their homes, indoctrinated in the tenets of revolution, and allowed to kill those held guilty of bourgeois crimes. Violence at all levels was sanctioned in the name of revolution. The legacies of the regime are both the emigration of surviving professionals, and one of the world's highest rates of orphans and widows.

Religious and ethnic tensions are minimal, though there is a traditional hostility in Khmer culture toward ethnic Vietnamese.

POPULATION AGE BREAKDOWN

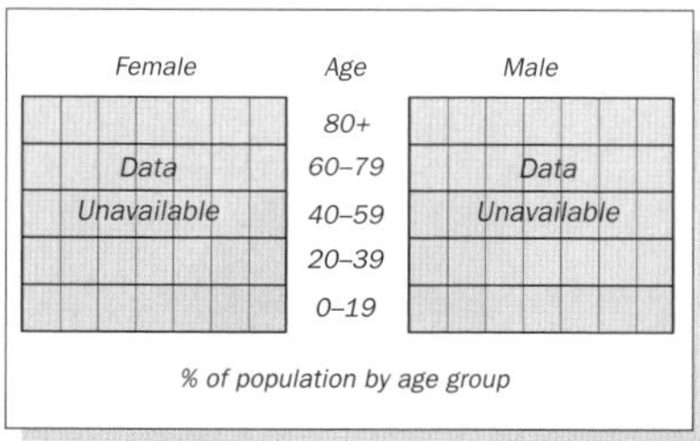
Female
Age
Male
80+
60–79
40–59
20–39
0–19
Data Unavailable
Data Unavailable
% of population by age group

C

POLITICS

Multiparty elections

L. House 2003/2008
U. House 1999/2004

H.M. King Norodom Sihanouk

AT THE LAST ELECTION

National Assembly 123 seats

55% **CPP** | **19%** **Funcinpec** | **19%** **SRP** | **6%** **ND**

CPP = Cambodian People's Party **Funcinpec** = United National Front for an Independent Neutral Peaceful and Cooperative Cambodia **SRP** = Sam Rainsy Party **ND** = Not declared

Senate 61 seats

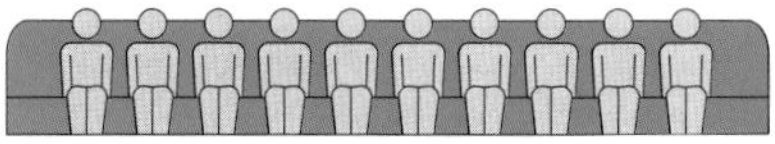

The membership of the Senate, first established in March 1999, was determined in proportion to the results of the 1998 legislative elections

Cambodia is a constitutional monarchy.

PROFILE

In 1975, a US-installed government was overthrown by the Maoist Khmer Rouge under Pol Pot. That extremist and murderous regime was ousted in 1979 thanks to a Vietnamese invasion. The Khmer Rouge then joined a Western-backed anti-Vietnamese exile coalition with the supporters of the then Prince Sihanouk and the Khmer People's National Liberation Front (KPNLF), gaining UN recognition against the Vietnam-backed regime in Phnom Penh. In 1989 Vietnam withdrew its forces, paving the way for UN-supervised elections in 1993. The royalist Funcinpec emerged as the main winners and King Sihanouk formed a coalition government; the Khmer Rouge remained outside this coalition and resumed armed resistance until its surrender in 1998. The strife-torn coalition meanwhile had descended into open hostility in 1997, when Hun Sen of the communist CPP ousted his co-prime minister Prince Ranariddh. Since then the CPP has failed to win the necessary two-thirds majority, forcing it into coalition (with Funcinpec 1998–2003).

MAIN POLITICAL ISSUES

Settling accounts with Khmer Rouge

The Khmer Rouge, which had resumed its armed struggle in 1993, surrendered in 1998, after mass defections and the death of Pol Pot earlier that year. The legislature in 2001 approved plans for a tribunal to try the surviving leaders for crimes against humanity.

Royalist–CPP rivalry

Power struggles between the Funcinpec and the CPP came to a head with CPP leader Hun Sen's mid-1997 coup. However, inconclusive elections in July 1998 led the two parties to re-form their uneasy coalition in November. Against expectations, that compromise lasted for the whole term.

Prime Minister Hun Sen, *who ousted his co-prime minister in 1997.*

King Norodom Sihanouk, *the pivotal figure in Cambodian society and politics.*

WORLD AFFAIRS

Joined UN in 1955

ASEAN | CP | OIF | Mekong River | NAM

During the civil war that followed the Vietnamese invasion of 1979, Cambodia was reduced to an international pariah. The Vietnam-puppet government was recognized by few countries outside the Soviet bloc, and its seat at the UN was allotted to the exiled resistance coalition, despite one of the components being the Khmer Rouge, which had inflicted appalling violence and suffering on Cambodians. The 1993 constitution aims to make the country a nonaligned "island of peace" with a neutral foreign policy.

Cambodia's relations with Vietnam remain problematic, fueled in part by the historic animosity between the two countries. The situation has improved since the late 1990s, and Cambodia's membership of ASEAN was confirmed in 1999.

Relations with Thailand were greatly affected by anti-Thai rioting in Phnom Penh in January 2003, after a Thai actress was (falsely) reported to have claimed that the Angkor Wat temples had been stolen from Thailand.

AID

Recipient

$409m (receipts) | Up 3% in 2001

Aid is crucial to Cambodia's economy, providing the bulk of government revenues. Widespread corruption and political instability prompted some countries to withhold assistance in the late 1990s, but NGOs continued working in the country, and Western donors made fresh pledges in 2000.

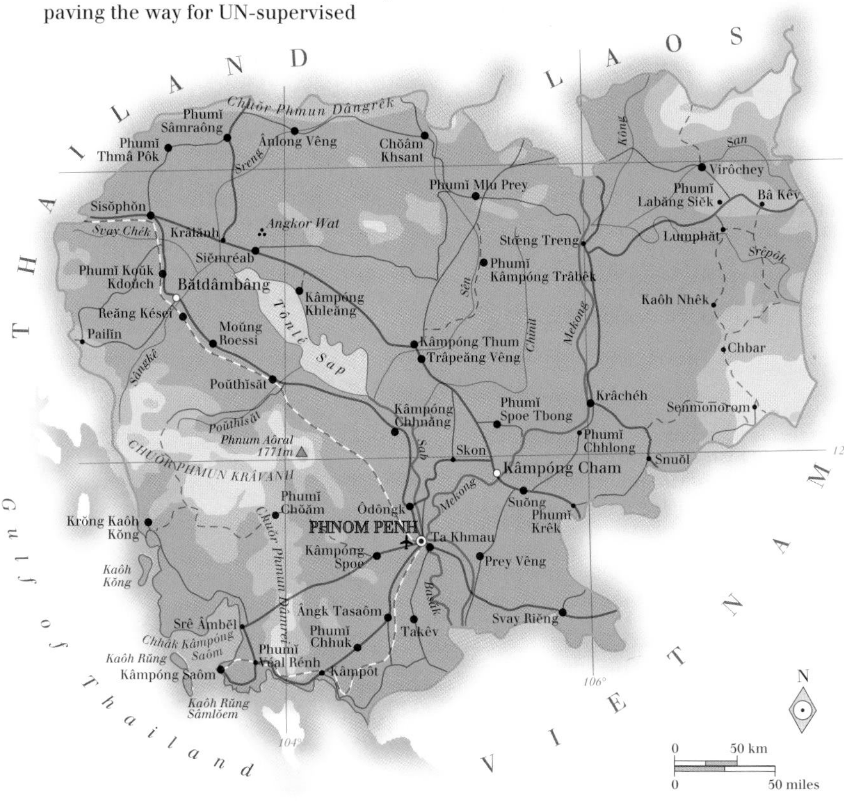
THAILAND
LAOS
VIETNAM
Gulf of Thailand
Chuŏr Phnum Dângrêk
Phumĭ Sâmraông
Phumĭ Thmâ Pŏk
Ânlong Vêng
Chŏâm Khsant
Sisŏphŏn
Svay Chék
Krâlănh
Angkor Wat
Siĕmréab
Phumĭ Koŭk Kdŏuch
Bătdâmbâng
Kâmpóng Khleăng
Reăng Kései
Pailĭn
Moŭng Roessei
Tônlé Sap
Poŭthĭsăt
Phnum Aôral 1771m
CHUŎR PHNUM KRÂVANH
Phumĭ Chŏâm
Ŏdôngk
Krŏng Kaôh Kŏng
Kaôh Kŏng
PHNOM PENH
Kâmpóng Spoe
Srê Âmbĕl
Chhâk Kâmpóng Saôm
Kaôh Rŭng
Kâmpóng Saôm
Kaôh Rŭng Sâmlŏem
Phumĭ Veal Rénh
Kâmpôt
Phumĭ Chhuk
Ângk Tasaôm
Takêv
Ta Khmau
Prey Vêng
Svay Riĕng
Suŏng
Phumĭ Krêk
Kâmpóng Cham
Skon
Kâmpóng Chhnăng
Phumĭ Spoe Tbong
Phumĭ Chhlong
Snuŏl
Krâchéh
Sênmonoŭrom
Chbar
Kaôh Nhêk
Kâmpóng Thum
Trâpeăng Vêng
Phumĭ Kâmpóng Trâbêk
Stœng Treng
Lumphăt
Phumĭ Mlu Prey
Phumĭ Labăng Siĕk
Virôchey
Bâ Kêv
Mekong
Kông
San
Srêpŏk
Sên
Chinit
Sângkê
Sab
Basăk
Sreng
14°
12°
104°
106°

CAMBODIA

Total Area : 181 040 sq. km (69 900 sq. miles)

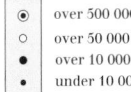

POPULATION: over 500 000; over 50 000; over 10 000; under 10 000

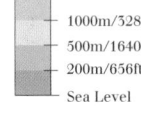

LAND HEIGHT: 1000m/3281ft; 500m/1640ft; 200m/656ft; Sea Level

0 — 50 km
0 — 50 miles

C

CHRONOLOGY

A former French protectorate, Cambodia gained independence in 1953 as a constitutional monarchy with Norodom Sihanouk as king.

- **1955** Sihanouk abdicates to pursue political career; takes title "prince."
- **1960** Sihanouk head of state.
- **1970** Right-wing coup led by Prime Minister Lon Nol deposes Sihanouk. Exiled Sihanouk forms Royal Government of National Union of Cambodia (GRUNC), backed by communist Khmer Rouge. Lon Nol proclaims Khmer Republic.
- **1975** GRUNC troops capture Phnom Penh. Prince Sihanouk head of state, Khmer Rouge assumes power. Huge numbers die under radical extremist regime.
- **1976** Country renamed Democratic Kampuchea. Elections. Sihanouk resigns; GRUNC dissolved. Khieu Samphan head of state; Pol Pot prime minister.
- **1978** December, Vietnam invades, supported by Cambodian communists opposed to Pol Pot.
- **1979** Vietnamese capture Phnom Penh. Khmer Rouge ousted by Kampuchean People's Revolutionary Party (KPRP), led by Pen Sovan. Khmer Rouge starts guerrilla war. Pol Pot held responsible for genocide and sentenced to death in absentia.
- **1982** Government-in-exile including Khmer Rouge and Khmer People's National Liberation Front, headed by Prince Sihanouk, is recognized by UN.
- **1989** Vietnamese troops withdraw.
- **1990** UN Security Council approves plan for UN-monitored cease-fire and elections.
- **1991** Signing of Paris peace accords. Sihanouk reinstated as head of state of Cambodia.
- **1993** UN-supervised elections won by royalist Funcinpec. Sihanouk takes title of "king."
- **1994** Khmer Rouge refuses to join peace process.
- **1995** Former finance minister Sam Rainsy forms opposition party.
- **1996** Leading Khmer Rouge member Ieng Sary defects.
- **1997** Joint prime minister Hun Sen mounts coup against royalist copremier Prince Ranariddh.
- **1998** April, death of Pol Pot; June, Khmer Rouge surrender; July, elections; November, Hun Sen heads coalition with Funcinpec.
- **2001** Law approved on trials of Khmer Rouge leaders for atrocities committed by regime.
- **2003** Relatively peaceful elections won by CPP.

DEFENSE

No compulsory military service

$188m

Down 4% in 2001

CAMBODIAN ARMED FORCES

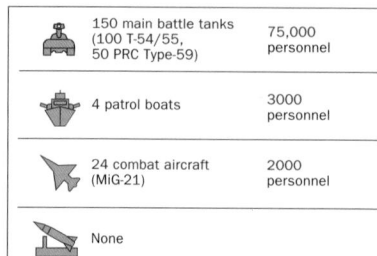

150 main battle tanks (100 T-54/55, 50 PRC Type-59)	75,000 personnel
4 patrol boats	3000 personnel
24 combat aircraft (MiG-21)	2000 personnel
None	

The coalition government's initial defense priority was to unify the command structures of armies under the control of diverse parties. The surrender of Khmer Rouge forces in mid-1998 and the disintegration of remaining pockets of Khmer resistance later that year improved the prospects for a unified national army. Plans for the demobilization of 30,000 soldiers over a three-year period began in 2000.

Under the nominal overall structure of the Royal Cambodian Armed Forces, there remain in existence three main armies – the CPP's Cambodian People's Armed Forces, Funcinpec's Armée Nationale Sihanoukiste, and the KPNLF's Khmer People's National Liberation Armed Forces. The rivalries between them remain intense, with the two first-named in open conflict as recently as 1997–1998. Though well equipped, their soldiers are poorly paid.

A system of conscription for five years between the ages of 18 and 35 has not been implemented since 1993.

ECONOMICS

Inflation 22% p.a. (1990–2001)

$3.34bn

3835 riels (3835)

SCORE CARD

- WORLD GNP RANKING........................127th
- GNP PER CAPITA..............................$270
- BALANCE OF PAYMENTS...................–$105m
- INFLATION..–0.6%
- UNEMPLOYMENT..................................3%

EXPORTS

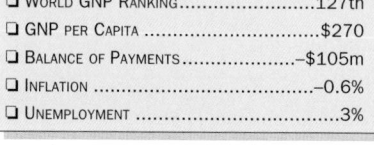

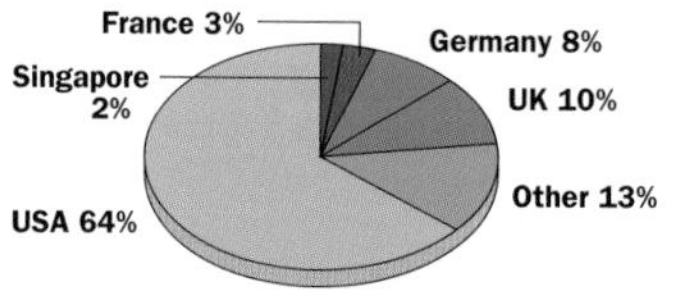
France 3%
Germany 8%
Singapore 2%
UK 10%
Other 13%
USA 64%

IMPORTS

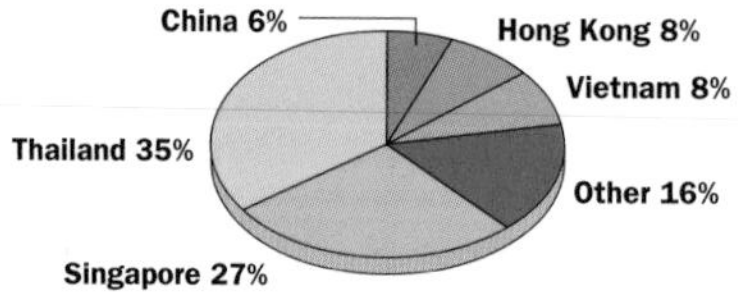
China 6%
Hong Kong 8%
Vietnam 8%
Thailand 35%
Other 16%
Singapore 27%

STRENGTHS

Currently very few, as economy still recovering from long-running conflicts. Considerable future potential. Growth in tourism. Relatively unbureaucratic mentality. Self-sufficiency in rice achieved by 1999. Gems, especially sapphires. Possible offshore oil wealth. Export-oriented garment industry.

WEAKNESSES

Tiny tax base makes economic reform hard to implement. Deflation since 2001. Dependence on overseas aid: corruption at most levels of government limits its effectiveness. Disputes over land ownership rights.

ECONOMIC PERFORMANCE INDICATOR

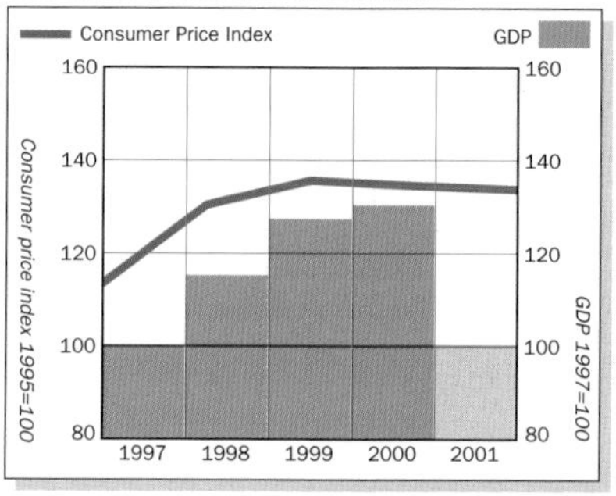
Consumer Price Index
GDP
160
140
120
100
80
Consumer price index 1995=100
GDP 1997=100
1997
1998
1999
2000
2001

PROFILE

A switch was made in the 1990s from Vietnamese-inspired central planning to encouragement of the private sector. The Asian financial crisis and internal turmoil affected funding after 1997. The country remains dependent on imports and growth has been slow. A period of deflation began in 2001.

CAMBODIA : MAJOR BUSINESSES

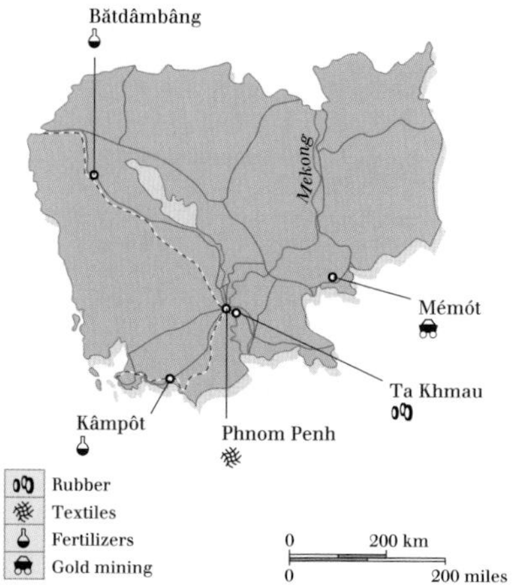
Bătdâmbâng
Mekong
Mémót
Ta Khmau
Kâmpôt
Phnom Penh
Rubber
Textiles
Fertilizers
Gold mining
0
200 km
0
200 miles

RESOURCES

Electric power 35,000 kW

298,798 tonnes

Not an oil producer

6.5m ducks, 2.92m cattle, 2.11m pigs, 16.7m chickens

Salt, phosphates, gemstones

Few resources are currently exploited, apart from tropical rainforest timber, particularly teak and rosewood, much of which is felled illegally.

ELECTRICITY GENERATION

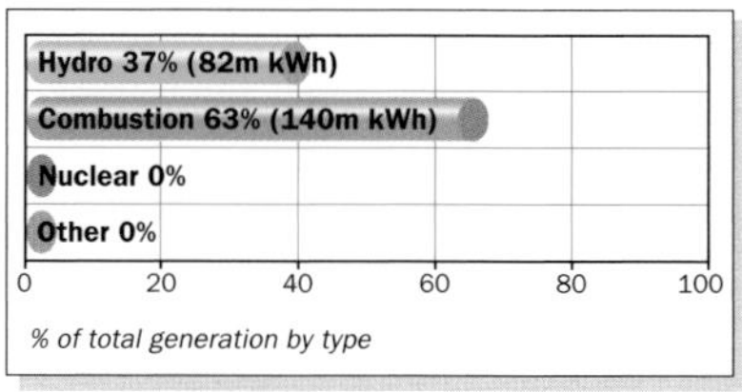
Hydro 37% (82m kWh)
Combustion 63% (140m kWh)
Nuclear 0%
Other 0%
0
20
40
60
80
100
% of total generation by type

CAMBODIA : LAND USE

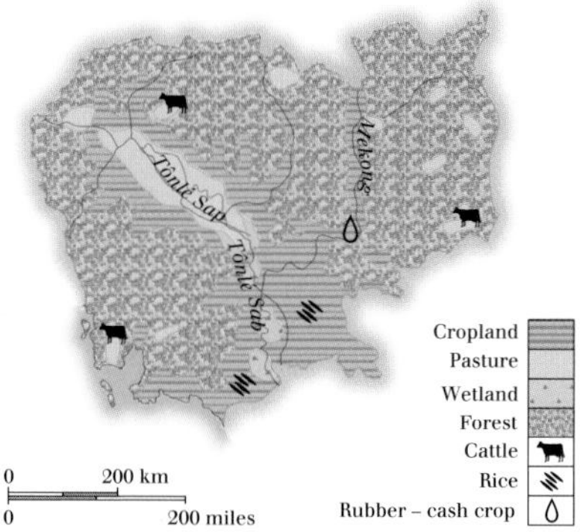
Tonle Sap
Tonle Sap
Mekong
Cropland
Pasture
Wetland
Forest
Cattle
Rice
Rubber – cash crop
0
200 km
0
200 miles

ENVIRONMENT

Sustainability rank: 97th

19% (14% partially protected)

0.05 tonnes per capita

ENVIRONMENTAL TREATIES

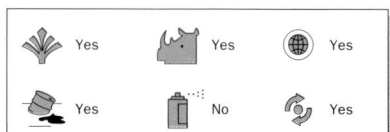

Yes Yes Yes

Yes No Yes

Deforestation is one of the most serious problems facing Cambodia. Illegal logging is the main culprit. Timber, one of the country's most valuable assets, was sold in huge quantities by all Cambodian factions to finance their war efforts. A moratorium on logging was declared at the end of 1992, but was largely ignored. Despite international pressure and efforts from 2000 to tighten controls, in many parts of the country logging is impossible to police. Tropical hardwoods extracted illegally from Cambodia find lucrative outlets through Thailand in particular. The environmental consequences – topsoil erosion and increased risk of flooding – are enormous and will hold back Cambodia's reconstruction.

MEDIA

TV ownership low

Daily newspaper circulation 2 per 1000 people

Phnom Penh has several independent TV stations in addition to the national network. However, many are reliant on party political support, which compromises their independence. The government has used a 1995 press law to prosecute numerous newspapers for defamation and disinformation.

PUBLISHING AND BROADCAST MEDIA

There are 2 daily newspapers; only 10 newspapers and magazines publish regularly

6 services: 1 state-run, 5 independent

10 services; 2 state-run, 8 independent

CRIME

No death penalty

6179 prisoners

Narcotics-related crime is rising

CRIME RATES

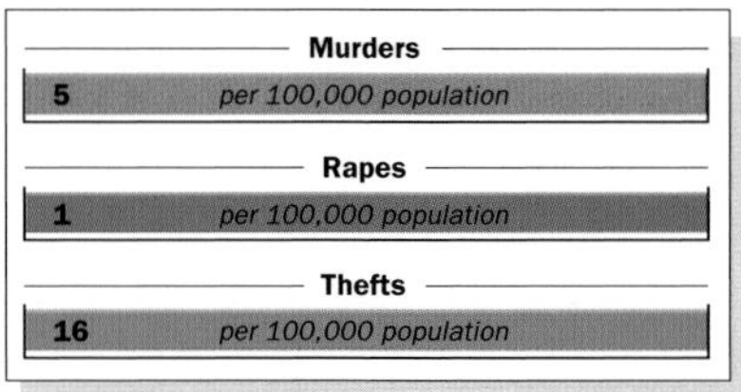
Murders
5 per 100,000 population
Rapes
1 per 100,000 population
Thefts
16 per 100,000 population

It is claimed that there has been a proliferation of narcotics trading, money laundering, and illegal banking operations. Mob killings go largely unremarked. Corruption in business is a major issue. Phnom Penh witnessed an increase in violent crime in the aftermath of the 1997 coup, owing to the spread of illegally owned firearms. Until the surrender of the Khmer Rouge in 1998, areas under its command, especially in the west around Pailin and Battambang, were particularly dangerous. Banditry remains rife and policing virtually nonexistent.

EDUCATION

School leaving age: 12

69%

25,416 students

THE EDUCATION SYSTEM

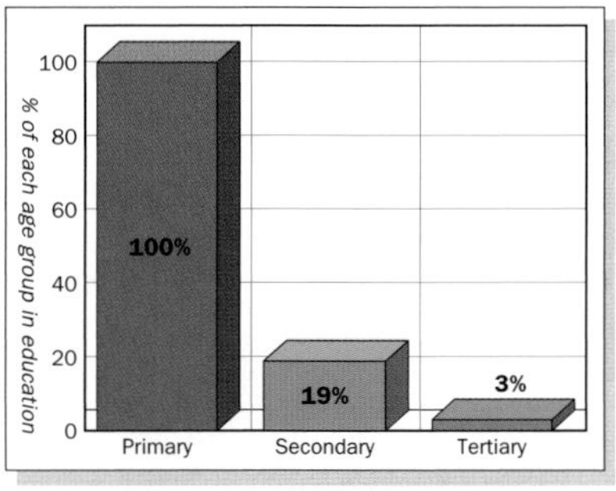
100
80
60
40
20
0
% of each age group in education
100%
19%
3%
Primary
Secondary
Tertiary

The government aims to provide a complete education system from primary to tertiary. Currently primary education is compulsory, and lasts for six years between the ages of six and 12. Only 5000 of Cambodia's 20,000 teachers survived the Pol Pot period; the Vietnamese-installed government trained or retrained about 40,000.

HEALTH

No welfare state health benefits

1 per 3333 people

Circulatory and infectious diseases, cancers

The Cambodian health system was effectively destroyed in the Pol Pot period; only 50 doctors survived, and Cambodia's health indicators were among the worst in the world.

Conditions have since improved, but AIDS is widespread, affecting even children in rural areas. Infant mortality remains high, and malaria and cholera are endemic. In 2000, UNICEF helped mount an immunization campaign against tetanus, a major cause of neonatal mortality.

SPENDING

GDP/cap. increase

CONSUMPTION AND SPENDING

26 per 1000 population

2 per 1000 population

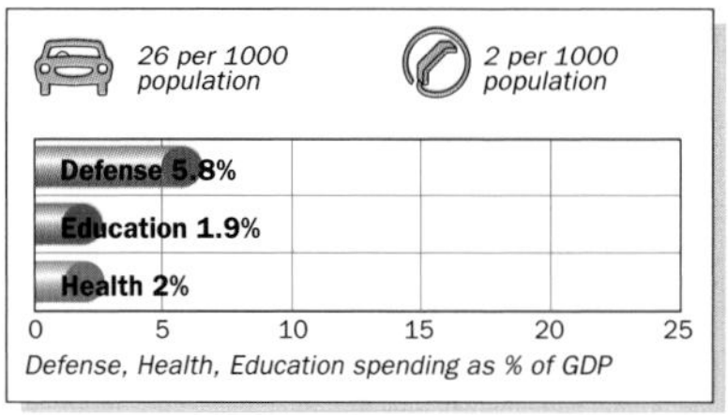
Defense 5.8%
Education 1.9%
Health 2%
0
5
10
15
20
25
Defense, Health, Education spending as % of GDP

New industries such as textiles, in which female garment workers may earn $40 a month in vast workshops, help to attract migrants to the towns, though they risk unemployment and homelessness. Cambodians in rural areas face more severe poverty, exacerbated by land shortage.

WORLD RANKING

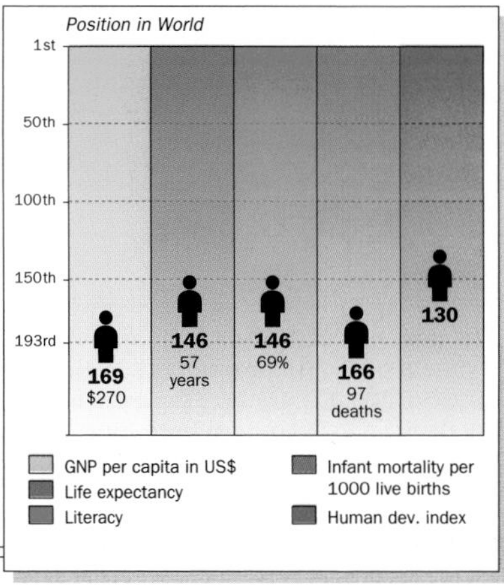
Position in World
1st
50th
100th
150th
193rd
169
$270
146
57 years
146
69%
166
97 deaths
130
GNP per capita in US$
Life expectancy
Literacy
Infant mortality per 1000 live births
Human dev. index

C

CAMEROON

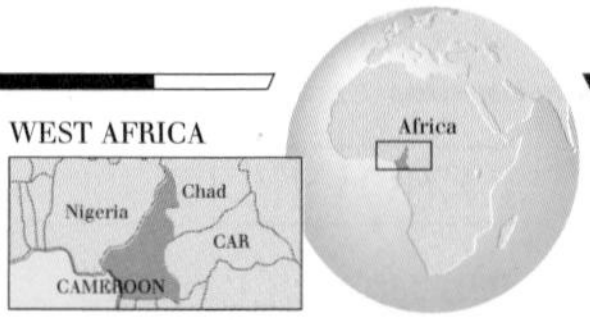
WEST AFRICA
Nigeria
Chad
CAR
CAMEROON
Africa

OFFICIAL NAME: Republic of Cameroon **CAPITAL:** Yaoundé
POPULATION: 15.5 million **CURRENCY:** CFA franc **OFFICIAL LANGUAGES:** French and English

C

1960 | 1961 | May 20 | CAM | +1 | +237 | .cm

LOCATED ON THE CENTRAL west African coast, over half of Cameroon is forested, with equatorial rainforest to the south and evergreen forest and wooded savanna north of the Sanaga River. Most cities are located in the south, although there are densely populated areas around Mount Cameroon, a dormant volcano. For 30 years Cameroon was effectively a one-party state. Democratic elections in 1992 returned the former ruling party to power.

Savanna landscape below Mindif Pic in Cameroon's far north. From here, the land slopes down to the hot, arid Lake Chad basin.

CLIMATE

Tropical equatorial

WEATHER CHART FOR YAOUNDE

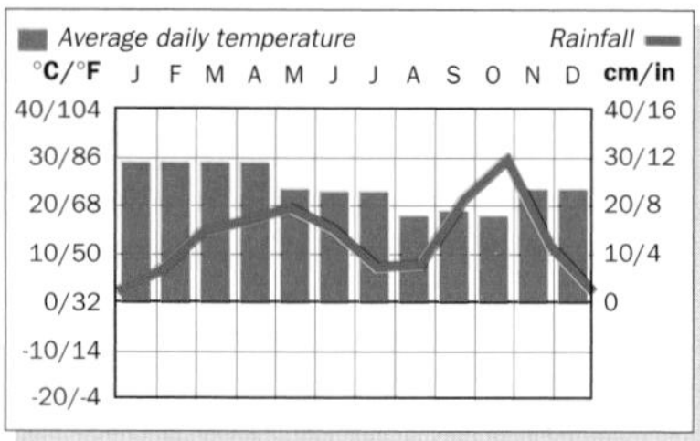
Average daily temperature
Rainfall
°C/°F J F M A M J J A S O N D cm/in
40/104
30/86
20/68
10/50
0/32
-10/14
-20/-4
40/16
30/12
20/8
10/4
0

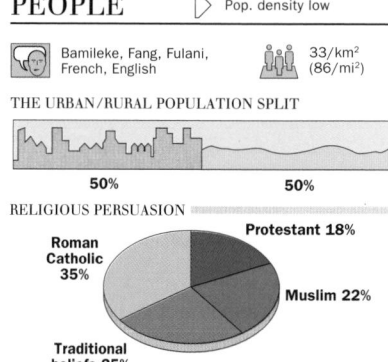

Climate varies from the equatorial south, with 500 cm (200 in) of rain a year, to the drought-beset Sahelian north.

TRANSPORTATION

Drive on right

Douala International 575,018 passengers

58 ships 13,600 grt

THE TRANSPORTATION NETWORK

4288 km (2664 miles)

Trans-African Highway

1016 km (631 miles)

2090 km (1299 miles)

Major projects are the east–west Trans-African Highway and the realigning of the Douala–Nkongsamba railroad.

TOURISM

Visitors : Population 1:263

59,000 visitors

Down 56% in 1999–2000

MAIN TOURIST ARRIVALS

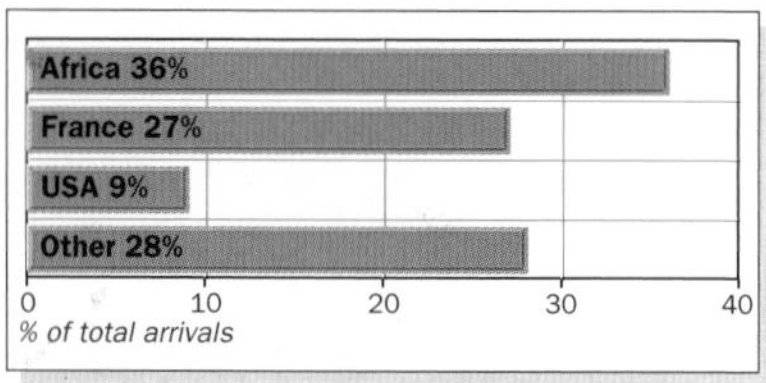
Africa 36%
France 27%
USA 9%
Other 28%
0 10 20 30 40
% of total arrivals

The government and Commonwealth are trying to boost visitor numbers, with a target of 500,000 a year. There are beach hotels near Kribi and package tours to northern game parks, but high levels of crime and corruption still deter many.

PEOPLE

Pop. density low

Bamileke, Fang, Fulani, French, English

33/km² (86/mi²)

THE URBAN/RURAL POPULATION SPLIT

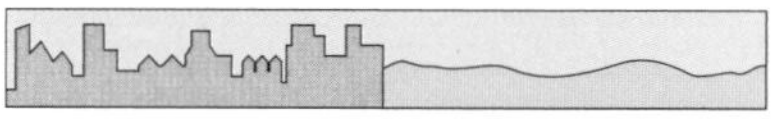
50%
50%

RELIGIOUS PERSUASION

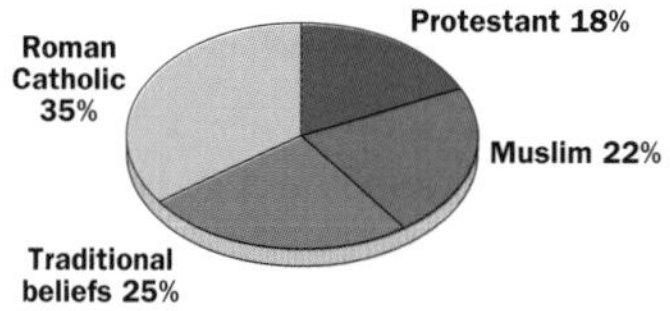
Protestant 18%
Roman Catholic 35%
Muslim 22%
Traditional beliefs 25%

Cameroon is ethnically diverse – there are 230 groups, no single group being dominant. The largest is the Bamileke of the center southwest, but this group has never held political power. When President Ahidjo, a northern Fulani, retired, he was replaced by Paul Biya of the southeastern Bulu-Beti group. The north–south enmity which affects many other west African states is also present here, albeit diminished by the great ethnic diversity. There is tension between the French- and minority English-speaking communities, as well as complaints from other sidelined groups.

POLITICS

Multiparty elections

2002/2007

President Paul Biya

AT THE LAST ELECTION

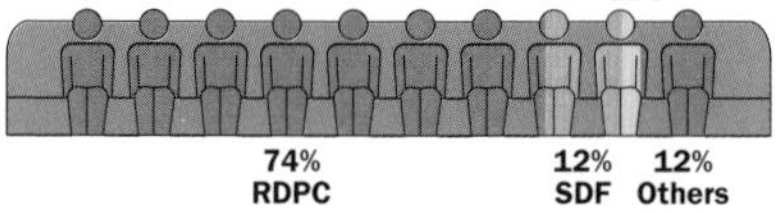
National Assembly 180 seats
2% CDU
74% RDPC
12% SDF
12% Others

RDPC = Cameroon People's Democratic Rally SDF = Social Democratic Front CDU = Cameroon Democratic Union

A Senate is to be created under the 1995 Constitution

Incumbent president Paul Biya's RDPC narrowly won control of the new parliament in multiparty elections in 1992 boycotted by the main opposition SDF. It has held on to power in the face of SDF claims of corruption, steadily increasing its majority in 1997 and again in 2002. Similarly, Biya's own reelections in 1992 and 1997 were condemned as the products of fraud and intimidation by SDF candidate John Fru Ndi.

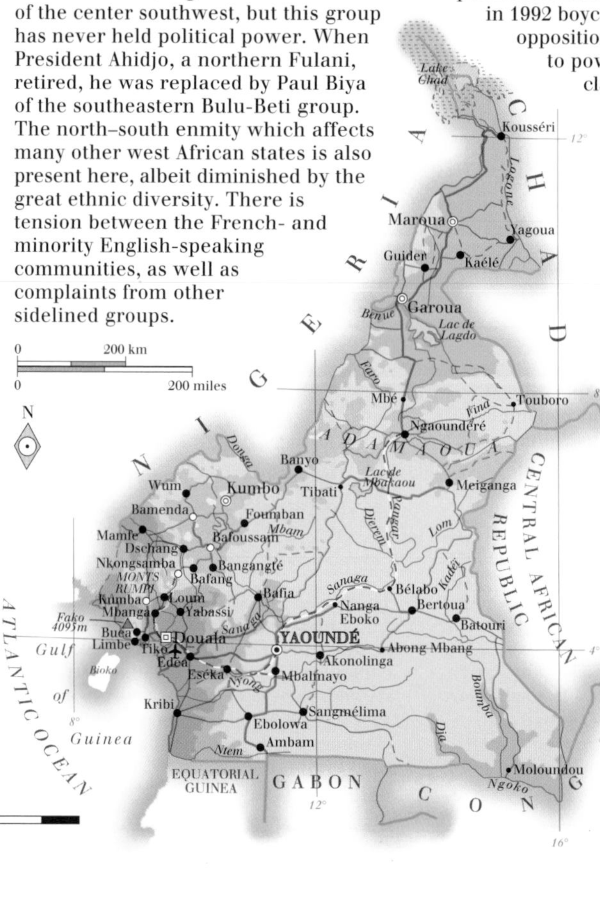
0 200 km
0 200 miles
N
Lake Chad
CHAD
NIGERIA
Kousséri
Logone
Maroua
Yagoua
Guider
Kaélé
Benue
Garoua
Lac de Lagdo
Faro
Mbé
Touboro
Ngaoundéré
ADAMAOUA
Banyo
Tibati
Lac de Mbakaou
Meiganga
Wum
Kumbo
Bamenda
Foumban
Mbam
Mamfe
Dschang
Bafoussam
Nkongsamba
MONTS RUMPI
Bafang
Bangangté
Kumba
Loum
Mbanga
Yabassi
Bafia
Fako 4095m
Buea
Limbe
Tiko
Douala
Edéa
Sanaga
YAOUNDÉ
Nanga Eboko
Bélabo
Bertoua
Batouri
Lom
Akonolinga
Abong Mbang
Eséka
Nyong
Mbalmayo
Gulf of Guinea
Bioko
ATLANTIC OCEAN
Kribi
Sangmélima
Ebolowa
Ambam
Ntem
Dja
Boumba
Moloundou
Ngoko
EQUATORIAL GUINEA
GABON
CONGO
CENTRAL AFRICAN REPUBLIC

CAMEROON

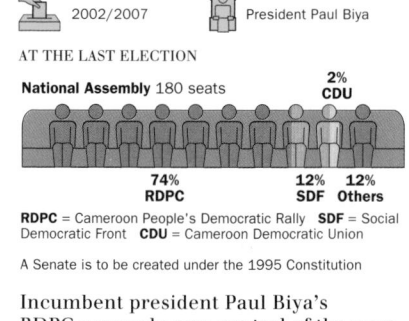

Total Area : 475 400 sq. km (183 567 sq. miles)

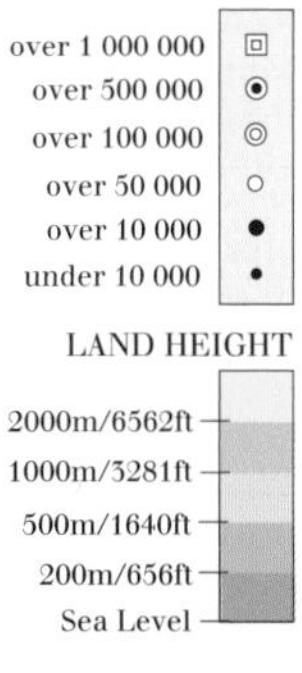
POPULATION
over 1 000 000
over 500 000
over 100 000
over 50 000
over 10 000
under 10 000
LAND HEIGHT
2000m/6562ft
1000m/3281ft
500m/1640ft
200m/656ft
Sea Level

C

WORLD AFFAIRS

Joined UN in 1960

BDEAC | Comm | OIC | LCBC | FZ

Cameroon's most important relationship is with France, but it has attempted to diversify its international and regional links. A territorial dispute with Nigeria over the oil-rich Bakassi peninsula, where there were clashes in 1996 and 1998, continues to be an issue, despite an international ruling in Cameroon's favor in 2002.

AID

Recipient

$398m (receipts) — Up 5% in 2001

France is by far the most important donor; it has twice paid Cameroon's back debts to the IMF to prevent its being blacklisted. The IMF agreed in 2000 to cancel $2 billion of debt if aid projects, many of which have been abandoned due to lack of funds, are completed.

DEFENSE

No compulsory military service

$120m — Down 2% in 2001

The 12,500-strong army has been active in supporting the regime and maintaining order in the face of prodemocratic protests since before independence. Military equipment and training come mainly from France. There is also a 9000-strong paramilitary gendarmerie.

ECONOMICS

Inflation 4.9% p.a. (1990–2001)

$8.74bn — 571.2 CFA francs (664.2)

SCORE CARD

❑ WORLD GNP RANKING	91st
❑ GNP PER CAPITA	$580
❑ BALANCE OF PAYMENTS	–$147m
❑ INFLATION	4.5%
❑ UNEMPLOYMENT	30%

STRENGTHS

French and US companies exploit moderate oil reserves. Very diversified agriculture includes timber, cocoa, bananas, and coffee. Self-sufficiency in food. Strong informal sector. Private sector in relatively good state. Electricity is 97% HEP.

WEAKNESSES

Massive fuel smuggling from Nigeria affects refinery profits. Inflated civil service. Widespread corruption.

EXPORTS

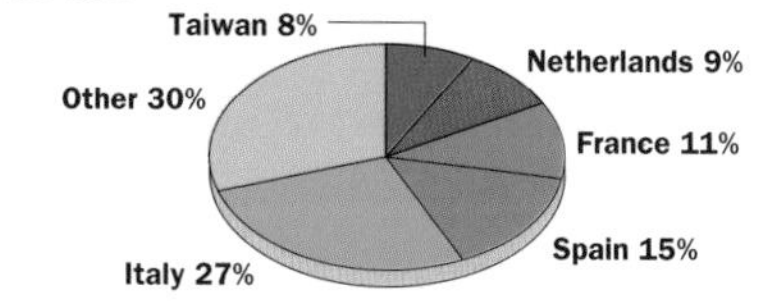
Taiwan 8%
Netherlands 9%
Other 30%
France 11%
Spain 15%
Italy 27%

IMPORTS

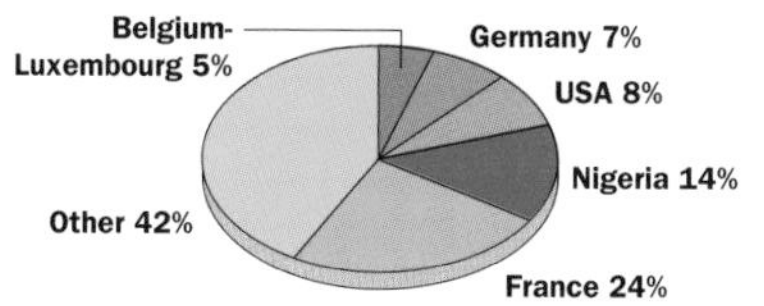
Belgium-Luxembourg 5%
Germany 7%
USA 8%
Nigeria 14%
Other 42%
France 24%

RESOURCES

Electric power 629,000 kW

112,159 tonnes — 72,000 b/d (reserves 400m barrels)

5.9m cattle, 4.4m goats, 3.8m sheep, 30m chickens — Oil, coal, tin, natural gas, bauxite, iron, uranium, gold

New oil discoveries may be able to bolster declining extraction rates. In spite of large bauxite deposits, much is imported for the Edea smelter, which uses a large share of electricity output.

ENVIRONMENT

Sustainability rank: 93rd

5% (2% partially protected) — 0.3 tonnes per capita

The rate of commercial logging and the planned Cameroon–Chad oil pipeline constitute major threats to Cameroon's environment.

MEDIA

TV ownership low

Daily newspaper circulation 0.5 per 1000 people

PUBLISHING AND BROADCAST MEDIA

There are 3 daily newspapers, *Politiks Matinal, Le Tribune du Cameroun,* and *Le Quotidien*

1 state-owned service — 1 state-owned service

There are frequent allegations of censorship and violence against journalists. English-language media are generally more outspoken.

CRIME

Death penalty in use

20,000 prisoners — Up sharply in 1996–1998

Armed robbery and burglary in Douala and Yaoundé are rising fast. The police are known to use torture.

EDUCATION

School leaving age: 12

72% — 68,495 students

The French-speaking majority has failed in its attempt to take over the bilingual system. Cameroon has a high literacy rate compared with much of the rest of west and central Africa.

CHRONOLOGY

One of the great trading emporia of west Africa, Cameroon was divided between the French and British in 1919, after 30 years of German rule.

- ❑ **1955** Revolt; French kill 10,000.
- ❑ **1960** French sector independent.
- ❑ **1961** British south joins Cameroon (north joins Nigeria).
- ❑ **1982** Ahmadou Ahidjo, first president, dies; succeeded by Biya.
- ❑ **1983–1984** Coup attempts. Heavy casualties; 50 plotters executed.
- ❑ **1990** Declaration of multiparty state.
- ❑ **1992** Multiparty elections.
- ❑ **1997** President and ruling RDPC returned in disputed elections.
- ❑ **2000** World Bank funds pipeline project, despite environmental fears.
- ❑ **2001** Over 80% of indigenous forests allocated for logging.
- ❑ **2002** RDPC increases its majority.

HEALTH

No welfare state health benefits

1 per 14,286 people — Malaria, diarrheal and respiratory diseases

A sharp fall in government health provision means that more people are using the private health sector or traditional practitioners.

SPENDING

GDP/cap. increase

CONSUMPTION AND SPENDING

7 per 1000 population — *7 per 1000 population*

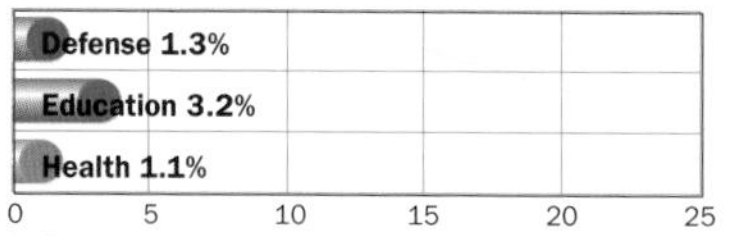
Defense 1.3%
Education 3.2%
Health 1.1%
0
5
10
15
20
25

Defense, Health, Education spending as % of GDP

Wealth is unevenly distributed and has been declining since the end of the 1980s oil boom. There is still a very wealthy, albeit small, sector of the population.

WORLD RANKING

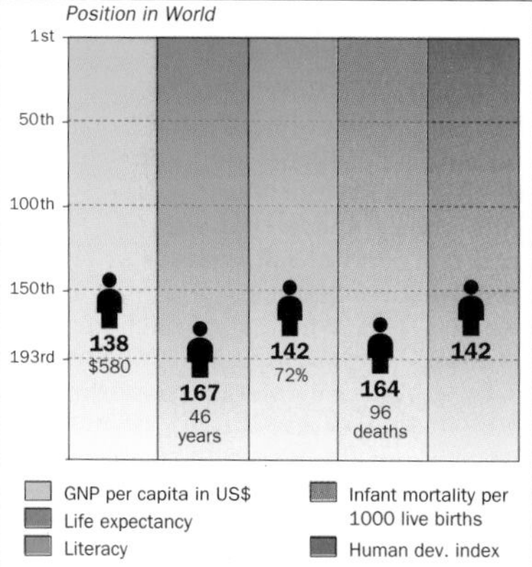
Position in World
1st
50th
100th
150th
193rd
138
$580
167
46 years
142
72%
164
96 deaths
142
GNP per capita in US$
Life expectancy
Literacy
Infant mortality per 1000 live births
Human dev. index

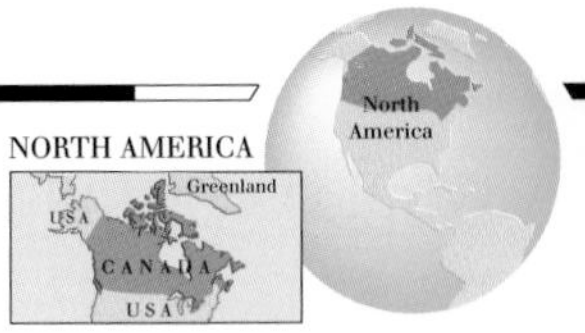
North America
NORTH AMERICA
Greenland
USA
CANADA
USA

CANADA

OFFICIAL NAME: Canada **CAPITAL:** Ottawa **POPULATION:** 31.3 million
CURRENCY: Canadian dollar **OFFICIAL LANGUAGES:** English and French

1867
1949
July 1
CDN
-3.5 to -8
+1
.ca

CANADA IS THE WORLD'S second-largest country, stretching north to Cape Columbia on Ellesmere Island, south to Lake Erie, and across six time zones from Newfoundland to the Pacific seaboard. The interior lowlands around Hudson Bay make up 80% of Canada's land area and include the vast Canadian Shield, with the plains of Saskatchewan and Manitoba and the Rocky Mountains to the west. The St. Lawrence, Yukon, Mackenzie, and Fraser Rivers are among the world's 40 largest. The Great Lakes–St. Lawrence River lowlands are the most populous areas. An Inuit homeland, Nunavut, formerly the eastern part of the Northwest Territories, was created in 1999, covering nearly a quarter of Canada's land area. French-speaking Québec's relationship with the rest of the country causes recurring constitutional arguments.

CLIMATE

Continental/subarctic/mountain

WEATHER CHART FOR OTTAWA

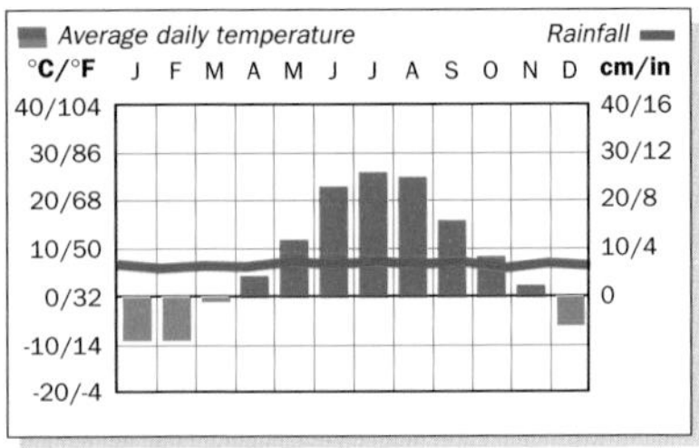
Average daily temperature
Rainfall
°C/°F
J F M A M J J A S O N D
cm/in
40/104
30/86
20/68
10/50
0/32
-10/14
-20/-4
40/16
30/12
20/8
10/4
0

Canada's climate ranges from polar and subpolar in the north, to cool in the south. Summers in the interior are hotter, and winters colder and longer than on the coast, with temperatures well below freezing and deep snow. The Pacific coast around Vancouver has the warmest winters, where temperatures rarely fall below zero.

TRANSPORTATION

Drive on right

Lester B. Pearson International, Toronto
25.9m passengers

875 ships
2.73m grt

THE TRANSPORTATION NETWORK

318,371 km (197,826 miles)

16,600 km (10,315 miles)

12,754 km (7925 miles)

3000 km (1864 miles)

The emergence of a national economy depended on the development of an efficient system of transportation. The Trans-Canada Highway and two transcontinental rail systems are the east–west backbones of the road and rail networks, which also reach into the far north. The Great Lakes–St. Lawrence Seaway system's cheap transportation helped Ontario and Québec dominate the economy for most of the 20th century. Air services were hit by the industry's crisis after September 11, 2001.

CANADA

Total Area : 9 984 670 sq. km (3 855 171 sq. miles)

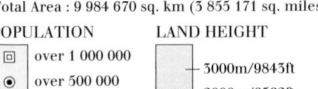

POPULATION	LAND HEIGHT
over 1 000 000	3000m/9843ft
over 500 000	2000m/6562ft
over 100 000	1000m/3281ft
over 50 000	500m/1640ft
over 10 000	200m/656ft
under 10 000	Sea Level

ARCTIC OCEAN
QUEEN ELIZABETH ISLANDS
Ellesmere
Axel Heiberg I.
Ellef Ringnes I.
Amund Ringnes I.
Isachsen
Prince Patrick I.
SVERDRUP ISLANDS
Mould Bay
PARRY ISLANDS
Melville I.
Bathurst I.
Cornwallis I.
Resolute
Beaufort Sea
Banks I.
Viscount Melville Sound
Sachs Harbour
Somerset I.
Prince of Wales I.
Inuvik
Amundsen Gulf
Victoria I.
M'Clintock Channel
Boothia Peninsula
Wollaston Peninsula
Cambridge Bay
King William I.
Gjoa Haven
Queen Maud Gulf
Kugluktuk
USA (ALASKA)
Yukon
Dawson
Klondike
MACKENZIE MOUNTAINS
YUKON TERRITORY
Great Bear Lake
NORTHWEST TERRITORIES
NUNAVUT
Mount Logan 5959m
Whitehorse
ROCKY MOUNTAINS
CASSIAR MOUNTAINS
Watson Lake
Mackenzie
Yellowknife
Great Slave Lake
Rankin Inlet
Hay River
Fort Smith
Dubawnt
PACIFIC OCEAN
COAST MOUNTAINS
BRITISH COLUMBIA
Peace
Lake Athabasca
Athabasca
Prince Rupert
Fort St. John
Churchill
Queen Charlotte Is
Grande Prairie
Fort McMurray
York Factory
Thompson
Nelson
ALBERTA
SASKATCHEWAN
MANITOBA
Ocean Falls
Prince George
Queen Charlotte Sound
St. Albert
Fort Saskatchewan
Edmonton
Flin Flon
Campbell River
Fraser
Leduc
Wetaskiwin
Camrose
Lloydminster
N. Saskatchewan
Red Deer
Prince Albert
Lake Winnipegosis
Lake Winnipeg
Vancouver I.
Kamloops
Airdrie
North Battleford
Saskatoon
Nanaimo
Vancouver
Vernon
Kelowna
Calgary
Victoria
Chilliwack
Penticton
S. Saskatchewan
Medicine Hat
Yorkton
Regina
Portage la Prairie
Cranbrook
Lethbridge
Swift Current
Moose Jaw
Brandon
Winnipeg
Weyburn
Estevan
Red R.
Lake of the Woods
UNITED STATES OF AMERICA
N
0
400 km
400 miles
140°
130°
120°
110°
100°

TOURISM

Visitors : Population 1:1.6

20m visitors

Up 2% in 2002

MAIN TOURIST ARRIVALS

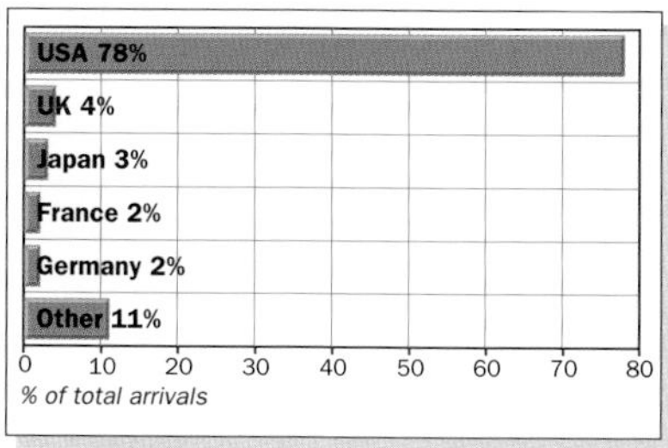
USA 78%
UK 4%
Japan 3%
France 2%
Germany 2%
Other 11%
0 10 20 30 40 50 60 70 80
% of total arrivals

Most tourist visitors come from the US, often on short tours. Efforts to attract European visitors center on campaigns emphasizing Canada's unpolluted natural beauty.

Bizarrely, the fictional home of the eponymous heroine of *Anne of Green Gables* on Prince Edward Island is a magnet for tourists from Japan, where the novels about her by L. M. Montgomery enjoy enormous popularity.

PEOPLE

Pop. density low

English, French, Chinese, Italian, German, Ukrainian, Portuguese, Inuktitut, Cree

3/km²
9/mi²

THE URBAN/RURAL POPULATION SPLIT

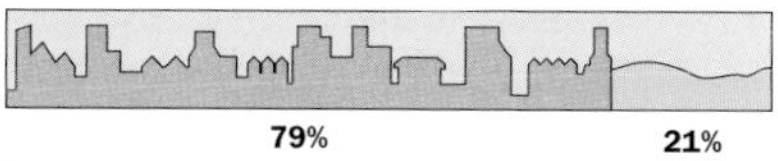
79%
21%

ETHNIC MAKEUP

Most Canadians are descended from immigrants from Britain, France, Ireland, and other European countries. Many now identify themselves simply as Canadian. In the 2001 census, which allowed multiple ethnic-origin answers, 6.7 million people chose only "Canadian" and 5 million more included it among their choices. Other responses included 14.3 million English, Scots, Irish, or Welsh, 4.7 million French, 8.7 million other European, 3 million Asian, and 1.3 million Amerindian, Métis, or Inuit.

RELIGIOUS PERSUASION

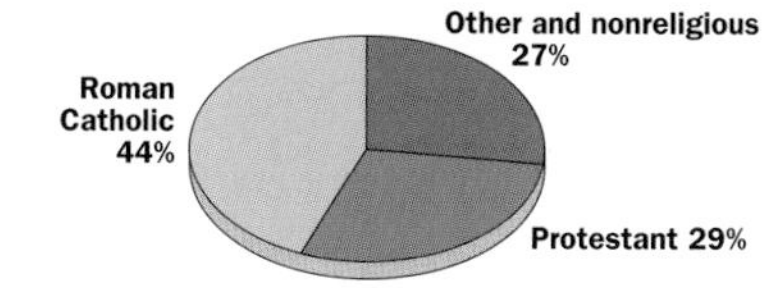
Other and nonreligious 27%
Roman Catholic 44%
Protestant 29%

Relations between French-speaking Québécois and the English-speaking majority in Canada have been the dominant ethnic issue of the past 40 years. Support for separatist parties increased mainly because of the failure of Canada's other provinces to deal with Québec's demand to be recognized as a "distinct society," with powers to preserve its culture and language from further anglicization.

Québec's still controversial 1977 language law made French the province's official language.

Two-thirds of Canada's population live in the 5% of its land area taken up by the Great Lakes–St. Lawrence lowlands. However, Canada's ethnic mix has changed significantly since the 1970s, due to a move from a restrictive immigration policy to one which welcomes those with money or skills. Significant numbers of Asians have moved to Canada. The government promotes a policy which encourages each group to maintain its own culture, creating a "mosaic" or a "community of communities."

The largest element of the indigenous population is the one million people of native Amerindian descent, known in Canada as First Nations. There are also 300,000 Métis (French-Amerindians) and an Inuit population of some 56,000 in the north. In 1992 the Inuit successfully settled their long-standing land claim, and in 1999 the Nunavut area, with only 25,000 mainly Inuit inhabitants, gained the status of a territory, the first part of Canada to be governed by indigenous Canadians in modern history. A Supreme Court land rights ruling in 1997, establishing the principle of "aboriginal title," opened the way for the return of ancestral lands claimed by native Amerindian nations, and in 1998 the federal government formally apologized for their past mistreatment.

Canada has a long tradition of state welfare more akin to Scandinavia than the US. Unemployment provision and health care, supported by high taxes, are still generous, despite recent cutbacks.

The government has sought to end inequalities. Measures include the "pay-equity" laws, which aim to specify equivalent pay rates for jobs done by men or women requiring a similar level of skill. Women are well represented at most levels of business and government.

A dude ranch in British Columbia. *Many tourists are attracted by Canada's wide choice of outdoor pursuits.*

POPULATION AGE BREAKDOWN

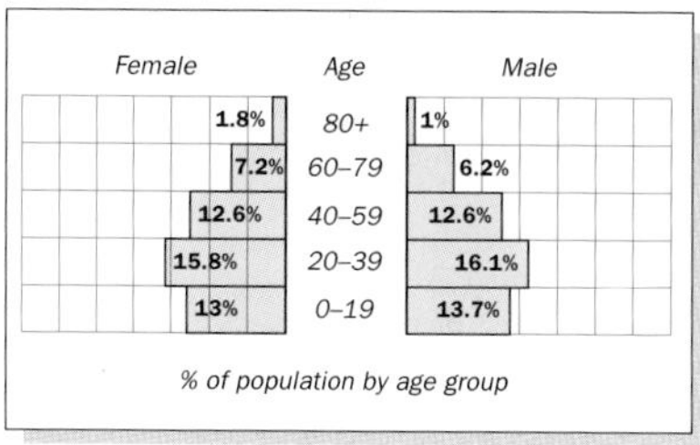
Female
Age
Male
1.8% 80+ 1%
7.2% 60–79 6.2%
12.6% 40–59 12.6%
15.8% 20–39 16.1%
13% 0–19 13.7%
% of population by age group

Baffin Bay
Davis Strait
Baffin Island
Cumberland Peninsula
Hall Peninsula
Foxe Peninsula
Iqaluit
Meta Incognita Peninsula
Coral Harbour
Ivujivik
Péninsula D'ungava
Ungava Bay
LABRADOR SEA
NEWFOUNDLAND & LABRADOR
Labrador
Happy Valley-Goose Bay
Schefferville
Smallwood Res.
QUEBEC
Belcher Is
Labrador City
Winisk
La Grande Rivière
LAURENTIAN MOUNTAINS
Corner Brook
St John's
Newfoundland
James Bay
Sept-Iles
Gulf of St. Lawrence
ST PIERRE & MIQUELON (to France)
Cabot Strait
PRINCE EDWARD ISLAND
Prince Edward I.
Sydney
Cape Breton I.
Moosonee
Péninsula de Gaspé
St. Lawrence
Chicoutimi
Jonquière
NEW BRUNSWICK
Charlottetown
Moncton
Fredericton
Saint John
Dartmouth
Halifax
NOVA SCOTIA
Yarmouth
Québec
Timmins
Trois-Rivières
Wawa
Laval
Hull
Sherbrooke
Montréal
Verdun
Superior
Sudbury
Sault Sainte Marie
North Bay
OTTAWA
Ottawa
Peterborough
L. Huron
Oshawa
Kingston
L. Ontario
Toronto
Kitchener
Hamilton
Niagara Falls
St Catherines
L. Michigan
Windsor
London
L. Erie
ATLANTIC OCEAN

C

CHRONOLOGY

Peopled for centuries by indigenous Amerindians and Inuit, Canada began to be settled by Europeans in the first half of the 17th century, following the English expedition led by John Cabot in 1497 and the landing of Frenchman Jacques Cartier in 1534.

- ❑ **1754–1760** British defeat French and Amerindian allies in Canada.
- ❑ **1763** Under Treaty of Paris, France cedes its St. Lawrence and Québec settlements to Britain.
- ❑ **1774** Act of Québec recognizes Roman Catholicism, French language, culture, and traditions.
- ❑ **1775–1783** American War of Independence. Canada becomes refuge for loyalists to British crown.
- ❑ **1867** Dominion of Canada created under British North America Act.
- ❑ **1885** Transcontinental railroad completed.
- ❑ **1897** Klondike gold rush begins.
- ❑ **1914–1918, 1939–1945** Canada supports Allies in both world wars.
- ❑ **1931** Autonomy within Commonwealth.
- ❑ **1949** Founder member of NATO. Newfoundland joins Canada.
- ❑ **1968** Liberal Party under Pierre Trudeau in power. Separatist Parti Québécois (PQ) formed.
- ❑ **1970s** Québec secessionist movement grows, accompanied by terrorist attacks.
- ❑ **1976** PQ wins Québec elections.
- ❑ **1977** French made official language in Québec.
- ❑ **1980** Referendum rejects secession of Québec. Trudeau prime minister.
- ❑ **1982** UK transfers all powers relating to Canada in British law.
- ❑ **1984** Trudeau resigns. Elections won by PCP. Brian Mulroney prime minister until 1993.
- ❑ **1987** Meech Lake Accord on provincial–federal relationship.
- ❑ **1989** Canadian–US Free Trade Agreement.
- ❑ **1992** Charlottetown Agreement on provincial–federal issues rejected in referendum. Canada, Mexico, and US finalize terms for NAFTA.
- ❑ **1993** Crushing election defeat of PCP, rise of regional parties. Jean Chrétien becomes prime minister.
- ❑ **1994** PQ regains power in Québec. NAFTA takes effect.
- ❑ **1995** Narrow "no" vote in second Québec sovereignty referendum.
- ❑ **1995** Fishing dispute with EU.
- ❑ **1997** Regionalism dominates federal election; Liberals retain power based on support in Ontario.
- ❑ **2000** Early elections: Liberals again retain power.
- ❑ **2003** PQ ousted by Liberals in Québec after nine years in power.

POLITICS

Multiparty elections

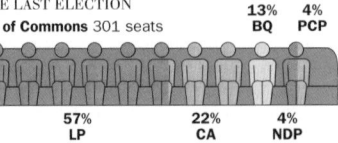

L. House 2000/2005 | H.M. Queen Elizabeth II

AT THE LAST ELECTION

House of Commons 301 seats

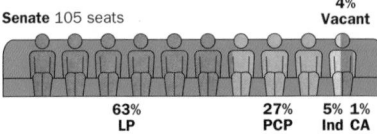

13% BQ
4% PCP
57% LP
22% CA
4% NDP

LP = Liberal Party **CA** = Canadian Reform Conservative Alliance **BQ** = Bloc Québécois **NDP** = New Democratic Party **PCP** = Progressive Conservative Party **Ind** = Independents

Senate 105 seats

4% Vacant
63% LP
27% PCP
5% Ind
1% CA

Senators are appointed by the governor-general on the recommendation of the prime minister, to a usual maximum of 105; the prime minister may also appoint an extra seven senators. Senators retain their seats until the age of 75

Canada is a federal multiparty democracy.

Profile

A major political shift has taken place with the eclipse of the once-powerful PCP, three victories for Jean Chrétien and the LP (1993, 1997, and 2000), and an eventual realignment on the right, based on the emergence of the populist Reform Party (RP) in the western provinces. However, the concurrent trend away from Canada-wide politics, toward parties representing strong regional interests, left the LP with few seats outside its strongholds in the east. The Bloc Québécois (BQ), espousing the separatist cause at federal level, was the second-largest party in the federal parliament between 1994 and 1997. Since the 1997 elections the official opposition has been the RP and then the conservative CA, into which the RP was incorporated in 2000. Chrétien has pledged to stand down in early 2004 to allow a new generation to take the LP into the next elections. Fomer finance minister Paul Martin is seen as his most likely successor.

Main Political Issues

The unity of the state

Opposition to federal government is not confined to Québec – the 1997 and 2000 federal elections confirmed support for greater autonomy for Canada's western provinces – but Canada has agonized over separatist tendencies in francophone Québec almost since the foundation of the state. Québec did not take part in the 1997 Calgary conference, where a Canadian unity framework was agreed by the other provinces, together with recognition of Québec's "unique character." A series of earlier proposals, to recognize Québec as a distinct society and strengthen the powers of all the federal provinces, had failed to gain ratification or been rejected by the electorate. The ambition of the Parti Québécois (PQ) to hold yet another referendum on separatism, despite losing those held in 1980 and 1995, was derailed when the party lost provincial elections to the LP in 2003. The popularity of the PQ suffered as voters were keen to focus on everyday issues, rather than the promise of more constitutional wrangling. Any future vote on secession will anyway require federal approval and the agreement of at least seven of the ten provinces, while the 2000 Clarity Act set strict criteria for the validation of any prosecession referendum.

North American integration

The North American Free Trade Agreement (NAFTA), a hotly debated issue in Canada when it was being negotiated in the early 1990s, produced a trade boom, especially for Ontario. However, Canadians have problems competing for foreign investment with Mexico, where labor costs, social welfare, and environmental standards are lower. Most Canadians oppose such ideas as a currency union and ever closer integration with the US.

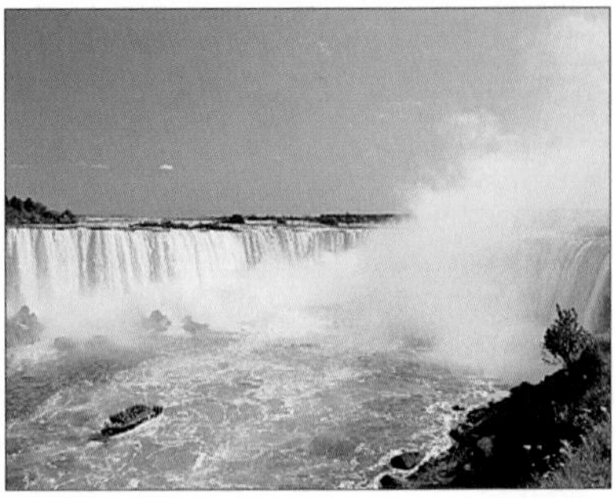

***The Niagara Falls** are situated between Lakes Erie and Ontario on the Canada–US border. Horseshoe Falls, in Canada, are 49 m (160 ft) high and 790 m (2591 ft) across.*

***Jean Charest**, the Liberal premier of Québec since 2003.*

***Stephen Harper** was elected leader of the CA in 2002.*

***Jean Chrétien**, prime minister since 1993.*

WORLD AFFAIRS

Joined UN in 1945

Comm | G8 | OECD | NAFTA | NATO

Canada's most important relationship is with the US. Though relations are on the whole good, there are tensions. Notably, Canada has protested over US duties on its softwood timber. At a more basic level Canadians are wary of the encroachment of US culture and of its concurrent social ills. Canada opposes the US sanctions imposed on Cuba and protests over its environmental lapses: there are concerns over the transportation of Alaskan oil and US resistance to international treaties (the US refuses to sign the Kyoto Protocol, signed by Canada in 2002). Canada has backed the US-led "war on terrorism," but refused to support the 2003 attack on Iraq.

In the forefront on debt relief for the poorest countries, Canada has also led the world campaign against antipersonnel mines.

AID

Donor

US$1.53bn (donations)

Down 12% in 2001

Canada's aid budget, earmarked for cuts in the 1990s, was given extra funding again at the end of the decade. NGOs supported by the Canadian International Development Agency (CIDA) are prominent on global development issues, and most Canadians approve of giving aid.

Aid now aims to provide know-how skills, rather than funding for large-scale development projects. CIDA has pioneered a theme-based approach, stressing health and nutrition, basic education, AIDS, and child protection. The regional focus of aid has gradually shifted, with less emphasis on Africa. Programs in the 1990s supported recovery and reform in former communist countries. Aid is now given to a range of countries; eastern Europe has become a particular focus.

DEFENSE

No compulsory military service

US$7.75bn

Down 7% in 2001

CANADIAN ARMED FORCES

114 main battle tanks (Leopard C-2)	19,300 personnel
2 submarines, 4 destroyers, 12 frigates, and 14 patrol boats	9000 personnel
140 combat aircraft (122 CF-18)	13,500 personnel
None	

Canada cooperates closely with the US on North American defense and security issues.

Defense spending was cut after the end of the Cold War. Recently the government has come under pressure to reinvest in the increasingly run-down armed forces. The focus of planning is now the creation of rapid reaction forces. Canadian troops have served in many UN peacekeeping operations, most recently in Kosovo, East Timor, and Sierra Leone. Their involvement in Somalia, however, which ended in 1993, was tarnished by a scandal over racism, torture, and murder which shocked Canadian society.

ECONOMICS

Inflation 1.5% p.a. (1990–2001)

US$682bn

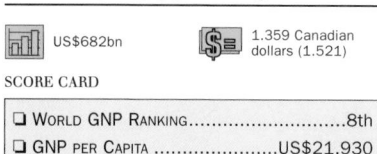

1.359 Canadian dollars (1.521)

SCORE CARD

❑ WORLD GNP RANKING	8th
❑ GNP PER CAPITA	US$21,930
❑ BALANCE OF PAYMENTS	US$19.5bn
❑ INFLATION	2.5%
❑ UNEMPLOYMENT	7%

EXPORTS

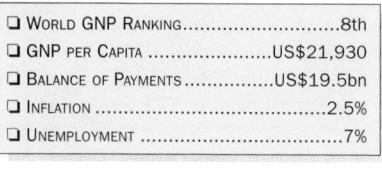

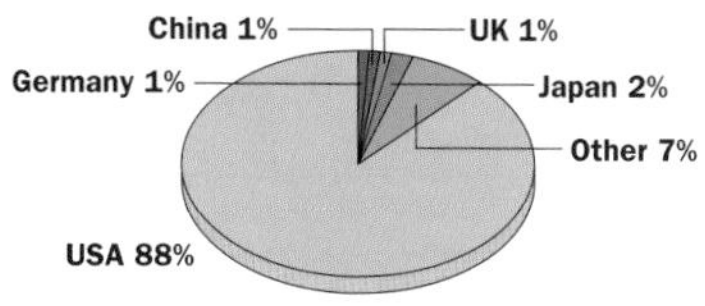
China 1%
UK 1%
Germany 1%
Japan 2%
Other 7%
USA 88%

IMPORTS

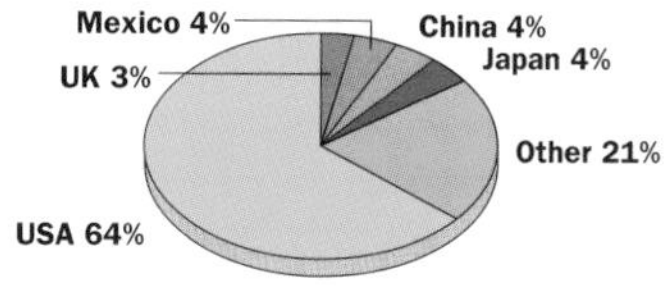
Mexico 4%
China 4%
Japan 4%
UK 3%
Other 21%
USA 64%

STRENGTHS

A broad and rich resource base. Provides exports, raw materials for manufacturing sector, and massive cheap energy, notably HEP; also large oil and gas reserves. Agriculture and forestry contribute 2% of GDP, mining 4%. Successful manufacturing sector, contributes 16% of GDP, especially forestry products, transportation equipment, and chemicals. Record budget surplus since 1997. Access to huge US and Mexican markets through NAFTA. Low inflation.

WEAKNESSES

Problems of competitiveness: higher taxes, more regulations, low productivity relative to NAFTA; other threats from globalization. Vulnerable to price fluctuations for raw material exports. Brain drain of professionals heading south.

ECONOMIC PERFORMANCE INDICATOR

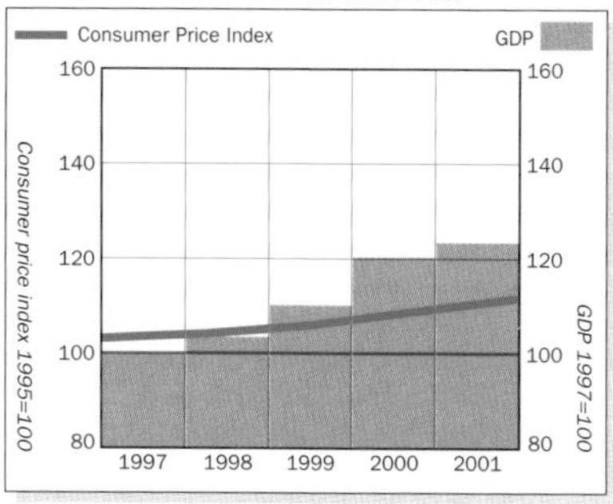
Consumer Price Index
GDP
160
140
120
100
80
Consumer price index 1995=100
GDP 1997=100
1997
1998
1999
2000
2001

PROFILE

Canada has an enormous resource base, and it has one of the highest standards of living in the world. Since the mid-1980s, however, manufactured exports have faced increasing competition, while prices for its primary exports fluctuate. Real growth averaged 3.5% a year for most of the 1980s, but then stagnated for five years, while budget deficits rose, forcing restructuring at both federal and provincial levels. Many welfare programs were cut back; the defense budget was sharply reduced. Growth resumed after 1993 and an unwieldy budget deficit was turned into a record surplus by 1997. Within NAFTA, Canadian firms have had to become more competitive to maintain exports. Most have been successful, with better productivity and a high-tech shift. Unemployment, at almost 10% in the mid-1990s, was reduced to just under 7% by 2001. Canada's close ties to the US left it hard hit by the 2001 slowdown.

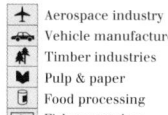

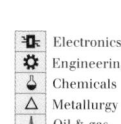

CANADA : MAJOR BUSINESSES

- Aerospace industry
- Vehicle manufacture
- Timber industries
- Pulp & paper
- Food processing
- Fish processing
- Electronics
- Engineering
- Chemicals
- Metallurgy
- Oil & gas

St John's
Edmonton
Vancouver
Halifax
Calgary
Regina
Québec
Winnipeg
ThunderBay
Montréal
Toronto
0 500 km
0 500 miles

C

C

RESOURCES

Electric power 116m kW

1.12m tonnes

2.88m b/d (reserves 6.9bn barrels)

14.4m pigs, 13.7m cattle, 5.9m turkeys, 160m chickens

Coal, oil, gas, gold, zinc, uranium, nickel, potash, asbestos, gypsum

ELECTRICITY GENERATION

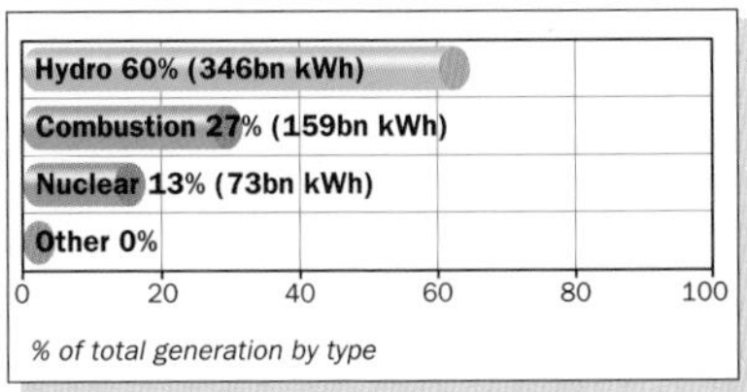
Hydro 60% (346bn kWh)
Combustion 27% (159bn kWh)
Nuclear 13% (73bn kWh)
Other 0%
0
20
40
60
80
100
% of total generation by type

Canada is a country of enormous natural resources. It is the world's largest exporter of forest products and a top exporter of fish, furs, and wheat. Minerals have played a key role in Canada's transformation into an urban–industrial economy. Alberta, British Columbia, Québec, and Saskatchewan are the principal mining regions. Ontario and the Northwest (NWT) and Yukon Territories are also significant producers. Canada is the world's largest producer of uranium and potash, the second-largest of nickel, and the third-largest of asbestos, gypsum, and zinc. Oil and gas are exploited in Alberta, off the Atlantic coast, and in the northwest – huge additional reserves are thought to exist in the high Arctic. Most exports go to the US. Canada is also one of the world's top hydroelectricity producers.

CANADA : LAND USE

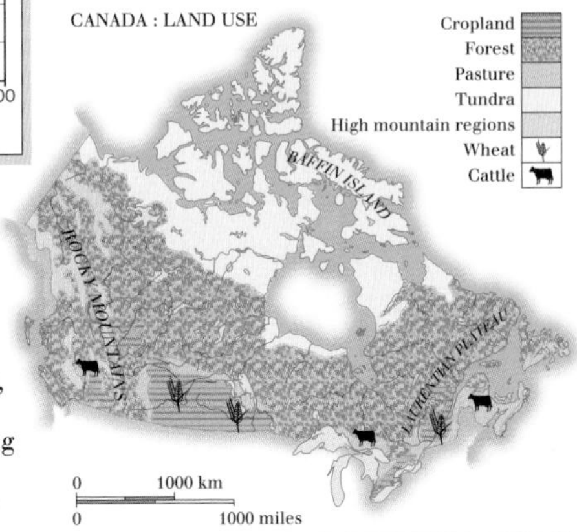
Cropland
Forest
Pasture
Tundra
High mountain regions
Wheat
Cattle
BAFFIN ISLAND
ROCKY MOUNTAINS
LAURENTIAN PLATEAU
0
1000 km
0
1000 miles

ENVIRONMENT

Sustainability rank: 4th

12% (5% partially protected)

18.6 tonnes per capita

ENVIRONMENTAL TREATIES

Yes Yes Yes

Yes Yes Yes

With a population of only some 31 million living in the world's second-largest country, Canada is justly renowned for vast tracts of wilderness untroubled by pollution either from industry or from intensive farming methods. A major conservation issue is the battle to stop the logging of virgin forest in northern Ontario and on the west coast. Notable successes were achieved in the late 1990s, pressuring timber companies to adopt more sustainable policies, and a landmark agreement in early 2001 promised protection for British Columbia's coastal Great Bear Rainforest.

Canadians have tighter pollution controls than the neighboring US. Ontario, the most polluted province, has imposed stricter limits on oil refineries and (from 2001) on electricity-generating plants. Carbon dioxide emissions (mainly from cars) are among the highest in the world per capita. Canada has accepted a target of a 6% cut by 2010. Production of hazardous waste is also higher than the European average.

MEDIA

TV ownership high

Daily newspaper circulation 159 per 1000 people

PUBLISHING AND BROADCAST MEDIA

There are 101 daily newspapers; over 80 daily or weekly publications appear in 20 languages, catering to immigrant

1 publicly owned service, many independent services

1 publicly owned service, many independent services

The public Canadian Broadcasting Corporation (CBC) runs two national TV channels, in English and French; the conservative opposition has called for its privatization. Local cable services often include multilingual or ethnic channels. Canadian TV is renowned for its news and sports coverage. *La Presse* is a leading French daily and the *Globe and Mail* is the leading national newspaper in English.

***Black spruce in autumn** in northern Canada. Whether due to global warming or localized temperature cycles, the tundra is retreating across Arctic Canada.*

CRIME

No death penalty

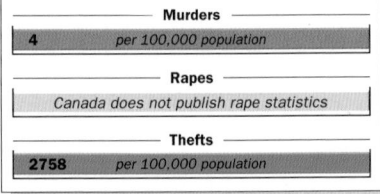

31,624 prisoners

Up 6% in 2000–2001

CRIME RATES

Murders

4 per 100,000 population

Rapes

Canada does not publish rape statistics

Thefts

2758 per 100,000 population

Rates for serious crime are lower in Canada than in the US. Canadians ascribe this to their far stricter gun control laws, which were further tightened in the 1990s.

Newfoundland police began carrying guns routinely only in 1998, the last force in North America to do so. There have been careful efforts to maintain the inner cities as crime-free zones.

To address the narcotics problem, innovative "drug treatment courts" in Toronto and Vancouver link criminal justice with treatment and social care.

EDUCATION

School leaving age: 16

99%

1.22m students

THE EDUCATION SYSTEM

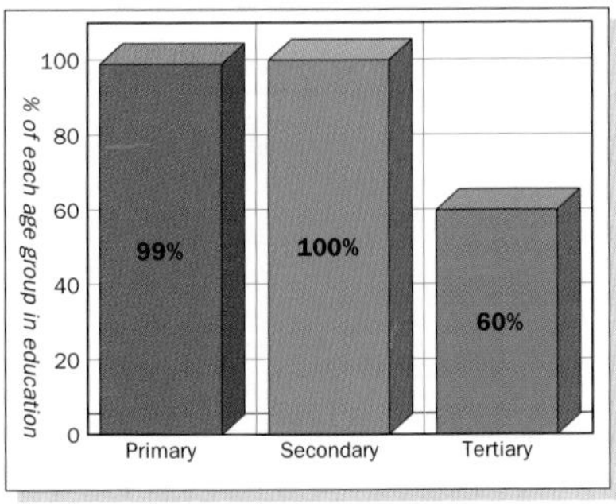
100
80
60
40
20
0
% of each age group in education
99%
100%
60%
Primary
Secondary
Tertiary

Education is a responsibility of the individual provinces, rather than the federal government, and is accorded a very high priority. The period of free compulsory school attendance varies, but is a minimum of nine years.

The prime medium of instruction is English in all provinces except francophone Québec. In several other provinces, French-speaking students are entitled to be taught in French. Multicultural education also helps maintain the cultural identity of immigrant groups.

Canada has 75 universities and some 200 other higher education institutions. Nearly all high school graduates go on to some form of tertiary or further education, one of the highest proportions in the industrialized world.

QUÉBEC'S DISTINCT SOCIETY AND SEPARATISM

QUÉBEC IS CANADA'S largest province, with an area of 1,667,926 sq. km (594,860 sq. miles). Its population, 7.2 million at the 2001 census, includes almost six million of Canada's 6.8 million French-speakers, most of them Roman Catholics. Its capital is Québec City. The leading commercial center, Montréal, has suffered a decline in prestige compared with Toronto, in neighboring Ontario, which is overwhelmingly English-speaking. Québec has massive hydroelectric power resources and vast areas of forest, and its principal industries include timber, pulp and paper, and mining, particularly for iron ore. Consequently, environmental protection legislation is relatively lax, and there is conflict with those seeking to protect First Nations lands from devastation by logging and massive dam schemes.

RESTAURANT
CAFÉ DE PARIS

***French shop signs** above the streets of Québec city.*

Conquered by the British in the 18th century, the Québécois retained the French civil code under the 1774 Québec Act, but French Canadians only gradually recovered minority language rights suppressed after an unsuccessful rebellion in the 1830s. A "quiet revolution" began in the 1960s, based initially on militant trade unionism, bringing far-reaching changes to the social, economic, and political balance in Québec. The wage gap closed, and francophones now slightly out-earn anglophones, partly because well-educated anglophones tend to leave the province. Francophone-owned businesses were built up through the "Québec Inc." project. Anglophone dominance in government and the civil service was reversed, and higher education opportunities expanded for francophones. Francophone militancy was also channeled into party politics, fueled by a harsh security clampdown in the early 1970s against the guerrilla Québec Liberation Front. The Parti Québécois (PQ) unexpectedly gained control of the provincial assembly in 1976; a French language charter, Bill 101, was enacted immediately. French became not only the official language but compulsory in government and on public signs. Nonfrancophones protested, and the Supreme Court ruled in 1988 that part of the language charter violated their human rights, but the provincial government managed to enforce the rules on a "temporary" basis.

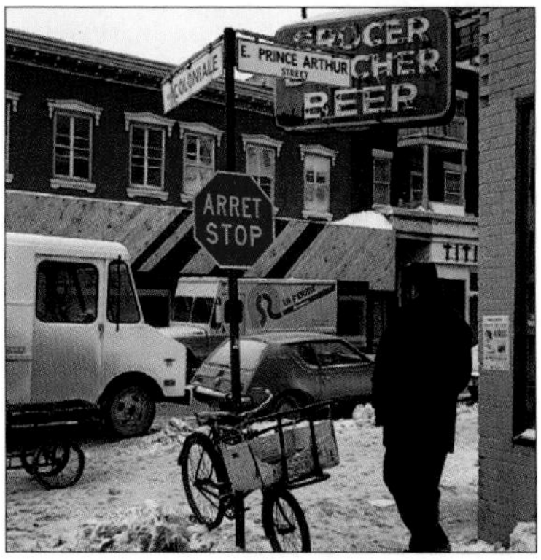
E. PRINCE ARTHUR STREET
BEER
ARRET
STOP

***Bilingual street signs** in Québec City have now largely been replaced by French-only signs.*

The PQ's main cause was sovereignty for Québec. After its defeat in a referendum in 1980, the idea was revived amid long-running disputes about the Canadian constitution and provincial–federal relationships in the 1990s. The PQ, promising a second referendum (and backed by its newly formed counterpart at federal level, the BQ), returned to power in Québec in 1994. The following year, 60% of Québec's francophone majority voted in favor of sovereignty in association with Canada, a high-water mark for separatism; the proposition was defeated by the narrowest of margins by the nonfrancophone vote. The PQ said that it would seek a third referendum, but federal legislation limits the conditions under which it can do so, and its commitment to separatism has lost much impetus. Francophones remain protective of their language and culture, but the declining political power of the PQ, and its relegation to an opposition role in 2003, suggest that the sovereignty issue may not dominate the 21st-century election agenda as it did in the closing decades of the last century.

HEALTH

Welfare state health benefits

1 per 538 people

Cancers, heart and respiratory diseases

The comprehensive state health service is funded from national insurance.

Rising costs are the result of an aging population and the spread of more sophisticated and expensive treatments. Health care was the main issue of the 2000 election campaign. Popular backing for retaining the present publicly funded system has encouraged the LP government to restore spending to earlier levels, after a period of cuts made in an effort to reduce the budget deficit. There is fierce debate over the possibility of privatization.

SPENDING

GDP/cap. increase

CONSUMPTION AND SPENDING

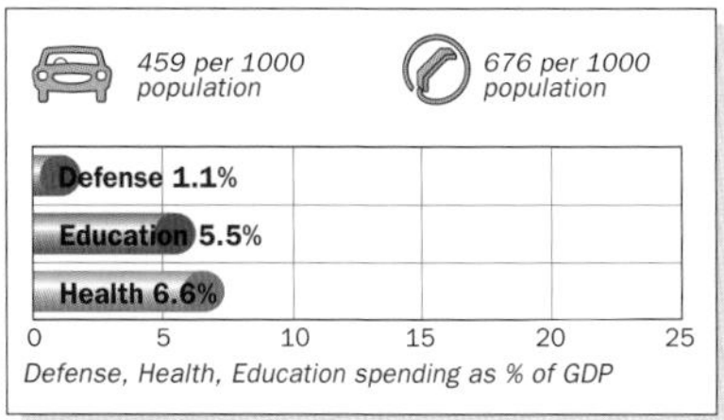
459 per 1000 population
676 per 1000 population
Defense 1.1%
Education 5.5%
Health 6.6%
0
5
10
15
20
25
Defense, Health, Education spending as % of GDP

Life for most Canadians is very good, despite strains caused by recession during the early 1990s – including a peak in unemployment at over 10%.

The UN ranks Canada as one of the best countries in the world in which to live. In its overall assessment of human development indicators such as income, education, and life expectancy, Canada was consistently top in the 1990s, but has now slipped to eighth.

However, disadvantaged groups do exist, in particular among indigenous Canadians. Unemployment, poor housing, and mortality rates for Amerindians and Inuit are well above those for other Canadians; the Inuit suicide rate is three times higher. Those Amerindians who live on reserves are the poorest group.

WORLD RANKING

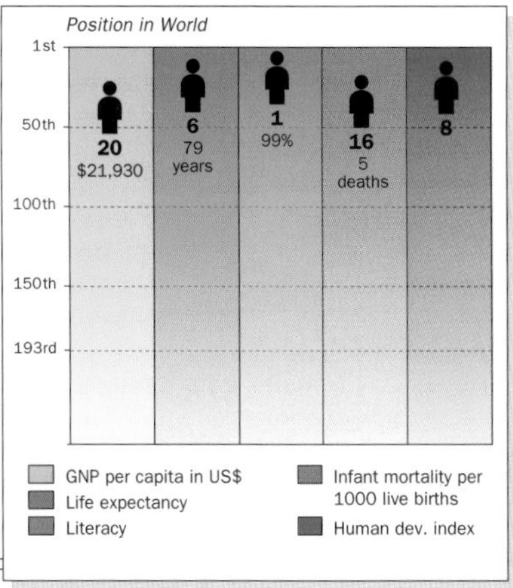
Position in World
1st
50th
100th
150th
193rd
20
$21,930
6
79 years
1
99%
16
5 deaths
8
GNP per capita in US$
Life expectancy
Literacy
Infant mortality per 1000 live births
Human dev. index

C

CAPE VERDE

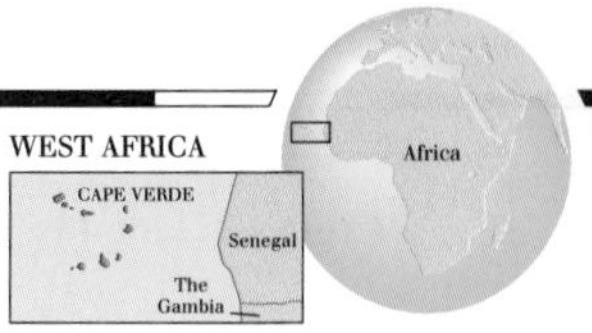
WEST AFRICA
CAPE VERDE
Senegal
The Gambia
Africa

OFFICIAL NAME: Republic of Cape Verde **CAPITAL:** Praia
POPULATION: 446,000 **CURRENCY:** Cape Verde escudo **OFFICIAL LANGUAGE:** Portuguese

C

1975 | 1975 | July 5 | CV | -1 | +238 | .cv

The Cape Verde archipelago off the west coast of Africa became independent of Portugal in 1975. Most of the islands are mountainous and volcanic; the low-lying islands of Sal, Boa Vista, and Maio have agricultural potential, though they are prone to debilitating droughts. Around 50% of the population live on Santiago. Following a period of single-party socialist rule, Cape Verde held its first multiparty elections in 1991.

CLIMATE

Tropical oceanic

WEATHER CHART FOR PRAIA

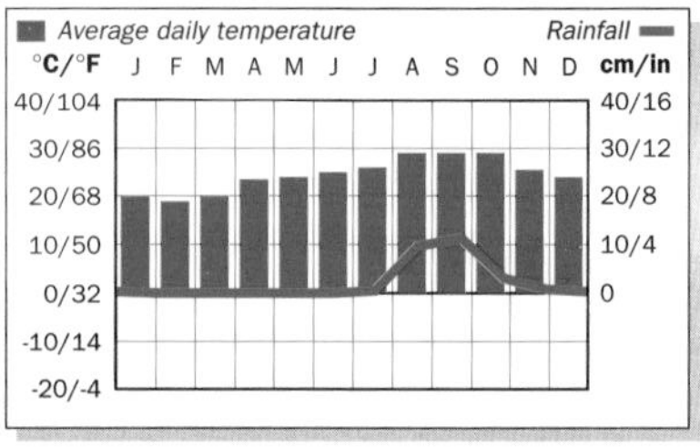
Average daily temperature
Rainfall
°C/°F
J F M A M J J A S O N D
cm/in
40/104
30/86
20/68
10/50
0/32
-10/14
-20/-4
40/16
30/12
20/8
10/4
0

Cape Verde has a very dry climate, subject to droughts that sometimes last for years at a time.

TRANSPORTATION

Drive on right

Amílcar Cabral, Sal Island
781,480 passengers

40 ships
16,500 grt

THE TRANSPORTATION NETWORK

858 km (533 miles)

None

None

None

Travel between the islands is either by ferry or the more expensive daily flights run by Cabo Verde Airlines.

TOURISM

Visitors : Population 1:6

74,000 visitors

Up 68% in 2000

MAIN TOURIST ARRIVALS

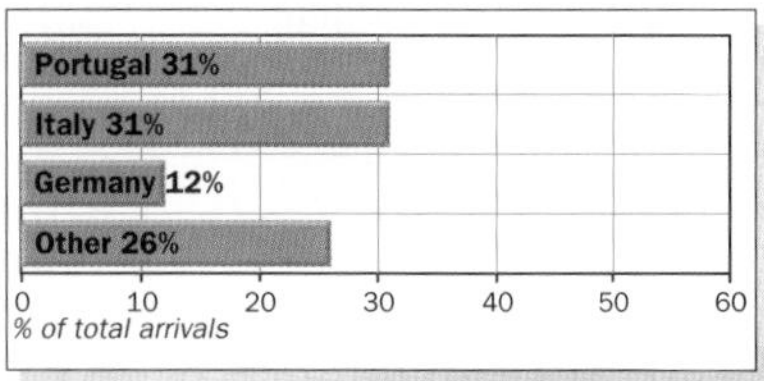
Portugal 31%
Italy 31%
Germany 12%
Other 26%
0
10
20
30
40
50
60
% of total arrivals

Tourism has not been a government priority and remains on a modest scale. The islands of Santiago, Santo Antão, Fogo, and Brava have tourist potential, offering a combination of mountain scenery and extensive beaches.

PEOPLE

Pop. density medium

Portuguese Creole, Portuguese

111/km² (287/mi²)

THE URBAN/RURAL POPULATION SPLIT

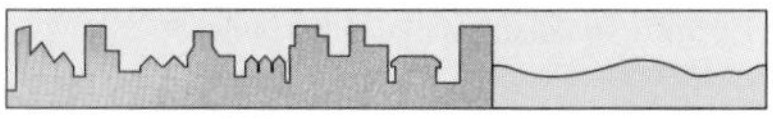
64%
36%

RELIGIOUS PERSUASION

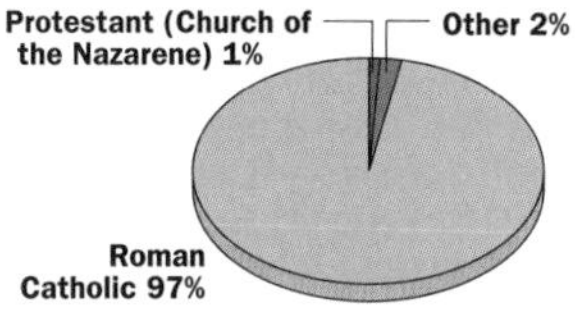
Protestant (Church of the Nazarene) 1%
Other 2%
Roman Catholic 97%

The majority of the population is Portuguese–African *mestiço*; the remainder is largely African, descended either from slaves or from more recent immigrants from the mainland. The Creolization of the culture has led to a relative lack of ethnic tension. African culture is influential on Santiago Island.

The extended family, as well as the Roman Catholic Church, have helped to ensure the vitality of family life. Some 600,000 Cape Verdean emigrants now live in communities around the world: overseas remittances are an important part of the economy.

POLITICS

Multiparty elections

2001/2006

President Pedro Pires

AT THE LAST ELECTION

National Assembly 72 seats

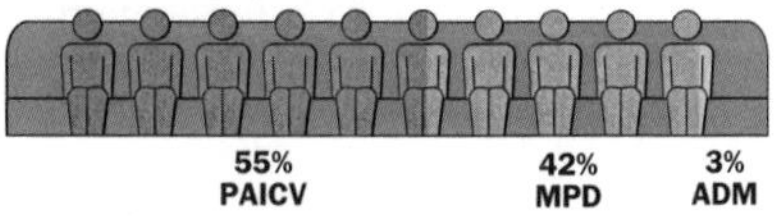
55% PAICV
42% MPD
3% ADM

PAICV = African Party for the Independence of Cape Verde
MPD = Movement for Democracy
ADM = Democratic Alliance for Change

Cape Verde experienced a peaceful transition to multipartyism in 1991, when elections brought the MPD to power. Although there had previously been a decade of single-party rule under the PAICV, it had in fact operated a liberal system in which opposition and dissent were tolerated. The large Cape Verdean diaspora had an important influence in effecting the transition to multiparty politics.

The MPD was defeated in legislative elections in January 2001, when the PAICV was returned to power with an absolute majority. Pedro Pires of the PAICV was elected president the following month, beating his MPD rival by just 17 votes. The main issues for the government are economic development, forging new international partnerships, and responding to drought.

WORLD AFFAIRS

Joined UN in 1975

CPLP | ECOWAS | OIF | NAM | AU

Cape Verde wishes to diversify its international contacts to secure aid and foreign investment, while maintaining good relations with Portugal. Regionally, it has improved relations with Guinea-Bissau, after withdrawing from a proposed union in 1980. Ties to other lusophone countries are important, including Angola and Brazil, as are links with "neighboring" Senegal and Gambia.

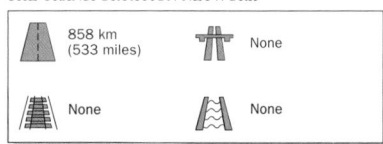

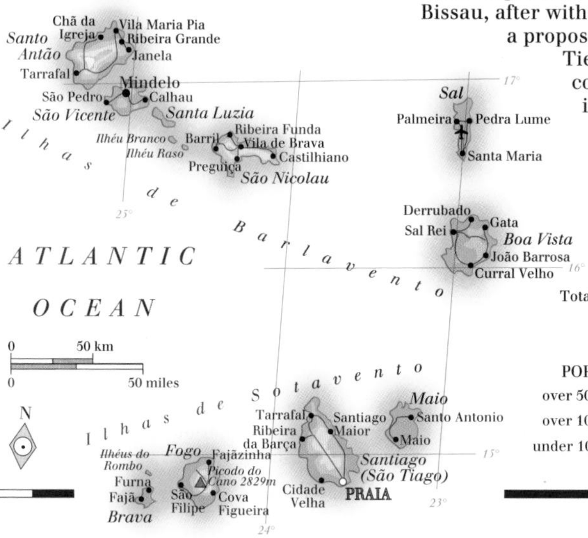
Chã da Igreja
Vila Maria Pia
Ribeira Grande
Santo Antão
Janela
Tarrafal
Mindelo
São Pedro
Calhau
São Vicente
Santa Luzia
Ilhas de Barlavento
Ilhéu Branco
Ilhéu Raso
Barril
Ribeira Funda
Vila de Brava
Castilhiano
Preguiça
São Nicolau
Sal
Palmeira
Pedra Lume
Santa Maria
Derrubado
Gata
Sal Rei
Boa Vista
João Barrosa
Curral Velho
ATLANTIC
OCEAN
0
50 km
50 miles
N
Ilhas de Sotavento
Tarrafal
Santiago
Maior
Ribeira da Barça
Maio
Santo Antonio
Ilhéus do Rombo
Fogo
Fajãzinha
Santiago (São Tiago)
Furna
Fajã
Brava
São Filipe
Pico do Cano 2829m
Cova Figueira
Cidade Velha
PRAIA

CAPE VERDE

Total Area : 4033 sq. km (1557 sq. miles)

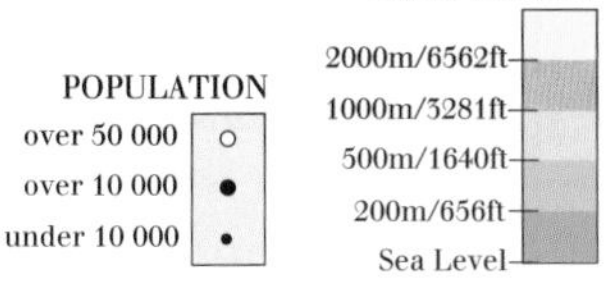
LAND HEIGHT
2000m/6562ft
1000m/3281ft
500m/1640ft
200m/656ft
Sea Level
POPULATION
over 50 000
over 10 000
under 10 000

AID

Recipient

$76m (receipts) — Down 19% in 2001

Aid finances almost all development in Cape Verde, which is one of the least industrialized countries in the world and is vulnerable to food shortages. Portugal is the main source of aid, while other major donors include the World Bank, the AfDB, and other European countries. The AfDB loaned $8 million in 2002 to finance an environment and food security project.

DEFENSE

Compulsory military service

$4m — No change in 2001

After independence, armed forces were established, now consisting of a 1000-strong army, a small air force, and a naval coastguard. They have never been called upon to play a political role; their main duties are to protect territorial waters against illegal fishing and to curb smuggling.

ECONOMICS

Inflation 4.8% p.a. (1990–2001)

$596m — 109 Cape Verde escudos (119.8)

SCORE CARD

- World GNP Ranking 166th
- GNP per Capita $1340
- Balance of Payments .... –$67m
- Inflation 3.7%
- Unemployment 24%

Strengths

Strategic location close to the mid-Atlantic where Africa is nearest to Latin America: military and economic advantages, including shipping maintenance and air travel. Low debt-servicing costs. Tourism and fishing. Privatization program.

Weaknesses

Permanent threat of drought and water supply problems, despite desalination plants. Lack of agricultural land and dependence on food aid. Difficulties of communications between islands.

EXPORTS

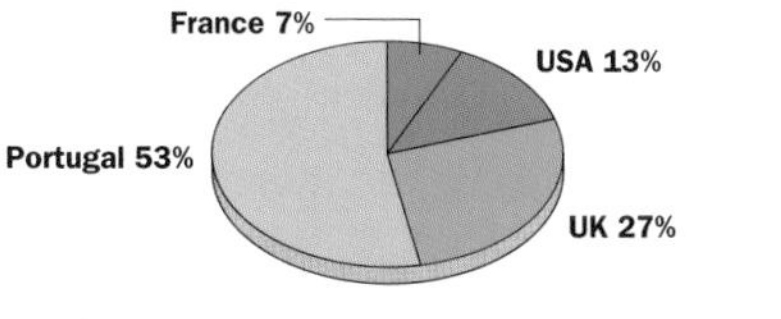
France 7%
USA 13%
Portugal 53%
UK 27%

IMPORTS

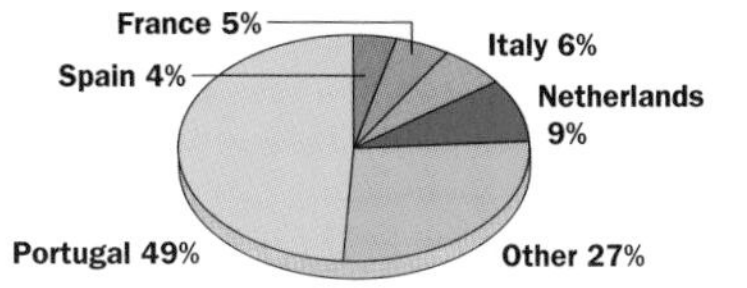
France 5%
Italy 6%
Spain 4%
Netherlands 9%
Portugal 49%
Other 27%

__Portuguese colonial-style architecture__ on Fogo, one of the larger islands. The volcano at its center is the highest point in Cape Verde.

RESOURCES

Electric power 7000 kW

10,821 tonnes — Not an oil producer

200,000 pigs, 112,000 goats, 480,000 chickens — Salt, limestone, pozzolana

Cape Verde has no known strategic resources. With no oil or gas and no possibility of hydroelectric power, it depends on imported petroleum for energy. However, experimental projects have been carried out to investigate the potential of wave power, windmills, and biogas.

ENVIRONMENT

Not available

None — 0.3 tonnes per capita

Cape Verde has recently suffered several years of persistent drought, which have affected food production and reduced livestock herds. It is a very active member of CILSS, which struggles against drought in the Sahel region. Environmental initiatives include reforestation, soil conservation, and a water resources program.

MEDIA

TV ownership low

There are no daily newspapers

PUBLISHING AND BROADCAST MEDIA

There are no daily newspapers. Independent publications suffer from financial pressures

1 state-controlled service — 1 state-controlled service

The government publishes three weeklies, but there are no daily newspapers. Press freedom is guaranteed by law. TV and radio broadcasting are in Portuguese and Creole, with the cooperation of the Portuguese service RTPI.

CRIME

No death penalty

775 prisoners — Little change from year to year

Crime is not a serious problem, even in urban centers, though smuggling is fairly widespread.

CHRONOLOGY

Cape Verde was a Portuguese colony from 1462 until 1975, and was ruled jointly with Guinea-Bissau.

- **1961** Joint struggle for independence of Cape Verde and Guinea-Bissau begins.
- **1974** Guinea-Bissau independent.
- **1975** Cape Verde independent.
- **1981** Final split from Guinea-Bissau.
- **1991** MPD wins first multiparty poll.
- **2001** General election returns PAICV to power.

C

EDUCATION

School leaving age: 12

75% — Not available

At independence, education became a priority; 99% of children now attend elementary school, although only half go on to secondary education.

HEALTH

No welfare state health benefits

1 per 5882 people — Heart disease, tuberculosis, typhoid, and accidents

Health care has improved since the colonial period, although there was an outbreak of polio in 2000.

SPENDING

GDP/cap. increase

CONSUMPTION AND SPENDING

31 per 1000 population — *143 per 1000 population*

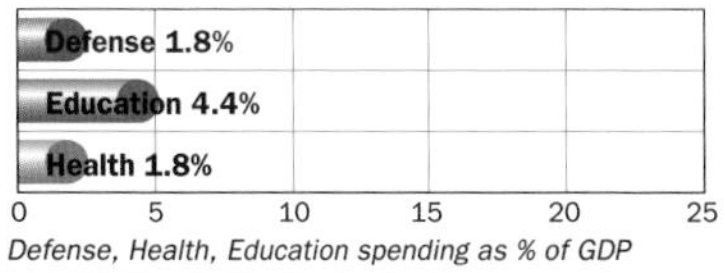
Defense 1.8%
Education 4.4%
Health 1.8%
0
5
10
15
20
25
Defense, Health, Education spending as % of GDP

Around 90% of the population of Cape Verde is engaged in primary production; by comparison, the small business class in Praia is well-off.

WORLD RANKING

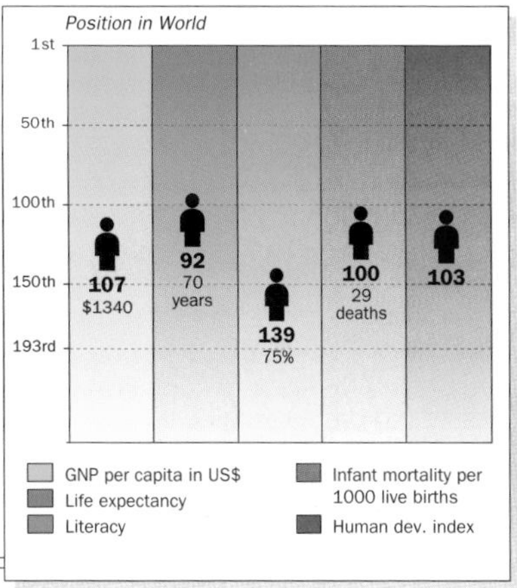
Position in World
1st
50th
100th
150th
193rd
107
$1340
92
70
years
139
75%
100
29
deaths
103
GNP per capita in US$
Life expectancy
Literacy
Infant mortality per 1000 live births
Human dev. index

CENTRAL AFRICAN REPUBLIC

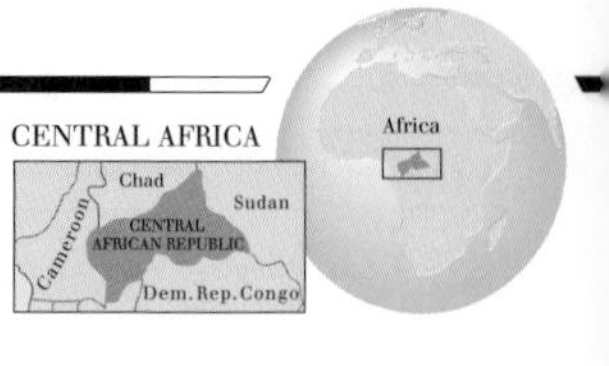
CENTRAL AFRICA
Chad
Sudan
Cameroon
CENTRAL AFRICAN REPUBLIC
Dem. Rep. Congo
Africa

OFFICIAL NAME: Central African Republic **CAPITAL:** Bangui
POPULATION: 3.8 million **CURRENCY:** CFA franc **OFFICIAL LANGUAGE:** French

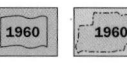

C

1960 | 1960 | Dec 1 | RCA | +1 | +236 | .cf

LANDLOCKED AT THE EASTERN end of the Sahel, the Central African Republic (CAR) is a low plateau stretching north from the Ubangi River. Almost all the population lives in the equatorial, rainforested south. "Emperor" Bokassa's eccentric rule from 1965 to 1979 was followed by military dictatorship. Democracy was restored in 1993. Any hopes for political stability have been shattered by a string of mutinies and coups since 1996.

CLIMATE

Tropical equatorial

WEATHER CHART FOR BANGUI

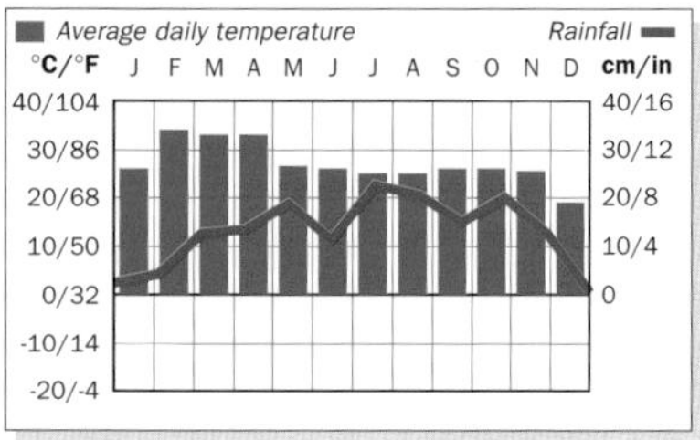
Average daily temperature
Rainfall
°C/°F J F M A M J J A S O N D cm/in
40/104
30/86
20/68
10/50
0/32
-10/14
-20/-4
40/16
30/12
20/8
10/4
0

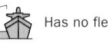

The south is equatorial, the north has a savanna-type climate, and the far north lies within the Sahel.

TRANSPORTATION

Drive on right

Mpoko, Bangui 56,038 passengers

Has no fleet

THE TRANSPORTATION NETWORK

429 km (267 miles)

Trans-African Highway

None

900 km (559 miles)

The CAR has a limited transportation system, depending on the river link to Brazzaville, Congo, and rail from there to Pointe-Noire and the Congo River ports.

TOURISM

Visitors : Population 1:380

10,000 visitors

Up 43% in 1999

MAIN TOURIST ARRIVALS

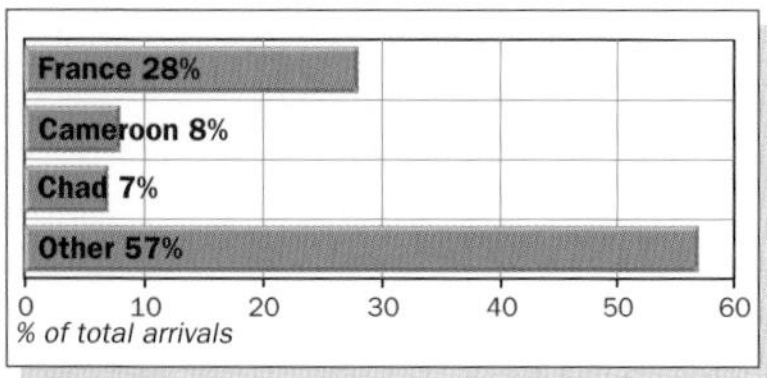
France 28%
Cameroon 8%
Chad 7%
Other 57%
0 10 20 30 40 50 60
% of total arrivals

High levels of insecurity and crime, particularly in recent years, have prevented the CAR from promoting tourism, despite the abundance of scenery and big game wildlife.

PEOPLE

Pop. density low

Sango, Banda, Gbaya, French

6/km² (16/mi²)

THE URBAN/RURAL POPULATION SPLIT

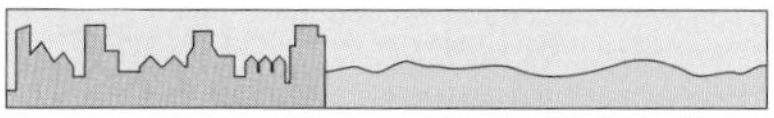
42%
58%

ETHNIC MAKEUP

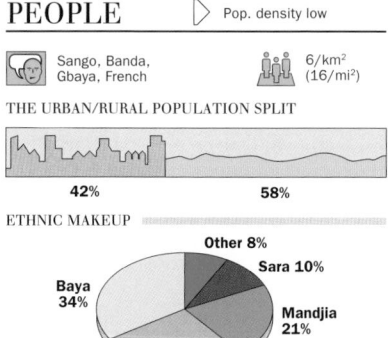

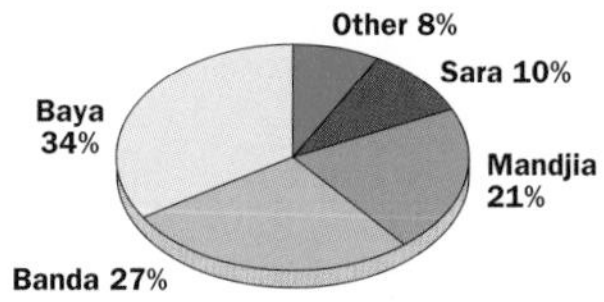
Other 8%
Sara 10%
Mandjia 21%
Banda 27%
Baya 34%

The Baya and Banda are the largest ethnic groups, but the lingua franca is Sango, a trading creole originating among the southern riverine minorities which provided the political leaders from independence until 1993 (Presidents Dacko and Kolingba and "Emperor" Bokassa). Resentment against the river peoples occasionally flares up, as happened after the coup attempt in 2001. As in other non-Muslim African countries, women have considerable power. Elizabeth Domitien was prime minister from 1975 to 1976 and Ruth Rolland ran for president in 1993.

WORLD AFFAIRS

Joined UN in 1960

BDEAC | CEMAC | FZ | LCBC | AU

Regional relations were altered by Gen. Bozizé's 2003 coup. While Chad had given him active support, Libya and factions from the neighboring DRC had emerged as the major allies of Patassé, becoming directly involved in the precoup conflicts. Bozizé is now keen to normalize relations, especially with other CEMAC countries and the DRC, but the AU is reluctant to recognize his regime.

AID

Recipient

$76m (receipts)

Little change in 2001

Almost all development projects are funded from external aid. France, the former colonial power, provides one-third of the total. Japan and the EU are other major donors. The CAR receives assistance from the World Bank and the IMF, which have provided funds to support its economic program. The Paris Club of creditor countries in 1998 rescheduled and reduced its debt.

DEFENSE

Compulsory military service

$15m

Up 7% in 2001

The well-equipped, 1400-strong army drains the budget and is a source of opposition to the government. Military rebellion resurfaced in 2001, a year after the withdrawal of a UN force. In 2001 and 2002 progovernment soldiers were supported by forces from Libya and Chad and rebel fighters from the DRC, but were unable to halt the 2003 coup.

POLITICS

In transition

1998/Not announced

President François Bozizé

AT THE LAST ELECTION

National Assembly (dissolved) 109 seats

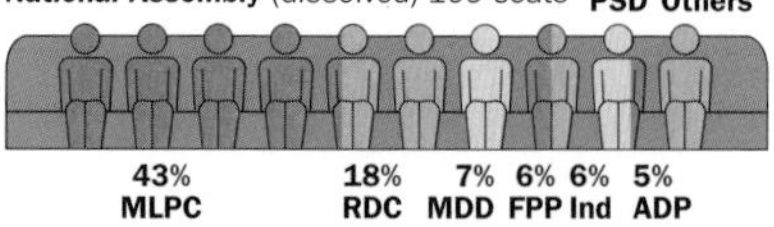
6% PSD
9% Others
43% MLPC
18% RDC
7% MDD
6% FPP
6% Ind
5% ADP

MLPC = Central African People's Liberation Movement **RDC** = Central African Democratic Rally **MDD** = Movement for Democracy and Development **FPP** = Patriotic Front for Progress **Ind** = Independents **PSD** = Social Democratic Party **ADP** = Alliance for Democracy and Progress

Elections in 1993 ended 12 years of single-party rule under Gen. André Kolingba. Former prime minister-turned-dissident Ange-Félix Patassé became president. His decade in power was dogged by army mutinies. The first major rebellion, in 1996, was only calmed after the intervention of a French-led multinational force in 1997. His party, the MLPC, remained the largest in parliament after the 1998 elections, but he was faced with yet more rebellion in 2001. Kolingba led a failed coup in May and was later supported by army chief Gen. François Bozizé. Patassé was kept in power with the assistance of Libyan and Congolese fighters in 2001, and again in 2002, but was finally toppled in a coup led by Gen. Bozizé in 2003. The new regime's main priority is tackling "corruption," in the form of the commercial ties established by its predecessor.

C

CENTRAL AFRICAN REPUBLIC

POPULATION

Total Area : 622 984 sq. km (240 534 sq. miles)

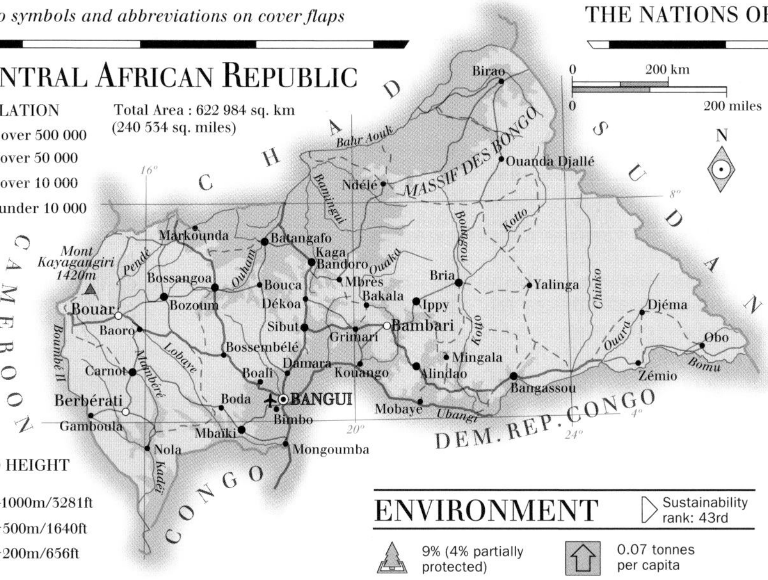
over 500 000
over 50 000
over 10 000
under 10 000
CHAD
SUDAN
CAMEROON
CONGO
DEM. REP. CONGO
Birao
Bahr Aouk
MASSIF DES BONGO
Ouanda Djallé
Ndélé
Bamingui
Markounda
Batangafo
Kaga Bandoro
Ouaka
Mbrès
Bakala
Mont Kayagangiri 1420m
Pendé
Bossangoa
Ouham
Bouca
Dékoa
Bouar
Bozoum
Baoro
Sibut
Bossembélé
Grimari
Bambari
Ippy
Bria
Yalinga
Kotto
Chinko
Djéma
Ouara
Obo
Bomu
Zémio
Mingala
Alindao
Bangassou
Kouango
Damara
Boali
Carnot
Mambéré
Lobaye
Berbérati
Gamboula
Boda
BANGUI
Bimbo
Mbaïki
Mobaye
Ubangi
Nola
Kadéï
Mongoumba
Boumbé II
0 200 km
0 200 miles
N
LAND HEIGHT
1000m/3281ft
500m/1640ft
200m/656ft

CHRONOLOGY

The French colony of Ubangi-Chari gained autonomy as the CAR in 1958.

- **1960** Independence under David Dacko; one-party state.
- **1965** Coup by Jean-Bédel Bokassa.
- **1977** Bokassa crowned "emperor."
- **1979** French help reinstate Dacko.
- **1981** Gen. Kolingba ousts Dacko.
- **1993** Democracy restored. Ange-Félix Patassé president.
- **1996–1997** Army rebellion.
- **2001–2003** Further mutinies.
- **2003** Gen. Bozizé leads coup.

ECONOMICS

Inflation 4.2% p.a. (1990–2001)

$999m

571.2 CFA francs (664.2)

SCORE CARD

World GNP Ranking	154th
GNP per Capita	$260
Balance of Payments	$16m
Inflation	3.6%
Unemployment	6%

Strengths

Self-sufficiency in food. Some diversity of export earnings (diamonds, cotton, timber, iron, coffee). Transit zone in central Africa.

Weaknesses

Instability. Landlocked. Government mismanagement. Poor infrastructure. Shortage of trained workers.

EXPORTS

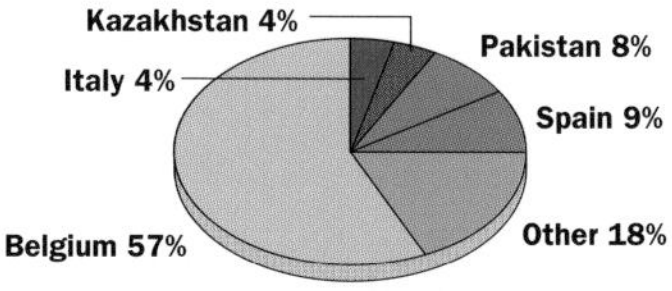
Kazakhstan 4%
Pakistan 8%
Italy 4%
Spain 9%
Other 18%
Belgium 57%

IMPORTS

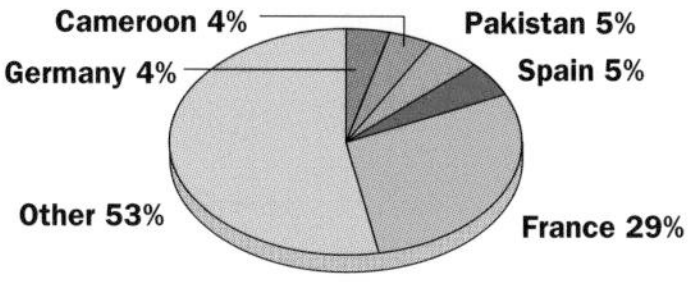
Cameroon 4%
Pakistan 5%
Germany 4%
Spain 5%
Other 53%
France 29%

RESOURCES

Electric power 43,000 kW

15,120 tonnes

Not an oil producer and has no refineries

3.27m cattle, 2.92m goats, 4.58m chickens

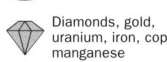

Diamonds, gold, uranium, iron, copper, manganese

Very little of the country's territory has been explored, and there is great potential for hidden resources.

ENVIRONMENT

Sustainability rank: 43rd

9% (4% partially protected)

0.07 tonnes per capita

Hunting elephants was banned in 1985, as numbers had fallen by 84% in a decade. The government empowered private antipoaching militias in 2002 to tackle the trade in bushmeat.

MEDIA

TV ownership low

Daily newspaper circulation 2 per 1000 people

PUBLISHING AND BROADCAST MEDIA

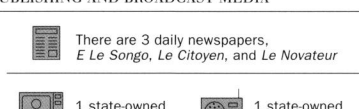

There are 3 daily newspapers, *E Le Songo, Le Citoyen*, and *Le Novateur*

1 state-owned service

1 state-owned service

The three weeklies and three daily newspapers have only limited circulation. A small opposition press has developed with multipartyism, but is inhibited by lack of resources.

CRIME

Death penalty not used in practice

4168 prisoners

Crime is rising

Human rights abuses have been reduced dramatically since the excesses of the Bokassa years. The level of criminality is usually low. The major criminal problem appears to be the increase in urban robbery which has escalated in parallel to political instability since 1996.

***Baskets of cotton,** Meme village. Cotton is one of the Central African Republic's most significant export crops.*

EDUCATION

School leaving age: 14

48%

6323 students

Schooling, on the French model, is compulsory, but in practice is only received by 55% of 6–14 year olds.

HEALTH

No welfare state health benefits

1 per 25,000 people

Communicable and parasitic diseases, malnutrition

Colonial neglect and postcolonial maladministration have resulted in a poorly developed health system.

SPENDING

GDP/cap. increase

CONSUMPTION AND SPENDING

1 per 1000 population

2 per 1000 population

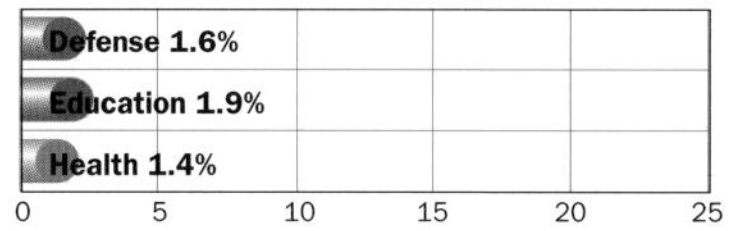
Defense 1.6%
Education 1.9%
Health 1.4%
0
5
10
15
20
25

Defense, Health, Education spending as % of GDP

There is a small political–military elite in the CAR, which came into being only in postcolonial days. For its members, Paris is the chosen destination and source of style.

WORLD RANKING

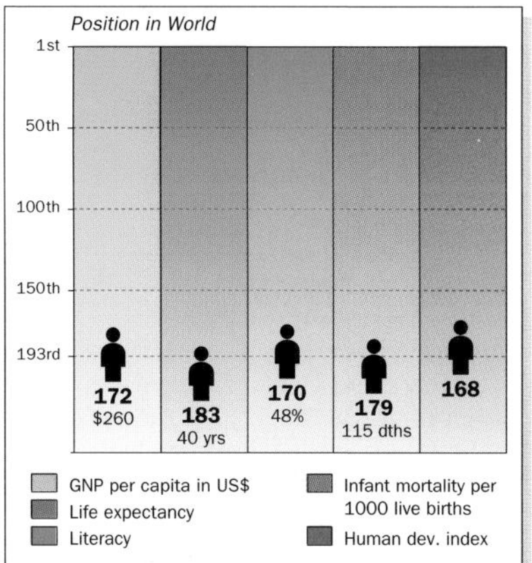
Position in World
1st
50th
100th
150th
193rd
172
$260
183
40 yrs
170
48%
179
115 dths
168
GNP per capita in US$
Life expectancy
Literacy
Infant mortality per 1000 live births
Human dev. index

CHAD

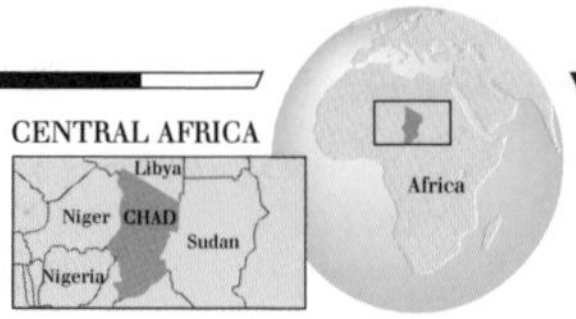
CENTRAL AFRICA
Libya
Niger
CHAD
Sudan
Nigeria
Africa

OFFICIAL NAME: Republic of Chad **CAPITAL:** N'Djamena **POPULATION:** 8.4 million
CURRENCY: CFA franc **OFFICIAL LANGUAGES:** Arabic and French

C

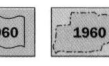

1960 | 1960 | Aug 11 | TCH | +1 | +235 | .td

LANDLOCKED IN NORTH central Africa, Chad has had a turbulent history since independence from France in 1960. Intermittent periods of civil war, involving French and Libyan troops, followed a coup in 1975. Another coup in 1990 preceded a transition to multipartyism, enshrined in a new constitution. The tropical, cotton-producing south is the most populous region. The discovery of large oil reserves could eventually have a dramatic impact on the economy.

CLIMATE

Hot desert/steppe

WEATHER CHART FOR N'DJAMENA

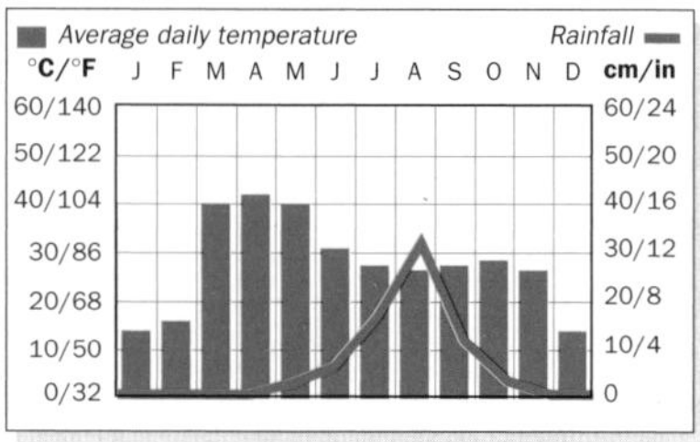
Average daily temperature
Rainfall
°C/°F
J F M A M J J A S O N D
cm/in
60/140
50/122
40/104
30/86
20/68
10/50
0/32
60/24
50/20
40/16
30/12
20/8
10/4
0

There are three distinct zones: the tropical south, the central semiarid Sahelian belt, and the desert north.

TRANSPORTATION

Drive on right

N'Djamena International 16,861 passengers

Has no fleet

THE TRANSPORTATION NETWORK

450 km (280 miles)

None

None

2000 km (1243 miles)

Chad has a limited transportation infrastructure. The nearest rail links are in Nigeria and Cameroon.

TOURISM

Visitors : Population 1:150

56,000 visitors

Up 40% in 2001

MAIN TOURIST ARRIVALS

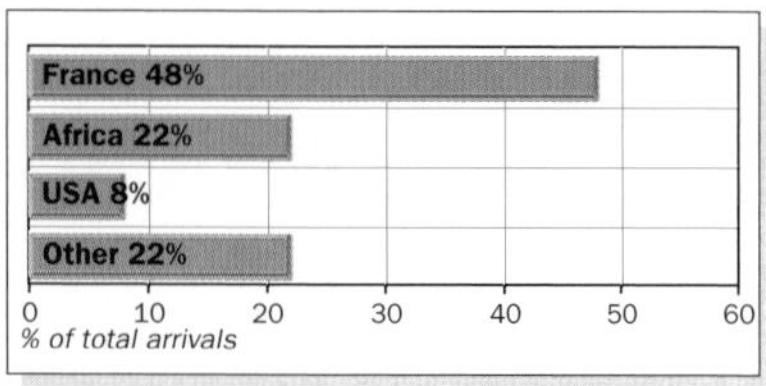
France 48%
Africa 22%
USA 8%
Other 22%
0
10
20
30
40
50
60
% of total arrivals

Tourism is virtually nonexistent due to poverty and years of war. Among potential attractions are national parks and game reserves, prehistoric rock painting in the Tibesti plateau, and the Muslim cities of the Sahara.

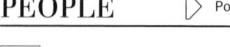

Watering hole at Oum Hadjer, a village on the Batha watercourse in central Chad, 145 km (90 miles) east of Ati.

PEOPLE

Pop. density low

French, Sara, Arabic, Maba

7/km² (17/mi²)

THE URBAN/RURAL POPULATION SPLIT

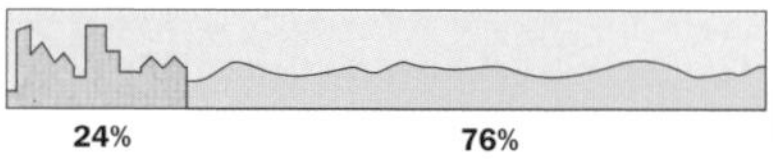
24%
76%

RELIGIOUS PERSUASION

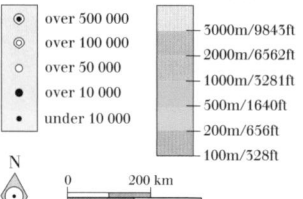

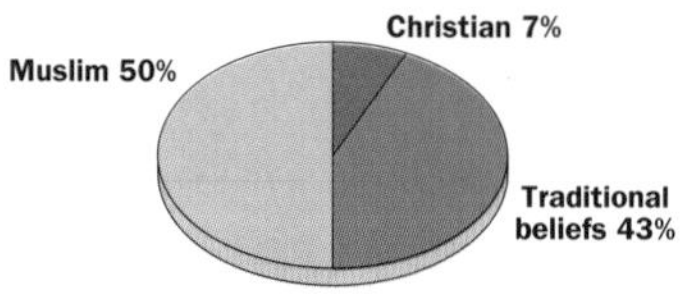
Christian 7%
Muslim 50%
Traditional beliefs 43%

About half the population, mainly the Sara-speaking and related peoples, is concentrated in the south in one-fifth of the national territory. Most of the rest are located in the central sultanates. The northern third of Chad has a population of only 100,000 people, mainly nomadic Muslim Toubou.

POLITICS

Multiparty elections

2002/2006

President Idriss Déby

AT THE LAST ELECTION

National Assembly 155 seats

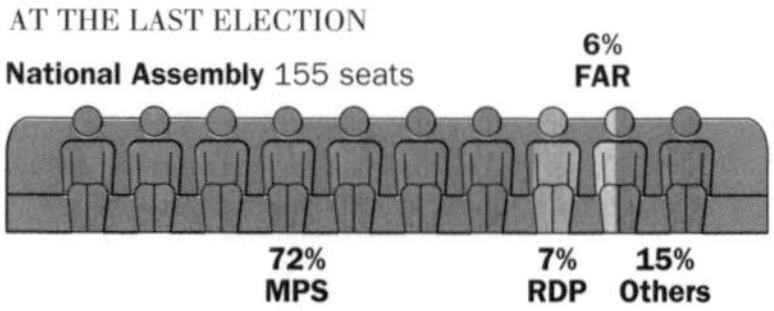
6%
FAR
72%
MPS
7%
RDP
15%
Others

MPS = Patriotic Salvation Movement
RDP = Rally for Democracy and Progress
FAR = Front of Action Forces for the Republic

Idriss Déby overthrew President Hissène Habré in 1990 after an armed invasion from Sudan. He promised multipartyism, and in 1992 – for the first time since the early 1960s – political parties were legalized. After many delays, the transitional process led to a successful referendum in 1996 on a new constitution based on the French model. President Déby was confirmed in office in elections in 1996 and again in 2001. His ruling MPS just achieved an overall majority in the 1997 elections, and expanded its share of seats further in 2002. A shaky Libyan-brokered peace deal in 2002 failed to end a rebellion in the north which had begun in 1999.

CHAD

Total Area : 1 284 000 sq. km (495 752 sq. miles)

POPULATION
- over 500 000
- over 100 000
- over 50 000
- over 10 000
- under 10 000

LAND HEIGHT
- 5000m/9843ft
- 2000m/6562ft
- 1000m/3281ft
- 500m/1640ft
- 200m/656ft
- 100m/328ft

0 200 km
0 200 miles

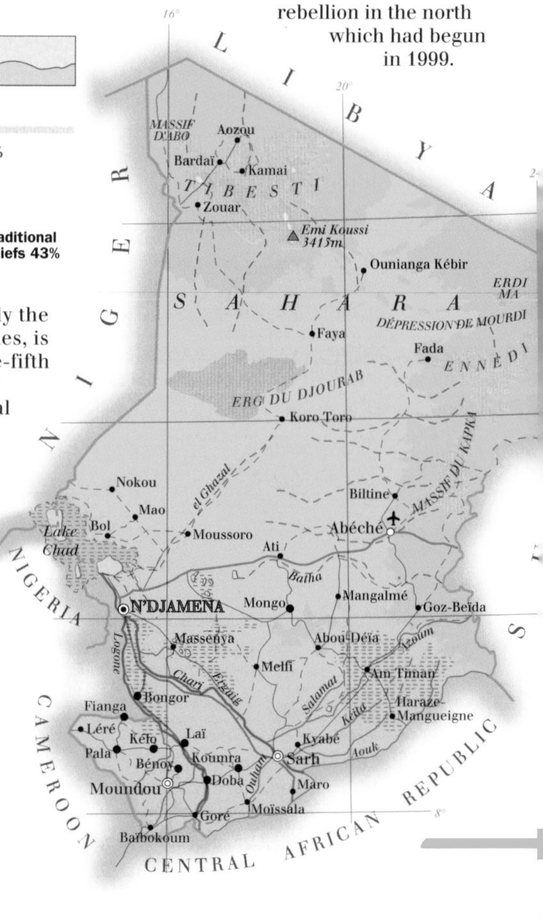
LIBYA
NIGER
SUDAN
NIGERIA
CAMEROON
CENTRAL AFRICAN REPUBLIC
MASSIF D'ABO
Aozou
Bardaï
Kamai
TIBESTI
Zouar
Emi Koussi 3415m
Ounianga Kébir
ERDI MA
SAHARA
DÉPRESSION DE MOURDI
Faya
Fada
ENNEDI
ERG DU DJOURAB
Koro Toro
MASSIF DU KAPKA
Nokou
Mao
Bol
Lake Chad
Moussoro
Biltine
Abéché
Ati
Batha
N'DJAMENA
Mongo
Mangalmé
Goz-Beïda
Massenya
Abou-Déïa
Melfi
Am Timan
Haraze-Mangueigne
Bongor
Fianga
Léré
Kélo
Laï
Pala
Bénoy
Koumra
Sarh
Kyabé
Doba
Moundou
Maro
Goré
Moïssala
Baïbokoum
Logone
Chari
Salamat
Aouk
Bahr el Ghazal
16°
20°
8°

WORLD AFFAIRS

Joined UN in 1960

CILSS FZ LCBC AU OIC

Chad's most important relationship is with France. Relations with the CAR are strained by cross-border skirmishes.

AID

Recipient

$179m (receipts)

Up 37% in 2001

France is the major donor. Other sources include the EU, the World Bank, Germany, and the Arab members of OPEC. The administration would probably have collapsed without assistance to cover civil servants' pay in recent years.

DEFENSE

Compulsory military service

$13m

Down 7% in 2001

On seizing power, Déby swelled the existing army with irregulars. This policy has now been reversed and the army reduced to 25,000, including former rebels. France provides military aid and personnel.

ECONOMICS

Inflation 6.7% p.a. (1990–2001)

$1.59bn

571.2 CFA francs (664.2)

SCORE CARD

❑ World GNP Ranking	145th
❑ GNP per Capita	$200
❑ Balance of Payments	–$660m
❑ Inflation	12.4%
❑ Unemployment	Widespread underemployment

STRENGTHS

Discovery of large oil deposits and Chad–Cameroon pipeline could transform economy. Cotton industry; potential for other agriculture in south. Strategic trading location in heart of Africa. Natron and uranium deposits.

WEAKNESSES

Underdevelopment and poverty. Lack of transportation infrastructure. Political instability. Frequent droughts.

EXPORTS

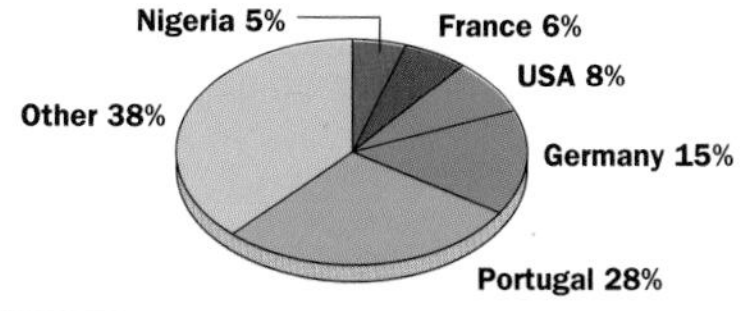
Nigeria 5%
France 6%
USA 8%
Other 38%
Germany 15%
Portugal 28%

IMPORTS

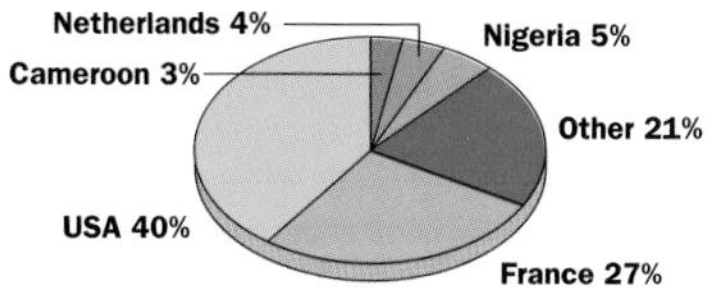
Netherlands 4%
Cameroon 3%
Nigeria 5%
Other 21%
USA 40%
France 27%

RESOURCES

Electric power 29,000 kW

84,000 tonnes

Oil production is beginning

5.9m cattle, 5.5m goats, 2.45m sheep, 5m chickens

Natron, uranium, oil, kaolin, soda, rock salt

The opening in 2003 of a pipeline to take oil from newly found reserves in the southern Doba region to the Cameroonian coast is set to make Chad a net oil exporter. Natron, a type of salt, is the only mineral currently exploited. There is uranium in the Aozou strip.

ENVIRONMENT

Sustainability rank: 96th

9% (8.6% partially protected)

0.02 tonnes per capita

President Déby's government has made protection of the environment a priority, with antidesertification measures such as tree-planting campaigns and aid-funded irrigation schemes. There is concern that environmental damage may result from oil production and from the planned Chad–Cameroon oil pipeline.

MEDIA

TV ownership low

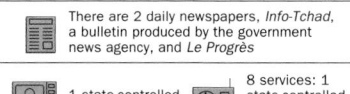

Daily newspaper circulation 0.2 per 1000 people

PUBLISHING AND BROADCAST MEDIA

There are 2 daily newspapers, *Info-Tchad*, a bulletin produced by the government news agency, and *Le Progrès*

1 state-controlled service

8 services: 1 state-controlled, 7 independent

Broadcasting is controlled by the government, which sometimes allows the airing of opposition views. There are a few independent publications, of which the best known is the weekly *N'Djamena-Hebdo*.

CRIME

Death penalty in use

3883 prisoners

Crime is rising

The easy availability of weapons in the region in the past two decades has meant that local disputes, usually over water or grazing, often now lead to gun battles. Armed robbery, smuggling, and vandalism are widespread. In several areas, the activities of disaffected former rebels threaten security.

EDUCATION

School leaving age: 11

44%

5901 students

All schools are underfunded and suffer from a lack of trained teachers. Chad has the lowest ratio of female enrollment in schools in Africa. Overall, only 55% of children attend classes and barely a third of them are girls.

CHRONOLOGY

France extended its domination of the area now known as Chad after ousting the last Arab ruler in 1900.

- ❑ **1960** Independence. One-party state.
- ❑ **1973–1994** Libyans occupy uranium-rich Aozou strip.
- ❑ **1975** Coup by Gen. Félix Malloum.
- ❑ **1979–1982** North–south civil war.
- ❑ **1980** Goukouni Oueddei in power.
- ❑ **1982** Hissène Habré (northerner) defeats Oueddei.
- ❑ **1990** Idriss Déby overthrows Habré, who flees to Senegal.
- ❑ **1996** National cease-fire; new constitution.
- ❑ **1997** Déby's MPS wins elections.
- ❑ **1999** Rebellion breaks out in north.
- ❑ **2001** Déby reelected.
- ❑ **2002** MPS increases its majority.

HEALTH

Welfare state health benefits

1 per 33,333 people

Diarrheal, parasitic, and communicable diseases

There are a few city hospitals and over 300 smaller health centers. One in five children die before the age of five.

SPENDING

GDP/cap. increase

CONSUMPTION AND SPENDING

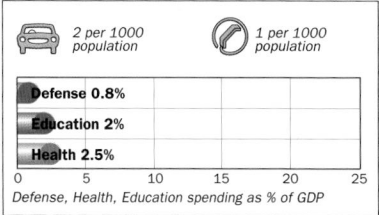

2 per 1000 population

1 per 1000 population

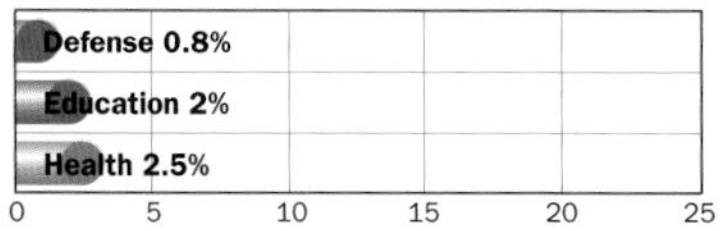
Defense 0.8%
Education 2%
Health 2.5%
0
5
10
15
20
25

Defense, Health, Education spending as % of GDP

Poverty is almost universal in Chad; the middle class is very small. There are few wealthy individuals. Habré looted the treasury when he was overthrown in 1990.

WORLD RANKING

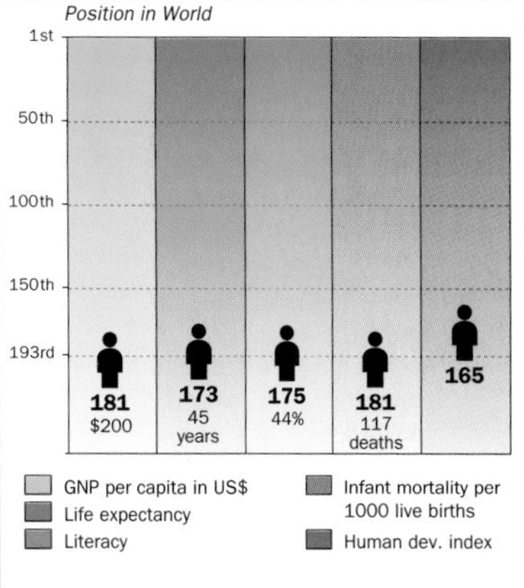
Position in World
1st
50th
100th
150th
193rd
181
$200
173
45 years
175
44%
181
117 deaths
165
GNP per capita in US$
Life expectancy
Literacy
Infant mortality per 1000 live births
Human dev. index

C

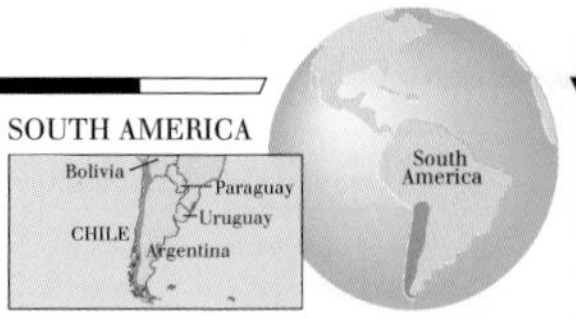
SOUTH AMERICA
Bolivia
Paraguay
Uruguay
CHILE
Argentina
South America

CHILE

OFFICIAL NAME: Republic of Chile **CAPITAL:** Santiago
POPULATION: 15.6 million **CURRENCY:** Chilean peso **OFFICIAL LANGUAGE:** Spanish

C

1818
1883
Sept 18
RCH
-4
+56
.cl

CHILE EXTENDS IN A narrow ribbon 4350 km (2700 miles) down the Pacific coast of South America. Its extraordinary shape means that its physical geography ranges from the deserts of the High Andes in the north to fertile valleys in the center, while in the south are the fjords, lakes, and deep sea channels of the Southern Andes. In 1989, Chile returned to elected civilian rule, following a popular rejection of the Pinochet dictatorship. A collapse in copper prices, coupled with weaker export markets, has interrupted the high growth seen in the 1990s.

General Pinochet, *a dictatorial president rejected by popular referendum in 1988.*

Ricardo Lagos *was narrowly elected president in 2000.*

CLIMATE

▷ Desert/mountain/maritime

WEATHER CHART FOR SANTIAGO

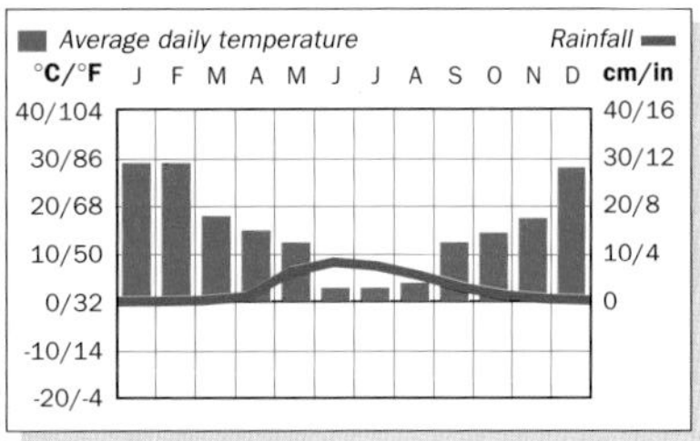
Average daily temperature
Rainfall
°C/°F J F M A M J J A S O N D cm/in
40/104
30/86
20/68
10/50
0/32
-10/14
-20/-4
40/16
30/12
20/8
10/4
0

Chile has an immensely varied climate. The north, which includes the world's driest desert, the Atacama, is frequently cloudy and cool for its latitude. The central regions have an almost Mediterranean climate, with changeable winters and hot, dry summers. The higher reaches of the Andes have a typically alpine climate, with glaciers and year-round snow. The south is the wettest region.

TRANSPORTATION

▷ Drive on right

Comodoro Arturo Merino Benítez, Santiago
5.65m passengers

480 ships
880,300 grt

THE TRANSPORTATION NETWORK

11,012 km (6843 miles)

3455 km (2147 miles)

2035 km (1264 miles)

725 km (450 miles)

The state railroad is being upgraded with private capital assistance: suburban services into Santiago are being improved, and line repairs and better rolling stock will shorten journey times from Santiago to Temuco. Sections of the Pan-American Highway, the sole arterial road running from the Peruvian border to Puerto Montt, are being upgraded. Chile has been given strong regional and international links by the 1999 open skies agreement with the US, its first with a South American country.

TOURISM

▷ Visitors : Population 1:11

1.41m visitors

Down 18% in 2002

MAIN TOURIST ARRIVALS

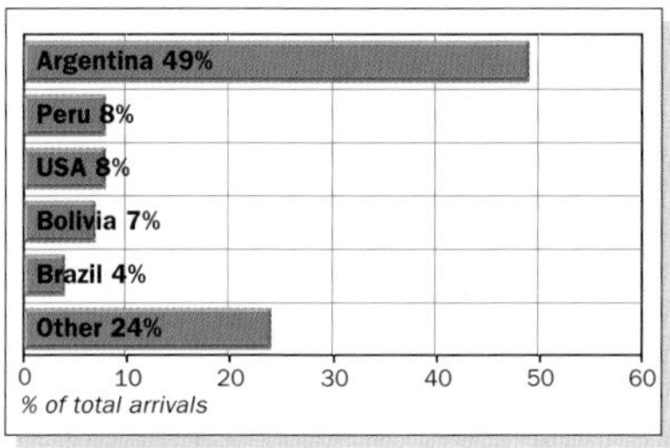
Argentina 49%
Peru 8%
USA 8%
Bolivia 7%
Brazil 4%
Other 24%
0 10 20 30 40 50 60
% of total arrivals

The Pinochet years saw a dramatic decline in tourists from the US and Europe, although the numbers from neighboring countries held up. Since 1989, visitors have returned, but over half of them still come from Argentina and Peru.

Investment in the sector totaled $2.17 billion in the first half of 2000, up 3.8% on the same period in 1999. Accordingly, Chile is making more of its stunning Andean scenery, its immensely long coastline, and a number of exceptional sites, including Chuquicamata, the world's largest copper mine, the Elqui Valley winegrowing region, and the spectacular glaciers and fjords of southern Chile. Easter Island in the Pacific is another major attraction.

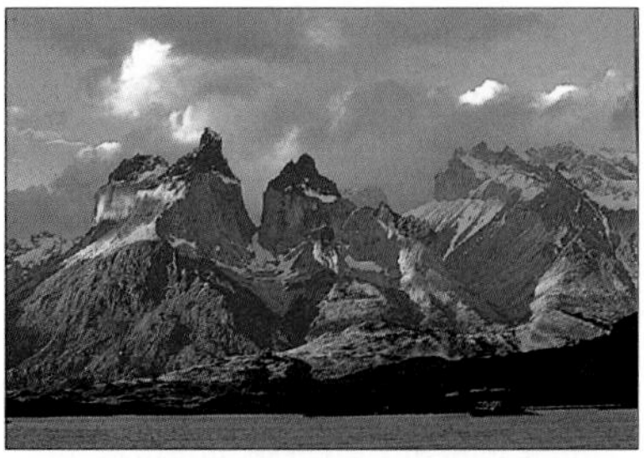

Peaks in the Paine range, southern Chile. *Fjords, glaciers, and myriad islands typify Chile's very wet, wild, and stormy south.*

PEOPLE

▷ Pop. density low

Spanish, Amerindian languages

21/km² (54/mi²)

THE URBAN/RURAL POPULATION SPLIT

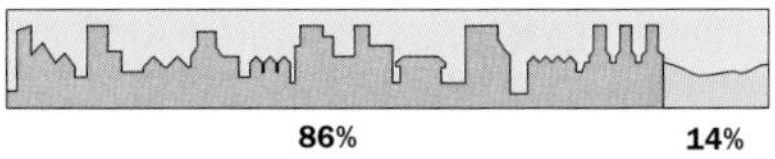
86%
14%

RELIGIOUS PERSUASION

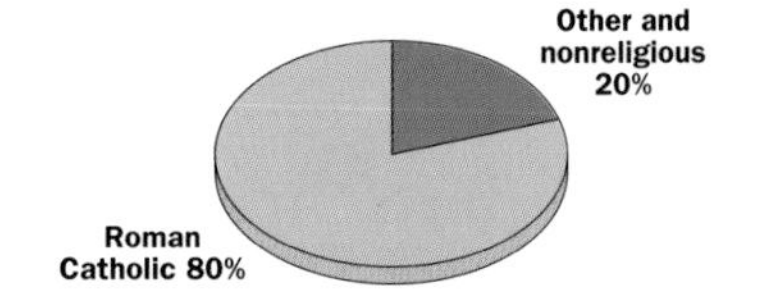
Other and nonreligious 20%
Roman Catholic 80%

ETHNIC MAKEUP

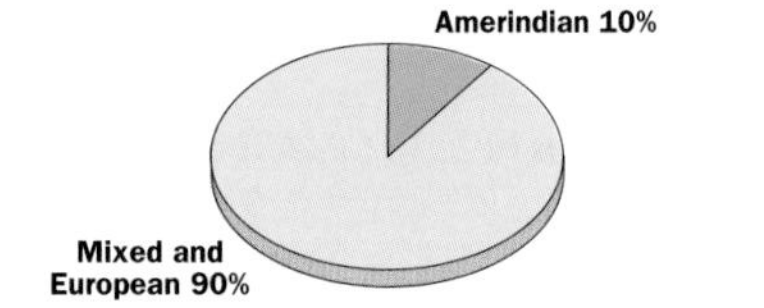
Amerindian 10%
Mixed and European 90%

One-third of Chile's population live in Santiago, where rapid growth has created large slums. Chile has relatively few immigrants; most people are of mixed Spanish–Amerindian descent. Problems analyzed by a Commission for Historic Truth, set up in 2000, have yet to be addressed. There are some 80,000 Mapuche Amerindians around Temuco in the south, 20,000 Aymara in the northern Chilean Andes, and 2000 Rapa Nui on Easter Island.

Over 25% of working women are employed in domestic service.

POPULATION AGE BREAKDOWN

Female
Age
Male
0.8% 80+ 0.4%
4.8% 60–79 3.8%
10.2% 40–59 9.8%
16.3% 20–39 16.4%
18.4% 0–19 19.1%
% of population by age group

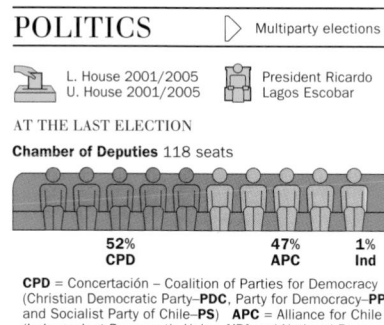

PERU
BOLIVIA
ARGENTINA
PACIFIC OCEAN
Juan Fernández Is
I. Alejandro Selkirk
San Juan Bautista
I. Robinson Crusoe
100 km
100 miles
Easter I.
Terevaka
Hanga Roa
10 km
10 miles
Arica
Iquique
Atacama Desert
Chuquicamata
Calama
Antofagasta
Chañaral
Nevado Ojos del Salado 6880m
Copiapó
Vallenar
La Serena
Coquimbo
Ovalle
Illapel
Los Andes
Viña del Mar
Valparaíso
Quilpué
Llolleo
SANTIAGO
San Bernardo
Puente Alto
Rancagua
Curicó
Rengo
Talca
San Javier de Loncomilla
Linares
Parral
Talcahuano
San Carlos
Concepción
Chillán
Los Ángeles
Curanilahue
Mulchén
Bío Bío
Traiguén
Victoria
Temuco
Lautaro
Valdivia
La Unión
Puerto Varas
Puerto Montt
Isla de Chiloé
Castro
Puerto Aisén
Coihaique
Lago General Carrera
Chile Chico
Isla Wellington
Cerro Paine
Puerto Natales
Magellan Strait
Punta Arenas
Porvenir
Beagle Channel
I. Picton
I. Nueva
I. Lennox
Cape Horn
Drake Passage
CHILE
Total Area : 756 950 sq. km (292 258 sq. miles)
POPULATION
over 1 000 000
over 100 000
over 50 000
over 10 000
under 10 000
LAND HEIGHT
4000m/13124ft
2000m/6562ft
1000m/3281ft
200m/656ft
Sea Level
N
300 km
300 miles

POLITICS

Multiparty elections

L. House 2001/2005
U. House 2001/2005

President Ricardo Lagos Escobar

AT THE LAST ELECTION

Chamber of Deputies 118 seats

52% CPD
47% APC
1% Ind

CPD = Concertación – Coalition of Parties for Democracy (Christian Democratic Party–**PDC**, Party for Democracy–**PPD**, and Socialist Party of Chile–**PS**) **APC** = Alliance for Chile (Independent Democratic Union–**UDI** and National Renewal Party–**RN**) **Ind** = Independents **App** = Appointed **SL** = Senator-for-Life

Senate 48 seats

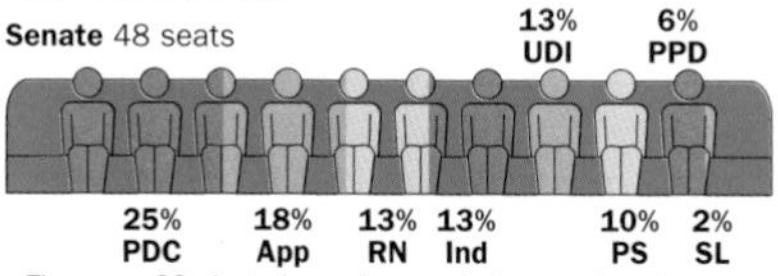
13% UDI
6% PPD
25% PDC
18% App
13% RN
13% Ind
10% PS
2% SL

There are 38 elected members and nine appointed senators. Former president Frei is a senator-for-life

After 16 years of military rule under Gen. Augusto Pinochet, Chile returned to multiparty democracy in 1989.

PROFILE

Chilean politics is still strongly affected by the legacy of the military dictatorship of 1973–1989, which began when Pinochet's coup overthrew the elected Marxist government of Salvador Allende.

The CIA backed the Pinochet coup, anxious to halt Allende's program of nationalization of the largely US-owned copper mines. As a result, thousands of Chileans were killed by the military or "disappeared," and a further 80,000 were taken as political prisoners.

Pinochet's nationalist politics drew on the example of Franco's Spain, while his economic policy was one of the first experiments in the free-market Chicago School of monetarism. Chile's business and middle classes prospered, while opposition, which was brutally suppressed by the DINA secret police, came most visibly from the Church and the urban poor.

In 1988 Pinochet, attempting to secure a popular mandate for continuing his regime, was surprised when the population emphatically voted for democracy. Pinochet stepped down, but remained head of the army. Patricio Aylwin won presidential elections held in 1989, heading Concertación, a center-left coalition.

Under Aylwin, politics became more stable, partly as a result of a cross-party consensus on economic policy. Continued growth and some progressive social measures attracted the support of the trade unions. These policies were continued under Eduardo Frei of the PS, who was elected president in 1993.

When Pinochet retired as army chief in 1998, heated disagreements over his entry to the Senate as a senator-for-life split Concertación along broadly left and right lines. Disagreements over Pinochet's subsequent arrest and detention in Europe on human rights charges further complicated the picture. Ricardo Lagos of the PS emerged as front-runner for the 1999 presidential elections, in which both the PS and the PDC presented themselves as the guarantors of peace and democracy. Right-wing opposition parties, however, also began to downplay their past links with Pinochet to broaden their electoral appeal. Lagos narrowly won a run-off poll in 2000. Facing a better organized opposition than hitherto, the ruling center-left Concertación performed reasonably well in the 2001 elections retaining its majority in the Chamber of Deputies but losing it in the Senate.

MAIN POLITICAL ISSUES

Future of the ruling alliance

Corruption scandals involving officials of all the member parties of the ruling Concertación coalition threatened its renegotiation or dissolution. Despite bills on probity, transparency, and modernization promoted by the government of the still popular President Lagos, observers suggested that Concertación had outserved its political usefulness now that democracy was maturing. A new understanding between the PDC and PS was one possible outcome, and fragmentation into right, center, and left parties, as before, was another.

Reform of the military

The resignation in 2002 of Gen. Patricio Ríos, the air force commander accused of covering up human rights abuses committed by some of his senior officers during military rule in the 1970s and 1980s, enhanced presidential authority and refocused attention on the efforts to reform the 1980 Constitution drafted by the military.

CHRONOLOGY

The Spanish tried to conquer the fierce indigenous Araucanian people in 1535. Conquest began in 1539, and Santiago was founded in 1541. Chile was under Spanish rule until independence in 1818.

- **1817–1818** Bernardo O'Higgins leads republican Army of the Andes in victories against royalist forces.
- **1879–1883** War of the Pacific with Bolivia and Peru. Chile gains valuable nitrate regions.
- **1891–1924** Parliamentary republic ends with growing political chaos.

C

CHRONOLOGY *continued*

- **1936–1946** Communist, Radical, and Socialist parties form influential Popular Front coalition.
- **1943** Chile backs US in World War II.
- **1946–1964** Right-wing Chilean presidents follow US McCarthy policy and marginalize the left.
- **1970** Salvador Allende elected president. Socialist reforms provoke strong reaction from the right.
- **1973** Allende dies in army coup. Brutal dictatorship of Gen. Pinochet begins.
- **1988** Referendum votes "no" to Pinochet staying in power.
- **1989** Democracy peacefully restored; Pinochet steps down after Aylwin election victory.
- **1998** Pinochet detained in UK pending extradition to Spain on human rights charges.
- **2000** Ricardo Lagos (PS) sworn in as president. Pinochet, deemed unfit to face trial, returns to Chile, where charges are suspended in 2001.

WORLD AFFAIRS

Joined UN in 1945

APEC | G15 | NAM | OAS | RG

During the Allende period in the early 1970s, the US actively worked against the government, fearing that the spread of socialism would jeopardize its investments in Latin America. The subsequent Pinochet regime's human rights record eventually became an embarrassment. In 1999, in response to Pinochet's detention in the UK and planned extradition to Spain to stand trial on human rights charges, Chile argued that this amounted to an infringement of its sovereignty. Relations with Spain and the UK improved in 2000 following Pinochet's return to Chile.

A nonpermanent member of the UN Security Council in 2003, Chile expressed reservations over war in Iraq and came under strong diplomatic pressure from the US and UK governments before efforts to gain a second UN resolution authorizing action ceased.

An associate member of Mercosur, Chile has free trade agreements with the EU, South Korea, and the US – its chief export market. Border disputes with Bolivia and Peru are ongoing.

AID

Recipient

$58m (receipts)

Up 18% in 2001

The majority of aid is in the form of debt rescheduling by the World Bank at the instigation of the US.

DEFENSE

Compulsory military service

$2.84bn

Down 10% in 2001

CHILEAN ARMED FORCES

290 main battle tanks (250 Leopard 1, 40 AMX-30)	45,000 personnel
3 submarines, 3 destroyers, 3 frigates, and 27 patrol boats	23,000 personnel
76 combat aircraft (15 F-5, 35 Mirage, 14 A-37B, 12 A-36)	12,500 personnel
None	

Most of the officers linked to human rights abuses under the dictatorship (1973–1989) are now retired, but dozens of them still face investigation and possible trial. The army has a moderate commander and in 2002, for the first time, a woman, a member of the PS, was appointed defense minister. Despite domestic concerns on pressing social needs, President Lagos signed up to reequip the air force with expensive, US-made F-16 fighters, still to be part-funded by 10% of copper exports under a controversial law inherited from the years of military rule. To dampen fears of arms escalation, Chile forewarned Argentina, Brazil, Peru, and Bolivia about the deal. Modernization of the navy, which was lobbying for four new frigates, is on hold.

ECONOMICS

Inflation 7.5% p.a. (1990–2001)

$70.6bn

700.8 Chilean pesos (688.8)

SCORE CARD

- World GNP Ranking 43rd
- GNP per Capita $4590
- Balance of Payments .... –$1.24bn
- Inflation 3.6%
- Unemployment 9%

EXPORTS

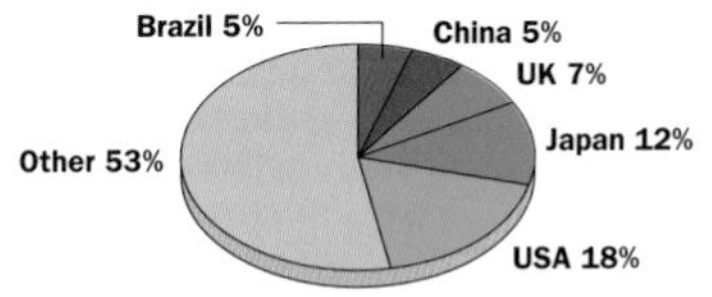

Brazil 5%
China 5%
UK 7%
Japan 12%
USA 18%
Other 53%

IMPORTS

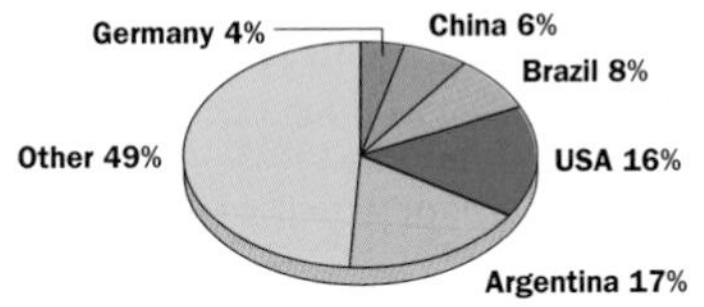

Germany 4%
China 6%
Brazil 8%
USA 16%
Argentina 17%
Other 49%

ECONOMIC PERFORMANCE INDICATOR

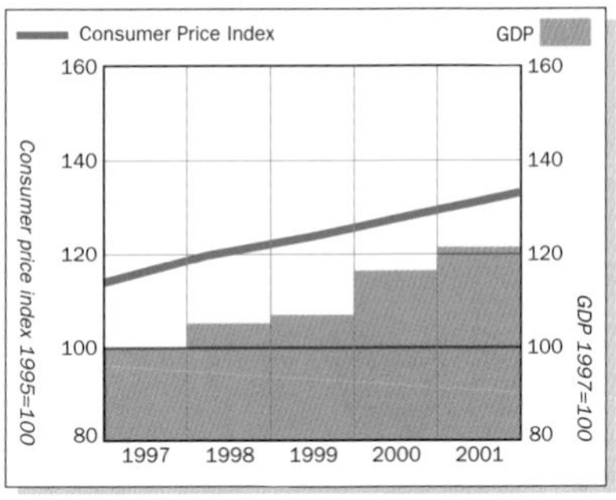

Consumer Price Index
GDP
160
140
120
100
80
1997
1998
1999
2000
2001
Consumer price index 1995=100
GDP 1997=100

Strengths
World's largest copper producer. Fresh fruit exports. Strong investment inflows allowing steady economic growth. Highest credit rating due to fiscal and monetary stability and highly liquid financial system. Development of nontraditional industries such as wine and fresh and prepared fish.

Weaknesses
Vulnerability of copper revenues (representing 40% of exports) and oil imports (90% of fuel consumed) to world price fluctuations. Dependence on US as single largest trading partner. Vulnerable peso.

Profile
Competing ideologies have battled over Chile's economy. Allende's socialism brought huge corporations into the state sector. Pinochet introduced radical monetarist policies. The selling-off of state enterprises at below market value led to large profits for investors and speculators. Tough economic measures, irrespective of the social consequences, brought Chile's inflation rate down from 400%.

The Aylwin and Frei governments continued with neoliberal policies, including privatizing the pension system. However, some 30 companies, including the large Codelco copper company, remain in the state sector.

Avoiding the worst of the Argentine crisis, domestic activity rose in 2003, but oil and copper prices remained a worry.

Iquique
Chuquica
Vina del Mar
Santiago
Teniente
Talcahuano
Concepción
Punta Arenas
Straits
Magella
0 300 km
0 300 miles

CHILE : MAJOR BUSINESSES

- Oil
- Oil refining
- Copper mining
- Manufacturing
- Pharmaceuticals
- Heavy engineering
- Fish processing
- Agribusiness

RESOURCES

Electric power 8.7m kW

4.69m tonnes

4792 b/d (reserves 289m barrels)

4.1m sheep, 3.57m cattle, 2.75m pigs, 74.7m chickens

Coal, copper, gold, silver, iron, lithium, molybdenum, iodine, natural gas, oil

ELECTRICITY GENERATION

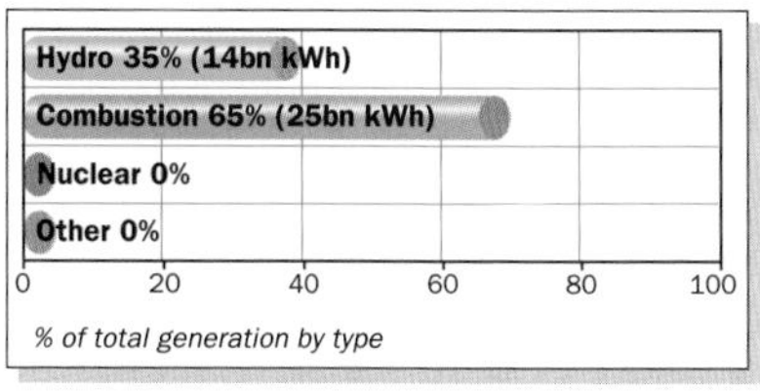

Hydro 35% (14bn kWh)
Combustion 65% (25bn kWh)
Nuclear 0%
Other 0%
0
20
40
60
80
100
% of total generation by type

Chile is the world's largest producer of copper, which accounts for almost 40% of its export revenues. There are important deposits of lithium, molybdenum, and especially of gold. Chile also has reserves of natural gas, oil, and coal, and plenty of hydroelectric potential. In addition, it is a leading producer of fishmeal, and has a flourishing wine industry.

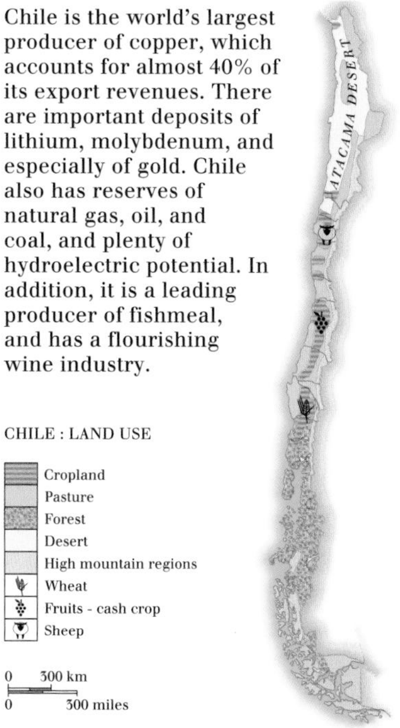

ATACAMA DESERT
CHILE : LAND USE
Cropland
Pasture
Forest
Desert
High mountain regions
Wheat
Fruits - cash crop
Sheep
0 300 km
0 300 miles

ENVIRONMENT

Sustainability rank: 35th

19% (7% partially protected)

4.2 tonnes per capita

ENVIRONMENTAL TREATIES

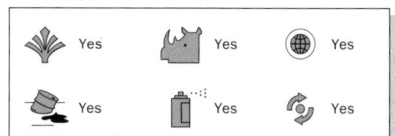

Yes Yes Yes

Yes Yes Yes

Environmental concerns do not rank high on the political agenda. Severe smogs still cover Santiago, due in part to diesel fumes from the city's 14,500 buses. The chief concern is logging in the south by Japanese and other foreign companies. The huge growth of the salmon industry, which fences off sea lakes, is resulting in dolphins losing their natural habitats. Overfishing of swordfish has led to friction with the EU, particularly Spain.

MEDIA

TV ownership high

Daily newspaper circulation 98 per 1000 people

PUBLISHING AND BROADCAST MEDIA

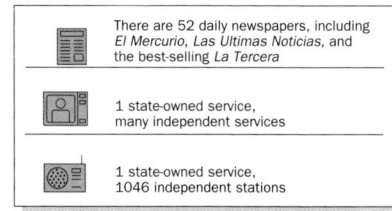

There are 52 daily newspapers, including *El Mercurio*, *Las Ultimas Noticias*, and the best-selling *La Tercera*

1 state-owned service, many independent services

1 state-owned service, 1046 independent stations

A long-delayed liberalized press law was finally introduced in 2001. Military courts will no longer be able to try journalists, and political authorities will be denied the special procedures used to sue reporters for slander.

CRIME

Death penalty not used in practice

31,600 prisoners

Up 12% in 2000

CRIME RATES

Murders	5	per 100,000 population
Rapes	12	per 100,000 population
Thefts	707	per 100,000 population

The judiciary has been slow to pursue human rights cases from the Pinochet regime, despite the discoveries during the 1990s of mass graves of victims of the DINA (secret police). Mapuche leaders were among the "disappeared." Levels of child abuse are exceptionally high, although now starting to fall.

EDUCATION

School leaving age: 14

96%

452,177 students

THE EDUCATION SYSTEM

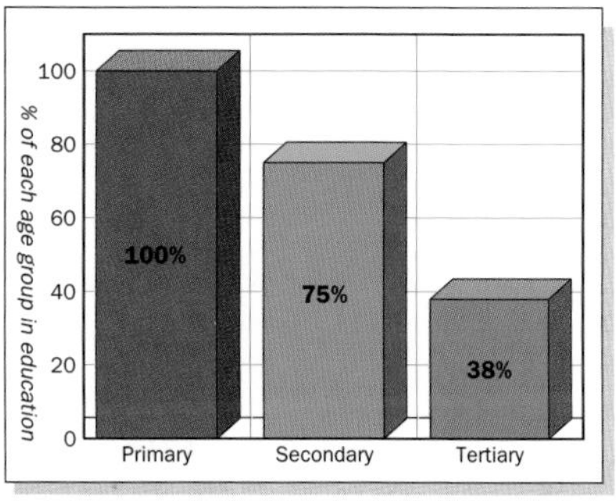

100
80
60
40
20
0
% of each age group in education
100%
75%
38%
Primary
Secondary
Tertiary

Economic growth has permitted public spending on education to increase substantially, but the sector suffers from budgetary cuts. Free primary education is officially compulsory for eight years. Human rights issues now appear in school curricula.

HEALTH

Welfare state health benefits

1 per 870 people

Cancers, respiratory, cerebrovascular, and heart diseases

Recent growth has meant increased public spending on health, but 2002 saw cuts. The public health service covers 80% of people, but is mostly found in urban areas. There is private care for the rich. Infant mortality has fallen to one-third of the 1980 level of 33 deaths per 1000.

SPENDING

GDP/cap. increase

CONSUMPTION AND SPENDING

87 per 1000 population

233 per 1000 population

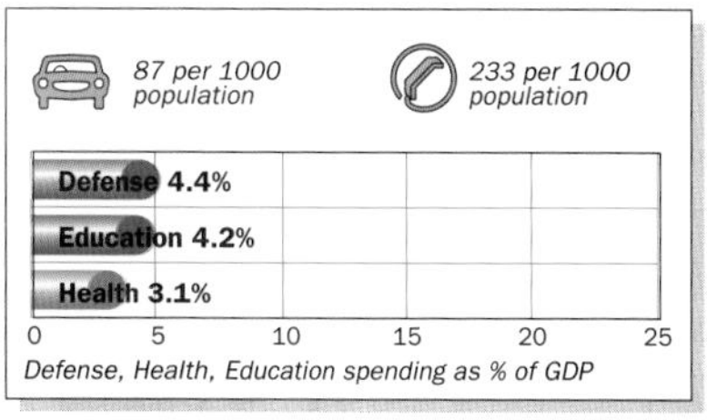

Defense 4.4%
Education 4.2%
Health 3.1%
0
5
10
15
20
25
Defense, Health, Education spending as % of GDP

Chile's traditionally large middle class did well under Pinochet and the economic policies of the Chicago School. The wealthiest sections benefited considerably from the sale of state assets at 40%–50% of their true market value. Five years into the regime, wealth had become highly concentrated, with just nine economic conglomerates controlling the assets of the top 250 businesses, 82% of banking, and 64% of all financial loans. The regime's artificially high domestic interest rates enabled those with access to international finance to earn an estimated $800 million between 1977 and 1980, simply by borrowing abroad and lending at home. These groups have retained their position.

The poor, by contrast, are over 15% worse off than in 1970, with millions of people living just above the UN poverty line and over 1.3 million below it. Poverty is concentrated among the native Amerindian community.

WORLD RANKING

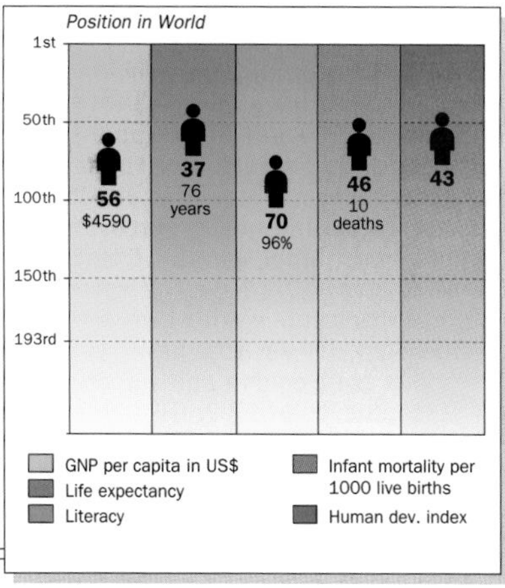

Position in World
1st
50th
100th
150th
193rd
56
$4590
37
76
years
70
96%
46
10
deaths
43
GNP per capita in US$
Life expectancy
Literacy
Infant mortality per 1000 live births
Human dev. index

CHINA

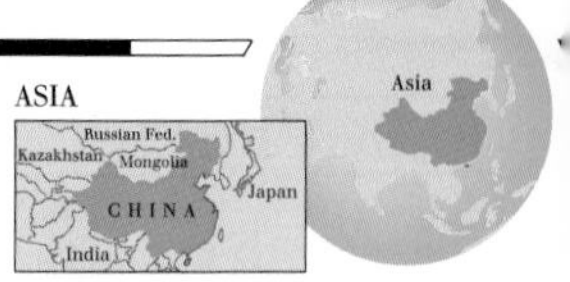
ASIA
Russian Fed.
Kazakhstan
Mongolia
CHINA
Japan
India
Asia

OFFICIAL NAME: People's Republic of China **CAPITAL:** Beijing
POPULATION: 1.29 billion **CURRENCY:** Renminbi (known as yuan) **OFFICIAL LANGUAGE:** Mandarin

960
1999
Oct 1
VRC
+8
+86
.cn

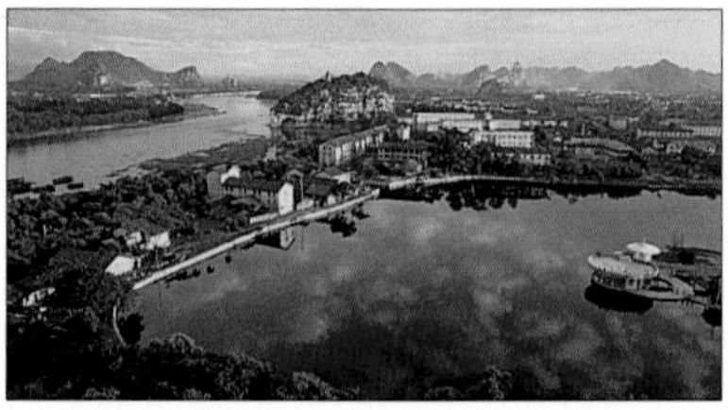

Li River (Xi Jiang), Guangxi, China's most beautiful region. Its spectacular scenery has encouraged large-scale tourist development.

COVERING A VAST AREA of eastern Asia and home to one-fifth of the world's population, China is bordered by 14 countries. Two-thirds of China is uplands: the southwestern mountains include the Tibetan Plateau; in the northwest, the Tien Shan Mountains separate the Tarim and Dzungarian basins. Two-thirds of the population live in the low-lying east. China was dominated by Chairman Mao Zedong from the founding in 1949 of the Communist People's Republic until his death in 1976. Despite the major disasters of the 1950s Great Leap Forward and the 1960s Cultural Revolution, it became an industrial and nuclear power. Today, China is rapidly developing a market-oriented economy. The current leadership remains set on achieving this without political liberalization, instead enforcing single-party rule as was advocated by "elder statesman" Deng Xiaoping, who died in 1997.

CLIMATE

Mountain/tropical/continental/steppe

WEATHER CHART FOR BEIJING

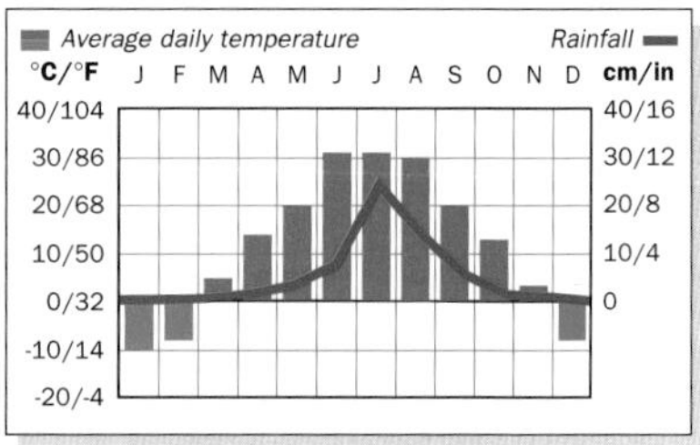
Average daily temperature
Rainfall
°C/°F
J F M A M J J A S O N D
cm/in
40/104
30/86
20/68
10/50
0/32
-10/14
-20/-4
40/16
30/12
20/8
10/4
0

China is divided into two main climatic regions. The north and west are semiarid or arid, with extreme temperature variations. The south and east are warmer and more humid, with year-round rainfall.

Winter temperatures vary with latitude and are warmest on the subtropical southeast coast, where they average about 16°C (60°F). Summer temperatures are more uniform, rising above 21°C (70°F) throughout China; on the southeast coast, the July average is about 30°C (86°F). In the north and west, temperate summers contrast with harsh winters. In northern Manchuria, rivers freeze for five months and temperatures can fall to –25°C (–13°F). In the deserts of Xinjiang province, temperatures range from –11°C (12°F) in winter to 33°C (91°F) in summer.

Summer and autumn are China's wettest seasons. Winds from the Pacific during the summer monsoon bring rains to most of the country. The south and east also have wet winters, but elsewhere the winter monsoon brings cold, dry air from Siberia.

Floods are frequent and sometimes catastrophic, as in 2002. Droughts can be even more devastating: that of 1959–1962 contributed to a famine which killed millions.

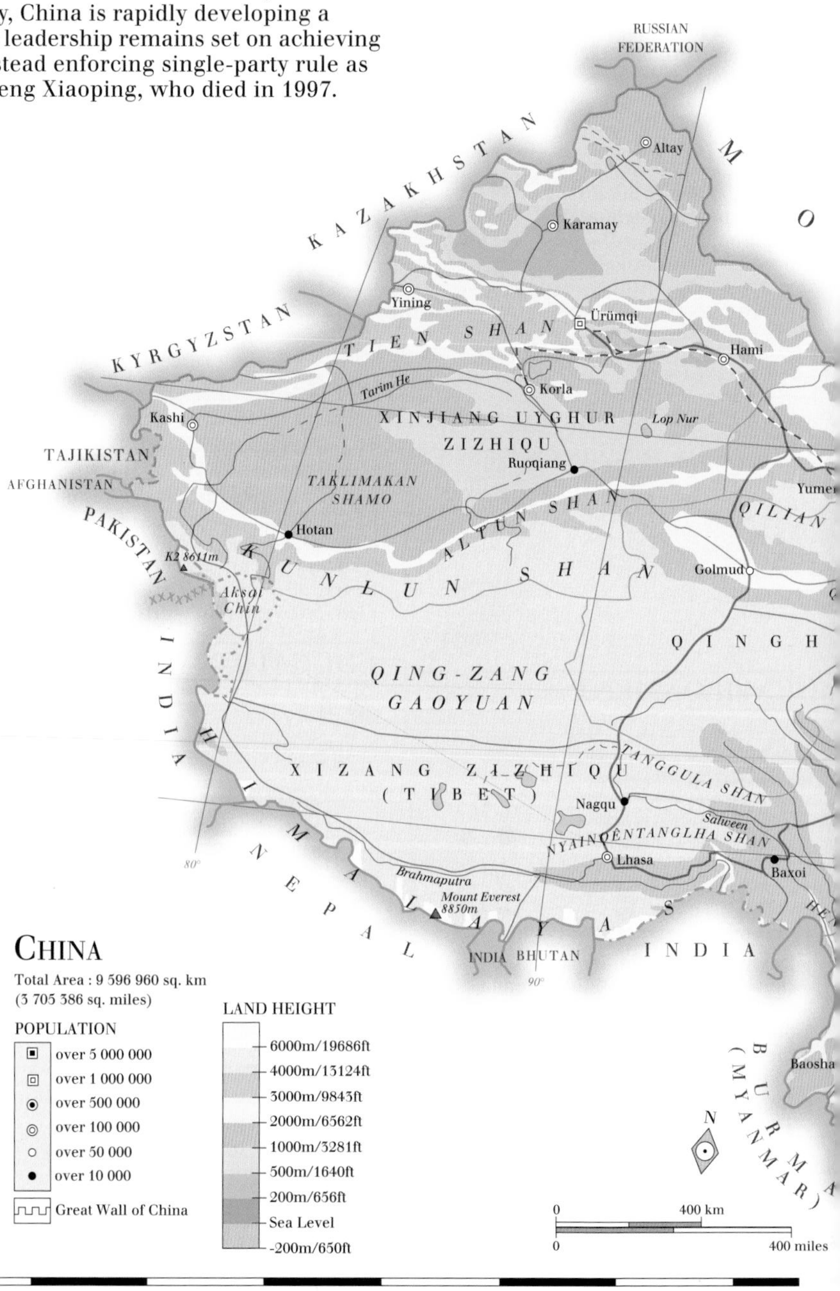
RUSSIAN FEDERATION
KAZAKHSTAN
Altay
Karamay
Yining
Ürümqi
KYRGYZSTAN
TIEN SHAN
Hami
Tarim He
Korla
Kashi
XINJIANG UYGHUR ZIZHIQU
Lop Nur
TAJIKISTAN
AFGHANISTAN
Ruoqiang
TAKLIMAKAN SHAMO
PAKISTAN
Hotan
ALTUN SHAN
QILIAN
K2 8611m
KUNLUN SHAN
Golmud
Aksai Chin
INDIA
QING-ZANG GAOYUAN
XIZANG ZIZHIQU (TIBET)
TANGGULA SHAN
Nagqu
Salween
NYAINQENTANGLHA SHAN
Lhasa
Baxoi
Brahmaputra
Mount Everest 8850m
HIMALAYAS
NEPAL
INDIA
BHUTAN
INDIA
BURMA (MYANMAR)
Baosha
80°
90°
CHINA
Total Area : 9 596 960 sq. km (3 705 386 sq. miles)
POPULATION
over 5 000 000
over 1 000 000
over 500 000
over 100 000
over 50 000
over 10 000
Great Wall of China
LAND HEIGHT
6000m/19686ft
4000m/13124ft
3000m/9843ft
2000m/6562ft
1000m/3281ft
500m/1640ft
200m/656ft
Sea Level
-200m/650ft
0
400 km
400 miles
N

C

TOURISM

Visitors : Population 1:35

36.8m visitors

Up 11% in 2002

MAIN TOURIST ARRIVALS

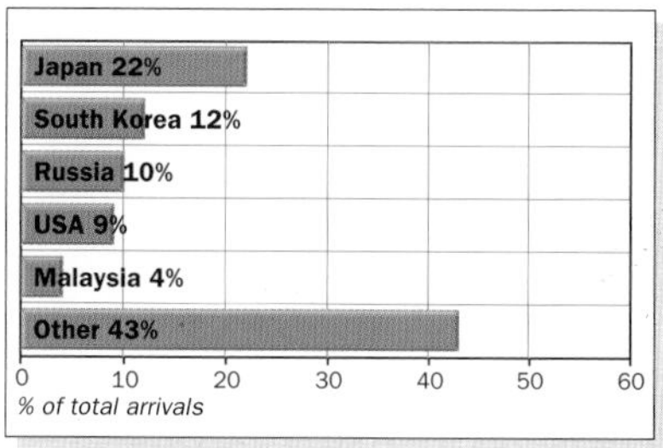
Japan 22%
South Korea 12%
Russia 10%
USA 9%
Malaysia 4%
Other 43%
0
10
20
30
40
50
60
% of total arrivals

The easing of restrictions since the 1980s has led to the rapid growth of all kinds of tourism, from luxury tours to budget packages and backpacking. Most of China is now open to visitors, and tourists are allowed into Tibet, though access to Xinjiang in western China, and other areas, is sometimes impossible. The Forbidden City and Tiananmen Square in Beijing, the modern splendor of Shanghai and Hong Kong, the Great Wall, and the terracotta warriors at Xi'an remain among the top attractions. The number of Chinese able to travel abroad now exceeds ten million.

RUSSIAN FEDERATION
XIAO HINGGAN LING
DA HINGGAN LING
Heihe
Manzhouli
Hulun Nur
Amur
Jiamusi
Qiqihar
HEILONGJIANG
MANCHURIA
Harbin
Jixi
L. Khanka
Baicheng
Mudanjiang
Xilinhot
Changchun
Jilin
JILIN
Siping
Shenyang
Tonghua
SEA OF JAPAN
Fushun
Fuxin
LIAONING
Benxi
Anshan
NORTH KOREA
Jinzhou
Dandong
Korea Bay
Hohhot
Zhangjiakou
Baotou
Huang He
BEIJING (PEKING)
Tangshan
Dalian
Liaodong Bandao
Datong
Baoding
Tianjin
Bo Hai
Yinchuan
Shijiazhuang
HEBEI
Yantai
Shandong Bandao
Taiyuan
Zibo
Weifang
NINGXIA
SHANXI
Jinan
Handan
Qingdao
YELLOW SEA
SHANDONG
Lanzhou
Luoyang
Kaifeng
Xuzhou
Lianyungang
GANSU
Baoji
Xi'an
Zhengzhou
HENAN
Hongze Hu
JIANGSU
SHAANXI
Nanyang
Bengbu
Huainan
Guangyuan
Nanjing
Xinyang
ANHUI
Wuxi
Suzhou
Hefei
Tai Hu
Shanghai
Wuhu
Shashi
Wuhan
Chang Jiang (Yangtze Kiang)
Hangzhou
EAST CHINA SEA
HUBEI
Ningbo
Zigong
Chongqing
Dongting Hu
Poyang Hu
ZHEJIANG
Chang Jiang
Nanchang
Xiangtan
Changsha
Wenzhou
JIANGXI
HUNAN
Guiyang
Hengyang
Fuzhou
FUJIAN
GUIZHOU
Quanzhou
Taiwan Strait
Shaoguan
TAIWAN
Liuzhou
Xi Jiang
Wuzhou
GUANGDONG
Shantou
GUANGXI
Guangzhou
Nanning
Hong Kong (Xianggang)
Macao (Aomen)
VIETNAM
Zhanjiang
Leizhou Bandao
Gulf of Tongking
SOUTH CHINA SEA
Haikou
HAINAN
Hainan Dao
MONGOLIA
INNER MONGOLIA (NEI MONGOL ZIZHIQU)
SICHUAN
30°
40°
50°
20°
110°
120°
130°

TRANSPORTATION

Drive on right

Chek Lap Kok, Hong Kong
33.9m passengers

3280 ships
16.6m grt

THE TRANSPORTATION NETWORK

271,300 km (168,578 miles)	24,474 km (15,207 miles)
58,656 km (36,447 miles)	110,000 km (68,351 miles)

Road and railroad networks are being modernized and expanded to support the push for economic growth. The planned 36-km (23-mile) Hangzhou Bay bridge, which will be the world's longest sea bridge, will drastically cut transit times between Ningbo and Shanghai when it is completed in 2009.

The world's first commercial maglev (magnetic train) route was opened in Shanghai in 2002. Plans have been announced to connect the Tibetan capital, Lhasa, to the railroad system by extending the track from Golmud. If and when it is completed, it will be one of the world's highest railroads.

Container shipping is growing fast. Shanghai handled one-third of all Chinese container traffic before the reversion of Hong Kong (which is the world's biggest container port) to Chinese rule in 1997. The inland waterway system, which was hitherto in a state of disrepair, is being upgraded and now handles one-third of all internal freight. The Yangtze River (Chang Jiang) is navigable by ships of over 1000 tonnes for more than 1000 km (620 miles) from the coast. This capacity is planned to increase under the Three Gorges Dam project.

Nine small airlines which had sprung up since 1988 were consolidated into three carriers in 2002. Hong Kong's new airport opened in 1999. Air transportation is growing rapidly, like private car ownership, as individual wealth increases. Bicycles still form the main mode of personal transportation.

Li River (Xi Jiang) valley. *Irrigation helps Chinese farmers to feed 20% of the world's people, using only 7% of the world's farmland.*

C

PEOPLE

Pop. density medium

Mandarin, Wu, Cantonese, Hsiang, Min, Hakka, Kan

139/km² (359/mi²)

THE URBAN/RURAL POPULATION SPLIT

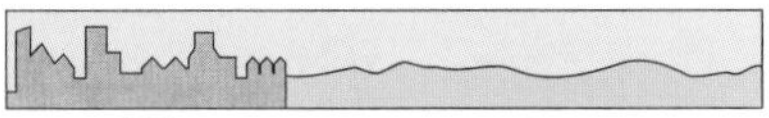

37%
63%

RELIGIOUS PERSUASION

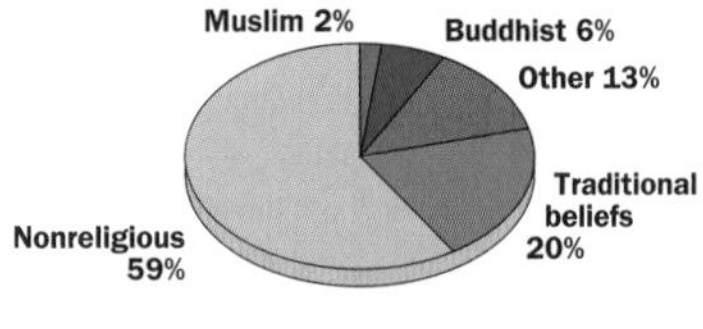

Muslim 2%
Buddhist 6%
Other 13%
Traditional beliefs 20%
Nonreligious 59%

ETHNIC MAKEUP

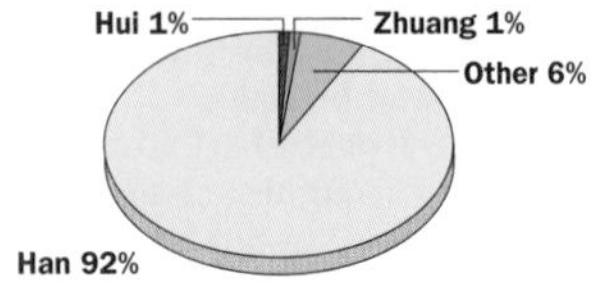

Hui 1%
Zhuang 1%
Other 6%
Han 92%

The vast majority of China's population is Han Chinese. The rest belong to one of 55 minority nationalities, or recognized ethnic groups. The minorities have disproportionate political significance because many, like the Mongolians, Tibetans, or Muslim Uyghurs in Xinjiang, live in strategic border areas.

The deeply resented policy of resettling Han Chinese in remote regions has led to ruthlessly suppressed uprisings in Xinjiang and Tibet. Han Chinese are now a majority in Xinjiang and Nei Mongol Zizhiqu (Inner Mongolia). Tibetan calls for greater political and cultural autonomy get much more international attention.

A one-child policy was adopted in 1979. Most Han Chinese still face strict family-planning controls, though these are widely flouted. Cases of female infanticide at birth have produced a demographic imbalance, and rules were relaxed for minorities after some small groups came near to extinction.

Chinese society is patriarchal in practice, and generations tend to live together. However, economic change is putting pressure on family life, breaking down the social controls of the Mao era. Divorce and unemployment are rising; materialism has replaced the puritanism of the past. The Falun Gong spiritual movement, perceived as a rival to CCP authority, was banned in 1999.

POPULATION AGE BREAKDOWN

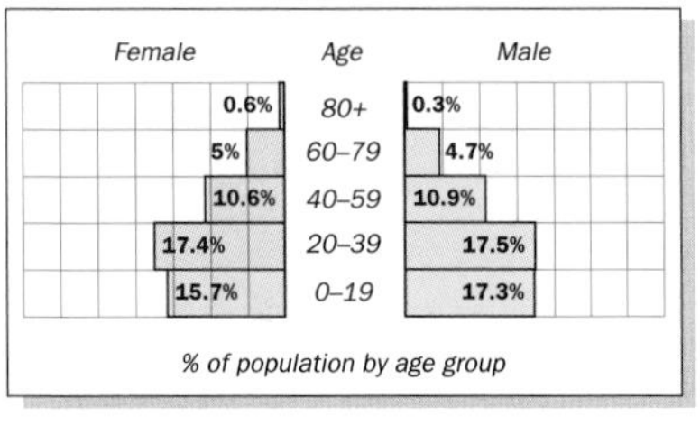

Female
Age
Male
0.6% 80+ 0.3%
5% 60–79 4.7%
10.6% 40–59 10.9%
17.4% 20–39 17.5%
15.7% 0–19 17.3%
% of population by age group

POLITICS

No multiparty elections

2003/2008

President Hu Jintao

AT THE LAST ELECTION

National People's Congress 2979 seats

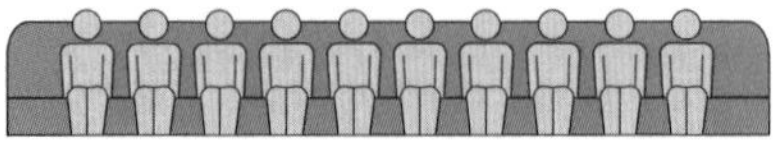

The Communist Party of China (CCP) is the only permitted party

China is a single-party state, dominated by the CCP, the world's largest political party. The National People's Congress, indirectly elected every five years, is theoretically the supreme organ of state power. It appoints the president and executive State Council, headed by the prime minister. The real focus of power, however, is the 22-member Politburo of the CCP and, in particular, its Standing Committee of seven.

PROFILE

The death in 1997 of Deng Xiaoping marked the passing of the dominance of the "Immortals" – those who took part with Mao in the 1934–1935 Long March. Deng, the architect of China's economic reforms, had worked hard behind the scenes forming alliances to promote his ideas and followers. His successor Jiang Zemin consolidated his position as president and CCP general secretary after Deng's death. A "fourth generation" leadership emerged at the 2002 party congress, with the new general secretary Hu Jintao appointed president in March 2003.

MAIN POLITICAL ISSUES

Economic change and CCP authority

After the death of Mao in 1976, China embarked on economic reform, while seeking to secure the dominance of the CCP and avoid political upheaval. The "great helmsman" of this process for two decades was Deng, China's paramount leader even after he had relinquished all official posts. Advocating a fast-track move to a "socialist market economy," he looked to South Korea and Taiwan as achieving high growth without political reform. At the 1997 party congress the reformers, led by Jiang, took their opportunity to realign formal party policy with their desire to privatize large areas of state-run industry. The transfer of much of the huge state economic system into private ownership has been a challenge to the CCP monopoly on power. The 22 provinces, particularly those in the southeast, are increasingly acting independently of Beijing. At a popular level, there is growing rural discontent over a widening wealth gap. However, the party has allowed no political opposition to surface.

Nanjing Donglu (Nanking Road), in central Shanghai, is one of China's most famous shopping streets. A magnet for foreign investment, Shanghai is China's largest city.

Shifting balances in the top leadership

The prodemocracy protests of 1989, culminating in the Tiananmen Square massacre, enabled conservatives within the party to gain the upper hand until Deng moved to restore the balance. His own longevity shifted the advantage toward his heir apparent, Jiang, who subsequently strengthened his own power base and international stature. A major overhaul of party ideology in 2001, under Jiang's "Three Represents" doctrine, encouraged the promotion equally of business, culture, and the rural masses. Jiang and his prime minister Zhu Rongji stood down from the Politburo at the 2002 party congress, handing over to the new generation of leaders, headed by President Hu, with Wen Jiabao as premier. However, Jiang retains considerable influence as armed forces chief, and Hu's accumulation of power is an ongoing process. He has so far done little to innovate politically.

Deng Xiaoping was China's paramount leader until his death in 1997.

Jiang Zemin, president until 2003, retains significant influence.

Wen Jiabao, premier of the State Council, appointed in 2003.

President Hu Jintao represents a "fourth generation" of leaders.

WORLD AFFAIRS

Joined UN in 1945

APEC | IAEA | WTO | ADB | SCO

The push for economic modernization and concerns about regional stability dominate. Investment, technology, and trade considerations outweigh ideology.

Despite lingering concerns over human rights, relations with the West have rebounded from the low of the 1989 Tiananmen Square massacre. China was awarded Most Favored Nation trading status by the US in 2000 and entered the WTO in 2001. Despite initial tensions in relations with the new US administration in 2001, the two countries had reached a "common understanding" by the end of the year on the issue of terrorism.

Regionally, ties have been normalized with Vietnam, and Himalayan territorial disputes with India were shelved in 2003, enabling the reopening of lucrative cross-border routes. China has strengthened ties with South Korea while maintaining a strongly paternalistic relationship with North Korea. Relations with Russia have improved steadily on the basis of shared opposition to certain Western, and particularly US, policies.

Taiwan remains a dark spot. Beijing strongly rejects any moves to recognize even de facto independence for the island, and cross-strait relations are frequently damaged by displays of military might and repetitive threats. Nonetheless, closer links have been forged since 2000, with an increase in tourist traffic and indirect trade.

AID

Recipient

$1.46bn (receipts) — Down 16% in 2001

In the 1970s aid was an important part of Chinese diplomacy, going mostly to Africa, but other communist and southeast Asian states were also recipients. Outward aid flows almost ceased in the late 1970s, as the economic reform process turned China itself into a major aid recipient. Japan is the biggest bilateral donor to China, but the potential of the Chinese market means that most developed states provide aid. A significant portion of funding is linked to a donor country's interest in opportunities created by China's huge infrastructure problems, and used to finance high-tech imports.

DEFENSE

Compulsory military service

$46bn — Up 10% in 2001

CHINESE ARMED FORCES

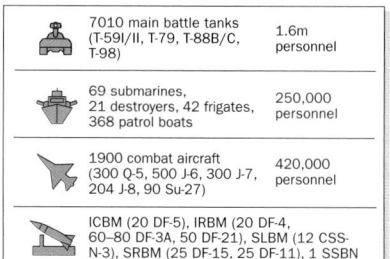

7010 main battle tanks (T-59I/II, T-79, T-88B/C, T-98)	1.6m personnel
69 submarines, 21 destroyers, 42 frigates, 368 patrol boats	250,000 personnel
1900 combat aircraft (300 Q-5, 500 J-6, 300 J-7, 204 J-8, 90 Su-27)	420,000 personnel
ICBM (20 DF-5), IRBM (20 DF-4, 60–80 DF-3A, 50 DF-21), SLBM (12 CSS-N-3), SRBM (25 DF-15, 25 DF-11), 1 SSBN	

The People's Liberation Army (PLA) is the basis of CCP control and is intimately entwined with the one-party state. It was used in 1967 to restore order during the chaos of the Cultural Revolution, and in 1989 to suppress prodemocracy protests in Tiananmen Square, as well as to stamp out dissent in Tibet. From a 1990s peak of three million personnel it is now being cut back as part of a modernization process, reducing both its numbers and its involvement in the economy through army-run industries.

China has a large weapons production and export industry, and has extended its nuclear weapons capability to include the neutron bomb. The government plans to have put a Chinese astronaut, or *taikonaut*, into space by 2004.

ECONOMICS

Inflation 6.2% p.a. (1990–2001)

$1131bn — 8.2775 yuan (8.2771)

SCORE CARD

- ❑ WORLD GNP RANKING 6th
- ❑ GNP PER CAPITA $890
- ❑ BALANCE OF PAYMENTS $17.4bn
- ❑ INFLATION 0.3%
- ❑ UNEMPLOYMENT .... 3% (official)

STRENGTHS

Huge domestic market. Food self-sufficiency. Mineral reserves. Diversified industrial sector. Low wage costs. Rapid sustained growth. Growing export sector. Hong Kong as financial center. Heavy investment in communications and IT.

ECONOMIC PERFORMANCE INDICATOR

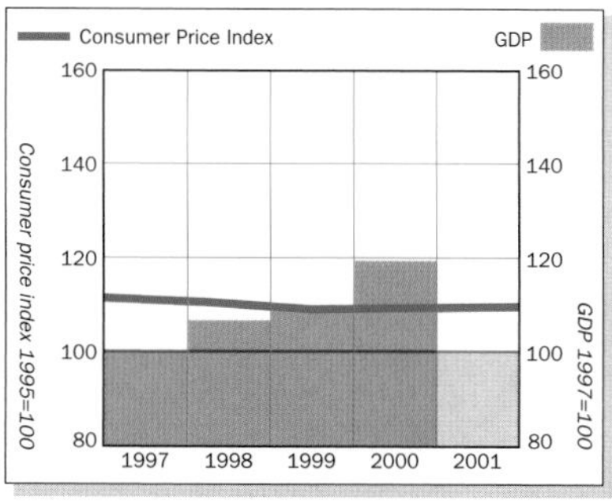
Consumer Price Index
GDP
160
140
120
100
80
1997
1998
1999
2000
2001
Consumer price index 1995=100
GDP 1997=100

EXPORTS

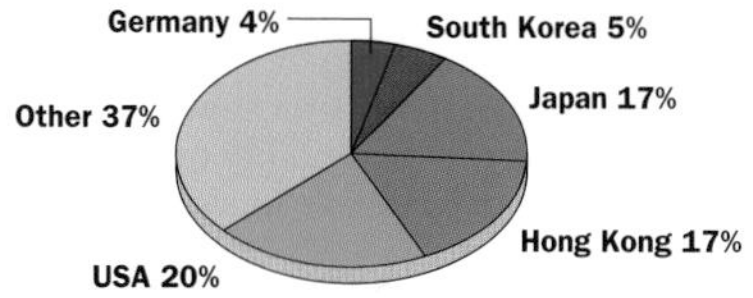
Germany 4%
South Korea 5%
Japan 17%
Hong Kong 17%
USA 20%
Other 37%

IMPORTS

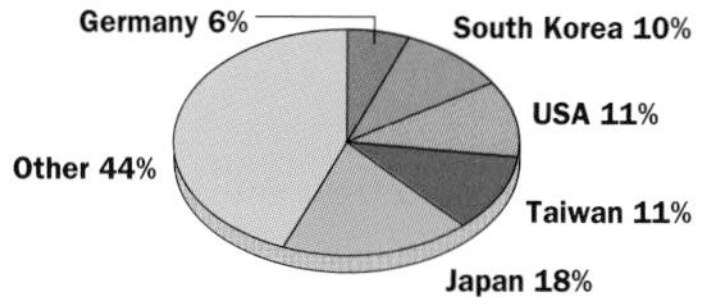
Germany 6%
South Korea 10%
USA 11%
Taiwan 11%
Japan 18%
Other 44%

WEAKNESSES

Poor transportation. Debt-ridden state sector. Massive underemployment, rising unemployment (132 million admitted in 2002). Unevenly distributed resources.

CHINA : MAJOR BUSINESSES

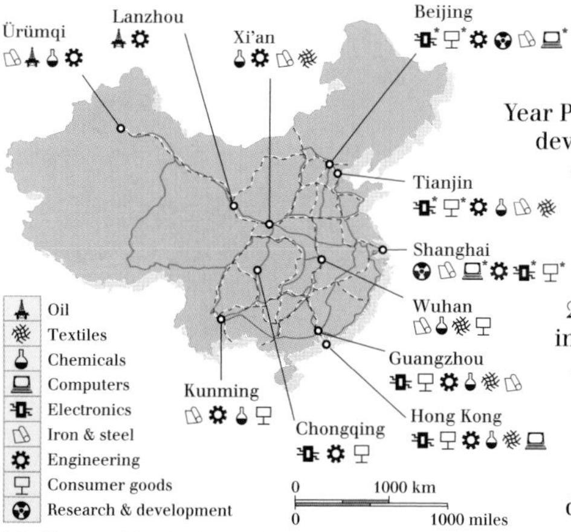
Ürümqi
Lanzhou
Xi'an
Beijing
Tianjin
Shanghai
Wuhan
Guangzhou
Hong Kong
Chongqing
Kunming
Oil
Textiles
Chemicals
Computers
Electronics
Iron & steel
Engineering
Consumer goods
Research & development
0
1000 km
0
1000 miles

* significant multinational ownership

PROFILE

China has shifted from a centrally planned to a market-oriented economy; liberalization has gone furthest in the south. In the Ninth Five-Year Plan (1996–2000) the government retained strict controls, promoting intensive growth and boosting privatization of the huge state-owned sector. The Tenth Five-Year Plan (2001–2005) emphasizes rapid development, reforms, and improving competitiveness. The government now runs a record deficit of almost $40 billion. GDP growth passed 7% in 2002.

Trade entered a new era in 2000–2001. A substantial growth in imports followed a deal with the EU and the normalization of US trade relations, while a boost in exports has aided the high growth rate in 2002. Even Taiwan has dropped its ban on direct trade with the mainland.

C

MINORITIES IN THE AUTONOMOUS REGIONS

Autonomous regions of China

XINJIANG UYGHUR ZIZHIQU
INNER MONGOLIA (NEI MONGOL ZIZHIQU)
NINGXIA
TIBET (XIZANG ZIZHIQU)
GUANGXI

China's constitution states that "regional autonomy is practiced in areas where people of minority nationalities live in compact communities." The Manchu, Miao, Yi, and many others among the 55 recognized ethnic minorities are not regarded as meeting this criterion, but there are five areas which do officially have the status of autonomous region or *zizhiqu*. The two most westerly such regions, sparsely populated Tibet and the home of the Uyghur people in Xinjiang, are both particularly sensitive border areas, and opposition to Chinese rule there has been suppressed.

Tibet

The vast mountainous region of Tibet has China's lowest population density, at only two inhabitants per sq. km (six per sq. mile), spread across an area of 1,221,600 sq. km (472,000 sq. miles). Lhasa is its capital. Tibetans were officially recorded as making up 2.41 million of its total population of 2.62 million at the 2000 census. Han Chinese, whose immigration has aroused strong local resentment, were recorded at under 6%.

In 1950, Chinese forces invaded Tibet, which had been part of the Chinese empire from the 18th century until 1911, and ruthlessly crushed the 1959 independence uprising. The Dalai Lama, spiritual head of Tibetan Buddhism, fled to India amid an exodus of refugees and established a government in exile, but he has recently come close to accepting Chinese rule – reestablishing direct relations with Beijing in September 2002 after a nine-year break – in an effort to win greater real self-government and cultural freedom for the Tibetan people. In 1965 Tibet was made a region of China, known as Xizang Zizhiqu. Opponents of Chinese rule were imprisoned or executed and many Buddhist monasteries were destroyed. Clashes between nationalists and Chinese troops in 1987 led to a renewed clampdown. In 1988, in an apparently more conciliatory spirit, the Chinese government accepted Tibetan as a "major official language."

Since 1995, the Chinese authorities have detained a young boy recognized by Tibetan Buddhists as the latest incarnation of their second-ranking spiritual leader, the Panchen Lama. The Chinese government named its own candidate to this office. Tibetans see this as unwarranted interference in their religious life. They are also alarmed by the promotion of Tibet as a tourist destination, and by the destruction involved in major "restoration" projects around the Potala and Norbulinka palaces in Lhasa.

Xinjiang Uyghur

Consisting largely of desert, and bordering on Kyrgyzstan and Kazakhstan, the Xinjiang Uyghur Zizhiqu has a total area of 1,646,900 sq. km (636,000 sq. miles), or nearly 18% of China's total land mass. Han Chinese are narrowly in the majority in its population of 19.25 million. Unrest among the mainly Muslim Uyghur minority has been met by strict security measures, especially since 2002, with a clampdown on "terrorists." The regional capital, Urumqi, is an industrial city noted for iron and steel, oil, and chemicals.

***The Kumbum dagoba** at the Palkhor Tschöde monastery, Gyangze (Chiang-tzu), Tibet. At the tip of this 15th-century structure is a Buddhist chapel.*

Inner Mongolia

Inner Mongolia, or Nei Mongol Zizhiqu, occupies most of the area of northern China along the long land border with Mongolia. This totals 1,177,500 sq. km (455,000 sq. miles). Han Chinese form the majority in a total population of 23.8 million, of whom fewer than a quarter are ethnic Mongolian.

Ningxia Hui

The smallest of all the autonomous regions, Ningxia Hui Zizhiqu occupies an area of 66,000 sq. km (25,000 sq. miles), just south of Nei Mongol Zizhiqu. Its capital is Yinchuan. The population was 5.6 million at the 2000 census. Many of the Hui people, the main local ethnic group, live outside the region.

Guangxi Zhuang

This autonomous region lies in the south, close to China's booming economic heartland. Relatively small in terms of area (220,000 sq. km – 85,000 sq. miles), it is by far the largest in terms of population, with a density of 204 per sq. km (528 per sq. mile) and 44.9 million inhabitants at the census. The capital is Nanning. The Zhuang people, China's largest ethnic minority, number only some 16 million, and thus are substantially in the minority in the region.

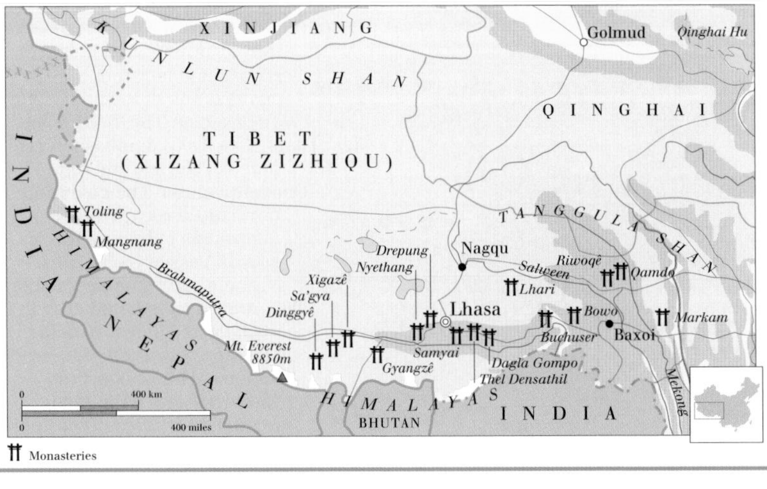
XINJIANG
KUNLUN SHAN
Golmud
Qinghai Hu
QINGHAI
TIBET (XIZANG ZIZHIQU)
INDIA
Toling
Mangnang
HIMALAYAS
Brahmaputra
NEPAL
Xigazê
Sa'gya
Dinggyê
Drepung
Nyethang
Nagqu
Lhasa
TANGGULA SHAN
Salween
Riwoqê
Qamdo
Lhari
Bowo
Markam
Baxoi
Buchuser
Samyai
Gyangzê
Dagla Gompo
Thel Densathil
Mt. Everest 8850m
HIMALAYAS
BHUTAN
INDIA
Mekong
0 400 km
0 400 miles
Monasteries

SPECIAL ECONOMIC ZONES, OPEN CITIES, AND SPECIAL ADMINISTRATIVE REGIONS

ECONOMIC REFORMS first instituted by Deng Xiaoping in 1978 began opening China to foreign business. This has spread from a small number of zones operating under special tax regimes to other cities all along the coastal belt and inland, and has fueled an extraordinary urban investment boom.

Nanchang
Changsha
HUNAN
JIANGXI
Hengyang
Ganzhou
Fuzhou
FUJIAN
Quanzhou
Shaoguan
Xiamen
GUANGXI
GUANGDONG
TAIWAN
Wuzhou
Xi Jiang
Guangzhou
Shantou
Shenzen
Zhuhai
SOUTH CHINA SEA
Zhanjiang
Macao
Hong Kong
Haikou
HAINAN
0 300 km
0 300 miles
Special Economic Zones (SEZs)
Special Administrative Regions (SARs)

SPECIAL ECONOMIC ZONES

The creation of five special economic zones (SEZs) on the south coast was a major early milestone. Shenzhen, the trailblazer for the concept, was established in 1980, adjoining Kowloon in Hong Kong. Also in Guangdong province are Zhuhai, adjoining Macao, and Shantou further east, while Xiamen SEZ is in Fujian province, facing Taiwan. These locations reflect the aim of attracting investment from the 30 million Chinese overseas, especially in Hong Kong and Taiwan, whose ancestral homes were in Guangdong and Fujian. The fifth and least dynamic of the SEZs, comprises the southern island province of Hainan.

FOREIGN INVESTMENT

Foreign direct investment dipped in the late 1990s, but turned upward again to reach $52.7 billion in 2002, when China overtook the US as the world's strongest magnet for investment. Most of this money goes into the Open Coastal Belt, based on 14 cities, from Dalian in the north to Zhanjiang and Beihai in the south, which were picked in the mid-1980s for the dual role of "windows," opening to the outside world, and "radiators," spreading the development of an export-oriented economy.

Among the most successful development areas is the great port of Shanghai, where the stock exchange reopened in 1990. Investors in the city's Pudong New Zone, on the east bank of the Huangpu River, enjoy more preferential conditions than do the SEZs, including the right to sell goods and financial services. Pudong has attracted major foreign companies keen to establish a foothold in the potentially massive Chinese market, including General Motors, NEC, Sharp, Hitachi, Siemens, Unilever, BASF, and Pilkington. Pudong also forms the "dragon head" for a chain of open cities, extending up the Yangtze River (Chang Jiang) valley, where foreign investment has been encouraged since 1990. China has also designated a new set of open cities since 1992, this time in areas near its land borders, adjoining Russia, Mongolia, Kazakhstan, Burma, and Vietnam, to develop infrastructure and promote trade and the growth of export-oriented industries.

INDUSTRIAL GROWTH IN GUANGDONG

Guangdong province, with Guangzhou and Shenzhen at its heart, is rapidly becoming Asia's largest industrial region. Many of the world's top multinational companies have invested in the Guangzhou Economic and Technical Development District (GET). Shenzhen, meanwhile, was the first Chinese city to start selling state-owned apartments freehold. It is being revamped as the science and technology city of the future, complete with parks, pedestrian precincts, civic amenities, and a sophisticated communications infrastructure. The process of reform was extended to politics in 2002 in an experiment to tackle rampant corruption.

HONG KONG AND MACAO SARS

Hong Kong, recession-hit after its reversion to Chinese sovereignty in mid-1997, recovered to record impressively high growth in 2000, but then suffered the knock-on effects of the global economic slowdown. As a British colony, Hong Kong had flourished through its textile industry, subsequently expanding into electronics, but it was above all a trade and financial services center. This role is preserved under its status as a special administrative region (SAR). Hong Kong's population is estimated at 6.78 million, in an area of only 1098 sq. km (424 sq. miles). Its Basic Law guarantees a high level of autonomy for 50 years under the "one country, two systems" formula. English and Chinese are both official languages, and the freely convertible Hong Kong dollar remains as the SAR's currency, while Hong Kong has its own separate membership of key international organizations, notably the WTO. Its Chinese-appointed chief executive, Tung Chee-hwa, has been unpopular, however – increasingly at odds with members of his administration and with the region's Legislative Council. The number of directly elected seats on the Council was increased somewhat (to 24 out of 60) for the September 2000 elections, half of which were won by the opposition Democratic Party. Two leading members of the executive resigned in mid-2003 amid increased unrest over a proposed antisubversion bill.

China's other SAR, Macao, ceased to be a Portuguese colony at midnight on December 19–20, 1999. Macao too has free port status, its own currency, the pataca, two official languages (Portuguese and Chinese), a partly elective Legislative Assembly, and a guarantee under its Basic Law that the "one country, two systems" formula will apply for 50 years. Macao's area of only 25.4 sq. km (9.8 sq. miles) was due to increase by 20% on completion of the Nam Van lakes project. The population was 440,000 at the 2000 census. The economy, based on tourism and gambling, has recently been in decline.

PHILIPS

Hong Kong's return to Chinese sovereignty after 157 years of British rule, took place at midnight on June 30, 1997.

C

CHRONOLOGY

China's recorded history began 4000 years ago with the Shang dynasty, founded in 1766 BCE; succeeding dynasties expanded its boundaries. The empire was reunified by the Sung dynasty in 960 CE after a period of dispersal, and reached its greatest extent under the Qing (Manchu) dynasty in the 18th century. For 3000 years China had been one of the world's most advanced nations, but, having fallen behind the industrializing West, its resistance to European trade was broken in a series of wars in the 19th century.

- **1839–1860** Opium Wars with Britain. China defeated; forced to open ports to foreigners.
- **1850–1873** Internal rebellions against Qing dynasty, including the large-scale Taiping rebellion.
- **1895** Defeat by Japan in war over Korean peninsula.
- **1900** Boxer Rebellion to expel all foreigners suppressed.
- **1911** Qing dynasty overthrown by nationalists led by Sun Yat-sen. Republic of China declared.
- **1912** Sun Yat-sen forms National People's Party (Guomindang).
- **1916** Nationalists factionalize. Sun Yat-sen sets up government in Guangdong. Rest of China under control of rival warlords.
- **1921** CCP founded in Shanghai.
- **1923** CCP joins Soviet-backed Guomindang to fight warlords.
- **1925** Chiang Kai-shek becomes Guomindang leader on death of Sun Yat-sen.
- **1927** Chiang turns on CCP. CCP leaders escape to rural south.
- **1930–1934** Mao Zedong formulates strategy of peasant-led revolution.
- **1931** Japan invades Manchuria.
- **1934** Chiang forces CCP out of its southern bases. Start of 12,000-km (7450-mile) Long March north.
- **1935** Long March ends. Mao becomes CCP leader.
- **1937–1945** War against Japan: CCP Red Army in north, Guomindang in south. Japan defeated.
- **1945–1949** War between Red Army and Guomindang. US-backed Guomindang retreats to Taiwan.
- **1949** 1st October, Mao proclaims People's Republic of China.
- **1950** Invasion of Tibet. Mutual assistance treaty with USSR.
- **1950–1958** Land reform; culminates in setting up of communes. First Five-Year Plan (1953–1958) fails.
- **1958** "Great Leap Forward" fails; contributes to millions of deaths during 1959–1961 famine. Mao resigns as CCP chairman; succeeded by Liu Shaoqi.

RESOURCES

Electric power 231m kW

43.1m tonnes

3.39m b/d (reserves 18.3bn barrels)

465m pigs, 661m ducks, 215m geese, 3.92bn chickens

Coal, oil, natural gas, salt, iron, molybdenum, titanium, tungsten

ELECTRICITY GENERATION

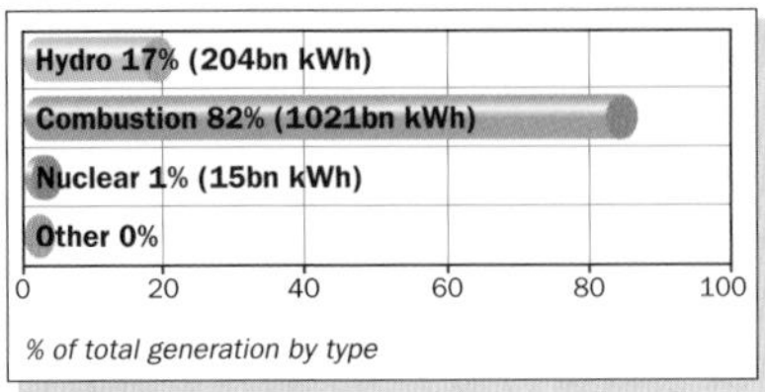
Hydro 17% (204bn kWh)
Combustion 82% (1021bn kWh)
Nuclear 1% (15bn kWh)
Other 0%
0
20
40
60
80
100
% of total generation by type

The world's biggest producer of steel and tungsten, with the world's largest deposits of more than a dozen minerals, and commercial deposits of most others, China plays a dominant role in the world mineral trade.

China is the world's largest producer and consumer of coal, though it has only 11% of world reserves. Annual output (around one billion tonnes) considerably exceeds demand; this and appalling safety records are forcing the closure of many mines.

Though demand is set to increase, there is currently an oversupply of power. Nuclear power capacity in 2002 was just over 2100 MW from three reactors, with major expansion to 50,000 MW planned by 2020. The world's largest HEP plant, the highly controversial Three Gorges Dam on the Yangtze River, began generating power in June 2003. Power provision was decentralized and opened to foreign investment in 2002.

Crude oil production has risen only slightly since reaching 160 million tonnes a year in 1997. Eastern oil fields are depleted, and hopes now center on enormous reserves in the Tarim basin in the far west. A 4000-km (2500-mile) pipeline is due to come on line in 2004.

CHINA : LAND USE

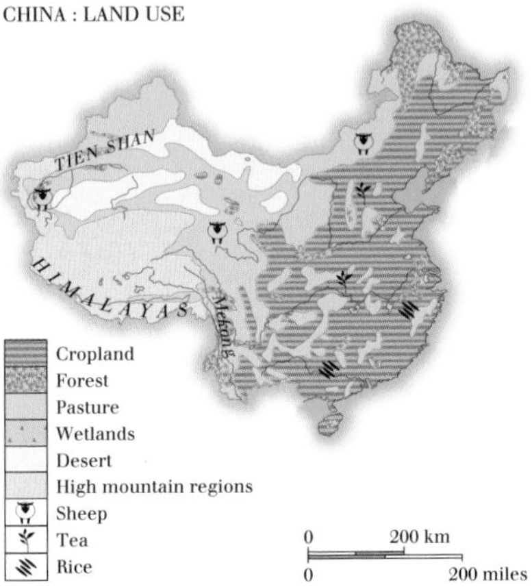
TIEN SHAN
HIMALAYAS
Mekong
Cropland
Forest
Pasture
Wetlands
Desert
High mountain regions
Sheep
Tea
Rice
0
200 km
0
200 miles

ENVIRONMENT

Sustainability rank: 129th

8% (2% partially protected)

2.2 tonnes per capita

ENVIRONMENTAL TREATIES

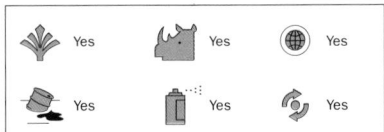

Yes	Yes	Yes
Yes	Yes	Yes

Climate and geology cause frequent natural disasters; their impact is often made worse by human actions. The economic policies of the 1950s turned drought into a devastating famine, while poor building standards pushed the death toll in the 1976 Tangshan earthquake to over 500,000.

Widespread industrial pollution and environmental degradation increase as China's leaders seek economic growth. However, the environment is a growing concern among educated Chinese. Becoming less suspicious of Western pressure, the government is taking steps to respond to acute problems of urban air pollution, deforestation, and water quality in particular. Nonetheless, grand schemes such as the Three Gorges Dam, and the diversion of Yangtze water to the parched north, continue to be pursued with devastating effects on existing ecosystems.

MEDIA

TV ownership high

Daily newspaper circulation 40 per 1000 people

PUBLISHING AND BROADCAST MEDIA

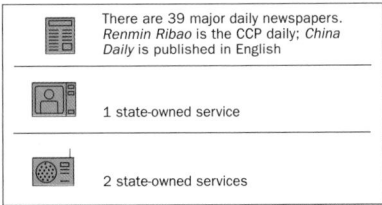

There are 39 major daily newspapers. *Renmin Ribao* is the CCP daily; *China Daily* is published in English

1 state-owned service

2 state-owned services

China's more open, market-oriented economy has created access to nonofficial sources of information. TV ownership is rising and those with satellite dishes can choose what to view, while growing Internet usage makes central control even more difficult. Since 2000, Internet sites have had to obtain official approval and have been held responsible for their content. Many Internet cafés were closed in 2001, and new rules in 2002 restricted the media's use of Internet sources.

The ideological influence of the huge-circulation party newspaper *Renmin Ribao* (*People's Daily*) and the trade union *Gongren Ribao* (*Workers' Daily*) is much diminished, but "undesirable" papers have their licenses removed in periodic cleanups. Beijing and most provinces have their own dailies.

CHRONOLOGY *continued*

- **1960** Sino-Soviet split.
- **1961–1965** More pragmatic economic approach led by Liu and Deng Xiaoping.
- **1966** Cultural Revolution initiated by Mao to restore his supreme power. Youthful Red Guards attack all authority. Mao rules, with Military Commission under Lin Biao and State Council under Zhou Enlai.
- **1967** Army intervenes to restore order amid countrywide chaos. Liu and Deng purged from party.
- **1969** Mao regains chair of CCP. Lin Biao designated his successor, but quickly attacked by Mao.
- **1971** Lin dies in plane crash.
- **1972** US president Nixon visits. More open foreign policy initiated.
- **1973** Mao's wife Jiang Qing, Zhang Chunqiao, and other "Gang of Four" members elected to CCP Politburo. Deng Xiaoping rehabilitated.
- **1976** Death of Zhou Enlai. Mao strips Deng of posts. September, Mao dies. October, Gang of Four arrested.
- **1977** Deng regains party posts, begins to extend power base.
- **1978** Decade of economic modernization launched. Open door policy to foreign investment; farmers allowed to farm for profit.
- **1980** Deng emerges as China's paramount leader. Economic reform gathers pace, but hopes for political change suppressed.
- **1983–1984** Conservative elderly leaders attempt to slow reform.
- **1984** Industrial reforms announced.
- **1989** Prodemocracy demonstrations in Tiananmen Square crushed by army; 1000–5000 dead.
- **1992–1995** Trials of prodemocracy activists continue. Plans for market economy accelerated.
- **1993** Jiang Zemin president.
- **1997** February, Deng Xiaoping dies at 92. June 30, UK hands back Hong Kong. September, party congress confirms reformist policies.
- **1998** Severe flooding: 3000 killed.
- **1999** China develops neutron bomb. Friction with Taiwan. Clampdown on Falun Gong sect. December 19, Portugal hands back Macao.
- **2000** US normalizes trade relations.
- **2001** Major diplomatic incident over downed US spy plane. "Strike Hard" campaign against corruption: executions increase. December, accession to WTO.
- **2002** Crackdown on Uyghur separatism.
- **2003** Hu Jintao president. SARS outbreak spreads globally, damaging economy. Flooding of Three Gorges Dam begins.

CRIME

Death penalty in use

1.44m prisoners

Little change in 1997

CRIME RATES

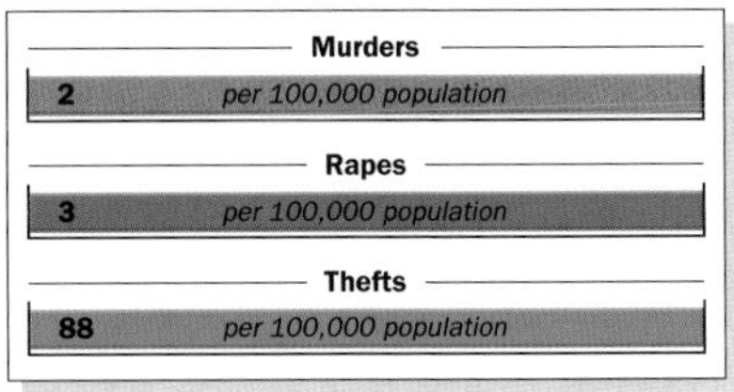
Murders
2
per 100,000 population
Rapes
3
per 100,000 population
Thefts
88
per 100,000 population

China's legal system is a mix of custom and statute. Judges have been required to hold law degrees only since 2002. A rise in corruption and violent crime has paralleled economic reform and social changes. In 2000 many party officials were convicted in the largest ever corruption trial. A crackdown on human trafficking followed the breaking of rings smuggling Chinese into Europe. The death penalty is used extensively – China carried out over 80% of the world's executions in 2001. Since a clampdown on dissent after the 1989 Tiananmen Square massacre many detainees have been released, but many more remain incarcerated.

EDUCATION

School leaving age: 14

86%

7.36m students

THE EDUCATION SYSTEM

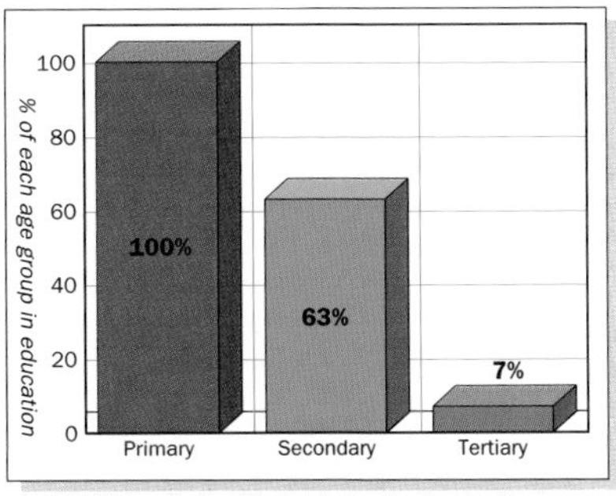
100
80
60
40
20
0
% of each age group in education
100%
63%
7%
Primary
Secondary
Tertiary

Despite the expansion of education since 1949, illiteracy and semiliteracy are still widespread. School attendance fell when fees at all levels were introduced in the 1980s, but now most children of secondary school age are in school – including those catching up with primary education.

Selection for higher education is now based on academic rather than political criteria, though fees can be prohibitive. Internet-based distance learning degrees, first allowed in 1998, are increasingly popular. In May 2001, the government legalized private schools (which have been tacitly permitted since the early 1980s) in an effort to regulate and profit from them. About seven million pupils are thought to attend them.

HEALTH

Welfare state health benefits

1 per 599 people

Cardiovascular and diarrheal diseases, cancers, tuberculosis

Primary health care combines Western and traditional medicine and extends to the remotest areas. For decades, free health care accompanied full state employment, and life expectancy was on a par with many richer countries. The change to a market-oriented economy, however, has produced a gaping divide between city and rural provision, and fees for treatment are rising. The UN estimated in 2002 that there would be over ten million HIV/AIDS sufferers in China by 2010. The outbreak of acute pneumonia (SARS) strained facilities in 2003. Suicide is a leading cause of death among the young.

SPENDING

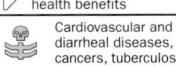

GDP/cap. increase

CONSUMPTION AND SPENDING

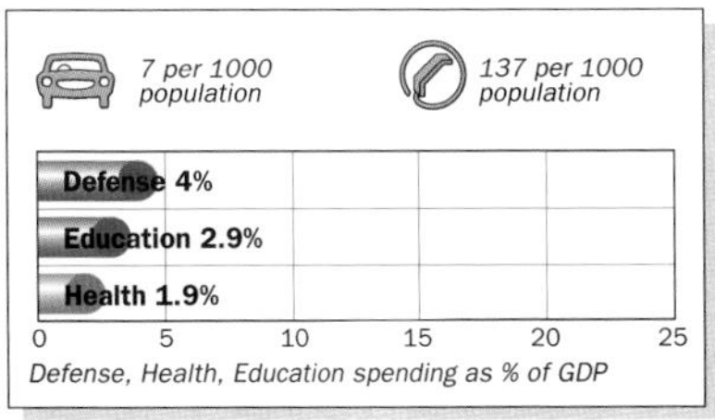
7 per 1000 population
137 per 1000 population
Defense 4%
Education 2.9%
Health 1.9%
0
5
10
15
20
25
Defense, Health, Education spending as % of GDP

The majority of Chinese are still farmers, whose living standards are threatened by rising production costs. Economic change has led to widening wealth disparities. The burgeoning small-business class and employees of companies with foreign investment have benefited most. They mainly live in the east, especially the southeast, where there are a number of dollar millionaires. The main losers are the 150 million "surplus" agricultural workers, many of whom have migrated to the cities in search of jobs. By July 2001, there were more mobile phones in China than in the US, 120.6 million in total – about one for every ten Chinese.

WORLD RANKING

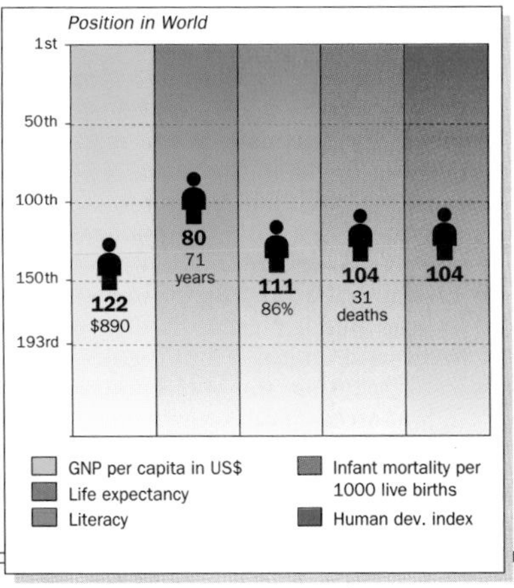
Position in World
1st
50th
100th
150th
193rd
122
$890
80
71
years
111
86%
104
31
deaths
104
GNP per capita in US$
Life expectancy
Literacy
Infant mortality per 1000 live births
Human dev. index

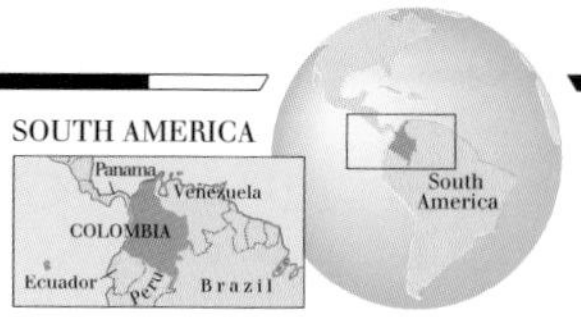
SOUTH AMERICA
Panama
Venezuela
COLOMBIA
Ecuador
Peru
Brazil
South America

COLOMBIA

OFFICIAL NAME: Republic of Colombia **CAPITAL:** Bogotá
POPULATION: 43.5 million **CURRENCY:** Colombian peso **OFFICIAL LANGUAGE:** Spanish

C

1819 | 1903 | July 20 | CO | -5 | +57 | .co

LYING IN NORTHWEST South America, Colombia has coastlines on both the Caribbean and the Pacific. The east is densely forested and sparsely populated, and separated from the western coastal plains by the Andes mountains. The Andes divide into three ranges (cordilleras) in Colombia. The eastern range is divided from the two western ranges by the densely populated Magdalena River valley. The Colombian lowlands are very wet, hot, and fertile, supporting two harvests and allowing many crops to be planted at any time of year. A state plagued by instability and violence, Colombia is noted for its coffee, emeralds, gold, and narcotics trafficking.

CLIMATE

Tropical/mountain

WEATHER CHART FOR BOGOTÁ

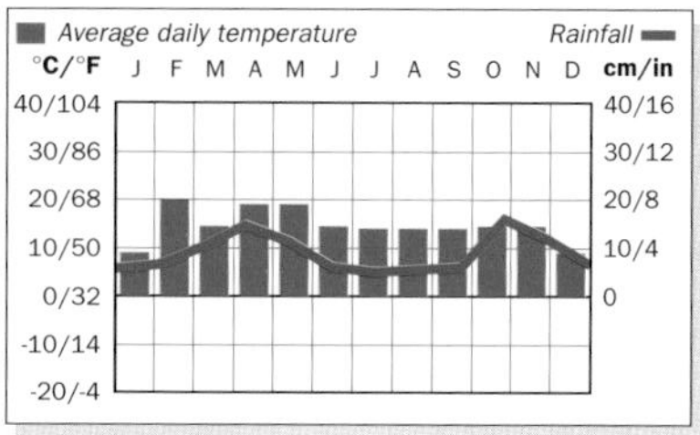
Average daily temperature
Rainfall
°C/°F J F M A M J J A S O N D cm/in
40/104
30/86
20/68
10/50
0/32
-10/14
-20/-4
40/16
30/12
20/8
10/4
0

Most of Colombia is wet, and the hot Pacific coastal areas receive up to 500 cm (200 in) of rain a year. The Caribbean coast is a little drier. The Andes have three climatic regions: the *tierra caliente* (hot lowlands), *tierra templada* (temperate uplands), and *tierra fría* (cold highlands); the last has year-round springlike conditions such as those found in Bogotá. The equatorial east has two wet seasons.

TRANSPORTATION

Drive on right

El Dorado, Bogotá
4.66m passengers

105 ships
65,600 grt

THE TRANSPORTATION NETWORK

26,000 km
(16,156 miles)

Caribbean Trunk Highway

3304 km
(2053 miles)

18,140 km
(11,272 miles)

Roads in the north are in reasonable condition. Those in the south and east tend to be rutted and badly affected by the frequent rains. Continuing instability means that roads are frequently blocked by the guerrillas and the military. Most of the railroad is closed.

Rivers are an important means of transportation; the Magdalena, Orinoco, Atrato, and Amazon river systems are all extensively navigable. Plans exist to connect Colombia to the Pan-American Highway.

TOURISM

Visitors : Population 1:71

616,000 visitors

Up 16% in 2001

MAIN TOURIST ARRIVALS

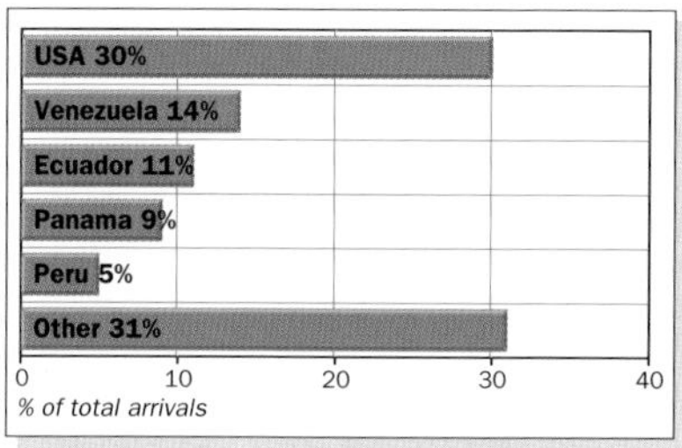
USA 30%
Venezuela 14%
Ecuador 11%
Panama 9%
Peru 5%
Other 31%
0 10 20 30 40
% of total arrivals

Tourism in Colombia is largely limited to the beaches of the Caribbean coast. Cartagena, Barranquilla, and Santa Marta are the main resorts. Cartagena has also been developed as a major Latin American conference center.

The expansion of tourism has been limited by Colombia's political instability and the prevalence of narcotics-related crime. The well-publicized activities of drugs cartels in Medellín and Cali, and instances of kidnappings in Bogotá, are major deterrents for travelers.

Limited infrastructure makes many regions of the country, particularly Amazonia to the east of the Andes, almost inaccessible. The Pacific coast is also barely exploited.

***Simón Bolívar and Cristóbal Colón**, twin peaks with a height of 5775 m (18,947 ft), are the highest in the Colombian Andes.*

PEOPLE

Pop. density low

Spanish, Amerindian languages, English Creole

42/km² (108/mi²)

THE URBAN/RURAL POPULATION SPLIT

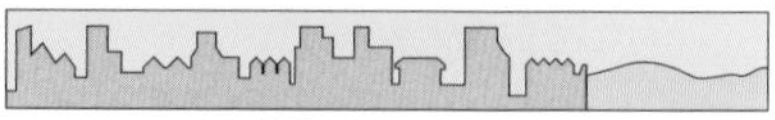
76%
24%

RELIGIOUS PERSUASION

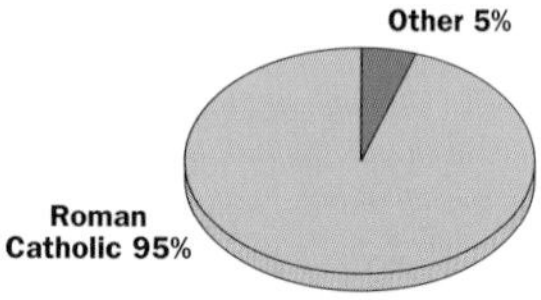
Other 5%
Roman Catholic 95%

ETHNIC MAKEUP

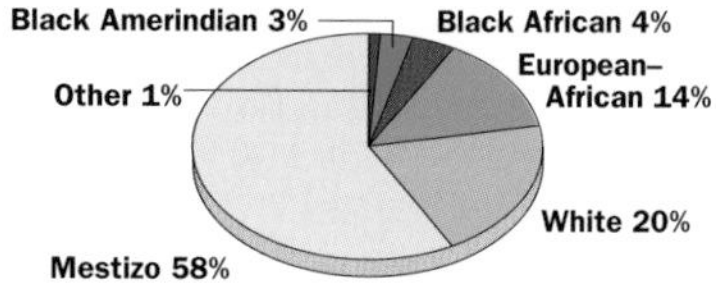
Black Amerindian 3%
Black African 4%
Other 1%
European–African 14%
White 20%
Mestizo 58%

Most Colombians are of mixed blood. An estimated 450,000 indigenous Amerindians are largely concentrated in the southwest and Amazonia. A small black population lives along both coasts, particularly in Chocó, Colombia's poorest region. Blacks are the most unrepresented group.

Some progress has been made in giving Amerindians a greater political voice. Since 1991, two seats in the Senate have been reserved for indigenous representatives, and pressure groups are increasingly active. Harassment by landowners and narcotics traffickers continues in Amazonia, and very few investigations into suspected human rights violations against Amerindians have led to prosecutions.

Women have a higher profile than in much of the rest of Latin America. Many are prominent in the professions, though few reach the top in politics. The traditional Roman Catholic extended family is still the norm.

NGOs estimate that civil conflict has displaced two million Colombians over the last 14 years and saw 1.2 million emigrate in the late 1990s.

POPULATION AGE BREAKDOWN

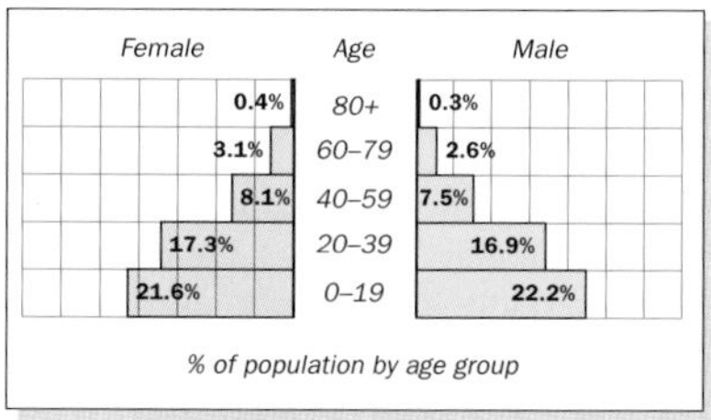
Female
Age
Male
0.4% 80+ 0.3%
3.1% 60–79 2.6%
8.1% 40–59 7.5%
17.3% 20–39 16.9%
21.6% 0–19 22.2%
% of population by age group

POLITICS

Multiparty elections

L. House 2002/2006
U. House 2002/2006

President Alvaro Uribe Velez

Colombia is a presidential democracy, with a bicameral Congress. Presidents may not serve two consecutive terms.

PROFILE

The two-party system which had held sway from the late 1950s appeared to have fractured by the 21st century. The dominance of the PCC and the PL, with few ideological differences, was undermined by electoral breakthroughs by new, smaller parties, culminating in the presidential victory of right-wing independent Alvaro Uribe Velez in 2002.

Pervasive official corruption and the violence associated with drugs cartels, guerrillas, paramilitaries, and the military have seriously weakened confidence in the state and the government, and have deterred foreign investors.

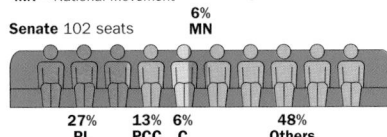

AT THE LAST ELECTION

House of Representatives 166 seats

33% PL
13% PCC
10% C
4% CR
3% AL
37% Others

PL = Liberal Party **PCC** = Colombian Conservative Party **C** = Coalition **CR** = Radical Change **AL** = Liberal Opening **MN** = National Movement

Senate 102 seats

6% MN
27% PL
13% PCC
6% C
48% Others

Two special representatives of the Amerindian communities are appointed to the Senate, and one is elected.

MAIN POLITICAL ISSUES

Elusive peace

Peace efforts pursued by President Andres Pastrana Arango (1998–2002) were abandoned in early 2002 as the country returned to full-scale civil conflict against the left-wing Armed Revolutionary Forces of Colombia (FARC) and the National Liberation Army (ELN). President Uribe, accused by the FARC of having connections to right-wing militias, has pushed the offensive with the aid of US military advisers.

Reforms

Uribe has made the most of his popularity to push IMF-sponsored reforms through Congress. Multilateral funding has been conditional on labor, pension, and tax reforms which, it is hoped, will reactivate the economy and increase investment. Plans to streamline government were also approved.

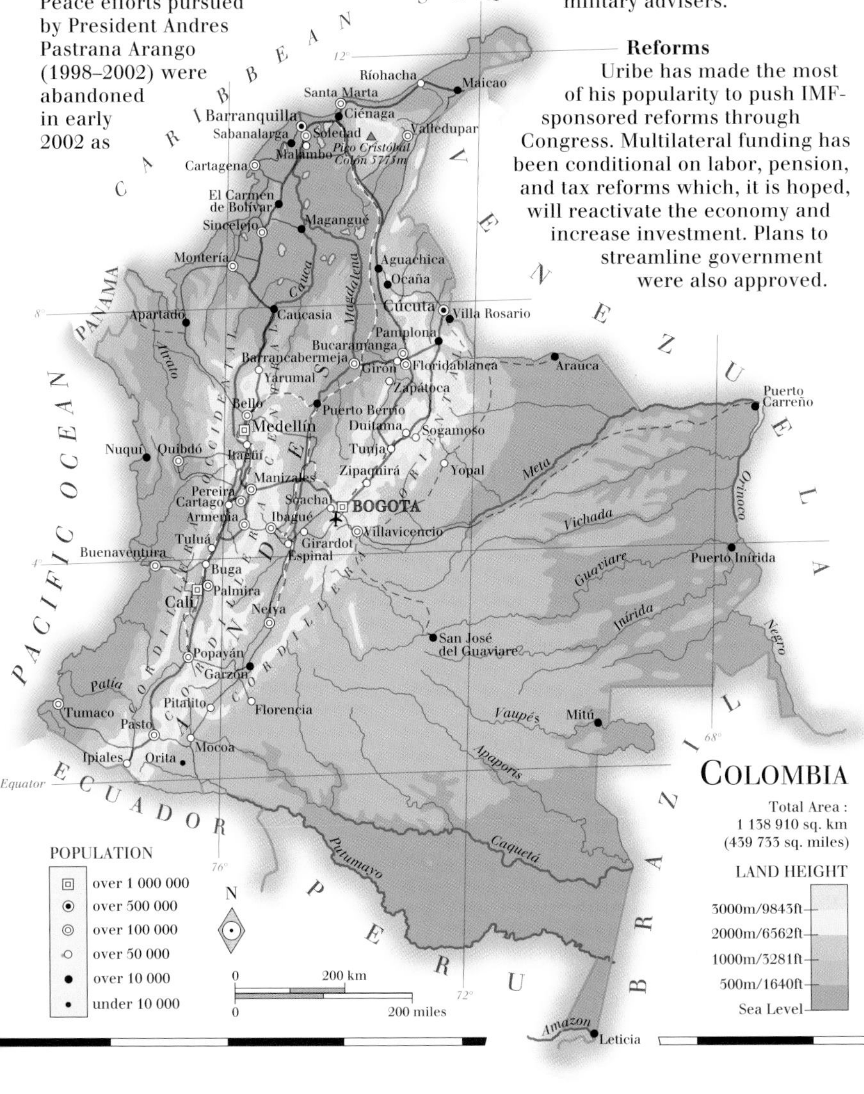
CARIBBEAN SEA
PACIFIC OCEAN
PANAMA
VENEZUELA
ECUADOR
PERU
BRAZIL
Ríohacha
Santa Marta
Maicao
Barranquilla
Ciénaga
Sabanalarga
Soledad
Valledupar
Pico Cristóbal Colón 5775m
Malambo
Cartagena
El Carmen de Bolívar
Sincelejo
Magangué
Montería
Aguachica
Ocaña
Cúcuta
Villa Rosario
Apartadó
Caucasia
Pamplona
Bucaramanga
Barrancabermeja
Girón
Floridablanca
Arauca
Yarumal
Zapátoca
Bello
Medellín
Puerto Berrío
Duitama
Sogamoso
Puerto Carreño
Nuquí
Quibdó
Itagüí
Tunja
Zipaquirá
Yopal
Manizales
Pereira
Cartago
Armenia
Soacha
BOGOTA
Ibagué
Villavicencio
Tuluá
Buenaventura
Girardot
Espinal
Puerto Inírida
Buga
Palmira
Cali
Neiva
San José del Guaviare
Popayán
Garzón
Pitalito
Florencia
Tumaco
Pasto
Mocoa
Mitú
Ipiales
Orita
Leticia
Equator
Cauca
Magdalena
Meta
Vichada
Guaviare
Inírida
Orinoco
Negro
Vaupés
Apaporis
Caquetá
Putumayo
Amazon
Patía
Atrato
COLOMBIA
Total Area : 1 138 910 sq. km (439 733 sq. miles)
LAND HEIGHT
3000m/9843ft
2000m/6562ft
1000m/3281ft
500m/1640ft
Sea Level
POPULATION
over 1 000 000
over 500 000
over 100 000
over 50 000
over 10 000
under 10 000
0 200 km
0 200 miles

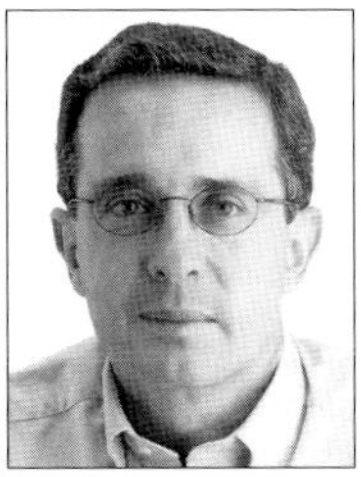

Alvaro Uribe Velez, the right-leaning independent elected president in 2002.

***Andres Pastrana Arango** launched the controversial "Plan Colombia."*

WORLD AFFAIRS

Joined UN in 1945

ACS AP AmCC OAS RG

Good relations with the US are conditional on tough measures to fight the narcotics trade. A $1.3 billion military aid package, approved in 2000, provided training, intelligence, and hardware, ostensibly to assist the "Plan Colombia" antidrugs program. The boundary between this aim and the targeting of guerrilla groups was always blurred. The army's invasion in 2002 of the demilitarized haven, granted to the FARC as part of peace efforts, was reportedly assisted by US military advisers. The US administration fought shy of describing events as a chapter in the US-led "war on terrorism," however, insisting that it was operating within legal limits set down by the Congress. Colombia's neighbors fear a "spillover" of violence and refugees.

AID

Recipient

$380m (receipts)

Up 103% in 2001

US military "antinarcotics aid" forms some 75% of total US aid. The IMF approved a standby loan of $2.1 billion in 2003 to act as security for other loans from international institutions.

CHRONOLOGY

In 1525, Spain began the conquest of Colombia, which became its chief source of gold.

- **1819** Simón Bolívar defeats the Spanish at Boyacá. Republic of Gran Colombia formed with Venezuela, Ecuador, and Panama.
- **1830** Venezuela and Ecuador split away during revolts and civil wars.
- **1849** The centralist Conservative and federalist Liberal parties are established.
- **1861–1886** Liberals hold monopoly on power.
- **1886–1930** Conservative rule.
- **1899–1903** Liberal "War of 1000 Days" revolt fails; 120,000 die.

C

C

CHRONOLOGY *continued*

- **1903** Panama secedes, but is not recognized by Colombia until 1921.
- **1930** Liberal President Olaya Herrera elected by coalition in first peaceful change of power.
- **1946** Conservatives take over.
- **1948** Shooting of Liberal mayor of Bogotá and riot – *El Bogotazo* – spark civil war – *La Violencia* – lasting until 1957; 300,000 killed.
- **1953–1957** Military dictatorship of Rojas Pinilla.
- **1958** Conservatives and Liberals agree to alternate government in a National Front until 1974. Other parties banned.
- **1965** Left-wing guerrilla National Liberation Army and Maoist Popular Liberation Army founded.
- **1966** Pro-Soviet FARC guerrilla group formed.
- **1968** Constitutional reform allows new parties, but two-party parity continues. Guerrilla groups proliferate from now on.
- **1984** Minister of justice assassinated for attempting to enforce antinarcotics campaign.
- **1985** M-19 guerrillas blast their way into ministry of justice; 11 judges and 90 others killed. Patriotic Union (UP) party formed.
- **1986** Liberal Virgilio Barco Vargas wins presidential elections, ending power-sharing. UP wins ten seats in parliament. Right-wing paramilitary start murder campaign against UP politicians. Violence by both left-wing groups and death squads run by narcotics cartels continues.
- **1989** M-19 reaches peace agreement with government, including the granting of a full pardon. Becomes legal party.
- **1990** Presidential candidates of UP and PL murdered during campaign. Liberal César Gaviria elected on antidrugs platform.
- **1991** New constitution legalizes divorce, prohibits extradition of Colombian nationals. Indigenous peoples' democratic rights guaranteed, but territorial claims are not addressed.
- **1992–1993** Medellín drugs cartel leader, Pablo Escobar, captured, escapes, and shot dead by police.
- **1995–1996** President Ernesto Samper cleared of charges of receiving drug funds for elections.
- **1999** Earthquake kills thousands.
- **2001** US-backed spraying of coca plantations and destruction of food crops by herbicides ("Plan Colombia") provokes resentment.
- **2002** Peace talks abandoned. Renewed military offensive. Independent candidate Alvaro Uribe Velez elected president.

DEFENSE

Compulsory military service

$2.86bn

Down 7% in 2001

COLOMBIAN ARMED FORCES

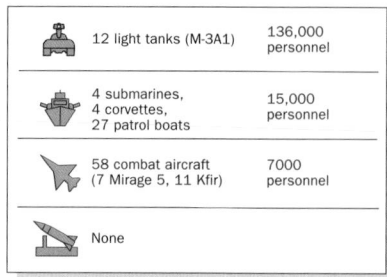

Army	12 light tanks (M-3A1)	136,000 personnel
Navy	4 submarines, 4 corvettes, 27 patrol boats	15,000 personnel
Air force	58 combat aircraft (7 Mirage 5, 11 Kfir)	7000 personnel
Missiles	None	

The military is powerful, but rarely intervenes directly in politics. Human rights groups accuse the armed forces and their paramilitary allies of gross and systematic abuses, involving torture and murder, in their fight against guerrilla groups and the production of narcotics. Although restructured in 1998, the army high command remained suspicious of peace negotiations and supported a tougher stance against the rebels, successfully exploiting tensions to expand substantially under President Pastrana, with numbers set to rise still more. Orders were given in 2002 to retake the FARC "safe haven."

Colombia participates in the joint Latin American Defense Force. The US supplies most arms and training, especially through "Plan Colombia."

ECONOMICS

Inflation 20% p.a. (1990–2001)

$81.6bn

2817 Colombian pesos (2399)

SCORE CARD

- WORLD GNP RANKING 40th
- GNP PER CAPITA $1890
- BALANCE OF PAYMENTS .... –$1.78bn
- INFLATION 8.7%
- UNEMPLOYMENT 20%

EXPORTS

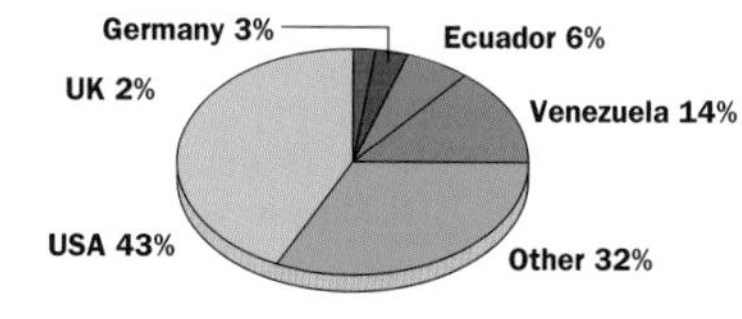
Germany 3%
Ecuador 6%
UK 2%
Venezuela 14%
USA 43%
Other 32%

IMPORTS

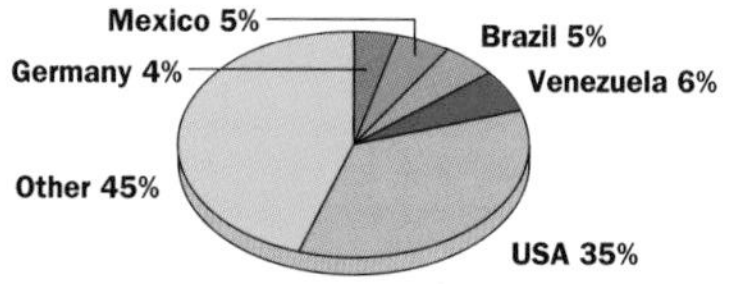
Mexico 5%
Brazil 5%
Germany 4%
Venezuela 6%
Other 45%
USA 35%

STRENGTHS

Substantial oil and coal deposits plus well-developed hydroelectric power make Colombia almost self-sufficient in energy. Diversified export sector – includes coffee and coal. Light manufactures. Worldwide market for cocaine.

WEAKNESSES

Narcotics-related violence, corruption, and political instability discourage foreign investors. Domestic industry uncompetitive owing to protection. High unemployment. Coffee and oil subject to world price fluctuations.

PROFILE

Of all the Latin American economies, Colombia's is probably the closest to the US model. The state has traditionally played a relatively minor role and

ECONOMIC PERFORMANCE INDICATOR

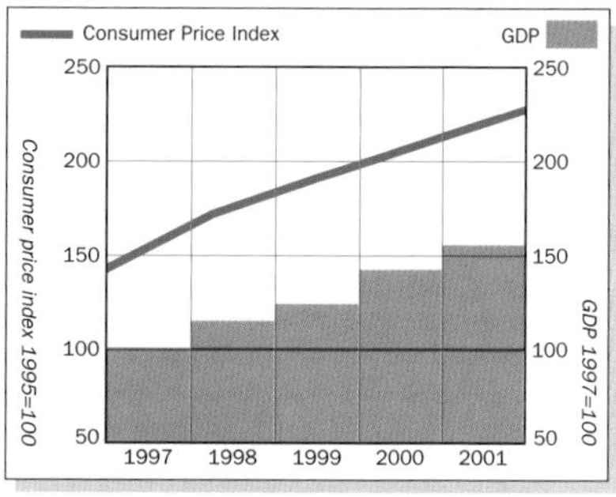
Consumer Price Index
GDP
Consumer price index 1995=100
GDP 1997=100
250
200
150
100
50
1997
1998
1999
2000
2001

Colombia has a successful private export sector. Reforms and austerity measures secured an IMF standby agreement in 2003 and $9 billion in multilateral pledges.

Regional disparities remain marked. Most wealth is found in the Bogotá, Medellín, and Cali regions. Rural areas are largely underdeveloped. The main obstacle to growth is the instability caused by the narcotics business and protracted conflict. Given stability and investment, Colombia's potential for growth is considerable.

COLOMBIA : MAJOR BUSINESSES

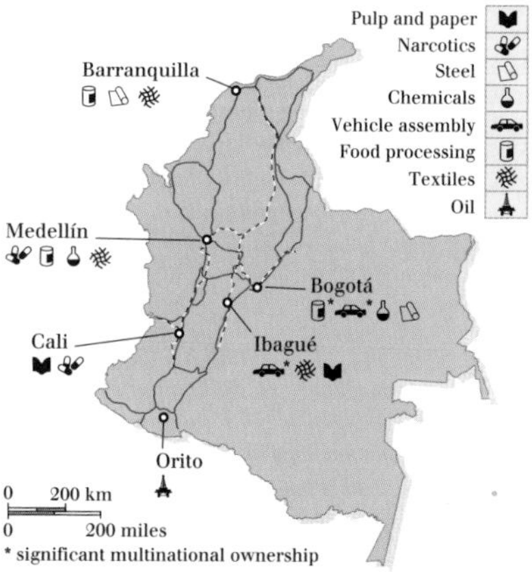
Pulp and paper
Narcotics
Steel
Chemicals
Vehicle assembly
Food processing
Textiles
Oil
Barranquilla
Medellín
Bogotá
Cali
Ibagué
Orito
0 200 km
0 200 miles
* significant multinational ownership

RESOURCES

Electric power 13.2m kW

191,430 tonnes

601,000 b/d (reserves 1.8bn barrels)

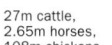

27m cattle, 2.65m horses, 108m chickens

Oil, coal, natural gas, silver, emeralds, gold, platinum

ELECTRICITY GENERATION

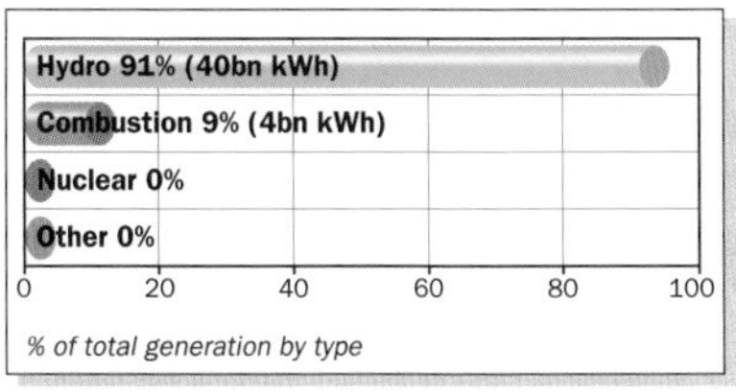

Hydro 91% (40bn kWh)
Combustion 9% (4bn kWh)
Nuclear 0%
Other 0%
0
20
40
60
80
100
% of total generation by type

Colombia has substantial oil reserves but needs increasing investment to maintain production. Coal and gas are important, and it is a major producer of gold, platinum, silver, and emeralds.

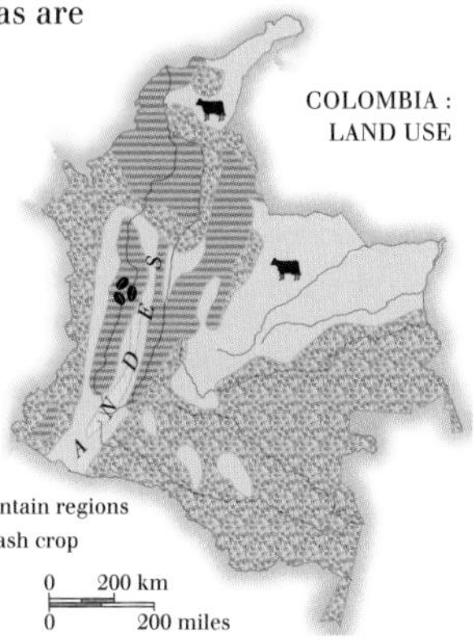

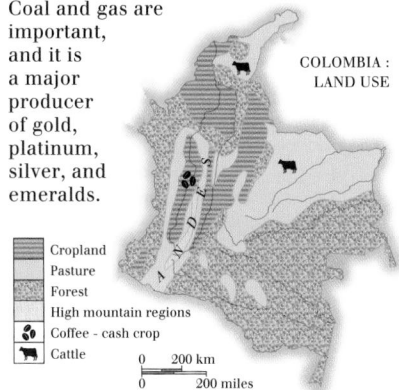

COLOMBIA : LAND USE
ANDES
Cropland
Pasture
Forest
High mountain regions
Coffee - cash crop
Cattle
0 200 km
0 200 miles

ENVIRONMENT

Sustainability rank: 22nd

9% (0.3% partially protected)

1.5 tonnes per capita

ENVIRONMENTAL TREATIES

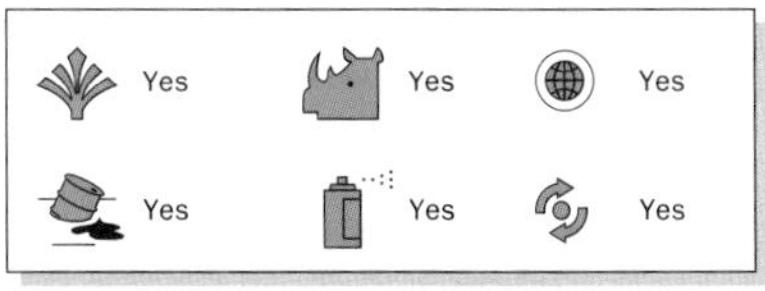

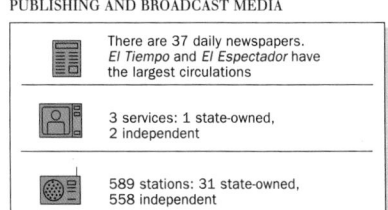

Yes
Yes
Yes
Yes
Yes
Yes

The government calculated in 2002 that 56% of the world's cocaine is produced in former Colombian rainforest.

MEDIA

TV ownership high

Daily newspaper circulation 26 per 1000 people

PUBLISHING AND BROADCAST MEDIA

There are 37 daily newspapers. *El Tiempo* and *El Espectador* have the largest circulations

3 services: 1 state-owned, 2 independent

589 stations: 31 state-owned, 558 independent

The independent press is very small. Journalists have been murdered by paramilitaries and held by guerrillas.

CRIME

No death penalty

57,068 prisoners

Crime is rising

CRIME RATES

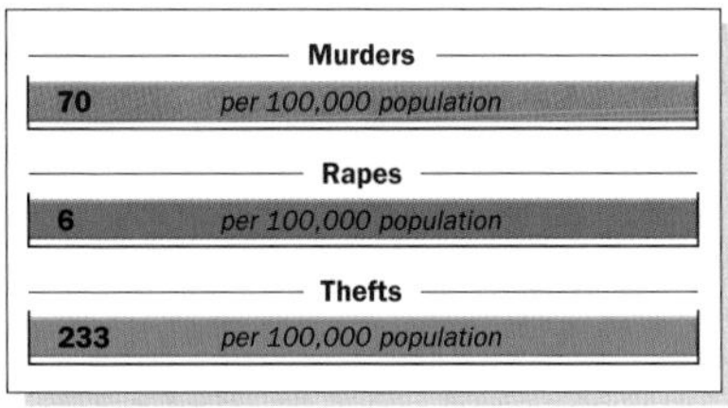

Murders
70 per 100,000 population
Rapes
6 per 100,000 population
Thefts
233 per 100,000 population

Colombia is one of the most violent countries in the world. Armed groups assassinated 20 mayoral candidates and 20 mayors, and kidnapped 200 other candidates in regional and local elections in 2000. The local monitoring group Fundación País Libre reported 2856 cases of kidnapping in 2001, mostly by guerrillas and paramilitaries, the rest blamed on other criminal groups. In 2002 anonymous gunmen murdered the Archbishop of Cali. Homicide is the main cause of death among young men in cities; overall, it rates second in the mortality stakes. Much of the violence is narcotics-related; the army, police, paramilitaries, and guerrillas are all accused of being involved. Police were empowered in 2002 to create "zones of rehabilitation and consolidation" and, in conjunction with the US-backed "Plan Colombia," coca production fell by 30% that year.

A relatively new phenomenon is that of "social cleansing" – the murder of street children and beggars by armed gangs, some in Bogotá funded by businesses.

Frequent armed robberies and kidnappings make wealthy residents extremely security conscious.

EDUCATION

School leaving age: 14

92%

934,085 students

THE EDUCATION SYSTEM

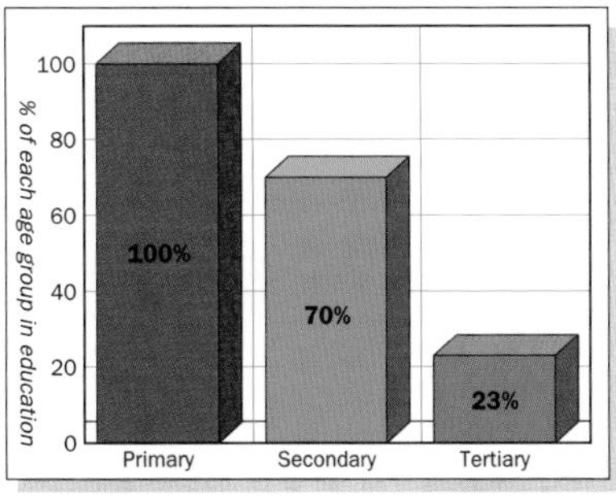

% of each age group in education
100
80
60
40
20
0
100%
70%
23%
Primary
Secondary
Tertiary

Education in Colombia is free and compulsory, and is a mix of French and US models, with a *baccalauréat*-style examination taken at the end of secondary school. A voucher system grants half the cost of private school fees to poor pupils. Where provided, public and university education is generally of a high standard, but the resources available to public education have decreased due to budget cuts. The rich send their children to private schools and universities in the US.

HEALTH

Welfare state health benefits

1 per 917 people

Heart diseases, murders, accidents, cancers

Budget cuts have reduced health spending; private care is growing. Medical care for pregnant mothers is underused and social security payments to the elderly are mostly uncollected. Rural areas have little health provision, since most doctors work in the larger cities. There are fewer than 600 hospitals. A polio vaccination campaign has largely eradicated the virus from Colombia.

SPENDING

GDP/cap. increase

CONSUMPTION AND SPENDING

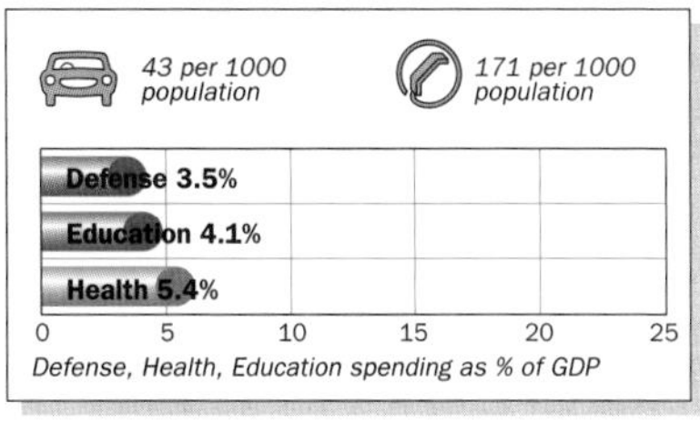

43 per 1000 population
171 per 1000 population
Defense 3.5%
Education 4.1%
Health 5.4%
0
5
10
15
20
25
Defense, Health, Education spending as % of GDP

There is little social mobility; the historically wealthy Spanish families are still dominant in political and business life, but the entry of narcotics-related money has created new layers of rich in cities and among landowners. Drug money also finances the import of consumer goods such as TV sets, computers, and perfume. The wealthy go to the US for medical treatment and educate their children overseas. The rural poor are mostly landless. The inhabitants of shanty towns in Barranquilla, Buenaventura, Cali, and Cartagena form the poorest groups.

WORLD RANKING

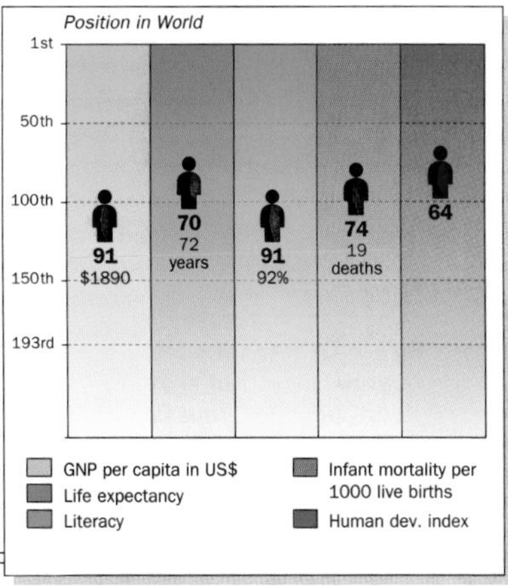

Position in World
1st
50th
100th
150th
193rd
91
$1890
70
72
years
91
92%
74
19
deaths
64
GNP per capita in US$
Life expectancy
Literacy
Infant mortality per 1000 live births
Human dev. index

Comoros

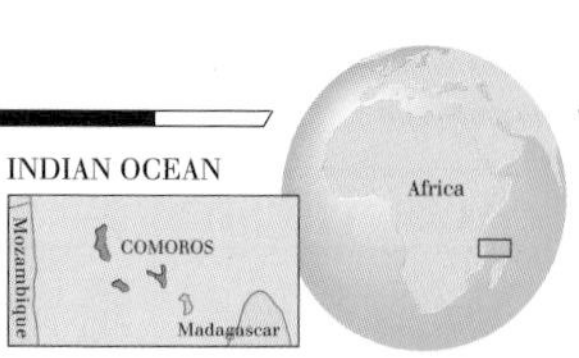
INDIAN OCEAN
Mozambique
COMOROS
Madagascar
Africa

Official Name: Union of the Comoros **Capital:** Moroni
Population: 749,000 **Currency:** Comoros franc **Official Languages:** Arabic, French, and Comoran

1975 | 1975 | July 6 | COM | +3 | +269 | .km

The archipelago republic of the Comoros lies off the east African coast, between Mozambique and Madagascar. It consists of three main islands and a number of islets. Most of the population are subsistence farmers. In 1975, the Comoros islands, except for Mayotte, became independent of France. Since then instability has plagued this poor country, with countless coups and countercoups, and repeated attempts at secession by smaller islands.

Moroni, the capital, on Grande Comore. *The Comoros islands are fertile and heavily forested. Many are ringed by coral reefs.*

CLIMATE

Tropical oceanic

WEATHER CHART FOR MORONI

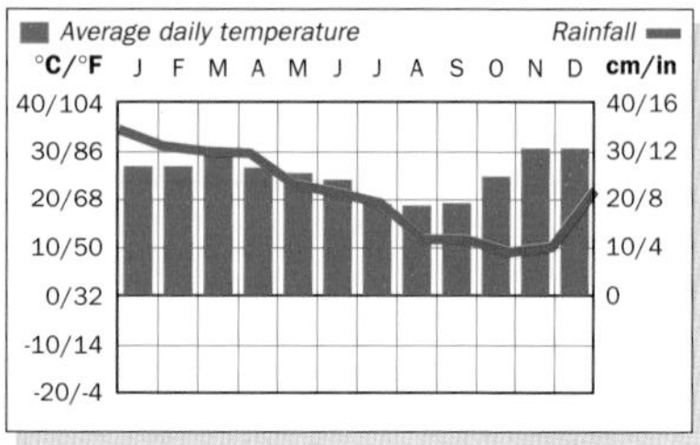
Average daily temperature
Rainfall
°C/°F
J F M A M J J A S O N D
cm/in
40/104
30/86
20/68
10/50
0/32
-10/14
-20/-4
40/16
30/12
20/8
10/4
0

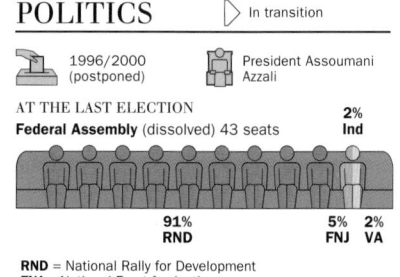

The islands are tropical; it is hot and humid on the coasts and cooler higher up, notably on Mount Kartala.

TRANSPORTATION

Drive on right

Moroni–Hahaya, Grande Comore 105,027 passengers

3 ships 2959 grt

THE TRANSPORTATION NETWORK

673 km (418 miles)	None
None	None

Ferries travel between the islands and also compensate for poor roads on Mohéli. Each island has an airfield.

TOURISM

Visitors : Population 1:31

24,000 visitors

Down 11% in 1999

MAIN TOURIST ARRIVALS

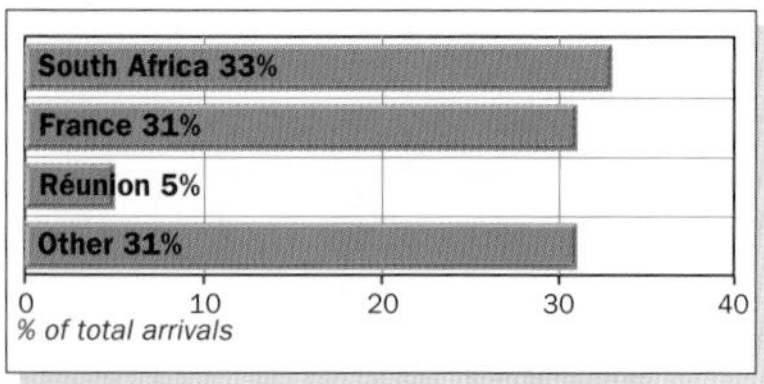
South Africa 33%
France 31%
Réunion 5%
Other 31%
0
10
20
30
40
% of total arrivals

Plans for tourism to take advantage of the islands' beautiful scenery, magnificent beaches, and fascinating history are fundamentally undermined by the country's chronic instability. Some cruise ships have begun to visit.

PEOPLE

Pop. density high

Arabic, Comoran, French

336/km² (870/mi²)

THE URBAN/RURAL POPULATION SPLIT

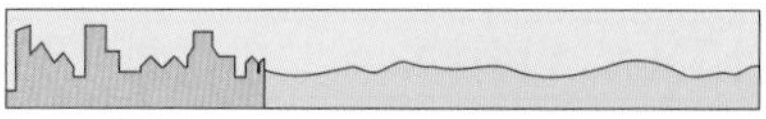
34%
66%

RELIGIOUS PERSUASION

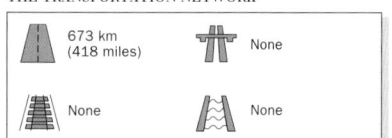

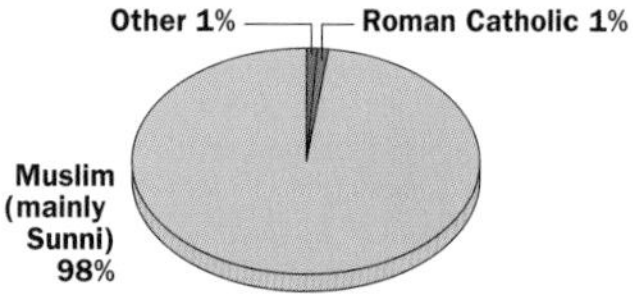
Other 1%
Roman Catholic 1%
Muslim (mainly Sunni) 98%

The Comoros has absorbed Polynesians, Africans, Indonesians, Persians, and Arabs over time, as well as immigrants from Portugal, the Netherlands, France, and India. Each island is named in French and Comoran – a mix of Kiswahili and Arabic. Some communities retain their individual character: Mohéli is still primarily African. Ethnic tension is rare; a more potent divisive factor, especially on Anjouan, is regionalism.

POLITICS

In transition

1996/2000 (postponed)

President Assoumani Azzali

AT THE LAST ELECTION

Federal Assembly (dissolved) 43 seats

2% Ind
91% RND
5% FNJ
2% VA

RND = National Rally for Development
FNJ = National Front for Justice
Ind = Independent **VA**= Votes annulled

The Senate was abolished under the 1996 Constitution

Comoran politics is characterized by chaos. Coups and countercoups have plagued the islands since independence. The key issue is the balance of power between the islands and the overarching government based on Grande Comore. Unrest followed declarations of independence on Anjouan and Mohéli in 1997 and renewed violence in 1999 prompted Col. Assoumani Azzali to assume power. He has since been the focus of politics, in 2002 forging a new loose "Union of the Comoros," of which he was elected president unopposed. All island governments contest Azzali's authoritarian use of his new constitutional powers.

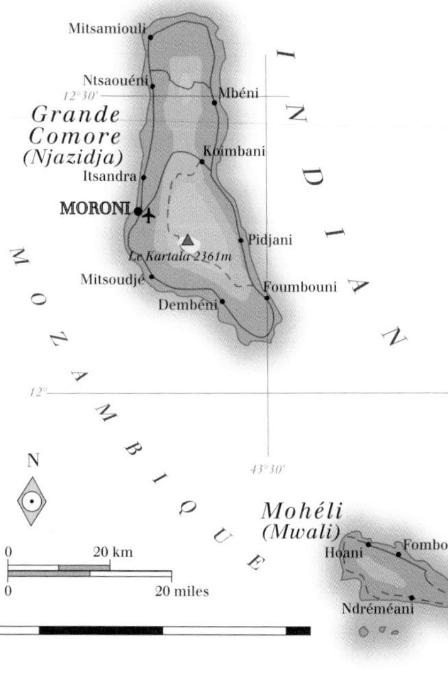
Mitsamiouli
Ntsaouéni
Mbéni
Grande Comore (Njazidja)
Koimbani
Itsandra
MORONI
Pidjani
Le Kartala 2361m
Mitsoudjé
Foumbouni
Dembéni
INDIAN OCEAN
MOZAMBIQUE CHANNEL
N
0 20 km
0 20 miles
Mohéli (Mwali)
Hoani
Fomboni
Itsamia
Ndréméani

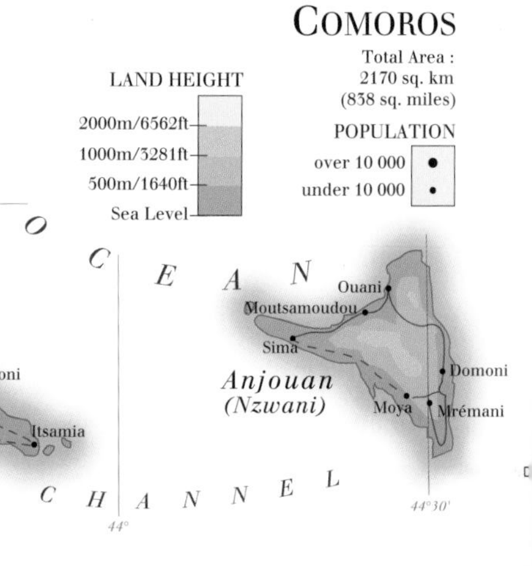
COMOROS
Total Area : 2170 sq. km (838 sq. miles)
LAND HEIGHT
2000m/6562ft
1000m/3281ft
500m/1640ft
Sea Level
POPULATION
over 10 000
under 10 000
Ouani
Moutsamoudou
Sima
Anjouan (Nzwani)
Domoni
Moya
Mrémani

C

WORLD AFFAIRS

Joined UN in 1975

AL | OIC | AU | COI | FZ

France remains the main aid donor, although economic ties with South Africa are strong. The turbulent situation on the war-torn islands forced a visiting OAU assessment team to flee Anjouan in 1999. An army of European mercenaries attempted to take over Mohéli in December 2001. The Comoros still claims sovereignty over Mayotte.

AID

Recipient

$28m (receipts)

Up 47% in 2001

Foreign aid, mainly from France, the World Bank, the EU, and the UN, accounts for over 40% of GDP. Because of its Islamic links, the Comoros also gets aid from Arab states and OPEC. In 1998, major donors attacked the government for spending more than 70% on "political superstructure."

DEFENSE

No compulsory military service

$3m (estimate)

No significant change

France and South Africa finance the small presidential guard, the principal security force. Mauritian aid was also sought after clashes on Anjouan.

ECONOMICS

Inflation 3.6% p.a. (1990–2001)

$219m

454.3 Comoros francs (495.4)

SCORE CARD

❑ WORLD GNP RANKING	182nd
❑ GNP PER CAPITA	$380
❑ BALANCE OF PAYMENTS	–$1m
❑ INFLATION	3.5%
❑ UNEMPLOYMENT	20%

STRENGTHS

Vanilla, ylang-ylang, and cloves main cash crops.

WEAKNESSES

Subsistence-level farming. Most food requirements imported. Lack of basic infrastructure, notably electricity and transportation. Poor education provision. Alleged financial mismanagement. Political instability – hinders growth of tourism. Dependence on aid.

EXPORTS

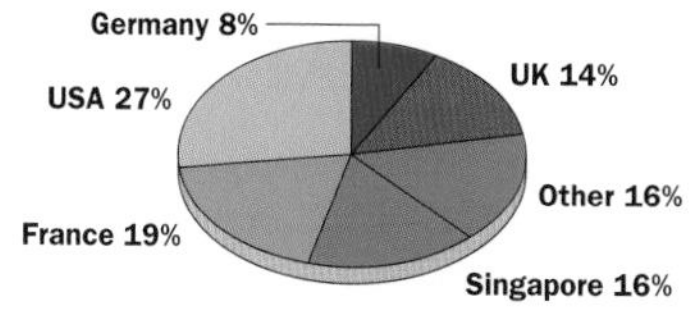
Germany 8%
UK 14%
USA 27%
Other 16%
France 19%
Singapore 16%

IMPORTS

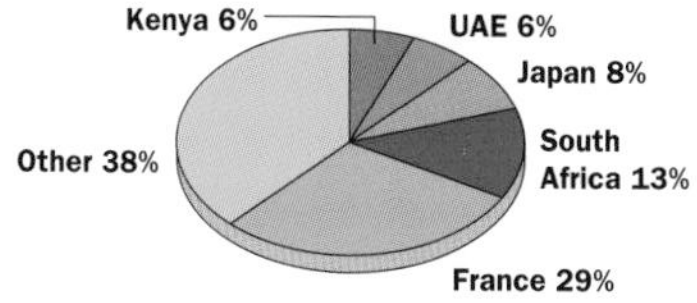
Kenya 6%
UAE 6%
Japan 8%
South Africa 13%
Other 38%
France 29%

RESOURCES

Electric power 6000 kW

13,200 tonnes

Not an oil producer

115,000 goats, 52,000 cattle, 490,000 chickens

None

There are few strategic resources. Most fuel for energy is imported, though there is potential for geothermal generation and HEP. Fishing remains a neglected source of future growth.

ENVIRONMENT

Not available

None

0.1 tonnes per capita

The environment is not a major priority in the Comoros; natural disasters, such as the volcanic eruption in 1977 which left 20,000 people homeless, are of more immediate concern. The government is promoting tourism and recognizes the long-term commercial value of imposing environmental controls on new developments.

MEDIA

TV ownership low

There are no daily newspapers

PUBLISHING AND BROADCAST MEDIA

There are 2 weekly newspapers, the state-owned *Al Watwan* and the independent *La Gazette des Comores*

1 state-owned service

1 state-controlled service, some independent services

China helped to fund the islands' first national TV station. Radio is strictly controlled, and there is no single national daily newspaper.

CRIME

Death penalty in use

200 prisoners

Crime is rising

A climate of lawlessness has been created by the continuing power struggles between rival militias – particularly on the island of Anjouan since 1997.

EDUCATION

School leaving age: 14

56%

714 students

There is a very limited education system beyond secondary level. Schools are equipped to teach only basic literacy, hygiene, and agricultural techniques. The ratio of pupils to teachers is high.

CHRONOLOGY

The Comoros was ruled by matrilineally inherited sultanates until shortly before becoming a French protectorate in 1886.

- ❑ **1961** Internal self-government.
- ❑ **1975** Independence.
- ❑ **1978** Mercenaries restore Ahmed Abdallah to power.
- ❑ **1989** Abdallah assassinated.
- ❑ **1992** Chaotic first multiparty polls.
- ❑ **1996** Mohammed Taki Abdoulkarim elected president.
- ❑ **1997** Anjouan separatists beat off government troops.
- ❑ **1999** Col. Azzali seizes power. Anjouan militias clash.
- ❑ **2000** Fomboni declaration signed with Anjouan.
- ❑ **2001** Successive coups on Anjouan.
- ❑ **2002** New constitution. Azzali returned to office.

HEALTH

No welfare state health benefits

1 per 14,286 people

Malaria, infectious intestinal and bacterial diseases

Although there are a good number of regional health centers, poor facilities deter potential patients.

SPENDING

GDP/cap. decrease

CONSUMPTION AND SPENDING

13 per 1000 population

12 per 1000 population

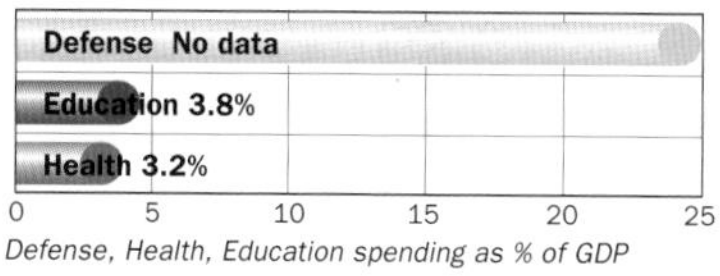
Defense No data
Education 3.8%
Health 3.2%
0
5
10
15
20
25

Defense, Health, Education spending as % of GDP

A political and business elite controls most of the wealth. Bridegrooms win social status according to the size of their wedding. Government workers often suffer from wage arrears.

WORLD RANKING

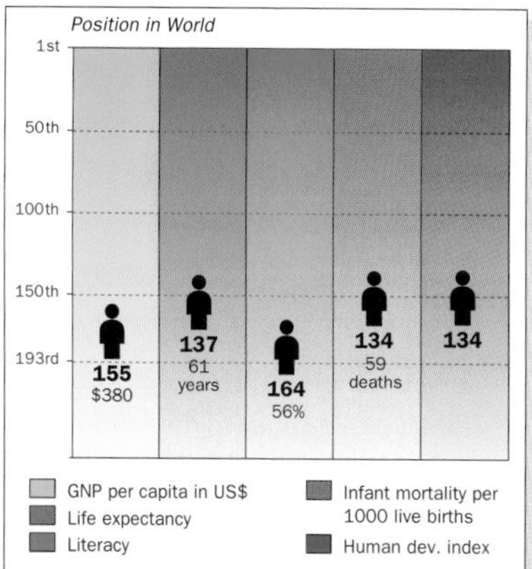
Position in World
1st
50th
100th
150th
193rd
155
$380
137
61 years
164
56%
134
59 deaths
134
GNP per capita in US$
Life expectancy
Literacy
Infant mortality per 1000 live births
Human dev. index

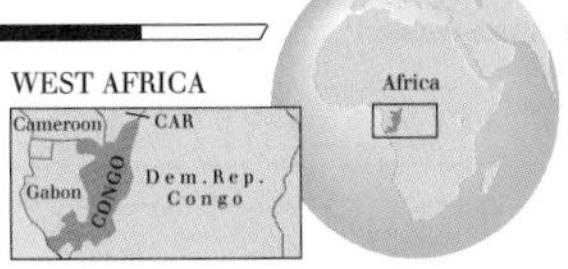
WEST AFRICA
Cameroon
CAR
Gabon
CONGO
Dem. Rep. Congo
Africa

CONGO

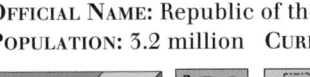

OFFICIAL NAME: Republic of the Congo **CAPITAL:** Brazzaville
POPULATION: 3.2 million **CURRENCY:** CFA franc **OFFICIAL LANGUAGE:** French

C

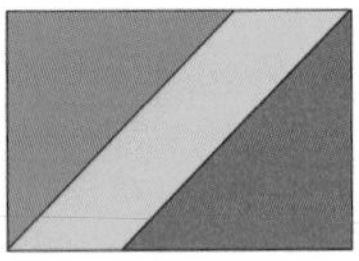

1960 | 1960 | Aug 15 | RCB | +1 | +242 | .cg

STRADDLING THE EQUATOR in west central Africa, Congo achieved independence from France in 1960, soon falling under a Marxist-Leninist form of government which discouraged much foreign investment. Multiparty democracy was achieved in 1991, but was soon overshadowed by years of violence.

CLIMATE

Tropical equatorial

WEATHER CHART FOR BRAZZAVILLE

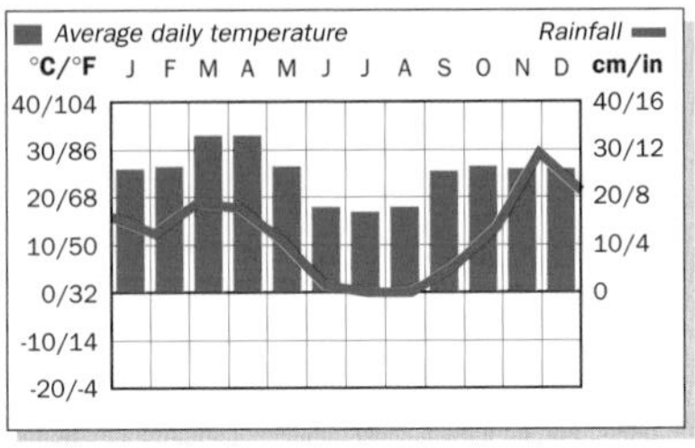
Average daily temperature
Rainfall
°C/°F J F M A M J J A S O N D cm/in
40/104 30/86 20/68 10/50 0/32 -10/14 -20/4
40/16 30/12 20/8 10/4 0

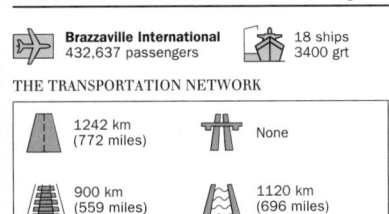

In most years there are two wet seasons and two dry seasons in Congo. The rainfall is heaviest in the coastal regions.

TRANSPORTATION

Drive on right

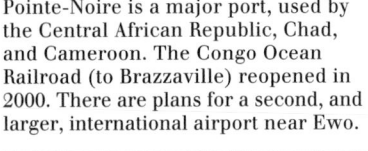

Brazzaville International 432,637 passengers

18 ships 3400 grt

THE TRANSPORTATION NETWORK

1242 km (772 miles)	None
900 km (559 miles)	1120 km (696 miles)

Pointe-Noire is a major port, used by the Central African Republic, Chad, and Cameroon. The Congo Ocean Railroad (to Brazzaville) reopened in 2000. There are plans for a second, and larger, international airport near Ewo.

TOURISM

Visitors : Population 1:123

26,000 visitors

Up 420% in 2000

MAIN TOURIST ARRIVALS

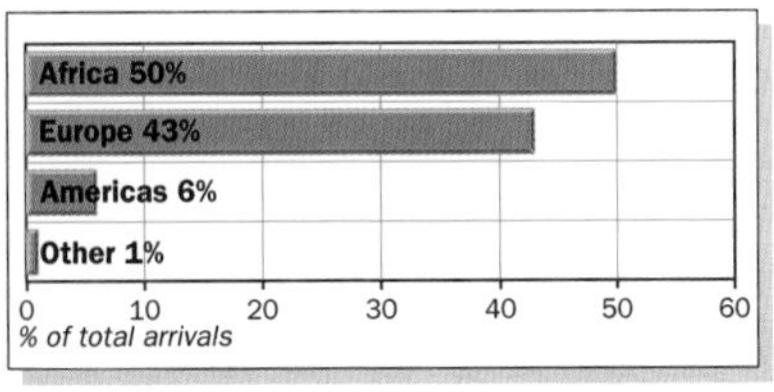
Africa 50%
Europe 43%
Americas 6%
Other 1%
0 10 20 30 40 50 60
% of total arrivals

The Marxist-Leninist regime did not seek to develop tourism, and visitors, mostly on safaris and business-related trips, are still rare, though increasing.

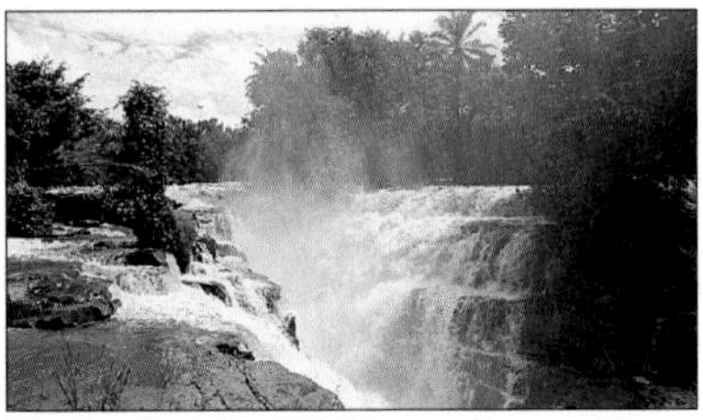

The Loufoulakari Falls, near Brazzaville. The Congo River is a key transportation artery for the region.

PEOPLE

Pop. density low

Kongo, Teke, Lingala, French

9/km² (24/mi²)

THE URBAN/RURAL POPULATION SPLIT

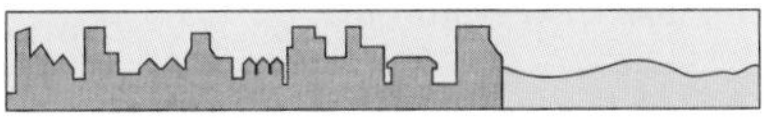
66%
34%

ETHNIC MAKEUP

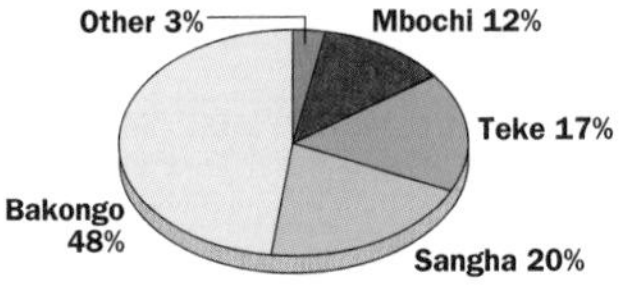
Other 3%
Mbochi 12%
Teke 17%
Sangha 20%
Bakongo 48%

Congo is one of the most tribally conscious countries in Africa. It is also one of the most urbanized in the region, most people living in Brazzaville, Pointe-Noire, and the area in between; to the north the country is dense jungle. Women have achieved considerable freedom during the period since the 1950s.

POLITICS

Multiparty elections

L. House 2002/2007
U. House 2002/2008

President Denis Sassou-Nguesso

AT THE LAST ELECTION

National Assembly 137 seats

4% UDR
61% PCT
6% Vacant
3% UPADS
26% Others

PCT = Congolese Labor Party and allies
UDR = Union for Democracy and the Republic
UPADS = Pan-African Union for Social Democracy

Senate 66 seats

9% Vacant
85% PCT
6% Others

Former Marxist dictator Denis Sassou-Nguesso seized power in 1997, amid intense fighting which left thousands dead. Relative peace was secured in 1999. A new constitution giving greater power to the presidency was approved in 2002, and Sassou-Nguesso was easily elected. Fighting broke out again later that year, but legislative elections were eventually held and were won by Sassou-Nguesso's supporters.

CONGO

Total Area : 342 000 sq. km (132 046 sq. miles)

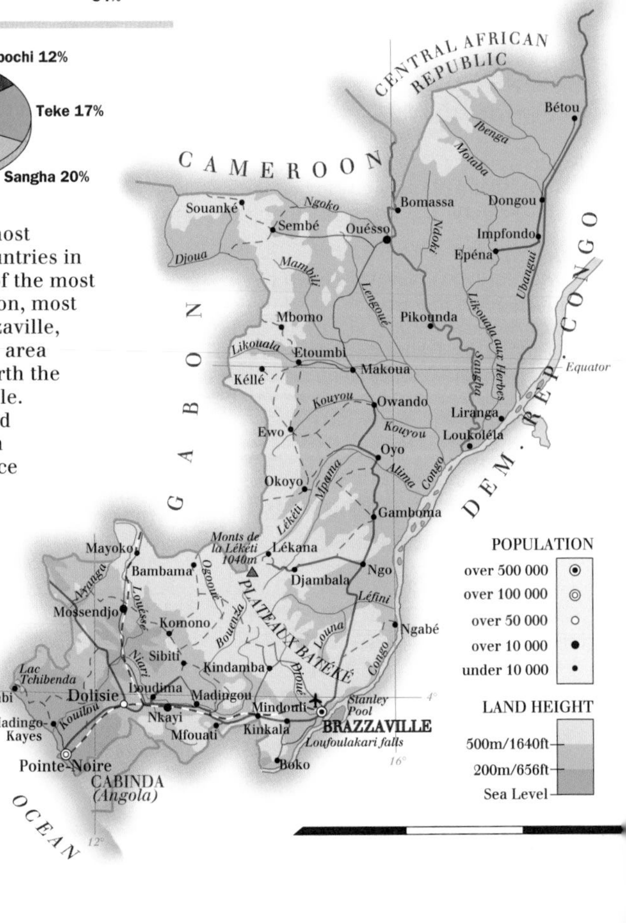
CENTRAL AFRICAN REPUBLIC
CAMEROON
GABON
DEM. REP. CONGO
ATLANTIC OCEAN
CABINDA (Angola)
Bétou
Souanké
Sembé
Ouésso
Bomassa
Dongou
Impfondo
Epéna
Mbomo
Pikounda
Etoumbi
Makoua
Kéllé
Owando
Liranga
Loukoléla
Ewo
Oyo
Okoyo
Gamboma
Mayoko
Lékana
Bambama
Djambala
Ngo
Mossendjo
Komono
Ngabé
Sibiti
Kindamba
Nzambi
Dolisie
Loudima
Madingou
Mindouli
BRAZZAVILLE
Madingo-Kayes
Nkayi
Mfouati
Kinkala
Stanley Pool
Loufoulakari falls
Pointe-Noire
Boko
Monts de la Lékéti 1040m
PLATEAUX BATÉKÉ
Lac Tchibenda
Equator
POPULATION
over 500 000
over 100 000
over 50 000
over 10 000
under 10 000
LAND HEIGHT
500m/1640ft
200m/656ft
Sea Level
N
0 100 km
0 100 miles

WORLD AFFAIRS

Joined UN in 1960

BDEAC | CEMAC | FZ | NAM | ACP

Balancing relations with France and the US is a priority, since both seek to extend their stakes in the oil industry.

Congo has been susceptible in recent years to political instability and wars in neighboring countries. It has hosted refugees from Angola, the DRC, the CAR, Chad, and Rwanda. Angola has been a key regional ally for Sassou-Nguesso.

AID

Recipient

$75m (receipts)

Up 127% in 2001

Until 1990, the USSR, Cuba, and China were major donors. Most aid now comes from France and the World Bank. The IMF has started moves to clear Congo's high levels of debt.

DEFENSE

No compulsory military service

$80m

Up 10% in 2001

The militias of the various political forces were being integrated into the 8000-strong army, until fighting broke out again between them in mid-1997. The air force numbers 1200, and is equipped with 12 MiG-21s.

ECONOMICS

Inflation 8.8% p.a. (1990–2001)

$1.99bn

571.2 CFA francs (664.2)

SCORE CARD

❑ World GNP Ranking	137th
❑ GNP per Capita	$640
❑ Balance of Payments	–$252m
❑ Inflation	0.1%
❑ Unemployment	Widespread underemployment

Strengths

Increase in importance of oil, now providing 95% of export revenues. Significant timber supplies. Skilled and well-trained workforce helps sustain substantial industrial base in the capital and Pointe-Noire.

Weaknesses

Massive debt burden. Top-heavy bureaucracy. Overdependence on oil. Political instability. Large refugee population.

EXPORTS

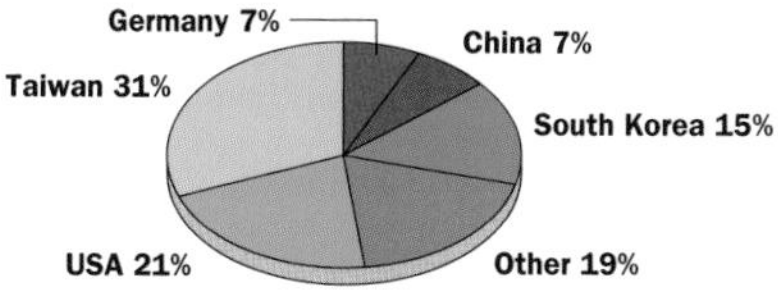
Germany 7%
China 7%
Taiwan 31%
South Korea 15%
USA 21%
Other 19%

IMPORTS

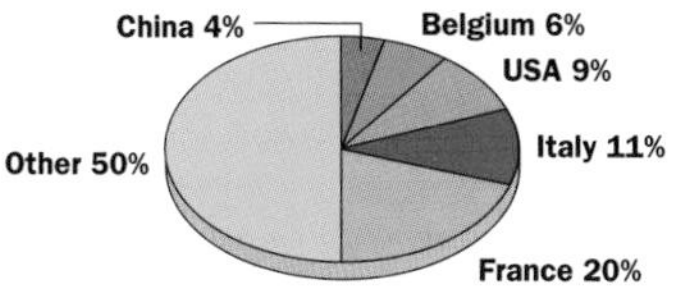
China 4%
Belgium 6%
USA 9%
Other 50%
Italy 11%
France 20%

RESOURCES

Electric power 121,000 kW

50,180 tonnes

258,000 b/d (reserves 1.5bn barrels)

294,150 goats, 96,000 sheep, 1.9m chickens

Oil, natural gas, zinc, gold, copper, potash, diamonds

Oil is by far the most important resource; the majority of oil is exported. Known natural gas reserves are not exploited due to a lack of dedicated facilities. Congo is a net importer of electricity, mostly from the neighboring DRC, despite an estimated HEP potential of 3000 MW. New dams are being considered; in the southwest, construction of one to power a large magnesium-mining project is under way.

ENVIRONMENT

Sustainability rank: 40th

5% (4% partially protected)

0.7 tonnes per capita

The 1999 Yaoundé Declaration should help control exploitation of tropical timber. Congo has been used in the past as a dumping ground for dangerous toxic waste from the West.

MEDIA

TV ownership low

Daily newspaper circulation 8 per 1000 people

PUBLISHING AND BROADCAST MEDIA

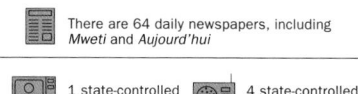

There are 64 daily newspapers, including *Mweti* and *Aujourd'hui*

1 state-controlled service

4 state-controlled services

With only moderate media control, the press often takes an antigovernment stance. During World War II, Radio Brazzaville, still the official state radio, was vital to de Gaulle's French forces.

CRIME

Death penalty not used in practice

918 prisoners

Crime is rising

Armed robbery and smuggling are widespread. Years of conflict and instability in neighboring countries mean that guns are easily available.

EDUCATION

School leaving age: 15

82%

13,403 students

Congo has one of the highest rates of literacy in Africa. There is one university, Marien Ngouabi, in Brazzaville.

CHRONOLOGY

The kingdoms of Teke and Loango were incorporated as the Middle Congo (part of French Equatorial Africa) between 1880 and 1883.

- ❑ **1960** Independence.
- ❑ **1964** Marxist-Leninist National Revolution Movement (MNR) sole legal party.
- ❑ **1977** Yhompi-Opango head of state after President Ngoumbi's murder.
- ❑ **1979** Col. Denis Sassou-Nguesso president.
- ❑ **1991** Multiparty democracy.
- ❑ **1992** Pascal Lissouba president.
- ❑ **1993** Elections: Lissouba's UPADS party gains majority.
- ❑ **1997** Sassou-Nguesso ousts Lissouba.
- ❑ **1999** Cease-fire signed.
- ❑ **2001** IMF starts to clear debt.
- ❑ **2002** New constitution approved. Sassou-Nguesso wins elections.

C

HEALTH

Welfare state health benefits

1 per 4000 people

Diarrheal, parasitic, and respiratory diseases, malaria

The health service, set up by French military doctors at the start of the 20th century, has been devastated by civil war.

SPENDING

GDP/cap. increase

CONSUMPTION AND SPENDING

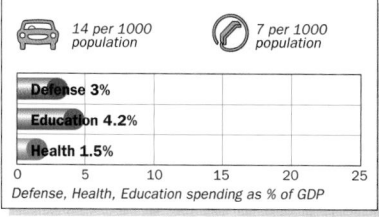

14 per 1000 population

7 per 1000 population

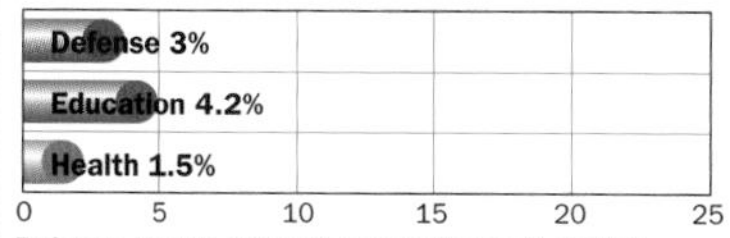
Defense 3%
Education 4.2%
Health 1.5%
0
5
10
15
20
25

Defense, Health, Education spending as % of GDP

Wealth generated from oil extraction has sustained an active and confident middle class. French-label products are considered to be status symbols.

WORLD RANKING

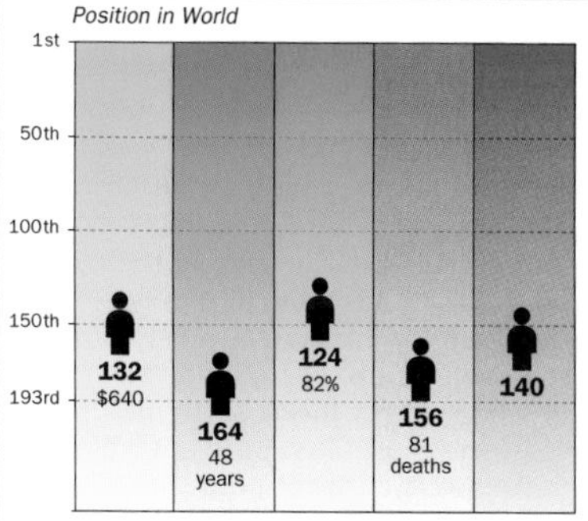
Position in World
1st
50th
100th
150th
193rd
132
$640
164
48
years
124
82%
156
81
deaths
140
GNP per capita in US$
Life expectancy
Literacy
Infant mortality per 1000 live births
Human dev. index

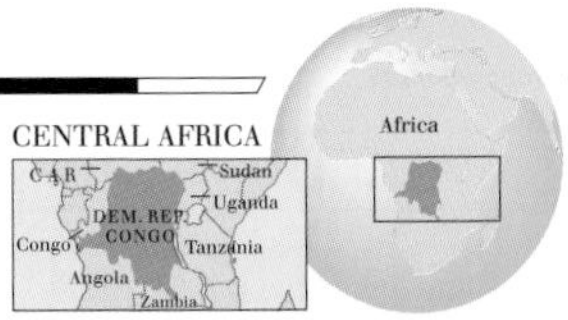
CENTRAL AFRICA
Africa
C.A.R.
Sudan
Uganda
DEM. REP. CONGO
Congo
Tanzania
Angola
Zambia

Congo (Democratic Republic)

Official Name: Democratic Republic of the Congo **Capital:** Kinshasa
Population: 54.3 million **Currency:** Congolese franc **Official Language:** French

C

1960 | 1960 | June 6 | CGO | +1 | +243 | .zr

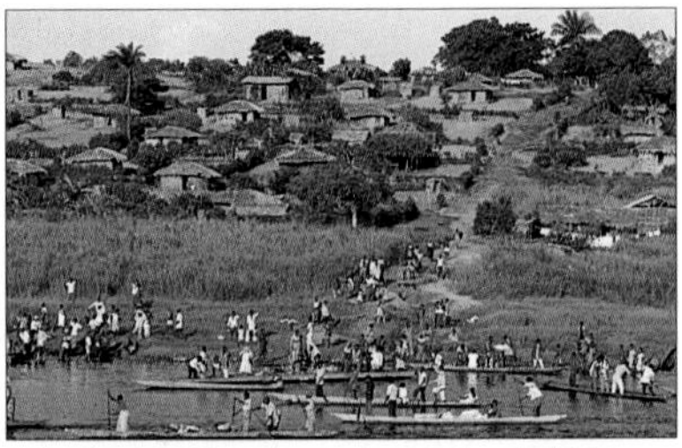

The Congo River is navigable for 1357 km (848 miles), and provides one of the most convenient ways of traveling in the country.

Lying in East Central Africa, the Democratic Republic of the Congo (DRC), known as Zaire from 1971 to 1997, is Africa's third-largest country. The rainforested basin of the Congo River occupies 60% of the land area. The notoriously corrupt Marshal Mobutu ruled from 1965 until his overthrow in 1997 by Laurent-Désiré Kabila. A rebellion launched in 1998 plunged the country into renewed chaos, and spiraled into regional conflict. Peace tentatively arrived two years after Joseph Kabila's succession in January 2001.

CLIMATE

Tropical equatorial/ wet and dry

WEATHER CHART FOR KINSHASA

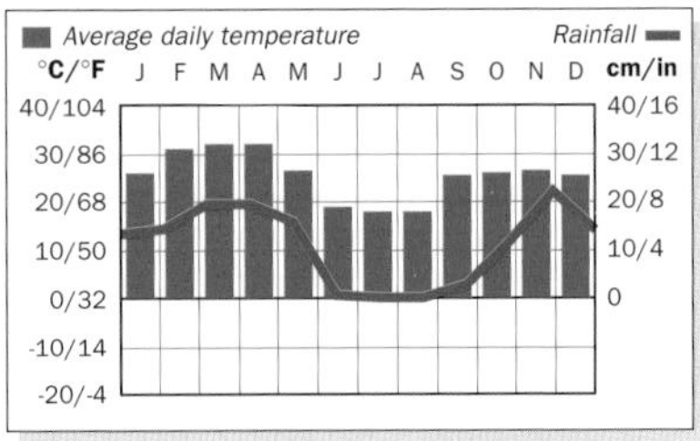
Average daily temperature
Rainfall
°C/°F
J F M A M J J A S O N D
cm/in
40/104
30/86
20/68
10/50
0/32
-10/14
-20/-4
40/16
30/12
20/8
10/4
0

The climate is tropical and humid. Temperatures average 25°C (77°F) and vary little through the year. Annual rainfall is around 150–200 cm (60–80 in); mountainous areas are wetter. The equator passes through the north of the country, causing marked regional variations. To its south, well-differentiated wet and dry seasons are October–May and June–September respectively. North of the equator, a short dry season lasts from December to February; the rest of the year is wet.

TRANSPORTATION

Drive on right

N'Djili, Kinshasa 358,833 passengers

20 ships 12,900 grt

THE TRANSPORTATION NETWORK

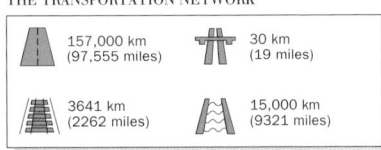

157,000 km (97,555 miles)

30 km (19 miles)

3641 km (2262 miles)

15,000 km (9321 miles)

The Congo River and its many tributaries provide the main means of communication. The size of the country and the fact that most of it is covered by dense rainforest have severely limited the development of road and rail networks. Many forest settlements are inaccessible except by air. Road maintenance, always poor, has virtually ceased outside the main towns since 1990, isolating even more settlements situated away from the main rivers.

TOURISM

Visitors : Population 1:527

103,000 visitors

Up 94% in 2000

MAIN TOURIST ARRIVALS

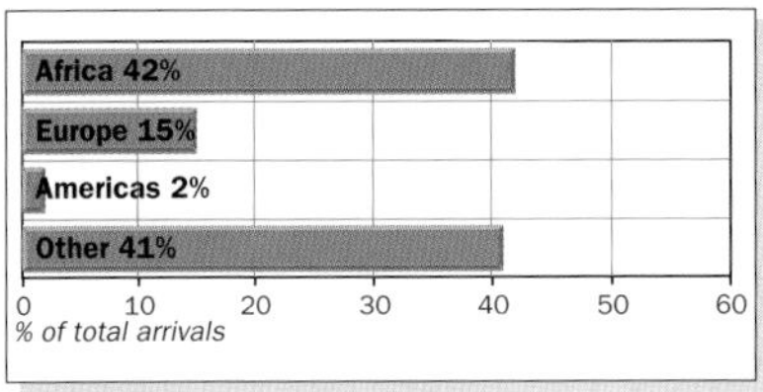
Africa 42%
Europe 15%
Americas 2%
Other 41%
0
10
20
30
40
50
60
% of total arrivals

Political turmoil and widespread anarchy since early 1997 ensure that the country remains off the itinerary for most travelers.

Potential tourist attractions consist mainly of scenery – mountains and lakes – and wildlife, but there are few facilities for tourists even in the capital. The Congo, 16 km (10 miles) wide in places, is Africa's second-longest river after the Nile. Visitors were formerly also attracted by the vibrant music of Kinshasa's many bands.

The once-large number of visitors on business has also collapsed as a consequence of the chronic instability of the 1990s.

PEOPLE

Pop. density low

Kiswahili, Tshiluba, Kikongo, Lingala, French

24/km² (62/mi²)

THE URBAN/RURAL POPULATION SPLIT

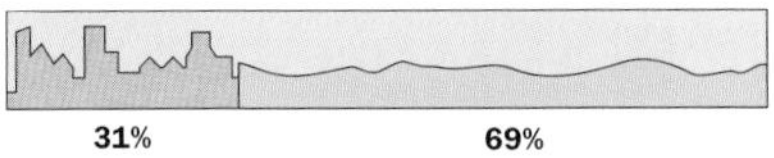
31%
69%

RELIGIOUS PERSUASION

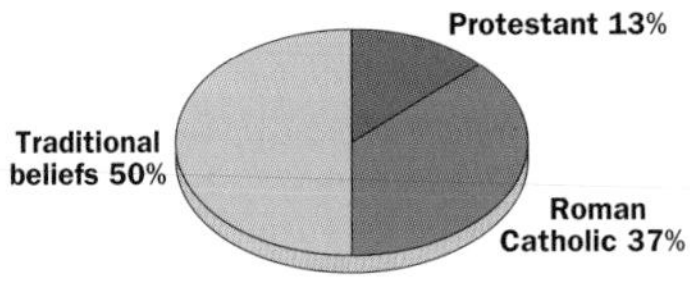
Protestant 13%
Traditional beliefs 50%
Roman Catholic 37%

ETHNIC MAKEUP

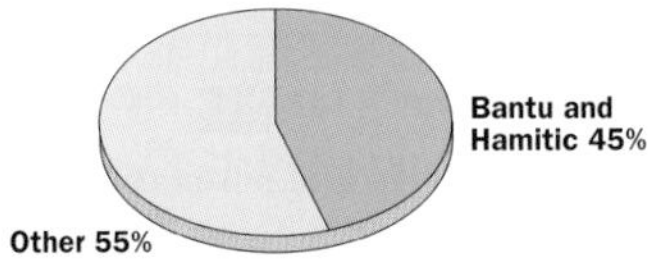
Bantu and Hamitic 45%
Other 55%

The southern Shaba mining area and major urban centers are densely populated, while the rainforests are relatively empty. There is great ethnic diversity, with more than 12 main groups and around 190 smaller ones. The majority are of Bantu origin, but there are also large Hamitic and Nilotic populations, mainly in the north and northeast. The original inhabitants, the forest pygmies, today form a tiny and marginalized group. They claim to have been hunted and eaten by all sides in the war. Cannibalism has been blamed on superstitious beliefs.

War, and consequent hunger, poverty, and disease have killed thousands of people. Much violence has an ethnic basis. In 1994 a Hutu refugee influx from Rwanda provoked serious tension among Tutsis in eastern areas; revenge killings became commonplace. Regarded by Mobutu as foreigners, Tutsis were the backbone of the 1996–1997 insurgency that overthrew him, and then turned against Laurent Kabila. Severe violence between Hema and Lendu tribes broke out in the northeast after the withdrawal of Ugandan and Rwandan troops in 2003.

POPULATION AGE BREAKDOWN

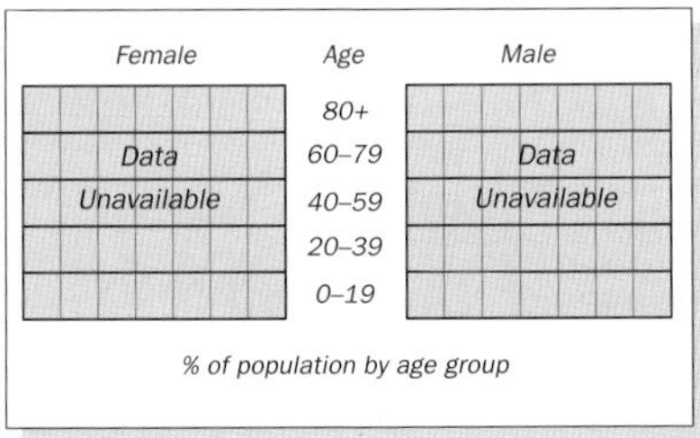
Female
Age
Male
80+
60–79
40–59
20–39
0–19
Data Unavailable
Data Unavailable
% of population by age group

CONGO, DEMOCRATIC REPUBLIC

Total Area : 2 345 410 sq. km
(905 563 sq. miles)

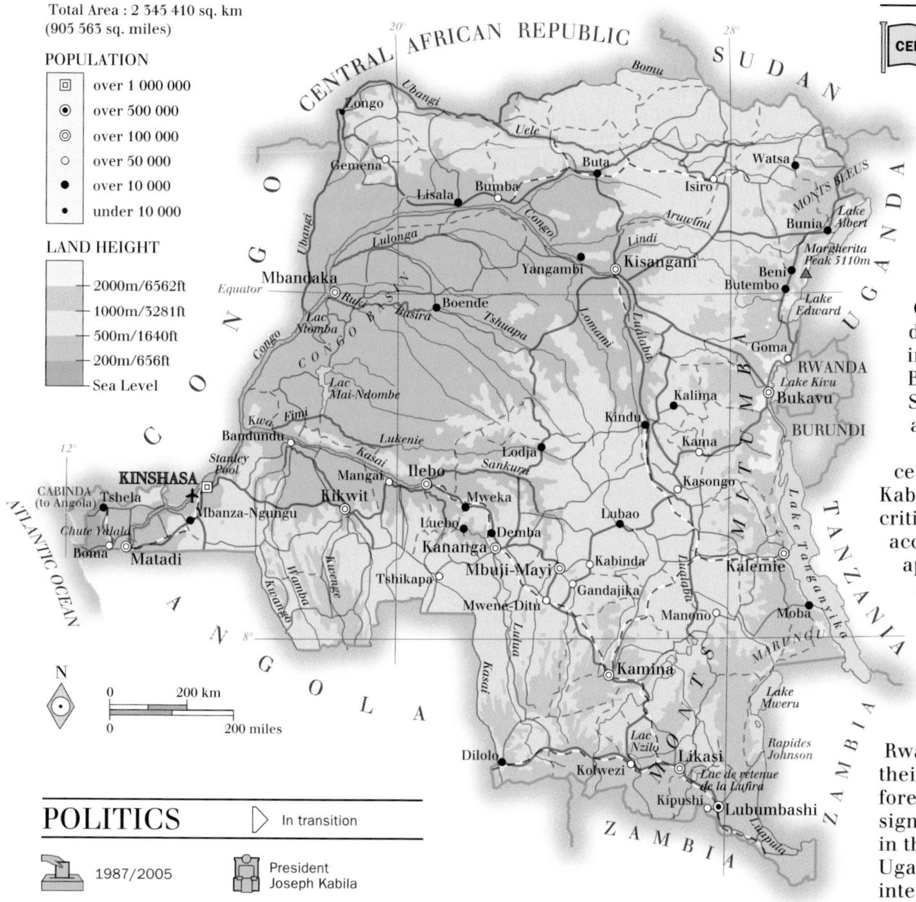
POPULATION
over 1 000 000
over 500 000
over 100 000
over 50 000
over 10 000
under 10 000
LAND HEIGHT
2000m/6562ft
1000m/3281ft
500m/1640ft
200m/656ft
Sea Level
CENTRAL AFRICAN REPUBLIC
SUDAN
UGANDA
RWANDA
BURUNDI
TANZANIA
ZAMBIA
ANGOLA
CONGO
ATLANTIC OCEAN
CABINDA (to Angola)
KINSHASA
Zongo
Gemena
Lisala
Bumba
Buta
Isiro
Watsa
Bunia
Beni
Butembo
Goma
Bukavu
Kisangani
Yangambi
Mbandaka
Boende
Bandundu
Kikwit
Ilebo
Mweka
Lodja
Kindu
Kalima
Kama
Kasongo
Lubao
Kabinda
Kananga
Luebo
Demba
Tshikapa
Mbuji-Mayi
Gandajika
Mwene-Ditu
Manono
Kalemie
Moba
Kamina
Dilolo
Kolwezi
Likasi
Kipushi
Lubumbashi
Matadi
Boma
Tshela
Mbanza-Ngungu
Mangai
Lake Albert
Lake Edward
Lake Kivu
Lake Tanganyika
Lake Mweru
Margherita Peak 5110m
Equator
0 200 km
0 200 miles

POLITICS

In transition

1987/2005

President Joseph Kabila

AT THE LAST ELECTION

Constituent and Legislative Assembly 300 seats

The last legislative poll was in 1987 when members were chosen from Mobutu's Popular Revolutionary Movement (**MPR**). An interim legislature was appointed in July/August 2000 with 300 members chosen by Laurent Kabila.

The authoritarian regime of Laurent-Désiré Kabila has been liberalized only slightly under his son.

PROFILE

The democratic credentials of Kabila, who overthrew Mobutu's 32-year dictatorial regime in 1997, came under question as he dissolved parliament and scrapped the constitution. A constituent assembly did not convene until 2000. Meanwhile in 1998 Kabila's ethnic Tutsi supporters, with the backing of Uganda and Rwanda, rose up against him.

Kabila's murder in 2001 left a vacuum exposing the true extent of his grip on power. His son Joseph, the armed forces head, was rapidly appointed as his successor. Talks were slowed by continued fighting, but the stalled UN peacekeeping force eventually arrived and cease-fires and troop withdrawals began. In April 2003 a Final Act providing for a transitional power-sharing government was agreed and democratic elections planned for 2005, though localized violence continued.

Joseph Kabila, who succeeded his father as president in 2001.

Mobutu, the ousted dictator, held power from 1965 to 1997.

MAIN POLITICAL ISSUE
Control of resources

The UN reported in 2002 that the rich mineral resources were still being heavily exploited by "civilianized" foreign armies, rebel groups, and even government officials. Ministers were dismissed and an investigation was launched. How to reclaim and distribute fairly the country's potential wealth is a major problem.

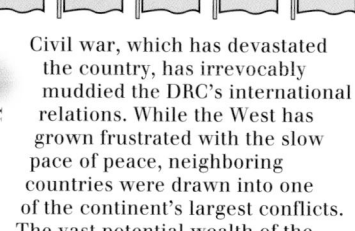

WORLD AFFAIRS

Joined UN in 1960

CEPGL | COMESA | OIF | G24 | AU

Civil war, which has devastated the country, has irrevocably muddied the DRC's international relations. While the West has grown frustrated with the slow pace of peace, neighboring countries were drawn into one of the continent's largest conflicts. The vast potential wealth of the Congolese forests and mineral deposits saw civil war quickly spiral into regional war by 1998. Angola, Burundi, Chad, Namibia, Rwanda, Sudan, Uganda, and Zimbabwe all sent troops.

Fighting continued despite a 1999 cease-fire signed in Lusaka. Laurent Kabila attracted intense international criticism in 2000 for suspending the accords, for taking an autocratic approach to a new transitional assembly, and for obstructing the arrival of the UN peacekeeping mission, MONUC. Kabila's death in 2001 and the accession of his son, Joseph, reinvigorated the peace process. Though fighting continued into 2002, with Rwanda and Uganda even reinforcing their troops, by the end of that year foreign forces had withdrawn to a significant extent. The vacuum created in the northeast by the departure of Ugandan forces was filled by intercommunal violence. French-led international forces spearheaded a limited peacekeeping mission there in 2003 amid rising concern about the worsening humanitarian situation.

The involvement of foreign firms in the running of the long-neglected mines in the south of the country has drawn sharp internal criticism, since profits rarely filter into the local economy.

AID

Recipient

$251m (receipts)

Up 36% in 2001

The regime's importance to the West during the Cold War brought in aid on a large scale. Between 1970 and 1989, it received $8.3 billion in economic aid and large-scale military assistance.

By 1990, changing political priorities prompted the US to act on long-deferred problems of human rights abuses and misappropriation of aid. It suspended all but humanitarian aid; most other donors followed suit, and the IMF declared the government to be "noncooperative" over its foreign debt. Joseph Kabila's accession in early 2001 improved the country's international standing; aid was resumed and debt cancellations followed: $10 billion (80% of the total) was forgiven in 2003.

C

CHRONOLOGY

The modern Congo was the site of the Kongo and other powerful African kingdoms, and a focus of the slave trade. Belgium's King Leopold II claimed most of the Congo basin after 1876 as his personal possession.

- **1885** Brutal colonization of Congo Free State (CFS) as Leopold's private fief.
- **1908** Belgium takes over CFS after international outcry.
- **1960** Independence as Republic of Congo (Democratic Republic of Congo from 1964). Katanga (Shaba) province secedes. UN intervenes.
- **1963** Katanga secession collapses.
- **1965** Marshal Joseph-Désiré Mobutu seizes power.
- **1970** Mobutu elected president; his MPR becomes sole legal party.
- **1971** Country renamed Zaire.
- **1977–1978** Two invasions by former Katanga separatists repulsed with Western help.
- **1982** Opposition parties set up Union for Democracy and Social Progress (UDPS).
- **1986–1990** Civil unrest and foreign criticism of human rights abuses.
- **1990** Belgium suspends aid after security forces kill prodemocracy demonstrators. Mobutu announces transition to multiparty rule.
- **1991** Opposition leader Etienne Tshisekedi heads short-lived "crisis government" formed by Mobutu.
- **1992–1993** Rival governments claim legitimacy.
- **1994** Combined High Council of the Republic–Transitional Parliament established.
- **1995** Regime demands international assistance to support a million Rwandan Hutu refugees.
- **1996** Major insurgency launched in east by Alliance of Democratic Forces for the Liberation of the Congo (AFDL) including Laurent Kabila's Popular Revolutionary Party (PRP), with disaffected ethnic Tutsi Banyamulunge.
- **1997** Forces led by Kabila sweep south and west. Kabila takes power. Country renamed DRC. Mobutu dies in exile.
- **1998** Banyamulunge join Kabila's opponents and launch rebellion in the east, backed by Rwanda and Uganda. Southern African states, give military backing to Kabila.
- **2000** UN approves peacekeeping mission; arrival stalled by Kabila.
- **2001** Kabila assassinated; succeeded by son Joseph. Peace talks restarted.
- **2003** April, Final Act peace accord signed. Hundreds massacred at Drodro in northeast during tribal conflict.

DEFENSE

No compulsory military service

$392m

Down 2% in 2001

The military strongly backed Mobutu's regime, but offered no real resistance when Laurent Kabila's insurgents swept the country in 1996–1997. Government troops, poorly paid and undisciplined, but supported by foreign allies, fought similar rebel adversaries in the 1998–2003 civil war. MONUC, the UN peacekeeping force, was doubled in size in 2002. Rebel forces are to be integrated into the regular army.

CONGOLESE ARMED FORCES

60 main battle tanks (20 PRC Type-59, 40 PRC Type-62)	79,000 personnel
2 patrol boats	900 personnel
No combat aircraft	1500 personnel
None	

ECONOMICS

Inflation 846% p.a. (1990–2001)

$4.16bn

421.5 Congolese francs (346)

SCORE CARD

- World GNP Ranking........................120th
- GNP per Capita.................................$80
- Balance of Payments....................–$798m
- Inflation.......................................358%
- Unemployment.............................Very high

EXPORTS

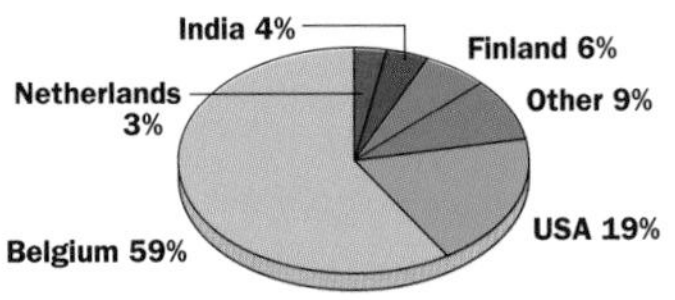
India 4%
Finland 6%
Netherlands 3%
Other 9%
USA 19%
Belgium 59%

IMPORTS

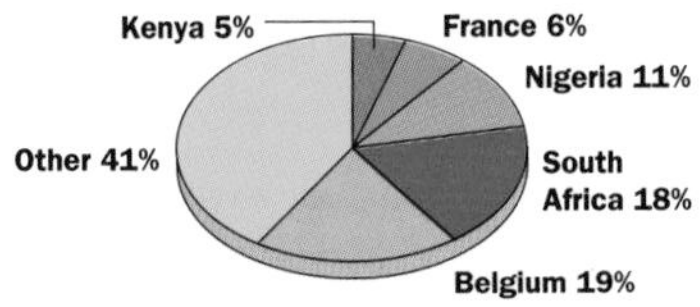
Kenya 5%
France 6%
Nigeria 11%
Other 41%
South Africa 18%
Belgium 19%

ECONOMIC PERFORMANCE INDICATOR

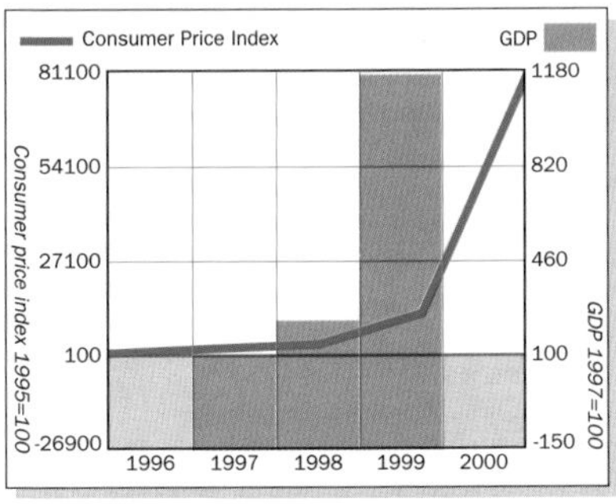
Consumer Price Index
GDP
81100
54100
27100
100
-26900
1180
820
460
100
-150
1996
1997
1998
1999
2000
Consumer price index 1995=100
GDP 1997=100

Strengths

Rich resource base. Minerals – notably copper, cobalt, diamonds – provide 85% of export earnings. 80% of debt canceled in 2003. Energy: oil; possibly Africa's largest hydropower potential. Rich soil; much unutilized arable land.

Weaknesses

Decades of mismanagement and corruption: inadequate, disintegrating infrastructure; non-self-sufficient in food. Political instability. Hyperinflation. Loss of export income. Mineral resources plundered by foreign powers.

Profile

Political instability, systematic corruption, long-term mismanagement, and outright civil war have brought what is potentially a leading African economy to a state of collapse.

By the mid-1990s real GDP was falling by 10% or more each year. The government budget ran record deficits, and inflation spiraled virtually out of control from 1994 onward. Lack of spares and power cuts have halted most industry and closed many mines. Strikes and riots over plummeting living standards hastened the flight of foreign capital. Subsistence farming and petty trade keep most people going. Restructuring state-owned enterprises in 2001 was aimed at attracting back foreign investment.

The Kabila regime, despite its originally Marxist background, claims to want an effective free-market economy. Resumption of essential large-scale aid, effective government, and tackling debt relief will depend on difficult reforms and arrears payments to the IMF and other creditors.

CONGO, DEM. REP. : MAJOR BUSINESSES

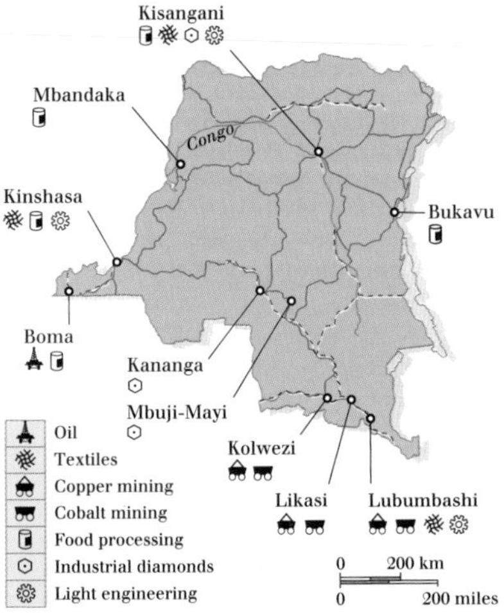
Kisangani
Mbandaka
Congo
Kinshasa
Bukavu
Boma
Kananga
Mbuji-Mayi
Kolwezi
Likasi
Lubumbashi
Oil
Textiles
Copper mining
Cobalt mining
Food processing
Industrial diamonds
Light engineering
0 200 km
0 200 miles

RESOURCES

Electric power 3.2m kW

208,862 tonnes

21,413 b/d (reserves 188m barrels)

4m goats, 953,066 pigs, 19.6m chickens

Copper, diamonds, oil, coltan, cobalt, zinc, uranium, manganese

ELECTRICITY GENERATION

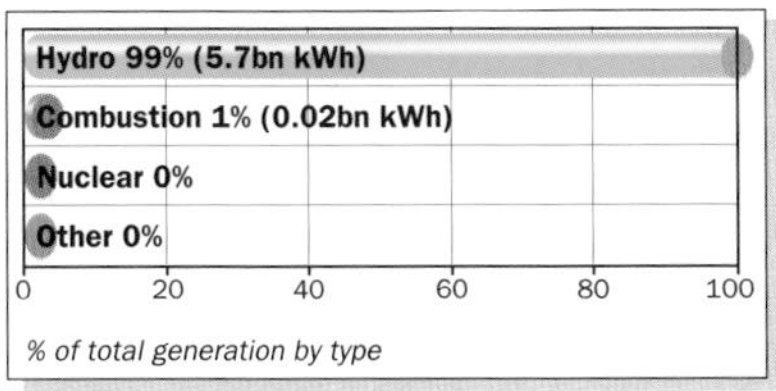

Hydro 99% (5.7bn kWh)
Combustion 1% (0.02bn kWh)
Nuclear 0%
Other 0%
0
20
40
60
80
100
% of total generation by type

What should be a prosperous country, with its rich resources, is instead one of the world's poorest states, exploited and mismanaged by its rulers for decades and plundered further by foreign forces during the civil war. In the 1980s, the country was the world's largest cobalt exporter and second-largest industrial diamond exporter. Since 1990, copper and cobalt output have collapsed and diamond smuggling is booming. There are oil reserves and hydroelectric installations with sufficient potential capacity to export power, but instead lack of maintenance has shut down many turbines and most urban areas face power cuts. Despite rich soils and the fact that 60% of people are involved in farming, the DRC is not even self-sufficient in food.

CONGO, DEM. REP. : LAND USE

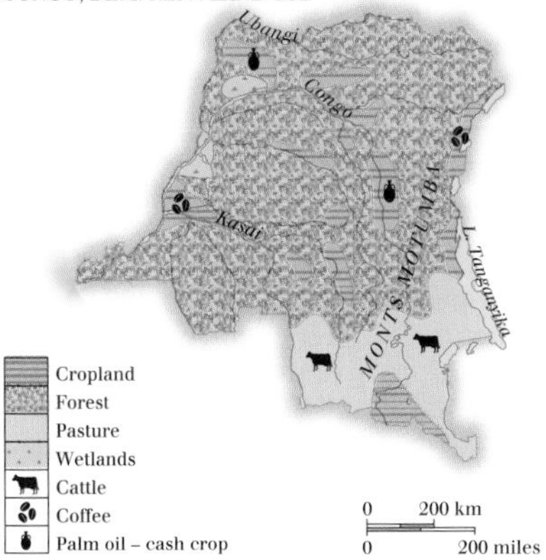

Ubangi
Congo
Kasai
MONTS MITUMBA
L. Tanganyika
Cropland
Forest
Pasture
Wetlands
Cattle
Coffee
Palm oil – cash crop
0 200 km
0 200 miles

ENVIRONMENT

Sustainability rank: 109th

7% (2% partially protected)

0.05 tonnes per capita

ENVIRONMENTAL TREATIES

Yes	Yes	Yes	Yes	Yes	No

Rainforests cover over 60% of the country, representing almost 6% of the world's and 50% of Africa's remaining woodlands. They are home to several endangered species. The poor transportation network has so far prevented large-scale commercial exploitation of timber, but clearance for fuelwood is a problem. The collapse of many urban refuse and sewage disposal systems has led to major health and pollution problems. Environmental damage caused by the civil war is estimated at $320 million.

MEDIA

TV ownership low

Daily newspaper circulation 3 per 1000 people

PUBLISHING AND BROADCAST MEDIA

There are 9 daily newspapers, including *Le Palmarès*, *Elima*, *Boyoma*, and *Mjumbe*

1 state-controlled service, some independent services

2 state-controlled services, some independent services

Fighting makes services less accessible outside the capital. Unlike the broadcast media, press outlets are privately owned, and many newspapers openly criticize the authorities, although self-preservation requires a degree of self-censorship. A ban on foreign radio broadcasts was lifted in 2001. MONUC operates the only countrywide radio station, Radio Okapi.

CRIME

Death penalty in use

The DRC does not publish prison figures

Violence and crime are rising rapidly

CRIME RATES

All types of crime are on the increase in the DRC

Civil war and remaining insecurity exacerbate long-standing problems of corruption and human rights abuses. Along the war's front line public order has largely broken down. Extortion, robbery, rape, and murder are widespread and on the increase. Ethnic violence, suppressed after 1965, resurfaced in the south and between the Hema and Lendu tribes in the northeast, leading to some gruesome atrocities. Crimes committed during combat in the civil war were pardoned in 2003.

EDUCATION

School leaving age: 14

63%

60,341 students

THE EDUCATION SYSTEM

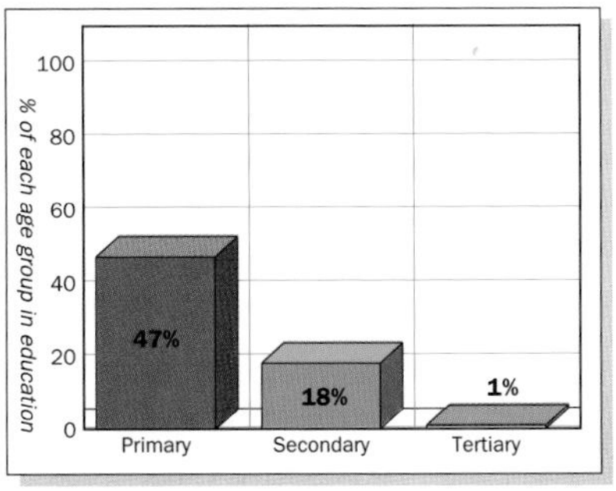

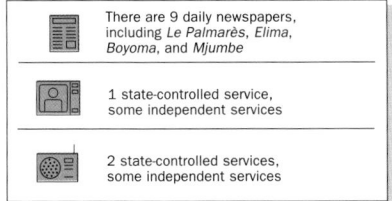

% of each age group in education
100
80
60
40
20
0
47%
18%
1%
Primary
Secondary
Tertiary

In 1997, just over 37% of secondary-age children were attending classes, but this figure dropped sharply during the civil war and has yet to recover. State provision, as with health care, is patchy and has faced sharp budget cuts since 1980. Most private schools are run by the Roman Catholic Church.

HEALTH

No welfare state health benefits

1 per 14,286 people

Malaria, respiratory and diarrheal diseases

State services have now virtually collapsed. Disease and death rates are rising, especially in rural areas. A new health insurance plan was announced in 2001, designed to enable greater access to health care. As of December 2001, just over one million people were estimated to be HIV/AIDS infected.

SPENDING

GDP/cap. decrease

CONSUMPTION AND SPENDING

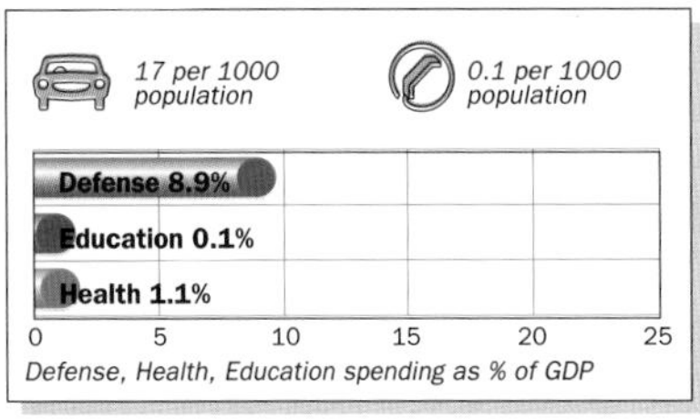

17 per 1000 population
0.1 per 1000 population
Defense 8.9%
Education 0.1%
Health 1.1%
0
5
10
15
20
25
Defense, Health, Education spending as % of GDP

Before his death in exile in 1997, ex-dictator Mobutu was one of the world's richest men, worth an estimated $4 billion. Most of his former subjects live in poverty exacerbated by civil war.

WORLD RANKING

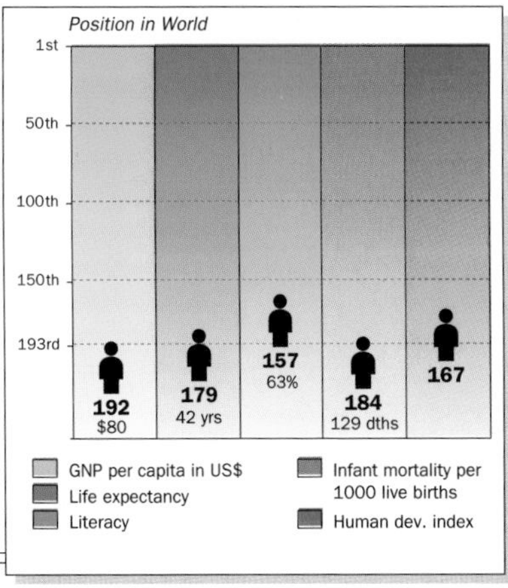

Position in World
1st
50th
100th
150th
193rd
192
$80
179
42 yrs
157
63%
184
129 dths
167
GNP per capita in US$
Life expectancy
Literacy
Infant mortality per 1000 live births
Human dev. index

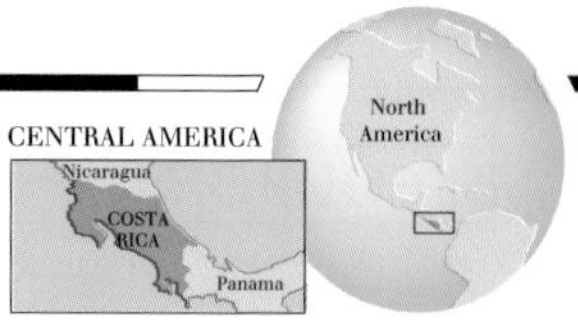
CENTRAL AMERICA
Nicaragua
COSTA RICA
Panama
North America

COSTA RICA

OFFICIAL NAME: Republic of Costa Rica **CAPITAL:** San José
POPULATION: 4.2 million **CURRENCY:** Costa Rican colón **OFFICIAL LANGUAGE:** Spanish

C

1838 | 1838 | Sept 15 | CR | -6 | +506 | .cr

SPANNING THE CENTRAL AMERICAN isthmus and wedged between Nicaragua and Panama, Costa Rica was under Spanish rule until 1821 and gained full independence in 1838. From 1948 until the end of the 1980s, it had the most developed welfare state in Central America. Costa Rica is nominally a multiparty democracy, but two parties dominate. Its army was abolished in 1948; the 1949 constitution then forbade national armies.

CLIMATE

Tropical wet & dry

WEATHER CHART FOR SAN JOSÉ

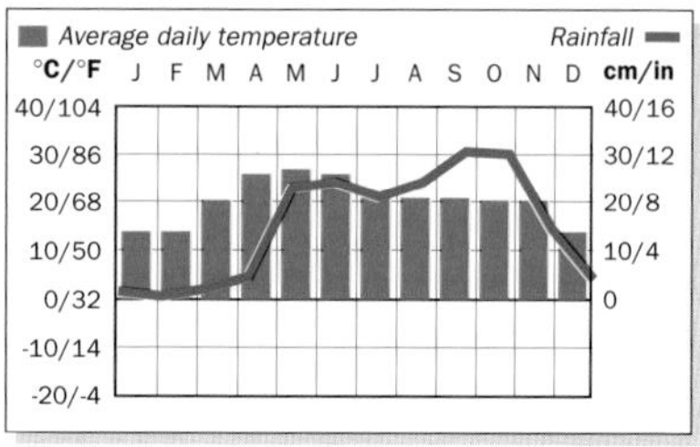
Average daily temperature
Rainfall
°C/°F J F M A M J J A S O N D cm/in
40/104
30/86
20/68
10/50
0/32
-10/14
-20/-4
40/16
30/12
20/8
10/4
0

The Caribbean coast has heavy rainfall, while the Pacific coast is much drier. The central uplands are temperate.

TRANSPORTATION

Drive on right

Juan Santamaría, San José
988,000 passengers

12 ships
3000 grt

THE TRANSPORTATION NETWORK

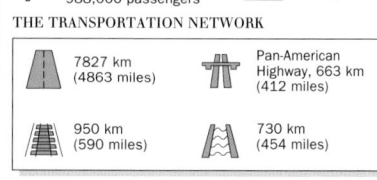

7827 km (4863 miles)

Pan-American Highway, 663 km (412 miles)

950 km (590 miles)

730 km (454 miles)

San José is the hub of a well-used bus network. Rail services have not recovered from an earthquake in 1991.

TOURISM

Visitors : Population 1:3.7

1.13m visitors

Up 4% in 2001

MAIN TOURIST ARRIVALS

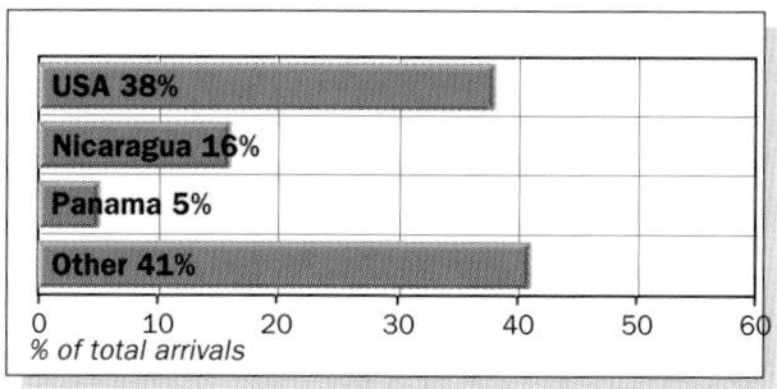
USA 38%
Nicaragua 16%
Panama 5%
Other 41%
0
10
20
30
40
50
60
% of total arrivals

Tourism has brought in over $1 billion each year since 1999, and is expanding with the help of both domestic and foreign investment. The country's tropical scenery and wildlife are promoted heavily for "eco-tourists."

PEOPLE

Pop. density medium

Spanish, English Creole, Bribri, Cabecar

82/km² (213/mi²)

THE URBAN/RURAL POPULATION SPLIT

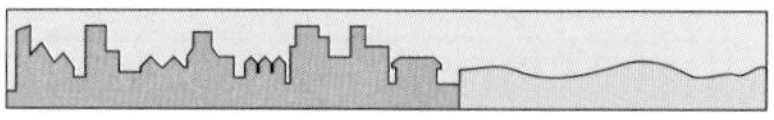
60%
40%

RELIGIOUS PERSUASION

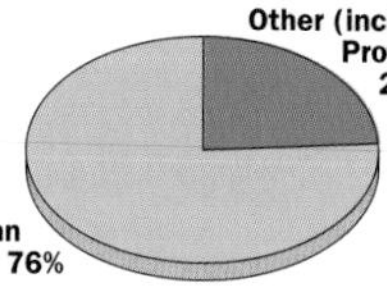
Other (including Protestant) 24%
Roman Catholic 76%

The majority of the population is *mestizo*, of partly Spanish origin. One-third of people in the Limón area are black and often English-speaking. There are only about 5000 indigenous Amerindians.

POLITICS

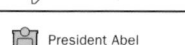

Multiparty elections

2002/2006

President Abel Pacheco de la Espriella

AT THE LAST ELECTION

Legislative Assembly 57 seats

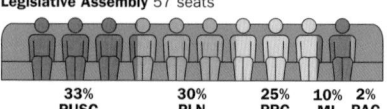

33% PUSC
30% PLN
25% PRC
10% ML
2% PAC

PUSC = Social Christian Unity Party **PLN** = National Liberation Party **PRC** = Costa Rican Renewal Party **ML** = Liberty Movement **PAC** = Citizens' Action Party

Politics has long been dominated by the PUSC and PLN, both of which have close ties to major banana- and coffee-growing families. Historically the US has exercised a very powerful influence on politics.

The PLN in 1994 promised reforms to its previous austerity policies, but soon came under pressure from international financial organizations to reduce the budget deficit. Harsh structural adjustment measures proved highly unpopular.

In 1998 the PUSC regained power. President Miguel Angel Rodríguez launched a three-year plan to reduce inflation and poverty, create thousands of jobs, and stimulate foreign investment in state companies. His chosen successor, Abel Pacheco, needed an unprecedented second round to clinch the presidency in 2002, when voter turnout hit an all-time low.

WORLD AFFAIRS

Joined UN in 1945

ACS | Geplac | RG | OAS | San José

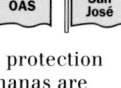

Trade ties with the US and protection of prices for coffee and bananas are priorities. Trade ties have also been agreed with Canada and Chile. Tensions with Nicaragua over their mutual border were resolved in 2000, but illegal immigrants remain an issue.

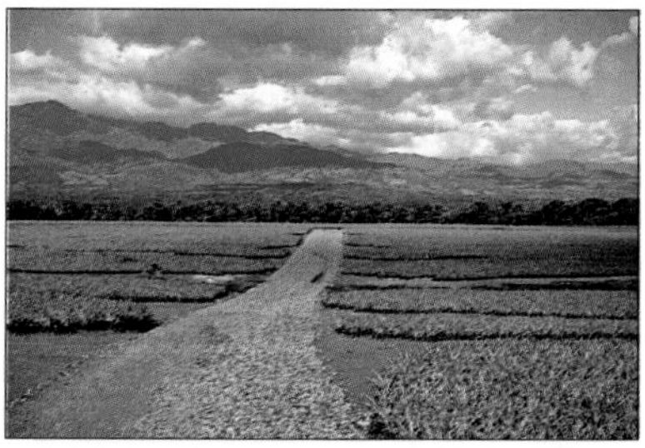

Pineapple plantation near Buenos Aires, crossed by the Pan-American Highway which runs for 663 km (412 miles) through Costa Rica.

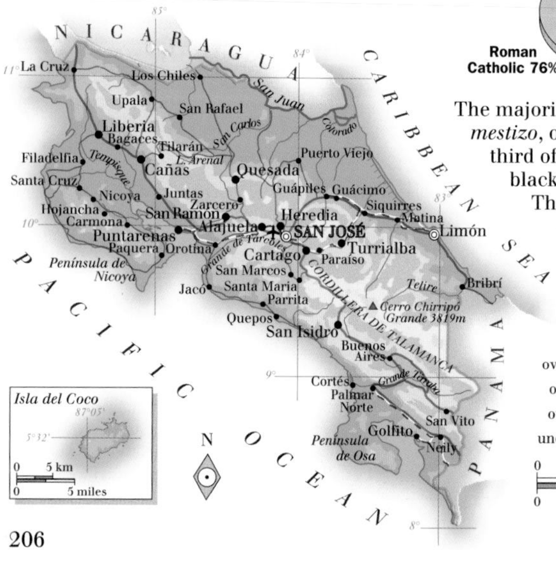
NICARAGUA
CARIBBEAN SEA
PACIFIC OCEAN
PANAMA
La Cruz
Los Chiles
Upala
San Rafael
Liberia
Bagaces
Filarán
Cañas
Filadelfia
Santa Cruz
Nicoya
Hojancha
Carmona
Juntas
Zarcero
San Ramón
Alajuela
Quesada
Puerto Viejo
Guápiles
Guácimo
Siquirres
Matina
Heredia
SAN JOSÉ
Limón
Puntarenas
Paquera
Orotina
Cartago
Paraíso
Turrialba
Península de Nicoya
San Marcos
Santa María
Jacó
Parrita
Quepos
San Isidro
Cerro Chirripó Grande 3819m
CORDILLERA DE TALAMANCA
Telire
Bribrí
Buenos Aires
Cortés
Palmar Norte
Golfito
San Vito
Neily
Península de Osa
Isla del Coco
0 5 km
0 5 miles
N

COSTA RICA

Total Area : 51 100 sq. km (19 730 sq. miles)

POPULATION
- over 100 000
- over 50 000
- over 10 000
- under 10 000

LAND HEIGHT
- 3000m/9843ft
- 2000m/6562ft
- 1000m/3281ft
- 500m/1640ft
- 200m/656ft
- Sea level

0 50 km
0 50 miles

AID

Recipient

$2m (receipts)

Down 83% in 2001

During the 1980s Costa Rica was a large recipient of US aid designed to inoculate it against left-wing insurgencies such as those in El Salvador, Guatemala, and neighboring Nicaragua. Peace in the region has led to a sharp decline in such aid, especially given the country's relatively high per capita income. World Bank aid has helped to modernize Juan Santamaría international airport.

DEFENSE

No compulsory military service

$76m

Down 8% in 2001

Costa Rica emerged from the 1948 civil war as a neutral, demilitarized modern state. A 4400-strong Civil Guard is complemented by a largely military-trained police force. Spending on security as a percentage of GDP has long been the lowest in the region. Lack of a common command structure hinders the influence of the security forces but also renders them less open to public control. Right-wing paramilitary groups are known to exist.

ECONOMICS

Inflation 16% p.a. (1990–2001)

$15.7bn

398.7 Costa Rican colones (359.2)

SCORE CARD

- ❑ WORLD GNP RANKING..........74th
- ❑ GNP PER CAPITA..........$4060
- ❑ BALANCE OF PAYMENTS..........–$702m
- ❑ INFLATION..........11.2%
- ❑ UNEMPLOYMENT..........5%

EXPORTS

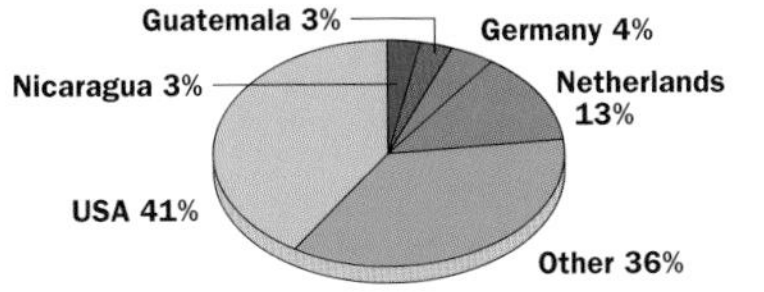
Guatemala 3%
Germany 4%
Nicaragua 3%
Netherlands 13%
USA 41%
Other 36%

IMPORTS

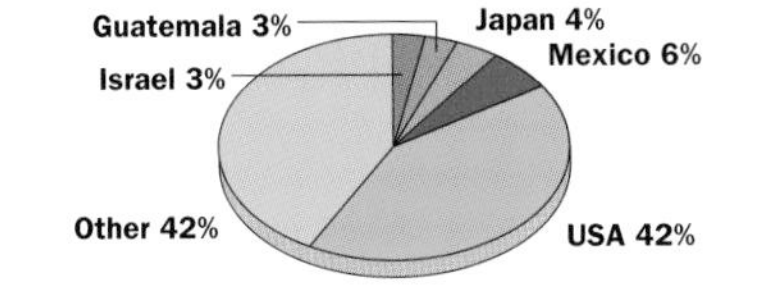
Guatemala 3%
Japan 4%
Israel 3%
Mexico 6%
Other 42%
USA 42%

STRENGTHS
Major coffee, beef, and banana exports. Expanding tourism also fueling construction. Strong inward investment. Favorable WTO ruling on banana access to EU market.

WEAKNESSES
Coffee, beef, and bananas all vulnerable to falling prices. History of high inflation. Dependence on imported oil. Large domestic debt. Competitiveness hindered by insufficient investment in infrastructure. State monopolies have deterred investment in energy, telecommunications, and insurance sectors. Inefficient management.

RESOURCES

Electric power 1.5m kW

37,658 tonnes

Not an oil producer; refines 280 b/d

1.22m cattle, 475,000 pigs, 17m chickens

Bauxite, gold, silver, manganese, mercury

Costa Rica has large bauxite deposits in the south – aluminum smelting is an important industry. Small quantities of gold, silver, manganese, and mercury are also mined. Self-sufficiency in energy is being pursued through the development of hydroelectric power, which now provides almost all energy.

MEDIA

TV ownership medium

Daily newspaper circulation 72 per 1000 people

PUBLISHING AND BROADCAST MEDIA

There are 8 daily newspapers, including *La Nación, La República, La Prensa Libre,* and *Diario Extra*

8 stations: 1 state-owned, 7 independent

State-owned and independent stations

The media are free but dominated by conservative opinion. Entry into journalism is strictly licensed.

ENVIRONMENT

Sustainability rank: 9th

24% (12% partially protected)

1.6 tonnes per capita

Despite good environmental regulation, reckless economic development has contributed to extensive deforestation. Forests now cover less than a third of the country. Pesticide abuse by agribusiness has poisoned rivers and threatened species. Urban sprawl has degraded the fertile central valley.

CRIME

No death penalty

8526 prisoners

Crime is rising

Costa Rica is the least violent Central American country. Attacks on and kidnappings of tourists are rare but have dented its image as a safe haven. Drugs cartels use the country to transfer cocaine to the US and Europe. Police show hostility toward immigrants from neighboring countries.

CHRONOLOGY

Costa Rica, ruled since the 16th century by Spain, became an independent state in 1838.

- ❑ **1948** Disputed elections lead to civil war; ended by Social Democratic Party (later the PLN) forming provisional government under José Ferrer. Army abolished.
- ❑ **1949** New constitution promulgated.
- ❑ **1987** Central American Peace Plan initiated by President Arias.
- ❑ **1998** PUSC returns to power.

EDUCATION

School leaving age: 15

96%

58,500 students

Costa Rica has the highest literacy rate in the isthmus, and is home to the University of Central America.

HEALTH

Welfare state health benefits

1 per 562 people

Cancers, respiratory diseases, accidents

The public health system is one of the most developed in Latin America. Some private clinics offer cosmetic surgery vacations.

SPENDING

GDP/cap. increase

CONSUMPTION AND SPENDING

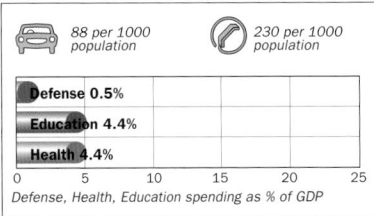

88 per 1000 population

230 per 1000 population

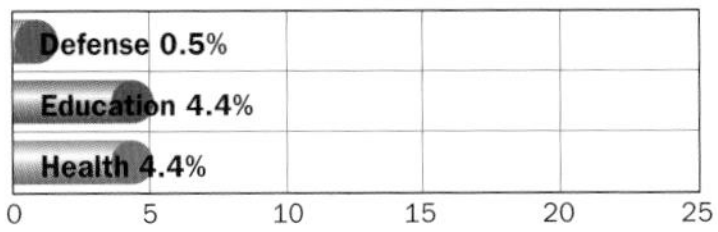
Defense 0.5%
Education 4.4%
Health 4.4%
0
5
10
15
20
25
Defense, Health, Education spending as % of GDP

Plantation-owners are the wealthiest group; over 25% of the population live in poverty. Nonetheless, Costa Rica has the region's highest standard of living.

WORLD RANKING

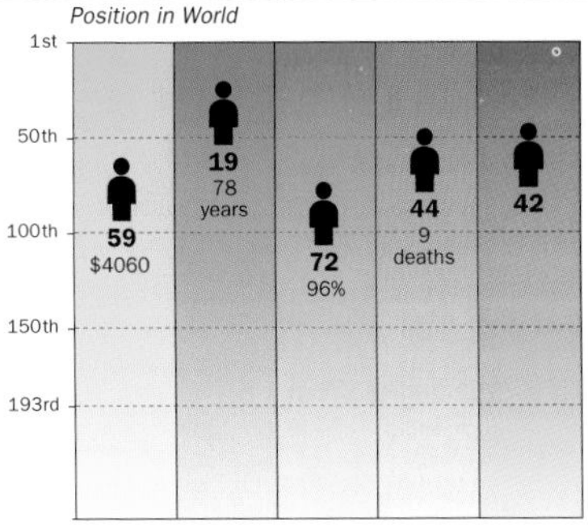
Position in World
1st
50th
100th
150th
193rd
59
$4060
19
78 years
72
96%
44
9 deaths
42
GNP per capita in US$
Life expectancy
Literacy
Infant mortality per 1000 live births
Human dev. index

C

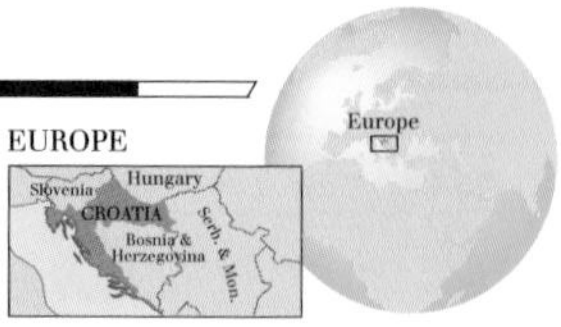
EUROPE
Europe
Hungary
Slovenia
CROATIA
Bosnia & Herzegovina
Serb. & Mon.

CROATIA

OFFICIAL NAME: Republic of Croatia **CAPITAL:** Zagreb
POPULATION: 4.7 million **CURRENCY:** Kuna **OFFICIAL LANGUAGE:** Croatian

1991 | 1991 | May 30 | HR | +1 | +385 | .hr

THOUGH IT WAS CONTROLLED by Hungary from medieval times and was a part of the Yugoslav state for much of the 20th century, Croatia still has a strong national identity. It includes the historic provinces of Slavonia, Istria, and Dalmatia (Dinara). Actively involved in the conflicts which broke up Yugoslavia in the early 1990s, Croatia only regained full control of Serb-occupied Eastern Slavonia, around Vukovar, in 1998.

Dubrovnik, Dalmatia. *This historic city on the Adriatic coast was shelled and besieged by the Yugoslav federal army in 1991.*

CLIMATE

Mediterranean/continental

WEATHER CHART FOR ZAGREB

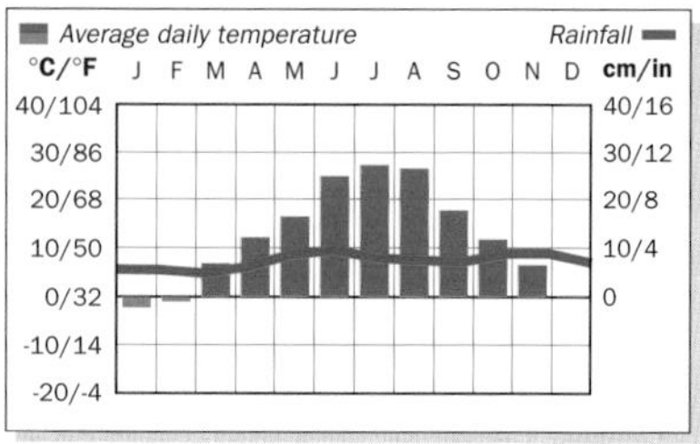
Average daily temperature
Rainfall
°C/°F
J F M A M J J A S O N D
cm/in
40/104
30/86
20/68
10/50
0/32
-10/14
-20/-4
40/16
30/12
20/8
10/4
0

Northern Croatia has a temperate continental climate. Its Adriatic coast has a Mediterranean climate.

TRANSPORTATION

Drive on right

Pleso International, Zagreb 1.2m passengers

243 ships 775,200 grt

THE TRANSPORTATION NETWORK

23,695 km (14,723 miles)

330 km (205 miles)

2727 km (1694 miles)

785 km (488 miles)

Zagreb has recovered from the effects of war, and of sanctions against Yugoslavia, and is once again an important regional road and rail hub. The Adriatic Highway affords fantastic views along the Dalmatian coast.

TOURISM

Visitors : Population 1.5:1

6.94m visitors

Up 6% in 2002

MAIN TOURIST ARRIVALS

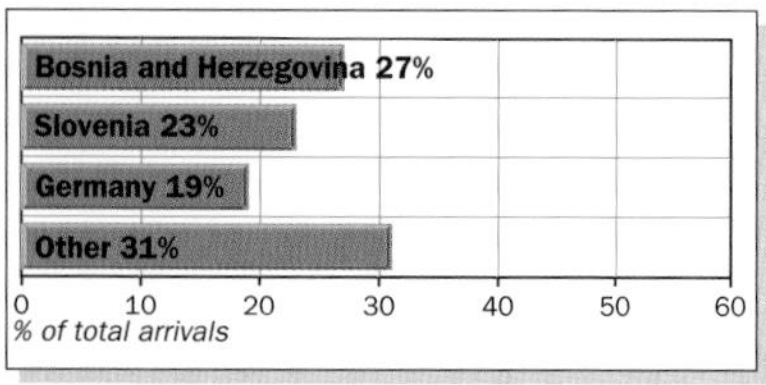
Bosnia and Herzegovina 27%
Slovenia 23%
Germany 19%
Other 31%
0 10 20 30 40 50 60
% of total arrivals

The Adriatic coast is regaining its popularity as a tourist destination. There are also many historical sites.

PEOPLE

Pop. density medium

Croatian

83/km² (215/mi²)

THE URBAN/RURAL POPULATION SPLIT

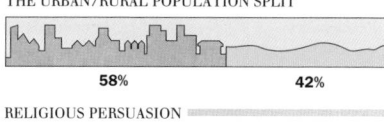

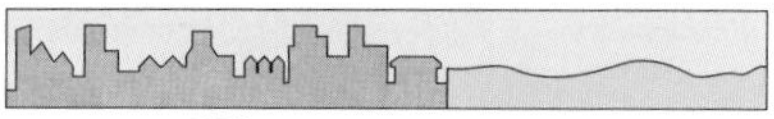
58%
42%

RELIGIOUS PERSUASION

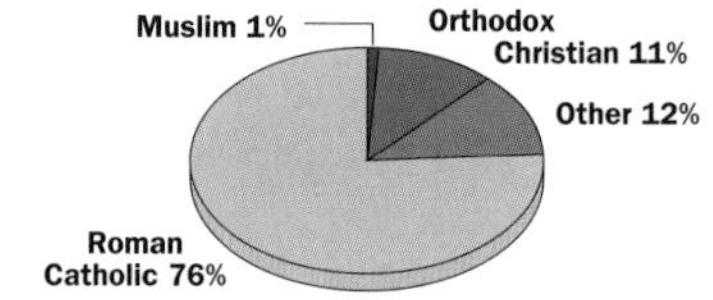
Muslim 1%
Orthodox Christian 11%
Other 12%
Roman Catholic 76%

War greatly altered the ethnic makeup. The Orthodox Christian Serb minority once constituted 12% of the population and had been based along the borders with Bosnia and Serbia. Alienated by Croatian nationalism, they established the Republic of Serbian Krajina in 1991. It was overrun by the Croatian army in 1995 and hundreds of thousands of Serbs were forced to flee east. Those who remained now make up just 4% of the population – not enough to warrant "minority rights" under the constitution. There was an influx of Croats and Bosniaks from Bosnia in the 1990s.

POLITICS

Multiparty elections

2000/2004

President Stipe Mesic

AT THE LAST ELECTION

House of Representatives 151 seats

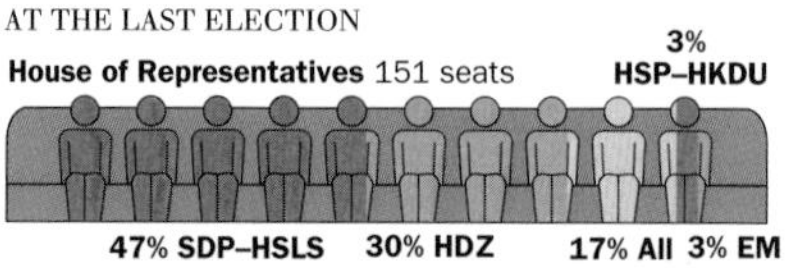
3% HSP–HKDU
47% SDP–HSLS
30% HDZ
17% All
3% EM

SDP–HSLS = Coalition of Social Democratic Party and Croatian Social Liberal Party **HDZ** = Croatian Democratic Union **All** = Alliance (led by Croatian Peasant Party–HSS) **HSP–HKDU** = Coalition of Croatian Party of Rights and Croatian Christian Democratic Union **EM** = Ethnic minorities

Six seats are reserved for representatives of Croats living abroad (all are currently held by the HDZ). Five seats are reserved for ethnic minorities (one is currently held by the HSS)

The nationalist HDZ, which had been in power from independence, was left rudderless in 1999 by the death of President Franjo Tudjman. Mired in corruption and spying scandals, the party was defeated in elections in 2000. The center-left SDP under Stipe Mesic won the presidency and also formed an eight-party coalition, headed by Prime Minister Ivica Racan.

Croatia had been internationally isolated for Tudjman's refusal to bring "war criminals" to justice. The SDP government has appeased the international community by arresting some, but has balked at extraditing the country's most popular "war heroes." Concern within the government over Croatia's acceptance of Slovenian nuclear waste forced the SDP to seek a fresh coalition without the HSLS in 2002.

WORLD AFFAIRS

Joined UN in 1992

CE | WTO | PfP | CEI | OSCE

The end of the Tudjman era cleared the way for a rapprochement with the international community and Croatia's neighbors. A dispute with Montenegro over the Prevlaka Peninsula was resolved in 2002. Croatia applied to join the EU in 2003, but still faces criticism for its unwillingness to extradite high-profile suspected war criminals.

AID

Recipient

$113m (receipts)

Up 71% in 2001

EU states have spent over $1 billion on reconstruction in Croatia since 1991.

DEFENSE

Compulsory military service

$512m

Down 8% in 2001

The army proved its effectiveness when in 1995 it recaptured territory held by Serb forces. Under 2002 proposals its size will be halved by 2005.

ECONOMICS

Inflation 72% p.a. (1990–2001)

$19.9bn

6.531 kuna (7.419)

SCORE CARD

- ❑ WORLD GNP RANKING..........63rd
- ❑ GNP PER CAPITA..........$4550
- ❑ BALANCE OF PAYMENTS..........–$642m
- ❑ INFLATION..........4.8%
- ❑ UNEMPLOYMENT..........20%

EXPORTS

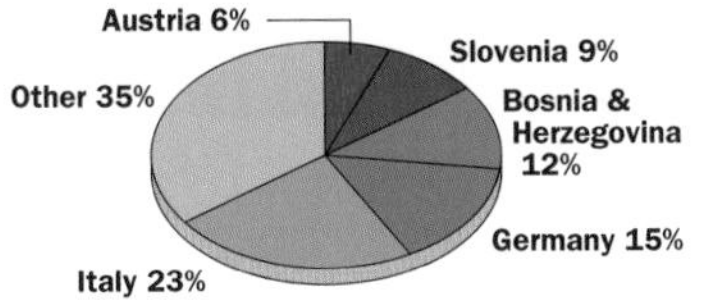

Austria 6%
Slovenia 9%
Other 35%
Bosnia & Herzegovina 12%
Germany 15%
Italy 23%

IMPORTS

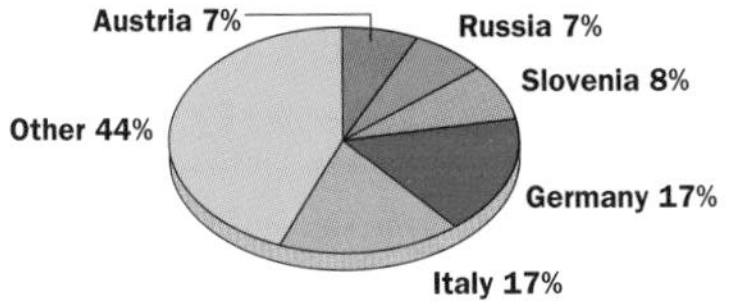

Austria 7%
Russia 7%
Slovenia 8%
Other 44%
Germany 17%
Italy 17%

STRENGTHS

Steady growth. Progress in reducing government overspending, backed by IMF. Recovery in tourism. Inflation brought under control.

WEAKNESSES

Slow privatization, until 2001, and trade union resistance to market reforms. War damage estimated at $50 billion. Persistent high unemployment.

RESOURCES

Electric power 3.8m kW

28,062 tonnes

25,925 b/d (reserves 47m barrels)

1.29m pigs, 710,000 turkeys, 11.7m chickens

Coal, bauxite, iron, oil, china clay, natural gas

Croatia generates 46% of its energy needs from combustion and 54% from hydroelectric sources. It has very few minerals, although it does have oil and gas fields. The rich fishing grounds of the Adriatic are a major resource.

ENVIRONMENT

Sustainability rank: 12th

8% (5% partially protected)

4.7 tonnes per capita

Croatia was the first Yugoslav republic to create reserves in order to protect endangered and unique wetlands.

MEDIA

TV ownership high

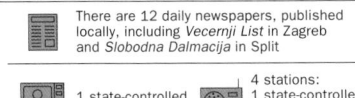

Daily newspaper circulation 114 per 1000 people

PUBLISHING AND BROADCAST MEDIA

There are 12 daily newspapers, published locally, including *Vecernji List* in Zagreb and *Slobodna Dalmacija* in Split

1 state-controlled service

4 stations: 1 state-controlled, 3 independent

The three TV channels are state-owned. Media freedoms, eroded under Tudjman, have gradually improved.

CRIME

No death penalty

2584 prisoners

Up 44% in 2000–2002

Under Tudjman, former Croat HOS militiamen escaped prosecution for "ethnic cleansing" in Bosnia, but the post-Tudjman government ordered a number of arrests.

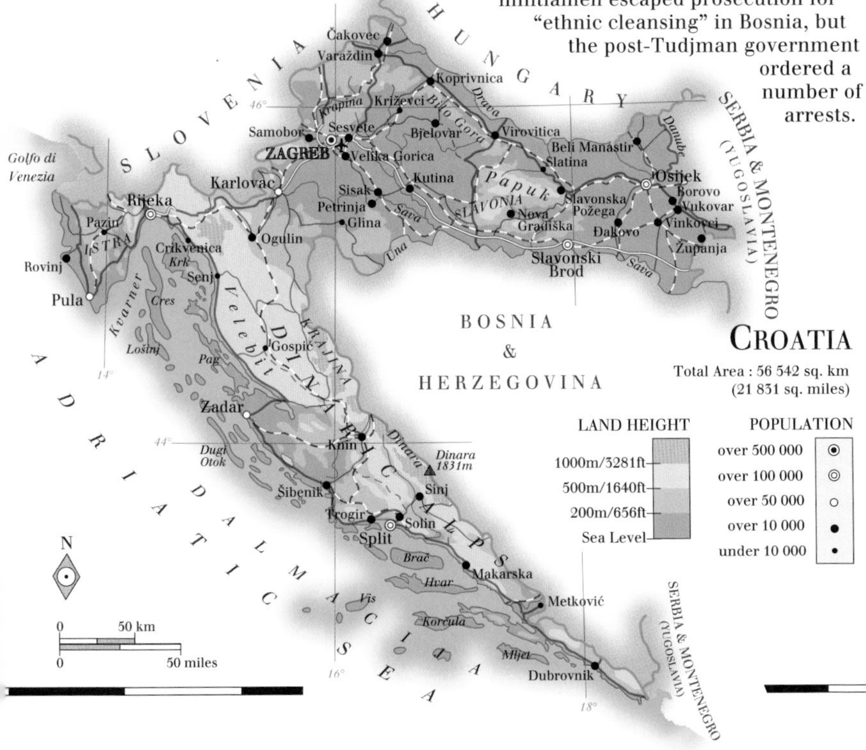

HUNGARY
SLOVENIA
SERBIA & MONTENEGRO (YUGOSLAVIA)
BOSNIA & HERZEGOVINA
ADRIATIC SEA
Golfo di Venezia
Čakovec
Varaždin
Koprivnica
Krapina
Križevci
Bilo Gora
Drava
Samobor
Sesvete
Bjelovar
Virovitica
Beli Manastir
Danube
ZAGREB
Velika Gorica
Slatina
Karlovac
Kutina
Osijek
Borovo
Vukovar
Vinkovci
Sisak
Petrinja
Glina
Sava
Papuk
SLAVONIA
Slavonska Požega
Nova Gradiška
Đakovo
Županja
Rijeka
Pazin
ISTRA
Crikvenica
Krk
Ogulin
Una
Slavonski Brod
Rovinj
Senj
Pula
Cres
Kvarner
Velebit
Gospić
DINARA
KRAJINA
Lošinj
Pag
Zadar
Dugi Otok
Knin
Dinara 1831m
DINARIC ALPS
Šibenik
Sinj
Trogir
Solin
Split
Brač
Hvar
Makarska
Vis
Korčula
Mljet
Metković
Dubrovnik
N
0 50 km
0 50 miles
CROATIA
Total Area : 56 542 sq. km (21 831 sq. miles)
LAND HEIGHT
1000m/3281ft
500m/1640ft
200m/656ft
Sea Level
POPULATION
over 500 000
over 100 000
over 50 000
over 10 000
under 10 000

CHRONOLOGY

Between 1945 and 1991 Croatia was a republic of the Yugoslav federation.

- ❑ **1991** Independence. Rebel Croatian Serb republic of Krajina proclaimed.
- ❑ **1992** Franjo Tudjman president. Involvement in Bosnian civil war.
- ❑ **1995** Krajina and Western Slavonia recaptured. Dayton agreement ends fighting.
- ❑ **1998** Eastern Slavonia reintegrated.
- ❑ **1999** Death of Tudjman.
- ❑ **2000** Center-left wins elections.

EDUCATION

School leaving age: 15

98%

104,168 students

The education system is well developed. There are four universities, at Zagreb, Rijeka, Osijek, and Split.

HEALTH

Welfare state health benefits

1 per 437 people

Cancers, heart and cerebrovascular diseases

Most Croats are covered by a health insurance scheme. However, an extra strain on already scarce funds is created by the demands of refugees and disabled war veterans.

SPENDING

GDP/cap. increase

CONSUMPTION AND SPENDING

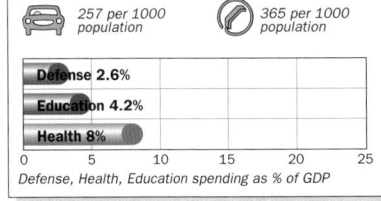

257 per 1000 population

365 per 1000 population

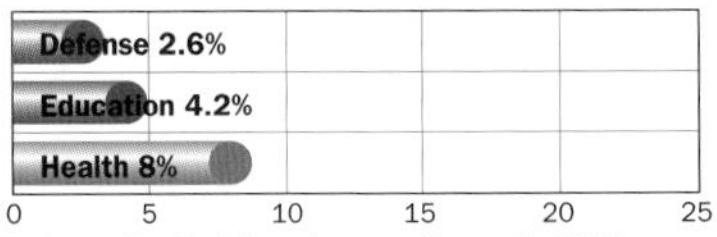

Defense 2.6%
Education 4.2%
Health 8%
0
5
10
15
20
25

Defense, Health, Education spending as % of GDP

Wage rises in the mid-1990s and again in 1999 led to spending booms. Consumers' high expectations were reined in by tighter wage policies.

WORLD RANKING

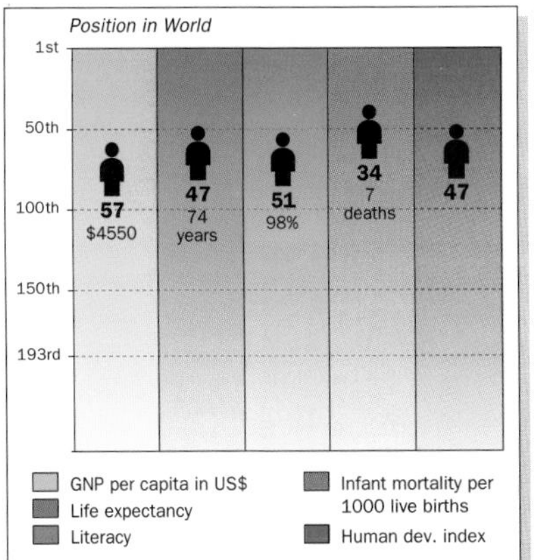

Position in World
1st
50th
100th
150th
193rd
57
$4550
47
74 years
51
98%
34
7 deaths
47
GNP per capita in US$
Life expectancy
Literacy
Infant mortality per 1000 live births
Human dev. index

C

CUBA

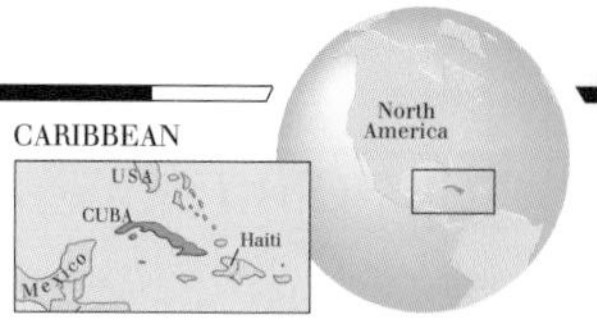
CARIBBEAN
USA
CUBA
Haiti
Mexico
North America

OFFICIAL NAME: Republic of Cuba **CAPITAL:** Havana
POPULATION: 11.3 million **CURRENCY:** Cuban peso **OFFICIAL LANGUAGE:** Spanish

C

1902 | 1902 | Jan 1 | C | -5 | +53 | .cu

THE CARIBBEAN'S LARGEST ISLAND, Cuba has widely cultivated lowlands which fall between three mountainous areas. The fertile soil of the lowlands supports the sugarcane, rice, and coffee plantations. Sugar, the country's major export, suffers from underinvestment, low yields, and fluctuating world prices. A former Spanish colony, Cuba in 1959 became the only communist state in the Americas. In 1962, the deployment of Soviet nuclear missiles on the island shocked the US and brought the two superpowers close to war. Veteran president Fidel Castro is still very much in control, but, since the collapse of the USSR, the US sees Cuba as less of a threat.

Valle de Viñales, Pinar del Río province. Cuba's undulating countryside is ideal for growing the main export crop, sugar.

CLIMATE

Tropical oceanic

WEATHER CHART FOR HAVANA

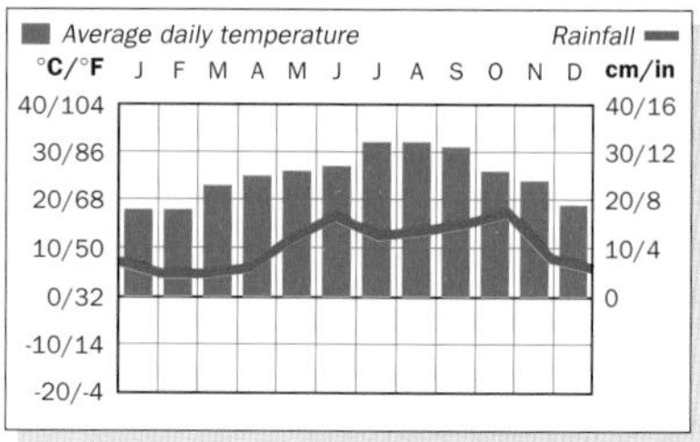
Average daily temperature
Rainfall
°C/°F
J F M A M J J A S O N D
cm/in
40/104
30/86
20/68
10/50
0/32
-10/14
-20/-4
40/16
30/12
20/8
10/4
0

Cuba's subtropical climate is hot all year round and very hot in the summer. Rainfall is heaviest in the mountains, which receive up to 250 cm (98 in) a year. Generally, the north is wetter than the south; the Guantánamo area receives only 20 cm (8 in) of rainfall annually. In winter, the west is affected sometimes by cold air from the US, but only for a day or two at a time.

TRANSPORTATION

Drive on right

José Martí, Havana 2.34m passengers

92 ships 101,000 grt

THE TRANSPORTATION NETWORK

29,820 km (18,529 miles)	638 km (396 miles)
11,969 km (7437 miles)	240 km (149 miles)

Public transportation in Cuba has been extremely cheap, though fuel shortages have made it increasingly erratic and unreliable. Cubans rely mostly on traditional black bicycles, imported by the thousand from China. Havana owes much of its charm to the number of 50-year-old Chevrolets and Oldsmobiles still being driven around. This is another result of sanctions, but keeps the many inventive local spare-parts workshops in business.

TOURISM

Visitors : Population 1:6.7

1.69m visitors

Down 5% in 2002

MAIN TOURIST ARRIVALS

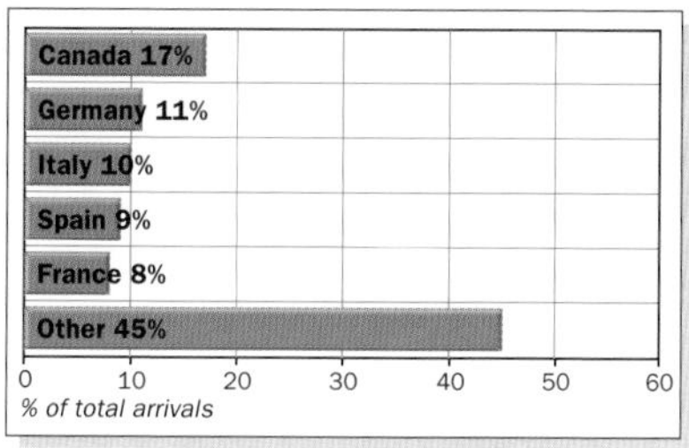
Canada 17%
Germany 11%
Italy 10%
Spain 9%
France 8%
Other 45%
0 10 20 30 40 50 60
% of total arrivals

Tourism began to develop after 1977 (when the US relaxed some travel restrictions), and Cuba is now among the Caribbean's most popular tourist destinations. Tourism has supplanted sugar as the most important motor of the economy and largest generator of foreign exchange. Official estimates are that the annual number of arrivals will exceed five million by 2010. The government seeks to promote family tourism by cracking down on prostitutes who target Havana's main hotels.

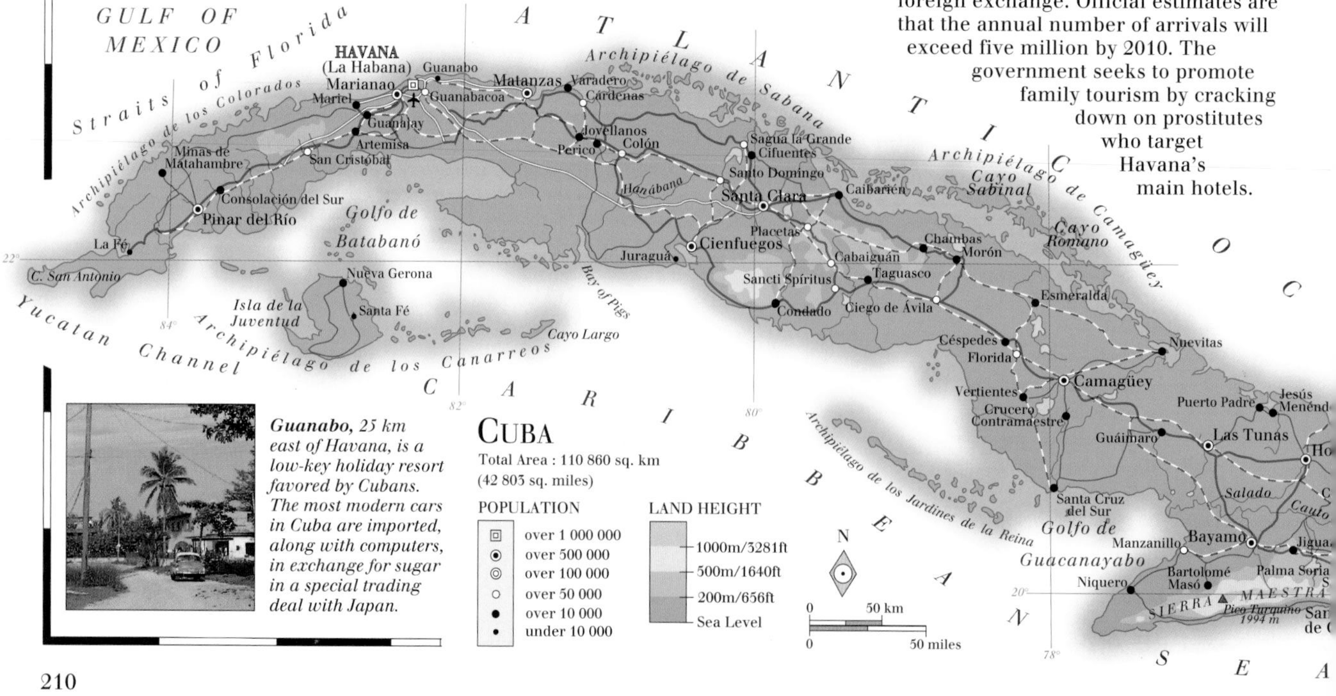
GULF OF MEXICO
Straits of Florida
HAVANA (La Habana)
Guanabo
Marianao
Mariel
Guanabacoa
Matanzas
Varadero
Cárdenas
Archipiélago de Sabana
Archipiélago de los Colorados
Guanajay
Artemisa
Minas de Matahambre
San Cristóbal
Consolación del Sur
Pinar del Río
La Fé
C. San Antonio
Golfo de Batabanó
Nueva Gerona
Isla de la Juventud
Santa Fé
Yucatan Channel
Archipiélago de los Canarreos
Cayo Largo
Jovellanos
Colón
Perico
Hanábana
Sagua la Grande
Cifuentes
Santo Domingo
Santa Clara
Caibarién
Placetas
Cienfuegos
Jaguará
Bay of Pigs
Cabaiguán
Sancti Spíritus
Taguasco
Condado
Ciego de Ávila
Chambas
Morón
Archipiélago Cayo Sabinal
Cayo Romano
Archipiélago de Camagüey
Esmeralda
Nuevitas
Céspedes
Florida
Camagüey
Vertientes
Crucero Contramaestre
Guáimaro
Las Tunas
Puerto Padre
Jesús Menéndez
Santa Cruz del Sur
Golfo de Guacanayabo
Archipiélago de los Jardines de la Reina
Manzanillo
Bayamo
Bartolomé Masó
Niquero
Palma Soriano
Salado
Cauto
Jiguaní
SIERRA MAESTRA
Pico Turquino 1994 m
ATLANTIC OCEAN
CARIBBEAN SEA
CUBA
Total Area : 110 860 sq. km (42 803 sq. miles)
POPULATION
over 1 000 000
over 500 000
over 100 000
over 50 000
over 10 000
under 10 000
LAND HEIGHT
1000m/3281ft
500m/1640ft
200m/656ft
Sea Level
N
0 50 km
0 50 miles

Guanabo, 25 km east of Havana, is a low-key holiday resort favored by Cubans. The most modern cars in Cuba are imported, along with computers, in exchange for sugar in a special trading deal with Japan.

PEOPLE

Pop. density medium

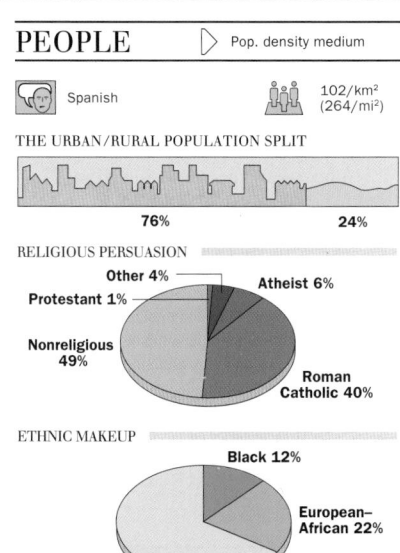

Spanish

102/km² (264/mi²)

THE URBAN/RURAL POPULATION SPLIT

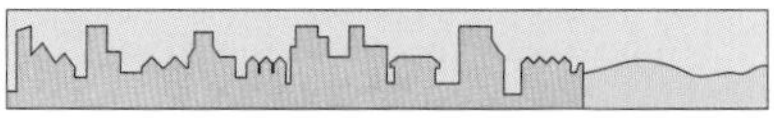
76%
24%

RELIGIOUS PERSUASION

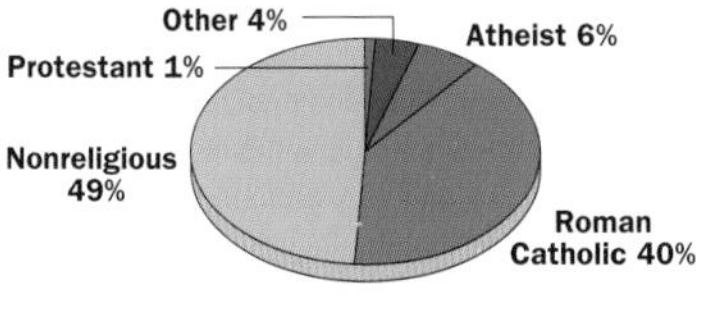
Other 4%
Atheist 6%
Protestant 1%
Nonreligious 49%
Roman Catholic 40%

ETHNIC MAKEUP

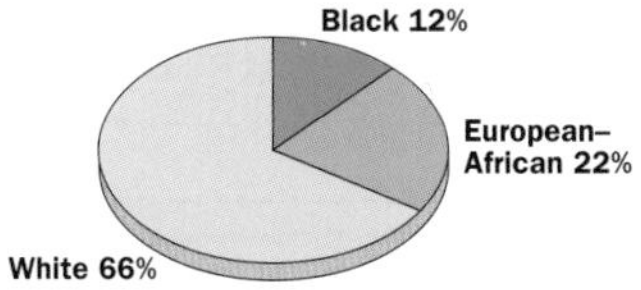
Black 12%
European–African 22%
White 66%

Ethnic tension in Cuba is minimal. About 70% of Cubans are of Spanish descent, mainly from the settlers, but also from the more recent influx of exiles from Franco's Spain. The black population is descended from the slaves and from migrants from neighboring states, in particular Jamaica.

Living standards in Cuba fell dramatically in the early 1990s after the collapse of the east European communist bloc, previously its main trading partner, and rationing for most basic foodstuffs was subsequently introduced. The "dollarization" of the economy in recent years has led to great divisions between those who survive on pesos and the more than 50% of the population who have access to dollars. Since the early 1990s the number of those trying to leave, legally or otherwise, has risen markedly.

An increasing number of women are playing a prominent role in politics, the professions, and the armed forces. Child-care facilities are widespread.

POPULATION AGE BREAKDOWN

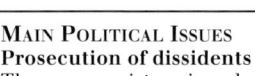

Female
Age
Male
0.5%
80+
0.4%
5.9%
60–79
5.7%
11.1%
40–59
10.9%
18%
20–39
18.2%
14.3%
0–19
15%
% of population by age group

WORLD AFFAIRS

Joined UN in 1945

ACP | IAEA | SELA | NAM | ACS

Since the 1959 revolution, and particularly after the 1962 stand-off over Soviet missiles, the US has considered Cuba a danger. The US trade blockade, first imposed in 1961, has left Cuba economically isolated despite regular votes in the UN condemning sanctions. The end of Soviet aid in the 1990s was another serious blow to Castro's embattled regime, but it has forced Cuba to soften its anti-Western stance in the search for alternative aid. Partly as a result, the US embargo has been progressively loosened since 1999 and now allows for more flights, direct mail, essential medicines, and more food imports.

Ties to Russia have been diluted further but relations with the US remain fraught, despite the arrival in 2001 of the first direct trade between the two countries' governments, in the form of emergency aid. In 2002 the US included Cuba in its "axis of evil" terrorist-sponsoring states and relations with the US and Europe were seriously dented in 2003 over the treatment of dissidents.

POLITICS

No multiparty elections

2003/2008

President Fidel Castro Ruz

AT THE LAST ELECTION

National Assembly of the People's Power 609 seats

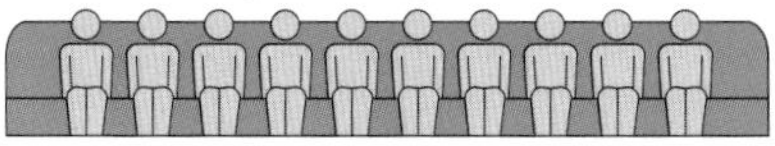
100%
PCC

PCC = Cuban Communist Party

Fidel Castro has led Cuba since 1959. The country's one-party communist system, set out in the 1976 constitution, was designated "untouchable" in 2002.

PROFILE

The 1959 popular revolution, led by Castro, toppled the corrupt Batista dictatorship and launched a far-reaching program of social, economic, and political reforms.

In the 1990s the revolution seemed under siege in the wake of the collapse of the Soviet Union and tightened trade sanctions by the US. Supporters continue to see Cuba as living proof of the triumph of socialist development over adversity, but critics offer the view that the Castro administration is an intolerant dictatorship.

N
Moa
Baracoa
El Salvador
Guantánamo
GUANTÁNAMO BAY (to US)
Windward Passage

MAIN POLITICAL ISSUES

Prosecution of dissidents

The communist regime does not tolerate dissent. The most recent crackdown on prodemocracy activists – the arrest and summary trial of 75 people in 2003 – attracted considerable international criticism. The US and the EU reacted by hardening diplomatic sanctions.

The succession

The aging Castro remains firmly in place, and debate about his successor is somewhat muted. While some predict that a younger, collective, and reform-minded leadership would normalize relations with the US and steer Cuba toward democracy, others warn of a period of unrest as reformers and communist hard-liners compete to fill the likely power vacuum.

Raúl Castro, *brother of Fidel and the minister of defense.*

Fidel Castro, *Cuba's charismatic communist leader since 1959.*

AID

Recipient

$51m (receipts)

Up 16% in 2001

Spain, France, and UNICEF have given aid, and China loaned $400 million in 2001. A cash purchase of food and supplies from the US was made after Hurricane Michelle in late 2001.

CHRONOLOGY

Originally inhabited by the Arawak people, Cuba was claimed for Spain by Columbus in 1492. Development of the sugar industry from the 18th century, using imported slave labor, made Cuba the world's third-largest producer by 1860.

- **1868** End of the slave trade.
- **1868–1878** Ten Years' War for independence from Spain.
- **1895** Second war of independence. Thousands die in Spanish concentration camps.
- **1898** In support of Cuban rebels US declares war on Spain to protect strong American financial interests in Cuba.
- **1899** US takes Cuba and installs military interim government.
- **1901** US is granted intervention rights and military bases, including Guantánamo Bay naval base.

C

CHRONOLOGY *continued*

- **1902** Tomás Estrada Palma takes over as first Cuban president. US leaves Cuba, but intervenes in 1906–1909 and 1919–1924.
- **1909** Liberal presidency of José Miguel Goméz. Economy prospers; US investment in tourism, gambling, and sugar.
- **1925–1933** Dictatorship of President Gerardo Machado.
- **1933** Years of guerrilla activity end in revolution. Sgt. Fulgencio Batista takes over; military dictatorship.
- **1955** Fidel Castro exiled after two years' imprisonment for subversion.
- **1956–1958** Castro returns to lead a guerrilla war in the Sierra Maestra.
- **1959** Batista flees. Castro takes over. Wholesale nationalizations; Cuba reorganized on Soviet model.
- **1960** US breaks off relations.
- **1961** US-backed invasion of Bay of Pigs by anti-Castro Cubans fails. Cuba declares itself Marxist-Leninist. US economic and political blockade.
- **1962** Missile crisis: Soviet deployment of nuclear weapons in Cuba leads to extreme Soviet–US tension; war averted by Khrushchev ordering withdrawal of weapons.
- **1965** One-party state formalized.
- **1972** Cuba joins COMECON (communist economic bloc).
- **1976** New socialist constitution. Cuban troops in Angola until 1991.
- **1977** Sends troops to Ethiopia.
- **1980** 125,000 Cubans, including "undesirables," flee to US.
- **1982** US tightens sanctions and bans flights and tourism to Cuba.
- **1983** US invasion of Grenada. Cuba involved in clashes with US forces.
- **1984** Agreement with US on Cuban emigration and repatriation of "undesirables" is short-lived.
- **1988** UN's second veto of US attempt to accuse Cuba of human rights violations. Diplomatic relations established with EC.
- **1989** Senior military executed for arms and narcotics smuggling.
- **1991** Preferential trade agreement with USSR ends. Severe rationing.
- **1992–1993** US tightens blockade. All former Soviet military leave.
- **1994–1995** Economic reforms to boost foreign trade and investment.
- **1996** US Helms-Burton Act tightens sanctions.
- **1998** Visit of Pope John Paul II.
- **1999** Leading moderate dissidents put on trial.
- **2001** Devastation by Hurricane Michelle.
- **2002** Guantánamo Bay used as high-security prison for captives from US "war on terrorism."
- **2003** Major crackdown on dissidents.

DEFENSE

▷ Compulsory military service

$735m

Down 2% in 2001

CUBAN ARMED FORCES

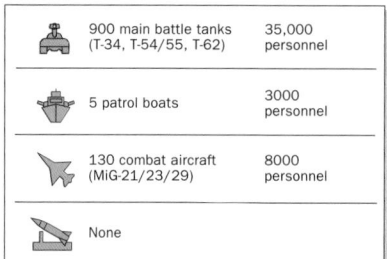

Tanks	900 main battle tanks (T-34, T-54/55, T-62)	35,000 personnel
Ships	5 patrol boats	3000 personnel
Aircraft	130 combat aircraft (MiG-21/23/29)	8000 personnel
Missiles	None	

From 1959 to the 1980s, Cuba's efficient military, well represented in the Council of Ministers and the Politburo, was one of the achievements of the revolution. Under Castro's brother Raúl, it succeeded in repelling the US-sponsored Bay of Pigs invasion in 1961, and saw effective action in Africa in the 1970s, preventing South Africa from taking control of Angola, and Somalia from occupying the Ogaden region in Ethiopia.

Today, communist regimes having collapsed around the world, the army has lost much of its prestige. Russia is still the main source of arms.

A siege mentality associated with the US economic embargo keeps the military on the alert for perceived internal and external threats.

ECONOMICS

▷ Inflation 1.1% p.a. (1990–1999)

$18bn

21 Cuban pesos (21)

SCORE CARD

❑ World GNP Ranking	69th
❑ GNP per Capita	$1600
❑ Balance of Payments	In deficit
❑ Inflation	0.5%
❑ Unemployment	6%

EXPORTS

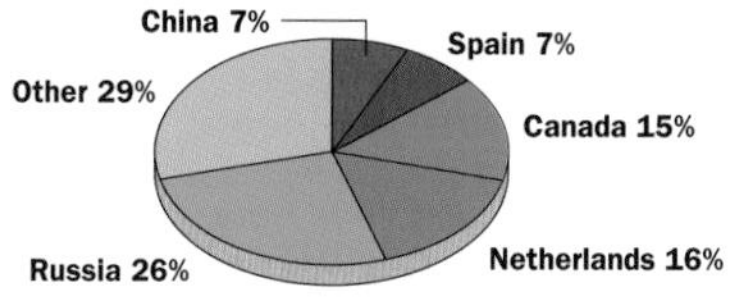
China 7%
Spain 7%
Other 29%
Canada 15%
Netherlands 16%
Russia 26%

IMPORTS

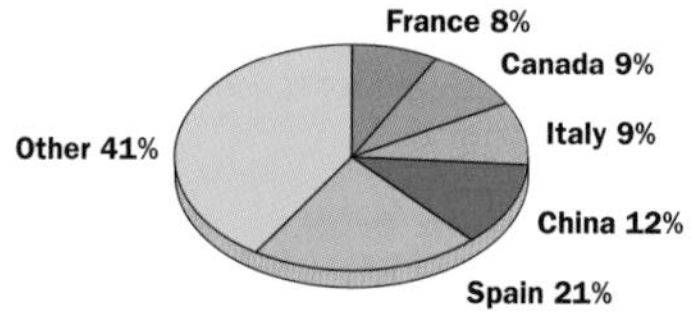
France 8%
Canada 9%
Other 41%
Italy 9%
China 12%
Spain 21%

Strengths

Tourism remains major growth sector, though ambitious targets are not being met. Nickel and cigars. Strengthening banking sector.

Weaknesses

Denied major market and investment capital by US trade embargo. Acute shortage of hard currency. Vulnerability of nickel to world price fluctuations. Collapse of sugar industry. Difficult terms of trade and weak legal framework deter investment. Infrastructure is deficient. Shortages of fuel, fertilizers, spare parts, and other inputs. Severe hurricane damage in 2001.

Profile

The collapse of the USSR meant the loss of some $5 billion in annual aid and led to a deep recession. A cautious adoption of some capitalist-style reforms in the mid-1990s, including the free use of the US dollar, stimulated the growth of a dollarized sector centered on tourism, which has attracted strong foreign investment. Tourism now dominates the economy, and benefits some 160,000 self-employed and small businesses. However, the once important sugar industry has collapsed, with the loss of around 100,000 jobs in recent years. Foreign companies are involved in joint ventures in banking and the oil and gas sectors. There is a very large informal sector. The government lost a significant source of revenue in 2001, when Russia terminated the lease of its information-gathering center.

ECONOMIC PERFORMANCE INDICATOR

Consumer Price Index
GDP
Consumer price index unavailable
GDP 1994=100
160
140
120
100
80
1994
1995
1996
1997
1998

CUBA : MAJOR BUSINESSES

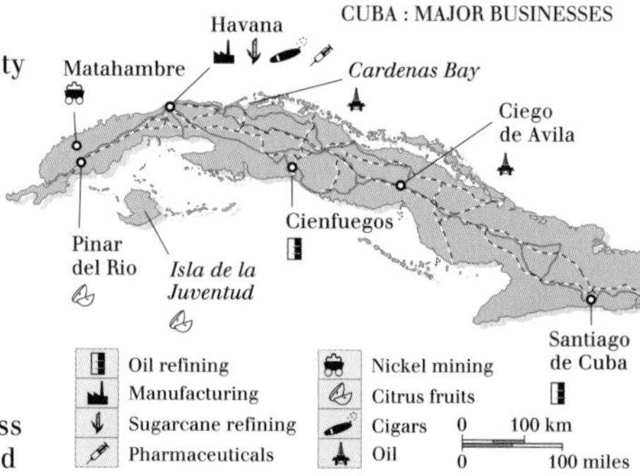
Havana
Matahambre
Cardenas Bay
Ciego de Avila
Cienfuegos
Pinar del Rio
Isla de la Juventud
Santiago de Cuba
Oil refining
Manufacturing
Sugarcane refining
Pharmaceuticals
Nickel mining
Citrus fruits
Cigars
Oil
0
100 km
0
100 miles

RESOURCES

Electric power 4.3m kW

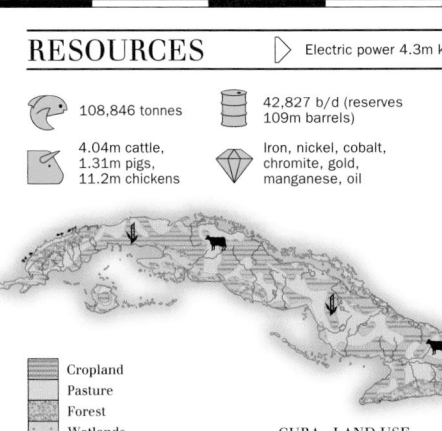

108,846 tonnes

42,827 b/d (reserves 109m barrels)

4.04m cattle, 1.31m pigs, 11.2m chickens

Iron, nickel, cobalt, chromite, gold, manganese, oil

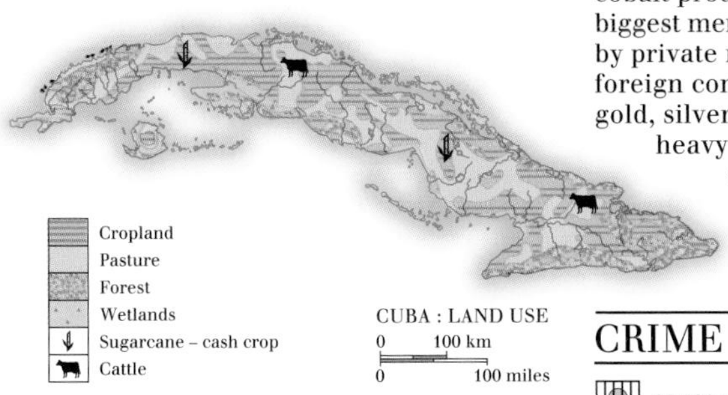
Cropland
Pasture
Forest
Wetlands
Sugarcane – cash crop
Cattle
CUBA : LAND USE
0 100 km
0 100 miles

The collapse of the USSR precipitated a steep decline in demand for sugar; production hit a 50-year low in 1998.

Cuba seeks to expand nickel and cobalt production, traditionally its biggest merchandise exports, assisted by private mining ventures. Several foreign companies are prospecting for gold, silver, and other metals, and for heavy crude oil and gas, through concessions. Work at Juraguá on a Russian-built nuclear reactor was abandoned in December 2000.

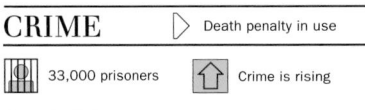

ELECTRICITY GENERATION

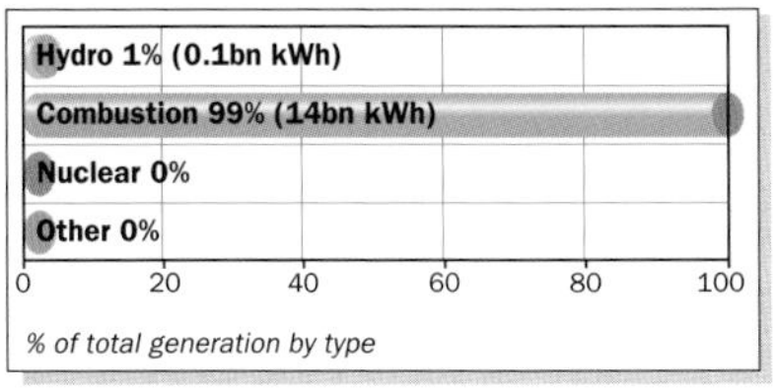
Hydro 1% (0.1bn kWh)
Combustion 99% (14bn kWh)
Nuclear 0%
Other 0%
0
20
40
60
80
100
% of total generation by type

ENVIRONMENT

Sustainability rank: 58th

17% (15% partially protected)

2.3 tonnes per capita

ENVIRONMENTAL TREATIES

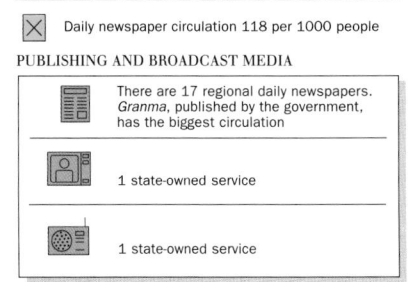

Yes Yes Yes

Yes Yes Yes

At the time of the revolution in 1959, only 14% of the country's forest cover remained, but a strong drive to replant has raised the tree cover level to over 20%. The intensive use of irrigation without adequate drainage has caused salinization and waterlogging. There is regional concern about the never-completed nuclear reactor at Juraguá.

MEDIA

TV ownership high

Daily newspaper circulation 118 per 1000 people

PUBLISHING AND BROADCAST MEDIA

There are 17 regional daily newspapers. *Granma*, published by the government, has the biggest circulation

1 state-owned service

1 state-owned service

A catch-all anticrime law restricts and penalizes investigative reporting by independent journalists which is judged to be assisting the US foreign policy against Cuba.

CRIME

Death penalty in use

33,000 prisoners

Crime is rising

CRIME RATES

Cuba does not publish official statistics for murders, rapes, or thefts

Violent crime is officially viewed as a threat to national stability. In 1999 the death penalty was extended to certain narcotics offenses, robbery involving firearms, attacks on security officers, and sexual corruption of minors. In the biggest crackdown in a decade, 75 prodemocracy activists were arrested in March 2003 and summarily tried. Shortly afterward a de facto three-year moratorium on executions was ended by the execution of three ferry hijackers.

EDUCATION

School leaving age: 14

97%

173,904 students

THE EDUCATION SYSTEM

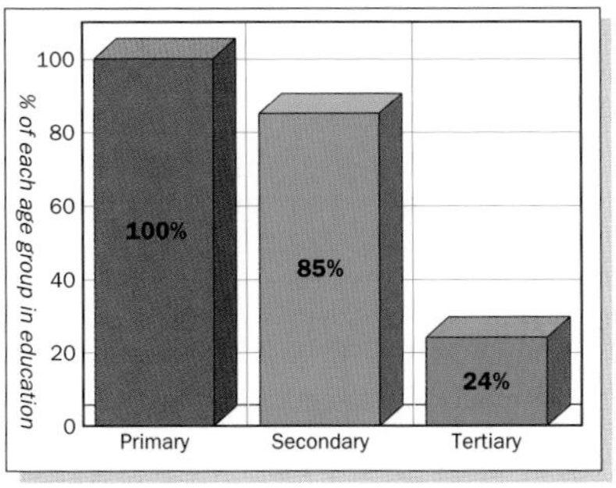
100
80
60
40
20
0
% of each age group in education
100%
85%
24%
Primary
Secondary
Tertiary

Education, which is universal and free at all levels, combines academic with manual work, in line with Marxist-Leninist principles. The importance given to education under Castro, which is reflected in the high literacy rate, is now being promoted to attract foreign investment in high-tech industries, particularly biotechnology. There are three large universities and more than 40 smaller tertiary institutions.

HEALTH

Welfare state health benefits

1 per 169 people

Cancers, heart and cerebrovascular diseases, pneumonia

Average life expectancy in Cuba is among the highest in Latin America, which is a reflection of its efficient, countrywide health service. The US trade embargo has led to shortages of hospital equipment and of raw materials for drugs, normally supplied by Havana's sizable pharmaceuticals industry. Cuba's advanced surgery techniques attract patients from overseas. The government's AIDS program has helped keep mortality of sufferers low and curtailed the spread of infection.

SPENDING

GDP/cap. increase

CONSUMPTION AND SPENDING

16 per 1000 population

51 per 1000 population

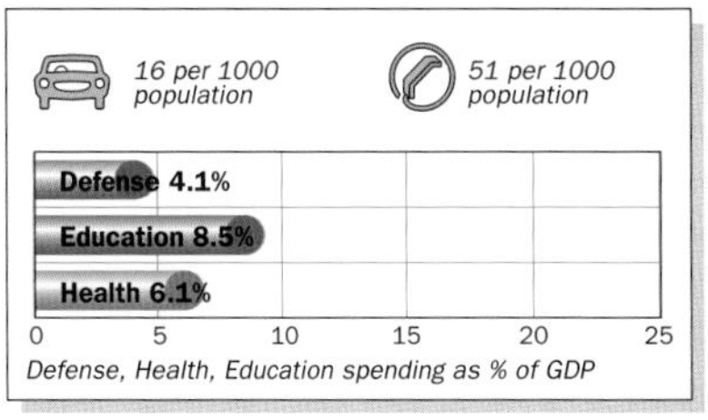
Defense 4.1%
Education 8.5%
Health 6.1%
0
5
10
15
20
25
Defense, Health, Education spending as % of GDP

Under Batista there were huge wealth disparities, and Cuba was a playground for the rich. The 1959 revolution succeeded in reducing the disparities, partly by taking over all businesses, from oil companies to barbershops, and partly by prescribing not only minimum but also maximum wages. Economic regulations have varied since then; for a brief period in 1985, different wage rates were allowed in an attempt to provide incentives for those who work hard, but this decision was reversed in 1986. Economic liberalization in the mid-1990s has created a large gulf between that half of the population with access to US dollars and those left in the peso economy who have to subsist on lower salaries.

WORLD RANKING

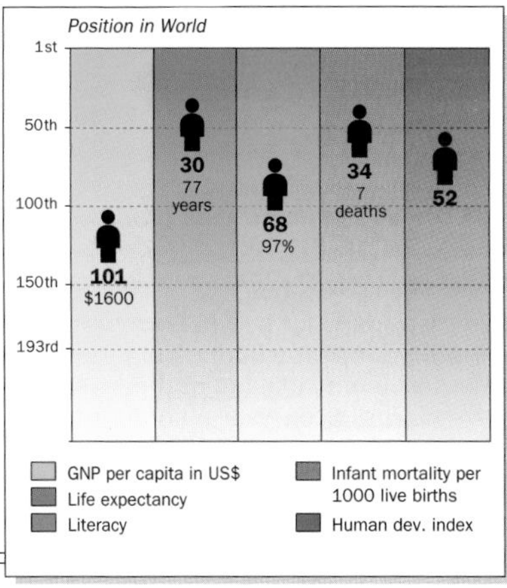
Position in World
1st
50th
100th
150th
193rd
101
$1600
30
77 years
68
97%
34
7 deaths
52
GNP per capita in US$
Life expectancy
Literacy
Infant mortality per 1000 live births
Human dev. index

CYPRUS

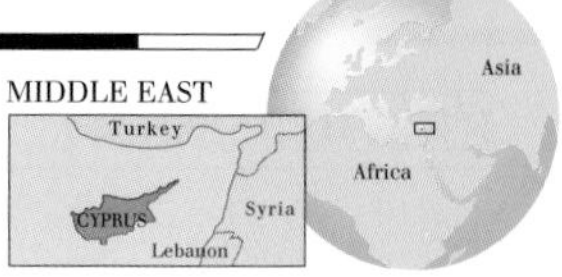
MIDDLE EAST
Turkey
CYPRUS
Syria
Lebanon
Asia
Africa

OFFICIAL NAME: Republic of Cyprus **CAPITAL:** Nicosia **POPULATION:** 797,000
CURRENCY: Cyprus pound (Turkish lira in TRNC) **OFFICIAL LANGUAGES:** Greek and Turkish

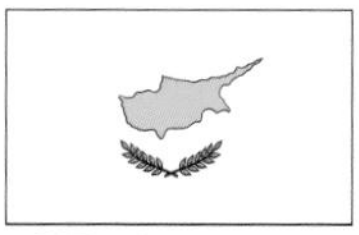

1960 | 1960 | Oct 1 | CY | +2 | +357 | .cy

THE ISLAND OF Cyprus, which rises from a central plateau to a high point at Mount Olympus, lies south of Turkey in the eastern Mediterranean. It was partitioned in 1974, following an invasion by Turkish troops. The south of the island is the Greek Cypriot Republic of Cyprus (Cyprus); the self-proclaimed Turkish Republic of Northern Cyprus (TRNC) is recognized only by Turkey.

CLIMATE

Mediterranean

WEATHER CHART FOR NICOSIA

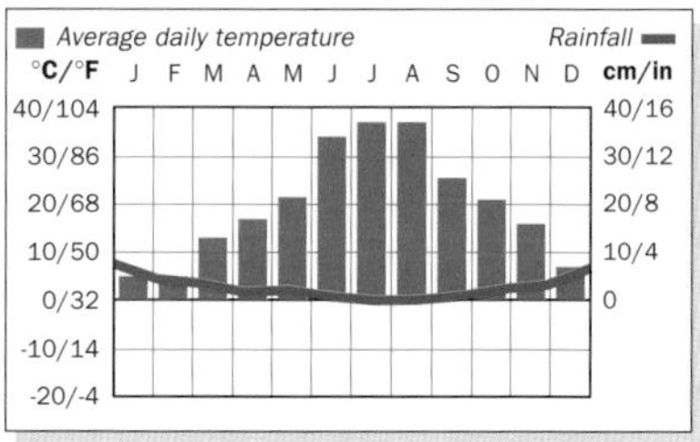
Average daily temperature
Rainfall
°C/°F J F M A M J J A S O N D cm/in
40/104
30/86
20/68
10/50
0/32
-10/14
-20/-4
40/16
30/12
20/8
10/4
0

The climate is typically Mediterranean: summers are hot and dry, and winters mild, though there is mountain snow.

TRANSPORTATION

Drive on left

Larnaca 4.96m passengers

1407 ships 22.8m grt

THE TRANSPORTATION NETWORK

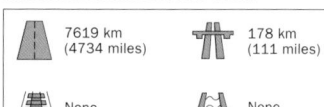

7619 km (4734 miles)

178 km (111 miles)

None

None

Cyprus views flights to the TRNC as illegal. People were allowed to cross the Green Line for the first time in 2003.

TOURISM

Visitors : Population 3:1

2.42m visitors

Down 10% in 2002

MAIN TOURIST ARRIVALS

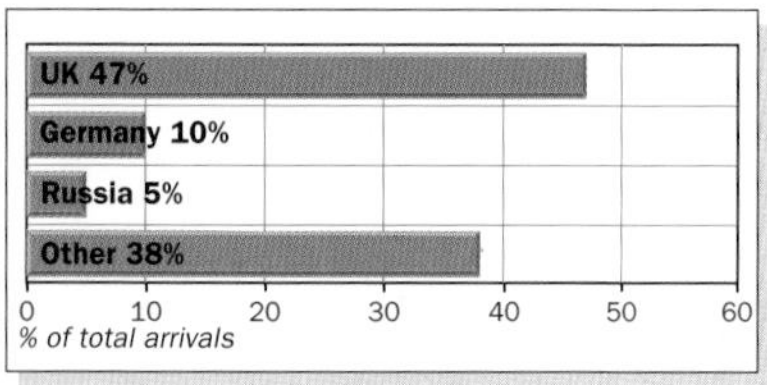
UK 47%
Germany 10%
Russia 5%
Other 38%
0 10 20 30 40 50 60
% of total arrivals

Tourists come for beaches, archaeology, or the abundant wildlife, notably on the Akamas peninsula and in the Troodos Mountains. A ten-year plan aims to double the number of visitors by 2010. The industry showed signs of a quick recovery following a slump in 2002.

PEOPLE

Pop. density medium

Greek, Turkish

86/km² (223/mi²)

THE URBAN/RURAL POPULATION SPLIT

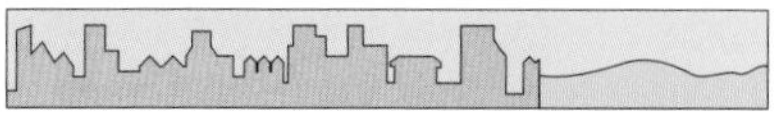
70%
30%

ETHNIC MAKEUP

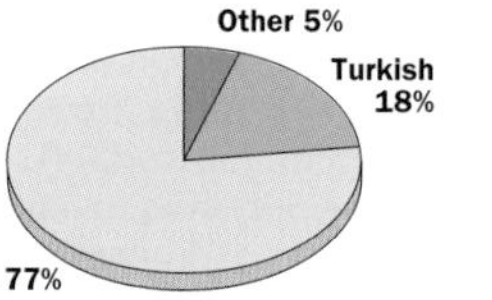
Other 5%
Turkish 18%
Greek 77%

Cyprus's Greek majority are Orthodox Christian. The Turkish minority are Muslim. They first arrived on the island as settlers in the 16th century, under the rule of the Ottoman Empire. Both Cypriot communities have suffered great upheavals: in 1974 the island was partitioned along what became the Green Line and 200,000 Greek Cypriots were forced to flee to the south, while 65,000 Turkish Cypriots fled in the other direction. Northern Cyprus is officially recognized as an independent entity only by Turkey. Over 100,000 mainland Turks have settled there and now outnumber indigenous Turkish Cypriots.

Contract labor, mainly from eastern Europe, is brought in to staff hotels in the south, where wage levels are at least three times higher than in the north. Unemployment levels in the north, meanwhile, are rising.

***The 2nd-century theater** at Curium, 14 km (19 miles) west of Limassol. Curium was the site of a flourishing Mycenaean colony before 1100 BCE.*

POLITICS

Multiparty elections

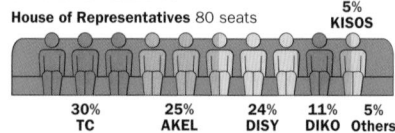

Cyprus 2001/2006
TRNC 1998/2003

President Tassos Papadopoulos (Cyprus)
President Rauf Denktash (TRNC)

AT THE LAST ELECTION

House of Representatives 80 seats

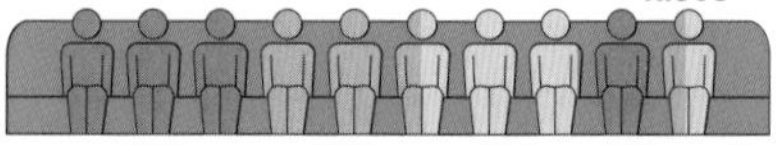
5% KISOS
30% TC
25% AKEL
24% DISY
11% DIKO
5% Others

TC = Reserved for Turkish Cypriots **AKEL** = Progressive Party of the Working People **DISY** = Democratic Rally **DIKO** = Democratic Party **KISOS** = Movement of Social Democrats

The 24 seats reserved for Turkish Cypriots have not been occupied since December 1963

Assembly (TRNC) 50 seats

48% UBP
26% DP
14% TKP
12% CTP

UBP = National Unity Party **DP** = Democrat Party
TKP = Social Welfare Party **CTP** = Republican Turkish Party

The UN-backed proposal for Cyprus would give each community its own territory while sharing a number of government functions. TRNC president Rauf Denktash, mindful of the Greek Cypriots' repression of the Turks prior to 1974 and backed by Turkey's military, is unwilling to accept a plan that does not ensure full sovereignty for Turks. Greek Cypriots, in turn, fear the plan would give too much influence over their affairs to the small Turkish minority. Such concerns led to the election of relative hard-liner Tassos Papadopoulos as president in 2003. A UN deadline for agreement was missed in 2003 despite the imminence of EU membership for Cyprus in 2004.

WORLD AFFAIRS

Joined UN in 1960

CE | Comm | IBRD | NAM | OSCE

Over 1000 UN troops staff the Green Line. Only Turkey recognizes the TRNC. The opening of the internal border in 2003 saw large numbers of people cross in both directions, but resolution of the basic dispute is unlikely before Cyprus joins the EU in 2004, in which case the TRNC will be excluded.

AID

Recipient

$50m (receipts)

Down 7% in 2001

Cyprus receives aid from international agencies, the EU, and individual countries such as the UK. The TRNC is dependent on aid from Turkey, which plans to give $500 million in 2003–2006.

CYPRUS

Total Area :
9250 sq. km
(3571 sq. miles)

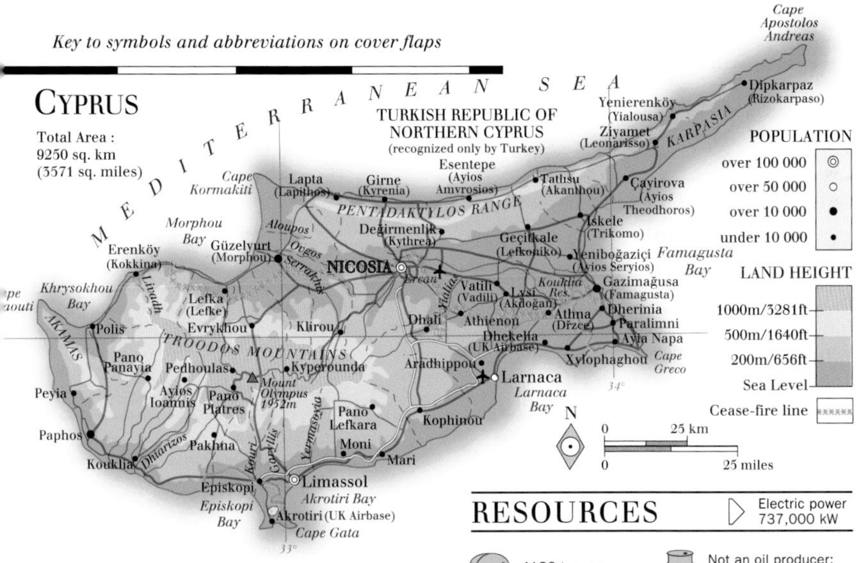
MEDITERRANEAN SEA
TURKISH REPUBLIC OF NORTHERN CYPRUS
(recognized only by Turkey)
Cape Apostolos Andreas
Dipkarpaz (Rizokarpaso)
Yenierenköy (Yialousa)
Ziyamet (Leonarisso)
KARPASIA
Esentepe (Ayios Amvrosios)
Tatlısu (Akanthou)
Cape Kormakiti
Lapta (Lapithos)
Girne (Kyrenia)
PENTADAKTYLOS RANGE
Çayirova (Ayios Theodhoros)
Iskele (Trikomo)
Morphou Bay
Erenköy (Kokkina)
Güzelyurt (Morphou)
Değirmenlik (Kythrea)
Geçitkale (Lefkoniko)
Yeniboğaziçi (Ayios Seryios)
Famagusta Bay
NICOSIA
Vatili (Vadili)
Lysi (Akdogan)
Gazimağusa (Famagusta)
Khrysokhou Bay
Lefka (Lefke)
Evrykhou
Klirou
Dhali
Athienou
Athna (Dirze)
Dherinia
Paralimni
Dhekelia (UK Airbase)
Ayia Napa
AKAMAS
Polis
TROODOS MOUNTAINS
Pano Panayia
Pedhoulas
Kyperounda
Aradhippou
Xylophaghou
Cape Greco
Larnaca
Larnaca Bay
Peyia
Ayios Ioannis
Pano Platres
Mount Olympus 1952m
Pano Lefkara
Kophinou
Paphos
Pakhna
Moni
Mari
Koukla
Limassol
Episkopi
Episkopi Bay
Akrotiri Bay
Akrotiri (UK Airbase)
Cape Gata
POPULATION
over 100 000
over 50 000
over 10 000
under 10 000
LAND HEIGHT
1000m/3281ft
500m/1640ft
200m/656ft
Sea Level
Cease-fire line
0 25 km
0 25 miles

CHRONOLOGY

Cyprus was dominated, in turn, by Egypt, Greece, the Byzantines, the Ottomans, and the UK, before independence in 1960.

- ❑ **1974** President Makarios deposed by Greek military junta. Turkey invades. Partition.
- ❑ **1983** Self-proclamation of TRNC.
- ❑ **1993** Glafcos Clerides president.
- ❑ **2002** EU approves membership for 2004.
- ❑ **2003** Tassos Papadopoulos elected president. Green Line opened.

C

DEFENSE

Compulsory military service

$315m — Down 13% in 2001

In addition to two sovereign British bases and UN forces, there are 36,000 Turkish troops in northern Cyprus and 1250 Greek troops in the buffer zone. The 10,000-strong Greek Cypriot army and the 5000-strong Turkish Cypriot army both rely heavily on conscripts.

ECONOMICS

Inflation 3.4% p.a. (1990–2001)

$9.37bn — 0.5101 Cyprus pounds (0.5865)

SCORE CARD

❑ World GNP Ranking	89th
❑ GNP per Capita	$12,320
❑ Balance of Payments	–$456m
❑ Inflation	2%
❑ Unemployment	4%

Strengths

Large tourism industry, accounting for over 20% of GDP. Manufacturing sector and provision of services to Middle Eastern countries. Integration with EU.

Weaknesses

Pressure for tighter supervision of offshore finance and crackdown on tax evasion. Slow pace of liberalization. TRNC starved of foreign investment.

EXPORTS

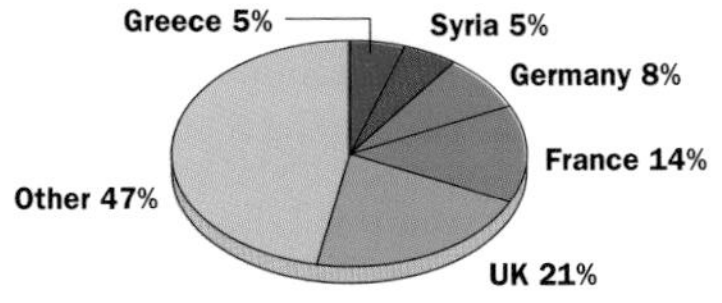
Greece 5%
Syria 5%
Germany 8%
France 14%
UK 21%
Other 47%

IMPORTS

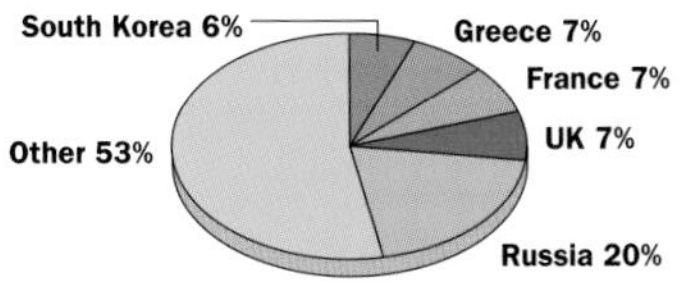
South Korea 6%
Greece 7%
France 7%
UK 7%
Russia 20%
Other 53%

RESOURCES

Electric power 737,000 kW

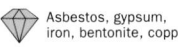

- 4186 tonnes
- Not an oil producer; refines 23,700 b/d
- 450,977 pigs, 447,100 goats, 3.4m chickens
- Asbestos, gypsum, iron, bentonite, copper

Cyprus continues to supply electricity to the TRNC; bills are unpaid. The possibility of offshore oil and gas to the south has attracted interest. Water is precious; desalinization plants and new reservoirs have boosted supplies.

ENVIRONMENT

Not available

- 8% (7% partially protected)
- 7.8 tonnes per capita

Campaigners demand that the 155 sq. km (60 sq. miles) of the Akamas peninsula be fully protected from the threat of being sold for tourist development. Akamas is home to an unusual variety of plant and bird life, and contains breeding sites of the rare green turtle.

MEDIA

TV ownership high

Daily newspaper circulation 111 per 1000 people

PUBLISHING AND BROADCAST MEDIA

There are 9 daily newspapers. *Phileleftheros* has the largest circulation; others include *Haravgi*, *Simerini*, and *Alithia*

6 services: 1 state-controlled, 5 independent

5 services: 1 state-controlled, 4 independent

The media in Cyprus are lively and tend to be highly politicized. In the TRNC, independent papers have faced harassment from the authorities.

CRIME

No death penalty

369 prisoners — Down 12% in 1999–2000

Crime rates are low and violence is rare. The unruly and sometimes violent behavior of foreign forces has on occasions led Cypriots to object to their presence. The arrest of a Cypriot politician during protests at a UK military base in 2001 provoked riots.

EDUCATION

School leaving age: 15

97% — 11,934 students

Education is free and compulsory to age 15 in the south and 14 in the north. Many Cypriots go abroad to university.

HEALTH

Welfare state health benefits

1 per 372 people — Heart diseases, accidents, cancers

Health care is more advanced in the south; sophisticated surgery is carried out at Lefkosia General Hospital.

SPENDING

GDP/cap. increase

CONSUMPTION AND SPENDING

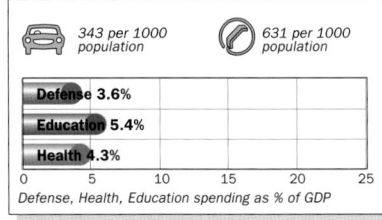

343 per 1000 population — 631 per 1000 population

Defense 3.6%
Education 5.4%
Health 4.3%
0
5
10
15
20
25

Defense, Health, Education spending as % of GDP

Average per capita income in the south is greater than in Greece or Portugal, and over three times higher than in the Turkish Cypriot north.

WORLD RANKING

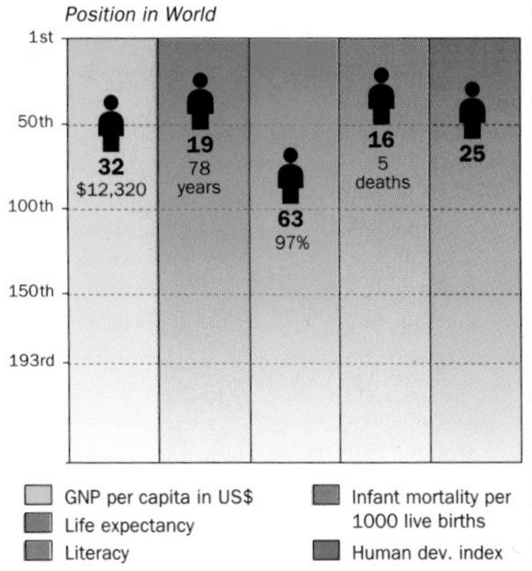
Position in World
1st
50th
100th
150th
193rd
32
$12,320
19
78 years
63
97%
16
5 deaths
25
GNP per capita in US$
Life expectancy
Literacy
Infant mortality per 1000 live births
Human dev. index

Czech Republic

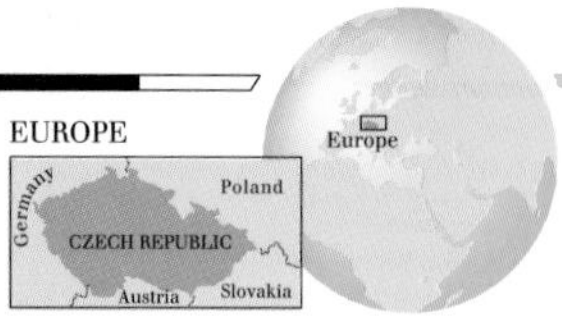
EUROPE
Europe
Germany
Poland
CZECH REPUBLIC
Austria
Slovakia

Official Name: Czech Republic **Capital:** Prague
Population: 10.3 million **Currency:** Czech koruna **Official Language:** Czech

C

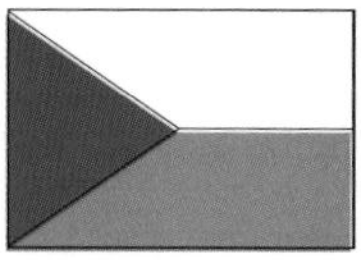

1993 | 1993 | Oct 28 | CZ | +1 | +420 | .cz

LANDLOCKED IN CENTRAL Europe, the Czech Republic comprises the territories of Bohemia and Moravia, and for most of the 20th century it was part of Czechoslovakia. In 1989, the "Velvet Revolution" ended four decades of communist rule, and free elections followed in 1990. In 1993 the Czech Republic and Slovakia peacefully dissolved their federal union to become two independent states.

CLIMATE

Continental

WEATHER CHART FOR PRAGUE

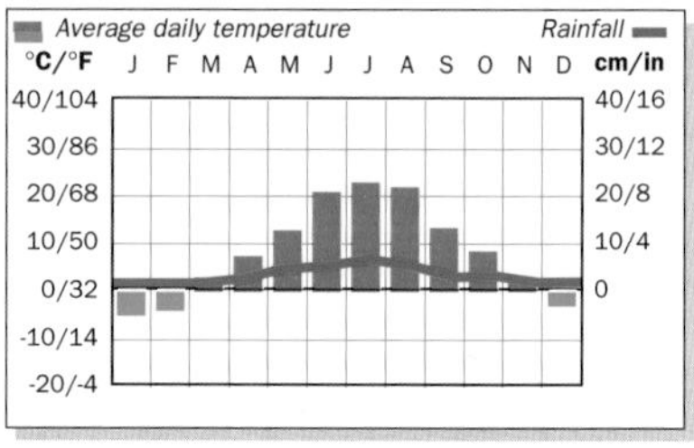
Average daily temperature
Rainfall
°C/°F
J F M A M J J A S O N D
cm/in
40/104
30/86
20/68
10/50
0/32
-10/14
-20/-4
40/16
30/12
20/8
10/4
0

The Czech climate is more moderate than that of Slovakia, though easterly winds bring low temperatures in winter.

TRANSPORTATION

Drive on right

Ruzyné, Prague 6.31m passengers

Has no fleet

THE TRANSPORTATION NETWORK

55,432 km (34,444 miles)	501 km (311 miles)
9365 km (5819 miles)	303 km (188 miles)

There are new expressways and rail links to Germany. Prague is a busy regional center for passenger air traffic.

TOURISM

Visitors : Population 1:2.2

4.58m visitors

Down 12% in 2002

MAIN TOURIST ARRIVALS

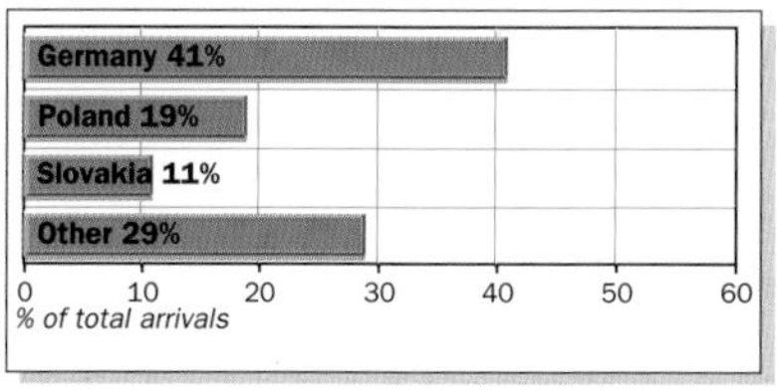
Germany 41%
Poland 19%
Slovakia 11%
Other 29%
0
10
20
30
40
50
60
% of total arrivals

Revenue from tourism amounts to nearly $3 billion a year, and tourism is an invaluable source of foreign earnings for the Czech economy. Germans are the most numerous among the millions of visiting tourists, mainly from Europe. Prague, which rivals Paris as the most beautiful capital in Europe, is still the main destination for visitors, although a growing proportion now seek other attractions such as spa towns and skiing.

PEOPLE

Pop. density medium

Czech, Slovak, Hungarian

131/km² (338/mi²)

THE URBAN/RURAL POPULATION SPLIT

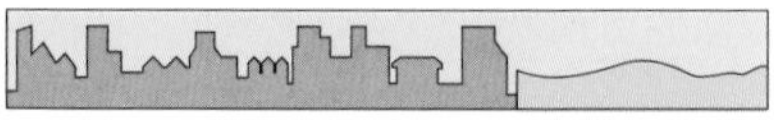
67%
33%

RELIGIOUS PERSUASION

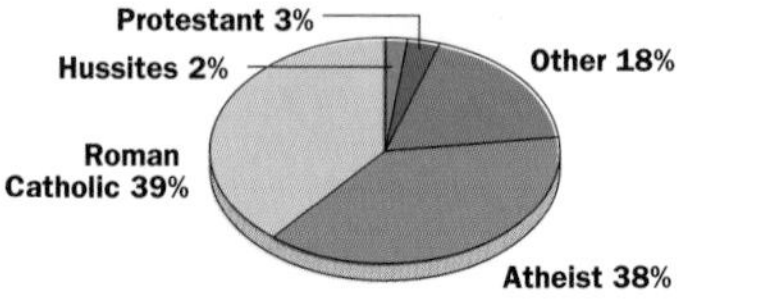
Protestant 3%
Hussites 2%
Other 18%
Roman Catholic 39%
Atheist 38%

Czechs make up over 80% of the population; Moravians are the next largest group. Some 300,000 Slovaks were left in the country after partition, and dual citizenship is now permitted. Ethnic tensions are few, except that the Roma community faces serious discrimination. Divorce rates are high.

POLITICS

Multiparty elections

L. House 2002/2006
U. House 2002/2004

President Vaclav Klaus

AT THE LAST ELECTION

Chamber of Deputies 200 seats

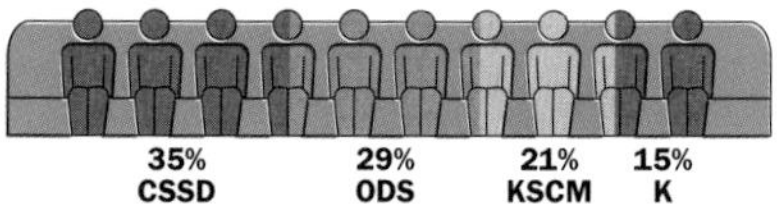
35% CSSD
29% ODS
21% KSCM
15% K

CSSD = Czech Social Democratic Party
ODS = Civic Democratic Party
KSCM = Communist Party of Bohemia and Moravia
K = Coalition of the Christian Democratic Union–Czech People's Party (**KDU–CSL**) and the Freedom Union (**US**)

Senate 81 seats

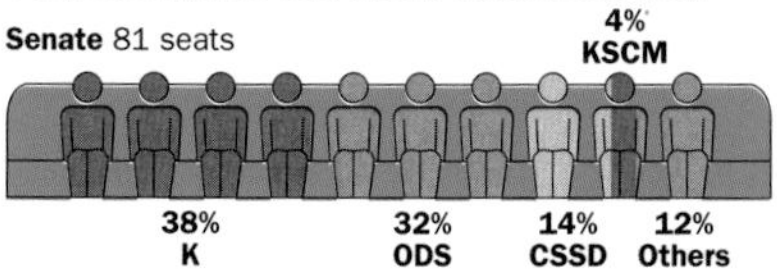
4% KSCM
38% K
32% ODS
14% CSSD
12% Others

The prodemocratic solidarity of 1989–1990, which saw the election of the Civic Forum and dissident playwright Vaclav Havel as president, soon gave way to a two-party system. The right-of-center ODS pursued market economics, and oversaw the split with the Slovak Republic in 1993. It then gave tacit support to the social-democratic CSSD's minority government from 1996. The CSSD under Vladimir Spidla was able to form a slender majority government, without ODS backing, in 2002. Havel retired in February 2003 with no obvious successor; he was eventually replaced by former prime minister Vaclav Klaus after a tortuous parliamentary election process.

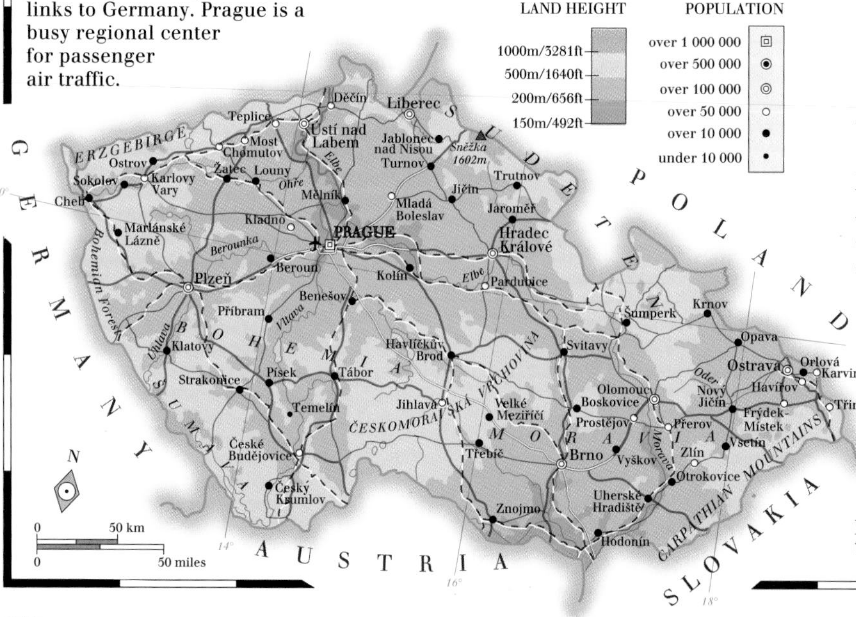
CZECH REPUBLIC
Total Area : 78 866 sq. km (30 450 sq. miles)
LAND HEIGHT
POPULATION
1000m/3281ft
500m/1640ft
200m/656ft
150m/492ft
over 1 000 000
over 500 000
over 100 000
over 50 000
over 10 000
under 10 000
GERMANY
POLAND
AUSTRIA
SLOVAKIA
ERZGEBIRGE
SUDETEN
BOHEMIA
MORAVIA
ŠUMAVA
Bohemian Forest
ČESKOMORAVSKÁ VRCHOVINA
CARPATHIAN MOUNTAINS
PRAGUE
Děčín
Liberec
Teplice
Ústí nad Labem
Most
Chomutov
Jablonec nad Nisou
Sněžka 1602m
Turnov
Ostrov
Karlovy Vary
Žatec
Louny
Sokolov
Cheb
Trutnov
Jičín
Mělník
Mladá Boleslav
Jaroměř
Kladno
Mariánské Lázně
Hradec Králové
Beroun
Plzeň
Kolín
Pardubice
Benešov
Příbram
Šumperk
Krnov
Opava
Klatovy
Písek
Tábor
Havlíčkův Brod
Svitavy
Ostrava
Orlová
Karviná
Havířov
Třinec
Strakonice
Temelín
Jihlava
Velké Meziříčí
Boskovice
Olomouc
Nový Jičín
Frýdek-Místek
Prostějov
Přerov
Vsetín
České Budějovice
Třebíč
Brno
Vyškov
Zlín
Otrokovice
Český Krumlov
Znojmo
Uherské Hradiště
Hodonín
Ohře
Elbe
Vltava
Berounka
Morava
Oder
N
0 50 km
0 50 miles

WORLD AFFAIRS

Joined UN in 1993

CE | CEFTA | NATO | OECD | OSCE

The Czech Republic has approved EU membership, due in the next wave of expansion in 2004. It joined NATO in 1999. Relations with Germany are a priority; the issue of the forced expulsion of Germans in 1945 remains a stumbling block. Austria and Germany strongly opposed the opening of the Temelín nuclear plant in 2000.

AID

Recipient

$314m (receipts) | Down 28% in 2001

Aid for economic restructuring has been crucial to upgrading infrastructure such as telecommunications.

DEFENSE

Phasing out conscription

$1.17bn | Up 2% in 2001

The split with Slovakia left an oversized, expensive army: professional soldiers with a communist past were the first to be demobilized. Conscription is to be phased out by 2006. The country's security was handed over to the US for the duration of a NATO summit in 2002. The Czech Republic is among the world's 20 largest arms exporters.

ECONOMICS

Inflation 11% p.a. (1990–2001)

$54.3bn | 27.5 Czech koruny (29.58)

SCORE CARD

❑ WORLD GNP RANKING	45th
❑ GNP PER CAPITA	$5310
❑ BALANCE OF PAYMENTS	–$2.64bn
❑ INFLATION	4.7%
❑ UNEMPLOYMENT	8%

STRENGTHS
Skilled industrial labor force. Good industrial base. Speed of privatization of state industries. Attractive to German investors. Draw of Prague for tourists.

WEAKNESSES
Lack of diversification. Limited restructuring, banking sector problems. Pressure to cut government expenditure to reduce serious budget deficit. $2–3 billion of flood damage in 2002.

EXPORTS

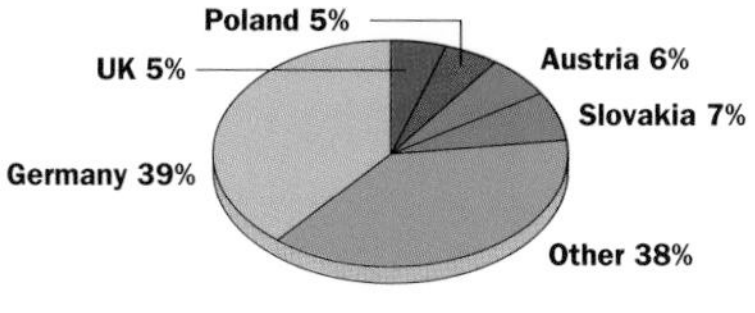
Poland 5%
UK 5%
Austria 6%
Slovakia 7%
Germany 39%
Other 38%

IMPORTS

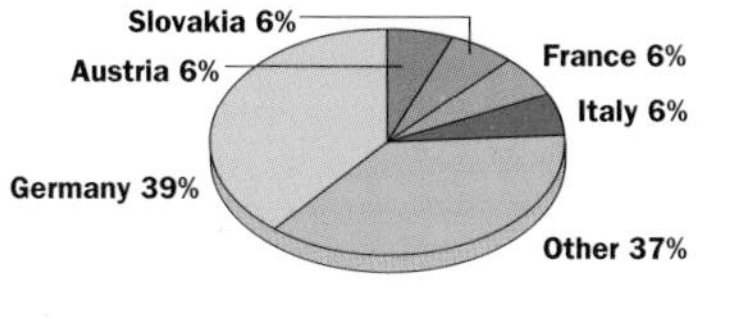
Slovakia 6%
Austria 6%
France 6%
Italy 6%
Germany 39%
Other 37%

RESOURCES

Electric power 14.5m kW

24,129 tonnes | 3669 b/d (reserves 88m barrels)

3.44m pigs, 1.52m cattle, 16.6m chickens | Oil, natural gas, copper, lead, zinc, coal, uranium

The Czech Republic now imports all metals. Brown coal is still exported. The government is aiming to phase out the worst-polluting coal-fired power plants. Opposition to a planned 2000 MW Soviet-designed nuclear power plant at Temelín delayed its completion until late 2000.

ENVIRONMENT

Sustainability rank: 64th

16% (15% partially protected) | 12.5 tonnes per capita

Pollution from the power, chemical, and cement industries and the new Temelín nuclear plant are key concerns.

MEDIA

TV ownership high

Daily newspaper circulation 254 per 1000 people

PUBLISHING AND BROADCAST MEDIA

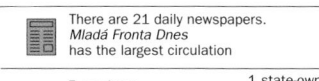

There are 21 daily newspapers. *Mladá Fronta Dnes* has the largest circulation

5 services: 2 state-owned, 3 independent | 1 state-owned service, over 44 independent services

Government-influenced appointments of senior media officials provoked mass protests and a change in the law in 2001.

CRIME

No death penalty

19,320 prisoners | Down 16% in 2000–2001

Prostitution is becoming a growing problem, especially in regions bordering Austria and Germany.

EDUCATION

School leaving age: 15

99% | 260,044 students

Schooling has reverted to the pre-1945 system. Charles University in Prague was founded in the 13th century.

HEALTH

Welfare state health benefits

1 per 325 people | Cancers, heart and cerebrovascular diseases

Government spending is high, and only a few hospitals are entirely privately owned. Wealthy Czechs travel to Germany for complex surgery.

***The Vltava River** in Prague. Millions of tourists, mainly from Europe, visit the beautiful city of Prague every year.*

CHRONOLOGY

Once part of the Austro-Hungarian Empire, Czechoslovakia was established in 1918.

- ❑ **1968** "Prague Spring." Invasion by Warsaw Pact countries.
- ❑ **1989** "Velvet Revolution."
- ❑ **1990** Free elections won by Civic Forum; Vaclav Havel president.
- ❑ **1993** Split with Slovakia.
- ❑ **1998** Elections: CSSD forms minority government.
- ❑ **1999** Joins NATO.
- ❑ **2002** CSSD reelected. Serious floods.
- ❑ **2003** Havel succeeded by former prime minister Vaclav Klaus.

SPENDING

GDP/cap. increase

CONSUMPTION AND SPENDING

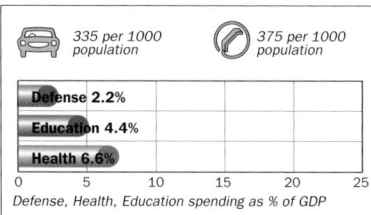

335 per 1000 population | *375 per 1000 population*

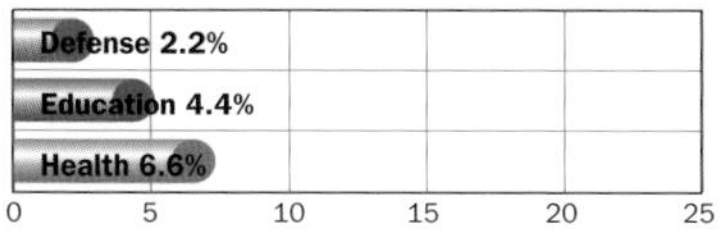
Defense 2.2%
Education 4.4%
Health 6.6%
0
5
10
15
20
25

Defense, Health, Education spending as % of GDP

An entrepreneurial class has emerged since 1989. Rapid privatization in the 1990s was achieved by offering ordinary Czechs coupons for shares.

WORLD RANKING

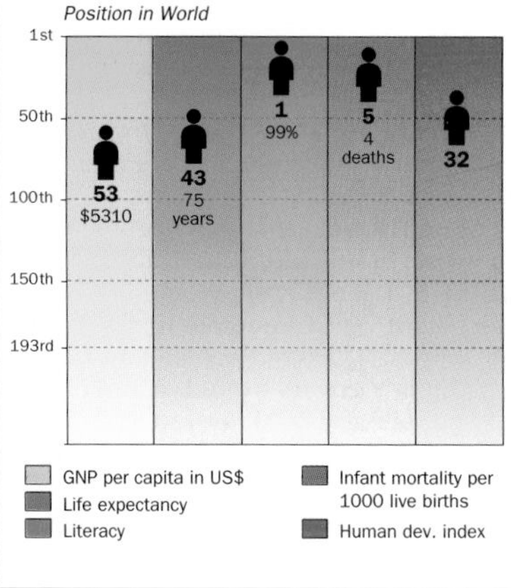
Position in World
1st
50th
100th
150th
193rd
53
$5310
43
75
years
1
99%
5
4
deaths
32
GNP per capita in US$
Life expectancy
Literacy
Infant mortality per 1000 live births
Human dev. index

C

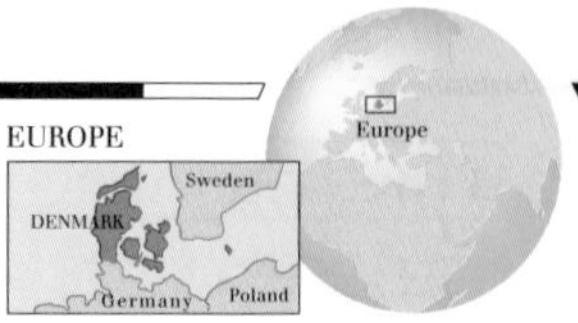
EUROPE
Europe
Sweden
DENMARK
Germany
Poland

D

Denmark

Official Name: Kingdom of Denmark **Capital:** Copenhagen
Population: 5.3 million **Currency:** Danish krone **Official Language:** Danish

950 | 1944 | April 16 | DK | +1 | +45 | .dk

THE MOST SOUTHERLY COUNTRY in Scandinavia, Denmark occupies the Jutland (Jylland) peninsula, the islands of Sjælland, Fyn, Lolland, and Falster, and more than 400 smaller islands. Its terrain is among the flattest in the world. The Faeroe Islands and Greenland in the North Atlantic are self-governing associated territories. Politically, Denmark is stable, despite a preponderance of minority governments since 1945. It possesses a long liberal tradition and was one of the first countries to establish a welfare system, in the 1930s.

TOURISM

Visitors : Population 1:2.6

2.01m visitors

Down 1% in 2002

MAIN TOURIST ARRIVALS

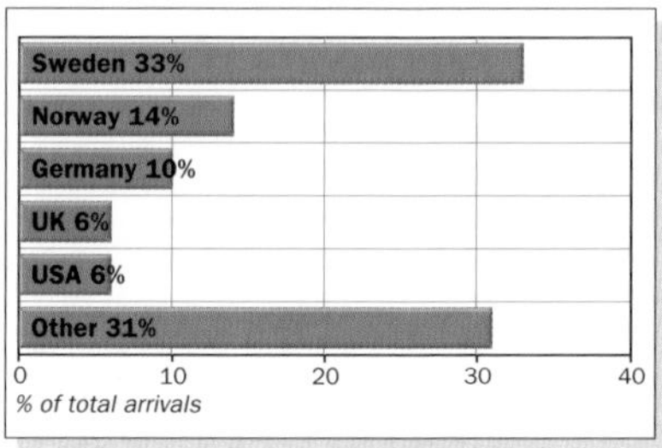
Sweden 33%
Norway 14%
Germany 10%
UK 6%
USA 6%
Other 31%
0
10
20
30
40
% of total arrivals

Principal attractions for tourists are Copenhagen (with its Tivoli Gardens and 18th-century architecture), Legoland, the countryside, and seaside resorts. Since 1959, only Danes have been allowed to own vacation homes.

CLIMATE

Maritime

WEATHER CHART FOR COPENHAGEN

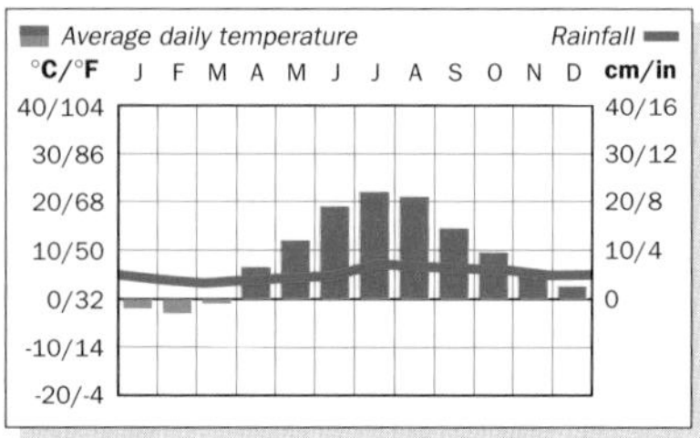
Average daily temperature
Rainfall
°C/°F
J F M A M J J A S O N D
cm/in
40/104
30/86
20/68
10/50
0/32
-10/14
-20/-4
40/16
30/12
20/8
10/4
0

Denmark's temperate, damp climate is one of the keys to its agricultural success. The Faeroes are windy, foggy, and cool. Greenland's climate ranges north–south from arctic to subarctic.

***The island of Fyn,** like the rest of Denmark, is flat and depends on coastal defenses to prevent flooding by the sea.*

TRANSPORTATION

Drive on right

Kastrup, Copenhagen
18.2m passengers

904 ships
6.91m grt

THE TRANSPORTATION NETWORK

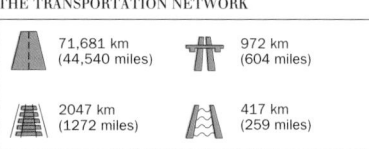

71,681 km (44,540 miles)	972 km (604 miles)
2047 km (1272 miles)	417 km (259 miles)

There is an extensive, well-integrated transportation network of bus, rail, and ferry services. State-owned companies predominate, though privatization of some ferry and rail services has been mooted. Denmark wishes to reduce significant state transportation subsidies. A few private companies operate in the Faeroes and Greenland with state support.

Major new construction projects focus on bridge and tunnel links, such as the Storebælt project connecting the islands of Fyn and Sjælland. A 16-km (10-mile) Øresund road and rail link by bridge and tunnel, connecting Copenhagen with Malmö in Sweden, opened in July 2000. Copenhagen's new Metro light rail system has now been completed.

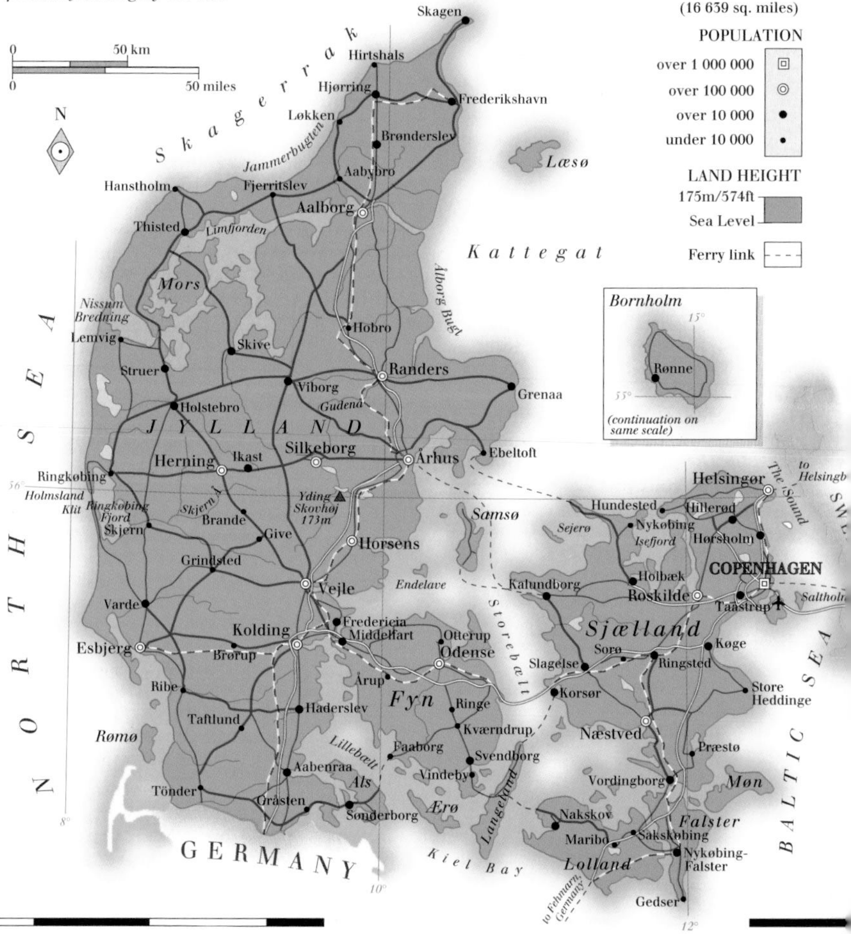
DENMARK
Total Area : 43 094 sq. km
(16 639 sq. miles)
POPULATION
over 1 000 000
over 100 000
over 10 000
under 10 000
LAND HEIGHT
175m/574ft
Sea Level
Ferry link
0
50 km
50 miles
N
Skagerrak
Kattegat
NORTH SEA
BALTIC SEA
GERMANY
Skagen
Hirtshals
Hjørring
Frederikshavn
Løkken
Brønderslev
Jammerbugten
Læsø
Aabybro
Hanstholm
Fjerritslev
Aalborg
Thisted
Limfjorden
Mors
Ålborg Bugt
Nissum Bredning
Hobro
Lemvig
Skive
Randers
Struer
Viborg
Grenaa
Holstebro
Gudenå
JYLLAND
Silkeborg
Ebeltoft
Herning
Ikast
Århus
Ringkøbing
Holmsland Klit
Ringkøbing Fjord
Skjern
Brande
Yding Skovhøj 173m
Samsø
Give
Horsens
Grindsted
Vejle
Endelave
Varde
Kolding
Fredericia
Middelfart
Esbjerg
Brørup
Odense
Otterup
Ribe
Haderslev
Fyn
Ringe
Tønder
Taftlund
Rømø
Kværndrup
Faaborg
Svendborg
Aabenraa
Als
Lillebælt
Gråsten
Sønderborg
Ærø
Vindeby
Langeland
Kiel Bay
Storebælt
Sejerø
Kalundborg
Slagelse
Korsør
Sorø
Ringsted
Sjælland
Næstved
Holbæk
Roskilde
Hundested
Nykøbing
Isefjord
Hillerød
Helsingør
to Helsingborg
The Sound
Hørsholm
COPENHAGEN
Tåstrup
Saltholm
Køge
Store Heddinge
Præstø
Vordingborg
Møn
Nakskov
Maribo
Sakskøbing
Falster
Nykøbing-Falster
Lolland
Gedser
to Fehmarn, Germany
Bornholm
Rønne
(continuation on same scale)

PEOPLE

Pop. density medium

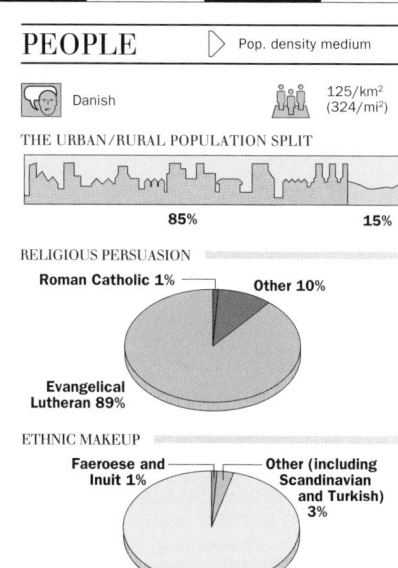

Danish

125/km² (324/mi²)

THE URBAN/RURAL POPULATION SPLIT

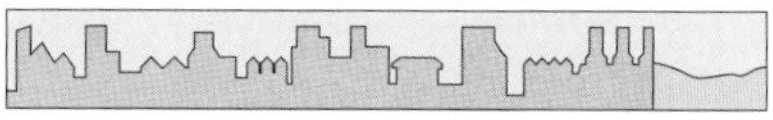
85%
15%

RELIGIOUS PERSUASION

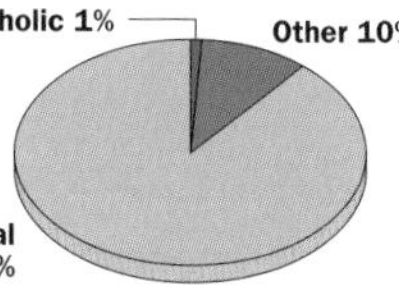
Roman Catholic 1%
Other 10%
Evangelical Lutheran 89%

ETHNIC MAKEUP

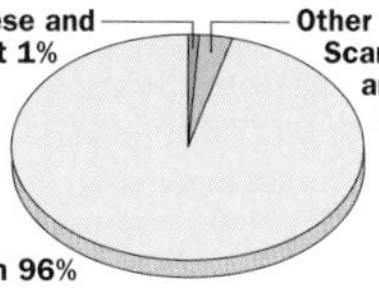
Faeroese and Inuit 1%
Other (including Scandinavian and Turkish) 3%
Danish 96%

Danish society is homogeneous, but the small population of foreign citizens doubled between 1984 and 1999, and the current right-leaning government has pledged to curb immigration. The most visible minority groups are the Inuit, Greenland's indigenous inhabitants, and the Turkish community. Rising unemployment has engendered some ethnic tension, though racially motivated attacks are still rare.

Helped by Denmark's extensive social and educational provision, almost all women now work in part-time or full-time jobs. Consequently, attendance at day nurseries is exceptionally high; 90% of three- to five-year-olds were enrolled in 2000.

Danish living arrangements have changed dramatically since the 1960s. Divorce rates are high and fewer people now live in extended families, while single-person households are increasing. Marriage is becoming less common and occurring later in life. Cohabiting couples now have equal legal rights. However, couples tend to marry when they have children, and 75% of children are raised by both parents. In 1989, Denmark became the first country to offer homosexual couples registered partnerships, effectively granting them the same legal status as heterosexual couples, though few have taken advantage of this.

POPULATION AGE BREAKDOWN

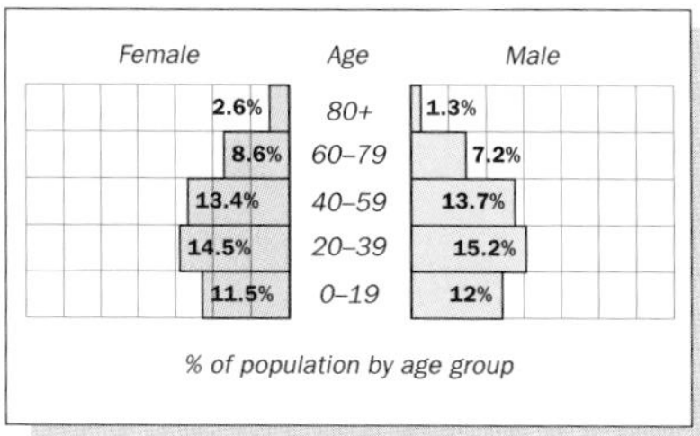
Female
Age
Male
2.6%
80+
1.3%
8.6%
60–79
7.2%
13.4%
40–59
13.7%
14.5%
20–39
15.2%
11.5%
0–19
12%
% of population by age group

POLITICS

Multiparty elections

2001/2005

H.M. Queen Margrethe II

AT THE LAST ELECTION

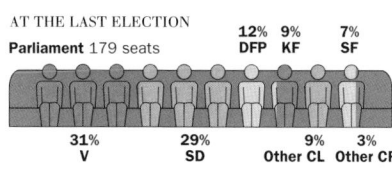

Parliament 179 seats

12% DFP
9% KF
7% SF
31% V
29% SD
9% Other CL
3% Other CR

V = Liberal Party (Venstre) **SD** = Social Democrats **DFP** = Danish People's Party **KF** = Conservative People's Party **Other CL** = Other Center Left **SF** = Socialist People's Party **Other CR** = Other Center Right

Greenland and the Faeroe Islands send two members each to the Parliament

Anders Fogh Rasmussen, heads a right-wing, minority coalition.

Queen Margrethe II, who succeeded to the throne in 1972.

Denmark is a constitutional monarchy and a multiparty democracy. The associated territories of Greenland and the Faeroe Islands have home rule. The latter are divided over the issue of independence.

Profile

The intricate proportional electoral system ensures that Parliament truly reflects voters' wishes, but also tends to lead to minority governments. After a decade of Conservative–Liberal rule, the SD regained power in 1993, at the head of a center-left coalition under Poul Nyrup Rasmussen. The pendulum swung back with a victory in 2001 for the Liberals and Anders Fogh Rasmussen. The Danish Confederation of Trade Unions voted in 2003 to cut its historic ties to the SD, ending over 100 years of political and financial support.

Main Political Issues

Relations with the EU

In recent years, Denmark's left-of-center parties have been suspicious of further EU integration. In 1992, ratification of the Maastricht Treaty, approved by Parliament, was rejected in a referendum, voters objecting to monetary union, a common defense force, and local election voting rights for European citizens living in Denmark. Later that year an EU summit allowed Denmark to opt out of monetary union, defense, and European citizenship. A referendum in 1993 finally approved the Maastricht Treaty, and voters approved the Amsterdam Treaty, its successor, in 1998, but a referendum in 2000 on adopting the euro (which Denmark had decided not to introduce from its outset in 1999) produced a highly significant, and unexpected, "no" result.

Immigration

Despite Danish liberal traditions, the position and integration into society of immigrants and refugees, who account for under 5% of the population, is a controversial issue. The election of a right-wing government in 2001 signaled support for an overtly restrictive policy and a greater emphasis on integration for those immigrants already there. The ruling coalition relies for support on the far-right, anti-immigrant Danish People's Party, which had almost doubled its representation. Legislation passed in 2002 prevents the foreign (non-EU) spouse of a Danish citizen living in or emigrating to Denmark.

WORLD AFFAIRS

Joined UN in 1945

CE | EU | NATO | OECD | OSCE

Relations with the rest of Europe are the major foreign policy concern, notably the issues of a common defense policy and monetary union. Denmark has decided against introducing the euro, but the krone is pegged to it and economic policies follow those of the participating states. Promoting economic ties with Norway, Sweden, and Finland is a priority, as are improving links with former Eastern bloc states, especially those on the Baltic – not least to assist pollution reduction, a serious concern. Denmark is also a strong supporter of Third World development, especially in Africa.

CHRONOLOGY

Founded in the 10th century, Denmark's monarchy is Europe's oldest. It was the dominant Baltic power until the 17th century, when it was eclipsed by Sweden.

- ❑ **1815** Denmark forced to cede Norway to Swedish rule.
- ❑ **1849** Creation of first democratic constitution.
- ❑ **1864** Denmark forced to cede provinces of Schleswig and Holstein after losing war with Prussia.
- ❑ **1914–1918** Denmark neutral in World War I.
- ❑ **1915** Universal adult suffrage introduced. Rise of SD.
- ❑ **1920** Northern Schleswig votes to return to Danish rule.

D

CHRONOLOGY *continued*

- **1929** First full SD government, Thorvald Stauning prime minister.
- **1930s** Implementation of advanced social welfare legislation and other liberal reforms under SD.
- **1939** Outbreak of World War II; Denmark reaffirms neutrality.
- **1940** Nazi occupation. National coalition government formed.
- **1943** Danish Resistance successes lead Nazis to take full control.
- **1944** Iceland declares independence from Denmark.
- **1945** Denmark recognizes Icelandic independence. After defeat of Nazi Germany, SD leads postwar coalition governments.
- **1948** Faeroes granted home rule.
- **1952** Founder member of the Nordic Council.
- **1953** Constitution reformed; single-chamber, proportionally elected parliament created.
- **1959** Denmark joins EFTA.
- **1972** Margrethe becomes queen.
- **1973** Denmark joins European Communities.
- **1979** Greenland granted home rule.
- **1975–1982** SD's Anker Jorgensen heads series of coalitions; elections in 1977, 1979, and 1981. Final coalition collapses over economic policy differences.
- **1982** Poul Schlüter first Conservative prime minister since 1894.
- **1992** Referendum rejects Maastricht Treaty on European Union.
- **1993** Schlüter resigns over “Tamilgate” scandal. Center-left government led by Poul Nyrup Rasmussen. Danish voters ratify revised Maastricht Treaty.
- **1994, 1998** Elections: Rasmussen heads SD-led minority coalition.
- **2000** Referendum rejects joining eurozone.
- **2001** Elections: Liberals regain power. Anders Fogh Rasmussen appointed prime minister.

AID

Donor

$1.63bn (donations)

Down 2% in 2001

During the 1990s, Denmark was the world's leading aid donor in GNP terms, contributing on average 1% of national income. It supports both economic and social development projects and policy reforms. The Liberal government elected in 2001 is committed to reducing the foreign aid budget.

Denmark provides aid to Asia and Latin America, but its closest ties are with Africa. Tanzania is the largest single aid recipient. Denmark has also provided considerable support to other southeast African states.

DEFENSE

Compulsory military service

$2.41bn

Up 1% in 2001

Denmark was neutral until 1945. Apart from NATO commitments, defense has a low priority; spending is less than 2% of GDP (well below the NATO average). Denmark provides troops for the NATO-led forces in the former Yugoslavia and observers for other UN peacekeeping operations. One-quarter of its armed forces are conscripts, and its reserves include a Home Guard. Denmark has observer status at the WEU.

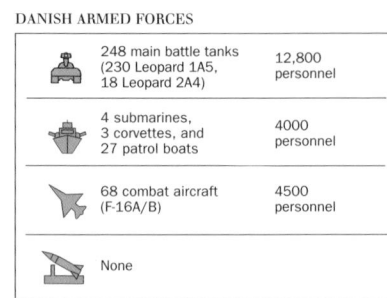

DANISH ARMED FORCES

248 main battle tanks (230 Leopard 1A5, 18 Leopard 2A4)	12,800 personnel
4 submarines, 3 corvettes, and 27 patrol boats	4000 personnel
68 combat aircraft (F-16A/B)	4500 personnel
None	

ECONOMICS

Inflation 2.2% p.a. (1990–2001)

$164bn

6.47 Danish kroner (7.522)

SCORE CARD

World GNP Ranking	25th
GNP per Capita	$30,600
Balance of Payments	$4.14bn
Inflation	2.4%
Unemployment	4%

EXPORTS

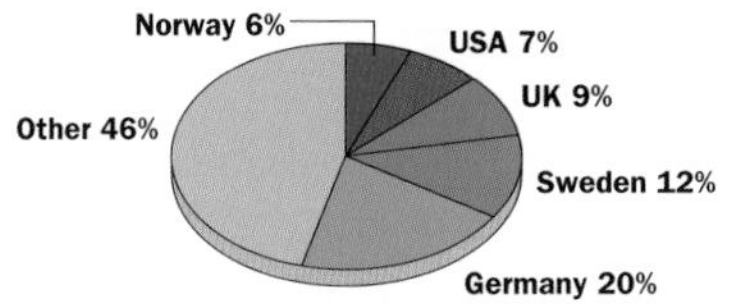
Norway 6%
USA 7%
UK 9%
Sweden 12%
Germany 20%
Other 46%

IMPORTS

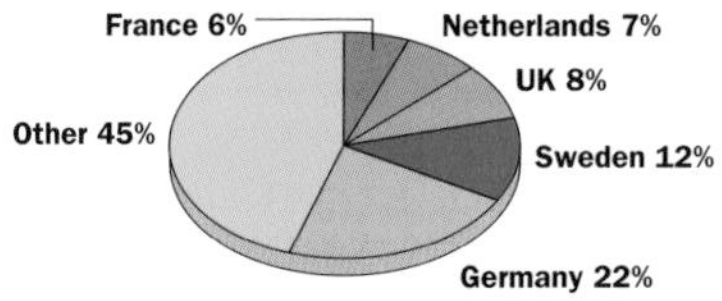
France 6%
Netherlands 7%
UK 8%
Sweden 12%
Germany 22%
Other 45%

Strengths

Low inflation and unemployment. Substantial balance-of-payments surplus. Gas and oil reserves. Strong high-tech, high-profit manufacturing sector. Skilled workforce.

Weaknesses

Heavy tax burden. Labor costs and historically strong currency affect competitiveness.

Profile

Denmark's mix of a large state sector and a private sector has been successful. GDP per capita is one of the highest among the OECD countries. However, total taxation, at about 50%, is among the world's highest. In November 2001 the Liberal government promised to fund increased welfare spending and lower taxation by extending privatization and reducing development aid.

In the 1980s the government stabilized the exchange rate and tightened budget controls in order to reduce inflation and reverse the balance-of-payments deficit. Growth slowed in the early 1990s, but an economic upturn between 1993 and 2000 was first led by private consumption and then buoyed by exports and business investment. Growth slowed significantly in 2001, but had regained momentum by mid-2002.

Voters have refused to accept EU monetary union, most recently in a “no” vote in 2000 in a referendum on the euro. However, Denmark meets the EU's convergence criteria for monetary union, the krone is pegged to the euro, and economic policies follow those of the participating states.

ECONOMIC PERFORMANCE INDICATOR

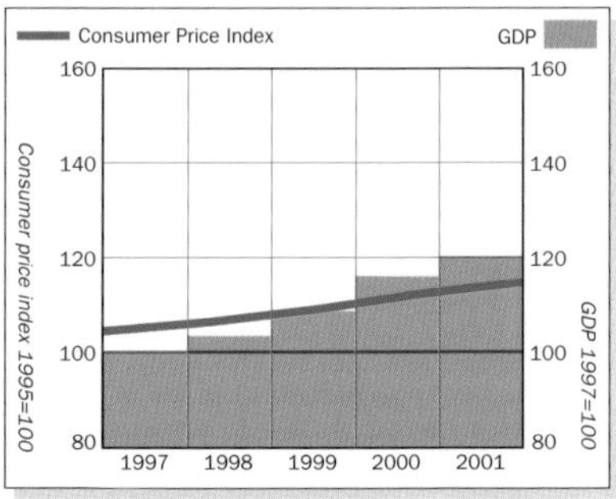
Consumer Price Index
GDP
Consumer price index 1995=100
GDP 1997=100
160
140
120
100
80
1997
1998
1999
2000
2001

DENMARK : MAJOR BUSINESSES

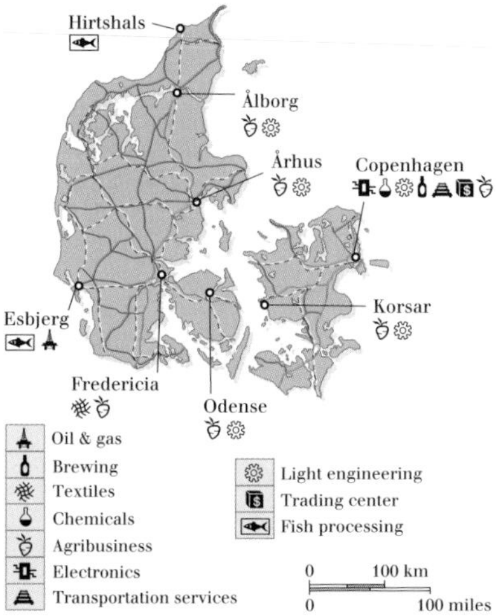
Hirtshals
Ålborg
Århus
Copenhagen
Esbjerg
Korsar
Fredericia
Odense
Oil & gas
Brewing
Textiles
Chemicals
Agribusiness
Electronics
Transportation services
Light engineering
Trading center
Fish processing
0 100 km
0 100 miles

RESOURCES

Electric power 12.7m kW

1.58m tonnes

371,000 b/d (reserves 1.3bn barrels)

13m pigs, 1.92m cattle, 20m chickens

Natural gas, oil

ELECTRICITY GENERATION

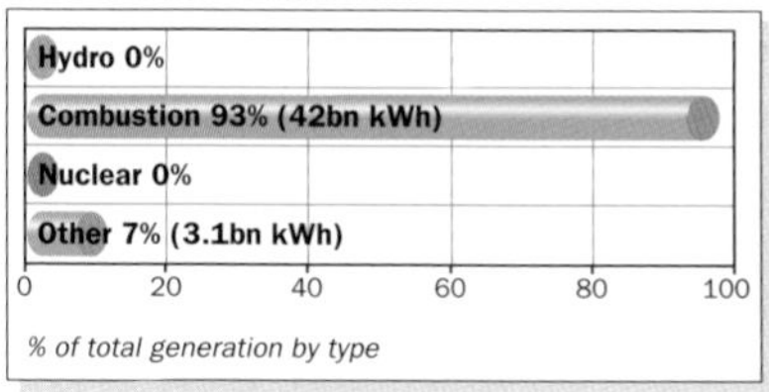
Hydro 0%
Combustion 93% (42bn kWh)
Nuclear 0%
Other 7% (3.1bn kWh)
0
20
40
60
80
100
% of total generation by type

Despite expansion of North Sea oil and gas output, Denmark is still an overall importer of energy. Agriculture is highly efficient, and Denmark is the world's biggest exporter of pork. The use of wind power is expanding rapidly; Denmark is a world leader in this technology.

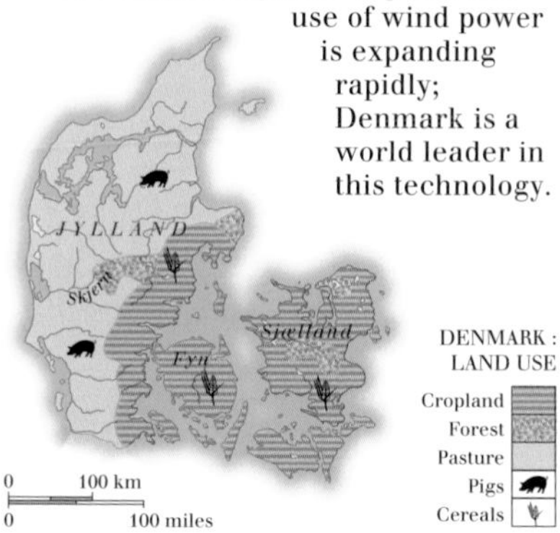
JYLLAND
Skjern
Fyn
Sjælland
DENMARK : LAND USE
Cropland
Forest
Pasture
Pigs
Cereals
0
100 km
0
100 miles

ENVIRONMENT

Sustainability rank: 31st

34% (31% partially protected)

9.9 tonnes per capita

ENVIRONMENTAL TREATIES

Yes Yes Yes

Yes Yes Yes

Denmark has some of the strictest regulations in Europe, including those aimed at reducing ozone-destroying emissions and water pollution, and met its 2000 target – recycling 54% of all waste – a year early. There was a marked change in policy under the incoming Liberal government of 2001. The bans on house-building in state forests and on the sale of beer in cans were lifted, three planned wind power plants were shelved, and the environment ministry's budget was cut by one-third.

MEDIA

TV ownership high

Daily newspaper circulation 283 per 1000 people

PUBLISHING AND BROADCAST MEDIA

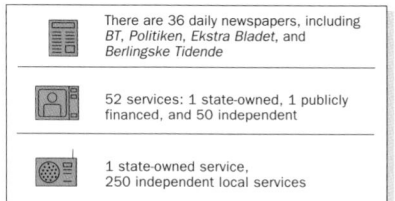

There are 36 daily newspapers, including *BT*, *Politiken*, *Ekstra Bladet*, and *Berlingske Tidende*

52 services: 1 state-owned, 1 publicly financed, and 50 independent

1 state-owned service, 250 independent local services

The media have a long history of political independence, and objectivity is prized. The tone of both TV and the press is serious; there is no scandal-mongering tabloid press as found in the US, the UK, and Germany. Invasion of privacy laws are strict. Legislation proposed in May 2002 would extend competition in broadcasting and prepare for the privatization of TV2.

CRIME

No death penalty

3150 prisoners

Down 5% in 2000–2001

CRIME RATES

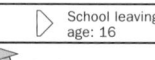

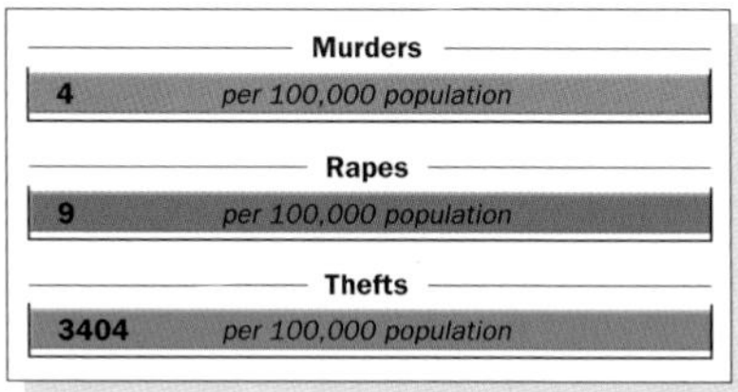
Murders
4 per 100,000 population
Rapes
9 per 100,000 population
Thefts
3404 per 100,000 population

Problems are the potential importing of Mafia-style organized crime from eastern Europe, computer hacking, and drug trafficking. In 2001, stricter penalties for violence and rape were promised.

EDUCATION

School leaving age: 16

99%

191,645 students

THE EDUCATION SYSTEM

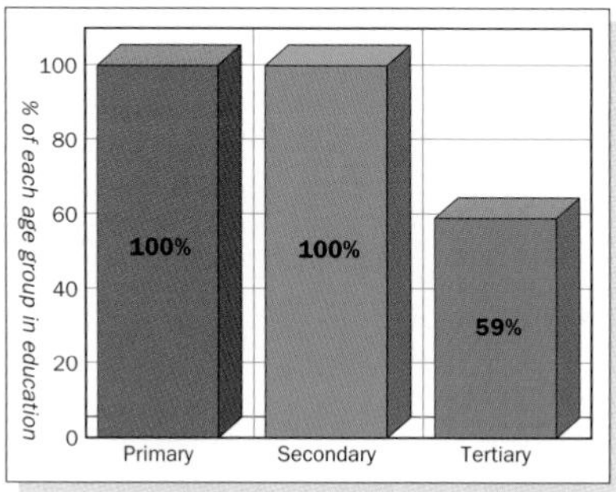
100
80
60
40
20
0
% of each age group in education
100%
100%
59%
Primary
Secondary
Tertiary

The educational level is generally high, in part reflecting the need for a skilled workforce. Formal schooling begins at age seven and is mandatory for nine years. However, most children receive preschool education, and around 90% of pupils go on at the age of 16 to further academic or vocational training. There are five main universities and six specialist institutions. The University of Copenhagen was founded in 1479.

HEALTH

Welfare state health benefits

1 per 295 people

Cancers, heart and cerebrovascular diseases, bronchitis

Denmark was one of the first countries to introduce a state social welfare system. The national health service, which still provides free treatment for almost everything, is the main reason for high taxes – in 2001 almost a quarter of government spending was allocated to social services. Any attempts to reduce expenditure will meet with strong opposition. Repeated surveys show that most Danes prefer their system to those based on private health insurance.

In the early 1980s, Denmark had the highest incidence of AIDS in Europe, but after peaking in 1993, the rate has dropped markedly, thanks to the free availability of drug therapies.

SPENDING

GDP/cap. increase

CONSUMPTION AND SPENDING

357 per 1000 population

719 per 1000 population

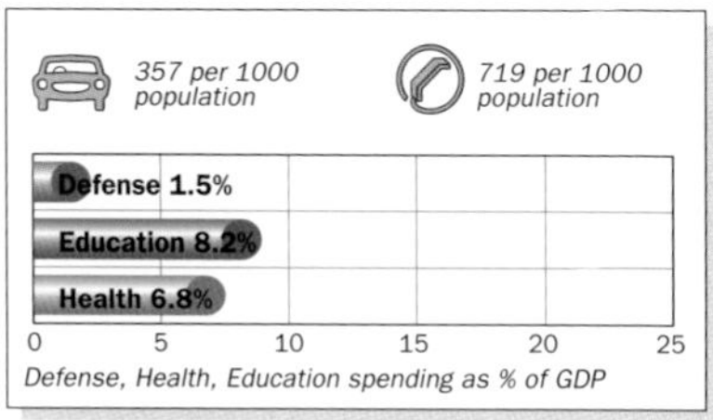
Defense 1.5%
Education 8.2%
Health 6.8%
0
5
10
15
20
25
Defense, Health, Education spending as % of GDP

Denmark forms one of the world's most egalitarian societies. Most Danes are comfortably off. Income distribution is the most even among Western countries and social mobility is high. Free higher education means that access to the professions is more a question of ability than wealth or connections. The generous social security system means that Danes suffer little from social deprivation. The SD government of 1994–2001 created more kindergarten places and increased time off for those with young children. Refugees and recent immigrants tend to be the most disadvantaged members of Danish society.

WORLD RANKING

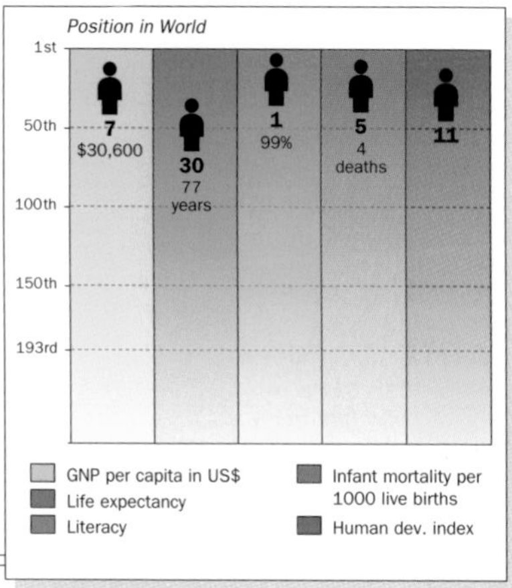
Position in World
1st
50th
100th
150th
193rd
7
$30,600
30
77
years
1
99%
5
4
deaths
11
GNP per capita in US$
Life expectancy
Literacy
Infant mortality per 1000 live births
Human dev. index

D

DJIBOUTI

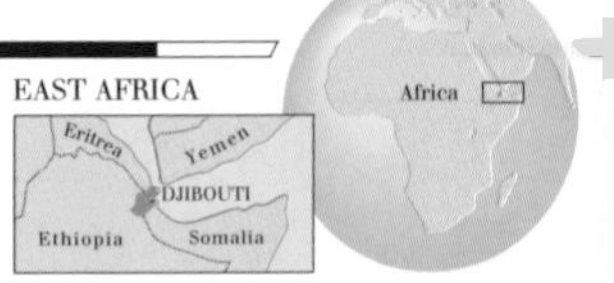
EAST AFRICA
Eritrea
Yemen
DJIBOUTI
Ethiopia
Somalia
Africa

OFFICIAL NAME: Republic of Djibouti **CAPITAL:** Djibouti
POPULATION: 652,000 **CURRENCY:** Djibouti franc **OFFICIAL LANGUAGES:** Arabic and French

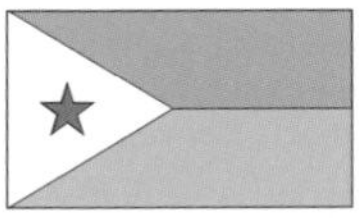

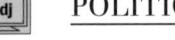

1977 | 1977 | June 27 | DJI | +3 | +253 | .dj

A CITY WITH A DESERT HINTERLAND, Djibouti lies in northeast Africa on the strait linking the Red Sea and the Indian Ocean. Known from 1967 as the French Territory of the Afars and Issas, Djibouti became independent in 1977. Its economy relies on the main port, the railroad to Addis Ababa, and French aid. A guerrilla war which erupted in 1991 as a result of tension between the Issas in the south and the Afars in the north has largely been resolved.

CLIMATE

Hot desert

WEATHER CHART FOR DJIBOUTI

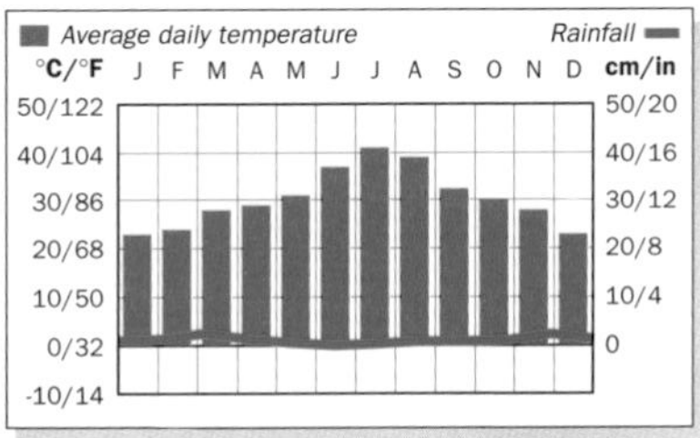
Average daily temperature
Rainfall
°C/°F
J F M A M J J A S O N D
cm/in
50/122
40/104
30/86
20/68
10/50
0/32
-10/14
50/20
40/16
30/12
20/8
10/4
0

Despite extremely low rainfall, the monsoon season is characterized by very humid conditions. Even locals find the heat in June–August hard to bear.

TRANSPORTATION

Drive on right

Ambouli International, Djibouti 168,224 passengers

10 ships 2493 grt

THE TRANSPORTATION NETWORK

364 km (226 miles)

None

100 km (62 miles)

None

Djibouti's port, created by the French in the 19th century and now a modern container facility, is its key asset. Landlocked Ethiopia's vital link to the sea is the Addis Ababa–Djibouti railroad.

TOURISM

Visitors : Population 1:31

21,000 visitors

Little change in 1995–1998

MAIN TOURIST ARRIVALS

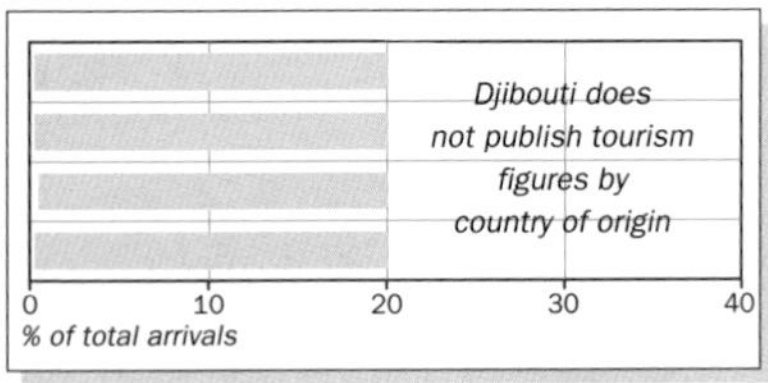
Djibouti does not publish tourism figures by country of origin
0
10
20
30
40
% of total arrivals

Most visitors are passing through on their way to Ethiopia, or coming to see relatives working in Djibouti port.

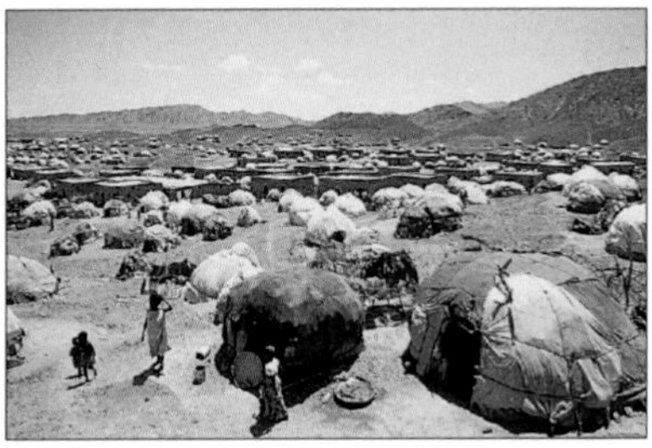

Nomadic Djiboutian village, close to Balho near the Ethiopian border.

PEOPLE

Pop. density low

Somali, Afar, French, Arabic

28/km² (73/mi²)

THE URBAN/RURAL POPULATION SPLIT

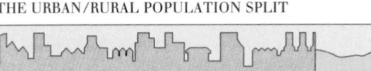

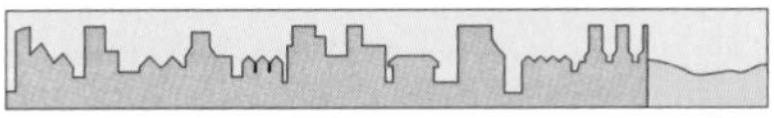
84%
16%

ETHNIC MAKEUP

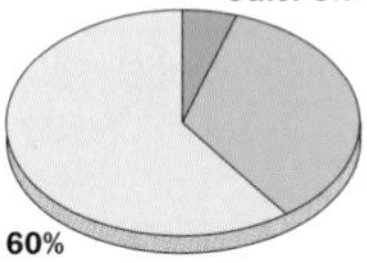
Other 5%
Afar 35%
Issa 60%

The main ethnic groups are the Afars and Issas; tension between these groups developed into a guerrilla war in 1991. The population was swelled in 1992 by 20,000 Somali refugees. The rural people are mostly nomadic.

POLITICS

Multiparty elections

2003/2008

President Ismael Omar Guelleh

AT THE LAST ELECTION

National Assembly 65 seats

100% UMP

UMP = Union for a Presidential Majority, composed of the Popular Rally for Progress (**RPP**), the Front for the Restoration of Unity and Democracy (**FRUD**), and two other parties

President Hassan Gouled Aptidon, an Issa, backed by France, dominated politics from independence in 1977 until his retirement in 1999. The Afar guerrilla group FRUD took control of much of the country in 1991. The French intervened militarily, but forced Gouled to hold multiparty elections in 1992. FRUD became a legal party after a 1994 peace deal. An alliance of the ruling RPP and FRUD won all seats in elections in 1997, and again within the UMP coalition in 2002, despite competition from recently unbanned opposition parties. Presidential elections in 1999 were won by Ismael Omar Guelleh, a former close aide of Gouled, amid opposition claims of electoral fraud.

DJIBOUTI

Total Area : 23 000 sq. km (8,880 sq. miles)

ERITREA
ETHIOPIA
SOMALIA
Bab el Mandeb
GULF OF ADEN
Bissidiro
Moulhoulé
Alaili Dadda'
Lâ'assa
Khôr 'Angar
Moussa 'Ali 2021m
Dadda'to
Assa Gaïla
Gaherré
Dorra
Ouaddi
Balho
Randa
Obock
Tadjoura
Gâlâfi
Lac 'Assal
Golfe de Tadjoura
Îles Moucha
DJIBOUTI
'Arta
Damêrdjôg
Loyada
Yoboki
Ghoubbet el-Kharâb
Goubétto
Holhol
Doudoub Bololé
Lake Abhe
Mouloud
Ali Sabieh
Dikhil
Guélilé
'Ali 'Addé
Koûta Boûyya
As Ela
Sankal
'Assâmo
N
0 30 km
0 30 mi
POPULATION
over 100 000
under 10 000
LAND HEIGHT
1000m/3281ft
500m/1640ft
200m/656ft
Sea Level
-200m/656ft

D

WORLD AFFAIRS

Joined UN in 1977

AL | OIF | IGAD | AU | OIC

France, with a key military presence, is pressing for greater democratization. Djibouti, Ethiopia, and Eritrea all seek to contain Afar secessionism. In 2000 the southern town of Arta hosted the Somali reconciliation conference.

AID

Recipient

$55m (receipts) | Down 23% in 2001

Djibouti is reliant on international aid, of which almost half is provided by France. Recent antipoverty projects have been funded by the AfDB.

DEFENSE

No compulsory military service

$22m | Down 4% in 2001

The size of the armed forces is a state secret, but is estimated at 9850 personnel; former FRUD guerrillas were integrated into the army. There is a 3200-strong French garrison.

ECONOMICS

Inflation 3.6% p.a. (1990–2001)

$572m | 175 Djibouti francs (164.9)

SCORE CARD

❑ World GNP Ranking	167th
❑ GNP per Capita	$890
❑ Balance of Payments	–$14m
❑ Inflation	2%
❑ Unemployment	50%

Strengths

Important location on Red Sea; continuing upgrading of Djibouti and Tadjoura port facilities. Development of information technology infrastructure.

Weaknesses

High poverty and unemployment levels. Dependence on French aid and garrison. Planned Saudi investment held back by civil war in 1990s. Stiff competition from other ports on Red Sea.

EXPORTS

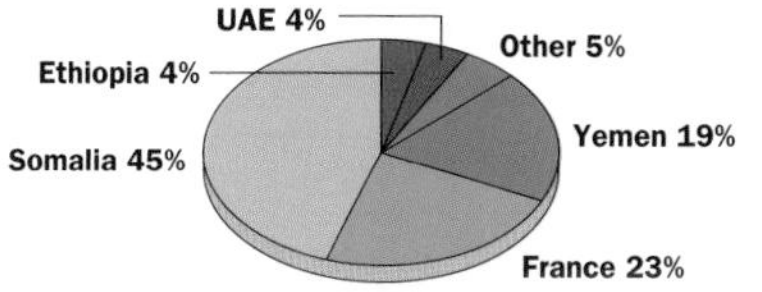
UAE 4%
Other 5%
Ethiopia 4%
Yemen 19%
Somalia 45%
France 23%

IMPORTS

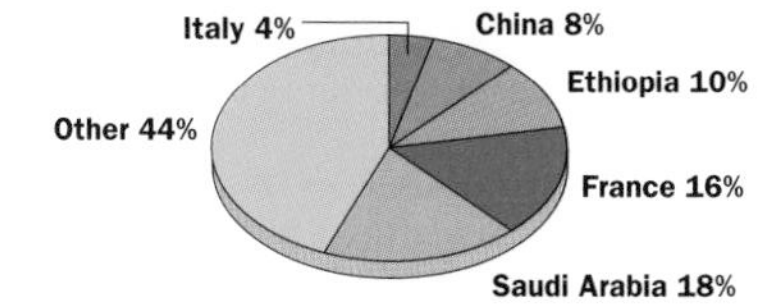
Italy 4%
China 8%
Ethiopia 10%
Other 44%
France 16%
Saudi Arabia 18%

RESOURCES

Electric power 85,000 kW

350 tonnes | Not an oil producer

512,000 goats, 475,000 sheep, 270,000 cattle | Gypsum, mica, amethyst, sulfur, natural gas

The few mineral resources are scarcely exploited. Geothermal energy is being developed and natural gas has recently been found. The guerrilla war delayed attempts to develop underground water supplies for agriculture.

ENVIRONMENT

Not available

0.4% | 0.6 tonnes per capita

The concentration of business around Djibouti port means that inland desert areas are largely untouched. Pollution from container ships is of concern.

MEDIA

TV ownership low

There are no daily newspapers

PUBLISHING AND BROADCAST MEDIA

There are no daily newspapers. The weekly *La Nation de Djibouti* is published by the government

1 state-controlled service | 1 state-controlled service

Djibouti is a member of the Arab Satellite Communications Organization. The media are largely state-controlled, but there is one opposition newspaper.

CRIME

No death penalty

384 prisoners | Up 74% in 1996–1998

The government accused the FRUD of atrocities, but the state's own human rights record has since been criticized by Amnesty International. While drug smuggling and prostitution are rife, petty crime, rather than violence, is the norm.

EDUCATION

School leaving age: 11

66% | 496 students

Schooling is mostly in French, while there is a growing emphasis on Islamic teaching. In 2000–2001 higher education was reorganized, with the creation of the core of a future University of Djibouti in association with French universities.

HEALTH

Welfare state health benefits

1 per 7692 people | Respiratory and heart diseases

AIDS is a growing problem in Djibouti port, with its large prostitute population. UN estimates for 1999 suggested that there were some 37,000 HIV/AIDS sufferers. Small French-financed hospitals cater for the urban elite.

CHRONOLOGY

The French set up a coaling station at Djibouti in the 1880s, to balance the British presence in Aden.

- ❑ **1917** Railroad from Addis Ababa reaches Djibouti port.
- ❑ **1977** Independence.
- ❑ **1981–1992** One-party state.
- ❑ **1989** Eruption of violence between Afars and Issas.
- ❑ **1991** FRUD launches armed insurrection.
- ❑ **1994** Peace agreement with FRUD.
- ❑ **1999** Ismael Omar Guelleh becomes president.
- ❑ **2000** Unsuccessful coup attempt by police officers.

SPENDING

GDP/cap. decrease

CONSUMPTION AND SPENDING

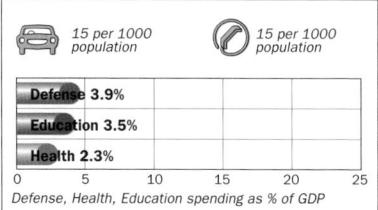

15 per 1000 population | *15 per 1000 population*

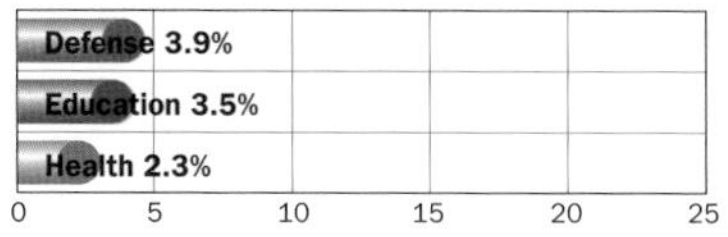
Defense 3.9%
Education 3.5%
Health 2.3%
0
5
10
15
20
25

Defense, Health, Education spending as % of GDP

As happens in many African states, the wealth in Djibouti tends to be concentrated among those closest to government. Djiboutians working in the ports also do well, though much port labor is expatriate. The guerrilla war had little effect on Djibouti city, since the capital is almost completely isolated from the rest of the country. The nomads of the interior are the poorest group.

Trade in the mild narcotic qat, or "green gold," which is grown in Ethiopia and shipped through Djibouti, is highly lucrative, to the extent that the state is now taking its share of the profits. In Djibouti, qat chewing is an age-old social ritual.

WORLD RANKING

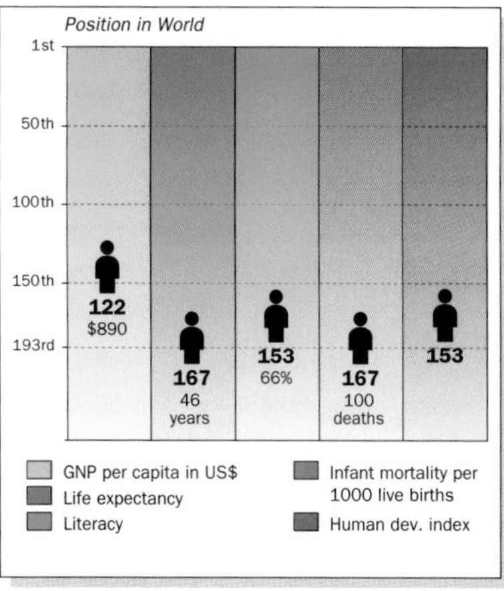
Position in World
1st
50th
100th
150th
193rd
122
$890
167
46 years
153
66%
167
100 deaths
153
GNP per capita in US$
Life expectancy
Literacy
Infant mortality per 1000 live births
Human dev. index

DOMINICA

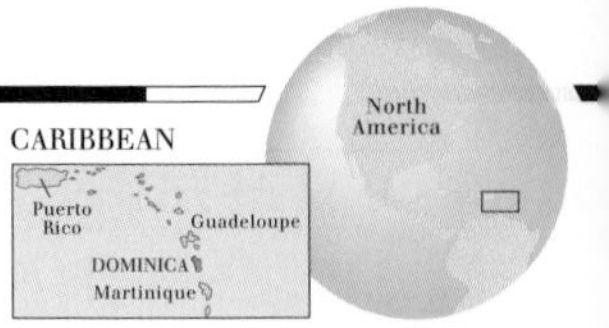
North America
CARIBBEAN
Puerto Rico
Guadeloupe
DOMINICA
Martinique

OFFICIAL NAME: Commonwealth of Dominica **CAPITAL:** Roseau
POPULATION: 70,158 **CURRENCY:** Eastern Caribbean dollar **OFFICIAL LANGUAGE:** English

1978 | 1978 | Nov 3 | WD | -4 | +1767 | .dm

DOMINICA IS RENOWNED as the Caribbean island that resisted European colonization until the 18th century, when it came under French control, passing to the UK in 1759. It is known as the "Nature Island" because of its spectacular, lush, and abundant flora and fauna, protected by extensive national parks. The most mountainous of the Lesser Antilles, Dominica is located between Guadeloupe and Martinique in the West Indian Windward Islands group. Its volcanic origin has given it very fertile soils and the second-largest boiling lake in the world.

CLIMATE

Tropical oceanic

WEATHER CHART FOR ROSEAU

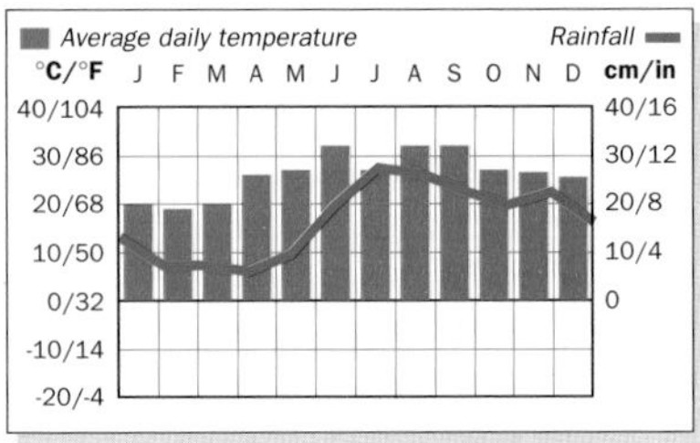
Average daily temperature
Rainfall
°C/°F
J F M A M J J A S O N D
cm/in
40/104
30/86
20/68
10/50
0/32
-10/14
-20/-4
40/16
30/12
20/8
10/4
0

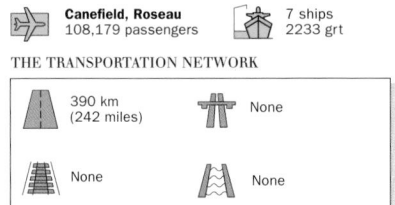

Like the other Windward Islands in the eastern Caribbean, Dominica is subject to constant trade winds. The rainy season is in the summer, and tropical depressions and hurricanes are likely between June and November. Short, thundery showers in the late afternoon and evening are common throughout the year.

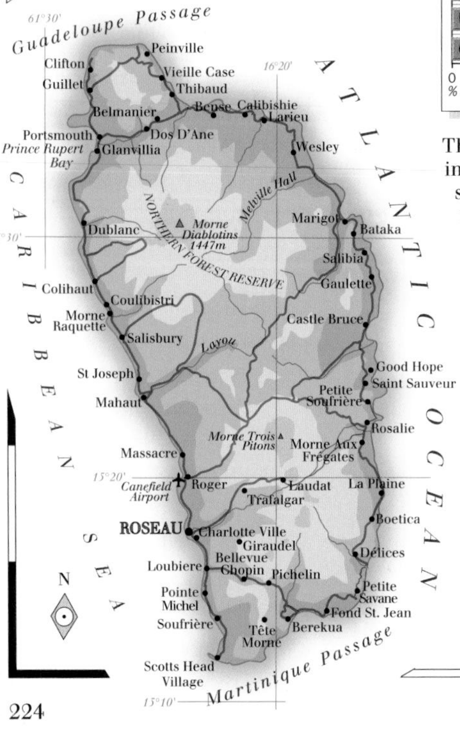
61°30'
Guadeloupe Passage
Peinville
Clifton
Guillet
Vieille Case
Thibaud
16°20'
ATLANTIC OCEAN
Belmanier
Bense
Calibishie
Marigot
Larieu
Portsmouth
Prince Rupert Bay
Dos D'Ane
Glanvillia
Wesley
Melville Hall
CARIBBEAN SEA
15°30'
Dublanc
Morne Diablotins 1447m
NORTHERN FOREST RESERVE
Bataka
Salibia
Colihaut
Coulibistri
Gaulette
Morne Raquette
Salisbury
Castle Bruce
Layou
St Joseph
Good Hope
Saint Sauveur
Mahaut
Petite Soufrière
Rosalie
Massacre
Morne Trois Pitons
Morne Aux Frégates
15°20'
Canefield Airport
Roger
Laudat
La Plaine
Trafalgar
ROSEAU
Charlotte Ville
Boetica
Giraudel
Loubiere
Bellevue Chopin
Délices
Pichelin
Pointe Michel
Petite Savane
Fond St. Jean
Soufrière
Tête Morne
Berekua
Scotts Head Village
Martinique Passage
15°10'
N

TRANSPORTATION

Drive on left

Canefield, Roseau
108,179 passengers

7 ships
2233 grt

THE TRANSPORTATION NETWORK

390 km (242 miles)

None

None

None

Both airports take only small propeller aircraft. Roads are well maintained. There is no speed limit in rural areas.

TOURISM

Visitors : Population 1.1:1

74,000 visitors

Up 12% in 1999

MAIN TOURIST ARRIVALS

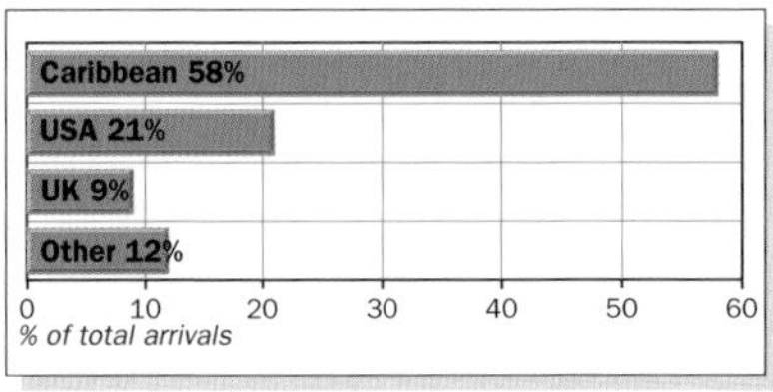
Caribbean 58%
USA 21%
UK 9%
Other 12%
0 10 20 30 40 50 60
% of total arrivals

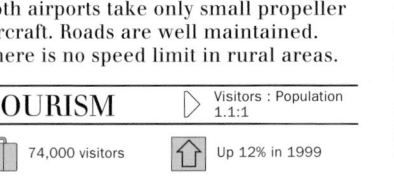

The national parks, with their rare indigenous birds, hot springs, and sulfur pools, are a major attraction for tourists. However, the lack of an airport able to take commercial jetliners (visitors use connecting flights from Barbados or Antigua) has made Dominica less accessible to mass-market tourism than its neighbors.

DOMINICA

Total Area : 754 sq. km (291 sq. miles)

LAND HEIGHT

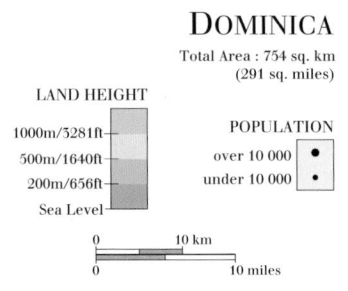

1000m/3281ft
500m/1640ft
200m/656ft
Sea Level

POPULATION

over 10 000
under 10 000

0 — 10 km
0 — 10 miles

PEOPLE

Pop. density medium

French Creole, English

94/km² (242/mi²)

THE URBAN/RURAL POPULATION SPLIT

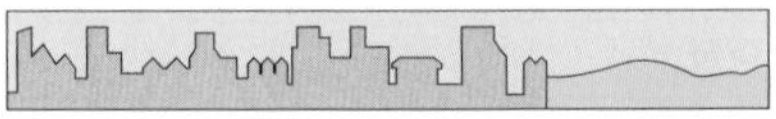
71%
29%

RELIGIOUS PERSUASION

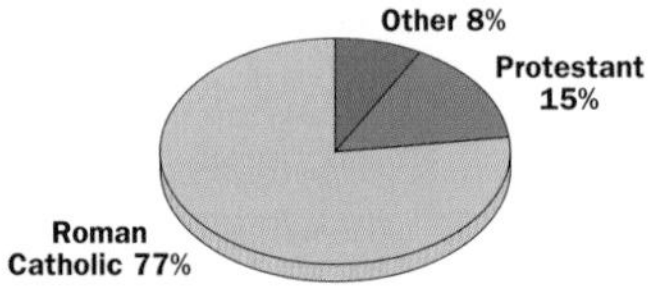
Other 8%
Protestant 15%
Roman Catholic 77%

The majority of Dominicans are descendants of Africans brought over to work the banana plantations. The Carib Territory on the northeast of the island contains the only surviving Carib population in the Caribbean.

POLITICS

Multiparty elections

2000/2005

President Vernon Shaw

AT THE LAST ELECTION

House of Assembly 30 seats

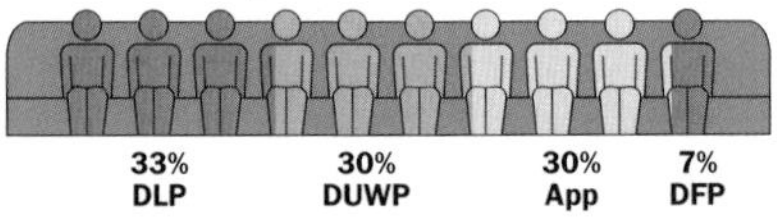
33% DLP
30% DUWP
30% App
7% DFP

DLP = Dominica Labour Party **DUWP** = Dominica United Workers' Party **App** = Appointed **DFP** = Dominica Freedom Party

Nine senators are appointed to the House of Assembly by the head of state

Politicians tend to come from the professional classes – usually young lawyers and doctors. The center-left DUWP narrowly won the 1995 elections, ending 15 years of rule by the right-wing DFP. A further swing to the left produced a DLP victory in 2000, and the party's leader Rosie Douglas became prime minister, Pierre Charles succeeding him on his sudden death a few months later. The contraction of the economy, due to difficulties in the banana trade and a global slowdown in tourism, is the main issue. An austerity budget imposed in 2002 led to widespread political protest.

WORLD AFFAIRS

Joined UN in 1978

ACS | Comm | Caricom | OAS | OECS

Dominica has close links with France and the US. Preferential access to EU markets for Caribbean bananas, crucial for Dominica's economy, was lost after a successful protest to the WTO in 1999 by the US.

Inshore fishing boats, *which mostly supply the domestic market, on a typical Dominican beach.*

AID

Recipient

US$20m (receipts) | Up 33% in 2001

A declining economy has left Dominica increasingly dependent on overseas assistance. Japan has given aid to ensure Dominican support for whaling.

DEFENSE

No compulsory military service

Defense forces were officially disbanded in 1981 | Not applicable

Dominica has no armed forces, but it does participate in the US-sponsored Regional Security System.

ECONOMICS

Inflation 2.8% p.a. (1990–2001)

US$230m | 2.67 Eastern Caribbean dollars (2.7)

SCORE CARD

❑ World GNP Ranking	181st
❑ GNP per Capita	US$3200
❑ Balance of Payments	–US69m
❑ Inflation	1%
❑ Unemployment	20%

Strengths

Bananas, though this sector has declined since the loss of EU preferential access. Growing services sector and "eco-tourism." IMF standby credit approved in 2002.

Weaknesses

Dependence on US and EU markets for its banana crop; access threatened by WTO ruling. Low productivity in public sector. Poor infrastructure.

EXPORTS

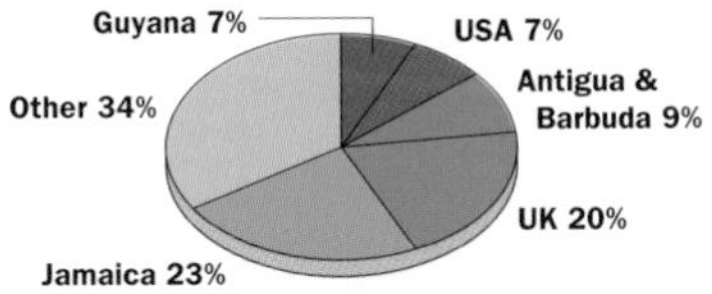
Guyana 7%
USA 7%
Antigua & Barbuda 9%
Other 34%
UK 20%
Jamaica 23%

IMPORTS

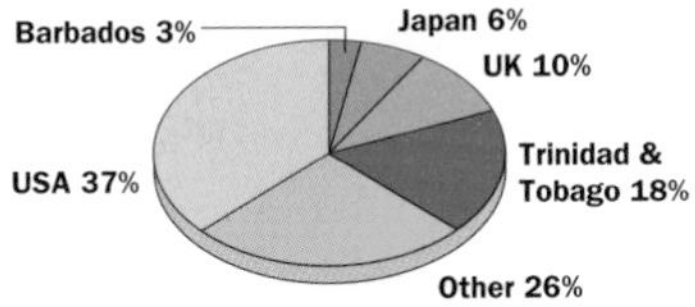
Barbados 3%
Japan 6%
UK 10%
Trinidad & Tobago 18%
USA 37%
Other 26%

RESOURCES

Electric power 10,000 kW

1157 tonnes | Not an oil producer

13,400 cattle, 9700 goats, 7600 sheep, 190,000 chickens | None

Dominica has no natural resources. A hydroelectric power plant in the Morne Trois Pitons national park provides half the island's power.

ENVIRONMENT

Not available

23% (13% partially protected) | 1 tonne per capita

Increased agriculture and timber harvesting is threatening Dominica's rainforest; already there is more land under cultivation than planned by the government. The current promotion of the rainforest as a tourist attraction poses a threat, as does a possible expansion in HEP generators. Two species of parrot – the imperial, or sisserou, and the red-necked – are threatened, despite conservation orders. Endangered hawksbill turtles, living on coral reefs off the island, are traditionally hunted.

MEDIA

TV ownership medium

There are no daily newspapers

PUBLISHING AND BROADCAST MEDIA

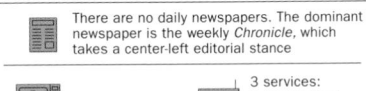

There are no daily newspapers. The dominant newspaper is the weekly *Chronicle,* which takes a center-left editorial stance

No TV service | 3 services: 1 state-owned, 2 independent

Local franchises, offering cable TV with selected US networks, serve one-third of the island. Broadcasts from other Caribbean states can also be received. There are four weekly newspapers.

CRIME

Death penalty in use

298 prisoners | Up 8% in 1999

Dominica has a lower crime rate than most of its Caribbean neighbors. Burglary and armed robbery are the major concerns; murders are rare. Justice is based on British common law and administered by the Eastern Caribbean Supreme Court, which is based on the island of St. Lucia.

EDUCATION

School leaving age: 17

96% | 461 students

Education is partly based on the old British model, and retains the selective 11-plus exam for entrance into high school. Students go on to the University of the West Indies or, increasingly, to colleges in the US and the UK.

CHRONOLOGY

Colonized first by the French, Dominica came under British control in 1759.

- ❑ **1975** Morne Trois Pitons national park established.
- ❑ **1978** Independence from UK. Patrick John first prime minister.
- ❑ **1980** Eugenia Charles becomes Caribbean's first woman prime minister.
- ❑ **1981** Two coup attempts, backed by Patrick John, foiled.
- ❑ **1995** Opposition DUWP defeats DFP. Dame Eugenia Charles retires after 27 years in politics.
- ❑ **1999** WTO ruling on preferential access for bananas to EU market.
- ❑ **2000** DLP wins elections.

D

HEALTH

Welfare state health benefits

1 per 2041 people | Cancers, heart, cerebrovascular, and infectious diseases

There are four hospitals, but surgery is carried out in only one. Difficult communications hamper emergency access in the interior.

SPENDING

GDP/cap. increase

CONSUMPTION AND SPENDING

90 per 1000 population | *299 per 1000 population*

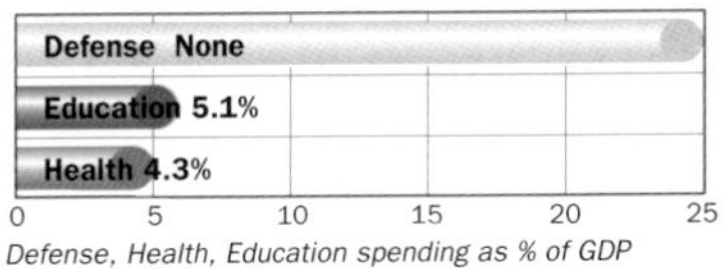
Defense None
Education 5.1%
Health 4.3%
0
5
10
15
20
25
Defense, Health, Education spending as % of GDP

Wealth disparities are not as marked in Dominica as they are on the larger Caribbean islands, but the alleviation of poverty has become a major plank of government policy. Measures taken include increased benefits and help for the country's pensioners.

WORLD RANKING

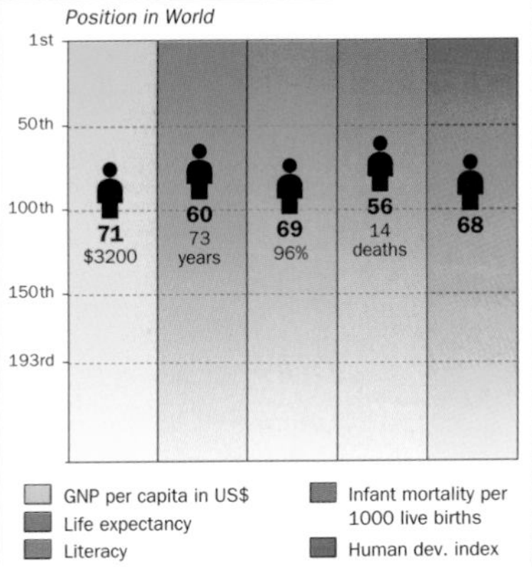
Position in World
1st
50th
100th
150th
193rd
71
$3200
60
73
years
69
96%
56
14
deaths
68
GNP per capita in US$
Life expectancy
Literacy
Infant mortality per 1000 live births
Human dev. index

Dominican Republic

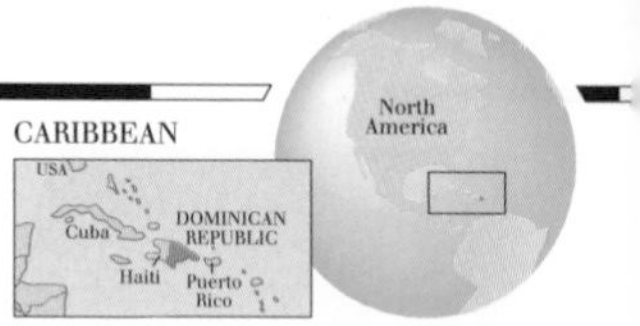
CARIBBEAN
USA
Cuba
Haiti
DOMINICAN REPUBLIC
Puerto Rico
North America

Official Name: Dominican Republic **Capital:** Santo Domingo
Population: 8.6 million **Currency:** Dominican Republic peso **Official Language:** Spanish

1865 | 1865 | Feb 27 | DOM | -4 | +1809 | .do

View south from Pico Duarte along the fertile banks of the Río Yaque del Norte.

THE MOST POPULAR tourist destination in the Caribbean, the Dominican Republic lies 970 km (600 miles) southeast of Florida. Once ruled by Spain, it occupies the eastern two-thirds of the island of Hispaniola and boasts both the region's highest point (Pico Duarte, 3088 m – 10,131 ft) and its lowest (Lake Enriquillo, 44 m – 144 ft – below sea level). Spanish-speaking, it seeks closer ties with the anglophone West Indies.

CLIMATE

Tropical equatorial/oceanic

WEATHER CHART FOR SANTO DOMINGO

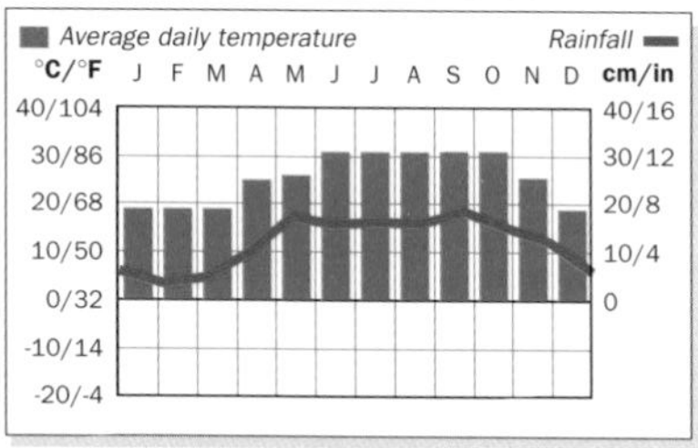
Average daily temperature
Rainfall
°C/°F
J F M A M J J A S O N D
cm/in
40/104
30/86
20/68
10/50
0/32
-10/14
-20/-4
40/16
30/12
20/8
10/4
0

The trade winds blow all year round, providing relief from the tropical heat and humidity. The hurricane season runs from June until November.

TRANSPORTATION

Drive on right

Aeropuerto Internacional de las Américas, Santo Domingo 2.43m passengers

20 ships 9400 grt

THE TRANSPORTATION NETWORK

Roads	6224 km (3867 miles)	Motorways	None
Railways	757 km (470 miles)	Waterways	None

Urban and rural transportation is poor; railroads are mainly for transporting sugarcane and ores. An international consortium in 1999 won a 30-year concession to operate four airports.

TOURISM

Visitors : Population 1:3.1

2.81m visitors

Down 3% in 2002

MAIN TOURIST ARRIVALS

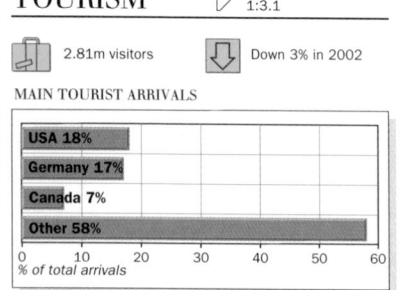

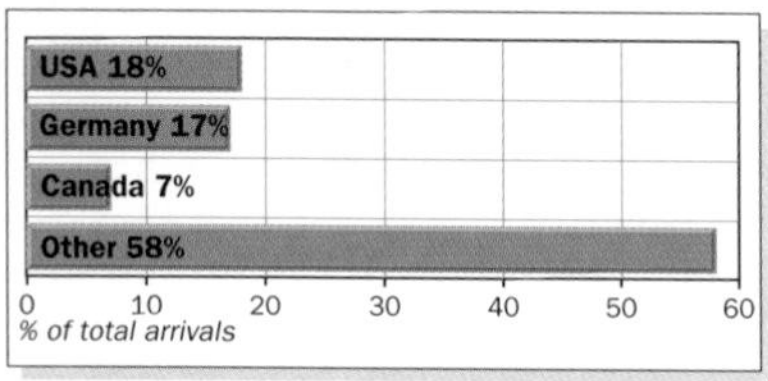
USA 18%
Germany 17%
Canada 7%
Other 58%
0
10
20
30
40
50
60
% of total arrivals

Ample accommodation and excellent beaches attract many tourists each year, mainly from Europe and North America.

PEOPLE

Pop. density medium

Spanish, French Creole

178/km² (460/mi²)

THE URBAN/RURAL POPULATION SPLIT

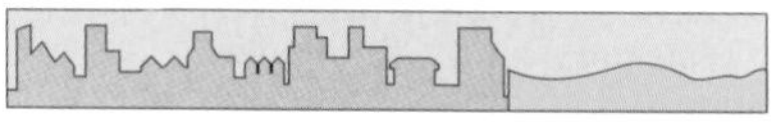
66%
34%

RELIGIOUS PERSUASION

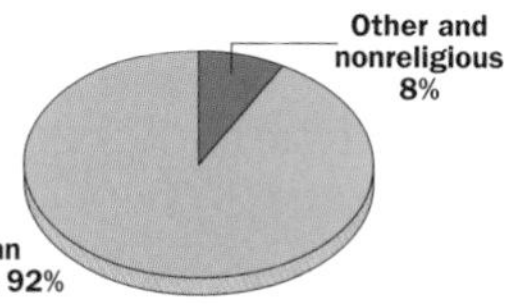
Other and nonreligious 8%
Roman Catholic 92%

The white population, primarily the descendants of Spanish settlers, still own most of the land. The mixed race majority – about 73% – controls much of the republic's commerce, and forms the bulk of the professional middle classes. Blacks, the descendants of Africans, are mainly small-scale farmers and often the victims of latent racism, especially in business. Women in the black community work the farms; in the white and mixed race communities women are starting to make professional careers.

POLITICS

Multiparty elections

L. House 2002/2006
U. House 2002/2006

President Hipolito Mejia

AT THE LAST ELECTION

Chamber of Deputies 150 seats

49% PRD
27% PLD
24% PRSC

PRD = Dominican Revolutionary Party **PLD** = Dominican Liberation Party **PRSC** = Christian Social Reform Party

Senate 32 seats

91% PRD
6% PRSC
3% PLD

Decades of conservative rule under Joaquín Balaguer ended in 1996. The election of President Hipolito Mejia in 2000 confirmed the dominance of the center-left PRD, which in 1998 had gained control of Congress. Despite initial successes, Mejia has seen his own popularity wane. Living costs have spiraled and unemployment has risen; chronic electricity shortages prompted mass demonstrations against his government. Under new rules introduced in 2001, Mejia will not be able to stand in 2004 for a second term.

Dominican Republic

Total Area : 48 730 sq. km (18 815 sq. miles)

ATLANTIC OCEAN
CARIBBEAN SEA
HAITI
Monte Cristi
Puerto Plata
Dajabón
Mao
Sabaneta
Esperanza
José E. Bisonó
Santiago
Moca
Salcedo
Nagua
San Francisco de Macorís
Samaná
La Vega
Pico Duarte 3175m
Jarabacoa
Cotuí
Yuna
Sabana de la Mar
Pedro Santana
Constanza
Bonao
Monte Plata
Hato Mayor
El Seibo
Comendador
San Juan
Villa Altagracia
SANTO DOMINGO
San Pedro de Macorís
Higüey
Malpasso
Lago Enriquillo
Jimaní
Neiba
Azua
S. José de Ocoa
San Cristóbal
Bajos de Haina
Intl Airport Las Américas
La Romana
Boca de Yuma
Vicente Noble
Baní
Barahona
Pedernales
Isla Saona
Mona Passage
Isla Beata
CORDILLERA CENTRAL
N
POPULATION
over 1 000 000
over 100 000
over 50 000
over 10 000
under 10 000
LAND HEIGHT
2000m/6562ft
1000m/3281ft
500m/1640ft
200m/656ft
Sea Level
50 km
50 miles

D

WORLD AFFAIRS

Joined UN in 1945

ACS | Geplac | IBRD | OAS | SELA

Relations with Haiti, which occupies the western third of Hispaniola, are important. The Dominican Republic favors a "strategic alliance" between the Caribbean and Central America.

AID

Recipient

$105m (receipts) | Up 69% in 2001

Multilateral and bilateral aid of some $235 million was granted in 1998 to repair severe hurricane damage.

DEFENSE

No compulsory military service

$156m | Down 8% in 2001

The military has economic and political interests, but no longer holds the defense portfolio. It focuses on illegal immigration from Haiti. The main arms supplier is the US.

ECONOMICS

Inflation 9.1% p.a. (1990–2001)

$19bn | 30.6 Dominican Republic pesos (17.2)

SCORE CARD

- ❑ WORLD GNP RANKING....................67th
- ❑ GNP PER CAPITA....................$2230
- ❑ BALANCE OF PAYMENTS....................–$839m
- ❑ INFLATION....................8.9%
- ❑ UNEMPLOYMENT....................14%

STRENGTHS

Sustained tourism growth. Mining – mainly of nickel and gold – and sugar major sectors. Hand-made cigars, which are biggest sellers in US. Large hidden economy based on transshipment of narcotics to US.

WEAKNESSES

Tourism vulnerable to global slumps, such as that after September 11, 2001. Peso falling in value. Massive bank fraud exposed in 2003 – $2.2 billion embezzled. Electricity shortages.

EXPORTS

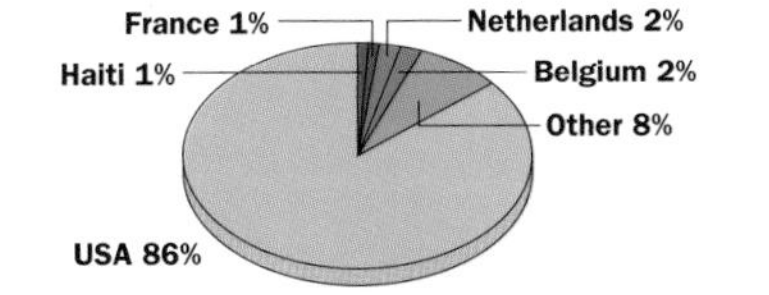
France 1%
Netherlands 2%
Haiti 1%
Belgium 2%
Other 8%
USA 86%

IMPORTS

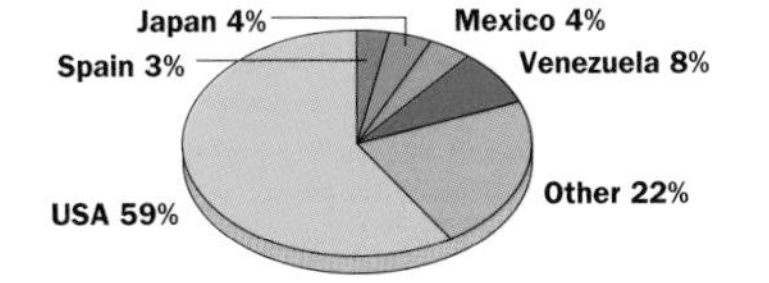
Japan 4%
Mexico 4%
Spain 3%
Venezuela 8%
USA 59%
Other 22%

RESOURCES

Electric power 3.1m kW

13,154 tonnes | Not an oil producer; refines 35,600 b/d

2.16m cattle, 577,000 pigs, 46m chickens | Ferro-nickel, bauxite, copper, gold, silver

The Dominican Republic is a net energy importer: hydroelectric generators are the only domestic source of power, and electricity blackouts can be a major problem. Oil prospecting has been unsuccessful, and oil is imported from Mexico and Venezuela on preferential terms under the San José Agreement. The Dominican Republic's quota from Venezuela was increased under the 2000 Caracas Accord.

ENVIRONMENT

Sustainability rank: 79th

174% (154% partially protected) including marine areas | 2.8 tonnes per capita

Forests are threatened by destructive agricultural practices and also by the use of wood as fuel by rural communities. Deforestation has accelerated soil erosion.

MEDIA

TV ownership medium

Daily newspaper circulation 27 per 1000 people

PUBLISHING AND BROADCAST MEDIA

There are 11 daily newspapers, including *Listín Diario*, *Ultima Hora*, *El Nacional*, and *El Caribe*

7 services: 1 state-owned, 6 independent | 131 services: 1 state-owned, 130 independent

Television broadcasts from both Mexico and the US can easily be received in the Dominican Republic.

CRIME

No death penalty

15,340 prisoners | Narcotics-related crime is rising

The Dominican Republic is increasingly used by narcotics cartels as a transit point to the US. Narcotics trafficking and arms smuggling are linked to the high levels of violent crime.

EDUCATION

School leaving age: 17

84% | 176,995 students

State schools are badly underfunded. The state university of Santo Domingo suffered a financial crisis in 1999. The rich send their children to study in the US and Spain.

HEALTH

Welfare state health benefits

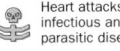

1 per 463 people | Heart attacks, infectious and parasitic diseases

Wealthy Dominicans fly to Cuba and the US for treatment. The poor rely on a basic public service, inadequately provided by some 20 state hospitals.

CHRONOLOGY

The 1697 Franco-Spanish partition of Hispaniola left Spain with the eastern two-thirds of the island, now the Dominican Republic.

- ❑ **1865** Independence from Spain.
- ❑ **1930–1961** Gen. Molina dictator.
- ❑ **1965** Civil war. US intervention.
- ❑ **1966** Conservative Joaquín Balaguer begins first of seven presidential terms over next 30 years.
- ❑ **1996** Candidate of moderate PLD succeeds Balaguer.
- ❑ **1998** Major hurricane damage.
- ❑ **2000** Hipolito Mejia of center-left PRD wins presidency.

SPENDING

GDP/cap. increase

CONSUMPTION AND SPENDING

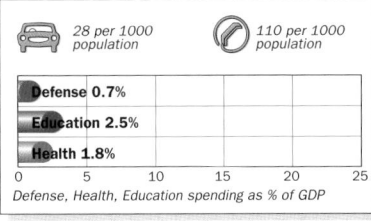

28 per 1000 population | *110 per 1000 population*

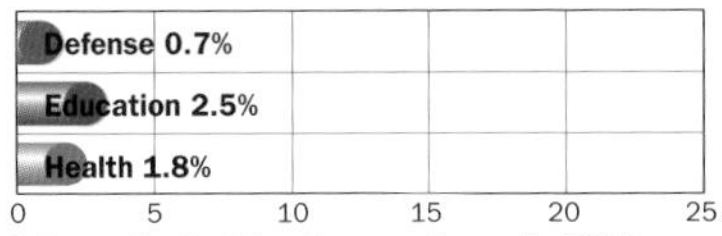
Defense 0.7%
Education 2.5%
Health 1.8%
0
5
10
15
20
25

Defense, Health, Education spending as % of GDP

Great disparities exist between rich and poor. The government in 1998 announced a seven-year plan to relieve poverty and reduce the level of malnutrition affecting well over two million people. Black Dominicans remain at the bottom of the economic and social ladder, accounting for the major proportion of small farmers and unemployed. Haitian immigrants are poorly paid, badly treated, and liable to be deported at short notice. Mixed races have shown most upward mobility in recent years, but, nevertheless, the old Spanish families still form the wealthiest section of society and retain their grip on valuable estates.

WORLD RANKING

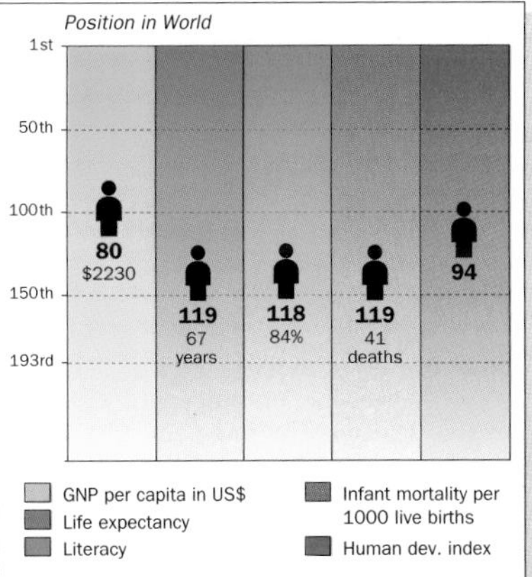
Position in World
1st
50th
100th
150th
193rd
80
$2230
119
67 years
118
84%
119
41 deaths
94
GNP per capita in US$
Life expectancy
Literacy
Infant mortality per 1000 live births
Human dev. index

EAST TIMOR

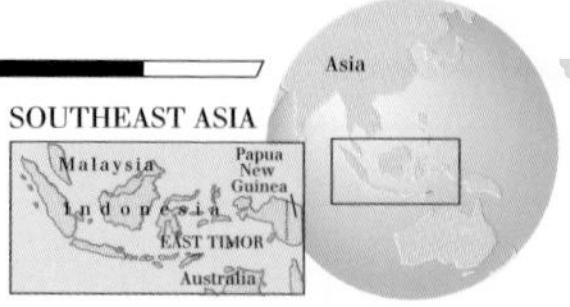
Asia
SOUTHEAST ASIA
Malaysia
Papua New Guinea
Indonesia
EAST TIMOR
Australia

OFFICIAL NAME: Democratic Republic of Timor Leste **CAPITAL:** Dili **POPULATION:** 779,000
CURRENCY: US dollar **OFFICIAL LANGUAGES:** Tetum (Portuguese/Austronesian) and Portuguese

2002 | 2002 | May 20 | n/a | +8 | +670 | .tp

LYING NORTH OF Australia across the Timor Sea, the island of Timor has a narrow coastal plain giving way to forested highlands. Its mountainous backbone rises to 2963 m (9715 ft). The eastern half was colonized for over 400 years by Portugal, then occupied from 1975 by Indonesia, whose forces hunted down all resistance. A referendum in 1999 launched a turbulent transition to independence in May 2002.

CLIMATE

Tropical equatorial

WEATHER CHART FOR DILI

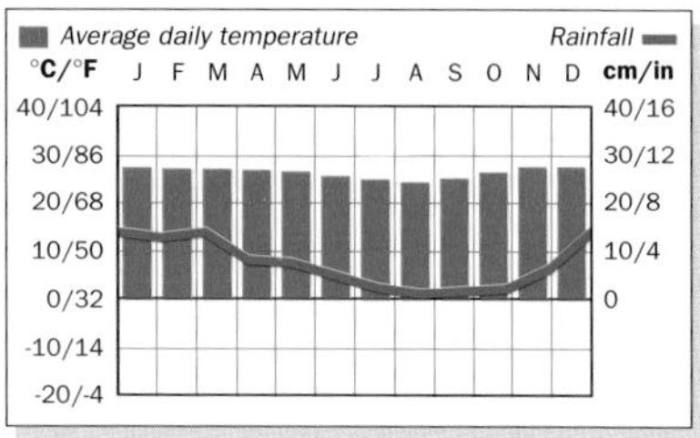
Average daily temperature
Rainfall
°C/°F J F M A M J J A S O N D cm/in
40/104
30/86
20/68
10/50
0/32
-10/14
-20/-4
40/16
30/12
20/8
10/4
0

The climate is tropical, with heavy rain from December to March, then dry and increasingly hot weather for the rest of the year, especially in the north.

TRANSPORTATION

Not available

Dili International — Not available

THE TRANSPORTATION NETWORK

1414 km (879 miles) — None — None — None

Roads are of poor quality and public transportation beyond Dili is unreliable and sparse.

TOURISM

Visitors : Population 1:260

3000 visitors — Down in 1999–2000

MAIN TOURIST ARRIVALS

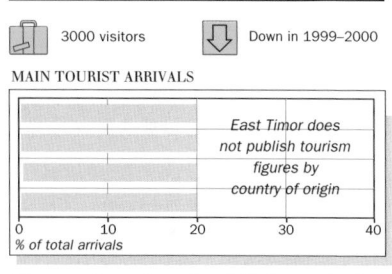

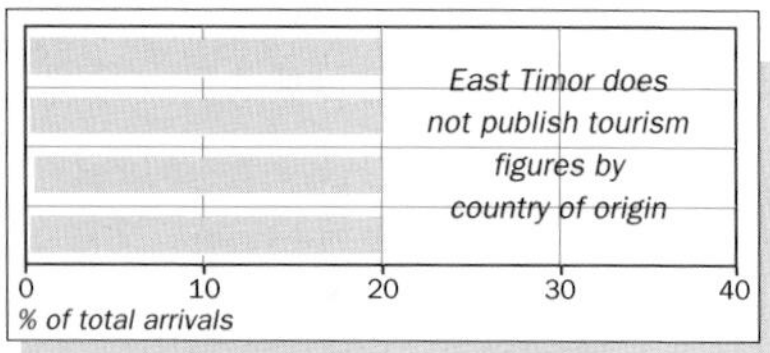
East Timor does not publish tourism figures by country of origin
0
10
20
30
40
% of total arrivals

The number of tourists fell dramatically after the preindependence violence in the region. Visitors are now generally discouraged by the high levels of crime and the almost complete lack of a tourist infrastructure.

PEOPLE

Pop. density medium

Tetum (Portuguese/Austronesian), Bahasa Indonesia, and Portuguese — 53/km² (138/mi²)

THE URBAN/RURAL POPULATION SPLIT

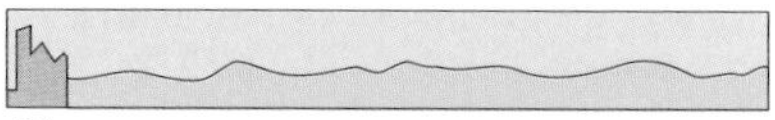
8%
92%

RELIGIOUS PERSUASION

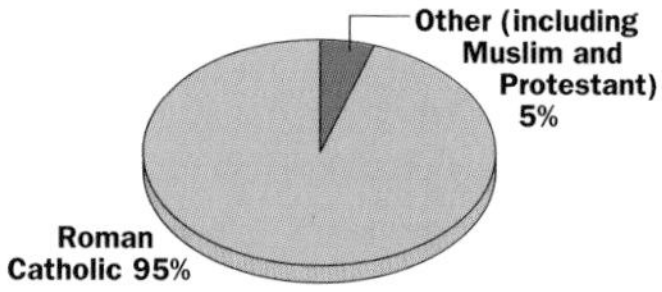
Other (including Muslim and Protestant) 5%
Roman Catholic 95%

East Timor is almost entirely Roman Catholic. The Timorese are a mix of Malay and Papuan peoples, and many indigenous Papuan tribes survive. There is an urban Chinese minority, and ethnic Indonesian settlers became numerous after annexation, constituting 20% of the population by 1999. Preindependence violence was politically rather than ethnically motivated.

Women do not enjoy a high profile in public life. The incidence of domestic violence is notably high.

EAST TIMOR

Total Area : 15,007 sq. km (5794 sq. miles)

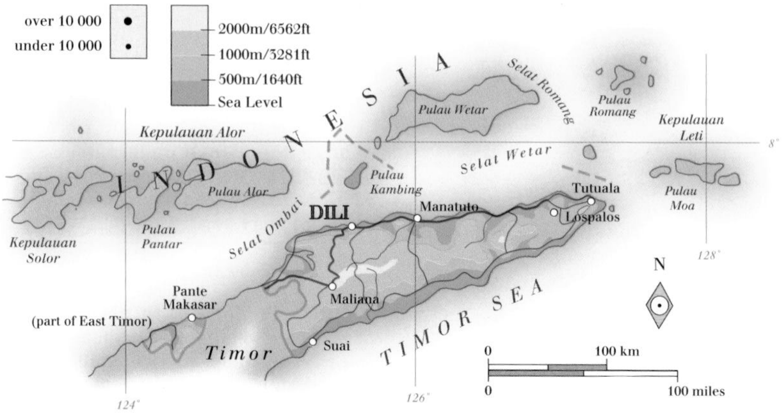
POPULATION
over 10 000
under 10 000
LAND HEIGHT
2000m/6562ft
1000m/3281ft
500m/1640ft
Sea Level
INDONESIA
Selat Romang
Pulau Wetar
Pulau Romang
Kepulauan Leti
Kepulauan Alor
Selat Wetar
Pulau Kambing
Pulau Alor
Tutuala
Pulau Moa
Manatuto
DILI
Lospalos
Selat Ombai
Pulau Pantar
Kepulauan Solor
Pante Makasar
Maliana
(part of East Timor)
Suai
Timor
TIMOR SEA
N
0
100 km
100 miles
124°
126°
128°
8°

POLITICS

Multiparty elections

2001/Transitional — President Xanana Gusmão

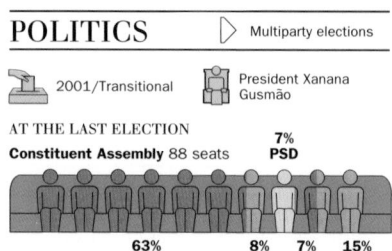

AT THE LAST ELECTION

Constituent Assembly 88 seats

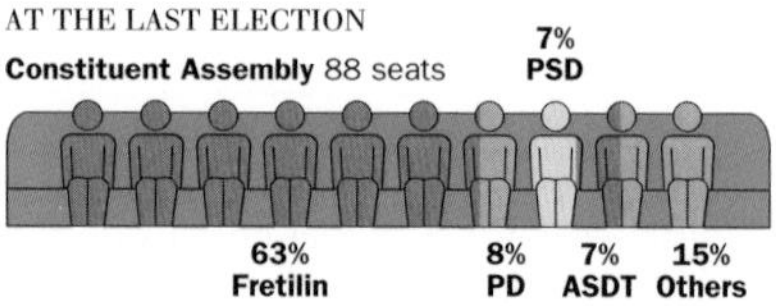
7% PSD
63% Fretilin
8% PD
7% ASDT
15% Others

Fretilin = Revolutionary Front of an Independent East Timor
PD = Democratic Party **PSD** = Social-Democratic Party
ASDT = Timorese Social-Democratic Association

East Timor is an emerging multiparty democracy. The Fretilin movement was the leading voice in the long struggle for independence. Turnout at recent elections was high.

After years of unrest and human rights abuses committed by the Indonesian army, the Indonesian government in 1999 conceded a referendum on East Timor's future. Pro-Indonesian militias went on the rampage, murdering hundreds of people in indiscriminate attacks, and forcing thousands into the Indonesian-controlled western half of the island. An Australian-led international peacekeeping force eventually secured relative calm and organized the promised vote on August 30, 1999. An overwhelming 80% of voters endorsed independence.

The UN Mission in East Timor was given full power over the territory in October 1999. Fretilin emerged as the outright victor in elections in late 2001 to the new Constituent Assembly. Its popular leader, Xanana Gusmão, reversed his decision to retire from politics and was duly elected president in 2002. Independence took effect on May 20 that year.

The new government, headed by Prime Minister Mari Alkatiri, pledged to concentrate spending on health and education.

WORLD AFFAIRS

Joined UN in 2002

IMF | ADB | IBRD

Relations with Indonesia remain strained over the issue of justice for past human rights abuses. Portugal, the former colonial power, had led international opposition to Indonesia's annexation of the territory. Australia, one of the few Western countries to recognize that annexation, later swung vital support behind the cause of independence. It is also a key player in providing future aid and assistance for reconstruction.

Since independence, East Timor has joined the UN and the ADB, and has applied to join ASEAN.

AID

Recipient

$195m (receipts)

Down 16% in 2001

International development aid provides the backbone of East Timor's GDP. Australia and Portugal are by far the biggest donors.

DEFENSE

No compulsory military service

Not available

Not available

The East Timorese Defense Force was established in 2001, formed from the remnants of proindependence militia. Its role is largely as an extension of the police force, as external defense is still provided by UN troops.

ECONOMICS

Not available

$391m

Currency is US dollar

SCORE CARD

❑ WORLD GNP RANKING	173rd
❑ GNP PER CAPITA	$520
❑ BALANCE OF PAYMENTS	$8m
❑ INFLATION	2.5%
❑ UNEMPLOYMENT	4%

STRENGTHS

Potential from oil and natural gas reserves in Timor Sea. Traditional agricultural base: coffee the main export.

WEAKNESSES

Infrastructure devastated by 1999 violence. Insecurity deterred investment. Undeveloped industrial sector.

EXPORTS/IMPORTS

Export and import figures are not available for East Timor

Despite its young age, *East Timor has a strong national identity, based largely on the domination of Roman Catholicism.*

RESOURCES

Electric power 14,400 kW

356 tonnes

Oil figures not available

343,072 pigs, 175,000 cattle, 2.1m chickens

Oil, natural gas, gold, manganese, marble

East Timor has few natural resources. Australia finally agreed in 2003 on the division of the substantial oil reserves under the Timor Sea.

ENVIRONMENT

Not available

Not available

Not available

Unrestricted logging under Indonesian rule has greatly diminished important species and contributed to erosion of the country's poor-quality soil.

MEDIA

TV ownership low

Daily newspaper circulation figures are not available

PUBLISHING AND BROADCAST MEDIA

There is 1 daily newspaper, the *Timor Post.* The UN Mission publishes the biweekly *Tais Timor*

1 service, run by the UN

4 stations: 1 UN-run, 1 run by the Catholic Church

Official newsletters have the highest circulation. A number of independent papers were established in 2000, including the *Timor Post*, managed by the editors and staff of *Suara Timor Timur*, the main preindependence daily.

CRIME

No death penalty

East Timor does not publish prison figures

Crime is rising

Petty and violent crimes are common. Most of the perpetrators of violence in 1999 have yet to be brought to justice.

EDUCATION

Not available

48%

7500 students

During Indonesian domination, classes were taught in Bahasa Indonesia. The number of students attending school and university has already begun to recover from the sharp decline in 1999.

CHRONOLOGY

The Portuguese arrived in Timor in the 1520s. It was formally divided by Portugal and the Netherlands in 1859.

- ❑ **1949** Dutch west Timor becomes part of Indonesia.
- ❑ **1975** Fretilin declares East Timor independent; Indonesia invades.
- ❑ **1991** Massacre of proindependence demonstrators in Dili.
- ❑ **1996** Timorese leaders receive Nobel Peace Prize, raising global awareness.
- ❑ **1999** Indonesian government agrees to hold referendum; resulting violence quelled by UN force.
- ❑ **2001** Elections to new Constituent Assembly; Fretilin wins majority.
- ❑ **2002** Xanana Gusmão elected president. Independence.

HEALTH

Not available

1 per 40,000 people

Not available

Life expectancy in East Timor has traditionally been lower than in the rest of the Indonesian archipelago. Most doctors left the province in 1999.

SPENDING

Not available

CONSUMPTION AND SPENDING

No data

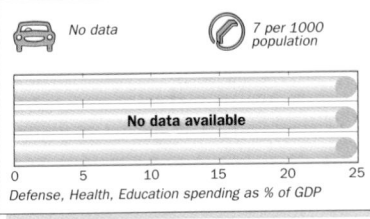

7 per 1000 population

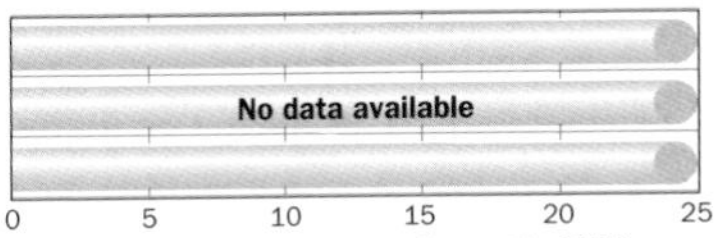
No data available
0
5
10
15
20
25

Defense, Health, Education spending as % of GDP

Living standards, already relatively low for the region, were made worse by the events of 1999. Thousands were left homeless. Well-paid UN staff enjoy a sharply contrasting lifestyle.

WORLD RANKING

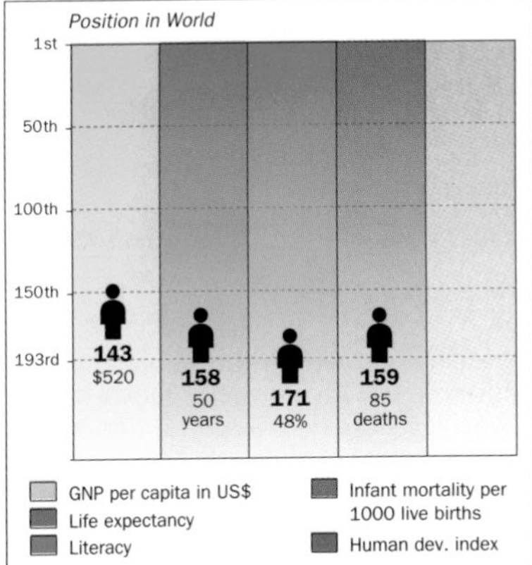
Position in World
1st
50th
100th
150th
193rd
143
$520
158
50 years
171
48%
159
85 deaths
GNP per capita in US$
Life expectancy
Literacy
Infant mortality per 1000 live births
Human dev. index

E

E

Ecuador

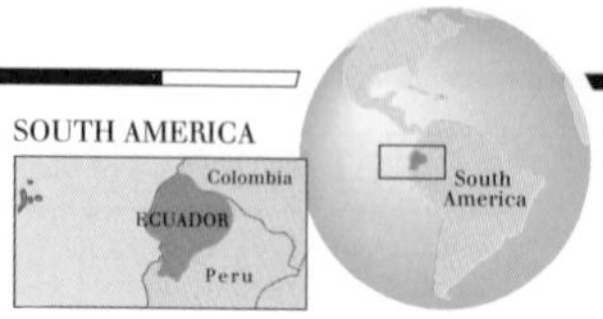
SOUTH AMERICA
Colombia
ECUADOR
Peru
South America

Official Name: Republic of Ecuador **Capital:** Quito
Population: 13.1 million **Currency:** US dollar **Official Language:** Spanish

1830 | 1941 | Aug 10 | EC | -5 | +593 | .ec

Once part of the Inca heartland, Ecuador lies on the western coast of South America. It was ruled by Spain from 1533, when the last Inca emperor was executed, until independence in 1830. Most Ecuadorians live either in the lowland coastal region or in the Andean Sierra. The Amazonian Amerindians are now pressing for their land rights to be recognized. Massive depreciation of the sucre forced the government to dollarize the currency in 2000.

CLIMATE

Tropical/mountain

WEATHER CHART FOR QUITO

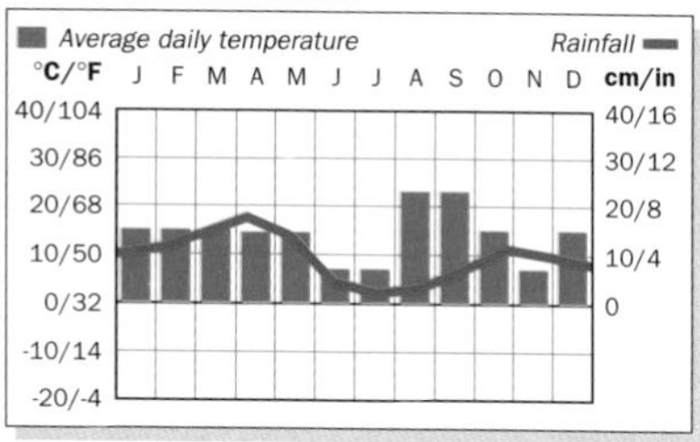
Average daily temperature
Rainfall
°C/°F J F M A M J J A S O N D cm/in
40/104 30/86 20/68 10/50 0/32 -10/14 -20/-4
40/16 30/12 20/8 10/4 0

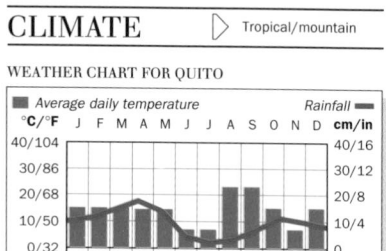

Climate varies from hot equatorial in the Amazon forests, to dry heat in the south and "perpetual spring" in Quito.

TRANSPORTATION

Drive on right

Mariscal Sucre, Quito
2.33m passengers

175 ships
305,900 grt

THE TRANSPORTATION NETWORK

8165 km (5073 miles)

Pan-American Highway

965 km (600 miles)

1500 km (932 miles)

The road network and railroad are grossly underfunded. Serious political unrest in 2000–2001 blocked roads.

TOURISM

Visitors : Population 1:20

654,000 visitors

Up 2% in 2002

MAIN TOURIST ARRIVALS

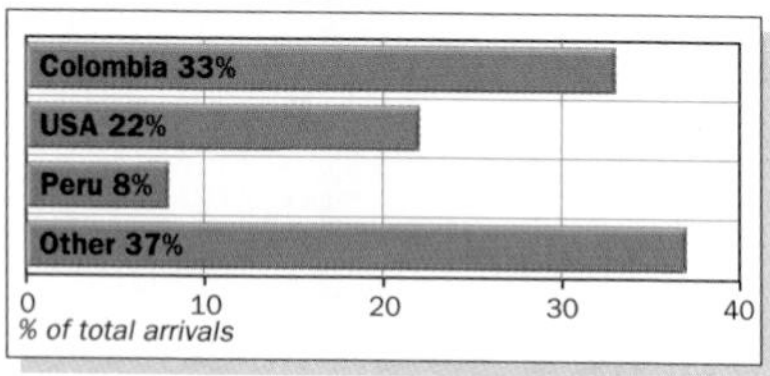
Colombia 33%
USA 22%
Peru 8%
Other 37%
0 10 20 30 40
% of total arrivals

Tourism is growing. Quito, once the capital of the Inca empire, has restored many of its Spanish imperial buildings, including 86 churches. Access to the unique wildlife on the Galapagos Islands is restricted to 60,000 visitors a year.

PEOPLE

Pop. density low

Spanish, Quechua, other Amerindian languages

47/km² (123/mi²)

THE URBAN/RURAL POPULATION SPLIT

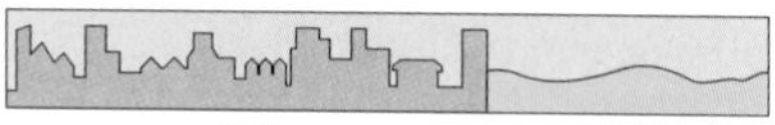
63%
37%

RELIGIOUS PERSUASION

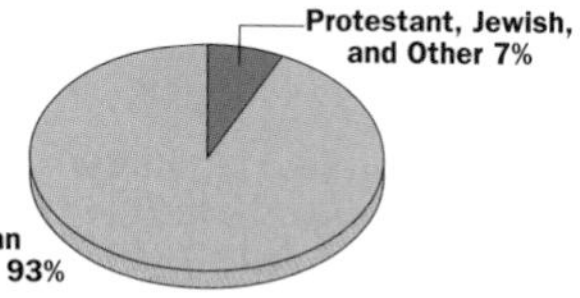
Protestant, Jewish, and Other 7%
Roman Catholic 93%

Over half of the population is of Amerindian–Spanish extraction (*mestizo*). Black communities exist on the coast. The Amerindians, who make up about one-quarter of the population, are pressing for Ecuador to be described as a plurinational state, within which the different indigenous communities are recognized as distinct nationalities. The strong and largely unified Amerindian movement is at the forefront of social protests.

POLITICS

Multiparty elections

2002/2006

President Lucio Gutiérrez

AT THE LAST ELECTION

National Congress 100 seats

26% PSC
15% PRE
13% ID
10% PRIAN
36% Others

PSC = Social Christian Party
PRE = Ecuadorian Roldosist Party **ID** = Democratic Left
PRIAN = Institutional Renewal Party of Democratic Action

The late 1990s were characterized by instability and corruption. Attempts to rescue the economy through austerity reforms and dollarization have provoked violent and widespread popular protests. In 2000 the army intervened and Vice President Gustavo Noboa took over the presidency. Coup leader Col. Lucio Gutiérrez went on to win presidential elections in 2002. He promised market-friendly policies, but faced opposition from Congress.

WORLD AFFAIRS

Joined UN in 1945

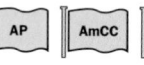

AP | AmCC | NAM | OAS | RG

Oil prices and access to US and EU markets for bananas are major concerns. There are serious security problems on the border with Colombia.

Ecuador

Total Area : 283 560 sq. km (109 483 sq. miles)

POPULATION

- over 1 000 000
- over 500 000
- over 100 000
- over 50 000
- over 10 000
- under 10 000

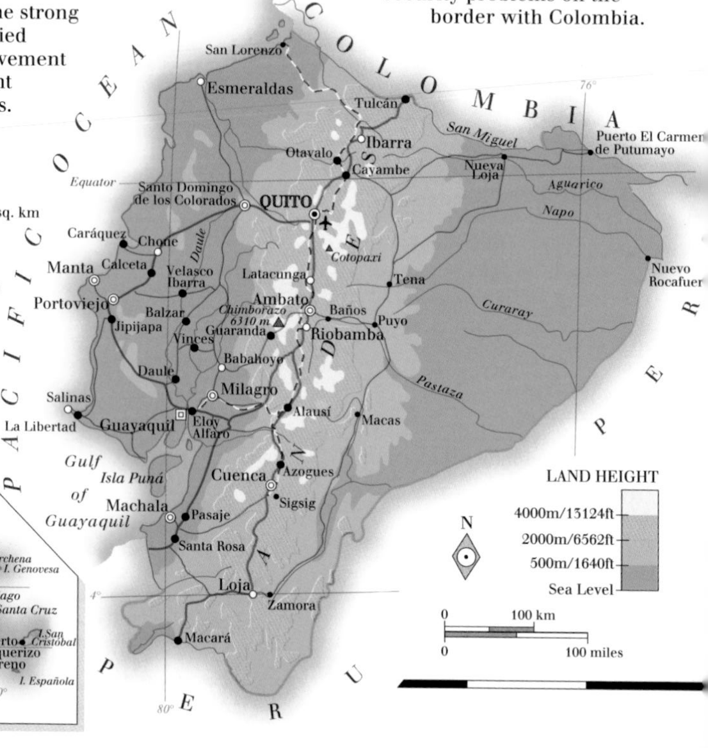
PACIFIC OCEAN
COLOMBIA
PERU
San Lorenzo
Esmeraldas
Tulcán
Ibarra
Otavalo
Cayambe
San Miguel
Nueva Loja
Puerto El Carmen de Putumayo
Aguarico
Napo
Equator
Santo Domingo de los Colorados
QUITO
Caráquez
Chone
Manta
Calceta
Portoviejo
Jipijapa
Velasco Ibarra
Daule
Latacunga
Cotopaxi
Tena
Nuevo Rocafuer
Ambato
Chimborazo 6310 m
Baños
Puyo
Curaray
Balzar
Guaranda
Riobamba
Vinces
Babahoyo
Pastaza
Milagro
Salinas
La Libertad
Guayaquil
Eloy Alfaro
Alausí
Macas
Gulf of Guayaquil
Isla Puná
Cuenca
Azogues
Machala
Sigsig
Pasaje
Santa Rosa
Loja
Zamora
Macará
76°
80°
4°
LAND HEIGHT
4000m/13124ft
2000m/6562ft
500m/1640ft
Sea Level
N
0 100 km
0 100 miles

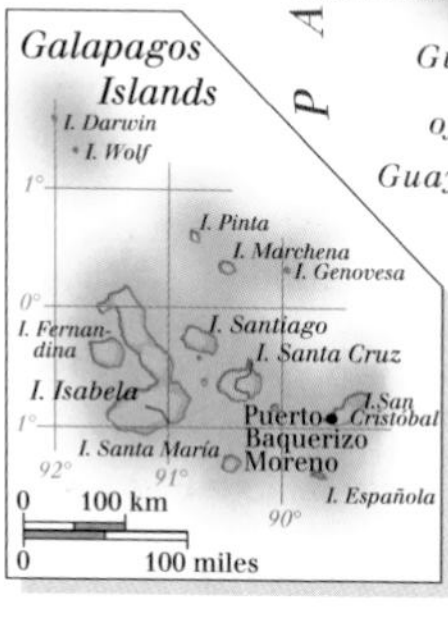
Galapagos Islands
I. Darwin
I. Wolf
I. Pinta
I. Marchena
I. Genovesa
I. Fernandina
I. Santiago
I. Santa Cruz
I. Isabela
I. San Cristóbal
Puerto Baquerizo Moreno
I. Santa María
I. Española
92°
91°
90°
1°
0°
0 100 km
0 100 miles

***Quito is the second-highest** capital in the world, after La Paz in Bolivia. It lies in an Andean valley lined with 30 volcanoes.*

AID

Recipient

$171m (receipts)

Up 16% in 2001

Aid from the US, Japan, Spain, and the IDB alleviates the heavy foreign debt burden. The Galapagos Islands receive generous grants from UNESCO.

DEFENSE

Compulsory military service

$507m

Up 6% in 2001

The army kept out of politics from the mid-1970s until its intervention in 2000. Moves to reduce the military's 50% "royalty" share of oil revenues, its prime source of funding, raised tensions.

ECONOMICS

Inflation 37% p.a. (1990–2001)

$14bn

Currency is US dollar

SCORE CARD

❑ World GNP Ranking	77th
❑ GNP per Capita	$1080
❑ Balance of Payments	–$800m
❑ Inflation	37.7%
❑ Unemployment	13%

Strengths

Net oil exporter. World's second-biggest banana producer. Fishing industry. US dollar offers stability, but removes control.

Weaknesses

Poor infrastructure and land productivity. Energy crises. High inflation. History of financial instability.

EXPORTS

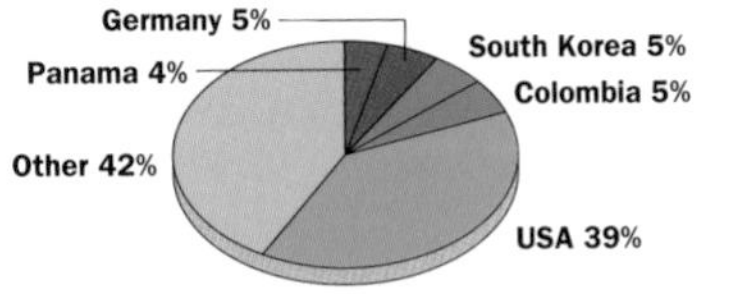
Germany 5%
Panama 4%
South Korea 5%
Colombia 5%
Other 42%
USA 39%

IMPORTS

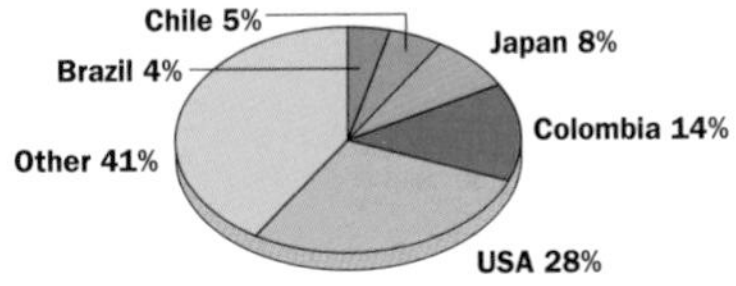
Chile 5%
Brazil 4%
Japan 8%
Colombia 14%
Other 41%
USA 28%

RESOURCES

Electric power 3.7m kW

654,658 tonnes

410,000 b/d (reserves 4.6bn barrels)

5.58m cattle, 2.81m pigs, 2.38m sheep, 140m chickens

Oil, natural gas, gold, silver, copper, zinc

The government is encouraging faster oil exploration and higher output. Ecuador left OPEC in 1992. Overfishing is threatening mackerel and squid stocks.

ENVIRONMENT

Sustainability rank: 41st

46% (25% partially protected)

1.9 tonnes per capita

Oil drilling in new areas of Amazonia threatens indigenous tribes. Tourism, some of it illegal, has upset the delicate ecosystems of the Galapagos Islands; the land iguana is endangered, and black coral is stolen in quantity for souvenirs. The breaching of the *Jessica* oil tanker just offshore in 2001 raised concerns about shipping oil through ecologically sensitive areas.

MEDIA

TV ownership medium

Daily newspaper circulation 96 per 1000 people

PUBLISHING AND BROADCAST MEDIA

There are 29 daily newspapers. The most popular are *El Universo* and *El Extra*

67 independent services

1 state-owned, 320 independent stations

The largely independent press is highly regionalized, based either in the Quito region or around Guayaquil on the coast, which is also a center for commercially run radio stations. There are ten cultural and ten religious radio stations.

CRIME

No death penalty

8520 prisoners

Up 1% in 1999

Right-wing paramilitaries were blamed for the murders of a trade union leader in 1998 and a left-wing congressman in 1999. The paramilitaries are rumored to be supported by Colombians. Left-wing urban guerrillas are also reported. Unprecedented numbers of citizens are applying for arms permits, while the illegal arms trade is thriving.

EDUCATION

School leaving age: 14

92%

206,541 students

Programs have been launched to combat high levels of adult illiteracy in rural areas. Secondary schools are badly underfunded.

There are three state universities, with branches across the country, and many private institutions.

CHRONOLOGY

Alternating republican and military governments ruled Ecuador from independence in 1830 to 1979.

- ❑ **1941–1942** Loss of mineral-rich El Oro region to Peru.
- ❑ **1948–1960** Prosperity from bananas.
- ❑ **1972** Oil production starts.
- ❑ **1979** Return to democracy.
- ❑ **1992** Amerindians win land in Amazonia.
- ❑ **1996–1997** Abdalá Bucarám Ortíz removed from presidency on grounds of mental incapacity.
- ❑ **1998–1999** Economic crisis.
- ❑ **2000** Army sides with Amerindian protestors. Vice President Gustavo Noboa replaces president.
- ❑ **2002** Lucio Gutiérrez, leader of 2000 coup, elected president.

E

HEALTH

Welfare state health benefits

1 per 725 people

Cancers, accidents, heart and infectious diseases

Health care is seriously underfunded. Some services exist in poor urban districts but are still unavailable in many rural areas. Severe budget cuts mean that any improvement will depend on more outside aid.

SPENDING

GDP/cap. increase

CONSUMPTION AND SPENDING

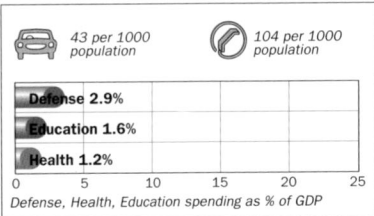

43 per 1000 population

104 per 1000 population

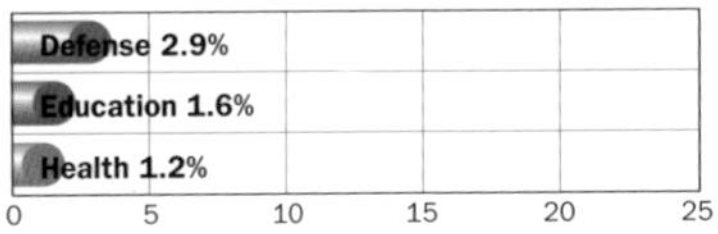
Defense 2.9%
Education 1.6%
Health 1.2%
0
5
10
15
20
25

Defense, Health, Education spending as % of GDP

The US state aid agency estimates that as much as 70% of the population lives in poverty. Most of these people are concentrated in urban areas.

WORLD RANKING

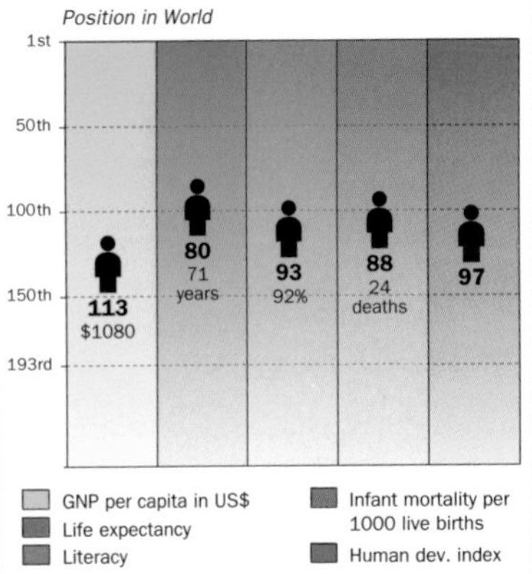
Position in World
1st
50th
100th
150th
193rd
113
$1080
80
71 years
93
92%
88
24 deaths
97
GNP per capita in US$
Life expectancy
Literacy
Infant mortality per 1000 live births
Human dev. index

EGYPT

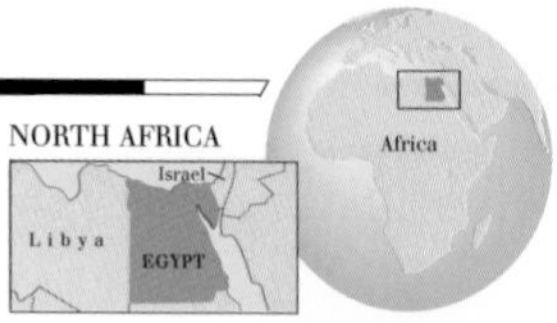
NORTH AFRICA
Israel
Libya
EGYPT
Africa

OFFICIAL NAME: Arab Republic of Egypt **CAPITAL:** Cairo
POPULATION: 70.3 million **CURRENCY:** Egyptian pound **OFFICIAL LANGUAGE:** Arabic

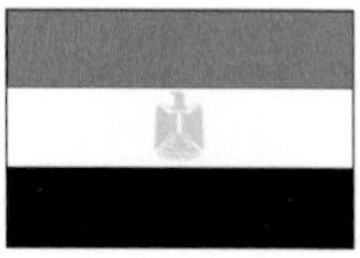

1936 | 1982 | July 23 | ET | +2 | +20 | .eg

OCCUPYING THE NORTHEAST corner of Africa, Egypt is divided by the highly fertile Nile valley separating the arid western desert from the smaller semiarid eastern desert. Egypt's 1979 peace treaty with Israel brought security, the return of the Sinai, and large injections of US aid. Its essentially pro-Western military-backed regime is now being challenged by an increasingly influential Islamic fundamentalist movement.

18th-Dynasty Temple of Queen Hatshepsut *dating from the Middle Kingdom, c.1480 BCE. It is at Deir el-Bahri on the west bank of the Nile opposite Thebes, Egypt's capital at the time.*

CLIMATE

Hot desert/ Mediterranean

WEATHER CHART FOR CAIRO

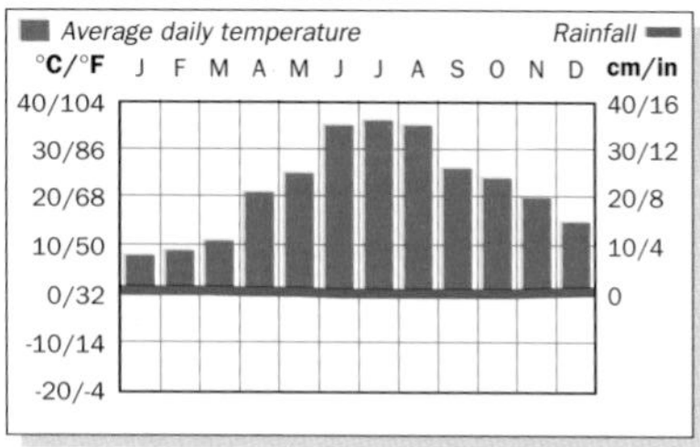
Average daily temperature
Rainfall
°C/°F
J F M A M J J A S O N D
cm/in
40/104
30/86
20/68
10/50
0/32
-10/14
-20/-4
40/16
30/12
20/8
10/4
0

Summers are very hot, especially in the south, but winters are cooler. The only significant rain falls in winter along the Mediterranean coast.

TRANSPORTATION

Drive on right

Cairo International 8.39m passengers

364 ships 1.35m grt

THE TRANSPORTATION NETWORK

49,684 km (30,872 miles)	None
5062 km (3145 miles)	3500 km (2175 miles)

Cities are linked by adequate roads, but the Nile and railroads are the main transportation arteries. Trains are frequently overcrowded. The Suez Canal is a vital international shipping lane.

TOURISM

Visitors : Population 1:14

4.91m visitors

Up 13% in 2002

MAIN TOURIST ARRIVALS

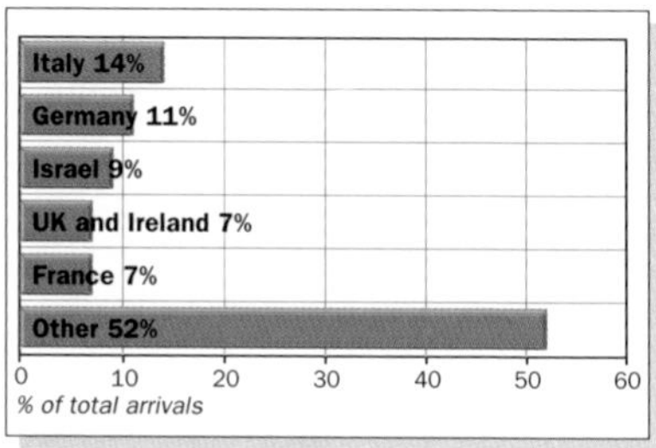
Italy 14%
Germany 11%
Israel 9%
UK and Ireland 7%
France 7%
Other 52%
0
10
20
30
40
50
60
% of total arrivals

Egypt's wealth of antiquities from its ancient civilizations have made it a key tourist destination since the 1880s. Today, it also offers Nile cruises and some of the world's best scuba diving, notably on the coral reefs near Hurghada on the Red Sea.

The industry went into sharp decline, however, when militant Islamists began targeting Western tourists in the mid-1990s; in an attack in Luxor in November 1997, 58 tourists were killed. Heightened security measures allowed a brief recovery, but the situation worsened following the September 2001 attacks in the US; the resultant contraction in the global tourism industry affected Islamic countries in particular.

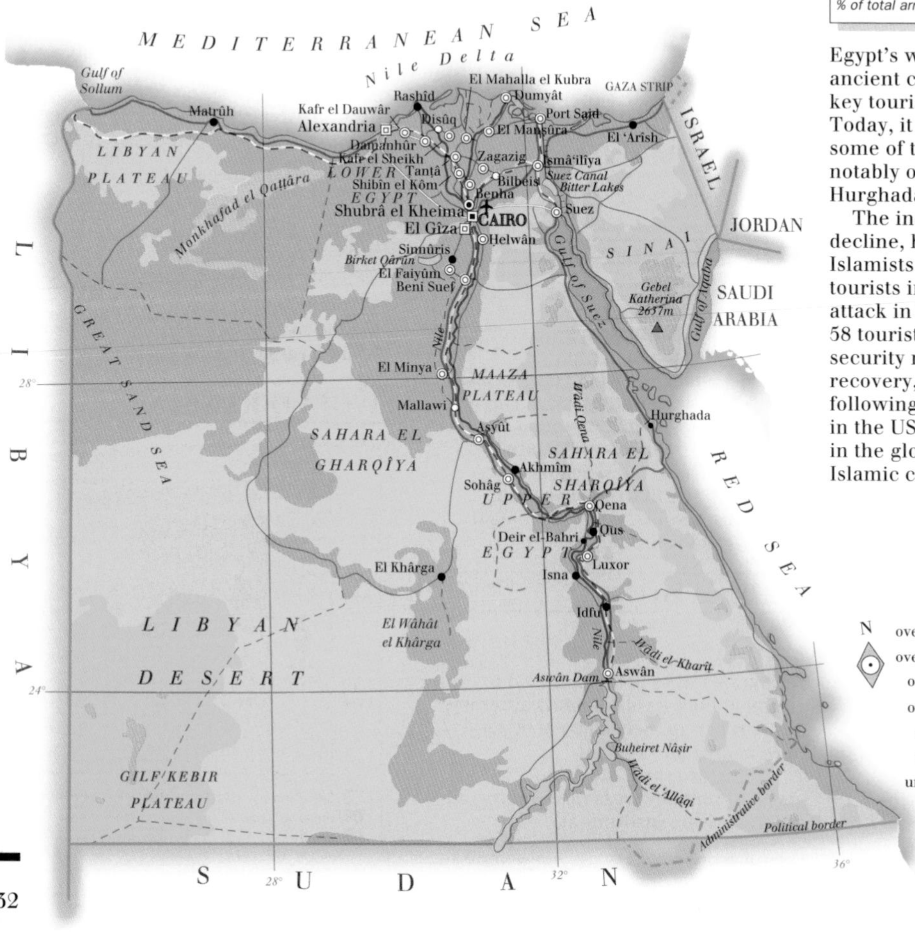
MEDITERRANEAN SEA
Nile Delta
Gulf of Sollum
Matrûh
Kafr el Dauwâr
Alexandria
Rashîd
Disûq
El Mahalla el Kubra
Dumyât
Port Said
GAZA STRIP
El 'Arish
El Mansûra
Damanhûr
Kafr el Sheikh
Tantâ
Zagazig
Ismâ'ilîya
Suez Canal
Bitter Lakes
Bilbeis
Shibîn el Kôm
LOWER EGYPT
Benha
Shubrâ el Kheima
CAIRO
El Gîza
Suez
Helwân
ISRAEL
JORDAN
LIBYAN PLATEAU
Monkhafad el Qattâra
Sinnûris
Birket Qârûn
El Faiyûm
Beni Suef
SINAI
Gulf of Suez
Gebel Katherina 2637m
Gulf of Aqaba
SAUDI ARABIA
LIBYA
GREAT SAND SEA
El Minya
MAAZA PLATEAU
Mallawi
Wadi Qena
Hurghada
Asyût
SAHARA EL GHARQÎYA
SAHARA EL SHARQÎYA
Akhmîm
Sohâg
UPPER EGYPT
Qena
Qus
Deir el-Bahri
Luxor
Isna
El Khârga
RED SEA
Idfu
Nile
El Wâhât el Khârga
LIBYAN DESERT
Wadi el-Kharît
Aswân Dam
Aswân
Buheiret Nâsir
Wadi el 'Allâqi
GILF KEBIR PLATEAU
Administrative border
Political border
SUDAN
28°
24°
32°
36°

EGYPT

Total Area : 1 001 450 sq. km (386 660 sq. miles)

POPULATION

over 5 000 000
over 1 000 000
over 500 000
over 100 000
over 50 000
over 10 000
under 10 000

LAND HEIGHT

2000m/6562ft
1000m/3281ft
500m/1640ft
200m/656ft
Sea Level
-200m/-656ft

0 200 km
0 200 miles

E

PEOPLE

Pop. density medium

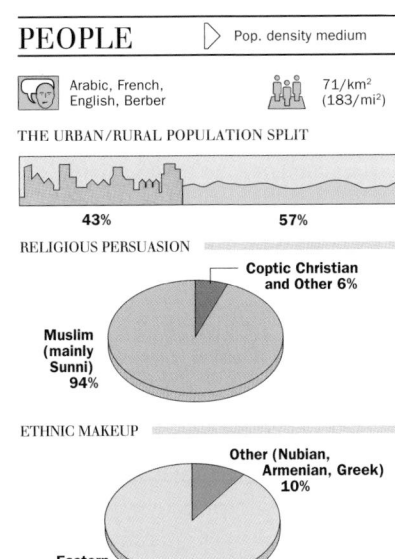

Arabic, French, English, Berber

71/km² (183/mi²)

THE URBAN/RURAL POPULATION SPLIT

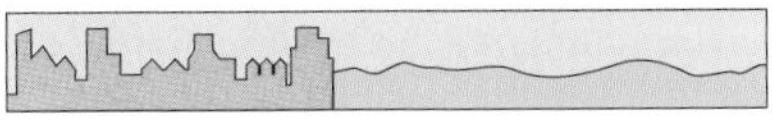
43%
57%

RELIGIOUS PERSUASION

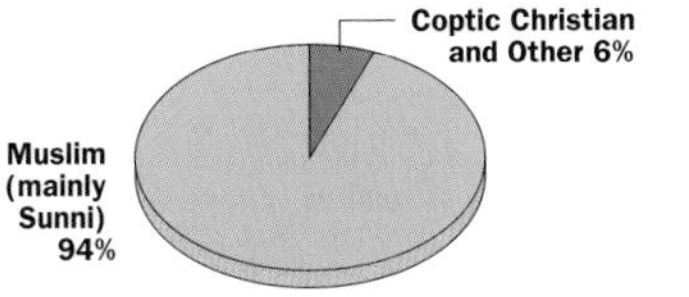
Coptic Christian and Other 6%
Muslim (mainly Sunni) 94%

ETHNIC MAKEUP

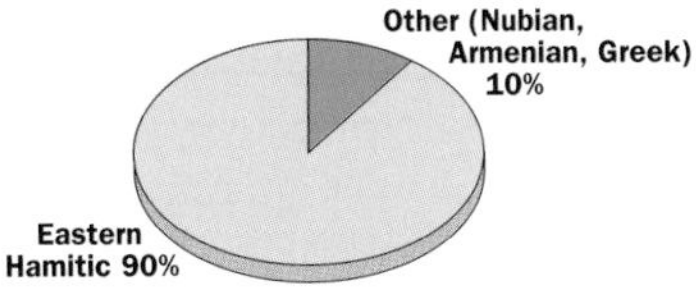
Other (Nubian, Armenian, Greek) 10%
Eastern Hamitic 90%

There is a long tradition of ethnic and religious tolerance, though the rise in Islamic fundamentalism has sparked sectarian clashes between Muslims and Copts (Coptic Christianity is one of the earliest branches of Christianity). Most Egyptians speak Arabic, though many also have French or English as a second language. There are Berber-speaking communities in the western oases. Small colonies of Greeks and Armenians live in the larger towns. Though many Jews left Egypt for Israel after 1948, a small community remains in Cairo.

Cairo is the second most populous city in Africa, and a key social question in Egypt is the high birthrate. In 1985 the government set up the National Population Council, which made birth control readily available. Since then, the birthrate has dropped from 39 to 25 per 1000 people, one of the lowest rates in Africa. Still, the population is predicted to reach almost 100 million by 2025. The growing influence of Islamic fundamentalists, who oppose contraception, could see the rate accelerate once more.

Egyptian women have been among the most liberated in the Arab world, and under a law passed in 2000 they now have the right to initiate divorce proceedings. Islamic fundamentalism, however, may threaten their position, particularly in rural areas.

POPULATION AGE BREAKDOWN

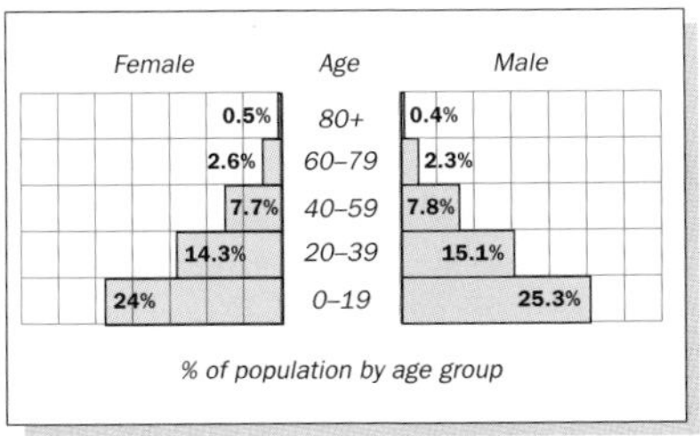
Female
Age
Male
0.5%
80+
0.4%
2.6%
60–79
2.3%
7.7%
40–59
7.8%
14.3%
20–39
15.1%
24%
0–19
25.3%
% of population by age group

POLITICS

Multiparty elections

2000/2005

President Mohammed Hosni Mubarak

AT THE LAST ELECTION

People's Assembly 454 seats

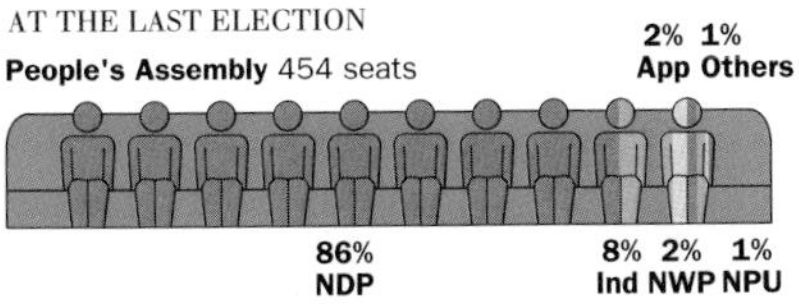
2% App
1% Others
86% NDP
8% Ind
2% NWP
1% NPU

NDP = National Democratic Party **Ind** = Independents **App** = Appointed **NWP** = New Wafd Party **NPU** = National Progressive Unionist Party

444 members of the Assembly are elected and ten are appointed by the head of state

Egypt is a multiparty system in theory. In practice, the ruling NDP, backed by the military, runs a one-party state.

PROFILE

Egypt has been politically stable since World War II, with just three leaders since 1954, when Gemal Abdel Nasser, the power behind a military coup in 1952, assumed the presidency. In 1981 President Anwar Sadat was assassinated, but was immediately replaced by Hosni Mubarak, a man in the same mold. The NDP retains its grip on the political process by means of the state of emergency. Elections in 2000 were more transparent than before and the Islamic opposition fared slightly better, but many candidates elected as independents then joined the NDP.

While Nasser promoted Arab socialism, influenced by the Soviet model, Sadat and Mubarak (whose fourth term began in 1999) encouraged private enterprise. However, there has been no parallel liberalization in politics.

MAIN POLITICAL ISSUES

Islamic fundamentalism

The NDP government is engaged in a struggle against Islamist terrorist groups seeking to turn Egypt into a Muslim theocracy. Extremists have been responsible for numerous attacks since 1994 on police and tourists, and attempted to assassinate Mubarak in 1995. The fundamentalist message, with promises of improved conditions, has proved attractive to both urban and rural poor. Mosques are often the main providers of education and health services that parallel those of the state.

***Hosni Mubarak,** president since the assassination of Anwar Sadat in 1981.*

***Gemal Abdel Nasser,** pan-Arab nationalist, president from 1954 to 1970.*

Although the government uses draconian measures to counter the terrorist threat, and banned the only legal Islamic party, the Labor Party, in 2000, it continues to allow religious organizations to pursue their social programs. A 1999 truce between the government and radicals still holds, although Egyptian Islamists have become more active in global terrorism.

The state of emergency

The NDP has repeatedly extended the national state of emergency, in force since the assassination of Sadat by Islamist terrorists in 1981, most recently in 2002 for a further three years. Emergency laws have been invoked to justify the ban on religious parties and groupings, especially the Muslim Brotherhood. Human rights groups claim that emergency powers are routinely used to silence the NDP's political opponents.

WORLD AFFAIRS

Joined UN in 1945

AL
Damasc
OAPEC
AU
OIC

Egypt has close relations with the West, particularly the US. Its support for the alliance against Iraq in the 1991 Gulf War was crucial, and Egypt received a massive economic reward from Saudi Arabia. It is also one of only two Arab countries to be technically at peace with Israel, for which it faces criticism from hard-line Islamic states. However, the Israeli military action in 2002 has weakened Egypt's support, and relations were consequently downgraded. Egypt continues to back Palestinian autonomy and has worked closely with liberals in the Palestinian National Authority.

Relations with Iran are particularly tense: Iran actively supports the Islamist groups operating against the NDP government, and characterizes Egypt as a corrupt state under US influence.

Egypt expressed concern over international treatment of Iraq, Mubarak advocating a diplomatic solution. He has urged restraint in the "war on terrorism" and that against Iraq in 2003.

Egypt's diplomatic service is the Arab world's largest, and many Egyptians have served on international bodies, such as former UN secretary-general Boutros Boutros Ghali.

AID

Recipient

$1.26bn (receipts)

Down 5% in 2001

Egypt has received much US military aid since the late 1970s, and is currently among the top three recipients of US aid, along with Israel and Russia. International aid was pledged in 2002 to make up for lost tourism revenue.

E

CHRONOLOGY

Egypt's centuries-long Ottoman occupation ended in 1914, when it came under direct British rule. It became fully independent in 1936. Army officers led by Lt. Col. Gemal Abdel Nasser seized power in 1952.

- **1953** Political parties dissolved, monarchy abolished. Republic proclaimed with Gen. Mohammed Neguib as president.
- **1954** Nasser deposes Neguib to become president.
- **1956** Suez Crisis following nationalization of Suez Canal. Israeli, British, and French forces invade, but withdraw after pressure from UN and US.
- **1957** Suez Canal reopens after UN salvage fleet clears blockade.
- **1958** Egypt merges with Syria as United Arab Republic.
- **1960–1970** Aswan High Dam built.
- **1961** Syria breaks away from union with Egypt.
- **1967** Six-Day War with Israel; loss of Sinai.
- **1970** Nasser dies; succeeded by Anwar Sadat.
- **1971** Readopts the name Egypt. Islam becomes state religion.
- **1972** Soviet military advisers dismissed from Egypt.
- **1974–1975** US brokers partial Israeli withdrawal from Sinai.
- **1977** Sadat visits Jerusalem: first ever meeting between Egyptian president and Israeli prime minister.
- **1978** Camp David accords, brokered by US, signed by Egypt and Israel.
- **1979** Egypt and Israel sign peace treaty, alienating most Arab states.
- **1981** Sadat assassinated; succeeded by Lt. Gen. Hosni Mubarak.
- **1982** Last Israeli troops leave Sinai.
- **1986** President Mubarak meets Israeli prime minister Shimon Peres to discuss Middle East peace.
- **1989** After 12-year rift, Egypt and Syria resume diplomatic relations.
- **1990–1991** Egypt participates in UN operation to liberate Kuwait.
- **1991** Damascus Declaration provides for a defense pact between Egypt, Syria, and GCC countries against Iraq.
- **1994–1998** Islamist extremists begin campaign of terrorism, killing civilians and tourists. Government steps up countermeasures.
- **1999** Banned Gamaat Islamiya ends campaign to overthrow government.
- **2000** Egypt recalls ambassador to Israel because of escalating Israeli aggression against Palestinians.
- **2001** Heavy decline in tourist numbers following September 2001 attack on US.

DEFENSE

Compulsory military service

$4.32bn — Up 5% in 2001

EGYPTIAN ARMED FORCES

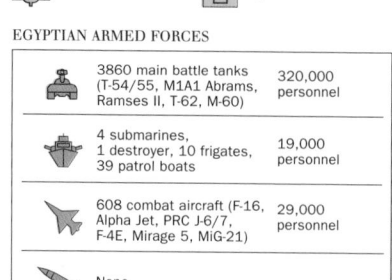

3860 main battle tanks (T-54/55, M1A1 Abrams, Ramses II, T-62, M-60)	320,000 personnel
4 submarines, 1 destroyer, 10 frigates, 39 patrol boats	19,000 personnel
608 combat aircraft (F-16, Alpha Jet, PRC J-6/7, F-4E, Mirage 5, MiG-21)	29,000 personnel
None	

Egypt's armed forces, the largest in the Arab world, are battle-hardened from successive wars with Israel and from participation in Operation Desert Storm to liberate Kuwait in 1991. More than 500,000 reservists augment the regular troops.

After the 1978 Camp David framework agreements were reached with Israel, Egypt stopped buying Soviet weapons and aircraft, and turned instead to Western suppliers. Cooperation with the US has reaped dividends in the form of access to more sophisticated defense equipment and improved training. Egypt has a small arms industry and sells light weapons, notably its version of the Soviet-developed AK-47 assault rifle, to other developing countries.

ECONOMICS

Inflation 7.8% p.a. (1990–2001)

$99.6bn

6.056 Egyptian pounds (4.644)

SCORE CARD

World GNP Ranking	37th
GNP per Capita	$1530
Balance of Payments	–$33m
Inflation	2.3%
Unemployment	12%

EXPORTS

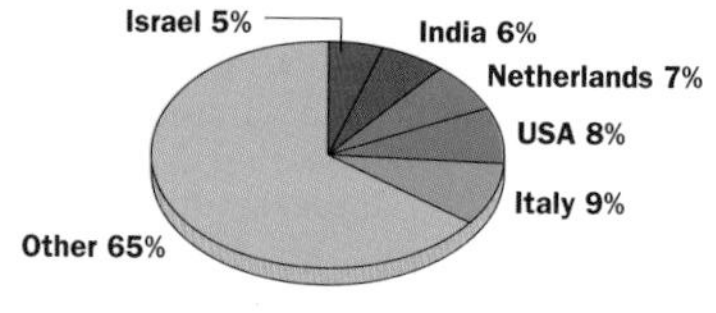
Israel 5%
India 6%
Netherlands 7%
USA 8%
Italy 9%
Other 65%

IMPORTS

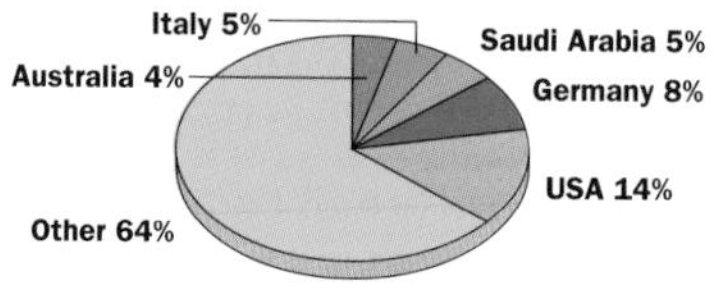
Italy 5%
Saudi Arabia 5%
Australia 4%
Germany 8%
USA 14%
Other 64%

ECONOMIC PERFORMANCE INDICATOR

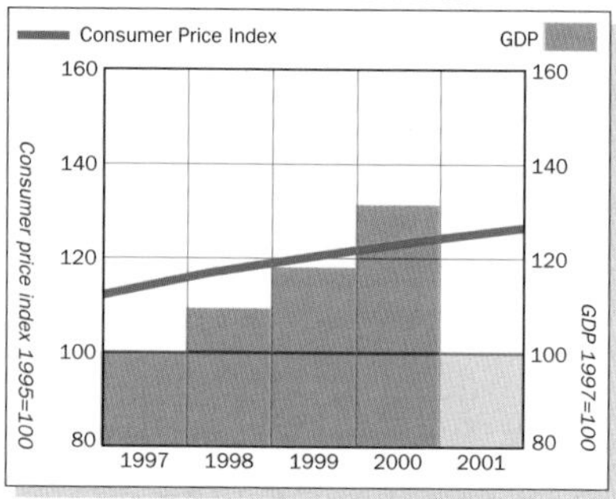
Consumer Price Index
GDP
160
140
120
100
80
Consumer price index 1995=100
GDP 1997=100
1997
1998
1999
2000
2001

Strengths

Oil and gas revenues. Well-developed tourist infrastructure. Remittances from Egyptians working throughout the region. Suez Canal tolls. Agricultural produce, especially cotton. Light industry and manufacturing. Planned gas pipeline to Lebanon.

Weaknesses

Tourism hit by "war on terrorism." Dependence on imported technology. High birthrate. Rural poverty.

Profile

The Soviet-inspired economic model pursued by Nasser was rigid and highly centralized. It gave Egypt one of the largest public sectors of all developing countries. Economic restrictions were first relaxed in 1974. President Sadat's "open-door" policy (*infitah*) allowed joint ventures with foreign partners for the first time, although only business classes profited. Most Egyptians suffered from new austerity measures.

Under President Mubarak, economic reform has quickened and there is more awareness of poverty and the high levels of unemployment. Priorities now are to encourage manufacturing, sustain economic growth, and reduce the gap between rich and poor.

EGYPT : MAJOR BUSINESSES

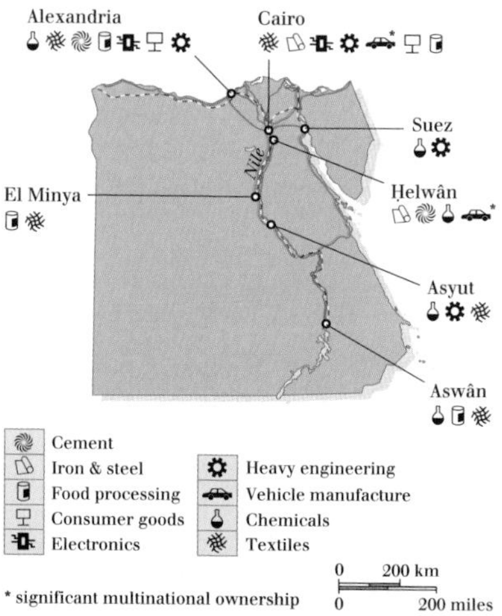
Alexandria
Cairo
Suez
Helwân
El Minya
Asyut
Aswân
Nile
Cement
Iron & steel
Food processing
Consumer goods
Electronics
Heavy engineering
Vehicle manufacture
Chemicals
Textiles
* significant multinational ownership
0 200 km
0 200 miles

RESOURCES

Electric power 17.6m kW

724,407 tonnes

751,000 b/d (reserves 3.7bn barrels)

9.1m ducks, 4.67m sheep, 9.1m geese, 92m chickens

Natural gas, oil, phosphates, manganese, uranium

ELECTRICITY GENERATION

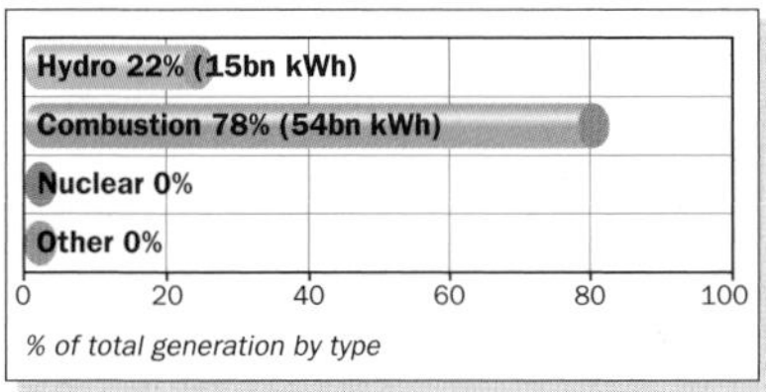
Hydro 22% (15bn kWh)
Combustion 78% (54bn kWh)
Nuclear 0%
Other 0%
0
20
40
60
80
100
% of total generation by type

Oil and gas are Egypt's most valuable resources. Oil multinationals are involved in new explorations, but more competitive oil-rich countries, such as Algeria and Yemen, are more profitable; 55% of Egypt's oil production is consumed locally.

Most electricity is derived from coal and hydroelectric power. The Aswan High Dam, built between 1960 and 1970 and with a maximum output of 10 billion kWh, provides the bulk of hydroelectricity. Within four years, revenue from it had covered its construction costs. The US gave aid in 2000 to upgrade the power plant, work going ahead in 2001.

EGYPT : LAND USE

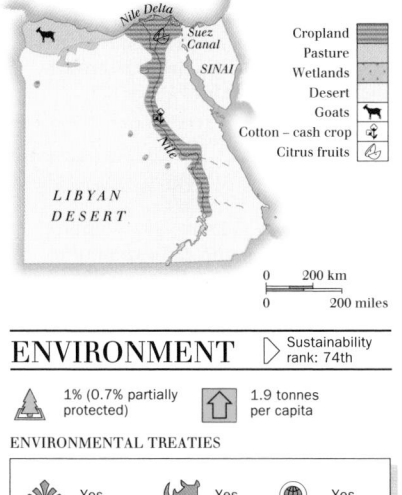

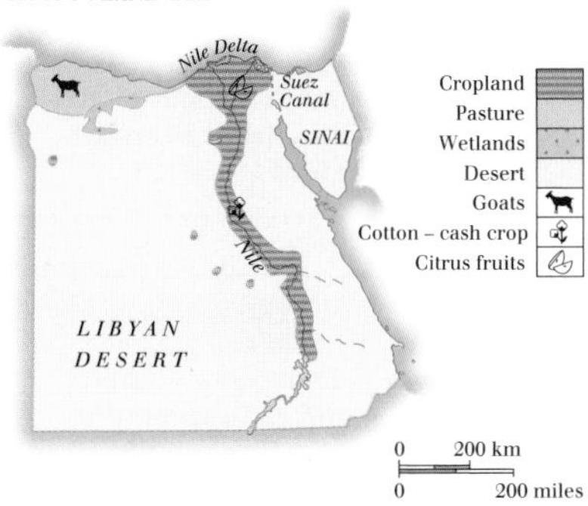
Nile Delta
Suez Canal
SINAI
Nile
LIBYAN DESERT
Cropland
Pasture
Wetlands
Desert
Goats
Cotton – cash crop
Citrus fruits
0 200 km
0 200 miles

ENVIRONMENT

Sustainability rank: 74th

1% (0.7% partially protected)

1.9 tonnes per capita

ENVIRONMENTAL TREATIES

Yes	Yes	Yes
Yes	Yes	No

Egypt suffers from a chronic lack of water. The Nile, the only perennial source, is increasingly saline because of its much-reduced flow, due to irrigation use and the Aswan High Dam. The main cities suffer heavy industrial pollution, and environmental controls are few. In Cairo a sewerage system has improved sanitary conditions.

MEDIA

TV ownership medium

Daily newspaper circulation 31 per 1000 people

Criticism of the government prompted severe restrictions in 1998. Pressure from Islamists has resulted in more airtime for Islamic sermons. Nilesat 101 was the Arab world's first satellite, and Egypt is now a center for satellite TV. A "free media zone" was launched in 2000 to attract foreign companies.

PUBLISHING AND BROADCAST MEDIA

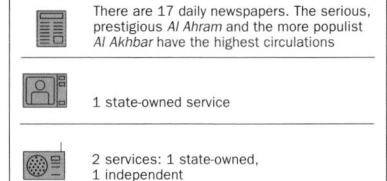

There are 17 daily newspapers. The serious, prestigious *Al Ahram* and the more populist *Al Akhbar* have the highest circulations

1 state-owned service

2 services: 1 state-owned, 1 independent

CRIME

Death penalty in use

80,000 prisoners

Crime is rising

CRIME RATES

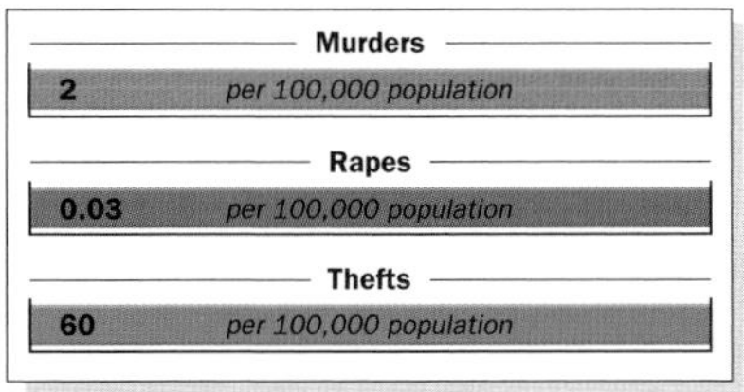
Murders
2 per 100,000 population
Rapes
0.03 per 100,000 population
Thefts
60 per 100,000 population

Terrorist attacks have tarnished Egypt's reputation as a law-abiding country. Street crime and muggings, previously rare, are increasing.

Intercommunity violence – in particular between Muslims and Christians – has become more common, as have attacks on Western tourists by Islamic extremists. Human rights groups have criticized the police for their abuse of current emergency laws, which results in the routine torture and/or death in police custody of scores of political prisoners.

EDUCATION

School leaving age: 14

56%

2.45m students

THE EDUCATION SYSTEM

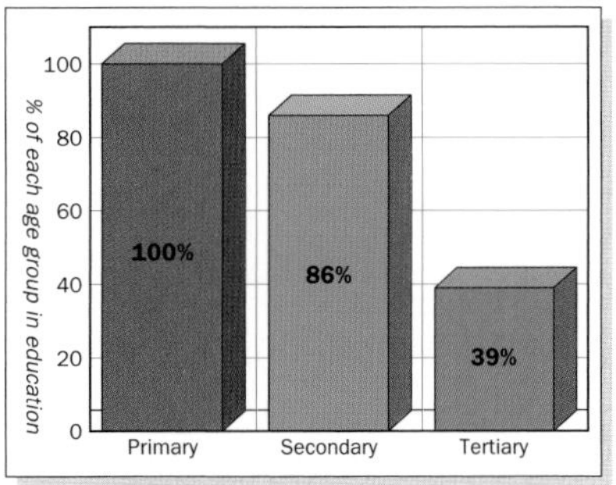
100
80
60
40
20
0
% of each age group in education
100%
86%
39%
Primary
Secondary
Tertiary

Most Egyptians attend elementary school until the age of 11, but not many complete secondary education. Two-thirds of men, but only a minority of women, are literate. A government initiative to improve girls' primary education was launched in 2000. The quality of the education given by Egyptian universities is widely respected in the Arab world.

HEALTH

Welfare state health benefits

1 per 459 people

Digestive, respiratory, and heart diseases, perinatal deaths

Health care, although improved, remains basic – there is only one hospital bed for every 500 people. Islamic medical centers based on the mosque organization are spreading, and are replacing the state system. In 1996 the government banned Pharaonic circumcision (female infibulation), a move upheld in 1997 by the Supreme Consitutional Court after being overturned by a lower court.

SPENDING

GDP/cap. increase

CONSUMPTION AND SPENDING

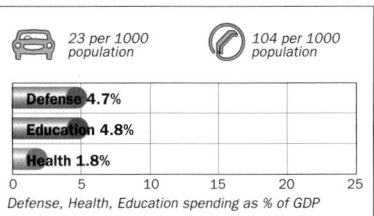

23 per 1000 population

104 per 1000 population

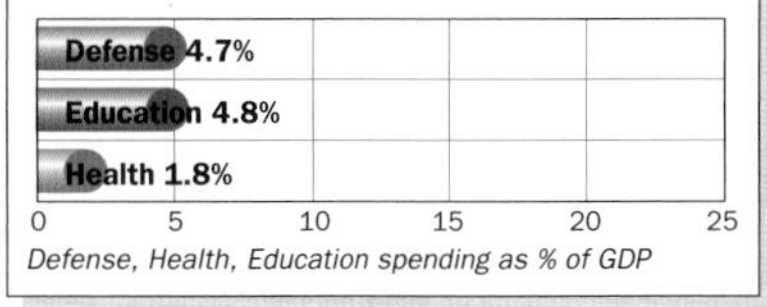
Defense 4.7%
Education 4.8%
Health 1.8%
0
5
10
15
20
25
Defense, Health, Education spending as % of GDP

A rapidly growing population and the introduction of market economics have combined to produce widespread poverty, particularly in the south, while concentrating wealth in the hands of a small urban elite. Poverty levels are highest in rural areas. Urban unemployment and internal migration have led to the creation of enormous slums around Cairo and other cities.

WORLD RANKING

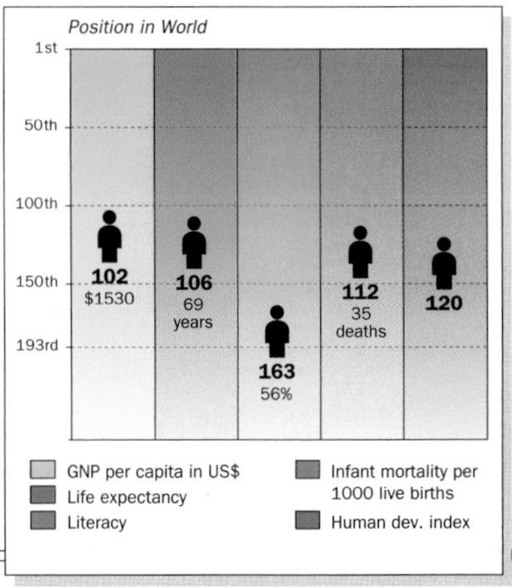
Position in World
1st
50th
100th
150th
193rd
102
$1530
106
69 years
163
56%
112
35 deaths
120
GNP per capita in US$
Life expectancy
Literacy
Infant mortality per 1000 live births
Human dev. index

E

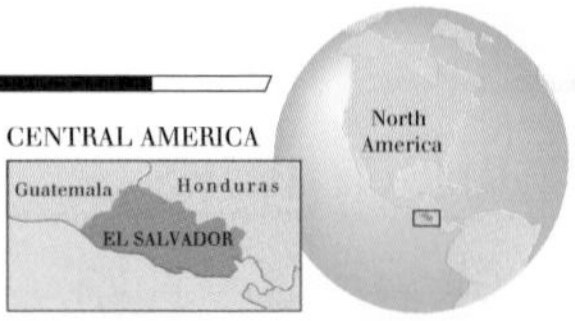
CENTRAL AMERICA
North America
Guatemala
Honduras
EL SALVADOR

EL SALVADOR

OFFICIAL NAME: Republic of El Salvador **CAPITAL:** San Salvador
POPULATION: 6.5 million **CURRENCIES:** Salvadorean colón & US dollar **OFFICIAL LANGUAGE:** Spanish

1841 | 1841 | Sept 15 | ES | -6 | +503 | .sv

THE SMALLEST AND MOST densely populated Central American republic, El Salvador won full independence in 1841. Located on the Pacific coast, it lies within a zone of seismic activity. Between 1979 and 1991, El Salvador was engulfed in a civil war between US-backed right-wing government forces and left-wing FMLN guerrillas. Since the UN-brokered peace agreement, the country has been concentrating on rebuilding its shattered economy.

View over the capital, San Salvador. It lies in a depression in the southern and higher of El Salvador's two mountain ranges, which is punctuated by more than 20 volcanoes.

CLIMATE

Tropical wet and dry

WEATHER CHART FOR SAN SALVADOR

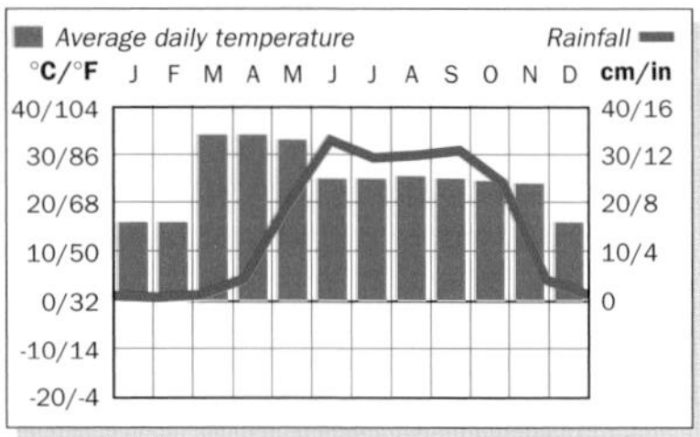
Average daily temperature
Rainfall
°C/°F
J F M A M J J A S O N D
cm/in
40/104
30/86
20/68
10/50
0/32
-10/14
-20/-4
40/16
30/12
20/8
10/4
0

The tropical coastal *tierra caliente* is very hot, with seasonal rains. The low hills are cooler at night; the higher *tierra templada* is drier and also cooler.

TRANSPORTATION

Drive on right

Cuscatlan, San Salvador 1.44m passengers

12 ships 1500 grt

THE TRANSPORTATION NETWORK

1986 km (1234 miles)

Pan-American Highway: 327 km (203 miles)

283 km (176 miles)

Rio Lempa partly navigable

Earthquakes in 2001 further damaged the already war-ravaged road and rail networks. Reconstruction will take many years.

TOURISM

Visitors : Population 1:6.8

951,000 visitors

Up 29% in 2002

MAIN TOURIST ARRIVALS

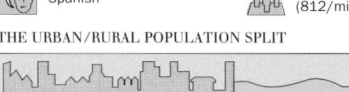

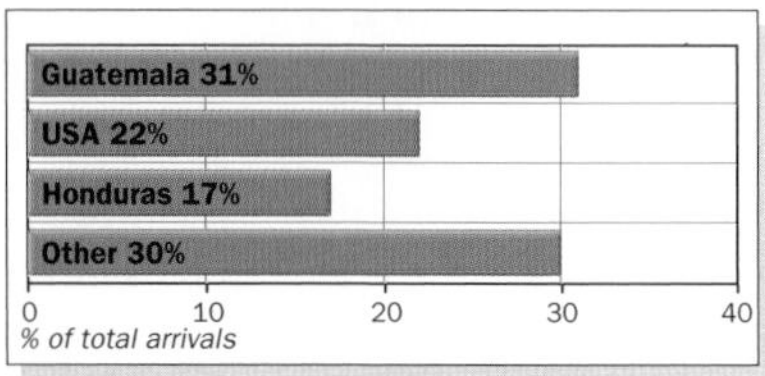
Guatemala 31%
USA 22%
Honduras 17%
Other 30%
0
10
20
30
40
% of total arrivals

Peace has brought visitors back to the unspoiled beach resorts, but crime, earthquakes, and high prices for rooms and air travel hinder tourist expansion.

PEOPLE

Pop. density high

Spanish

314/km² (812/mi²)

THE URBAN/RURAL POPULATION SPLIT

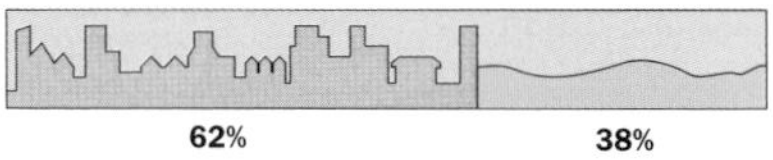
62%
38%

RELIGIOUS PERSUASION

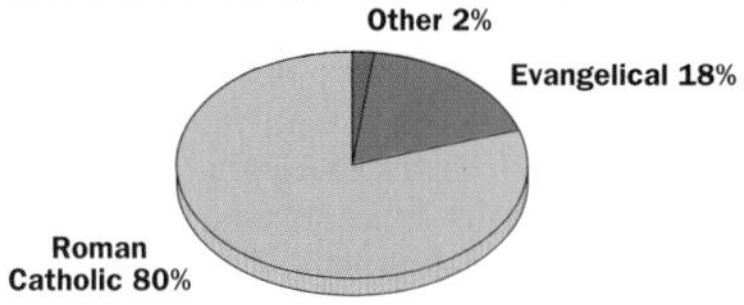
Other 2%
Evangelical 18%
Roman Catholic 80%

Salvadorans are largely *mestizo* (mixed race); there are few ethnic tensions. The civil war was fought over gross economic disparities, which still exist.

POLITICS

Multiparty elections

2003/2006

President Francisco Flores

AT THE LAST ELECTION

Legislative Assembly 84 seats

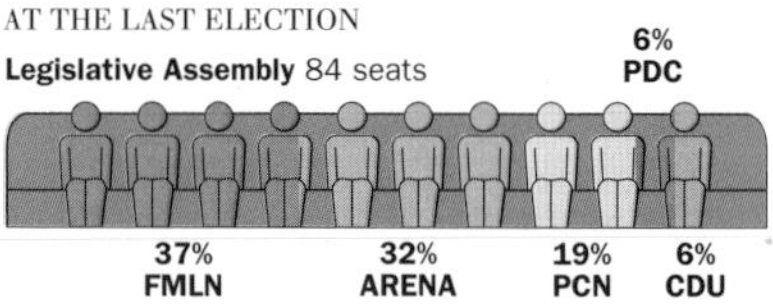
6%
PDC
37%
FMLN
32%
ARENA
19%
PCN
6%
CDU

FMLN = Farabundo Martí National Liberation Front **ARENA** = Nationalist Republican Alliance **PCN** = National Conciliation Party **PDC** = Christian Democratic Party **CDU** = United Democratic Center

El Salvador was dominated by the centrist PDC and right-wing ARENA until the rise in the late 1990s of the FMLN, the leftist former guerrillas. In 1997 the FMLN won the mayorship of San Salvador and half the state capitals.

In the 1999 presidential election a divided FMLN came a poor second to ARENA's Francisco Flores, who promised reduced poverty and the redistribution of income. In 2000 and 2003, however, with the economy in difficulties, voters punished ARENA by returning the FMLN as the largest party in parliament.

Major political issues are violent crime and the prosecution of human rights cases from the 1980s.

WORLD AFFAIRS

Joined UN in 1945

ACS | Geplac | IBRD | OAS | San José

El Salvador was an international pariah in the 1980s because of the human rights abuses committed by military death squads. Today it cooperates with its neighbors in pressing the US on key issues such as trade and immigration. It relied heavily on US aid in 2001 after three devastating earthquakes. In 2000 it cosigned a free trade treaty with Guatemala, Honduras, and Mexico. Long-standing border disputes exist with Honduras, and El Salvador contests the sovereignty of islands in the Gulf of Fonseca.

AID

Recipient

$234m (receipts)

Up 30% in 2001

Post–civil-war aid focused on efforts to secure peace and achieve national reconciliation by funding rebuilding and refugee resettlement programs. The current emphasis is on a shift toward supporting growth.

The UN received a slow international response in 2001 to its appeal for $34.8 million in emergency housing, medicine, and disaster prevention programs after El Salvador's devastating earthquakes.

DEFENSE

Compulsory military service

$165m

Down 2% in 2001

Between 1979 and 1991, the role of the US-backed military was to fight an unrestricted war against the FMLN. Human rights were in effect suspended and governments that opposed the military were overthrown. Under the peace accords the military agreed to withdraw from politics and internal security matters, but it remains a potent force capable of intervention.

E

ECONOMICS

Inflation 6.8% p.a. (1990–2001)

$13bn

8.752 Salvadorean colones (8.747)

SCORE CARD

- ❑ World GNP Ranking 80th
- ❑ GNP per Capita $2040
- ❑ Balance of Payments .... –$177m
- ❑ Inflation 3.8%
- ❑ Unemployment 10%

Strengths

Coffee. Foreign investment. Family remittances from US. Dollarization.

Weaknesses

Exports uncompetitive. High tax evasion and unemployment. Low savings. Vast reconstruction needed after earthquakes in 2001. International concern over conditions in *maquilas* (assembly plants).

EXPORTS

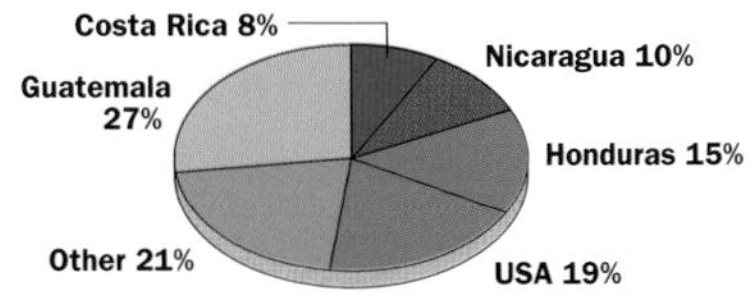

Costa Rica 8%
Nicaragua 10%
Guatemala 27%
Honduras 15%
Other 21%
USA 19%

IMPORTS

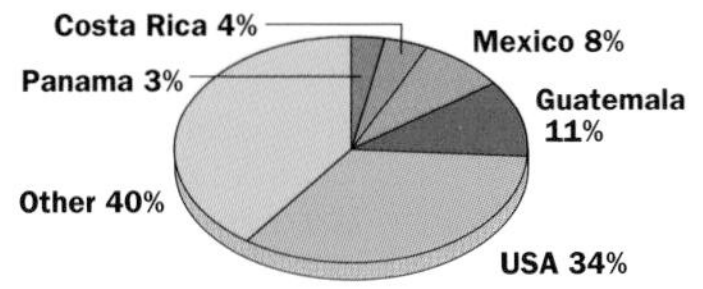

Costa Rica 4%
Mexico 8%
Panama 3%
Guatemala 11%
Other 40%
USA 34%

RESOURCES

Electric power 583,000 kW

9851 tonnes

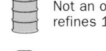

Not an oil producer; refines 19,000 b/d

1.39m cattle, 153,463 pigs, 8.1m chickens

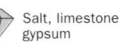

Salt, limestone, gypsum

No significant resources. Several volcanoes facilitate abundant and relatively cheap geothermal energy.

ENVIRONMENT

Sustainability rank: 75th

0.4% (0.2% partially protected)

0.9 tonnes per capita

Deforestation has led to erosion and desertification – worsening landslides during the earthquakes of 2001. Overuse of pesticides is a major problem.

MEDIA

TV ownership medium

Daily newspaper circulation 28 per 1000 people

PUBLISHING AND BROADCAST MEDIA

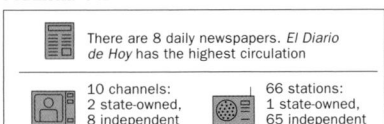

There are 8 daily newspapers. *El Diario de Hoy* has the highest circulation

10 channels: 2 state-owned, 8 independent

66 stations: 1 state-owned, 65 independent

The media are constitutionally free, but are mainly owned by powerful groups such as the Dutriz family.

CRIME

Death penalty not used in practice

6914 prisoners

Down 43% in 2000–2001

A corrupt judiciary and police force have failed to stem a postwar crime wave fueled by readily available arms; armed robberies, kidnappings, and murders deter investment and tourism. Uncompleted elements of the peace accords, particularly land transfers, often lead to violence.

EDUCATION

School leaving age: 15

79%

118,491 students

Education is based on the US system and is limited in rural areas. During the civil war, state universities were closed, prompting the creation of private universities which continue to thrive despite their low standards. A 1995 reform bill tried to address the negative impact of deregulation.

CHRONOLOGY

El Salvador was a Spanish colony until 1821. Part of the United Provinces of Central America in 1823–1839, it became fully independent in 1841.

- ❑ **1932** Army crushes popular insurrection led by Farabundo Martí.
- ❑ **1944–1979** Army rules through PCN.
- ❑ **1979** Reformist officers overthrow PCN government.
- ❑ **1981** Left-wing FMLN launches civil war.
- ❑ **1991** UN-brokered peace. FMLN recognized as a political party.
- ❑ **1999** ARENA retains presidency.
- ❑ **2000, 2003** FMLN wins Assembly elections.
- ❑ **2001** Devastating earthquakes kill hundreds. Dollarization of economy.

HEALTH

Welfare state health benefits

1 per 826 people

Heart disease, cancers, homicide, infectious diseases

Health problems were worsened after the 2001 earthquakes. Plans to privatize the health service are unpopular.

SPENDING

GDP/cap. increase

CONSUMPTION AND SPENDING

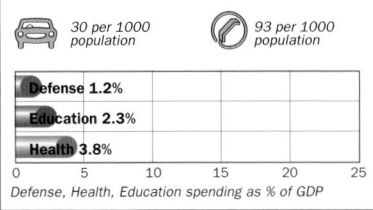

30 per 1000 population

93 per 1000 population

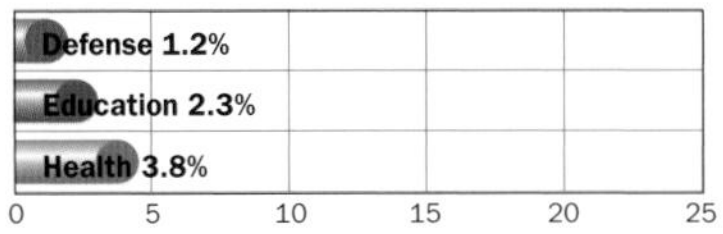

Defense 1.2%
Education 2.3%
Health 3.8%
0
5
10
15
20
25

Defense, Health, Education spending as % of GDP

Although there is a growing middle class, much of the country's wealth is controlled by just a few hundred families. Land distribution remains highly skewed, and nearly half the population live in poverty.

WORLD RANKING

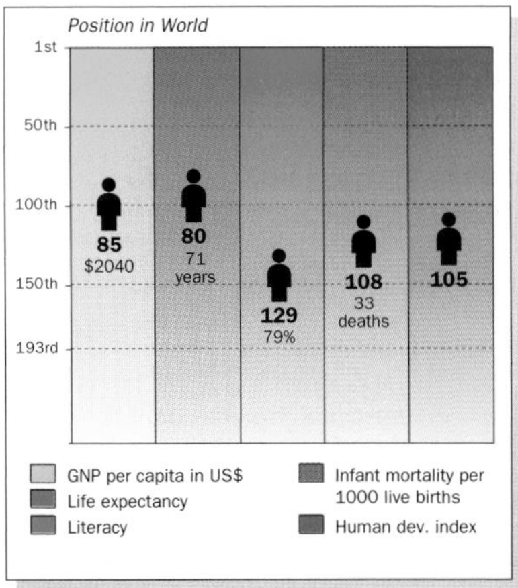

Position in World
1st
50th
100th
150th
193rd
85
$2040
80
71 years
129
79%
108
33 deaths
105
GNP per capita in US$
Life expectancy
Literacy
Infant mortality per 1000 live births
Human dev. index

EL SALVADOR

Total Area : 21 040 sq. km (8124 sq. miles)

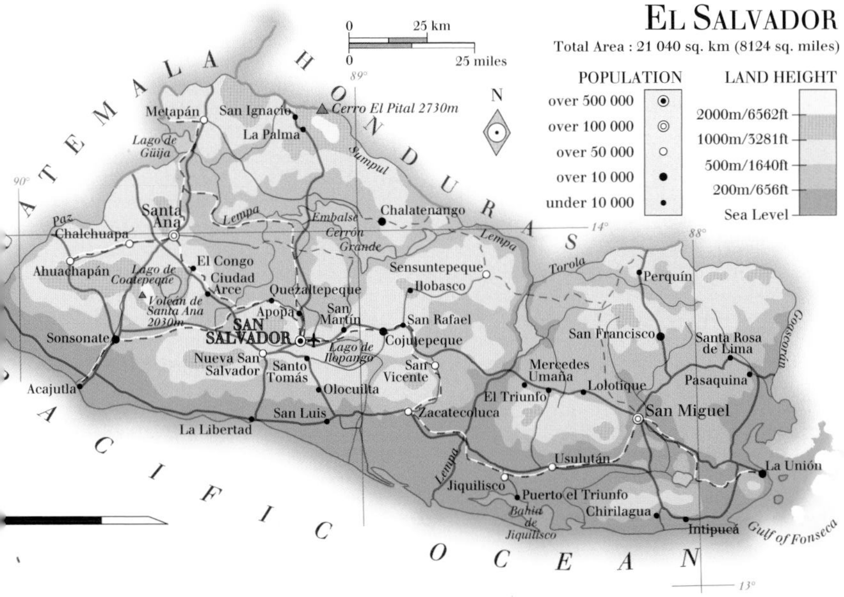

0
25 km
0
25 miles
POPULATION
LAND HEIGHT
over 500 000
over 100 000
over 50 000
over 10 000
under 10 000
2000m/6562ft
1000m/3281ft
500m/1640ft
200m/656ft
Sea Level
N
GUATEMALA
HONDURAS
PACIFIC OCEAN
Metapán
San Ignacio
La Palma
Cerro El Pital 2730m
Lago de Güija
Sumpul
Lempa
Santa Ana
Chalchuapa
Embalse Cerrón Grande
Chalatenango
Ahuachapán
El Congo
Lago de Coatepeque
Ciudad Arce
Quezaltepeque
Volcán de Santa Ana 2030m
Apopa
San Martín
Sensuntepeque
Ilobasco
Torola
Perquín
Sonsonate
SAN SALVADOR
Lago de Ilopango
Cojutepeque
San Rafael
San Francisco
Santa Rosa de Lima
Goascorán
Nueva San Salvador
Santo Tomás
San Vicente
Mercedes Umaña
Lolotique
Pasaquina
Acajutla
Olocuilta
El Triunfo
San Luis
Zacatecoluca
San Miguel
La Libertad
Usulután
La Unión
Jiquilisco
Puerto el Triunfo
Bahía de Jiquilisco
Chirilagua
Intipucá
Gulf of Fonseca

EQUATORIAL GUINEA

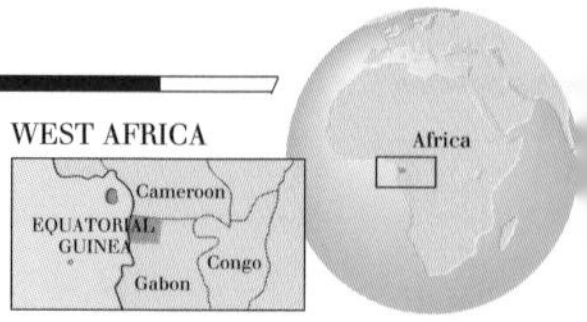
WEST AFRICA
Cameroon
EQUATORIAL GUINEA
Gabon
Congo
Africa

OFFICIAL NAME: Republic of Equatorial Guinea **CAPITAL:** Malabo
POPULATION: 483,000 **CURRENCY:** CFA franc **OFFICIAL LANGUAGES:** Spanish and French

1968
1968
Oct 12
GQ
+1
+240
.gq

COMPRISING FIVE ISLANDS and the territory of Río Muni on the west coast of Africa, Equatorial Guinea lies just north of the equator. Mangrove swamps border the mainland coast. The republic gained its independence in 1968 after 190 years of Spanish rule. Multipartyism was accepted in 1991, but the fairness of subsequent general elections has been questioned.

Bioko, formerly Fernando Po. Though the volcanic land is very fertile, cocoa production fell by 90% during the Macías years.

CLIMATE

Tropical equatorial

WEATHER CHART FOR MALABO

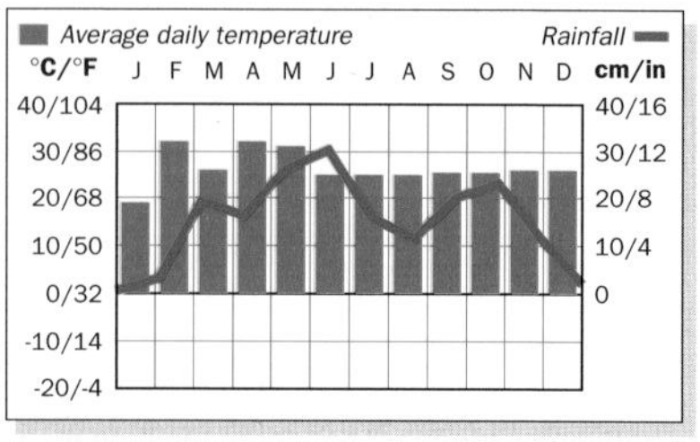
Average daily temperature
Rainfall
°C/°F J F M A M J J A S O N D cm/in
40/104
30/86
20/68
10/50
0/32
-10/14
-20/4
40/16
30/12
20/8
10/4
0

The island of Bioko is extremely wet and humid, with an annual rainfall of 200 cm (80 in), while the mainland is only marginally drier and cooler.

TRANSPORTATION

Drive on right

Malabo International 187,474 passengers

60 ships 37,225 grt

THE TRANSPORTATION NETWORK

508 km (316 miles)	None
None	None

There are six flights a week between Malabo and Bata. Mainland public transportation is restricted to minibuses. There is only one properly paved road, serving the president's hometown.

TOURISM

Not available

Tourism receipts totaled $2m in 1998

Numbers are increasing slowly

MAIN TOURIST ARRIVALS

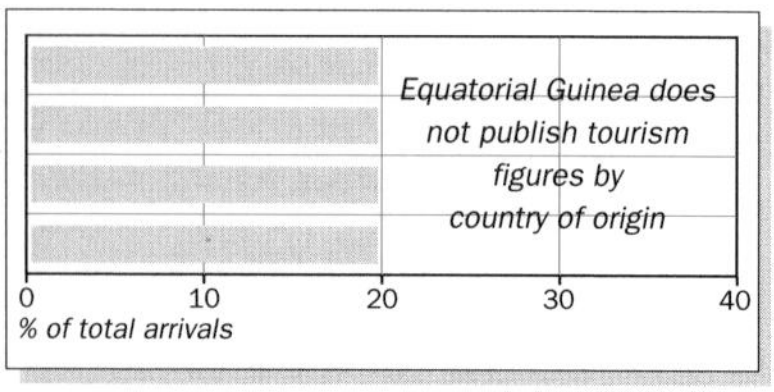
Equatorial Guinea does not publish tourism figures by country of origin
0
10
20
30
40
% of total arrivals

Equatorial Guinea is only of interest to the adventurous, independent tourist, despite the potential attraction of its beaches and the island of Bioko's spectacular mountain scenery.

PEOPLE

Pop. density low

Spanish, Fang, Bubi

17/km² (45/mi²)

THE URBAN/RURAL POPULATION SPLIT

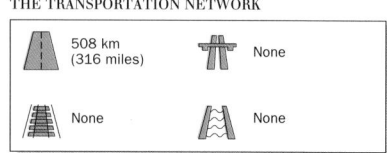

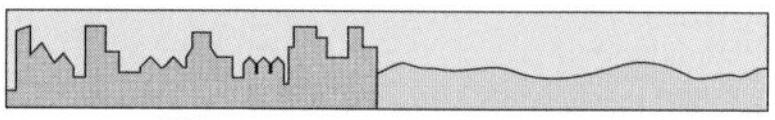
49%
51%

RELIGIOUS PERSUASION

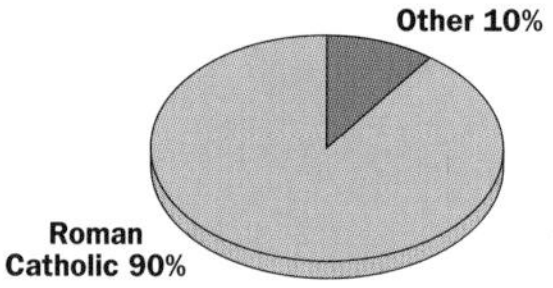
Other 10%
Roman Catholic 90%

Equatorial Guinea is the only Spanish-speaking country in Africa. The mainland has a majority of Fang, a people also found in Cameroon and north Gabon. Bioko is populated by a majority of Bubi and a minority of Creoles, known as Fernandinos. Tensions between the mainland and Bioko have been reignited since the discovery of oil reserves off Bioko. The Fang dominated politically under the Macías dictatorship. The extended family has maintained its importance.

POLITICS

Multiparty elections

1999/2004

President Teodoro Obiang Nguema Mbasogo

AT THE LAST ELECTION

House of Representatives of the People 80 seats

94%
PDGE
5%
UP
1%
CDS

PDGE = Equatorial Guinea Democratic Party **UP** = Popular Union **CDS** = Convergence for Social Democracy

Despite its officially being a multiparty state since 1991, some exiled parties have not yet found it safe to return to Equatorial Guinea. The ruling PDGE was set up in 1987 by Teodoro Obiang Nguema Mbasogo, nephew of the dictator Francisco Macías Nguema, whom he overthrew in 1979. It replaced Macías's National Workers' Party (PUNT). The PDGE benefits from heavy government patronage, receiving 3% of all salaries.

The gradual movement toward multipartyism – which was initiated in 1988 following the first elections for 20 years – has been marked by instability. The 1993 parliamentary elections were boycotted by the main opposition parties, while the presidential polls in 1996 and 2002, in which Obiang Nguema was effectively the only candidate, were declared farcical by foreign observers. The 1999 legislative elections were won easily by the PDGE, but denounced by the opposition. Dozens of opposition figures were detained in 2002–2003 over a 1997 plot to overthrow the government.

EQUATORIAL GUINEA

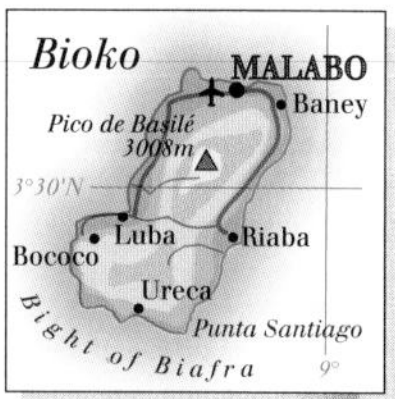
Bioko
MALABO
Baney
Pico de Basilé 3008m
3°30'N
Luba
Riaba
Bococo
Ureca
Punta Santiago
Bight of Biafra

Total Area : 28 051 sq. km (10 830 sq. miles)

POPULATION

over 10 000

under 10 000

LAND HEIGHT

2000m/6562ft

1000m/3281ft

500m/1640ft

200m/656ft

Sea Level

0 50 km

0 50 miles

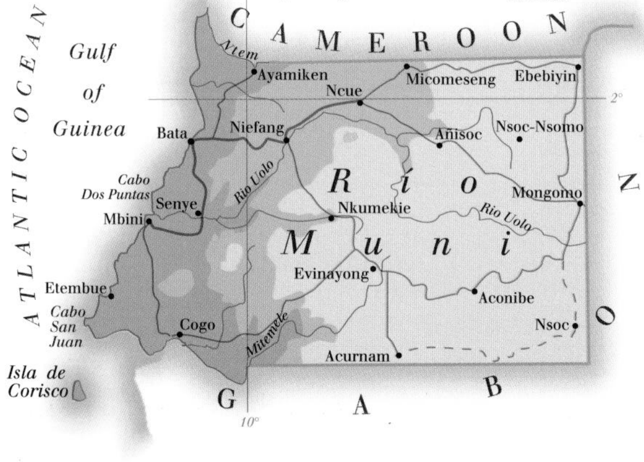
ATLANTIC OCEAN
Gulf of Guinea
CAMEROON
GABON
Ntem
Ayamiken
Ncue
Micomeseng
Ebebiyin
Bata
Niefang
Añisoc
Nsoc-Nsomo
Río Uolo
Río Muni
Cabo Dos Puntas
Senye
Mbini
Nkumekie
Mongomo
Evinayong
Etembue
Aconibe
Cabo San Juan
Cogo
Mitemele
Nsoc
Acurnam
Isla de Corisco

WORLD AFFAIRS

Joined UN in 1968

BDEAC | ACP | FZ | NAM | AU

After its extreme isolation during the Macías dictatorship, Equatorial Guinea sought to rebuild links, especially with Spain, traditionally a haven for political dissenters. A maritime border dispute with Nigeria was finally settled in 2000, paving the way for the exploitation of large oil reserves in the Gulf of Guinea. Oil potential has also stimulated the interest of the US, in turn prompting its concern over the country's poor human rights record.

AID

Recipient

$13m (receipts) | Down 38% in 2001

Equatorial Guinea is poorly developed and therefore heavily dependent on aid. Inefficiency, corruption, and a shortage of skilled people hinder the planning and implementation of projects, and the government's political record threatens funding. Spain and France are the main donors, while aid from UN agencies is also important. An IMF program was suspended in 1997 after the government failed to implement reforms.

DEFENSE

No compulsory military service

$4m | No change in 2001

The main concern is internal security. Cuba and North Korea provided Macías with a presidential guard, while Obiang Nguema has been protected by Moroccan troops. Nigeria, Cameroon, and Gabon have interests in maintaining the autonomy of the Malabo and Río Muni regions.

RESOURCES

Electric power 18,000 kW

3634 tonnes | 237,000 b/d (reserves 71m barrels)

37,600 sheep, 30,000 ducks, 320,000 chickens | Oil, natural gas, gold

Oil production levels doubled between 1998 and the end of 2001. President Obiang Nguema has pledged to use income from oil to promote development. The region around Bata is served by a 3.2 MW hydropower station.

ENVIRONMENT

Not available

None | 1.5 tonnes per capita

The government has failed to impose any serious measures to stop timber companies depleting the rainforest.

MEDIA

TV ownership low

Daily newspaper circulation 5 per 1000 people

PUBLISHING AND BROADCAST MEDIA

There is no regular daily press. The formerly daily newspaper *Poto Poto* now appears irregularly

1 state-owned service | 3 services: 1 state-owned, 2 independent

The press remains tightly controlled, despite the state's adoption of multipartyism. In 2003, state radio declared President Obiang Nguema to be "like God in Heaven."

CRIME

Death penalty in use

Equatorial Guinea does not publish prison figures | Little change from year to year

The level of recorded crime is relatively low, but many offenses are not reported. Many human rights abuses still occur.

CHRONOLOGY

Equatorial Guinea remained a backwater of Spanish colonialism until development began after 1939.

- ❑ **1968** Independence. President Macías begins reign of terror.
- ❑ **1979** Coup puts nephew in power.
- ❑ **1991** Multiparty constitution.
- ❑ **1999** PDGE wins denounced poll.
- ❑ **2001** Ministers resign in corruption scandal.
- ❑ **2002** Obiang Nguema reelected in disputed vote.

EDUCATION

School leaving age: 11

84% | 1003 students

Education declined in the Macías years, when attendance rates fell from 90% to 55%. Although education is declared the state's first priority, funding is poor.

HEALTH

No welfare state health benefits

1 per 4000 people | Diarrheal and respiratory diseases, malaria

Life expectancy – just 37 years in 1960 – had risen substantially by 2000. There are 25 doctors to every 100,000 people.

SPENDING

GDP/cap. increase

CONSUMPTION AND SPENDING

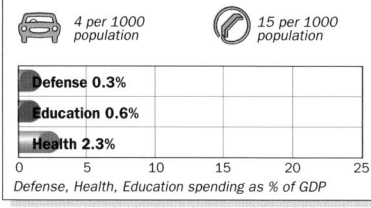

4 per 1000 population | *15 per 1000 population*

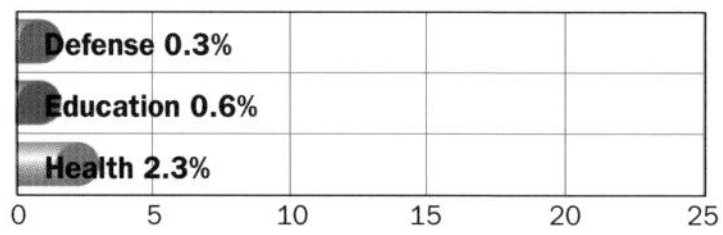
Defense 0.3%
Education 0.6%
Health 2.3%
0
5
10
15
20
25

Defense, Health, Education spending as % of GDP

What wealth there is in Equatorial Guinea tends to be concentrated in the ruling clan. There is also a remnant of the former Spanish plutocracy.

ECONOMICS

Inflation 17% p.a. (1990–2001)

$327m | 571.2 CFA francs (664.2)

SCORE CARD

- ❑ World GNP Ranking 175th
- ❑ GNP per Capita $700
- ❑ Balance of Payments .... –$344m
- ❑ Inflation 6%
- ❑ Unemployment 30%

Strengths

Fertile soils. Timber. Cocoa and coffee. Extensive territorial waters, with potential for fisheries. The economy is strengthening as oil and gas reserves are exploited.

Weaknesses

Lasting effects of economic regression under Macías dictatorship. Maladministration and ideological attacks on the educated have restricted growth; under Macías, cocoa production slumped by 90%. Deterioration of rural economy under successive brutal regimes. Undeveloped natural resources.

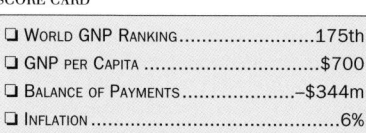

EXPORTS

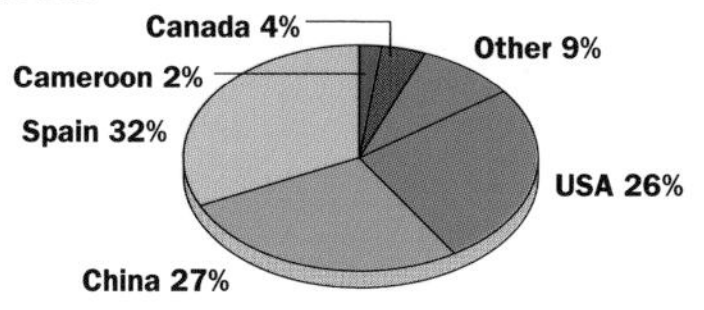
Canada 4%
Other 9%
Cameroon 2%
Spain 32%
USA 26%
China 27%

IMPORTS

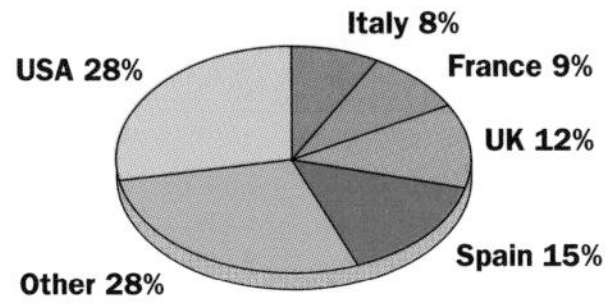
Italy 8%
USA 28%
France 9%
UK 12%
Spain 15%
Other 28%

WORLD RANKING

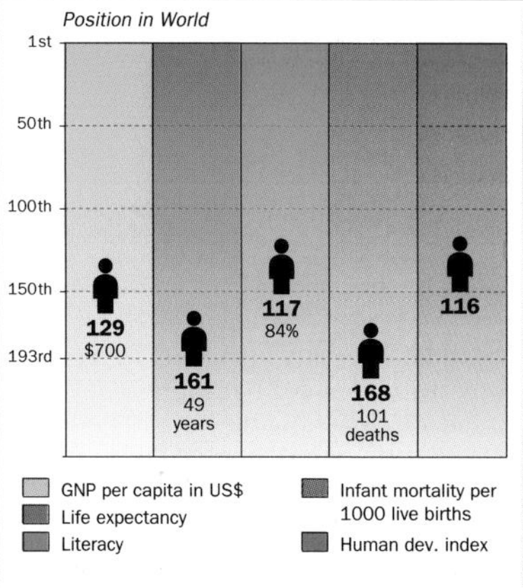
Position in World
1st
50th
100th
150th
193rd
129
$700
161
49 years
117
84%
168
101 deaths
116
GNP per capita in US$
Life expectancy
Literacy
Infant mortality per 1000 live births
Human dev. index

ERITREA

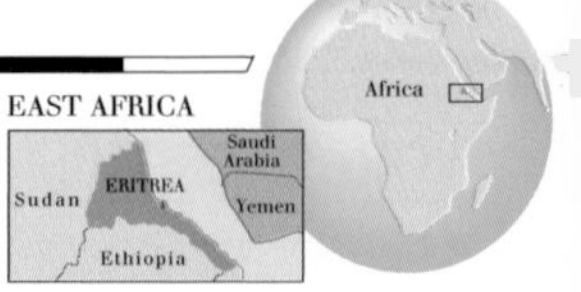

EAST AFRICA
Africa
Saudi Arabia
Sudan
ERITREA
Yemen
Ethiopia

OFFICIAL NAME: State of Eritrea **CAPITAL:** Asmara
POPULATION: 4 million **CURRENCY:** Nakfa **OFFICIAL LANGUAGE:** Tigrinya, English, and Arabic

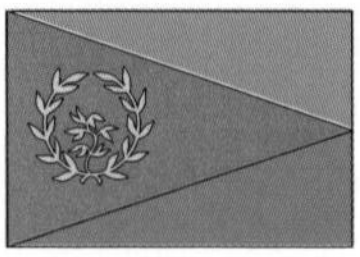

1993 | 2002 | May 24 | ER | +3 | +291 | .er

LYING ALONG THE SHORE of the Red Sea, Eritrea has a landscape of rugged mountains, bush, and desert. A former Italian colony later annexed by Ethiopia, Eritrea fought a long war to win independence in 1993. It is the only country successfully to have seceded in postcolonial Africa. Like its southern neighbor, Eritrea is prone to recurring droughts and the threat of famine. War with Ethiopia in 1998–2000 brought heavy losses on both sides.

CLIMATE

Hot desert/mountain

WEATHER CHART FOR ASMARA

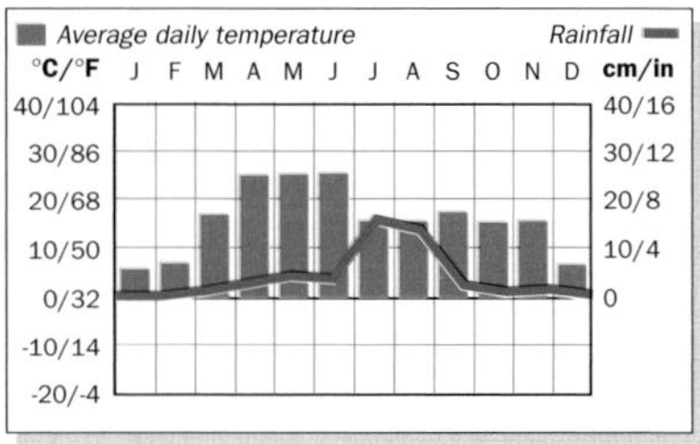

Average daily temperature
Rainfall
°C/°F J F M A M J J A S O N D cm/in
40/104
30/86
20/68
10/50
0/32
-10/14
-20/-4
40/16
30/12
20/8
10/4
0

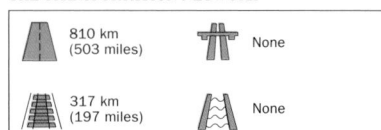

Eritrea's harvest is dependent on mid-year rainfall in the highlands. Lowland temperatures may exceed 50°C (122°F).

TRANSPORTATION

Drive on right

Yohannes IV, Asmara 128,622 passengers

12 ships 20,686 grt

THE TRANSPORTATION NETWORK

810 km (503 miles)		None	
317 km (197 miles)		None	

All transportation infrastructure requires massive investment. Ports have potential as transit points for Ethiopia.

TOURISM

Visitors : Population 1:35

113,000 visitors

Up 61% in 2001

MAIN TOURIST ARRIVALS

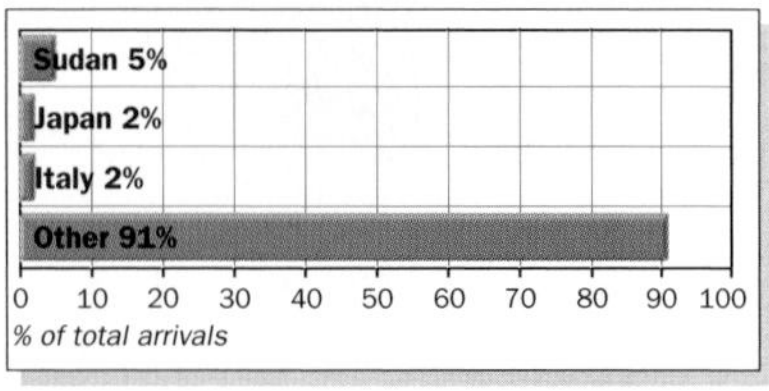

Sudan 5%
Japan 2%
Italy 2%
Other 91%
0 10 20 30 40 50 60 70 80 90 100
% of total arrivals

There is currently very little tourism, but Eritrea has considerable long-term potential, especially along the Red Sea coast, with its underwater attractions, and in the spectacular Danakil depression. Guides are essential.

PEOPLE

Pop. density low

Tigrinya, English, Tigre, Afar, Arabic, Bilen, Kunama, Nara, Saho, Hadareb

34/km² (88/mi²)

THE URBAN/RURAL POPULATION SPLIT

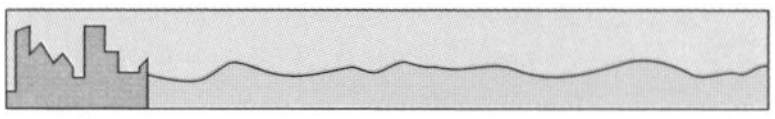

19%
81%

RELIGIOUS PERSUASION

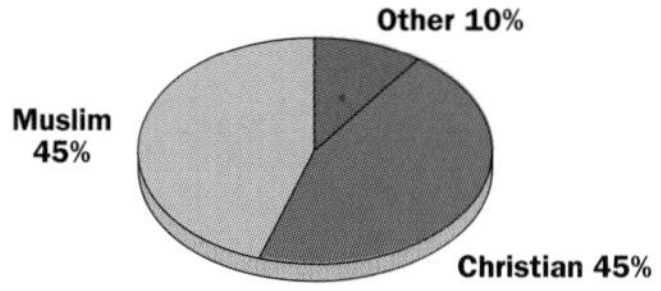

Other 10%
Muslim 45%
Christian 45%

Tigrinya-speakers, mainly Orthodox Christians, form the largest of Eritrea's nine main ethnic groups. A strong sense of nationhood has been forged by the 30-year struggle for independence. Women played an important role in the war; from 1973, 30,000 fought alongside men, some in positions of command. The nomadic peoples of the Danakil desert remain fiercely independent. Subsistence farmers account for 80% of the population.

ERITREA

Total Area : 121 320 sq. km (46 842 sq. miles)

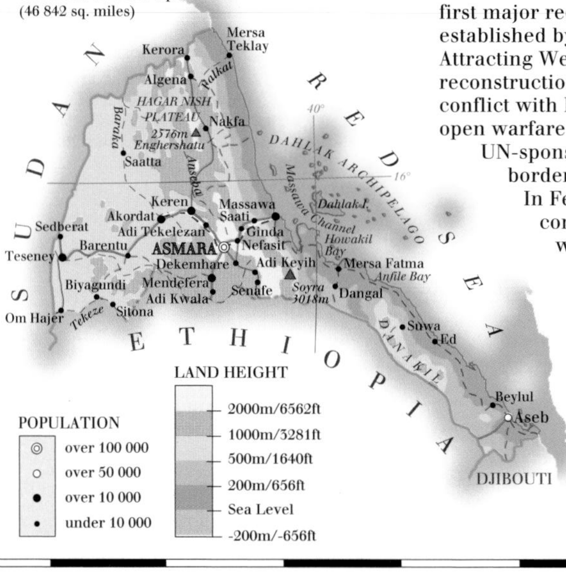

SUDAN
Mersa Teklay
Kerora
Algena
HAGAR NISH PLATEAU
Barka
Nakfa
2376m Enghershatu
Saatta
Anseba
Keren
Massawa
Saati
Akordat
Adi Tekelezan
Sedberat
Barentu
ASMARA
Ginda
Nefasit
Teseney
Dekemhare
Adi Keyih
Biyagundi
Mendefera
Adi Kwala
Senafe
Soyra 3018m
Om Hajer
Tekeze
Sitona
ETHIOPIA
RED SEA
DAHLAK ARCHIPELAGO
Dahlak I.
Massawa Channel
Howakil Bay
Mersa Fatma
Anfile Bay
Dangal
Sawa
Ed
DANAKIL
Beylul
Aseb
DJIBOUTI
40°
16°
LAND HEIGHT
2000m/6562ft
1000m/3281ft
500m/1640ft
200m/656ft
Sea Level
-200m/-656ft
POPULATION
over 100 000
over 50 000
over 10 000
under 10 000

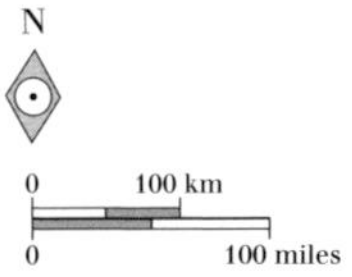

N
0 100 km
0 100 miles

POLITICS

No legislative elections

Elections not yet held

President Issaias Afewerki

LEGISLATIVE OR ADVISORY BODIES

National Assembly 150 seats

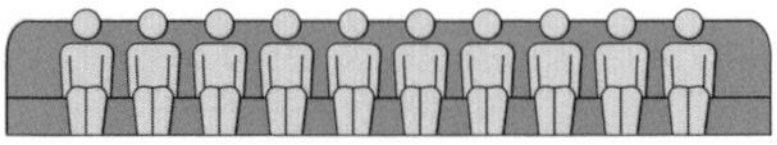

The National Assembly comprises 75 People's Front for Democracy and Justice (**PFDJ**) central committee members and 75 directly elected members, including 11 seats reserved for women. Elections expected in 1997 under the new constitution have not yet taken place

A former Italian colony, Eritrea was dominated by Ethiopia in a federation set up in 1952. Within ten years Ethiopia had reduced Eritrea to a province, prompting a long secessionist struggle. The Eritrean People's Liberation Front (EPLF) and its Tigrean allies helped defeat the Ethiopian regime in 1991. In 1993 a referendum gave overwhelming support to independence.

Pending elections, the country is run by a core leadership from the EPLF (now the PFDJ), with the National Assembly convening only sporadically. The 1997 constitution forbids parties based on religious or ethnic affiliations. Issaias Afewerki, a Christian, has been careful to include Muslims in his cabinet. He lashed out at opponents in 2001 and faced unprecedented criticism, even from within the PFDJ.

WORLD AFFAIRS

Joined UN in 1993

COMESA | IAEA | IGAD | NAM | AU

Eritrea's secession represented the first major redrawing of borders established by Africa's colonizers. Attracting Western and Arab aid for reconstruction is a priority. A border conflict with Ethiopia erupted into open warfare in 1998. Under the 2000 UN-sponsored peace accord, a new border was to be established. In February 2001 Ethiopia completed its troop withdrawal. Work on a physical demarcation of the border is due to finish in mid-2004.

AID

Recipient

$280m (receipts) | Up 59% in 2001

The economy is highly aid-dependent, and millions of Eritreans survive on food aid. This is an obvious and pressing need, given the country's vulnerability to famine, but Western donors have been less generous with aid for the $2 billion cost of reconstruction. Emergency UN aid was requested in mid-2000 to assist over a million people displaced by the Ethiopian incursion. WHO supplied emergency medical aid.

DEFENSE

Compulsory military service

$173m | Down 12% in 2001

Defense expenditure is massive. Vast numbers of conscripts swell the 50,000-strong permanent army. During the independence struggle a third of soldiers were women. Troops were being rehabilitated on "food for work" schemes until the latest war with Ethiopia, which inflicted heavy losses. Mass demobilization was restarted in 2002.

ECONOMICS

Inflation 9% p.a. (1993–2001)

$679m | 13.552 nakfa (13.551)

SCORE CARD

- World GNP Ranking 162nd
- GNP per Capita $160
- Balance of Payments ....–$206m
- Inflation 15%
- Unemployment ....Widespread underemployment

STRENGTHS

Strategic position on Red Sea – tourism and transportation. Asmara–Massawa railroad reopened in 2003. Potential for mining and oil industry. Commitment to cutting dependence on food aid.

WEAKNESSES

Destruction of infrastructure and equipment; port of Massawa heavily bombed. Dependent on aid. Most of population living at subsistence level. Susceptibility to drought and famine. Return of some 750,000 refugees.

EXPORTS

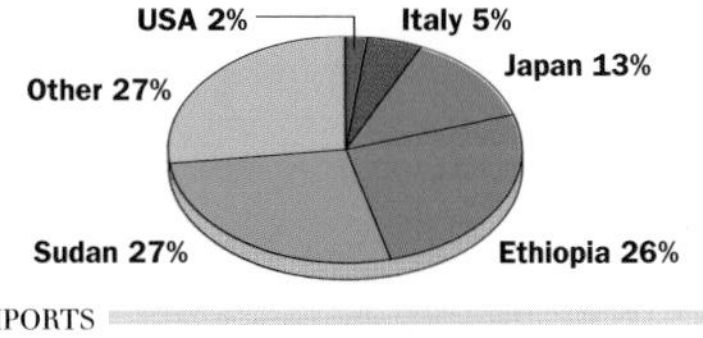
USA 2%
Italy 5%
Japan 13%
Other 27%
Sudan 27%
Ethiopia 26%

IMPORTS

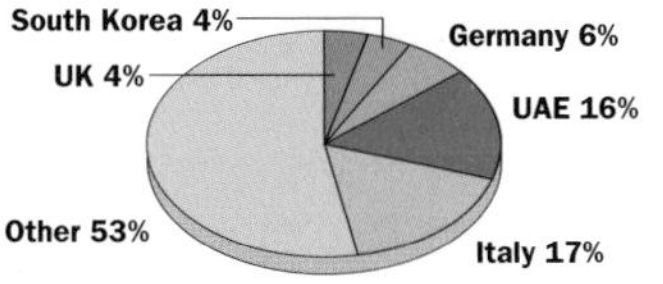
South Korea 4%
Germany 6%
UK 4%
UAE 16%
Other 53%
Italy 17%

RESOURCES

Electric power 172,000 kW

12,612 tonnes | Not an oil producer; oil refinery at Assab

2.2m cattle, 1.7m goats, 1.58m sheep, 1.37m chickens | Copper, potash, gold, iron, silver, zinc, oil, silica, granite, marble

Eritrea has substantial copper reserves, and lesser ones of silver, zinc, and gold. Building materials are exported. Onshore and offshore oil deposits are believed to exist. There is potential for power generation from geothermal sources, though most now comes from a new diesel-powered plant in Massawa.

ENVIRONMENT

Not available

5% | 0.1 tonnes per capita

Deforestation and soil erosion are major problems. The Ethiopian army uprooted trees to destroy the cover they provided for Eritrean soldiers. Since 1991, around 70 million seedlings have been grown in a replanting scheme. The Red Sea coast is a conservation priority.

MEDIA

TV ownership low

There are no daily newspapers

PUBLISHING AND BROADCAST MEDIA

New Eritrea, owned by the PFDJ, is published every 3 days in English, Tigrinya, and Arabic

1 state-controlled service | 1 state-controlled service

The media are largely controlled by the PFDJ, which runs both the radio and TV services. Independent newspapers are not encouraged.

CRIME

Death penalty in use

Eritrea does not publish prison figures | Crime levels remain low

Crime has not been a major problem since independence. The judiciary and police answer to the PFDJ. There are several political prisoners.

EDUCATION

School leaving age: 13

57% | 5505 students

Very few schools functioned during the war. There is one university. In an attempt to reduce potential ethnic tension, all children above the age of 11 are taught in English or Arabic.

HEALTH

No welfare state health benefits

1 per 20,000 people | Malaria, potential risk of famine

The risk of famine overrides normal health concerns. Eritreans built their own hospitals during the independence struggle. Health provision is basic.

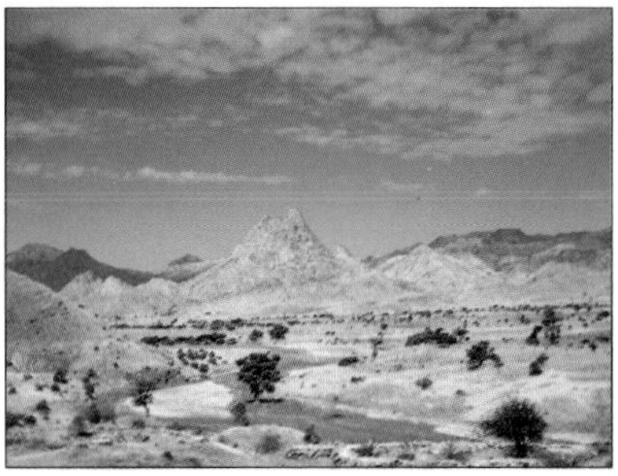

***Seasonal river beds** carry rain from the Ethiopian highlands into Eritrea, providing essential irrigation for agriculture.*

CHRONOLOGY

British military rule replaced Italian colonial authority in 1941.

- **1952** Ethiopia absorbs Eritrea.
- **1961** Beginning of armed struggle.
- **1987** EPLF refuses offer of autonomy; fighting intensifies.
- **1991** EPLF takes Asmara.
- **1993** Formal independence.
- **1998** Border war with Ethiopia.
- **2000** OAU peace treaty signed.
- **2001** Ethiopia completes troop withdrawal.
- **2002** Border demarcation begins.

SPENDING

GDP/cap. increase

CONSUMPTION AND SPENDING

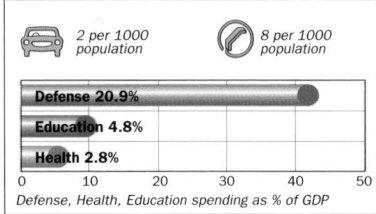

2 per 1000 population | *8 per 1000 population*

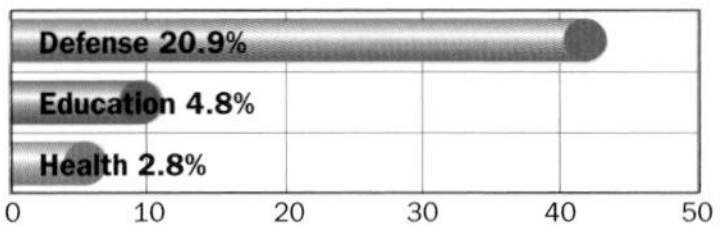
Defense 20.9%
Education 4.8%
Health 2.8%
0
10
20
30
40
50

Defense, Health, Education spending as % of GDP

Some 80% of Eritrea's population are subsistence farmers. A few of the many thousands of refugees who fled to Arab and Western countries have built up some personal savings.

WORLD RANKING

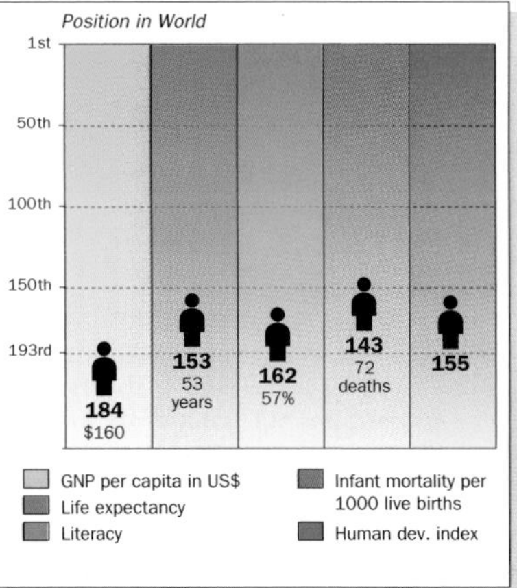
Position in World
1st
50th
100th
150th
193rd
184
$160
153
53 years
162
57%
143
72 deaths
155
GNP per capita in US$
Life expectancy
Literacy
Infant mortality per 1000 live births
Human dev. index

ESTONIA

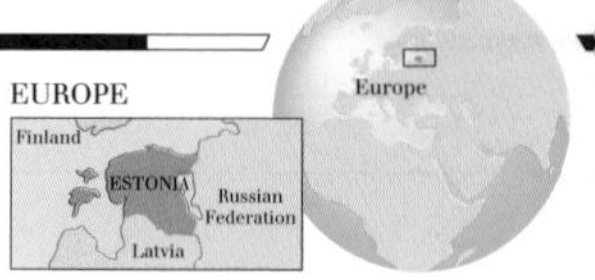

EUROPE
Europe
Finland
ESTONIA
Russian Federation
Latvia

OFFICIAL NAME: Republic of Estonia **CAPITAL:** Tallinn
POPULATION: 1.4 million **CURRENCY:** Kroon **OFFICIAL LANGUAGE:** Estonian

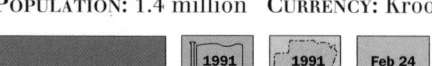

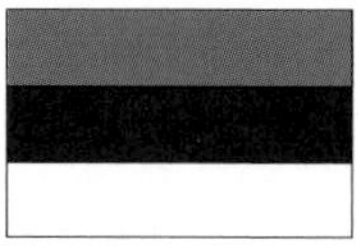

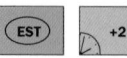

1991 | 1991 | Feb 24 | EST | +2 | +372 | .ee

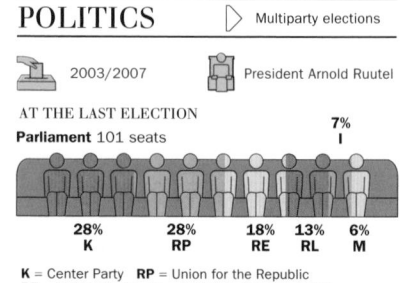

TRADITIONALLY THE MOST Western-oriented of the Baltic states, Estonia is bordered by Latvia and the Russian Federation. Its terrain is flat, boggy, and partly wooded, and includes more than 1500 islands. Estonia formally regained its independence as a multiparty democracy in 1991. In contrast to the peoples of Latvia and Lithuania, Estonians are Finno-Ugric, speaking a language related to Finnish.

CLIMATE

Continental

WEATHER CHART FOR TALLINN

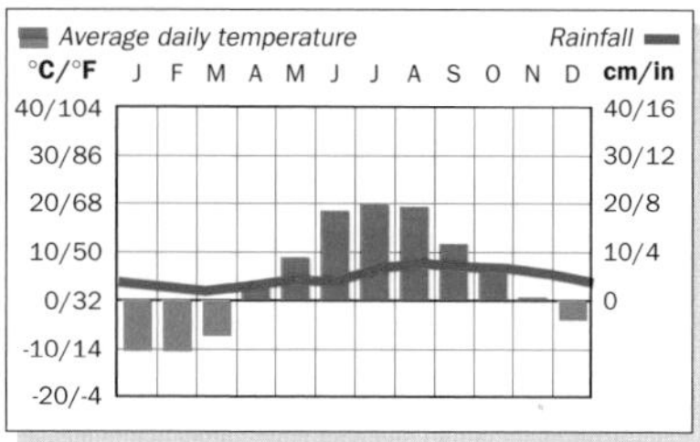

Average daily temperature
Rainfall
°C/°F
J F M A M J J A S O N D
cm/in
40/104
30/86
20/68
10/50
0/32
-10/14
-20/-4
40/16
30/12
20/8
10/4
0

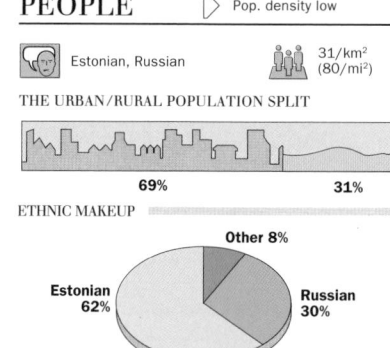

Estonia's coastal location gives it cool summers, and cold winters when the Baltic Sea freezes.

TRANSPORTATION

Drive on right

Tallinn Ulemiste 606,787 passengers

191 ships 346,600 grt

THE TRANSPORTATION NETWORK

29,200 km (18,144 miles)

75 km (47 miles)

968 km (601 miles)

320 km (199 miles)

Railroads have improved and buses are reliable. Baltic ferries link Tallinn with Finland, Sweden, and Germany.

TOURISM

Visitors : Population 1:1

1.36m visitors

Up 3% in 2002

MAIN TOURIST ARRIVALS

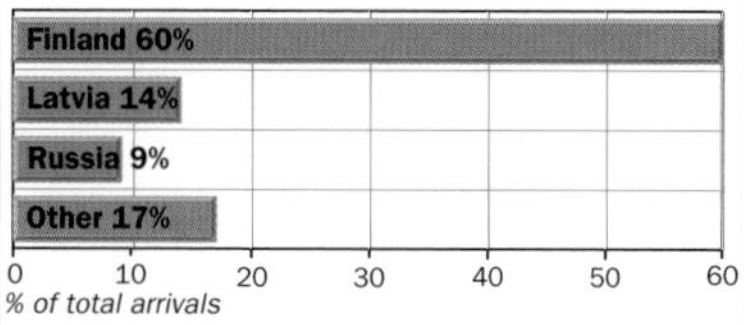

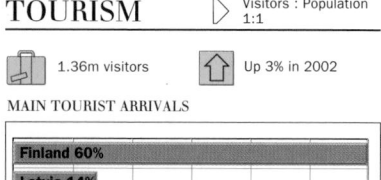

Finland 60%
Latvia 14%
Russia 9%
Other 17%
0 10 20 30 40 50 60
% of total arrivals

Estonia is particularly popular with Finns. Water sports, winter sports, folk and architectural heritage, and nature tours are the main attractions. Tallinn's medieval center draws tourists on short visits and Baltic cruises.

PEOPLE

Pop. density low

Estonian, Russian

31/km² (80/mi²)

THE URBAN/RURAL POPULATION SPLIT

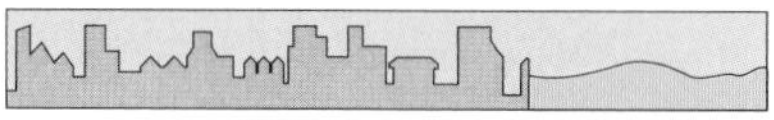

69%
31%

ETHNIC MAKEUP

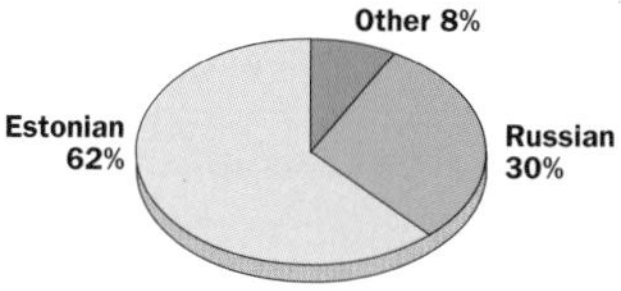

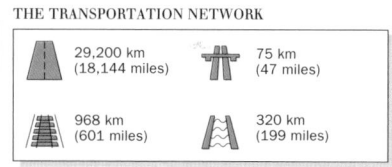

Other 8%
Estonian 62%
Russian 30%

After the decades of Soviet rule, the relationship between Estonians and the Russian minority was problematic. Rules on citizenship, introduced in 1992 and 1995, excluded many ethnic Russians who could not meet the Estonian language and minimum residency requirements. Over 100,000 took Russian rather than Estonian citizenship. A 2000 language law met international demands for an end to discrimination against the Russian-speaking minority. Estonians are predominantly Lutheran. Families are small; divorce rates are high.

POLITICS

Multiparty elections

2003/2007

President Arnold Ruutel

AT THE LAST ELECTION

Parliament 101 seats

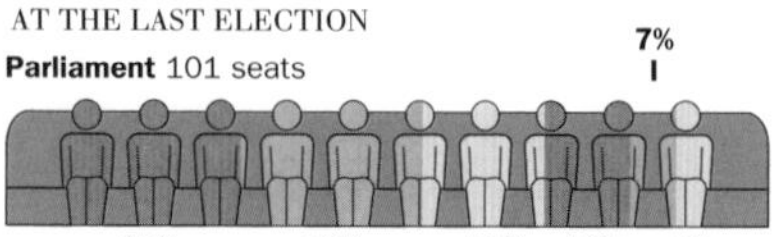

7% I
28% K
28% RP
18% RE
13% RL
6% M

K = Center Party **RP** = Union for the Republic
RE = Reform Party **RL** = Estonian People's Union
I = Pro Patria Union **M** = Moderates

Coalitions have been the norm since the end of communist rule. The left-wing Center Party dominated parliament from 1999, but was initially kept from power. Instead Mart Laar, of the center-right Pro Patria Union, became prime minister. Although hindered by a slim majority, his efforts to pursue free-market reforms became easier as the economy grew strongly from the beginning of 2000. However, cracks in his coalition led to its collapse in 2002, enabling the Center Party to enter the RE-led government. The 2003 elections resulted in a tie between the Center Party and the new right-wing RP, whose leader Juhan Parts became prime minister. He formed a new center-right coalition with the RE and the RL.

ESTONIA

Total Area : 45 226 sq. km (17 462 sq. miles)

LAND HEIGHT
200m/565ft
Sea Level

POPULATION
over 500 000
over 100 000
over 50 000
over 10 000
under 10 000

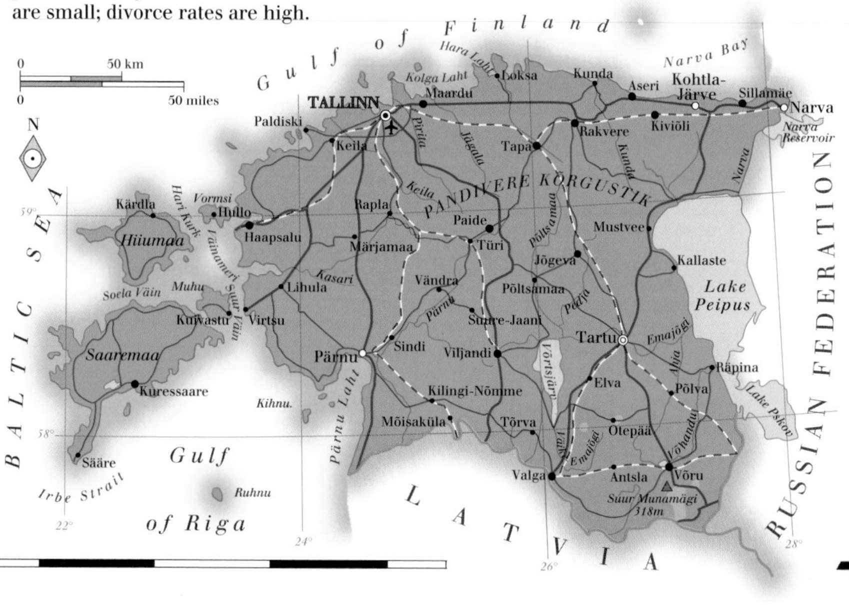

Gulf of Finland
0 50 km
0 50 miles
N
BALTIC SEA
Hara Laht
Kolga Laht
Loksa
Kunda
Narva Bay
Aseri
Kohtla-Järve
Sillamäe
Narva
Narva Reservoir
TALLINN
Maardu
Paldiski
Keila
Tapa
Rakvere
Kiviõli
Pirita
Jägala
Kunda
Narva
Keila
PANDIVERE KÕRGUSTIK
Vormsi
Hullo
Kärdla
Hiiumaa
Hari Kurk
Väinameri
Haapsalu
Rapla
Märjamaa
Paide
Türi
Põltsamaa
Mustvee
Kallaste
Jõgeva
Lake Peipus
Kasari
Lihula
Vändra
Põltsamaa
Soela Väin
Muhu
Suur Väin
Kuivastu
Virtsu
Pärnu
Pedja
Suure-Jaani
Tartu
Emajõgi
Saaremaa
Pärnu
Sindi
Viljandi
Võrtsjärv
Räpina
Elva
Põlva
Kuressaare
Kihnu
Kilingi-Nõmme
Mõisaküla
Tõrva
Otepää
Lake Pskov
Pärnu Laht
Väike Emajõgi
Võhandu
Sääre
Gulf of Riga
Valga
Antsla
Võru
Irbe Strait
Ruhnu
Suur Munamägi 318m
LATVIA
RUSSIAN FEDERATION

WORLD AFFAIRS

Joined UN in 1991

CBSS | CE | EAPC | OSCE | PfP

Estonia's trade with the West has been growing, and ties with other Baltic countries and with Scandinavia have been particularly emphasized.

Integration with the EU and NATO is the top priority; full membership of both organizations is expected in 2004.

Estonia has now accepted the de facto border with Russia, having effectively ceded a portion of its territory during the Soviet period.

AID

Recipient

$69m (receipts) — Up 8% in 2001

Although an aid recipient, since 1997 Estonia has also been an aid donor, mainly through technical assistance.

DEFENSE

Compulsory military service

$92m — Up 18% in 2001

The government agreed in 2000 to shorten compulsory military service from 12 to eight months. Initial US opposition to full membership of NATO has now been changed to support for the Baltic states' entry into the organization.

ECONOMICS

Inflation 46% p.a. (1990–2001)

$5.27bn — 13.62 krooni (15.85)

SCORE CARD

- ❑ WORLD GNP RANKING........110th
- ❑ GNP PER CAPITA........$3870
- ❑ BALANCE OF PAYMENTS........–$339m
- ❑ INFLATION........5.7%
- ❑ UNEMPLOYMENT........13%

STRENGTHS

Improved productivity and stable currency are pegged to the euro. Simplicity of tax regime. More advantage is being taken of natural resources, including timber and oil shale. Transportation infrastructure has been upgraded. Exports growing.

WEAKNESSES

Poor raw materials base. Dependence on imported energy supplies.

EXPORTS

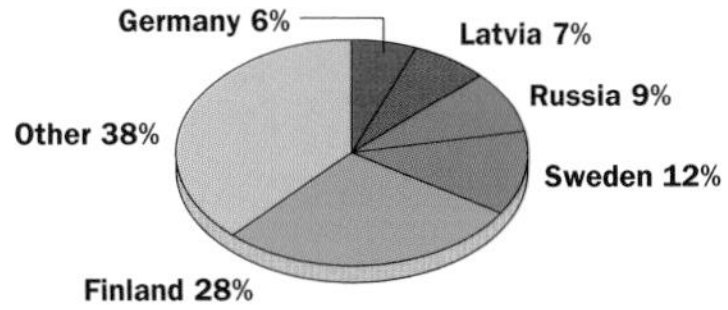
Germany 6%
Latvia 7%
Russia 9%
Sweden 12%
Finland 28%
Other 38%

IMPORTS

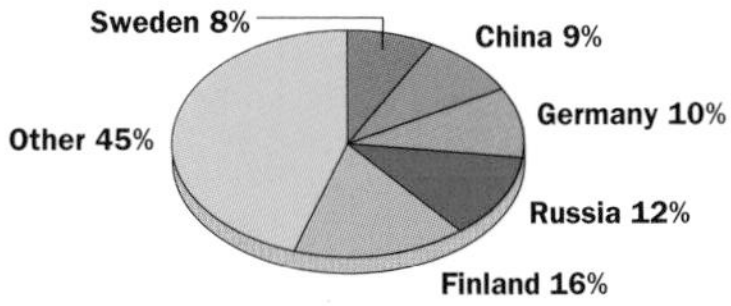
Sweden 8%
China 9%
Germany 10%
Russia 12%
Finland 16%
Other 45%

RESOURCES

Electric power 2.6m kW

113,371 tonnes — Oil figures not published

345,000 pigs, 260,500 cattle, 2.3m chickens — Oil shale, coal, peat, phosphorite

The chief energy resource is oil shale. Phosphorite mining has been stopped. Timber is processed to make paper.

ENVIRONMENT

Sustainability rank: 18th

12% (8% partially protected) — 12.3 tonnes per capita

Industrial pollution comes especially from power stations burning oil shale. Danger of radioactive leaks from former Soviet bases remains. Water supply and sewage treatment have improved.

MEDIA

TV ownership high

Daily newspaper circulation 176 per 1000 people

PUBLISHING AND BROADCAST MEDIA

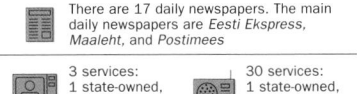

There are 17 daily newspapers. The main daily newspapers are *Eesti Ekspress*, *Maaleht*, and *Postimees*

3 services: 1 state-owned, 2 independent — 30 services: 1 state-owned, 29 independent

The media are mostly progovernment. The number of Russian-language programs is declining. Estonians have been able to receive Finnish satellite TV for some years.

CRIME

No death penalty

4723 prisoners — Up 21% in 2000–2001

Robbery and narcotics are the main crime problems. Generally, however, crime levels are still relatively low.

EDUCATION

School leaving age: 15

99% — 57,778 students

Education is becoming increasingly Westernized. There are two main universities, in Tallinn and Tartu.

HEALTH

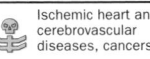

Welfare state health benefits

1 per 326 people — Ischemic heart and cerebrovascular diseases, cancers

The health system, improved since the collapse of communism, is better than that of most former Soviet republics.

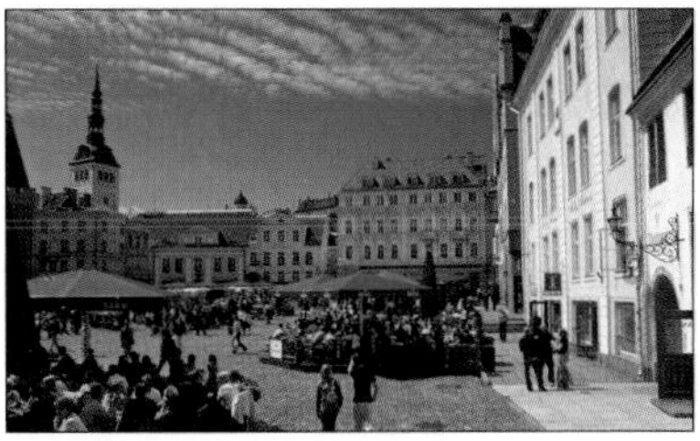

***The historical center** of Tallinn was restored after much of the city was destroyed during World War II.*

E

CHRONOLOGY

After Swedish and then Russian rule, Estonia briefly enjoyed independence from 1921 until its incorporation into the Soviet Union in 1940.

- ❑ **1990** Unilateral declaration of independence; achieved in 1991.
- ❑ **1992** First multiparty elections: center-right government formed.
- ❑ **1992–2001** Lennart Meri president.
- ❑ **1999** Left-wing K wins elections, but center-right forms new coalition.
- ❑ **2001** Communist-era leader Arnold Ruutel elected president.
- ❑ **2002** K joins new ruling coalition. EU approves 2004 membership.
- ❑ **2003** K and RP tie in elections.

SPENDING

GDP/cap. increase

CONSUMPTION AND SPENDING

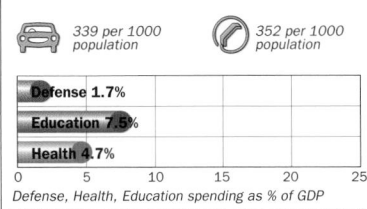

339 per 1000 population — *352 per 1000 population*

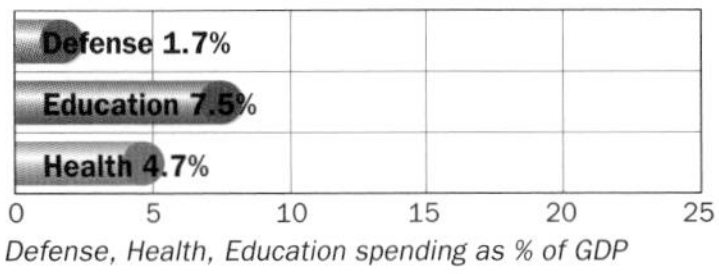
Defense 1.7%
Education 7.5%
Health 4.7%
0
5
10
15
20
25
Defense, Health, Education spending as % of GDP

Market reforms have led to increased prosperity. A few people have become very rich. Average wages are higher than in other Baltic states.

WORLD RANKING

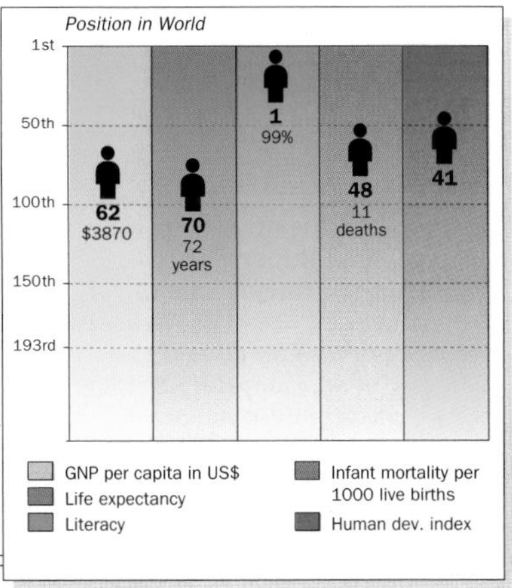
Position in World
1st
50th
100th
150th
193rd
62
$3870
70
72
years
1
99%
48
11
deaths
41
GNP per capita in US$
Life expectancy
Literacy
Infant mortality per 1000 live births
Human dev. index

ETHIOPIA

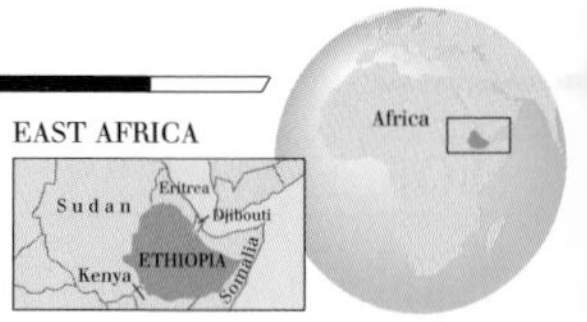
EAST AFRICA
Africa
Sudan
Eritrea
Djibouti
ETHIOPIA
Kenya
Somalia

OFFICIAL NAME: Federal Democratic Republic of Ethiopia **CAPITAL:** Addis Ababa
POPULATION: 66 million **CURRENCY:** Ethiopian birr **OFFICIAL LANGUAGE:** Amharic

1896 | 2002 | May 28 | ETH | +3 | +251 | .et

THE FORMER EMPIRE OF Ethiopia, the only African country to escape colonization, is the cradle of an ancient civilization which adopted Orthodox Christianity in the 4th century. It has been landlocked since 1993, when Eritrea seceded. Ethiopia is mountainous except for desert lowlands in the northeast and southeast, and is prone to devastating drought and famine. A long civil war ended in 1991 with the defeat of the Stalinist military dictatorship that had ruled since 1974. A free-market, multiparty democratic system now provides substantial regional autonomy. War with Eritrea in 1998–2000 brought heavy losses on both sides before a peace agreement was signed in December 2000. Arbitrators began redefining the border in spring 2002.

CLIMATE

Mountain/steppe

WEATHER CHART FOR ADDIS ABABA

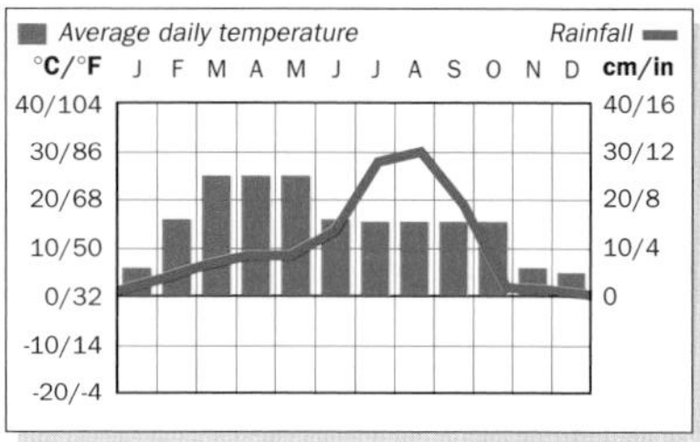
Average daily temperature
Rainfall
°C/°F
J F M A M J J A S O N D
cm/in
40/104
30/86
20/68
10/50
0/32
-10/14
-20/-4
40/16
30/12
20/8
10/4
0

In general, the climate is moderate, except in the lowlands of the Danakil and the Ogaden deserts, which are hot all year round and can suffer severe drought. The highlands are temperate, with night frost in the mountains. The single rainy season in the west brings twice as much rain as do the two wet seasons in the east. During these cloudy periods, thunderstorms occur almost daily.

TRANSPORTATION

Drive on right

Bole International, Addis Ababa
1.23m passengers

9 ships
81,933 grt

THE TRANSPORTATION NETWORK

3290 km (2044 miles)

Trans-East Africa Highway

681 km (423 miles)

None

The single railroad linking Addis Ababa with Djibouti has grown in strategic importance due to tensions with Eritrea. Ethiopia's main access to the sea by road has been through the Red Sea ports of Assab and Massawa, now part of an independent Eritrea. Inland, pack mules and donkeys are widely used. Ethiopian Airlines has good services to much of Africa, and to major cities around the world.

TOURISM

Visitors : Population 1:423

156,000 visitors

Up 5% in 2002

MAIN TOURIST ARRIVALS

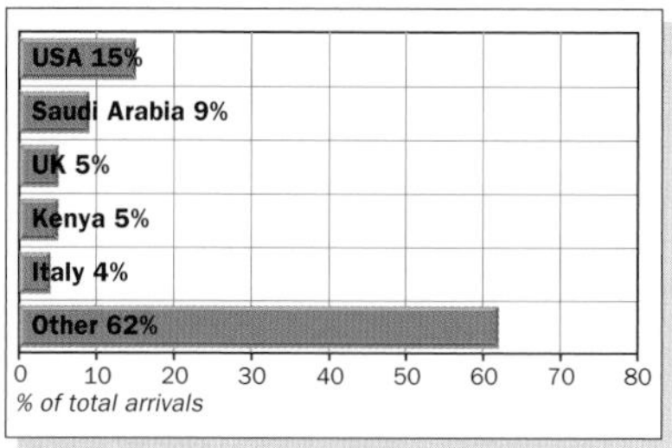
USA 15%
Saudi Arabia 9%
UK 5%
Kenya 5%
Italy 4%
Other 62%
0 10 20 30 40 50 60 70 80
% of total arrivals

Despite Ethiopia's unique attractions, tourism is on a small scale, though since 1991 there has been a sizable increase in the number of visitors, mostly on organized tours. Several new hotels are being built. The Rift Valley lakes, Lake Tana, the Gonder castles, and the Blue Nile gorge, with its spectacular scenery, are popular destinations, but guides are essential. Ancient rock-hewn churches, and cities such as Aksum, the royal capital of the first Ethiopian kingdom, are now accessible. There are nine national parks.

***Lalibela** lies 120 km (75 miles) northwest of Desē in Ethiopia's plateau region, and is famous for the rock-hewn churches created by King Lalibela of the Zagwe dynasty.*

PEOPLE

Pop. density medium

Amharic, Tigrinya, Galla, Sidamo, Somali, English, Arabic

59/km² (154/mi²)

THE URBAN/RURAL POPULATION SPLIT

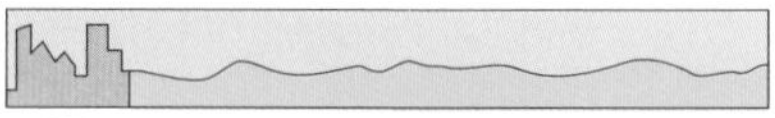
16%
84%

RELIGIOUS PERSUASION

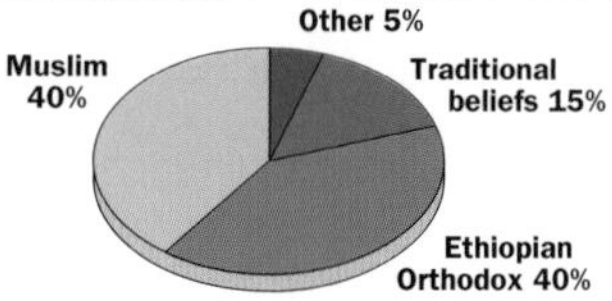
Other 5%
Muslim 40%
Traditional beliefs 15%
Ethiopian Orthodox 40%

ETHNIC MAKEUP

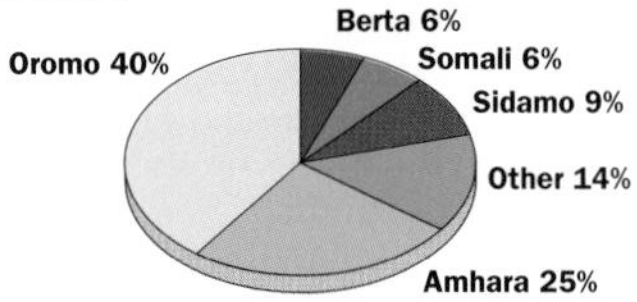
Berta 6%
Oromo 40%
Somali 6%
Sidamo 9%
Other 14%
Amhara 25%

There are 76 ethnic nations in Ethiopia, speaking 286 languages. Oromos (or Gallas) form the largest group, whereas less than 5% of the population are Tigreans.

Civil war was sparked by fighting between different ethnic groups, but they later united in opposition to the Mengistu regime. Ethnic tensions are still near the surface in spite of the new federal structure, and there have been reports of boundary disputes in several regions. The Oromos withdrew from the Tigrean-dominated government in 1992. Hostility to the government has also been voiced by disaffected Amharas, who had been dominant for several centuries, and by the Orthodox Church. The aspirations of ethnic Somalis in the southeast are another source of tension.

Most of the small Jewish community, which has lived in Ethiopia for 2000 years, was evacuated to Israel in 1991, but more than 20,000 remain, waiting for Israel to offer them citizenship.

The participation of women in rural organizations is increasing, reflecting the key role women played in the war.

POPULATION AGE BREAKDOWN

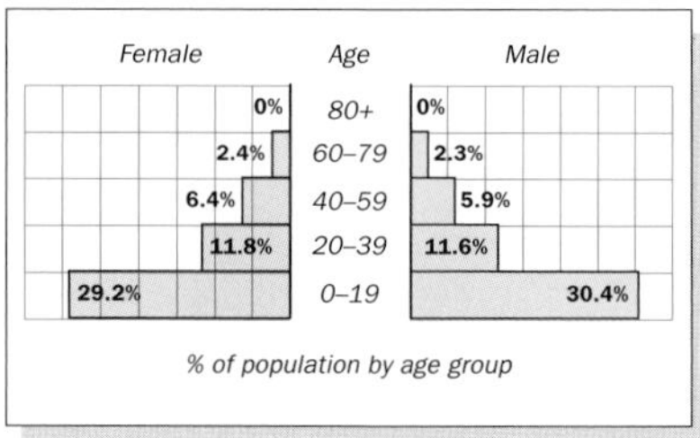
Female
Age
Male
0%
80+
0%
2.4%
60–79
2.3%
6.4%
40–59
5.9%
11.8%
20–39
11.6%
29.2%
0–19
30.4%
% of population by age group

Key to symbols and abbreviations on cover flaps

ETHIOPIA

Total Area :
1 127 127 sq. km
(435 184 sq. miles)

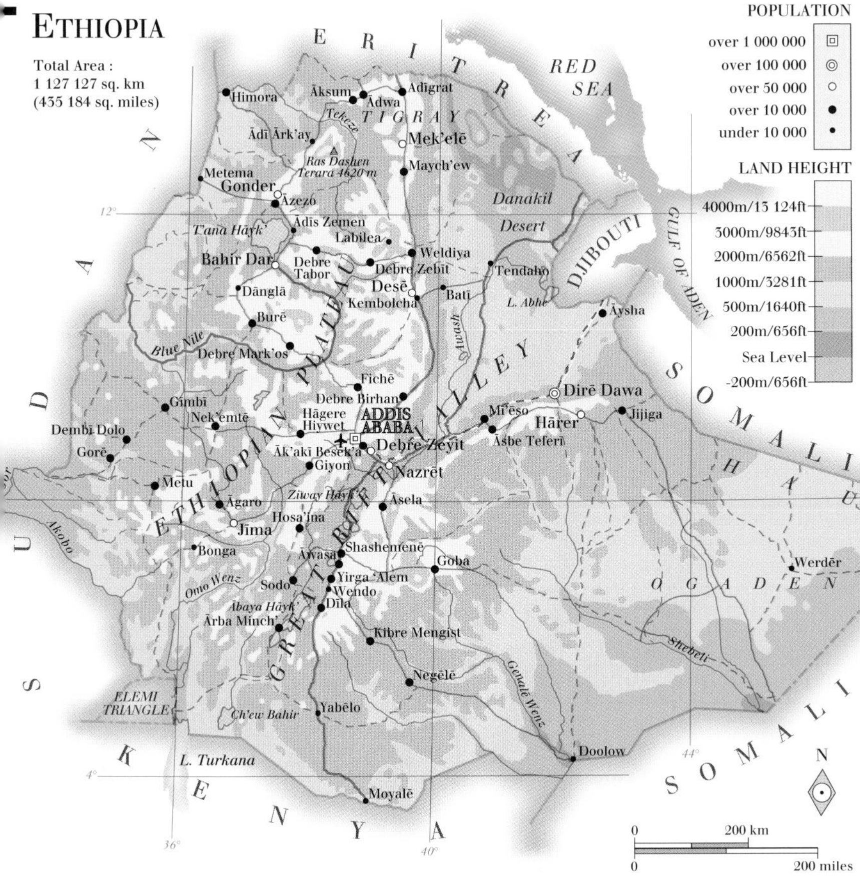

POPULATION
over 1 000 000
over 100 000
over 50 000
over 10 000
under 10 000
LAND HEIGHT
4000m/13 124ft
3000m/9843ft
2000m/6562ft
1000m/3281ft
500m/1640ft
200m/656ft
Sea Level
-200m/656ft
E R I T R E A
RED SEA
DJIBOUTI
GULF OF ADEN
S O M A L I A
K E N Y A
S U D A N
Himora
Āksum
Adwa
Ādīgrat
T I G R A Y
Ādī Ārk'ay
Tekezē
Ras Dashen Terara 4620 m
Mek'elē
Maych'ew
Metema
Gonder
Āzezo
Danakil Desert
T'ana Hāyk'
Ādīs Zemen
Labilea
Weldiya
Bahir Dar
Debre Tabor
Debre Zebīt
Tendaho
Desē
Kembolcha
Batī
L. Abhe
Dānglā
Burē
Āysha
Blue Nile
Debre Mark'os
Awash
Fichē
Debre Birhan
Dirē Dawa
Gīmbī
Nek'emtē
Hāgere Hiywet
ADDIS ABABA
Mī'ēso
Hārer
Jījiga
Dembī Dolo
Āsbe Teferī
Gorē
Āk'ak'ī Besek'a
Debre Zeyit
Gīyon
Nazrēt
H A U D
Metu
Ziway Hāyk'
Āsela
Āgaro
Jīma
Hosa'ina
ETHIOPIAN PLATEAU
GREAT RIFT VALLEY
Bonga
Shashemenē
Āwasa
Goba
Werdēr
Omo Wenz
Sodo
Yirga 'Alem
Wendo
O G A D E N
Ābaya Hāyk'
Dīla
Ārba Minch'
Kibre Mengist
Shebeli
Negēlē
Genalē Wenz
ELEMI TRIANGLE
Ch'ew Bahir
Yabēlo
Doolow
L. Turkana
Moyalē
Akobo
0 200 km
0 200 miles
N

WORLD AFFAIRS

Joined UN in 1945

COMESA | G24 | IGAD | NAM | AU

Landlocked since the secession of Eritrea, Ethiopia needs to have continued access to the Red Sea ports of Massawa and Assab. Relations with Eritrea remained cordial until a border dispute escalated into armed conflict in 1998. A peace accord reached two years later allowed for the demarcation of a new border.

Addis Ababa is the headquarters of the AU and of the UN Economic Commission for Africa. Ethiopia is active in regional diplomacy, including numerous attempts at brokering peace in Somalia, though tension with Somali factions has escalated into armed intervention by Ethiopia, provoking considerable resentment in Somalia.

The Ethiopian government's official policy is one of noninterference in the affairs of neighboring countries, though both Sudan and Somalia have accused Ethiopia of supporting rebels. Links with other African states have been strengthened, as have those with the US, the EU, and Israel.

E

POLITICS

Multiparty elections

L. House 2000/2005
U. House 2000/2005

President Girma Wolde Giorgis

AT THE LAST ELECTION

House of People's Representatives 550 seats **8% Vacant** **2% Ind**

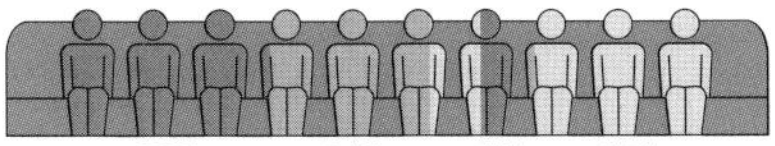

32% OPDO **24% ANDM** **7% TPLF** **27% Others**

OPDO = Oromo People's Democratic Organization
ANDM = Amhara National Democratic Movement
TPLF = Tigre People's Liberation Front **Ind** = Independents

The Ethiopian People's Revolutionary Democratic Front (**EPRDF**) includes all the main parties and controls over 90% of the lower house

House of the Federation 108 seats

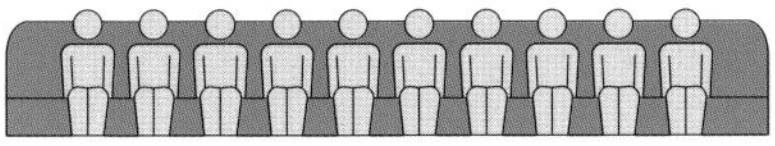

The upper house is elected indirectly on a nonparty basis

The transitional period which followed the collapse of the Mengistu military dictatorship in 1991 ended in 1995 with multiparty elections.

Profile

The current government, first elected in 1995, succeeded that set up in 1991 by the EPRDF, the strongest of the groups that fought Mengistu's Marxist regime and chiefly responsible for winning the civil war. Prime Minister Meles Zenawi is the leader of the Tigrean People's Liberation Front, the largest group within the EPRDF. There is growing opposition from the Oromos and Amharas to the dominance of Tigreans. The nine states are run by elected governments mainly headed by local liberation movements.

Main Political Issue
Ethnic representation

The 1994 constitution establishing a nine-state federation grants the states considerable autonomy, including the right to secede, as Eritrea had done in 1993. The EPRDF government believes this to be the best way to prevent secessionist conflict and maintain national unity. The ruling broad-based coalition is dominated ideologically by Tigrean politicians.

***Prime Minister Meles Zenawi**, leader of the EPRDF, which ousted the Mengistu regime.*

***Emperor Haile Selassie**, revered by Rastafarians as a god.*

CHRONOLOGY

After repelling a devastating Muslim invasion in 1523, Ethiopia developed as an isolated empire until Egyptian and Sudanese incursions in the 1850s led to its renewed political power under Emperor Teodros. His successor, Menelik II, doubled the empire southward and eastward.

- **1896** Italian invasion of Tigre defeated. Europeans recognize Ethiopia's independence.
- **1913** Menelik II dies.
- **1916** His son, Lij Iyasu, is deposed for his conversion to Islam and a proposed alliance with Turkey. Menelik's daughter, Zauditu, becomes empress with Ras (Prince) Tafari as regent.
- **1923** Joins League of Nations.
- **1930** Zauditu dies. Ras Tafari crowned Emperor Haile Selassie.
- **1936** Italians occupy Ethiopia. League of Nations fails to react.
- **1941** British oust Italians and restore Haile Selassie, who sets up a constitution, parliament, and cabinet, but retains personal power and the feudal system.
- **1952** Eritrea, ruled by Italy until 1941, then under British mandate, federated with Ethiopia.

E

CHRONOLOGY *continued*

- **1962** Unitary state created; Eritrea loses its autonomy despite demands of secessionists.
- **1972–1974** Famine kills 200,000.
- **1974** Strikes and army mutinies at Haile Selassie's autocratic rule and country's economic decline. Dergue (Military Committee) stages coup.
- **1975** Becomes socialist state: nationalizations, worker cooperatives, and health reforms.
- **1977** Col. Mengistu Haile Mariam takes over. Somali invasion of Ogaden defeated with Soviet and Cuban help.
- **1978–1979** Thousands of political opponents killed or imprisoned.
- **1984** Workers' Party of Ethiopia (WPE) set up on Soviet model. One million die in famine after drought and years of war. Live Aid concert raises funds for relief.
- **1986** Eritrean rebels now control entire northeastern coast.
- **1987** Serious drought again threatens famine.
- **1988** Eritrean and Tigrean People's Liberation Fronts (EPLF and TPLF) begin new offensives. Mengistu's budget is for "Everything to the War Front." Diplomatic relations with Somalia restored.
- **1989** Military coup attempt fails. TPLF controls most of Tigre. TPLF and Ethiopian People's Revolutionary Movement form alliance – EPRDF.
- **1990** Military gains by opponents of Mengistu regime. Moves toward market economy and restructuring of ruling party to include non-Marxists. Distribution of food aid for victims of new famine is hampered by government and rebel forces.
- **1991** Mengistu accepts military defeat and flees country. EPRDF enters Addis Ababa, sets up provisional government, promising representation for all ethnic groups. Outbreaks of fighting continue, between mainly Tigrean EPRDF and opposing groups.
- **1993** Eritrean independence recognized following referendum.
- **1995** Transitional rule ends. EPRDF wins landslide in multiparty elections, sets up first democratic government. New nine-state federation is formed.
- **1998–2000** Border war with Eritrea.
- **2000** OAU peace treaty signed. Haile Selassie's remains buried in Trinity Cathedral, Addis Ababa.
- **2001** Ethiopia completes troop withdrawal from Eritrea.
- **2002** Over 120 human rights demonstrators killed by police.

AID

Recipient

$1.08bn (receipts) | Up 56% in 2001

Aid plays an increasingly important role in the economy. The World Bank, the US, and the EU are the largest sources of assistance. The World Bank donated $3.6 billion in 2002 toward tackling poverty. However, emphasis has shifted from infrastructure development back to straightforward food aid since recurring and prolonged droughts hit the country from 2000. Contributions have consistently fallen short of the country's needs, and failed to prevent a new famine in early 2003, despite months of warnings.

DEFENSE

No compulsory military service

$580m | Down 13% in 2001

Ethiopia is one of the most heavily militarized states in Africa. Its sizable standing army is boosted by conscription at times of crisis. Heavy losses have been sustained in fighting with Eritrea, and a 12-month international arms embargo was imposed following the Ethiopian advance in 2000. The government is trying to gain control of the many ethnic and clan-based militias throughout the country.

ETHIOPIAN ARMED FORCES

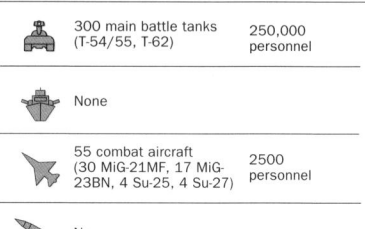

300 main battle tanks (T-54/55, T-62)	250,000 personnel
None	
55 combat aircraft (30 MiG-21MF, 17 MiG-23BN, 4 Su-25, 4 Su-27)	2500 personnel
None	

ECONOMICS

Inflation 6.1% p.a. (1990–2001)

$6.68bn | 8.575 Ethiopian birr (8.3)

SCORE CARD

- World GNP Ranking 103rd
- GNP per Capita $100
- Balance of Payments ....–$272m
- Inflation ....–11.2%
- Unemployment...................................63%

ECONOMIC PERFORMANCE INDICATOR

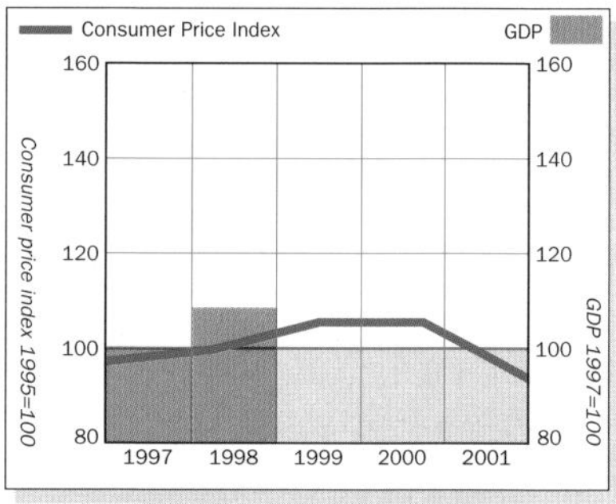
Consumer Price Index
GDP
160
140
120
100
80
Consumer price index 1995=100
GDP 1997=100
1997
1998
1999
2000
2001

EXPORTS

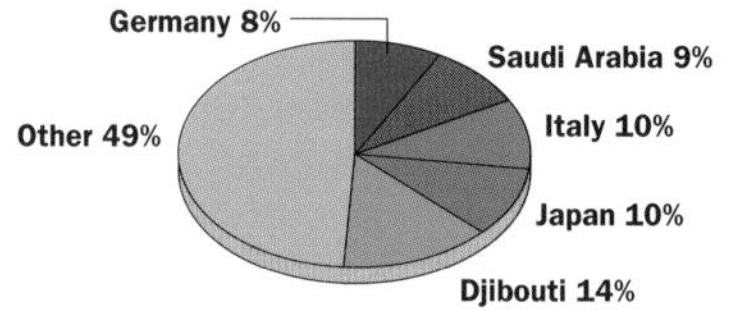
Germany 8%
Saudi Arabia 9%
Italy 10%
Japan 10%
Djibouti 14%
Other 49%

IMPORTS

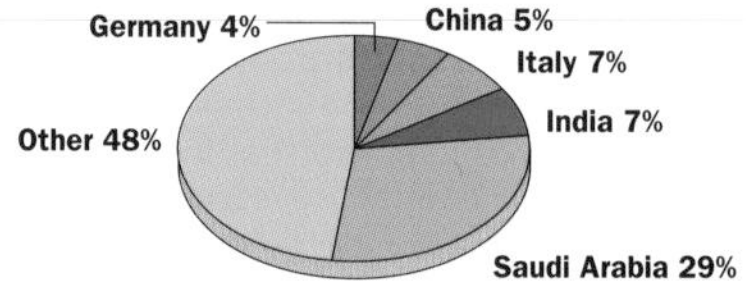
Germany 4%
China 5%
Italy 7%
India 7%
Saudi Arabia 29%
Other 48%

Strengths

Increased economic aid in 1990s. End of total state control. Coffee production.

Weaknesses

Overwhelming dependence on agriculture. Periodic serious droughts and famine. Massive displacement of population by war and drought. War-damaged infrastructure. Small industrial base. Lack of skilled workers. Growing problem of AIDS infections.

Profile

After the end of the civil war in 1991, Ethiopia began moving toward a market economy by encouraging foreign investment and reforming land tenure. Economic decline was reversed in 1993 as agricultural and industrial output grew, with foreign aid used to fund the purchase of parts and raw materials for manufacturing. These gains were undermined by war with Eritrea in 1998–2000 and the renewed danger of severe drought-related famine from 2000.

ETHIOPIA : MAJOR BUSINESSES

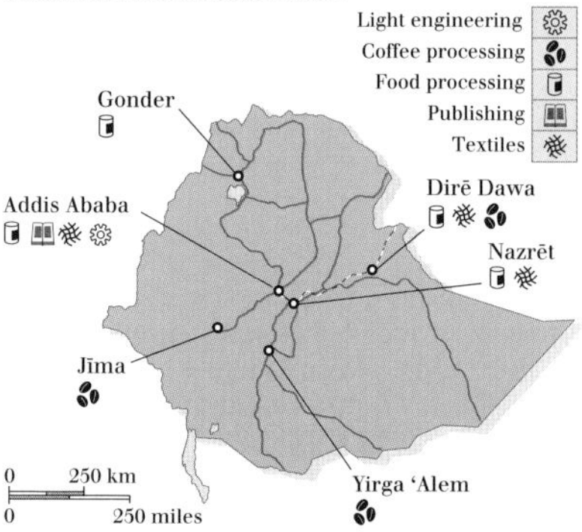
Light engineering
Coffee processing
Food processing
Publishing
Textiles
Gonder
Addis Ababa
Dirē Dawa
Nazrēt
Jīma
Yirga 'Alem
0 250 km
0 250 miles

RESOURCES

Electric power 459,000 kW

15,681 tonnes

Oil reserves currently unexploited

35.5m cattle, 11.4m sheep, 9.62m goats, 38m chickens

Oil, gold, platinum, copper, potash, iron, natural gas

ELECTRICITY GENERATION

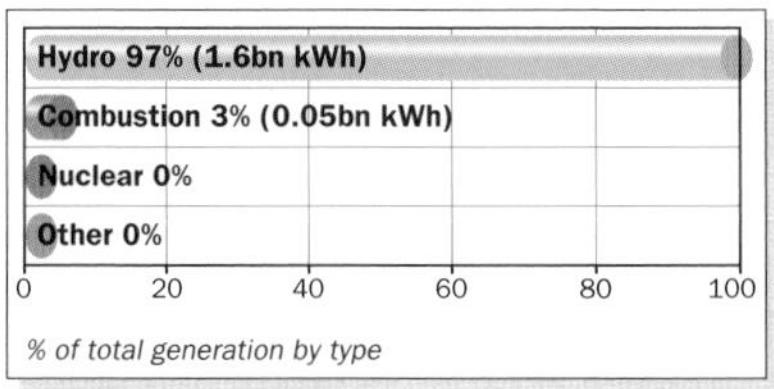

Hydro 97% (1.6bn kWh)
Combustion 3% (0.05bn kWh)
Nuclear 0%
Other 0%
0
20
40
60
80
100
% of total generation by type

Manpower and financial constraints have prevented a systematic survey of mineral resources. Mining contributes less than 1% of GDP. Ethiopia has great potential for HEP which, in the long run, could offset domestic reliance on fuelwood and slow massive deforestation and soil erosion. Construction of the 300 MW Tekeze Dam began in 2002 and is expected to be completed by 2007. The potential for geothermal energy production along the Rift Valley is estimated at 700 MW. The Malaysian oil firm Petronas won the right in 2003 to explore western Ethiopia.

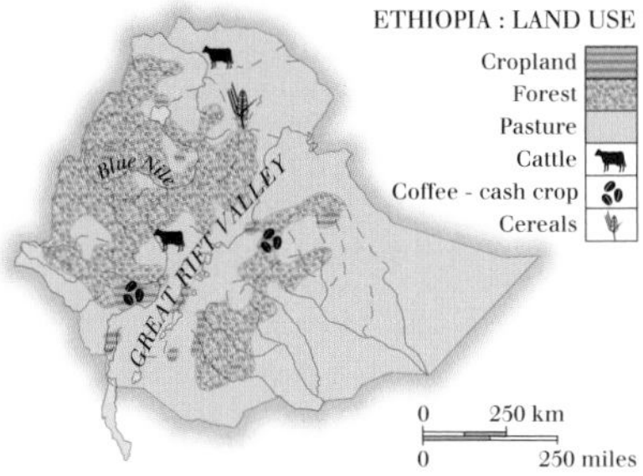

ETHIOPIA : LAND USE
Cropland
Forest
Pasture
Cattle
Coffee - cash crop
Cereals
Blue Nile
GREAT RIFT VALLEY
0 250 km
0 250 miles

ENVIRONMENT

Sustainability rank: 113th

23% (14% partially protected)

0.09 tonnes per capita

ENVIRONMENTAL TREATIES

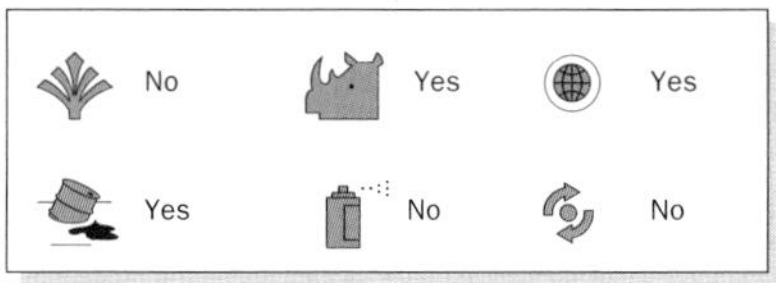

No
Yes
Yes
Yes
No
No

Deforestation for fuelwood and the resultant rapid soil erosion, particularly in the highlands, are serious problems. Forest cover has fallen from 40% in 1900 to only 5% today. Dung is being used for fuel, instead of as a fertilizer. Local projects include terracing hillsides to prevent soil and water run-off – 36,000 km (22,370 miles) of terraces were built in Tigre in 1992. Thousands of people invaded the Bale Mountains National Park in 2002 in search of water, threatening its delicate ecosystem.

MEDIA

TV ownership low

Daily newspaper circulation 0.4 per 1000 people

The government remains uneasy about the post-Mengistu independent press, which has become prolific and critical, though circulation is small. Legal action has been taken to silence several publications. All main newspapers and the TV broadcasting station are government-owned and operated.

PUBLISHING AND BROADCAST MEDIA

There are 3 daily newspapers, including *Addis Zemen* and *Ethiopian Herald* published by the government

1 state-owned service

4 services: 1 state-owned, 3 independent

CRIME

Death penalty in use

13,585 prisoners

Up 12% in 2000–2001

CRIME RATES

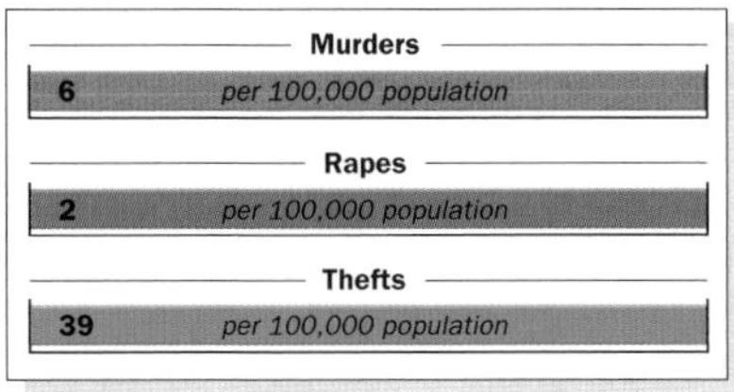

Murders
6 per 100,000 population
Rapes
2 per 100,000 population
Thefts
39 per 100,000 population

A number of human rights abuses by the transitional government have been documented by the independent Ethiopian Human Rights Council. These include detention without trial, "disappearances," and extrajudicial killings. There is some concern over indiscipline among EPRDF forces, who provide a de facto police force in many regions. In rural areas the state system has yet to replace traditional forms of justice.

EDUCATION

School leaving age: 13

40%

87,431 students

THE EDUCATION SYSTEM

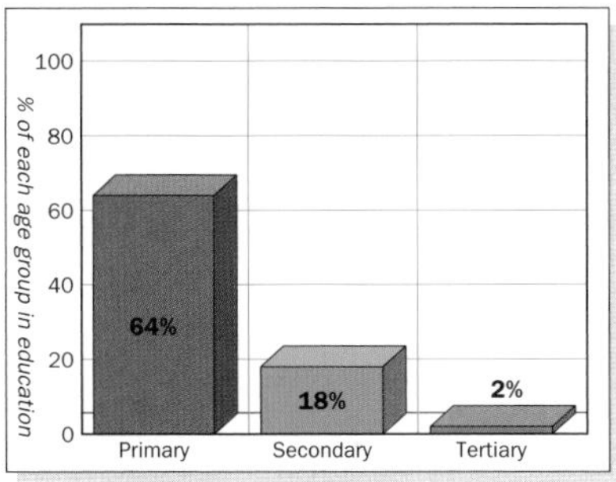

100
80
60
40
20
0
% of each age group in education
64%
18%
2%
Primary
Secondary
Tertiary

Education is free, but classes are crowded and schooling has been severely disrupted by war. Only a small minority of children attend secondary school. Addis Ababa University, a center of political activity (usually anti-EPRDF), suffers periodic closures and the dismissal of leading academics.

HEALTH

No welfare state health benefits

1 per 33,333 people

Diarrheal and respiratory diseases, tuberculosis, malaria

Starvation after severe drought is the principal concern. Malnutrition is increasingly widespread, causing growth problems and allowing the rapid spread of infectious diseases among the weakened. HIV affects 6.4% of the population – over four million people. Fewer than one in four Ethiopians have access to clean water. The use of traditional remedies is widespread.

SPENDING

GDP/cap. increase

CONSUMPTION AND SPENDING

1 per 1000 population

4 per 1000 population

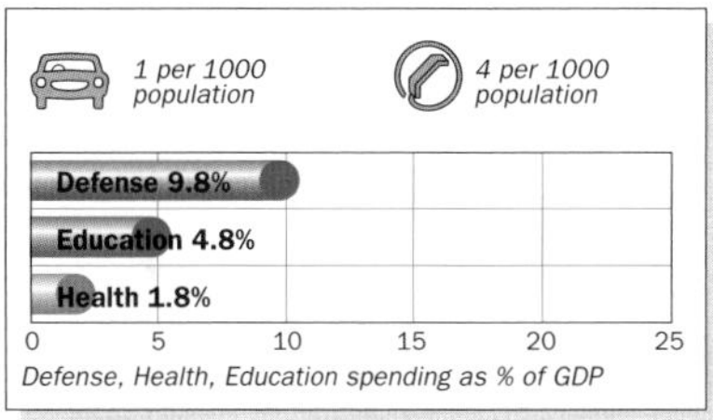

Defense 9.8%
Education 4.8%
Health 1.8%
0
5
10
15
20
25
Defense, Health, Education spending as % of GDP

Most Ethiopians are extremely poor, many of the country's wealthier families having fled into exile in recent years. Ethiopian Christian culture places more value on maintaining traditional social structures than on realizing individual ambition. Living at subsistence level and a reliance on traditional agriculture remain the general expectation.

WORLD RANKING

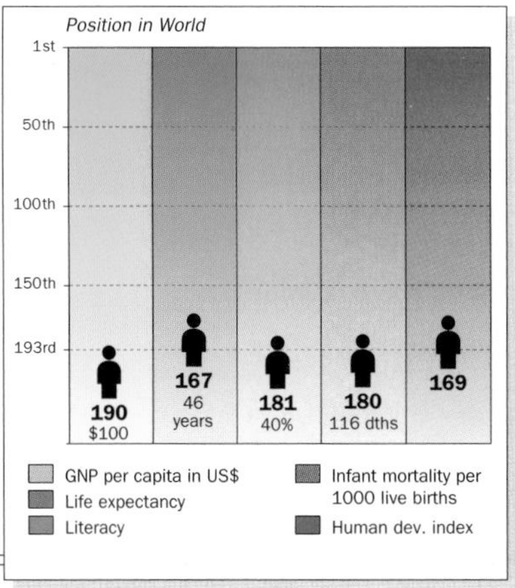

Position in World
1st
50th
100th
150th
193rd
190
$100
167
46
years
181
40%
180
116 dths
169
GNP per capita in US$
Life expectancy
Literacy
Infant mortality per 1000 live births
Human dev. index

E

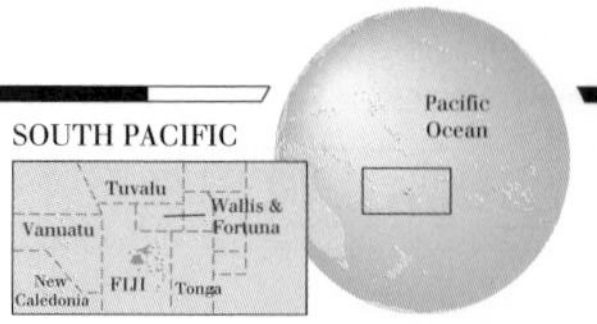
SOUTH PACIFIC
Pacific Ocean
Tuvalu
Wallis & Futuna
Vanuatu
New Caledonia
FIJI
Tonga

Fiji

OFFICIAL NAME: Republic of the Fiji Islands **CAPITAL:** Suva
POPULATION: 832,000 **CURRENCY:** Fiji dollar **OFFICIAL LANGUAGE:** English

1970 | 1970 | Oct 10 | FJI | +12 | +679 | .fj

FIJI IS A VOLCANIC archipelago in the southern Pacific Ocean, comprising two main islands and nearly 900 smaller islands and islets. The Melanesian Fijian population was outnumbered in the post-1945 period by ethnic Indians, descended from workers brought over by the British in 1879–1916. Coups led by Fijian supremacists between 1987 and 2000 led to a mass exodus of Indo-Fijians, reversing the ethnic balance and seriously damaging the economy.

F

CLIMATE

Tropical oceanic

WEATHER CHART FOR SUVA

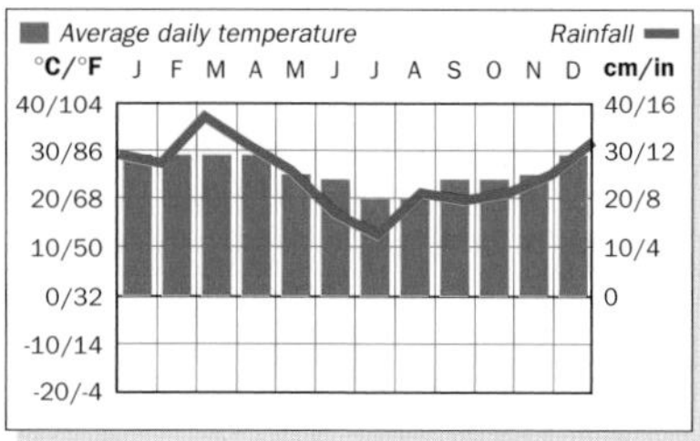
Average daily temperature
Rainfall
°C/°F J F M A M J J A S O N D cm/in
40/104
30/86
20/68
10/50
0/32
-10/14
-20/4
40/16
30/12
20/8
10/4
0

The eastern sides of the main islands are wettest, having more than twice the annual rainfall of the western flanks. Fiji lies in a cyclone path.

TRANSPORTATION

Drive on left

Nadi International 1.07m passengers

50 ships 28,700 grt

THE TRANSPORTATION NETWORK

1692 km (1051 miles)	None
597 km (371 miles)	203 km (126 miles)

On the axis of Australian–west coast US air routes, Fiji is well served by international flights. An international airport is proposed for Vanua Levu.

TOURISM

Visitors : Population 1:2.1

397,000 visitors

Up 14% in 2002

MAIN TOURIST ARRIVALS

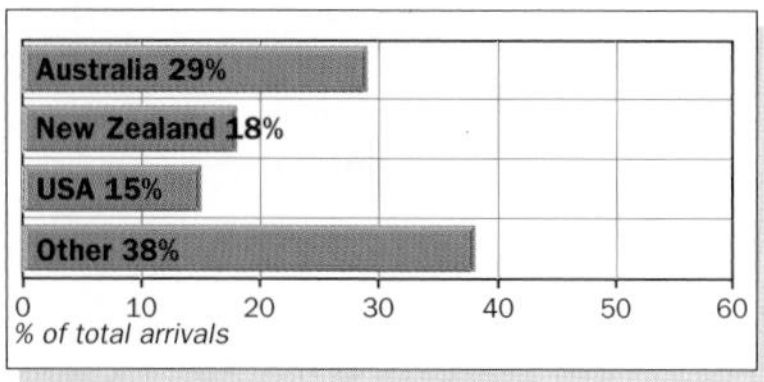
Australia 29%
New Zealand 18%
USA 15%
Other 38%
0 10 20 30 40 50 60
% of total arrivals

Tourism – Fiji's largest earner – is greatly affected by political instability: 7500 jobs were lost in 2000 alone. Recovery has been rapid.

PEOPLE

Pop. density low

Fijian, English, Hindi, Urdu, Tamil, Telugu

46/km² (118/mi²)

THE URBAN/RURAL POPULATION SPLIT

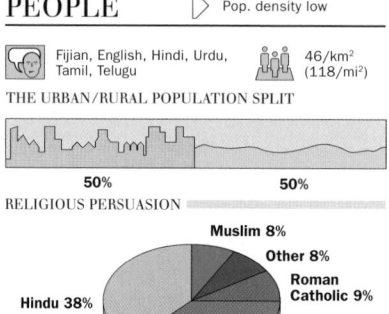

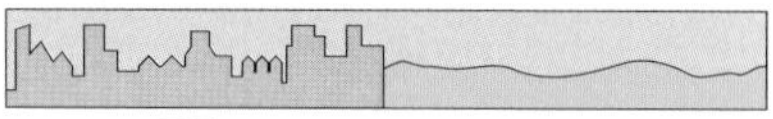
50%
50%

RELIGIOUS PERSUASION

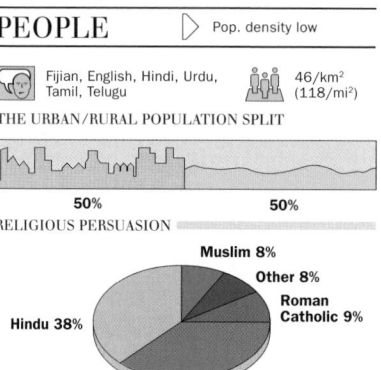

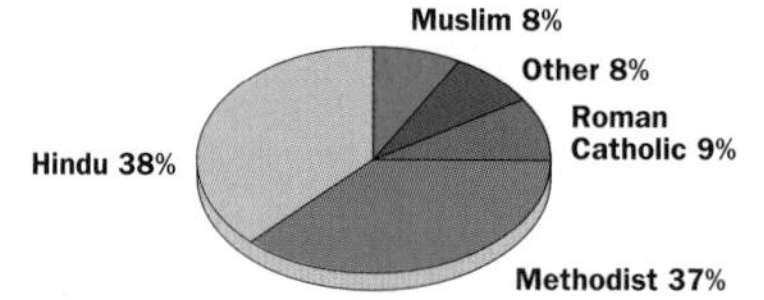
Muslim 8%
Other 8%
Roman Catholic 9%
Hindu 38%
Methodist 37%

A delicate ethnic balance was shattered by the exodus of Indo-Fijians in 1987–1989 and again in 2000–2001. The lawlessness accompanying the recent upheavals exaggerated ethnic tensions and brought racist rhetoric back to the political mainstream. A substantial population of Polynesians live on Rotuma and have a great degree of autonomy. Women are lobbying for more rights.

POLITICS

Multiparty elections

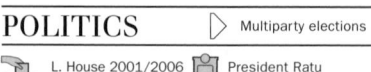

L. House 2001/2006
U. House 2001/2006

President Ratu Josefa Iloilo

AT THE LAST ELECTION

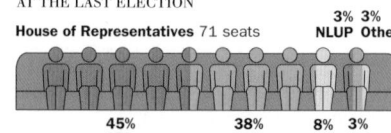

House of Representatives 71 seats

3% NLUP
3% Others
45% SDL
38% FLP
8% MV
3% Ind

SDL = Fijian People's Party **FLP** = Fiji Labor Party **MV** = Conservative Alliance (Matanitu Vanua) **NLUP** = New Labor Unity Party **Ind** = Independents

Senate 32 seats

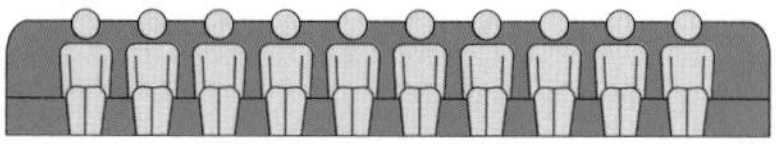

The Senate is appointed by the president

The Great Council of Chiefs emerged as the power broker after the 2000 coup, preventing the FLP from returning to power and upholding the ban on the multiethnic 1997 Constitution. The new Fijian-nationalist SDL government, led by Laisenia Qarase, refused to let the FLP join the cabinet, despite its right to do so after winning over 10% of votes in new elections in 2001. Former FLP prime minister Mahendra Chaudhry rejected the role of opposition leader. The courts have backed the FLP, ruling in 2003 that it must be given cabinet seats.

FIJI

Total Area : 18 270 sq. km (7054 sq. miles)

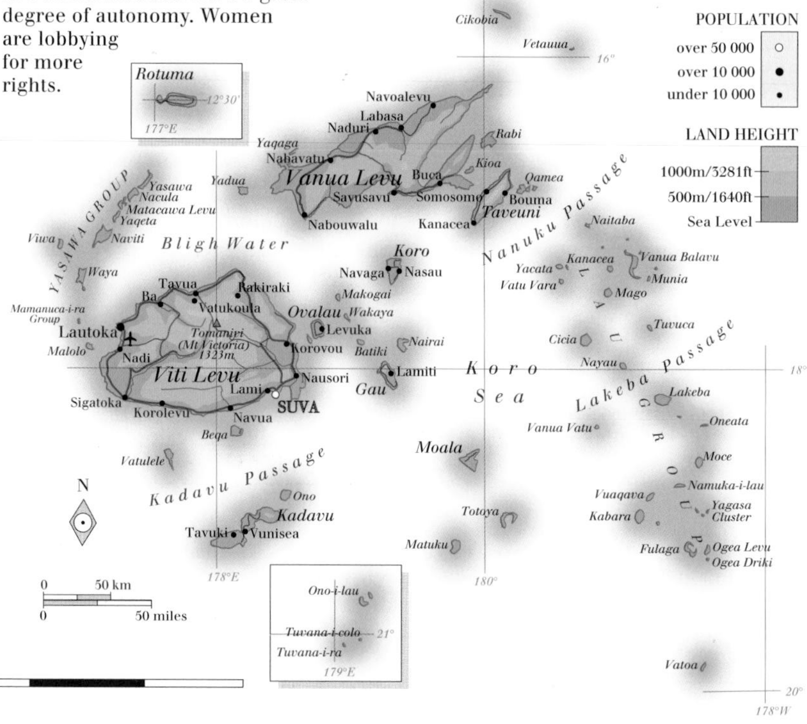
POPULATION
over 50 000
over 10 000
under 10 000
LAND HEIGHT
1000m/3281ft
500m/1640ft
Sea Level
Rotuma
177°E
Cikobia
Vetauua
Navoalevu
Labasa
Naduri
Nabavatu
Vanua Levu
Savusavu
Nabouwalu
Rabi
Kioa
Buca
Somosomo
Qamea
Bouma
Taveuni
Kanacea
Yaqaga
Yadua
Yasawa
Nacula
Matacawa Levu
Yaqeta
Naviti
Viwa
Waya
YASAWA GROUP
Bligh Water
Mamanuca-i-ra Group
Tavua
Ba
Rakiraki
Vatukoula
Lautoka
Nadi
Malolo
Tomanivi (Mt Victoria) 1323m
Viti Levu
Korovou
Nausori
Lami
SUVA
Sigatoka
Korolevu
Navua
Beqa
Vatulele
Kadavu Passage
Ono
Kadavu
Tavuki
Vunisea
Koro
Navaga
Nasau
Makogai
Ovalau
Wakaya
Levuka
Batiki
Nairai
Lamiti
Gau
Koro Sea
Moala
Totoya
Matuku
Nanuku Passage
Naitaba
Kanacea
Vanua Balavu
Munia
Yacata
Vatu Vara
Mago
Tuvuca
Cicia
Nayau
Lakeba Passage
Lakeba
Vanua Vatu
Oneata
Moce
Namuka-i-lau
Yagasa Cluster
Vuaqava
Kabara
Fulaga
Ogea Levu
Ogea Driki
Vatoa
Ono-i-lau
Tuvana-i-colo
Tuvana-i-ra
179°E
21°
16°
18°
20°
178°E
180°
178°W
N
0 50 km
0 50 miles

WORLD AFFAIRS

Joined UN in 1970

ACP | CP | Comm | PC | PIF

Fiji's international reputation has been severely damaged by its discrimination against Indo-Fijians and the recent coups. Fiji has been intermittently suspended from the Commonwealth.

AID

Recipient

US$26m (receipts) — Down 10% in 2001

Fiji traditionally received a lot of overseas aid, but international reaction to the 2000 coup prompted drastic cuts.

DEFENSE

No compulsory military service

US$26m — Down 21% in 2001

Of the almost entirely ethnic Fijian military, significant numbers – around 20% – are assigned to UN duties and have served in Lebanon and Egypt.

ECONOMICS

Inflation 3.1% p.a. (1990–2001)

US$1.76bn — 1.873 Fiji dollars (2.106)

SCORE CARD

❑ World GNP Ranking	141st
❑ GNP per Capita	US$2150
❑ Balance of Payments	US$13m
❑ Inflation	4.3%
❑ Unemployment	5%

Strengths

Diversification. Strong and resilient tourist infrastructure. Location on Pacific air routes. Many regional and international organizations located in Suva.

Weaknesses

2000 coup caused dramatic contraction in economy – 12.5%. Migration of many Indo-Fijian professionals. Sugar crops vulnerable to drought. Major exports – sugar, copra, and gold – subject to large fluctuations in world prices.

EXPORTS

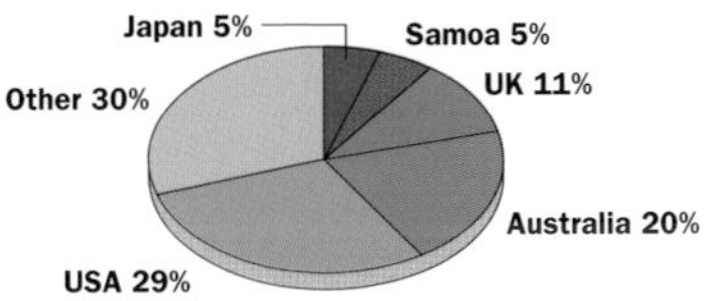
Japan 5%
Samoa 5%
UK 11%
Other 30%
Australia 20%
USA 29%

IMPORTS

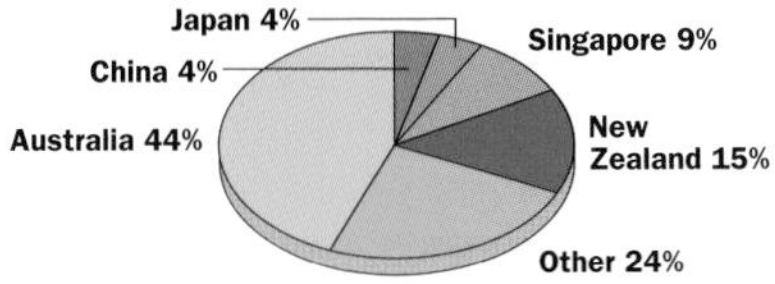
Japan 4%
Singapore 9%
China 4%
Australia 44%
New Zealand 15%
Other 24%

Cane field *on the west side of Viti Levu, between Nadi and Lautoka. Sugar accounts for just over a fifth of Fiji's exports.*

RESOURCES

Electric power 200,000 kW

39,379 tonnes — Not an oil producer

340,000 cattle, 247,000 goats, 3.7m chickens — Gold, silver

The varied terrain allows diversified agriculture. Gold and minerals are mined. A hydroelectric plant at Monasavu provides 79% of electricity.

ENVIRONMENT

Not available

1.1% — 0.9 tonnes per capita

Fiji's governments are environmentally aware. Tourism is damaging coral reefs. Fiji was downwind of French Pacific nuclear tests. Fertilizers are overused.

MEDIA

TV ownership low

Daily newspaper circulation 51 per 1000 people

PUBLISHING AND BROADCAST MEDIA

There are 2 English-language dailies, *Fiji Times* and *Fiji Daily Post*. *Nai Lalakai* and *Shanti Dut* are Fijian and Indian weeklies

2 services: 1 state-owned, 1 independent — 4 services: 1 state-controlled, 3 independent

Freedom of the press is championed by the government, and cases of corruption are often reported in the media. However, the police have blocked politically sensitive broadcasts.

CRIME

Death penalty not used in practice

1102 prisoners — Up in 2000

Usually theft and drink-related violence top the crime list. The 2000 coup spurred Fijians to settle old scores by force.

EDUCATION

School leaving age: 15

93% — 9208 students

Education, originally modeled on the British system, is now mostly run by local committees and is increasingly racially segregated. The use of the birch in schools was banned in 2002.

CHRONOLOGY

The British decision to import Indian sugar workers in 1879–1916 dramatically changed Fijian society.

- ❑ **1970** Independence from Britain.
- ❑ **1987** Election win for Indo-Fijian coalition. Sitiveni Rabuka's coups secure minority ethnic Fijian rule. Ejected from Commonwealth.
- ❑ **1989** Mass Indo-Fijian emigration.
- ❑ **1990** Constitution discriminating against Indo-Fijians introduced.
- ❑ **1992** Rabuka wins legislative polls.
- ❑ **1997** Census shows ethnic Fijians outnumber Indo-Fijians. Fiji rejoins Commonwealth. New constitution.
- ❑ **1999** General election won by FLP. First Indo-Fijian prime minister.
- ❑ **2000** Civilian-led coup; new ethnic Fijian government.
- ❑ **2001** Nationalists win elections.

F

HEALTH

Welfare state health benefits

1 per 2778 people — Cerebrovascular and heart diseases, cancers, accidents

Medical treatment is provided for all at a nominal charge. There is a shortfall of native health workers. Suicide is rising, particularly among ethnic Indians.

SPENDING

GDP/cap. increase

CONSUMPTION AND SPENDING

59 per 1000 population — *112 per 1000 population*

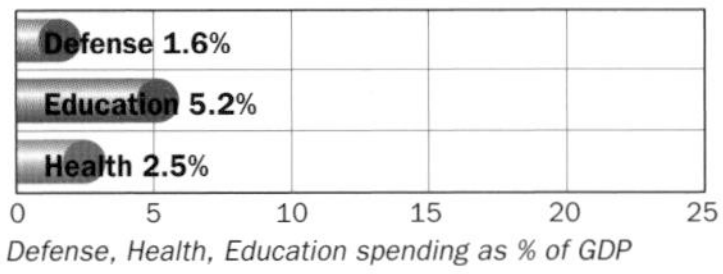
Defense 1.6%
Education 5.2%
Health 2.5%
0
5
10
15
20
25
Defense, Health, Education spending as % of GDP

Ostentatious displays of wealth are rare in Fiji; prestige derives from family and landholdings. The professional middle class, traditionally dominated by Indo-Fijians, is becoming more mixed.

WORLD RANKING

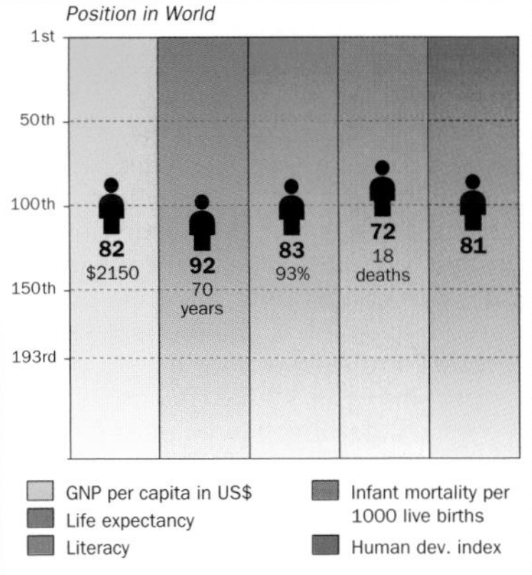
Position in World
1st
50th
100th
150th
193rd
82
$2150
92
70
years
83
93%
72
18
deaths
81
GNP per capita in US$
Life expectancy
Literacy
Infant mortality per 1000 live births
Human dev. index

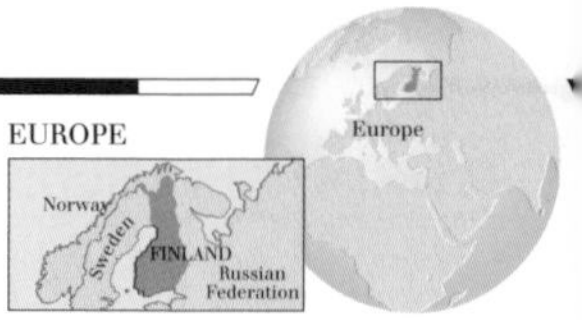
EUROPE
Europe
Norway
Sweden
FINLAND
Russian Federation

FINLAND

OFFICIAL NAME: Republic of Finland **CAPITAL:** Helsinki
POPULATION: 5.2 million **CURRENCY:** Euro **OFFICIAL LANGUAGES:** Finnish and Swedish

1917 | 1947 | Dec 6 | FIN | +2 | +358 | .fi

BORDERED TO THE north and west by Norway and Sweden, and to the east by Russia, Finland is a low-lying country of forests and 187,888 lakes. Politics is based on consensus, and the country has been stable despite successive short-lived coalitions. Russia annexed Finland in 1809, ruling it until 1917, and subsequently Finland accepted a close relationship with the USSR as the price of maintaining its independence. It joined the EU in 1995 and, despite popular suspicion of Brussels bureaucracy, Finland was among the 12 EU states to adopt the euro from 2002.

CLIMATE

Subarctic/continental

WEATHER CHART FOR HELSINKI

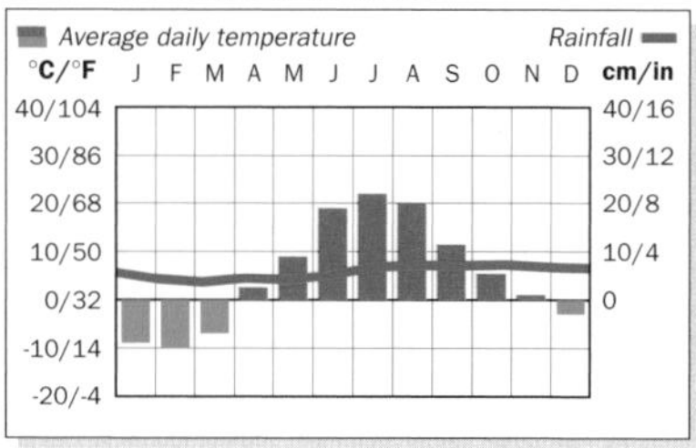
Average daily temperature
Rainfall
°C/°F
J F M A M J J A S O N D
cm/in
40/104
30/86
20/68
10/50
0/32
-10/14
-20/-4
40/16
30/12
20/8
10/4
0

North of the Arctic Circle the climate is extreme. Temperatures fall to –30°C (–22°F) in the six-month winter and rise to 27°C (81°F) during the 73 days of summer midnight sun. In the south, summers are mild and short, winters are cold.

TRANSPORTATION

Drive on right

Helsinki–Vantaa, 9.6m passengers

284 ships 1.6m grt

THE TRANSPORTATION NETWORK

49,789 km (30,937 miles)

549 km (341 miles)

5854 km (3637 miles)

6675 km (4148 miles)

The transportation system is well integrated. The railroad connects with the Swedish and Russian networks. There are frequent air services to most neighboring states, and links with Baltic states are being expanded. With one of the densest domestic networks in Europe, internal air travel is important, particularly north of the Arctic Circle. Finland has Europe's largest inland waterway system, now used mainly for recreation. Its international ports handle around 70 million tonnes a year. Kotka is the chief export port. Helsinki's specialized harbors handle most imports, but construction of a new harbor at Vuosaari is under way, and cargo traffic is due to move there in 2008.

TOURISM

Visitors : Population 1:1.8

2.88m visitors

Up 2% in 2002

MAIN TOURIST ARRIVALS

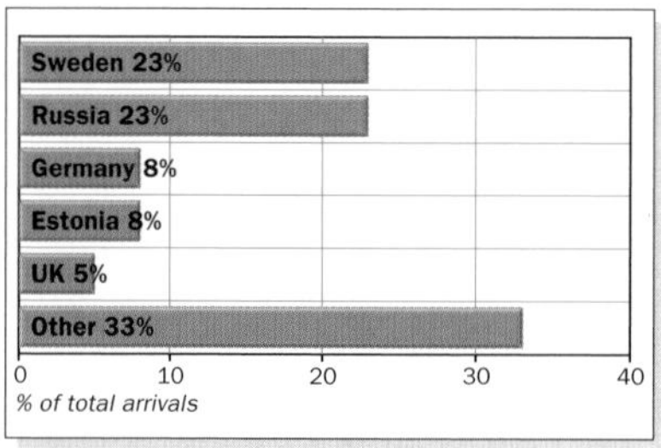
Sweden 23%
Russia 23%
Germany 8%
Estonia 8%
UK 5%
Other 33%
0
10
20
30
40
% of total arrivals

The scenery of the southern lakes and the vast forests of its Arctic north are Finland's main attractions. Helsinki is an important cultural center and hosts an annual arts festival. There are many first-class restaurants and its opera house has an international reputation. Most tourists try a sauna, a Finnish invention, and the local vodka, which is reputedly among the world's finest.

Visitors come largely from Sweden, Russia, the Baltic states, and Germany. In 2001 Finland was ranked the seventh most popular European destination for employers offering vacations as an incentive to their workforce.

A summer's night at Kilpisjärvi, "The Way of the Four Winds," which lies at the point where Finland, Sweden, and Norway meet.

PEOPLE

Pop. density low

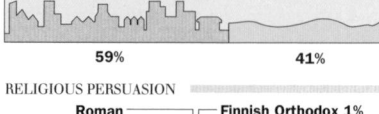

Finnish, Swedish, Sami

17/km² (44/mi²)

THE URBAN/RURAL POPULATION SPLIT

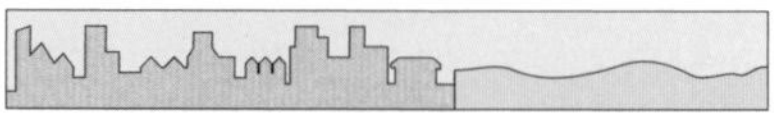
59%
41%

RELIGIOUS PERSUASION

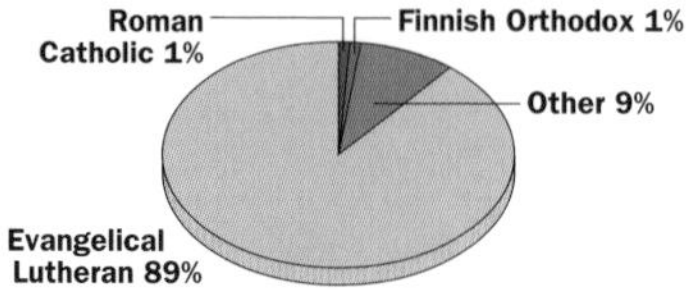
Roman Catholic 1%
Finnish Orthodox 1%
Other 9%
Evangelical Lutheran 89%

ETHNIC MAKEUP

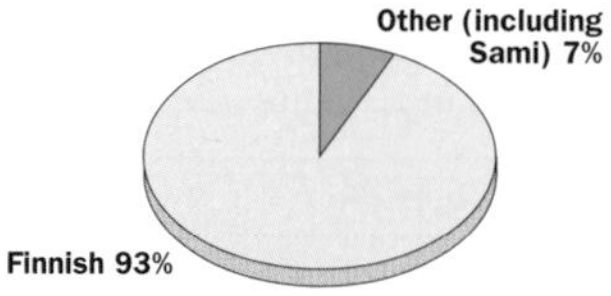
Other (including Sami) 7%
Finnish 93%

Most Finns are of Scandinavian–Baltic extraction. Finnish, part of the small Finno-Ugric linguistic group, is a legacy of the country's early Asian invaders. These tribes integrated with local and surrounding European peoples, but preserved their distinct language. Sami, also a Finno-Ugric language, is spoken by the small Sami population which lives within the Arctic Circle. Swedish speakers make up around 6% of the population and mostly live in the southwest coastal regions and on the Åland Islands.

More than half of Finns live in the five southernmost districts around Helsinki. Families tend to be close-knit, though divorce rates are high. The sauna is an integral part of everyday life; there are 1.5 million saunas among 5.2 million Finns.

Finnish women have a long tradition of political and economic participation. They were the first in Europe to get the vote, in 1906, and the first in the world able to stand for parliament. In 2003 Finland became for a short time the only European country to have both a female president and prime minister.

POPULATION AGE BREAKDOWN

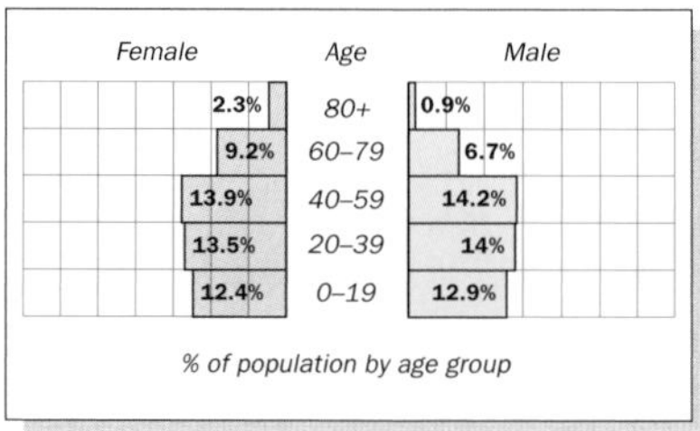
Female
Age
Male
2.3%
80+
0.9%
9.2%
60–79
6.7%
13.9%
40–59
14.2%
13.5%
20–39
14%
12.4%
0–19
12.9%
% of population by age group

POLITICS

Multiparty elections

2003/2007

President Tarja Halonen

Finland's constitution combines parliamentary government with a strong presidency. The Swedish-speaking Åland Islands external territory has internal self-government.

PROFILE

Proportional representation has led to government by coalition, usually dominated by the SDP or KESK. The emphasis on consensus favors stability but slows decision-making. The KESK led a new coalition from 2003. KESK leader Anneli Jäätteenmäki became the country's first female premier, but resigned after only two months in office, and was replaced by Matti Vanhanen.

AT THE LAST ELECTION

Parliament 200 seats
7% G
5% Others
28% KESK
27% SDP
20% KOK
9% VL
4% SFP

KESK = Center Party **SDP** = Social Democratic Party **KOK** = National Coalition Party **VL** = Left-wing Alliance **G** = Greens **SFP** = Swedish People's Party

MAIN POLITICAL ISSUES

EU membership

Finland joined the EU in 1995. The small but influential farming community was hostile to membership, while others feared that welfare cuts would be more far-reaching if the economy was liberalized in line with EU expectations. In the event, after a dose of austerity, EU membership became associated with greater prosperity from the late 1990s. However, public opinion regarding the EU remains evenly divided between its supporters and detractors. Finland's decision to join the eurozone was in contrast to the nonmembership of its closest EU neighbor, Sweden.

Nuclear power

In 2002 parliament narrowly approved the construction of a fifth nuclear reactor. It will be the first to be built in western Europe since 1991 and the first in Finland for 30 years. The vote was divisive, and the Green Party, a junior coalition partner, pulled out of the SDP-led government in protest. KESK Prime Minister Vanhanen had previously expressed his opposition to the plan.

FINLAND
Total Area :
337 030 sq. km
(130 127 sq. miles)
POPULATION
over 100 000
over 50 000
over 10 000
LAND HEIGHT
500m/1640ft
200m/656ft
Sea Level
NORWAY
SWEDEN
RUSSIAN FEDERATION
LAPLAND
BARENTS SEA
Gulf of Bothnia
Gulf of Finland
BALTIC SEA
Lake Ladoga
Haltiatunturi 1328m
Kilpisjärvi
Inarijärvi
Sodankylä
Salla
Kemijärvi
Rovaniemi
Arctic Circle
Kuusamo
Tornio
Kemi
Pudasjärvi
Hailuoto
Oulu
Raahe
Kajaani
Kuhmo
Kokkola
Jakobstad
Vallgrund
Vaasa
Iisalmi
Nurmes
Lieksa
Kuopio
Seinäjoki
Joensuu
Närpes
Varkaus
Jyväskylä
Savonlinna
Jämsä
Mikkeli
Tampere
Pori
Nokia
Valkeakoski
Rauma
Hämeenlinna
Lahti
Kuusankoski
Imatra
Lappeenranta
Forssa
Riihimäki
Hyvinkää
Kouvola
Åland
Turku
Vantaa
Järvenpää
Kerava
Kotka
Mariehamn
Espoo
HELSINKI
Hanko
0 100 km
0 100 miles

President Tarja Halonen (left) and former prime minister Anneli Jäätteenmäki. Briefly in 2003 Finland was the only country in Europe with a female head of state and government.

WORLD AFFAIRS

Joined UN in 1955

CE | EU | OECD | OSCE | PfP

After carefully balancing its relations with the USSR and the West during the Cold War, Finland has now decided that its national interest lies with western Europe. In addition to joining the EU, it has observer status at the WEU. However, acknowledging historical and geographic realities, the government is also keen to maintain a special relationship with Russia.

AID

Donor

$389m (donations)

Up 5% in 2001

Finland's aid budget is still well below the UN target of 0.7% of GNP, despite vigorous campaigning. The recipients, spread across the globe, include the Balkans and southern Africa.

CHRONOLOGY

Finland's history has been closely linked with the competing interests of Sweden and Russia.

- **1323** Treaty of Pähkinäsaari. Finland part of Swedish Kingdom.
- **1809** Ceded to Russia; Finland becomes a Grand Duchy enjoying considerable autonomy.
- **1812** Helsinki becomes capital.
- **1863** Finnish becomes an official language alongside Swedish.
- **1865** Grand Duchy acquires its own monetary system.
- **1879** Conscription law lays the foundation for a Finnish army.
- **1899** Russification begins. Labor Party founded.
- **1900** Gradual imposition of Russian as the official language begins.
- **1901** Finnish army disbanded, Finns ordered into Russian units. Disobedience campaign prevents men being drafted into the army.
- **1903** Labor Party becomes SDP.
- **1905** National strike forces

CHRONOLOGY *continued*

restoration of 1899 status quo.

- **1906** Parliamentary reform. Universal suffrage introduced.
- **1910** Responsibility for important legislation passed to Russian parliament.
- **1917** Russian revolution allows Finland to declare independence.
- **1918** Civil war between Bolsheviks and right-wing government. Gen. Gustav Mannerheim leads government to victory at Battle of Tampere.
- **1919** Finland becomes republic. Kaarlo Ståhlberg elected president with wide political powers.
- **1920** Treaty of Tartu: USSR recognizes Finland's borders.
- **1921** London Convention. Åland Islands become part of Finland.
- **1939** August, Hitler–Stalin nonaggression pact gives USSR a free hand in Finland. November, Soviet invasion; strong Finnish resistance in ensuing Winter War.
- **1940** Treaty of Moscow. Finland cedes a tenth of national territory.
- **1941** Finnish troops join Germany in its invasion of USSR.
- **1944** June, Red Army invades. August, President Risto Ryti resigns. September, Finland, led by Marshal Mannerheim, signs armistice.
- **1946** President Mannerheim resigns, Juho Paasikivi president.
- **1948** Signs friendship treaty with USSR. Agrees to resist any attack on USSR made through Finland by Germany or its allies.
- **1952** Payment of $570 million in war reparations completed.
- **1956** Uhro Kekkonen, leader of the Agrarian Party, becomes president.
- **1956–1991** A series of coalition governments involving SDP and Agrarians (renamed KESK in 1965).
- **1981** President Kekkonen resigns.
- **1982** Mauno Koivisto president.
- **1989** USSR recognizes Finnish neutrality for first time.
- **1991** Non-SDP government elected. Austerity measures.
- **1992** Signs ten-year agreement with Russia which, for first time since World War II, involves no military agreement.
- **1994** SDP candidate Martti Ahtisaari elected president.
- **1995** Finland joins EU. General election returns SDP-led coalition under Paavo Lipponen (reelected in 1999).
- **2000** Tarja Halonen elected as first woman president.
- **2002** Euro fully adopted. Fifth nuclear power plant approved.
- **2003** KESK wins elections. Anneli Jäätteenmäki, first female prime minister, resigns after two months.

F

DEFENSE

Compulsory military service

$1.43bn

Down 8% in 2001

Finland is a neutral country. Its armed forces, the majority of whom are conscripts, are backed up by over 400,000 reservists and 3100 border guards. Russia's relative instability in the 1990s reinforced concern about border security, the main defense issue. Finland participates in NATO's Partnership for Peace program and has WEU observer status. Military service lasts for up to 12 months.

FINNISH ARMED FORCES

268 main battle tanks (33 T-54, 74 T-55, 161 T-72)	24,550 personnel
9 patrol boats	4600 personnel
63 combat aircraft (F/A-18C/D)	2700 personnel
None	

ECONOMICS

Inflation 1.9% p.a. (1990–2001)

$123bn

0.871 euros (1.013)

SCORE CARD

World GNP Ranking	29th
GNP per Capita	$23,780
Balance of Payments	$8.36bn
Inflation	2.6%
Unemployment	9%

EXPORTS

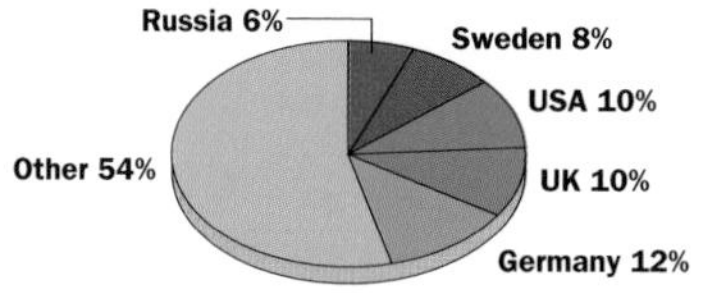
Russia 6%
Sweden 8%
USA 10%
UK 10%
Germany 12%
Other 54%

IMPORTS

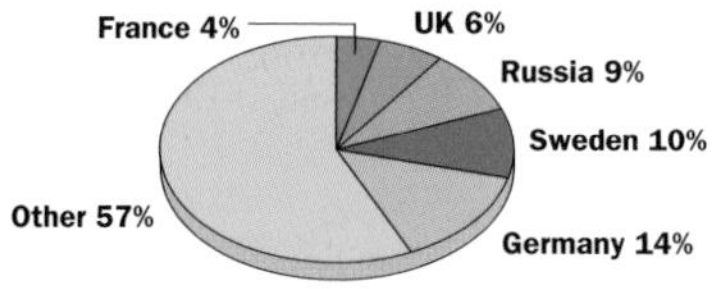
France 4%
UK 6%
Russia 9%
Sweden 10%
Germany 14%
Other 57%

Strengths

Industry export- and quality-oriented. Large high-tech sector, especially Nokia mobile phones and Internet services. World leader in pulp and paper. Exports quick to recover from recession. Relatively low inflation. Improved foreign investment incentives. Gateway to Russian and Baltic economies. Membership of eurozone. Competitive economy.

Weaknesses

Slowdown in economy from 2001; telecommunications industry hit particularly badly by global slump. Rapidly aging population and low retirement age. High level of public and foreign debt. High unemployment. Small domestic market. Peripheral position in Europe.

Profile

Finland is a wealthy market economy. In the early 1990s it experienced the worst recession in 60 years, chiefly as a result of the collapse of the former Soviet Union. Russia took only 4% of Finland's exports in 1999, compared with over 25% to the Soviet Union before 1990.

A rapid rise in unemployment and business failures after 1990 pushed up government spending. The floating of the markka in 1992 and austerity measures improved competitiveness, overturned substantial fiscal deficits, and allowed tax cuts in 2002. Though it has fallen, unemployment is still around 9%. Rapid growth in 2000 was followed by a slowdown in 2001. Finland fully adopted the euro in 2002, and in 2003 was named as the world's most competitive small country.

ECONOMIC PERFORMANCE INDICATOR

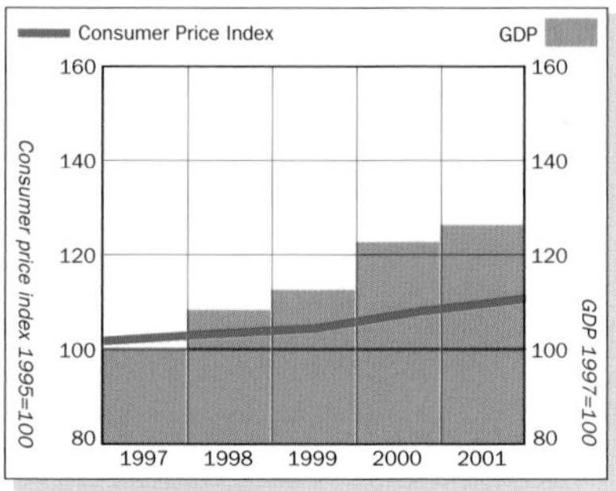
Consumer Price Index
GDP
160
140
120
100
80
1997
1998
1999
2000
2001
Consumer price index 1995=100
GDP 1997=100

FINLAND : MAJOR BUSINESSES

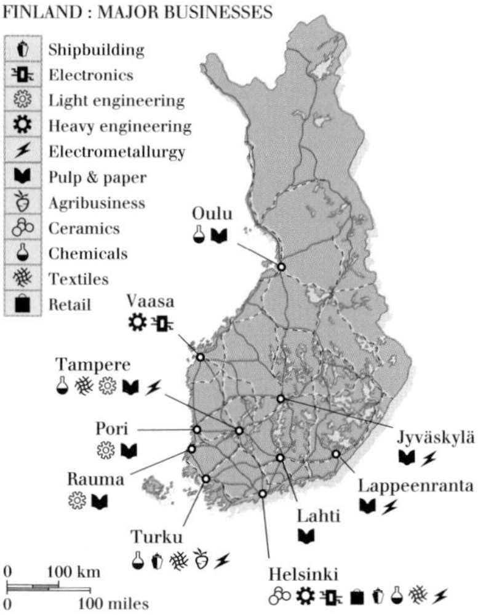
Shipbuilding
Electronics
Light engineering
Heavy engineering
Electrometallurgy
Pulp & paper
Agribusiness
Ceramics
Chemicals
Textiles
Retail
Oulu
Vaasa
Tampere
Pori
Rauma
Turku
Helsinki
Lahti
Lappeenranta
Jyväskylä
0 100 km
0 100 miles

RESOURCES

Electric power 16.2m kW

178,306 tonnes

Not an oil producer; refines 259,000 b/d

1.32m pigs, 95,884 sheep, 1.03m cattle, 5.77m chickens

Gold, copper, zinc, iron, lead, silver

ELECTRICITY GENERATION

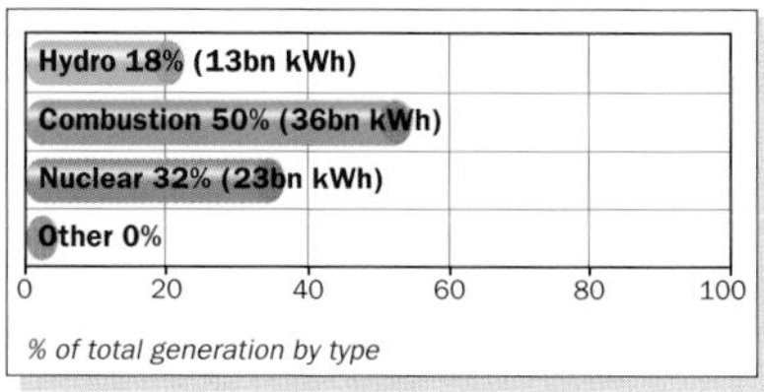
Hydro 18% (13bn kWh)
Combustion 50% (36bn kWh)
Nuclear 32% (23bn kWh)
Other 0%
0
20
40
60
80
100
% of total generation by type

Finland's trees are its prime natural resource. Commercial forests cover 65% of the land, and wood products account for over 20% of exports. Finland has no oil, but has significant hydroelectric resources. The high energy demands of industry are met chiefly by combustion and nuclear power. A fifth nuclear power plant was approved in 2002. Oil import costs have risen since 1990, when the collapse of the USSR ended a 42-year agreement on the exchange of Finnish manufactures for Soviet oil.

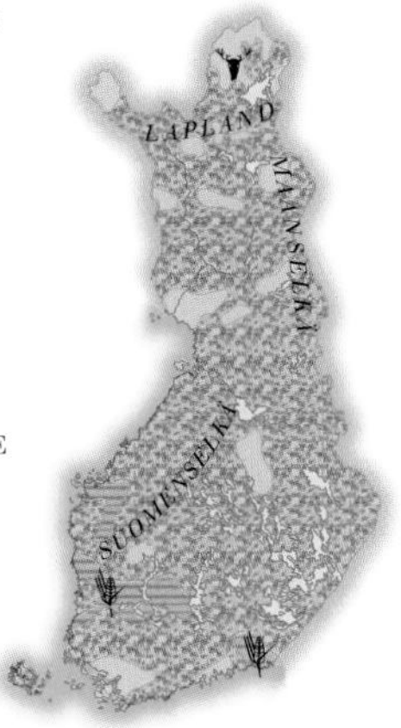
LAPLAND
MAANSELKÄ
SUOMENSELKÄ

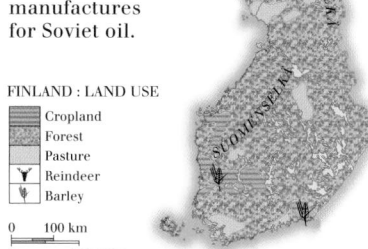

FINLAND : LAND USE

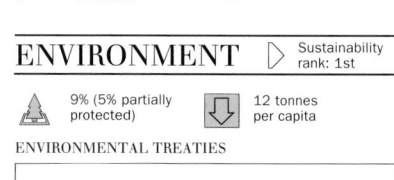

- Cropland
- Forest
- Pasture
- Reindeer
- Barley

0 100 km
0 100 miles

ENVIRONMENT

Sustainability rank: 1st

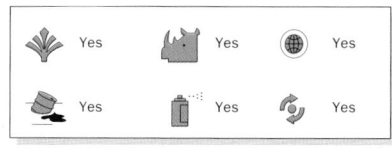

9% (5% partially protected)

12 tonnes per capita

ENVIRONMENTAL TREATIES

Yes	Yes	Yes
Yes	Yes	Yes

Finland has strict laws on industrial emissions. Energy efficiency is a priority; nearly half of all homes are connected to district heating systems. Though there is opposition to the fifth nuclear plant, proponents argue that it will help the country meet its target emissions for greenhouse gases. The government is funding nuclear safety programs in Russia. Rising levels of pollution in the Baltic have given rise to concern.

MEDIA

TV ownership high

Daily newspaper circulation 445 per 1000 people

PUBLISHING AND BROADCAST MEDIA

There are 200 daily newspapers. The most important are *Helsingin Sanomat, Aamulehti, Ilta-Sanomat, Turun Sanomat,* and *Kaleva*

3 services: 1 state-owned, 2 independent

5 services: 1 state-owned, 4 independent

Nine out of ten adult Finns read a daily paper, the world's fourth-highest per capita ratio. Regional papers dominate; the only national is the independent *Helsingin Sanomat*. There is no censorship, but the press shows restraint in criticizing the government.

CRIME

No death penalty

3040 prisoners

Up 73% in 2000–2001

CRIME RATES

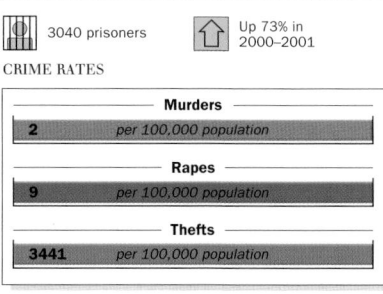

Murders
2 per 100,000 population

Rapes
9 per 100,000 population

Thefts
3441 per 100,000 population

The jump in unemployment in the early 1990s was seen as one of the causes of rising crime. There is concern about links with organized crime in Russia.

EDUCATION

School leaving age: 16

99%

279,628 students

THE EDUCATION SYSTEM

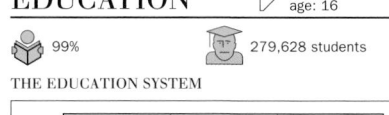

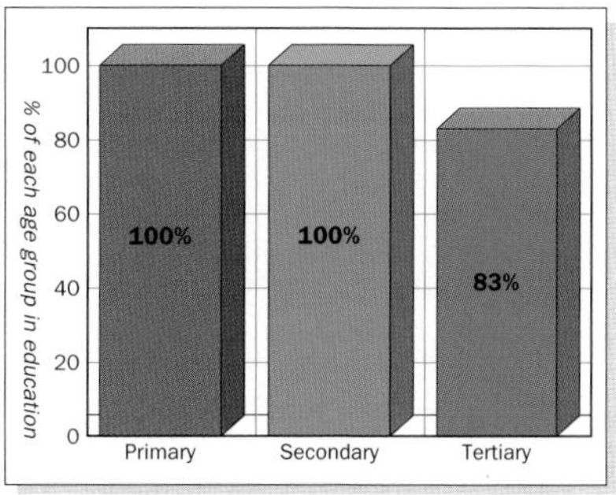
100
80
60
40
20
0
% of each age group in education
100%
100%
83%
Primary
Secondary
Tertiary

Compulsory education, introduced in 1921, lasts from seven to 16 years of age. The comprehensive system dates from the 1970s. Almost all children receive preschool education and also go on to three years of upper secondary education. Tough examinations mean that only around 40% of entrants qualify to attend one of the 20 universities. There are also 29 polytechnics.

HEALTH

Welfare state health benefits

1 per 327 people

Heart diseases, cancers, cerebro-vascular diseases

Of total government expenditure, almost 20% is spent on Finland's well-developed health system. Every Finn is legally guaranteed access to a local health center which is staffed by up to four doctors, as well as nurses and a midwife. Most nonhospital medical costs are covered by national health insurance; hospital fees are moderate. Diabetes and osteoporosis are increasing, and obesity is a growing health problem.

SPENDING

GDP/cap. increase

CONSUMPTION AND SPENDING

403 per 1000 population

548 per 1000 population

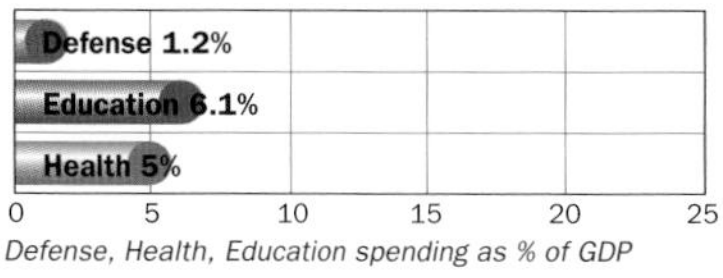
Defense 1.2%
Education 6.1%
Health 5%
0
5
10
15
20
25
Defense, Health, Education spending as % of GDP

The economic boom and labor shortages of the 1980s helped living standards to soar. Personal consumption reached Swedish levels, and many families were able to take two vacations a year. Social security benefits were extended.

During the deep recession which began in 1990, this improvement was reversed. Wealth disparities widened and expenditure cuts led to lower social security benefits for the jobless. Those in work had to accept lower pay rises and higher taxes. Average real disposable incomes dropped sharply. The situation started to improve in 2000, with a temporary downturn in 2001. Income disparities fell again and are now as low as in other Scandinavian countries.

Ethnic Ingrian immigrants from the former USSR were the poorest group in Finnish society in the 1990s.

WORLD RANKING

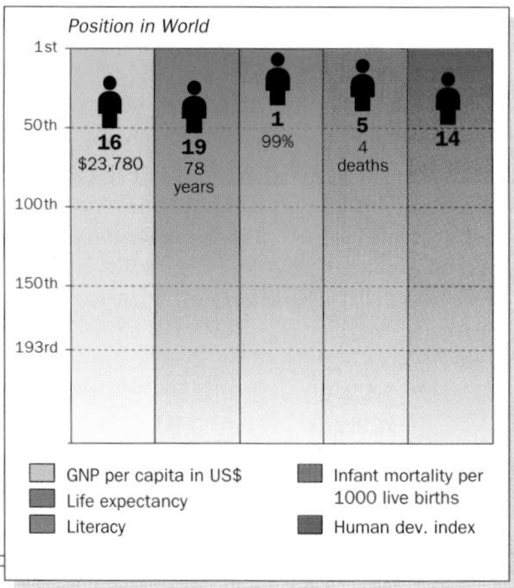
Position in World
1st
50th
100th
150th
193rd
16
$23,780
19
78 years
1
99%
5
4 deaths
14
GNP per capita in US$
Life expectancy
Literacy
Infant mortality per 1000 live births
Human dev. index

F

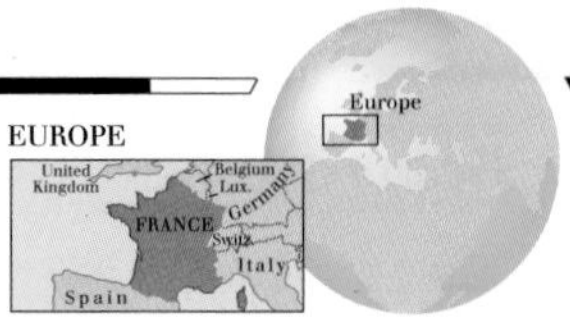
EUROPE
Europe
United Kingdom
Belgium
Lux.
Germany
FRANCE
Switz.
Italy
Spain

FRANCE

OFFICIAL NAME: French Republic **CAPITAL:** Paris
POPULATION: 59.7 million **CURRENCY:** Euro **OFFICIAL LANGUAGE:** French

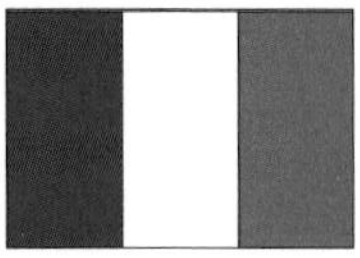

987 | 1919 | July 14 | F | +1 | +33 | .fr

STRADDLING WESTERN EUROPE from the English Channel (La Manche) to the Mediterranean, France was Europe's first modern republic, and possessed a colonial empire second only to that of the UK. Today, it is one of the world's major industrial powers and its fourth-largest exporter. Industry is the leading economic sector, but the agricultural lobby remains powerful – French farmers will mount the barricades in defense of their interests. France's focus is very much on Europe. Together with Germany it was a founder member of the European Economic Community (EEC), and has supported successive steps to build a more closely integrated European Union. Paris, the French capital, is generally considered to be one of the world's most beautiful cities. Some of the most influential artists, writers, and filmmakers of the modern era have lived there.

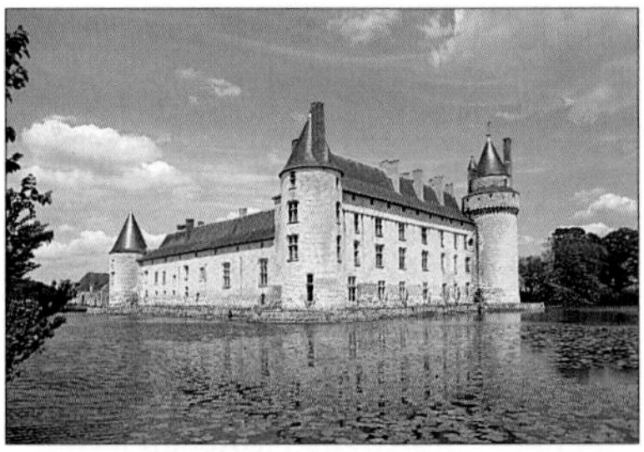

Le Plessis-Bourré, Loire Valley. *The region is famous for its many chateaux, which attract thousands of visitors every year.*

CLIMATE

Maritime/Mediterranean/mountain/continental

WEATHER CHART FOR PARIS

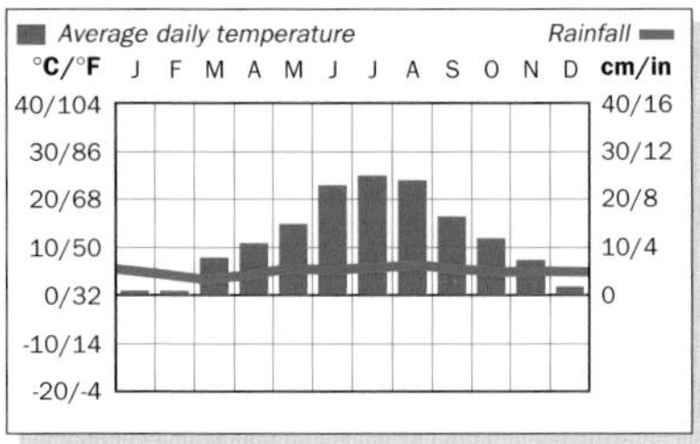
Average daily temperature
Rainfall
°C/°F J F M A M J J A S O N D cm/in
40/104
30/86
20/68
10/50
0/32
-10/14
-20/-4
40/16
30/12
20/8
10/4
0

France's climate differs significantly from region to region. The northwest, in particular Brittany, is mild but damp. The east has hot summers and stormy winters, while in the south summers are dry and hot, and forest fires are a frequent occurrence.

TRANSPORTATION

Drive on right

Charles de Gaulle, Paris 48.3m passengers

699 ships 1.41m grt

THE TRANSPORTATION NETWORK

892,900 km (554,821 miles)

9632 km (5985 miles)

29,343 km (18,233 miles)

14,932 km (9278 miles)

France led the world in high-speed train technology in 1983 with the TGV (*train à grande vitesse*) from Paris to Lyon. TGV lines have since been extended, and also link up with Belgium, Italy, Spain, the Channel Tunnel, and the Mediterranean; a Paris–Strasbourg line is planned for 2005. Traffic through Paris's two airports is set to leap to 140 million by 2020, but plans for a third airport at Chaulnes, 130 km (80 miles) to the north, have become a political football.

TOURISM

Visitors : Population 1.3:1

76.7m visitors

Up 2% in 2002

MAIN TOURIST ARRIVALS

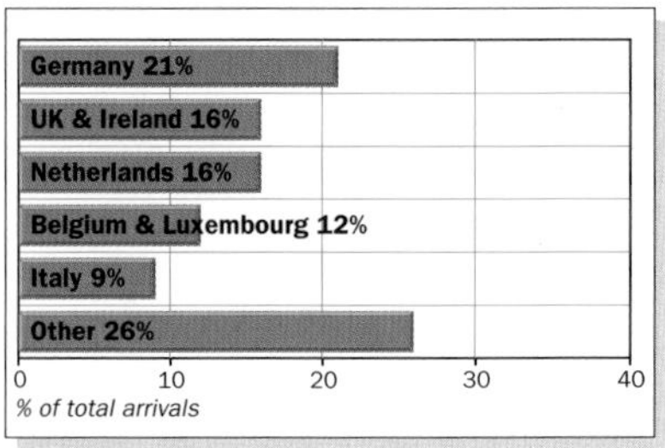
Germany 21%
UK & Ireland 16%
Netherlands 16%
Belgium & Luxembourg 12%
Italy 9%
Other 26%
0
10
20
30
40
% of total arrivals

France is the world's leading tourist destination, with over 76 million visitors a year. It ranks high as a destination for visitors from neighboring countries, particularly Germany and the UK. Most French people also prefer to take vacations in their own country, though many do visit Spain and Italy.

Paris is the most visited city in Europe. Its attractions include the Eiffel Tower, Nôtre Dame cathedral, Eurodisney, the Pompidou Center, and the Louvre, the world's most popular art museum.

The Côte d'Azur in the southeast became a byword for fashionable tourism when royalty and other notables flocked to resorts such as Nice at the end of the 19th century. Today Cannes hosts the world's leading film festival, and has a growing business convention trade. Other destinations throughout the country attract tourists for a variety of reasons such as wine production, historic and archaeological sites, and good beaches. There are resorts for skiing and hiking in the Alps and Pyrenees, and sailing off the varied coastline is also popular.

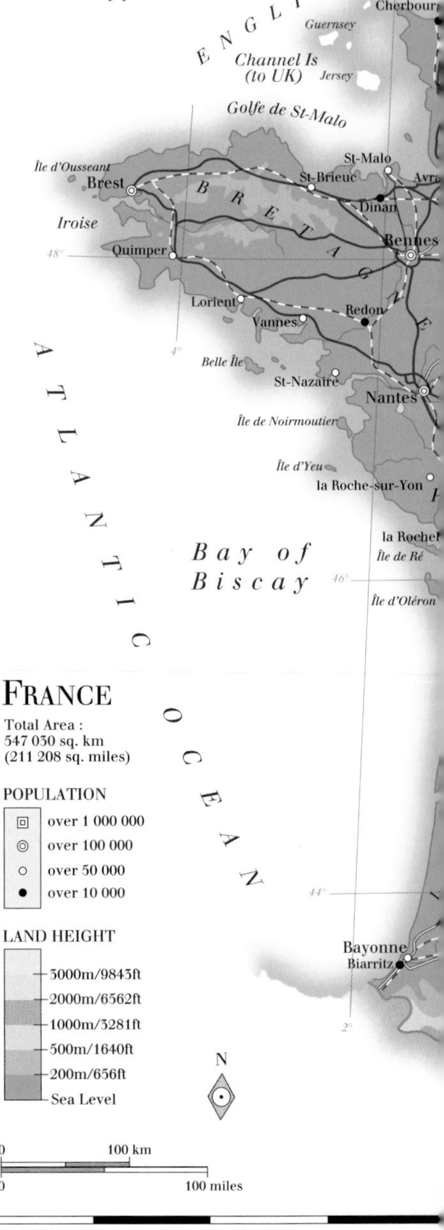
ENGLISH
Cherbourg
Guernsey
Channel Is (to UK)
Jersey
Golfe de St-Malo
Île d'Ousseant
Brest
St-Malo
St-Brieuc
Dinan
Iroise
BRETAGNE
Rennes
Quimper
Lorient
Vannes
Redon
Belle Île
St-Nazaire
Nantes
Île de Noirmoutier
Île d'Yeu
la Roche-sur-Yon
la Rochelle
Île de Ré
Île d'Oléron
Bay of Biscay
ATLANTIC OCEAN
Bayonne
Biarritz
FRANCE
Total Area : 547 030 sq. km (211 208 sq. miles)
POPULATION
over 1 000 000
over 100 000
over 50 000
over 10 000
LAND HEIGHT
3000m/9843ft
2000m/6562ft
1000m/3281ft
500m/1640ft
200m/656ft
Sea Level
N
0 100 km
0 100 miles

F

PEOPLE

Pop. density medium

French, Provençal, German, Breton, Catalan, Basque

109/km² (281/mi²)

THE URBAN/RURAL POPULATION SPLIT

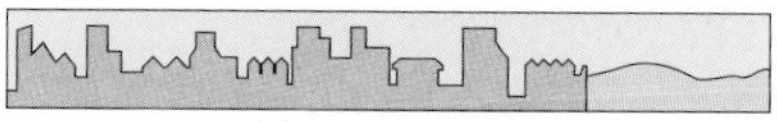
76%
24%

POPULATION AGE BREAKDOWN

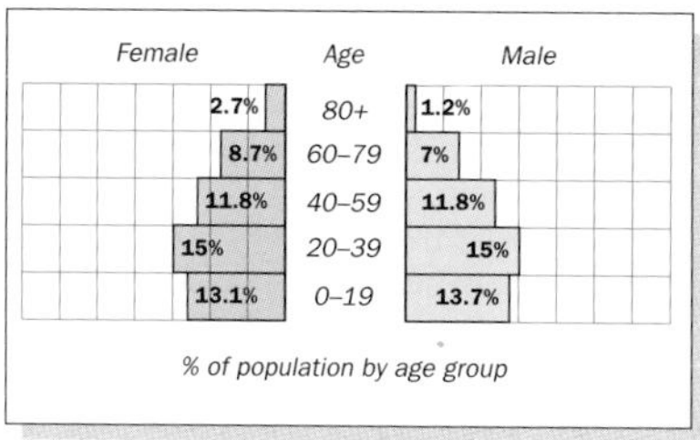
Female
Age
Male
2.7% 80+ 1.2%
8.7% 60–79 7%
11.8% 40–59 11.8%
15% 20–39 15%
13.1% 0–19 13.7%
% of population by age group

RELIGIOUS PERSUASION

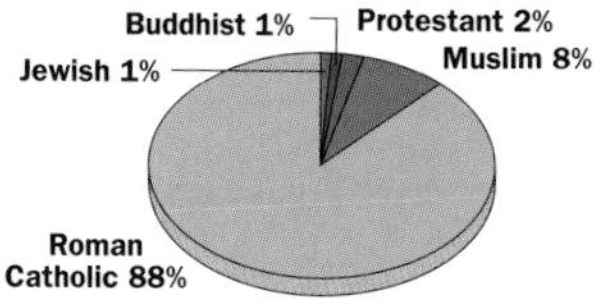
Buddhist 1%
Protestant 2%
Muslim 8%
Jewish 1%
Roman Catholic 88%

ETHNIC MAKEUP

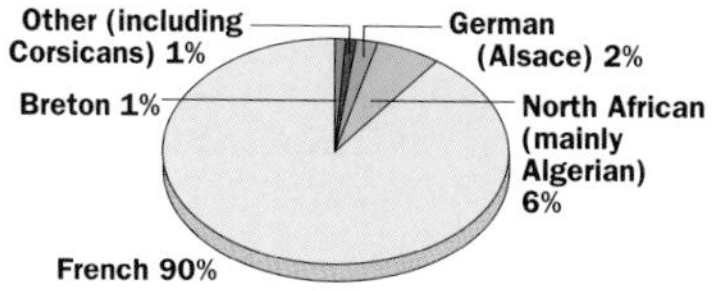
Other (including Corsicans) 1%
German (Alsace) 2%
Breton 1%
North African (mainly Algerian) 6%
French 90%

There is a strong sense of national identity, and compulsory use of French has traditionally been promoted as a unifying force. The cultural traditions of Bretons, Flemings, Alsatians, Basques, Occitans, Catalans, and Corsicans are now respected, but the Constitutional Court has struck down legislation on the use of regional language in government.

France encouraged immigration until the early 1970s, but laws have since become more restrictive. The 1999 census recorded 3.26 million resident foreigners (5.6% of the population) and a similar number of foreign-born immigrants have been naturalized. Racist National Front (FN) propaganda has periodically whipped up anti-immigrant feeling, but there is also a strong current of youth solidarity among "black, blanc, beur" ("black, white, Arab"), boosted by the prevalence of black and Arab stars in music and football, the focus of youth culture.

The Roman Catholic Church is still dominant, but there are sizable Muslim, Protestant, Buddhist, and Jewish minorities. Abortion and birth control were both legalized in the 1970s, despite strong Catholic opposition, and couples now commonly live together before marriage. Some two million unmarried couples of two or more years' standing, including gay couples, gained legal status with social and tax rights under 1998 legislation recognizing the civil solidarity pact.

Women did not get the vote until 1944. Though there has been a woman prime minister, Edith Cresson (1991–1992), and some women have held cabinet posts, there have been no female leaders of the main parties and there were relatively few women in parliament until the introduction of a "parity" law in 2000, requiring an equal number of male and female candidates on party electoral lists.

Strait of Dover
Channel Tunnel
Calais
Dunkerque
BELGIUM
Boulogne-sur-Mer
Lille
Lens
Douai
Arras
ARTOIS
Abbeville
Somme
Amiens
Dieppe
Charleville-Mézieres
LUXEMBOURG
GERMANY
Rouen
Seine
Beauvais
Oise
Laon
PICARDIE
Reims
Thionville
Metz
Lisieux
Charles-de-Gaulle Airport
Pontoise
Nanterre
Évreux
Bobigny
Mantes-la-Jolie
Versailles
PARIS
Créteil
Évry
Melun
Châlons-en-Champagne
Bar-le-Duc
Nancy
LORRAINE
Strasbourg
Chartres
CHAMPAGNE
Troyes
Chaumont
Marne
Moselle
Épinal
VOSGES
ALSACE
Colmar
Mulhouse
Rhine
Orléans
ORLÉANAIS
Loir
Blois
Loire
Yonne
Auxerre
Vesoul
Belfort
Montbéliard
Tours
Bourges
Nevers
MORVAN
Dijon
Besançon
BOURGOGNE
Saône
JURA MOUNTAINS
SWITZERLAND
Indre
Châteauroux
Cher
Poitiers
Vienne
Creuse
Moulins
Digoin
Lons-le-Saunier
Lake Geneva
Mâcon
Bourg-en-Bresse
Guéret
MARCHE
Roanne
Vichy
Annecy
Mont Blanc 4807m
Limoges
LIMOUSIN
Clermont-Ferrand
Lyon
Rhône
Angoulême
St-Chamond
Chambéry
MASSIF CENTRAL
AUVERGNE
St-Étienne
Grenoble
Isère
Périgueux
Tulle
Le Puy
Valence
ALPS
ITALY
Isle
Dordogne
Aurillac
CÉVENNES
Privas
Gap
Lot
Cahors
Rodez
Mende
Aveyron
Agen
Tarn
Digne
Montauban
Albi
Avignon
PROVENCE
Durance
Nîmes
Montpellier
Arles
MONACO
Ligurian Sea
Auch
Toulouse
Salon-de-Provence
Aix-en-Provence
Antibes
Nice
Cannes
Marseille
Martigues
Tarbes
Béziers
Ciotat
Toulon
Carcassonne
Narbonne
Golfe du Lion
la Seyne-sur-Mer
Hyères
Côte d'Azur
Îles d'Hyères
Bastia
Foix
PYRENEES
Perpignan
ANDORRA
SPAIN
MEDITERRANEAN SEA
Corse (Corsica)
Ajaccio
Strait of Bonifacio

CHRONOLOGY

The French Revolution of 1789–1794 overthrew a monarchy that had lasted for more than 800 years. It ushered in successive periods of republicanism, Napoleonic imperialism, and monarchism. In 1870 the founding of the Third Republic established France firmly in the republican tradition.

- **1914–1918** 1.4 million Frenchmen killed in World War I.
- **1918–1939** Economic recession and political instability: 20 prime ministers and 44 governments.
- **1940** Capitulation to Germany. Puppet Vichy regime. Abroad, Gen. de Gaulle leads "Free French."
- **1944** Liberation of France.
- **1946–1958** Fourth Republic. Political instability: 26 governments. Nationalizations. France takes leading role in EEC formation.
- **1958** Fifth Republic. De Gaulle president with strong powers.
- **1960** Most French colonies gain independence.
- **1962** Algerian independence after bitter war with France.
- **1966** France withdraws from NATO military command.
- **1968** General strike and riots over education policy and low wages. National Assembly dissolved; Gaullist victory in June elections.
- **1969** De Gaulle resigns after defeat in referendum on regional reform; replaced by Georges Pompidou.
- **1974** Valéry Giscard d'Estaing president. Center-right coalition.
- **1981** Left wins elections; François Mitterrand president.
- **1983–1986** Government U-turn on economic policy.
- **1986** Cohabitation between socialist president and new right-wing government led by Jacques Chirac. Privatization program introduced.
- **1988** Mitterrand wins second term. PS-led coalition returns.
- **1991** Edith Cresson becomes first woman prime minister.
- **1993** Center right wins elections. Second period of cohabitation.
- **1995** Jacques Chirac president.
- **1995–1996** Controversial series of Pacific nuclear tests.
- **1996** Unpopular austerity measures to prepare for adopting euro.
- **1997** PS-led government takes office in reversed cohabitation.
- **1999** France introduces euro.
- **2000** 35-hour week becomes law.
- **2002** January, euro fully adopted. April–June, center-right victory in presidential and legislative elections.
- **2003** Strikes over pension reform. Heatwave kills 3000 people.

F

POLITICS

Multiparty elections

L. House 2002/2007
U. House 2001/2004

President Jacques Chirac

AT THE LAST ELECTION

National Assembly 577 seats

4% PCF
62% UMP
24% PS
5% UDF
5% Others

UMP = Union for a Presidential Majority (Rally for the Republic – **RPR** and Liberal Democracy – **DL**)
PS = Socialist Party **UDF** = Union for French Democracy
PCF = Communist Party of France **UC** = Centrist Union
Rep = Republicans and Independents **RCC** = Republicans, Communists, and Citizens **RDSE** = European Democratic and Social Rally **Ind** = Independents **G** = Greens

Senate 321 seats

7% RCC
2% Ind
30% RPR
26% PS
16% UC
12% Rep
6% RDSE
1% G

France is a multiparty democracy. The constitution of the Fifth Republic, framed by Charles de Gaulle in 1958, ensures that the president has strong executive powers, but rules in tandem with a government and prime minister chosen by the National Assembly. Under changes agreed in 2000, the president and parliament are no longer elected according to separate timetables; the 2002 elections chose both for a five-year term. Traditionally the president attends to foreign policy and defense issues, while the government focuses on domestic and economic policy.

Profile

Apart from François Mitterrand of the PS (1981–1995), French presidents of the Fifth Republic have all been right-of-center. Between 1986 and 2002, however, both Mitterrand and his successor Jacques Chirac served for much of the time with a government and parliament dominated by political opponents. Thus Chirac, a conservative Gaullist, had to appoint Lionel Jospin of the PS as prime minister in 1997–2002, heading a government coalition with the Communists, Greens, and Radical Socialists. In 2002, however, after Chirac was reelected as president in May, the sweeping victory of his UMP in legislative elections the following month marked a decisive rejection of so-called "cohabitation." Later that year the UMP coalition was formalized as a single party, the Union for a Popular Movement.

The far left has declined since 1945, when the PCF had 25% of the vote. The Greens suffered a serious setback in the 2002 elections, winning just three Assembly seats. The racist National Front (FN) failed to win any seats, but had created a major shock in the first round of the presidential poll when its leader Jean-Marie Le Pen came second. The "democratic" parties united to ensure that he was trounced by Chirac in the run-off, but his taking almost 18% of the vote has remained a high-water mark for the FN.

Main Political Issues

Liberal economic reform

The center right elected in 2002 promised immediate income tax cuts and probusiness measures. In 2003 a controversial cost-cutting pension reform, effectively delaying retirement by two years, was introduced despite a wave of strike action.

Racism and "exclusion"

Exploiting concerns about crime, urban violence, and unemployment, the racist right several times turned such fears to its political advantage. Legislation on immigration has been tightened. Inner-city deprivation and "exclusion" of the unemployed and homeless, though widely recognized as divisive, were issues on which the PS-led government of 1997–2002 failed to find effective policies. The new government in 2002 promoted a tough line on law and order.

European integration and globalization

A current of opposition to European integration grew in the 1990s, fueled by fears of the loss of French sovereignty. Opponents of "globalization" tap into similar concerns that French jobs and culture are under threat. When France joined the eurozone, many saw giving up the franc as losing a symbolic part of their national identity. The most strident opponent of EU integration is the FN, but the center right is also a stout defender of French interests, notably over agricultural reform and in backing French economic interests abroad.

Jacques Chirac, *president of France since 1995.*

Jean-Marie Le Pen, *leader of the far-right FN and presidential runner-up in 2002.*

Jean-Pierre Raffarin *was appointed prime minister by Chirac in 2002.*

WORLD AFFAIRS

Joined UN in 1945

EU | G8 | NATO | OECD | OSCE

There have been two strands to foreign policy since World War II – strong independence and furtherance of French interests in a united Europe. France's role in the EU is seen as a way of combining them. It also seeks to maintain its influence over its former empire, especially francophone Africa.

Traditional enmity with Germany has been dropped; the Franco–German alliance now forms the heart of an expanding EU, and there are plans to harmonize laws across the two states. Relations with the UK are more troublesome, with friction over agricultural imports and the passage of immigrants across the Channel.

France has long been concerned with US dominance in both foreign affairs and culture. It left NATO's military command in 1966 and maintained an independent nuclear deterrent throughout the Cold War (conducting nuclear tests in the Pacific in 1995–1996 despite international criticism). It was vilified by the US for opposing war on Iraq in 2003, especially after threatening to use its veto in the UN Security Council. France (and Germany) were dismissed as "old Europe" over this issue, whereas the majority of existing and prospective EU member states were more supportive of the US.

AID

Donor

$4.2bn (donations) | Up 2% in 2001

As a major global donor, France's motives are not simply commercial: it wishes to maintain the influence of the French language, particularly in Africa, though the main aid recipients remain its overseas territories. Médecins sans Frontières is part of a tradition of active involvement through NGO aid agencies.

ECONOMICS

Inflation 1.5% p.a. (1990–2001)

$1381bn | 0.871 euros (1.013)

SCORE CARD

❑ WORLD GNP RANKING	5th
❑ GNP PER CAPITA	$22,730
❑ BALANCE OF PAYMENTS	$21.4bn
❑ INFLATION	1.6%
❑ UNEMPLOYMENT	9%

EXPORTS

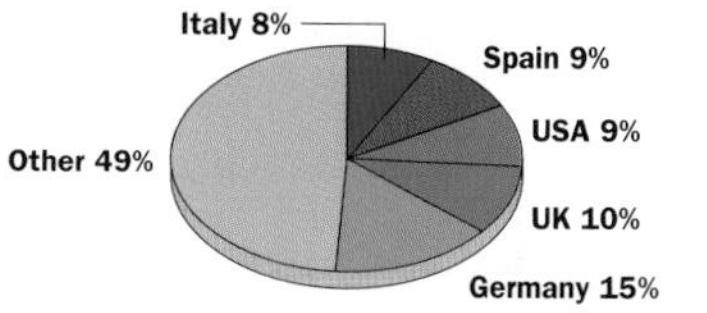

Italy 8%
Spain 9%
USA 9%
UK 10%
Germany 15%
Other 49%

IMPORTS

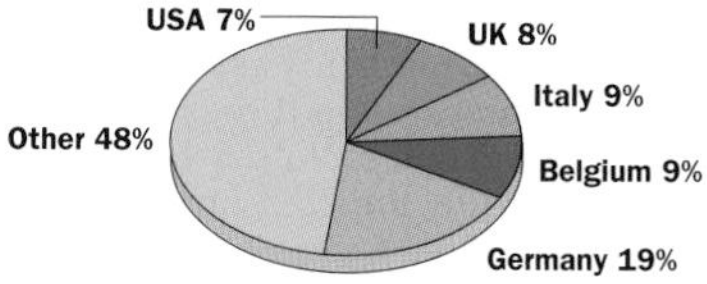

USA 7%
UK 8%
Italy 9%
Belgium 9%
Germany 19%
Other 48%

STRENGTHS

Engineering, reflected in TGV and nuclear industries. Specializations: cars (Citroën, Peugeot, and Renault) and telecommunications (Alcatel). Major exporter: defense sector, pharmaceuticals, and chemicals. Success in attracting inward investment. Strong technocratic traditions: unlike in US or UK, top graduates are attracted into engineering. Luxury goods, cosmetics, perfumes, and quality wines. Most agriculture well modernized: France is Europe's leading agricultural producer. Strong in utilities and water companies.

WEAKNESSES

High taxes, social charges, and labor costs. France has lost its positions in traditional industries such as iron and steel, metallurgy, and textiles. Some major high-tech industries, such as telecommunications, are run partly to further national pride rather than strictly on a commercial basis; France Telecom has faced major financial difficulties.

ECONOMIC PERFORMANCE INDICATOR

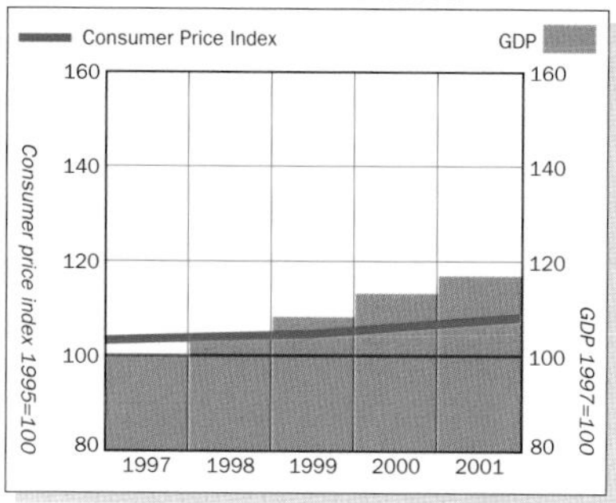

Consumer Price Index
GDP
160
140
120
100
80
Consumer price index 1995=100
GDP 1997=100
1997
1998
1999
2000
2001

F

PROFILE

Protectionist France, at first slow to industrialize, started competing in world markets and modernizing its industry in the 1950s. Integration in western Europe, starting with coal and steel in the 1950s, placed France at the heart of the EU. It was one of the 12 EU countries to adopt the euro in 2002 (though it has dragged its feet on opening up key markets). France has a long tradition of state involvement in running the economy. Nationalization of key industries began in the late 1930s, with a fresh burst in 1981–1983, but since then right-of-center and socialist governments have vigorously pursued privatization. Regional hubs are of growing economic significance. France is the EU's largest agricultural producer; its farmers form a powerful political lobby. Active trade unions succeeded in getting a 35-hour week introduced in 2000, but lost a major battle over pension reform in 2003.

FRANCE : MAJOR BUSINESSES

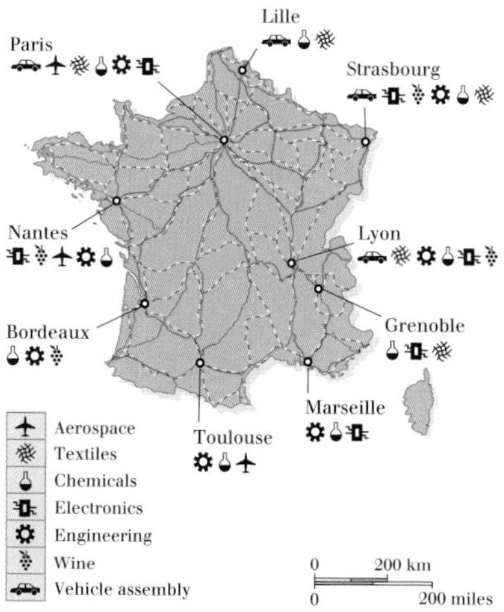

Lille
Paris
Strasbourg
Nantes
Lyon
Bordeaux
Grenoble
Marseille
Toulouse
Aerospace
Textiles
Chemicals
Electronics
Engineering
Wine
Vehicle assembly
0
200 km
0
200 miles

DEFENSE

No compulsory military service

$32.9bn | Down 3% in 2001

FRENCH ARMED FORCES

786 main battle tanks (471 AMX-30B2, 315 Leclerc)	137,000 personnel
1 carrier, 10 submarines, 1 cruiser, 3 destroyers, 30 frigates, 35 patrol boats	45,600 personnel
449 combat aircraft (339 Mirage F-1B/1C/1CR/2000B/C/5F/N/D)	64,000 personnel
64 SLBM in 4 SSBN	

France was a founder member of NATO, but left its military command in 1966 in opposition to US domination. It maintained an independent nuclear deterrent through the Cold War, but went though a rapprochement with NATO in the 1990s. Joint participation between France and Germany in European army units is partly symbolic of reconciliation, as well as an expression of the need for an EU defense structure.

The influence of the army, which was once very strong, is now much diminished. Compulsory military service ended in 2001.

France has one of the world's largest and most export-oriented defense industries, producing its own tanks, jet fighter aircraft, and missiles.

F

RESOURCES

Electric power 115m kW

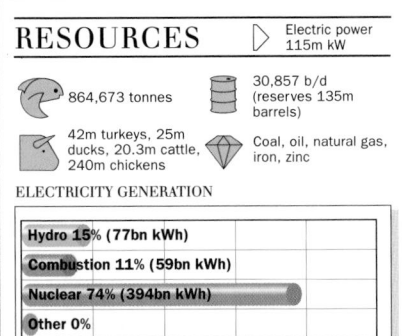

864,673 tonnes

30,857 b/d (reserves 135m barrels)

42m turkeys, 25m ducks, 20.3m cattle, 240m chickens

Coal, oil, natural gas, iron, zinc

ELECTRICITY GENERATION

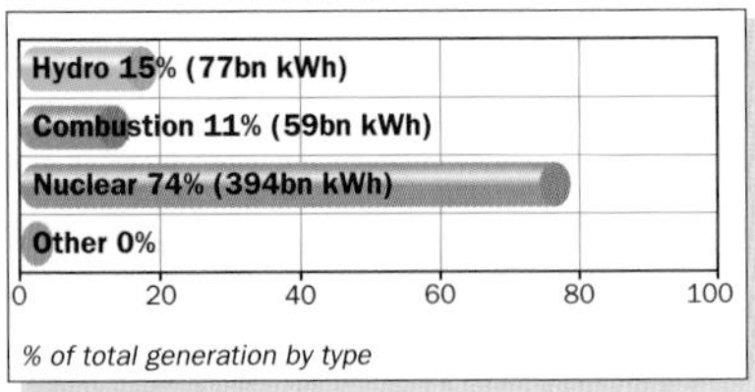
Hydro 15% (77bn kWh)
Combustion 11% (59bn kWh)
Nuclear 74% (394bn kWh)
Other 0%
0 20 40 60 80 100
% of total generation by type

France is the world's most committed user of nuclear energy, which provides over three-quarters of its electricity requirements. The policy reflects a desire for national energy self-sufficiency. Coal, once plentiful in the north and Lorraine, is now mostly exhausted, as are the gas fields off the southwest coast.

FRANCE : LAND USE

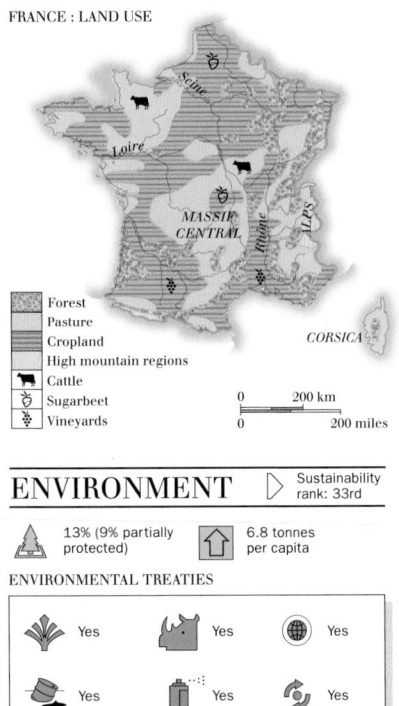

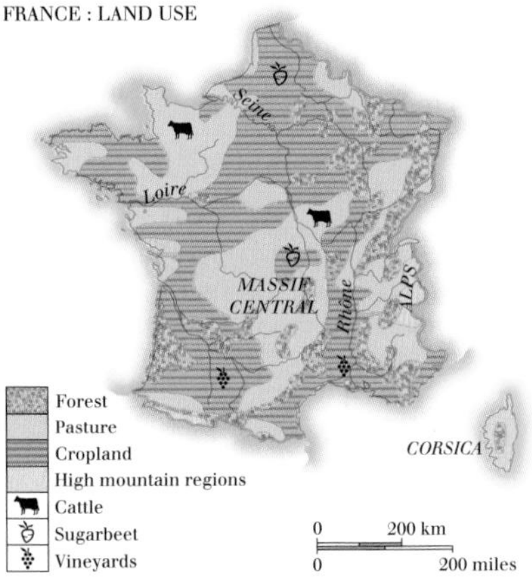
Seine
Loire
MASSIF CENTRAL
Rhône
ALPS
CORSICA
Forest
Pasture
Cropland
High mountain regions
Cattle
Sugarbeet
Vineyards
0 200 km
0 200 miles

ENVIRONMENT

Sustainability rank: 33rd

13% (9% partially protected)

6.8 tonnes per capita

ENVIRONMENTAL TREATIES

Yes	Yes	Yes
Yes	Yes	Yes

Awareness of "green" issues has risen with a series of campaigns against major infrastructure projects. Nuclear power's importance, however, puts the environmentalist lobby in perspective. Transportation of oil by sea poses the threat of pollution of the Atlantic coast. Brittany's beaches and fisheries were badly affected by the wreck of the *Erika* in 1999. Severe storms devastated woodlands in 2000, focusing attention on the dangers of global warming.

THE IMPACT OF MODERN TRANSPORTATION

While the French regions retain distinctive characteristics, the country's modern transportation and telecommunications network, with Paris at its hub, has brought the main provincial cities within easy reach of the capital. It also helps France to play a central role in European business.

The autoroute network

The toll-charging *autoroutes*, or freeways, with a speed limit of 130 km/h (81 mph), now reach almost every corner of the map except the Cherbourg peninsula and Brittany in the northwest. They have relieved the previous generation of town-to-town highways of much of their former traffic congestion, but have also encouraged the upsurge in trans-European heavy freight vehicle movement, carrying through traffic to and from Spain, Italy, Switzerland, Germany, the Benelux countries, and the Channel ports. There has been much controversy about the environmental impact of several as yet uncompleted cross-country links, notably the E11 route south from Clermont-Ferrand to join the Mediterranean network.

French leadership in high-speed trains

French pride in leading-edge engineering, and a capacity for ambitious centralized planning and state-backed investment, have been apparent in its high-speed train system, the *train à grande vitesse* (TGV). Rivaled only by the Japanese bullet train as the fastest in passenger service, the TGV can run at sustained speeds of over 300 km/h (186 mph). The first element was the TGV southeast. Construction began in 1975 and the Paris–Lyon section came into service in 1983, with subsequent extensions southward, culminating in the high-profile opening in 2001 of the direct service from Paris to Marseille. By the end of the 1980s a western route from Paris, initially to Le Mans, was also in service. The northern Paris–Lille route opened in 1993 with extensions to Brussels, Calais, and the Channel Tunnel. During the 1990s, some double-decker trains were introduced to help meet high demand for seats, and a new generation of TGV trains was unveiled by the engineers Alstom in 1998–1999. The TGV has hit domestic airline

Calais
Lille
Le Havre
Rouen
PARIS
Metz
Strasbourg
Brest
Le Mans
Nantes
Orléans
Tours
Dijon
Poitiers
Limoges
Lyon
Bordeaux
Nîmes
Nice
Toulouse
Marseille
Autoroute
TGV route
Other rail

FRANCE : ROAD AND RAIL

traffic hard on some of the prime routes, by offering a combination of comfort and shorter door-to-door journey times in many instances.

Extending the train network

The existing TGV lines, which use mainly modernized but also some purpose-built track, are a highly profitable part of the French rail network. Seeing the likely economic benefits, many towns have lobbied hard to be included. The next planned line, however, from Paris east to Strasbourg, has faced more opposition as well as escalating cost estimates. Construction began in early 1999, aiming for completion in six to seven years. To make money, this line will need to provoke a big shift in existing traveling habits. The French government's commitment is also in part a strategic political decision, designed to reinforce Strasbourg's role "at the heart of European integration."

A link via Tours to Bordeaux is intended to be part of the next stage, along with further international links – from Lyon to Turin, from Marseille and Montpellier to Barcelona, and via Strasbourg to Stuttgart and Frankfurt and thus linking into the German high-speed ICE train network.

The Antigone development *in Montpellier, a city whose new dynamic image owes much to its transportation links and investment in communications technology.*

MEDIA

TV ownership high

Daily newspaper circulation 201 per 1000 people

PUBLISHING AND BROADCAST MEDIA

There are 117 daily newspapers, including *Le Monde, Libération*, and *Le Figaro. Ouest-France* has the highest circulation

10 services: 5 state-controlled, 5 independent

7 services: 3 state-controlled, 4 independent

TV and radio were freed from direct state influence in the 1980s. Two of the main TV channels are still state-owned, but TF1 was privatized in 1987. Canal Plus mixes pay-per-view and advertising-backed services. A Breton-language station started up in 2000. Commercial channels have multiplied with the growth of satellite and cable.

The once innovative Minitel electronic communications system is now overshadowed by the Internet. Circulation of prestigious national newspapers has dwindled and regional papers too have suffered from a gradual shift to electronic media.

CRIME

No death penalty

59,155 prisoners

Up 14% in 2000–2002

CRIME RATES

Crime	Rate
Murders	4 per 100,000 population
Rapes	18 per 100,000 population
Thefts	4225 per 100,000 population

The Code Napoléon, enacted in 1804, still forms the basis of French law. Criminal justice is based on inquisitorial rather than adversarial principles: the judge has considerable powers to examine witnesses and assess evidence. There are no *sub judice* restrictions on reporting trials. Political corruption cases, reaching into government, attract much attention.

Public concern about rising petty crime and violence has encouraged tough policing. Harsh laws targeting beggars, prostitutes, and squatters were introduced in 2002, and have been held responsible for a sudden increase in the prison population.

HEALTH

Welfare state health benefits

1 per 330 people

Cancers, heart and cerebrovascular diseases, accidents

The French consume more medicines per capita than any other nation, and a significant number take medically approved, and prescribed, cures at health spas. French health care was rated the most efficient in the world by WHO in 2000. Under the national health system patients pay for treatment, and then get the majority of the cost reimbursed by an insurance company paid by the social services. Though health awareness has risen in recent years, a culture of tobacco and alcohol abuse prevails. Cirrhosis of the liver is not uncommon as a cause of death. In 2003 a 500 million antismoking campaign was launched.

SPENDING

GDP/cap. increase

CONSUMPTION AND SPENDING

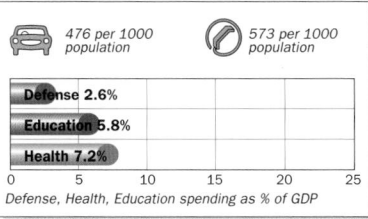

476 per 1000 population

573 per 1000 population

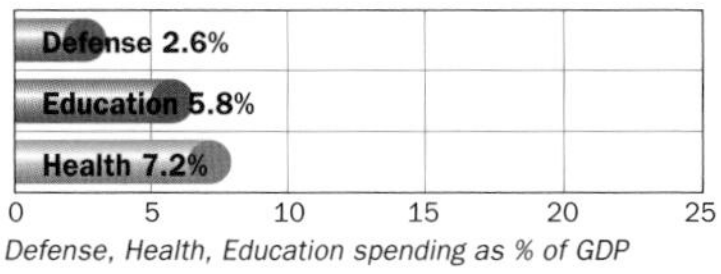

Defense 2.6%
Education 5.8%
Health 7.2%
0
5
10
15
20
25
Defense, Health, Education spending as % of GDP

Wealth and income disparities in France are higher than in most OECD states. The Socialists narrowed the gap a little in the 1980s with the introduction of the legal minimum wage (*le SMIC*). Most tax is indirect – a result of a long French tradition of income-tax evasion. Major tax cuts announced in 2000 aimed to redress the imbalance of income tax on the rich and poor. The wealthy take exotic vacations to the Himalayas, the Andes, and Polynesia. The French lag behind their European neighbors in using the Internet; fewer than one-fifth of the population had done so by 2001.

EDUCATION

School leaving age: 16

99%

2.03m students

THE EDUCATION SYSTEM

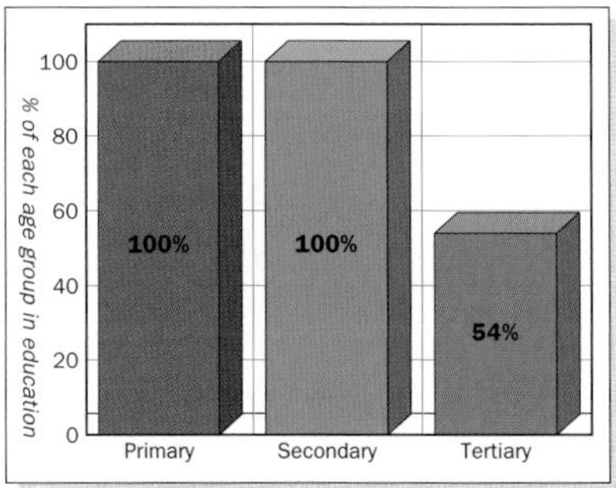

100
80
60
40
20
0
% of each age group in education
100%
100%
54%
Primary
Secondary
Tertiary

Education is highly centralized, a situation which is slowly generating a desire for greater flexibility. The education ministry organizes the curriculum, sets examinations, and decides staffing issues. Roman Catholic schools, which take most of the 17% of privately educated children (but are not fee paying and receive large state subsidies), are the exception. However, they are still obliged to follow the national curriculum.

The focus in the classroom remains the acquisition of a broad range of knowledge. Pupils' academic records are impressive, despite frequent staff strikes.

France has more than 70 universities and higher education bodies, with 1.2 million students. The famous Sorbonne in Paris was split into 13 separate universities in 1971. Entry is not competitive, but based on passing the secondary-level exam, the *baccalauréat*. Most students attend the university nearest to home. The universities have been given neither the funds nor the staff to cope with the huge increase in student numbers in recent years. The Grandes Ecoles, the most influential tertiary institutions, are outside the university system, and each takes just a few hundred carefully selected students. They groom the future governing elite, opening the way for their successful graduates to gain the top civil service and professional jobs.

Massif Central, Auvergne. *The Massif's lonely granite plateaus and extinct volcanoes are France's oldest rock formations.*

WORLD RANKING

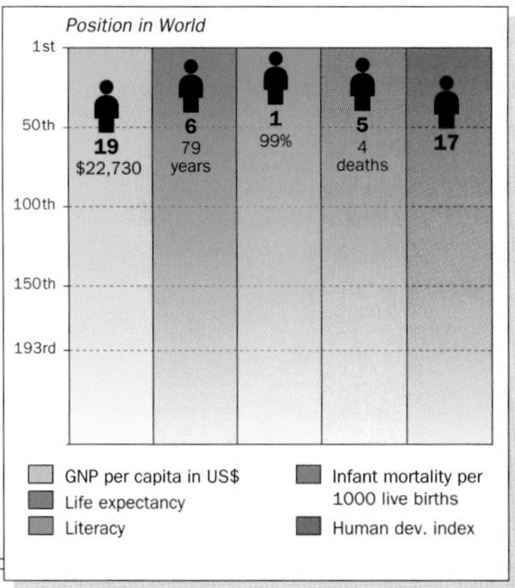

Position in World
1st
50th
100th
150th
193rd
19
$22,730
6
79
years
1
99%
5
4
deaths
17
GNP per capita in US$
Life expectancy
Literacy
Infant mortality per 1000 live births
Human dev. index

See also OVERSEAS TERRITORIES *p.640*

GABON

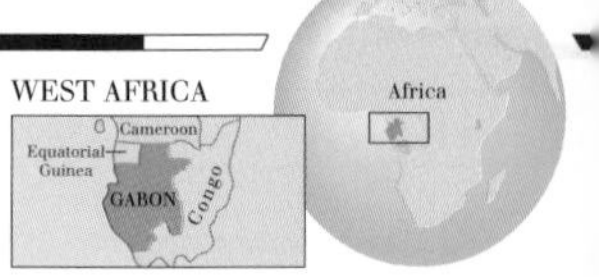
WEST AFRICA
Africa
Cameroon
Equatorial Guinea
GABON
Congo

OFFICIAL NAME: Gabonese Republic **CAPITAL:** Libreville
POPULATION: 1.3 million **CURRENCY:** CFA franc **OFFICIAL LANGUAGE:** French

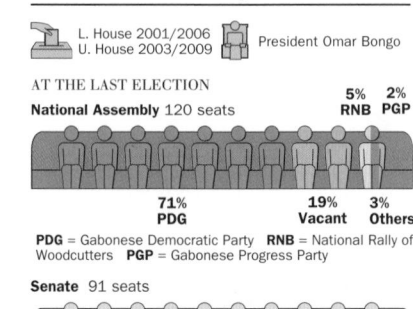

1960 | 1960 | Aug 17 | G | +1 | +241 | .ga

AN EQUATORIAL COUNTRY on the west coast of Africa, Gabon has an economy based on the production of oil. Only a small area of Gabon is cultivated, and more than two-thirds of it constitutes one of the world's finest virgin rainforests. Gabon became independent of France in 1960. A single-party state from 1968, it returned to multiparty democracy in 1990. Gabon's population is small, and the government is encouraging its increase.

CLIMATE

Tropical equatorial

WEATHER CHART FOR LIBREVILLE

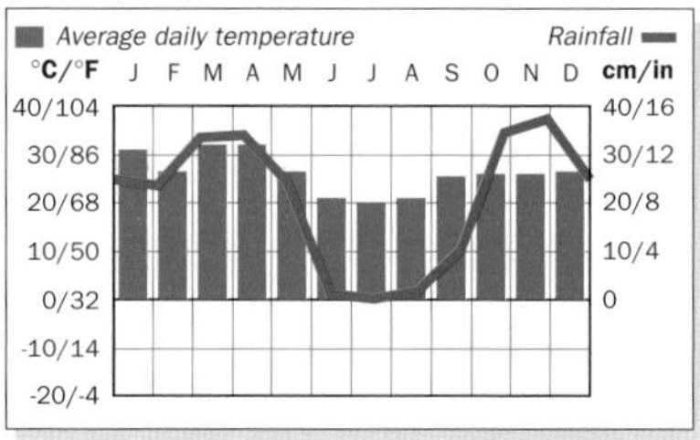
Average daily temperature
Rainfall
°C/°F
J F M A M J J A S O N D
cm/in
40/104
30/86
20/68
10/50
0/32
-10/14
-20/-4
40/16
30/12
20/8
10/4
0

The climate is heavily equatorial – hot all year round with a long rainy season from October to May. The cold Benguela current lowers coastal temperatures.

TRANSPORTATION

Drive on right

Léon M'ba, Libreville 838,087 passengers

12,541 grt

THE TRANSPORTATION NETWORK

838 km (521 miles)

30 km (19 miles)

731 km (454 miles)

1600 km (994 miles)

The Trans-Gabon Railroad from Owendo port near Libreville to Massoukou is the key transportation link.

Air transportation is well developed, and most big companies have airstrips.

TOURISM

Visitors : Population 1:7.7

169,000 visitors

Up 9% in 2001

MAIN TOURIST ARRIVALS

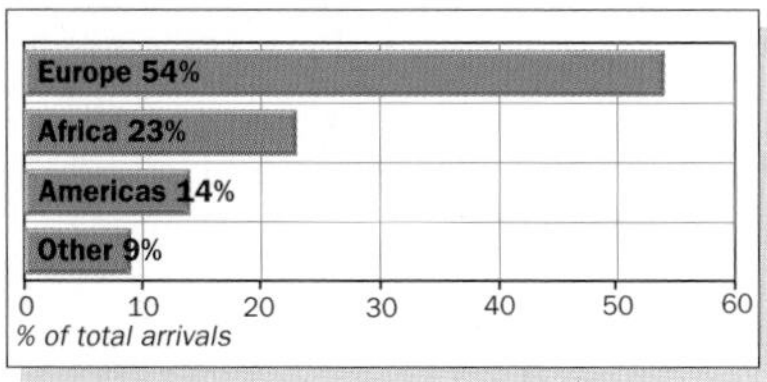
Europe 54%
Africa 23%
Americas 14%
Other 9%
0
10
20
30
40
50
60
% of total arrivals

Despite Libreville's many hotels, Gabon has little tourism, in part a reflection of its lack of good beaches.

PEOPLE

Pop. density low

Fang, French, Punu, Sira, Nzebi, Mpongwe

5/km² (13/mi²)

THE URBAN/RURAL POPULATION SPLIT

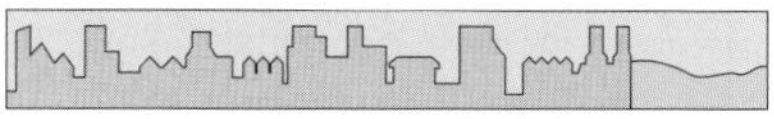
82%
18%

ETHNIC MAKEUP

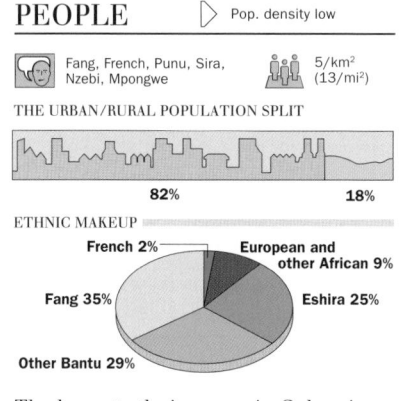

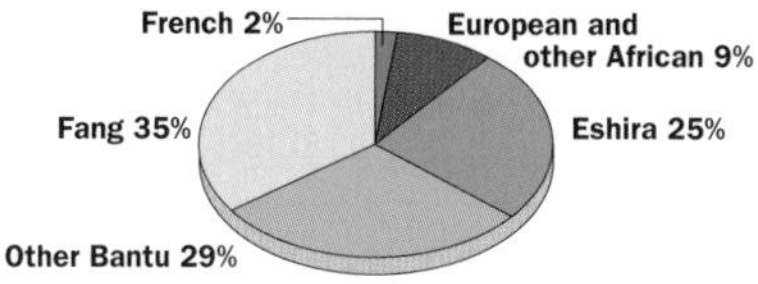
French 2%
European and other African 9%
Fang 35%
Eshira 25%
Other Bantu 29%

The largest ethnic group in Gabon is the Fang, who live mainly in the north. President Omar Bongo, from a subgroup of the Bateke in the southeast, has artfully united the common interests of other ethnic groups to keep the Fang from government. The Myene group around Port-Gentil consider themselves as the aristocrats of Gabonese society owing to their long-standing ex-colonial contacts. Oil wealth has led to the growth of a distinct bourgeoisie. Gabon is one of Africa's most urbanized countries.

POLITICS

Multiparty elections

L. House 2001/2006
U. House 2003/2009

President Omar Bongo

AT THE LAST ELECTION

National Assembly 120 seats

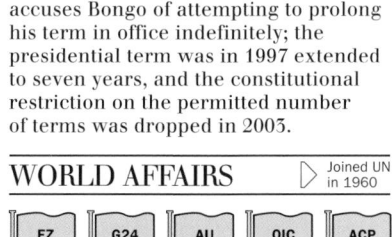

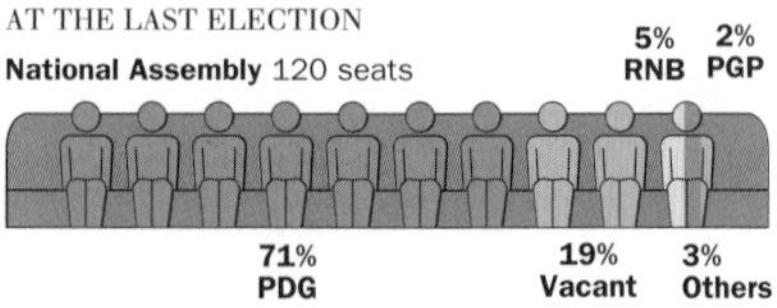
5% RNB
2% PGP
71% PDG
19% Vacant
3% Others

PDG = Gabonese Democratic Party **RNB** = National Rally of Woodcutters **PGP** = Gabonese Progress Party

Senate 91 seats

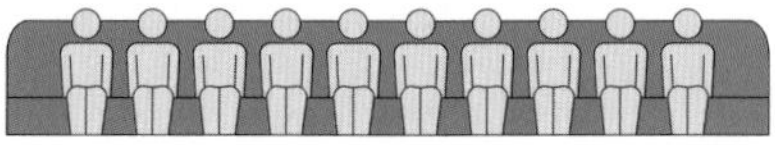

The Senate is indirectly elected by regional councils

Omar Bongo has been in power since 1967, running a single-party state from 1968 until a multiparty system was introduced in 1990. Elections since then have confirmed Bongo in power, along with the former sole ruling party, the PDG. The fairness of the polls has been widely disputed. The opposition accuses Bongo of attempting to prolong his term in office indefinitely; the presidential term was in 1997 extended to seven years, and the constitutional restriction on the permitted number of terms was dropped in 2003.

WORLD AFFAIRS

Joined UN in 1960

FZ | G24 | AU | OIC | ACP

Gabon maintains close links with France, although US companies are also making inroads into Gabon's oil-rich economy. Gabon remains influential regionally (the Gulf of Guinea Commission was launched in Libreville in 2001), and relations further afield, particularly with OPEC, are also important.

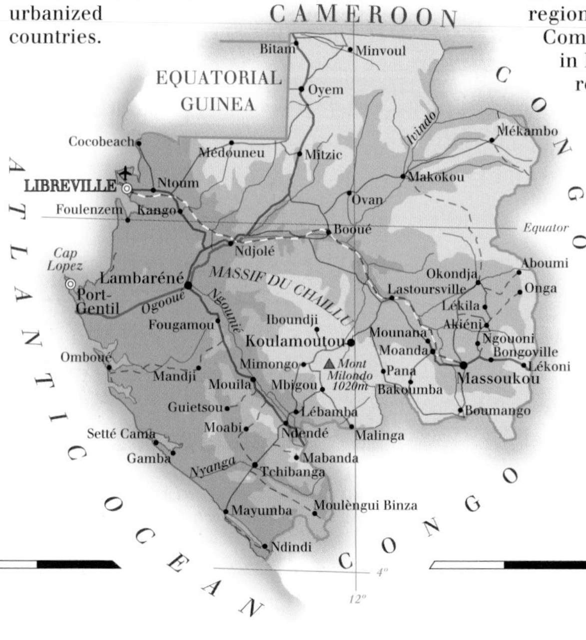
CAMEROON
EQUATORIAL GUINEA
CONGO
ATLANTIC OCEAN
Bitam
Minvoul
Oyem
Cocobeach
Médouneu
Mitzic
Ivindo
Mékambo
Makokou
LIBREVILLE
Ntoum
Foulenzem
Kango
Ovan
Booué
Equator
Cap Lopez
Port-Gentil
Lambaréné
Ndjolé
MASSIF DU CHAILLU
Okondja
Lastoursville
Aboumi
Onga
Ogooué
Ngounié
Lékila
Akiéni
Fougamou
Iboundji
Koulamoutou
Mounana
Moanda
Ngouoni
Bongoville
Lékoni
Omboué
Mimongo
Mont Milondo 1020m
Pana
Mandji
Mouila
Mbigou
Bakoumba
Massoukou
Guietsou
Lébamba
Boumango
Moabi
Ndendé
Malinga
Setté Cama
Gamba
Mabanda
Nyanga
Tchibanga
Mayumba
Moulèngui Binza
Ndindi
4°
12°

GABON

Total Area : 267 667 sq. km (103 346 sq. miles)

POPULATION

over 100 000
over 10 000
under 10 000

LAND HEIGHT

500m/1640ft
200m/656ft
Sea Level

N

0 100 km
0 100 miles

AID

Recipient

$9m (receipts)

Down 25% in 2001

France is by far the major aid donor, providing over two-thirds of total receipts. For a middle-income country with one of the highest GNPs per capita in the developing world, Gabon has benefited from considerable aid. Its indebtedness is the result of excessive borrowing, which was encouraged by Western banks in the 1970s. Much aid goes to servicing this debt.

DEFENSE

No compulsory military service

$120m

Down 4% in 2001

President Bongo's background in the military is reflected in Gabon's large defense budget and prestige weaponry, which includes French Mirage jets. France guarantees Gabon's security and keeps a small garrison in Libreville. Military service is voluntary, and in 2001 a recruitment drive was launched to recruit 1500 18- to 25-year-olds by 2006.

ECONOMICS

Inflation 5.6% p.a. (1990–2001)

$3.99bn

571.2 CFA francs (664.2)

SCORE CARD

❑ World GNP Ranking	121st
❑ GNP per Capita	$3160
❑ Balance of Payments	$435m
❑ Inflation	1.5%
❑ Unemployment	21%

STRENGTHS

Oil and relatively small population: high per capita GNP. Abundant resources – including some of the world's best tropical hardwoods.

WEAKNESSES

Large debt burden incurred in the 1970s. Continuing dependence on French technical assistance. Reliance on oil wealth leaves Gabon vulnerable to price fluctuations.

EXPORTS

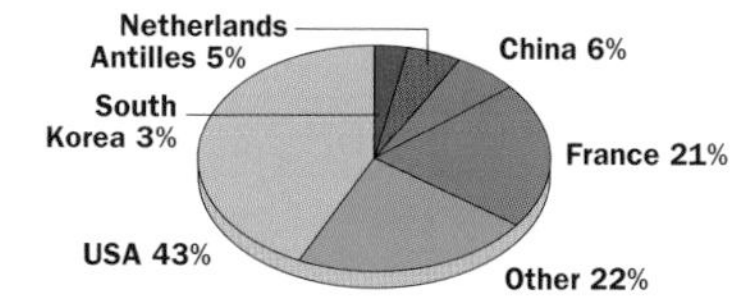
Netherlands Antilles 5%
China 6%
South Korea 3%
France 21%
USA 43%
Other 22%

IMPORTS

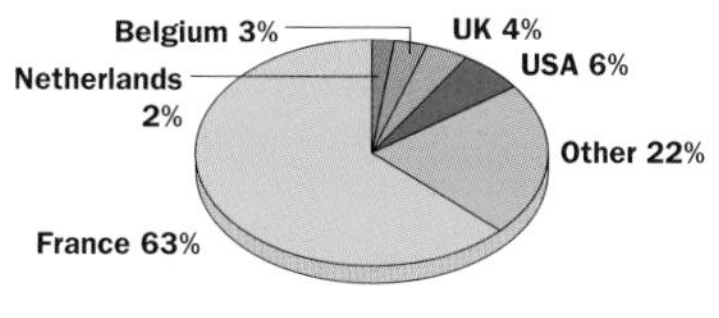
Belgium 3%
UK 4%
USA 6%
Netherlands 2%
Other 22%
France 63%

RESOURCES

Electric power 402,000 kW

48,028 tonnes

295,000 b/d (reserves 2.5bn barrels)

212,000 pigs, 195,000 sheep, 3.1m chickens

Oil, manganese, uranium, gold, iron, natural gas

Oil is the major export earner. Gabon also has large deposits of uranium and over 100 years' reserves of manganese. The unexploited iron ore deposits at Bélinga are among the world's largest.

ENVIRONMENT

Sustainability rank: 36th

3% partially protected

2.9 tonnes per capita

The Trans-Gabon Railroad has sliced through one of the world's finest virgin rainforests and has opened the interior to indiscriminate exploitation of rare woods such as oleoirme. Gabon abandoned plans for nuclear power following the 1986 Chernobyl disaster.

MEDIA

TV ownership high

Daily newspaper circulation 30 per 1000 people

PUBLISHING AND BROADCAST MEDIA

There are 2 daily newspapers, *L'Union* and *Gabon-Matin*

3 services: 1 state-owned, 2 independent

7 services: 2 state-controlled, 5 independent

The media are mostly government-controlled. There was a crackdown in 1998 on independent media – which in the 1990s had become quite diverse – raising concerns about freedom of expression.

CRIME

Death penalty in use

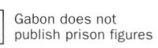

Gabon does not publish prison figures

Crime is rising

Gabon's human rights record has improved in recent years.

A campaign to combat child trafficking was launched in 2001.

Urban crime rates are rising.

***Albert Schweitzer Hospital,** Lambaréné, on the lower Ogooué River. Schweitzer won the Nobel Peace Prize in 1952.*

CHRONOLOGY

Gabon became a French colony in 1886, administered as part of French Equatorial Africa.

- ❑ **1960** Independence. Léon M'ba president.
- ❑ **1967** Albert-Bernard (later Omar) Bongo president.
- ❑ **1968** Single-party state instituted.
- ❑ **1990** Multiparty democracy.
- ❑ **1998** Bongo reelected president.
- ❑ **2001** Elections: ruling PDG retains majority.

G

EDUCATION

School leaving age: 16

71%

7473 students

Education follows the French system. Université Omar Bongo in Libreville, founded in the 1970s, now has more than 4000 students.

HEALTH

No welfare state health benefits

1 per 5000 people

Heart and diarrheal diseases, pneumonia, accidents

Oil revenues have allowed substantial investment in the health service, which is now among the best in Africa.

SPENDING

GDP/cap. increase

CONSUMPTION AND SPENDING

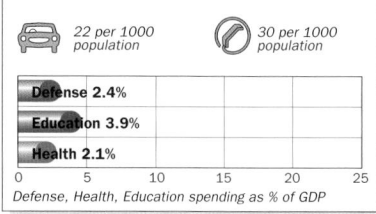

22 per 1000 population

30 per 1000 population

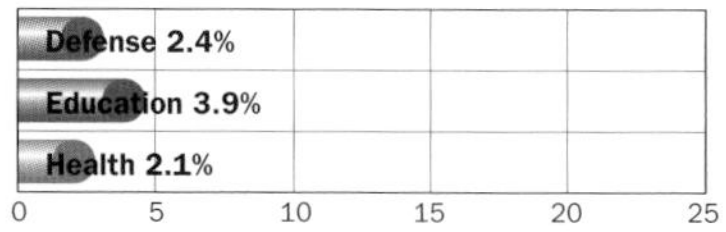
Defense 2.4%
Education 3.9%
Health 2.1%
0
5
10
15
20
25

Defense, Health, Education spending as % of GDP

Oil wealth has created an affluent bourgeoisie. Immigrants take on menial and low-income jobs. The cost of living in Libreville is surprisingly high.

WORLD RANKING

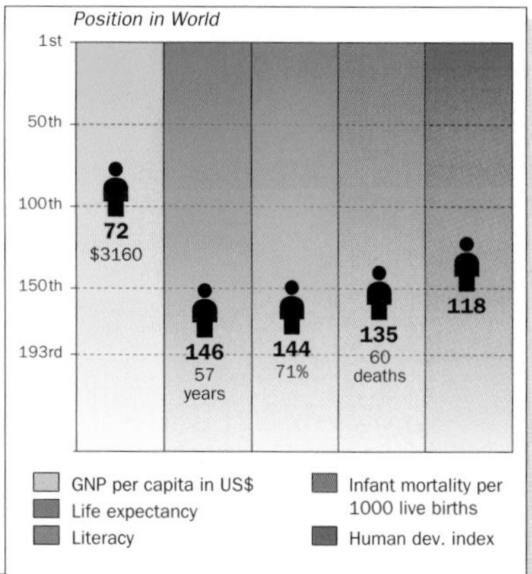
Position in World
1st
50th
100th
150th
193rd
72
$3160
146
57 years
144
71%
135
60 deaths
118
GNP per capita in US$
Life expectancy
Literacy
Infant mortality per 1000 live births
Human dev. index

GAMBIA

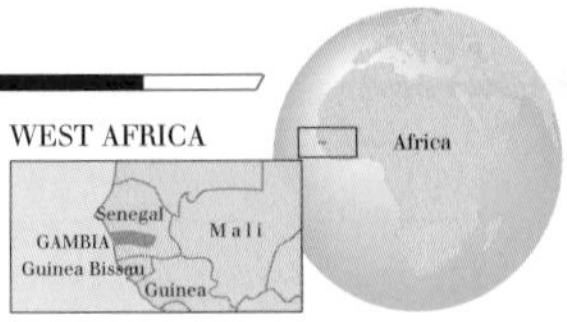
WEST AFRICA
Africa
Senegal
GAMBIA
Guinea Bissau
Mali
Guinea

OFFICIAL NAME: Republic of the Gambia **CAPITAL:** Banjul
POPULATION: 1.4 million **CURRENCY:** Dalasi **OFFICIAL LANGUAGE:** English

1965 | 1965 | Feb 18 | WAG | 0 | +220 | .gm

A NARROW COUNTRY on the western coast of Africa, the Gambia was renowned as a stable democracy until an army coup in 1994. Agriculture accounts for 65% of GDP, yet many Gambians are leaving rural areas for the towns, where average incomes are four times higher. Its position as an enclave within Senegal seems likely to endure, following the failure of an experiment in federation in the 1980s.

CLIMATE

Tropical wet and dry

WEATHER CHART FOR BANJUL

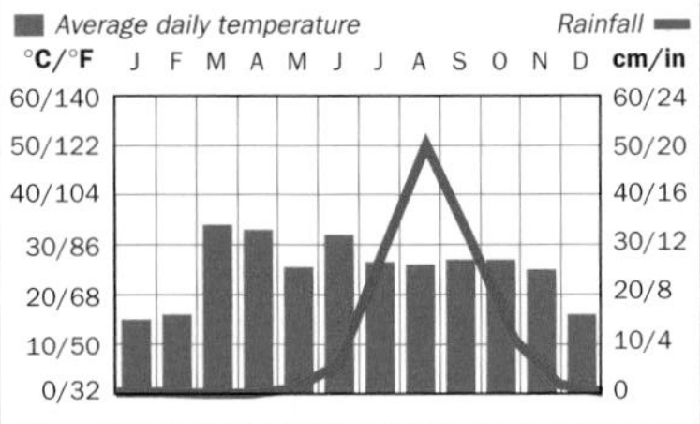
Average daily temperature
Rainfall
°C/°F J F M A M J J A S O N D cm/in
60/140 50/122 40/104 30/86 20/68 10/50 0/32
60/24 50/20 40/16 30/12 20/8 10/4 0

The subtropical and sunny dry season is punctuated by intermittent hot *harmattan* winds.

TRANSPORTATION

Drive on right

Yundum International, Banjul
302,841 passengers

8 ships
1884 grt

THE TRANSPORTATION NETWORK

956 km (594 miles)

None

None

400 km (249 miles)

The Gambia River carries more traffic than the roads – ships of up to 3000 tonnes can reach Georgetown. Yundum airport was upgraded by NASA in 1989 for US space shuttle emergency landings.

TOURISM

Visitors : Population 1:15

96,000 visitors

Up 5% in 1999

MAIN TOURIST ARRIVALS

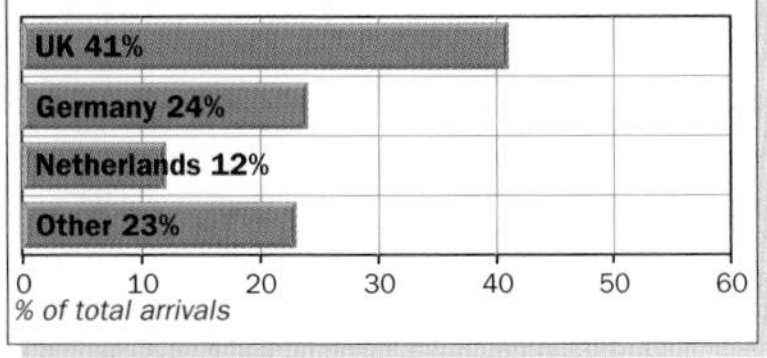
UK 41%
Germany 24%
Netherlands 12%
Other 23%
0 10 20 30 40 50 60
% of total arrivals

"Eco-tourism" is being developed, but most of those enjoying the beaches and resort hotel life are Europeans escaping winter, including many single women.

PEOPLE

Pop. density medium

Mandinka, Fulani, Wolof, Jola, Soninke, English

140/km² (363/mi²)

THE URBAN/RURAL POPULATION SPLIT

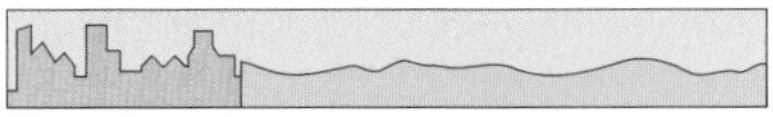
31%
69%

ETHNIC MAKEUP

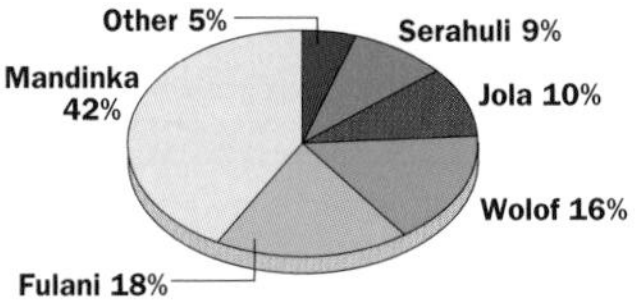
Other 5%
Serahuli 9%
Mandinka 42%
Jola 10%
Wolof 16%
Fulani 18%

The Mandinka have traditionally dominated politically. Potential resentment among the smaller ethnic groups was offset under the regime of President Sir Dawda Jawara by the distribution of political offices fairly according to ethnic origins. President Jammeh, a fervent Muslim, is from the minority Jola (or Diola) community, numerous across the border in Senegal, where they are active in a local rebellion. About 85% of Gambians follow Islam, though there is no official state religion. There is a yearly influx of migrants, who come from Senegal, Guinea, and Mali to trade in groundnuts, and a small UK expatriate community along the coast. Gambia is still a poor country, with 80% of the labor force engaged in agriculture. Women are active as traders in an otherwise male-dominated society.

***Fishing village.** Overfishing in the waters off the Gambia and Senegal, mainly by foreign vessels, is a growing problem.*

POLITICS

Multiparty elections

2002/2007

President Yahya Jammeh

AT THE LAST ELECTION

National Assembly 53 seats

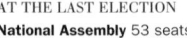

4% PDOIS
85% APRC
9% Nom
2% NRP

APRC = Alliance for Patriotic Reorientation and Construction
Nom = Nominated **PDOIS** = People's Democratic Organization for Independence and Socialism
NRP = National Reconciliation Party

The People's Progressive Party (PPP) was in government from 1962 until 1994, for most of which time the Gambia was one of Africa's few democracies. A ban, imposed after the 1994 coup on the PPP and the three main parties which had been in opposition, was lifted in 2001 in time for elections.

During the army's coup, Sir Dawda Jawara took refuge aboard a visiting US warship, and he then went into exile in Britain. The coup's leaders claimed that it had been initiated in a bid to end corruption and pledged to preserve democracy. In the new government several portfolios went to civil servants who had served in the Jawara administration. Military leader Yahya Jammeh was elected president in controversial elections in September 1996, and the following January his APRC won the majority of seats in a parliamentary election. Jammeh and the APRC were reelected in 2001–2002; the PPP won no seats.

WORLD AFFAIRS

Joined UN in 1965

CILSS | Comm | ECOWAS | AU | OIC

International criticism of the 1994 coup which brought President Jammeh to power has softened in recent years, but an apparent crackdown on opponents following Jammeh's reelection in 2001 reawakened concern. Relations with Senegal have been strained by the rebellion of the Jola community in the province of Casamance.

AID

Recipient

$51m (receipts)

Up 4% in 2001

Western aid flows, suspended after the 1994 coup, have largely resumed. International agencies are the major donors. 2002/03 was officially declared a year of crop failure in an effort to attract emergency food aid.

GAMBIA

Total Area : 11 300 sq. km (4363 sq. miles)

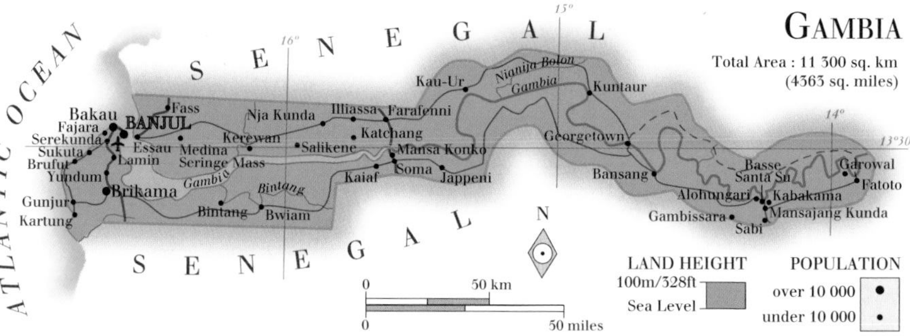

ATLANTIC OCEAN
SENEGAL
SENEGAL
Bakau
Fajara
Serekunda
Sukuta
Brufut
Yundum
Gunjur
Kartung
BANJUL
Fass
Essau
Lamin
Brikama
Medina
Seringe Mass
Kerewan
Nja Kunda
Illiassa
Farafenni
Katchang
Salikene
Mansa Konko
Soma
Kaiaf
Jappeni
Bintang
Bwiam
Kau-Ur
Nianija Bolon
Gambia
Kuntaur
Georgetown
Bansang
Basse Santa Su
Garowal
Fatoto
Alohungari
Kabakama
Mansajang Kunda
Gambissara
Sabi
N
0
50 km
50 miles
LAND HEIGHT
100m/328ft
Sea Level
POPULATION
over 10 000
under 10 000

CHRONOLOGY

Mandinka traders brought Islam in the 13th century and were the main influence until the 18th century. The 1700s and 1800s saw colonial rivalry between Britain and France.

- **1888** British possession.
- **1959** Dawda Jawara founds PPP.
- **1965** Independence from Britain.
- **1970** Republic; Jawara president.
- **1982–1989** Federation with Senegal.
- **1994** Jawara ousted in army coup.
- **1996** Yahya Jammeh wins presidential election.
- **2000** Military coup foiled.
- **2001** $2 million antipoverty program launched by government.
- **2002** Jammeh's party sweeps parliamentary elections.

G

DEFENSE

No compulsory military service

$3m

No change in 2001

The 800-strong Gambia National Army includes a small marine unit and a presidential guard. There is also a 600-strong gendarmerie. Most arms are bought from the UK, though supplies are now increasingly coming from Nigeria too. A defense pact with Senegal collapsed along with the federation in 1989.

ECONOMICS

Inflation 4.1% p.a. (1990–2001)

$426m

26 dalasis (18.8)

SCORE CARD

WORLD GNP RANKING	172nd
GNP PER CAPITA	$320
BALANCE OF PAYMENTS	–$53m
INFLATION	4%
UNEMPLOYMENT	Widespread underemployment

STRENGTHS

Low tariffs promote regional trade. Natural deepwater harbor at Banjul, one of the finest on the west African coast. Well-managed economy, favorably viewed by donors. Agriculture, particularly livestock. Tourism.

WEAKNESSES

Small market inhibits investment. Smuggling. Lack of resources, little agricultural diversification; consequent overreliance on groundnuts. Decline of fish stocks. Major crop failure in 2002.

EXPORTS

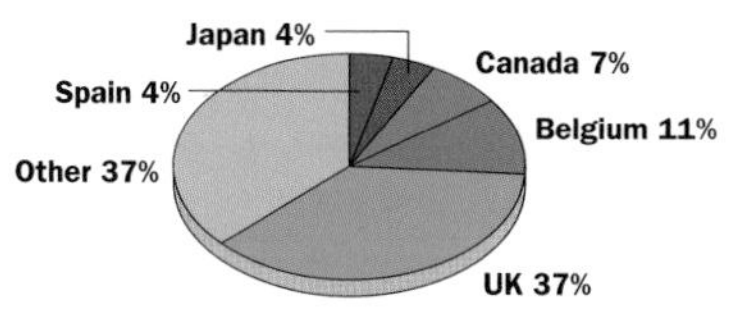

Japan 4%
Canada 7%
Spain 4%
Belgium 11%
Other 37%
UK 37%

IMPORTS

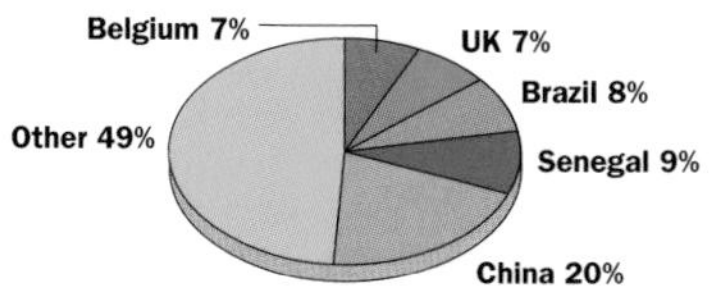

Belgium 7%
UK 7%
Brazil 8%
Other 49%
Senegal 9%
China 20%

RESOURCES

Electric power 29,000 kW

29,016 tonnes

Not an oil producer

326,556 cattle, 261,965 goats, 591,000 chickens

Ilmenite, zirconium, rutile, kaolin, tin, oil

The Gambia River is one of Africa's few good waterways, but it is underused owing to its separation from its natural hinterland by the Gambia–Senegal border. Irrigation is at present provided by a single dam; plans for further dams for power generation have met with opposition. Oil deposits are believed to exist offshore.

ENVIRONMENT

Sustainability rank: 103rd

2% (0.4% partially protected)

0.2 tonnes per capita

The impact of tourism and of overfishing in Gambian waters are major concerns, as are desertification and deforestation.

MEDIA

TV ownership low

Daily newspaper circulation 2 per 1000 people

PUBLISHING AND BROADCAST MEDIA

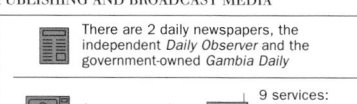

There are 2 daily newspapers, the independent *Daily Observer* and the government-owned *Gambia Daily*

1 state-owned service

9 services: 1 state-owned, 8 independent

The independent media are restricted. Radio news broadcasts are dominated by state-controlled Radio Gambia, and the government runs the only national television station.

CRIME

Death penalty not used in practice

450 prisoners

General crime levels are low, but rising

Crime levels are relatively low in what is a peaceful society compared with many other states in the region.

EDUCATION

Schooling is not compulsory

38%

1702 students

Efforts to increase enrollment have been successful. Levels are now over 80% for primary and over 35% for secondary. A university was established in 1998.

HEALTH

No welfare state health benefits

1 per 25,000 people

Malaria, tuberculosis, parasitic diseases

Most people have access to basic medicines, but these are no longer free. Advanced medical care in the public sector is limited. An HIV/AIDS awareness campaign was launched in 2002.

SPENDING

GDP/cap. increase

CONSUMPTION AND SPENDING

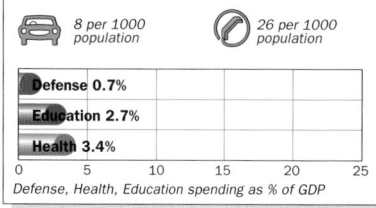

8 per 1000 population

26 per 1000 population

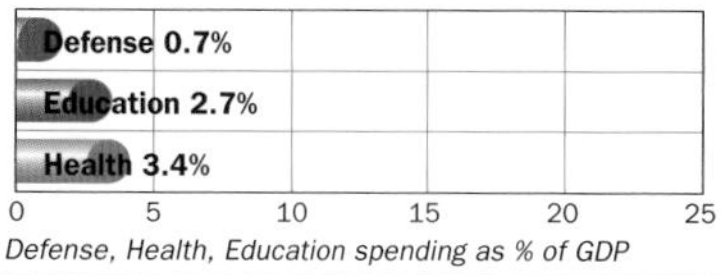

Defense 0.7%
Education 2.7%
Health 3.4%
0
5
10
15
20
25

Defense, Health, Education spending as % of GDP

Public service and the professions have created wealth and some people are comfortably off, but great wealth is not a feature of Gambian life. Unemployed young men in Banjul are regarded as the underclass.

WORLD RANKING

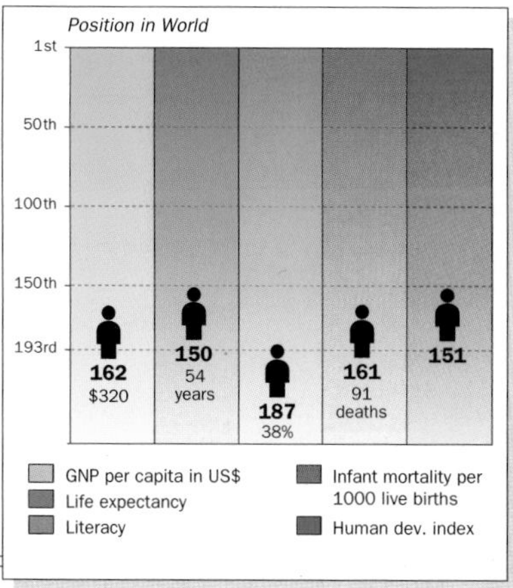

Position in World
1st
50th
100th
150th
193rd
162
$320
150
54 years
187
38%
161
91 deaths
151
GNP per capita in US$
Life expectancy
Literacy
Infant mortality per 1000 live births
Human dev. index

GEORGIA

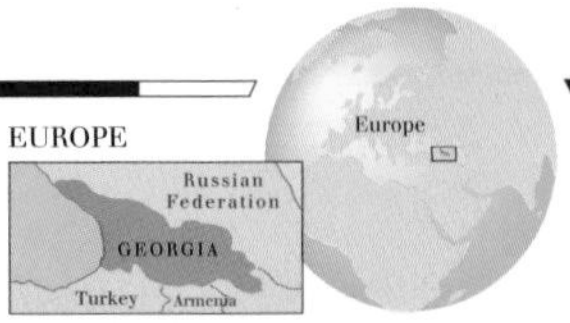

EUROPE
Europe
Russian Federation
GEORGIA
Turkey
Armenia

OFFICIAL NAME: Georgia **CAPITAL:** Tbilisi
POPULATION: 4.6 million **CURRENCY:** Lari **OFFICIAL LANGUAGE:** Georgian; Abkhazian (in Abkhazia)

1991 | 1991 | May 26 | GE | +4 | +995 | .ge

SANDWICHED BETWEEN the Greater and Lesser Caucasus, Georgia is a mountainous country, with a Black Sea coastline running north–south from Abkhazia to Ajaria. Georgia was one of the first republics to demand independence from the Soviet Union, but has been plagued over recent years by civil war and ethnic disputes in Abkhazia and South Ossetia. Georgia is a primarily agricultural country, and is noted for its wine.

CLIMATE

Mountain/subtropical

WEATHER CHART FOR TBILISI

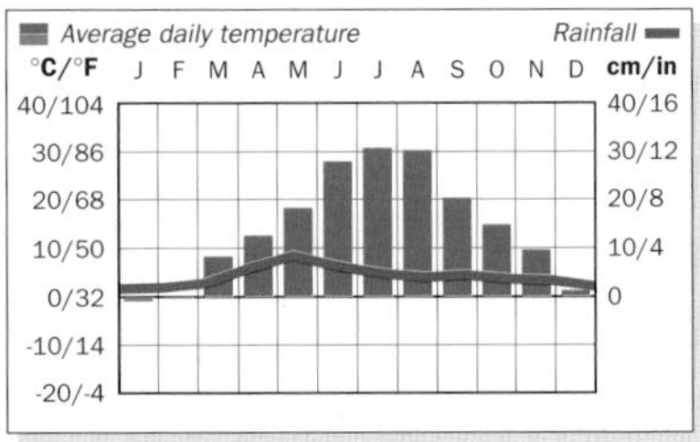

Average daily temperature
Rainfall
°C/°F
J F M A M J J A S O N D
cm/in
40/104
30/86
20/68
10/50
0/32
-10/14
-20/-4
40/16
30/12
20/8
10/4
0

Georgia's climate is continental inland and subtropical along the coast, where grapes, citrus fruit, and tea are grown.

Tbilisi, Georgia's capital since the 5th century. Its buildings rise in steep terraces from both banks of the Kura River.

TRANSPORTATION

Drive on right

Novo Alexeyevka, Tbilisi 249,649 passengers

201 ships 276,600 grt

THE TRANSPORTATION NETWORK

19,354 km (12,026 miles)	None
1562 km (971 miles)	None

Transportation was seriously disrupted by civil war. A new rail route and oil pipeline from Baku to the Black Sea ports of Poti and Supsa was opened in 1999.

TOURISM

Visitors : Population 1:15

302,000 visitors

Down 21% in 2000–2001

MAIN TOURIST ARRIVALS

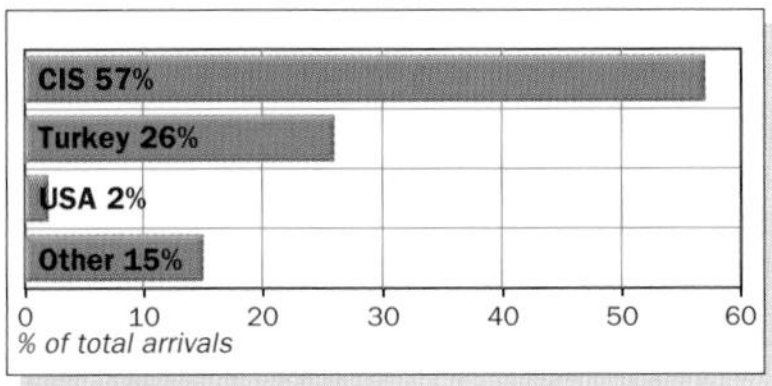

CIS 57%
Turkey 26%
USA 2%
Other 15%
0
10
20
30
40
50
60
% of total arrivals

The volatile political situation has discouraged tourism, but numbers are rising again. Most tourists still come from former Soviet states.

PEOPLE

Pop. density medium

Georgian, Russian, Azeri, Armenian, Mingrelian, Ossetian, Abkhazian

66/km² (171/mi²)

THE URBAN/RURAL POPULATION SPLIT

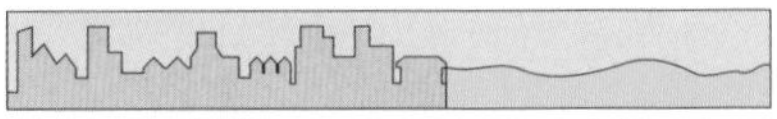

57%
43%

ETHNIC MAKEUP

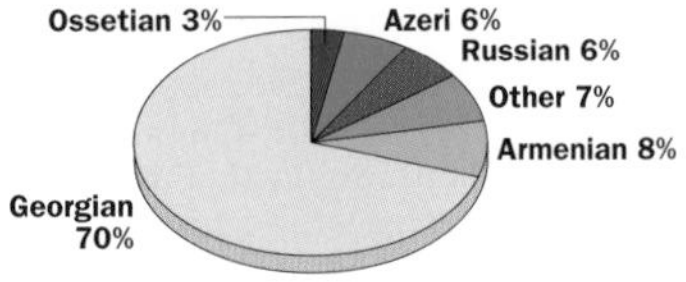

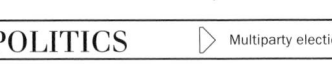

Ossetian 3%
Azeri 6%
Russian 6%
Other 7%
Armenian 8%
Georgian 70%

Georgia was converted to (Orthodox) Christianity in 326 CE. Conflict with the partly Muslim Abkhaz and Ossets in the 1990s displaced over 300,000 people. The Muslim–Georgian Ajarians have a level of autonomy, while among the poorest of the population are the Armenians of Javakheti, in the south.

POLITICS

Multiparty elections

1999/2003

President Eduard Shevardnadze

AT THE LAST ELECTION

Parliament of Georgia 235 seats

56% CUG
24% AGUR
7% ISG
5% AD
8% Others

CUG = Citizens' Union of Georgia **AGUR** = All Georgian Union of Revival **ISG** = Industry Will Save Georgia **AD** = Abkhazian Deputies

Ten Abkhazian seats were not contested in 1999.

Georgia has a strong presidential system; party allegiances are fluid and liable to change. President Eduard Shevardnadze, a former foreign minister of the Soviet Union, has dominated since coming to power amid civil war in 1992. His position has been challenged ever since – there have been several assassination attempts. Recently he has backed calls for reform, supporting the idea of an executive prime minister. Effective independence is exercised by the regions of Abkhazia and South Ossetia. Georgians expelled from Abkhazia during the 1992–1993 war now form a powerful lobby group in Tbilisi, the capital.

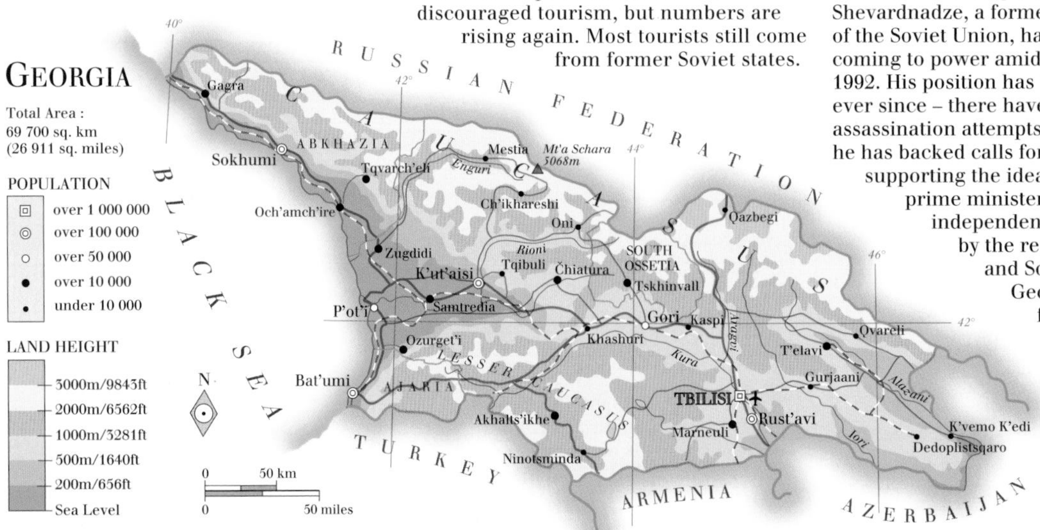

GEORGIA
Total Area : 69 700 sq. km (26 911 sq. miles)
POPULATION
over 1 000 000
over 100 000
over 50 000
over 10 000
under 10 000
LAND HEIGHT
3000m/9843ft
2000m/6562ft
1000m/3281ft
500m/1640ft
200m/656ft
Sea Level
0 50 km
0 50 miles
RUSSIAN FEDERATION
BLACK SEA
TURKEY
ARMENIA
AZERBAIJAN
CAUCASUS
LESSER CAUCASUS
ABKHAZIA
AJARIA
SOUTH OSSETIA
Gagra
Sokhumi
Och'amch'ire
Tqvarch'eli
Mestia
Mt'a Schara 5068m
Enguri
Ch'ikhareshi
Oni
Zugdidi
Rioni
K'ut'aisi
Tqibuli
Chiatura
Tskhinvali
P'ot'i
Samtredia
Gori
Kaspi
Qazbegi
Ozurget'i
Khashuri
Kura
Aragvi
Qvareli
T'elavi
Gurjaani
Alazani
Bat'umi
TBILISI
Rust'avi
Akhalts'ikhe
Marneuli
Iori
K'vemo K'edi
Dedoplists'qaro
Ninotsminda

WORLD AFFAIRS

Joined UN in 1992

BSEC | CIS | CE | OSCE | PfP

The US and Russia struggle for influence over Georgia. Both fear the presence of Islamist militants.

AID

Recipient

$290m (receipts)

Up 71% in 2001

As well as aid for infrastructure projects, Georgia receives Western support for institutional and financial sector reform.

DEFENSE

Compulsory military service

$265m

Down 9% in 2001

The army's main focus remains Abkhazia. However, US concerns over the presence of Islamist terrorists prompted the arrival in 2002 of US forces to train the regular Georgian army; the security service is already CIA-trained. Russian troops, once numbering over 9000, have been steadily withdrawn since 2000.

ECONOMICS

Inflation 279% p.a. (1990–2001)

$3.1bn

2.155 lari (2.233)

SCORE CARD

❑ World GNP Ranking	130th
❑ GNP per Capita	$590
❑ Balance of Payment	–$162m
❑ Inflation	4.6%
❑ Unemployment	15%

Strengths

Gateway to West for Azeri oil through pipelines to Black Sea and Mediterranean ports. Traditional and well-established wine industry providing exports, mainly to Russia.

Weaknesses

Political instability deters investment. Large black economy and influential Mafia. Drought and currency crisis in 1998. Serious budget deficit problems. Negative trade balance.

EXPORTS

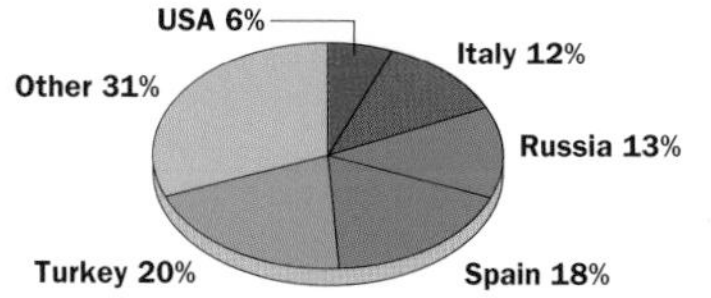
USA 6%
Italy 12%
Other 31%
Russia 13%
Turkey 20%
Spain 18%

IMPORTS

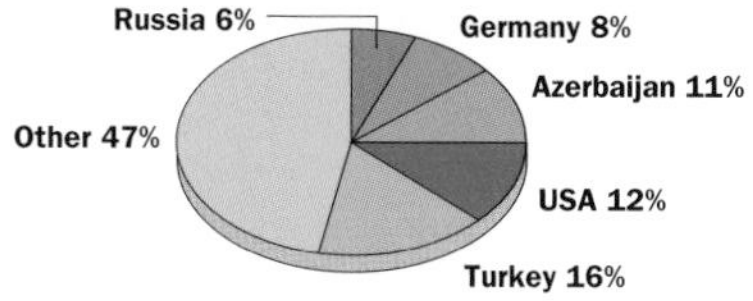
Russia 6%
Germany 8%
Azerbaijan 11%
Other 47%
USA 12%
Turkey 16%

RESOURCES

Electric power 4.6m kW

2536 tonnes

2145 b/d (reserves 37m barrels)

1.18m cattle, 567,500 sheep, 8.5m chickens

Manganese, coal, oil, natural gas, zinc, cobalt, vanadium

Known oil reserves are as yet barely developed. Georgia is dependent on Russia for much of its energy supply, although a new US–Georgian oil refinery was opened in eastern Georgia in 1998. Georgia is a predominantly agricultural country, and food processing and wine production continue to be the major industries. Manganese and small quantities of zinc, cobalt, and vanadium are mined.

ENVIRONMENT

Not available

3%

1 tonne per capita

Radiation from materials left by departing Russian soldiers is a growing problem, as is Black Sea pollution and ensuring protection of upland pastures.

MEDIA

TV ownership high

Daily newspaper circulation 5 per 1000 people

PUBLISHING AND BROADCAST MEDIA

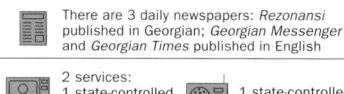

There are 3 daily newspapers: *Rezonansi* published in Georgian; *Georgian Messenger* and *Georgian Times* published in English

2 services: 1 state-controlled, 1 independent

1 state-controlled service

Government newspapers are subsidized. The independent TV channel, Rustavi–2, was permitted to reopen in 1998, but has faced harassment.

CRIME

No death penalty

7688 prisoners

Up 5% in 1999–2001

Organized crime under the control of Mafia-style groups has flourished since independence in 1991. The police force, accused of corruption and human rights abuses, was purged in 2002.

EDUCATION

School leaving age: 14

99%

140,627 students

Since independence, education has stressed Georgian language and history. All levels of education are seriously underfunded. Tbilisi University was formerly of a high standard.

HEALTH

Welfare state health benefits

1 per 205 people

Cerebrovascular and heart diseases, cancers, liver disease

The health system was limited under the control of the Soviet Union. Internal strife and a lack of resources have prevented any recent investment.

CHRONOLOGY

A Russian protectorate from 1763, Georgia was absorbed into the Russian Empire in 1801. It was established as an independent state under a Menshevik socialist government in 1918.

- ❑ **1920** Recognized by Soviet Russia as an independent state.
- ❑ **1921** Soviet Red Army invades. Effectively part of USSR.
- ❑ **1922–1936** Incorporated into Transcaucasian Soviet Federative Socialist Republic (TSFSR).
- ❑ **1989** Proindependence riots in Tbilisi put down by Soviet troops.
- ❑ **1990** Declares sovereignty.
- ❑ **1991** Independence. Zviad Gamsakhurdia elected president.
- ❑ **1992** Gamsakhurdia flees Tbilisi. Shevardnadze elected chair of Supreme Soviet and State Council.
- ❑ **1992–1993** Abkhazia conflict.
- ❑ **1995** Shevardnadze narrowly survives assassination attempt, subsequently elected president.
- ❑ **1999** Opening of pipeline from Caspian to Black Sea.
- ❑ **2000** Shevardnadze reelected. Russian troop withdrawal begins.

G

SPENDING

GDP/cap. decrease

CONSUMPTION AND SPENDING

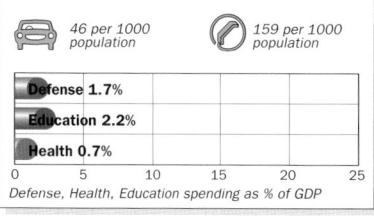

46 per 1000 population

159 per 1000 population

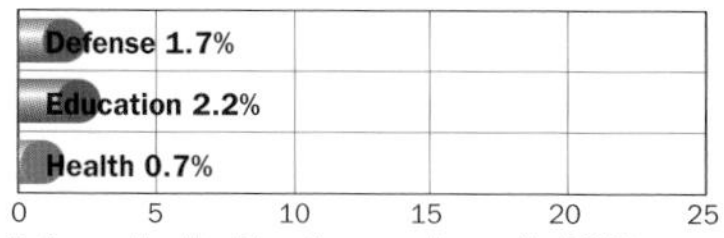
Defense 1.7%
Education 2.2%
Health 0.7%
0
5
10
15
20
25

Defense, Health, Education spending as % of GDP

There is a wealthy and extravagant urban elite, but most depend on small incomes from agriculture. Wages and welfare are often in arrears.

WORLD RANKING

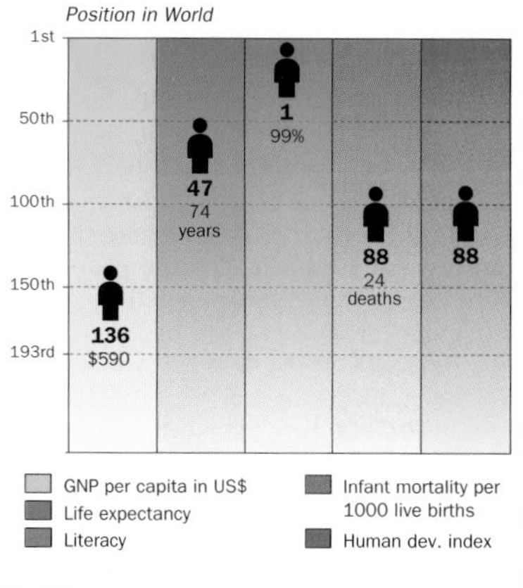
Position in World
1st
50th
100th
150th
193rd
136
$590
47
74 years
1
99%
88
24 deaths
88
GNP per capita in US$
Life expectancy
Literacy
Infant mortality per 1000 live births
Human dev. index

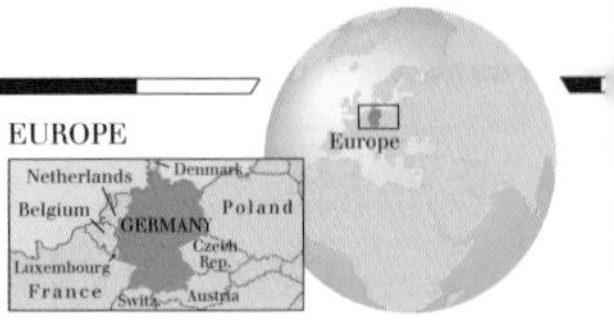
EUROPE
Europe
Netherlands
Denmark
Belgium
GERMANY
Poland
Czech Rep.
Luxembourg
France
Switz.
Austria

GERMANY

OFFICIAL NAME: Federal Republic of Germany **CAPITAL:** Berlin
POPULATION: 82 million **CURRENCY:** Euro **OFFICIAL LANGUAGE:** German

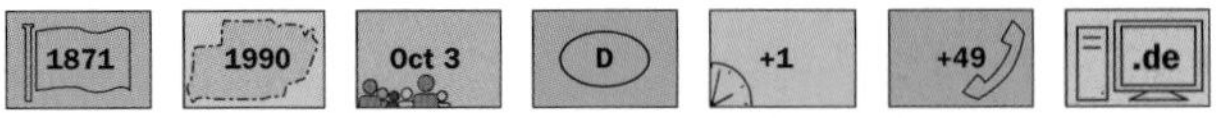
1871
1990
Oct 3
D
+1
+49
.de

WITH COASTLINES on both the Baltic and North Seas, Germany is bordered by nine countries. Plains and rolling hills in the north give way to more mountainous terrain in the south. Europe's foremost industrial power, and its most populous country apart from Russia, Germany is the world's second-biggest exporter. Unified in the 1870s, it was divided after the defeat of the Nazi regime in 1945. The communist-ruled east was part of the Soviet bloc until the collapse of the East German regime in 1989, which paved the way for reunification in 1990. Tensions created by wealth differences between east and west were then exacerbated by record levels of unemployment. The government committed itself to European union and adopted the single currency, the euro, even though the stable deutsche mark had been a symbol of German pride.

CLIMATE

Continental/maritime

WEATHER CHART FOR BERLIN

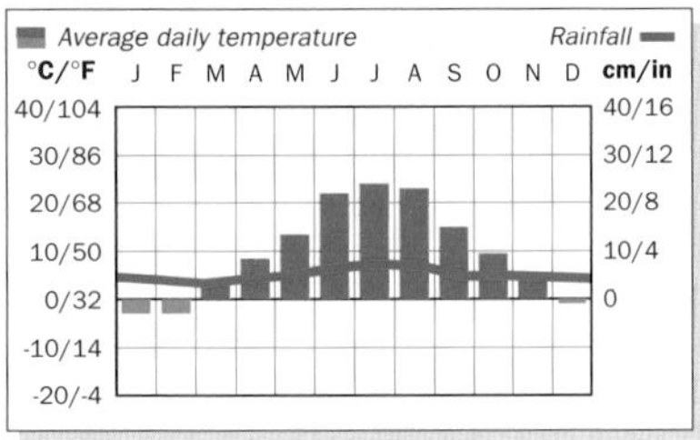
Average daily temperature
Rainfall
°C/°F
J F M A M J J A S O N D
cm/in
40/104
30/86
20/68
10/50
0/32
-10/14
-20/-4
40/16
30/12
20/8
10/4
0

Germany has a broad climatic range. The upper Rhine valley is very mild and suitable for wine making. The Bavarian Alps, the Harz Mountains, and the Black Forest are by contrast cold, with heavy falls of snow in winter.

TRANSPORTATION

Drive on right

Frankfurt/Main International
48.5m passengers

906 ships
6.3m grt

THE TRANSPORTATION NETWORK

650,891 km (404,444 miles)

11,712 km (7277 miles)

36,652 km (22,774 miles)

7500 km (4660 miles)

Germany virtually invented the modern highway with the first *Autobahnen* in the 1930s. These have since become Europe's most elaborate highway network; there are generally no tolls and few speed limits, despite protests from environmentalists. The efficient railroad system has been restructured as a first step toward privatization. Germany's high-speed ICE railroad opened its main north–south routes in 1991 and has expanded greatly since then. Urban transportation systems are highly efficient.

TOURISM

Visitors : Population
1:4.6

18m visitors

Up 1% in 2002

MAIN TOURIST ARRIVALS

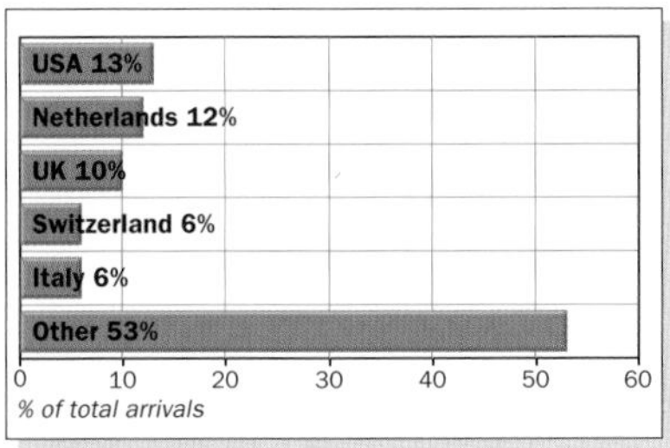
USA 13%
Netherlands 12%
UK 10%
Switzerland 6%
Italy 6%
Other 53%
0 10 20 30 40 50 60
% of total arrivals

Northerly beaches and a colder climate make Germany less of a tourist destination than France or Italy. Skiing in the Bavarian Alps, the historic castles of the Rhine valley, the Black Forest, and Germany's excellent beer are all major attractions. Berlin, even before 1989, drew tourists with its rich cultural life and its Wall separating capitalist West and communist East. Now capital of the reunified Germany, and with a dynamic and vibrant atmosphere, it has undergone massive reconstruction.

The Stillach Valley, Allgäu Alps, Bavaria (Bayern). Alarm at acid rain damage to Germany's forests sparked off the rise of the Greens, who joined the government in 1998.

GERMANY
Total Area : 357 021 sq. km
(137 846 sq. miles)
POPULATION
over 1 000 000
over 500 000
over 100 000
over 10 000
0 50 km
0 50 miles
N
LAND HEIGHT
2000m/6562ft
1000m/3281ft
500m/1640ft
200m/656ft
Sea Level
NORTH SEA
Helgoland
German Bight
Ostfriesische Inseln
Nordfriesische Inseln
Helgoländer Bucht
Cuxhaven
Wilhelmshaven
Bremerhaven
Emden
Oldenburg
NETHERLANDS
NORDDEUTSCHES
NIEDERSACHSEN
Ems
Osnabrück
Münster
Bielefeld
NORDRHEIN-WESTFALEN
Recklinghausen
Herne
Hamm
Gelsenkirchen
Bochum
Oberhausen
Dortmund
Duisburg
Essen
RUHR
Hagen
Mülheim
Wuppertal
Mönchengladbach
Düsseldorf
Solingen
VALLEY
Leverkusen
Köln
Siegen
Aachen
Bonn
RHEINISCHES SCHIEFERGEBIRGE
Marburg an der Lahn
HESSEN
BELGIUM
EIFEL
Koblenz
Frankfurt am Main
Offenbach
Wiesbaden
Mainz
Darmstadt
LUXEMBOURG
Mosel
RHEINLAND-PFALZ
Trier
Kaiserslautern
SAARLAND
Ludwigshafen
Mannheim
Neckar
Heidelberg
Saarbrücken
Heilbronn
Karlsruhe
Baden-Baden
BADEN-WÜRTTEMBERG
Offenburg
FRANCE
SCHWARZWALD
BLACK FOREST
Freiburg im Breisgau
Friedrichshafen
SWITZERLAND

PEOPLE

Pop. density high

German, Turkish

235/km² (608/mi²)

THE URBAN/RURAL POPULATION SPLIT

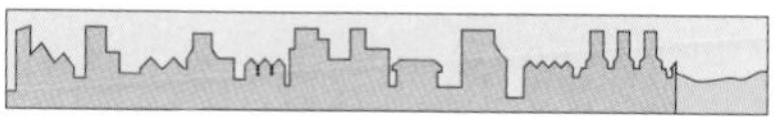
88%
12%

RELIGIOUS PERSUASION

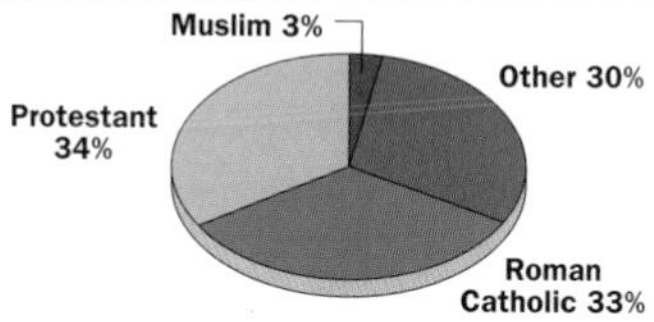
Muslim 3%
Other 30%
Protestant 34%
Roman Catholic 33%

ETHNIC MAKEUP

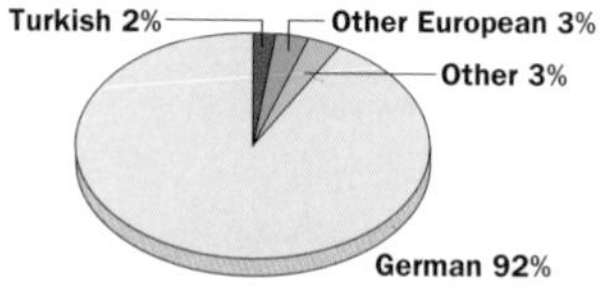
Turkish 2%
Other European 3%
Other 3%
German 92%

BALTIC SEA
Fehmarnbelt
Fehmarn
Lübecker Bucht
Sassnitz
Stralsund
Pomeranian Bay
Greifswald
Rostock
Lübeck
Wismar
MECKLENBURG-VORPOMMERN
Stettiner Haff
Schwerin
Schweriner See
Neubrandenburg
Plauer See
Müritz
BRANDENBURG
Oder
Wolfsburg
Brandenburg
BERLIN
Frankfurt an der Oder
Braunschweig
Potsdam
Magdeburg
SACHSEN-ANHALT
Dessau
Cottbus
Nordhausen
Halle
Saale
Elbe
Spree
Meissen
Görlitz
Leipzig
Dresden
Erfurt
SACHSEN
Jena
Gera
Chemnitz
Zwickau
CZECH REPUBLIC
Hof
Bayreuth
Weiden
Erlangen
Nürnberg
BAYERN
Regensburg
Ingolstadt
Danube
Landshut
Passau
Augsburg
Inn
München
Rosenheim
Chiemsee
Zugspitze 2962m

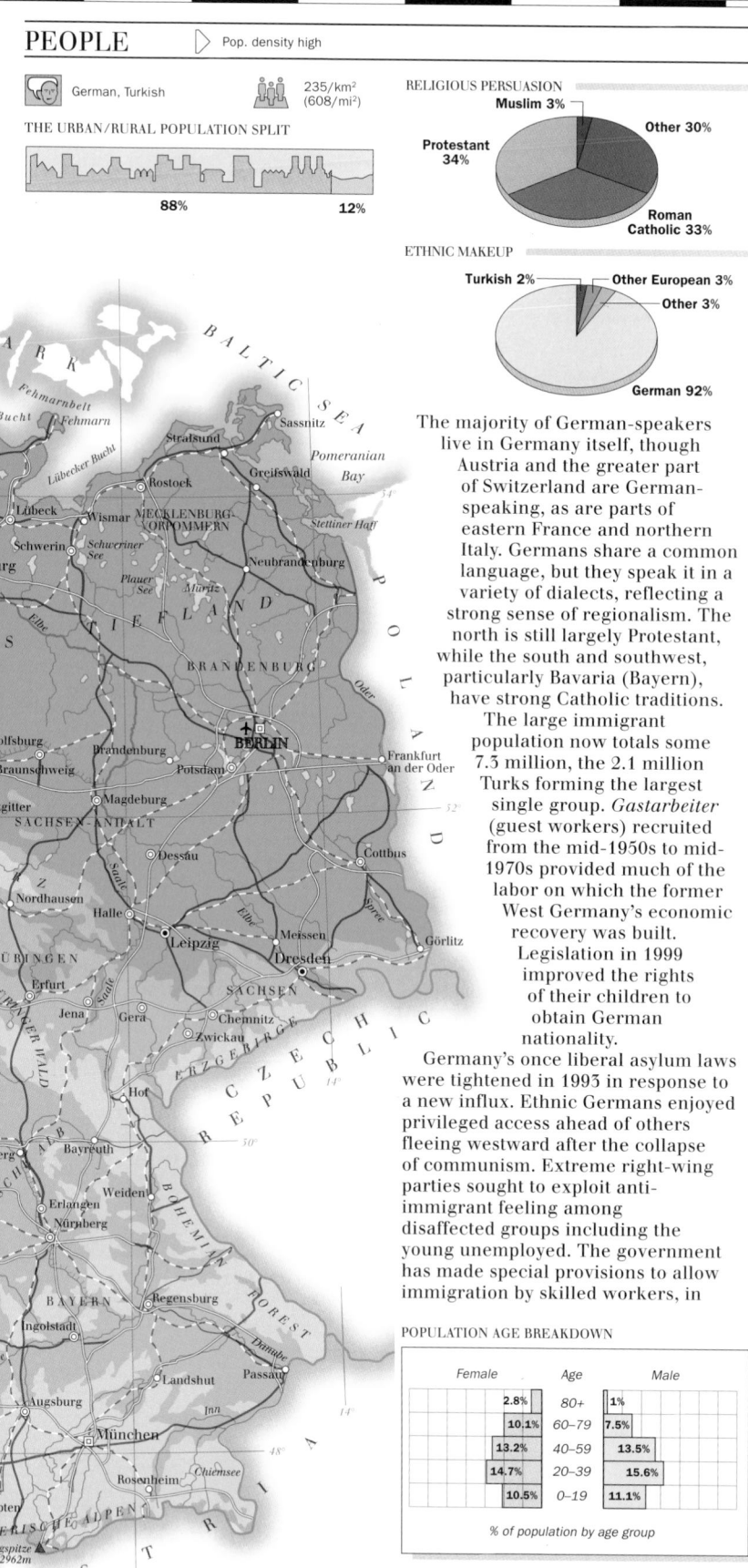

The majority of German-speakers live in Germany itself, though Austria and the greater part of Switzerland are German-speaking, as are parts of eastern France and northern Italy. Germans share a common language, but they speak it in a variety of dialects, reflecting a strong sense of regionalism. The north is still largely Protestant, while the south and southwest, particularly Bavaria (Bayern), have strong Catholic traditions.

The large immigrant population now totals some 7.3 million, the 2.1 million Turks forming the largest single group. *Gastarbeiter* (guest workers) recruited from the mid-1950s to mid-1970s provided much of the labor on which the former West Germany's economic recovery was built. Legislation in 1999 improved the rights of their children to obtain German nationality.

Germany's once liberal asylum laws were tightened in 1993 in response to a new influx. Ethnic Germans enjoyed privileged access ahead of others fleeing westward after the collapse of communism. Extreme right-wing parties sought to exploit anti-immigrant feeling among disaffected groups including the young unemployed. The government has made special provisions to allow immigration by skilled workers, in recognition of the need for specific talents, while concurrently tightening the asylum procedure.

Family ties in Germany are little different from those in the US or the UK. Millions of couples live together in common-law arrangements, though this is frowned on by the Roman Catholic Church. In rural districts, notably in Bavaria (Bayern), more traditional habits are still observed. The birthrate is one of Europe's lowest, and the population would have fallen were it not for the influx of immigrants since the 1950s.

Germany has a tradition of strong feminism. Women have full rights under the law and play a bigger role in politics than in most other European countries. Over 30% of Bundestag (Federal Assembly) members elected in 2002 were women, and women ministers occupy several top cabinet posts. From 2001, women were permitted to take on combat roles in the armed forces. However, they are less well represented in top jobs in business and industry. Abortion remains a charged issue. Women in the former East Germany had the right to abortion on demand, but the Constitutional Court, after strong Catholic lobbying, overruled a relatively liberal 1992 compromise law for the whole country. The current regulations, dating from mid-1995, allow abortions (but only after counseling) within three months of conception.

POPULATION AGE BREAKDOWN

Female
Age
Male
2.8%
80+
1%
10.1%
60–79
7.5%
13.2%
40–59
13.5%
14.7%
20–39
15.6%
10.5%
0–19
11.1%
% of population by age group

G

CHRONOLOGY

German unification in the 19th century brought together a mosaic of states with a common linguistic, but varied cultural, heritage.

- **1815** German Confederation under nominal Austrian leadership.
- **1834** Zollverein Customs Union of 18 states, including Prussia.
- **1862** Otto von Bismarck appointed Prussian chancellor.
- **1864–1870** Prussia defeats Austrians, Danes, and French; north German states under Prussian control.
- **1871** Southern states join Prussian-led unified German Empire under Wilhelm I.
- **1870s** Rapid industrialization.
- **1890** Kaiser Wilhelm II accedes, with aspirations to German world role. Bismarck sacked.
- **1914–1918** World War I.
- **1918** Germany signs armistice; Weimar Republic created.
- **1919** Treaty of Versailles: colonies lost and reparations paid. Rhineland demilitarized.

CHRONOLOGY *continued*

- **1923** France occupies Ruhr; financial collapse, hyperinflation.
- **1933** Hitler chancellor after Nazis elected largest party. One-party rule; rearmament.
- **1935** Nuremberg Laws; official persecution of Jews begins.
- **1936** German entry into Rhineland. Axis alliance with Italy.
- **1938** Annexation of Austria and Sudetenland.
- **1939** Invasion of Poland starts World War II.
- **1940** France, Belgium, Netherlands, and Norway invaded.
- **1941** USSR invaded.
- **1942–1943** Germans defeated by Red Army at Stalingrad.
- **1945** German surrender; Allies control four occupation zones.
- **1949** Germany divided: communist East led by Walter Ulbricht 1951–1971, Erich Honecker 1971–1989; liberal democratic West led by CDU's Konrad Adenauer, first Chancellor, 1949–1963.
- **1955** West Germany joins NATO.
- **1961** Berlin Wall built.
- **1966–1969** West German "grand coalition" of CDU and SPD.
- **1969–1982** SPD-led West German governments under Willy Brandt (1969–1974) and Helmut Schmidt (1974–1982).
- **1973** Both Germanies join UN.
- **1982** Helmut Kohl West German chancellor, CDU–FDP coalition.
- **1989** Fall of Berlin Wall.
- **1990** Reunification of Germany. First all-German elections since 1933; Kohl heads government.
- **1998** Gerhard Schröder heads coalition of SPD and Greens.
- **2000** Disgrace of Kohl in party funding scandal.
- **2001** Historic Berlin city government coalition of SPD and former communist PDS.
- **2002** Euro fully adopted. SPD–Green coalition reelected.

The Messeturm, Frankfurt, is the second-tallest office building in Europe. Frankfurt is Germany's financial services center, and many leading companies are located there.

POLITICS

Multiparty elections

L. House 2002/2006
U. House varying

President
Johannes Rau

AT THE LAST ELECTION

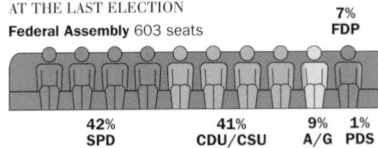

Federal Assembly 603 seats

7% FDP

42% SPD · 41% CDU/CSU · 9% A/G · 1% PDS

SPD = Social Democratic Party of Germany **CDU/CSU** = Christian Democratic Union/Christian Social Union **A/G** = Alliance 90/Greens **FDP** = Free Democratic Party **PDS** = Party of Democratic Socialism

Federal Council 69 seats

Each of the 16 states (*Länder*) is represented by between three and six members in the Federal Council (Bundesrat), who are appointed after the elections in each *Land*

Germany is a federal democratic republic of 16 *Länder* (states). The government is led by the federal chancellor, elected by the Bundestag (Federal Assembly). The president's role is largely ceremonial. The "Basic Law" of West Germany, drawn up in 1948, became the 1990 federal constitution of reunified Germany.

PROFILE

Germany's politics are now strongly democratic, with a long tradition of federative association. Before 1871, Germany was a mass of separate principalities, kingdoms, and city-states, a situation in many ways respected by Bismarck's unification constitution. The 1933–1945 Nazi period, during which the federal system was abolished, was very much a hiatus. The Allies reestablished the federal system in West Germany in 1949; in the east, the *Länder* were restored after reunification in 1990. In many ways, the *Länder* are at the heart of German political life, each with its own elected parliament and largely controlling its finances. By general consensus the system delivers efficient and commercially astute government. There have been few major differences on domestic policy between the postwar ruling coalitions. All parties support the social market economy on which prosperity was built.

Germany has enjoyed stable governments, with coalitions of the center left and center right each holding sway since the "grand coalition" of 1966–1969. In 1998 the electorate chose moderate SPD leader Gerhard Schröder in a vote for change, ousting long-serving CDU chancellor Helmut Kohl. In opposition the CDU was beset by a party-funding scandal. Kohl was disgraced. Edmund Stoiber, leader of the CDU's Bavarian-based sister party, the CSU, challenged Schröder for the chancellorship in September 2002, but he fell short of toppling the "red–green" coalition. However, economic problems, high unemployment, and the "Agenda 2010" package that Schröder introduced in response caused him to lose popularity rapidly thereafter.

MAIN POLITICAL ISSUES

The economy

Recession was a shock to Germany, used to constant growth since the 1950s. Spending was reined in to meet targets for European monetary union in the late 1990s. Unrest ensued as unemployment topped four million. A brief return to growth enabled the SPD to start tackling pension reform, but the economy still dominates the political agenda.

East and west

Most Germans supported reunification after the fall of the Berlin Wall in 1989, but feelings soured as the true costs became clear. Many billions of euros have been spent on reconstruction in the east, financed partly by a "solidarity surcharge" on income tax, but the tenth anniversary of reunification in November 2000 was less a celebration than a reflection on past mistakes. The east remains poorer, and people moving west, still seen as "Ossis," may find it hard to fit in. Support for the former communist PDS is strong in, but confined almost entirely to, the east.

Far-right violence

Unemployment and resentment of "foreigners" led to a rise in support for far-right parties. Foreign workers, particularly Turks, and asylum seekers have been subject to shocking attacks. The problem of racism, even if no worse than in many other European states, is particularly sensitive, given Germany's history.

***Helmut Kohl**, long-serving chancellor until 1998.*

***Gerhard Schröder**, chancellor from 1998, reelected in 2002.*

***Joschka Fischer**, leading Green politician and a popular foreign minister from 1998.*

G

WORLD AFFAIRS

Joined UN in 1973

EU G8 NATO OECD OSCE

During the Cold War, a Germany divided since the end of World War II was inevitably forced to play a subservient role in international affairs. West Germany closely adhered to US interests, while East Germany took its orders directly from the Soviet Union. After reunification in 1990 the emphasis changed, and Germany began to voice a foreign policy which reflects its position as the most powerful country in Europe.

In 2001 Germany was given command of the NATO peacekeeping mission in Macedonia, and German troops were involved in the "war on terrorism" in Afghanistan. Extremely critical of the US-led assault on Iraq in 2003, Germany continues to champion EU enlargement, and, because of large-scale investment, has considerable influence in eastern Europe.

AID

Donor

$4.99bn (donations)

Down 1% in 2001

Unlike the US, the UK, and France, Germany's aid programs are not directly motivated by its desire for political influence in the world's poorer regions. Most are multilateral, though there is also a strong tradition of direct aid. Much comes from church organizations such as the Protestant Brot für die Welt. Many German volunteers and missionaries work overseas on aid programs.

DEFENSE

Compulsory military service

$26.9bn

Down 4% in 2001

The armed forces are being reduced, to focus more on mobility and providing support to allied states. In 1994 the Constitutional Court ruled that military units could participate in collective defense activities abroad, opening the way for Germany to take part in NATO operations; the 1999 action against Serbia was a landmark. In 2002–2003 Germany led the peacekeeping force in Afghanistan.

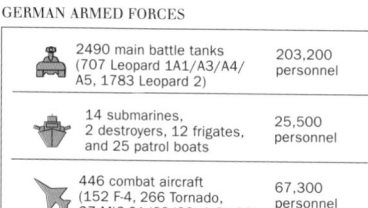

GERMAN ARMED FORCES

2490 main battle tanks (707 Leopard 1A1/A3/A4/A5, 1783 Leopard 2)	203,200 personnel
14 submarines, 2 destroyers, 12 frigates, and 25 patrol boats	25,500 personnel
446 combat aircraft (152 F-4, 266 Tornado, 27 MiG-21/23/29, 1 Su-22)	67,300 personnel
None	

ECONOMICS

Inflation 1.8% p.a. (1990–2001)

$1940bn

0.871 euros (1.013)

SCORE CARD

❑ WORLD GNP RANKING	3rd
❑ GNP PER CAPITA	$23,560
❑ BALANCE OF PAYMENTS	$3.82bn
❑ INFLATION	2.5%
❑ UNEMPLOYMENT	10%

EXPORTS

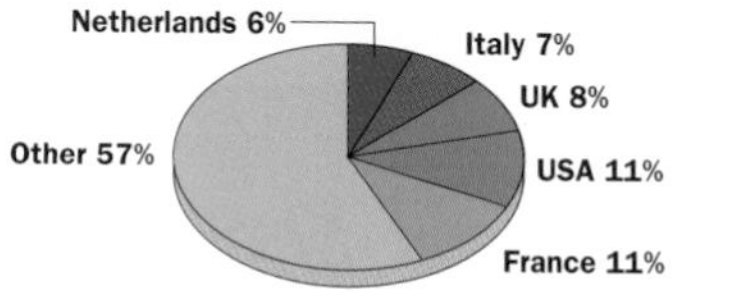

Netherlands 6%
Italy 7%
UK 8%
USA 11%
France 11%
Other 57%

IMPORTS

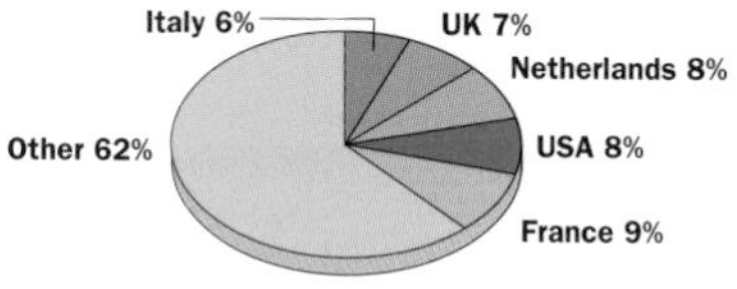

Italy 6%
UK 7%
Netherlands 8%
USA 8%
France 9%
Other 62%

STRENGTHS

Europe's major industrial power. Cars, heavy engineering, electronics, and chemicals. Efficient industry benefits from low inflation. Strong work ethic.

WEAKNESSES

Underestimation of costs of updating inefficient east German economy. High welfare costs and potentially crippling pension obligations (despite reforms in 2001) with an aging population. Rising unemployment. Relatively few small firms, short working week in terms of hours, poorly developed service sector.

ECONOMIC PERFORMANCE INDICATOR

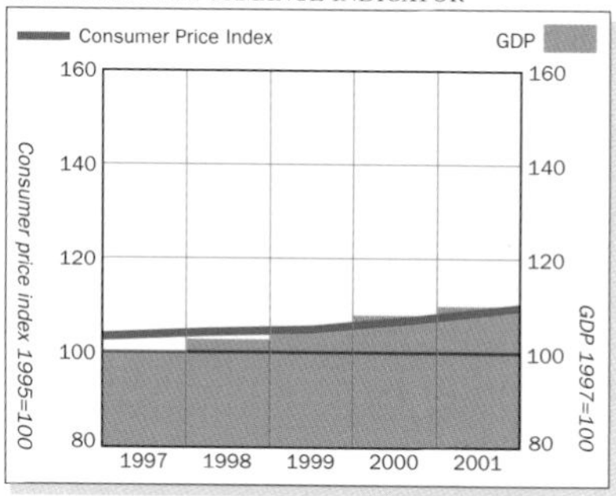

Consumer Price Index
GDP
160
140
120
100
80
1997 1998 1999 2000 2001
Consumer price index 1995=100
GDP 1997=100

PROFILE

West Germany's remarkable postwar recovery, to become the world's third-strongest economy, was based on the concept of a social market economy, under which the state provided welfare and ensured workers' rights, while the economy was largely in private hands. Major banks and businesses are privately owned, except for the partly state-owned Volkswagen. After reunification in 1990, massive investment went into the former East Germany, where state concerns were sold off.

Germany was one of the 12 EU states to adopt the euro in 2002. The SPD-led government elected in 1998 undertook to tackle unemployment and to maintain growth, which reached a ten-year high of 3.1% in 2000. Major tax reforms aimed to balance the budget by 2006. The government received $46 billion from the sale of "third generation" mobile phone operators' licenses in 2001, but global economic slowdown hit employment levels hard. The jobless figure rose again, exceeding four million in late 2002, and in 2003 the EU threatened sanctions over the rising budget deficit. Tax cuts were brought forward in an attempt to boost consumer spending. The economy entered a recession in mid-2003.

GERMANY : MAJOR BUSINESSES

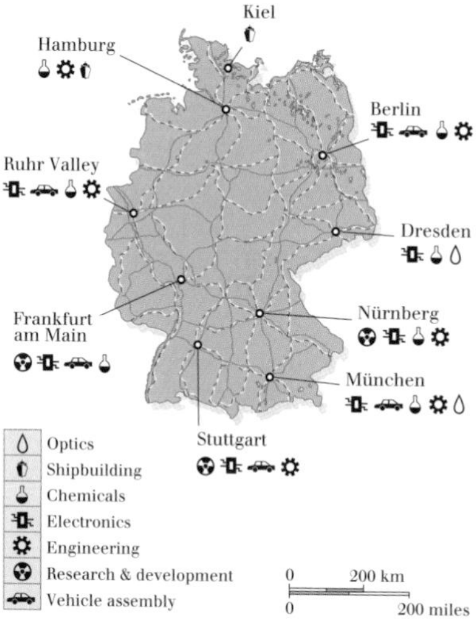

Kiel
Hamburg
Berlin
Ruhr Valley
Dresden
Frankfurt am Main
Nürnberg
München
Stuttgart
Optics
Shipbuilding
Chemicals
Electronics
Engineering
Research & development
Vehicle assembly
0 200 km
0 200 miles

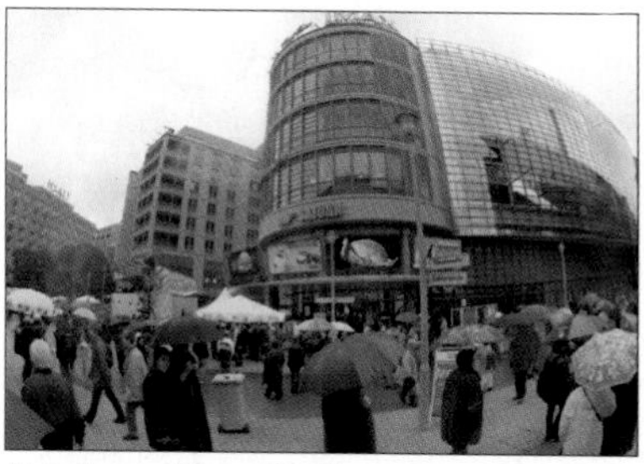

***Potsdamer Platz, Berlin,** was rapidly reconstructed after reunification and is once again the commercial center of the capital.*

G

G

RESOURCES

Electric power 117m kW

265,580 tonnes

55,057 b/d (reserves 201m barrels)

26m pigs, 14.2m cattle, 110m chickens

Coal, oil, natural gas, copper, salt, potash, tin, nickel

ELECTRICITY GENERATION

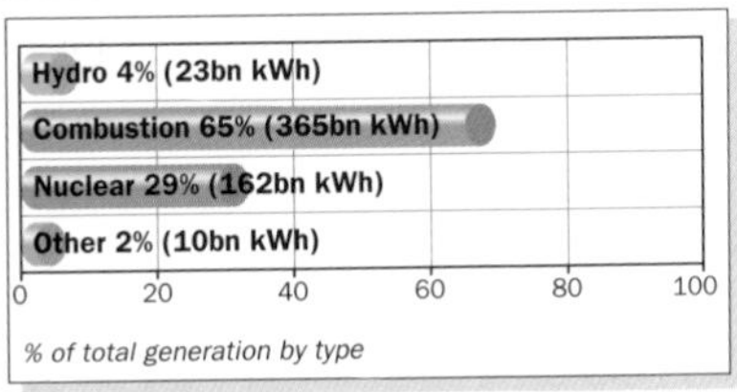
Hydro 4% (23bn kWh)
Combustion 65% (365bn kWh)
Nuclear 29% (162bn kWh)
Other 2% (10bn kWh)
0
20
40
60
80
100
% of total generation by type

With relatively few natural resources, Germany imports over 60% of its energy needs, mainly oil and gas. Coal, the basis of industrialization, now accounts for under a quarter of energy consumption. West Germany invested less heavily than France in nuclear power, and Soviet-built plants in the east have been shut down. The "red–green" coalition government decided in mid-2000 to phase out nuclear power (which provides over 25% of electricity). Renewable resources, particularly wind, account for 4% of primary energy consumption (with a target of 50% by 2050); Germany is the world's leading user of wind power.

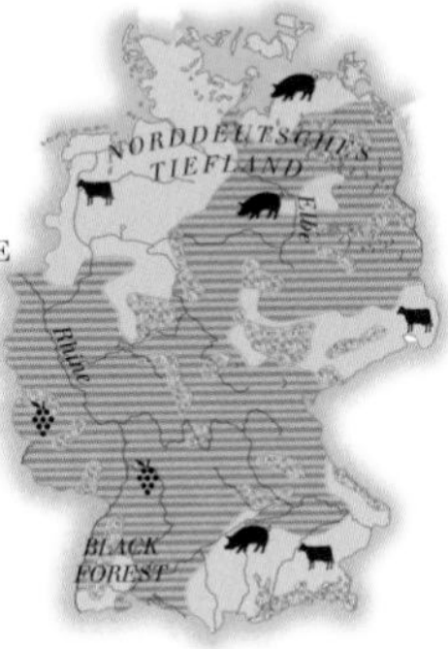
NORDDEUTSCHES TIEFLAND
Elbe
Rhine
BLACK FOREST
GERMANY : LAND USE
Cropland
Forest
Pasture
Vineyards
Pigs
Cattle
0 200 km
0 200 miles

ENVIRONMENT

Sustainability rank: 50th

31% (27% partially protected)

10.4 tonnes per capita

ENVIRONMENTAL TREATIES

Yes Yes Yes

Yes Yes Yes

Germans are among the world's most environmentally conscious people. Campaigns led by the Green Party, which emerged as a powerful political force in the 1980s, have influenced the policies of all major parties. The Greens are a significant force in the Bundestag; they joined the SPD-led federal government coalition in 1998, and are strongly represented in *Land* parliaments and local councils.

Germany has some of the strictest pollution controls in the world, with ambitious targets for reducing carbon dioxide emissions, compelling businesses to become more energy-efficient. Germans recycle around 80% of their waste paper and glass, and three-quarters of their used tires.

The nuclear debate has been vigorously fought and won by the Greens; a gradual program of closing existing nuclear power plants was approved in 2001, though waste disposal is still an issue. Fears in the 1980s that up to 50% of trees were sick or dying because of car fumes and industrial pollution led to Germany becoming the first European country to insist that new cars be fitted with catalytic converters. The east had the highest per capita rate of sulfur emissions in the world, but these have been reduced by the closure of industrial plants and the elimination of the noxious Trabant cars.

MEDIA

TV ownership high

Daily newspaper circulation 300 per 1000 people

PUBLISHING AND BROADCAST MEDIA

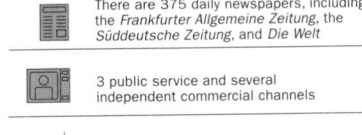

There are 375 daily newspapers, including the *Frankfurter Allgemeine Zeitung*, the *Süddeutsche Zeitung*, and *Die Welt*

3 public service and several independent commercial channels

13 public service and several independent networks

TV is supervised by the political parties to ensure a balance of views. Satellite and cable TV have taken much of the audience once shared between the main public service channels, ARD and ZDF. Media conglomerates such as Bertelsmann are major international players. Newspapers are mostly regional and serious. An exception is *Bild*, a right-wing, sensationalist tabloid, which sells 4.4 million copies daily.

***Neuschwanstein Castle**, Bavaria (Bayern), one of Germany's major tourist attractions. It was built for the eccentric King Ludwig II.*

EDUCATION

School leaving age: 18

99%

2.09m students

THE EDUCATION SYSTEM

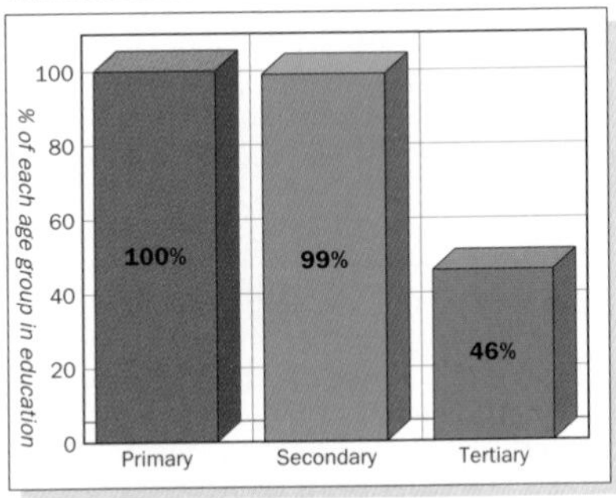
100
80
60
40
20
0
% of each age group in education
100%
99%
46%
Primary
Secondary
Tertiary

Nearly one-tenth of total government expenditure goes on education, which is run by the *Länder*. They coordinate teaching policies, but have autonomy within their borders. The German approach to education stresses academic and vocational achievement. Sporting or cultural activities tend to be organized informally. Nearly all schools have Internet access.

Young people wanting to leave school must continue studying at least part-time until 18. Those who wish to go to university attend the upper-secondary *Gymnasien* to prepare for the *Abitur* exam. Students were taking an average of seven years to complete degrees, until new legislation added shorter bachelor's and master's degrees as in other countries. Research is done as much by major companies as by the universities.

CRIME

No death penalty

78,707 prisoners

Up 3% in 2000–2002

CRIME RATES

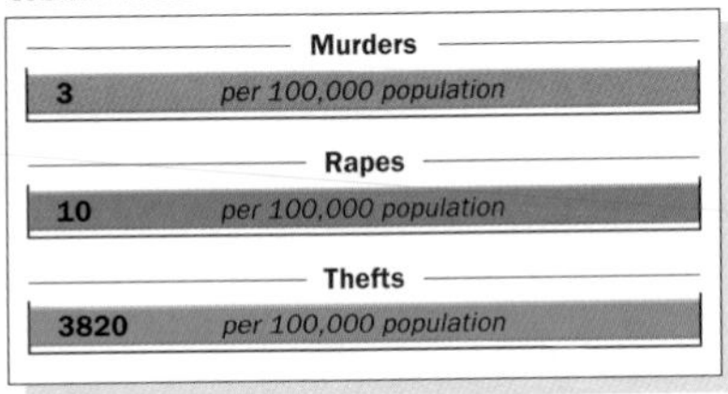
Murders
3 per 100,000 population
Rapes
10 per 100,000 population
Thefts
3820 per 100,000 population

Crime rates in Germany are lower than in most other European countries. This is largely the result of a genuine respect for the law, coupled with a strong police force. Recently, however, higher unemployment has led to an increase in petty theft and a wave of violence, notably against immigrants.

German politicians, once with an enviably clean reputation, have suffered several corruption scandals. Civil service corruption remains rare. People convicted under environmental laws can face ten-year jail sentences.

BERLIN, REUNIFICATION, AND CENTRAL EUROPE

THE SO-CALLED "BONN REPUBLIC," created in West Germany in the postwar period, ended symbolically in September 1999. Bonn could justifiably claim to have been home for some 50 years to Germany's only enduringly successful parliamentary democracy. The decision to move the capital to Berlin, however, symbolizing German unity, was enshrined in the 1990 unification treaty only months after the fall of the Berlin Wall in November 1989. It took time to confirm that both government and parliament would be transferred – the lower house of parliament, the Bundestag, only voted in 1994 to move – but five years after that vote, in the same month that Federal Chancellor Schröder moved into his office in Berlin, the Bundestag held its first full session there.

***The dramatic glass dome** of the new Reichstag building in Berlin.*

PROSPECTS FOR BERLIN

The parliament's new home is the former Reichstag building, impressively redesigned by English architect Norman Foster. Topped with a transparent dome and lit up at night from within, it epitomizes the emphasis on architectural and engineering achievements in modern Berlin. New government, commercial, and tourist facilities have brought a lengthy construction boom in Berlin, which with a population of some 4.2 million is Germany's largest city. The proliferation of cultural and artistic activity has also contributed to a strong sense of excitement, boosting the city's image with the international media and the public. Berlin nevertheless faces many problems, including the threat of bankruptcy, unemployment well above the national average, and the need to revitalize its declining industrial base. The outward movement of business and population, from central urban areas to surrounding regions, has been an established trend for decades in major western German cities, but is happening much more rapidly in Berlin, whose western half was for years an enclave within East Germany. The city also has a long way to go in attracting major companies to make their headquarters there: far fewer of the largest German companies are located in Berlin than in Hamburg, Munich, or Frankfurt.

COSTLY REUNIFICATION

The costs of reconstruction of the former East Germany far outweighed initial expectations. Achievements stand out in telecommunications and rail transportation, but most infrastructure in the east is still well below the standard of the west, despite subsidies amounting to the transfer to the east of some 7% of GDP of western *Länder* per year for a decade. Unemployment is nearly twice as high, labor productivity lower, and living conditions less attractive to the majority of Germans.

GERMANY'S NEW CENTER OF GRAVITY

The transfer of the capital has reinforced the shift in the center of gravity brought about by reunification. Coinciding with the collapse of communism across the whole former Soviet bloc came a revival of interest in Germany's role in central Europe or *Mitteleuropa*. In the former communist countries German economic influence is now particularly strong. West Germany was firmly anchored in western Europe, in economic terms by the European Economic Community (now the EU), and in a political–military sense by its membership of NATO. The imminent eastward expansion of the EU, however, suggests the emergence of France–Germany–Poland as a new and powerful axis in the Europe of the 21st century.

Arbeit!

***Unemployed** Germans demonstrate for the right to work.*

HEALTH

Welfare state health benefits

1 per 282 people

Cancers, heart, cerebrovascular, and respiratory diseases

The German social security system, pioneered by Bismarck, is one of the most comprehensive in the world. Health insurance is compulsory, and employer and employee contributions are high. Though most hospitals are run by the *Länder*, some are still owned by Germany's wealthy churches. Almost one-quarter of health spending is now private.

Germans are increasingly health-conscious, paying great attention to diet. Nearly a million people go on cures every year to the country's 200-plus spas. In the east there is a higher incidence of lung diseases, the legacy of industrial pollution.

SPENDING

GDP/cap. increase

CONSUMPTION AND SPENDING

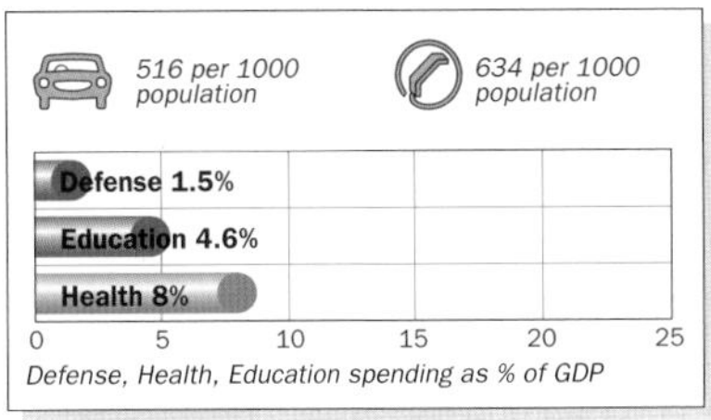
516 per 1000 population
634 per 1000 population
Defense 1.5%
Education 4.6%
Health 8%
0
5
10
15
20
25
Defense, Health, Education spending as % of GDP

The effects of the Nazi period, which discredited many of the ruling class, and the destruction of the property of millions of families in the war, explain the relatively classless nature of society. Status is now more closely linked to wealth than to birth. In the west, there are fewer disparities than in most of Europe; workers are generally well paid and social security is generous. Wages in the east, however, are 10% below western rates, and a disproportionate number of unemployed live on welfare benefit. Most Germans own a mobile phone, and almost a third of them had accessed the Internet by 2001.

WORLD RANKING

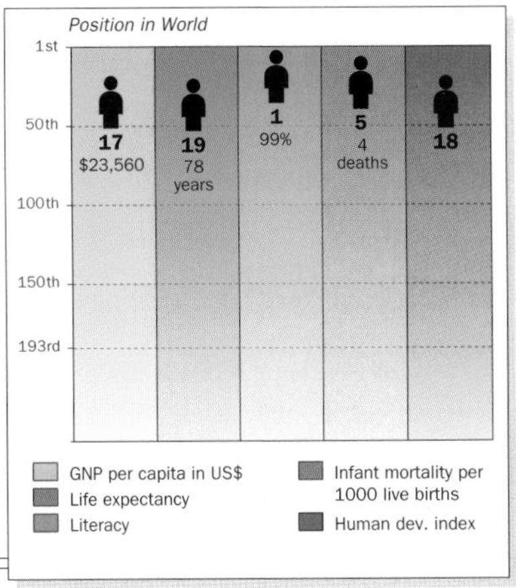
Position in World
1st
50th
100th
150th
193rd
17
$23,560
19
78
years
1
99%
5
4
deaths
18
GNP per capita in US$
Life expectancy
Literacy
Infant mortality per 1000 live births
Human dev. index

G

GHANA

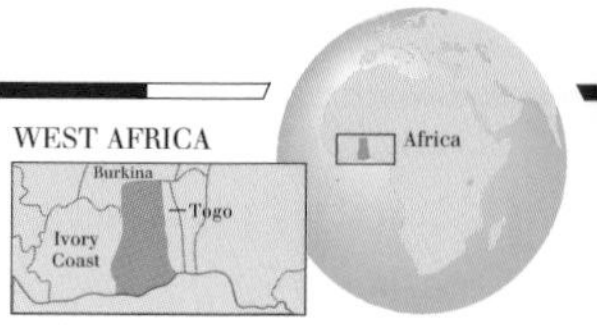
WEST AFRICA
Burkina
Togo
Ivory Coast
Africa

OFFICIAL NAME: Republic of Ghana **CAPITAL:** Accra
POPULATION: 20.2 million **CURRENCY:** Cedi **OFFICIAL LANGUAGE:** English

1957 | 1957 | March 6 | GH | 0 | +233 | .gh

THE HEARTLAND OF THE ancient Ashanti kingdom, modern Ghana is a union of the former British colony of the Gold Coast and the British-administered part of the UN Trust Territory of Togoland. Ghana gained independence in 1957, the first west African colony to do so. Multiparty democracy was embraced in 1992, and the handover of power to the main opposition party in 2000 confirmed the shift from a recent history of intermittent military rule.

CLIMATE

Tropical wet and dry/ equatorial

WEATHER CHART FOR ACCRA

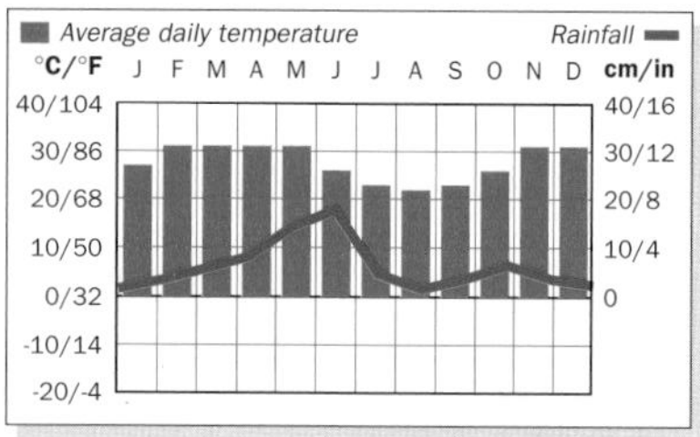
Average daily temperature
Rainfall
°C/°F J F M A M J J A S O N D cm/in
40/104
30/86
20/68
10/50
0/32
-10/14
-20/-4
40/16
30/12
20/8
10/4
0

Southern Ghana has two rainy seasons: from April to July and September to November. The drier north has just one, from April to September.

TRANSPORTATION

Drive on right

Kotoka International, Accra
702,281 passengers

212 ships
123,100 grt

THE TRANSPORTATION NETWORK

9346 km (5807 miles)
30 km (19 miles)
953 km (592 miles)
1293 km (803 miles)

In 1983, work began to restore Ghana's roads, which had fallen into disrepair in the 1960s and 1970s; the network is now improving.

TOURISM

Visitors : Population 1:46

439,000 visitors

Up 18% in 2000–2001

MAIN TOURIST ARRIVALS

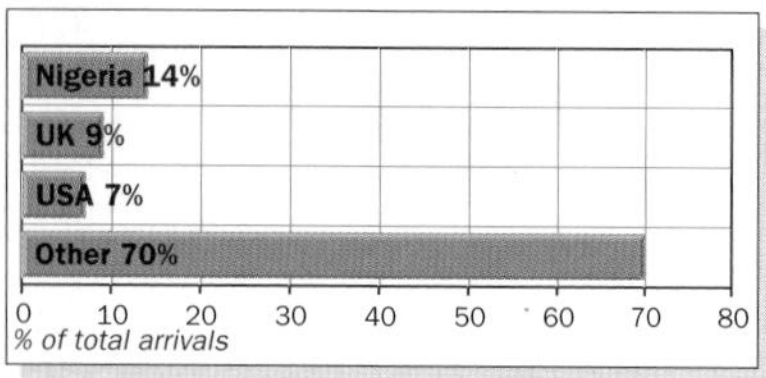
Nigeria 14%
UK 9%
USA 7%
Other 70%
0 10 20 30 40 50 60 70 80
% of total arrivals

Tourism is still small-scale; most visitors come from the rest of Africa, the UK, and the US. Good beaches and old coastal forts are major attractions.

PEOPLE

Pop. density medium

Twi, Fanti, Ewe, Ga, Adangbe, Gurma, Dagomba (Dagbani)

88/km² (227/mi²)

THE URBAN/RURAL POPULATION SPLIT

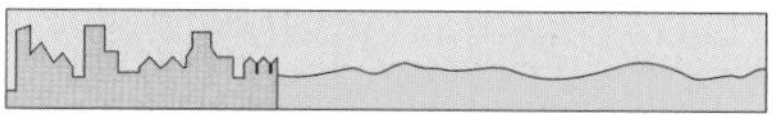
36%
64%

RELIGIOUS PERSUASION

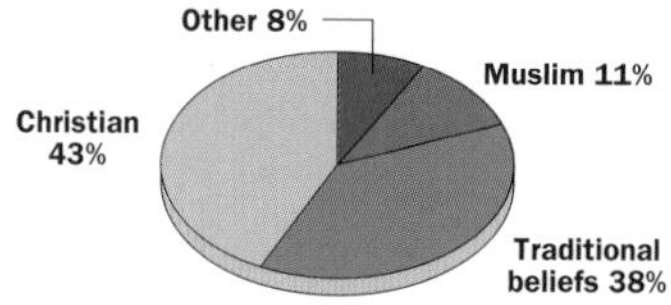
Other 8%
Muslim 11%
Christian 43%
Traditional beliefs 38%

The largest ethnic group is the coastal Akan, who include the Ashanti and Fanti peoples. Other important groups are the Mole-Dagbani in the north, Ga-Adangbe around Accra, and Ewe in the southeast. Though the north is less developed than the south, ethnic tensions are relatively rare.

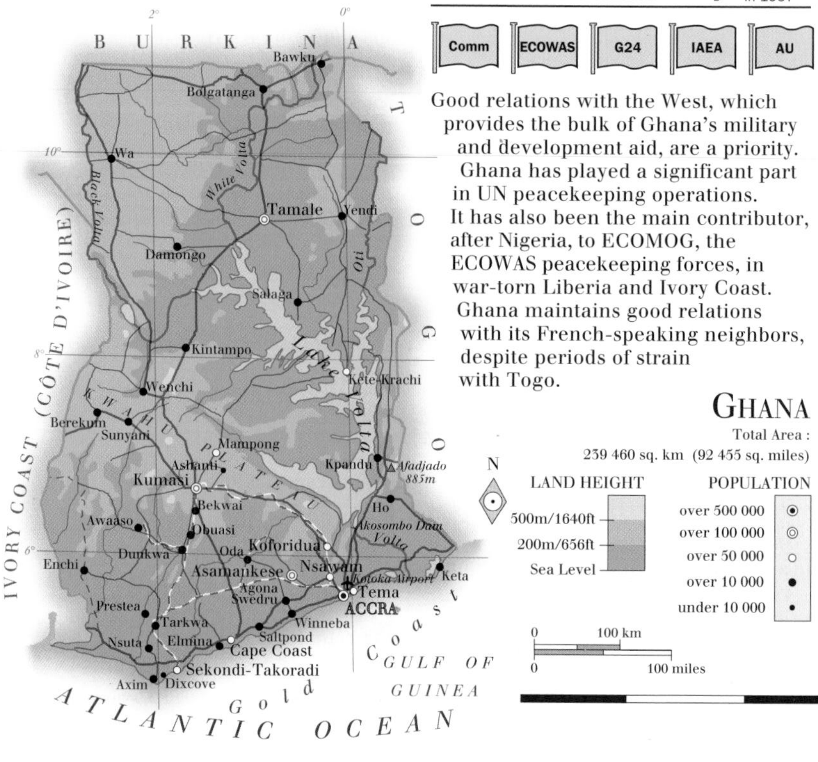
BURKINA
TOGO
IVORY COAST (CÔTE D'IVOIRE)
Bawku
Bolgatanga
Wa
Black Volta
White Volta
Tamale
Yendi
Oti
Damongo
Salaga
Kintampo
Lake Volta
Kete-Krachi
Wenchi
Berekum
Sunyani
KWAHU PLATEAU
Mampong
Ashanti
Kumasi
Kpandu
Afadjado 885m
Bekwai
Awaaso
Obuasi
Ho
Akosombo Dam
Volta
Dunkwa
Oda
Koforidua
Enchi
Asamankese
Nsawam
Kotoka Airport
Keta
Agona Swedru
Tema
ACCRA
Prestea
Tarkwa
Winneba
Nsuta
Elmina
Saltpond
Cape Coast
Sekondi-Takoradi
Axim
Dixcove
Gold Coast
GULF OF GUINEA
ATLANTIC OCEAN
GHANA
Total Area : 239 460 sq. km (92 455 sq. miles)
LAND HEIGHT
500m/1640ft
200m/656ft
Sea Level
POPULATION
over 500 000
over 100 000
over 50 000
over 10 000
under 10 000
0 100 km
0 100 miles

POLITICS

Multiparty elections

2000/2004

President John Kufuor

AT THE LAST ELECTION

Parliament 200 seats

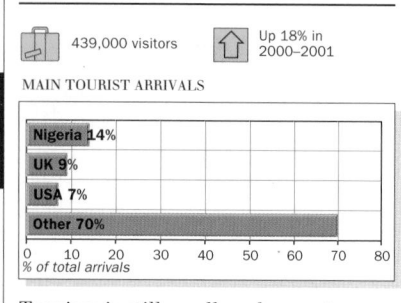

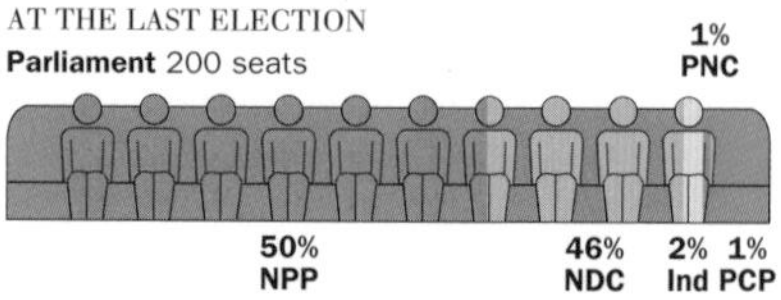
1% PNC
50% NPP
46% NDC
2% Ind
1% PCP

NPP = New Patriotic Party **NDC** = National Democratic Congress **Ind** = Independents **PNC** = People's National Convention **PCP** = People's Convention Party

Ghana's return to multiparty rule in 1992 marked the legitimization of the military government of Jerry Rawlings. An air force flight-lieutenant of Ewe–Scottish descent and one of the great survivors of African politics, Rawlings staged coups in 1979 and 1981, and led the 1981–1992 Provisional National Defense Council (PNDC) military government. As the NDC candidate, Rawlings won 58% of the vote in the 1992 presidential election. Opposition parties boycotted the following parliamentary elections, which the NDC won easily. Elections in 1996 gave Rawlings a further and final term of office. In December 2000 the opposition NPP gained a historic victory when it stripped the NDC of its parliamentary majority and NPP candidate John Kufuor won the presidency.

WORLD AFFAIRS

Joined UN in 1957

Comm | ECOWAS | G24 | IAEA | AU

Good relations with the West, which provides the bulk of Ghana's military and development aid, are a priority. Ghana has played a significant part in UN peacekeeping operations. It has also been the main contributor, after Nigeria, to ECOMOG, the ECOWAS peacekeeping forces, in war-torn Liberia and Ivory Coast. Ghana maintains good relations with its French-speaking neighbors, despite periods of strain with Togo.

AID

Recipient

$652m (receipts) | Up 7% in 2001

Ghana receives most of its aid from the World Bank, which has supported a largely successful economic recovery program which began in 1983. Aid is now channeled to antipoverty programs. The most recent World Bank/IMF debt relief program started in 2001.

DEFENSE

No compulsory military service

$34m | Down 15% in 2001

In 1966, 1972, 1979, and 1981, the military mounted successful coups, and there have also been several unsuccessful coups. Outside Ghana, the 5000-strong army has been deployed mainly in UN and ECOWAS operations. Ghana's navy is small, with four patrol boats. The air force has 19 combat aircraft.

ECONOMICS

Inflation 27% p.a. (1990–2001)

$5.75bn | 8675 cedis (7923)

SCORE CARD

❑ WORLD GNP RANKING	108th
❑ GNP PER CAPITA	$290
❑ BALANCE OF PAYMENTS	–$251m
❑ INFLATION	32.9%
❑ UNEMPLOYMENT	20%

STRENGTHS

Relatively well-developed industrial base. Second-largest gold producer in Africa – Ashanti Goldfields Company: multinational active in 12 African countries. Cocoa production accounts for around 14% of world total. Steady economic growth during 1990s.

WEAKNESSES

High budget deficits and debt repayments; the cedi has generally declined in value since devaluation in 1983. Foreign investment largely restricted to gold mining. High inflation levels. Underdevelopment in north. High unemployment.

EXPORTS

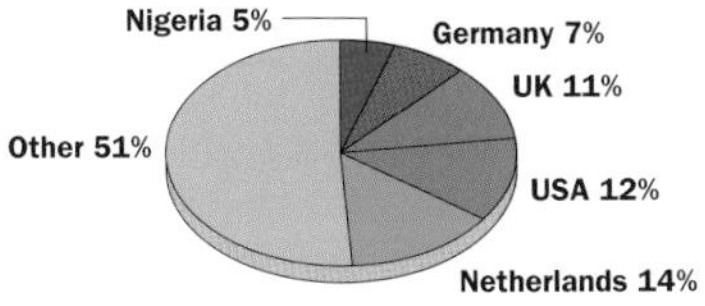
Nigeria 5%
Germany 7%
UK 11%
Other 51%
USA 12%
Netherlands 14%

IMPORTS

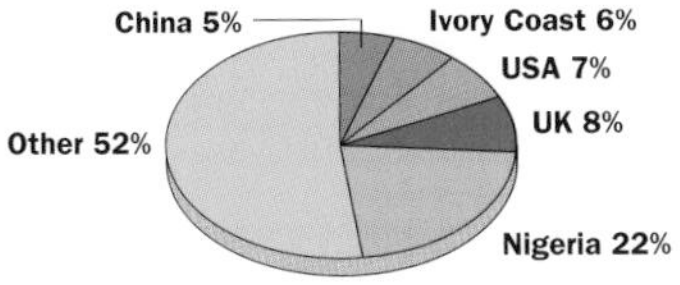
China 5%
Ivory Coast 6%
USA 7%
UK 8%
Other 52%
Nigeria 22%

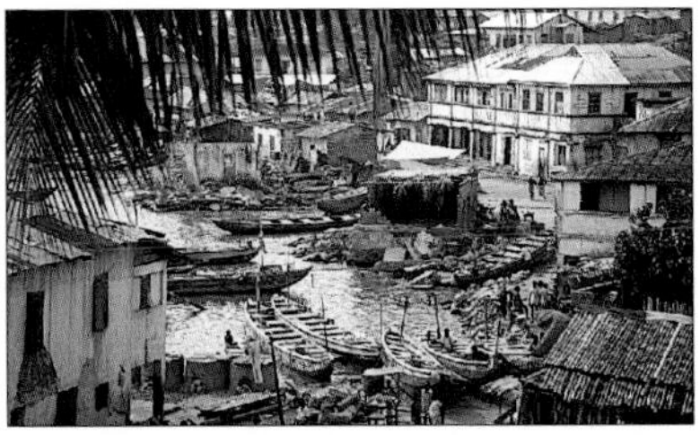

Dixcove harbor, close to Ghana's most southerly cape. The majority of Ghanaians lead a traditional subsistence existence.

RESOURCES

Electric power 1.2m kW

452,581 tonnes | 180 b/d (reserves 15m barrels)

3.41m goats, 2.97m sheep, 1.43m cattle, 22m chickens | Gold, diamonds, bauxite, manganese

Gold production has expanded strongly since the mid-1980s; by 1993, gold had overtaken cocoa as the major export. Diamonds, bauxite, and manganese are also exported. Hydropower from the Volta Dam is exported to Togo and Benin, but is hit by periodic droughts.

ENVIRONMENT

Sustainability rank: 65th

6% (0.7% partially protected) | 0.3 tonnes per capita

Cutting wood for fuel, timber, and farming has destroyed 70% of forests since 1981. Devastation caused by mining is now being tackled under a World Bank project.

MEDIA

TV ownership medium

Daily newspaper circulation 14 per 1000 people

PUBLISHING AND BROADCAST MEDIA

There are 2 daily newspapers, the *Ghanaian Times* and the *Daily Graphic*

1 state-controlled service | 1 state-controlled service

New independent weeklies reflect the increase in private press ownership. Radio and TV tend to follow government reporting guidelines.

CRIME

Death penalty in use

11,624 prisoners | Up 61% in 2000–2001

The judiciary has little independence and the government often resorts to ad hoc "people's tribunals." Corruption is now less of a problem.

EDUCATION

School leaving age: 14

73% | 64,098 students

The "Vision 2020" program aims to improve access to education and to redress existing gender imbalances. There are five universities.

CHRONOLOGY

In 1874 Kumasi, capital of the Ashanti kingdom, was sacked by a British force to create the Gold Coast colony.

- ❑ **1957** Independence under Kwame Nkrumah.
- ❑ **1964** Single-party state.
- ❑ **1966** Army coup.
- ❑ **1972–1979** "Kleptocracy" of Gen. Acheampong. Executed 1979.
- ❑ **1979** Flt. Lt. Jerry Rawlings leads coup. Civilian Hilla Limann wins elections.
- ❑ **1981** Rawlings takes power again.
- ❑ **1992, 1996** Rawlings and NDC win multiparty elections.
- ❑ **2000** Opposition NPP wins elections; John Kufuor wins presidency.

G

HEALTH

No welfare state health benefits

1 per 16,667 people | Malaria, diarrheal diseases, tuberculosis

The health of most of the population has benefited more from improvements in public hygiene than those in medical care. Private health care is available.

SPENDING

GDP/cap. increase

CONSUMPTION AND SPENDING

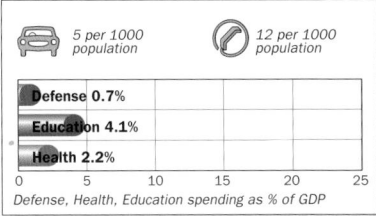

5 per 1000 population | *12 per 1000 population*

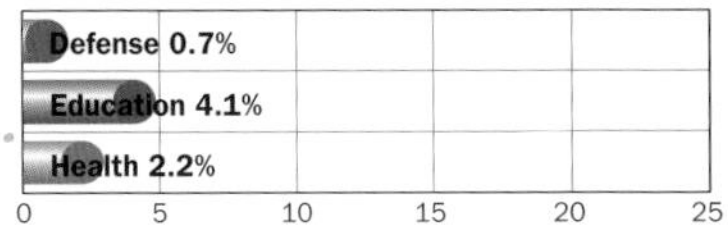
Defense 0.7%
Education 4.1%
Health 2.2%
0
5
10
15
20
25

Defense, Health, Education spending as % of GDP

Political uncertainty brought few opportunities for advancement, and many Ghanaians emigrated, but the situation is now improving. The main economic disparity is still between the poorer rural north and the richer, more urban, south.

WORLD RANKING

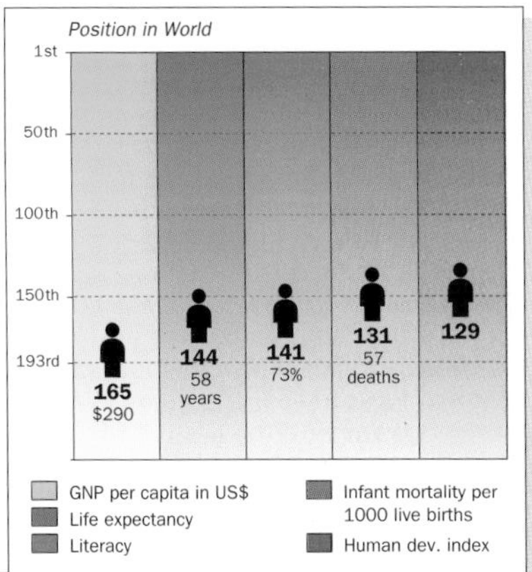
Position in World
1st
50th
100th
150th
193rd
165
$290
144
58 years
141
73%
131
57 deaths
129
GNP per capita in US$
Life expectancy
Literacy
Infant mortality per 1000 live births
Human dev. index

GREECE

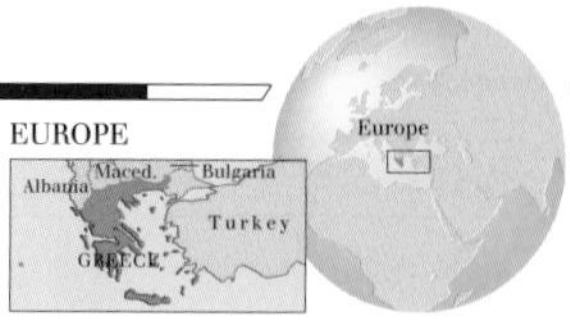
EUROPE
Maced.
Bulgaria
Albania
Turkey
GREECE
Europe

OFFICIAL NAME: Hellenic Republic **CAPITAL:** Athens
POPULATION: 10.6 million **CURRENCY:** Euro **OFFICIAL LANGUAGE:** Greek

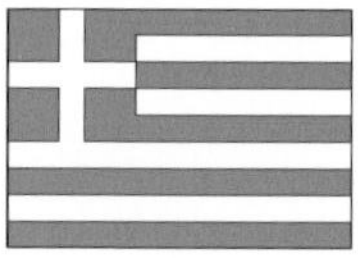

1829 | 1947 | March 25 | GR | +2 | +30 | .gr

THE SOUTHERNMOST COUNTRY of the Balkans, Greece is embraced by the Aegean, Ionian, and Cretan Seas. Its mainly mountainous territory includes more than 2000 islands. Only one-third of the land is cultivated. There is a strong seafaring tradition, and some of the world's biggest shipowners are Greek. Greece is rich in minerals – including chromium, whose occurrence is rare. Relations with Turkey, marked by conflict and territorial disputes, have improved in recent years. To the north, however, upheavals in Albania and the conflicts in former Yugoslavia have made for greater instability.

G

CLIMATE

Mediterranean

WEATHER CHART FOR ATHENS

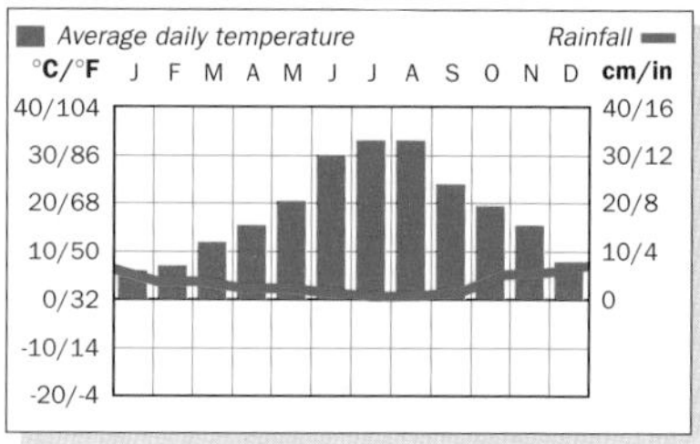
Average daily temperature
Rainfall
°C/°F J F M A M J J A S O N D cm/in
40/104
30/86
20/68
10/50
0/32
-10/14
-20/-4
40/16
30/12
20/8
10/4
0

The climate varies from region to region. The northwest is alpine, while parts of Crete border on the subtropical. The large central plain experiences high summer temperatures. Water is a problem, particularly on the many barren Aegean islands.

TRANSPORTATION

Drive on right

Athinai, Athens
11.8m passengers

1529 ships
28.7m grt

THE TRANSPORTATION NETWORK

107,406 km (66,739 miles)

470 km (292 miles)

2299 km (1429 miles)

80 km (50 miles)

The easiest and cheapest method of transportation between the islands and the mainland is by boat or hovercraft. A major ferry disaster in 2000 prompted government moves to improve standards. Greece has 444 ports, of which Piraeus is the main one, and 123 are large enough to handle passenger or freight traffic. A new airport at Spata, 30 km east of Athens, opened in 2001. Greece has a good, if increasingly congested, road network. Expressway routes have been upgraded and two lines have been added to the Athens metro with the help of EU funds. An interurban bus system and a fleet of air-conditioned tourist Pullmans offer an extensive service.

TOURISM

Visitors : Population 1.2:1

13.1m visitors

Up 3% in 2000

MAIN TOURIST ARRIVALS

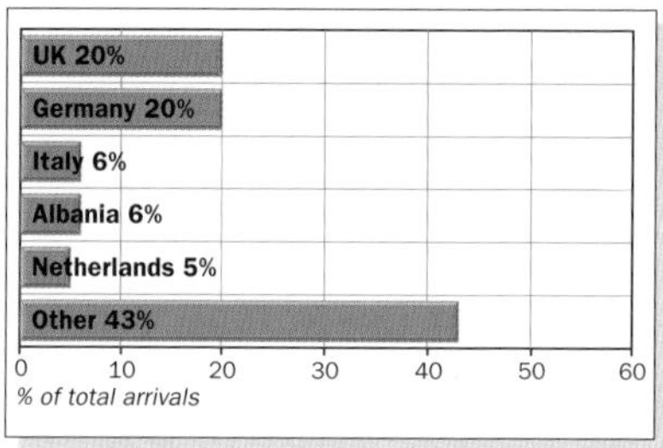
UK 20%
Germany 20%
Italy 6%
Albania 6%
Netherlands 5%
Other 43%
0 10 20 30 40 50 60
% of total arrivals

Tourism is a mainstay of the Greek economy, with an annual turnover of some $10 billion, and is a major source of foreign exchange. Until recently, the state gave grants for hotel development and many third-grade hotels were built, especially on Crete and Rhodes. Smaller islands often lack sufficient water supplies or sandy beaches. To offset falling visitor numbers in the mid-1990s the industry has been encouraged to move upmarket, and is also promoting year-round activity vacations and conference tourism. The 2004 Olympics, to be held in Athens, are a stimulus to upgrade the city's facilities. A museum is planned to house the Parthenon Marbles, currently held in the British Museum (UK).

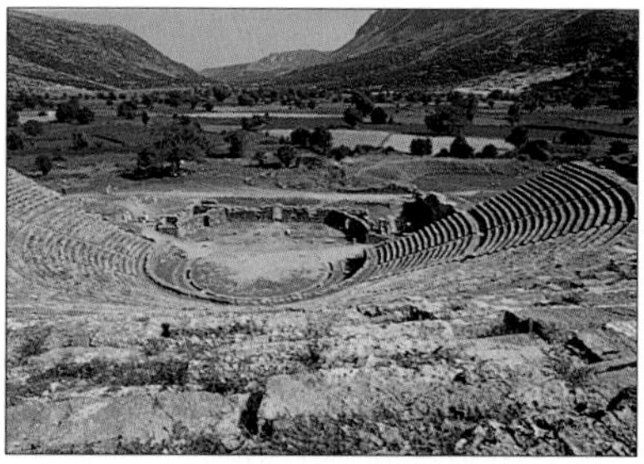

The theater at Dodona. *Classical sites, such as this theater in northwestern Greece, have helped to make tourism one of the country's most important industries.*

PEOPLE

Pop. density medium

Greek, Turkish, Macedonian, Albanian

81/km² (210/mi²)

THE URBAN/RURAL POPULATION SPLIT

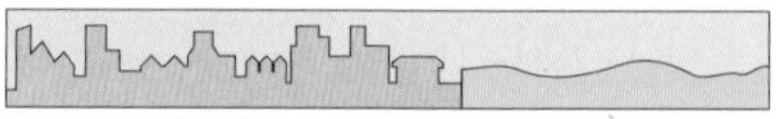
60%
40%

RELIGIOUS PERSUASION

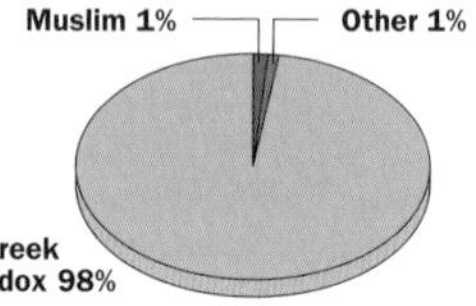
Muslim 1%
Other 1%
Greek Orthodox 98%

ETHNIC MAKEUP

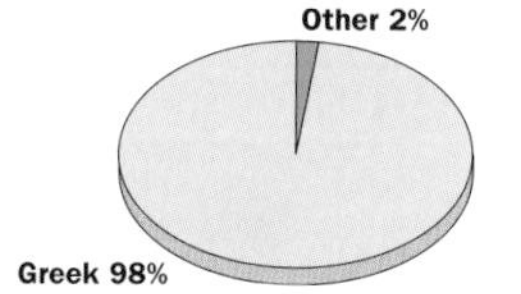
Other 2%
Greek 98%

The Greeks were for many centuries a largely agrarian and seafaring nation. The German occupation during World War II, and the civil war that followed, destroyed much of the fabric of rural life and there was rapid urbanization after the 1950s. There was also extensive emigration in the 1950s and 1960s to northern Europe, Australia, the US, Canada, and southern Africa. However, many people returned to Greece in the 1980s, putting pressure on the labor market. The socialist PASOK governments of 1981–1989 spent large sums, mostly from EU sources, on developing the infrastructure and business life of the rural regions with a view to halting migration to the cities. The policy was partly successful, but a majority still lives in or near the capital, Athens, and Thessaloníki in the north.

Some 98% of the population belong to the Greek Orthodox Church. Civil marriage and divorce only became legal in 1982. There are minorities of Muslims, Roman Catholics, and Jews, and a recent influx of illegal immigrants, mainly from Albania.

POPULATION AGE BREAKDOWN

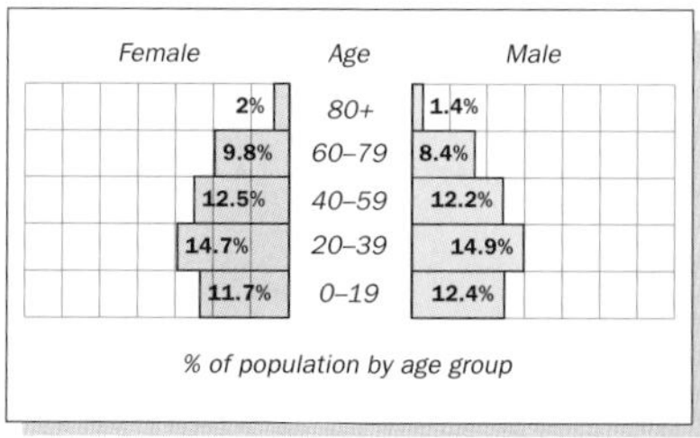
Female
Age
Male
2%
80+
1.4%
9.8%
60–79
8.4%
12.5%
40–59
12.2%
14.7%
20–39
14.9%
11.7%
0–19
12.4%
% of population by age group

POLITICS

Multiparty elections

2000/2004 President Costas Stephanopoulos

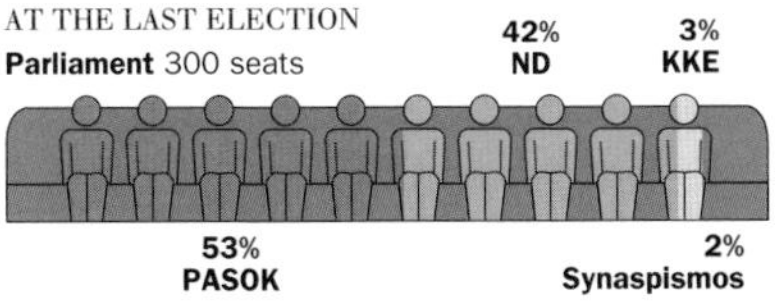

AT THE LAST ELECTION
Parliament 300 seats
42% ND
3% KKE
53% PASOK
2% Synaspismos

PASOK = Pan-Hellenic Socialist Movement
ND = New Democracy **KKE** = Communist Party of Greece
Synaspismos = Left Coalition

Greece is a multiparty democracy. A military regime held power in 1967–1974.

PROFILE

On PASOK's election victory in 1981 its founder Andreas Papandreou headed Greece's first socialist government, which remained in power until 1989. Since 1993, PASOK has held power continuously, but its economic policies have differed little from the previous conservative government; it only narrowly won the 2000 election. Kostas Simitis has led the party since Papandreou's resignation and death in 1996.

MAIN POLITICAL ISSUES

Closer European union

Greece joined the eurozone in 2001, but only after stringent austerity policies, which evoked widespread protests. Greece is in favor of EU enlargement, and backed EU membership for Cyprus, to the annoyance of Turkey. Currently the poorest EU country, Greece could lose funding to new members.

Relations with FYRM

In 1995, Greece, with a northern province also named Macedonia, finally agreed to recognize the sovereignty of the Former Yugoslav Republic of Macedonia. The crisis in that country in 2001 over ethnic Albanian separatism increased Greek concerns over regional security.

Albanian refugees

Thousands of Albanians of Greek descent entered Greece illegally after 1990. Willing to work for very low wages, they swelled the thriving black economy. A legalization program was implemented in 1998, resulting in the registration of 375,000 Albanians.

Kostas Simitis, *prime minister since January 1996.*

President Costas Stephanopoulos, *elected with right- and left-wing support.*

G

WORLD AFFAIRS

Joined UN in 1945

EU NATO OECD OSCE CE

Though part of the Western alliance, Greece has sympathies with Russians and Serbs, who share its Orthodox heritage. Cyprus remains a sore point in Greece's otherwise improving ties with Turkey. Friction with Macedonia over the use of the name "Macedonia" (also the name of a province in Greece) has eased, but relations remain tense. The current priority is Greece's role within an expanding EU. Greece held the EU presidency in the first half of 2003, when deep EU divisions over Iraq remained unresolved.

AID

Donor

$202m (donations) Down 11% in 2001

Greece's contribution to overseas development aid is the lowest per capita among major donors. However, Greek companies have invested elsewhere in the southern Balkans, and increasingly in Turkey since 1999.

Greece receives regional development assistance from the EU, especially from the EU's structural and cohesion funds, its share of which was estimated to amount to around $3.5 billion over the period 1994–1999. Some of the money was used to reverse the decline of northeast Greece – then the EU's least developed region.

Emergency humanitarian aid was given to Turkey following the severe earthquake there in 1999.

GREECE

Total Area : 131 940 sq. km (50 942 sq. miles)

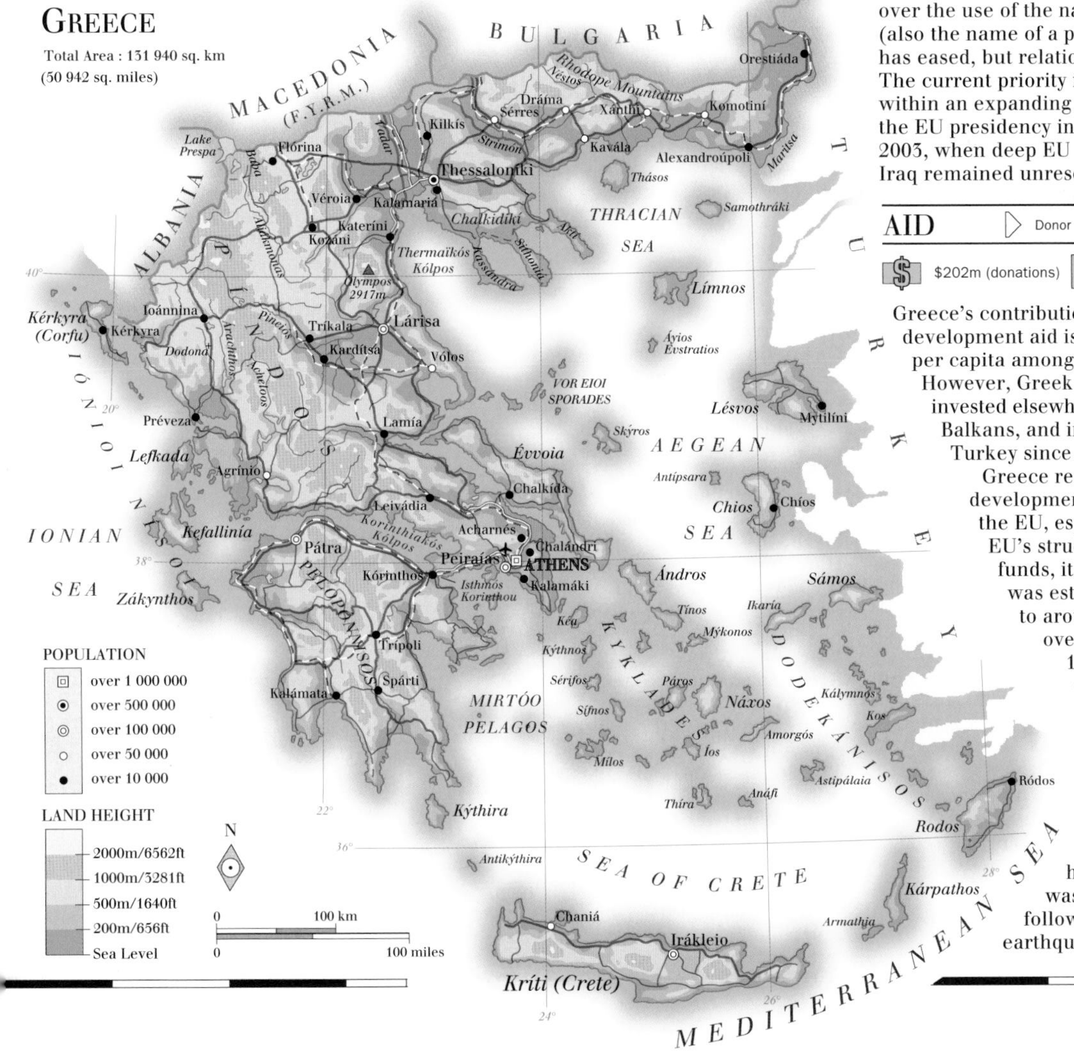

BULGARIA
MACEDONIA (F.Y.R.M.)
ALBANIA
TURKEY
THRACIAN SEA
AEGEAN SEA
IONIAN SEA
SEA OF CRETE
MIRTÓO PELAGOS
MEDITERRANEAN SEA
Thessaloníki
ATHENS
Peiraiás
Pátra
Lárisa
Irákleio
Vólos
Ioánnina
Kérkyra (Corfu)
Kríti (Crete)
Ródos
Límnos
Lésvos
Chíos
Sámos
Náxos
Kýthira
Kefallinía
Zákynthos
Lefkada
Évvoia
Olympos 2917m
POPULATION
over 1 000 000
over 500 000
over 100 000
over 50 000
over 10 000
LAND HEIGHT
2000m/6562ft
1000m/3281ft
500m/1640ft
200m/656ft
Sea Level
N
100 km
100 miles

G

CHRONOLOGY

Greece was occupied by Nazi Germany between 1941 and 1944. After liberation by the Allies, communists and royalists fought a five-year civil war. This ended with communist defeat, and King Paul became the constitutional monarch.

- ❑ **1964** King Constantine succeeds his father, King Paul.
- ❑ **1967** Military coup. King in exile. Col. Giorgios Papadopoulos premier.
- ❑ **1973** Greece declared a republic, with Papadopoulos as president. Papadopoulos overthrown in military coup. Lt. Gen. Ghizikis becomes president, Adamantios Androutsopoulos prime minister.
- ❑ **1974** Greece leaves NATO in protest at Turkish occupation of northern Cyprus. "Colonels' regime" falls. Constantinos Karamanlis becomes premier and his ND party wins subsequent elections.
- ❑ **1975** Konstantinos Tsatsou becomes president.
- ❑ **1977** Elections: ND reelected.
- ❑ **1980** Karamanlis president. Georgios Rallis prime minister. Greece rejoins NATO.
- ❑ **1981** PASOK wins elections. Andreas Papandreou first socialist premier. Greece joins European Communities.
- ❑ **1985** Proposals to limit power of president. Karamanlis resigns. Christos Sartzetakis president. Greece and Albania reopen borders, closed since 1940.
- ❑ **1985–1989** Civil unrest caused by economic austerity program.
- ❑ **1988** Cabinet implicated in financial scandal. Leading members resign.
- ❑ **1989** Defense agreement with US. Two inconclusive elections lead to formation of all-party coalition.
- ❑ **1990** Coalition government collapses. ND wins elections. Konstantinos Mitsotakis prime minister, Karamanlis president.
- ❑ **1990–1992** Strikes against economic reform.
- ❑ **1992** EU persuaded not to recognize independent Macedonia.
- ❑ **1993** PASOK wins election, Andreas Papandreou premier.
- ❑ **1995** Costas Stephanopoulos elected president; recognition of sovereignty of Former Yugoslav Republic of Macedonia (FYRM).
- ❑ **1996** Andreas Papandreou resigns as prime minister; succeeded by Kostas Simitis.
- ❑ **1999** Earthquakes in Greece and Turkey. Sympathetic response shows improvement in relations.
- ❑ **2000** PASOK wins general election.
- ❑ **2001** Armed conflict in FYRM.
- ❑ **2002** Euro fully adopted.

DEFENSE

Compulsory military service

$5.52bn

No change in 2001

Greece spends a higher percentage of GDP on defense than any other NATO country except Turkey, whose perceived threat is its main concern, though tensions with that country are now less acute. In 1998 a law was passed on the conscription of women (for four days a year) for the defense of border regions. Greece has committed 3500 troops to the planned European rapid response force.

GREEK ARMED FORCES

1735 main battle tanks (695 M-48, 628 M-60, 412 Leopard 1)	114,000 personnel
8 submarines, 2 destroyers, 12 frigates, and 40 patrol boats	19,000 personnel
418 combat aircraft (A-7, F-5, F-4E, F-16, Mirage F-1, Mirage 2000)	33,000 personnel
None	

ECONOMICS

Inflation 8.5% p.a. (1990–2001)

$121bn

0.871 euros (1.013)

SCORE CARD

❑ World GNP Ranking	31st
❑ GNP per Capita	$11,430
❑ Balance of Payments	–$9.4bn
❑ Inflation	3.4%
❑ Unemployment	10%

EXPORTS

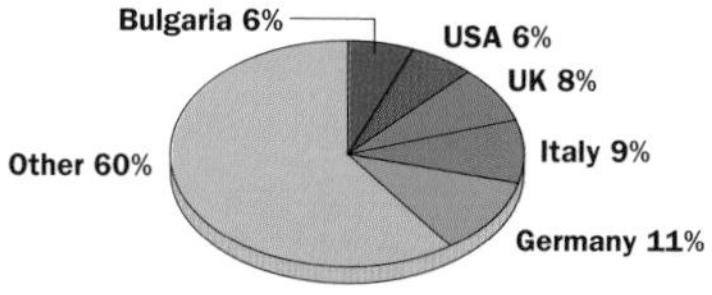
Bulgaria 6%
USA 6%
UK 8%
Italy 9%
Germany 11%
Other 60%

IMPORTS

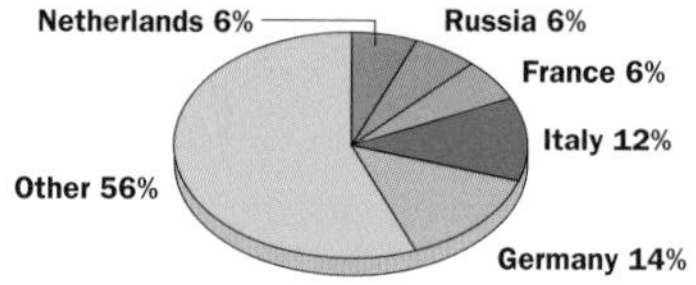
Netherlands 6%
Russia 6%
France 6%
Italy 12%
Germany 14%
Other 56%

ECONOMIC PERFORMANCE INDICATOR

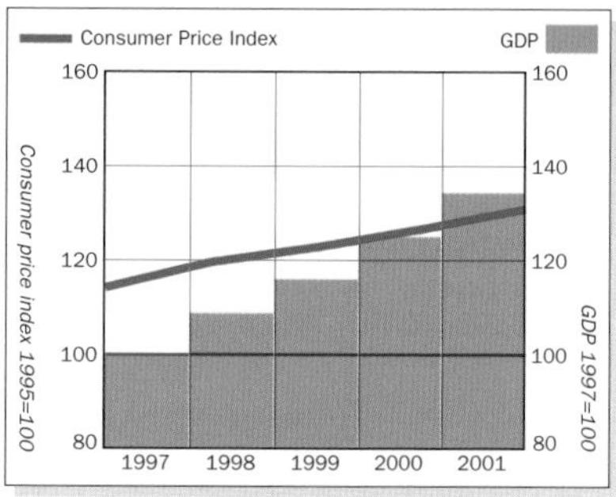
Consumer Price Index
GDP
160
140
120
100
80
1997
1998
1999
2000
2001
Consumer price index 1995=100
GDP 1997=100

Strengths

One of the major tourist destinations in Europe. Efficient agricultural exporter. Shipping: the world's largest beneficially owned fleet.

Weaknesses

High levels of public debt. Until recently, interest rates and bureaucratic banking system discouraged private initiative. State-owned sector, like black economy, remains large. Loss of jobs to low-wage ex-communist neighbouring states.

Profile

Greece took longer than most other countries to recover from World War II. It was not until the 1960s that any substantial investment occurred. The Colonels' dictatorship curbed inflationary pressures with a wage freeze. When civilian government was restored in 1974, a spate of high wage settlements and the oil price shocks of 1973 and 1979 drove inflation over 20%. Greece's largest companies made substantial losses until the socialists' controversial austerity program of 1986–1987 reined in labor costs.

Greece failed in 1999 to meet the economic convergence criteria for introducing the euro. It then tackled the problems with determination, balancing the budget and bringing inflation under control, although public-sector debt remains high. In 2001 Greece became the 12th member of the eurozone, and fully adopted the currency in 2002. Unemployment is still high and GDP per capita is the lowest in the EU.

GREECE : MAJOR BUSINESSES

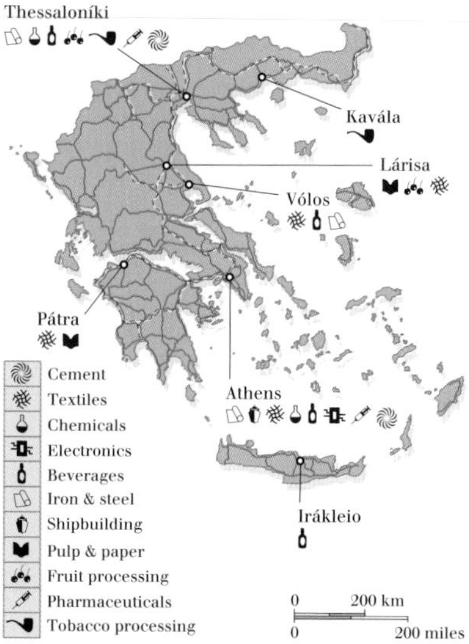
Thessaloníki
Kavála
Lárisa
Vólos
Pátra
Athens
Irákleio
Cement
Textiles
Chemicals
Electronics
Beverages
Iron & steel
Shipbuilding
Pulp & paper
Fruit processing
Pharmaceuticals
Tobacco processing
0 200 km
0 200 miles

RESOURCES

Electric power 10.3m kW

179,159 tonnes

301 b/d (reserves 15m barrels)

9.2m sheep, 5.02m goats, 938,000 pigs, 28m chickens

Oil, gas, coal, iron, bauxite, marble, nickel, magnesite, chromium

ELECTRICITY GENERATION

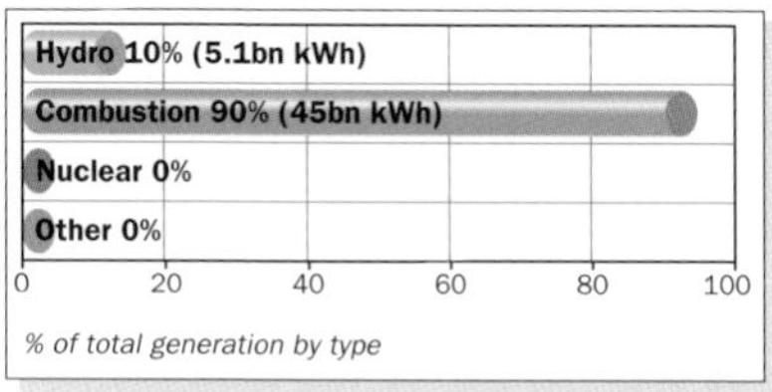
Hydro 10% (5.1bn kWh)
Combustion 90% (45bn kWh)
Nuclear 0%
Other 0%
0
20
40
60
80
100
% of total generation by type

There is an oil and gas field off the coast of the island of Thasos. There may also be exploitable reserves in eastern waters, whose ownership is contested by Turkey. Coal, iron, and other mining contribute less than 1% to GDP. Greece is a leading producer of marble.

GREECE : LAND USE

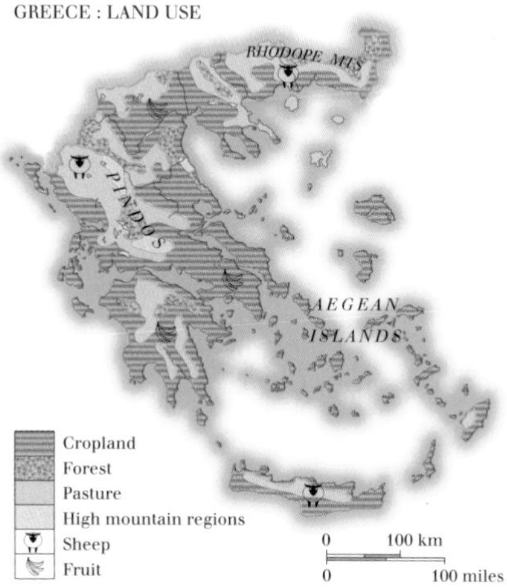
RHODOPE MTS
PINDOS
AEGEAN ISLANDS
Cropland
Forest
Pasture
High mountain regions
Sheep
Fruit
0
100 km
0
100 miles

ENVIRONMENT

Sustainability rank: 60th

4% (1% partially protected)

9.5 tonnes per capita

ENVIRONMENTAL TREATIES

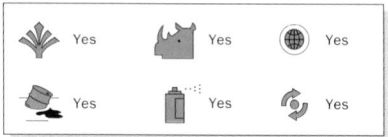

Yes — Yes — Yes

Yes — Yes — Yes

Local fishing interests have formed a successful antipollution organization, HELMEPA. Smog in Athens is irritating to the eyes and throat and highly damaging to ancient monuments: the Parthenon in Athens has suffered more erosion in the last two decades than in the previous 2000 years. Forest fires regularly cause havoc, damaging flora and fauna.

MEDIA

TV ownership high

Daily newspaper circulation 64 per 1000 people

PUBLISHING AND BROADCAST MEDIA

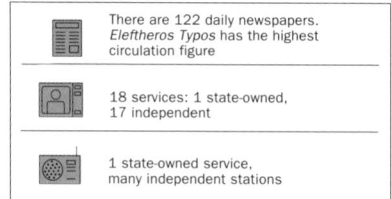

There are 122 daily newspapers. *Eleftheros Typos* has the highest circulation figure

18 services: 1 state-owned, 17 independent

1 state-owned service, many independent stations

After the state broadcasting monopoly ended in 1990, many private TV and radio networks emerged. Commercial broadcasting has made politicians more answerable to the public, and has also had a cultural impact, with the import of more foreign programs, particularly from the US. Many private radio and TV broadcasters are unlicensed.

CRIME

Death penalty not used in practice

8343 prisoners

Down 1% in 2000

CRIME RATES

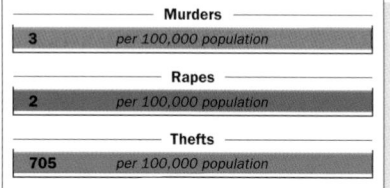

Murders	3	*per 100,000 population*
Rapes	2	*per 100,000 population*
Thefts	705	*per 100,000 population*

An influx of migrants is blamed for an increase in violent crime. The terrorist group November 17, which had carried out high-profile assassinations, was finally tracked down in 2002.

EDUCATION

School leaving age: 14

97%

363,150 students

THE EDUCATION SYSTEM

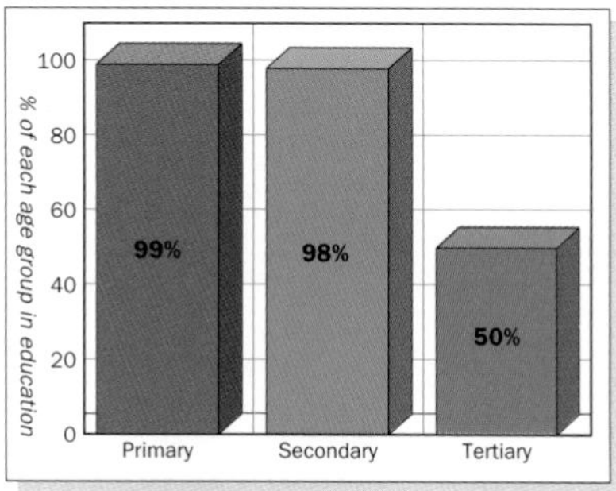
100
80
60
40
20
0
% of each age group in education
99%
98%
50%
Primary
Secondary
Tertiary

Some 9% of total government spending is on education, which is free and officially compulsory for nine years. The use of informal Greek (*demotiki*) replaced the formal *katharevoussa* in Greek schools when it became the country's official language in 1976. There are 18 universities and 74 other institutions of higher education.

HEALTH

Welfare state health benefits

1 per 255 people

Cerebrovascular and heart diseases, cancers

The first PASOK government introduced a national health service and a national pharmaceuticals industry. Some 15% of government expenditure goes on health, and every Greek is entitled to sickness benefit. Greece now has one of the highest numbers of doctors per head of population in the EU. In the early 1990s the ND attempted to upgrade private medicine and to incorporate its activities with those in state hospitals. Overall, provision has improved greatly, but private clinics now offer better facilities than state-run centers.

G

SPENDING

GDP/cap. increase

CONSUMPTION AND SPENDING

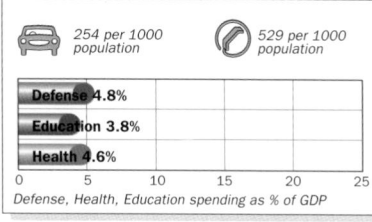

254 per 1000 population

529 per 1000 population

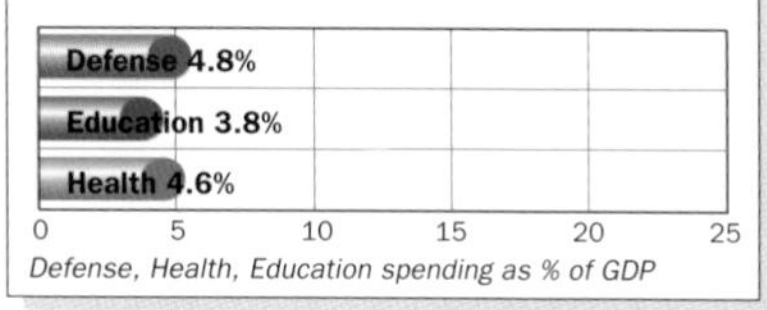
Defense 4.8%
Education 3.8%
Health 4.6%
0
5
10
15
20
25
Defense, Health, Education spending as % of GDP

Greek society changed dramatically in the postwar period. Formerly a largely agricultural society living in isolated communities, it was rapidly urbanized in the 1950s. Former agricultural workers made fortunes, many by grabbing opportunities presented by the shipping industry. Among these were the now prominent Niarchos and Onassis families.

The advent of the republic in 1973 reflected the social changes which had occurred since the war. New wealth and success became more admired than aristocratic birth or prestige. Greece is now a socially mobile society. Living standards have improved universally since the 1950s.

WORLD RANKING

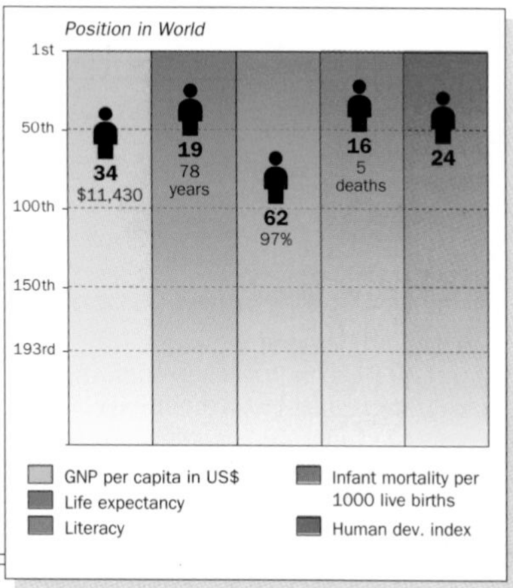
Position in World
1st
50th
100th
150th
193rd
34
$11,430
19
78
years
62
97%
16
5
deaths
24
GNP per capita in US$
Life expectancy
Literacy
Infant mortality per 1000 live births
Human dev. index

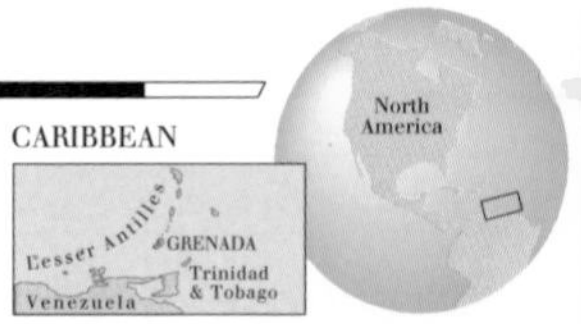
CARIBBEAN
North America
Lesser Antilles
GRENADA
Trinidad & Tobago
Venezuela

GRENADA

OFFICIAL NAME: Grenada **CAPITAL:** St. George's

POPULATION: 89,211 **CURRENCY:** Eastern Caribbean dollar **OFFICIAL LANGUAGE:** English

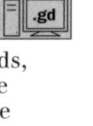

1974 | 1974 | Feb 7 | WG | -4 | +1473 | .gd

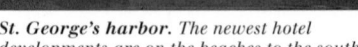

THE MOST SOUTHERLY of the Windward Islands, Grenada also includes the southern Grenadine islands of Carriacou and Petite Martinique. It is the world's second-largest nutmeg producer. One of the seven members of the OECS, Grenada became a focus of international attention in 1983 when the US, with token backing from several Caribbean states, mounted an invasion to sever its growing links with Castro's Cuba.

***St. George's harbor.** The newest hotel developments are on the beaches to the south.*

CLIMATE

Tropical oceanic

WEATHER CHART FOR ST. GEORGE'S

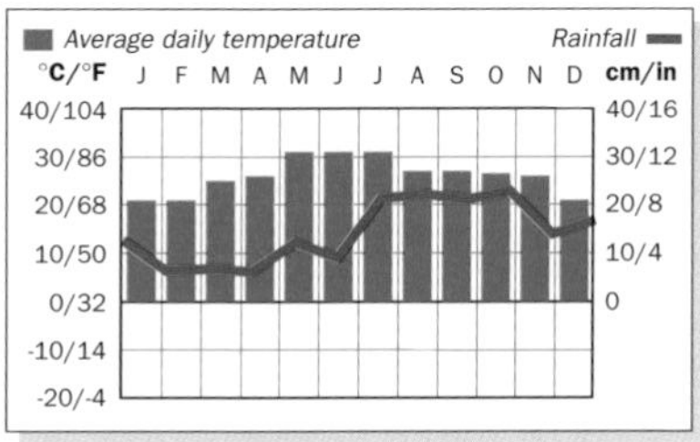
Average daily temperature
Rainfall
°C/°F J F M A M J J A S O N D cm/in
40/104
30/86
20/68
10/50
0/32
-10/14
-20/-4
40/16
30/12
20/8
10/4
0

Rainfall totals 150 cm (60 in) on the coast, and twice that in the mountains. Hurricanes occur in the rainy season.

TRANSPORTATION

Drive on left

Point Salines, St. George's 427,753 passengers

6 ships 1009 grt

THE TRANSPORTATION NETWORK

638 km (396 miles)	None
None	None

Roads in the interior are poor. Catamarans provide the fastest link between Grenada and Carriacou.

TOURISM

Visitors : Population 1.5:1

132,000 visitors

Up 8% in 2002

MAIN TOURIST ARRIVALS

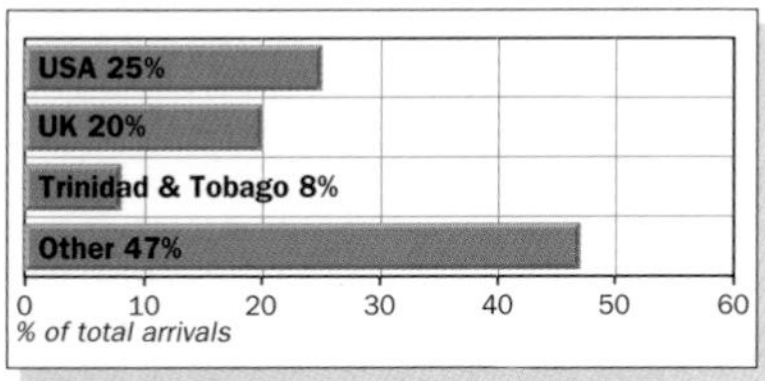
USA 25%
UK 20%
Trinidad & Tobago 8%
Other 47%
0 10 20 30 40 50 60
% of total arrivals

Tourism has developed since the 1984 completion of the international airport, though there has been a concurrent decline in cruise ship arrivals. A ten-year development plan aims to increase hotel capacity to 2500 rooms by 2007.

PEOPLE

Pop. density high

English, English Creole

262/km² (681/mi²)

THE URBAN/RURAL POPULATION SPLIT

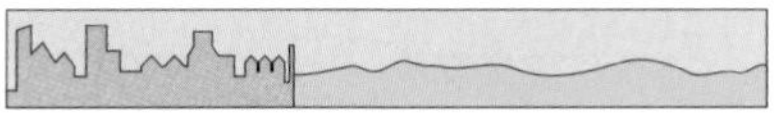
38%
62%

RELIGIOUS PERSUASION

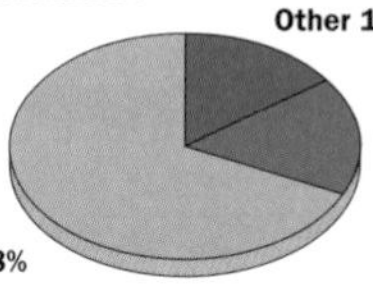
Other 15%
Anglican 17%
Roman Catholic 68%

Most Grenadians are descendants of Africans brought over to work sugar plantations in the 16th to 19th centuries. The black community now comprises over 80% of the population, and intermarriage has negated any serious racial tension. As in other Caribbean states, extended families with absentee fathers are not uncommon.

POLITICS

Multiparty elections

L. House 1999/2004
U. House 1999/2004

H.M. Queen Elizabeth II

AT THE LAST ELECTION

House of Representatives 15 seats

100% NNP

NNP = New National Party

Senate 13 seats

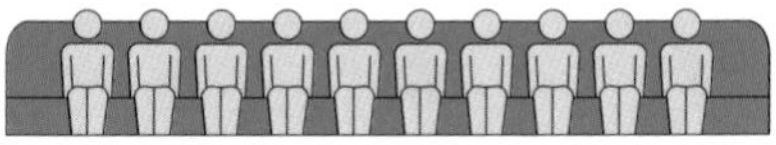

The members of the Senate are appointed by the prime minister and the leader of the opposition

Sir Eric Gairy dominated politics as prime minister until his overthrow in 1979. His successor, the charismatic socialist Maurice Bishop, was in turn deposed and then executed in 1983. This latter coup was the pretext for a US invasion, the primary motive of which was to end the perceived Cuban influence in Grenada. Politics has since been center right, and there is little to choose ideologically between the major parties. The NNP, led by Keith Mitchell, gained power in 1995, and went on to achieve an unparalleled victory over a divided opposition in the early general election held in 1999, taking all 15 seats.

GRENADA

Total Area : 340 sq. km (131 sq. miles)

POPULATION
- over 10 000
- under 10 000

LAND HEIGHT
- 500m/1640ft
- 200m/656ft
- Sea Level

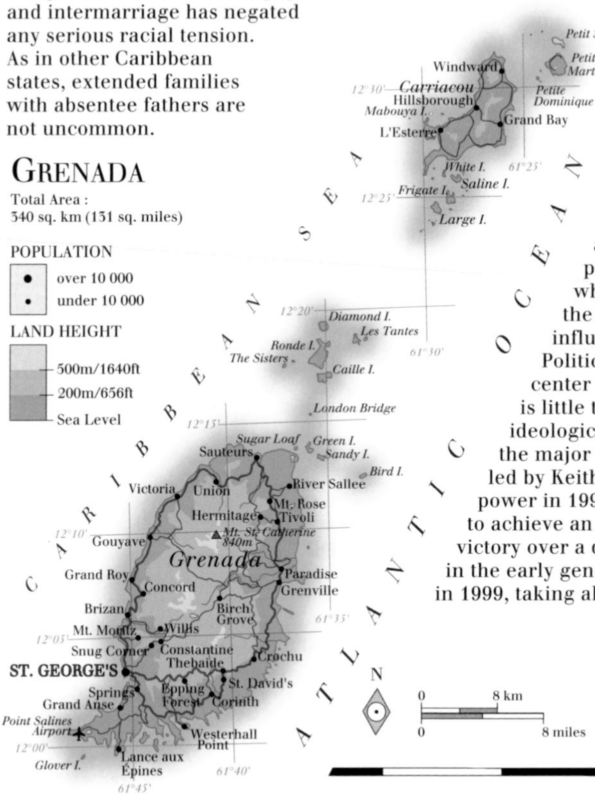
CARIBBEAN SEA
ATLANTIC OCEAN
Petit St Vincent I.
Petite Martinique
Petite Dominique
Windward
Carriacou
Hillsborough
Mabouya I.
Grand Bay
L'Esterre
White I.
Saline I.
Frigate I.
Large I.
Diamond I.
Les Tantes
Ronde I.
The Sisters
Caille I.
London Bridge
Sugar Loaf
Green I.
Sandy I.
Bird I.
Sauteurs
Victoria
Union
River Sallee
Hermitage
Mt. Rose
Tivoli
Mt. St. Catherine 840m
Gouyave
Grenada
Paradise
Grenville
Grand Roy
Concord
Brizan
Birch Grove
Mt. Moritz
Willis
Snug Corner
Constantine
Thebaide
Crochu
ST. GEORGE'S
St. David's
Springs
Grand Anse
Epping Forest
Corinth
Point Salines Airport
Westerhall Point
Lance aux Epines
Glover I.
N
0 8 km
0 8 miles

WORLD AFFAIRS

Joined UN in 1974

ACS | Caricom | Comm | OAS | OECS

Key priorities are relations with the rest of the Windward Islands group, promoting Grenada as a tourist destination, and maintaining close links with the EU. Since 1983, Grenada has supported US policy, but it restored links with Cuba in 2002.

AID

Recipient

US$12m (receipts)

Down 29% in 2001

Main aid sources are Japan and the Caribbean Development Bank. Before the 1983 invasion, Cuba helped build the international airport at Point Salines.

DEFENSE

No compulsory military service

Minimal expenditure

Defense spending is falling

The People's Revolutionary Army, created by Maurice Bishop in the wake of his 1979 coup, was replaced in 1983 by a paramilitary defense unit trained by the US and the UK.

ECONOMICS

Inflation 2.3% p.a. (1990–2001)

US$363m

2.67 Eastern Caribbean dollars (2.7)

SCORE CARD

❑ World GNP Ranking	174th
❑ GNP per Capita	US$3610
❑ Balance of Payments	–US$79m
❑ Inflation	2.8%
❑ Unemployment	15%

STRENGTHS

Second-largest producer of nutmeg after Indonesia. Important sectors are tourism, cocoa, bananas, construction, and financial services.

WEAKNESSES

Weak tax base, lack of diversification. Poor infrastructure. Low productivity. Large avoidance of customs duties. Smuggling. High unemployment.

EXPORTS

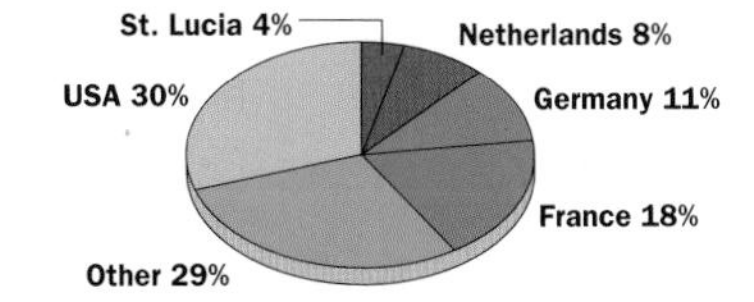
St. Lucia 4%
Netherlands 8%
USA 30%
Germany 11%
France 18%
Other 29%

IMPORTS

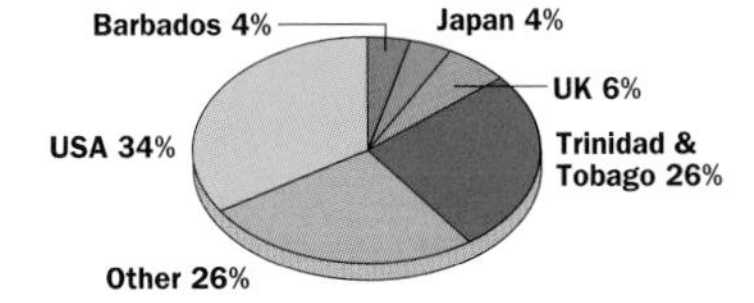
Barbados 4%
Japan 4%
UK 6%
USA 34%
Trinidad & Tobago 26%
Other 26%

RESOURCES

Electric power 17,000 kW

1700 tonnes

Not an oil producer

13,100 sheep, 7100 goats, 168,000 chickens

None

Grenada has no strategic resources and has to import most of its energy. The major asset is Grenadian nutmeg, which is highly prized for its quality, but production levels fluctuate.

ENVIRONMENT

Not available

1.7% partially protected

2.6 tonnes per capita

Tourism threatens some key environmental sites, including a remnant of rainforest. Resort projects have caused serious beach erosion, in turn requiring costly coastal defenses. An environmental levy on visitors is opposed by cruise companies.

MEDIA

TV ownership high

There are no daily newspapers

PUBLISHING AND BROADCAST MEDIA

There are no daily newspapers. The *Grenadian Voice* and the *Grenada Guardian* are published weekly

1 state-owned service

3 services: 1 partly state-owned, 2 independent

The government sold a 60% share in the then Grenada Broadcasting Corporation (GBC) in 1999. There is an independent private press.

CRIME

Death penalty not used in practice

297 prisoners

Thefts rose sharply in 1997

The doubling of poverty during the 1990s and high unemployment have contributed to a rising crime rate. Narcotics trafficking is also a growing problem. However, while there is street crime, the level of violence is low.

EDUCATION

School leaving age: 16

94%

651 students

Education follows the former British selective 11-plus system. Many students go on to the University of the West Indies, or to college in the US.

HEALTH

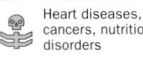

Welfare state health benefits

1 per 2000 people

Heart diseases, cancers, nutritional disorders

After 1979, Cuban physicians provided a basic health care system. There are free weekly clinics in each district, and treatment in subsidized state hospitals now matches the Caribbean average. In 1999 Cuba began its promised expansion of the general hospital.

CHRONOLOGY

Sighted, and named, by Columbus in 1498, Grenada was a French colony from 1650. Captured by the British in 1762, it formally became a part of the British Empire in 1783.

- ❑ **1885–1958** Grenada acts as administrative center for the Windward Islands.
- ❑ **1950** Eric Gairy founds Grenada United Labour Party.
- ❑ **1951** Universal suffrage introduced.
- ❑ **1967** Internal self-government.
- ❑ **1974** Full independence. Gairy prime minister.
- ❑ **1979** Coup. Maurice Bishop prime minister. Growing links with Cuba.
- ❑ **1983** After improving ties with US, Bishop is ousted and executed by former allies. US invasion establishes pro-US administration.
- ❑ **1995** Keith Mitchell of NNP becomes prime minister.
- ❑ **1999** NNP reelected, taking all 15 seats in House of Representatives.
- ❑ **2001–2002** Grenada is blacklisted as tax haven.
- ❑ **2002** Full diplomatic ties with Cuba restored.

G

SPENDING

GDP/cap. increase

CONSUMPTION AND SPENDING

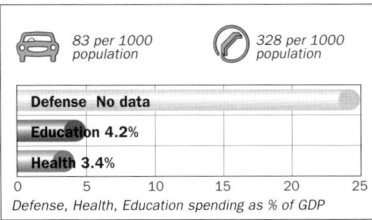

83 per 1000 population

328 per 1000 population

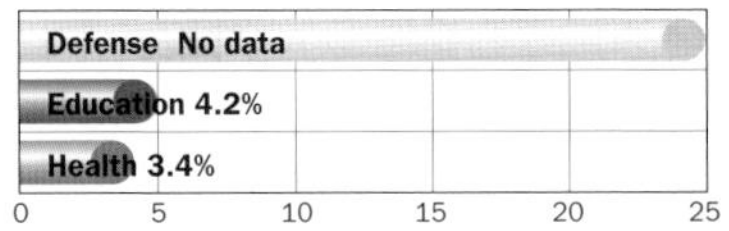
Defense No data
Education 4.2%
Health 3.4%
0
5
10
15
20
25

Defense, Health, Education spending as % of GDP

Wealth disparities in Grenada are less marked than in most Caribbean states, but poverty is growing. The wealthiest groups are those in control of the nutmeg trade.

WORLD RANKING

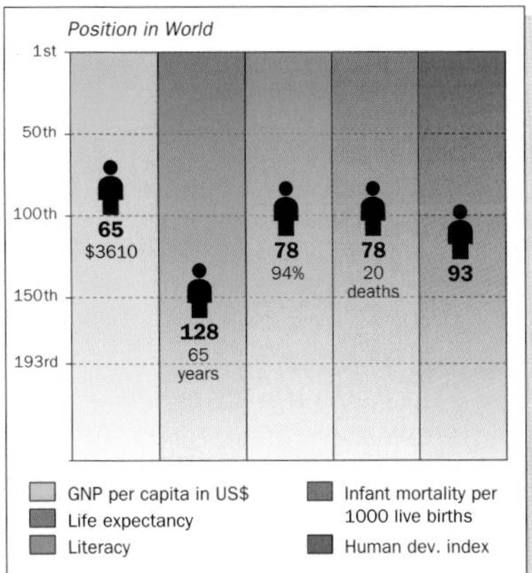
Position in World
1st
50th
100th
150th
193rd
65
$3610
128
65
years
78
94%
78
20
deaths
93
GNP per capita in US$
Life expectancy
Literacy
Infant mortality per 1000 live births
Human dev. index

GUATEMALA

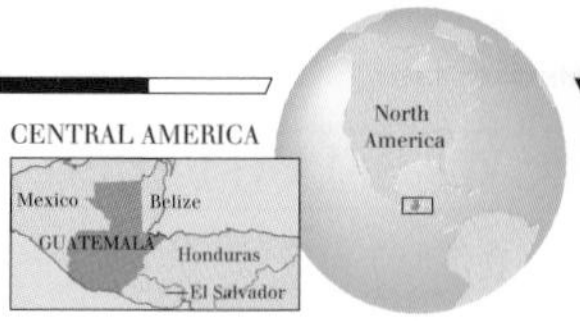
CENTRAL AMERICA
North America
Mexico
Belize
GUATEMALA
Honduras
El Salvador

OFFICIAL NAME: Republic of Guatemala **CAPITAL:** Guatemala City
POPULATION: 12 million **CURRENCY:** Quetzal **OFFICIAL LANGUAGE:** Spanish

1838 | 1838 | Sept 15 | GCA | -6 | +502 | .gt

THE LARGEST AND MOST POPULOUS of the states of the Central American isthmus, Guatemala was home to the ancient Mayan civilization. Its fertile Pacific and Caribbean coastal lowlands give way to the highlands which dominate the country. Independent since 1838, Guatemala fell under military rule in 1954. Civilian rule was not restored for over three decades, in 1986. Some 60% of people live below the poverty line.

CLIMATE

Tropical equatorial/ wet and dry

WEATHER CHART FOR GUATEMALA CITY

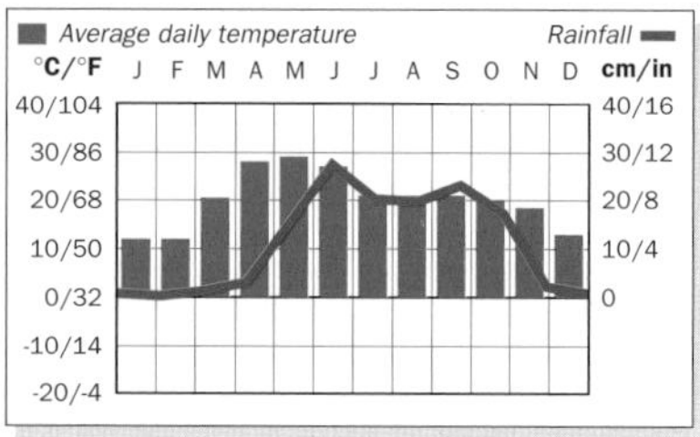
Average daily temperature
Rainfall
°C/°F
J F M A M J J A S O N D
cm/in
40/104
30/86
20/68
10/50
0/32
-10/14
-20/-4
40/16
30/12
20/8
10/4
0

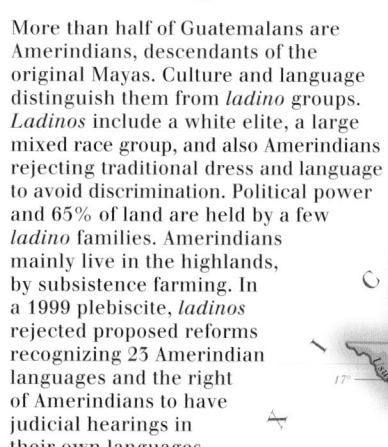

The climate varies with altitude: daytime temperatures average 28°C (82°F) in tropical coast areas and 20°C (68°F) in the more temperate central highlands.

TRANSPORTATION

Drive on right

La Aurora, Guatemala City 939,000 passengers

8 ships 4600 grt

THE TRANSPORTATION NETWORK

4370 km (2715 miles)

140 km (87 miles)

884 km (549 miles)

990 km (615 miles)

Good roads link the major towns. The railroad and two international airports are attracting foreign investment.

TOURISM

Visitors : Population 1:14

835,000 visitors

Up 1% in 2001

MAIN TOURIST ARRIVALS

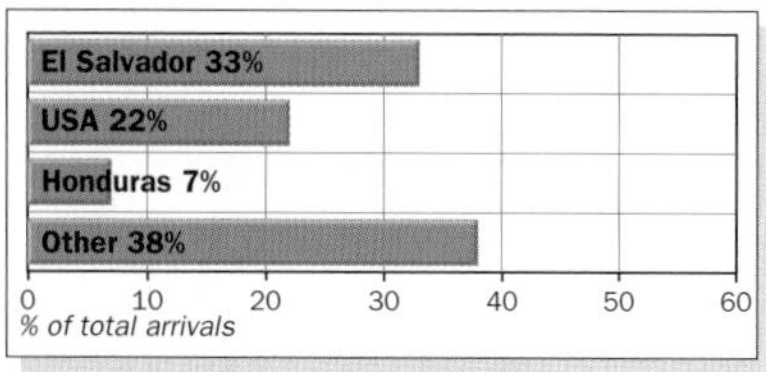
El Salvador 33%
USA 22%
Honduras 7%
Other 38%
0
10
20
30
40
50
60
% of total arrivals

Tourism rapidly revived after the military excesses in the 1980s, but postwar crime, including an increase in mob violence, deters visitors. Mayan ruins are the top attractions.

PEOPLE

Pop. density medium

Quiché, Mam, Cakchiquel, Kekchí, Spanish

111/km² (287/mi²)

THE URBAN/RURAL POPULATION SPLIT

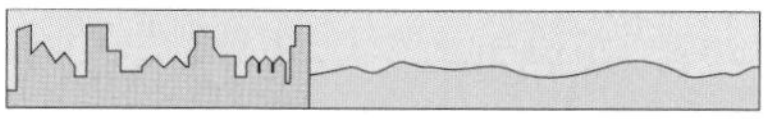
40%
60%

ETHNIC MAKEUP

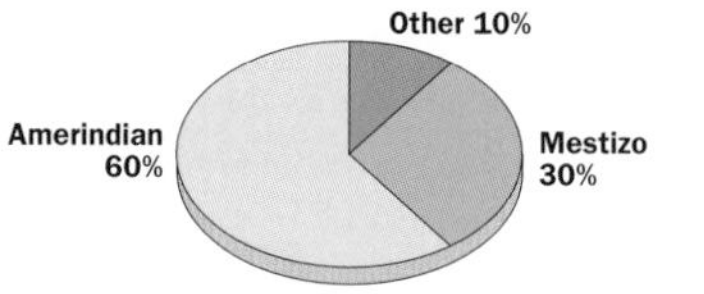
Other 10%
Amerindian 60%
Mestizo 30%

More than half of Guatemalans are Amerindians, descendants of the original Mayas. Culture and language distinguish them from *ladino* groups. *Ladinos* include a white elite, a large mixed race group, and also Amerindians rejecting traditional dress and language to avoid discrimination. Political power and 65% of land are held by a few *ladino* families. Amerindians mainly live in the highlands, by subsistence farming. In a 1999 plebiscite, *ladinos* rejected proposed reforms recognizing 23 Amerindian languages and the right of Amerindians to have judicial hearings in their own languages.

POLITICS

Multiparty elections

1999/2003

President Alfonso Portillo

AT THE LAST ELECTION

Congress of the Republic 113 seats

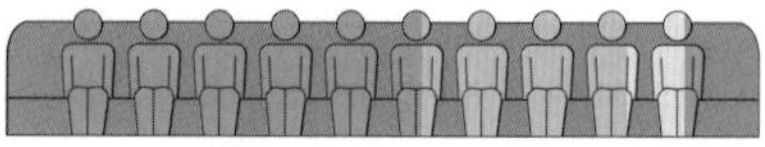
56% FRG
32% PAN
9% NNA
3% Others

FRG = Guatemalan Republican Front **PAN** = National Advancement Party **NNA** = New Nation Alliance

The military government which came to power in 1954 with US backing brutally suppressed opposition and persecuted the highland Amerindians, until the return of democracy in 1986. Civil war effectively continued until President Arzú of the PAN concluded a peace agreement with the Guatemalan National Revolutionary Unity (URNG) guerrillas in 1996. The 36-year war had claimed 200,000 lives, mostly innocent civilians. In presidential elections in 1999 Alfonso Portillo of the right-wing FRG, running on a strong law and order platform, defeated the PAN candidate.

Efraín Ríos Montt, military ruler in 1982–1986, remains a force in politics, despite being investigated by a Spanish court on charges of genocide. After a protracted legal struggle he was accepted as the 2003 presidential candidate for the FRG.

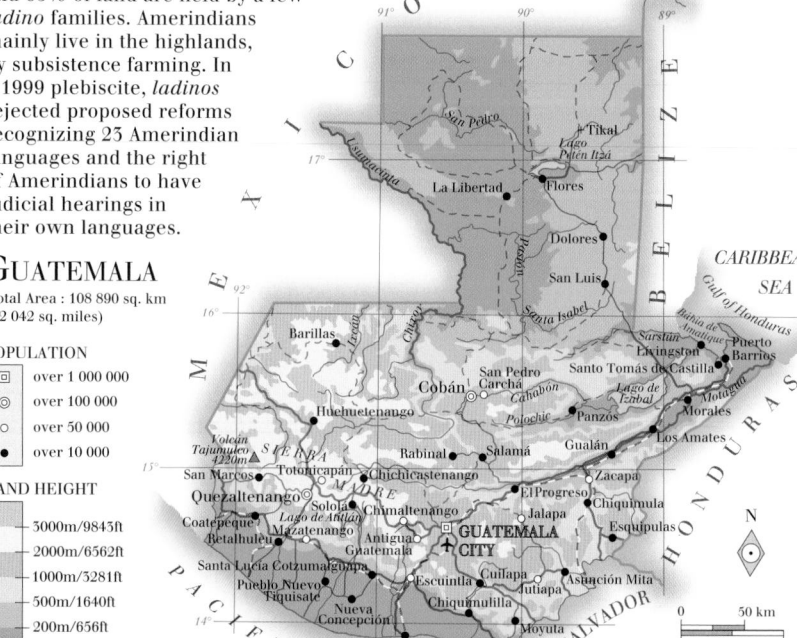

GUATEMALA

Total Area : 108 890 sq. km (42 042 sq. miles)

POPULATION

- over 1 000 000
- over 100 000
- over 50 000
- over 10 000

LAND HEIGHT

- 3000m/9843ft
- 2000m/6562ft
- 1000m/3281ft
- 500m/1640ft
- 200m/656ft
- Sea Level

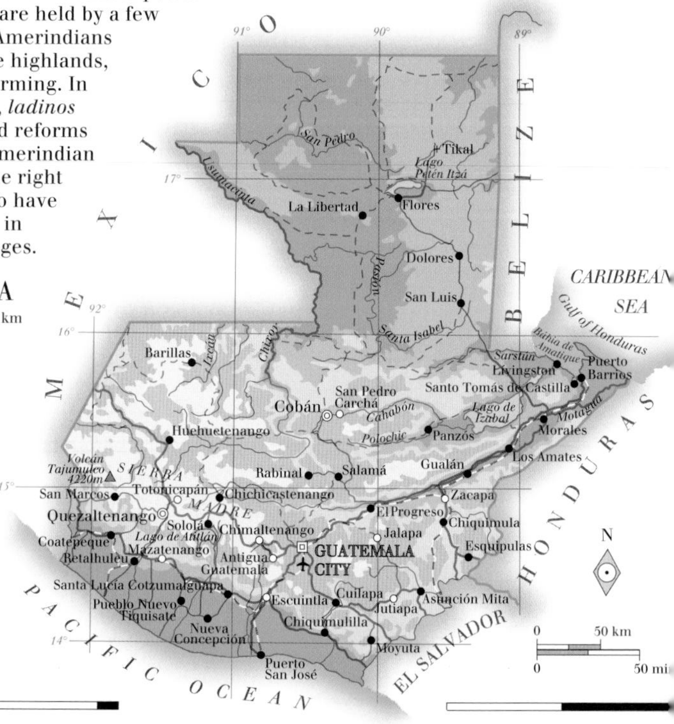
MEXICO
BELIZE
HONDURAS
EL SALVADOR
CARIBBEAN SEA
Gulf of Honduras
PACIFIC OCEAN
SIERRA MADRE
Tikal
Lago Petén Itzá
Flores
La Libertad
San Pedro
Usumacinta
Pasión
Dolores
San Luis
Santa Isabel
Chixoy
Barillas
Cobán
San Pedro Carchá
Cahabón
Santo Tomás de Castilla
Puerto Barrios
Livingston
Sarstún
Lago de Izabal
Motagua
Morales
Los Amates
Panzós
Polochic
Gualán
Huehuetenango
Volcán Tajumulco 4220m
Rabinal
Salamá
Totonicapán
Chichicastenango
San Marcos
Quezaltenango
Zacapa
El Progreso
Chiquimula
Sololá
Chimaltenango
Lago de Atitlán
Coatepeque
Retalhuleu
Mazatenango
Antigua Guatemala
GUATEMALA CITY
Jalapa
Esquipulas
Santa Lucía Cotzumalguapa
Escuintla
Cuilapa
Jutiapa
Asunción Mita
Pueblo Nuevo Tiquisate
Nueva Concepción
Chiquimulilla
Moyuta
Puerto San José
91°
90°
89°
92°
17°
16°
15°
14°
N
0 50 km
0 50 mi

WORLD AFFAIRS

Joined UN in 1945

ACS | Geplac | NAM | OAS | San José

Economic relations with the US and neighboring states are priorities. A UN mission was deployed for six months to oversee the 1996 peace accord. Guatemala lays claim to half of Belize.

AID

Recipient

$225m (receipts) | Down 15% in 2001

In 1998 the government agreed the disbursement of the second half of $1.9 billion pledged by the international donors for postwar reconstruction. In the same year $1.4 million were also loaned as hurricane relief.

DEFENSE

Compulsory military service

$186m | Up 20% in 2001

A damning "truth commission" report in 1999 found the armed forces and their allies guilty of 93% of human rights violations during the civil war. The army remains largely unreformed and a potent sociopolitical force.

ECONOMICS

Inflation 9.9% p.a. (1990–2001)

$19.6bn | 7.93 quetzales (7.889)

SCORE CARD

- ❑ WORLD GNP RANKING..........64th
- ❑ GNP PER CAPITA..........$1680
- ❑ BALANCE OF PAYMENTS..........-$1.24bn
- ❑ INFLATION..........7.6%
- ❑ UNEMPLOYMENT..........8%

STRENGTHS

Main exports are coffee, sugar, beef, bananas, and cardamom. Privatizations boost foreign investor confidence.

WEAKNESSES

Traditional exports vulnerable to world price changes. Natural disasters. Shaky financial system. Wealth inequalities limit domestic market. Tax evasion.

EXPORTS

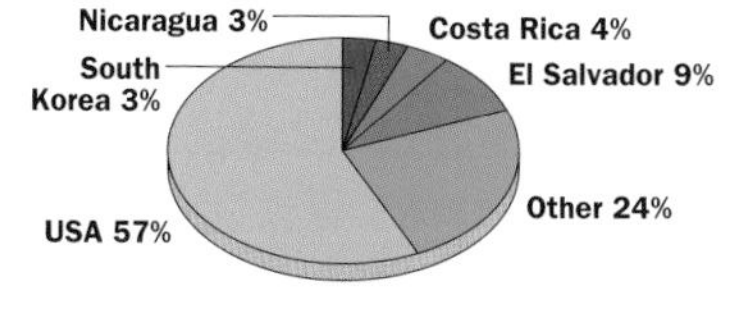
Nicaragua 3%
Costa Rica 4%
South Korea 3%
El Salvador 9%
Other 24%
USA 57%

IMPORTS

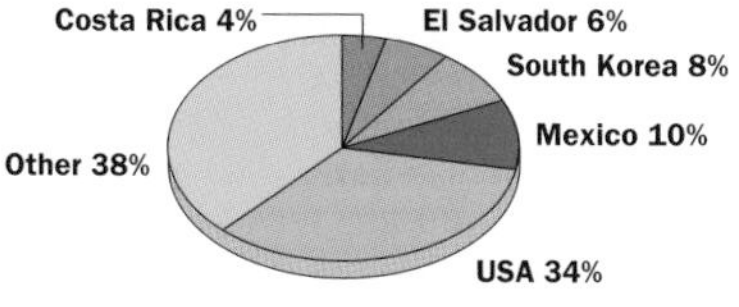
Costa Rica 4%
El Salvador 6%
South Korea 8%
Mexico 10%
Other 38%
USA 34%

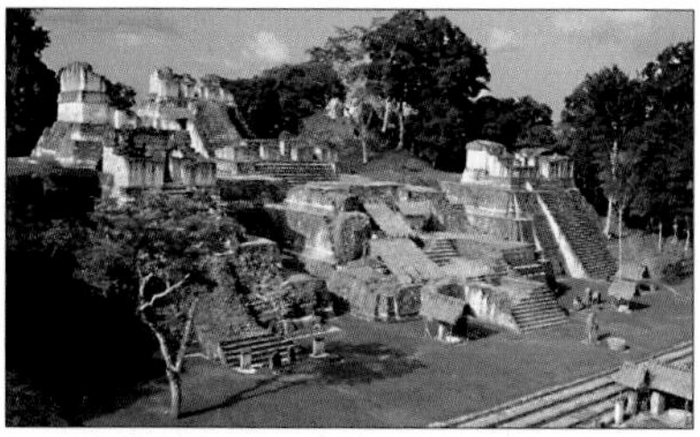

North Acropolis, Tikal, Petén. *One of the largest lowland Mayan cities, Tikal was virtually abandoned by about 900 CE.*

RESOURCES

Electric power 1.4m kW

44,041 tonnes | 23,318 b/d (reserves 196m barrels)

2.54m cattle, 778,000 pigs, 26m chickens | Oil, antimony, lead, tungsten, nickel, copper

Agriculture provides over 20% of GDP and over 50% of export earnings. Guatemala is the world's largest producer of cardamom. The civil war hindered the exploitation of oil reserves and hydroelectric potential.

ENVIRONMENT

Sustainability rank: 67th

20% (3% partially protected) | 0.9 tonnes per capita

Forest cover has fallen dramatically since 1954 to 26%, due to intensive agriculture. The excessive use of pesticides, many banned in the US, threatens health. In rural areas indoor pollution from traditional stoves is a major concern.

MEDIA

TV ownership medium

Daily newspaper circulation 33 per 1000 people

PUBLISHING AND BROADCAST MEDIA

There are 7 daily newspapers, including *Prensa Libre, Siglo Veintiuno, El Periódico,* and the state *Diario de Centroamérica*

5 services: 1 state-owned, 4 independent | 85 stations: 5 state-owned, 80 independent

Powerful groups own the media, but newspapers can be hard-hitting. The four independent TV stations are controlled by a single owner.

CRIME

Moratorium on death penalty

8460 prisoners | Crime is rising

Violence is high. In 2000 the interior ministry purged the police, which had been corrupted by drug trafficking.

EDUCATION

School leaving age: 15

69% | 146,291 students

Education is only for the privileged. Guatemala has one of the lowest literacy rates in Latin America; only 69% of women are literate.

CHRONOLOGY

The site of the Mayan civilization, Guatemala declared independence from Spain in 1821. It became a fully independent nation in 1838.

- ❑ **1954** US-backed coup topples reformist government.
- ❑ **1966–1984** Counterinsurgency war; highlands "pacification."
- ❑ **1986–1993** Return of civilian rule; President Serrano elected. Flees country after abortive "self-coup."
- ❑ **1996** President Arzú elected; peace deal with URNG guerrillas, ending 36 years of civil war.
- ❑ **1998** Bishop Juan Gerardi, human rights campaigner, murdered.
- ❑ **1999** "Truth Commission" blames army for most human rights abuses. Portillo and FRG win elections.

G

HEALTH

Welfare state health benefits

1 per 1111 people | Gastrointestinal infections, tuberculosis, heart disease, violence

Health spending is a budget priority as a result of pressure from the UN and multilateral lenders. Gastrointestinal and other infections directly linked to poverty remain the main causes of death.

SPENDING

GDP/cap. increase

CONSUMPTION AND SPENDING

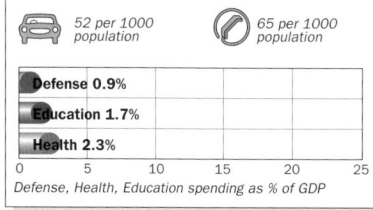

52 per 1000 population | *65 per 1000 population*

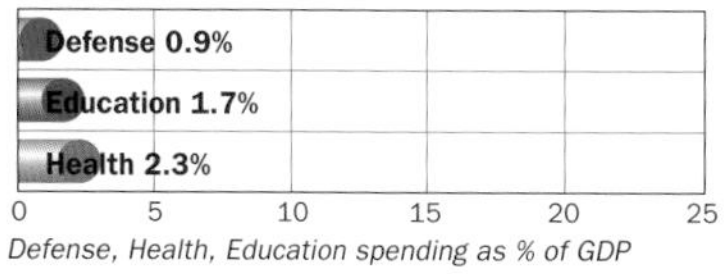
Defense 0.9%
Education 1.7%
Health 2.3%
0
5
10
15
20
25
Defense, Health, Education spending as % of GDP

Poverty in Guatemala has risen since 1980: a third of the population now live below the poverty line. The richest 10% control an estimated 46% of the national wealth.

WORLD RANKING

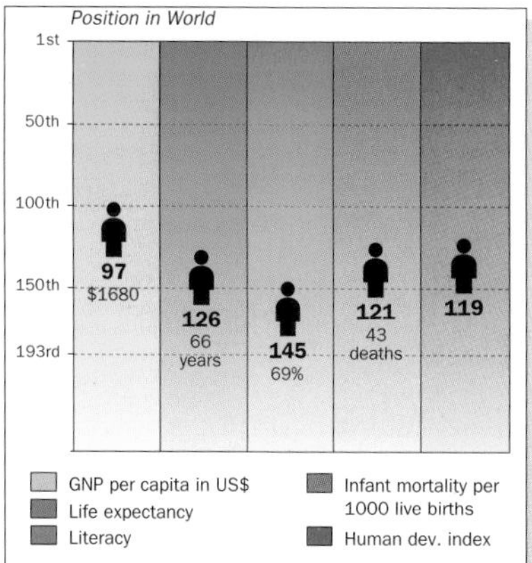
Position in World
1st
50th
100th
150th
193rd
97
$1680
126
66 years
145
69%
121
43 deaths
119
GNP per capita in US$
Life expectancy
Literacy
Infant mortality per 1000 live births
Human dev. index

GUINEA

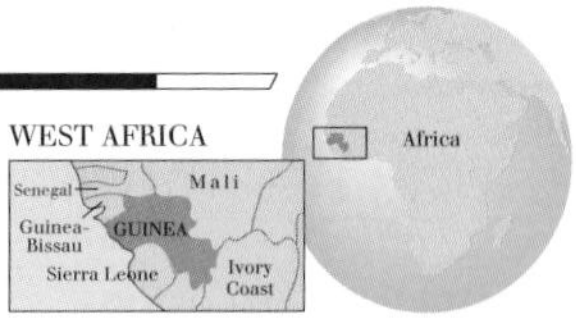
WEST AFRICA
Africa
Senegal
Mali
Guinea-Bissau
GUINEA
Sierra Leone
Ivory Coast

OFFICIAL NAME: Republic of Guinea **CAPITAL:** Conakry
POPULATION: 8.4 million **CURRENCY:** Guinea franc **OFFICIAL LANGUAGE:** French

1958 | 1958 | Apr 3 | RG | 0 | +224 | .gn

GUINEA LIES ON the western coast of Africa. Central highlands, either densely forested or savanna covered, slope down to coastal plains and swamps; the north is semidesert. Military rule from 1984 ended with disputed elections in 1995. Neighboring civil wars have spilled over into domestic conflict in Guinea.

CLIMATE

Tropical monsoon

WEATHER CHART FOR CONAKRY

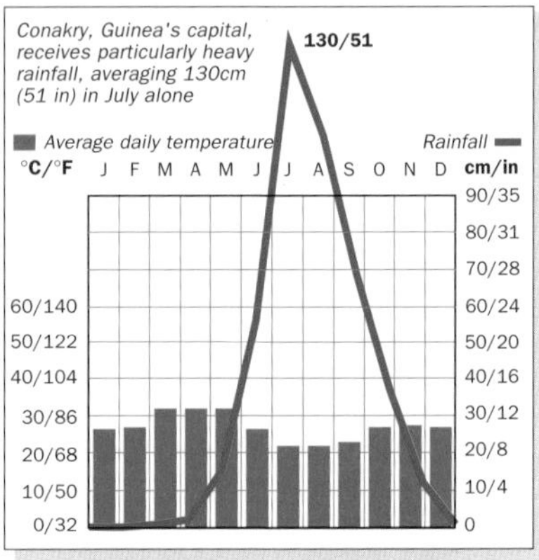
Conakry, Guinea's capital, receives particularly heavy rainfall, averaging 130cm (51 in) in July alone
130/51
Average daily temperature
Rainfall
°C/°F J F M A M J J A S O N D cm/in
90/35
80/31
70/28
60/140 60/24
50/122 50/20
40/104 40/16
30/86 30/12
20/68 20/8
10/50 10/4
0/32 0

Dusty *harmattan* winds govern the dry season. A six-month rainy season begins in April.

TRANSPORTATION

Drive on right

Conakry–Gbessia 263,454 passengers

33 ships 11,400 grt

THE TRANSPORTATION NETWORK

5033 km (3127 miles)

None

1086 km (675 miles)

1295 km (805 miles)

Major roads and rail lines are being rebuilt with World Bank and French aid. Much of the rail network is exclusively for the use of the bauxite industry.

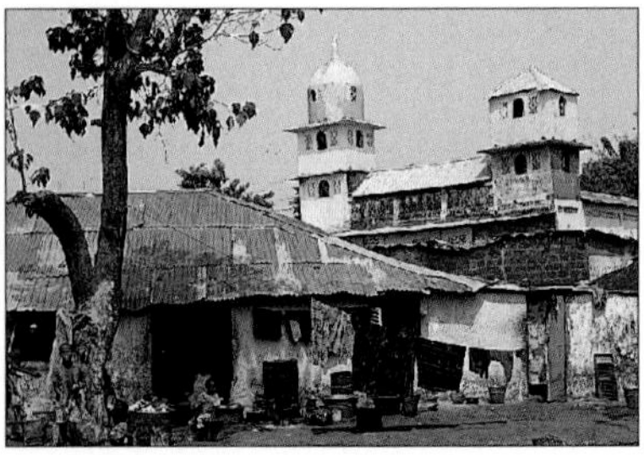

A small mosque in Conakry. *Muslims make up 85% of the population; 8% are Christian. The remainder follow traditional beliefs.*

TOURISM

Visitors : Population 1:227

37,000 visitors

Up 12% in 2001

MAIN TOURIST ARRIVALS

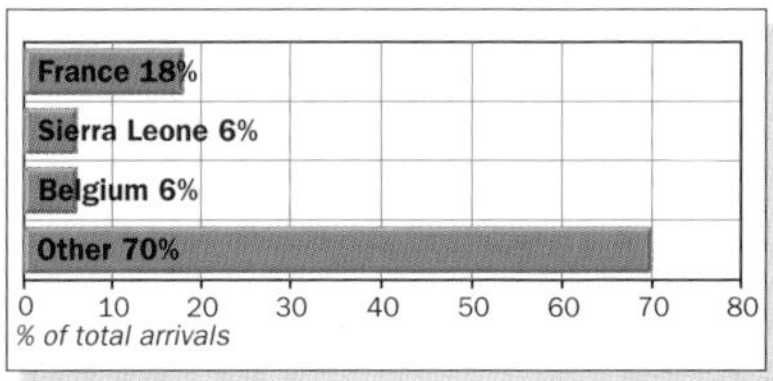
France 18%
Sierra Leone 6%
Belgium 6%
Other 70%
0 10 20 30 40 50 60 70 80
% of total arrivals

Limited infrastructure means that Guinea cannot exploit the tourist potential of its beaches, scenery, and rich culture.

PEOPLE

Pop. density low

Fulani, Malinke, Soussou, French

34/km² (88/mi²)

THE URBAN/RURAL POPULATION SPLIT

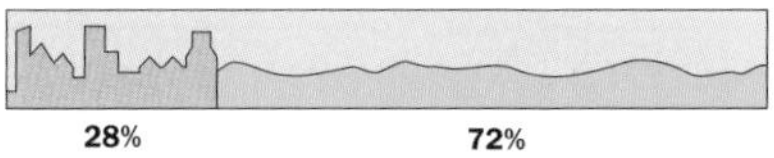
28%
72%

ETHNIC MAKEUP

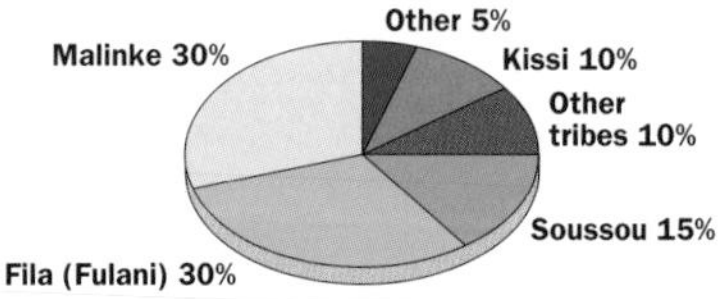
Other 5%
Malinke 30%
Kissi 10%
Other tribes 10%
Soussou 15%
Fila (Fulani) 30%

Since the death of Marxist dictator Sekou Touré in 1984, traditional rivalries have reemerged between ethnic groups. The two largest groups are the Fulani, based in the highland region of Fouta Djallon, and the Malinke, who lost the power they had held under Touré, and have suffered reprisals. Today, the coastal peoples, including the Soussou, are dominant, benefiting from renewed rivalry between the Malinke and Fulani.

The extended family system survived the climate of suspicion generated by paid informers under Sekou Touré. Women acquired influence within his Marxist party, but a Muslim revival since 1984 has reversed this trend.

Hundreds of thousands of refugees, fleeing from conflicts in neighboring countries, are now caught up in fighting in the southern border region.

POLITICS

Multiparty elections

2002/2007

President Lansana Conté

AT THE LAST ELECTION

National Assembly 114 seats

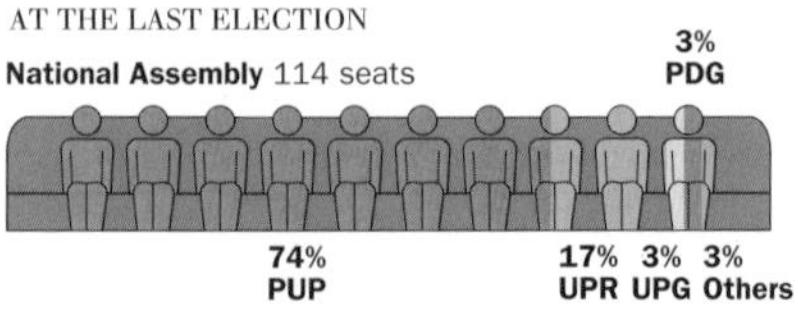
3% PDG
74% PUP
17% UPR
3% UPG
3% Others

PUP = Party of Unity and Progress **UPR** = Union for Progress and Renewal **UPG** = Union for the Progress of Guinea **PDG** = Democratic Party of Guinea

The transition to democracy following the death in 1984 of Marxist dictator Sekou Touré was postponed by the military until 1993. Serious violence broke out that year following the presidential election, amid accusations of vote rigging leveled at the incumbent junta, headed by Gen. Lansana Conté. A disputed victory for Conté's PUP in the 1995 legislative elections was followed by his own reelection in 1998. Fighting escalated into civil war in 2000, with incursions from rebels based in Sierra Leone and Liberia. A controversial constitutional referendum in 2001 granted the ailing Conté the option of standing for a third term in 2003.

The PUP increased its majority in much-delayed legislative polls in July 2002 and a prodemocracy conference, organized by veteran opposition and Malinke leader Alpha Condé, was outlawed in 2003. The PUP government is consistently accused of widespread repression and the general limitation of freedoms.

WORLD AFFAIRS

Joined UN in 1958

ECOWAS | OIF | AU | OIC | OMVG

Guinea has been deeply involved in regional crises in neighboring Sierra Leone, Liberia, and Ivory Coast. Though relations were symbolically patched up in 2002, tensions remain over the region's porous borders.

AID

Recipient

$272m (receipts)

Up 78% in 2001

In 1969, the World Bank funded the Boké bauxite project, then one of its most ambitious projects. Since 1986, Western aid has grown to finance over 85% of all development projects. The 1997–2000 World Bank/IMF structural reform program foresees an annual growth rate of 5%.

GUINEA

Total Area : 245 857 sq. km (94 925 sq. miles)

POPULATION

- ⊙ over 500 000
- ○ over 50 000
- ● over 10 000
- • under 10 000

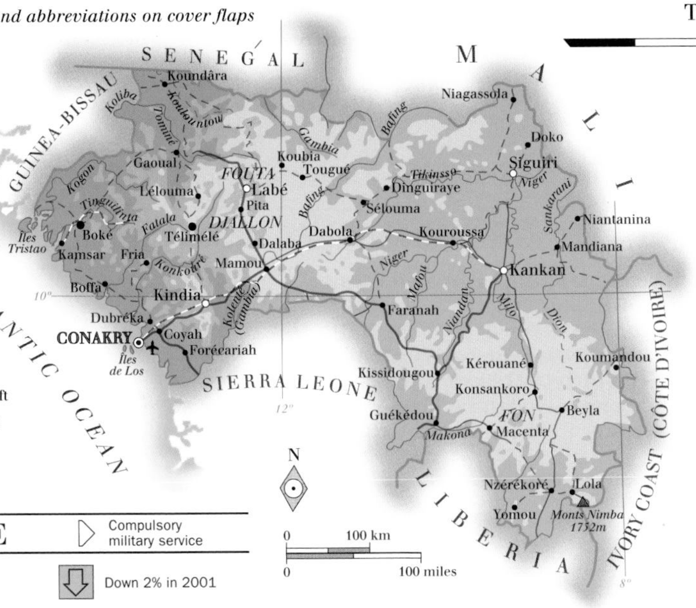
SENEGAL
MALI
GUINEA-BISSAU
Koundâra
Niagassola
Doko
Siguiri
Koubia
Tougué
Labé
Pita
Gaoual
Lélouma
FOUTA DJALLON
Dinguiraye
Sélouma
Boké
Télimélé
Dabola
Kouroussa
Niantanina
Mandiana
Kankan
Kamsar
Fria
Dalaba
Mamou
Îles Tristao
Boffa
Kindia
Faranah
Dubréka
CONAKRY
Coyah
Forécariah
Îles de Los
ATLANTIC OCEAN
SIERRA LEONE
Kissidougou
Kérouané
Koumandou
Konsankoro
Guékédou
Beyla
FON
Macenta
Nzérékoré
Lola
Yomou
Monts Nimba 1752m
LIBERIA
IVORY COAST (CÔTE D'IVOIRE)
Gambia
Niger
Bafing
Milo
Dion
Sankarani
Konkouré
Kogon
N
0 100 km
0 100 miles

LAND HEIGHT

- 1000m/3281ft
- 500m/1640ft
- 200m/656ft
- Sea Level

DEFENSE

Compulsory military service

$45m | Down 2% in 2001

Defense forces consist of an army and a militia (partly merged since the 1984 coup) a gendarmerie, and a tiny navy and air force. China, North Korea, and the Soviet bloc used to be the main arms procurement markets. Weaponry is now supplied by France and the US.

ECONOMICS

Inflation 5.1% p.a. (1990–2001)

$3.14bn | 1990 Guinea francs (1976.5)

SCORE CARD

❑ WORLD GNP RANKING	129th
❑ GNP PER CAPITA	$410
❑ BALANCE OF PAYMENTS	–$60m
❑ INFLATION	5.1%
❑ UNEMPLOYMENT	Widespread underemployment

STRENGTHS

Natural resources including bauxite, gold, and diamonds. Major iron ore deposits at Mount Nimba. Good soil and climate give high cash-crop yields. Relatively low inflation.

WEAKNESSES

Instability. Legacy of maladministration under Touré. Poor infrastructure. Conflict in Liberia has set back major joint projects. Refugee influx a drain on resources. Electricity shortages.

EXPORTS

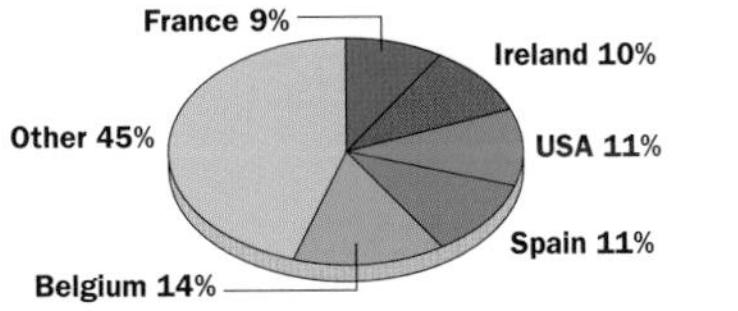
France 9%
Ireland 10%
Other 45%
USA 11%
Spain 11%
Belgium 14%

IMPORTS

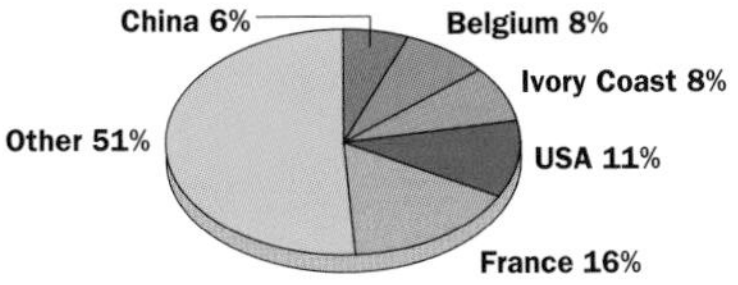
China 6%
Belgium 8%
Ivory Coast 8%
Other 51%
USA 11%
France 16%

RESOURCES

Electric power 197,000 kW

91,513 tonnes | Not an oil producer

3.13m cattle, 1.12m goats, 13.3m chickens | Bauxite, diamonds, gold, iron

Bauxite provides the majority of export earnings, though gold production has increased significantly. Guinea, with 30% of the world's known bauxite reserves, is the world's largest producer after Australia. Demand for electricity for bauxite processing is high.

ENVIRONMENT

Sustainability rank: 98th

0.7% | 0.2 tonnes per capita

Uncontrolled deforestation, particularly of large areas of rainforest, is the major long-term problem.

MEDIA

TV ownership low

Daily newspaper circulation 2 per 1000 people

PUBLISHING AND BROADCAST MEDIA

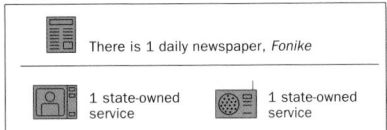

There is 1 daily newspaper, *Fonike*

1 state-owned service | 1 state-owned service

Guinea's limited broadcast media are state-owned. The main newspaper, *Horoya*, is a weekly. There has been a slight relaxation in censorship.

CRIME

Death penalty in use

3070 prisoners | Crime is rising

The death penalty was reintroduced in 2001 in an attempt to crack down on spiraling crime. Cross-border diamond smuggling is at the root of anarchy in the south.

CHRONOLOGY

France colonized Guinea in 1890, strongly opposed by the Fulani Muslim empire of Fouta Djallon.

- ❑ **1958** Full independence under Sekou Touré.
- ❑ **1984** Touré dies. Army coup.
- ❑ **1993–1995** Disputed elections.
- ❑ **1998** Conté reelected president.
- ❑ **2000** Cross-border rebel attacks place Guinea in a state of civil war.
- ❑ **2002** PUP wins delayed elections.

EDUCATION

School leaving age: 12

41% | 8151 students

French was readopted as the main teaching language in 1984, after Sekou Touré's Marxist-inspired experiments.

HEALTH

No welfare state health benefits

1 per 7692 people | Malaria, diarrheal and respiratory diseases, tuberculosis

Health provision is very poor, reflected in Guinea's high infant mortality rate and low average life expectancy. Private health care was legalized in 1984.

SPENDING

GDP/cap. increase

CONSUMPTION AND SPENDING

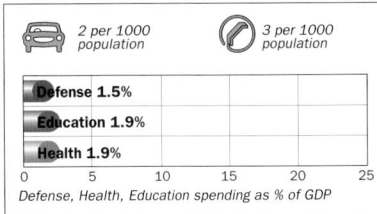

2 per 1000 population | *3 per 1000 population*

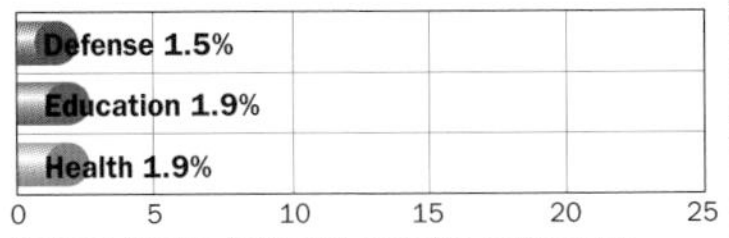
Defense 1.5%
Education 1.9%
Health 1.9%
0
5
10
15
20
25

Defense, Health, Education spending as % of GDP

Private enterprise has brought with it a new business class and Guinea now has some wealthy exiles, but much of the country remains poor and underdeveloped; GNP is below $500 per capita.

WORLD RANKING

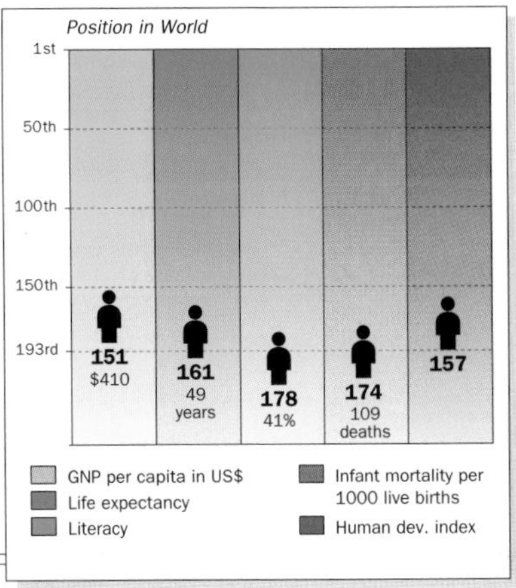
Position in World
1st
50th
100th
150th
193rd
151
$410
161
49 years
178
41%
174
109 deaths
157
GNP per capita in US$
Life expectancy
Literacy
Infant mortality per 1000 live births
Human dev. index

G

GUINEA-BISSAU

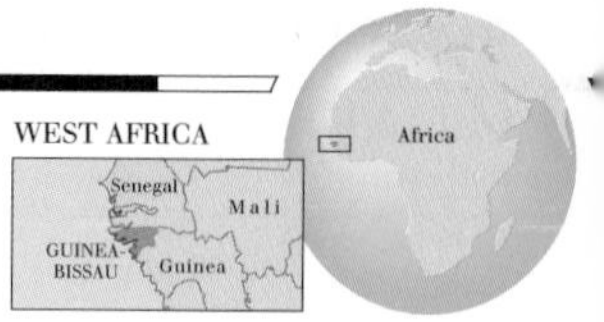
WEST AFRICA
Senegal
Mali
GUINEA-BISSAU
Guinea
Africa

OFFICIAL NAME: Republic of Guinea-Bissau **CAPITAL:** Bissau
POPULATION: 1.3 million **CURRENCY:** CFA franc **OFFICIAL LANGUAGE:** Portuguese

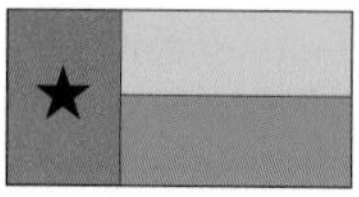

1974 | 1974 | Sept 24 | GNB | 0 | +245 | .gw

LYING ON AFRICA'S west coast, impoverished Guinea-Bissau is a former Portuguese territory. Apart from savanna highlands in the northeast, the country is low-lying. The PAIGC initiated a process of transition to multiparty democracy in 1990, and elections were held in 1994. A military coup in 1999 followed an army rebellion the previous year, but legislative and presidential elections have since been held. There are plans to move the capital east to Buba.

G

CLIMATE

Tropical monsoon

WEATHER CHART FOR BISSAU

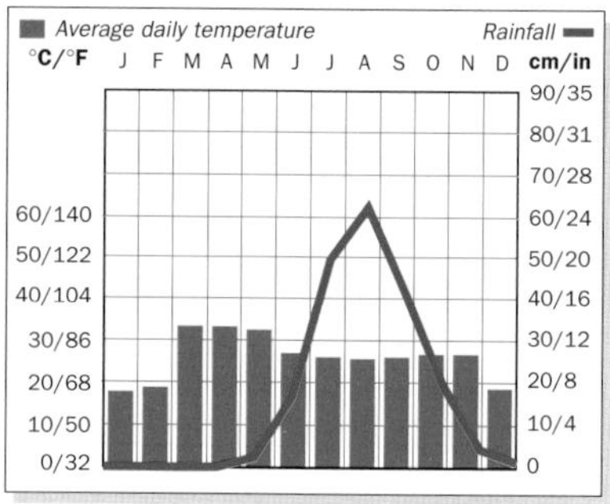
Average daily temperature
Rainfall
°C/°F
J F M A M J J A S O N D
cm/in
90/35
80/31
70/28
60/24
50/20
40/16
30/12
20/8
10/4
0
60/140
50/122
40/104
30/86
20/68
10/50
0/32

The climate is tropical. The north is affected by the Sahel, the wetter south by the Atlantic. Droughts can occur.

TRANSPORTATION

Drive on right

Bissalanca International, Bissau

24 ships 6459 grt

THE TRANSPORTATION NETWORK

453 km (281 miles)

None

None

Scattered stretches important to coastal commerce

The many waterways and islands make water transportation as vital as the roads. Both are being improved.

TOURISM

Visitors : Population 1:162

8000 visitors

No significant change from year to year

MAIN TOURIST ARRIVALS

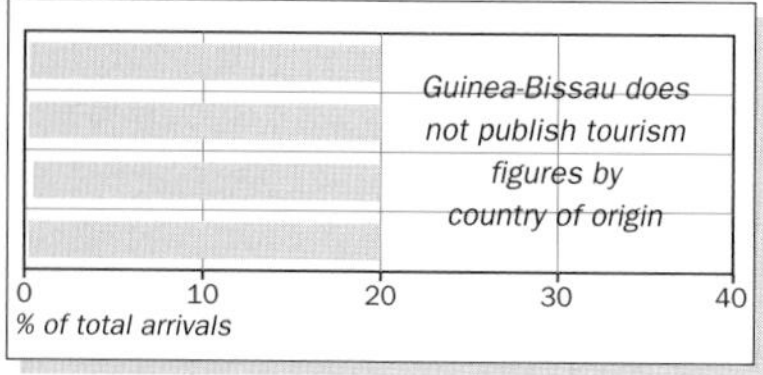
Guinea-Bissau does not publish tourism figures by country of origin
0
10
20
30
40
% of total arrivals

The lack of tourist facilities means that the country remains a destination for only the most independent of travelers.

PEOPLE

Pop. density low

Portuguese Creole, Balante, Fulani, Malinke, Portuguese

46/km² (120/mi²)

THE URBAN/RURAL POPULATION SPLIT

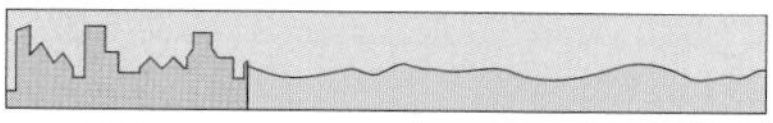
32%
68%

RELIGIOUS PERSUASION

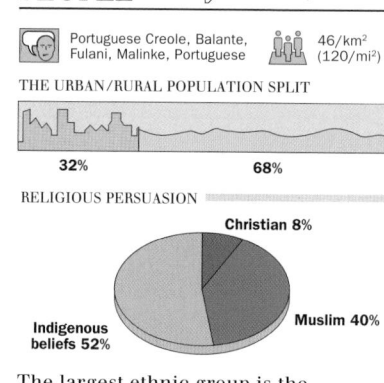

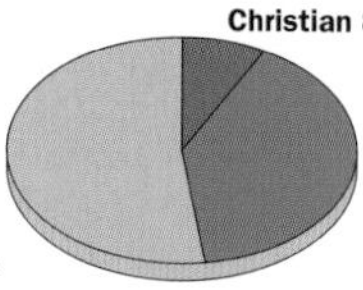
Christian 8%
Muslim 40%
Indigenous beliefs 52%

The largest ethnic group is the southern Balante, which forms almost one-third of the population. Mixed-race *mestiço* and European minorities make up just 2% of the population. Though small in number, the *mestiços* – many of whom derive from Cape Verde, Portugal's other former west African colony – still dominate the bureaucracy. Resentment at this, especially among the Balante, who provided most of the PAIGC troops in the independence war, was one cause of the 1980 coup. The majority of the population live and work on small family farms, grouped in self-contained villages. Most of the urban population live in the capital, Bissau, where they face economic hardship and increasing political instability.

POLITICS

Multiparty elections

1999/2003 (postponed)

President Kumba Yalla

AT THE LAST ELECTION

National People's Assembly (dissolved) 102 seats

37% PRS
27% RGB
24% PAIGC
4% AD
8% Others

PRS = Party for Social Renewal **RGB** = Guinea-Bissau Resistance **PAIGC** = African Party for the Independence of Guinea and Cape Verde **AD** = Alliance for Democracy

Twenty years of one-party rule ended in 1994 with the holding of multiparty elections. However, opposition groups disputed the ruling PAIGC's victory.

A period of instability led to an army rebellion in 1998 and eight months of fighting between those loyal to President João Bernardo Vieira and to the army chief, Gen. Ansumane Mane; about half the population was displaced as a result. ECOWAS troops intervened and a national unity government was formed, only to be overthrown by an army coup in 1999.

Fresh elections were won by the PRS, and its candidate Kumba Yalla went on to be elected president in 2000. Mane was killed in another coup attempt later that year. The erratic Yalla is under intense pressure to institute widespread liberal reforms, starting with fresh elections which have been persistently postponed.

WORLD AFFAIRS

Joined UN in 1974

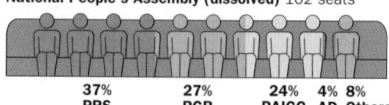

ECOWAS | CPLP | OIF | AU | OIC

Relations with neighboring states are extremely tense due to the activities of various rebel militias on the borders. There is mounting international concern over the lack of effective democracy and reports of repression.

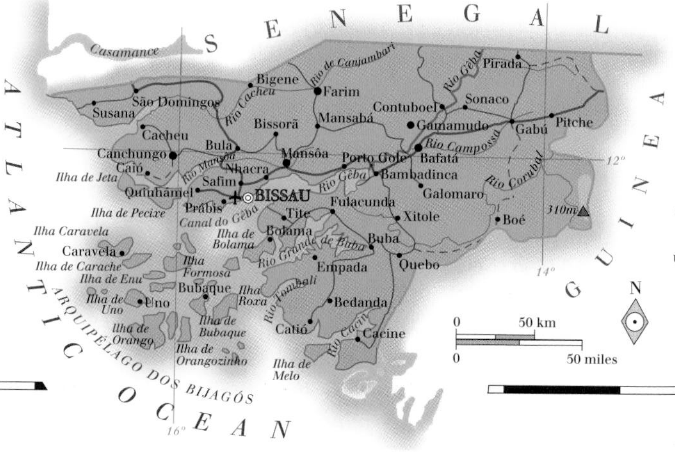
SENEGAL
Casamance
ATLANTIC OCEAN
ARQUIPÉLAGO DOS BIJAGÓS
GUINEA
Pirada
Sonaco
Pitche
Gabu
Bigene
Farim
Contuboel
São Domingos
Susana
Cacheu
Bissorã
Mansabá
Gamamudo
Rio Cacheu
Rio Geba
Rio Corubal
Bula
Canchungo
Mansôa
Porto Gole
Bafatá
Caió
Nhacra
Bambadinca
Ilha de Jeta
Safim
Quinhámel
Galomaro
Prabis
BISSAU
Fulacunda
Ilha de Pecixe
Tite
Xitole
Boé
310m
Canal do Gêba
Bolama
Ilha de Bolama
Buba
Ilha Caravela
Caravela
Ilha de Carache
Ilha Formosa
Empada
Quebo
Ilha de Enu
Bubaque
Ilha Roxa
Ilha de Uno
Uno
Bedanda
Ilha de Orango
Ilha de Bubaque
Catió
Cacine
Ilha de Orangozinho
Ilha de Melo
12°
14°
16°
0
50 km
50 miles
N

GUINEA-BISSAU

Total Area : 36 120 sq. km (13 946 sq. miles)

POPULATION

over 100 000

over 10 000

under 10 000

LAND HEIGHT

200m/656ft

Sea Level

AID

Recipient

$59m (receipts)

Down 26% in 2001

After the EU, Portugal is the most important single aid donor. Balance-of-payments support is critical to the economy. Export earnings are small compared with the costs of imports and debt servicing. Donor support was frozen in 1991 because of the country's World Bank arrears, but the government pushed ahead with economic reforms begun in the mid-1980s, and the World Bank and the IMF agreed a $790 million debt-relief package in 2001. Education, infrastructure, and health care are the main targets of project aid.

DEFENSE

Compulsory military service

$3m

No change in 2001

There are around 9000 troops. The army led coups in 1980 and 1999, and suffered internal rebellions in 1998 and 2000, continuing a history of military interference in politics. ECOWAS soldiers have intervened to restore order on a number of occasions.

ECONOMICS

Inflation 29% p.a. (1990–2001)

$199m

571.2 CFA francs (664.2)

SCORE CARD

❑ WORLD GNP RANKING	184th
❑ GNP PER CAPITA	$160
❑ BALANCE OF PAYMENTS	–$27m
❑ INFLATION	3.3%
❑ UNEMPLOYMENT	Widespread underemployment

STRENGTHS

Minimal at present, but good potential in fisheries and timber. Hydropower and offshore oil potential.

WEAKNESSES

Instability. Lack of sufficiency in rice staple. Fish stocks depleted by poaching. Few exports, mainly cashew nuts, groundnuts. Minimal industry. High illiteracy. Poor state economic management.

EXPORTS

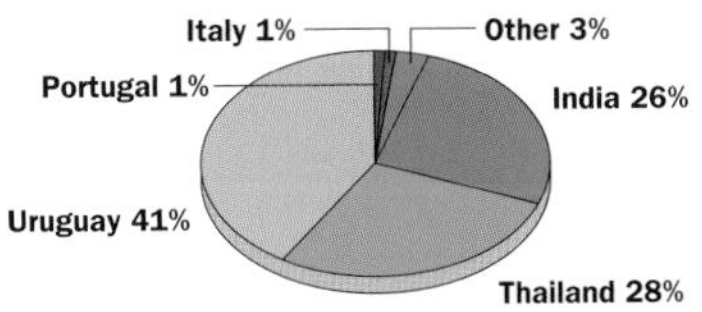
Italy 1%
Other 3%
Portugal 1%
India 26%
Uruguay 41%
Thailand 28%

IMPORTS

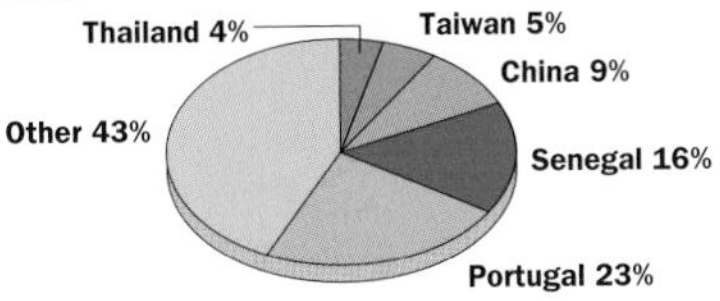
Thailand 4%
Taiwan 5%
China 9%
Other 43%
Senegal 16%
Portugal 23%

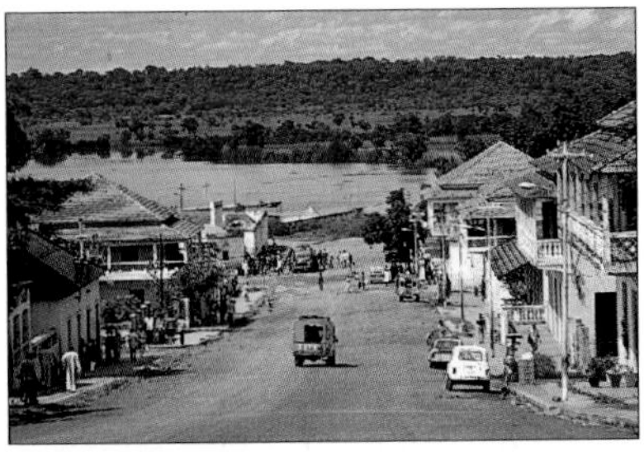

Bafatá, the chief town in central Guinea-Bissau. It lies on the Gêba River and is also an important inland port.

RESOURCES

Electric power 21,000 kW

5000 tonnes

Not an oil producer

515,000 cattle, 350,000 pigs, 1.5m chickens

Bauxite, phosphates

Fish and timber are the main natural resources, but local exploitation is only a tiny proportion of the sustainable levels. There is considerable potential for developing hydropower and for offshore oil production.

ENVIRONMENT

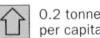

Sustainability rank: 127th

None

0.2 tonnes per capita

Drought and locust plagues are serious natural hazards. A small population and minimal industry mean that there are few serious environmental problems.

MEDIA

TV ownership low

Daily newspaper circulation 5 per 1000 people

PUBLISHING AND BROADCAST MEDIA

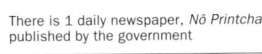

There is 1 daily newspaper, *Nô Printcha*, published by the government

1 state-owned service

3 services: 1 state-owned, 2 independent

Three independent newspapers publish intermittently due to high costs. There is one state-owned TV channel. The Portuguese-run RTP-Africa broadcasts two hours of programming a day.

CRIME

No death penalty

Guinea-Bissau does not publish prison figures

Crime is rising

Human rights abuses increased during the instability in the late 1990s, but crime levels are relatively low. Separatist conflict in neighboring Senegal makes the border region dangerous.

EDUCATION

School leaving age: 12

40%

463 students

Civil war has left school buildings damaged and a lack of trained teachers. Female education is a priority.

CHRONOLOGY

Explored by the Portuguese in the 15th century, Portuguese Guinea was established in 1879. A war for independence began in the 1960s.

- ❑ **1974** Independence. PAIGC takes power.
- ❑ **1980** Military coup.
- ❑ **1990** Multiparty politics accepted.
- ❑ **1994** Multiparty elections.
- ❑ **1998** Army rebellion led by Gen. Mane. ECOWAS intervention.
- ❑ **1999** Transitional government. May, army seizes power. November, PRS defeats PAIGC in elections.
- ❑ **2000** Kumba Yalla president. Mane killed in failed coup attempt.

G

HEALTH

No welfare state health benefits

1 per 5882 people

Parasitic, diarrheal, and communicable diseases, malaria

Guinea-Bissau's health statistics are among the world's worst, due partly to the minimal medical facilities. What had been available was severely affected by civil war, leading to outbreaks of diseases such as meningitis. In mid-2000 the AfDB provided $500,000 in funding for an emergency health program.

SPENDING

GDP/cap. increase

CONSUMPTION AND SPENDING

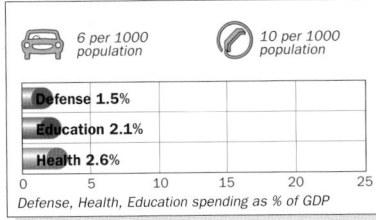

6 per 1000 population

10 per 1000 population

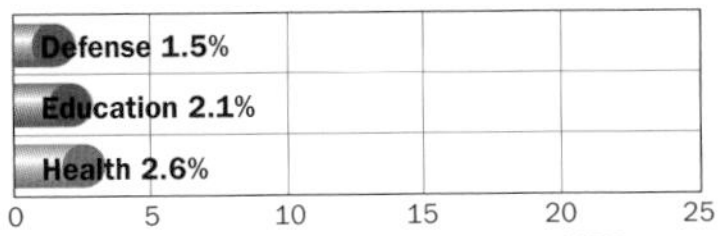
Defense 1.5%
Education 2.1%
Health 2.6%
0
5
10
15
20
25

Defense, Health, Education spending as % of GDP

Living conditions for the majority of Guinea-Bissau's people are extremely poor; around 50% of the population are unable to meet their basic needs. The tiny elite is mainly *mestiço*.

WORLD RANKING

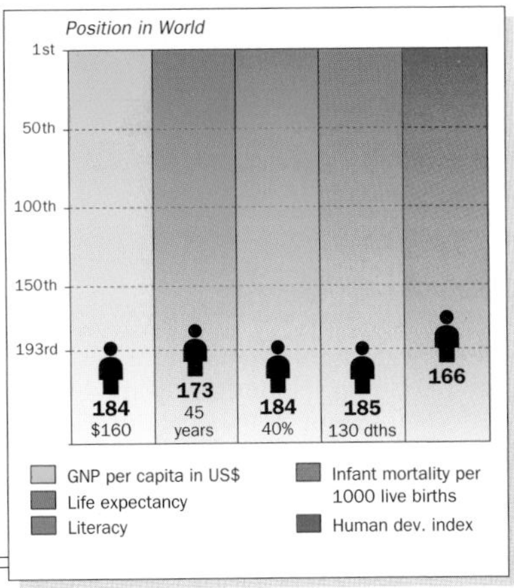
Position in World
1st
50th
100th
150th
193rd
184
$160
173
45
years
184
40%
185
130 dths
166
GNP per capita in US$
Life expectancy
Literacy
Infant mortality per 1000 live births
Human dev. index

GUYANA

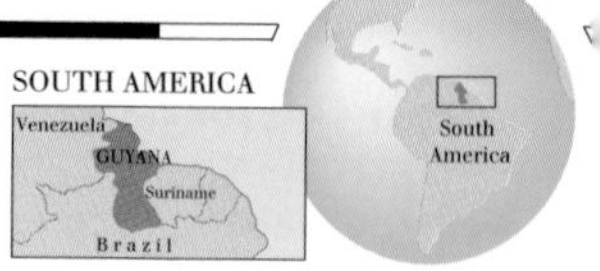
SOUTH AMERICA
Venezuela
GUYANA
Suriname
Brazil
South America

OFFICIAL NAME: Cooperative Republic of Guyana **CAPITAL:** Georgetown
POPULATION: 765,000 **CURRENCY:** Guyana dollar **OFFICIAL LANGUAGE:** English

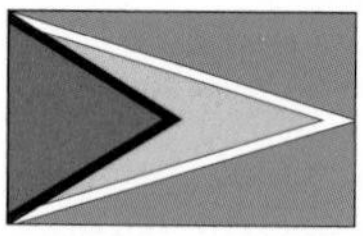

1966 | 1966 | Feb 23 | GUY | -4 | +592 | .gy

LYING ON THE NORTHERN EDGE of South America, Guyana stretches 600 km (375 miles) from dense tropical rainforests, through broad savanna and mountains dotted with waterfalls, to the narrow Atlantic coastal plain where most of the population lives. A British colony from 1814 until independence in 1966, Guyana has closer ties with the mostly anglophone Caribbean than with its Spanish-, Portuguese-, and Dutch-speaking neighbors.

CLIMATE

Tropical equatorial

WEATHER CHART FOR GEORGETOWN

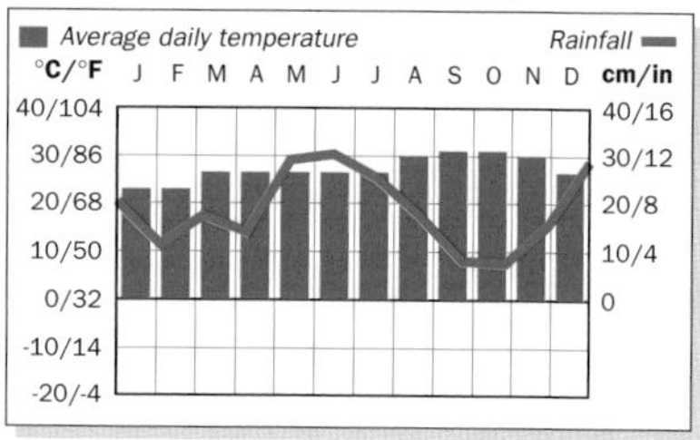
Average daily temperature
Rainfall
°C/°F
J F M A M J J A S O N D
cm/in
40/104
30/86
20/68
10/50
0/32
-10/14
-20/-4
40/16
30/12
20/8
10/4
0

The lowlands are very humid, with a constant temperature. The highlands are a little cooler, especially at night.

TRANSPORTATION

Drive on left

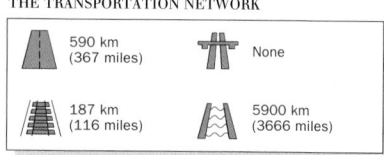

Timehri International, Georgetown 270,500 passengers

59 ships 15,169 grt

THE TRANSPORTATION NETWORK

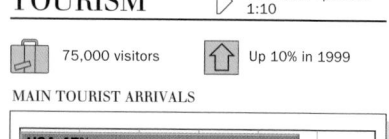

590 km (367 miles)	None
187 km (116 miles)	5900 km (3666 miles)

Reliable travel to the interior is by air or river; most paved roads are coastal. The only international airport is Timehri.

TOURISM

Visitors : Population 1:10

75,000 visitors

Up 10% in 1999

MAIN TOURIST ARRIVALS

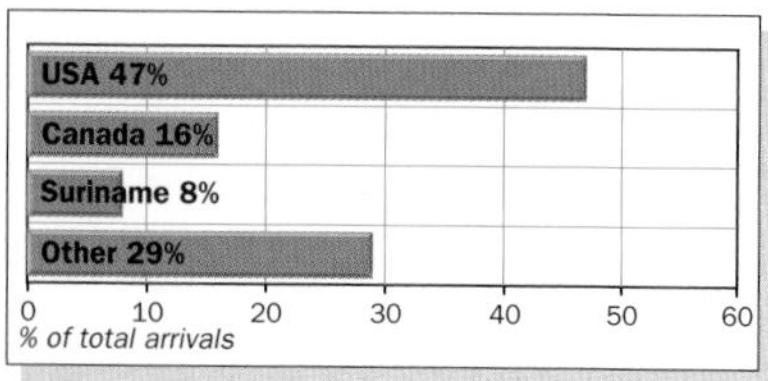
USA 47%
Canada 16%
Suriname 8%
Other 29%
0 10 20 30 40 50 60
% of total arrivals

The government promotes tourism, but the number of tourists is modest. "Guyana" means "Land of Many Waters"; the Kaieteur Falls are among the world's most impressive. Old Dutch wooden architecture characterizes Georgetown.

Modest homes, Georgetown. *Most buildings are made of wood. The cathedral is one of the world's tallest freestanding wooden buildings.*

PEOPLE

Pop. density low

English Creole, Hindi, Tamil, Amerindian languages, English

4/km² (10/mi²)

THE URBAN/RURAL POPULATION SPLIT

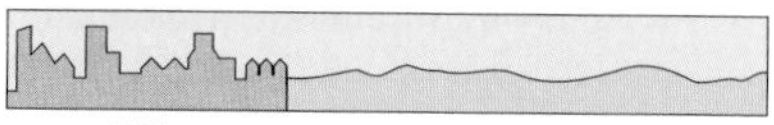
37%
63%

ETHNIC MAKEUP

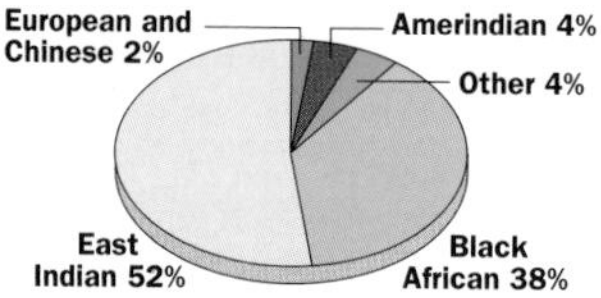
European and Chinese 2%
Amerindian 4%
Other 4%
East Indian 52%
Black African 38%

Guyana is a complex multiracial society. Tension exists between the Afro-Guyanese, descended from slaves brought over in the 17th to 19th centuries, and the Indo-Guyanese, descendants of laborers brought from India in the 19th century. This is currently displayed in the hostility existing between the PNC, representing Afro-Guyanese, and the PPP, traditionally representing the Indo-Guyanese.

POLITICS

Multiparty elections

2001/2006

President Bharrat Jagdeo

AT THE LAST ELECTION

National Assembly 65 seats

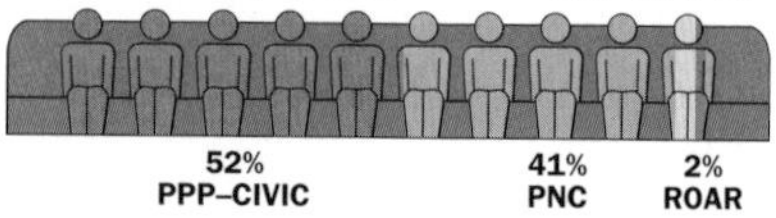
3% GAP–WPA
2% TUF
52% PPP–CIVIC
41% PNC
2% ROAR

PPP–CIVIC = People's Progressive Party–CIVIC
PNC = People's National Congress
GAP–WPA = Guyana Action Party–Working People's Alliance
ROAR = Rise, Organize, and Rebuild **TUF** = The United Force

The success of the PPP in 1992, in what was widely seen as the first fair poll since independence, ended the dominance of the PNC. Politics since has been characterized by serious animosity between the two main parties. The PNC violently contested the succession of Janet Jagan as president in 1997 following the death of her husband, veteran PPP leader Cheddi, and open hostility erupted once again in 2001 when Bharrat Jagdeo won the presidency. Interparty hostility has eased somewhat since the death of PNC leader and former president Desmond Hoyte in 2003.

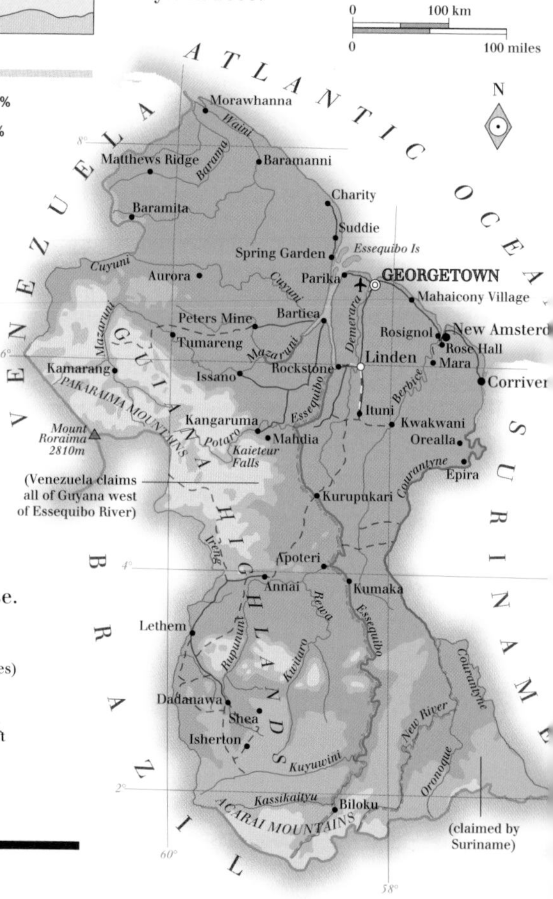
0 100 km
0 100 miles
ATLANTIC OCEAN
N
VENEZUELA
SURINAME
BRAZIL
Morawhanna
Waini
Matthews Ridge
Barama
Baramanni
Charity
Baramita
Suddie
Essequibo Is
Spring Garden
Cuyuni
Aurora
Parika
GEORGETOWN
Mahaicony Village
Peters Mine
Bartica
Tumareng
Mazaruni
Rosignol
New Amsterdam
Rose Hall
Linden
Mara
Demerara
Kamarang
Issano
Rockstone
Berbice
Corriverton
GUIANA
PAKARAIMA MOUNTAINS
Ituni
Kwakwani
Kangaruma
Orealla
Mount Roraima 2810m
Potaro
Mahdia
Kaieteur Falls
Epira
Courantyne
(Venezuela claims all of Guyana west of Essequibo River)
Kurupukari
Apoteri
Iwokrama
Annai
Kumaka
Rewa
Lethem
Essequibo
Rupununi
Kwitaro
Dadanawa
Shea
Isherton
New River
Kuyuwini
Oronoque
Kassikaityu
Biloku
ACARAI MOUNTAINS
(claimed by Suriname)
HIGHLANDS

GUYANA

Total Area : 214 970 sq. km (83 000 sq. miles)

POPULATION	LAND HEIGHT
over 100 000	1000m/3281ft
over 50 000	500m/1640ft
over 10 000	200m/656ft
under 10 000	Sea Level

WORLD AFFAIRS

Joined UN in 1966

ACS | OIC | Caricom | Comm | OAS

Rescheduling debt with Western creditor states is paramount. Long-standing border disputes with Venezuela and Suriname and closer integration with the Caribbean are also important.

AID

Recipient

US$102m (receipts) | Down 6% in 2001

Most aid comes from the IDB, the UK, and the US. Recent grants covered public health projects, business development, and protection of the rainforest.

DEFENSE

No compulsory military service

US$6m | Down 14% in 2001

The security forces, which include a small land army, benefit from financial support and training provided by the US and UK governments.

ECONOMICS

Inflation 12% p.a. (1990–2001)

US$641m | 179 Guyana dollars (180.5)

SCORE CARD

❑ WORLD GNP RANKING	163rd
❑ GNP PER CAPITA	US$840
❑ BALANCE OF PAYMENTS	–US$117m
❑ INFLATION	2.6%
❑ UNEMPLOYMENT	12%

STRENGTHS

Diverse exports: gold, rice, sugar, diamonds, bauxite, and timber production. Debt reduction agreed with multilateral agencies.

WEAKNESSES

High per capita foreign debt. Political instability dents investor confidence. Bauxite industry weakened by departure of major US investor, Alcoa. Sugar exports threatened by end of preferential access to EU markets. High unemployment.

EXPORTS

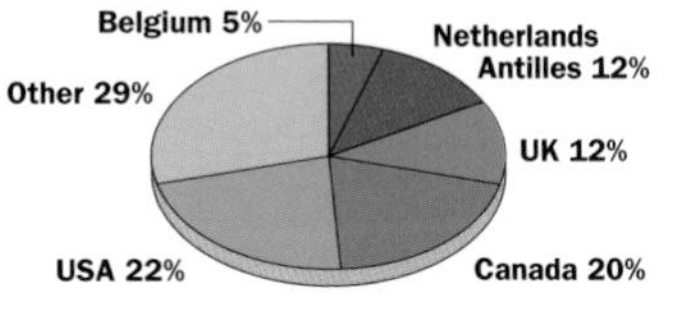
Belgium 5%
Netherlands Antilles 12%
Other 29%
UK 12%
USA 22%
Canada 20%

IMPORTS

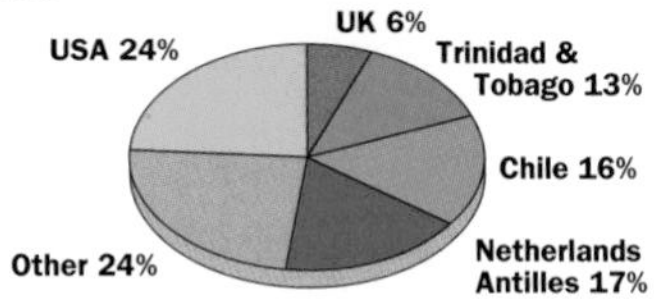
UK 6%
USA 24%
Trinidad & Tobago 13%
Chile 16%
Other 24%
Netherlands Antilles 17%

RESOURCES

Electric power 302,000 kW

49,424 tonnes | Minimal oil production

130,000 sheep, 100,000 cattle, 12.5m chickens | Gold, diamonds, bauxite, gemstones, oil, manganese, uranium

Gold, diamonds, bauxite, and timber are major resources. Offshore and onshore prospecting for oil has not reduced the need for petroleum imports for electricity generation. More hydroelectric power plants are being constructed.

ENVIRONMENT

Not available

0.3% | 2.2 tonnes per capita

The state of disrepair of the 18th-century sea defense system endangers the urbanized coastline that lies below sea level. Commercial logging threatens to deplete the rainforest. The pollution of rivers caused by mining activities is now a serious problem.

MEDIA

TV ownership medium

Daily newspaper circulation 75 per 1000 people

PUBLISHING AND BROADCAST MEDIA

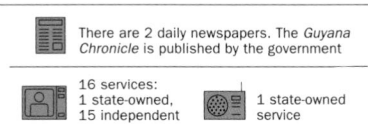

There are 2 daily newspapers. The *Guyana Chronicle* is published by the government

16 services: 1 state-owned, 15 independent | 1 state-owned service

The PPP and the PNC both publish periodicals. The government owns one TV service and the sole radio service as well as publishing a daily newspaper.

CRIME

Death penalty in use

1507 prisoners | Thefts increased in 2000–2001

The police are strongly criticized for corruption and ineffectiveness in the face of rising urban crime. Serious violence between PNC and PPP–CIVIC supporters erupted in 1998, 1999, and 2001.

EDUCATION

School leaving age: 15

99% | 8965 students

Education is based on the former British system. Entry to high schools is by examination at 11 years. There is a state-financed university, though many students go to the US or the UK.

HEALTH

Welfare state health benefits

1 per 2083 people | Heart diseases, violence, accidents, cancers

Nearly all of the population have access to the mainly state-run health service, though this is hindered by poor transportation links.

CHRONOLOGY

During the 17th and 18th centuries, the Dutch founded three colonies, Essequibo, Demerara, and Berbice, in the region. In 1814, these came under British control, and were later combined to form British Guiana.

- ❑ **1953** First universal elections won by PPP under Cheddi Jagan; parliament later suspended by UK.
- ❑ **1966** Independence from UK.
- ❑ **1973** PPP boycotts parliament, accusing PNC of electoral fraud.
- ❑ **1992** Fair elections won by PPP. Jagan president.
- ❑ **1997–1998** Jagan dies in office; PNC rejects his widow's election victory. Political crisis.
- ❑ **1999** Caricom-brokered peace deal. Janet Jagan resigns; Bharrat Jagdeo takes over as president.
- ❑ **2001** Jagdeo and PPP reelected. Political violence flares again.

G

SPENDING

GDP/cap. increase

CONSUMPTION AND SPENDING

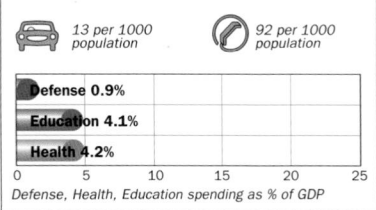

13 per 1000 population | *92 per 1000 population*

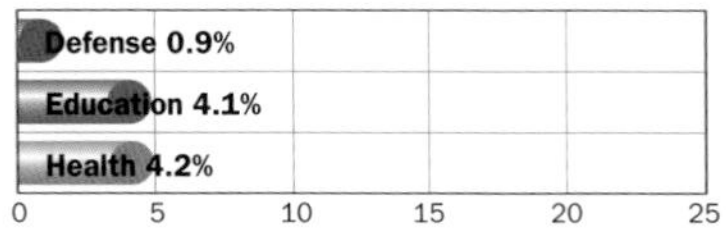
Defense 0.9%
Education 4.1%
Health 4.2%
0
5
10
15
20
25

Defense, Health, Education spending as % of GDP

Significant urban and rural poverty in Guyana has forced the government to make provision in the budget for poverty alleviation. Redundancies in the public sector exacerbate the problem. The poorest group in society are Amerindian subsistence farmers. There are a few very affluent urban families who derive their wealth not only from business but also from rural farming interests.

WORLD RANKING

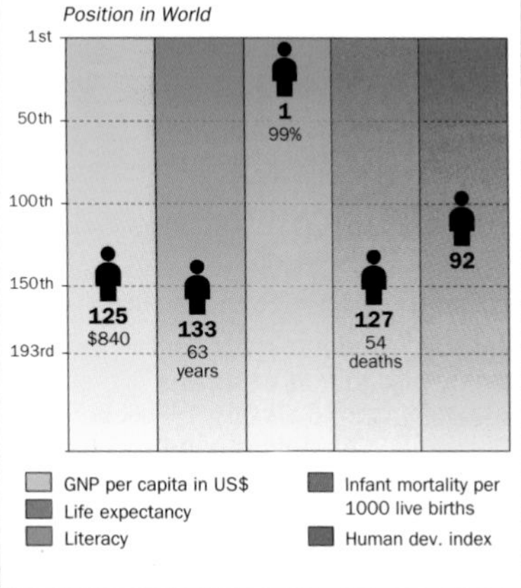
Position in World
1st
50th
100th
150th
193rd
125
$840
133
63 years
1
99%
127
54 deaths
92
GNP per capita in US$
Life expectancy
Literacy
Infant mortality per 1000 live births
Human dev. index

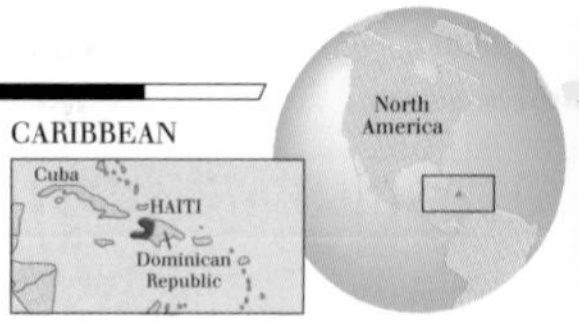
CARIBBEAN
Cuba
HAITI
Dominican Republic
North America

HAITI

OFFICIAL NAME: Republic of Haiti **CAPITAL:** Port-au-Prince **POPULATION:** 8.4 million
CURRENCY: Gourde **OFFICIAL LANGUAGES:** French and French Creole

1804 | 1844 | Jan 1 | RH | -5 | +509 | .ht

HAITI OCCUPIES the western third of the Caribbean island of Hispaniola. A colony first of Spain and then of France, in 1804 it was the first Caribbean state to become independent, and has been in a state of political chaos virtually ever since. Democracy did not materialize with the exile of the dictator Jean-Claude Duvalier in 1986. Elections were held in 1990, but by 1991 the army was back in power and was ousted in 1994 only through US intervention.

CLIMATE

Tropical equatorial/ oceanic

WEATHER CHART FOR PORT-AU-PRINCE

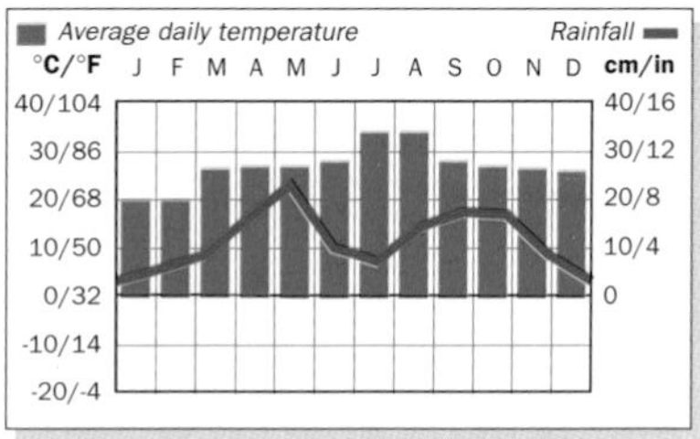
Average daily temperature
Rainfall
°C/°F J F M A M J J A S O N D cm/in
40/104
30/86
20/68
10/50
0/32
-10/14
-20/-4
40/16
30/12
20/8
10/4
0

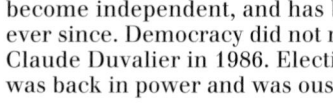

Humidity is lower than the Caribbean average, as Haiti lies in the rain shadow of Hispaniola's central mountains.

TRANSPORTATION

Drive on right

Port-au-Prince 962,599 passengers

4 ships 1200 grt

THE TRANSPORTATION NETWORK

1011 km (628 miles)	None
40 km (25 miles)	100 km (62 miles)

Roads are poor, especially in the interior. Ferries provide the main transportation to the southern peninsula.

TOURISM

Visitors : Population 1:60

140,000 visitors

Down 2% in 2000

MAIN TOURIST ARRIVALS

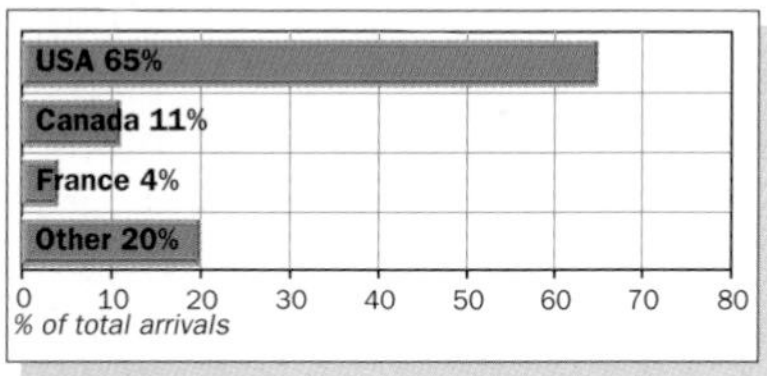
USA 65%
Canada 11%
France 4%
Other 20%
0 10 20 30 40 50 60 70 80
% of total arrivals

Haiti's location, history, and culture provided much of its attraction for tourists in the 1960s and 1970s. Political instability and violence in the 1980s, however, led to the industry's near collapse and it has yet to recover.

PEOPLE

Pop. density high

French Creole, French

305/km² (789/mi²)

THE URBAN/RURAL POPULATION SPLIT

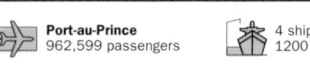

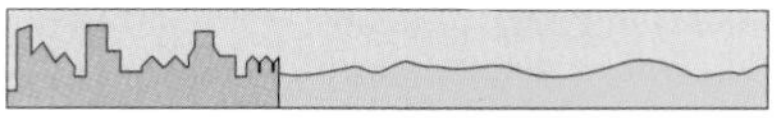
36%
64%

RELIGIOUS PERSUASION

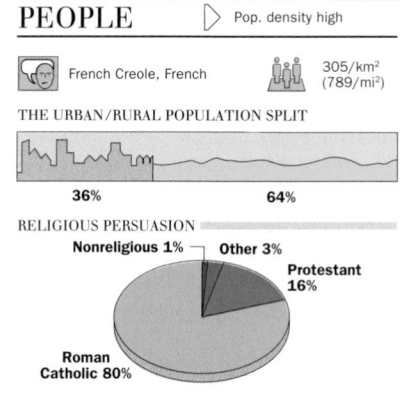

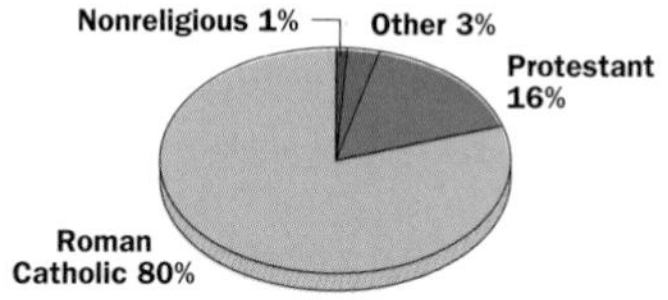
Nonreligious 1%
Other 3%
Protestant 16%
Roman Catholic 80%

Most Haitians are of African descent; a few have European roots, primarily French. Haiti is one of the poorest countries in the Americas. Social tensions run high, focusing on class rather than race. Political repression and a collapsing economy have led many to emigrate legally, or illegally, to North America and the neighboring Caribbean, particularly the Dominican Republic. As well as being Christians, a majority of Haitians practice voodoo, which was given the status of an official religion only in 2003.

POLITICS

Multiparty elections

L. House 2000/2004
U. House 2000/2002 (postponed)

President Jean-Bertrand Aristide

AT THE LAST ELECTION

Chamber of Deputies 83 seats

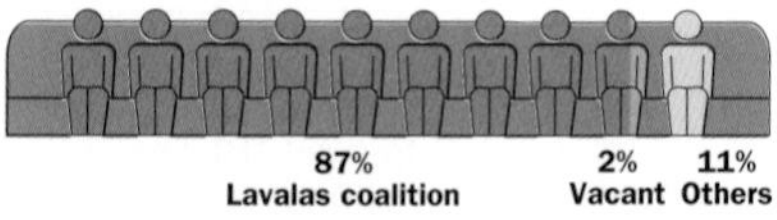
87% Lavalas coalition
2% Vacant
11% Others

Senate 27 seats

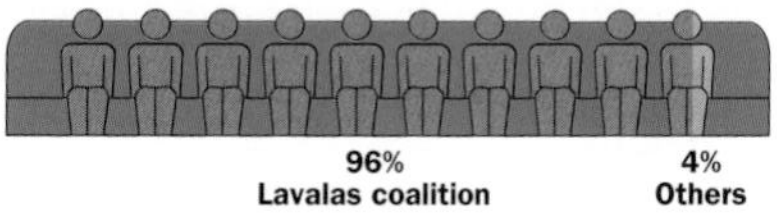
96% Lavalas coalition
4% Others

A wealthy elite, backed by the military, supported the Duvalier dictatorships and regularly financed coups after "Baby Doc" Duvalier's overthrow in 1986. UN sanctions followed the 1991 coup and US forces restored the elected president, Jean-Bertrand Aristide, in 1994. His left-wing Lavalas party won legislative elections in 1995. A backlash against austerity policies insisted on by the US soured relations between the presidency and the legislature. New elections, finally held in 2000, resulted in a strongly disputed but decisive victory for the Lavalas coalition, while a similarly controversial presidential poll was won by Aristide. The opposition rejected his victory, effectively creating political stalemate. Both Aristide and the opposition have refused to agree to internationally backed compromises. Popular unrest has steadily increased.

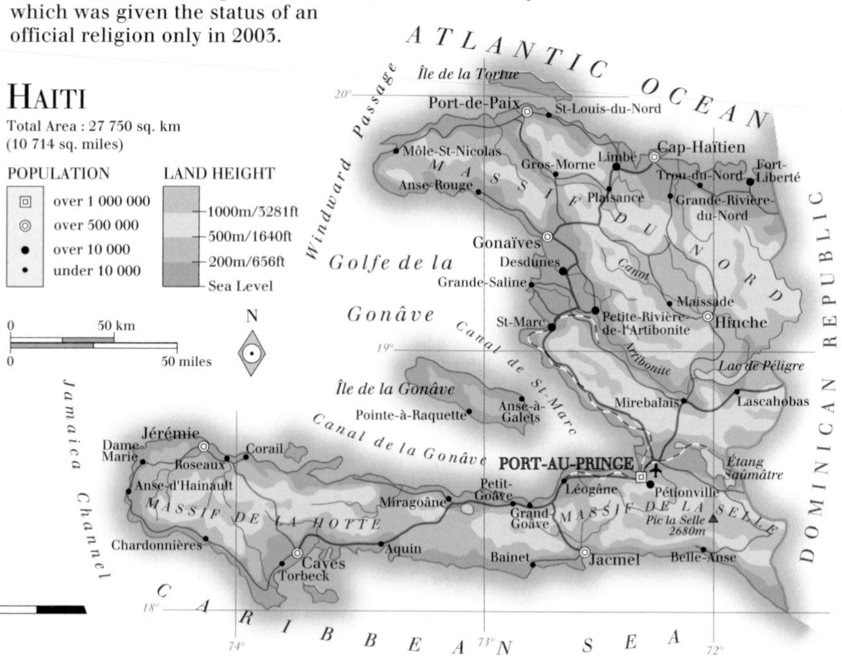
HAITI
Total Area : 27 750 sq. km (10 714 sq. miles)
POPULATION
over 1 000 000
over 500 000
over 10 000
under 10 000
LAND HEIGHT
1000m/3281ft
500m/1640ft
200m/656ft
Sea Level
0 50 km
0 50 miles
N
ATLANTIC OCEAN
Île de la Tortue
Port-de-Paix
St-Louis-du-Nord
Windward Passage
Môle-St-Nicolas
Cap-Haïtien
Limbé
Gros-Morne
Fort-Liberté
Trou-du-Nord
Anse-Rouge
MASSIF DU NORD
Plaisance
Grande-Rivière-du-Nord
Gonaïves
Desdunes
Golfe de la Gonâve
Grande-Saline
Maissade
Petite-Rivière-de-l'Artibonite
Hinche
St-Marc
Canal de St-Marc
Artibonite
Lac de Péligre
Île de la Gonâve
Anse-à-Galets
Mirebalais
Lascahobas
Pointe-à-Raquette
Canal de la Gonâve
Jérémie
Dame-Marie
Corail
Roseaux
PORT-AU-PRINCE
Étang Saumâtre
Anse-d'Hainault
Petit-Goâve
Léogâne
Pétionville
Miragoâne
MASSIF DE LA HOTTE
Grand-Goâve
MASSIF DE LA SELLE
Pic la Selle 2680m
Chardonnières
Aquin
Cayes
Torbeck
Bainet
Jacmel
Belle-Anse
Jamaica Channel
CARIBBEAN SEA
DOMINICAN REPUBLIC
20°
19°
18°
74°
73°
72°

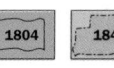

WORLD AFFAIRS

Joined UN in 1945

ACS | ACP | Caricom | OAS | WTO

Continued political instability has led to cuts in international aid and in ties with major donors. Relations with the US have deteriorated over Aristide's refusal to accept political compromise.

AID

Recipient

$166m (receipts) | Down 20% in 2001

The IMF granted $21 million in emergency aid in 1998 for hurricane damage. The IDB approved loans for water and health projects, and Taiwan granted $60.4 million in aid.

DEFENSE

No compulsory military service

$40m | Down 7% in 2001

In 1994, the military was ousted and democracy was restored. The armed forces and police were disbanded and an interim public security force was created. A 5300-strong new national police force has now been formed, funded and trained by the US.

ECONOMICS

Inflation 20% p.a. (1990–2001)

$3.9bn | 39.15 gourdes (27.5)

SCORE CARD

❑ World GNP Ranking	122nd
❑ GNP per Capita	$480
❑ Balance of Payments	–$177m
❑ Inflation	14.2%
❑ Unemployment	70%

Strengths

Few. Coffee exports. Remittances from Haitians living abroad. Large profits from transshipment of narcotics to US.

Weaknesses

Political instability has destroyed investor confidence. $500 million of US aid frozen since 2000. Massive unemployment and underemployment.

EXPORTS

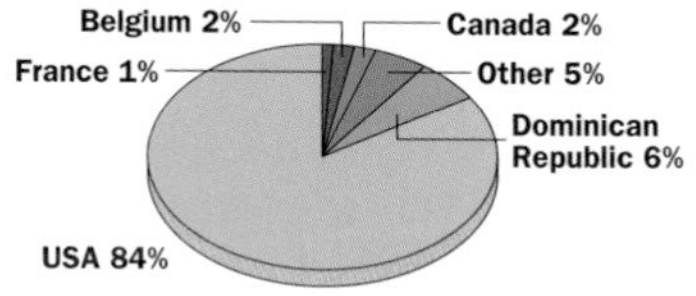
Belgium 2%
Canada 2%
France 1%
Other 5%
Dominican Republic 6%
USA 84%

IMPORTS

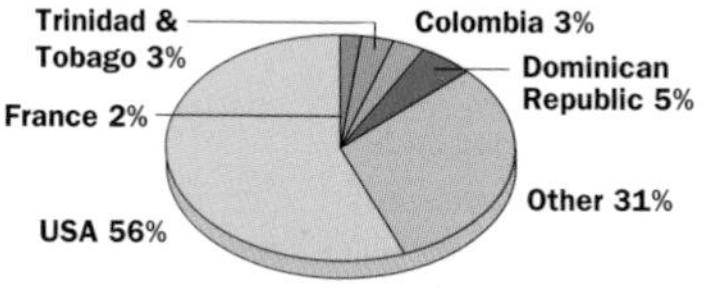
Trinidad & Tobago 3%
Colombia 3%
Dominican Republic 5%
France 2%
Other 31%
USA 56%

***In remote villages in Haiti,** most houses are made of earth and do not have glass in their windows.*

RESOURCES

Electric power 264,000 kW

5000 tonnes | Not an oil producer

1.94m goats, 1.45m cattle, 1m pigs, 5.6m chickens | Marble, limestone, clay, silver, gold, natural asphalt

Haiti has no strategic resources. Under prolonged economic sanctions, it had to find unofficial sources of oil; much was imported from Europe.

ENVIRONMENT

Sustainability rank: 137th

0.4% (0.1% partially protected) | 0.2 tonnes per capita

Diminishing forests now cover only 3.2% of total land area, resulting in severe soil erosion. The removal of 4000 tonnes of toxic waste, illegally dumped in 1988 near Gonaïves, finally began in 1998.

MEDIA

TV ownership low

Daily newspaper circulation 3 per 1000 people

PUBLISHING AND BROADCAST MEDIA

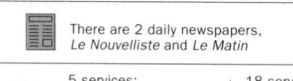

There are 2 daily newspapers, *Le Nouvelliste* and *Le Matin*

5 services: 1 state-owned, 4 independent | 18 services: 1 state-owned, 17 independent

Under military rule, the media were largely controlled through intimidation. The transition to democracy promised, but failed to deliver, a more open press.

CRIME

No death penalty

4152 prisoners | Crime is rising

Extrajudicial killings, torture, and brutality continue, despite the ending of military dictatorship. Narcotics trafficking is highly organized. Police are inexperienced and the judicial system is slow and open to corruption.

EDUCATION

School leaving age: 11

51% | 6288 students

In the run-down state system under 10% of students pass the *baccalauréat* exam. Church-run private schools perform better, but fees are beyond most Haitians.

CHRONOLOGY

In 1697, Spain ceded the west of Hispaniola to France. Ex-slave Toussaint Louverture's rebellion in 1791 led to independence in 1804.

- ❑ **1915–1934** US occupation.
- ❑ **1957–1971** François "Papa Doc" Duvalier's brutal dictatorship.
- ❑ **1971–1986** His son Jean-Claude, "Baby Doc," rules; eventually flees.
- ❑ **1986–1988** Military rule.
- ❑ **1990** Jean-Bertrand Aristide elected; exiled in 1991 coup.
- ❑ **1994–1995** US forces oust military. Aristide reinstated; elections.
- ❑ **1997–1999** Political deadlock.
- ❑ **2000** Lavalas coalition and Aristide reelected.

H

HEALTH

No welfare state health benefits

1 per 4000 people | Malaria, other parasitic diseases, tuberculosis

Most Haitians cannot afford health care. In rural areas, help is often sought from voodoo priests.

SPENDING

GDP/cap. decrease

CONSUMPTION AND SPENDING

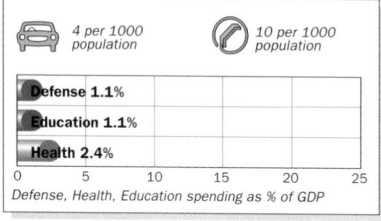

4 per 1000 population | *10 per 1000 population*

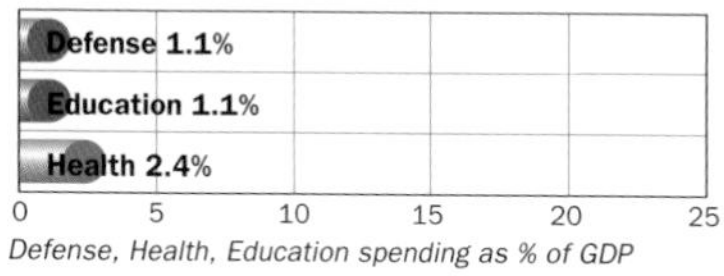
Defense 1.1%
Education 1.1%
Health 2.4%
0
5
10
15
20
25
Defense, Health, Education spending as % of GDP

Haiti's rigid class structure maintains extreme disparities of wealth between a few affluent families and the mass of the population, who live in slums without running water or proper sanitation. Two-thirds of the population fall below the national poverty level laid down by the government.

WORLD RANKING

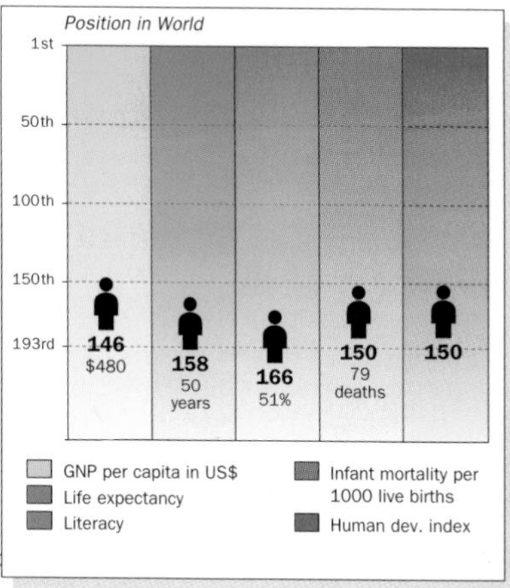
Position in World
1st
50th
100th
150th
193rd
146
$480
158
50 years
166
51%
150
79 deaths
150
GNP per capita in US$
Life expectancy
Literacy
Infant mortality per 1000 live births
Human dev. index

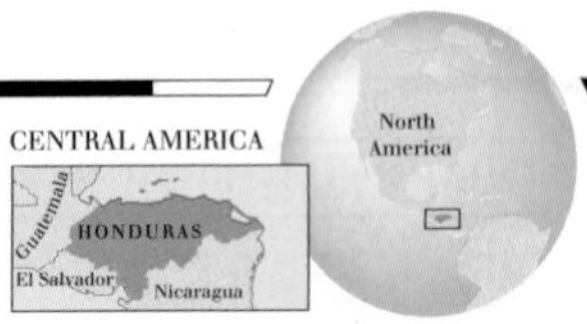
CENTRAL AMERICA
HONDURAS
Guatemala
El Salvador
Nicaragua
North America

HONDURAS

OFFICIAL NAME: Republic of Honduras **CAPITAL:** Tegucigalpa
POPULATION: 6.7 million **CURRENCY:** Lempira **OFFICIAL LANGUAGE:** Spanish

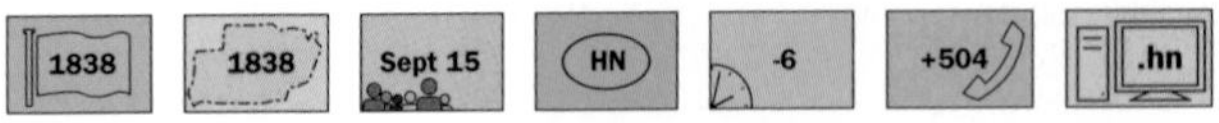
1838
1838
Sept 15
HN
-6
+504
.hn

MOST OF HONDURAS is mountainous terrain, with a small sheltered Pacific coast to the south and a broad Caribbean shoreline to the north, including part of the virtually uninhabited Mosquito Coast. After a succession of military governments it returned to full civilian rule in 1984. In 1998 Honduras was devastated by Hurricane Mitch, which resulted in the death of at least 5600 people and damage estimated at some $3 billion.

CLIMATE

Tropical equatorial

WEATHER CHART FOR TEGUCIGALPA

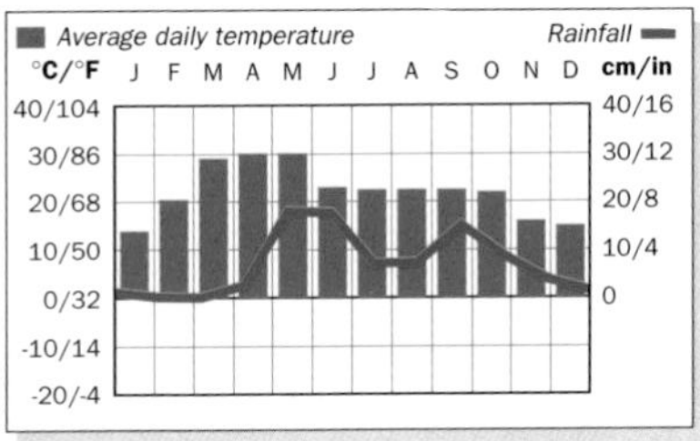
Average daily temperature
Rainfall
°C/°F
J F M A M J J A S O N D
cm/in
40/104
30/86
20/68
10/50
0/32
-10/14
-20/-4
40/16
30/12
20/8
10/4
0

Honduras's Caribbean coastline is generally extremely hot. The rest of the country is much cooler.

TRANSPORTATION

Drive on right

La Mesa, San Pedro Sula 502,414 passengers

1183 ships 966,500 grt

THE TRANSPORTATION NETWORK

3126 km (1942 miles)	None
595 km (370 miles)	465 km (289 miles)

In 1998 Hurricane Mitch destroyed roads and bridges across the country; reconstruction will take many years.

TOURISM

Visitors : Population 1:12

550,000 visitors

Up 6% in 2002

MAIN TOURIST ARRIVALS

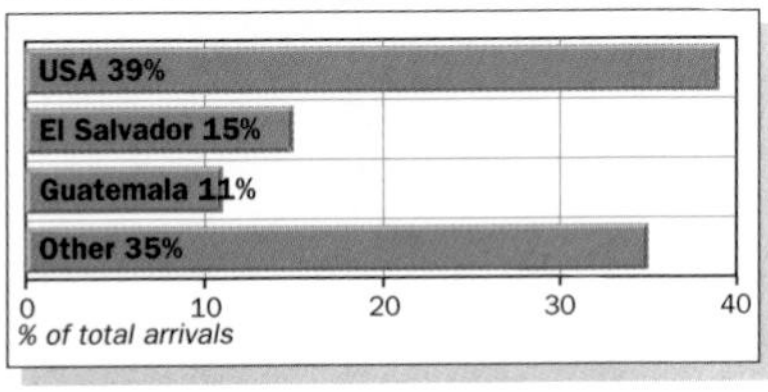
USA 39%
El Salvador 15%
Guatemala 11%
Other 35%
0
10
20
30
40
% of total arrivals

Caribbean coast resorts and the Bay Islands are popular, while exploring the remote region inland from the Mosquito Coast and jungle rafting appeal to the adventurous. The ruined Mayan temples of Copán are a major draw.

PEOPLE

Pop. density medium

Spanish, Black Carib, English Creole

60/km² (155/mi²)

THE URBAN/RURAL POPULATION SPLIT

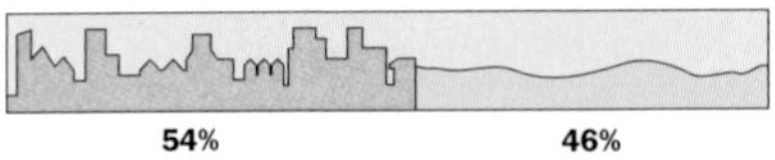
54%
46%

ETHNIC MAKEUP

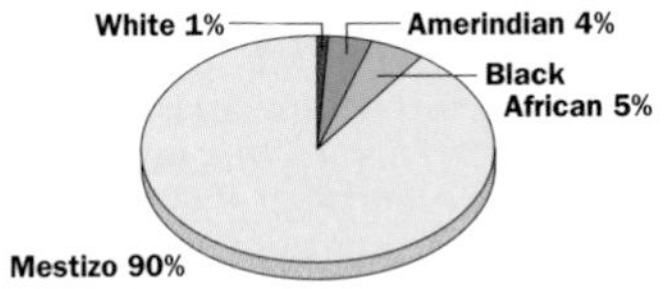
White 1%
Amerindian 4%
Black African 5%
Mestizo 90%

As in most of Central America, very few pure indigenous groups remain. The estimated 45,000 Miskito Amerindians, and an English-speaking *garífuna* (black) population on the Caribbean coast united in 1999 to oppose a constitutional amendment allowing foreigners to buy land in coastal areas, traditionally their communal lands. Poverty is at the root of social tension; whites still have the best opportunities.

Rural poverty and strong Roman Catholicism (97% are Roman Catholic) mean that the family is a powerful unifying force. The status of women is low; many work in domestic service.

POLITICS

Multiparty elections

2001/2005

President Ricardo Maduro

AT THE LAST ELECTION

National Congress 128 seats

3%
PINU–SD
48%
PNH
43%
PLH
4%
PDU
2%
PDCH

PNH = National Party of Honduras **PLH** = Liberal Party of Honduras **PDU** = Party of Democratic Unification **PINU–SD** = Innovation and Unity Party–Social Democracy **PDCH** = Honduran Christian Democratic Party

The traditional power brokers have been the military, the US embassy, and the United Fruit Company (now called Chiquita), the country's biggest banana producer. The military held power intermittently from the mid-1950s, until pressure from the US government forced it to restore civilian rule in 1984. During the 1980s, US military aid and political influence increased sharply. The armed forces retained a strong political hold. Attempts continue to bring human rights cases from the 1980s to trial.

The PNH and PLH have few real ideological differences. Presidents, able to serve only one four-year term, have tended to be weak. The PLH introduced unpopular austerity measures in 1994, but also began reducing the autonomy of the military by abolishing conscription. President Carlos Flores of the PLH, elected in 1997, continued this "demilitarization" process by naming a civilian defense minister in 1999. The presidency was won back by the PNH when Ricardo Maduro was elected in 2001.

Reconstruction after the devastation of Hurricane Mitch in 1998 will be a long-term undertaking.

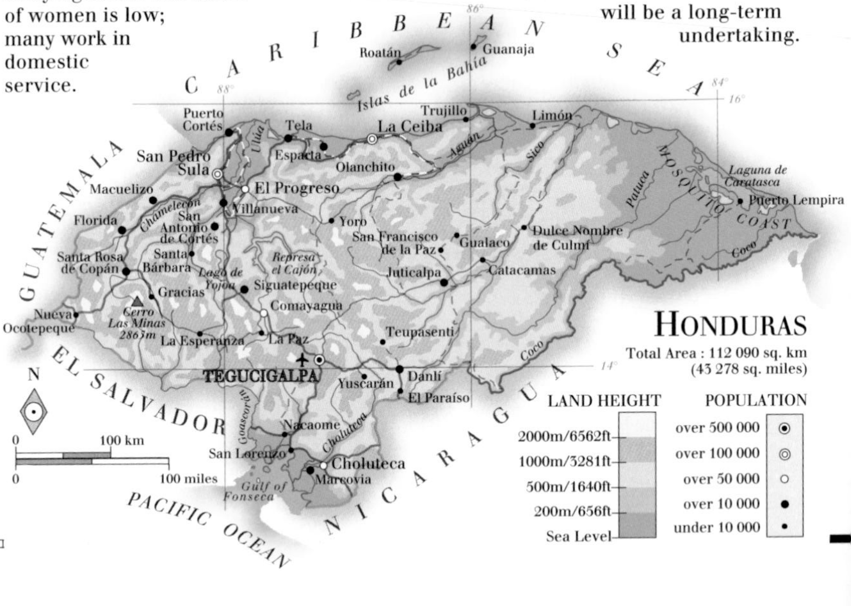
CARIBBEAN SEA
Roatán
Guanaja
Islas de la Bahía
Puerto Cortés
Tela
Trujillo
Limón
La Ceiba
San Pedro Sula
Esparta
Olanchito
Macuelizo
El Progreso
Villanueva
Laguna de Caratasca
Puerto Lempira
MOSQUITO COAST
Florida
San Antonio de Cortés
Yoro
San Francisco de la Paz
Gualaco
Dulce Nombre de Culmí
Santa Rosa de Copán
Santa Bárbara
Lago de Yojoa
Represa el Cajón
Juticalpa
Catacamas
Gracias
Siguatepeque
Comayagua
Cerro Las Minas 2865m
Nueva Ocotepeque
La Esperanza
La Paz
Teupasenti
TEGUCIGALPA
Yuscarán
Danlí
El Paraíso
GUATEMALA
EL SALVADOR
NICARAGUA
Nacaome
San Lorenzo
Choluteca
Marcovia
Gulf of Fonseca
PACIFIC OCEAN
0 100 km
0 100 miles
HONDURAS
Total Area : 112 090 sq. km (43 278 sq. miles)
LAND HEIGHT
2000m/6562ft
1000m/3281ft
500m/1640ft
200m/656ft
Sea Level
POPULATION
over 500 000
over 100 000
over 50 000
over 10 000
under 10 000

WORLD AFFAIRS

Joined UN in 1945

ACS | IAEA | NAM | OAS | San José

Relations with the US are key. In 2001 free trade was agreed with El Salvador, Guatemala, and Mexico. Border disputes exist with El Salvador and Nicaragua.

AID

Recipient

$678m (receipts) — Up 51% in 2001

Aid from the IMF and the World Bank on favorable terms followed the 1998 hurricane. Western countries agreed debt relief of $1.2 billion.

DEFENSE

No compulsory military service

$96m — Up 1% in 2001

Until 1994 the military operated with virtual impunity. The first civilian defense minister was appointed in 1999, completing the "demilitarization" process begun with the return to civilian rule in 1984.

ECONOMICS

Inflation 18% p.a. (1990–2001)

$5.93bn — 17.33 lempiras (16.4)

SCORE CARD

❑ WORLD GNP RANKING	105th
❑ GNP PER CAPITA	$900
❑ BALANCE OF PAYMENTS	–$325m
❑ INFLATION	9.7%
❑ UNEMPLOYMENT	28%

STRENGTHS

Coffee, flowers, fruit. Economic boost due to hurricane reconstruction. Overseas remittances. Barely exploited mineral deposits. Hardwoods.

WEAKNESSES

Foreign debt. Vulnerable coffee exports. Banana industry affected by hurricane damage. Lack of land reform. Slow rate of privatizations. High unemployment and underemployment. Corruption. Weak industrial base. Overdependence on HEP.

EXPORTS

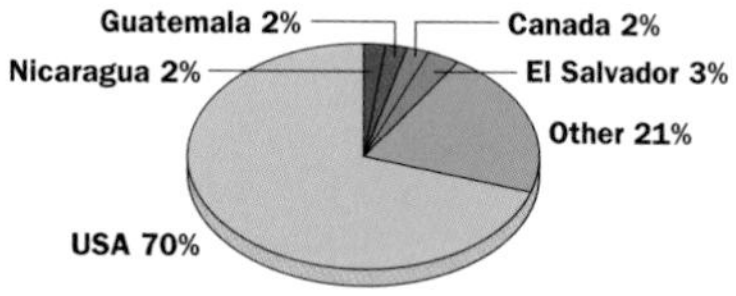
Guatemala 2%
Canada 2%
Nicaragua 2%
El Salvador 3%
Other 21%
USA 70%

IMPORTS

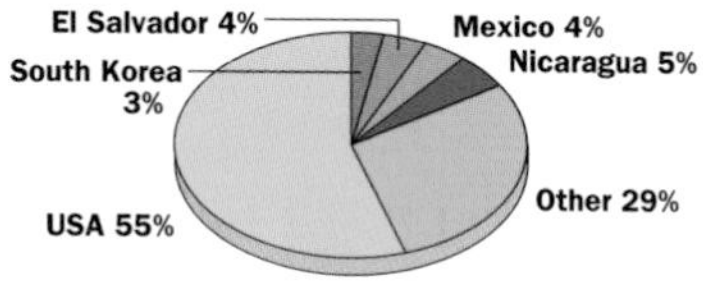
El Salvador 4%
Mexico 4%
South Korea 3%
Nicaragua 5%
Other 29%
USA 55%

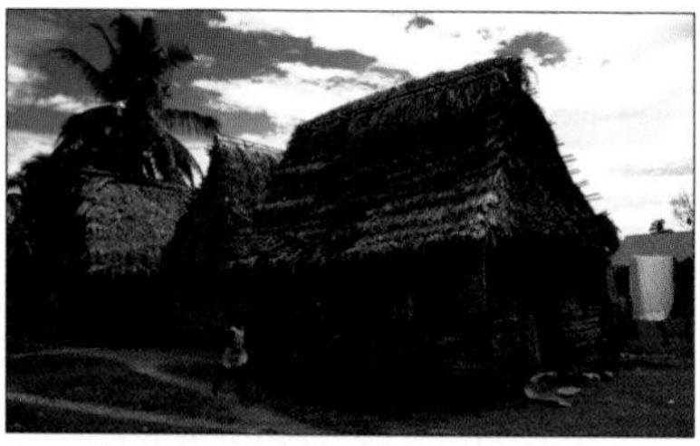

A ***garífuna settlement*** *on Honduras's long Caribbean coast.*

RESOURCES

Electric power 715,000 kW

23,862 tonnes — Not an oil producer

1.86m cattle, 538,033 pigs, 18.6m chickens — Lead, zinc, silver, gold, copper, iron, tin, coal

Coffee exports dropped dramatically in 2001, due to low world prices. Oil exploration is under way. Most energy is produced hydroelectrically.

ENVIRONMENT

Sustainability rank: 47th

10% (4% partially protected) — 0.8 tonnes per capita

The unregulated timber, cotton, and cattle industries, land colonization, and pesticides have led to ecological crisis.

MEDIA

TV ownership medium

Daily newspaper circulation 55 per 1000 people

PUBLISHING AND BROADCAST MEDIA

There are 9 daily newspapers, including *La Prensa*, *El Heraldo*, and *La Tribuna*

6 independent services — 5 services: 1 state-owned, 4 independent

Self-censorship, dependence on US sources, corruption, and intimidation guarantee a largely compliant media.

CRIME

No death penalty

10,869 prisoners — Violent crime is rising

Overzealous security forces are frequently accused of murdering child members of violent street gangs.

EDUCATION

School leaving age: 13

76% — 90,620 students

The drop-out rate of students is very high: almost half of all children do not complete primary school.

HEALTH

Welfare state health benefits

1 per 1205 people — Circulatory, infectious, and parasitic diseases, malaria

A third of Hondurans have no access to health services. Plans to privatize the social security system are unpopular.

CHRONOLOGY

Honduras was a Spanish possession until 1821. In 1823, it formed the United Provinces of Central America with four neighboring nations.

- ❑ **1838** Declares full independence.
- ❑ **1890s** US banana plantations set up.
- ❑ **1932–1949** Dictatorship of Gen. Tiburcio Carías Andino of PNH.
- ❑ **1954–1957** Elected PLH president Villeda Morales deposed, reelected.
- ❑ **1963** Military coup.
- ❑ **1969** 13-day Soccer War with El Salvador sparked by World Cup.
- ❑ **1980–1983** PLH wins elections but Gen. Gustavo Alvarez holds real power. Military maneuvers with US. Trades unionists arrested; death squads operate.
- ❑ **1984** Return to democracy.
- ❑ **1988** 12,000 Contra rebels forced out of Nicaragua into Honduras.
- ❑ **1995** Military defies human rights charges.
- ❑ **1998** Hurricane Mitch wreaks havoc.
- ❑ **1999** Appointment of first civilian defense minister.

H

SPENDING

GDP/cap. increase

CONSUMPTION AND SPENDING

52 per 1000 population — *47 per 1000 population*

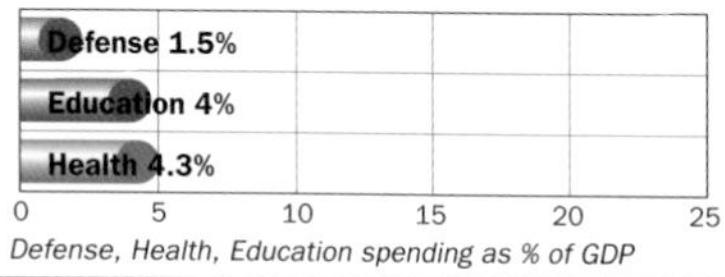
Defense 1.5%
Education 4%
Health 4.3%
0
5
10
15
20
25

Defense, Health, Education spending as % of GDP

Honduran society is characterized by great inequalities: the richest 5% own two-thirds of the land. As many as 85% of the population were thrown into poverty in 1998 by Hurricane Mitch. Some 45% are still existing on less than $2 a day.

WORLD RANKING

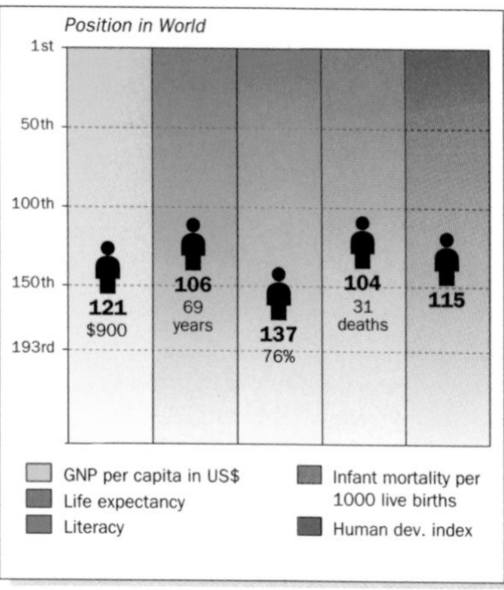
Position in World
1st
50th
100th
150th
193rd
121
$900
106
69
years
137
76%
104
31
deaths
115
GNP per capita in US$
Life expectancy
Literacy
Infant mortality per 1000 live births
Human dev. index

Europe
EUROPE
Slovakia
Ukraine
Austria
HUNGARY
Romania
Slovenia
Croatia
S & Mon.

HUNGARY

OFFICIAL NAME: Republic of Hungary **CAPITAL:** Budapest
POPULATION: 10.2 million **CURRENCY:** Forint **OFFICIAL LANGUAGE:** Hungarian

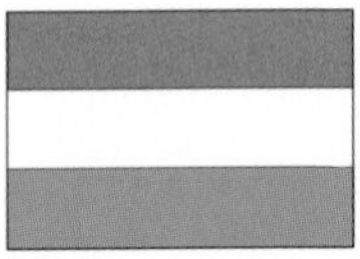

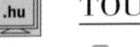

1918 | 1947 | Aug 20 | H | +1 | +36 | .hu

LYING AT THE HEART of central Europe, Hungary is landlocked and has borders with seven states. Historically, Hungary has been a cosmopolitan cultural center, and during its years of market socialism was more prosperous than the other Eastern Bloc countries. Economic and political reforms have brought it closer to the EU, which it has been invited to join in the next wave of enlargement in 2004; Hungary has also become a member of NATO. In foreign policy it is particularly sensitive about the treatment of Hungarian minorities in neighboring states.

CLIMATE

Continental

WEATHER CHART FOR BUDAPEST

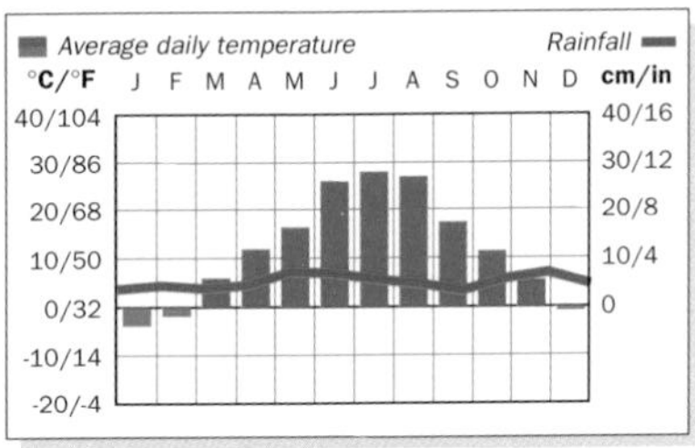
Average daily temperature
Rainfall
°C/°F
J F M A M J J A S O N D
cm/in
40/104
30/86
20/68
10/50
0/32
-10/14
-20/-4
40/16
30/12
20/8
10/4
0

Hungary has a continental climate, with wet springs, late summers, and cold, cloudy winters. There are no great differences of weather and climate within the country. Conditions in summer and winter may, however, differ greatly from one year to the next. The transition between seasons tends to be sudden.

TRANSPORTATION

Drive on right

Budapest Ferihegy
4.47m passengers

Has no fleet

THE TRANSPORTATION NETWORK

81,680 km (50,754 miles)

448 km (278 miles)

8005 km (4974 miles)

1373 km (853 miles)

Freight travels mainly via the rail link from Budapest to the Austrian border. Most foreign investment is located along this corridor. A direct link to Slovenia opened in mid-2001. The Budapest–Vienna expressway was the first of four big EU-backed road projects to be completed.

TOURISM

Visitors : Population 1.6:1

15.9m visitors

Up 4% in 2002

MAIN TOURIST ARRIVALS

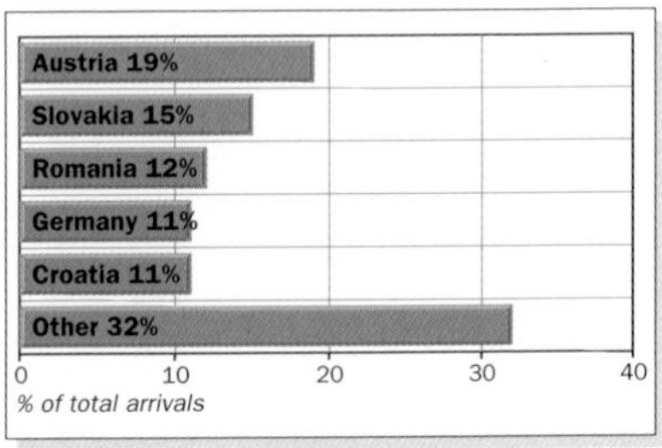
Austria 19%
Slovakia 15%
Romania 12%
Germany 11%
Croatia 11%
Other 32%
0
10
20
30
40
% of total arrivals

Lake Balaton, the traditional summer vacation destination, was a magnet for east European visitors during the communist period. Since then, Hungary has invested heavily in its tourist facilities, and the number of travel agents and hotels has risen dramatically. Austrians and Slovakians are most numerous among those whom the country now attracts. Budapest's baths, some of which date from the Ottoman period, are a distinctive feature, and the capital also promotes itself as an international business convention center.

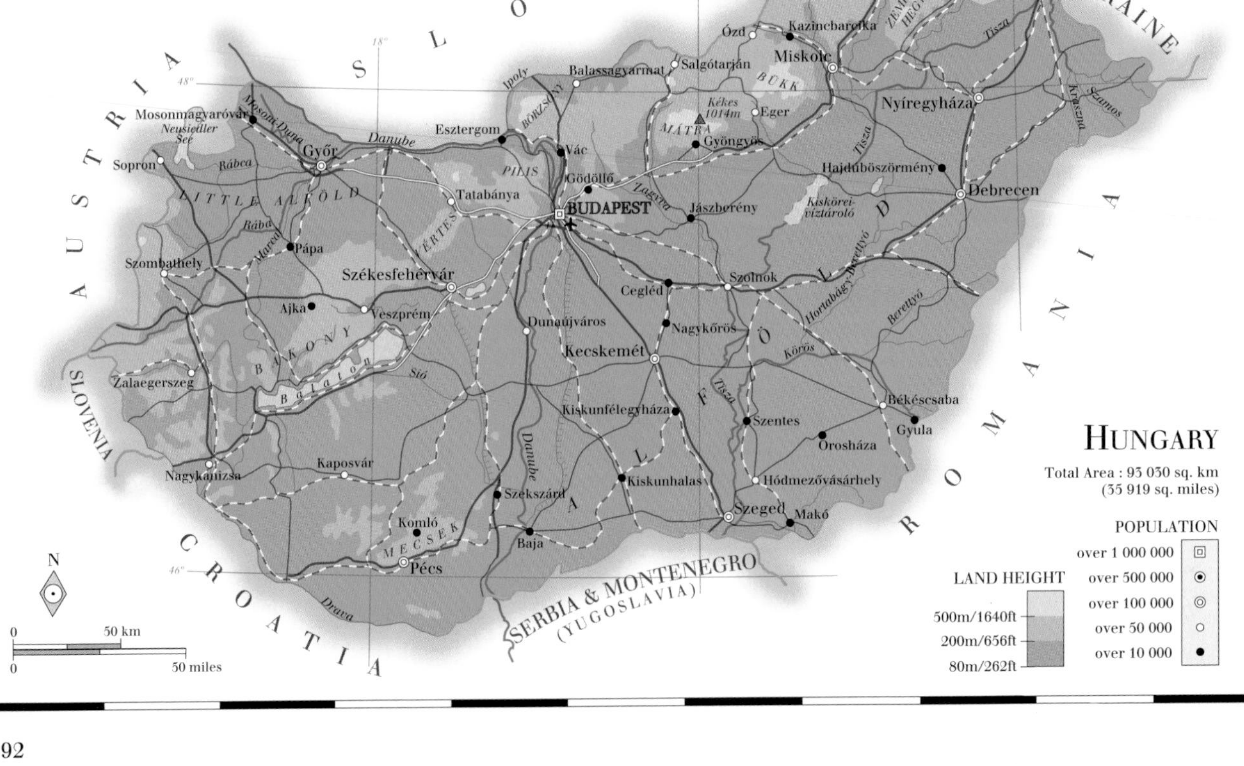
S L O V A K I A
UKRAINE
A U S T R I A
SLOVENIA
C R O A T I A
SERBIA & MONTENEGRO
(YUGOSLAVIA)
R O M A N I A
BUDAPEST
Miskolc
Debrecen
Nyíregyháza
Győr
Székesfehérvár
Kecskemét
Szeged
Pécs
Szolnok
Tatabánya
Sopron
Szombathely
Zalaegerszeg
Nagykanizsa
Kaposvár
Veszprém
Pápa
Ajka
Mosonmagyaróvár
Esztergom
Vác
Gödöllő
Salgótarján
Ózd
Kazincbarcika
Eger
Gyöngyös
Jászberény
Cegléd
Nagykőrös
Dunaújváros
Kiskunfélegyháza
Kiskunhalas
Szekszárd
Baja
Komló
Szentes
Orosháza
Hódmezővásárhely
Makó
Békéscsaba
Gyula
Hajdúböszörmény
Balassagyarmat
Danube
Tisza
Drava
Balaton
Neusiedler See
Kékes 1014m
MÁTRA
BÜKK
BAKONY
MECSEK
PILIS
VÉRTES
BÖRZSÖNY
LITTLE ALFÖLD
A L F Ö L D
ZEMPLÉNI HEGYSÉG
Kiskörei-víztároló
Rába
Rábca
Marcal
Sió
Zagyva
Ipoly
Körös
Berettyó
Hortobágy-Berettyó
Kraszna
Szamos
Mosoni-Duna
18°
20°
22°
48°
46°
N
0
50 km
50 miles
HUNGARY
Total Area : 93 030 sq. km
(35 919 sq. miles)
POPULATION
over 1 000 000
over 500 000
over 100 000
over 50 000
over 10 000
LAND HEIGHT
500m/1640ft
200m/656ft
80m/262ft

PEOPLE

Pop. density medium

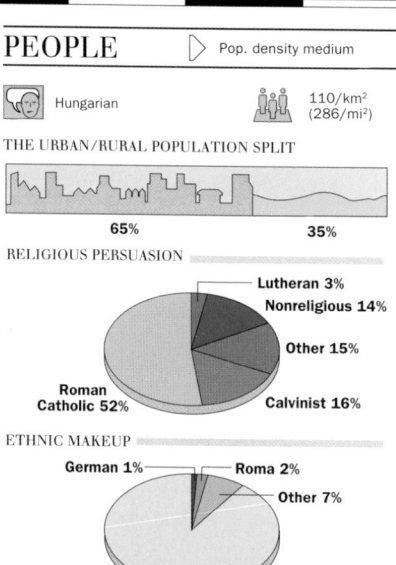

Hungarian

110/km² (286/mi²)

THE URBAN/RURAL POPULATION SPLIT

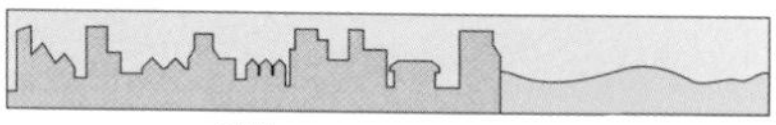
65%
35%

RELIGIOUS PERSUASION

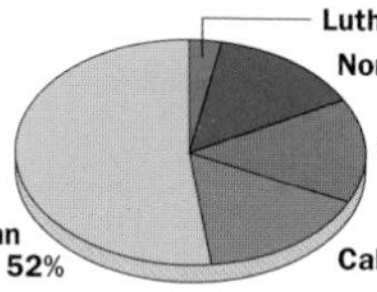
Lutheran 3%
Nonreligious 14%
Other 15%
Roman Catholic 52%
Calvinist 16%

ETHNIC MAKEUP

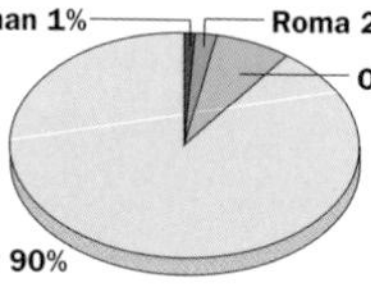
German 1%
Roma 2%
Other 7%
Magyar 90%

Hungary's population is shrinking, having reached a peak of just under 11 million in 1980.

An almost ethnically homogeneous society means that tensions are rare. There are small minorities of Roma, Germans, Jews, Romanians, Serbs, Slovaks, and Croats. The government is greatly concerned about the treatment of Hungarian minorities in Romanian Transylvania, Serbian Vojvodina, and Slovakia. New legislation gave them special status in Hungary from 2002, including the right to work there for three months a year. Prejudice against Roma is widespread, despite official drives to stamp it out. Over two-thirds of the prewar Jewish community were murdered by the Nazis. Antisemitism has reemerged since 1989. Overall, religious adherence is falling and the 2001 census showed an increase in the numbers of the nonreligious. A new bourgeoisie has emerged, but for the unskilled and unemployed life is often tougher than under communism.

POPULATION AGE BREAKDOWN

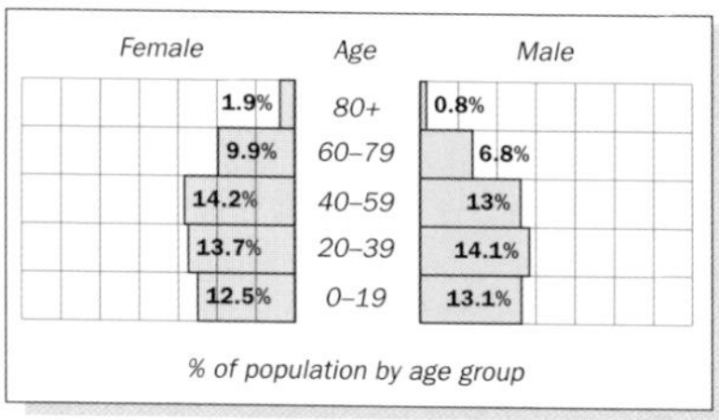
Female
Age
Male
1.9%
80+
0.8%
9.9%
60–79
6.8%
14.2%
40–59
13%
13.7%
20–39
14.1%
12.5%
0–19
13.1%
% of population by age group

POLITICS

Multiparty elections

2002/2006

President Ferenc Mádl

AT THE LAST ELECTION

National Assembly 386 seats

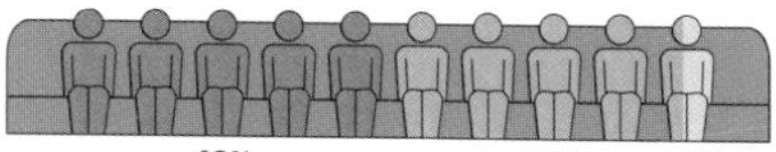
49% Fidesz–MPP–MDF
46% MSzP
5% SzDSz

Fidesz–MPP–MDF = Federation of Young Democrats–Hungarian Civic Party and Hungarian Democratic Forum
MSzP = Hungarian Socialist Party
SzDSz = Alliance of Free Democrats

Hungary has been a multiparty democracy since 1990.

Profile

Hungary's governments since the fall of communism have been relatively stable coalitions. The electoral pendulum has swung at four-yearly intervals between right and left.

József Antall, leader of the Christian-democratic nationalist MDF and prime minister from 1990, was the dominant figure in Hungarian democratic politics until his death in 1993. However, party disintegrations and disappointing economic results increased apathy and disillusionment among voters, who returned the former communists to power in 1994. The victorious MSzP under Gyula Horn nevertheless preferred to work in coalition in order to ease the passage of economic and social reforms through parliament.

The right-of-center Fidesz–MPP coalition led by Viktor Orbán, which took office after the 1998 election, drove the country toward completing its transition to a market economy ready for EU membership. However, Orbán was narrowly defeated by a coalition of the MSzP and the SzDSz in the 2002 elections. Peter Medgyessy was appointed prime minister.

Main Political Issue

Social welfare versus free-market economics

Reforms to assist transition to a market economy have led to strong economic recovery in the Budapest area and the western part of the country. Widening income differentials between young, skilled workers and those in education, health, and other state sectors have provoked protests and strikes, as the new prosperity eludes others.

***Ferenc Mádl**, known as "Mr. Professor," was elected president in 2000.*

***Peter Medgyessy**, leader of the center-left MSzP and prime minister since 2002.*

***The majestic Danube River** divides the modern city of Budapest, flowing between the ancient towns of Buda (foreground) and Pest.*

WORLD AFFAIRS

Joined UN in 1955

CE | CEFTA | NATO | OECD | OSCE

Hungary gained WEU associate status in 1994. In a 1997 referendum 85% of voters endorsed joining NATO, and in 1999 Hungary became a full member. Joining the EU is a slower process, from an association agreement in 1994 to expected membership in 2004.

Hungary has a cooperation and friendship treaty with Russia, but relations have been strained by Hungary's open courting of the West. Difficult relations with Slovakia and Romania were eased by friendship treaties concluded in the mid-1990s, but were troubled again by the controversial Status Law which provides benefits to ethnic Hungarians resident abroad.

CHRONOLOGY

The region today occupied by Hungary was first settled by the Finno-Ugrian Magyar peoples from the 8th century. In the 16th century, it was divided between Austria and the Ottoman Empire and was controlled by Austria until 1867, when Austria-Hungary was formed.

- **1918** Hungarian Republic created as successor state to Austria-Hungary.
- **1919** Béla Kún leads a short-lived communist government. Romania intervenes militarily and hands power to Adm. Horthy.
- **1938–1941** Hungary gains territory from Czechoslovakia, Yugoslavia, and Romania in return for supporting Nazi Germany.
- **1941** Hungary drawn into World War II on Axis side when Hitler attacks Soviet Union.
- **1944** Nazi Germany preempts Soviet advance on Hungary by invading. Deportation of Hungarian Jews and Roma to extermination camps begins. Soviet Red Army enters in October. Horthy forced to resign.
- **1945** Liberated by Red Army. Soviet-formed provisional government

H

CHRONOLOGY *continued*

installed. Imre Nagy introduces land reform.

- 1947 Communists emerge as largest party in second postwar election.
- 1948 Forcible merger of Social Democrats with communists; known as Hungarian Socialist Workers' Party (HSWP) from 1956.
- 1949 New constitution; formally becomes People's Republic.
- 1950–1951 First Secretary Mátyás Rákosi uses authoritarian powers to collectivize agriculture and industrialize the economy.
- 1953 Nagy, Rákosi's rival, becomes premier and reduces political terror.
- 1955 Nagy deposed by Rákosi.
- 1956 Rákosi out. Student demonstrations, demanding withdrawal of Soviet troops and Nagy's return, become popular uprising. Nagy appointed premier and János Kádár First Secretary. Nagy announces Hungary will leave Warsaw Pact. Three days later, Soviet forces suppress protests. About 25,000 killed. Kádár becomes premier.
- 1958 Nagy executed.
- 1968 Kádár introduces New Economic Mechanism to bring market elements to socialism.
- 1986 Police suppress commemoration of 1956 uprising. Democratic opposition demands Kádár's resignation.
- 1987 Party reformers establish MDF as a political movement.
- 1988 Kádár ousted. Protests force suspension of plans for Nagymaros Dam on the Danube.
- 1989 Parliament votes to allow independent parties. Posthumous rehabilitation of Nagy, who is given state funeral. Round table talks between HSWP and opposition.
- 1990 József Antall's MDF wins multiparty elections decisively. Speed of economic reform hotly debated. Árpád Göncz president.
- 1991 Warsaw Pact dissolved. Last Soviet troops leave.
- 1994 Hungary joins NATO's Partnership for Peace program. Former communist MSzP wins general election. Austerity program prompts protests.
- 1998 Elections: Viktor Orbán (Fidesz–MPP) forms right-of-center coalition.
- 1999 Joins NATO. Airspace used in NATO bombing of Yugoslavia.
- 2000 Ferenc Mádl succeeds Göncz as president.
- 2002 Elections won by socialist and free democrat alliance. Peter Medgyessy prime minister. EU approves membership for 2004.

H

AID

Recipient

$418m (receipts)

Up 66% in 2001

Hungary received substantial Western aid in 1990–1996, but by the end of the decade was considered able to attract investment mainly on commercial terms. EU and World Bank assistance moved to focus on targeting disadvantaged social groups, raising environmental standards, and strengthening market institutions.

DEFENSE

Phasing out conscription

$909m

Up 13% in 2001

Troop numbers were more than halved and conventional arms and the military hierarchy were updated in advance of NATO membership in 1999. The emphasis has switched toward more flexibility and rapid response. Almost immediately on joining NATO, Hungary permitted that organization to use its airspace to bomb Serbia. Military service, already shortened to six months, is to be phased out by 2006.

HUNGARIAN ARMED FORCES

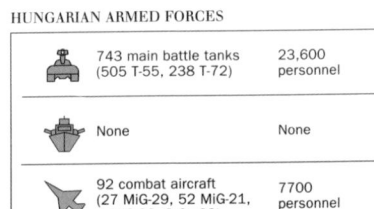

743 main battle tanks (505 T-55, 238 T-72)	23,600 personnel
None	None
92 combat aircraft (27 MiG-29, 52 MiG-21, 4 MiG-23, 9 Su-22)	7700 personnel
None	

ECONOMICS

Inflation 18% p.a. (1990–2001)

$49.2bn

231.9 forint (247.9)

SCORE CARD

World GNP Ranking	50th
GNP per Capita	$4830
Balance of Payments	–$1.1bn
Inflation	9.1%
Unemployment	6%

ECONOMIC PERFORMANCE INDICATOR

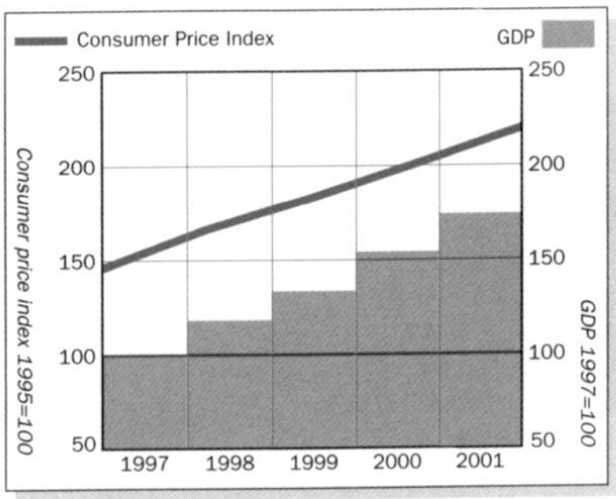
Consumer Price Index
GDP
250
200
150
100
50
1997
1998
1999
2000
2001
Consumer price index 1995=100
GDP 1997=100

EXPORTS

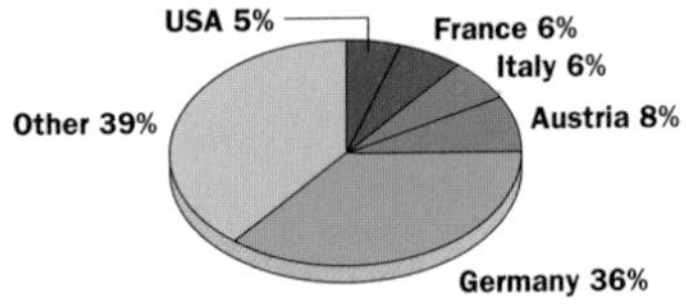
USA 5%
France 6%
Italy 6%
Austria 8%
Other 39%
Germany 36%

IMPORTS

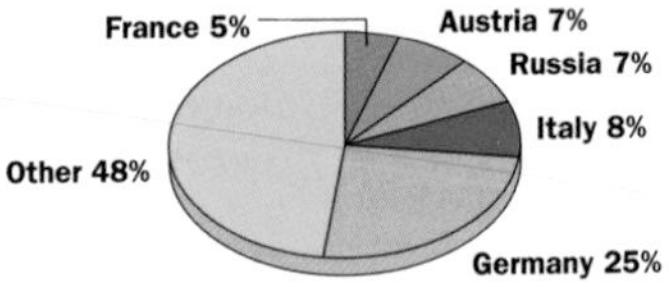
France 5%
Austria 7%
Russia 7%
Italy 8%
Other 48%
Germany 25%

Profile

The collapse of COMECON (communist economic bloc) caused a reorientation of trade toward western Europe. Exports increased rapidly and competitiveness has improved. However, the economy did not recover to its pre-1989 level until 1999. Privatization has reduced the state-owned share of the economy from 85% to 15%, and has helped cut external debt.

Strengths

Openness to foreign direct investment, especially since 1998. Favorable tax regime, streamlined bureaucracy. Strong export-led growth since late 1990s. High industrial production, especially at new, state-of-the-art factories. Currency fully convertible from mid-2001. Inflation dropping.

Weaknesses

Low energy efficiency. East–west split as development bypasses rural eastern areas. Widening income differentials. Money laundering a challenge to finance industry regulators; Hungary has featured on OECD blacklists.

HUNGARY : MAJOR BUSINESSES

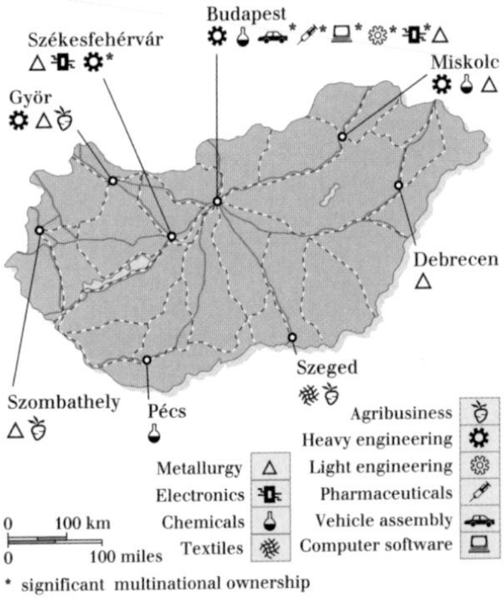
Budapest
Székesfehérvár
Miskolc
Györ
Debrecen
Szeged
Szombathely
Pécs
Agribusiness
Heavy engineering
Light engineering
Pharmaceuticals
Vehicle assembly
Computer software
Metallurgy
Electronics
Chemicals
Textiles
0 100 km
0 100 miles
* significant multinational ownership

RESOURCES

Electric power 7.8m kW

19,987 tonnes

24,922 b/d (reserves 55m barrels)

4.82m pigs, 3.92m turkeys, 34.3m chickens

Bauxite, coal, oil, natural gas, lignite

ELECTRICITY GENERATION

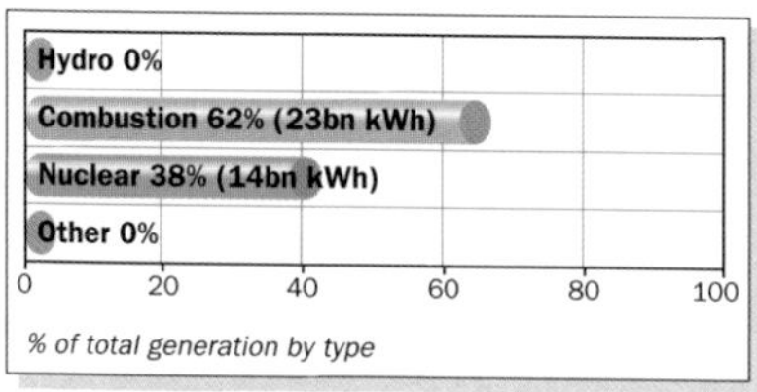
Hydro 0%
Combustion 62% (23bn kWh)
Nuclear 38% (14bn kWh)
Other 0%
0
20
40
60
80
100
% of total generation by type

HUNGARY : LAND USE

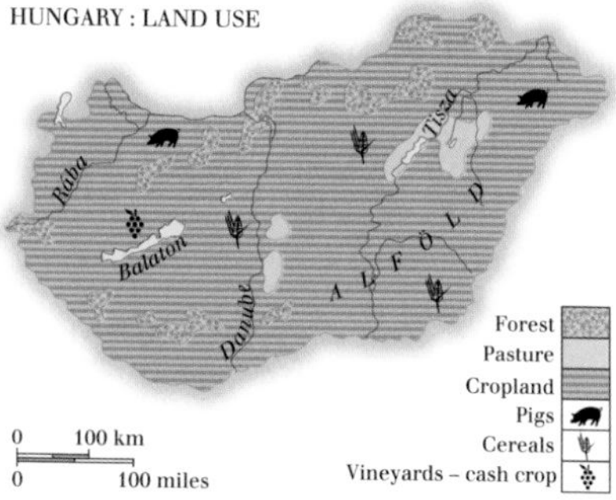
Raba
Balaton
Danube
Tisza
A L F Ö L D
Forest
Pasture
Cropland
Pigs
Cereals
Vineyards – cash crop
0 100 km
0 100 miles

Hungary has bauxite, brown coal, lignite, and natural gas reserves. It depends for about 40% of its electricity on nuclear energy from the Paks complex, north of Baja. Fertile farmlands provide grains, sugar beet, and potatoes. Wine production is also important.

ENVIRONMENT

Sustainability rank: 11th

7% (5% partially protected)

5.9 tonnes per capita

ENVIRONMENTAL TREATIES

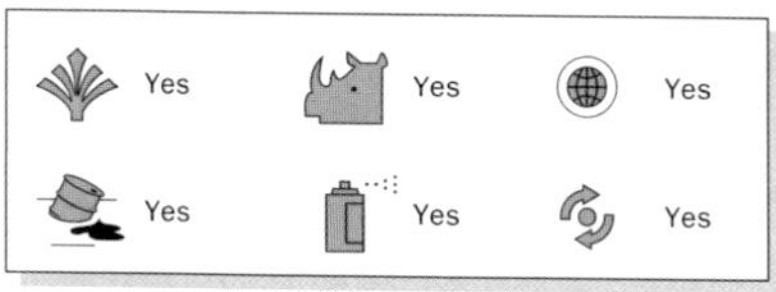
Yes
Yes
Yes
Yes
Yes
Yes

A high sulfur content in Hungary's fossil fuels exacerbates the serious air pollution in industrial zones. A "green card" system favors the use of cars with catalytic converters, reducing the serious levels of pollution from older vehicles.

The ecologically sensitive wetlands and lake systems of the Tisza River were contaminated with cyanide by a factory in Romania in 2000. An EU-sponsored program now oversees the river's management.

MEDIA

TV ownership high

Daily newspaper circulation 465 per 1000 people

PUBLISHING AND BROADCAST MEDIA

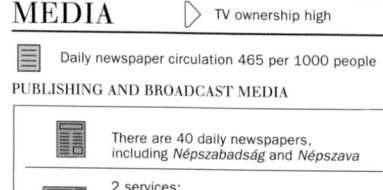

There are 40 daily newspapers, including *Népszabadság* and *Népszava*

2 services: 1 state-owned, 1 independent

4 services: 1 state-owned, 3 independent

Newspapers and magazines are fiercely independent and critical of government policy. In 1994, the Constitutional Court declared that state interference in the media was unlawful, but allegations of interference persist. The boards controlling state TV and radio must have equal representation from government and opposition under a 1996 media law, but the Orbán government was accused of bending or ignoring the rules.

CRIME

No death penalty

17,890 prisoners

Down 7% in 2000–2001

CRIME RATES

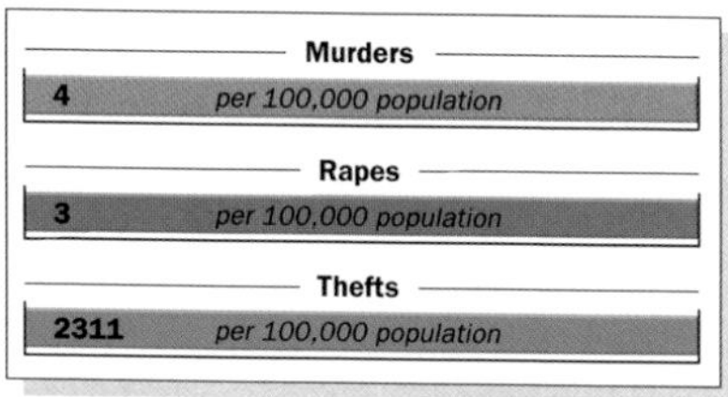
Murders
4 per 100,000 population
Rapes
3 per 100,000 population
Thefts
2311 per 100,000 population

An alarming trend in the late 1990s was the increase in murders of elderly people for financial gain. Organized crime, money laundering, and smuggling of illegal immigrants are rising.

EDUCATION

School leaving age: 16

99%

330,549 students

THE EDUCATION SYSTEM

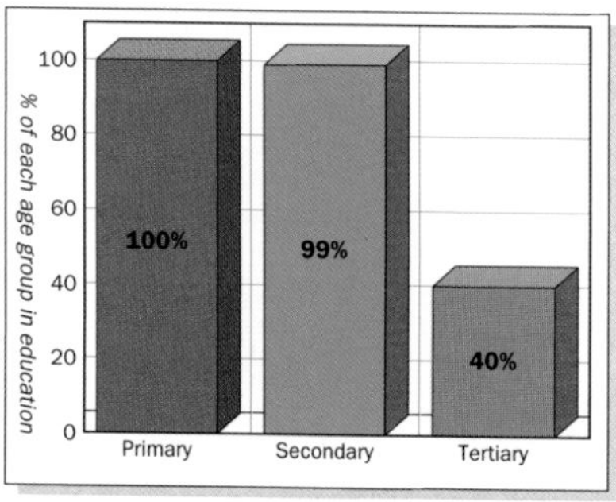
100
80
60
40
20
0
% of each age group in education
100%
99%
40%
Primary
Secondary
Tertiary

Education is free and compulsory from the age of six to 16. Bilingual schools have been established in southern Hungary to promote the languages of the national minorities. In 1999–2000 a major transformation of the education system took place, as a result of which there are 30 universities and colleges run by the state and 26 run by the Roman Catholic Church; a further six colleges are run by various foundations.

HEALTH

Welfare state health benefits

1 per 277 people

Cancers, heart and cerebrovascular diseases, accidents

Medical treatment has traditionally been free to all, although there is a contribution to prescription costs. State sickness benefits remain relatively generous. Spending on the health service has fallen in recent years in real terms; at around $800 per capita, it is only 40% of the OECD average, and there is concern that Hungary's health care sector is among the least developed of OECD countries. The ratio of doctors to patients is high, but there is a shortage of nurses. Family physician services are being privatized rapidly under a law passed in 2000.

SPENDING

GDP/cap. increase

CONSUMPTION AND SPENDING

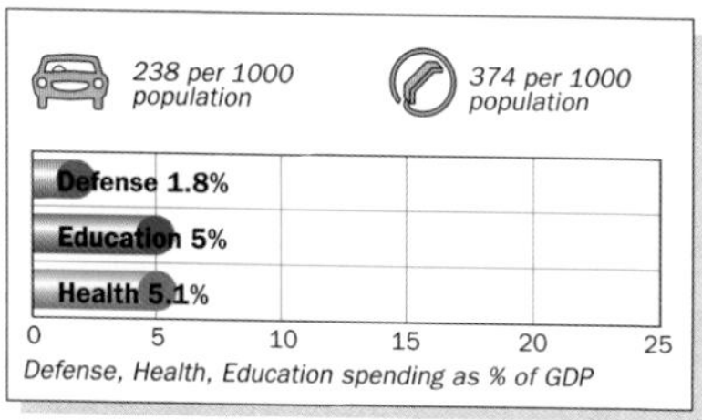
238 per 1000 population
374 per 1000 population
Defense 1.8%
Education 5%
Health 5.1%
0
5
10
15
20
25
Defense, Health, Education spending as % of GDP

Hungary enjoys one of the highest standards of living among the former communist countries and the most even distribution of wealth in the world. Mobile phone and Internet access is relatively high. Real wages, which fell by 15% in the mid-1990s, had largely regained ground by 2000. To earn enough to buy basic consumer goods, Hungarians still have to work longer hours than workers in western Europe. Public services pay has not kept pace with the rising cost of living, and there is a growing disparity with the private sector. The Roma minority suffers particularly over access to housing and has a life expectancy 10–15 years lower than the Hungarian average.

WORLD RANKING

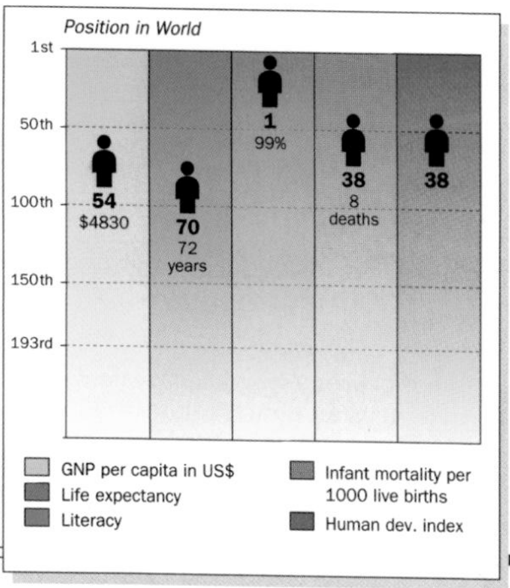
Position in World
1st
50th
100th
150th
193rd
54
$4830
70
72 years
1
99%
38
8 deaths
38
GNP per capita in US$
Life expectancy
Literacy
Infant mortality per 1000 live births
Human dev. index

H

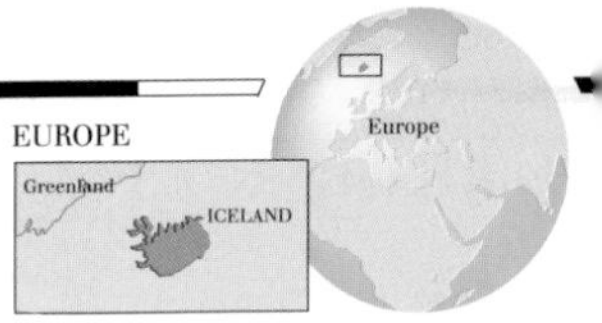
EUROPE
Europe
Greenland
ICELAND

ICELAND

OFFICIAL NAME: Republic of Iceland **CAPITAL:** Reykjavík
POPULATION: 283,000 **CURRENCY:** Icelandic króna **OFFICIAL LANGUAGE:** Icelandic

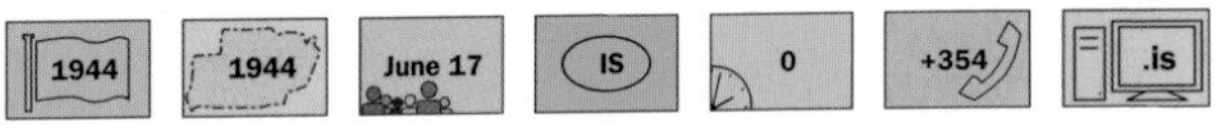
1944
1944
June 17
IS
0
+354
.is

EUROPE'S WESTERNMOST country, Iceland has a strategic location in the North Atlantic, just south of the Arctic Circle. Its position, on the rift where the North American and European continental plates are pulling apart, accounts for its 200 volcanoes and its numerous geysers and solfataras. Previously a Danish possession, Iceland became fully independent in 1944. Most settlements are along the coast, where ports remain ice-free in winter.

CLIMATE

Subarctic

WEATHER CHART FOR REYKJAVÍK

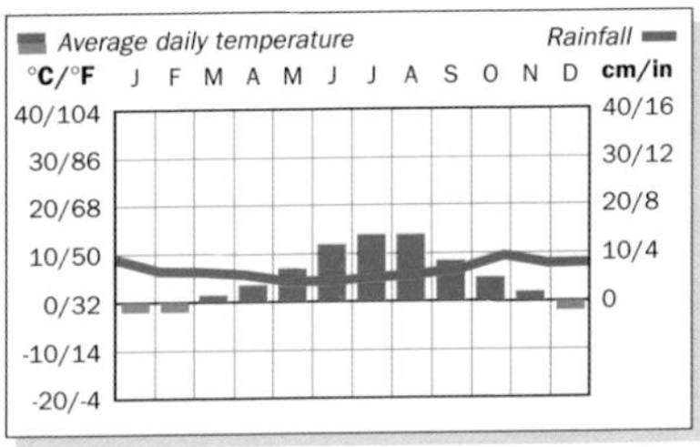
Average daily temperature
Rainfall
°C/°F
J F M A M J J A S O N D
cm/in
40/104
30/86
20/68
10/50
0/32
-10/14
-20/-4
40/16
30/12
20/8
10/4
0

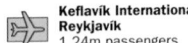

Iceland sits in the Gulf Stream. Winters are consequently mild. Summers are cool, with fine, long sunny days.

TRANSPORTATION

Drive on right

Keflavík International, Reykjavík 1.24m passengers

1135 ships 232,682 grt

THE TRANSPORTATION NETWORK

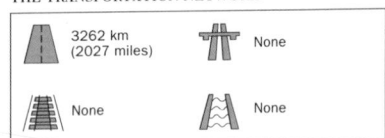

3262 km (2027 miles)

None

None

None

During winter Icelanders rely on internal flights to cross the country. Most freight moves by sea. The only main road circles the island.

TOURISM

Visitors : Population 1.1:1

303,000 visitors

Up 15% in 2000

MAIN TOURIST ARRIVALS

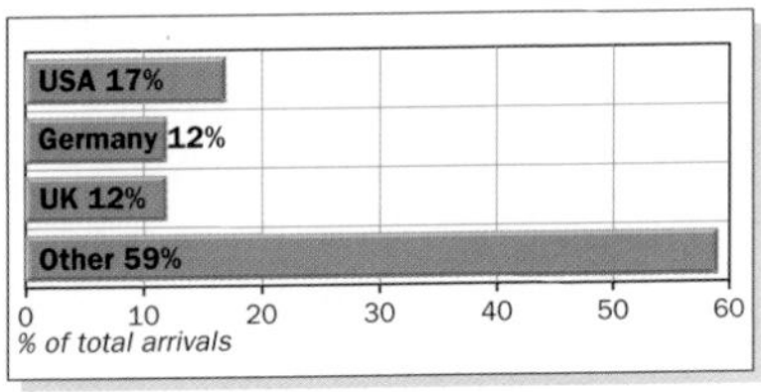
USA 17%
Germany 12%
UK 12%
Other 59%
0
10
20
30
40
50
60
% of total arrivals

Iceland is promoting itself, especially in Japan, as an upmarket destination for tourists who are attracted by its spectacular scenery, glaciers, green valleys, fjords, and hot springs.

PEOPLE

Pop. density low

Icelandic

3/km² (7/mi²)

THE URBAN/RURAL POPULATION SPLIT

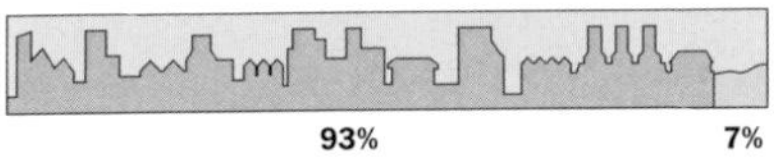
93%
7%

RELIGIOUS PERSUASION

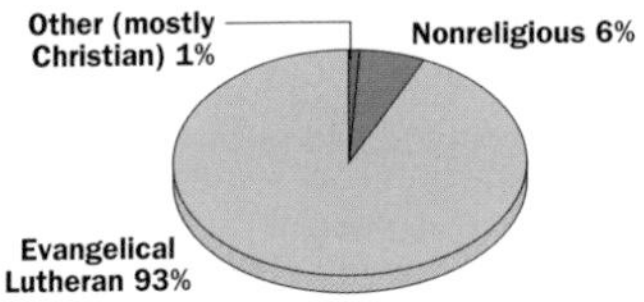
Other (mostly Christian) 1%
Nonreligious 6%
Evangelical Lutheran 93%

Descended from Norwegians and Celts, Icelanders are ethnically homogeneous. Almost all belong to the Evangelical Lutheran Church. More than half the population live in or near Reykjavík. Living standards are high, and there are few social tensions. The Icelandic language has changed little in 700 years, in part due to Iceland's isolation.

POLITICS

Multiparty elections

2003/2007

President Olafur Ragnar Grimsson

AT THE LAST ELECTION

Parliament 63 seats

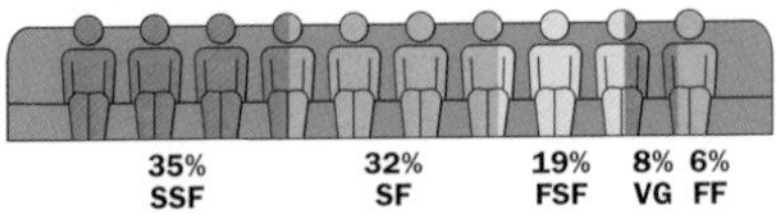
35% SSF
32% SF
19% FSF
8% VG
6% FF

SSF = Independence Party **SF** = Alliance
FSF = Progressive Party **VG** = Left-Green Alliance
FF = Liberal Party

Iceland has always been ruled by coalitions, but the traditional four-party system began to splinter in the 1980s. Arguments over whether or not to join the EU were defused in 1992 with the successful negotiation of the EEA, giving Iceland access to the key EU market.

David Oddsson became leader of the Independence Party and prime minister in 1991. He switched from a center-left to a center-right coalition, with the Progressive Party, in 1995. This partnership was reelected in 1999 and 2003, despite losses for the Independence Party in the most recent poll. Oddsson, now Europe's longest-serving prime minister, has successfully built on an economic recovery based on market-led reforms.

ICELAND

Total Area : 103 000 sq. km (39 768 sq. miles)

POPULATION
over 50 000
over 10 000
under 10 000

LAND HEIGHT
1000m/3281ft
500m/1640ft
200m/656ft
Sea Level
Ice Cap

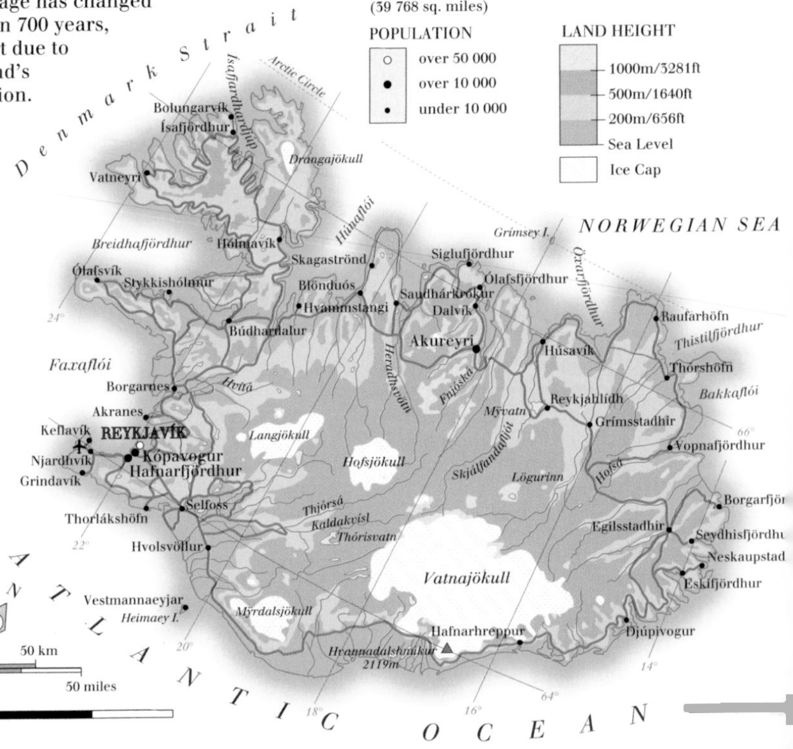
Denmark Strait
Arctic Circle
Ísafjardhardjúp
Bolungarvík
Ísafjördhur
Drangajökull
Vatneyri
Húnaflói
Breidhafjördhur
Hólmavík
Skagaströnd
Grímsey I.
NORWEGIAN SEA
Siglufjördhur
Ólafsvík
Stykkishólmur
Blönduós
Ólafsfjördhur
Saudhárkrókur
Hvammstangi
Dalvík
Öxarfjördhur
Raufarhöfn
Thistilfjördhur
Búdhardalur
Akureyri
Húsavík
Heradhsvötn
Thórshöfn
Faxaflói
Hvítá
Fnjóská
Bakkaflói
Borgarnes
Reykjahlídh
Mývatn
Akranes
Grímsstadhir
Keflavík
REYKJAVÍK
Langjökull
Vopnafjördhur
Njardhvík
Kópavogur
Hafnarfjördhur
Hofsjökull
Skjálfandafljót
Grindavík
Lögurinn
Jökulsá
Borgarfjördhur
Thorlákshöfn
Selfoss
Thjórsá
Kaldakvísl
Thórisvatn
Egilsstadhir
Seydhisfjördhur
Hvolsvöllur
Neskaupstad
Vatnajökull
Eskifjördhur
ATLANTIC OCEAN
Vestmannaeyjar
Heimaey I.
Mýrdalsjökull
Hafnarhreppur
Djúpivogur
Hvannadalshnúkur 2119m
0 50 km
0 50 miles
24°
22°
20°
18°
16°
14°
66°
64°

WORLD AFFAIRS

Joined UN in 1946

CE | NATO | OECD | OSCE | EFTA

As a member of EFTA, Iceland has access to European markets through the EEA, undermining the need to join the EU. Iceland's creation in 1975 of an exclusive fishing zone of 200 nautical miles ended serious disputes concerning fishing rights. Iceland's desire to restart large-scale whaling provokes much international criticism.

AID

Donor

$10m (donations)

Up 11% in 2001

Aid donations are modest, and form a smaller proportion of the budget than in other Scandinavian states.

DEFENSE

No compulsory military service

Coastguard is only military force

Not applicable

Despite being a member of NATO, Iceland has no armed forces. There is a 120-strong coastguard.

ECONOMICS

Inflation 3.4% p.a. (1990–2001)

$8.15bn

76.28 Icelandic krónur (86.83)

SCORE CARD

- ❑ World GNP Ranking 94th
- ❑ GNP per Capita $28,910
- ❑ Balance of Payments .... –$848m
- ❑ Inflation 6.4%
- ❑ Unemployment 2%

Strengths

High-tech fishing industry with exclusive access to prime fishing grounds. Low inflation and unemployment. Very cheap HEP and geothermal power, potential for use of hydrogen for fuel.

Weaknesses

Over 70% of export earnings derived from single source: fish. State-owned banking sector restricts flexibility.

EXPORTS

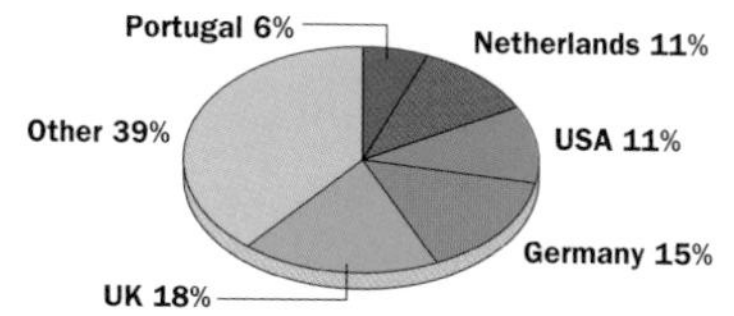
Portugal 6%
Netherlands 11%
Other 39%
USA 11%
Germany 15%
UK 18%

IMPORTS

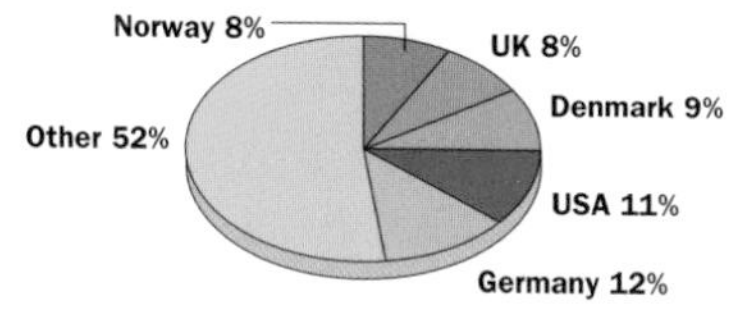
Norway 8%
UK 8%
Denmark 9%
Other 52%
USA 11%
Germany 12%

***Lava towers**, near Lake Mývatn in northern Iceland – an area of grassy lowlands. Iceland's center consists of lava desert and glaciers.*

RESOURCES

Electric power 1.3m kW

1.99m tonnes

Not an oil producer

470,000 sheep, 73,000 horses, 180,000 chickens

Diatomite

Iceland has virtually no minerals. All energy needs are met by geothermal and hydroelectric sources. It has implemented measures to try to restore once abundant fish stocks.

ENVIRONMENT

Sustainability rank: 8th

10% (8% partially protected)

8.7 tonnes per capita

Iceland has no nuclear or coal-fired power plants. Believing that minke whales are abundant and eat valuable cod stocks, Iceland warns that it will resume commercial whaling in 2006. The volcanic eruption in 1996 under the Vatna glacier caused extensive flooding and damage.

MEDIA

TV ownership high

Daily newspaper circulation 336 per 1000 people

PUBLISHING AND BROADCAST MEDIA

There are 4 daily newspapers, including *Dagbladid-Visir* and *Morgunbladid*, which has the largest circulation

11 services: 1 state-owned, 10 independent

17 services: 1 state-owned, 16 independent

Iceland is renowned for having one of the highest per capita newspaper circulations in the world.

CRIME

No death penalty

110 prisoners

Crime rates are rising

Crime rates are comparatively low. Violent crime is rising, especially on weekends in Reykjavík.

EDUCATION

School leaving age: 16

99%

10,184 students

Icelanders buy more books per capita than any other nation. Education is state-run; some 46% of school students go on to one of the country's four universities, or to a college abroad.

CHRONOLOGY

Settled by Norwegians in the 9th century, Iceland was ruled by Denmark from 1380 to 1944, becoming fully self-governing in 1918.

- ❑ **1940–1945** Occupied by UK and US.
- ❑ **1944** Independence as republic.
- ❑ **1949** Founder member of NATO.
- ❑ **1951** US air base built at Keflavík despite strong local opposition.
- ❑ **1972–1976** Extends fishing limits to 50 miles; two "cod wars" with UK.
- ❑ **1975** Sets 200-mile fishing limit.
- ❑ **1980** Vigdís Finnbogadóttir world's first elected woman head of state.
- ❑ **1985** Declares nuclear-free status.
- ❑ **1991** David Oddsson prime minister.
- ❑ **1995** Center-right coalition formed: reelected in 1999 and 2003.

I

HEALTH

Welfare state health benefits

1 per 307 people

Cancers, heart, cerebrovascular, and respiratory diseases

The state health system is free to all Icelanders. Iceland has one of the lowest infant mortality rates and one of the highest longevity rates in the world.

SPENDING

GDP/cap. increase

CONSUMPTION AND SPENDING

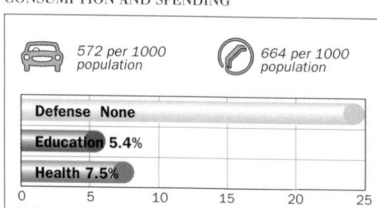

572 per 1000 population

664 per 1000 population

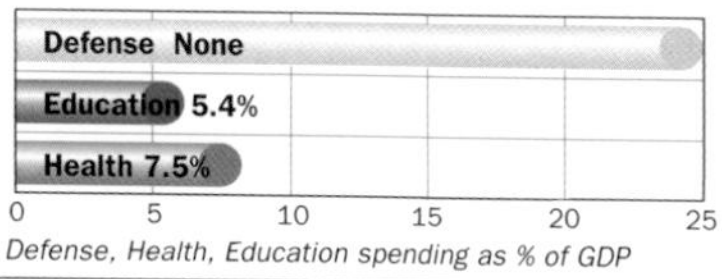
Defense None
Education 5.4%
Health 7.5%
0
5
10
15
20
25

Defense, Health, Education spending as % of GDP

The cost of living is high, but wealth distribution is fairly even, and there is ease of social mobility. Domestic heating, provided from geothermal sources, is provided at very low cost.

WORLD RANKING

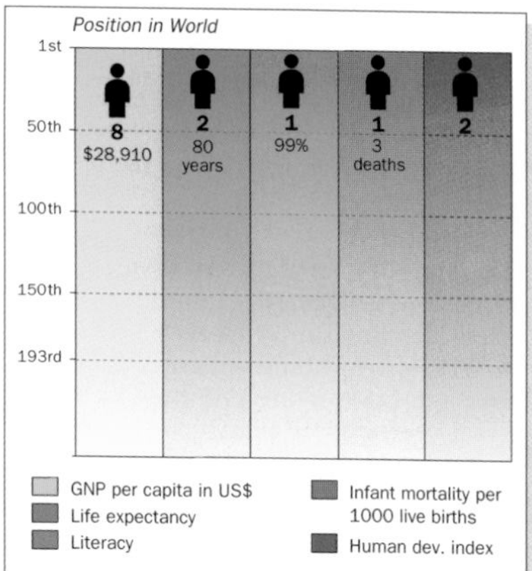
Position in World
1st
50th
100th
150th
193rd
8
$28,910
2
80 years
1
99%
1
3 deaths
2
GNP per capita in US$
Life expectancy
Literacy
Infant mortality per 1000 live births
Human dev. index

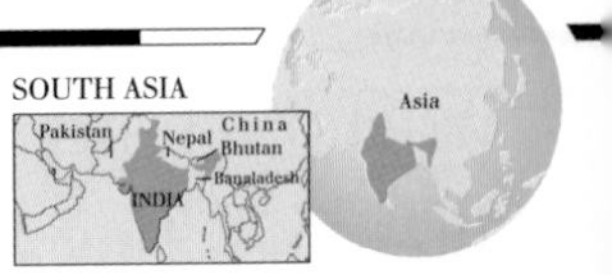
SOUTH ASIA
Pakistan
Nepal
China
Bhutan
Bangladesh
INDIA
Asia

INDIA

OFFICIAL NAME: Republic of India **CAPITAL:** New Delhi
POPULATION: 1.04 billion **CURRENCY:** Indian rupee **OFFICIAL LANGUAGES:** Hindi and English

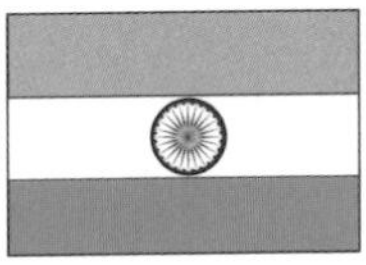

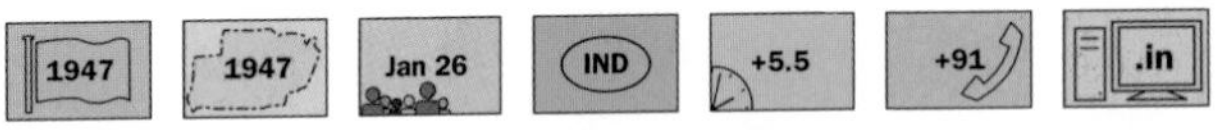
1947
1947
Jan 26
IND
+5.5
+91
.in

SEPARATED FROM the rest of Asia by the Himalaya mountain range, India forms the bulk of a subcontinent. As well as the Himalayas, there are two other main geographic regions, the Indo-Gangetic plain, which lies between the foothills of the Himalayas and the Vindhya Mountains, and the central-southern plateau. India is the world's largest democracy and second most populous country after China. The birthrate has recently been falling, but even at its current level India's population will probably overtake China's by 2030. After years of protectionism, India is opening up its economy to the outside world in the hope that the free market will go some way to alleviating one of the country's major problems – poverty.

CLIMATE

Tropical/subtropical/desert/mountain/monsoon

WEATHER CHART FOR NEW DELHI

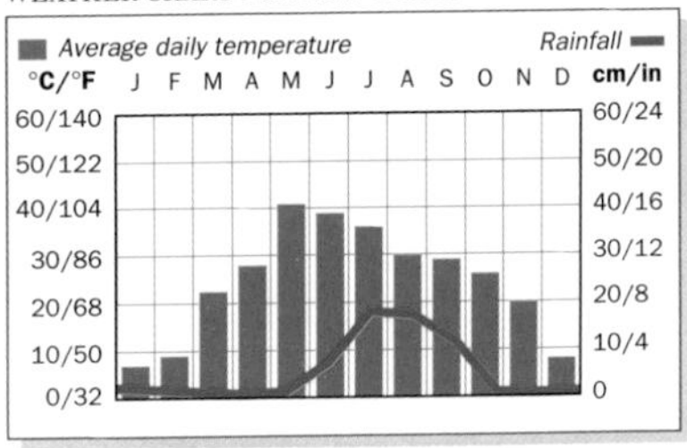
Average daily temperature
Rainfall
°C/°F
J F M A M J J A S O N D
cm/in
60/140
50/122
40/104
30/86
20/68
10/50
0/32
60/24
50/20
40/16
30/12
20/8
10/4
0

Temperatures in the north vary between 5°C (41°F) and 40°C (104°F). Heavy monsoon rains break in June, bringing severe flooding, and peter out by October. The south has a less variable climate. Chennai (Madras) is always hot: average temperatures range from 24°C (75°F) in January to 32°C (90°F) in May and June. Annual heatwaves in the southeast can be unbearable: over 1000 people died in 2003.

TRANSPORTATION

Drive on left

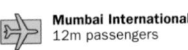

Mumbai International 12m passengers

1018 ships 6.69m grt

THE TRANSPORTATION NETWORK

1.52m km (942,666 miles)

33,500 km (20,816 miles)

62,759 km (38,997 miles)

16,180 km (10,054 miles)

The state-owned railroad system, the largest in Asia, carries 13 million people every day and employs over 1.5 million. Strict controls on diesel emissions from cars and buses were enforced in 2001. Cycle and scooter rickshaws abound in urban centers. Kolkata (Calcutta), site of India's first metro system, still has rickshaws pulled by hand.

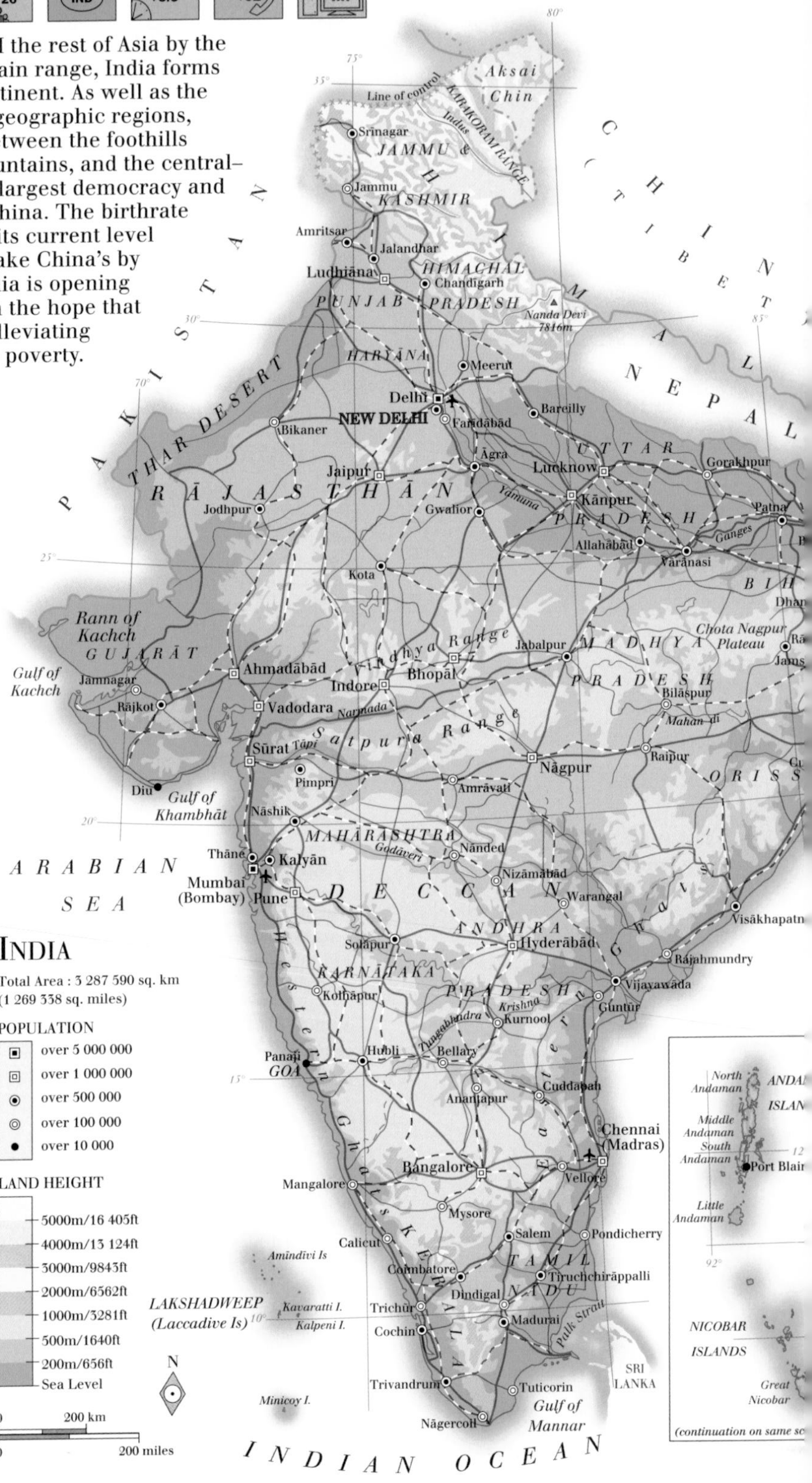
Aksai Chin
Line of control
KARAKORAM RANGE
Indus
Srinagar
JAMMU & KASHMIR
Jammu
Amritsar
Jalandhar
Ludhiana
HIMACHAL PRADESH
Chandigarh
PUNJAB
Nanda Devi 7816m
HARYANA
Meerut
Delhi
NEW DELHI
Faridabad
Bareilly
Bikaner
THAR DESERT
PAKISTAN
CHINA
TIBET
NEPAL
Jaipur
RAJASTHAN
Jodhpur
Agra
Lucknow
Kanpur
UTTAR PRADESH
Gorakhpur
Patna
Ganges
Gwalior
Yamuna
Allahabad
Varanasi
Kota
Rann of Kachch
GUJARAT
Gulf of Kachch
Jamnagar
Rajkot
Ahmadabad
Vadodara
Indore
Bhopal
Vindhya Range
Jabalpur
MADHYA PRADESH
Chota Nagpur Plateau
Bilaspur
Mahanadi
Narmada
Surat
Tapi
Satpura Range
Raipur
Nagpur
Pimpri
Amravati
Diu
Gulf of Khambhat
Nashik
MAHARASHTRA
Godavari
Thane
Kalyan
Nanded
Nizamabad
Mumbai (Bombay)
Pune
DECCAN
Warangal
Visakhapatnam
ARABIAN SEA
Solapur
ANDHRA PRADESH
Hyderabad
Rajahmundry
KARNATAKA
Kolhapur
Vijayawada
Guntur
Krishna
Kurnool
Tungabhadra
Panaji
GOA
Hubli
Bellary
Anantapur
Cuddapah
Chennai (Madras)
Bangalore
Vellore
Mangalore
Mysore
Salem
Pondicherry
Calicut
Amindivi Is
TAMIL NADU
Coimbatore
Tiruchchirappalli
LAKSHADWEEP (Laccadive Is)
Kavaratti I.
Kalpeni I.
Trichur
Dindigal
Cochin
Madurai
Palk Strait
KERALA
Trivandrum
Tuticorin
SRI LANKA
Minicoy I.
Nagercoil
Gulf of Mannar
INDIAN OCEAN
North Andaman
Middle Andaman
South Andaman
Port Blair
Little Andaman
ANDAMAN ISLANDS
NICOBAR ISLANDS
Great Nicobar
(continuation on same scale)

INDIA

Total Area : 3 287 590 sq. km (1 269 338 sq. miles)

POPULATION
- over 5 000 000
- over 1 000 000
- over 500 000
- over 100 000
- over 10 000

LAND HEIGHT
- 5000m/16 405ft
- 4000m/13 124ft
- 3000m/9843ft
- 2000m/6562ft
- 1000m/3281ft
- 500m/1640ft
- 200m/656ft
- Sea Level

0 200 km
0 200 miles

A religious festival. *Such festivals are a frequent occurrence and form an important part of Hindu culture.*

90°
95°
BHUTAN
chenjunga
8598m
rjiling
uliguri
ARUNACHAL PRADESH
Brahmaputra
Guwāhāti
ASSAM
Imphāl
BANGLADESH
Ganges
Kolkata
(Calcutta)
Mouths of the Ganges
BURMA
(MYANMAR)
BAY OF
BENGAL

TOURISM

Visitors : Population 1:439

2.37m visitors

Down 7% in 2002

MAIN TOURIST ARRIVALS

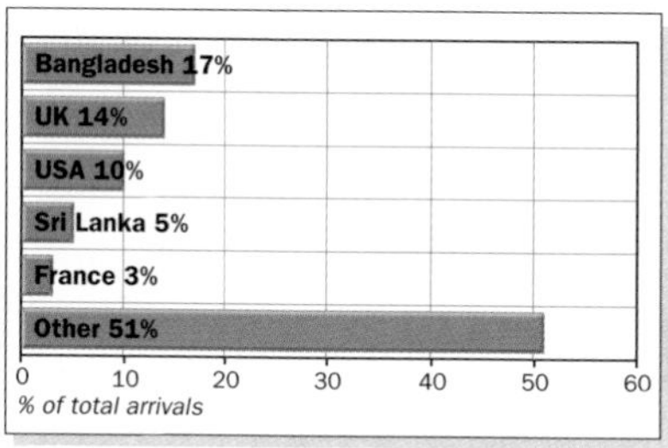
Bangladesh 17%
UK 14%
USA 10%
Sri Lanka 5%
France 3%
Other 51%
0
10
20
30
40
50
60
% of total arrivals

Tourism is India's fourth-largest foreign exchange earner. More luxury hotels are being built, and wildlife and adventure tourism are being promoted. However, India has only a small share of the world tourism market, and has suffered recently from security worries over the repercussions of the US-led "war on terrorism" and acute tensions with Pakistan, particularly over Kashmir.

PEOPLE

Pop. density high

Hindi, English, Urdu, Bengali, Marathi, Telugu, Tamil, Bihari, Gujarati, Kanarese

350/km² (907/mi²)

THE URBAN/RURAL POPULATION SPLIT

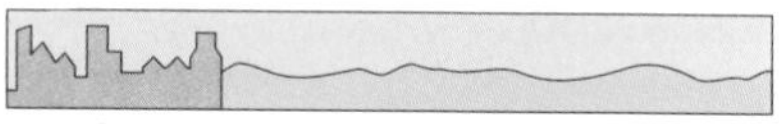
28%
72%

RELIGIOUS PERSUASION

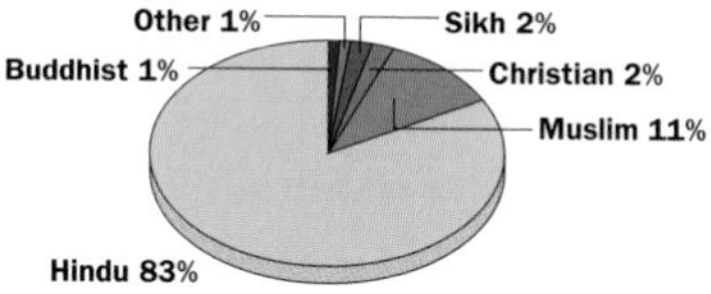
Other 1%
Sikh 2%
Buddhist 1%
Christian 2%
Muslim 11%
Hindu 83%

ETHNIC MAKEUP

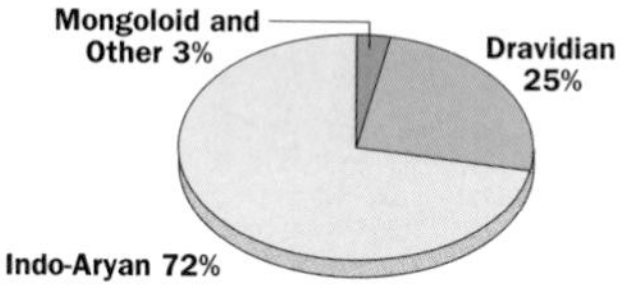
Mongoloid and Other 3%
Dravidian 25%
Indo-Aryan 72%

India is the world's second most populous country after China, officially passing the one-billion mark in 2000. Despite a major birth control program, the decrease in population growth has been marginal. Nationwide awareness campaigns aim to promote the idea of smaller families. India's planners consider the rise in the population to be the most significant brake on development. Cultural and religious pressures encourage large families, however, and the extended family is seen as essential security for old age.

The fertile rice-growing areas of the Gangetic plain and delta are very densely populated. The northern state of Uttar Pradesh has the largest population, followed by the western state of Maharashtra and the eastern state of Bihar. Maharashtra is also the most urbanized state, with more than half of its people living in towns or cities. Elsewhere, most Indians live in rural areas, though poverty continues to drive many to the swelling cities.

The overwhelming majority of the population are Hindus, who belong to thousands of castes and subcastes, which largely determine status, occupation, and whom they marry. Tension between Hindus and Muslims has grown in recent years, and escalated sharply in 2002 during violent clashes in Gujarat.

POPULATION AGE BREAKDOWN

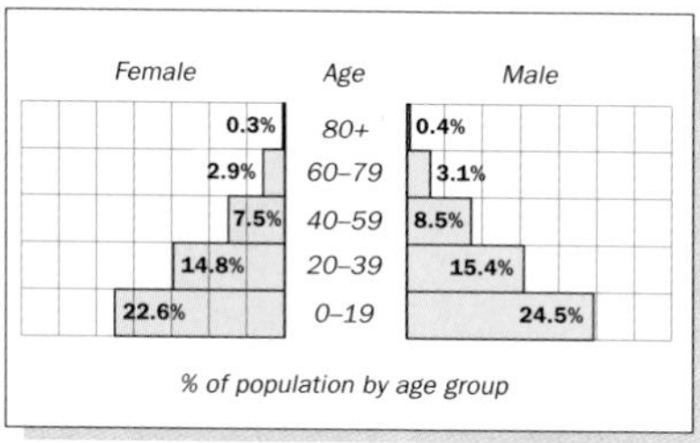
Female
Age
Male
0.3%
80+
0.4%
2.9%
60–79
3.1%
7.5%
40–59
8.5%
14.8%
20–39
15.4%
22.6%
0–19
24.5%
% of population by age group

CHRONOLOGY

The origins of an Indus Valley civilization may be traced back to the third millennium BCE. By the 3rd century BCE, the Mauryan kingdom under Ashoka encompassed most of modern India. Following the Battle of Plassey in 1757, British rule – through the East India Company – was consolidated.

- ❑ **1885** Formation of Indian National Congress.
- ❑ **1919** Act of Parliament introduces "responsible government."
- ❑ **1920–1922** Mahatma Gandhi's first civil disobedience campaign.
- ❑ **1935** Government of India Act grants autonomy to provinces.
- ❑ **1936** First elections under new constitution.
- ❑ **1942–1943** "Quit India" movement.
- ❑ **1947** August, independence and partition into India and Pakistan. Jawarhalal Nehru becomes first prime minister.
- ❑ **1948** Assassination of Mahatma Gandhi. War with Pakistan over Kashmir. India becomes a republic.
- ❑ **1951–1952** First general election won by Congress party.
- ❑ **1957** Congress party reelected. First elected communist state government installed in Kerala.
- ❑ **1960** Bombay divided into states of Gujarat and Maharashtra.
- ❑ **1962** Congress party reelected. Border war with China.
- ❑ **1964** Death of Nehru. Lal Bahadur Shastri becomes prime minister.
- ❑ **1965** Second war with Pakistan over Kashmir.
- ❑ **1966** Shastri dies; Indira Gandhi (daughter of Jawarhalal Nehru) becomes prime minister.
- ❑ **1969** Congress party splits into two factions; larger faction led by Indira Gandhi.
- ❑ **1971** Indira Gandhi's Congress party wins elections. Third war with Pakistan, over creation of Bangladesh.
- ❑ **1972** Simla (peace) Agreement signed with Pakistan.
- ❑ **1974** Explosion of first nuclear device in underground test.
- ❑ **1975–1977** State of emergency: Ghandi guilty of electoral fraud.
- ❑ **1977** Congress loses general election. People's Party (JD) takes power at the center.
- ❑ **1978** New political group, Congress (Indira) – Congress (I) – formally established.
- ❑ **1980** Indira Gandhi's C(I) wins general election.
- ❑ **1984** Indian troops storm Sikh Golden Temple in Amritsar. Assassination of Indira Gandhi ⇨

I

CHRONOLOGY *continued*

by Sikh bodyguard; her son Rajiv becomes prime minister and C(I) leader. Gas explosion at US-owned Union Carbide Corporation plant in Bhopal kills 2000 people in India's worst industrial disaster.

- **1985** Peace accords with militant separatists in Assam and Punjab.
- **1987** Deployment of Indian peacekeeping force in Sri Lanka to combat Tamil Tigers.
- **1989** General election; National Front forms minority government with BJP support. C(I) implicated in Bofors scandal.
- **1990** Withdrawal of troops from Sri Lanka.
- **1991** Rajiv Gandhi assassinated. Narasimha Rao becomes prime minister of a C(I) minority government and initiates economic liberalization.
- **1992** Demolition of the Babri Masjid mosque at Ayodhya by Hindu extremists triggers widespread violence; 1200 people die.
- **1993** Resurgence of Hindu–Muslim riots. Bomb explosions in Bombay (Mumbai). Border troop agreement with China.
- **1994** Rupee made fully convertible. C(I) routed in key state elections amid increasing allegations of corruption in ruling party. Outbreak of pneumonic plague.
- **1995** Punjab chief minister assassinated by Sikh extremists.
- **1996** Corruption scandal triggers political crisis. C(I) suffers its worst electoral defeat. Leftist United Front coalition government takes office.
- **1997** Successive governments fall as C(I) withdraws support.
- **1998** General election; BJP led by Atal Bihari Vajpayee forms coalition government. Sonia Gandhi, widow of Rajiv Gandhi, becomes president of C(I). India tests nuclear bomb.
- **1999** Vajpayee travels to Pakistan to inaugurate bus service between India and Pakistan. India and Pakistan test nuclear missiles, and engage in violent confrontation in Kashmir. BJP returned to power after elections triggered by vote of no confidence.
- **2001** Earthquake kills more than 25,000 in Gujarat. BJP government implicated in major bribery scandal.
- **2001–2002** Terrorist attacks by Kashmiri separatists precipitate crisis with Pakistan.
- **2002** More than 2000, mainly Muslims, killed in Gujarat following worst intercommunal riots since independence.
- **2003** Heatwave kills over 1400.

POLITICS

Multiparty elections

L. House 1999/2003
U. House 2002/2004

President A. P. J. Abdul Kalam

AT THE LAST ELECTION

House of the People (Lok Sabha) 545 seats

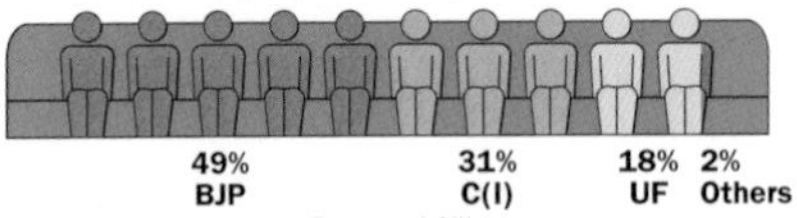
49% BJP
31% C(I)
18% UF
2% Others

BJP = Bharatiya Janata Party and Allies, including the All-India Anna Dravida Munnetra Kazhagam
C(I) = Congress (I) and Allies
UF = United Front and Allies, including the Communist Party of India (Marxist) – **CPI(M)**
Nom = Nominated

Others include the Rashtriya Janata Dal, independents, and two appointed seats reserved for Anglo-Indians

Council of States (Rajya Sabha) 245 seats

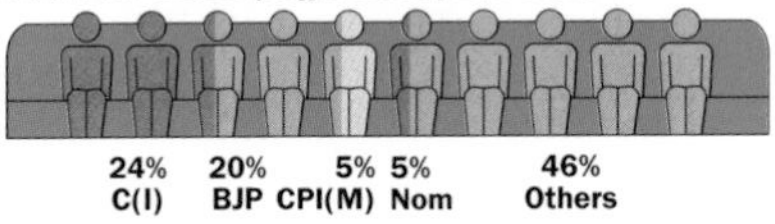
24% C(I)
20% BJP
5% CPI(M)
5% Nom
46% Others

233 members are elected to the Rajya Sabha by State Legislative Assemblies, and 12 "distinguished citizens" are nominated by the head of state

India is a multiparty democracy. The Lok Sabha (lower house) is directly elected by universal adult suffrage, while the Rajya Sabha (upper house) is indirectly elected by the state assemblies. There are 28 self-governing states. Of the seven union territories, Delhi and Pondicherry have their own assemblies.

PROFILE

The ascendancy of the Hindu nationalist BJP, in government since 1998, has relegated C(I) – founded in 1978 as successor to the historic Congress party which led India to independence in 1947 – to an unprecedented period of opposition at union level.

Under Prime Minister P. V. Narasimha Rao of C(I) in 1991–1996, a bold program of economic liberalization had broken with C(I)'s traditionally left-of-center policies. However, allegations of corruption undermined the party, resulting in heavy electoral defeats in 1996–1999.

The 1998 election established the BJP with a mandate strong enough to challenge C(I) effectively and form a coalition government headed by its leader, A. B. Vajpayee. Elections held in 1999 returned the coalition to power with an overall majority and the BJP has made a strong showing in regional polls, particularly in strife-torn Gujarat. Hopes for C(I)'s political revival rest on Sonia Gandhi, its president, who, as the widow of the assassinated former prime minister Rajiv Gandhi, restored the influence of the Nehru dynasty over the party.

MAIN POLITICAL ISSUES

Hindu militancy

The right-wing Hindu BJP has emerged as a credible alternative to C(I). In 1996 it won the most seats in parliament, despite being tainted by corruption allegations. Though it failed to form a viable administration on that occasion, the BJP did take office in 1998. Its rise has encouraged the spread of Hindu nationalism and raised fears about the future of India's secular constitution. In 2002 the BJP state government in Gujarat was accused by its critics of sanctioning mob attacks against the minority Muslim community in Ahmadabad during communal riots in the state.

Political corruption

Allegations of political corruption have dominated Indian politics. In 1989, C(I) prime minister Rajiv Gandhi was accused of accepting bribes from Bofors, a Swedish arms company, and the party was also implicated in a financial scandal in 1992. In 1996, corruption forced the resignations of several C(I) government ministers and the leader of the opposition BJP. The issue resurfaced in 2001, when the BJP government was implicated in the "Tehelka scandal" over arms sales, which led to the resignation of the defense minister.

The free market

The introduction of the free-market economy has been controversial. Critics contend that free trade would undermine local production and participation by foreign companies would damage the national economy. In the 1990s governments increased spending on rural development programs in order to soften the impact of economic liberalization. The BJP-led coalition, though more sympathetic to urban interests, is generally opposed to competition from foreign businesses.

A. B. Vajpayee, BJP leader and prime minister since 1998.

***A. P. J. Abdul Kalam**, a Muslim nuclear scientist, elected president in 2002.*

***Sonia Gandhi** has revived the fortunes of the opposition Congress (I).*

WORLD AFFAIRS

Joined UN in 1945

Comm | G15 | G24 | NAM | SAARC

The overriding preoccupation in foreign policy is the dispute with Pakistan over Kashmir, which has sparked two wars, in 1948 and 1965, and intensified the nuclear race between the two countries. In 1998, India carried out nuclear weapons tests, prompting Pakistan to follow suit and sparking international condemnation. India has not yet signed the Comprehensive Test Ban Treaty, but nonetheless, the US imposed sanctions against India for ignoring the ban. Sanctions were lifted in 2001 following India's support for the "war on terrorism," but the US has pushed India to renew negotiations over Kashmir. Despite these efforts, border clashes continue. In 2002 a series of attacks across the Line of Control pushed the two countries to the brink of war. India now accuses Pakistan of waging a "proxy terrorist war" against it.

AID

Recipient

$1.71bn (receipts)

Up 14% in 2001

India does not depend on aid. The US suspended donations following nuclear tests in 1998, but restored payments in late 2001. The World Bank withdrew its funding for the Narmada Dam project. International relief aid helped victims of the 2001 Gujarat earthquake.

DEFENSE

No compulsory military service

$14.2bn

Down 4% in 2001

INDIAN ARMED FORCES

3898 main battle tanks (700 T-55, 1900 T-72 M1, 1200 Vijayanta, 84 T-90S)	1.1m personnel
16 submarines, 1 carrier, 8 destroyers, 11 frigates, 7 corvettes, 39 patrol boats	53,000 personnel
701 combat aircraft (35 Jaguar S(I), MiG-21/23/27/29)	145,000 personnel
Capability undisclosed; weapons tested in 1998	

India considers a nuclear deterrent to be vital, and tested weapons in 1998. It has the world's third-largest military, and produces its own hardware. In 2001 the Agni-II intermediate-range missile, which is able to carry a nuclear warhead anywhere in Pakistan, went into production, while the long-delayed Light Combat Aircraft began flight tests. Virtual nuclear tests became possible in 2003 with the construction of the Param Padma supercomputer. India aims to send its own probe to the Moon in 2008.

ECONOMICS

Inflation 7.6% p.a. (1990–2001)

$477bn

46.47 Indian rupees (48.86)

SCORE CARD

- ❑ WORLD GNP RANKING..........12th
- ❑ GNP PER CAPITA..........$460
- ❑ BALANCE OF PAYMENTS..........$1.3bn
- ❑ INFLATION..........3.7%
- ❑ UNEMPLOYMENT......Widespread underemployment

EXPORTS

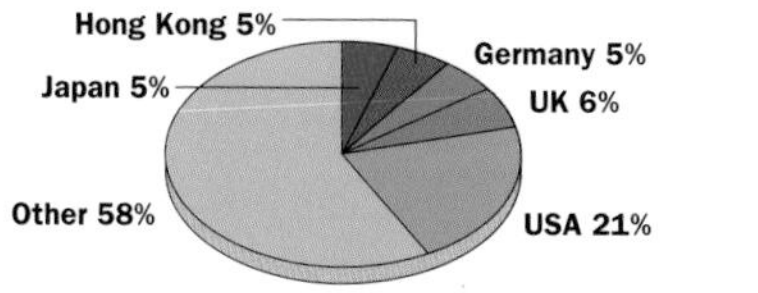
Hong Kong 5%
Germany 5%
Japan 5%
UK 6%
Other 58%
USA 21%

IMPORTS

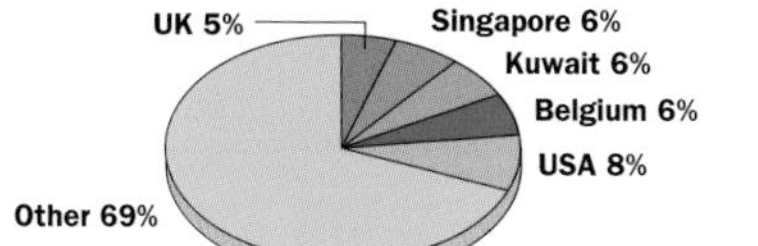
UK 5%
Singapore 6%
Kuwait 6%
Belgium 6%
USA 8%
Other 69%

STRENGTHS

Massive home market of over one billion people. Cheap labor. Some of the workforce possess skills for new high-tech industries such as software programming, a major boom area of the economy. Vibrant film industry: "Bollywood." Highly efficient textile sector and garment manufacturers. Growing competitiveness in world market, reflected in strong export growth. Competition encouraging improvement in manufacturing standards. Despite strong objections from opposition parties, India ratified the GATT world trade agreement in 1995.

Since the economy was opened up to foreign competition in 1991, foreign direct investment has risen massively. Much of this has gone into the power sector. Large multinationals, such as Coca-Cola and IBM, are expanding, despite protests from some sections of the ruling BJP hostile to the growing presence of foreign businesses.

WEAKNESSES

A large budget deficit dogs the economy. Governments have found it politically difficult to move away from the old system of widespread subsidies. The value of the rupee has declined sharply. Poor communications systems and power shortages hinder growth. The prestige of Bollywood has been damaged by allegations of underworld connections.

PROFILE

India has the fastest-growing economy in Asia after China. From a highly protectionist mixed economy, which succeeded in building the basis of a modern industrial state, India has to a large extent converted to a free-market economy and is entering the global marketplace. Wide-ranging reforms, from lowering trade barriers to attracting foreign investment, have been put in place. The United Front and BJP-led governments in power since 1996 have not undone these reforms, though they have been criticized for not being wholehearted about driving them forward. Meanwhile, in the rural economy millions of people grapple with the problems of subsistence farming.

ECONOMIC PERFORMANCE INDICATOR

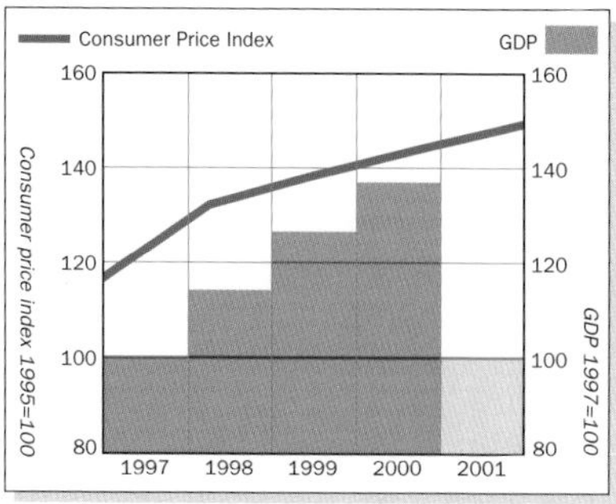
Consumer Price Index
GDP
160
140
120
100
80
Consumer price index 1995=100
GDP 1997=100
1997
1998
1999
2000
2001

INDIA : MAJOR BUSINESSES

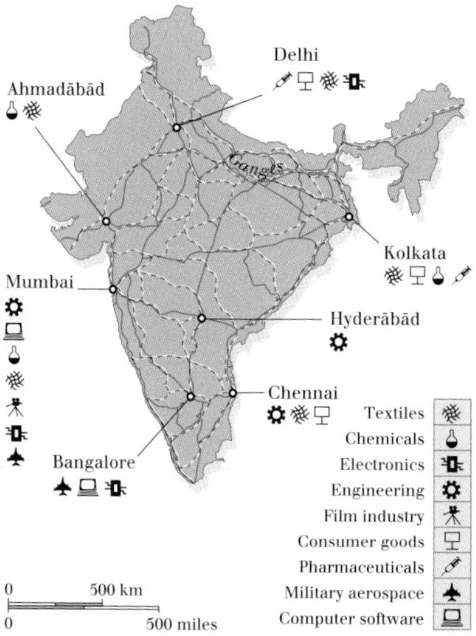
Delhi
Ahmadābād
Ganges
Kolkata
Mumbai
Hyderābād
Chennai
Bangalore
Textiles
Chemicals
Electronics
Engineering
Film industry
Consumer goods
Pharmaceuticals
Military aerospace
Computer software
0
500 km
0
500 miles

Hillside monastery in Ladakh, *Kashmir, northern India. The Ladakhi Buddhists maintain their traditional farming existence and are known for their friendliness.*

I

RESOURCES

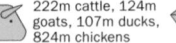

Electric power 113m kW

5.69m tonnes

793,000 b/d (reserves 5.4bn barrels)

222m cattle, 124m goats, 107m ducks, 824m chickens

Iron, diamonds, coal, limestone, zinc, lead, gems, natural gas

ELECTRICITY GENERATION

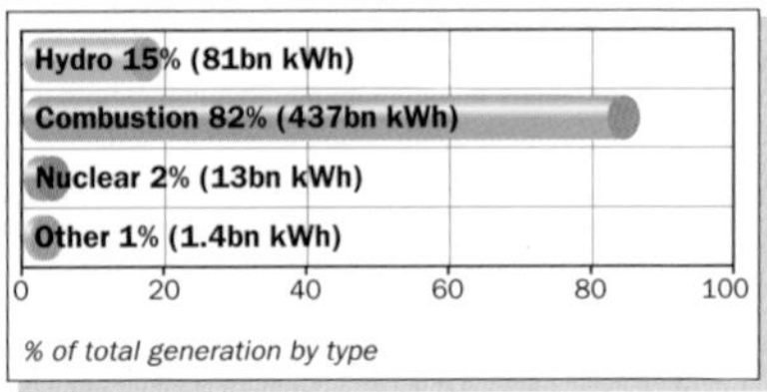
Hydro 15% (81bn kWh)
Combustion 82% (437bn kWh)
Nuclear 2% (13bn kWh)
Other 1% (1.4bn kWh)
0 20 40 60 80 100
% of total generation by type

Agriculture still dominates the economy. It provides 25% of GDP and employs over 60% of the workforce. Tea, cotton, and rice are the principal cash crops, and account for over 10% of exports. Assam and Darjeeling are among the country's most famous types of tea, while cotton and jute provide the raw material for the strong textile industry.

Precious gems and jewelry, including cut diamonds, are the most valuable mineral exports, though iron ore is also important. In addition, there are large coal reserves: India is the world's third-largest coal producer. Despite this, and discoveries of new gas reserves, India is unable to meet its own domestic energy needs. Petroleum and coal dominate imports. Efforts to increase power production through a series of "mega projects" to construct large power plants have been hit by financial mismanagement and a lack of investor confidence. The government hopes to make over $1 billion from the part-privatization of the oil industry.

INDIA - LAND USE

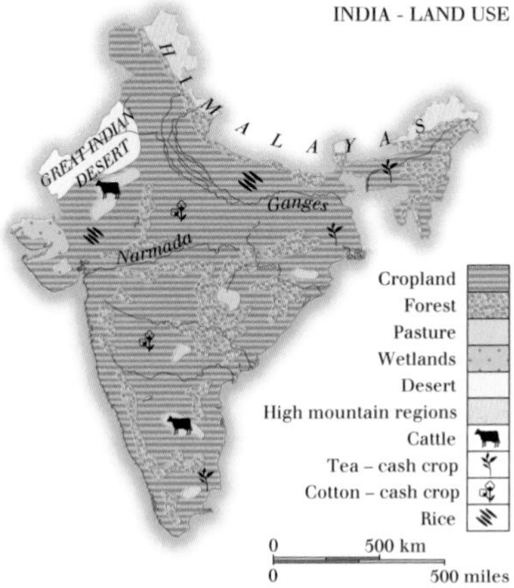
HIMALAYAS
GREAT INDIAN DESERT
Ganges
Narmada
Cropland
Forest
Pasture
Wetlands
Desert
High mountain regions
Cattle
Tea – cash crop
Cotton – cash crop
Rice
0 500 km
0 500 miles

ENVIRONMENT

Sustainability rank: 116th

5% (3% partially protected)

1.1 tonnes per capita

ENVIRONMENTAL TREATIES

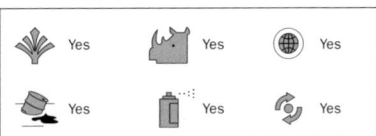

Yes Yes Yes

Yes Yes Yes

Deforestation is one of India's most pressing environmental problems. Industrial and agricultural pressures have felled almost 90% of original forest cover. This results in major soil erosion, the silting up of dams, and landslides. Unusually serious flooding in eastern states in 2000 was largely attributed to deforestation. On the other hand, dealing with water scarcities, such as the drought which affected much of the northwest in 2000, has become a major public policy issue.

MEDIA

TV ownership medium

Daily newspaper circulation 28 per 1000 people

PUBLISHING AND BROADCAST MEDIA

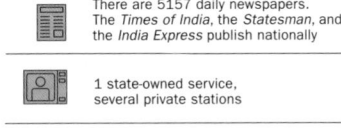

There are 5157 daily newspapers. The *Times of India*, the *Statesman*, and the *India Express* publish nationally

1 state-owned service, several private stations

1 state-owned service, several music and educational stations

Viewing figures for the state-run Doordarshan television channels have fallen since the arrival of satellite TV and private broadcasters. More than seven million households are estimated to have acquired dishes. Critics fear a Western onslaught on Indian values. Indian films, produced traditionally in "Bollywood" (Mumbai), are now a major part of the economy, with millions of devotees worldwide as well as within India. There are literally thousands of newspapers; the *Times of India* has almost two million readers.

CRIME

Death penalty in use

281,380 prisoners

Crime is rising

CRIME RATES

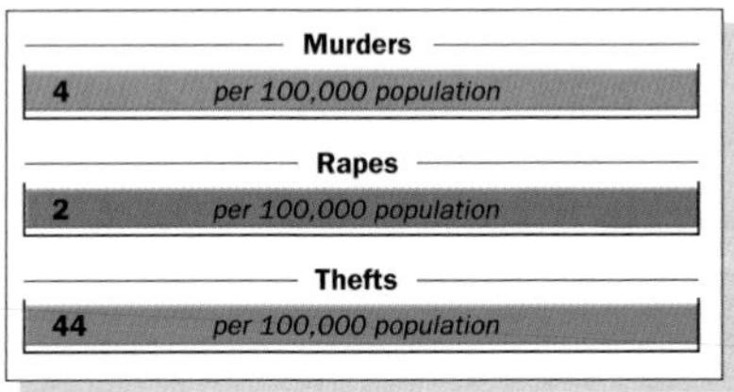
Murders
4 per 100,000 population
Rapes
2 per 100,000 population
Thefts
44 per 100,000 population

Interreligious violence is sporadic but serious. Attacks on Christians draw particular attention, but were overshadowed by Hindu–Muslim violence in Gujarat in 2002. Security forces gained increased powers that year under the Prevention of Terrorism Ordinance, passed in response to Kashmiri separatist attacks in Delhi and other cities.

Violent crime is increasing, especially in the big cities. Gangs have made vast profits from smuggling, prostitution, narcotics, and protection and extortion rackets. Theft has risen sharply as consumer spending increases, and Internet crime is a problem.

Dacoits still operate in large areas of central India. Modeled on the *thugee* gangs of the 19th century, they are outlaws who live by highway robbery and terrorizing small rural communities.

EDUCATION

School leaving age: 12

58%

9.4m students

THE EDUCATION SYSTEM

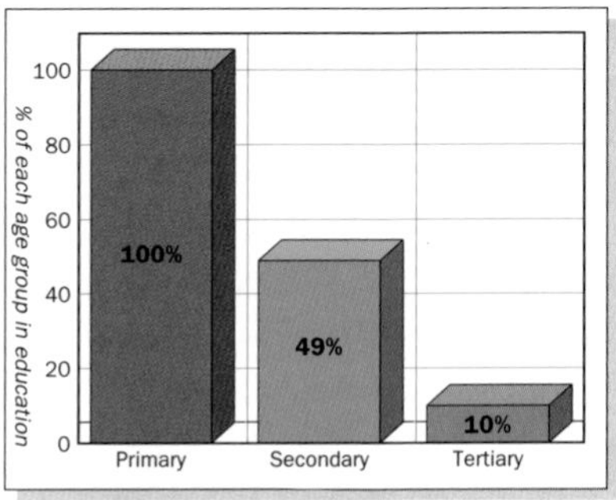
100
80
60
40
20
0
% of each age group in education
100%
49%
10%
Primary
Secondary
Tertiary

Education is primarily the responsibility of the individual state governments. There is now a primary school in every village across the subcontinent, but many children drop out of school to provide supplementary income for their families. There are more than 40 million students at secondary level, and an estimated 20 million graduates from more than 200 universities. Women make up around a third of those enrolled in higher education: a good percentage for a low-income economy. Though the high level of illiteracy is a brake on development, India has one of the largest pools of science graduates anywhere in the world.

***Terraced fields** in central India. In addition to rice, wheat, sorghum, maize, millet, and barley are also important cereal crops.*

THE SANGH MOVEMENT FOR A HINDU NATIONAL IDENTITY

THE IDEA OF *HINDUTVA*, a specifically Hindu-based national identity, has, since preindependence days existed in Indian politics. For decades, however, its supporters were no more than a minor strand of the opposition to the secularist Congress party, which ruled almost uninterruptedly for over 40 years. In the late 1980s, however, the rise of the BJP made *Hindutva* a national issue. When the party came to power, heading its first coalition government in 1998, Prime Minister A. B. Vajpayee kept its ideology in the background, but it is pressed by the nationalist Sangh movement to deliver on its pro-Hindu aims. The so-called "saffron brigade" calls in particular for a Hindu temple to be built in place of a Muslim mosque at Ayodhya, Uttar Pradesh, the supposed birthplace of the Hindu god Rama. In 1992 Hindu activists destroyed the mosque, setting off communal rioting in which 1200 people died. Another major flare-up came in 2002, sparked by plans to begin construction of the proposed temple. When Hindu activists returning from Ayodhya were massacred on a train, revenge attacks set off intercommunal violence in Gujarat in which some 2000 people died.

Multifaith demonstrators *condemned the intercommunal violence which left 2000 people dead in Gujarat in early 2002.*

THE SANGH MOVEMENT

The BJP's ideological origins lay in the Sangh movement built around the Rashtriya Swayamsevak Sangh (RSS). The RSS, whose name translates as the National Union of Selfless Servants, was first formed in Nagpur in 1925 to recruit men and women as *swayemsevaks*, volunteers dedicated to the creation of a Hindu nation (Hindu *rashtra*). Banned briefly in 1948 over its association with the Hindu extremist assassin of Mahatma Gandhi, the RSS has no clear organizational structure or membership. It has educational and trade union-based arms, and a religious wing in the militant World Hindu Council (VHP). The Sangh's influence is still strong in the BJP, though in 2000 the BJP-led government was compelled by the strength of pro-secular parties to reaffirm a ban on RSS members in the civil service. The BJP also tried to distance itself from the Sangh leader K. S. Sudarshan's increasingly vocal campaign for the expulsion of Christian missionaries and the replacement of "foreign churches" with a Hindu national church. The movement is linked with fringe organizations blamed for attacks on Christians.

REGIONAL APPEAL

The appeal of *Hindutva* is strongest in the Hindi-speaking heartland, the "cow belt," centered on Uttar Pradesh and Madhya Pradesh, with Bihar and Orissa to the east and in the west Maharashtra and Gujarat. While seeking to be inclusive and to appeal to all Hindus, the movement is rooted in Brahmin culture, and faces rivalry in some states from parties combating the oppression of the lowest castes (*dalits*).

In Maharashtra, the RSS inspires a more extreme local rival Hindu chauvinist party, Shiv Sena (the "army of Shivaji," a 17th-century warrior king). Shiv Sena leader Bal Thackeray, an open admirer of Adolf Hitler, is the main force in local politics. He led the campaign for Bombay's change of name to Mumbai in 1995.

The growth of regional parties has made coalition building a feature of government, and has been a major restraint on the BJP's more militant ideologues at national level. The party under Vajpayee's leadership at first downplayed controversial policies, but he provoked a storm in 2000 by describing the temple-building movement as embodying national sentiment and part of an unfinished agenda.

Hindu militants *on a pilgrimage to Ayodhya in Uttar Pradesh, northern India.*

HEALTH

Welfare state health benefits

1 per 2083 people

Respiratory, nutritional, and diarrheal diseases, malaria

Malnutrition is extremely common, increasing infant mortality, much of which is due to preventable diseases. Air pollution from the domestic use of solid fuel kills half a million children every year. HIV infection rates are rising: almost four million people were living with HIV/AIDS by end-2001. State governments are responsible for most health programs, but various national health projects include a huge polio eradication program. Plans to subsidize health insurance for the poorest of the poor were announced in 2000.

SPENDING

GDP/cap. increase

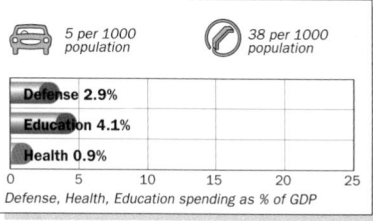

CONSUMPTION AND SPENDING

5 per 1000 population

38 per 1000 population

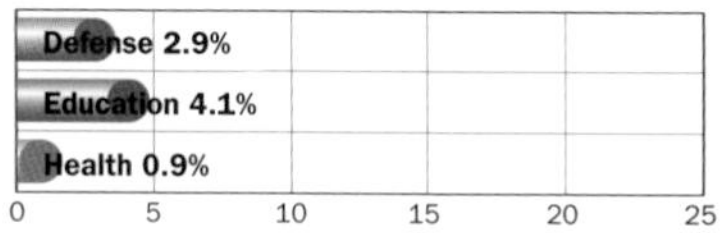
Defense 2.9%
Education 4.1%
Health 0.9%
0
5
10
15
20
25

Defense, Health, Education spending as % of GDP

India has become steadily more wealthy since independence, but distribution of this wealth has been far from even. Officially almost 300 million people – just under a third of the population – live in poverty. However, under the UN's $2-a-day guide the number is more like 800 million. Poverty is worse in the countryside, but more visible in the sprawling slums and on the crowded streets of the big cities.

Perched above the poverty line are the increasingly affluent middle classes, making up the bulk of the remaining population. With access to the new economy, the richest enjoy a standard of living comparable to that in the West, and have high expectations for their children.

WORLD RANKING

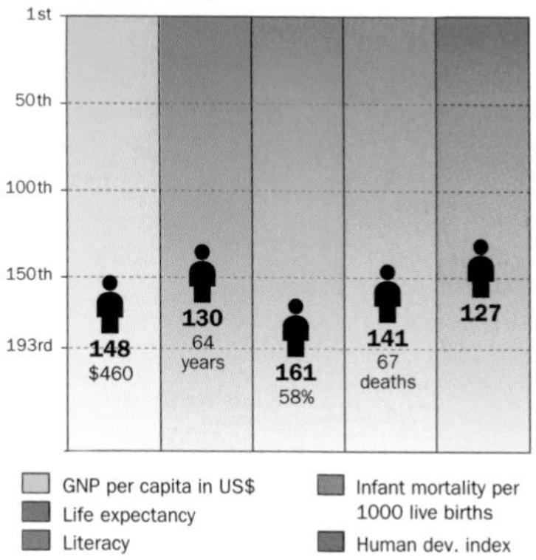
Position in World
1st
50th
100th
150th
193rd
148
$460
130
64 years
161
58%
141
67 deaths
127
GNP per capita in US$
Life expectancy
Literacy
Infant mortality per 1000 live births
Human dev. index

Asia
SOUTHEAST ASIA
Malaysia
Papua New Guinea
INDONESIA
East Timor
Australia

INDONESIA

OFFICIAL NAME: Republic of Indonesia **CAPITAL:** Jakarta
POPULATION: 218 million **CURRENCY:** Rupiah **OFFICIAL LANGUAGE:** Bahasa Indonesia

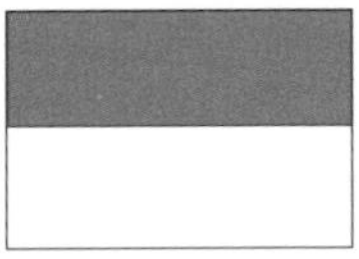

1949 | 1999 | Aug 17 | RI | +7 to +9 | +62 | .id

INDONESIA IS THE WORLD'S largest archipelago. Its 18,108 islands stretch 5000 km (3100 miles) from the Indian Ocean to New Guinea. Java, Kalimantan, Papua, Sulawesi, and Sumatra are mountainous, volcanic, and densely forested. Politics after independence was dominated by the military for over three decades, until the fall of the Suharto regime in 1998, when a partial "civilianization" began. In outlying regions, the forcibly suppressed demands for greater autonomy have flared up, bringing renewed violence. East Timor, which Indonesia invaded in 1975 and then annexed, voted for independence in 1999 and became a fully sovereign state in 2002.

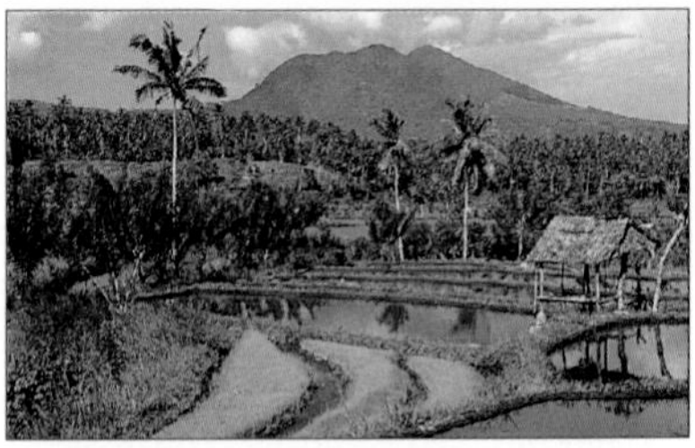

Rice terraces on Bali, *one of Indonesia's many islands and its most popular tourist destination. Rice is the staple food crop.*

CLIMATE

Tropical equatorial/ monsoon

WEATHER CHART FOR JAKARTA

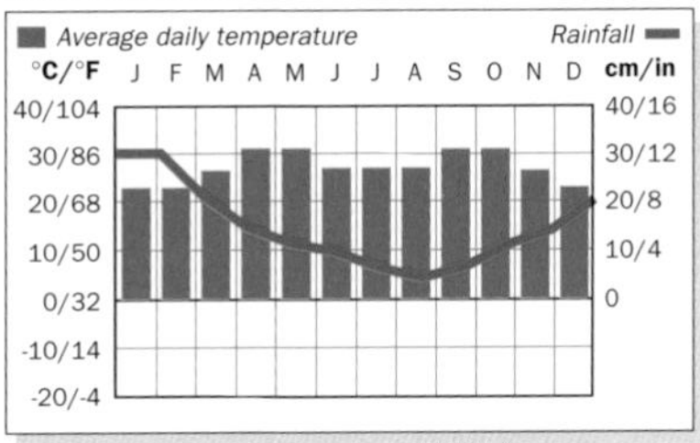
Average daily temperature
Rainfall
°C/°F
J F M A M J J A S O N D
cm/in
40/104
30/86
20/68
10/50
0/32
-10/14
-20/-4
40/16
30/12
20/8
10/4
0

Indonesia's climate is predominantly tropical. Variations relate mainly to differences in latitude, but hilly areas are cooler overall. Rain falls throughout the year, often in thunderstorms, but there is a relatively dry season from June to September. December to March is the wettest period, except in the Moluccas, which receive the bulk of their rain between June and September.

TRANSPORTATION

Drive on left

Sukarno–Hatta, Jakarta 14.8m passengers

2528 ships 3.61m grt

THE TRANSPORTATION NETWORK

158,670 km (98,593 miles)

200 km (124 miles)

6458 km (4013 miles)

21,579 km (13,409 miles)

For a multi-island state spread across three time zones, communications are an obvious government priority. Indonesia was an early entrant into satellite communications, providing an international satellite-based telephone system as early as 1976.

However, provisions vary greatly in the different provinces. Road surfaces in Java and Sumatra are excellent. Rail services are restricted to these two islands. In contrast, roads in Kalimantan and Papua are poor, and most travel is by air or river.

TOURISM

Visitors : Population 1:43

5.03m visitors

Down 2% in 2002

MAIN TOURIST ARRIVALS

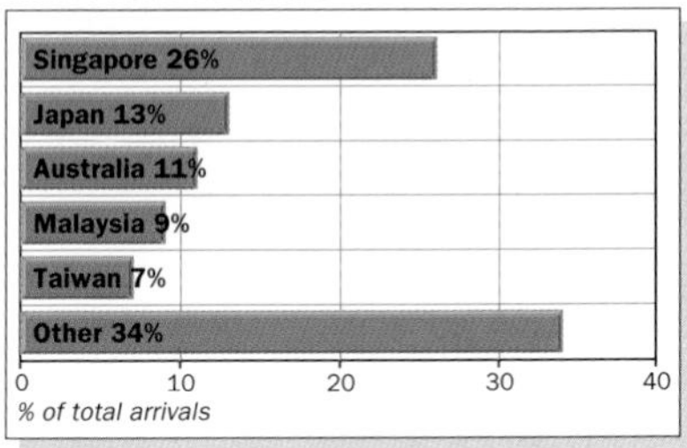
Singapore 26%
Japan 13%
Australia 11%
Malaysia 9%
Taiwan 7%
Other 34%
0
10
20
30
40
% of total arrivals

Tourism took off during the 1980s. The number of tourists now exceeds five million, though political unrest and the rise of Islamist militancy have discouraged many visitors. Expansion has been encouraged by major investment in hotels and the opening of Bali to airlines other than the national carrier, Garuda Indonesia. Tourism on Bali recovered quickly from the 2002 bombing.

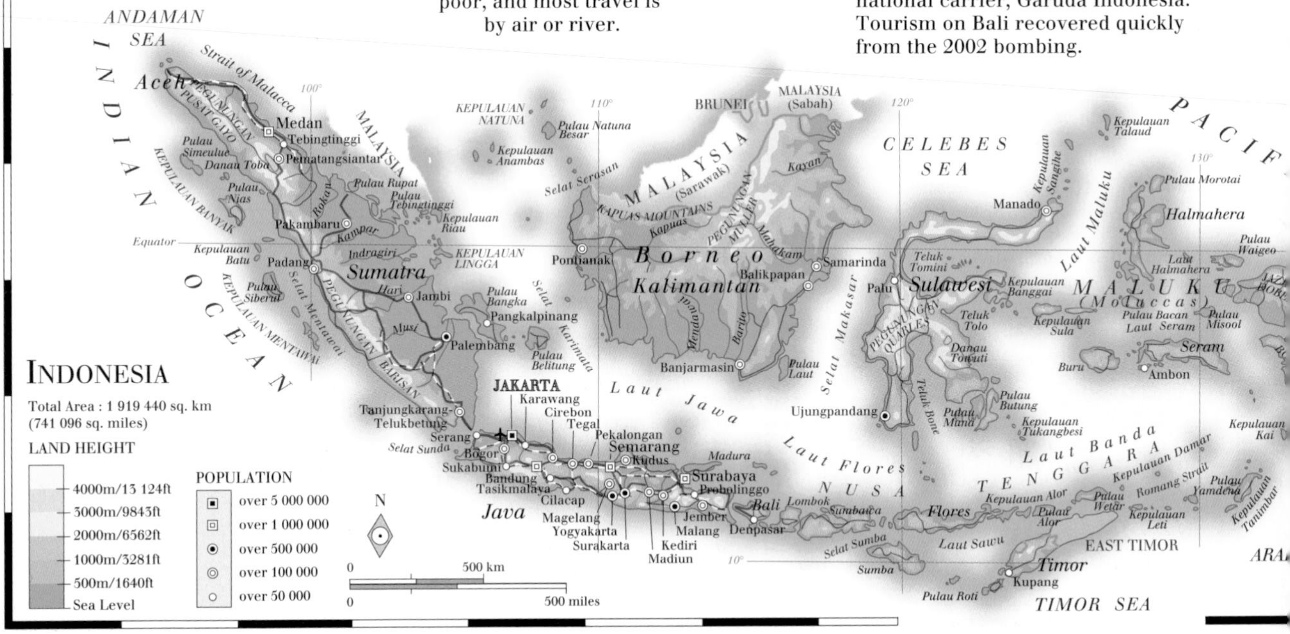
ANDAMAN SEA
INDIAN OCEAN
Strait of Malacca
MALAYSIA
Aceh
Medan
Tebingtinggi
Pematangsiantar
Pulau Simeulue
Danau Toba
Pulau Nias
KEPULAUAN BANYAK
Pakambaru
Pulau Rupat
Pulau Tebingtinggi
Kepulauan Riau
Equator
Kepulauan Batu
Padang
Pulau Siberut
Selat Mentawai
KEPULAUAN MENTAWAI
Sumatra
Indragiri
Jambi
Musi
Palembang
PEGUNUNGAN BARISAN
Pulau Bangka
Pangkalpinang
Pulau Belitung
KEPULAUAN NATUNA
Pulau Natuna Besar
Kepulauan Anambas
KEPULAUAN LINGGA
Pontianak
BRUNEI
MALAYSIA (Sabah)
MALAYSIA (Sarawak)
KAPUAS MOUNTAINS
Borneo
Kalimantan
Balikpapan
Samarinda
Banjarmasin
Laut Jawa
JAKARTA
Karawang
Cirebon
Tegal
Pekalongan
Semarang
Kudus
Serang
Bogor
Sukabumi
Bandung
Tasikmalaya
Cilacap
Java
Magelang
Yogyakarta
Surakarta
Madiun
Kediri
Malang
Jember
Probolinggo
Surabaya
Madura
Bali
Denpasar
Tanjungkarang-Telukbetung
Selat Sunda
CELEBES SEA
Manado
Sulawesi
Palu
Teluk Tomini
Selat Makasar
Ujungpandang
Teluk Bone
Pulau Buton
Kepulauan Tukangbesi
Laut Flores
NUSA TENGGARA
Lombok
Sumbawa
Flores
Sumba
Selat Sumba
Laut Sawu
Timor
Kupang
Pulau Roti
EAST TIMOR
TIMOR SEA
Laut Banda
Kepulauan Alor
Pulau Wetar
Kepulauan Leti
Pulau Yamdena
Kepulauan Tanimbar
MALUKU (Moluccas)
Halmahera
Pulau Morotai
Pulau Waigeo
Laut Halmahera
Laut Maluku
Kepulauan Talaud
Kepulauan Sangihe
Kepulauan Banggai
Kepulauan Sula
Buru
Seram
Ambon
Pulau Misool
Laut Seram
Kepulauan Kai
PACIFIC
INDONESIA
Total Area : 1 919 440 sq. km (741 096 sq. miles)
LAND HEIGHT
4000m/13 124ft
3000m/9843ft
2000m/6562ft
1000m/3281ft
500m/1640ft
Sea Level
POPULATION
over 5 000 000
over 1 000 000
over 500 000
over 100 000
over 50 000
N
0 500 km
0 500 miles

PEOPLE

Pop. density medium

Javanese, Sundanese, Madurese, Bahasa Indonesia, Dutch

121/km² (314/mi²)

THE URBAN/RURAL POPULATION SPLIT

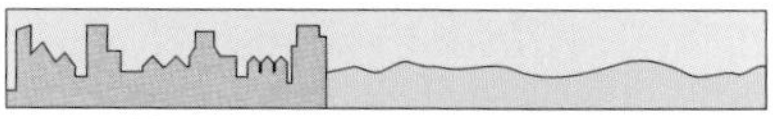
42%
58%

RELIGIOUS PERSUASION

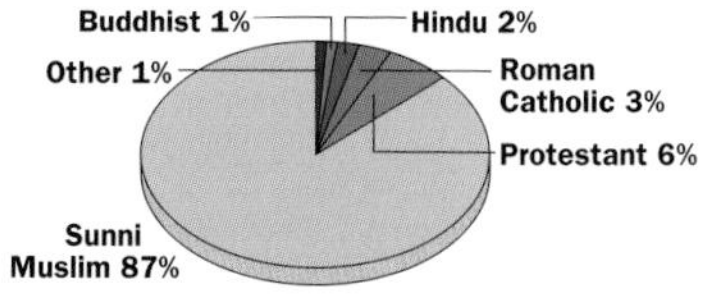
Buddhist 1%
Hindu 2%
Other 1%
Roman Catholic 3%
Protestant 6%
Sunni Muslim 87%

ETHNIC MAKEUP

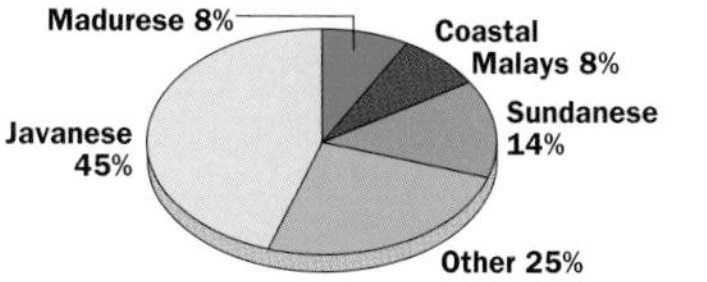
Madurese 8%
Coastal Malays 8%
Sundanese 14%
Javanese 45%
Other 25%

The basic Melanesian–Malay ethnic division disguises a diverse society. The national language, Bahasa Indonesia, coexists with at least 250 other spoken languages or dialects. Attempts by the Javanese political elite to suppress local cultures have been vigorously opposed, especially by the Aceh of northern Sumatra, and the Papuans of New Guinea.

Religious and interethnic hostility is increasing. Since 1998 there have been violent clashes between Muslims and Christians on Sulawesi, and in the Moluccas. Similar clashes occurred in Kalimantan in 1999 and 2001 between indigenous Dayaks and ethnic Madurese immigrants. Aceh introduced *sharia* (Islamic law) in 2000.

Discrimination against ethnic Chinese has encouraged vicious attacks on their businesses, as in Jakarta in 1998.

Gender equality is enshrined in law, and women are active in public life.

POPULATION AGE BREAKDOWN

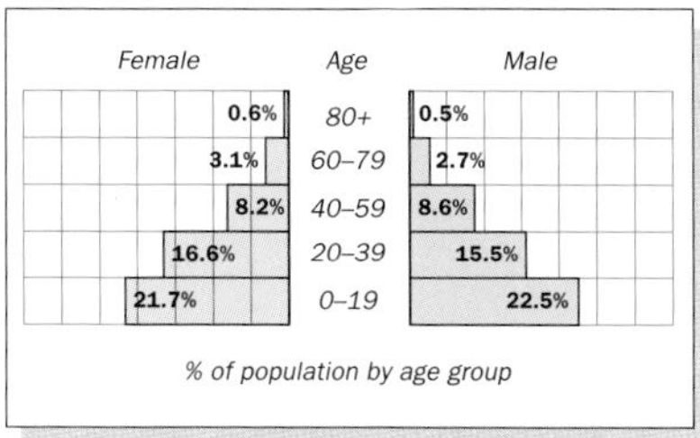
Female
Age
Male
0.6% 80+ 0.5%
3.1% 60–79 2.7%
8.2% 40–59 8.6%
16.6% 20–39 15.5%
21.7% 0–19 22.5%
% of population by age group

WORLD AFFAIRS

Joined UN in 1950

APEC ASEAN G15 OIC OPEC

Indonesia pursues a largely pro-Western foreign policy, though the government is under pressure to improve its human rights record, and it opposed the 2003 invasion of Iraq. The scale and nature of the East Timor massacres in 1999 severely damaged its standing. Internal security in the far-flung provinces tests regional relations.

China remains a concern, despite the restoration of diplomatic ties in 1990. Indonesia and Australia have cooperated on security since 1995, but the movement of illegal immigrants through Indonesia and recent Islamist terrorism create tensions.

AID

Recipient

$1.5bn (receipts)

Down 13% in 2001

Japan accounts for the bulk of bilateral aid. Multilateral aid comes above all from the World Bank, though it called for urgent reform in late 2001 before loaning more money. Aid has been notoriously subject to "leakage."

POLITICS

Multiparty elections

1999/2004

President Megawati Sukarnoputri

AT THE LAST ELECTION

House of Representatives 500 seats

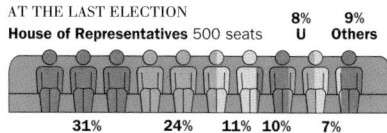

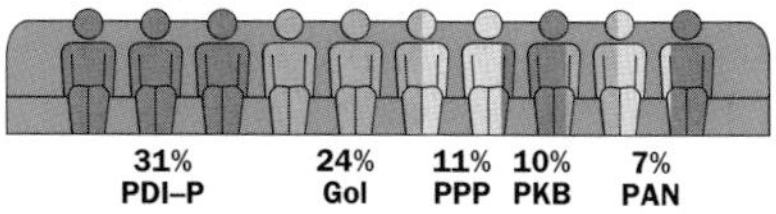
8% U
9% Others
31% PDI–P
24% Gol
11% PPP
10% PKB
7% PAN

PDI–P = Indonesian Democratic Party of Struggle
Gol = Golkar **PPP** = United Development Party
PKB = National Awaking Party **U** = Unelected (army) seats
PAN = National Mandate Party

Indonesia is a multiparty democracy.

PROFILE

Under Gen. Suharto, in power from 1966, Golkar and the army were dominant. Suharto was forced to resign in 1998 amid widespread protest over corruption, economic mismanagement, and denial of democratic rights. After his fall, the mainly Muslim PDI–P, led by Megawati Sukarnoputri, daughter of the first president, won elections, but Abdurrahman Wahid of the PKB was appointed president; Megawati became vice president. Increasingly vehement opposition to Wahid in parliament culminated in his removal in 2001 whereupon Megawati was made president. She has pledged further democratic reforms, and faces stiff competition in the country's first direct presidential elections, due in October 2004.

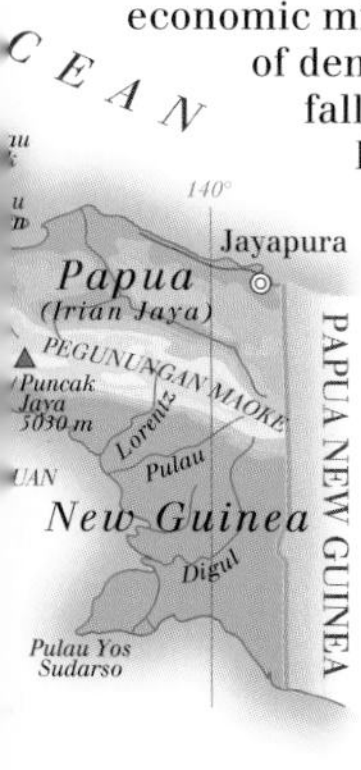
CEAN
140°
Jayapura
Papua
(Irian Jaya)
PEGUNUNGAN MAOKE
Puncak Jaya 5030 m
Lorentz
Pulau
New Guinea
Digul
Pulau Yos Sudarso
PAPUA NEW GUINEA

MAIN POLITICAL ISSUES

The army

The army's involvement in politics remains a serious problem. In early 2000, the influential Gen. Wiranto left the government, but the army refused to relinquish its 38-seat entitlement in the legislature any earlier than 2009.

Separatist movements

Separatism and religious violence threaten national unity. Though greater autonomy was granted to both Papua and Aceh in 2001, tensions persist. In Papua there is anger over plans to divide the province administratively, while in Aceh an all-out offensive against separatists was launched by the government in 2003.

Dr. Sukarno, *Indonesia's "father of independence."*

President Megawati Sukarnoputri, *Sukarno's daughter.*

CHRONOLOGY

Hindu, Buddhist, and Islamic interest preceded 16th-century European rivalries over valuable spices. The Dutch had won control by the 17th century, when colonization began on Java. By 1910, the Dutch East Indies encompassed present-day Indonesia.

- ❑ **1920** Indonesian Communist Party (PKI) formed; leads revolt in West Java (1926) and Sumatra (1927).
- ❑ **1927** Indonesian National Party formed under Dr. Sukarno.
- ❑ **1930s** Dutch repress nationalists.
- ❑ **1942–1945** Japanese occupation. Autonomy within "Greater East Asia" state promised. Sukarno works with Japanese while promoting independence.
- ❑ **1945** Sukarno declares Indonesian independence. Dutch forces attempt to reassert control.
- ❑ **1945–1949** Nationalist guerrilla war.
- ❑ **1949** Dutch grant independence to federal-style United States of Indonesia under Sukarno as president.
- ❑ **1950** Union dissolved, Sukarno grows increasingly authoritarian.
- ❑ **1950s** Moluccas declare independence: unsuccessful separatist war.
- ❑ **1957–1959** Sukarno introduces authoritarian Guided Democracy.
- ❑ **1959** Sukarno extends

⇨

CHRONOLOGY *continued*

presidential powers. Civilian legislature replaced by military. Extreme nationalist and pro-Chinese policies.

- ❑ **1962** Dutch relinquish Western New Guinea.
- ❑ **1965** Communist PKI alliance with military ends. Army led by Gen. Suharto crushes abortive coup and acts to eliminate the now banned PKI; up to one million killed.
- ❑ **1966** Sukarno hands over power to Gen. Suharto temporarily; becomes permanent in 1967.
- ❑ **1968** Suharto becomes president: declares "New order"; introduces pro-Western liberal economic policies while transferring real power to small group of officers.
- ❑ **1971** First elections for 16 years. Government-sponsored Golkar wins landslide. Opposition parties now passive partners of government.
- ❑ **1975** Invasion of East Timor; its incorporation in 1976 as 27th province is not recognized by UN.
- ❑ **1984** Muslim protesters clash with troops in Jakarta. Start of resurgence of Islamic protest.
- ❑ **1985** Fretilin movement declares East Timor independent.
- ❑ **1989** Growing discontent with authoritarian government; student protests, unrest in Java and Sumbawa. Demands for Suharto to retire. Low-key official response.
- ❑ **1991** Indonesian troops massacre proindependence demonstrators in East Timor. New organizations, including Democratic Forum and League for Restoration of Democracy, allowed to form in response to growing demands for "openness."
- ❑ **1993** Suharto wins sixth term.
- ❑ **1996** Antigovernment demonstrations in Jakarta.
- ❑ **1997** Economic recession. Smog across region from forest fires.
- ❑ **1998** Suharto resigns amid unrest.
- ❑ **1999** Election victory for opposition led by Megawati Sukarnoputri. East Timor referendum backing independence triggers violent backlash. Abdurrahman Wahid of PKB elected president, Megawati named vice president.
- ❑ **2000** Aceh becomes first province to introduce *sharia*. Violence erupts again in Moluccas.
- ❑ **2001** Wahid removed, replaced by Megawati.
- ❑ **2002** January, autonomy officially granted to Papua. May, East Timor independent. October, terrorist attack in Bali kills over 200, mostly Western holidaymakers.
- ❑ **2003** Major offensive against Aceh separatists.

DEFENSE

Compulsory military service

$860m — Up 40% in 2001

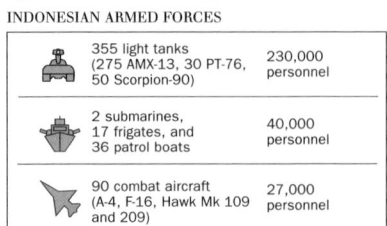

INDONESIAN ARMED FORCES

355 light tanks (275 AMX-13, 30 PT-76, 50 Scorpion-90)	230,000 personnel
2 submarines, 17 frigates, and 36 patrol boats	40,000 personnel
90 combat aircraft (A-4, F-16, Hawk Mk 109 and 209)	27,000 personnel
None	

Defense spending is low by regional standards, despite the military's high profile. The constitution enshrines the military's political role. The civilianization of political parties, the bureaucracy, and state companies has reduced the presence of the military in these areas, if not their influence. The army is accused of human rights abuses, particularly in separatist regions. High-ranking officers have been imprisoned for their role in violence in Timor and West Papua, though their sentences are often very short. Western arms sales are increasingly being made dependent on the improvement of Indonesia's human rights record. There are tensions between the army and nonmilitary security forces.

Military service is selective and lasts for two years.

ECONOMICS

Inflation 16% p.a. (1990–2001)

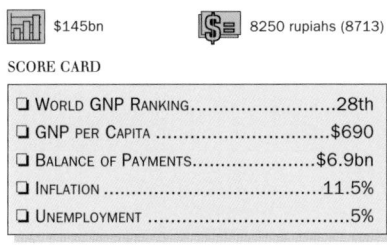

$145bn — 8250 rupiahs (8713)

SCORE CARD

- ❑ WORLD GNP RANKING..........28th
- ❑ GNP PER CAPITA..........$690
- ❑ BALANCE OF PAYMENTS..........$6.9bn
- ❑ INFLATION..........11.5%
- ❑ UNEMPLOYMENT..........5%

EXPORTS

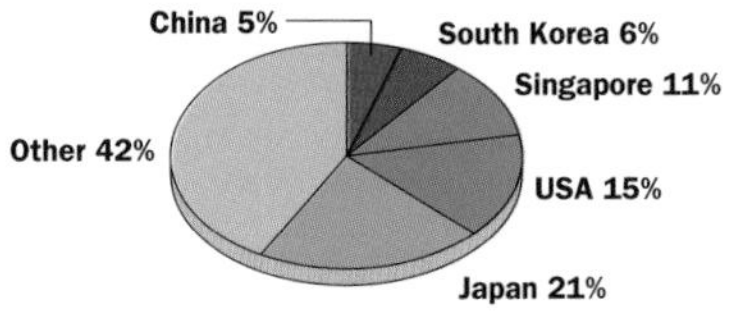
China 5%
South Korea 6%
Singapore 11%
USA 15%
Japan 21%
Other 42%

IMPORTS

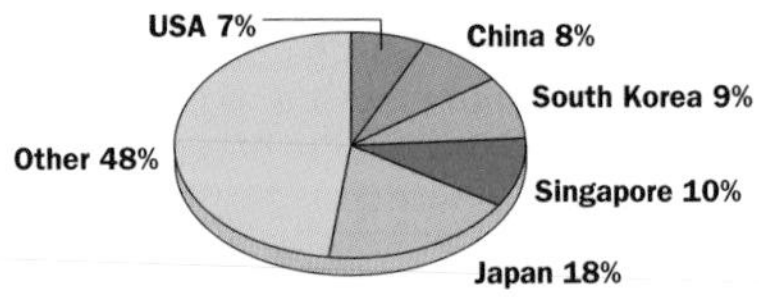
USA 7%
China 8%
South Korea 9%
Singapore 10%
Japan 18%
Other 48%

STRENGTHS

Varied resources, especially oil. Signs of return to high growth. Debt successfully rescheduled. International credit rating improved.

WEAKNESSES

High level of bureaucracy. Endemic corruption. Huge wealth disparities. Regional insecurity deters investment. High underemployment. Piracy.

ECONOMIC PERFORMANCE INDICATOR

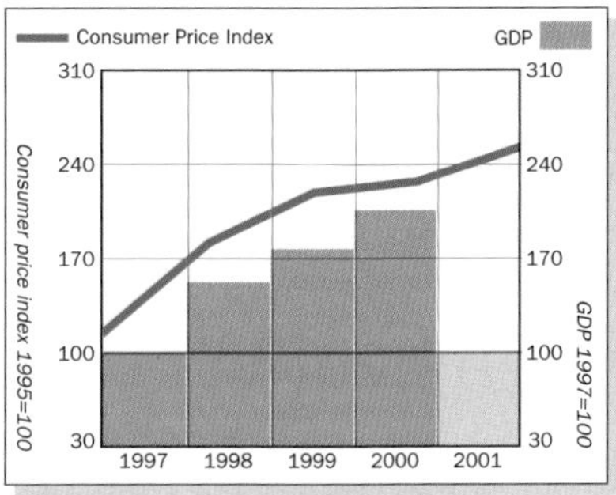
Consumer Price Index
GDP
Consumer price index 1995=100
GDP 1997=100
310
240
170
100
30
1997
1998
1999
2000
2001

PROFILE

Under Suharto the economy grew rapidly, fueled largely by oil, until its collapse in the 1997–1998 Asian crisis. State-owned corporations, protected from foreign competition, had played a significant role in the expansion. Exports were diversified, but the debt burden used up a third of export earnings. Reform was delayed by conflict between "technologists" favoring industrialization over profit for state concerns and advocates of deregulation. Further reforms have been stalled by opposition in parliament. Corruption remains rife, embroiling incumbent president Wahid in 2001. However, relations with the IMF and other donors were sufficiently improved by 2002 for Indonesia's international credit rating to be upgraded, and GDP growth that year was barely affected by the Bali bombing.

INDONESIA : MAJOR BUSINESSES

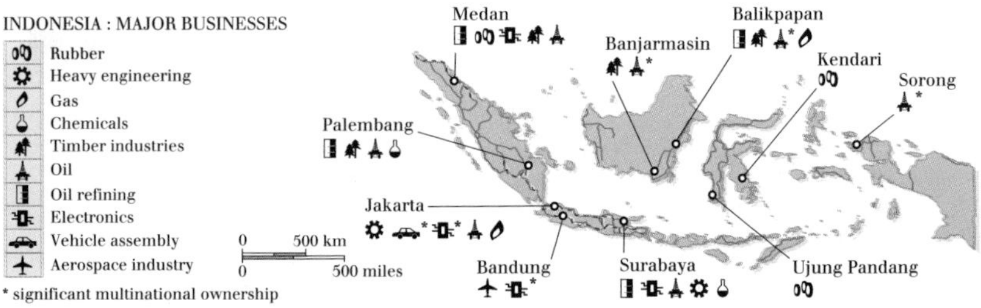
Rubber
Heavy engineering
Gas
Chemicals
Timber industries
Oil
Oil refining
Electronics
Vehicle assembly
Aerospace industry
* significant multinational ownership
0 500 km
0 500 miles
Medan
Balikpapan
Banjarmasin
Kendari
Sorong
Palembang
Jakarta
Bandung
Surabaya
Ujung Pandang

RESOURCES

Electric power 25.2m kW

4.93m tonnes

1.28m b/d (reserves 5bn barrels)

30m ducks, 12.4m goats, 870m chickens

Oil, natural gas, coal, bauxite, nickel, copper, gold, tin

ELECTRICITY GENERATION

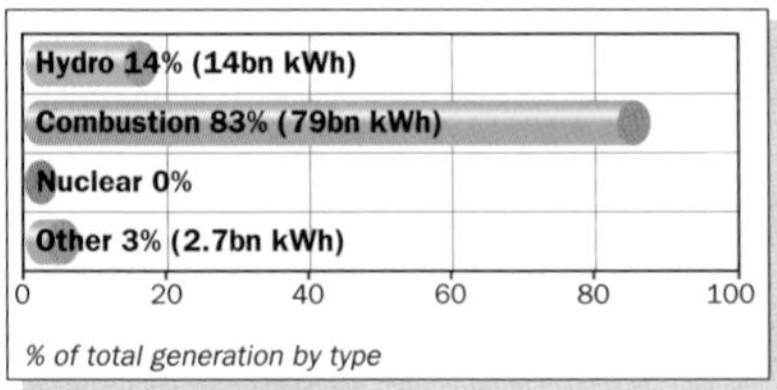
Hydro 14% (14bn kWh)
Combustion 83% (79bn kWh)
Nuclear 0%
Other 3% (2.7bn kWh)
0
20
40
60
80
100
% of total generation by type

INDONESIA : LAND USE

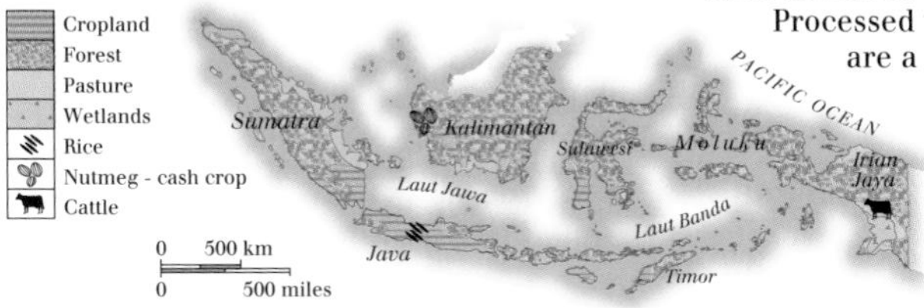
Cropland
Forest
Pasture
Wetlands
Rice
Nutmeg - cash crop
Cattle
Sumatra
Kalimantan
Sulawesi
Moluku
Irian Jaya
PACIFIC OCEAN
Laut Jawa
Laut Banda
Java
Timor
0 500 km
0 500 miles

Indonesia is rich in energy sources. The main export earners are liquefied natural gas (LNG), of which it is the world's largest exporter, and oil. However, oil output has been falling, and combined with rapid growth in domestic energy demand, this could turn Indonesia into an oil importer in the next decade. The government is therefore encouraging oil exploration in remote regions. It is also considering developing existing geothermal and hydroelectric energy sources. Indonesia's other main resources are coal, bauxite, and nickel, and agricultural products such as rubber and palm oil. Processed wood products are a significant export commodity; the rapid depletion of the rainforests has given rise to attempts to control timber exports.

ENVIRONMENT

Sustainability rank: 100th

20% (10% partially protected)

1.1 tonnes per capita

ENVIRONMENTAL TREATIES

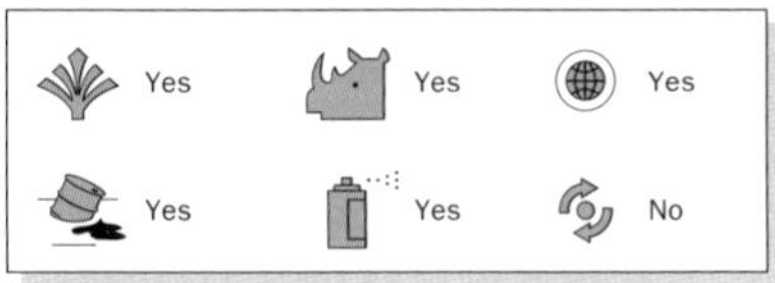
Yes
Yes
Yes
Yes
Yes
No

Environmental legislation is poorly enforced: the rich tropical forests suffer from excessive logging, and rare species, such as orangutans, are disappearing. Greenpeace helps monitor illegal logging in remote areas. Smog from forest fires seriously contributes to global levels of greenhouse gases. The World Bank warned in 2003 of massive health problems from pollution, particularly in urban areas.

MEDIA

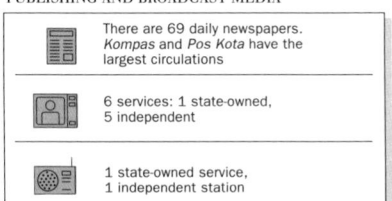

TV ownership medium

Daily newspaper circulation 23 per 1000 people

PUBLISHING AND BROADCAST MEDIA

There are 69 daily newspapers. *Kompas* and *Pos Kota* have the largest circulations

6 services: 1 state-owned, 5 independent

1 state-owned service, 1 independent station

The 1999 press law prohibits censorship, but journalists can still be fined for violating "religious and moral norms." Independent press and broadcasting have flourished since 1998.

CRIME

Death penalty in use

62,886 prisoners

Up 17% in 1999

CRIME RATES

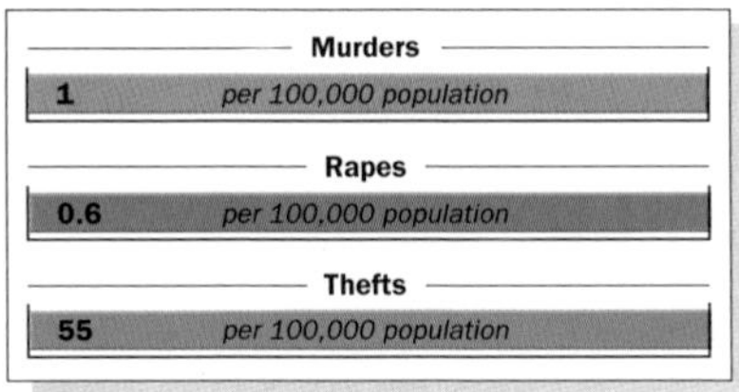
Murders
1 per 100,000 population
Rapes
0.6 per 100,000 population
Thefts
55 per 100,000 population

Suppression of secessionists is harsh. There is brutal ethnic violence in the provinces. Piracy is rife.

EDUCATION

School leaving age: 15

87%

3.02m students

THE EDUCATION SYSTEM

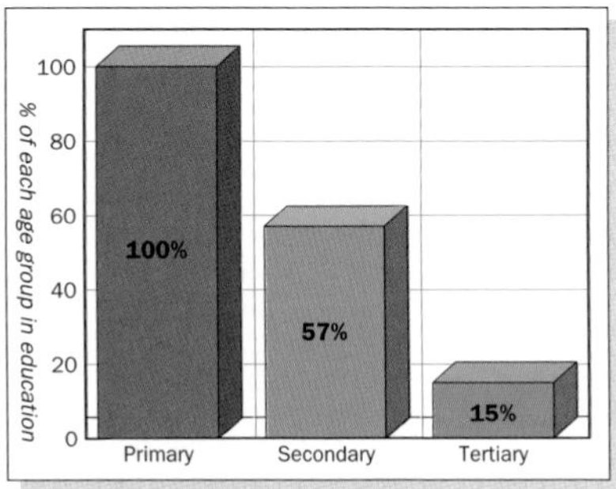
100
80
60
40
20
0
% of each age group in education
100%
57%
15%
Primary
Secondary
Tertiary

Primary education is subsidized by the state, compulsory, and often provided by Islamic schools. In contrast, good secondary education is hard to find in rural areas. University students come predominantly from the richer elites.

HEALTH

Welfare state health benefits

1 per 6250 people

Lower respiratory and diarrheal diseases

An extensive network of clinics, down to village level, means that access to health care is reasonable, and health indicators have improved significantly. The death rate declined from 2% in 1965 to 0.7% in 2000, thus helping to increase life expectancy, while infant mortality has more than halved over this period. However, malnutrition and pollution-related health problems, which were estimated in 2003 to affect 30% of all children, remain a real problem. The World Bank has warned of massive poisoning from pollution. The rate of HIV infection among intravenous drug users, particularly in prisons, is rising.

SPENDING

GDP/cap. increase

CONSUMPTION AND SPENDING

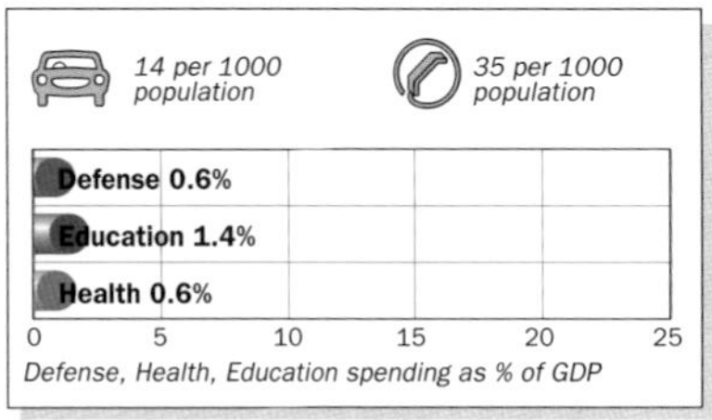
14 per 1000 population
35 per 1000 population
Defense 0.6%
Education 1.4%
Health 0.6%
0
5
10
15
20
25
Defense, Health, Education spending as % of GDP

Many Indonesians live in relative poverty and those on the peripheral islands in real poverty; large wealth disparities exist between the Javanese middle classes and the subsistence farmers and tribesmen of Papua and Kalimantan. This reflects both a concentration of wealth in the hands of a limited number of key political and business figures, and a concentration of development and investment on the main islands, particularly Java. Since 1998 attempts have been made in the courts to tackle the issues of corruption and concentration of wealth in the hands of close associates and relatives of former president Suharto and his political successors.

WORLD RANKING

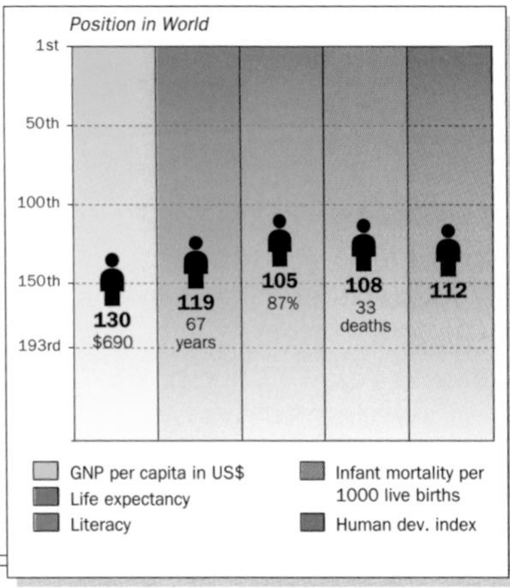
Position in World
1st
50th
100th
150th
193rd
130
$690
119
67
years
105
87%
108
33
deaths
112
GNP per capita in US$
Life expectancy
Literacy
Infant mortality per 1000 live births
Human dev. index

I

IRAN

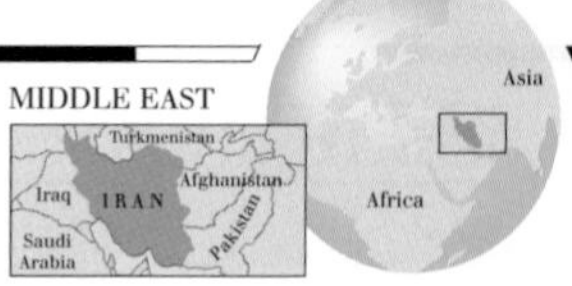

MIDDLE EAST
Turkmenistan
Afghanistan
Iraq
IRAN
Pakistan
Saudi Arabia
Asia
Africa

OFFICIAL NAME: Islamic Republic of Iran **CAPITAL:** Tehran
POPULATION: 72.4 million **CURRENCY:** Iranian rial **OFFICIAL LANGUAGE:** Farsi

1502 | 1990 | Feb 11 | IR | +3.5 | +98 | .ir

TURBULENT NEIGHBORS surround Iran; there are republics of the former Soviet Union to the north, Afghanistan and Pakistan to the east, and Iraq and Turkey to the west. The south faces the Persian Gulf and the Gulf of Oman. Since 1979, when a revolution led by Ayatollah Khomeini deposed the shah, Iran has become the world's largest theocracy and the leading center for militant Shi'a Islam. Iran's active support for Islamic fundamentalist movements has led to strained relations with central Asian, Middle Eastern, and north African states, as well as with the US and Europe.

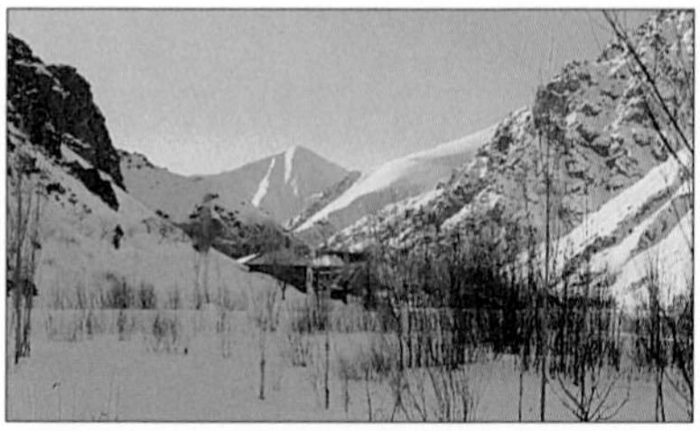

*The **Reshteh-ye Kuhhā-ye Alborz** (Elburz Mountains). Their Caspian Sea slopes are rainy and forested; the southern slopes are dry.*

CLIMATE

Mountain/cold desert

WEATHER CHART FOR TEHRAN

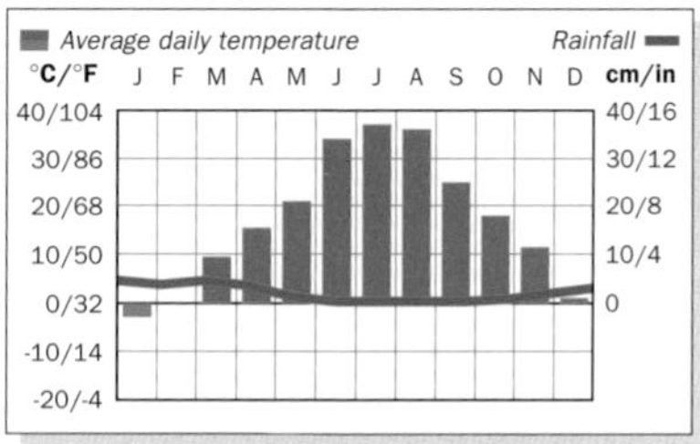

Average daily temperature
Rainfall
°C/°F
J F M A M J J A S O N D
cm/in
40/104
30/86
20/68
10/50
0/32
-10/14
-20/-4
40/16
30/12
20/8
10/4
0

The area bordering the Caspian Sea is Iran's most temperate region. Most of the country has a desert climate.

TRANSPORTATION

Drive on right

Mehrabad International, Tehran
8.47m passengers

389 ships
3.94m grt

THE TRANSPORTATION NETWORK

49,440 km (30,721 miles)

470 km (292 miles)

6688 km (4156 miles)

904 km (562 miles)

Adequate roads link main towns, but rural areas are less well served. Most freight travels by rail. A ferry runs from Bandar-e Abbas to the UAE.

PEOPLE

Pop. density low

Farsi, Azeri, Gilaki, Mazanderani, Kurdish, Baluchi, Arabic, Turkmen

44/km² (115/mi²)

THE URBAN/RURAL POPULATION SPLIT

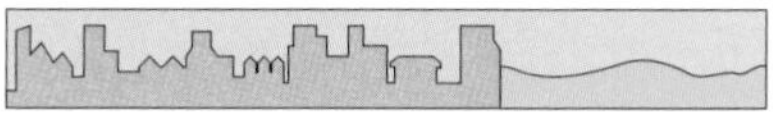

65%
35%

RELIGIOUS PERSUASION

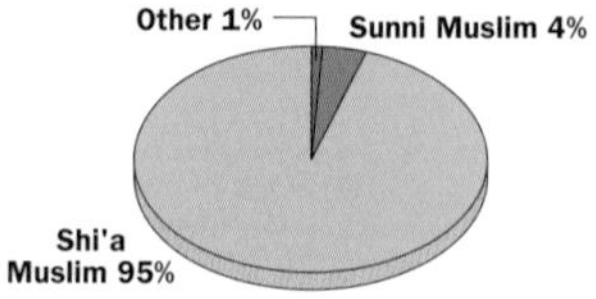

Other 1%
Sunni Muslim 4%
Shi'a Muslim 95%

ETHNIC MAKEUP

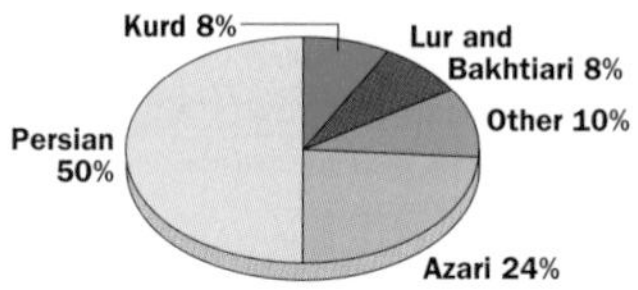

Kurd 8%
Lur and Bakhtiari 8%
Other 10%
Persian 50%
Azari 24%

The people of the north and center of Iran – about half of all Iranians – speak Farsi (Persian), while about a quarter speak related languages, including Kurdish in the west and Baluchi in the southeast. Another quarter of the population speaks Turkic languages, primarily the Azaris and the Turkmen in the northwest. Smaller groups, such as the Circassians and Georgians, are found in the northern provinces.

Until the 16th century, much of Iran followed the Sunni interpretation of Islam, but since then the Shi'a sect has been dominant. Religious minorities, accounting for just 1% of the population, include followers of the Bahai faith, who suffer discrimination, Zoroastrians, Christians, and Jews. The regime has a remarkably liberal attitude to refugees of the Muslim faith. Nearly three million Afghan refugees were received during the height of the Afghan civil war in the 1980s–1990s, though many have since returned. In Khorosan province in the east, refugees account for nearly a quarter of the population; near the Turkish border they constitute half the total population. Many are young, resulting in intense competition with Iranians for jobs and consequent ethnic tensions.

One of the main consequences of the 1979 Islamic revolution was to reverse the policy of female emancipation. The revolution restricted the public role of women and enforced a strict dress code, obliging women to cover themselves from head to foot in the chador (veil). More liberal attitudes have gradually emerged. Reform of the divorce laws, so that the wife could initiate proceedings, is backed by the reformist parliament, but strongly opposed by the conservative judiciary as un-Islamic.

POPULATION AGE BREAKDOWN

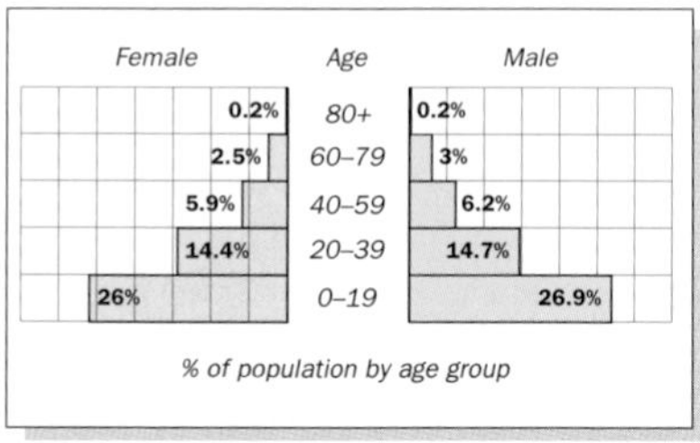

Female
Age
Male
0.2% 80+ 0.2%
2.5% 60–79 3%
5.9% 40–59 6.2%
14.4% 20–39 14.7%
26% 0–19 26.9%
% of population by age group

TOURISM

Visitors : Population 1:52

1.4m visitors

Up 5% in 2001

MAIN TOURIST ARRIVALS

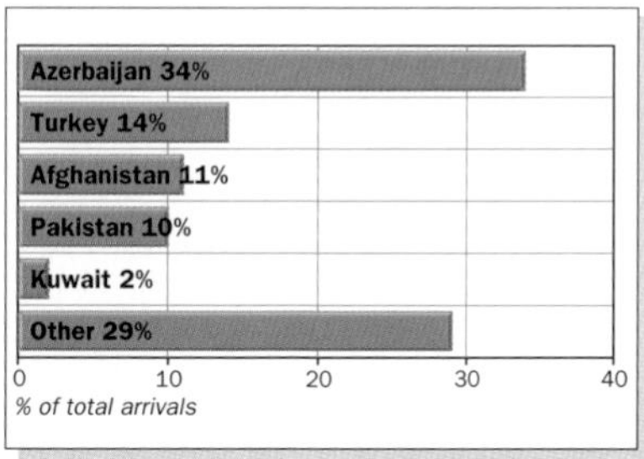

Azerbaijan 34%
Turkey 14%
Afghanistan 11%
Pakistan 10%
Kuwait 2%
Other 29%
0
10
20
30
40
% of total arrivals

Iran's historical heritage, mosques, and bazaars formerly attracted sizable numbers of tourists. This flow was cut off by the 1979 revolution, which deterred visitors, especially from the West. In the 1990s, however, there was a rise in the number of business people visiting Iran. Procedures at Tehran's Mehrabad airport have been simplified and the capital's hotels refurbished. In late 1998 President Khatami's more liberal regime welcomed a delegation of US tourists, despite opposition from conservative groups.

POLITICS

Multiparty elections

2000/2004

President Mohammad Khatami

AT THE LAST ELECTION

Consultative Council (Majlis al-Shoura) 290 seats

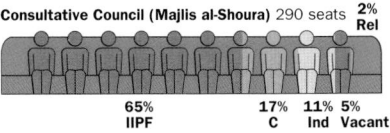

2%
Rel
65%
IIPF
17%
C
11%
Ind
5%
Vacant

IIPF = Islamic Iran Participation Front (reformists)
C = Coalition of Followers of the Line of Imam (conservatives)
Ind = Independents **Rel** = Religious Minorities

Iran is a theocracy. Tension exists between the conservative mullahs and the reformist government.

Profile

Iran's religious revolution of 1979 was fueled by popular outrage at the corruption, repression, and inequalities of the shah's regime. Since the time of Ayatollah Khomeini, successive Iranian governments have maintained that the clergy have a religious duty to establish a just social system. Accordingly, the legislature, the executive, and the judiciary may, in theory, be overruled by the religious leadership; former president Hashemi Rafsanjani's moderate policies were questioned by radical clergymen advocating "permanent revolution." However, the mullahs' failure to address Iran's economic problems has eroded their political standing. Reformists were encouraged by the election of President Mohammad Khatami in 1997, but the clergy remains powerful. Huge student demonstrations in 1999 and 2000 in favor of reform were offset by crackdowns on reformist politicians and newspapers. The mullahs, so far unbowed by reformist election victories, have continued to confront the modernizers.

Ayatollah Khamenei, *who became spiritual leader after the death of Ayatollah Khomeini.*

Mohammad Khatami, *reformist president, in office since 1997.*

Main Political Issue

Mosque versus secular state

A power struggle between the clergy and the secular state has arisen from the ill-defined division of power between the two. The conservative faction in parliament lost its overall majority in 1996 and has been steadily displaced by reformists, who in 2000 made sweeping gains in parliamentary elections. In 2001 reformist president Mohammad Khatami was reelected, this time with an overwhelming 77% of the vote.

Khatami is committed to modernizing the economy, but is strongly opposed by the mullahs, for whom adherence to religious values is more important than material welfare. Student proreform protests were harshly suppressed by hard-liners, who remain a force, despite their losses in the 2000 elections, through the powerful Council of Guardians.

WORLD AFFAIRS

Joined UN in 1945

ECO | G24 | NAM | OIC | OPEC

Following the 1979 revolution, Iran assumed international significance as the voice of militant Shi'a Islam. Iran is accused of backing terrorist activity carried out by Muslim extremists and of fostering unrest throughout the Middle East and central Asia.

Under President Khatami, Iran has tried to convey a less confrontational image. Improved relations with Saudi Arabia, troubled since Iran's seizure of the islands of Abu Musa and the Tunbs in 1970, resulted in the signing of a pact in 2001. Relations with the US remain tense. In 2002 US President George W. Bush cast Iran (with Iraq and North Korea) as part of an international "axis of evil," and since then has accused Iran of covertly seeking to develop weapons of mass destruction, particularly nuclear weapons.

Iraq under the regime of Saddam Hussein had been Iran's main security preoccupation; following his removal in 2003, the political and security uncertainties thrown up by the US-led occupation continue to cause concern.

AZERBAIJAN
ARMENIA
AZERBAIJAN
TURKEY
CASPIAN SEA
TURKMENISTAN
IRAQ
AFGHANISTAN
PAKISTAN
KUWAIT
THE GULF
GULF OF OMAN
U.A.E.
OMAN
Khvoy
Tabrīz
Ardabīl
Orūmīyeh
Marāgheh
Rasht
Zanjān
Qazvīn
Bījār
Sanandaj
Karaj
TEHRĀN
Tajrīsh
Rey
Gorgān
Sārī
Āmol
Shāhrūd
Sabzevār
Mashhad
Hamadān
Qom
Bākhtarān
Malāyer
Borūjerd
Arāk
Kāshān
DASHT-E KAVĪR
Gonābād
Deyhūk
Mūd
Khorramābād
Khomeynīshahr
Dezfūl
Najafābād
Eşfahān
Masjed-e Soleymān
PLATEAU OF IRAN
Yazd
Ahvāz
Khorramshahr
Ābādān
Nūrābād
Kermān
Zāhedān
Shīrāz
Sīrjān
Bam
Bandar-e Būshehr
Kangān
Īrānshahr
Bandar-e 'Abbās
Strait of Hormuz
Qeshm
Makran Coast
Konārak
Dasht-e Lūt
Daryācheh-ye Namak
Kavīr-e Namak
Daryācheh-ye Sīstān
Hāmūn-e Jaz Mūrīān
IRAN
Total Area : 1 648 000 sq. km
(636 293 sq. miles)
POPULATION
over 1 000 000
over 500 000
over 100 000
over 50 000
over 10 000
under 10 000
LAND HEIGHT
3000m/9843ft
2000m/6562ft
1000m/3281ft
500m/1640ft
200m/656ft
Sea Level
200 km
200 miles

CHRONOLOGY

Persia was ruled by the shahs as an absolute monarchy until 1906, when the first constitution was approved. The Pahlavis took power in 1925 and changed the country's name to Iran in 1935.

- ❑ **1957** SAVAK, shah's secret police, established to control opposition.
- ❑ **1964** Ayatollah Khomeini is exiled to Iraq for criticizing secular state.
- ❑ **1971** Shah celebrates 2500th anniversary of Persian monarchy.
- ❑ **1975** Agreement with Iraq over Shatt al Arab waterway.
- ❑ **1977** Khomeini's son dies. Anti-shah demonstrations during mourning.
- ❑ **1978** Riots and strikes. Khomeini settles in Paris.
- ❑ **1979** Shah goes into exile. Ayatollah Khomeini returns, declares an Islamic republic. Students seize 63 hostages at US embassy in Tehran.
- ❑ **1980** Shah dies in exile. Start of eight-year Iran–Iraq war.
- ❑ **1981** US hostages released. Hojatoleslam Ali Khamenei elected president.
- ❑ **1985** Khamenei reelected.
- ❑ **1987** Around 275 Iranian pilgrims killed in riots in Mecca.
- ❑ **1988** USS *Vincennes* shoots down Iranian airliner; 290 killed. End of Iran–Iraq war.
- ❑ **1989** Khomeini issues *fatwa* condemning UK author Salman Rushdie to death for blasphemy. Khomeini dies. President Ali Khamenei appointed Supreme Religious Leader. Hashemi Rafsanjani elected president.
- ❑ **1990** Earthquake in northern Iran kills 45,000 people.
- ❑ **1992** Majlis elections.
- ❑ **1993** Rafsanjani reelected president.
- ❑ **1995** Imposition of US sanctions.
- ❑ **1996** Majlis elections. Society for Combatant Clergy loses ground to more liberal Servants of Iran's Construction.
- ❑ **1997** Earthquake south of Mashhad kills 1500 people. Mohammad Khatami elected president.
- ❑ **1998** Khatami government dissociates itself from *fatwa* against Salman Rushdie.
- ❑ **1999** First nationwide local elections since 1979. President Khatami visits Italy: first Iranian leader to be welcomed by a Western government since 1979.
- ❑ **2000** Sweeping election victory for reformists. Crackdown on reformist newspapers.
- ❑ **2001** Khatami reelected, winning 77% of vote.

I

AID

Recipient

$115m (receipts) | Down 12% in 2001

As an oil exporter, Iran does not qualify for much aid, and hard-liners are opposed to money from the West. However, Iran receives some UN aid for its millions of refugees from Afghanistan and Iraq. Concern that Iran supports Islamist terrorism has affected aid programs. In 1994, the World Bank suspended loans. US sanctions imposed since 1995 have curtailed donations, but humanitarian assistance was provided after an earthquake in 2002.

DEFENSE

Compulsory military service

$4.7bn | Up 19% in 2001

Iran has more than 500,000 men under arms, including the 125,000-strong Revolutionary Guard Corps (*Pasdaran Inqilab*), and is regarded by neighboring states as a serious military threat. The testing of medium-range cruise and ballistic missiles has heightened concern over Iran's possible military objectives: it can now theoretically strike as far as Israel.

Before the 1979 revolution Iran was part of a pro-Western alliance structure. The long war with Iraq in the 1980s diminished the military power of the revolutionary regime. A new defense agreement with Russia allowing for the sale of arms to Iran was reached in 2000.

IRANIAN ARMED FORCES

1565 main battle tanks (M-47/48/60A1, Chieftain Mk3/5, T-54/55/62/72)	325,000 personnel
6 submarines, 3 frigates, 56 patrol boats	18,000 personnel
306 combat aircraft (F-4D/E, F-5E/F, Su-24, F-14, F-7, MiG-29, Mirage F-1E)	52,000 personnel
None	

ECONOMICS

Inflation 26% p.a. (1990–2001)

$109bn | 8185 Iranian rials (1750)

SCORE CARD

❑ World GNP Ranking	35th
❑ GNP per Capita	$1680
❑ Balance of Payments	$4.75bn
❑ Inflation	11.3%
❑ Unemployment	25%

EXPORTS

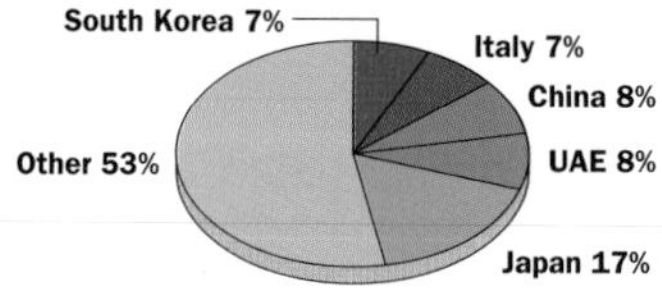
South Korea 7%
Italy 7%
China 8%
UAE 8%
Japan 17%
Other 53%

IMPORTS

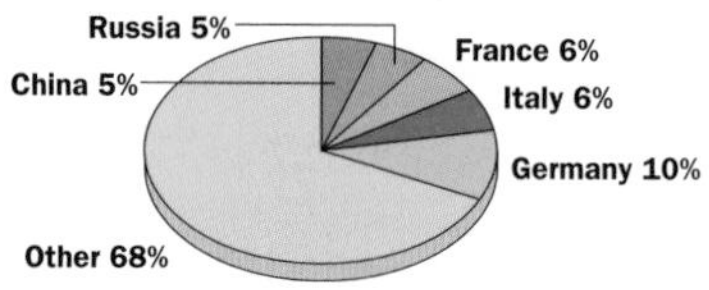
Russia 5%
China 5%
France 6%
Italy 6%
Germany 10%
Other 68%

ECONOMIC PERFORMANCE INDICATOR

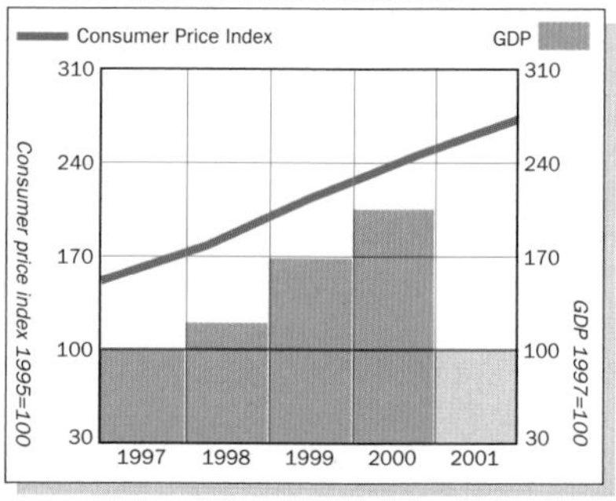
Consumer Price Index
GDP
Consumer price index 1995=100
GDP 1997=100
310
240
170
100
30
1997
1998
1999
2000
2001

Profile

With few industries other than oil, US sanctions and fluctuations in oil prices made foreign earnings volatile; higher prices in 2000 held out the prospect of being able to invest in diversification.

IRAN : MAJOR BUSINESSES

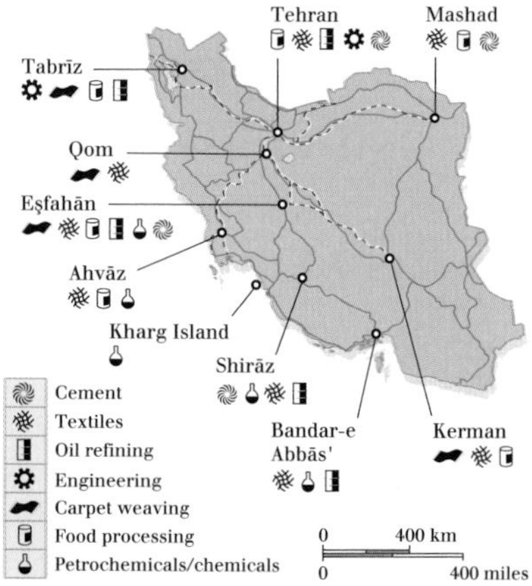
Tehran
Mashad
Tabrīz
Qom
Eşfahān
Ahvāz
Kharg Island
Shirāz
Bandar-e Abbās'
Kerman
Cement
Textiles
Oil refining
Engineering
Carpet weaving
Food processing
Petrochemicals/chemicals
0
400 km
0
400 miles

Strengths

OPEC's second-biggest oil producer. Second-largest natural gas reserves in the world. Potential for related industries and increased production of traditional exports: carpets, pistachio nuts, and caviar.

Weaknesses

Theocratic authorities restrict contact with West and access to technology. High unemployment and inflation. Excessive foreign debts.

RESOURCES

Electric power 30.6m kW

452,050 tonnes

3.37m b/d (reserves 89.7bn barrels)

53.9m sheep, 25.8m goats, 8.74m cattle, 270m chickens

Iron, copper, lead, oil, natural gas, zinc, chromite, coal, manganese, gypsum

ELECTRICITY GENERATION

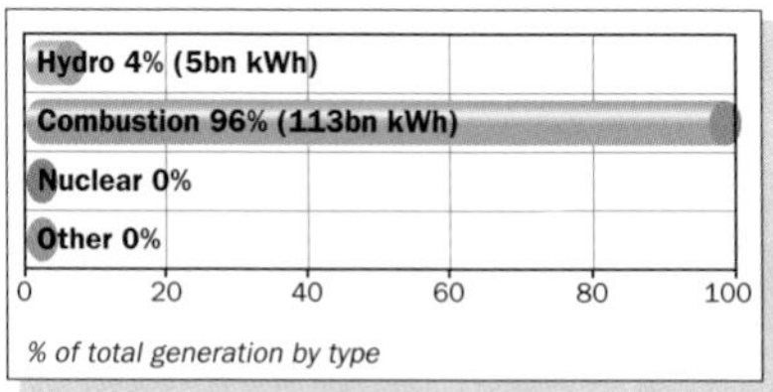

Hydro 4% (5bn kWh)
Combustion 96% (113bn kWh)
Nuclear 0%
Other 0%
0
20
40
60
80
100
% of total generation by type

Iran has substantial oil and natural gas reserves, plus relatively undeveloped deposits of metal, coal, and salt. A Russian-built nuclear power plant is set to open in 2004, powered by uranium mined in Iran. There is international concern over the government's aims.

The agricultural sector is a major part of the economy. Principal crops are fruit, wheat, barley, rice, sugar, and pistachio nuts. The Caspian Sea fisheries are controlled by the state, which sells caviar for export. Iran was once an opium exporter, but its cultivation and use have since been banned. The vodka industry has also been closed down.

IRAN : LAND USE

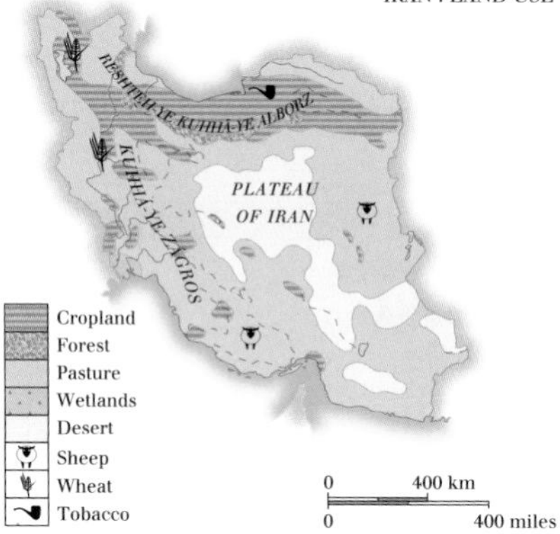

RESHTEH-YE KUHHA-YE ALBORZ
KUHHA-YE ZAGROS
PLATEAU OF IRAN
Cropland
Forest
Pasture
Wetlands
Desert
Sheep
Wheat
Tobacco
0
400 km
0
400 miles

ENVIRONMENT

Sustainability rank: 104th

5% (4% partially protected)

4.6 tonnes per capita

ENVIRONMENTAL TREATIES

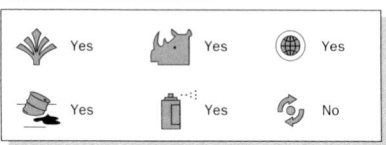

Yes	Yes	Yes
Yes	Yes	No

Environmental issues have been seriously neglected. The growing population, an overreliance on old cars, and the abundance of cheap gasolene have combined to destroy urban air quality. Pollution from oil exploration in the Caspian Sea is of major concern.

MEDIA

TV ownership medium

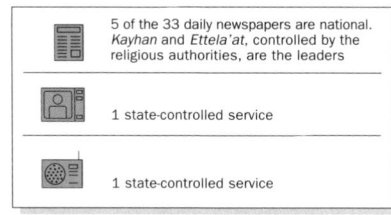

Daily newspaper circulation 28 per 1000 people

PUBLISHING AND BROADCAST MEDIA

5 of the 33 daily newspapers are national. *Kayhan* and *Ettela'at*, controlled by the religious authorities, are the leaders

1 state-controlled service

1 state-controlled service

Radio and TV are state-controlled. Satellite dishes are banned. Closures of reformist newspapers by the conservative Council of Guardians, and prosecutions of their editors, continue.

CRIME

Death penalty in use

163,526 prisoners

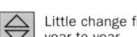

Little change from year to year

CRIME RATES

Iran does not publish crime statistics. However, general crime rates are relatively low.

Revolutionary guards enforce order. More than 100 offenses carry the death sentence. Executions are common for political "crimes." Murderers can avoid the death penalty by paying a $19,000 "blood price" – or half if the victim was female. Narcotics addiction, prostitution, and the violent abuse of women are rife. Iran is accused by Western governments of supporting Islamist terrorism.

EDUCATION

School leaving age: 11

77%

733,527 students

THE EDUCATION SYSTEM

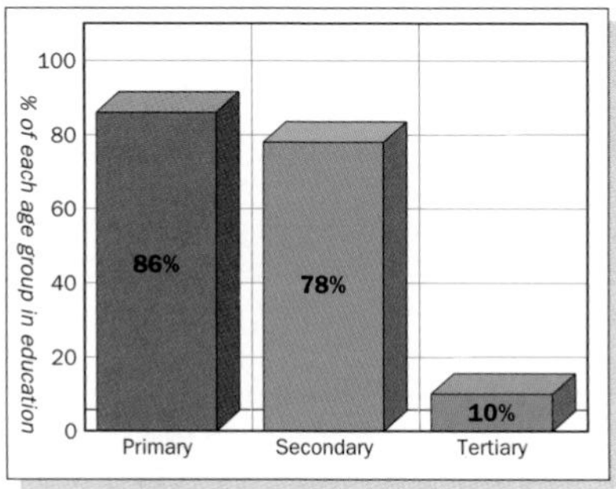

100
80
60
40
20
0
% of each age group in education
86%
78%
10%
Primary
Secondary
Tertiary

Primary education, which lasts for five years from the age of six, is free, as are universities. Most schools are single-sex. Since 2002, female students and staff in Tehran's classrooms have been permitted to lower their veils. There are 36 universities; their students are strong supporters of liberalization and reform.

HEALTH

Welfare state health benefits

1 per 909 people

Heart and respiratory diseases, injuries, neonatal deaths

Though an adequate system of primary health care exists in the cities, conditions in rural areas are basic. Under Khomeini, having children became a political and religious duty, but the high birthrate has now forced the introduction of birth control programs, and sterilization and contraception are now officially promoted. Growing drug addiction has resulted in rehabilitation programs and antidrugs propaganda. AIDS is spreading; some 20,000 adults were estimated to be living with HIV/AIDS in 2001.

SPENDING

GDP/cap. increase

CONSUMPTION AND SPENDING

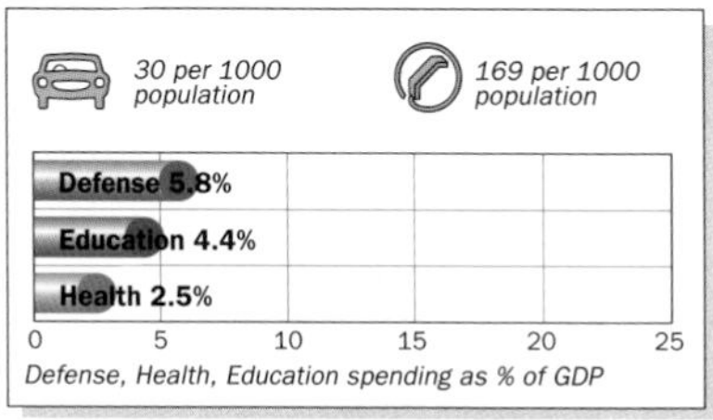

30 per 1000 population
169 per 1000 population
Defense 5.8%
Education 4.4%
Health 2.5%
0
5
10
15
20
25
Defense, Health, Education spending as % of GDP

After the 1979 revolution, living standards in Iran declined markedly. A shortage of foreign exchange has stifled imports of consumer goods. Rationing, brought in during the war with Iraq, is still partly in force, and smuggling from the Arab Gulf states is rife. Unemployment is high, and few Iranians are able to gain access to modern technology such as telephones. Official figures for income per capita do not relate to conditions on the ground. In reality, oil wealth fails to reach the economically deprived. Private businesses have gradually emerged in Iran since the launch in 1994 of the country's first private savings and loans associations.

WORLD RANKING

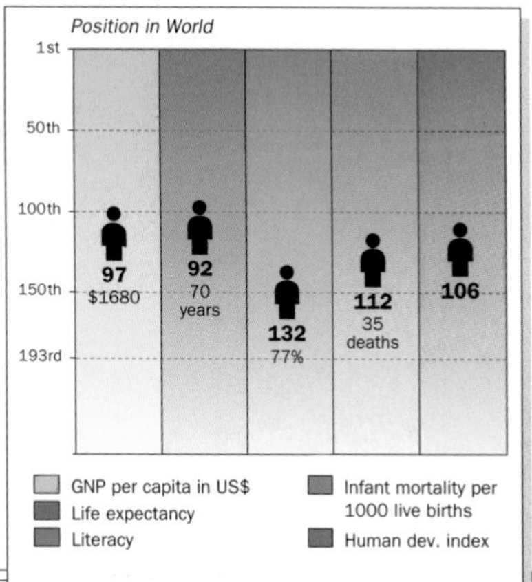

Position in World
1st
50th
100th
150th
193rd
97
$1680
92
70 years
132
77%
112
35 deaths
106
GNP per capita in US$
Life expectancy
Literacy
Infant mortality per 1000 live births
Human dev. index

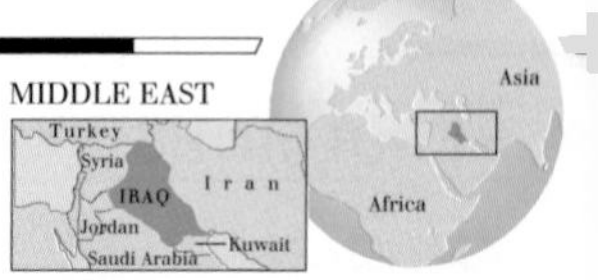
MIDDLE EAST
Turkey
Syria
IRAQ
Iran
Jordan
Kuwait
Saudi Arabia
Asia
Africa

IRAQ

OFFICIAL NAME: Republic of Iraq **CAPITAL:** Baghdad
POPULATION: 24.2 million **CURRENCY:** Iraqi dinar **OFFICIAL LANGUAGE:** Arabic

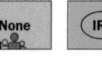

1932 | 1990 | None | IRQ | +3 | +964 | .iq

OIL-RICH IRAQ is divided by the Euphrates and Tigris Rivers. Mesopotamia, the region between them, saw the beginnings of writing and mathematics, and the invention of the wheel. While the river valleys are fertile, most of the country is inhospitable desert or mountains. The modern state encompasses Kurds in the north, Sunni Muslims largely in the center, and a Shi'a Muslim majority to the south. Saddam Hussein seized power in 1979 and maintained it through fear until his ouster in the rapid 2003 US-led invasion.

Golden Mosque at Sāmarrā' on the Tigris. Among the extensive remains of its ancient city are those of the Great Mosque built in 847 CE.

CLIMATE

Hot desert/steppe

WEATHER CHART FOR BAGHDAD

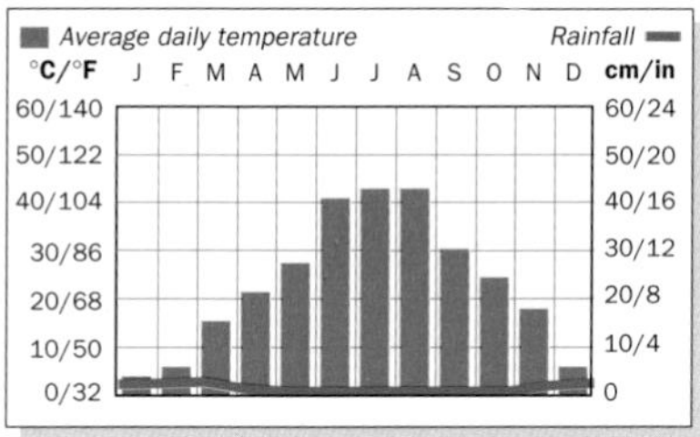
Average daily temperature
Rainfall
°C/°F
J F M A M J J A S O N D
cm/in
60/140
50/122
40/104
30/86
20/68
10/50
0/32
60/24
50/20
40/16
30/12
20/8
10/4
0

The weather is dry and rainfall is low and unreliable, except in the north. Iraq experiences a wide range of temperatures. The south has a desert climate, with hot, dry summers and mild winters. In mountainous Iranian and Turkish border regions winters can be harsh, with frost and heavy falls of snow. In the Mesopotamian plain huge dust storms are a regular feature of the summer.

TRANSPORTATION

Drive on right

Baghdad International

91 ships 240,600 grt

THE TRANSPORTATION NETWORK

38,400 km (23,861 miles)

1264 km (785 miles)

2603 km (1617 miles)

1015 km (631 miles)

Infrastructure was damaged during the 2003 invasion, though the rapid defeat of the Iraqi forces spared many key bridges and roads.

TOURISM

Visitors : Population 1:191

127,000 visitors

Up 63% in 2001

MAIN TOURIST ARRIVALS

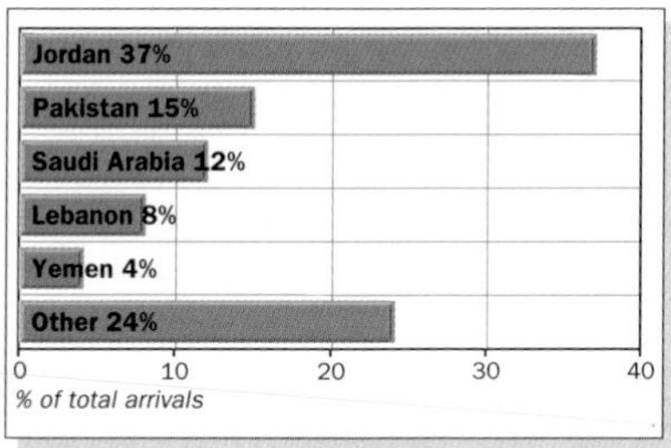
Jordan 37%
Pakistan 15%
Saudi Arabia 12%
Lebanon 8%
Yemen 4%
Other 24%
0
10
20
30
40
% of total arrivals

International isolation and war have prevented Iraq from making the most of its spectacular tourist potential, though the Shi'a holy shrines still attract thousands of pilgrims each year. Visitors used to also be attracted by Iraq's wealth of archaeological remains, in particular the ruins of Babylon and its fabled hanging gardens, near Al Hillah. The ecologically important southern marshes, once rich in wildlife, were largely drained to suppress dissent among the Shi'a Marsh Arabs.

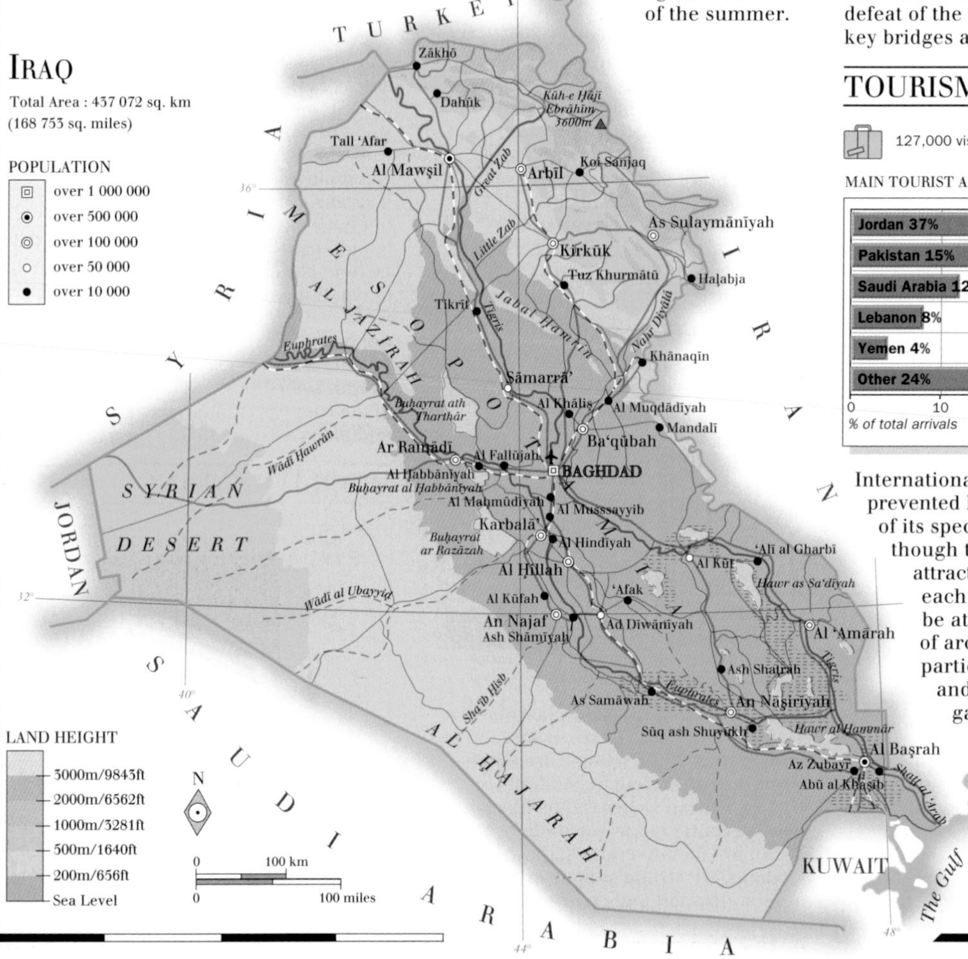
IRAQ
Total Area : 437 072 sq. km
(168 753 sq. miles)
POPULATION
over 1 000 000
over 500 000
over 100 000
over 50 000
over 10 000
LAND HEIGHT
3000m/9843ft
2000m/6562ft
1000m/3281ft
500m/1640ft
200m/656ft
Sea Level
N
100 km
100 miles
TURKEY
SYRIA
IRAN
JORDAN
KUWAIT
SAUDI ARABIA
AL JAZIRAH
MESOPOTAMIA
SYRIAN DESERT
AL HAJARAH
The Gulf
Zākhō
Dahūk
Kūh-e Hājī Ebrāhīm 3600m
Tall 'Afar
Al Mawşil
Arbīl
Koi Sanjaq
As Sulaymānīyah
Kirkūk
Tuz Khurmātū
Halabja
Tikrīt
Jabal Ḩamrīn
Khānaqīn
Sāmarrā'
Al Khāliş
Al Muqdādīyah
Mandalī
Ba'qūbah
Ar Ramādī
Al Fallūjah
BAGHDAD
Al Ḩabbānīyah
Buḩayrat al Ḩabbānīyah
Buḩayrat ath Tharthār
Al Maḩmūdīyah
Al Musayyib
Karbalā'
Al Hindīyah
Buḩayrat ar Razāzah
Al Ḩillah
Al Kūfah
An Najaf
Ash Shāmīyah
'Afak
Ad Dīwānīyah
Al Kūt
'Alī al Gharbī
Hawr as Sa'dīyah
Al 'Amārah
Ash Shaţrah
As Samāwah
An Nāşirīyah
Sūq ash Shuyūkh
Hawr al Ḩammār
Al Başrah
Az Zubayr
Abū al Khaşīb
Shaţţ al 'Arab
Euphrates
Tigris
Great Zab
Little Zab
Nahr Diyālā
Wādī Ḩawrān
Wādī al Ubayyid
Sha'īb Hisb

PEOPLE

Pop. density medium

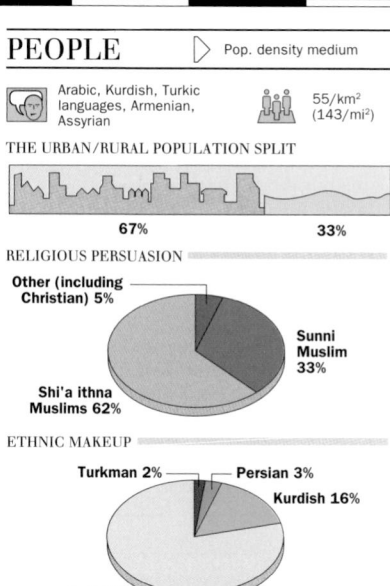

Arabic, Kurdish, Turkic languages, Armenian, Assyrian

55/km² (143/mi²)

THE URBAN/RURAL POPULATION SPLIT

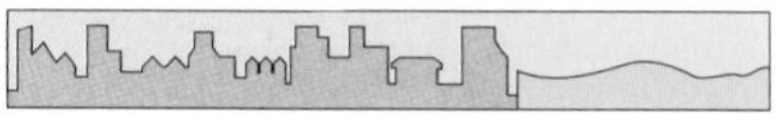
67%
33%

RELIGIOUS PERSUASION

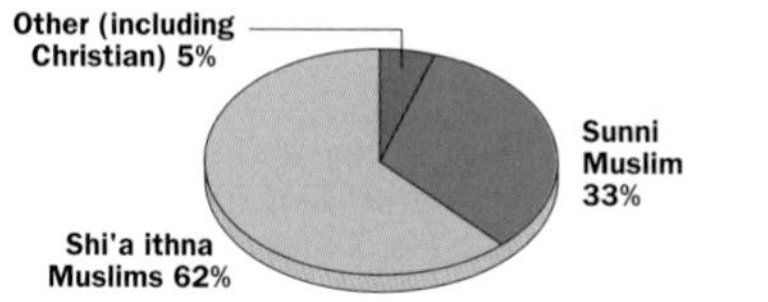
Other (including Christian) 5%
Sunni Muslim 33%
Shi'a ithna Muslims 62%

ETHNIC MAKEUP

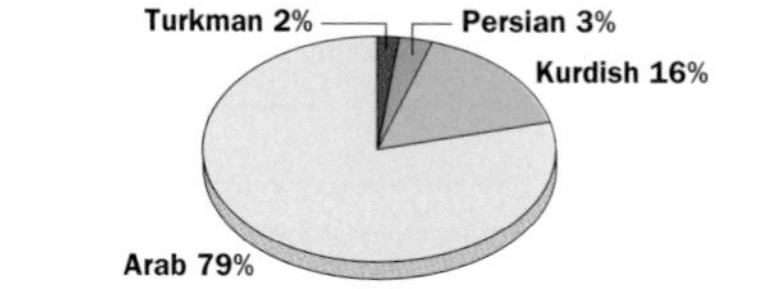
Turkman 2%
Persian 3%
Kurdish 16%
Arab 79%

Carved out of remnants of the Ottoman Empire, Iraq is home to three distinct ethno-religious groups as well as smaller minorities, including Turkmen and Persians. There are several Christian sects, but all but a handful of Iraq's Jews have emigrated to Israel.

The Arab Muslims are divided between the Shi'a and Sunni sects; some of the holiest sites of Shi'a Islam are in Iraq. Religious tensions have been largely suppressed, but resentment exists over previous minority Sunni control of government. The homeland and culture of the Shi'a Marsh Arabs were specifically targeted and largely destroyed after an abortive uprising in 1991.

The Kurdish community, based in the north, was granted de facto self-rule under the protection of the no-fly zones after 1991, but was riven by internal conflict. The long-held desire for a separate Kurdish homeland has been politically suppressed to ensure the viability of postwar Iraq.

POPULATION AGE BREAKDOWN

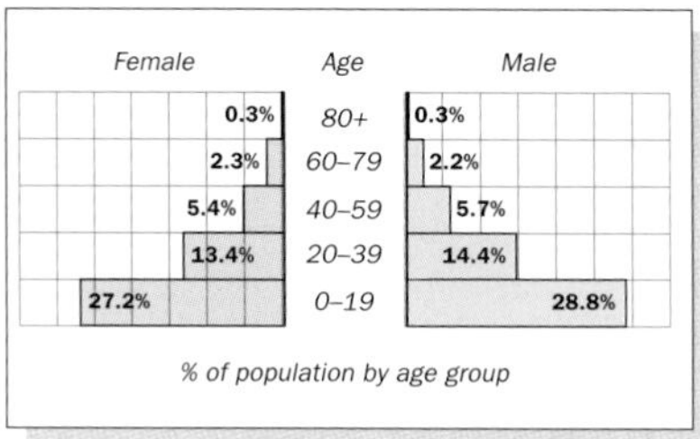
Female
Age
Male
0.3%
80+
0.3%
2.3%
60–79
2.2%
5.4%
40–59
5.7%
13.4%
20–39
14.4%
27.2%
0–19
28.8%
% of population by age group

WORLD AFFAIRS

Joined UN in 1945

AL | NAM | OAPEC | OIC | OPEC

Iraq's strategic importance rests on its vast oil reserves.

During the 1980–1988 Iran–Iraq war, Saddam Hussein was armed by the West as an ally against Islamic fundamentalism. However, his invasion of Kuwait in 1990 was condemned the world over. A US-led force, assisted by several Arab states, repelled Iraq in 1991. While Russia and France led the way in undermining the resultant UN sanctions on humanitarian grounds, the US increased the pressure on Saddam Hussein after 2001, counting Iraq among the "axis of evil" states sponsoring international terrorism on the assumption that it had the potential to provide weapons of mass destruction to terrorists. France, Germany, and Russia were joined by most of Iraq's neighbors in opposing the war launched, without UN backing, by the US in 2003. The postwar regime is likely to have close ties to the US. Iran, Syria, and Muslim extremists are deeply suspicious of a potential US client state in their midst, while Turkey fears a resurgence of pan-Kurdish nationalism.

I

POLITICS

In transition

2000/In transition

Vacant

AT THE LAST ELECTION

National Assembly (suspended) 250 seats

The National Assembly is composed of Ba'athists and their allies. Thirty seats representing the Kurdish region were not elected.

Saddam Hussein dominated politics after overthrowing his predecessor in 1979, and held power through a brutal dictatorship until his dramatic removal following a US-led invasion in 2003.

PROFILE

Saddam Hussein's period in power was dominated by warfare and its consequences: he launched a ten-year war against neighboring Iran within a year of coming to power, and in 1990 invaded Kuwait. A US-led alliance forced him to withdraw in 1991 and a harsh policy of international sanctions was imposed. Viciously crushing dissent, he remained in power throughout the 1990s, and even succeeded in drawing support against the sanctions from previously hostile Arab neighbors and other countries. In March 2003, with UN weapons inspectors still failing to uncover his alleged arsenal of weapons of mass destruction (WMD), a US-led coalition invaded Iraq and ousted Saddam Hussein within three weeks.

The removal of the Ba'athist regime and the ensuing power vacuum raised major concerns over the security and structure of a postwar, post–Saddam-Hussein Iraq.

MAIN POLITICAL ISSUES

Postwar reconstruction

The standard of living had dropped dramatically under the UN sanctions in the 1990s, and this, coupled with the brutality of the Ba'athist regime, paved the way for the government's rapid fall in 2003. While many welcomed the ouster of Saddam Hussein, few were happy at the prospect of a US-controlled regime, and estimates of the 2003 civilian death toll are as high as 10,000. Potential future leaders for Iraq are likely to be drawn from the previously exiled, and often US-backed, opposition. Fears that US companies would benefit from reconstruction contracts prompted accusations of a new economic imperialism. UN Resolution 1483 confirmed the Coalition as the governing "Authority" until a new Iraqi administration can be built with the help of the UN.

Ethnic and religious tensions

Though the Ba'athist regime drew its members from across Iraqi society and began by asserting its secularity, in reality much power was concentrated in the hands of the Sunni Muslim Tikriti tribe of Saddam Hussein.

***Ayatollah Ali Sistani**, the Shi'a cleric who has led opposition to US occupation.*

***Saddam Hussein**, Iraq's dictatorial leader in power from 1979 to 2003.*

Domestic opposition became centered on the Kurds in the north and the Shi'a Marsh Arabs in the south. Suppression was ruthless. Chemical agents were used against the Kurds in the late 1980s and the ecosystem of the southern marshes was deliberately destroyed in the early 1990s. It was feared that the 2003 invasion would unleash the potential for ethnic tensions.

AID

Recipient

$122m (receipts)

Up 21% in 2001

Under UN sanctions, Iraq was officially entitled only to humanitarian and food aid under the oil-for-food program, though there was probably substantial covert trading via neighboring states. The US and its allies have pledged to help reconstruct Iraq.

CHRONOLOGY

Iraq became independent in 1932. In 1958, the Hashemite dynasty was overthrown when King Faisal died in a coup led by the military under Brig. Kassem. He was initially supported by the Iraqi Ba'ath Party.

- **1961** Start of Kurdish rebellion. Iraq claims sovereignty over Kuwait on the eve of Kuwait's independence.
- **1963** Kassem overthrown. Col. Abd as-Salem Muhammad Aref takes power. Kuwait's sovereignty recognized.
- **1964** Ayatollah Khomeini, future leader of Iran, takes refuge at Najaf in Iraq.
- **1966** Aref is succeeded by his brother, Abd ar-Rahman.
- **1968** Ba'athists under Ahmad Hassan al-Bakr take power.
- **1970** Revolutionary Command Council agrees manifesto on Kurdish autonomy.
- **1972** Nationalization of Western-controlled Iraq Petroleum Company.
- **1978** Iraq and Syria form economic and political union.
- **1979** Saddam Hussein replaces al-Bakr as president.
- **1980** Outbreak of Iran–Iraq war.
- **1982** Shi'a leader Mohammed Baqir al-Hakim, exiled in Tehran, forms Supreme Council of the Islamic Revolution in Iraq.
- **1988** Iraq and Iran agree cease-fire. Iraqi chemical weapons attack on Kurdish village of Halabja.
- **1990** British journalist Farzad Bazoft hanged for spying. Iraq and Iran restore diplomatic relations. Iraq invades Kuwait. UN imposes trade sanctions.
- **1991** Gulf War. US-led military coalition defeats Iraq. Shi'a rebellion brutally suppressed. Northern no-fly zone enforced.
- **1992** Western powers proclaim air exclusion zone over south.
- **1994** Outbreak of Kurdish civil war. Iraq recognizes Kuwaiti sovereignty.
- **1995** Government minister Gen. Hussein Kamil defects to Jordan, and is murdered on his return to Iraq in January 1996.
- **1996** First legislative elections since 1989 won by ruling Ba'ath Party. UN supervises limited sales of Iraqi oil to purchase humanitarian supplies.
- **1998–1999** UN weapons inspection teams refused reentry into Iraq; US and UK mount punitive air strikes.
- **2002** Weapons inspectors return.
- **2003** Coalition forces invade. Saddam Hussein overthrown.

I

DEFENSE

Compulsory military service

$1.37bn

Down 2% in 2001

IRAQI ARMED FORCES

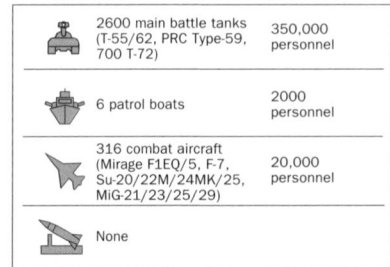

2600 main battle tanks (T-55/62, PRC Type-59, 700 T-72)	350,000 personnel
6 patrol boats	2000 personnel
316 combat aircraft (Mirage F1EQ/5, F-7, Su-20/22M/24MK/25, MiG-21/23/25/29)	20,000 personnel
None	

Under Saddam Hussein the military was intertwined with the regime. The elite Republican Guard received the best equipment and training available. In contrast the regular, conscripted army was poorly trained, with chronically low morale. In the face of superior Coalition firepower in 2003, both forces quickly melted away, with low-level resistance left to the Fedayeen militia.

After the 1991 war Iraq's arsenal of weapons of mass destruction (WMD), many originally supplied by the West, was set for destruction under UN sanctions. The regime's obstructiveness in its dealings with weapons inspectors prompted the invasion of 2003.

The creation of a new army was put into the hands of the private US Vinnel corporation.

ECONOMICS

Not available

$14.8bn

0.311 Iraqi dinars (0.311)

SCORE CARD

- World GNP Ranking..........................76th
- GNP per Capita $625
- Balance of Payments ....Not available
- Inflation 60%
- Unemployment.........................Not available

EXPORTS

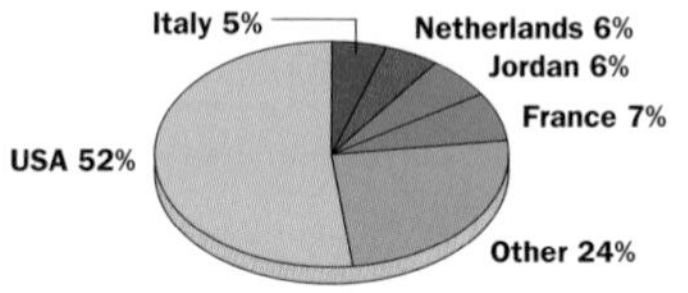
Italy 5%
Netherlands 6%
Jordan 6%
France 7%
USA 52%
Other 24%

IMPORTS

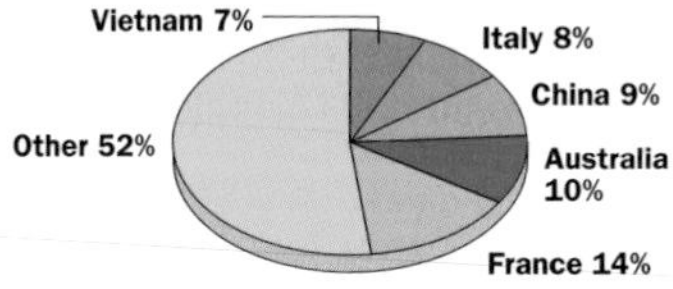
Vietnam 7%
Italy 8%
China 9%
Other 52%
Australia 10%
France 14%

STRENGTHS

Second-largest crude oil reserves in OPEC. Sizable natural gas reserves. US promises aid. Large labor force.

WEAKNESSES

Infrastructure devastated by war. Legacy of sanctions. War-ravaged agricultural sector.

PROFILE

Before 1990, Iraq was the world's third-largest oil supplier. Under sanctions, oil was produced only for domestic consumption. Limited oil exports under strict UN supervision were resumed for the first time in 1996, and in 2000 the UN permitted Iraq to buy parts and equipment for the oil industry.

The denial of Western assistance after the 1991 Gulf War stifled Iraq's economy. Agriculture, once thriving, was devastated. Manufacturing remains at a standstill. Harsh penalties, including the death sentence, failed to curb the black market or halt the sharp depreciation of the dinar. Efforts at recovery, such as the resumption of some informal economic links and the revision of UN sanctions in 2002, were undermined by the return of war in 2003. Hopes for the postwar economy will rest on the sale of oil and rebuilt infrastructure. A new dinar was set for circulation from October 2003.

ECONOMIC PERFORMANCE INDICATOR

Consumer Price Index
GDP
Consumer price index unavailable
13600
9100
4600
100
-4400
GDP 1991=100
1991
1992
1993
1994
1995

IRAQ : MAJOR BUSINESSES

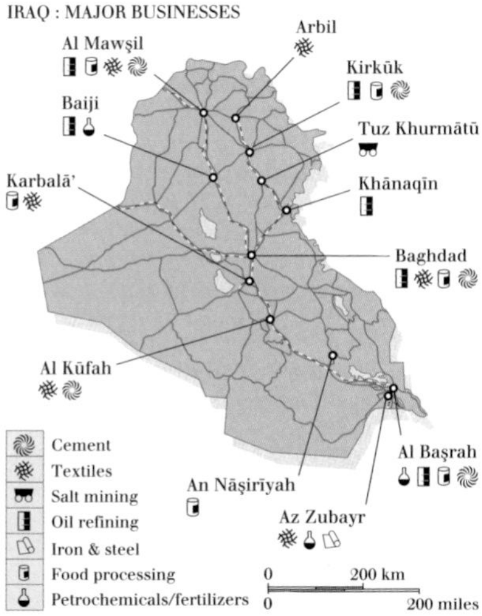
Al Mawşil
Arbil
Kirkūk
Baiji
Tuz Khurmātū
Karbalā'
Khānaqīn
Baghdad
Al Kūfah
Al Başrah
An Nāşirīyah
Az Zubayr
Cement
Textiles
Salt mining
Oil refining
Iron & steel
Food processing
Petrochemicals/fertilizers
0
200 km
0
200 miles

RESOURCES

Electric power 9.5m kW

22,511 tonnes

2.03m b/d (reserves 113bn barrels)

6.2m sheep, 1.65m goats, 1.4m cattle, 23m chickens

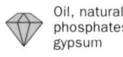

Oil, natural gas, phosphates, sulfur, gypsum

ELECTRICITY GENERATION

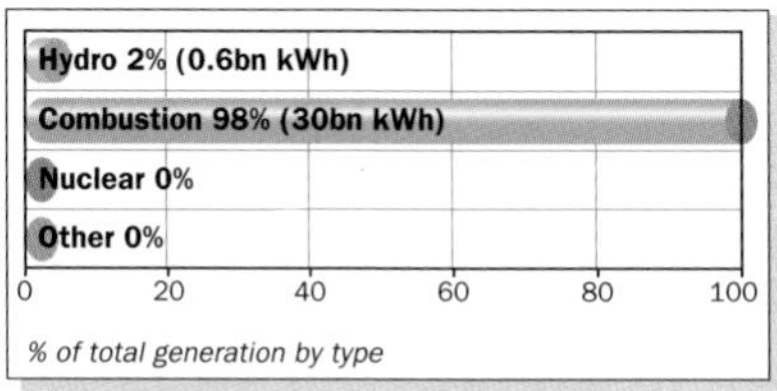
Hydro 2% (0.6bn kWh)
Combustion 98% (30bn kWh)
Nuclear 0%
Other 0%
0
20
40
60
80
100
% of total generation by type

Iraq has huge reserves of oil and natural gas (the second-largest in the world). Total gas reserves, many of which are associated with oil, are proven to be 3.11 trillion cu. m (110 trillion cu. ft), with estimates of a further 4.25 trillion cu. m (150 trillion cu. ft). The capture of oil fields was a key priority for the invading Coalition forces in 2003, ostensibly to provide a firm economic future for a postwar Iraq. US companies are likely to be at the forefront of reconstruction.

Before the 1990 invasion of Kuwait and the subsequent war, Iraq supplied 80% of the world's trade in dates. After the imposition of sanctions, food was produced simply for domestic consumption, and Iraq achieved a degree of self-sufficiency in such crops as wheat, rice, and sugarcane.

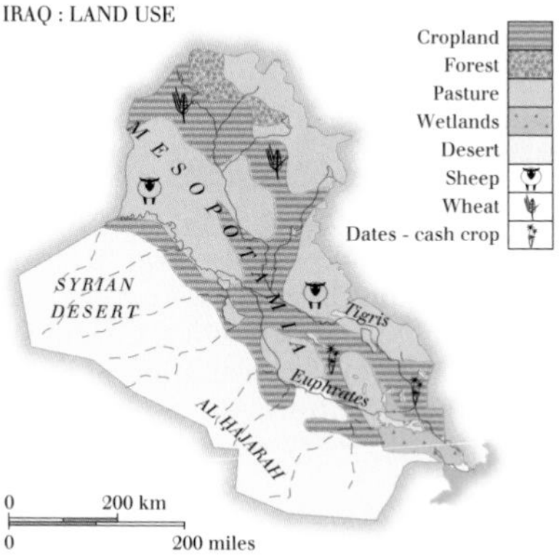
IRAQ : LAND USE
Cropland
Forest
Pasture
Wetlands
Desert
Sheep
Wheat
Dates - cash crop
MESOPOTAMIA
SYRIAN DESERT
Tigris
Euphrates
AL HAJARAH
0
200 km
0
200 miles

ENVIRONMENT

Sustainability rank: 139th

None

3.3 tonnes per capita

ENVIRONMENTAL TREATIES

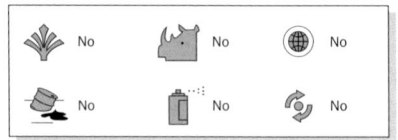

No No No

No No No

War has led to massive environmental damage. As a specific legacy of the first Gulf War, hundreds of thousands of land mines remain in the south, and there is concern about the long-term effects of the depleted uranium shells used by the US and its allies. The north has been affected by chemical weapons, used by Saddam Hussein's regime against the Kurds. In the southeast, an entire wetland ecosystem was largely destroyed by a program to drain the marshes for political reasons.

MEDIA

TV ownership medium

Daily newspaper circulation 19 per 1000 people

PUBLISHING AND BROADCAST MEDIA

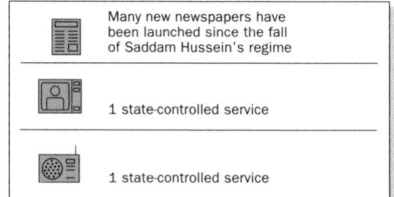

Many new newspapers have been launched since the fall of Saddam Hussein's regime

1 state-controlled service

1 state-controlled service

The media were strictly controlled under Saddam Hussein, his son Uday in charge of two major newspapers.

The 2003 war was covered by the international media in unprecedented detail. Journalists were even "embedded" with invading troops. In the war's aftermath a flurry of new newspapers, most controlled by aspiring political and social groups, emerged in Baghdad.

CRIME

Death penalty in use

Iraq does not publish prison figures

Crime is rising

CRIME RATES

Murders

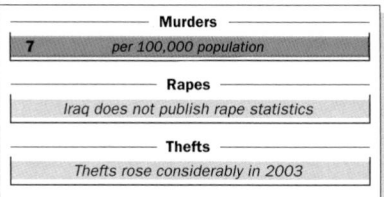

7 *per 100,000 population*

Rapes

Iraq does not publish rape statistics

Thefts

Thefts rose considerably in 2003

Crime rates soared in the 1990s due to economic collapse, despite brutal punishments. During the 2003 war, looters targeted government property but also hospitals, museums, and shops. Mass graves were discovered in 2003.

EDUCATION

School leaving age: 11

40%

288,670 students

THE EDUCATION SYSTEM

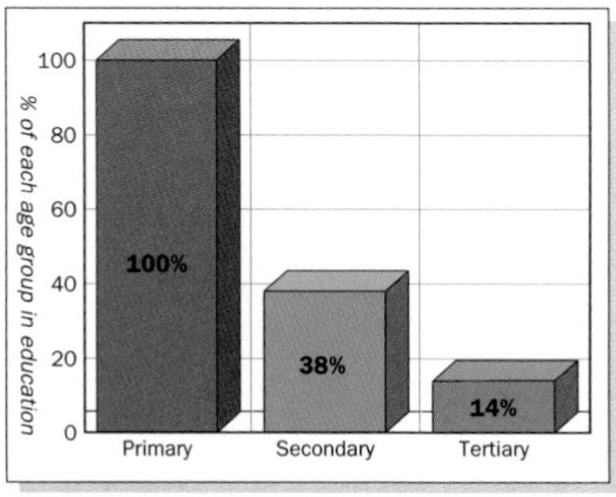
100
80
60
40
20
0
% of each age group in education
100%
38%
14%
Primary
Secondary
Tertiary

The Ba'athist regime controlled the education system, using it to instill loyalty. University scientists worked closely with the regime on weapons research programs. Many priceless museum artefacts were stolen by looters in 2003, and the Baghdad Library lies in ashes. In postwar Iraq the reconstruction of the education system was not immediately prioritized.

HEALTH

Welfare state health benefits

1 per 1667 people

Pneumonia, influenza, cancers, heart diseases

Deaths among children and the elderly had spiraled sharply before 2003, as UN sanctions led to shortages of medical supplies and equipment. Hospitals in major cities were damaged by looters in the aftermath of hostilities. Increases in birth defects since 1991 are attributed to the Allies' use of depleted uranium shells during the first Gulf War.

SPENDING

GDP/cap. decrease

CONSUMPTION AND SPENDING

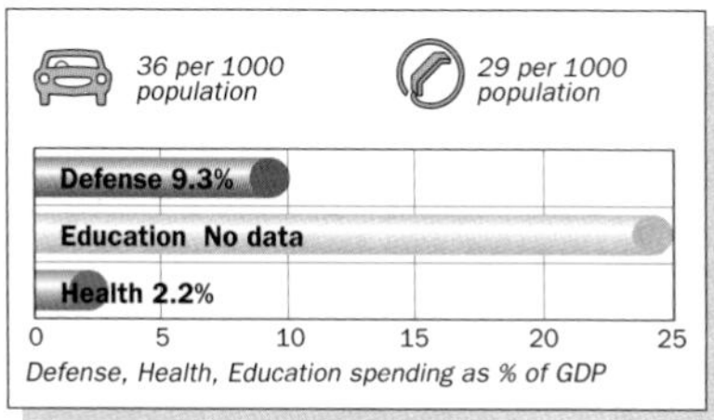
36 per 1000 population
29 per 1000 population
Defense 9.3%
Education No data
Health 2.2%
0
5
10
15
20
25
Defense, Health, Education spending as % of GDP

The most vulnerable sections of society were disproportionately affected by the decade of UN sanctions. The elite of the Ba'athist regime displayed their wealth ostentatiously.

WORLD RANKING

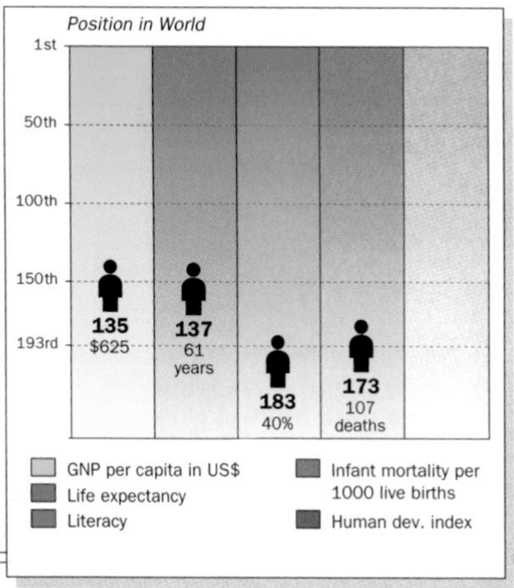
Position in World
1st
50th
100th
150th
193rd
135
$625
137
61 years
183
40%
173
107 deaths
GNP per capita in US$
Life expectancy
Literacy
Infant mortality per 1000 live births
Human dev. index

I

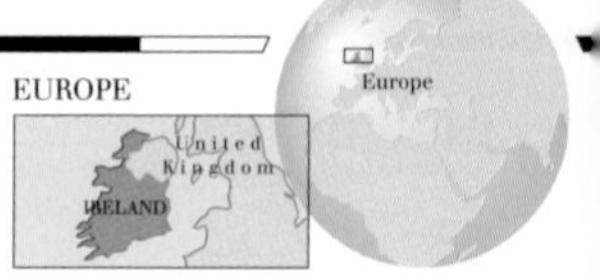
EUROPE
United Kingdom
IRELAND
Europe

IRELAND

OFFICIAL NAME: Ireland **CAPITAL:** Dublin
POPULATION: 3.9 million **CURRENCY:** Euro **OFFICIAL LANGUAGES:** Irish and English

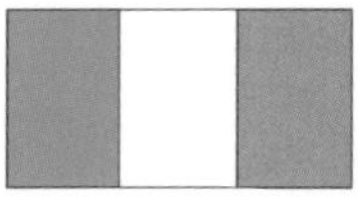

1922 | 1922 | March 17 | IRL | 0 | +353 | .ie

LYING IN THE Atlantic Ocean, off the west coast of Great Britain, the Irish republic occupies about 85% of the island of Ireland. Low coastal ranges surround a central basin with lakes, hills, and peat bogs. Centuries of struggle against English domination led in 1922 to the formation of the Irish Free State and in 1937 to full sovereignty. Efforts to resolve the Northern Ireland conflict center on the 1998 Good Friday accord, under which Ireland gave up its territorial claim.

CLIMATE

Maritime

WEATHER CHART FOR DUBLIN

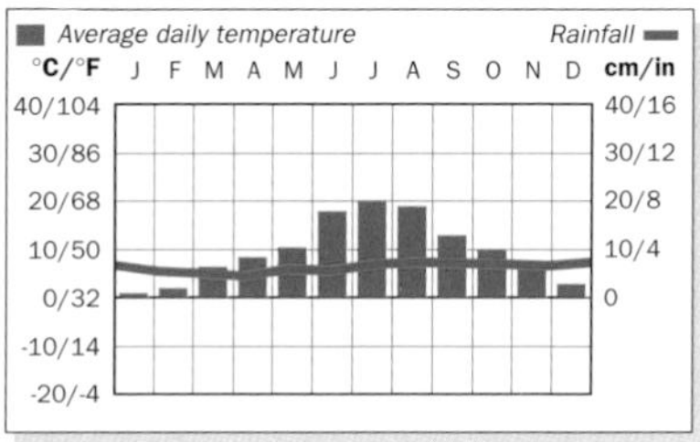
Average daily temperature
Rainfall
°C/°F
J F M A M J J A S O N D
cm/in
40/104
30/86
20/68
10/50
0/32
-10/14
-20/-4
40/16
30/12
20/8
10/4
0

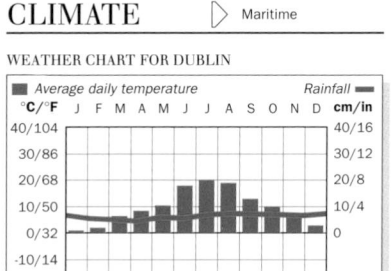

Moderated by the Gulf Stream, the Irish climate is mild, equable, and wet. The mean annual temperature is 12°C (54°F).

TRANSPORTATION

Drive on left

Dublin International
15m passengers

193 ships
300,289 grt

THE TRANSPORTATION NETWORK

87,043 km
(54,086 miles)

125 km
(78 miles)

1919 km
(1192 miles)

700 km
(435 miles)

EU funds have improved road networks, especially around Dublin, which still, however, suffers from congestion.

TOURISM

Visitors : Population
1.5:1

5.76m visitors

Up 2% in 2002

MAIN TOURIST ARRIVALS

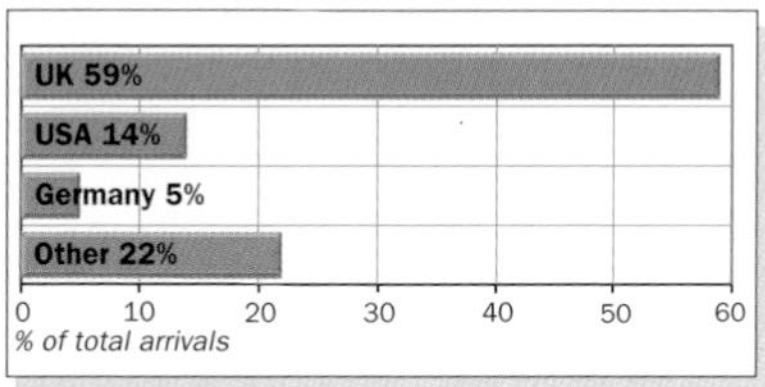
UK 59%
USA 14%
Germany 5%
Other 22%
0
10
20
30
40
50
60
% of total arrivals

Tourist numbers have increased steadily in recent years, approaching six million a year. Vibrant Dublin attracts many on city breaks. Other draws are scenery, Ireland's "clean" environmental image, and the relaxed lifestyle.

PEOPLE

Pop. density medium

English, Irish Gaelic

57/km²
(147/mi²)

THE URBAN/RURAL POPULATION SPLIT

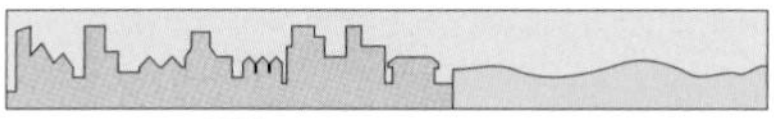
59%
41%

RELIGIOUS PERSUASION

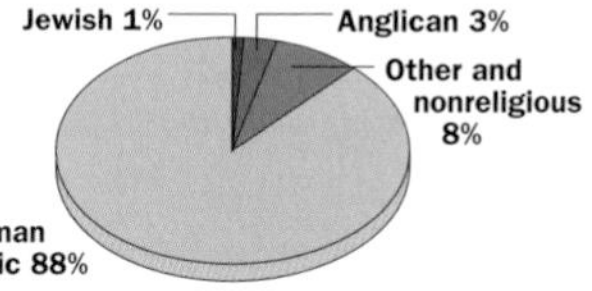
Jewish 1%
Anglican 3%
Other and nonreligious 8%
Roman Catholic 88%

The population is 95% ethnic Irish. The influence of the Roman Catholic Church is declining. Ireland is now a country of net immigration, against the trend of the past 150 years.

POLITICS

Multiparty elections

L. House 2002/2007
U. House 2002/2007

President Mary McAleese

AT THE LAST ELECTION

House of Representatives 166 seats

5% PD
3% SF
49% FF
19% FG
12% LP
4% GP
8% Others

FF = Fianna Fail FG = Fine Gael LP = Labour Party
PD = Progressive Democrats GP = Green Party
SF = Sinn Fein Ind = Independents

Senate 60 seats

8% Ind
2% Others
50% FF
25% FG
8% LP
7% PD

Coalition governments have been the norm in recent decades, the *taoiseach* (prime minister) coming either from FG or FF. The latter, once seen as the traditional party of government, has dominated a coalition under Bertie Ahern since the 1997 elections. Though it improved its position in the April 2002 elections, Ahern's FF remains just short of an outright majority of seats in the legislature and so continues to depend on its PD junior partner.

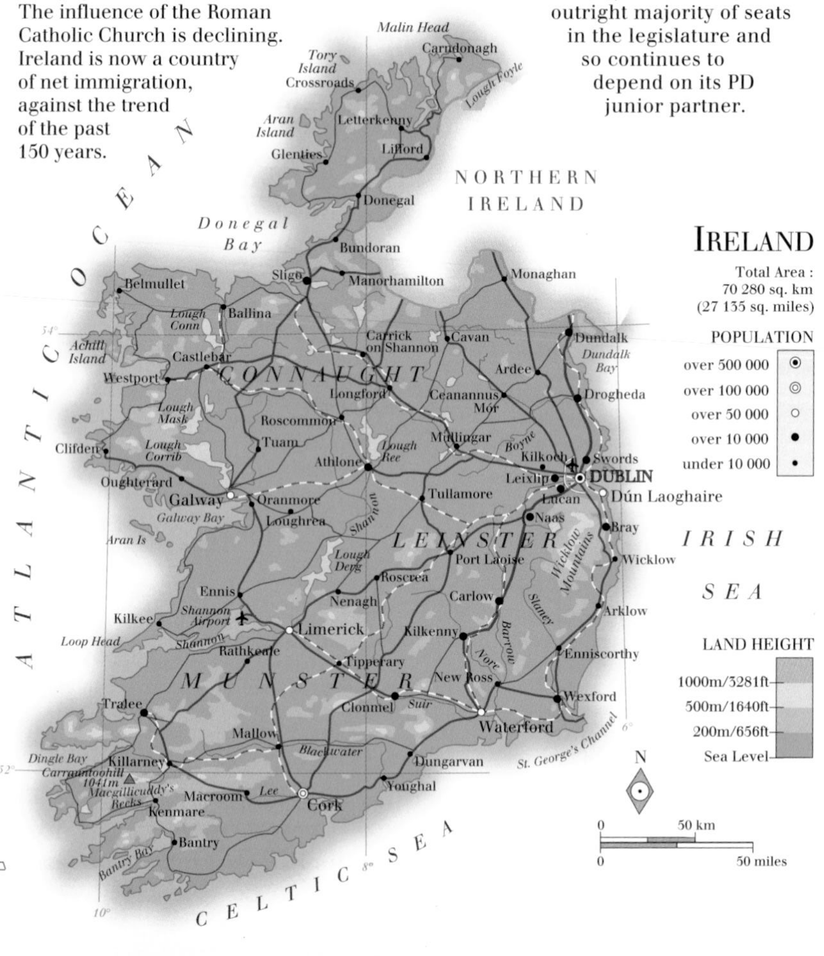
IRELAND
Total Area : 70 280 sq. km (27 135 sq. miles)
POPULATION
over 500 000
over 100 000
over 50 000
over 10 000
under 10 000
LAND HEIGHT
1000m/3281ft
500m/1640ft
200m/656ft
Sea Level
50 km
50 miles
ATLANTIC OCEAN
CELTIC SEA
IRISH SEA
NORTHERN IRELAND
CONNAUGHT
LEINSTER
MUNSTER
Malin Head
Carndonagh
Tory Island
Crossroads
Letterkenny
Aran Island
Glenties
Lifford
Donegal
Donegal Bay
Bundoran
Sligo
Manorhamilton
Monaghan
Belmullet
Ballina
Lough Conn
Achill Island
Castlebar
Westport
Carrick on Shannon
Cavan
Dundalk
Dundalk Bay
Ardee
Drogheda
Longford
Ceanannus Mór
Lough Mask
Roscommon
Tuam
Lough Corrib
Clifden
Mullingar
Lough Ree
Athlone
Boyne
Kilkock
Swords
DUBLIN
Leixlip
Dún Laoghaire
Lucan
Oughterard
Galway
Galway Bay
Oranmore
Loughrea
Tullamore
Naas
Bray
Aran Is
Shannon
Lough Derg
Port Laoise
Wicklow Mountains
Wicklow
Roscrea
Ennis
Nenagh
Carlow
Slaney
Arklow
Kilkee
Shannon Airport
Limerick
Kilkenny
Barrow
Loop Head
Rathkeale
Nore
Enniscorthy
Tipperary
New Ross
Suir
Wexford
Tralee
Clonmel
Waterford
St. George's Channel
Mallow
Blackwater
Dingle Bay
Carrauntoohill 1041m
Killarney
Dungarvan
Macgillicuddy's Reeks
Macroom
Lee
Cork
Youghal
Kenmare
Bantry
Bantry Bay

WORLD AFFAIRS

Joined UN in 1955

CE | ESA | EU | OECD | OSCE

Northern Ireland dominates relations with the UK. Ireland accepted the 2001 Treaty of Nice on EU enlargement only after a second referendum.

AID

Donor

$287m (donations) — Up 22% in 2001

Africa is the main recipient of Irish aid. Ireland itself benefits from EU funding.

DEFENSE

No compulsory military service

$623m — Down 1% in 2001

Ireland is determined to maintain its neutrality, despite EU moves to establish a common European defense policy. It has observer status at the WEU.

ECONOMICS

Inflation 3.7% p.a. (1990–2001)

$87.7bn — 0.871 euros (1.013)

SCORE CARD

❑ WORLD GNP RANKING	39th
❑ GNP PER CAPITA	$22,850
❑ BALANCE OF PAYMENTS	–$1.04bn
❑ INFLATION	4.9%
❑ UNEMPLOYMENT	4%

STRENGTHS

Size of economy doubled during EU-backed "Celtic tiger" growth phase up to 2001, achieving trade surplus and full employment. Efficient agriculture and food processing. Foreign investment in high-tech sector: electronics account for 25% of exports. Highly educated workforce.

WEAKNESSES

End of boom after 2001. Many key sectors owned by overseas multinationals. Housing shortages and strains on other infrastructure. Return of higher unemployment, and rising inflation.

EXPORTS

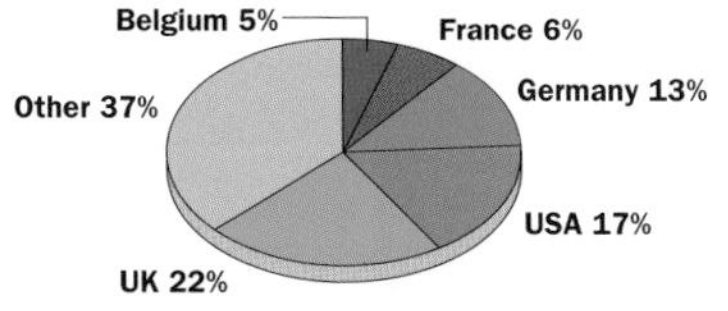

Belgium 5%
France 6%
Germany 13%
Other 37%
USA 17%
UK 22%

IMPORTS

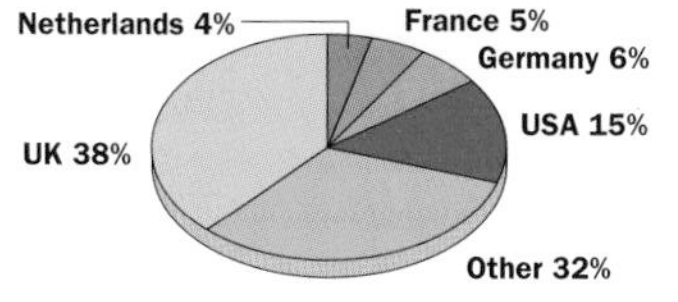

Netherlands 4%
France 5%
Germany 6%
USA 15%
UK 38%
Other 32%

RESOURCES

Electric power 4.4m kW

324,478 tonnes — Not an oil producer; refines 57,000 b/d

6.41m cattle, 4.81m sheep, 1.76m pigs, 11.3m chickens — Lead, zinc, natural gas, silver, coal, oil

Zinc and lead are the most important mineral resources and Ireland is one of the EU's major producers.

ENVIRONMENT

Sustainability rank: 37th

1% (0.3% partially protected) — 11.5 tonnes per capita

The main environmental concerns are overexploitation of the country's peat bogs for fuel and the recent expansion of conifer plantations, even though this increases forest cover. In 1994 stringent new laws increased pollution controls. Work began in 2003 on the world's largest offshore wind farm, off the coast of Arklow.

MEDIA

TV ownership high

Daily newspaper circulation 150 per 1000 people

PUBLISHING AND BROADCAST MEDIA

There are 6 daily newspapers. These include the *Irish Times* and the *Irish Independent*

TV: 2 services: 1 state-owned, 1 independent — Radio: 3 services: 1 state-owned, 2 independent

The national Radio Telefís Éireann (RTE) dominates broadcasting. Radió na Gaeltachta and TG4 broadcast in Irish. Access to UK media is widespread.

CRIME

No death penalty

3378 prisoners — Up 41% in 2000–2001

Rural Ireland has one of the EU's lowest crime rates. Urban crime and narcotics are a problem in Dublin and Cork.

EDUCATION

School leaving age: 15

99% — 166,600 students

The Roman Catholic Church runs many schools. Increased education spending has resulted in a skilled workforce.

Clew Bay in County Mayo, *on the western coast of Connaught, viewed from the slopes of neighboring Croagh Patrick.*

CHRONOLOGY

English colonization, begun in 1167, was reinforced after 1558 by anti-Catholic legislation and settlement of Scottish Protestants in the north.

- ❑ **1845–1855** Famine. One million die, 1.5 million emigrate.
- ❑ **1919–1921** Anglo-Irish war after Sinn Fein proclaims independence.
- ❑ **1922** Irish Free State established.
- ❑ **1973** FG/LP alliance wins elections, ending FF's ascendancy since 1932.
- ❑ **1990** Mary Robinson elected first woman president.
- ❑ **1995** Referendum favors divorce.
- ❑ **1997** Bertie Ahern appointed *taioseach* (prime minister).
- ❑ **1998** Good Friday accord on Northern Ireland.
- ❑ **2002** Euro fully adopted.

I

HEALTH

Welfare state health benefits

1 per 442 people — Cancers, heart, cerebrovascular, and respiratory diseases

Free care is means tested; about one-third of people qualify. Others pay to visit their doctor and for prescriptions, and there is a modest charge for hospital care.

SPENDING

GDP/cap. increase

CONSUMPTION AND SPENDING

296 per 1000 population — 485 per 1000 population

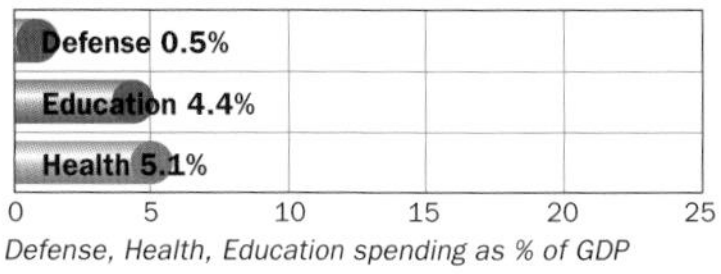

Defense 0.5%
Education 4.4%
Health 5.1%
0 5 10 15 20 25
Defense, Health, Education spending as % of GDP

Living standards for those with jobs are rising steadily. Welfare for those not in work is low by OECD standards.

WORLD RANKING

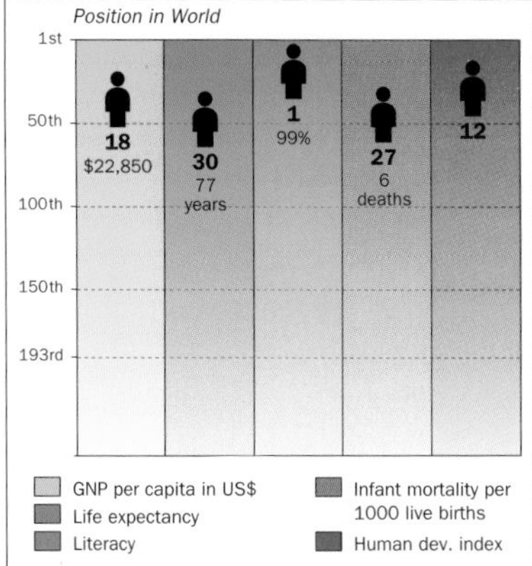

Position in World
1st
50th
100th
150th
193rd
18
$22,850
30
77 years
1
99%
27
6 deaths
12
GNP per capita in US$
Life expectancy
Literacy
Infant mortality per 1000 live births
Human dev. index

ISRAEL

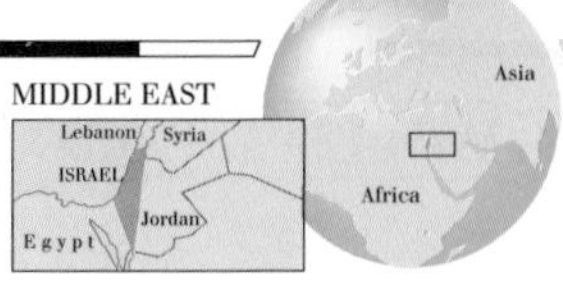
MIDDLE EAST
Lebanon
Syria
ISRAEL
Jordan
Egypt
Asia
Africa

OFFICIAL NAME: State of Israel **CAPITAL:** Jerusalem (not internationally recognized)
POPULATION: 6.6 million **CURRENCY:** Shekel **OFFICIAL LANGUAGES:** Hebrew and Arabic

1948 | 1994 | May 12 | IL | +2 | +972 | .il

THE CREATION OF ISRAEL in 1948 in the then British mandate of Palestine fulfilled the Zionist ambition for a Jewish state. Subsequent military victories over its Arab neighbors enabled Israel to annex or occupy additional territory, some of which it returned to Egypt under the 1978 Camp David agreement. Hopes in the 1990s for a "land for peace" deal to end the Israeli–Palestinian conflict became mired in a cycle of violence.

CLIMATE

Hot desert/ Mediterranean

WEATHER CHART FOR JERUSALEM

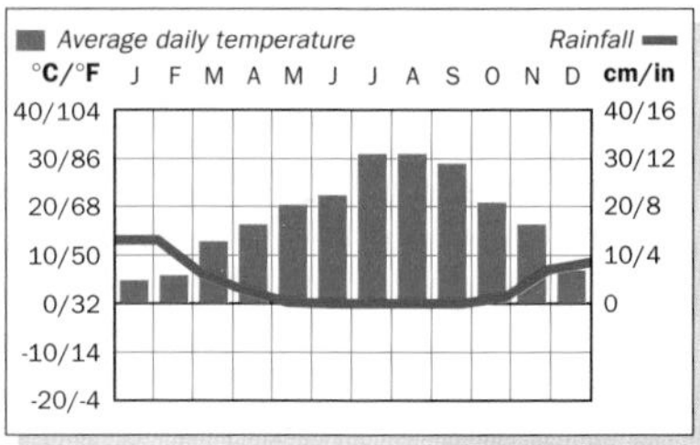
Average daily temperature
Rainfall
°C/°F
J F M A M J J A S O N D
cm/in
40/104
30/86
20/68
10/50
0/32
-10/14
-20/-4
40/16
30/12
20/8
10/4
0

Summers are hot and dry. The wet season is between November and March, when the weather is mild.

TRANSPORTATION

Drive on right

Ben-Gurion International, Tel Aviv–Yafo 7.31m passengers

48 ships 611,400 grt

THE TRANSPORTATION NETWORK

15,965 km (9920 miles)	56 km (35 miles)
669 km (416 miles)	None

Railroads are being extended. There are three commercial ports. Ben-Gurion international airport has been expanded.

TOURISM

Visitors : Population 1:7.7

862,300 visitors

Down 28% in 2002

MAIN TOURIST ARRIVALS

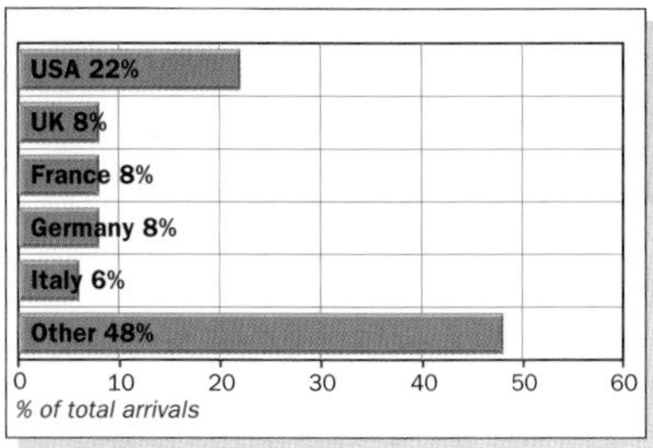
USA 22%
UK 8%
France 8%
Germany 8%
Italy 6%
Other 48%
0
10
20
30
40
50
60
% of total arrivals

Tourism has been damaged by the sustained violence of the Israeli–Palestinian conflict.

PEOPLE

Pop. density high

Hebrew, Arabic, Yiddish, German, Russian, Polish, Romanian, Persian

325/km² (841/mi²)

THE URBAN/RURAL POPULATION SPLIT

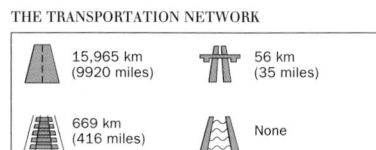

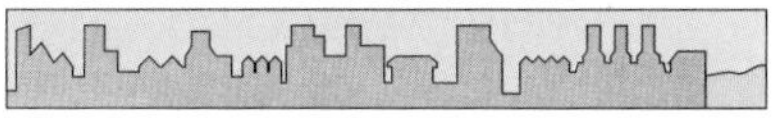
92%
8%

RELIGIOUS PERSUASION

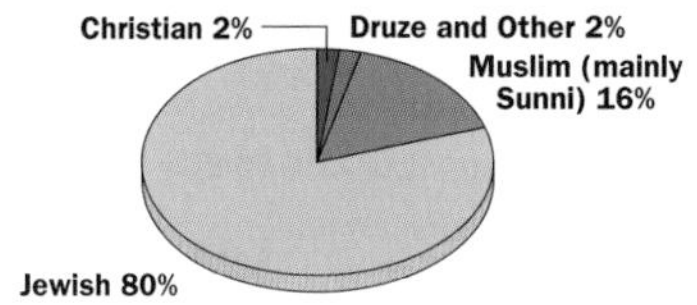
Christian 2%
Druze and Other 2%
Muslim (mainly Sunni) 16%
Jewish 80%

ETHNIC MAKEUP

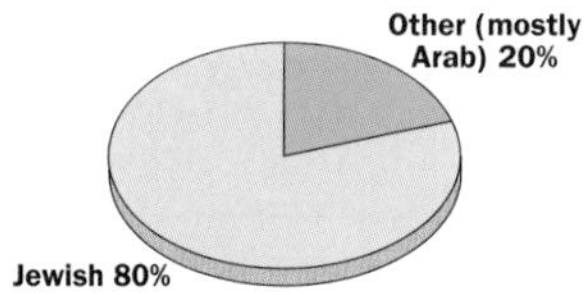
Other (mostly Arab) 20%
Jewish 80%

Large numbers of Jewish immigrants settled in Palestine before Israel was founded. Sephardi Jews from the Middle East and Mediterranean are now probably in the majority, but Ashkenazi Jews, most of central European origin, still dominate society. Hundreds of thousands of Russian Jews have arrived since 1989. Israel's minority, non-Jewish population – mostly Arab and predominantly Muslim (with Christian and Druze minorities) – totals more than one million but remains sidelined in Israeli life. There are tensions between secular and Orthodox Jews and between left and right over the pursuit of peace with the Palestinians.

POPULATION AGE BREAKDOWN

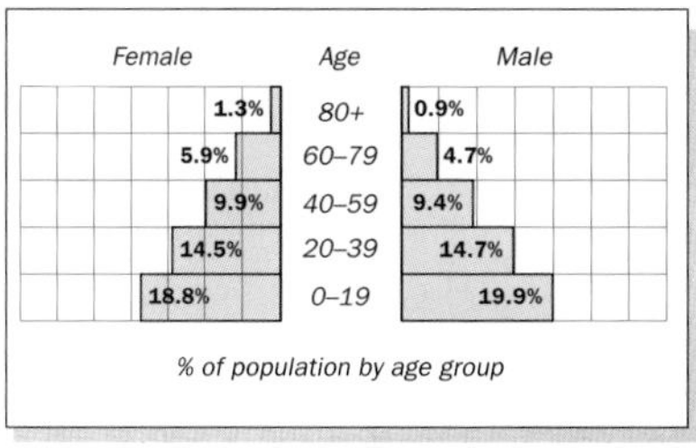
Female
Age
Male
1.3%
80+
0.9%
5.9%
60–79
4.7%
9.9%
40–59
9.4%
14.5%
20–39
14.7%
18.8%
0–19
19.9%
% of population by age group

POLITICS

Multiparty elections

2003/2007

President Moshe Katzav

AT THE LAST ELECTION

Parliament 120 seats

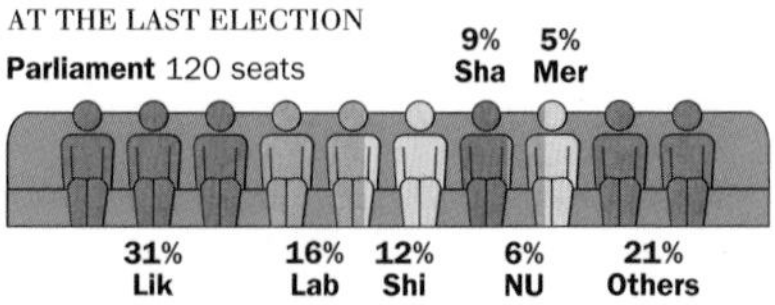
9% Sha
5% Mer
31% Lik
16% Lab
12% Shi
6% NU
21% Others

Lik = Likud **Lab** = Labor **Shi** = Shinui **Sha** = Shas
NU = National Union **Mer** = Meretz

Israel is a multiparty democracy.

PROFILE

Recent governments have alternated between right-wing Likud or left-of-center Labor leadership. Since neither can win an overall majority they must either join in a unity government, or bridge the religious–secular divide in fractious coalitions with smaller parties. Likud, under Prime Minister Ariel Sharon from 2001, doubled its presence in the Knesset in 2003 after the collapse of the previous "government of national unity." Labor refused to join the new coalition.

MAIN POLITICAL ISSUE

Peace with the Palestinians

The central question is whether Israel's security should be based on armed strength, or on agreements with Palestinians and neighboring countries. Small but influential religious parties support Jewish settlement of the occupied territories, the main obstacle to any "land for peace" deal. Sharon came to power backing a hard-line stance, insisting on a change in the Palestinian leadership and an end to violence before talks could even begin. The renewed *intifada* (uprising), with Palestinian terror attacks and suicide bombings of civilian targets, reinforced skepticism about prospects for peace, but negotiations resumed in 2003 under the US-initiated "roadmap" process.

Ariel Sharon, *Israel's hard-line prime minister elected in 2001.*

Yasser Arafat, *the militant-turned-moderate leader of the PLO.*

WORLD AFFAIRS

Joined UN in 1949

EBRD | IAEA | IBRD | WTO | IMF

Israel is technically at war with all Arab states except Egypt and Jordan. In 2000 it withdrew from southern Lebanon. Israel maintains close ties with the US, but its harsh response to Palestinian attacks leaves it increasingly isolated.

AID

Recipient

$172m (receipts) | Down 78% in 2001

Israel receives massive military and economic aid from the US. Large ad hoc donations are also received from Jewish NGOs.

DEFENSE

Compulsory military service

$10.4bn | Up 9% in 2001

Israel, the only known nuclear-armed power in the Middle East, has a small regular defense force, which can be boosted by over 400,000 reservists. Equipped with some of the latest US technology, it is vastly superior to the forces of its Arab neighbors in firepower (and training). To counter the Palestinian *intifada* (uprising) it uses punitive strikes and counterinsurgency methods, including targeted assassinations.

ISRAELI ARMED FORCES

3750 main battle tanks (Centurion, M-60A1/3, Magach 7, Merkava I–III)	120,000 personnel
3 submarines and 48 patrol boats	6500 personnel
704 combat aircraft (50 F-4E/2000, 86 F-15, 232 F-16)	35,000 personnel
Widely believed that Israel has a nuclear capacity with up to 100 warheads. Delivery via Jericho 1 and Jericho 2 missiles	

ECONOMICS

Inflation 9.3% p.a. (1990–2001)

$107bn | 4.324 sheqalim (4.755)

STRENGTHS

Modern infrastructure; educated population. Huge potential of agriculture, manufacturing, and high-tech industry. Banking sector. Trade with the EU.

WEAKNESSES

Violence. Large defense budget. Cost of subsidizing settlement and initial integration of immigrants. Little trade with Arab neighbors. Collapse of tourism. Corruption. Rising unemployment.

PROFILE

The government seeks ways to reduce massive state spending. The state owns most of the land and controls over 20% of all industries and services. Public companies are being privatized and there are plans to end restrictive labor practices. Agriculture, highly specialized and profitable, has been eclipsed by high-tech industries. The state aims to boost the service sector.

Israel's economy expanded through the 1990s, benefiting from mass immigration of Jews, many highly educated, from the former Soviet Union. Though unemployment rose as a result, new skills and contacts also helped the Israeli economy toward sustained export-led growth. Pockets of poverty remain in "development towns."

ECONOMIC PERFORMANCE INDICATOR

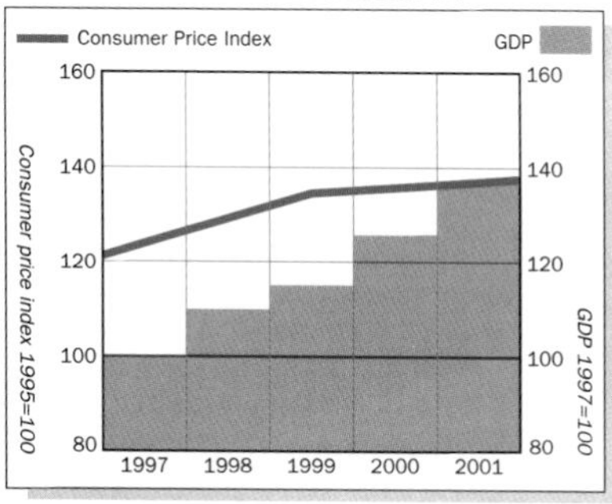
Consumer Price Index
GDP
Consumer price index 1995=100
GDP 1997=100
160
140
120
100
80
1997
1998
1999
2000
2001

SCORE CARD

❑ WORLD GNP RANKING	36th
❑ GNP PER CAPITA	$16,750
❑ BALANCE OF PAYMENTS	–$1.85bn
❑ INFLATION	1.1%
❑ UNEMPLOYMENT	9%

EXPORTS

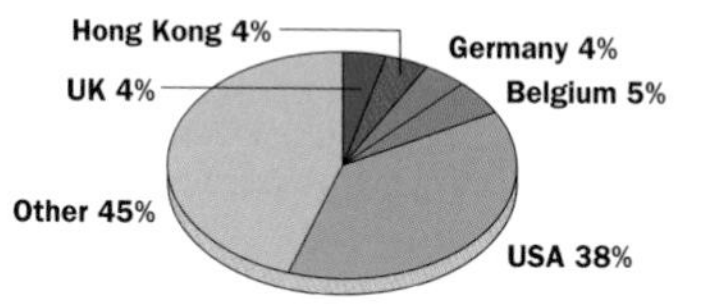
Hong Kong 4%
Germany 4%
UK 4%
Belgium 5%
Other 45%
USA 38%

IMPORTS

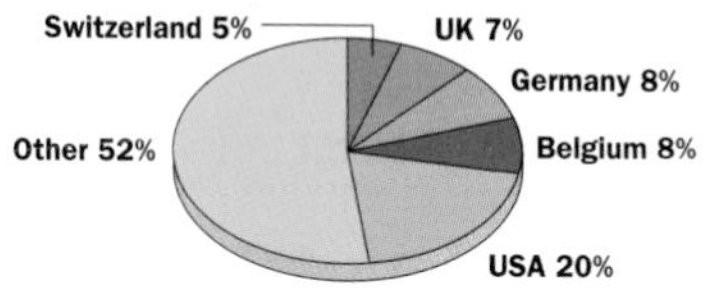
Switzerland 5%
UK 7%
Germany 8%
Other 52%
Belgium 8%
USA 20%

The Palestinian uprising which began in 2000 has sent the economy into recession, hitting trade, tourism, and investment. The military response has eaten into the Israeli budget and has inflicted damage in the West Bank and Gaza Strip estimated at over $300 million.

ISRAEL : MAJOR BUSINESSES

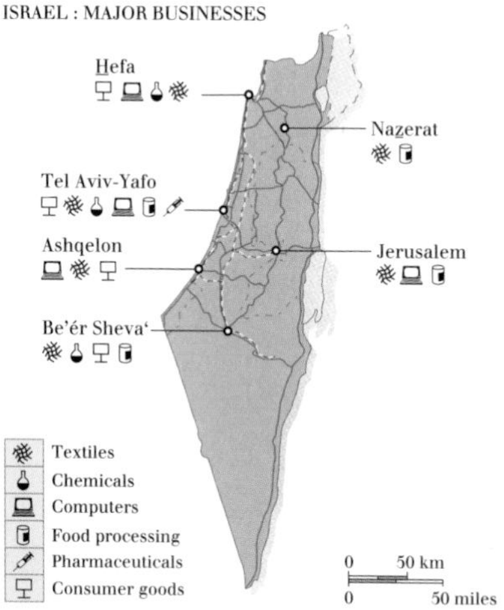
Hefa
Nazerat
Tel Aviv-Yafo
Ashqelon
Jerusalem
Be'ér Sheva'
Textiles
Chemicals
Computers
Food processing
Pharmaceuticals
Consumer goods
0 50 km
0 50 miles

ISRAEL

Total Area : 20 770 sq. km (8019 sq. miles)

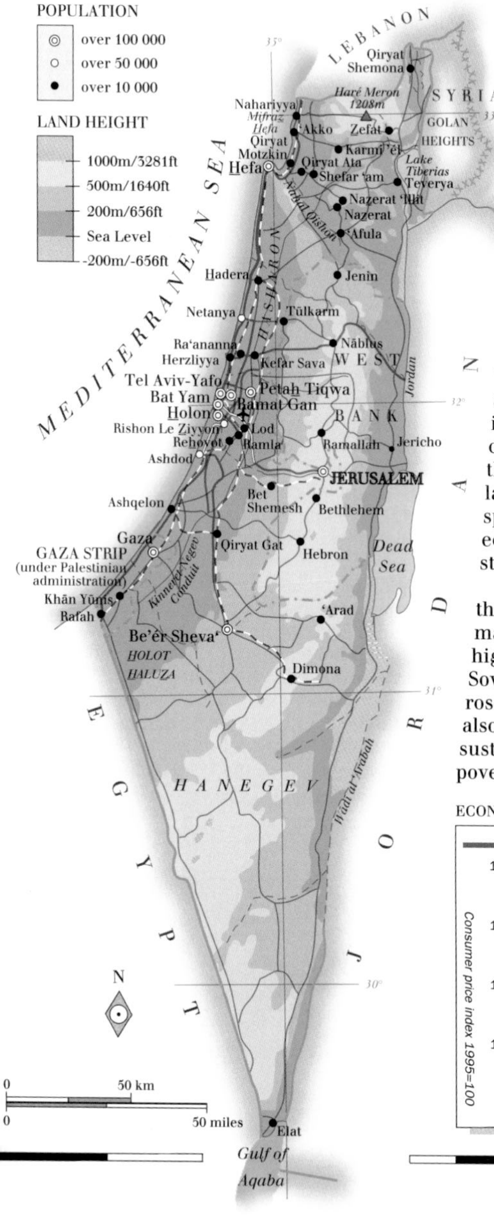
POPULATION
over 100 000
over 50 000
over 10 000
LAND HEIGHT
1000m/3281ft
500m/1640ft
200m/656ft
Sea Level
-200m/-656ft
LEBANON
SYRIA
GOLAN HEIGHTS
MEDITERRANEAN SEA
WEST BANK
GAZA STRIP
(under Palestinian administration)
JORDAN
EGYPT
HANEGEV
Qiryat Shemona
Nahariyya
Haré Meron 1208m
'Akko
Zefat
Hefa
Karmi'él
Lake Tiberias
Teverya
Nazerat
Afula
Hadera
Jenin
Netanya
Tulkarm
Nablus
Kefar Sava
Herzliyya
Tel Aviv-Yafo
Petah Tiqwa
Bat Yam
Ramat Gan
Holon
Rishon Le Ziyyon
Lod
Rehovot
Ramla
Ramallah
Jericho
Ashdod
JERUSALEM
Bet Shemesh
Bethlehem
Ashqelon
Gaza
Qiryat Gat
Hebron
Dead Sea
Khan Yunis
Rafah
'Arad
Be'ér Sheva'
HOLOT HALUZA
Dimona
Wadi al 'Arabah
Elat
Gulf of Aqaba
N
0 50 km
0 50 miles

I

ISRAEL AND THE PALESTINIANS

THE CONFLICT between Israel and the Palestinians is crucial in Middle East politics. The creation of Israel in 1948 effectively turned the almost one million Arabs living in the former British Mandate of Palestine into refugees overnight. Some 300,000 more left territories occupied by Israel in 1967. Not until the 1993 accords were the Palestinians granted limited self-rule in the West Bank and Gaza – inhabited by two million Palestinians and 300,000 Jewish settlers – under the jurisdiction of the Palestinian National Authority (PNA), headed by Palestine Liberation Organization (PLO) leader Yasser Arafat. Hopes of a resolution of "permanent status" issues, and accession to full statehood, were lost from sight after 2000 amid a return to violent conflict, but a US-initiated "roadmap" for peace, put forward in 2003, opened a fresh round of contacts.

I

BACKGROUND

In 1947 a UN plan partitioned Palestine into separate Jewish and Arab states. When the British Mandate ended in 1948, Arab countries (which had all rejected the plan) invaded Palestine, but were pushed back well beyond the UN partition lines by Israeli forces. The 1949 armistices left only East Jerusalem, the West Bank (5900 sq. km – 2300 sq. miles), and the Egyptian-administered Gaza Strip (1000 sq. km – 400 sq. miles) outside Israel. Jordan declared East Jerusalem and the West Bank to be part of its territory, only renouncing this claim formally in 1988. Israel annexed the Palestinian territories after the 1967 Six-Day War, and Jewish settlers began moving to what they regard as part of the biblical-era "Land of Israel."

***Poor slum housing** in Gaza.*

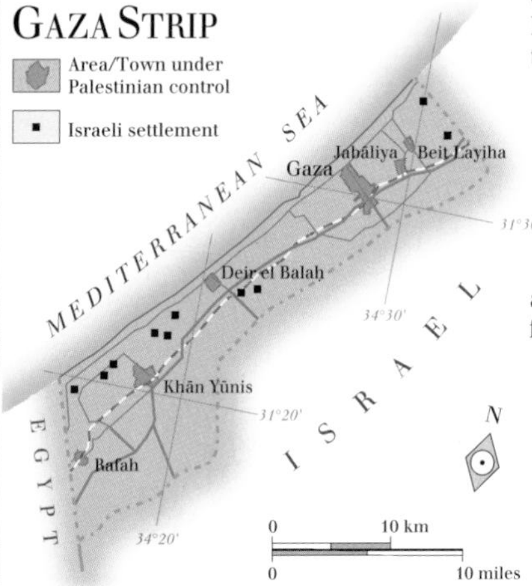
GAZA STRIP
Area/Town under Palestinian control
Israeli settlement
MEDITERRANEAN SEA
Gaza
Jabāliya
Beit Lāyjha
Deir el Balah
Khān Yūnis
Rafah
EGYPT
ISRAEL
N
31°30′
34°30′
31°20′
34°20′
0
10 km
0
10 miles

Palestinian autonomy, part of the 1978 Camp David agreement, did not happen; there was diplomatic deadlock. Not until 1988 did the PLO recognize Israel's right to exist, while Israel refused to "negotiate with terrorists."

PALESTINIAN AUTONOMY

Turning away from armed struggle, the PLO concluded a historic "land for peace" deal with Israel in 1993, known as the Oslo Accords. The two sides formally recognized one another, and Arafat and Israeli prime minister Yitzhak Rabin signed a Declaration of Principles in Washington D.C. A five-year timetable for "permanent status" negotiations would tackle the future of Jewish settlements and the Palestinian demand for East Jerusalem as their capital. Palestinians were to get interim self-rule, initially in Gaza and Jericho (achieved in 1994), and gradually in the whole West Bank. Palestinian police were to take over from the Israeli military, who had been struggling since 1987 to end an uprising (*intifada*) led by the radical Islamic organization Hamas. The PNA was established, based in Gaza, and Arafat returned in triumph in July 1994. He was elected president of the newly created 88-member Palestinian Legislative Council in January 1996.

THE DERAILING OF THE PEACE PROCESS

The "Oslo B" accord in 1995 extended PNA rule to six more West Bank towns. After repeated delays Israel also gave up control of Hebron (but not of rural areas). Mutual mistrust and violence, however, threatened to derail the peace process before the stage of "final status" talks, and Arafat risked losing credibility among radical Palestinians. Attacks by Hamas guerrillas, including suicide bombings, dominated mid-1996 elections in Israel. A new right-wing government took a tougher stance and did little to restrain Jewish settlers, fierce opponents of "land for peace."

A Labor-led government, in power from 2000, laid out an ambitious timetable for a permanent agreement with the PNA. Intensive US diplomacy helped keep this plan alive until the eleventh hour, but heavy-handed Israeli retaliation to violent incidents in September–

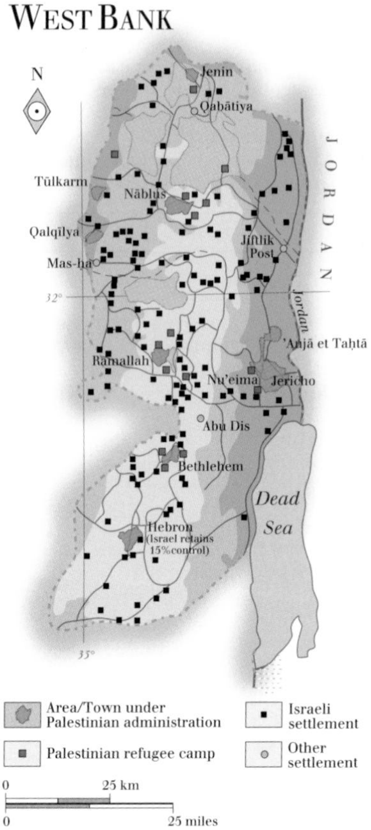
WEST BANK
N
Jenin
Qabātiya
Tūlkarm
Nāblus
Qalqīlya
Mas-ha
Jiftlik Post
JORDAN
Jordan
32°
'Anjā et Taḥtā
Ramallah
Nu'eima
Jericho
Abu Dis
Bethlehem
Dead Sea
Hebron (Israel retains 15% control)
35°
Area/Town under Palestinian administration
Israeli settlement
Palestinian refugee camp
Other settlement
0
25 km
0
25 miles

October provoked Palestinian rage and a fresh *intifada*. In a bitter climate of atrocity, retaliation, and counterstrike, Ariel Sharon, elected prime minister in 2001, formed a new Israeli government. Denouncing Palestinian militants for suicide bomb attacks on civilian targets, Sharon blamed Arafat for failing to control them, while instituting a brutal policy of military reprisals and "targeted assassinations." He gained US support in mid-2002 for the idea that only a Palestinian leadership change could bring Israel back to the negotiating table. A new role of Palestinian prime minister, created in 2003, sidelined Arafat sufficiently to initiate fresh contacts based on the US "roadmap."

***Bethlehem,** situated in the troubled West Bank.*

RESOURCES

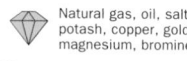

Electric power 8.6m kW

25,916 tonnes

80 b/d (reserves 7.3m barrels)

5m turkeys, 1.4m geese, 30m chickens

Natural gas, oil, salt, potash, copper, gold, magnesium, bromine

ELECTRICITY GENERATION

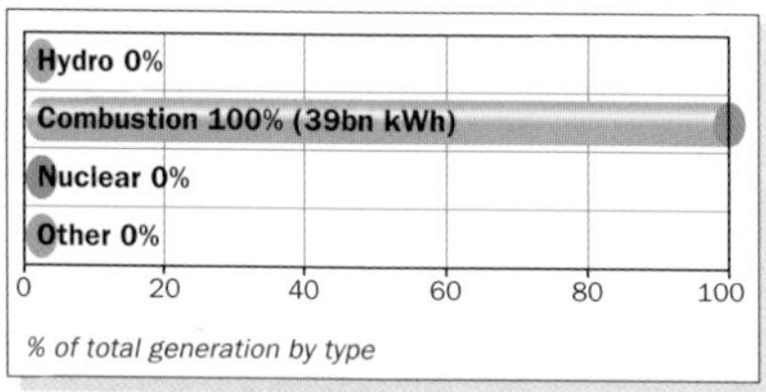
Hydro 0%
Combustion 100% (39bn kWh)
Nuclear 0%
Other 0%
0
20
40
60
80
100
% of total generation by type

Israel's most critical resource is water. The water of the River Jordan is shared by Jordan and Israel, and Israel buys water from Turkey.

The country's most valuable mineral deposits are potash salts, bromine (of which Israel is the world's largest exporter), and other salts mined near the Dead Sea. Reserves of copper ore and gold were discovered in 1988. In the coastal plain, mixed farming, vineyards, and citrus groves are plentiful. Former desert areas now have extensive irrigation systems supporting specialized agriculture.

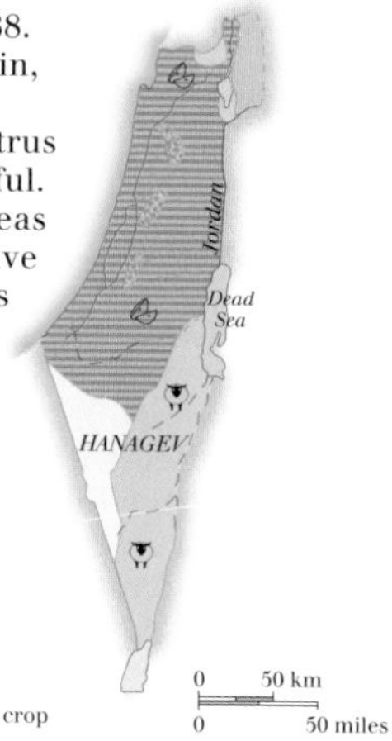
Jordan
Dead Sea
HANAGEV
ISRAEL : LAND USE
Cropland
Forest
Pasture
Desert
Sheep
Citrus fruit – cash crop
0
50 km
0
50 miles

ENVIRONMENT

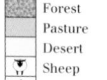

Sustainability rank: 63rd

16% partially protected

10.3 tonnes per capita

Government environmental efforts focus on recycling and the cleanup of towns and rivers. In an effort to halt the depletion of the Dead Sea, water is to be piped from the Red Sea.

ENVIRONMENTAL TREATIES

Yes — Yes — Yes

Yes — Yes — No

MEDIA

TV ownership high

Daily newspaper circulation 290 per 1000 people

PUBLISHING AND BROADCAST MEDIA

There are 34 daily newspapers. The leading papers are the Hebrew *Ha'aretz*, and the English *Jerusalem Post*

2 services: 1 state-owned, 1 independent

2 state-owned services, many independent stations

The left-wing press favors the peace process. The number of private radio stations, many right-wing, is rising.

CRIME

Death penalty not used in practice

9421 prisoners

Violent crime rose in 2000–2001

CRIME RATES

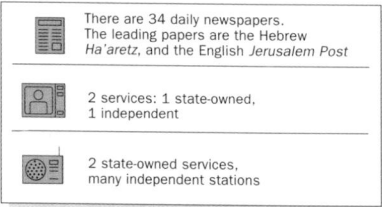

Murders	3	per 100,000 population
Rapes	10	per 100,000 population
Thefts	3221	per 100,000 population

The vast majority of violent attacks are due to the Israeli–Palestinian conflict. Car theft is a rising concern.

EDUCATION

School leaving age: 16

95%

270,979 students

THE EDUCATION SYSTEM

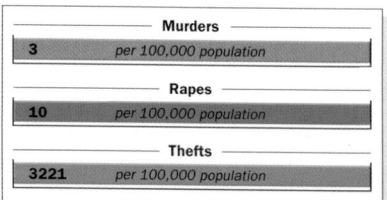

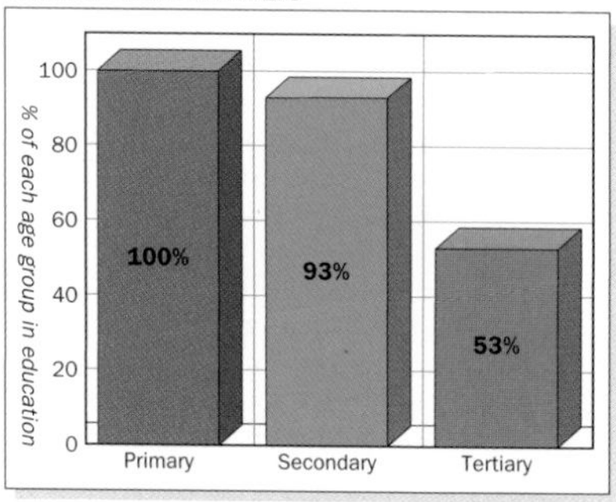
100
80
60
40
20
0
% of each age group in education
100%
93%
53%
Primary
Secondary
Tertiary

A highly educated population has been the engine of Israel's economic growth. State schools have religious (Jewish), secular, and Arab streams. Ultraorthodox and Sephardi Jews increasingly run their own private establishments.

HEALTH

Welfare state health benefits

1 per 265 people

Cancers, heart and cerebrovascular diseases

The ratio of doctors to the total population in Israel is one of the highest in the world. Primary health care reaches all communities. Israel's hospitals have pioneered many innovative treatments.

CHRONOLOGY

War with the neighboring Arab states followed immediately upon the creation of the state of Israel in 1948.

- **1967** Israeli victory in Six-Day War.
- **1973** Egypt and Syria attack Israel.
- **1978** Camp David accords with Egypt.
- **1979** Formal peace treaty, Sinai returned to Egypt.
- **1982** Israel invades Lebanon.
- **1987** Palestinians launch *intifada*.
- **1993** Oslo Accords.
- **1994** Palestinian autonomy begins in Gaza and Jericho.
- **1995** Prime Minister Yitzhak Rabin assassinated.
- **1996** Palestinian elections.
- **1998** Government stalls on US-backed plan to revive peace process.
- **1999** Ehud Barak (Labor) prime minister. Renewed peace process with Palestinians and Syria.
- **2000** Israel withdraws from Lebanon. *Intifada* relaunched.
- **2001** Ariel Sharon (Likud) prime minister; forms unity government.
- **2002** Suicide attacks and Israeli reprisals intensify. Unity government collapses.
- **2003** Likud wins elections. US peace "roadmap" published.

SPENDING

GDP/cap. increase

CONSUMPTION AND SPENDING

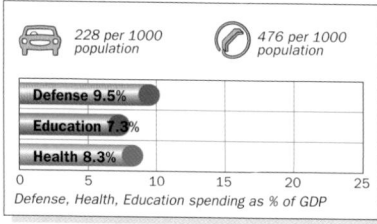

228 per 1000 population

476 per 1000 population

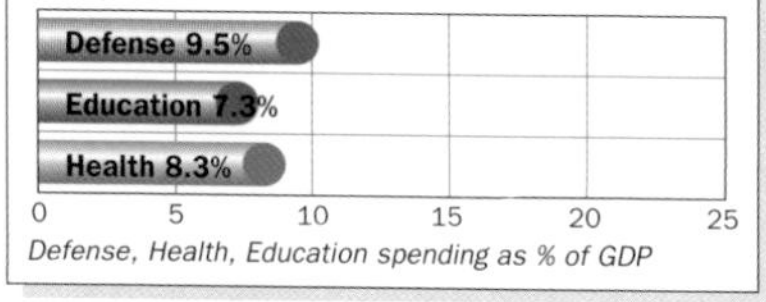
Defense 9.5%
Education 7.3%
Health 8.3%
0
5
10
15
20
25
Defense, Health, Education spending as % of GDP

Income per head is high, but taxation is heavy. In theory, those living in communes (*kibbutzim*) eschew personal material wealth.

WORLD RANKING

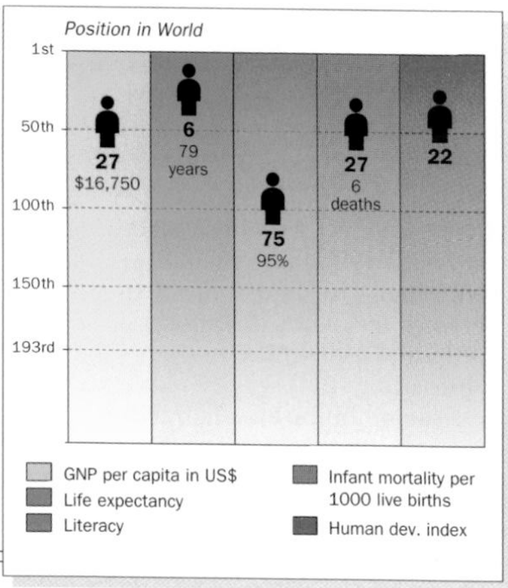
Position in World
1st
50th
100th
150th
193rd
27
$16,750
6
79 years
75
95%
27
6 deaths
22
GNP per capita in US$
Life expectancy
Literacy
Infant mortality per 1000 live births
Human dev. index

I

ITALY

OFFICIAL NAME: Italian Republic **CAPITAL:** Rome
POPULATION: 57.4 million **CURRENCY:** Euro **OFFICIAL LANGUAGE:** Italian

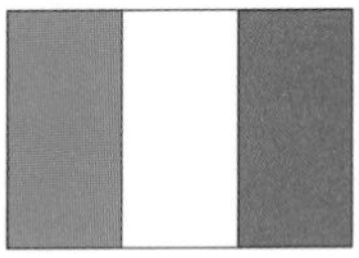

1861
1947
June 2
I
+1
+39
.it

THE BOOT-SHAPED Italian peninsula stretches 800 km (500 miles) southward into the Mediterranean, while the Alps form a natural boundary to the north. Italy also includes Sicily, Sardinia, and several smaller islands. The south is an area of seismic activity, with two famous volcanoes, Vesuvius and Etna. Rival city-states flourished in Renaissance Italy, a unified country only in Roman times and since 1861. Fascist rule under Mussolini from 1922 ended with Italy's defeat in World War II. The Christian Democrats (DC) then dominated Italy's notoriously short-lived governments for decades, until in the 1990s the established parties and patronage systems were shaken up by corruption investigations. New groupings emerged, power alternating between a right-wing coalition and a broad center-left Olive Tree alliance.

CLIMATE

Mediterranean/mountain

WEATHER CHART FOR ROME

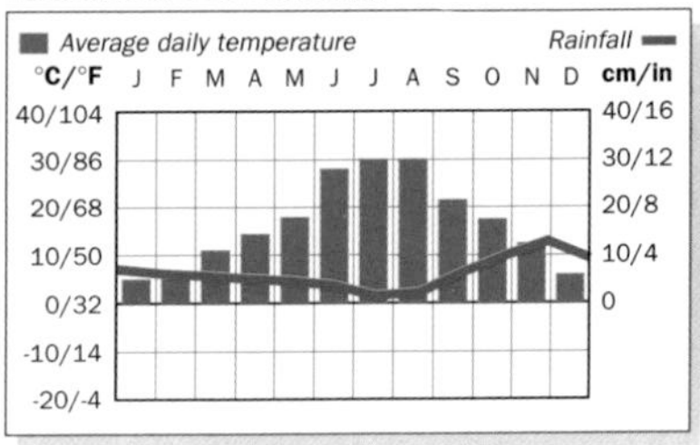

Average daily temperature
Rainfall
°C/°F
J F M A M J J A S O N D
cm/in
40/104
30/86
20/68
10/50
0/32
-10/14
-20/-4
40/16
30/12
20/8
10/4
0

A Mediterranean climate in the south contrasts with more temperate conditions in the north. Summers are hot and dry, especially in the south; Sardinia and Sicily have highs of more than 30°C (86°F). The Adriatic coast suffers from cold winds such as the *bora*. Southern winters are mild; northern ones are cooler and wetter, with heavy snow in the mountains.

TRANSPORTATION

Drive on right

Leonardo da Vinci (Fiumicino), Rome
25.3m passengers

1476 ships
9.66m grt

THE TRANSPORTATION NETWORK

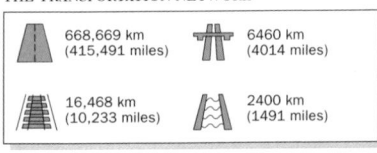

668,669 km (415,491 miles)	6460 km (4014 miles)
16,468 km (10,233 miles)	2400 km (1491 miles)

Roads, which carry most of Italy's trade via Switzerland and Austria, are badly congested. The *autostrada* (expressway) network lacks key links, and serious bottlenecks affect the main north–south artery. Rail services are extensive and cheap. Luxurious Pendolino trains link Rome and Milan, but the high-speed TAV (*treno alta velocità*) project is behind schedule and over budget.

TOURISM

Visitors : Population 1:1.4

39.8m visitors

Up 1% in 2002

MAIN TOURIST ARRIVALS

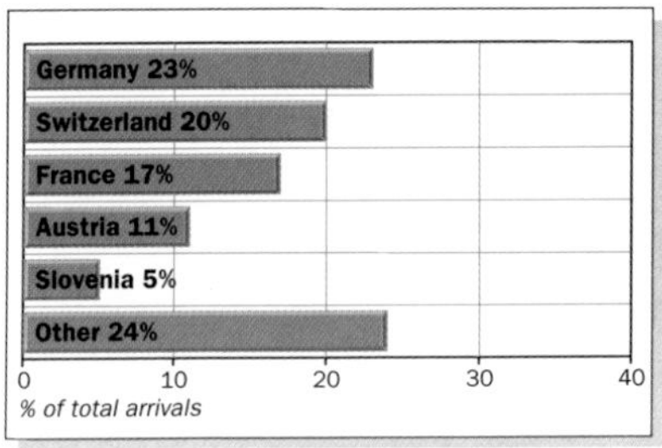

Germany 23%
Switzerland 20%
France 17%
Austria 11%
Slovenia 5%
Other 24%
0
10
20
30
40
% of total arrivals

Italy has been a tourist destination since the 16th century. Roman popes consciously aimed to make their city the most beautiful in the world to attract travelers. In the 18th century, Italy was the focus of any Grand Tour. Today, its many unspoiled centers of Renaissance and ancient culture continue to make Italy one of the world's major tourism destinations. The industry accounts for 3% of Italy's GDP, and employs a million people – 5% of the workforce.

Most visitors travel to the northern half of Italy, to cities such as Venice and Florence, and to Rome. Tourists are also drawn to the northern lakes, while beach resorts such as Rimini attract a large, youthful crowd in summer. Italy is also growing in popularity as a skiing destination. In the south the breathtaking ruins of Roman Pompeii are a particular magnet for visitors.

Fears have been expressed about the detrimental impact of tourism on Italy's environment. The pressure of visitors to Venice is such that in summer one-way systems for pedestrians have to be introduced and day-trippers are often turned away.

EUROPE
Europe
Switz.
Austria
France
ITALY
Tunisia
Greece
SWITZERLAND
FRANCE
Mont Blanc 4807m
Gran Paradiso 4061m
Lago di Como
Lake Maggiore
Varese
Lecco
Bergamo
Lago di Garda
Aosta
Biella
Como
Monza
Brescia
Vercelli
Novara
Milano
Ticino
Tanaro
Torino
Asti
Piacenza
Mantova
Alessandria
Parma
Reggio nell' Emilia
Modena
Appennino Ligure
Genova
Rapallo
Cueno
Savona
Golfo di Genova
La Spezia
Carrara
Massa
MONACO
Imperia
San Remo
Viareggio
Pisa
Arno
Livorno
LIGURIAN SEA
Isola d'Elba
Arcipelago Toscano
Corsica (FRANCE)
Porto Torres
Olbia
Sassari
Alghero
Tirso
Macomer
Nuoro
Sardegna (Sardinia)
Monti del Gennargentu
Oristano
Arbatax
Iglesias
Carbonia
Cagliari
Sant Antioco

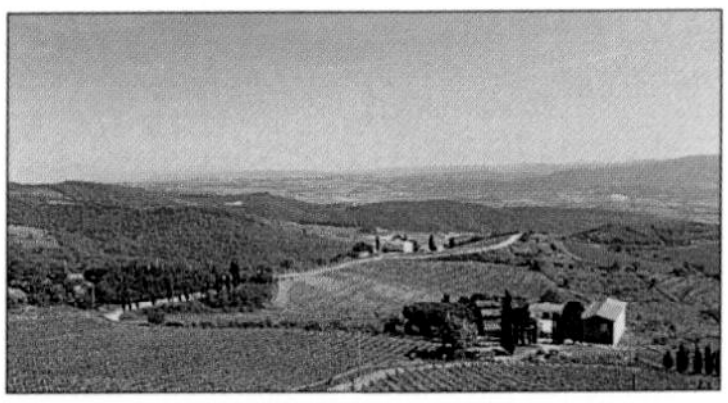

***Tuscan landscape.** Chianti wine is produced in this region, where many northern Europeans own holiday homes.*

ITALY

Total Area : 301 230 sq. km (116 305 sq. miles)

POPULATION
over 1 000 000
over 500 000
over 100 000
over 50 000
over 10 000
LAND HEIGHT
3000m/9843ft
2000m/6562ft
1000m/3281ft
500m/1640ft
200m/656ft
Sea Level
SLOVENIA
Udine
Monfalcone
Trieste
Venezia
Golfo di Venezia
Ravenna
Rimini
SAN MARINO
Pesaro
Fano
Sengallia
Ancona
Fabriano
Perugia
Assisi
Lago Trasimeno
Ascoli Piceno
Teramo
Terni
Pescara
L'Aquila
ADRIATIC SEA
ROME
CITY
Ostia
Tivoli
Avezzano
Vasto
Rodi Garganico
San Severo
Manfredonia
Foggia
Campobasso
Latina
Teracina
Barletta
Benevento
Andria
Bari
Monopoli
Golfo di Gaeta
Isloe Ponziane
Napoli
Vesuvio
Avellino
Torre del Greco
I. d'Ischia
Castellammare di Stabia
Isola di Capri
Salerno
Potenza
La Murge
Brindisi
Taranto
Lecce
Strait of Otranto
Golfo di Salerno
Penisola Salentina
Golfo di Taranto
Castrovillari
RRHENIAN SEA
Rossano
Paola
Cosenza
La Sila
Crotone
Nicastro
Catanzaro
I. de Ustica
Isole Eolie
I. Lupari
Vulcano
Stretto di Messina
IONIAN SEA
Messina
Locri
Reggio di Calabria
Palermo
Trapani
Alcamo
Barcellona
Marsala
Corleone
Sicilia (Sicily)
Mt Etna 3323m
Taormina
Acireale
Castelvetrano
Sciacca
Enna
Caltanissetta
Catania
Caltagirone
Augusta
Agrigento
Licata
Gela
Siracusa
Vittoria
Ragusa
Pantelleria
RANEAN SEA
N
0 100 km
0 100 miles

PEOPLE

Pop. density medium

Italian, German, French, Rhaeto-Romanic, Sardinian

195/km² (506/mi²)

THE URBAN/RURAL POPULATION SPLIT

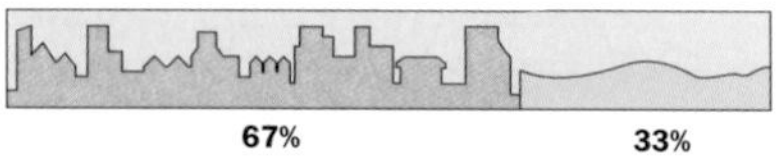
67%
33%

RELIGIOUS PERSUASION

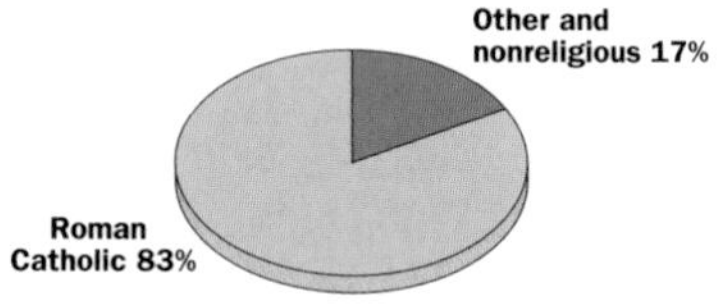
Other and nonreligious 17%
Roman Catholic 83%

ETHNIC MAKEUP

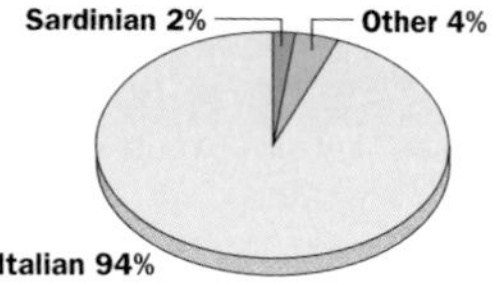
Sardinian 2%
Other 4%
Italian 94%

Italy is a remarkably homogeneous society. Most Italians are Roman Catholics and Italy has far fewer ethnic minorities than its EU neighbors; most are fairly recent immigrants from Ethiopia, the Philippines, and Egypt. A sharp rise in illegal immigration in the 1980s and 1990s, from north and west Africa, Turkey, and Albania, became a major election issue and a factor in the rise of the federalist Northern League. Despite stringent measures introduced in 1995 against illegal immigrants, the number of new arrivals continues to increase.

Difficult economic conditions caused many Italians to emigrate in the 1950s and 1960s. There are now five million Italians living abroad. About half live in other EU countries, the rest mainly in the US, South America, and Australia. Most migrants then, as now, are from the poorer south – the Mezzogiorno. Within Italy, prejudice still exists in the north against southern Italians.

Sport – especially soccer – has an unusual ability to bring out a strong sense of national identity among Italians. In other spheres, with state institutions viewed as inefficient and corrupt, most people feel a stronger allegiance to the region, or the community, and above all to the family. The extended family remains Italy's key social and economic support system. Most Italians live at home before marriage. Marriage rates are among the highest in Europe and divorce rates the lowest. Catholicism, however, has not stopped Italy having the lowest birthrate and one of the highest abortion rates in the EU.

Italians tend to dress well. Their preoccupation with style reflects the traditional importance of *bella figura* – image, cutting a dash – in Italian life as much as the high living standards which most now enjoy.

POPULATION AGE BREAKDOWN

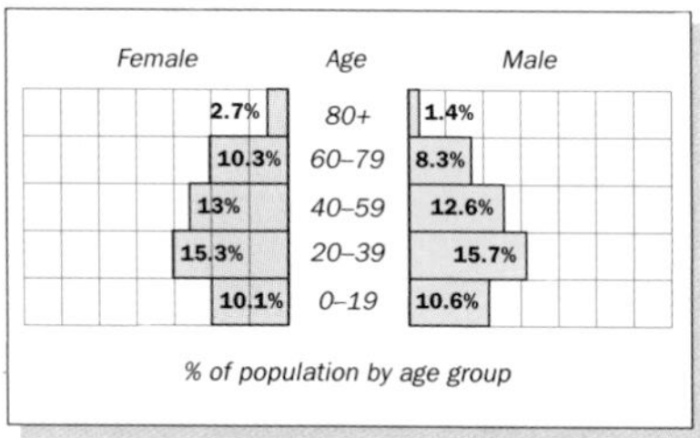
Female
Age
Male
2.7%
80+
1.4%
10.3%
60–79
8.3%
13%
40–59
12.6%
15.3%
20–39
15.7%
10.1%
0–19
10.6%
% of population by age group

CHRONOLOGY

Previously a collection of independent city-states, dukedoms, and monarchies, Italy became a unified state in 1861.

- **1922** Mussolini asked to form government by king.
- **1928** One-party rule by Fascists.
- **1929** Lateran Treaties with Vatican recognize sovereignty of Holy See.
- **1936–1937** Axis formed with Nazi Germany. Abyssinia (Ethiopia) conquered.
- **1939** Albania annexed.
- **1940** Italy enters World War II on German side.
- **1943** Invaded by Allies. Mussolini imprisoned by Victor Emmanuel III. Armistice with Allies. Italy declares war on Germany.

I

CHRONOLOGY *continued*

- **1945** Mussolini released; establishes puppet regime in north; executed by Italian partisans.
- **1946** Referendum votes in favor of Italy becoming a republic.
- **1947** Italy signs peace treaty, ceding border areas to France and Yugoslavia, Dodecanese to Greece, and giving up colonies.
- **1948** Elections: De Gaspieri of Christian Democrats (DC) heads coalition.
- **1949** Founder member of NATO.
- **1950** Agreement reached on US bases in Italy.
- **1951** Joins European Coal and Steel Community.
- **1957** Founder member of European Economic Community. Aided by funds from that organization and by Marshall Aid, industrial growth accelerates.
- **1964** DC government under Aldo Moro forms coalition with Socialist Party (PSI).
- **1969** Red Brigades, extreme left terrorist group, formed.
- **1972** Support for extreme right reaches postwar peak (9%). Rise in urban terrorism by both extreme left and right.
- **1976** Communist Party (PCI) support reaches a peak of 34% under Enrico Berlinguer's Eurocommunist philosophy.
- **1978** Aldo Moro abducted and murdered by Red Brigades.
- **1980** Extreme right bombing of Bologna station kills 84, wounds 200.
- **1983–1987** Center-left coalition formed under Bettino Craxi.
- **1990** LN attacks immigration policies and subsidies for the south.
- **1992** Corruption scandal, involving bribes for public contracts, uncovered in Milan. Government members accused.
- **1994** General election: DC support collapses; coalition government formed between Silvio Berlusconi's Forza Italia, LN, and "post-fascists."
- **1995–1996** Technocrat government tackles budget, pensions, media, and regional issues.
- **1996** Center-left Olive Tree alliance wins general election; Romano Prodi prime minister.
- **1998** May, Italy qualifies to join euro currency from January 1999. October, Prodi government falls, Massimo D'Alema prime minister.
- **1999** Carlo Ciampi president.
- **2000** D'Alema replaced by Giuliano Amato.
- **2001** May, Berlusconi victory in general election. June, right-wing government includes post-fascist National Alliance.
- **2002** Euro fully adopted.

POLITICS

Multiparty elections

L. House 2001/2006
U. House 2001/2006

President Carlo Azeglio Ciampi

AT THE LAST ELECTION

Chamber of Deputies 630 seats

1%
U–SVP
58%
PdL
38%
U
2% 1%
PRC Others

PdL = Freedom Alliance (includes Forza Italia, National Alliance – **AN**, and Northern League – **LN**)
U = Olive Tree alliance (includes Democrats of the Left – **DS** and Party of Italian Communists – **PdCI**)
PRC = Communist Refoundation Party
U–SVP = Olive Tree–South Tyrolese People's Party
Nom = Nominated

Senate of the Republic 324 seats

1% 2%
U–SVP Others
55%
PdL
38%
U
3% 1%
Nom PRC

The Senate of the Republic comprises 315 elected members and several life senators

Italy is a multiparty democracy.

Profile

The May 2001 electoral triumph of the right-wing Forza Italia allowed Silvio Berlusconi to return as head of government after six years out of office. His coalition revives the short-lived 1994 alliance between Forza Italia, Gianfranco Fini's "post-fascist" AN, and Umberto Bossi's xenophobic, northern-based LN. In the interim, Italy had had a spell of nonparty technocratic government and then five years of a center-left coalition, ushered in by the victory of the Olive Tree alliance at the 1996 election. Meanwhile, Bossi had failed to rouse mass support for his declaration in 1996 of an independent northern state of "Padania."

Italy's success in qualifying for membership of the single European currency had crowned the center-left government's achievements in the economic sphere. After two years in office, Romano Prodi was ousted in 1998 when the communists challenged his budget. The premiership passed to Massimo D'Alema of the DS (one of the successor groups to the Communist Party – PCI), then to Giuliano Amato, retaining a broadly similar coalition formula. Aware of the strength of the challenge from Berlusconi and the right, Amato then stood aside so that the popular mayor of Rome, Francesco Rutelli, could lead the ultimately unsuccessful center-left campaign in the May 2001 elections.

There were mass public protests in 2002 against proposed reforms of labor law.

Romano Prodi, ex-premier (1996–1998) who heads European Commission.

Umberto Bossi, LN leader and minister in the Berlusconi government.

Silvio Berlusconi, conservative prime minister, elected for a second time in 2001.

The church of Santa Maria della Salute marks the entrance to Venice. The city-state managed to retain its independence until Napoleon Bonaparte's invasion of Italy.

Main Political Issues

Corruption

Berlusconi's return to power in 2001 brought the corruption issue back to the very heart of public life, as he pushed through reforms which gave him immunity as prime minister and meant that outstanding bribery-related charges against him could be quashed. Paradoxically, he himself had emerged as a leading figure in the country's new political makeup in the wake of the 1990s *mani pulite* (clean hands) investigations, which revealed a nationwide network of corruption and destroyed the old political order.

Institutional reform

The old proportional representation (PR) electoral system, blamed for a lack of strong government, was much modified in the early 1990s, but the process then lost impetus. Twice, in 1999 and in 2000, referenda failed to abolish the 25% of seats still elected by PR, not because voters opposed this, but merely due to inadequate turnout. Berlusconi favors a system with greater presidential powers, akin to that in France (and has made explicit his desire to go on to be head of state under such a system).

I

WORLD AFFAIRS

Joined UN in 1955

EU | G8 | NATO | OECD | OSCE

Italy was one of the founders of the EU, but the return of a right-wing government in 2001 encouraged the opponents of further integration. Tasteless remarks by Berlusconi in mid-2003 caused a rift with Germany just as Italy began its six-month spell holding the EU presidency. The NATO South European Command is based in Naples. Despite pro-Western orientation, Italy often contributes to mediation in eastern Europe and the Middle East.

Major concerns in the 1990s were upheaval in Albania and conflict in the former Yugoslavia. NATO used Italian bases for air strikes against Yugoslavia in 1999, and Italy has backed the US-led "war on terrorism," and the invasion of Iraq in 2003.

AID

Donor

$1.63bn (donations)

Up 18% in 2001

A relatively small aid program makes major use of international organizations. In 2002, $4 billion of developing country debt was canceled. The countries of the former Yugoslavia and Albania have received funding to stave off a feared influx of economic migrants.

DEFENSE

Phasing out conscription

$21bn

Down 7% in 2001

ITALIAN ARMED FORCES

1253 main battle tanks (440 Leopard 1, 378 Centauro B-1, 200 Ariete)	128,000 personnel
6 submarines, 1 carrier, 1 cruiser, 4 destroyers, 14 frigates, 16 patrol boats	38,000 personnel
326 combat aircraft (115 Tornado, 65 F-104, 103 AMX)	50,800 personnel
None	

Since the ending of the Cold War, conflicts in former Yugoslavia have helped refocus defense priorities. A "New Model Defense" was announced in 1992, and in 2000 the legislature approved a law ending conscription by 2005 and introducing women soldiers. The envisaged professional army is to play a rapid-intervention role on NATO's southern flank, while the navy fulfills Mediterranean coastal functions rather than retaining ocean-going capabilities. Defense spending remains low, despite pressures to modernize weapons systems. In 2001, 2700 troops were deployed in the "war on terrorism."

ECONOMICS

Inflation 3.6% p.a. (1990–2001)

$1124bn

0.871 euros (1.013)

SCORE CARD

❑ WORLD GNP RANKING	7th
❑ GNP PER CAPITA	$19,390
❑ BALANCE OF PAYMENTS	–$163m
❑ INFLATION	2.8%
❑ UNEMPLOYMENT	10%

EXPORTS

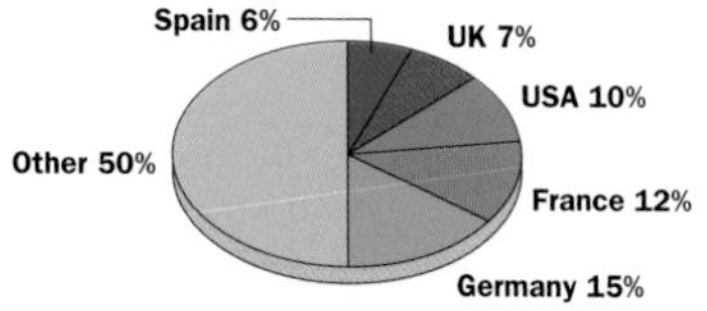
Spain 6%
UK 7%
USA 10%
France 12%
Germany 15%
Other 50%

IMPORTS

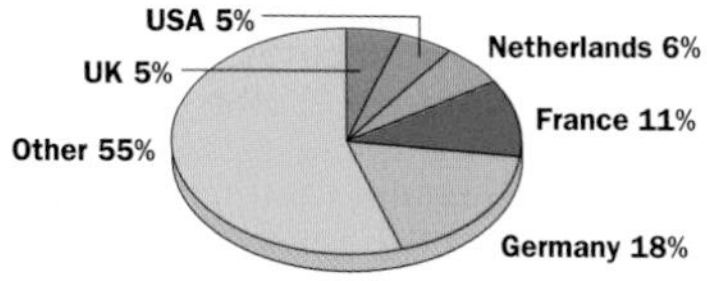
USA 5%
UK 5%
Netherlands 6%
France 11%
Germany 18%
Other 55%

STRENGTHS

Highly competitive, innovative small- to medium-size business sector. World leader in industrial and product design, textiles, and household appliances. Several highly innovative firms include Fiat (cars), Montedison (plastics), Olivetti (communications), and Benetton (clothes). Strong tourism and agriculture sectors, prestigious fashion houses.

WEAKNESSES

Public deficit and government debt remain high. Recession in 2003. Inefficient public sector undergoing major privatizations. Uneven wealth distribution: northern Italy far richer than the south, which suffers three times more unemployment. Poor record on tax collection, though now much improved. Relatively small companies facing foreign competition. Heavy dependence on imported energy.

PROFILE

Since World War II, Italy has developed from a mainly agricultural society into a world industrial power. The economy is characterized by a large state sector, a mass of family-owned businesses, relatively high levels of protectionism, and strong regional differences. Italy also has relatively few multinationals compared with other G7 economies.

The Institute for Industrial Reconstruction (IRI), a state-owned holding company dating from the Fascist era, progressively privatized its electronics, steel, engineering, shipbuilding, telecommunications, transportation, and aerospace companies, until closing down itself in 2000. The National Hydrocarbons Group (ENI), one of the world's top players in the energy and chemicals sectors, has been privatized, as has Telecom Italia and the electricity corporation Enel. City and regional authorities own utilities, banks, and other businesses.

Family-owned businesses, which are the backbone of the private sector, include Fiat, whose interests include aero engines, telecommunications, and bioengineering, as well as cars. Similar businesses tend to congregate, encouraging local competition which has translated into national success.

The Mezzogiorno remains an exception. State attempts to attract new investment have met with success in areas immediately south of Rome, but elsewhere organized crime has deterred investors and siphoned off state funds. Anger at the misuse of state funds in the south was a powerful factor in the growth of the LN, with its demands for autonomy. One-third of Italian tax revenue is generated in Italy's industrial heartland of Milan.

ECONOMIC PERFORMANCE INDICATOR

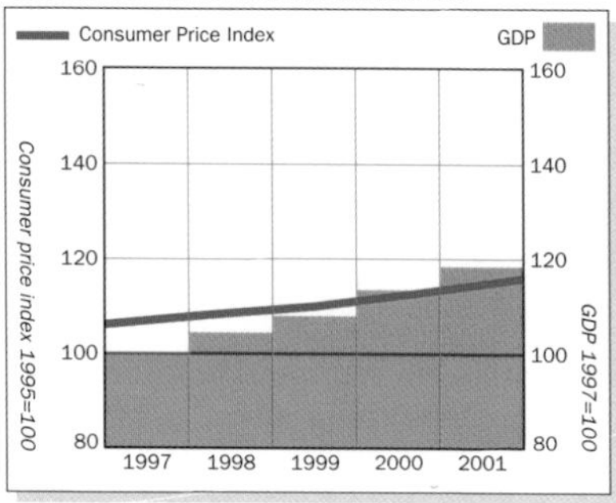
Consumer Price Index
GDP
160
140
120
100
80
Consumer price index 1995=100
GDP 1997=100
1997
1998
1999
2000
2001

ITALY : MAJOR BUSINESSES

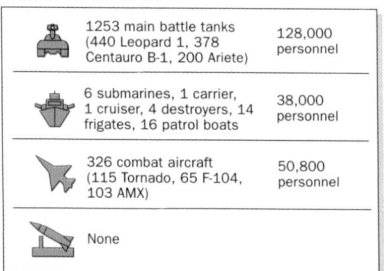

Milano
Torino
Venezia
Bologna
Genova
Firenze
Rome
Napoli
Palermo
Textiles
Chemicals
Garments
Electronics
Pharmaceuticals
Light engineering
Defence industries
Vehicle manufacture
Aerospace industries
0
200 km
0
200 miles

I

I

***Remains of the Greek theater** at Taormina, eastern Sicily. It was rebuilt by the Romans in the 2nd century CE. Today, the theater is the venue for an annual arts festival.*

RESOURCES

Electric power 71m kW

513,474 tonnes

103,000 b/d (reserves 600m barrels)

25m turkeys, 11m sheep, 8.41m pigs, 100m chickens

Coal, oil, lignite, pyrites, fluorite, barytes, bauxite

ELECTRICITY GENERATION

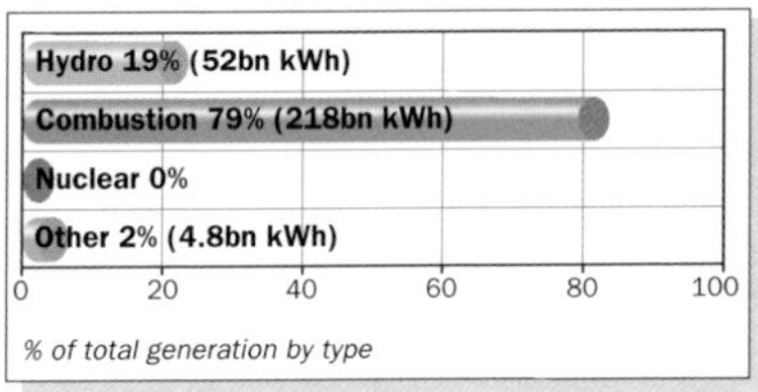
Hydro 19% (52bn kWh)
Combustion 79% (218bn kWh)
Nuclear 0%
Other 2% (4.8bn kWh)
0
20
40
60
80
100
% of total generation by type

Italy has very few natural resources. Its mineral assets are small and the sector contributes little to national wealth. Italy produces less than 10% of its oil needs and is highly vulnerable to both fluctuations in world prices and political instability in its traditional north African suppliers. Keen to diversify in areas of dependence, it has switched increasingly to natural gas, in the last 30 years cutting its reliance on oil from 71% of its energy needs to around 50%. Nuclear power was rejected in a 1987 referendum, and development has effectively been abandoned.

ITALY : LAND USE

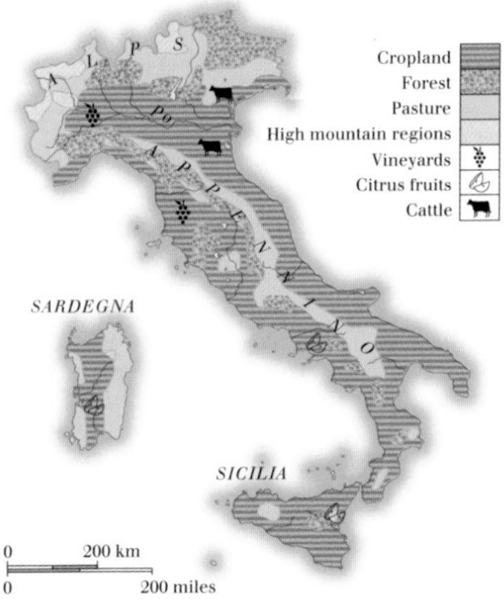
Cropland
Forest
Pasture
High mountain regions
Vineyards
Citrus fruits
Cattle
SARDEGNA
SICILIA
0
200 km
0
200 miles

ENVIRONMENT

Sustainability rank: 84th

8% (6% partially protected)

8.1 tonnes per capita

ENVIRONMENTAL TREATIES

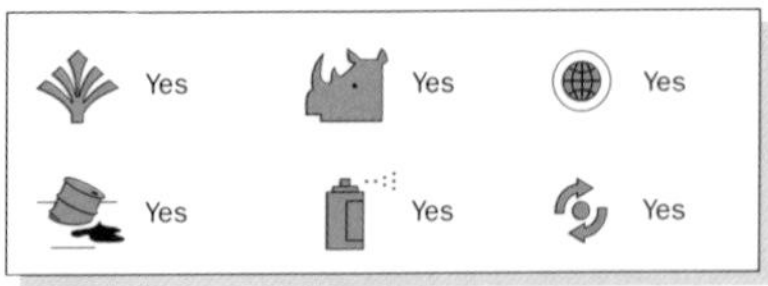
Yes
Yes
Yes
Yes
Yes
Yes

Italy has extensive environmental legislation, but has faced problems in enforcing directives. Wildlife successes include the return of the endangered lynx and brown bear, and growing numbers of wolves in the Appenines. The hunting of migrant birds, a popular sport in Italy, attracts international criticism. The use of drift nets, prone to catching dolphins and turtles as well as fish, has been made illegal under EU law. The right-wing government of the mid-1990s, returned to office in 2001, is suspicious of energy taxes and laws on waste recycling, not wanting to restrict business competitiveness. Green Party members in government in the Olive Tree alliance from 1996 to 2001 had insisted on a more active environmental stance.

Pollution in cities such as Naples and Rome is a major concern. Bans on traffic for up to seven hours during windless days are not uncommon. Acid rain has damaged forests and historic buildings.

MEDIA

TV ownership high

Daily newspaper circulation 104 per 1000 people

PUBLISHING AND BROADCAST MEDIA

There are 78 daily newspapers. The leading nationals are *Corriere della Serra* and *La Repubblica*

1 publicly owned service, 16 independent national networks, over 900 independent stations

1 publicly owned service, over 2100 independent stations

Mediaset, owned by Prime Minister Silvio Berlusconi, is the main commercial operator. The state-operated Rai TV channels were traditionally highly politicized; until reforms in the 1990s, Rai Uno was apportioned to the Christian Democrats, Rai Due to the Socialists, and Rai Tre to the Communists. Now they cover general programming, entertainment, and education respectively. News Corporation bought out Vivendi in 2002 to gain a near-monopoly of pay-TV. All the media reflect the Italian love of sport, especially soccer: *La Gazzetta dello Sport* has one of the largest circulations of the national dailies. The press is highly regionalized.

CRIME

No death penalty

55,136 prisoners

Down 11% in 1999–2001

CRIME RATES

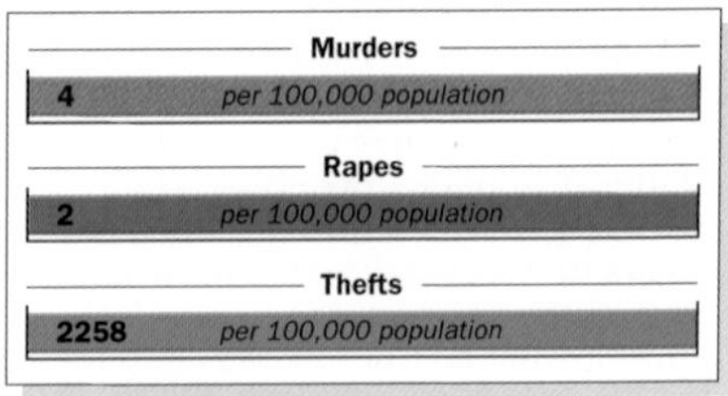
Murders
4 per 100,000 population
Rapes
2 per 100,000 population
Thefts
2258 per 100,000 population

Over 25% of prisoners are foreigners, many held for narcotics offenses. There is a huge backlog of cases. Organized crime has been weakened by the anticorruption drive and a cleaned-up bureaucracy. In particular, the Sicilian Mafia, the Cosa Nostra, was hit hard by arrests and trials in which former members provided key evidence. However, the Cosa Nostra and its counterparts in Naples and Calabria – Camorra and 'ndrangheta – still control wholesale agricultural markets and much of the narcotics trade, bleed businesses of protection money, and manipulate public works contracts.

EDUCATION

School leaving age: 16

99%

1.81m students

THE EDUCATION SYSTEM

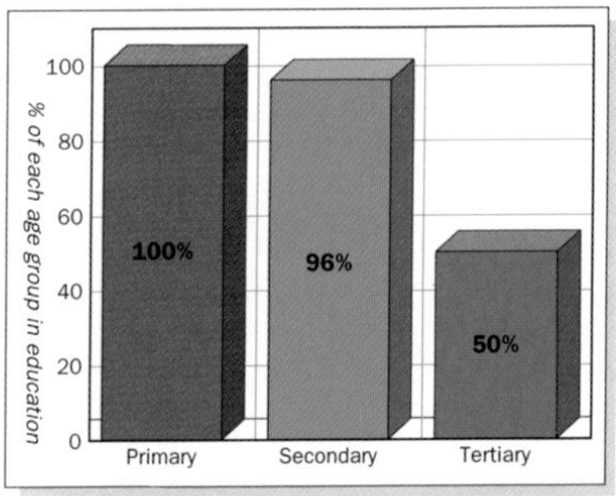
100
80
60
40
20
0
% of each age group in education
100%
96%
50%
Primary
Secondary
Tertiary

Schooling is state-run, apart from a few religious and elite private institutions. The pupil–teacher ratio in Italian schools is one of the best in Europe. In 1993, the minimum school leaving age was raised from 14 to 16 years, bringing Italy into line with most of Europe. An educational credit system aims to tackle shortcomings in information technology training.

Higher education is restricted to pupils who pass the *esamo di Stato*. There are almost 800 university-level institutions, including the University of Bologna – the oldest university in Europe, established in 1088. The government hopes to increase spending on research, which, at little more than 1% of GNP in recent years, has been less than half the European average.

REGIONALISM AND NORTHERN SEPARATISM

THE DIVISION OF Italy into the more dynamic and prosperous north and the impoverished south, or Mezzogiorno, is a source of continuing tension. It helps to explain why, in a country as homogeneous as Italy in terms of ethnicity, language, and religion, there is a strong demand for more devolution of power to regional level. In the mid-1990s, a political party calling for the breakup of the country was able to gain a significant following. The Northern League (LN), created in 1991 and built around the earlier Lombard League, won over 10% of the vote in the 1996 elections. Though it has lost momentum since then, regional feeling remained sufficient for the LN to be drafted into the right-wing government formed after the 2001 elections, and for a referendum to secure the first step toward limited devolution.

Run-down housing in the poor, rural region of Calabria in southern Italy.

REGIONS WITH MORE DYNAMIC ECONOMIES

GDP per capita is almost three times higher in the richest northern areas, such as Bologna in Emilia-Romagna and Milan in Lombardy, than in southern areas such as Reggio di Calabria. After the 1996 recession, the north achieved more rapid growth, creating more new jobs faster. Lombardy and Piedmont attract the lion's share of inward investment. Turin, the capital of Piedmont and home of Fiat, is boosting its industrial image by completing high-speed rail links and staging the Winter Olympics in 2006. Some southern areas try to attract investment by emphasizing that labor is cheaper there, and getting unions to accept lower wages locally in so-called "territorial pacts," but poor infrastructure remains a major obstacle. A road–rail bridge project linking Sicily to the Italian mainland was only revived in 2002.

PADANIA

The LN championed the idea of creating a "Republic of Padania" to secede from the rest of Italy (Rome,

Aosta
Trento
Milano
Venezia
Trieste
Torino
Genova
Bologna
Firenze
Ancona
PADANIA
Perugia

its surrounding Lazio region, and the south). The LN leader Umberto Bossi declared Padania's "independence" in a ceremony in 1996 after a pilgrimage the length of the river Po, the symbolic artery of "Padania," from Piedmont in northwest Italy to the Adriatic south of Venice. The LN set up a self-styled government and parliament, a national guard, and a flag, while allowing a year to "negotiate" terms of separation with the Italian government. Mantua was described as the Padanian capital, but it remained unclear precisely how far its intended territory extended. Usually understood to refer to the nine most northerly regions, as far south as Florence and the rest of Tuscany, it was sometimes defined by the LN as also including the Umbria and Marche regions.

The Italian government refused to take the Padania idea seriously, dismissing it as a publicity stunt. LN leaders were subsequently persuaded, by a series of bad local election results including losing the mayorships of Mantua and Milan, that the time was not right to press forward with their project. Some of its impetus – the desire of northern businesses to be at the center of European Union integration, not held back by the south – also disappeared when Italy qualified to join the euro, in 1999. The euro replaced the lira in 2002.

Shopping center in Milan, Italy's center of fashion and commerce.

HEALTH

Welfare state health benefits

1 per 176 people

Cancers, heart, cerebrovascular, and respiratory diseases

Italy's health care system was rated by WHO in 2000 as the second most efficient in the world.

The state-run national health system was created in 1978, with authority based in the regions, and standards of care vary across the country. The system was further decentralized in 1999 in an effort to iron out irregularities. Charges are levied for some dental and prescription costs; patients also have to pay a daily hospital charge and a yearly health fee. AIDS patients are exempt.

SPENDING

GDP/cap. increase

CONSUMPTION AND SPENDING

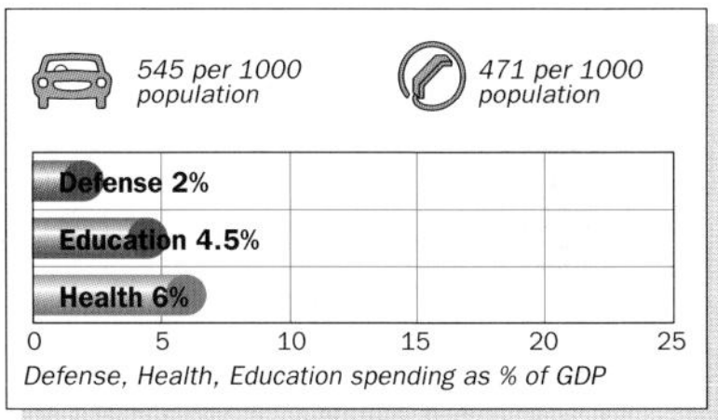
545 per 1000 population
471 per 1000 population
Defense 2%
Education 4.5%
Health 6%
0
5
10
15
20
25
Defense, Health, Education spending as % of GDP

Italians, particularly in the north, are today among the world's wealthiest people in terms of disposable income. This is a result not only of economic growth, but also of the structure of Italian society.

Many Italians, particularly in the south, have more than one job. The extended families in which most people still live often have access to more than one income. Few people have mortgages, and tax avoidance levels are high.

The main exceptions are in parts of the south. Though inward investment has been attracted to the Bari area, many people still live in poverty in other places, such as Naples and the Calabria region, where investment has been lowest, unemployment is highest, and even tourism is underdeveloped.

WORLD RANKING

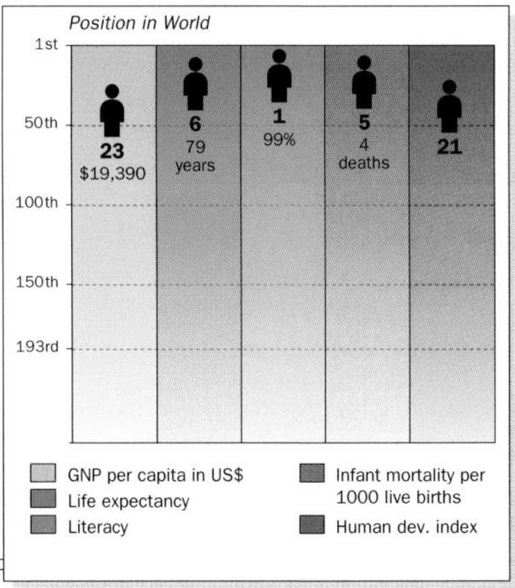
Position in World
1st
50th
100th
150th
193rd
23
$19,390
6
79 years
1
99%
5
4 deaths
21
GNP per capita in US$
Life expectancy
Literacy
Infant mortality per 1000 live births
Human dev. index

I

Ivory Coast

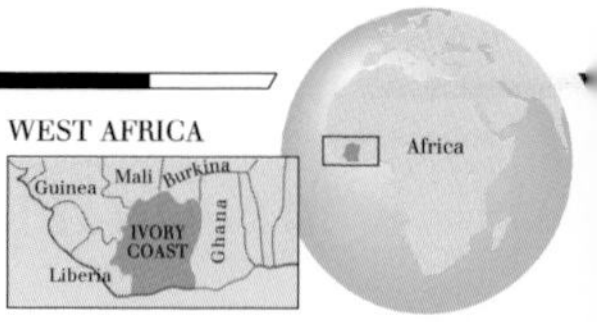
WEST AFRICA
Guinea
Mali
Burkina
IVORY COAST
Ghana
Liberia
Africa

Official Name: Republic of Côte d'Ivoire **Capital:** Yamoussoukro
Population: 16.7 million **Currency:** CFA franc **Official Language:** French

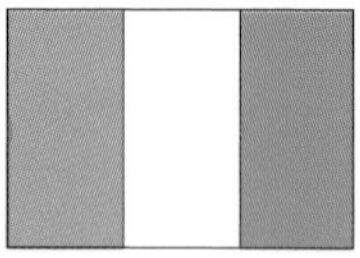

1960 | 1960 | Aug 7 | CI | 0 | +225 | .ci

One of the larger countries on the shores of west Africa, Ivory Coast – officially Côte d'Ivoire – is the world's biggest cocoa producer. Its reputation as an island of stability in a continent of chaos was largely due to the pro-Western and long-term president Félix Houphouët-Boigny (1960–1993). This image was shattered in 1999 by a military coup which was in turn followed by a popular uprising in 2000 and outright civil conflict in 2002–2003.

Climate

Tropical wet and dry

WEATHER CHART FOR YAMOUSSOUKRO

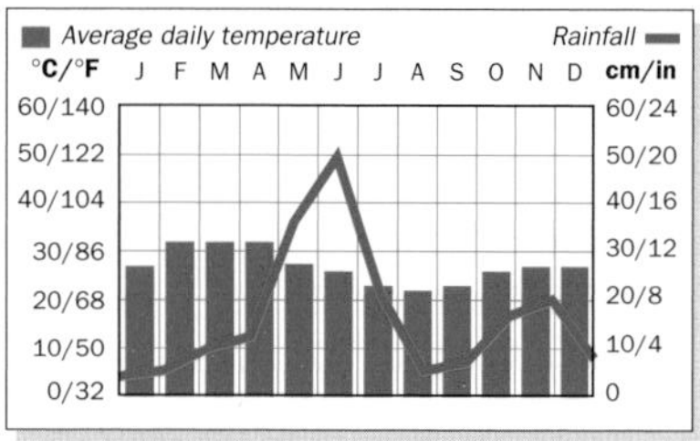
Average daily temperature
Rainfall
°C/°F
J F M A M J J A S O N D
cm/in
60/140
50/122
40/104
30/86
20/68
10/50
0/32
60/24
50/20
40/16
30/12
20/8
10/4
0

The south's four seasons – two rainy and two dry – merge in the north into a single wet season with lower rainfall.

Transportation

Drive on right

Abidjan (Port-Bouët) 819,938 passengers

32 ships 8600 grt

THE TRANSPORTATION NETWORK

4889 km (3038 miles)

None

639 km (397 miles)

980 km (609 miles)

The relatively good transportation system focuses on Abidjan, the premier port of francophone west Africa.

Tourism

Visitors : Population 1:55

301,000 visitors

Up 10% in 1998

MAIN TOURIST ARRIVALS

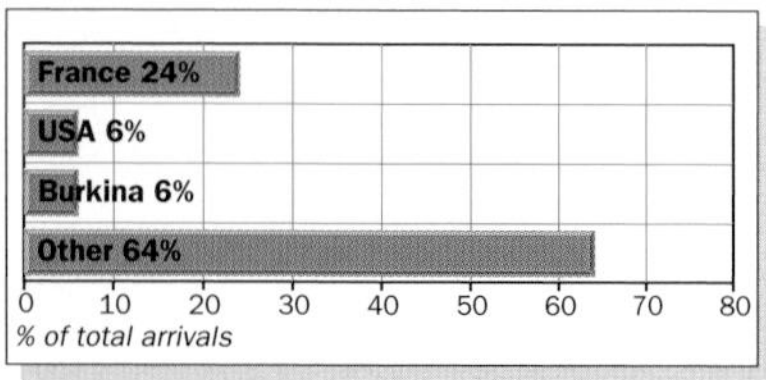
France 24%
USA 6%
Burkina 6%
Other 64%
0 10 20 30 40 50 60 70 80
% of total arrivals

Ambitious plans for an "African Riviera" east of Abidjan and the opening of a hotel by the French Club Méditerranée have been undermined by recent instability. The giant Roman Catholic basilica at Yamoussoukro is an attraction.

People

Pop. density medium

Akan, French, Kru, Voltaic

53/km² (136/mi²)

THE URBAN/RURAL POPULATION SPLIT

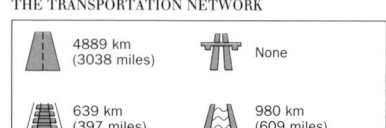

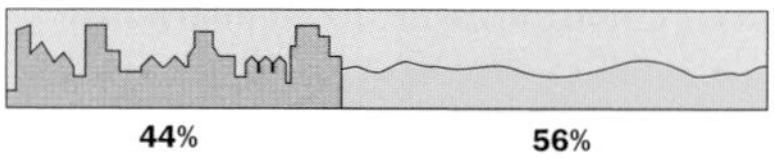
44%
56%

RELIGIOUS PERSUASION

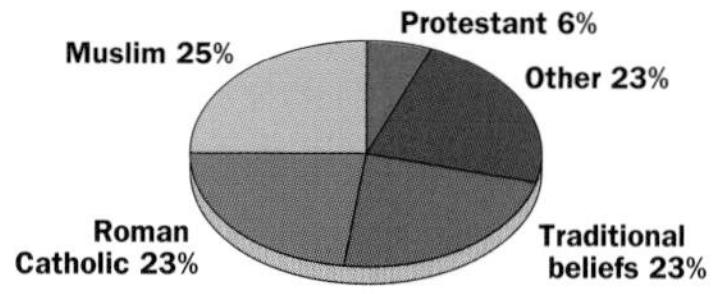
Protestant 6%
Muslim 25%
Other 23%
Roman Catholic 23%
Traditional beliefs 23%

There are more than 60 tribes in Ivory Coast. Larger groups among them can be recognized on the basis of cultural identity, the key ones being the Baoulé in the center, the Agri in the east, the Senufo in the north, the Dioula in the northwest and west, the Bété in the center-west, and the Dan-Yacouba in the west.

Migrants from other west African countries account for up to 40% of the population. Their presence has stirred tensions in recent years leading to a growth in "identity politics" and xenophobic popularism. In addition, Christians in the south harbor resentment against non-Ivorian Muslims in the north.

Politics

Multiparty elections

2000/2005

President Laurent Gbagbo

AT THE LAST ELECTION

National Assembly 225 seats

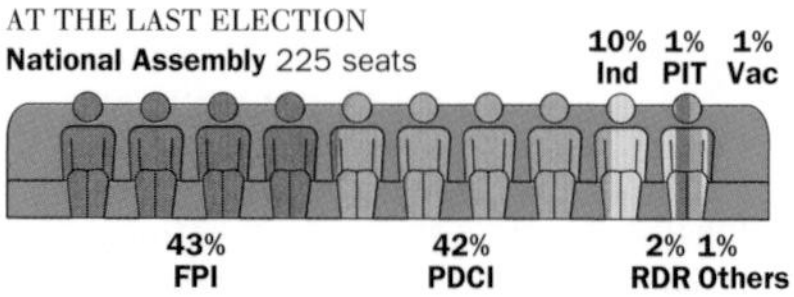
10% Ind
1% PIT
1% Vac
43% FPI
42% PDCI
2% RDR
1% Others

FPI = Ivorian Popular Front **PDCI** = Democratic Party of Ivory Coast **Ind** = Independents **RDR** = Rally of the Republicans **PIT** = Ivorian Labor Party **Vac** = Vacant

Since the death of President Houphouët-Boigny in 1993, Ivorian politics has become increasingly polarized. Attempts by his successor, Henri Konan Bédié, to ban the Muslim northerner, and RDR leader, Alassane Ouattara from the 1999 elections prompted a coup by Gen. Robert Guei, who in turn barred Ouattara from the 2000 election. Guei's fraudulent attempt to claim victory in the vote led to an uprising which carried the poll's actual victor, Laurent Gbagbo of the socialist FPI, to power and was followed by violent political clashes. Again Ouattara became the focus of the opposition. An uprising in September 2002 by disgruntled soldiers quickly escalated into civil war, with Guei a prominent early casualty. The conflict tapped the country's latent ethnic tensions, with support divided between north and south, immigrants and Ivorians. As part of peace initiatives a power-sharing government was formed in 2003.

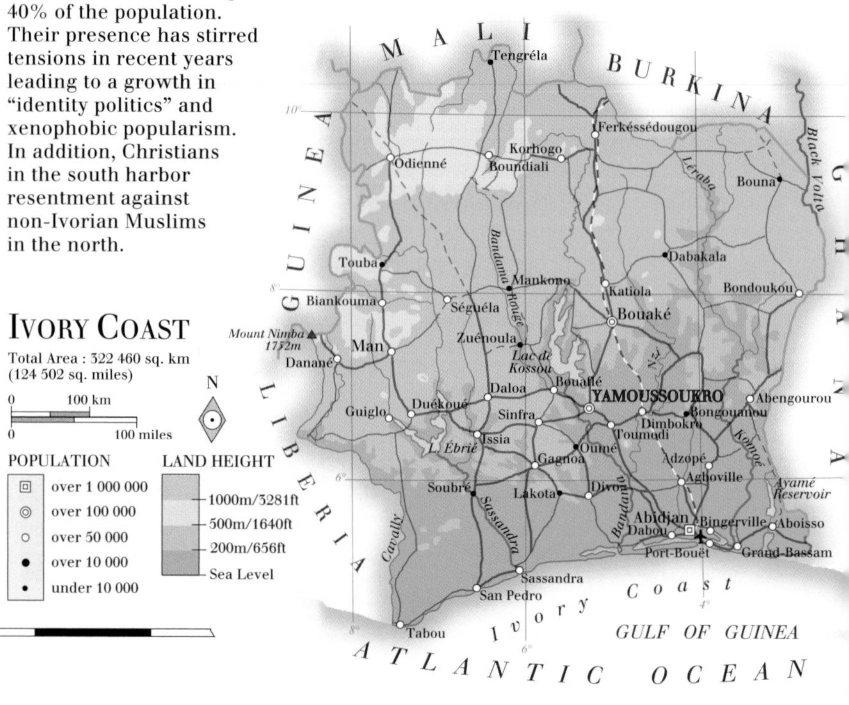
IVORY COAST
Total Area : 322 460 sq. km (124 502 sq. miles)
0 100 km
0 100 miles
N
POPULATION
over 1 000 000
over 100 000
over 50 000
over 10 000
under 10 000
LAND HEIGHT
1000m/3281ft
500m/1640ft
200m/656ft
Sea Level
MALI
BURKINA
GUINEA
LIBERIA
GHANA
Tengréla
Ferkéssédougou
Odienné
Korhogo
Boundiali
Bouna
Black Volta
Dabakala
Touba
Mankono
Katiola
Bondoukou
Biankouma
Séguéla
Bouaké
Mount Nimba 1752m
Man
Danané
Zuénoula
Lac de Kossou
Bouaflé
Daloa
YAMOUSSOUKRO
Abengourou
Guiglo
Duékoué
Sinfra
Dimbokro
Bongouanou
Toumodi
Issia
Oumé
Gagnoa
Adzopé
Agboville
Soubré
Lakota
Divo
Ayamé Reservoir
Abidjan
Bingerville
Aboisso
Dabou
Port-Bouët
Grand-Bassam
Sassandra
San Pedro
Tabou
Ivory Coast
GULF OF GUINEA
ATLANTIC OCEAN
Bandama
Sassandra
Cavally
Komoé
Nzi
Lérraba
Bandama Rouge
L. Ébrié

WORLD AFFAIRS

Joined UN in 1960

ECOWAS FZ G24 OIC AU

Good relations with donors are vital and will be key to hopes of stability. Regional violence has fueled tensions in Ivory Coast, enabling the movement of arms and troops across porous borders. ECOWAS and French troops mediated in the recent civil war. Ivory Coast has influence in international cocoa and coffee organizations.

AID

Recipient

$187m (receipts)

Down 47% in 2001

France is by far the largest source of bilateral aid. Structural adjustment loans from the World Bank were particularly important in easing the acute burden of a debt accumulated on the strength of overinflated oil hopes.

DEFENSE

Compulsory military service

$80m

Down 2% in 2001

France trains officers for the Ivorian army and is the main supplier of equipment, though at the start of the 2002–2003 conflict the government purchased arms and equipment from Angola.

ECONOMICS

Inflation 8.4% p.a. (1990–2001)

$10.3bn

571.2 CFA francs (664.2)

SCORE CARD

- ❑ WORLD GNP RANKING........................85th
- ❑ GNP PER CAPITA $630
- ❑ BALANCE OF PAYMENTS......................–$58m
- ❑ INFLATION 4.3%
- ❑ UNEMPLOYMENT.................................13%

STRENGTHS

Well-developed agriculture: major cocoa and coffee producer. Relatively good infrastructure. Expanding oil and gas industries. Successful debt rescheduling.

WEAKNESSES

Instability. Failure to invest adequately in education and professional training. Overdependence on cocoa and coffee. Slave labor on plantations.

EXPORTS

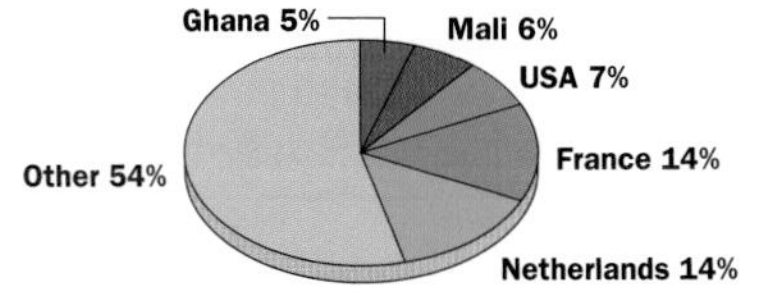

Ghana 5%
Mali 6%
USA 7%
France 14%
Netherlands 14%
Other 54%

IMPORTS

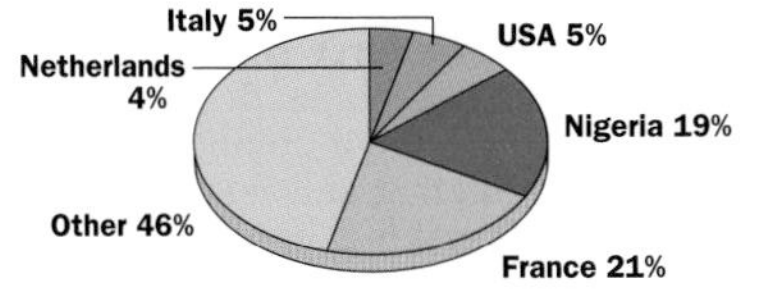

Italy 5%
USA 5%
Netherlands 4%
Nigeria 19%
France 21%
Other 46%

RESOURCES

Electric power 1.2m kW

81,519 tonnes

29,754 b/d (reserves 98m barrels)

1.52m sheep, 1.48m cattle, 32.6m chickens

Oil, diamonds, cobalt, gold, iron, manganese, nickel

There are significant offshore oil and gas reserves. Most fuel is currently imported. Forest resources are badly depleted.

ENVIRONMENT

Sustainability rank: 108th

6% (0.3% partially protected)

0.8 tonnes per capita

Deforestation remains a problem in the Ivory Coast, despite a 1995 government ban on unprocessed timber exports.

MEDIA

TV ownership medium

Daily newspaper circulation 16 per 1000 people

PUBLISHING AND BROADCAST MEDIA

There are 16 daily newspapers, including *Fraternité Matin* and *Ivoir Soir*, both published by the government

2 services: 1 state-owned, 1 independent

8 services: 1 state-owned, 7 independent

Though heavy censorship in Ivory Coast has eased since the early 1990s, there are still cases of official harassment of the media.

EDUCATION

School leaving age: 15

50%

96,681 students

Baccalauréat pass rates are low. Cuts in spending have triggered student protests. Primary education fees ended in 2001.

CRIME

No death penalty

10,355 prisoners

Up sharply in 1997–2002

Foreign immigrants are often blamed for the widespread crime in Abidjan. Human rights abuses are common.

***The basilica, Yamoussoukro.** Built in the new capital, Houphouët-Boigny's birthplace, it is modeled on St. Peter's, Rome.*

CHRONOLOGY

One of the great trading emporia of west Africa, the Ivory Coast was made a French colony in 1893. By 1918, the French had defeated the Malinke empire and the forest peoples of the interior.

- ❑ **1903–1935** Plantations developed.
- ❑ **1960** Independence. Houphouët-Boigny president.
- ❑ **1990** First contested polls: Houphouët-Boigny and PDCI win.
- ❑ **1993** Houphouët-Boigny dies.
- ❑ **1998** Power of president increased, Ouattara apparently barred from standing in presidential elections.
- ❑ **1999** Military coup by Gen. Guei.
- ❑ **2000** Guei ousted after false election victory claim. Gbagbo president.
- ❑ **2002–2003** Military uprising turns into major rebellion. Guei killed.

I

HEALTH

No welfare state health benefits

1 per 11,111 people

Malaria, communicable diseases, neonatal deaths

The incidence of HIV/AIDS is high, affecting around 10% of adults. In 2001 drugs companies agreed to cut the prices of treatments by 80–90%.

SPENDING

GDP/cap. increase

CONSUMPTION AND SPENDING

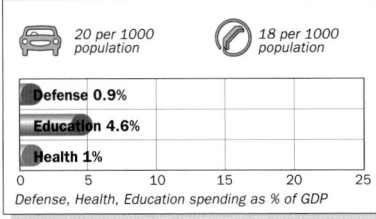

20 per 1000 population

18 per 1000 population

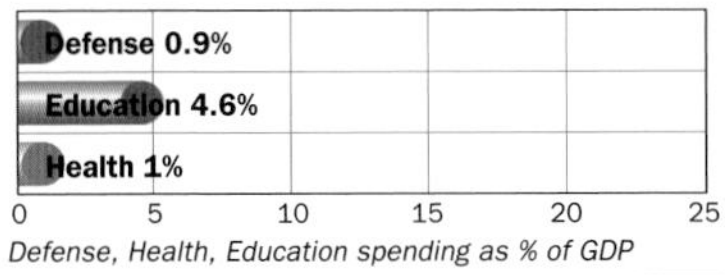

Defense 0.9%
Education 4.6%
Health 1%
0
5
10
15
20
25
Defense, Health, Education spending as % of GDP

A large bourgeoisie emerged after independence. Recent economic and security problems have eroded wealth generated through trade.

WORLD RANKING

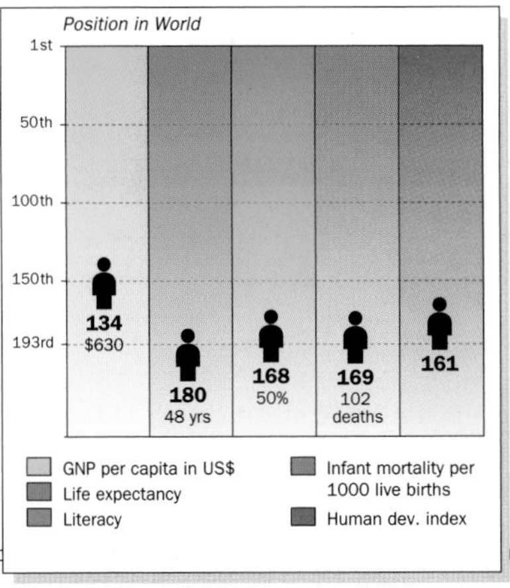

Position in World
1st
50th
100th
150th
193rd
134
$630
180
48 yrs
168
50%
169
102 deaths
161
GNP per capita in US$
Life expectancy
Literacy
Infant mortality per 1000 live births
Human dev. index

JAMAICA

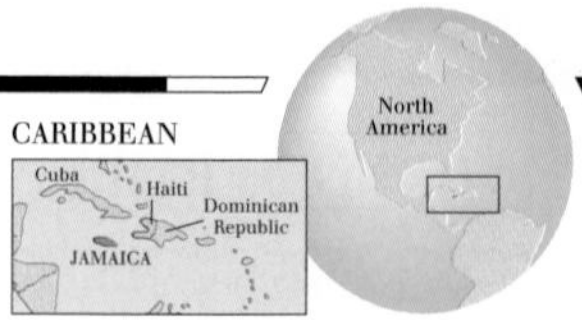
North America
CARIBBEAN
Cuba
Haiti
Dominican Republic
JAMAICA

OFFICIAL NAME: Jamaica **CAPITAL:** Kingston
POPULATION: 2.6 million **CURRENCY:** Jamaican dollar **OFFICIAL LANGUAGE:** English

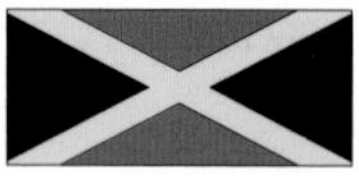

1962 | 1962 | Aug 5 | JA | -5 | +1876 | .jm

FIRST COLONIZED BY the Spanish and then, from 1655, by the English, Jamaica is located in the Caribbean, 145 km (90 miles) south of Cuba. It was the first of the Caribbean island countries to become independent in the postwar years, and remains an active force in Caribbean politics. Jamaica is also influential on the world music scene: reggae, ska, and ragga (or dancehall) developed in the tough conditions of Kingston's poor districts.

CLIMATE

Tropical oceanic

WEATHER CHART FOR KINGSTON

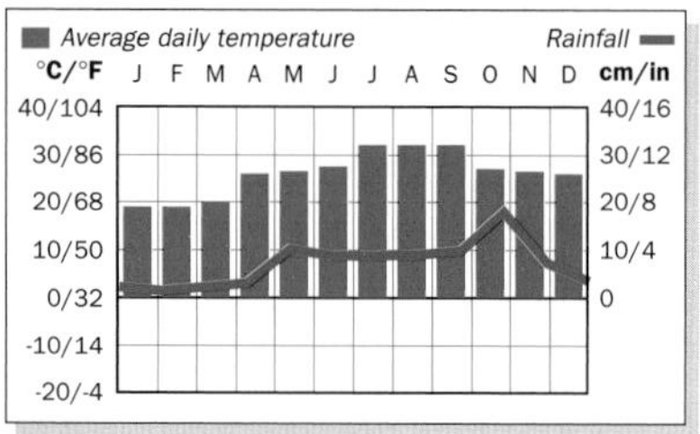
Average daily temperature
Rainfall
°C/°F J F M A M J J A S O N D cm/in
40/104 30/86 20/68 10/50 0/32 -10/14 -20/-4
40/16 30/12 20/8 10/4 0

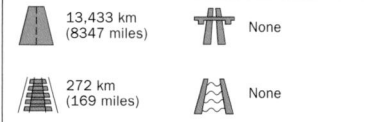

Tropical and humid conditions at sea level give way to temperate weather in mountain areas. Rainfall is seasonal, with marked regional variations.

TRANSPORTATION

Drive on left

Donald Sangster International, Montego Bay
3.12m passengers

7 ships
3100 grt

THE TRANSPORTATION NETWORK

13,433 km (8347 miles)	None
272 km (169 miles)	None

Kingston's harbor has been expanded and its airport improved. The road network is extensive. Private buses provide public transportation.

TOURISM

Visitors : Population 1:2.1

1.27m visitors

Down 1% in 2002

MAIN TOURIST ARRIVALS

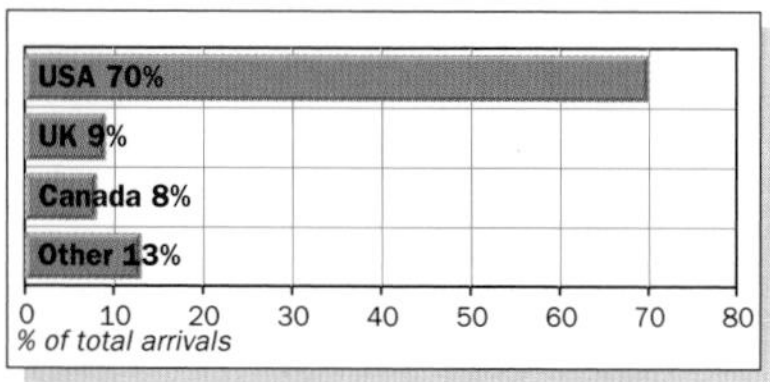
USA 70%
UK 9%
Canada 8%
Other 13%
0 10 20 30 40 50 60 70 80
% of total arrivals

Tourism is the major earner of foreign exchange. Most tourists stay in large, enclosed beach resorts. Recent bouts of social unrest have damaged the sector.

PEOPLE

Pop. density high

English Creole, English

240/km² (622/mi²)

THE URBAN/RURAL POPULATION SPLIT

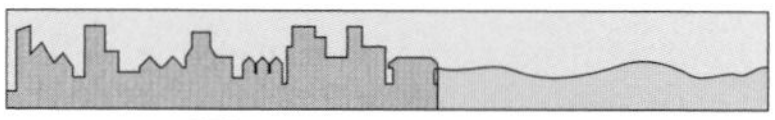
57%
43%

RELIGIOUS PERSUASION

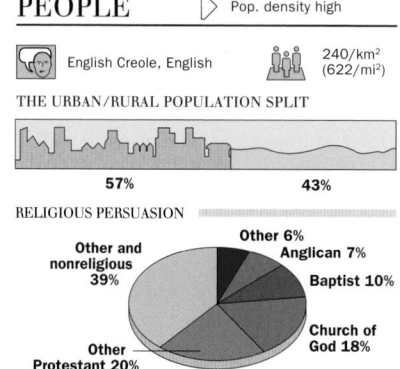

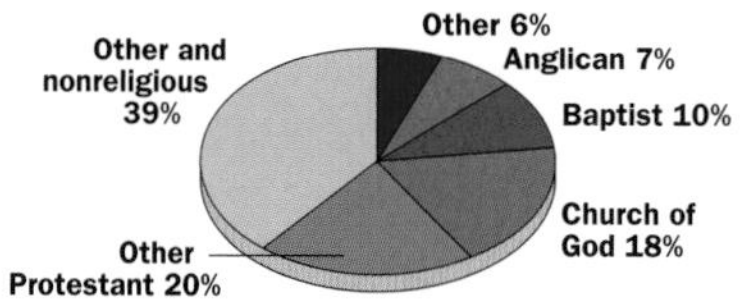
Other and nonreligious 39%
Other 6%
Anglican 7%
Baptist 10%
Church of God 18%
Other Protestant 20%

Most Jamaicans are the descendants of Africans brought to the island between the 16th and 19th centuries, but there are small minorities of Europeans, Indians, Chinese, and Arabs.

Most social tension is the result of the marked disparities in wealth. The Caribbean women's rights movement originated in Jamaica, and today many Jamaican women hold senior positions in economic and political life.

Life in the ghettos of Kingston is often violent and based largely on gun law; the capital has one of the highest murder rates in the world.

Jamaican music styles, including ska, ragga, and reggae, have become popular across the world. Reggae is particularly connected to Jamaica's Rastafarians, followers of the former Ethiopian emperor Haile Selassie.

***Bauxite mine and terminal,** Runaway Bay. Bauxite – from which aluminum is extracted – is the main source of foreign income.*

POLITICS

Multiparty elections

L. House 2002/2007
U. House 2002/2007

H.M. Queen Elizabeth II

AT THE LAST ELECTION

House of Representatives 60 seats

57% PNP
43% JLP

PNP = People's National Party **JLP** = Jamaica Labour Party

Senate 21 seats

The members of the Senate are appointed. Thirteen members are chosen by the prime minister and eight by the leader of the opposition

The country's political complexion changed markedly in the late 1980s, as the ideologies of the once socialist PNP and the conservative JLP converged toward a moderate free-market economic approach.

Violent disturbances in 1998 and 1999 were in response to the PNP government's attempts to deal with economic recession and a large fiscal deficit. The unrest, which led to several deaths, gave new life to the internally troubled JLP, as it then identified itself with opposition to fuel tax increases. It increased its representation in the 2002 election, but failed to unseat the PNP, which entered a historic fourth consecutive term in office.

WORLD AFFAIRS

Joined UN in 1962

ACS | Caricom | Geplac | Comm | OAS

The main issue is Jamaica's position as a major transshipment point for narcotics heading for the US and the UK.

AID

Recipient

US$54m (receipts)

Up 440% in 2001

Most aid comes from the EU, the US, and Canada. It includes both project loans and balance-of-payments support.

DEFENSE

No compulsory military service

US$40m

Down 5% in 2001

Jamaica's defense force is trained with the assistance of Canada, the UK, and the US. Its main role is combating narcotics smuggling and assisting the police in breaking up unrest, as in 1999 and 2001.

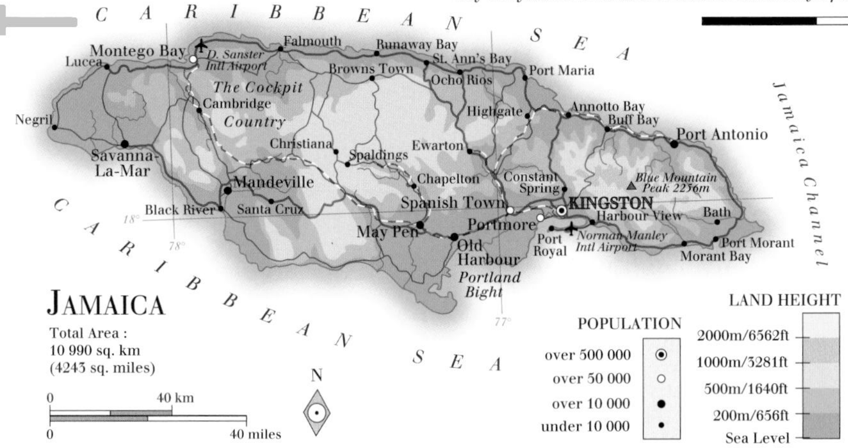
CARIBBEAN SEA
Montego Bay
Lucea
D. Sanster Intl Airport
Falmouth
Runaway Bay
St. Ann's Bay
Port Maria
Browns Town
Ocho Rios
The Cockpit Country
Cambridge
Negril
Highgate
Annotto Bay
Buff Bay
Port Antonio
Jamaica Channel
Christiana
Ewarton
Spaldings
Savanna-La-Mar
Mandeville
Chapelton
Constant Spring
Blue Mountain Peak 2256m
Black River
Santa Cruz
Spanish Town
KINGSTON
Harbour View
Bath
May Pen
Portmore
Port Royal
Norman Manley Intl Airport
Port Morant
Morant Bay
Old Harbour
Portland Bight
JAMAICA
Total Area :
10 990 sq. km
(4243 sq. miles)
0 40 km
0 40 miles
N
POPULATION
over 500 000
over 50 000
over 10 000
under 10 000
LAND HEIGHT
2000m/6562ft
1000m/3281ft
500m/1640ft
200m/656ft
Sea Level

CHRONOLOGY

Spain occupied the island in 1510, wiping out the indigenous Arawak population. Britain seized it in 1655.

- **1958–1961** West Indies Federation.
- **1962** Independence under JLP.
- **1972** PNP elected. Reforms fail; street violence begins.
- **1980** Unpopular IMF austerity measures lead to JLP election win.
- **1989–2002** PNP wins elections and austerity continues.
- **1999** Violent protests over fuel tax increases.

ECONOMICS

Inflation 22% p.a. (1990–2001)

US$7.26bn

58.7 Jamaican dollars (48.25)

SCORE CARD

World GNP Ranking	100th
GNP per Capita	US$2800
Balance of Payments	–US$788m
Inflation	7%
Unemployment	16%

Strengths

Relatively diversified economy. Tourism. Mining and refining of bauxite for aluminum. Agriculture, including sugar, bananas, rum, and coffee. Light manufacturing.

Weaknesses

Banking and insurance sectors. Climbing debt burden, now around 150% of GDP, dominates budget. Financing of sugar production. Stagnant growth. High unemployment.

EXPORTS

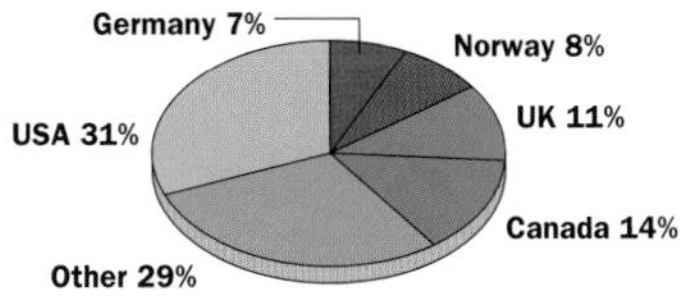
Germany 7%
Norway 8%
UK 11%
USA 31%
Canada 14%
Other 29%

IMPORTS

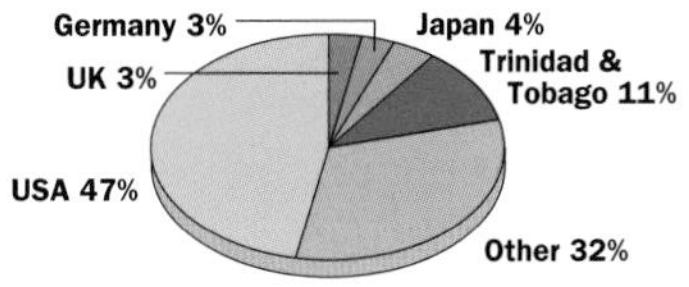
Germany 3%
Japan 4%
UK 3%
Trinidad & Tobago 11%
USA 47%
Other 32%

RESOURCES

Electric power 1.3m kW

10,188 tonnes

Not an oil producer; refines 11,000 b/d

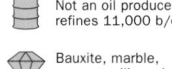

440,000 goats, 400,000 cattle, 11m chickens

Bauxite, marble, gypsum, silica, clay

Jamaica is the world's fourth-largest producer of bauxite. Sugar and bananas are major exports.

ENVIRONMENT

Sustainability rank: 122nd

9% partially protected

4 tonnes per capita

Acidic dust from bauxite processing is a major problem, as is urban pollution in Kingston and its bay. Broad-leaved tropical forests have largely disappeared.

MEDIA

TV ownership medium

Daily newspaper circulation 75 per 1000 people

PUBLISHING AND BROADCAST MEDIA

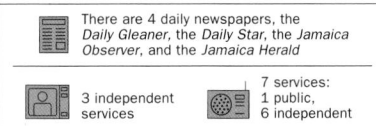

There are 4 daily newspapers, the *Daily Gleaner*, the *Daily Star*, the *Jamaica Observer*, and the *Jamaica Herald*

3 independent services

7 services: 1 public, 6 independent

The government has loosened its hold on broadcasting. The Jamaican press is one of the most influential in the Caribbean.

CRIME

Death penalty in use

4288 prisoners

Down 31% in 1999–2001

Armed crime is a major problem. Many murders are the result of armed robberies linked to narcotics gangs competing for territory. Much of the world crack trade is still controlled from Jamaica. Large areas of Kingston are ruled by violent gang leaders. The armed police are also frequently accused of the arbitrary shooting of suspects. An agreement to create a new Caribbean Court of Justice increased the likelihood of executions being carried out. The last hangings were in 1988, but death sentences are still being imposed.

EDUCATION

School leaving age: 12

87%

42,502 students

Education is based on the former British 11-plus selection system. Jamaica hosts the largest of the three campuses of the University of the West Indies.

HEALTH

Welfare state health benefits

1 per 714 people

Cerebrovascular and heart diseases, cancers, diabetes

The once-efficient state health service is now seriously underfunded. Hospitals generally have a shortage of drugs and there is only rudimentary medical equipment. The incidence of HIV is small but growing fast.

SPENDING

GDP/cap. increase

CONSUMPTION AND SPENDING

41 per 1000 population

197 per 1000 population

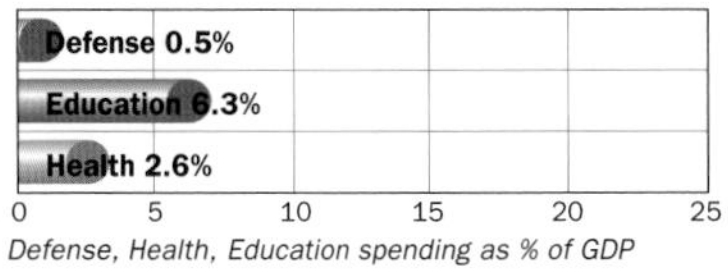
Defense 0.5%
Education 6.3%
Health 2.6%
0
5
10
15
20
25
Defense, Health, Education spending as % of GDP

Wealth disparities are very marked in Jamaica, though better education has seen an increase in the number of Afro-Jamaicans taking more lucrative, white-collar jobs. The poorest in Jamaica, mostly migrants from rural areas, live in the slums of Kingston.

WORLD RANKING

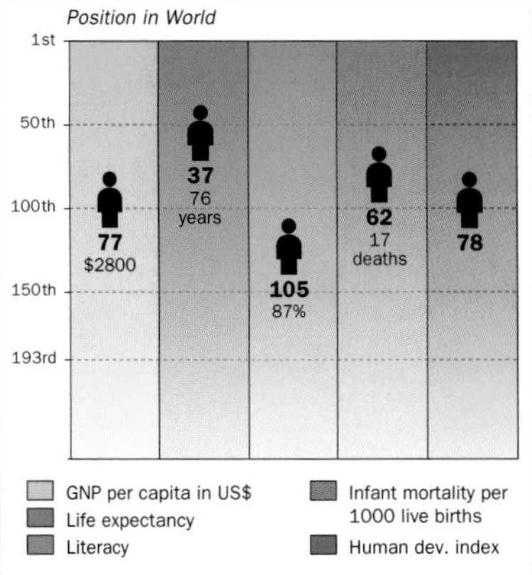
Position in World
1st
50th
100th
150th
193rd
77
$2800
37
76 years
105
87%
62
17 deaths
78
GNP per capita in US$
Life expectancy
Literacy
Infant mortality per 1000 live births
Human dev. index

J

JAPAN

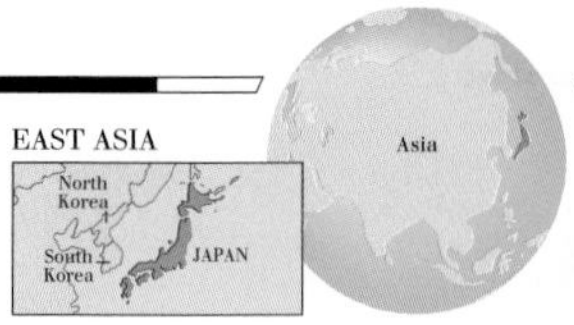
EAST ASIA
Asia
North Korea
South Korea
JAPAN

OFFICIAL NAME: Japan **CAPITAL:** Tokyo
POPULATION: 128 million **CURRENCY:** Yen **OFFICIAL LANGUAGE:** Japanese

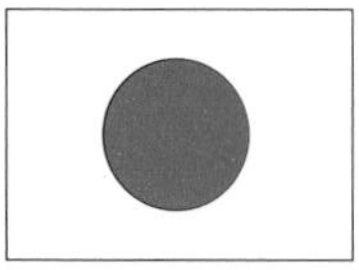

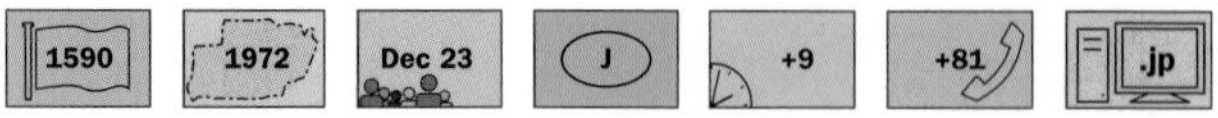
1590
1972
Dec 23
J
+9
+81
.jp

A CONSTITUTIONAL MONARCHY, with an emperor as ceremonial head of state, Japan is located off the east Asian coast in the north Pacific. It comprises four principal islands and more than 3000 smaller islands. Sovereignty over the most southerly and northerly islands is disputed with China and the Russian Federation respectively. The terrain is mostly mountainous, with fertile coastal plains; over two-thirds is woodland. The Pacific coast is vulnerable to tsunamis – tidal waves triggered by submarine earthquakes. Most cities are located by the sea; Tokyo, Kawasaki, and Yokohama together constitute the most populous and heavily industrialized area. Hokkaido is the most rural of the main islands. Japan's power in the global economy, with annual trade surpluses exceeding $100 billion and massive overseas investments, has been shaken since the early 1990s by a series of bad debt crises, bankruptcies in the financial sector, and two recessions.

The Shinkansen bullet train *is the second-fastest train in the world. Its speed is matched by its punctuality.*

CLIMATE

Continental/subtropical

WEATHER CHART FOR TOKYO

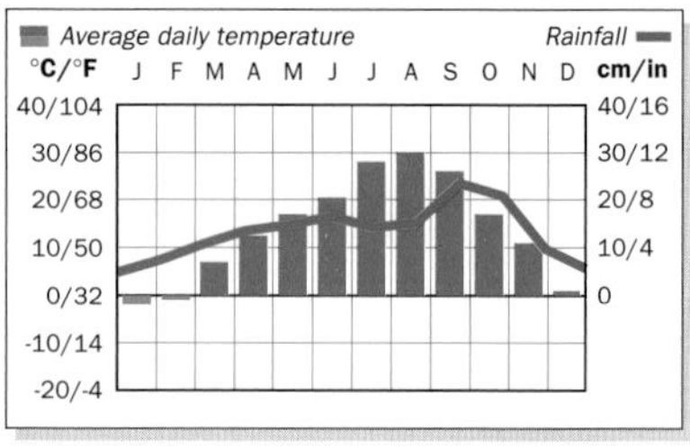
Average daily temperature
Rainfall
°C/°F
J F M A M J J A S O N D
cm/in
40/104
30/86
20/68
10/50
0/32
-10/14
-20/-4
40/16
30/12
20/8
10/4
0

The Sea of Japan has a moderating influence on the climate. Winters are less cold than on the Asian mainland, and rainfall is much higher. Spring is perhaps the most pleasant season, with warm, sunny days without the sultry, oppressive heat and rainfall of the summer. Recent freak storms and heavy floods have raised concern over the implications of global climate change.

TRANSPORTATION

Drive on left

Haneda, Tokyo 61.1m passengers

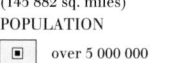

7924 ships 16.7m grt

THE TRANSPORTATION NETWORK

863,003 km (536,244 miles)

6617 km (4112 miles)

20,160 km (12,527 miles)

1770 km (1100 miles)

Railroads are the most important means of transportation in Japan. The Shinkansen, known in the West as the bullet train, is the second-fastest in the world. It is renowned as much for its reliability – timed to the second – as for its speed. The Tokyo–Sapporo air route is the busiest in the world.

JAPAN

Total Area : 377 835 sq. km (145 882 sq. miles)

POPULATION

- over 5 000 000
- over 1 000 000
- over 500 000
- over 100 000
- over 50 000
- over 10 000

LAND HEIGHT

- 1500m/4921ft
- 1000m/3281ft
- 500m/1640ft
- Sea Level

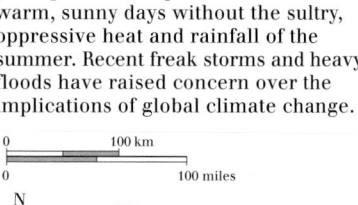

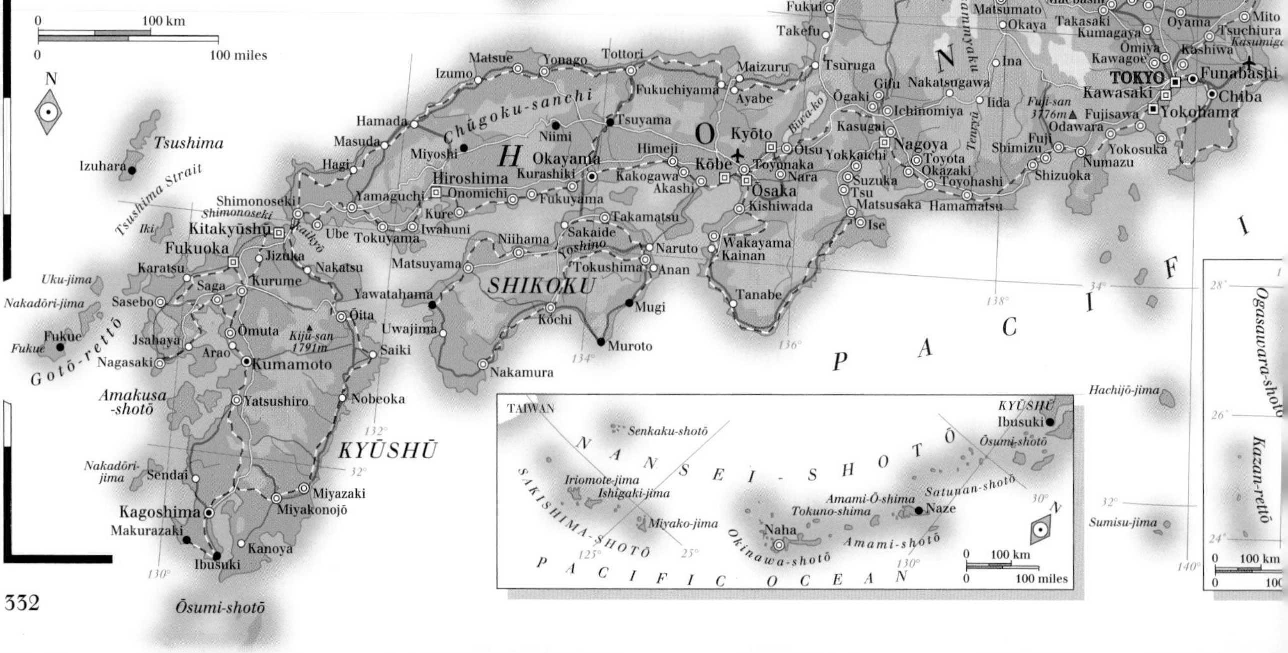
0 100 km
0 100 miles
N
SEA OF JAPAN
PACIFIC
Tsushima
Izuhara
Tsushima Strait
Oki
Dōzen
Sado
Okushiri-tō
Hakodate
Goshogawara
Hirosaki
Noshiro
Ogata
Akita
Sakata
Tsuruoka
Tendō
Yamagata
Yonegama
Shibata
Niigata
Fukushima
Aizu-Wakamatsu
Kōriya
Nagaoka
Inawashiro-ko
Sukagawa
Kashiwazaki
Nanao
Arai
Nagano
Takaoka
Kanazawa
Komatsu
Toyama
Uozu
Hida-sammyaku
Mikuni-sammyaku
Ueda
Maebashi
Kiryū
Ashikaga
Utsunomiya
Hitachi
Mito
Tsuchiura
Matsumoto
Okaya
Takasaki
Kumagaya
Oyama
Kashiwa
Omiya
Kawagoe
TOKYO
Funabashi
Kawasaki
Chiba
Yokohama
Fujisawa
Odawara
Yokosuka
Fukui
Takefu
Tsuruga
Ina
Nakatsugawa
Gifu
Iida
Fuji-san 3776m
Ichinomiya
Ōgaki
Kasugai
Nagoya
Toyota
Okazaki
Toyohashi
Shimizu
Fuji
Numazu
Shizuoka
Hamamatsu
Yokkaichi
Suzuka
Tsu
Matsusaka
Ise
Maizuru
Fukuchiyama
Ayabe
Biwa-ko
Kyōto
Ōtsu
Kōbe
Toyonaka
Nara
Ōsaka
Kishiwada
Himeji
Kakogawa
Akashi
Wakayama
Kainan
Tanabe
Matsue
Yonago
Tottori
Izumo
Hamada
Masuda
Chūgoku-sanchi
Tsuyama
Niimi
Miyoshi
Hagi
Okayama
Kurashiki
Hiroshima
Onomichi
Fukuyama
Kure
Iwakuni
Yamaguchi
Tokuyama
Ube
Shimonoseki
Kitakyūshū
Fukuoka
Iki
Jizuka
Karatsu
Kurume
Saga
Nakatsu
Uku-jima
Nakadōri-jima
Sasebo
Fukue
Gotō-rettō
Isahaya
Nagasaki
Ōmuta
Arao
Kumamoto
Kujū-san 1791m
Ōita
Uwajima
Saiki
Amakusa-shotō
Yatsushiro
Nobeoka
KYŪSHŪ
Nakadōri-jima
Sendai
Miyazaki
Miyakonojō
Kagoshima
Makurazaki
Kanoya
Ibusuki
Ōsumi-shotō
Takamatsu
Sakaide
Niihama
Matsuyama
Naruto
Tokushima
Anan
SHIKOKU
Yawatahama
Kōchi
Mugi
Muroto
Nakamura
TAIWAN
Senkaku-shotō
NANSEI-SHOTŌ
Iriomote-jima
Ishigaki-jima
SAKISHIMA-SHOTŌ
Miyako-jima
Okinawa-shotō
Naha
Tokuno-shima
Amami-Ō-shima
Amami-shotō
Naze
Satsunan-shotō
KYŪSHŪ
Ibusuki
Ōsumi-shotō
PACIFIC OCEAN
Hachijō-jima
Ogasawara-shotō
Kazan-rettō
Sumisu-jima

Iturup
Kuril'sk
PACIFIC OCEAN
0 50 km
0 50 miles
Kunashir
KKAIDO
KURILE IS
Kitami
Asahikawa
Kussharo-ko
Asahi-dake 2290m
HABOMAI IS
Kushiro
Obihiro
Horoshiri-dake 2051m
The Kurile islands are administered by the Russian Federation, but claimed by Japan
PACIFIC
OCEAN

TOURISM

Visitors : Population 1:24

5.24m visitors

Up 10% in 2002

MAIN TOURIST ARRIVALS

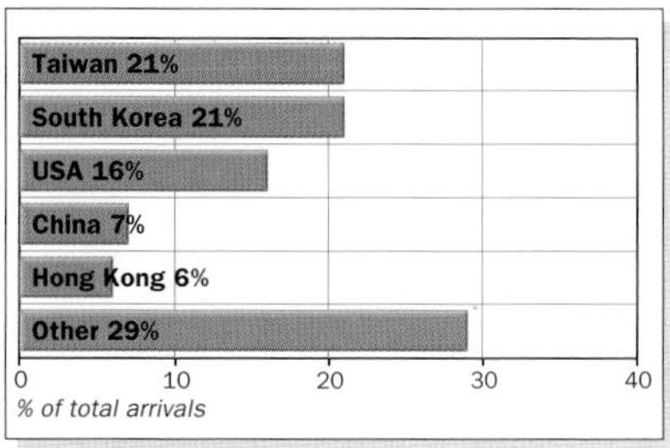
Taiwan 21%
South Korea 21%
USA 16%
China 7%
Hong Kong 6%
Other 29%
0
10
20
30
40
% of total arrivals

Japan is expensive for foreign tourists, despite reductions in the yen exchange rate. An increasing number of tourists are now coming from China. The ancient imperial capital, Kyoto, and the temples and gardens of Nara are popular tourist destinations. Other attractions include Mount Fuji and the extraordinary variety of energetic high-tech urban living in Tokyo and Osaka. Traditional agricultural life can be found in rural areas such as Tohoku in northern Honshu. Wilderness areas of Hokkaido attract mainly Japanese climbers and hikers.

High Street, Ginza District, Tokyo. *Japan's well-policed cities are among the safest in the world.*

PEOPLE

Pop. density high

Japanese, Korean, Chinese

339/km² (877/mi²)

THE URBAN/RURAL POPULATION SPLIT

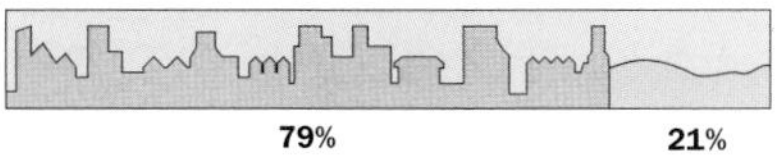
79%
21%

RELIGIOUS PERSUASION

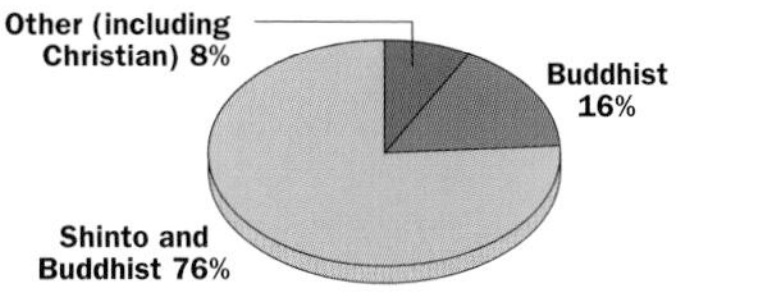
Other (including Christian) 8%
Buddhist 16%
Shinto and Buddhist 76%

ETHNIC MAKEUP

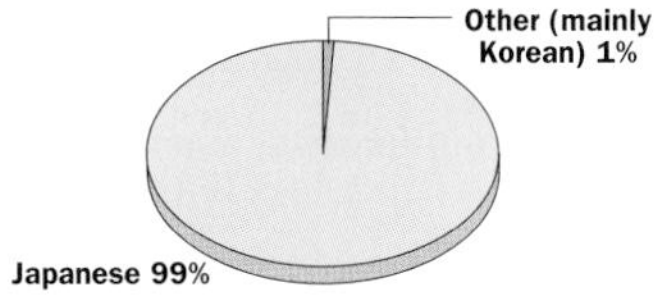
Other (mainly Korean) 1%
Japanese 99%

Japan is racially one of the most homogeneous societies in the world, its sense of order reflected in the tradition of the lifetime employer. Many Japanese men define themselves by the company they work for rather than their job. An employer's influence stretches into employees' social time, and even to encouraging and approving marriages.

Traditionally, women run the home and supervise the all-important education of their children. Many pursue careers until marriage, then continue to work part-time. However, some women are beginning to take on long-term careers, particularly in the medical and legal professions. Makiko Tanaka, the first-ever female foreign minister in 2001–2002, remains a very popular political figure.

Social form remains extremely important in Japanese society. Respect for elders and for social and business superiors is strongly ingrained. There is little tradition of generation rebellion, but the youth market is powerful and current fashions are geared toward teenagers. Many may still follow their parents' lifestyles, but established attitudes are under challenge. Working for the same company for life, and giving up evenings and weekends to entertain company clients, have become harder to justify amid economic turbulence.

POPULATION AGE BREAKDOWN

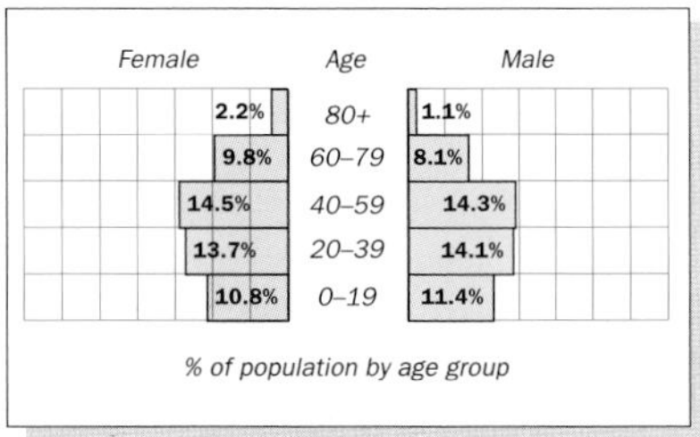
Female
Age
Male
2.2%
80+
1.1%
9.8%
60–79
8.1%
14.5%
40–59
14.3%
13.7%
20–39
14.1%
10.8%
0–19
11.4%
% of population by age group

CHRONOLOGY

Japan's tendency to limit its contacts with the outside world ended in 1853, when a US naval squadron forced trading concessions from the last of the Tokugawa shoguns.

- **1868** Meiji Restoration; overthrow of Tokugawa regime and restoration of imperial power.
- **1872** Modernization along Western lines. Japan's strong military tradition becomes state-directed.
- **1889** Constitution modeled on Bismarck's Germany adopted.
- **1894–1895** War with China, ending in Japanese victory.
- **1904–1905** War with Russia, ending in Japanese victory. Formosa (Taiwan) and Korea later annexed.
- **1914** Joins World War I on Allied side. Sees limited naval action.
- **1919** Versailles peace conference gives Japan limited territorial gains in the Pacific.
- **1923** Yokohama earthquake kills 140,000.
- **1927** Japan enters period of radical nationalism, and introduces the notion of a "coprosperity sphere" in southeast Asia under Japanese control. Interpreted in the US as a threat to its Pacific interests.
- **1931** Chinese Manchuria invaded and renamed Manchukuo.
- **1937** Japan launches full-scale invasion of China proper.
- **1938** All political parties placed under one common banner; Japan effectively ruled by militarists.
- **1939** Undeclared border war with Soviet Union; Japan defeated.
- **1940** Fall of France in Europe; Japan occupies French Indo-China.
- **1941** US imposes total trade embargo, including oil, on Japan thereby threatening to stifle its military machine. Japan responds in December by launching attack on US fleet at Pearl Harbor and invading US, British, and Dutch possessions in the Pacific.
- **1942** Japan loses decisive naval battle of Midway.
- **1945** Huge US bombing campaign culminates in atomic bombing of Hiroshima and Nagasaki: over 200,000 die. Soviet Union declares war on Japan. Emperor Hirohito surrenders, gives up divine status. Japan placed under US military government with Gen. MacArthur as supreme commander.
- **1947** New US-style constitution: retains emperor in ceremonial role.
- **1950** Korean War. US army contracts lead to quick expansion of Japanese economy.
- **1952** Treaty of San Francisco. Japan regains independence.

J

CHRONOLOGY *continued*

Industrial production recovers to 15% above 1936 levels.

- ❑ **1955** Formation of LDP, which governs for next 38 years.
- ❑ **1964** Tokyo Olympics. Bullet train (Shinkansen) inaugurated. Japan admitted to OECD.
- ❑ **1973** Oil crisis. Economic growth falls. Government-led economic reassessment decides to concentrate on high-tech industries.
- ❑ **1976** LDP shaken by Lockheed bribery scandal; in subsequent election it remains in power but loses outright majority for first time.
- ❑ **1979** Second oil crisis. Growth continues at 6% per year.
- ❑ **1980** Elections: restoration of LDP overall majority.
- ❑ **1982** Honda establishes first car factory in US.
- ❑ **1988** Japan becomes world's largest aid donor and overseas investor.
- ❑ **1989** Death of Emperor Hirohito. Accession of son, Akihito. Recruit–Cosmos bribery scandal leads to resignation of Prime Minister Noburo Takeshita; replaced by Sosuke Uno, in turn forced to resign over sex scandal.
- ❑ **1990** Tokyo stock market crash.
- ❑ **1991–1992** LDP torn by factional disputes, further financial scandals, and the issue of electoral reform.
- ❑ **1993** Reformists split from LDP and create new parties. Elections; LDP loses power. Morihiro Hosokawa becomes prime minister at head of seven-party coalition.
- ❑ **1994** Hosokawa resigns. Withdrawal of SDPJ causes collapse of coalition. New three-party coalition includes LDP and SDPJ. Opposition parties unified by creation of Shinshinto. Implementation of far-reaching political and electoral reforms designed to eradicate "money politics."
- ❑ **1995** Kobe earthquake kills more than 5000 people.
- ❑ **1996** Elections: LDP minority government. Copper trader Yasuo Yamanaka sentenced to eight years in prison for incurring losses of $2.6 billion while acting for the Sumitomo Corporation.
- ❑ **1997** Severe economic recession.
- ❑ **1998** Crisis over reform of banking and financial system.
- ❑ **2000** Prime Minister Keizo Obuchi falls into coma, replaced by Yoshiro Mori. LDP loses overall majority in general election.
- ❑ **2001** LDP turns to populist right-winger Junichiro Koizumi as prime minister; five women appointed to cabinet.
- ❑ **2002** Japan cohosts soccer World Cup.

POLITICS

▷ Multiparty elections

L. House 2000/2004
U. House 2001/2004

Emperor Tsegu no Miya Akihito

AT THE LAST ELECTION

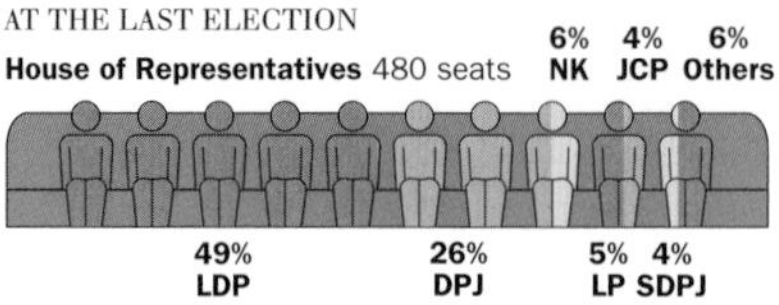
House of Representatives 480 seats
6% NK
4% JCP
6% Others
49% LDP
26% DPJ
5% LP
4% SDPJ

LDP = Liberal Democratic Party DPJ = Democratic Party of Japan NK = New Komeito LP = Liberal Party JCP = Japan Communist Party SDPJ = Social Democratic Party of Japan

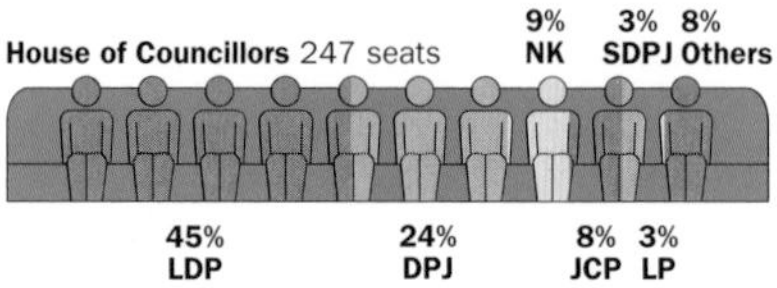
House of Councillors 247 seats
9% NK
3% SDPJ
8% Others
45% LDP
24% DPJ
8% JCP
3% LP

Japan is a multiparty democracy. The emperor has a purely ceremonial role.

Profile

The right-of-center LDP has dominated Japanese politics since its formation in 1955. For the first 21 years its parliamentary majority was untouched, but it has had to rely on occasionally shaky coalitions since 1976. In 1993 it lost power altogether, but recovered the following year and has remained in control ever since. The seven-party government which held power in 1993–1994 proved unworkable in the long run and the later Shinshinto coalition was unable to challenge the LDP despite the dire economic situation of the late 1990s.

Indeed, the LDP's position is threatened less by external opposition than by the machinations of its various internal factions. Prime Minister Yoshiro Mori led a lack-luster campaign in a general election in 2000, from which the LDP emerged with a reduced representation but still as the largest party and the main force in government. Mori's unpopularity finally led to his replacement as LDP leader (and prime minister) in 2001 by charismatic newcomer Junichiro Koizumi.

With the economy stagnating, Koizumi took it upon himself to push a radical reformist agenda, making the most of his immense public popularity. However, though he promised much, he has delivered little in the way of significant change, especially in the political sphere. The inertia of the faction system and the fierce conservatism of the grass-roots LDP have forced him to scale down his visions and settle into the familiar routine of gentle persuasion and appeasement. His popularity has consequently suffered. He was particularly criticized for sidelining the popular but controversial foreign minister Makiko Tanaka in 2002.

Junichiro Koizumi, *populist premier who has promised economic reform.*

Yoshiro Mori, *prime minister in 2000–2001, but not liked by the voters.*

Emperor Akihito. *He acceded in 1989 on the death of his father, Hirohito.*

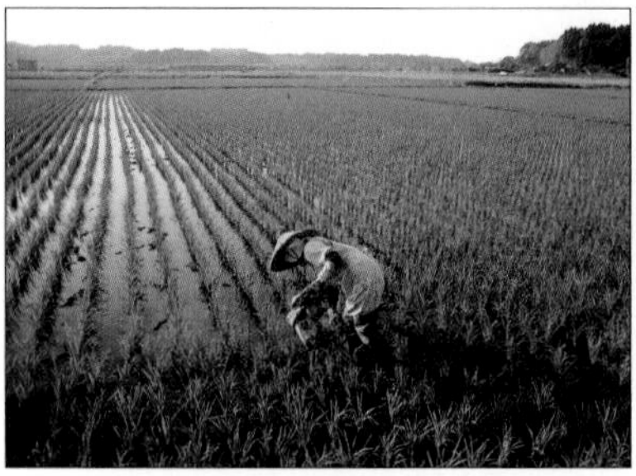

Traditional paddy field *in Hokkaido. Rice farming is among the most protected sectors of the Japanese economy.*

Main Political Issues

Economic reform

Efforts to restructure the way in which government money is spent have met stiff resistance. The changes that Koizumi did make in 2001–2002 have done little to offset the stagnation of the Japanese economy. While he has pledged that there will be "no economic crisis in Japan," he admitted in early 2003 that his reforms had been "derailed" and would take more time than had been anticipated.

LDP strength and opposition weakness

The LDP has close links, built up through a system of patronage, with big business and government bureaucracy which have left it virtually unassailable. Defeat at the polls in 1993 prompted an overhaul of the electoral system, aimed at stamping out "money politics," and ensured that the party would rise again soon after, easily outmaneuvering the Shinshinto alliance which briefly hoped to establish two-party politics in Japan.

J

WORLD AFFAIRS

Joined UN in 1956

APEC | G8 | IAEA | WTO | OECD

Having spent decades limiting its international role, Japan has become more assertive. Its eventual aim is a seat on the UN's Security Council, commensurate with its economic influence. Tentative moves toward greater participation were made in 1993, when Japanese forces joined UN peacekeepers in Cambodia, and in 2001, when Japan assisted in the US-led "war on terrorism." It has also become bolder in its dealings with North Korea. Relations with the West are seriously strained over Japan's continuing to carry out "scientific" whale hunts. In Asia, Japan remains burdened by the legacy of its wartime aggression, exacerbated by revision of Japanese school history texts downplaying its crimes.

AID

Donor

$9.85bn (donations) — Down 27% in 2001

Japan's aid donations are the largest of any single country in the world. Most aid goes to Asia and the Pacific, particularly China. Polynesian islands are heavily dependent on Japanese aid in support of their main livelihood, fishing. In 2001, Japan admitted to "buying" support for whaling.

DEFENSE

No compulsory military service

$39.5bn — Down 13% in 2001

JAPANESE ARMED FORCES

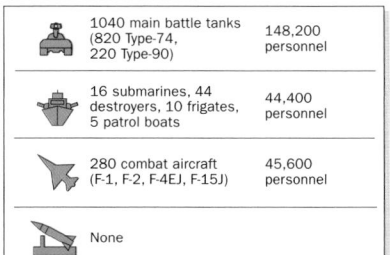

1040 main battle tanks (820 Type-74, 220 Type-90)	148,200 personnel
16 submarines, 44 destroyers, 10 frigates, 5 patrol boats	44,400 personnel
280 combat aircraft (F-1, F-2, F-4EJ, F-15J)	45,600 personnel
None	

Article 9 of the constitution renounces war as a means of settling international disputes, and military activity arouses fierce debate. Even UN peacekeeping duties are hotly contested. The Self-Defense Forces, however, have grown quite large; main concerns are North Korea and the threat of terrorism. Since 1999 force has been used to deter intrusions by North Korean vessels. In 2001 a bill allowed noncombat assistance specifically to the "war on terrorism," and two years later parliament discussed, for the first time since World War II, how Japan would respond to future attacks.

ECONOMICS

Inflation –0.1% p.a. (1990–2001)

$4523bn — 120.08 yen (119.86)

ECONOMIC PERFORMANCE INDICATOR

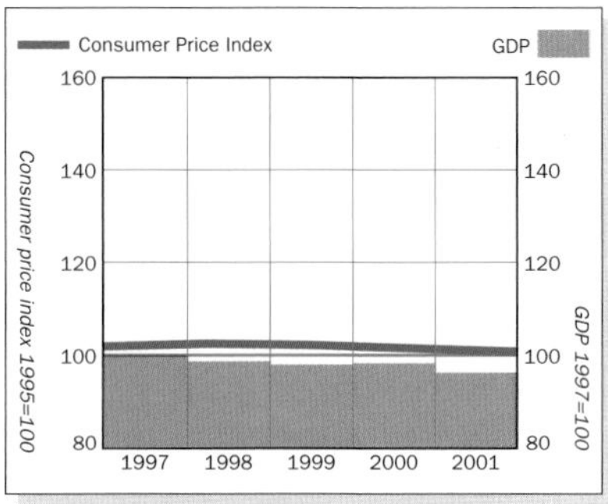

Consumer Price Index
GDP
160
140
120
100
80
Consumer price index 1995=100
GDP 1997=100
1997
1998
1999
2000
2001

STRENGTHS

Established market leader in high-tech products and cars. Commitment to long-term research. Talent for capitalizing on imported ideas. Manufacturing plants already established in the West. Domestic economy heavily protected from outside competition. Weak yen has promoted exports.

WEAKNESSES

Recent recession. Dependence on oil imports. Secretive and debt-ridden financial system. Falling industrial production, high-profile bankruptcies, and record unemployment levels. Trade surplus damages international relations.

PROFILE

Once among the world's strongest performing economies, Japan's strengths have been overshadowed for a decade by growing weaknesses.

The 1990 crash of the Tokyo stock market marked the end of a period of remarkable growth. The government managed to spend its way out of disaster, effectively delaying the full impact of the downturn. Japan entered a brief recession for the second time in five years in 2001.

In an attempt to appease Western discontent over a huge trade surplus, the government encouraged a move away from a dependence on export revenues through stimulation of the domestic economy. However, the contracting trade balance remains above $100 billion a year. Bilateral trade has been promoted and Japan entered its first free trade agreement – with Singapore from April 2002.

However, the domestic situation remains critical. The financial sector is in desperate need of reform. The prominent corporate collapses of 1997 were repeated in 2001, with record losses reported across the high-tech industries in particular. Koizumi has promised radical change, rejecting the standard increase in government spending in favor of basic structural reform. Banks' bad loans have been cleared and the system of privileged "special public institutions" has been overhauled. Despite these measures, traditional economic power brokers have put a brake on the pace of reform and the overall economy continues to underachieve. Plans to tackle the banking sector were criticized as not being hard enough on poor performers. A government injection of $24 billion in 2002 was ridiculed as insufficient to solve the continuing problems.

SCORE CARD

❑ WORLD GNP RANKING	2nd
❑ GNP PER CAPITA	$35,610
❑ BALANCE OF PAYMENTS	$89.3bn
❑ INFLATION	–0.7%
❑ UNEMPLOYMENT	5%

EXPORTS

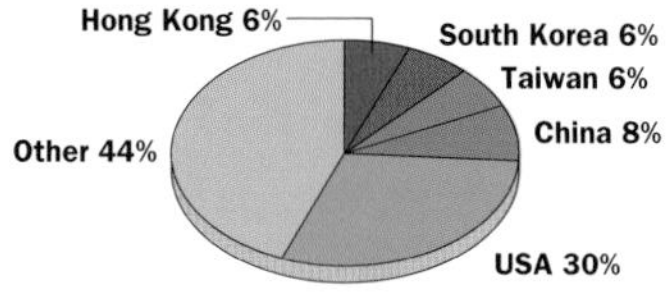

Hong Kong 6%
South Korea 6%
Taiwan 6%
China 8%
USA 30%
Other 44%

IMPORTS

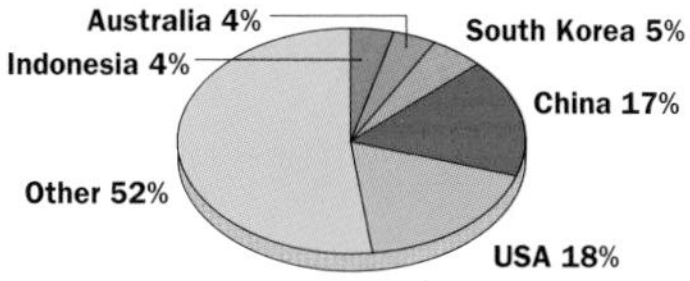

Australia 4%
Indonesia 4%
South Korea 5%
China 17%
USA 18%
Other 52%

J

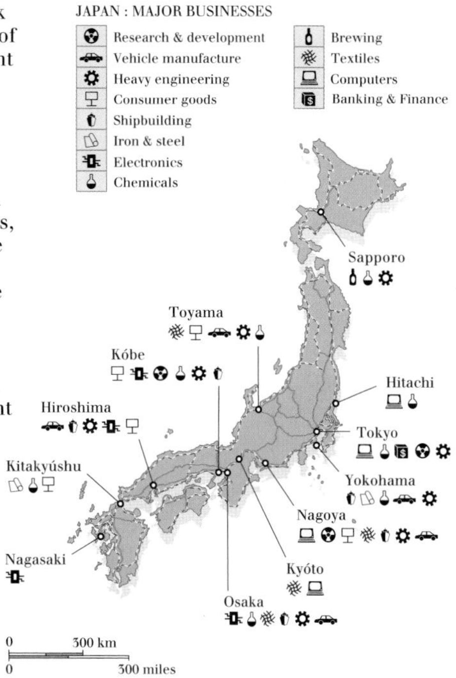

JAPAN : MAJOR BUSINESSES
Research & development
Vehicle manufacture
Heavy engineering
Consumer goods
Shipbuilding
Iron & steel
Electronics
Chemicals
Brewing
Textiles
Computers
Banking & Finance
Sapporo
Toyama
Kobe
Hitachi
Hiroshima
Tokyo
Kitakyúshu
Yokohama
Nagoya
Nagasaki
Kyóto
Osaka
0 300 km
0 300 miles

RESOURCES

Electric power 247m kW

5.75m tonnes

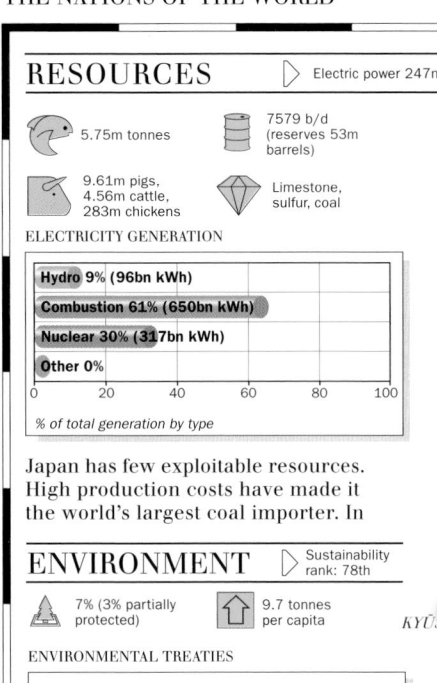

7579 b/d (reserves 53m barrels)

9.61m pigs, 4.56m cattle, 283m chickens

Limestone, sulfur, coal

ELECTRICITY GENERATION

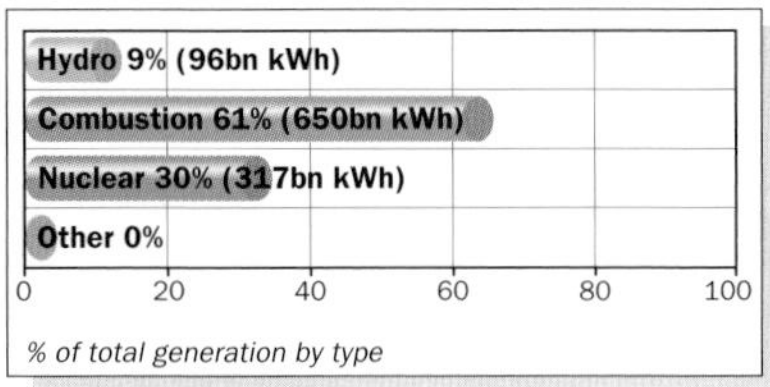
Hydro 9% (96bn kWh)
Combustion 61% (650bn kWh)
Nuclear 30% (317bn kWh)
Other 0%
0
20
40
60
80
100
% of total generation by type

Japan has few exploitable resources. High production costs have made it the world's largest coal importer. In an attempt to reduce dependence on imported fuels, Japan has developed alternative energy sources. It is now the world's third-biggest generator of nuclear power. However, environmentalists strongly oppose any expansion of this sector. Nuclear safety became a priority issue after a serious accident at the Tokaimura plant in 1999.

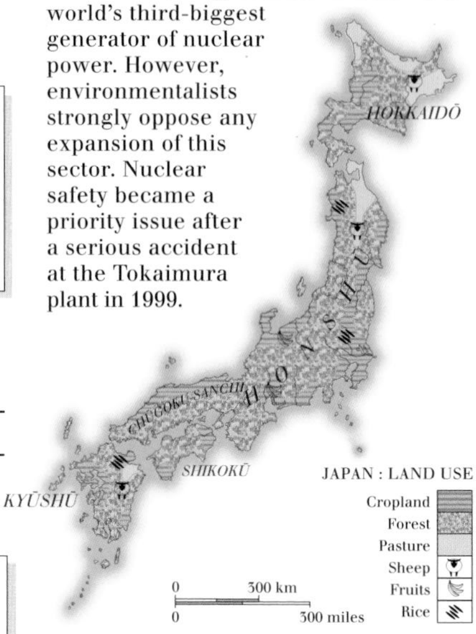
HOKKAIDŌ
HONSHU
CHUGOKU-SANCHI
SHIKOKU
KYŪSHŪ
JAPAN : LAND USE
Cropland
Forest
Pasture
Sheep
Fruits
Rice
0
300 km
0
300 miles

ENVIRONMENT

Sustainability rank: 78th

7% (3% partially protected)

9.7 tonnes per capita

ENVIRONMENTAL TREATIES

Yes Yes Yes

Yes Yes Yes

Japan supports moves to establish a global foundation to aid sustainable development in the Third World. In 1997 it played host to the Kyoto climate conference, though it only agreed to a modest cut in its "greenhouse gas" emissions. It faces strong criticism for its consumption of tropical timber, overfishing, and continuing to catch whale species under the umbrella of "scientific research."

Traditional Japanese respect for nature has spawned a vigorous grassroots ecological movement, which prevented a second runway at Tokyo's Narita airport, and opposes nuclear power expansion and waste processing. The most serious environmental disasters have been a nuclear accident at Tokaimura in 1999 and the breakup in early 1997 of a Russian oil tanker along Japan's western shoreline.

***Datsetsusan National Park**, Hokkaido. Japan's northerly island is the least populous of the main group.*

MEDIA

TV ownership high

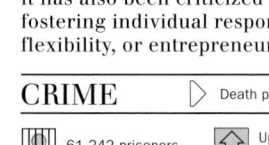

Daily newspaper circulation 574 per 1000 people

PUBLISHING AND BROADCAST MEDIA

There are 122 daily newspapers. *Asahi Shimbun, Mainichi Shimbun*, and *Yomiuri Shimbun* are among the most popular

128 services: 1 publicly owned, 127 commercial

100 services: 1 publicly owned, 99 commercial

The Japanese are among the world's most avid newspaper readers. Major papers are issued in simultaneous editions in the main urban centers. Most dailies are owned by large media groups who also have TV and cable interests. Weekly newspapers carry more tabloid journalism. *Manga*, Japanese comics, are massively popular, with their characteristic artwork influencing design and art across Japanese culture. They now account for 40% of all published material in Japan; the most popular title, *Shonen Jump*, sells over three million copies a week.

Japanese technology has defined the world's media. Along with the personal stereo, Japanese companies effectively created the huge international computer games market. Nintendo, a leading games company, is among the most profitable in Japan. Ironically, the Internet was slow to take off, though by 2001 Japan had the third-highest number of people "online." That year also saw Japan launch the world's first "third-generation" mobile phone service.

EDUCATION

School leaving age: 15

99%

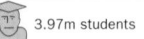

3.97m students

THE EDUCATION SYSTEM

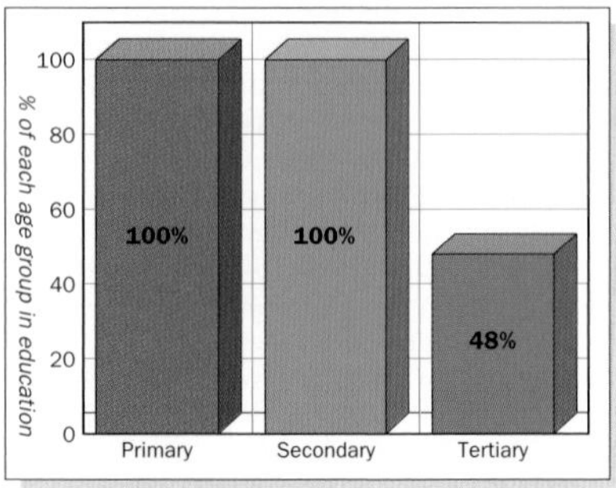
100
80
60
40
20
0
% of each age group in education
100%
100%
48%
Primary
Secondary
Tertiary

The Japanese education system is highly pressurized and competitive. One of the key dividing lines is between university graduates, who get the most coveted white-collar jobs, and nongraduates, who have difficulty reaching management level.

Competition for university places is intense, and starts with the choice of kindergarten, which the Japanese attend from the age of four. Academic pressure diminishes once at university. Graduates from Tokyo, Kyoto, Waseda, and Keio, which are the most prestigious universities, have access to top civil service and business jobs. The system succeeds in producing a uniformly well-educated workforce. However, it has also been criticized for not fostering individual responsibility, flexibility, or entrepreneurship.

CRIME

Death penalty in use

61,242 prisoners

Up 25% in 2000–2001

CRIME RATE

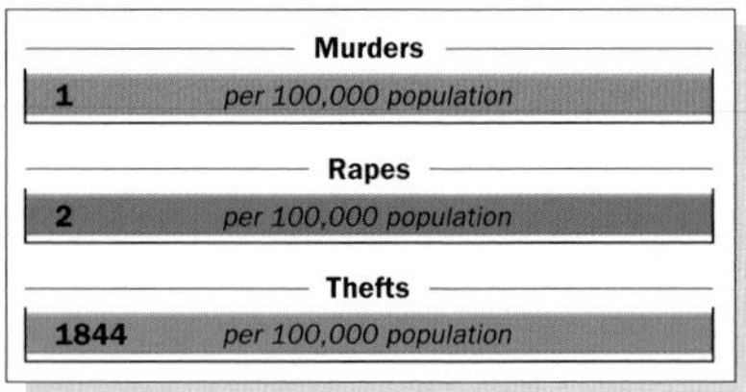
Murders
1 per 100,000 population
Rapes
2 per 100,000 population
Thefts
1844 per 100,000 population

Japan has one of the Western world's lowest crime rates, despite petty crime levels being at a 50-year high. Cities are safe, with police kiosks at frequent intervals on street corners. However, crime is involving more young people, and narcotics abuse is increasing.

The major crime problem is fraud and the activities of the *kumi*, organized Mafia-style syndicates. The authorities have been reluctant to challenge these groups, seeking to contain rather than halt their activities. *Kumi* are suspected of having connections with the political extreme right.

THE 2002 WORLD CUP: A GAME OF TWO HALVES

SEEKING BOTH AN economic boost, and a way of improving rocky relations across the Korea Strait, in 2002 Japan cohosted the world's premier soccer tournament, the FIFA World Cup, with South Korea. It was the first World Cup to be held in Asia and the first to be staged by two countries. It was also expected that the tournament would boost the popularity of soccer in Japan, a country where it had only recently became a professional game. The Japanese Professional Football League itself (popularly known as the J League) has been in existence only since 1993.

CAUGHT OFFSIDE

The principle behind sharing the monthlong competition was to spread both the cost and the expected economic rewards. However, the 2002 World Cup was by far the most costly ever staged in the tournament's history, and the much-vaunted financial benefits failed to materialize. Under FIFA rules at least eight stadiums must be supplied for each tournament. Japan and its neighbor went well beyond this minimum requirement. Each built eight brand new arenas from scratch, refurbished a further two, and upgraded local facilities and infrastructure. The cost for Japan alone was estimated at $4.5 billion. To offset this outlay the authorities predicted rewards totaling somewhere near $30 billion from ticket sales, advertising, and "soccer tourists." In the event, though companies selling televisions saw a 38% increase in trade, and imports of foreign beer tripled, actual revenues were far less spectacular. An embarrassing mix-up with ticketing left each game being played before a significant number of empty seats. Advertisers declined to risk the early morning/midnight exposure which the time difference imposed on key Western audiences, and "soccer tourists" came in far fewer numbers than the extravagant 800,000 predicted. Those who did come

*The **Sapporo Dome** features a "floating" pitch, which is kept outside when not in use.*

spent little, and left quickly. Of the new Japanese stadiums, few have hosted professional soccer since the tournament and they now face multi-million-dollar yearly running costs. The Saitama Stadium has resorted to offering itself as a wedding venue, while International Stadium Yokohama has offered to be renamed in honor of the highest bidder.

THE FAILED FRIENDLY

The World Cup had also been expected to contribute to a warming of relations between its ambitious cohosts. However, in the year leading up to the opening match the intensified press attention seemed only to put greater strain on the two neighbors. Junichiro Koizumi's new populist administration in Japan stirred Korean ire by staging visits to the Yasakuni war shrine (which includes Japanese war criminals among those whom it commemorates) and by approving "revisionist" school textbooks which, in Korean eyes, glossed over the Imperial army's war crimes in occupied east Asia during World War II. Korean fans took the opportunity presented by the Cup to publicize the popular campaign to reinstate their country's English-language spelling as "Corea." The "K" spelling, they claim, came about through a conspiracy by their imperial overlords after 1910, designed to give Japan precedence in alphabetical ranking.

Though the ailing Japanese economy saw little overall benefit, and relations with Korea (or Corea) failed to transcend traditional enmities, the tournament itself was celebrated around the world. Expected underdogs, including Japan and South Korea, did well enough to challenge the supposed supremacy of European and South American teams. In the end, however, the competition had a fitting finale as the world's most celebrated team, Brazil, won through to take the title for a record fifth time.

COREA

*A **"Corean" fan** at the World Cup in 2002.*

HEALTH

Welfare state health benefits

1 per 508 people

Cancers, respiratory, cerebrovascular, and heart diseases

Japan's health care system, which is ranked by WHO as the best in the world, delivers the highest longevity and lowest infant mortality rates. The poorest in society receive free treatment; expensive high-tech hospital facilities can also offer the latest techniques. Contributory national health insurance is based on earnings-related premiums, and the cost of medical care for the elderly and the self-employed is subsidized, though the rapidly aging population presents a major future funding challenge.

SPENDING

GDP/cap. increase

CONSUMPTION AND SPENDING

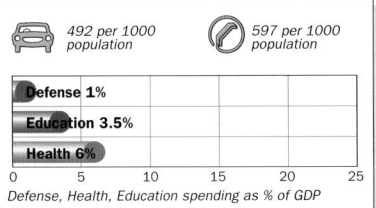

492 per 1000 population

597 per 1000 population

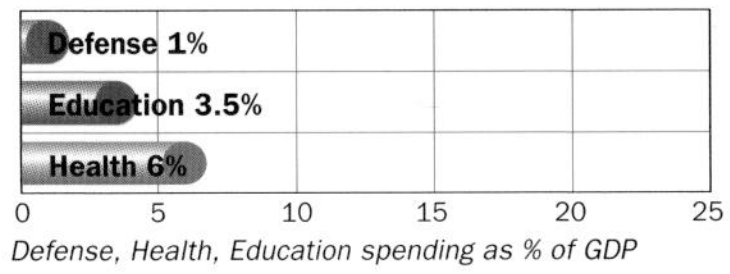
Defense 1%
Education 3.5%
Health 6%
0
5
10
15
20
25
Defense, Health, Education spending as % of GDP

Measured in consumer goods, the Japanese are wealthy; car ownership is only low because city parking is so restricted. Most households have substantial savings, enabling them to withstand economic recession.

The country's wealthiest men have seen their wealth decline markedly: the fortunes of the top ten averaged $3.7 billion in 2003, down from $7 billion in 2000. The richest, Nobutada Saji, is worth $7.1 billion. Tokyo's living costs are high and most who work there live outside the city center, facing long, cramped commuter journeys to work and back. Girls and young women still living in their parents' homes are one group with high disposable income.

WORLD RANKING

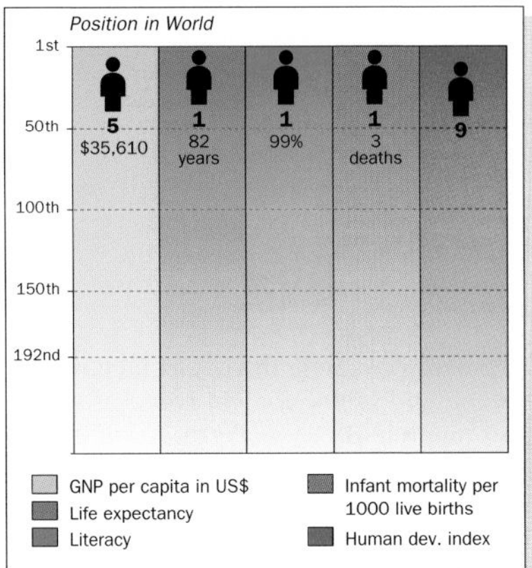
Position in World
1st
50th
100th
150th
192nd
5
$35,610
1
82 years
1
99%
1
3 deaths
9
GNP per capita in US$
Life expectancy
Literacy
Infant mortality per 1000 live births
Human dev. index

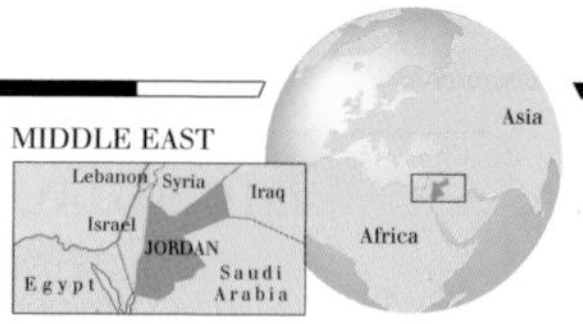
MIDDLE EAST
Lebanon
Syria
Iraq
Israel
JORDAN
Egypt
Saudi Arabia
Asia
Africa

JORDAN

OFFICIAL NAME: Hashemite Kingdom of Jordan **CAPITAL:** Amman
POPULATION: 5.2 million **CURRENCY:** Jordanian dinar **OFFICIAL LANGUAGE:** Arabic

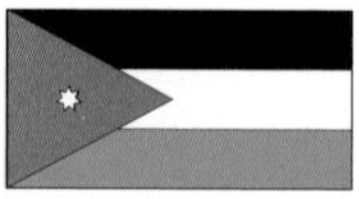

1946 | 1967 | May 25 | HKJ | +2 | +962 | .jo

SURROUNDED by the deserts of the Middle East, Jordan has just 26 km (16 miles) of maritime coastline on the Gulf of Aqaba. The vast majority of the population lives in the northwest, on the east bank of the River Jordan. Jordan ceded its claim to the West Bank of the river to the aspiring Palestinian state in 1988. Tourism, associated with important historical sites such as Petra, and phosphates are the mainstays of the economy.

CLIMATE

Hot desert/steppe/ Mediterranean

WEATHER CHART FOR AMMAN

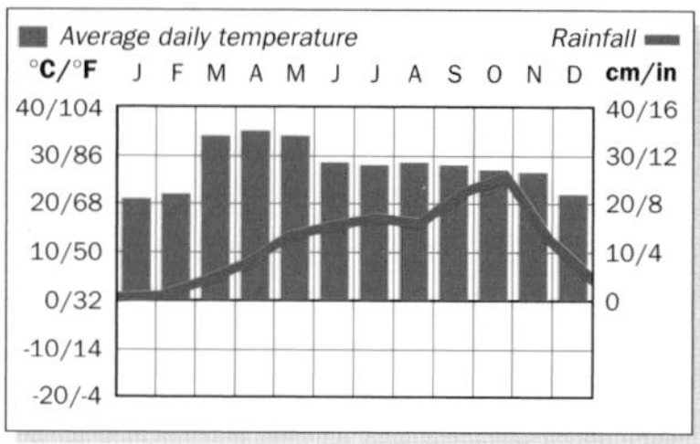
Average daily temperature
Rainfall
°C/°F
J F M A M J J A S O N D
cm/in
40/104
30/86
20/68
10/50
0/32
-10/14
-20/-4
40/16
30/12
20/8
10/4
0

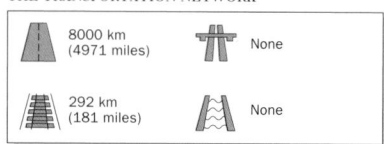

Summers are hot and dry, winters cool and wet. Areas below sea level are very hot in summer and warm in winter.

TRANSPORTATION

Drive on right

Queen Alia International, Amman
2.33m passengers

10 ships
42,100 grt

THE TRANSPORTATION NETWORK

8000 km (4971 miles) | None
292 km (181 miles) | None

Adequate roads link main cities. A railroad links the port of Aqaba with the Syrian capital, Damascus.

TOURISM

Visitors : Population 1:3.2

1.62m visitors

Up 10% in 2002

MAIN TOURIST ARRIVALS

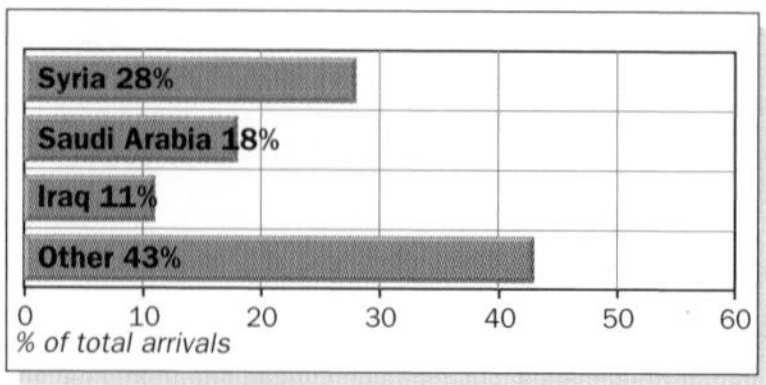
Syria 28%
Saudi Arabia 18%
Iraq 11%
Other 43%
0
10
20
30
40
50
60
% of total arrivals

Attractions include the resort facilities of Aqaba and archaelogical remains such as the ancient city of Petra. Amman is developing as a center for Arab culture. Visitor numbers dropped sharply after September 11, 2001.

PEOPLE

Pop. density medium

Arabic

58/km² (151/mi²)

THE URBAN/RURAL POPULATION SPLIT

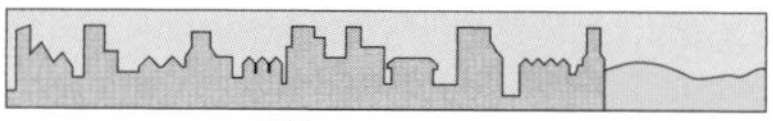
79%
21%

ETHNIC MAKEUP

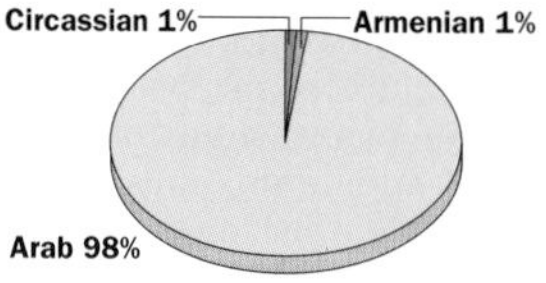
Circassian 1%
Armenian 1%
Arab 98%

Jordan is a predominantly Muslim country with Bedouin roots; there are Arab Christian and Muslim Circassian minorities. About half the population are Palestinian in origin. The monarchy's power base lies among the rural tribes, which provide the backbone of the military.

POLITICS

Multiparty elections

L. House 2003/2007
U. House 2001/2005

H.M. King Abdullah II

AT THE LAST ELECTION
House of Deputies 110 seats

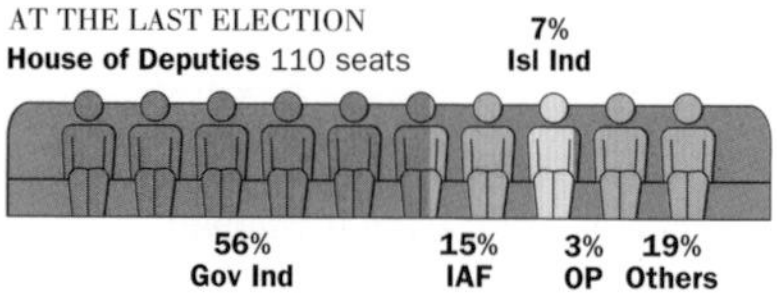
7%
Isl Ind
56%
Gov Ind
15%
IAF
3%
OP
19%
Others

Gov Ind = Progovernment independents
IAF = Islamic Action Front **Isl Ind** = Islamist independents
OP = Other parties
Nine seats are reserved for Christians, six for women, and three for Circassians

Senate 40 seats

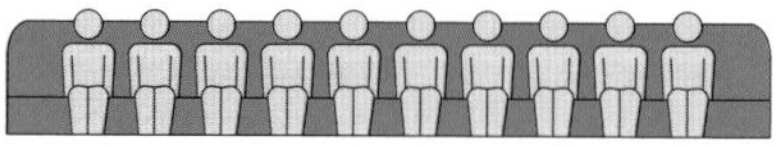

The members of the Senate (Majlis al-Aayan) are appointed by the king

King Abdullah II acceded in 1999. He enjoys the support of tribal leaders and the army. Multiparty elections, initiated in 1993, have benefited progovernment parties, despite a strong Islamist opposition. The appointment in 2000 of Prime Minister Ali Abu ar-Ragheb marked a shift toward a modernizing government. Clashes between police and Islamists in Ma'an in 2002 led to armed intervention and raised concern over the impact of regional tensions on the volatile populace.

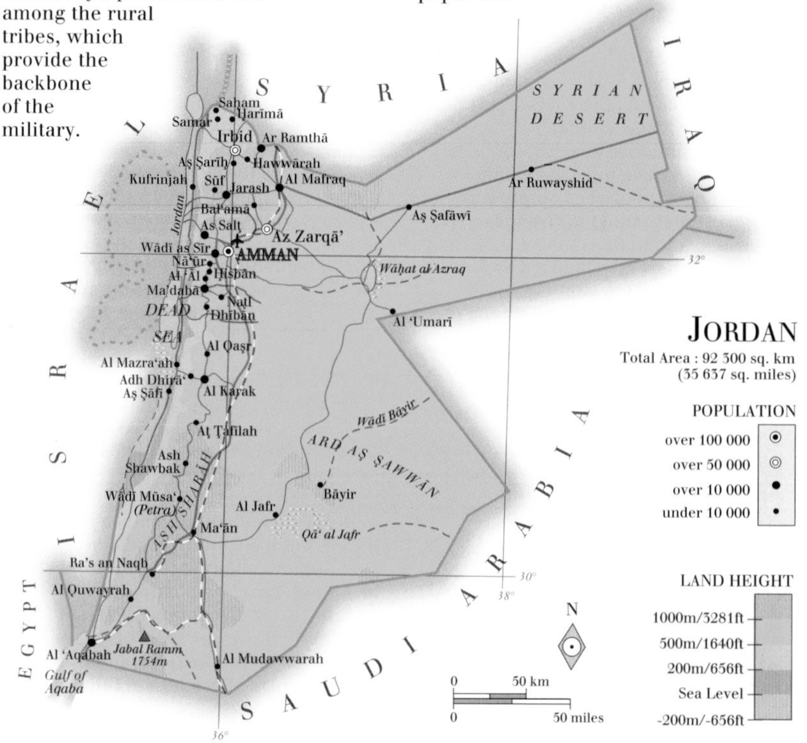
SYRIA
SYRIAN DESERT
IRAQ
ISRAEL
SAUDI ARABIA
EGYPT
Saham
Harimā
Samar
Irbid
Ar Ramthā
Aş Şarīḩ
Ḩawwārah
Kufrinjah
Şūf
Jarash
Al Mafraq
Jordan
Ar Ruwayshid
Aş Şafāwī
Bal'amā
As Salţ
Az Zarqā'
Wādī as Sīr
AMMAN
Nā'ūr
Ḩisbān
Al 'Āl
Wāḩat al Azraq
Mādabā
Nā'ūr
Dhībān
DEAD SEA
Al 'Umarī
Al Qaşr
Al Mazra'ah
Adh Dhirā'
Aş Şāfī
Al Karak
Aţ Ţafīlah
Wādī Bāyir
ARD AŞ ŞAWWĀN
Ash Shawbak
Bāyir
Wādī Mūsā (Petra)
ASH SHARĀH
Al Jafr
Ma'ān
Qā' al Jafr
Ra's an Naqb
Al Quwayrah
Al 'Aqabah
Jabal Ramm 1754m
Al Mudawwarah
Gulf of Aqaba
32°
30°
36°
38°
N
0
50 km
50 miles
JORDAN
Total Area : 92 300 sq. km (35 637 sq. miles)
POPULATION
over 100 000
over 50 000
over 10 000
under 10 000
LAND HEIGHT
1000m/3281ft
500m/1640ft
200m/656ft
Sea Level
-200m/-656ft

WORLD AFFAIRS

Joined UN in 1955

AL · AMF · WTO · NAM · OIC

Jordan's position as a key player in Middle East politics is under question. It actively supports US peace initiatives, while Jordan's relations with Israel remain much less aggressive than those of other Arab countries. The US signed a ten-year free trade agreement with Jordan in 2000.

Jordan refused to join the anti-Iraq coalition formed by the Gulf states in 1991. Prior to the US invasion in 2003 it called for Iraq's rehabilitation, and went on to condemn the invasion.

AID

Recipient

$432m (receipts) — Down 22% in 2001

The US is by far the biggest single donor, reflected in the government's largely pro-US line in regional relations.

DEFENSE

No compulsory military service

$740m — Down 7% in 2001

The military is loyal to the monarchy. It has a reputation for thorough training and professionalism. The forces are dependent on Western support for credit for purchasing advanced arms and equipment, but Jordan, unlike many Arab neighbors, played no part in the 1991 Gulf War.

ECONOMICS

Inflation 2.9% p.a. (1990–2001)

$8.79bn — 0.709 Jordanian dinars (0.705)

SCORE CARD

❑ WORLD GNP RANKING	90th
❑ GNP PER CAPITA	$1750
❑ BALANCE OF PAYMENTS	–$4m
❑ INFLATION	1.8%
❑ UNEMPLOYMENT	15%

STRENGTHS

Major exporter of phosphates. Skilled workforce. Port of Aqaba a special economic zone.

WEAKNESSES

Unemployment, exacerbated by influx of refugees from Kuwait after Gulf crisis. Reliance on energy imports. Poor export-to-import ratio. Tourism badly affected by regional insecurity. Little arable land.

EXPORTS

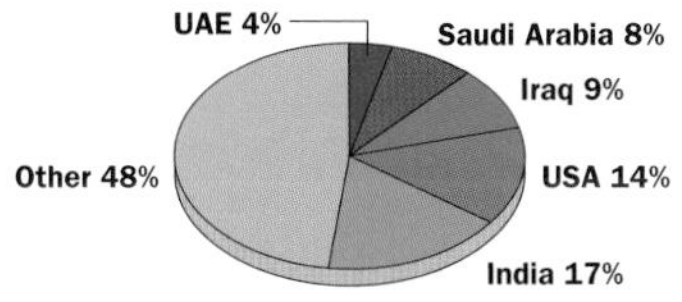
UAE 4%
Saudi Arabia 8%
Iraq 9%
USA 14%
India 17%
Other 48%

IMPORTS

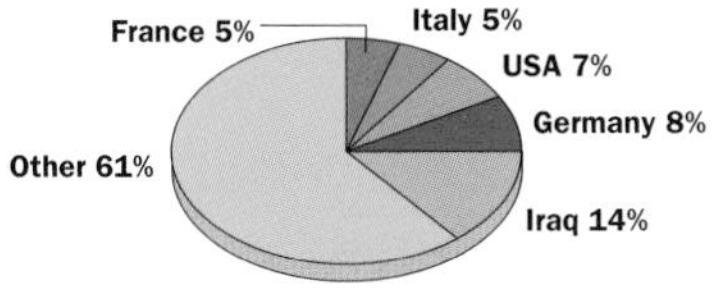
France 5%
Italy 5%
USA 7%
Germany 8%
Iraq 14%
Other 61%

RESOURCES

Electric power 1.7m kW

1119 tonnes — 40 b/d

1.46m sheep, 557,260 goats, 24m chickens — Oil, phosphates, potash

Oil, phosphates, livestock, and crops such as tomatoes, wheat, and olives are the main resources. The electricity grid is shared with Egypt and Syria.

ENVIRONMENT

Sustainability rank: 53rd

3% partially protected — 3 tonnes per capita

Conservation is a government priority. Rare animals are protected and species that became extinct in the wild in the 1950s are being reintroduced into controlled environments.

MEDIA

TV ownership medium

Daily newspaper circulation 42 per 1000 people

PUBLISHING AND BROADCAST MEDIA

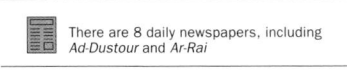

There are 8 daily newspapers, including *Ad-Dustour* and *Ar-Rai*

1 state-controlled service — 1 state-controlled service

A restrictive press and publications law was enacted in 1998. Radio and TV are controlled by the state.

CRIME

Death penalty in use

5448 prisoners — Up 7% in 1999

Jordan is largely peaceful. Crime levels are generally low, although theft in urban areas is rising.

EDUCATION

School leaving age: 15

90% — 142,190 students

There is no gender discrimination in education. Jordanian teachers work all over the Middle East.

HEALTH

Welfare state health benefits

1 per 488 people — Heart, digestive, and respiratory diseases, accidents, cancers

Health care is subsidized by the government. Hospitals are well distributed throughout the country.

CHRONOLOGY

Jordan, previously the British-mandated territory of Transjordan, became independent in 1946.

- ❑ **1953** Hussein becomes king.
- ❑ **1967** Israel seizes West Bank territories.
- ❑ **1970** Massive crackdown on Palestine Liberation Organization.
- ❑ **1988** Jordan cedes claims to West Bank to PLO.
- ❑ **1994** Peace treaty with Israel.
- ❑ **1999** Death of King Hussein; succession of King Abdullah II.

The King's Highway, *seen from the castle at Al Karak, a strategic fortress built by Crusader knights in the 12th century.*

SPENDING

GDP/cap. increase

CONSUMPTION AND SPENDING

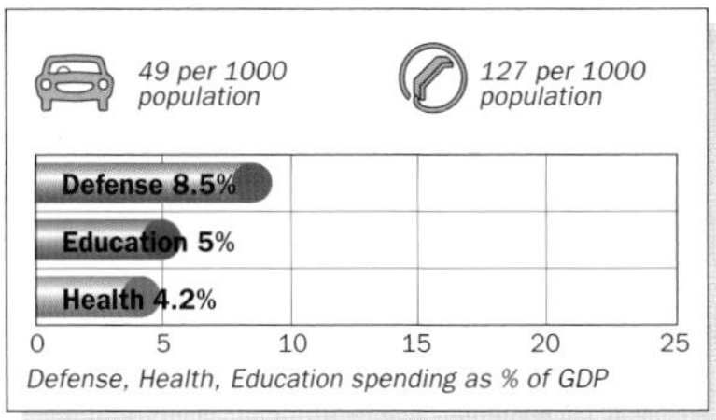
49 per 1000 population
127 per 1000 population
Defense 8.5%
Education 5%
Health 4.2%
0
5
10
15
20
25
Defense, Health, Education spending as % of GDP

Poverty is relatively rare, though refugee camps still exist and 25% unemployment affected many family incomes in the late 1990s.

WORLD RANKING

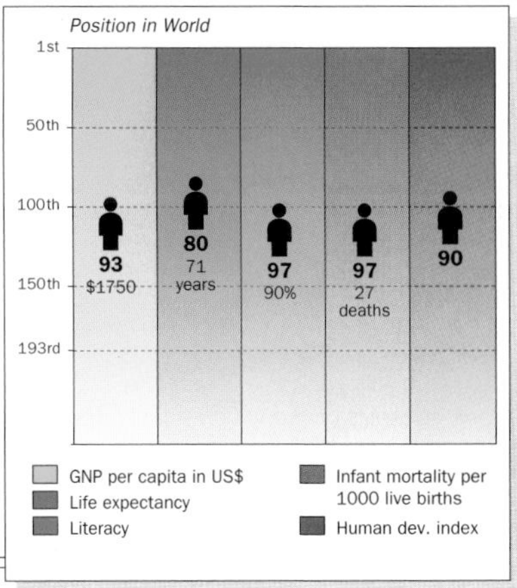
Position in World
1st
50th
100th
150th
193rd
93
$1750
80
71 years
97
90%
97
27 deaths
90
GNP per capita in US$
Life expectancy
Literacy
Infant mortality per 1000 live births
Human dev. index

J

KAZAKHSTAN

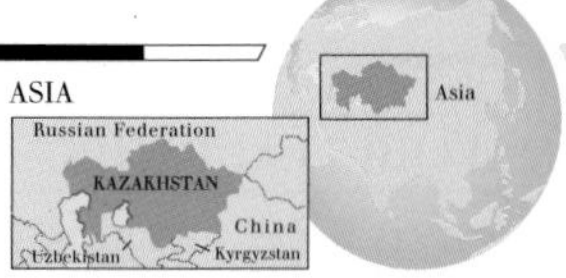
ASIA
Russian Federation
KAZAKHSTAN
China
Uzbekistan
Kyrgyzstan
Asia

OFFICIAL NAME: Republic of Kazakhstan **CAPITAL:** Astana
POPULATION: 16 million **CURRENCY:** Tenge **OFFICIAL LANGUAGE:** Kazakh

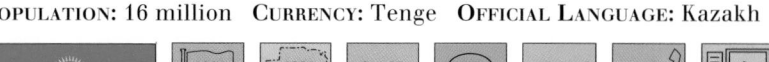

1991 | 1991 | Oct 25 | KZ | +5 to +6 | +7 | .kz

THE SECOND-LARGEST of the former Soviet republics, Kazakhstan extends almost 3000 km (1900 miles) from the Caspian Sea in the west to the Altai Mountains in the east and 1600 km (1000 miles) north to south. It borders Russia to the north and China to the east. Kazakhstan was the last Soviet republic to declare its independence, in 1991. In 1999, elections confirmed the former communist Nursultan Nazarbayev and his supporters in power. Kazakhstan has considerable economic potential, and many Western companies seek to exploit its mineral resources.

***The Altai Mountains**, eastern Kazakhstan. Subject to harsh continental winters, the Altai range is a cold, inhospitable place. Rivers carry meltwater down onto the vast steppe.*

CLIMATE

Cold desert/steppe

WEATHER CHART FOR ASTANA

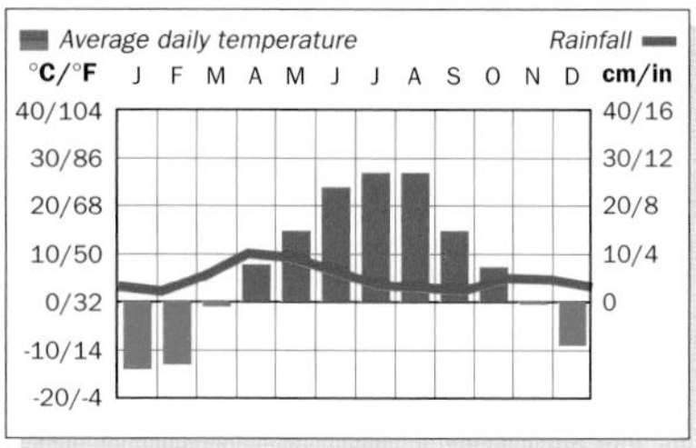
Average daily temperature
Rainfall
°C/°F
J F M A M J J A S O N D
cm/in
40/104
30/86
20/68
10/50
0/32
-10/14
-20/-4
40/16
30/12
20/8
10/4
0

Kazakhstan has a continental climate with large temperature variations: average January temperatures range from –18°C (0°F) on the northern Kazakh steppe to –3°C (27°F) in the deserts 1600 km (1000 miles) to the south; July temperatures average 19°C (66°F) and 30°C (86°F) respectively. The Caspian Sea never freezes, and winters are mildest on Kazakhstan's southwestern coast.

TRANSPORTATION

Drive on right

Astana 340,817 passengers

21 ships 13,096 grt

THE TRANSPORTATION NETWORK

103,272 km (64,170 miles)	None
13,601 km (8452 miles)	3900 km (2423 miles)

Transportation networks focus on the north and east as the key economic areas. Most of the roads in Kazakhstan are in urgent need of repair. In 1998, measures to restructure and privatize the railroad were announced. The railroad system links into that of the Russian Federation. Helicopters are frequently used to reach remote destinations.

TOURISM

Visitors : Population 1:8.7

1.85m visitors

Gradually increasing

MAIN TOURIST ARRIVALS

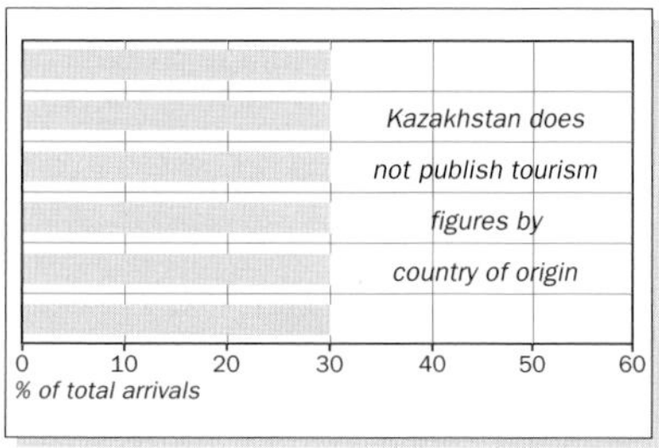
Kazakhstan does not publish tourism figures by country of origin
0
10
20
30
40
50
60
% of total arrivals

The number of visitors to Kazakhstan is increasing, but very few come solely as tourists. The majority are business travelers, and a dense web of contacts with foreign companies has evolved. Of the central Asian states, Kazakhstan has cultivated the closest links with the West. Most foreign businesses are concentrated in Almaty.

KAZAKHSTAN

Total Area : 2 717 300 sq. km (1 049 150 sq. miles)

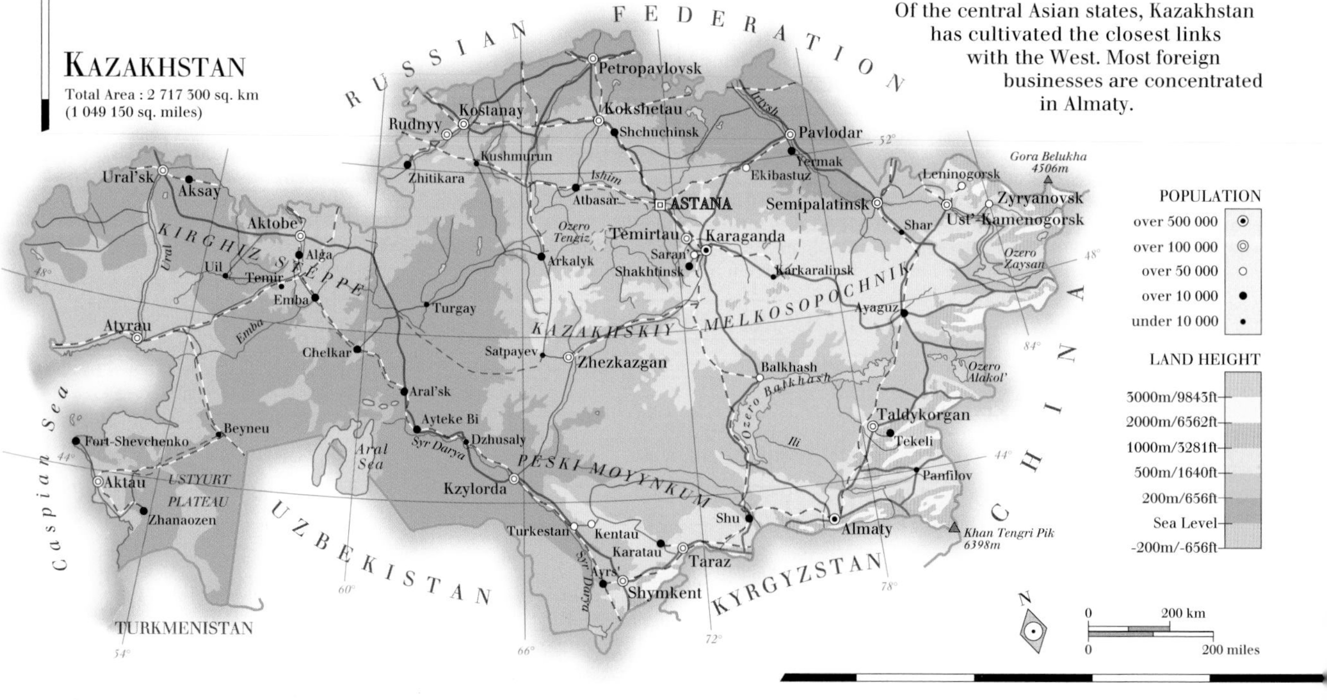
RUSSIAN FEDERATION
Petropavlovsk
Kostanay
Rudnyy
Kokshetau
Shchuchinsk
Pavlodar
Irtysh
Kushmurun
Zhitikara
Yermak
Ekibastuz
Ishim
Atbasar
ASTANA
Semipalatinsk
Leninogorsk
Gora Belukha 4506m
Zyryanovsk
Ust'-Kamenogorsk
Shar
Ural'sk
Aksay
Aktobe
KIRGHIZ STEPPE
Alga
Uil
Temir
Emba
Ural
Ozero Tengiz
Temirtau
Karaganda
Saran
Arkalyk
Shakhtinsk
Karkaralinsk
Ozero Zaysan
MELKOSOPOCHNIK
Ayaguz
Turgay
KAZAKHSKIY
Atyrau
Emba
Chelkar
Satpayev
Zhezkazgan
Balkhash
Ozero Balkhash
Ozero Alakol'
Aral'sk
Caspian Sea
Beyneu
Ayteke Bi
Fort-Shevchenko
Aral Sea
Syr Darya
Dzhusaly
Taldykorgan
Tekeli
Ili
PESKI MOYYNKUM
Aktau
USTYURT PLATEAU
Kzylorda
Panfilov
Zhanaozen
Shu
Almaty
UZBEKISTAN
Turkestan
Kentau
Karatau
Taraz
Khan Tengri Pik 6398m
Arys'
Shymkent
KYRGYZSTAN
CHINA
TURKMENISTAN
POPULATION
over 500 000
over 100 000
over 50 000
over 10 000
under 10 000
LAND HEIGHT
3000m/9843ft
2000m/6562ft
1000m/3281ft
500m/1640ft
200m/656ft
Sea Level
-200m/-656ft
0 200 km
0 200 miles

PEOPLE

Pop. density low

Kazakh, Russian, Uighur, Korean, German

6/km² (15/mi²)

THE URBAN/RURAL POPULATION SPLIT

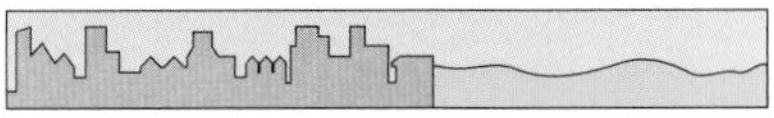
56%
44%

RELIGIOUS PERSUASION

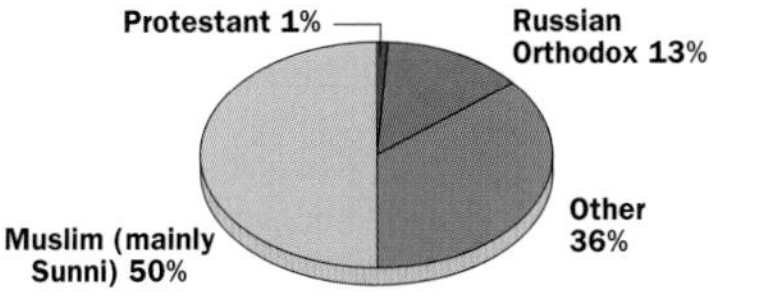
Protestant 1%
Russian Orthodox 13%
Other 36%
Muslim (mainly Sunni) 50%

ETHNIC MAKEUP

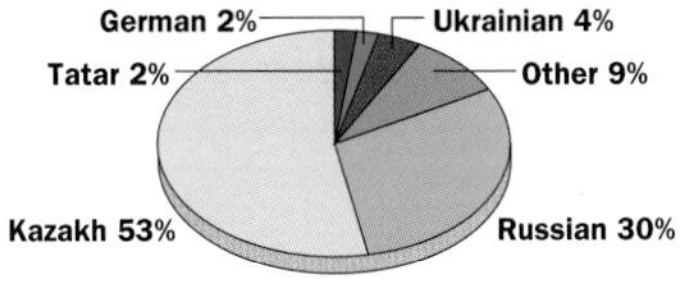
German 2%
Ukrainian 4%
Tatar 2%
Other 9%
Kazakh 53%
Russian 30%

POPULATION AGE BREAKDOWN

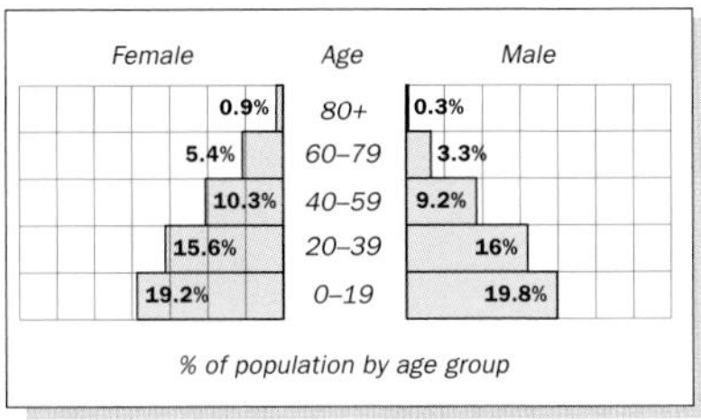
Female
Age
Male
0.9%
80+
0.3%
5.4%
60–79
3.3%
10.3%
40–59
9.2%
15.6%
20–39
16%
19.2%
0–19
19.8%
% of population by age group

Kazakhstan's ethnic diversity arose mainly from forced settlement of Tatars, Germans, and Russians during the Soviet era. By 1959, Kazakhs were outnumbered by ethnic Russians. This balance has been redressed by the immigration of ethnic Kazakhs from neighboring states and the departure in the 1990s of some 1.5 million ethnic Russians. In addition, a majority of ethnic Germans have opted to live in Germany, though in 2000 the government announced a campaign to try to lure some of them back.

In 1995, ethnic Russians criticized the country's new constitution for preventing dual citizenship with Russia and refusing to recognize Russian as an official language. Central control over ethnic Russians has been reinforced by shifting the capital to Astana (formerly Akmola) in the north, where the majority of ethnic Russians reside.

Few Kazakhs retain their traditional nomadic life. Commitment to Islam and loyalty to the clan remain strong.

POLITICS

Multiparty elections

L. House 1999/2004
U. House 2002/2005

President Nursultan Nazarbayev

AT THE LAST ELECTION

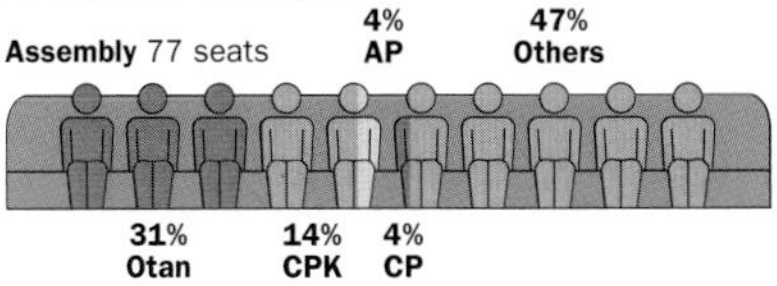
Assembly 77 seats
4% AP
47% Others
31% Otan
14% CPK
4% CP

Otan = Fatherland Republican Party of Kazakhstan
CPK = Civil Party of Kazakhstan **AP** = Agrarian Party
CP = Communist Party of Kazakhstan

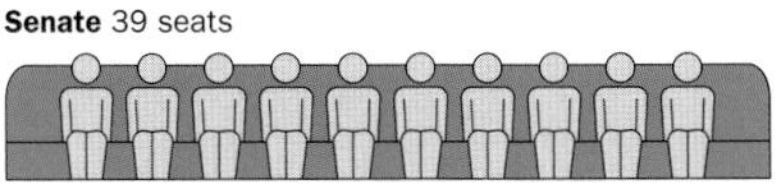
Senate 39 seats

Two members are elected by each of 16 districts and seven are nominated by the president

Legislative authority is vested in the bicameral Parliament. The president has supreme executive power.

PROFILE

Despite a democratic government, the president enjoys political dominance, and the patronage of the Kazakh clans is still important. Since coming to power in 1989, President Nursultan Nazarbayev has concentrated on market reforms and increasing his own powers at the expense of any political opposition. In 2000 the Assembly granted him special powers to advise future presidents after his term expires in 2006, and opposition parties were effectively neutered in 2002 by reform of the party registration process. Opposition leaders are often the focus of corruption charges.

MAIN POLITICAL ISSUES

Presidential powers

Critics accuse Nazarbayev of developing a personality cult. The 1995 constitution strengthened his powers, conferring the right to veto Constitutional Council decisions, and resulting in his being able to ride out a number of controversies. His reelection in early elections in 1999 was tarnished by accusations of voting irregularities and in 2002 he was able to shrug off the revelation that he had moved $1 billion of state oil revenues into a secret overseas bank account, without parliament's knowledge.

The sale of farmland

Legislation allowing the sale of farmland, key to Nazarbayev's economic liberalization, met stiff opposition in 2003. After its ultimately successful struggle to get it passed the government resigned, to be largely reappointed.

President Nursultan Nazarbayev*, who steered Kazakhstan to independence.*

WORLD AFFAIRS

Joined UN in 1992

CIS | SCO | EAPC | OIC | OSCE

Relations with Russia are good but sometimes strained by concerns over Kazakhstan's ethnic Russians. However, Kazakhstan's earlier enthusiasm for greater integration of the former Soviet states has cooled.

The country's location, bridging Europe and Asia, has led to close relations with a variety of partners, and its rich mineral resources have attracted investors from Europe, the US, and Asia. Relations with China have improved, with agreements in 1998 and 1999 on border issues, and it joins China, Russia, and three other central Asian republics in the Shanghai Cooperation Organization. However, it competes with Uzbekistan to be the acknowledged central Asian regional power. Kazakhstan's southern borders were only officially delimited in 2003; its boundary with Russia remains disputed.

K

AID

Recipient

$148m (receipts)

Down 22% in 2001

Kazakhstan joined the IMF and the World Bank in 1992, and is also a member of the EBRD. Most multilateral and bilateral aid is aimed at supporting economic reform and improving health care, transportation, and communications.

CHRONOLOGY

Once part of the Mongol empire, Kazakhstan was absorbed by the Russian Empire in the 19th century. Ethnic Russians began to settle on land used by nomadic Kazakhs. Russian settlement intensified after the 1917 Revolution, and Kazakhstan was subjected to intensive industrial and agricultural development.

- **1916** Rebellion against Russian rule brutally suppressed.
- **1917** Russian Revolution inspires civil war in Kazakhstan between Bolsheviks, anti-Bolsheviks, and Kazakh nationalists.
- **1918** Kazakh nationalists set up autonomous republic.
- **1920** Bolsheviks take control. Kirghiz Autonomous Soviet Socialist Republic (ASSR) set up within Russian Soviet Federative Socialist Republic.
- **1925** Kirghiz ASSR renamed Kazakh ASSR.
- **1936** Kazakhstan becomes full union republic of the USSR as Kazakh SSR.

CHRONOLOGY *continued*

- ❑ **1930s** Stalin's collectivization program leads to increase in Russian settlement and deaths of an estimated one million Kazakhs. Large penal settlements established for victims of Stalinist purges.
- ❑ **1941–1945** Large-scale deportations from Russia of Germans, Jews, Crimean Tatars, and others to Kazakhstan.
- ❑ **1949–1989** Nuclear test site at Semipalatinsk carries out nearly 500 nuclear explosions.
- ❑ **1954–1960** Khrushchev's policy to plow "Virgin Lands" for grain most vigorously followed in Kazakhstan. Russian settlement reaches peak.
- ❑ **1986** Riots in Almaty after ethnic Russian Gennadi Kolbin appointed head of Kazakhstan Communist Party (CPK) to replace Kazakh Dinmukhamed Kunyev.
- ❑ **1989** Kolbin replaced by Nursultan Nazarbayev, ethnic Kazakh and chair of Council of Ministers. Reform of political and administrative system.
- ❑ **1990** CPK wins elections to Supreme Soviet by overwhelming majority. Nazarbayev appointed first president of Kazakhstan. Kazakhstan declares sovereignty.
- ❑ **1991** Kazakhstan votes to preserve USSR as union of sovereign states. USSR authorities hand over control of enterprises in Kazakhstan to Kazakh government. CPK ordered to cease activities in official bodies following abortive August coup in Moscow. CPK restructures itself as Socialist Party of Kazakhstan (SPK). Independence of Republic of Kazakhstan declared; joins CIS. Announcement of closure of Semipalatinsk nuclear test site.
- ❑ **1992** Opposition demonstrations against dominance of reformed communists in Supreme Soviet, now Supreme Kenges. Nationalist groups form Republican Party, Azat.
- ❑ **1993** Adoption of new constitution. Introduction of new currency, the tenge.
- ❑ **1994** Legislative elections annulled after proof of widespread voting irregularities.
- ❑ **1995** Adoption of new constitution broadening presidential powers; referendum extends Nazarbayev's term of office.
- ❑ **1998** Legislature approves constitutional amendments, including early presidential election.
- ❑ **1999** Nazarbayev reelected president for seven more years.
- ❑ **2003** Sale of farmland legalized.

DEFENSE

Phasing out conscription

$1.27bn

Up 2% in 2001

KAZAKH ARMED FORCES

Army	930 main battle tanks (650 T-72, 280 T-62)	41,000 personnel
Navy	None	None
Air force	164 combat aircraft (MiG-29, Su-24/25/27)	19,000 personnel
Missiles	None	

As a former nuclear power and the largest of the five former Soviet central Asian republics, Kazakhstan is a potential guarantor of regional peace and stability. Kazakhstan ratified the START-I nuclear reduction treaty in 1992 and the NPT in 1993. The US agreed in 1993 to grant Kazakhstan $84 million to enable it to dismantle its nuclear weapons armory. In 1995, Kazakhstan announced that all its nuclear weapons had been transferred to Russia or else had been destroyed.

A restructuring of Kazakhstan's armed forces was launched in 2001. This included moves to end conscription, the duration of which had been halved in 1998 from two years to one. It was expected that the restructuring process would last for least three years.

ECONOMICS

Inflation 169% p.a. (1990–2001)

$20.1bn

147.5 tenge (153.3)

SCORE CARD

❑ World GNP Ranking	61st
❑ GNP per Capita	$1350
❑ Balance of Payments	–$1.75bn
❑ Inflation	8.4%
❑ Unemployment	4%

EXPORTS

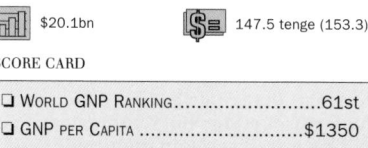

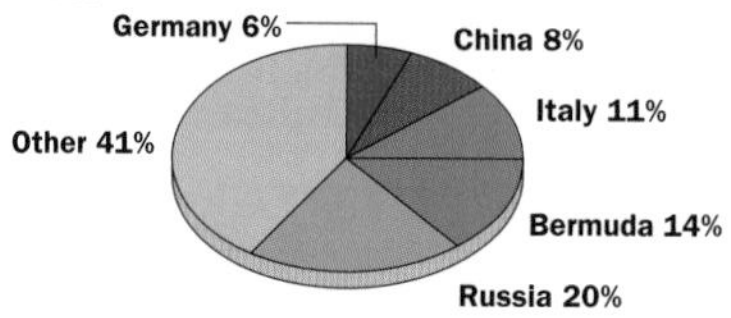
Germany 6%
China 8%
Italy 11%
Bermuda 14%
Russia 20%
Other 41%

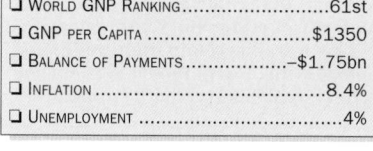

IMPORTS

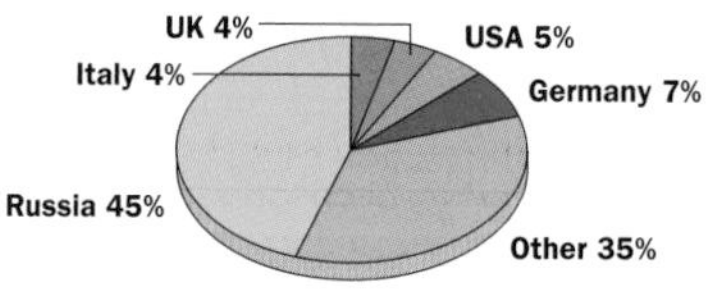
UK 4%
USA 5%
Italy 4%
Germany 7%
Russia 45%
Other 35%

ECONOMIC PERFORMANCE INDICATOR

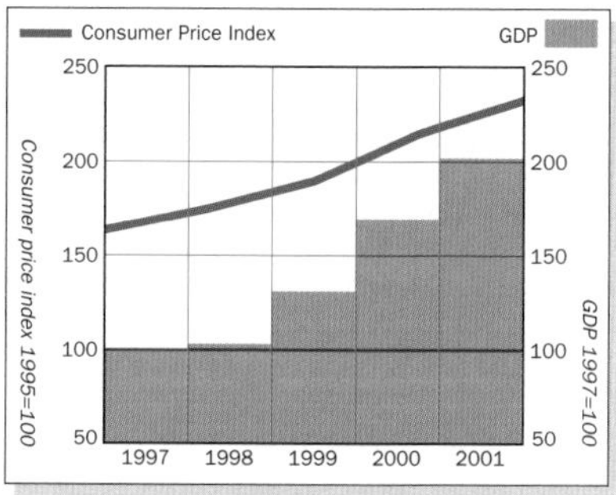
Consumer Price Index
GDP
250
200
150
100
50
Consumer price index 1995=100
GDP 1997=100
1997
1998
1999
2000
2001

Strengths

Mineral resources: oil, gas, bismuth, cadmium (used in electronics industry). Joint oil and gas ventures with Western companies. Privatization and liberalization. Baikonur space center.

Weaknesses

Collapse of former Soviet economic and trading system. Reliance on imported consumer goods. Rapid introduction of new currency, the tenge, in 1993 increased instability and fueled sharp price rises. Inefficient industrial plants.

Profile

Kazakhstan has moved faster than other former Soviet republics to establish a market economy. Prices have been freed, foreign trade deregulated, and the tax system reformed. Oil revenues have been the main engine of growth, and inflation, at one time rising sharply, has been brought under control.

Foreign direct investment is mainly in the energy sector. Outdated equipment and inadequate distribution networks mean that energy has to be imported, though Kazakhstan exports fossil fuel.

An oil price boom set the tone for the country's first "five-year plan" in 2000, part of President Nazarbayev's "Kazakhstan 2030" program. The sale of agricultural land and property was legalized in 2003.

KAZAKHSTAN : MAJOR BUSINESSES

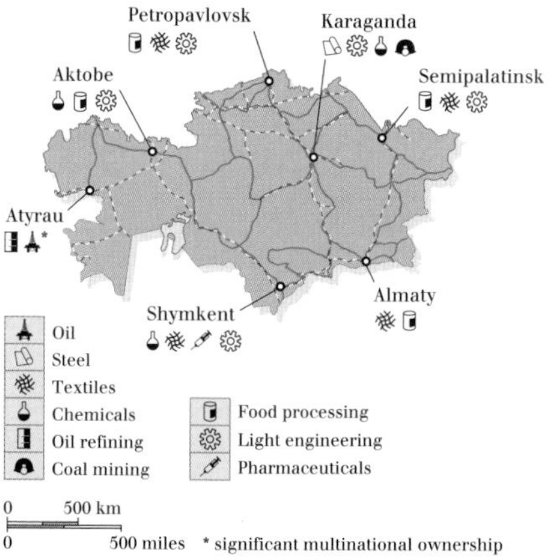
Petropavlovsk
Karaganda
Aktobe
Semipalatinsk
Atyrau
Shymkent
Almaty
Oil
Steel
Textiles
Chemicals
Oil refining
Coal mining
Food processing
Light engineering
Pharmaceuticals
0 500 km
0 500 miles
* significant multinational ownership

RESOURCES

Electric power 19m kW

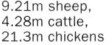

26,927 tonnes

989,000 b/d (reserves 9bn barrels)

9.21m sheep, 4.28m cattle, 21.3m chickens

Oil, gas, manganese, gold, silver, coal, iron, tungsten, chromite, bismuth, cadmium

ELECTRICITY GENERATION

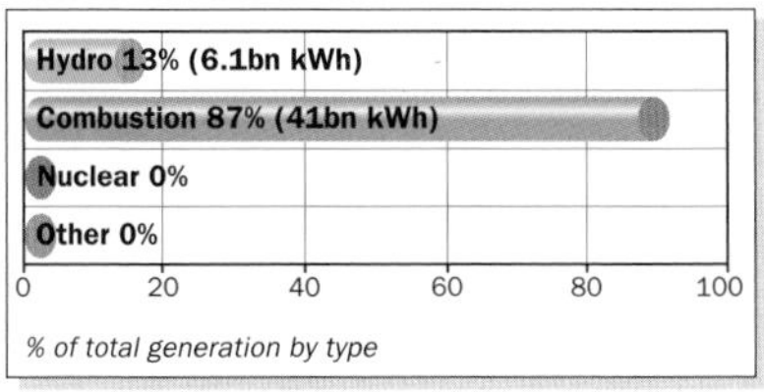
Hydro 13% (6.1bn kWh)
Combustion 87% (41bn kWh)
Nuclear 0%
Other 0%
0
20
40
60
80
100
% of total generation by type

Mining is the single most important industry in Kazakhstan. The US company Chevron has been developing the huge Tengiz oil field since 1993. Joint ventures to exploit substantial oil and gas reserves in the Caspian Sea were agreed with Russia in 1995, and the US and Japan in 1998. Kazakhstan also possesses vast iron ore and gold reserves.

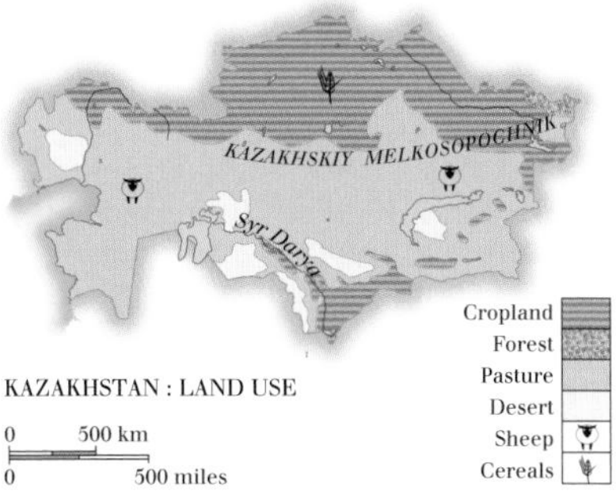
KAZAKHSKIY MELKOSOPOCHNIK
Syr Darya
Cropland
Forest
Pasture
Desert
Sheep
Cereals
0
500 km
0
500 miles

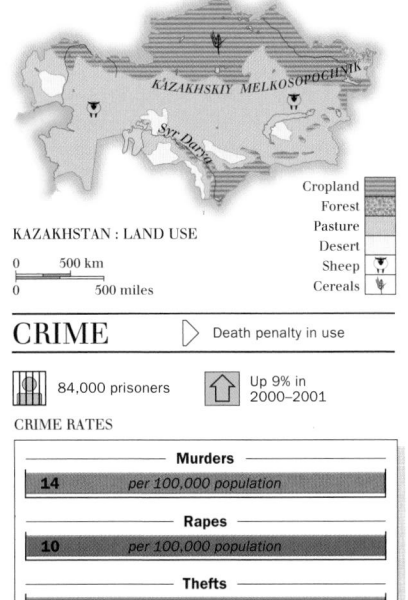

KAZAKHSTAN : LAND USE

ENVIRONMENT

Sustainability rank: 88th

3% (2% partially protected)

7.1 tonnes per capita

ENVIRONMENTAL TREATIES

No	Yes	Yes
Yes	No	No

Environmental damage caused by intensive industrial and agricultural development is a major concern. The eastern cities are heavily polluted and farmlands are being eroded. The Aral Sea, polluted by overuse of fertilizers, has shrunk by 50% because rivers have been diverted for irrigation. Half of the country is threatened by desertification.

Environmental groups succeeded in ending nuclear testing at Semipalatinsk and the green lobby is now pressing for tighter pollution controls.

MEDIA

TV ownership medium

Daily newspaper circulation 30 per 1000 people

PUBLISHING AND BROADCAST MEDIA

There are 7 principal daily newspapers and over 900 other registered newspapers

1 state-owned service, several private services

1 state-owned service, several private stations

The state-owned media operate alongside independent publications and privately owned radio and television stations. Amendments in 2001 to the Media Law strengthened state control over small broadcast outlets and Internet sites, and created more grounds for libel charges against editors and proprietors. Such state pressure has produced a drastic decline in the number of media outlets.

CRIME

Death penalty in use

84,000 prisoners

Up 9% in 2000–2001

CRIME RATES

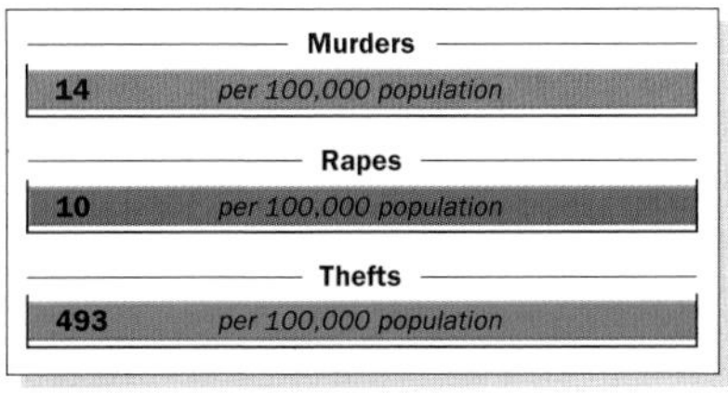
Murders
14 per 100,000 population
Rapes
10 per 100,000 population
Thefts
493 per 100,000 population

Narcotics smuggling is increasing. Corruption is rife. Political opponents are frequently jailed. Kazakhstan uses the death penalty, but does not publish statistics on its use.

EDUCATION

School leaving age: 17

99%

445,651 students

THE EDUCATION SYSTEM

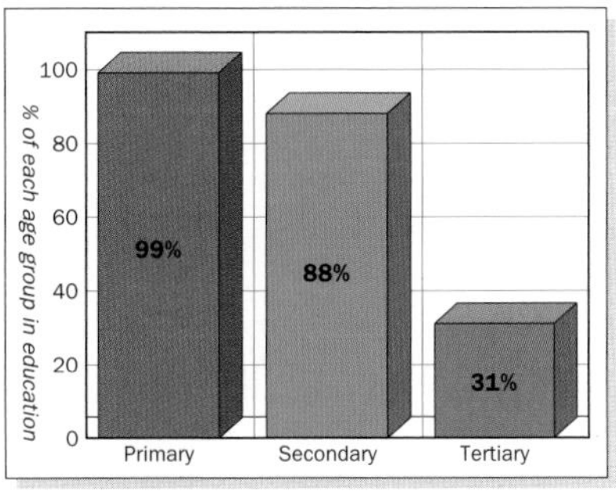
100
80
60
40
20
0
% of each age group in education
99%
88%
31%
Primary
Secondary
Tertiary

Education remains based on the Soviet model. Since its adoption as the state language in 1995, Kazakh is gradually replacing Russian as the main instruction medium in schools, but there is a shortage of Kazakh textbooks and Kazakh-speaking teachers. There are a large number of higher-education institutions and medical schools.

HEALTH

Welfare state health benefits

1 per 295 people

Cerebrovascular and heart diseases, cancers, accidents, violence

Kazakhstan's ill-equipped and poorly funded health system has produced the lowest average life expectancy in central Asia.

The health system is limited in terms of both facilities and coverage. Rural people have minimal access to clinics. The country's size means that extending coverage and improving the quality of care will be costly. Attempts are therefore being made to attract foreign investment into the health sector. Many doctors have emigrated to Russia.

SPENDING

GDP/cap. decrease

CONSUMPTION AND SPENDING

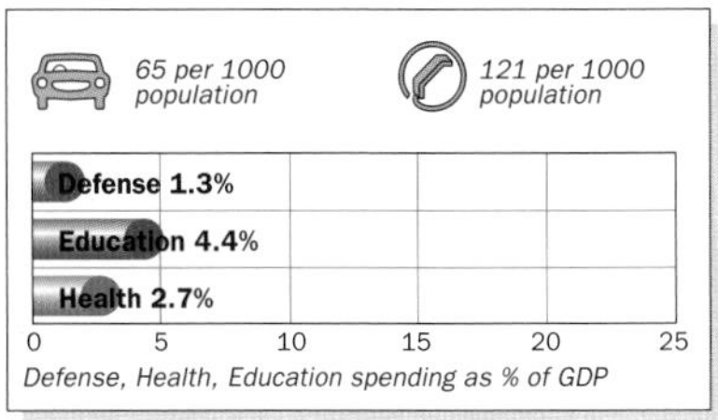
65 per 1000 population
121 per 1000 population
Defense 1.3%
Education 4.4%
Health 2.7%
0
5
10
15
20
25
Defense, Health, Education spending as % of GDP

Life for the majority of Kazakhs has always been hard, and has grown even more difficult since 1989. Unemployment rose and living standards deteriorated as a result of the market-oriented reforms within Kazakhstan in the 1990s. In addition, the liberalization of the economy has had the effect of fueling sharp price rises for essential commodities.

The rural population, the poorest group in Kazakhstan, has been badly affected. The small wealthy elite is made up mainly of former communist officials, many of whom have benefited from privatization, or are members of President Nazarbayev's clan.

WORLD RANKING

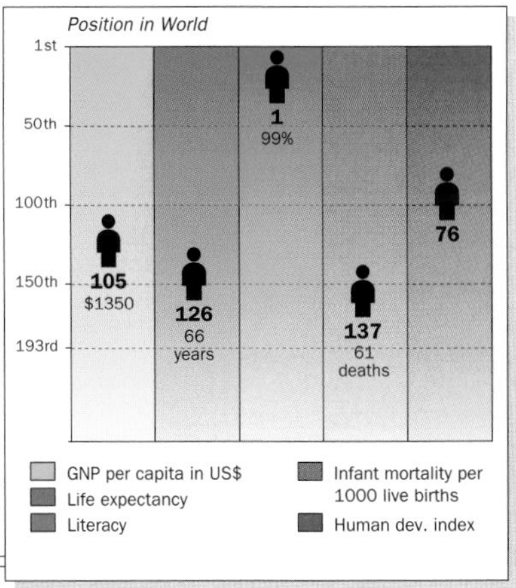
Position in World
1st
50th
100th
150th
193rd
105
$1350
126
66
years
1
99%
137
61
deaths
76
GNP per capita in US$
Life expectancy
Literacy
Infant mortality per 1000 live births
Human dev. index

K

KENYA

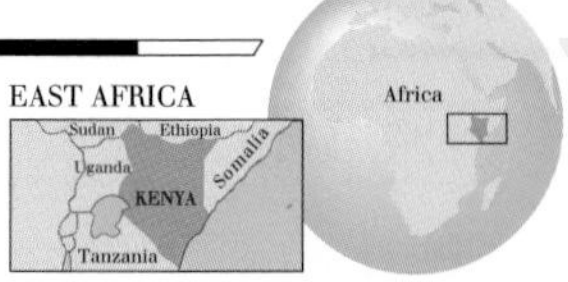
EAST AFRICA
Africa
Sudan
Ethiopia
Uganda
KENYA
Somalia
Tanzania

OFFICIAL NAME: Republic of Kenya **CAPITAL:** Nairobi
POPULATION: 31.9 million **CURRENCY:** Kenya shilling **OFFICIAL LANGUAGES:** Kiswahili and English

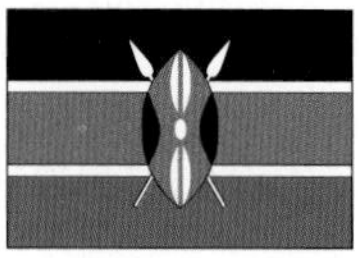

1963 | 1963 | Dec 12 | EAK | +3 | +254 | .ke

KENYA STRADDLES the equator on Africa's east coast. Its central plateau is bisected by the Great Rift Valley. The land to the north is desert, while to the east lies a fertile coastal belt. After independence from the UK in 1963, politics was dominated by Jomo Kenyatta. He was succeeded as president in 1978 by Daniel arap Moi, whose divide-and-rule policies drew accusations of favoritism and of fomenting ethnic hatreds. After 40 years in power, his KANU was finally defeated in 2002. Economic mainstays are tourism and agriculture, but high population growth is a major problem.

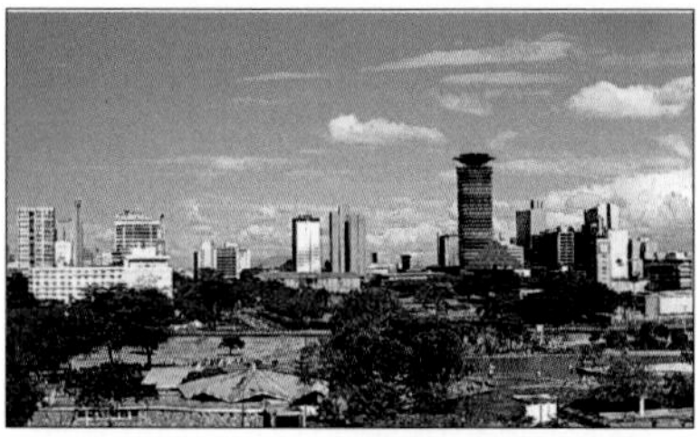

Kenyatta Conference Center, Nairobi. The modern skyline of the business center contrasts sharply with the slums on the city's outskirts.

CLIMATE

Steppe/mountain/tropical

WEATHER CHART FOR NAIROBI

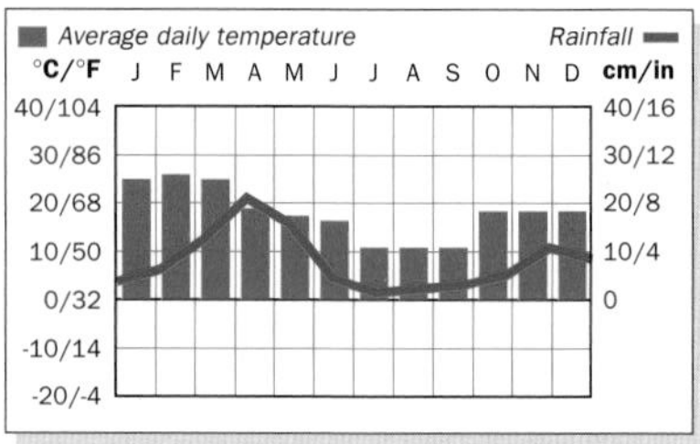
Average daily temperature
Rainfall
°C/°F
J F M A M J J A S O N D
cm/in
40/104
30/86
20/68
10/50
0/32
-10/14
-20/-4
40/16
30/12
20/8
10/4
0

The coast and Great Rift Valley are hot and humid, the plateau interior is temperate, and the northeastern desert hot and dry. Rain generally falls from April to May and October to November.

TRANSPORTATION

Drive on left

Jomo Kenyatta, Nairobi 3.06m passengers

36 ships 19,100 grt

THE TRANSPORTATION NETWORK

8940 km (5555 miles)

None

2634 km (1637 miles)

Lake Victoria is navigable

Road conditions in Kenya vary greatly, though most are still unpaved. The main railroad connects Mombasa with the highland interior. There are over 200 airstrips across the country.

Great Rift Valley, Kenya. This huge crack in the Earth's crust runs from the Jordan right through Africa to the Zambezi River.

TOURISM

Visitors : Population 1:38

838,000 visitors

Little change in 2002

Tourism is vital to the economy and a key foreign exchange earner. After a boom in package safaris and beach vacations during the 1980s, Kenya has seen a general decline in visitor numbers since. World recession, reports of instability, the much-publicized murder of several tourists in the 1990s, and, more recently, a series of Islamist terrorist attacks have been to blame.

MAIN TOURIST ARRIVALS

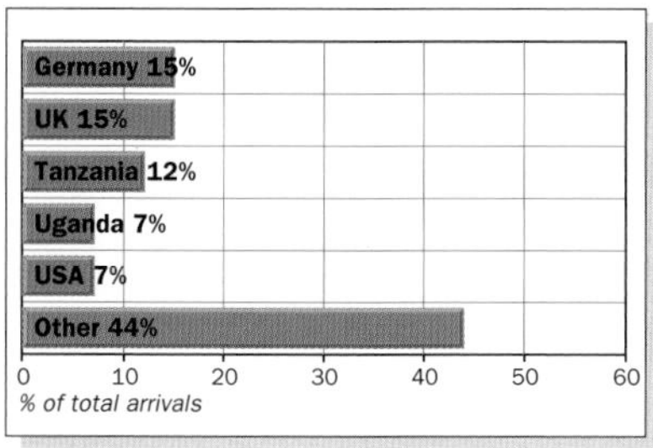
Germany 15%
UK 15%
Tanzania 12%
Uganda 7%
USA 7%
Other 44%
0
10
20
30
40
50
60
% of total arrivals

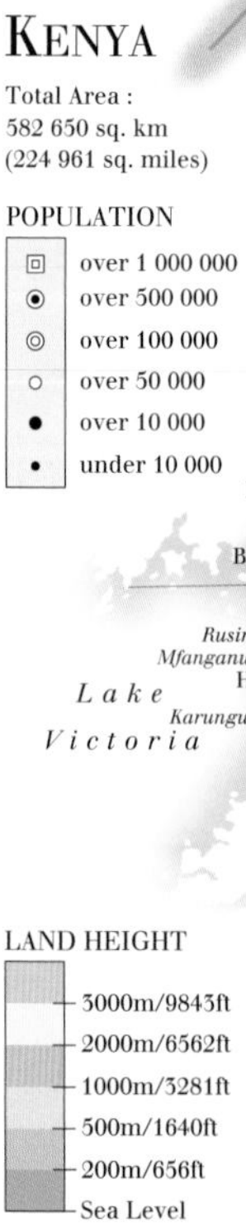
KENYA
Total Area :
582 650 sq. km
(224 961 sq. miles)
POPULATION
over 1 000 000
over 500 000
over 100 000
over 50 000
over 10 000
under 10 000
LAND HEIGHT
3000m/9843ft
2000m/6562ft
1000m/3281ft
500m/1640ft
200m/656ft
Sea Level

SUDAN
ETHIOPIA
UGANDA
SOMALIA
TANZANIA
ELEMI TRIANGLE
Lokitaung
Lake Turkana
(Lake Rudolf)
Lodwar
CHALBI DESERT
Moyale
Marsabit
Daua
Mande
HAWAR PLAIN
BOKHOL PLAIN
Wajir
BOJI PLAIN
GREAT RIFT VALLEY
Kapenguria
Kitale
Maralal
Chandlers Falls
Ewaso Ngiro
Lorian Swamp
Bungoma
Tambach
Lake Baringo
Isiolo
Eldoret
Kakamega
Kabarnet
Meru
Busia
Kisumu
Kapsabet
Nyahururu
Nanyuki
Kirinyaga 5199m
Equator
Tana
Winam Gulf
Londiani
Nakuru
Nyeri
Garissa
Rusinga I.
Mfangano I.
Kericho
Njoro
Embu
Grand Falls
Homa Bay
Elburgon
Murang'a
Masinga Reservoir
Lake Victoria
Karungu Bay
Kisii
Naivasha
Lake Naivasha
Thika
Narok
NAIROBI
Kitui
Machakos
LOITA HILLS
Lake Magadi
Magadi
NYIKA
NYIRI DESERT
YATTA PLATEAU
Lamu
Pate Island
Manda Island
Garsen
Namanga
Oloitokitok
Ungama Bay
Galana
Lugards Falls
Malindi
Voi
Taveta
Kilifi
Mombasa
Kwale
INDIAN OCEAN
N
0
100 km
100 miles

PEOPLE

Pop. density medium

Kiswahili, English, Kikuyu, Luo, Kamba

56/km² (146/mi²)

THE URBAN/RURAL POPULATION SPLIT

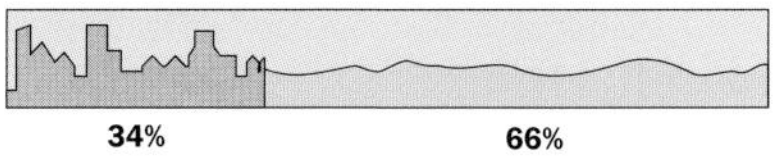
34%
66%

RELIGIOUS PERSUASION

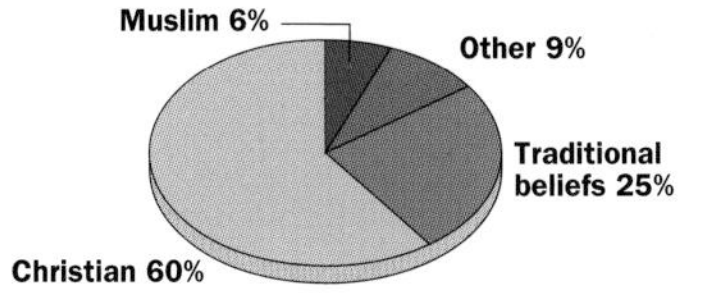
Muslim 6%
Other 9%
Traditional beliefs 25%
Christian 60%

ETHNIC MAKEUP

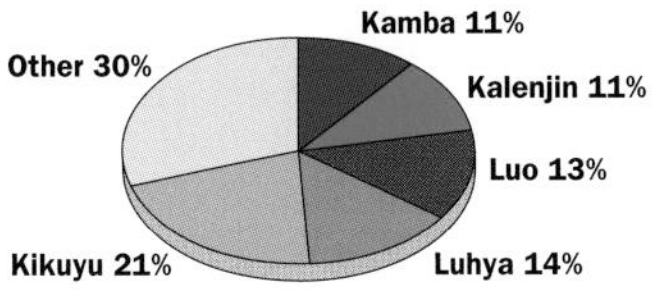
Kamba 11%
Other 30%
Kalenjin 11%
Luo 13%
Kikuyu 21%
Luhya 14%

Kenya's ethnic diversity, with about 70 different groups, reflects its past as a focus of population movements. Asians, Europeans, and Arabs form 1% of the population. The rural majority retains strong clan and extended family links, though these are being weakened by urban migration. Poverty, severe drought, and a high population growth rate are behind a land hunger which has fueled a surge in ethnic violence. In the 1990s, violence was concentrated in western Kenya, where Kikuyu, the formerly dominant tribe, were the main targets of attacks. Several hundred thousand Kikuyu are believed to have been displaced from their villages.

Female genital mutilation, criminalized in 2001, remains widespread.

POPULATION AGE BREAKDOWN

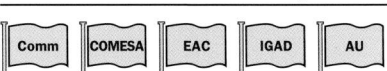

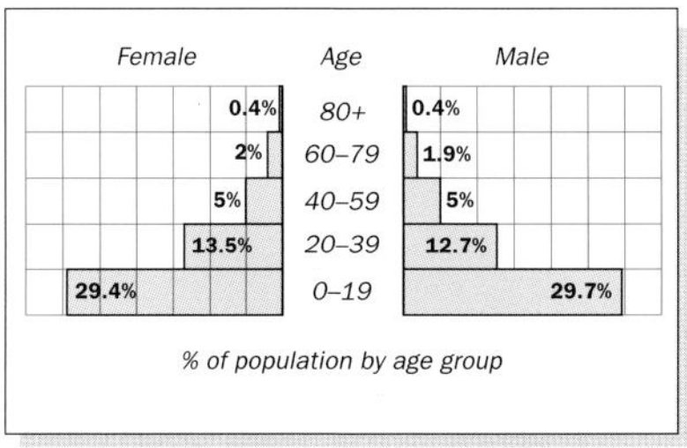
Female
Age
Male
0.4%
80+
0.4%
2%
60–79
1.9%
5%
40–59
5%
13.5%
20–39
12.7%
29.4%
0–19
29.7%
% of population by age group

POLITICS

Multiparty elections

2002/2007

President Mwai Kibaki

AT THE LAST ELECTION

National Assembly 224 seats

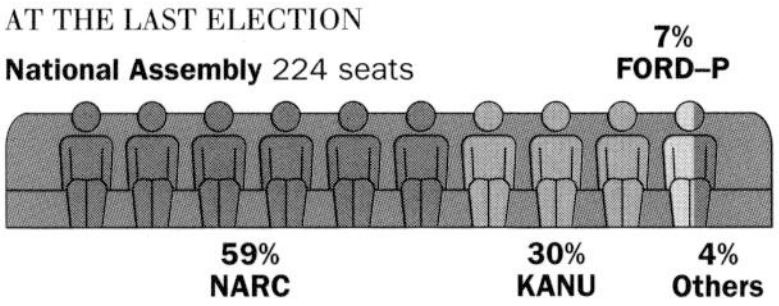
7%
FORD–P
59%
NARC
30%
KANU
4%
Others

NARC = National Rainbow Coalition (including **FORD–Kenya** and the Democratic Party–**DP**)
KANU = Kenya African National Union
FORD–P = Forum for the Restoration of Democracy–People
Others include FORD–Asili, Sisi Kwa Sisi, Safina, Shirikisho, and two ex officio members.

The National Assembly comprises 210 elected members, 12 nominated by the president, and two ex officio members

KANU dominated Kenya for four decades, from independence in 1963 until its defeat in elections in 2002.

PROFILE

International criticism of human rights abuses, and internal unrest in response to President Daniel arap Moi's attempt to entrench KANU's power, forced the introduction of multipartyism in 1992. Despite increasing unpopularity, KANU and Moi remained in power in the face of a divided opposition and amid widespread allegations of electoral irregularities. Under Moi's presidency smaller ethnic groups had gained ascendancy in the ruling party and government, while the majority Kikuyu increasingly supported the opposition.

Moi's attempt to impose Uhuru, the son of Jomo Kenyatta, Kenya's first president, as KANU candidate for the 2002 elections alienated many senior KANU members. The party was heavily defeated by the NARC in legislative elections, and Mwai Kibaki was elected president.

MAIN POLITICAL ISSUE

Government corruption

High-level corruption is entrenched in Kenyan politics and culture, and international donors pressed Moi to address the problem. In 2001 an anticorruption drive headed by former opposition figure Richard Leakey produced a "list of shame" which included senior government ministers. President Kibaki has promised to usher in a new corruption-free era.

Daniel arap Moi, *dictatorial president 1978–2002.*

President Mwai Kibaki, *opposition figure elected in 2002.*

AID

Recipient

$453m (receipts)

Down 12% in 2001

Kenya has been a major recipient of aid from the World Bank, Japan, the UK, and the EU. Little, however, has trickled down to the majority of the population. This is partly because of the high proportion of aid tied to contracts for firms from donor countries, and partly because of mismanagement and corruption. In 1996 aid disbursements were linked to improvements in human rights, and in 2001 the IMF and the World Bank withheld all aid pending anticorruption reforms. A budget deficit of almost $1 billion prompted a call in 2003 for financial aid.

CHRONOLOGY

From the 10th century, Arab coastal settlers mixed with indigenous peoples in the region. Britain's need for a route to landlocked Uganda led to the formation in 1895 of the British East African Protectorate in the coastal region.

- **1900–1918** White settlement.
- **1920** Interior becomes UK colony.
- **1930** Jomo Kenyatta goes to UK; stays 14 years.
- **1944** Kenyan African Union (KAU) formed; Kenyatta returns to lead it.
- **1952–1956** Mau Mau, Kikuyu-led violent campaign to restore African lands. State of emergency; 13,000 people killed.
- **1953** KAU banned. Kenyatta jailed.
- **1960** State of emergency ends. Tom Mboya and Oginga Odinga form KANU.
- **1961** Kenyatta freed; takes up presidency of KANU.
- **1963** KANU wins elections. Kenyatta prime minister. Full independence declared.
- **1964** Republic of Kenya formed with Kenyatta as president and Odinga as vice president.
- **1966** Odinga defects from KANU to form Kenya People's Union (KPU).

WORLD AFFAIRS

Joined UN in 1963

Comm | COMESA | EAC | IGAD | AU

Relations with neighboring states and with key Western donors are Kenya's priorities. In 1991, human rights issues were partly responsible for a two-year suspension of aid.

Kenya has become increasingly concerned about its apparent status as a "soft target" for terrorists seeking to attack the US and its allies. When the US embassy was destroyed by a car bomb in 1998, 254 people were killed and over 5000 injured, and in 2002, 15 died when a hotel was bombed in Mombasa in an attack aimed at Israelis.

Kenya is wary of the volatile security situations in neighboring states. It has recently sought to mediate in the many-sided conflict in Somalia, and hosted peace talks in 2002.

K

CHRONOLOGY *continued*

- **1969** KANU sole party to contest elections (also 1974). Tom Mboya of KANU assassinated. Unrest. KPU banned and Odinga arrested.
- **1978** Kenyatta dies. Vice President Daniel arap Moi succeeds him.
- **1982** Kenya declared a one-party state. Opposition to Moi. Abortive air force coup. Odinga rearrested.
- **1986** Open "queue-voting" replaces secret ballot in first stage of general elections. Other measures to extend Moi's powers stir up opposition.
- **1988** Moi wins third term and extends his control over judiciary.
- **1990** Government implicated in deaths of Foreign Minister Robert Ouko and Anglican archbishop. Riots. Odinga and others form FORD, outlawed by government.
- **1991** Arrest of FORD leaders, attempts to stop prodemocracy demonstrations. Donors suspend aid. Moi agrees to introduce multiparty system. Ethnic violence increases.
- **1992** FORD splits into factions. Opposition weakness helps Moi win elections.
- **1994** Odinga dies.
- **1997** Widely criticized elections.
- **1998** Bomb at US embassy kills 254.
- **1999** Moi appoints paleontologist Richard Leakey to lead government drive against corruption.
- **2000–2001** Worst drought since 1947 threatens millions with starvation.
- **2002** Thousands displaced by recurrence of major floods. Israeli tourists targeted in terrorist attacks. December, elections: KANU defeated by NARC and Mwai Kibaki elected president.

DEFENSE

No compulsory military service

$308m

Down 91% in 2001

KENYAN ARMED FORCES

78 main battle tanks (Vickers Mk 3)	20,000 personnel
4 patrol boats	1400 personnel
29 combat aircraft (9 F-5E/F)	3000 personnel
None	

The destabilization of the northeastern border by insecurity in Somalia is the main defense issue. The army has recently been deployed to suppress tribal fighting in the Rift Valley. Military assistance is given by the UK and the US.

ECONOMICS

Inflation 13% p.a. (1990–2001)

$10.7bn

73.8 Kenya shillings (78.76)

SCORE CARD

World GNP Ranking	84th
GNP per Capita	$350
Balance of Payments	–$318m
Inflation	0.8%
Unemployment	50%

EXPORTS

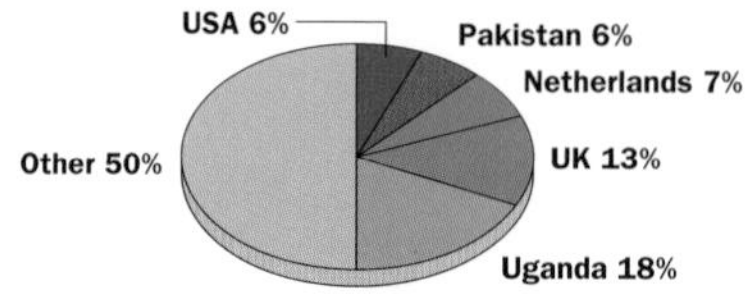
USA 6%
Pakistan 6%
Netherlands 7%
UK 13%
Uganda 18%
Other 50%

IMPORTS

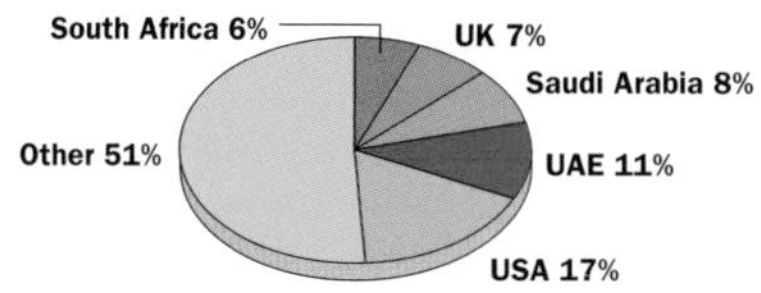
South Africa 6%
UK 7%
Saudi Arabia 8%
UAE 11%
USA 17%
Other 51%

Strengths

Tourism – largest foreign exchange earner. Broad agricultural base, especially cash crops such as coffee and tea. East Africa's largest, most diversified manufacturing sector.

Weaknesses

Fluctuating world prices for coffee and tea. Corruption. Poor recent GDP growth. High population growth. Land shortage means uneconomic small units. Country's image problem affects tourism.

Profile

Kenya has been hailed as an example to the rest of Africa of the benefits of a mainly free-market economy. Government involvement has been relatively limited, and recently further reduced by privatization. Foreign investment has been encouraged, with some success. Tourism has become the leading foreign exchange earner over the past 20 years, despite suffering serious setbacks since the 1990s. Manufacturing now accounts for 21% of GDP, and is the most diversified sector in east Africa, but needs to expand rapidly in order to create more jobs.

Economic growth was good by African standards during the 1980s, averaging over 4% a year. However, it was barely sufficient to compensate for one of the world's highest population growth rates, approximately 3.5%, though the UN estimates that this rate will have almost halved by 2015. For the majority of Kenyans, farming ever-smaller landholdings or earning a living in the informal sector, life has become harsher. The situation was exacerbated in 2001 by a ban on all trade with Somalia, which affects exports of the mild narcotic, qat, widely grown in Kenya. Severe drought from 2000 crippled the agricultural sector and put 20 million people at risk of starvation.

Other problems, including inflation, a heavy debt burden, and growing dependence on balance-of-payments support had come to a head in the early 1990s, when economic growth gave way to recession. Real GDP growth fell to 0.4% in 1992 and has remained low, falling to –0.2% in 2000. The rise in poverty-linked violence and political unrest hit tourism; earnings fell by 15% in the early 1990s, and the industry has yet to recover fully, a global downturn causing further problems in 2001.

Partly as a response to pressure from donors, the government has implemented some economic liberalization measures. These include floating the Kenya shilling, raising interest rates, and giving exporters direct access to their hard currency earnings. However, sustained growth is likely to remain elusive until Kenya overcomes the official corruption which drains vital resources, and the poor image affecting its tourist industry.

ECONOMIC PERFORMANCE INDICATOR

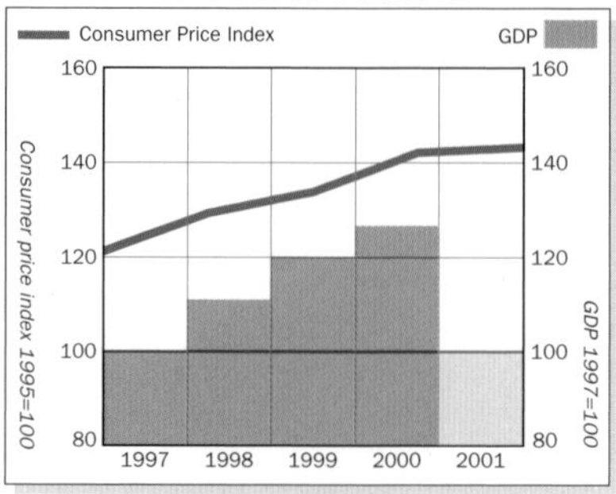
Consumer Price Index
GDP
160
140
120
100
80
1997
1998
1999
2000
2001
Consumer price index 1995=100
GDP 1997=100

KENYA : MAJOR BUSINESSES

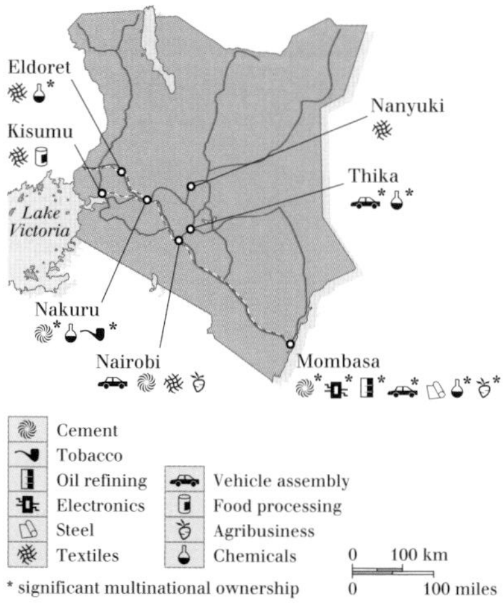
Eldoret
Kisumu
Lake Victoria
Nakuru
Nairobi
Nanyuki
Thika
Mombasa
Cement
Tobacco
Oil refining
Electronics
Steel
Textiles
Vehicle assembly
Food processing
Agribusiness
Chemicals
0 100 km
0 100 miles
* significant multinational ownership

RESOURCES

Electric power 942,000 kW

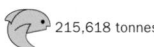

215,618 tonnes

Oil reserves not currently exploited

13.5m cattle, 9m goats, 8m sheep, 32m chickens

Soda ash, fluorite, limestone, rubies, gold, vermiculite, oil

ELECTRICITY GENERATION

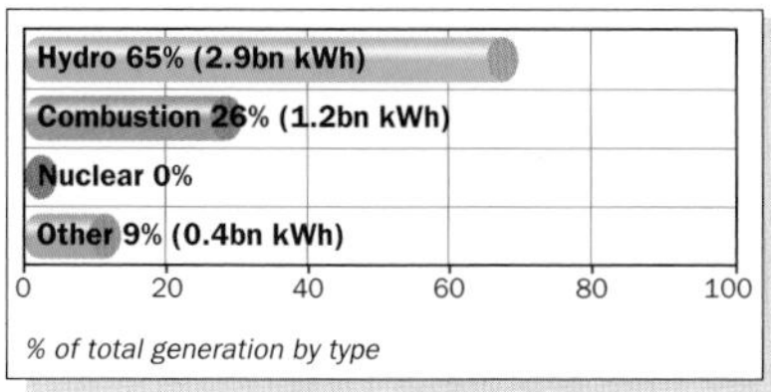
Hydro 65% (2.9bn kWh)
Combustion 26% (1.2bn kWh)
Nuclear 0%
Other 9% (0.4bn kWh)
0
20
40
60
80
100
% of total generation by type

Agriculture is still the largest sector of the economy. Kenya's varied topography means that tropical, subtropical, and temperate crops may be grown. Coffee and tea, the main export crops, have been affected by falling world prices. Efforts to reduce dependence on these have led to the growth of a successful export-oriented horticultural industry.

Kenya has few mineral resources, though oil exploration has revealed deposits in Turkana District. Hydroelectric and geothermal sources are being developed to reduce energy imports – currently 70% of total requirements. However, droughts caused power shortages in 2000 and 2001, leading to the imposition of daily power cuts.

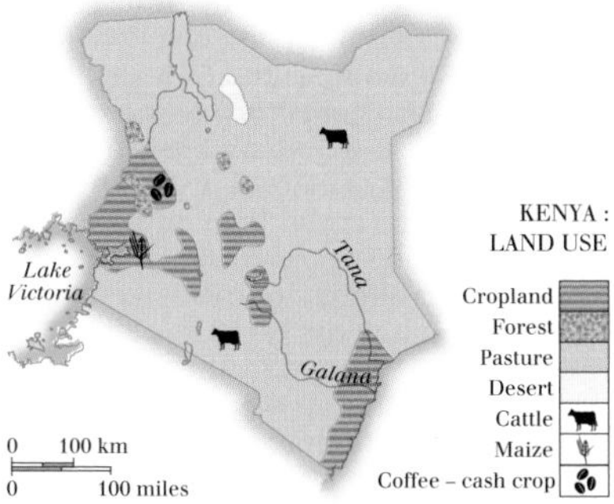
KENYA : LAND USE
Lake Victoria
Tana
Galana
Cropland
Forest
Pasture
Desert
Cattle
Maize
Coffee – cash crop
0 100 km
0 100 miles

ENVIRONMENT

Sustainability rank: 89th

8% (2% partially protected)

0.3 tonnes per capita

ENVIRONMENTAL TREATIES

Yes Yes Yes

Yes Yes No

The importance to tourism of wildlife conservation is recognized, and recent elephant protection schemes have been a success, but proposed national reserves compete with agriculture for land. Opposition to government plans to reallocate some national park land to squatters is growing.

MEDIA

TV ownership low

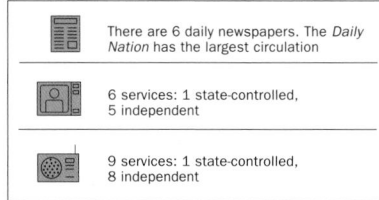

Daily newspaper circulation 8 per 1000 people

PUBLISHING AND BROADCAST MEDIA

There are 6 daily newspapers. The *Daily Nation* has the largest circulation

6 services: 1 state-controlled, 5 independent

9 services: 1 state-controlled, 8 independent

Government intolerance of criticism is long-standing and includes plays and novels as well as the media. Ngugi wa Thiongo, Kenya's most famous novelist, was exiled for his criticism of KANU.

CRIME

Death penalty in use

35,278 prisoners

Crime is rising

CRIME RATES

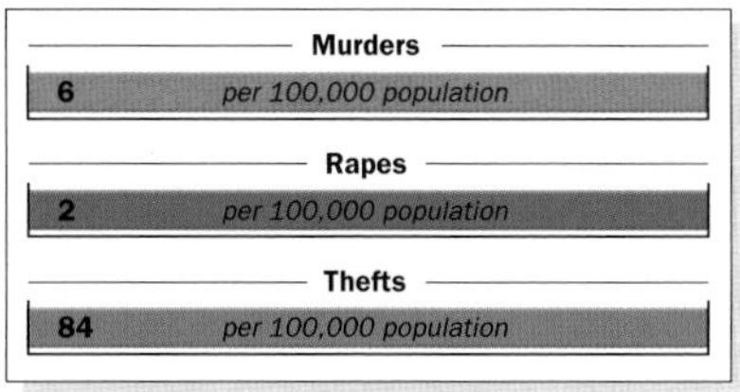
Murders
6 per 100,000 population
Rapes
2 per 100,000 population
Thefts
84 per 100,000 population

Nairobi's high crime levels are spreading countrywide as a result of worsening poverty, ethnic violence, and rising banditry in the northeast. An increase in the use of guns underlies the rapid increase in violent crime.

EDUCATION

School leaving age: 14

83%

98,583 students

THE EDUCATION SYSTEM

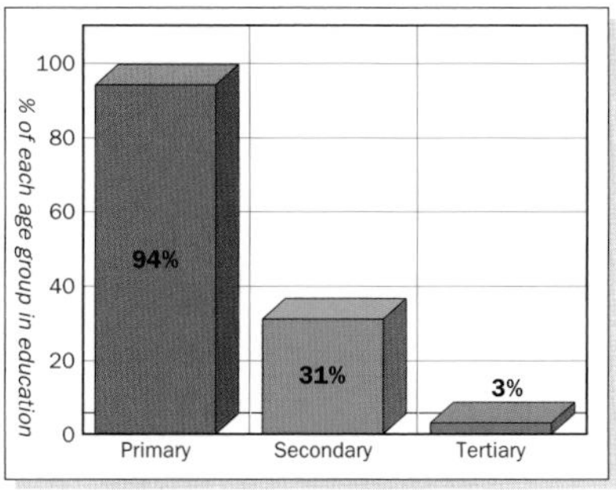
100
80
60
40
20
0
% of each age group in education
94%
31%
3%
Primary
Secondary
Tertiary

The education system is loosely based on the British model. Primary education, which lasts for eight years from the age of six, is free and compulsory; some 70% of children attend. The drop-out rate at secondary level is high, with only about 23% attendance. In higher education, the emphasis is on vocational training. There are 20 universities.

HEALTH

Welfare state health benefits

1 per 7143 people

Respiratory and diarrheal diseases, malaria, AIDS

The health system comprises a mixture of state and private facilities, the latter mainly run by charities and missions. The state system has been badly hit by recession, worsening the already limited access of the rural majority. Poverty-related illnesses, particularly among women and children, are increasing. HIV and AIDS reached epidemic proportions in some areas in the 1990s. Estimates of the level of infection with HIV continue to be around 14% of the adult population, and the government calculated that by 2002 there were 1.1 million AIDS orphans.

SPENDING

GDP/cap. increase

CONSUMPTION AND SPENDING

10 per 1000 population

10 per 1000 population

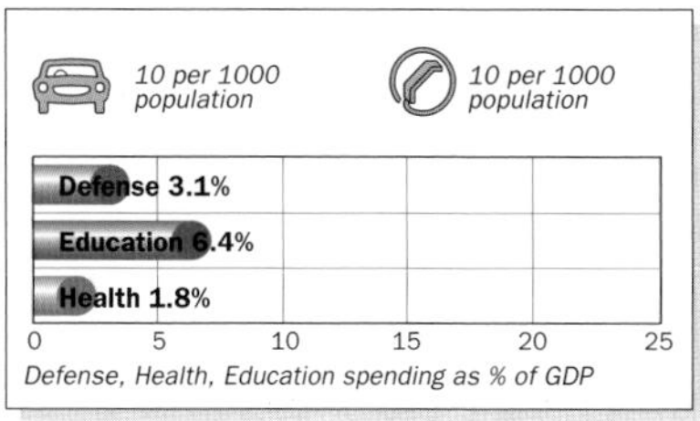
Defense 3.1%
Education 6.4%
Health 1.8%
0
5
10
15
20
25
Defense, Health, Education spending as % of GDP

Wealth disparities in Kenya are large and growing, exacerbated by land hunger and migration to the cities, where jobs are few and existence depends on the informal economy. More than half of all town dwellers live in slums, and the slum dwellers of Nairobi's Amarthi Valley are among Africa's poorest, worst-nourished people. Their lives contrast sharply with those of the country's elite – top government officials with access to patronage; white Kenyans, who derive their wealth largely from agricultural estates; and the largely Asian business community. Landless peasants have pushed for a redistribution of land similar to that in Zimbabwe.

WORLD RANKING

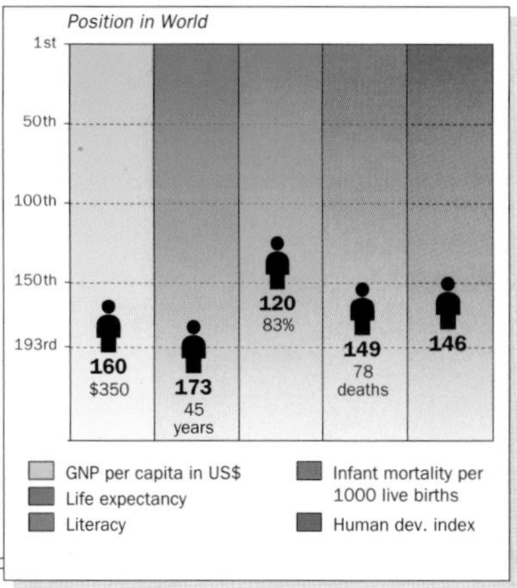
Position in World
1st
50th
100th
150th
193rd
160
$350
173
45
years
120
83%
149
78
deaths
146
GNP per capita in US$
Life expectancy
Literacy
Infant mortality per 1000 live births
Human dev. index

K

KIRIBATI

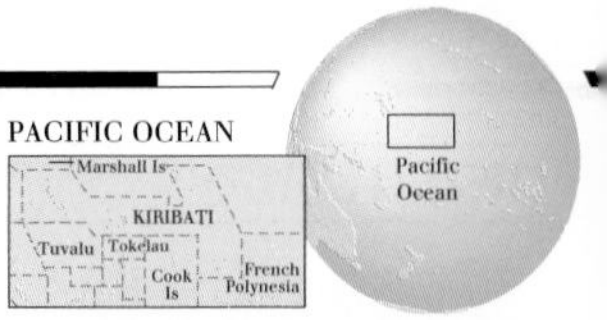
PACIFIC OCEAN
Marshall Is
KIRIBATI
Tuvalu
Tokelau
Cook Is
French Polynesia
Pacific Ocean

OFFICIAL NAME: Republic of Kiribati **CAPITAL:** Bairiki (Tarawa Atoll)
POPULATION: 96,335 **CURRENCY:** Australian dollar **OFFICIAL LANGUAGE:** English

1979 | 1979 | July 12 | KIR | +12 | +686 | .ki

FORMERLY PART OF THE colony of the Gilbert and Ellice Islands, the Gilberts became independent from Britain in 1979 and took the name Kiribati (pronounced "Keer-ee-bus"). British interest in the Gilbert Islands rested solely on the exploitation of the phosphate deposits on Banaba; these ran out in 1980. In 1981, Kiribati won damages (but not the costs of litigation) from the British for decades of phosphate exploitation.

***Banreaba Island, Tarawa Atoll.** None of the atolls are more than 8 m (26 ft) high except Banaba, once the source of phosphates.*

CLIMATE

Tropical oceanic

WEATHER CHART FOR BAIRIKI

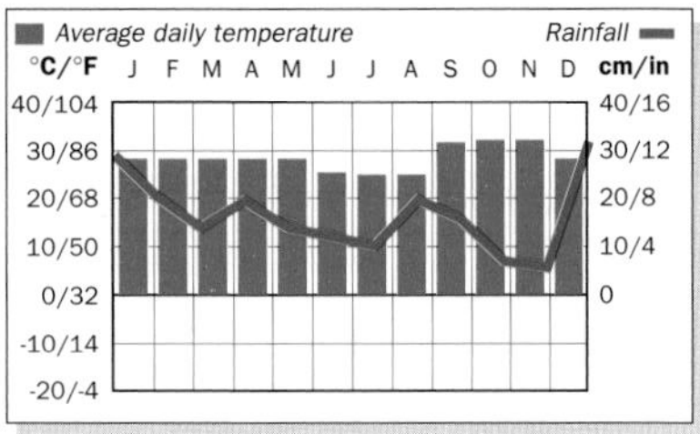
Average daily temperature
Rainfall
°C/°F
J F M A M J J A S O N D
cm/in
40/104
30/86
20/68
10/50
0/32
-10/14
-20/-4
40/16
30/12
20/8
10/4
0

Kiribati's small land area in the vast Pacific means that some atolls can often go for months without rain. In 1999, a nationwide drought emergency was declared.

TRANSPORTATION

Drive on right

Bonriki International, Tarawa 51,000 passengers

8 ships 4198 grt

THE TRANSPORTATION NETWORK

483 km (300 miles)

None

None

5 km (3 miles)

Kiribati has a limited air link with Fiji. Transportation around and between the atolls is provided mostly by small canoes.

TOURISM

Visitors : Population 1:96

1000 visitors

No change in 2000

MAIN TOURIST ARRIVALS

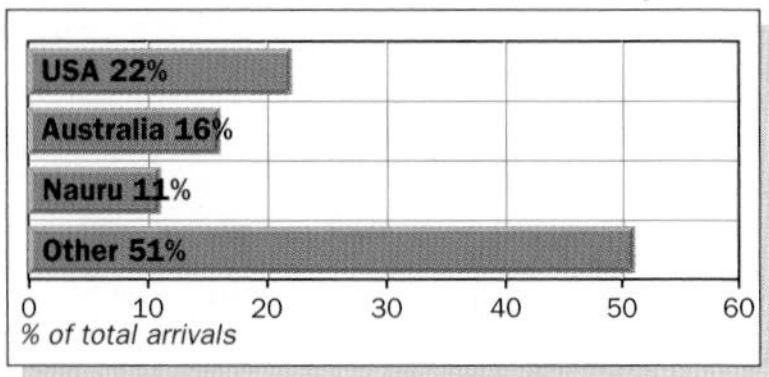
USA 22%
Australia 16%
Nauru 11%
Other 51%
0
10
20
30
40
50
60
% of total arrivals

A weekly flight from Honolulu to Kiritimati (Christmas) Island ensures a small but steady stream of visitors.

PEOPLE

Pop. density medium

English, Kiribati

136/km² (352/mi²)

THE URBAN/RURAL POPULATION SPLIT

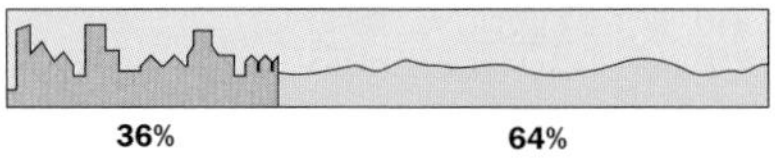
36%
64%

RELIGIOUS PERSUASION

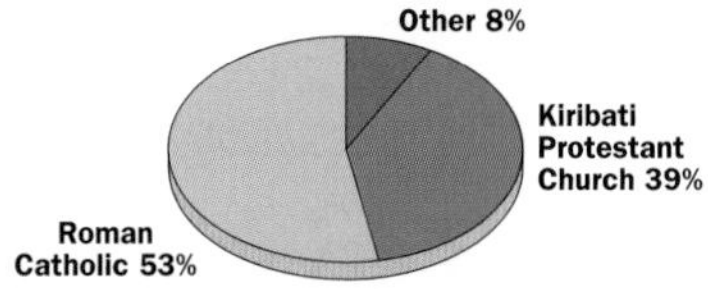
Other 8%
Kiribati Protestant Church 39%
Roman Catholic 53%

Almost all I-Kiribati (as the Gilbertese have been known since independence) are Micronesian, although the Banabans employed anthropologists to establish their racial distinctness. Tension with the Banabans is intense, mostly fueled by the historic value of Banaba's phosphate deposits. Most I-Kiribati are poor. Many go to Nauru as guest workers, living in barrack-room conditions, or work as merchant shipping crew. Those who stay at home go through a circular migration from the outlying islands to Tarawa, returning to see relatives. Women play a prominent role, especially on outlying islands, where they run most of the farms.

POLITICS

Nonparty elections

2003/2007

President Anote Tong

AT THE LAST ELECTION

House of Assembly 42 seats

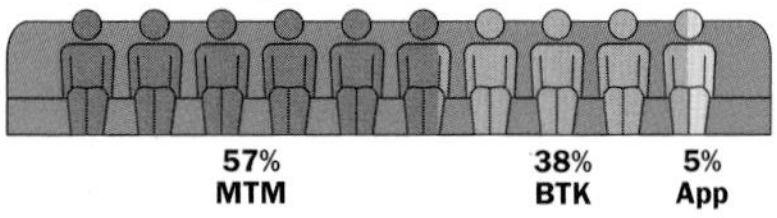
57% MTM
38% BTK
5% App

MTM = Protect the Maneaba **BTK** = Pillars of Truth
App = Appointed

The House of Assembly has one appointed member (for the Banaban community in Fiji) and one ex-officio member

The traditional chiefs still effectively rule Kiribati. A period of political uncertainty followed the election victory of the opposition BTK in 2002. The party succeeded in ousting the incumbent president, and its candidate Anote Tong was elected president in 2003. In the meantime, however, the MTM had regained control of the House of Assembly in fresh elections. Overpopulation on Tarawa is a major issue, in part caused by the poverty and lack of opportunity on the outer islands; a resettlement program began in 1998. The economy's overdependence on coconut products is also of concern.

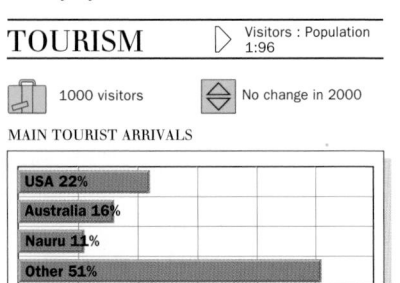

KIRIBATI

Total Area : 811 sq. km (313 sq. miles)

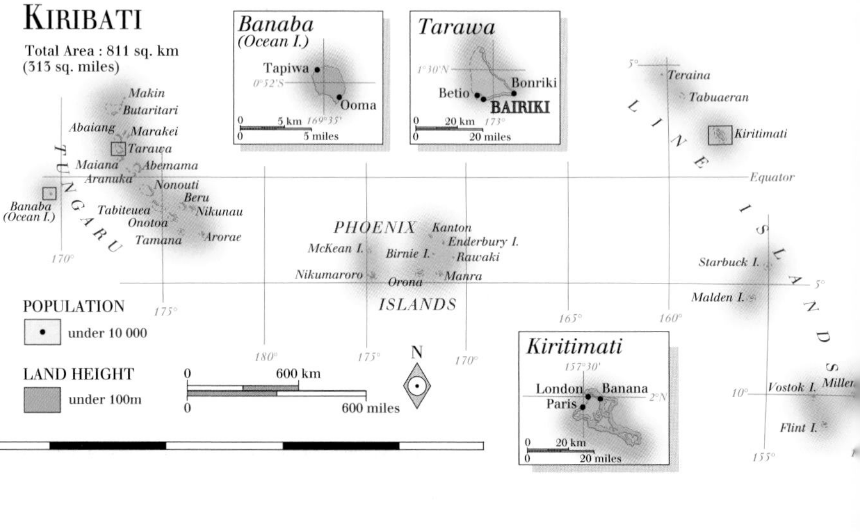
Banaba (Ocean I.)
Tapiwa
Ooma
5 km
5 miles
Tarawa
Betio
Bonriki
BAIRIKI
20 km
20 miles
Makin
Butaritari
Abaiang
Marakei
Tarawa
Maiana
Abemama
Aranuka
Nonouti
Beru
Nikunau
Tabiteuea
Onotoa
Tamana
Arorae
Banaba (Ocean I.)
TUNGARU
PHOENIX ISLANDS
Kanton
Enderbury I.
McKean I.
Birnie I.
Rawaki
Nikumaroro
Orona
Manra
Teraina
Tabuaeran
Kiritimati
LINE ISLANDS
Equator
Starbuck I.
Malden I.
Vostok I.
Millet
Flint I.
Kiritimati
London
Banana
Paris
20 km
20 miles
POPULATION
under 10 000
LAND HEIGHT
under 100m
0
600 km
600 miles
N

WORLD AFFAIRS

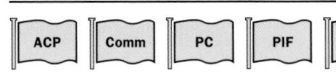

Joined UN in 1999

ACP | Comm | PC | PIF | ADB

Kiribati has little international significance because of its tiny size and remote location, but is able to make its voice heard regionally through the Pacific Islands Forum. In 1986, Kiribati was a signatory to a deal between the US and a number of Pacific Island states that resulted in the US paying US$60 million in return for access to Pacific fishing grounds. In the Cold War era Kiribati played the USSR off against the US, extracting a high price for fishing leases, which allowed boats to spy on US nuclear testing on the neighboring Kwajalein Atoll in the Marshall Islands.

AID

Recipient

US$12m (receipts) | Down 33% in 2001

Aid is mostly channeled to infrastructure projects. Japan is a major donor and provided US$22 million for the upgrade of Betio port.

DEFENSE

No compulsory military service

Kiribati has no defense budget | Not applicable

Australia and New Zealand provide de facto protection, with regular antisubmarine patrols.

ECONOMICS

Inflation 3.3% p.a. (1990–2001)

US$77m | 1.491 Australian dollars (1.781)

SCORE CARD

- WORLD GNP RANKING........................189th
- GNP PER CAPITA ....US$830
- BALANCE OF PAYMENTS ....US$1m
- INFLATION 2.5%
- UNEMPLOYMENT 2%

STRENGTHS

Subsistence economy; only Tarawa imports food. Coconuts provide some export income, mostly from the EU. Fisheries have limited potential. Upgraded port facilities at Betio.

WEAKNESSES

Lack of resources. High levels of poverty. Isolation, and large distances between islands. Heavy dependence on international aid. Almost no economic potential.

EXPORTS

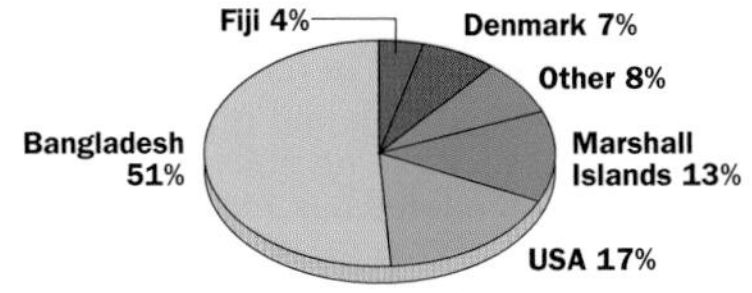
Fiji 4%
Denmark 7%
Other 8%
Marshall Islands 13%
USA 17%
Bangladesh 51%

IMPORTS

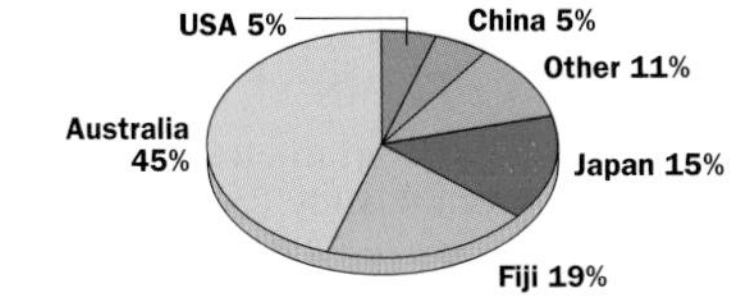
USA 5%
China 5%
Other 11%
Japan 15%
Fiji 19%
Australia 45%

RESOURCES

Electric power 2000 kW

40,009 tonnes | Not an oil producer

12,000 pigs, 450,000 chickens | None

Phosphate deposits on Banaba ran out in 1980. All energy supplies have to be imported. An underwater agriculture scheme is under development.

ENVIRONMENT

Not available

39% (including marine and semi-protected areas) | 0.3 tonnes per capita

Rising sea levels cause coastal erosion and ultimately threaten Kiribati's existence. Global warming is a critical issue both for this reason and because of its damaging effects on the coral reef which protects Tarawa from the sea and holds important inshore fish stocks in the lagoon. The coral has also suffered from pollution by untreated effluent.

MEDIA

TV ownership low

There are no daily newspapers

PUBLISHING AND BROADCAST MEDIA

There are no daily newspapers. The weekly newspapers are *Butim'aea Manin te Euangkerio, Kiribati Newstar,* and *Te Uekera*

1 state-owned service | 1 state-owned service

The independent *Kiribati Newstar* competes with the state-owned *Te Uekera* and the Protestant Church's paper *Butim'aea Manin te Euangkerio.*

CRIME

No death penalty

63 prisoners | Crime is minimal

Crime, apart from brawls resulting from drunkenness, is minimal. The islands' judicial system is based on the British model.

EDUCATION

School leaving age: 15

99% | 568 students

Education is British-inspired and compulsory from six to 15. The best students go on to university in Fiji.

CHRONOLOGY

In 1892, the British established the phosphate-producing colony of the Gilbert and Ellice Islands.

- **1957** British nuclear tests take place near Kiritimati.
- **1979** Independence as two states, Kiribati and Tuvalu.
- **1981** Kiribati wins damages for phosphate mining from UK.
- **1986** Kiribati–US fishing deal.
- **1994** Teburoro Tito president.
- **1999** National drought emergency.
- **2002** BTK wins elections.
- **2003** Anote Tong of BTK president, despite MTM parliamentary majority.

HEALTH

Welfare state health benefits

1 per 3333 people | Heart diseases, diabetes

Most I-Kiribati are healthy despite the high levels of poverty. Free medical care is provided to all. Nutrition is becoming a problem on Tarawa, where overpopulation limits agriculture.

SPENDING

GDP/cap. increase

CONSUMPTION AND SPENDING

2 per 1000 population | *40 per 1000 population*

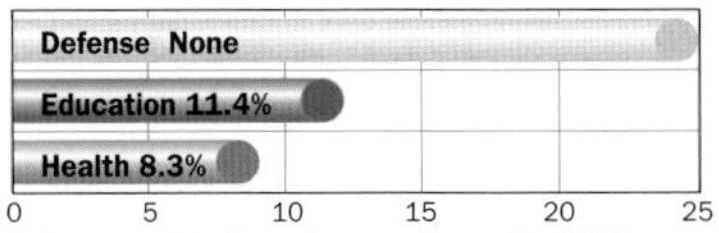
Defense None
Education 11.4%
Health 8.3%
0
5
10
15
20
25

Defense, Health, Education spending as % of GDP

Life in Kiribati is modest. Most I-Kiribati live by subsistence farming and fishing. Civil servants in Bairiki form the wealthiest group. The cost of living on Tarawa is higher than that on the outlying islands due to the need to import food, though fish is abundant and cheap everywhere.

WORLD RANKING

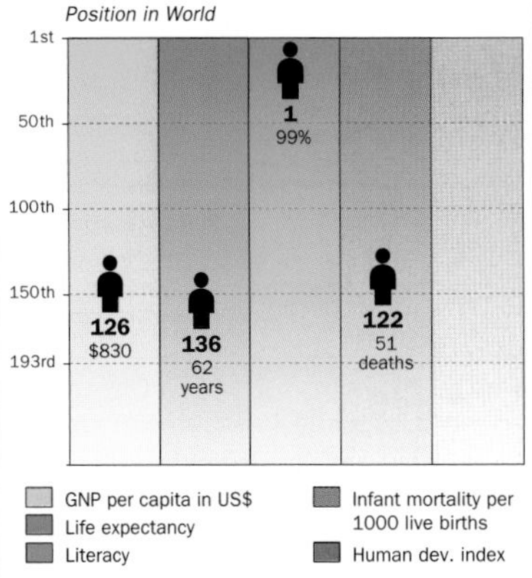
Position in World
1st
50th
100th
150th
193rd
126
$830
136
62 years
1
99%
122
51 deaths
GNP per capita in US$
Life expectancy
Literacy
Infant mortality per 1000 live births
Human dev. index

K

NORTH KOREA

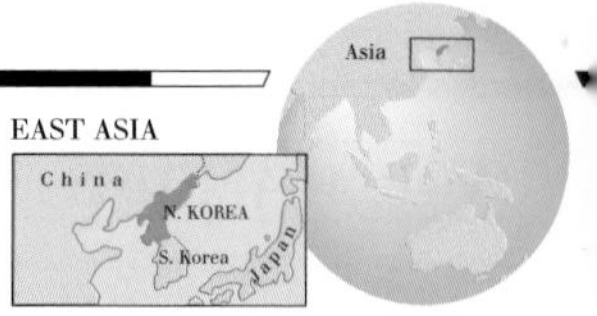
Asia
EAST ASIA
China
N. KOREA
S. Korea
Japan

OFFICIAL NAME: Democratic People's Republic of Korea **CAPITAL:** Pyongyang
POPULATION: 22.6 million **CURRENCY:** North Korean won **OFFICIAL LANGUAGE:** Korean

1948 | 1953 | Sept 9 | DRK | +9 | +850 | .kp

COMPRISING THE NORTHERN half of the Korean peninsula, North Korea is separated from the US-backed South by an armistice line straddling the 38th parallel. Much of the country is mountainous; the Chaeryong and Pyongyang plains in the southwest are the most fertile regions. An independent communist republic from 1948, it remains largely isolated. With its economy starved of capital, it now faces a food crisis requiring large-scale international assistance.

CLIMATE

Continental

WEATHER CHART FOR PYONGYANG

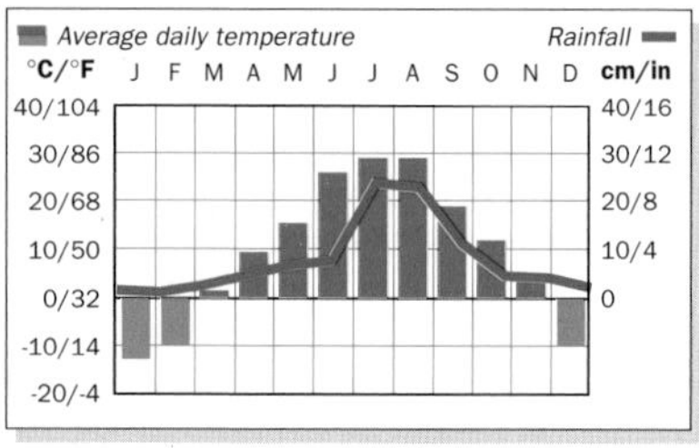
Average daily temperature
Rainfall
°C/°F
J F M A M J J A S O N D
cm/in
40/104
30/86
20/68
10/50
0/32
-10/14
-20/-4
40/16
30/12
20/8
10/4
0

North Korea has a typically continental climate, but with wet summers. Winters in the north can be extreme.

TRANSPORTATION

Drive on right

Sunan, Pyongyang | 176 ships 697,800 grt

THE TRANSPORTATION NETWORK

1997 km (1241 miles)	524 km (326 miles)
5214 km (3240 miles)	2253 km (1400 miles)

The heavily used railroads were built by the occupying Japanese after 1910. Highways are open only to very limited, officially approved traffic. Improving relations with South Korea in 2000 led to projects for cross-border links.

TOURISM

Visitors : Population 1:174

130,000 visitors | Up 2% in 1995–1998

MAIN TOURIST ARRIVALS

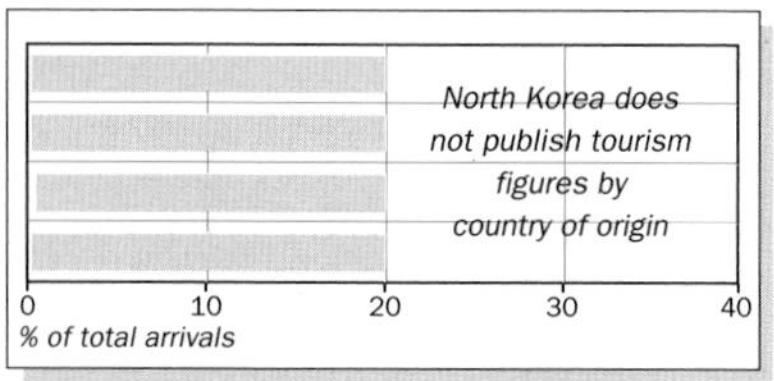
North Korea does not publish tourism figures by country of origin
0
10
20
30
40
% of total arrivals

Economic need has forced limited tourism. South Korean firms have developed resorts such as Mt. Kumgang.

Paddy field. *The hot, wet summers are ideal for rice growing. Most farms are run as cooperatives.*

PEOPLE

Pop. density medium

Korean, Chinese | 188/km² (486/mi²)

THE URBAN/RURAL POPULATION SPLIT

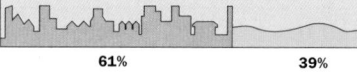

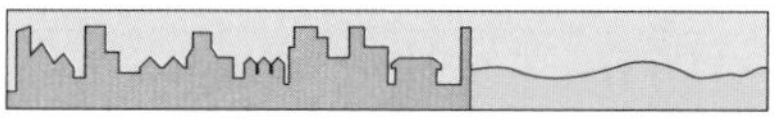

61% **39%**

ETHNIC MAKEUP

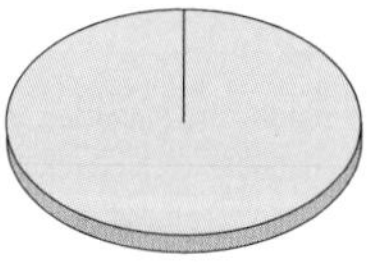
Korean 100%

The Korean peninsula is unusual in having been inhabited by a single ethnic group for the last 2000 years. There is a tiny Chinese minority in North Korea.

The religions practiced under strict control are Buddhism, Christianity, and Chondogyo, a combination of Taoism, Confucianism, Buddhism, shamanism, and Christianity peculiar to Korea.

North Koreans live highly regulated lives. Divorce is nonexistent and extramarital sex highly frowned upon. Women form more than 50% of the workforce, but are also expected to run the home; it is not uncommon for them to rise at 4 a.m., and end their working day at 7 p.m. From an early age, children are looked after by an extensive system of state-run crèches. The privileged lifestyle of the political elite – some 200,000 in number – is rumored to be a source of popular resentment.

POLITICS

No multiparty elections

2003/2008 | Eternal President Kim Il Sung

AT THE LAST ELECTION

Supreme People's Assembly 687 seats

100% KWP

KWP = Korean Workers' Party

The three million-strong KWP is the only legal party; membership is essential for individual advancement. State control is total.

After almost 50 years as leader Kim Il Sung, subject of a lavish personality cult, died in 1994. Kim Jong Il, his son and chosen successor, lacks his father's authority and has yet to seal the succession; in 1998 Kim Il Sung, by then four years dead, was declared "Eternal President." Nonetheless, Kim Jong Il is officially known as "Dear Leader" and is guaranteed 100% of the vote in elections.

WORLD AFFAIRS

Joined UN in 1991

NAM

China has been North Korea's closest ally since the collapse in 1991 of Soviet communism. The key relationship is with South Korea, with which the North is still notionally at war. A breakthrough in relations in 2000 has since been undermined by mutual suspicion. There has also been a growing antagonism with the US administration, particularly over North Korea's nuclear missile program. In 2002 the US designated North Korea part of an "axis of evil" and has intensified pressure ever since.

AID

Recipient

$119m (receipts) | Up 59% in 2001

Droughts and floods in the 1990s caused famine; international aid levels are insufficient to stave off starvation. Fuel aid was suspended from 2002 over North Korea's nuclear program.

DEFENSE

Compulsory military service

$2.05bn | Down 2% in 2001

North Korea has continued its nuclear missile program despite the 1994 agreement to freeze its research. It develops and exports missiles.

NORTH KOREA

Total Area : 120 540 sq. km (46 540 sq. miles)

0
100 km
0
100 miles
N
CHINA
RUSSIAN FEDERATION
Onsŏng
Kyŏnghŭng
Hoeryŏng
Najin
Musan
Komusan
Tumen
Paektu-san 2744 m
Ch'ŏngjin
Hyesan
Myŏngch'ŏn
Kilchu
Manp'o
Kanggye
Yalu
Sup'ung-ho
Sakchu
Hŭich'ŏn
HAMGYŎNG-SANMAEK
Tanch'ŏn
Kimch'aek
Pukch'ŏng
Iwŏn
Sinŭiju
Kusŏng
Kujang
Orori
Sinp'o
Hongwŏn
Hamhŭng
Hŭngnam
Pakch'ŏn
Chŏngju
Anju
Kunu-ri
Tŏkch'ŏn
Sunch'ŏn
Yŏnghŭng
Kowŏn
Munch'ŏn
Wŏnsan
Tongjosŏn-man
Sŏjosŏn-man
Sukch'ŏn
Yangdŏk
KOREA BAY
PYONGYANG
Nam
Kosan
Kuŭm
Kosŏng
Songnim
Namp'o
Sariwŏn
Chaeryŏng
Changyŏn
Haeju
Kŭmch'ŏn
Kaesŏng
Ongjin
Kyŏnggi-man
YELLOW SEA
SOUTH KOREA
SEA OF JAPAN
42°
40°
38°
130°
128°
126°
124°

POPULATION

- over 1 000 000
- over 100 000
- over 50 000
- over 10 000

LAND HEIGHT

- 1500m/4920ft
- 1000m/3281ft
- 500m/1640ft
- 200m/656ft
- Sea Level

CHRONOLOGY

Annexed by Japan in 1910, the peninsula was divided in 1945 at the 38th parallel; North Korea was made an independent state in 1948.

- ❑ **1950–1953** Korean War.
- ❑ **1994** Withdrawal from IAEA. Kim Il Sung dies; declared "Eternal President" four years later.
- ❑ **1997** Threat of famine worsens. Kim Jong Il becomes party leader.
- ❑ **2000** Historic North–South summit.

ECONOMICS

Not available

$18.2bn

2.2 North Korean won (2.2)

SCORE CARD

- ❑ WORLD GNP RANKING..........................68th
- ❑ GNP PER CAPITA..............................$760
- ❑ BALANCE OF PAYMENTS..........*Closed economy;*
- ❑ INFLATION..........................*does not publish*
- ❑ UNEMPLOYMENT..........................*any figures*

STRENGTHS

Other than minerals, North Korea's economy has few strengths.

WEAKNESSES

GNP has declined steadily since 1990. The acute shortage of foreign capital and technology has been catastrophic.

EXPORTS

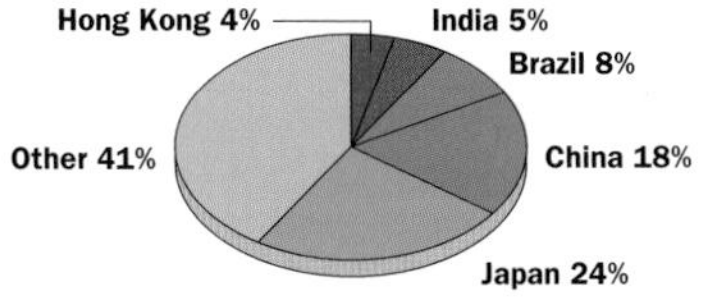
Hong Kong 4%
India 5%
Brazil 8%
China 18%
Japan 24%
Other 41%

IMPORTS

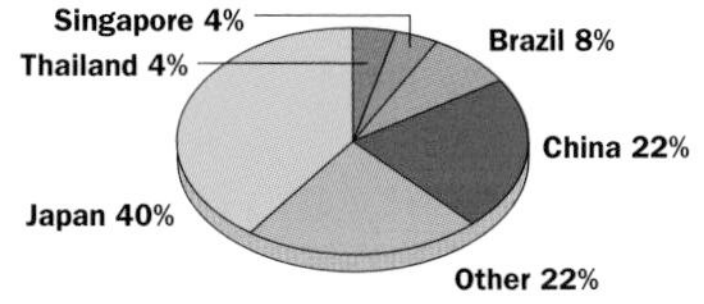
Singapore 4%
Thailand 4%
Brazil 8%
China 22%
Other 22%
Japan 40%

RESOURCES

Electric power 9.5m kW

267,550 tonnes

Not an oil producer; refines 50,000 b/d

4.19m ducks, 3.15m pigs, 2.69m goats, 18.5m chickens

Coal, iron, lead, gold, copper, zinc, tungsten, silver, tin, uranium

North Korea is rich in minerals. Electricity supply remains a major problem; blackouts are frequent. The nuclear power program was restarted in 2003, antagonizing the US, which suspects that the power plants are being used to manufacture weapons-grade material.

ENVIRONMENT

Sustainability rank: 140th

3% (1% partially protected)

9.4 tonnes per capita

Excessive use of fertilizers and unchecked pollution from heavy industry are the major problems.

MEDIA

TV ownership medium

Daily newspaper circulation 208 per 1000 people

PUBLISHING AND BROADCAST MEDIA

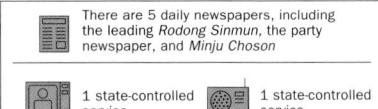

There are 5 daily newspapers, including the leading *Rodong Sinmun*, the party newspaper, and *Minju Choson*

1 state-controlled service

1 state-controlled service

TV consists mostly of musical shows praising Kim Il Sung and Kim Jong Il, and anti-American tirades directed against the Korean War.

CRIME

Death penalty in use

North Korea does not publish prison figures

Low level of violent street crime

At an individual level, crime is officially said hardly to exist. The criminal code is weighted to protect the state against "subversion," rather than the rights of the individual. North Korea has a very poor human rights record and there is a *gulag* of more than 100,000 "subversives," where whole families are sent along with those accused, and where torture is routine.

EDUCATION

School leaving age: 16

99%

390,000 students

English is compulsory as a second language at the age of 14. Kim Il Sung, Pyongyang, is the main university.

HEALTH

Welfare state health benefits

1 per 333 people

Heart disease, cancers, digestive diseases

Health care is free. Reasonable life expectancy is now threatened by malnutrition and outright starvation.

SPENDING

GDP/cap. decrease

CONSUMPTION AND SPENDING

No data

22 per 1000 population

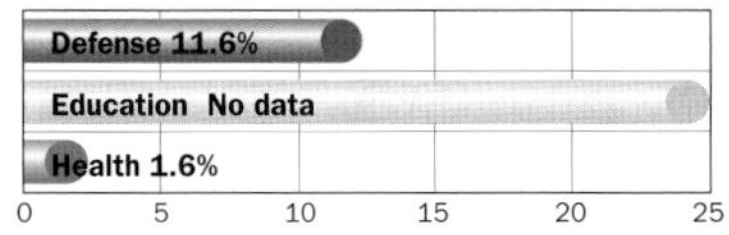
Defense 11.6%
Education No data
Health 1.6%
0
5
10
15
20
25

Defense, Health, Education spending as % of GDP

Most people live in poverty. An elite within the KWP lives well, with access to specialist shops and high-tech consumer goods. Personal ownership of telephones, private cars, and, in many areas, bicycles, is forbidden.

WORLD RANKING

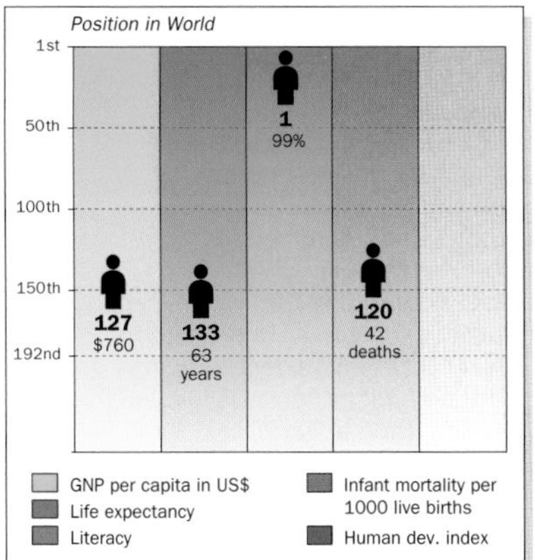
Position in World
1st
50th
100th
150th
192nd
127
$760
133
63
years
1
99%
120
42
deaths
GNP per capita in US$
Life expectancy
Literacy
Infant mortality per 1000 live births
Human dev. index

K

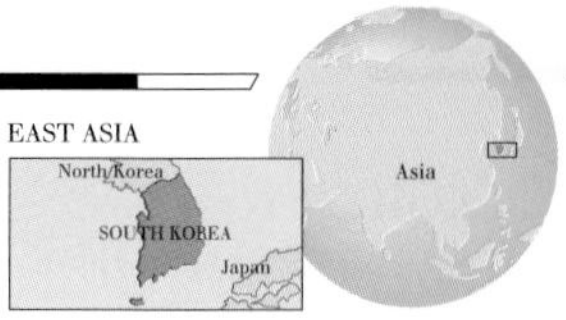
EAST ASIA
North Korea
SOUTH KOREA
Japan
Asia

South Korea

Official Name: Republic of Korea **Capital:** Seoul
Population: 47.4 million **Currency:** South Korean won **Official Language:** Korean

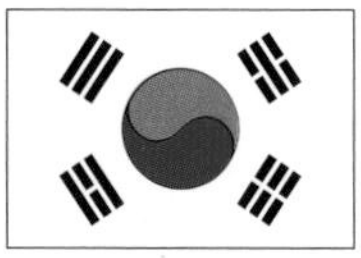

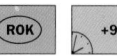

1948 | 1953 | Aug 15 | ROK | +9 | +82 | .kr

Occupying the southern half of the Korean peninsula in East Asia, over 80% of South Korea is mountainous and two-thirds is forested. Rice is the major agricultural product, grown by over 85% of South Korea's three million farmers. The whole peninsula was annexed by Japan from 1910 to 1945, and the split between South Korea and the communist North originated with the arrival of rival US and Soviet armies in 1945. Though the two states have discussed reunification, the legacy of hostility arising from the 1950–1953 Korean War remains a major obstacle.

CLIMATE

Continental

WEATHER CHART FOR SEOUL

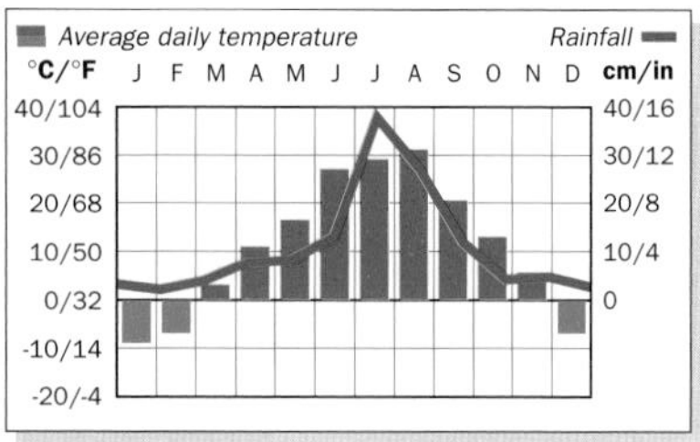
Average daily temperature
Rainfall
°C/°F
J F M A M J J A S O N D
cm/in
40/104
30/86
20/68
10/50
0/32
-10/14
-20/-4
40/16
30/12
20/8
10/4
0

South Korea has four distinct seasons. Winters are dry and can be bitterly cold. Summers are hot and humid, especially during July and August.

TRANSPORTATION

Drive on right

Kimpo International, Seoul
21.1m passengers

2426 ships
6.4m grt

THE TRANSPORTATION NETWORK

65,388 km (40,630 miles)
2567 km (1595 miles)
3123 km (1941 miles)
1609 km (1000 miles)

The public transportation system is efficient and highly integrated. Buses, trains, boats, and planes are all included in one timetable, and have a reputation for punctuality. A toll-based nationwide motor expressway network links most major cities. Air travel has expanded rapidly as a convenient way to traverse the mountainous interior. A high-speed rail link will connect Seoul and Busan (Pusan) in 2010.

Improving relations with North Korea in 2000 led to projects for cross-border rail and road links and connecting flights. The first flights since 1953 took place in mid-2002, albeit limited to specific teams of construction workers in the nuclear industry, and the land border was opened for the first time in early 2003 for a South Korean tourist bus. Continuing political uncertainty has slowed the progress of other projects.

TOURISM

Visitors : Population 1:8.9

5.35m visitors

Up 4% in 2002

MAIN TOURIST ARRIVALS

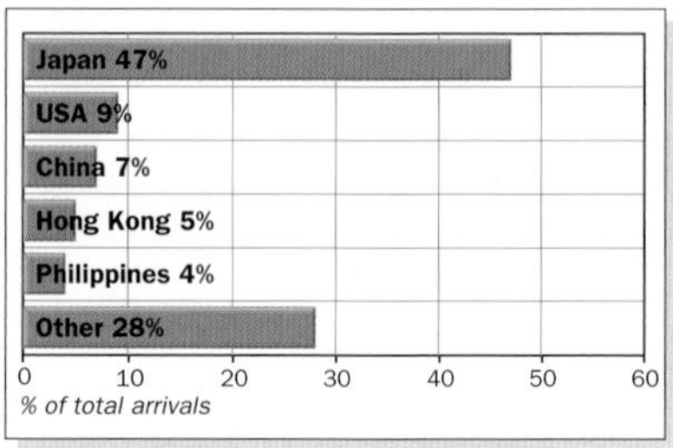
Japan 47%
USA 9%
China 7%
Hong Kong 5%
Philippines 4%
Other 28%
0 10 20 30 40 50 60
% of total arrivals

Overseas tourism to South Korea has increased ten-fold since 1969. Most visitors are Japanese, who come for the golf and Seoul's nightlife; Jeju-do (Cheju-do) is a favored honeymoon destination. Whereas visiting relations of US army personnel once made up 13% of all tourists, today Los Angeles-based Korean–Americans make up the greatest proportion of US visitors. However, despite the publicity generated by the 1988 Seoul Olympics and the 2002 soccer World Cup, South Korea is still not seen in the West as a prime tourist destination.

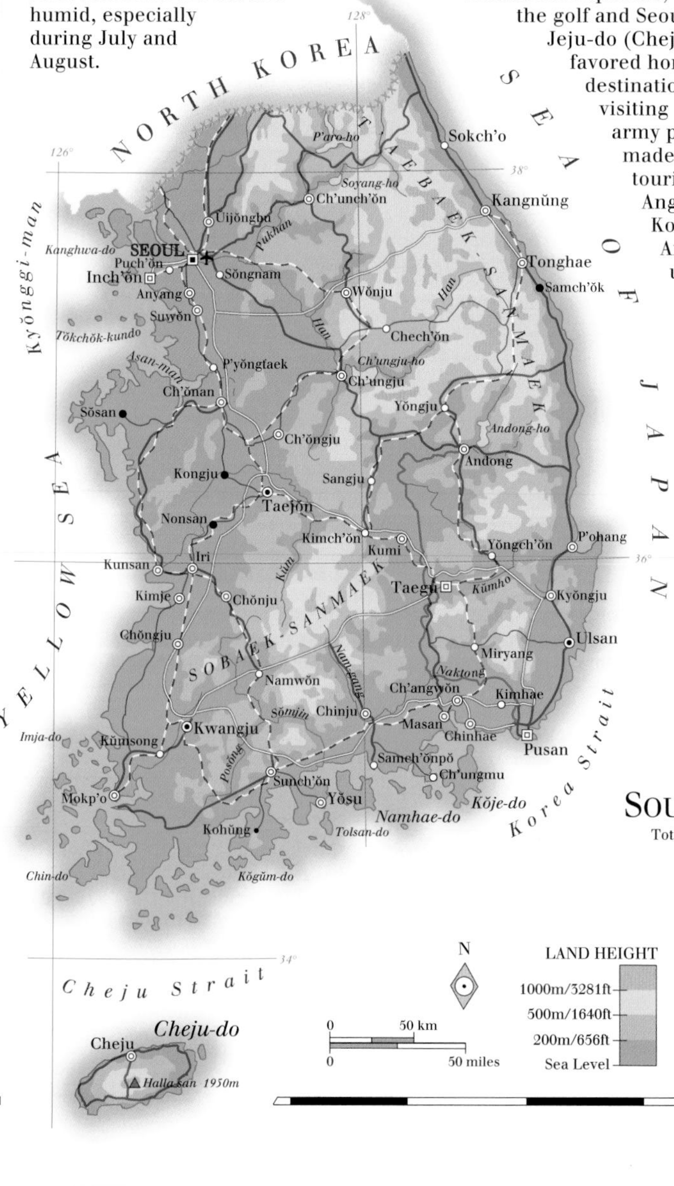
NORTH KOREA
SEA OF JAPAN
YELLOW SEA
Kyŏnggi-man
Korea Strait
Cheju Strait
SEOUL
Inch'ŏn
Taejŏn
Taegu
Kwangju
Pusan
Ulsan
Cheju-do
Halla-san 1950m
SOUTH KOREA
Total Area : 98 480 sq. km (38 023 sq. miles)
POPULATION
over 5 000 000
over 1 000 000
over 500 000
over 100 000
over 50 000
over 10 000
under 10 000
LAND HEIGHT
1000m/3281ft
500m/1640ft
200m/656ft
Sea Level
N
0 50 km
0 50 miles

PEOPLE

Pop. density high

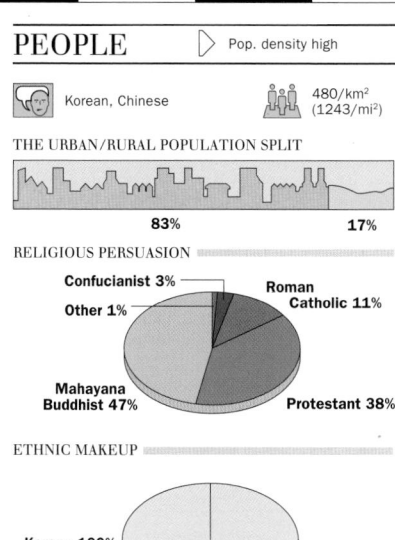

Korean, Chinese

480/km² (1243/mi²)

THE URBAN/RURAL POPULATION SPLIT

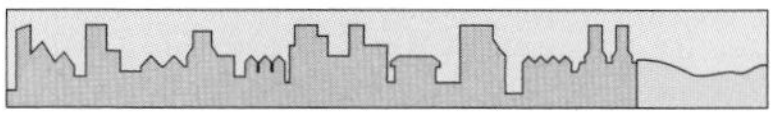
83%
17%

RELIGIOUS PERSUASION

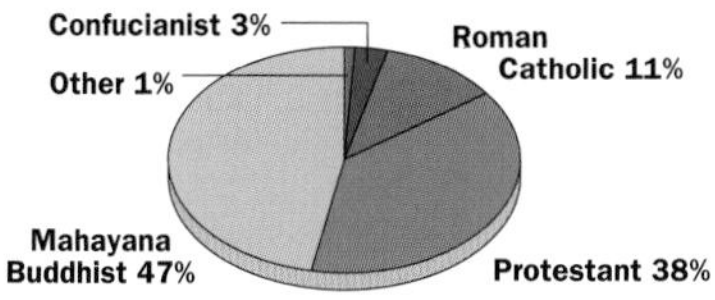
Confucianist 3%
Other 1%
Roman Catholic 11%
Mahayana Buddhist 47%
Protestant 38%

ETHNIC MAKEUP

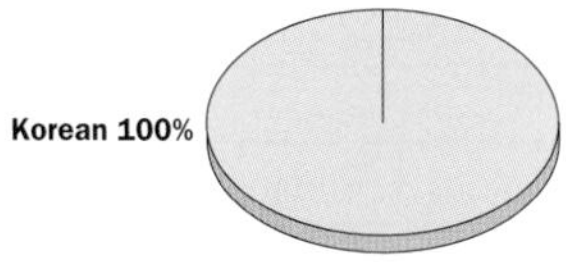
Korean 100%

Korean culture is strongly colored by its unusual racial homogeneity. Family life is a central and clearly defined part of society, though the nuclear family model is becoming the norm rather than the old-style household of the extended family. Most Koreans can trace their ancestry back thousands of years. Regional origin is important in determining blood heritage, since there are only 270 Korean surnames and half the population is named Kim, Lee, Park, or Choi.

Chondogyo, combining elements of Confucianism, Buddhism, shamanism, Taoism, and Christianity, is peculiar to the Koreas but has only a tiny following. Traditional values condition attitudes to women, and it is still not respectable for those who are married to have a job.

Economic growth has attracted illegal immigrants from the poorer Asian countries, who take menial jobs that South Koreans now refuse to do.

POPULATION AGE BREAKDOWN

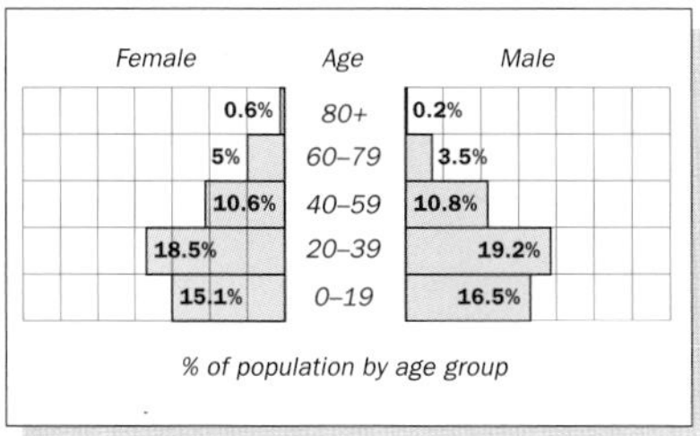
Female
Age
Male
0.6%
80+
0.2%
5%
60–79
3.5%
10.6%
40–59
10.8%
18.5%
20–39
19.2%
15.1%
0–19
16.5%
% of population by age group

POLITICS

Multiparty elections

2000/2004

President Roh Moo Hyun

AT THE LAST ELECTION

National Assembly 273 seats

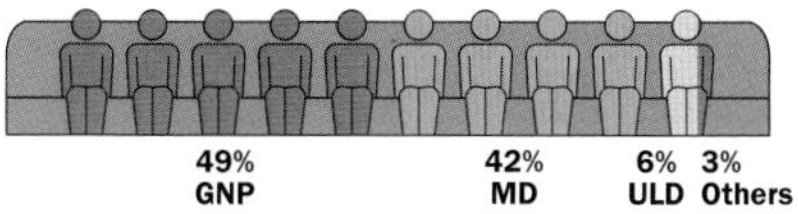
49% GNP
42% MD
6% ULD
3% Others

GNP = Grand National Party **MD** = Millennium Democratic Party **ULD** = United Liberal Democrats

Officially a democracy since its inception, South Korea was in practice ruled by military dictators until 1987.

PROFILE

Direct presidential elections and a parliament with enhanced powers were introduced in 1987.

In 1993, Kim Young Sam became the first nonmilitary leader in 30 years. He launched a popular anticorruption campaign, targeting former presidents. His New Korea Party (NKP), returned to power with a reduced majority in 1996, was brought down amid a steel scandal in 1997. Veteran opposition leader Kim Dae Jung was elected president later that year in the first peaceful transfer of power to the opposition. His supporters gained ground in elections in 2000, but political instability continued, with frequent changes of prime minister and opposition byelection victories.

Although President Kim's final year in office was marred by corruption scandals, Roh Moo Hyun, the candidate of the ruling MD, was in December 2002 elected president to continue his policies.

MAIN POLITICAL ISSUES

The economy

The Asian financial crisis of 1997–1998 was followed by a period of global slowdown from 2001, with unsuccessful efforts to recover during the intervening period by means of severe financial austerity and retrenchment. Industrial action is frequent and effective.

Relations with North Korea

The sudden flowering of North–South relations in 2000 soon lost popularity. Expensive cross-border projects, and promises of aid, raised fears over the mounting costs, while erratic North Korean diplomacy has done little to improve mutual trust.

Kim Dae Jung, *president (1998–2003) and Nobel Peace Prize winner.*

President Roh Moo Hyun *found renown as a human rights lawyer in the 1980s.*

WORLD AFFAIRS

Joined UN in 1991

APEC | CP | IAEA | OECD | WTO

Since the division of Korea, relations with the North have dominated foreign policy. A historic summit meeting in 2000 in the North Korean capital, Pyongyang, opened a new phase, and cross-border diplomatic and economic cooperation briefly flourished. Reunification remains the ultimate goal of both Koreas, but with doubts about its social and economic costs. Military tensions persist, and a large detachment of US troops remains on the border – the most heavily defended in the world. Relations with China, the closest ally of North Korea, have improved. Japan is a major trading partner, though South Koreans continue to harbor resentment over the 1910–1945 Japanese annexation.

AID

Donor

$265m (donations)

Up 25% in 2001

Once a massive recipient of US aid, and then of Japanese war reparations, South Korea emerged in the 1970s and 1980s as a major aid donor. However, the economic crisis in 1997–1998 forced it to seek international financial assistance to salvage key sectors of its threatened economy.

CHRONOLOGY

The Yi dynasty, founded in Seoul in 1392, ruled the kingdom of Korea until 1910. Korea became a vassal state of China in 1644.

- **1860** Korea reacts to French and British occupation of Peking by preventing Western influence: becomes the "Hermit Kingdom."
- **1904–1905** Russo-Japanese War. Japan conquers Korea.
- **1910** Japan annexes Korea.
- **1919** Independence protests violently suppressed.
- **1945** US and Soviet armies arrive. Korea split at 38°N. South comes under de facto US rule.
- **1948** Republic of South Korea created; Syngman Rhee becomes president at head of an increasingly authoritarian regime.
- **1950** Hostilities between North and South, each aspiring to rule a united Korea. North invades, sparking Korean War. US, with UN backing, enters on South's side; China unofficially assists North. In 1951 fighting stabilizes near 38th parallel.
- **1953** Armistice; de facto border at cease-fire line, close to 38th parallel.

CHRONOLOGY *continued*

- **1960** Syngman Rhee resigns in face of popular revolt.
- **1961** Military coup leads to authoritarian junta led by Park Chung Hee.
- **1963** Pressure for civilian government. Park elected as president (reelected in 1967 and 1971). Strong manufacturing base and exports drive massive economic development program.
- **1965** Links restored with Japan.
- **1966** 45,000 troops engaged in South Vietnam.
- **1972** Martial law. New constitution with greater presidential powers.
- **1979** Park assassinated. Gen. Chun Doo Hwan, intelligence chief, leads coup. Kim Young Sam, opposition leader, expelled from parliament.
- **1980** Chun chosen as president. Kim Dae Jung and other opposition leaders arrested.
- **1986** Car exports start.
- **1987** Emergence of prodemocracy movement. Roh Tae Woo, Chun's chosen successor, elected president.
- **1988** Inauguration of Sixth Republic which offers genuine multiparty democracy. Restrictions on foreign travel lifted.
- **1990** Government party and two opposition parties, including Kim Young Sam's, merge.
- **1991** South Korea joins UN.
- **1992** Diplomatic links with China established. Kim Young Sam elected president.
- **1996** Chun sentenced to death on charges of organizing 1979–1980 overthrow of government; Roh given a lengthy prison term. Both sentences were rescinded.
- **1997** Violent protests against new labor laws. Steel scandal brings down government. Economic crisis.
- **1998** Kim Dae Jung president.
- **2000** Historic North–South summit in Pyongyang.
- **2002** Roh Moo Hyun of the ruling MD elected president.
- **2003** 182 die in subway arson attack.

Seoul lit up at night. *The city is home to over ten million people – more than one-fifth of the country's population. Seoul means "capital."*

K

DEFENSE

Compulsory military service

$11.2bn

Down 12% in 2001

SOUTH KOREAN ARMED FORCES

2258 main battle tanks (Type 88, M-47, M-48, T-80U)	560,000 personnel
20 submarines, 6 destroyers, 9 frigates, 24 corvettes, 84 patrol boats	63,000 personnel
538 combat aircraft (153 F-16C/D, 185 F-5E/F, 130 F-4D/E)	63,000 personnel
None	

The military has retreated from politics since a major corruption investigation in the mid-1990s. The main defense concern is North Korea. South Korea has fewer troops, tanks, artillery, and aircraft than the North, but claims parity through superior technology and the permanent presence of 35,000 US troops on its territory. The manufacture of missiles capable of striking any target in North Korea was legalized in 2001. However, South Korea's ability to resist an invasion by the North is questionable, since Seoul is only 55 km (35 miles) from the demilitarized zone (DMZ). Stumbling efforts at improving cross-border relations led to a commitment in 2002 to clear land mines from the DMZ to allow the construction of transportation links.

ECONOMICS

Inflation 4.5% p.a. (1990–2001)

$448bn

1195 South Korean won (1203)

SCORE CARD

- WORLD GNP RANKING..........13th
- GNP PER CAPITA..........$9460
- BALANCE OF PAYMENTS..........$8.62bn
- INFLATION..........4.3%
- UNEMPLOYMENT..........4%

EXPORTS

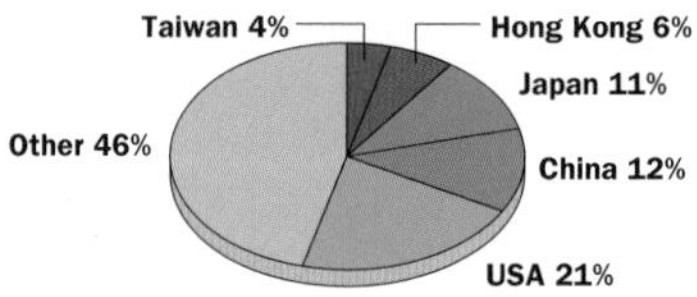
Taiwan 4%
Hong Kong 6%
Japan 11%
China 12%
USA 21%
Other 46%

IMPORTS

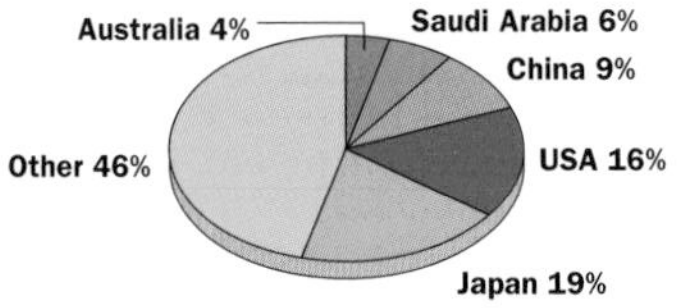
Australia 4%
Saudi Arabia 6%
China 9%
USA 16%
Japan 19%
Other 46%

ECONOMIC PERFORMANCE INDICATOR

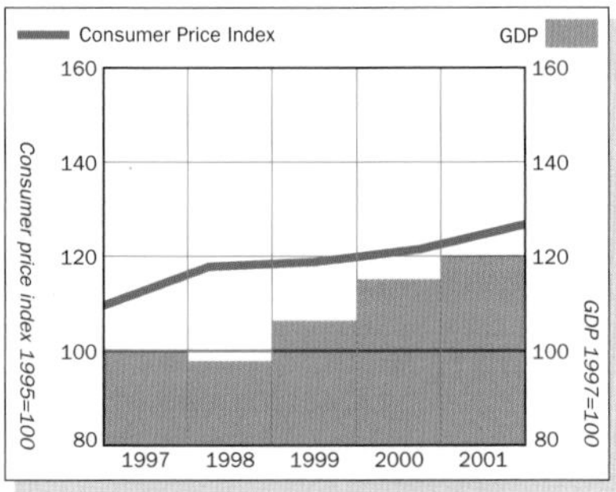
Consumer Price Index
GDP
160
140
120
100
80
Consumer price index 1995=100
GDP 1997=100
1997
1998
1999
2000
2001

STRENGTHS

World's most successful shipbuilder, with bulk of the market. Demand from China, particularly for cars. Well-developed high-tech industry.

WEAKNESSES

High level of indebtedness and vulnerability to international capital movements. Increasingly militant workforce since 1997. State sector a burden on the economy. Strong competition from Japan, especially as the yen weakens.

PROFILE

South Korea's economic miracle began with centralized planning. Chaebol (conglomerates) such as Samsung achieved impressive growth rates in strategic industries such as car manufacturing, shipbuilding, and semiconductors. Cheap state credit and a well-educated workforce gave South Korea a competitive edge. The government then encouraged foreign investment and an emphasis on smaller industries to maintain growth. In 1997, however, a major financial crisis and the threat of a debt implosion forced the government to turn to the IMF for a huge credit agreement. Though the banking system had shown signs of recovery by 2001, private debt increased in 2002 and the economy contracted in early 2003.

SOUTH KOREA : MAJOR BUSINESSES

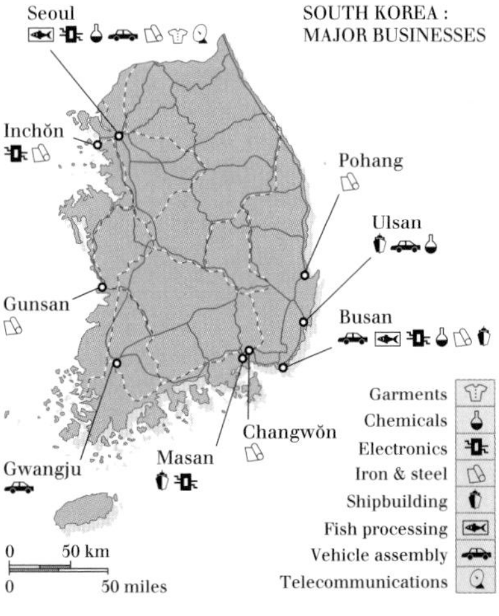
Seoul
Inchŏn
Pohang
Ulsan
Gunsan
Busan
Changwŏn
Masan
Gwangju
0 50 km
0 50 miles
Garments
Chemicals
Electronics
Iron & steel
Shipbuilding
Fish processing
Vehicle assembly
Telecommunications

RESOURCES

Electric power 51.6m kW

2.15m tonnes

Not an oil producer; refines 2.37m b/d

8.81m pigs, 8m ducks, 107m chickens

Coal, iron, lead, zinc, tungsten, gold, graphite, fluorite

ELECTRICITY GENERATION

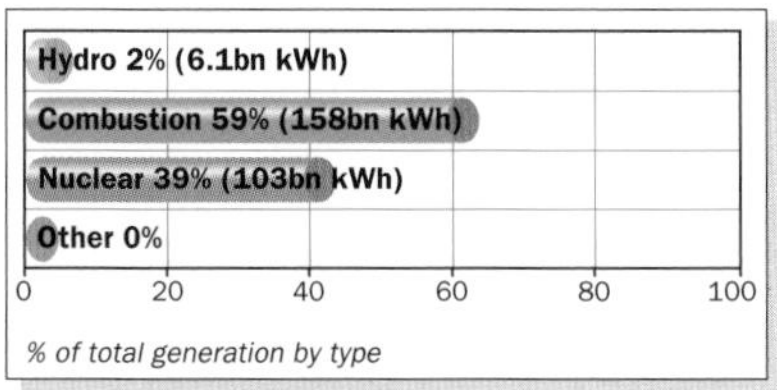
Hydro 2% (6.1bn kWh)
Combustion 59% (158bn kWh)
Nuclear 39% (103bn kWh)
Other 0%
0
20
40
60
80
100
% of total generation by type

South Korea has few natural resources. It has to import all of its oil and has built a series of nuclear reactors for generating electricity. Under the terms of the 1994 agreement between North Korea and the US, South Korea is constructing two reactors in the North which, in the event of reunification, will be connected to the national grid.

Agriculture remains a highly protected sector of the economy. Plans to open up the rice market have in the past provoked massive demonstrations in Seoul.

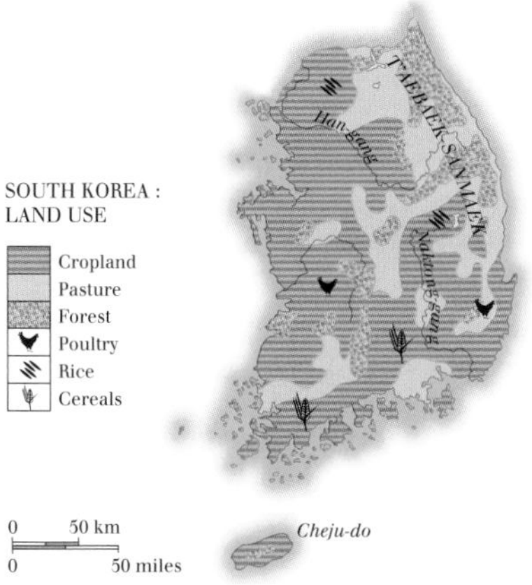
SOUTH KOREA : LAND USE
Cropland
Pasture
Forest
Poultry
Rice
Cereals
Han-gang
TAEBAEK-SANMAEK
Naktong-gang
Cheju-do
0 50 km
0 50 miles

ENVIRONMENT

Sustainability rank: 135th

7% partially protected

8.5 tonnes per capita

ENVIRONMENTAL TREATIES

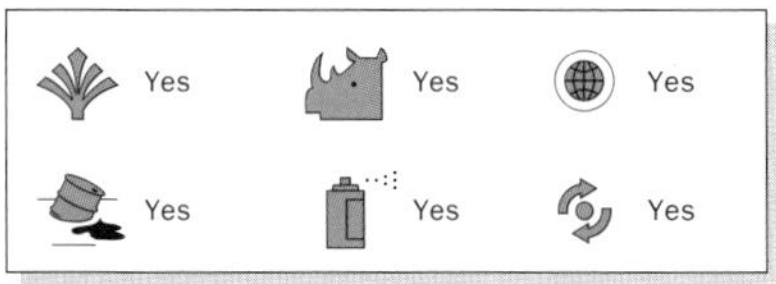
Yes
Yes
Yes
Yes
Yes
Yes

Environmental groups remain hostile to South Korea's nuclear power program. Rapid industrialization has resulted in environmental problems, especially pollution. The government only ratified the Kyoto Protocol, which aims to reduce carbon dioxide emissions, as late as November 2002. Steps have recently been taken to address the severe problem of air pollution in urban areas, particularly in Seoul. Rivers in rural areas have been polluted by fertilizers and chemicals.

CRIME

Death penalty in use

62,732 prisoners

Down 52% in 2000–2001

CRIME RATES

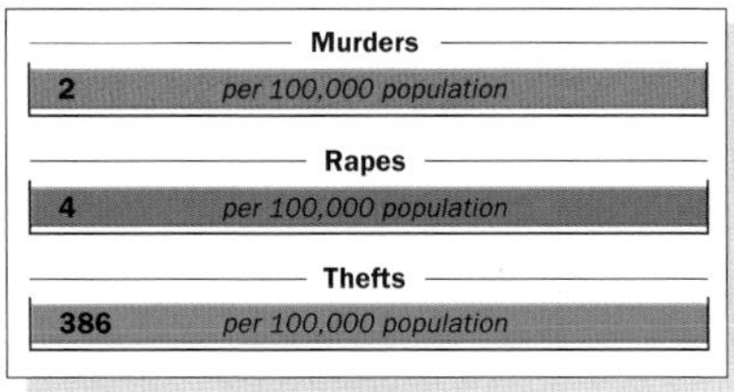
Murders
2 per 100,000 population
Rapes
4 per 100,000 population
Thefts
386 per 100,000 population

Violent crime is relatively uncommon. Since 1987, the internal security forces' operations have been restricted, though left-wing activists are still harassed. Striking workers and student demonstrators encounter – and prepare for – confrontational and forceful crowd control. Police brutality was highlighted by the death of a detained suspect in 2002.

HEALTH

Welfare state health benefits

1 per 578 people

Cancers, cerebrovascular disease, senility, accidents

The health service has improved in line with economic growth. Most hospitals are equipped with modern facilities, and many offer advanced treatments comparable with those in the US and western Europe. Health indicators such as infant mortality and longevity have likewise improved.

SPENDING

GDP/cap. increase

CONSUMPTION AND SPENDING

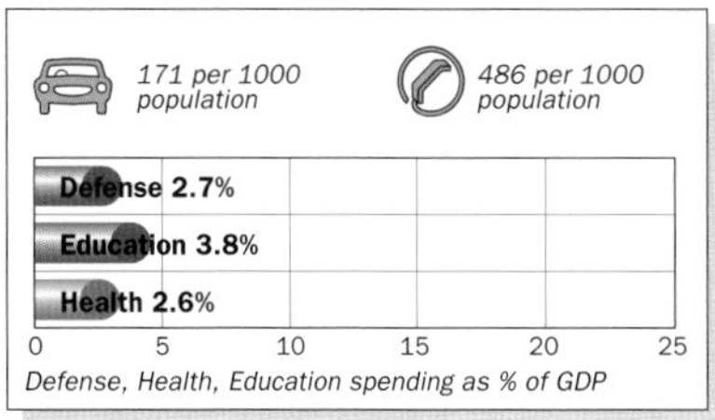
171 per 1000 population
486 per 1000 population
Defense 2.7%
Education 3.8%
Health 2.6%
0
5
10
15
20
25
Defense, Health, Education spending as % of GDP

An increase in credit-card spending had created massively bloated levels of private debt by 2002. Wealth is unevenly distributed; the Jolla (Cholla) region in the southwest remains the poorest.

MEDIA

TV ownership high

Daily newspaper circulation 393 per 1000 people

PUBLISHING AND BROADCAST MEDIA

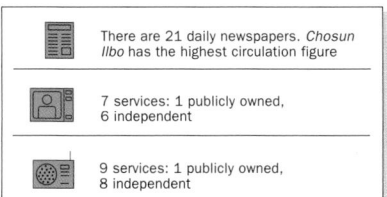

There are 21 daily newspapers. *Chosun Ilbo* has the highest circulation figure

7 services: 1 publicly owned, 6 independent

9 services: 1 publicly owned, 8 independent

South Korea's media have been freed of most restrictions since the advent of full democracy. However, criticisms of the armed forces and their role in society are still frowned upon, and generally avoided. Caution also has to be exercised in reporting facts about North Korea. In the past, South Korean journalists who made favorable mention of the North Korean regime suffered harassment. Plans to break into the satellite industry by 2015 were boosted by the successful launch in 2003 of the first domestically built rocket.

EDUCATION

School leaving age: 15

98%

3m students

THE EDUCATION SYSTEM

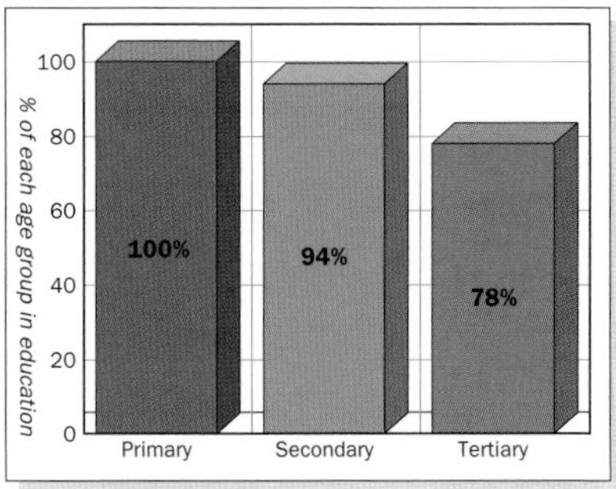
100
80
60
40
20
0
% of each age group in education
100%
94%
78%
Primary
Secondary
Tertiary

South Korea began a concentrated education program in the 1950s, and a well-educated workforce has been the foundation of impressive economic growth. Education is compulsory from age five to 15. The final three-year cycle of secondary school is voluntary but attendance is high. Tertiary enrollment is nearly 80% – one of the highest rates in the world.

WORLD RANKING

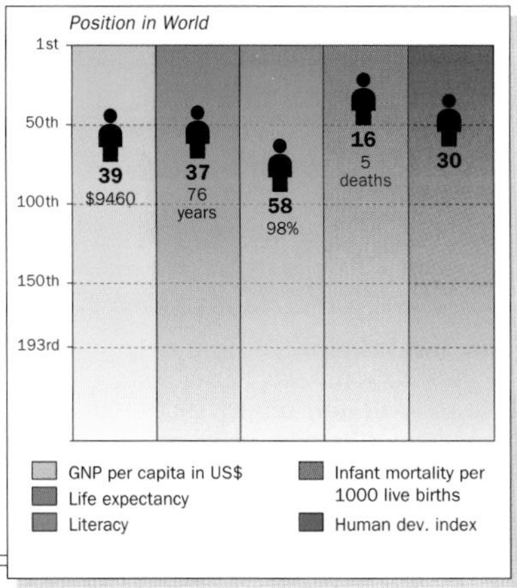
Position in World
1st
50th
100th
150th
193rd
39
$9460
37
76 years
58
98%
16
5 deaths
30
GNP per capita in US$
Life expectancy
Literacy
Infant mortality per 1000 live births
Human dev. index

K

KUWAIT

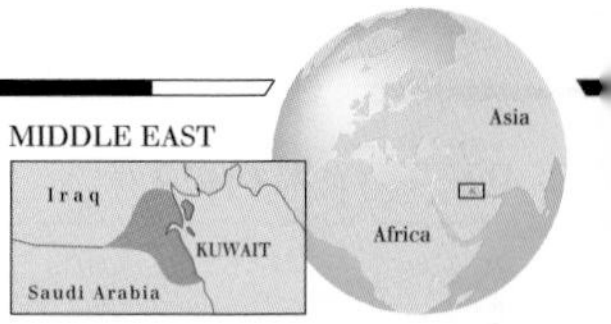
MIDDLE EAST
Asia
Iraq
KUWAIT
Africa
Saudi Arabia

OFFICIAL NAME: State of Kuwait **CAPITAL:** Kuwait City
POPULATION: 2 million **CURRENCY:** Kuwaiti dinar **OFFICIAL LANGUAGE:** Arabic

1961 | 1961 | Feb 25 | KWT | +3 | +965 | .kw

AT THE NORTHWEST EXTREME of the Gulf, Kuwait is dwarfed by its neighbors. The flat, almost featureless landscape conceals huge oil and gas reserves which put Kuwait among the world's first oil-rich states. In 1990 Iraq invaded, claiming it as its 19th province. A US-led alliance, under the aegis of the UN, expelled Iraqi forces following a short war in 1991 and restored the rule of the al-Sabah dynasty. Kuwait served as the launching point for the 2003 invasion of Iraq.

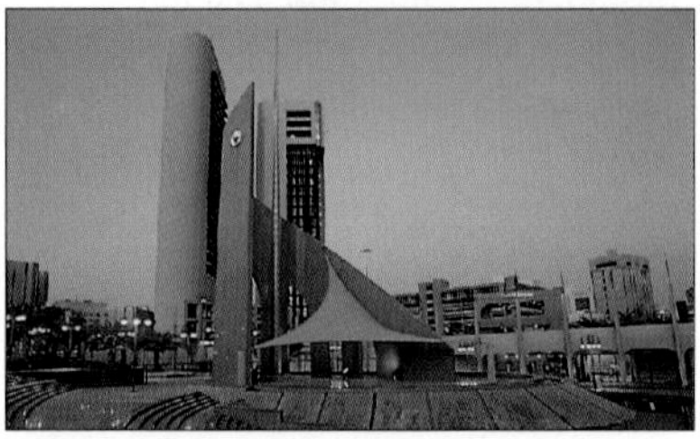

Saffar Towers in the business center of Kuwait City. Rebuilding Kuwait's postwar economy is estimated to have cost $25 billion.

CLIMATE

Hot desert

WEATHER CHART FOR KUWAIT CITY

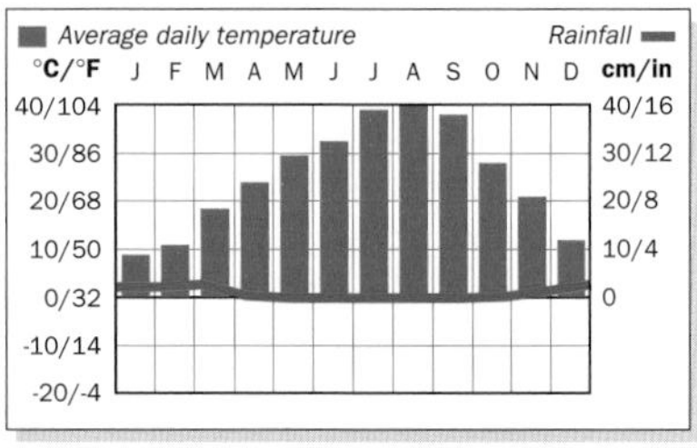
Average daily temperature
Rainfall
°C/°F J F M A M J J A S O N D cm/in
40/104
30/86
20/68
10/50
0/32
-10/14
-20/-4
40/16
30/12
20/8
10/4
0

Summer temperatures can soar to over 40°C (104°F), but winters can be cold, with frost at night.

TRANSPORTATION

Drive on right

Kuwait International, Kuwait City
4.27m passengers

200 ships
2.29m grt

THE TRANSPORTATION NETWORK

3590 km (2231 miles)

280 km (174 miles)

None

None

Kuwait has a system of radial expressways around the capital and good connecting roads to Saudi Arabia.

TOURISM

Visitors : Population 1:25

79,000 visitors

Up 3% in 1999–2000

MAIN TOURIST ARRIVALS

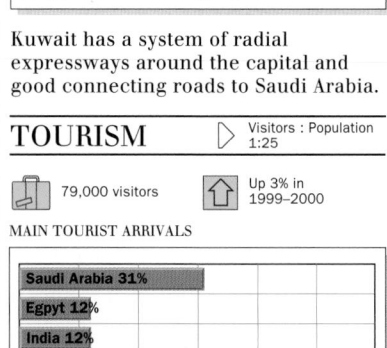

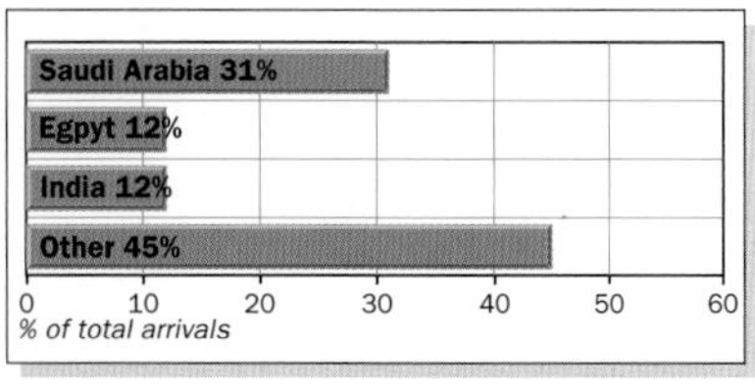
Saudi Arabia 31%
Egypt 12%
India 12%
Other 45%
0 10 20 30 40 50 60
% of total arrivals

The limited tourism from neighboring Arab states, notably Saudi Arabia, has not recovered from the 1990–1991 Gulf War. Most Western visitors to Kuwait go specifically to see relatives working in the oil industry.

PEOPLE

Pop. density medium

Arabic, English

112/km² (291/mi²)

THE URBAN/RURAL POPULATION SPLIT

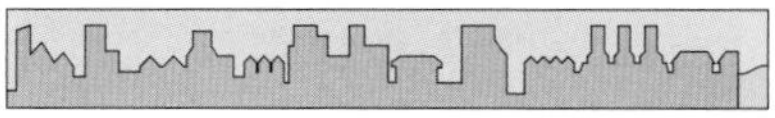
96%
4%

ETHNIC MAKEUP

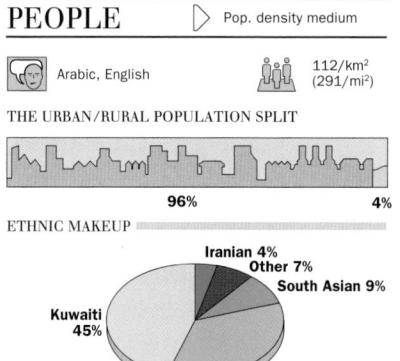

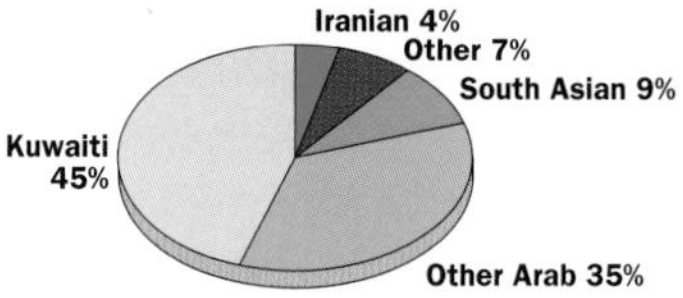
Iranian 4%
Other 7%
South Asian 9%
Kuwaiti 45%
Other Arab 35%

Kuwait is a conservative Sunni Muslim society (27% of the population are Shi'a). Women have considerable freedom, although the amir's decree providing for female enfranchisement has been repeatedly rejected by the National Assembly.

Kuwait's oil wealth has drawn in thousands of workers from other Arab countries and south Asia. The Palestine Liberation Organization's support for the Iraqi invasion led to most Palestinians, hitherto more numerous in Kuwait than elsewhere in the Arabian peninsula, being driven out. Native Kuwaitis are outnumbered by resident foreign nationals.

POLITICS

Nonparty elections

2003/2007

Amir Shaikh Jabir al-Ahmad al-Jabir al-Sabah

AT THE LAST ELECTION

National Assembly 50 seats

The electorate comprises civilian men over 21 years of age whose families have been resident in Kuwait since before 1921. Elections on July 5, 2003, were contested by independents: Islamists won just under half of the seats and government supporters won just over a quarter.

In 1992 Amir Shaikh Jabir restored the National Assembly. Since 1999 nonparty elections have strengthened the amir's Islamist opponents. Crown Prince Shaikh Saad was dismissed as prime minister in 2003 after 25 years, and was replaced by the amir's half brother Shaikh Sabah in the first separation of the roles of crown prince and premier.

KUWAIT

Total Area : 17 820 sq. km (6880 sq. miles)

POPULATION
- ◎ over 100 000
- ○ over 50 000
- ● over 10 000
- • under 10 000

LAND HEIGHT
- 200m/656ft
- Sea Level

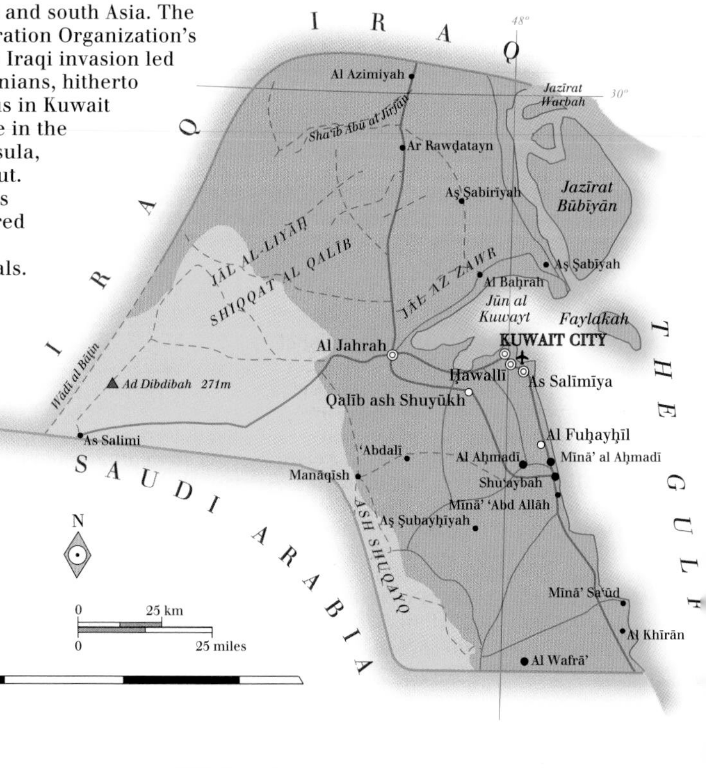
IRAQ
Al Azimiyah
Jazīrat Warbah
Sha'īb Abū al Jīrfān
Ar Rawḑatayn
Aş Şabiriyah
Jazīrat Būbiyān
JĀL AL-LIYĀḨ
SHIQQAT AL QALĪB
JĀL AZ ZAWR
Aş Şabīyah
Al Bahrah
Jūn al Kuwayt
Faylakah
Al Jahrah
KUWAIT CITY
Ḩawallī
As Salīmīya
Ad Dibdibah 271m
Wādī al Bāţin
Qalīb ash Shuyūkh
As Salimi
'Abdalī
Al Aḩmadī
Al Fuḩayḩīl
Mīnā' al Aḩmadī
Manāqīsh
Shu'aybah
Mīnā' 'Abd Allāh
Aş Şubayḩīyah
ASH SHUQAYQ
SAUDI ARABIA
THE GULF
Mīnā' Sa'ūd
Al Khīrān
Al Wafrā'
N
0 25 km
0 25 miles

WORLD AFFAIRS

Joined UN in 1963

AL | Damasc | GCC | OIC | OPEC

Strategically important as a major exporter of crude oil and natural gas, Kuwait has close links with the West. These were strengthened by the 1991 war which secured Iraq's withdrawal from Kuwait after its invasion the previous year. In March 2003 the US-led Coalition forces used Kuwait as a launchpad for their invasion of Iraq.

AID

Donor

$73m (donations) — Down 56% in 2001

The Kuwait Fund for Arab Economic Development continued to give aid even during the invasion crisis.

DEFENSE

Compulsory military service

$5.03bn — Up 36% in 2001

In August 1990 Kuwait's 11,000-strong, partly volunteer army was easily overrun by vastly superior Iraqi forces. Since its liberation, defense pacts have been signed with the US, the UK, France, and Russia. Kuwait rearmed fast, with weapons purchased from major Western suppliers.

ECONOMICS

Inflation 1.9% p.a. (1990–2000)

$37.4bn — 0.3003 Kuwaiti dinars (0.302)

SCORE CARD

- ❑ WORLD GNP RANKING..........54th
- ❑ GNP PER CAPITA..........$18,270
- ❑ BALANCE OF PAYMENTS..........$8.57bn
- ❑ INFLATION..........1.7%
- ❑ UNEMPLOYMENT..........2%

STRENGTHS

Oil and gas. Large overseas investments. Stable banking system. Healthy trade.

WEAKNESSES

Overreliance of economy on oil and gas. Adverse consequences of 1990 Iraqi invasion, including debt to Western liberators. Strategic vulnerability deters investment. Reliance on imported skilled labor, food, and raw materials. Delays in enacting privatization package.

EXPORTS

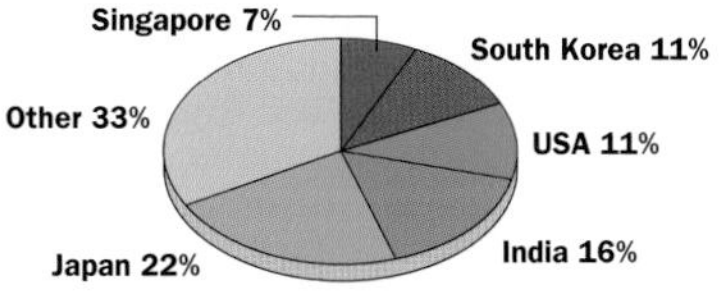

Singapore 7%
South Korea 11%
Other 33%
USA 11%
India 16%
Japan 22%

IMPORTS

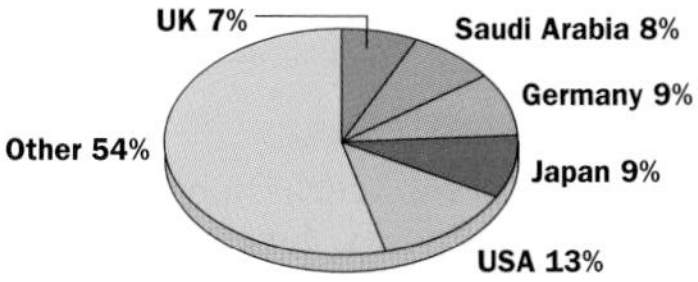

UK 7%
Saudi Arabia 8%
Germany 9%
Other 54%
Japan 9%
USA 13%

RESOURCES

Electric power 8.5m kW

6676 tonnes — 1.87m b/d (reserves 96.5bn barrels)

800,000 sheep, 130,000 goats, 32.5m chickens — Oil, natural gas, salt

The oil industry is Kuwait's most profitable sector, accounting for around 90% of export earnings. Although badly hit by the Gulf War, when a number of wells were deliberately fired, it was quickly rehabilitated. Kuwait also possesses valuable reserves of natural gas. Other resources are dates, fish, ammonia, and chemicals.

ENVIRONMENT

Sustainability rank: 142nd

2% (1% partially protected) — 22.7 tonnes per capita

The Iraqi invasion in 1990 and the subsequent war caused an ecological disaster. Although the effects of this did not prove as grave as some observers first feared, marine life was damaged and many thousands of hectares of cultivated land were obliterated. Millions of land mines were left strewn across border areas. Water is scarce.

MEDIA

TV ownership high

Daily newspaper circulation 374 per 1000 people

PUBLISHING AND BROADCAST MEDIA

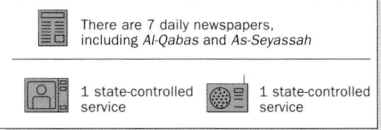

There are 7 daily newspapers, including *Al-Qabas* and *As-Seyassah*

1 state-controlled service — 1 state-controlled service

Radio and TV are state-controlled, but satellite TV is freely available. Press freedom exists in theory.

CRIME

Death penalty in use

1735 prisoners — Up 8% in 1996–1998

Isolated acts of terrorism occur. There have been complaints of human rights abuses.

EDUCATION

School leaving age: 14

82% — 32,320 students

Kuwaiti citizens receive free education from nursery to university. Since the liberation, more emphasis has been placed on technology in the curriculum.

CHRONOLOGY

Kuwait traces its independence to 1710, but was under British rule from the late 18th century until 1961. The government denies any historical link with Iraq.

- ❑ **1961** Independence from UK. Iraq claims Kuwait.
- ❑ **1976** Amir suspends National Assembly.
- ❑ **1990** Iraqi invasion.
- ❑ **1991** Liberation following Gulf War.
- ❑ **1992** National Assembly elections.
- ❑ **1999, 2003** Elections: opposition Islamists win most seats.

HEALTH

Welfare state health benefits

1 per 625 people — Heart diseases, cancers, car accidents, diabetes

Despite theft of equipment during the Iraqi invasion, Kuwait has restored its Western-standard health care service. Nationals receive free treatment.

SPENDING

GDP/cap. increase

CONSUMPTION AND SPENDING

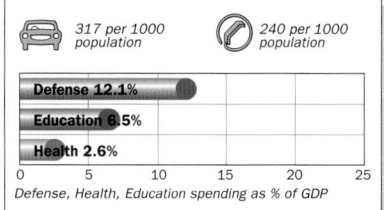

317 per 1000 population — *240 per 1000 population*

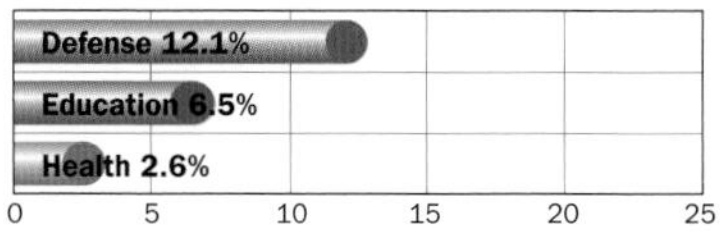

Defense 12.1%
Education 6.5%
Health 2.6%
0
5
10
15
20
25

Defense, Health, Education spending as % of GDP

Most Kuwaitis – not only the oil-rich elite – enjoy high incomes, and the government has repeatedly rescued citizens who have suffered stock market or other financial losses. School and university leavers are guaranteed jobs. Capital is easily transferred abroad and there are effectively no exchange controls.

WORLD RANKING

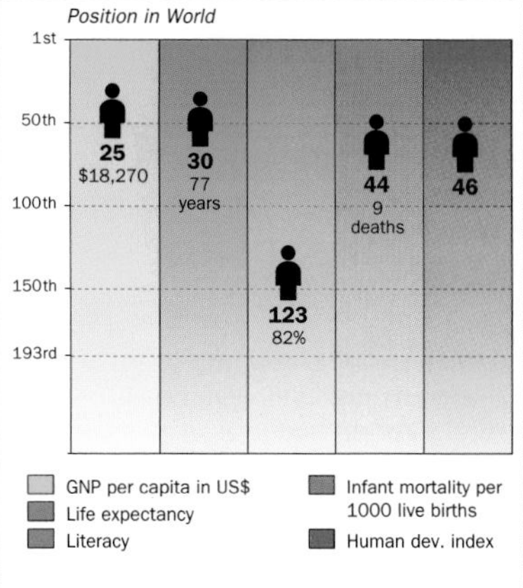

Position in World
1st
50th
100th
150th
193rd
25
$18,270
30
77
years
123
82%
44
9
deaths
46
GNP per capita in US$
Life expectancy
Literacy
Infant mortality per 1000 live births
Human dev. index

K

KYRGYZSTAN

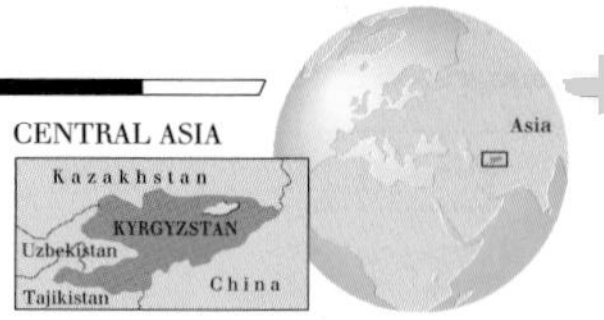
CENTRAL ASIA
Kazakhstan
KYRGYZSTAN
Uzbekistan
Tajikistan
China
Asia

OFFICIAL NAME: Kyrgyz Republic **CAPITAL:** Bishkek
POPULATION: 5 million **CURRENCY:** Som **OFFICIAL LANGUAGES:** Kyrgyz and Russian

1991 | 1991 | Aug 31 | KS | +6 | +996 | .kg

KYRGYZSTAN IS A SMALL and very mountainous state in central Asia. It is one of the least urbanized of the former Soviet republics (the rural population is growing faster than that in the towns) and was among the last to develop its own cultural nationalism. Its increasingly autocratic government tries to steer between Kyrgyz nationalist pressures and ensuring that the Russian minority is not alienated, since it tends to possess the skills necessary to run a market-based economy.

CLIMATE

Mountain

WEATHER CHART FOR BISHKEK

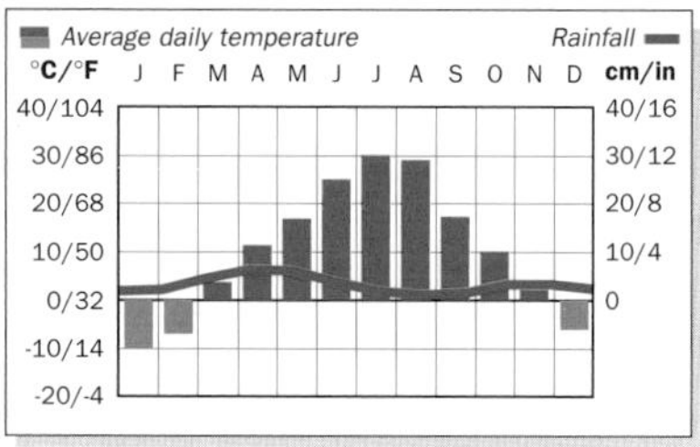
Average daily temperature
Rainfall
°C/°F
J F M A M J J A S O N D
cm/in
40/104
30/86
20/68
10/50
0/32
-10/14
-20/-4
40/16
30/12
20/8
10/4
0

Conditions vary from permanent snow and cold deserts at altitude to hot deserts in lower regions. Intermediate slopes and valleys receive some rain.

TRANSPORTATION

Drive on right

Bishkek International

Has no fleet

THE TRANSPORTATION NETWORK

16,854 km (10,473 miles)

140 km (87 miles)

417 km (259 miles)

600 km (373 miles)

Kyrgyzstan does not have the necessary finances to improve its poor mountain road network.

TOURISM

Visitors : Population 1:72

69,000 visitors

Up 17% in 1999

MAIN TOURIST ARRIVALS

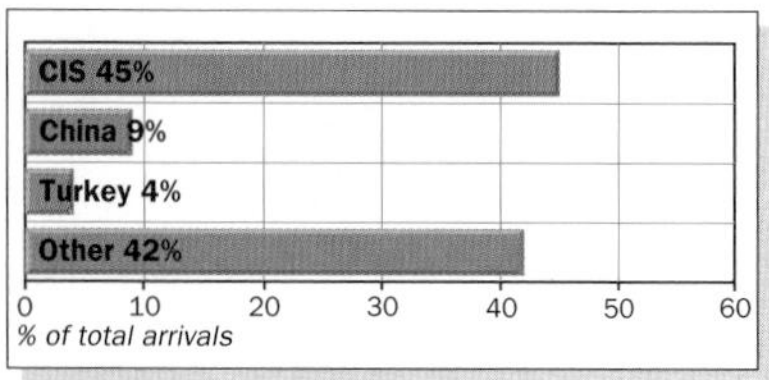
CIS 45%
China 9%
Turkey 4%
Other 42%
0
10
20
30
40
50
60
% of total arrivals

Tourism is undeveloped; most visitors are on business or working on multilateral aid projects. Tourism promotion centers on Kyrgyzstan's position on the Silk Road.

PEOPLE

Pop. density low

Kyrgyz, Russian

25/km² (65/mi²)

THE URBAN/RURAL POPULATION SPLIT

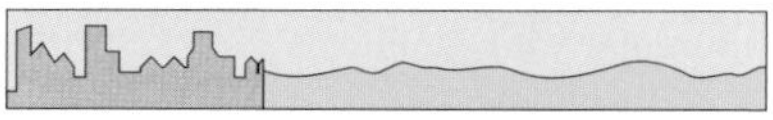
34%
66%

ETHNIC MAKEUP

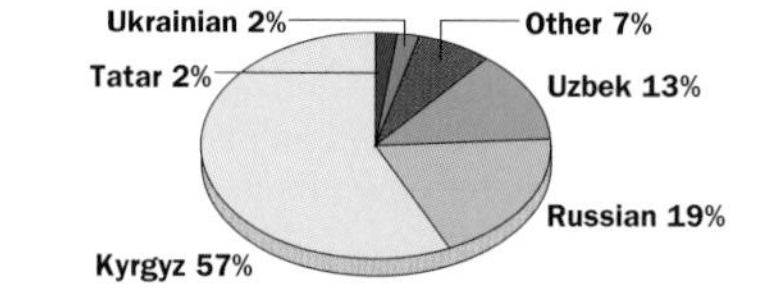
Ukrainian 2%
Other 7%
Tatar 2%
Uzbek 13%
Russian 19%
Kyrgyz 57%

Like other former Soviet republics, Kyrgyzstan has witnessed the rise of militant nationalism. Relations are most strained with the large Uzbek minority. The preference given to Kyrgyz in the political system and in particular in the land laws, which exclude all others from full title, has aggravated ethnic tensions. The trend in politics is toward greater Islamization, which is linking religion and race issues more closely and adding social pressure on "foreigners," particularly ethnic Russians, to leave.

Since 1989 a high birthrate has enabled the Kyrgyz to resume their position as the main ethnic group, replacing the Russian community which until recently controlled the economy. However, the government moved to stem the tide of Russian emigration by declaring Russian to be an official language, with full equal status with effect from 2000.

Loess landscape, Naryn valley. *Kyrgyzstan is dominated by the ice-capped Tien Shan mountains, but valleys are green and fertile.*

POLITICS

Multiparty elections

L. House 2000/2005
U. House 2000/2005

President Askar Akayev

AT THE LAST ELECTION

Legislative Assembly 60 seats

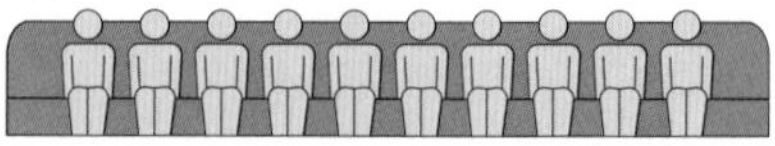

Election results by party were announced only for the 15 national list seats. The other 45 seats are elected on a constituency basis. The Party of Communists of Kyrgyzstan is the largest party and the Union of Democratic Forces the second-largest.

Assembly of People's Representatives 45 seats

The members represent Kyrgyzstan's different regional and ethnic communities

President Akayev's administration has become increasingly autocratic, ending Kyrgyzstan's reputation as one of the region's most liberal societies. Already damaged democratic credentials were destroyed by accusations of fraud during the 2000 legislative and presidential elections. The main opposition leader, Felix Kulov, was imprisoned only weeks before the presidential poll (in which Akayev won his third term in office). In 2002, the death of protestors during demonstrations over the temporary imprisonment of Kulov's successor ultimately forced the entire cabinet to resign. In February 2003 a number of constitutional changes were approved by 75% of voters in a hastily called referendum. Among them were the scrapping of the upper house and, as a rebuff to Akayev's opponents, a clause confirming that he should remain in power until the end of his current term.

WORLD AFFAIRS

Joined UN in 1992

CIS | SCO | OIC | OSCE | EAPC

Kyrgyzstan is working to reduce its dependence on Russia. Turkey is developing close links based on ethnic similarities and aimed at restraining Iranian influence. Relations with Uzbekistan, which allegedly supports some of the antigovernment forces in Kyrgyzstan, are tense, though in 2000 both countries joined with Tajikistan to combat Islamist militants in the region.

AID

Recipient

$188m (receipts)

Down 13% in 2001

The ADB and the World Bank are the main aid donors. Japan is also an important source of financial assistance.

K

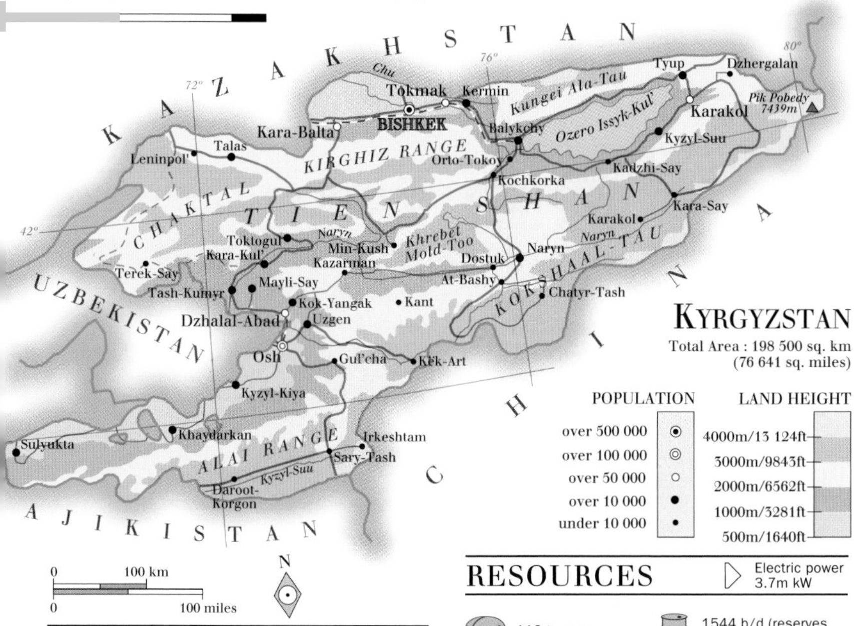
KAZAKHSTAN
UZBEKISTAN
TAJIKISTAN
CHINA
TIEN SHAN
KIRGHIZ RANGE
CHAKTAL
Khrebet Mold-Too
KOKSHAAL-TAU
ALAI RANGE
Ozero Issyk-Kul'
Kungei Ala-Tau
Chu
Naryn
Kyzyl-Suu
BISHKEK
Tokmak
Kemin
Kara-Balta
Talas
Leninpol'
Balykchy
Orto-Tokoy
Kochkorka
Tyup
Dzhergalan
Karakol
Pik Pobedy 7439m
Kyzyl-Suu
Kadzhi-Say
Kara-Say
Karakol
Naryn
Dostuk
At-Bashy
Chatyr-Tash
Toktogul
Kara-Kul'
Min-Kush
Kazarman
Terek-Say
Tash-Kumyr
Mayli-Say
Kok-Yangak
Kant
Dzhalal-Abad
Uzgen
Osh
Gul'cha
Kek-Art
Kyzyl-Kiya
Khaydarkan
Sulyukta
Irkeshtam
Sary-Tash
Daroot-Korgon
72°
76°
80°
42°
KYRGYZSTAN
Total Area : 198 500 sq. km
(76 641 sq. miles)
POPULATION
over 500 000
over 100 000
over 50 000
over 10 000
under 10 000
LAND HEIGHT
4000m/13 124ft
3000m/9843ft
2000m/6562ft
1000m/3281ft
500m/1640ft
0
100 km
100 miles
N

DEFENSE

Phasing out conscription

$255m

Up 11% in 2001

A national army was set up in 1992. Conscription is to be phased out by 2005. Kyrgyzstan is home to the new military alliance of six ex-Soviet states.

ECONOMICS

Inflation 95% p.a. (1990–2001)

$1.38bn

41.18 soms (46.52)

SCORE CARD

❑ World GNP Ranking	148th
❑ GNP per Capita	$280
❑ Balance of Payments	–$20m
❑ Inflation	6.9%
❑ Unemployment	6%

Strengths

Agricultural self-sufficiency. Private land ownership since 2000. Gold and mercury exports. Hydropower potential.

Weaknesses

Dominant state and collective farming mentality. Sharp economic decline since USSR's breakup. History of high inflation. Increasing political instability.

EXPORTS

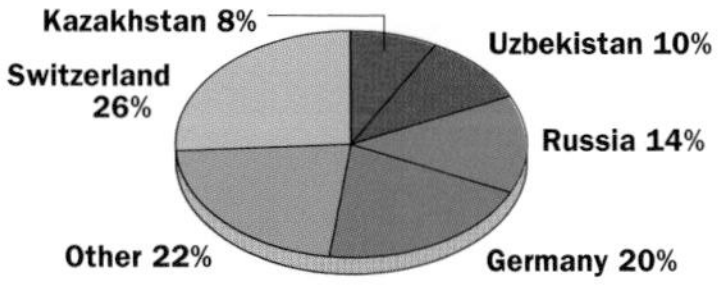
Kazakhstan 8%
Uzbekistan 10%
Switzerland 26%
Russia 14%
Other 22%
Germany 20%

IMPORTS

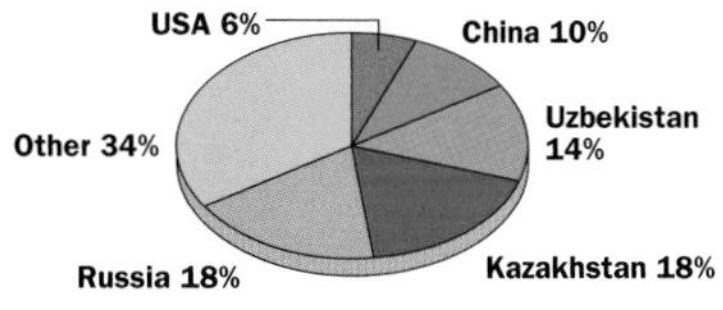
USA 6%
China 10%
Other 34%
Uzbekistan 14%
Russia 18%
Kazakhstan 18%

RESOURCES

Electric power 3.7m kW

110 tonnes

1544 b/d (reserves 37m barrels)

3.1m sheep, 988,016 cattle, 3.4m chickens

Coal, antimony, gas, oil, tin, mercury, iron, uranium, zinc, gold

Kyrgyzstan has small quantities of commercially exploitable coal, oil, and gas, and great hydroelectric power potential. Energy policy, which relies on Western aid and technology, is primarily aimed at developing these further in order to reduce dependence on supplies from Russia, and eventually to achieve self-sufficiency in energy.

ENVIRONMENT

Sustainability rank: 56th

4% (2% partially protected)

1 tonne per capita

The major problem is the salination of the soil caused by excessive irrigation of cotton crops. Kyrgyzstan has a poor record in limiting industrial pollution.

MEDIA

TV ownership low

Daily newspaper circulation 27 per 1000 people

PUBLISHING AND BROADCAST MEDIA

There are 4 daily newspapers, including *Kyrgyz Tuusu*, *Slovo Kyrgyzstana*, and *Vechernii Bishkek*

2 services: 1 state-owned, 1 independent

1 state-owned, several independent services

The Kyrgyz press is increasingly under pressure from the government's efforts to silence opposition.

CRIME

Moratorium on death penalty

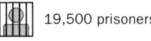

19,500 prisoners

Down 5% in 1995–1997

Ethnic tension fuels violence. The narcotics trade flourishes. Prison overcrowding is a serious problem: 786 prisoners were amnestied in 2003.

CHRONOLOGY

The Kyrgyz first developed a recognizable ethnic consciousness in the late 18th century.

- ❑ **1860s** Expansion of Russian Empire into Kyrgyz lands.
- ❑ **1924–1991** Incorporated in USSR.
- ❑ **1995** New constitution adopted.
- ❑ **2000** Legislative and presidential elections; Askar Akayev reelected.
- ❑ **2002** Government resigns after police shoot demonstrators.

EDUCATION

School leaving age: 16

97%

49,744 students

Replacing Russian as the main teaching language is proving an enormous task. Russian is likely to survive at tertiary level, as the Kyrgyz language lacks key technical and scientific terms.

HEALTH

Welfare state health benefits

1 per 347 people

Cerebrovascular and heart diseases, cancers, accidents

Infant mortality is high. Kyrgyzstan has one of the least developed public health systems in central Asia.

SPENDING

GDP/cap. decrease

CONSUMPTION AND SPENDING

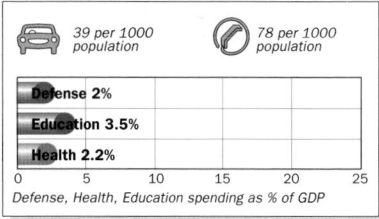

39 per 1000 population

78 per 1000 population

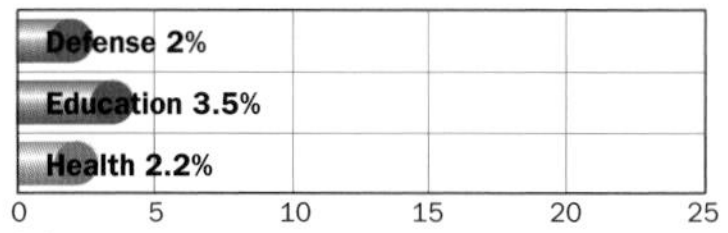
Defense 2%
Education 3.5%
Health 2.2%
0
5
10
15
20
25

Defense, Health, Education spending as % of GDP

Poverty levels peaked in 2000 at almost 90% of the population. The old Communist Party *nomenklatura* have benefited from privatization.

WORLD RANKING

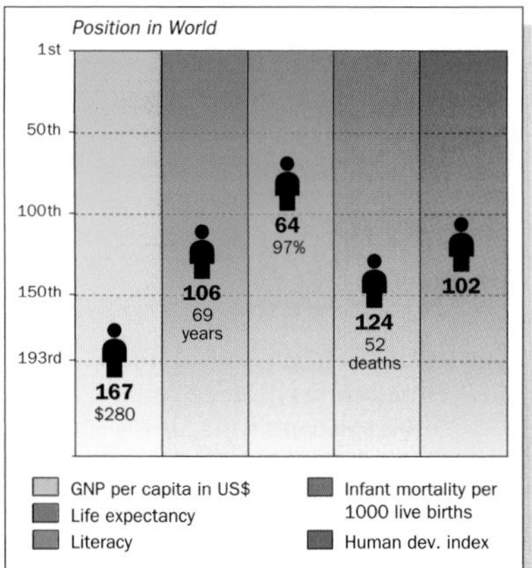
Position in World
1st
50th
100th
150th
193rd
167
$280
106
69 years
64
97%
124
52 deaths
102
GNP per capita in US$
Life expectancy
Literacy
Infant mortality per 1000 live births
Human dev. index

K

LAOS

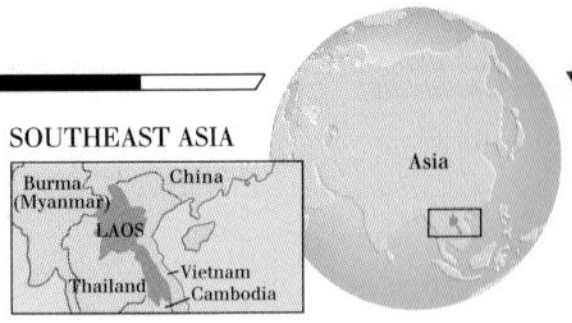
SOUTHEAST ASIA
Asia
Burma (Myanmar)
China
LAOS
Vietnam
Thailand
Cambodia

OFFICIAL NAME: Lao People's Democratic Republic **CAPITAL:** Vientiane
POPULATION: 5.5 million **CURRENCY:** New kip **OFFICIAL LANGUAGE:** Lao

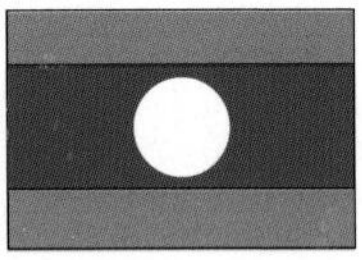

1953 | 1953 | Dec 2 | LAO | +7 | +856 | .la

THE MEKONG RIVER forms Laos's main thoroughfare and feeds the fertile lowlands of the Mekong valley. Two decades of civil war followed independence from France in 1953, and Laos was bombed heavily during the Vietnam War. The communist LPRP has held power since 1975. Market-oriented reforms began to be introduced in 1986. A transfer of power to a younger generation within the LPRP took place during the 1990s.

CLIMATE

Tropical monsoon

WEATHER CHART FOR VIENTIANE

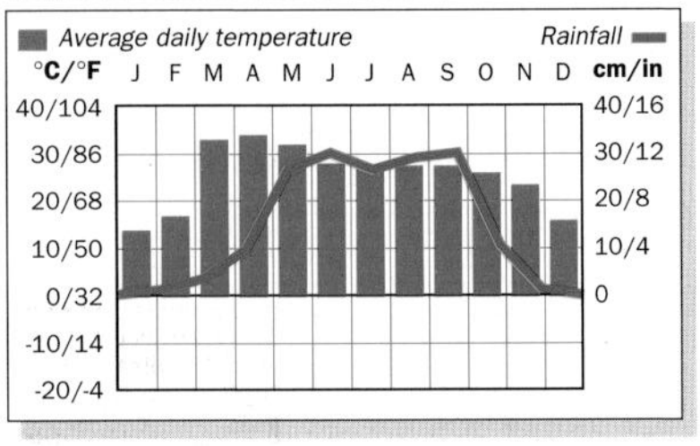
Average daily temperature
Rainfall
°C/°F J F M A M J J A S O N D cm/in
40/104 30/86 20/68 10/50 0/32 -10/14 -20/-4
40/16 30/12 20/8 10/4 0

The tropical southerly monsoon brings heavy rains from May to September.

TRANSPORTATION

Drive on right

Wattay, Vientiane 165,000 passengers

1 ship 2400 grt

THE TRANSPORTATION NETWORK

9674 km (6011 miles)	None
None	4587 km (2850 miles)

A major new Thailand–Vietnam road is planned via Savannakhét. Freight goes mainly by river; there is no railroad and roads are poor and few.

TOURISM

Visitors : Population 1:33

169,000 visitors

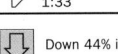

Down 44% in 2001

MAIN TOURIST ARRIVALS

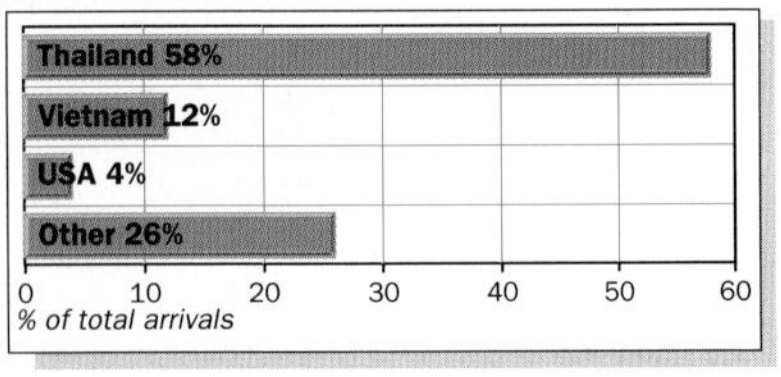
Thailand 58%
Vietnam 12%
USA 4%
Other 26%
0 10 20 30 40 50 60
% of total arrivals

Tourists were first allowed into Laos in 1989; numbers have risen rapidly since then. Mass tourism is discouraged and preference given to small package tours. Hotels are few, and travel outside Vientiane is difficult.

PEOPLE

Pop. density low

Lao, Mon-Khmer, Yao, Vietnamese, Chinese, French

24/km² (62/mi²)

THE URBAN/RURAL POPULATION SPLIT

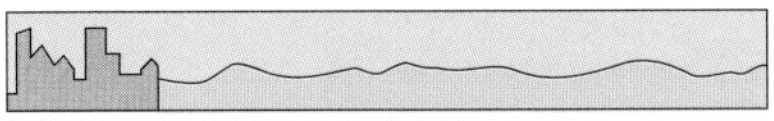
20%
80%

RELIGIOUS PERSUASION

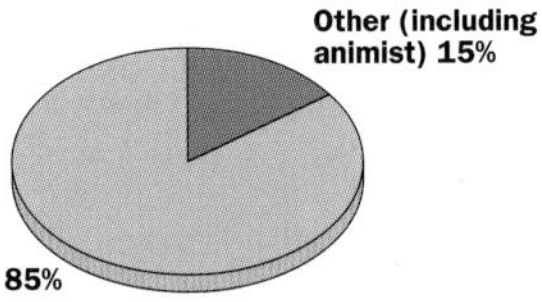
Other (including animist) 15%
Buddhist 85%

There are more than 60 ethnic groups in Laos and this considerable diversity has hindered national integration. Society is broadly divided by geography, but by altitude rather than by region. The lowland Laotians (*Lao Loum*) make up some 60% of the population. The upland Laotians (*Lao Theung*), who live in the hills above the valleys, account for 30%. The small minority of highland Laotians (*Lao Soung*), among whom are included the Hmong, Yao, and Man groups, have resisted government efforts to introduce substitutes for traditional cash crops such as opium. The government continues to face small pockets of Hmong resistance.

Two-thirds of Laotians speak Lao, and many tribal dialects are also spoken. Buddhism is the main religion, but there are some Christians and animists.

POLITICS

No multiparty elections

2002/2007

President Khamtay Siphandone

AT THE LAST ELECTION

National Assembly 109 seats

99% LPRP
1% Ind

LPRP = Lao People's Revolutionary Party (the sole legal political party) **Ind** = Independent

All candidates were approved by the LPRP

Though a new nomenklatura came to power in the 1990s, the established pillars of the military, the LPRP, and the executive branch remain closely intertwined. Party chairman Gen. Khamtay Siphandone became the country's president in February 1998. Despite limited moves toward political reform, the LPRP, which is modeled on the Communist Party of Vietnam, continues to dominate political life at every level. The long-standing problem of corruption, sometimes at high levels, has become a matter of concern as Laos has opened up to foreign investors. Economic reform has not been accompanied by political liberalization. Tensions continue to be felt between the government and the rural areas, where there is particular resistance to attempts to alter traditional farming methods.

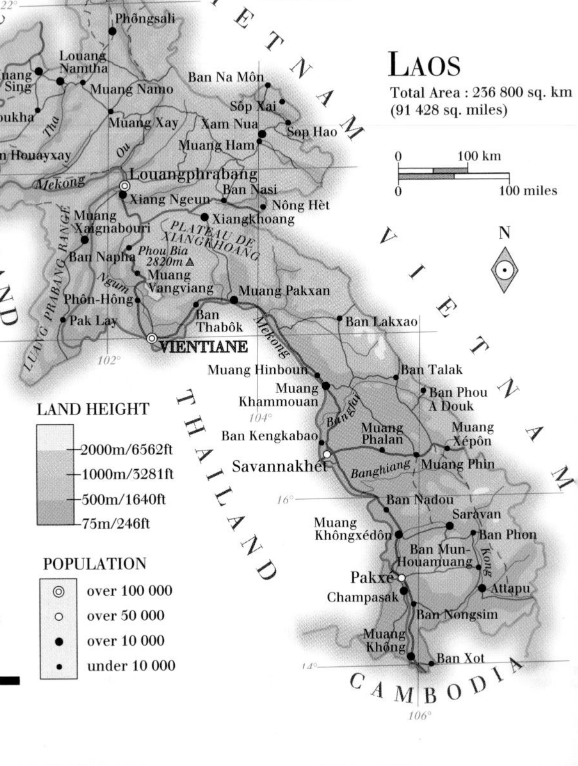
LAOS
Total Area : 236 800 sq. km (91 428 sq. miles)
0 100 km
0 100 miles
CHINA
VIETNAM
BURMA (MYANMAR)
THAILAND
CAMBODIA
Phôngsali
Louang Namtha
Muang Sing
Muang Namo
Ban Na Môn
Sôp Xai
Xam Nua
Sop Hao
Muang Xay
Muang Ham
Viangphoukha
Ban Houayxay
Louangphrabang
Ban Nasi
Nông Hèt
Xiang Ngeun
Xiangkhoang
Muang Xaignabouri
PLATEAU DE XIANGKHOANG
Phou Bia 2820m
Ban Napha
Muang Vangviang
Muang Pakxan
Phôn-Hông
Pak Lay
Ban Thabôk
VIENTIANE
Ban Lakxao
Muang Hinboun
Ban Talak
Muang Khammouan
Ban Phou A Douk
Ban Kengkabao
Muang Phalan
Muang Xépôn
Savannakhét
Muang Phin
Ban Nadou
Saravan
Muang Khôngxédôn
Ban Phon
Ban Mun-Houamuang
Pakxé
Champasak
Attapu
Ban Nongsim
Muang Không
Ban Xot
Mekong
LUANG PRABANG RANGE
LAND HEIGHT
2000m/6562ft
1000m/3281ft
500m/1640ft
75m/246ft
POPULATION
over 100 000
over 50 000
over 10 000
under 10 000

WORLD AFFAIRS

Joined UN in 1955

ASEAN | CP | OIF | Mekong River | NAM

Vietnam was Laos's most important ally from 1975 until the late 1980s, when the LPRP began to seek improved relations with Thailand and the West.

The change was mainly due to the need for foreign aid. In 1992, Laos acceded to the Treaty of Amity and Concord of ASEAN, marking the beginning of a new relationship with former adversaries. Laos was admitted to full membership of ASEAN in 1997.

AID

Recipient

$243m (receipts) — Down 14% in 2001

Laos has one of the highest per capita aid inflows in south or east Asia, Japan being the major donor.

DEFENSE

Compulsory military service

$19m — Down 5% in 2001

The armed forces are estimated by the West to number around 30,000 personnel. This total is further swelled by a paramilitary militia. Eighteen months' military service is compulsory for all Laotian men.

ECONOMICS

Inflation 29% p.a. (1990–2001)

$1.63bn — 7600 new kips (7600)

SCORE CARD

- ❑ WORLD GNP RANKING........................143rd
- ❑ GNP PER CAPITA..............................$300
- ❑ BALANCE OF PAYMENTS......................–$82m
- ❑ INFLATION..7.8%
- ❑ UNEMPLOYMENT..................................6%

EXPORTS

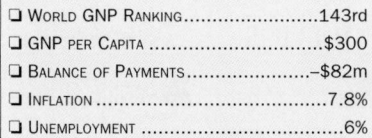

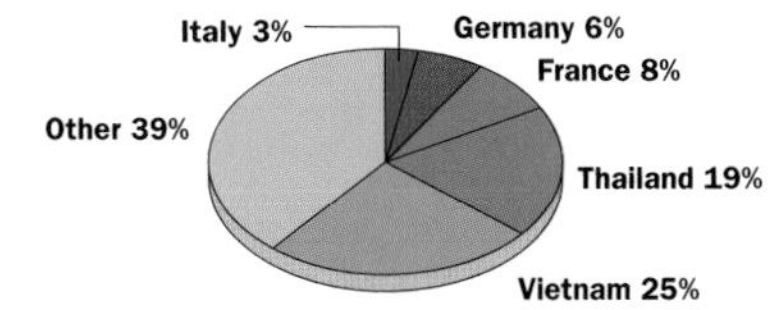
Italy 3%
Germany 6%
France 8%
Other 39%
Thailand 19%
Vietnam 25%

IMPORTS

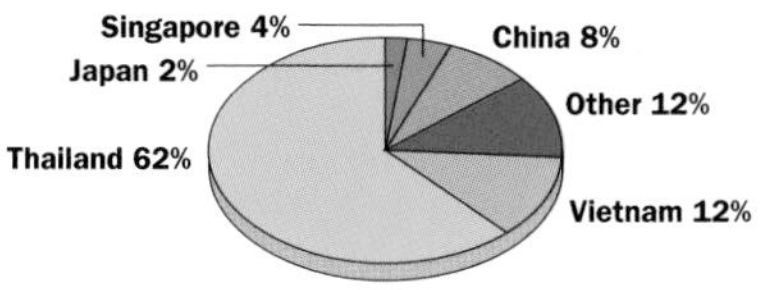
Singapore 4%
Japan 2%
China 8%
Other 12%
Thailand 62%
Vietnam 12%

STRENGTHS

Rising levels of investment from overseas. Potential of garment manufacturing, timber plantations, mining, wood processing, tourism, banking, and aviation. Minerals and possible oil and gas deposits.

WEAKNESSES

One of the world's least developed countries. Lack of technical expertise. Imbalance in sources of foreign investment – most is Thai. Problems in targeting aid efficiently.

RESOURCES

Electric power 256,000 kW

71,316 tonnes — Not an oil producer

1.9m ducks, 1.43m pigs, 1.15m cattle, 15m chickens — Tin, gypsum, iron, coal, copper, potash, lead, limestone, antimony

Laos's most important agricultural resources are timber and coffee. It has awarded foreign countries concessions to mine for gold and precious stones.

ENVIRONMENT

Sustainability rank: 32nd

13% (12% partially protected) — 0.08 tonnes per capita

Bombing and the use of defoliants in the Vietnam War did serious ecological damage. Slash and burn farming and illegal logging are destroying forests.

MEDIA

TV ownership medium

Daily newspaper circulation 4 per 1000 people

PUBLISHING AND BROADCAST MEDIA

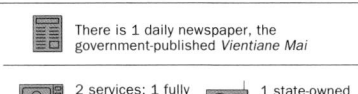

There is 1 daily newspaper, the government-published *Vientiane Mai*

2 services: 1 fully state-owned, 1 30% state-owned — 1 state-owned service

Newspapers are owned and controlled by the LPRP; one is published by the Lao People's Army. Revelations of corruption by state officials are not uncommon, but criticism of the party and its leaders remains taboo.

CRIME

Death penalty in use

Laos does not publish prison figures — Rising overall, particularly corruption

Laos is the world's third-largest opium producer. The US has provided funds to replace poppies with alternative cash crops in the northeast provinces.

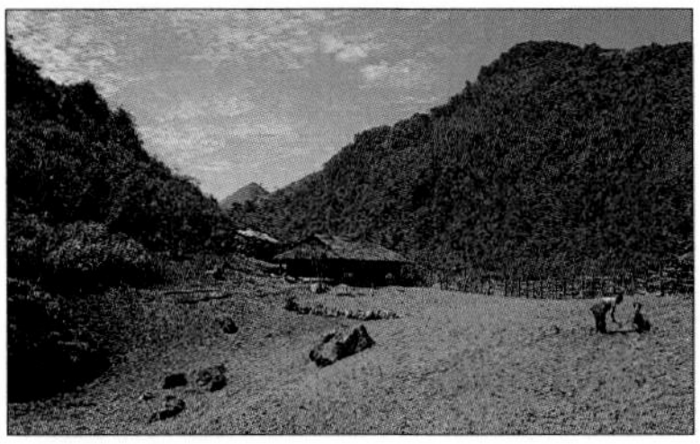

***Farm in northeastern Laos.** The only lowlands are along the Mekong River. Three-quarters of Laotians are subsistence farmers.*

CHRONOLOGY

In 1899, the three small Lao kingdoms were unified under the French.

- ❑ **1953** Independence.
- ❑ **1963** Left-wing armed struggle, overshadowed by Vietnam War.
- ❑ **1975** LPRP seizes power.
- ❑ **1986** Market-oriented reforms.
- ❑ **1997** Accession to ASEAN.
- ❑ **1999** Protests demanding greater political freedom.
- ❑ **2001** Prime minister resigns over economic mismanagement.

EDUCATION

School leaving age: 10

66% — 16,621 students

Adult education is being expanded. Since 1990, private schools have been allowed, in order to help meet demand.

HEALTH

Welfare state health benefits

1 per 1639 people — Diarrheal, respiratory, and parasitic diseases, malaria, influenza

Since 1975, public health care has developed steadily. Malaria and hemorrhagic fever are on the increase.

SPENDING

GDP/cap. increase

CONSUMPTION AND SPENDING

3 per 1000 population — *10 per 1000 population*

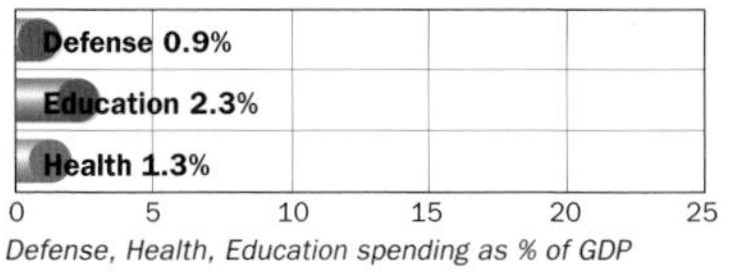
Defense 0.9%
Education 2.3%
Health 1.3%
0
5
10
15
20
25
Defense, Health, Education spending as % of GDP

While a rapidly expanding group of entrepreneurs profits from the gradual liberalization of the country's economy, many in highland and mountainous regions lead a subsistence existence.

WORLD RANKING

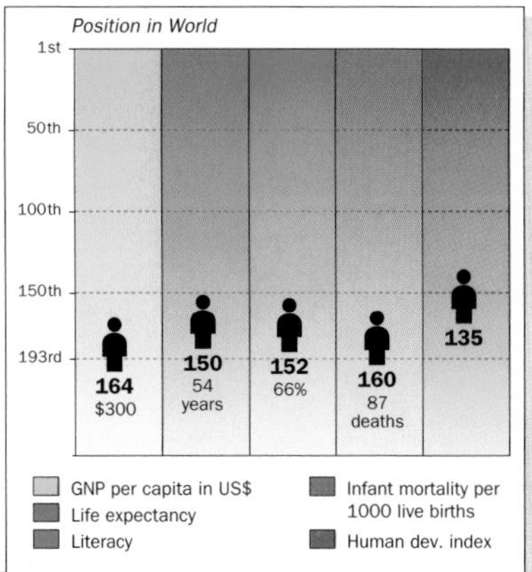
Position in World
1st
50th
100th
150th
193rd
164
$300
150
54 years
152
66%
160
87 deaths
135
GNP per capita in US$
Life expectancy
Literacy
Infant mortality per 1000 live births
Human dev. index

L

LATVIA

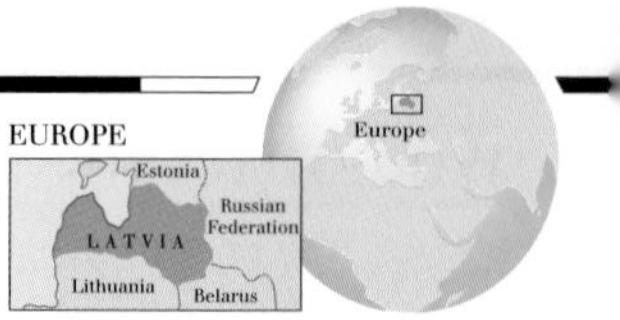
EUROPE
Estonia
Russian Federation
LATVIA
Lithuania
Belarus
Europe

OFFICIAL NAME: Republic of Latvia **CAPITAL:** Riga
POPULATION: 2.4 million **CURRENCY:** Lats **OFFICIAL LANGUAGE:** Latvian

1991 | 1991 | Nov 18 | LV | +2 | +371 | .lv

LATVIA IS ONE of the three Baltic states (with Estonia to the north and Lithuania to the south) which regained independence from Soviet rule in 1991. It lies on a low plain, which nowhere rises above 300 m (975 ft). Almost one-third of the population lives in the capital, Riga. Defense-related industries and agriculture play an important role in the economy. Only just over half of the population are ethnic Latvians.

CLIMATE

Continental

WEATHER CHART FOR RIGA

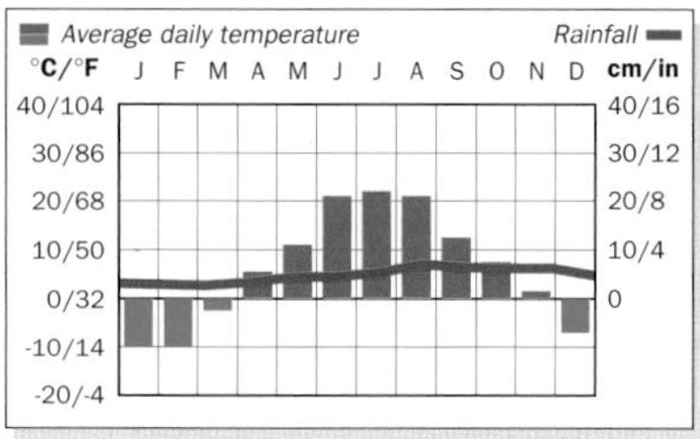
Average daily temperature
Rainfall
°C/°F J F M A M J J A S O N D cm/in
40/104
30/86
20/68
10/50
0/32
-10/14
-20/-4
40/16
30/12
20/8
10/4
0

Latvia's coastal position moderates its continental-type climate and summers are cool, but winters are cold.

TRANSPORTATION

Drive on right

Riga International 633,631 passengers

160 ships 68,300 grt

THE TRANSPORTATION NETWORK

22,843 km (14,194 miles)	None
2331 km (1448 miles)	300 km (186 miles)

Riga has the busiest container port in the Baltic. The EU-backed Via Baltica highway, linking Poland and Finland, runs north–south through Latvia. An east–west link of a similar standard is a priority.

Riga, the Latvian capital. The Russian Orthodox cathedral in the foreground was used as a planetarium during the Soviet era.

TOURISM

Visitors : Population 1:4.1

591,000 visitors

Up 21% in 2000–2001

MAIN TOURIST ARRIVALS

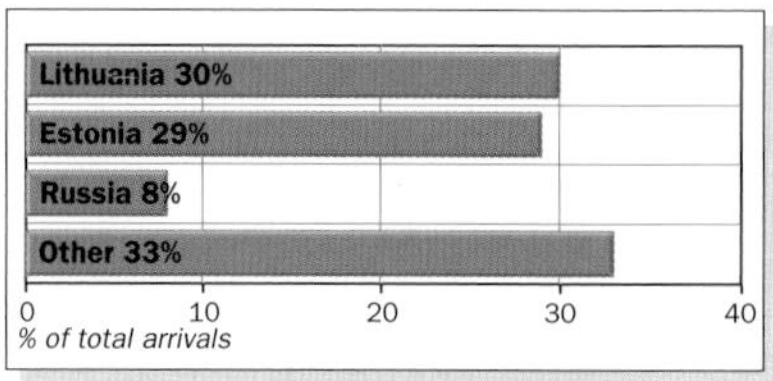
Lithuania 30%
Estonia 29%
Russia 8%
Other 33%
0 10 20 30 40
% of total arrivals

Riga is the main tourist destination, with many hotels and restaurants. Its medieval center is being restored.

PEOPLE

Pop. density low

Latvian, Russian

37/km² (96/mi²)

THE URBAN/RURAL POPULATION SPLIT

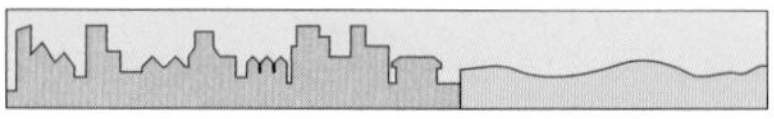
60%
40%

ETHNIC MAKEUP

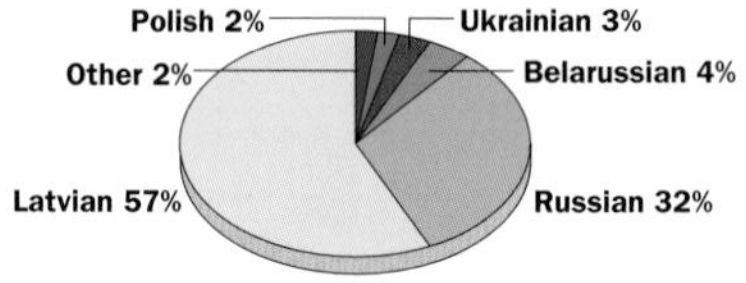
Polish 2%
Ukrainian 3%
Other 2%
Belarussian 4%
Latvian 57%
Russian 32%

Latvians (who form the minority in Riga and are mostly Lutheran) have been effectively favored by the state since 1991 over the Orthodox Russian minority (which was boosted by Soviet-era migrations). The naturalization process was simplified in 1998, but Latvian was proclaimed the only official language for state and private sectors in 2000 and will be used exclusively in schools from 2004.

POLITICS

Multiparty elections

2002/2006

President Vaira Vike-Freiberga

AT THE LAST ELECTION
Parliament 100 seats

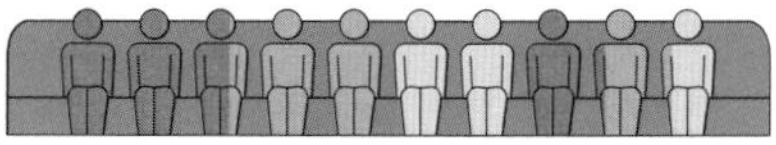
10% LPP
26% JL
25% PCTVL
20% TP
12% ZZS
7% TB/LNNK

JL = New Era **PCTVL** = For Human Rights in a United Latvia (including the National Harmony Party–**TSP**) **TP** = People's Party **ZZS** = Green and Farmers' Union **LPP** = Latvia's First Party **TB/LNNK** = Fatherland and Freedom

Recent elections have boosted center-right parties, all in favor of EU membership and continuing market reforms. Coalitions have been short-lived, with four different governments between 1998 and 2002. Former premier Andris Skele's TP won the 1998 elections, was initially excluded from power, and later failed to hold together its own coalition. Riga's high-profile mayor, Andris Berzins, was prime minister until the 2002 elections, but saw his Latvia's Way routed. The JL, led by Einars Repse, went on to build a four-party center-right coalition.

LATVIA

Total Area : 64 589 sq. km (24 938 sq. miles)

POPULATION
- over 500 000
- over 100 000
- over 50 000
- over 10 000
- under 10 000

LAND HEIGHT
- 200m/656ft
- Sea Level

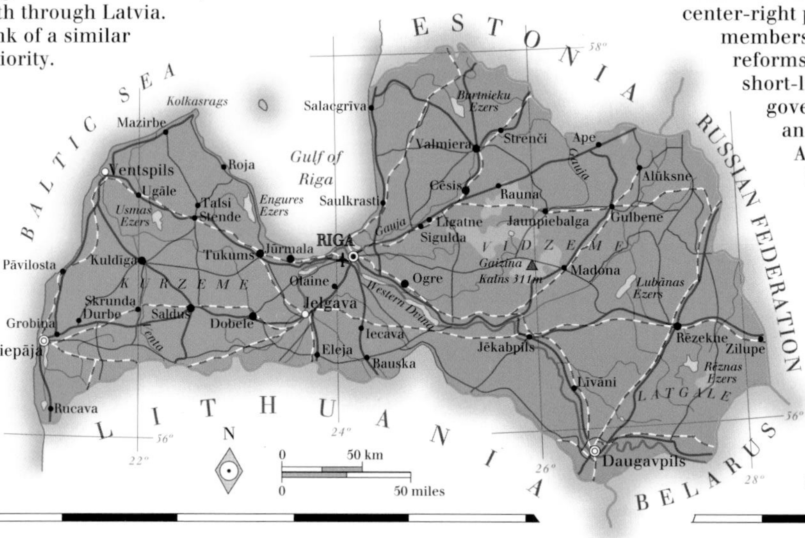
ESTONIA
RUSSIAN FEDERATION
BALTIC SEA
LITHUANIA
BELARUS
Kolkasrags
Mazirbe
Ventspils
Ugāle
Usmas Ezers
Roja
Talsi
Stende
Gulf of Riga
Engures Ezers
Saulkrasti
Salacgrīva
Burtnieku Ezers
Valmiera
Strenči
Ape
Gauja
Alūksne
Cēsis
Rauna
Ligatne
Sigulda
Jaunpiebalga
Gulbene
RIGA
Jūrmala
Tukums
Kuldīga
Pāvilosta
KURZEME
VIDZEME
Gaiziņa Kalns 311m
Madona
Lubānas Ezers
Ogre
Olaine
Jelgava
Skrunda
Durbe
Saldus
Dobele
Grobiņa
Liepāja
Venta
Iecava
Western Dvina
Eleja
Bauska
Jēkabpils
Rēzekne
Zilupe
Rēznas Ezers
Līvāni
LATGALE
Rucava
Daugavpils
N
0 50 km
0 50 miles
58°
56°
22°
24°
26°
28°

WORLD AFFAIRS

Joined UN in 1991

CE | CBSS | OSCE | EAPC | PfP

Latvia is one of ten candidate countries invited to become full members of the EU in the 2004 expansion. It also has US backing for entry to NATO, due the same year. Discrimination against Russian-speakers, exemplified by laws passed in 2000 making Latvian the only official language, have strained relations with Russia.

AID

Recipient

$106m (receipts)

Up 16% in 2001

Aid to Latvia comes mainly from the EU and individual member states. Most is spent on improving the country's infrastructure.

DEFENSE

Compulsory military service

$85m

Up 20% in 2001

Building up the military is a priority, and NATO membership is expected in 2004; Latvia has been participating in NATO's Partnership for Peace program. In February 2000, Russian forces finished dismantling their last military installation in Latvia, the Skrunda radar station.

ECONOMICS

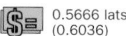

Inflation 42% p.a. (1990–2001)

$7.63bn

0.5666 lats (0.6036)

SCORE CARD

- World GNP Ranking........................98th
- GNP per Capita $3230
- Balance of Payments..................–$758m
- Inflation 2.5%
- Unemployment 8%

Strengths

Thriving service sector: now provides over 70% of GDP. Buoyant manufacturing industries. Low inflation. Foreign investment.

Weaknesses

Dependence on imports for energy. Lack of raw materials. Farming technically backward after dismantling of collective farms. Sizable current account deficit.

EXPORTS

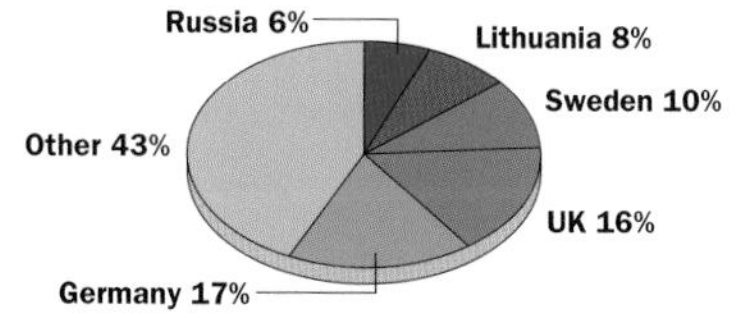
Russia 6%
Lithuania 8%
Sweden 10%
Other 43%
UK 16%
Germany 17%

IMPORTS

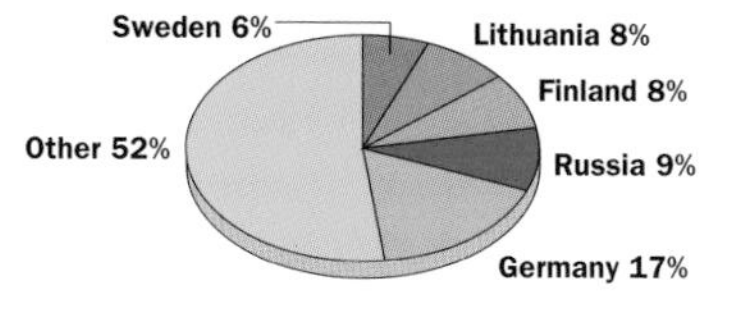
Sweden 6%
Lithuania 8%
Finland 8%
Other 52%
Russia 9%
Germany 17%

RESOURCES

Electric power 2.1m kW

136,728 tonnes

Not an oil producer

453,200 pigs, 450,000 turkeys, 3.88m chickens

Amber, dolomite, gravel, gypsum, limestone, peat, sand

Latvia has limited natural resources, and is dependent on imports (including Russian oil and gas) to meet much of its energy needs. Electricity comes chiefly from hydroelectric power and regular imports from Lithuania and Estonia. Offshore oil exploration is planned, with Ventspils deepwater port being promoted as an important oil terminal.

ENVIRONMENT

Sustainability rank: 10th

13% (12% partially protected)

2.9 tonnes per capita

Peat extraction has damaged valuable bog habitat. Pollution of the Baltic Sea and air and water quality in industrial centers are also of concern.

In 2001 Latvia committed to full enforcement of EU environmental directives by 2010.

MEDIA

TV ownership high

Daily newspaper circulation 135 per 1000 people

PUBLISHING AND BROADCAST MEDIA

There are 5 daily newspapers, including *Diena* and *Neatkariga Rita Avize*

2 services: 1 state-owned, 1 independent

15 services: 1 state-owned, 14 independent

The press is now relatively free from state interference. Previously, the media were predominantly in Russian. Since 1991 the state, aiming to broaden the use of the official language, has actively promoted Latvian publications.

CRIME

Death penalty not used in practice

8486 prisoners

Up 3% in 2000–2001

General crime levels are lower than in Russia, but are on the rise. Organized crime is a growing problem.

EDUCATION

School leaving age: 15

99%

102,783 students

Latvian is replacing Russian as the main language of instruction in schools, and is set to become universal by 2005.

CHRONOLOGY

Governed in turn by Teutons, Poles, and Swedes, Latvia was conquered by Russia in 1795.

- **1917** Declares independence.
- **1918–1920** Invaded by Bolsheviks and Germany.
- **1920** Gains independence.
- **1944** Incorporated into USSR.
- **1989** Popular Front wins elections; declares independence.
- **1991** Independence recognized.
- **1998** Elections; LC-led coalition. Naturalization procedure eased.
- **1999** Vaira Vike-Freiberga elected first woman president. Andris Skele of TP returns as premier.
- **2000** Skele resigns.
- **2002** JL wins elections, Einars Repse prime minister.

HEALTH

Welfare state health benefits

1 per 319 people

Cerebrovascular and heart diseases, cancers, car accidents, suicide

The state-run system suffers shortages of medicines and equipment. Some improvements have been made, but it is still seriously underfunded.

SPENDING

GDP/cap. decrease

CONSUMPTION AND SPENDING

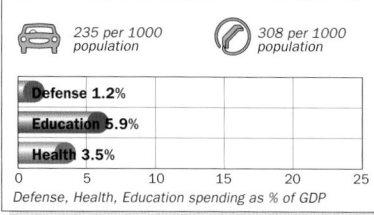

235 per 1000 population

308 per 1000 population

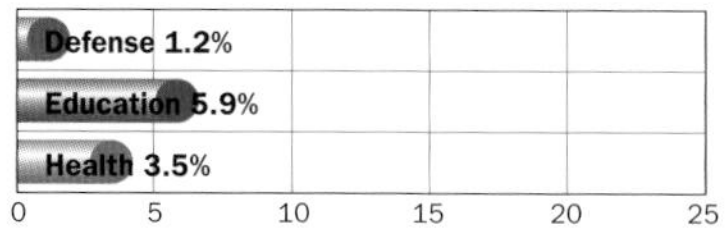
Defense 1.2%
Education 5.9%
Health 3.5%
0
5
10
15
20
25

Defense, Health, Education spending as % of GDP

The old bureaucracy has retained its privileged status and contacts, and remains the wealthiest group. Farmers are among the poorest.

WORLD RANKING

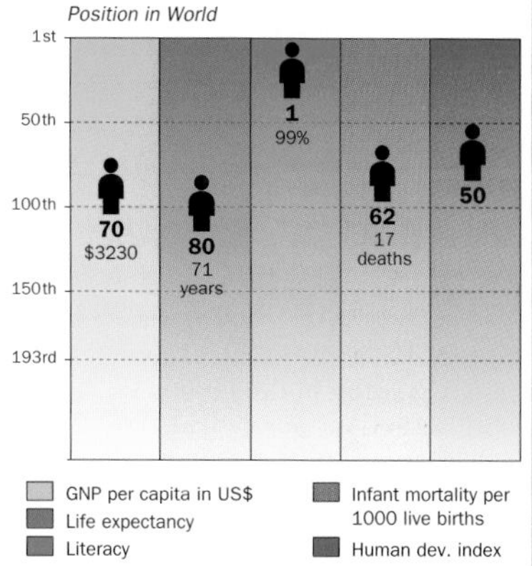
Position in World
1st
50th
100th
150th
193rd
70
$3230
80
71
years
1
99%
62
17
deaths
50
GNP per capita in US$
Life expectancy
Literacy
Infant mortality per 1000 live births
Human dev. index

L

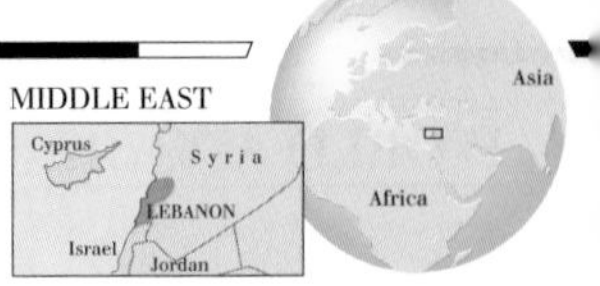
MIDDLE EAST
Cyprus
Syria
LEBANON
Israel
Jordan
Asia
Africa

LEBANON

OFFICIAL NAME: Republic of Lebanon **CAPITAL:** Beirut
POPULATION: 3.6 million **CURRENCY:** Lebanese pound **OFFICIAL LANGUAGE:** Arabic

1941 | 1941 | Nov 22 | RL | +2 | +961 | .lb

LEBANON LIVES in the shadow of its powerful neighbors, Syria and Israel. The coastal strip is fertile and the hinterland mountainous. The minority Maronite Christians have traditionally dominated the government. Civil war between Muslim and Christian factions from 1975, complicated by an Israeli invasion in 1982, threatened a breakup of the state, until Saudi Arabia brokered a peace deal in 1989. Greater political stability and reconstruction have ensued.

CLIMATE

Mediterranean/ mountain

WEATHER CHART FOR BEIRUT

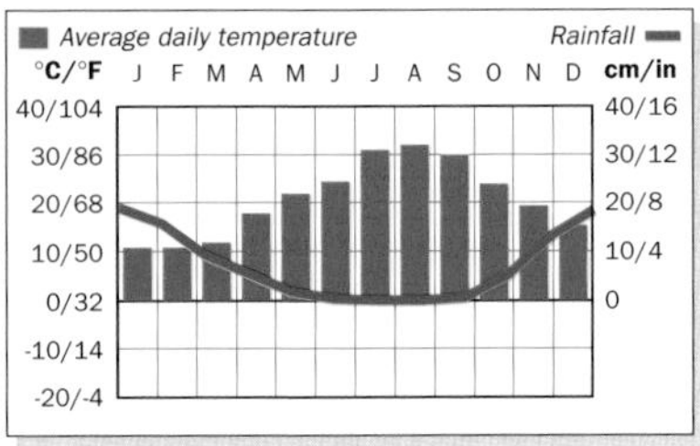
Average daily temperature
Rainfall
°C/°F J F M A M J J A S O N D cm/in
40/104
30/86
20/68
10/50
0/32
-10/14
-20/-4
40/16
30/12
20/8
10/4
0

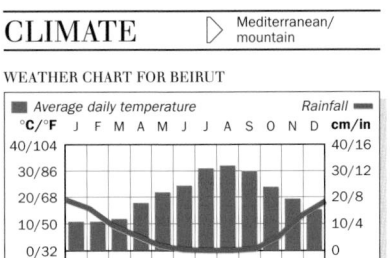

Winters are mild and summers hot, with high humidity on the coast. Snow falls on high ground in the winter.

TRANSPORTATION

Drive on right

Beirut International, Khaldeh
2.61m passengers

99 ships
301,700 grt

THE TRANSPORTATION NETWORK

6350 km (3946 miles)

None

399 km (248 miles)

None

The redevelopment of Beirut could see it regain its position as one of the Middle East's major entrepôts.

TOURISM

Visitors : Population 1:3.8

956,000 visitors

Up 14% in 2002

MAIN TOURIST ARRIVALS

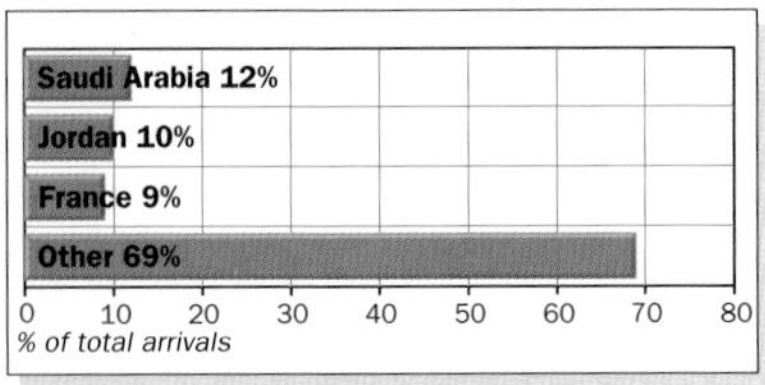
Saudi Arabia 12%
Jordan 10%
France 9%
Other 69%
0 10 20 30 40 50 60 70 80
% of total arrivals

Tourists have gradually returned since the devastation of the civil war. The main attractions are Beirut, Tripoli, Crusader castles, the Roman remains and the festival at Baalbek, and the Phoenician city of Gubla (Byblos).

PEOPLE

Pop. density high

Arabic, French, Armenian, Assyrian

352/km² (911/mi²)

THE URBAN/RURAL POPULATION SPLIT

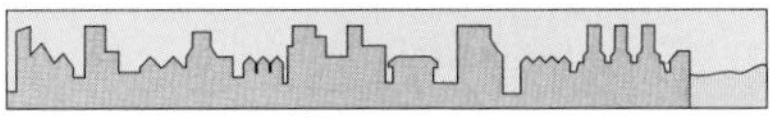
90%
10%

RELIGIOUS PERSUASION

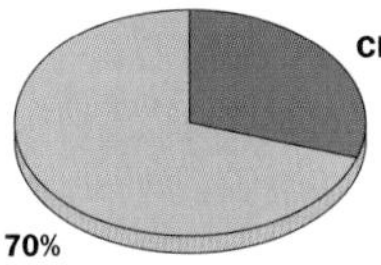
Christian 30%
Muslim 70%

The Lebanese population is fragmented in religious terms into subsects of Christians and Muslims, but retains a strong sense of national identity. There has been a large Palestinian refugee population in the country since 1948. Islamic fundamentalism is influential among poorer Shi'a Muslims, who constitute the largest single group.

LEBANON

Total Area : 10 400 sq. km (4015 sq. miles)

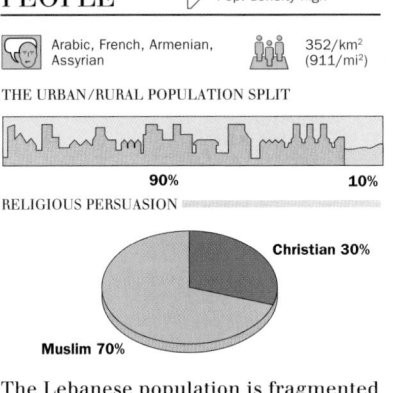

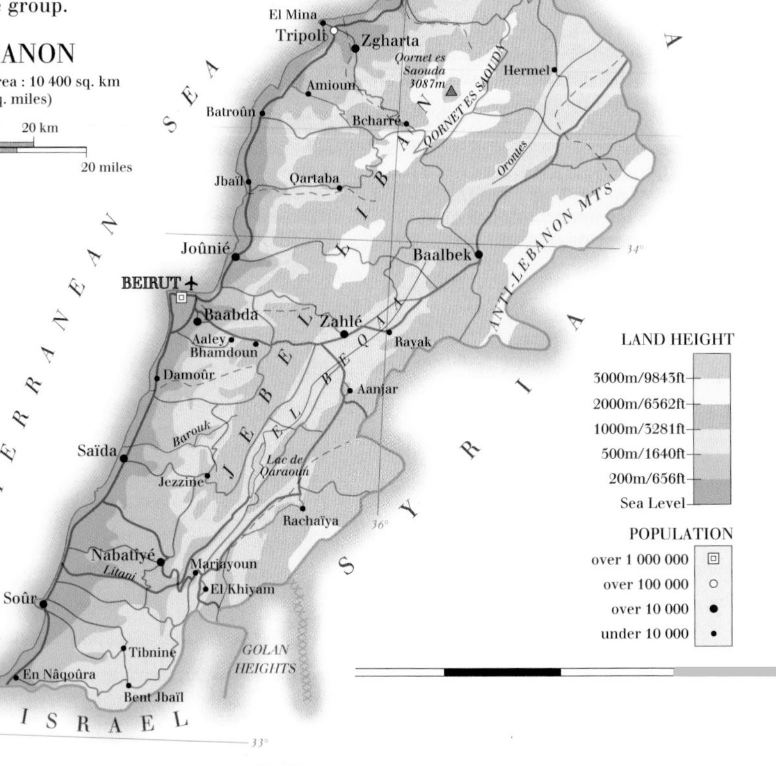
0 20 km
0 20 miles
N
SYRIA
MEDITERRANEAN SEA
ISRAEL
El Mina
Tripoli
Zgharta
Qoubaïyât
Qornet es Saouda 3087m
Hermel
Amioun
Batroûn
Bcharré
QORNET ES SAOUDA
LIBAN
Orontes
Jbaïl
Qartaba
Joûnié
Baalbek
ANTI-LEBANON MTS
BEIRUT
Baabda
Zahlé
BEQAA
Aaley
Bhamdoun
Rayak
Damoûr
Aanjar
Barouk
JEBEL
Saïda
Lac de Qaraoun
Jezzine
Rachaïya
Nabatîyé
Litani
Marjayoun
El Khiyam
Soûr
Tibnine
GOLAN HEIGHTS
En Nâqoûra
Bent Jbaïl
34°
36°
33°
LAND HEIGHT
3000m/9843ft
2000m/6562ft
1000m/3281ft
500m/1640ft
200m/656ft
Sea Level
POPULATION
over 1 000 000
over 100 000
over 10 000
under 10 000

POLITICS

Multiparty elections

2000/2004

President Emile Lahoud

AT THE LAST ELECTION

National Assembly 128 seats

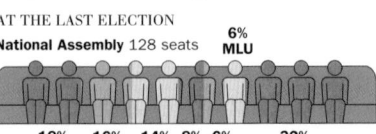

6% MLU
18% RD
16% Ind
14% D
8% BH
6% NS
32% Others

RD = Resistance and Development List **Ind** = Independents **D** = Dignity **BH** = Baalbek–Hermel List **NS** = National Struggle List **MLU** = Mount Lebanon Unity

The Arab-brokered 1989 Taif peace agreement ending the civil war redressed the constitutional balance between Christians and Muslims and guaranteed power-sharing. Syria remains the main power broker in Lebanon, especially following the withdrawal of Israeli troops in 2000. A once popular campaign for the removal of Syrian forces has abated. The first postwar legislative elections were held in 1992, and Rafiq al-Hariri was appointed prime minister. He took office for a third term in 2000, after his supporters had won three-quarters of the seats in the Assembly. However, a worsening economic situation has led to clashes between Hariri and Gen. Emile Lahoud, president since 1998.

L

WORLD AFFAIRS

Joined UN in 1945

AL | G24 | OIF | NAM | OIC

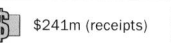

The 1989 Taif Agreement left Syria with enormous influence in Lebanese politics. Anti-Israeli rhetoric remains the political lingua franca. The Hezbollah militia fought frequent and bloody skirmishes with Israeli occupying forces (and their proxy militias) until Israel withdrew in 2000. A UN force now patrols the still-volatile border. In 2002 tensions mounted after Israel accused Lebanon of diverting shared water sources.

AID

Recipient

$241m (receipts) | Up 22% in 2001

The World Bank has become an increasingly important source of loans for improving Lebanon's infrastructure.

DEFENSE

Compulsory military service

$576m | No change in 2001

The army has over 70,000 troops. Hezbollah guerrillas rapidly regained control of southern Lebanon after the Israeli withdrawal in 2000. There is a UN peacekeeping force on the Israeli border. Syrian forces, whose dominant security role had been formalized in 1991, withdrew from Beirut in 2001.

ECONOMICS

Inflation 15% p.a. (1990–2001)

$17.6bn | 1514 Lebanese pounds (1513.5)

SCORE CARD

❑ World GNP Ranking	70th
❑ GNP per Capita	$4010
❑ Balance of Payments	–$3.98bn
❑ Inflation	0.5%
❑ Unemployment	18%

Strengths

Financial services industry. Potential for wine and fruit production. Low inflation. Lifting of US financial restrictions.

Weaknesses

Dependent on imported oil and gas. Agriculture still below prewar levels. High public debt. Alleged Syrian "dumping" of cheap produce. Reports of narcotics handling and corruption harm investor confidence.

EXPORTS

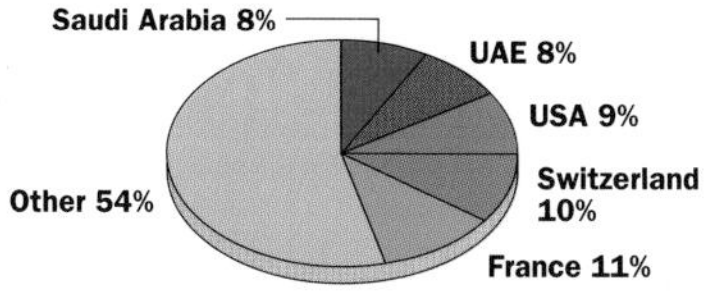
Saudi Arabia 8%
UAE 8%
USA 9%
Switzerland 10%
France 11%
Other 54%

IMPORTS

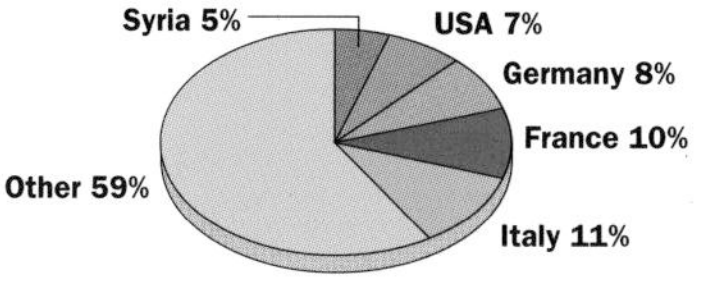
Syria 5%
USA 7%
Germany 8%
France 10%
Italy 11%
Other 59%

RESOURCES

Electric power 2.3m kW

4066 tonnes | Not an oil producer

385,000 goats, 350,000 sheep, 33m chickens | Lignite, iron ore

Wine, cotton, fruit, and vegetables are the main crops. Power plants are fueled by imported petroleum.

ENVIRONMENT

Sustainability rank: 106th

0.5% | 5 tonnes per capita

Lack of central authority during the civil war allowed unregulated building, logging, and quarrying to flourish.

MEDIA

TV ownership high

Daily newspaper circulation 74 per 1000 people

PUBLISHING AND BROADCAST MEDIA

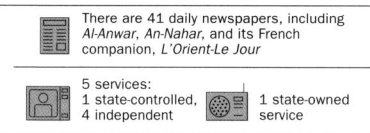

There are 41 daily newspapers, including *Al-Anwar*, *An-Nahar*, and its French companion, *L'Orient-Le Jour*

5 services: 1 state-controlled, 4 independent | 1 state-owned service

In the late 1990s the government banned news and political programs on private satellite television channels.

CRIME

Death penalty in use

8285 prisoners | Down 1% in 2000

The kidnapping of hostages and the breakdown of law during the civil war made Beirut a dangerous city for visitors.

Politically motivated violence has largely declined, though the risk of urban terrorism remains. Rural areas, which were untouched by the conflict, have maintained low levels of crime.

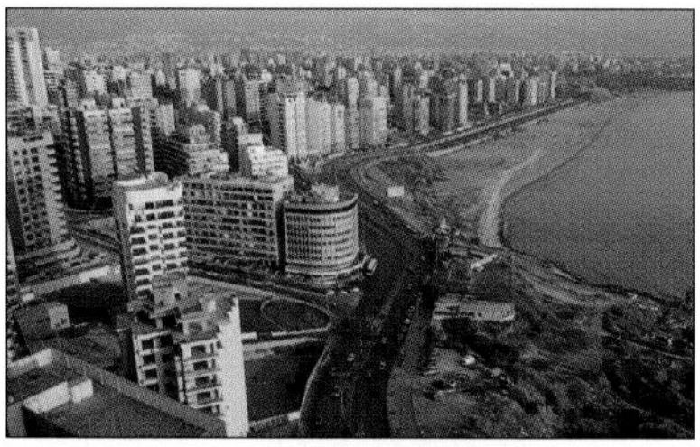

***The Corniche, Beirut,** was rebuilt after the civil war by US consultant engineers and architects in a privately financed scheme.*

CHRONOLOGY

Under French mandate from 1920, Lebanon declared independence in 1941, achieving full autonomy in 1946.

- ❑ **1975** Civil war erupts.
- ❑ **1982** Israeli invasion.
- ❑ **1989** Taif Agreement ends civil war.
- ❑ **1992** First election in 20 years. Rafiq al-Hariri prime minister.
- ❑ **1996** Israeli attack kills over 100 civilians at UN base in Qana.
- ❑ **1998** Emile Lahoud president.
- ❑ **2000** Israeli forces withdraw. Hariri reelected by a landslide.

EDUCATION

School leaving age: 12

87% | 134,018 students

Lebanon has one of the highest literacy rates in the Arab world. Education was severely disrupted by the war.

HEALTH

Welfare state health benefits

1 per 365 people | Heart disease, infectious and parasitic diseases

An adequate system of primary health care exists. Hospital staffing is returning to prewar levels.

SPENDING

GDP/cap. increase

CONSUMPTION AND SPENDING

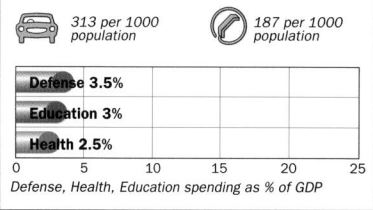

313 per 1000 population | *187 per 1000 population*

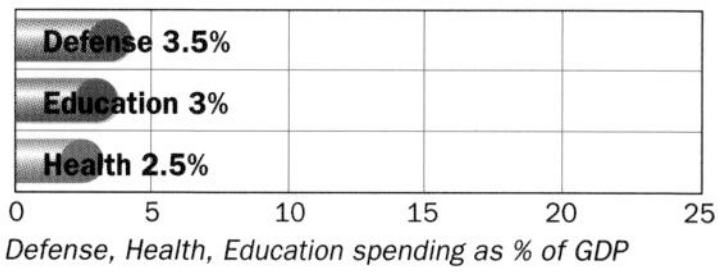
Defense 3.5%
Education 3%
Health 2.5%
0
5
10
15
20
25
Defense, Health, Education spending as % of GDP

Average income per capita statistics conceal the fact that a huge gulf exists between the poor and a small, massively rich elite.

WORLD RANKING

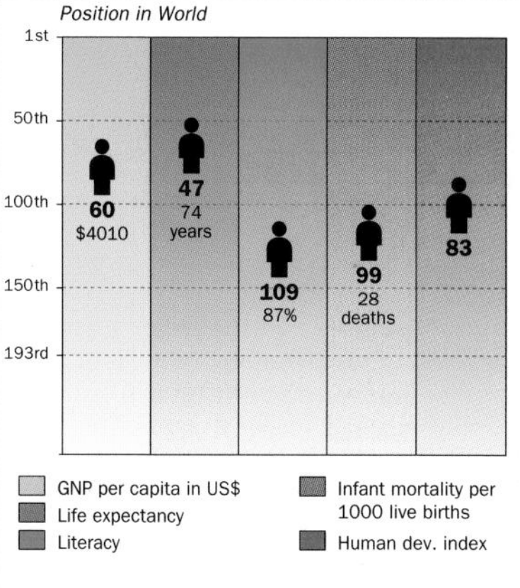
Position in World
1st
50th
100th
150th
193rd
60
$4010
47
74
years
109
87%
99
28
deaths
83
GNP per capita in US$
Life expectancy
Literacy
Infant mortality per 1000 live births
Human dev. index

L

LESOTHO

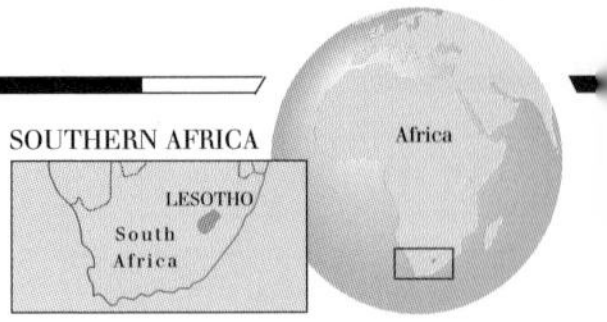
SOUTHERN AFRICA
Africa
LESOTHO
South Africa

OFFICIAL NAME: Kingdom of Lesotho **CAPITAL:** Maseru
POPULATION: 2.1 million **CURRENCY:** Loti **OFFICIAL LANGUAGES:** English and Sesotho

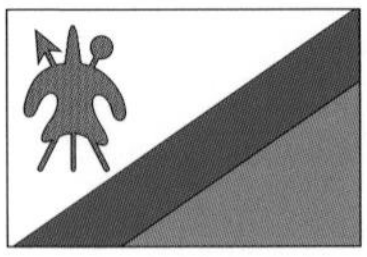

1966 | 1966 | Oct 4 | LS | +2 | +266 | .ls

A MOUNTAINOUS AND landlocked country entirely surrounded by South Africa, Lesotho is economically dependent on its larger neighbor. However, Lesotho is beginning to benefit from the export of energy from the recently completed Highlands Water Scheme. Elections in 1993 ended a period of military rule, but South Africa had to send in its troops when serious political unrest erupted in 1998.

CLIMATE

Mountain

WEATHER CHART FOR MASERU

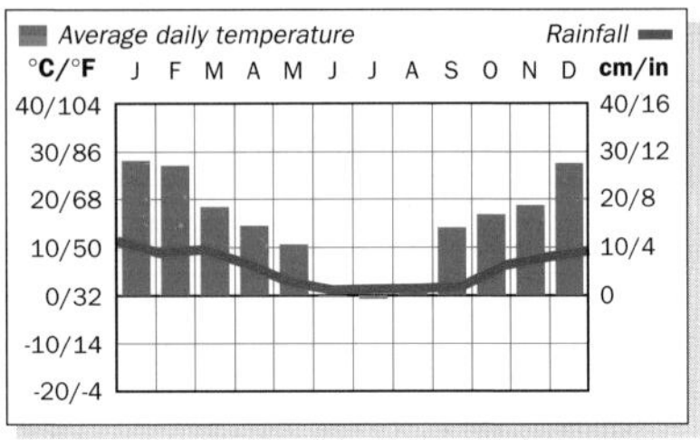
Average daily temperature
Rainfall
°C/°F J F M A M J J A S O N D cm/in
40/104 30/86 20/68 10/50 0/32 -10/14 -20/-4
40/16 30/12 20/8 10/4 0

Drought is often followed by torrential rain storms. Snow is frequent in winter in the mountains.

TRANSPORTATION

Drive on left

Moshoeshoe International, Maseru 43,000 passengers

Has no fleet

THE TRANSPORTATION NETWORK

887 km (551 miles)

None

3 km (2 miles)

None

Lesotho has to rely on South African road and rail outlets. New roads have been constructed to service the Highlands Water Scheme.

TOURISM

Visitors : Population 1:9.1

231,000 visitors

Up 24% in 2000

MAIN TOURIST ARRIVALS

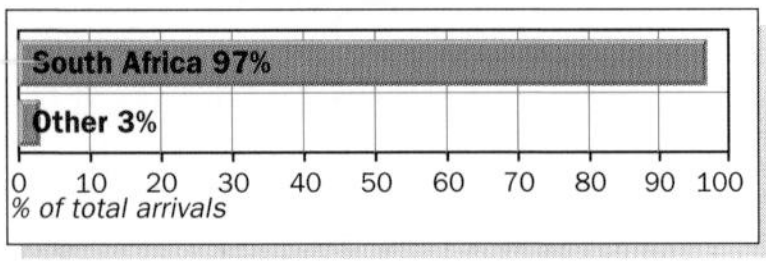
South Africa 97%
Other 3%
0 10 20 30 40 50 60 70 80 90 100
% of total arrivals

Tourists, mainly South African, are attracted to the dramatic mountain scenery and watersports on artificially created lakes. Another draw is Thaba-Bosiu, King Moshoeshoe the Great's mountain stronghold. Political violence in 1998 deterred many visitors.

PEOPLE

Pop. density medium

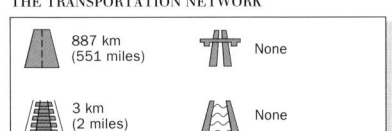

English, Sesotho, isiZulu

69/km² (179/mi²)

THE URBAN/RURAL POPULATION SPLIT

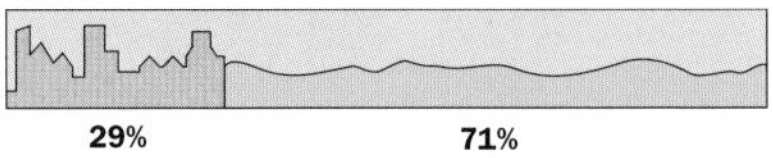
29%
71%

ETHNIC MAKEUP

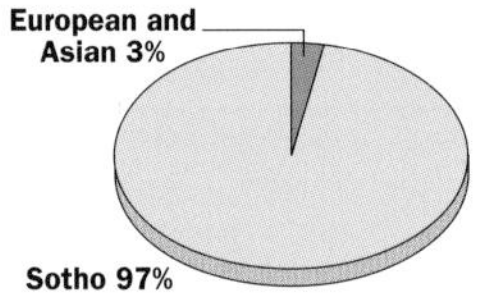
European and Asian 3%
Sotho 97%

The overwhelming majority of the population are Sotho, though there is a small community of European origin, as well as south Asian and Chinese minorities, which are active in the retailing business. Ethnic homogeneity and a strong sense of national identity have tended to minimize ethnic tension.

The export of male contract labor to South African mines means that women head the majority of households; they also run farming, regarded by Lesotho men as "women's work."

POLITICS

Multiparty elections

L. House 2002/2007
U. House 2002/2007

H.M. King Letsie III

AT THE LAST ELECTION

National Assembly 120 seats

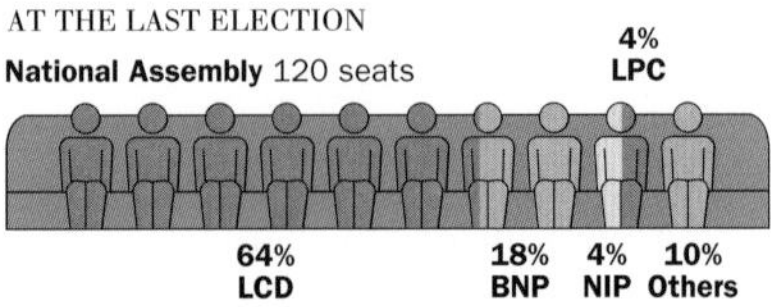
4% LPC
64% LCD
18% BNP
4% NIP
10% Others

LCD = Lesotho Congress for Democracy **BNP** = Basotho National Party **NIP** = National Independent Party **LPC** = Lesotho People's Congress

Senate 33 seats

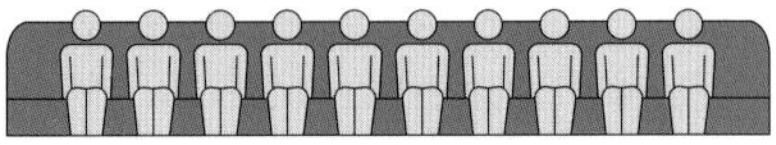

The Senate comprises 22 principal chiefs and 11 other members named by the king

The armed forces have played a key role in Lesotho since a bloodless coup in 1986. Direct military rule ended in 1993, and a free and peaceful general election resulted in a sweeping victory for the Basotho Congress Party (BCP), though the army maintained its powers over national security. Tensions escalated in 1994, when mutinous troops killed the deputy prime minister. King Moshoeshoe II was restored to the throne, and was succeeded by his son Letsie III in 1996.

Accusations of vote rigging and mass protests greeted a general election win in 1998 by the LCD (a splinter of the BCP). After an attempted coup in September, the South African military intervened to restore democracy, brokering an agreement between the king and Lesotho's 12 parties. When elections were finally held in 2002, the LCD, under Prime Minister Bethuel Mosisili, retained its majority.

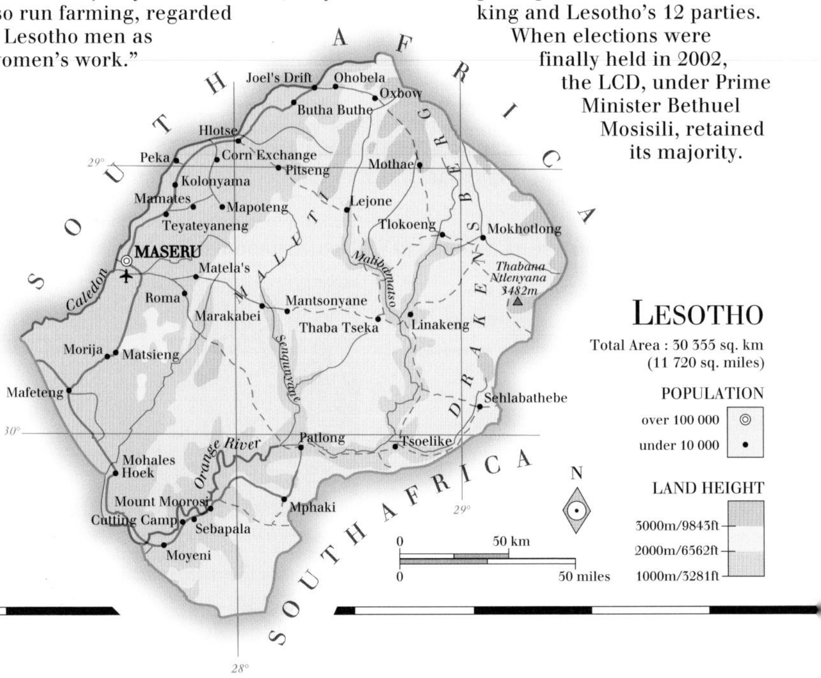
SOUTH AFRICA
Joel's Drift
Ohobela
Oxbow
Butha Buthe
Hlotse
Peka
Corn Exchange
Pitseng
Mothae
Kolonyama
Mamates
Mapoteng
Lejone
Teyateyaneng
Tlokoeng
Mokhotlong
MASERU
Matela's
MALOTI
Malibamatso
DRAKENSBERG
Thabana Ntlenyana 3482m
Caledon
Roma
Mantsonyane
Marakabei
Thaba Tseka
Linakeng
Senqunyane
Morija
Matsieng
Mafeteng
Sehlabathebe
Orange River
Patlong
Tsoelike
Mohales Hoek
Mount Moorosi
Mphaki
Cutting Camp
Sebapala
Moyeni
29°
30°
28°
N
0 50 km
0 50 miles
LESOTHO
Total Area : 30 355 sq. km (11 720 sq. miles)
POPULATION
over 100 000
under 10 000
LAND HEIGHT
3000m/9843ft
2000m/6562ft
1000m/3281ft

WORLD AFFAIRS

Joined UN in 1966

Comm | ACP | NAM | AU | SADC

Foreign policy is dominated by the nature of Lesotho's relationship with South Africa. Lesotho currently has duty-free access to the EU for most manufactured goods, and also has preferential access to US and Scandinavian markets.

AID

Recipient

$54m (receipts) | Up 32% in 2001

Aid has become less important as a proportion of GNP, and mostly comes from the EU and the World Bank. A national famine was formally declared in 2002 to encourage donations of emergency assistance.

DEFENSE

No compulsory military service

$24m | Down 11% in 2001

Lesotho's 2000-strong army relied on South African assistance to quell political violence in 1998.

ECONOMICS

Inflation 9.5% p.a. (1990–2001)

$1.1bn | 7.51 maloti (10.31)

SCORE CARD

❑ WORLD GNP RANKING	153rd
❑ GNP PER CAPITA	$530
❑ BALANCE OF PAYMENTS	–$95m
❑ INFLATION	–9.6%
❑ UNEMPLOYMENT	45%

STRENGTHS

Textiles and other manufacturing. Educated workforce. Water as commodity: exports and HEP sales.

WEAKNESSES

Dependence on South Africa. Loss of workforce to South African mines. Weak agricultural sector. Sporadic disturbances in retail sector. 2002 corruption in Development Authority. Spread of AIDS.

EXPORTS

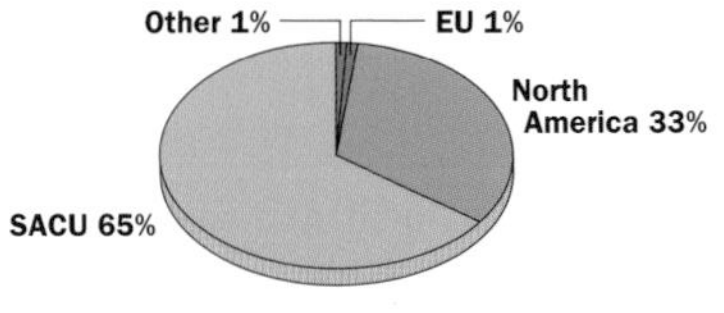
Other 1%
EU 1%
North America 33%
SACU 65%

IMPORTS

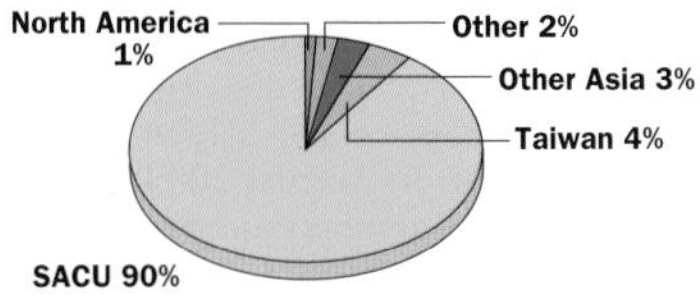
North America 1%
Other 2%
Other Asia 3%
Taiwan 4%
SACU 90%

***Landscape near Mohales Hoek** in Lesotho's lowest lands – over 1300 m (4260 ft) above sea level.*

RESOURCES

Electric power: Included in South African total

40 tonnes | Included in South African total

850,000 sheep, 650,000 goats, 1.8m chickens | Diamonds

The Highlands Water hydroelectric scheme has the capacity to supply all of Lesotho's energy requirements, as well as 62 cu. m (2200 cu. ft) of water per second for South African use. Diamonds are mined in the northeast.

ENVIRONMENT

Not available

0.2% partially protected | Negligible emissions per capita

Climate and overgrazing have seriously eroded the land. The Highlands Water Scheme has flooded acres of peasant farmland. Supporters of this massive dam project stress encouragement for wildlife in reservoirs and on bird-friendly pylons.

MEDIA

TV ownership low

Daily newspaper circulation 8 per 1000 people

PUBLISHING AND BROADCAST MEDIA

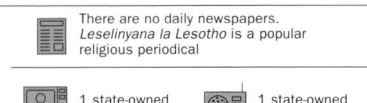

There are no daily newspapers. *Leselinyana la Lesotho* is a popular religious periodical

1 state-owned service | 1 state-owned service

In 1998 state-controlled media were used for political ends. The six independent papers often carry opposition views.

CRIME

Death penalty in use

3000 prisoners | Up sharply in 1998–1999

The 1998 political crisis increased crime levels, which previously were much lower than in South Africa.

EDUCATION

School leaving age: 13

84% | 4976 students

Schools have very high enrollment levels, and Lesotho has one of the highest literacy rates in Africa.

CHRONOLOGY

As Basutoland, Lesotho became a British Crown colony in 1884.

- ❑ **1966** Independent kingdom.
- ❑ **1986** Military coup.
- ❑ **1990** King Moshoeshoe II exiled. Son installed as Letsie III.
- ❑ **1993** Free elections.
- ❑ **1994** Return of Moshoeshoe II.
- ❑ **1996** Letsie III succeeds to throne.
- ❑ **1998** New LCD wins polls. South Africa intervenes after coup attempt, and reconciles king and parties.
- ❑ **2002** Food emergency follows successive poor harvests. LCD wins long-postponed elections.

HEALTH

Welfare state health benefits

1 per 14,286 people | Tuberculosis, AIDS, parasitic diseases, nutritional disorders

Private health organizations and NGOs account for half of all health services. A government-operated flying doctor service covers the highlands. An estimated 31% of adults are HIV positive and life expectancy is declining. Food shortages in 2002 exacerbated the country's health problems.

SPENDING

GDP/cap. increase

CONSUMPTION AND SPENDING

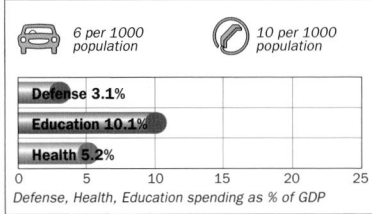

6 per 1000 population | *10 per 1000 population*

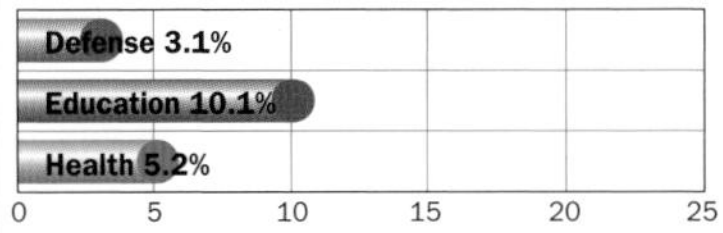
Defense 3.1%
Education 10.1%
Health 5.2%
0
5
10
15
20
25

Defense, Health, Education spending as % of GDP

Social mobility is limited in Lesotho; the ruling elite keeps a tight hold on power and wealth. Around 66% of the population live below the UN poverty line and many are migrant laborers.

WORLD RANKING

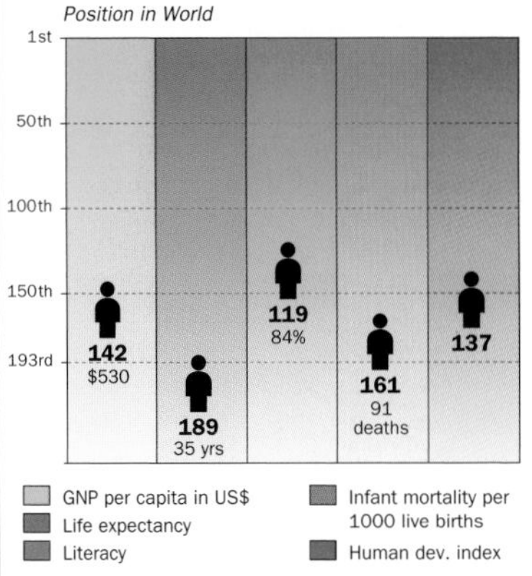
Position in World
1st
50th
100th
150th
193rd
142
$530
189
35 yrs
119
84%
161
91 deaths
137
GNP per capita in US$
Life expectancy
Literacy
Infant mortality per 1000 live births
Human dev. index

L

LIBERIA

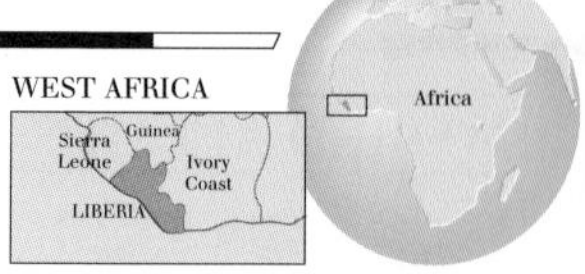
WEST AFRICA
Guinea
Sierra Leone
Ivory Coast
LIBERIA
Africa

OFFICIAL NAME: Republic of Liberia **CAPITAL:** Monrovia
POPULATION: 3.3 million **CURRENCY:** Liberian dollar **OFFICIAL LANGUAGE:** English

1847 | 1847 | July 26 | LB | 0 | +231 | .lr

FACING THE ATLANTIC in equatorial west Africa, most of Liberia's coastline is characterized by lagoons and mangrove swamps. Inland, a grassland plateau supports the limited agriculture. Founded in 1847 by freed US slaves, Liberia today has largely been reduced to anarchy after a renewed offensive by rebel factions opposed to the government of former coup leader Charles Taylor. Hundreds of civilians were killed in 2003 alone as fighting reached Monrovia.

CLIMATE

Tropical equatorial

WEATHER CHART FOR MONROVIA

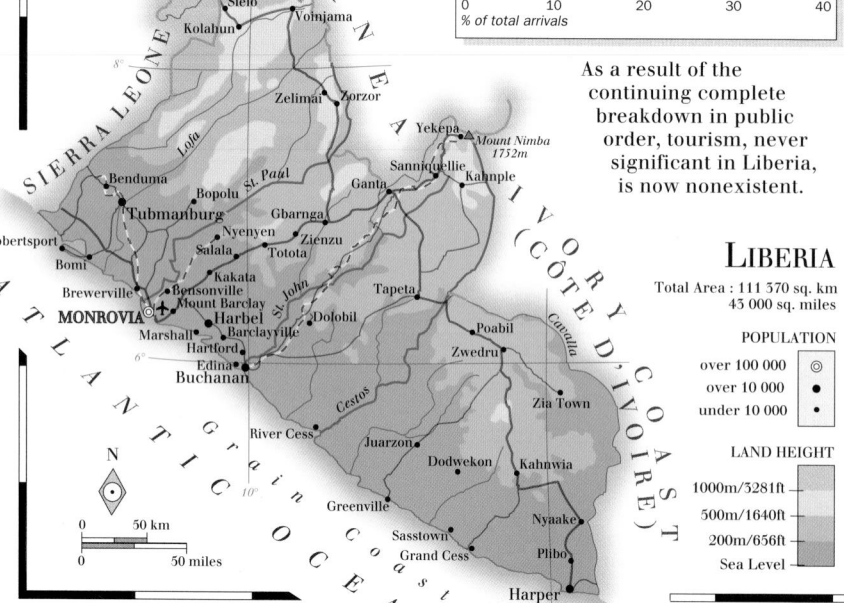

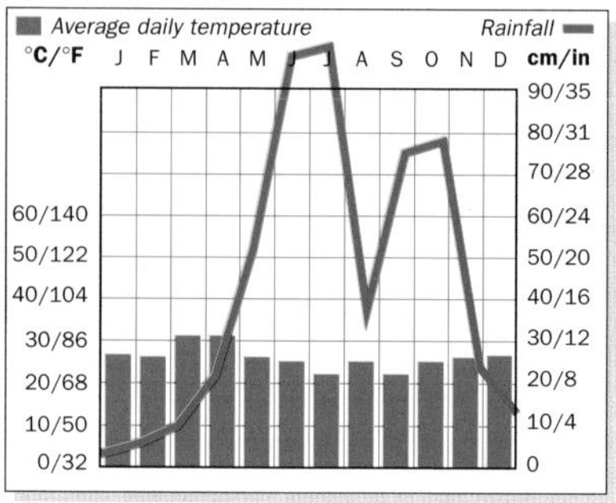
Average daily temperature
Rainfall
°C/°F
J F M A M J J A S O N D
cm/in
90/35
80/31
70/28
60/140
60/24
50/122
50/20
40/104
40/16
30/86
30/12
20/68
20/8
10/50
10/4
0/32
0

There is one long rainy season from May to October, with a brief interlude in most of the country of about two weeks in August.

Temperatures are consistently high. During the dry season, when the dust-laden *harmattan* wind blows, they rise even higher inland.

TRANSPORTATION

Drive on right

Roberts Field International, Monrovia

1556 ships 51.8m grt

THE TRANSPORTATION NETWORK

657 km (408 miles)

None

490 km (304 miles)

None

Most roads in Liberia are unpaved. The railroad was built to transport iron ore and carries little other traffic. Roberts Field airport was built by the US during World War II.

TOURISM

Not available

Tourists deterred by civil war

Little change from year to year

MAIN TOURIST ARRIVALS

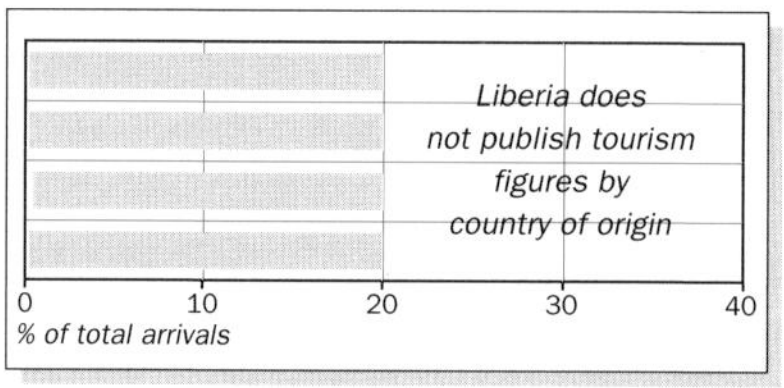
Liberia does not publish tourism figures by country of origin
0
10
20
30
40
% of total arrivals

As a result of the continuing complete breakdown in public order, tourism, never significant in Liberia, is now nonexistent.

PEOPLE

Pop. density low

Kpelle, Vai, Bassa, Kru, Grebo, Kissi, Gola, Loma, English

34/km² (89/mi²)

THE URBAN/RURAL POPULATION SPLIT

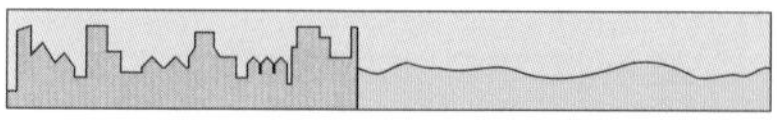
46%
54%

ETHNIC MAKEUP

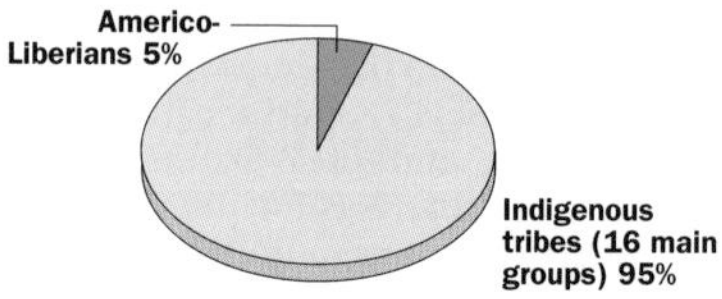
Americo-Liberians 5%
Indigenous tribes (16 main groups) 95%

A key distinction has been between Americo-Liberians, the descendants of those freed from slavery (known as "civilized persons"), and the majority indigenous "tribals." The latter were long held in contempt by the Americos, but intermarriage and political assimilation since 1944 have softened attitudes. Intertribal tension in Liberia is now a far more serious problem, and has been the main cause of conflict.

Christianity and Islam are practiced alongside traditional beliefs.

POLITICS

Multiparty elections

L. House 1997/2003
U. House 1997/2006

President Moses Blah

AT THE LAST ELECTION

House of Representatives 64 seats

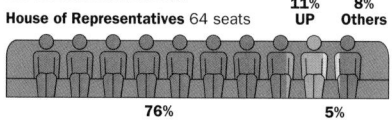

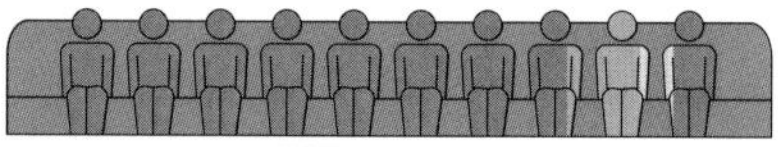
11% UP
8% Others
76% NPP
5% ALCP

NPP = National Patriotic Party **UP** = Unity Party
ALCP = All Liberia Coalition Party

Senate 26 seats

81% NPP
11% UP
8% ALCP

A chaotic, bloody, and many-sided conflict erupted in 1990. Instability continued despite elections in 1997 (won by rebel leader Charles Taylor and his NPP), and intense fighting broke out in the north in 2000. The rebel Liberians United for Reconciliation and Democracy (LURD) and its splinter Movement for Democracy in Liberia (Model) had gained control of much of the country by mid-2003, when heavy fighting reached Monrovia. Under intense international pressure, Taylor eventually stepped down in August 2003, after the arrival of peacekeepers. He was replaced by his deputy, Moses Blah.

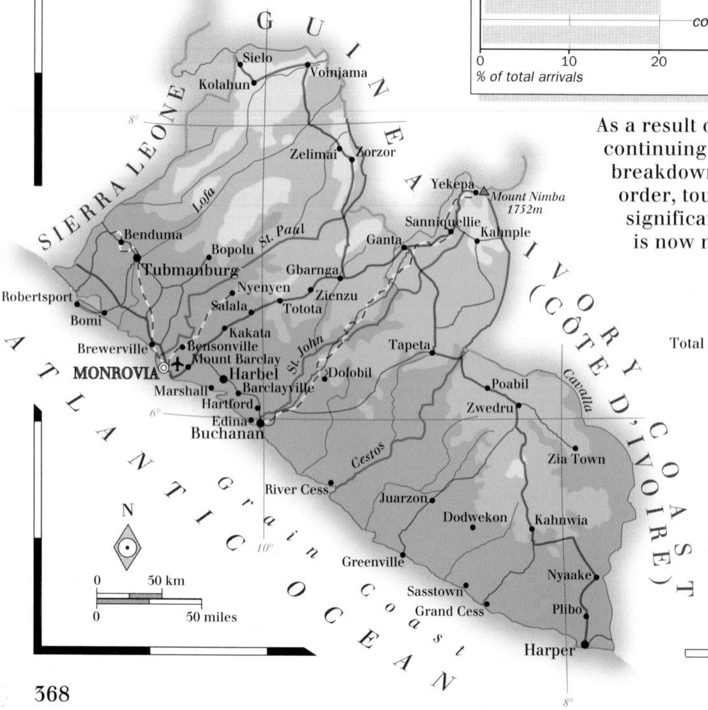
GUINEA
SIERRA LEONE
IVORY COAST (CÔTE D'IVOIRE)
ATLANTIC OCEAN
Grain Coast
Sielo
Kolahun
Voinjama
Zelimai
Zorzor
Yekepa
Mount Nimba 1752m
Sanniquellie
Kahnple
Ganta
Lofa
St. Paul
Bendumа
Bopolu
Tubmanburg
Gbarnga
Nyenyen
Zienzu
Salala
Totota
Robertsport
Bomi
Kakata
Brewerville
Bensonville
Mount Barclay
MONROVIA
Harbel
St. John
Dolobil
Tapeta
Marshall
Barclayville
Hartford
Poabil
Zwedru
Cavalla
Edina
Buchanan
Cestos
Zia Town
River Cess
Juarzon
Dodwekon
Kahnwia
Greenville
Nyaake
Sasstown
Grand Cess
Plibo
Harper
N
0 50 km
0 50 miles

LIBERIA

Total Area : 111 370 sq. km
43 000 sq. miles

POPULATION
over 100 000
over 10 000
under 10 000

LAND HEIGHT
1000m/3281ft
500m/1640ft
200m/656ft
Sea Level

WORLD AFFAIRS

Joined UN in 1945

ACP | ECOWAS | IAEA | NAM | AU

The UN imposed sanctions in 2001, accusing Liberia of fomenting war in west Africa. Relations with neighboring states have been badly affected by these conflicts, and Liberian fighters have been directly implicated in conflicts in Sierra Leone and Ivory Coast. The arrival in 2003 of ECOWAS and US peacekeepers had been delayed as the fighting in Liberia intensified.

AID

Recipient

US$37m (receipts) — Down 46% in 2001

Regional and civil war have seriously disrupted aid flows. The EU cut funds in 2000, accusing Liberia of supporting rebels in Sierra Leone.

DEFENSE

No compulsory military service

US$24m — Down 4% in 2001

The government admitted in 2003 that it had contravened a UN weapons embargo in order to boost its defenses against the rebel LURD.

ECONOMICS

Inflation 53% p.a. (1990–2001)

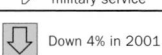

US$459m — 1 Liberian dollar (1)

SCORE CARD

- WORLD GNP RANKING........................171st
- GNP PER CAPITA ....US$140
- BALANCE OF PAYMENTS................–US$145m
- INFLATION 8%
- UNEMPLOYMENT.................................70%

STRENGTHS

Potential for reviving the Firestone rubber plantation and huge LAMCO iron ore mine. Tropical timber.

WEAKNESSES

Severe instability. Internal population displacement. Little commercial activity, and low confidence. UN sanctions on diamond trade.

EXPORTS

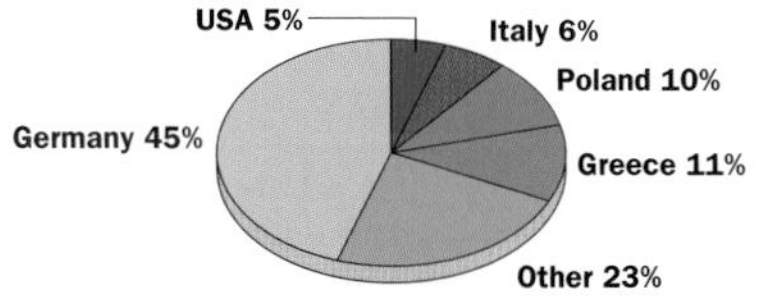
USA 5%
Italy 6%
Poland 10%
Germany 45%
Greece 11%
Other 23%

IMPORTS

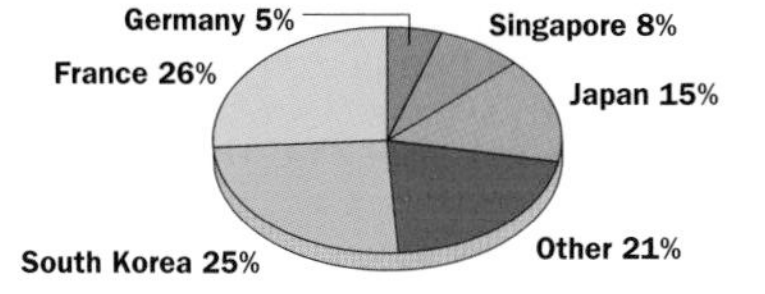
Germany 5%
Singapore 8%
France 26%
Japan 15%
South Korea 25%
Other 21%

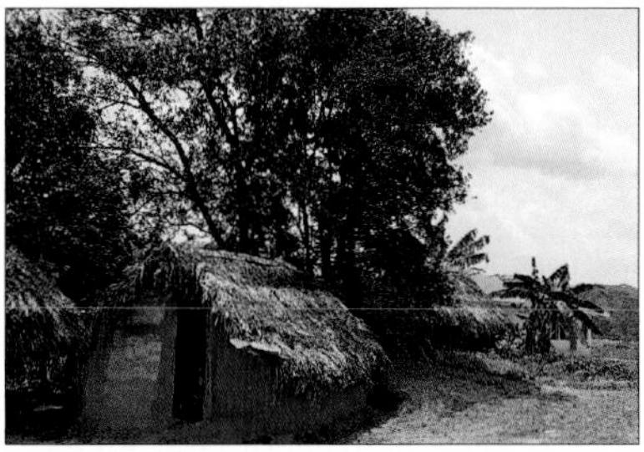

***Village near Gbarnga.** The Kpelle, the largest of Liberia's 16 indigenous ethnic groups, are concentrated in this part of Liberia.*

RESOURCES

Electric power 334,000 kW

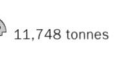

11,748 tonnes — Not an oil producer

220,000 goats, 210,000 sheep, 5m chickens — Iron ore, diamonds, gold, barytes, kyanite, columbite, manganese

Liberia has an estimated billion tonnes of iron ore reserves at Mount Nimba. In 2000, Liberia's involvement in unrest in Sierra Leone caused the UN to call for an embargo on all diamond exports.

ENVIRONMENT

Sustainability rank: 130th

3% — 0.1 tonnes per capita

Insurgents on all sides of the conflict have plundered Liberia's natural resources to finance their armies.

MEDIA

TV ownership low

Daily newspaper circulation 12 per 1000 people

PUBLISHING AND BROADCAST MEDIA

There are 4 daily newspapers, including the independents *Monrovia Guardian*, *The Inquirer*, and *News*

1 state-owned service — 4 services: 2 state-owned, 2 independent

The dominant Liberian Communication Network (LCN) is owned by the ruling NPP. Independent newspapers use LCN-owned printing presses.

CRIME

Death penalty in use

Liberia does not publish prison figures — Crime is rampant. There are no enforcing agencies

In the 1990s warring factions regularly massacred civilians, press-ganged armies, and displaced thousands into seeking refuge in neighboring states. As fighting escalated again in 2001, government forces were accused of human rights abuses.

EDUCATION

School leaving age: 16

55% — 20,804 students

Originally based on the US model, the education system effectively collapsed during the civil war.

CHRONOLOGY

Between 1816 and 1892, 22,000 liberated slaves, most from the US, settled in Liberia, established as a republic in 1847.

- **1980** Coup. President assassinated by Samuel Doe.
- **1990** Outbreak of civil war.
- **1991** Doe assassinated.
- **1996** Second peace agreement.
- **1997** Charles Taylor president.
- **2001** Conflict with rebels escalates.
- **2002** State of emergency declared.
- **2003** Rebels reach Monrovia. Taylor goes into exile in Nigeria.

HEALTH

No welfare state health benefits

1 per 20,000 people — Communicable, diarrheal, parasitic, and heart diseases

A large increase in the number of internally displaced persons (IDPs) within Liberia has had a detrimental effect on already low health standards.

SPENDING

GDP/cap. increase

CONSUMPTION AND SPENDING

3 per 1000 population — *2 per 1000 population*

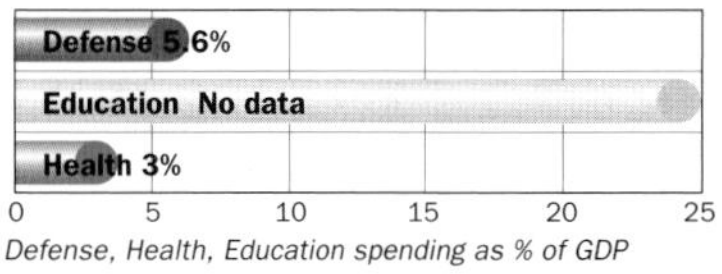
Defense 5.6%
Education No data
Health 3%
0
5
10
15
20
25
Defense, Health, Education spending as % of GDP

By 1996, real GDP was as low as one-tenth of its prewar level. Real income per capita remains at about one-third of prewar levels. Any increase will depend on the government carrying out major reforms of Liberia's war-ravaged economy, including the encouragement of foreign investment. Most ordinary Liberians continue to live in rural poverty.

WORLD RANKING

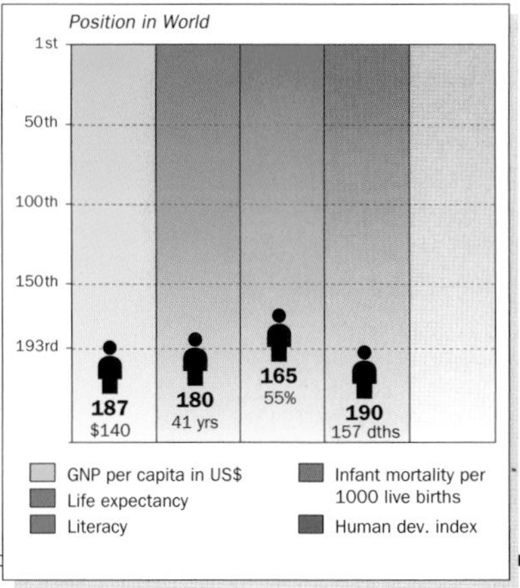
Position in World
1st
50th
100th
150th
193rd
187
$140
180
41 yrs
165
55%
190
157 dths
GNP per capita in US$
Life expectancy
Literacy
Infant mortality per 1000 live births
Human dev. index

L

LIBYA

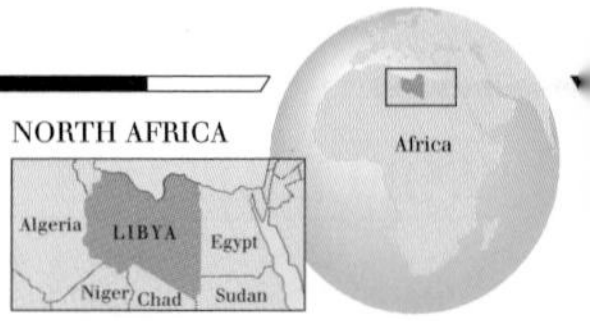
NORTH AFRICA
Africa
Algeria
LIBYA
Egypt
Niger
Chad
Sudan

OFFICIAL NAME: Great Socialist People's Libyan Arab Jamahiriyah
CAPITAL: Tripoli **POPULATION:** 5.5 million **CURRENCY:** Libyan dinar **OFFICIAL LANGUAGE:** Arabic

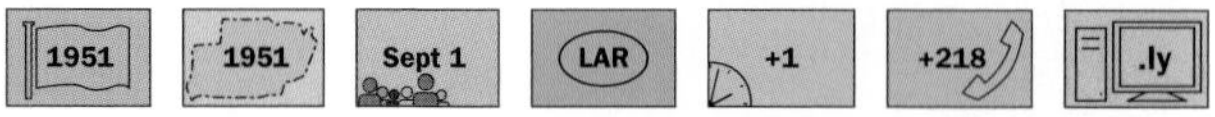
1951
1951
Sept 1
LAR
+1
+218
.ly

LIBYA IS SITUATED in north Africa between Egypt and Algeria, with the Mediterranean to the north and Chad and Niger on its southern borders. Apart from the coastal strip and the mountains in the south, it is desert or semidesert. Libya's strategic position in north Africa and its abundant oil and gas resources made it an important trading partner for European states. It has for many years been politically marginalized by the West for its links with terrorist groups, but UN sanctions were suspended in 1999 when it handed over for trial the two men suspected of the 1988 Lockerbie bombing.

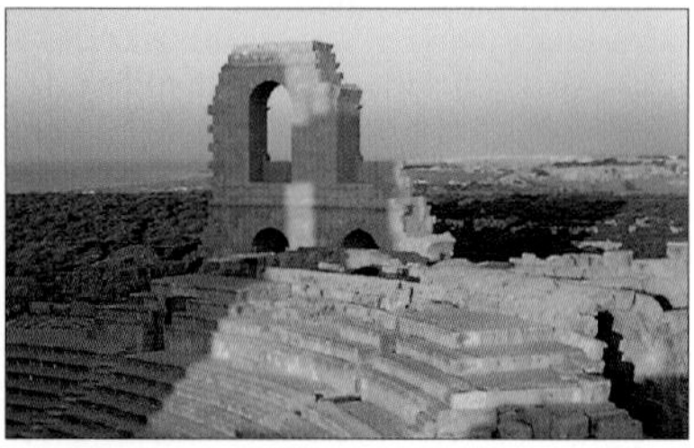

Roman theater, Sabrata. *Libya's impressive classical heritage testifies to its importance in ancient times.*

CLIMATE

Hot desert

WEATHER CHART FOR TRIPOLI

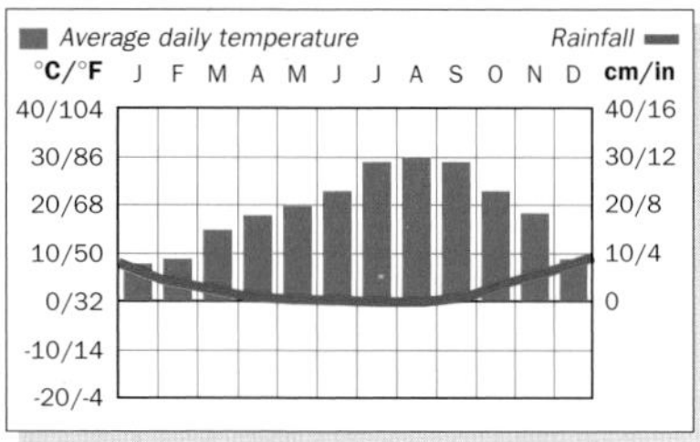
Average daily temperature
Rainfall
°C/°F
J F M A M J J A S O N D
cm/in
40/104
30/86
20/68
10/50
0/32
-10/14
-20/4
40/16
30/12
20/8
10/4
0

The coastal region has a warm, temperate climate, with mild, wet winters and hot, dry summers.

TRANSPORTATION

Drive on right

Tripoli International

140 ships 250,800 grt

THE TRANSPORTATION NETWORK

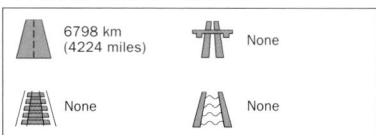

6798 km (4224 miles)	None
None	None

The National Coast Road runs 1825 km (1135 miles) between the Tunisian and Egyptian borders, linking the principal urban centers. There are no railroads, but some are planned. Since sanctions were suspended in 1999, international airlines have resumed flights to Libya.

Al Kufrah Oasis. *As 90% of Libya is arid rock and sand, oases provide essential agricultural land, besides being tourist attractions.*

TOURISM

Visitors : Population 1:32

174,000 visitors

Up sharply in 2000

Libya possesses a rich Roman and Greek heritage, centered on the ancient Roman coastal towns of Labdah (Leptis Magna) and Sabrata near Tripoli, and Shahhat (Cyrene) further east. There are fine beaches at Tripoli. A $2–3 billion investment program launched in 2000 aims to attract thousands of visitors. Western tourists have begun to return since sanctions were lifted in 1999.

MAIN TOURIST ARRIVALS

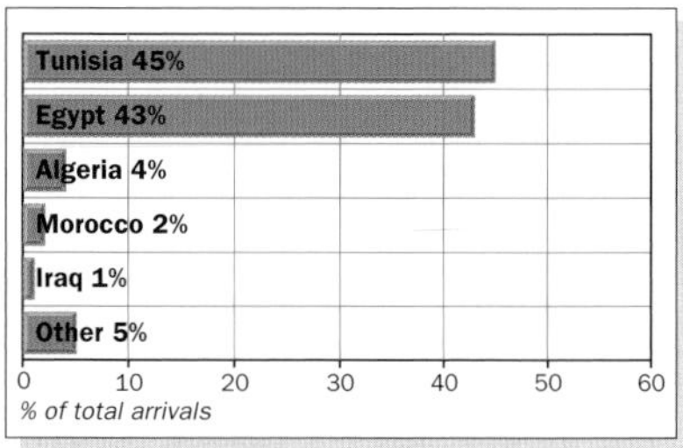
Tunisia 45%
Egypt 43%
Algeria 4%
Morocco 2%
Iraq 1%
Other 5%
0 10 20 30 40 50 60
% of total arrivals

PEOPLE

Pop. density low

Arabic, Tuareg

3/km² (8/mi²)

THE URBAN/RURAL POPULATION SPLIT

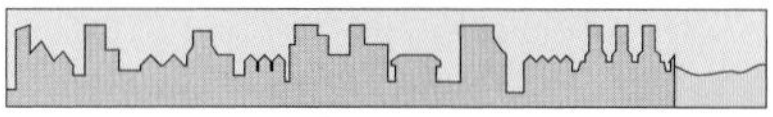
88%
12%

RELIGIOUS PERSUASION

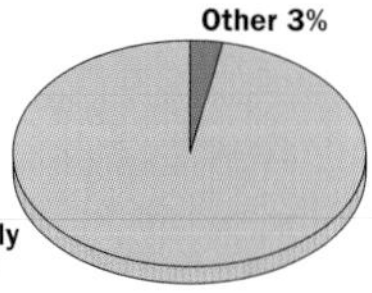
Other 3%
Muslim (mainly Sunni) 97%

ETHNIC MAKEUP

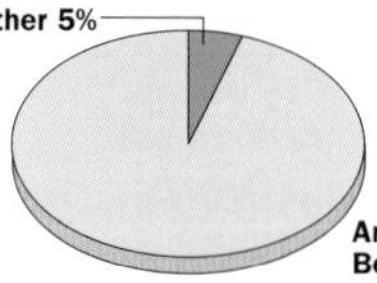
Other 5%
Arab and Berber 95%

POPULATION AGE BREAKDOWN

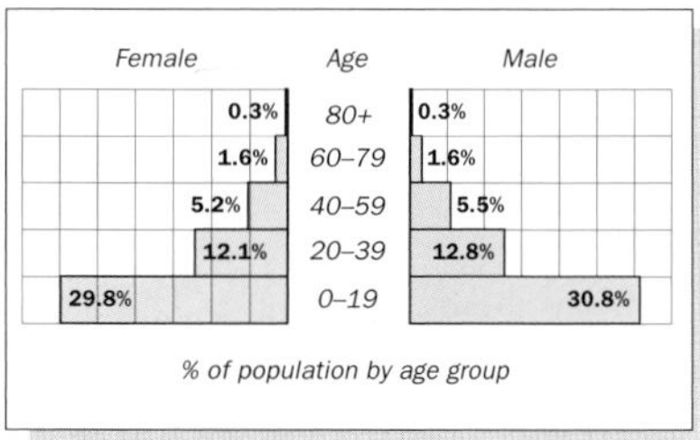
Female
Age
Male
0.3%
80+
0.3%
1.6%
60–79
1.6%
5.2%
40–59
5.5%
12.1%
20–39
12.8%
29.8%
0–19
30.8%
% of population by age group

Arabs and Berbers, split into many tribal groupings, form 95% of the population. They were artificially brought together when Libya was created in 1951 by the unification of three historic Ottoman provinces. The newly established pro-Western monarchy then perpetuated the dominance of Cyrenaican tribes and the Sanusi religious order.

The 1969 revolution brought to the fore Arab nationalist Col. Muammar al-Gaddafi, who embodied the character and aspirations of the rural Sirtica tribes from Fazzan: fierce independence, deep Islamic convictions, belief in a communal lifestyle, and hatred for the urban rich. His revolution wiped out private enterprise and the middle class, banished European settlers and Jews, undermined the religious Muslim establishment, and imposed a form of popular democracy through the *jamahiriyah* (state of the masses). However, resentment of the regime grew as it became clear that power now lay mainly with the Sirtica tribes, especially Gaddafi's own clan, the Qadhadhfa.

Since the revolution, Libya has become a society where most are city dwellers. Jews have been invited to return as investors, and immigrants from sub-Saharan Africa have been drawn in to provide low-cost labor. However, clashes in 2000, in which 100 died, highlighted unresolved social issues.

POLITICS

No multiparty elections

Not applicable

Leader of the Revolution Col. Muammar al-Gaddafi

LEGISLATIVE OR ADVISORY BODIES

General People's Congress 750 seats

The constitution makes no provision for direct elections.
Last renewal May 2000

Executive power is exercised by the General People's Committee. The General People's Congress elects the head of state, the Leader of the Revolution.

PROFILE

In 1977, a new form of direct democracy was promulgated, through which some 2000 People's Congresses sought to involve every adult in policy-making. In theory, their wishes are carried out by popular committees. In practice, ultimate control rests with Col. Gaddafi and his collaborators, many of whom were involved in the 1969 revolution. In recent years some are thought to have been alienated from Gaddafi, including his deputy, Maj. Abdessalem Jalloud, who in 1994 was reportedly marginalized after expressing differences with him. In 1995, another of Gaddafi's close associates, Khoueldi Hamidi, a defense commander, was also said to have become disillusioned with him. In 2000, Gaddafi embraced African unity – an unpopular concept among most Libyans, increasing his alienation from former associates. He is now believed to rely on members of his own clan, particularly his five sons.

MAIN POLITICAL ISSUES

Repression

Political dissidents, including Islamist militants, have been violently suppressed. Libyan dissidents have been murdered abroad, allegedly by government agents. Political parties were banned in 1971, but opposition groups are active in Egypt and Sudan.

The regime's public image

In the past few years, the regime has made an effort to improve its image. Measures have included freeing political prisoners, welcoming back exiles, permitting foreign travel, and accepting responsibility for past acts of terrorism.

Col. Gaddafi, Libya's leader since 1969, shies from official titles.

Ex-king Idris was deposed by Col. Gaddafi in 1969.

WORLD AFFAIRS

Joined UN in 1955

AL | AU | NAM | OIC | OPEC

Gaddafi has attempted to style himself as the champion of African integration and regional stability. He was a chief architect of the African Union, and has hosted various peace negotiations in the trans-Saharan area. This transformation has also involved a less confrontational stance toward the West, dropping key policies which had left Libya internationally isolated in the past – support for various terrorist groups and strong opposition to Israel – and pursuing a crackdown on internal corruption. In 1999 UN sanctions imposed in 1992 were suspended, and relations with the UK were resumed. Gaddafi tacitly approved the US-led "war on terrorism" in 2001, but the US still added Libya to the "axis of evil" in 2002.

L

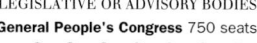

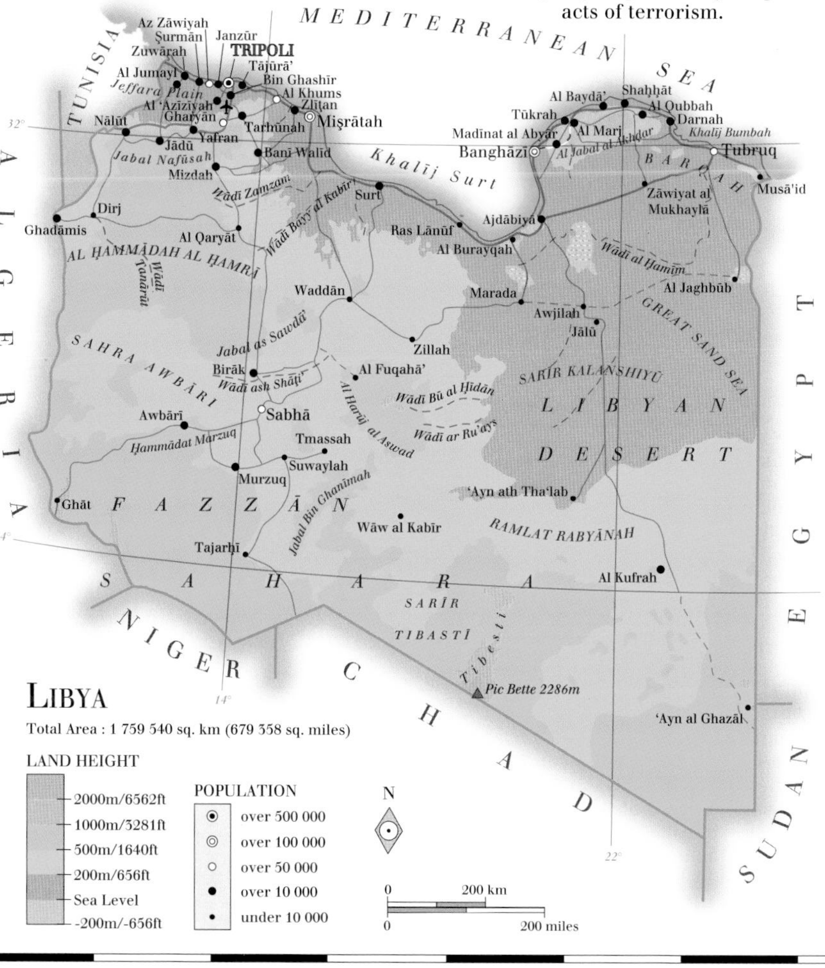
MEDITERRANEAN SEA
TRIPOLI
Az Zāwiyah
Şurmān
Janzūr
Zuwārah
Tājūrā'
Bin Ghashīr
Al Jumayl
Zlītan
Al Khums
Jeffara Plain
Al 'Azīzīyah
Gharyān
Mişrātah
Tarhūnah
Nālūt
Jādū
Yafran
Jabal Nafūsah
Banī Walīd
Mizdah
Khalīj Surt
Wādī Zamzam
Wādī Bayy al Kabīr
Surt
Dirj
Ghadāmis
Al Qaryāt
Ras Lānūf
Al Burayqah
Ajdābiyā
AL HAMMĀDAH AL HAMRĀ'
Wādī Tānīrāt
Waddān
Marada
Awjilah
Jālū
Zillah
Jabal as Sawdā'
Birāk
Wādī ash Shāţi'
Al Fuqahā'
SAHRĀ AWBĀRĪ
Awbārī
Sabhā
Ḩammādat Marzūq
Tmassah
Wādī Bū al Ḩidān
Al Harūj al Aswad
Wādī ar Ru'ays
Suwaylah
Murzuq
Ghāt
FAZZĀN
Jabal Bin Ghanīmah
Wāw al Kabīr
Tajarhī
SAHARA
SARĪR TIBASTĪ
Tibesti
Pic Bette 2286m
Al Bayḑā'
Shaḩḩāt
Al Qubbah
Darnah
Ţūkrah
Madīnat al Abyār
Al Marj
Banghāzī
Al Jabal al Akhḑar
Khalīj Bumbah
Tubruq
BARQAH
Mūsā'id
Zāwiyat al Mukhaylā
Wādī al Ḩamīm
Al Jaghbūb
GREAT SAND SEA
SARĪR KALANSHIYŪ
LIBYAN DESERT
'Ayn ath Tha'lab
RAMLAT RABYĀNAH
Al Kufrah
'Ayn al Ghazāl
TUNISIA
ALGERIA
NIGER
CHAD
SUDAN
EGYPT
32°
24°
14°
22°
LIBYA
Total Area : 1 759 540 sq. km (679 358 sq. miles)
LAND HEIGHT
2000m/6562ft
1000m/3281ft
500m/1640ft
200m/656ft
Sea Level
-200m/-656ft
POPULATION
over 500 000
over 100 000
over 50 000
over 10 000
under 10 000
N
0
200 km
0
200 miles

CHRONOLOGY

Italy occupied Libya and expelled the Turks in 1911. Britain and France agreed to a UN plan for an independent monarchy in 1951.

- **1969** King Idris deposed in coup led by Col. Gaddafi. Revolution Command Council established. Tripoli Charter sets up revolutionary alliance with Egypt and Sudan.
- **1970** UK and US military ordered out. Property belonging to Italians and Jews confiscated. Western oil company assets nationalized, a process completed in 1973.
- **1973** Libya forms abortive union with Egypt. Libya occupies Aozou Strip in Chad.
- **1974** Libya proposes union of Libya and Tunisia.
- **1977** Official name changed to Great Socialist People's Libyan Arab Jamahiriyah. Revolution Command Council dissolved. Gaddafi elected Leader of the Revolution. Council of Ministers replaced by General People's Committee.

CHRONOLOGY *continued*

- **1981** US shoots down two Libyan aircraft over Gulf of Sirte.
- **1984** Gunman at Libyan embassy in UK kills British policewoman; UK severs diplomatic relations (until 1999). Oudja Accord signed with Morocco for Arab Africa Federation.
- **1985** Libya expels 30,000 foreign workers. Tunisia cuts diplomatic links.
- **1986** US aircraft bomb Libya, killing 101 people and destroying Gaddafi's residence.
- **1988** Pan-Am airliner explodes over Lockerbie, Scotland; allegations of Libyan complicity.
- **1988–1989** Army restructured.
- **1989** Arab Maghreb Union established with Algeria, Morocco, Mauritania, and Tunisia. Cease-fire in Aozou Strip.
- **1990** Libya expels Palestinian splinter group led by Abu Abbas.
- **1991** Opening of first branch of Great Man-Made River project.
- **1992–1993** UN sanctions imposed as Libya fails to hand over Lockerbie suspects; sanctions made stricter.
- **1994** Religious leaders obtain right to issue religious decrees (*fatwas*) for first time since 1969. Return of Aozou strip to Chad.
- **1996** US legislation imposes penalties on foreign companies investing in Libya's energy sector.
- **1999** Lockerbie suspects handed over for trial in the Netherlands under Scottish law; UN sanctions suspended.
- **2001** Lockerbie trial verdict: one suspect convicted.
- **2002** US–Libya talks aim to mend relations, but Libya added to "axis of evil." Lockerbie bomber begins life sentence.

AID

Recipient

$10m (receipts) | Down 33% in 2001

As an oil-exporting state, Libya fails to qualify for much international aid, despite being a developing country. During the 1970s, Col. Gaddafi aided several African liberation movements, notably the ANC in South Africa. He has backed factions during civil conflicts in neighboring countries, including Chad and the Central African Republic, and helped dissidents by training them in his Pan-African legion. He has also financed or supplied arms to the Palestine Liberation Organization in the Middle East, Irish republicans in Northern Ireland, the Moros in the southern Philippines, and Basques, Corsicans, and other separatist groups in Europe.

DEFENSE

Compulsory military service

$546m | Up 29% in 2001

LIBYAN ARMED FORCES

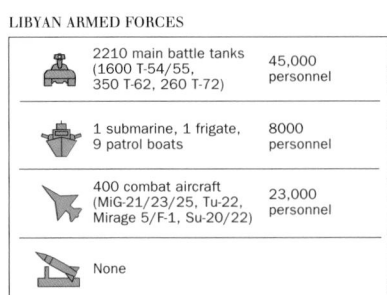

2210 main battle tanks (1600 T-54/55, 350 T-62, 260 T-72)	45,000 personnel
1 submarine, 1 frigate, 9 patrol boats	8000 personnel
400 combat aircraft (MiG-21/23/25, Tu-22, Mirage 5/F-1, Su-20/22)	23,000 personnel
None	

The armed forces suffered a blow in 1987 with the loss of thousands of men and equipment worth $1.4 billion when Libya became embroiled in the Chad civil war; in 1994 it agreed to hand back to Chad the Aozou Strip, which it had first occupied in 1973. In 1988–1989 the armed forces were replaced by "the Armed People." Conscription is selective, and can last up to two years. In addition, there is a 40,000-strong People's Militia.

Attempts to depoliticize the army received a setback following confirmation of an abortive military coup in 1993. UN sanctions resulted in military hardware becoming outdated. Despite the suspension of the sanctions in 1999, fresh arms contracts would still be too controversial for most potential suppliers.

ECONOMICS

Not available

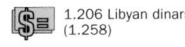

$31bn | 1.206 Libyan dinars (1.258)

SCORE CARD

- World GNP Ranking..........59th
- GNP per Capita..........$5540
- Balance of Payments..........$1.98bn
- Inflation..........13.6%
- Unemployment..........30%

EXPORTS

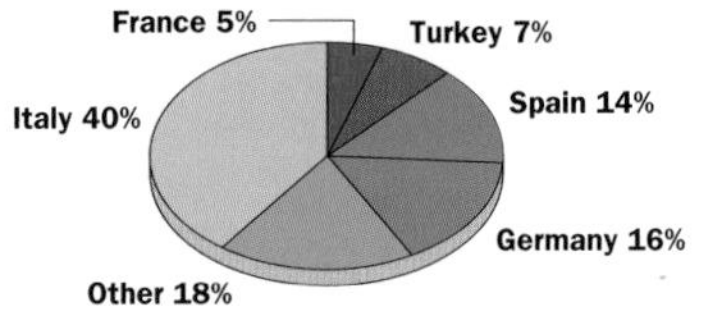
France 5%
Turkey 7%
Italy 40%
Spain 14%
Germany 16%
Other 18%

IMPORTS

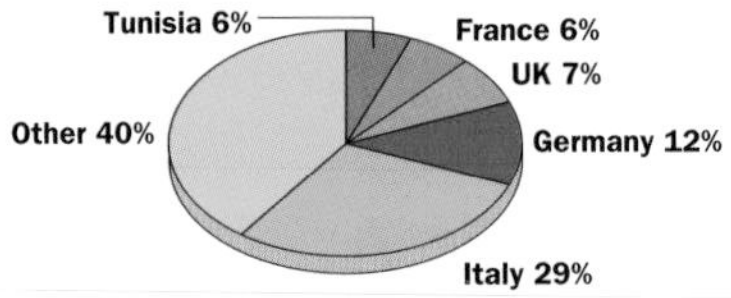
Tunisia 6%
France 6%
UK 7%
Other 40%
Germany 12%
Italy 29%

Strengths

Oil and gas production. High levels of investment in downstream industries: petrochemicals, refineries, fertilizers, and aluminum smelting.

Weaknesses

Single-resource economy: subject to oil-market fluctuations. Most food imported. Reliance on foreign labor. Lack of water for agriculture. History of international unreliability.

Profile

Western oil companies had close business ties with Libya until the imposition in 1992 of UN sanctions over the Lockerbie affair. In 1993, Gaddafi called for the program of privatization, authorized by the General People's Congress in 1992, to be revived, but there have been few tangible results.

ECONOMIC PERFORMANCE INDICATOR

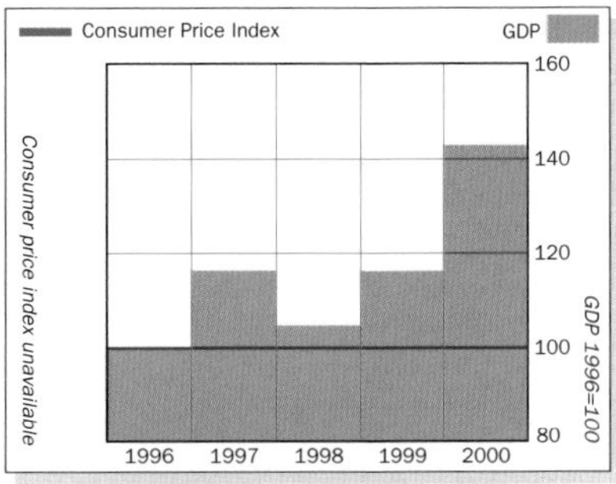
Consumer Price Index
GDP
160
140
120
100
80
Consumer price index unavailable
GDP 1996=100
1996
1997
1998
1999
2000

In the 1970s, an ambitious program of industrialization was launched. Gaddafi's most controversial economic project has been the Great Man-Made River. Started in 1984 and engineered by European and Korean companies, this scheme was designed to bring underground water from the Sahara to the coast, but the pipes are already corroding, with water leaking into the sand.

LIBYA : MAJOR BUSINESSES

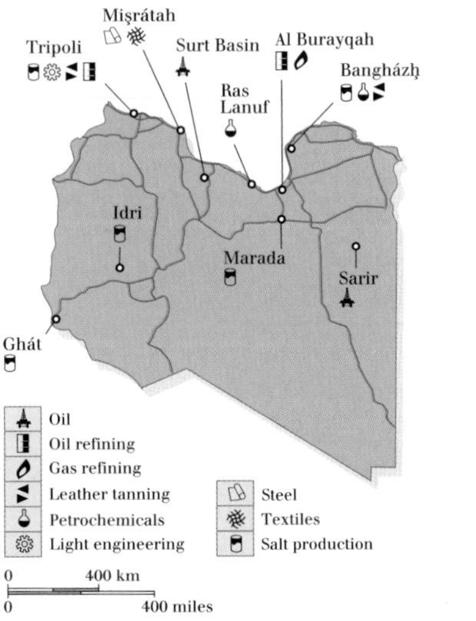
Mişrātah
Tripoli
Surt Basin
Al Burayqah
Banghāzī
Ras Lanuf
Idri
Marada
Sarir
Ghát
Oil
Oil refining
Gas refining
Leather tanning
Petrochemicals
Light engineering
Steel
Textiles
Salt production
0
400 km
0
400 miles

RESOURCES

Electric power 4.6m kW

33,487 tonnes

1.38m b/d (reserves 29.5bn barrels)

4.13m sheep, 1.26m goats, 25m chickens

Oil, natural gas, iron, potassium, sulfur, magnesium, gypsum

ELECTRICITY GENERATION

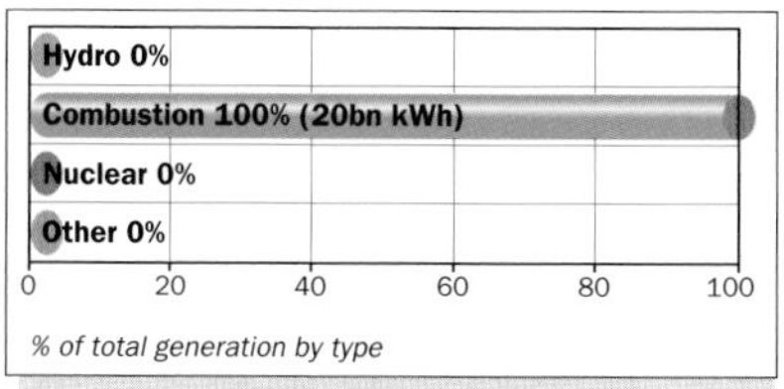
Hydro 0%
Combustion 100% (20bn kWh)
Nuclear 0%
Other 0%
0
20
40
60
80
100
% of total generation by type

Libya's economy depends almost entirely on its oil and natural gas resources. It has considerable crude oil reserves and is likely to remain an oil-exporting country for many decades. Natural gas potential is more limited but, provided links are developed with other north African states, the future is assured. Libya also has reserves of iron ore, potassium, sulfur, magnesium, and gypsum, though these contribute little to the overall economy and most minerals are imported.

The aging Great Man-Made River project means that the area of irrigated land has grown, but 90% of Libya is desert. Animal husbandry, particularly of sheep, is the basis of farming, but some cereal crops are grown, as well as dates, olives, and citrus fruits.

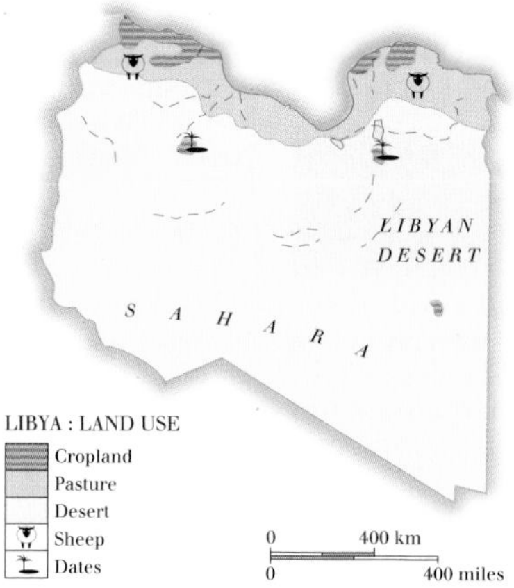
LIBYAN DESERT
S A H A R A
LIBYA : LAND USE
Cropland
Pasture
Desert
Sheep
Dates
0
400 km
0
400 miles

ENVIRONMENT

Sustainability rank: 124th

0.1% partially protected

8.3 tonnes per capita

ENVIRONMENTAL TREATIES

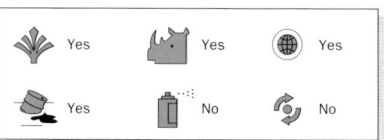

Yes	Yes	Yes
Yes	No	No

The UN Development Program has described Libya as more than 90% "wasteland." Both nature and man have conspired against the environment. Apart from two coastal strips – the Jeffara Plain and the Jabal al Akhdar in Cyrenaica – together with the Fazzan Oasis, most of Libya is desert. Much of the irrigated area is saline because of unwise use of naturally occurring water from artesian wells. Near Tripoli, seawater has penetrated the water table as far as 20 km (12 miles) inland.

MEDIA

TV ownership medium

Daily newspaper circulation 15 per 1000 people

PUBLISHING AND BROADCAST MEDIA

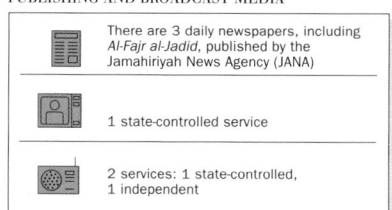

There are 3 daily newspapers, including *Al-Fajr al-Jadid*, published by the Jamahiriyah News Agency (JANA)

1 state-controlled service

2 services: 1 state-controlled, 1 independent

Libya's press and TV are a mouthpiece for the leadership. Satellite TV and the Internet are widely available, but heavily censored. The main daily newspaper is published in Arabic and has a circulation of 40,000 readers. The TV station broadcasts mostly in Arabic. Radio broadcasts in Kiswahili, Hausa, Fulani, and Amharic were due to begin in 1999, but were postponed.

CRIME

Death penalty in use

6750 prisoners

Up 10% in 1999

CRIME RATES

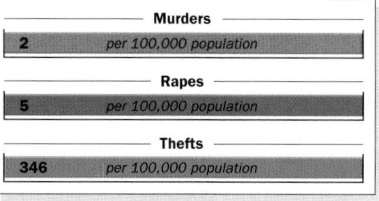

Crime	Rate
Murders	2 per 100,000 population
Rapes	5 per 100,000 population
Thefts	346 per 100,000 population

Policing is often in the hands of gangs appointed by Gaddafi's lieutenants to root out student protestors and other dissidents. Hit squads allegedly operate abroad against Libyan exiles.

EDUCATION

School leaving age: 15

81%

287,172 students

THE EDUCATION SYSTEM

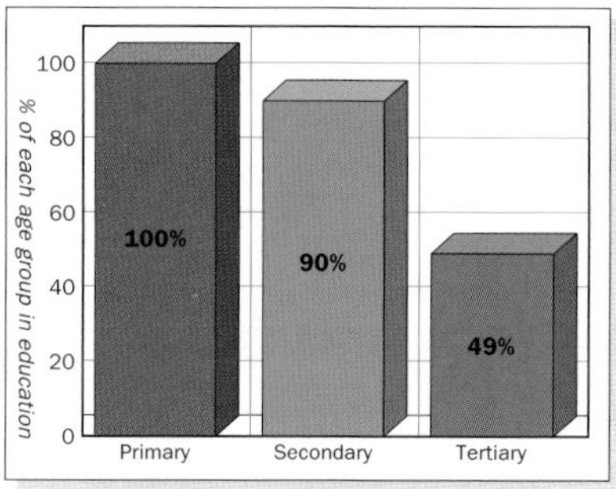
100
80
60
40
20
0
% of each age group in education
100%
90%
49%
Primary
Secondary
Tertiary

Some 1.5 million Libyans are in formal education. It is compulsory for nine years from the age of six and rates of attendance are very high, but it varies in quality and can be rudimentary in rural areas. Secondary education, from the age of 15, lasts for three years. There are 13 universities, and several institutes for vocational training. The literacy rate has more than doubled from a level of 39% in 1970.

HEALTH

Welfare state health benefits

1 per 833 people

Pneumonia, diarrheal diseases, accidents, cancers

An adequate system of free primary health care exists except in remote areas, and there are two big hospitals, in Benghazi and Tripoli. Sanctions have led to a lack of equipment and a shortage of medical supplies.

SPENDING

GDP/cap. decrease

CONSUMPTION AND SPENDING

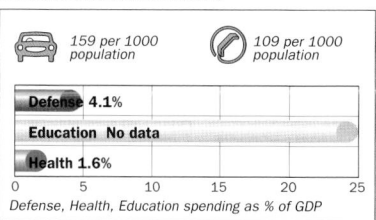

159 per 1000 population

109 per 1000 population

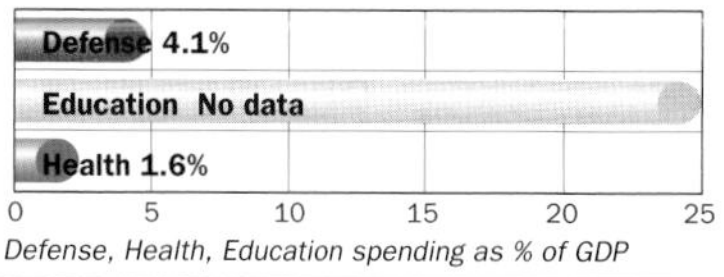
Defense 4.1%
Education No data
Health 1.6%
0
5
10
15
20
25
Defense, Health, Education spending as % of GDP

There is widespread poverty after years of import constraints; UN sanctions worsened the situation. Gaddafi refuses to use oil revenues for basic expenses, such as salaries – teachers earn about $1200 a year.

WORLD RANKING

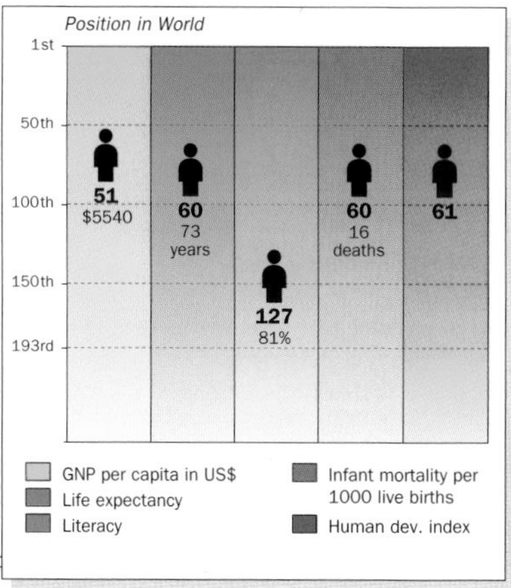
Position in World
1st
50th
100th
150th
193rd
51
$5540
60
73 years
127
81%
60
16 deaths
61
GNP per capita in US$
Life expectancy
Literacy
Infant mortality per 1000 live births
Human dev. index

L

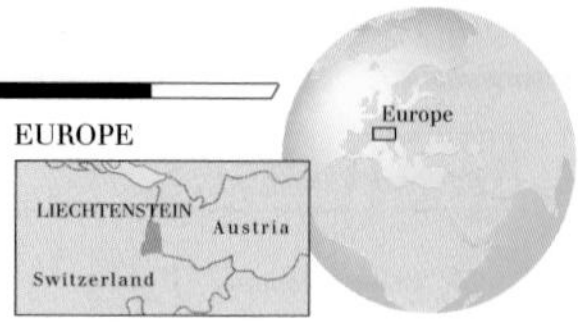

EUROPE
Europe
LIECHTENSTEIN
Austria
Switzerland

LIECHTENSTEIN

OFFICIAL NAME: Principality of Liechtenstein **CAPITAL:** Vaduz
POPULATION: 32,842 **CURRENCY:** Swiss franc **OFFICIAL LANGUAGE:** German

1719 | 1719 | Aug 15 | FL | +1 | +423 | .li

PERCHED IN THE ALPS, Liechtenstein is rare among small states in having both a thriving banking sector and a well-diversified manufacturing economy. It is closely allied to Switzerland, which handles its foreign relations and defense. Life in Liechtenstein is stable and conservative. The traditional secrecy surrounding the country's financial industry, and low taxes, means that many overseas trusts, banks, and investment companies are located there.

CLIMATE

Mountain

WEATHER CHART FOR VADUZ

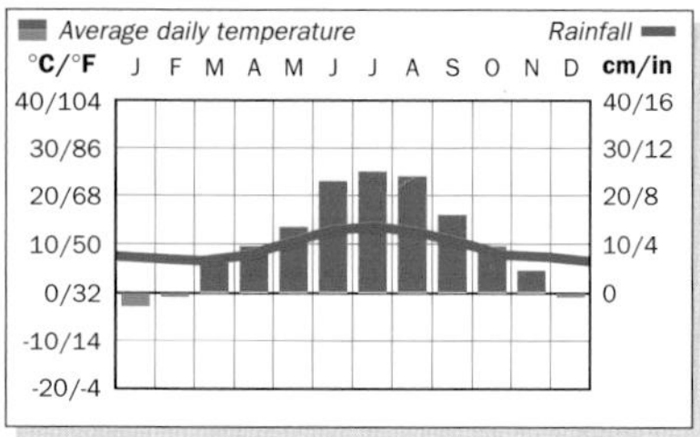

Average daily temperature
Rainfall
°C/°F
J F M A M J J A S O N D
cm/in
40/104
30/86
20/68
10/50
0/32
-10/14
-20/-4
40/16
30/12
20/8
10/4
0

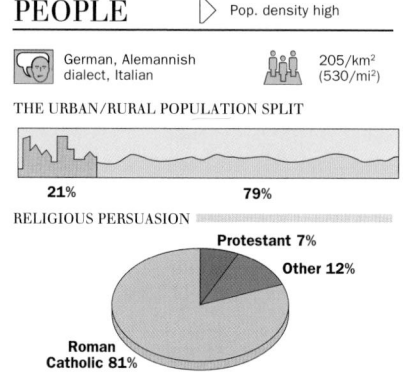

Climate varies with altitude. Excellent skiing conditions are the result of heavy settling snow from December to March. Summers are warm and wet.

TRANSPORTATION

Drive on right

None

Has no fleet

THE TRANSPORTATION NETWORK

250 km (155 miles)

None

19 km (12 miles)

26 km (16 miles)

Public transportation in Liechtenstein is mostly by the postal bus network. The single-track railroad has few stops. Zürich, a two-hour drive away, is the nearest airport.

TOURISM

Visitors : Population 1.5:1

49,000 visitors

Down 13% in 2002

MAIN TOURIST ARRIVALS

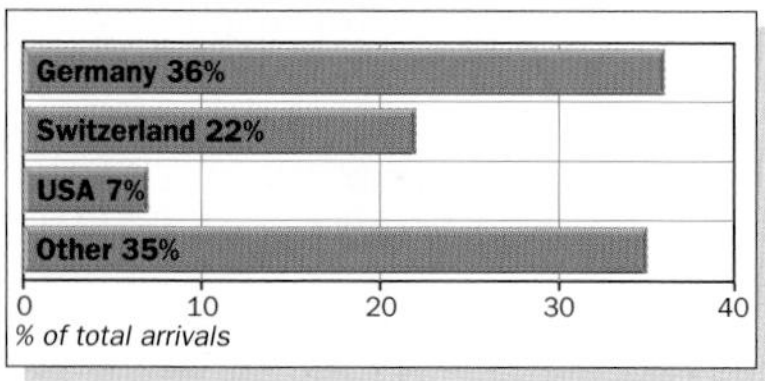

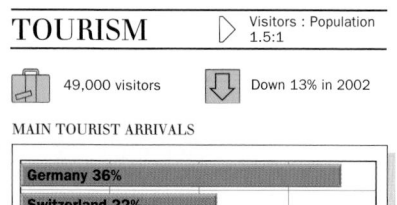

Germany 36%
Switzerland 22%
USA 7%
Other 35%
0
10
20
30
40
% of total arrivals

Liechtenstein's alpine scenery attracts skiers in the winter, and climbers and hikers in the summer.

PEOPLE

Pop. density high

German, Alemannish dialect, Italian

205/km² (530/mi²)

THE URBAN/RURAL POPULATION SPLIT

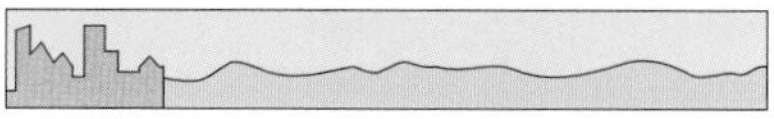

21%
79%

RELIGIOUS PERSUASION

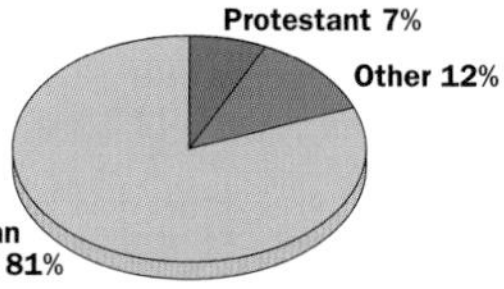

Protestant 7%
Other 12%
Roman Catholic 81%

Liechtenstein's role as a financial center accounts for the many foreign residents (over 35% of the population), of whom half are Swiss and the rest mostly German. Family life is highly traditional; women received the vote only in 1984, after much controversy. A proposal to enshrine equal rights for women in the constitution was rejected in a referendum in 1985 by a large majority and only finally passed in 1992. Abortion laws are restrictive but rarely enforced in practice.

POLITICS

Multiparty elections

2001/2005

Prince Hans-Adam II von und zu Liechtenstein

AT THE LAST ELECTION

Parliament 25 seats

52% FBP
44% VU
4% FL

FBP = Progressive Citizens' Party **VU** = Fatherland Union
FL = Free List

From 1938 to 1997 the VU and the FBP alternated as coalition leaders. Mario Frick, who in 1993 at the age of 28 had become Europe's youngest premier, formed a VU-only government in 1997, ending the partnership. In elections in 2001 the FBP under Otmar Hasler overtook the VU. In 2003 Prince Hans-Adam II won greater political powers after threatening to emigrate.

WORLD AFFAIRS

Joined UN in 1990

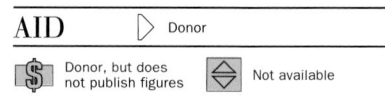

CE | EFTA | IAEA | OSCE | WTO

Liechtenstein effectively gave up control of its external relations in 1924 when it signed a Customs Union Treaty with Switzerland. This agreement requires Swiss approval for any treaty arrangements between Liechtenstein and a third state. Liechtenstein became a member of the UN only in 1990. It joined EFTA and the EBRD in 1991, and has been a participant in the EEA since 1995. However, Swiss rejection of EU membership in 1992 effectively ended any prospect of Liechtenstein joining the EU in the foreseeable future.

AID

Donor

Donor, but does not publish figures

Not available

Though overseas aid donations are small and aid issues have little political importance, Liechtenstein has helped to fund shelter and reconstruction projects in the former Yugoslavia and local development projects in Bulgaria.

LIECHTENSTEIN

Total Area : 160 sq. km (62 sq. miles)

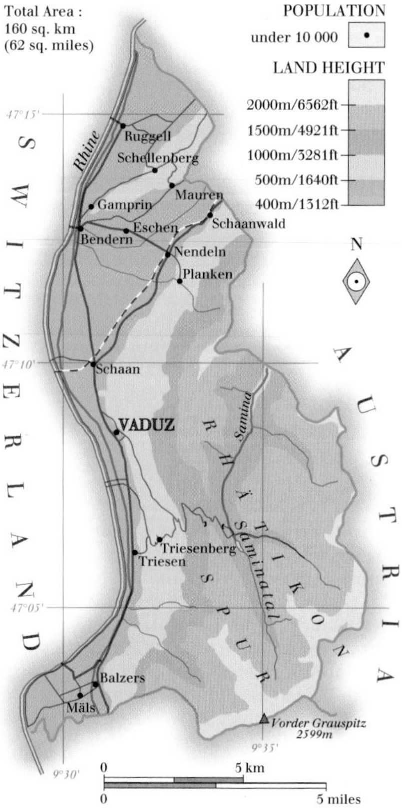

POPULATION
under 10 000
LAND HEIGHT
2000m/6562ft
1500m/4921ft
1000m/3281ft
500m/1640ft
400m/1312ft
N
SWITZERLAND
AUSTRIA
Rhine
Ruggell
Schellenberg
Mauren
Gamprin
Eschen
Schaanwald
Bendern
Nendeln
Planken
Schaan
VADUZ
Samina
RHÄTIKON
Triesenberg
Triesen
Saminatal
SPUR
Balzers
Mäls
Vorder Grauspitz
2599m
47°15'
47°10'
47°05'
9°30'
9°35'
0
5 km
0
5 miles

***Alpine scenery near Vaduz.** The state budget includes 2% allocated to restoring mountain vegetation and coordinating land use.*

DEFENSE

No compulsory military service

No defense force — Not applicable

There has been no standing army since 1868, and there is only a small police force. De facto protection is provided by Switzerland. In theory, any male under 60 is liable for military service during a national emergency, though this law has never been invoked.

ECONOMICS

Inflation 2.9% p.a. (1985–1996)

$1.6bn — 1.355 Swiss francs (1.488)

SCORE CARD

- ❑ WORLD GNP RANKING........................144th
- ❑ GNP PER CAPITA $50,000
- ❑ BALANCE OF PAYMENTS.....Included in Swiss total
- ❑ INFLATION 1%
- ❑ UNEMPLOYMENT 2%

STRENGTHS

Stability and customs union with Switzerland make Liechtenstein a favored tax haven; its lack of EU membership makes the banking sector less vulnerable to future changes in EU banking laws. The economy is well diversified: chemicals, furniture, coatings for the electro-optical industry, construction services, and precision instruments are all thriving sectors.

WEAKNESSES

Very few. Need to balance integration with other countries with safeguarding economic independence.

EXPORTS

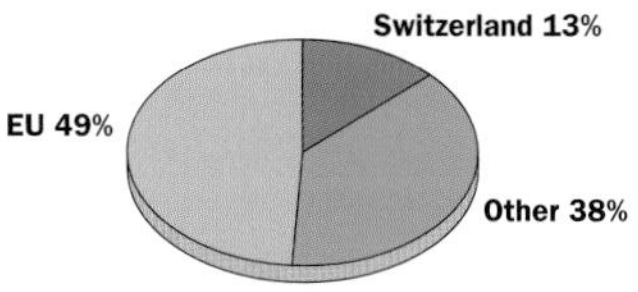
Switzerland 13%
EU 49%
Other 38%

IMPORTS

With a limited domestic market, Liechtenstein's industry is export-oriented. Liechtenstein has a customs union with Switzerland and does not publish separate import figures.

RESOURCES

Electric power: Included in Swiss total

None — Not an oil producer

6000 cattle, 3000 pigs, 2900 sheep, 280 goats — None

Liechtenstein has to import most of its energy. Almost all of its electricity comes from German power plants.

ENVIRONMENT

Not available

38% partially protected — 6.1 tonnes per capita

Protection of Liechtenstein's alpine scenery is high enough on the political agenda for one of the five councillors, or ministers, to have responsibility for the environment. As in Switzerland, the greatest worry is the effect of high rates of car use and of through traffic. However, a 1988 trial in providing free public bus transportation proved a failure, as Liechtensteiners remained firmly wedded to their automobiles.

MEDIA

TV ownership high

Daily newspaper circulation 602 per 1000 people

PUBLISHING AND BROADCAST MEDIA

There are 2 daily newspapers, *Liechtensteiner Vaterland* and *Liechtensteiner Volksblatt*

No TV service — 1 radio service

The two daily newspapers, though free of formal state control, are both run by political parties: the *Vaterland*, with the larger circulation (over 10,000), by the VU, the *Volksblatt* by the FBP.

CRIME

No death penalty

24 prisoners — Crime does not pose any great problems

Crime is a minor problem, a result of the relatively even distribution of wealth and high average living standard. Liechtenstein has also taken great care to protect its tax-haven status by careful regulation of its financial sector. It has avoided major scandals, and took steps in 2000 to tighten precautions against the growing problem of money laundering.

EDUCATION

School leaving age: 16

99% — Not available

Education, modeled on the German system, includes two types of school at secondary level – the more academic *Gymnasium* and the *Realschule*. Liechtenstein has no university; students go on to colleges in Austria, Switzerland, or Germany, or to business schools in the US.

CHRONOLOGY

In 1719 Liechtenstein became an independent principality of the Holy Roman Empire.

- ❑ **1924** Customs union with Switzerland.
- ❑ **1992** Women given equal rights.
- ❑ **1997** End of VU–FBP coalition dominant since 1938. Mario Frick heads VU government.
- ❑ **2001** FBP wins majority in elections; Otmar Hasler premier.
- ❑ **2003** Prince wins greater powers.

HEALTH

Welfare state health benefits

1 per 763 people — Heart and respiratory diseases, cancers

Though clinics and hospitals are few, the health system provides advanced care. Many Liechtensteiners have private health insurance arrangements, so that they have access to Swiss medical expertise and facilities as well as their own.

SPENDING

GDP/cap. increase

CONSUMPTION AND SPENDING

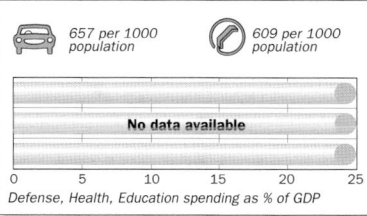

657 per 1000 population — 609 per 1000 population

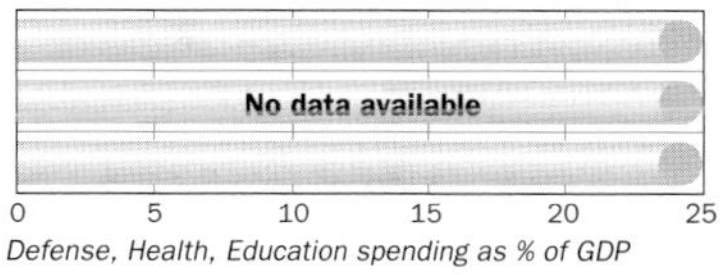
No data available
0
5
10
15
20
25
Defense, Health, Education spending as % of GDP

Unlike other tax havens, Liechtenstein displays a more conservative prosperity. Private deposit accounts are not a key part of its banking business, but an increase in money-laundering activities and the country's appearance on a blacklist of financial centers led to a ban on anonymous accounts in mid-2000.

WORLD RANKING

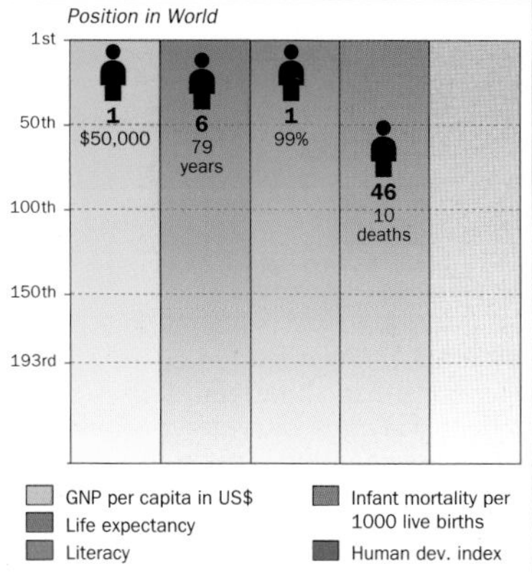
Position in World
1st
50th
100th
150th
193rd
1
$50,000
6
79 years
1
99%
46
10 deaths
GNP per capita in US$
Life expectancy
Literacy
Infant mortality per 1000 live births
Human dev. index

L

LITHUANIA

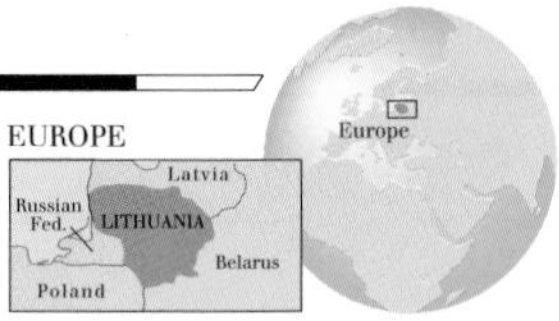
EUROPE
Europe
Latvia
Russian Fed.
LITHUANIA
Belarus
Poland

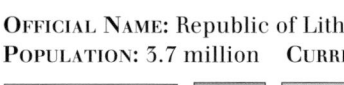

OFFICIAL NAME: Republic of Lithuania **CAPITAL:** Vilnius
POPULATION: 3.7 million **CURRENCY:** Litas and euro **OFFICIAL LANGUAGE:** Lithuanian

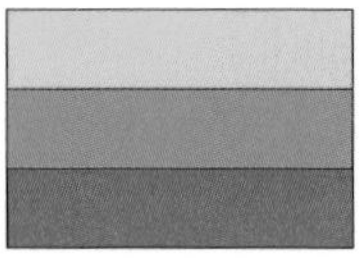

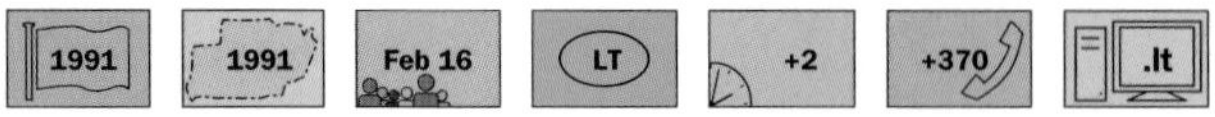
1991
1991
Feb 16
LT
+2
+370
.lt

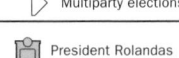

LYING ON THE EASTERN COAST of the Baltic Sea, Lithuania was the last European country formally to embrace Christianity, in about 1400. Its terrain is mostly flat, with many lakes, moors, and bogs. Now a multiparty democracy, Lithuania regained independence from the former USSR in 1991. Industrial production and agriculture are the mainstays of the economy. Russia finally withdrew all its troops from Lithuania in 1993.

CLIMATE

Continental

WEATHER CHART FOR VILNIUS

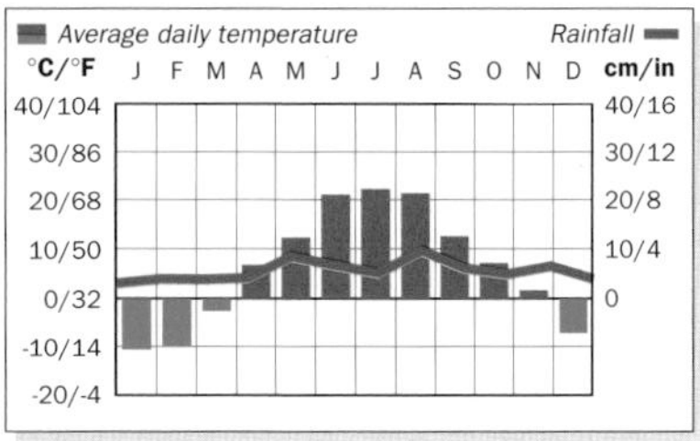
Average daily temperature
Rainfall
°C/°F J F M A M J J A S O N D cm/in
40/104
30/86
20/68
10/50
0/32
-10/14
-20/-4
40/16
30/12
20/8
10/4
0

Lithuania's coastal position moderates an otherwise continental-type climate. Summers are cool.

TRANSPORTATION

Drive on right

Vilnius International
634,991 passengers

175 ships
393,300 grt

THE TRANSPORTATION NETWORK

35,500 km (22,059 miles)

417 km (259 miles)

1905 km (1184 miles)

600 km (373 miles)

Lithuania is crossed by international rail routes, and Klaipeda provides extensive connections to other Baltic ports.

TOURISM

Visitors : Population 1:2.6

1.43m visitors

Up 13% in 2002

MAIN TOURIST ARRIVALS

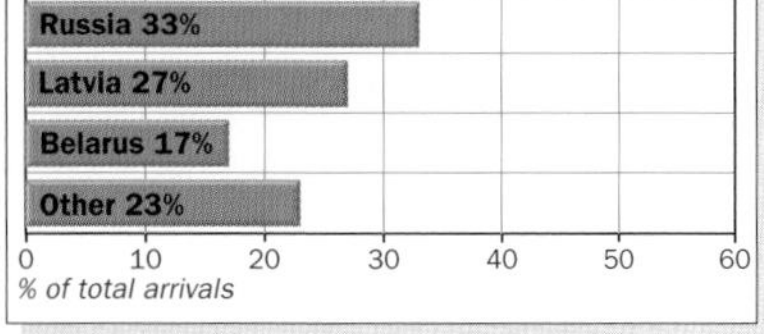
Russia 33%
Latvia 27%
Belarus 17%
Other 23%
0 10 20 30 40 50 60
% of total arrivals

The tourist industry boomed after independence. Vilnius is well preserved; its historic center survived German and Russian occupation. Trakai, the capital of the Grand Duchy in the 16th century, is also popular with visitors.

PEOPLE

Pop. density medium

Lithuanian, Russian

57/km² (147/mi²)

THE URBAN/RURAL POPULATION SPLIT

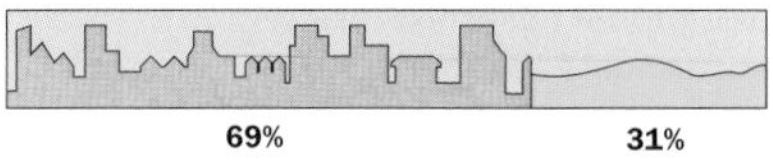
69%
31%

ETHNIC MAKEUP

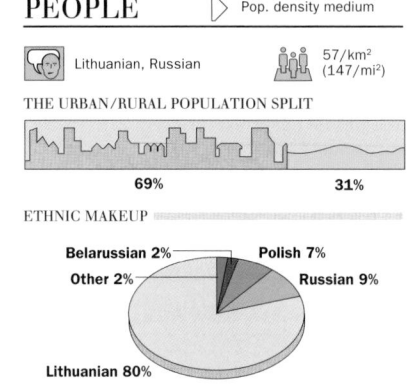

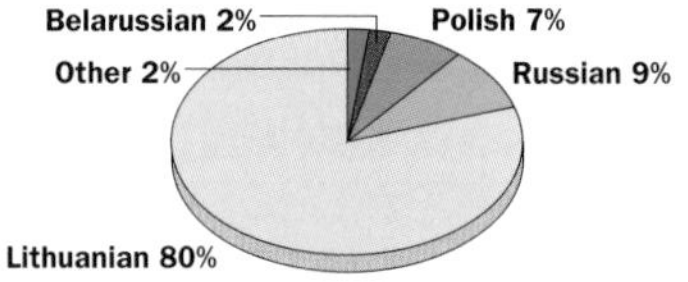
Belarussian 2%
Polish 7%
Other 2%
Russian 9%
Lithuanian 80%

With a mainly Catholic population, Lithuania has strong historical links with Poland, with which it was once united, though there is tension between ethnic Lithuanians and Poles. Relations with the Jewish minority are strained. More than 90% of nonethnic Lithuanians have been granted citizenship. Of all the Baltic states, Lithuania has the best relations with ethnic Russians, but they form a smaller minority there than in Estonia or Latvia.

POLITICS

Multiparty elections

2000/2004

President Rolandas Paksas

AT THE LAST ELECTION

Parliament 141 seats

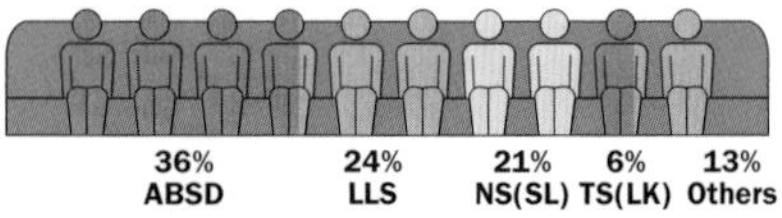
36% ABSD
24% LLS
21% NS(SL)
6% TS(LK)
13% Others

ABSD = A. Brazauskas Social Democratic Coalition
LLS = Lithuanian Liberal Union
NS(SL) = New Union (Social Liberals)
TS(LK) = Homeland Union (Lithuanian Conservatives)

Though governments have proved somewhat shortlived in recent years and personalities dominate politics, Lithuania's overall drive since independence in 1991 toward market reform and integration with the West has been unhindered. Former communist and conservative parties have led coalitions, with increasing levels of fractiousness – there were four different governments between 1999 and 2001. On the collapse in 2001 of an avowedly promarket coalition headed by Rolandas Paksas of the LLS, a new government was formed by the largest bloc in the Parliament, the ABSD, headed by former president and reformed communist Algirdas Brazauskas. He has promised to maintain the country's economic reforms while pursuing more socially oriented policies. Paksas unexpectedly won the presidential elections in January 2003, defeating the incumbent ex-emigré businessman Valdas Adamkus.

LITHUANIA

Total Land Area : 65 200 sq. km (25 174 sq. miles)

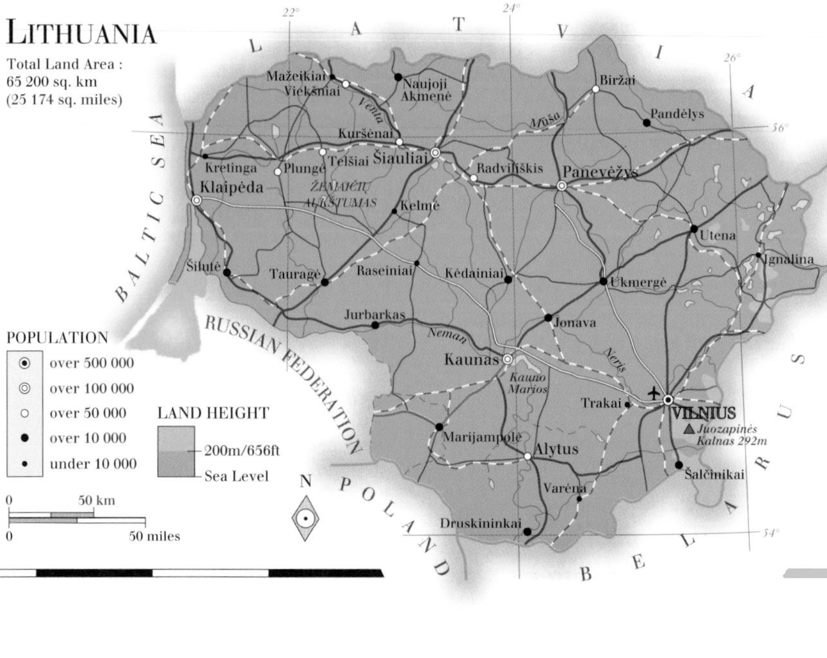
LATVIA
BALTIC SEA
RUSSIAN FEDERATION
POLAND
BELARUS
Mažeikiai
Viekšniai
Naujoji Akmenė
Biržai
Pandėlys
Kuršėnai
Venta
Mūša
Kretinga
Plungė
Telšiai
Šiauliai
Radviliškis
Panevėžys
Klaipėda
ŽEMAIČIŲ AUKŠTUMAS
Kelmė
Utena
Ignalina
Šilutė
Tauragė
Raseiniai
Kėdainiai
Ukmergė
Jurbarkas
Jonava
Neman
Neris
Kaunas
Kauno Marios
Trakai
VILNIUS
Juozapinės Kalnas 292m
Marijampolė
Alytus
Šalčininkai
Varėna
Druskininkai
22°
24°
26°
56°
54°
POPULATION
over 500 000
over 100 000
over 50 000
over 10 000
under 10 000
LAND HEIGHT
200m/656ft
Sea Level
0 50 km
0 50 miles
N

L

WORLD AFFAIRS

Joined UN in 1991

CE | CBSS | WTO | OSCE | PfP

Lithuania is one of ten candidates due to become full members of the EU in 2004. It currently has the best relations with Russia of all the Baltic states, while being set to join NATO, also in 2004.

AID

Recipient

$130m (receipts)

Up 31% in 2001

Aid, mostly from the IMF and the EU, is used for infrastructure projects and to promote private enterprise.

DEFENSE

Compulsory military service

$211m

Up 6% in 2001

A large National Guard patrols the country's frontiers. Legislation was passed in 2003 to cut active troop numbers from 22,000 to 17,000 by 2008 through a reduction in both the length of military service (from one year) and the size of the active reserve force.

ECONOMICS

Inflation 63% p.a. (1990–2001)

$11.7bn

3.007 litai (3.495); 0.871 euros (1.013)

SCORE CARD

- ❑ WORLD GNP RANKING 82nd
- ❑ GNP PER CAPITA $3350
- ❑ BALANCE OF PAYMENTS ....–$574m
- ❑ INFLATION 1.2%
- ❑ UNEMPLOYMENT.................................11%

STRENGTHS

Successful transition to stable market economy. Increase in foreign investment. Low inflation. Litas pegged to euro (legal tender from 2002).

WEAKNESSES

Agriculture slow to recover from decollectivization. Exports dependent on health of Russian economy. Poor raw materials base. Widening external current account deficit.

EXPORTS

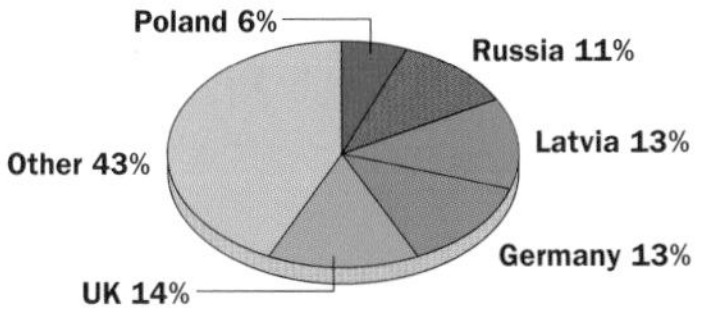
Poland 6%
Russia 11%
Other 43%
Latvia 13%
Germany 13%
UK 14%

IMPORTS

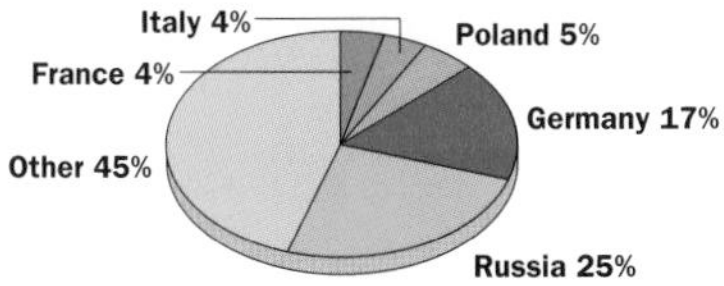
Italy 4%
Poland 5%
France 4%
Germany 17%
Other 45%
Russia 25%

One of Lithuania's 3000 lakes. *The entire country is low-lying. Its coast, fringed by dunes and pine forests, is famous for amber.*

RESOURCES

Electric power 5.8m kW

80,983 tonnes

4652 b/d (reserves 15m barrels)

1.01m pigs, 751,700 cattle, 6.58m chickens

Sand, gravel, clay, limestone, gypsum

Lithuania has significant reserves of peat and of materials used in the construction industry. The Ignalina nuclear plant provides more than 75% of the country's electricity. Oil is mostly imported from Russia.

ENVIRONMENT

Sustainability rank: 27th

10% (7% partially protected)

3.8 tonnes per capita

Radioactive leaks and the risk of accident at the giant Chernobyl-type nuclear plant at Ignalina cause much concern. In 2002 the government agreed to decommission it by 2009, after pressure from the EU, which will share the $2.6 billion cost.

MEDIA

TV ownership high

Daily newspaper circulation 29 per 1000 people

PUBLISHING AND BROADCAST MEDIA

There are 9 daily newspapers, including *Lietuvos Rytas* and *Respublika*

10 services: 1 state-owned, 9 independent

26 services: 1 state-owned, 25 independent

The mainstream media now publish and broadcast mainly in Lithuanian, having been in Russian under communism.

CRIME

No death penalty

11,216 prisoners

Down 20% in 2000–2001

Levels of crime are lower than in the other Baltic states. However, robbery is a growing problem.

EDUCATION

School leaving age: 15

99%

135,923 students

Teaching at all levels is in Lithuanian, making access to higher education harder for minorities; 8% of the population are graduates.

CHRONOLOGY

The commonwealth of Lithuania and Poland formed the largest state in Europe until Lithuania was annexed by Russia in 1795.

- ❑ **1915** Occupied by German troops.
- ❑ **1918** Independence declared.
- ❑ **1926** Military coup; one-party rule.
- ❑ **1940** Annexed by Soviet Union.
- ❑ **1941–1944** Nazi occupation.
- ❑ **1945** Incorporated into USSR.
- ❑ **1991** Achieves full independence.
- ❑ **1992** First multiparty elections.
- ❑ **1993** Russian troops withdraw.
- ❑ **1996** General election follows banking scandal; TS(LK) wins.
- ❑ **2000** Brief center-left coalition.
- ❑ **2001** Ex-president Brazauskas becomes prime minister.
- ❑ **2003** Former prime minister Paksas becomes president.

HEALTH

Welfare state health benefits

1 per 254 people

Heart diseases, cancers, cerebrovascular diseases, accidents

The reorganization of the health service, begun in 1997, is replacing state funding with finance from insurance funds.

SPENDING

GDP/cap. decrease

CONSUMPTION AND SPENDING

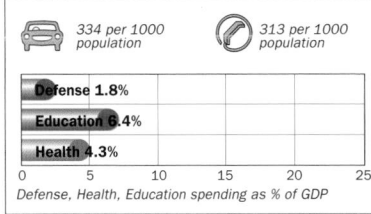

334 per 1000 population

313 per 1000 population

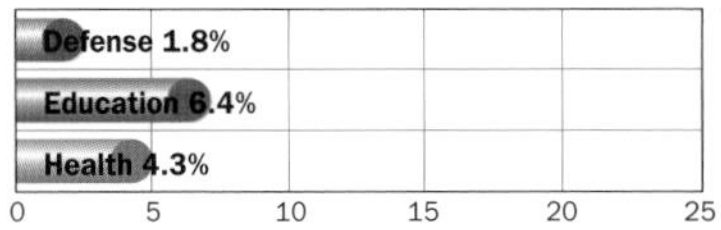
Defense 1.8%
Education 6.4%
Health 4.3%
0
5
10
15
20
25

Defense, Health, Education spending as % of GDP

High unemployment and weak consumption have held back growth. Since 1991 a large gap has opened between the incomes of rich and poor.

WORLD RANKING

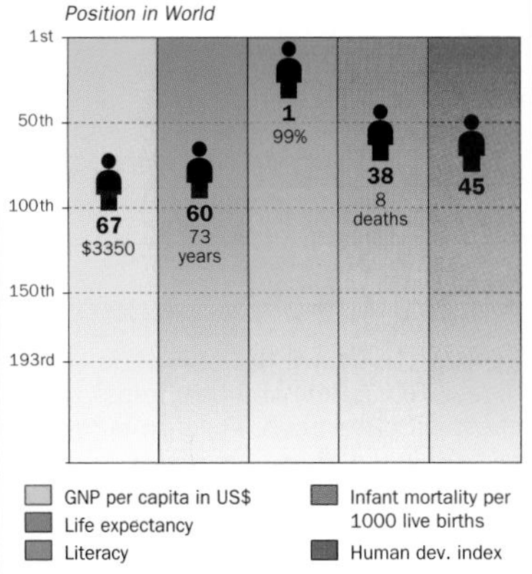
Position in World
1st
50th
100th
150th
193rd
67
$3350
60
73
years
1
99%
38
8
deaths
45
GNP per capita in US$
Life expectancy
Literacy
Infant mortality per 1000 live births
Human dev. index

L

LUXEMBOURG

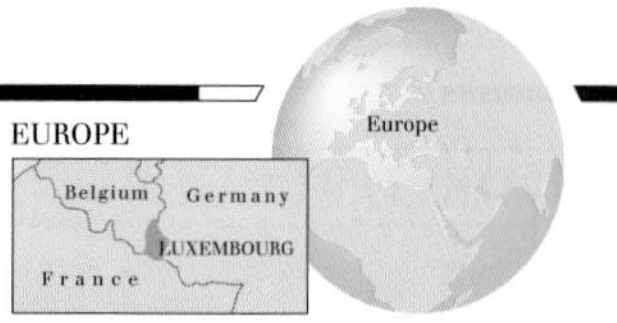
EUROPE
Belgium
Germany
LUXEMBOURG
France
Europe

OFFICIAL NAME: Grand Duchy of Luxembourg **CAPITAL:** Luxembourg-Ville
POPULATION: 448,000 **CURRENCY:** Euro **OFFICIAL LANGUAGES:** French, German, and Luxembourgish

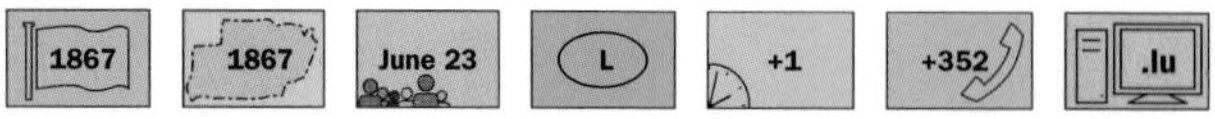
1867
1867
June 23
L
+1
+352
.lu

LUXEMBOURG SHARES BORDERS with the industrial regions of Germany, France, and Belgium, and has the highest per capita income in the EU. The northern Ösling region is part of the plateau of the Ardennes, and is undulating and forested. Luxembourg's prosperity was once based on steel; before World War II it produced more per capita than the US. Today, it is known as the headquarters of key EU institutions and as a banking center.

CLIMATE

Maritime

WEATHER CHART FOR LUXEMBOURG-VILLE

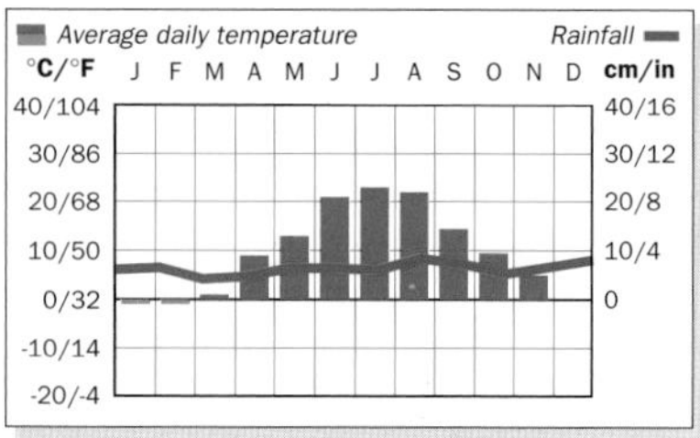
Average daily temperature
Rainfall
°C/°F
J F M A M J J A S O N D
cm/in
40/104
30/86
20/68
10/50
0/32
-10/14
-20/-4
40/16
30/12
20/8
10/4
0

The south, where vines grow, is the warmest area. Winter is cold and snowy, especially in the Ardennes.

TRANSPORTATION

Drive on right

Findel, Luxembourg-Ville
1.62m passengers

Has no fleet

THE TRANSPORTATION NETWORK

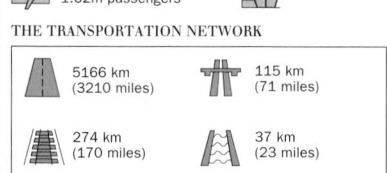

5166 km (3210 miles)

115 km (71 miles)

274 km (170 miles)

37 km (23 miles)

There is an excellent road network, though congestion is a problem. Rail and bus services are integrated.

TOURISM

Visitors : Population 1.8:1

807,000 visitors

Down 3% in 2000

MAIN TOURIST ARRIVALS

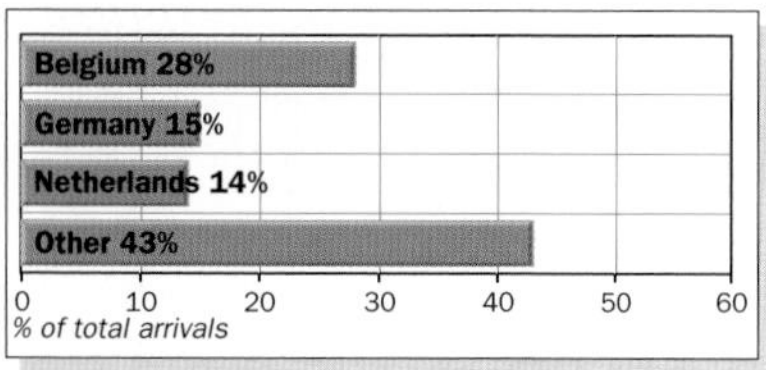
Belgium 28%
Germany 15%
Netherlands 14%
Other 43%
0
10
20
30
40
50
60
% of total arrivals

Key attractions are the mountains and forests, 76 castles, and the Benedictine abbey at Echternach. Foreign hotel workers learn about the history, language, and culture of the duchy under a government initiative.

PEOPLE

Pop. density medium

Luxembourgish, German, French

173/km² (449/mi²)

THE URBAN/RURAL POPULATION SPLIT

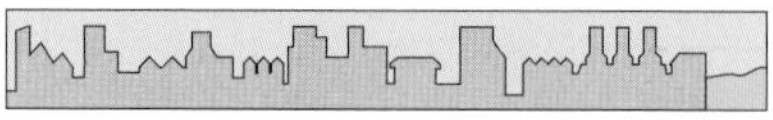
92%
8%

RELIGIOUS PERSUASION

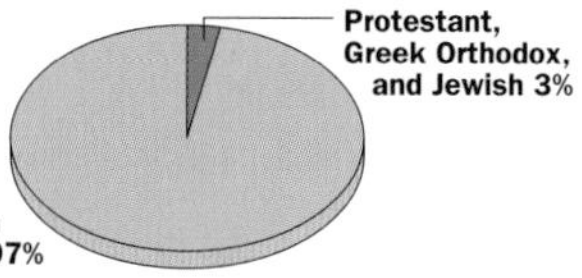
Protestant, Greek Orthodox, and Jewish 3%
Roman Catholic 97%

Nearly a third of its residents and half of Luxembourg's workers are foreigners. Integration has been straightforward; most are fellow western Europeans and Roman Catholics, mainly from Italy and Portugal. Life in Luxembourg is comfortable. Salaries are high, unemployment very low, and social tensions few.

POLITICS

Multiparty elections

L. House 1999/2004

Grand Duke Henri

AT THE LAST ELECTION

Chamber of Deputies 60 seats

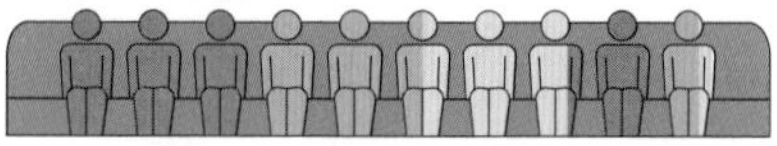
12% ACDJ
2% L
32% CSV/PCS
25% DP/PD
21% LSAP/POSL
8% G

CSV/PCS = Christian Social Party **DP/PD** = Democratic Party **LSAP/POSL** = Luxembourg Socialist Workers' Party **ACDJ** = Action Committee for Democracy and Justice **G** = Greens **L** = The Left

Council of State 21 seats

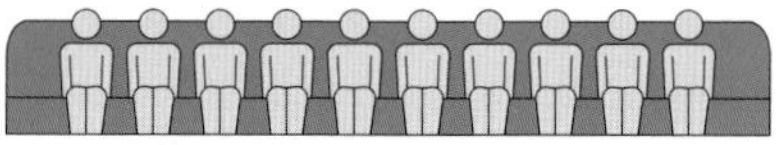

The members of the Council of State are appointed for life by the grand duke

There is remarkable political consensus, and governments are characterized by coalitions and long-serving prime ministers; the grand duke's role is mostly ceremonial. Main issues relate to European integration.

WORLD AFFAIRS

Joined UN in 1945

Benelux | EU | NATO | OECD | OSCE

Luxembourg has long been the keenest member of the EU. It was during its EU presidency that the Maastricht agreement for closer European union was brokered, and Luxembourg was not only the first member state to meet all the economic, financial, and legal requirements of union under Maastricht, but did so a year early. This commitment to the EU reflects the tremendous benefits Luxembourg has gained from membership. It is home to both the Secretariat of the European Parliament and the Court of Justice. In 1995, Prime Minister Jacques Santer left office to become president of the European Commission, but had to resign in 1999 amid allegations of corruption in the Commission.

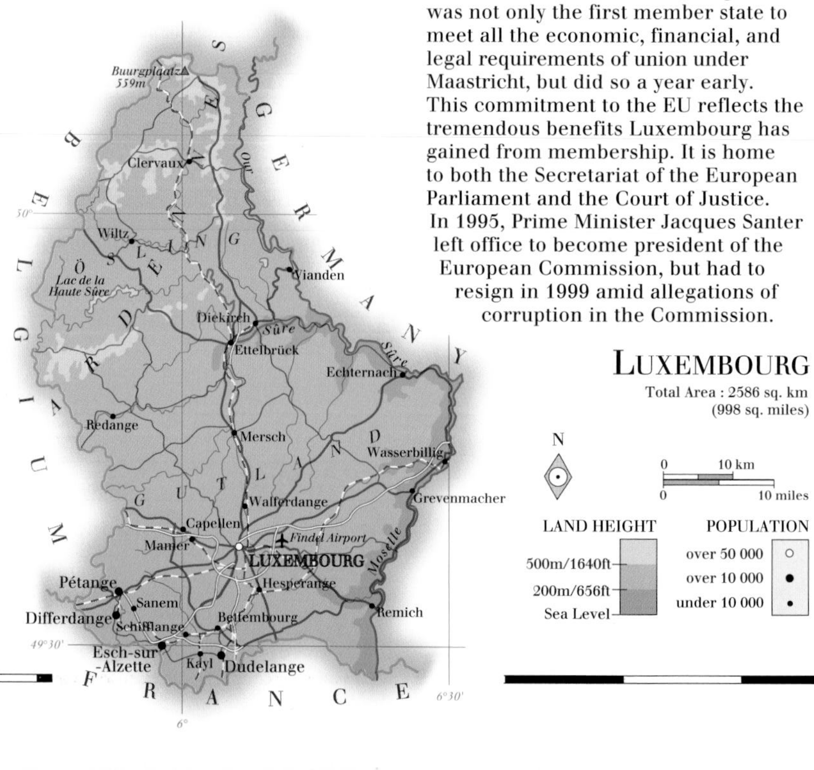
Buurgplaatz 559m
BELGIUM
GERMANY
FRANCE
ÖSLING
ARDENNES
GUTLAND
Clervaux
Wiltz
Lac de la Haute Sûre
Vianden
Diekirch
Sûre
Ettelbrück
Echternach
Redange
Mersch
Wasserbillig
Grevenmacher
Walferdange
Capellen
Mamer
Findel Airport
LUXEMBOURG
Moselle
Pétange
Hesperange
Sanem
Differdange
Schifflange
Bettembourg
Remich
Esch-sur-Alzette
Kayl
Dudelange
Our
50°
49°30'
6°
6°30'
LUXEMBOURG
Total Area : 2586 sq. km (998 sq. miles)
N
0
10 km
10 miles
LAND HEIGHT
500m/1640ft
200m/656ft
Sea Level
POPULATION
over 50 000
over 10 000
under 10 000

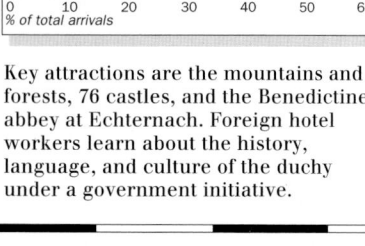

Charlotte Bridge, Luxembourg. The modern road system provides excellent links with the rest of Europe.

AID

Donor

$141m (donations)

Up 11% in 2001

Aid has been increased substantially and equaled 0.82% of GNP in 2001. Most goes to sub-Saharan Africa.

DEFENSE

No compulsory military service

$145m

Up 12% in 2001

A few members of the 900-strong army assist in international peacekeeping missions. There is no navy or air force.

ECONOMICS

Inflation 2.2% p.a. (1990–2001)

$17.6bn

0.871 euros (1.013)

SCORE CARD

- ❑ WORLD GNP RANKING.........................71st
- ❑ GNP PER CAPITA $39,840
- ❑ BALANCE OF PAYMENTS... ....$884m
- ❑ INFLATION 2.7%
- ❑ UNEMPLOYMENT 3%

STRENGTHS

Location for some EU institutions. Banking secrecy and expertise make the capital home to around 1000 investment funds and over 200 banks – more than in any other city in the world.

WEAKNESSES

International service industries account for 65% of GDP, making Luxembourg vulnerable to changing conditions overseas. Downturn in steel market.

EXPORTS

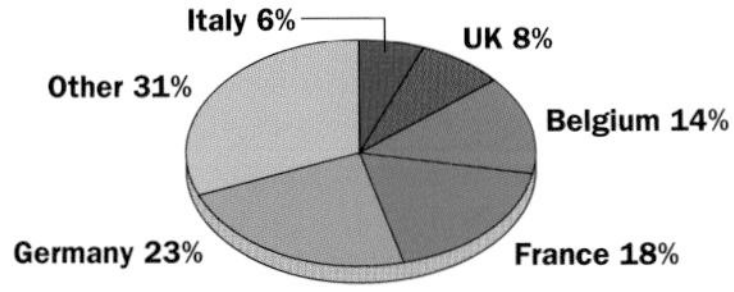
Italy 6%
UK 8%
Other 31%
Belgium 14%
Germany 23%
France 18%

IMPORTS

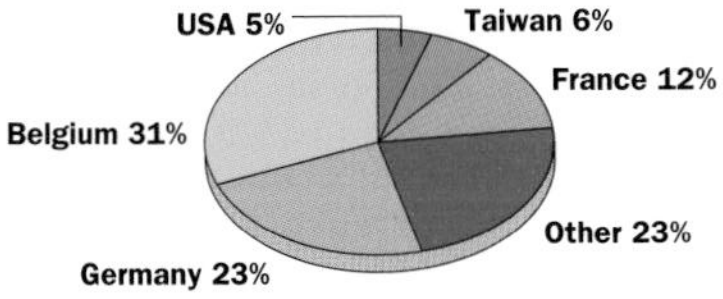
USA 5%
Taiwan 6%
France 12%
Belgium 31%
Other 23%
Germany 23%

RESOURCES

Electric power 1.3m kW

Not available

Not an oil producer

198,000 cattle, 85,830 pigs, 8220 sheep, 2818 horses

Iron

Most energy is imported; Luxembourg produces only a small amount of hydroelectricity. Arbed is part of the world's third-largest steel producing company.

ENVIRONMENT

Not available

14% partially protected

12.4 tonnes per capita

Acid rain from European industry has affected 20% of Luxembourg's trees and, in the worst cases, 30% of trees in mature stands. Luxembourg is a member of an international committee on reducing pollution of the Rhine.

MEDIA

TV ownership high

Daily newspaper circulation 328 per 1000 people

PUBLISHING AND BROADCAST MEDIA

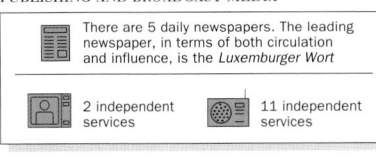

There are 5 daily newspapers. The leading newspaper, in terms of both circulation and influence, is the *Luxemburger Wort*

2 independent services

11 independent services

Broadcasting is dominated by RTL (Radio–Television Luxembourg), one of the largest media groups in Europe, which exports its programs in a variety of languages.

CRIME

No death penalty

357 prisoners

Down 7% in 2000–2002

Luxembourg's banking secrecy rules have provoked international criticism, as they can provide a cover for both tax evasion and fraud. Violent crime remains uncommon.

EDUCATION

School leaving age: 15

99%

2533 students

Teaching is mainly in German at primary and French at secondary level. Higher education is limited and many students go to universities in other European countries. Training given by Luxembourg banks is reputed to be the best in Europe.

HEALTH

Welfare state health benefits

1 per 395 people

Cancers, heart and cerebrovascular diseases, accidents

There are no private commercial hospitals in Luxembourg; they are run either by the state or by nuns. Patients' fees are refunded from the state sickness fund.

CHRONOLOGY

Until 1867, Luxembourg was ruled by a succession of neighboring European powers.

- ❑ **1890** Link with Dutch throne ends.
- ❑ **1921** Economic union with Belgium. End of German ties.
- ❑ **1940–1944** German occupation.
- ❑ **1948** Benelux treaty (1944) creating a customs union comes into effect.
- ❑ **1957** One of six signatories of Treaty of Rome, the principal foundation of what develops into the EU.
- ❑ **1995** Premier Jacques Santer is president of European Commission.
- ❑ **1999** Santer resigns amid corruption allegations. Socialist election losses.
- ❑ **2000** Grand Duke Jean abdicates in favor of his son, Henri.
- ❑ **2002** Euro fully adopted.

SPENDING

GDP/cap. increase

CONSUMPTION AND SPENDING

588 per 1000 population

780 per 1000 population

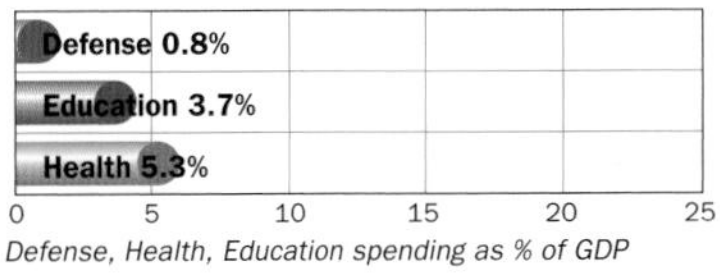
Defense 0.8%
Education 3.7%
Health 5.3%
0
5
10
15
20
25
Defense, Health, Education spending as % of GDP

With the world's second-highest per capita income, Luxembourgers enjoy a comfortable lifestyle. Recent strong economic performance has allowed them to benefit both from lower taxes and increased social security spending. Low unemployment has led to the recruitment of foreign workers, mainly from neighboring countries or from other EU countries such as Portugal and Italy, to take less well-paid jobs. As elsewhere in western Europe, financing care of the aging population is likely to be a burden in the future.

WORLD RANKING

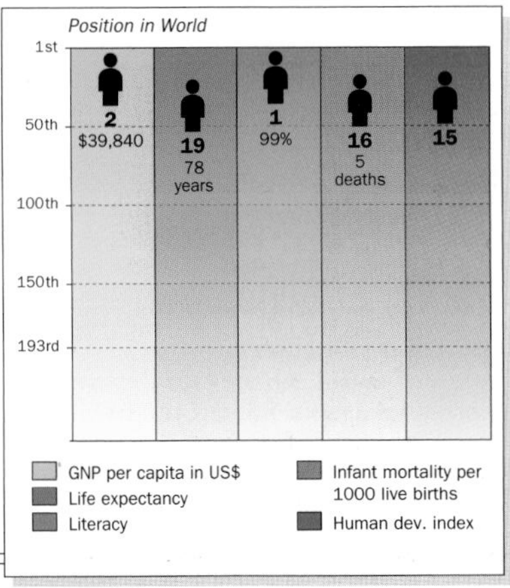
Position in World
1st
50th
100th
150th
193rd
2
$39,840
19
78
years
1
99%
16
5
deaths
15
GNP per capita in US$
Life expectancy
Literacy
Infant mortality per 1000 live births
Human dev. index

L

MACEDONIA

EUROPE
Serbia & Montenegro
Bulgaria
Albania
MACEDONIA
Greece
Europe

OFFICIAL NAME: Republic of Macedonia **CAPITAL:** Skopje
POPULATION: 2.1 million **CURRENCY:** Macedonian denar **OFFICIAL LANGUAGES:** Macedonian and Albanian

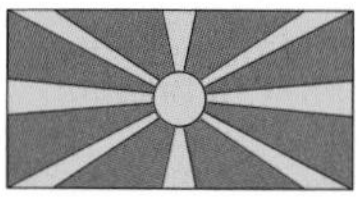

1991 | 1991 | Aug 2 | MK | +1 | +389 | .mk

THE FORMER YUGOSLAV REPUBLIC of Macedonia (FYRM) is landlocked in southeastern Europe. Despite the signing of an accord in 1995, Greece remains suspicious that it harbors ambitions about absorbing northern Greece – also called Macedonia – in a "Greater Macedonia." A militant movement among ethnic Albanians erupted into violent conflict in March–September 2001, but a peace agreement was reached after the involvement of a NATO force.

A ***fisherman's hut*** *on Lake Dojran. The lake lies on the border with Greece in southeastern Macedonia and is shared by the two countries.*

CLIMATE

Continental

WEATHER CHART FOR SKOPJE

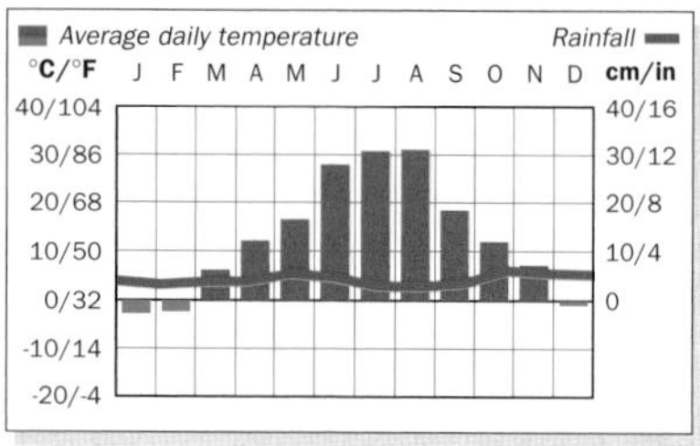
Average daily temperature
Rainfall
°C/°F
J F M A M J J A S O N D
cm/in
40/104
30/86
20/68
10/50
0/32
-10/14
-20/-4
40/16
30/12
20/8
10/4
0

The FYRM has a continental climate. Winter snow supports skiing.

TRANSPORTATION

Drive on right

Skopje International 520,497 passengers

Has no fleet

THE TRANSPORTATION NETWORK

5540 km (3442 miles)

133 km (83 miles)

699 km (434 miles)

Only lakes navigable

An east–west road and rail route from Tirana in Albania through Macedonia to Sofia in Bulgaria is planned, to reduce reliance on routes through Serbia.

PEOPLE

Pop. density medium

Macedonian, Albanian, Serbo-Croat

82/km² (212/mi²)

THE URBAN/RURAL POPULATION SPLIT

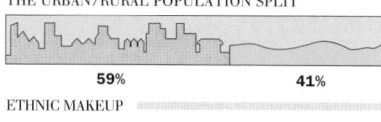

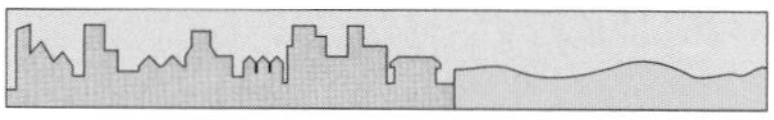
59%
41%

ETHNIC MAKEUP

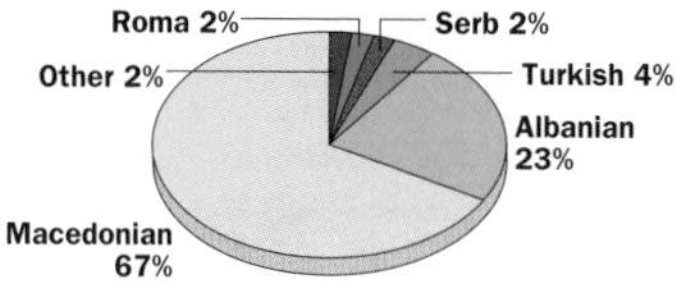
Roma 2%
Serb 2%
Other 2%
Turkish 4%
Albanian 23%
Macedonian 67%

Slav Macedonians, speaking a language akin to Bulgarian, are in the majority. The large Albanian minority, claiming to amount to over one-third of the population, maintains strong links with Albanians in neighboring states. Months of violent conflict sparked by ethnic Albanian insurgents seeking greater rights resulted in a new constitution in 2001 guaranteeing equality.

Macedonians are mostly Orthodox Christians, but there are a substantial number of Slavic Muslims (Pomaks), whose ancestors converted during the Ottoman occupation. Ethnic Albanians are mostly Muslim.

WORLD AFFAIRS

Joined UN in 1993

CE | WTO | EAPC | PfP | OSCE

Macedonia's hosting of NATO troops in the Kosovo conflict in 1999 placed it firmly in the Western fold. In 2003 the EU took charge of the international peacekeeping force in Macedonia.

AID

Recipient

$248m (receipts)

Down 2% in 2001

The World Bank, the US, and the EU are the main channels for economic development assistance. The EU and the US pledged $515 million for reconstruction in 2002. Regional security fears limit foreign investment.

DEFENSE

Compulsory military service

$73m

Up 3% in 2001

The army relies heavily on officer training in NATO countries. A major overhaul has been announced, with the aim being to tackle weaknesses revealed by the 2001 conflict.

TOURISM

Visitors : Population 1:21

99,000 visitors

Down 56% in 2001

MAIN TOURIST ARRIVALS

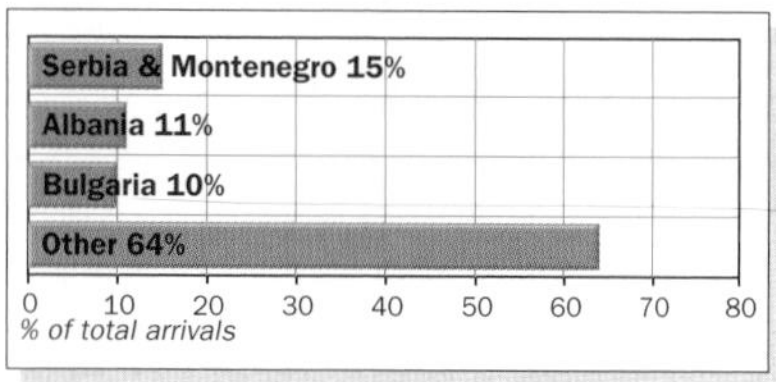
Serbia & Montenegro 15%
Albania 11%
Bulgaria 10%
Other 64%
0 10 20 30 40 50 60 70 80
% of total arrivals

The major attraction is the ecclesiastical center of Ohrid, situated on Europe's deepest lake, with Roman and Byzantine ruins. Other lake resorts and skiing in the Sara mountains in the northwest, have potential once stability is restored.

POLITICS

Multiparty elections

2002/2006

President Boris Trajkovski

AT THE LAST ELECTION

Assembly 120 seats

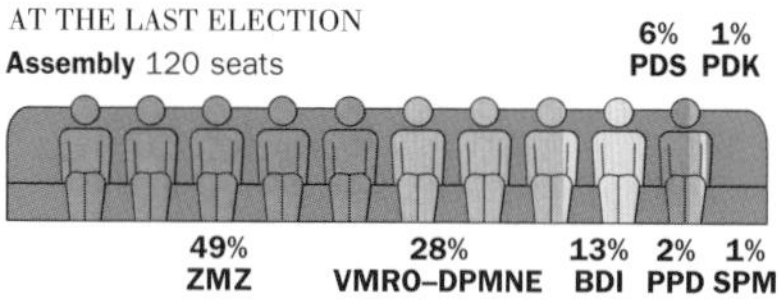
6% PDS
1% PDK
49% ZMZ
28% VMRO–DPMNE
13% BDI
2% PPD
1% SPM

ZMZ = Together for Macedonia, headed by the Social Democratic Alliance of Macedonia (**SDSM**) **VMRO–DPMNE** = Internal Macedonian Revolutionary Organization–Democratic Party for Macedonian National Unity **BDI** = Democratic Union for Integration **PDS** = Democratic Party of Albanians **PPD** = Party for Democratic Prosperity **PDK** = National Democratic Party **SPM** = Socialist Party of Macedonia

Political parties follow ethnic lines. The Social Democrats and the right-wing VMRO–DPMNE are predominantly Slav, while Albanians vote mainly for the BDI, the PDS, and the smaller PPD.

VMRO–DPMNE Prime Minister Ljubco Georgievski led a fragile "national unity" government through an armed insurrection by the Albanian rebel National Liberation Army (UCK). A peace deal in August 2001 ushered in a new, more equal constitution and guarantees on minority rights. With peace secured at the end of 2001, the "unity" government fractured, but Georgievski remained in power until the 2002 polls. The Social Democrat-led ZMZ alliance fell just short of a majority, and formed a coalition with the BDI. Branko Crvenkovski was appointed prime minister.

ECONOMICS

Inflation 66% p.a. (1990–2001)

$3.46bn

53.69 Macedonian denari (61.12)

SCORE CARD

- WORLD GNP RANKING........................126th
- GNP PER CAPITA $1690
- BALANCE OF PAYMENTS...................–$324m
- INFLATION 5.3%
- UNEMPLOYMENT..................................32%

EXPORTS

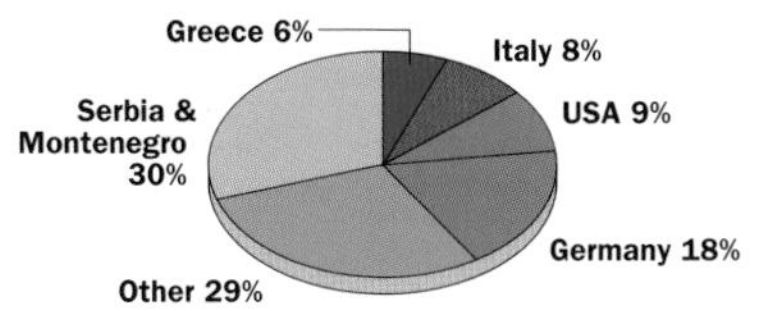
Greece 6%
Italy 8%
USA 9%
Serbia & Montenegro 30%
Germany 18%
Other 29%

IMPORTS

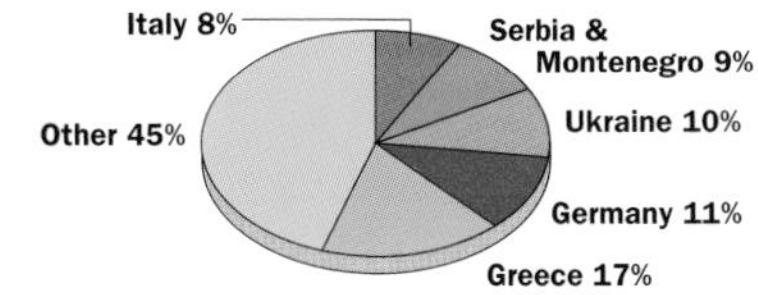
Italy 8%
Serbia & Montenegro 9%
Ukraine 10%
Other 45%
Germany 11%
Greece 17%

STRENGTHS

Growth in private sector and foreign investment. Mineral resources.

WEAKNESSES

Among poorest of former Yugoslav republics. Loss of trade in mid-1990s due to sanctions and Greek embargo. Dependence on oil, gas, and machinery imports. Disruption caused by Kosovo conflict and 2001 violence.

RESOURCES

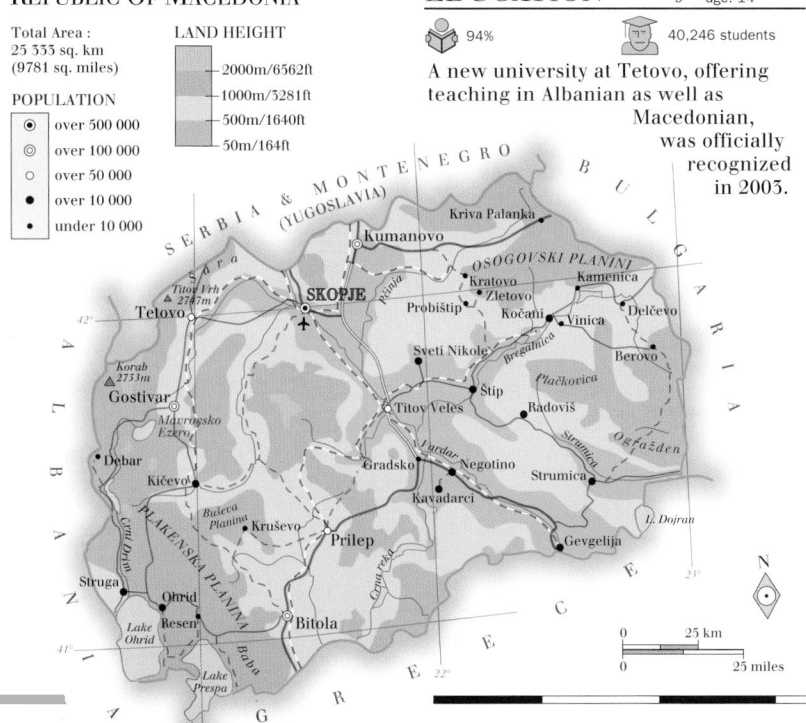

Electric power 1.5m kW

1834 tonnes

Not an oil producer

1.23m sheep, 259,000 cattle, 2.9m chickens

Coal, copper, bauxite, iron, antimony, chromium, lead, zinc

Minerals remain underexploited. South-facing fertile plains produce early fruit and vegetables for EU markets.

ENVIRONMENT

Sustainability rank: 83rd

7% (0.7% partially protected)

5.7 tonnes per capita

Industrial pollution affects water quality. The Titov Veles lead and zinc smelter is the worst culprit for toxic waste.

MEDIA

TV ownership high

Daily newspaper circulation 53 per 1000 people

PUBLISHING AND BROADCAST MEDIA

There are 6 daily newspapers, including the government-funded Albanian *Flaka e Vellazerimit*

3 services: 1 state-owned, 2 independent

1 state-owned, also independent services

Newspaper sales have expanded rapidly. In 2001, two independent newspapers "voluntarily" ceased publication.

CRIME

No death penalty

1413 prisoners

Down 18% in 1999–2002

Cigarette smuggling is dominated by Albanian gangs also involved in the illegal arms trade and heroin trafficking.

EDUCATION

School leaving age: 14

94%

40,246 students

A new university at Tetovo, offering teaching in Albanian as well as Macedonian, was officially recognized in 2003.

CHRONOLOGY

The end of Ottoman rule saw historic Macedonia divided between Serbia, Bulgaria, and Greece in 1912–1913. What is now the FYRM was incorporated into Serbia.

- **1944** Tito establishes republic, stressing Macedonian identity.
- **1989–1990** Multiparty elections.
- **1991** Independence declared. EU recognition delayed by Greeks.
- **1995** Accord with Greece.
- **1998–1999** Right-wing VMRO–DPMNE coalition wins elections.
- **1999** Upheaval over Kosovo conflict.
- **2001** Conflict with ethnic Albanian militants. NATO intervenes. New, more egalitarian constitution.
- **2002** Left-of-center ZMZ alliance wins elections.

HEALTH

Welfare state health benefits

1 per 333 people

Pulmonary, cerebro-vascular and heart diseases, cancers

In theory, the state guarantees universal health care, but effective and speedy treatment is increasingly only available in the private sector.

SPENDING

GDP/cap. decrease

CONSUMPTION AND SPENDING

139 per 1000 population

263 per 1000 population

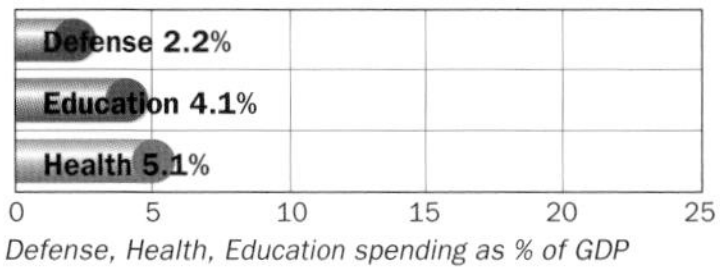
Defense 2.2%
Education 4.1%
Health 5.1%
0
5
10
15
20
25
Defense, Health, Education spending as % of GDP

Incomes have fallen by more than two-thirds since 1990, though smuggling and organized crime have made a few people conspicuously wealthy.

WORLD RANKING

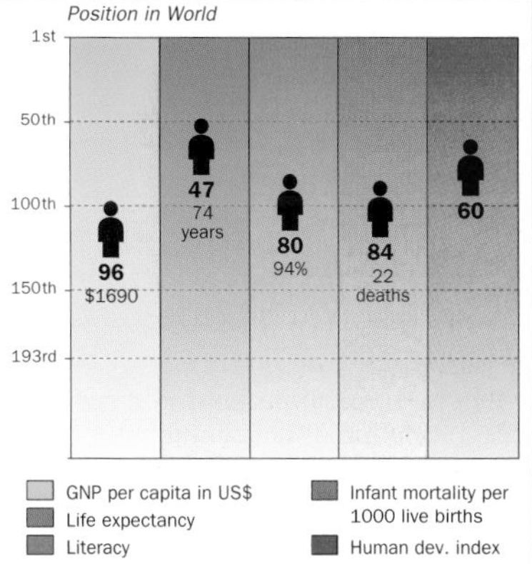
Position in World
1st
50th
100th
150th
193rd
96
$1690
47
74 years
80
94%
84
22 deaths
60
GNP per capita in US$
Life expectancy
Literacy
Infant mortality per 1000 live births
Human dev. index

M

FORMER YUGOSLAV REPUBLIC OF MACEDONIA

Total Area : 25 333 sq. km (9781 sq. miles)

POPULATION

- over 500 000
- over 100 000
- over 50 000
- over 10 000
- under 10 000

LAND HEIGHT

- 2000m/6562ft
- 1000m/3281ft
- 500m/1640ft
- 50m/164ft

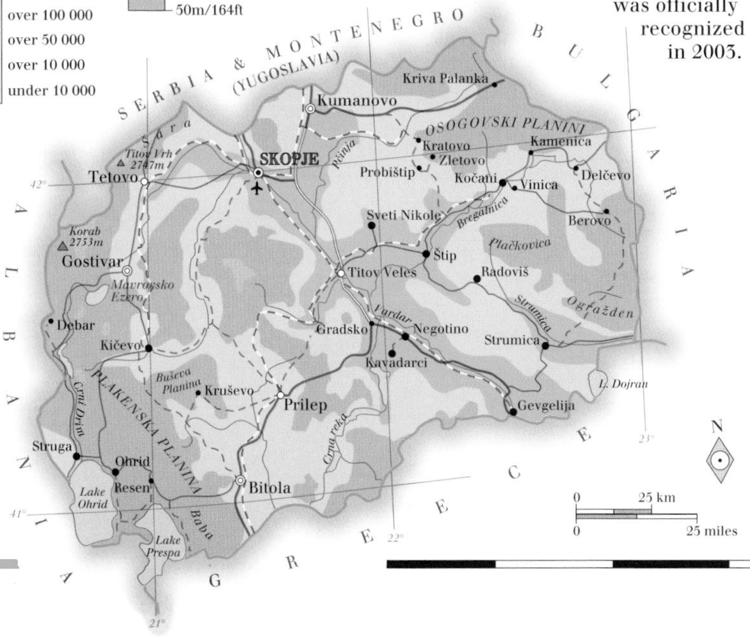
SERBIA & MONTENEGRO (YUGOSLAVIA)
BULGARIA
ALBANIA
GREECE
SKOPJE
Kumanovo
Kriva Palanka
Osogovski Planini
Kratovo
Zletovo
Kamenica
Delčevo
Probištip
Kočani
Vinica
Tetovo
Titov Vrh 2747m
Šar Planina
Pčinja
Sveti Nikole
Bregalnica
Berovo
Korab 2753m
Gostivar
Mavrovsko Ezero
Štip
Plačkovica
Titov Veles
Radoviš
Strumica
Ogražden
Debar
Gradsko
Vardar
Negotino
Strumica
Kičevo
Kavadarci
Buševa Planina
Kruševo
Prilep
L. Dojran
Gevgelija
Crni Drim
Plakenska Planina
Crna reka
Struga
Ohrid
Lake Ohrid
Resen
Bitola
Baba
Lake Prespa
42°
41°
21°
22°
23°
N
0
25 km
25 miles

MADAGASCAR

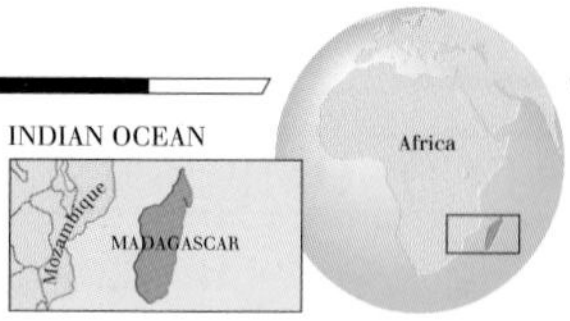
INDIAN OCEAN
Mozambique
MADAGASCAR
Africa

OFFICIAL NAME: Republic of Madagascar **CAPITAL:** Antananarivo
POPULATION: 16.9 million **CURRENCY:** Malagasy franc **OFFICIAL LANGUAGES:** French and Malagasy

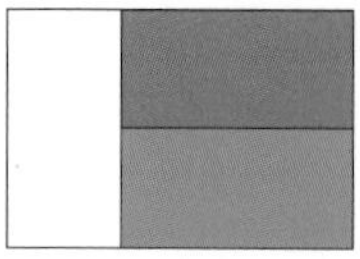

1960 | 1960 | June 26 | RM | +3 | +261 | .mg

LYING IN THE INDIAN Ocean, Madagascar is the world's fourth-largest island. Its isolation means that there is a host of unique wildlife and plants. To the east, the large central plateau drops precipitously through forested cliffs to the coast; in the west, gentler gradients give way to fertile plains. After 18 years of radical socialism, it became a multiparty democracy in 1993. Internal conflict over disputed elections in 2002 seriously damaged the economy.

CLIMATE

Tropical

WEATHER CHART FOR ANTANANARIVO

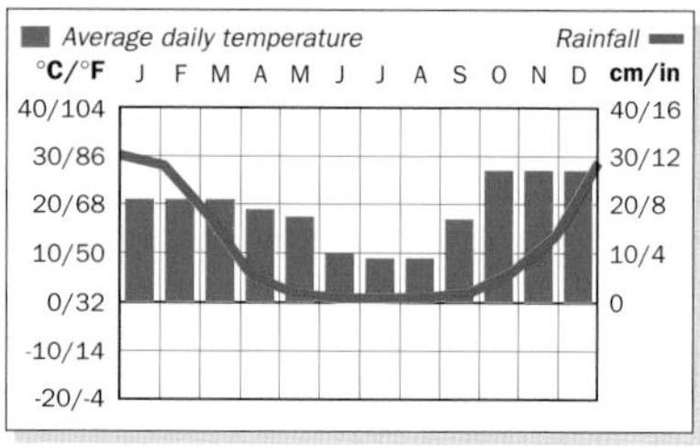
Average daily temperature
Rainfall
°C/°F J F M A M J J A S O N D cm/in
40/104 30/86 20/68 10/50 0/32 -10/14 -20/-4
40/16 30/12 20/8 10/4 0

Tropical Madagascar often has cyclones. The coastal lowlands are humid, while the central plateau is cooler.

TRANSPORTATION

Drive on right

Ivato, Antananarivo 336,711 passengers

104 ships 43,400 grt

THE TRANSPORTATION NETWORK

5781 km (3592 miles)	None
883 km (549 miles)	600 km (373 miles)

An extensive domestic air network – due for privatization – compensates for a very limited rail network and roads that are impassable during the rains.

TOURISM

Visitors : Population 1:99

170,000 visitors

Up 6% in 2001

MAIN TOURIST ARRIVALS

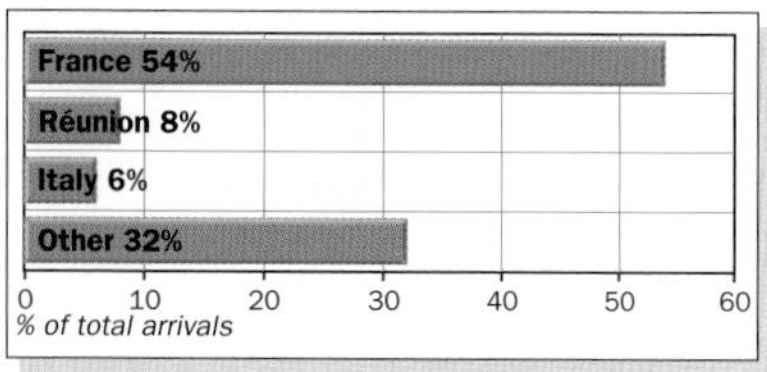
France 54%
Réunion 8%
Italy 6%
Other 32%
0 10 20 30 40 50 60
% of total arrivals

Extensive tropical beaches and unique flora and fauna offer great tourism potential. Political stability after 1993 led to a marked increase in arrivals which was threatened by the chaos in 2002.

PEOPLE

Pop. density low

Malagasy, French

29/km² (75/mi²)

THE URBAN/RURAL POPULATION SPLIT

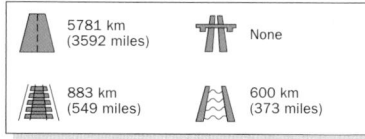

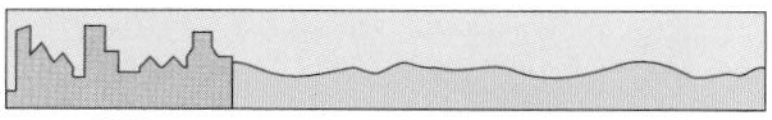
30%
70%

RELIGIOUS PERSUASION

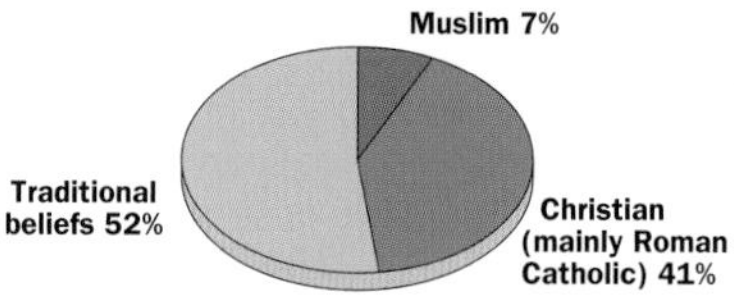
Muslim 7%
Traditional beliefs 52%
Christian (mainly Roman Catholic) 41%

Madagascans are largely Malay–Indonesian in origin. Their ancestors migrated across the Indian Ocean from the 1st century CE. Later migrants from the African mainland intermixed. Arab traders added another ingredient to the racial blend. The main ethnic division is between the central plateau and *côtier* peoples. Of more pronounced Malay extraction, the plateau Merina were Madagascar's historic rulers. They remain the social elite – to the resentment of the poorer *côtiers*, who were championed by former president Ratsiraka. The extended family remains the focus of social life for the rural majority.

POLITICS

Multiparty elections

L. House 2002/2007
U. House 2001/2007

President Marc Ravalomanana

AT THE LAST ELECTION

National Assembly 160 seats

3% RPSD
3% Others
64% TIM
14% FP
14% Ind
2% Arema

TIM = I Love Madagascar **FP** = National Unity **Ind** = Independents **RPSD** = Rally for Socialism and Democracy **Arema** = Association for the rebirth of Madagascar

Senate 90 seats

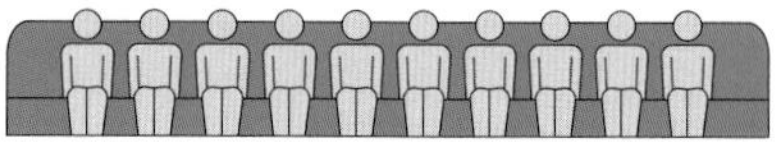

Two-thirds of Senate members are elected by regional governments; the remainder are nominated by the president

From 1975 until 2002 politics was dominated by radical socialist Didier Ratsiraka. He refused to accept the election victory of business tycoon Marc Ravalomanana in 2001 and the resulting power struggle violently divided the island. Eventually support for Ravalomanana proved overwhelming and he was internationally recognized as president in June 2002. His TIM party decisively won legislative elections later that year, but he now faces growing opposition from former paramilitary supporters. An ineffectual military coup was foiled in 2003.

A key issue is decentralization of power.

MADAGASCAR

Total Area : 587 040 sq. km (226 656 sq. miles)

0 200 km
0 200 miles

POPULATION	LAND HEIGHT
over 500 000	2000m/6562ft
over 100 000	1000m/3281ft
over 50 000	500m/1640ft
over 10 000	200m/656ft
under 10 000	Sea Level

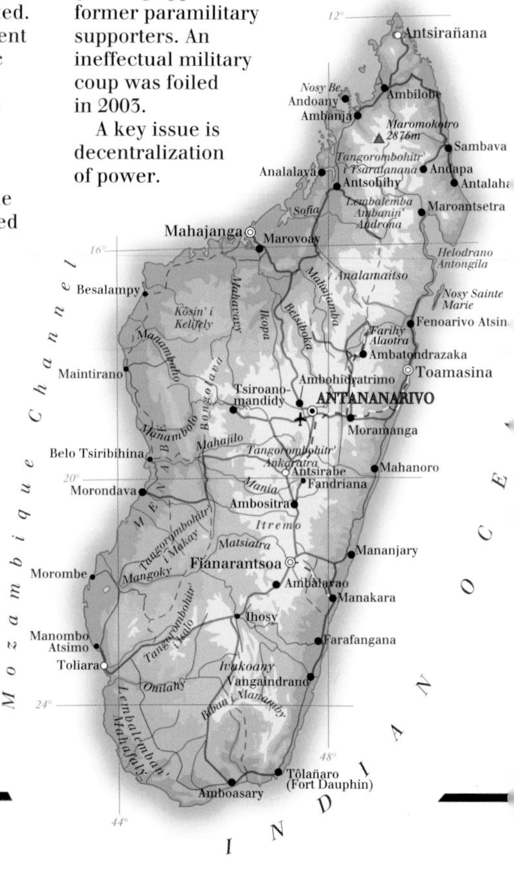
Antsirañana
Ambilobe
Nosy Be
Andoany
Ambanja
Maromokotro 2876m
Sambava
Andapa
Antalaha
Analalava
Antsohihy
Maroantsetra
Mahajanga
Marovoay
Besalampy
Helodrano Antongila
Nosy Sainte Marie
Fenoarivo Atsinanana
Ambatondrazaka
Toamasina
Maintirano
Tsiroanomandidy
ANTANANARIVO
Moramanga
Belo Tsiribihina
Antsirabe
Mahanoro
Morondava
Fandriana
Ambositra
Fianarantsoa
Mananjary
Morombe
Ambalavao
Manakara
Ihosy
Manombo Atsimo
Toliara
Farafangana
Vangaindrano
Tôlañaro (Fort Dauphin)
Amboasary
Mozambique Channel
INDIAN OCEAN

WORLD AFFAIRS

Joined UN in 1960

COMESA | OIF | IAEA | COI | AU

Once-close ties with Moscow and North Korea waned as Madagascar cemented relations with its main Western trading partners, especially France and the US. Since 1997 cooperation with the IMF has improved too. In 2003 the AU gave belated recognition to Ravalomanana's government. Traditional links with francophone Africa also remain strong.

AID

Recipient

$354m (receipts)

Up 10% in 2001

International donors pledged $2.3 billion in July 2002 in a four-year emergency aid package to support the new government and fund reconstruction.

DEFENSE

Compulsory military service

$47m

No change in 2001

The army was briefly divided during the 2002 turmoil and was implicated in an abortive coup in 2003.

ECONOMICS

Inflation 18% p.a. (1990–2001)

$4.19bn

5880 Malagasy francs (6030)

SCORE CARD

- World GNP Ranking 119th
- GNP per Capita $260
- Balance of Payments .... –$17m
- Inflation 6.9%
- Unemployment .... Widespread underemployment

Strengths

Varied agricultural base: vanilla, coffee, and clove exports. Offshore oil and gas. Prawns. Literate workforce. Chromium. Fabrics.

Weaknesses

Disruption caused by instability in 2002. Undercut by cheaper vanilla exporters. Vulnerability to drought and cyclones. Not self-sufficient in rice, the food staple.

EXPORTS

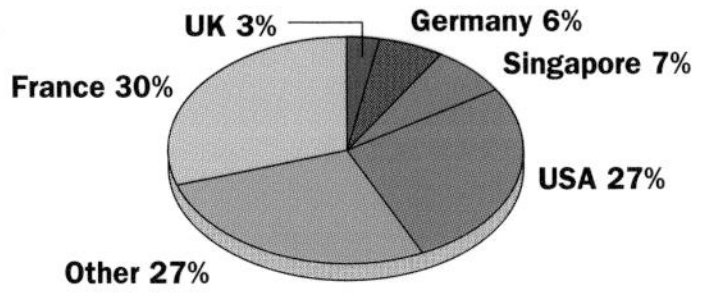
UK 3%
Germany 6%
Singapore 7%
France 30%
USA 27%
Other 27%

IMPORTS

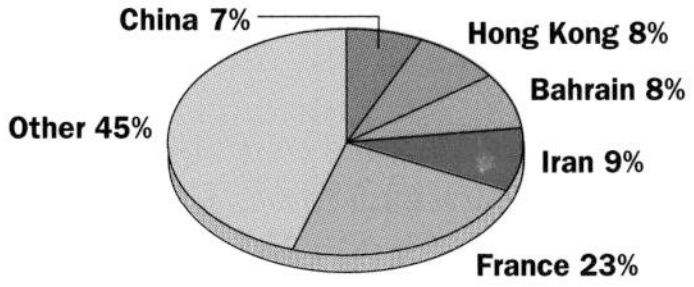
China 7%
Hong Kong 8%
Bahrain 8%
Other 45%
Iran 9%
France 23%

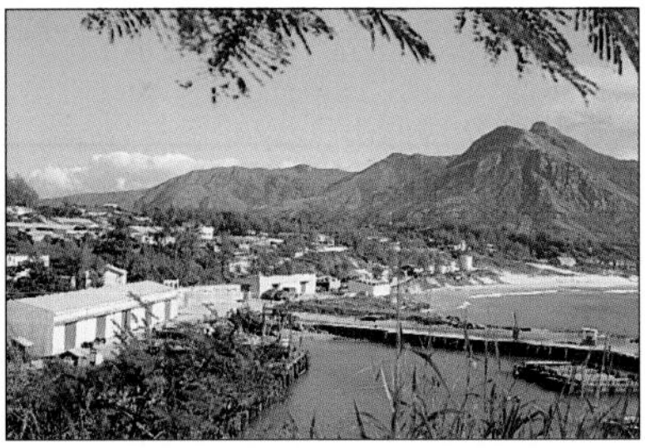

Tôlañaro (also known as Fort Dauphin), a port on the southeast coast. This was the area first settled by the French in the 16th century.

RESOURCES

Electric power 228,000 kW

139,373 tonnes

Not an oil producer; refines 6200 b/d

11m cattle, 3.8m ducks, 3m geese, 20m chickens

Chromite, graphite, oil, mica, iron, bitumen, gemstones, marble, gas

Electricity is produced by waterpower. There are underexploited mineral reserves and offshore oil and gas. High-quality sapphires were found in 1998.

ENVIRONMENT

Sustainability rank: 128th

2% (1% partially protected)

0.1 tonnes per capita

Madagascar's environment is a unique resource; 80% of its plant species and many animal species, such as the lemur, are found nowhere else. Aid helps to combat deforestation and soil erosion.

MEDIA

TV ownership low

Daily newspaper circulation 5 per 1000 people

PUBLISHING AND BROADCAST MEDIA

There are 6 daily newspapers, including the *Madagascar Tribune* and *Midi Madagasikara*

1 state-owned service

1 state-owned service, many independent stations

Even before the return of multiparty democracy in 1993, there was a flourishing opposition press. There are 127 local radio stations.

CRIME

Death penalty not used in practice

20,109 prisoners

Crime is rising

Urban crime levels are rising, with theft a particular concern. The army faces accusations of abusing human rights and of shooting federalists in 1993.

EDUCATION

School leaving age: 14

67%

31,386 students

Primary education will soon be based on French, not Malagasy. Attendance at secondary level is rising, as is the number of teachers; the government has increased spending in recent years.

CHRONOLOGY

Increasing European contacts after the 16th century culminated in the 1895 French invasion. Madagascar became a French colony and the Merina monarchy was abolished.

- **1947–1948** French troops kill thousands in nationalist uprisings.
- **1960** Independence.
- **1975** Radical socialist Didier Ratsiraka takes power.
- **1991** Forces Vives (CFV) coalition set up, led by Albert Zafy. Mass strikes.
- **1992** Civilian rule restored.
- **1993** Zafy's CFV defeats Ratsiraka's coalition in free elections.
- **1996** Zafy impeached.
- **1997** Ratsiraka reelected president.
- **2002** Country divided after opposition leader Marc Ravalomanana claims victory in 2001 presidential election.

HEALTH

Welfare state health benefits

1 per 9091 people

Malaria, enteric and respiratory diseases

Private health care was legalized in 1993. State care is free but inadequate. Malaria is at epidemic levels. There are outbreaks of bubonic plague.

SPENDING

GDP/cap. increase

CONSUMPTION AND SPENDING

4 per 1000 population

4 per 1000 population

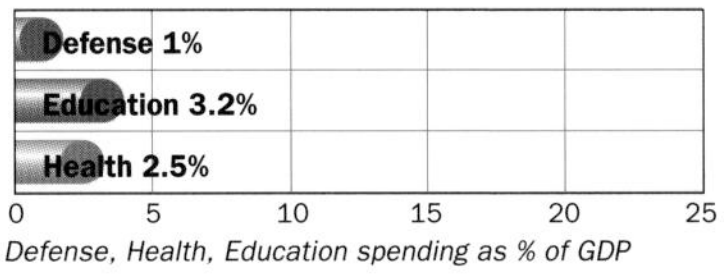
Defense 1%
Education 3.2%
Health 2.5%
0
5
10
15
20
25
Defense, Health, Education spending as % of GDP

Most of Madagascar's people are terribly poor, though those who live on the central plateau are richer than the *côtier* farmers and fishermen.

WORLD RANKING

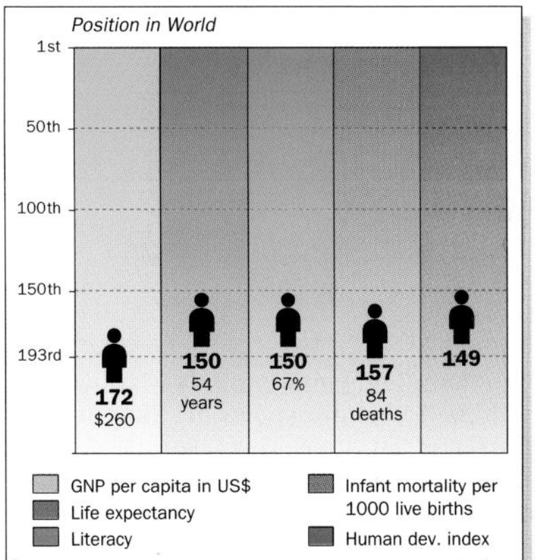
Position in World
1st
50th
100th
150th
193rd
172
$260
150
54 years
150
67%
157
84 deaths
149
GNP per capita in US$
Life expectancy
Literacy
Infant mortality per 1000 live births
Human dev. index

M

MALAWI

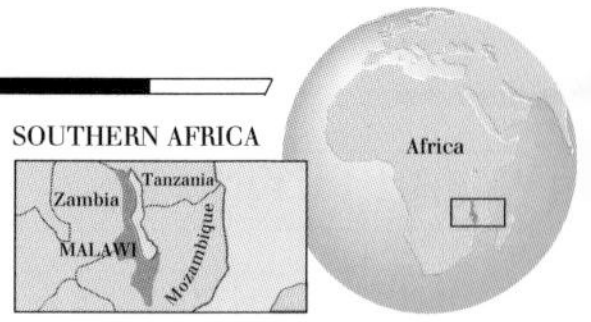
SOUTHERN AFRICA
Tanzania
Zambia
MALAWI
Mozambique
Africa

OFFICIAL NAME: Republic of Malawi **CAPITAL:** Lilongwe
POPULATION: 11.8 million **CURRENCY:** Malawi kwacha **OFFICIAL LANGUAGE:** English

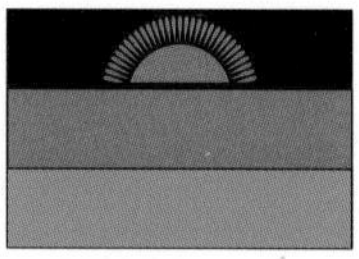

1964
1964
July 6
MW
+2
+265
.mw

LANDLOCKED IN SOUTHEAST Africa, Malawi lies on the Great Rift Valley and is dominated by Lake Nyasa, Africa's third-largest expanse of water. In the 1980s Malawi hosted large numbers of Mozambican refugees, at some cost to its fragile economy; food shortages are a recurrent and serious threat. Democracy was established in Malawi, a former British colony, in 1994, after three decades of one-party rule under Hastings Banda.

CLIMATE

Tropical wet and dry

WEATHER CHART FOR LILONGWE

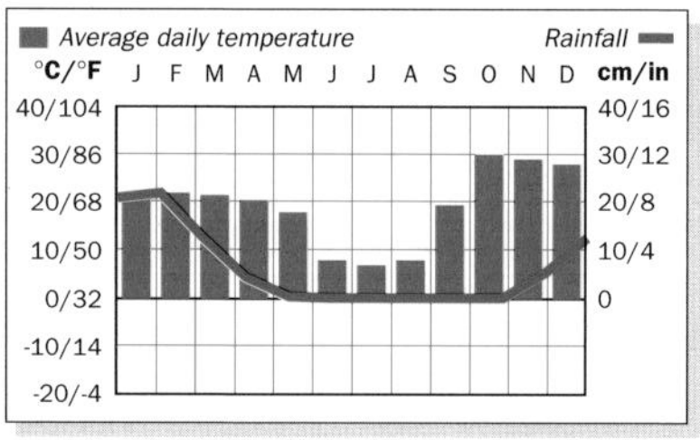
Average daily temperature
Rainfall
°C/°F
J F M A M J J A S O N D
cm/in
40/104
30/86
20/68
10/50
0/32
-10/14
-20/-4
40/16
30/12
20/8
10/4
0

The south is hot and humid. The rest of Malawi is warm and very sunny in the dry season, but cooler in the highlands.

TRANSPORTATION

Drive on left

Kamuzu International, Lilongwe 181,259 passengers

Has no fleet

THE TRANSPORTATION NETWORK

2773 km (1723 miles)	None
797 km (495 miles)	144 km (89 miles)

The Kamuzu Highway has been upgraded, and the Nacala Rail Corridor, a vital link to the distant sea, has attracted private investment.

TOURISM

Visitors : Population 1:52

228,000 visitors

Down 10% in 2000

MAIN TOURIST ARRIVALS

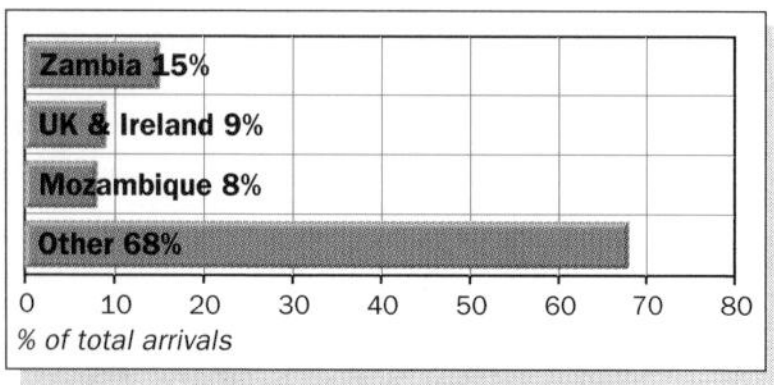
Zambia 15%
UK & Ireland 9%
Mozambique 8%
Other 68%
0 10 20 30 40 50 60 70 80
% of total arrivals

The national parks and Lake Nyasa's fishing and water sports are the main tourist attractions. The opening of international airports at Blantyre and Lilongwe has increased accessibility.

PEOPLE

Pop. density medium

Chewa, Lomwe, Yao, Ngoni, English

125/km² (325/mi²)

THE URBAN/RURAL POPULATION SPLIT

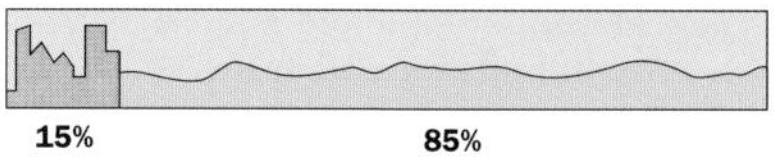
15%
85%

RELIGIOUS PERSUASION

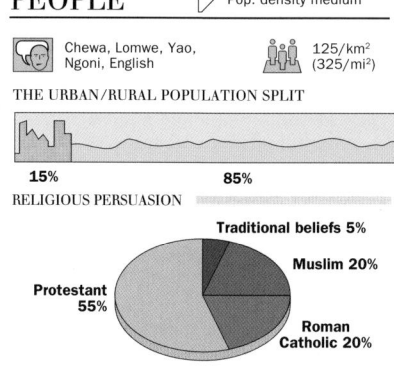

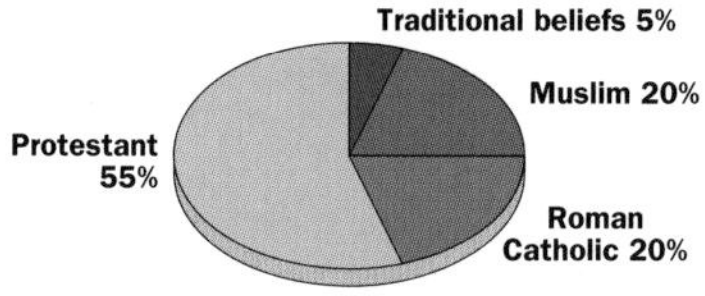
Traditional beliefs 5%
Muslim 20%
Protestant 55%
Roman Catholic 20%

Ethnicity has not been exploited for political ends in Malawi as has been the case in neighboring states. Most Malawians share a common Bantu origin. Of the various groups, the Chewa are dominant in the central region, Nyanja in the south, Tumbuka in the north, the mostly Muslim Yao in the southeast, and the Ngoni, a Zulu offshoot, in the lowlands. Other groups include the Chieoka and Tonga. Northerners felt ignored by Banda and his MCP, but the UDF government has largely succeeded in reducing tensions.

The election in 1994 of President Muluzi, a member of Malawi's Muslim minority, arguably signaled the failure of Banda's plan to enforce Protestant domination in Malawi. Many Muslim Asians work in the retail sector.

Society is strongly patriarchal. Women form the majority of farmers.

***Fruit and vegetable sellers** offering their wares on the Mozambican border. The south of the country is intensively cultivated.*

POLITICS

Multiparty elections

1999/2004

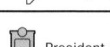

President Bakili Muluzi

AT THE LAST ELECTION

National Assembly 193 seats

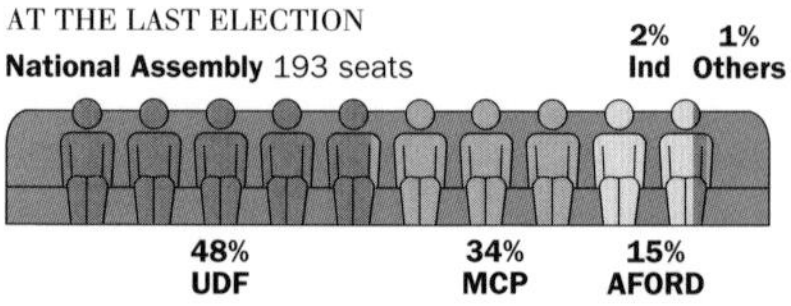
2% Ind
1% Others
48% UDF
34% MCP
15% AFORD

UDF = United Democratic Front **MCP** = Malawi Congress Party **AFORD** = Alliance for Democracy **Ind** = Independents

For 30 years from independence in 1964 Malawi was ruled by the autocratic Hastings Banda. His single-party regime outlawed dissent; torture and imprisonment without trial were common. A referendum forced Banda to introduce multiparty politics in 1994, when the mainly southern-based UDF scored a dramatic victory. Its leader Bakili Muluzi won the presidency and shrewdly recruited several prominent MCP politicians to his team. He vowed to restore personal freedoms and to revive and liberalize the shattered economy.

Muluzi was narrowly reelected in 1999, but the MCP contested the results, and violence against Muslims and UDF supporters erupted in the north. He has since also been accused of corruption. Muluzi's bid to choose his own successor in 2003, after failing to push through changes allowing himself a third term, prompted major criticism from within the UDF. A "national unity" cabinet was later formed with AFORD.

WORLD AFFAIRS

Joined UN in 1964

Comm COMESA NAM AU SADC

Relations with potential aid donors are key. The West backs the government's reformist policies, but accuses it of mismanagement. Malawi also wants to preserve its close ties with South Africa. One in ten Mozambicans fled to Malawi as refugees in the 1980s. A 2002 ban on "foreign" ownership of land concerns investors and the Asian minority.

AID

Recipient

$402m (receipts)

Down 10% in 2001

Nonhumanitarian aid resumed with the advent of democracy. However, the EU, the US, and the UK suspended aid in late 2001 in response to corruption and economic mismanagement. Emergency food aid was granted in May 2002.

M

DEFENSE

No compulsory military service

$6m

No change in 2001

Muluzi's government has the backing of the 5300-strong army. In the last days of Banda's rule, the military lost confidence in the ruling MCP, forcing the pace of democratization. In 1993, it disarmed the Young Pioneers, a militarized section of the MCP.

ECONOMICS

Inflation 33% p.a. (1990–2001)

$1.71bn

89.5 Malawi kwacha (76.28)

SCORE CARD

- ❑ WORLD GNP RANKING 142nd
- ❑ GNP PER CAPITA $160
- ❑ BALANCE OF PAYMENTS....................–$531m
- ❑ INFLATION 28.6%
- ❑ UNEMPLOYMENT 1%

STRENGTHS

Tobacco, earning 76% of foreign exchange. Tea and sugar production. Growing contribution of industry to GDP. Unexploited bauxite, asbestos, and coal reserves. Much tourism potential.

WEAKNESSES

Agriculture vulnerable to drought and price fluctuations: severe famine in 2002. Small domestic market, few skilled workers.

EXPORTS

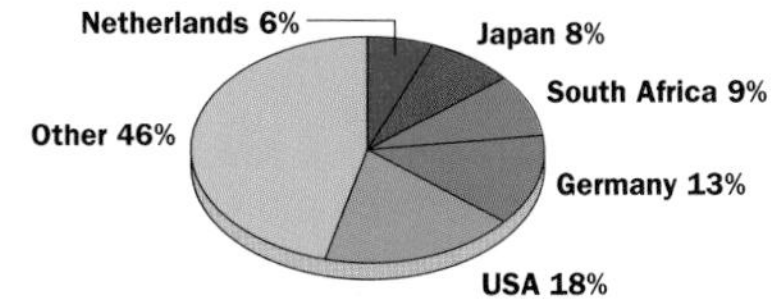
Netherlands 6%
Japan 8%
South Africa 9%
Other 46%
Germany 13%
USA 18%

IMPORTS

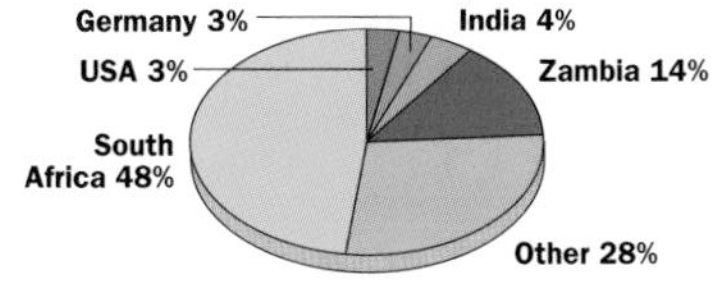
Germany 3%
India 4%
USA 3%
Zambia 14%
South Africa 48%
Other 28%

RESOURCES

Electric power 250,000 kW

45,530 tonnes

Not an oil producer

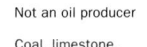

1.7m goats, 750,000 cattle, 15.2m chickens

Coal, limestone, gemstones, bauxite, graphite, uranium

Hydropower plants on the Shire River account for nearly 85% of generating capacity, but only 3% of total energy use. Most people rely on fuelwood for their energy needs. Malawi now encourages privatization, crop diversification, improved irrigation, and regional economic integration via the SADC to exploit its naturally limited resources. A deep-seam coal mine is currently being worked at Rumphi.

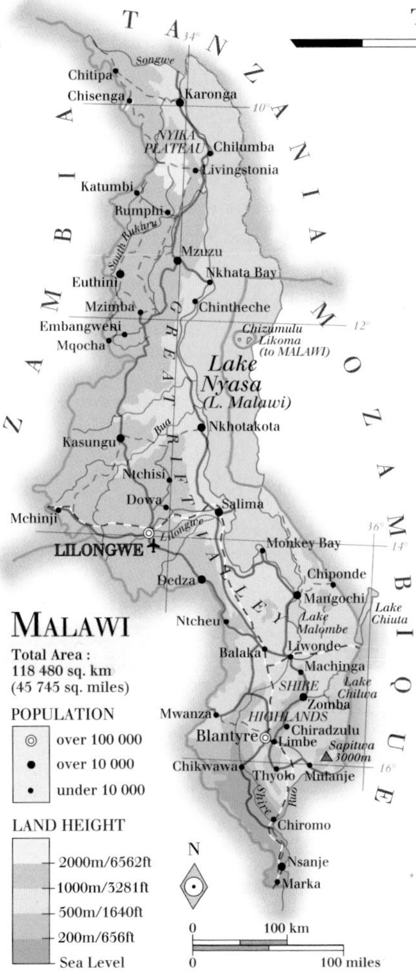
TANZANIA
ZAMBIA
MOZAMBIQUE
Chitipa
Chisenga
Karonga
Songwe
NYIKA PLATEAU
Chilumba
Livingstonia
Katumbi
Rumphi
South Rukuru
Mzuzu
Nkhata Bay
Euthini
Mzimba
Chintheche
Embangweni
Mqocha
Chizumulu
Likoma (to MALAWI)
GREAT RIFT VALLEY
Lake Nyasa (L. Malawi)
Kasungu
Bua
Nkhotakota
Ntchisi
Dowa
Salima
Mchinji
Lilongwe
LILONGWE
Monkey Bay
Dedza
Chiponde
Mangochi
Lake Malombe
Lake Chiuta
Ntcheu
Balaka
Liwonde
Machinga
SHIRE HIGHLANDS
Lake Chilwa
Zomba
Mwanza
Chiradzulu
Blantyre
Limbe
Sapitwa 3000m
Chikwawa
Thyolo
Mulanje
Shire
Ruo
Chiromo
Nsanje
Marka
MALAWI
Total Area : 118 480 sq. km (45 745 sq. miles)
POPULATION
over 100 000
over 10 000
under 10 000
LAND HEIGHT
2000m/6562ft
1000m/3281ft
500m/1640ft
200m/656ft
Sea Level
N
0 100 km
0 100 miles

ENVIRONMENT

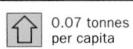

Sustainability rank: 82nd

11% (4% partially protected)

0.07 tonnes per capita

Drought, with its devastating effects on agriculture, eclipses all other problems. Ecological husbandry attracts tourism.

MEDIA

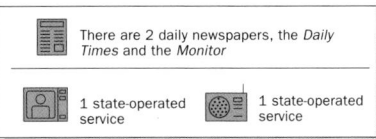

TV ownership low

Daily newspaper circulation 3 per 1000 people

PUBLISHING AND BROADCAST MEDIA

There are 2 daily newspapers, the *Daily Times* and the *Monitor*

1 state-operated service

1 state-operated service

Violence against the staff of privately owned newspapers causes concern among human rights groups.

CRIME

Death penalty in use

8769 prisoners

Crime is rising

Urban crime is on the increase. The proliferation of weapons, particularly guns, is contributing to a rise in cases of armed robbery.

CHRONOLOGY

After strong Scottish missionary activity, Malawi came under British rule as Nyasaland in 1891.

- ❑ **1964** Independence under Hastings Banda.
- ❑ **1966** One-party state.
- ❑ **1992** Antigovernment riots. Illegal prodemocracy groups unite.
- ❑ **1993** Referendum for multipartyism.
- ❑ **1994** Muluzi's UDF wins elections.
- ❑ **2002** Severe cholera epidemic, exacerbated by food shortages.

EDUCATION

School leaving age: 14

61%

3179 students

Primary-level education is widespread, with 73% of boys and 60% of girls attending school regularly.

HEALTH

Welfare state health benefits

1 per 20,000 people

Infectious, parasitic, and respiratory diseases, AIDS

A cholera epidemic, exacerbated by malnutrition, killed 1000 people in 2002.

SPENDING

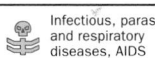

GDP/cap. increase

CONSUMPTION AND SPENDING

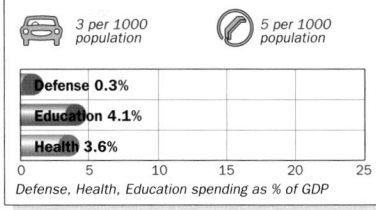

3 per 1000 population

5 per 1000 population

Defense 0.3%
Education 4.1%
Health 3.6%
0
5
10
15
20
25

Defense, Health, Education spending as % of GDP

The ousted MCP elite grew wealthy, allegedly through embezzlement. However, 80% of Malawians remain mired in poverty, and are forced to survive on less than $2 a day.

WORLD RANKING

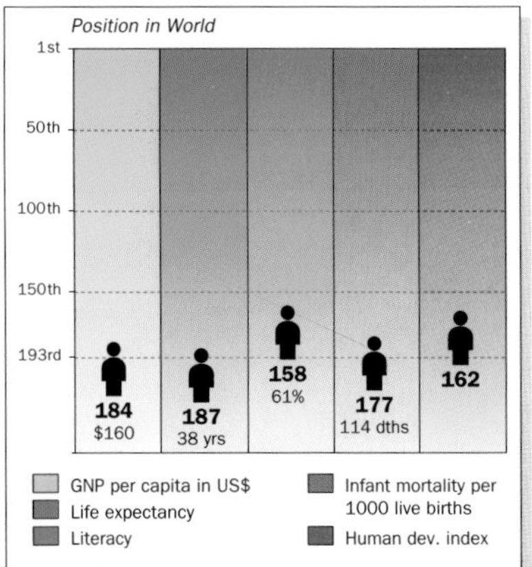
Position in World
1st
50th
100th
150th
193rd
184
$160
187
38 yrs
158
61%
177
114 dths
162
GNP per capita in US$
Life expectancy
Literacy
Infant mortality per 1000 live births
Human dev. index

M

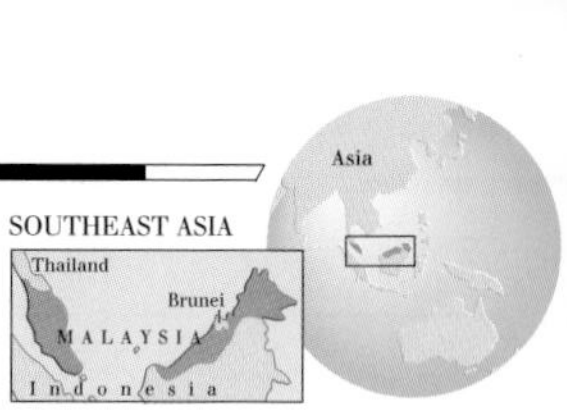
Asia
SOUTHEAST ASIA
Thailand
Brunei
MALAYSIA
Indonesia

MALAYSIA

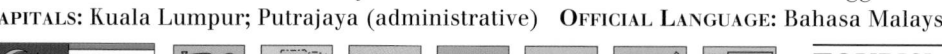

OFFICIAL NAME: Federation of Malaysia **POPULATION:** 23 million **CURRENCY:** Ringgit
CAPITALS: Kuala Lumpur; Putrajaya (administrative) **OFFICIAL LANGUAGE:** Bahasa Malaysia

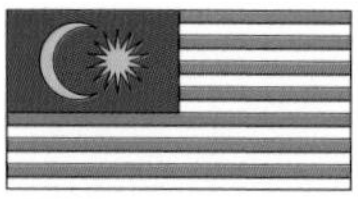

1963 | 1965 | Aug 31 | MAL | +8 | +60 | .my

MALAYSIA COMPRISES the three territories of Peninsular Malaysia, Sarawak, and Sabah, stretching over 2000 km (1240 miles) from the edge of the Indian Ocean to the northeastern end of the island of Borneo. A central mountain chain separates the coastal lowlands of Peninsular Malaysia; Sarawak and Sabah have swampy coastal plains rising to mountains on the border with Indonesia. Putrajaya, just south of Kuala Lumpur, is a high-tech new development intended as the home of government. The United Malays National Organization (UMNO) has dominated politics since independence.

CLIMATE

Tropical equatorial

WEATHER CHART FOR KUALA LUMPUR

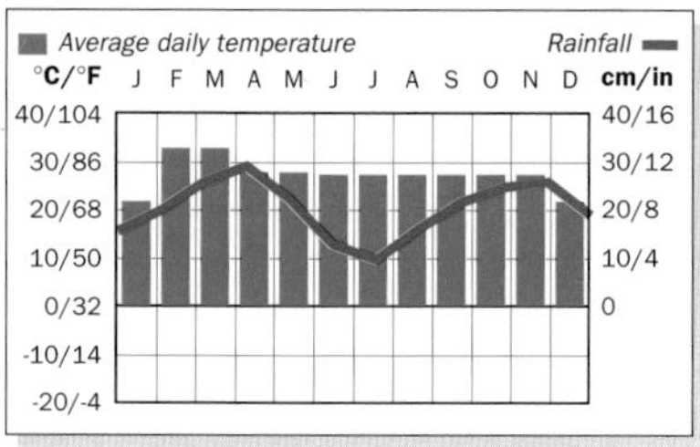
Average daily temperature
Rainfall
°C/°F
J F M A M J J A S O N D
cm/in
40/104
30/86
20/68
10/50
0/32
-10/14
-20/-4
40/16
30/12
20/8
10/4
0

The whole of Malaysia has an equatorial climate: very hot and very humid all year round. While there are two distinct rainy seasons, from March to May and from September to November, there is rain throughout the year: almost everywhere has rain on between 150 and 200 days a year. Coastal areas are also subject to monsoon winds, which alternate in direction between the southwest and northeast.

***Tea plantations** and colonial-style houses and gardens make Cameron Highlands, in Peninsular Malaysia, one of Asia's most popular mountain resorts.*

TRANSPORTATION

Drive on left

Subang International, Kuala Lumpur
16.4m passengers

882 ships
5.21m grt

THE TRANSPORTATION NETWORK

48,707 km (30,265 miles)	1192 km (741 miles)
1670 km (1038 miles)	7296 km (4534 miles)

Transportation in Peninsular Malaysia is well developed. A major north–south highway connects the urban centers of the west coast. Roads in Sabah are also good, with an efficient bus network linking the towns. Travel in Sarawak, on the other hand, is hindered by poorly maintained roads and a lack of public transportation. East Malaysia is most effectively traversed by air.

TOURISM

Visitors : Population 1:1.7

13.3m visitors

Up 4% in 2002

MAIN TOURIST ARRIVALS

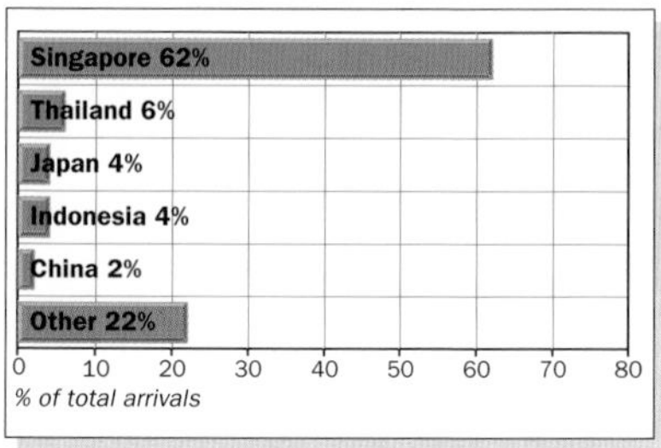
Singapore 62%
Thailand 6%
Japan 4%
Indonesia 4%
China 2%
Other 22%
0 10 20 30 40 50 60 70 80
% of total arrivals

Malaysia is southeast Asia's major tourist destination. Most tourists come for the excellent tropical beaches on the peninsula's east coast, to hike in the Cameron Highlands, or to trek in the world's oldest rainforests in Borneo. There has recently been an increase in the international business convention trade, and hotel capacity has been growing at 10% a year.

By 1990, when the government ran the Visit Malaysia Year campaign, tourism had become Malaysia's third-biggest foreign exchange earner. Two other such campaigns were launched in 1994 and 1998. However, the resurgence since 1999 of pro-Islamic parties, which favor stricter dress codes for women and a ban on alcohol, has deterred some Western tourists. In 2000 Malaysia backed an integrated tourism package with Thailand, Indonesia, and Singapore to enable tourists to visit the four countries under a common program.

MALAYSIA

Total Area : 329 750 sq. km (127 316 sq. miles)

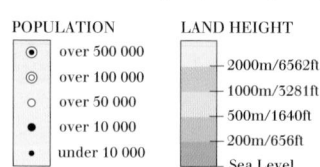

POPULATION	LAND HEIGHT
over 500 000	2000m/6562ft
over 100 000	1000m/3281ft
over 50 000	500m/1640ft
over 10 000	200m/656ft
under 10 000	Sea Level

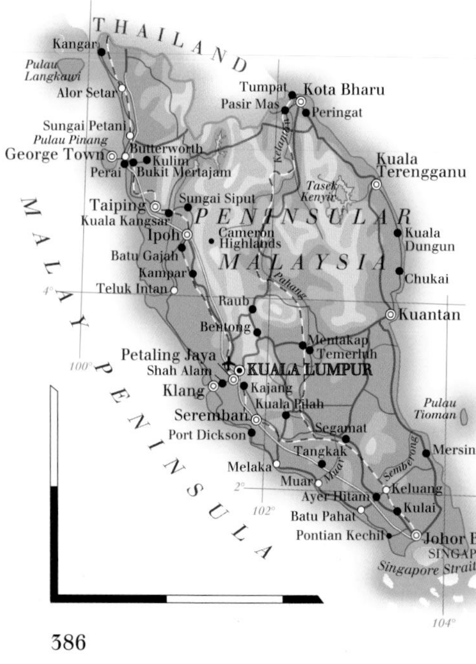
THAILAND
Kangar
Pulau Langkawi
Alor Setar
Tumpat
Kota Bharu
Pasir Mas
Peringat
Sungai Petani
Pulau Pinang
George Town
Butterworth
Kulim
Perai
Bukit Mertajam
Kuala Terengganu
Taiping
Sungai Siput
Tasek Kenyir
Kuala Kangsar
PENINSULAR MALAYSIA
Ipoh
Cameron Highlands
Kuala Dungun
Batu Gajah
Kampar
Chukai
Teluk Intan
Raub
Kuantan
Bentong
Mentakab
Temerluh
Petaling Jaya
Shah Alam
KUALA LUMPUR
Klang
Kajang
Kuala Pilah
Pulau Tioman
Seremban
Port Dickson
Segamat
Mersing
Melaka
Tangkak
Muar
Keluang
Ayer Hitam
Kulai
Batu Pahat
Pontian Kechil
Johor Bahru
SINGAPORE
Singapore Strait
MALAY PENINSULA

Kepulauan Anambas (INDONESIA)
Kepulauan Natuna (INDONESIA)
SOUTH CHINA SEA
Selat Serasan
Teluk Datu
Kuching
Bandar Sri Aman
Pulau Beruit
SARAWAK
Bintulu
Sibu
Rajang
Kepulauan Tambelan (INDONESIA)
INDON
EAST

PEOPLE

Pop. density medium

Bahasa Malaysia, Malay, Chinese, Tamil, English

70/km² (181/mi²)

THE URBAN/RURAL POPULATION SPLIT

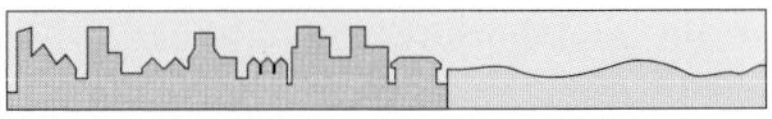
58%
42%

RELIGIOUS PERSUASION

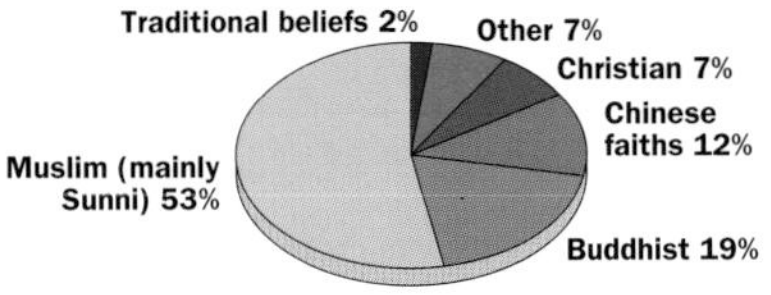
Traditional beliefs 2%
Other 7%
Christian 7%
Chinese faiths 12%
Muslim (mainly Sunni) 53%
Buddhist 19%

ETHNIC MAKEUP

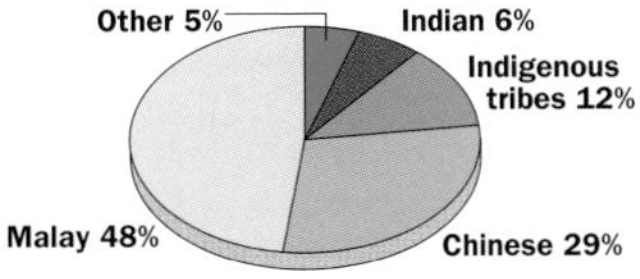
Other 5%
Indian 6%
Indigenous tribes 12%
Malay 48%
Chinese 29%

POPULATION AGE BREAKDOWN

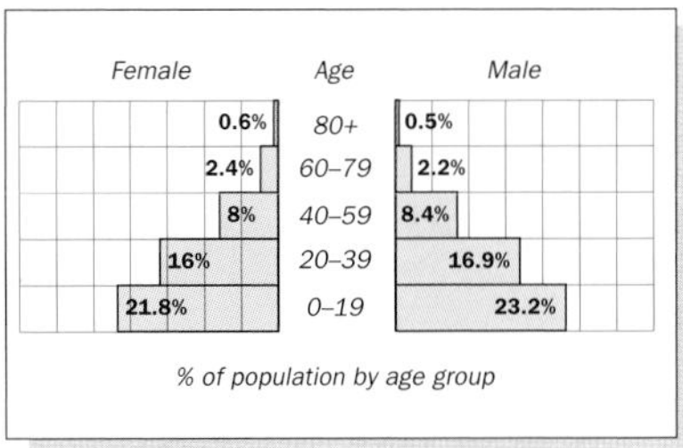
Female
Age
Male
0.6%
80+
0.5%
2.4%
60–79
2.2%
8%
40–59
8.4%
16%
20–39
16.9%
21.8%
0–19
23.2%
% of population by age group

The key distinction in Malaysian society is between the indigenous Malays, termed the Bumiputras ("sons of the soil"), and the Chinese. The Malays form the largest group, accounting for just under half of the population. However, the Chinese have traditionally controlled most business activity. The New Economic Policy (NEP), introduced in the 1970s, was designed to address this imbalance by offering positive opportunities to the Malays through the education system and by making jobs available to them in both the state and private sectors. There are estimated to be more than one million Indonesian and Filipino immigrants in Malaysia, a dearth of employment in their own countries giving additional attraction to Malaysia's need for labor. In addition, nearly 255,000 Vietnamese refugees were offered temporary refuge in Malaysia between 1975 and 1997; most have now been resettled in third countries, but several thousand remain. Gender discrimination was only outlawed in 2001. Muslim women are encouraged to wear a veil.

POLITICS

Multiparty elections

L. House 1999/2004
U. House varying

Raja Tuanku Syed Sirajuddin ibni al-Marhum Syed Putra Jamalullail

AT THE LAST ELECTION

House of Representatives 193 seats

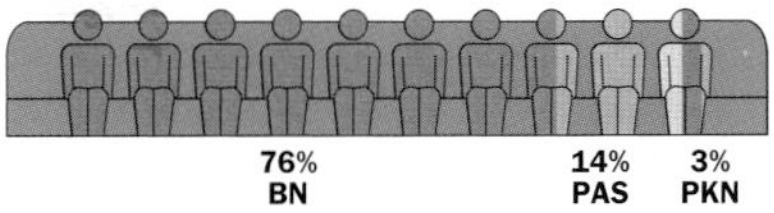
5% DAP
2% PBS
76% BN
14% PAS
3% PKN

BN = National Front (dominated by the United Malays National Organization – **UMNO**) **PAS** = Pan-Malaysian Islamic Party **DAP** = Democratic Action Party **PKN** = National Justice Party (Keadilan) **PBS** = Sabah United Party

The DAP, the PAS, and the PKN form the Alternative Front

Senate 69 seats

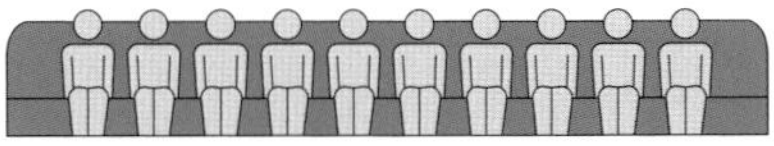

The Senate comprises 26 members indirectly elected by the State Legislative Assemblies, and 43 appointed by the head of state

Balabac Strait
Pulau Banggi
Kudat
SULU SEA
Gunung Kinabalu 4094m
Teluk Labuk
Kota Kinabalu
Labuk
Sandakan
Pulau Labuan
Sibutu Passage
Kinabatangan
Brunei Bay
SABAH
Banjaran Brassey
Telukan Lahad Datu
Tawau
CELEBES SEA
Borneo
116°
118°
4°
2°
N
0
100 km
0
100 miles

Supreme power rests in theory with the monarch, acting on the advice of parliament. In practice, the prime minister wields executive authority. Opposition parties, while legal, are under tight control.

Profile

Malaysia has been dominated by UMNO, part of the ruling BN coalition, since Malay independence in 1957. It controls a huge network of patronage. In 2002, Prime Minister Mahathir Mohamed shocked the country by tearfully announcing that he would retire in 2003, after 22 years at the helm. He had appeared unassailable, though his authority had been shaken by the economic crisis of 1997–1998 and dissent within the ruling coalition. In 1998, Anwar Ibrahim, deputy prime minister and once Mahathir's chosen successor, was dismissed after challenging the government's economic policy and calling for political reform. He was convicted in 1999 on corruption charges; his prison sentence was lengthened to 15 years in 2000 after his conviction for sodomy. The initial verdict sparked riots and gained support for the new opposition PKN headed by Anwar's wife, Wan Azizah. PKN activists have been hounded by the government. In the 1999 elections, the BN coalition retained its large majority but Mahathir's own UMNO lost ground.

***Anwar Ibrahim,** in 1998 controversially dismissed by Mahathir.*

***Mahathir Mohamed,** prime minister since 1981.*

Main Political Issue

Malay dominance of government

Mahathir's administration has declared that it no longer wishes to discriminate positively in favor of Malays, but the Chinese community accuses the government of corruption and uncompetitive practices, declaring that Malays are still favored for the placing of government contracts. The Chinese are further alienated by the more restrictive nature of Islamic society.

WORLD AFFAIRS

Joined UN in 1957

APEC | ASEAN | Comm | G15 | OIC

Mahathir sees himself as one of the developing world's leading voices. He maintains a strongly anti-US line in his public speeches and has chastised the West for singling out Islamic countries in its campaign against international terrorism. Mahathir's pro-Malay policies have caused tensions with Singapore, exacerbated by the latter's dependence on Malaysia for water.

AID

Recipient

$27m (receipts)

Down 40% in 2001

Most Western aid to Malaysia was used until recently to finance large infrastructure projects. The economic crisis which affected southeast Asia in 1997–1998 forced Malaysia to seek foreign assistance to support an economic recovery program.

M

CHRONOLOGY

The former British protectorate of Malaya gained independence in 1957. The federation of Malaysia, incorporating Singapore, Sarawak, and Sabah, was founded in 1963.

- ❑ **1965** Singapore leaves federation, reducing Malaysian states to 13.
- ❑ **1970** Malay–Chinese ethnic tension forces resignation of Prime Minister Tunku Abdul Rahman. New prime minister, Tun Abdul Razak, creates the BN coalition.
- ❑ **1976–1978** Guerrilla attacks by banned Communist Party of Malaya (CPM), based in southern Thailand.
- ❑ **1976** Death of Tun Abdul Razak.
- ❑ **1977** Unrest in Kelantan following expulsion of its chief minister from Pan-Malaysian Islamic Party (PAS). National emergency declared. PAS expelled from BN.
- ❑ **1978** Elections consolidate BN power. PAS marginalized. Government rejects plans for Chinese university.
- ❑ **1978–1989** Unrestricted asylum given to Vietnamese refugees.
- ❑ **1981** Mahathir Mohamed becomes prime minister.
- ❑ **1982** General election returns BN with increased majority.
- ❑ **1985** BN defeated by PBS in Sabah state elections.
- ❑ **1986** PBS joins BN coalition. Dispute between Mahathir and his deputy, Dakuk Musa, triggers general election, won by BN.
- ❑ **1987** Detention without trial of 106 politicians from all parties suspected of Chinese sympathies. Media censored.
- ❑ **1989** Disaffected UMNO members join PAS. Screening of Vietnamese refugees introduced. CPM signs peace agreement with Malaysian and Thai governments.
- ❑ **1990** General election. BN returned to power with reduced majority.
- ❑ **1993** Sultans lose powers, including legal immunity.
- ❑ **1995** BN wins landslide victory in the country's ninth general election.
- ❑ **1997** Major financial crisis ends decade of spectacular economic growth.
- ❑ **1998–1999** Deputy Prime Minister Anwar Ibrahim dismissed from office. Launches Reformasi (Reform) movement. Found guilty of corruption, later convicted of sodomy: 15-year sentence. His wife, Wan Azizah, forms National Justice Party (PKN).
- ❑ **1999** UMNO loses ground in general election.
- ❑ **2002** Mahathir announces that he will step down in 2003. Chinese university opened.

M

DEFENSE

No compulsory military service

$3.25bn

Up 26% in 2001

MALAYSIAN ARMED FORCES

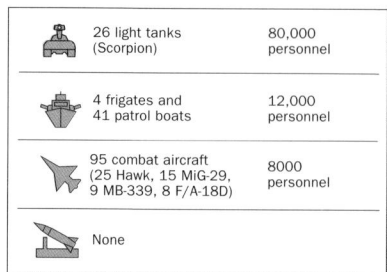

26 light tanks (Scorpion)	80,000 personnel
4 frigates and 41 patrol boats	12,000 personnel
95 combat aircraft (25 Hawk, 15 MiG-29, 9 MB-339, 8 F/A-18D)	8000 personnel
None	

Malaysia's armed forces are predominantly composed of Malays. Main defense concerns are Singapore, with its large and highly mechanized army, and more recently, though to a lesser extent, Indonesia. Also important to Malaysia is the growing Chinese influence in the South China Sea. Patrolling east and west Malaysia is a key function of the navy.

Malaysia is an important market for international arms suppliers and has purchased equipment from all over the world, including over 200 armored vehicles bought from Turkey in 2000.

ECONOMICS

Inflation 3.6% p.a. (1990–2001)

$79.3bn

3.8 ringgits (3.8)

SCORE CARD

- ❑ World GNP Ranking 42nd
- ❑ GNP per Capita $3330
- ❑ Balance of Payments....................$7.29bn
- ❑ Inflation 1.4%
- ❑ Unemployment 3%

EXPORTS

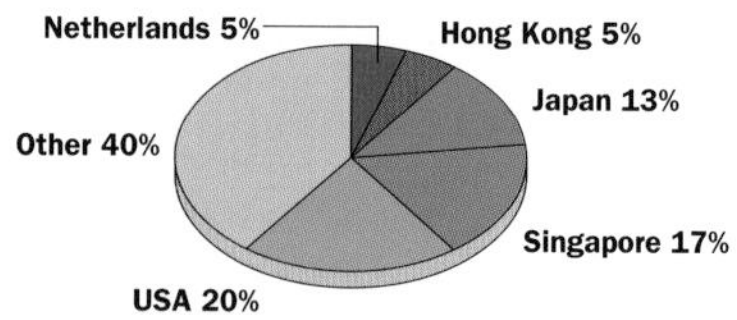

Netherlands 5%
Hong Kong 5%
Japan 13%
Other 40%
Singapore 17%
USA 20%

IMPORTS

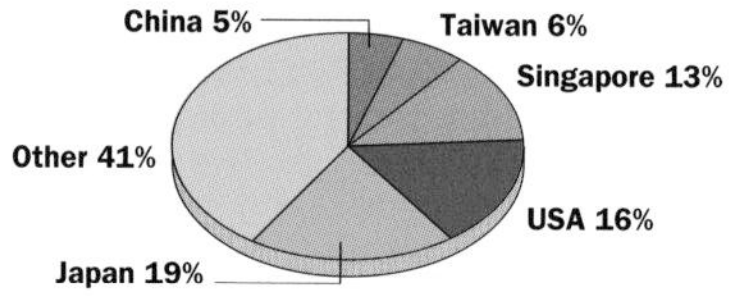

China 5%
Taiwan 6%
Singapore 13%
Other 41%
USA 16%
Japan 19%

Strengths

Electronics, computer hardware, and electrical appliances. Tourism. Heavy industries such as steel. Palm oil. Latex, rubber, chemical products. Success of "national car," the Proton. Ringgit pegged to US dollar.

ECONOMIC PERFORMANCE INDICATOR

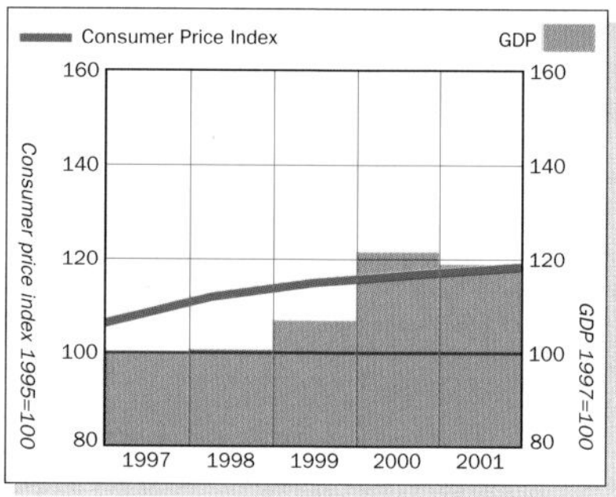

Consumer Price Index
GDP
160
140
120
100
80
1997
1998
1999
2000
2001
Consumer price index 1995=100
GDP 1997=100

Weaknesses

High level of debt. Shortage of skilled labor. High interest rates deter private investors. High government budget spending. Competition from NICs.

Profile

From 1987, for almost a decade, Malaysia expanded faster than any other southeast Asian nation, at an average yearly rate of 8%, with much of the growth state-directed. However, plans for full industrialization, named "Vision 2020," were revised after the 1997 financial crisis. The construction of Putrajaya provided a renewed stimulus to growth at the end of the 1990s. A project for a Multimedia Super Corridor (MSC), located south of Kuala Lumpur and aimed at attracting world-class companies, is expected to be completed in 2003.

MALAYSIA : MAJOR BUSINESSES

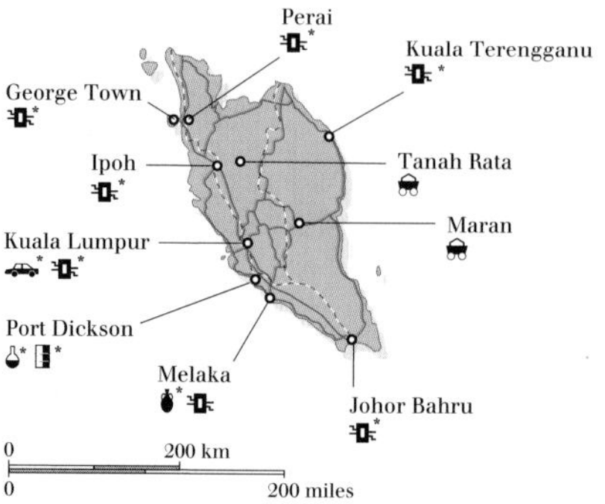

Perai
Kuala Terengganu
George Town
Ipoh
Tanah Rata
Maran
Kuala Lumpur
Port Dickson
Melaka
Johor Bahru
0
200 km
0
200 miles

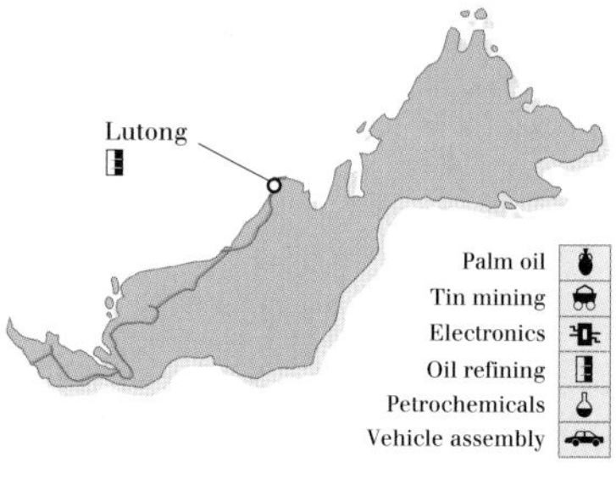

Lutong
Palm oil
Tin mining
Electronics
Oil refining
Petrochemicals
Vehicle assembly

* significant multinational ownership

RESOURCES

Electric power 12.7m kW

1.44m tonnes

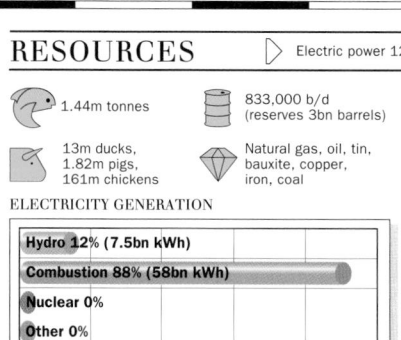

833,000 b/d (reserves 3bn barrels)

13m ducks, 1.82m pigs, 161m chickens

Natural gas, oil, tin, bauxite, copper, iron, coal

ELECTRICITY GENERATION

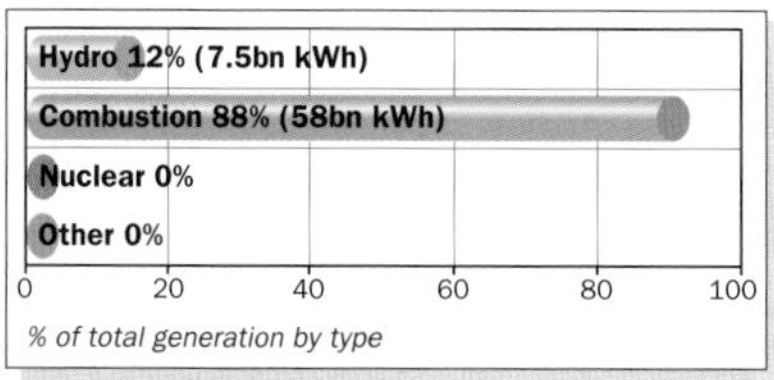
Hydro 12% (7.5bn kWh)
Combustion 88% (58bn kWh)
Nuclear 0%
Other 0%
0
20
40
60
80
100
% of total generation by type

Palm oil, of which Malaysia is the world's largest producer, and petroleum are the key resources. Chemical products from both are now the major resource-based export. Gas and petroleum reserves lie offshore from Sabah and Sarawak. The petroleum is high grade; most is exported, while crude imports are refined. Malaysia has the world's second-largest tin reserves, but low world prices hold back production. Timber, mostly from Sarawak, accounts for nearly half of world exports.

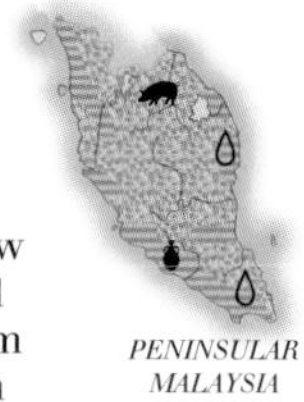
PENINSULAR MALAYSIA

MALAYSIA : LAND USE

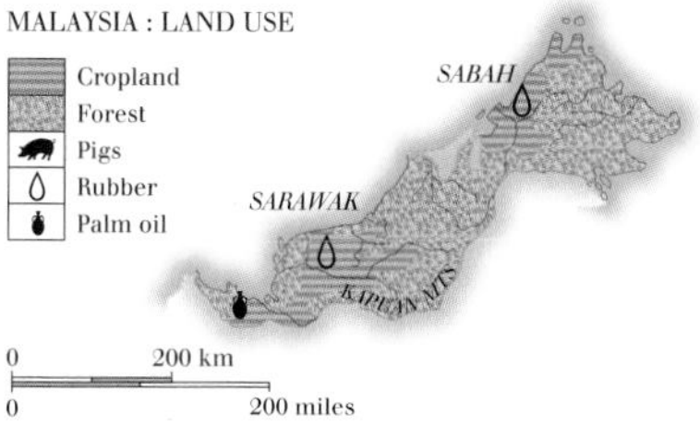
Cropland
Forest
Pigs
Rubber
Palm oil
SABAH
SARAWAK
KAPUAS MTS
0
200 km
0
200 miles

ENVIRONMENT

Sustainability rank: 68th

5% (2% partially protected)

5.5 tonnes per capita

ENVIRONMENTAL TREATIES

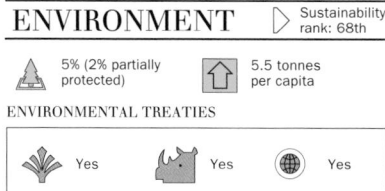

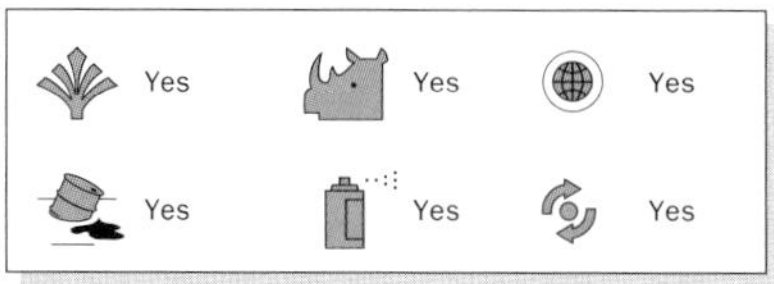
Yes
Yes
Yes
Yes
Yes
Yes

Logging is the overwhelming concern. Indigenous forest communities are being destroyed, and some species of tree are near extinction. The government launched a program in 1997 to plant 20 million trees by 2020. 100,000 were planted simultaneously to draw attention to the scheme in 2000.

Periodic forest fires in the region produce dramatic smog clouds covering whole countries. As well as damaging woodland, the smog poses very serious health problems.

Traditional lifestyles are threatened by grandiose modernization schemes. The Bakun Dam project, shelved in 1997 due to a lack of investment confidence, was restarted in 2000.

MEDIA

TV ownership medium

Daily newspaper circulation 112 per 1000 people

PUBLISHING AND BROADCAST MEDIA

There are 38 daily newspapers. The most influential are the *New Straits Times*, *Utusan Malaysia*, and *Sin Chew Jit Poh*

7 services: 3 state-controlled, 4 independent

6 services: 3 state-controlled, 3 independent

Almost all newspapers, TV stations, and radio broadcasts are strictly controlled by the state and UMNO, which claim a need to protect the country from un-Islamic influences. A series of laws passed in the 1980s regulate content. The Internet provides a medium for free reporting. One of the leading websites is Malaysiakini.

CRIME

Death penalty in use

27,299 prisoners

Up 21% in 1999–2002

CRIME RATES

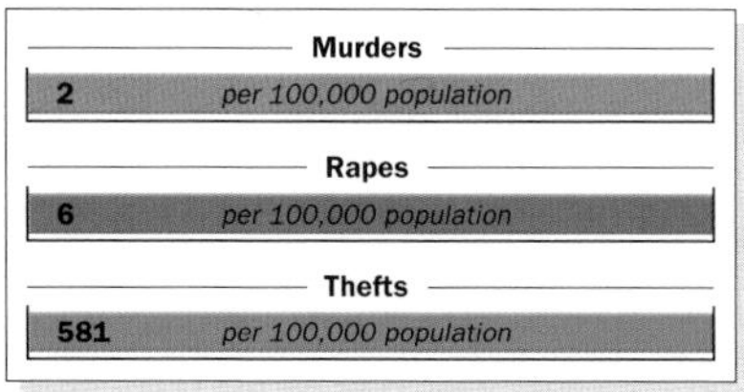
Murders
2 per 100,000 population
Rapes
6 per 100,000 population
Thefts
581 per 100,000 population

Migrants found working without the proper documentation can now be imprisoned or whipped. The death sentence for possession of narcotics is mandatory. The Internal Security Act allows detention without trial, and convictions cannot be challenged.

EDUCATION

School leaving age: 15

88%

549,205 students

THE EDUCATION SYSTEM

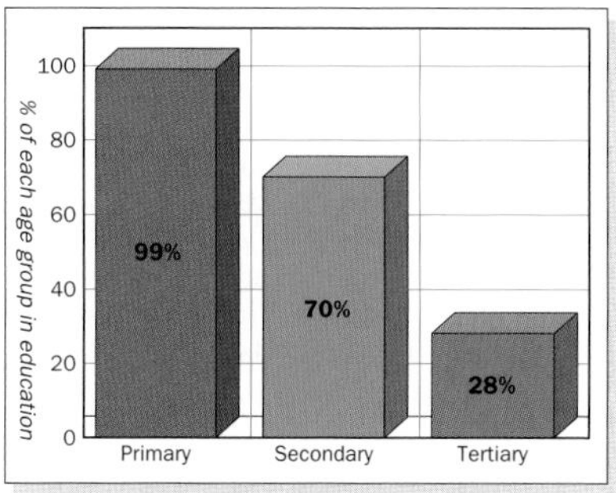
100
80
60
40
20
0
% of each age group in education
99%
70%
28%
Primary
Secondary
Tertiary

Racial integration in multiethnic schools is encouraged, but teaching is to remain in separate languages.

At tertiary level a quota system gives Malays preference for places. The Chinese community has its own schools, and plans for a private Chinese university were finally realized in 2002. Many students, particularly the Chinese, complete their studies in the UK or the US. From 2002, university students and staff have had to swear allegiance to the state.

HEALTH

Welfare state health benefits

1 per 1471 people

Heart diseases, cancers

There is growing disparity between the modern facilities available in cities and the traditional medicine practiced in rural and outlying areas. Traditional practices such as acupuncture and herbal medicine continue to be used by the Chinese community.

SPENDING

GDP/cap. increase

CONSUMPTION AND SPENDING

181 per 1000 population

196 per 1000 population

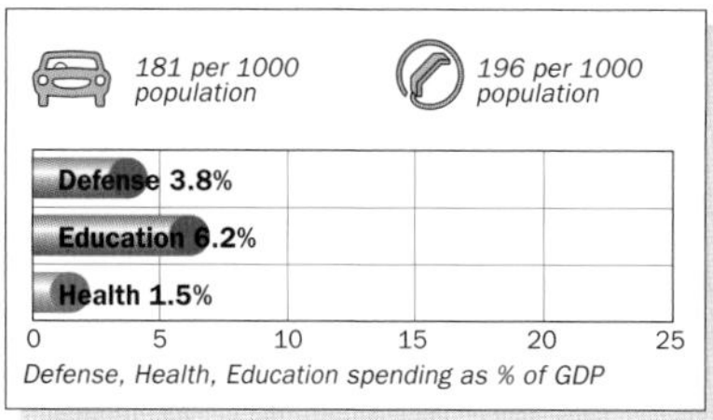
Defense 3.8%
Education 6.2%
Health 1.5%
0
5
10
15
20
25
Defense, Health, Education spending as % of GDP

The Chinese remain the wealthiest community in Malaysia. However, following riots in 1970, the UMNO government embarked on a deliberate program of achieving 30% Malay ownership of the corporate sector. The "extremely rich" were barred from government service in 2001 in an effort to stamp out "money politics."

WORLD RANKING

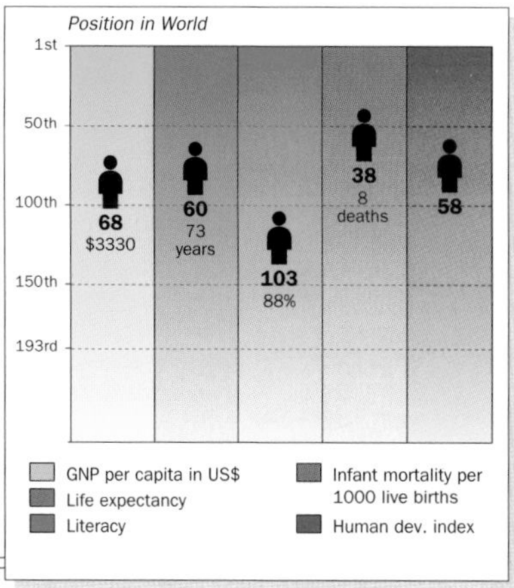
Position in World
1st
50th
100th
150th
193rd
68
$3330
60
73
years
103
88%
38
8
deaths
58
GNP per capita in US$
Life expectancy
Literacy
Infant mortality per 1000 live births
Human dev. index

M

MALDIVES

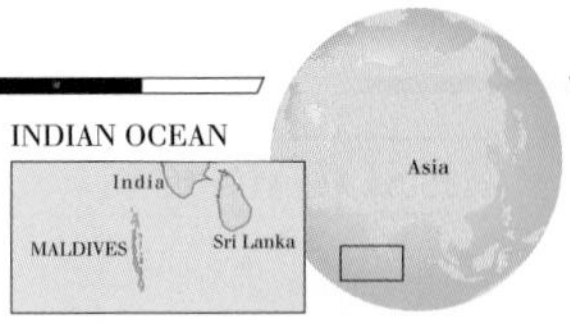

INDIAN OCEAN
India
Sri Lanka
MALDIVES
Asia

OFFICIAL NAME: Republic of Maldives **CAPITAL:** Male'
POPULATION: 309,000 **CURRENCY:** Rufiyaa **OFFICIAL LANGUAGE:** Dhivehi

1965 | 1965 | July 26 | MV | +5 | +960 | .mv

AN ISLAMIC SULTANATE until 1968, the Maldives is an archipelago of 1190 small coral islands or atolls (a word derived from the local Dhivehi language), set in the Indian Ocean southwest of India. The islands, none of which rise above 1.8 m (6 ft), are protected by encircling reefs or faros. Only 200 are inhabited. Tourism has grown in recent years, though vacation islands are separate from settled islands.

Traditional Maldivian trading yacht. *The 1190 coral islands are grouped in atolls, a word derived from the Dhivehi word "atolu."*

CLIMATE

Tropical oceanic

WEATHER CHART FOR MALE'

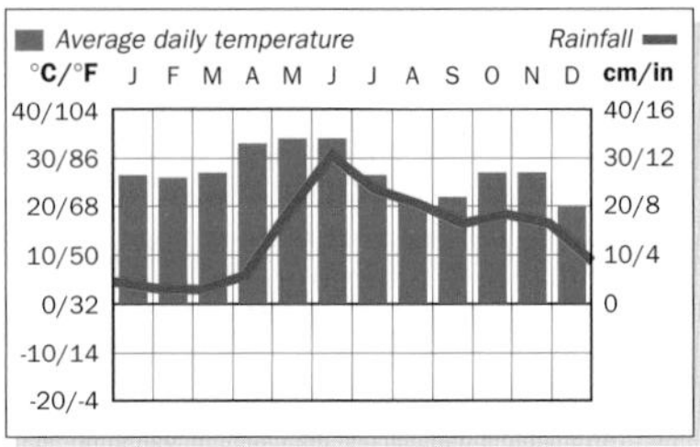

Average daily temperature
Rainfall
°C/°F
J F M A M J J A S O N D
cm/in
40/104
30/86
20/68
10/50
0/32
-10/14
-20/-4
40/16
30/12
20/8
10/4
0

The Maldives has a tropical climate, with abundant rainfall and high temperatures throughout the year. The northern islands are occasionally affected by violent storms caused by tropical cyclones. Most rain falls in the southern islands.

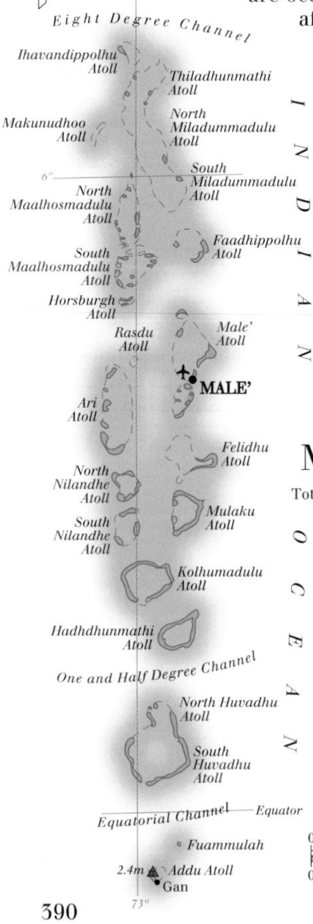

Eight Degree Channel
Ihavandippolhu Atoll
Thiladhunmathi Atoll
Makunudhoo Atoll
North Miladummadulu Atoll
South Miladummadulu Atoll
North Maalhosmadulu Atoll
Faadhippolhu Atoll
South Maalhosmadulu Atoll
Horsburgh Atoll
Rasdu Atoll
Male' Atoll
MALE'
Ari Atoll
Felidhu Atoll
North Nilandhe Atoll
Mulaku Atoll
South Nilandhe Atoll
Kolhumadulu Atoll
Hadhdhunmathi Atoll
One and Half Degree Channel
North Huvadhu Atoll
South Huvadhu Atoll
Equatorial Channel
Equator
Fuammulah
2.4m
Addu Atoll
Gan
INDIAN OCEAN

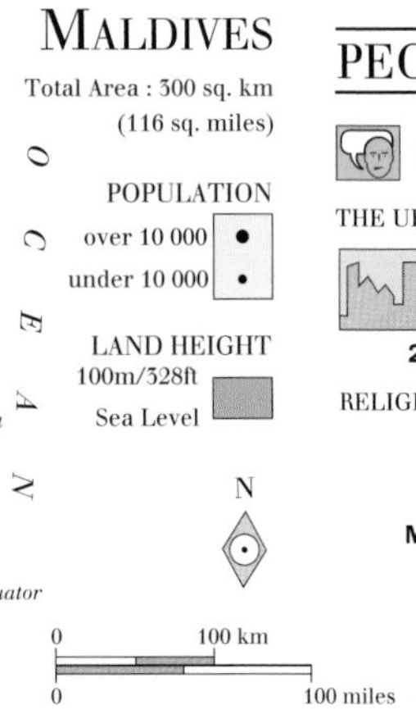

MALDIVES
Total Area : 300 sq. km (116 sq. miles)
POPULATION
over 10 000
under 10 000
LAND HEIGHT
100m/328ft
Sea Level
N
0
100 km
0
100 miles

TRANSPORTATION

Drive on left

Male' International, Hulule Island 1.82m passengers

68 ships 66,600 grt

THE TRANSPORTATION NETWORK

10 km (6 miles) | None
None | None

It is possible to walk across Male' island in 20 minutes. Interisland travel is mostly by ferry and traditional *dhoni*.

TOURISM

Visitors : Population 1.6:1

485,000 visitors

Up 5% in 2002

MAIN TOURIST ARRIVALS

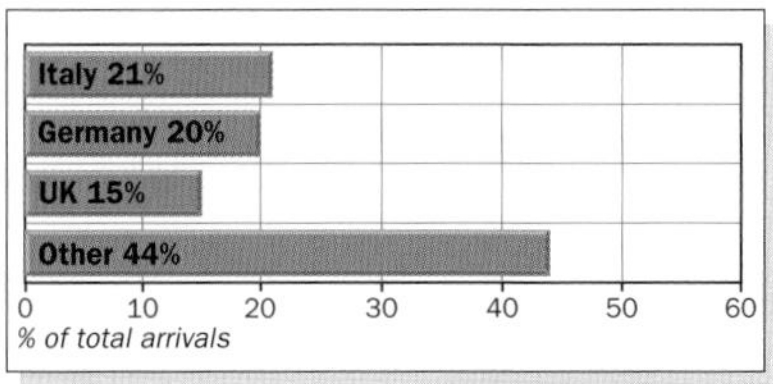

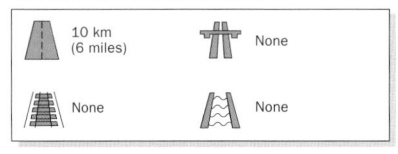

Italy 21%
Germany 20%
UK 15%
Other 44%
0
10
20
30
40
50
60
% of total arrivals

Tourism is the largest source of foreign exchange, accounting for almost 20% of GDP. The first resort was opened in 1972, and hotels financed by local and foreign capital have since been built on the uninhabited islands. There are now nearly half a million visitors a year.

POLITICS

Nonparty elections

1999/2004

President Maumoon Abdul Gayoom

AT THE LAST ELECTION

People's Assembly 50 seats

There are no political parties. 42 members of the Majlis (Assembly) are elected, and eight appointed by the president

Politics in the Maldives is the preserve of a small group of influential families. Most were already dominant under the sultanate. Formal parties with ideological objectives are virtually nonexistent, politics being organized around family and clan loyalties.

Former president Ibrahim Nasir abolished the premiership in 1975 and substantially strengthened the presidency. The main figure now is Maumoon Abdul Gayoom, a wealthy businessman who has been president since 1978. His brother-in-law, Ilyas Ibrahim, is regarded as his main rival.

A young Westernized elite has increased the pressure for political reform. Under a constitution effective since 1998, rival candidates may seek to be parliament's presidential nominee; only one name then goes forward for popular endorsement in a referendum.

PEOPLE

Pop. density high

Dhivehi (Maldivian)

1030/km² (2664/mi²)

THE URBAN/RURAL POPULATION SPLIT

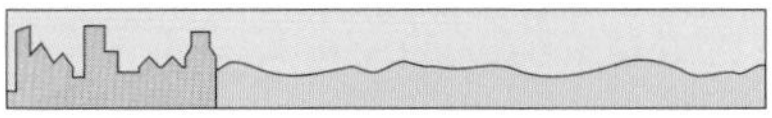

28%
72%

RELIGIOUS PERSUASION

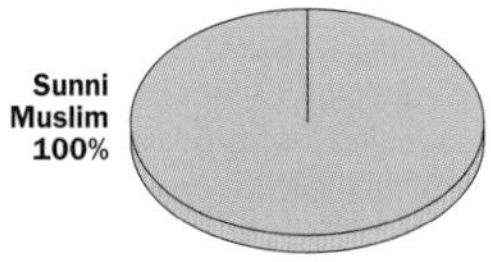

Sunni Muslim 100%

It is believed that the islands were inhabited as early as 1500 BCE. Aryan immigrants arrived around 500 BCE. The islands were then discovered by Arab traders. The people, who are all Sunni Muslims, live on only 200 of the 1190 islands. About 25% of the total population live on the island capital of Male'. It is estimated that 12,000 guest workers from neighboring Sri Lanka and India work in the Maldives. The country's newfound prosperity has seen the emergence of a commercial elite.

M

WORLD AFFAIRS

Joined UN in 1965

Comm | NAM | OIC | SAARC | WTO

The Maldives is a long-standing member of the Non-Aligned Movement. A strong Islamic lobby close to President Gayoom favors closer ties with other Muslim countries, particularly in the Middle East. The Maldives' international standing was enhanced in 1990, when it hosted the fifth SAARC summit meeting, held in Male'.

AID

Recipient

$25m (receipts) — Up 32% in 2001

Aid has helped to finance the development of port and airport facilities. Japan is the most important bilateral aid donor. The Maldives is classed by the UN as a Least Developed Country, which grants it access to special financial programs; it hopes to graduate from this listing.

DEFENSE

No compulsory military service

$36m — Up 3% in 2001

The British military presence ended in 1975, when troops were withdrawn from the staging post on Gan, in the Addu Atoll. The Maldives follows a policy of nonalignment, but in 1988 called on India for military assistance to help suppress a coup attempt.

ECONOMICS

Inflation 1.8% p.a. (1990–2000)

$562m — 12.8 rufiyaa (11.77)

SCORE CARD

- ❑ WORLD GNP RANKING........168th
- ❑ GNP PER CAPITA........$2000
- ❑ BALANCE OF PAYMENTS........–$53m
- ❑ INFLATION........0.6%
- ❑ UNEMPLOYMENT........1%

STRENGTHS

Boom in tourism. Thriving fishing industry, especially tuna. Shipping. Clothing. Coconut production. Economic reforms since 1989 have eased import restrictions and encouraged foreign investment.

WEAKNESSES

Too dependent on fluctuating tourist industry. Growing trade deficit. Skilled labor shortage. Small manufacturing base. Cottage industries employ 25% of workforce; little scope for expansion.

EXPORTS

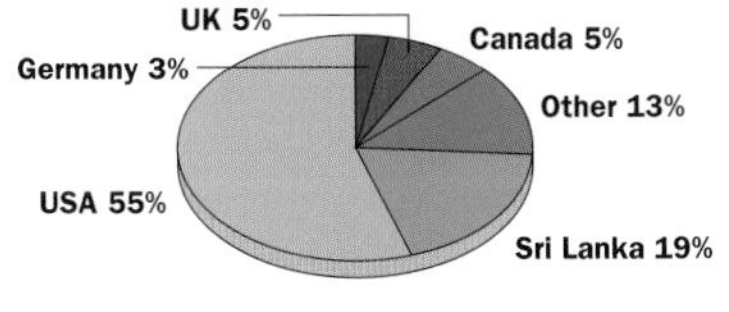
UK 5%
Canada 5%
Germany 3%
Other 13%
USA 55%
Sri Lanka 19%

IMPORTS

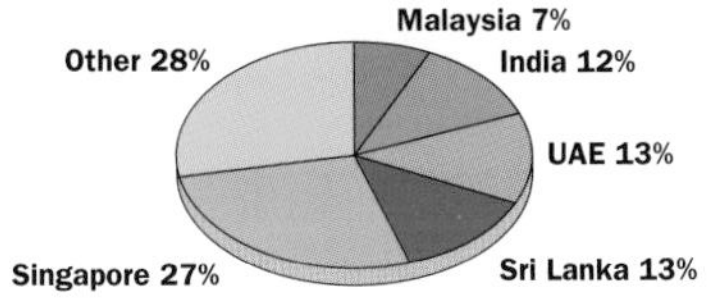
Malaysia 7%
Other 28%
India 12%
UAE 13%
Singapore 27%
Sri Lanka 13%

RESOURCES

Electric power 33,000 kW

132,427 tonnes — Not an oil producer

31,000 cattle, 20,000 goats, 11,000 sheep — None

Natural resources include abundant stocks of fish, particularly tuna. Fishing, still carried out by the traditional pole and line method to help conserve stocks, employs over 10% of the working population. Coconut production is also important. All oil products and virtually all staple foods are imported.

ENVIRONMENT

Not available

None — 1.6 tonnes per capita

Rising sea levels due to global warming and climate change threaten the islands, which have an average height of just 1.5 m (5 ft). A sea wall has been built around the capital island.

Other environmental concerns are sewerage, waste disposal, and the mining of coral for building.

MEDIA

TV ownership low

Daily newspaper circulation 19 per 1000 people

PUBLISHING AND BROADCAST MEDIA

There are 3 daily newspapers, including *Haveeru Daily* and *Aafathis Daily News*, published in Dhivehi and English

1 state-owned service — 3 services

There is a marked degree of press self-censorship; in the past, journalists have been imprisoned. An Internet café opened in Male' in 1998.

CRIME

Death penalty not used in practice

1098 prisoners — Up 34% in 1997

The Maldives is a strict Islamic society. Narcotics crimes are heavily punished. Political prisoners are banished to outer islands. The country was dropped from the OECD's tax haven list in 2002.

CHRONOLOGY

The Maldives was a British protectorate from 1887 and gained its independence in 1965.

- ❑ **1932** First written constitution.
- ❑ **1968** Sultanate abolished. Declared a republic. Ibrahim Nasir elected as first president.
- ❑ **1978** Gayoom becomes president.
- ❑ **1994** Nonparty legislative elections.
- ❑ **1998** New constitution; Gayoom reelected for fifth five-year term.

EDUCATION

School leaving age: 12

97% — Not available

Primary education has been improved. Secondary education is less developed in the outer islands; the first school outside Male' was opened in 1992.

HEALTH

Welfare state health benefits

1 per 2500 people — Infectious and parasitic diseases, tuberculosis, perinatal deaths

There is a lack of general equipment and facilities. Health care is less developed on the outlying islands.

SPENDING

GDP/cap. increase

CONSUMPTION AND SPENDING

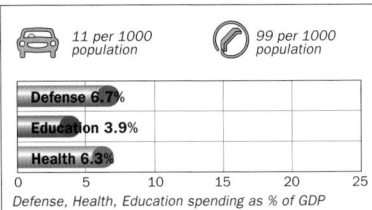

11 per 1000 population — *99 per 1000 population*

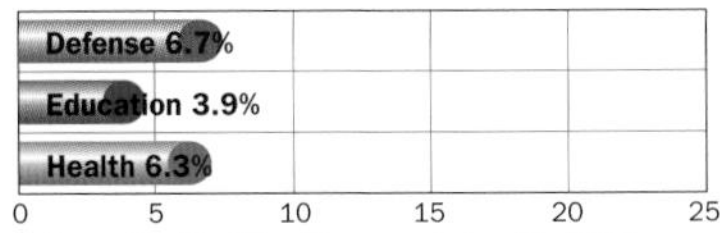
Defense 6.7%
Education 3.9%
Health 6.3%
0
5
10
15
20
25

Defense, Health, Education spending as % of GDP

Great disparities of wealth exist between the people who live in Male' and those who live on the more distant outer islands.

WORLD RANKING

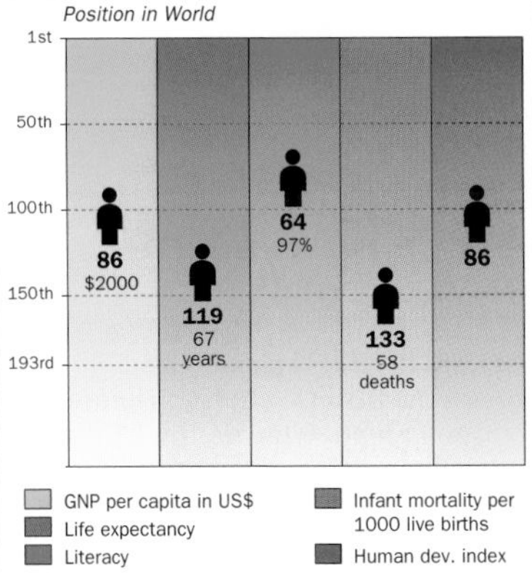
Position in World
1st
50th
100th
150th
193rd
86
$2000
119
67
years
64
97%
133
58
deaths
86
GNP per capita in US$
Life expectancy
Literacy
Infant mortality per 1000 live births
Human dev. index

M

MALI

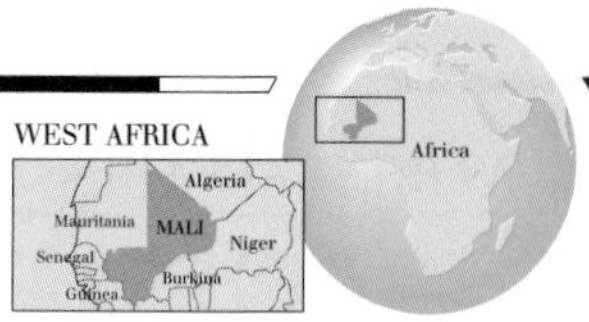
WEST AFRICA
Algeria
Mauritania
MALI
Niger
Senegal
Burkina
Guinea
Africa

OFFICIAL NAME: Republic of Mali **CAPITAL:** Bamako
POPULATION: 12 million **CURRENCY:** CFA franc **OFFICIAL LANGUAGE:** French

1960 | 1960 | Sept 22 | RMM | 0 | +223 | .ml

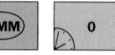

MALI IS LANDLOCKED in the heart of west Africa. Its mostly flat terrain comprises virtually uninhabited Saharan plains in the north and more fertile savanna land in the south, where most of the population live. The Niger River irrigates the central and southwestern regions. Mali achieved independence from France in 1960. Multiparty democratic elections under a new constitution, in 1992 and then in 1997, provoked accusations of severe irregularities.

CLIMATE

Hot desert/steppe

WEATHER CHART FOR BAMAKO

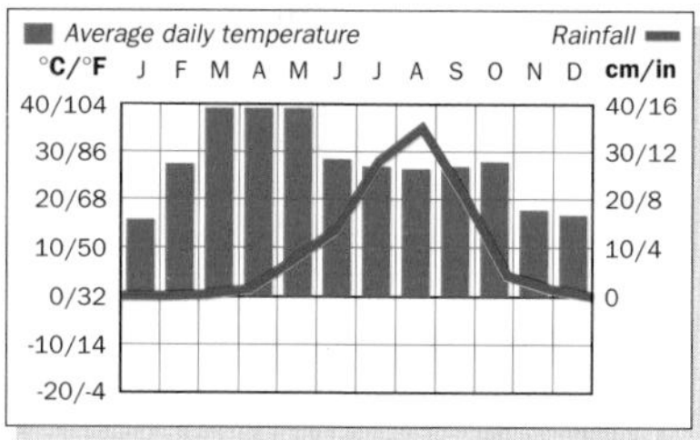
Average daily temperature
Rainfall
°C/°F
J F M A M J J A S O N D
cm/in
40/104
30/86
20/68
10/50
0/32
-10/14
-20/-4
40/16
30/12
20/8
10/4
0

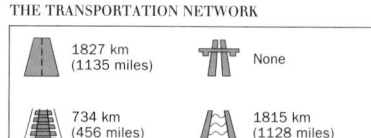

In the south, intensely hot, dry weather precedes the westerly rains. Mali's northern half is almost rainless.

TRANSPORTATION

Drive on right

Bamako–Senou
336,508 passengers

Has no fleet

THE TRANSPORTATION NETWORK

1827 km (1135 miles)	None
734 km (456 miles)	1815 km (1128 miles)

Mali is linked by rail with the port of Dakar in Senegal, and by good roads to the port of Abidjan in Ivory Coast.

TOURISM

Visitors : Population 1:135

89,000 visitors

Down 2% in 2001

MAIN TOURIST ARRIVALS

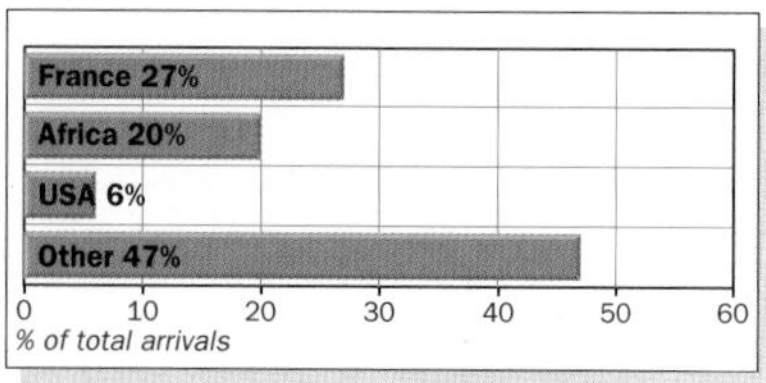
France 27%
Africa 20%
USA 6%
Other 47%
0
10
20
30
40
50
60
% of total arrivals

Tourism is largely safari-oriented, though the historic cities of Djénné, Gao, and Mopti, lying on the banks of the Niger River, also attract visitors. A national domestic airline began operating in 1990.

PEOPLE

Pop. density low

Bambara, Fulani, Senufo, Soninke, French

10/km² (25/mi²)

THE URBAN/RURAL POPULATION SPLIT

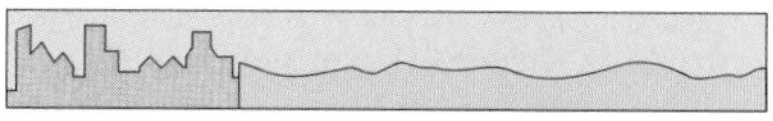
31%
69%

RELIGIOUS PERSUASION

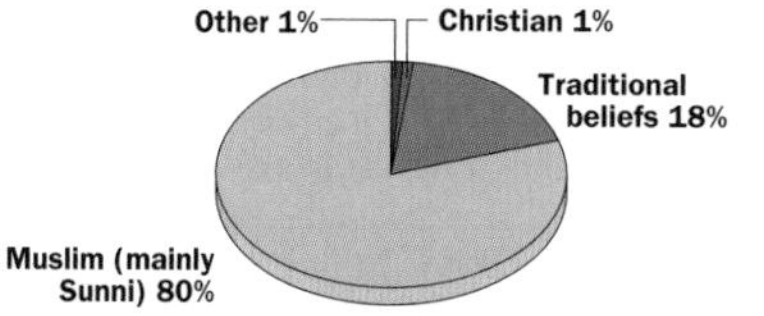
Other 1%
Christian 1%
Traditional beliefs 18%
Muslim (mainly Sunni) 80%

Mali's most significant ethnic group, the Bambara, is also politically dominant. The Bambara speak the lingua franca of the Niger River; other groups using it include the Malinke. The relationship between the Bambara–Malinke majority and the Tuareg nomads of the Saharan north is tense and sometimes violent. The extended family is a vital social security system and link between the urban and rural poor. Though there are a few powerful women in Mali, in general women have little status.

POLITICS

Multiparty elections

2002/2007

President Amadou Toumani Touré

AT THE LAST ELECTION

National Assembly 147 seats

5% Vacant
4% SADI
45% Espoir 2002
35% ARD
7% ACC
4% Ind

Espoir 2002 = Hope 2002 (led by the Rally for Mali – **RPM**)
ARD = Alliance for the Republic and Democracy (led by the Alliance for Democracy in Mali – **ADEMA**)
ACC = Convergence for Rotation and Change
Ind = Independents **SADI** = Party for African Solidarity, Democracy, and Integration

The successful transition to multiparty politics in 1992 followed the overthrow the previous year of Moussa Traoré, Mali's dictator for 23 years. The army's role was crucial in leading the coup, while Col. Amadou Toumani Touré, who acted as interim president, was responsible for the swift return to civilian rule in less than a year. For a decade the ADEMA government of President Alpha Oumar Konaré attempted to alleviate poverty while placating the opposition. However, its economic austerity measures eventually proved unpopular, and Touré was returned to power in the 2002 presidential elections. He was supported by all the main opposition parties, and in the legislative polls ADEMA saw its majority disappear.

Maintaining good relations with the Tuareg remains a key issue.

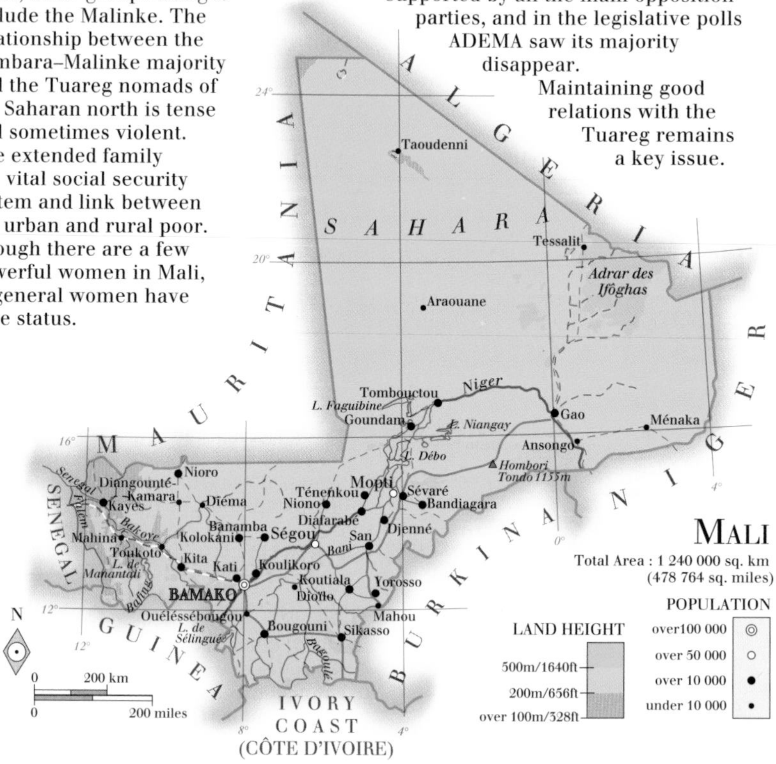
ALGERIA
MAURITANIA
SAHARA
NIGER
BURKINA
SENEGAL
GUINEA
IVORY COAST (CÔTE D'IVOIRE)
Taoudenni
Tessalit
Adrar des Ifôghas
Araouane
Tombouctou
Niger
L. Faguibine
Goundam
L. Niangay
Gao
Ménaka
Ansongo
L. Débo
Hombori Tondo 1155m
Nioro
Diangounté-Kamara
Kayes
Diéma
Ténenkou
Mopti
Sévaré
Bandiagara
Niono
Diafarabé
Djenné
Banamba
Ségou
San
Bani
Kolokani
Mahina
Toukoto
Kita
L. de Manantali
Bafing
Bakoye
Kati
Koulikoro
Koutiala
Diolla
Yorosso
BAMAKO
Ouéléssébougou
L. de Sélingué
Bougouni
Bagoé
Mahou
Sikasso
Falémé
24°
20°
16°
12°
4°
0°
8°
N
0 200 km
0 200 miles

MALI

Total Area : 1 240 000 sq. km (478 764 sq. miles)

LAND HEIGHT
500m/1640ft
200m/656ft
over 100m/328ft

POPULATION
over 100 000
over 50 000
over 10 000
under 10 000

WORLD AFFAIRS

Joined UN in 1960

ECOWAS | FZ | AU | OIC | OIF

Apart from a brief war with Burkina in 1985, Mali has been on relatively peaceful terms with its neighbors. It concentrates on maintaining good relations with ECOWAS and northern neighbors such as Algeria. Relations with Libya, which is suspected of fomenting Tuareg revolt, are tense.

AID

Recipient

$350m (receipts) — Down 3% in 2001

Mali is highly dependent on foreign aid, which principally comes from the World Bank, France, the US, Germany, the Netherlands, Japan, and the EU.

DEFENSE

Compulsory military service

$63m — Down 2% in 2001

Mali's 7800-strong armed forces have stayed out of politics since the overthrow of President Traoré in 1991.

ECONOMICS

Inflation 6.9% p.a. (1990–2001)

$2.51bn — 571.2 CFA francs (664.2)

SCORE CARD

- ❑ WORLD GNP RANKING........134th
- ❑ GNP PER CAPITA........$230
- ❑ BALANCE OF PAYMENTS........–$178m
- ❑ INFLATION........5.2%
- ❑ UNEMPLOYMENT........Widespread underemployment

STRENGTHS

Producer of high-quality cotton. Irrigation potential from the Niger and Senegal Rivers. Expansion of gold production.

WEAKNESSES

Serious poverty and underdevelopment. Overdependence on cotton: falling world prices. Communications difficulties of vast landlocked country. Drought-prone climate.

EXPORTS

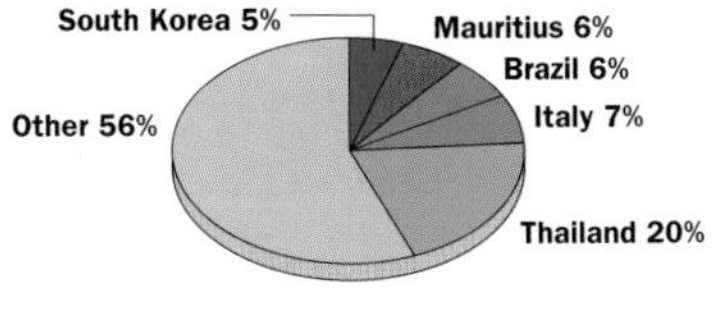
South Korea 5%
Mauritius 6%
Brazil 6%
Italy 7%
Other 56%
Thailand 20%

IMPORTS

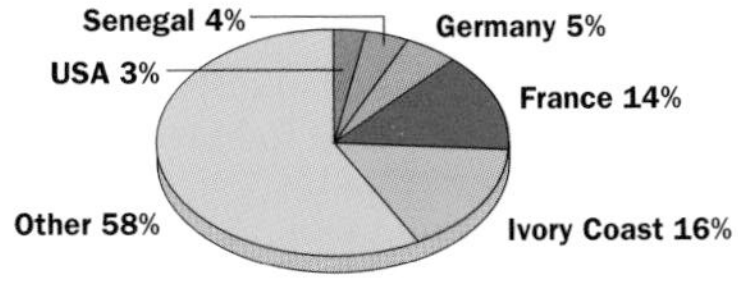
Senegal 4%
Germany 5%
USA 3%
France 14%
Other 58%
Ivory Coast 16%

Village near Bandiagara. The low, broken hills typical of the east and southeast of Mali are the homeland of the Dogon people.

RESOURCES

Electric power 114,000 kW

- 109,900 tonnes
- Oil reserves not yet exploited
- 8.85m goats, 6.82m cattle, 6.15m sheep, 25.5m chickens
- Gold, salt, marble, phosphates, tungsten, diamonds, oil

Gold deposits are now being mined, and prospecting is under way for tungsten, diamonds, and oil. Exploitation of natural resources is hampered by Mali's poor infrastructure and landlocked situation. Electric power comes from the Selingue Dam on the Niger and the Manantali Dam on the Senegal. The latter produced its first electricity in 2001 – 13 years after it was completed.

ENVIRONMENT

Sustainability rank: 85th

4% (3% partially protected) — 0.04 tonnes per capita

Severe drought in 1983 destroyed herds and accelerated desertification and deforestation. The Selingue Dam seriously affects the levels of the Niger, even in years of good rainfall.

MEDIA

TV ownership low

Daily newspaper circulation 1 per 1000 people

PUBLISHING AND BROADCAST MEDIA

There are 5 daily newspapers, including the progovernment *L'Essor – La Voix du Peuple*

3 services: 1 state-owned, 2 independent — 1 state-owned service, about 100 private stations

Even before the 1991 coup, previously rigid controls were being relaxed. The 1992 constitution guarantees the freedom of the press, and Mali's broadcast and print media are now among the freest in Africa.

CRIME

Death penalty not used in practice

4040 prisoners — Crime is rising slowly

Crime is not particularly prevalent compared with some other countries in the region, owing at least in part to the relative lack of urbanization. In towns, robbery, juvenile delinquency, and smuggling are problems.

CHRONOLOGY

Mali was a major trans-Saharan trading empire. The French colonized the area between 1881 and 1895.

- ❑ **1960** Independence.
- ❑ **1968** Coup by Gen. Moussa Traoré.
- ❑ **1990** Prodemocracy demonstrations.
- ❑ **1991** Traoré arrested.
- ❑ **1992** Free multiparty elections.
- ❑ **1997** President Konaré and ADEMA party reelected in disputed polls.
- ❑ **2002** Elections: Col. Touré president; ADEMA loses majority.

EDUCATION

School leaving age: 15

26% — 18,662 students

Just over half of children go to primary school and only 15% to secondary school. A ten-year program to raise education levels for girls was launched in 2001.

HEALTH

No welfare state health benefits

1 per 20,000 people — Malaria, pneumonia, parasitic and diarrheal diseases

A health program began in 1998, with the aim of higher immunization rates for children and more health care access.

SPENDING

GDP/cap. increase

CONSUMPTION AND SPENDING

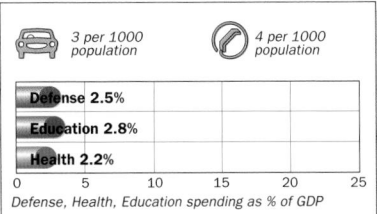

3 per 1000 population — *4 per 1000 population*

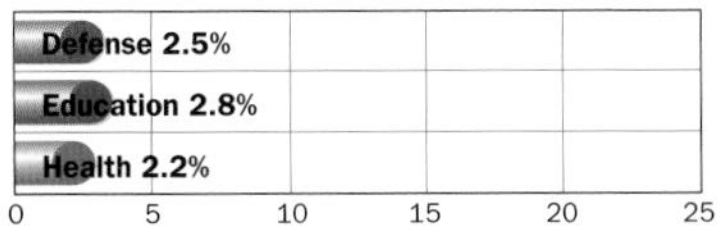
Defense 2.5%
Education 2.8%
Health 2.2%
0
5
10
15
20
25

Defense, Health, Education spending as % of GDP

Poverty is widespread, and wealth is limited to a very small group. Malians disapprove of flaunted wealth and public ostentation is rare.

WORLD RANKING

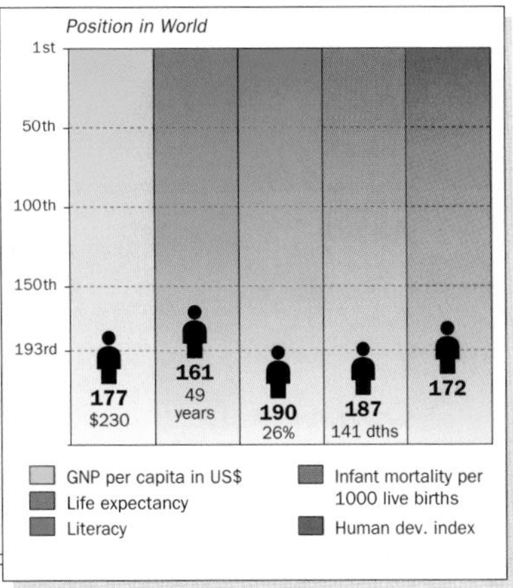
Position in World
1st
50th
100th
150th
193rd
177
$230
161
49 years
190
26%
187
141 dths
172
GNP per capita in US$
Life expectancy
Literacy
Infant mortality per 1000 live births
Human dev. index

M

MALTA

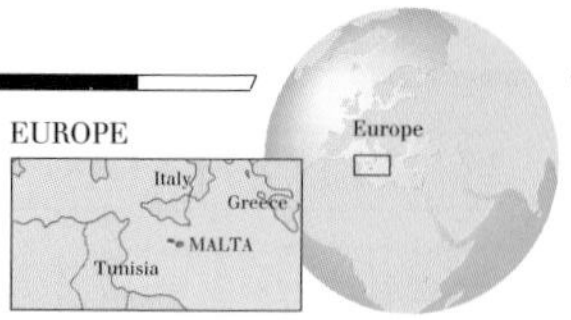
EUROPE
Europe
Italy
Greece
MALTA
Tunisia

OFFICIAL NAME: Republic of Malta **CAPITAL:** Valletta
POPULATION: 393,000 **CURRENCY:** Maltese lira **OFFICIAL LANGUAGES:** Maltese and English

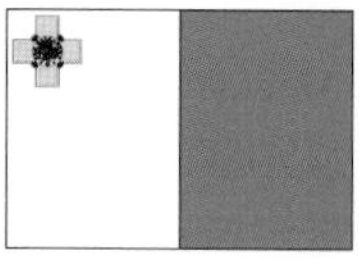

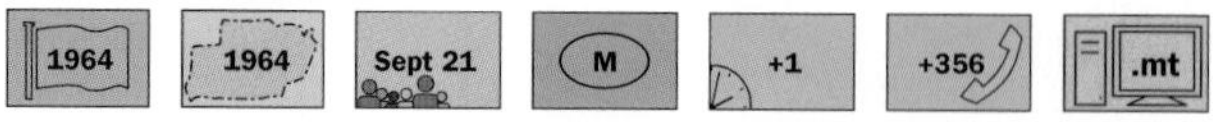
1964
1964
Sept 21
M
+1
+356
.mt

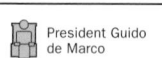

THE MALTESE ARCHIPELAGO is strategically located, lying between Europe and north Africa. Controlled throughout its history by successive colonial powers, Malta finally gained independence from the UK in 1964. The islands are mainly low-lying, with rocky coastlines; only Malta, Gozo (Ghawdex), and Kemmuna are inhabited. Tourism is Malta's chief source of income, with an influx of tourists each year of over three times the islands' population.

CLIMATE

Mediterranean

WEATHER CHART FOR VALLETTA

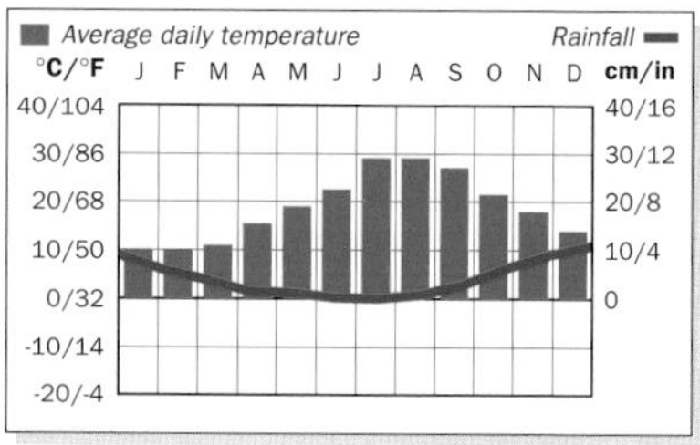
Average daily temperature
Rainfall
°C/°F J F M A M J J A S O N D cm/in
40/104
30/86
20/68
10/50
0/32
-10/14
-20/-4
40/16
30/12
20/8
10/4
0

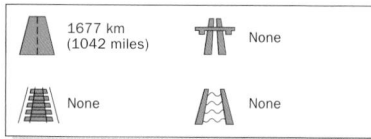

The climate is typical of the southern Mediterranean – with at least six hours of sunshine a day, even in winter.

TRANSPORTATION

Drive on left

Luqa International, Valletta
2.62m passengers

1421 ships
27.1m grt

THE TRANSPORTATION NETWORK

1677 km (1042 miles)

None

None

None

Malta Freeport at Marsaxlokk exploits Malta's strategic shipping location in the Mediterranean. In summer, a five-minute helicopter flight from the international airport links the islands of Malta and Gozo. There is a well-developed public transportation system, with ferry and hovercraft services and buses on both islands.

***Traditionally painted* luzzus** *in St. Julian's harbor. The fish caught are now only for domestic and tourist consumption.*

TOURISM

Visitors : Population 3.1:1

1.22m visitors

No change in 2000

MAIN TOURIST ARRIVALS

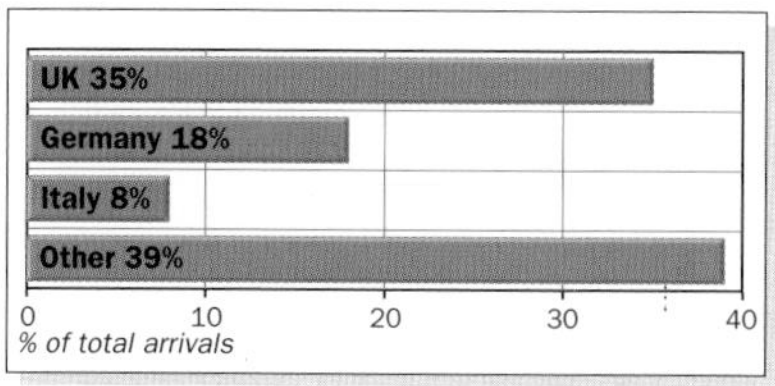
UK 35%
Germany 18%
Italy 8%
Other 39%
0
10
20
30
40
% of total arrivals

Tourism is vital to the economy and accounts for more than 30% of GDP, even though most visitors are budget vacationers. In addition to beaches and scenery, there are the historical attractions of Mdina and Valletta. Development on the quieter island of Gozo is limited to luxury-grade hotels.

PEOPLE

Pop. density high

Maltese, English

1228/km² (3169/mi²)

THE URBAN/RURAL POPULATION SPLIT

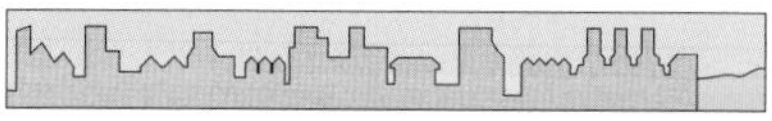
91%
9%

RELIGIOUS PERSUASION

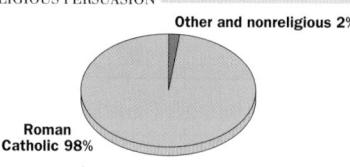

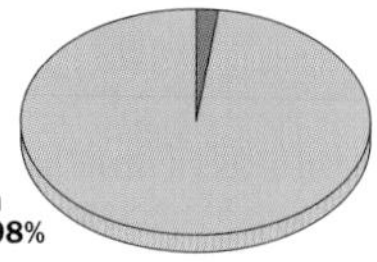
Other and nonreligious 2%
Roman Catholic 98%

Malta's population has been subject over the centuries to diverse Arabic, Sicilian, Norman, Spanish, British, and Italian influences. Today, much of the younger Maltese population goes abroad to find work, especially to the US or Australia; opportunities for them on the islands are few.

The Maltese are staunch Roman Catholics, on a percentage basis more so than virtually any other nation. The remainder are mainly Anglicans, who are included within the diocese of Gibraltar. Divorce is not allowed.

POLITICS

Multiparty elections

2003/2008

President Guido de Marco

AT THE LAST ELECTION

House of Representatives 65 seats

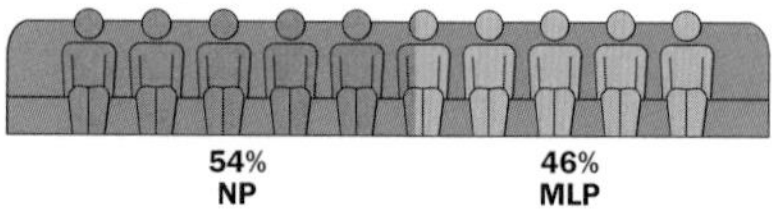
54% NP
46% MLP

NP = Nationalist Party **MLP** = Malta Labour Party

Maltese politics is strongly adversarial and evenly split between the right-wing NP and the left-wing MLP. The latter was in power during the 1970s and most of the 1980s, ensuring state control of industry and pursuing a nonaligned foreign policy.

The late 1980s and 1990s saw a switch to the NP. Prime Minister Edward Fenech Adami's government moved toward ever closer ties with Europe, and favored a free-market approach to the economy. The NP secured reelection in 1992, largely as a result of a rise in living standards. A modernized MLP ended the NP's nine-year reign in 1996. Under Alfred Sant, a leading writer and Harvard MBA, it weakened traditional links with the unions and stalled Malta's EU application. However, the MLP's small parliamentary majority undermined the government, and the NP won early elections in 1998. Fenech Adami has since secured Malta's membership of the EU, and his party was reelected in 2003.

WORLD AFFAIRS

Joined UN in 1964

CE | Comm | IBRD | NAM | OSCE

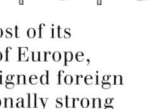

Malta has made the most of its location on the fringe of Europe, with a staunchly nonaligned foreign policy. Ties are traditionally strong with the Arab world and north Africa, and relations with Libya remain good. There are also close commercial links with Russia and China.

However, it is the island's relationship with Europe that has dominated recent policy. Malta's formal application for EU membership, made in 1990, was derailed by the anti-EU MLP government in 1996. With the application frozen, Malta was initially denied a place in the "first wave" of potential EU members. However, the return to power of the pro-EU NP in 1998 restarted the bid, and Malta's accession to the union is now scheduled for 2004.

M

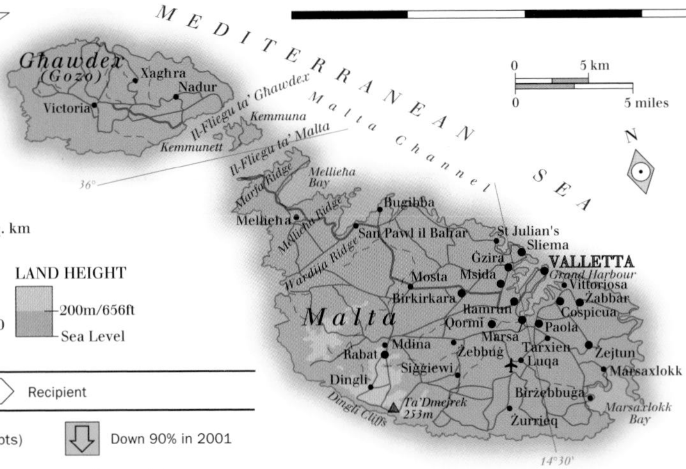
MEDITERRANEAN SEA
Ghawdex (Gozo)
Xaghra
Nadur
Victoria
Il-Fliegu ta' Ghawdex
Kemmuna
Kemmunett
Il-Fliegu ta' Malta
Malta Channel
0 5 km
0 5 miles
N
Mellieha Bay
Marfa Ridge
Mellieha
Mellieha Ridge
Bugibba
San Pawl il Bahar
St Julian's
Sliema
Gzira
VALLETTA
Grand Harbour
Vittoriosa
Wardija Ridge
Mosta
Msida
Birkirkara
Zabbar
Hamrun
Cospicua
Malta
Qormi
Paola
Mdina
Marsa
Rabat
Zebbug
Tarxien
Zejtun
Siggiewi
Luqa
Marsaxlokk
Dingli
Birzebbuga
Dingli Cliffs
Ta'Dmejrek 253m
Zurrieq
Marsaxlokk Bay
36°
14°30'

MALTA

Total Area : 316 sq. km
(122 sq. miles)

POPULATION	LAND HEIGHT
● over 10 000	200m/656ft
• under 10 000	Sea Level

AID

Recipient

$2m (receipts) — Down 90% in 2001

Malta receives economic assistance under an agreement with the EU. Italy is the main bilateral source of aid.

DEFENSE

No compulsory military service

$24m — Down 11% in 2001

The Maltese army, advised by the Libyans in the 1980s, now receives training and equipment from Italy, Germany, and the UK.

ECONOMICS

Inflation 2.8% p.a. (1990–2001)

$3.64bn — 0.372 Maltese liri (0.4225)

SCORE CARD

- ❑ WORLD GNP RANKING........................124th
- ❑ GNP PER CAPITA $9210
- ❑ BALANCE OF PAYMENTS...................–$172m
- ❑ INFLATION 2.9%
- ❑ UNEMPLOYMENT 5%

STRENGTHS

Tourism and naval dockyards. Schemes to attract foreign high-tech industry. Malta Freeport container distribution center. Offshore banking. Strategic position between Europe and Africa, on main Mediterranean shipping lines.

WEAKNESSES

Cut-rate competition from Africa and Asia in traditional textile industry. Almost all material needs imported.

EXPORTS

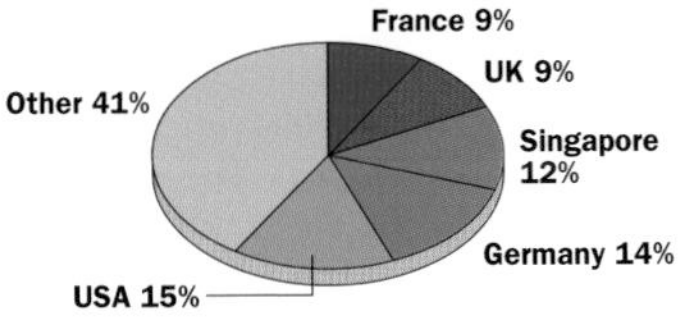
France 9%
UK 9%
Other 41%
Singapore 12%
Germany 14%
USA 15%

IMPORTS

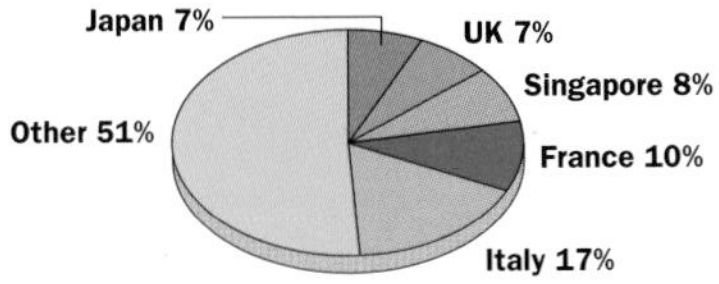
Japan 7%
UK 7%
Singapore 8%
Other 51%
France 10%
Italy 17%

RESOURCES

Electric power 570,000 kW

2785 tonnes — Reserves under exploration

79,303 pigs, 18,000 cattle, 1m chickens — Stone, sand, oil

Malta is dependent on desalination plants for most of its water supply. All oil has to be imported, mostly from Libya. However, there are petroleum reserves currently under exploration in Maltese waters.

ENVIRONMENT

Not available

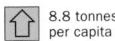

0.6% partially protected — 8.8 tonnes per capita

The main environmental concern is linked to the tourist industry. A lack of planning controls in the 1970s was responsible for unsightly beach developments. These are now tightly controlled, particularly on Gozo.

MEDIA

TV ownership high

Daily newspaper circulation 127 per 1000 people

PUBLISHING AND BROADCAST MEDIA

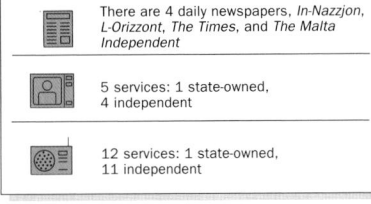

There are 4 daily newspapers, *In-Nazzjon*, *L-Orizzont*, *The Times*, and *The Malta Independent*

5 services: 1 state-owned, 4 independent

12 services: 1 state-owned, 11 independent

The Maltese press is largely party politically oriented. Two of the three main press groups are affiliated to the NP or MLP; one is independent.

CRIME

No death penalty

257 prisoners — Up 89% in 1997–2000

Crime rates are low compared with those on the European mainland. There has been an increase in narcotics transshipment and associated crimes.

CHRONOLOGY

Malta has been dominated by a host of rulers: Phoenicians, Greeks, Romans, Arabs, Norman Sicily, Spain, France, and, finally, the UK.

- ❑ **1964** Full independence from UK.
- ❑ **1971–1987** Dom Mintoff and MLP government push nonaligned status.
- ❑ **1987–1996** Ruling NP in EU talks.
- ❑ **1998** NP and Prime Minister Edward Fenech Adami reelected after brief MLP interlude.
- ❑ **2003** Future EU accession approved in referendum. NP reelected.

EDUCATION

School leaving age: 16

92% — 6315 students

One-third of pupils attend non-state schools, including heavily subsidized church-run institutions. There is a state university in Valletta.

HEALTH

Welfare state health benefits

1 per 380 people — Heart diseases, cancers, cerebrovascular and pulmonary diseases

Malta has five state-run and a couple of private hospitals. Diabetes is prevalent, as on other Mediterranean islands.

SPENDING

GDP/cap. increase

CONSUMPTION AND SPENDING

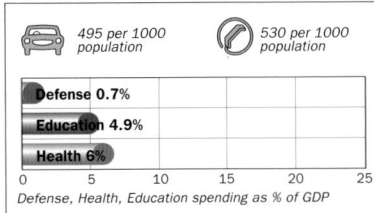

495 per 1000 population — *530 per 1000 population*

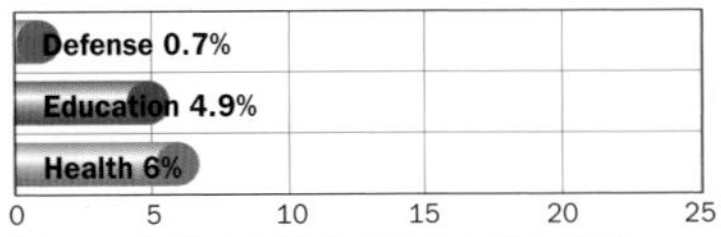
Defense 0.7%
Education 4.9%
Health 6%
0
5
10
15
20
25

Defense, Health, Education spending as % of GDP

Remittances from Maltese working abroad are an important source of income for many island families.

WORLD RANKING

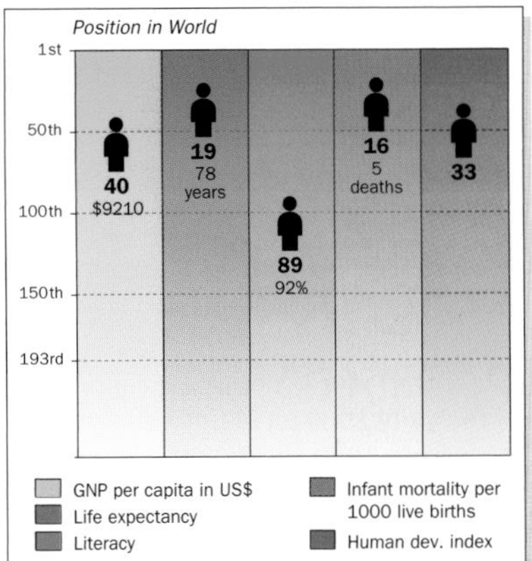
Position in World
1st
50th
100th
150th
193rd
40
$9210
19
78 years
89
92%
16
5 deaths
33
GNP per capita in US$
Life expectancy
Literacy
Infant mortality per 1000 live births
Human dev. index

M

MARSHALL ISLANDS

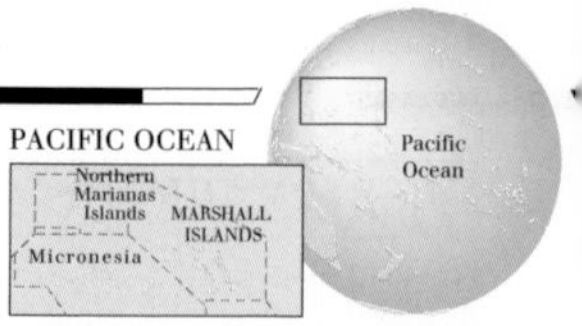
PACIFIC OCEAN
Northern Marianas Islands
MARSHALL ISLANDS
Micronesia
Pacific Ocean

OFFICIAL NAME: Republic of the Marshall Islands **CAPITAL:** Majuro
POPULATION: 73,630 **CURRENCY:** US dollar **OFFICIAL LANGUAGES:** English and Marshallese

1986 | 1986 | May 1 | MH | +12 | +692 | .mh

THE MARSHALL ISLANDS comprises a group of 34 widely scattered atolls in the central Pacific Ocean, formerly under US rule as part of the UN Trust Territory of the Pacific Islands. An agreement which granted internal sovereignty in free association with the US became operational in 1986, and the Trust was formally dissolved in 1990. The economy is almost entirely dependent on US aid and rent for the US missile base on Kwajalein Atoll.

Ebeye District on Kwajalein Atoll. *Population pressures on the island have led to the disappearance of most tree and grass cover.*

CLIMATE

Tropical oceanic

WEATHER CHART FOR MAJURO

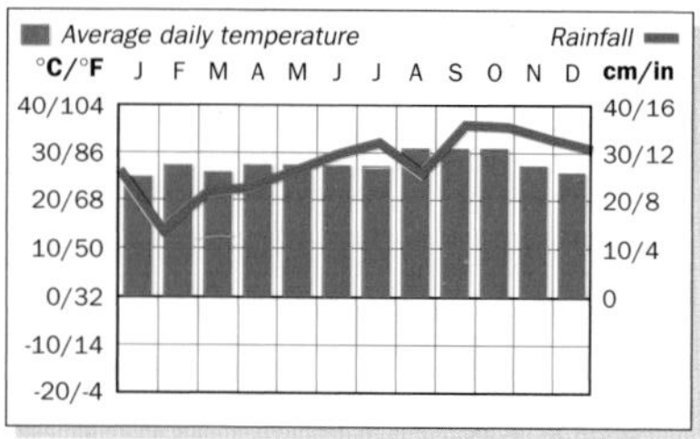
Average daily temperature
Rainfall
°C/°F
J F M A M J J A S O N D
cm/in
40/104
30/86
20/68
10/50
0/32
-10/14
-20/-4
40/16
30/12
20/8
10/4
0

The climate is tropical oceanic with little seasonal variation; temperatures average just under 30°C (86°F).

TRANSPORTATION

Drive on right

Majuro International

360 ships 11.7m grt

THE TRANSPORTATION NETWORK

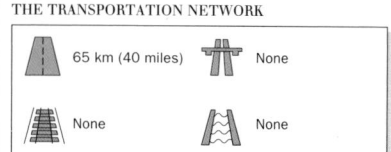

65 km (40 miles) | None
None | None

The transportation system is limited, though there is some interisland shipping. State carrier Air Marshalls has experienced economic difficulties.

TOURISM

Visitors : Population 1:15

5000 visitors

No change in 2000

MAIN TOURIST ARRIVALS

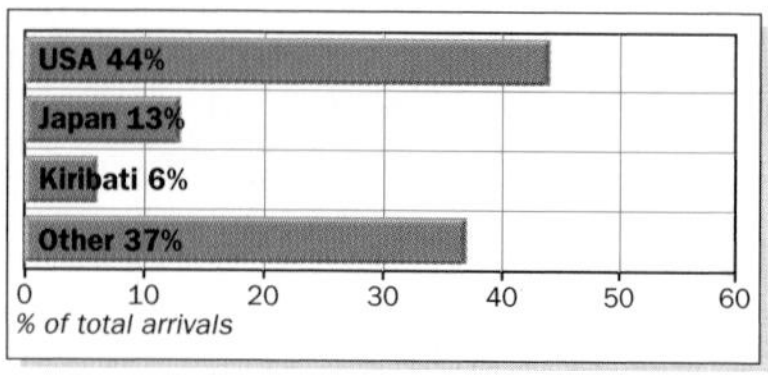
USA 44%
Japan 13%
Kiribati 6%
Other 37%
0
10
20
30
40
50
60
% of total arrivals

In the late 1990s major resort complexes were established on Majuro and on Mili Atoll. Attractions include diving, game fishing, and exploring the sites and relics of World War II battles.

PEOPLE

Pop. density high

Marshallese, English, Japanese, German

407/km² (1052/mi²)

THE URBAN/RURAL POPULATION SPLIT

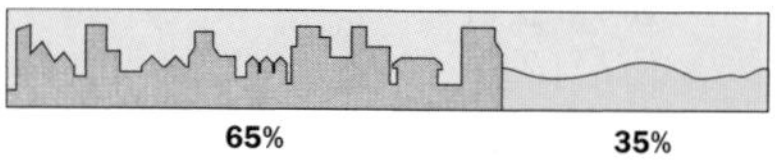
65%
35%

ETHNIC MAKEUP

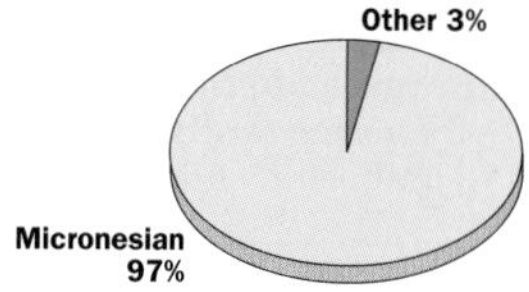
Other 3%
Micronesian 97%

Of the 34 atolls making up the Marshall Islands, 24 are inhabited. Majuro, the capital and commercial center, is home to almost half of the population, many of whom live in its overcrowded slums. The other main center of population is Ebeye Island in the Kwajalein Atoll, where tensions are high due to poor living conditions. Most of Kwajalein Atoll's inhabitants were forcibly relocated to Ebeye in 1947 to make way for a US missile tracking, testing, and interception base; many still travel daily to work at the base. Life on the outlying islands is still centered on subsistence agriculture and fishing. Society is traditionally matrilineal.

POLITICS

Multiparty elections

L. House 1999/2003

President Kessai Note

AT THE LAST ELECTION

Parliament 33 seats

55% UDP
45% K

UDP = United Democratic Party **K** = Pro-Kabua Grouping
The 33 members are elected from 25 districts

Council of Chiefs 12 seats

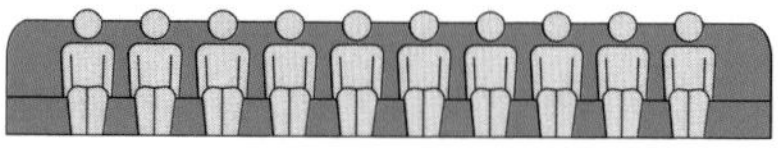

All 12 members are high chiefs

Politics is traditionally dominated by chiefs. Amata Kabua, the islands' high chief and first president until his death in 1996, was succeeded in early 1997 by his cousin Imata Kabua. However, the 1999 elections were won by the United Democratic Party, whose presidential candidate, commoner and former parliamentary speaker Kessai Note, was elected in early January 2000. Just over a year later Imata Kabua initiated an unsuccessful vote of no confidence in Note's administration – only the second in the islands' history. The vote was motivated by criticism of the government's approach to the crucial renegotiation of the Compact of Free Association with the US. The original treaty, which provided most of the islands' revenue and defense, expired in 2001; a new 20-year treaty was signed in 2003.

MARSHALL ISLANDS

Total Area : 181 sq. km (70 sq. miles)

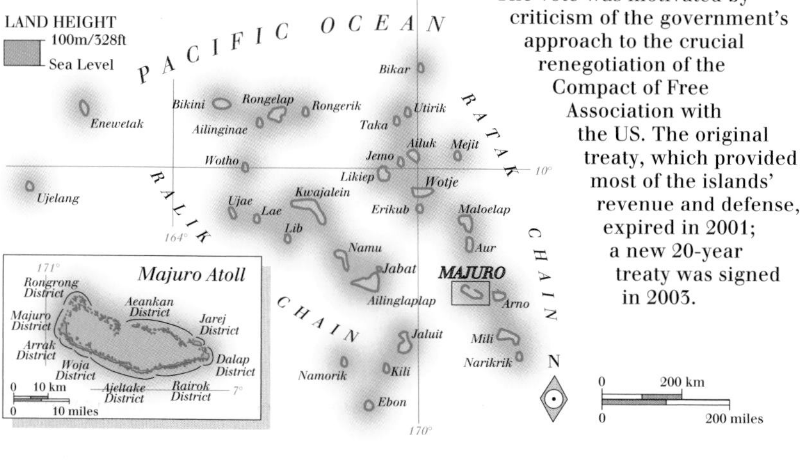
LAND HEIGHT
100m/328ft
Sea Level
PACIFIC OCEAN
Bokak
Bikar
Bikini
Rongelap
Rongerik
Utirik
Enewetak
Ailinginae
Taka
Ailuk
Mejit
Wotho
Jemo
Likiep
Wotje
Ujelang
Kwajalein
Ujae
Lae
Erikub
Maloelap
Lib
Aur
Namu
Jabat
MAJURO
Ailinglaplap
Arno
Jaluit
Mili
Narikrik
Namorik
Kili
Ebon
RATAK CHAIN
RALIK CHAIN
10°
164°
170°
N
0
200 km
200 miles
Majuro Atoll
171°
Rongrong District
Majuro District
Aeankan District
Jarej District
Arrak District
Woja District
Dalap District
Ajeltake District
Rairok District
7°
10 km
10 miles

WORLD AFFAIRS

Joined UN in 1991

IAEA | PIF | ACP | PC | ADB

The Compact of Free Association has made ties to the US of central importance. From 1986 the US provided $1 billion in return for the use of Kwajalein Atoll as a missile range and has determined the islands' foreign and defense policies. A new Compact was signed in 2003. Taiwan has become a source of funding for development, provoking controversy on the issue of diplomatic recognition.

AID

Recipient

$74m (receipts)

Up 30% in 2001

US aid accounts for 60% of revenue. A trust fund was created under the 2003 Compact to provide aid after 2023.

DEFENSE

No compulsory military service

US is responsible for defense

Not applicable

There is no defense force; all defense is provided by the US under the Compact of Free Association. The US does not have offensive weapons sited in the Marshalls, but its navy patrols regularly.

ECONOMICS

Inflation 5.3% p.a. (1990–2001)

$115m

Currency is US dollar

SCORE CARD

❑ WORLD GNP RANKING	188th
❑ GNP PER CAPITA	$2190
❑ BALANCE OF PAYMENTS	$21m
❑ INFLATION	2%
❑ UNEMPLOYMENT	31%

STRENGTHS

US guarantee against economic collapse to preserve strategic influence. Aid from the US, on which islands almost totally depend. Huge tourism potential.

WEAKNESSES

High unemployment. Dependence on imports, which are twice as large as exports. All fuel has to be imported. Vulnerability to storms. Large state sector. Drop in world copra trade.

EXPORTS

The Marshall Islands' main export partners are the US, Australia, and Japan.

IMPORTS

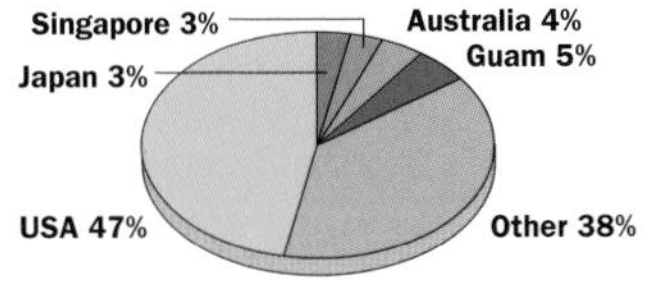
Singapore 3%
Australia 4%
Japan 3%
Guam 5%
USA 47%
Other 38%

RESOURCES

Not available

7960 tonnes

Not an oil producer

Not available

Phosphates

There are few known strategic resources. Exploratory tests have revealed some high-grade phosphate deposits, but not in economically viable quantities. Small diesel generators are used for electricity production.

ENVIRONMENT

Not available

None

Not available

Between 1946 and 1958, Bikini, Enewetak, and neighboring atolls were rendered uninhabitable by a series of US nuclear military tests. Enewetak residents were allowed to return in 1980, and Rongelap was declared habitable in 2001. A 1999 tribunal adopted stringent standards for further decontamination. The US has now paid out over $101 million to victims of nuclear testing. Nuclear waste imports were banned in 1999. The effects of rising sea levels are a major concern. Erosion affects beaches and soil is being lost and also contaminated by brackish water.

MEDIA

TV ownership low

There are no daily newspapers

PUBLISHING AND BROADCAST MEDIA

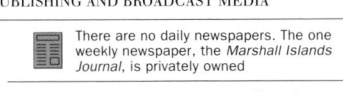

There are no daily newspapers. The one weekly newspaper, the *Marshall Islands Journal*, is privately owned

2 independent services

2 services: 1 state-owned, 1 independent

Radio is the major source of information in the Marshalls. The main TV service is subscription-only. The US personnel stationed on Kwajalein have their own TV and radio stations.

CRIME

No death penalty

23 prisoners

Crime levels are rising slightly

Crime levels are generally low; however, the rate is up in Ebeye. Outlying islands are crime-free.

EDUCATION

School leaving age: 14

91%

251 students

Education, compulsory between the ages of six and 14 years, is based on the US model. The number of secondary school graduates exceeds the availability of suitable employment in the Marshall Islands. Many go on to university in the US.

CHRONOLOGY

After a period under Spanish rule, the Marshall Islands became a German protectorate in 1885; Japan took possession at the start of World War I. The islands were transferred to US control in 1945.

- ❑ **1946** US nuclear testing begins.
- ❑ **1947** UN Trust Territory of the Pacific Islands established.
- ❑ **1961** Kwajalein becomes US army missile range.
- ❑ **1979** Constitution approved in referendum. Government set up.
- ❑ **1986** Compact of Free Association with US operational.
- ❑ **1990** Trust terminated by UN.
- ❑ **1997** President Amata Kabua dies: succeeded by his cousin, Imata.
- ❑ **2000** Kessai Note president after opposition election victory.
- ❑ **2003** New Compact agreed.

HEALTH

No welfare state health benefits

1 per 2381 people

Respiratory, heart, and diarrheal diseases

Medical facilities are rudimentary. Complex operations are performed in Hawaii. Levels of malnutrition and vitamin A deficiency are high.

SPENDING

Not available

CONSUMPTION AND SPENDING

No data

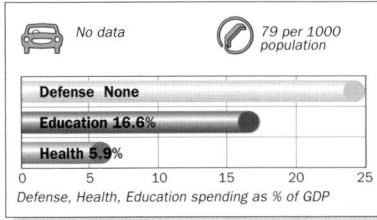

79 per 1000 population

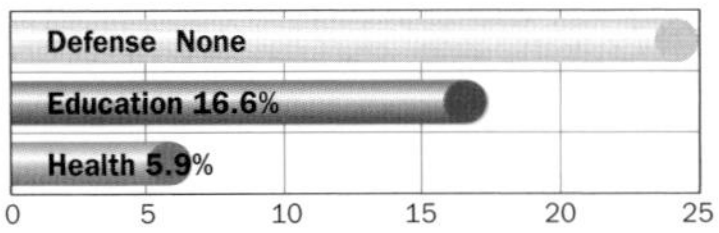
Defense None
Education 16.6%
Health 5.9%
0
5
10
15
20
25

Defense, Health, Education spending as % of GDP

Wealth disparities are small. Very few citizens can afford luxuries such as air conditioning and cars.

WORLD RANKING

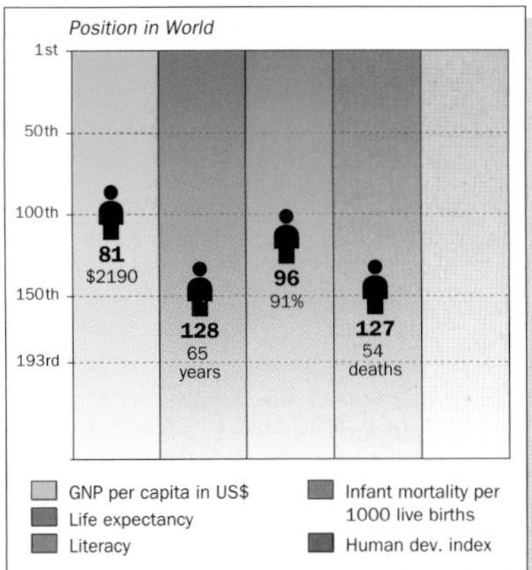
Position in World
1st
50th
100th
150th
193rd
81
$2190
128
65 years
96
91%
127
54 deaths
GNP per capita in US$
Life expectancy
Literacy
Infant mortality per 1000 live births
Human dev. index

M

MAURITANIA

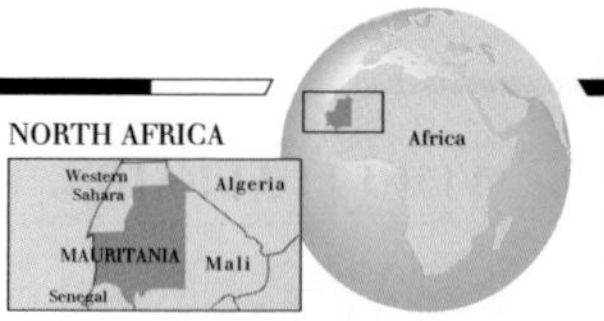
NORTH AFRICA
Africa
Western Sahara
Algeria
MAURITANIA
Mali
Senegal

OFFICIAL NAME: Islamic Republic of Mauritania **CAPITAL:** Nouakchott
POPULATION: 2.8 million **CURRENCY:** Ouguiya **OFFICIAL LANGUAGE:** Arabic

1960 | 1960 | Nov 28 | RIM | 0 | +222 | .mr

LOCATED IN NORTHWEST AFRICA, Mauritania is a member of both the AU and the Arab League. Formerly a French colony, the country has taken a strongly Arab direction since 1964; today, it is the Maures who control political life and dominate the minority black population. The Sahara extends across two-thirds of Mauritania's territory; the only productive land is that drained by the Senegal River in the south and southwest.

CLIMATE

Hot desert

WEATHER CHART FOR NOUAKCHOTT

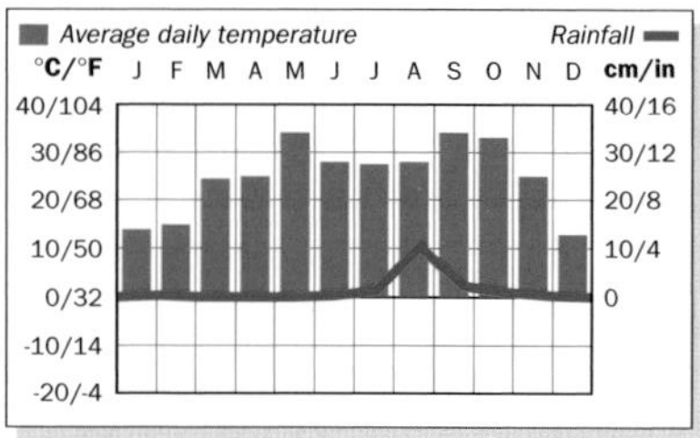
Average daily temperature
Rainfall
°C/°F J F M A M J J A S O N D cm/in
40/104
30/86
20/68
10/50
0/32
-10/14
-20/-4
40/16
30/12
20/8
10/4
0

The dusty Saharan *harmattan* wind often aggravates the very hot, dry conditions. Some rain falls in the south.

TRANSPORTATION

Drive on right

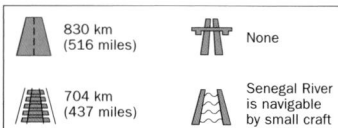

Nouakchott 226,096 passengers

141 ships 47,400 grt

THE TRANSPORTATION NETWORK

830 km (516 miles)	None
704 km (437 miles)	Senegal River is navigable by small craft

The transportation system is limited and unevenly developed. There are two major roads, but shifting sands mean that they require constant maintenance.

TOURISM

Visitors : Population 1:93

30,000 visitors

Up 25% in 2000

MAIN TOURIST ARRIVALS

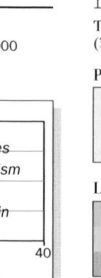

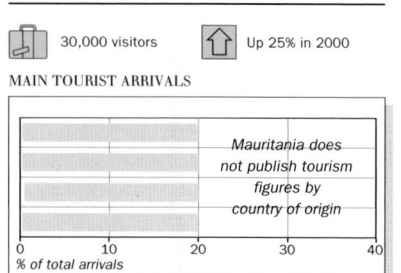

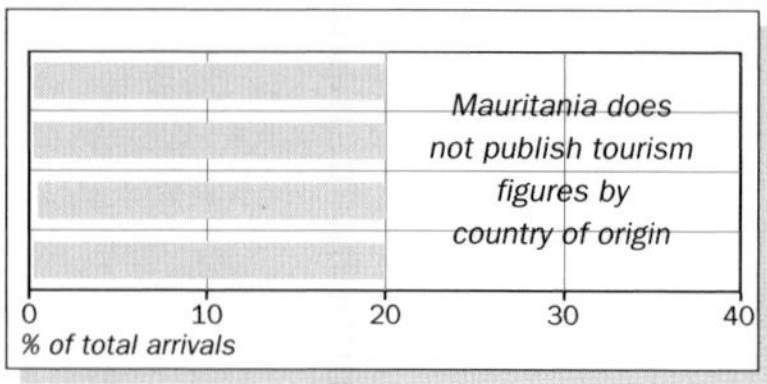
Mauritania does not publish tourism figures by country of origin
0
10
20
30
40
% of total arrivals

There are few tourists apart from desert safari enthusiasts. The more mountainous areas are especially dramatic, but access is difficult. Nouakchott has some hotels.

PEOPLE

Pop. density low

Hassaniyah Arabic, Wolof, French

3/km² (7/mi²)

THE URBAN/RURAL POPULATION SPLIT

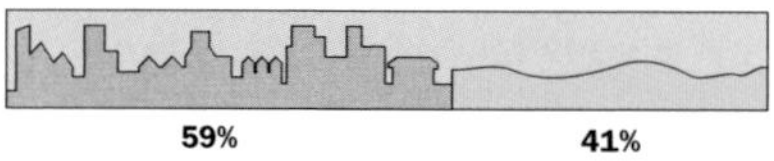
59%
41%

RELIGIOUS PERSUASION

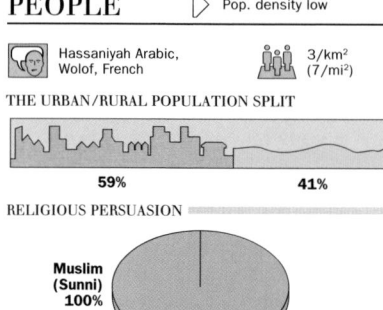

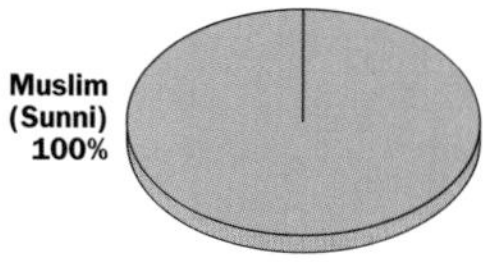
Muslim (Sunni) 100%

The Maure majority is also politically dominant. Ethnic tension centers on their oppression of the black minority, which comprises the Havalin, the Senegalese, and the Peulh, Tukolor, and Wolof groups. The old black bourgeoisie has now been superseded by a Maurish class; tens of thousands of blacks are estimated to be in slavery. The arrival of 200,000 Maures from Senegal in 1989 caused ethnic tension to come to a head: there were attacks on Senegalese in Mauritania and many fled or were deported to refugee camps along the Senegal River.

Family solidarity among nomads is particularly strong.

POLITICS

Multiparty elections

L. House 2001/2006
U. House 2002/2004

President Maaouya ould Sid Ahmed Taya

AT THE LAST ELECTION

National Assembly 81 seats

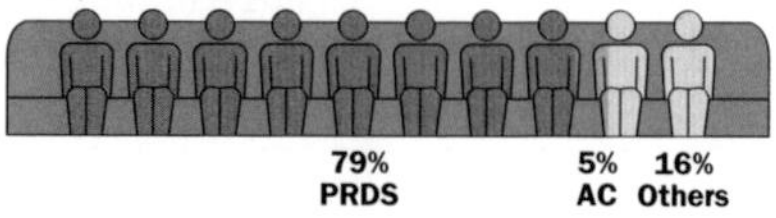
79% PRDS
5% AC
16% Others

PRDS = Democratic and Social Republican Party **AC** = Action for Change **Rep** = Representatives of Mauritanians living abroad **Ind** = Independents

Senate 56 seats

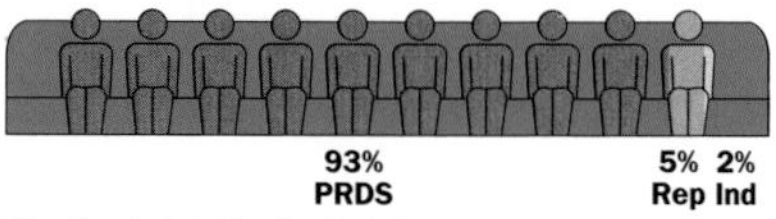
93% PRDS
5% Rep
2% Ind

The Senate is indirectly elected

Mauritania officially adopted multiparty democracy in 1991. However, the 1992 and 1997 presidential elections simply returned to power the incumbent military ruler, President Maaouya ould Sid Ahmed Taya, with around 90% of the vote. Opposition parties have accused the government of electoral fraud; initially boycotting legislative elections, they increased their representation in the 2001 poll, but the AC was subsequently banned. An apparently Islamist-backed coup was foiled in 2003.

The blacks of the south support exiled parties, such as the Senegal-based African Liberation Forces of Mauritania (FLAM).

MAURITANIA

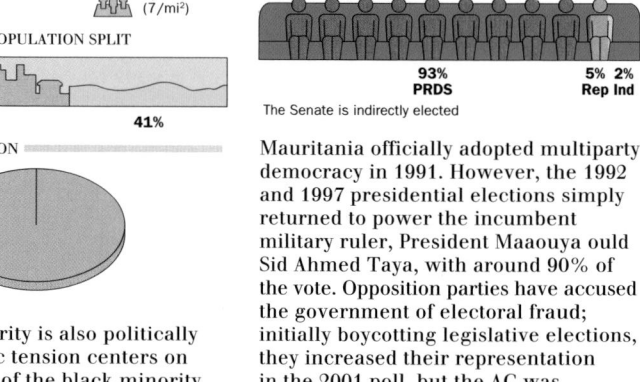

Total Area : 1 030 700 sq. km (397 953 sq. miles)

POPULATION
- over 500 000
- over 10 000
- under 10 000

LAND HEIGHT
- 500m/1640ft
- 200m/656ft
- Sea Level

N

0 200 km
0 200 miles

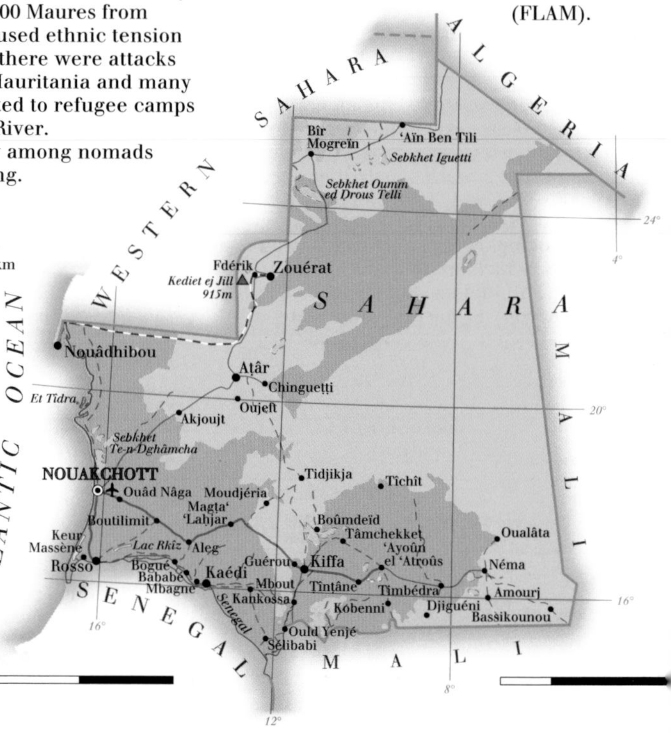
WESTERN SAHARA
ALGERIA
MALI
SENEGAL
ATLANTIC OCEAN
SAHARA
Bîr Mogreïn
'Aïn Ben Tili
Sebkhet Iguetti
Sebkhet Oumm ed Drous Telli
Fdérik
Zouérat
Kediet ej Jill 915m
Nouâdhibou
Atâr
Chinguetti
Ouâdâne
Et Tidra
Akjoujt
Sebkhet Te-n-Dghâmcha
NOUAKCHOTT
Ouâd Nâga
Moudjéria
Tidjikja
Tîchît
Magta' Lahjar
Boutilimit
Boûmdeïd
Tâmchekket
'Ayoûn el 'Atroûs
Oualâta
Keur Massène
Rosso
Lac Rkiz
Aleg
Bogué
Bababé
Mbagne
Kaédi
Guérou
Kiffa
Mbout
Kankossa
Tîntâne
Timbédra
Néma
Kobenni
Djiguéni
Amourj
Bassikounou
Ould Yenjé
Sélibabi
Senegal
24°
20°
16°
16°
12°
8°
4°

WORLD AFFAIRS

Joined UN in 1961

AL | CILSS | AU | OIF | OIC

Mauritania seeks to maintain a balance between sub-Saharan Africa and the Arab world, but has had tense relations with all its neighbors. It has now effectively withdrawn from the Western Sahara dispute. Mauritania maintains good relations with Israel and the West.

AID

Recipient

$262m (receipts) | Up 24% in 2001

The EU, the World Bank, and Japan are the main donors. Most aid is used for development projects, such as the EU-funded Trans-Mauritanian Highway.

DEFENSE

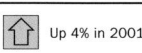

Compulsory military service

$25m | Up 4% in 2001

The 15,000-strong army is a strain on Mauritania's budget. Troops are used increasingly in public works projects. France is the main arms supplier.

ECONOMICS

Inflation 6.2% p.a. (1990–2001)

$999m | 266.7 ouguiyas (276)

SCORE CARD

- ❑ WORLD GNP RANKING........................154th
- ❑ GNP PER CAPITA..............................$360
- ❑ BALANCE OF PAYMENTS......................$65m
- ❑ INFLATION..4.7%
- ❑ UNEMPLOYMENT.................................23%

STRENGTHS

Iron from the Cominor mine at Zouérat. Largest gypsum deposits in the world. Copper, yet to be properly exploited. Offshore fishing among the best in West Africa. Significant debt cancellations in 2002.

WEAKNESSES

Poor land. Drought, locust attacks. Fluctuating commodity prices. Very hot, dry desert climate.

EXPORTS

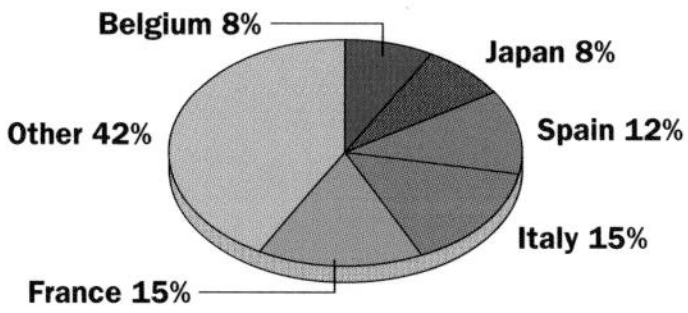
Belgium 8%
Japan 8%
Other 42%
Spain 12%
Italy 15%
France 15%

IMPORTS

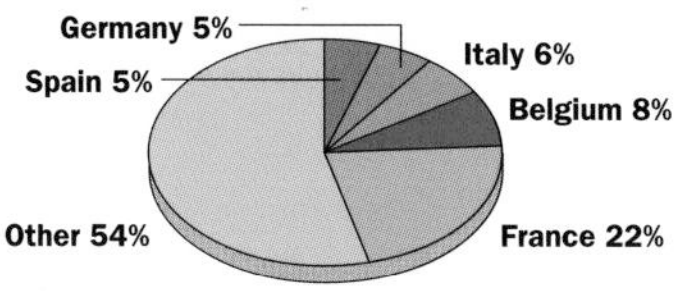
Germany 5%
Spain 5%
Italy 6%
Belgium 8%
Other 54%
France 22%

***Mauritania's extreme aridity** means that only 1% of the land is arable. Two-thirds of the country are part of the Sahara Desert; sparse vegetation over the rest supports some livestock.*

RESOURCES

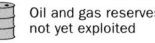

Electric power 115,000 kW

38,096 tonnes | Oil and gas reserves not yet exploited

7.6m sheep, 5.1m goats, 1.5m cattle, 4.1m chickens | Iron, gypsum, copper, gold, diamonds, oil, phosphates, yttrium,

Iron continues to be exploited, despite low world prices. There are some gold and diamond deposits. Phosphates have been found near the Senegal River. Offshore oil exploration yielded finds in 2001. Mining and fisheries represent 99.7% of exports. Electricity generation expanded by 40% between 1989 and 1996, and further expansion is expected to come from the Manantali Dam.

ENVIRONMENT

Sustainability rank: 126th

2% (0.2% partially protected) | 1.2 tonnes per capita

The chief environmental problem in Mauritania is that of the encroaching Sahara Desert, a situation worsened by the droughts of 1973 and 1983, which caused widespread loss of grazing land. The consequent exodus of people away from the land and into the towns has raised Nouakchott's population from 20,000 in 1960 to over 600,000.

MEDIA

TV ownership medium

Daily newspaper circulation 0.5 per 1000 people

PUBLISHING AND BROADCAST MEDIA

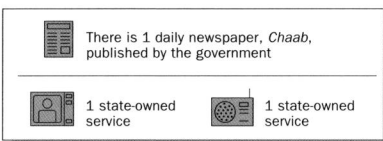

There is 1 daily newspaper, *Chaab*, published by the government

1 state-owned service | 1 state-owned service

The press is heavily censored, and the broadcast media are state-owned. *Chaab*, the government newspaper, is also published in French (*Horizons*).

CRIME

Death penalty in use

1354 prisoners | Down 45% in 1997–1999

Key issues are smuggling, robbery, and a growing number of abandoned children in Nouakchott and other towns.

CHRONOLOGY

Once part of the Islamic Almoravid state, Mauritania became a French colony in 1814.

- ❑ **1960** Independence; one-party state.
- ❑ **1972** Peace with Polisario in war waged over Western Sahara.
- ❑ **1984** Col. Maaouya Taya takes power in bloodless coup.
- ❑ **1992** First multiparty elections.
- ❑ **2003** Coup attempt fails.

EDUCATION

School leaving age: 14

41% | 9033 students

Though over half the population is still illiterate, primary school enrollment rates have increased from 49% in 1987 to 83% in 2000.

HEALTH

No welfare state health benefits

1 per 7143 people | Diarrheal and respiratory diseases, influenza, tuberculosis

Historic regional inequalities persist and the best facilities are in the capital. The overall level of care is on a par with neighboring states.

SPENDING

GDP/cap. increase

CONSUMPTION AND SPENDING

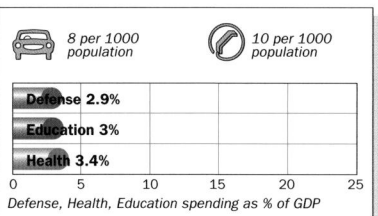

8 per 1000 population | *10 per 1000 population*

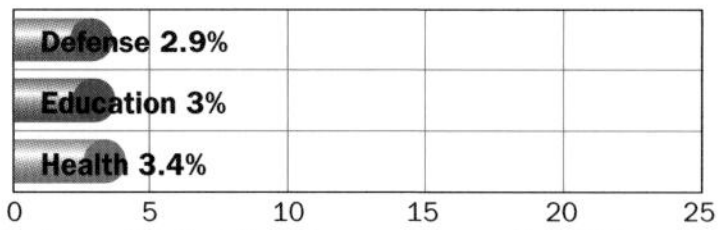
Defense 2.9%
Education 3%
Health 3.4%
0
5
10
15
20
25

Defense, Health, Education spending as % of GDP

The small ruling Maurish elite forms the richest sector. Wealthy Maures travel to Mecca, Saudi Arabia, to perform the *haj* (Muslim pilgrimage).

WORLD RANKING

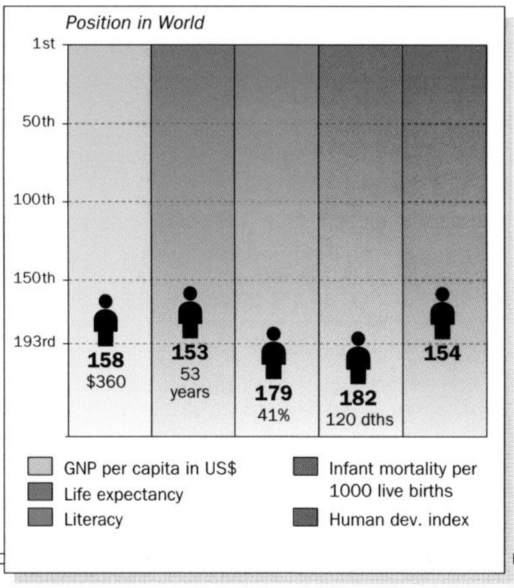
Position in World
1st
50th
100th
150th
193rd
158
$360
153
53 years
179
41%
182
120 dths
154
GNP per capita in US$
Life expectancy
Literacy
Infant mortality per 1000 live births
Human dev. index

M

MAURITIUS

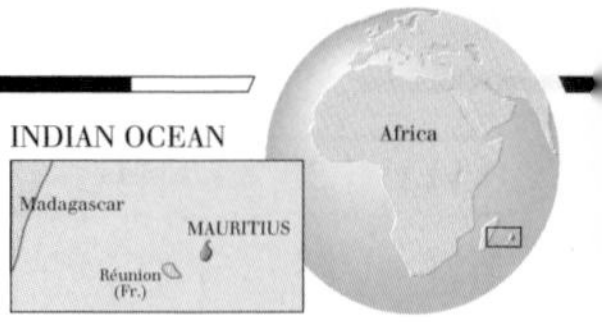
INDIAN OCEAN
Madagascar
MAURITIUS
Réunion (Fr.)
Africa

OFFICIAL NAME: Republic of Mauritius **CAPITAL:** Port Louis
POPULATION: 1.2 million **CURRENCY:** Mauritian rupee **OFFICIAL LANGUAGE:** English

1968 | 1968 | March 12 | MS | +4 | +230 | .mu

THE ISLANDS THAT MAKE UP Mauritius lie in the Indian Ocean east of Madagascar. The main island, from which the country takes its name, is of volcanic origin and surrounded by coral reefs. Along with Rodrigues to the east, the country includes the Agalega Islands and the Cargados Carajos Shoals, 500 km (300 miles) to the north. Mauritius has enjoyed considerable economic success following recent industrial diversification and the expansion of tourism.

CLIMATE

Tropical oceanic

WEATHER CHART FOR PORT LOUIS

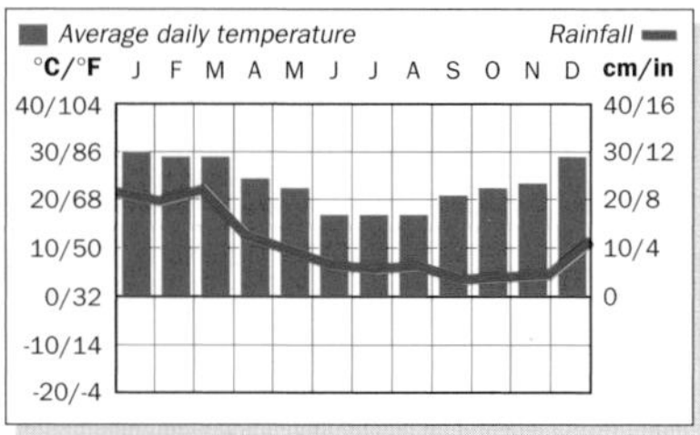
Average daily temperature
Rainfall
°C/°F J F M A M J J A S O N D cm/in
40/104
30/86
20/68
10/50
0/32
-10/14
-20/-4
40/16
30/12
20/8
10/4
0

The climate is subtropical and humid. December to March are the hottest and wettest months. Tropical cyclones are an occasional threat during this time.

TRANSPORTATION

Drive on left

Sir Seewoosagur Ramgoolam International 1.9m passengers

42 ships 96,900 grt

THE TRANSPORTATION NETWORK

1786 km (1110 miles)

36 km (22 miles)

None

None

Roads are extensive, but often congested. Plans exist for a monorail link between Port Louis and Curepipe.

TOURISM

Visitors : Population 1:1.8

681,000 visitors

Up 3% in 2002

MAIN TOURIST ARRIVALS

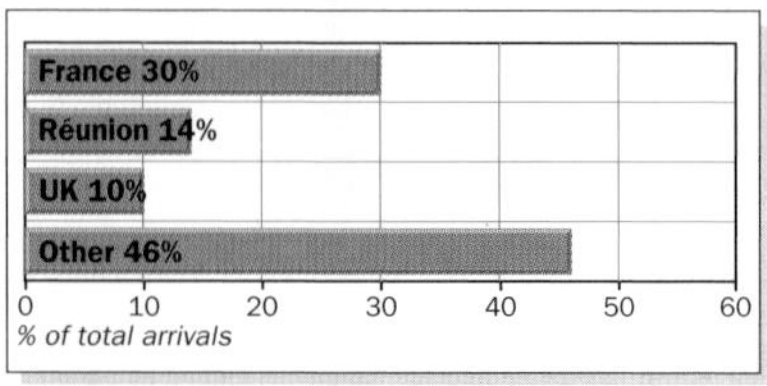
France 30%
Réunion 14%
UK 10%
Other 46%
0 10 20 30 40 50 60
% of total arrivals

Tourism expanded rapidly in the 1990s. Spectacular beaches, water sports, and big game fishing are major attractions. Around 30% of visitors each year come from France.

PEOPLE

Pop. density high

French Creole, Hindi, Urdu, Tamil, Chinese, English, French

645/km² (1671/mi²)

THE URBAN/RURAL POPULATION SPLIT

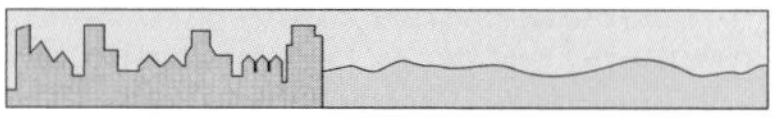
42%
58%

RELIGIOUS PERSUASION

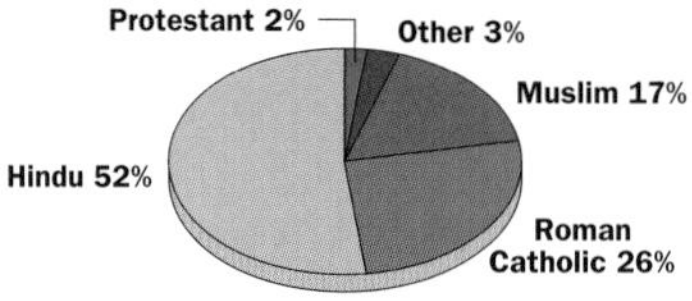
Protestant 2%
Other 3%
Muslim 17%
Hindu 52%
Roman Catholic 26%

Mauritius is one of the world's most densely populated countries. Most Mauritians are descended from indentured laborers brought from India. Creoles, the descendants of African slaves, make up a third of the population. There is also a small Chinese minority. Clashes between the main ethnic groups no longer occur, though Creoles complain of discrimination.

POLITICS

Multiparty elections

2000/2005

President Karl Offmann

AT THE LAST ELECTION
National Assembly 70 seats

11% PTr–PMXD
3% MR
83% MSM–MMM
3% OPR

MSM–MMM = Mauritian Socialist Movement–Mauritian Militant Movement **PTr–PMXD** = Labour Party–Mauritian Social Democratic Party of Xavier Duval **OPR** = Organization of the People of Rodrigues **MR** = Mouvement Rodriguais

Rodrigues has its own legislature which exercises local power

Mauritius became a republic in 1992. Sir Anerood Jugnauth of the MSM had been prime minister for 13 years before losing elections in 1995 to the PTr. He was returned to power when corruption scandals led to early elections in 2000; under the coalition deal that he made with the MMM, Jugnauth will step aside in favor of MMM leader Paul Bérenger in late 2003, halfway through the government's term in office.

WORLD AFFAIRS

Joined UN in 1968

Comm | COMESA | COI | AU | SADC

Mauritius hosted a francophone nations summit in 1995, and the first OAU human rights conference in 1999. Links with South Africa and India are important. Disputes persist over UK-administered Diego Garcia and the French-ruled island of Tromelin.

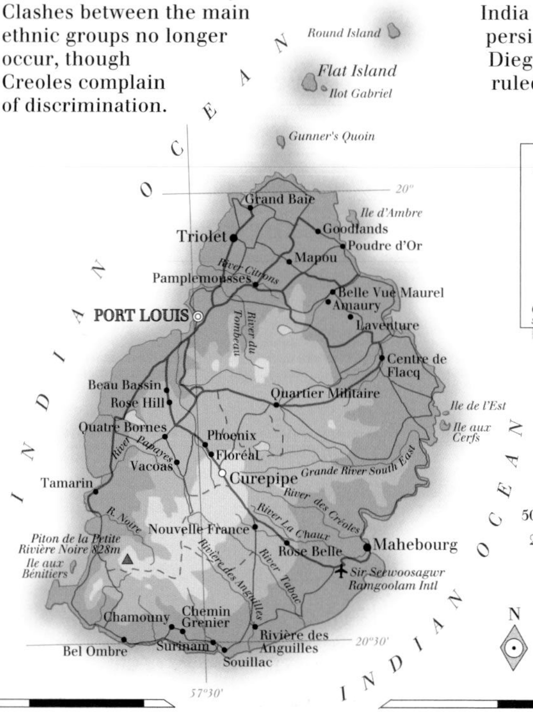
INDIAN OCEAN
INDIAN OCEAN
Round Island
Flat Island
Ilot Gabriel
Gunner's Quoin
Grand Baie
Triolet
Ile d'Ambre
Goodlands
Poudre d'Or
Mapou
Pamplemousses
PORT LOUIS
Belle Vue Maurel
Amaury
Laventure
Centre de Flacq
Beau Bassin
Rose Hill
Quartier Militaire
Quatre Bornes
Phoenix
Floréal
Vacoas
Curepipe
Tamarin
Ile de l'Est
Ile aux Cerfs
Grande River South East
Nouvelle France
Mahebourg
Rose Belle
Sir Seewoosagur Ramgoolam Intl
Piton de la Petite Rivière Noire 828m
Ile aux Bénitiers
Chamouny
Chemin Grenier
Bel Ombre
Surinam
Souillac
Rivière des Anguilles
20°
20°30'
57°30'

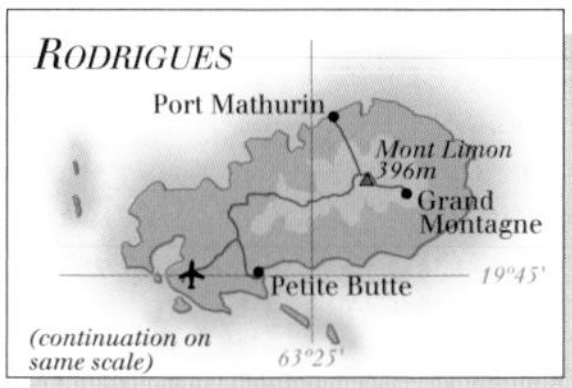
RODRIGUES
Port Mathurin
Mont Limon 396m
Grand Montagne
Petite Butte
19°45'
63°25'
(continuation on same scale)

MAURITIUS

Total Area : 2400 sq. km (788 sq. miles)

LAND HEIGHT: 500m/1640ft, 200m/656ft, Sea Level

POPULATION: over 100 000, over 50 000, over 10 000, under 10 000

0 10 km
0 10 miles

AID

Recipient

$22m (receipts) — Up 10% in 2001

Aid is predominantly bilateral, with the EU and France as the main donors. Mauritius also receives aid from Arab aid agencies and Japan, and from the UN and other international organizations. The World Bank assisted a five-year conservation program, starting in 1990, and promised $53 million toward transforming Port Louis into a free port.

DEFENSE

No compulsory military service

$9m — No change in 2001

Mauritius has no standing defense forces. There is, however, a 1100-strong special police mobile unit to ensure internal security. There is also a coastguard numbering 500.

ECONOMICS

Inflation 6.2% p.a. (1990–2001)

$4.59bn — 29.15 Mauritian rupees (30.03)

SCORE CARD

❑ World GNP Ranking	116th
❑ GNP per Capita	$3830
❑ Balance of Payments	$247m
❑ Inflation	5.4%
❑ Unemployment	6%

Strengths

Strong economic growth. Export processing zone (EPZ), especially for clothing manufacture. Sugar industry. Tourism. Highly educated workforce. Offshore financial services. Ranked as the most competitive economy in Africa by the World Eonomic Forum in 1999.

Weaknesses

Vulnerability to droughts. Most food has to be imported: few crops other than sugar can be grown. Banking scandals have dented investor confidence. Enduring pockets of poverty. Lack of strategic resources. Remoteness.

EXPORTS

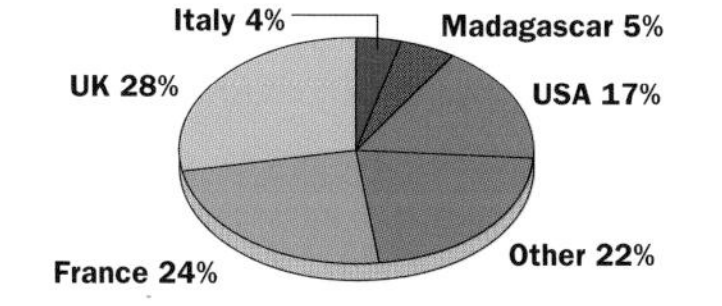
Italy 4%
Madagascar 5%
UK 28%
USA 17%
France 24%
Other 22%

IMPORTS

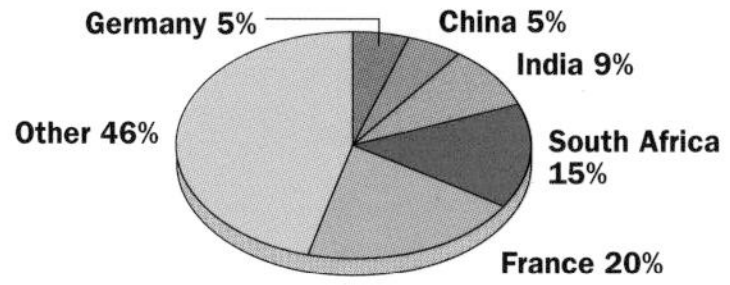
Germany 5%
China 5%
India 9%
Other 46%
South Africa 15%
France 20%

Villagers at a water source in the center of Mauritius Island. Mauritius's main rivers are used for hydropower generation.

RESOURCES

Electric power 529,000 kW

9386 tonnes — Not an oil producer

93,000 goats, 28,000 cattle, 7.7m chickens — None

Mauritius has to import oil, so the government has invested heavily in alternative indigenous energy schemes, including HEP generation and power plants fueled by bagasse (a by-product of the sugar industry). An $800,000 solar energy project was launched in 2000 for street and government office lighting.

ENVIRONMENT

Not available

8% (5% partially protected) — 2.1 tonnes per capita

Rapid industrialization as well as unchecked hotel building have caused environmental problems. Coral reefs are under threat from both coral sand mining and the discharging of untreated sewage into the sea.

MEDIA

TV ownership high

Daily newspaper circulation 119 per 1000 people

PUBLISHING AND BROADCAST MEDIA

There are 10 daily newspapers. *Le Quotidien, L'Express,* and *Le Mauricien* have the largest circulations

1 independent service — 4 independent services

Mauritius has an active press, which is subject to few regulations and has a wide readership. Newspapers are published in English, French, Creole, Hindi, Chinese, and Tamil. The creation of several "cybercities" is planned, with high-tech Internet and telecommunications facilities.

CRIME

No death penalty

2438 prisoners — Up 23% in 2000–2001

Crime rates on the main island are fairly low. There has been a small increase in thefts and narcotics smuggling. Outlying islands are virtually crime-free.

CHRONOLOGY

Mauritius was colonized and ruled by the Dutch in the 17th century, the French (1710–1810), and the British.

- ❑ **1959** First full elections.
- ❑ **1968** Independence. Riots between Creoles and Muslims.
- ❑ **1982–1995** Sir Anerood Jugnauth prime minister; forms MSM.
- ❑ **1992** Becomes a republic.
- ❑ **1995** Elections won by PTr–MMM.
- ❑ **2000** Return of Jugnauth.

EDUCATION

School leaving age: 12

85% — 12,481 students

Educational provision is good, and over 90% of Mauritians under the age of 30 are literate. The University of Mauritius has about 4000 students.

HEALTH

Welfare state health benefits

1 per 1176 people — Cerebrovascular and heart diseases, cancers

In Mauritius free health care is universally available. There are 14 state hospitals and six private clinics.

SPENDING

GDP/cap. increase

CONSUMPTION AND SPENDING

73 per 1000 population — *257 per 1000 population*

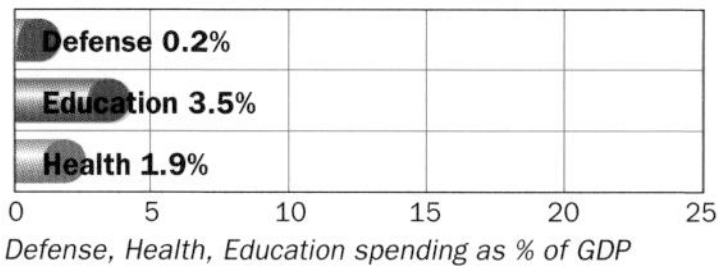
Defense 0.2%
Education 3.5%
Health 1.9%
0
5
10
15
20
25
Defense, Health, Education spending as % of GDP

French-descended hotel and plantation owners form the country's wealthiest social group. Government employees are well paid.

WORLD RANKING

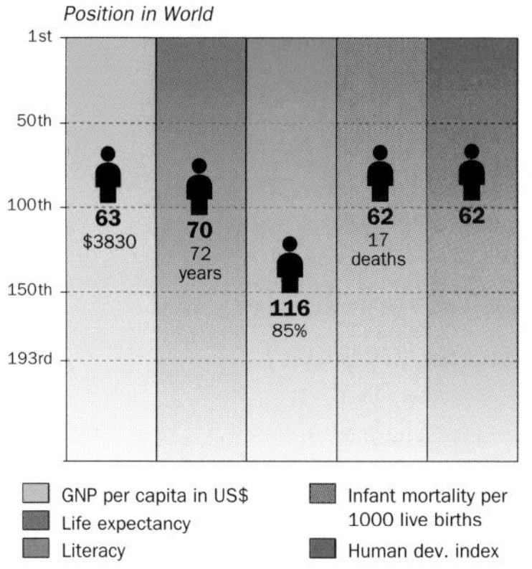
Position in World
1st
50th
100th
150th
193rd
63
$3830
70
72 years
116
85%
62
17 deaths
62
GNP per capita in US$
Life expectancy
Literacy
Infant mortality per 1000 live births
Human dev. index

M

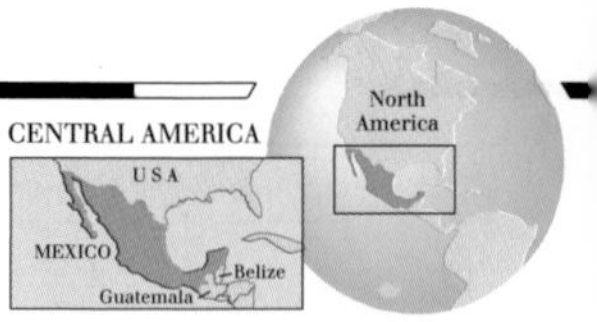
CENTRAL AMERICA
USA
MEXICO
Belize
Guatemala
North America

Mexico

Official Name: United Mexican States **Capital:** Mexico City
Population: 102 million **Currency:** Mexican peso **Official Language:** Spanish

1836 | 1848 | Sept 16 | MEX | -6 | +52 | .mx

INCREASINGLY CONSIDERED a part of North rather than Central America, Mexico separates the US from the rest of Latin America. Coastal plains along its Pacific and Caribbean seaboards rise into an arid central plateau, which includes one of the world's biggest conurbations, Mexico City, built on the site of the Aztec capital, Tenochtitlán. Colonized by the Spanish for its silver mines, Mexico achieved independence in 1836. In the "Epic Revolution" of 1910–1920, in which 250,000 died, much of modern Mexico's structure was established. In 1994, Mexico signed the North American Free Trade Agreement (NAFTA).

The cathedral of Santa Prisca at Taxco near Cuernavaca. It was built in Spanish Churriguera style between 1748 and 1758.

CLIMATE

Tropical/mountain/desert

WEATHER CHART FOR MEXICO CITY

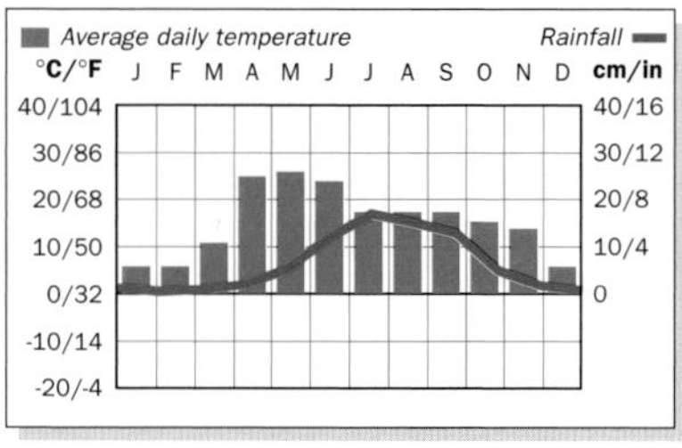
Average daily temperature
Rainfall
°C/°F J F M A M J J A S O N D cm/in
40/104
30/86
20/68
10/50
0/32
-10/14
-20/-4
40/16
30/12
20/8
10/4
0

The plateau and high mountains are warm for much of the year. The Pacific coast has a tropical climate.

TRANSPORTATION

Drive on right

Benito Juárez International, Mexico City
20.3m passengers

633 ships
908,100 grt

THE TRANSPORTATION NETWORK

96,221 km (59,789 miles)

6335 km (3936 miles)

18,000 km (11,185 miles)

2900 km (1802 miles)

A privately financed $14 billion road network – some 6000 km (3730 miles) of toll roads – is seriously underused and a commercial failure. Regional travel is mainly by bus; the unreliable railroad is largely for freight. Plans to construct a new international airport serving Mexico City were abandoned in 2002 as local farmers staged violent protests against the implied acquisition of their lands.

TOURISM

Visitors : Population 1:5.2

19.7m visitors

Down 1% in 2002

MAIN TOURIST ARRIVALS

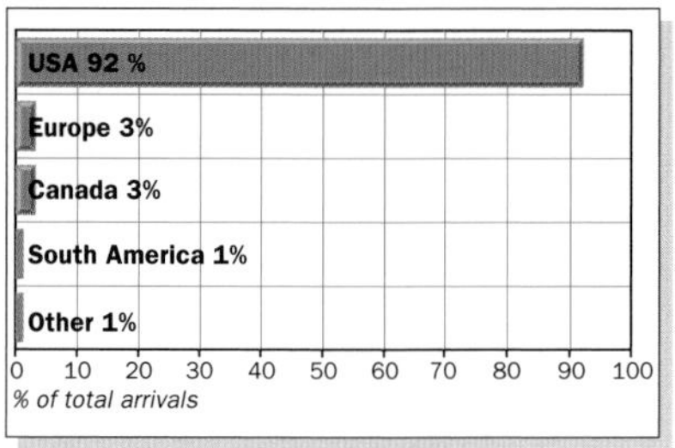
USA 92 %
Europe 3%
Canada 3%
South America 1%
Other 1%
0 10 20 30 40 50 60 70 80 90 100
% of total arrivals

Tourism is one of the largest employment sectors in Mexico, and a major source of foreign exchange. Attractions include excellent beach resorts such as Acapulco on the Pacific coast, and the new resorts of the Peninsula de Yucatán on the Caribbean coast. Impressive coastal scenery, volcanoes, the Sierra Madre, and archaeological remains of Aztec and Mayan civilizations, designated as World Heritage sites, are major draws, as are the many Spanish colonial cities, such as Morelia and Guadalajara, which have remained virtually intact since their construction after the conquest.

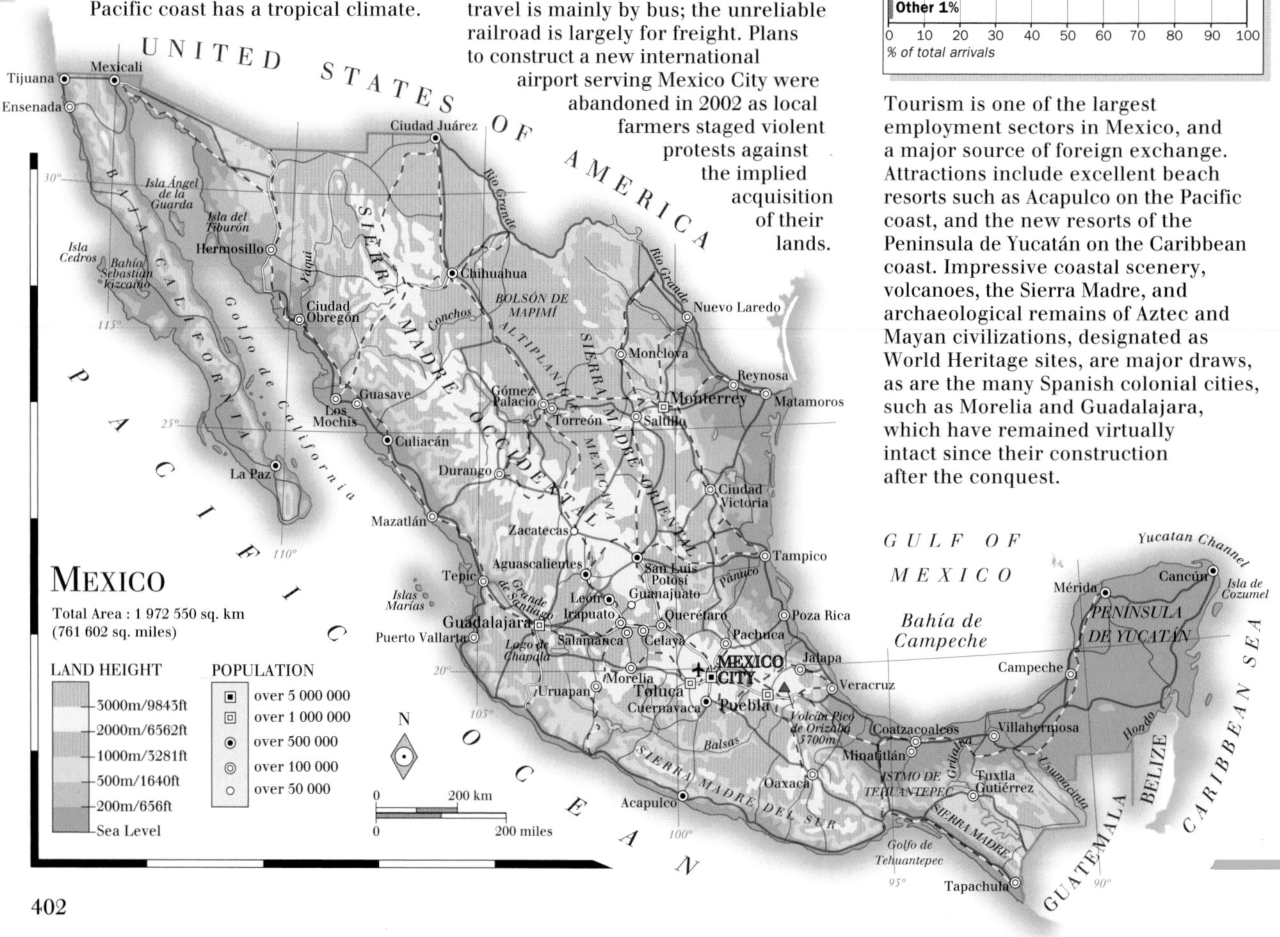
UNITED STATES OF AMERICA
Tijuana
Mexicali
Ensenada
Ciudad Juárez
Isla Ángel de la Guarda
Isla del Tiburón
Hermosillo
Isla Cedros
Bahía Sebastián Vizcaíno
BAJA CALIFORNIA
Golfo de California
Chihuahua
BOLSÓN DE MAPIMÍ
SIERRA MADRE OCCIDENTAL
ALTIPLANICIE MEXICANA
SIERRA MADRE ORIENTAL
Río Grande
Conchos
Yaqui
Ciudad Obregón
Nuevo Laredo
Monclova
Reynosa
Monterrey
Matamoros
Guasave
Los Mochis
Gómez Palacio
Torreón
Saltillo
Culiacán
La Paz
Durango
Ciudad Victoria
Mazatlán
Zacatecas
Tampico
Aguascalientes
San Luis Potosí
Pánuco
Tepic
Islas Marías
Grande de Santiago
León
Guanajuato
Irapuato
Querétaro
Poza Rica
Guadalajara
Puerto Vallarta
Lago de Chapala
Salamanca
Celaya
Pachuca
Jalapa
MEXICO CITY
Morelia
Uruapan
Toluca
Cuernavaca
Puebla
Veracruz
Volcán Pico de Orizaba 5700m
Balsas
Coatzacoalcos
Minatitlán
Villahermosa
ISTMO DE TEHUANTEPEC
Oaxaca
Tuxtla Gutiérrez
Acapulco
SIERRA MADRE DEL SUR
SIERRA MADRE
Golfo de Tehuantepec
Tapachula
Grijalva
Usumacinta
Hondo
GULF OF MEXICO
Bahía de Campeche
Campeche
Mérida
Cancún
Isla de Cozumel
Yucatan Channel
PENÍNSULA DE YUCATÁN
BELIZE
GUATEMALA
CARIBBEAN SEA
PACIFIC OCEAN
MEXICO
Total Area : 1 972 550 sq. km (761 602 sq. miles)
LAND HEIGHT
3000m/9843ft
2000m/6562ft
1000m/3281ft
500m/1640ft
200m/656ft
Sea Level
POPULATION
over 5 000 000
over 1 000 000
over 500 000
over 100 000
over 50 000
N
0 200 km
0 200 miles

PEOPLE

Pop. density medium

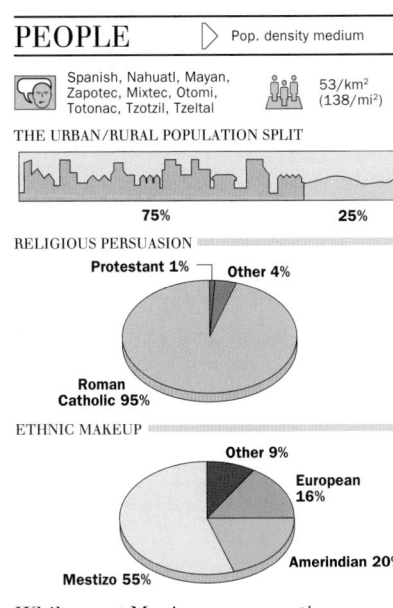

Spanish, Nahuatl, Mayan, Zapotec, Mixtec, Otomi, Totonac, Tzotzil, Tzeltal

53/km² (138/mi²)

THE URBAN/RURAL POPULATION SPLIT

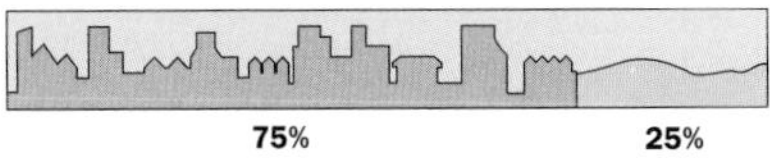
75%
25%

RELIGIOUS PERSUASION

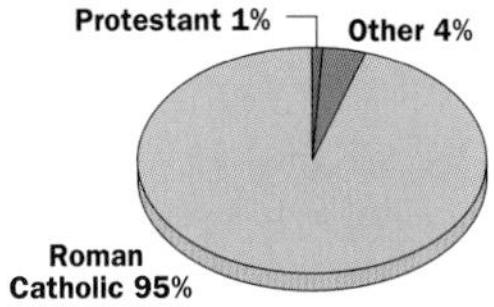
Protestant 1%
Other 4%
Roman Catholic 95%

ETHNIC MAKEUP

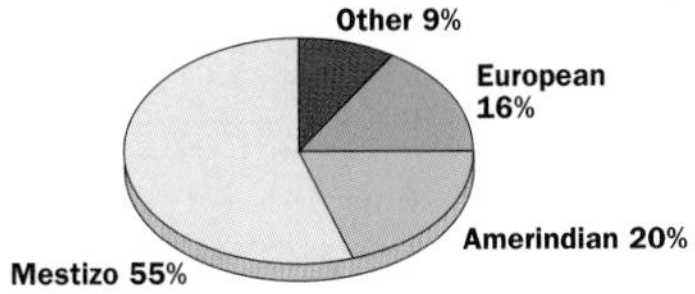
Other 9%
European 16%
Amerindian 20%
Mestizo 55%

While most Mexicans are *mestizo* (mixed race), it is Mexico's Amerindian culture which is promoted by the state. This obscures the fact that rural Amerindians are largely segregated from Hispanic society, a situation that dates back to the Spanish colonial period and which has only recently been seriously challenged. The 1994 Zapatista (EZLN) guerrilla uprising in Chiapas was on behalf of Amerindian rights, and in protest against the poverty of landless Amerindians. President Vicente Fox promised to act, but the Indigenous Rights and Culture Bill, watered down by a hostile Congress and enacted in 2001, was rejected by the EZLN and all the main indigenous groups.

The small black community, which is concentrated along the eastern coast, is well integrated.

As in much of Latin America, men retain their dominance in business and relatively few women take part in the political process.

POPULATION AGE BREAKDOWN

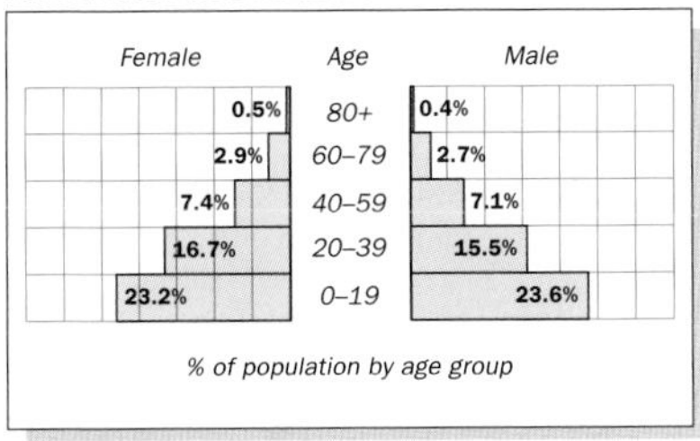
Female
Age
Male
0.5%
80+
0.4%
2.9%
60–79
2.7%
7.4%
40–59
7.1%
16.7%
20–39
15.5%
23.2%
0–19
23.6%
% of population by age group

WORLD AFFAIRS

Joined UN in 1945

G15 | NAFTA | OECD | OAS | RG

NAFTA has bonded the economies of Mexico and the US. Progress on economic migrants remains stalled, but long-running disputes with the US on tuna and trucking are all but resolved. Huge US farm subsidies remain a great source of bilateral tension following the lifting of most tariffs on agricultural products in 2003, as required under NAFTA. Unable to compete, far poorer Mexican farmers have staged border protests and demanded protection. The Mexican government has promised renegotiation, but the US and Canada remain strongly opposed. Tariffs on Mexican beans and corn are to be removed in 2008.

Under Fox, traditional support for Cuba has diminished in favor of the US. Mexico has free trade agreements with 32 countries, as well as with the EU and EFTA, and competes with Brazil to play a leading negotiating role for Latin America in the formation of a Free Trade Area of the Americas (FTAA) due to be signed in 2005.

AID

Recipient

$75m (receipts)

Up 103% in 2001

In 2002 the IDB made its biggest loan – $1 billion – to support a six-year antipoverty project in Mexico. European and US NGOs provide assistance.

M

POLITICS

Multiparty elections

L. House 2003/2006
U. House 2000/2006

President Vicente Fox

AT THE LAST ELECTION

Chamber of Deputies 500 seats

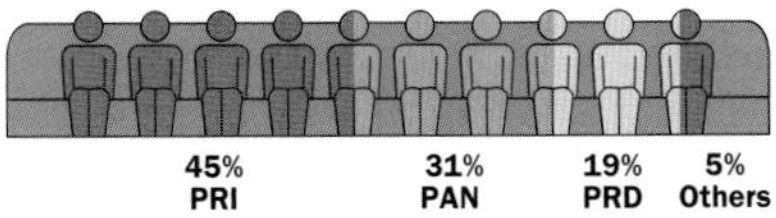
45% PRI
31% PAN
19% PRD
5% Others

PRI = Institutional Revolutionary Party **PAN** = National Action Party **PRD** = Party of the Democratic Revolution **PAN–PVEM** = Alliance for Change (PAN and Green Party) **PRD–PT** = Alliance for Mexico (PRD and Labor Party)

Senate of the Republic 128 seats

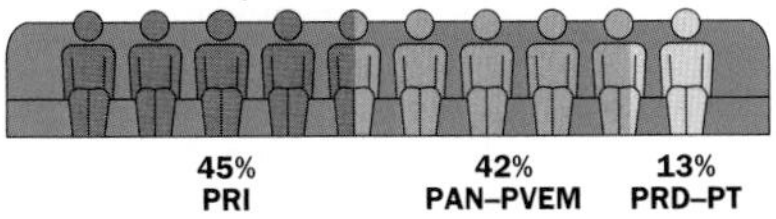
45% PRI
42% PAN–PVEM
13% PRD–PT

Mexico was a multiparty democracy in name only until 1997; reforms culminated in a PAN presidency in 2000.

PROFILE

The PRI dominated Mexico from 1929. The strength of opposition parties grew during the 1990s, and, after grudging electoral reform, the PRI lost its monopoly on power in 1997. After the 2000 elections the PAN was the largest party in the Chamber of Deputies, but it lacked an overall majority and was overtaken once more by the PRI in the 2003 midterm poll.

MAIN POLITICAL ISSUES

President Fox's administration

The first half of President Fox's six-year term was uneven. His failure to consult and build consensus, coupled with PRI opposition in Congress, resulted in key policy failures, notably in the areas of electricity, telecommunications, and fiscal reform. Promises on job creation went unmet but government accountability and transparency improved. An economic downturn was also seen off without the specter of hyperinflation. Fox's position was made all the more difficult when the PRI emerged as the victors in the July 2003 Congressional elections.

Future of the PRI

Election defeats in the late 1990s left the PRI rudderless and faction-ridden. It turned to hard-liner Roberto Madrazo, party leader from 2002, to translate public disillusionment with the PAN into popular support for the PRI.

Vicente Fox, elected president in 2000, ending 70 years of PRI dominance.

***Subcomandante Marcos,** leader of the Zapatista National Liberation Army.*

CHRONOLOGY

The Aztec kingdom of Montezuma II was defeated in war by the Spaniard, Hernán Cortés, in 1521. By 1546, the Spaniards had discovered large silver mines at Zacatecas. Mexico, then known as New Spain, became a key part of the Spanish colonial empire.

- **1810** Fr. Miguel Hidalgo leads abortive rising against Spanish.
- **1821** Spanish viceroy forced to leave by Agustín de Iturbide.
- **1822** Federal Republic established.
- **1823** Texas opened to US immigration.
- **1829** Spanish military expedition fails to regain control.
- **1836** US is first country to recognize Mexico's independence. Spain follows suit. Texas declares its independence from Mexico.
- **1846** War breaks out with US.
- **1848** Loses modern-day New Mexico, Arizona, Nevada, Utah, California, and part of Colorado.
- **1858–1861** War of Reform won by anticlerical Liberals.
- **1862** France, Britain, and Spain launch military expedition.

CHRONOLOGY *continued*

- **1863** French troops capture Mexico City. Maximilian of Austria established as Mexican emperor.
- **1867** Mexico recaptured by Benito Juárez. Maximilian shot.
- **1876** Porfirio Díaz president. Economic growth; rail system built.
- **1901** First year of oil production.
- **1910–1920** Epic Revolution provoked by excessive exploitation by foreign companies and desire for land reform. 250,000 killed.
- **1911** Díaz overthrown by Francisco Madero. Guerrilla war breaks out in north. Emilio Zapata leads peasant revolt in the south.
- **1913** Madero murdered.
- **1917** New constitution limits power of Church. Minerals and subsoil rights reserved for the nation.
- **1926–1929** Cristero rebellion led by militant Catholic priests.
- **1929** National Revolutionary Party (later PRI) formed.
- **1934** Gen. Cárdenas president. Land reform accelerated, cooperative farms established, railroads nationalized, and US and UK oil companies expelled.
- **1940s** US war effort helps Mexican economy to grow.
- **1970** Accelerating population growth reaches 3% a year.
- **1982** Mexico declares it cannot repay its foreign debt of over $800 billion. IMF insists on economic reforms to reschedule the debt.
- **1984** Government contravenes constitution by relaxing laws on foreign investment.
- **1985** Earthquake in Mexico City. Official death toll 7000. Economic cost estimated at $425 million.
- **1988** Carlos Salinas de Gortari, minister of planning during the earthquake, elected president.
- **1990** Privatization program begins.
- **1994–1995** Guerrilla rebellion in southern Chiapas state brutally suppressed by army: 100 dead. Mexico joins NAFTA. PRI presidential candidate Luis Colosio murdered. Ernesto Zedillo replaces him and is elected. Economic crisis.
- **1997–1999** PRI's monopoly on power in Congress ended. Banks bailed out.
- **2000** July, PAN wins presidency and elections, ending 70 years of PRI rule. December, President Vicente Fox takes office.
- **2001** EZLN guerrillas and supporters make 16-day motorcade from Chiapas to Mexico City to push for indigenous rights law.
- **2002** Hard-liner Roberto Madrazo elected PRI leader.
- **2003** PRI gain in midterm elections.

DEFENSE

Compulsory military service

$5.73bn

Up 8% in 2001

Mexico has no ambitions beyond its borders, and the army acts to defend internal security. The military has, on the whole, avoided direct interference in politics. Most arms procurement is from the US. In 1994, the role of controlling the border with the US was passed to the police.

The Zapatista rebellion in Chiapas in 1994 elicited a brutal response from the army, acting on PRI orders. The increasing militarization of the state over the next six years hindered the peace process and led to a proliferation of paramilitaries, with the tacit blessing of the local PRI, who were blamed by human rights groups for the massacre of Amerindians. The PAN government has withdrawn some forces from key areas of the state.

MEXICAN ARMED FORCES

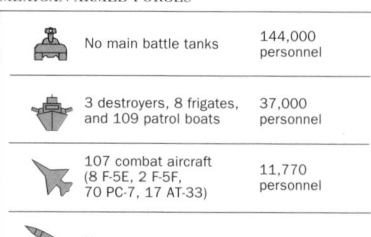

No main battle tanks	144,000 personnel
3 destroyers, 8 frigates, and 109 patrol boats	37,000 personnel
107 combat aircraft (8 F-5E, 2 F-5F, 70 PC-7, 17 AT-33)	11,770 personnel
None	

ECONOMICS

Inflation 18% p.a. (1990–2001)

$550bn

10.42 Mexican pesos (9.945)

SCORE CARD

- World GNP Ranking 10th
- GNP per Capita $5530
- Balance of Payments .... –$17.7bn
- Inflation 6.4%
- Unemployment 3%

EXPORTS

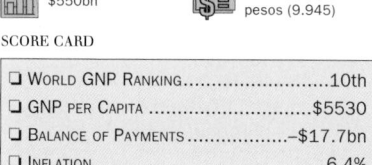

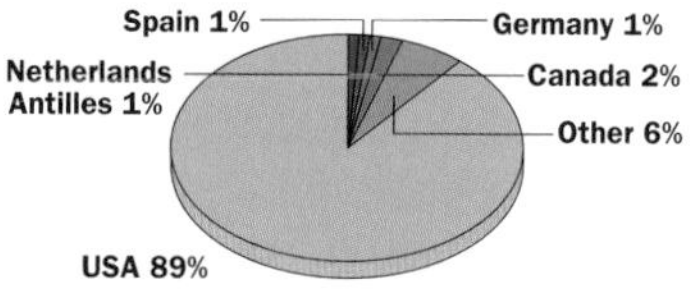
Spain 1%
Germany 1%
Netherlands Antilles 1%
Canada 2%
Other 6%
USA 89%

IMPORTS

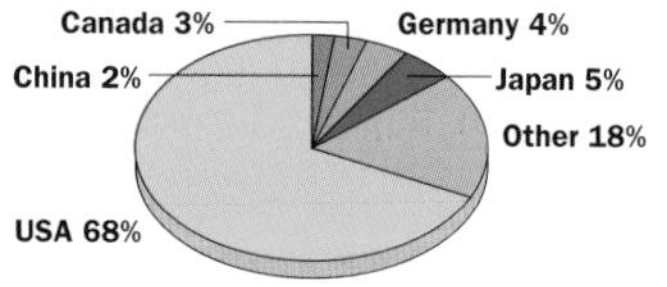
Canada 3%
Germany 4%
China 2%
Japan 5%
Other 18%
USA 68%

Strengths
Global oil producer, with substantial reserves. Extensive mineral resources. Strong foreign direct investment. Diversification of exports. NAFTA membership. Low overheads.

Weaknesses
Debt burden. Vulnerable currency. Corruption. Affected by oil price changes and US slowdown. Weak tax system.

Profile
While in power, the PRI effectively ran the economy. The debt crisis of the 1980s, however, forced privatizations. The 1994 peso crisis needed a US-led $20 billion international bailout and resulted in a severe slump. The Zedillo government launched tough reforms, but a global loss of confidence in emerging markets affected growth. Tighter fiscal management was rewarded by 2000, when investor confidence improved. The Fox government's tight fiscal and monetary stance secured the approval of the IMF and major credit agencies, giving the country greater access to cheaper foreign capital. However, pledges on social spending and poverty relief suffered, and promises of large job creation projects also went unfulfilled, as the export-led economy echoed the slowdown in the US from 2001.

ECONOMIC PERFORMANCE INDICATOR

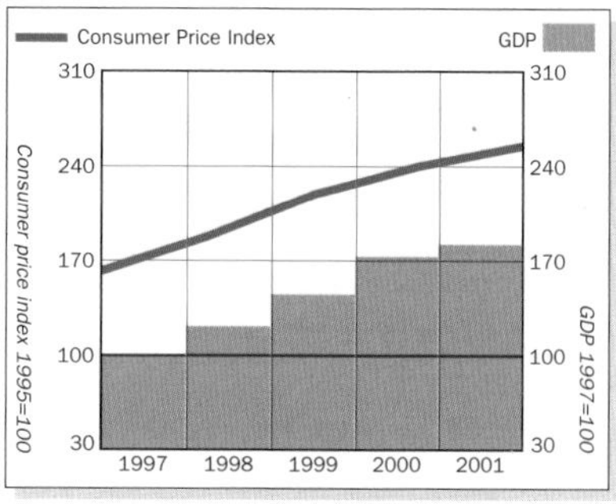
Consumer Price Index
GDP
310
240
170
100
30
Consumer price index 1995=100
GDP 1997=100
1997
1998
1999
2000
2001

MEXICO : MAJOR BUSINESSES

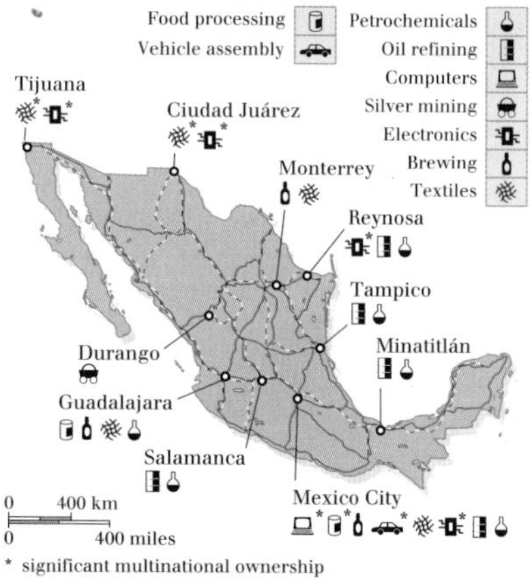
Food processing
Vehicle assembly
Petrochemicals
Oil refining
Computers
Silver mining
Electronics
Brewing
Textiles
Tijuana
Ciudad Juárez
Monterrey
Reynosa
Tampico
Durango
Minatitlán
Guadalajara
Salamanca
Mexico City
0 400 km
0 400 miles
* significant multinational ownership

M

RESOURCES

Electric power 46.3m kW

1.37m tonnes

3.59m b/d (reserves 12.6bn barrels)

30.6m cattle, 17m pigs, 9.4m goats, 521m chickens

Oil, gas, gold, silver, copper, coal, fluorite, mercury, antimony

ELECTRICITY GENERATION

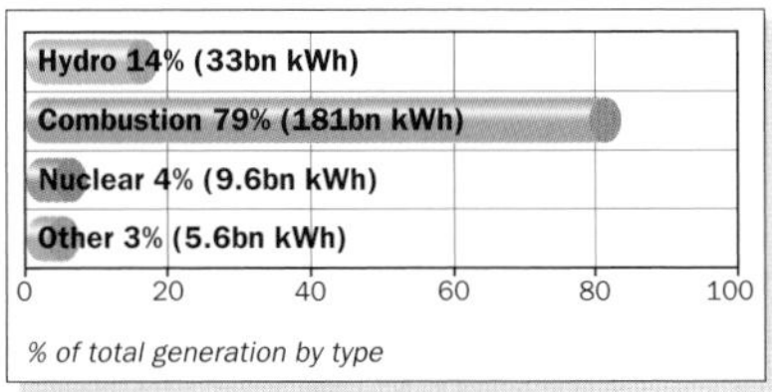
Hydro 14% (33bn kWh)
Combustion 79% (181bn kWh)
Nuclear 4% (9.6bn kWh)
Other 3% (5.6bn kWh)
0 20 40 60 80 100
% of total generation by type

Mexico is one of the largest oil exporters outside OPEC. Most oil production comes from offshore drilling platforms in the Gulf of Mexico. The industry was state-owned and state-run by PEMEX, the world's fifth-largest oil company, employing 120,000 people. The decision to privatize petrochemical plants has provoked serious social unrest, and further sell-offs and deregulation remain politically highly sensitive. Despite its oil reserves, Mexico has embarked on a nuclear power program and projects to modernize the national electricity grid and boost natural gas production to overcome an energy crisis.

MEXICO : LAND USE

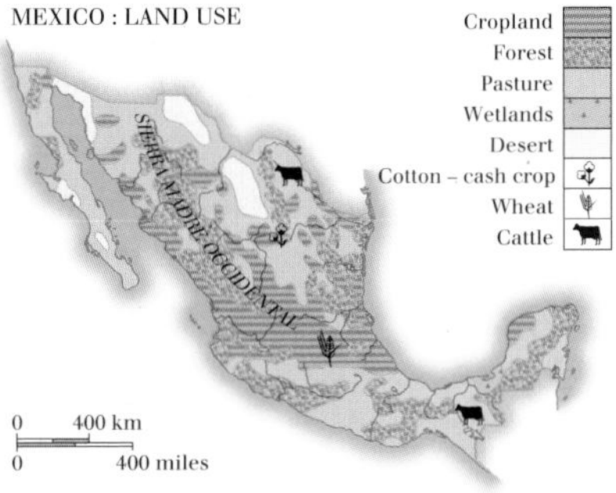
Cropland
Forest
Pasture
Wetlands
Desert
Cotton – cash crop
Wheat
Cattle
SIERRA MADRE OCCIDENTAL
0 400 km
0 400 miles

ENVIRONMENT

Sustainability rank: 92nd

10% (7% partially protected)

3.9 tonnes per capita

ENVIRONMENTAL TREATIES

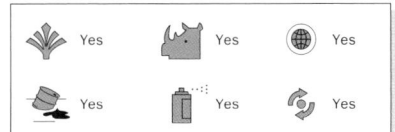

Yes Yes Yes

Yes Yes Yes

Mexico City, largely unplanned, struggles to accommodate around 20 million inhabitants as the absence of environmental controls contributes to perhaps the world's worst air quality and waste problems. PEMEX (the state petroleum company) stands accused of massive pollution. *Maquiladoras* – assembly plants on the Mexico–US border – have no effective environmental controls and are usually surrounded by slums. Environmentalists oppose the intense development of tourism along the coast and are concerned about high rates of deforestation.

MEDIA

TV ownership high

Daily newspaper circulation 94 per 1000 people

PUBLISHING AND BROADCAST MEDIA

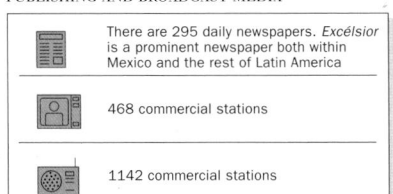

There are 295 daily newspapers. *Excélsior* is a prominent newspaper both within Mexico and the rest of Latin America

468 commercial stations

1142 commercial stations

The PRI in particular has historically manipulated the media, being accused of denying electoral opponents airtime.

CRIME

Death penalty not used in practice

154,765 prisoners

Crime is rising

CRIME RATES

Mexico does not publish official statistics for murders, rapes, or thefts

Northern Mexico is a major center for narcotics shipments to the US. Antidrugs police are accused by the US of corruption. Guns are rife and minor incidents may end in shootings. The high crime rate in Mexico City is a major political issue. Reforms of the corrupt judiciary and the whole police force are perennial issues.

EDUCATION

School leaving age: 14

91%

2.05m students

THE EDUCATION SYSTEM

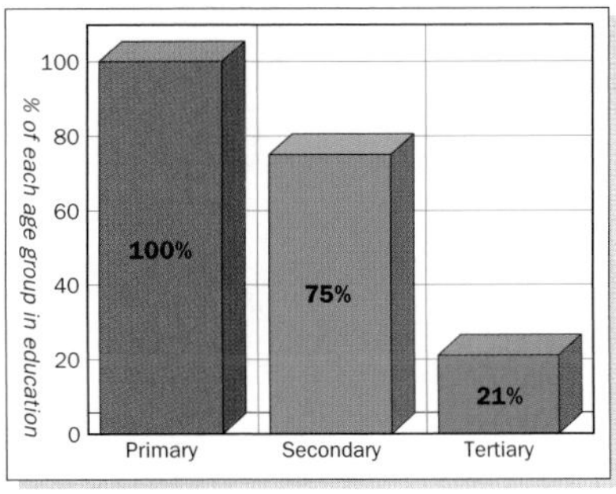
% of each age group in education
100
80
60
40
20
0
100%
75%
21%
Primary
Secondary
Tertiary

Public education, officially compulsory for the first six years, is underfunded and rural provision is poor. The system is a mixture of the French and US models. There is a well-developed public university system.

HEALTH

Welfare state health benefits

1 per 769 people

Cancers, diabetes, heart and respiratory diseases, accidents

The national health care system is basic and badly underfunded, although an ambitious scheme was launched in 1996 to improve access to health services in marginalized areas. Mexico has a good reputation for surgery and dentistry, but this is mostly in the private sector. The rich also go to the US for treatment.

SPENDING

GDP/cap. increase

CONSUMPTION AND SPENDING

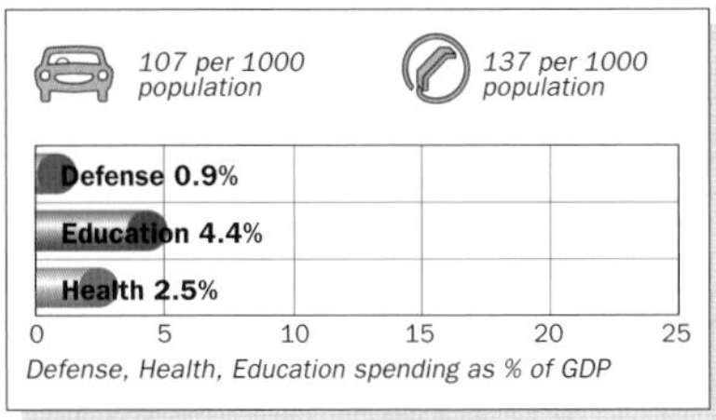
107 per 1000 population
137 per 1000 population
Defense 0.9%
Education 4.4%
Health 2.5%
0 5 10 15 20 25
Defense, Health, Education spending as % of GDP

Mexico has enormous wealth disparities. Preliminary official figures in 2002 had six million families, or 26 million people, in extreme poverty. There is little social mobility; the old Spanish families retain their hold on institutions. In the past, the wealthy did not generally pay taxes and often benefited from the large state machine. Tax evasion remains a serious problem.

Rural Amerindians are probably the most disadvantaged group. In the last decade, poverty has forced them into city slums to work in factories or *maquiladoras*, where conditions and pay are poor. The 1994 Chiapas rebellion was fed by demands for more land and more assistance in farming it. The flow of poor rural migrants to the US stems largely from the need to subsidize families back home.

WORLD RANKING

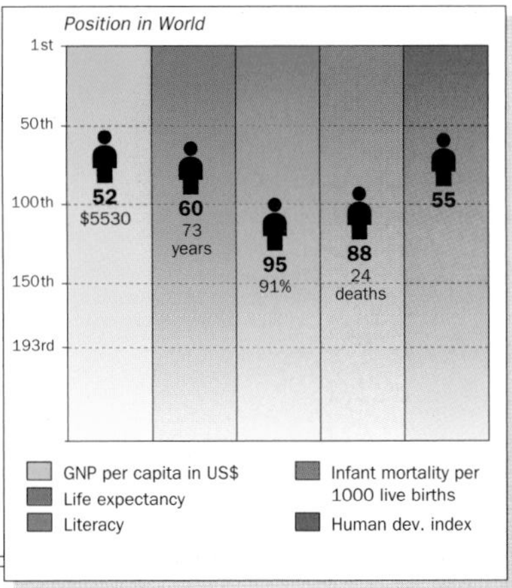
Position in World
1st
50th
100th
150th
193rd
52
$5530
60
73
years
95
91%
88
24
deaths
55
GNP per capita in US$
Life expectancy
Literacy
Infant mortality per 1000 live births
Human dev. index

M

MICRONESIA

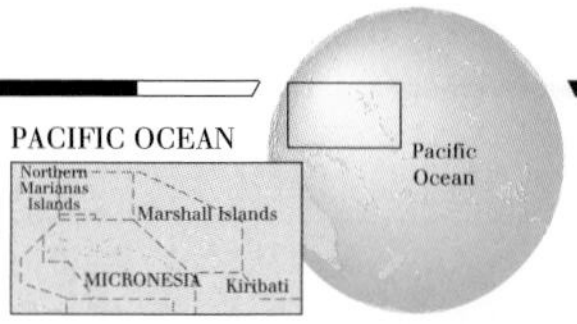
PACIFIC OCEAN
Northern Marianas Islands
Marshall Islands
MICRONESIA
Kiribati
Pacific Ocean

OFFICIAL NAME: Federated States of Micronesia **CAPITAL:** Palikir (Pohnpei Island)
POPULATION: 135,869 **CURRENCY:** US dollar **OFFICIAL LANGUAGE:** English

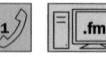

1986 | 1986 | May 10 | FSM | +10 to +11 | +691 | .fm

SITUATED IN THE PACIFIC OCEAN, the Federated States of Micronesia (FSM) encompasses all the Caroline Islands except Palau. It is composed of four island cluster states: Pohnpei, Kosrae, Chuuk, and Yap. The FSM was formerly under US rule as part of the UN Trust Territory of the Pacific Islands. An agreement which granted internal sovereignty in free association with the US became operational in 1986, and the Trust was formally dissolved in 1990. The islands continue to receive considerable aid from the US.

CLIMATE

Tropical oceanic

WEATHER CHART FOR PALIKIR

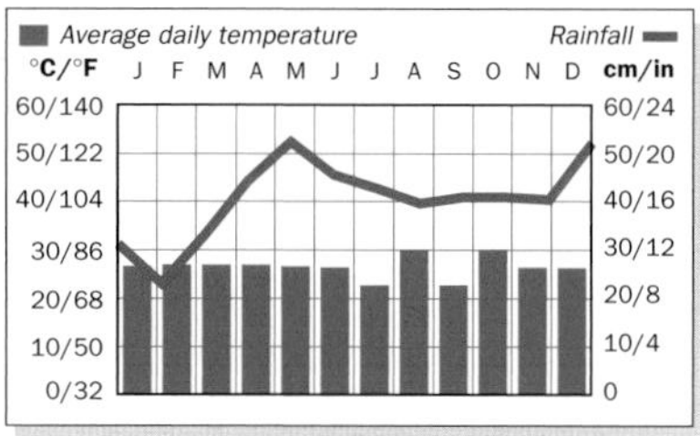
Average daily temperature
Rainfall
°C/°F
J F M A M J J A S O N D
cm/in
60/140
50/122
40/104
30/86
20/68
10/50
0/32
60/24
50/20
40/16
30/12
20/8
10/4
0

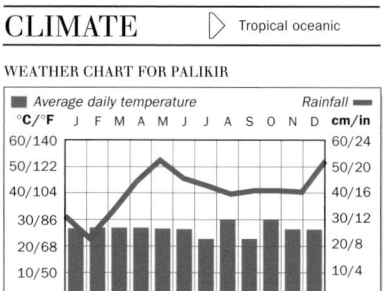

The islands are humid and fairly hot all year round, and the daily temperature range is small. Rainfall is abundant.

TRANSPORTATION

Drive on right

Pohnpei 58,029 passengers

18 ships 9200 grt

THE TRANSPORTATION NETWORK

42 km (26 miles)	None
None	None

The inauguration in 2000 of flights by a Boeing 737 opened the way for greater air traffic between the islands. Shipping is mainly used for bulk cargoes and copra. Some island roads are surfaced with coral.

Micronesia, aerial view of rock islands. *Like many Pacific states, Micronesia fears rising sea levels as a result of global warming.*

TOURISM

Visitors : Population 1:4.1

33,000 visitors

Up 65% in 1997–2000

MAIN TOURIST ARRIVALS

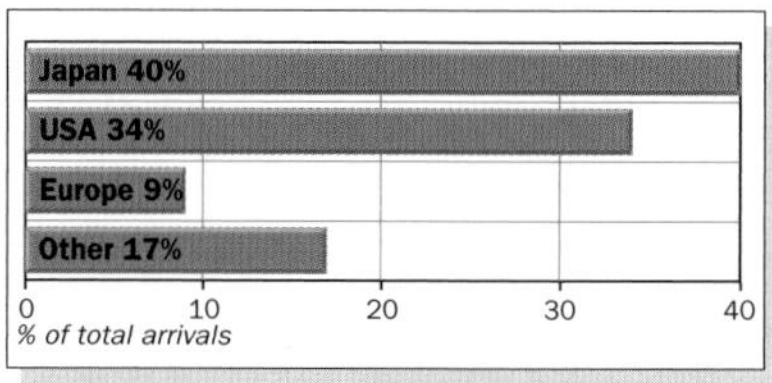
Japan 40%
USA 34%
Europe 9%
Other 17%
0
10
20
30
40
% of total arrivals

Outlying islands remain untouched and unspoilt. Chuuk's underwater war wreckage and Kosrae's beaches attract visitors. Lack of infrastructure tends to hinder the growth of tourism.

PEOPLE

Pop. density medium

Trukese, Pohnpeian, Mortlockese, Kosraean, English

194/km² (501/mi²)

THE URBAN/RURAL POPULATION SPLIT

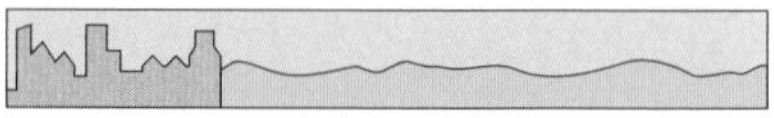
28%
72%

RELIGIOUS PERSUASION

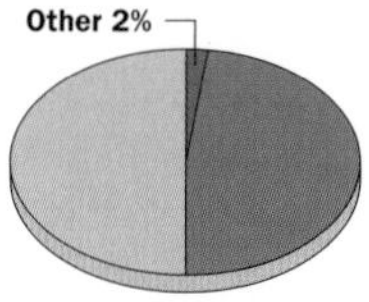
Other 2%
Roman Catholic 50%
Protestant 48%

The Micronesians are physically, linguistically, and culturally diverse. Melanesians live on Yap, and Polynesians occupy southwestern atolls in Pohnpei state. Most islanders live without electricity or running water, and many are effectively recipients of US welfare. Society is traditionally matrilineal.

POLITICS

Nonparty elections

2003/2005

President Joseph J. Urusemal

AT THE LAST ELECTION

Congress 14 seats

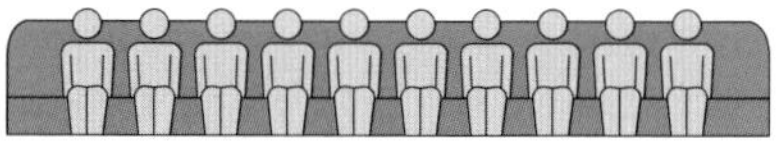

There are no political parties. Ten senators are directly elected for a two-year term and four "at-large" senators (one from each state) are elected for a four-year term

The executive is drawn from the "at-large" senators, but the power of the traditional chiefs remains very strong. The country's relationship with the US is vital and the negotiation of the new Compact of Free Association – which was agreed in 2003 – dominated recent politics. The Faichuk islands, in the western corner of the Chuuk Lagoon, have pressed for the status of a full state, or even independence, complaining of long-term economic neglect.

MICRONESIA

Total Area : 702 sq. km (271 sq. miles)

POPULATION

• under 10 000

LAND HEIGHT

100m/328ft

Sea Level

0 200 km

0 200 miles

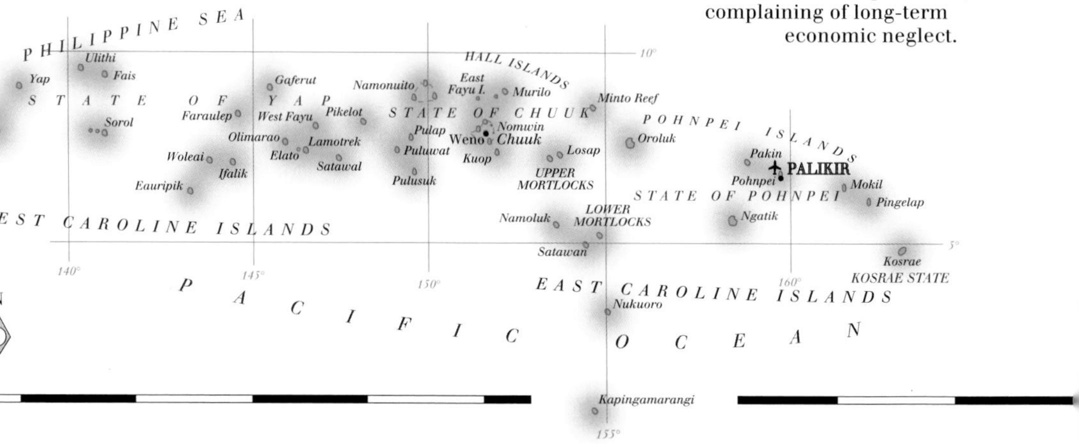
PHILIPPINE SEA
Ulithi
Fais
Yap
STATE OF YAP
Ngulu
Sorol
Gaferut
Faraulep
West Fayu
Pikelot
Olimarao
Lamotrek
Woleai
Elato
Satawal
Ifalik
Eauripik
Namonuito
HALL ISLANDS
East Fayu I.
Murilo
Minto Reef
STATE OF CHUUK
Nomwin
Pulap
Weno
Chuuk
Puluwat
Kuop
Losap
Pulusuk
UPPER MORTLOCKS
Namoluk
LOWER MORTLOCKS
Satawan
POHNPEI ISLANDS
Oroluk
Pakin
PALIKIR
Pohnpei
Mokil
Pingelap
STATE OF POHNPEI
Ngatik
Kosrae
KOSRAE STATE
WEST CAROLINE ISLANDS
EAST CAROLINE ISLANDS
Nukuoro
PACIFIC OCEAN
Kapingamarangi
N
140°
145°
150°
155°
160°
10°
5°

WORLD AFFAIRS

Joined UN in 1991

ADB | PIF | ACP | PC | IBRD

Micronesia's most important relationship is with the US, which administered the islands from 1947 as part of the UN Trust Territory of the Pacific Islands. Under the Compact of Free Association, the US has control over the FSM's foreign and defense policies. Alternative financial assistance is an increasing priority as the new 20-year Compact, which was agreed in May 2003, will not be renewed. Japan is also important, the Tokyo government providing aid, and the FSM has recently cultivated strong links with China.

AID

Recipient

$138m (receipts)

Up 35% in 2001

The US is the principal donor of aid, which is used to fund hospitals, schools, food stamps, and construction projects.

DEFENSE

No compulsory military service

US is responsible for defense

Not applicable

Defense is entirely in the hands of the US. Airstrips in the FSM were used by the US in the Vietnam War.

ECONOMICS

Inflation 3% p.a. (1990–2001)

$258m

Currency is US dollar

SCORE CARD

- ❑ World GNP Ranking.......179th
- ❑ GNP Per Capita.......$2150
- ❑ Balance of Payments.......$67m
- ❑ Inflation.......2.5%
- ❑ Unemployment.......16%

STRENGTHS

Access to US economy, especially for garment manufacture, through preferential trading rights. Large construction industry. Tourism, fishing, and copra production. US strategic interest in Micronesia, and US budget subsidies.

WEAKNESSES

Lack of resources. Dependence on US for imports, especially for fuel. Heavy indebtedness. Acute shortage of water limits development potential. High levels of underemployment.

EXPORTS

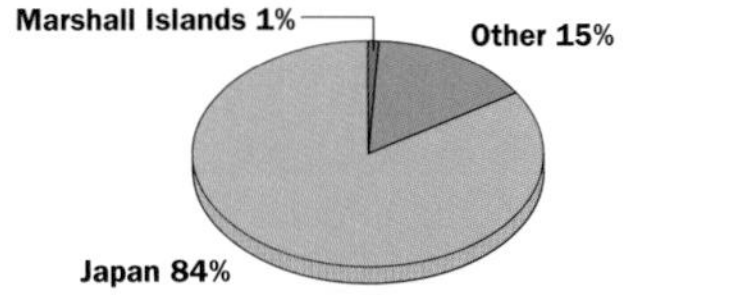
Marshall Islands 1%
Other 15%
Japan 84%

IMPORTS

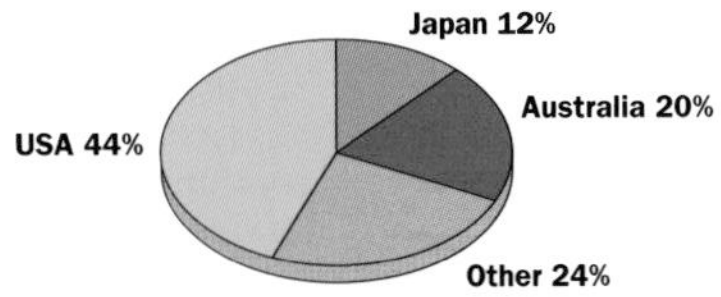
Japan 12%
Australia 20%
USA 44%
Other 24%

RESOURCES

Not available

27,974 tonnes

Not an oil producer

32,000 pigs, 13,900 cattle, 4000 goats, 185,000 chickens

None

The FSM is entirely dependent on external sources for its energy supply. Almost all electricity is produced by small diesel generators. The main resources are copra and valuable fish stocks, especially tuna.

ENVIRONMENT

Not available

None

1.3 tonnes per capita

The FSM does not face pollution on the scale of that in the neighboring Marshall Islands. However, Chuuk suffers serious droughts; occasionally water rationing has had to be introduced for short periods. The growth of marine-based tourism is monitored by the South Pacific Environment Program, which aims to promote sustainable development.

MEDIA

TV ownership medium

There are no daily newspapers

PUBLISHING AND BROADCAST MEDIA

There are no daily newspapers. *The National Union* is a popular biweekly

4 services: 1 state-owned, 3 independent

1 state-owned service

Press freedoms have not been infringed since the strongly criticized expulsion of a Canadian journalist in 1997.

CRIME

No death penalty

39 prisoners

Little change from year to year

Crime is rare and the outlying islands are crime-free. Some alcohol-related assault occurs on Chuuk.

EDUCATION

School leaving age: 13

81%

1510 students

Education is compulsory from the age of six for seven years. Most university students are supported by US grants and a large number attend US colleges.

CHRONOLOGY

The Caroline Islands were first colonized by the Spanish. Sold to Germany in 1899, the islands were occupied by Japan from 1914 and served as an important base in World War II. US control of the islands began in 1945.

- ❑ **1947** UN Trust Territory of the Pacific Islands established.
- ❑ **1979** Independence.
- ❑ **1986** Compact of Free Association with US operational.
- ❑ **1990** Official termination of trusteeship agreement.
- ❑ **1991** Joins UN.
- ❑ **2001** Submerged remains of USS *Mississinewa* causes oil leak in Yap.
- ❑ **2003** Joseph Urusemal elected president. New Compact agreed.

HEALTH

Welfare state health benefits

1 per 1754 people

Cerebrovascular, heart, and intestinal diseases

Basic health care is accessible to all. Diabetes and drug abuse are growing problems. An increase in imported food has led to dietary problems.

SPENDING

GDP/cap. decrease

CONSUMPTION AND SPENDING

No data

80 per 1000 population

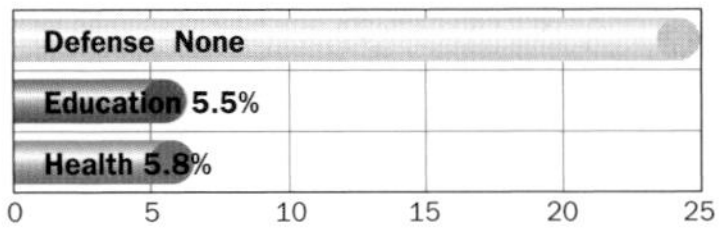
Defense None
Education 5.5%
Health 5.8%
0
5
10
15
20
25

Defense, Health, Education spending as % of GDP

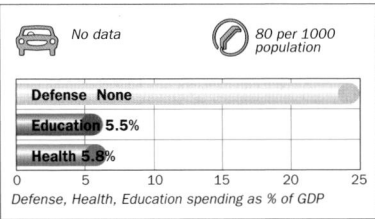

The gap between rich and poor is increasing as Micronesia's businessmen and local officials exploit US aid donations.

WORLD RANKING

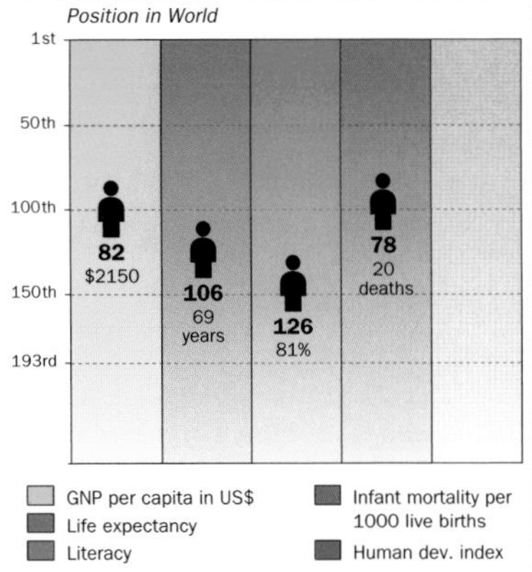
Position in World
1st
50th
100th
150th
193rd
82
$2150
106
69 years
126
81%
78
20 deaths
GNP per capita in US$
Life expectancy
Literacy
Infant mortality per 1000 live births
Human dev. index

M

EUROPE
Europe
Ukraine
MOLDOVA
Romania

MOLDOVA

OFFICIAL NAME: Republic of Moldova **CAPITAL:** Chisinau
POPULATION: 4.3 million **CURRENCY:** Moldovan leu **OFFICIAL LANGUAGE:** Moldovan

1991 | 1991 | Aug 27 | MD | +2 | +373 | .md

MOSTLY UNDULATING steppe country, Moldova is the most densely populated of the former Soviet republics. Once a part of Romania, it was incorporated into the Soviet Union in 1940. Independence in 1991 brought with it the expectation that Moldova would be reunited with Romania. In a 1994 plebiscite, however, Moldovans voted against the proposal. Most of Moldova's population is engaged in intensive agriculture.

Agricultural landscape. *Warm summers and even rainfall are ideal for cereal and fruit farming. Moldova is famous for its wine.*

CLIMATE

Continental

WEATHER CHART FOR CHISINAU

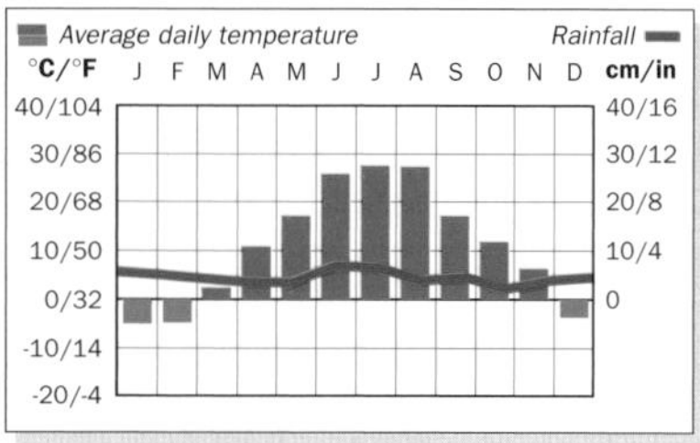
Average daily temperature
Rainfall
°C/°F
J F M A M J J A S O N D
cm/in
40/104
30/86
20/68
10/50
0/32
-10/14
-20/-4
40/16
30/12
20/8
10/4
0

Warm summers, mild winters, and moderate rainfall give Moldova an ideal climate for cultivation.

TRANSPORTATION

Drive on right

Chisinau International 274,662 passengers

Small Black Sea fleet

THE TRANSPORTATION NETWORK

10,738 km (6672 miles)

None

1139 km (708 miles)

424 km (263 miles)

The transportation infrastructure is to be part of a planned "Transport Corridor Europe–Caucasus–Asia" (TRACECA).

TOURISM

Visitors : Population 1:269

16,000 visitors

Down 6% in 2001

MAIN TOURIST ARRIVALS

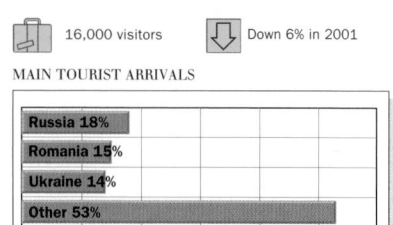

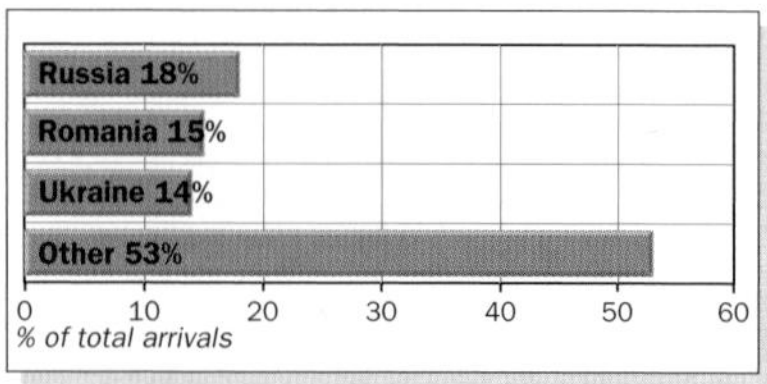
Russia 18%
Romania 15%
Ukraine 14%
Other 53%
0
10
20
30
40
50
60
% of total arrivals

Few tourists go to Moldova, although some visitors to Romania do combine the two. Hopes for the expansion of tourism focus on vineyards and underground wine vault "streets" as the main attractions.

PEOPLE

Pop. density medium

Moldovan, Romanian, Russian

128/km² (330/mi²)

THE URBAN/RURAL POPULATION SPLIT

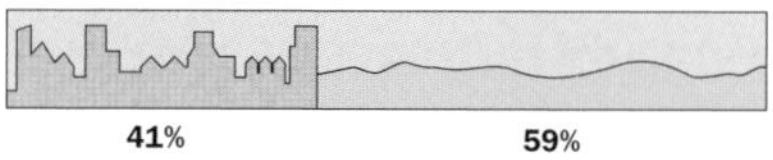
41%
59%

ETHNIC MAKEUP

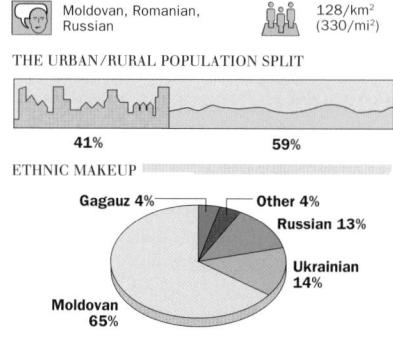

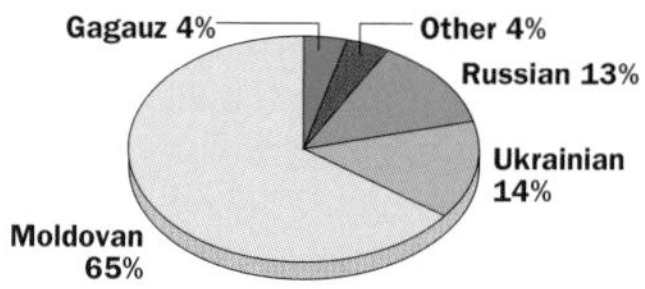
Gagauz 4%
Other 4%
Russian 13%
Ukrainian 14%
Moldovan 65%

Moldovans are ethnically identical to Romanians. There are 153,000 Gagauz (Orthodox Christian Turks) in the south, and a population of mixed Russian–Moldovan–Ukrainian parentage on the eastern bank of the Dniester.

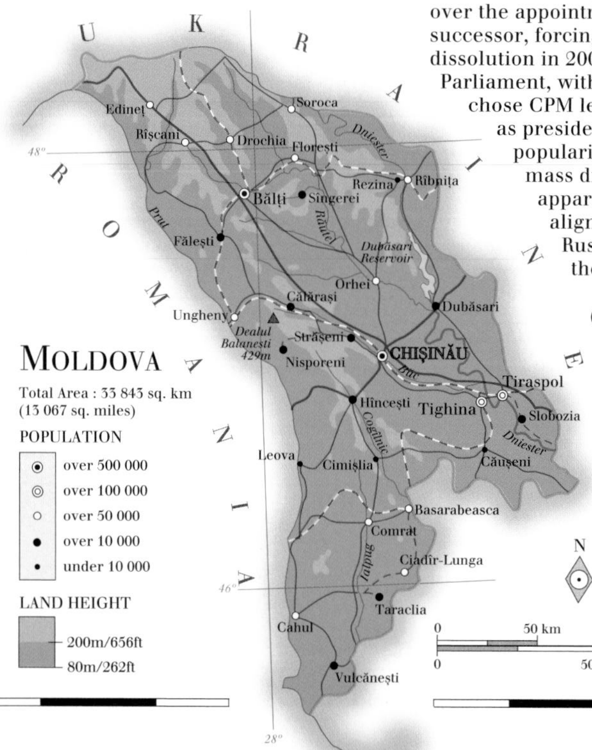
U K R A I N E
R O M A N I A
Edineț
Soroca
Rîșcani
Drochia
Florești
Dniester
Rezina
Rîbnița
Bălți
Sîngerei
Prut
Răut
Fălești
Dubăsari Reservoir
Orhei
Călărași
Dubăsari
Ungheny
Dealul Balanesti 429m
Strășeni
CHIȘINĂU
Nisporeni
Bîc
Tiraspol
Hîncești
Tighina
Slobozia
Cogîlnic
Leova
Cimișlia
Căușeni
Basarabeasca
Comrat
Ialpug
Ciadîr-Lunga
Taraclia
Cahul
Vulcănești
48°
46°
28°
N
0
50 km
0
50 miles

MOLDOVA

Total Area : 33 843 sq. km (13 067 sq. miles)

POPULATION

- over 500 000
- over 100 000
- over 50 000
- over 10 000
- under 10 000

LAND HEIGHT

- 200m/656ft
- 80m/262ft

POLITICS

Multiparty elections

2001/2005

President Vladimir Voronin

AT THE LAST ELECTION

Parliament 101 seats

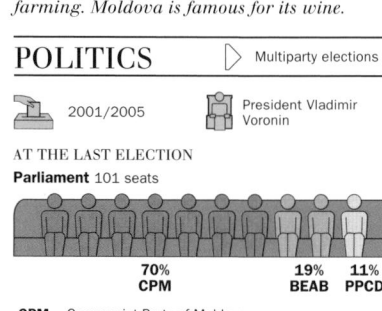

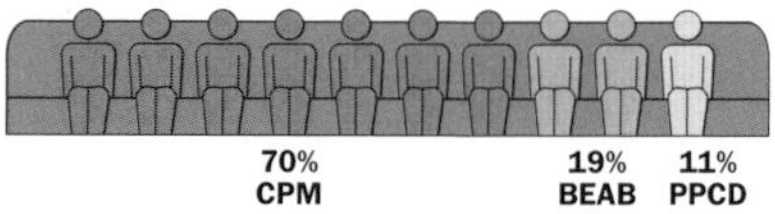
70% CPM
19% BEAB
11% PPCD

CPM = Communist Party of Moldova
BEAB = Electoral Bloc Braghis Alliance
PPCD = Christian-Democratic People's Party

Moldova declared its independence in 1991. Reformist Petru Lucinschi was elected president in 1996 but faced stiff opposition from the increasingly powerful left: the revived CPM won most seats in the 1998 elections. Parliament ended direct presidential elections in 2000, but deadlock ensued over the appointment of Lucinschi's successor, forcing Parliament's dissolution in 2001. The new Parliament, with a big CPM majority, chose CPM leader Vladimir Voronin as president. However, the left's popularity has faltered, with mass discontent over its apparent eagerness to align Moldova with Russia rather than the West.

Transdniestria (on the eastern bank of the river Dniester) and Gagauzia (in the south) declared themselves to be republics in 1990. While Gagauzia accepted autonomous status as provided for in the 1994 Constitution, Transdniestria continues to seek independence.

WORLD AFFAIRS

Joined UN in 1992

BSEC | CE | CIS | EAPC | OSCE

Moldova has not sought NATO membership, and in 2001 showed interest in joining a Union State with Russia and Belarus. Ties with countries in the Black Sea Economic Zone, including Romania and Ukraine, are being developed. The creation of a free economic zone near the mouth of the Danube is under discussion.

AID

Recipient

$119m (receipts)

Down 3% in 2001

The World Bank resumed lending in 2002, granting $30 million. The US, the EU states, and the IMF are also important sources of aid.

DEFENSE

Compulsory military service

$147m

Up 5% in 2001

In 1999 plans were announced to cut army personnel by 30%; military service has been reduced. In 2003 the Transdniestrian authorities finally permitted the full withdrawal of Russian forces.

ECONOMICS

Inflation 103% p.a. (1990–2001)

$1.45bn

14.1 Moldovan lei (13.85)

SCORE CARD

❑ WORLD GNP RANKING	146th
❑ GNP PER CAPITA	$400
❑ BALANCE OF PAYMENTS	–$118m
❑ INFLATION	9.8%
❑ UNEMPLOYMENT	11%

STRENGTHS

Agriculture (wine, tobacco, and cotton) and food processing. Light manufacturing. Signs of economic improvement.

WEAKNESSES

Instability, particularly over Transdniestria, deters investment. Dependent on Russia for raw materials and fuel, and as market for exports. Isolated location; weak transportation network. Slow pace of reform. Cumbersome bureaucracy. Strong black economy. Massive foreign debt eats into export earnings.

EXPORTS

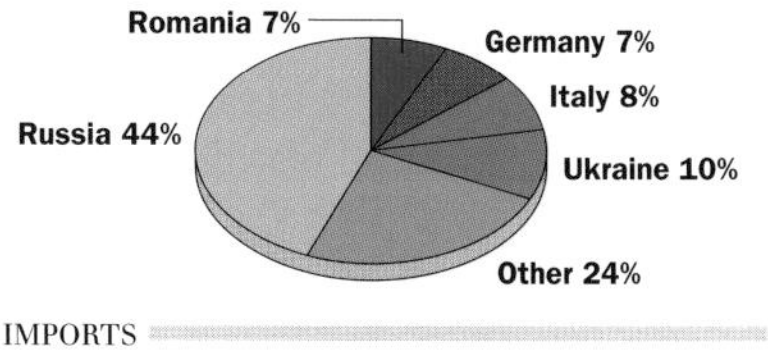
Romania 7%
Germany 7%
Italy 8%
Russia 44%
Ukraine 10%
Other 24%

IMPORTS

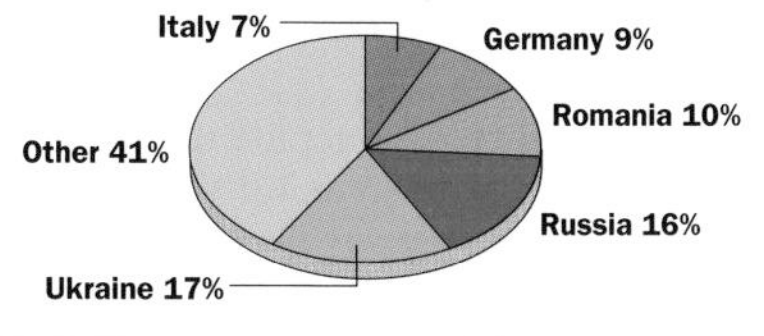
Italy 7%
Germany 9%
Romania 10%
Other 41%
Russia 16%
Ukraine 17%

RESOURCES

Electric power 1m kW

1319 tonnes

Oil and gas reserves not exploited

834,870 sheep, 448,898 pigs, 14.1m chickens

Lignite, phosphates, gypsum, oil, natural gas

Moldova has few mineral resources. It has to import all its fuel and most of its electricity.

ENVIRONMENT

Sustainability rank: 39th

1.5% (0.9% partially protected)

1.5 tonnes per capita

Overuse of agricultural chemicals and pesticides on tobacco farms is a problem, as is soil erosion. There is little spending on environmental improvement.

MEDIA

TV ownership high

Daily newspaper circulation 153 per 1000 people

PUBLISHING AND BROADCAST MEDIA

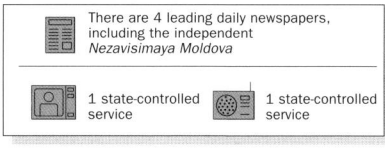

There are 4 leading daily newspapers, including the independent *Nezavisimaya Moldova*

1 state-controlled service

1 state-controlled service

The many new publications represent widely differing interest groups. Russian-language broadcasting is restricted.

CRIME

No death penalty

10,633 prisoners

Up 9% in 1999–2001

Economic decline has caused crime to increase. The unstable situation in Transdniestria has encouraged smuggling, particularly of Russian arms. The Council of Europe has accused the police of routinely using torture.

EDUCATION

School leaving age: 16

99%

102,825 students

Education has followed a Romanian (French-inspired) system since 1991. Mass protests met plans in 2002 to make Russian compulsory in schools.

HEALTH

Welfare state health benefits

1 per 308 people

Cerebrovascular and heart diseases, cancers, liver disease

The centralized health service is poor by regional standards. There are serious shortages of medical supplies.

CHRONOLOGY

Modern Moldova corresponds roughly to the eastern part of the Romanian principality of Moldavia, which existed for 500 years from 1359. Most of it was annexed by Russia in 1812 as Bessarabia.

- ❑ **1918** Bessarabia joins Romania.
- ❑ **1924** Moldovan Autonomous Soviet Republic formed within USSR.
- ❑ **1940** Romania cedes Bessarabia to Ukrainian and Moldovan SSRs.
- ❑ **1941–1945** Bessarabia again under Romanian control.
- ❑ **1945** Returns to Soviet control.
- ❑ **1990** Declares sovereignty.
- ❑ **1991** Independence.
- ❑ **1993–1994** Prounification parties' election defeat; referendum rejects Romanian unification. Rejoins CIS.
- ❑ **1998** Elections: communist revival.
- ❑ **2001** CPM wins big majority. Vladimir Voronin becomes president.
- ❑ **2002** Mass protests over education plans.

SPENDING

GDP/cap. decrease

CONSUMPTION AND SPENDING

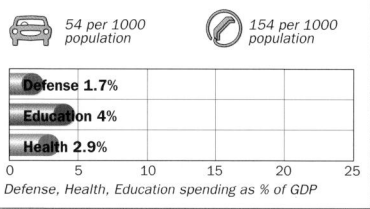

54 per 1000 population

154 per 1000 population

Defense 1.7%
Education 4%
Health 2.9%
0
5
10
15
20
25

Defense, Health, Education spending as % of GDP

Former communist officials have been well placed to benefit from the sale of state-owned businesses. Car ownership is low but rising. However, pensions and wages are often months in arrears. In 1998 the benefits for low-income families and veterans were scrapped. Ethnic Gagauz (Orthodox Christian Turks) are the poorest group.

WORLD RANKING

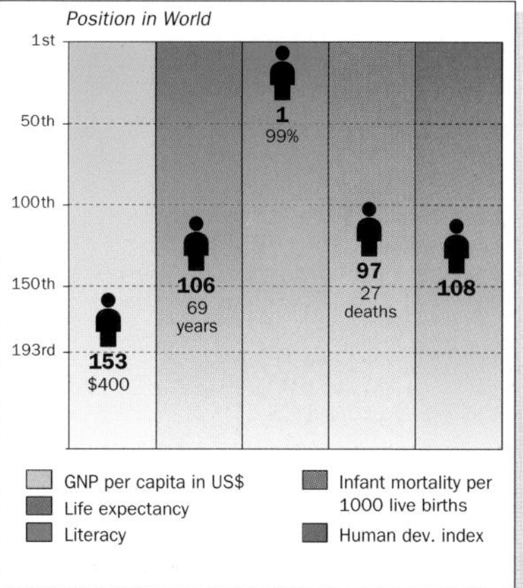
Position in World
1st
50th
100th
150th
193rd
153
$400
106
69
years
1
99%
97
27
deaths
108
GNP per capita in US$
Life expectancy
Literacy
Infant mortality per 1000 live births
Human dev. index

M

MONACO

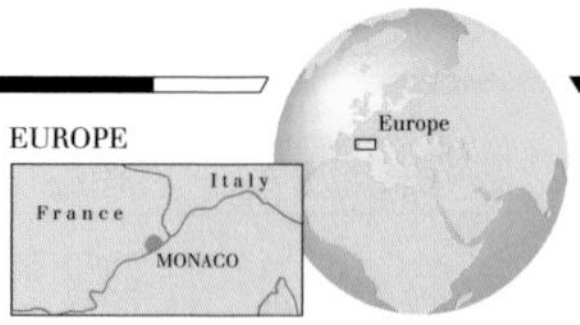
EUROPE
Europe
Italy
France
MONACO

OFFICIAL NAME: Principality of Monaco **CAPITAL:** Monaco-Ville
POPULATION: 31,987 **CURRENCY:** Euro **OFFICIAL LANGUAGE:** French

1861
1861
Nov 19
MC
+1
+377
.mc

MONACO IS A TINY ENCLAVE on the French Côte d'Azur. Its destiny changed radically in 1863, when Prince Charles III, after whom Monte Carlo is named, opened the casino there. Today, Monaco is a lucrative banking and services center, as well as a tourist destination. Prince Rainier's marriage to film star Grace Kelly, and some astute management of the economy, successfully transformed Monaco into a center for the international jet set. In 1962, the prince's absolute authority was abolished by a new, democratic constitution.

CLIMATE

Mediterranean

WEATHER CHART FOR MONACO-VILLE

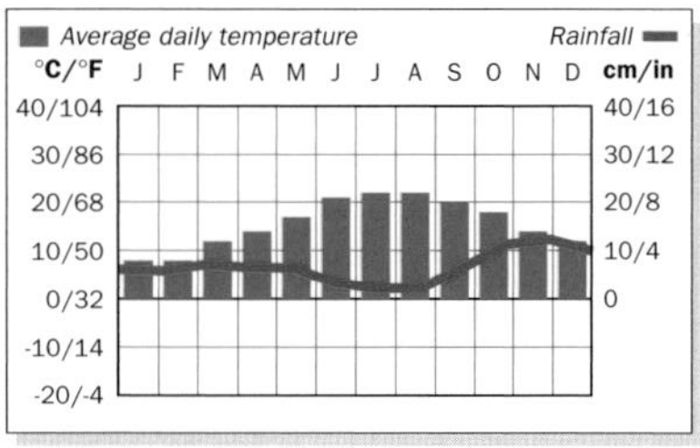
Average daily temperature
Rainfall
°C/°F J F M A M J J A S O N D cm/in
40/104
30/86
20/68
10/50
0/32
-10/14
-20/-4
40/16
30/12
20/8
10/4
0

Summers are hot and dry; days with 12 hours of sunshine are not uncommon. Winters are mild and sunny.

TRANSPORTATION

Drive on right

Héliport de Monaco, Fontvieille
126,755 passengers

8 ships

THE TRANSPORTATION NETWORK

50 km (31 miles)

None

2 km (1 mile)

None

An underground railroad system opened in 1999, with the consequence that 2% of Monaco's area could be reclaimed. Part of the network of roads and tunnels is used for the Grand Prix each year. Air Monaco provides helicopter flights from Nice airport.

TOURISM

Visitors : Population 9.4:1

300,000 visitors

Up 8% in 2000

MAIN TOURIST ARRIVALS

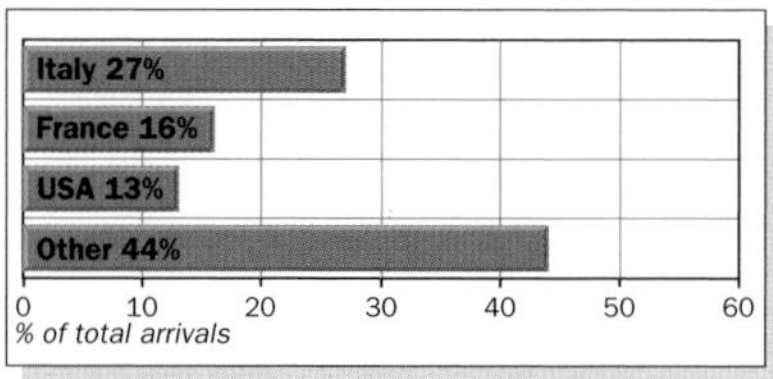
Italy 27%
France 16%
USA 13%
Other 44%
0 10 20 30 40 50 60
% of total arrivals

Huge numbers of tourists, greatly outnumbering the inhabitants, are attracted to Monaco, most coming from Italy and France. Almost all are day-trippers drawn by the casinos and Monaco's conspicuous high society. Around 75% of hotel rooms are classed as "four-star deluxe," and the principality is a particular favorite of wealthy Italians. The Grimaldi Forum conference center, which opened in 2000, hopes to attract more business travelers.

A number of social and sporting events draw particularly large crowds each spring, including the Rose Ball (March), the Tennis Open (April), and the Grand Prix (May).

PEOPLE

Pop. density high

French, Italian, Monégasque, English

16,404/km² (42,649/mi²)

THE URBAN/RURAL POPULATION SPLIT

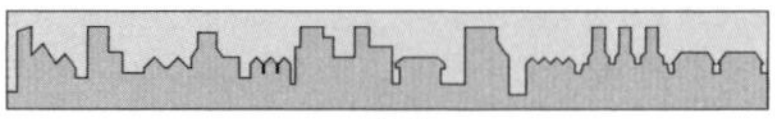
100%

RELIGIOUS PERSUASION

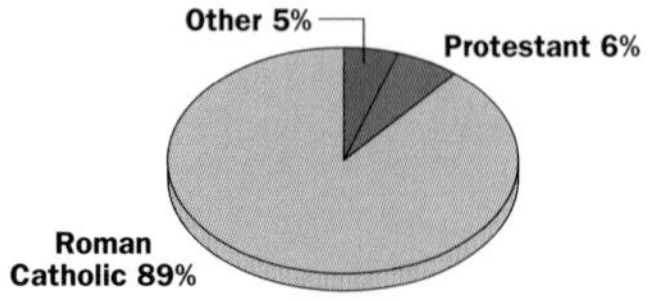
Other 5%
Protestant 6%
Roman Catholic 89%

Fewer than a fifth of Monaco's residents are Monégasque. Around half are French, the rest Italian, American, British, and Belgian. Monégasques enjoy considerable privileges, including housing subsidies to protect them from Monaco's high property prices, and the right of first refusal before a job can be offered to a foreigner. Women have equal status, but only acquired the vote in the constitutional changes of 1962.

POLITICS

Multiparty elections

2003/2008

H.S.H. Prince Rainier III

AT THE LAST ELECTION

National Council 24 seats

88% UPM
12% UND

UPM = Union for Monaco
UND = National and Democratic Union
There are no formal political parties

Prince Rainier III retains considerable power, appointing the government head from a list of French diplomats. The 2003 election, ending 40 years of UND rule, was seen as a vote of no confidence in UND leader Jean-Louis Campora, who is also president of the AS Monaco soccer team. Its troubled finances were a major campaign issue.

WORLD AFFAIRS

Joined UN in 1993

IWC IAEA OSCE OIF

A key concern is to protect both banking secrecy and the liberal tax regime from EU regulation, though the principality has adopted the euro. France is particularly critical, and French citizens have been banned from banking in Monaco since 1962.

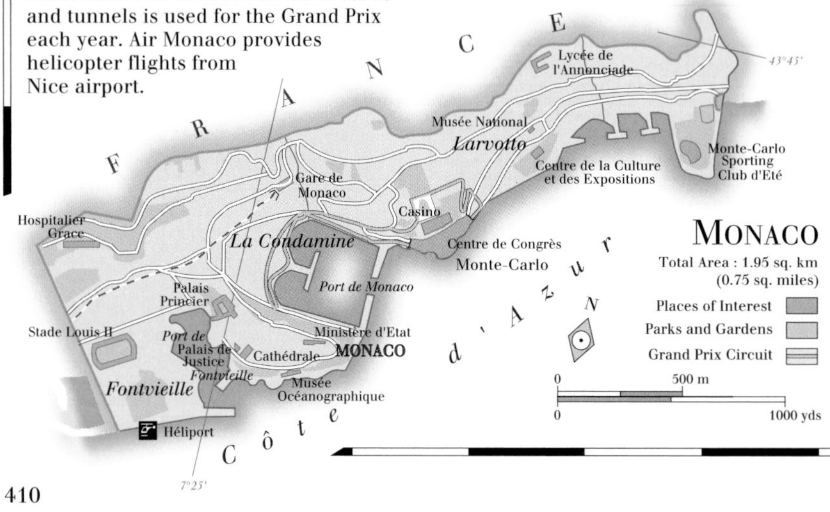
FRANCE
Lycée de l'Annonciade
43°45'
Musée National
Larvotto
Monte-Carlo Sporting Club d'Eté
Centre de la Culture et des Expositions
Gare de Monaco
Casino
Hospitalier Grace
La Condamine
Centre de Congrès
Monte-Carlo
Port de Monaco
Palais Princier
Stade Louis II
Port de Palais de Justice
Fontvieille
Ministère d'Etat
Cathédrale
MONACO
Musée Océanographique
Fontvieille
Héliport
Côte d'Azur
N
7°25'
MONACO
Total Area : 1.95 sq. km (0.75 sq. miles)
Places of Interest
Parks and Gardens
Grand Prix Circuit
0 500 m
0 1000 yds

***Monte Carlo** with its luxury hotels and yacht harbor. The only space for new development is on land reclaimed from the sea.*

AID

Not applicable

Monaco has no aid receipts or donations

Not applicable

Monaco neither receives nor gives aid, and the issue is not of concern to Monégasques.

DEFENSE

No compulsory military service

France responsible for defense

Not applicable

Monaco has no armed forces and no defense budget. France, as the protecting power, bears responsibility for the defense of the principality.

ECONOMICS

Inflation 2.6% p.a. (1985–1996)

$800m

0.871 euros (1.013)

SCORE CARD

❑ WORLD GNP RANKING	157th
❑ GNP PER CAPITA	$25,000
❑ BALANCE OF PAYMENTS	Included in French total
❑ INFLATION	Included in French total
❑ UNEMPLOYMENT	3%

STRENGTHS

Strong tourism sector. Strict banking confidentiality and low taxes attract billions of dollars of overseas deposits. Assets managed by Monaco banks increased by 18% a year in the late 1990s. Very low unemployment. No formal debt and reserves of over €2.3 billion. Main port expanded in 2002.

WEAKNESSES

Continuing vulnerability to money laundering despite the 1994 accord with France obliging banks to furnish details of suspicious accounts. Subject to fluctuations of French and Italian economies. Dependence on VAT for bulk of revenues. Pressure from EU states to end privileged banking and tax laws. Lack of natural resources means total dependence on imports.

EXPORTS/IMPORTS

Monaco has a full customs union with France

RESOURCES

Electric power: Included within French total

3 tonnes

Not an oil producer

Included within French total

None

Monaco has no strategic resources and imports all its energy from France. It has no agricultural land.

ENVIRONMENT

Not available

None

4.1 tonnes per capita

Monaco has built the most extensive underground car parking facilities in the world to tackle congestion. The quality of the built environment around the harbor occasionally arouses local passions. Important populations of red coral are under threat from land reclamation and pollution.

MEDIA

TV ownership high

Daily newspaper circulation 251 per 1000 people

PUBLISHING AND BROADCAST MEDIA

There is 1 daily newspaper. *Nice-Matin*, a regional French newspaper, publishes a Monaco edition

2 services

4 services: 1 part-owned by French state, 3 independent

In addition to its domestic radio and TV, Monaco receives all the mainstream French and Italian channels.

CRIME

No death penalty

13 prisoners

Up 35% in 2000–2001

Monaco was censured in 2002 by the OECD as one of seven "uncooperative tax havens" failing to respond to a campaign for greater financial transparency.

EDUCATION

School leaving age: 15

99%

Not available

The education system is essentially the same as that of France, with students studying for the *baccalauréat* exam. Most go on to university in France, but then return to claim good jobs in Monaco. The Catholic Church exerts considerable influence and is still responsible for primary schooling.

HEALTH

Welfare state health benefits

1 per 151 people

cerebrovascular and heart diseases, cancers

Most medical care is provided by private health insurance. Doctors train in France. The Princess Grace Hospital can serve 60,000 people, also catering for patients from outside Monaco.

CHRONOLOGY

In 1297, the Grimaldis first seized control of the territory of which they became hereditary rulers.

- ❑ **1861** Independent under French protection.
- ❑ **1863** Monte Carlo casino opens.
- ❑ **1949** Rainier III accedes to throne.
- ❑ **1962** Constitution rewritten: end of absolute authority of the prince.
- ❑ **1963** Democratic legislative elections held for first time.
- ❑ **1982** Princess Grace dies following car accident.
- ❑ **2002** Euro introduced.

SPENDING

GDP/cap. increase

CONSUMPTION AND SPENDING

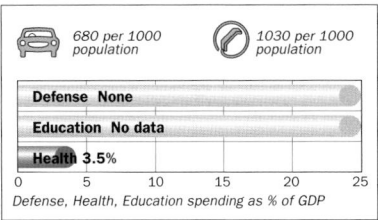

680 per 1000 population

1030 per 1000 population

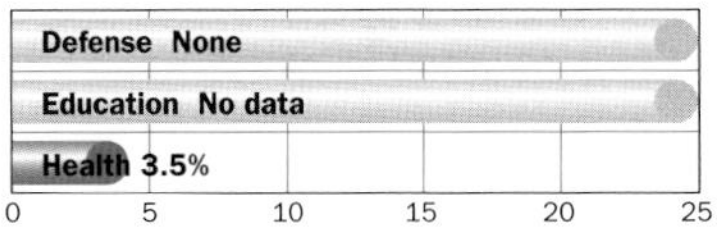

Defense None
Education No data
Health 3.5%
0
5
10
15
20
25

Defense, Health, Education spending as % of GDP

Monaco's image abroad has changed dramatically since Prince Rainier acceded in 1949. From being considered simply as a gambling spot, it is now ranked as one of the world's most glamorous international jet-set destinations. In part, this was the result of Prince Rainier's marriage to Grace Kelly, then a leading Hollywood star, which brought Monaco to the attention of US high society. More important was the prince's work in turning Monaco into a major tax haven and an upmarket resort, by making the most of its Mediterranean coastal location. Many celebrities are residents, among them Luciano Pavarotti, Ringo Starr, and racing drivers David Coulthard and Jenson Button.

WORLD RANKING

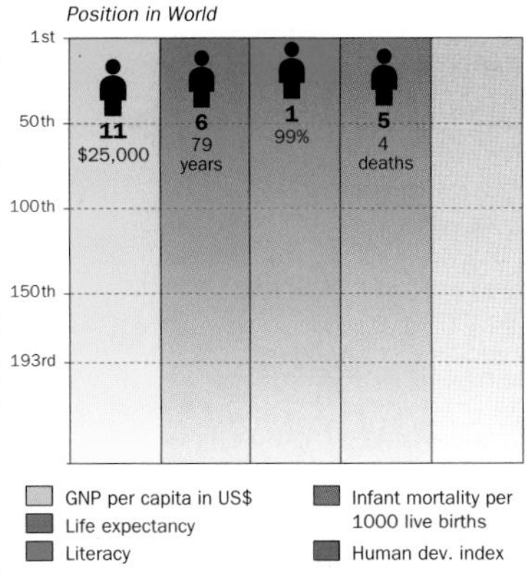

Position in World
1st
50th
100th
150th
193rd
11
$25,000
6
79 years
1
99%
5
4 deaths
GNP per capita in US$
Life expectancy
Literacy
Infant mortality per 1000 live births
Human dev. index

M

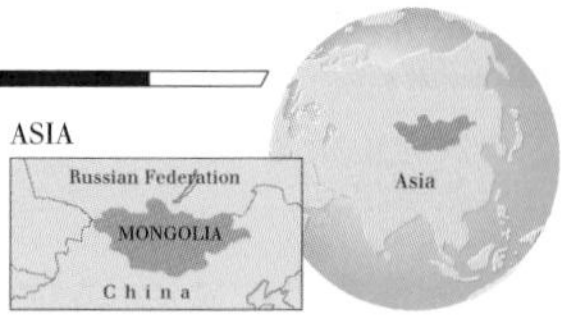
ASIA
Russian Federation
MONGOLIA
China
Asia

MONGOLIA

OFFICIAL NAME: Mongolia **CAPITAL:** Ulan Bator **POPULATION:** 2.6 million
CURRENCY: Tugrik (tögrög) **OFFICIAL LANGUAGE:** Khalkha Mongolian

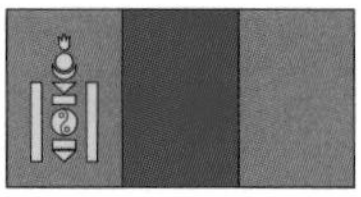

1924 | 1924 | July 11 | MGL | +8 | +976 | .mn

LANDLOCKED BETWEEN Siberia and China's Mongolian provinces, Mongolia rises from the semiarid Gobi Desert to mountainous steppe. The traditionally nomadic Mongols were first unified by Genghis Khan in 1206. "Outer" Mongolia achieved independence from China as a communist state in 1924 and was officially aligned with the USSR from 1936. In 1990, it abandoned communist rule; widespread poverty ensued. Extremely harsh winters in 1999–2001 devastated the rural economy.

CLIMATE

Mountain/cold desert/steppe

WEATHER CHART FOR ULAN BATOR

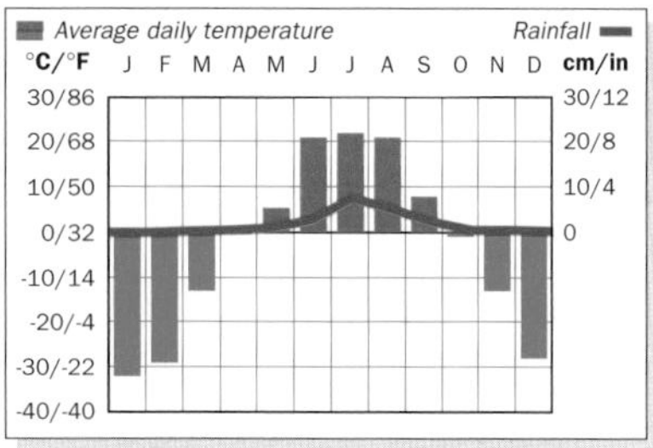
Average daily temperature
Rainfall
°C/°F
J F M A M J J A S O N D
cm/in
30/86
20/68
10/50
0/32
-10/14
-20/-4
-30/-22
-40/-40
30/12
20/8
10/4
0

Temperature variations are extreme. Dry summers combine with severe winters, known as *zud*, to devastate livestock, as happened in 1999 and 2000.

TRANSPORTATION

Drive on right

Buyant-Ukhaa, Ulan Bator | Has no fleet

THE TRANSPORTATION NETWORK

1563 km (971 miles)	None
1810 km (1125 miles)	400 km (249 miles)

Lack of investment has left Mongolia's infrastructure to decay, increasing transportation and distribution costs. Links to China and the Pacific are priorities. Gasoline shortages have meant a large increase in the use of animals for transportation.

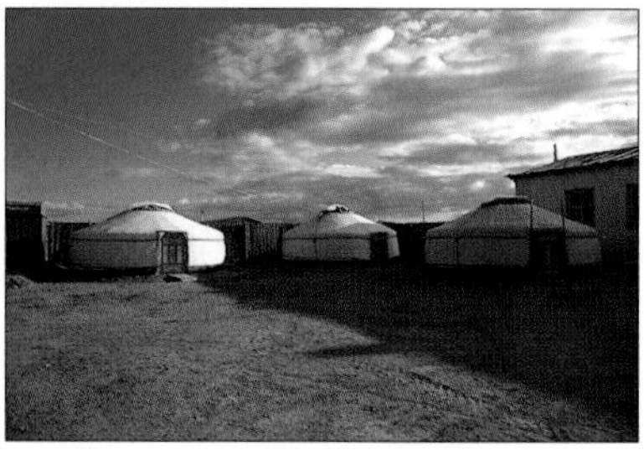

Traditional gers in the Gobi Desert. *Many Mongolians still choose to pursue a nomadic lifestyle, living in felt tents or* gers.

TOURISM

Visitors : Population 1:14

192,000 visitors | Up 22% in 2001

MAIN TOURIST ARRIVALS

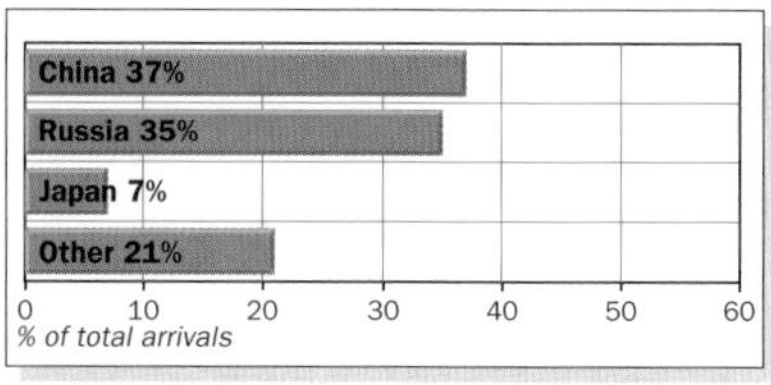
China 37%
Russia 35%
Japan 7%
Other 21%
0
10
20
30
40
50
60
% of total arrivals

Tourism has expanded overall since the easing of visa restrictions in 1991. Under communism, all travel was arranged through the state agency, Zhuuichin, but private companies are now entering the market.

PEOPLE

Pop. density low

Khalkha Mongolian, Kazakh, Chinese, Russian | 2/km² (4/mi²)

THE URBAN/RURAL POPULATION SPLIT

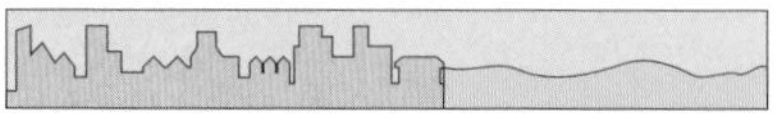
57%
43%

ETHNIC MAKEUP

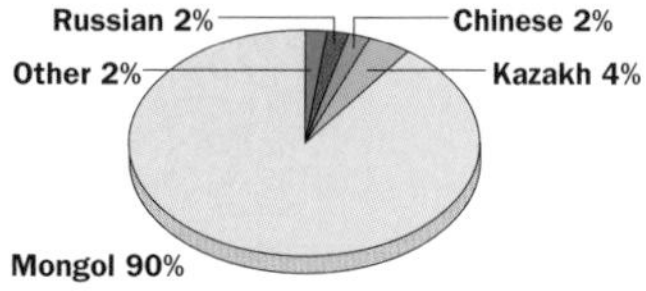
Russian 2%
Chinese 2%
Other 2%
Kazakh 4%
Mongol 90%

Khalkh Mongols, who adhere to Tibetan Buddhism, are the main ethnic group. Though economic pressures keep many people near urban centers, most remain nomadic. One-third live in Ulan Bator. Turkic Kazakhs in the west form the largest minority, but emigration to Kazakhstan since 1990 has reduced their numbers. Tensions exist with the Chinese and Russian minorities.

POLITICS

Multiparty elections

2000/2004 | President Natsagyn Bagabandi

AT THE LAST ELECTION

State Great Hural 76 seats

95%
MPRP
4%
Ind
1%
MNDP

MPRP = Mongolian People's Revolutionary Party
Ind = Independents
MNDP = Mongolian National Democratic Party

The end of communism and the advent of democracy in 1990 revolutionized Mongolian politics. The shock of economic reform led many Mongolians to regret the lost certainties of the communist era. In 1992 the democrats lost power to the renamed communists (MPRP), but their failure to revive the economy swung the pendulum back in favor of a democratic coalition in 1996. An uneasy cohabitation between President Natsagyn Bagabandi of the MPRP, who took office in 1997, and an MNDP-led government existed until the sweeping MPRP election victory in 2000.

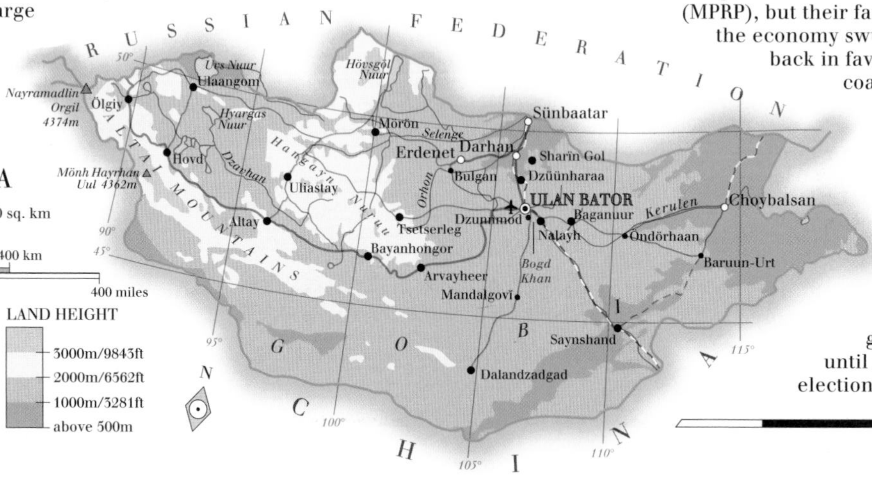
RUSSIAN FEDERATION
CHINA
GOBI
ALTAI MOUNTAINS
Hangayn Nuruu
Nayramadlin Orgil 4374m
Mönh Hayrhan Uul 4362m
Uvs Nuur
Ulaangom
Hövsgöl Nuur
Ölgiy
Hyargas Nuur
Mörön
Selenge
Sünbaatar
Darhan
Erdenet
Sharin Gol
Bulgan
Dzüünharaa
Hovd
Dzavhan
Uliastay
Orhon
ULAN BATOR
Kerulen
Choybalsan
Baganuur
Dzuunmod
Nalayh
Öndörhaan
Altay
Tsetserleg
Bayanhongor
Baruun-Urt
Arvayheer
Bogd Khan
Mandalgovĭ
Saynshand
Dalandzadgad
50°
45°
90°
95°
100°
105°
110°
115°
N

MONGOLIA

Total Area : 1 565 000 sq. km (604 247 sq. miles)

0 400 km
0 400 miles

POPULATION
- over 500 000
- over 50 000
- over 10 000
- under 10 000

LAND HEIGHT
- 3000m/9843ft
- 2000m/6562ft
- 1000m/3281ft
- above 500m

M

WORLD AFFAIRS

Joined UN in 1961

IAEA | IBRD | NAM | ADB | WTO

Closer relations with Japan and other east Asian states have failed to weaken Mongolia's ties with Russia and China. There are residual tensions with China, since the majority of ethnic Mongols actually reside in the adjoining Chinese province of Inner Mongolia, but there is no longer a fear of Chinese designs on Mongolian sovereignty.

AID

Recipient

$212m (receipts) — Down 2% in 2001

A balance-of-payments deficit and severe weather make aid vital. The main donors are Japan and the ADB.

DEFENSE

Compulsory military service

$25m — Up 9% in 2001

The last Soviet forces left in 1992. However, ties are still strong, and under agreements reached in 2000 and 2001, Russia is helping to reform the greatly reduced and poorly equipped Mongolian forces.

ECONOMICS

Inflation 51% p.a. (1990–2001)

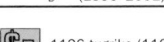

$963m — 1126 tugriks (1105)

SCORE CARD

- World GNP Ranking 156th
- GNP per Capita $400
- Balance of Payments ....-$79m
- Inflation 8.7%
- Unemployment 5%

Strengths

Copper and cashmere. Largely untapped coal and oil reserves. Traditional and efficient rural economy.

Weaknesses

Harsh winters ravaged livestock between 1999 and 2001. Decaying infrastructure. Rising poverty.

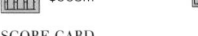

EXPORTS

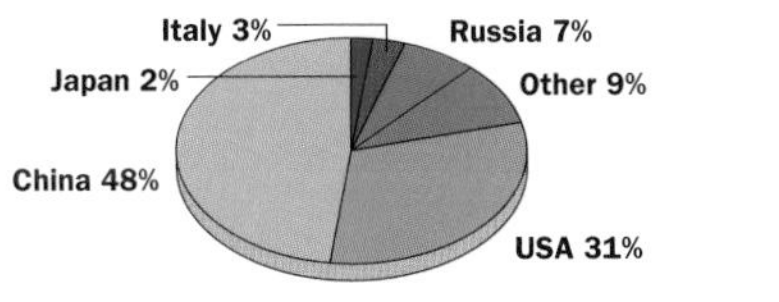

Italy 3%
Russia 7%
Japan 2%
Other 9%
China 48%
USA 31%

IMPORTS

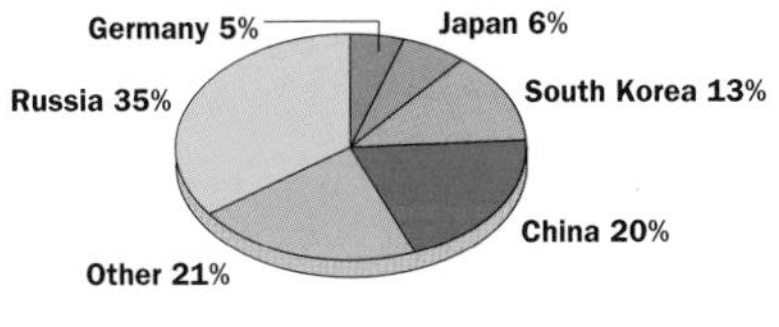

Germany 5%
Japan 6%
Russia 35%
South Korea 13%
China 20%
Other 21%

RESOURCES

Electric power 901,000 kW

425 tonnes — Contracts have been signed with oil prospectors

11.9m sheep, 8.86m goats, 3.1m horses — Oil, coal, copper, lead, fluorite, tungsten, tin, gold, uranium

Under communism, Mongolia's vast mineral resources were barely exploited, and prospecting has only recently begun. A uranium-mining joint venture with Russia has been established. Mongolia is rich in oil, with sufficient reserves to meet future domestic needs. In 1999 an oil extraction agreement was signed with China.

ENVIRONMENT

Sustainability rank: 42nd

12% — 3.1 tonnes per capita

The air in Ulan Bator is heavily polluted as a result of burning soft coal in power plants and the nonenforcement of environmental laws. In 2001 efforts were renewed to preserve the Bogd Khan, the world's oldest protected area, from illegal logging, hunting, and air pollution.

MEDIA

TV ownership medium

Daily newspaper circulation 17 per 1000 people

PUBLISHING AND BROADCAST MEDIA

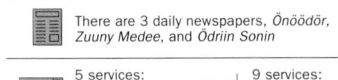

There are 3 daily newspapers, *Önöödör, Zuuny Medee,* and *Ödriin Sonin*

5 services: 1 state-owned, 4 independent — 9 services: 1 state-owned, 8 independent

Slander and libel laws were abolished in 1990, and legislation enacted in 1999 eased curbs on the media. However, paper and fuel shortages have restricted the number of publications and their distribution. Several independent radio and TV stations compete with the state-owned service.

CRIME

Death penalty in use

6656 prisoners — Down 1% in 2000–2001

Crime rose rapidly in the early 1990s, particularly organized crime and muggings by knife gangs. Ulan Bator is the most dangerous area, especially for foreigners; Russians, Chinese, and dollar-carrying US tourists are the main targets.

EDUCATION

School leaving age: 15

99% — 84,970 students

Education is modeled on the former Soviet system. The majority of teachers are women on low salaries. Private-sector schools emphasizing Mongol culture are beginning to open.

CHRONOLOGY

In the 17th century, the Manchus took control of Mongolia. It stayed in Chinese hands until 1911.

- **1919** China reoccupies Mongolia.
- **1924** Independent communist state.
- **1989–1990** Prodemocracy protests; communist election defeat.
- **1992** Former communists, renamed MPRP, returned to power.
- **1996** Democratic Union coalition wins general election.
- **1997** MPRP wins presidency.
- **1999–2001** Severe winters.
- **2000** Landslide electoral victory for MPRP.

HEALTH

Welfare state health benefits

1 per 394 people — Heart, parasitic, and respiratory diseases

Shortages of drugs and equipment have renewed interest in traditional Mongolian herbal medicine. As well as the state-run system, some Buddhist monasteries provide health care.

SPENDING

GDP/cap. increase

CONSUMPTION AND SPENDING

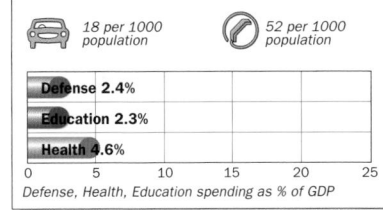

18 per 1000 population — *52 per 1000 population*

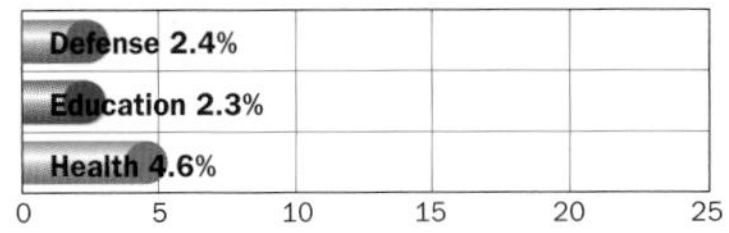

Defense 2.4%
Education 2.3%
Health 4.6%
0
5
10
15
20
25

Defense, Health, Education spending as % of GDP

Economic liberalization has fueled great disparities in wealth. An estimated 50% of the population live below the poverty line; the poorest cannot even afford to buy bread. Starvation threatened after the severe winters of 1999–2001.

WORLD RANKING

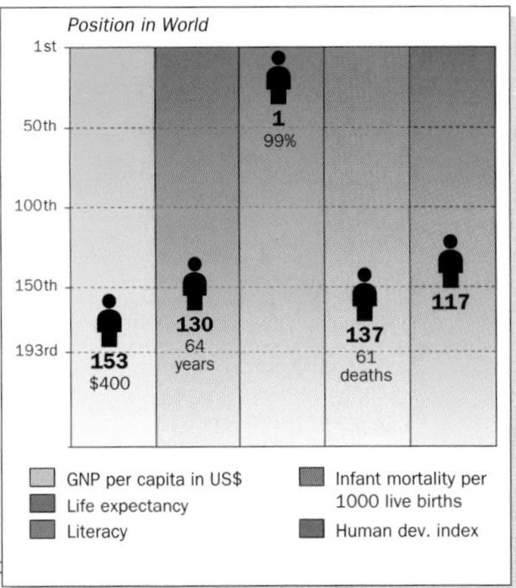

Position in World
1st
50th
100th
150th
193rd
153
$400
130
64
years
1
99%
137
61
deaths
117
GNP per capita in US$
Life expectancy
Literacy
Infant mortality per 1000 live births
Human dev. index

M

MOROCCO

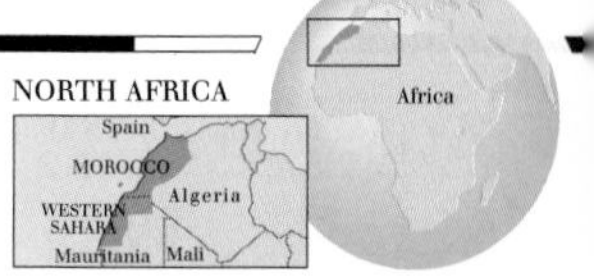
NORTH AFRICA
Spain
MOROCCO
Algeria
WESTERN SAHARA
Mauritania
Mali
Africa

OFFICIAL NAME: Kingdom of Morocco **CAPITAL:** Rabat
POPULATION: 31 million **CURRENCY:** Moroccan dirham **OFFICIAL LANGUAGE:** Arabic

1956 | 1956 | July 30 | MA | 0 | +212 | .ma

MOROCCO IS SITUATED in north Africa, but at its northernmost point lies only 12 km (8 miles) from mainland Europe, across the Strait of Gibraltar. The northern regions have a Mediterranean climate, while the south comprises semiarid desert. The late King Hassan's international prestige gave Morocco status out of proportion to its wealth. The main issues facing the country are the internal threat of Islamist militancy and the stalled political process in Western Sahara, the former Spanish colony occupied by Morocco since 1975. Key economic strengths are tourism, phosphates, and agriculture.

CLIMATE

Hot desert/mountain/ Mediterranean

WEATHER CHART FOR RABAT

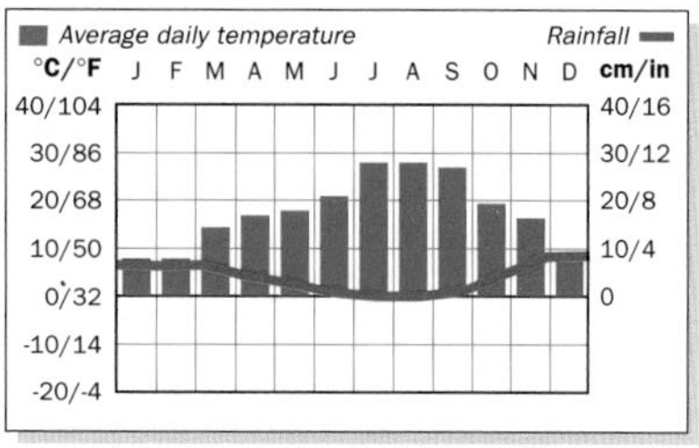
Average daily temperature
Rainfall
°C/°F
J F M A M J J A S O N D
cm/in
40/104
30/86
20/68
10/50
0/32
-10/14
-20/-4
40/16
30/12
20/8
10/4
0

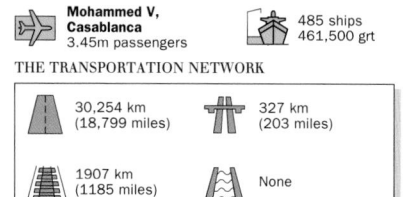

The climate ranges from warm and temperate in the north to semiarid in the south, but temperatures are cooler in the mountains, especially in the high Atlas. During the summer, the effects of the *sirocco* and *chergui*, hot winds from the Sahara, are felt.

TRANSPORTATION

Drive on right

Mohammed V, Casablanca
3.45m passengers

485 ships
461,500 grt

THE TRANSPORTATION NETWORK

30,254 km (18,799 miles)

327 km (203 miles)

1907 km (1185 miles)

None

Morocco has three main international airports. A highway links Rabat and Casablanca, and plans for a new trans-Sahara highway from Tangier to Lagos, Nigeria, were announced in mid-2000. In rural areas, however, roads tend to peter out.

TOURISM

Visitors : Population 1:7.4

4.19m visitors

Down 1% in 2002

MAIN TOURIST ARRIVALS

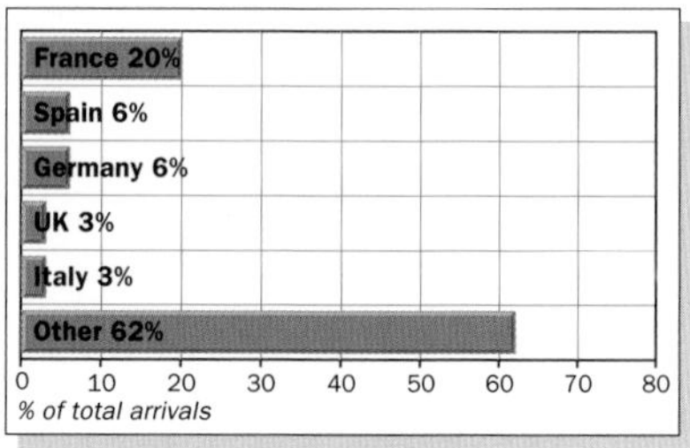
France 20%
Spain 6%
Germany 6%
UK 3%
Italy 3%
Other 62%
0 10 20 30 40 50 60 70 80
% of total arrivals

Tourism is vital to the Moroccan economy. Good beaches abound; Agadir has 300 days of sunshine a year. Fès and Marrakech offer cultural interest, while the Atlas Mountains attract walkers and skiers. Desert safaris are offered in the Sahara. Most Western tourists come from France, Germany, and Spain.

M

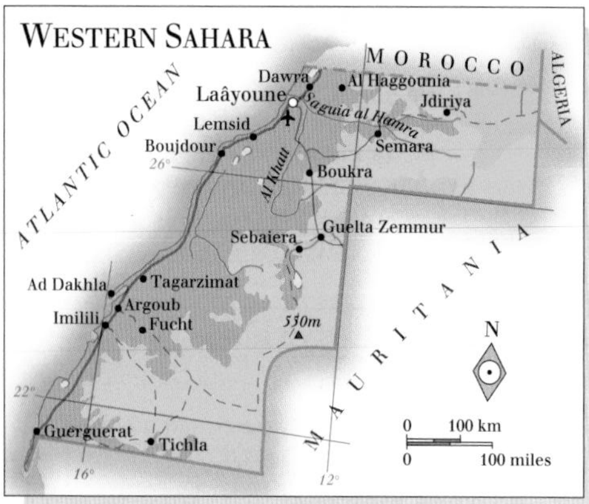
WESTERN SAHARA
MOROCCO
ALGERIA
ATLANTIC OCEAN
MAURITANIA
Dawra
Al Haggounia
Laâyoune
Jdiriya
Saguia al Hamra
Lemsid
Semara
Boujdour
Boukra
Al Khatt
Sebaiera
Guelta Zemmur
Ad Dakhla
Tagarzimat
Argoub
Imilili
Fucht
550m
Guerguerat
Tichla
N
0 100 km
0 100 miles

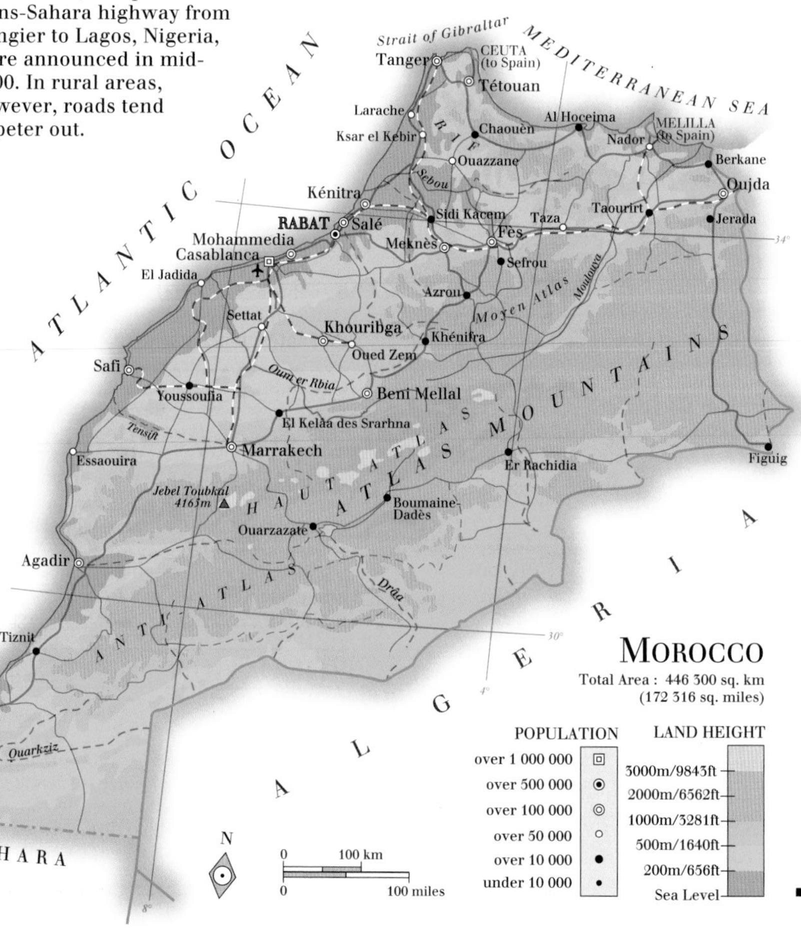
Strait of Gibraltar
MEDITERRANEAN SEA
ATLANTIC OCEAN
Tanger
CEUTA (to Spain)
Tétouan
Larache
Ksar el Kebir
Chaouèn
Al Hoceima
Nador
MELILLA (to Spain)
Berkane
Oujda
Ouazzane
Sebou
Kénitra
Sidi Kacem
Taza
Taourirt
Jerada
RABAT
Salé
Fès
Mohammedia
Casablanca
Meknès
Sefrou
El Jadida
Azrou
Moyen Atlas
Settat
Khouribga
Khénifra
Oued Zem
Safi
Oum er Rbia
Beni Mellal
Youssoufia
El Kelâa des Srarhna
Tensift
Marrakech
Essaouira
Er Rachidia
Figuig
Jebel Toubkal 4165m
HAUT ATLAS
ATLAS MOUNTAINS
Boumaine-Dadès
Ouarzazate
Agadir
ANTI ATLAS
Drâa
Tiznit
ALGERIA
Tan-Tan
Ouarkziz
WESTERN SAHARA
N
0 100 km
0 100 miles
MOROCCO
Total Area : 446 300 sq. km (172 316 sq. miles)
POPULATION
over 1 000 000
over 500 000
over 100 000
over 50 000
over 10 000
under 10 000
LAND HEIGHT
3000m/9843ft
2000m/6562ft
1000m/3281ft
500m/1640ft
200m/656ft
Sea Level

PEOPLE

Pop. density medium

Arabic, Tamazight, French, Spanish

69/km² (180/mi²)

THE URBAN/RURAL POPULATION SPLIT

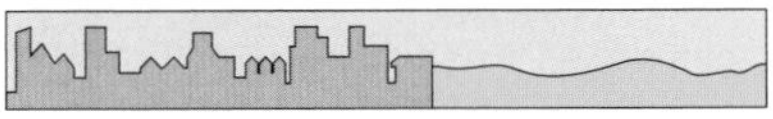

56%
44%

RELIGIOUS PERSUASION

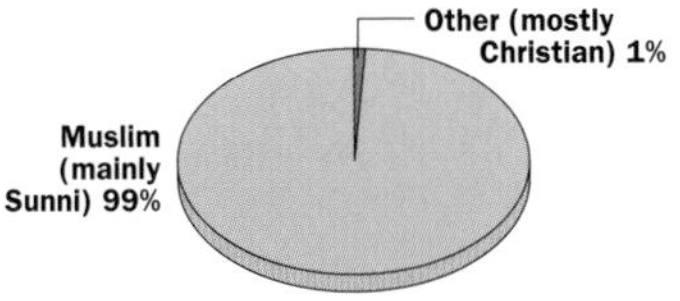

Other (mostly Christian) 1%
Muslim (mainly Sunni) 99%

ETHNIC MAKEUP

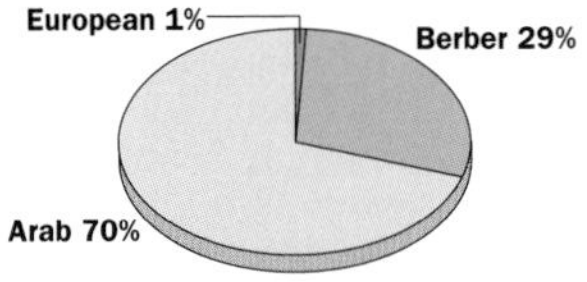

European 1%
Berber 29%
Arab 70%

Morocco, the westernmost of the Maghreb states, is the main refuge for descendants of the original Berber inhabitants of northwest Africa. About 35% of Moroccans speak Berber (Tamazight is the main dialect). They live mainly in mountain villages, while the Arab majority inhabit the lowlands. Before independence from France, 450,000 Europeans lived in Morocco; numbers have since greatly diminished. Some 45,000 Jews enjoy religious freedom and full civil rights – a position in society unique among Arab countries. Most people speak Arabic, and French is also spoken in urban areas.

Sunni Islam is the religion of almost all of the population. The king is the spiritual leader through his position as Commander of the Faithful.

Female emancipation has been slow to take root in Morocco, but women are starting to take a more prominent role in society.

POPULATION AGE BREAKDOWN

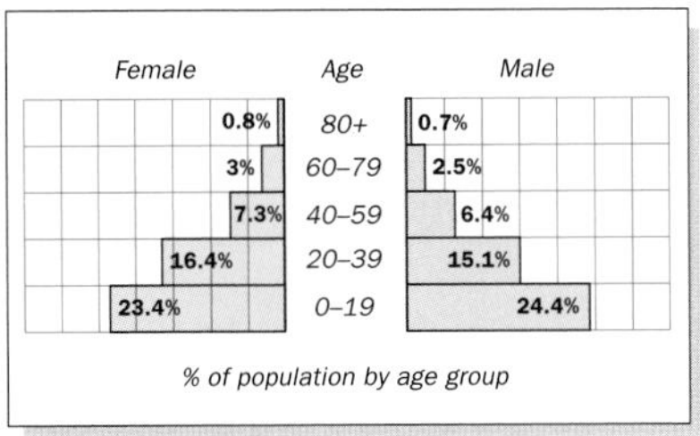

Female
Age
Male
0.8%
80+
0.7%
3%
60–79
2.5%
7.3%
40–59
6.4%
16.4%
20–39
15.1%
23.4%
0–19
24.4%
% of population by age group

POLITICS

Multiparty elections

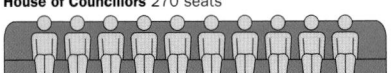

L. House 2002/2007
U. House 2000/2003

H.M. King Mohammed VI

AT THE LAST ELECTION

House of Representatives 325 seats

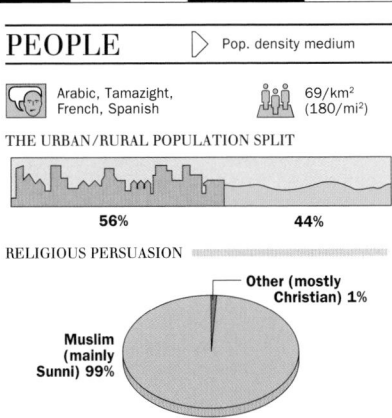

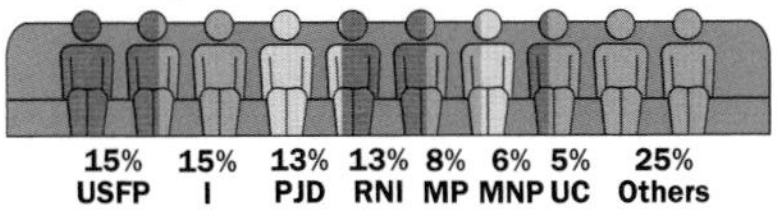

15% USFP
15% I
13% PJD
13% RNI
8% MP
6% MNP
5% UC
25% Others

USFP = Socialist Union of Popular Forces **I** = Istiqlal (Independence) **PJD** = Justice and Development Party **RNI** = National Rally of Independents **MP** = Popular Movement **MNP** = National Popular Movement **UC** = Constitutional Union

House of Councillors 270 seats

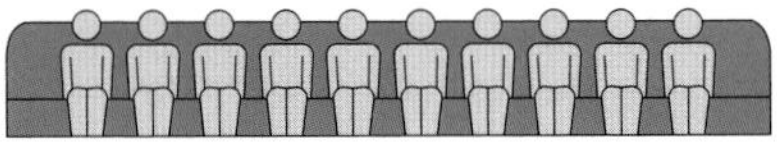

An indirectly elected House of Councillors was formed in 1997

Morocco is a constitutional monarchy with a bicameral legislature. The king appoints (and may dismiss) the prime minister and, on the prime minister's recommendation, other members of the cabinet.

PROFILE

The formation of a socialist-led government after the elections in 1997 was seen as a breakthrough in terms of indicating the growing role of the party system. The ruling parties maintained their strength in the 2002 elections, with the USFP and Istiqlal gaining most seats, but support for Islamists (the PJD) rose dramatically. Independent Driss Jettou was appointed prime minister.

MAIN POLITICAL ISSUES

The post-Hassan monarchy

King Mohammed VI is seen as a less dominating figure than his father, Hassan II, and his accession raised hopes for change. The king's marriage in 2002 to computer engineer Salma Bennani was presented as evidence of a more modern and open outlook. The queen is expected to provide a role model for Moroccan women.

Islamist militancy

There is now a more tolerant stance toward Islamist activists. In 2000, Abdessalam Yassine, spiritual leader of the banned Justice and Good Deeds movement, was released after ten years in prison without trial. Pro-Islamist rallies have far outnumbered those by supporters of greater rights for women. In 2003, suicide bombings in Casablanca were linked to al-Qaida, suggesting a widening of Moroccan Islamist activities.

***Prime Minister Driss Jettou**, appointed in 2002.*

***King Mohammed VI**, who succeeded his father, Hassan II.*

***The town of Boumaine-Dadès** lies in the southern foothills of the Atlas Mountains. The region's outstanding scenery makes it one of Morocco's major tourist attractions.*

WORLD AFFAIRS

Joined UN in 1956

AL | AMU | NAM | OIC | OIF

Morocco's important role in the quest for lasting peace in the Middle East was underlined by Israeli prime minister Yitzhak Rabin's visit to Rabat following the signing in Washington D.C. of the 1993 peace accord with the Palestine Liberation Organization. King Hassan's foreign policy was ambiguous, for while he negotiated with Israel he also headed the Jerusalem Committee of the Organization of the Islamic Conference (OIC). Generally more pro-Western than other Arab states, Morocco has also earned respect by protecting its Jewish minority.

International disapproval has focused on Morocco's occupation since 1975 of the former Spanish colony of Western Sahara. Resistance by Polisario Front guerrillas, who are fighting for an independent Western Sahara, began in 1983 and has continued, despite a 1991 UN-brokered peace plan. Since then, UN proposals have included a referendum on self-determination and autonomy for Western Sahara under Moroccan sovereignty. The process remained stalled in 2003, the UN repeatedly extending its mandate.

Relations with the EU were strengthened with the signing of an association agreement in late 1995, envisaging free trade in industrial goods within 12 years.

Sovereignty disputes with Spain over rocky islets in the Mediterranean were at the heart of a high-profile confrontation in 2002.

AID

Recipient

$517m (receipts)

Up 23% in 2001

Saudi Arabia wrote off $2.7 billion of Moroccan debt after the 1991 Gulf War. The World Bank has given help to Morocco, but it receives little aid.

M

CHRONOLOGY

Independence from France in 1956 ended colonial rule over the oldest monarchy in the Arab world. The present Alaoui dynasty has ruled Morocco since 1666.

- ❑ **1956** France recognizes Moroccan independence under Sultan Mohammed ibn Yousif. Morocco joins UN. Spain renounces control over most of its territories.
- ❑ **1957** Sultan Mohammed king.
- ❑ **1961** Hassan succeeds his father.
- ❑ **1967** Morocco backs Arab cause in Six-Day War with Israel.
- ❑ **1969** Spain returns Ifni to Morocco.
- ❑ **1972** King Hassan survives assassination attempt.
- ❑ **1975** International Court of Justice grants right of self-determination to Western Saharan people. Moroccan forces seize Saharan capital.
- ❑ **1976** Morocco and Mauritania partition Western Sahara.
- ❑ **1979** Mauritania renounces claim to part of Western Sahara, which is added to Morocco's territory.
- ❑ **1984** King Hassan signs Oujda Treaty with Col. Gaddafi of Libya as first step toward Maghreb union. Morocco leaves OAU after criticism of its role in Western Sahara.
- ❑ **1986** Morocco abrogates Oujda Treaty.
- ❑ **1987** Defensive wall built around Western Sahara.
- ❑ **1989** Arab Maghreb Union (AMU) creates tariff-free zone between Morocco, Algeria, Tunisia, Libya, and Mauritania.
- ❑ **1990** Morocco condemns Iraq's invasion of Kuwait.
- ❑ **1991** Morocco accepts UN plan for referendum in Western Sahara.
- ❑ **1992** New constitution grants majority party in parliament right to choose government.
- ❑ **1993** First general election for nine years. After major parties refuse his invitation, king appoints nonparty government.
- ❑ **1994** King Hassan replaces veteran prime minister Karim Lamrani with Abdellatif Filali.
- ❑ **1995** Islamist opposition leader Mohamed Basri returns after 28 years of exile. Severe drought.
- ❑ **1998** Socialists enter government; Abderrahmane el Youssoufi prime minister.
- ❑ **1999** Death of King Hassan. Mohammed VI enthroned. Liberalization program announced.
- ❑ **2000–2003** Polisario repeatedly rejects UN proposals for autonomy for Western Sahara as part of Morocco.
- ❑ **2002** Islamists gain in elections.

M

DEFENSE

▷ Compulsory military service

$1.32bn

Down 8% in 2001

MOROCCAN ARMED FORCES

Army	744 main battle tanks (224 M-48A5, 420 M-60, 100 T-72)	175,000 personnel
Navy	2 frigates and 27 patrol boats	7800 personnel
Air force	95 combat aircraft (39 F-5, 29 Mirage F-1, 4 OV-10, 23 Alpha Jet)	13,500 personnel
Missiles	None	

Morocco's long struggle in Western Sahara against Polisario Front guerrillas has given the kingdom's forces a formidable reputation. Moroccans have also fought as mercenaries in the Gulf. In the 1980s, Moroccan sappers constructed a 2500-km (1550-mile) defensive wall to cordon off Western Sahara in an attempt to prevent incursions from Polisario guerrillas based in Algeria. The Polisario forces themselves number some 3000–6000.

Morocco's pro-Western stance has allowed its forces access to sophisticated weapons and training from the West, particularly the US – unlike other north African states, which have been dependent on the former Soviet bloc.

The air force was formed in 1956 and flies US and European aircraft, notably Mirage interceptors. The navy uses Western-supplied ships, but is insignificant in regional terms. In addition, there are 50,000 paramilitaries.

Spending on defense as a percentage of gross national income is relatively high for a developing country.

Military service, lasting 18 months, is compulsory.

ECONOMICS

▷ Inflation 2.7% p.a. (1990–2001)

$34.7bn

9.455 Moroccan dirhams (10.645)

SCORE CARD

❑ World GNP Ranking	57th
❑ GNP per Capita	$1190
❑ Balance of Payments	$1.61bn
❑ Inflation	0.6%
❑ Unemployment	23%

EXPORTS

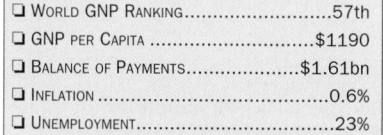

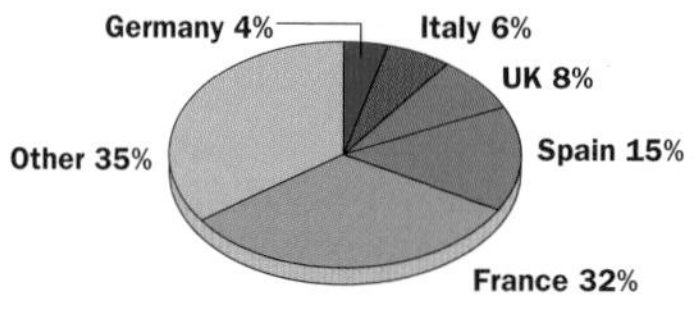
Germany 4%
Italy 6%
UK 8%
Spain 15%
France 32%
Other 35%

IMPORTS

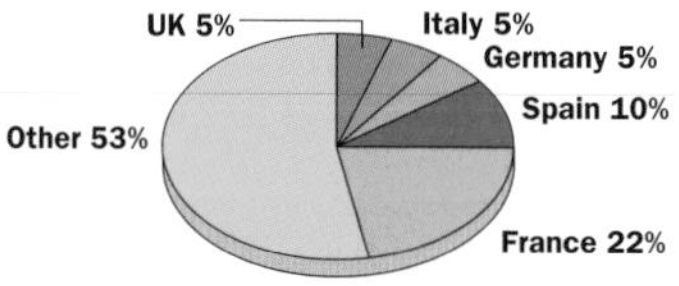
UK 5%
Italy 5%
Germany 5%
Spain 10%
France 22%
Other 53%

ECONOMIC PERFORMANCE INDICATOR

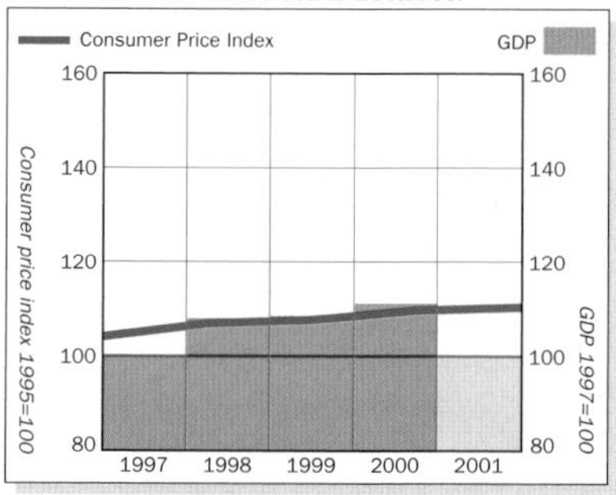
Consumer Price Index
GDP
160
140
120
100
80
Consumer price index 1995=100
GDP 1997=100
1997
1998
1999
2000
2001

Strengths

Probusiness policies and abundant labor attract foreign investment. Low inflation. Great potential for tourist industry (already important), phosphates, and agriculture.

Weaknesses

High unemployment and population growth. Droughts have hit agriculture. Cannabis production (providing Europe's main source of resin) complicates closer EU links.

Profile

The government's large-scale privatization program, which began in 1992, was designed to attract investment, particularly from Europe. Severe drought in 1995 made austerity measures necessary. Socialist-led governments have given social policy a higher priority. Expected revenue from oil reserves will be channeled into the development of rural areas.

MOROCCO : MAJOR BUSINESSES

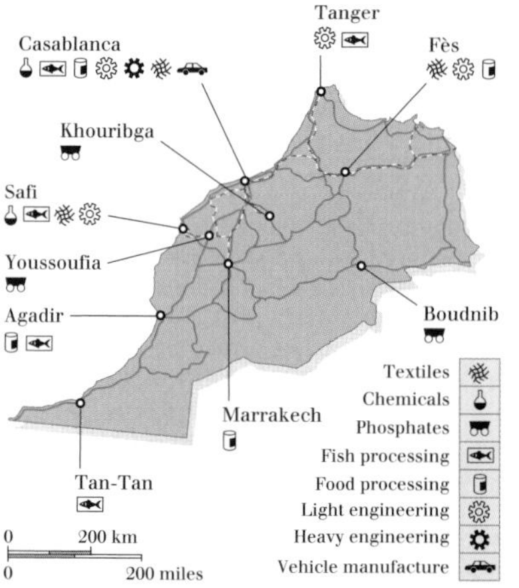
Tanger
Casablanca
Fès
Khouribga
Safi
Youssoufia
Agadir
Boudnib
Marrakech
Tan-Tan
Textiles
Chemicals
Phosphates
Fish processing
Food processing
Light engineering
Heavy engineering
Vehicle manufacture
0
200 km
0
200 miles

RESOURCES

Electric power 4m kW

898,467 tonnes

221 b/d (reserves 659m barrels)

16.3m sheep, 5.09m goats, 137m chickens

Phosphates, oil, gas, coal, iron, barytes, lead, copper, zinc

ELECTRICITY GENERATION

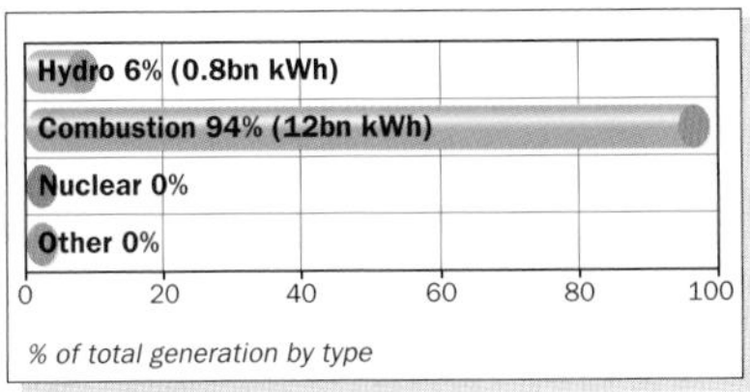
Hydro 6% (0.8bn kWh)
Combustion 94% (12bn kWh)
Nuclear 0%
Other 0%
0
20
40
60
80
100
% of total generation by type

Morocco possesses over a third of the world's phosphate reserves. The discovery of large oil and gas deposits in the northeastern desert in mid-2000 could yield an annual revenue of $400 million.

MOROCCO : LAND USE

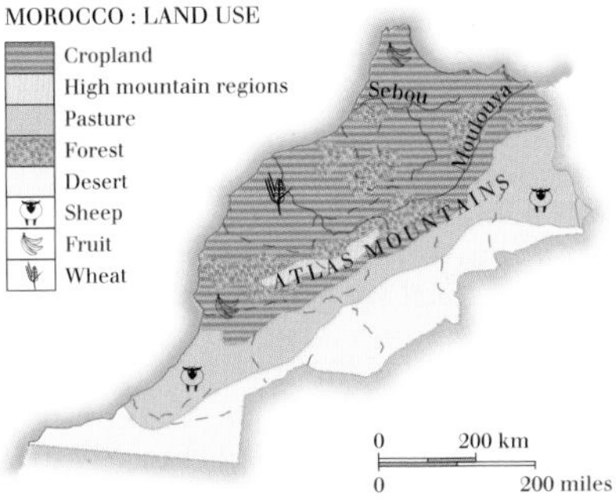
Cropland
High mountain regions
Pasture
Forest
Desert
Sheep
Fruit
Wheat
Sebou
Moulouya
ATLAS MOUNTAINS
0
200 km
0
200 miles

ENVIRONMENT

Sustainability rank: 73rd

0.7% partially protected

1.3 tonnes per capita

ENVIRONMENTAL TREATIES

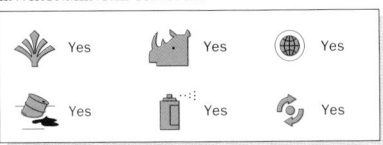

Yes	Yes	Yes
Yes	Yes	Yes

Morocco's wealth of plant and animal life has suffered severely from long periods of drought, most recently in the early 1980s and early 1990s. The unplanned development of tourist resorts is posing a threat to fragile coastal ecosystems.

MEDIA

TV ownership medium

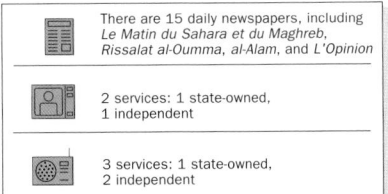

Daily newspaper circulation 28 per 1000 people

PUBLISHING AND BROADCAST MEDIA

There are 15 daily newspapers, including *Le Matin du Sahara et du Maghreb*, *Rissalat al-Oumma*, *al-Alam*, and *L'Opinion*

2 services: 1 state-owned, 1 independent

3 services: 1 state-owned, 2 independent

The succession of Mohammed VI fueled hopes of a more liberal climate, but the media remain strictly controlled, particularly over reporting of the Western Sahara issue. In 2000, the outspoken French-language weekly *Demain* was banned. The sports pages, especially the soccer reports, are the most dynamic sections of the press. State-owned TV began transmissions in Arabic and French in 1962. Radio broadcasts are in Arabic, Berber, French, Spanish, and English from Rabat and Tangier. Morocco can receive broadcasts from Spanish radio and television stations.

CRIME

Death penalty in use

54,288 prisoners

Crime has risen sharply

CRIME RATES

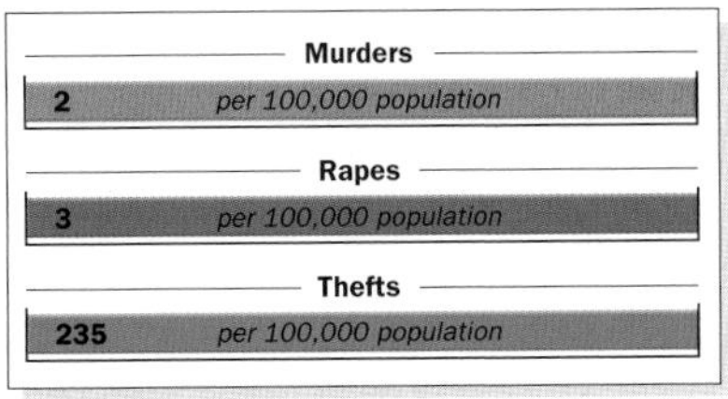
Murders
2
per 100,000 population
Rapes
3
per 100,000 population
Thefts
235
per 100,000 population

Urban crime is increasing, but muggings are rare. There is little civil unrest. Prisons are overcrowded, and conditions are poor. Civil occasions are used to pardon thousands of prisoners at a time.

EDUCATION

School leaving age: 14

50%

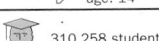

310,258 students

THE EDUCATION SYSTEM

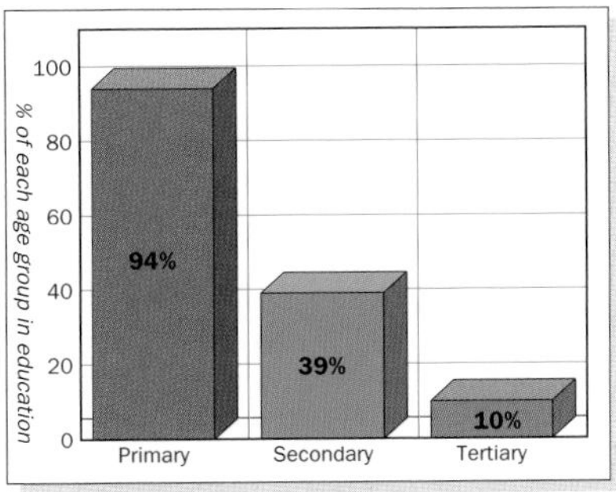
% of each age group in education
100
80
60
40
20
0
94%
39%
10%
Primary
Secondary
Tertiary

Literacy rates are lowest in rural areas, and girls are particularly affected. The literacy level and elementary school net enrollment rates are well below average for countries with similar living standards; child labor is widely used. There are both state-controlled and private schools. In 1988 the secondary school graduation examination, the *baccalauréat*, was replaced by a system of continuous assessment.

HEALTH

Welfare state health benefits

1 per 2041 people

Neonatal causes, cerebrovascular and heart diseases

There is one hospital bed for every 1000 people. Despite recent progress, child mortality and nutritional standards for the poorest Moroccans remain substantially below the average. Outside the cities, primary health care is virtually nonexistent, with the result that people depend on traditional remedies for illnesses. All employees are required to contribute to a social welfare fund, which operates a system of benefits in the event of illness, occupational accidents, and old age.

SPENDING

GDP/cap. increase

CONSUMPTION AND SPENDING

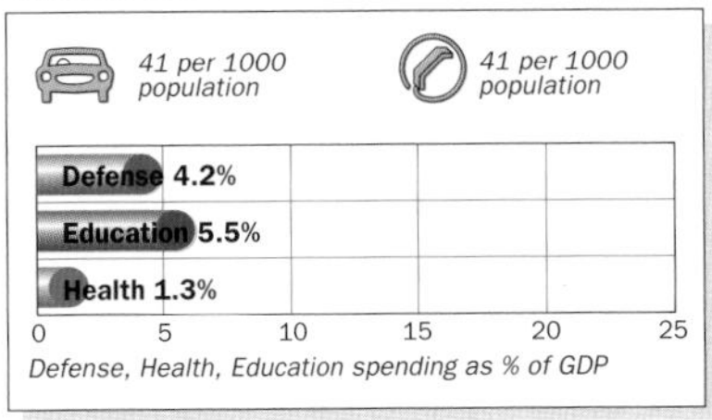
41 per 1000 population
41 per 1000 population
Defense 4.2%
Education 5.5%
Health 1.3%
0
5
10
15
20
25
Defense, Health, Education spending as % of GDP

Average income per head is much lower than in the neighboring countries of Algeria and Tunisia. Over 14% of Moroccans live below the UN poverty line, and the rural–urban gap in wealth is considerable; just under half of the population live in rural areas. A period of drought in the 1990s encouraged urban drift.

Unrest has largely been avoided owing to the fact that Morocco has a thriving informal sector. This provides jobs in food processing, clothes manufacturing, goods transportation, and the hotel and building trades. In addition, there is work to be found in the illegal hashish trade and the smuggling of alcohol and Western goods.

WORLD RANKING

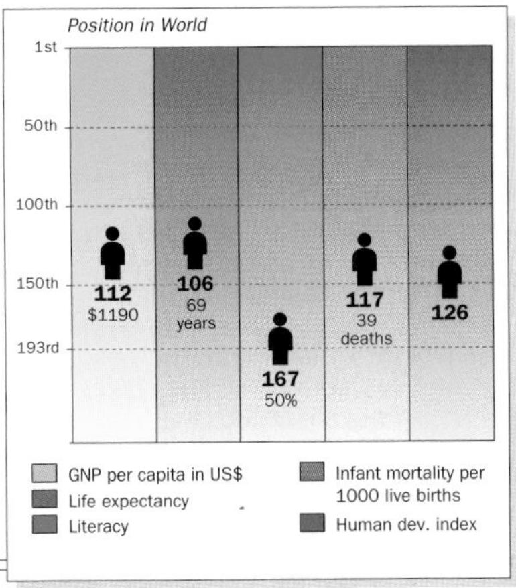
Position in World
1st
50th
100th
150th
193rd
112
$1190
106
69
years
167
50%
117
39
deaths
126
GNP per capita in US$
Life expectancy
Literacy
Infant mortality per 1000 live births
Human dev. index

M

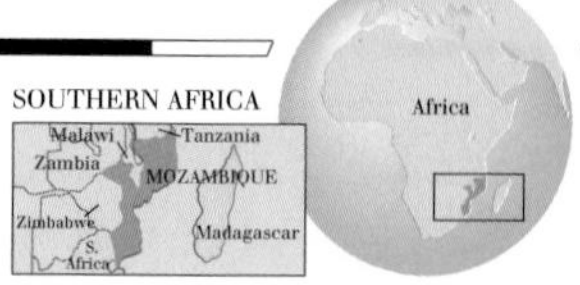
SOUTHERN AFRICA
Malawi
Tanzania
Zambia
MOZAMBIQUE
Zimbabwe
S. Africa
Madagascar
Africa

MOZAMBIQUE

OFFICIAL NAME: Republic of Mozambique **CAPITAL:** Maputo
POPULATION: 19 million **CURRENCY:** Metical **OFFICIAL LANGUAGE:** Portuguese

1975 | 1975 | June 25 | MOC | +2 | +258 | .mz

SITUATED ON THE SOUTHEAST African coast, Mozambique is bisected by the Zambezi River. South of the Zambezi lies a semiarid savanna lowland. The more fertile north-central delta provinces around Tete are home to most of Mozambique's ethnically diverse population. Following independence from Portugal in 1975, Mozambique was torn apart by civil war between the (then Marxist) Frelimo government and the South African-backed Mozambique National Resistance (Renamo). The conflict finally ended in 1992 after UN arbitration. Multiparty elections in 1994 returned Frelimo to power. Devastating floods in 2000 and 2001 created a desperate situation for this impoverished country, with famine a major threat.

CLIMATE

Tropical wet and dry

WEATHER CHART FOR MAPUTO

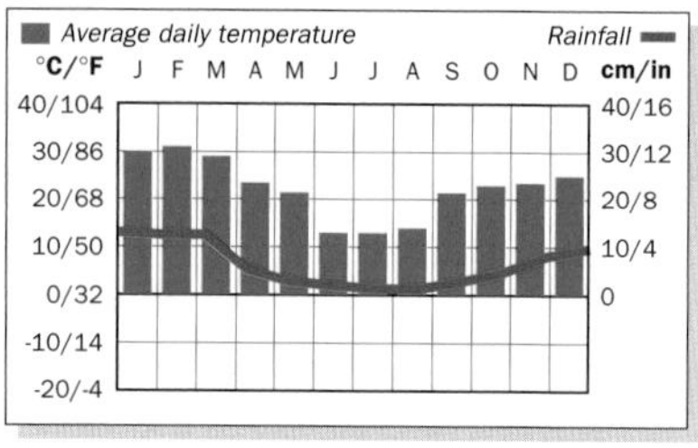
Average daily temperature
Rainfall
°C/°F
J F M A M J J A S O N D
cm/in
40/104
30/86
20/68
10/50
0/32
-10/14
-20/-4
40/16
30/12
20/8
10/4
0

In theory, Mozambique has a rainy season and a dry season. The coast at Beira and at Quelimane and the highlands west of Nampula are the wettest areas. The Zambezi valley is the hottest region.

Mozambique is prone to extremes of rainfall. In the 1980s, frequent failure of the rains contributed to two disastrous famines, while devastating floods occurred in 2000 and 2001.

TRANSPORTATION

Drive on left

Mavalane International, Maputo
437,798 passengers

131 ships
38,000 grt

THE TRANSPORTATION NETWORK

5685 km (3532 miles)

None

3114 km (1935 miles)

3750 km (2330 miles)

The billion-dollar Maputo Corridor, launched in 1995, reconnects South African industrial centers with the Mozambican coast, and has also facilitated port modernization. CFM, the state-owned railroad company, is cooperating with other neighboring states. The national airline is returning profits. Even so, millions of land mines still hamper access, damaged bridges have yet to be rebuilt, and remote communities remain isolated.

Tea picking. *Other important cash crops are cashew nuts, cotton, sugar, copra, and citrus fruits. Agriculture employs 83% of workers.*

TOURISM

Not available

Tourism has still not recovered after war

Little change from year to year

MAIN TOURIST ARRIVALS

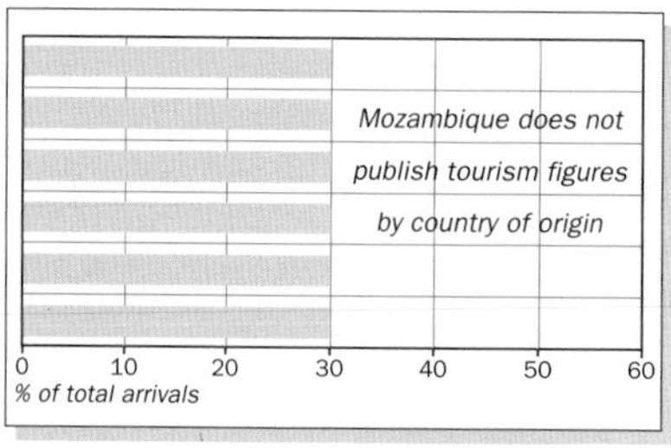
Mozambique does not publish tourism figures by country of origin
0
10
20
30
40
50
60
% of total arrivals

Mozambique used to attract around 300,000 South Africans and Rhodesians a year in the 1970s, but the tourist industry was destroyed by the civil war and is only slowly being rebuilt. Land mines still render travel outside the capital hazardous, while food shortages, poor infrastructure, and costly international flights are added obstacles. Further setbacks followed the floods in 2000 and 2001.

Given political stability, though, Mozambique could yet exploit its excellent beaches and game reserves, which include the Gorongosa Game Park. Some hotel groups are once more targeting Maputo as a luxury tourist and conference venue.

PEOPLE

Pop. density low

Makua, Xitsonga, Sena, Lomwe, Portuguese

24/km² (63/mi²)

THE URBAN/RURAL POPULATION SPLIT

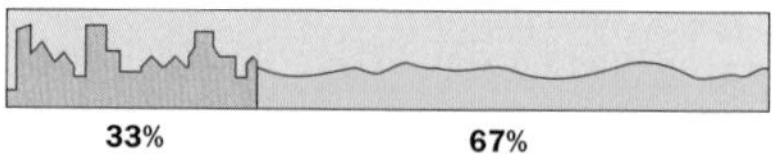
33%
67%

RELIGIOUS PERSUASION

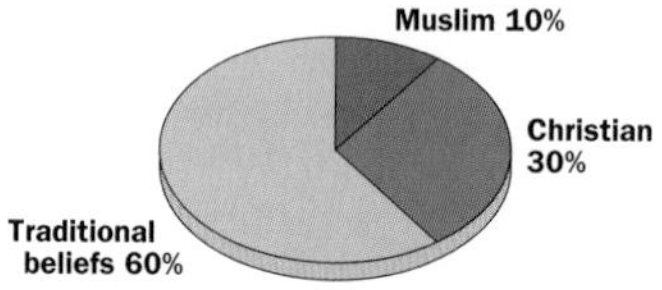
Muslim 10%
Christian 30%
Traditional beliefs 60%

ETHNIC MAKEUP

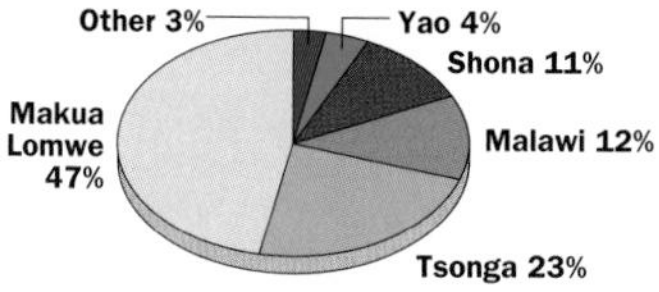
Other 3%
Yao 4%
Shona 11%
Makua Lomwe 47%
Malawi 12%
Tsonga 23%

The very large black African majority is divided into numerous groups. There are tiny minorities of whites, mixed-race groups, and Asians. However, the predominant social tensions are regional: Renamo, strong in the north and the center, accuses the Frelimo government of consistently favoring the south. Antiwhite feelings are growing too, as "Africanists" claim that whites enjoy disproportionate political and economic influence.

Society centers on the extended family. In some northern provinces this is matriarchal. Polygamy is fairly widespread among men who can support second wives. Frelimo emphasizes women's rights. Many women served in Frelimo armies, and are now protected by divorce, child-custody, and husband-desertion laws. The Mozambican Women's Organization encourages political participation.

The death of almost a million people during 17 years of civil war has seriously affected the economy and society. The sheer loss of manpower is exacerbated by the parallel increase in the number of orphans, widows, and amputees.

POPULATION AGE BREAKDOWN

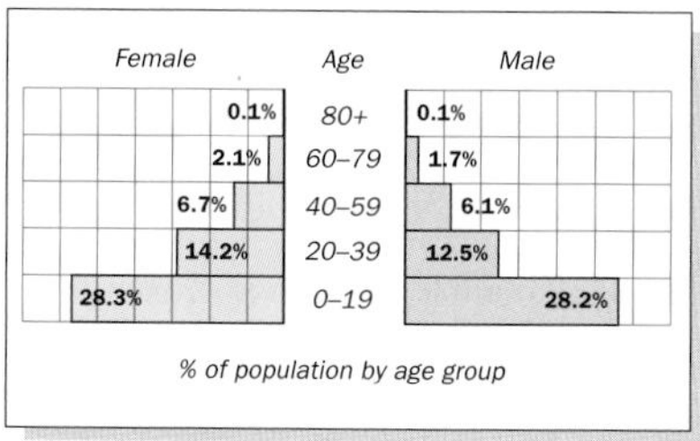
Female
Age
Male
0.1%
80+
0.1%
2.1%
60–79
1.7%
6.7%
40–59
6.1%
14.2%
20–39
12.5%
28.3%
0–19
28.2%
% of population by age group

M

POLITICS

Multiparty elections

1999/2004

President Joaquim Alberto Chissano

AT THE LAST ELECTION

Assembly of the Republic 250 seats

53% **Frelimo** **47%** **Renamo**

Frelimo = Front for the Liberation of Mozambique
Renamo = Mozambique National Resistance

Mozambique held its first multiparty elections in 1994.

PROFILE

Changing international realities in 1990 at the end of the Cold War persuaded the previously Soviet-backed Frelimo government to adopt a democratic constitution. Its civil-war rival Renamo lost the support of South Africa after the fall of apartheid there in the same year, and today little distinguishes the two parties ideologically. Though Frelimo is the larger party in the Assembly, Renamo is clearly popular, and demands recognition for its 15 years of struggle. New groups, such as the antiwhite Palmo, Coinmo, and Unamo, have recently emerged; Frelimo is pushing ahead with plans to decentralize power. Fears for the future of Mozambican democracy have been rekindled since 1999 amid worsening disputes between Renamo and Frelimo. Contentious issues include provincial representation, the murder of a prominent journalist in 2000, and parliamentary defections between parties. There has been occasional violent rioting.

Joaquim Chissano, president since 1986, has pushed toward political pluralism.

Afonso Dhlakama, Renamo leader, has turned from militarism to politics.

MAIN POLITICAL ISSUES

The move to democracy

The country's first democratic elections were held in 1994 and returned Frelimo to power. However, support for Renamo was stronger than had been expected. Their leader Afonso Dhlakama polled strongly in the presidential elections in both 1994 and 1999, contesting Joaquim Chissano's claim of victory. In 2002 Frelimo chose Armando Guebeza as its candidate for the 2004 presidential elections to replace incumbent Chissano.

Reconstruction

The government is slowly rebuilding a country where devastating floods in 2000 and 2001, and severe drought in 2002, have simply added to the ravages of civil war. The fighting had left 900,000 dead, one million refugees, and an estimated 80% of the remaining population living below the national poverty line.

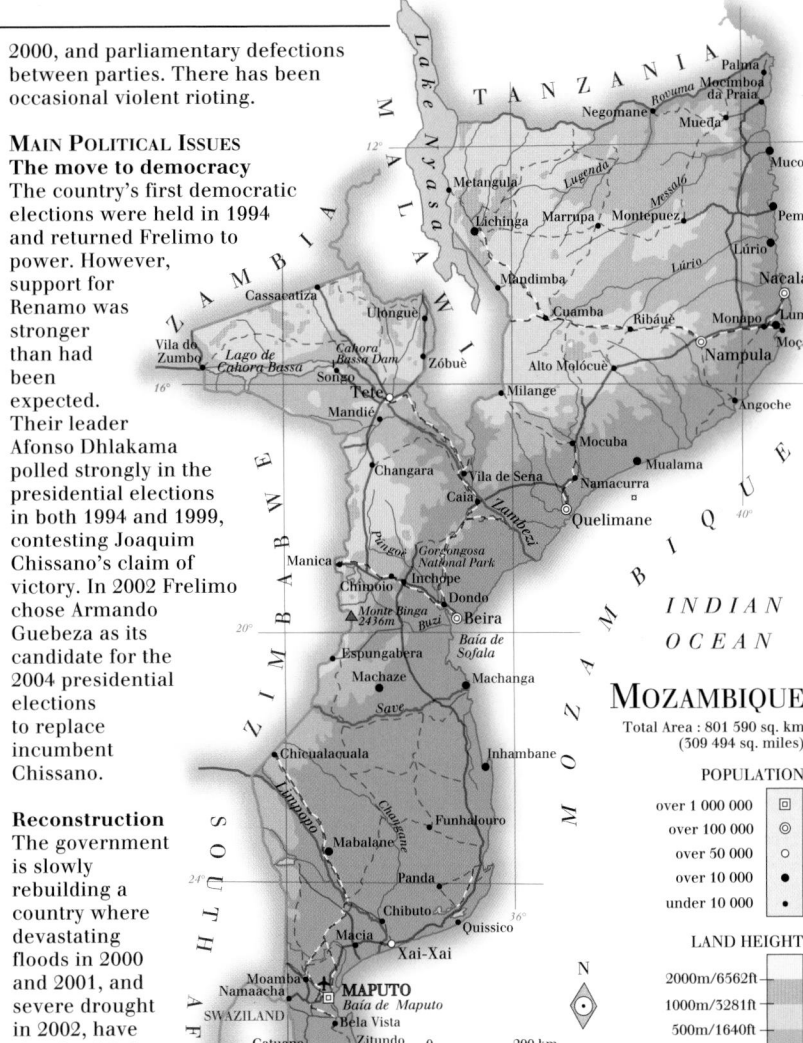

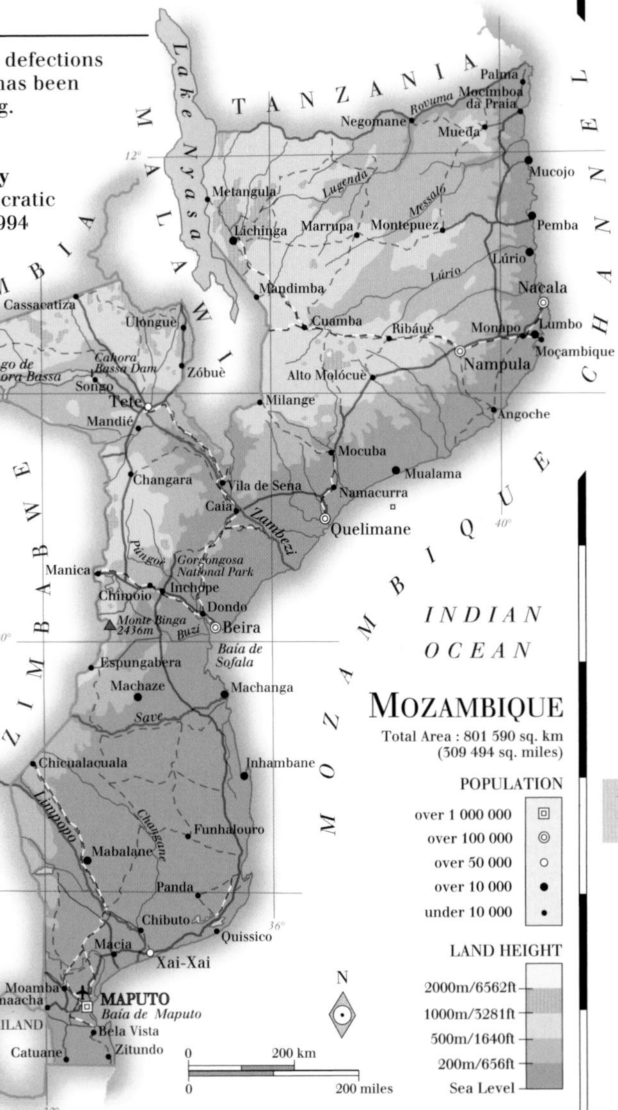
TANZANIA
Lake Nyasa
MALAWI
ZAMBIA
ZIMBABWE
SOUTH AFRICA
SWAZILAND
MOZAMBIQUE CHANNEL
INDIAN OCEAN
Palma
Mocimboa da Praia
Rovuma
Negomane
Mueda
Mucojo
Metangula
Lugenda
Messalo
Lichinga
Marrupa
Montepuez
Pemba
Lúrio
Mandimba
Nacala
Cuamba
Ribáuè
Monapo
Lumbo
Moçambique
Nampula
Cassacatiza
Ulongue
Vila do Zumbo
Lago de Cahora Bassa
Cahora Bassa Dam
Songo
Zóbuè
Alto Molócuè
Tete
Milange
Angoche
Mandié
Mocuba
Mualama
Changara
Vila de Sena
Namacurra
Caia
Zambezi
Quelimane
Pungoè
Gorongosa National Park
Manica
Chimoio
Inchope
Dondo
Monte Binga 2436m
Buzi
Beira
Baía de Sofala
Espungabera
Machaze
Machanga
Save
Chicualacuala
Inhambane
Limpopo
Changane
Funhalouro
Mabalane
Panda
Chibuto
Quissico
Macia
Xai-Xai
Moamba
Namaacha
MAPUTO
Baía de Maputo
Bela Vista
Catuane
Zitundo
12°
16°
20°
24°
32°
36°
40°
N
0 200 km
0 200 miles
MOZAMBIQUE
Total Area : 801 590 sq. km (309 494 sq. miles)
POPULATION
over 1 000 000
over 100 000
over 50 000
over 10 000
under 10 000
LAND HEIGHT
2000m/6562ft
1000m/3281ft
500m/1640ft
200m/656ft
Sea Level

CHRONOLOGY

The Portuguese tapped the local trade in slaves, gold, and ivory in the 16th century and made Mozambique a colony in 1752. Large areas were run by private companies until 1929.

- **1964** Frelimo starts war of liberation.
- **1975** Independence. Frelimo leader Samora Machel is president.
- **1976** Rhodesians set up Renamo resistance movement inside Mozambique.
- **1976–1980** Mozambique closes Rhodesian border and supports Zimbabwean freedom fighters. Reprisals by Renamo.
- **1977** Frelimo constitutes itself as Marxist-Leninist party.
- **1980** South Africa takes over backing of Renamo.

WORLD AFFAIRS

Joined UN in 1975

Comm | CPLP | AU | OIC | SADC

Mozambique was a key Cold War battleground between Soviet-backed Marxism and capitalism sponsored by the US and South Africa. The resulting civil war devastated the country until peace in 1992.

In the early 1980s, however, the Frelimo government's position began to shift as Soviet aid became erratic. Responding to President Samora Machel's overtures, the US lifted its ban on economic assistance in 1984. Britain agreed to train Frelimo's forces in 1987. South Africa continued tacitly to support Renamo until at least 1990. Zimbabwean troops helped Mozambique guard the strategically important Beira and Limpopo corridors, but left in 1993.

In 1995, the UN withdrew its peacekeepers and a democratic Mozambique joined the Commonwealth, despite having no formal links with the old British Empire. President Chissano became deputy head of the SADC, but regional tensions persisted, with Mozambique accusing South Africans of gun-running, and Swaziland claiming Maputo Province as its own.

M

CHRONOLOGY *continued*

- **1982** Zimbabwean troops arrive to guard Mutare–Beira corridor.
- **1984** Nkomati Accord: South Africa agrees to stop support for Renamo, and Mozambique for ANC, but fighting continues.
- **1986** Renamo declares war on Zimbabwe. Tanzanian troops reinforce Frelimo. Machel dies in mysterious air crash in South Africa. Joaquim Chissano replaces him.
- **1988** Nkomati Accord reactivated. Mozambicans allowed back to work in South African mines.
- **1989** War and malnutrition said to claim one million lives. Frelimo drops Marxism-Leninism.
- **1990** Multipartyism and free-market economy in new constitution. Renamo breaches cease-fire.
- **1992** Chissano signs peace agreement with Renamo.
- **1994** Democratic elections return Frelimo to power.
- **1995** Joins Commonwealth. Economic reforms begun.
- **1999** G7 chooses Mozambique as flagship for international debt relief initiative. Renamo disputes results of December elections.
- **2000–2001** Thousands displaced by devastating floods.

AID

Recipient

$935m (receipts) | Up 7% in 2001

Mozambique is one of the most aid-dependent countries in the world. Aid accounts for over 50% of national earnings, and pays for the food needs of some seven million people. In 1999, Mozambique became one of only four countries to receive the G7 debt relief scheme for HIPCs, which is worth nearly $3 billion. Debt servicing still accounts for 20% of aid. The main donor states are the UK, Portugal, the US, the World Bank, and other EU member states. Debts from earlier Soviet aid have been written off.

DEFENSE

Compulsory military service

$71m | Down 22% in 2001

About 2.5 million men were deemed "fit for military service" in 1998, but since the civil war ended in 1992, the military's once dominant role in society has greatly diminished. Military figures, once prominent in the Frelimo government, have been largely stripped of political influence.

Mozambique's new postwar, British-trained permanent army was formally inaugurated in 1994. Truly national in character, and only around 10,000 strong, it contains both former government and Renamo troops.

However, one by-product of reorganization was the demobilization of some 75,000 battle-hardened soldiers. Their severance pay ended in mid-1996, and it has not been easy to retrain them, or reintegrate them into civilian life. Some have turned to banditry.

The end of the war also saw the departure of external forces, such as UN peacekeepers and the Zimbabwean troops who once guarded strategic railroads against Renamo attack.

MOZAMBICAN ARMED FORCES

80 main battle tanks (T-54/55)	10,000 personnel
Some patrol boats	150 personnel
No combat aircraft	1000 personnel
None	

ECONOMICS

Inflation 30% p.a. (1990–2001)

$3.8bn | 23,345 meticais (23,224)

SCORE CARD

- World GNP Ranking.......................123rd
- GNP per Capita..............................$210
- Balance of Payments....................–$1.6bn
- Inflation...10%
- Unemployment..................................21%

EXPORTS

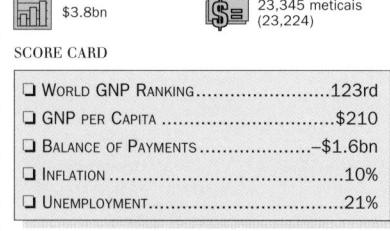

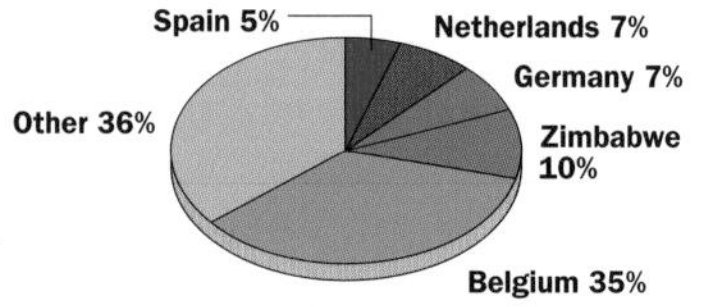
Spain 5%
Netherlands 7%
Germany 7%
Other 36%
Zimbabwe 10%
Belgium 35%

IMPORTS

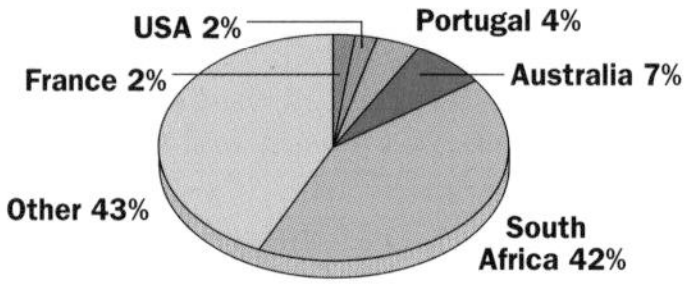
USA 2%
Portugal 4%
France 2%
Australia 7%
Other 43%
South Africa 42%

Strengths

IMF-sponsored program of privatization, exchange rate reforms, and trade liberalization have helped attract aid and increase exports. Relative political stability. Massive rural development programs target agriculture, which employs 85% of the workforce. Fisheries industry has great potential. Improved transportation links with Maputo, Africa's second-largest harbor, will help to service southern Africa's landlocked regions. The go-ahead for a new port at Dobela, in the south, was given in 2002.

ECONOMIC PERFORMANCE INDICATOR

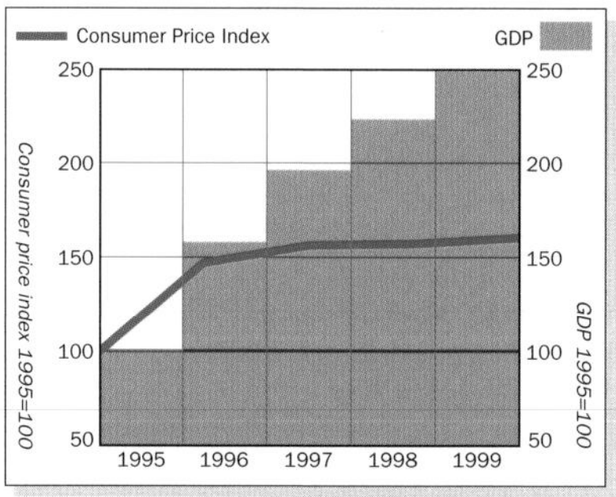
Consumer Price Index
GDP
250
200
150
100
50
1995
1996
1997
1998
1999
Consumer price index 1995=100
GDP 1995=100

Weaknesses

Overseas aid is essential to prevent at least half the population starving. Overdependence on foreign donors and companies is another long-term concern. The country is susceptible to drought, floods, and cyclones. Skilled workers often choose to work in other countries, impeding Mozambique's return to normal economic activity. Increase in corruption.

Profile

Though Mozambique has enormous problems, the government in 1995 produced an optimistic plan, based on World Bank recommendations, to eradicate poverty and raise annual GDP growth to 8–9% by 2000. Devastation resulting from the floods of 2000 and 2001 has effectively destroyed such hopes, and GDP growth in 2000 was only 2.1%.

MOZAMBIQUE: MAJOR BUSINESSES

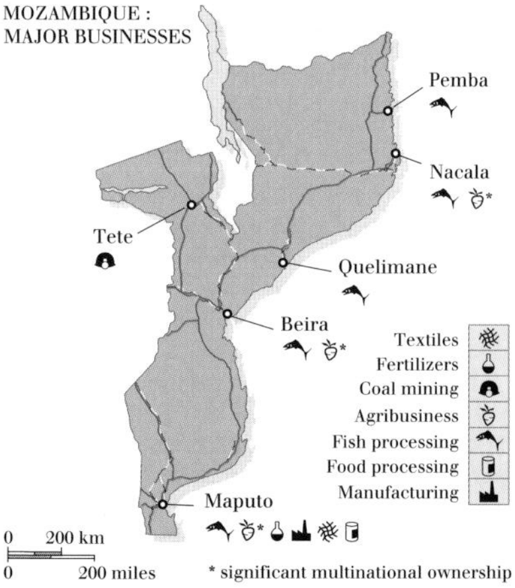
Pemba
Nacala
Tete
Quelimane
Beira
Maputo
Textiles
Fertilizers
Coal mining
Agribusiness
Fish processing
Food processing
Manufacturing
0 200 km
0 200 miles
* significant multinational ownership

RESOURCES

Electric power 2.4m kW

39,065 tonnes

Not an oil producer

1.32m cattle, 670,000 ducks, 28m chickens

Coal, iron, tantalite, uranium, gold, bauxite, titanium, copper, gas

ELECTRICITY GENERATION

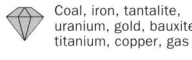

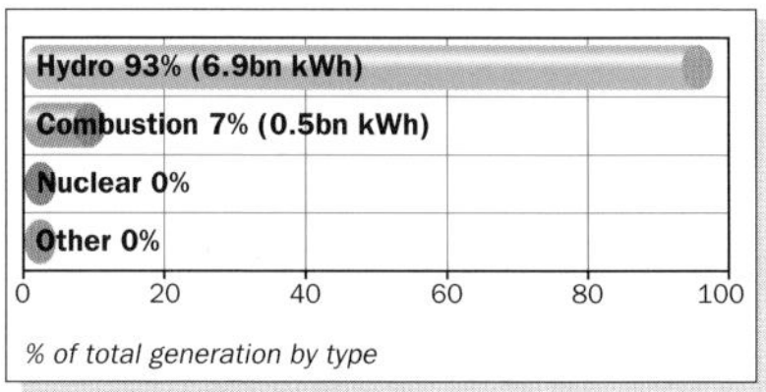
Hydro 93% (6.9bn kWh)
Combustion 7% (0.5bn kWh)
Nuclear 0%
Other 0%
0
20
40
60
80
100
% of total generation by type

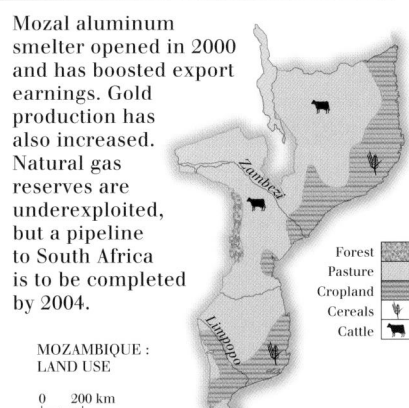

Cotton vies with cashew nuts as the chief crop. Fishing is a vital sector; shrimps are a lucrative export. The Mozal aluminum smelter opened in 2000 and has boosted export earnings. Gold production has also increased. Natural gas reserves are underexploited, but a pipeline to South Africa is to be completed by 2004.

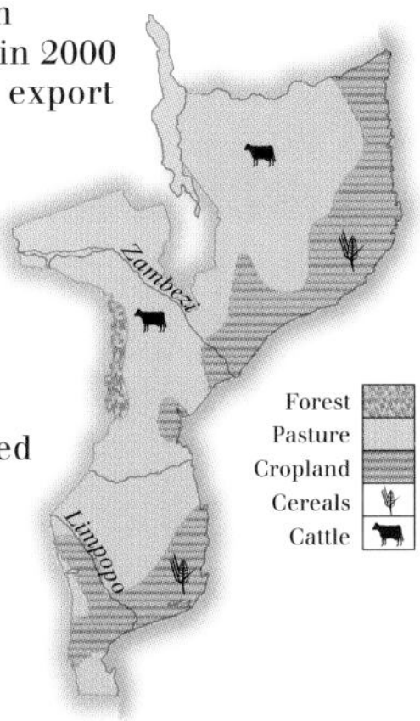
Zambezi
Limpopo
Forest
Pasture
Cropland
Cereals
Cattle
MOZAMBIQUE : LAND USE
0 200 km
0 200 miles

HEALTH

Welfare state health benefits

1 per 16,667 people

Tuberculosis, gastroenteric infections, pneumonia, AIDS

Thousands of people lost limbs from land mines, or suffered other appalling injuries and psychological trauma, during Mozambique's savage civil war. Health services have improved since the end of the war, and preventive medicines and antenatal care are provided free. Doctors serve a mandatory two years in rural areas. Many private clinics have been established since 1987. However, cholera, a lingering by-product of war, is still a serious issue in the far northern province of Cabo Delgado. An estimated 1.1 million Mozambicans have contracted HIV.

ENVIRONMENT

Sustainability rank: 59th

9% (6% partially protected)

0.08 tonnes per capita

ENVIRONMENTAL TREATIES

No	Yes	Yes
Yes	Yes	No

Floods followed by droughts are often devastating. Floods in 2000 and 2001, resulting from a combination of cyclones and torrential rain, affected around one million people. Civil war had pushed people toward the cities and coasts, causing overcrowding, disease, pollution, and desertification of abandoned farms. The Great Limpopo Transfrontier Park opened in 2002. Straddling the border with South Africa and Zimbabwe and covering 35,000 sq. km (13,500 sq. miles), it is Africa's largest reserve. However, ecological concerns are still low on the national agenda.

MEDIA

TV ownership low

Daily newspaper circulation 2 per 1000 people

PUBLISHING AND BROADCAST MEDIA

There are 5 daily newspapers, including *Notícias* and *Diário de Moçambique*

2 services: 1 state-owned, 1 independent

3 services: 1 state-owned, 2 independent

The press, hitherto a Frelimo publicity machine, has enjoyed greater freedom in the 1990s. The killing in 2000 of a popular and outspoken editor, Carlos Cardoso, shocked the country. TV sets are still a rarity. The state-owned radio station broadcasts in Portuguese, English, and vernacular languages.

CRIME

No death penalty

8812 prisoners

Little change from year to year

CRIME RATES

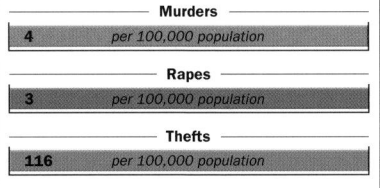

Murders
4 *per 100,000 population*

Rapes
3 *per 100,000 population*

Thefts
116 *per 100,000 population*

Weapons are easily obtainable. In rural areas there are many bandits, often former soldiers; road travel is unsafe. Senior officials stand accused of misappropriating food aid money.

EDUCATION

School leaving age: 12

45%

9774 students

THE EDUCATION SYSTEM

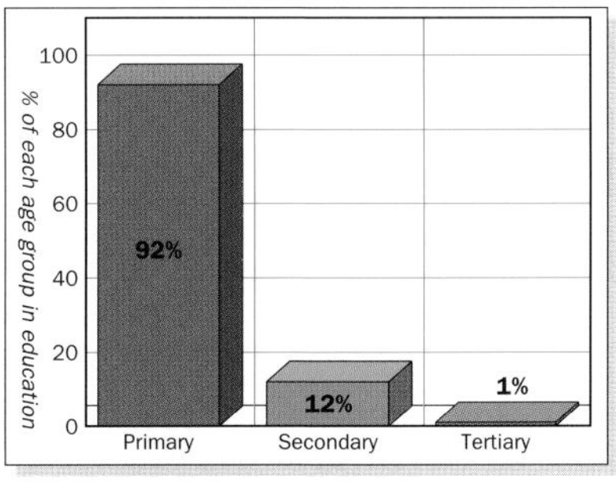
100
80
60
40
20
0
% of each age group in education
92%
12%
1%
Primary
Secondary
Tertiary

At independence, between 85% and 95% of the adult population were illiterate, and school closures during the civil war created a lost generation of uneducated people. In 2001, around two-thirds of youths (15–24) could read thanks to a concerted literacy campaign. The government used World Bank/IMF debt relief to strengthen the education budget in 2001.

SPENDING

GDP/cap. increase

CONSUMPTION AND SPENDING

1 per 1000 population

4 per 1000 population

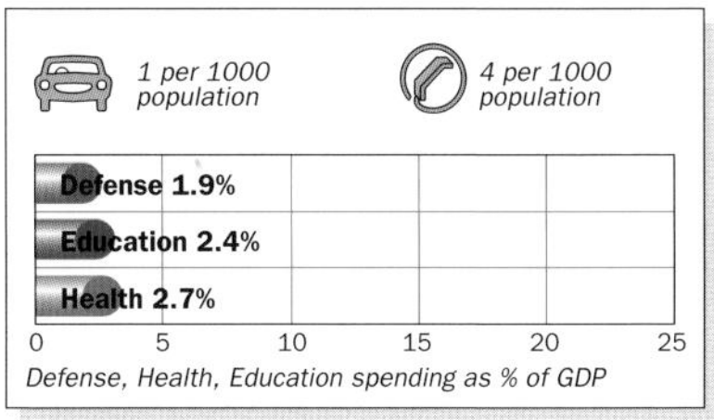
Defense 1.9%
Education 2.4%
Health 2.7%
0
5
10
15
20
25
Defense, Health, Education spending as % of GDP

Mozambique is one of the world's poorest countries, with around 80% of the people living below the national poverty line even before the floods of 2000 and 2001, which left thousands homeless. Measures adopted in the 1990s to attract Western aid made conditions tougher, raising the price of rice by 600%. The recent export boom has generally bypassed the traditional subsistence farmer. Only the higher echelons of Frelimo, Renamo, and other political parties have cars, air-conditioning, and brick-built apartments. Free-market reforms, however, are gradually increasing access to consumer goods.

WORLD RANKING

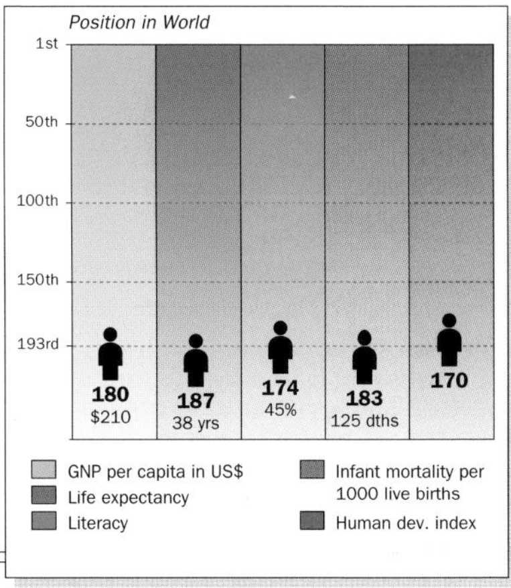
Position in World
1st
50th
100th
150th
193rd
180
$210
187
38 yrs
174
45%
183
125 dths
170
GNP per capita in US$
Life expectancy
Literacy
Infant mortality per 1000 live births
Human dev. index

M

NAMIBIA

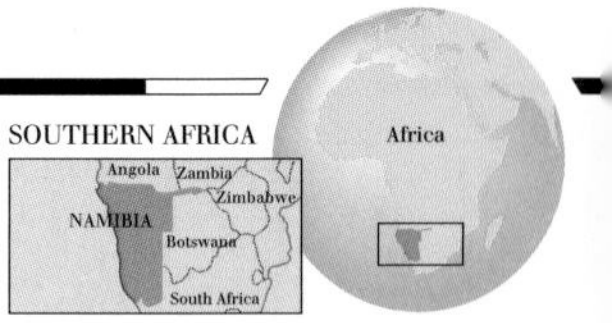
SOUTHERN AFRICA
Africa
Angola
Zambia
Zimbabwe
NAMIBIA
Botswana
South Africa

OFFICIAL NAME: Republic of Namibia **CAPITAL:** Windhoek
POPULATION: 1.8 million **CURRENCY:** Namibian dollar **OFFICIAL LANGUAGE:** English

1990 | 1994 | March 21 | NAM | +2 | +264 | .na

NAMIBIA LIES IN SOUTHWEST Africa, the ecologically unique Namib Desert extending the length of its long coastline. After many years of guerrilla warfare, Namibia won independence from South Africa in 1990. Despite the move away from apartheid, Namibia's economy remains reliant on the expertise of the small white population, a legacy of the previously poor education for blacks. Namibia is Africa's fourth-largest minerals producer.

CLIMATE

▷ Hot desert/steppe

WEATHER CHART FOR WINDHOEK

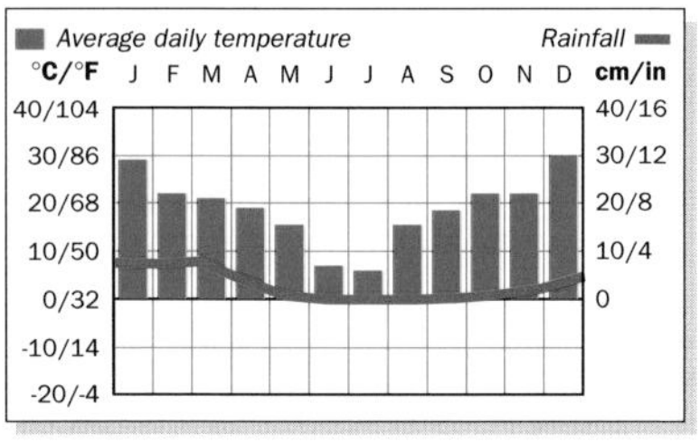
Average daily temperature
Rainfall
°C/°F J F M A M J J A S O N D cm/in
40/104
30/86
20/68
10/50
0/32
-10/14
-20/-4
40/16
30/12
20/8
10/4
0

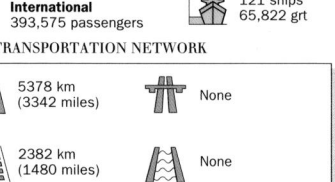

Namibia is almost rainless. The coast is usually shrouded in thick, cold fog unless the hot, very dry *berg* blows.

TRANSPORTATION

▷ Drive on left

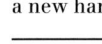

Windhoek International 393,575 passengers

121 ships 65,822 grt

THE TRANSPORTATION NETWORK

5378 km (3342 miles)

None

2382 km (1480 miles)

None

Large-scale industry is well served by road and rail. Plans exist to build a new harbor at Walvis Bay.

TOURISM

▷ Visitors : Population 1:2.1

861,000 visitors

Up 40% in 1999–2001

MAIN TOURIST ARRIVALS

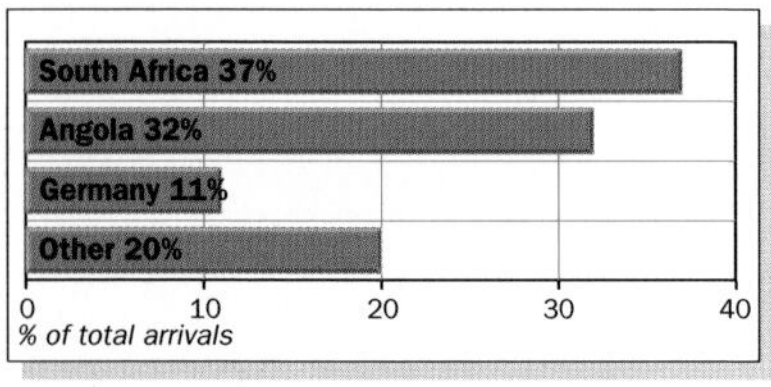
South Africa 37%
Angola 32%
Germany 11%
Other 20%
0
10
20
30
40
% of total arrivals

Tourists, mainly from neighboring countries and Germany, the former colonial power, make a very limited contribution to GDP. There are plans to limit tourists to 300,000 a year to preserve the fragile desert ecology.

Spitzkoppe, west of Karibib. *Unique scenery such as this is attracting increasing numbers of tourists to Namibia.*

PEOPLE

▷ Pop. density low

Ovambo, Kavango, English, Bergdama, German, Afrikaans

2/km² (6/mi²)

THE URBAN/RURAL POPULATION SPLIT

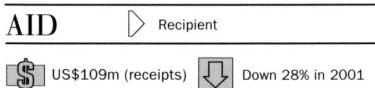

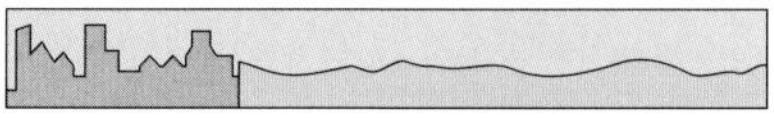
31%
69%

ETHNIC MAKEUP

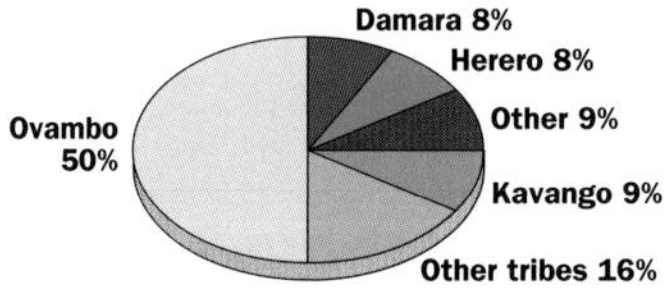
Damara 8%
Herero 8%
Other 9%
Kavango 9%
Other tribes 16%
Ovambo 50%

The largest ethnic group, the Ovambo, tend to live in the sparsely populated north. Smaller groups, such as the Herero and the Afrikaans-speaking Basters, are politically vocal. Whites – most of whom speak Afrikaans – are concentrated in Windhoek. The capital is also home to a wealthy century-old German community. Namibia's original inhabitants, the San and Khoi (once called Bushmen) now constitute a tiny, marginalized minority. The ethnic strife predicted in 1990 has not materialized.

Black Namibians are predominantly subsistence farmers. Many black women have six or more children. The constitution supports gender equality and discriminates in favor of women; few, however, have official jobs or own property. Homosexuality is not tolerated.

POLITICS

▷ Multiparty elections

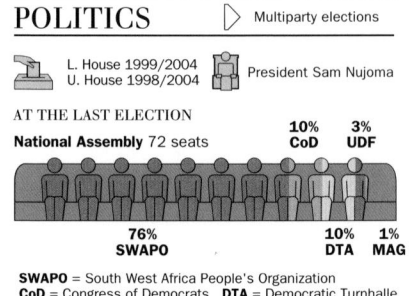

L. House 1999/2004
U. House 1998/2004

President Sam Nujoma

AT THE LAST ELECTION

National Assembly 72 seats

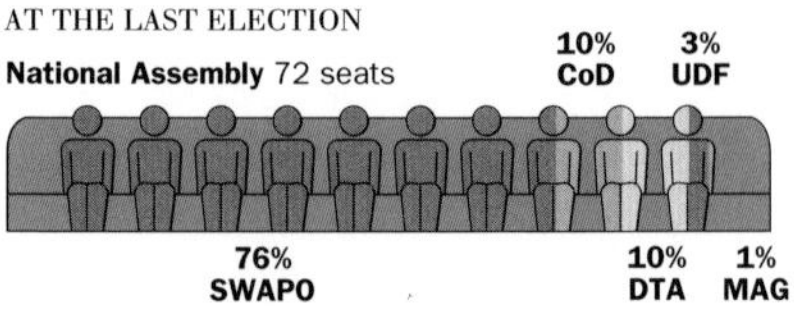
10% CoD
3% UDF
76% SWAPO
10% DTA
1% MAG

SWAPO = South West Africa People's Organization
CoD = Congress of Democrats **DTA** = Democratic Turnhalle Alliance **UDF** = United Democratic Front **MAG** = Monitor Action Group
Six additional nonvoting members may be appointed to the National Assembly by the president

National Council 26 seats

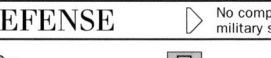

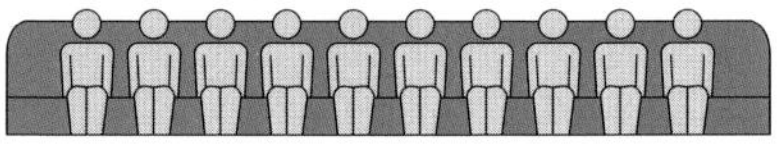

Two members are elected by each of the 13 Regional Councils to the National Council

Namibia became a multiparty democracy at independence in 1990. The center-left SWAPO, the former guerrilla force, has dominated politics ever since. In 1998 an amendment to the constitution allowed President Sam Nujoma to run for a third term, which he duly won in 1999, despite violence among separatists in the Caprivi Strip. Theo-Ben Gurirab, prime minister since 2002, has made land reform a priority amid increasing calls for redistribution.

WORLD AFFAIRS

▷ Joined UN in 1990

Comm | COMESA | NAM | AU | SADC

In 1994 South Africa relinquished control of Walvis Bay – Namibia's only deepwater port. South Africa has also written off Namibia's earlier debts. Remaining border disputes were settled in the late 1990s. Namibian troops withdrew from the war-torn Democratic Republic of the Congo in 2001.

AID

▷ Recipient

US$109m (receipts)

Down 28% in 2001

The EU provides most aid; Germany is the main unilateral donor. Around one-fifth of aid is spent on education.

DEFENSE

▷ No compulsory military service

US$91m

Down 17% in 2001

Fishing grounds are patrolled to prevent raids by foreign trawlers. Namibian soldiers performed a peacekeeping role in the DRC.

N

ANGOLA
ZAMBIA
ZIMBABWE
BOTSWANA
SOUTH AFRICA
ATLANTIC OCEAN
Skeleton Coast
NAMIB DESERT
Kalahari Desert
Ruacana
Opuwo
Oshakati
Oshikango
Ondangwa
Okavango
Rundu
Caprivi Strip
Zambezi
Katima Mulilo
Etosha Pan
Namutoni
Tsumeb
Kamanjab
Grootfontein
Tsumkwe
Outjo
Otavi
Khorixas
Kalkfeld
Otjiwarongo
Okakarara
Brandberg 2573m
Uis
Spitzkopje
Omaruru
Otjinene
Karibib
Okahandja
Hentiesbaai
Usakos
Gobabis
Walvis Bay
Swakopmund
WINDHOEK
Rehoboth
Leonardville
Stampriet
Aranos
Hardap Dam
Maltahöhe
Mariental
Gibeon
Gochas
Nossob
Koes
Bethanien
Fish
Lüderitz
Aus
Keetmanshoop
Seeheim Noord
Aroab
Grünau
Rosh Pinah
Karasburg
Ariamsvlei
Oranjemund
Warmbad
Orange River
Noordoewer
0 200 km
0 200 miles

NAMIBIA

Total Area : 825 418 sq. km (318 694 sq. miles)

LAND HEIGHT
- 2000m/6562ft
- 1000m/3281ft
- 500m/1640ft
- 200m/656ft
- Sea Level

POPULATION
- over 100 000
- over 10 000
- under 10 000

CHRONOLOGY

In 1915, South Africa took over the former German colony as a League of Nations' mandate known as South West Africa.

- ❑ **1966** Apartheid laws imposed. SWAPO begins armed struggle.
- ❑ **1968** Renamed Namibia.
- ❑ **1973** UN recognizes SWAPO.
- ❑ **1990** Independence.
- ❑ **1994** South Africa relinquishes Walvis Bay.
- ❑ **1999** President Sam Nujoma wins third term.

ECONOMICS

Inflation 8.5% p.a. (1990–2001)

US$3.51bn

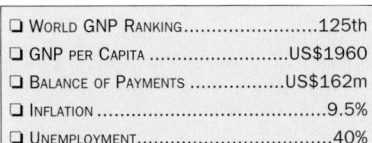

7.51 Namibian dollars (10.31)

SCORE CARD

❑ WORLD GNP RANKING	125th
❑ GNP PER CAPITA	US$1960
❑ BALANCE OF PAYMENTS	US$162m
❑ INFLATION	9.5%
❑ UNEMPLOYMENT	40%

STRENGTHS

Varied mineral resources. Rich fishing grounds. Potential of Walvis Bay as conduit for landlocked neighbors. Low external debt. Foreign investment.

WEAKNESSES

Most goods imported. Fluctuations in mineral prices. Lack of skilled labor; high unemployment. Potential for disruption from land redistribution, favoring smaller farms over large white-owned estates. AIDS epidemic.

EXPORTS

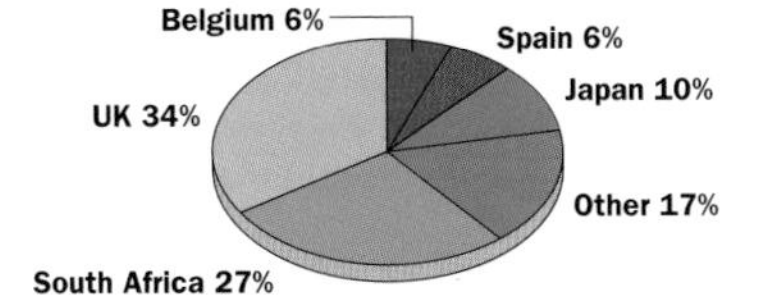
Belgium 6%
Spain 6%
Japan 10%
UK 34%
Other 17%
South Africa 27%

IMPORTS

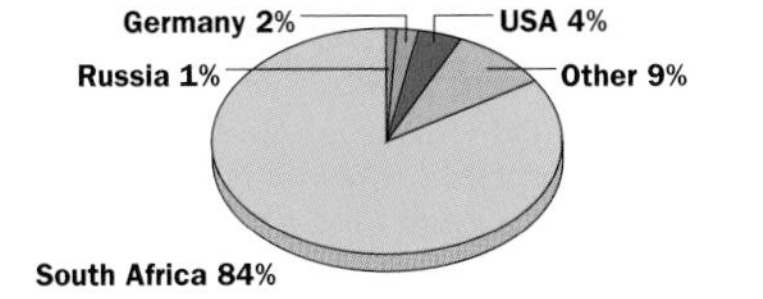
Germany 2%
USA 4%
Russia 1%
Other 9%
South Africa 84%

RESOURCES

Electric power: Included in South African total

283,015 tonnes

Included in South African total

2.51m cattle, 2.37m sheep, 1.77m goats, 2.6m chickens

Uranium, lead, gold, cadmium, oil, copper, diamonds, zinc, silver,

Namibia has abundant uranium, lead, and cadmium resources. Large oil deposits were discovered in 2000. Hydroelectric power and offshore diamond mining have huge potential. The Okavango river system carries more water than all South Africa's rivers combined.

ENVIRONMENT

Sustainability rank: 26th

14% (2% partially protected)

0.07 tonnes per capita

Illegal poaching and the presence of anthrax threaten the unique Namibian desert-adapted elephant (fewer than 50 remain) and the black rhino. Vast expanses of the fragile, unspoiled Namib and Kalahari Desert ecosystems are protected. The government is generally sensitive to environmental issues (the annual seal cull to protect fish stocks is an exception) and wishes to attract "eco-tourists" rather than invest in mass-market developments.

MEDIA

TV ownership low

Daily newspaper circulation 19 per 1000 people

PUBLISHING AND BROADCAST MEDIA

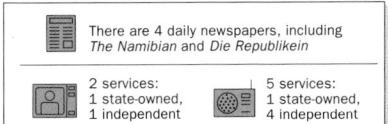

There are 4 daily newspapers, including *The Namibian* and *Die Republikein*

2 services: 1 state-owned, 1 independent

5 services: 1 state-owned, 4 independent

An active press targets corrupt politicians, but foreign TV programs are banned. State radio transmits in 11 languages.

CRIME

No death penalty

4814 prisoners

Down 51% in 1999

Burglary and theft are rising, particularly in urban areas. Ostrich smuggling to the US is common.

EDUCATION

School leaving age: 16

83%

9561 students

Most children attend primary school, but illiteracy among black adults remains a legacy of apartheid.

HEALTH

Welfare state health benefits

1 per 3448 people

AIDS, respiratory, heart, and intestinal diseases

Preventive care and rural health care have top priority. Most areas lack safe water. AIDS is the leading cause of death.

SPENDING

GDP/cap. increase

CONSUMPTION AND SPENDING

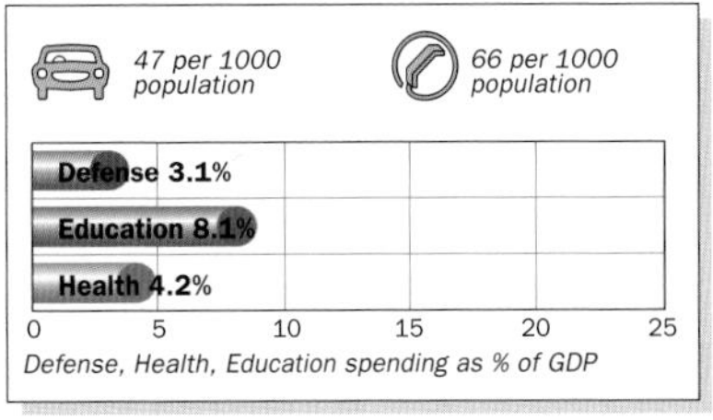
47 per 1000 population
66 per 1000 population
Defense 3.1%
Education 8.1%
Health 4.2%
0
5
10
15
20
25
Defense, Health, Education spending as % of GDP

Gross disparities in wealth persist throughout Namibia: the top 0.5% of households consumes as much as the poorest 57%.

WORLD RANKING

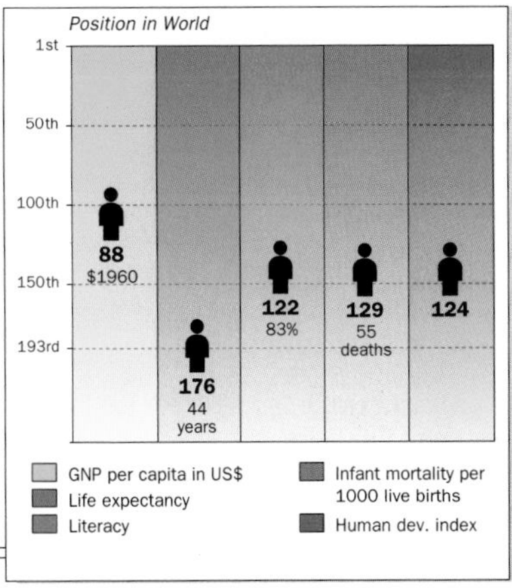
Position in World
1st
50th
100th
150th
193rd
88
$1960
176
44 years
122
83%
129
55 deaths
124
GNP per capita in US$
Life expectancy
Literacy
Infant mortality per 1000 live births
Human dev. index

N

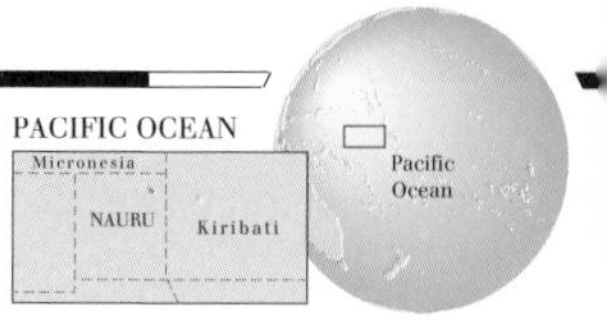
PACIFIC OCEAN
Micronesia
NAURU
Kiribati
Pacific Ocean

NAURU

OFFICIAL NAME: Republic of Nauru **CAPITAL:** *No official capital*
POPULATION: 12,329 **CURRENCY:** Australian dollar **OFFICIAL LANGUAGE:** Nauruan

1968 | 1968 | Jan 31 | NAU | +12 | +674 | .nr

THE WORLD'S SMALLEST REPUBLIC, Nauru lies in the Pacific Ocean, 4000 km (2480 miles) northeast of Australia. Once a British colony exploited for its phosphates by the UK, Australia, and New Zealand, it became independent in 1968. The phosphates industry made Nauruans among the wealthiest people in the world, but economic mismanagement and the imminent end of phosphate reserves have left Nauru facing financial ruin, prompting economic reform.

CLIMATE

Tropical oceanic

WEATHER CHART FOR NAURU

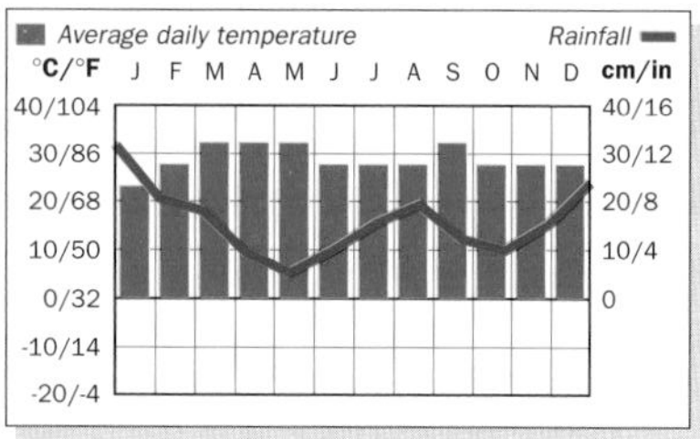
Average daily temperature
Rainfall
°C/°F J F M A M J J A S O N D cm/in
40/104
30/86
20/68
10/50
0/32
-10/14
-20/-4
40/16
30/12
20/8
10/4
0

Nauru's tiny size means that rain clouds often miss the island; years can pass without rain.

TRANSPORTATION

Drive on left

Nauru Island International

3 ships 1000 grt

THE TRANSPORTATION NETWORK

24 km (15 miles) | None

5 km (3 miles) | None

Nauru operates its own airline with a Boeing 737 flown by Australian pilots. The Nauru Pacific Line provides infrequent commercial services to Australia. However, all external travel is very expensive. Nauru has no harbor: to load cargoes of phosphates, ships have to dock, engines still running, with huge concrete caissons floating out at sea. The circular ring road is often littered with abandoned cars, as it has been much cheaper for Nauruans to import new vehicles than to attempt to repair existing ones. The number of car accident fatalities is one of the highest in the South Pacific.

TOURISM

Not available

Minimal tourist arrivals

Little variation from year to year

MAIN TOURIST ARRIVALS

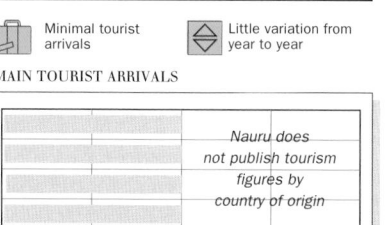

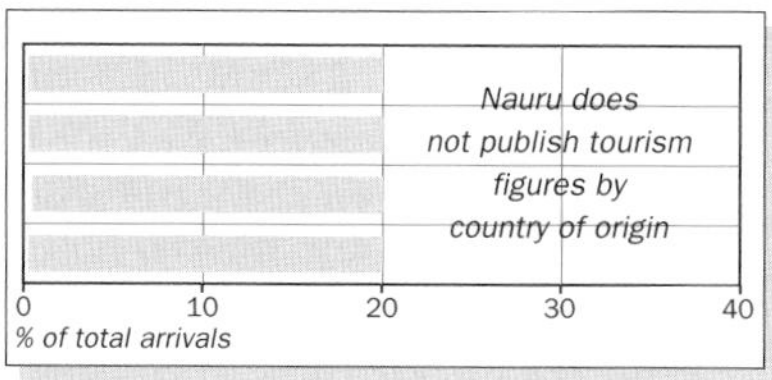
Nauru does not publish tourism figures by country of origin
0
10
20
30
40
% of total arrivals

Even if Nauru had any conventional tourist attractions, the enormous cost of getting there would dissuade most tourists from making the journey. The main feature of interest on the island is the bizarre lunar landscape created by over 90 years of phosphate extraction. There are few beaches and only a handful of hotels.

NAURU

Total Area : 21 sq. km (8.1 sq. miles)

LAND HEIGHT
200m/565ft
Sea Level

Urban area
Phosphate mineworks

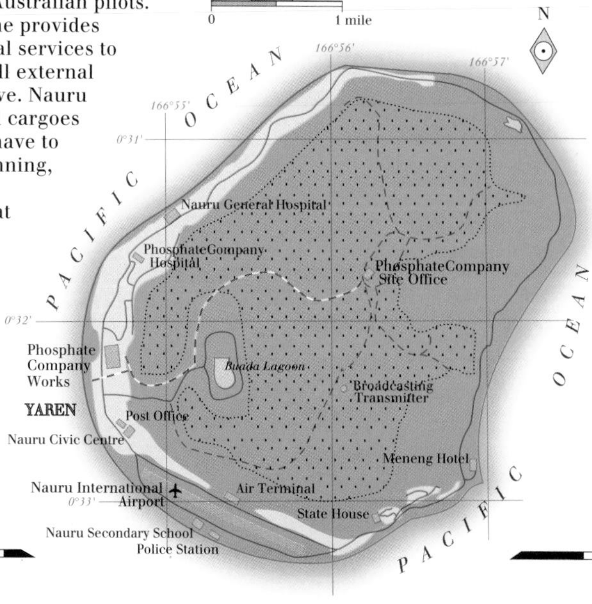
0
1 km
0
1 mile
N
166°55'
166°56'
166°57'
0°31'
0°32'
0°33'
PACIFIC OCEAN
PACIFIC
OCEAN
PACIFIC
Nauru General Hospital
Phosphate Company Hospital
Phosphate Company Site Office
Phosphate Company Works
Buada Lagoon
Broadcasting Transmitter
YAREN
Post Office
Nauru Civic Centre
Meneng Hotel
Nauru International Airport
Air Terminal
State House
Nauru Secondary School
Police Station

PEOPLE

Pop. density high

Nauruan, Kiribati, Chinese, Tuvaluan, English

587/km² (1522/mi²)

THE URBAN/RURAL POPULATION SPLIT

Nauru is 100% semiurban

ETHNIC MAKEUP

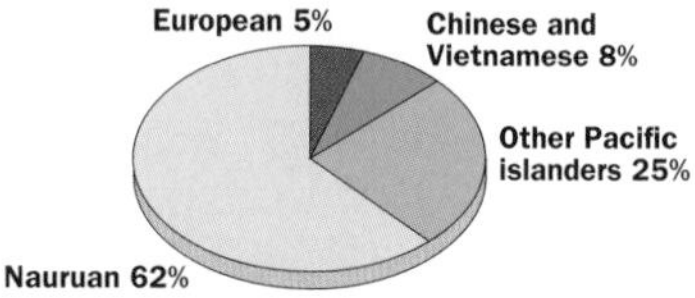
European 5%
Chinese and Vietnamese 8%
Other Pacific islanders 25%
Nauruan 62%

Indigenous Nauruans are a homogeneous blend of Melanesian, Micronesian, and Polynesian strands. They have traditionally held posts in government service, while a large imported workforce – mainly from Kiribati – mines the phosphates.

A society of just over 12,000 people, Nauru is mostly self-regulating. There is some tension between younger Nauruans, who go to Australia to study but have little incentive to do well, and their parents, who fought hard for independence. As the phosphates run out, an increasing feeling of futility is gripping the young. Many see their future in Australia or New Zealand, but fear a drop in living standards and the loss of the luxury of sovereignty. These fears led Nauruans to reject the offer of resettlement on an island off the Queensland coast of Australia.

POLITICS

Multiparty elections

2003/2006

President Rene Harris

AT THE LAST ELECTION
Parliament 18 seats

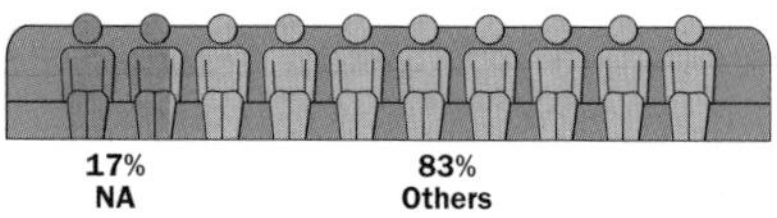
17% NA
83% Others

NA = Nauru First **Others** includes independents

Parliament is based on the British model, but traditional leaders are the dominant figures. Politics revolves around personalities rather than ideologies, leading to direct conflict between the president and the legislature and a high turnover at the top. There have been 24 changes of president since independence (though only ten different presidents), while two men – Bernard Dowiyogo and Rene Harris – alternated as president six times between 1999 and 2003. Harris returned to the post in August 2003.

N

WORLD AFFAIRS

Joined UN in 1999

Comm | PC | PIF | ADB | ACP

The case for compensation for phosphate exploitation brought by Nauru against the UK government was rejected in 1992 after the longest suit in British legal history. However, an Australian settlement that year brought payments eventually totaling US$79 million. Nauru's main concern is participation in the PIF and the management of trust funds to support Nauruans when phosphate income runs out. Nauru joined the UN in 1999. It seeks to have a voice on environmental issues.

AID

Recipient

US$7m (receipts) — Up 75% in 2001

Nauru receives or donates little aid, except as a member of the PIF.

DEFENSE

No compulsory military service

Australia responsible for defense — Not applicable

Nauru has no defense force. Australia, under a de facto arrangement, is responsible for the island's security.

ECONOMICS

Not available

US$42m — 1.491 Australian dollars (1.781)

SCORE CARD

- ❑ WORLD GNP RANKING........................191st
- ❑ GNP PER CAPITA.........................US$3540
- ❑ BALANCE OF PAYMENTS................Not available
- ❑ INFLATION.....................................-3.6%
- ❑ UNEMPLOYMENT...........Minimal unemployment

STRENGTHS

Considerable investments overseas. Trust funds for post-phosphate era. Strong Australian dollar.

WEAKNESSES

Phosphate revenues due to end in 2003. High cost of rehabilitating the 80% of the island where mining occurred. Virtually no other resources. Bad investment decisions in 1990s. Loss of offshore banking industry.

EXPORTS

Nauru's only export commodity is phosphates, in which it trades with Australia and New Zealand.

IMPORTS

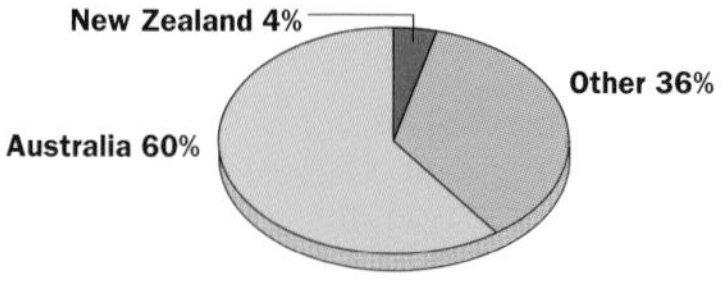
New Zealand 4%
Other 36%
Australia 60%

RESOURCES

Electric power 10,000 kW

250 tonnes — Not an oil producer

2800 pigs, 5000 chickens — Guano (phosphates)

Nauru has been exploited for its valuable phosphate reserves by Germans, the British, Australians, and New Zealanders since 1906, and recently by Nauruans themselves. Extraction has destroyed four-fifths of the island, and the deposits are almost exhausted. Nauru has no other mineral resources.

The island is entirely dependent on outside energy supplies, and the cost of oil is 50% higher than the Pacific average, since Nauru does not lie on any shipping routes. Most electricity is produced by small diesel generators.

ENVIRONMENT

Not available

None — 11.4 tonnes per capita

Nauru is an environmental disaster area. Mining has destroyed 80% of its ecosystem and, like other Pacific islands, it faces the increasing threat of rising sea levels. Also of concern is contamination from the nearby former French nuclear test sites in the Pacific.

MEDIA

TV ownership low

There are no daily newspapers

PUBLISHING AND BROADCAST MEDIA

There are no daily newspapers. The *Nasero Bulletin* is published biweekly

1 state-owned service — 1 state-owned service

Nauru has one national TV broadcasting service and one radio station. Both are state-run.

CRIME

Death penalty not used in practice

Nauru does not publish prison figures — Crime levels are rising slightly

Theft is almost nonexistent. Assaults and dangerous driving as a result of drunkenness are the major problems.

Nauru is almost circular, *with a 16-km (10-mile) ring road. The overcrowded coastal strip is the sole habitable land.*

CHRONOLOGY

Colonized by Germany in 1888, from 1919 the island was administered by the UK, Australia, and New Zealand.

- ❑ **1968** Independence.
- ❑ **1992** Australia agrees compensation for phosphate extraction.
- ❑ **1998–2003** Rene Harris and Bernard Dowiyogo alternate presidency.

EDUCATION

School leaving age: 16

95% — Not available

Many Nauruans attend boarding school in Australia from a young age. Few go on to university.

HEALTH

Welfare state health benefits

1 per 637 people — Tuberculosis, vitamin deficiencies, diabetes

A diet largely of processed imported foods and widespread obesity are the major problems. Over one-third of the population suffers from non-insulin-dependent diabetes. Industrial accidents are treated in Australia.

SPENDING

GDP/cap. increase

CONSUMPTION AND SPENDING

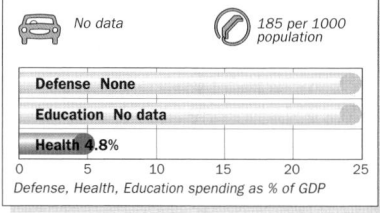

No data — *185 per 1000 population*

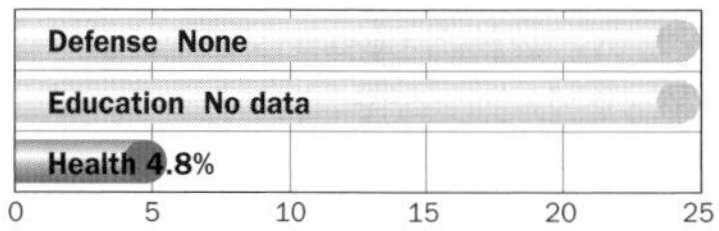
Defense None
Education No data
Health 4.8%
0
5
10
15
20
25

Defense, Health, Education spending as % of GDP

Nauru is carrying out a major economic adjustment program, to be funded by the ADB. The program is intended to allow it to adjust to the loss of income now that its phosphate reserves are near exhaustion.

WORLD RANKING

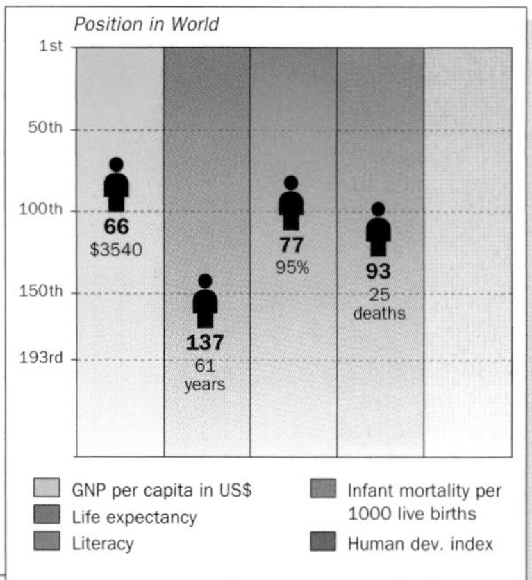
Position in World
1st
50th
100th
150th
193rd
66
$3540
137
61
years
77
95%
93
25
deaths
GNP per capita in US$
Life expectancy
Literacy
Infant mortality per 1000 live births
Human dev. index

N

NEPAL

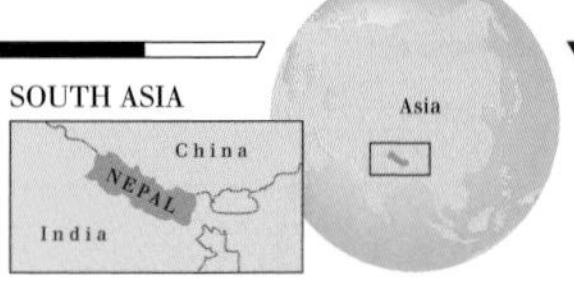
SOUTH ASIA
China
NEPAL
India
Asia

OFFICIAL NAME: Kingdom of Nepal **CAPITAL:** Kathmandu
POPULATION: 24.2 million **CURRENCY:** Nepalese rupee **OFFICIAL LANGUAGE:** Nepali

1769 | 1769 | Dec 28 | NEP | +5.75 | +977 | .np

LYING ALONG the southern Himalayas, Nepal was an absolute monarchy until 1990, since when its politics became increasingly turbulent. The mainly agricultural economy depends heavily on the prompt arrival of the monsoon. Hopes for development have been invested in hydropower, despite the adverse impact of large dams. A Maoist insurgency, begun in 1999, threw the country into chaos in 2001.

CLIMATE

▷ Mountain/subtropical

WEATHER CHART FOR KATHMANDU

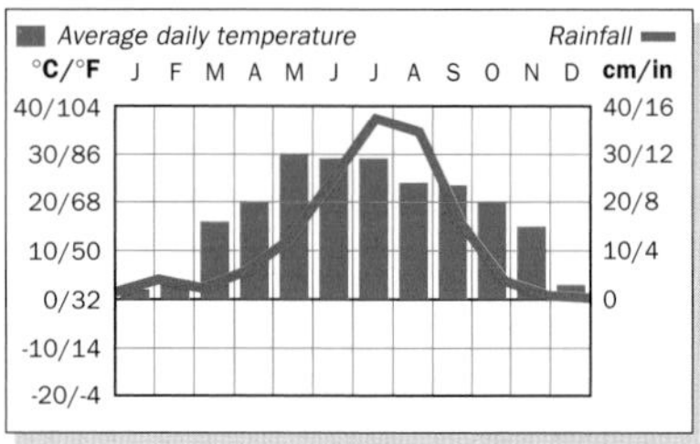
Average daily temperature
Rainfall
°C/°F
J F M A M J J A S O N D
cm/in
40/104
30/86
20/68
10/50
0/32
-10/14
-20/-4
40/16
30/12
20/8
10/4
0

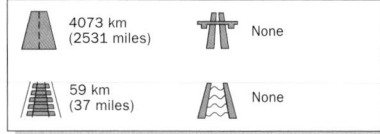

The warm July to October monsoon affects the whole country, causing flooding in the hot Terai plain, but generally decreases northward and westward. The rest of the year is dry, sunny, and mild, except in the Himalayas, where valley temperatures in winter may average –10°C (14°F).

TRANSPORTATION

▷ Drive on left

Tribhuvan International, Kathmandu 1.6m passengers

Has no fleet

THE TRANSPORTATION NETWORK

4073 km (2531 miles) | None
59 km (37 miles) | None

Domestic flights link the main towns. There are paved roads in the south and in the Kathmandu valley; only one runs north to China. Two short stretches of railroad cross into India.

Himalayan harvest. *Steep mountainsides and easily eroded soils mean that most fields are terraced. A majority of Nepalese are farmers.*

TOURISM

▷ Visitors : Population 1:67

363,000 visitors

Down 22% in 2001

MAIN TOURIST ARRIVALS

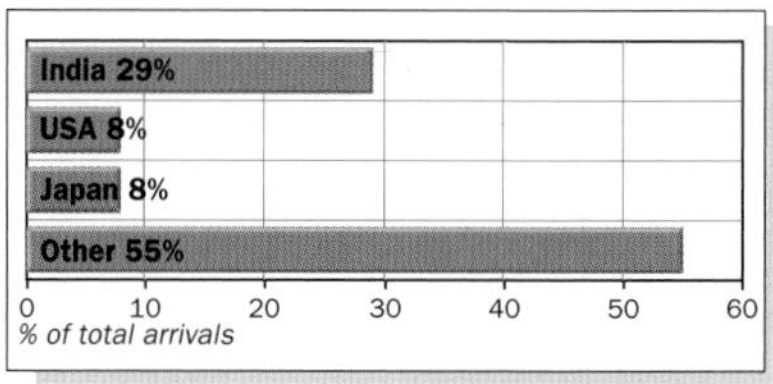
India 29%
USA 8%
Japan 8%
Other 55%
0
10
20
30
40
50
60
% of total arrivals

The Maoist insurgency has devastated the country's important and previously healthy tourism industry. A steady stream of backpackers from the West has dried up, though tourist numbers from neighboring India have actually increased.

The wish to preserve the environment conflicts with the desire for tourist revenue. Child labor was banned in the tourism industry from 2000.

PEOPLE

▷ Pop. density medium

Nepali, Maithilli, Bhojpuri

177/km² (458/mi²)

THE URBAN/RURAL POPULATION SPLIT

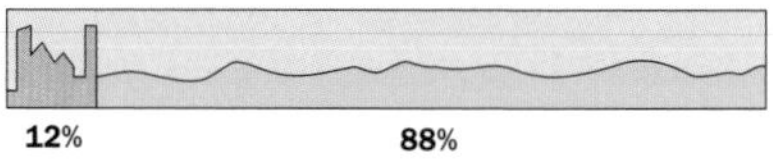
12%
88%

RELIGIOUS PERSUASION

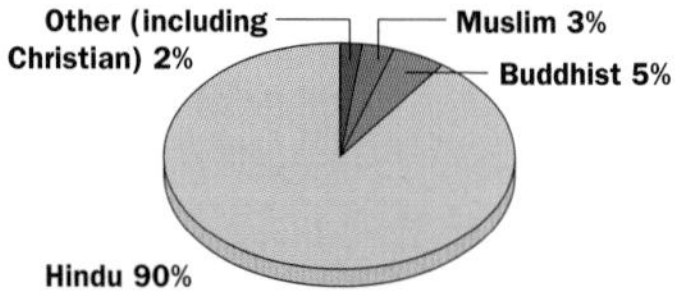
Other (including Christian) 2%
Muslim 3%
Buddhist 5%
Hindu 90%

There are few tensions among diverse ethnic groups such as the Sherpas in the north, "Hill Hindu" Brahmins and Chhettris, Newars, and others in the Kathmandu valley, and Terai in the south. The Sherpa and other Buddhist women are less restricted than Hindus. Polygamy is practiced in the hills. Since 1990 many ethnic Nepali refugees from Bhutan have settled in Nepal.

POLITICS

▷ Multiparty elections

L. House 1999/2002
U. House 2001/2003
(both postponed)

H.M. King Gyanendra Bir Bikram Shah Dev

AT THE LAST ELECTION

House of Representatives 205 seats

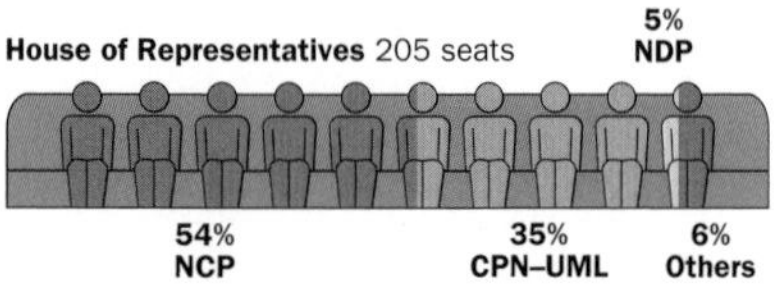
5% NDP
54% NCP
35% CPN–UML
6% Others

NCP = Nepali Congress Party **CPN–UML** = Communist Party of Nepal–United Marxist-Leninist **NDP** = National Democratic Party **App** = Appointed by the king

National Council 60 seats

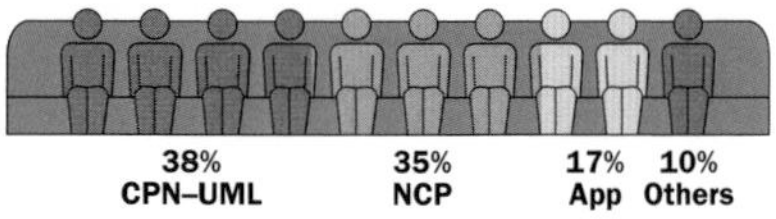
38% CPN–UML
35% NCP
17% App
10% Others

Multipartyism, reinstated in 1990, produced a short-lived communist government in 1994, then a series of unstable coalitions until the NCP won elections in 1999. Instability returned in 2001: the royal family was murdered, and the Maoist rebel insurgency intensified. A controversial nationwide state of emergency was imposed. Unpopular new King Gyanendra caused a political crisis in 2002 when he dismissed the elected NCP government and appointed an NDP administration in its place; S. B. Thapa was made prime minister in 2003.

WORLD AFFAIRS

▷ Joined UN in 1955

CP | IBRD | NAM | SAARC | ADB

The NCP government revived relations with India but there are tensions over India's alleged links with Maoist rebels, some of whom are said to operate from over the border. Relations with Bhutan are strained over the issue of ethnic Nepali Bhutanese refugees in Nepal.

AID

▷ Recipient

$388m (receipts)

Down 1% in 2001

Nepal's strategic position has made it a focus for powerful donors, including Japan, the ADB, the World Bank, and member states of the EU.

DEFENSE

▷ No compulsory military service

$142m

Up 34% in 2001

The army, at 46,000 men, is small and has no tanks or combat aircraft. Weapons come from India and the UK, in whose own army the Nepalese Gurkhas serve.

N

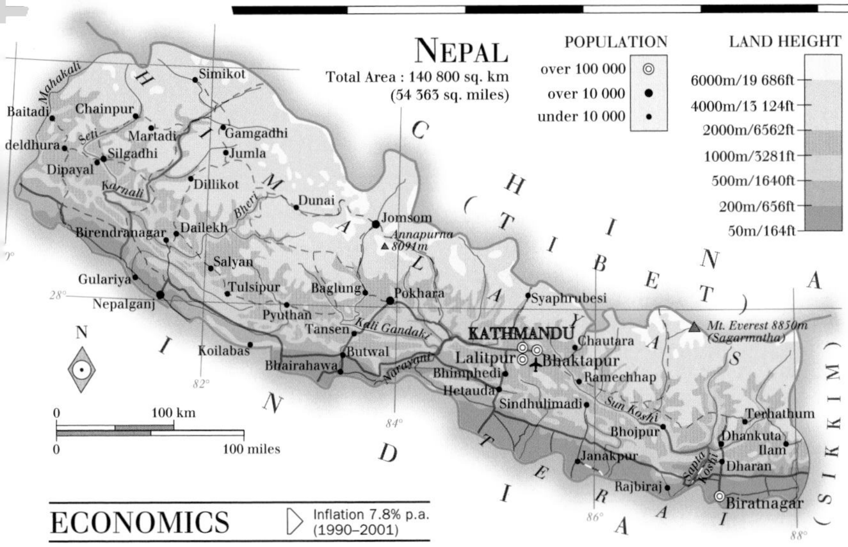
NEPAL
Total Area : 140 800 sq. km (54 363 sq. miles)
POPULATION
over 100 000
over 10 000
under 10 000
LAND HEIGHT
6000m/19 686ft
4000m/13 124ft
2000m/6562ft
1000m/3281ft
500m/1640ft
200m/656ft
50m/164ft
KATHMANDU
Lalitpur
Bhaktapur
Pokhara
Biratnagar
Mt. Everest 8850m (Sagarmatha)
Annapurna 8091m
CHINA (TIBET)
INDIA
SIKKIM
0 100 km
0 100 miles

ECONOMICS

Inflation 7.8% p.a. (1990–2001)

$5.83bn

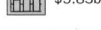

75.65 Nepalese rupees (77.61)

SCORE CARD

❑ WORLD GNP RANKING	107th
❑ GNP PER CAPITA	$250
❑ BALANCE OF PAYMENTS	$172m
❑ INFLATION	2.8%
❑ UNEMPLOYMENT	1%

STRENGTHS

Self-sufficiency in grain most years. Economic liberalization under NCP government. Potential for hydroelectric power generation. Low debt level.

WEAKNESSES

Instability. Agricultural dependency: only 10% of GDP from manufacturing. Landlocked. Low savings rate. Absence of active entrepreneurial class.

EXPORTS

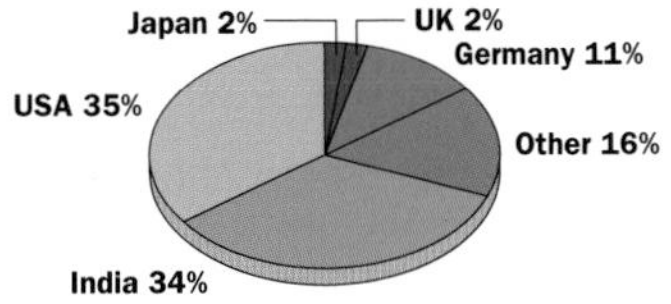
Japan 2%
UK 2%
Germany 11%
USA 35%
Other 16%
India 34%

IMPORTS

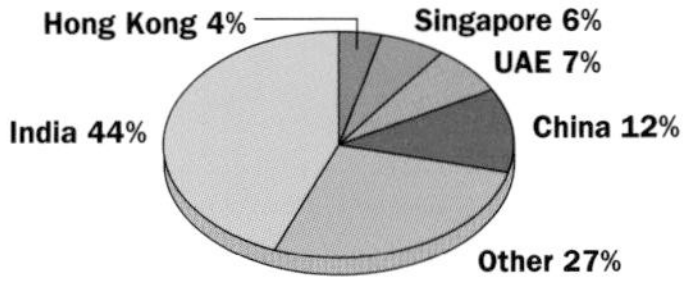
Hong Kong 4%
Singapore 6%
UAE 7%
India 44%
China 12%
Other 27%

RESOURCES

Electric power 458,000 kW

31,723 tonnes

Not an oil producer

6.98m cattle, 6.61m goats, 4m buffaloes, 21.4m chickens

Mica, lignite, copper, cobalt, iron

The first privately owned power plant, situated near Ramechhap, opened in mid-2000. HEP is being developed.

ENVIRONMENT

Sustainability rank: 99th

9% (2% partially protected)

0.1 tonnes per capita

Kathmandu has chronic traffic and pollution problems. Deforestation and soil erosion are serious. The native tiger is fast disappearing. Approval of the controversial Arun III hydroelectric project was granted in mid-2000.

MEDIA

TV ownership low

Daily newspaper circulation 12 per 1000 people

PUBLISHING AND BROADCAST MEDIA

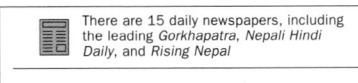

There are 15 daily newspapers, including the leading *Gorkhapatra*, *Nepali Hindi Daily*, and *Rising Nepal*

1 limited state-owned service

1 state-owned service

The Nepal TV service began in 1986; under 25% of the population receives it. The press is mainly Kathmandu-based with low circulations. Press watchdogs warned of censorship under the state of emergency imposed in 2001.

CRIME

No death penalty

5878 prisoners

Up slightly in 2000

Petty theft and smuggling are the main problems. The legal provision for detention without trial is used, and police suppression of demonstrations is often brutal.

EDUCATION

School leaving age: 11

43%

103,290 students

Nearly 80% of boys attend school in Nepal, but still only two-thirds of girls. Nepal's literacy rate is among the lowest in the world.

CHRONOLOGY

The foundations of the Nepalese state were laid in 1769, when King Prithvi Narayan Shah conquered the region.

- ❑ **1816–1923** Quasi-British protectorate.
- ❑ **1959** First multiparty constitution.
- ❑ **1960** Constitution suspended.
- ❑ **1962–1990** *Panchayat* nonparty system.
- ❑ **1972** Birendra succeeds to throne.
- ❑ **1991** NCP victory in elections.
- ❑ **1994–1995** Communist government.
- ❑ **1999** NCP election victory. Maoist insurgency in rural areas.
- ❑ **2001** King and family shot by crown prince; Gyanendra crowned amid unrest. Upsurge in Maoist violence; state of emergency declared.
- ❑ **2002** Gyanendra dismisses NCP government.

HEALTH

Welfare state health benefits

1 per 25,000 people

Respiratory and diarrheal diseases, maternal deaths

There are about 100 *dharmi-jhankri* (faith healers) for every health worker. Maternal mortality is high, the result of harmful traditional birth practices; a reeducation program for midwives has been established.

SPENDING

GDP/cap. increase

CONSUMPTION AND SPENDING

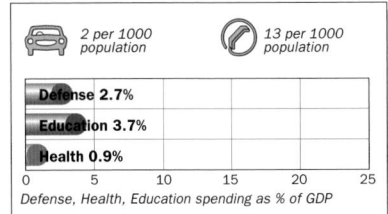

2 per 1000 population

13 per 1000 population

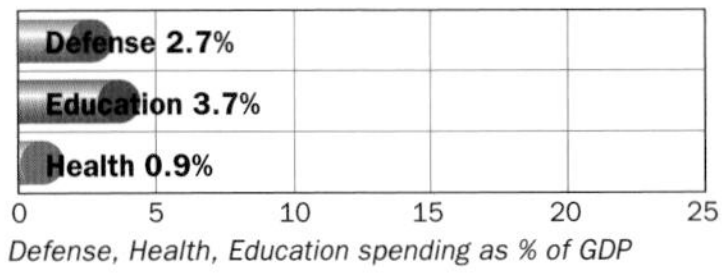
Defense 2.7%
Education 3.7%
Health 0.9%
0 5 10 15 20 25
Defense, Health, Education spending as % of GDP

Nepal is one of the poorest countries in the world. Bonded labor was abolished in mid-2000, releasing 36,000 people.

WORLD RANKING

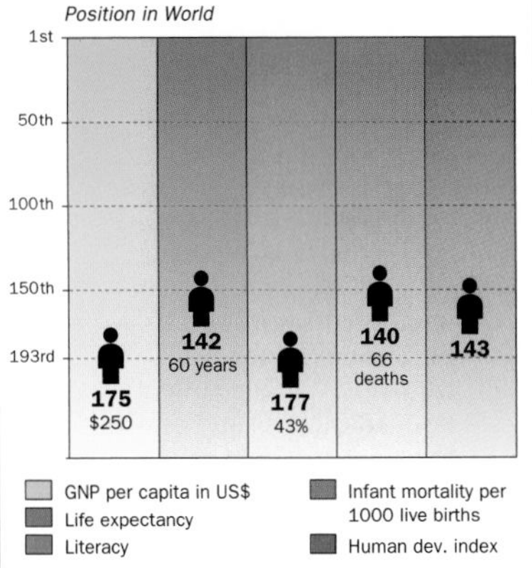
Position in World
1st
50th
100th
150th
193rd
175
$250
142
60 years
177
43%
140
66 deaths
143
GNP per capita in US$
Life expectancy
Literacy
Infant mortality per 1000 live births
Human dev. index

N

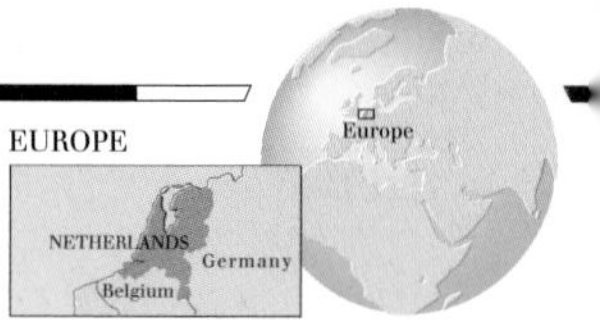
EUROPE
Europe
NETHERLANDS
Germany
Belgium

NETHERLANDS

OFFICIAL NAME: Kingdom of the Netherlands **POPULATION:** 16.2 million
CAPITALS: Amsterdam; The Hague (administrative) **CURRENCY:** Euro **OFFICIAL LANGUAGE:** Dutch

1648 | 1839 | April 30 | NL | +1 | +31 | .nl

THE NETHERLANDS IS LOCATED at the delta of four major rivers in northwest Europe. The few hills in the eastern and southern part of the country descend to a flat coastal area, bordered by the North Sea to the north and west. This is protected by a giant infrastructure of dunes, dikes, and canals, since 27% of the coast is below sea level. The Netherlands became one of the world's first confederative republics after Spain recognized its independence in 1648. Its highly successful economy has a long trading tradition, and Rotterdam is the world's largest port.

CLIMATE

Maritime

WEATHER CHART FOR AMSTERDAM

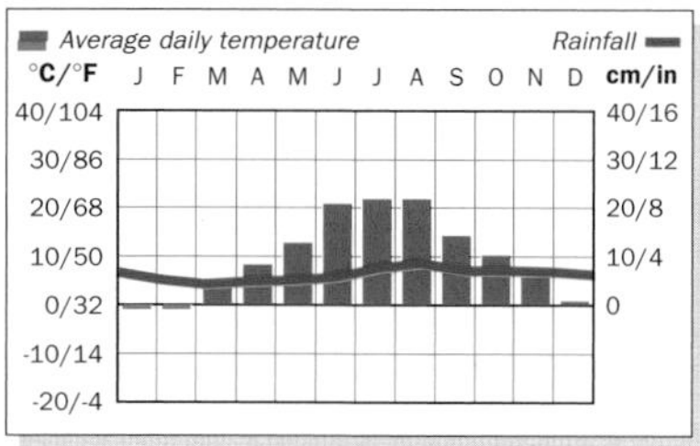
Average daily temperature
Rainfall
°C/°F J F M A M J J A S O N D cm/in
40/104
30/86
20/68
10/50
0/32
-10/14
-20/-4
40/16
30/12
20/8
10/4
0

The Netherlands has a temperate climate, with mild winters which rarely fall much below freezing, and cool summers with a mean temperature of 20°C (68°F). The country's coastal areas have the mildest climate, though northerly gales are fairly frequent, particularly in autumn and winter.

TRANSPORTATION

Drive on right

Schiphol, Amsterdam 40.7m passengers

1337 ships 5.61m grt

THE TRANSPORTATION NETWORK

104,850 km (65,151 miles)

2256 km (1402 miles)

2802 km (1741 miles)

5046 km (3135 miles)

Rotterdam, the key transshipment port for northern Europe, is also the world's largest. Schiphol airport is one of the air transportation hubs of Europe. A high-speed passenger rail line is due to link Amsterdam and Rotterdam with Brussels and Paris in 2003, and a high-speed freight line from Rotterdam to Germany should be completed in 2004.

TOURISM

Visitors : Population 1:1.7

9.6m visitors

Up 1% in 2002

MAIN TOURIST ARRIVALS

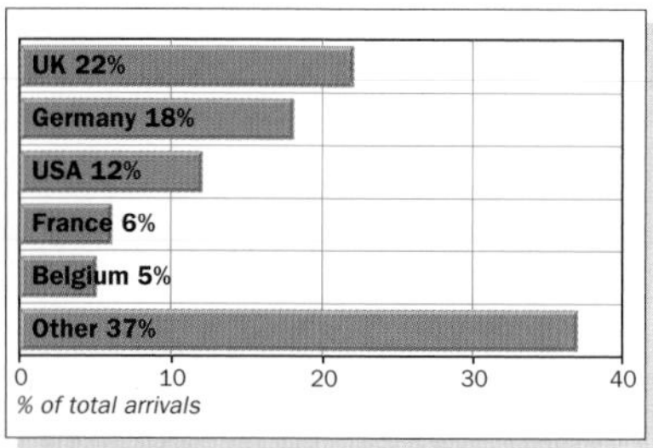
UK 22%
Germany 18%
USA 12%
France 6%
Belgium 5%
Other 37%
0
10
20
30
40
% of total arrivals

Tourism is a major business in the Netherlands. Visitors go mainly to Amsterdam, though cities such as Groningen and Maastricht are growing in popularity. Amsterdam caters for a diverse tourism market. Its world-famous museums include the Rijksmuseum, with its collection of Vermeers and Rembrandts, while its network of canals is popular. Amsterdam is also renowned for its liberal attitude to sex; its red-light district attracts millions every year. In the past decade, the city has become a center for the European gay community, with celebrations on April 30 (Queen's Day – the monarch's official birthday) and in August (Amsterdam Pride). A thriving club scene and liberal drug laws draw enthusiasts from neighboring countries. In spring and summer, the tulip fields and North Sea beaches attract large numbers of visitors.

***Windmill at Baambrugge,** near Amsterdam. A century ago there were 10,000 in the country compared with today's 1000. A protective ring of 900 mills kept Amsterdam from flooding.*

PEOPLE

Pop. density high

Dutch, Frisian

478/km² (1237/mi²)

THE URBAN/RURAL POPULATION SPLIT

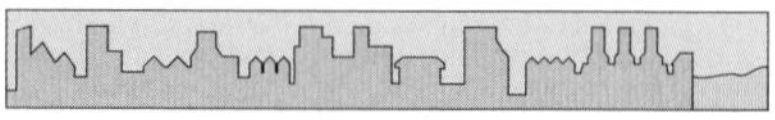
90%
10%

RELIGIOUS PERSUASION

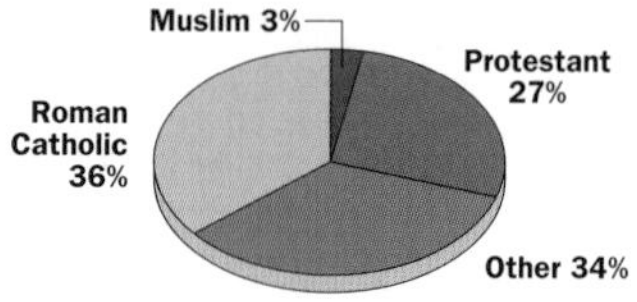
Muslim 3%
Protestant 27%
Roman Catholic 36%
Other 34%

ETHNIC MAKEUP

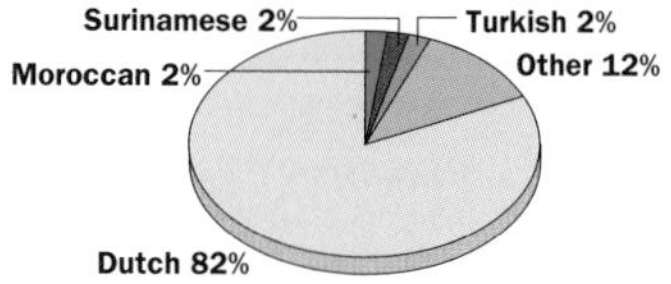
Surinamese 2%
Turkish 2%
Moroccan 2%
Other 12%
Dutch 82%

The Dutch see their country as the most tolerant in Europe, and it has a long history of welcoming refugees seeking religious and political asylum. In the 20th century, immigrants from former colonies settled in the Netherlands and became fully accepted as citizens. They came first from Indonesia and then from Suriname, the Netherlands Antilles, and Morocco. The small Turkish community, however, does not enjoy full citizenship.

The tradition of tolerance is reflected in liberal attitudes to sexuality. In 2001 same-sex marriages were legalized, giving gay couples full equality, including the right of adoption (after three years of marriage).

The state does not try to impose a particular morality on its citizens. Drug taking is seen as a matter of personal choice, and in 2001 the Netherlands became the first country in the world to legalize euthanasia, albeit under strict conditions.

Women enjoy equal rights and hold 37% of seats in the Second Chamber of the States-General, but are not well represented in boardrooms.

POPULATION AGE BREAKDOWN

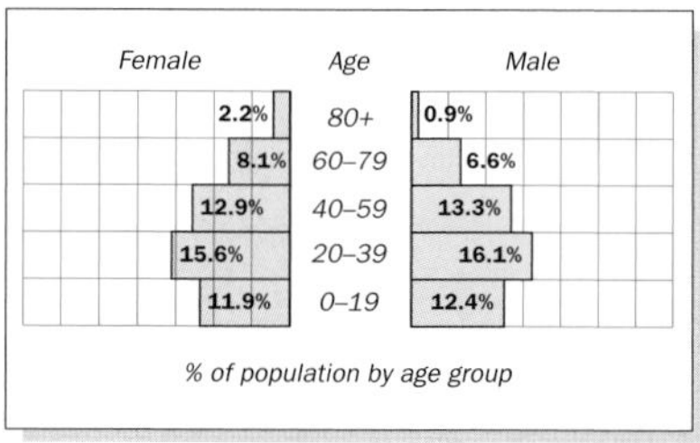
Female
Age
Male
2.2% 80+ 0.9%
8.1% 60–79 6.6%
12.9% 40–59 13.3%
15.6% 20–39 16.1%
11.9% 0–19 12.4%
% of population by age group

N

POLITICS

Multiparty elections

L. House 2003/2007
U. House 2003/2007

H.M. Queen Beatrix

AT THE LAST ELECTION

Second Chamber of the States-General 150 seats

29% CDA	28% PvdA	19% VVD	6% SP	5% GL	5% LPF	8% Others

CDA = Christian Democratic Appeal **PvdA** = Labor Party
VVD = People's Party for Freedom and Democracy
SP = Socialist Party **GL** = Green Left
LPF = Pim Fortuyn List **D66** = Democrats 66

First Chamber of the States-General 75 seats

31% CDA	25% PvdA	20% VVD	7% GL	5% SP	4% D66	8% Others

The First Chamber of the States-General is indirectly elected

The Netherlands is a constitutional monarchy. Legislative power is vested in parliament, and the monarch has only nominal power.

PROFILE

Dutch politics show a high degree of consensus. Since the early 1980s, governments have employed the "polder model," which focuses on pay moderation, job creation, economic deregulation, and generous social protection.

The CDA has traditionally led two-party coalitions, with either the left-of-center PvdA or the right-wing VVD. However, after the 1994 election the PvdA under Wim Kok led the government, in coalition with the VVD and the left-liberal D66.

In 2002 the emergence of the ultranationalist Pim Fortuyn challenged current policy on immigration and integration. Fortuyn also argued that the polder model had made the political establishment complacent. His murder prompted a strong sympathy vote and a swing to the right in the May election. The LPF came second to the CDA, under Jan Peter Balkenende. However, the resulting coalition collapsed within 100 days as a result of the LPF's political inexperience. Fresh elections in January 2003 saw support for the LPF demolished and a reemergence of the PvdA. The CDA remained the largest party, but took four months to organize a new coalition with the VVD and the small D66.

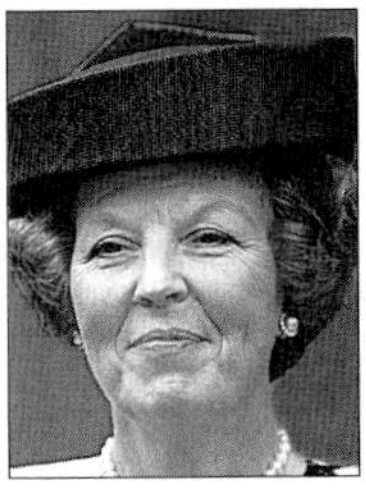

Queen Beatrix, who acceded in 1980 and rebuilt support for the Dutch monarchy.

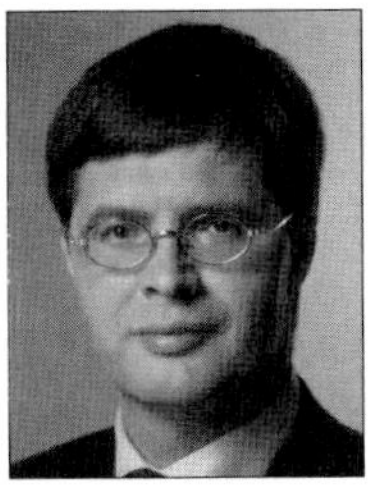

CDA leader Jan Peter Balkenende *was appointed prime minister in 2002.*

MAIN POLITICAL ISSUES

The future of social welfare
Despite cutbacks in the 1980s, the Dutch still have one of Europe's most generous welfare systems. Most parties accepted that levels of welfare could not be maintained indefinitely. The debate thus focuses on how much and in which areas cuts should be made.

Refugees and asylum seekers
Asylum laws have been tightened since 1994 as the number of immigrants has risen. First- and second-generation immigrants made up 18% of the national population in 2002, but 40% (30% non-European) in Rotterdam, where support for the LPF was greatest in 2002. Concern focuses not so much on the number of immigrants as on the extent of their integration into Dutch society.

NETHERLANDS

Total Area :
41 526 sq. km
(16 033 sq. miles)

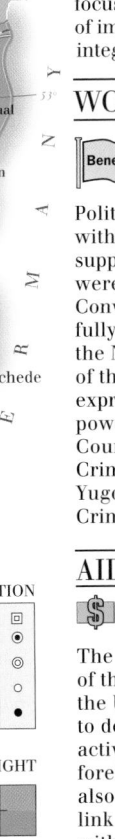

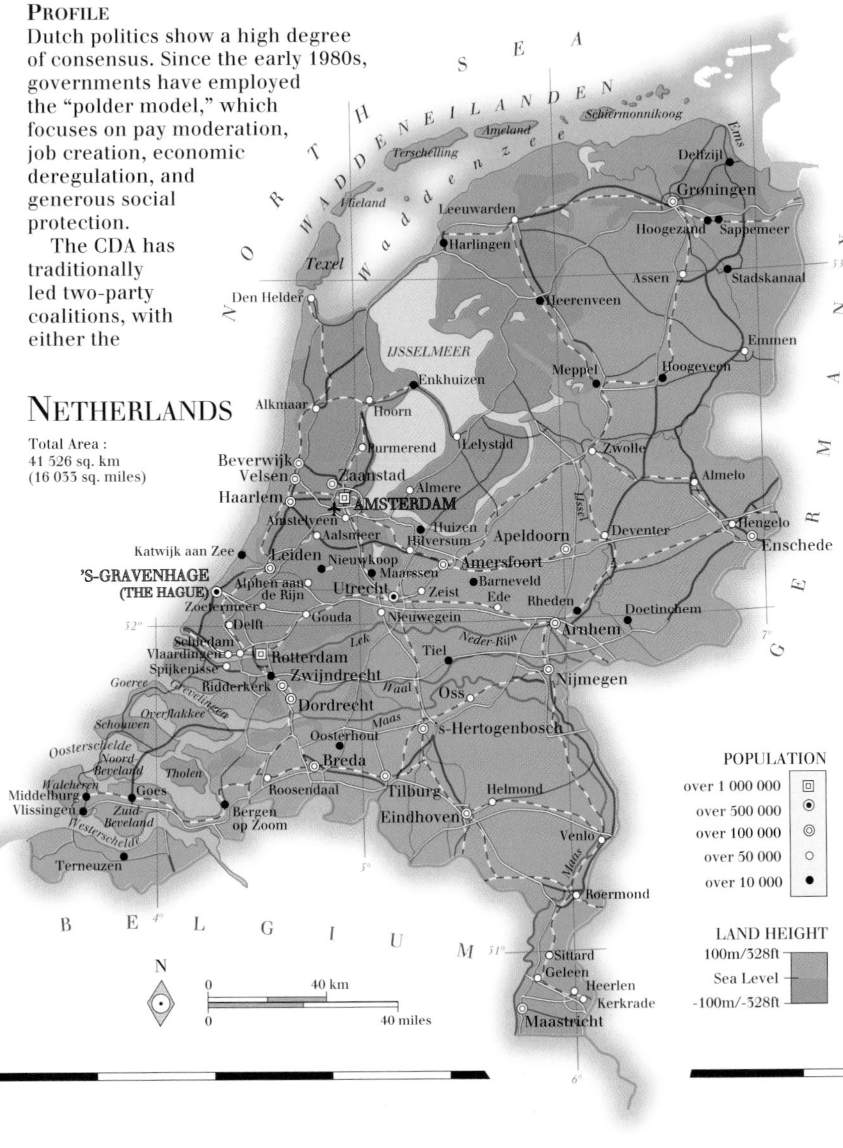
NORTH SEA
WADDENEILANDEN
Waddenzee
Schiermonnikoog
Ameland
Terschelling
Vlieland
Texel
Delfzijl
Groningen
Leeuwarden
Hoogezand
Sappemeer
Harlingen
Assen
Stadskanaal
Den Helder
Heerenveen
Emmen
IJSSELMEER
Enkhuizen
Meppel
Hoogeveen
Alkmaar
Hoorn
Purmerend
Lelystad
Zwolle
Beverwijk
Velsen
Zaanstad
Almelo
Haarlem
Almere
AMSTERDAM
Amstelveen
Huizen
Hilversum
Apeldoorn
Deventer
Hengelo
Enschede
Aalsmeer
Katwijk aan Zee
Leiden
Nieuwkoop
Maarssen
Amersfoort
'S-GRAVENHAGE (THE HAGUE)
Alphen aan de Rijn
Utrecht
Zeist
Barneveld
Ede
Rheden
Zoetermeer
Gouda
Nieuwegein
Doetinchem
Delft
Arnhem
Schiedam
Vlaardingen
Rotterdam
Spijkenisse
Tiel
Nijmegen
Ridderkerk
Zwijndrecht
Goeree
Dordrecht
Waal
Oss
Overflakkee
Schouwen
Oosterhout
Maas
's-Hertogenbosch
Oosterschelde
Noord-Beveland
Tholen
Breda
Walcheren
Goes
Roosendaal
Tilburg
Helmond
Middelburg
Vlissingen
Zuid-Beveland
Bergen op Zoom
Eindhoven
Westerschelde
Venlo
Terneuzen
Roermond
BELGIUM
GERMANY
Sittard
Geleen
Heerlen
Kerkrade
Maastricht
N
0 40 km
0 40 miles
POPULATION
over 1 000 000
over 500 000
over 100 000
over 50 000
over 10 000
LAND HEIGHT
100m/328ft
Sea Level
-100m/-328ft

WORLD AFFAIRS

Joined UN in 1945

Benelux | EU | NATO | OECD | OSCE

Political and monetary integration within the EU have strong popular support. In 1995, internal border controls were lifted under the Schengen Convention and in 2002 the Netherlands fully adopted the euro. Traditionally the Netherlands favored enlargement of the EU, but the CDA government expressed reservations when it came to power in May 2002. The International Court of Justice, the International Criminal Tribunal for the former Yugoslavia, and the International Criminal Court sit in The Hague.

AID

Donor

$3.17bn (donations)

Up 1% in 2001

The Netherlands continues to be one of the few countries which exceeds the UN target of devoting 0.7% of GNP to development aid. The government actively pursues a policy of linking foreign aid and human rights. It also gives priority to projects which link longer-term development goals with efforts to manage and reduce intergroup conflict.

N

CHRONOLOGY

Suppression of Protestantism by the ruling Spanish Habsburgs led to the revolt of the Netherlands and the declaration of independence of the northern provinces as a republic in 1581, recognized by Spain in 1648.

- **1813** Dutch oust French after 18 years of French rule and choose to become a constitutional monarchy.
- **1815** United Kingdom of Netherlands formed to include Belgium and Luxembourg.
- **1839** Recognition of 1830 secession of Catholic southern provinces as Belgium.
- **1848** New constitution – ministers to be accountable to parliament.
- **1897–1901** Wide-ranging social legislation enacted. Development of strong trade unions.
- **1898** Wilhelmina succeeds to throne, ending Luxembourg union, where male hereditary Salic Law is in force.
- **1914–1918** Dutch neutrality respected in World War I.
- **1922** Women fully enfranchised.
- **1940** Dutch assert neutrality in World War II, but Germany invades. Fierce resistance.
- **1942** Japan invades Dutch East Indies.
- **1944–1945** "Winter of starvation" in German-occupied western provinces.
- **1945** Liberation. International Court of Justice set up in The Hague.
- **1946–1958** PvdA leads coalitions. Marshall Aid speeds reconstruction.
- **1948** Juliana becomes queen.
- **1949** Joins NATO. Most of East Indies colonies gain independence as Indonesia.
- **1957** Founder member of EEC.
- **1960** Economic union with Belgium and Luxembourg comes into effect.
- **1973** PvdA wins power after 15 years spent mainly in opposition. Center-left coalition until 1977.
- **1980** CDA alliance of the "confessional" parties forms a single party. Beatrix becomes queen.
- **1982–1994** CDA-led coalitions under Ruud Lubbers.
- **1990** 20-year National Environment Policy (NEP) introduced.
- **1992** Licensed brothels legalized.
- **1994** Elections: Wim Kok of PvdA heads coalition with VVD and D66.
- **2001** Euthanasia and gay marriage legalized.
- **2002** January, euro fully adopted. April, government resigns after publication of report blaming Dutch military in Bosnia for Srebrenica massacre in 1995. May, ultra-nationalist leader Pim Fortuyn assassinated. Elections. October, CDA-led coalition collapses.
- **2003** CDA reelected.

N

DEFENSE

No compulsory military service

$6.26bn

Up 4% in 2001

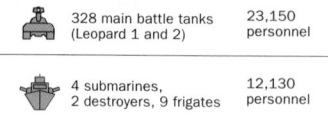

DUTCH ARMED FORCES

328 main battle tanks (Leopard 1 and 2)	23,150 personnel
4 submarines, 2 destroyers, 9 frigates	12,130 personnel
143 combat aircraft (F-16A/B)	8850 personnel
None	

The Dutch military has undergone major restructuring since the end of the Cold War with the aim of making it a rapidly deployable, more flexible military force as befits a NATO member state. Compulsory military service was abolished in 1996 and personnel cut by 44%, with the number of army divisions reduced from three to two. In 1995, a joint Dutch–German, 28,000-strong army corps was inaugurated. The Dutch army has been criticized for failing to prevent the massacre at Srebrenica, Bosnia, in 1995, but it has continued to play a role in other international peacekeeping efforts since.

The Netherlands also has a large defense industry, which specializes in submarines, weapons systems, and aircraft.

ECONOMICS

Inflation 2.1% p.a. (1990–2001)

$390bn

0.871 euros (1.013)

SCORE CARD

World GNP Ranking	14th
GNP per Capita	$24,330
Balance of Payments	$12.4bn
Inflation	4.5%
Unemployment	2%

EXPORTS

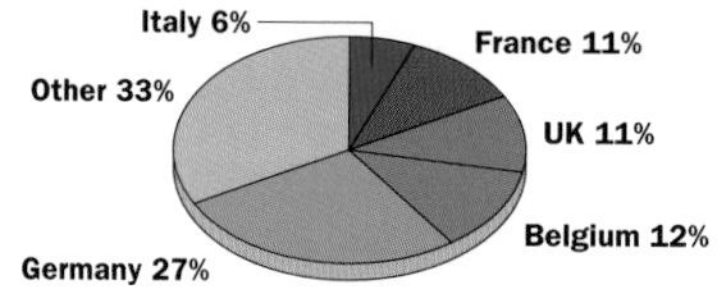
Italy 6%
France 11%
Other 33%
UK 11%
Belgium 12%
Germany 27%

IMPORTS

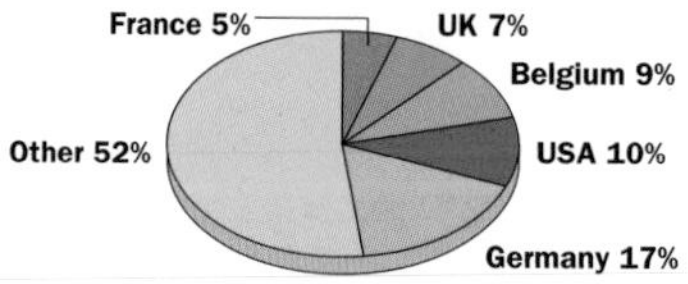
France 5%
UK 7%
Belgium 9%
Other 52%
USA 10%
Germany 17%

ECONOMIC PERFORMANCE INDICATOR

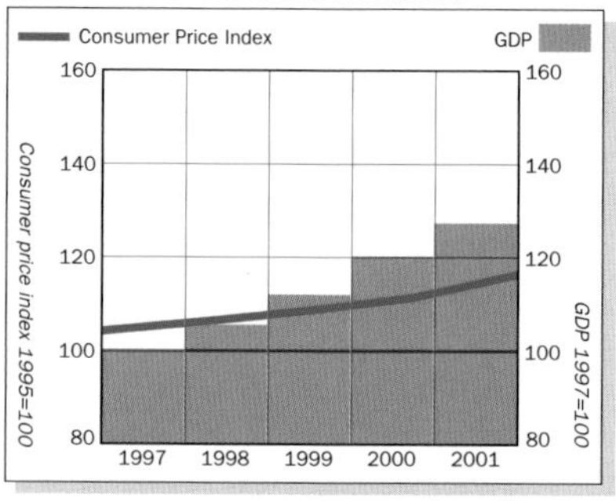
Consumer Price Index
GDP
160
140
120
100
80
Consumer price index 1995=100
GDP 1997=100
1997
1998
1999
2000
2001

Strengths

Highly skilled, educated, multilingual workforce. Sophisticated infrastructure. Many blue-chip multinationals, including Philips and Shell. Harmony between employers and employees. Low inflation and unemployment. Tradition of high-tech innovation, including development of music cassette and CD.

Weaknesses

Costly welfare system, resulting in high taxes and social insurance premiums; one-third of national income spent on social security. Aging population. High labor costs.

Profile

Trade has been central to the success of the economy of the Netherlands since the 16th century. Most goods travel through Rotterdam, the world's biggest port. As well as high-tech industries such as electronics, telecommunications, and chemicals, there is a successful and intensive agricultural sector. Dependence on trade makes the economy vulnerable to world economic fluctuations; thus high growth rates in 1997–2000 were followed by a marked downturn in 2001.

NETHERLANDS : MAJOR BUSINESSES

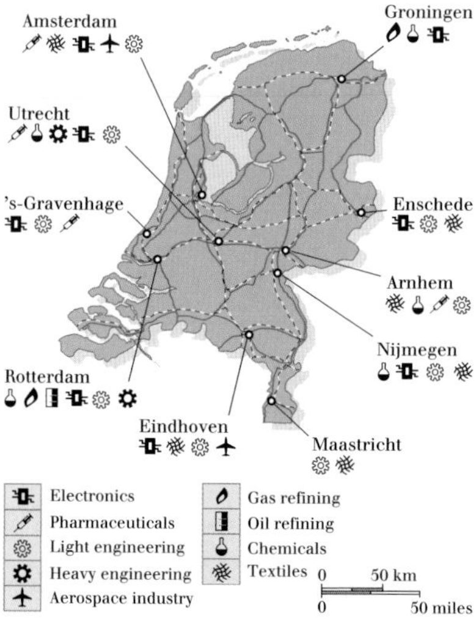
Amsterdam
Groningen
Utrecht
's-Gravenhage
Enschede
Arnhem
Nijmegen
Rotterdam
Eindhoven
Maastricht
Electronics
Pharmaceuticals
Light engineering
Heavy engineering
Aerospace industry
Gas refining
Oil refining
Chemicals
Textiles
0
50 km
0
50 miles

RESOURCES

Electric power 20.6m kW

571,143 tonnes

31,960 b/d (reserves 105m barrels)

13m pigs, 1.52m turkeys, 4.05m cattle, 98m chickens

Natural gas, oil

ELECTRICITY GENERATION

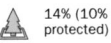

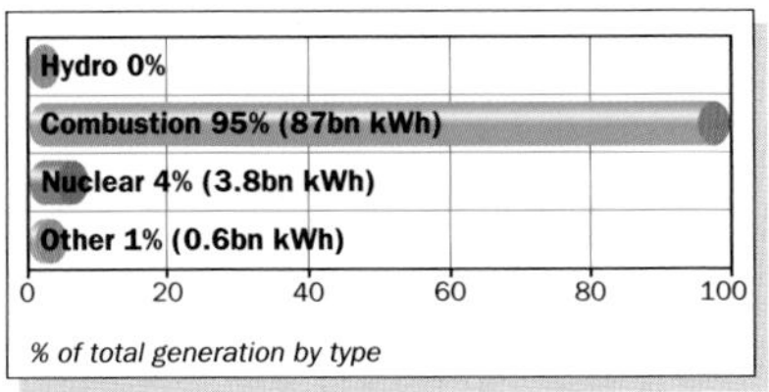
Hydro 0%
Combustion 95% (87bn kWh)
Nuclear 4% (3.8bn kWh)
Other 1% (0.6bn kWh)
0
20
40
60
80
100
% of total generation by type

There are large natural gas reserves in the north. A 22.5 MW wind power station near Rotterdam began operation in 2002.

NETHERLANDS : LAND USE

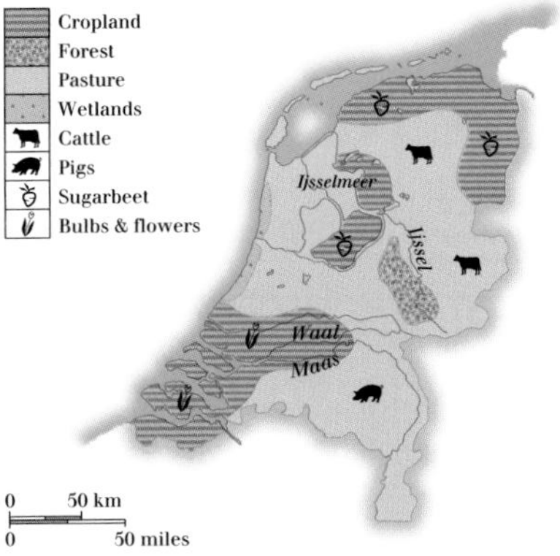
Cropland
Forest
Pasture
Wetlands
Cattle
Pigs
Sugarbeet
Bulbs & flowers
IJsselmeer
IJssel
Waal
Maas
0
50 km
0
50 miles

ENVIRONMENT

Sustainability rank: 34th

14% (10% partially protected)

10.9 tonnes per capita

ENVIRONMENTAL TREATIES

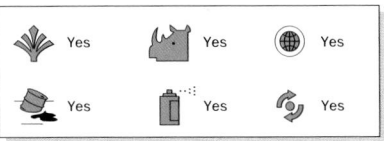

Yes | Yes | Yes

Yes | Yes | Yes

There is a strong environmental tradition, a legacy in part of living in one of the most densely populated states in the world. NGOs such as Greenpeace are well supported and the Green Left party is represented in parliament.

The Dutch recycle domestic trash, have a good record on energy efficiency, and have developed innovative projects in housing and local transportation. An eco-tax on energy users was introduced in 1996 – the first of its kind in the West – though big businesses are exempt.

Serious flooding of the rivers Maas and Waal (an arm of the Rhine) in 1993 and 1995 raised concern about the state of the country's flood defenses and the use of floodplains for development.

MEDIA

TV ownership high

Daily newspaper circulation 306 per 1000 people

PUBLISHING AND BROADCAST MEDIA

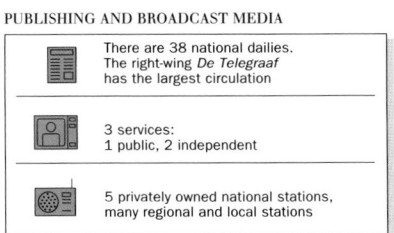

There are 38 national dailies. The right-wing *De Telegraaf* has the largest circulation

3 services:
1 public, 2 independent

5 privately owned national stations, many regional and local stations

Newspaper circulation is high. While editorially independent, broadcasting is strongly regulated. Dutch law does not recognize a right of reply or a right to protect information sources.

CRIME

No death penalty

14,968 prisoners

Down 16% in 1996–1998

CRIME RATES

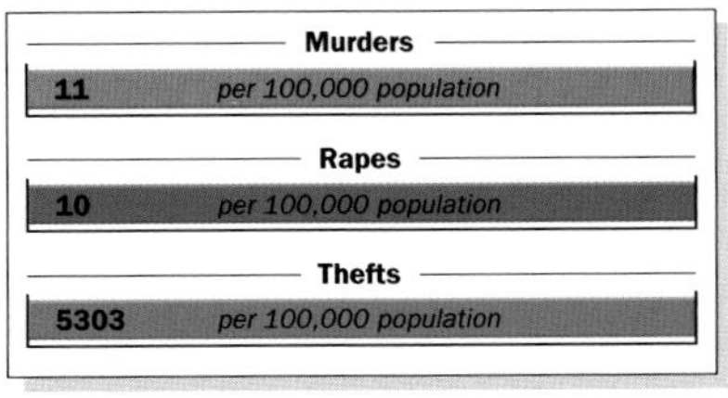
Murders
11 per 100,000 population
Rapes
10 per 100,000 population
Thefts
5303 per 100,000 population

The Netherlands treats the use of hard drugs more as a medical and social issue than a criminal one. Other member states of Europe's Schengen Convention, particularly France, fear that this makes Dutch ports a soft point of entry for narcotics. Possessing cannabis for personal use has been decriminalized – stopping short of actual legalization.

EDUCATION

School leaving age: 18

99%

504,042 students

THE EDUCATION SYSTEM

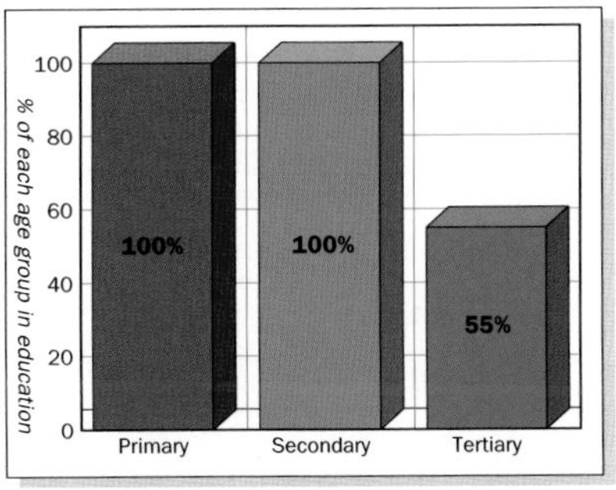
100
80
60
40
20
0
% of each age group in education
100%
100%
55%
Primary
Secondary
Tertiary

Private schools take 65% of students; most of them are run by the various religious denominations. Both public and private institutions are state-funded.

There are 13 universities in the Netherlands. Corporate funding plays an important part in research.

HEALTH

Welfare state health benefits

1 per 398 people

Cancers, heart, cerebrovascular, and respiratory diseases

Health care is largely funded by the state, though around 33% of funding comes from private sources. The quality of care provided, currently among the best in the world, is threatened by a rapidly aging population. The Netherlands was the first country to legalize abortion, but has the lowest rate of terminations in the world. Major health problems are similar to those in the rest of western Europe. Incidence of AIDS is higher than in Sweden or the UK but lower than in Switzerland, France, or Spain.

SPENDING

GDP/cap. increase

CONSUMPTION AND SPENDING

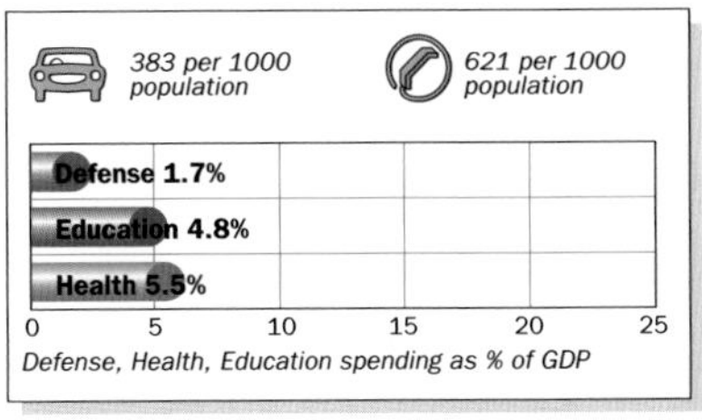
383 per 1000 population
621 per 1000 population
Defense 1.7%
Education 4.8%
Health 5.5%
0
5
10
15
20
25
Defense, Health, Education spending as % of GDP

The Netherlands is, per capita, one of the richest countries in the world. Oil executives, stock market traders, and businessmen are among the wealthiest sector of the population. A progressive taxation system and extensive social welfare mean that wealth is reasonably evenly distributed. A small elite have considerable inherited wealth, but extravagant displays of affluence are rare.

Class does not play a big part in Dutch society. Most citizens would consider themselves middle class. Immigrant communities are the exception; they often live on the edges of towns in deprived areas. The poorest group of all are the illegal immigrants.

WORLD RANKING

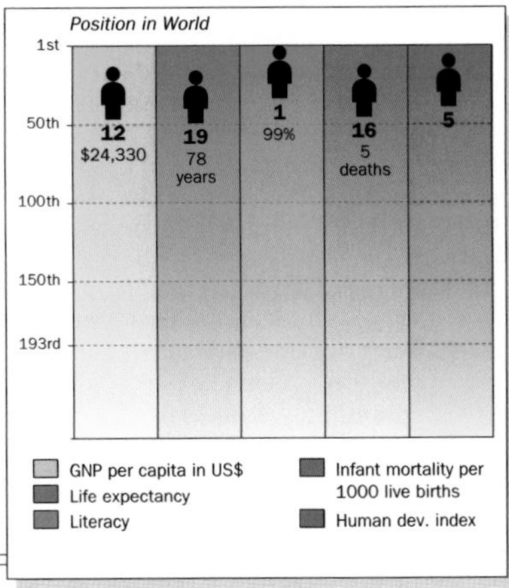
Position in World
1st
50th
100th
150th
193rd
12
$24,330
19
78
years
1
99%
16
5
deaths
5
GNP per capita in US$
Life expectancy
Literacy
Infant mortality per 1000 live births
Human dev. index

N

NEW ZEALAND

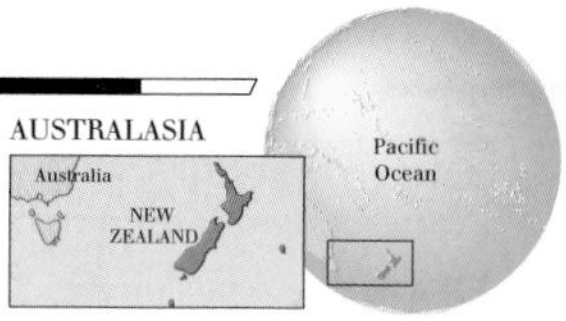
AUSTRALASIA
Australia
NEW ZEALAND
Pacific Ocean

OFFICIAL NAME: New Zealand **CAPITAL:** Wellington **POPULATION:** 4 million
CURRENCY: New Zealand dollar **OFFICIAL LANGUAGES:** English and Maori

1947
1947
Feb 6
NZ
+12
+64
.nz

LYING IN THE SOUTH PACIFIC, 1600 km (992 miles) southeast of Australia, New Zealand comprises the main North and South Islands, separated by the Cook Strait, and a number of smaller islands. South Island is the more mountainous; North Island contains hot springs and geysers, and the bulk of the population. The political tradition is liberal and egalitarian, and has been dominated by the National and Labour parties. Radical, and often unpopular, reforms since 1984 have restored economic growth, speeded up economic diversification, and strengthened New Zealand's position within the Pacific Rim countries.

CLIMATE

Maritime/subtropical

WEATHER CHART FOR WELLINGTON

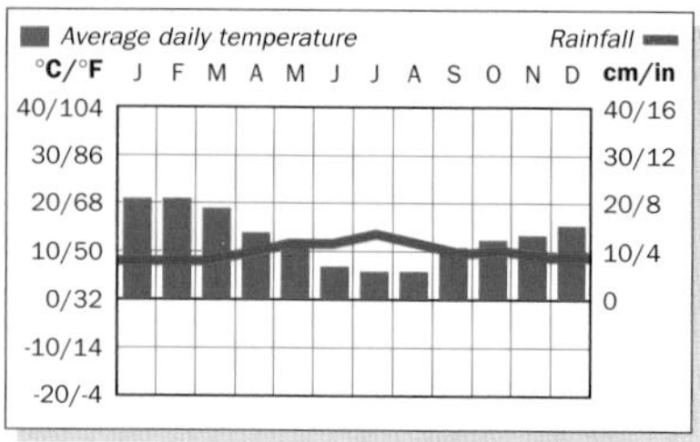
Average daily temperature
Rainfall
°C/°F J F M A M J J A S O N D cm/in
40/104
30/86
20/68
10/50
0/32
-10/14
-20/-4
40/16
30/12
20/8
10/4
0

New Zealand's climate is generally temperate and damp, with an average temperature of 12°C (54°F). There are differences between the islands, which extend north–south nearly 2000 km (1240 miles). The extreme north is almost subtropical; southern winters are cold. It is windy: Wellington, in particular, is known for bouts of blustery weather that can last for days.

TRANSPORTATION

Drive on left

Auckland International 8.37m passengers

159 ships 174,942 grt

THE TRANSPORTATION NETWORK

53,568 km (33,286 miles)

167 km (104 miles)

3908 km (2428 miles)

1609 km (1000 miles)

Though both the main islands are well provided with transportation services, the more populous North Island's road and rail network is more extensive than the South's. Air and ferry services complement the land networks and provide links between the North and South Islands, as well as with the numerous smaller islands. Cargo ferry services are particularly important for Antarctic bases in the Ross Dependency. Links with New Zealand's other associated territories – the Cook Islands, Niue, and the atolls of Tokelau – are underdeveloped.

TOURISM

Visitors : Population 1:2

2.05m visitors

Up 7% in 2002

MAIN TOURIST ARRIVALS

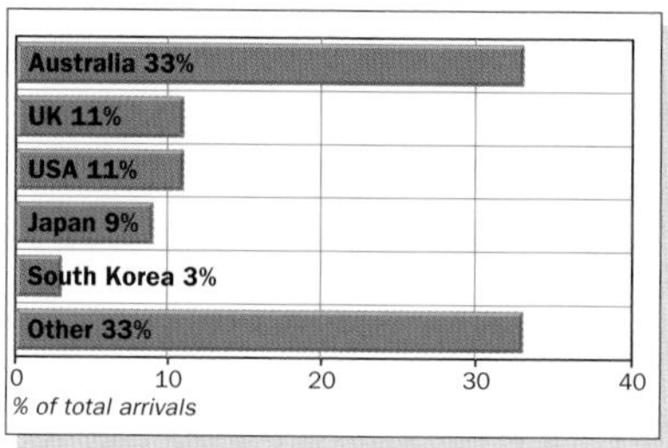
Australia 33%
UK 11%
USA 11%
Japan 9%
South Korea 3%
Other 33%
0
10
20
30
40
% of total arrivals

New Zealand's prime attraction is its scenery. Unspoiled and, relative to the country's size, the most varied in the world, it offers mountains, fjords and lakes, glaciers, rainforests, beaches, boiling mud pools, and geysers. Other attractions are the Maori culture and outdoor activities such as river rafting, fishing, skiing, whale watching, and bungee jumping – a local invention.

Tourists come mainly from Australia, the US, the UK, and Japan. Tourism, the largest single foreign-exchange earner, continues to grow, though the 1997–1998 Asian economic crisis saw the number of Asian tourists drop by 10%. An increase in visitor numbers has followed the huge success of the *Lord of the Rings* films: the whole series was shot in New Zealand.

***Mount Egmont,** an extinct volcano, is one of the numerous popular natural attractions of New Zealand's North Island.*

PEOPLE

Pop. density low

English, Maori

15/km² (39/mi²)

THE URBAN/RURAL POPULATION SPLIT

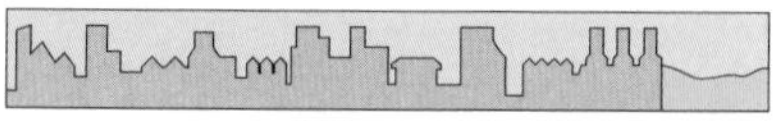
86%
14%

RELIGIOUS PERSUASION

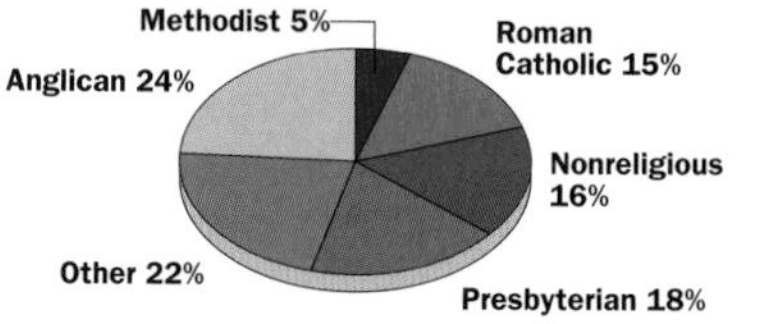
Methodist 5%
Roman Catholic 15%
Anglican 24%
Nonreligious 16%
Other 22%
Presbyterian 18%

ETHNIC MAKEUP

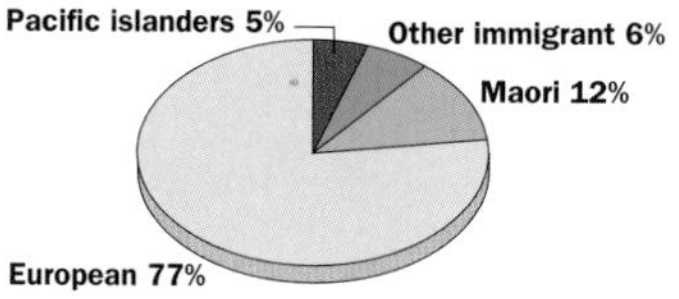
Pacific islanders 5%
Other immigrant 6%
Maori 12%
European 77%

New Zealand is a country of migrants. The first settlers, the Maoris, migrated from Polynesia about 1200 years ago. Today's majority European population is mainly descended from British migrants who settled after 1840. Newer migrants include Asians from Hong Kong and Malaysia, and Polynesians. The government is keen to attract skilled South Americans, Russians, Chinese, and Africans to revitalize the economy.

The living standards and unemployment rates of the Maoris compare adversely with those of the European-descended majority, and relations can be tense. The Waikato Raupatu Claims Settlement Act was signed in 1995 and an official apology to the Maoris was made. In 1998 the Waitangi Tribunal ordered the return of confiscated land.

New Zealand became the first country in the world to give women the vote – in 1893. In 2001, the posts of prime minister, leader of the opposition, and governor-general were all held by women.

POPULATION AGE BREAKDOWN

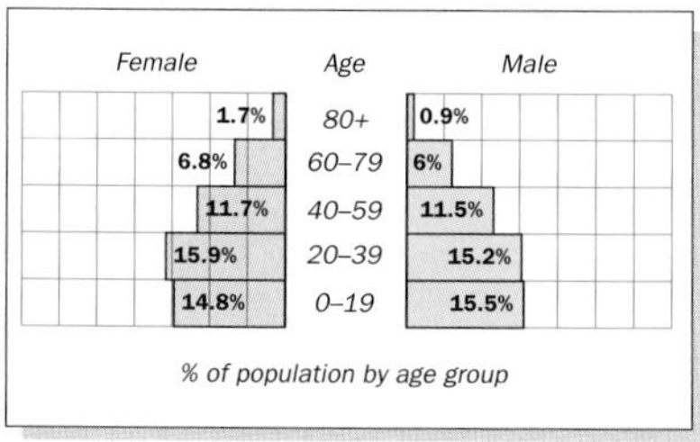
Female
Age
Male
1.7%
80+
0.9%
6.8%
60–79
6%
11.7%
40–59
11.5%
15.9%
20–39
15.2%
14.8%
0–19
15.5%
% of population by age group

N

POLITICS

Multiparty elections

2002/2005

H.M. Queen Elizabeth II

AT THE LAST ELECTION

House of Representatives 120 seats

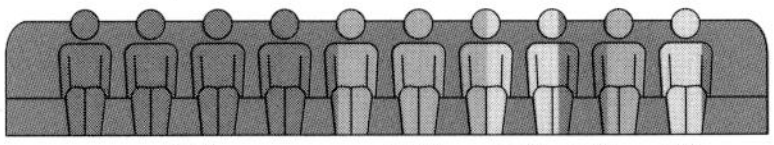
8% GP
2% PC
43% LP
22% NP
11% NZF
8% ACT
6% UFNZ

LP = Labour Party **NP** = National Party **NZF** = New Zealand First Party **ACT** = ACT New Zealand (Association of Consumers and Taxpayers) **GP** = Green Party **UFNZ** = United Future **PC** = Progressive Coalition

Helen Clark, LP leader and prime minister since 1999.

Jenny Shipley, the first woman prime minister (NP, 1997–1999).

New Zealand is a parliamentary democracy. The Cook Islands and Niue are self-governing territories.

PROFILE

Since 1984 the economy has undergone massive reforms; cuts to the welfare system and privatization of public assets have been unpopular. The NP and the LP dominated politics until proportional representation (PR) was first used in 1996. Former NP leader Jenny Shipley became the country's first woman prime minister in 1997 at the head of a coalition with the small NZF, and from 1998 led a minority administration when the NZF withdrew. A new minority coalition of the LP and the Alliance assumed power under LP leader Helen Clark in 1999. The LP remained in power after the 2002 elections, forming a minority coalition with the PC.

MAIN POLITICAL ISSUE

Electoral reform

New Zealand shifted from a first-past-the-post electoral system to PR for the 1996 general election. Endorsement of this reform in a referendum in 1993 had reflected widespread disillusionment with the NP and LP. The new German-style system strengthened the role of smaller parties. As predicted, the first election to use the system in 1996 produced a coalition government, led by the NP. Forced into opposition in 1998, the NP has, unsuccessfully, called for a review of the PR system.

WORLD AFFAIRS

Joined UN in 1945

Comm | APEC | OECD | PIF | PC

Many New Zealanders are strongly committed to the British monarchy and the Commonwealth, but the UK's EU involvement has forced New Zealand to reorient its trade and foreign policy toward its Pacific Rim neighbors, especially Australia, now New Zealand's single largest trading partner. Their 1983 Closer Economic Relationship (CER) treaty was strengthened in 1996 by the signing of a mutual recognition agreement.

Relations with Asia are growing in importance. The 1997–1998 Asian economic crisis significantly affected trade, particularly tourism.

Relations with the US are improving after a low point when New Zealand's antinuclear stance led to its exclusion from the ANZUS pact. Official ties with France, cut in 1985 after French agents bombed Greenpeace's *Rainbow Warrior* in Auckland harbor, were restored in 1997.

AID

Donor

US$112m (donations)

Down 1% in 2001

Over 75% of New Zealand's overseas aid is bilateral. Particular areas of focus are the Pacific states and Pacific-wide organizations. New Zealand is a major supporter of the Pacific Islands Forum, the University of the South Pacific, and the Pacific Environment Program. It also offers scholarships to overseas students for study or training in New Zealand.

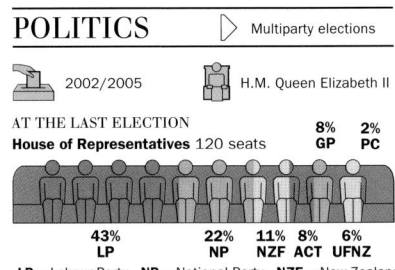

NORTH ISLAND
SOUTH ISLAND
TASMAN SEA
SOUTH PACIFIC OCEAN
Kaitaia
Whangarei
Dargaville
Auckland
Manurewa
Hamilton
Tauranga
Rotorua
Taupo
Gisborne
New Plymouth
Napier
Hastings
Wanganui
Palmerston North
WELLINGTON
Nelson
Blenheim
Westport
Greymouth
Hokitika
Kaikoura
Christchurch
Ashburton
Timaru
Oamaru
Dunedin
Queenstown
Invercargill
Halfmoon Bay
Stewart Island
Foveaux Strait
Cook Strait
SOUTHERN ALPS
Aoraki (Mount Cook) 3744m
Chatham Is
Chatham I.
Pitt I.
(continuation on same scale)
NEW ZEALAND
Total Area : 268 680 sq. km (103 737 sq. miles)
LAND HEIGHT
2000m/6562ft
1000m/3281ft
500m/1640ft
200m/656ft
Sea Level
POPULATION
over 500 000
over 100 000
over 50 000
over 10 000
under 10 000
100 km
100 miles

CHRONOLOGY

A former British colony, New Zealand became a dominion in 1907, self-governing from 1926, and fully independent in 1947.

- **1962** Western Samoa (now Samoa) gains independence.
- **1965** Cook Islands gain autonomy.
- **1975** Conservative NP wins elections. Economic austerity program introduced.
- **1976** Immigration cut by over 80%.
- **1984** LP elected; David Lange prime minister. Auckland harbor headland restored to Maoris.
- **1985** New Zealand prohibits nuclear vessels from ports and waters. French agents sink Greenpeace ship *Rainbow Warrior* in Auckland harbor.
- **1986** US suspends military obligations under ANZUS Treaty.
- **1987** LP wins elections. Introduction of controversial privatization plan. Nuclear ban enshrined in legislation.
- **1990** LP defeated by NP in elections. James Bolger prime minister.
- **1991** Widespread protests at spending cuts.
- **1992** Maoris win South Island fishing rights. Majority vote for electoral reform in referendum.
- **1993** Docking of first French naval ship for eight years. NP returned with single-seat majority in election. Proportional representation introduced by referendum.
- **1994** Senior-level US contacts restored; agrees not to send nuclear-armed ships to New Zealand ports. Maoris reject government ten-year land claims settlement of US$660 million.
- **1995** Waitangi Day celebrations abandoned after Maori protests. Crown apologizes to Maoris and signs Waikato Raupatu Claims Act. UK warship visits resume.
- **1996** NP forms coalition to preserve overall legislative majority. First general election under new proportional representation system.
- **1997** NP forms coalition with New Zealand First (NZF) party. Bolger resigns. Jenny Shipley becomes first woman prime minister.
- **1998** Shipley sacks NZF leader Winston Peters as deputy prime minister. Waitangi Tribunal orders government to return to Maoris US$3.3 million of confiscated land.
- **1999** LP led by Helen Clark wins general election.
- **2001** Air New Zealand renationalized.
- **2002** Combat wing of air force taken out of service. July, elections: LP reelected.

N

DEFENSE

No compulsory military service

US$664m

Down 17% in 2001

Military cuts announced in May 2001 emphasized the aim to refocus defense policy on small-scale peacekeeping, protection against low-level economic threats, and terrorism. As part of cutbacks the combat wing of the air force was taken out of active service in 2002. The move put renewed stress on the 1951 security pact with Australia and the US (ANZUS). The 1984 decision to refuse access to nuclear warships from 1985 damaged defense cooperation with the US and other Western powers for a decade, forcing New Zealand to seek closer links with Australia. Senior-level contacts were resumed in 1994. Since then, the US and the UK have resumed naval visits, though not with nuclear-armed vessels.

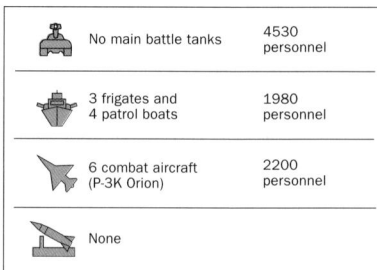

NEW ZEALAND ARMED FORCES

No main battle tanks	4530 personnel
3 frigates and 4 patrol boats	1980 personnel
6 combat aircraft (P-3K Orion)	2200 personnel
None	

ECONOMICS

Inflation 1.6% p.a. (1990–2001)

US$51bn

1.708 New Zealand dollars (2.059)

SCORE CARD

World GNP Ranking	48th
GNP per capita	US$13,250
Balance of payments	–US$1.59bn
Inflation	2.6%
Unemployment	5%

EXPORTS

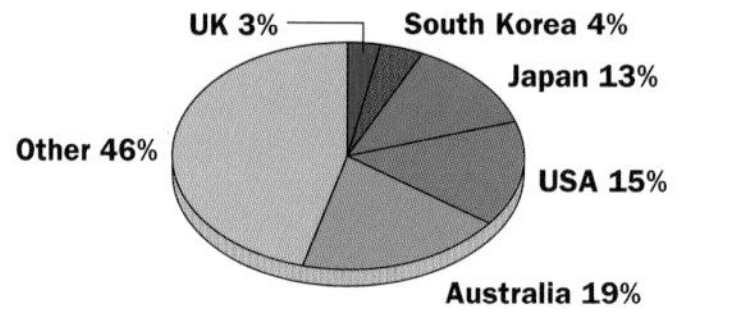
UK 3%
South Korea 4%
Japan 13%
USA 15%
Australia 19%
Other 46%

IMPORTS

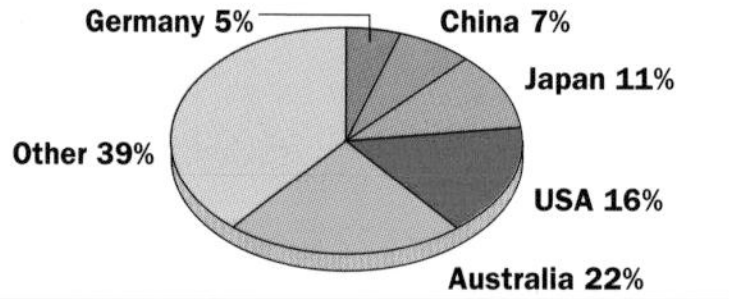
Germany 5%
China 7%
Japan 11%
USA 16%
Australia 22%
Other 39%

ECONOMIC PERFORMANCE INDICATOR

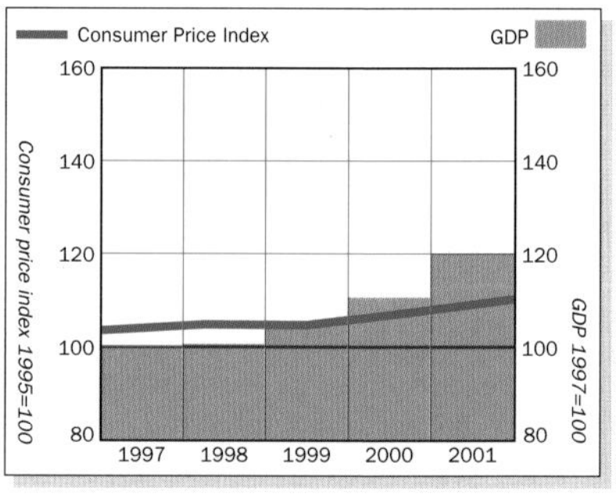
Consumer Price Index
GDP
160
140
120
100
80
Consumer price index 1995=100
GDP 1997=100
1997
1998
1999
2000
2001

Strengths

Modern agricultural sector; one of the five biggest exporters of dairy products. Rapidly expanding tourist sector. Manufacturing, with emphasis on high-tech. One of world's most open economies. Strong trade links within Pacific Rim.

Weaknesses

One of the highest levels of public debt outside developing world. Continuing reliance on imported manufactured goods and foreign investment.

Profile

Since 1984, New Zealand has changed from being one of the most regulated to one of the most open economies in the world. Radical reforms and drastic cuts in social security and related government spending helped to restore growth and cut inflation to a minimum. Diversification into new markets and products recovered after the 1997–1998 Asian economic crisis. Prime Minister Clark dropped objections in 2001 to the idea of a unified Australia–New Zealand dollar. High public debt and poor levels of private investment remain a problem.

NEW ZEALAND : MAJOR BUSINESSES

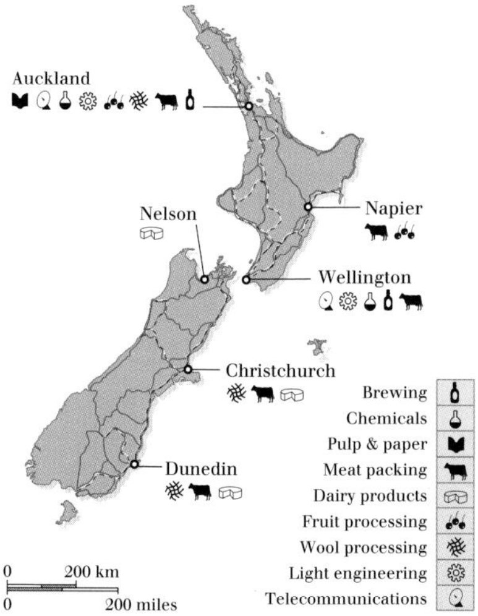
Auckland
Nelson
Napier
Wellington
Christchurch
Dunedin
Brewing
Chemicals
Pulp & paper
Meat packing
Dairy products
Fruit processing
Wool processing
Light engineering
Telecommunications
0 200 km
0 200 miles

RESOURCES

Electric power 8.2m kW

646,964 tonnes

36,311 b/d (reserves 106m barrels)

43.1m sheep, 9.63m cattle, 13m chickens

Coal, oil, natural gas, iron, gold, silica sand

ELECTRICITY GENERATION

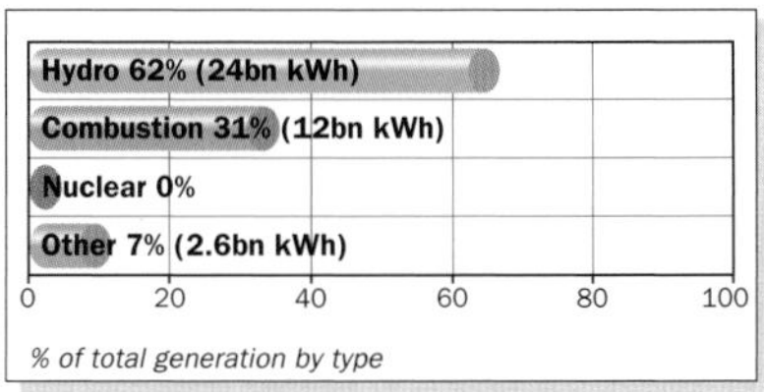
Hydro 62% (24bn kWh)
Combustion 31% (12bn kWh)
Nuclear 0%
Other 7% (2.6bn kWh)
0
20
40
60
80
100
% of total generation by type

New Zealand's rich pastures, a result of even rainfall throughout the year, have traditionally been its key resource. The sheep, wool, and dairy products on which the country's wealth was built are still important. Newer export industries include products such as fruit, vegetables, fish, cork, wood, wine, and textile fibers.

New Zealand is well endowed with energy resources. It has coal, oil, and natural gas reserves, but most energy is generated by hydroelectric plants.

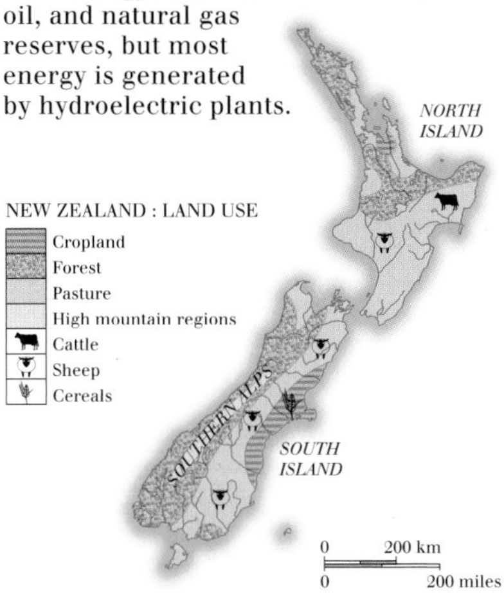
NORTH ISLAND
NEW ZEALAND : LAND USE
Cropland
Forest
Pasture
High mountain regions
Cattle
Sheep
Cereals
SOUTHERN ALPS
SOUTH ISLAND
0
200 km
0
200 miles

ENVIRONMENT

Sustainability rank: 19th

24% (6% partially protected)

8.2 tonnes per capita

ENVIRONMENTAL TREATIES

Yes Yes Yes

Yes Yes Yes

New Zealand's isolation, small population, and limited industry have helped to keep it one of the world's most pollution-free countries. It was a leading opponent of French nuclear testing in the Pacific and has banned nuclear vessels from its ports. Ozone depletion over Antarctica, deforestation, and protection of native flora and fauna are major issues.

MEDIA

TV ownership high

Daily newspaper circulation 362 per 1000 people

PUBLISHING AND BROADCAST MEDIA

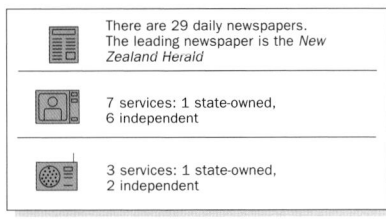

There are 29 daily newspapers. The leading newspaper is the *New Zealand Herald*

7 services: 1 state-owned, 6 independent

3 services: 1 state-owned, 2 independent

Deregulated in 1988, New Zealand television is one of the most liberal media in the world. Ruia Mai, the first Maori-language radio station, began broadcasting in 1996.

CRIME

No death penalty

5980 prisoners

Crime is rising

CRIME RATES

Murders	4 per 100,000 population
Rapes	20 per 100,000 population
Thefts	6978 per 100,000 population

Crime rates in New Zealand's urban areas have increased in recent years. However, overall, the country remains one of the world's safest and most peaceful places in which to live.

EDUCATION

School leaving age: 16

99%

171,962 students

THE EDUCATION SYSTEM

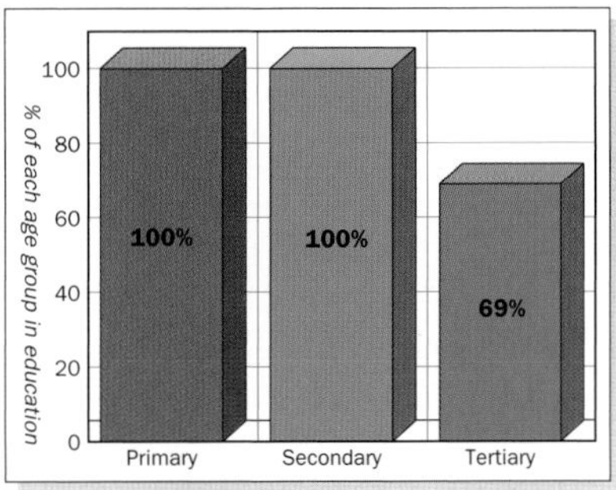
100
80
60
40
20
0
% of each age group in education
100%
100%
69%
Primary
Secondary
Tertiary

Education is free, and compulsory between six and 16. A number of schools are composite, providing both primary and secondary education. New Zealand has one of the highest proportions of the population with tertiary qualifications in the OECD. Nearly all adults are literate, but the level of literacy is not always very high: a government initiative, More than Words, was launched in 2000.

HEALTH

Welfare state health benefits

1 per 442 people

Cancers, respiratory, cerebrovascular, and heart diseases

In 1936, New Zealand became the first country to introduce a full welfare state. Government efforts since 1991 to impose UK-style market systems on the health service have been very unpopular. While life expectancy continues to improve, the nation's OECD health ranking has fallen. In comparison with other OECD countries, New Zealand has high mortality rates for heart diseases, respiratory disease, breast and bowel cancer, motor vehicle accidents, and suicide.

SPENDING

GDP/cap. increase

CONSUMPTION AND SPENDING

580 per 1000 population

477 per 1000 population

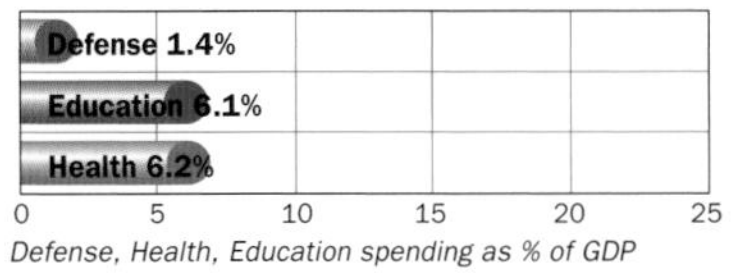
Defense 1.4%
Education 6.1%
Health 6.2%
0
5
10
15
20
25
Defense, Health, Education spending as % of GDP

The years since 1984 have been very difficult for New Zealanders, who are used to affluence within a generous welfare state. A rash of economic and social reforms has held back wages, raised unemployment, and cut welfare benefits. Even so, average living standards are still high, and a strong egalitarian tradition means that wealth remains relatively evenly distributed.

The quality of life in New Zealand is among the best in the world, in terms of access to basic necessities, and a pure, healthy, urban and rural environment. Social mobility is fairly high. Wealthier people tend to spend their money on houses close to the water. Yachts are a major status symbol.

WORLD RANKING

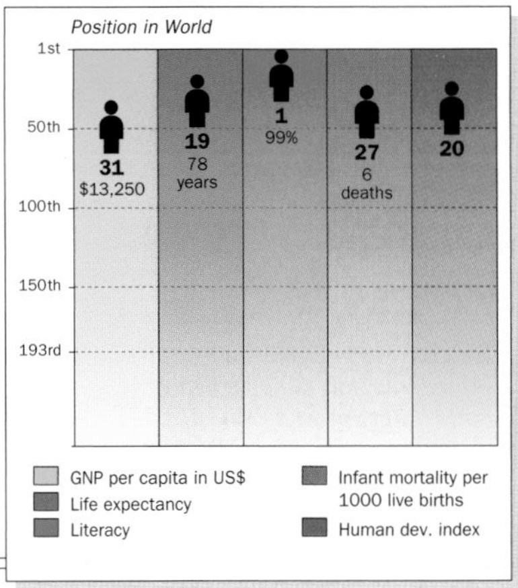
Position in World
1st
50th
100th
150th
193rd
31
$13,250
19
78 years
1
99%
27
6 deaths
20
GNP per capita in US$
Life expectancy
Literacy
Infant mortality per 1000 live births
Human dev. index

N

NICARAGUA

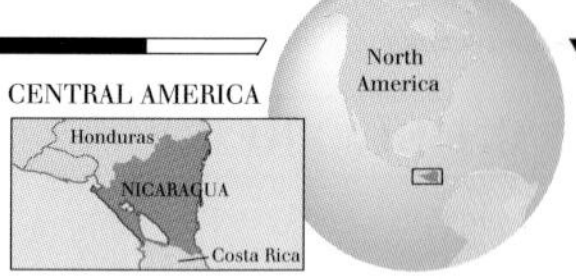
CENTRAL AMERICA
Honduras
NICARAGUA
Costa Rica
North America

OFFICIAL NAME: Republic of Nicaragua **CAPITAL:** Managua
POPULATION: 5.3 million **CURRENCY:** Córdoba oro **OFFICIAL LANGUAGE:** Spanish

1838 | 1838 | Sept 15 | NIC | -6 | +505 | .ni

Oil refinery at Bluefields, on the Caribbean coast. Under the Sandinistas, most crude oil came from the Soviet Union, via Cuba.

BOUNDED BY the Pacific Ocean to the west and the Caribbean Sea to the east, Nicaragua lies at the heart of Central America. After more than 40 years of dictatorship, the Sandinista revolution in 1978 led to social reforms, but also to 11 years of civil war, which almost destroyed the economy. Right-wing parties have held power since the Sandinistas unexpectedly lost the 1990 elections. Despite the devastation of Hurricane Mitch in 1998, the economy is slowly strengthening.

CLIMATE

Tropical equatorial/ wet and dry

WEATHER CHART FOR MANAGUA

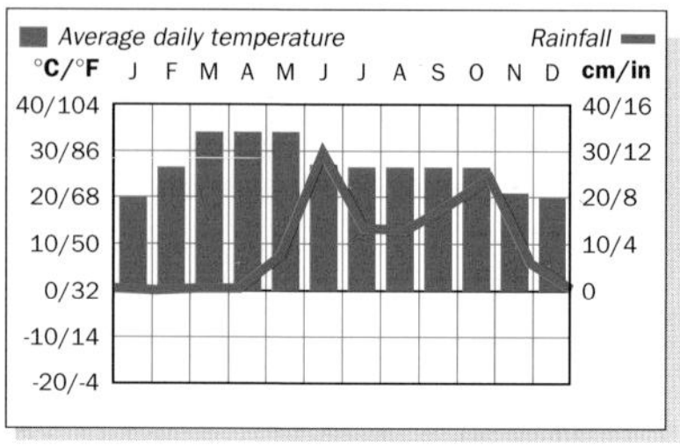
Average daily temperature
Rainfall
°C/°F
J F M A M J J A S O N D
cm/in
40/104
30/86
20/68
10/50
0/32
-10/14
-20/-4
40/16
30/12
20/8
10/4
0

The climate is tropical and often violent, as evidenced by seasonal hurricanes, such as Hurricane Mitch in 1998.

TRANSPORTATION

Drive on right

Augusto C. Sandino International, Managua 833,389 passengers

26 ships 3600 grt

THE TRANSPORTATION NETWORK

1818 km (1130 miles)

Pan-American Highway: 384 km (239 miles)

6 km (4 miles)

2220 km (1379 miles)

Nicaragua lacks a Caribbean deepwater port. Hurricane Mitch damaged major roads and destroyed 35 key bridges.

TOURISM

Visitors : Population 1:11

472,000 visitors

Down 2% in 2002

MAIN TOURIST ARRIVALS

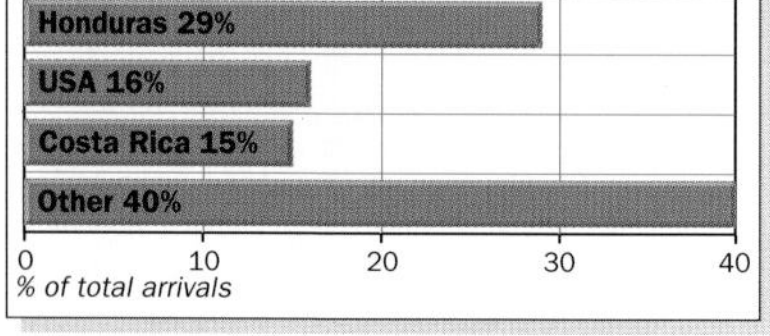
Honduras 29%
USA 16%
Costa Rica 15%
Other 40%
0
10
20
30
40
% of total arrivals

The civil war caused the near-collapse of tourism, and slow recovery has been interrupted by the devastation caused by Hurricane Mitch. Foreign direct investment in the sector grew in 1997–1998.

PEOPLE

Pop. density low

Spanish, English Creole, Miskito

45/km² (116/mi²)

THE URBAN/RURAL POPULATION SPLIT

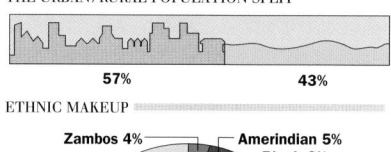

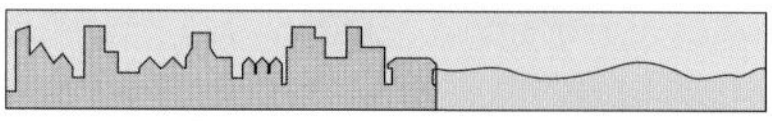
57%
43%

ETHNIC MAKEUP

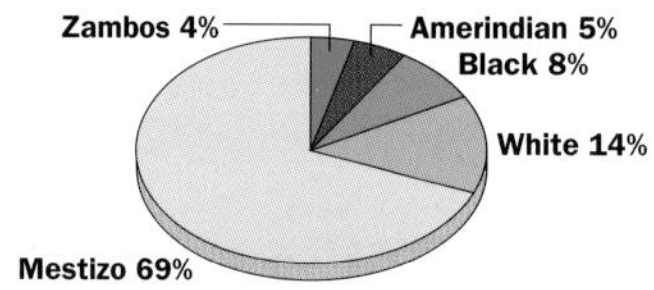
Zambos 4%
Amerindian 5%
Black 8%
White 14%
Mestizo 69%

The Caribbean regions, which in 1987 achieved limited autonomy, are isolated from the more populous Pacific regions. The indigenous Miskito tribes and the descendants of Africans, brought over by Spanish colonists in the 18th century to work the plantations, are concentrated along the Caribbean coast, where English Creole is widely spoken. The Sandinista revolution improved the status of women through changes in the legal system and the incorporation of women into economic and political life. However, poverty and lack of permanent employment have since forced many women into prostitution.

POLITICS

Multiparty elections

2001/2006

President Enrique Bolaños

AT THE LAST ELECTION

National Assembly 92 seats

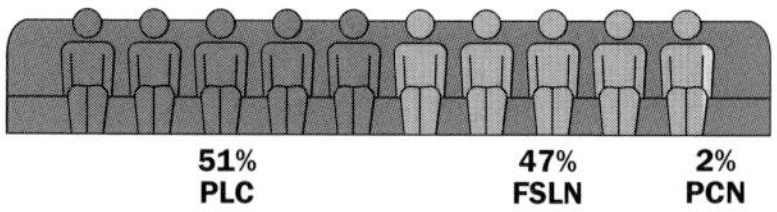
51% PLC
47% FSLN
2% PCN

PLC = Liberal Constitutionalist Party
FSLN = Sandinista National Liberation Front
PCN = Conservative Party of Nicaragua

Right-wing coalitions have held power since 1990. The PLC took office in 1997, promising to unite the country but quickly became unpopular due to austerity measures and allegations of corruption. Recent two-party domination of politics, shared between the PLC and the FSLN, has strained democracy. Charges of corruption, backed by PLC President Enrique Bolaños and leveled against former PLC president and party leader Arnoldo Alemán, polarized Congress and the party in 2003.

NICARAGUA

Total Area : 129 494 sq. km (49 998 sq. miles)

POPULATION
- over 500 000
- over 100 000
- over 50 000
- over 10 000
- under 10 000

LAND HEIGHT
- 1000m/3281ft
- 500m/1640ft
- 200m/656ft
- Sea Level

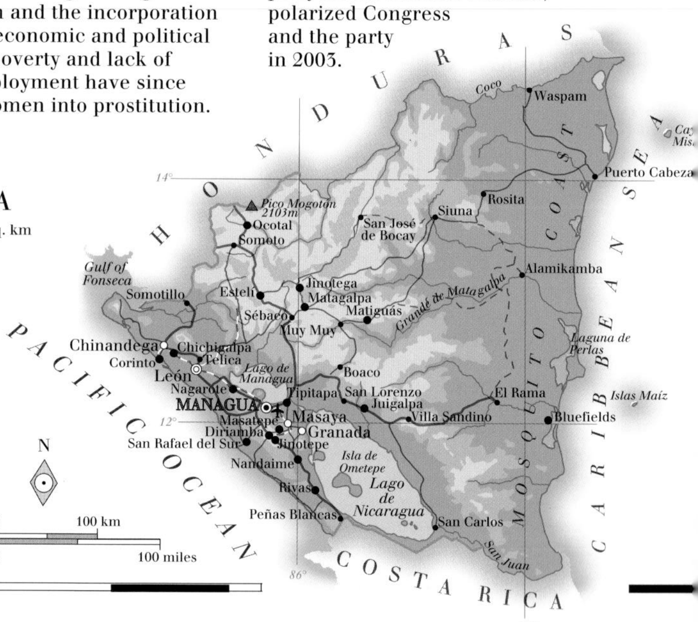
HONDURAS
PACIFIC OCEAN
CARIBBEAN SEA
MOSQUITO COAST
COSTA RICA
Waspam
Puerto Cabezas
Rosita
Siuna
Pico Mogotón 2103m
Ocotal
Somoto
San José de Bocay
Gulf of Fonseca
Somotillo
Estelí
Jinotega
Matagalpa
Matiguás
Alamikamba
Sébaco
Muy Muy
Río Grande de Matagalpa
Chinandega
Chichigalpa
Telica
Corinto
León
Lago de Managua
Nagarote
Boaco
MANAGUA
Tipitapa
San Lorenzo
Juigalpa
El Rama
Masatepe
Masaya
Granada
Villa Sandino
Bluefields
Diriamba
Jinotepe
San Rafael del Sur
Nandaime
Isla de Ometepe
Lago de Nicaragua
Rivas
Peñas Blancas
San Carlos
San Juan
Laguna de Perlas
Islas Maíz
Coco
N
0
100 km
100 miles
14°
12°
86°
84°

WORLD AFFAIRS

Joined UN in 1945

ACS · Geplac · NAM · OAS · San José

Main issues are debt relief in the wake of Hurricane Mitch, cooperation with neighboring countries for increased US trade access, and the treatment of over 300,000 Nicaraguan immigrants in Costa Rica. A free trade agreement with Mexico is important. A dispute over the common border with Costa Rica was resolved in 2000. Ongoing border and navigation rights disputes exist with Honduras and Colombia.

AID

Recipient

$928m (receipts) — Up 65% in 2001

Hurricane Mitch damage elicited new World Bank and IDB loans. Cuba, France, Finland, and Spain pardoned all or part of Nicaragua's debt. The US and other Western creditors canceled outstanding obligations when the IMF included Nicaragua in the Highly Indebted Poor Countries initiative.

DEFENSE

Compulsory military service

$27m — Up 12% in 2001

FSLN forces once formed the basis of the army, which was cut from a civil war peak of 134,000 to 10,000 by 1995. Senior Sandinistas were among officers retired in 1998. The army is to be involved in more community-based roles focused on the defense of natural resources and mine clearance. Russia agreed in 2001 to help upgrade the military.

ECONOMICS

Inflation 45% p.a. (1990–2000)

$1.78bn — 15 córdobas oro (14.19)

SCORE CARD

- World GNP Ranking 140th
- GNP per Capita $370
- Balance of Payments .... –$557m
- Inflation 7.4%
- Unemployment 11%

STRENGTHS

Coffee, sugar, and grain exports. Foreign aid and public and private reconstruction work after Hurricane Mitch will benefit tourism, energy, services, and construction.

WEAKNESSES

Heavy debt burden. Main exports subject to price fluctuations. High unemployment. Poor energy supply and infrastructure. Lack of investment and diversification. Weak banks. Delays in privatization. Skewed land ownership and protracted property disputes. Corruption. Frequent natural disasters.

EXPORTS

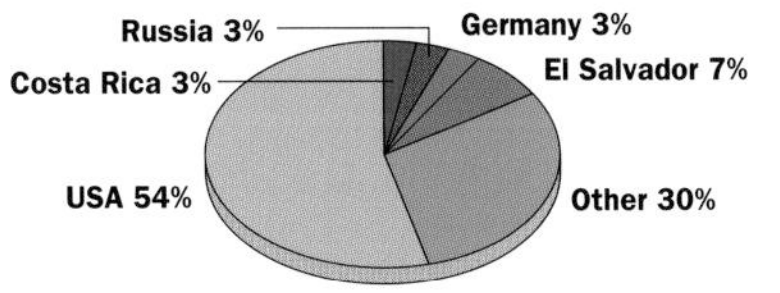

Russia 3%
Germany 3%
Costa Rica 3%
El Salvador 7%
USA 54%
Other 30%

IMPORTS

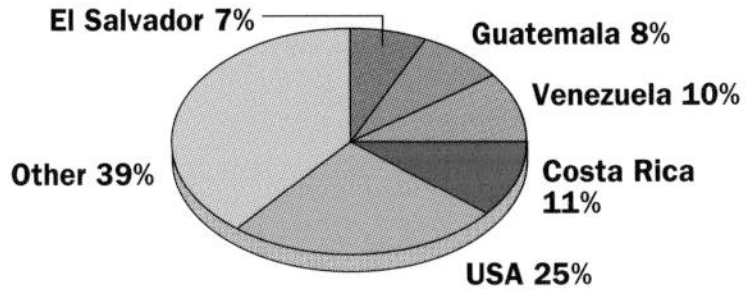

El Salvador 7%
Guatemala 8%
Venezuela 10%
Other 39%
Costa Rica 11%
USA 25%

RESOURCES

Electric power 628,000 kW

33,437 tonnes — Not an oil producer; refines 16,700 b/d

3.35m cattle, 420,000 pigs, 15.5m chickens — Gold, silver, lead, zinc, copper, tungsten, salt

Nicaragua has small quantities of gold and silver. New thermal generation projects are planned to overcome energy deficits. There is possible offshore oil.

ENVIRONMENT

Sustainability rank: 52nd

18% (8% partially protected) — 0.8 tonnes per capita

Deforestation over large areas and the widespread use of pesticides are major problems.

MEDIA

TV ownership medium

Daily newspaper circulation 30 per 1000 people

PUBLISHING AND BROADCAST MEDIA

There are 8 daily newspapers, including *La Prensa* and *El Nuevo Diario*

7 services — 62 stations: 1 state-owned, 61 independent

Since the civil war, radio, TV, and newspapers have tended to ally themselves with the government or the opposition; there is little room for political neutrality.

CRIME

No death penalty

7198 prisoners — Up 23% in 1997–1998

Former combatants have menaced parts of central and northern regions. Violent crime is rising, as is drug trafficking.

CHRONOLOGY

Nicaragua became an independent state in 1838. Guerrilla forces, led by Gen. Sandino, opposed the US marine presence in the early 1930s.

- **1978** FSLN, formed in 1961, ends 44-year Somoza dictatorship; ensuing conflict between FSLN and Contras.
- **1984** Daniel Ortega, FSLN leader, elected president.
- **1990** End of civil war. Center-right National Opposition Union (UNO) unexpectedly wins elections.
- **1998** Hurricane Mitch causes havoc.
- **2002** Bolaños becomes president.

EDUCATION

School leaving age: 12

67% — 56,558 students

Nicaragua's adult literacy rate is one of the lowest in Latin America; few students complete fifth grade.

HEALTH

Welfare state health benefits

1 per 1639 people — Cancers, heart diseases, perinatal causes, accidents

Real spending on health fell by 71% between 1988 and 1993, and still has to recover.

SPENDING

GDP/cap. increase

CONSUMPTION AND SPENDING

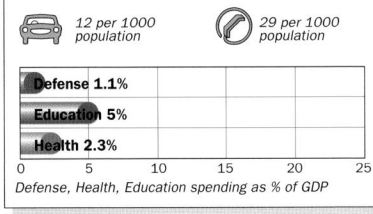

12 per 1000 population — *29 per 1000 population*

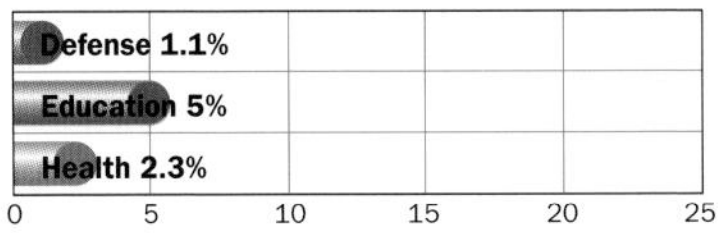

Defense 1.1%
Education 5%
Health 2.3%
0
5
10
15
20
25

Defense, Health, Education spending as % of GDP

Just under half of Nicaragua's population live below the national poverty line, rising to 69% in rural areas.

WORLD RANKING

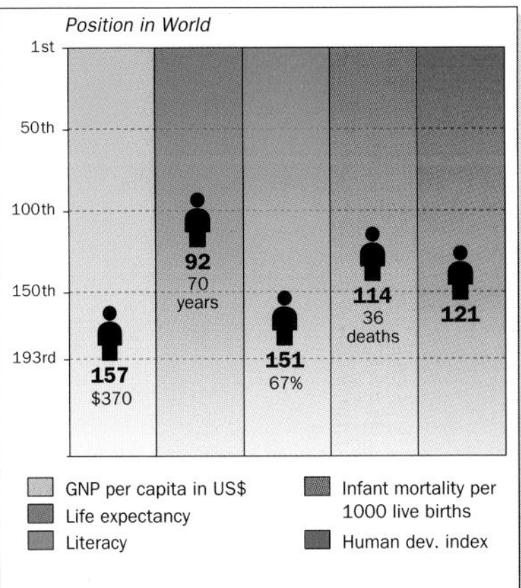

Position in World
1st
50th
100th
150th
193rd
157
$370
92
70
years
151
67%
114
36
deaths
121
GNP per capita in US$
Life expectancy
Literacy
Infant mortality per 1000 live births
Human dev. index

N

NIGER

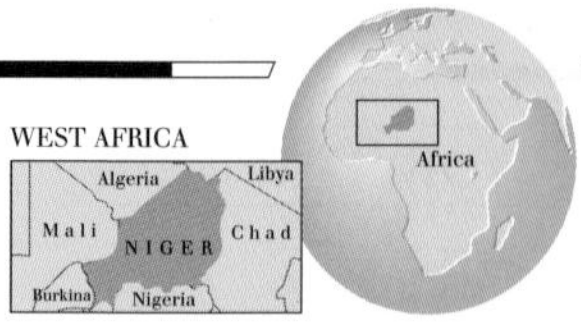
WEST AFRICA
Algeria
Libya
Mali
NIGER
Chad
Burkina
Nigeria
Africa

OFFICIAL NAME: Republic of Niger **CAPITAL:** Niamey
POPULATION: 11.6 million **CURRENCY:** CFA franc **OFFICIAL LANGUAGE:** French

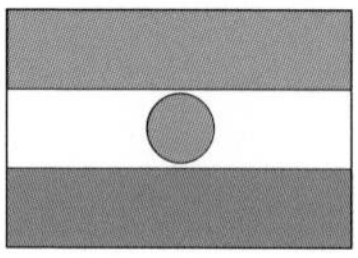

1960 | 1960 | Dec 18 | RN | +1 | +227 | .ne

LANDLOCKED IN THE WEST of Africa, Niger is linked to the sea by the Niger River. Saharan conditions prevail in the northern regions, in the area around the Aïr Mountains, and, particularly, in the vast uninhabited northeast. Niger was ruled by one-party or military regimes until 1992. A much-troubled democratic process was then disrupted by military coups in 1996 and 1999. Niger is one of the poorest countries in Africa.

CLIMATE

Hot desert/steppe

WEATHER CHART FOR NIAMEY

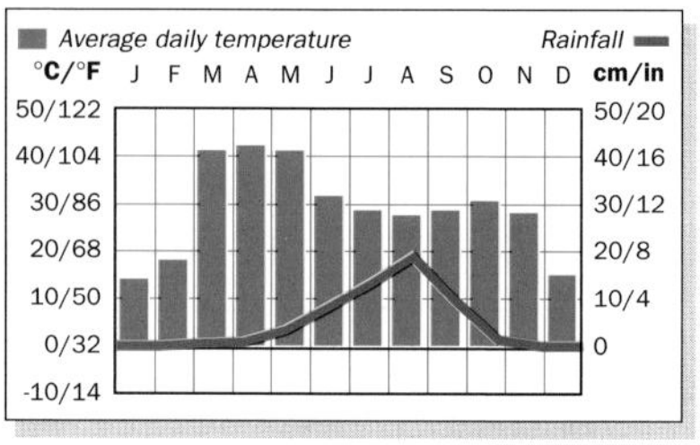
Average daily temperature
Rainfall
°C/°F J F M A M J J A S O N D cm/in
50/122 40/104 30/86 20/68 10/50 0/32 -10/14
50/20 40/16 30/12 20/8 10/4 0

The Saharan north is virtually rainless. The south, in the Sahel belt, has an unreliable rainy season, preceded by a period of extreme daytime heat.

TRANSPORTATION

Drive on right

Niamey International 79,789 passengers

Has no fleet

THE TRANSPORTATION NETWORK

798 km (496 miles)

Trans-Sahara Highway: 428 km (266 miles)

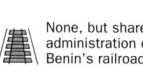

None, but shares administration of Benin's railroad

300 km (186 miles)

A very small proportion of Niger's road network is paved. There are international airports at Niamey and Agadez. There is no railroad.

TOURISM

Visitors : Population 1:223

52,000 visitors

Up 4% in 2001

MAIN TOURIST ARRIVALS

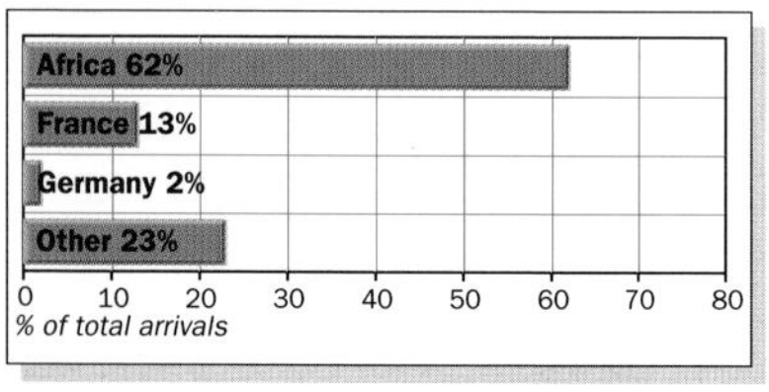
Africa 62%
France 13%
Germany 2%
Other 23%
0 10 20 30 40 50 60 70 80
% of total arrivals

The Aïr Mountains, southern Hausa cities, and Saharan Tuareg culture attract some tourists in spite of Niger's limited infrastructure and its instability.

PEOPLE

Pop. density low

Hausa, Djerma, Fulani, Tuareg, Teda, French

9/km² (24/mi²)

THE URBAN/RURAL POPULATION SPLIT

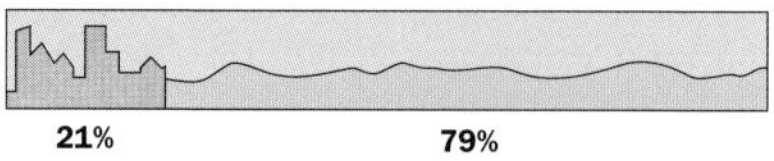
21%
79%

ETHNIC MAKEUP

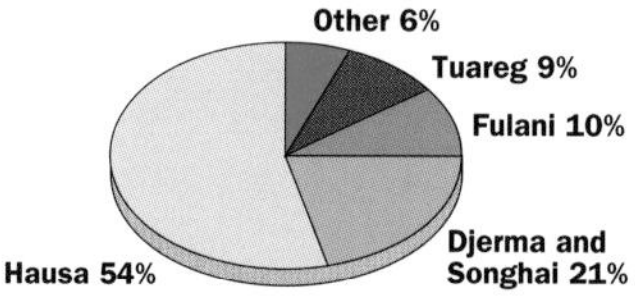
Other 6%
Tuareg 9%
Fulani 10%
Djerma and Songhai 21%
Hausa 54%

Considerable tensions exist in Niger between the Tuaregs in the north and the southern groups. The Tuaregs' sense of alienation from mainstream Nigerien politics has increased since the 1973 and 1984 droughts, which disrupted the Tuaregs' nomadic way of life. A five-year rebellion by northern Tuaregs ended in 1995 with a peace agreement. In eastern Niger, Toubou and Arab groups have also been in revolt.

A more subtle antagonism exists between the Djerma and Hausa groups. The Djerma elite from the southwest dominated politics for many years until 1993, when control passed to the Hausa majority.

Niger is an overwhelmingly Islamic society. Women have, on the whole, only limited rights and restricted access to education.

***Testing boating poles in the market** at Ayorou on the Niger River, the country's only major permanent watercourse.*

POLITICS

Multiparty elections

1999/2004

President Mamadou Tandja

AT THE LAST ELECTION

National Assembly 83 seats

5% ANDP
46% MNSD
20% CDS
19% PNDS
10% RDP

MNSD = National Movement for the Development of Society **CDS** = Democratic and Social Convention **PNDS** = Niger Party for Democracy and Socialism **RDP** = Rally for Democracy and Progress **ANDP** = Niger Alliance for Democracy and Progress

Multiparty elections in 1993 were achieved after six years of prodemocracy demonstrations following the death in 1987 of the military dictator Seyni Kountché. An ensuing power struggle between President Mahamane Ousmane and his political opponents provoked a military coup in 1996. Gen. Ibrahim Barre Mainassara promulgated a new constitution and won a presidential election condemned as fraudulent by the opposition. Mainassara was assassinated by his presidential guard in early 1999. The new military leadership drew up yet another constitution. Mamadou Tandja won the presidential poll later that year. His MNSD is allied to Ousmane's CDS, and the two dominate the National Assembly. Tandja is accused of authoritarianism by the opposition.

WORLD AFFAIRS

Joined UN in 1960

CILSS | ECOWAS | FZ | AU | OIC

Relations with Libya and Algeria have improved since the end of the Tuareg rebellion in 1995. ECOWAS members and the OAU condemned the 1999 coup, as did all key donors, led by France.

AID

Recipient

$249m (receipts)

Up 18% in 2001

The World Bank is the principal donor, followed by France and the EU. Most aid was frozen immediately following the 1999 coup, but in late 2000 the IMF approved a three-year loan under its Poverty Reduction and Growth Facility.

DEFENSE

Compulsory military service

$29m

Up 7% in 2001

Niger's armed forces and paramilitary elements total 10,700. A brief army mutiny was quelled in August 2002.

N

NIGER

Total Area : 1 267 000 sq. km (489 188 sq. miles)

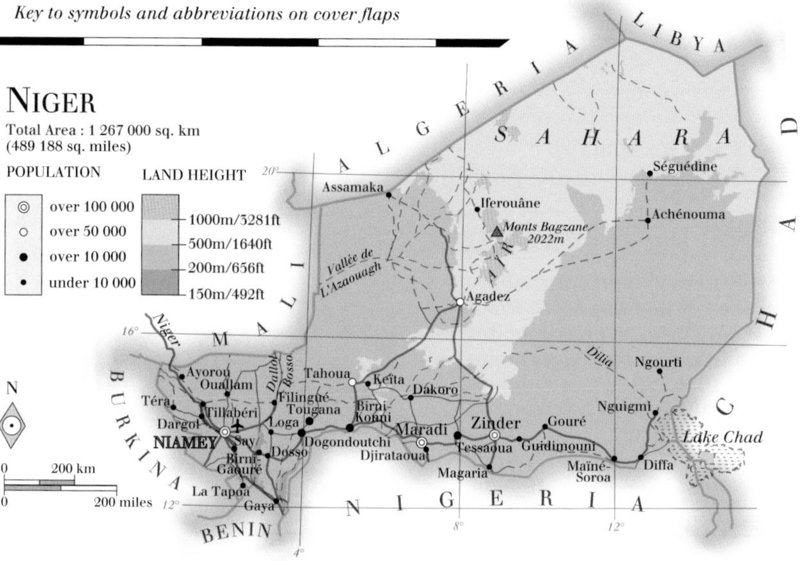
POPULATION
over 100 000
over 50 000
over 10 000
under 10 000
LAND HEIGHT
1000m/3281ft
500m/1640ft
200m/656ft
150m/492ft
N
0 200 km
0 200 miles
LIBYA
ALGERIA
MALI
BURKINA
BENIN
NIGERIA
CHAD
SAHARA
Séguédine
Assamaka
Iferouâne
Achénouma
Monts Bagzane 2022m
AÏR
Vallée de L'Azaouagh
Agadez
Niger
Dilia
Ngourti
Ayorou
Ouallam
Tahoua
Keita
Téra
Filingué
Dakoro
Tillabéri
Tougana
Birni-Konni
Nguigmi
Dargol
Loga
Maradi
Zinder
Gouré
NIAMEY
Say
Dogondoutchi
Tessaoua
Guidimouni
Lake Chad
Dosso
Djirataoua
Birni-Gaouré
Magaria
Mainé-Soroa
Diffa
La Tapoa
Gaya
20°
16°
12°
4°
8°
12°

CHRONOLOGY

The powerful Islamic Sokoto empire dissolved as the French took over Niger between 1883 and 1901.

- ❑ **1960** Independence.
- ❑ **1968** French open uranium mines.
- ❑ **1973** Drought; 60% of livestock die.
- ❑ **1974** Military coup. Gen. Seyni Kountché bans political parties.
- ❑ **1984** New drought; Niger River dries up. Uranium boom ends.
- ❑ **1987** Kountché dies. Gen. Ali Saibou begins transition to democracy.
- ❑ **1990–1995** Tuareg rebellion.
- ❑ **1992** Multiparty constitution.
- ❑ **1993** Democratic elections.
- ❑ **1996** Military coup. Staged elections.
- ❑ **1999** New constitution. Gen. Mainassara assassinated. Multiparty elections won by Mamadou Tandja.
- ❑ **2001** Hunting banned in effort to save wildlife.

ECONOMICS

▷ Inflation 5.8% p.a. (1990–2001)

$1.98bn

571.2 CFA francs (664.2)

SCORE CARD

❑ WORLD GNP RANKING	138th
❑ GNP PER CAPITA	$180
❑ BALANCE OF PAYMENTS	–$170m
❑ INFLATION	4%
❑ UNEMPLOYMENT	3%

STRENGTHS

Vast uranium deposits. Gold and oil discoveries in late 1990s revived hopes for economic viability.

WEAKNESSES

Aid-dependent. Collapse of uranium prices in 1980s created large debt burden. Only 3% of land cultivable. Weak infrastructure. Frequent droughts. Political instability.

EXPORTS

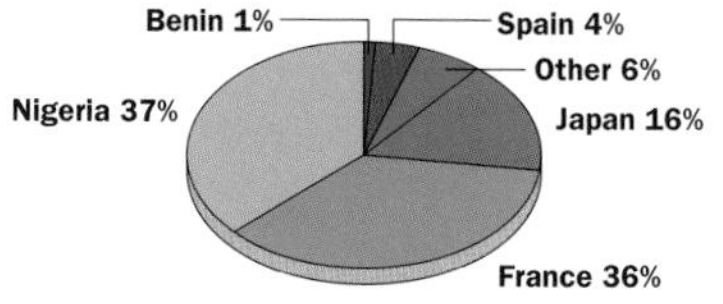
Benin 1%
Spain 4%
Other 6%
Nigeria 37%
Japan 16%
France 36%

IMPORTS

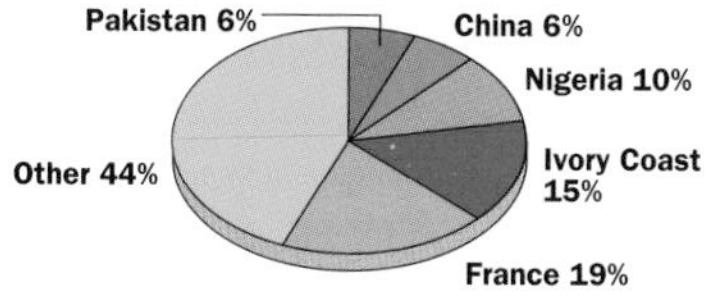
Pakistan 6%
China 6%
Nigeria 10%
Other 44%
Ivory Coast 15%
France 19%

ENVIRONMENT

▷ Sustainability rank: 123rd

8% (7% partially protected)

0.1 tonnes per capita

Serious droughts intensify desertification. Hunting was banned in 2001, in an effort to preserve wildlife numbers.

MEDIA

▷ TV ownership low

Daily newspaper circulation 0.2 per 1000 people

PUBLISHING AND BROADCAST MEDIA

There is 1 daily newspaper, *Le Sahel*, published by the government

2 services: 1 state-owned, 1 independent

3 services: 1 state-owned, 2 independent

The government controls most broadcasting. The BBC World Service's Hausa programming is influential.

CRIME

▷ Death penalty not used in practice

6000 prisoners

Down 36% in 1996–1998

Rural banditry is common, often involving access to grazing and water. Urban crime levels are low, but in border areas smuggling is a way of life.

EDUCATION

▷ School leaving age: 12

17%

13,400 students

Local languages are emphasized more strongly than in most francophone states. School attendance is only 30%.

HEALTH

▷ No welfare state health benefits

1 per 25,000 people

Malaria, tuberculosis, meningitis, measles, malnutrition

Rural health care has improved, but progress in immunization, malaria control, and child nutrition is limited.

SPENDING

▷ GDP/cap. increase

CONSUMPTION AND SPENDING

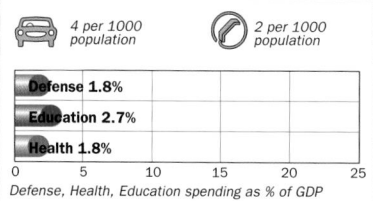

4 per 1000 population

2 per 1000 population

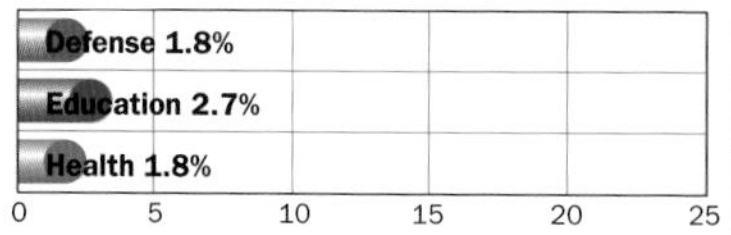
Defense 1.8%
Education 2.7%
Health 1.8%
0
5
10
15
20
25

Defense, Health, Education spending as % of GDP

A small circle of secretive trading families controls much of Niger's wealth and tends to evade taxation. Over 870,000 people live in slavery.

WORLD RANKING

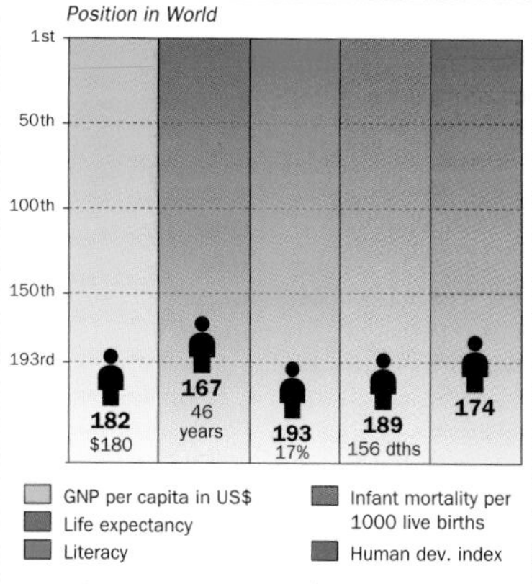
Position in World
1st
50th
100th
150th
193rd
182
$180
167
46 years
193
17%
189
156 dths
174
GNP per capita in US$
Life expectancy
Literacy
Infant mortality per 1000 live births
Human dev. index

RESOURCES

▷ Electric power 105,000 kW

16,265 tonnes

Not an oil producer

6.9m goats, 4.5m sheep, 2.26m cattle, 24.5m chickens

Uranium, tin, gypsum, coal, salt, tungsten, oil, iron, phosphates, gold

During the 1970s, Niger's uranium mines boomed, but output collapsed in the 1980s when world prices slumped. Other mining is small-scale and oil reserves, discovered in the Lake Chad area, are not yet commercially viable. Salt is a traditionally exploited resource, as are such plant resources as the doum and palmyra palms.

N

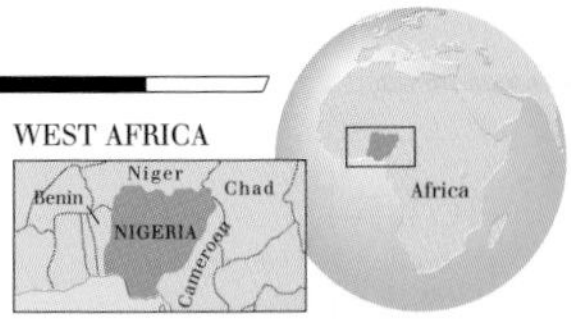

WEST AFRICA
Niger
Benin
Chad
NIGERIA
Cameroon
Africa

NIGERIA

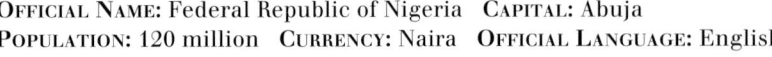

OFFICIAL NAME: Federal Republic of Nigeria **CAPITAL:** Abuja
POPULATION: 120 million **CURRENCY:** Naira **OFFICIAL LANGUAGE:** English

1960
1961
Oct 1
NGR
+1
+234
.ng

AFRICA'S MOST POPULOUS state, Nigeria gained its independence from the UK in 1960. Bordered by Benin, Niger, Chad, and Cameroon, its terrain varies from tropical rainforest and swamps in the south to savanna in the north. Nigeria has been dominated by military governments since 1966. After many delays, a promised return to civilian rule came about in 1999, with the election as president of Olusegun Obasanjo, a former general who had been head of state from 1976 to 1979. Nigeria is a major OPEC oil producer, but it experienced a fall in living standards after the end of the 1970s oil boom.

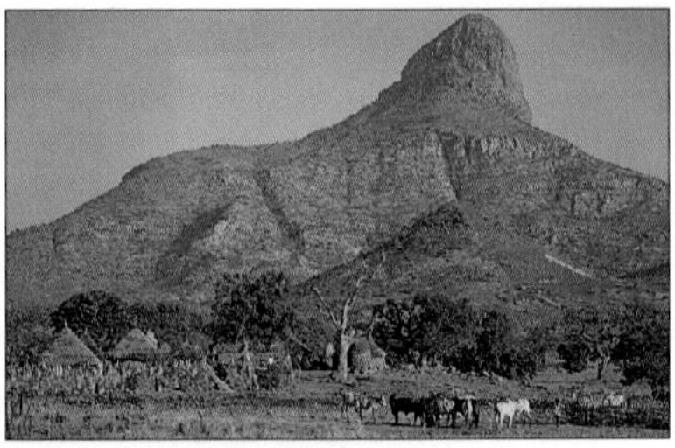

***Village beneath Tengele Peak** in Bauchi State. A large proportion of Nigerians live by subsistence agriculture.*

CLIMATE

Tropical/steppe

WEATHER CHART FOR ABUJA

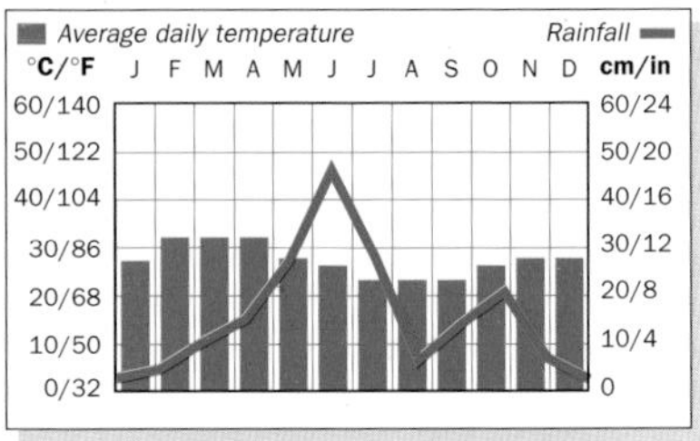

Average daily temperature
Rainfall
°C/°F
J F M A M J J A S O N D
cm/in
60/140
50/122
40/104
30/86
20/68
10/50
0/32
60/24
50/20
40/16
30/12
20/8
10/4
0

The south is hot, rainy, and humid for most of the year. The arid north experiences only one, uncomfortably humid, rainy season from May to September. Its very hot dry season is marked by the *harmattan* wind. The Jos Plateau and the eastern highlands are cooler than the rest of Nigeria. Forcados, in the Niger Delta, gets most rain, with 380 cm (150 in) a year.

TRANSPORTATION

Drive on right

Murtala Muhammad, Lagos
3.26m passengers

293 ships
404,200 grt

THE TRANSPORTATION NETWORK

59,892 km (37,215 miles)

1194 km (742 miles)

3557 km (2210 miles)

8575 km (5328 miles)

Nigeria relies almost entirely on road transportation. During the oil-boom years of the 1970s, new long-distance roads and stretches of freeway were built. The road network is now badly maintained and in urgent need of repair. The road accident rate is among the world's highest and there is severe and chronic traffic congestion in Lagos. In mid-2000, plans for a new trans-Sahara highway from Lagos to Tangiers, Morocco, were announced. Work started in 2001 on a $40 million ports project to boost the development of the five southeastern states.

TOURISM

Visitors : Population 1:126

955,000 visitors

Up 18% in 2001

Nigeria has attempted to build a tourist industry, but numbers remain low. Year-round tropical temperatures and poor infrastructure have limited its growth. The major deterrent to visitors, however, is crime. Travel can be hazardous, and Lagos has one of the world's highest crime rates.

MAIN TOURIST ARRIVALS

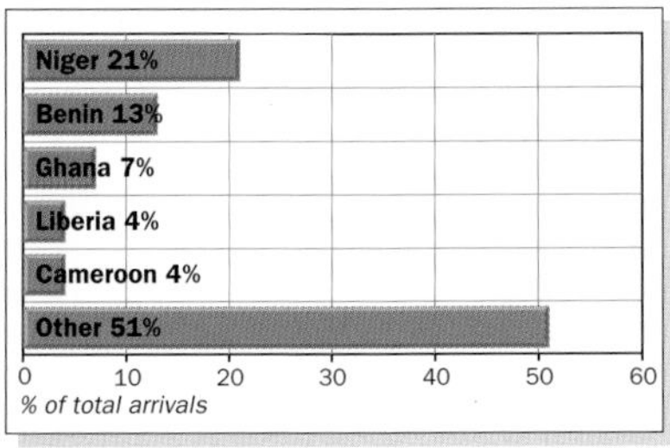

Niger 21%
Benin 13%
Ghana 7%
Liberia 4%
Cameroon 4%
Other 51%
0
10
20
30
40
50
60
% of total arrivals

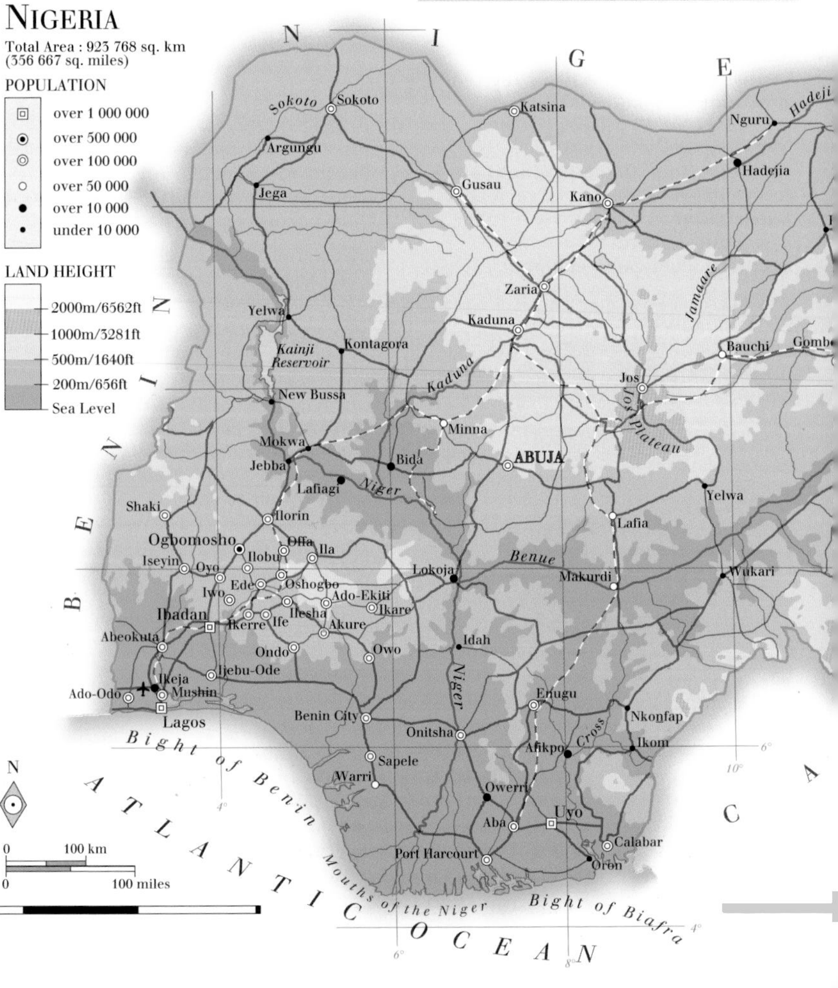

NIGERIA
Total Area : 923 768 sq. km (356 667 sq. miles)
POPULATION
over 1 000 000
over 500 000
over 100 000
over 50 000
over 10 000
under 10 000
LAND HEIGHT
2000m/6562ft
1000m/3281ft
500m/1640ft
200m/656ft
Sea Level
N I G E R
BENIN
ATLANTIC OCEAN
Bight of Benin
Bight of Biafra
Mouths of the Niger
Sokoto
Katsina
Nguru
Hadejia
Argungu
Jega
Gusau
Kano
Zaria
Kaduna
Yelwa
Kainji Reservoir
Kontagora
Bauchi
Jos
Jos Plateau
New Bussa
Minna
Mokwa
Jebba
Bida
ABUJA
Lafiagi
Shaki
Ilorin
Lafia
Ogbomosho
Offa
Ila
Iseyin
Oyo
Ilobu
Oshogbo
Lokoja
Benue
Makurdi
Wukari
Iwo
Ede
Ado-Ekiti
Ikare
Ibadan
Ikerre
Ife
Ilesha
Akure
Abeokuta
Ondo
Owo
Idah
Ijebu-Ode
Ikeja
Mushin
Ado-Odo
Lagos
Benin City
Enugu
Nkonfap
Onitsha
Ikom
Afikpo
Sapele
Warri
Owerri
Uyo
Aba
Calabar
Port Harcourt
Oron
Niger
Kaduna
Sokoto
Jamaare
Cross
0
100 km
100 miles

PEOPLE

Pop. density medium

Hausa, English, Yoruba, Ibo

132/km² (341/mi²)

THE URBAN/RURAL POPULATION SPLIT

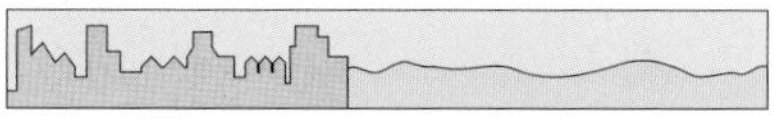
45%
55%

RELIGIOUS PERSUASION

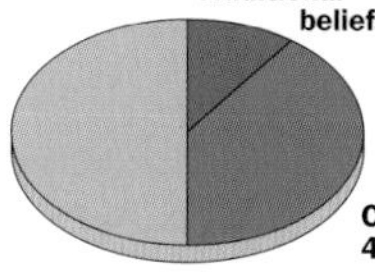
Traditional beliefs 10%
Muslim 50%
Christian 40%

ETHNIC MAKEUP

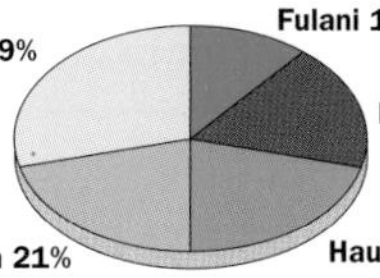
Other 29%
Fulani 11%
Ibo 18%
Yoruba 21%
Hausa 21%

Nigeria had been fairly successful in containing tensions caused by ethnic and religious diversity until fighting erupted between Hausas and Yorubas in the southwest in 1999. There is also rivalry between these two and the third main ethnic group, the Ibo. There are 245 smaller groups. Allegations of repression in order to favor multinational companies cause unrest in the oil-rich Niger Delta region.

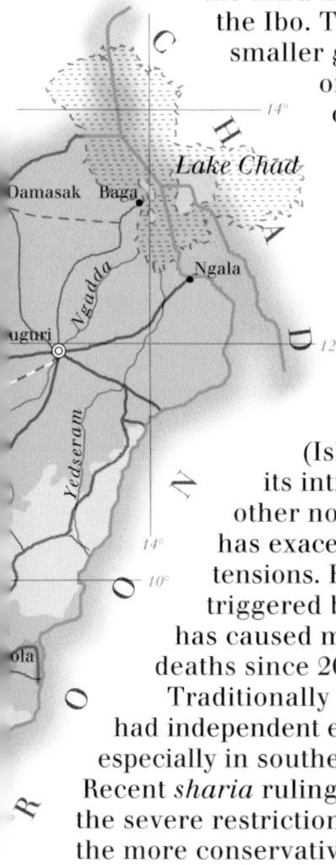
Lake Chad
Damasak
Baga
Ngala
Yedseram
Ngadda

The northern state of Zamfara was, in 1999, the first state to adopt *sharia* (Islamic law), and its introduction in other northern states has exacerbated religious tensions. Rioting ostensibly triggered by these tensions has caused more than 1000 deaths since 2000.

Traditionally women have had independent economic status, especially in southern urban areas. Recent *sharia* rulings have exposed the severe restrictions imposed in the more conservative Islamic north.

POPULATION AGE BREAKDOWN

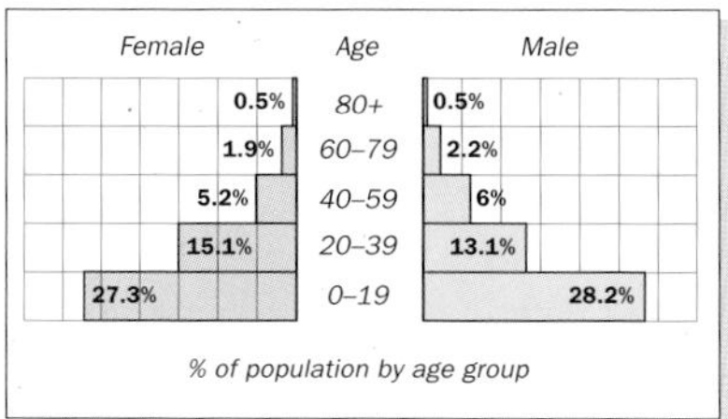
Female
Age
Male
0.5% 80+ 0.5%
1.9% 60–79 2.2%
5.2% 40–59 6%
15.1% 20–39 13.1%
27.3% 0–19 28.2%
% of population by age group

POLITICS

Multiparty elections

L. House 2003/2007
U. House 2003/2007

President Olusegun Obasanjo

AT THE LAST ELECTION

House of Representatives 360 seats

4% Vacant
59% PDP
26% ANPP
9% AD
2% Others

PDP = People's Democratic Party **ANPP** = All Nigeria People's Party **AD** = Alliance for Democracy

Senate 109 seats

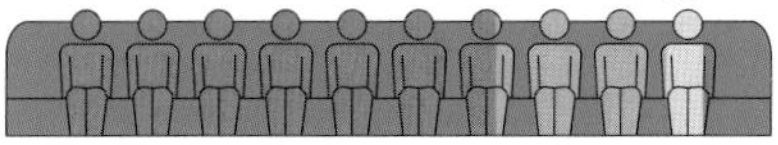
5% AD
67% PDP
26% ANPP
2% Vacant

Since May 1999 Nigeria has had a civilian constitution, after 16 years of military dictatorships. President Olusegun Obasanjo and his PDP promise national reconciliation.

PROFILE

The sudden death of military ruler Sani Abacha in 1998, followed by that of the imprisoned Chief Moshood Abiola, the presumed winner of the annulled 1993 presidential elections, left Gen. Abdulsalam Aboubakar to usher in civilian rule. Olusegun Obasanjo, a popular general who was head of state in 1976–1979, won elections held in 1999 and 2003. His PDP won a contested majority in legislative elections in April 2003.

MAIN POLITICAL ISSUES

Corruption

Corruption is a major cause of Nigeria's debt levels. Accusations at all levels of government peaked in 2000 with the impeachment of the Senate president.

Ethnic tensions and human rights

The Obasanjo regime faces difficulties in stemming the rivalries between the Hausa, Yoruba, and Ibo. Despite regional pressure, it shows little willingness to address the problem by devolving more power to the states. The introduction of often brutal *sharia* punishments has heightened international concern over human rights, which had previously focused on the apparent repression of the local population in the southern delta region.

Olusegun Obasanjo, *elected president in 1999.*

Gen. Sani Abacha, *head of state from 1993 until 1998.*

CHRONOLOGY

Before formal colonization by the British, begun only in 1861, Nigeria was a collection of African states owing their considerable wealth to trans-Saharan and transatlantic trade. During the 18th century the principal commodity was slaves: over 15,000 people a year were exported from the Bight of Benin and another 15,000 from the Bight of Biafra.

- ❏ **1885** Royal Niger Company given official responsibility for British sphere of influence along Niger and Benue Rivers. British armed forces coerce local rulers into accepting British rule.
- ❏ **1897** West Africa Frontier Force (WAFF) established; subjugation of the north begins.
- ❏ **1900** British Protectorate of Northern Nigeria established.
- ❏ **1906** Lagos incorporated into the Protectorate of Southern Nigeria.
- ❏ **1914** Protectorates of Northern and Southern Nigeria joined to form colony of Nigeria.
- ❏ **1960** Independence. Nigeria established as a federation.
- ❏ **1961** Northern part of UK-administered UN Trust Territory of the Cameroons incorporated as part of Nigeria's Northern Region.
- ❏ **1966** January, first military coup, led by Maj. Gen. Ironsi. July, countercoup mounted by group of northern army officers. Ironsi murdered. Thousands of Ibo in Northern Region massacred. Gen. Gowon in control of north and west.
- ❏ **1967–1970** Civil war. Lt. Col. Ojukwu calls for secession of oil-rich east under the new name Biafra. Over one million Nigerians die before secessionists defeated by federal forces.
- ❏ **1970** Gen. Gowon in power.
- ❏ **1975** Gowon toppled in bloodless coup. Brig. Mohammed takes power.
- ❏ **1976** Mohammed murdered in abortive coup. Succeeded by Gen. Olusegun Obasanjo.
- ❏ **1978** Political parties legalized, on condition they represent national, not tribal, interests.
- ❏ **1979** Elections won by Alhaji Shehu Shagari and the National Party of Nigeria (NPN), marking return to civilian government.
- ❏ **1983** Military coup. Maj. Gen. Mohammed Buhari heads Supreme Military Council.
- ❏ **1985** Maj. Gen. Ibrahim Babangida heads bloodless coup, promising a return to democracy.
- ❏ **1993** August, elections annulled; Babangida resigns; military sets up Interim National Government (ING). November, ING dissolved. ➪

N

CHRONOLOGY *continued*

Military, headed by Gen. Sani Abacha, takes over.

- **1994** Moshood Abiola arrested, opposition harassed.
- **1995** Ban on parties lifted. Obasanjo and 39 others convicted of plotting coup. Execution of Ken Saro-Wiwa and eight other Ogoni activists: EU sanctions, suspension of Commonwealth membership.
- **1998** Abacha dies; Abiola dies; return to civilian rule timetabled.
- **1999** Elections: presidency won by Obasanjo. Sanctions lifted, Commonwealth membership restored. Zamfara becomes first state to introduce *sharia*.
- **2000** Ethnic violence escalates, threatens national unity.
- **2001** 200 villagers massacred by army in apparent revenge killing.
- **2002** 1000 killed in Lagos munitions dump explosion and ensuing chaos. 700 killed in clashes between Muslims and Christians in Jos.
- **2003** PDP majority and Obasanjo reelected in disputed elections.

WORLD AFFAIRS

Joined UN in 1960

Comm | ECOWAS | AU | OIC | OPEC

Nigeria sees itself as one of Africa's leading voices alongside South Africa – a position commensurate with its large population. It is a strong supporter of ECOWAS and of the AU, and has been the main contributor to regional peacekeeping forces. Recently it has played a key role in attempting to mediate in Zimbabwe's internal political strife. Marine oil reserves have been the cause of border tensions with Cameroon. A similar dispute with Equatorial Guinea was settled in 2001.

Human rights abuses under the military regime (most notoriously the murder of human rights campaigner Ken Saro-Wiwa in 1995) led to Nigeria's suspension from the Commonwealth. It rejoined after civilian rule was restored in 1999, but concerns remain.

AID

Recipient

$185m (receipts)

Little change in 2001

The 1981 drop in world oil prices turned Nigeria from an aid donor into a major receiver of World Bank assistance. Aid flows were interrupted in late 1995, but were resumed in 2000. Aid agreed at the G8 summit in 2002 was welcomed by President Obasanjo, one of the architects of the New Partnership for Africa's Development (Nepad) plan.

DEFENSE

No compulsory military service

$516m

No change in 2001

The Nigerian government has contributed a significant number of forces to ECOMOG, the regional peacekeeping force set up in 1990 by ECOWAS, initially to restore order in Liberia. Nigerian forces served there until 1999 and in 2003, and in Sierra Leone in 1993–2000 and from 2002.

Since 2001 the armed forces have also been deployed to restore internal control after outbreaks of religious unrest in northern and central states, in which hundreds of civilians have been killed. However, government troops themselves were reported to have massacred some 200 villagers in the eastern state of Benue in 2001, in retaliation for the abduction of 19 members of the armed forces who had been deployed to quell unrest.

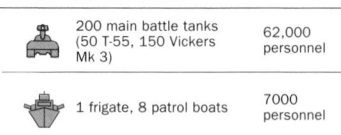

NIGERIAN ARMED FORCES

200 main battle tanks (50 T-55, 150 Vickers Mk 3)	62,000 personnel
1 frigate, 8 patrol boats	7000 personnel
86 combat aircraft (19 Alpha Jet, 17 MiG-21, 15 Jaguar)	9500 personnel
None	

ECONOMICS

Inflation 27% p.a. (1990–2001)

$37.1bn

130.1 naira (119.9)

SCORE CARD

World GNP Ranking	55th
GNP per Capita	$290
Balance of Payments	$6.98bn
Inflation	16.5%
Unemployment	28%

EXPORTS

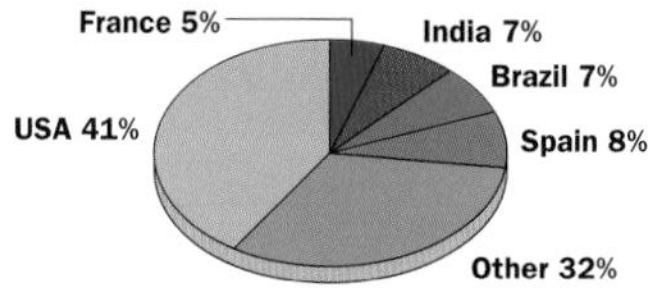
France 5%
India 7%
Brazil 7%
USA 41%
Spain 8%
Other 32%

IMPORTS

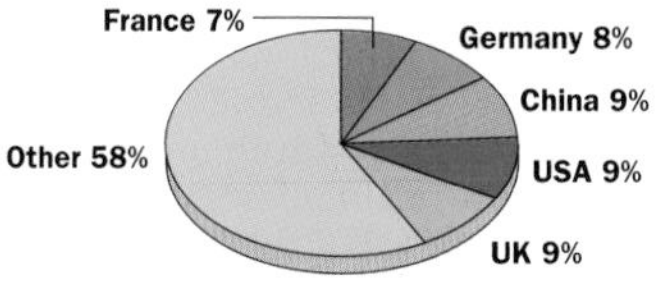
France 7%
Germany 8%
China 9%
Other 58%
USA 9%
UK 9%

Strengths

One of world's top oil producers. Vast reserves of natural gas, still only partly exploited. Soaring world oil prices in 2000 signified recovery from 1986 collapse. Almost self-sufficient in food. Strong entrepreneurial class. Large population, provides workforce and domestic market.

Weaknesses

Overdependence since the 1970s on oil, which encourages massive state inefficiency. Advantages of a large domestic market mitigated by low per capita purchasing power and high unit transportation costs. Entrepreneurs focus on trade rather than production. Of Nigeria's traditional agricultural exports only cocoa remains. Notorious corruption and maladministration undermine investors' confidence.

ECONOMIC PERFORMANCE INDICATOR

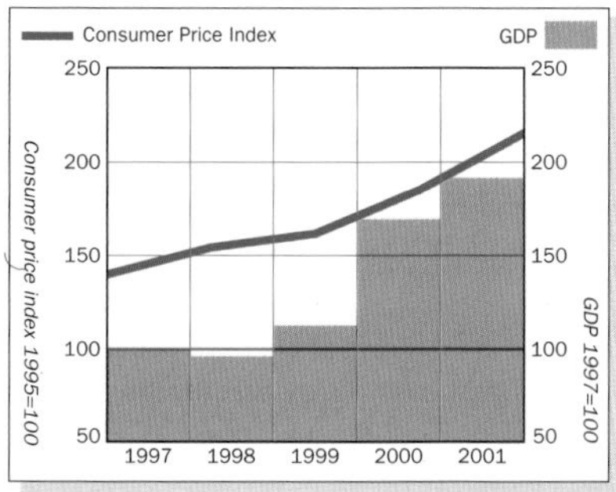
Consumer Price Index
GDP
250
200
150
100
50
1997
1998
1999
2000
2001
Consumer price index 1995=100
GDP 1997=100

Profile

Massive government spending ran up huge debts which could not be serviced after the 1981 oil price fall. Led by the IMF, creditors want major cuts in spending – especially on loss-making public-sector companies – and subsidies. Gasoline subsidies alone are estimated to have cost $2.4 billion a year, but tampering with the price of fuel in particular is politically fraught, leading to a week of strikes in 2003. Economic policy is likely to focus on building on recent limited gains.

NIGERIA : MAJOR BUSINESSES

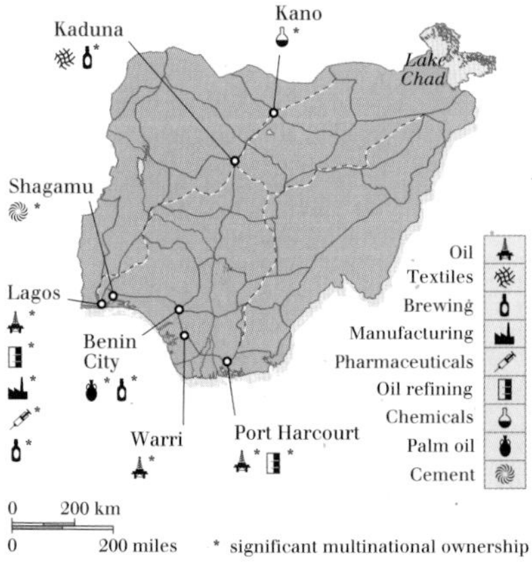
Kaduna
Kano
Lake Chad
Shagamu
Lagos
Benin City
Warri
Port Harcourt
Oil
Textiles
Brewing
Manufacturing
Pharmaceuticals
Oil refining
Chemicals
Palm oil
Cement
0 200 km
0 200 miles
* significant multinational ownership

RESOURCES

Electric power 5.9m kW

467,095 tonnes

2.01m b/d (reserves 24bn barrels)

27m goats, 22m sheep, 20m cattle, 140m chickens

Oil, natural gas, coal, tin, iron, bauxite, columbite, lead

ELECTRICITY GENERATION

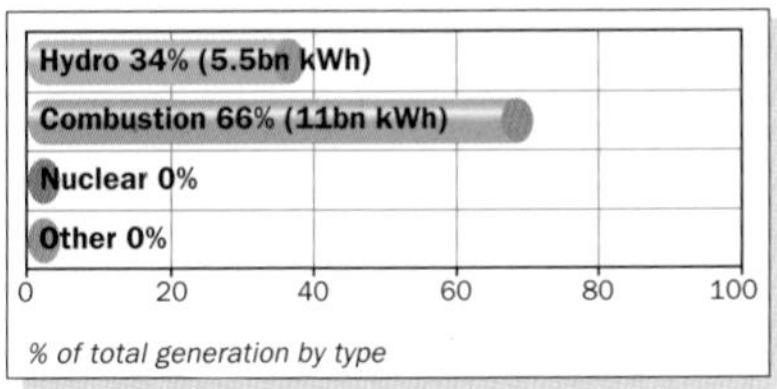
Hydro 34% (5.5bn kWh)
Combustion 66% (11bn kWh)
Nuclear 0%
Other 0%
0
20
40
60
80
100
% of total generation by type

Oil has been the main resource since the 1970s, and Nigeria is one of Africa's largest producers. The state retains 60% control of the industry. Shell is the main foreign shareholder, but most oil multinationals are represented. Production is frequently interrupted by regional unrest. As much as 300,000 b/d is smuggled to neighboring countries. Nigeria's vast gas deposits are still underexploited.

Nigeria has sizable iron ore deposits. These are not yet utilized in the state-run steel industry; imported ore is used instead. Bauxite deposits are also currently underexploited. There are, however, plans for establishing an aluminum industry. Nigeria also has deposits of coal and tin.

NIGERIA : LAND USE

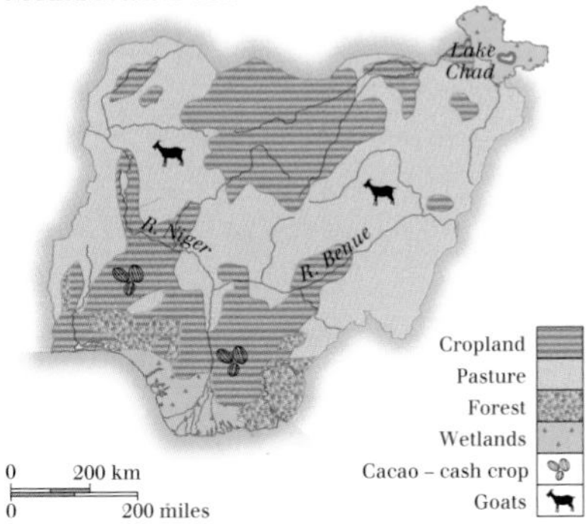
Lake Chad
R. Niger
R. Benue
Cropland
Pasture
Forest
Wetlands
Cacao – cash crop
Goats
0
200 km
0
200 miles

ENVIRONMENT

Sustainability rank: 133rd

3% (1% partially protected)

0.4 tonnes per capita

ENVIRONMENTAL TREATIES

Yes | Yes | Yes

Yes | Yes | No

Oil industry pollution in the Niger Delta, a major local concern, came to international attention in 1995; Shell has been particularly condemned. Before the discovery of a highly toxic cargo in 1988, Nigeria was a dumping ground for European chemical waste.

MEDIA

TV ownership medium

Daily newspaper circulation 24 per 1000 people

The Nigerian press is traditionally one of Africa's liveliest. Media freedom has improved since the return to civilian government. There are over 100 TV stations; the state-run Nigerian Television Authority runs 67, having introduced digital channels in 2003.

PUBLISHING AND BROADCAST MEDIA

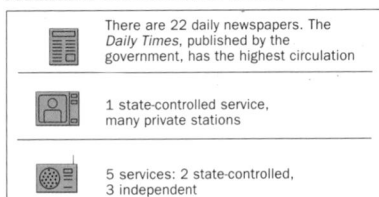

There are 22 daily newspapers. The *Daily Times*, published by the government, has the highest circulation

1 state-controlled service, many private stations

5 services: 2 state-controlled, 3 independent

CRIME

Death penalty in use

39,368 prisoners

Crime is rising

CRIME RATES

Murders

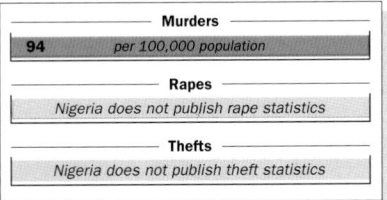

94 per 100,000 population

Rapes

Nigeria does not publish rape statistics

Thefts

Nigeria does not publish theft statistics

Nigeria has one of the highest crime rates in the world. Murder often accompanies even minor burglaries. Rich Nigerians live in high-security compounds. Police in some states are empowered to "shoot on sight" violent criminals. Brutal *sharia* punishments are claimed to have reduced crime in northern states. Vigilante gangs are used to fight crime in the southeastern states.

EDUCATION

School leaving age: 12

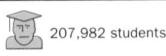

65%

207,982 students

THE EDUCATION SYSTEM

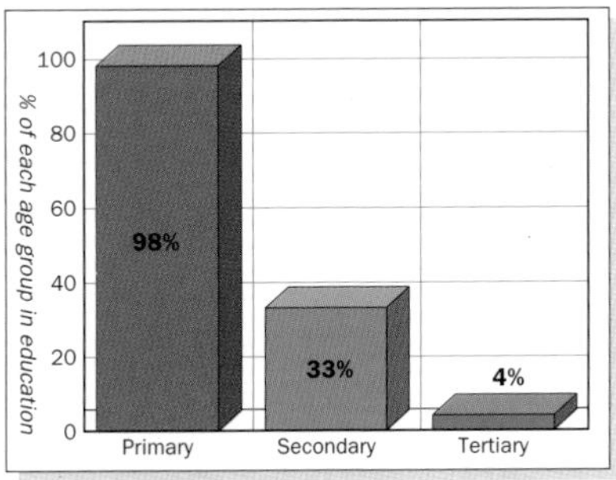
100
80
60
40
20
0
% of each age group in education
98%
33%
4%
Primary
Secondary
Tertiary

Responsibility for education is shared between the federal and the state governments. Education has suffered from the government's massive debt repayment burden. During the oil-boom years, Nigeria concentrated on creating 31 universities with prestigious medical and scientific schools. However, standards in primary education, which has not received the same level of investment, have fallen since the 1970s. Almost all children attend primary school, but only about one-third receive secondary education.

HEALTH

Welfare state health benefits

1 per 5263 people

Yellow fever, malaria, trachoma, yaws

The health service functions mainly in urban areas and has suffered from the crisis in government revenues; a 1999 government report stated that only 49% of people had access to water and health services. More than 3.5 million Nigerians were living with HIV/AIDS as at end-2001. Free generic versions of AIDS treatments became available in 2001 and the government supports a successful AIDS awareness strategy.

SPENDING

GDP/cap. increase

CONSUMPTION AND SPENDING

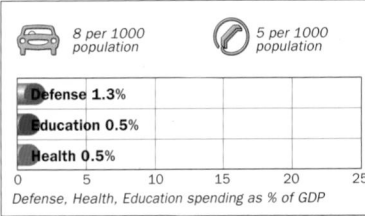

8 per 1000 population

5 per 1000 population

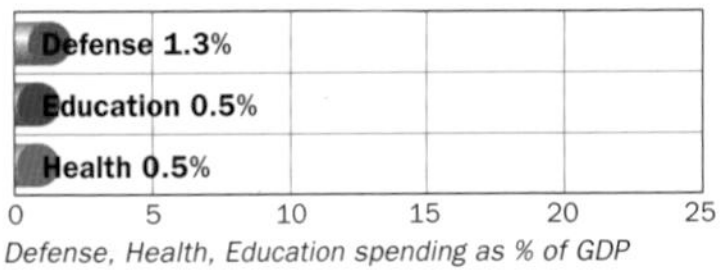
Defense 1.3%
Education 0.5%
Health 0.5%
0
5
10
15
20
25
Defense, Health, Education spending as % of GDP

Nigerians with access to the rich pickings of political office spent on a massive scale during the country's oil boom – on expensive cars and on overseas education for their children. Much was financed by government loans. Habits have not changed with the fall in oil revenues: borrowing has simply grown.

WORLD RANKING

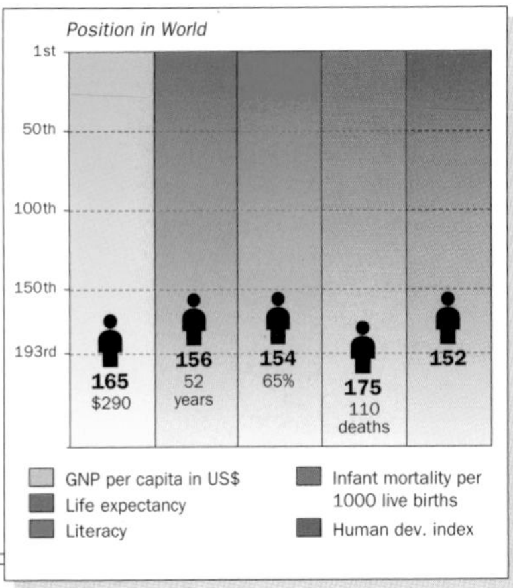
Position in World
1st
50th
100th
150th
193rd
165
$290
156
52 years
154
65%
175
110 deaths
152
GNP per capita in US$
Life expectancy
Literacy
Infant mortality per 1000 live births
Human dev. index

N

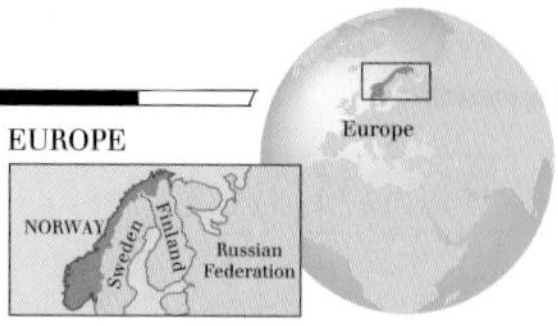
EUROPE
NORWAY
Sweden
Finland
Russian Federation
Europe

NORWAY

OFFICIAL NAME: Kingdom of Norway **CAPITAL:** Oslo
POPULATION: 4.5 million **CURRENCY:** Norwegian krone **OFFICIAL LANGUAGE:** Norwegian

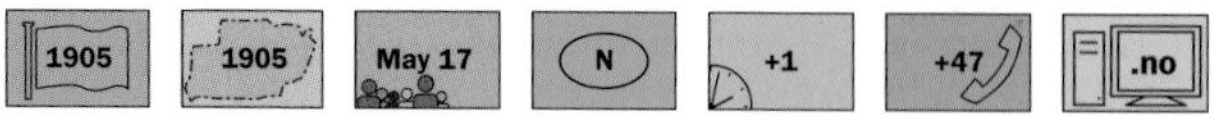
1905
1905
May 17
N
+1
+47
.no

OCCUPYING THE WESTERN PART of Scandinavia, Norway's western coastline is characterized by numerous fjords and islands. Large oil and gas revenues have brought prosperity. Gro Harlem Brundtland, Norway's first woman prime minister, went on to take top UN posts. Despite the Europe-wide recession in the early 1990s, Norway was able to contain rising unemployment, which peaked at 6% in 1993. A constitutional requirement is that government creates conditions that enable every person to find work.

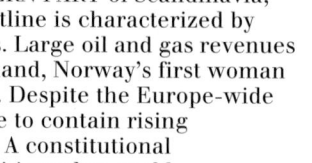

***The village of Reine** on Moskenesøya, deep inside the Arctic Circle in the Lofoten Islands. It is a popular destination for summer visitors.*

CLIMATE

Maritime/subarctic

WEATHER CHART FOR OSLO

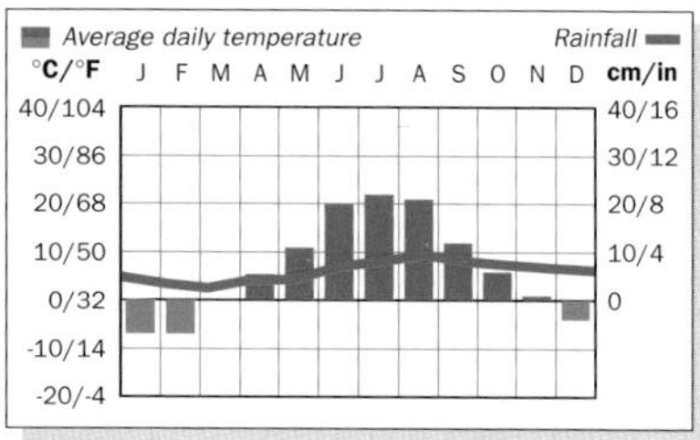
Average daily temperature
Rainfall
°C/°F
J F M A M J J A S O N D
cm/in
40/104
30/86
20/68
10/50
0/32
-10/14
-20/-4
40/16
30/12
20/8
10/4
0

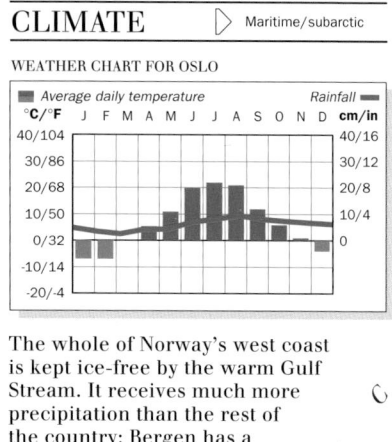

The whole of Norway's west coast is kept ice-free by the warm Gulf Stream. It receives much more precipitation than the rest of the country; Bergen has a yearly average of 225 cm (89 in). Norway enjoys the highest mean temperatures in Scandinavia, but in winter the temperature in Oslo can fall as low as –25°C (–13°F).

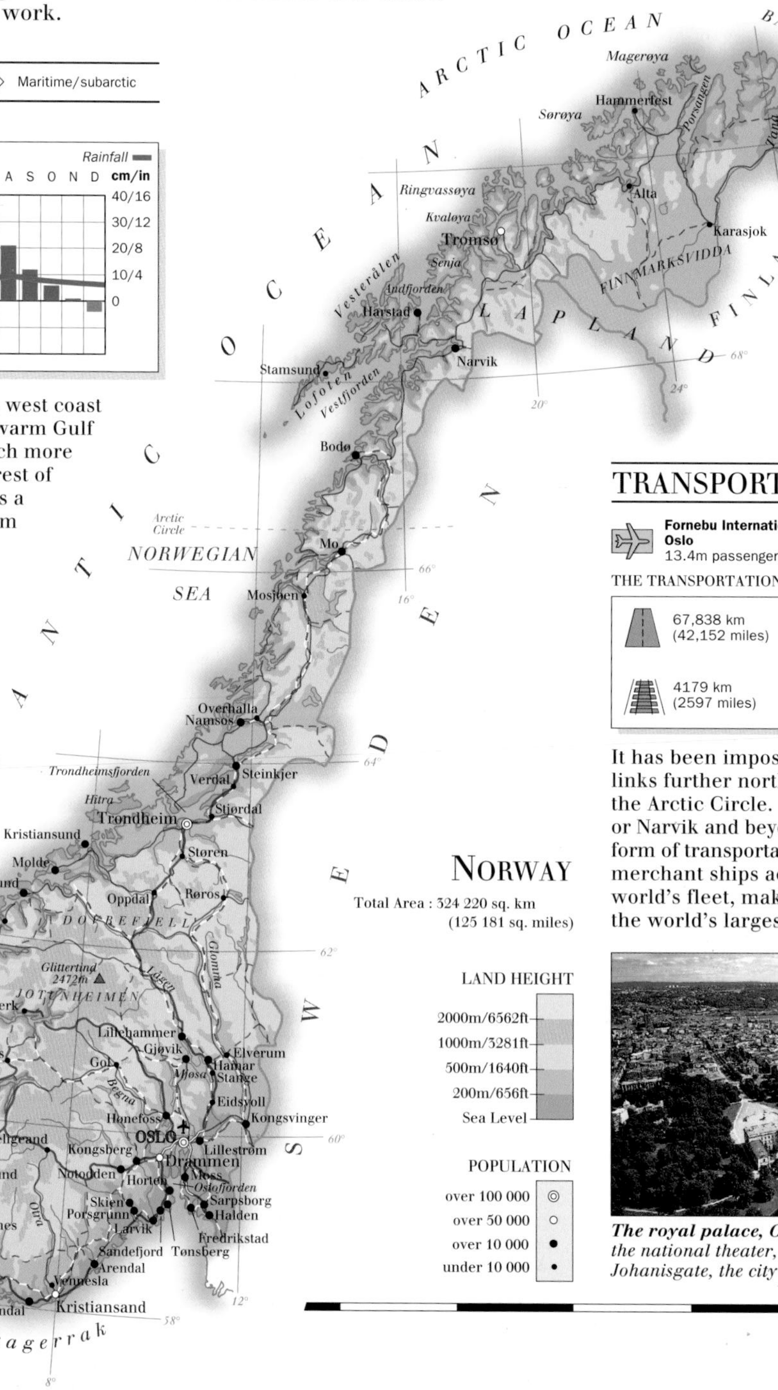
ARCTIC OCEAN
BARENTS SEA
Magerøya
Hammerfest
Sørøya
Porsangen
Tana
Tana Bru
Varangerfjorden
Kirkenes
Ringvassøya
Kvaløya
Tromsø
Senja
Alta
Karasjok
FINNMARKSVIDDA
RUSSIAN FEDERATION
FINLAND
LAPLAND
Vesterålen
Andfjorden
Harstad
Narvik
Stamsund
Lofoten
Vestfjorden
Bodø
ATLANTIC OCEAN
NORWEGIAN SEA
Arctic Circle
Mo
Mosjøen
SWEDEN
Overhalla
Namsos
Trondheimsfjorden
Verdal
Steinkjer
Hitra
Trondheim
Stjørdal
Kristiansund
Støren
Molde
Ålesund
Oppdal
Røros
Ørsta
DOVREFJELL
Glomma
Glittertind 2472m
Lågen
JOTUNHEIMEN
Hermansverk
Sognefjorden
Lillehammer
Gjøvik
Elverum
Hamar
Mjøsa
Stange
Voss
Gol
Bergen
Hardangerfjorden
Begna
Eidsvoll
Hønefoss
Kongsvinger
NORTH SEA
Haukeligrend
OSLO
Lillestrøm
Kongsberg
Drammen
Åkrehamn
Haugesund
Notodden
Horten
Moss
Oslofjorden
Boknafjorden
Stavanger
Skien
Sarpsborg
Porsgrunn
Halden
Sola
Sandnes
Otra
Larvik
Fredrikstad
Sandefjord
Tønsberg
Egersund
Arendal
Vennesla
Mandal
Kristiansand
Skagerrak
0 100 km
0 100 miles

NORWAY

Total Area : 324 220 sq. km (125 181 sq. miles)

LAND HEIGHT

- 2000m/6562ft
- 1000m/3281ft
- 500m/1640ft
- 200m/656ft
- Sea Level

POPULATION

- over 100 000
- over 50 000
- over 10 000
- under 10 000

TRANSPORTATION

Drive on right

Fornebu International, Oslo 13.4m passengers

2363 ships 22.6m grt

THE TRANSPORTATION NETWORK

67,838 km (42,152 miles)	173 km (107 miles)
4179 km (2597 miles)	1577 km (980 miles)

It has been impossible to extend rail links further north than Bodø, inside the Arctic Circle. To reach the Lofotens or Narvik and beyond, the most common form of transportation is air. Norwegian merchant ships account for 10% of the world's fleet, making Norway one of the world's largest shipping nations.

***The royal palace, Oslo.** This is situated near the national theater, at one end of the Karl Johanisgate, the city's main thoroughfare.*

N

TOURISM

Visitors : Population 1:1.4

3.11m visitors

Up 1% in 2002

Norway is a popular destination, receiving most visitors from Germany, Sweden, Denmark, the UK, and the US. Its winter tourism industry is based on skiing and was boosted by the 1994 Winter Olympics taking place in Lillehammer. Cruising along the fjords is popular with summer visitors. Areas within the Arctic Circle are a particular attraction in June, when tourists go in search of the midnight sun. Oslo has a reputation for good classical music and jazz. However, the strength of the krone and the high cost of living make Norway expensive.

MAIN TOURIST ARRIVALS

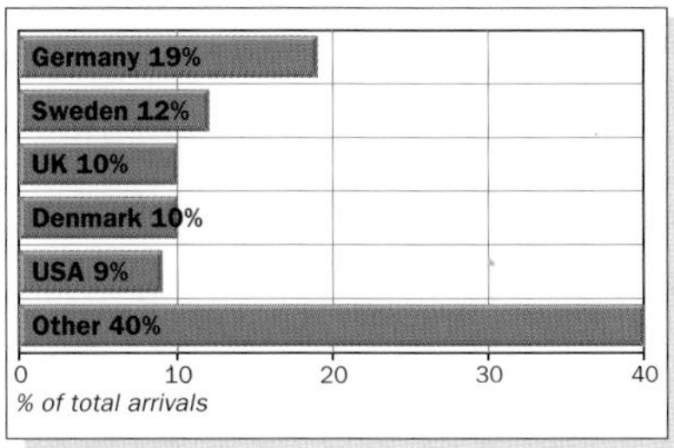
Germany 19%
Sweden 12%
UK 10%
Denmark 10%
USA 9%
Other 40%
0
10
20
30
40
% of total arrivals

PEOPLE

Pop. density low

Norwegian (*Bokmål* "book language" and *Nynorsk* "new Norsk"), Sami

15/km² (38/mi²)

THE URBAN/RURAL POPULATION SPLIT

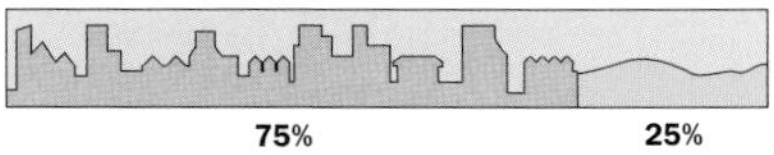
75%
25%

RELIGIOUS PERSUASION

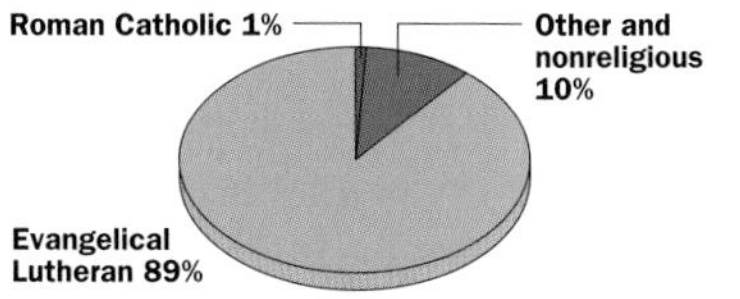
Roman Catholic 1%
Other and nonreligious 10%
Evangelical Lutheran 89%

ETHNIC MAKEUP

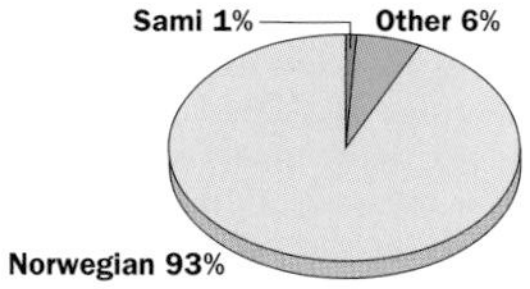
Sami 1%
Other 6%
Norwegian 93%

Norway has a small but growing immigrant population, forming 5.6% of the population in 2001. In the early 1990s the number of asylum seekers increased, especially as a result of the Bosnian conflict. Some refugees have been attacked by right-wing groups.

The family is traditionally close and nuclear. Men are expected to share responsibility for raising children, who frequently attend day schools from under the age of two years. Women enjoy considerable power and freedom, and comprise at least 40% of members of the government. Over half of marriages end in divorce.

POPULATION AGE BREAKDOWN

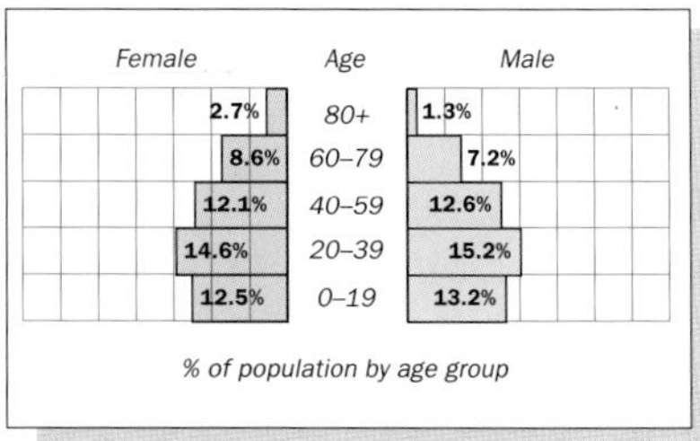
Female
Age
Male
2.7%
80+
1.3%
8.6%
60–79
7.2%
12.1%
40–59
12.6%
14.6%
20–39
15.2%
12.5%
0–19
13.2%
% of population by age group

POLITICS

Multiparty elections

2001/2005

H.M. King Harald V

AT THE LAST ELECTION

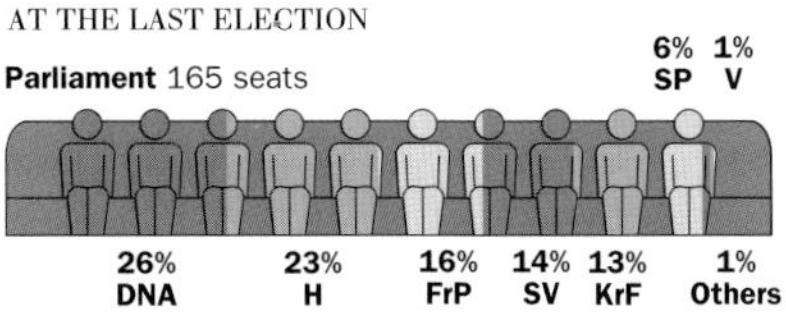
Parliament 165 seats
6% SP
1% V
26% DNA
23% H
16% FrP
14% SV
13% KrF
1% Others

DNA = Norwegian Labor Party **H** = Hoeyre (Conservative Party) **FrP** = Progress Party **SV** = Socialist Left Party **KrF** = Christian Democratic Party **SP** = Center Party **V** = Venstre (Liberal Party)

The Parliament (Storting) is elected as one body but divides itself for most legislative purposes into an upper chamber (Lagting, with 42 members) and a lower chamber (Odelsting, with 123 members)

Norway is a constitutional monarchy, with a king as head of state and an elected parliament.

PROFILE

Political decisions are based on consensus building between the government, parliament, and the strong trade unions. In 1993, opposition to EU membership boosted support for the SP, but the DNA remained the largest party.

In 1997 the DNA lost ground to the center right, which formed a coalition led by Kjell Magne Bondevik of the KrF. Returned to office in 2000, the DNA suffered heavy losses in the 2001 polls, and Bondevik, who had campaigned for using oil revenues to fund tax cuts and public service improvements, was reappointed prime minister. He heads a minority government, in coalition with the Conservatives and the Liberals.

MAIN POLITICAL ISSUE

The rise of the far right

The anti-immigration FrP, originally formed in 1973, grew in popularity during the 1990s as the number of asylum seekers rose. It emerged as the third-largest party in the 2001 election, and is now a significant force in parliamentary politics. The minority government was forced to rely on its support to pass the 2003 budget, promising further tax cuts in return for FrP backing.

WORLD AFFAIRS

Joined UN in 1945

CE | NATO | OECD | OSCE | EFTA

A founder member of NATO, Norway continues to offer it strong support. It became an associate member of the WEU in 1992. The 1994 referendum rejecting EU membership means that the European Economic Area (EEA) offers Norway its main access to the European single market. As a Nordic Council member it is associated with the Schengen Convention on passport-free borders. In January 2002 Bondevik stated that there would be no referendum on joining the EU, but a concurrent opinion poll suggested that a majority now favored membership.

Norway has played peacemaker on a number of occasions, notably in attempting to mediate in the Israeli–Palestinian conflict during the mid-1990s, and in Sri Lanka from 2002.

The government has been unable to control the ecological effects of acid rain, which is destroying its forests. Representatives of 25 European countries and Canada met in Oslo in 1994 and signed a UN protocol on reducing sulfur emissions.

King Harald V, who succeeded his father King Olav V in 1991.

Prime Minister Kjell Magne Bondevik, reelected in 2002.

CHRONOLOGY

Norway gained independence from the Swedish crown in 1905 and elected its own king, Håkon VII.

- **1935** DNA forms government.
- **1940–1945** Nazi occupation. Puppet regime led by Vidkun Quisling.
- **1945** DNA resumes power.
- **1949** Founder member of NATO.
- **1957** King Håkon dies. Succeeded by son, Olav V.
- **1960** Becomes member of EFTA.
- **1962** Unsuccessfully applies to join European Communities (EC).
- **1965** DNA electoral defeat by SP coalition led by Per Borten.
- **1967** Second bid for EC membership.
- **1971** Borten resigns following disclosure of secret negotiations to join EC; DNA government, led by Trygve Bratteli.

N

CHRONOLOGY *continued*

- **1972** EC membership rejected in popular referendum by 5% majority. Bratteli resigns. Center coalition government takes power. Lars Korvald prime minister.
- **1973** Elections. Bratteli returns to power as prime minister.
- **1976** Bratteli succeeded by Odvar Nordli.
- **1981** Nordli resigns owing to ill health. Gro Harlem Brundtland becomes first woman prime minister. Elections bring to power Conservative Party (H) government for first time in 53 years. Kare Willoch prime minister.
- **1983** Conservatives form coalition with SP and KrF.
- **1985** Election. Willoch's H–SP–KrF coalition returned. Norway agrees to suspend commercial whaling.
- **1986** 100,000 demonstrate for better working conditions. Brundtland forms minority DNA government. Currency devalued by 12%.
- **1989** Brundtland resigns. H–KrF coalition in power. USSR agrees exchange of information after fires break out on Soviet nuclear submarines off Norwegian coast.
- **1990** H–KrF coalition breaks up over closer ties with EU (formerly EC). Brundtland and DNA in power.
- **1991** Olav V dies; succeeded by son, Harald V.
- **1994** EEA comes into effect. Referendum rejects EU membership.
- **1996** Brundtland resigns; replaced by Thorbjørn Jagland (also DNA).
- **1997** Kjell Magne Bondevik forms center-right coalition.
- **2000** Jens Stoltenberg (DNA) heads three-party coalition.
- **2001** Right-wing victory in elections. Bondevik heads coalition government.

AID

Donor

$1.35bn (donations)

Up 6% in 2001

Norway has been granting more than the UN development target of 0.7% of GNP in aid every year since 1975. Though Norway's ratio of aid to GNP has declined somewhat, to 0.83% in 2001, it remains one of the highest in the world. The vast majority of Norway's bilateral aid goes to the least developed countries of southeast Africa, south Asia, and the Balkans. In 1999 the largest single recipient of Norwegian aid was Kosovo (Serbia). The government also allocates funds to various multilateral assistance programs. The 1999 budget included a debt-relief program to help reduce developing country indebtedness.

DEFENSE

Compulsory military service

$2.97bn

Up 2% in 2001

Plans have been announced to almost halve Norway's conscript army, which traditionally has absorbed most of the defense budget. Norway joined NATO in 1949. The overriding defense issue is the stability of Russia and the security of their common border. Five Russian diplomats were expelled in 1998 after a double agent revealed that Russia had extensive information on Norway's defenses and its oil industry.

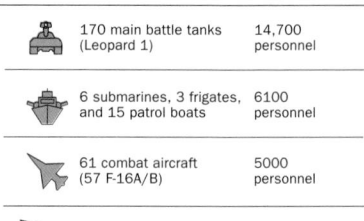

NORWEGIAN ARMED FORCES

170 main battle tanks (Leopard 1)	14,700 personnel
6 submarines, 3 frigates, and 15 patrol boats	6100 personnel
61 combat aircraft (57 F-16A/B)	5000 personnel
None	

ECONOMICS

Inflation 3.2% p.a. (1990–2001)

$161bn

7.218 Norwegian kroner (7.504)

SCORE CARD

WORLD GNP RANKING	27th
GNP PER CAPITA	$35,630
BALANCE OF PAYMENTS	$26bn
INFLATION	3%
UNEMPLOYMENT	4%

EXPORTS

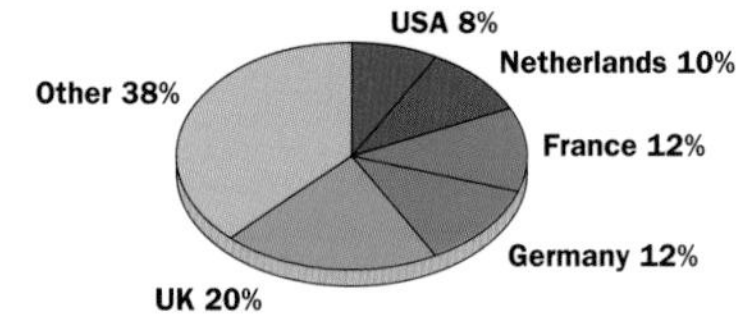
USA 8%
Netherlands 10%
France 12%
Germany 12%
UK 20%
Other 38%

IMPORTS

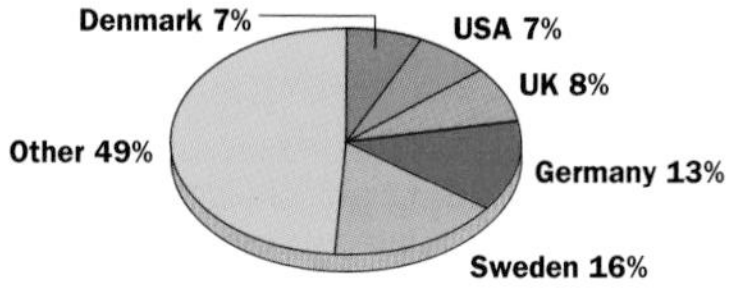
Denmark 7%
USA 7%
UK 8%
Germany 13%
Sweden 16%
Other 49%

ECONOMIC PERFORMANCE INDICATOR

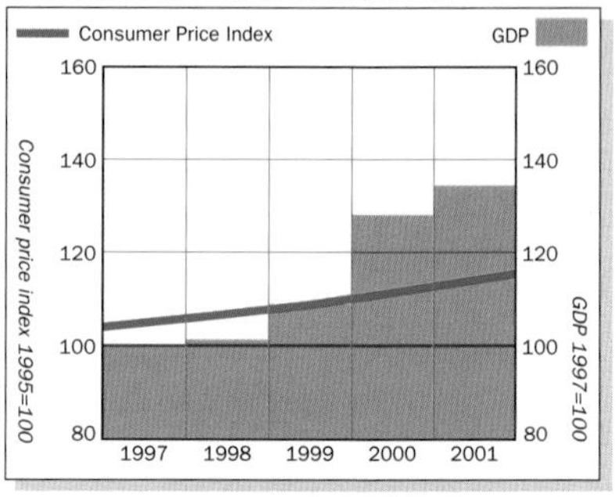
Consumer Price Index
GDP
160
140
120
100
80
1997
1998
1999
2000
2001
Consumer price index 1995=100
GDP 1997=100

STRENGTHS

Western Europe's biggest producer and exporter of oil and natural gas. Mineral reserves. Hydroelectric power satisfies much of country's energy demands, allowing most oil to be exported. Petroleum fund to ensure current profits provide for future generations. Large merchant shipping fleet. Low inflation and unemployment compared with rest of Europe.

WEAKNESSES

Overdependence on oil revenue. Small home market and relatively remote location. Shortage of skilled labor. Harsh climate limits agriculture.

PROFILE

The state is interventionist by nature. In 1991, it stepped in to rescue most of the main commercial banks, which had been hit by bad loans. It began returning them to the private sector in 1994. The state also manages the distribution of offshore oil and gas licenses, and owns 45% of the Norsk Hydro conglomerate. In 2000 the state sold a 20% share in its oil and telecommunications companies.

Norway's immediate future prosperity is guaranteed by its offshore oil sector. There is a shortage of skilled labor, which has partly been eased by the arrival of workers from other Scandinavian countries, but has created upward pressure on wages. Continuing the strong regional policy of redirecting resources from the more prosperous south to the isolated north is likely to remain a priority, both for social and strategic reasons.

NORWAY : MAJOR BUSINESSES

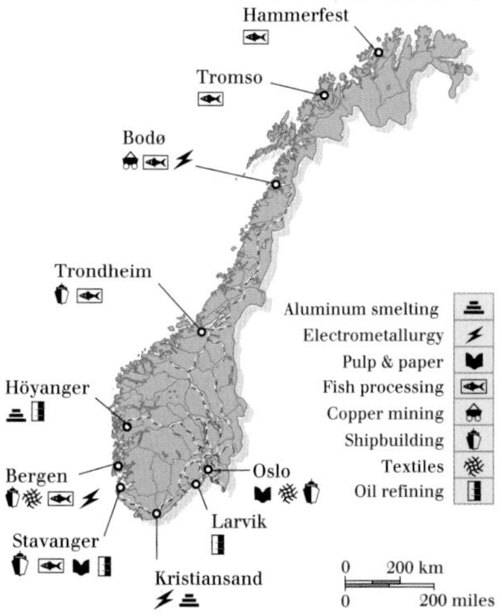
Hammerfest
Tromso
Bodø
Trondheim
Höyanger
Bergen
Oslo
Larvik
Stavanger
Kristiansand
Aluminum smelting
Electrometallurgy
Pulp & paper
Fish processing
Copper mining
Shipbuilding
Textiles
Oil refining
0 200 km
0 200 miles

RESOURCES

Electric power 27.9m kW

3.19m tonnes

3.33m b/d (reserves 10.3bn barrels)

2.4m sheep, 967,200 cattle, 3.2m chickens

Oil, natural gas, iron, coal, copper, lead, zinc

ELECTRICITY GENERATION

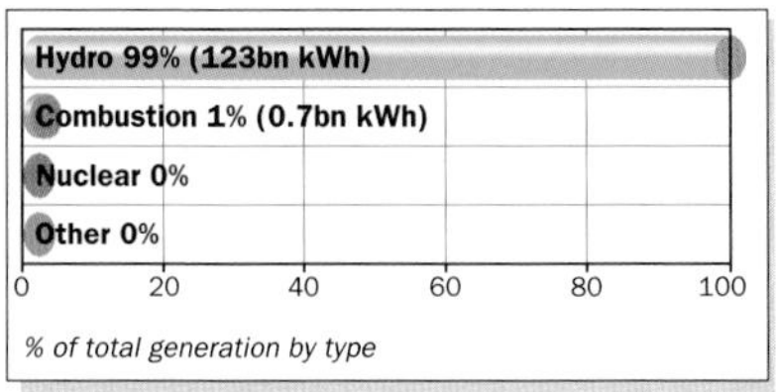

Hydro 99% (123bn kWh)
Combustion 1% (0.7bn kWh)
Nuclear 0%
Other 0%
0 20 40 60 80 100
% of total generation by type

Norway is Europe's largest oil producer, and it also has sizable gas reserves, yet most of Norway's electricity is produced by hydropower. In summer, the HEP surplus is exported. Fish and forestry are traditionally significant sectors – salmon farming, managed with particular efficiency, has grown rapidly – though together with agriculture they account for only 2.5% of GDP and 5% of the workforce.

A 2002 report warned that cod stocks in the North Sea were under threat from oil-drilling waste products.

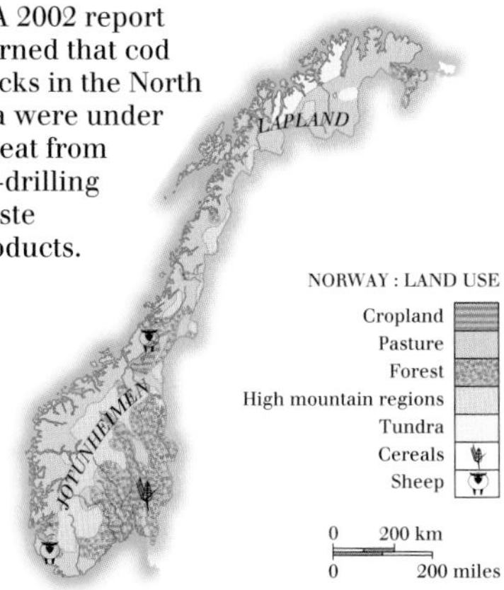

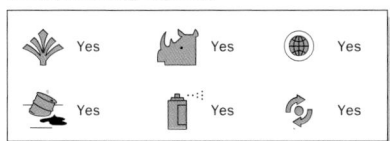

LAPLAND
JOTUNHEIMEN
NORWAY : LAND USE
Cropland
Pasture
Forest
High mountain regions
Tundra
Cereals
Sheep
0 200 km
0 200 miles

ENVIRONMENT

Sustainability rank: 2nd

7% (2% partially protected)

9.2 tonnes per capita

ENVIRONMENTAL TREATIES

Yes	Yes	Yes
Yes	Yes	Yes

In 1986 northern Norway suffered radioactive contamination after the Chernobyl nuclear disaster. Norway has a tax on carbon dioxide emissions and was instrumental in securing agreement on the 1997 Kyoto Protocol on greenhouse gas emissions. In 1993, it lifted a ban on fishing minke whales, and in 2001 it allowed the export of whale products. It was also criticized in 2001 for a cull of (endangered) gray wolves and for plans to develop a coalfield on Svalbard.

MEDIA

TV ownership high

Daily newspaper circulation 569 per 1000 people

PUBLISHING AND BROADCAST MEDIA

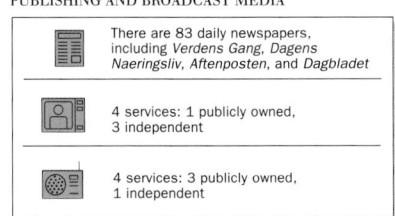

There are 83 daily newspapers, including *Verdens Gang, Dagens Naeringsliv, Aftenposten*, and *Dagbladet*

4 services: 1 publicly owned, 3 independent

4 services: 3 publicly owned, 1 independent

The state broadcaster NRK enjoys comparatively generous funding and attracts around a third of viewers. Newspapers have the second-highest proportion of readers in the world.

CRIME

No death penalty

2666 prisoners

Up 3% in 2000

CRIME RATES

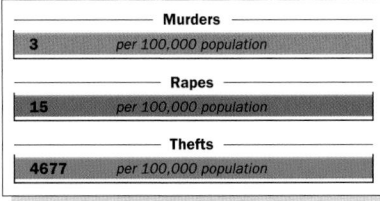

Crime	Rate
Murders	3 per 100,000 population
Rapes	15 per 100,000 population
Thefts	4677 per 100,000 population

Norway has low levels of crime, even by Scandinavian standards. Violent crime barely exists – the murder rate is one-third of that of Sweden, and there are considerably fewer assaults and robberies.

EDUCATION

School leaving age: 16

99%

189,947 students

THE EDUCATION SYSTEM

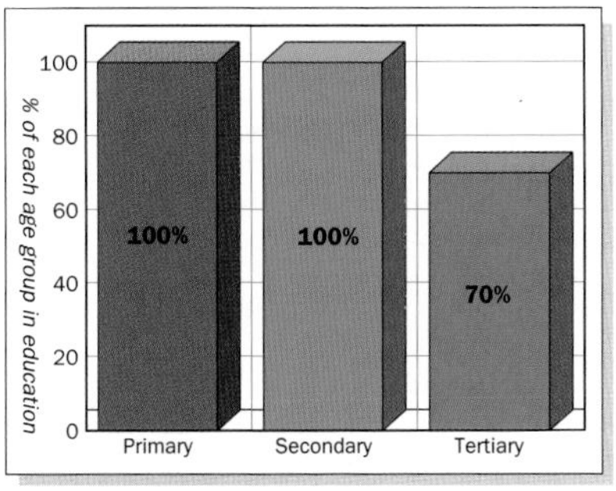

% of each age group in education
100
80
60
40
20
0
100%
100%
70%
Primary
Secondary
Tertiary

The period of compulsory schooling was increased from nine to ten years, with effect from the school year 1997/1998. Most schools are run by municipalities. There are four universities; specialized colleges include the Nordic College of Fisheries. Promotion of continuing education kept youth unemployment down during the early 1990s recession.

HEALTH

Welfare state health benefits

1 per 242 people

Cancers, heart and respiratory diseases, accidental falls

Norway's health system is ranked by the WHO as the best in Scandinavia and 11th in the world. The country's infant mortality rate is among the world's lowest, and life expectancy at birth is one of the highest. Spending on health care is among the highest by OECD states. A new health plan announced in 2002 will place the high-spending hospitals under central control.

Telemedicine (online remote audio and image diagnosis) allows remote northern hospitals to obtain specialist consultations without having to send patients to the regional hospital.

SPENDING

GDP/cap. increase

CONSUMPTION AND SPENDING

412 per 1000 population

720 per 1000 population

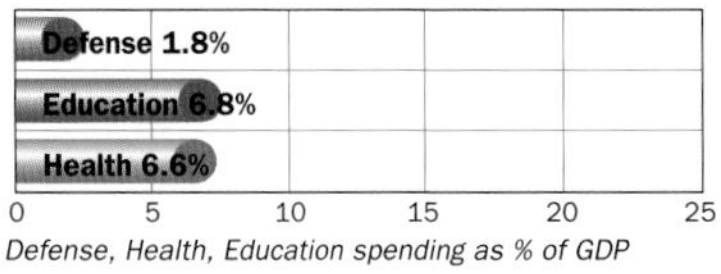

Defense 1.8%
Education 6.8%
Health 6.6%
0 5 10 15 20 25
Defense, Health, Education spending as % of GDP

In terms of income distribution, the Scandinavian countries are the most egalitarian in the world, and the richest 10% of Norway's population owns much less of the country's wealth than is the case in other developed countries. The cost of living is high, and Oslo is one of the world's most expensive cities. Refugees from the Bosnian conflict are the most disadvantaged group.

The discrepancy between pay for men and women is greater than in either Sweden or Finland, though still well below the European average. Social provision has been maintained even through economic recession. Benefits are generous.

WORLD RANKING

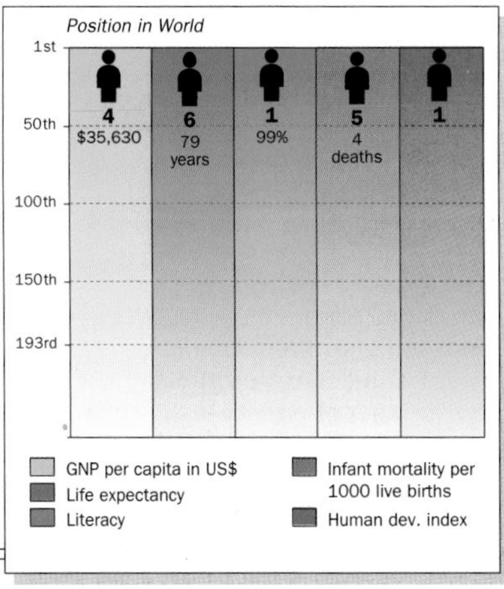

Position in World
1st
50th
100th
150th
193rd
4
$35,630
6
79 years
1
99%
5
4 deaths
1
GNP per capita in US$
Life expectancy
Literacy
Infant mortality per 1000 live births
Human dev. index

N

OMAN

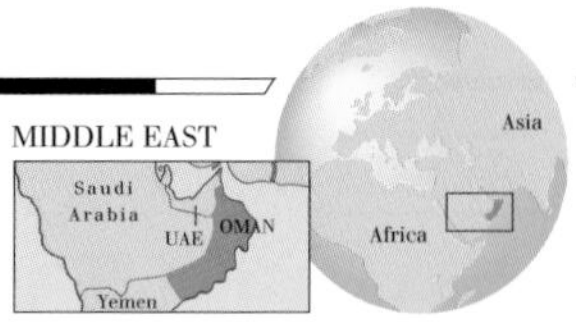

MIDDLE EAST
Saudi Arabia
UAE
OMAN
Yemen
Asia
Africa

OFFICIAL NAME: Sultanate of Oman **CAPITAL:** Muscat
POPULATION: 2.7 million **CURRENCY:** Omani rial **OFFICIAL LANGUAGE:** Arabic

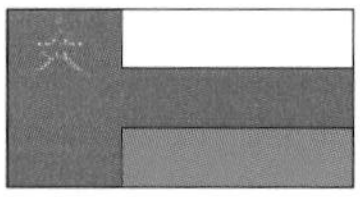

1951 | 1951 | Nov 18 | OM | +4 | +968 | .om

OCCUPYING THE EASTERN corner of the Arabian peninsula, Oman commands a strategic position at the entrance to the Persian Gulf. It is the least developed of the Gulf states. The most densely populated areas are the northern coast and the southern Salalah plain. Oil exports have given Oman modest prosperity under a paternalistic sultan. A Marxist-led insurgency supported by southern Dhofaris was defeated in the 1970s.

CLIMATE

Hot desert

WEATHER CHART FOR MUSCAT

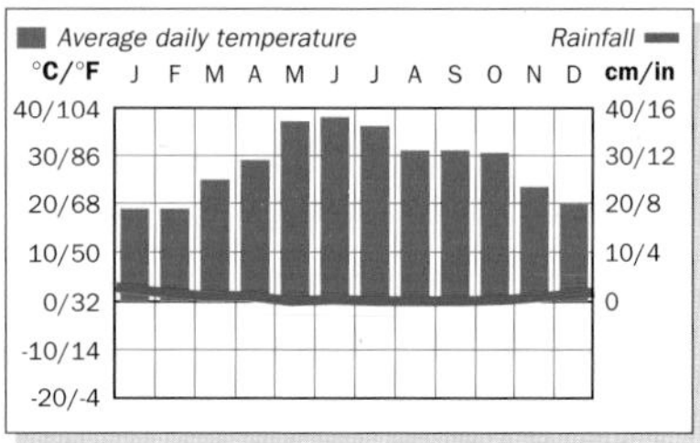

Average daily temperature
Rainfall
°C/°F J F M A M J J A S O N D cm/in
40/104
30/86
20/68
10/50
0/32
-10/14
-20/-4
40/16
30/12
20/8
10/4
0

In the north temperatures often climb above 45°C (113°F) in summer. The south has a monsoon climate.

TRANSPORTATION

Drive on right

Seeb International, Muscat 2.46m passengers

28 ships 19,700 grt

THE TRANSPORTATION NETWORK

9840 km (6114 miles)

550 km (342 miles)

None

None

Northern cities are well served by good roads, but some places, in the south particularly, are best reached by air.

TOURISM

Visitors : Population 1:4.8

562,000 visitors

Up 12% in 2000–2001

MAIN TOURIST ARRIVALS

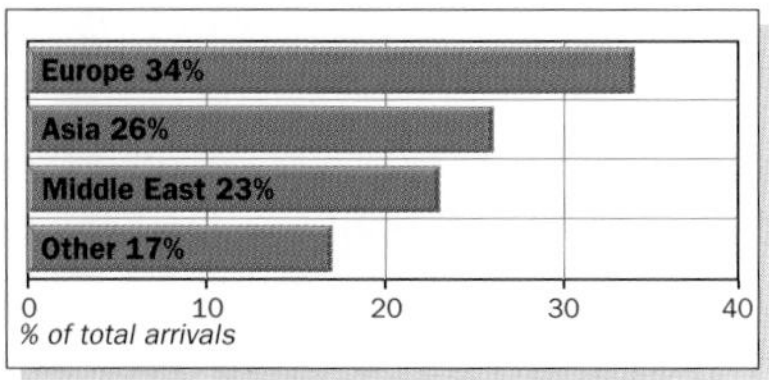

Europe 34%
Asia 26%
Middle East 23%
Other 17%
0
10
20
30
40
% of total arrivals

Until the late 1980s, Oman was closed to all but business or official visitors. The number of visitors to the sultanate's rich cultural heritage, fine beaches, and luxury hotels has been badly affected by the 2003 war on Iraq.

PEOPLE

Pop. density low

Arabic, Baluchi

13/km² (33/mi²)

THE URBAN/RURAL POPULATION SPLIT

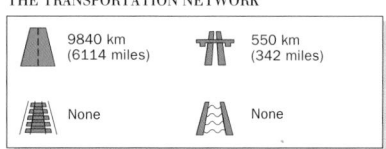

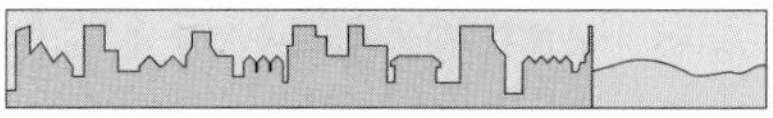

77%
23%

RELIGIOUS PERSUASION

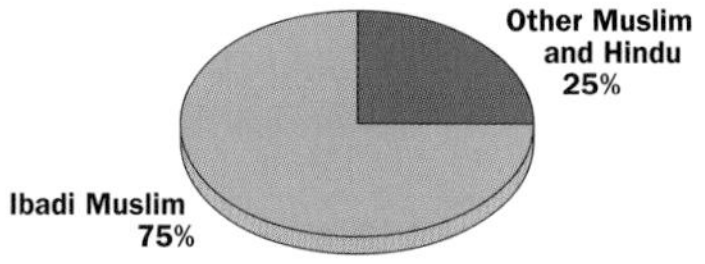

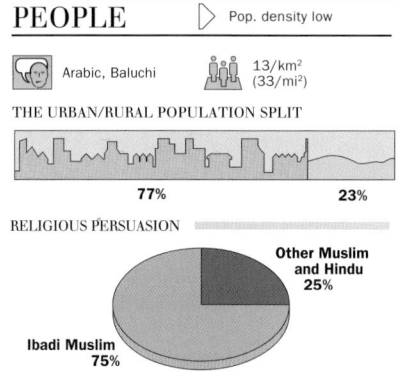

Other Muslim and Hindu 25%
Ibadi Muslim 75%

Native Omanis, who include Arab refugees who fled Zanzibar in the 1960s, make up three-quarters of the population. Baluchis, from Pakistan, are the largest foreign grouping among large numbers of foreign workers employed in the building and service industries on two-year contracts. A process of urban drift means that most Omanis now live in cities. Oman has a number of distinct minorities: the most numerous are the Jebalis in Dhofar – nomadic herdsmen who speak a language resembling Ethiopian. Many Dhofaris supported the Marxist-led insurgents in the 1970s, but they are now considered to be loyal.

Most Omanis are Ibadi Muslims who follow an appointed leader, the imam. Ibadism does not oppose freedom for women, and a few enjoy positions of authority; suffrage was extended to women in 2002.

POLITICS

No legislative elections

2000/2003

Sultan Qaboos bin Said

LEGISLATIVE OR ADVISORY BODIES

Consultative Council 82 seats

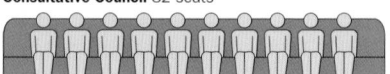

There are no political parties. The members of the Consultative Council (Majlis al-Shoura) were directly elected for the first time in 2000 by electoral committees in each province, and included two women.

Sultan Qaboos, ruler since 1970, is an authoritarian but paternalistic monarch. He is head of state, prime minister, and minister for foreign affairs, defense, and finance. Family members hold other key positions. Civil rights were enshrined in the 1996 Constitution. The regime faces no serious challenge, although Qaboos keeps a careful eye on the religious right wing. Qaboos has no immediate heirs, raising concern for the succession.

The Consultative Council was created in 1991, giving a semblance of democracy. Since 2000 its members have been directly elected. Major political issues include the planned privatization of medium-sized government projects, and improving Oman's self-defense capability.

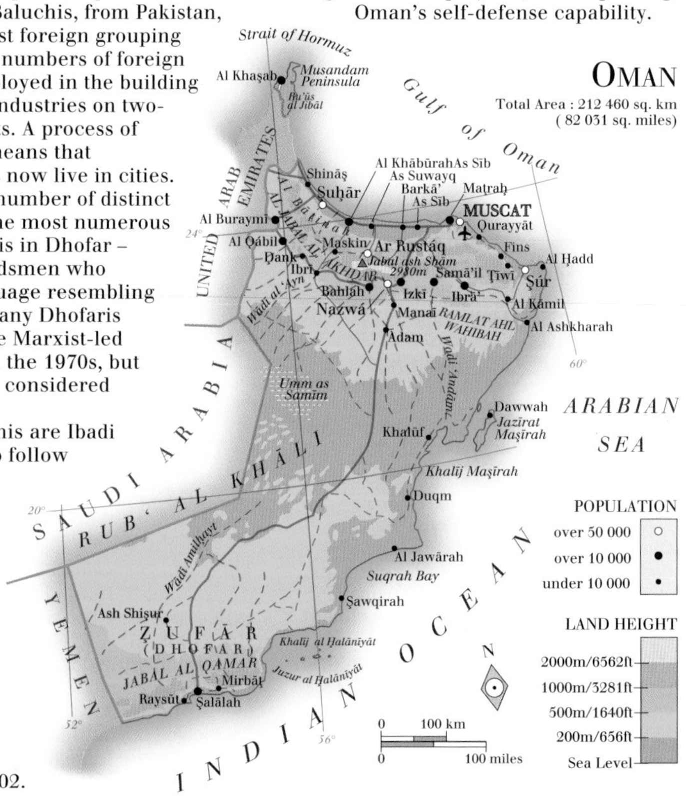

OMAN
Total Area : 212 460 sq. km (82 031 sq. miles)
Strait of Hormuz
Musandam Peninsula
Al Khaşab
Gulf of Oman
UNITED ARAB EMIRATES
Shināş
Şuḩār
Al Khābūrah
As Suwayq
As Sīb
Barkā'
Maţraḩ
MUSCAT
Qurayyāt
Al Buraymī
Al Qābil
Þank
Ibrī
Maskin
Ar Rustāq
Jabal ash Shām 2980m
Fins
Al Ḩadd
Samā'il
Ţīwī
Şūr
Bahlah
Izkī
Ibrā'
Al Kāmil
Nazwá
Manaḩ
RAMLAT AHL WAHIBAH
Al Ashkharah
Adam
Umm as Samīm
Dawwah
Jazirat Maşīrah
ARABIAN SEA
Khalūf
Khalīj Maşīrah
Duqm
SAUDI ARABIA
RUB' AL KHĀLĪ
Al Jawārah
Suqrah Bay
Shawqirah
Ash Shişur
ZUFĀR (DHOFAR)
JABAL AL QAMAR
Mirbāţ
Raysūt
Şalālah
YEMEN
INDIAN OCEAN
Khalīj al Ḩalānīyāt
Juzur al Ḩalānīyāt
0 100 km
0 100 miles
POPULATION
over 50 000
over 10 000
under 10 000
LAND HEIGHT
2000m/6562ft
1000m/3281ft
500m/1640ft
200m/656ft
Sea Level

WORLD AFFAIRS

Joined UN in 1971

AL | AMF | Damasc | GCC | OIC

Border disputes with the UAE were resolved in 1999. Relations with Israel were cut off after the outbreak of the Palestinian *intifada* in 2000. Oman has ties with Iran and called for easing sanctions against Iraq, but supported the US-led military actions in 1991 and 2003.

A watchtower above an oasis. *Most of Oman is gravelly desert. The only large area of cultivation is the 20-km-wide Al Batinah plain.*

CHRONOLOGY

The present Albusaidi dynasty has ruled in Oman since 1749.

- ❑ **1932** Sultan bin Taimur in power.
- ❑ **1951** Sovereignty recognized by UK.
- ❑ **1970** Sultan Qaboos bin Said seizes power from his father.
- ❑ **1975** Suppression of Dhofar revolt.
- ❑ **1991** Consultative Council set up.
- ❑ **2000** Consultative Council members elected for first time.

AID

Recipient

$2m (receipts) — Down 96% in 2001

Aid used to come mainly from the West, and particularly the US, but Japanese aid is now of greater significance. The UN is also a contributor. Oman makes occasional donations of its own to Arab and Muslim causes.

DEFENSE

No compulsory military service

$2.83bn — Up 35% in 2001

The UK is the main equipment supplier. Oman has provided communications and services to US and UK forces in their campaigns against Iraq. Oman's Defense Council, established in 1996, has replenished tanks, ships, and aircraft in recent years. Baluchi mercenaries supplement army strength.

EDUCATION

Schooling is not compulsory

73% — 19,297 students

Education has improved, but rural illiteracy is still high. Between 1996 and 2000, over 200 new schools were built.

HEALTH

Welfare state health benefits

1 per 730 people — Cerebrovascular and heart diseases, accidents

There is a policy of replacing expatriate medical staff with Omani nationals. Rural areas are served by clinics.

ECONOMICS

Inflation 1.8% p.a. (1990–2000)

$14.9bn — 0.385 Omani rials (0.385)

SCORE CARD

- ❑ WORLD GNP RANKING........................75th
- ❑ GNP PER CAPITA $6180
- ❑ BALANCE OF PAYMENTS....................$2.32bn
- ❑ INFLATION ....–1.1%
- ❑ UNEMPLOYMENT 5%

STRENGTHS

Oil industry, led by Royal Dutch/Shell: has benefited from staying out of OPEC and selling oil at spot prices without quotas. Exports of liquefied petroleum gas from new pipeline and terminal. Stable agriculture. Potential for sizable fishing industry.

WEAKNESSES

Overdependence on oil (90% of GNP), with fewer than 20 years' known reserves. Services sector could be better developed. Foreign workers needed in all economic sectors.

EXPORTS

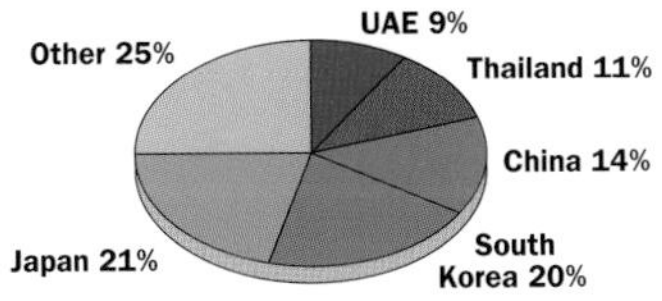
UAE 9%
Thailand 11%
China 14%
South Korea 20%
Japan 21%
Other 25%

IMPORTS

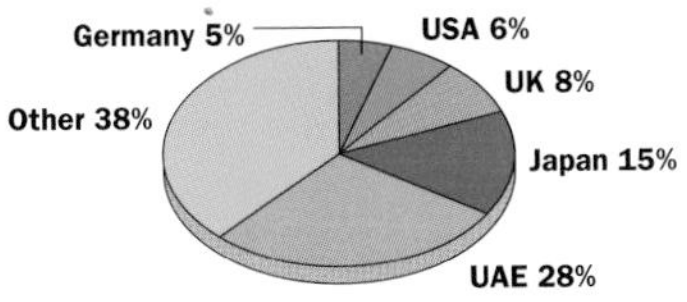
Germany 5%
USA 6%
UK 8%
Japan 15%
UAE 28%
Other 38%

RESOURCES

Electric power 2.4m kW

123,706 tonnes — 902,000 b/d (reserves 5.5bn barrels)

998,000 goats, 354,000 sheep, 3.4m chickens — Oil, natural gas, copper, chromite, marble, gypsum

The government invested $3 billion in 2003 in a number of projects to encourage diversification and cut down dependence on oil revenues.

ENVIRONMENT

Sustainability rank: 120th

13% — 7.9 tonnes per capita

Overpumping of groundwater causes seawater to seep into traditional irrigation areas. Nature reserves and antihunting laws protect rich wildlife.

MEDIA

TV ownership high

Daily newspaper circulation 29 per 1000 people

PUBLISHING AND BROADCAST MEDIA

There are 6 daily newspapers, including *Al-Watan, Oman Daily Newspaper*, and the English-language *Oman Daily Observer*

1 state-controlled service — 2 state-controlled services

Nothing critical of the government may be published in Oman, despite a 1984 law allowing for "freedom of opinion."

CRIME

Death penalty in use

2020 prisoners — Up 25% in 2000

Reckless driving by young Omani males is a problem. A "flying court" serves remote communities.

SPENDING

GDP/cap. increase

CONSUMPTION AND SPENDING

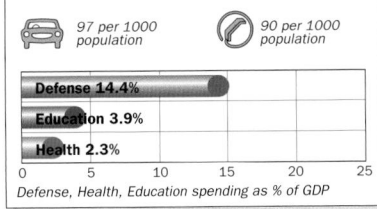

97 per 1000 population — *90 per 1000 population*

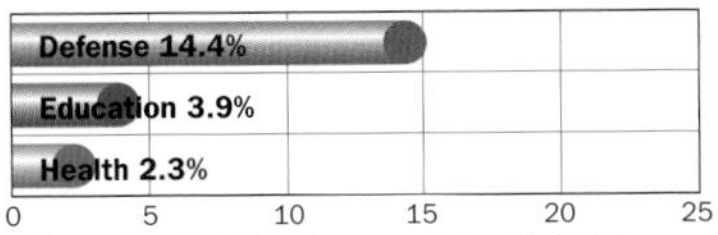
Defense 14.4%
Education 3.9%
Health 2.3%
0
5
10
15
20
25

Defense, Health, Education spending as % of GDP

Omanis in urban areas enjoy the same high living standards that are to be found in other Gulf states. Hunting trips to Pakistan are popular among the rich Omani elite, and a *khanjar*, a curved dagger, is seen as a status symbol.

WORLD RANKING

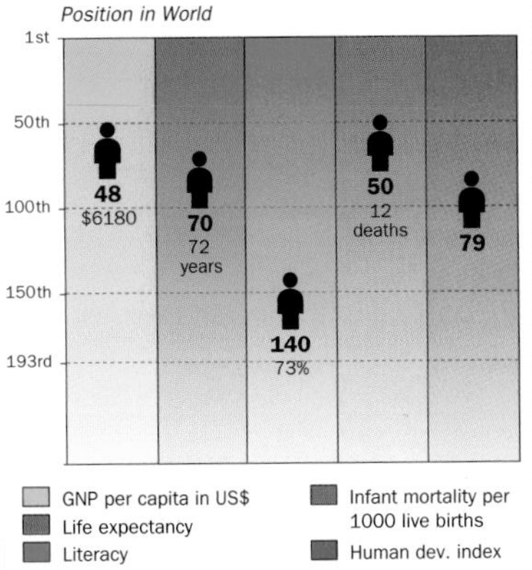
Position in World
1st
50th
100th
150th
193rd
48
$6180
70
72 years
140
73%
50
12 deaths
79
GNP per capita in US$
Life expectancy
Literacy
Infant mortality per 1000 live births
Human dev. index

PAKISTAN

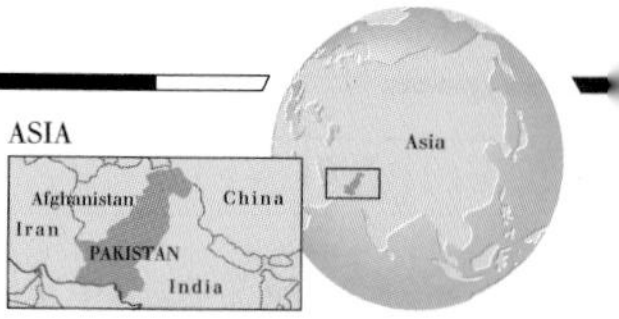
ASIA
Afghanistan
Iran
PAKISTAN
China
India
Asia

OFFICIAL NAME: Islamic Republic of Pakistan **CAPITAL:** Islamabad
POPULATION: 149 million **CURRENCY:** Pakistani rupee **OFFICIAL LANGUAGE:** Urdu

1947 | 1971 | March 23 | PK | +5 | +92 | .pk

ONCE A PART OF BRITISH INDIA, Pakistan was created in 1947 in response to the demand for an independent and predominantly Muslim Indian state. Initially the new nation included East Pakistan, present-day Bangladesh, which seceded from Pakistan in 1971. Eastern and southern Pakistan, the flood plain of the Indus River, is highly fertile and produces cotton, the basis of the large textile industry.

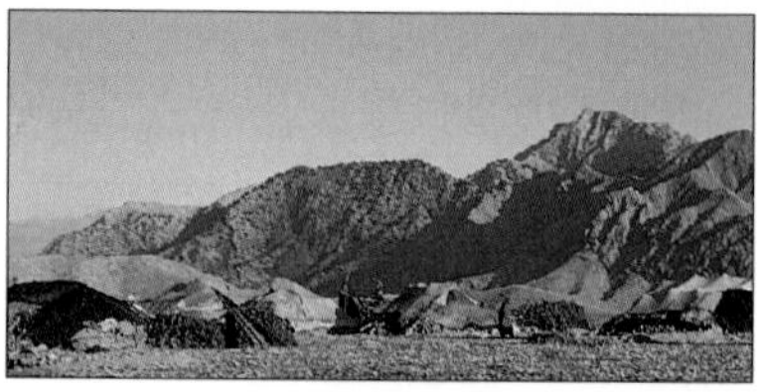

Barren landscape in Kachhi, Baluchistan. *This area of Pakistan has some of the highest May–September temperatures in the world.*

CLIMATE

Mountain/steppe/hot desert

WEATHER CHART FOR ISLAMABAD

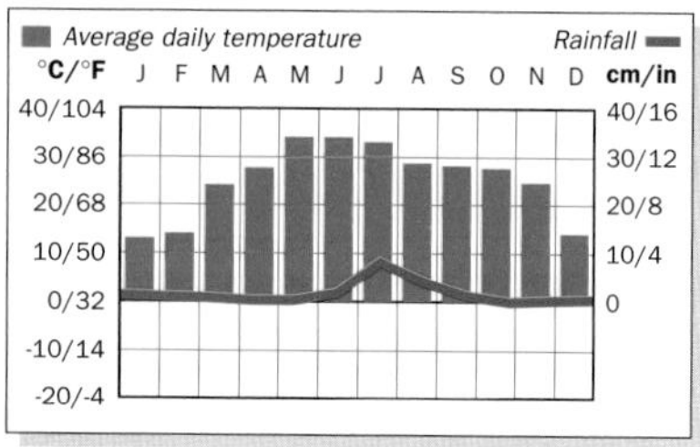
Average daily temperature
Rainfall
°C/°F
J F M A M J J A S O N D
cm/in
40/104
30/86
20/68
10/50
0/32
-10/14
-20/-4
40/16
30/12
20/8
10/4
0

Temperatures can soar to 50°C (122°F) in Sindh and Baluchistan and fall to –20°C (–4°F) in the northern mountains.

TRANSPORTATION

Drive on left

Karachi International 5.03m passengers

49 ships 247,400 grt

THE TRANSPORTATION NETWORK

141,252 km (87,770 miles)

339 km (211 miles)

7791 km (4841 miles)

None

Most roads are poorly maintained. A modern highway linking Islamabad and Lahore was inaugurated in 1997.

TOURISM

Visitors : Population 1:297

500,000 visitors

Down 10% in 2001

MAIN TOURIST ARRIVALS

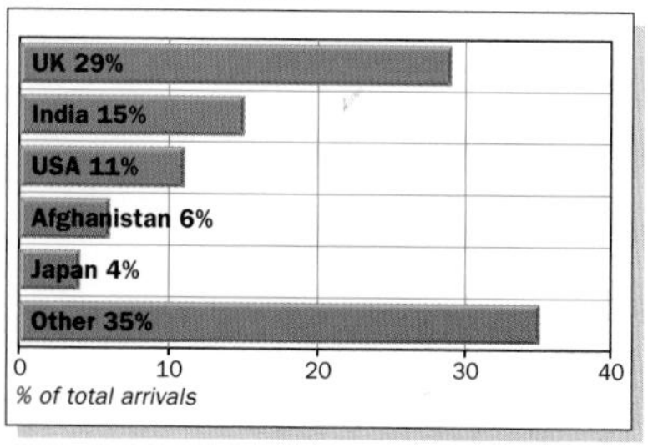
UK 29%
India 15%
USA 11%
Afghanistan 6%
Japan 4%
Other 35%
0
10
20
30
40
% of total arrivals

Relatively few tourists visit Pakistan, despite its rich cultural heritage and unspoiled natural beauty.

PEOPLE

Pop. density medium

Punjabi, Sindhi, Pashtu, Urdu, Baluchi, Brahui

193/km² (500/mi²)

THE URBAN/RURAL POPULATION SPLIT

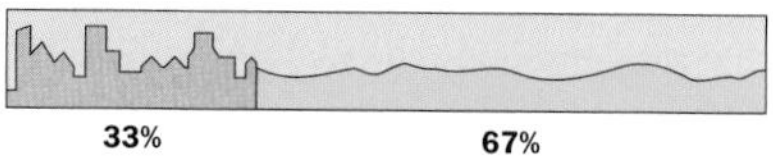
33%
67%

RELIGIOUS PERSUASION

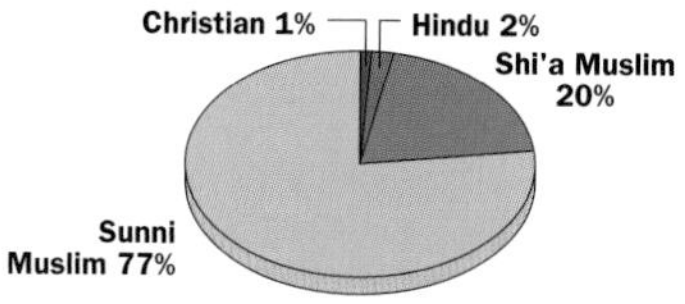
Christian 1%
Hindu 2%
Shi'a Muslim 20%
Sunni Muslim 77%

ETHNIC MAKEUP

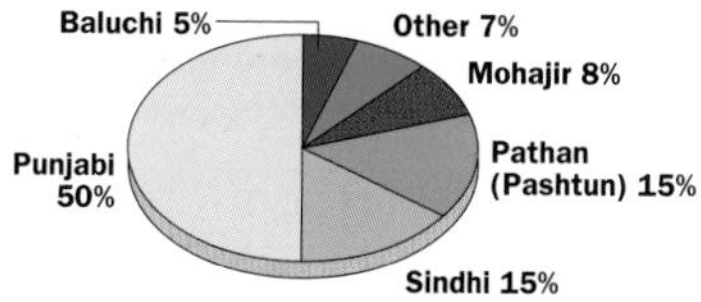
Baluchi 5%
Other 7%
Mohajir 8%
Pathan (Pashtun) 15%
Punjabi 50%
Sindhi 15%

Punjabis account for 50% of the population, while Sindhis, Pathans (Pashtuns), and Baluchi are also prominent. *Mohajirs* – Urdu-speaking immigrants from prepartition India – predominate in Karachi and Hyderabad. Punjabi political and military dominance of the centralized state has spawned many separatist and autonomy movements. Pathans have frequently threatened to establish a homeland with ethnic kin in Afghanistan. Tensions between the Baluchi and Pashtun refugees from Afghanistan sporadically erupt into violence, as do those between native Sindhis and immigrant *mohajirs.*

The gap between rich and poor, for example between the feudal landowning class and their serfs, is considerable. There is an expanding middle class of small-scale traders and manufacturers.

Recent years have witnessed a marked increase in Islamist militancy, accompanied by sectarian conflict between Sunnis and Shi'as and by growing discrimination against religious minorities. After the 1999 coup, the Musharraf regime trod a fine line in trying to avoid conflict with Islamist militants, both over issues such as the strict application of *sharia* (Islamic law) and over foreign policy.

The extended family is an enduring institution, and ties between its members are strong, reflected in the dynastic and nepotistic nature of the political system. Though some women hold prominent positions, and Benazir Bhutto has twice been prime minister, relatively few are allowed to work by their religiously conservative menfolk. Pakistan has one of the world's lowest ratios of females to males, implying widespread neglect and some female infanticide. Amnesty International has criticized Pakistan for its failure to give women's rights sufficient protection. Women's rights groups are mainly based in cities, and have made little overall impact.

POPULATION AGE BREAKDOWN

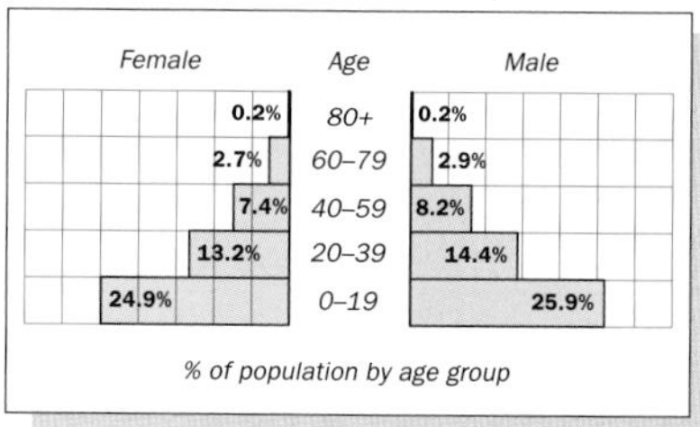
Female
Age
Male
0.2%
80+
0.2%
2.7%
60–79
2.9%
7.4%
40–59
8.2%
13.2%
20–39
14.4%
24.9%
0–19
25.9%
% of population by age group

IRAN
CHĀGAI HILLS
Hāmūn-i Māshkel
SANDY D
BALUC
SIĀHĀN
CENTRAL M
Turbat
Dasht Kaur
Gwādar
ARABIA

POLITICS

Multiparty elections

L. House 2002/2007
U. House 2003/2006

President Pervez Musharraf

AT THE LAST ELECTION

National Assembly
342 seats

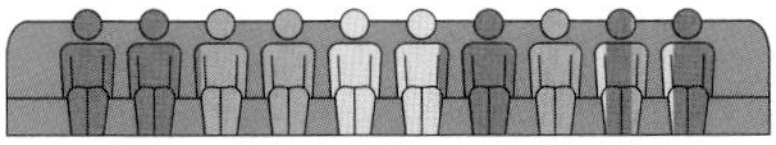
22% PML(Q)
18% PPP
18% W
13% MMA
8% Ind
4% NA
3% MQM
4% PML(N)
3% N-M
7% Others

PML(Q) = Pakistan Muslim League (Quaid-e-Azam)
PPP = Pakistan People's Party (Parliamentarians)
W = Women **MMA** = Muttahida Majlis-e-Amal
Ind = Independents **PML(N)** = Pakistan Muslim League (Nawaz) **NA** = National Alliance **N-M** = Non-Muslim minorities **MQM** = Muttahida Qaumi Movement

Senate 100 seats

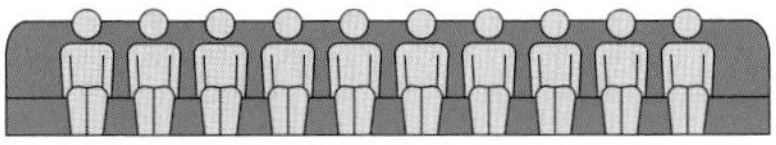

The Senate is indirectly elected. Seventeen seats are reserved for women

Multiparty democracy was suspended from 1999 to 2002, when a series of constitutional reforms was implemented. The military-dominated National Security Council advises the president.

PROFILE

Throughout the 1990s fragile coalitions had to rule in cooperation with the president and the army, and were hampered by a large bureaucracy. The popularity of the 1999 coup, which removed PML Prime Minister Nawaz Sharif, indicated the loss of respect for the country's much-abused democratic institutions. In 2001, coup leader Gen. Musharraf appointed himself president, and has since restored, and also enlarged, the post's constitutional powers. He faces intense opposition pressure to step down as head of the army.

The 2002 elections were won by the pro-Musharraf PML(Q), which outmaneuvered the PPP and the Islamist MMA to secure the appointment of Zafarullah Jamali as prime minister.

MAIN POLITICAL ISSUE
Militant Islam

Pressure to curb the ambitions of Islamists in Kashmir is balanced by the popularity in domestic politics of militant Islam, which has a powerful grip on the poor. In 2002 the MMA became the third-largest group in parliament, and in 2003 its North West Frontier Province government imposed *sharia* (Islamic law).

***Benazir Bhutto,** PPP leader and former prime minister.*

***Pervez Musharraf,** self-appointed president.*

WORLD AFFAIRS

Joined UN in 1947

IAEA | ECO | NAM | OIC | SAARC

In 1998, Pakistan carried out a series of nuclear tests in response to similar tests by India, provoking international condemnation and three years of US sanctions. The last of three wars between India and Pakistan was more than three decades ago, but their dispute over Kashmir has repeatedly stoked tensions. In late 2001–early 2002, attacks by Muslim Kashmiri separatists, allegedly supported by Pakistan, pushed the two countries again to the brink of war.

Since the fall of the *taliban* in Afghanistan, Pakistan has courted the US-installed interim regime. Central to relations is a potential gas pipeline bringing Turkmen gas to Pakistan. There are tensions, however, over support in Pakistan's northern regions for Islamist movements in Afghanistan.

Pakistan's membership of the Commonwealth was suspended after the 1999 coup.

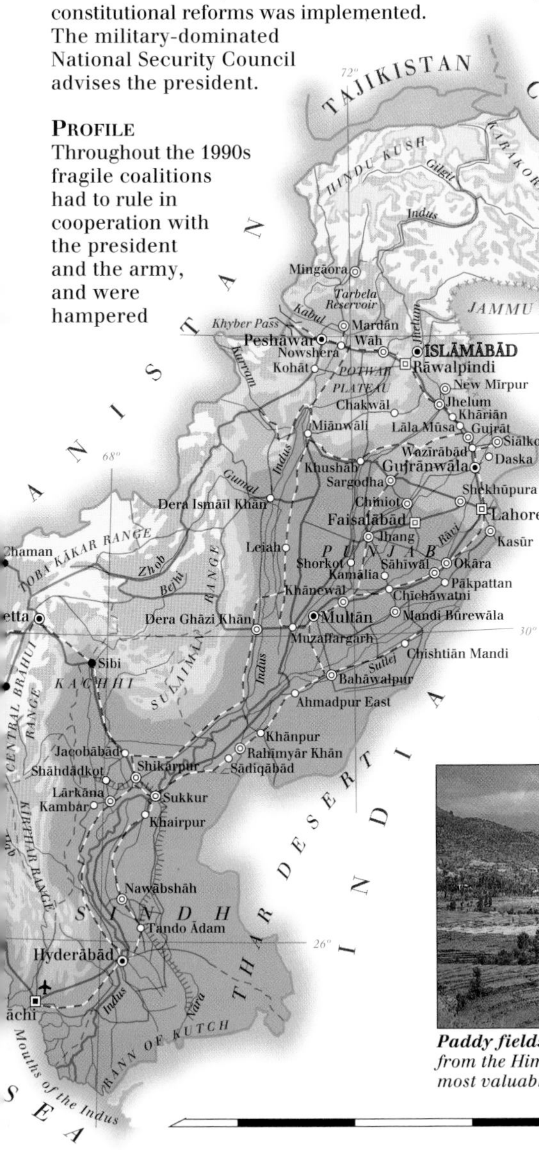
TAJIKISTAN
CHINA
AFGHANISTAN
INDIA
JAMMU AND KASHMIR
HINDU KUSH
KARAKORAM RANGE
Mt Godwin Austen (K2) 8611m
Gilgit
Indus
Mingāora
Tarbela Reservoir
Khyber Pass
Kabul
Mardān
Peshāwar
Nowshera
Wah
ISLĀMĀBĀD
Kohāt
Rāwalpindi
POTWAR PLATEAU
New Mīrpur
Chakwāl
Jhelum
Khāriān
Miānwāli
Lāla Mūsa
Gujrāt
Sialkot
Wazīrābād
Daska
Khushāb
Gujrānwāla
Sargodha
Shekhūpura
Dera Ismāil Khān
Chiniot
Lahore
Faisalābād
Jhang
Kasūr
Chaman
TOBA KAKAR RANGE
Zhob
Leiah
PUNJAB
Shorkot
Sāhiwāl
Okāra
Kamālia
Khānewāl
Pākpattan
Chīchāwatni
Dera Ghāzi Khān
Multān
Mandi Būrewāla
Muzaffargarh
SULAIMAN RANGE
Sibi
KACHHI
Sutlej
Chishtiān Mandi
Bahāwalpur
Ahmadpur East
CENTRAL BRAHUI RANGE
Khānpur
Jacobābād
Rahīmyār Khān
Shāhdādkot
Shikārpur
Sādiqābād
Lārkāna
Sukkur
Kambar
Khairpur
KIRTHAR RANGE
THAR DESERT
Nawābshāh
SINDH
Tando Ādam
Hyderābād
Nāra
RANN OF KUTCH
Mouths of the Indus
SEA
PAKISTAN
Total Area : 803 940 sq. km (310 401 sq. miles)
LAND HEIGHT
6000m/19 686ft
4000m/13 124ft
3000m/9843ft
2000m/6562ft
1000m/3281ft
500m/1640ft
200m/656ft
Sea Level
POPULATION
over 5 000 000
over 1 000 000
over 500 000
over 100 000
over 50 000
over 10 000
N
0 200 km
0 200 miles

***Paddy fields,** with monsoon rains threatening from the Himalaya mountains. Rice is the second most valuable agricultural export after cotton.*

CHRONOLOGY

From the 8th to the 16th centuries, Islamic rule extended to northwest and northeast India. Punjab and Sindh, annexed by the British East India Company in the 1850s, were ceded to the British Raj in 1857.

- **1906** Muslim League founded as organ of Indian Muslim separatism.
- **1947** Partition of India. Pakistan divided by 1600 km (994 miles) of Indian territory into East and West Pakistan. Millions displaced by large-scale migration. Muhammad Ali Jinnah first governor-general.
- **1948** First India–Pakistan war over Kashmir.
- **1949** New Awami League (AL) demands East Pakistan's autonomy.
- **1956** Constitution establishes Pakistan as an Islamic republic.
- **1958** Martial law. Gen. Muhammad Ayub Khan takes over; elected president two years later.

P

CHRONOLOGY *continued*

- **1965** Second India–Pakistan war over Kashmir.
- **1970** Ayub Khan resigns. Gen. Agha Yahya Khan takes over. First direct elections won by AL; West Pakistani parties reject results. War with India over East Pakistan.
- **1971** East Pakistan secedes as Bangladesh. PPP leader Zulfikar Ali Bhutto president.
- **1972** Simla (peace) Agreement with India.
- **1973** Bhutto, now prime minister, initiates Islamic socialism.
- **1977** General election. Riots over allegations of vote rigging. Gen. Zia ul-Haq stages military coup.
- **1979** Bhutto executed.
- **1986** Bhutto's daughter Benazir returns from exile to lead PPP.
- **1988** Zia killed in air crash. PPP wins general election.
- **1990** Ethnic violence in Sindh. President dismisses Benazir Bhutto. Nawaz Sharif of PML premier.
- **1991** Islamic *sharia* incorporated in legal code.
- **1992** Violence between Sindhis and *mohajirs* escalates in Sindh.
- **1993** President Khan and Prime Minister Sharif resign. Elections; Bhutto returns to power.
- **1996** President dismisses Bhutto.
- **1997** PML wins landslide election victory; Sharif prime minister.
- **1998** Nuclear tests.
- **1999–2000** Military coup. Sharif found guilty of treason.
- **2001** Parliament suspended, Gen. Musharraf appoints himself president. Pakistan key ally in US-led "war on terrorism."
- **2002** US and French nationals killed in terrorist attacks. Threat of war with India over Kashmir. October, PML(Q) wins elections. November, Zafarullah Jamali prime minister.

AID

Recipient

$1.94bn (receipts) | Up 176% in 2001

Pakistan is heavily dependent on aid, though the government has a long history of misdirecting aid payments. Aid intended for major projects has regularly been used to fund the current-account deficit. In mid-1998 the IMF agreed to help Pakistan meet its international debt obligations after the US and other Western aid donors cut off aid in protest against Pakistan's nuclear tests. The US subsequently agreed to resume aid, and boosted its support in late 2001 to reward the regime for supporting the "war on terrorism." Japan and Germany are among other main bilateral donors.

DEFENSE

No compulsory military service

$2.4bn | Down 5% in 2001

Pakistan has emerged as a significant regional arms trader. It established itself as a nuclear power by conducting a number of successful nuclear tests in 1998. Defense spending has a high priority, accounting for about a quarter of all government expenditure. The US, once the most important arms supplier, in 2001 lifted the sanctions imposed in 1990 and 1998. The army has been highly involved in politics throughout the period since independence, even when a military regime was not actually in power. Two years before the 1999 coup, its inclusion in a National Security Council assured it of a formal role in civilian decision-making.

Pakistan's army test-fired its own Prithvi surface-to-surface missile in March 2003.

PAKISTANI ARMED FORCES

2357 main battle tanks (PRC Type-59/69/85, M-47/48A5, T-54/55/80)	550,000 personnel
10 submarines, 8 frigates, 9 patrol boats	25,000 personnel
366 combat aircraft (52 Mirage 5, 42 Q-5)	45,000 personnel
Capability undisclosed; weapons tested in 1998	

ECONOMICS

Inflation 9.6% p.a. (1990–2001)

$60bn | 57.86 Pakistani rupees (60.01)

SCORE CARD

World GNP Ranking	44th
GNP per Capita	$420
Balance of Payments	–$1.11bn
Inflation	3.1%
Unemployment	6%

EXPORTS

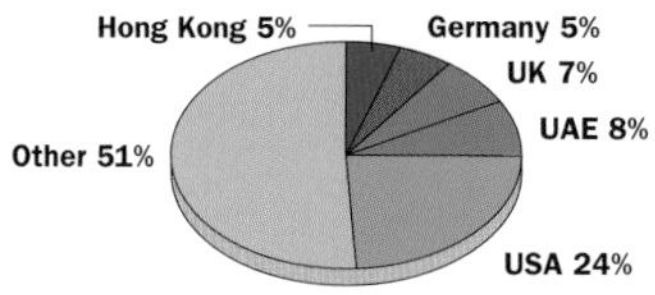
Hong Kong 5%
Germany 5%
UK 7%
UAE 8%
Other 51%
USA 24%

IMPORTS

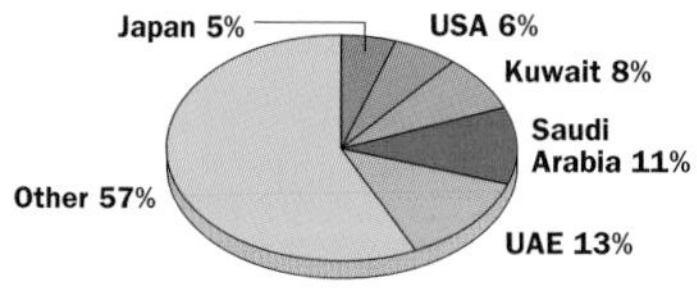
Japan 5%
USA 6%
Kuwait 8%
Saudi Arabia 11%
Other 57%
UAE 13%

Strengths
Gas, water, coal, oil. Substantial untapped natural resources. Low labor costs. Potentially huge market. One of the world's leading producers of cotton and a major exporter of rice.

Weaknesses
Production of cotton and rice vulnerable to weather conditions. History of inefficient and haphazard government economic policies. Weak and overstretched infrastructure.

Profile
Pakistan has yet to show progress in tackling its considerable economic problems. Though successive governments have reversed the nationalization policies instituted in the 1970s, private enterprise has been stifled by the rules of a massive bureaucracy. There is some foreign investment in previously state-only sectors such as banking, and water and other utilities. However, corruption at all levels of government undermined economic confidence throughout the 1990s, and it was particularly acute under the administration of Benazir Bhutto. Efforts by the military government to tackle corruption and poverty were praised by the World Bank in 2001. Defense spending remains high.

ECONOMIC PERFORMANCE INDICATOR

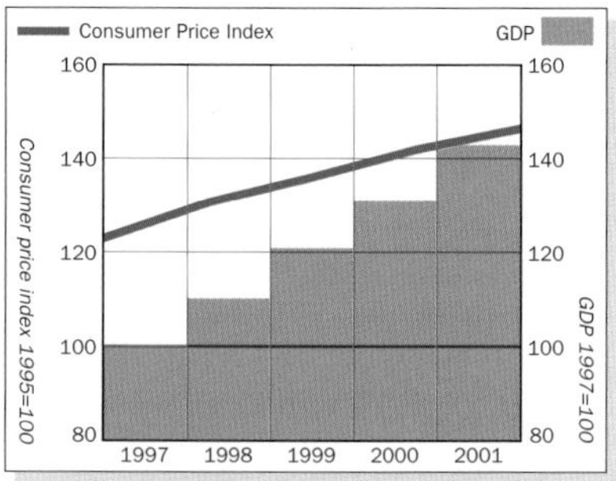
Consumer Price Index
GDP
160
140
120
100
80
Consumer price index 1995=100
GDP 1997=100
1997
1998
1999
2000
2001

PAKISTAN : MAJOR BUSINESSES

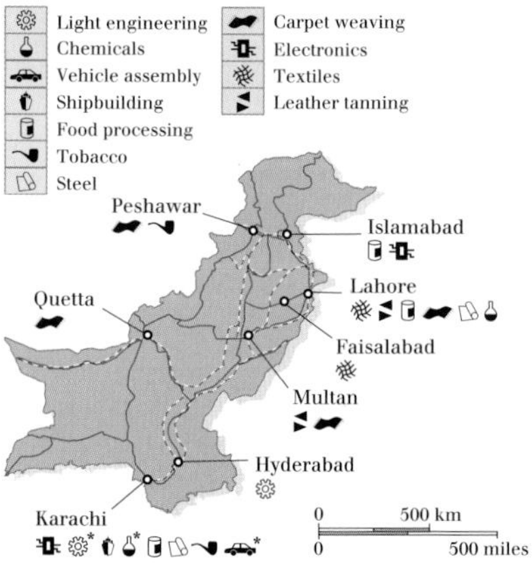
Light engineering
Chemicals
Vehicle assembly
Shipbuilding
Food processing
Tobacco
Steel
Carpet weaving
Electronics
Textiles
Leather tanning
Peshawar
Islamabad
Lahore
Quetta
Faisalabad
Multan
Hyderabad
Karachi
0
500 km
0
500 miles

* significant multinational ownership

RESOURCES

Electric power 15.7m kW

627,314 tonnes

53,754 b/d (reserves 216m barrels)

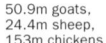

50.9m goats, 24.4m sheep, 153m chickens

Oil, natural gas, coal, limestone, salt, gypsum, silica sand

ELECTRICITY GENERATION

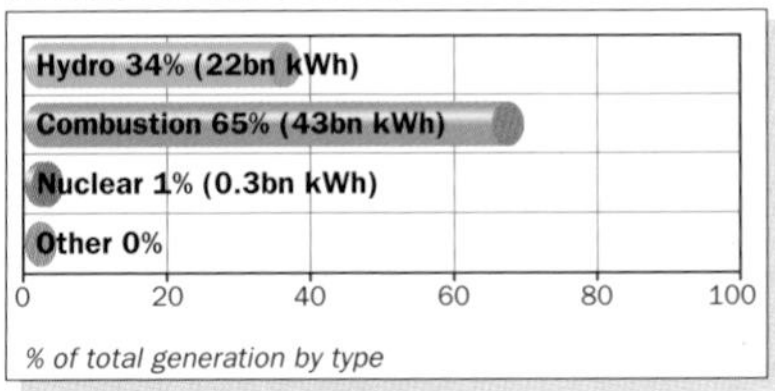

Hydro 34% (22bn kWh)
Combustion 65% (43bn kWh)
Nuclear 1% (0.3bn kWh)
Other 0%
0
20
40
60
80
100
% of total generation by type

Apart from cotton and rice, Pakistan's major resources are oil, coal, gas, and water. Oil-refining capacity is well below present demand. The French firm Total was awarded a $3 billion contract in 2003 to explore for offshore oil and gas.

Power theft is a problem, constituting a sizable proportion of the overall 30% power loss rate, and army units were assigned to investigate illegal connections in 1999. China agreed in 2003 to help build a second nuclear reactor at the existing Chashma plant.

PAKISTAN : LAND USE

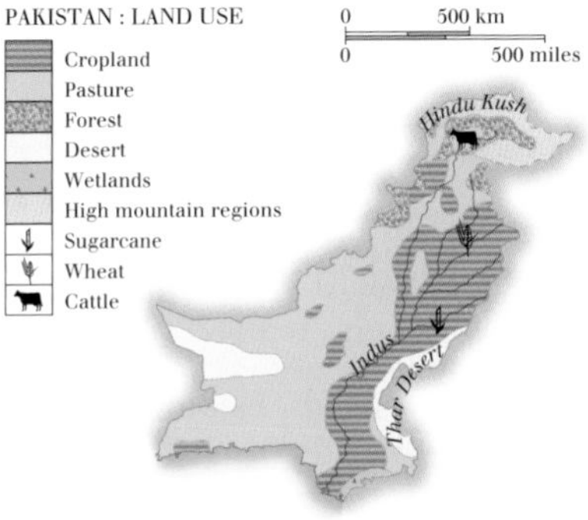

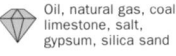

0
500 km
0
500 miles
Cropland
Pasture
Forest
Desert
Wetlands
High mountain regions
Sugarcane
Wheat
Cattle
Hindu Kush
Indus
Thar Desert

ENVIRONMENT

Sustainability rank: 112th

5% (4% partially protected)

0.7 tonnes per capita

ENVIRONMENTAL TREATIES

Yes Yes Yes

Yes Yes No

Tough measures are in force to curb illegal logging. Urban pollution affects many cities. Local groups increasingly voice environmental concerns.

MEDIA

TV ownership medium

Daily newspaper circulation 40 per 1000 people

PUBLISHING AND BROADCAST MEDIA

There are 264 daily newspapers. The best-selling paper is *Daily Jang*, published in Urdu

2 services: 1 state-owned, 1 state-controlled

3 services: 2 state-owned, 1 independent

Private broadcasts were licensed in 2003. Journalists who challenge official views are systematically harassed.

EDUCATION

Schooling is not compulsory

44%

1.14m students

THE EDUCATION SYSTEM

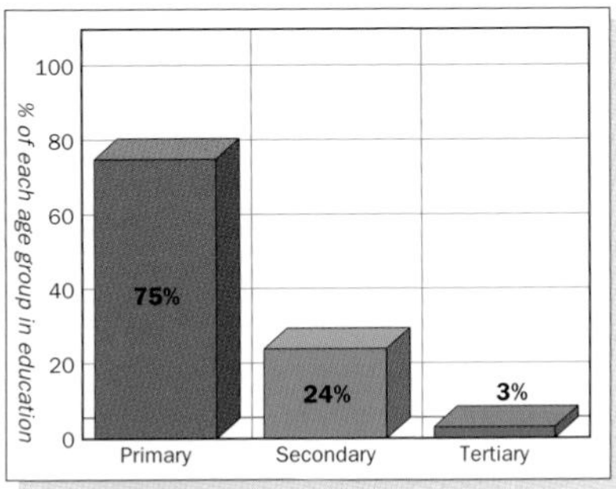

100
80
60
40
20
0
% of each age group in education
75%
24%
3%
Primary
Secondary
Tertiary

Though universal free primary education is a constitutional right, it is not compulsory. Literacy rates are among the lowest in the world. The education system is heavily Islamized, and weighted toward educating males: a large majority of children enrolled in primary schools are boys.

There are 26 universities, 853 arts and sciences colleges, and 308 professional colleges, all of which have a heavy preponderance of arts students. Wealthy parents frequently choose to send their children abroad for higher education, mainly to colleges in the UK or the US.

HEALTH

No welfare state health benefits

1 per 1471 people

Malaria, tuberculosis, diarrheal diseases

Availability of doctors and hospital beds is low, and there is a shortage of equipment and medicines. Uncontrolled counterfeit drugs are common. A specialized cancer hospital in Lahore, opened in 1995, offers modern facilities and advanced treatment. Pakistan has a high incidence of heroin addicts, due largely to its proximity to Afghanistan.

SPENDING

GDP/cap. increase

CONSUMPTION AND SPENDING

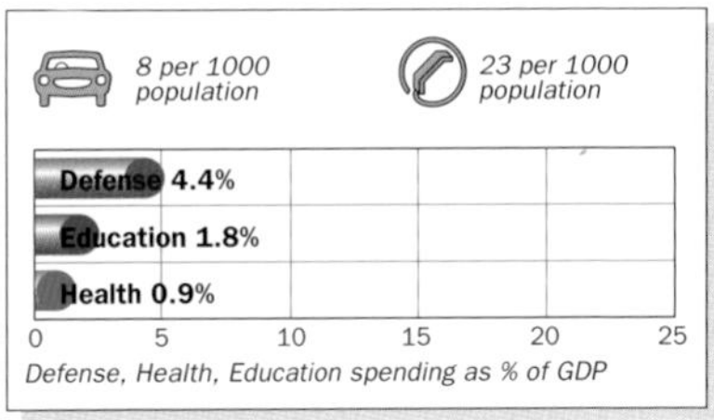

8 per 1000 population
23 per 1000 population
Defense 4.4%
Education 1.8%
Health 0.9%
0
5
10
15
20
25
Defense, Health, Education spending as % of GDP

Members of the bureaucratic and political elite tend to be extremely rich, as are some of the top military. Despite Pakistan's considerable economic potential, many people live below the poverty line.

P

CRIME

Death penalty in use

78,938 prisoners

Down 27% in 2000

CRIME RATES

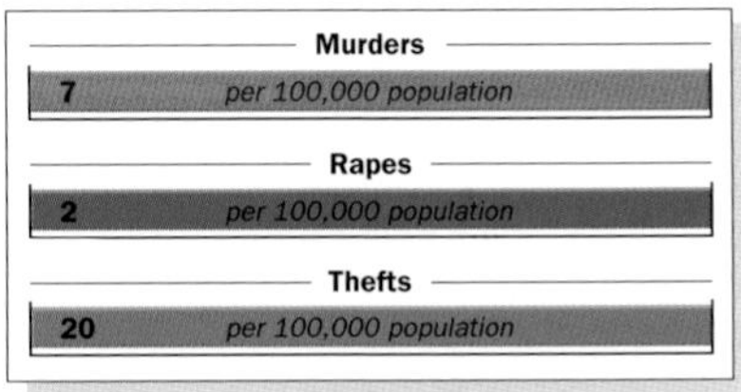

Murders
7 per 100,000 population
Rapes
2 per 100,000 population
Thefts
20 per 100,000 population

Compared with similar Islamic states, rates of murder, kidnapping, narcotics trafficking, rape, and robbery are high, though offical reporting of crime is low.

Corruption and the abuse of women are major causes for concern; reports of deaths or death threats for refusing to accept arranged marriages are rising. Torture and rape of prisoners and deaths in custody are frequent. The most dangerous area is Sindh: Karachi is terrorized by severe factional violence. Militant sectarian groups are also blamed for a recent rise in crime in Punjab. Special part-military courts were established in 2002 to combat terrorism and other "serious" crimes. The MMA provincial government of North West Frontier Province fulfilled its electoral promise to impose *sharia* (Islamic law) in 2003.

WORLD RANKING

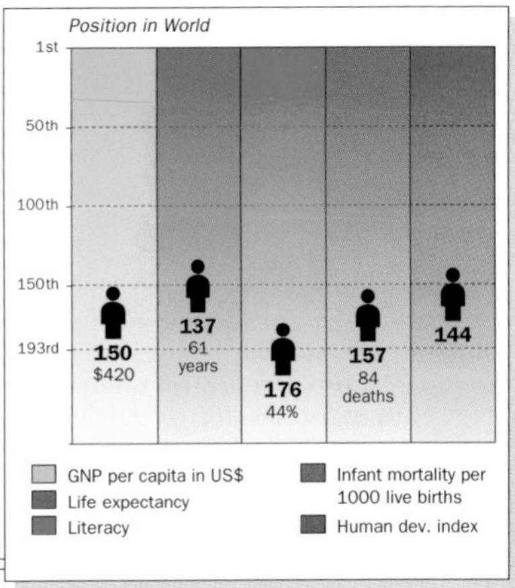

Position in World
1st
50th
100th
150th
193rd
150
$420
137
61
years
176
44%
157
84
deaths
144
GNP per capita in US$
Life expectancy
Literacy
Infant mortality per 1000 live births
Human dev. index

PALAU

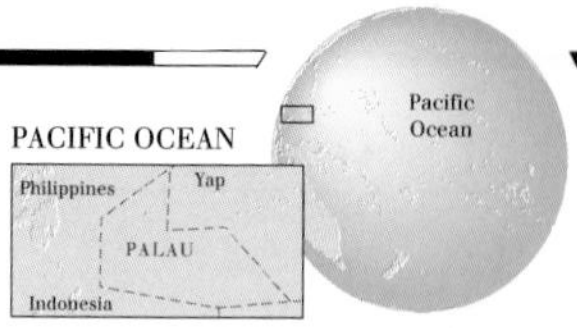
PACIFIC OCEAN
Pacific Ocean
Philippines
Yap
PALAU
Indonesia

OFFICIAL NAME: Republic of Palau **CAPITAL:** Koror
POPULATION: 19,409 **CURRENCY:** US dollar **OFFICIAL LANGUAGES:** Palauan and English

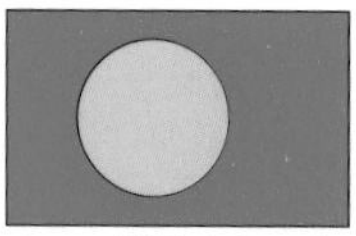

1994 | 1994 | Oct 1 | PAL | +9 | +680 | .pw

THE REPUBLIC OF PALAU (locally known as Belau) is situated in the western Pacific and comprises more than 300 islands in the Caroline Islands archipelago, only nine of which are inhabited. Formerly a part of the US-administered Trust Territory of the Pacific Islands, Palau became independent in association with the US in 1994, but continues to be heavily dependent on the US.

CLIMATE

Tropical oceanic

WEATHER CHART FOR KOROR

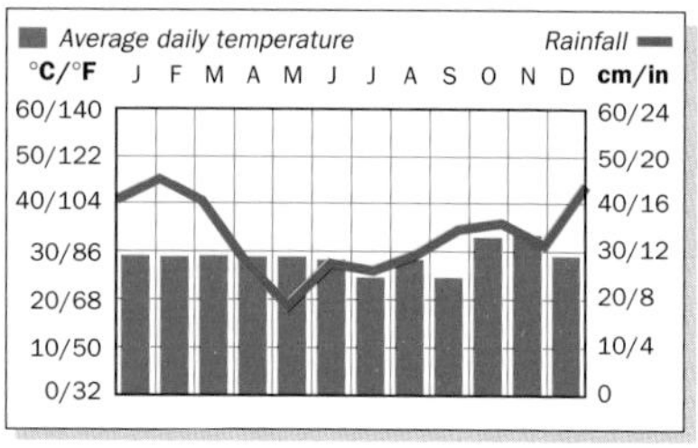
Average daily temperature
Rainfall
°C/°F J F M A M J J A S O N D cm/in
60/140 50/122 40/104 30/86 20/68 10/50 0/32
60/24 50/20 40/16 30/12 20/8 10/4 0

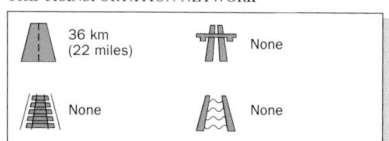

The islands are humid, with fairly constant temperatures and heavy rainfall all year round. The mean temperature is 27°C (81°F).

TRANSPORTATION

Drive on right

Palau International, Koror

Has no fleet

THE TRANSPORTATION NETWORK

36 km (22 miles)

None

None

None

There are limited air and sea links between islands. A new bridge, opened in 2002, connects Koror to Babelthuap.

TOURISM

Visitors : Population 3:1

59,000 visitors

Up 9% in 2002

MAIN TOURIST ARRIVALS

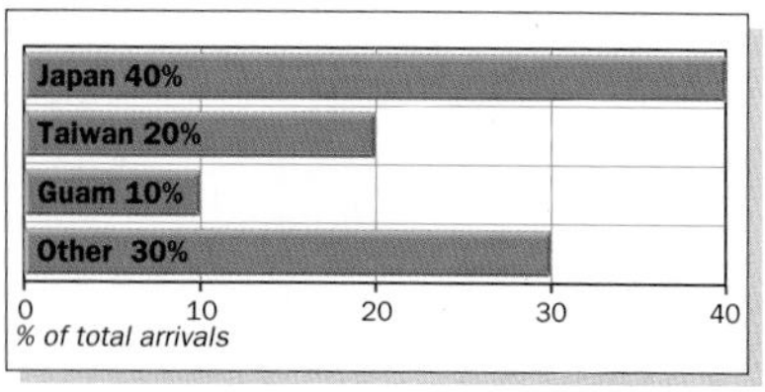
Japan 40%
Taiwan 20%
Guam 10%
Other 30%
0 10 20 30 40
% of total arrivals

Tourism is important, though there are concerns about its impact on traditional culture. Some islands have battle sites from the Pacific War. A drop in visitors in early 2003 was blamed on the outbreak in Asia of acute pneumonia (SARS).

PEOPLE

Pop. density low

Palauan, English, Japanese, Angaur, Tobi, Sonsorolese

38/km² (99/mi²)

THE URBAN/RURAL POPULATION SPLIT

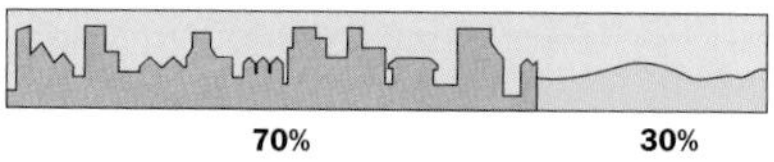
70%
30%

RELIGIOUS PERSUASION

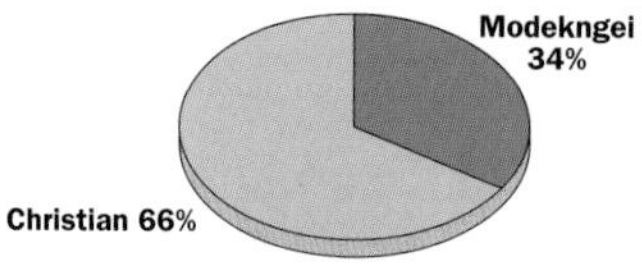
Modekngei 34%
Christian 66%

Palau was first colonized by southeast Asian peoples some 3000 years ago. There has also been mixing with other Melanesian and Polynesian peoples. The recent influx of migrants from Asia has raised tensions. Low-skilled Filipinos now make up over 16% of the population. Immigration from south Asia was explicitly banned in 2001.

Some 70% of Palauans live on the island city of Koror (a new capital is being constructed on neighboring Babelthuap). The thinly scattered remaining population are linguistically diverse, with distinct languages in the south. Cultural influence from the US and Japan has been strong, though traditional culture has been maintained on the more remote islands. Society remains largely matrilineal. The indigenous Modekngei religion is a blend of traditional beliefs and Christianity.

Palau's islands *have many idyllic beaches, but a lack of resources means that tourism remains underdeveloped.*

POLITICS

Nonparty elections

L. House 2000/2004
U. House 2000/2004

President Tommy Remengesau

AT THE LAST ELECTION

House of Delegates 16 seats

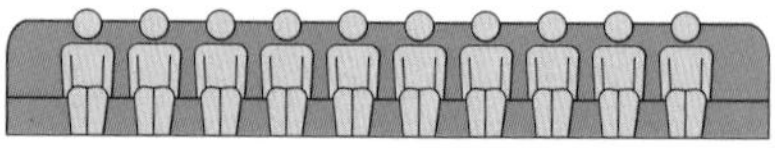

One member is elected to the House of Delegates to represent each of the 16 states

Senate 14 seats

The 14 senators represent geographical districts, according to population

Palau's independence was delayed until 1994, after a 1993 referendum had finally accepted the transit and storage of US nuclear materials as stipulated under the Compact of Free Association with the US. Vice President Tommy Remengesau was elected president in 2000. He has clashed with the legislature over control of the budget. Overcrowding in Koror and immigration are main issues.

WORLD AFFAIRS

Joined UN in 1994

PC | PIF | IBRD | ACP | IWC

The US has exclusive control over Palau's foreign affairs and defense policies under the conditions of the 1994 Compact of Free Association. Cordial relations with the Pacific Islands Forum were restored in 1999 after tensions caused by Palau's bid to give Japan the right to veto the establishment of a whale sanctuary in the South Pacific.

AID

Recipient

$34m (receipts)

Down 13% in 2001

Palau is heavily dependent on aid, which accounts for around 30% of GDP. Under the 15-year Compact of Free Association, signed with the US in 1994, Palau is set to receive up to $700 million in return for the use of military facilities. However, in recent years Japan has overtaken the US as the country's major donor.

DEFENSE

No compulsory military service

There are no armed forces

Not applicable

Under the 1994 Compact of Free Association, the US is responsible for Palau's defense.

P

ECONOMICS

Inflation 2.8% p.a. (1994–2001)

$132m

Currency is US dollar

SCORE CARD

- ❑ WORLD GNP RANKING........................187th
- ❑ GNP PER CAPITA $6780
- ❑ BALANCE OF PAYMENTS....................$17.2bn
- ❑ INFLATION 2.6%
- ❑ UNEMPLOYMENT 2%

STRENGTHS

Relationship with aid donors – US and Japan – provides economic stability and access to lucrative markets. Tourism industry growing. Transportation infrastructure improving. Fishing and copra production important. Increasing regional trade. Trust funds established from Compact money.

EXPORTS

Palau does not publish export figures by country

IMPORTS

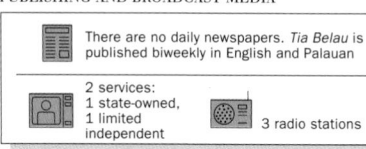

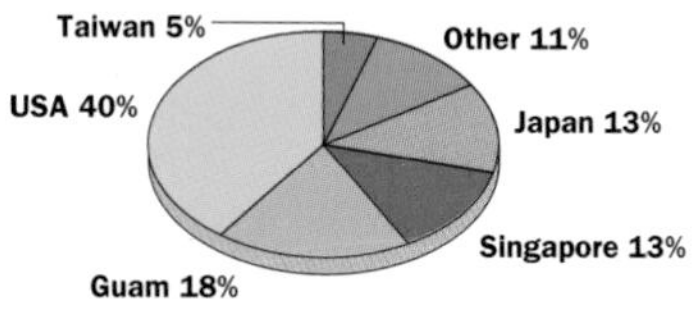
Taiwan 5%
Other 11%
USA 40%
Japan 13%
Singapore 13%
Guam 18%

WEAKNESSES

Heavy dependence on aid. Remote location. Underemployment. Poor transportation links between islands and to other countries. Few resources.

RESOURCES

Electric power 62,000 kW

2002 tonnes

Not an oil producer

Not available

Gold

On some islands the soil is highly fertile, though the terrain of the larger islands makes farming difficult. Some islands are densely forested. Palau has copra and some gold deposits. There is also the possibility of exploitation of reserves of minerals on the seabed. Palau has a small fishing industry with the potential for development.

ENVIRONMENT

Not available

8% (6% partially protected)

12.9 tonnes per capita

Palau suffers from inadequate facilities for the disposal of solid waste. Sand and coral dredging, and illegal fishing practices pose a significant threat to the marine ecosystem. Palau and its surrounding waters are Micronesia's richest habitat; however, there is concern about the commercial export of fruit bats to neighboring islands as a delicacy. Typhoons sometimes cause severe damage to infrastructure.

PALAU

Total Area : 458 sq. km (177 sq. miles)

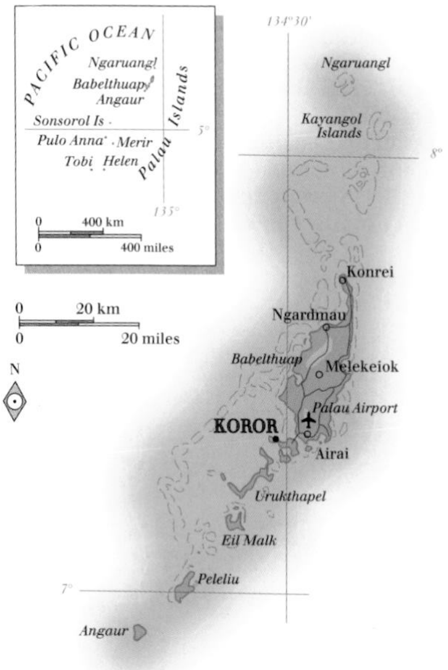
PACIFIC OCEAN
Ngaruangl
Babelthuap
Angaur
Sonsorol Is
Pulo Anna
Merir
Tobi
Helen
Palau Islands
400 km
400 miles
Ngaruangl
Kayangol Islands
Konrei
Ngardmau
Babelthuap
Melekeiok
Palau Airport
KOROR
Airai
Urukthapel
Eil Malk
Peleliu
Angaur
20 km
20 miles
N

MEDIA

TV ownership high

There are no daily newspapers

PUBLISHING AND BROADCAST MEDIA

There are no daily newspapers. *Tia Belau* is published biweekly in English and Palauan

2 services: 1 state-owned, 1 limited independent

3 radio stations

The country's TV and radio stations tend to deal in material which is largely derived from the US.

CRIME

No death penalty

Palau does not publish prison figures

Little change from year to year

There is a little alcohol-related crime, but much of the country, particularly the outlying islands, is crime-free.

EDUCATION

School leaving age: 14

98%

305 students

Elementary education is compulsory between the ages of six and 14. The Micronesian Occupational College, based in Palau, provides two-year training programs.

CHRONOLOGY

The Caroline Islands were colonized in turn by Spain, Germany, and Japan, coming under US control in 1945.

- ❑ **1947** UN Trust Territory of the Pacific Islands established.
- ❑ **1982** Compact of Free Association with US signed.
- ❑ **1993** Compact finally approved.
- ❑ **1994** Independence in free association with US.
- ❑ **2001** Tommy Remengesau takes office as president.

HEALTH

Welfare state health benefits

1 per 909 people

Cerebrovascular, heart, and intestinal diseases

Basic health care is available. Many outlying islands do not have easy access to qualified doctors and therefore often rely on nurses or traditional health remedies. An epidemic of mosquito-borne dengue fever hit Palau in 2000.

SPENDING

Not available

CONSUMPTION AND SPENDING

No data

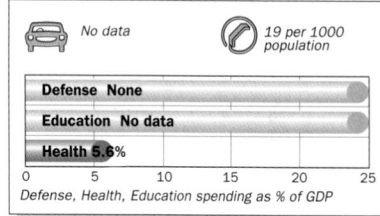

19 per 1000 population

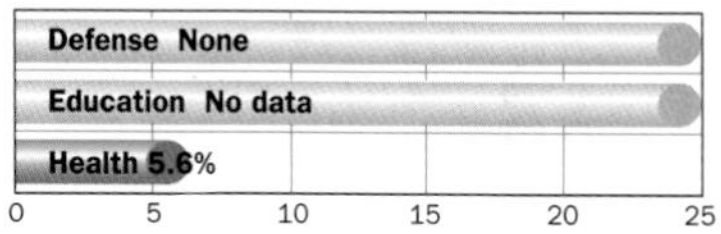
Defense None
Education No data
Health 5.6%
0
5
10
15
20
25

Defense, Health, Education spending as % of GDP

The gap between rich and poor is growing steadily, as entrepreneurs and government officials exploit aid and develop the tourist industry. In 2001, a program providing cheap rental housing for low-income families received a US grant of $200,000.

WORLD RANKING

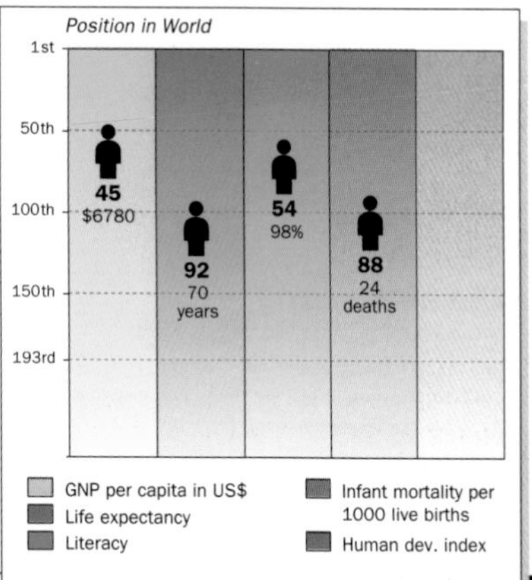
Position in World
1st
50th
100th
150th
193rd
45
$6780
92
70 years
54
98%
88
24 deaths
GNP per capita in US$
Life expectancy
Literacy
Infant mortality per 1000 live births
Human dev. index

P

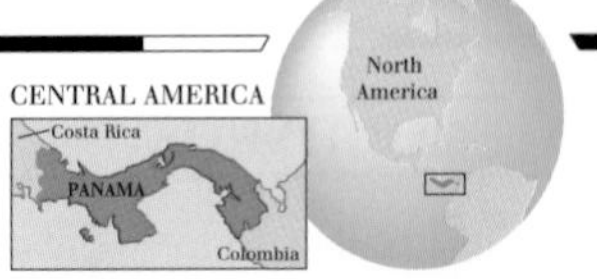
CENTRAL AMERICA
North America
Costa Rica
PANAMA
Colombia

PANAMA

OFFICIAL NAME: Republic of Panama **CAPITAL:** Panama City
POPULATION: 2.9 million **CURRENCY:** Balboa **OFFICIAL LANGUAGE:** Spanish

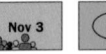

1903 | 1903 | Nov 3 | PA | -5 | +507 | .pa

PANAMA IS THE SOUTHERNMOST of the seven countries occupying the isthmus that joins North and South America. The rainforests of the southeastern Darien region are some of the wildest areas left in the Americas. Elected governments have held power since the US invasion of 1989. Panama's traditional economic strength is its banking sector. The US returned control of the Panama Canal Zone to Panama on December 31, 1999.

Cruise liner on the Panama Canal. The canal shortens the sea route between the east coast of the US and Japan by 4800 km (3000 miles).

CLIMATE

Tropical wet and dry

WEATHER CHART FOR PANAMA CITY

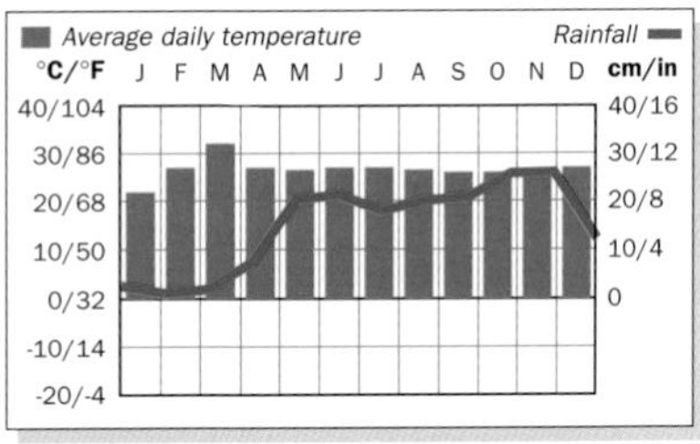
Average daily temperature
Rainfall
°C/°F
J F M A M J J A S O N D
cm/in
40/104
30/86
20/68
10/50
0/32
-10/14
-20/-4
40/16
30/12
20/8
10/4
0

Panama has a humid tropical climate; rainfall is twice as heavy on the Caribbean coast as on the Pacific coast.

TRANSPORTATION

Drive on right

Tocumen International, Panama City 898,000 passengers

6245 ships 122m grt

THE TRANSPORTATION NETWORK

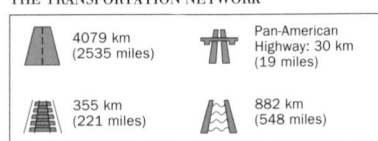

4079 km (2535 miles)

Pan-American Highway: 30 km (19 miles)

355 km (221 miles)

882 km (548 miles)

The 80-km (50-mile) Panama Canal cuts around two weeks off the voyage between the Atlantic and Pacific Oceans. Boats form the most convenient means of transportation for the coastal regions. Many roads are in disrepair.

TOURISM

Visitors : Population 1:5.4

534,000 visitors

Up 3% in 2002

MAIN TOURIST ARRIVALS

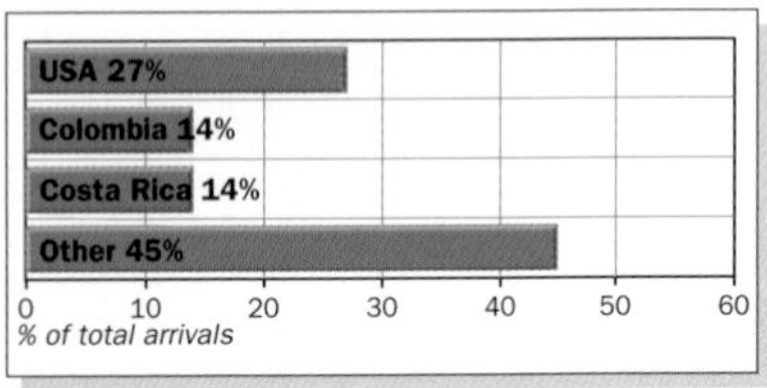
USA 27%
Colombia 14%
Costa Rica 14%
Other 45%
0
10
20
30
40
50
60
% of total arrivals

Portobelo and Panama City have old Spanish colonial buildings. In 2000, new cruise-ship facilities opened in Colón.

PEOPLE

Pop. density low

English Creole, Spanish, Amerindian languages, Chibchan

38/km² (99/mi²)

THE URBAN/RURAL POPULATION SPLIT

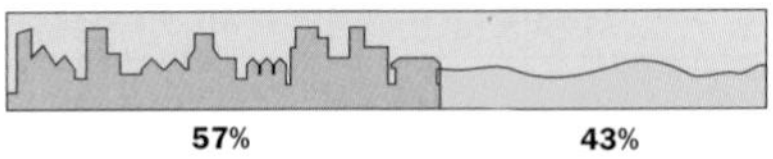
57%
43%

ETHNIC MAKEUP

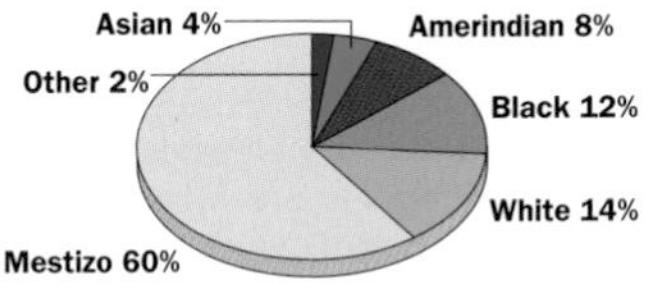
Asian 4%
Amerindian 8%
Other 2%
Black 12%
White 14%
Mestizo 60%

The northwest coast has a large black community, mostly descended from African immigrants who worked the plantations. The majority speak English Creole rather than Spanish. About 8% of the population are Amerindians mainly from the Guaymies, Chocoes, Kunas, and Ngobe-Buglé tribes. Roman Catholicism and the extended family remain strong, though the canal and the former US military bases have given society a cosmopolitan outlook.

PANAMA

Total Area : 78 200 sq. km (30 193 sq. miles)

POPULATION	LAND HEIGHT
over 500 000	2000m/6562ft
over 100 000	1000m/3281ft
over 50 000	500m/1640ft
over 10 000	200m/656ft
under 10 000	Sea Level

CARIBBEAN SEA
PACIFIC OCEAN
COSTA RICA
COLOMBIA
0 50 km
0 50 miles
N
Changuinola
Bocas del Toro
Almirante
Laguna de Chiriquí
Volcán Barú 3475m
Golfo de los Mosquitos
Chiriquí Grande
Río Sereno
Volcán
Boquete
La Concepción
David
Pedregal
Puerto Armuelles
Guabalá
Golfo de Chiriquí
Sona
Isla de Coiba
El Tigre de San Lorenzo
Isla Cébaco
Arenas
SERRANÍA DE TABASARÁ
Santa Fé
Santiago
Divisa
Aguadulce
Bahía de Parita
Monagrillo
Chitré
Las Tablas
Pocrí
Tonosí
PENÍNSULA DE AZUERO
Portobelo
Colón
Cristóbal
Lago Gatún
El Porvenir
Narganá
CORDILLERA DE SAN BLAS
Alcalde Díaz
Chepo
San Miguelito
Tocumen
PANAMA CITY
Arraiján
La Chorrera
Guadalupe
Balboa
El Copé
Penonomé
Bahía de Panamá
Punta Chame
Archipiélago de las Perlas
Isla del Rey
San Miguel
Golfo de San Miguel
La Palma
Yaviza
Ailigandí
Lago Bayano
SERRANÍA DEL DARIÉN
Golfo de Panamá
Istmo de Panamá

POLITICS

Multiparty elections

1999/2004

President Mireya Moscoso

AT THE LAST ELECTION
Legislative Assembly 71 seats

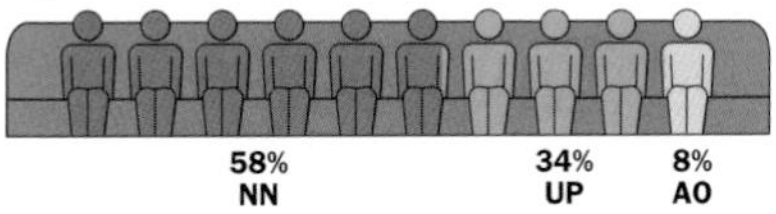
58%
NN
34%
UP
8%
AO

NN = New Nation (led by the Democratic Revolutionary Party–**PRD**) **UP** = Union for Panama (led by the Arnulfista Party–**PA**) **AO** = Action for the Opposition (led by the Christian Democratic Party–**PDC**)

In 1989, the US invaded Panama and arrested its ruler, Gen. Manuel Noriega, for narcotics smuggling. US forces installed the compliant Endara government, criticized for corruption. The 1994 presidential and legislative elections were won by Ernesto Pérez Balladares and the PRD, Noriega's old party, but the new government was largely pro-US and its economic reforms attracted widespread discontent. A 1998 referendum denied Pérez Balladares a second consecutive term. In 1999 opposition leader Mireya Moscoso of the PA was elected Panama's first woman president. Lacking a congressional majority until mid-2002, she struggled to address economic problems and meet promises to help the poor.

P

WORLD AFFAIRS

Joined UN in 1945

RG | Geplac | NAM | OAS | San José

The Canal Zone reverted to Panama on December 31, 1999, and US forces vacated their 14 military bases there.

Spillover from the Colombian civil war is a major concern. Border incidents have increased since 1999, and Panama is accused of involvement in arms and narcotics smuggling, and forced repatriations of Colombian refugees.

AID

Recipient

$28m (receipts)

Up 65% in 2001

The IDB pledged $3.3 million in 2000 to rehabilitate a former US base; Japan has loaned $1 million for the project.

DEFENSE

No compulsory military service

$132m

Up 2% in 2001

The National Guard and defense forces were disbanded in 1990 following the 1989 US invasion. They were replaced by the Panamanian Public Force, numbering some 11,800 and comprising the National Police, the National Air Service, and the National Maritime Service.

ECONOMICS

Inflation 1.9% p.a. (1990–2001)

$9.46bn

1 balboa (1)

SCORE CARD

❑ World GNP Ranking	87th
❑ GNP per Capita	$3260
❑ Balance of Payments	–$499m
❑ Inflation	0.3%
❑ Unemployment	13%

Strengths

Colón Free Trade Zone: second-largest in the world. Income from Canal. Financial services. Banana, shrimp exports. Merchant shipping payments for sailing under the Panamanian flag. Tourism potential.

Weaknesses

History of political instability and corruption. Large foreign debt. High unemployment, underemployment. Poor infrastructure.

EXPORTS

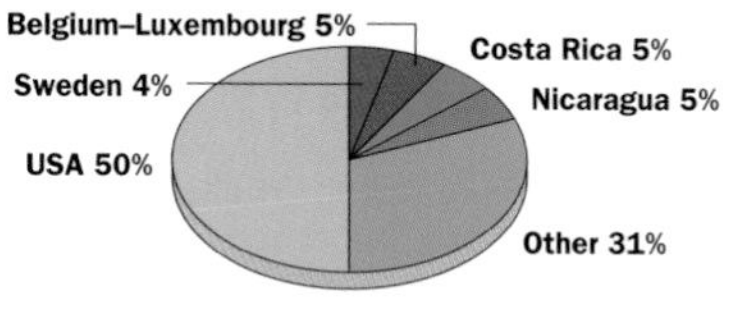
Belgium–Luxembourg 5%
Costa Rica 5%
Sweden 4%
Nicaragua 5%
USA 50%
Other 31%

IMPORTS

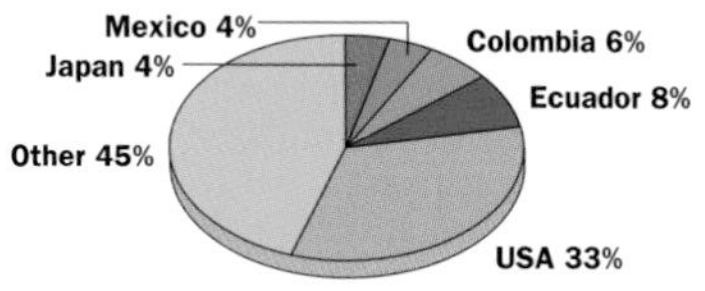
Mexico 4%
Colombia 6%
Japan 4%
Ecuador 8%
Other 45%
USA 33%

RESOURCES

Electric power 1.2m kW

225,896 tonnes

Not an oil producer; refines 45,900 b/d

1.53m cattle, 280,000 pigs, 14.1m chickens

Copper, coal, gold, silver, manganese, salt, clay

The Petaquilla area, west of the canal, has great copper and gold potential. To reduce the country's dependence on oil imports, the government has stepped up hydroelectric production; four state energy plants were privatized in 1999. Tropical hardwoods are being cut down at an alarming rate.

ENVIRONMENT

Sustainability rank: 17th

23% (2% partially protected)

2.9 tonnes per capita

The destruction of rainforests is proceeding at an increasingly rapid rate, resulting in widespread soil erosion. Large numbers of rare bird and animal species are threatened. Sewage from Panama City and Colón is discharged directly into coastal waters, canals, and ditches. Stretches of mangrove swamps are cut down for urban development, shrimp farms, and resorts.

MEDIA

TV ownership medium

Daily newspaper circulation 62 per 1000 people

PUBLISHING AND BROADCAST MEDIA

There are 8 daily newspapers, including *La Prensa* and *La Estrella de Panamá*

7 independent services

1 state-owned service, over 200 independent stations

A more independent press has flourished since Noriega's overthrow. Radio reaches the greatest number.

CRIME

No death penalty

8290 prisoners

Crime is rising

Panama City and Colón have high crime levels. Money laundering, narcotics trafficking, and corruption are rife.

EDUCATION

School leaving age: 11

92%

89,352 students

Schooling is based on the US model. Provision for the urban poor, blacks, and indigenous people is limited.

CHRONOLOGY

On independence from Spain in 1821, Panama was incorporated into Gran Colombia. Panama gained independence from Colombia with US support in 1903.

- ❑ **1903** US buys concession for Panama Canal.
- ❑ **1914–1939** Canal opens to traffic. US protectorate status ended.
- ❑ **1968–1981** Rule of Col. Torrijos Herrera.
- ❑ **1989** Indicted narcotics trafficker Gen. Noriega annuls elections to retain power. US invasion.
- ❑ **1994** PRD wins presidency and is largest party in parliament.
- ❑ **1999** PA's Mireya Moscoso elected first woman president. December, control of Canal Zone reverts from US to Panama.

HEALTH

Welfare state health benefits

1 per 855 people

Cancers, heart, cerebro-vascular, and infectious diseases, accidents

Primary health care is accessible to some two-thirds of the rural population. The isolation of many villages hinders efforts to improve the system.

SPENDING

GDP/cap. increase

CONSUMPTION AND SPENDING

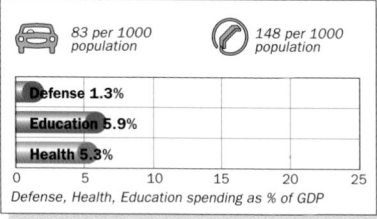

83 per 1000 population

148 per 1000 population

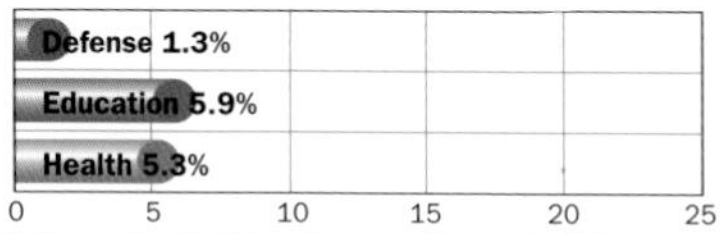
Defense 1.3%
Education 5.9%
Health 5.3%
0
5
10
15
20
25

Defense, Health, Education spending as % of GDP

Wealth disparities are large. Almost 30% of the population are estimated to live below the poverty line – clustered in the cities rather than in rural areas.

WORLD RANKING

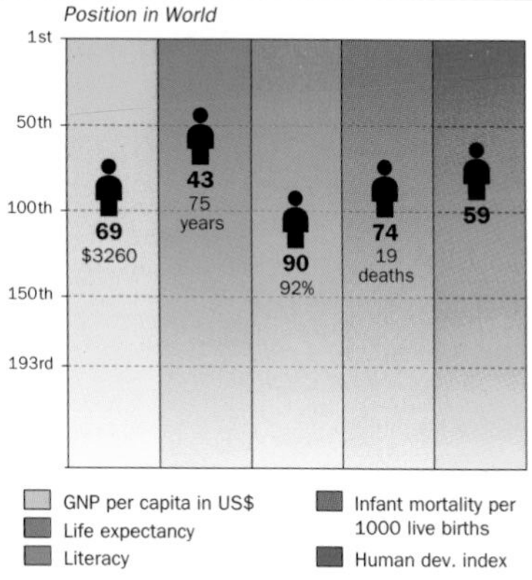
Position in World
1st
50th
100th
150th
193rd
69
$3260
43
75 years
90
92%
74
19 deaths
59
GNP per capita in US$
Life expectancy
Literacy
Infant mortality per 1000 live births
Human dev. index

P

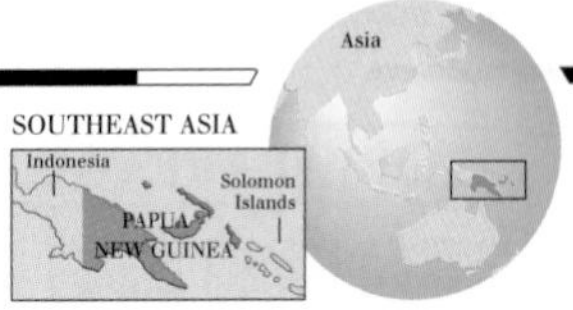
Asia
SOUTHEAST ASIA
Indonesia
Solomon Islands
PAPUA NEW GUINEA

PAPUA NEW GUINEA

OFFICIAL NAME: Independent State of Papua New Guinea **CAPITAL:** Port Moresby
POPULATION: 5 million **CURRENCY:** Kina **OFFICIAL LANGUAGE:** English

1975 | 1975 | Sept 16 | PNG | +10 | +675 | .pg

THE MOST LINGUISTICALLY diverse country in the world, with approximately 750 languages, Papua New Guinea (PNG) achieved independence from Australia in 1975. It occupies the eastern end of New Guinea, the world's third-largest island, and several other groups of islands. Much of the country is still isolated, and in rural areas living conditions are often basic. Bougainville has been promised autonomy.

CLIMATE

Tropical equatorial/monsoon

WEATHER CHART FOR PORT MORESBY

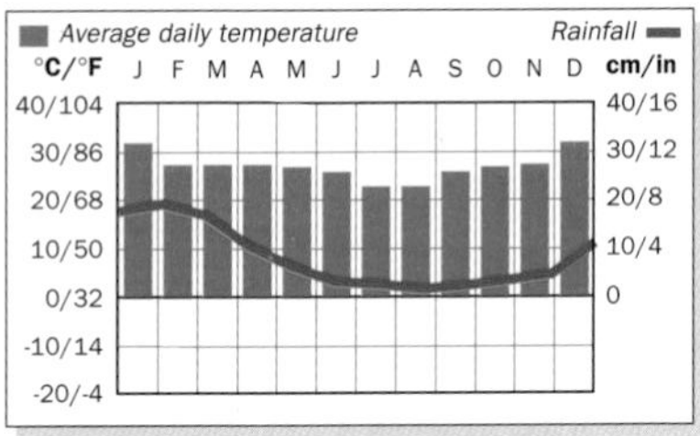
Average daily temperature
Rainfall
°C/°F
J F M A M J J A S O N D
cm/in
40/104
30/86
20/68
10/50
0/32
-10/14
-20/-4
40/16
30/12
20/8
10/4
0

Unvaryingly hot lowlands contrast with snow on Mount Victoria. Severe weather followed El Niño of 1997–1998.

TRANSPORTATION

Drive on left

Jacksons, Port Moresby
745,000 passengers

114 ships
77,000 grt

THE TRANSPORTATION NETWORK

686 km (426 miles)

None

None

10,940 km (6798 miles)

Infrastructure is improving with the construction and upgrading of major link roads, airports, and port facilities.

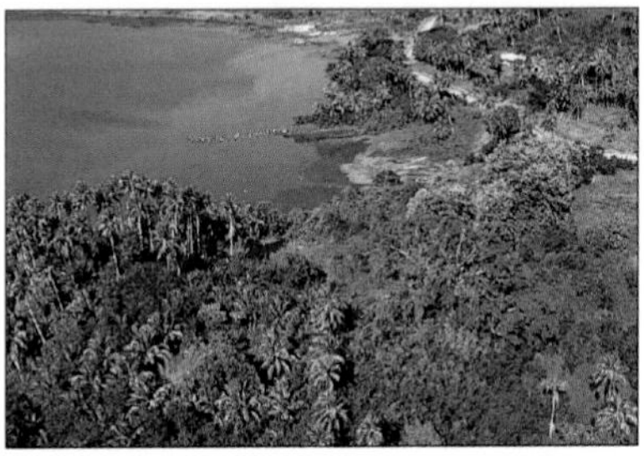

Papua New Guinea's 600 or so outer islands are mainly mountainous and volcanic, with lush vegetation and fringing coral reefs.

TOURISM

Visitors : Population 1:93

54,000 visitors

Down 7% in 2001

MAIN TOURIST ARRIVALS

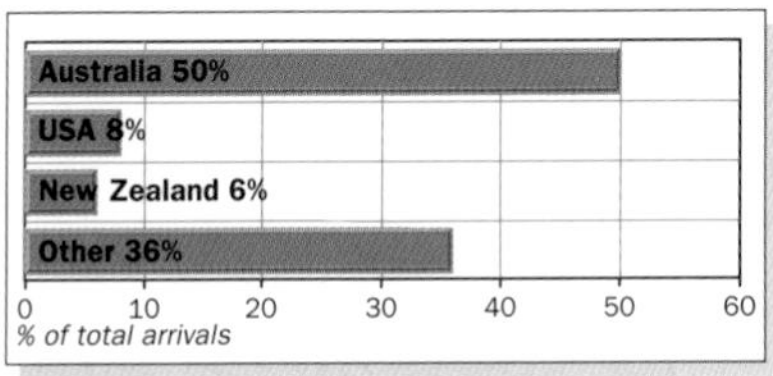
Australia 50%
USA 8%
New Zealand 6%
Other 36%
0
10
20
30
40
50
60
% of total arrivals

Tourism has great potential. However, it is hampered by the high rates of poverty-related violent crime, particularly in urban centers.

PEOPLE

Pop. density low

Pidgin English, Papuan, English, Motu, 750 (est.) native languages

11/km² (29/mi²)

THE URBAN/RURAL POPULATION SPLIT

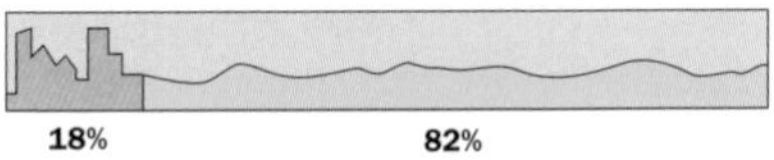
18%
82%

RELIGIOUS PERSUASION

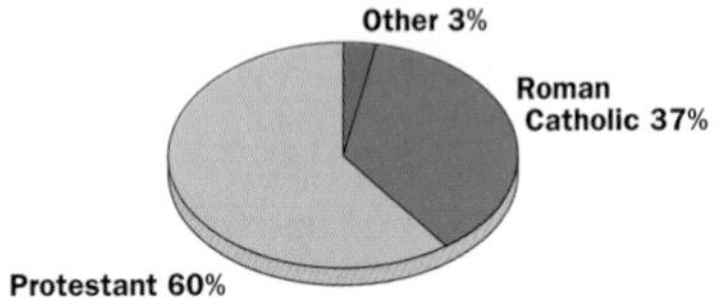
Other 3%
Roman Catholic 37%
Protestant 60%

PNG has an extraordinary diversity of peoples, with around 750 different languages and even more tribes. The key distinction is between the low-landers, who have frequent contact with the outside world, and the very isolated highlanders. Highland tribes see all strangers as potentially hostile. Vendettas can last for generations and tribal battles are not infrequent. A majority of people are nominally Christian, but indigenous beliefs and practices are widespread.

POLITICS

Multiparty elections

2002/2007

H.M. Queen Elizabeth II

AT THE LAST ELECTION
National Parliament 109 seats

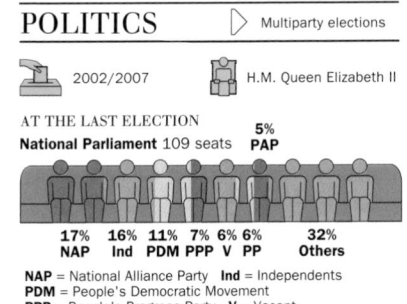

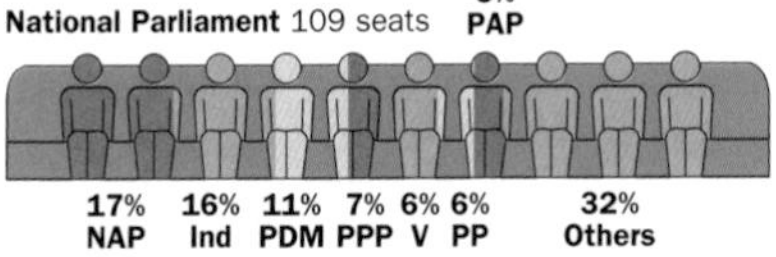
5%
PAP
17%
NAP
16%
Ind
11%
PDM
7%
PPP
6%
V
6%
PP
32%
Others

NAP = National Alliance Party **Ind** = Independents
PDM = People's Democratic Movement
PPP = People's Progress Party **V** = Vacant
PP = Pangu Pati **PAP** = People's Action Party

The many parties lack clear ideological foundations, creating long-term political instability. The patronage required to maintain coalitions bred corruption. A PDM-led government worked to overhaul the system, and claimed the first simple majority in 2001. However, the party was overshadowed in the 2002 elections by the NAP. Veteran NAP leader Sir Michael Somare returned as prime minister.

A ten-year insurgency by separatists on Bougainville ended with the 1998 cease-fire. Autonomy has been promised, along with a future referendum on independence. Elsewhere, strong local traditions and communications problems have made centralization difficult.

PAPUA NEW GUINEA

Total Area : 462 840 sq. km (178 703 sq. miles)

POPULATION
over 100 000
over 50 000
over 10 000
under 10 000
LAND HEIGHT
3000m/9843ft
2000m/6562ft
1000m/3281ft
500m/1640ft
200m/656ft
Sea Level
0 200 km
0 200 miles
N
NORTH PACIFIC OCEAN
INDONESIA (PAPUA)
Ninigo Group
Hermit Is
Manus I.
Lorengau
Mussau I.
ADMIRALTY ISLANDS
Ysabel Channel
BISMARCK ARCHIPELAGO
Kavieng
Vanimo
Aitape
Lumi
Wewak
Angoram
Sepik
BISMARCK SEA
New Ireland
Namatanai
Rabaul
New Guinea
CENTRAL RANGE
Karkar I.
Madang
Ramu
New Britain
GREEN IS
Buka I.
Ok Tedi
Sologomik
Porgera
Wabag
Mt Wilhelm 4509m
Arop I. Umboi
Vitiaz Strait
Pomio
Kimbe
Kiunga
Mendi
Mount Hagen
Kundiawa
Goroka
Lae
Kandrian
Bougainville Island
SOLOMON IS
Arawa
Kieta
Panguna
Buin
Lake Murray
Strickland
Kikori
Purari
Bulolo
Wau
Huon Gulf
Fly
Balimo
Kerema
SOLOMON SEA
OWEN STANLEY RANGE
Morehead
Gulf of Papua
Mt Victoria
Popondetta
KIRIWINA ISLANDS
Goodenough I.
Murua Island
Daru
PORT MORESBY
Torres Strait
Fergusson I.
D'ENTRECASTEAUX IS
Esa'ala
Great Barrier Reef
Kupiano
Alotau
Normanby I.
Samarai
CORAL SEA
LOUISIADE ARCHIPELAGO
Tagula I.
145°
150°
155°
5°
10°

WORLD AFFAIRS

Joined UN in 1975

APEC | Comm | NAM | PC | PIF

Accusations of PNG support for separatists in Papua, the neighboring Indonesian province, have strained relations. A pro-Taiwan policy, in return for aid funding, provoked Chinese anger in 1999.

AID

Recipient

$203m (receipts) | Down 26% in 2001

Australia is the major aid donor. The World Bank in 2000 endorsed government reforms with a $90 million loan.

DEFENSE

No compulsory military service

$27m | Down 13% in 2001

The army has expressed its doubts over political and economic reforms, most recently in a mutiny in March 2001.

ECONOMICS

Inflation 7.3% p.a. (1990–2001)

$3.03bn | 3.497 kina (3.977)

SCORE CARD

❑ World GNP Ranking	131st
❑ GNP per Capita	$580
Balance of Payments	$286m
❑ Inflation	9.3%
❑ Unemployment	8%

Strengths

Significant copper, gold, nickel, cobalt, oil, and natural gas reserves. Proposed gas pipeline between highlands and Australia expected to net annually $219 million. Agriculture sustains population.

Weaknesses

Agricultural production and mining prone to disruption from occasional drought. High spending: government close to bankruptcy in 2002. Poor transportation and banking infrastructures. Political instability. Foreign exploitation of resources.

EXPORTS

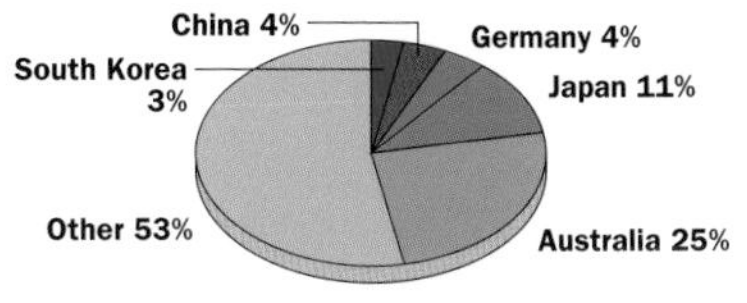
China 4%
Germany 4%
South Korea 3%
Japan 11%
Other 53%
Australia 25%

IMPORTS

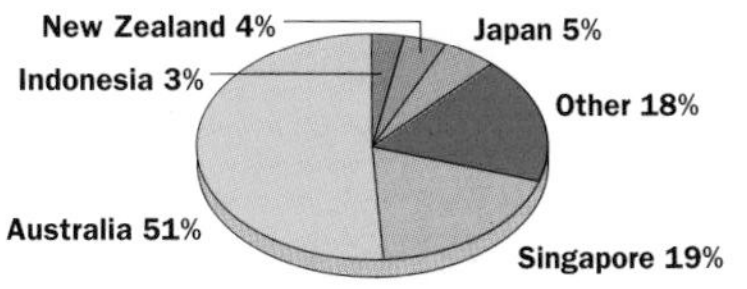
New Zealand 4%
Japan 5%
Indonesia 3%
Other 18%
Australia 51%
Singapore 19%

RESOURCES

Electric power 543,000 kW

50,556 tonnes | 46,000 b/d (reserves 200m barrels)

1.65m pigs, 89,000 cattle, 3.8m chickens | Copper, gold, silver, gas, oil, nickel, chromite, cobalt

PNG is rich in minerals. The Ok Tedi gold/copper mine in the Star Mountains is the most productive in the country; the Porgera gold mine is one of the world's largest. The severity of the 1998 drought significantly affected production at both. Prospecting has revealed extensive oil and natural gas reserves.

ENVIRONMENT

Sustainability rank: 51st

2% partially protected | 0.5 tonnes per capita

Deforestation and heavy-metal pollution are major issues. Cyanide poisoning from an Australian-owned mine in 2000 caused serious water pollution. Subduction of continental plates has forced the relocation of thousands of people from the more low-lying islands.

MEDIA

TV ownership low

Daily newspaper circulation 14 per 1000 people

PUBLISHING AND BROADCAST MEDIA

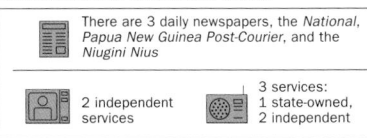

There are 3 daily newspapers, the *National*, *Papua New Guinea Post-Courier*, and the *Niugini Nius*

2 independent services | 3 services: 1 state-owned, 2 independent

The dismissal of the head of the National Broadcasting Commission in 2001 raised concerns over the freedom of the media.

CRIME

Death penalty not used in practice

3296 prisoners | Crime is rising

Violent crime by gangs of "Rascals" is very common. A cultural tradition of vendettas persists in rural communities.

EDUCATION

Schooling is not compulsory

65% | 9859 students

Education is not compulsory. Equipment charges and fees have been introduced. Universities are suffering funding cuts.

HEALTH

Welfare state health benefits

1 per 14,286 people | Malaria, pneumonia, diarrheal diseases, tuberculosis

The health system has suffered from recent cuts. HIV and tuberculosis co-infections are at crisis level. Life expectancy rates are among the lowest in the Pacific. Access to clean water and sanitation are major issues.

CHRONOLOGY

The British annexed the southeast and the Germans the northeast of the island of New Guinea in 1884.

- ❑ **1904** Australia takes over British sector; renamed Papua in 1906.
- ❑ **1914** German sector occupied by Australia.
- ❑ **1942–1945** Japanese occupation.
- ❑ **1964** National Parliament created.
- ❑ **1971** Renamed Papua New Guinea.
- ❑ **1975** Independence under Michael Somare, leader since 1972.
- ❑ **1988** Bougainville Revolutionary Army begins guerrilla campaign.
- ❑ **1997** El Niño causes severe drought and tsunamis. Prime Minister Julius Chan resigns over use of Western-led mercenaries in Bougainville.
- ❑ **2000** Loloata Understanding promises autonomy for Bougainville.
- ❑ **2001** PDM claims parliamentary majority. Final peace accord with Bougainville ratified after three-year cease-fire.
- ❑ **2002** NAP wins elections. Somare returns as prime minister.

SPENDING

GDP/cap. increase

CONSUMPTION AND SPENDING

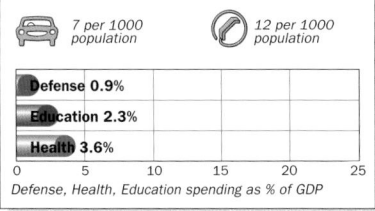

7 per 1000 population | *12 per 1000 population*

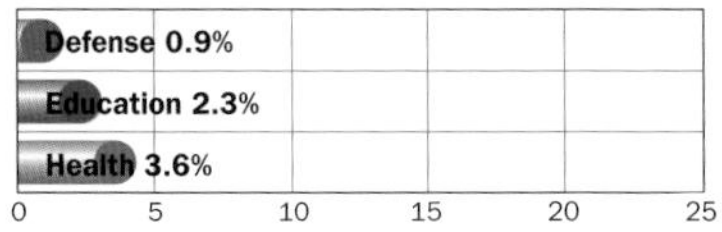
Defense 0.9%
Education 2.3%
Health 3.6%
0
5
10
15
20
25

Defense, Health, Education spending as % of GDP

There is a growing gap between rich and poor, particularly in urban areas. Spending on education and health was cut in 1998, when the kina dropped in value, but it was increased again in 2000, and the 2002 budget proposed the reintroduction of free schooling.

WORLD RANKING

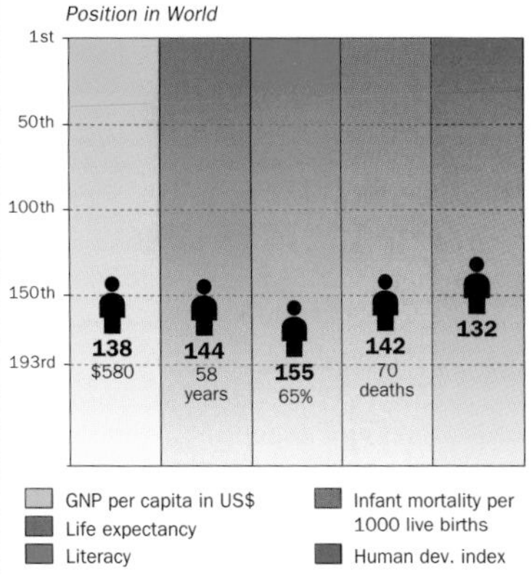
Position in World
1st
50th
100th
150th
193rd
138
$580
144
58 years
155
65%
142
70 deaths
132
GNP per capita in US$
Life expectancy
Literacy
Infant mortality per 1000 live births
Human dev. index

P

Paraguay

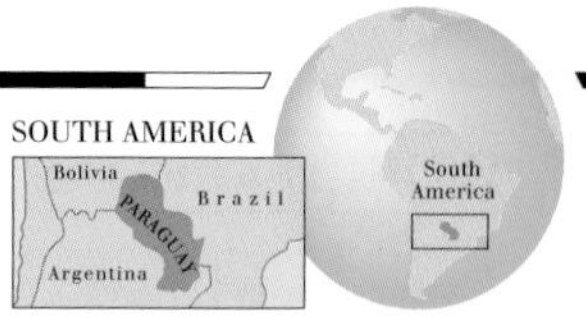
SOUTH AMERICA
Bolivia
PARAGUAY
Brazil
Argentina
South America

Official Name: Republic of Paraguay **Capital:** Asunción
Population: 5.8 million **Currency:** Guaraní **Official Language:** Spanish

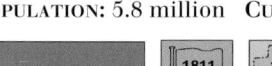

1811 | 1938 | May 14 | PY | -4 | +595 | .py

LANDLOCKED IN SOUTH America and a Spanish possession until 1811, Paraguay gained large tracts of land from Bolivia in 1938. From then until the overthrow in 1989 of Gen. Alfredo Stroessner, South America's longest-surviving dictator, it experienced periods of anarchy and military rule. The Paraguay River divides the eastern hills and fertile plains, where 90% of people live, from the almost uninhabited Chaco in the west. Paraguay's economy is largely agricultural.

CLIMATE

Tropical/subtropical

WEATHER CHART FOR ASUNCIÓN

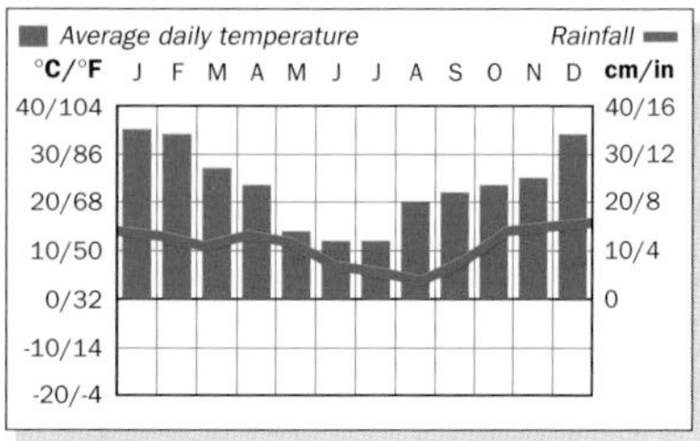
Average daily temperature
Rainfall
°C/°F
J F M A M J J A S O N D
cm/in
40/104
30/86
20/68
10/50
0/32
-10/14
-20/-4
40/16
30/12
20/8
10/4
0

Paraguay is subtropical, with all parts experiencing floods and droughts, but the Chaco is generally drier and hotter.

TRANSPORTATION

Drive on right

Silvio Pettirossi International, Asunción 465,664 passengers

44 ships 47,100 grt

THE TRANSPORTATION NETWORK

3067 km (1906 miles)

Pan-American Highway: 700 km (435 miles)

971 km (603 miles)

3100 km (1926 miles)

Roads badly need upgrading. The government wants to part-privatize the near-paralyzed FCCAL (railroad).

TOURISM

Visitors : Population 1:20

295,000 visitors

Up 33% in 2001

MAIN TOURIST ARRIVALS

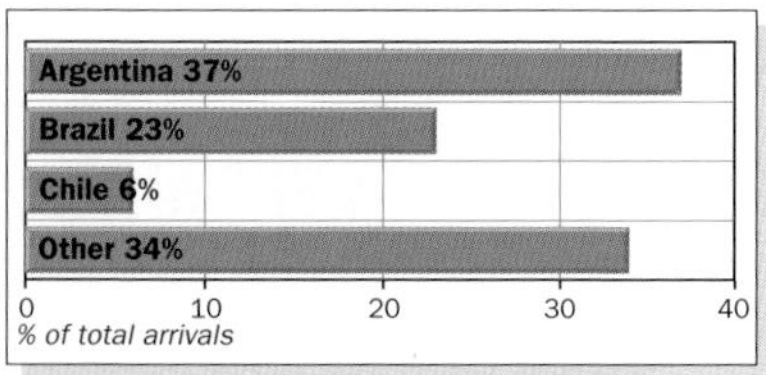
Argentina 37%
Brazil 23%
Chile 6%
Other 34%
0
10
20
30
40
% of total arrivals

Tourist numbers are small. Most visitors are cross-border day-trippers from Brazil and Argentina, who flock to Ciudad del Este to buy cheap, mainly Far Eastern, electrical goods. The Chaco attracts tourists for safaris.

PEOPLE

Pop. density low

Guaraní, Spanish

15/km² (38/mi²)

THE URBAN/RURAL POPULATION SPLIT

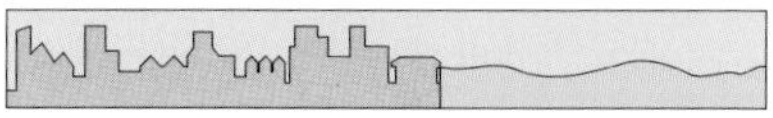
57%
43%

ETHNIC MAKEUP

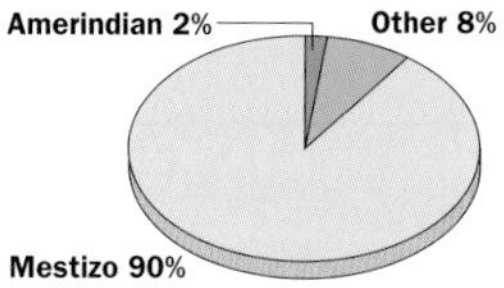
Amerindian 2%
Other 8%
Mestizo 90%

Most Paraguayans are of combined Spanish and native Guaraní origin. The majority are bilingual, though outside the large cities Guaraní is spoken almost exclusively. Rural Guaraní, deprived of ancestral lands, have been forced into marginal labor and prostitution. While most immigrants historically have been European, Japanese, Koreans, and South Africans are recent arrivals.

POLITICS

Multiparty elections

L. House 2003/2008
U. House 2003/2008

President Nicanor Duarte Frutos

AT THE LAST ELECTION

Chamber of Deputies 80 seats

13% UNACE
46% ANR–PC
26% PLRA
13% MPQ
2% PPS

ANR–PC = National Republican Association–Colorado Party **PLRA** = Authentic Radical Liberal Party **MPQ** = Beloved Fatherland Movement **UNACE** = National Union of Ethical Citizens **PPS** = Party of a United Country **PEN** = National Encounter Party

Senate 45 seats

4% PPS
36% ANR–PC
26% PLRA
16% MPQ
16% UNACE
2% PEN

A 1989 coup ended Gen. Stroessner's 34-year dictatorship. In 1993, his PC won the first free elections in 60 years, but with continued reliance on the military. Former army chief Gen. Lino Oviedo was pivotal to the country's instability, leading three failed coups between 1993 and 2000. He went into exile in 1999 after the assassination of his main opponent in the PC, Vice President Luis Argaña. Vice-presidential elections in 2000 created an unprecedented cohabitation between the PC president, Luis Gonzalez Macchi, and his PLRA deputy. Gonzalez Macchi's personal unpopularity failed to undermine the PC, whose candidate Nicanor Duarte Frutos won the presidency in 2003.

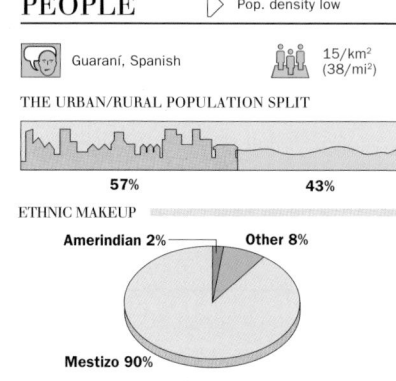

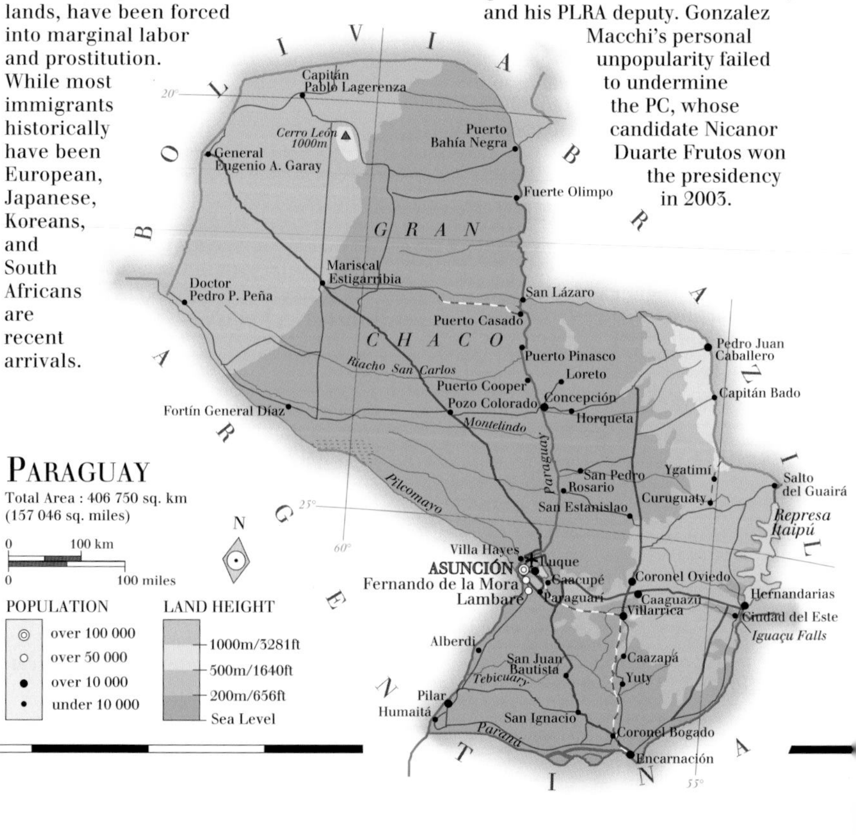
BOLIVIA
BRAZIL
ARGENTINA
Capitán Pablo Lagerenza
Cerro León 1000m
Puerto Bahía Negra
General Eugenio A. Garay
Fuerte Olimpo
GRAN CHACO
Mariscal Estigarribia
Doctor Pedro P. Peña
San Lázaro
Puerto Casado
Puerto Pinasco
Loreto
Pedro Juan Caballero
Riacho San Carlos
Puerto Cooper
Pozo Colorado
Concepción
Horqueta
Capitán Bado
Fortín General Díaz
Montelindo
Paraguay
Pilcomayo
San Pedro
Rosario
Ygatimí
Curuguaty
Salto del Guairá
San Estanislao
Represa Itaipú
Villa Hayes
ASUNCIÓN
Luque
Fernando de la Mora
Caacupé
Lambaré
Paraguarí
Coronel Oviedo
Caaguazú
Villarrica
Hernandarias
Ciudad del Este
Iguaçu Falls
Alberdi
San Juan Bautista
Tebicuary
Caazapá
Yuty
Pilar
Humaitá
San Ignacio
Paraná
Coronel Bogado
Encarnación
PARAGUAY
Total Area : 406 750 sq. km (157 046 sq. miles)
0 100 km
0 100 miles
POPULATION
over 100 000
over 50 000
over 10 000
under 10 000
LAND HEIGHT
1000m/3281ft
500m/1640ft
200m/656ft
Sea Level

WORLD AFFAIRS

Joined UN in 1945

IBRD | IAEA | Geplac | Mercosr | RG

The main aims are fairer integration in the Mercosur common market and good relations with the US.

AID

Recipient

$61m (receipts) — Down 26% in 2001

Japan offers most development aid; the IMF provides conditional loans. NGOs run small programs in rural areas.

DEFENSE

Compulsory military service

$76m — Down 16% in 2001

Under Stroessner, the military controlled political and economic life. In 1994–1995, Congress tried to limit its powers, but President Juan Carlos Wasmosy endorsed its political and institutional role. The pact between the military and the PC, in power since 1947, has been weakened by factionalism.

ECONOMICS

Inflation 12% p.a. (1990–2001)

$7.6bn — 6200 guaraníes (5845)

SCORE CARD

- ❑ WORLD GNP RANKING..........99th
- ❑ GNP PER CAPITA..........$1350
- ❑ BALANCE OF PAYMENTS..........–$207m
- ❑ INFLATION..........7.3%
- ❑ UNEMPLOYMENT..........16%

STRENGTHS

Electricity exporter – earnings obtain foreign exchange. Self-sufficiency in wheat and other staple foodstuffs. Cotton, oilseeds, notably soybeans.

WEAKNESSES

Reliance on agriculture and shaky Brazilian and Argentine markets. No hydrocarbons produced. Weak banking and financial sectors. High unemployment. Political instability deters foreign investment.

EXPORTS

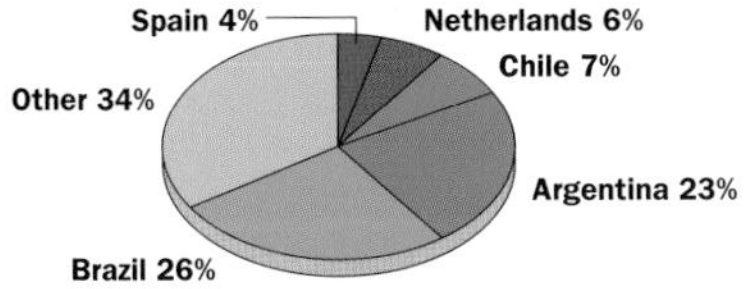
Spain 4%
Netherlands 6%
Chile 7%
Other 34%
Argentina 23%
Brazil 26%

IMPORTS

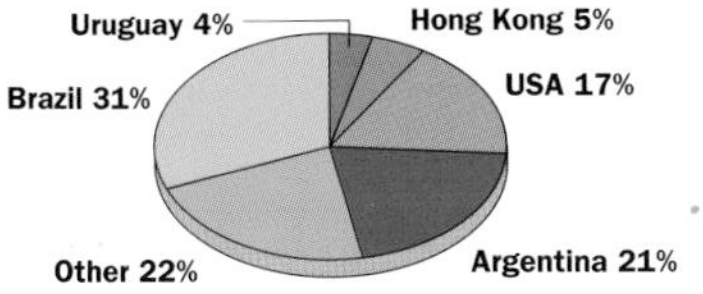
Uruguay 4%
Hong Kong 5%
Brazil 31%
USA 17%
Other 22%
Argentina 21%

The Iguaçu Falls, on the border with Brazil and Argentina, comprise over 20 cataracts, separated by rocks and tree-covered islands.

RESOURCES

Electric power 7.4m kW

25,103 tonnes — Not an oil producer; refines 2300 b/d

9.9m cattle, 2.75m pigs, 720,000 ducks, 15.5m chickens — Gypsum, marble, clay, kaolin, iron, manganese, uranium

The joint Paraguay–Brazil Itaipú hydroelectric dam is the world's largest. The massive Yacyretá Dam is operated with Argentina.

ENVIRONMENT

Sustainability rank: 25th

4% (0.1% partially protected) — 0.8 tonnes per capita

Apart from the destruction of forests for farming and for dams, a major ecological worry is the smuggling abroad of endangered species.

MEDIA

TV ownership medium

Daily newspaper circulation 43 per 1000 people

PUBLISHING AND BROADCAST MEDIA

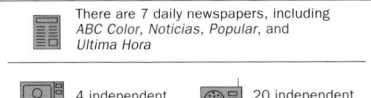

There are 7 daily newspapers, including *ABC Color, Noticias, Popular,* and *Ultima Hora*

4 independent services — 20 independent services

The media, historically sponsored by political parties, flourished after the fall of Stroessner, publishing details of corruption and abuses of human rights. The constitution nominally protects the rights of columnists to air their views.

CRIME

No death penalty

4088 prisoners — Up 10% in 2000–2001

Paraguay is the contraband capital of Latin America, with trade in everything from cars to cocaine. Jungle airstrips near Brazil provide a route for narcotics.

EDUCATION

School leaving age: 12

94% — 42,302 students

Education is compulsory only to the age of 12, and fewer than half of children go on to secondary school. Provision is limited in remote rural areas.

CHRONOLOGY

Paraguay was controlled by Spain from 1536 until 1811.

- ❑ **1864–1870** Loses War of the Triple Alliance against Argentina, Brazil, and Uruguay.
- ❑ **1928–1935** Two Chaco Wars against Bolivia over disputed territory.
- ❑ **1938** Boundary with Bolivia fixed; Paraguay awarded large tracts.
- ❑ **1954–1989** Rule of Gen. Stroessner: repressive military regime.
- ❑ **1993** First democratic elections.
- ❑ **1993–2000** Three coup attempts by Gen. Lino Oviedo.
- ❑ **1998–1999** Raúl Cubas elected president; resigns after assassination of vice president; Cubas and Oviedo leave country.
- ❑ **2003** Nicanor Duarte Frutos of PC wins presidency.

HEALTH

Welfare state health benefits

1 per 855 people — Cerebrovascular and heart diseases, cancers, infectious diseases

Hepatitis, typhoid, dysentery, and tuberculosis are endemic and leprosy is common. Medical care is expensive.

SPENDING

GDP/cap. increase

CONSUMPTION AND SPENDING

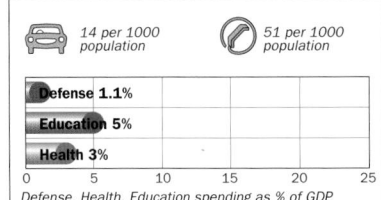

14 per 1000 population — *51 per 1000 population*

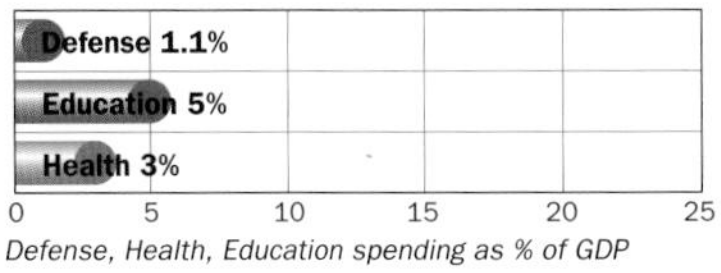
Defense 1.1%
Education 5%
Health 3%
0
5
10
15
20
25
Defense, Health, Education spending as % of GDP

Income inequality is great and rural poverty serious. Top military ranks, business leaders, and landed elites control wealth.

WORLD RANKING

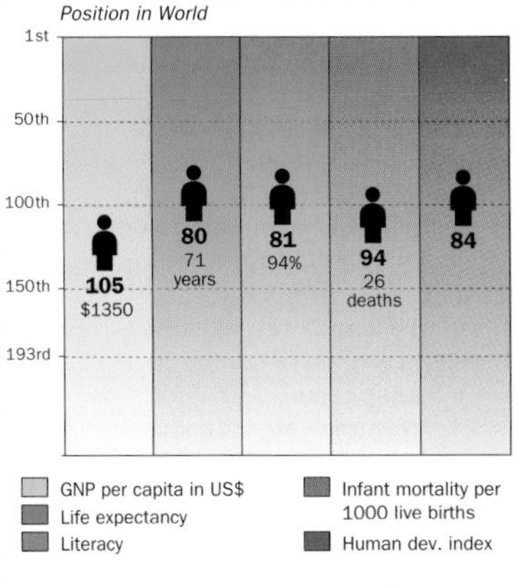
Position in World
1st
50th
100th
150th
193rd
105
$1350
80
71
years
81
94%
94
26
deaths
84
GNP per capita in US$
Life expectancy
Literacy
Infant mortality per 1000 live births
Human dev. index

P

PERU

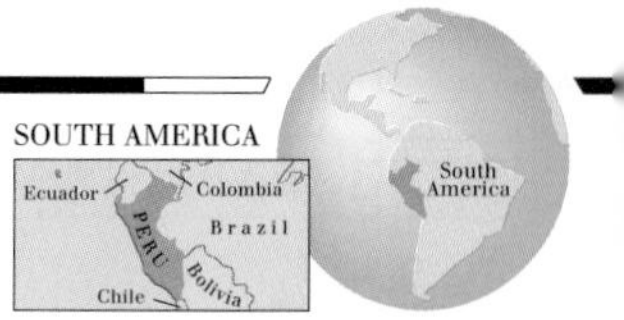
SOUTH AMERICA
Ecuador
Colombia
Brazil
PERU
Bolivia
Chile
South America

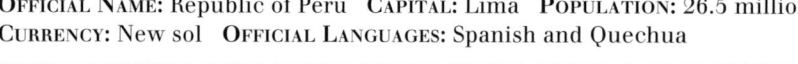

OFFICIAL NAME: Republic of Peru **CAPITAL:** Lima **POPULATION:** 26.5 million
CURRENCY: New sol **OFFICIAL LANGUAGES:** Spanish and Quechua

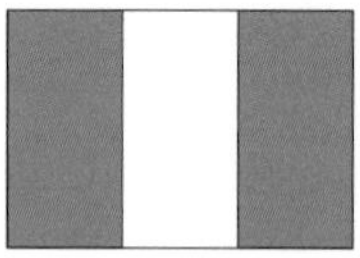

1824
1941
July 28
PE
-5
+51
.pe

LYING JUST SOUTH of the equator, on the Pacific coast of South America, Peru became independent of Spain in 1824. It rises from an arid coastal strip to the Andes, dominated in the south by volcanoes; about half of Peru's population live in mountain regions. Peru's border with Bolivia to the south runs through Lake Titicaca, the highest navigable lake in the world. In 1995, Peru was involved in a brief border war with Ecuador, its northern neighbor, and the issue was finally settled in 1998.

CLIMATE

Tropical/mountain/desert

WEATHER CHART FOR LIMA

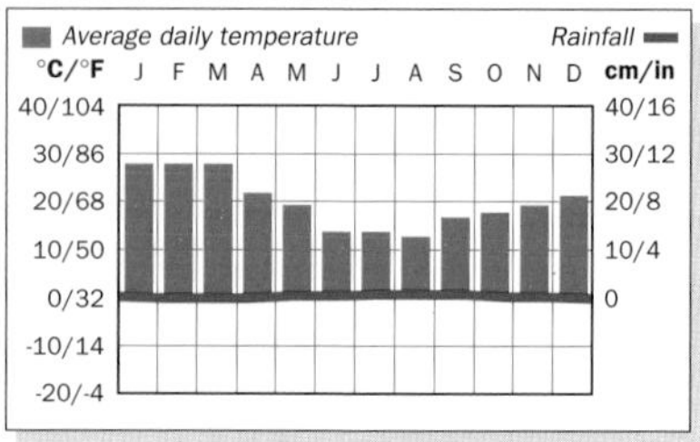
Average daily temperature
Rainfall
°C/°F
J F M A M J J A S O N D
cm/in
40/104
30/86
20/68
10/50
0/32
-10/14
-20/-4
40/16
30/12
20/8
10/4
0

Peru has several distinct climatic regions. The arid or desert coastal region experiences the *garúa*, persistent low cloud and fog, giving Lima cool "winters" even though it is close to the equator. The temperate slopes of the Andes have large daily temperature ranges and one rainy season, while the tropical Amazon Basin receives year-round rains.

TRANSPORTATION

Drive on right

Jorge Chávez International, Lima
4.31m passengers

717 ships
239,600 grt

THE TRANSPORTATION NETWORK

8700 km (5406 miles)

Pan-American Highway: 2495 km (1550 miles)

1639 km (1018 miles)

8808 km (5473 miles)

The World Bank in 2001 estimated that Peru had a public infrastructure deficit of $7 billion. Most roads remain unpaved. Work on a transcontinental highway from Ilo, a free port on the Pacific, via Puerto Suárez in Bolivia, to the port of Portos in Brazil is ongoing. The two rail networks, the Central and Southern, are as yet unconnected. The La Oroya–Huancayo line is the world's highest stretch of standard-gauge railroad. River transportation provides major access to Iquitos in Amazonia. As well as four important international airports, there are more than 130 airstrips scattered throughout the country.

Spanish colonial church near Urubamba. *The Urubamba River with its deep gorges was known to the Incas as the Sacred Valley.*

TOURISM

Visitors : Population 1:32

823,000 visitors

Up 3% in 2002

MAIN TOURIST ARRIVALS

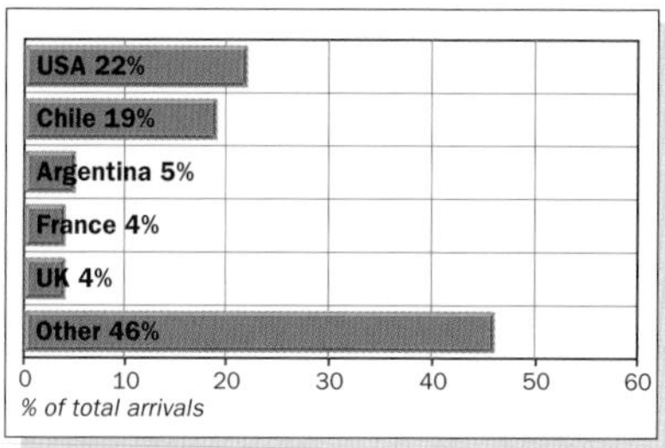
USA 22%
Chile 19%
Argentina 5%
France 4%
UK 4%
Other 46%
0
10
20
30
40
50
60
% of total arrivals

Tourism is gradually recovering after being plunged into crisis in the early 1990s by guerrilla activity, crime, and cholera fears. The heavily indebted industry has been unable to take full advantage of new investment opportunities, but privatization programs have seen the sale of state hotels. Visitors brave poor infrastructure and accommodation to see incomparable sites such as the Inca ruins at Machu Picchu in the Andes. The patterns in the desert made by the Nazca people (known as the Nazca lines), dating from the 2nd century BCE, are also a major attraction. Tourism to the Amazon is growing, but environmentalists are concerned about the impact on indigenous peoples. Lake Titicaca and the Spanish colonial architecture of Lima are other draws.

PEOPLE

Pop. density low

Spanish, Quechua, Aymara

21/km² (54/mi²)

THE URBAN/RURAL POPULATION SPLIT

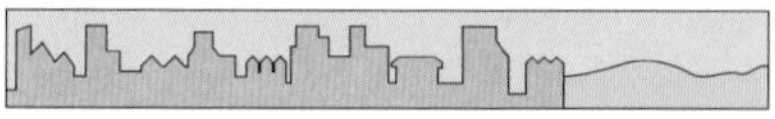
73%
27%

RELIGIOUS PERSUASION

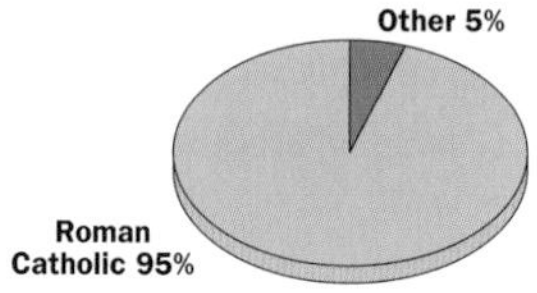
Other 5%
Roman Catholic 95%

ETHNIC MAKEUP

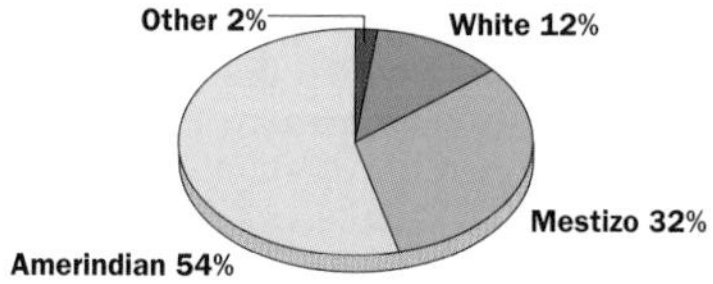
Other 2%
White 12%
Mestizo 32%
Amerindian 54%

Most Peruvians are Amerindian or *mestizo* (mixed race). The small elite of Spanish descendants retain a strong hold on the economy, power, and social standing. A few Chinese and Japanese live in the northern cities.

Previously remote Andean Amerindians are increasingly informed of events in Lima and the coastal strip by radio and by relatives in cities. This has compensated for problems associated with the marginalization of their native Quechua and Aymara languages in a Spanish-speaking culture. A further 250,000 Amazonian Amerindians live in the eastern lowlands. Together with the small community of Africans (descendants of plantation workers), they tend to suffer the worst discrimination in towns.

The extended family remains strong. A part of traditional native Amerindian traditions, its role as a social bond was strengthened by Roman Catholicism. In recent years, economic difficulties have raised its profile as the key social support system for most Peruvians.

POPULATION AGE BREAKDOWN

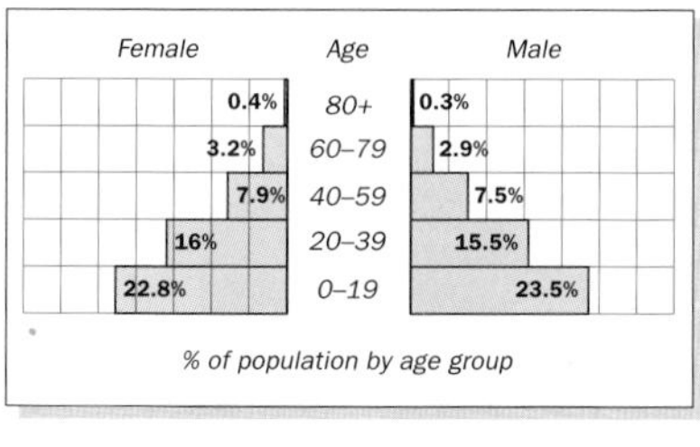
Female
Age
Male
0.4%
80+
0.3%
3.2%
60–79
2.9%
7.9%
40–59
7.5%
16%
20–39
15.5%
22.8%
0–19
23.5%
% of population by age group

P

POLITICS

Multiparty elections

2001/2006

President Alejandro Toledo

Alberto Fujimori, *president 1990–2000, ran an increasingly autocratic regime.*

President Alejandro Toledo, *Peru's first Amerindian head of state, elected in 2001.*

Peru is a multiparty democracy in which the president holds executive power.

PROFILE

The long tradition of large parties dominating politics ended with Alberto Fujimori's election as president in 1990. His "self-coup" created a compliant legislature and judiciary, and approval of a new constitution permitted his reelection in 1995. His popularity was greatly boosted by successes against hyperinflation and the Sendero

AT THE LAST ELECTION

Congress of the Republic 120 seats

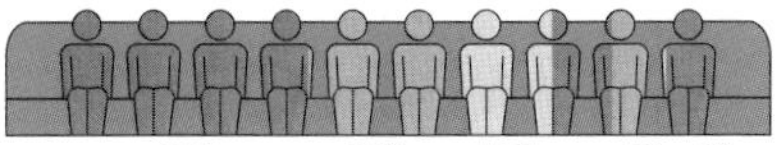
9% FIM
3% SP
38% PP
23% APRA
14% NU
5% UPP
8% Others

PP = Peru Posible **APRA** = American Popular Revolutionary Alliance **NU** = National Unity **FIM** = Independent Moralizing Front **UPP** = Union for Peru **SP** = Somos Peru

Luminoso (Shining Path) guerrillas. It faded in the late 1990s as he tightened his personal control of the government, and appeared increasingly reliant on the army. Few checks on the executive remained, and Fujimori was able to obtain his third term in 2000. However, blatant electoral fraud and the corrupt use of power were exposed when his security service chief Vladimiro Montesinos was videoed bribing opposition legislators. Fujimori's position was irrevocably damaged, and he resigned in November, having fled to Japan. Fresh presidential and legislative elections in April 2001 were won by populist Alejandro Toledo and his Peru Posible (PP) party.

MAIN POLITICAL ISSUES

Disenchantment with Toledo

President Toledo promised a new start for Peru, but his low ratings in opinion polls testified to early impatience with his administration. Respondents expressed disappointment that he had failed to fulfill election promises, especially on job creation, as the government committed itself to IMF goals on structural reform and fiscal restraint.

Toledo's popularity picked up somewhat on the back of good economic results posted in 2002. He was also given credit for more direct speaking and his perceived tough stance on corruption and terrorism. Newly created regional governments threatened to increase pressure on his still weak government with a possible negative impact on fiscal stability.

The resurgence of APRA

APRA won 12 of the new regional presidencies in 2002, compared with 11 won by independents and one each by PP and SP. APRA leader Alán García, who as president had presided over a bankrupt country in the 1980s, used the result to increase pressure on Toledo for more budgetary clout for regional government, but did not press for a PP–APRA coalition. Distancing himself from a potentially unpopular government will improve his chances in the 2006 presidential elections.

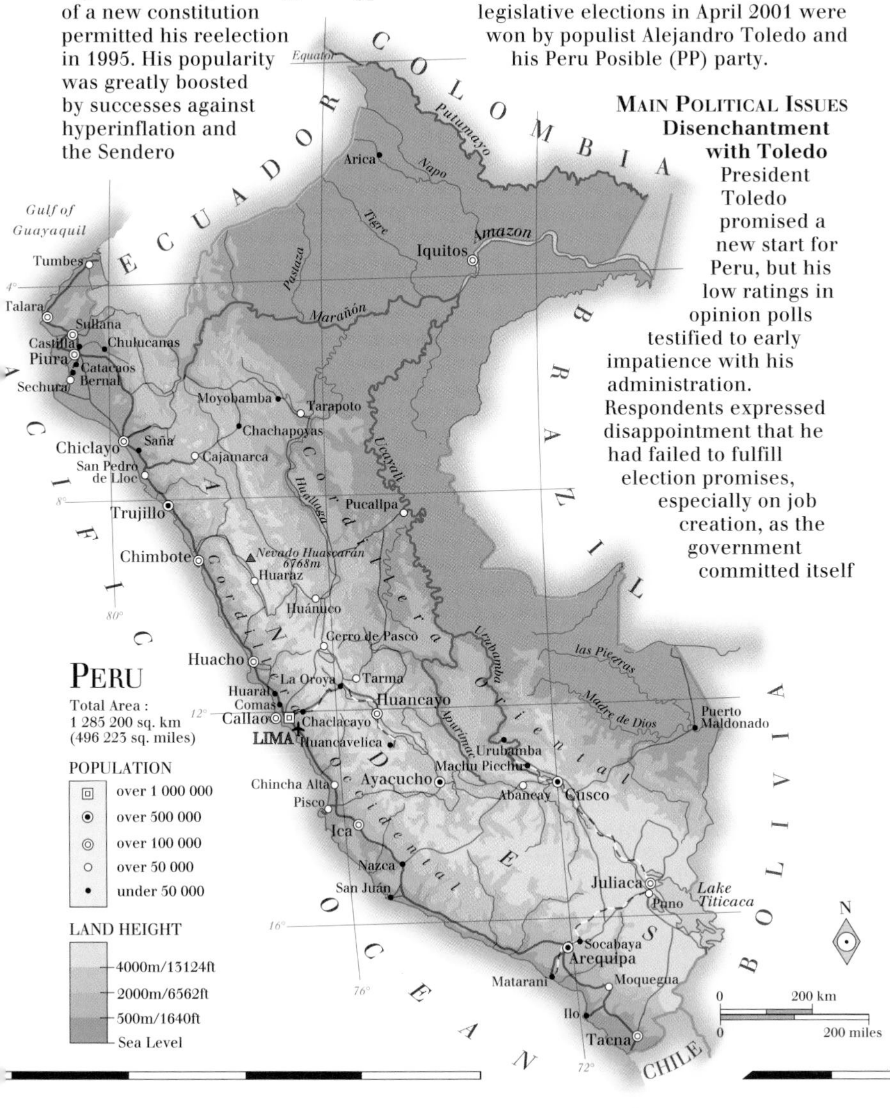
PERU
Total Area : 1 285 200 sq. km (496 223 sq. miles)
POPULATION
over 1 000 000
over 500 000
over 100 000
over 50 000
under 50 000
LAND HEIGHT
4000m/13124ft
2000m/6562ft
500m/1640ft
Sea Level
COLOMBIA
ECUADOR
BRAZIL
BOLIVIA
CHILE
PACIFIC OCEAN
Equator
Gulf of Guayaquil
Tumbes
Talara
Sullana
Castilla
Chulucanas
Piura
Catacaos
Bernal
Sechura
Chiclayo
Saña
San Pedro de Lloc
Trujillo
Chimbote
Moyobamba
Tarapoto
Chachapoyas
Cajamarca
Pucallpa
Nevado Huascarán 6768m
Huaraz
Huánuco
Cerro de Pasco
Huacho
La Oroya
Tarma
Huaral
Comas
Callao
LIMA
Chaclacayo
Huancayo
Huancavelica
Chincha Alta
Pisco
Ayacucho
Ica
Nazca
San Juan
Machu Picchu
Urubamba
Abancay
Cusco
Puerto Maldonado
Juliaca
Puno
Lake Titicaca
Socabaya
Arequipa
Matarani
Moquegua
Ilo
Tacna
Arica
Iquitos
Amazon
Putumayo
Napo
Tigre
Pastaza
Marañón
Ucayali
Huallaga
Urubamba
Apurímac
las Piedras
Madre de Dios
Cordillera Oriental
Cordillera Occidental
N
200 km
200 miles

CHRONOLOGY

Francisco Pízarro's arrival in 1532 during a war of succession between two Inca rulers marked the start of the Spanish colonization of Peru and the end of the Inca empire.

- ❑ **1821** Independence proclaimed in Lima after its capture by Argentine liberator, José de San Martín, who had just freed Chile.
- ❑ **1824** Spain defeated at battles of Junín and Ayacucho by Simón Bolívar and Gen. Sucre, liberators of Venezuela and Colombia.
- ❑ **1836–1839** Peru and Bolivia joined in short-lived confederation.
- ❑ **1866** Peruvian–Spanish War.
- ❑ **1879–1884** War of the Pacific. Chile defeats Peru and Bolivia. Peru loses territory in south.
- ❑ **1908** Augusto Leguía y Salcedo's dictatorial rule begins.
- ❑ **1924** Dr. Víctor Raúl Haya de la Torre founds nationalist APRA in exile in Mexico.
- ❑ **1930** Leguía ousted. APRA moves to Peru as first political party.
- ❑ **1931–1945** APRA banned.
- ❑ **1939–1945** Moderate, pro-US civilian government.
- ❑ **1948** Gen. Manuel Odría takes power. APRA banned again.
- ❑ **1956** Civilian government restored.
- ❑ **1962–1963** Two military coups.
- ❑ **1963** Election of Fernando Belaúnde Terry. Land reform, but military used to suppress communist-inspired insurgency.
- ❑ **1968** Military junta takes over.

➪

P

CHRONOLOGY *continued*

Attempts to alleviate poverty. Large-scale nationalizations.

- ❑ **1975–1978** New right-wing junta.
- ❑ **1980** Belaúnde reelected. Maoist Sendero Luminoso (Shining Path) begins armed struggle.
- ❑ **1981–1998** Border war with Ecuador over Cordillera del Cóndor, given to Peru by a 1942 protocol. Ecuador wants access to Amazon.
- ❑ **1982** Deaths and "disappearances" start to escalate as army cracks down on guerrillas and narcotics.
- ❑ **1985** Electoral win for left-wing APRA under Alán García Pérez.
- ❑ **1987** Peru bankrupt. Plans to nationalize banks blocked by new Libertad movement led by writer Mario Vargas Llosa.
- ❑ **1990** Over 3000 political murders. Alberto Fujimori, an independent, elected president on anticorruption platform. Severe austerity program.
- ❑ **1992–95** Fujimori "self-coup." New constitution. Fujimori reelected.
- ❑ **1996–1997** Left-wing Tupac Amarú guerrillas seize hundreds of hostages at Japanese ambassador's residence in four-month siege.
- ❑ **2000** November, Fujimori seeks refuge in Japan and resigns amid corruption scandal despite having won controversial third term in May.
- ❑ **2001** Fresh presidential elections: Alejandro Toledo defeats García.
- ❑ **2003** Beatriz Merino appointed first female prime minister.

P

WORLD AFFAIRS

▷ Joined UN in 1945

AP | AmCC | NAM | OAS | RG

Cooperation with the US, which is the main source of aid, extends to the war on cocaine, though Peru remains one of the world's largest coca producers.

Reported incursions by guerrillas, paramilitaries, and narcotics traffickers highlight the security of the border, with Colombia as a key problem.

Peru competes with Chile for an alliance with Bolivia to process and pipe natural gas.

AID

▷ Recipient

$451m (receipts) — Up 12% in 2001

Aid from the US is mostly directed at antinarcotics activity. Loans worth some $1.3 billion in recent years from the IDB, the World Bank, and Japan were conditional on Peru's meeting specific health and educational targets and on making progress on privatizations.

DEFENSE

▷ Compulsory military service

$896m — Up 1% in 2001

The military, in power from 1968 to 1980, supported President Fujimori's 1992 presidential coup. A quarter of national territory remained under states of emergency until early 2000, despite the apparent defeat of the Sendero Luminoso guerrillas. Fujimori's control over promotions and the National Intelligence Service (SIN) guaranteed a loyal armed forces leadership. After his resignation and the dissolution of the SIN in late 2000, the interim government moved to cut back military influence. Bomb attacks in Lima prior to US president Bush's 2002 visit were widely blamed on guerrillas, but an option studied by the Interior Ministry was that elements within the military, intelligence, or police still sympathetic to Montesinos were responsible.

PERUVIAN ARMED FORCES

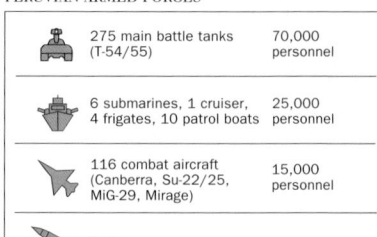

275 main battle tanks (T-54/55)	70,000 personnel
6 submarines, 1 cruiser, 4 frigates, 10 patrol boats	25,000 personnel
116 combat aircraft (Canberra, Su-22/25, MiG-29, Mirage)	15,000 personnel
None	

ECONOMICS

▷ Inflation 23% p.a. (1990–2001)

$52.2bn — 3.472 new soles (3.512)

SCORE CARD

- ❑ World GNP Ranking..........46th
- ❑ GNP per Capita..........$1980
- ❑ Balance of Payments..........–$1.1bn
- ❑ Inflation..........2%
- ❑ Unemployment..........8%

EXPORTS

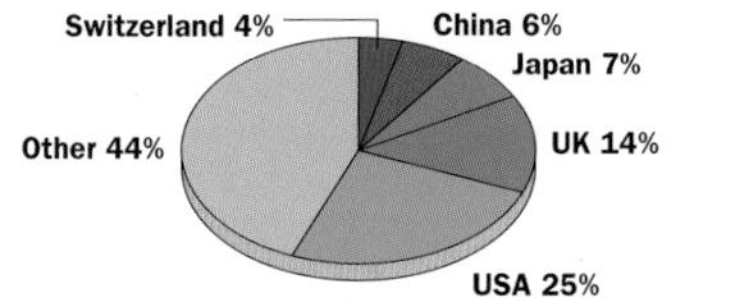
Switzerland 4%
China 6%
Japan 7%
UK 14%
Other 44%
USA 25%

IMPORTS

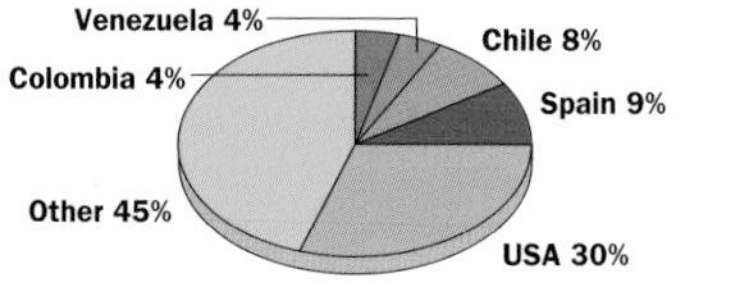
Venezuela 4%
Chile 8%
Colombia 4%
Spain 9%
Other 45%
USA 30%

ECONOMIC PERFORMANCE INDICATOR

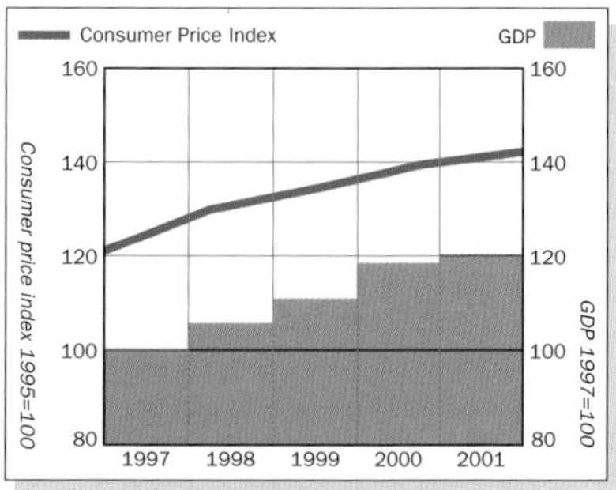
Consumer Price Index
GDP
160
140
120
100
80
Consumer price index 1995=100
GDP 1997=100
1997
1998
1999
2000
2001

Strengths
Abundant mineral resources, including oil. Rich Pacific fish stocks. Wide climatic variation allows diverse and productive agriculture; cotton and coffee are important. Well-developed textile industry.

Weaknesses
Overdependence on metals and commodities whose fluctuating prices undermine trade and investment. Stalled privatization. Corruption and poor infrastructure deterring investment. Weak banks.

Profile
Wealth and economic activity are largely confined to the cities of the coastal plain. The inhabitants of the Andean uplands are subsistence farmers or coca producers. Peru's strict fiscal and monetary policy continued under Fujimori. Growth was hit hard in 1998 by the disruption of fishing by El Niño-generated storms, the Asian economic crises, Russian-provoked turmoil in emerging markets, and depressed world commodity prices. In 1999 the IMF granted a three-year loan package, extended in 2002, to support comprehensive structural reform and fiscal restraint. Strong growth in 2002, led by mining, construction, and manufacturing, aided recovery.

PERU : MAJOR BUSINESSES

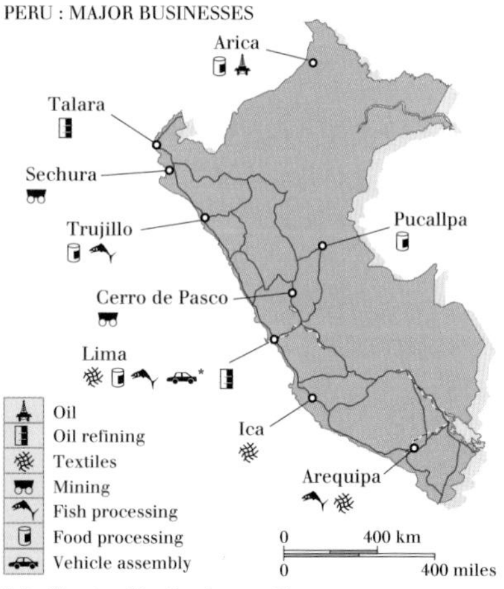
Arica
Talara
Sechura
Trujillo
Pucallpa
Cerro de Pasco
Lima
Ica
Arequipa
Oil
Oil refining
Textiles
Mining
Fish processing
Food processing
Vehicle assembly
0
400 km
0
400 miles

* significant multinational ownership

RESOURCES

Electric power 5.7m kW

10.7m tonnes

98,000 b/d (reserves 300m barrels)

14.3m sheep, 4.95m cattle, 2.8m pigs, 90m chickens

Oil, coal, lead, zinc, silver, iron, gold, copper

ELECTRICITY GENERATION

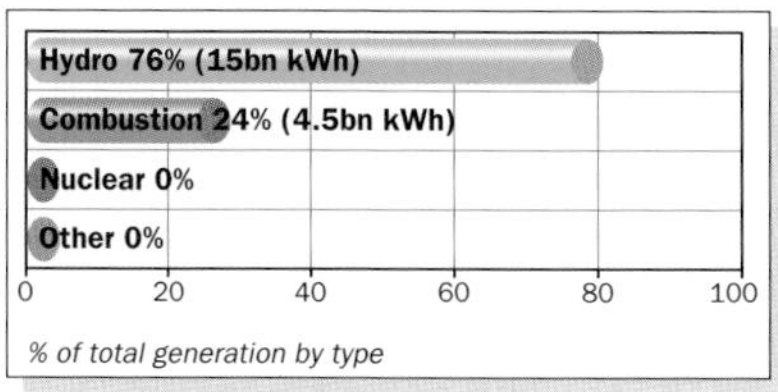
Hydro 76% (15bn kWh)
Combustion 24% (4.5bn kWh)
Nuclear 0%
Other 0%
0
20
40
60
80
100
% of total generation by type

Peru is an important exporter of copper and lead. Development of the huge Antamina copper and zinc deposit is under way, and the $3 billion Camisea hydrocarbon project is in construction. Peru is attempting to reduce its dependence on hydroelectric power because inconsistent rainfall patterns cause output to fluctuate.

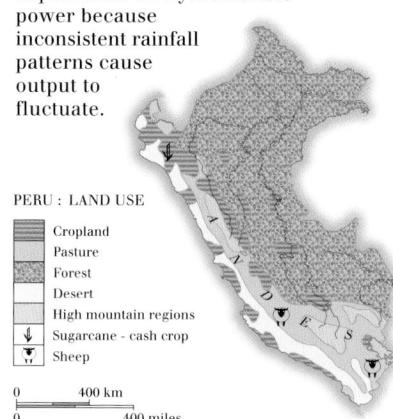

A N D E S
PERU : LAND USE
Cropland
Pasture
Forest
Desert
High mountain regions
Sugarcane - cash crop
Sheep
0 400 km
0 400 miles

ENVIRONMENT

Sustainability rank: 29th

6% (3% partially protected)

1.2 tonnes per capita

ENVIRONMENTAL TREATIES

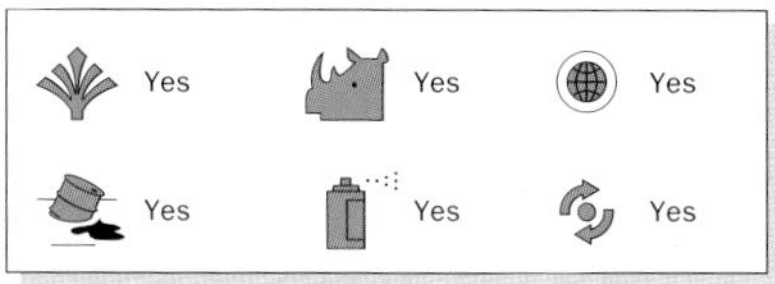
Yes
Yes
Yes
Yes
Yes
Yes

Environmentalists have long been concerned about coastal industrial pollution and the activities of the fishing industry. Overfishing of anchovies almost resulted in their extinction in the 1970s. Today, attention has switched to the rising number of dolphins being caught in drift nets. Unchecked urban and industrial pollution, especially in Lima, is a major problem.

Environmentalists fear that the policy of using powerful air-sprayed herbicides to destroy coca crops is adding to river pollution in the Andes, where mining also causes severe environmental problems.

MEDIA

TV ownership medium

Daily newspaper circulation 4 per 1000 people

PUBLISHING AND BROADCAST MEDIA

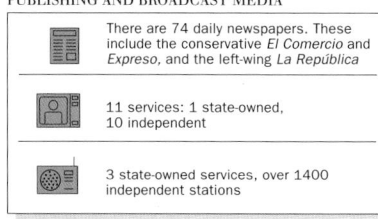

There are 74 daily newspapers. These include the conservative *El Comercio* and *Expreso*, and the left-wing *La República*

11 services: 1 state-owned, 10 independent

3 state-owned services, over 1400 independent stations

Main cities have their own newspapers; Lima's papers cater to diverse political readerships. State TV is not popular.

CRIME

Death penalty not used in practice

27,452 prisoners

Urban crime levels are high

CRIME RATES

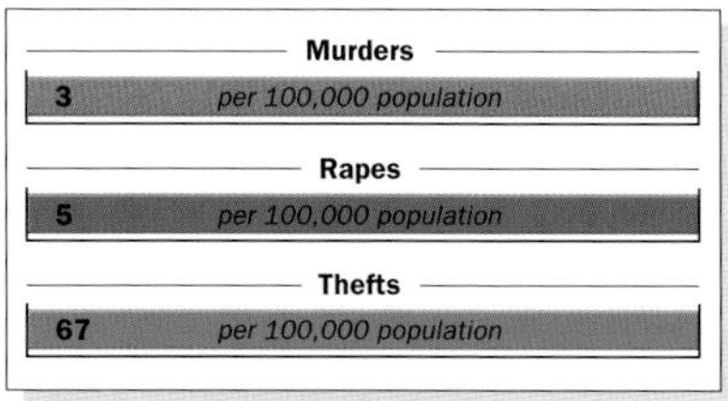
Murders
3 per 100,000 population
Rapes
5 per 100,000 population
Thefts
67 per 100,000 population

Kidnappings, murders, armed robberies, and drugs-related crime remain serious problems, especially in Lima. Corruption is deep-seated in the police and security forces, and was a major political issue throughout the 1990s. Despite the near-destruction of the Sendero Luminoso and Tupac Amarú guerrilla groups, main cities frequently have curfews. Peru has not yet succeeded in halting coca production.

EDUCATION

School leaving age: 16

90%

734,392 students

THE EDUCATION SYSTEM

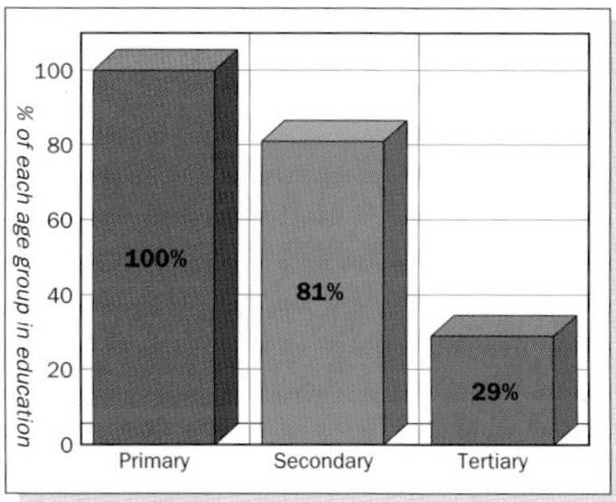
% of each age group in education
100
80
60
40
20
0
100%
81%
29%
Primary
Secondary
Tertiary

Education is based on the US system; spending has been declining. The provision of state education, especially for the poor, remains a major challenge. State and private universities are accessible to a small minority.

HEALTH

Welfare state health benefits

1 per 855 people

Cancers, pneumonia, accidents, infectious diseases

The poor public health system almost collapsed in the 1980s. In many areas primary care is nonexistent. Advanced treatment is available only to private patients in city clinics. Goiter, a thyroid abnormality, is widespread, especially in mountain areas. Infant mortality is rising due to social deprivation, diarrheal diseases, and tuberculosis. Malaria is again widespread, and cholera reached epidemic proportions in 1994. Thousands of poor women were forcibly sterilized in the late 1990s as part of a government program to lower the birthrate. Social welfare is compulsory, and benefits cover sickness, disability, and old age.

SPENDING

GDP/cap. increase

CONSUMPTION AND SPENDING

27 per 1000 population

78 per 1000 population

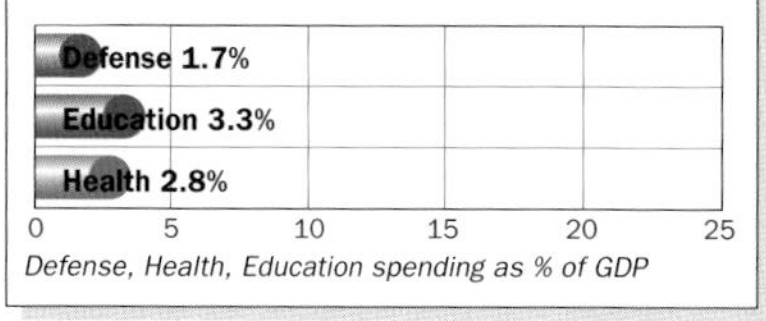
Defense 1.7%
Education 3.3%
Health 2.8%
0
5
10
15
20
25
Defense, Health, Education spending as % of GDP

Most wealth and power in Peru is still retained by old Spanish families. Indigenous peoples remain excluded from both. The rich live in a state of siege; a key status symbol is the number of armed guards and security cameras protecting family property. Overpopulation and rural migration accentuate poverty in Lima, where some 2.7 million people live in shanty towns, many of them lacking such basic utilities as running water and electricity. The UN estimates that nearly half of the population live below the poverty line.

WORLD RANKING

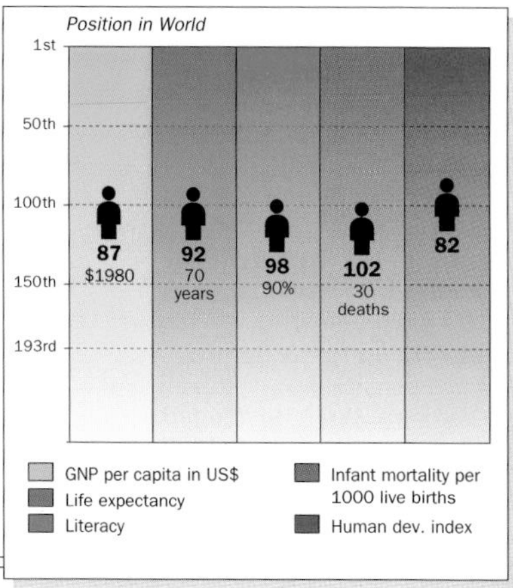
Position in World
1st
50th
100th
150th
193rd
87 $1980
92 70 years
98 90%
102 30 deaths
82
GNP per capita in US$
Life expectancy
Literacy
Infant mortality per 1000 live births
Human dev. index

P

PHILIPPINES

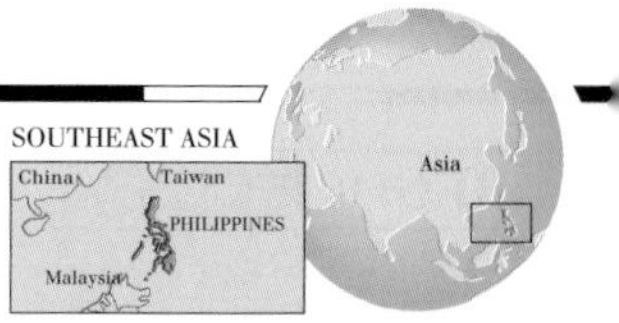
SOUTHEAST ASIA
China
Taiwan
PHILIPPINES
Malaysia
Asia

OFFICIAL NAME: Republic of the Philippines **CAPITAL:** Manila
POPULATION: 78.6 million **CURRENCY:** Philippine peso **OFFICIAL LANGUAGES:** English and Filipino

1946 | 1946 | June 12 | RP | +8 | +63 | .ph

LYING ON THE WESTERN RIM of the Pacific Ocean, the Philippines is the world's second-largest archipelago-state. Of its 7107 islands, 4600 are named and 1000 inhabited. There are three main island groupings: Luzon, Visayan, and the Mindanao and Sulu islands. Located on the Pacific "ring of fire," it is thus subject to frequent earthquakes and volcanic activity. Economic growth outstripped population increase in the 1990s, until the 1997–1998 Asian crisis, but efforts to build a stable democracy have been compromised by high-level corruption, leading to the ouster of President Estrada in 2001.

***Bohol Island** has over 1000 of these famous mounds, known as "the chocolate hills."*

CLIMATE

Tropical monsoon/equatorial

WEATHER CHART FOR MANILA

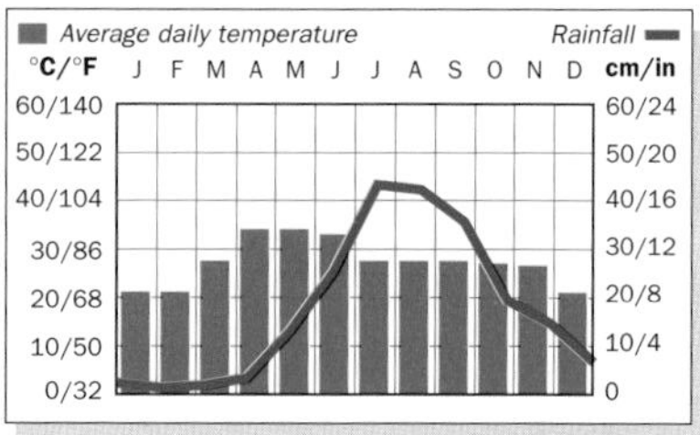
Average daily temperature
Rainfall
°C/°F
J F M A M J J A S O N D
cm/in
60/140
50/122
40/104
30/86
20/68
10/50
0/32
60/24
50/20
40/16
30/12
20/8
10/4
0

The Philippines is warm and humid all year. The rainy season lasts from June to October. Humidity falls from 85% in September to 71% in March.

TRANSPORTATION

Drive on right

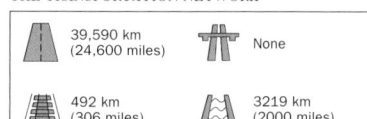

Ninoy Aquino International, Manila 12.8m passengers

1697 ships 6.03m grt

THE TRANSPORTATION NETWORK

39,590 km (24,600 miles)	None
492 km (306 miles)	3219 km (2000 miles)

Basic infrastructure lacks investment and many main roads are in desperate need of repair. Chronic traffic congestion in Manila holds back economic growth.

Air travel is the only means of getting around the islands quickly. Philippines Airlines, privatized in 1992, has invested heavily in new aircraft and in expanding its regional route network. Work on a new 28-gate terminal at Manila's international airport ran into financial difficulties in 2002.

Subic Bay, a massive US naval base until 1992, is now being exploited as a commercial asset, thanks to its prime location. Opening on to the South China Sea, its deep natural harbor has been developed as a free port and enterprise zone. The Taiwanese are the biggest investors in this project.

TOURISM

Visitors : Population 1:41

1.93m visitors

Up 8% in 2002

MAIN TOURIST ARRIVALS

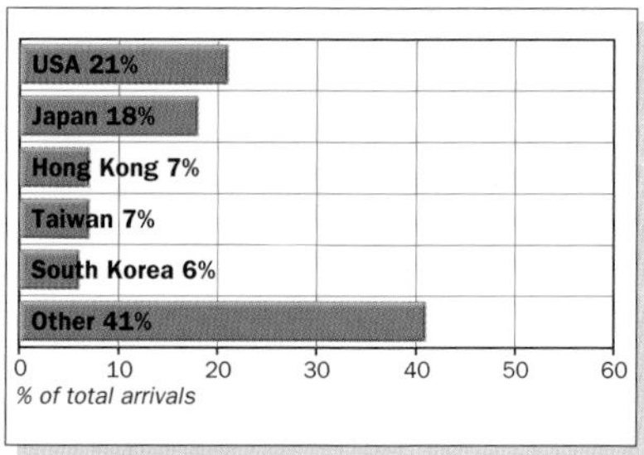
USA 21%
Japan 18%
Hong Kong 7%
Taiwan 7%
South Korea 6%
Other 41%
0
10
20
30
40
50
60
% of total arrivals

There is less tourism in the Philippines than in other regional NICs. Dubious images conveyed by sex tourism have become a liability. International pressure to end this abuse has intensified. Muslim secessionists have seized tourists on nearby Malaysian islands as hostages.

The tiny island of Boracay, off Panay, is a popular resort, and Palawan retains most of its tropical rainforest and coral lagoons, though coral reefs elsewhere are badly damaged. The rice terraces of northern Luzon are another attraction.

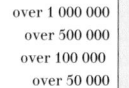

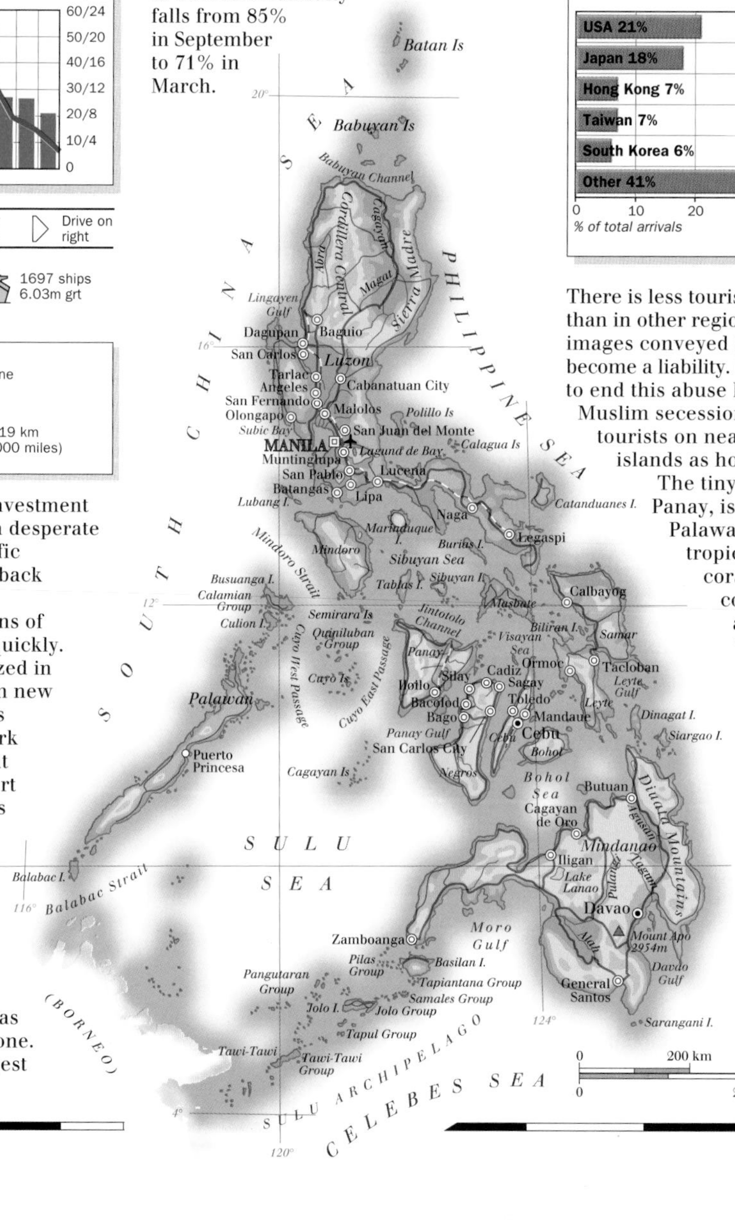
Batan Is
Babuyan Is
Babuyan Channel
Cordillera Central
Cagayan
Sierra Madre
Abra
Magat
Lingayen Gulf
Dagupan
Baguio
San Carlos
Luzon
Tarlac
Angeles
Cabanatuan City
San Fernando
Olongapo
Malolos
Polillo Is
Subic Bay
MANILA
San Juan del Monte
Muntinglupa
Laguna de Bay
Calagua Is
San Pablo
Lucena
Batangas
Lipa
Lubang I.
Naga
Catanduanes I.
Legaspi
Marinduque I.
Burias I.
Mindoro
Sibuyan Sea
Mindoro Strait
Tablas I.
Sibuyan I.
Busuanga I.
Calamian Group
Culion I.
Masbate
Calbayog
Semirara Is
Jintotolo Channel
Quiniluban Group
Biliran I.
Samar
Visayan Sea
Panay
Ormoc
Tacloban
Cuyo West Passage
Cuyo East Passage
Leyte Gulf
Cuyo Is
Sagay
Cadiz
Iloilo
Silay
Toledo
Leyte
Dinagat I.
Bacolod
Bago
Mandaue
Palawan
Cebu
Siargao I.
Panay Gulf
San Carlos City
Bohol
Puerto Princesa
Negros
Cagayan Is
Bohol Sea
Butuan
Cagayan de Oro
Mindanao
Diuata Mountains
Agusan
Iligan
Lake Lanao
Pulangi
Tagum
Davao
Mount Apo 2954m
Balabac I.
Balabac Strait
Moro Gulf
Mati
Davao Gulf
Zamboanga
Pilas Group
Basilan I.
Pangutaran Group
Tapiantana Group
Samales Group
General Santos
Jolo I.
Jolo Group
Sarangani I.
Tapul Group
Tawi-Tawi
Tawi-Tawi Group
SOUTH CHINA SEA
PHILIPPINE SEA
SULU SEA
SULU ARCHIPELAGO
CELEBES SEA
(BORNEO)
20°
16°
12°
8°
4°
116°
120°
124°
PHILIPPINES
Total Area : 300 000 sq. km (115 830 sq. miles)
POPULATION
over 1 000 000
over 500 000
over 100 000
over 50 000
LAND HEIGHT
2000m/6562ft
1000m/3281ft
500m/1640ft
200m/656ft
Sea Level
N
0
200 km
0
200 miles

PEOPLE

Pop. density high

Filipino, Tagalog, Cebuano, Hiligaynon, Samaran, Ilocano, Bicolano, English

264/km² (683/mi²)

THE URBAN/RURAL POPULATION SPLIT

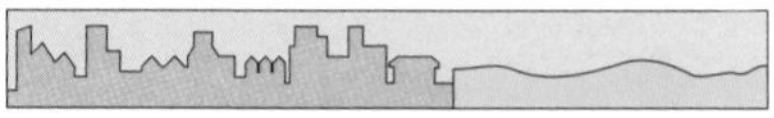
59%
41%

RELIGIOUS PERSUASION

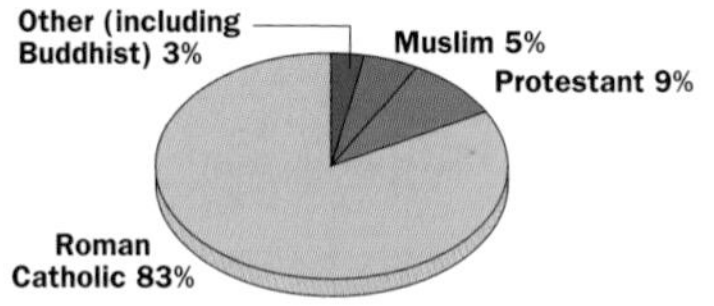
Other (including Buddhist) 3%
Muslim 5%
Protestant 9%
Roman Catholic 83%

ETHNIC MAKEUP

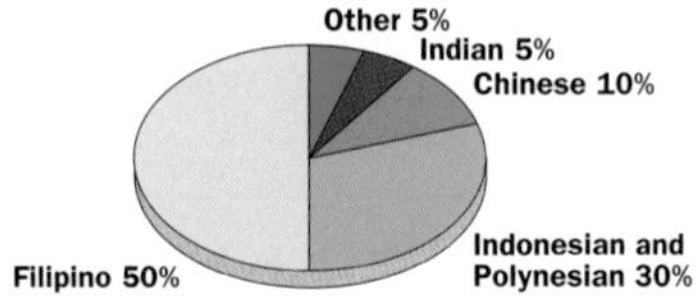
Other 5%
Indian 5%
Chinese 10%
Indonesian and Polynesian 30%
Filipino 50%

POPULATION AGE BREAKDOWN

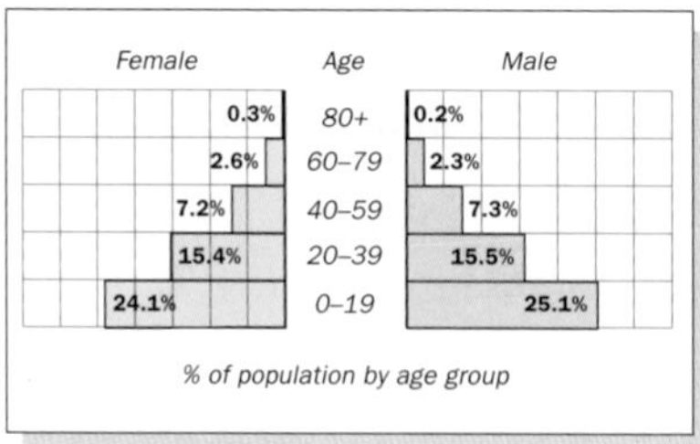
Female
Age
Male
0.3%
80+
0.2%
2.6%
60–79
2.3%
7.2%
40–59
7.3%
15.4%
20–39
15.5%
24.1%
0–19
25.1%
% of population by age group

The Philippines encompasses more than 100 distinct ethnic groups, many of Malay origin. The national language, Filipino, is based on Tagalog, spoken by the largest of the various groups. Other groups include Cebuano, Ilocan, Longgo, Bicolano, Waray, Pampangan, and Pangasinan. They are concentrated on the main island, Luzon, and are also a majority on Mindanao. Most Muslims live on Mindanao, but many are also found in the Sulu archipelago. The Chinese minority, which was well established by 1603, has remained significant in business and trade. More than 120 Chinese schools have ensured that it has retained a distinct identity.

There are also a number of cultural minorities who practice animist religions. They include the Ifugaos, Bontocks, Kalingas, and Ibalois on Luzon, the Manobo and Bukidnon on Mindanao, and the Mangyans on Palawan. Many of these groups speak Malayo-Polynesian dialects. Limited intermarriage with other peoples has meant that groups in the more remote regions have managed to retain their traditional ways of life.

The Philippines is one of only two Christian states in Asia. Over 80% of Filipinos are Roman Catholics, and the Church is the dominant cultural force. It opposes state-sponsored preventive family planning programs aimed at curbing accelerating population growth. Abortion is illegal but widespread.

Women have traditionally played a prominent part in Philippine public and professional life. Inheritance laws give them equal rights to men. Many go into politics, banking, and business, and in several professional sectors they form a majority.

POLITICS

Multiparty elections

L. House 2001/2004
U. House 2001/2004

President Gloria Macapagal Arroyo

AT THE LAST ELECTION

House of Representatives 216 seats

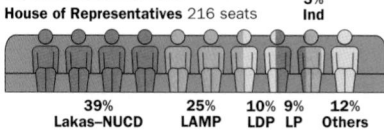

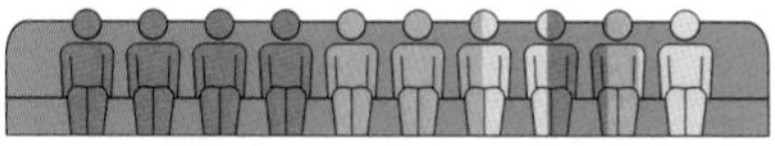
5%
Ind
39%
Lakas–NUCD
25%
LAMP
10%
LDP
9%
LP
12%
Others

Lakas–NUCD = Lakas – National Union of Christian Democrats **LAMP** = Party of the Filipino Masses
LDP = Fight of Democratic Filipinos **LP** = Liberal Party
Ind = Independents **PP** = People's Power (coalition led by Lakas–NUCD and including the LP)
PnM = Strength of the Masses (coalition of LAMP and LDP)

Senate 24 seats

50%
PP
46%
PnM
4%
Ind

The Philippines is a multiparty democracy.

PROFILE

By 1986, the 21-year dictatorship of Ferdinand Marcos had no popular backing. A massive "people power" movement supported his opponent Corazon Aquino, who was declared the true winner of the presidential elections. Losing the backing of the US, Marcos was forced into exile.

Former film star Joseph Estrada of LAMP was elected president in 1998. Accusations that he was involved in a gambling syndicate led to impeachment proceedings in late 2000. A repeat of the mass demonstrations of 1986 forced him to relinquish power in 2001. Vice President Gloria Macapagal Arroyo of the NUCD, who had led the united political opposition to Estrada, was appointed to replace him. She has pledged not to stand in the 2004 polls.

MAIN POLITICAL ISSUES

Political stability

After the downfall of the Marcos regime, the subsequent two presidents passed on power smoothly to an elected successor, but Estrada was quickly mired in corruption scandals. Moves for his impeachment were overtaken by mass rallies in Manila. Out of office he retains widespread support among the rural poor, who question the legitimacy of Arroyo's appointment. She has since also faced popular discontent and a failed military rebellion in July 2003.

Insurgency and separatism

Communists and Muslim separatists have been fighting government forces for over 30 years, with more than 10,000 armed confrontations with rebels recorded by the army. Support for secession has been fueled by government failure to alleviate poverty.

The communist New People's Army (NPA), once regarded as a heroic army of the oppressed and as an alternative to traditional politics, has declined in significance, but launched new offensives in 2000. Of greater importance is the Muslim insurrection on Mindanao and other southern islands. The Moro National Liberation Front (MNLF) signed a peace agreement in 1996. The splinter Muslim Islamic Liberation Front (MILF) continued fighting, but also joined the peace process in mid-2001. Nonetheless, the government launched a major offensive against MILF headquarters in February 2003. The smaller, but internationally backed, Abu Sayyaf continues low-level fighting in the Sulu region.

Joseph Estrada, film-star-turned-president, ousted in 2001.

Gloria Arroyo, president after a popular uprising.

Suggested links with international Islamist terrorists have brought full military assistance from the US in its "war on terrorism." The presence of US troops on Philippine soil has provoked controversy.

WORLD AFFAIRS

Joined UN in 1945

APEC | ASEAN | G24 | NAM | WTO

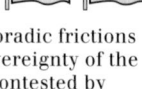

Regionally, there are sporadic frictions with Malaysia, while sovereignty of the Spratly Islands is hotly contested by China. The resumption of US naval visits since 1999 indicates improved security cooperation. President Arroyo quickly pledged her country's support for the US-led "war on terrorism" in 2001.

CHRONOLOGY

Ceded to the US by Spain in 1898, the Philippines became self-governing in 1935, and an independent republic in 1946.

- ❑ **1965** Ferdinand Marcos president.
- ❑ **1972** Marcos declares martial law. Opposition leaders arrested, parliament suspended, press censored.
- ❑ **1977** Ex-Liberal Party leader Benigno Aquino sentenced to death. Criticism forces Marcos to delay execution.
- ❑ **1978** Elections won by Marcos's New Society (KBL). He is named president and prime minister.
- ❑ **1980** Aquino allowed to travel to US for medical treatment.
- ❑ **1981** Martial law ends. Marcos reelected president by referendum.
- ❑ **1983** Aquino shot dead on return from US. Inquiry blames military conspiracy.
- ❑ **1986** US compels presidential election. Result disputed. Army rebels led by Gen. Fidel Ramos, and public demonstrations, bring Aquino's widow, Corazon, to power. Marcos exiled to US.
- ❑ **1987** New constitution. Aquino-led coalition wins Congress elections.
- ❑ **1988** Marcos and wife Imelda indicted for massive racketeering.
- ❑ **1989** Marcos dies in US.
- ❑ **1990** Imelda Marcos acquitted of fraud charges in US. Earthquake in Baguio city leaves 1600 dead.
- ❑ **1991** Mt. Pinatubo erupts. US leaves Clark Air Base.
- ❑ **1992** Ramos wins presidential election. US withdrawal from Subic Bay base.
- ❑ **1996** Peace agreement with Muslim MNLF secessionists.
- ❑ **1998** Joseph Estrada president.
- ❑ **1999** First execution in 22 years.
- ❑ **2000** Tourists kidnapped by Islamic extremists.
- ❑ **2001** Estrada overthrown by popular protest. Gloria Macapagal Arroyo assumes presidency. August, Muslim MILF joins peace process.
- ❑ **2002** Local elections, described as "peaceful" despite 86 deaths.

AID

Recipient

$577m (receipts)

Little change in 2001

The Philippines' main bilateral aid donors are Japan and the US. Many NGOs operate in the outlying islands. Large remittances are also received from Filipinos working overseas: funds received from these hundreds of thousands of emigrant workers exceeded $6 billion in 2000.

DEFENSE

No compulsory military service

$1.07bn

Down 22% in 2001

The military retains political influence. An abortive army mutiny called for President Arroyo's resignation in 2003.

The historic tie to the US has been translated in modern times into a close strategic relationship; US forces were deployed to help the government combat Muslim rebels in the south from 2001. Modernization of the armed forces is being undertaken with US assistance.

PHILIPPINE ARMED FORCES

40 light tanks (Scorpion)	66,000 personnel
1 frigate and 58 patrol boats	24,000 personnel
49 combat aircraft (14 F-5A/B)	16,000 personnel
None	

ECONOMICS

Inflation 8.2% p.a. (1990–2001)

$80.8bn

53.45 Philippine pesos (50.33)

SCORE CARD

❑ World GNP Ranking	41st
❑ GNP per Capita	$1030
❑ Balance of Payments	$4.5bn
❑ Inflation	6.1%
❑ Unemployment	10%

EXPORTS

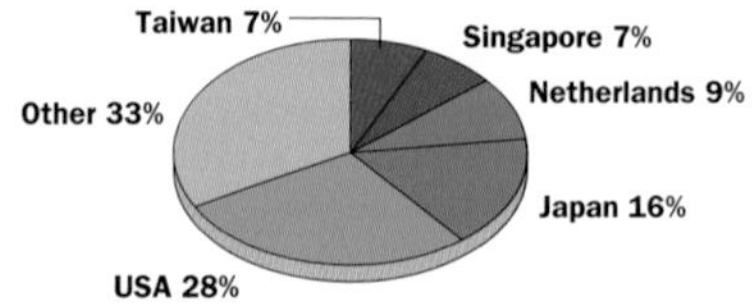
Taiwan 7%
Singapore 7%
Netherlands 9%
Other 33%
Japan 16%
USA 28%

IMPORTS

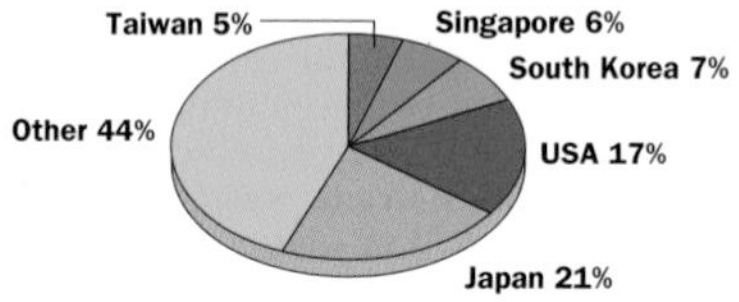
Taiwan 5%
Singapore 6%
South Korea 7%
Other 44%
USA 17%
Japan 21%

Strengths

Now fully open to outside investment. Agricultural productivity rising. Strong pineapple and banana export industries. Substantial remittances from Filipinos working overseas.

Weaknesses

Power failures limit scope for expansion. Rudimentary infrastructure. Low domestic savings rates mean reliance on foreign finance.

Profile

Once one of Asia's strongest economies, the Philippines has now fallen behind once much poorer countries such as Thailand, Malaysia, and South Korea. Around half of the population live below the UN poverty line, on less than $2 a day, fueling many of the secessionist movements that have undermined the stability of successive governments.

The financial successes of the early 1990s – opening up to foreign investment, cutting back private monopolies – were effectively nullified by the crippling 1997–1998 Asian economic and financial crises. The government of Joseph Estrada failed to shore up the economy and ran up a crippling budget deficit, and investor confidence vanished amid political scandals. His successor, President Arroyo, has done much to regain the approval of the IMF and the international community, mainly through further deregulation and privatization. Growth is back on track, thanks mainly to increased agricultural production, but many public works projects have simply been put on hold.

ECONOMIC PERFORMANCE INDICATOR

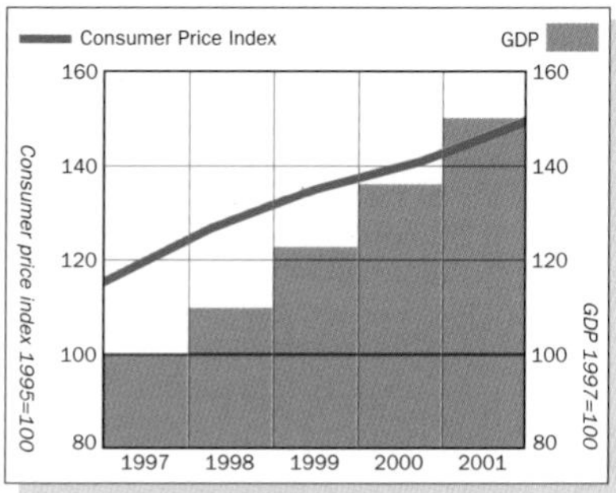
Consumer Price Index
GDP
160
140
120
100
80
Consumer price index 1995=100
GDP 1997=100
1997
1998
1999
2000
2001

PHILIPPINES : MAJOR BUSINESSES

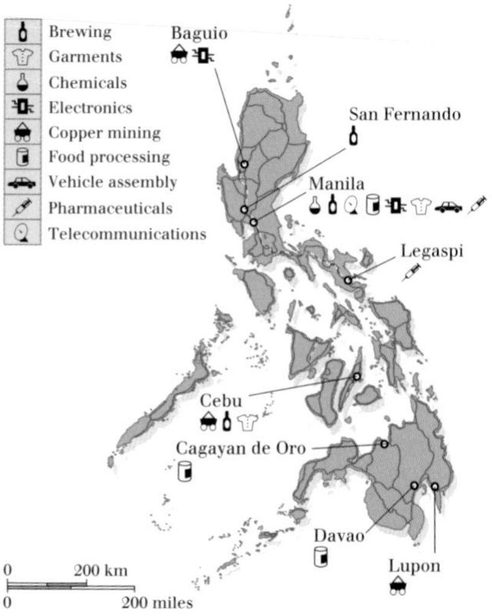
Brewing
Garments
Chemicals
Electronics
Copper mining
Food processing
Vehicle assembly
Pharmaceuticals
Telecommunications
Baguio
San Fernando
Manila
Legaspi
Cebu
Cagayan de Oro
Davao
Lupon
0 200 km
0 200 miles

P

RESOURCES

Electric power 11.9m kW

2.28m tonnes

942 b/d (reserves 205m barrels)

12m ducks, 11.7m pigs, 6.25m goats, 126m chickens

Coal, copper, nickel, chromium, silver, gas, manganese, gold, oil

ELECTRICITY GENERATION

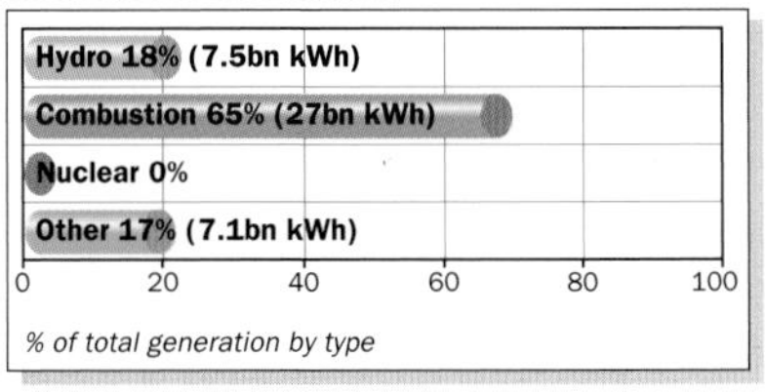
Hydro 18% (7.5bn kWh)
Combustion 65% (27bn kWh)
Nuclear 0%
Other 17% (7.1bn kWh)
0 20 40 60 80 100
% of total generation by type

The Philippines is the world's biggest supplier of refractory chrome. Copper is also a significant export. Substantial gold reserves have been mined since 1996. However, more than 90% of mineral potential remains undeveloped. Oil production off Palawan began in 1979. A major natural gas discovery in the Malampaya field, officially inaugurated in October 2001, could prove to have a significant impact. Though timber exports were halted in 1989, illegal logging continues to cause deforestation.

PHILIPPINES : LAND USE

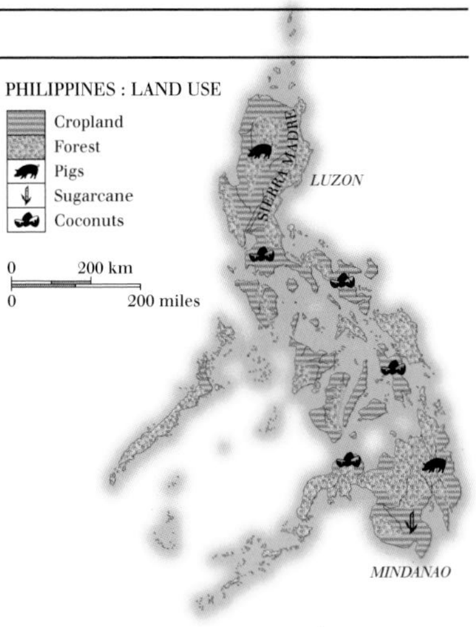
Cropland
Forest
Pigs
Sugarcane
Coconuts
0 200 km
0 200 miles
SIERRA MADRE
LUZON
MINDANAO

ENVIRONMENT

Sustainability rank: 117th

6% (3% partially protected)

1 tonne per capita

ENVIRONMENTAL TREATIES

Yes	Yes	Yes
Yes	Yes	No

The environment has become a major issue. Most of the tropical rainforest has been destroyed, except for pockets such as the island of Palawan. Unique coral habitats have been dynamited, and fishermen continue to use cyanide and *muro-ami* (reef-hunting) techniques to increase the size of their catches.

The government recognizes the costs of environmental damage, as soil run-off silts rivers and reduces the power generated by hydroelectric dams, and fast-depleting coral habitats reduce the attraction of the Philippines for tourists.

Enforcement of a ban on logging is difficult; many loggers have their own private armies. In addition, continued use of slash-and-burn farming has contributed to deforestation.

MEDIA

TV ownership medium

Daily newspaper circulation 63 per 1000 people

PUBLISHING AND BROADCAST MEDIA

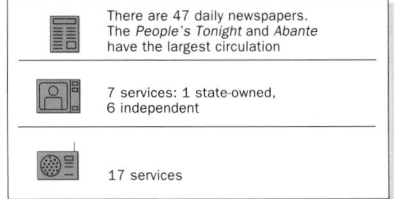

There are 47 daily newspapers. The *People's Tonight* and *Abante* have the largest circulation

7 services: 1 state-owned, 6 independent

17 services

Censorship was lifted under the 1987 constitution, but harassment of journalists still occurs. As well as the lively national press, there are more than 250 regional newspapers in local dialects. State TV and radio broadcast in English and Filipino. Powerful families control many independentoutlets.

CRIME

Moratorium on death penalty

70,383 prisoners

Little change in 1999–2000

CRIME RATES

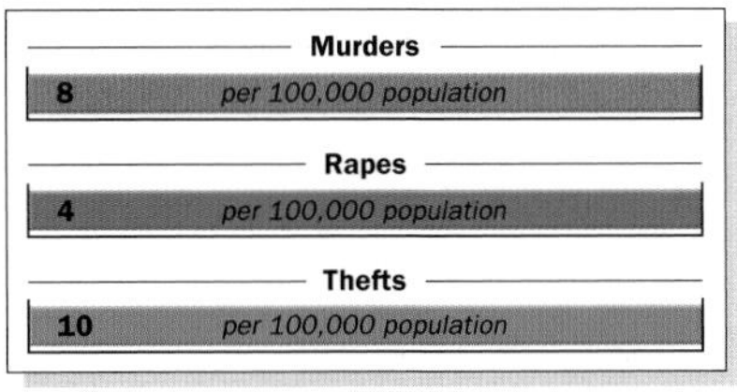
Murders
8 per 100,000 population
Rapes
4 per 100,000 population
Thefts
10 per 100,000 population

The death penalty, reinstated in 1993, was suspended again in 2000, but President Arroyo made an exception for 95 kidnappers in 2001.

EDUCATION

School leaving age: 12

95%

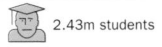

2.43m students

THE EDUCATION SYSTEM

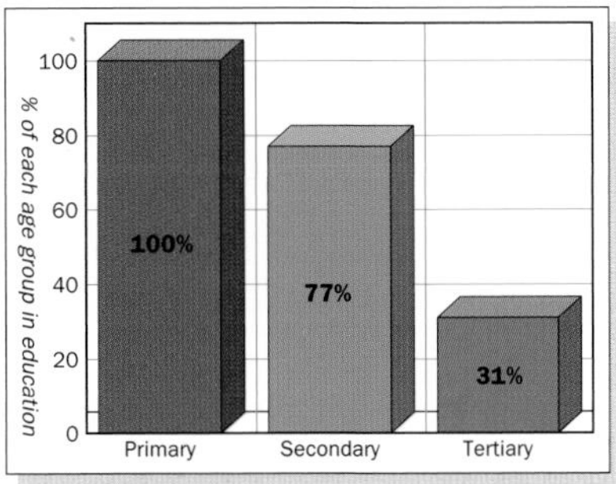
100
80
60
40
20
0
% of each age group in education
100%
77%
31%
Primary
Secondary
Tertiary

The Philippines has one of the highest literacy rates among developing countries. The education system is based on the US model, but with a higher proportion of private schools. The main teaching languages are English and Filipino/Tagalog.

Though there is a national curriculum up to age 15, sectarianism is common; the Chinese community has its own schools. Most colleges and universities are also run privately. The universities of San Carlos in Cebu and Santo Tomas in Manila are Spanish colonial foundations, dating from 1595 and 1611 respectively.

HEALTH

No welfare state health benefits

1 per 806 people

Pneumonia, tuberculosis, violence, accidents, malaria, typhoid

Most general hospitals are privately run. Malaria, which was once a major problem, has been eradicated in all but remote areas. Poor sanitation and disease are common in the sprawling slums around Manila.

SPENDING

GDP/cap. increase

CONSUMPTION AND SPENDING

10 per 1000 population

42 per 1000 population

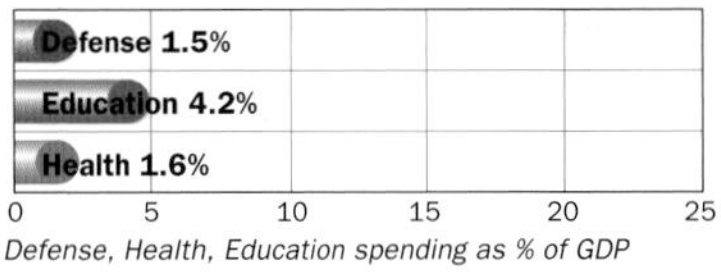
Defense 1.5%
Education 4.2%
Health 1.6%
0 5 10 15 20 25
Defense, Health, Education spending as % of GDP

The contrast between extremes of wealth and poverty is particularly marked. Wealth remains highly concentrated in a few select business families which are based in Manila.

WORLD RANKING

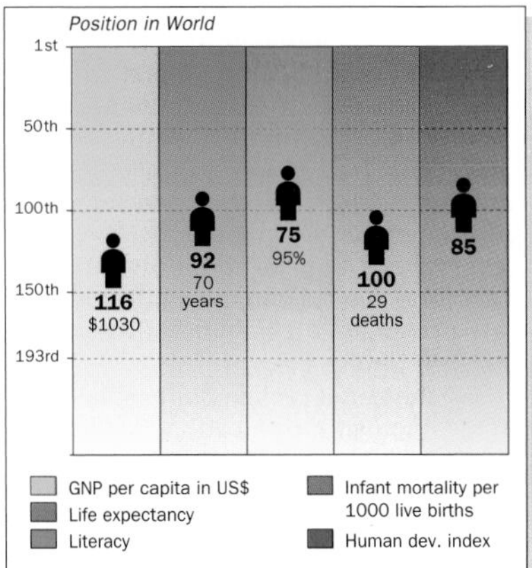
Position in World
1st
50th
100th
150th
193rd
116
$1030
92
70
years
75
95%
100
29
deaths
85
GNP per capita in US$
Life expectancy
Literacy
Infant mortality per 1000 live births
Human dev. index

P

POLAND

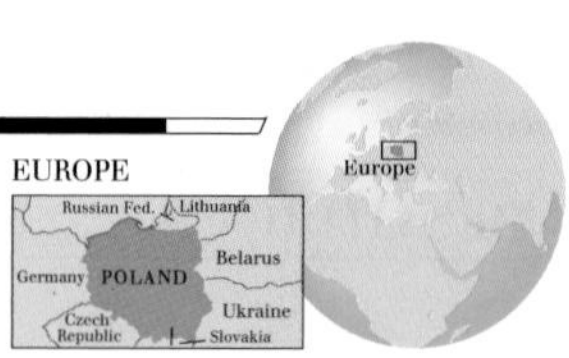
EUROPE
Europe
Russian Fed.
Lithuania
Belarus
Germany
POLAND
Czech Republic
Ukraine
Slovakia

OFFICIAL NAME: Republic of Poland **CAPITAL:** Warsaw
POPULATION: 38.2 million **CURRENCY:** Zloty **OFFICIAL LANGUAGE:** Polish

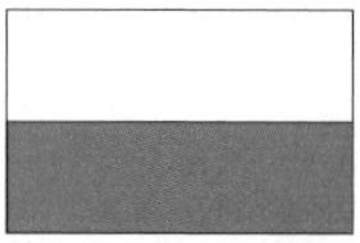

1918 | 1945 | May 3 | PL | +1 | +48 | .pl

LOCATED IN THE HEART of Europe, Poland's low-lying plains extend from the Baltic shore in the north to the Tatra Mountains on its southern border with Slovakia. Since the collapse of communism, Poland has undergone massive social, economic, and political change. Opting for a radical form of economic "shock therapy" in the early 1990s to kick-start the switch to a market economy, it has experienced rapid growth, is one of the ten countries set to join the EU in 2004, and has already been accepted as a member of NATO.

CLIMATE

Continental

WEATHER CHART FOR WARSAW

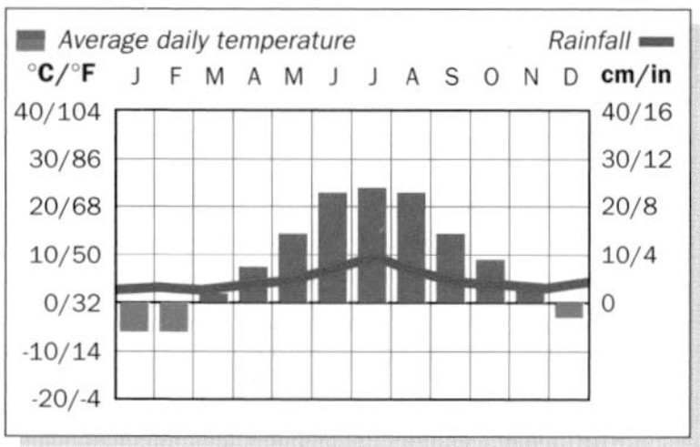
Average daily temperature
Rainfall
°C/°F
J F M A M J J A S O N D
cm/in
40/104
30/86
20/68
10/50
0/32
-10/14
-20/-4
40/16
30/12
20/8
10/4
0

Most of the country has the same climate. Summers are hot, with heavy rainfall often accompanied by thunder. Winters are severe, with snow covering the ground on the southern mountains, for as much as 60–70 days in the east.

TRANSPORTATION

Drive on right

Okecie International, Warsaw
4.94m passengers

393 ships
618,300 grt

THE TRANSPORTATION NETWORK

249,966 km (155,321 miles)

336 km (209 miles)

22,560 km (14,018 miles)

3812 km (2369 miles)

The national airline LOT has increased its charter business as more middle-class Poles vacation abroad. Russian aircraft have all been replaced with Western models. A 15-year roads expansion program was begun in 1997. "Fast tram" systems for cities and long-distance high-speed rail links need major investment. The government plans to slim down the rail workforce and to commercialize and part-privatize Polish State Railways (PKP) by 2003.

The advent of mobile phones has affected telecommunications, as has the privatization of Telekomunikacja Polska and the end of its monopoly on long-distance calls.

***The medieval administrative center of Lublin** lies in Poland's southeastern agricultural heartland.*

TOURISM

Visitors : Population 1:2.7

14m visitors

Down 7% in 2002

MAIN TOURIST ARRIVALS

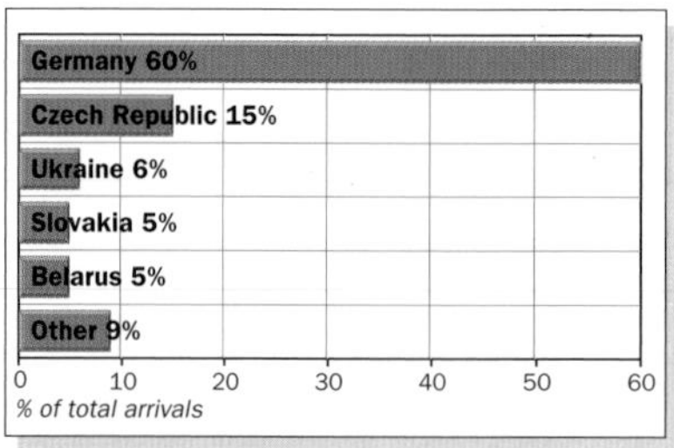
Germany 60%
Czech Republic 15%
Ukraine 6%
Slovakia 5%
Belarus 5%
Other 9%
0
10
20
30
40
50
60
% of total arrivals

Despite environmental problems, Poland is renowned for its skiing and hiking, especially in the Tatra Mountains. Kraków's medieval core has been preserved, while Toruń has restored its historic German Hanseatic buildings.

Warsaw's historic center has been reconstructed following the destruction of 80% of it by the German army in 1944. More hotels and restaurants are being opened.

Poznań has exploited its location between Warsaw and Berlin to create an international exhibition and business convention industry.

Airlines have increased their flights from the West to take advantage of the country's tourist potential.

PEOPLE

Pop. density medium

Polish

125/km² (325/mi²)

THE URBAN/RURAL POPULATION SPLIT

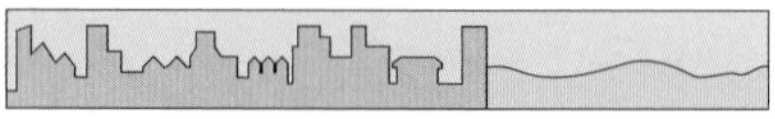
63%
37%

RELIGIOUS PERSUASION

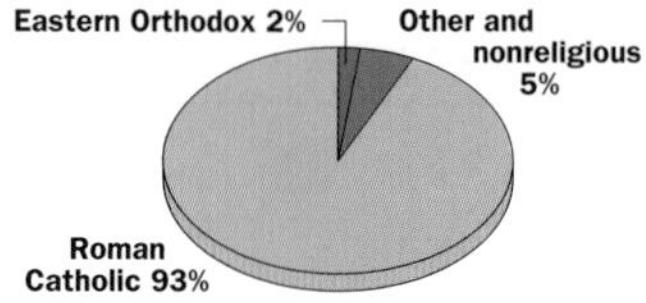
Eastern Orthodox 2%
Other and nonreligious 5%
Roman Catholic 93%

ETHNIC MAKEUP

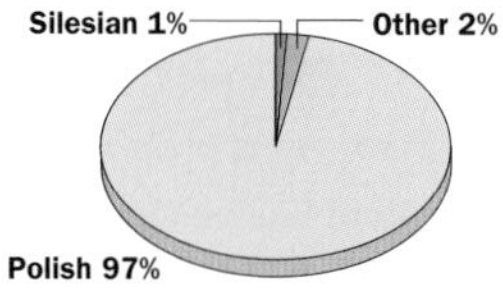
Silesian 1%
Other 2%
Polish 97%

Poland has a strongly Roman Catholic population, and in addition there is little ethnic diversity. The Church believes that stronger links with the West, especially through joining the EU, will weaken its influence. Abortion is still a major issue, and attempts to liberalize the law in 1996 were overturned by the Constitutional Tribunal.

Some small ethnic groups have opened schools and cultural and religious centers. Others, particularly ethnic Germans and German-dialect speakers in Silesia, are becoming more assertive. Jews are still resentful of past discrimination, and there is some evidence of residual antisemitism at a high level. Disputes over the special significance of the site of the Auschwitz concentration camp, near Kraków, has caused conflict between Jews and Catholics.

Wealth disparities are small, though the growing wealth of the entrepreneurial class is causing tension. The major political parties on left and right agree on continuing economic reform.

POPULATION AGE BREAKDOWN

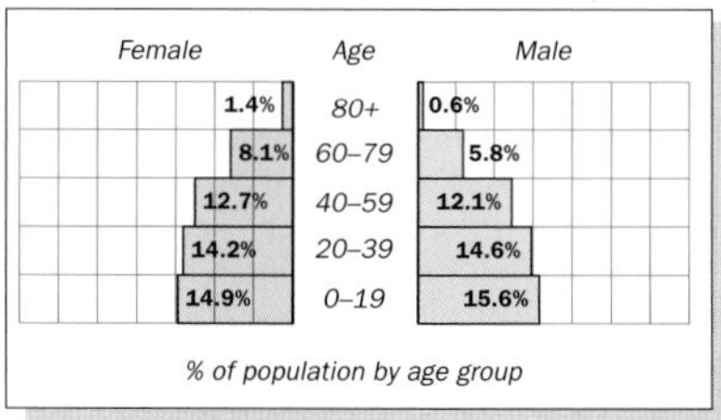
Female
Age
Male
1.4%
80+
0.6%
8.1%
60–79
5.8%
12.7%
40–59
12.1%
14.2%
20–39
14.6%
14.9%
0–19
15.6%
% of population by age group

P

POLITICS

Multiparty elections

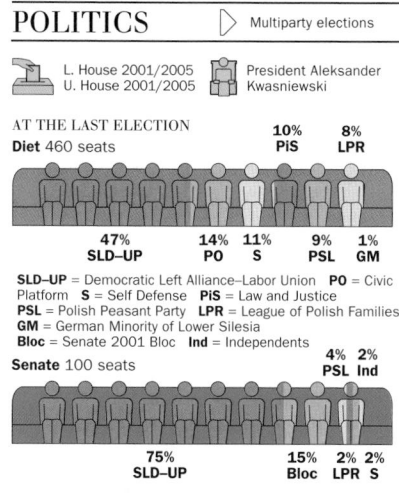

L. House 2001/2005
U. House 2001/2005

President Aleksander Kwasniewski

AT THE LAST ELECTION

Diet 460 seats

10% PiS
8% LPR
47% SLD–UP
14% PO
11% S
9% PSL
1% GM

SLD–UP = Democratic Left Alliance–Labor Union **PO** = Civic Platform **S** = Self Defense **PiS** = Law and Justice **PSL** = Polish Peasant Party **LPR** = League of Polish Families **GM** = German Minority of Lower Silesia **Bloc** = Senate 2001 Bloc **Ind** = Independents

Senate 100 seats

4% PSL
2% Ind
75% SLD–UP
15% Bloc
2% LPR
2% S

Since 1989, Poland has been a multiparty parliamentary democracy.

PROFILE

The reformed communists of the SLD and the PSL pursued a policy of market reforms in successive governments from 1993 until 1997. Aleksander Kwasniewski of the SLD was elected president in 1995, and reelected in 2000. More right-wing groups held sway for the 1997–2001 parliamentary term, with Jerzy Buzek as prime minister. His Solidarity Electoral Action (AWS) alliance, a right-wing grouping with vocal Catholic and nationalist elements, formed a coalition with the liberal Freedom Union (UW), but remained in office as a minority government after the UW withdrew in 2000. Buzek, who resisted pressure for early elections, came under attack from within the AWS itself.

In 2001 the Solidarity trade union wing voted to withdraw from politics, and the AWS lost all its seats in the legislative elections that September. A new left-of-center coalition was brought together under former communist Leszek Miller of the SLD. Since dismissing the PSL from his coalition in March 2003, Miller also has headed a minority government.

MAIN POLITICAL ISSUES

Minority rule

A superfluity of political parties has meant that fractious coalitions are the norm. Both Buzek and Miller were forced to lead minority governments after the loss of quarrelsome partners, leaving them reliant on parliamentary maneuvering to ensure the day-to-day survival of their governments.

***Leszek Miller**, a reformed communist, appointed prime minister in 2001.*

***President Aleksander Kwasniewski** of the SLD, elected in 1995.*

Church–state relations

Debates over abortion, worship in schools, values in the media, and even membership of the EU have fueled a heated dialogue over the proper role of the Church, which has been outspoken in its views – Pope John Paul II openly backs Poland's accession to the EU. However, the eclipse of Solidarity and the AWS has left the Church without its previous outlet in parliament.

POLAND

Total Area : 312 685 sq. km (120 728 sq. miles)

BALTIC SEA
Pomeranian Bay
Gulf of Danzig
Vistula Lagoon
RUSSIAN FEDERATION
LITHUANIA
BELARUS
UKRAINE
SLOVAKIA
CZECH REPUBLIC
GERMANY
Słupsk
Gdynia
Gdańsk
Koszalin
Elbląg
Olsztyn
MAZURY
Szczecin
Grudziądz
Piła
Bydgoszcz
Toruń
Białystok
Gorzów Wielkopolski
Włocławek
Płock
Poznań
WARSAW
Zielona Góra
Kalisz
Łódź
Głogów
Legnica
Radom
Lublin
Wrocław
Jelenia Góra
Wałbrzych
Kielce
Ostrowiec Świętokrzyski
Częstochowa
Opole
Chorzów
Bytom
Katowice
Dąbrowa Górnicza
Gliwice
Zabrze
Sosnowiec
Rybnik
Tychy
Wodzisław Śląski
Jastrzębie Zdrój
Ruda Śląska
Kraków
Tarnów
Rzeszów
Przemyśl
Bielsko Biała
Nowy Sącz
CARPATHIAN MOUNTAINS
Tatra Mts
Rysy 2499 m
Małopolska
Wyżyna Lubelska
Sudeten
Oder
Wisła
Warta
Noteć
Narew
Bug
San
Oderhaff
POPULATION
over 1 000 000
over 500 000
over 100 000
over 50 000
LAND HEIGHT
1000m/3281ft
500m/1640ft
200m/656ft
Sea Level
N
100 km
100 miles

WORLD AFFAIRS

Joined UN in 1945

CE | CEFTA | OECD | NATO | OSCE

Poland is keen to integrate with the West. It was admitted to NATO in 1999 and is set to join the EU in 2004. Membership of the latter rested on negotiating restrictions on the sale of Polish land to foreigners and the migration of Poles westward. Poland was an active part of the Coalition against Iraq in 2003 and as an ccupying force was given control over one of the military commands established there.

CHRONOLOGY

Poland was the second country in Europe to have a written constitution. In 1795, it was partitioned between Austria-Hungary, Prussia, and Russia.

- **1918** Polish state recreated.
- **1921** Democratic constitution.
- **1926–1935** Marshal Jozef Pilsudski heads military coup. Nine years of authoritarian rule.
- **1939** Germany invades and divides Poland with Russia.
- **1941** First concentration camps built on Polish soil.
- **1944** Warsaw Uprising.
- **1945** Potsdam and Yalta Conferences set present borders and determine political allegiance to Soviet Union.
- **1947** Communists manipulate elections to gain power.

P

CHRONOLOGY *continued*

- ❑ **1956** More than 50 killed in rioting in Poznań.
- ❑ **1970** Food price increases lead to strikes and riots in the Baltic port cities. Hundreds are killed.
- ❑ **1979** Cardinal Karol Wojtyla of Kraków is elected pope (John Paul II).
- ❑ **1980** Strikes force government to negotiate with Solidarity union. Resulting Gdańsk Accords grant right to strike and to form free trade unions.
- ❑ **1981** Gen. Wojciech Jaruzelski becomes prime minister.
- ❑ **1981–1983** Martial law. Solidarity forced into underground existence. Many of its leaders, including Lech Walesa, interned.
- ❑ **1983** Walesa awarded Nobel Peace Prize.
- ❑ **1986** Amnesty for political prisoners.
- ❑ **1987** Referendum rejects government austerity program.
- ❑ **1988** Renewed industrial unrest.
- ❑ **1989** Ruling party holds talks with Solidarity, which is relegalized. Partially free elections held. First postwar noncommunist government formed.
- ❑ **1990** Launch of market reforms. Walesa elected president.
- ❑ **1991** Free elections lead to fragmented parliament.
- ❑ **1992** Last Russian troops leave.
- ❑ **1993** Elections: reformed communists head coalition government.
- ❑ **1994** Launch of mass privatization.
- ❑ **1995** Aleksander Kwasniewski, leader of reformed communists, elected president.
- ❑ **1996** Historic Gdańsk shipyard declared bankrupt and closed down.
- ❑ **1997** Parliament finally adopts new postcommunist constitution. Legislative elections end former communist majority with big swing to right-wing AWS coalition.
- ❑ **1999** Joins NATO.
- ❑ **2001** Elections: AWS routed, left-of-center coalition formed under Leszek Miller.
- ❑ **2002** EU approves membership for 2004.

AID

Recipient

$966m (receipts) — Down 31% in 2001

Large-scale aid for economic transformation was a phenomenon of the early 1990s. The IMF, the EBRD, and the EU all supported Poland's stabilization and reform program. EU aid now focuses on debt-servicing and helping Poland to prepare to meet the environmental standards required of EU members.

DEFENSE

Compulsory military service

$3.41bn — Up 10% in 2001

Poland joined NATO in March 1999. Its standing army is among the largest in Europe, and there are also large paramilitary units, including border guards. A 15-year program to modernize the armed forces was introduced by the government in 1997. A civilian alternative to military service was first offered in 1998, and military service was reduced from 18 months to a year from 1999.

POLISH ARMED FORCES

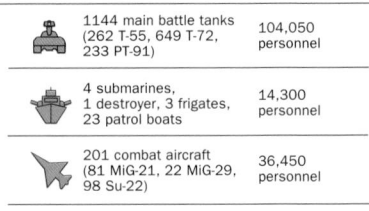

1144 main battle tanks (262 T-55, 649 T-72, 233 PT-91)	104,050 personnel
4 submarines, 1 destroyer, 3 frigates, 23 patrol boats	14,300 personnel
201 combat aircraft (81 MiG-21, 22 MiG-29, 98 Su-22)	36,450 personnel
None	

ECONOMICS

Inflation 21% p.a. (1990–2001)

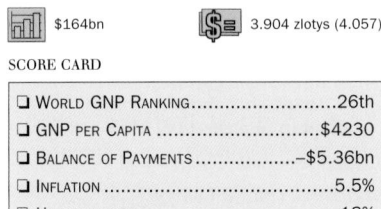

$164bn — 3.904 zlotys (4.057)

SCORE CARD

❑ World GNP Ranking	26th
❑ GNP per capita	$4230
❑ Balance of Payments	–$5.36bn
❑ Inflation	5.5%
❑ Unemployment	18%

EXPORTS

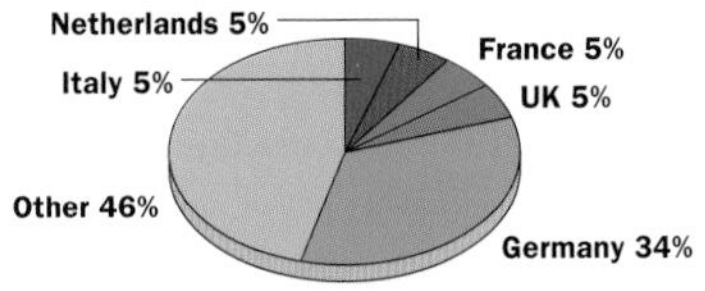

Netherlands 5%
Italy 5%
France 5%
UK 5%
Other 46%
Germany 34%

IMPORTS

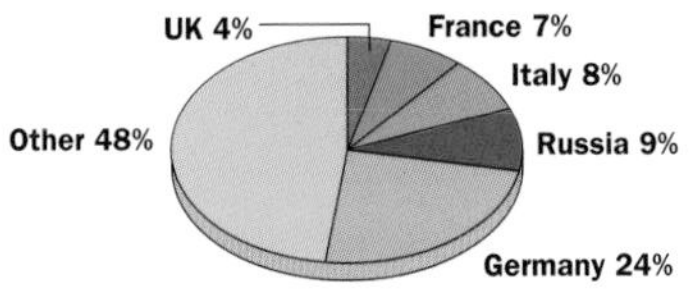

UK 4%
France 7%
Italy 8%
Other 48%
Russia 9%
Germany 24%

Strengths

Restructuring of loss-making coal industry began in 1998. Successful privatizations accelerated again in late 1990s. High rates of foreign investment reflect status as largest market in central Europe. Booming construction industry.

Weaknesses

High and rising unemployment. Agriculture suffers from overmanning, tiny farms, and lack of investment. Compensation for communist-era property expropriations unresolved. Heavy industries not competitive.

Profile

After a decade of economic crisis, the postcommunist government in 1990 drove through the most determined plan in the whole region to make the transition to a market economy. Most prices were freed, trade was opened and the zloty was made convertible. Economic growth and foreign investment soared, especially after

ECONOMIC PERFORMANCE INDICATOR

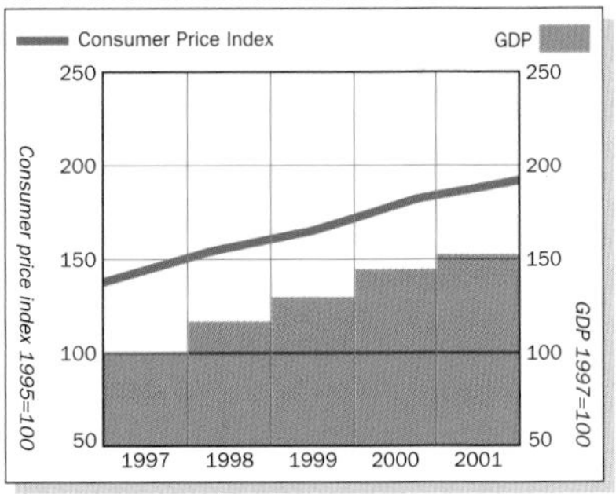

Consumer Price Index
GDP
250
200
150
100
50
1997
1998
1999
2000
2001
Consumer price index 1995=100
GDP 1997=100

Western creditors agreed to cancel half of the country's foreign debt in 1994. Poland now attracts the most foreign capital in central and eastern Europe.

There are still large-scale heavy industrial plants left over from the communist era, but some have been converted or reorganized successfully. Many state farms have been liquidated, but agricultural efficiency is improving only slowly. Some 26% of the workforce is employed in farming. Economic growth slowed at the end of the 1990s, but was back to 4% in 2000. Inflation has fallen since the 1990s, but unemployment hit a postcommunist record level in 2002, exceeding 18%.

POLAND : MAJOR BUSINESSES

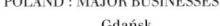

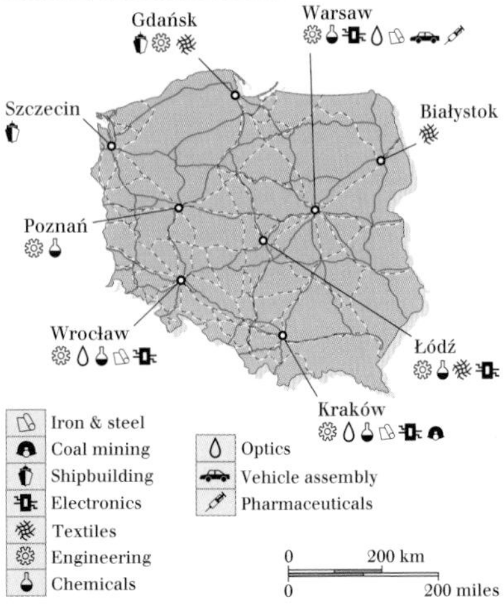

Gdańsk
Warsaw
Szczecin
Białystok
Poznań
Wrocław
Łódź
Kraków
Iron & steel
Coal mining
Shipbuilding
Electronics
Textiles
Engineering
Chemicals
Optics
Vehicle assembly
Pharmaceuticals
0 200 km
0 200 miles

P

RESOURCES

Electric power 30.7m kW

254,149 tonnes

8702 b/d (reserves 38m barrels)

18.7m pigs, 5.5m cattle, 3.57m ducks, 50.7m chickens

Coal, copper, silver, sulfur, natural gas, lead, salt, iron

ELECTRICITY GENERATION

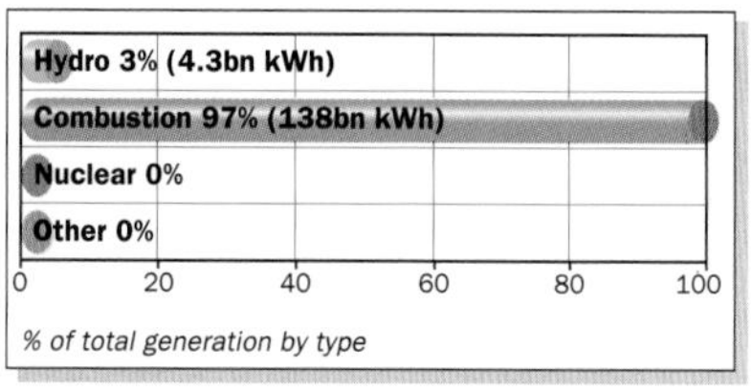
Hydro 3% (4.3bn kWh)
Combustion 97% (138bn kWh)
Nuclear 0%
Other 0%
0
20
40
60
80
100
% of total generation by type

Poland has significant quantities of coal, copper, silver, sulfur, natural gas, lead, and salt. The government's aim is to achieve self-sufficiency in energy resources and eventually to be able to export them; plans are in place to privatize the fuel and energy industries. The government also intends to reduce dependence on coal and to generate more electricity from natural gas.

POLAND : LAND USE

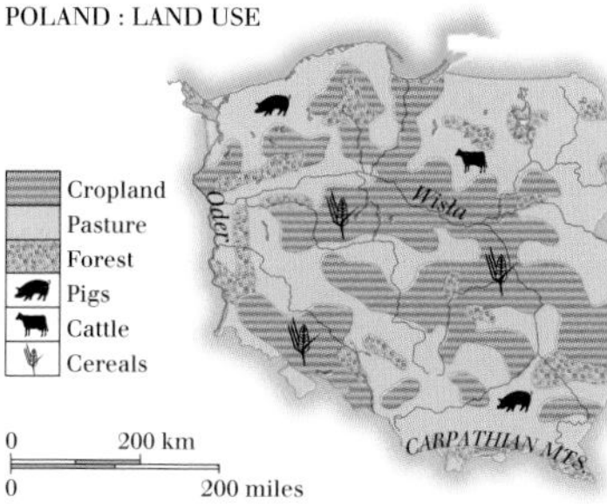
Cropland
Pasture
Forest
Pigs
Cattle
Cereals
Oder
Wisła
CARPATHIAN MTS.
0
200 km
0
200 miles

ENVIRONMENT

Sustainability rank: 87th

12% (9% partially protected)

8.1 tonnes per capita

ENVIRONMENTAL TREATIES

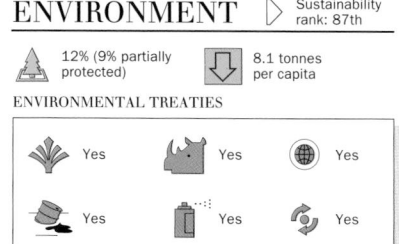

Yes	Yes	Yes
Yes	Yes	Yes

Pollution problems are serious, but lessening. Upper Silesia and the Kraków area are still badly affected, but industry there only emits a third of the pollutants it emitted in 1990. Now that much heavy industry has been cleaned up or closed down, there is more concern about small factories, domestic coal fires, and the increased use of private cars.

Water pollution, mainly from untreated sewage and industrial discharges, is a major problem. Rivers flowing into the Baltic are badly affected by nitrates and phosphates used in farming. Polish standards, themselves widely disregarded, need to be raised to meet EU minimum requirements.

MEDIA

TV ownership high

Daily newspaper circulation 102 per 1000 people

The constitution guarantees media freedom. *Gazeta Wyborcza*, set up by Solidarity in 1989, is still the leading daily, and its owners are expanding into other media. In 2003 the government ordered the bugging of all telecommunications, including e-mail, citing security concerns.

PUBLISHING AND BROADCAST MEDIA

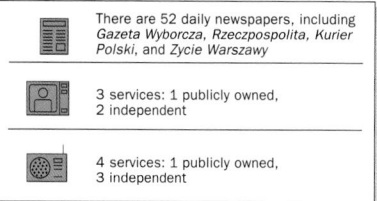

There are 52 daily newspapers, including *Gazeta Wyborcza, Rzeczpospolita, Kurier Polski,* and *Zycie Warszawy*

3 services: 1 publicly owned, 2 independent

4 services: 1 publicly owned, 3 independent

CRIME

No death penalty

82,173 prisoners

Up 24% in 2000–2001

CRIME RATES

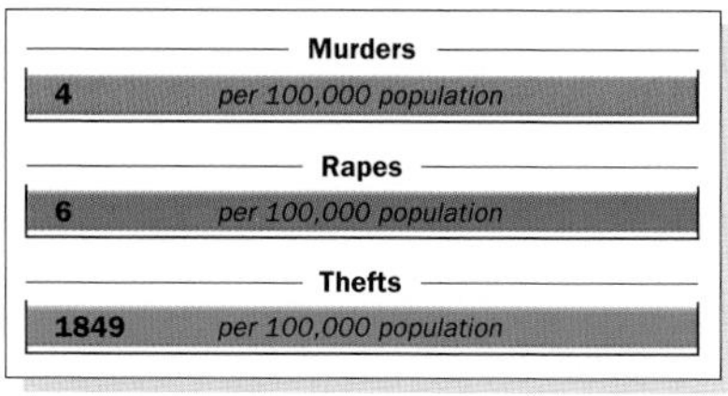
Murders
4
per 100,000 population
Rapes
6
per 100,000 population
Thefts
1849
per 100,000 population

Smuggling is the most significant problem, and Warsaw is a main center for this. Narcotics are transferred westward to Germany and expensive cars eastward to Russia. A National Remembrance Institute was set up in mid-2000 to investigate and prosecute the Nazi- and communist-era crimes of 1939–1989.

EDUCATION

School leaving age: 16

99%

1.77m students

THE EDUCATION SYSTEM

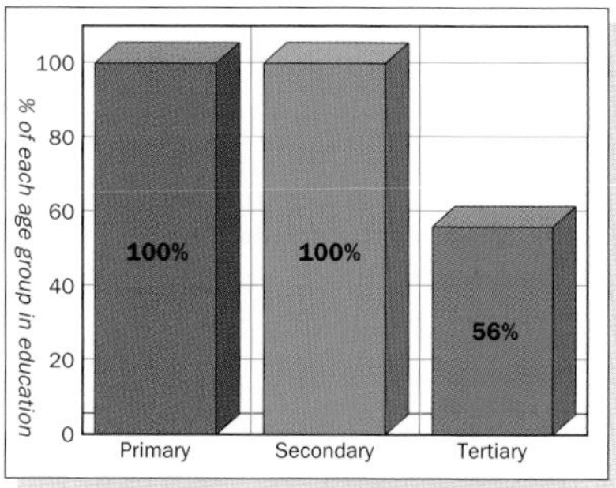
100
80
60
40
20
0
% of each age group in education
100%
100%
56%
Primary
Secondary
Tertiary

Primary education lasts from the age of seven to 13; lower secondary level follows until 16. At upper secondary level, exam-based selection separates the academic, technical, and vocational schools. A standard curriculum is followed in all schools. Despite the high official literacy figures, a relatively large proportion of school-leavers still lack basic skills. Public spending on education fell in real terms in the 1990s. Since 1989 the Roman Catholic Church has been allowed to operate schools. Most of the higher education institutions offer business-related courses.

HEALTH

Welfare state health benefits

1 per 429 people

Cancers, heart and cerebrovascular diseases

Fundamental reforms introduced in 1999 created a "market" health system, giving patients the right to choose where to go for treatment. Intended to be decentralized and less bureaucratic, the new system was confusing for some patients, with hospitals and doctors competing for business. Medical care is free for most people, but there are now a number of private health clinics.

SPENDING

GDP/cap. increase

CONSUMPTION AND SPENDING

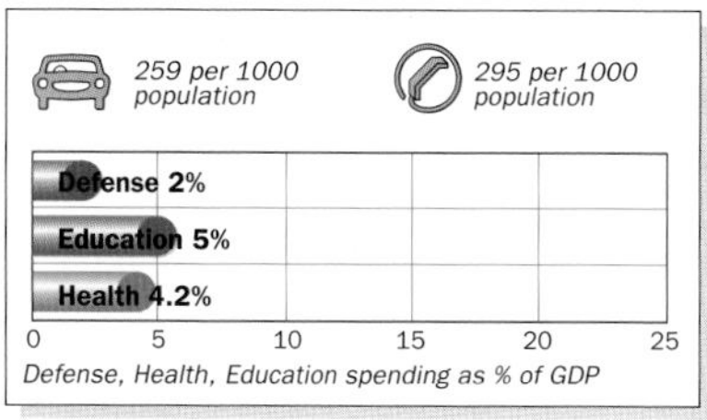
259 per 1000 population
295 per 1000 population
Defense 2%
Education 5%
Health 4.2%
0
5
10
15
20
25
Defense, Health, Education spending as % of GDP

Market reforms have led to some structural unemployment, and the inevitable hardship that this represents. More restructuring of heavy industry is planned. Pensioners have enjoyed benefits amounting to a higher percentage of GDP than in most countries, but state cutbacks are making private pensions more necessary.

WORLD RANKING

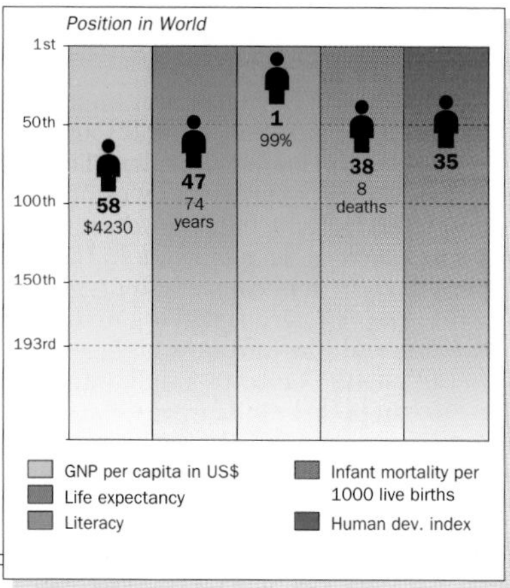
Position in World
1st
50th
100th
150th
193rd
58
$4230
47
74
years
1
99%
38
8
deaths
35
GNP per capita in US$
Life expectancy
Literacy
Infant mortality per 1000 live births
Human dev. index

P

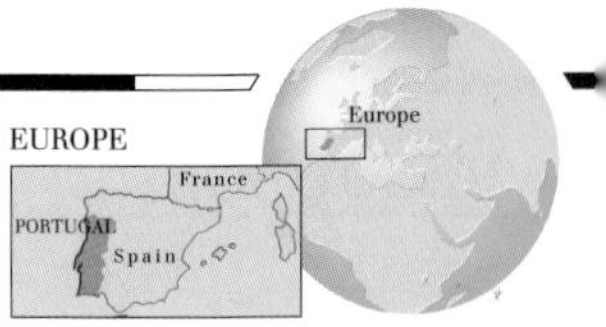
EUROPE
Europe
France
PORTUGAL
Spain

PORTUGAL

OFFICIAL NAME: Republic of Portugal **CAPITAL:** Lisbon
POPULATION: 10 million **CURRENCY:** Euro **OFFICIAL LANGUAGE:** Portuguese

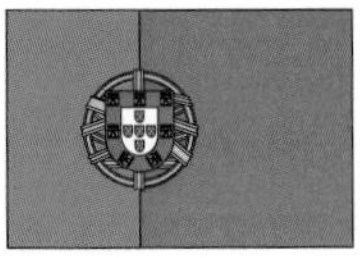

1139 | 1640 | June 10 | P | 0 | +351 | .pt

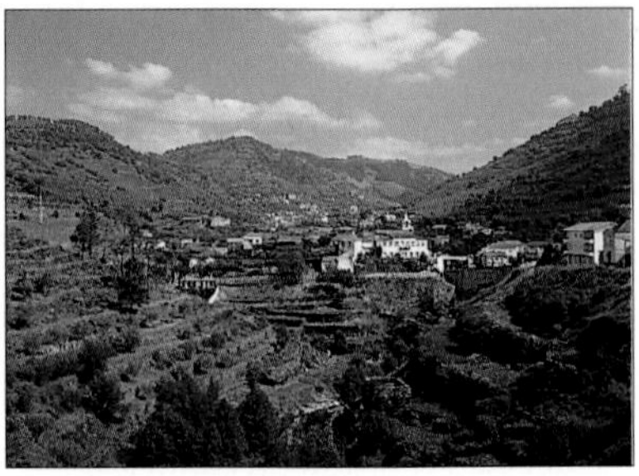

Santa Marta de Penaguiao, a small village in the heart of Portugal's wine-producing region, which is centered on the Douro valley.

PORTUGAL, WITH ITS long Atlantic coast, lies on the western side of the Iberian peninsula. The River Tagus divides the more mountainous north from the lower, undulating terrain to the south. In 1974, a bloodless military coup overthrew a long-standing conservative dictatorship. A constituent assembly was elected in 1975 and the armed forces withdrew from politics thereafter. Portugal then began a substantial program of economic modernization and accompanying social change. Membership of the EU has helped underpin this process.

CLIMATE

Mediterranean/ maritime

WEATHER CHART FOR LISBON

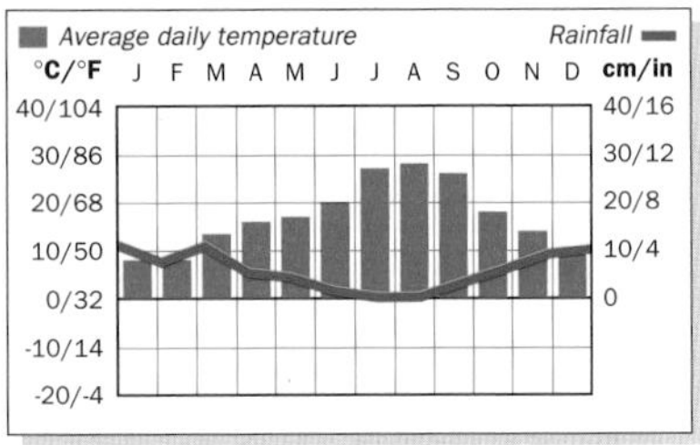
Average daily temperature
Rainfall
°C/°F J F M A M J J A S O N D cm/in
40/104
30/86
20/68
10/50
0/32
-10/14
-20/-4
40/16
30/12
20/8
10/4
0

Portugal has a mild, Mediterranean climate, which is moderated by the influence of the Atlantic. Summers can be hot and sultry, while winters are relatively mild. Inland areas have more variable weather than coastal regions. Rainfall is generally higher in the mountainous north, while the central areas are more temperate. The southern Algarve region is predominantly dry and sunny.

TRANSPORTATION

Drive on right

Portela de Sacavém, Lisbon 9.37m passengers

456 ships 1.2m grt

THE TRANSPORTATION NETWORK

59,110 km (36,729 miles)

883 km (549 miles)

2814 km (1749 miles)

820 km (510 miles)

Road links with Spain remain limited, despite modernization schemes and the new southern Guadiana bridge. The Lisbon–Madrid expressway was finally completed in 1999, the year after the 17-km Vasco da Gama bridge in Lisbon opened. Poor road construction, heavy traffic, and dangerous driving mean that Portugal has Europe's highest rate of road deaths. Lisbon's small, efficient metro complements its trams, but Porto's metro remains uncompleted. A high speed rail link with Spain is due for completion in 2008.

TOURISM

Visitors : Population 1.2:1

11.7m visitors

Down 4% in 2002

MAIN TOURIST ARRIVALS

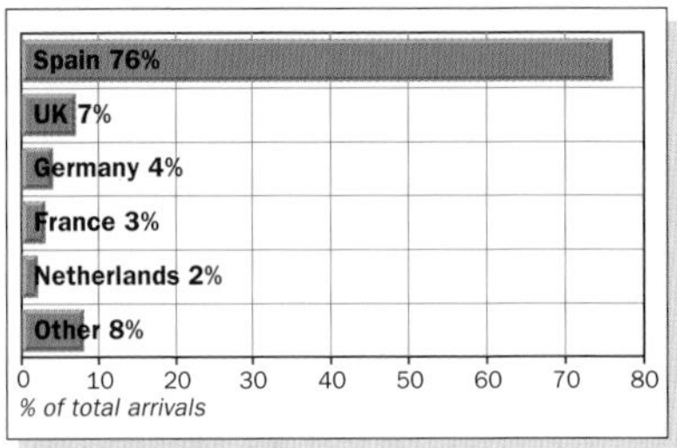
Spain 76%
UK 7%
Germany 4%
France 3%
Netherlands 2%
Other 8%
0 10 20 30 40 50 60 70 80
% of total arrivals

From the 1960s, Portugal's popularity as a tourist destination has been linked in part to qualities which reflected its relatively poor economic development, such as low prices and little crime. Thus some of the consequences of its substantial economic growth may have eroded part of Portugal's appeal, but since it now has a healthy number of visitors each year, tourism remains a major income-earner. The most popular destination is the Algarve, the southernmost province, followed by the western resorts of Figueira da Foz and the Tróia Peninsula. Visitors are also attracted by Portugal's architecture, notably that dating from the Manueline period (1490–1520), by its wine and port, and by its handicrafts, such as ceramics, lace, and tapestries. In addition, Portugal is noted for being the location of some of Europe's finest golf courses.

PORTUGAL

Total Area : 92 391 sq. km (35 672 sq. miles)

Minho
Viana do Castelo
Braga
Chaves
Bragança
Póvoa de Varzim
Vila do Conde
Matosinhos
Guimarães
Porto
Vila Real
Douro
Vila Nova de Gaia
Gondomar
Aveiro
Viseu
Mondego
Estrela 1991m
Coimbra
Figueira da Foz
Covilhã
Zêzere
Castelo Branco
Tagus
Caldas da Rainha
Fátima
Tomar
Peniche
Santarém
Portalegre
Amadora
Queluz
Sintra
Sacavém
Estoril
LISBON
Almada
Montijo
Barreiro
Setúbal
SERRA DE OSSA
Elvas
Évora
Tróia Peninsula
Alcácer do Sal
Bahía de Setúbal
Beja
Sines
Guadiana
ALGARVE
Lagos
Portimão
Faro
Olhão
Gulf of Cadiz
SPAIN

Azores
Ponta do Pico 2351m
Corvo
Flores
São Jorge
Graciosa
Terceira
Faial
Pico
São Miguel
Ponta Delgada
Santa Maria
0 200 km
0 200 miles

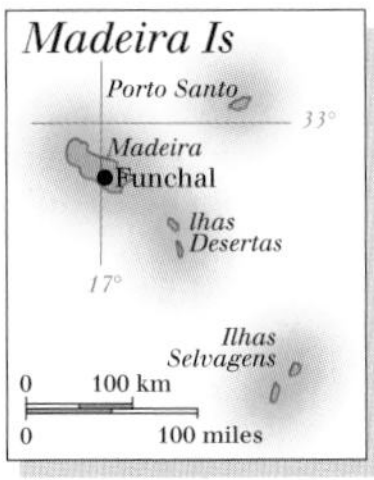
Madeira Is
Porto Santo
Madeira
Funchal
Ilhas Desertas
Ilhas Selvagens
0 100 km
0 100 miles

POPULATION

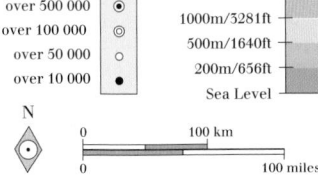

over 500 000
over 100 000
over 50 000
over 10 000

LAND HEIGHT

1000m/3281ft
500m/1640ft
200m/656ft
Sea Level

N

0 100 km
0 100 miles

P

PEOPLE

Pop. density medium

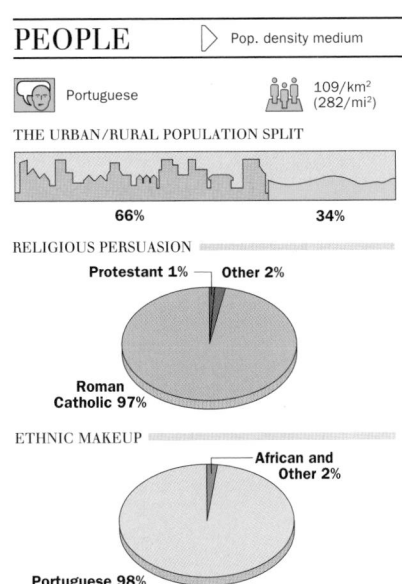

Portuguese

109/km² (282/mi²)

THE URBAN/RURAL POPULATION SPLIT

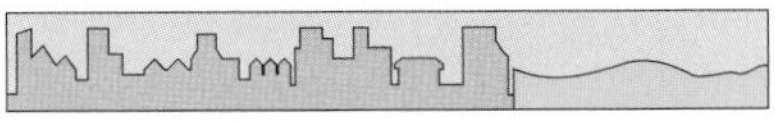
66%
34%

RELIGIOUS PERSUASION

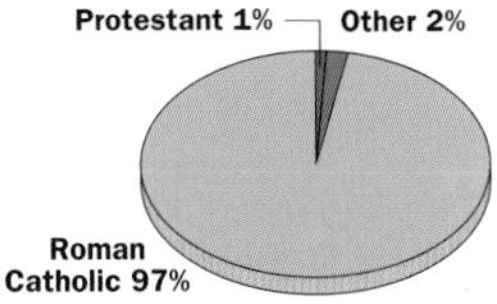
Protestant 1%
Other 2%
Roman Catholic 97%

ETHNIC MAKEUP

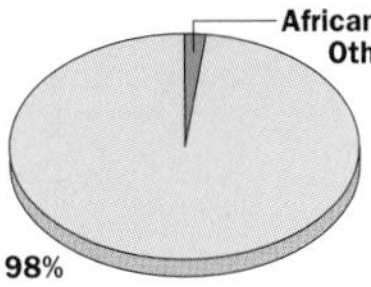
African and Other 2%
Portuguese 98%

Portuguese society, once regarded as rather inward-looking, has become much more egalitarian since the 1974 revolution. It is increasingly integrated into the rest of western Europe.

The Roman Catholic Church has lost some of its social influence, as shown by falling birthrates and more liberal attitudes to abortion, divorce, and unmarried mothers (almost one in five children are born outside marriage). Apart from urban areas, the north is still devoutly Catholic. Family ties remain all-important.

Ethnic and religious tensions are limited. Immigration increased after 1974, and foreigners now constitute 2% of the population. Early arrivals came from the former African colonies, but recently there has been an influx of east European workers.

Women got the vote only in 1976; now 60% of university students are women, and 63% of women of working age have jobs.

POPULATION AGE BREAKDOWN

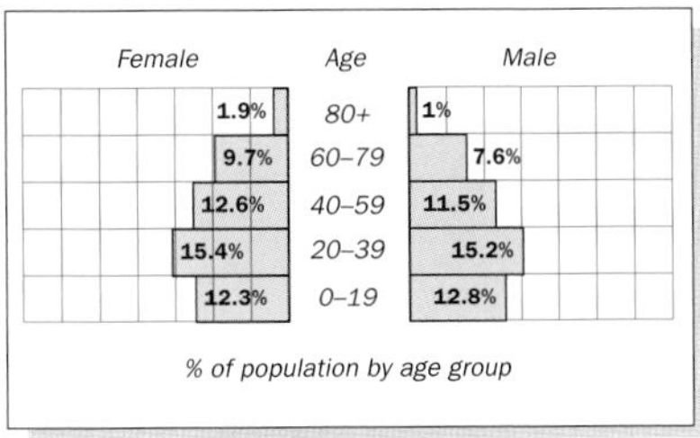
Female
Age
Male
1.9%
80+
1%
9.7%
60–79
7.6%
12.6%
40–59
11.5%
15.4%
20–39
15.2%
12.3%
0–19
12.8%
% of population by age group

WORLD AFFAIRS

Joined UN in 1955

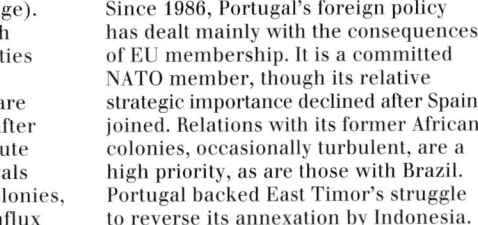

EU | CE | NATO | OECD | OSCE

Since 1986, Portugal's foreign policy has dealt mainly with the consequences of EU membership. It is a committed NATO member, though its relative strategic importance declined after Spain joined. Relations with its former African colonies, occasionally turbulent, are a high priority, as are those with Brazil. Portugal backed East Timor's struggle to reverse its annexation by Indonesia. Relations with China were cordial enough to ensure the smooth return of Macao to the latter at the end of 1999.

AID

Donor

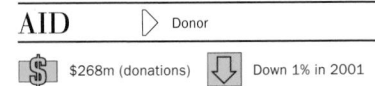

$268m (donations)

Down 1% in 2001

Portugal is a major beneficiary of EU aid from the so-called structural funds. It currently earmarks 0.25% of its GNP for aid to developing countries. More than 60% goes to former colonies in Africa, especially Mozambique, where Portuguese funding helped rebuild the massive war-damaged Cahora Bassa Dam and power plant.

POLITICS

Multiparty elections

2002/2006

President Jorge Sampãio

AT THE LAST ELECTION

Assembly of the Republic 230 seats
5% CDU
46% PSD
42% PS
6% PP
1% BE

PSD = Social Democratic Party
PS = Socialist Party **PP** = People's Party
CDU = United Democratic Coalition **BE** = Left Bloc

Portugal is a multiparty democracy.

PROFILE

A decade of center-right government ended in the 1995 elections, when the PSD lost to the PS. Having campaigned on a platform of social reform, the PS, under António Guterres, gave priority to fiscal control. Despite a privatization program, however, the size of the public sector actually increased in 1995–1999. The PS was reelected in 1999, but soon lost popularity, and was ousted by the PSD in early elections in March 2002. PSD leader José Manuel Durão Barroso was appointed prime minister. Lacking an overall majority, the PSD allied with the right-wing PP. The new government pledged to cut public spending and accelerate privatization.

MAIN POLITICAL ISSUES

Transformation

Portugal has been transformed in recent decades. The consolidation of democracy since the 1974 "Carnation Revolution" and EU membership since 1986 have brought Portugal into the European mainstream. There are high expectations about completing the "catching-up" process. Expo '98 in Lisbon showed off the new confidence. In 2002 Portugal was among the first 12 EU countries fully to adopt the euro.

Presidency and parliament

For ten years up to 1995, the presidency and the government were controlled by opposing parties, a situation which encouraged conflict and obstruction. A succession of PS presidents and minority governments then followed. Former PS leader Jorge Sampãio, who succeeded Mário Soares as president in 1996, was reelected comfortably in early 2001, but was to see a PSD government take office a year later, returning the executive to an uneasy "cohabitation."

***President Jorge Sampãio**, socialist president since 1996.*

***José Manuel Durão Barroso**, PSD prime minister since 2002.*

CHRONOLOGY

Portugal has existed as a nation state since 1139, though it was frequently challenged by Spain. It reached its zenith in the 16th century, before being annexed by Spain in 1580.

- **1640** Independence from Spain.
- **1755** Earthquake destroys Lisbon.
- **1793** Joins coalition against revolutionary France.
- **1807** France invades; royal family flees to Brazil.
- **1808** British troops arrive under Wellington. Start of Peninsular War.
- **1810** French leave Portugal.
- **1820** Liberal revolution.
- **1822** King João VI returns and accepts first Portuguese constitution. His son Dom Pedro declares independence of Brazil.
- **1834** Dom Pedro returns to Portugal to end civil war and installs his daughter as Queen Maria II.
- **1875–1876** Republican and Socialist parties founded.
- **1891** Republican uprising in Porto.
- **1908** Assassination of King Carlos I and heir to the throne.
- **1910** Abdication of Manuel II and proclamation of the Republic. Church and state separated.
- **1916** Portugal joins Allies in World War I.
- **1917–1918** New Republic led by Sidónio Pais.

➪

CHRONOLOGY *continued*

- **1926** Army overturns republic.
- **1928** António Salazar joins government as finance minister. Economy improves significantly.
- **1932** Salazar prime minister.
- **1933** Promulgation of the constitution of the "New State," instituting right-wing dictatorship.
- **1936–1939** Salazar assists Franco in Spanish Civil War.
- **1939–1945** Portugal neutral during World War II, but lets UK use air bases in Azores.
- **1949** Founder member of NATO.
- **1955** Joins UN.
- **1958** Américo Thómas appointed president, following fraudulent defeat of Gen. Humberto Delgado.
- **1961** India annexes Goa. Guerrilla warfare breaks out in Angola, Mozambique, and Guinea.
- **1970** Death of Salazar, incapacitated since 1968; succeeded by Marcelo Caetano.
- **1971** Caetano attempts liberalization.
- **1974** "Carnation Revolution" – left-wing Armed Forces Movement overthrows Caetano.
- **1974–1975** Portuguese possessions in Africa attain independence. Some 750,000 Portuguese expatriates return to Portugal.
- **1975** Communist takeover foiled by moderates and Mário Soares's PS.
- **1975** Indonesia seizes former Portuguese East Timor unopposed.
- **1976** Gen. António Eanes elected president. New constitution. Soares appointed prime minister.
- **1978** Period of nonparty technocratic government instituted.
- **1980** Center-right wins elections. Gen. Eanes reelected.
- **1982** Full civilian government formally restored.
- **1983** Soares caretaker prime minister, PS majority party.
- **1985** Anibal Cavaco Silva prime minister, minority PSD government.
- **1986** Soares elected president. Portugal joins EU, which funds major infrastructure and construction projects.
- **1987** Cavaco Silva wins absolute majority in parliament.
- **1991** Soares reelected president.
- **1995** PS wins elections; António Guterres prime minister.
- **1996** Former PS leader Jorge Sampãio elected president.
- **1999** PS strengthens its position in general election. December, Macao returned to China.
- **2001** Sampãio reelected.
- **2002** Euro fully adopted. PSD wins early elections, forms coalition with PP. José Manuel Durão Barroso prime minister.

P

DEFENSE

Phasing out conscription

$2.23bn

No change in 2001

Portugal has been a member of NATO since 1949. It has a small but relatively modern navy, while army and air force equipment is less up to date. Compulsory military service (currently of four to eight months (army) or four to 12 months (navy and air force), with a civilian alternative) is to be abolished in 2004. The US, which is the major arms supplier, has a strategic air base in the Azores.

PORTUGUESE ARMED FORCES

187 main battle tanks (86 M-48A5, 101 M-60)	25,400 personnel
2 submarines, 6 frigates, 28 patrol boats	10,800 personnel
65 combat aircraft (40 Alpha Jet, 6 P-3P, 19 F-16A/B)	7400 personnel
None	

ECONOMICS

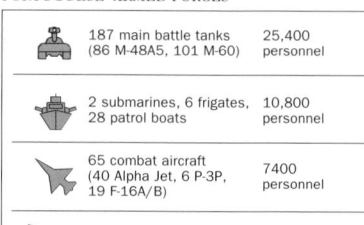

Inflation 5.1% p.a. (1990–2001)

$109bn

0.871 euros (1.013)

SCORE CARD

- World GNP Ranking 34th
- GNP per Capita $10,900
- Balance of Payments .... –$9.96bn
- Inflation 4.4%
- Unemployment 4%

EXPORTS

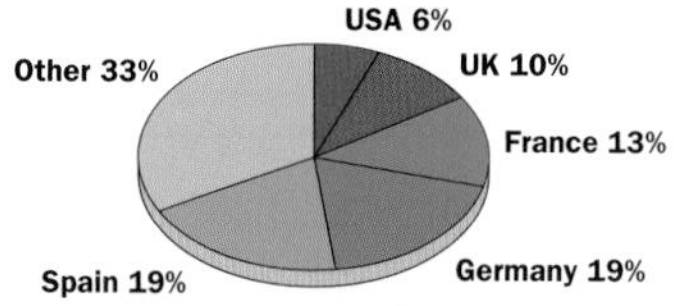
USA 6%
UK 10%
France 13%
Germany 19%
Spain 19%
Other 33%

IMPORTS

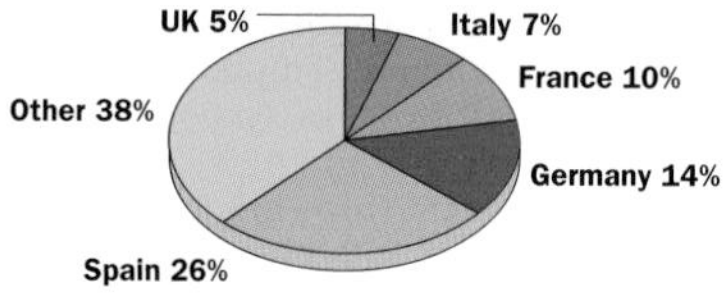
UK 5%
Italy 7%
France 10%
Germany 14%
Spain 26%
Other 38%

Strengths

Flexible labor market. High domestic and direct foreign investment. Strong banking sector. Tourism, now earning 6% of GDP – highest ratio in EU. Clothing and shoe manufacturing now joined by cars (notably Volkswagens) and machinery as major exports. Fast-track improvement of transportation infrastructure. Good deepwater port at Lisbon. Wine, especially port. Tomatoes, citrus fruit, cork, sardines.

Weaknesses

High dependence on imported oil. Reliance on public works to drive economic growth. Large agricultural sector (4% of GDP, 13% of workforce) is most inefficient in EU; product prices undercut by Spain. Concern over Spanish control of industries, banking in particular. Rising labor costs: manufacturers moving to eastern Europe.

Profile

EU membership in 1986 brought a sharp increase in foreign investment to largely rural Portugal. Exports rose dramatically and the economy grew steadily in the late 1990s. In a bid to boost foreign investment, the PSD government tightened labor legislation in 2002.

Though Portugal was among the 12 EU countries which fully adopted the euro, it has had difficulty meeting EU economic targets. Sanctions were imposed in 2002 when it was shown that the budget deficit had reached over 4% in 2001 – much higher than the EU's 3% limit. While Portuguese wages are about 70% of the EU average, the unemployment rate is among the lowest in the EU.

ECONOMIC PERFORMANCE INDICATOR

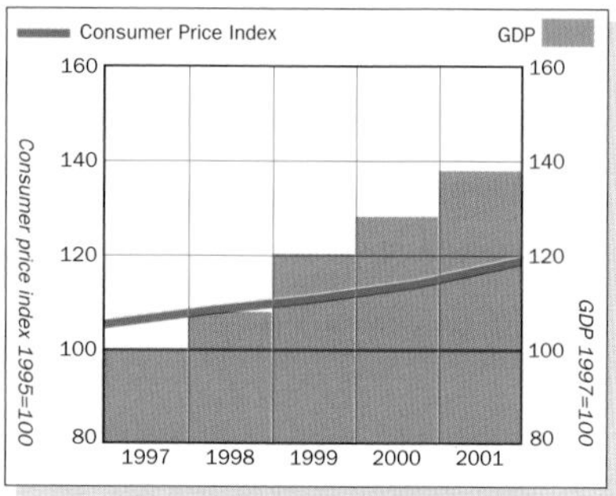
Consumer Price Index
GDP
160
140
120
100
80
1997
1998
1999
2000
2001
Consumer price index 1995=100
GDP 1997=100

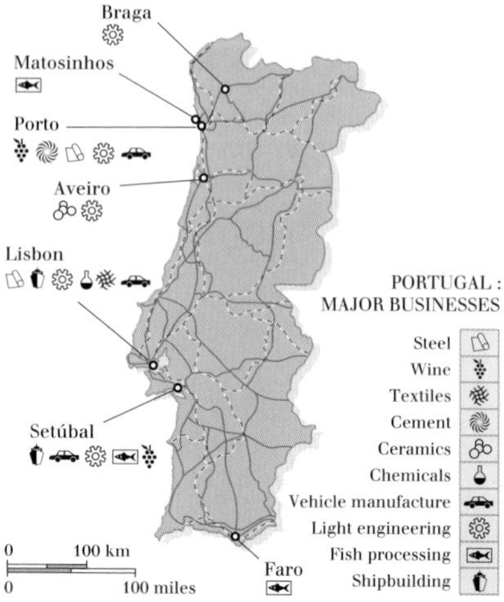
Braga
Matosinhos
Porto
Aveiro
Lisbon
Setúbal
Faro
0 100 km
0 100 miles
PORTUGAL : MAJOR BUSINESSES
Steel
Wine
Textiles
Cement
Ceramics
Chemicals
Vehicle manufacture
Light engineering
Fish processing
Shipbuilding

RESOURCES

Electric power 10.8m kW

194,691 tonnes

Not an oil producer; refines 270,000 b/d

7m turkeys, 5.48m sheep, 2.39m pigs, 35m chickens

Coal, limestone, granite, marble, tin, copper, tungsten

ELECTRICITY GENERATION

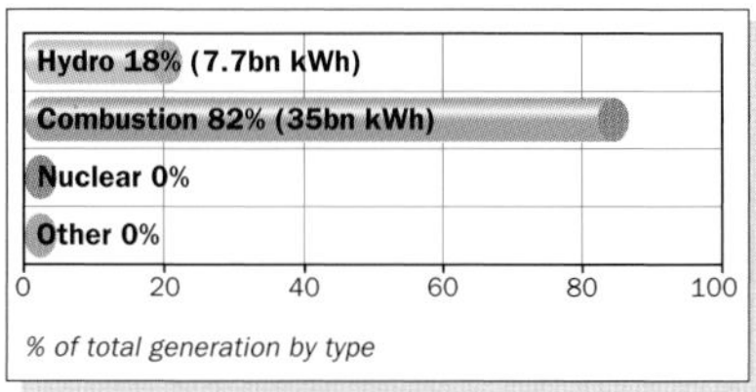

Hydro 18% (7.7bn kWh)
Combustion 82% (35bn kWh)
Nuclear 0%
Other 0%
0
20
40
60
80
100
% of total generation by type

Portugal is disadvantaged by a lack of natural resources, including water. Mining has historically been important, notably for tungsten, copper, and tin. The last coal mine closed in the mid-1990s. The fish catch, once central to the economy, has been declining in recent years.

PORTUGAL : LAND USE

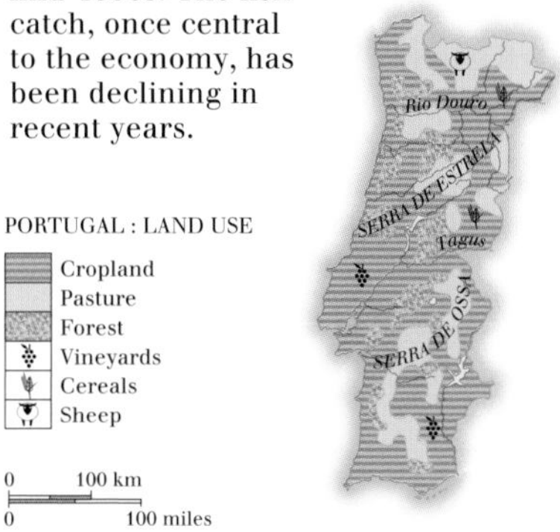

Cropland
Pasture
Forest
Vineyards
Cereals
Sheep
0 100 km
0 100 miles
Rio Douro
SERRA DE ESTRELA
Tagus
SERRA DE OSSA

ENVIRONMENT

Sustainability rank: 28th

7% (6% partially protected)

6.3 tonnes per capita

ENVIRONMENTAL TREATIES

Yes	Yes	Yes
Yes	Yes	Yes

The unrestricted development of tourist resorts in the Algarve and major infrastructure projects are having a detrimental effect on natural habitats. EU agricultural grants for projects such as draining meadows, and monoculture afforestation, notably of eucalyptus and pine, are degrading biodiversity. Concerns include air pollution caused by industrial and vehicle emissions, and water pollution in coastal areas. New waste management regulations are being introduced.

MEDIA

TV ownership high

Daily newspaper circulation 73 per 1000 people

PUBLISHING AND BROADCAST MEDIA

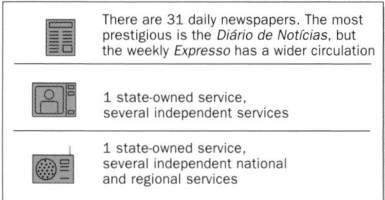

There are 31 daily newspapers. The most prestigious is the *Diário de Notícias*, but the weekly *Expresso* has a wider circulation

1 state-owned service, several independent services

1 state-owned service, several independent national and regional services

Most newspapers have only regional distribution. TV is the dominant medium. The Roman Catholic TVI was sold in 1998 to Media Capital, one of four groups that control most of the press and broadcasting. In 2002, the government strengthened its control over the state-owned RTP raising fears for its political independence.

CRIME

No death penalty

13,384 prisoners

Up sharply in 2000–2002

CRIME RATES

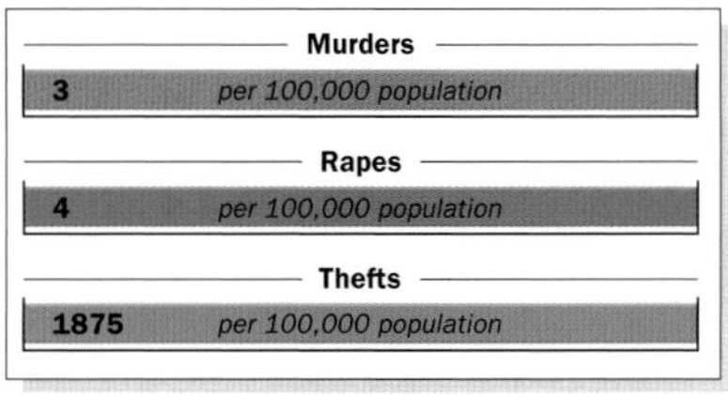

Murders
3 per 100,000 population
Rapes
4 per 100,000 population
Thefts
1875 per 100,000 population

Thefts have increased in recent years, raising the low crime rate. Possession and consumption of small quantities of narcotics were decriminalized in mid-2000 and legalized a year later.

EDUCATION

School leaving age: 15

93%

387,703 students

THE EDUCATION SYSTEM

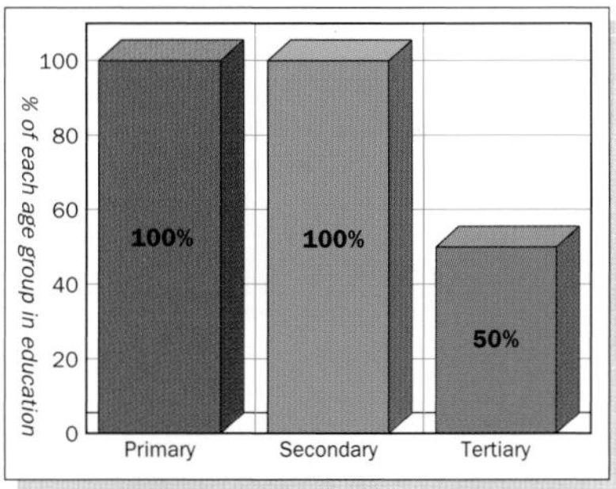

100
80
60
40
20
0
% of each age group in education
100%
100%
50%
Primary
Secondary
Tertiary

Portuguese is the sixth most widely spoken language in the world.

Free state education is available to all pupils between the ages of three and 15. Nursery provision has been greatly expanded, though the preschool stage is not compulsory. Middle-class parents rely heavily on the private sector. State universities have been expanded to ease the pressure on places. There are several prestigious private universities.

HEALTH

Welfare state health benefits

1 per 321 people

Cancers, cerebro-vascular, respiratory, and heart diseases

Of total government expenditure nearly 10% is spent on health.

Portugal has had a publicly funded, free national health service since 1979; Spending on health has increased markedly in recent years, but care remains below the EU average. There are strong regional differences in facilities. Larger urban hospitals are modern and well equipped. Private health care schemes, which are allowed to coexist, are both affordable and good value for money; over 40% of the population use the private system.

SPENDING

GDP/cap. increase

CONSUMPTION AND SPENDING

321 per 1000 population

427 per 1000 population

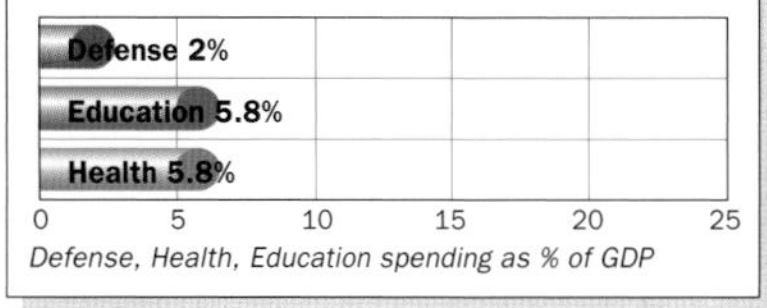

Defense 2%
Education 5.8%
Health 5.8%
0
5
10
15
20
25
Defense, Health, Education spending as % of GDP

Wealth differentials in Portugal are smaller than in most EU countries. The 1976 Constitution committed Portugal to making the transition to socialism, and since then governments have introduced limited wealth redistribution measures.

Internal investment is directed chiefly through the property market, and there was a surge of purchases in the late 1990s. External investment goes to the EU and Brazil. In 2000, 14.5% of the population held shares directly. Average incomes, which were just over half the EU average in 1986, are now around three-quarters of the EU average. Portugal pioneered prepayment systems for mobile phones, which are widely owned.

WORLD RANKING

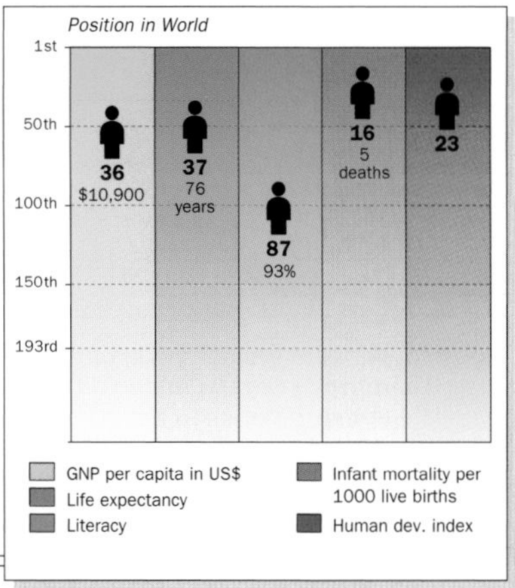

Position in World
1st
50th
100th
150th
193rd
36
$10,900
37
76
years
87
93%
16
5
deaths
23
GNP per capita in US$
Life expectancy
Literacy
Infant mortality per 1000 live births
Human dev. index

P

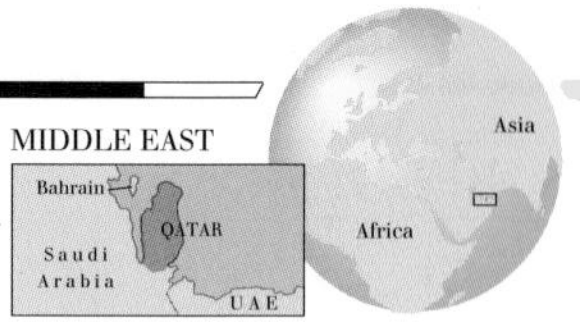
MIDDLE EAST
Bahrain
QATAR
Saudi Arabia
UAE
Asia
Africa

QATAR

OFFICIAL NAME: State of Qatar **CAPITAL:** Doha
POPULATION: 584,000 **CURRENCY:** Qatar riyal **OFFICIAL LANGUAGE:** Arabic

1971 | 1971 | Sept 3 | Q | +3 | +974 | .qa

PROJECTING NORTH FROM the Arabian peninsula into the Gulf, Qatar is mostly flat, semiarid desert. Oil production began in the late 1940s and quickly transformed Qatar from an impoverished pearl producer into a prosperous shaikhdom and a founder member of OPEC. Plentiful oil and gas reserves have made it one of the wealthiest states in the region. Politics is being democratized gradually under the ruling al-Thani clan.

CLIMATE

Hot desert

WEATHER CHART FOR DOHA

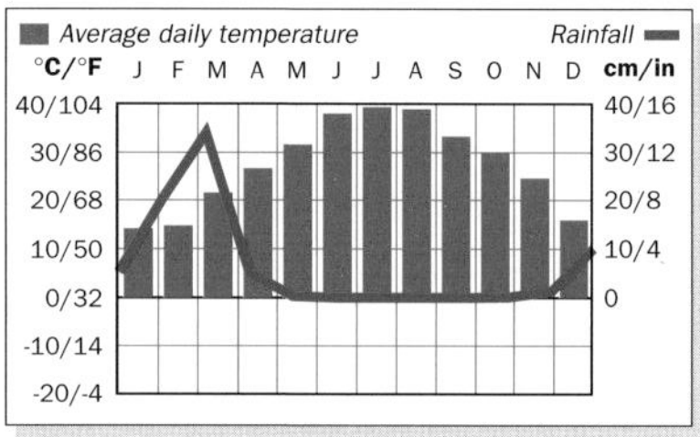
Average daily temperature
Rainfall
°C/°F
J F M A M J J A S O N D
cm/in
40/104
30/86
20/68
10/50
0/32
-10/14
-20/-4
40/16
30/12
20/8
10/4
0

The climate is hot and sultry, with midsummer temperatures reaching 44°C (111°F). Rainfall is rare.

TRANSPORTATION

Drive on right

Doha International 2.95m passengers

68 ships 690,812 grt

THE TRANSPORTATION NETWORK

1107 km (688 miles)

None

None

None

A 45-km "Friendship Bridge," the world's longest fixed link, is planned to connect Qatar to Bahrain.

TOURISM

Visitors : Population 1:1.3

451,000 visitors

Up 6% in 1998

MAIN TOURIST ARRIVALS

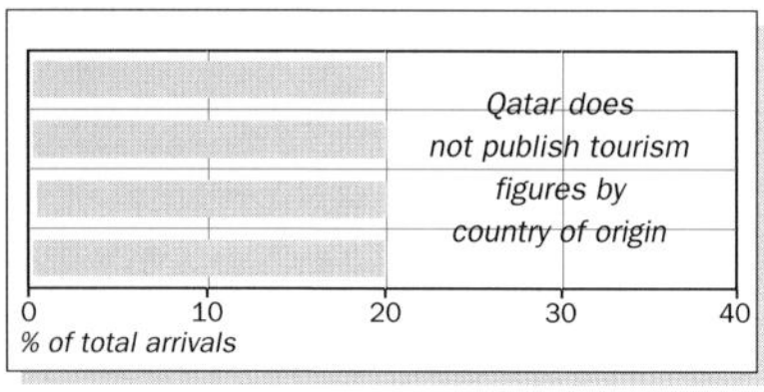
Qatar does not publish tourism figures by country of origin
0
10
20
30
40
% of total arrivals

Tourism is expanding. A government drive to improve Qatar's image as a tourist destination aims to net more than 1.5 million tourists a year by 2010. Attractions include unspoiled beaches, duty-free shopping, and modern hotels.

PEOPLE

Pop. density medium

Arabic

53/km² (138/mi²)

THE URBAN/RURAL POPULATION SPLIT

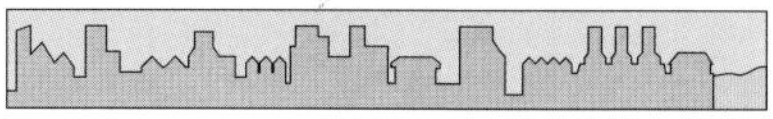
93%
7%

ETHNIC MAKEUP

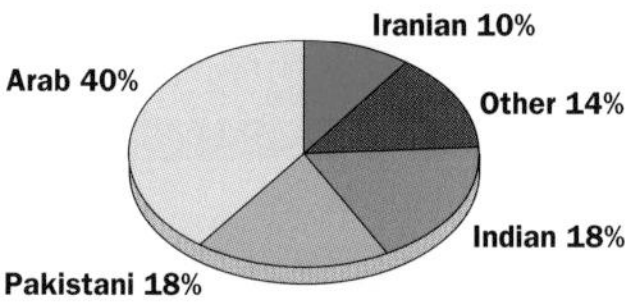
Iranian 10%
Arab 40%
Other 14%
Indian 18%
Pakistani 18%

Only one in five inhabitants is native-born. Most are guest workers from the Indian subcontinent, Iran, and north African countries. Western expatriates enjoy a high standard of living and take no part in politics.

Most Qataris are followers of the Wahhabi interpretation of Sunni Islam and espouse conservative religious views. However, women are not obliged to wear a veil and can hold a driving license. Expatriate Christians are allowed freedom to worship but not to promote Christianity.

Since the advent of oil wealth, the Qataris, who were formerly nomadic Bedouins, have become a nation of city dwellers. Almost 90% of the population now inhabit the capital Doha and its suburbs. As a result, northern Qatar is dotted with depopulated and abandoned villages.

Doha, the capital. *Though desert covers the whole country, Qatar now grows most of its own vegetables by tapping groundwater.*

POLITICS

In transition

Not applicable

Amir Shaikh Hamad bin Khalifa al-Thani

LEGISLATIVE OR ADVISORY BODIES

Advisory Council 35 seats

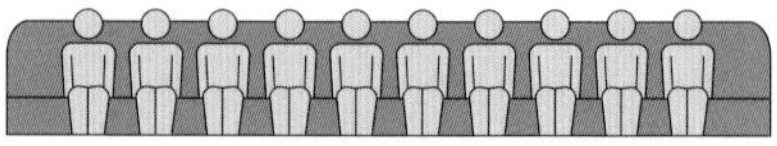

Qatar is an absolute monarchy. The amir rules with the assistance of the Council of Ministers and the Advisory Council. A partially elected 45-member parliament is to be created, with elections expected in 2004.

Qatar is a traditional emirate. The government and religious establishment are dominated by the amir, Shaikh Hamad, who ousted his father, Shaikh Khalifa, in 1995. A failed coup against Hamad in early 1996 was linked with efforts by Khalifa to regain power. The prodemocracy movement has called for reform of the 35-member Advisory Council. Shaikh Hamad responded by authorizing Qatar's first elections, to a new municipal council for Doha, in 1999. All adults, including women, were able to vote and stand as candidates. The creation of a partially elected 45-seat legislature was approved overwhelmingly in a 2003 referendum.

WORLD AFFAIRS

Joined UN in 1971

AL | OIC | GCC | OAPEC | OPEC

Though Qatar was a founder member of the GCC, Shaikh Hamad has adopted a somewhat ambivalent stance toward it. However, Qatar entered into the region's first mutual defense pact, under the aegis of the GCC, in 2000. In 2001 Qatar reached an agreement on the border with Saudi Arabia, but lost its claim to the Hawar Islands when the International Court of Justice ruled in Bahrain's favor.

Qatar supplied liquefied natural gas (LNG) to Israel in the late 1990s, but relations, previously the most cordial of the Gulf states, have suffered greatly since the renewal of the Palestinian *intifada* in 2000. The amir had criticized previous US and UK air strikes on Iraq, but allowed the country to be used as a base for the US Central Command during the 2003 invasion.

AID

Recipient

$1m (receipts)

Up slightly in 2001

Qatar was an aid donor in the 1970s and early 1980s. Now it receives small amounts of aid, mainly from France; around 70% is allocated to education.

Q

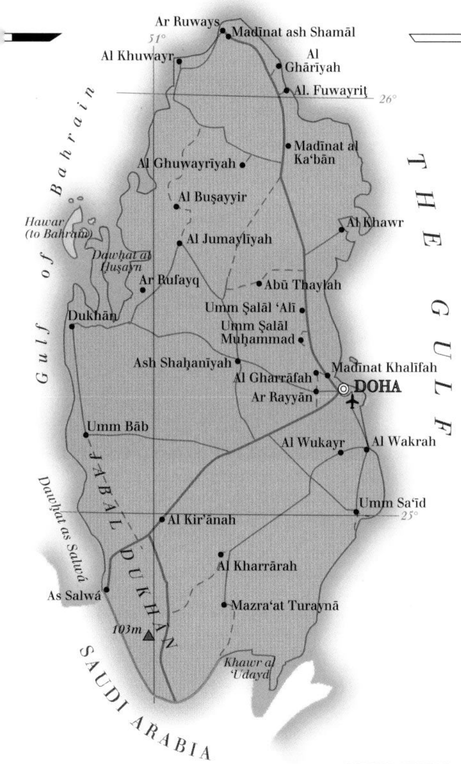

Ar Ruways
Madīnat ash Shamāl
Al Khuwayr
Al Ghārīyah
Al Fuwayriṭ
Madīnat al Ka'bān
Al Ghuwayrīyah
Al Buşayyir
Al Khawr
Hawar (to Bahrain)
Gulf of Bahrain
Dawhat al Ḩusayn
Al Jumaylīyah
Ar Rufayq
Abū Thaylah
THE GULF
Dukhān
Umm Şalāl 'Alī
Umm Şalāl Muḩammad
Ash Shaḩanīyah
Madīnat Khalīfah
Al Gharrāfah
DOHA
Ar Rayyān
Umm Bāb
Al Wukayr
Al Wakrah
JABAL DUKHĀN
Umm Sa'īd
Dawhat as Salwá
Al Kir'ānah
Al Kharrārah
As Salwá
Mazra'at Turaynā
103m
Khawr al 'Udayd
SAUDI ARABIA

QATAR

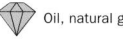

Total Area : 11 437 sq. km (4416 sq. miles)

POPULATION
over 100 000
under 10 000

LAND HEIGHT
200m/1640ft
Sea Level

0 20 km
0 20 miles

DEFENSE

No compulsory military service

$1.24bn

Up 5% in 2001

The armed forces are too small – at an estimated 12,000 – to play a significant role in Qatari affairs, even in the event of political turmoil. A defense agreement with the US, extended in 2002, provides for joint exercises, stockpiling of US equipment, and US access to bases.

RESOURCES

Electric power 1.9m kW

7142 tonnes

755,000 b/d (reserves 15.2bn barrels)

200,000 sheep, 179,000 goats, 4m chickens

Oil, natural gas

Qatar has the third-smallest reserves of crude oil within OPEC but abundant reserves of gas (the third-largest in the world), including the world's largest field of gas unassociated with oil.

ENVIRONMENT

Not available

0.1% partially protected

90.7 tonnes per capita

The desert hinterland supports little plant or animal life. Most native species are extinct in the wild. Oil pollution has damaged marine life. There are salt flats in the south.

MEDIA

TV ownership high

Daily newspaper circulation 161 per 1000 people

PUBLISHING AND BROADCAST MEDIA

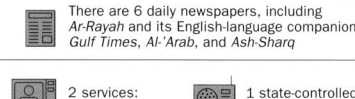

There are 6 daily newspapers, including *Ar-Rayah* and its English-language companion *Gulf Times*, *Al-'Arab*, and *Ash-Sharq*

2 services: 1 state-controlled

1 state-controlled service

Qatari TV is the most independent in the region; Al-Jazeera offers the leading Arab perspective internationally, especially since the events of 2001.

CRIME

Death penalty in use

570 prisoners

Up 19% in 1999

Traditional Islamic punishments have deterred crime. However, narcotics trafficking is on the increase. The incidence of street crime is low.

CHRONOLOGY

The al-Thanis, related to the Khalifa family of Bahrain, took control of the Qatar peninsula in the 18th century.

- ❑ 1971 Sovereignty recognized by UK.
- ❑ 1972 Accession of Amir Khalifa.
- ❑ 1995 Shaikh Hamad takes power.
- ❑ 1999 First ever (municipal) polls.
- ❑ 2003 Referendum approves creation of partially elected legislature.

EDUCATION

School leaving age: 11

82%

7808 students

Education is free from primary to university level. The government finances students to study overseas.

HEALTH

Welfare state health benefits

1 per 455 people

Heart, circulatory, and infectious diseases, cancers

Primary health care is free to Qataris. Hospitals operate to Western standards of care and the government also funds treatment abroad.

SPENDING

GDP/cap. increase

CONSUMPTION AND SPENDING

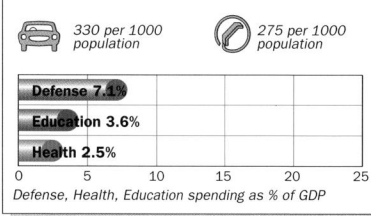

330 per 1000 population

275 per 1000 population

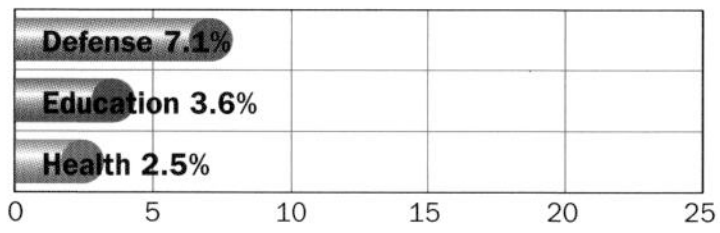

Defense 7.1%
Education 3.6%
Health 2.5%
0
5
10
15
20
25

Defense, Health, Education spending as % of GDP

Qataris have a high per capita income. There is no income tax, public services are free, and the government guarantees jobs for school-leavers. There are no exchange controls.

ECONOMICS

Inflation 2.5% p.a. (1990–2000)

$8.4bn

3.639 Qatar riyals (3.641)

SCORE CARD

- ❑ WORLD GNP RANKING........................92nd
- ❑ GNP PER CAPITA.........................$12,000
- ❑ BALANCE OF PAYMENTS.................–$1.66bn
- ❑ INFLATION...2%
- ❑ UNEMPLOYMENT.........................Not available

STRENGTHS

Steady supply of crude oil and huge gas reserves, plus related industries. Modern infrastructure. Budget surplus.

WEAKNESSES

Dependence on foreign workforce. Oil price fluctuations. All raw materials imported. Virtually all water has to be desalinated. Large foreign reserves, but new industries depend on cementing agreements with foreign partners. Potential threats to security from Iraq and Iran make some multinationals wary of investment.

EXPORTS

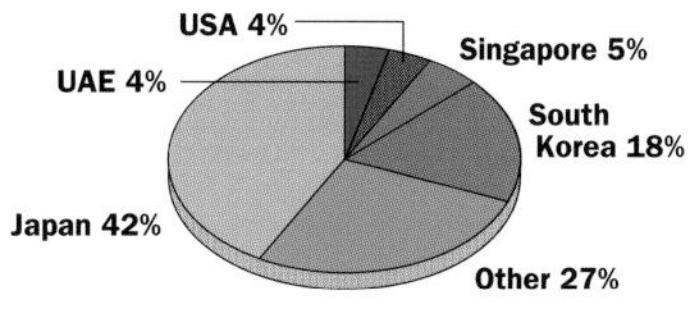

USA 4%
Singapore 5%
UAE 4%
South Korea 18%
Japan 42%
Other 27%

IMPORTS

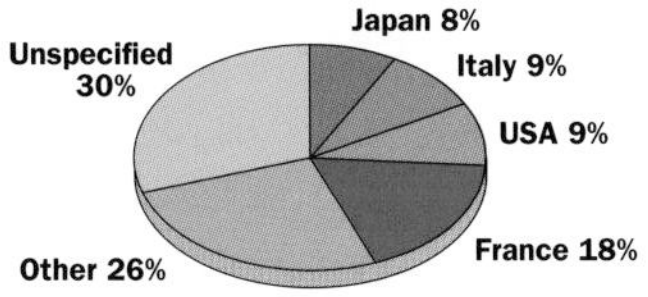

Japan 8%
Unspecified 30%
Italy 9%
USA 9%
France 18%
Other 26%

WORLD RANKING

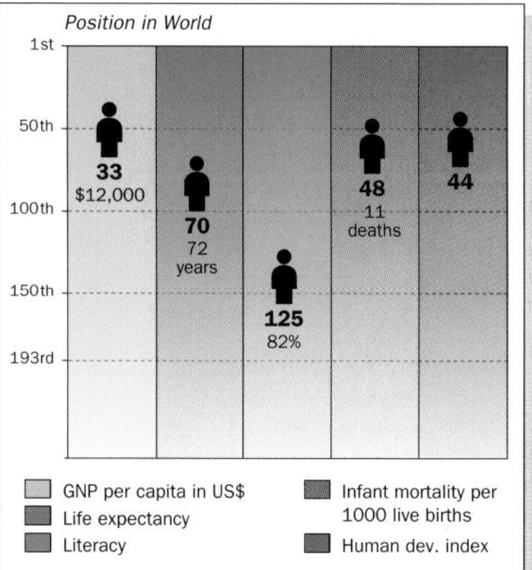

Position in World
1st
50th
100th
150th
193rd
33
$12,000
70
72 years
125
82%
48
11 deaths
44
GNP per capita in US$
Life expectancy
Literacy
Infant mortality per 1000 live births
Human dev. index

Q

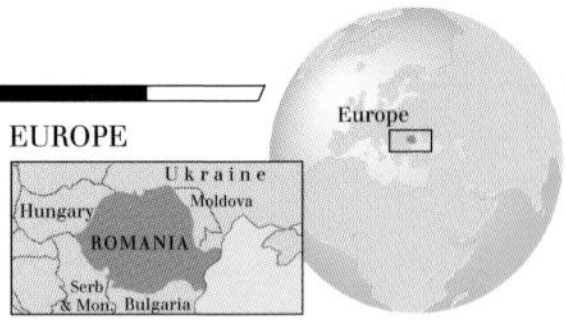

EUROPE
Europe
Ukraine
Moldova
Hungary
ROMANIA
Serb & Mon.
Bulgaria

ROMANIA

OFFICIAL NAME: Romania **CAPITAL:** Bucharest
POPULATION: 21.7 million **CURRENCY:** Romanian leu **OFFICIAL LANGUAGE:** Romanian

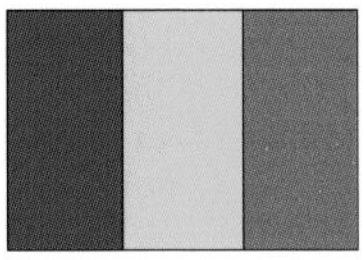

1878 | 1947 | Dec 1 | RO | +2 | +40 | .ro

ROMANIA LIES ON THE Black Sea coast, with the Danube as its southern border. The Carpathian Mountains form an arc across the country, curving around the upland basin of Transylvania. Long dominated by Poles, Hungarians, and Ottomans, Romania became an independent monarchy in 1878. After World War II, this was supplanted by a communist People's Republic, headed from 1965 by Nicolae Ceauşescu. A coup in 1989 resulted in his execution and a limited democracy under Ion Iliescu. Defeated in elections in 1996, Iliescu was returned to office in 2000.

Village in northeastern Romania, in the foothills of the Carpathian Mountains, close to the border with Ukraine. Corn and wheat are Romania's main crops.

CLIMATE

Continental

WEATHER CHART FOR BUCHAREST

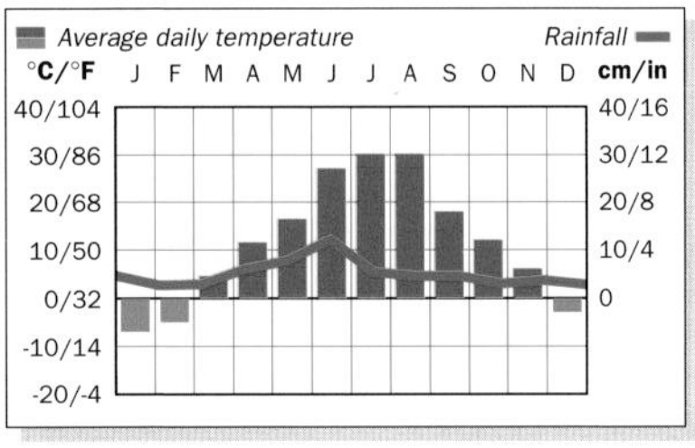

Average daily temperature
Rainfall
°C/°F
J F M A M J J A S O N D
cm/in
40/104
30/86
20/68
10/50
0/32
-10/14
-20/-4
40/16
30/12
20/8
10/4
0

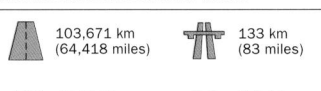

Romania has a continental climate with two growing seasons. Rainfall is generally moderate, with most rain falling in spring and early summer. Very heavy spring rains occasionally destroy new crops. Snow is frequent in winter, which can be bitterly cold.

TRANSPORTATION

Drive on right

Bucharest–Otopeni International
2.12m passengers

240 ships
637,700 grt

THE TRANSPORTATION NETWORK

103,671 km (64,418 miles)

133 km (83 miles)

11,364 km (7061 miles)

1724 km (1071 miles)

The road network is inadequate, and traffic levels are rising. EBRD, EU, World Bank, and Japanese funding has focused on the expressway from Bucharest to Hungary, and on improving major roads. Modernization of the port of Constanţa to include a container port and new grain silo is also under way.

TOURISM

Visitors : Population 1:7.7

2.82m visitors

Down 14% in 2001

MAIN TOURIST ARRIVALS

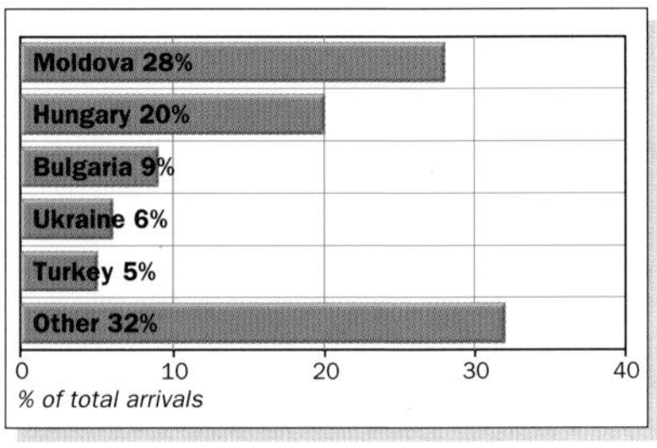

Moldova 28%
Hungary 20%
Bulgaria 9%
Ukraine 6%
Turkey 5%
Other 32%
0
10
20
30
40
% of total arrivals

The Black Sea and the Carpathian Mountains are the primary natural attractions, while Transylvania has a rich historical heritage. However, tourist facilities are poor. A proposal to build a theme park to exploit the Dracula legend was shelved in 2002 after an international outcry over its proposed location in a historic town. Under Ceauşescu, the need for foreign currency meant that tourist facilities were prioritized over housing. Today, privatization of property and an acute housing shortage have reduced the accommodation available to visitors.

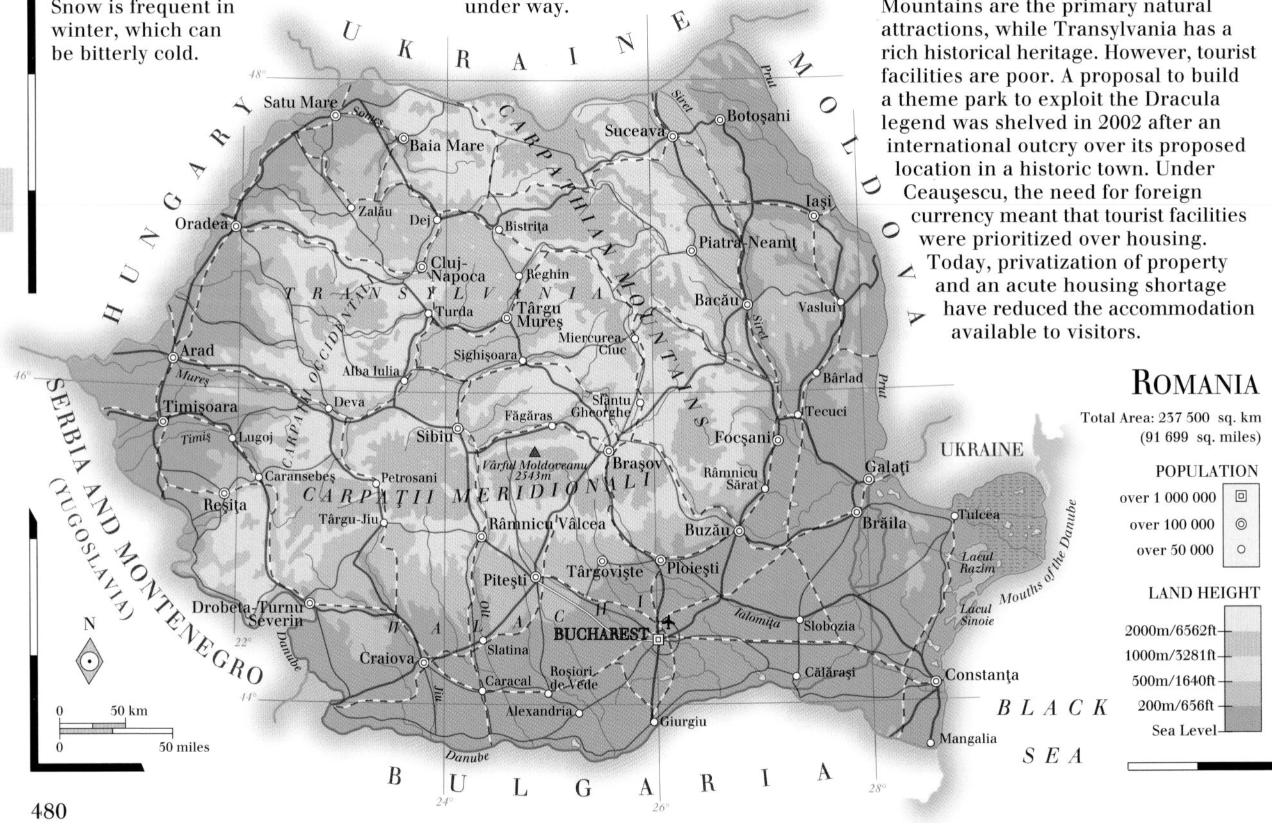

UKRAINE
MOLDOVA
HUNGARY
SERBIA AND MONTENEGRO (YUGOSLAVIA)
BULGARIA
BLACK SEA
UKRAINE
Satu Mare
Baia Mare
Suceava
Botoşani
Iaşi
Oradea
Zalău
Dej
Bistriţa
Cluj-Napoca
Reghin
Piatra-Neamţ
Bacău
Vaslui
TRANSYLVANIA
CARPATHIAN MOUNTAINS
CARPAŢII OCCIDENTALI
CARPAŢII MERIDIONALI
Turda
Târgu Mureş
Miercurea-Ciuc
Arad
Alba Iulia
Sighişoara
Bârlad
Timişoara
Deva
Sfântu Gheorghe
Tecuci
Lugoj
Sibiu
Făgăraş
Focşani
Braşov
Vârful Moldoveanu 2543m
Caransebeş
Petrosani
Râmnicu Sărat
Galaţi
Reşiţa
Târgu-Jiu
Râmnicu Vâlcea
Buzău
Brăila
Tulcea
Piteşti
Târgovişte
Ploieşti
Drobeta-Turnu Severin
BUCHAREST
Slobozia
Slatina
Craiova
Caracal
Roşiori de Vede
Călăraşi
Constanţa
Alexandria
Giurgiu
Mangalia
Lacul Razim
Lacul Sinoie
Mouths of the Danube
Danube
Mureş
Timiş
Someş
Siret
Prut
Ialomiţa
Olt
Jiu
N
0 50 km
0 50 miles
48°
46°
44°
22°
24°
26°
28°

ROMANIA

Total Area: 237 500 sq. km (91 699 sq. miles)

POPULATION

over 1 000 000

over 100 000

over 50 000

LAND HEIGHT

2000m/6562ft

1000m/3281ft

500m/1640ft

200m/656ft

Sea Level

R

PEOPLE

Pop. density medium

Romanian, Hungarian, Romani, German

94/km² (244/mi²)

THE URBAN/RURAL POPULATION SPLIT

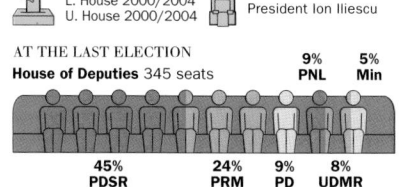

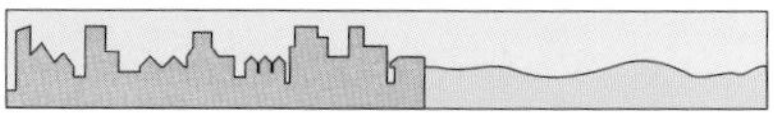

55% 45%

RELIGIOUS PERSUASION

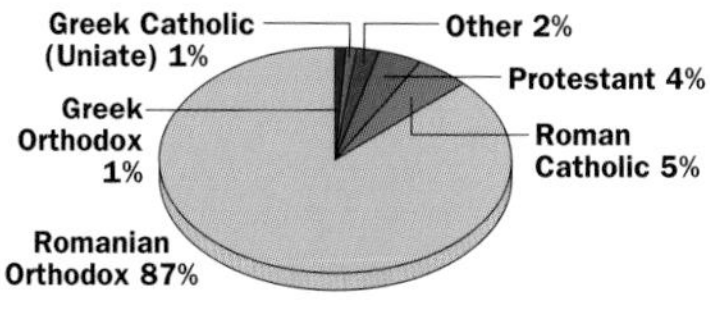
Greek Catholic (Uniate) 1%
Other 2%
Protestant 4%
Greek Orthodox 1%
Roman Catholic 5%
Romanian Orthodox 87%

ETHNIC MAKEUP

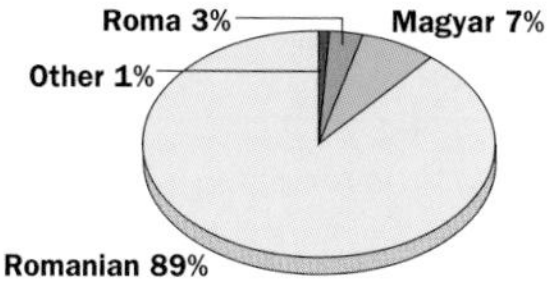
Roma 3%
Magyar 7%
Other 1%
Romanian 89%

Since 1989, Romanian nationalism has increased, aggravated by economic austerity measures. The incidence of ethnic violence has also risen, toward Roma and Hungarians in particular. Ethnic Hungarians, or Magyar, who form the largest minority group, are partly protected by the influence of Hungary, whereas the Roma do not have any similar support and tend to suffer greater discrimination.

The population is currently shrinking, due to rising emigration since 1989, mainly for economic reasons, and to a falling birthrate since the early 1990s. The latter trend is in sharp contrast to the 1980s, when the Ceauşescu regime enforced a "pronatalist" policy, banning abortion and contraception; the birthrate rose, but the population as a whole did not grow significantly due to an increase in the mortality rate. Abortion was legalized in 1989 and maternal death rates have since declined. Adoptions by foreigners, spurred partly by shocking conditions in orphanages, were banned in 2001, amid concerns over a "trade in children." Romania, the last country in Europe to lift its ban on homosexuality, only properly did so in 2001; public prejudice against homosexuals remains high.

POPULATION AGE BREAKDOWN

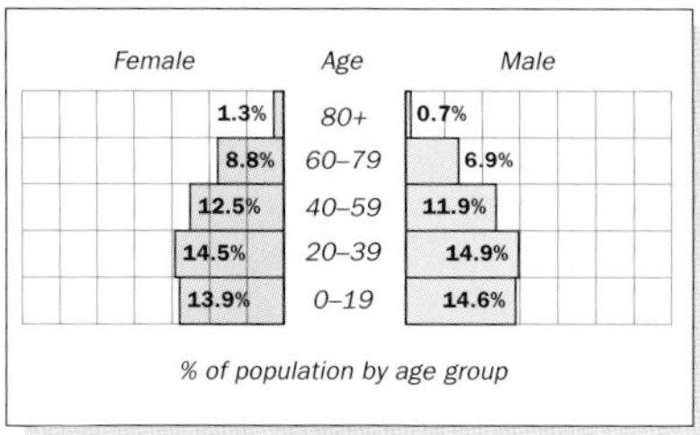
Female
Age
Male
1.3% 80+ 0.7%
8.8% 60–79 6.9%
12.5% 40–59 11.9%
14.5% 20–39 14.9%
13.9% 0–19 14.6%
% of population by age group

WORLD AFFAIRS

Joined UN in 1955

BSEC | CE | EBRD | OSCE | CEFTA

Romania's priority is building closer links with western Europe. In 1993, it signed an association agreement with the EU, and in 1995 formally applied for membership. Though not one of the front-runners with which the EU opened negotiations in 1998, it was told in 2002 that it could expect membership in 2007.

Relations with Hungary remain tense over the treatment of the Magyar minority. Romania has rejected calls for greater autonomy in Transylvania, while the Hungarian authorities have extended special rights to the Magyars.

Relations with Ukraine have been hampered by a lingering territorial dispute over Serpent's Island in the Black Sea, which controls potentially rich oil deposits.

AID

Recipient

$648m (receipts) Up 50% in 2001

Western aid declined after the mid-1990s, reflecting uncertainty about the implementation of reform. In October 2001 the World Bank announced that it would loan $1 billion between 2002 and 2004 for a series of social and environmental projects.

POLITICS

Multiparty elections

L. House 2000/2004
U. House 2000/2004

President Ion Iliescu

AT THE LAST ELECTION

House of Deputies 345 seats

45% PDSR, 24% PRM, 9% PD, 8% UDMR, 9% PNL, 5% Min

PDSR = Social Democratic Pole of Romania (led by the Social Democracy Party of Romania) **PRM** = Greater Romania Party **PD** = Democratic Party **PNL** = National Liberal Party **UDMR** = Hungarian Democratic Union of Romania **Min** = Minority representatives: 18 seats in the House of Deputies are reserved for national minorities

Senate 140 seats

46% PDSR, 27% PRM, 9% PD, 9% PNL, 9% UDMR

Romania is a multiparty democracy led by a directly elected president.

PROFILE

The 1989 "revolution" left an old communist elite in power, with no group ready to introduce reform. Only the victory of the center right in 1996 brought more far-reaching change.

Many of the state assets privatized under the first regime of Ion Iliescu remained closely linked to the ruling clique. Now a declared social democrat, Iliescu retains the support of such conservative groups as miners and rural workers. The coalition parties in power after 1996 came a poor third in the 2000 elections behind Iliescu's PDSR and the extreme nationalist PRM; Iliescu won the presidential vote. In mid-2001 the PDSR electoral coalition was formalized in a merger of its two main constituent parties to form the Social Democrat Party (PSD), which is headed by Prime Minister Adrian Nastase.

MAIN POLITICAL ISSUES

The pace of liberalization

The success of the left in 2000 was based on a commitment to promote social concerns alongside economic reform. However, amid pressure from the IMF and other lending bodies, the government has been forced to maintain and even increase the pace of economic liberalization, creating serious tensions within government.

Ethnic tensions

The economic difficulties of the 1990s saw far-right political gains and increased nationalism. Roma have been victims of violent, racially motivated attacks. Benefits given to ethnic Magyars by the Hungarian government have provoked an outcry in Romania.

Ion Iliescu, Romania's first postcommunist president, reelected in 2000.

Adrian Nastase, prime minister since December 2000.

CHRONOLOGY

Dominated by Hungary and the Ottoman Empire for centuries, the Romanian provinces of Wallachia and Moldavia were united for the first time in 1859, forming the basis of the modern Romanian state.

- ❑ **1878** Independence, but at cost of losing eastern Moldavia to Russia.
- ❑ **1916–1918** Enters World War I on Allied side. At end of war gains substantial territory, including Transylvania from Hungary.
- ❑ **1924** Communists banned in unstable political arena. Rise

R

CHRONOLOGY *continued*

of fascist "Iron Guard."

- **1938** King Carol establishes royal autocracy.
- **1940** Territory forcibly ceded to Soviet Union, Bulgaria, and Hungary. Coup by Iron Guard. King Carol abdicates in favor of son, Michael. Tripartite Pact with Germany.
- **1941** Enters war on Axis side, hoping to recover Moldavian lands.
- **1944** Romania switches sides as Soviet troops reach border.
- **1945** Soviet-backed regime installed. Romanian Communist Party plays an increasing role.
- **1946–1947** Romania regains Transylvania. Eastern Moldavia reverts to USSR, which also demands huge reparations. Communist-led National Democratic Front wins majority in disputed elections.
- **1947** Michael forced to abdicate.
- **1948–1953** Centrally planned economy put in place.
- **1953** Leaders of Jewish community prosecuted for Zionism.
- **1958** Soviet troops withdraw.
- **1964** Prime Minister Gheorghiu-Dej declares national sovereignty. Proposes joint planning by all communist countries to lessen Soviet economic control.
- **1965** Ceauşescu party secretary after death of Gheorghiu-Dej.
- **1968–1980** Condemns Soviet invasion of Czechoslovakia; courts US and European Communities.
- **1982** Ceauşescu vows to pay off foreign debt.
- **1989** Demonstrations; many killed by military. Armed forces join with opposition in National Salvation Front (NSF) to form government. Ion Iliescu declared president. Ceauşescu summarily tried and shot.
- **1990** NSF election victory. Political prisoners freed.
- **1991** New constitution, providing for market reform, approved.
- **1992** Second free elections. NSF splits. Nicolae Vacaroiu forms minority government.
- **1994** General strike demands faster economic reform. Referendum in Moldova rejects reunification with Romania.
- **1996** Reconciliation treaty with Hungary. Center right wins elections, breaking with communist past; Emil Constantinescu president.
- **2000** Ion Iliescu and social democrats win elections.
- **2001** Repeal of Article 200: Romania becomes last country in Europe to decriminalize homosexuality.

DEFENSE

Compulsory military service

$969m

Up 3% in 2001

The military received limited funding under the Ceauşescu regime, and troops were routinely deployed as cheap labor. Romania was the first country to join NATO's Partnership for Peace program in 1994. Since 1996 the government has actively sought membership of NATO itself. Romanian soldiers were deployed in the US-led "war on terrorism" in Afghanistan from 2002.

ROMANIAN ARMED FORCES

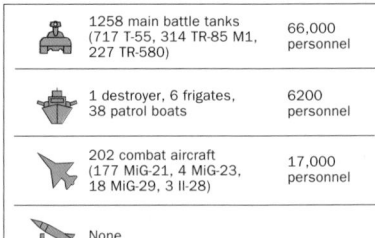

1258 main battle tanks (717 T-55, 314 TR-85 M1, 227 TR-580)	66,000 personnel
1 destroyer, 6 frigates, 38 patrol boats	6200 personnel
202 combat aircraft (177 MiG-21, 4 MiG-23, 18 MiG-29, 3 Il-28)	17,000 personnel
None	

ECONOMICS

Inflation 91% p.a. (1990–2001)

$38.6bn

32,788 Romanian lei (33,458)

SCORE CARD

World GNP Ranking	53rd
GNP per Capita	$1720
Balance of Payments	–$2.32bn
Inflation	34.5%
Unemployment	7%

EXPORTS

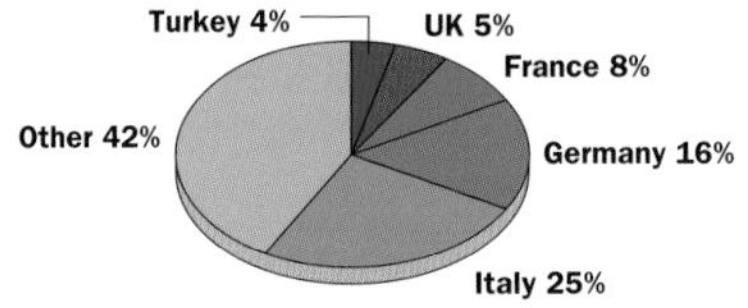
Turkey 4%
UK 5%
France 8%
Germany 16%
Italy 25%
Other 42%

IMPORTS

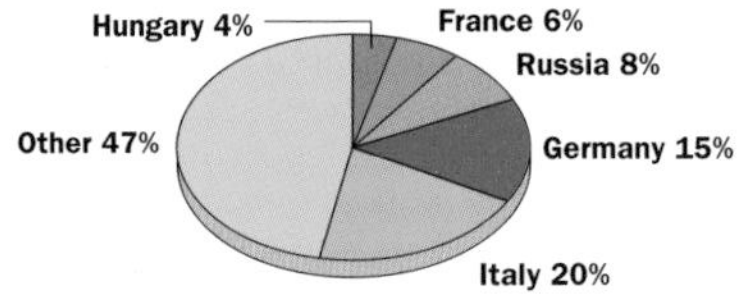
Hungary 4%
France 6%
Russia 8%
Germany 15%
Italy 20%
Other 47%

Strengths

Oil reserves. Tourism potential. Steady export-led recovery since 2000.

Weaknesses

High inflation. Slow transition from centrally planned to market economy. Delays in economic reform. Low foreign investment confidence.

Profile

Despite being the first east European country to open its economy to foreign investment, Romania was relatively slow to launch economic reforms, and suffered severe recession for most of the 1990s. Priority areas for structural overhaul and liberalization are the chemical, petrochemical, transportation, metal, and food industries. Efforts from 1996 to curb inflation and the budget deficit had little impact. Output fell sharply, worsened by disruption to trade during the 1999 Kosovo conflict.

Most farmland has been restored to private hands. Agriculture, severely undermechanized, still employs over 40% of the workforce. The worst drought for 50 years severely affected production in 2000.

From 1990, 100% foreign ownership of ventures was permitted. Joint ventures, while now numerous, are small in scale; larger investors are put off by bureaucracy and doubts about stability. Privatization, a priority for government since 1996, was delayed by problems in the sale of larger companies, but by 2000 the private sector accounted for over 60% of GDP and a renewed drive to privatize was begun in 2001. 2000 saw an export-led recovery after three straight years of recession. Falling gasoline prices have also since helped to boost GDP.

ECONOMIC PERFORMANCE INDICATOR

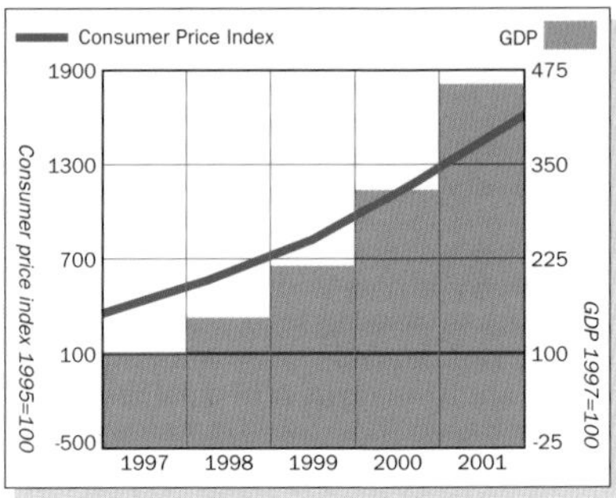
Consumer Price Index
GDP
1900
1300
700
100
-500
475
350
225
100
-25
1997
1998
1999
2000
2001
Consumer price index 1995=100
GDP 1997=100

ROMANIA : MAJOR BUSINESSES

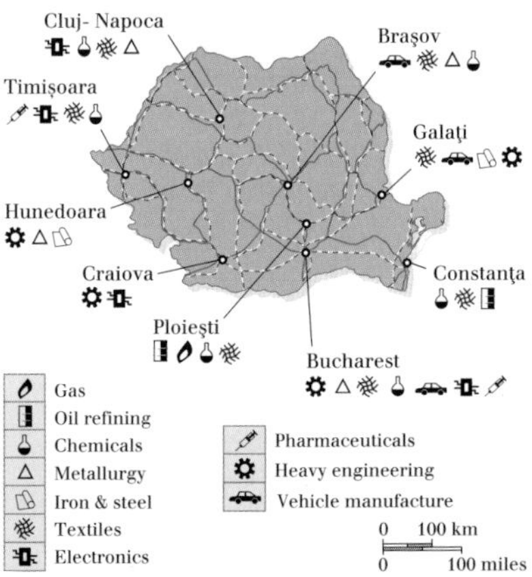
Cluj- Napoca
Braşov
Timişoara
Galaţi
Hunedoara
Craiova
Constanţa
Ploieşti
Bucharest
Gas
Oil refining
Chemicals
Metallurgy
Iron & steel
Textiles
Electronics
Pharmaceuticals
Heavy engineering
Vehicle manufacture
0 100 km
0 100 miles

R

RESOURCES

Electric power 22.6m kW

17,099 tonnes

127,000 b/d (reserves 1bn barrels)

7.25m sheep, 4m geese, 4.45m pigs, 71.4m chickens

Oil, coal, salt, natural gas, methane, bauxite, iron, copper, lead, zinc

ELECTRICITY GENERATION

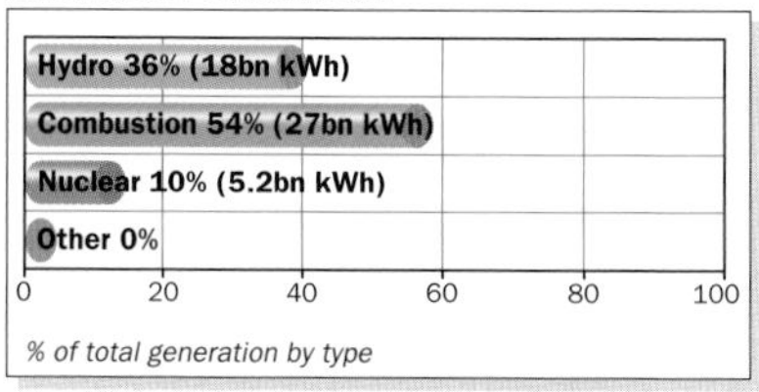

Hydro 36% (18bn kWh)
Combustion 54% (27bn kWh)
Nuclear 10% (5.2bn kWh)
Other 0%
0
20
40
60
80
100
% of total generation by type

Romania has large reserves of oil, but there is little left of proven gas reserves. Oil and gas production from onshore fields has fallen since 1976, and the country is a net oil importer. Since the mid-1990s efforts have been concentrated on developing offshore reserves in the Black Sea, opening up exploration and processing to foreign investors. Deposits of other minerals are small and contribute little to export earnings. Many coal mines have been shut down.

The electricity industry is outdated but does produce a surplus for export. An agreement in 2000 connected the national grid with that of Bulgaria. The removal of price ceilings since 1997, with a consequent doubling of prices, provides strong incentives to users to improve poor efficiency.

ENVIRONMENT

Sustainability rank: 66th

5% (0.2% partially protected)

3.6 tonnes per capita

ENVIRONMENTAL TREATIES

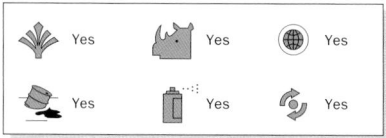

Yes Yes Yes

Yes Yes Yes

Saddled with the disastrous legacy of its communist-era industry, Romania needs help with a major cleanup. Air pollution, mainly from emissions from cement and power plants but also from exhaust fumes and low-quality coal, is most serious in the south. Cyanide and heavy metal leaked from a gold mine in Baia Mare in 2000, creating a transboundary pollution catastrophe in the Tisza River in Hungary. The Danube delta, despite serious pollution, was designated a UNESCO biosphere reserve in 1998.

MEDIA

TV ownership high

Daily newspaper circulation 300 per 1000 people

PUBLISHING AND BROADCAST MEDIA

There are 106 daily newspapers, including *Evenimentul Zilei, Adevărul, România Liberă, Curierul Național*, and *Cotidianul*

5 services: 2 state-owned, 3 independent

4 services: 3 state-owned, 1 independent

Newspapers proliferated after 1989, but have since struggled to compete for readers. The government-controlled national TV service faces a strong challenge from commercial channels Pro TV and Antena Independenta. Pro TV dominates urban viewing, and cable TV is common in the capital. The first exclusively Hungarian-language radio station began broadcasting in 1999.

CRIME

No death penalty

51,528 prisoners

Little change in 2000

CRIME RATES

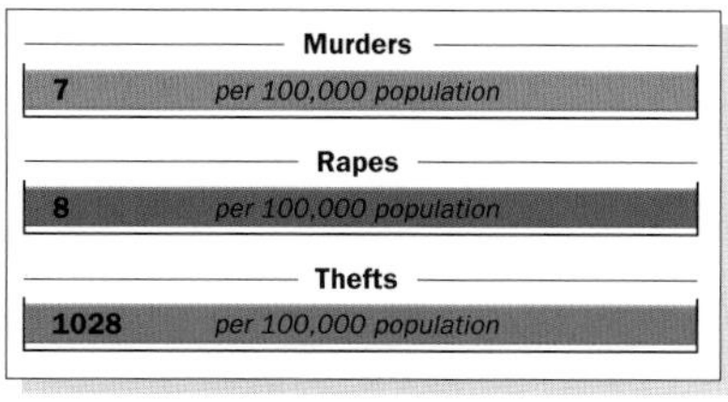

Murders
7 per 100,000 population
Rapes
8 per 100,000 population
Thefts
1028 per 100,000 population

The black economy is the main source of income for a third of the population. Levels of tax evasion are extremely high. Romania is a source and transit country for people trafficking.

EDUCATION

School leaving age: 14

98%

533,152 students

THE EDUCATION SYSTEM

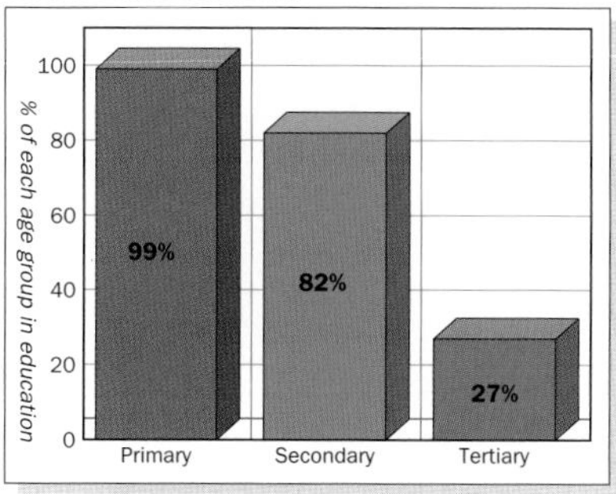

100
80
60
40
20
0
% of each age group in education
99%
82%
27%
Primary
Secondary
Tertiary

Attendance at secondary schools is below the European average. As university enrollment is no longer restricted, the number of tertiary students has risen rapidly. The government increased education expenditure in early 2000, pledging to devote at least 4% of GDP in future years and going some way to meet criticisms over the chronic underfunding of the school system.

ROMANIA : LAND USE

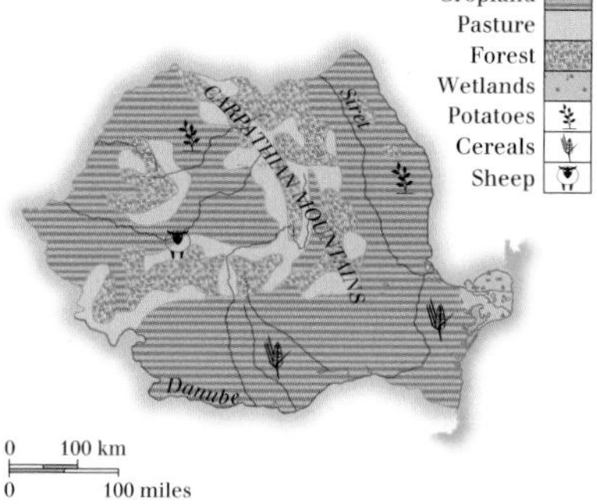

Cropland
Pasture
Forest
Wetlands
Potatoes
Cereals
Sheep
CARPATHIAN MOUNTAINS
Siret
Danube
0 100 km
0 100 miles

HEALTH

Welfare state health benefits

1 per 524 people

Heart, respiratory, and cerebrovascular diseases, cancers

Average life expectancy is among the lowest in Europe; in the worst-polluted parts of Transylvania it is as low as 61 years. The incidence of tuberculosis is the highest in Europe. After years of chronic state underfunding, there was a shift in 1999–2001 toward an insurance-based system.

SPENDING

GDP/cap. decrease

CONSUMPTION AND SPENDING

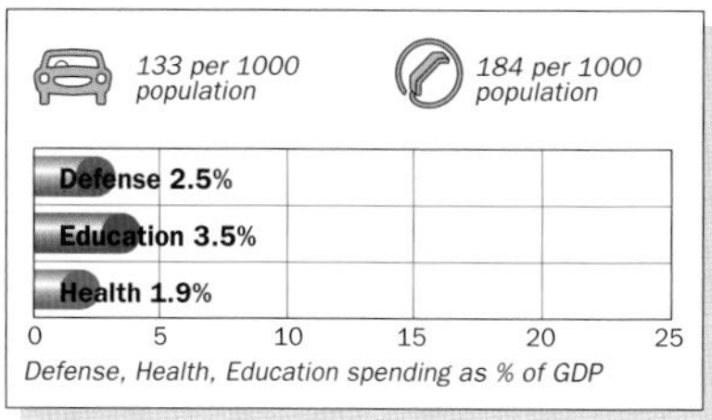

133 per 1000 population
184 per 1000 population
Defense 2.5%
Education 3.5%
Health 1.9%
0
5
10
15
20
25
Defense, Health, Education spending as % of GDP

Real income has been hit hard by a decade of economic decline: 20% of people live below the national poverty line. Most families own their own homes (often overcrowded) and many have small plots of land. Few rural homes have running water or sewerage.

WORLD RANKING

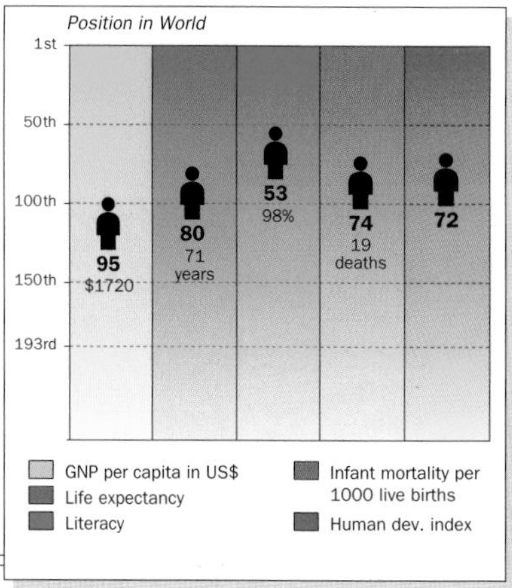

Position in World
1st
50th
100th
150th
193rd
95
$1720
80
71 years
53
98%
74
19 deaths
72
GNP per capita in US$
Life expectancy
Literacy
Infant mortality per 1000 live births
Human dev. index

R

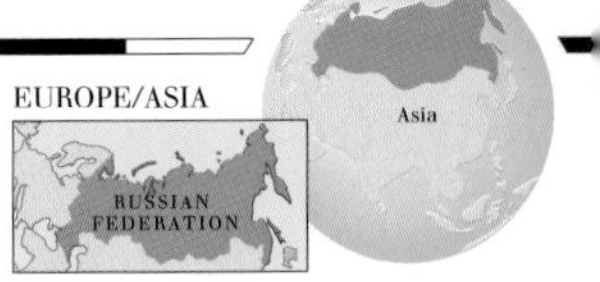
EUROPE/ASIA
RUSSIAN FEDERATION
Asia

RUSSIAN FEDERATION

OFFICIAL NAME: Russian Federation **CAPITAL:** Moscow
POPULATION: 143 million **CURRENCY:** Russian rouble **OFFICIAL LANGUAGE:** Russian

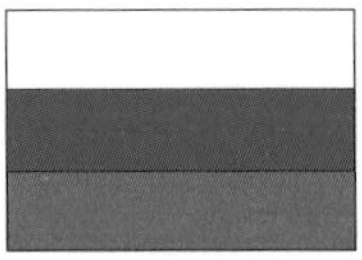

1480 | 1991 | June 12 | RUS | +1 to +11 | +7 | .ru

BOUNDED BY THE ARCTIC and Pacific Oceans to the north and east, Russia extends over 17 million sq. km (6.6 million sq. miles). By far the world's largest state, it is almost twice as big as either the US or China. With the modern borders of the Russian federative state established in 1954, the sovereign status of the Russian Federation itself dates from 1991 – the dissolution of the USSR. Within the CIS it maintains a traditionally dominant role in central Asia and the Caucasus. Ethnic Russians make up 82% of the population, but there are around 150 smaller ethnic groups, many with their own national territories within Russia's borders. Regionalism and separatism are major political issues. The situation is complicated by the fact that many of these territories are rich in key resources such as oil, gas, gold, and diamonds.

The Kremlin, Moscow. *Rebuilt in 1475 by Ivan the Great, who commissioned architects from Pskov and Italy, it is enclosed by walls 4 km (1.5 miles) long and lies on the Moscow River.*

CLIMATE

Subarctic/continental/mountain/steppe

WEATHER CHART FOR MOSCOW

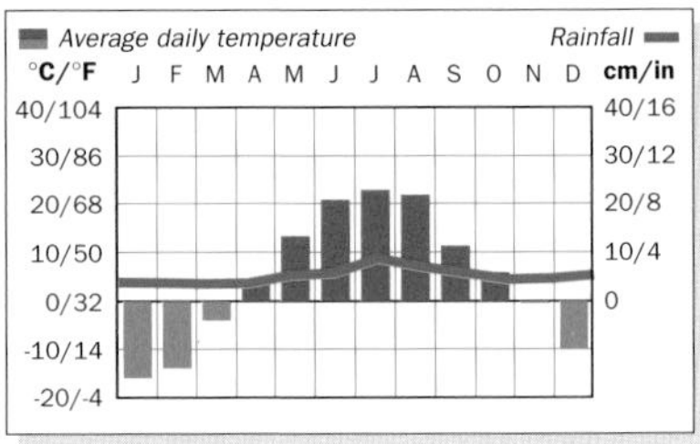
Average daily temperature
Rainfall
°C/°F
J F M A M J J A S O N D
cm/in
40/104
30/86
20/68
10/50
0/32
-10/14
-20/-4
40/16
30/12
20/8
10/4
0

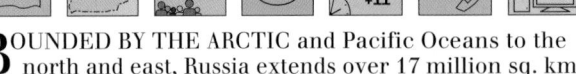

Russia has a cold continental climate, characterized by two widely divergent main seasons. Spring and autumn are very brief periods of transition between warm summers and freezing winters. The country is open to the influences of the Arctic and Atlantic to the north and west. However, mountains to the south and east prevent any warming effects from the Indian and Pacific Oceans filtering across. Severe winters affect most regions. Winter temperatures vary surprisingly little from north to south, but fall sharply in eastern regions. The January temperature of –70°C (–94°F) recorded at Verkhoyansk in Siberia is the world record low outside Antarctica.

Housing in Moscow. *Living conditions in major cities can be cramped, with families often sharing their small apartments.*

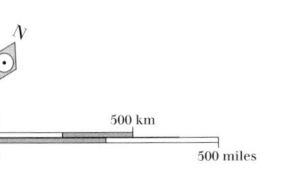

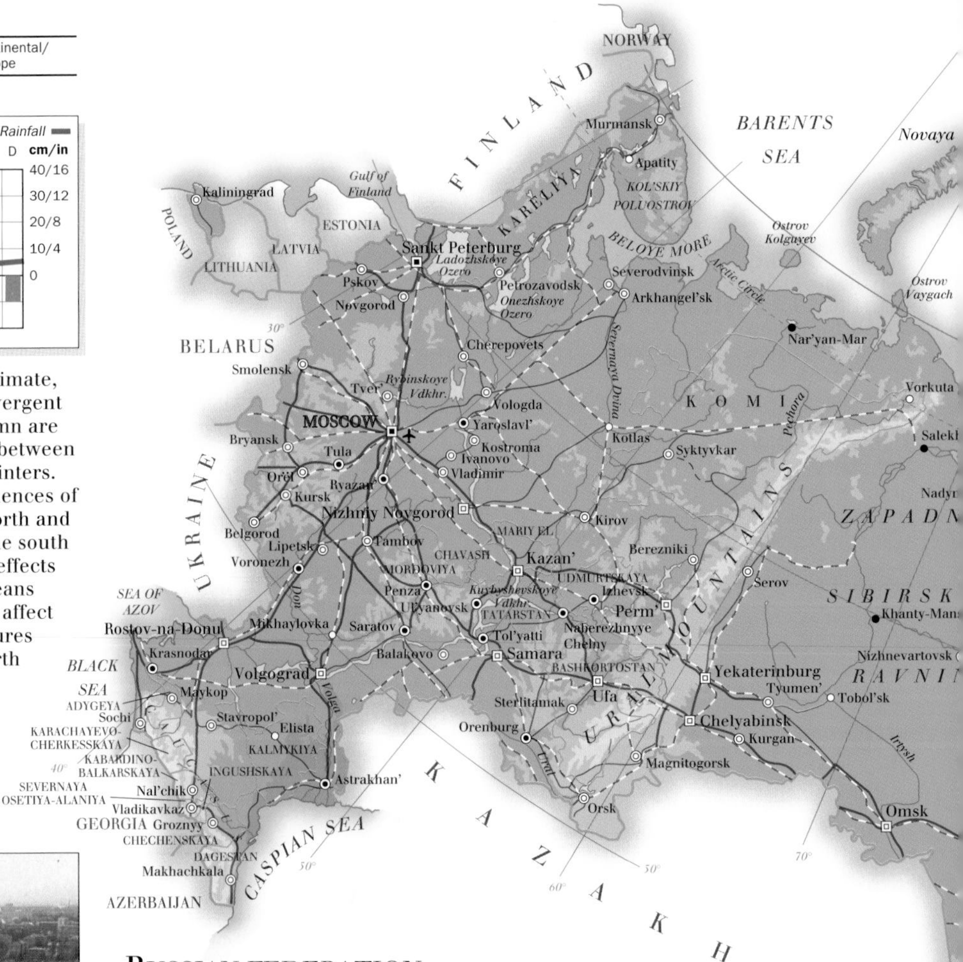
NORWAY
FINLAND
BARENTS SEA
Novaya
Zemlya
Murmansk
Apatity
KOL'SKIY POLUOSTROV
KARELIYA
Kaliningrad
Gulf of Finland
POLAND
ESTONIA
LATVIA
LITHUANIA
Sankt Peterburg
Ladozhskoye Ozero
Ostrov Kolguyev
BELOYE MORE
Severodvinsk
Arkhangel'sk
Arctic Circle
Ostrov Vaygach
Pskov
Novgorod
Petrozavodsk
Onezhskoye Ozero
BELARUS
Cherepovets
Nar'yan-Mar
Smolensk
Rybinskoye Vdkhr.
Tver'
Vologda
Severnaya Dvina
KOMI
Pechora
Vorkuta
MOSCOW
Yaroslavl'
Kotlas
Salekh
Bryansk
Kostroma
Tula
Ivanovo
Syktyvkar
Vladimir
Orël
Ryazan'
Kursk
Nizhniy Novgorod
Kirov
ZAPADN
UKRAINE
Belgorod
MARIY EL
Lipetsk
Tambov
CHAVASH
Kazan'
Bereznik
Voronezh
MORDOVIYA
UDMURTSKAYA
Izhevsk
Serov
SEA OF AZOV
Penza
Kuybyshevskoye Vdkhr.
Ul'yanovsk
TATARSTAN
Perm'
SIBIRSK
Khanty-Man
Rostov-na-Donu
Mikhaylovka
Saratov
Naberezhnyye Chelny
Tol'yatti
Krasnodar
Balakovo
Samara
Nizhnevartovsk
BLACK SEA
Volgograd
BASHKORTOSTAN
Yekaterinburg
RAVNI
ADYGEYA
Maykop
Sterlitamak
Ufa
Tyumen'
Tobol'sk
Sochi
Stavropol'
Chelyabinsk
KARACHAYEVO-CHERKESSKAYA
Elista
Orenburg
Kurgan
KABARDINO-BALKARSKAYA
KALMYKIYA
Irtysh
INGUSHSKAYA
Magnitogorsk
SEVERNAYA OSETIYA-ALANIYA
Nal'chik
Astrakhan'
Vladikavkaz
GEORGIA
Groznyy
CHECHENSKAYA
Orsk
Omsk
CASPIAN SEA
DAGESTAN
Makhachkala
AZERBAIJAN
KAZAKHSTAN
URAL MOUNTAINS
Volga
Don
Ural
Rubts
N
0 500 km
0 500 miles

RUSSIAN FEDERATION

Total Area :
17 075 200 sq. km
(6 592 735 sq. miles)

POPULATION

- over 5 000 000
- over 1 000 000
- over 500 000
- over 100 000
- over 50 000
- over 10 000

LAND HEIGHT

- 3000m/9843ft
- 2000m/6562ft
- 1000m/3281ft
- 500m/1640ft
- 200m/656ft
- Sea Level
- -200m/-656ft

TRANSPORTATION

Drive on right

Sheremetyevo-2, Moscow 10.9m passengers

4727 ships 10.2m grt

THE TRANSPORTATION NETWORK

336,000 km (208,780 miles)	Not available
86,075 km (53,484 miles)	95,900 km (59,589 miles)

Russia has a comprehensive transportation network. However, since 1991, all systems have seen some decline due to lack of funding. Cities are still served by good trolley and bus systems and Moscow has one of the most impressive subway systems in the world. In rural areas, car ownership is low and the population relies on an extensive bus service.

About 20% of the railroad track should be renewed annually owing to frost and other damage. Shortage of funds means that this is no longer done. The railroads are heavily used but seriously overburdened and liable to accidents and delays. New track has been laid for the Sokol (Falcon) high-speed rail link between Moscow and St. Petersburg; the first trains to use it in 2000 cut over an hour off the previous minimum journey time and further dramatic reductions are expected.

Roads in major cities are deteriorating, as are interurban highways. Crime is a problem on railroads – notably the Trans-Siberian – and roads.

The former Aeroflot monopoly of air transportation has been broken up. Aeroflot now competes as Aeroflot Russian Airlines, but hundreds of regional "babyflot" airlines run mainly domestic routes, some with alarming accident records.

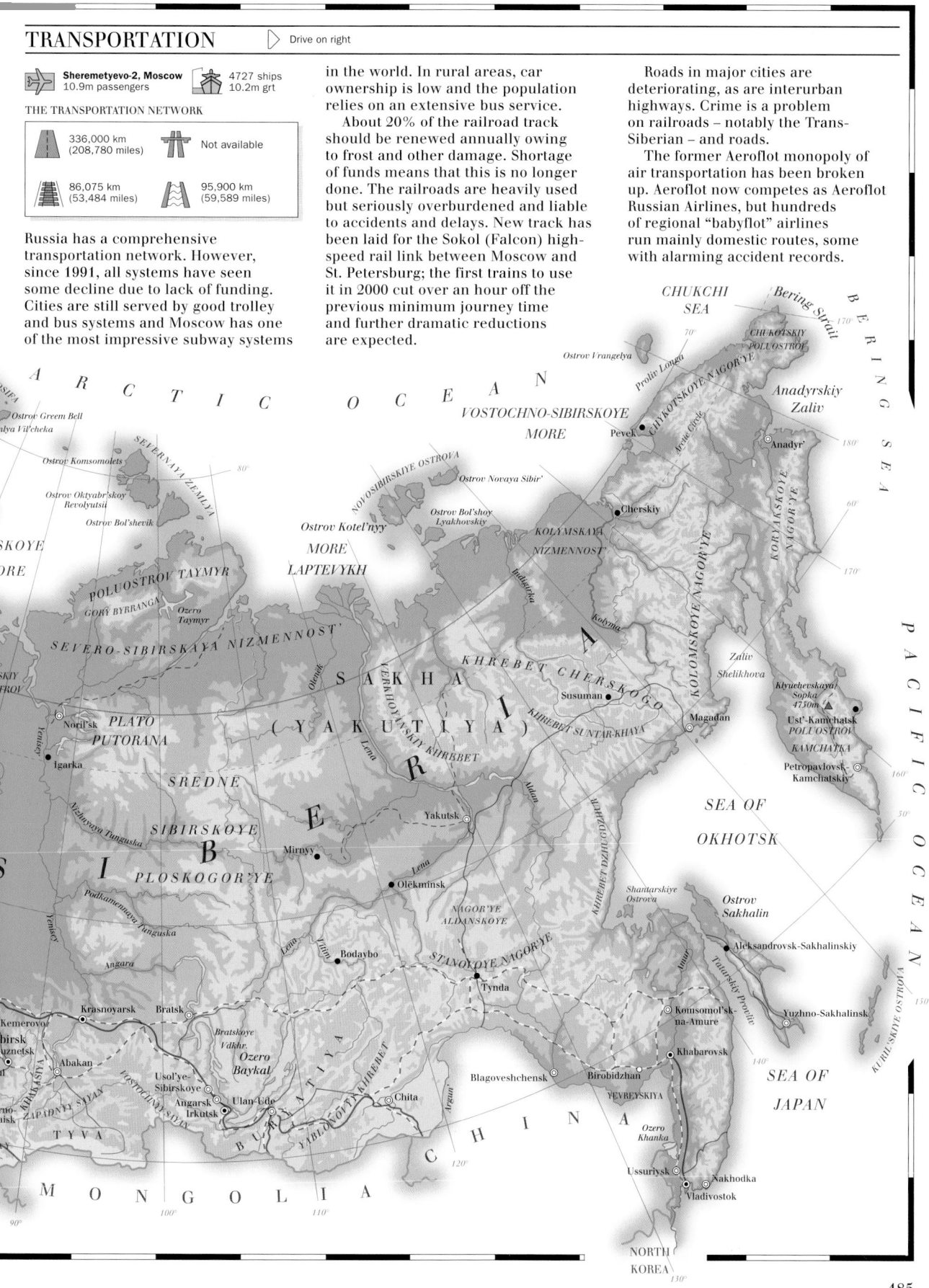

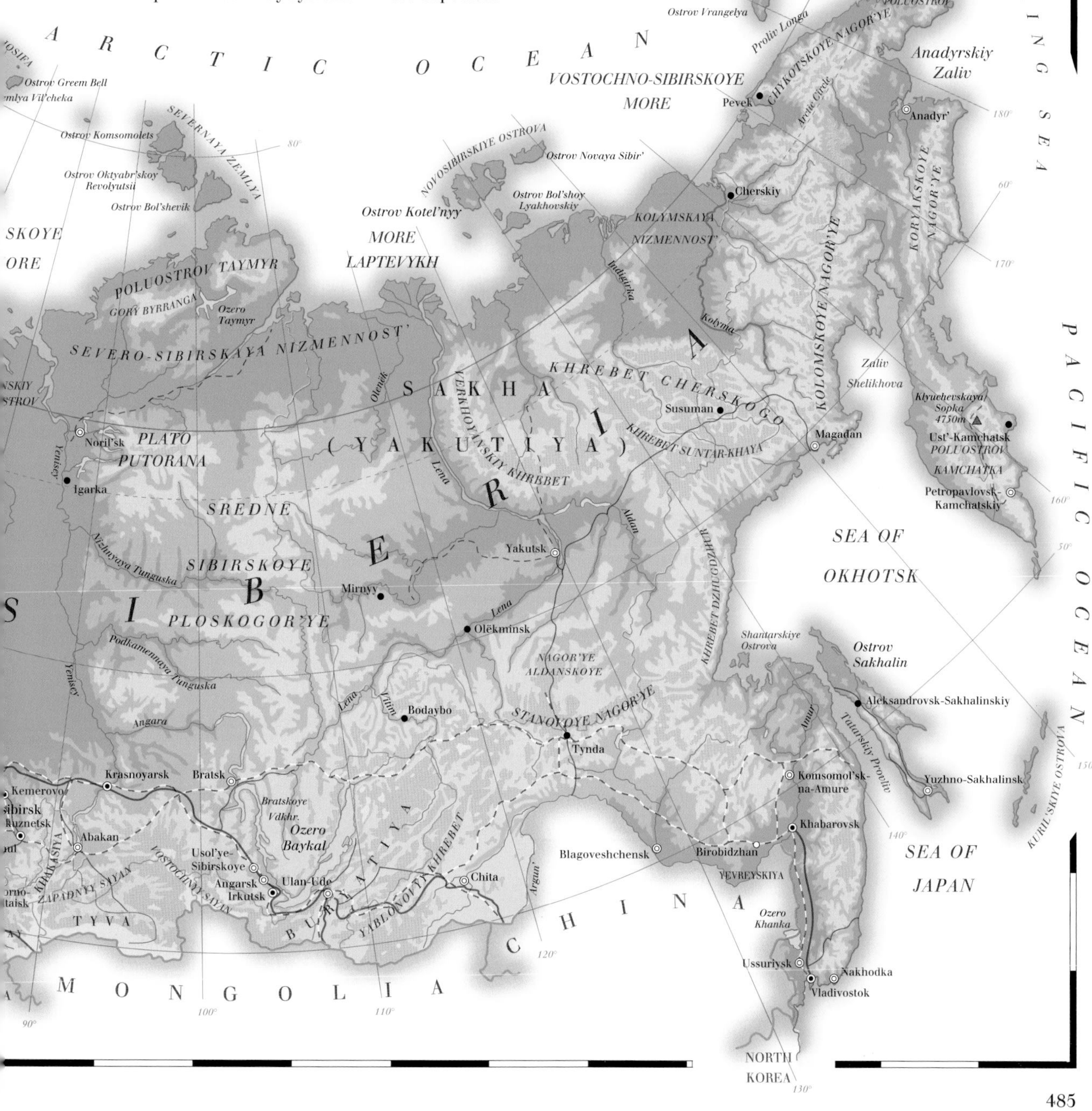
CHUKCHI SEA
Bering Strait
BERING SEA
CHUKOTSKIY POLUOSTROV
Ostrov Vrangelya
Proliv Longa
CHUKOTSKOYE NAGOR'YE
Anadyrskiy Zaliv
ARCTIC OCEAN
VOSTOCHNO-SIBIRSKOYE MORE
Pevek
Anadyr'
Ostrov Greem Bell
Ostrov Komsomolets
SEVERNAYA ZEMLYA
Ostrov Oktyabr'skoy Revolyutsii
Ostrov Bol'shevik
NOVOSIBIRSKIYE OSTROVA
Ostrov Novaya Sibir'
Ostrov Bol'shoy Lyakhovskiy
Ostrov Kotel'nyy
MORE LAPTEVYKH
Cherskiy
KOLYMSKAYA NIZMENNOST'
KORYAKSKOYE NAGOR'YE
KOLOMSKOYE NAGOR'YE
POLUOSTROV TAYMYR
GORY BYRRANGA
Ozero Taymyr
SEVERO-SIBIRSKAYA NIZMENNOST'
Indigirka
Kolyma
PACIFIC OCEAN
Zaliv Shelikhova
KHREBET CHERSKOGO
SAKHA (YAKUTIYA)
Olenëk
VERKHOYANSKIY KHREBET
Susuman
KHREBET SUNTAR-KHAYA
Magadan
Klyuchevskaya Sopka 4750m
Ust'-Kamchatsk
POLUOSTROV KAMCHATKA
Petropavlovsk-Kamchatskiy
Noril'sk
PLATO PUTORANA
Igarka
Yenisey
Lena
SREDNE SIBIRSKOYE PLOSKOGOR'YE
SIBERIA
Aldan
KHREBET DZHUGDZHUR
SEA OF OKHOTSK
Yakutsk
Nizhnyaya Tunguska
Mirnyy
Olëkminsk
Podkamennaya Tunguska
NAGOR'YE ALDANSKOYE
Shantarskiye Ostrova
Ostrov Sakhalin
Angara
Vitim
Bodaybo
STANOVOYE NAGOR'YE
Tynda
Amur
Aleksandrovsk-Sakhalinskiy
Tatarskiy Proliv
KURIL'SKIYE OSTROVA
Krasnoyarsk
Bratsk
Kemerovo
Komsomol'sk-na-Amure
Yuzhno-Sakhalinsk
Bratskoye Vdkhr.
Ozero Baykal
Abakan
Usol'ye-Sibirskoye
Angarsk
Irkutsk
Ulan-Ude
Chita
Blagoveshchensk
Birobidzhan
Khabarovsk
SEA OF JAPAN
KHAKASIYA
ZAPADNYY SAYAN
VOSTOCHNYY SAYAN
BURYATIYA
YABLONOVYY KHREBET
Argun'
YEVREYSKIYA
TYVA
CHINA
Ozero Khanka
MONGOLIA
Ussuriysk
Nakhodka
Vladivostok
NORTH KOREA

TOURISM

Visitors : Population 1:6.8

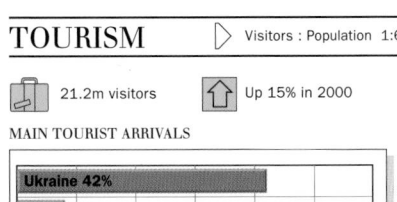

21.2m visitors

Up 15% in 2000

MAIN TOURIST ARRIVALS

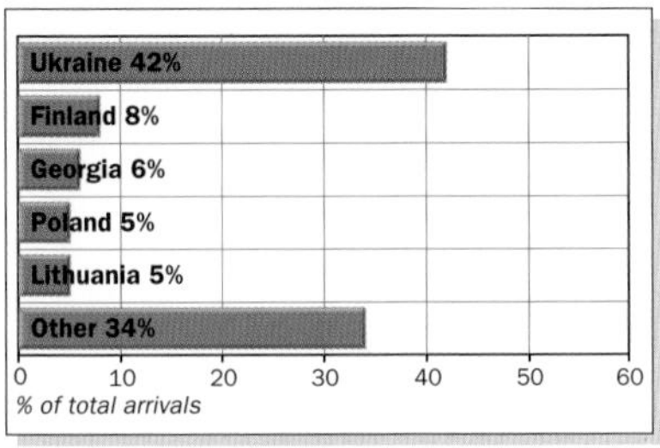
Ukraine 42%
Finland 8%
Georgia 6%
Poland 5%
Lithuania 5%
Other 34%
0
10
20
30
40
50
60
% of total arrivals

The breakup of the previous monopoly tourist agency, Intourist, has led to a vast expansion of tourism opportunities: each region is keen to earn hard currency and to attract rich visitors. Russia now ranks seventh in the world as a tourist destination.

Moscow and St. Petersburg remain favorite destinations, where hotels tend either to be for the well-off or of a basic standard. Near St. Petersburg, Novgorod has many fine churches, and the Pskov area is celebrated as the setting for many of Pushkin's works, including *Eugene Onegin* and *Boris Godunov*.

At the luxury end of the market, trips from St. Petersburg to Tashkent on former president Brezhnev's official train are now available. River trips down the Volga and visits to medieval monasteries are increasingly popular. Tourists can also explore forests or fish for salmon in the Kola Peninsula. The defense sector has opened up to tourism and now offers flights in MiG jets, or rides in Russian T-80 tanks. Even the space industry has branched into tourism.

Many parts of Russia remain inaccessible to most tourists. The communist-era ban on foreigners visiting the Urals has been lifted, but the area still has very few facilities. Resorts such as the subtropical Sochi on the Black Sea, where powerful Russians have *dachas* (country houses), have experienced a building boom.

PEOPLE

Pop. density low

Russian, Tatar, Ukrainian, Chavash, various other national languages

8/km² (22/mi²)

THE URBAN/RURAL POPULATION SPLIT

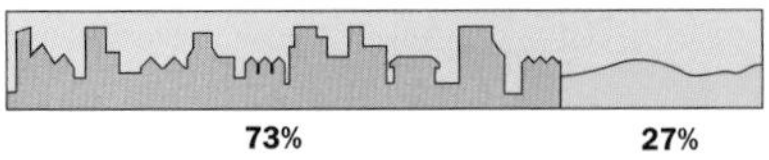
73%
27%

RELIGIOUS PERSUASION

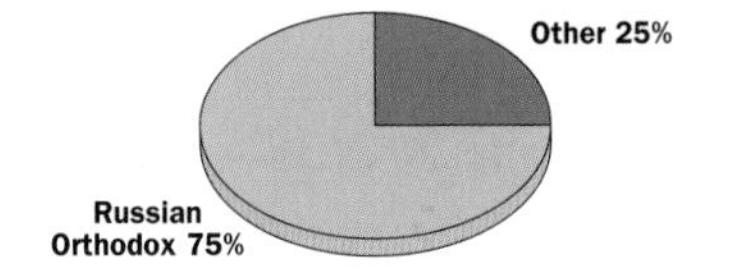
Other 25%
Russian Orthodox 75%

ETHNIC MAKEUP

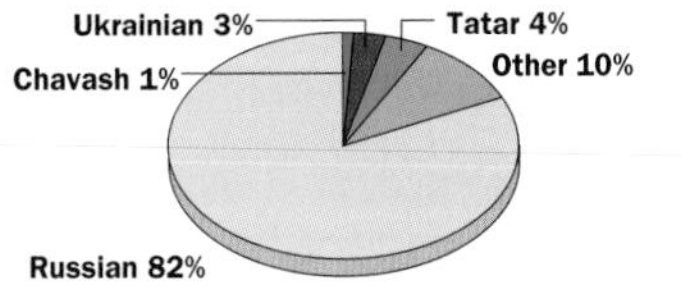
Ukrainian 3%
Tatar 4%
Chavash 1%
Other 10%
Russian 82%

Within the Russian Federation there are 57 "nationalities" with their own republic or territory, and a further 95 (who make up just 6% of the population) without a territory. The boundaries of the republics, and Soviet-era persecution, ensure that ethnic Russians are dominant almost everywhere. The minorities include Turkic-speakers, Finno-Ugrians, Muslims, Buddhists, indigenous Arctic peoples, and the various peoples of the Caucasus. Russians form by far the largest single group, and the dominance of Russian culture and Orthodox Christianity is supported by the federal state. The forced use of Cyrillic script is one of a number of points of conflict between the republics and Moscow.

The greatest hostility in Russian society is reserved for the Muslim populations of the north Caucasus, principally the Chechens. Since the outbreak of the separatist war in Chechnya in the 1990s, tensions have risen sharply, helping to fuel a growth in right-wing extremist groups.

The collapse of the Soviet Union has been followed by a marked increase in materialism and a greater expression of sexuality and of political and religious views. The expensive rebuilding of Moscow's Church of Christ the Savior symbolized this change. The strong revival of Russian Orthodoxy is boosted by legal recognition of its "special role" in Russia's history. Many small minority faiths have been unable to meet strict new registration requirements.

The position of women has changed little since the fall of communism. Many have suffered from the rise in unemployment, but this reflects the demise of part-time or badly paid jobs, rather than gender-motivated social change. Most Russians have very modest living standards and were further impoverished by the collapse of the economy in the late 1990s.

POPULATION AGE BREAKDOWN

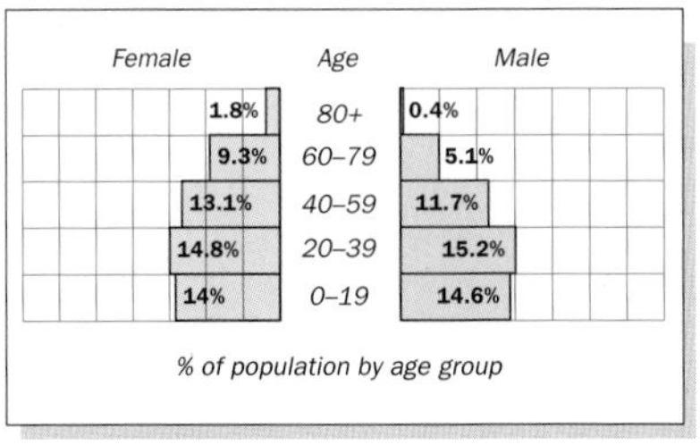
Female
Age
Male
1.8%
80+
0.4%
9.3%
60–79
5.1%
13.1%
40–59
11.7%
14.8%
20–39
15.2%
14%
0–19
14.6%
% of population by age group

POLITICS

Multiparty elections

L. House 1999/2003
U. House varying

President
Vladimir Putin

AT THE LAST ELECTION

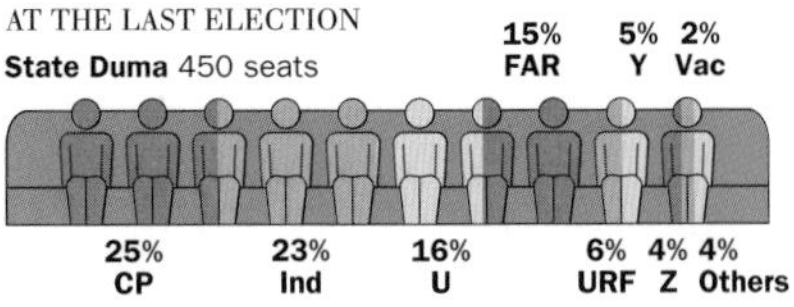
State Duma 450 seats
15% FAR
5% Y
2% Vac
25% CP
23% Ind
16% U
6% URF
4% Z
4% Others

CP = Communist Party **Ind** = Independents **U** = Unity **FAR** = Fatherland–All Russia **URF** = Union of Right Forces **Y** = Yabloko **Z** = Zhirinovsky's Bloc **Vac** = Vacant

Council of the Federation 178 seats

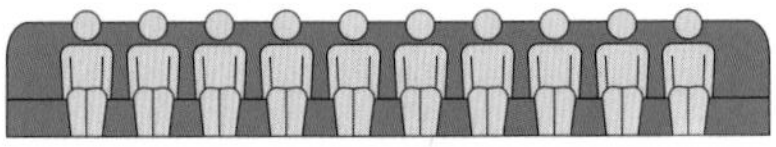

Each of 89 regions is represented in the Council of the Federation (Soviet Federatsii) by two members chosen by the regional legislature

The government is responsible to the Duma, but executive power lies firmly with the president.

Profile

President Boris Yeltsin's second term (1996–1999) was overshadowed by his health problems, economic crisis, and corruption. Dramatic changes of government personnel were a characteristic of this period, as Yeltsin confronted the Duma in both 1998 and 1999 over his choice of prime minister. The confrontation ended with the appointment of Vladimir Putin, a little-known former head of the Federal Security Service (FSB), who became Yeltsin's favorite to succeed him.

Putin has greatly consolidated his position since becoming acting president at the end of 1999. Having stormed to victory in the first round of the 2000 presidential elections, he has tackled the power of the business "oligarchs," and of Russia's 89 regional governors, with his program of centralization. His support within the Duma has been consolidated by the transformation of the Unity bloc (which Putin had formed for the 1999 legislative elections) into an official party. A merger with the Fatherland bloc in April 2001 made Unity the largest single party in parliament.

The conflict in Chechnya, though internationally damaging to Putin's

Former president Boris Yeltsin, *renowned for his erratic behavior, stepped down in 1999.*

Mikhail Gorbachev, *whose restructuring ultimately led to the breakup of the Soviet Union.*

R

POLITICS *continued*

image, has by contrast been a key element in his domestic appeal as a strong leader. His popularity was shaken by criticism of his handling of the *Kursk* submarine disaster, in which 118 sailors died in August 2000. However, the marked improvement in the economy during his first year in office stood greatly to his credit in popular opinion, as it also did to that of Prime Minister Mikhail Kasyanov, appointed in 2000 with revitalizing the economy as his central task.

The Communist Party, which until 2001 was the single largest party in the Duma, remains powerful because of its effective organization and its ability to appeal to those who have suffered from the upheavals of the post-Soviet period. However, even with parliamentary allies, it has been unable to take power. Its leader Gennady Zyuganov has three times been beaten to the presidency.

MAIN POLITICAL ISSUES

Regionalism and separatism
Nation-based separatism is brutally suppressed. Nowhere has this been made clearer than by the ferocious military campaign in Chechnya.

Influence accumulated under the Yeltsin regime by Russia's 89 regional governors was reversed by Putin's efforts to concentrate power in the presidency. Control of police and taxation has been centralized in seven huge federal districts, responsible only to Putin, and the governors have been stripped of their seats in the upper house, the Council of the Federation.

Living standards
The 1990s were characterized by uneven and crisis-prone efforts at introducing a market economy under Yeltsin, which created much insecurity. The fall of communism swept away the securities which used to underpin life – long-term employment, guaranteed housing, and a basic diet – hitting the old particularly hard. Putin and Kasyanov have more credibility running the economy, and by 2002 living standards had recovered from the 1998 crash.

Vladimir Putin *was handed power by Yeltsin in 1999, and was elected president in 2000.*

Mikhail Kasyanov, *economic reformist appointed prime minister in 2000.*

Crime and corruption
Crime levels rose alarmingly under the post-Soviet regime, and visitors began to be warned against walking the streets of St. Petersburg or Moscow after dark. Widespread bureaucratic corruption was countered by the power acquired by business tycoons, the so-called "oligarchs," who snapped up privatized industries at bargain prices. Putin launched a crusade against them, but has shied away from a full-scale review of the privatization process.

Political violence
A number of high-profile murders of Duma members and regional administrators has rocked Russian politics in recent years. Always blamed immediately on contract killings, the assassinations attest to the apparent links between organized crime and the political mainstream.

WORLD AFFAIRS

Joined UN in 1945

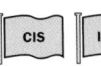

CE | CIS | IAEA | G8 | OSCE

The September 11, 2001, terrorist attacks on the US laid the foundations for a massive change in Russia's relations with the West. By pledging immediate support to the US-led "war on terrorism," President Putin secured unqualified backing for the Chechnya campaign. Once strongly criticized by the West, this conflict was recast as a legitimate battle against "terrorism." By agreeing to share intelligence information as part of the new global war, Russia and NATO appeared to have buried their grievances, and in 2002 a new NATO–Russia Council was established. In return Russia dropped its fundamental objection to the US missile defense system and agreed to a new nuclear disarmament treaty which was widely seen as favoring the US. However, Russia is uneasy over the growth of US influence in central Asia and the Caucasus in the course of its campaign against Islamism.

The successor states of the USSR, the "near abroad," retain close links with Russia and are still viewed, at least domestically, as Russia's sphere of influence. A "joint economic space" comprising Russia, Belarus, Kazakhstan, and Ukraine was announced in 2003. Belarus is eager for full reunification, but plans for monetary and political union have stalled in recent years. Relations with the Baltic states are the least cordial, but are improving after tension over discrimination against ethnic Russians there. Special transit passes for the people of Kaliningrad will come into force when the EU expands up to Russia's border in 2004.

St. Basil's Cathedral, Moscow. *Commissioned by Ivan the Terrible, it was built in 1555–1561. The exterior domes were decorated in the 1670s.*

AID

Recipient

$1.11bn (receipts) | Down 29% in 2001

Russia has received billions of dollars in aid from Western countries on several occasions to stave off government debt and to promote economic restructuring. Large-scale IMF credits were obtained during the economic crises of the mid- and late 1990s.

DEFENSE

Phasing out conscription

$63.7bn | Up 22% in 2001

RUSSIAN ARMED FORCES

21,870 main battle tanks (T-34, T-55, T-62, T-64, T-72, T-80, T-90)	321,000 personnel
53 submarines, 1 carrier, 14 destroyers, 7 cruisers, 10 frigates, 88 patrol boats	171,500 personnel
2434 combat aircraft (MiG-25/29/31, Su-24/25/27, Tu-22)	184,600 personnel
735 ICBM, 13 SSBN, 100 ABM	

The loss of the 118-man *Kursk* nuclear submarine in August 2000 symbolized the long-term decline in Russia's military might. Maintaining and using the enormous former communist war machine has proved too expensive. There are plans to axe hundreds of thousands of troops in 2003, and conscription is set to be abolished by 2005. Public anger at conditions within the services has led to pay increases.

Spending on nuclear forces is limited to physical protection of warheads. In 2002, Russia agreed to cut its nuclear arsenal further, expanding on the 2000 Start II Treaty, and slashing the number of warheads by 60%. It also dropped previous objections to the proposed US national missile defense system.

The Northern and Pacific navy fleets are inactive and deteriorating fast. Fourteen admirals were disciplined in 2001 for the "failings" of the Northern fleet.

THE RUSSIAN FEDERATION: A MODERN EMPIRE

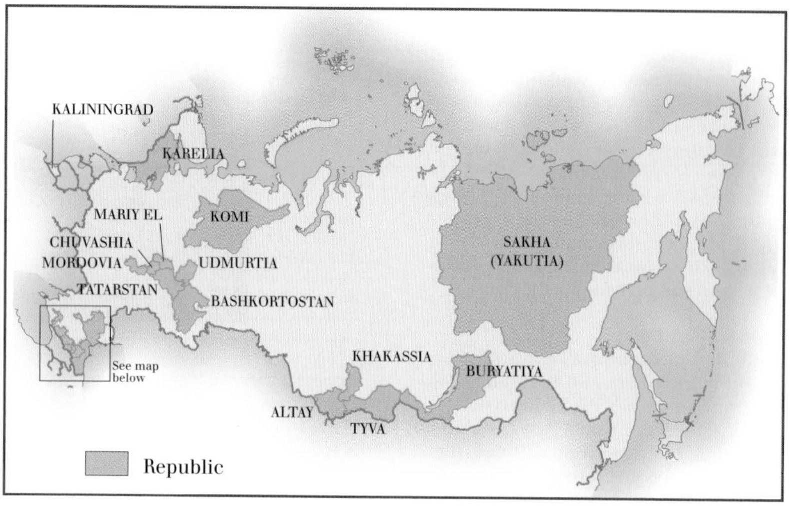
KALININGRAD
KARELIA
KOMI
MARIY EL
CHUVASHIA
MORDOVIA
UDMURTIA
TATARSTAN
BASHKORTOSTAN
SAKHA
(YAKUTIA)
See map
below
KHAKASSIA
BURYATIYA
ALTAY
TYVA
Republic

THE RUSSIAN FEDERATION (RF) is divided into seven federal districts, covering 89 separate federal "units": 49 *oblasti* (regions), 21 republics, ten autonomous *okrugi* (districts), six *kraya* (territories), two federal cities (Moscow and St. Petersburg), and one autonomous *oblast* (Yevreyskaya).

Russian control west and east of the Ural Mountains was secured during waves of imperial expansion from the 16th century. By the beginning of the 20th century the empire had spread so far that it included Finnish-speaking Karelians in the northwest, the various Caucasian peoples of the south, and the Eskimo and Mongolian-related tribes of Arctic Siberia. To ensure Russian authority across the enormous distances, the Russian Empire encouraged a process of physical and cultural russification, sending thousands of colonists to spread Russian commerce, language, and the Orthodox Christian religion. Under the Soviet Union this process – but promoting communism instead of Christianity – was accelerated, despite the official liberation of the ethnic peasants and their "national determination." Nomadic peoples were forced to adopt sedentary and cooperative lifestyles and religion was discouraged if not suppressed outright.

By the time the USSR collapsed in 1991 the process of liberalization had unleashed a wave of nationalist sentiment among many of the country's ethnic minorities. The Union had been subdivided and the larger Soviet Socialist Republics (SSRs) became the independent successor states which crowd Russia's borders. The smaller, ethnically based Autonomous SSRs were granted the status of republics within the new Russian Federation. These 20 republics (21 after the separation of Ingushetia and Chechnya) were granted the right to draft their own constitutions and pass their own legislation provided they acknowledged the supremacy of the federal constitution.

While few of the republics would be viable as separate countries, many held on strongly to the idea of cultural, political, and economic independence. The resources of the Urals and Siberia, and the strategic significance of the Caucasus and far east, made the republic–federal relationship of paramount importance to the emerging state. In many cases ethnic republics cover regions rich in oil and the industrial infrastructure established by the Soviets to process it. Most republics were quick to sign federation treaties confirming their position within the RF, but in some cases a power struggle soon broke out.

Tatarstan

Tatars form the second-largest ethnic group in the RF after the Russians themselves. Their culture is Turkic and Muslim and they have been at the forefront of calls for greater regional autonomy. In 1990 a sovereign Tatar republic was declared covering the Soviet-era ASSR of Tataria, and in 1992 the republican authorities not only refused to sign the federation treaty but actually declared the country's independence after a referendum in favor. However, independence was not recognized internationally and was not a viable option, surrounded as Tatarstan is by Russia, and with its own 43% Russian minority. A power-sharing agreement was eventually signed in 1994, Tatarstan accepting its place within the RF. Relations have not run smoothly since; Tatarstan was one of the four republics named in 2001 as having local laws at odds with the federal constitution. A new 2002 constitution sought to resolve conflicts, and the local authorities have toned down their policy of "Tatarization," but tensions remain. The Tatarstani government has held back from the process of privatization embraced elsewhere and, significantly, retains control of the Tatneft oil company.

The Caucasus and Chechnya

The north Caucasus region is one of the most ethnically diverse regions in the world. The precipitous Greater Caucasus Mountains divide the region and its people into many separate, though often related, linguistic, cultural, and even religious groups. There are now eight separate republics in the region, including Europe's only Buddhist state (Kalmykia); however, Islam dominates among the republics. The most easterly republic, Dagestan, acts as a microcosm of the whole region and is the local religious center. Home to over 32 ethnic groups itself, it is the most diverse state in Europe.

Despite being made a full SSR just before the collapse of the Soviet Union, Dagestan became a constituent Russian republic. Nonetheless, separatism from Russia, centered on the popularity of conservative Sunni Islam, and even interethnic tensions within Dagestan itself are the source of serious tension. An attempted Islamist uprising in 1999, fueled by the presence of battle-hardened Muslim fighters from neighboring Chechnya, was brutally suppressed by the Russian authorities, but served as a pretext for a renewed offensive in Chechnya.

Chechen nationalism in the Checheno-Ingushetia region flourished under the liberalism of *perestroika* in the 1980s,

Elista
KALMYKIA
Caspian Depression
ADYGEYA
Maykop
Cherkessk
KABARDINO-
BALKARIA
KARACHAI-
CHERKESSIA
CHECHNYA
DAGESTAN
Caspian Sea
Nal'chik
Groznyy
NORTH
OSSETIA
Vladikavkaz
Makhachkala
Black Sea
Caucasus
INGUSHETIA
GEORGIA

and a separate Chechen republic declared its sovereignty as Ichkeria under Dzhokar Dudayev, a former air force general, in November 1991. Constrained by a reluctant parliament, the then Russian president Boris Yeltsin was unable to launch a military offensive to reassert control for three years. By 1994 Dudayev's authoritarian rule had provoked civil war in Chechnya (a separate federal republic of Ingushetia having been established in 1992) and Yeltsin, buoyed by a recent victory against his opponents, sent Russian troops to intervene.

The Chechen capital Grozny was razed in a brutal offensive which crushed the Chechen separatists and led to a cease-fire in 1996. However, three years later, following the unsuccessful rebellion in neighboring Dagestan mentioned above, violence broke out once again. This time Yeltsin placed his new prime minister, Vladimir Putin, in charge of responding and a major new offensive

A golomo (winter dwelling) of the Evenk people from Yakutia, northeastern Siberia. Russia is home to 152 different nationalities.

was launched in October 1999. Despite claiming victory in early 2000 and again in mid-2002, Russian forces have been subjected to intense guerrilla action ever since. At the peak of hostilities in mid-2000 as many as 160 Russian soldiers were being killed every day.

A new constitution for Chechnya was endorsed by a 95% majority in a referendum held in March 2003 in an effort to draw a line under the conflict. The republic was designated an autonomous part of the RF. However, separatists and terrorist groups have rejected the new regime with characteristic disdain and attacks continue. High-profile incidents in Russia itself, such as the 2002 Moscow theater siege and the bombing of a rock concert in 2003, receive the most media attention, but a near-constant stream of attacks in Chechnya go largely unreported by the global press.

ECONOMICS

Inflation 140% p.a. (1990–2001)

$253bn

30.35 Russian roubles (official rate) (31.52)

SCORE CARD

- World GNP Ranking..........19th
- GNP per Capita..........$1750
- Balance of Payments..........$34.6bn
- Inflation..........21.5%
- Unemployment..........11%

EXPORTS

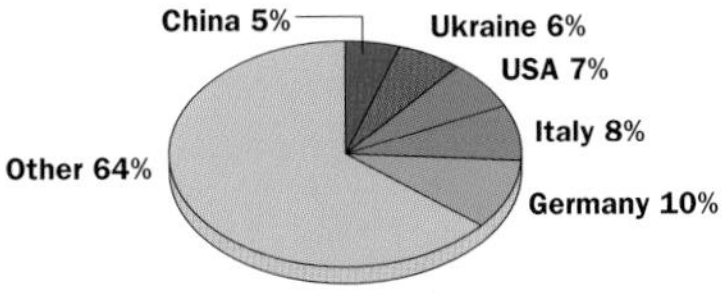
China 5%
Ukraine 6%
USA 7%
Italy 8%
Germany 10%
Other 64%

IMPORTS

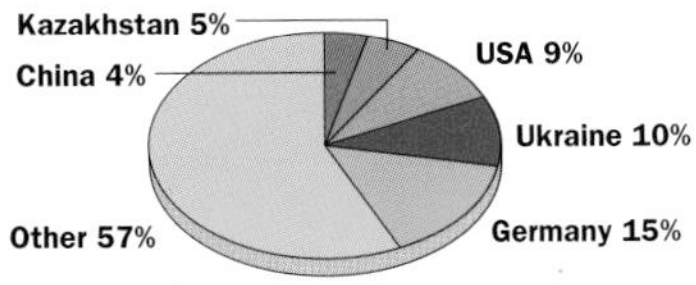
Kazakhstan 5%
China 4%
USA 9%
Ukraine 10%
Germany 15%
Other 57%

Strengths

Huge natural resources, in particular hydrocarbons, precious metals, fuel, timber. Potential from future international oil pipelines. Enormous engineering and scientific base. Massive arms export industry: world's largest in 2002. Government revenue increased by tax reforms. Lucrative privatizations. Recognized as a market economy in 2002, encouraging foreign investment.

Weaknesses

Oil profits vulnerable to fluctuating world prices. Crumbling infrastructure. Slow transition to market economy. Privatized companies asset-stripped by former managers. Organized crime controls huge areas of the economy. Regional investment hindered by uneven implementation of federal laws. Tax evasion and corruption remain

ECONOMIC PERFORMANCE INDICATOR

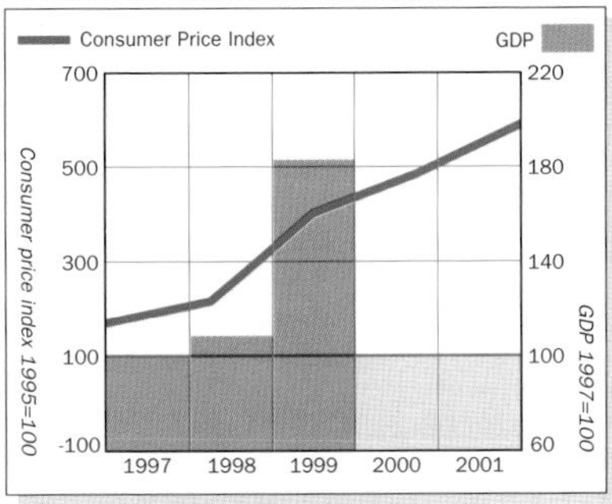
Consumer Price Index
GDP
Consumer price index 1995=100
GDP 1997=100
700
500
300
100
-100
220
180
140
100
60
1997
1998
1999
2000
2001

widespread. Rising wages and strengthening rouble have promoted boom in imports, narrowing trade gap, harming local production, and stifling small enterprises.

Profile

The few gains made in the early postcommunist era were swept aside in the 1998 economic crisis. Powerful financial "oligarchs" emerged, and organized crime moved into most areas of the economy. However, the devaluation of the rouble ironically served to promote a miniboom in the last years of the 20th century. Real wages fell, encouraging small enterprises to expand, while the devaluation made imports too expensive for the average consumer – promoting local production. Industrial production increased and GDP grew by 7.6% in 2000. Putin has moved to dismantle the power of the economic elites. The private sale of land was permitted from 2001, and a new 13% flat rate of income tax promised to help reduce widespread tax evasion. However, while the economy weathered the 2001 global slowdown, the rise in real wages and the strengthening of the rouble have begun to offset the previous years' gains. Some 50% of the economy is conducted on the black market.

RUSSIAN FEDERATION : MAJOR BUSINESSES

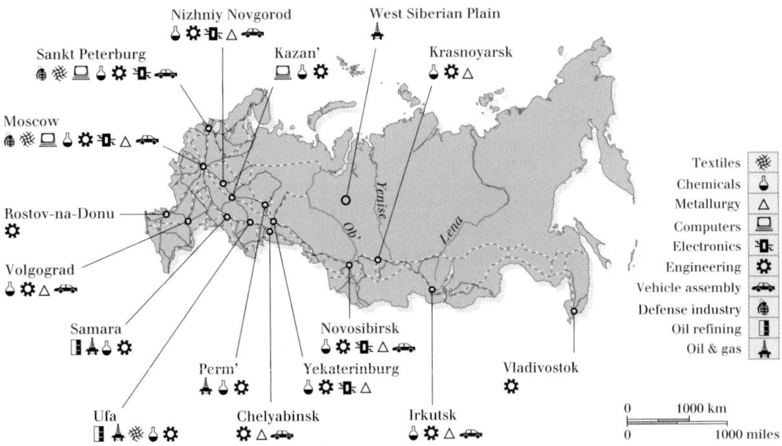
Nizhniy Novgorod
West Siberian Plain
Sankt Peterburg
Kazan'
Krasnoyarsk
Moscow
Rostov-na-Donu
Volgograd
Samara
Perm'
Ufa
Chelyabinsk
Yekaterinburg
Novosibirsk
Irkutsk
Vladivostok
Ob'
Yenisey
Lena
Textiles
Chemicals
Metallurgy
Computers
Electronics
Engineering
Vehicle assembly
Defense industry
Oil refining
Oil & gas
0
1000 km
0
1000 miles

R

CHRONOLOGY

The first Russian state (Rus) was in present-day Ukraine. Occupation by the Tatars (1240–1480) marked the Russian language and character. From the 17th century, the Romanovs ruled an expanding empire.

- **1904–1905** Russian war against Japan; ends in defeat for Russia.
- **1905** "Bloody Sunday" revolution.
- **1909–1914** Rapid economic expansion.
- **1914** Enters World War I against Germany.
- **1917** February Revolution; abdication of Nicholas II. October Revolution; Bolsheviks take over with Lenin as leader.
- **1918** Nicholas II and family shot.
- **1918–1920** Civil war.
- **1921** New Economic Policy; retreat from socialism.
- **1922** USSR established.
- **1924** Lenin dies. Leadership struggle eventually won by Stalin.
- **1928** First Five-Year Plan: forced industrialization and collectivization.
- **1936–1938** Show trials and campaigns against actual and suspected members of opposition. Millions sent to gulags in Siberia and elsewhere. Purges widespread.
- **1939** Hitler–Stalin pact gives USSR Baltic states, eastern Poland, and Bessarabia (Moldova).
- **1941** Germany attacks USSR.
- **1943** February, tide of war turns with lifting of siege of Stalingrad.
- **1944–1945** Soviet offensive penetrates Balkans.
- **1945** Germany defeated. Under Yalta and Potsdam agreements eastern and southeastern Europe are Soviet zone of influence.
- **1947** Cold War begins; Stalin on defensive and fears penetration of Western capitalist values.
- **1953** Stalin dies.
- **1956** Hungarian uprising crushed. Krushchev's "secret speech" attacking Stalin at party congress.
- **1957** Krushchev consolidates power. *Sputnik* launched.
- **1961** Yuri Gagarin first man in space.
- **1962** Cuban missile crisis.
- **1964** Krushchev ousted in coup, replaced by Leonid Brezhnev.
- **1975** Helsinki Final Act; confirms European frontiers as at end of World War II. Soviets agree human rights are concern of international community.
- **1979** Soviets invade Afghanistan. New intensification of Cold War.
- **1982** Brezhnev dies.
- **1985** Gorbachev in power. Start of *perestroika*, "restructuring." First of three US–USSR summits, resulting in arms ⇨

RESOURCES

Electric power 211m kW

4.05m tonnes

7.7m b/d (reserves 60bn barrels)

27.1m cattle, 16m pigs, 13m sheep, 340m chickens

Coal, oil, gas, gold, diamonds, iron, aluminum, manganese

ELECTRICITY GENERATION

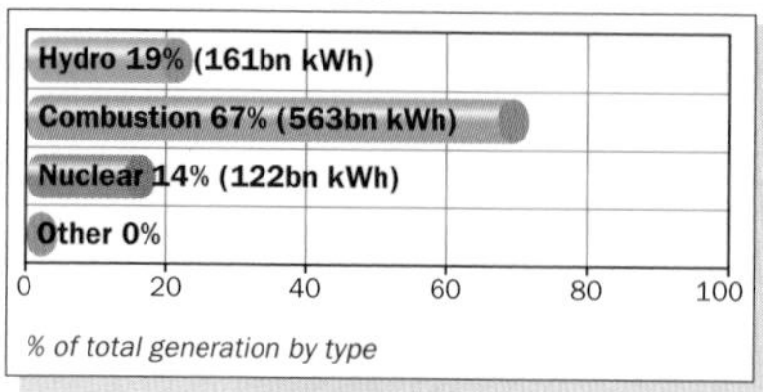

Hydro 19% (161bn kWh)
Combustion 67% (563bn kWh)
Nuclear 14% (122bn kWh)
Other 0%
0
20
40
60
80
100
% of total generation by type

Russia is a major producer of oil, natural gas, and electricity, among other resources. Confirmed reserves make Russia the world's leading country in terms of hydrocarbons, gold, other precious metals, diamonds, and timber.

Russia has been slow to open its resources up to foreign concerns, but is starting to realize the potential of its vast resources. In 2003 foreign firms invested in a mammoth $10 billion liquefied natural gas plant in Sakhalin – set to be the world's largest integrated oil and gas project.

However, geographic remoteness has held back exploitation, while the fact that some of the richest deposits are located in national territories such as Tatarstan and Sakha (Yakutia) in Siberia has turned the ownership of these resources into a delicate political issue.

RUSSIAN FEDERATION : LAND USE

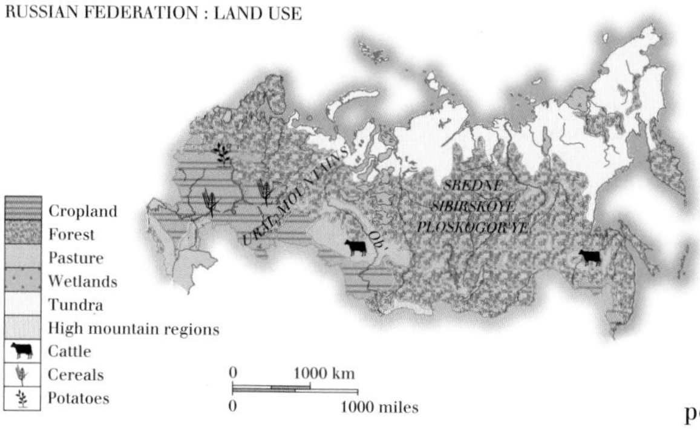

Cropland
Forest
Pasture
Wetlands
Tundra
High mountain regions
Cattle
Cereals
Potatoes
0
1000 km
0
1000 miles
URAL MOUNTAINS
Ob'
SREDNE SIBIRSKOYE PLOSKOGOR'YE

ENVIRONMENT

Sustainability rank: 72nd

8% (0.8% partially protected)

9.8 tonnes per capita

ENVIRONMENTAL TREATIES

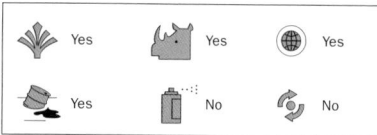

Yes	Yes	Yes
Yes	No	No

Though awareness of Russia's environmental problems has risen sharply, the resources, political will, and know-how to tackle them are still lacking. While Russia now has an active green movement, it has not as yet won significant support in general elections.

Each region has its own particular problems. The northwest risks contamination from the neglected Soviet-era nuclear submarine fleet and from nuclear waste containers dumped in the Barents Sea. Thousands of tonnes of chemical weapons have been dumped in the Baltic, though their exact location has not been revealed. Several fish species are now extinct in the Volga River in central Russia. In the Urals and the cities of European Russia, many chemical and heavy industrial plants do not treat their effluents at all. In 2001 parliament approved a bill to allow the atomic energy ministry Minatom to earn $2 billion a year from storing and reprocessing foreign nuclear waste.

MEDIA

TV ownership high

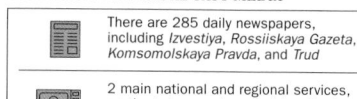

Daily newspaper circulation 105 per 1000 people

PUBLISHING AND BROADCAST MEDIA

There are 285 daily newspapers, including *Izvestiya*, *Rossiiskaya Gazeta*, *Komsomolskaya Pravda*, and *Trud*

2 main national and regional services, partly state-owned, several localized independent channels

1 main state-run service, broadcasting 2 channels, 1 foreign broadcasting service, several independents

There is growing concern over state control of the media. Bias in TV reporting, rife under Yeltsin, continues under Putin. Reporting on Chechnya is subject to particular pressure. The NTV network, flagship of exiled magnate Vladimir Gusinsky, was taken over in 2001 by the state-run gas company Gazprom, while the remaining independent national broadcaster, TVS, was shut down due to poor finances in 2003. Critical editorial staff have been dismissed from the daily *Sevodnya* and weekly *Itogi*. Many Russians have satellite dishes and tune in to CNN and other Western channels.

Argumenty i Fakty is the best-selling weekly paper, with a circulation of nearly three million. *Komsomolskaya Pravda* is the biggest-selling daily. The Soviet state organ *Izvestiya* is now independent.

Overall, 9% of the population have access to the Internet, but use is concentrated among Muscovites.

R

CHRONOLOGY *continued*

reduction treaties. Nationality conflicts surface.

- ❏ **1988** Law of State Enterprises gives more power to enterprises; inflation and dislocation of economy.
- ❏ **1990** Gorbachev becomes Soviet president. First partly freely elected parliament (Supreme Soviet) meets.
- ❏ **1991** Boris Yeltsin elected president of Russia. Yeltsin and Muscovites resist hard-line communist coup. Gorbachev sidelined. CIS established; demise of USSR.
- ❏ **1992** Economic shock therapy.
- ❏ **1993** Yeltsin decrees dissolution of Supreme Soviet and uses force to disband parliament. Elections return conservative State Duma.
- ❏ **1994** First Russian military offensive against Chechnya.
- ❏ **1995** Communists win elections.
- ❏ **1996** Yeltsin reelected despite strong Communist challenge. Peace accord in Chechnya.
- ❏ **1998** Economic turmoil forces devaluation of rouble. Severe recession, rampant inflation.
- ❏ **1998–1999** Yeltsin repeatedly changes prime minister in successive political crises.
- ❏ **1999** Parliamentary elections. Yeltsin resigns; prime minister Putin is acting president.
- ❏ **1999–2000** Terrorist violence blamed on Islamic separatists in Dagestan and Chechnya. Military offensive against Chechnya; fall of Chechen capital Grozny to Russian forces.
- ❏ **2000** Putin wins presidential election, consolidates power. Attack on "oligarchs" in big business. Improvement in economy. *Kursk* nuclear submarine disaster.
- ❏ **2001** Party mergers: Putin's Unity party largest grouping in parliament. Russian–Chinese friendship treaty.
- ❏ **2002** April, Putin declares Chechen war "over." May, Cam Ranh Bay base in Vietnam, last Russian outpost beyond former USSR, closed. October, Moscow theater hostage crisis: Chechen separatists and 128 hostages killed during rescue.

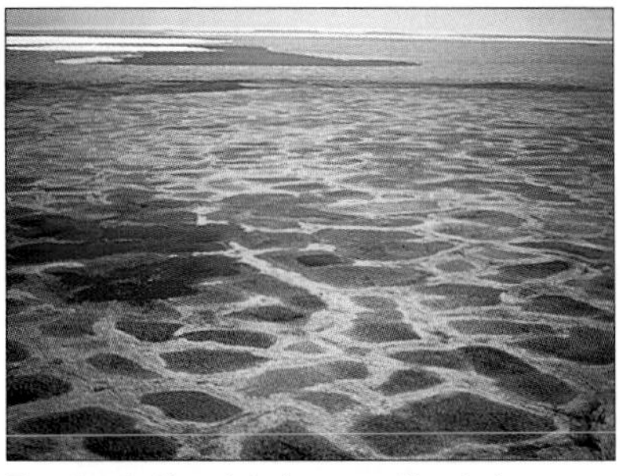

Tundra in Russia's far east. *Russia has some of the largest uninhabited tracts of land in the world.*

CRIME

Death penalty not used in practice

919,330 prisoners

Down 14% in 2000–2002

CRIME RATES

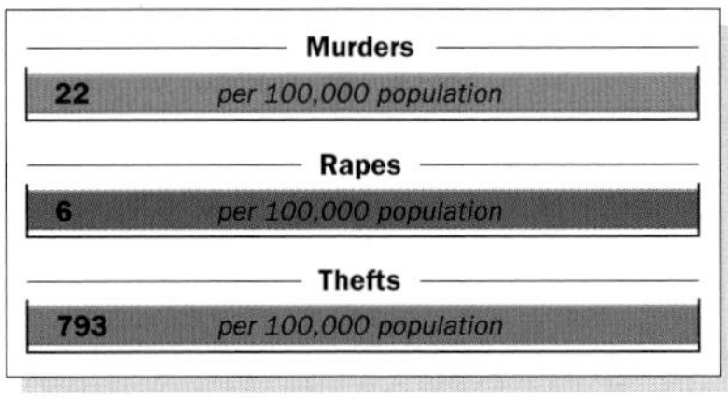
Murders
22
per 100,000 population
Rapes
6
per 100,000 population
Thefts
793
per 100,000 population

Policing cannot keep pace with the formidable levels of crime in Russia.

Intergang violence accounts for a recent rise in the murder rate. Street crime has also increased in the larger cities. Corruption is rife, particularly in the regions. The Russian mafia profits from protection rackets, prostitution, smuggling operations, and narcotics, and is also active in western Europe.

Public fear resulting from level of crime contributed to a temporary rise in popularity for authoritarian political platforms.

With around one million inmates in prison, overcrowding, poor conditions, and disease are major problems.

EDUCATION

School leaving age: 15

99%

7.22m students

THE EDUCATION SYSTEM

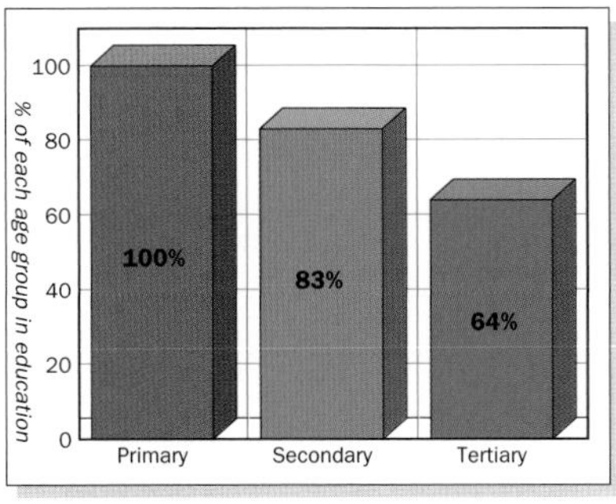
% of each age group in education
100
80
60
40
20
0
100%
83%
64%
Primary
Secondary
Tertiary

Schooling is free, and is compulsory for nine years up to age 15.

Attempts to change the Soviet-based curriculum, still widely in use, are hampered by lack of funds. Hundreds of private lycées, such as those run by the Orthodox Church, offer courses in west European languages. German in particular has made a comeback as a key language for international commerce. The state-subsidized higher education system is seriously underfunded, and some institutions have begun charging students. Prestigious institutions such as the Academy of Sciences have been forced to cut staff and research. Most academics have to rely on extramural earnings.

HEALTH

Welfare state health benefits

1 per 236 people

Cerebrovascular and heart diseases, accidents, cancers

The health care system is in crisis and medicines are often in short supply. Nearly two-thirds of children are deemed "unhealthy."

Until 1991, state enterprises provided considerable health care for employees. Employers should now make payments through the Medical Insurance Fund, but many privatized concerns seek to cut costs. Bribing medical staff to obtain treatment is commonplace, and there is a lack of pharmaceutical products and drugs. Alcoholism is increasing as a cause of death.

SPENDING

GDP/cap. decrease

CONSUMPTION AND SPENDING

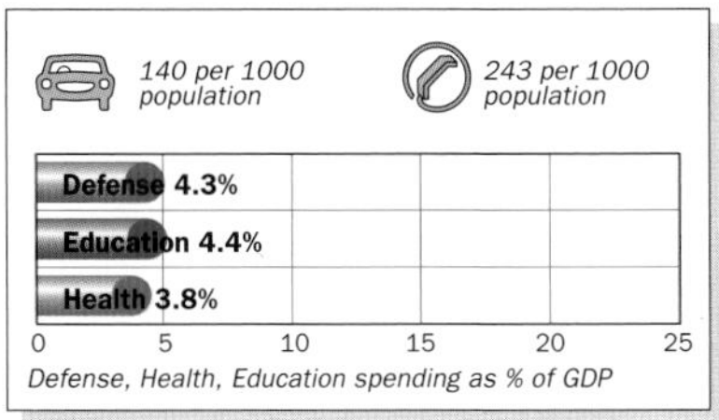
140 per 1000 population
243 per 1000 population
Defense 4.3%
Education 4.4%
Health 3.8%
0
5
10
15
20
25
Defense, Health, Education spending as % of GDP

Wealth disparities in Russia have increased sharply. A small minority made huge profits from the dismantling of the old Soviet command economy, while a quarter of the population now live in poverty.

A growing number of dollar millionaires flaunt their wealth, especially in Moscow. The bosses of organized crime are Russian society's wealthiest group. Russia is now the biggest buyer of Rolls Royces, while BMWs, Mercedes, and Volvos are relatively common in Moscow and St. Petersburg. A considerable amount of wealth is deposited abroad. There are thousands of Russian offshore bank accounts; the Turkish Republic of Northern Cyprus is a favorite location.

WORLD RANKING

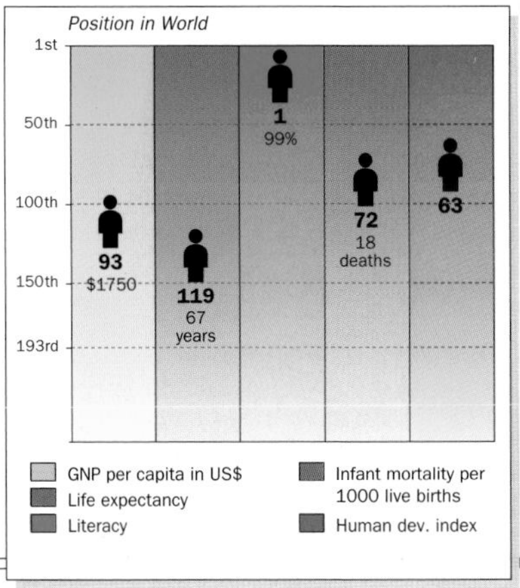
Position in World
1st
50th
100th
150th
193rd
93
$1750
119
67
years
1
99%
72
18
deaths
63
GNP per capita in US$
Life expectancy
Literacy
Infant mortality per 1000 live births
Human dev. index

R

RWANDA

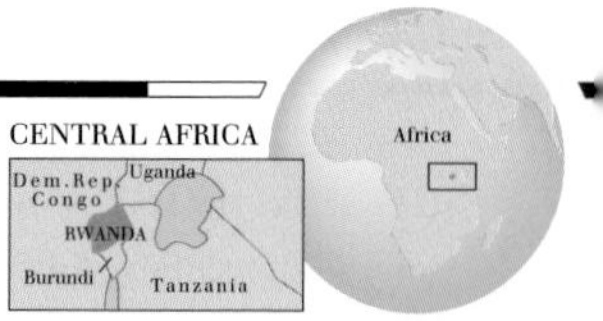
CENTRAL AFRICA
Dem. Rep. Congo
Uganda
RWANDA
Burundi
Tanzania
Africa

OFFICIAL NAME: Republic of Rwanda **CAPITAL:** Kigali **POPULATION:** 8.16 million
CURRENCY: Rwanda franc **OFFICIAL LANGUAGES:** French, English, and Kinyarwanda

1962 | 1962 | July 1 | RWA | +2 | +250 | .rw

LANDLOCKED RWANDA lies just south of the equator in east central Africa. Since independence in 1962, ethnic tensions have dominated politics. In 1994, the violent death of the president led to appalling political and ethnic violence. Over half of the surviving population were displaced. The perpetrators of the genocide held sway in desperately overcrowded refugee camps in adjacent countries, greatly complicating the process of eventual repatriation and reintegration.

CLIMATE
Tropical wet and dry

WEATHER CHART FOR KIGALI

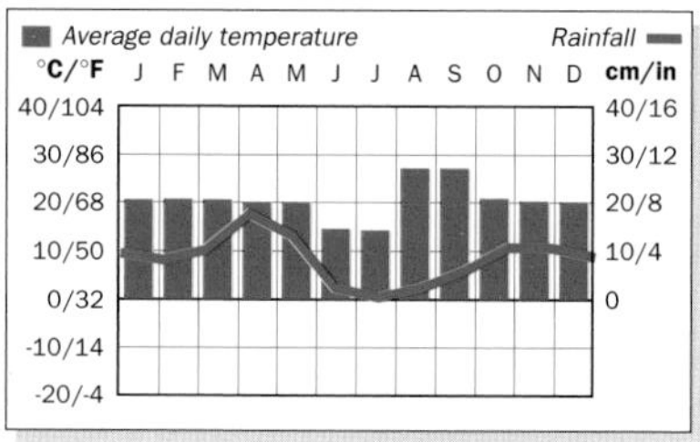
Average daily temperature
Rainfall
°C/°F J F M A M J J A S O N D cm/in
40/104 30/86 20/68 10/50 0/32 -10/14 -20/4
40/16 30/12 20/8 10/4 0

Rwanda's climate is tropical, tempered by altitude. Two wet seasons allow for two harvests each year.

TRANSPORTATION
Drive on right

Kanombe International, Kigali
113,336 passengers

Has no fleet

THE TRANSPORTATION NETWORK

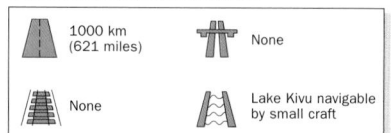

1000 km (621 miles)

None

None

Lake Kivu navigable by small craft

The road network is well developed, and Rwanda has access by road to the Tanzanian railroad system.

TOURISM
Visitors : Population 1:4080

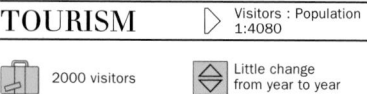

2000 visitors

Little change from year to year

MAIN TOURIST ARRIVALS

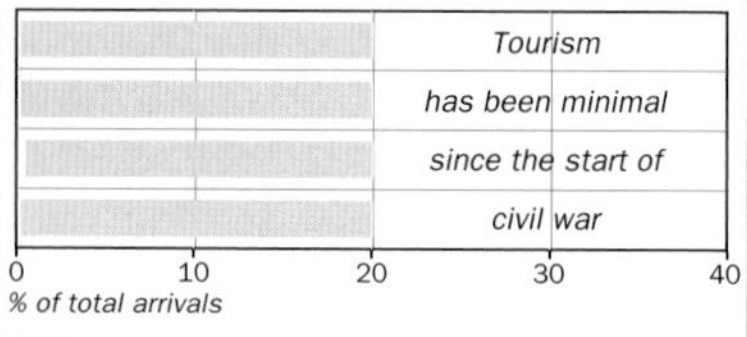
Tourism has been minimal since the start of civil war
0 10 20 30 40
% of total arrivals

Tourism has effectively ceased as a result of the civil war. When peace is secured, Rwanda may be able to regain its status as a destination for wildlife enthusiasts. Top attractions are the mountain gorillas and Lake Kivu.

PEOPLE
Pop. density high

Kinyarwanda, French, Kiswahili, English

327/km² (847/mi²)

THE URBAN/RURAL POPULATION SPLIT

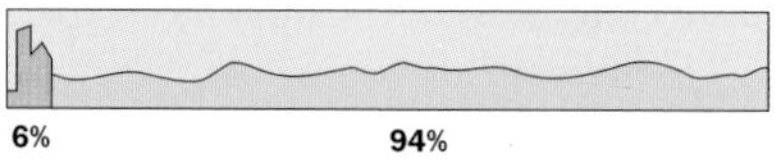
6%
94%

ETHNIC MAKEUP

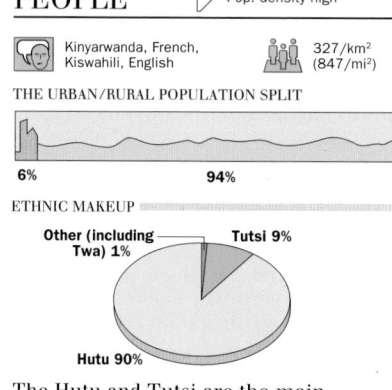

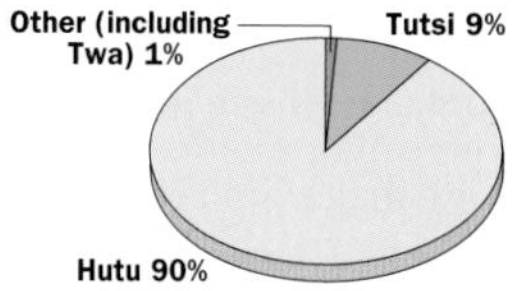
Other (including Twa) 1%
Tutsi 9%
Hutu 90%

The Hutu and Tutsi are the main groups; few of the Twa pygmies, the original inhabitants, remain. For more than 500 years, the cattle-owning Tutsi were politically dominant, oppressing the landowning Hutu majority. In 1959, violent revolt led to a reversal of the roles. The two groups have since been waging a spasmodic war. It is estimated that 800,000 people were killed in the violence of the mid-1990s, the majority of them Tutsi victims massacred by Hutus.

POLITICS
In transition

1988/2003

President Paul Kagame

AT THE LAST ELECTION

Transitional National Assembly 74 seats

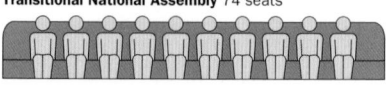

The last legislative election, to the National Development Council, took place in December 1988.
A Transitional National Assembly was set up in 1994. Polls due in 1999 were postponed until 2003. A new constitution, approved by referendum in May 2003, will allow for the creation of a bicameral legislature.

A peace accord ending a three-year rebellion by the Tutsi-dominated Rwandan Patriotic Front (FPR) was signed in 1993, but the fragile peace process was shattered in 1994 by the death of the president in a plane crash. Genocidal violence was unleashed by the mainly Hutu supporters of the old regime on their mainly, but not exclusively, Tutsi opponents. The FPR eventually gained control in the conflict. In an effort to balance the government, Hutu were allocated key government posts, including the presidency. An attempt to increase Tutsi representation prompted President Pasteur Bizimungu to resign in 2000. His deputy, Vice President Paul Kagame, succeeded him. A draft new constitution was approved by referendum in 2003. It includes safeguards against ethnic hatred and one-party dominance, but allows the curtailment of free speech. Elections are scheduled to follow.

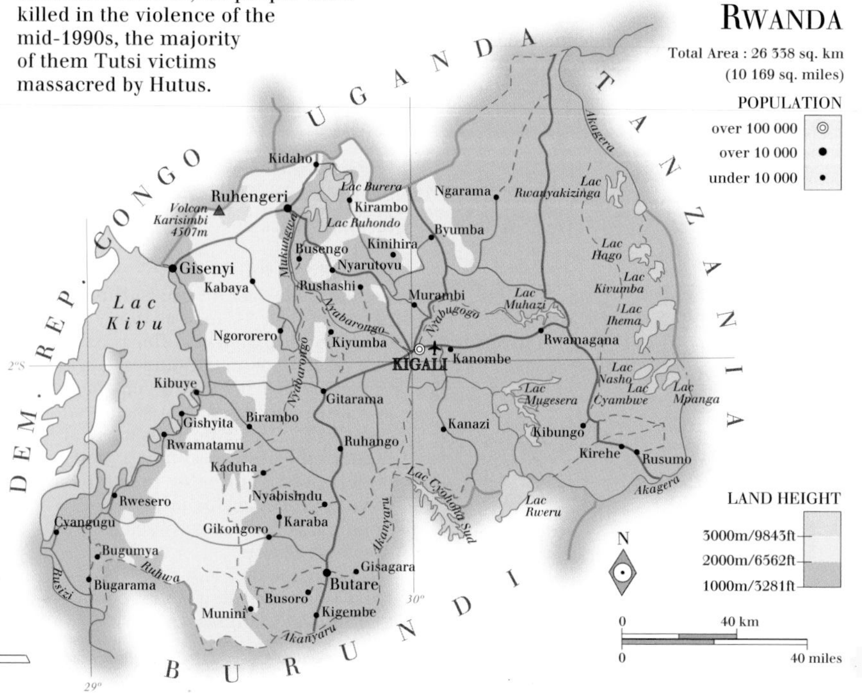
RWANDA
Total Area : 26 338 sq. km (10 169 sq. miles)
POPULATION
over 100 000
over 10 000
under 10 000
LAND HEIGHT
3000m/9843ft
2000m/6562ft
1000m/3281ft
0 40 km
0 40 miles
UGANDA
TANZANIA
BURUNDI
DEM. REP. CONGO
Lac Kivu
KIGALI
Kanombe
Ruhengeri
Gisenyi
Kidaho
Volcan Karisimbi 4507m
Lac Burera
Kirambo
Lac Ruhondo
Busengo
Kinihira
Byumba
Ngarama
Lac Rwanyakizinga
Nyarutovu
Kabaya
Rushashi
Murambi
Lac Muhazi
Lac Hago
Lac Kivumba
Lac Ihema
Rwamagana
Ngororero
Kiyumba
Kibuye
Gitarama
Gishyita
Birambo
Rwamatamu
Kanazi
Kibungo
Lac Mugesera
Lac Nasho
Lac Cyambwe
Lac Mpanga
Kirehe
Rusumo
Ruhango
Kaduha
Nyabisindu
Karaba
Gikongoro
Rwesero
Cyangugu
Bugumya
Bugarama
Gisagara
Butare
Busoro
Kigembe
Munini
Lac Rweru
Lac Cyohoha Sud
Akagera
Akanyaru
Nyabarongo
Mukungwa
Rusizi
Ruhwa
2°S
29°
30°

WORLD AFFAIRS

Joined UN in 1962

COMESA | CEPGL | OIF | NAM | AU

Relations with neighboring Uganda are particularly tense, especially over the recent conflict in the DRC – from where Rwandan troops only withdrew in 2002. Ethnic strife in neighboring Burundi has a destablizing effect.

AID

Recipient

$291m (receipts) | Down 10% in 2001

Large amounts of aid are required, particularly for the agricultural sector, which had been severely disrupted by fighting. Aid donors in November 2000 urged Rwanda to withdraw its troops from the DRC.

DEFENSE

No compulsory military service

$98m | No change in 2001

The Rwandan army is sufficiently powerful to make it a strong influence in the war-torn region. A national police force was established in 1999.

ECONOMICS

Inflation 13% p.a. (1990–2001)

$1.89bn | 525.1 Rwanda francs (460.8)

SCORE CARD

❑ World GNP Ranking	139th
❑ GNP per Capita	$220
❑ Balance of Payments	–$118m
❑ Inflation	3.3%
❑ Unemployment	Few have formal employment

Strengths

Currently few. With stability, Rwanda can produce coffee and tea (the main export). Possible oil and gas reserves. Tourism potential. Mining.

Weaknesses

Economic activity completely disrupted by 1994 violence. Distance to nearest ports raises transportation costs. Few resources. Border instability.

EXPORTS

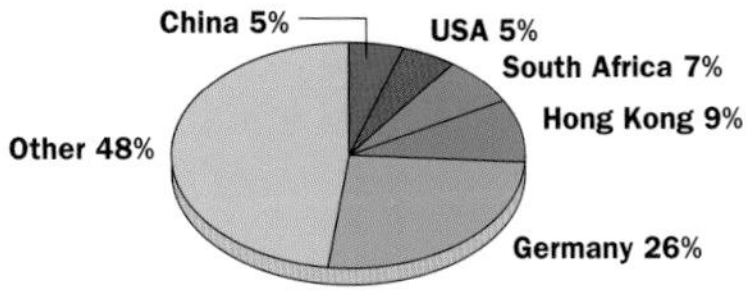
China 5%
USA 5%
South Africa 7%
Hong Kong 9%
Other 48%
Germany 26%

IMPORTS

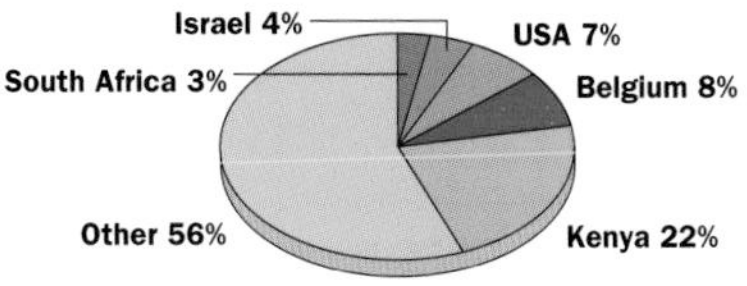
Israel 4%
USA 7%
South Africa 3%
Belgium 8%
Other 56%
Kenya 22%

Terraced hillside. *Before the war, Rwanda was the most densely populated country in Africa and its land was intensively cultivated.*

RESOURCES

Electric power 43,000 kW

6996 tonnes | Not an oil producer

815,000 cattle, 760,000 goats, 1.2m chickens | Tin, tungsten, gold, columbo-tantalite, methane gas

There are plans to extract natural gas from Lake Kivu: the reserves could potentially supply Rwanda's electricity needs for 400 years.

ENVIRONMENT

Sustainability rank: 119th

15% (5% partially protected) | 0.08 tonnes per capita

Apart from the effects of war, soil erosion and forest loss are the major environmental problems. The tourist industry underpinned the preservation of the mountain gorilla.

MEDIA

TV ownership low

Daily newspaper circulation 0.1 per 1000 people

PUBLISHING AND BROADCAST MEDIA

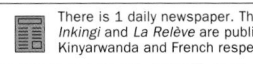

There is 1 daily newspaper. The monthly *Inkingi* and *La Relève* are published in Kinyarwanda and French respectively

1 state-controlled service | 2 services: 1 state-controlled 1 independent

The media have been used as an important propaganda tool by both sides in the political conflict.

CRIME

Death penalty in use

112,000 prisoners | Crime is rising

Rehabilitation centers have opened for those who have admitted to taking part in the genocide and who are being released from prison, reeducated, and sent back to their communities.

EDUCATION

School leaving age: 12

68% | 12,802 students

Schools are run by the state and by Christian missions. Primary education is officially compulsory, but only 78% of children attended in 1997; just 12% go on to secondary schooling.

CHRONOLOGY

The Hutu majority began to arrive in the 14th century, the warrior Tutsi in the 15th. From 1890, German and then Belgian colonizers acted to reinforce Tutsi dominance.

- ❑ **1962** Independence. Hutu-led government.
- ❑ **1960s** Tutsi revolt; massacres by Hutu; thousands of Tutsis in exile.
- ❑ **1973** Coup by Gen. Habyarimana.
- ❑ **1994** Habyarimana dies in plane crash. Genocidal violence unleashed by Hutu extremist regime, ousted by Tutsi-led FPR. Hutu refugee exodus.
- ❑ **1995** Start of war crimes tribunal.
- ❑ **1997** Refugees forcibly repatriated.
- ❑ **2000** Prominent Hutus leave office.
- ❑ **2001–2002** Troop withdrawal from DRC.

HEALTH

Welfare state health benefits

1 per 20,000 people | Malaria, measles, diarrheal diseases, violence

Rwanda has a network of 34 hospitals and 188 health centers. At the end of 2001, 9% of the population was estimated to be HIV-positive.

SPENDING

GDP/cap. increase

CONSUMPTION AND SPENDING

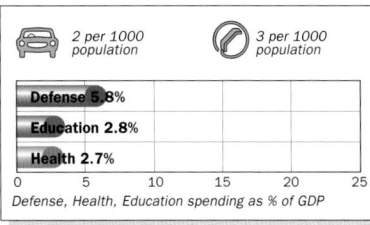

2 per 1000 population | *3 per 1000 population*

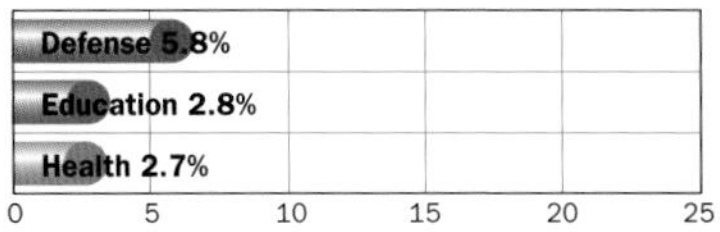
Defense 5.8%
Education 2.8%
Health 2.7%
0
5
10
15
20
25

Defense, Health, Education spending as % of GDP

Wealth is limited to the country's political elite. Most Rwandans are poor farmers; Twa pygmies and refugees are poorer still.

WORLD RANKING

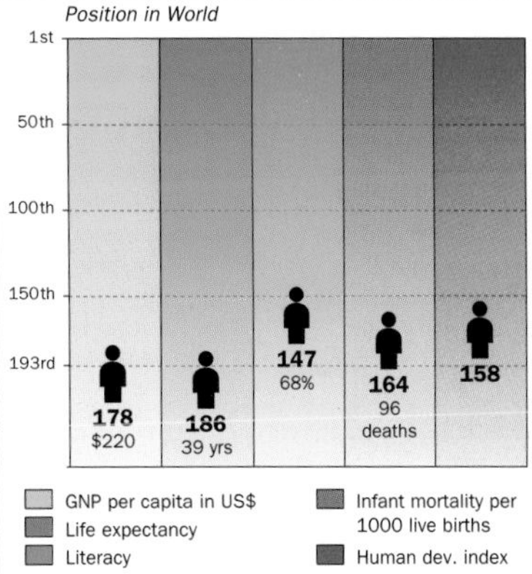
Position in World
1st
50th
100th
150th
193rd
178
$220
186
39 yrs
147
68%
164
96
deaths
158
GNP per capita in US$
Life expectancy
Literacy
Infant mortality per 1000 live births
Human dev. index

R

St. Kitts & Nevis

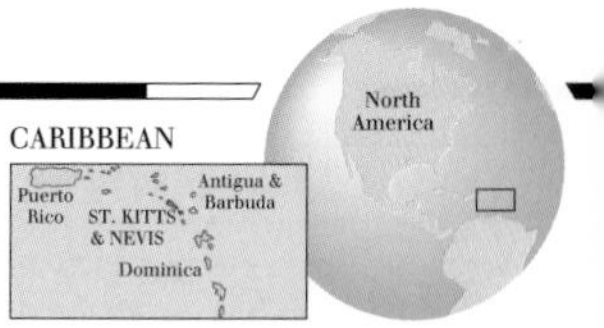
North America
CARIBBEAN
Puerto Rico
ST. KITTS & NEVIS
Antigua & Barbuda
Dominica

Official Name: Federation of Saint Christopher and Nevis **Capital:** Basseterre
Population: 38,736 **Currency:** Eastern Caribbean dollar **Official Language:** English

1983 | 1983 | Sept 19 | KN | -4 | +1869 | .kn

ONE OF THE CARIBBEAN'S most popular tourist destinations, St. Kitts and Nevis, a former British colony, lies at the northern end of the Leeward Islands chain. St. Kitts is of volcanic origin; Mount Liamuiga, a dormant volcano with a crater 227 m (745 ft) deep, is the highest point on the island. Nevis, separated from St. Kitts by a channel 3 km (2 miles) wide, is the lusher but less developed of the two islands. In the 18th century, its famed hot and cold springs gained Nevis the title "the Spa of the Caribbean."

CLIMATE

Tropical oceanic

WEATHER CHART FOR BASSETERRE

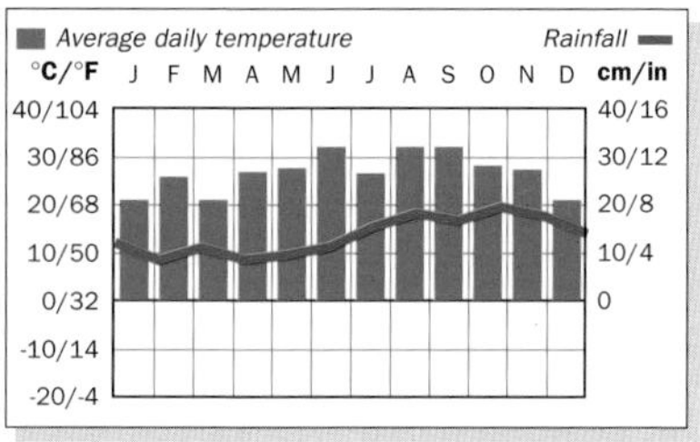
Average daily temperature
Rainfall
°C/°F
J F M A M J J A S O N D
cm/in
40/104
30/86
20/68
10/50
0/32
-10/14
-20/-4
40/16
30/12
20/8
10/4
0

A combination of high temperatures, trade breezes, and moderate rainfall in summer constitute St. Kitts's typically Caribbean climate.

TRANSPORTATION

Drive on left

Golden Rock International, Basseterre

1 ship 600 dwt

THE TRANSPORTATION NETWORK

136 km (85 miles)

None

58 km (36 miles)

None

Most roads on the islands follow the coast; just a few cross the interior. Access to the remote southeastern peninsula of St. Kitts has been improved. The airport on St. Kitts takes large jets; Nevis airport accepts only light aircraft. Regular ferries connect the islands.

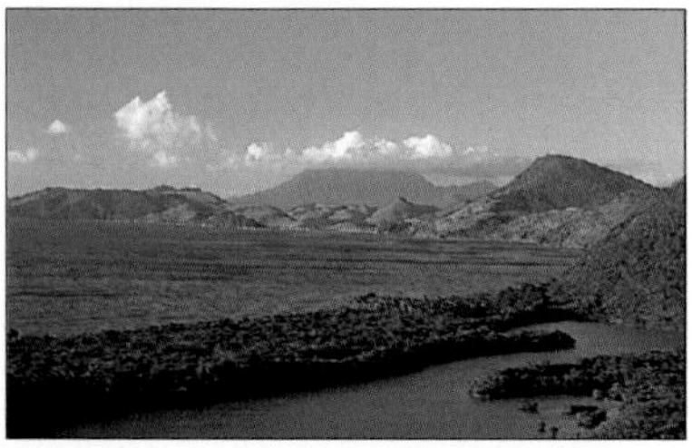

The southeastern peninsula of St. Kitts, looking across to Nevis in the background, on a typical December evening.

TOURISM

Visitors : Population 2.2:1

84,000 visitors

Down 10% in 1999

MAIN TOURIST ARRIVALS

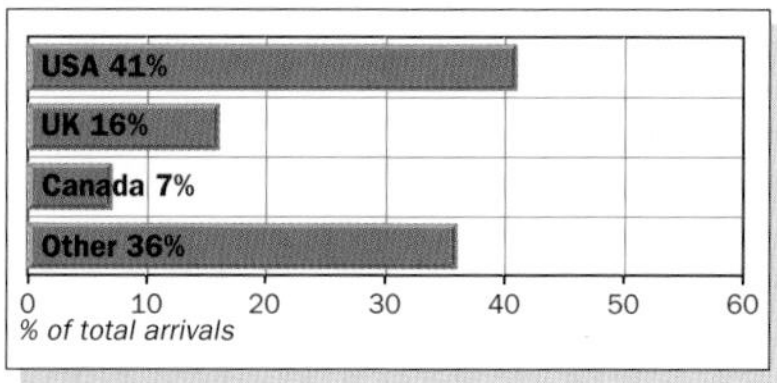
USA 41%
UK 16%
Canada 7%
Other 36%
0 10 20 30 40 50 60
% of total arrivals

St. Kitts has long targeted the mass US tourist market. Improvements to boost tourism include the opening up of the St. Kitts southern peninsula to large-scale tourist developments, and the expansion of the main port to accommodate two cruise ships simultaneously. Most visitors come for sand, sun, and the Caribbean mood, though in recent years safaris inland to see local wildlife and mineral springs have become more popular. On St. Kitts, the old Brimstone Hill fortress has been converted into a museum, as has the Nevis birthplace of Alexander Hamilton, one of the architects of the US constitution.

PEOPLE

Pop. density medium

English, English Creole

108/km² (279/mi²)

THE URBAN/RURAL POPULATION SPLIT

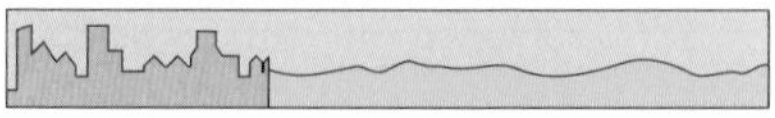
34%
66%

RELIGIOUS PERSUASION

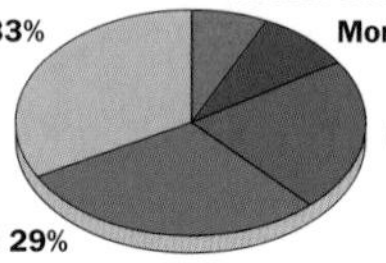
Roman Catholic 7%
Anglican 33%
Moravian 9%
Other 22%
Methodist 29%

Most of the population is descended from Africans brought over as slaves in the 17th century. There are small numbers of Europeans and South Asians, and a community of Lebanese. Levels of emigration are high; remittances from abroad provide an important source of revenue.

POLITICS

Multiparty elections

2000/2005

H.M. Queen Elizabeth II

AT THE LAST ELECTION

National Assembly 15 seats

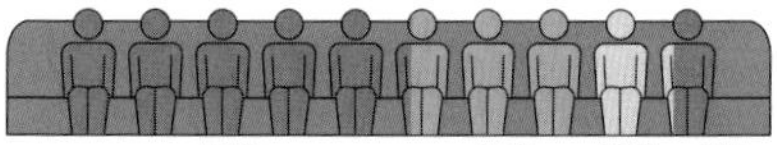
53% SKLP
27% App
13% CCM
7% NRP

SKLP = St. Kitts Labour Party **CCM** = Concerned Citizens' Movement **NRP** = Nevis Reformation Party **App** = Appointed

Nevis has its own executive and legislature, the Nevis Island Assembly, which exercise local power

Fifteen years of rule by the People's Action Movement ended in 1995 amid concerns over narcotics trafficking. The center-left SKLP has held power since, and in the 2000 election won all the seats contested on St. Kitts itself. The secessionist movement on Nevis remains an issue.

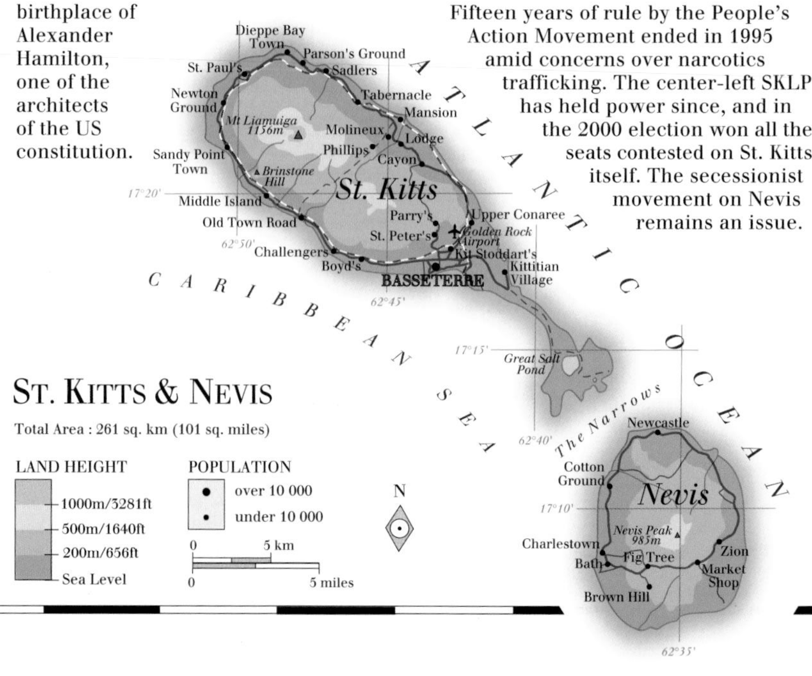
Dieppe Bay Town
Parson's Ground
Sadlers
St. Paul's
Newton Ground
Tabernacle
Mansion
Mt Liamuiga 1156m
Molineux
Lodge
Phillips
Cayon
Sandy Point Town
Brimstone Hill
St. Kitts
Middle Island
Parry's
Upper Conaree
Old Town Road
St. Peter's
Golden Rock Airport
Kit Stoddart's
Challengers
Boyd's
BASSETERRE
Kittitian Village
ATLANTIC OCEAN
CARIBBEAN SEA
Great Salt Pond
The Narrows
Newcastle
Cotton Ground
Nevis
Nevis Peak 985m
Charlestown
Bath
Fig Tree
Zion
Market Shop
Brown Hill
ST. KITTS & NEVIS
Total Area : 261 sq. km (101 sq. miles)
LAND HEIGHT
1000m/3281ft
500m/1640ft
200m/656ft
Sea Level
POPULATION
over 10 000
under 10 000
0 5 km
0 5 miles
N

WORLD AFFAIRS

Joined UN in 1983

ACS | Comm | Caricom | OAS | OECS

Suspected money laundering earned St. Kitts condemnation from G7 in 2000. St. Kitts is an active member of the OECS, and Basseterre is the headquarters for the Eastern Caribbean Central Bank.

AID

Recipient

US$11m (receipts) | Up 175% in 2001

International aid in 1999 supported an economic recovery and relief program, following hurricanes Georges and Lenny, which significantly damaged buildings and infrastructure. About 50% of aid is through the CDB.

DEFENSE

No compulsory military service

Not available | Little change from year to year

An army existed for six years before it was disbanded to cut government spending in 1981. In 1997 the National Assembly approved the reestablishment of a full-time defense force; it has around 200 personnel, plus reserves.

ECONOMICS

Inflation 3% p.a. (1990–2001)

US$299m | 2.67 Eastern Caribbean dollars (2.7)

SCORE CARD

- ❑ World GNP Ranking........................177th
- ❑ GNP per Capita.........................US$6630
- ❑ Balance of Payments..................–US$62m
- ❑ Inflation..1.7%
- ❑ Unemployment...................................5%

Strengths

Tourism industry. Growth in light manufacturing and financial services.

Weaknesses

Tourism sector vulnerable to downturns in key US market. Islands prone to hurricane damage. Declining sugar production may soon be stopped altogether.

EXPORTS

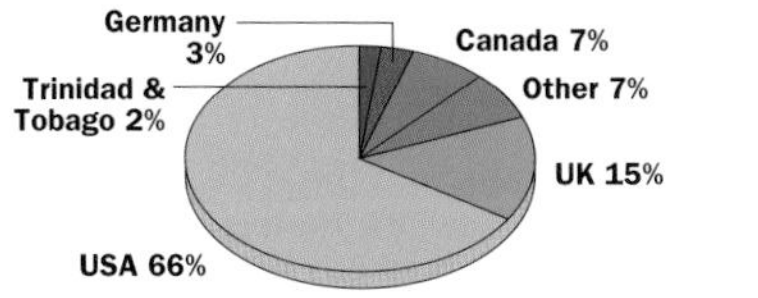
Germany 3%
Canada 7%
Trinidad & Tobago 2%
Other 7%
UK 15%
USA 66%

IMPORTS

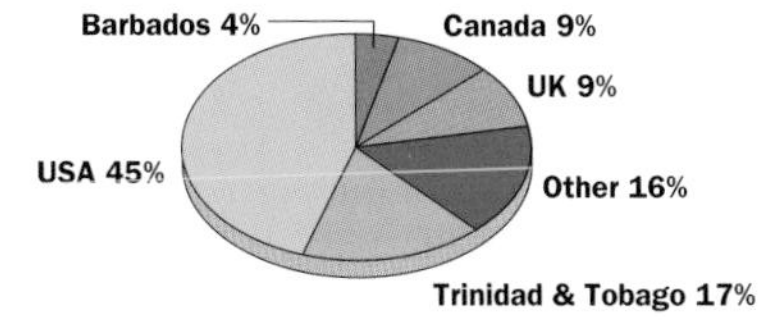
Barbados 4%
Canada 9%
UK 9%
USA 45%
Other 16%
Trinidad & Tobago 17%

RESOURCES

Electric power 20,000 kW

262 tonnes | Not an oil producer

14,400 goats, 14,000 sheep, 60,000 chickens | None

St. Kitts has no strategic resources. Almost all energy has to be imported (mainly oil from Venezuela and Mexico). The government is attempting to close down the loss-making sugar industry, retrain the workforce, and diversify, including growing Sea Island cotton.

ENVIRONMENT

Not available

10% | 2.4 tonnes per capita

Hurricanes are the greatest environmental threat. Hurricane Georges alone caused damage in 1998 estimated at US$400 million. It was followed in 1999 by Hurricane Lenny. As in the rest of the Caribbean, benefits from encouraging tourism must be set against potential ecological damage. The government has shown sensitivity, with strict preservation orders on the remaining rainforest and on indigenous monkeys.

MEDIA

TV ownership high

There are no daily newspapers

PUBLISHING AND BROADCAST MEDIA

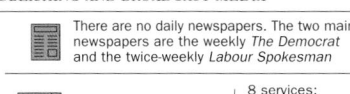

There are no daily newspapers. The two main newspapers are the weekly *The Democrat* and the twice-weekly *Labour Spokesman*

1 state-owned service | 8 services: 1 state-owned, 7 independent

Opposition parties have difficulty broadcasting their views on state-owned TV and radio. However, dissent is expressed in the printed press. The two main papers are run by political parties.

CRIME

Death penalty in use

135 prisoners | Down 31% in 1999

The judicial system is based on British common law. Hanging was resumed in 1998, and plans agreed in 2001 to replace the role of the UK Privy Council with a Caribbean Court of Justice raised fears of more executions. Money laundering and narcotics-related crime are increasing.

EDUCATION

School leaving age: 17

98% | 997 students

Education is free, and the government is keen to promote information technology subjects. Students attend the regional University of the West Indies, or go on to colleges in the US and the UK.

CHRONOLOGY

A British colony since 1783, the islands were a part of the Leeward Islands Federation until 1956.

- ❑ **1932** Proindependence St. Kitts–Nevis–Anguilla Labour Party set up.
- ❑ **1967** Internal self-government.
- ❑ **1980** Anguilla formally separates from St. Kitts and Nevis.
- ❑ **1983** Independence.
- ❑ **1995** Opposition SKLP wins election.
- ❑ **1998** Nevis referendum narrowly rejects secession.
- ❑ **2000** Prime Minister Denzil Douglas and SKLP reelected. Blacklisted by G7 for financial dealings.

HEALTH

Welfare state health benefits

1 per 855 people | Heart and respiratory diseases, cancers

The government-run health service now provides rudimentary care on both St. Kitts and Nevis. The EU and France provided EC$8 million in 1998 for repairs to the main hospital at Basseterre, which was badly damaged by Hurricane Georges.

SPENDING

GDP/cap. increase

CONSUMPTION AND SPENDING

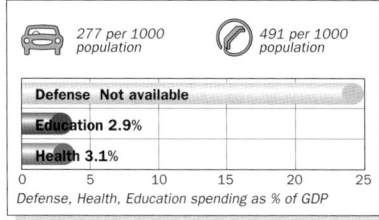

277 per 1000 population | *491 per 1000 population*

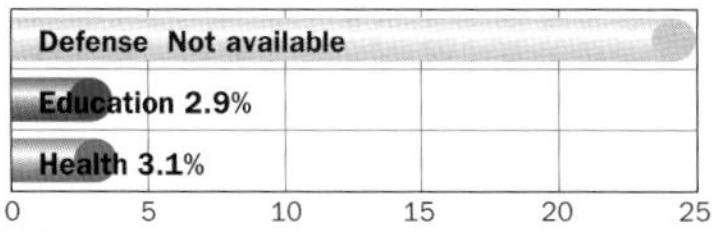
Defense Not available
Education 2.9%
Health 3.1%
0
5
10
15
20
25

Defense, Health, Education spending as % of GDP

Native professionals and civil servants have replaced expatriates over the years since independence. They are now the best-paid group, but there are no great extremes of income.

WORLD RANKING

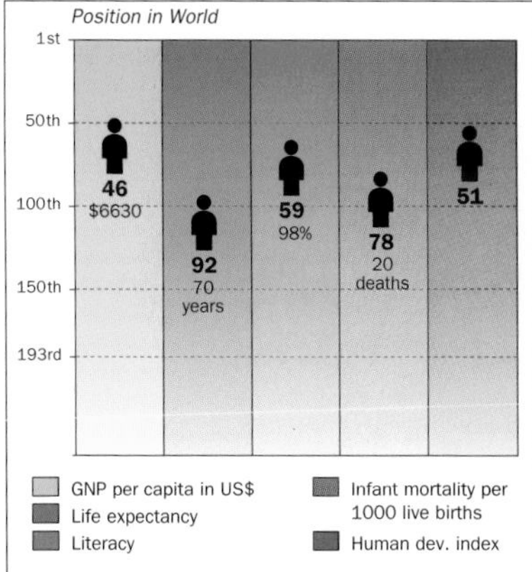
Position in World
1st
50th
100th
150th
193rd
46
$6630
92
70
years
59
98%
78
20
deaths
51
GNP per capita in US$
Life expectancy
Literacy
Infant mortality per 1000 live births
Human dev. index

S

St. Lucia

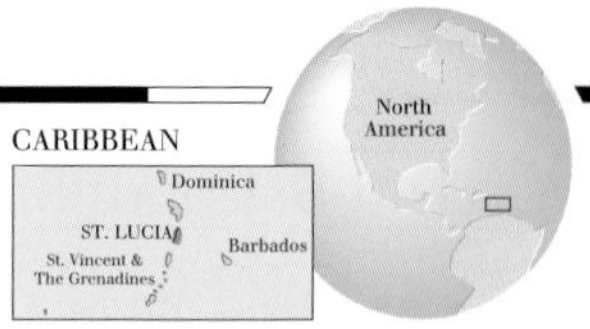
CARIBBEAN
North America
Dominica
ST. LUCIA
Barbados
St. Vincent & The Grenadines

Official Name: Saint Lucia **Capital:** Castries **Population:** 160,145
Currency: Eastern Caribbean dollar **Official Language:** English

1979 | 1979 | Feb 22 | WL | -4 | +1758 | .lc

St. Lucia is one of the most beautiful islands of the Windward group of the Antilles. The twin Pitons, south of Soufrière, are among the most striking natural features in the Caribbean. Ruled by the French and the British at different times in its past, St. Lucia retains the character of both. A multiparty democracy, its economy is based on bananas and tourism, with enticing beaches and a rich variety of wildlife in the rainforest.

CLIMATE

Tropical oceanic

WEATHER CHART FOR CASTRIES

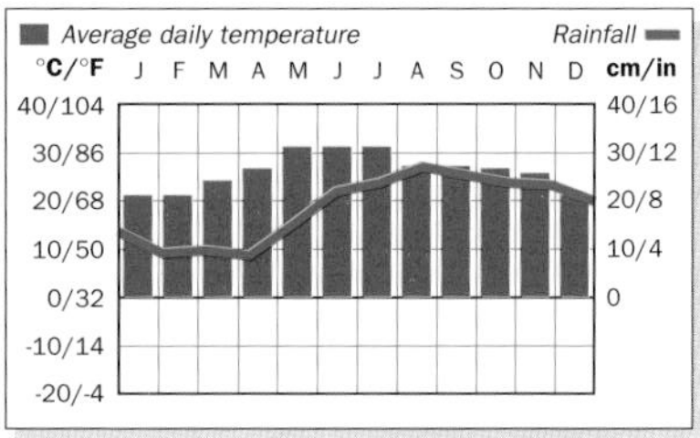
Average daily temperature
Rainfall
°C/°F J F M A M J J A S O N D cm/in
40/104
30/86
20/68
10/50
0/32
-10/14
-20/-4
40/16
30/12
20/8
10/4
0

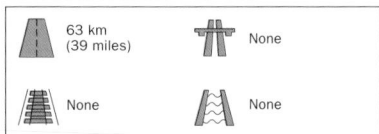

The dry season, from January to April, brings intense heat to sheltered parts of St. Lucia. During the rainy season, short warm showers can be expected daily. Rainfall is highest in the mountains.

TRANSPORTATION

Drive on left

Vigie Field, Castries 468,053 passengers

3 ships 911 grt

THE TRANSPORTATION NETWORK

63 km (39 miles)

None

None

None

Roads are confined to the west and southeast coasts; only half are paved. Flights arrive from major European and North American cities, and other Caribbean locations. Direct passage to South America is largely by sea.

One of the twin Pitons south of Soufrière, marking the entrance to the Jalousie Plantation harbor.

TOURISM

Visitors : Population 1.6:1

253,000 visitors

Up 1% in 2002

MAIN TOURIST ARRIVALS

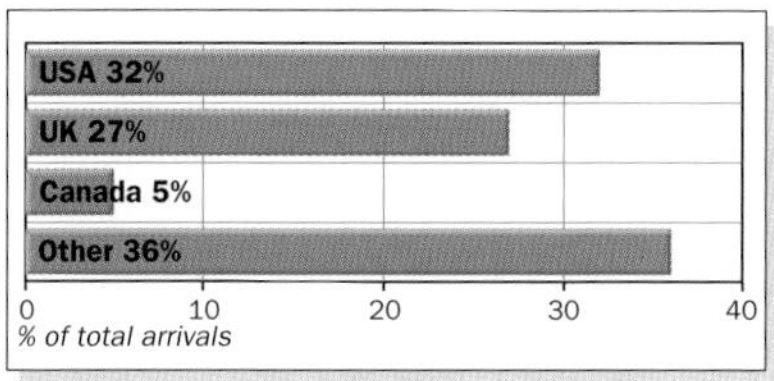
USA 32%
UK 27%
Canada 5%
Other 36%
0
10
20
30
40
% of total arrivals

Tropical beaches and typical Caribbean towns make St. Lucia a favorite destination for cruise ships and stay-over tourists. The number of hotel rooms continues to rise. The pristine rainforest has become the focus of nature tourism, with tours often organized by the National Trust.

PEOPLE

Pop. density high

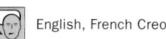

English, French Creole

263/km² (679/mi²)

THE URBAN/RURAL POPULATION SPLIT

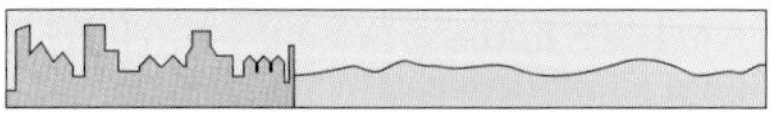

38% 62%

RELIGIOUS PERSUASION

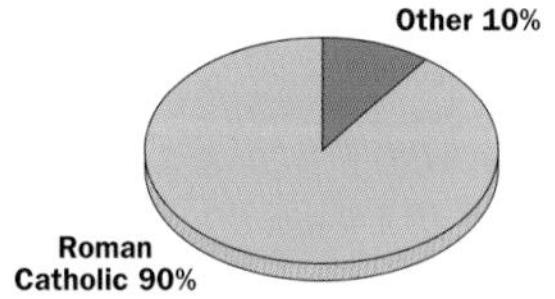
Other 10%
Roman Catholic 90%

St. Lucia has a rich, tension-free racial mix of descendants of Africans, Caribs, and European settlers. Despite relaxed attitudes, family life is central to most St. Lucians, many of whom are practicing Roman Catholics. Small families are the norm. In rural districts, where women run many of the farms, absentee fathers are fairly common. In recent years, women have had greater access to higher education and have moved into professions. A bill to permit the occasional use of Creole in parliament was passed in 1998.

POLITICS

Multiparty elections

L. House 2001/2006
U. House 2001/2006

H.M. Queen Elizabeth II

AT THE LAST ELECTION

House of Assembly 18 seats

78% SLP | 17% UWP | 5% App

SLP = St. Lucia Labour Party **UWP** = United Workers' Party
App = Appointed

Senate 11 seats

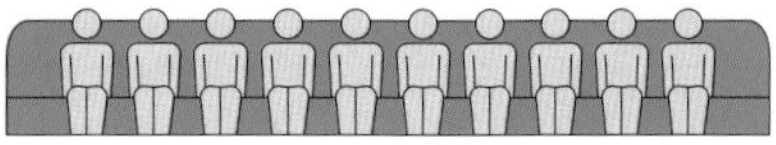

Six Senate members are nominated by the government, three by the opposition, and two by the governor-general on a nonparty basis

St. Lucian politics was long dominated by personalities, particularly John Compton of the conservative UWP. The election victory in 1997 of the SLP, led by Kenny Anthony, ending 15 years of UWP government, saw a shift in the political climate. Divided and factionalized, the UWP was unable to prevent the SLP's reelection in 2001.

WORLD AFFAIRS

Joined UN in 1979

ACS | Comm | Caricom | OECS | OAS

St. Lucia took a leading role in 1999 in the unsuccessful campaign to preserve preferential access to the EU market for bananas from the Windward Islands. Good relations with the UK and EU remain central, but it is feared that from 2006 the Caribbean will be unable to compete with cheaper fruit from US-owned growers in Latin America. St. Lucia is active in the OECS and hosts the regional secretariat. It also supports Japan, an aid donor, in its bid for a permanent seat on the UN Security Council.

AID

Recipient

US$16m (receipts)

Up 45% in 2001

The EU, Japan, and the CDB are the main donors. China has also given aid and grant loans in recent years.

DEFENSE

No compulsory military service

US$5m

Little change from year to year

The police force is supported by a small paramilitary unit. Training is provided by the US and the UK.

S

ST. LUCIA

Total Area : 620 sq. km (239 sq. miles)

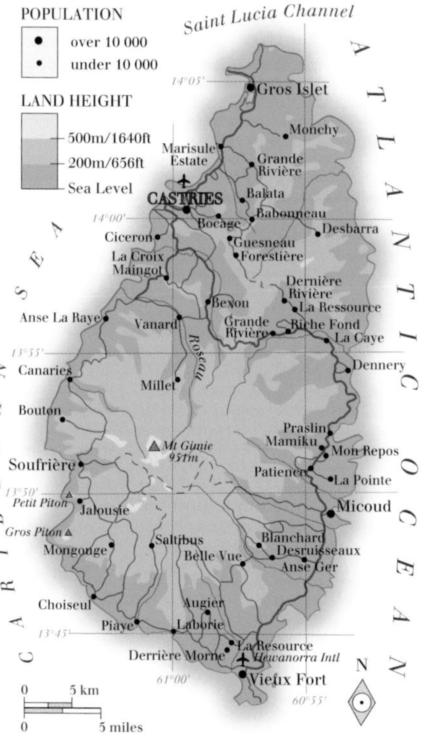
POPULATION
over 10 000
under 10 000
LAND HEIGHT
500m/1640ft
200m/656ft
Sea Level
Saint Lucia Channel
ATLANTIC OCEAN
CARIBBEAN SEA
Gros Islet
Monchy
Marisule Estate
Grande Rivière
Castries
Balata
Babonneau
Bocage
Desbarra
Ciceron
Guesneau
Forestière
La Croix Maingot
Dernière Rivière
La Ressource
Bexon
Anse La Raye
Vanard
Grande Rivière
Riche Fond
La Caye
Roseau
Dennery
Canaries
Millet
Bouton
Praslin
Mamiku
Mt Gimie 951m
Mon Repos
Soufrière
Patience
La Pointe
Petit Piton
Jalousie
Micoud
Gros Piton
Saltibus
Blanchard
Mongonge
Belle Vue
Desruisseaux
Anse Ger
Choiseul
Augier
Piaye
Laborie
La Resource
Derrière Morne
Hewanorra Intl
Vieux Fort
0 5 km
0 5 miles
N

ECONOMICS

Inflation 2.7% p.a. (1990–2001)

US$619m

2.67 Eastern Caribbean dollars (2.7)

SCORE CARD

- ❑ WORLD GNP RANKING........165th
- ❑ GNP PER CAPITA........US$3950
- ❑ BALANCE OF PAYMENTS........–US$82m
- ❑ INFLATION........3%
- ❑ UNEMPLOYMENT........16%

STRENGTHS

Banana industry (privatized in 1998). Tourism and services.

WEAKNESSES

Preferential banana trade with EU to be phased out. Global slumps affect tourism.

EXPORTS

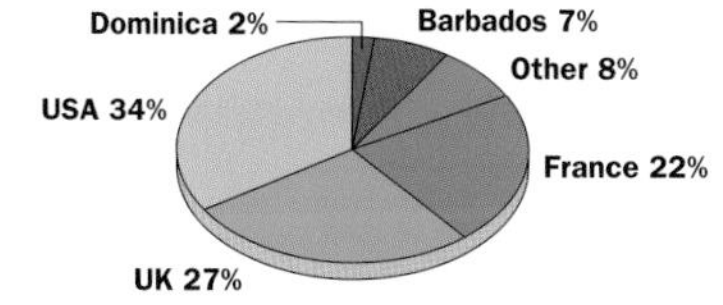
Dominica 2%
Barbados 7%
Other 8%
USA 34%
France 22%
UK 27%

IMPORTS

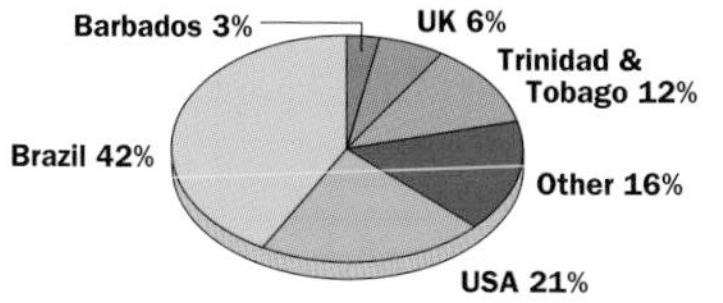
Barbados 3%
UK 6%
Trinidad & Tobago 12%
Brazil 42%
Other 16%
USA 21%

RESOURCES

Electric power 60,000 kW

1760 tonnes

Not an oil producer

14,950 pigs, 12,500 sheep, 240,000 chickens

None

St. Lucia has no mineral resources and imports most of its energy. Plans exist to develop geothermal energy from the hot springs in the volcanic interior.

ENVIRONMENT

Not available

16% partially protected

2.2 tonnes per capita

St. Lucians are proud of their island, and environmental questions arouse fierce debate. In recent years the greatest controversy surrounded the decision to allow a luxury hotel development on the ecologically important Jalousie Plantation, which encompasses the extraordinary twin Pitons and includes an important Amerindian archaeological site. The issue illustrates a key problem in St. Lucia, where business pressures to develop tourism can outweigh vital environmental concerns. One notable conservation success has been the St. Lucia parrot. In 1978, there were 150 birds; strict laws against the trade in parrots ensured that by 2000 numbers had risen to over 800.

MEDIA

TV ownership medium

There are no daily newspapers

PUBLISHING AND BROADCAST MEDIA

There are no daily newspapers. *The Star* and *The Mirror* are published weekly

5 independent services

5 services: 1 state-owned, 4 independent

The privately owned press is free from government intervention. It is possible to receive TV programs from US, Mexican, and some Caribbean stations.

CRIME

Death penalty in use

365 prisoners

Crime is rising

Murder is rare, but narcotics-related deaths are increasing, as is violence in schools. The government has strengthened the police force to combat rising urban crime.

EDUCATION

School leaving age: 16

90%

3881 students

Education is based on the British system. Nobel prizewinners Sir Arthur Lewis (economics) and Derek Walcott (literature) give St. Lucia the world's highest per capita ratio of laureates.

CHRONOLOGY

An excellent naval raiding base in the Caribbean in the 17th and 18th centuries, St. Lucia was fought over by France and Britain. Ownership alternated before it was finally ceded to Britain in 1814. French influence survives in St. Lucian patois and the local cuisine.

- ❑ **1958** Joins West Indies Federation.
- ❑ **1964** Sugar growing ceases.
- ❑ **1979** Gains independence and joins Commonwealth.
- ❑ **1990** Establishes body with Dominica, Grenada, and St. Vincent to discuss forming a Windward Islands Federation.
- ❑ **1997** Hitherto ruling UWP reduced to one seat in general election.
- ❑ **2000** Blacklisted by OECD as international tax haven.

HEALTH

Welfare state health benefits

1 per 193 people

Heart and respiratory diseases, cancers

The National Insurance Scheme provides free medical cover for all. Work on a new general hospital began in 2001.

SPENDING

GDP/cap. increase

CONSUMPTION AND SPENDING

115 per 1000 population

317 per 1000 population

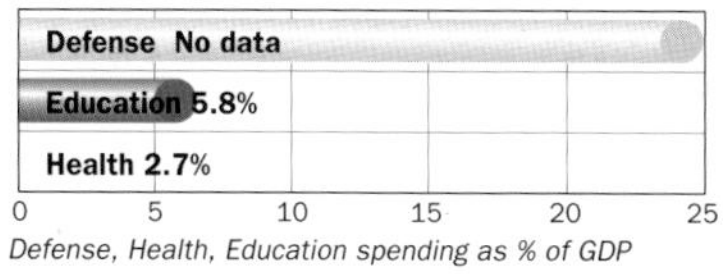
Defense No data
Education 5.8%
Health 2.7%
0
5
10
15
20
25
Defense, Health, Education spending as % of GDP

The island's large-scale banana growers and hotel owners form the richest section of society. Nearly one-fifth of households are considered to be poor.

WORLD RANKING

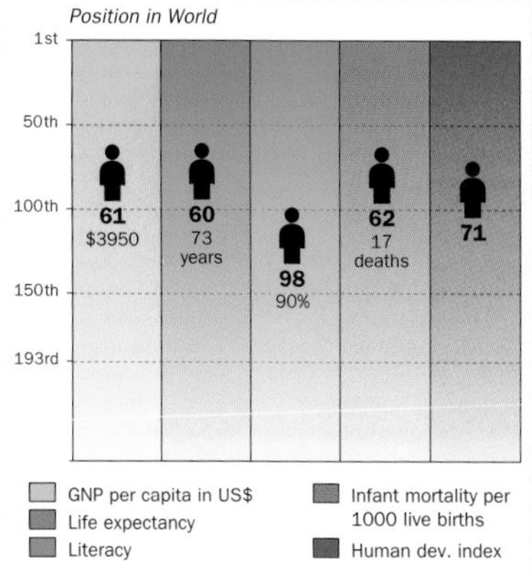
Position in World
1st
50th
100th
150th
193rd
61 $3950
60 73 years
98 90%
62 17 deaths
71
GNP per capita in US$
Life expectancy
Literacy
Infant mortality per 1000 live births
Human dev. index

S

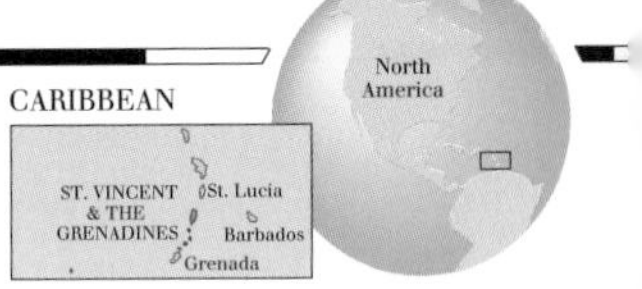
North America
CARIBBEAN
ST. VINCENT & THE GRENADINES
St. Lucia
Barbados
Grenada

St. Vincent & the Grenadines

Official Name: Saint Vincent and the Grenadines **Capital:** Kingstown
Population: 116,394 **Currency:** Eastern Caribbean dollar **Official Language:** English

1979 | 1979 | Oct 27 | WV | -4 | +1784 | .vc

PART OF THE WINDWARD ISLANDS group, and bounded by submerged coral reefs, St. Vincent and the Grenadines is the Caribbean playground of the international celebrity circuit. Tourism and bananas are the economic mainstays; St. Vincent is also the world's largest arrowroot producer. It is mostly volcanic; the one remaining active volcano, La Soufrière, last erupted in 1979. The Grenadines are flat, mainly bare, coral islands.

CLIMATE

Tropical oceanic

WEATHER CHART FOR KINGSTOWN

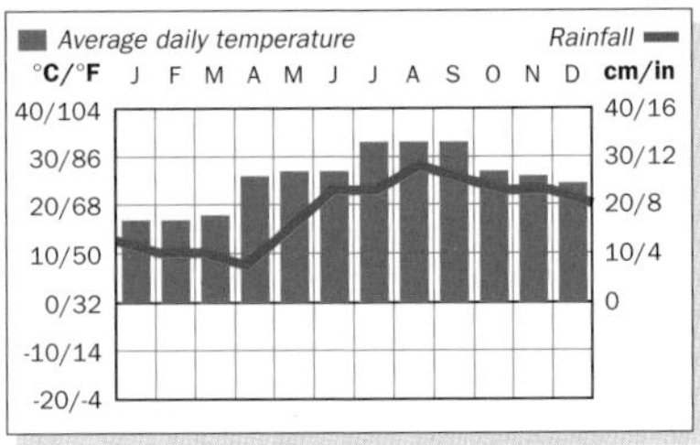
Average daily temperature
Rainfall
°C/°F J F M A M J J A S O N D cm/in
40/104
30/86
20/68
10/50
0/32
-10/14
-20/-4
40/16
30/12
20/8
10/4
0

Constant trade winds moderate St. Vincent's tropical climate. Rainfall is heaviest during the summer months. Deep depressions and hurricanes are likely between June and November.

TRANSPORTATION

Drive on left

Arnos Vale, Kingstown

1318 ships 7.07m grt

THE TRANSPORTATION NETWORK

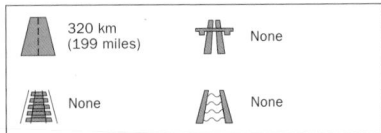

320 km (199 miles)

None

None

None

Access by air is via neighboring islands. Only one-third of roads are paved; there are few roads in the interior. Port improvements have been completed in recent years. In 1992, an airport capable of taking executive jets was completed on the island of Bequia.

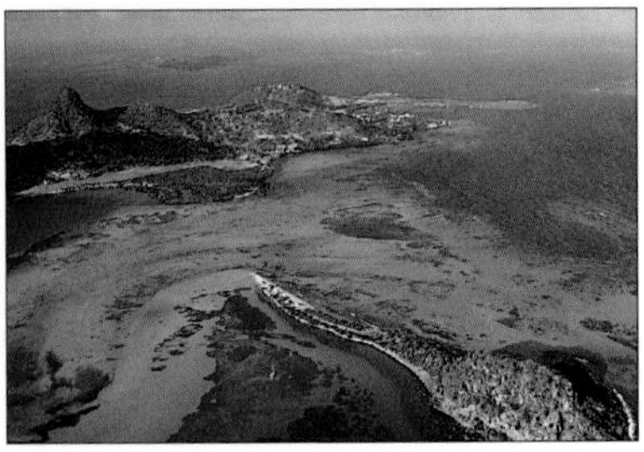

Aerial view of Union Island in the Grenadines chain. The government is developing the island as a major yachting center.

TOURISM

Visitors : Population 1:1.6

73,000 visitors

Up 7% in 2000

MAIN TOURIST ARRIVALS

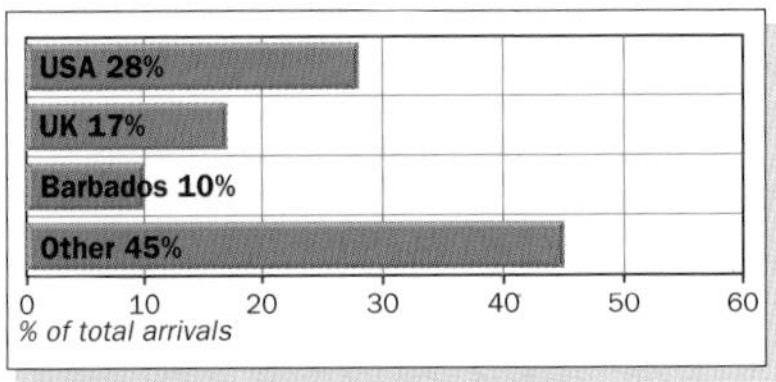
USA 28%
UK 17%
Barbados 10%
Other 45%
0 10 20 30 40 50 60
% of total arrivals

Tourism is targeted at celebrities and cruise ships rather than the mass market, and is concentrated on the Grenadines. Mustique, long associated with the UK's Princess Margaret, has a rock music clientele. Union Island draws the yachting rich, and luxury villas, apartments, a golf course, and a casino have been built on Canouan. Layou, on St. Vincent, is the site of pre-Columbian Amerindian petroglyphs.

PEOPLE

Pop. density high

English, English Creole

342/km² (889/mi²)

THE URBAN/RURAL POPULATION SPLIT

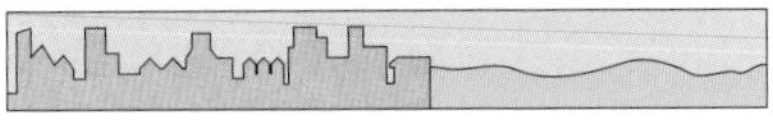
56%
44%

RELIGIOUS PERSUASION

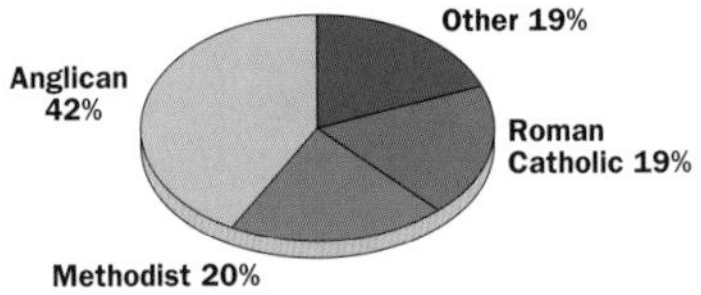
Anglican 42%
Other 19%
Roman Catholic 19%
Methodist 20%

The majority of people are descendants of Africans brought over in the 18th century. Racial tensions are few, and intermarriage has meant that the original communities of descendants of African slaves, Europeans, and the few indigenous Caribs can no longer be distinguished. Many locals fear that traditional island life is being threatened by the expanding tourist industry.

POLITICS

Multiparty elections

2001/2006

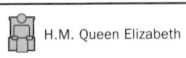

H.M. Queen Elizabeth II

AT THE LAST ELECTION

House of Assembly 21 seats

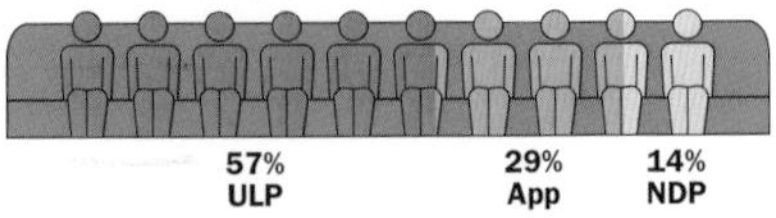
57% ULP
29% App
14% NDP

ULP = Unity Labour Party **App** = Appointed
NDP = New Democratic Party
Six senators are appointed to the House of Assembly by the governor-general

In 2001, 17 years of NDP rule ended with a crushing electoral defeat. The leader of the long-term opposition ULP, Ralph Gonsalves, became prime minister. He has launched a number of initiatives aimed at modernizing the economy and government, and restructuring the banana industry. Ties to the UK remain, though republicanism is strong.

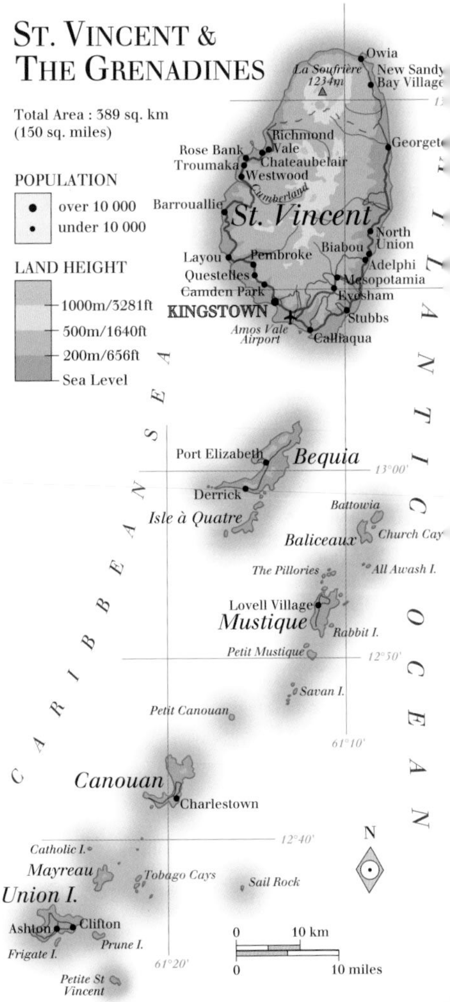
ST. VINCENT & THE GRENADINES
Total Area : 389 sq. km (150 sq. miles)
POPULATION
over 10 000
under 10 000
LAND HEIGHT
1000m/3281ft
500m/1640ft
200m/656ft
Sea Level
La Soufrière 1234m
Owia
New Sandy Bay Village
Richmond
Vale
Rose Bank
Troumaka
Chateaubelair
Westwood
Georgetown
Barrouallie
St. Vincent
North Union
Biabou
Layou
Pembroke
Questelles
Adelphi
Mesopotamia
Camden Park
Evesham
KINGSTOWN
Stubbs
Arnos Vale Airport
Calliaqua
CARIBBEAN SEA
ATLANTIC OCEAN
Port Elizabeth
Bequia
13°00'
Derrick
Isle à Quatre
Battowia
Baliceaux
Church Cay
The Pillories
All Awash I.
Lovell Village
Mustique
Rabbit I.
Petit Mustique
12°50'
Savan I.
Petit Canouan
61°10'
Canouan
Charlestown
12°40'
Catholic I.
Mayreau
Tobago Cays
Sail Rock
Union I.
Ashton
Clifton
Prune I.
Frigate I.
61°20'
Petite St Vincent
N
0 10 km
0 10 miles

WORLD AFFAIRS

Joined UN in 1980

ACS | Comm | Caricom | OAS | OECS

The most important external links are the EU and the UK. The government promotes regional integration and has played a leading role in Caribbean affairs. The successful US bid to end EU preferential treatment of Caribbean banana imports has strained relations.

AID

Recipient

US$9m (receipts) | Up 50% in 2001

The Caribbean Development Bank and the EU are the major sources of development aid. Significant funds also come from Japan and France.

DEFENSE

No compulsory military service

US$3m (estimate) | No significant change from year to year

St. Vincent has no army. Its small police force, trained by the US and the UK, is part of the Windward and Leeward Islands' Regional Security System.

ECONOMICS

Inflation 2.1% p.a. (1990–2001)

US$317m | 2.67 Eastern Caribbean dollars (2.7)

SCORE CARD

❑ World GNP Ranking	176th
❑ GNP per Capita	US$2740
❑ Balance of Payments	–US$26m
❑ Inflation	0.8%
❑ Unemployment	22%

Strengths
Bananas, but preferential access to EU markets will end in 2006. Top producer of arrowroot starch. Tourist potential. Improving infrastructure.

Weaknesses
Little diversification. Development of financial services hit by OECD blacklisting for money laundering. Vulnerable to hurricane damage.

EXPORTS

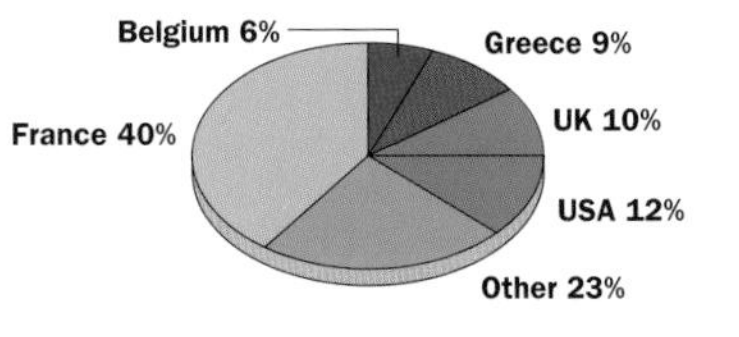
Belgium 6%
Greece 9%
France 40%
UK 10%
USA 12%
Other 23%

IMPORTS

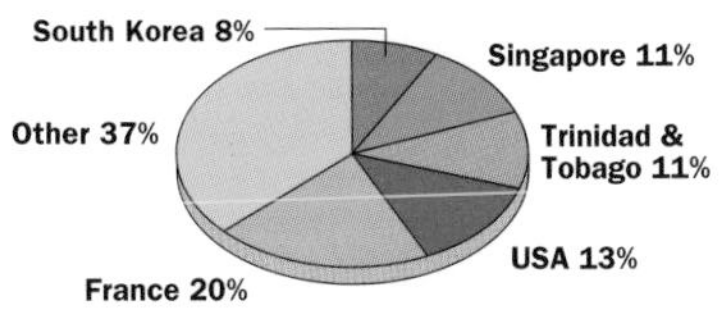
South Korea 8%
Singapore 11%
Other 37%
Trinidad & Tobago 11%
USA 13%
France 20%

RESOURCES

Electric power 16,000 kW

7294 tonnes | Not an oil producer

13,000 sheep, 9500 pigs, 200,000 chickens | None

There is a hydroelectric plant on the Cumberland River. Virtually all other energy requirements have to be imported. Some of the Grenadines have no fresh water sources.

ENVIRONMENT

Not available

21% partially protected | 1.4 tonnes per capita

Hurricanes are the main environmental threat, sometimes destroying as much as 70% of the banana crop. The former inaccessibility of St. Vincent and the Grenadines meant that tourism was a minor environmental threat, and the untouched, idyllic landscape of islands such as Mustique was their attraction. Mustique is reasonably well protected – building has been restricted and further development is limited since fresh water has to be shipped in. On Bequia, the new airport and consequent increase in visitors are seen as a mixed blessing. Some development schemes on Canouan have been opposed by locals.

MEDIA

TV ownership medium

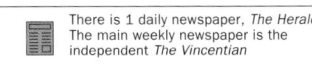

Daily newspaper circulation 9 per 1000 people

PUBLISHING AND BROADCAST MEDIA

There is 1 daily newspaper, *The Herald*. The main weekly newspaper is the independent *The Vincentian*

1 state-owned service | 1 state-owned service

Of the many periodicals, three are published by the political parties; the rest are independent. Freedom of the press is written into the constitution.

CRIME

Death penalty in use

302 prisoners | Little change from year to year

The incidence of rape and robbery causes most concern, though on the outlying islands both crimes are very rare. St. Vincent is used for narcotics transshipment to the US.

EDUCATION

School leaving age: 15

89% | 677 students

State schools follow the former British 11-plus selective system. There are a few private schools. University students go on to the regional University of the West Indies in Jamaica, though increasing numbers are also studying in the US and the UK.

CHRONOLOGY

In 1795, the local Carib population staged a revolt against the British, who deported them, leaving a largely black African population.

- ❑ **1951** Universal suffrage.
- ❑ **1969** Internal self-government.
- ❑ **1972** James Mitchell premier; holds balance of power between People's Political Party (PPP) and St. Vincent Labour Party (SVLP).
- ❑ **1974** PPP–SVLP coalition.
- ❑ **1979** Full independence under Milton Cato of SVLP. La Soufrière volcano erupts.
- ❑ **1984** NDP, founded by Mitchell in 1975, wins first of four terms.
- ❑ **2000** Mitchell resigns premiership.
- ❑ **2001** ULP wins landslide victory. Ralph Gonsalves prime minister.

HEALTH

Welfare state health benefits

1 per 1136 people | Heart and respiratory diseases, cancers

Doctors train at the University of the West Indies. The system is a mixture of state and private hospitals and clinics; facilities are scarcer on the Grenadines.

SPENDING

GDP/cap. increase

CONSUMPTION AND SPENDING

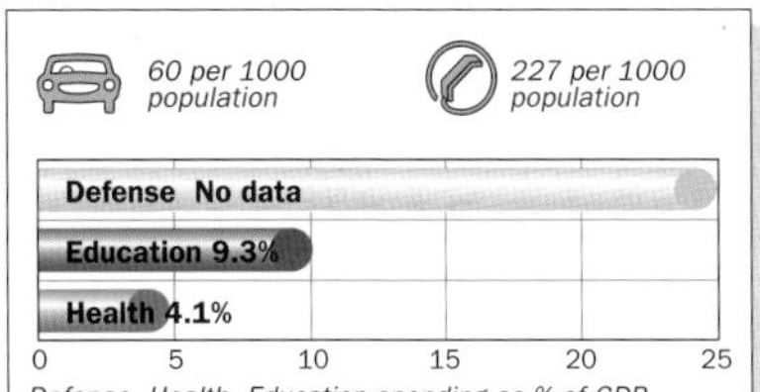
60 per 1000 population
227 per 1000 population
Defense No data
Education 9.3%
Health 4.1%
0
5
10
15
20
25

Defense, Health, Education spending as % of GDP

Jet-set wealth in the islands coexists with the low wages paid to most local workers. Union Island and Mustique in particular attract the wealthy, with their motor yachts and jeeps.

WORLD RANKING

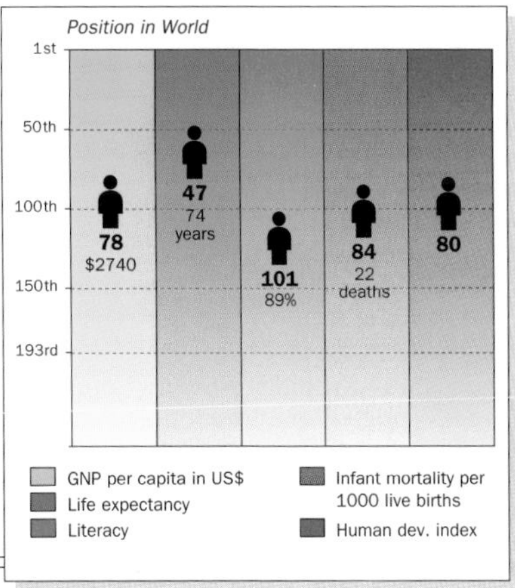
Position in World
1st
50th
100th
150th
193rd
78
$2740
47
74 years
101
89%
84
22 deaths
80
GNP per capita in US$
Life expectancy
Literacy
Infant mortality per 1000 live births
Human dev. index

S

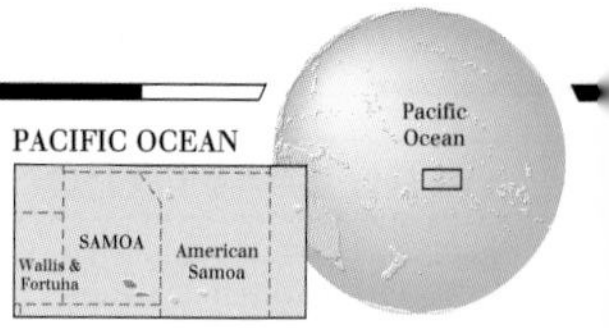
PACIFIC OCEAN
SAMOA
Wallis & Futuna
American Samoa
Pacific Ocean

SAMOA

OFFICIAL NAME: Independent State of Samoa **CAPITAL:** Apia
POPULATION: 176,848 **CURRENCY:** Tala **OFFICIAL LANGUAGES:** Samoan and English

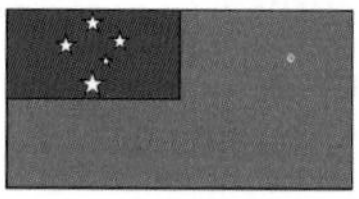

1962 | 1962 | June 1 | WS | -11 | +685 | .ws

SAMOA, LYING IN THE HEART of the South Pacific, 2400 km (1500 miles) north of New Zealand, comprises nine volcanic islands. Four are inhabited – Apolima, Manono, Savai'i, and Upolu (where 72% of the population live). Rainforests cloak the mountains; vegetable gardens and coconut plantations thrive around the coasts. A relative boom in the economy in recent years has not lifted Samoa from the ranks of the UN's Least Developed Countries.

CLIMATE

Tropical oceanic

WEATHER CHART FOR APIA

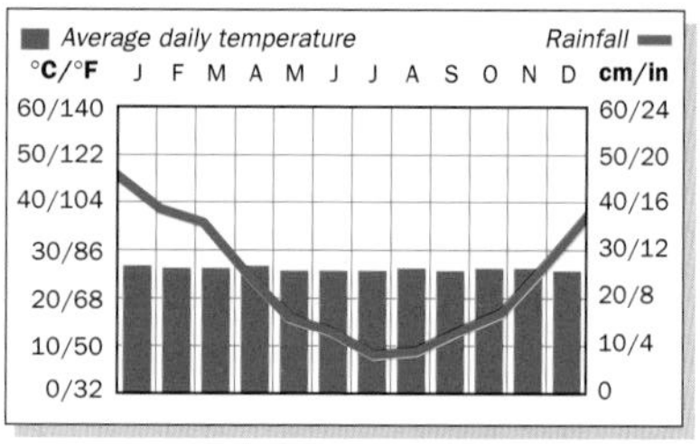
Average daily temperature
Rainfall
°C/°F J F M A M J J A S O N D cm/in
60/140
50/122
40/104
30/86
20/68
10/50
0/32
60/24
50/20
40/16
30/12
20/8
10/4
0

The climate is humid and temperatures rarely drop below 25°C (77°F). December to March is the hurricane season.

TRANSPORTATION

Drive on right

Faleolo Apia 162,807 passengers

7 ships 9700 grt

THE TRANSPORTATION NETWORK

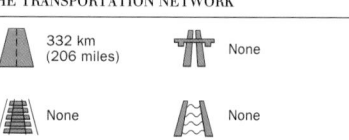

332 km (206 miles)	None
None	None

Apia port has been improved with Japanese aid. International links are mainly by air. Ferries provide interisland connections.

TOURISM

Visitors : Population 1:2

88,000 visitors

Up 4% in 2000

MAIN TOURIST ARRIVALS

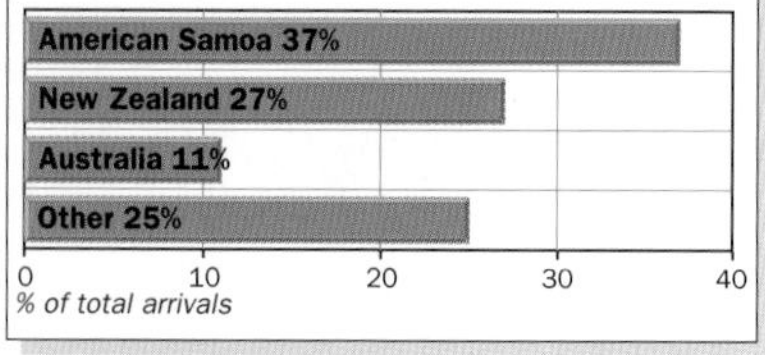
American Samoa 37%
New Zealand 27%
Australia 11%
Other 25%
0
10
20
30
40
% of total arrivals

Tourism is a rapidly growing industry. Small-scale village-based tourism is encouraged. Tourists are attracted by the climate and the easygoing *fa'a Samoa* (Samoan way of life).

PEOPLE

Pop. density medium

Samoan, English

62/km² (162/mi²)

THE URBAN/RURAL POPULATION SPLIT

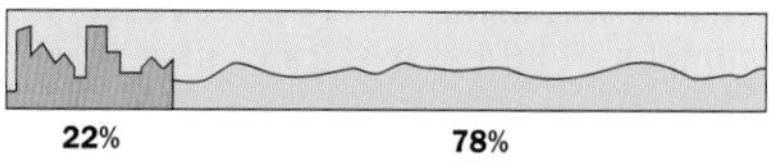
22%
78%

ETHNIC MAKEUP

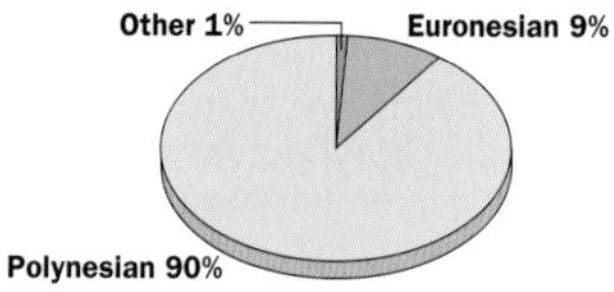
Other 1%
Euronesian 9%
Polynesian 90%

Ethnic Samoans form the world's second-largest Polynesian group. Euronesians, making up 9% of the population, are those of mixed European/Polynesian descent. The *fa'a Samoa* – Samoan way of life – is communal and conservative. Extended family groups, in which most people live, own 80% of the land and cannot sell it. Each is headed by a *matai*, or elected chief, who looks after its social and political interests. Conflict between the *fa'a Samoa* and modern life is strongest among the young, who have a high suicide rate.

Almost 100% of Samoans are nominally Christian.

POLITICS

Multiparty elections

2001/2006

H.H. Susuga Malietoa Tanumafili II

AT THE LAST ELECTION

Legislative Assembly 49 seats

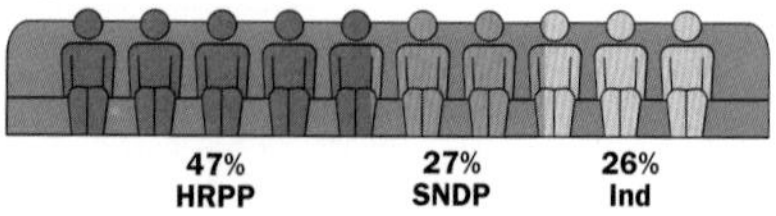
47% HRPP
27% SNDP
26% Ind

HRPP = Human Rights Protection Party **SNDP** = Samoan National Development Party **Ind** = Independents

The conservatism of the *fa'a Samoa* and the Church underpins Samoa's political stability. Allegiance to the two main parties is quite fluid. Until 1990, only the 1800 elected chiefs, or *matai*, could vote for the 47 ethnic Samoan seats in the Assembly; the other two seats are elected by non-Samoans. Universal suffrage was introduced at the 1991 elections. Tofilau Eti Alesana of the HRPP, prime minister twice since 1988, resigned in 1998 amid widespread protest against the government's autocratic style. His successor, Tuilaepa Sailele Malielegaoi, also of the HRPP, was reappointed in 2001.

WORLD AFFAIRS

Joined UN in 1976

ACP | Comm | IBRD | PC | PIF

Australia is Samoa's main trading partner. The US, New Zealand, Indonesia, Japan, and American Samoa are also important. Relations with China are well established. Samoa has trade links with the Cook Islands, and supports a Polynesian free trade agreement.

AID

Recipient

$43m (receipts)

Up 59% in 2001

Japan, Australia, and the EU are Samoa's main donors. Import costs are many times higher than export earnings and there is a heavy debt burden, so that aid is vital to the survival of the economy.

S

SAMOA

Total Area : 2944 sq. km (1137 sq. miles)

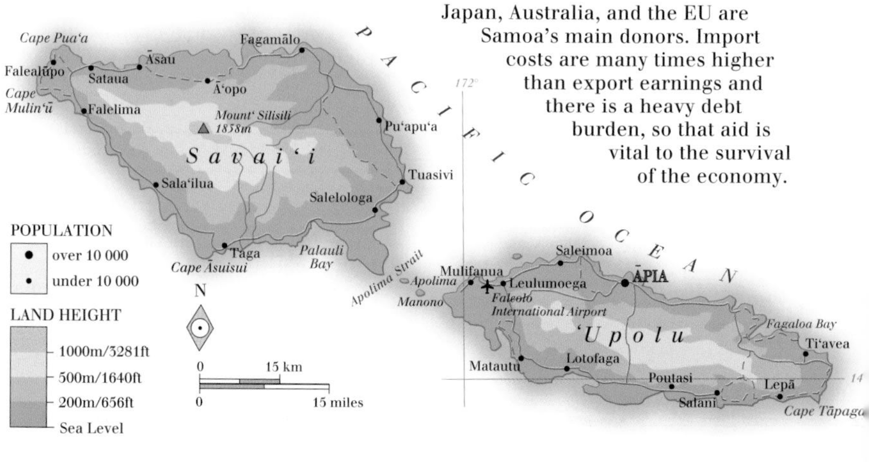
Cape Pua'a
Fagamālo
Falealupo
Āsau
Sataua
A'opo
Cape Mulin'ū
Falelima
Mount Silisili 1858m
Pu'apu'a
Savai'i
Tuasivi
Sala'ilua
Salelologa
Tāga
Cape Asuisui
Palauli Bay
Apolima Strait
Apolima
Manono
Mulifanua
Leulumoega
Faleolo International Airport
Saleimoa
ĀPIA
Upolu
Fagaloa Bay
Ti'avea
Matautu
Lotofaga
Poutasi
Salani
Lepā
Cape Tāpaga
PACIFIC OCEAN
POPULATION
over 10 000
under 10 000
LAND HEIGHT
1000m/3281ft
500m/1640ft
200m/656ft
Sea Level
N
0 15 km
0 15 miles

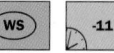

DEFENSE

No compulsory military service

Samoa has no army and few police

Not applicable

New Zealand looks after defense under a 1962 treaty. Internal order is mostly maintained by the *matai* (chiefs).

ECONOMICS

Inflation 3.8% p.a. (1990–2001)

$260m

2.892 tala (3.242)

SCORE CARD

- ❑ WORLD GNP RANKING........................178th
- ❑ GNP PER CAPITA.............................$1490
- ❑ BALANCE OF PAYMENTS......................–$19m
- ❑ INFLATION..4%
- ❑ UNEMPLOYMENT.......Widespread underemployment

STRENGTHS

Light manufacturing expanding, attracting foreign, especially Japanese, firms. Tourism growing rapidly with improved infrastructure. Services expanding rapidly since 1989 launch of offshore banking. Tropical agriculture: taro, coconut products (cream, oil, copra) main exports. Large fishing potential.

WEAKNESSES

Development adversely affected by cyclones. Fluctuating international markets for coconut products. Dependence on aid and expatriate remittances.

EXPORTS

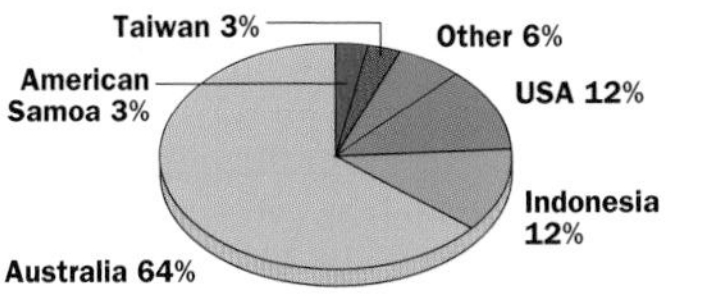
Taiwan 3%
Other 6%
American Samoa 3%
USA 12%
Indonesia 12%
Australia 64%

IMPORTS

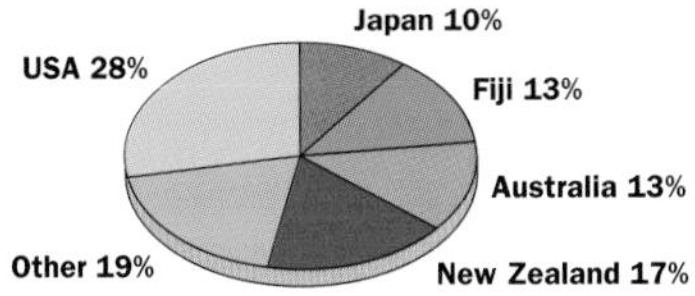
Japan 10%
USA 28%
Fiji 13%
Australia 13%
Other 19%
New Zealand 17%

RESOURCES

Electric power 20,000 kW

13,004 tonnes

Not an oil producer

201,000 pigs, 28,000 cattle, 450,000 chickens

None

With no minerals, Samoa's main resources are its forests and tropical agriculture. The rainforests in lower-lying areas are increasingly exploited for timber. Mahogany and teak plantations are being developed. The volcanic soils, particularly on Upolu, support a wide range of staple and export crops. Two-thirds of the population work in agriculture.

***Apia, the capital**, on Upolu, Samoa's second-largest island. It has a central volcanic range of mountains and many rivers.*

ENVIRONMENT

Not available

4% (3% partially protected)

0.8 tonnes per capita

Strict logging regulations have been introduced to halt irreparable damage to the environment; over 80% of forests have been replaced by plantations. Overhunting and loss of habitat have endangered rare species of fruit bat and pigeon. Samoa is concerned about its marine resources and has taken a firm stance against driftnet fishing.

MEDIA

TV ownership medium

Daily newspaper circulation figures are not available

PUBLISHING AND BROADCAST MEDIA

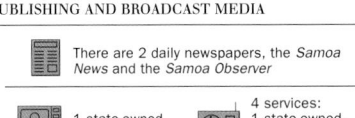

There are 2 daily newspapers, the *Samoa News* and the *Samoa Observer*

1 state-owned service

4 services: 1 state-owned, 3 independent

The independent media, notably the *Samoa Observer*, can face strong governmental opposition.

CRIME

Death penalty not used in practice

176 prisoners

Crime is rising slowly

Alcohol-related violence is a problem at weekends; otherwise, violent crime is almost unknown. Theft is increasing in urban areas.

EDUCATION

School leaving age: 14

99%

1874 students

Education is based on the New Zealand system. School attendance is universal. A university was established in Samoa in 1988. There is widespread use of corporal punishment.

HEALTH

No welfare state health benefits

1 per 1429 people

Cerebrovascular and heart diseases, pneumonia, suicide

The Samoan preference for being big went well with traditional diets. Diabetes and heart disease are rising as people change to Western-style foods.

CHRONOLOGY

Polynesians settled Samoa in about 1000 BCE. Western rivalry after 1830 led to the 1899 division of the islands into German Western and American Eastern Samoa.

- ❑ **1914** New Zealand occupies Western Samoa.
- ❑ **1962** Becomes first independent Polynesian nation.
- ❑ **1990** Cyclone Ofa leaves 10,000 people homeless.
- ❑ **1991** HRPP retains power in first election under universal adult suffrage.
- ❑ **1996, 2001** HRPP returned to power in elections.
- ❑ **1997** Country's name changed from Western Samoa to Samoa.

SPENDING

GDP/cap. increase

CONSUMPTION AND SPENDING

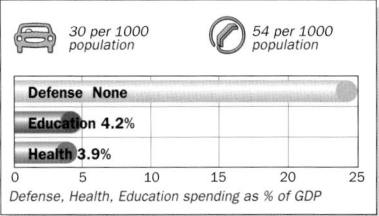

30 per 1000 population

54 per 1000 population

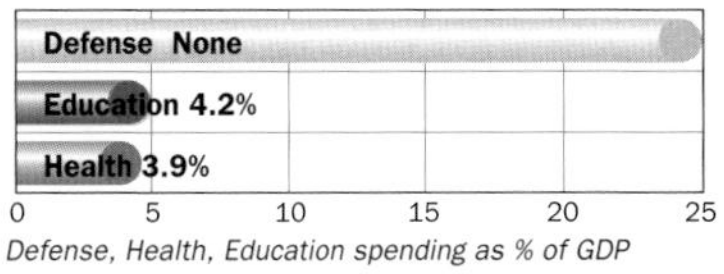
Defense None
Education 4.2%
Health 3.9%
0
5
10
15
20
25
Defense, Health, Education spending as % of GDP

Most of the population depend on subsistence farming and the remittances of relatives for their livelihood. Samoa is classified by the UN as a Least Developed Country. Two-thirds of those with a permanent job work for the government. The prospect of earning higher wages by working in other, wealthier countries in the Pacific region, notably in the tuna canneries of American Samoa, the neighboring US dependency, leads thousands of young Samoans to emigrate every year.

WORLD RANKING

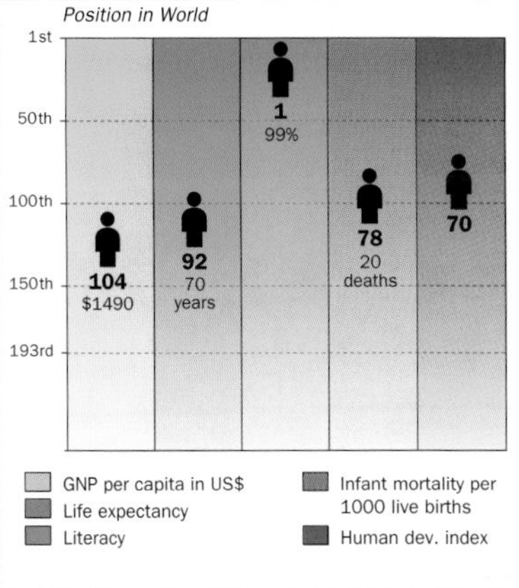
Position in World
1st
50th
100th
150th
193rd
104
$1490
92
70
years
1
99%
78
20
deaths
70
GNP per capita in US$
Life expectancy
Literacy
Infant mortality per 1000 live births
Human dev. index

S

San Marino

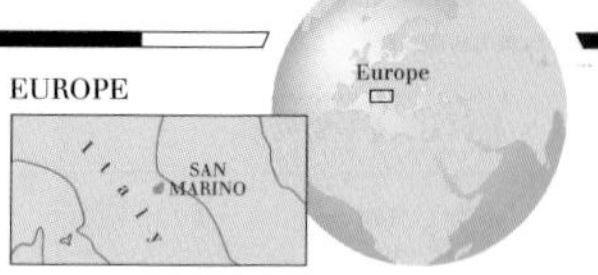
EUROPE
ITALY
SAN MARINO
Europe

Official Name: Republic of San Marino **Capital:** San Marino
Population: 27,730 **Currency:** Euro **Official Language:** Italian

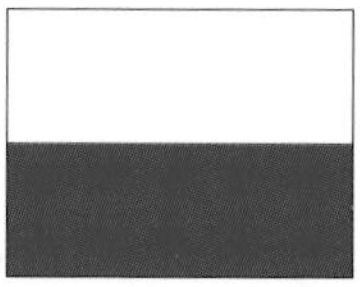

1631 | 1631 | Sept 3 | RSM | +1 | +378 | .sm

PERCHED ON THE SLOPES of Monte Titano in the Italian Appennines, tiny San Marino is the world's oldest republic and claims a lineage dating back to the 4th century. The territory is divided into nine castles, or districts. One-third of Sammarinesi live in the northern town of Serravalle. Today San Marino makes its living through agriculture, tourism, philately, and limited industry. Italy effectively controls most of its affairs.

San Marino's second fortress, la Cesta, built in the 13th century, dominates the republic from its pinnacle, 755 m (2477 ft) above sea level.

CLIMATE

Mediterranean

WEATHER CHART FOR SAN MARINO

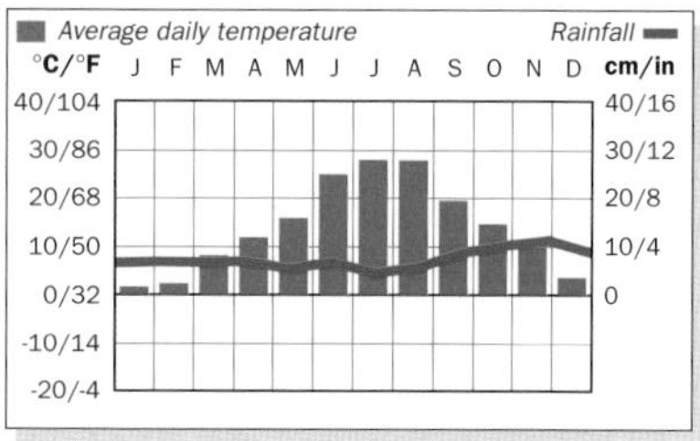
Average daily temperature
Rainfall
°C/°F
J F M A M J J A S O N D
cm/in
40/104
30/86
20/68
10/50
0/32
-10/14
-20/-4
40/16
30/12
20/8
10/4
0

San Marino's Mediterranean climate is moderated by cool sea breezes and its height above sea level. In summer, temperatures can reach 27°C (81°F), while in winter they fall to 2°C (35°F). There is rarely ever any snow.

TRANSPORTATION

Drive on right

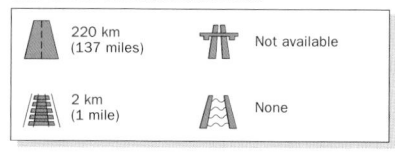

None

Has no fleet

THE TRANSPORTATION NETWORK

220 km (137 miles)

Not available

2 km (1 mile)

None

The 24-km (15-mile) highway to Rimini, which has the nearest airport, is San Marino's most important link. Congestion is a major problem, especially during the annual Mille Miglia car rally. A funicular railroad climbs the east side of Monte Titano. The railroad to Rimini has been closed since World War II.

PEOPLE

Pop. density high

Italian

455/km² (1155/mi²)

THE URBAN/RURAL POPULATION SPLIT

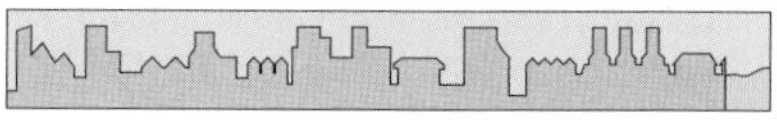
94%
6%

RELIGIOUS PERSUASION

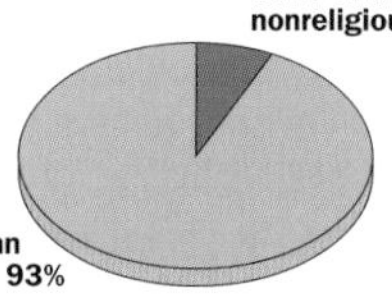
Other and nonreligious 7%
Roman Catholic 93%

Citizenship requires 30 years' residence; it is no longer transmissible by marriage. Women gained the vote in 1960, but could not stand for public office until 1973. Around 20,000 live abroad, mainly in Italy. Some Sammarinesi speak a distinct regional dialect.

TOURISM

Visitors : Population 19:1

532,000 visitors

Little change in 1999

MAIN TOURIST ARRIVALS

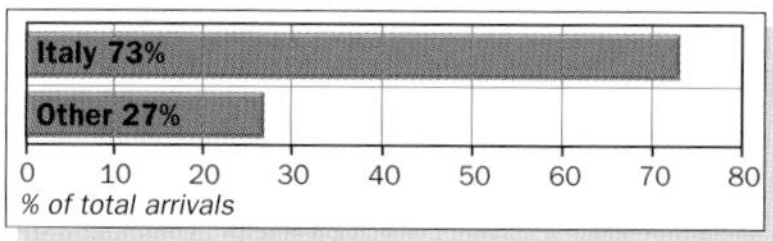
Italy 73%
Other 27%
0 10 20 30 40 50 60 70 80
% of total arrivals

Tourism is the mainstay of San Marino's economy, contributing about 60% of government revenue and employment for almost 20% of the workforce. Earnings from tourism are the largest share of GDP. Every year around three million visitors pass through San Marino, though most do not stay overnight. They are drawn by its mild climate and contrasting scenery, and come to sample its folklore and museums. The fortresses of Monte Titano – la Rocca, la Cesta, and Montale – built during the Middle Ages, command superb views and are the main attractions, along with the medieval city of San Marino itself. Many visitors to San Marino are day-trippers from Italy, though tourism is also boosted by the close proximity of the international airport at Rimini.

The San Marino tourist bureau also attracts thousands of sports enthusiasts to the republic by hosting a series of top international sporting events. In March, both the Rimini–San Marino marathon and the Mille Miglia veteran car meeting are held. May heralds the San Marino Grand Prix, when thousands of Formula One fans descend on the country. June, meanwhile, attracts more motor-racing fans for the World Motocross Championships. A renowned crossbow competition is held to mark San Marino's national day, September 3.

Efforts have been made to attract business meetings and conferences by means of extensive publicity in the Italian media.

***Religious procession.** The official state religion of San Marino is Roman Catholicism, in contrast to Italy, which has no state religion.*

San Marino

Total Area : 61 sq. km (23.6 sq. miles)

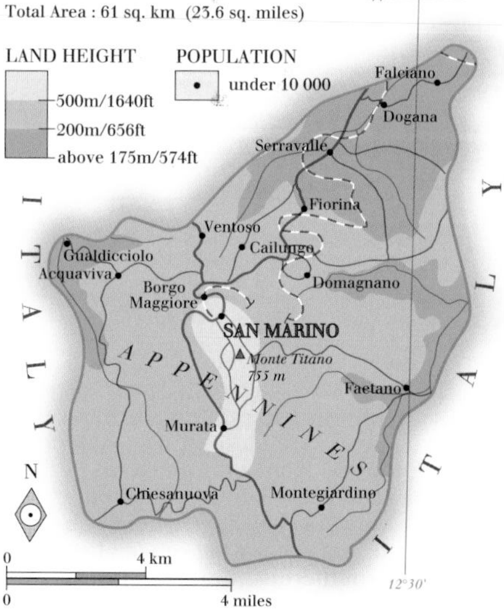
LAND HEIGHT
500m/1640ft
200m/656ft
above 175m/574ft
POPULATION
under 10 000
Falciano
Dogana
Serravalle
Fiorina
Ventoso
Cailungo
Gualdicciolo
Acquaviva
Borgo Maggiore
Domagnano
SAN MARINO
Monte Titano 755 m
Faetano
APPENNINES
Murata
Chiesanuova
Montegiardino
ITALY
ITALY
N
0 4 km
0 4 miles
44°
12°30'

S

POLITICS

Multiparty elections

2001/2006

Captains-Regent Pier Marino Menicucci and Giovanni Giannoni

San Marino is a parliamentary democracy headed by two captains-regent elected every six months. Though the PDCS is the largest single party, it is not guaranteed a place in the ever-shifting ruling coalition. The most recent government, formed in 2002, is headed by the PSS.

AT THE LAST ELECTION

Great and General Council 60 seats

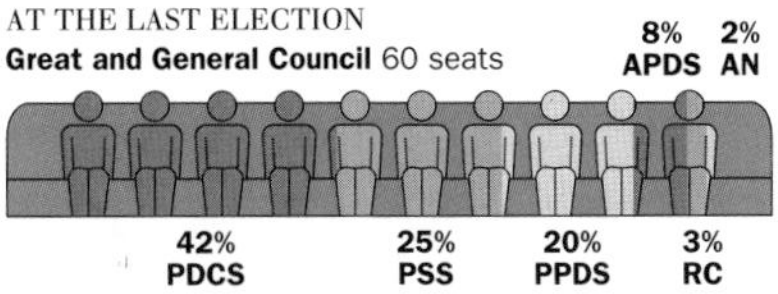
8% APDS
2% AN
42% PDCS
25% PSS
20% PPDS
3% RC

PDCS = San Marino Christian Democratic Party **PSS** = Socialist Party of San Marino **PPDS** = Progressive Democratic Party **APDS** = Popular Democratic Alliance **RC** = Communist Refoundation **AN** = National Alliance

WORLD AFFAIRS

Joined UN in 1992

CE | OSCE | IBRD | IMF | IWC

Foreign affairs are effectively decided by Italy, on which San Marino is entirely dependent. In 1992, San Marino acquired a seat at the UN.

AID

Neither

Neither an aid donor nor receiver

Not applicable

San Marino does not receive aid. However, annual subsidies from Italy and free access to the Italian market are essential to the economy.

DEFENSE

No compulsory military service

$1m

Little change from year to year

San Marino has a small territorial army and fortification guards. There is no compulsory military service, but males aged 16–55 may be called up in a national emergency.

ECONOMICS

Inflation 5.9% p.a. (1985–1996)

$190m

0.871 euros (1.013)

SCORE CARD

- World GNP Ranking........185th
- GNP per capita........$7830
- Balance of Payments........$11m
- Inflation........3.3%
- Unemployment........3%

Strengths

Tourism, providing 60% of government revenue. Light industry, notably mechanical engineering and clothing, with emphasis on sportswear and high-quality prestige lines. Philately.

Weaknesses

Need to import all raw materials.

EXPORTS/IMPORTS

San Marino does not publish independent trade statistics; trade movements are included in the Italian totals.

RESOURCES

Electric power: Included in Italian total

None

Not an oil producer

Small numbers of cattle, pigs, sheep, and horses

None

San Marino has to import all its energy from Italy. It has no exploitable mineral resources now that the stone quarry on Monte Titano has been exhausted.

ENVIRONMENT

Not available

None

Not available

Monte Titano is a unique limestone outcrop in the surrounding Italian plain. It thus has a very localized ecosystem.

MEDIA

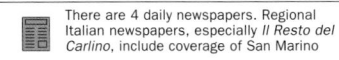

TV ownership high

Daily newspaper circulation 70 per 1000 people

PUBLISHING AND BROADCAST MEDIA

There are 4 daily newspapers. Regional Italian newspapers, especially *Il Resto del Carlino*, include coverage of San Marino

1 state-run service

2 services: 1 state-run, 1 independent

In 1993, a local TV station, San Marino RTV, began broadcasting. Sammarinesi can also receive Italian TV.

CRIME

No death penalty

San Marino does not publish prison figures

Little change from year to year

San Marino has a low crime rate. Justice is mainly administered in Italy. Until mid-1997 homosexuality was illegal.

EDUCATION

School leaving age: 14

99%

942 students

All teachers are trained abroad, mostly in Italy. Secondary school pupils can go on to Italian universities.

HEALTH

Welfare state health benefits

1 per 397 people

Circulatory system diseases, cancers

Health care is free and available to all. There is a hospital, but those requiring difficult operations normally go to Rimini for treatment.

CHRONOLOGY

Traditionally held to have been founded in the 4th century, the Republic of San Marino, one of many medieval Italian city-states, was recognized by the papacy in 1631.

- **1797** San Marino rejects expansion offered by Napoléon.
- **1861** Refuses to join unified Italy.
- **1914–1918** Fights for Italy in World War I.
- **1940** Supports Axis powers and declares war on Allies.
- **1943** Declares neutrality shortly before Italy surrenders.
- **1960** Women obtain vote.
- **1978** Coalition of San Marino Communist Party (PCS) and PSS: sole communist-led government in Western Europe.
- **1986** Financial scandals lead to new PDCS–PCS government.
- **1988** Joins Council of Europe.
- **1990** PCS renames itself PPDS.
- **1992** Joins UN. Collapse of communism in Europe sees PDCS–PPDS alliance replaced by PDCS–PSS coalition.
- **2002** Adoption of euro.

SPENDING

GDP/cap. increase

CONSUMPTION AND SPENDING

No data

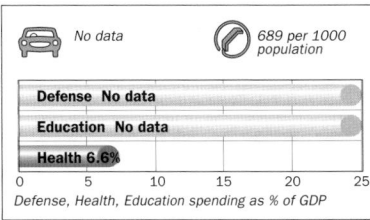

689 per 1000 population

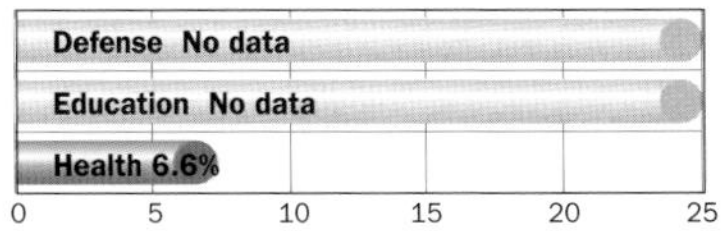
Defense No data
Education No data
Health 6.6%
0
5
10
15
20
25

Defense, Health, Education spending as % of GDP

Living standards are similar to those of northern Italy, while the unemployment rate is well below the Italian average.

WORLD RANKING

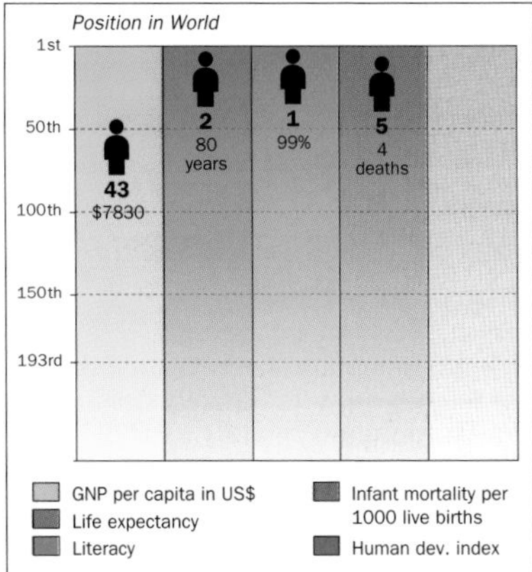
Position in World
1st
50th
100th
150th
193rd
43
$7830
2
80 years
1
99%
5
4 deaths
GNP per capita in US$
Life expectancy
Literacy
Infant mortality per 1000 live births
Human dev. index

S

São Tomé & Príncipe

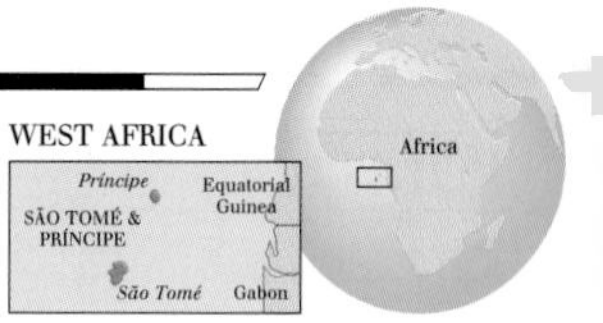
WEST AFRICA
Príncipe
SÃO TOMÉ & PRÍNCIPE
Equatorial Guinea
São Tomé
Gabon
Africa

Official Name: Democratic Republic of São Tomé and Príncipe **Capital:** São Tomé
Population: 170,372 **Currency:** Dobra **Official Language:** Portuguese

1975 | 1975 | July 12 | STP | 0 | +239 | .st

COMPOSED OF TWO main islands and their surrounding islets, São Tomé and Príncipe is situated off the west coast of Africa. In 1975, a classic Marxist single-party regime was established following independence from Portugal, but a referendum in 1990 resulted in a 72% vote in favor of democracy. São Tomé's main concerns are relations with Portugal and seeking closer ties with the EU and the US.

CLIMATE

Tropical equatorial

WEATHER CHART FOR SÃO TOMÉ

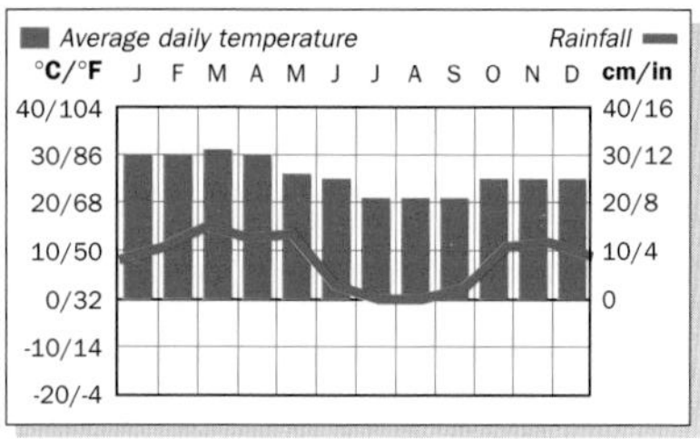
Average daily temperature
Rainfall
°C/°F J F M A M J J A S O N D cm/in
40/104
30/86
20/68
10/50
0/32
-10/14
-20/-4
40/16
30/12
20/8
10/4
0

The humid islands straddle the equator. The southwest of São Tomé is much wetter than the northern lowlands.

TRANSPORTATION

Drive on right

São Tomé International 23,000 passengers

64 ships 190,428 grt

THE TRANSPORTATION NETWORK

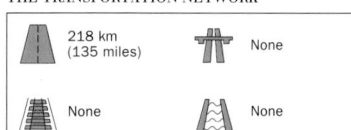

218 km (135 miles)

None

None

None

There are plans to construct a deepwater port and free trade zone at Agulhas Bay on Príncipe.

TOURISM

Visitors : Population 1:34

5000 visitors

Down 17% in 1995–1998

MAIN TOURIST ARRIVALS

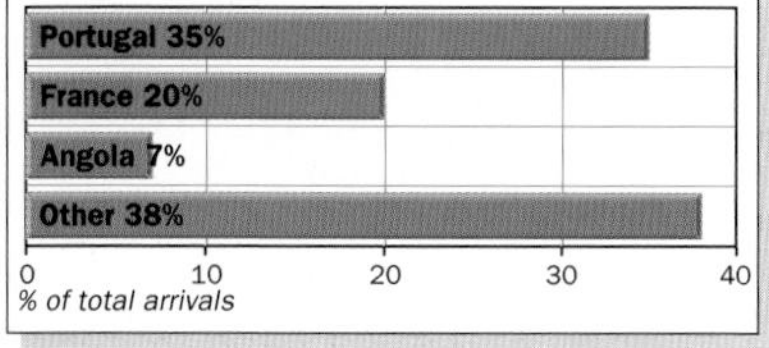
Portugal 35%
France 20%
Angola 7%
Other 38%
0 10 20 30 40
% of total arrivals

Despite recent foreign investment, the islands attract relatively few tourists annually, mainly wealthy Africans and Europeans. Attractions include snorkling, scenery, and wildlife. The first modern hotel opened in 1986.

PEOPLE

Pop. density medium

Portuguese Creole, Portuguese

177/km² (459/mi²)

THE URBAN/RURAL POPULATION SPLIT

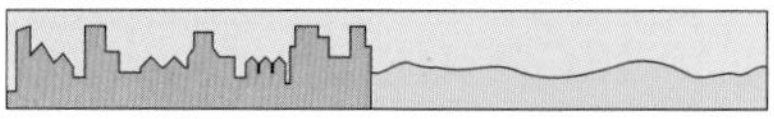
48%
52%

ETHNIC MAKEUP

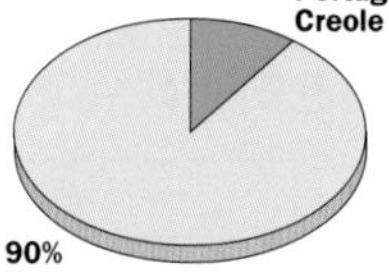
Portuguese and Creole 10%
Black 90%

The population is entirely descended from immigrants, since the islands were uninhabited when the Portuguese arrived in 1470. As the Portuguese settled, they imported Africans as slaves to work the sugar and cocoa plantations. The abolition of slavery in the 19th century, and the departure of 4000 Portuguese at independence, has resulted in a population which is 10% Portuguese and Creole and 90% black African, though Portuguese culture predominates. Blacks run the political parties. Society is well integrated and free of racial tensions. The main conflicts relate to class or differing ideologies. The extended family still offers the best, if not the only, form of social security. Women have a higher status than in most other African states; in 2002, Maria das Neves de Souza became the first female prime minister.

Lush vegetation on São Tomé. *The tropical climate is slightly moderated by the cool Benguela current.*

POLITICS

Multiparty elections

2002/2006

President Fradique de Menezes

AT THE LAST ELECTION

National Assembly 55 seats

44%
MLSTP–PSD
42%
MDFM–PCD
14%
UK

MLSTP–PSD = São Tomé and Príncipe Liberation Movement –Social Democratic Party **MDFM–PCD** = Force for Change Democratic Movement–Democratic Convergence Party **UK** = Ue Kedadji coalition

In 1990, a new multiparty constitution was introduced, ending the Marxist single-party state that had existed since independence in 1975. The opposition PCD was swept to victory in 1991, and later that year Miguel Trovoada returned from 11 years' exile to be elected as an independent to the presidency. Early elections in 1994 saw the return to power of the MLSTP as the renamed MLSTP–PSD. In the 2001 presidential elections, businessman Fradique de Menezes defeated former Marxist president Manuel Pinto da Costa. However, de Menezes was forced to negotiate the formation of a coalition government with the MLSTP–PSD after the party won elections in 2002. Conflict with the legislature developed over the president's power to control policy, especially in relation to the undersea oil reserves. A brief army takeover in 2003 forced de Menezes to promise greater cooperation with parliament.

WORLD AFFAIRS

Joined UN in 1975

CPLP | ACP | OIF | NAM | AU

São Tomé has achieved rapprochement with Portugal and seeks to maintain links with other former Portuguese colonies, notably Angola. It has always had close ties with Gabon and, while not dropping its ex-communist links, seeks closer relations with other central African states, France, and the US.

AID

Recipient

$38m (receipts)

Up 9% in 2001

São Tomé has one of the highest aid-to-population ratios in Africa. The government was granted $200 million in debt relief in 2001 by the World Bank Group's International Development Fund and the International Monetary Fund under the Initiative for Heavily Indebted Poor Countries program.

S

DEFENSE

No compulsory military service

$400,000

Little change

Since independence, the armed forces have figured prominently in national life. There have been a number of attempted coups, notably in 1978 (after which 2000 Angolan troops plus Soviet and Cuban advisers were invited in), 1988, and 1995. The most recent, in 2003, saw the brief establishment of a military junta. The national armed forces are believed to number 2000. With the collapse of the Eastern bloc, São Tomé now receives military assistance from the West.

RESOURCES

Electric power 6000 kW

3500 tonnes

Reserves currently unexploited

30,000 ducks, 4800 goats, 350,000 chickens

Oil

An offshore oil exploration agreement with Nigeria was signed in 2001. There are no mineral resources on the islands. São Tomé is very fertile; cocoa estates are finally back to pre-1975 productivity, and diversification of crops is now a priority. Príncipe has better ports, but its wild scenery makes it more suitable for tourism than farming.

CHRONOLOGY

The entire preindependence history of the islands was as a Portuguese colony exploited by plantation owners.

- ❑ **1972–1973** Strikes by plantation workers.
- ❑ **1975** Independence as Marxist state. Plantations nationalized.
- ❑ **1990** New democratic constitution.
- ❑ **1991–2000** Miguel Trovoada president for two terms.
- ❑ **1995** Príncipe granted autonomy.
- ❑ **2001** De Menezes wins presidency.
- ❑ **2003** Brief military takeover.

ECONOMICS

Inflation 47% p.a. (1990–2001)

$43m

8700 dobras (9020)

SCORE CARD

❑ World GNP Ranking	190th
❑ GNP per Capita	$280
❑ Balance of Payments	–$9m
❑ Inflation	7%
❑ Unemployment	50%

EXPORTS

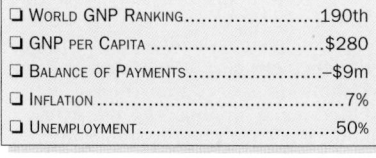

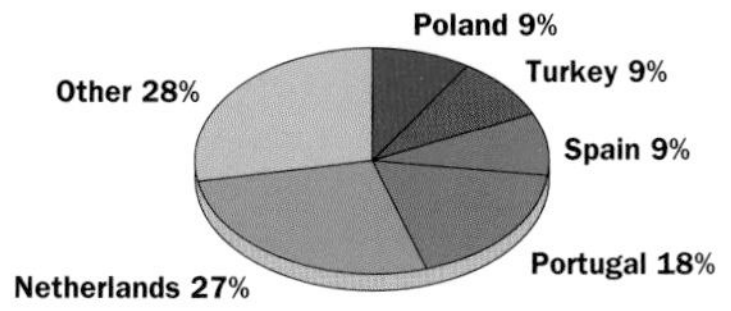
Poland 9%
Turkey 9%
Spain 9%
Portugal 18%
Netherlands 27%
Other 28%

IMPORTS

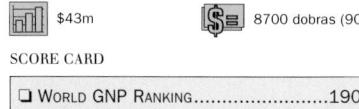

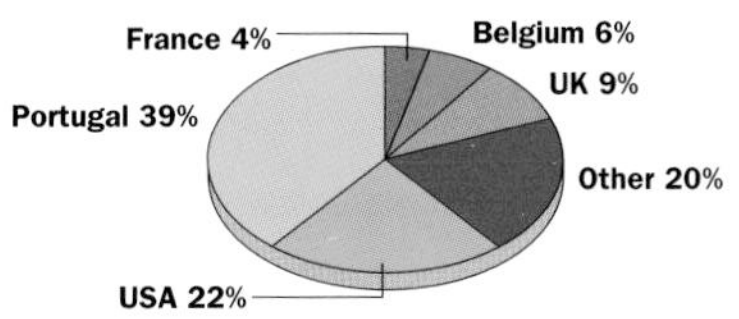
France 4%
Belgium 6%
UK 9%
Other 20%
USA 22%
Portugal 39%

STRENGTHS

Legacy of Portuguese-built infrastructure. Potential for development of fisheries, agriculture, tourism, and oil. Able to attract substantial aid.

WEAKNESSES

Cocoa accounts for 90% of export earnings. Skillful diplomacy has attracted high levels of aid, but mismanagement of these funds has resulted in severe debt. Weak currency.

EDUCATION

School leaving age: 15

83%

Not available

Education is officially compulsory only for a four-year period between the ages of seven and 14.

HEALTH

No welfare state health benefits

1 per 2128 people

Malaria, other parasitic diseases, respiratory and diarrheal diseases

Health care is not free, but São Tomé has a better system of basic care than other African countries.

SPENDING

GDP/cap. decrease

CONSUMPTION AND SPENDING

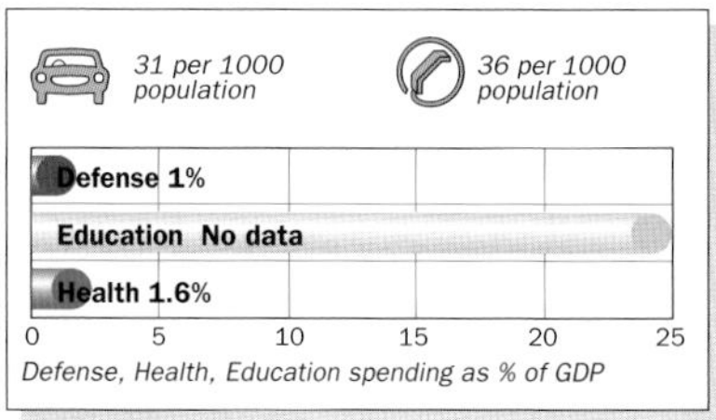
31 per 1000 population
36 per 1000 population
Defense 1%
Education No data
Health 1.6%
0
5
10
15
20
25
Defense, Health, Education spending as % of GDP

Wealth disparities are not conspicuous. There is a growing business class. Cocoa workers form the country's poorest group.

WORLD RANKING

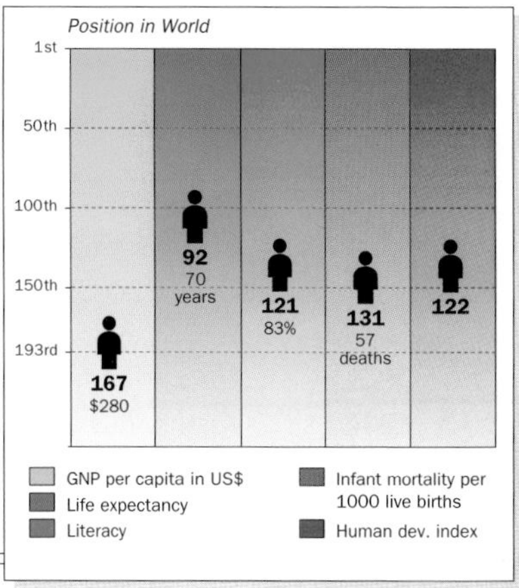
Position in World
1st
50th
100th
150th
193rd
167
$280
92
70 years
121
83%
131
57 deaths
122
GNP per capita in US$
Life expectancy
Literacy
Infant mortality per 1000 live births
Human dev. index

SÃO TOMÉ & PRÍNCIPE

Total Area : 1001 sq. km (386 sq. miles)

POPULATION

- over 10 000
- under 10 000

LAND HEIGHT

- 1000m/3281ft
- 500m/1640ft
- 200m/656ft
- Sea Level

0 10 km
0 10 miles

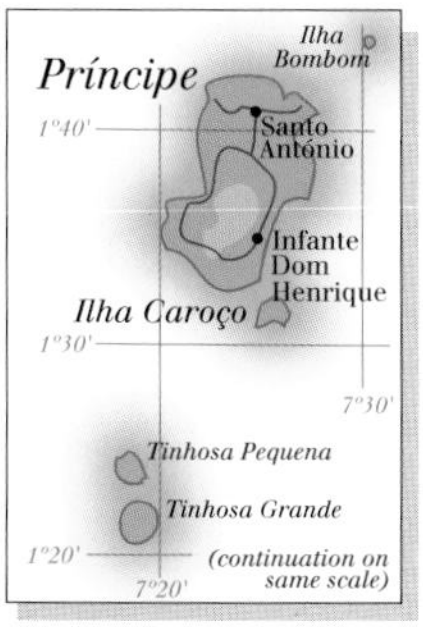
Príncipe
Ilha Bombom
Santo António
Infante Dom Henrique
Ilha Caroço
1°40'
1°30'
1°20'
7°30'
7°20'
Tinhosa Pequena
Tinhosa Grande
(continuation on same scale)

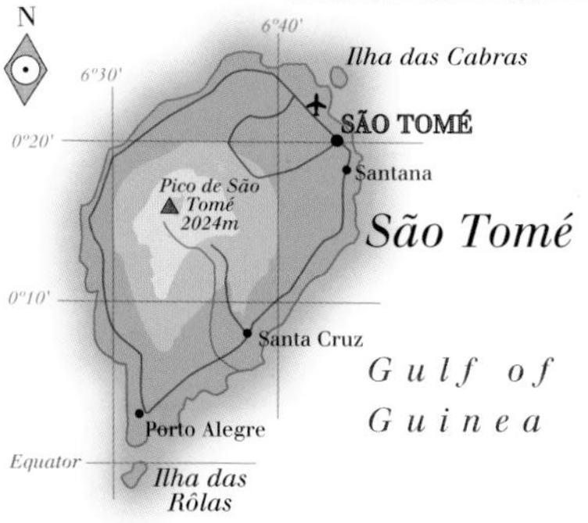
N
6°40'
6°30'
0°20'
0°10'
Ilha das Cabras
SÃO TOMÉ
Santana
Pico de São Tomé 2024m
São Tomé
Santa Cruz
Gulf of Guinea
Porto Alegre
Equator
Ilha das Rôlas

ENVIRONMENT

Not available

None

0.6 tonnes per capita

Fish conservation, deforestation for fuelwood, and potential tourism expansion are the major issues.

MEDIA

TV ownership medium

There are no daily newspapers

PUBLISHING AND BROADCAST MEDIA

There are no daily newspapers. *Diário da República* and *Notícias* are published weekly by the government

1 state-controlled service

1 state-controlled service

Freedom of expression is respected. The state controls radio and TV stations. Radio ownership is high for Africa.

CRIME

No death penalty

130 prisoners

Little change in 1999

Crime levels are fairly low owing to the tight-knit nature of communities. Robbery is a problem in urban areas.

S

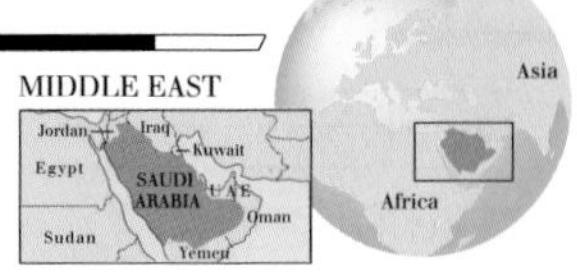
MIDDLE EAST
Jordan
Iraq
Kuwait
Egypt
SAUDI ARABIA
UAE
Oman
Sudan
Yemen
Asia
Africa

SAUDI ARABIA

OFFICIAL NAME: Kingdom of Saudi Arabia **CAPITAL:** Riyadh; Jiddah (administrative)
POPULATION: 21.7 million **CURRENCY:** Saudi riyal **OFFICIAL LANGUAGE:** Arabic

1932 | 1932 | Sept 23 | SA | +3 | +966 | .sa

OCCUPYING MOST OF THE Arabian peninsula, Saudi Arabia covers an area as large as western Europe. Over 95% of its land is desert, with the most arid part, known as the Empty Quarter or Rub al Khali, being in the southeast. Saudi Arabia has the world's largest oil reserves. It includes Islam's holiest cities, Medina and Mecca, visited each year by two million Muslims performing the pilgrimage known as the *haj*. The al-Sa'ud family have been Saudi Arabia's absolutist rulers since 1932. In theory, Islamic *sharia* underpins the constitution.

CLIMATE

Hot desert

WEATHER CHART FOR RIYADH

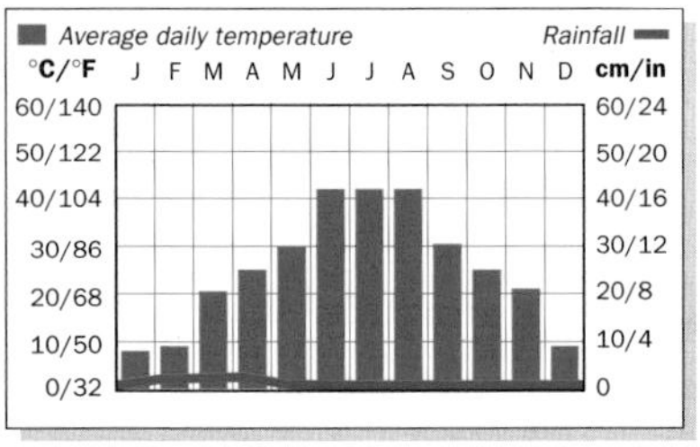
Average daily temperature
Rainfall
°C/°F
J F M A M J J A S O N D
cm/in
60/140
50/122
40/104
30/86
20/68
10/50
0/32
60/24
50/20
40/16
30/12
20/8
10/4
0

The kingdom's only reliable rainfall is in the southern Asir province, making agriculture viable there. The central plateau requires deep artesian wells to water crops. Inland, summer temperatures often soar above 48°C (118°F), but in winter, especially in the northwest, they may fall to freezing point.

TRANSPORTATION

Drive on right

King Abd al-Aziz International, Jiddah
10.9m passengers

274 ships
1.13m grt

THE TRANSPORTATION NETWORK

44,104 km (27,405 miles)

Trans-Arabian Highway

958 km (595 miles)

None

A modern transportation infrastructure links the main population centers to the Gulf states and Jordan. Saudi Arabia has the only rail system in the Arabian peninsula.

TOURISM

Visitors : Population 1:3.4

6.3m visitors

Up 70% in 1999–2000

MAIN TOURIST ARRIVALS

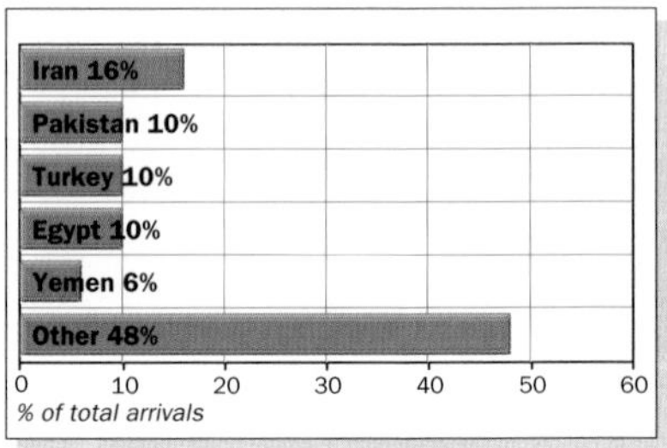
Iran 16%
Pakistan 10%
Turkey 10%
Egypt 10%
Yemen 6%
Other 48%
0
10
20
30
40
50
60
% of total arrivals

Foreign tourism is discouraged. Until a limited relaxation in 2000, only Muslim pilgrims, business people, and foreign workers were permitted entry. Non-Muslims are banned from the holy cities of Mecca and Medina. Though strict quotas have been imposed to avoid overcrowding, stampedes of *haj* pilgrims in 1990, 1997, and 2001 killed or injured thousands. Many choose the port of Jiddah as a base from which to begin the pilgrimage. Also popular is the *umra*, or little pilgrimage, since it can be made at any time of year. An estimated $2.5 billion has been spent on improving *haj* facilities in recent years.

Jizan on the Red Sea offers superb scuba diving. The Hejaz railroad and the Nabatean ruins at Medain Salih are of archaeological interest. To escape the summer heat, the government relocates to mountainous Taif, used as a resort by the Saudis.

SAUDI ARABIA

Total Area : 1 960 582 sq. km (756 981 sq. miles)

POPULATION
- over 1 000 000
- over 500 000
- over 100 000
- over 50 000
- over 10 000
- under 10 000

LAND HEIGHT
- 3000m/9843ft
- 2000m/6562ft
- 1000m/3281ft
- 500m/1640ft
- Sea Level

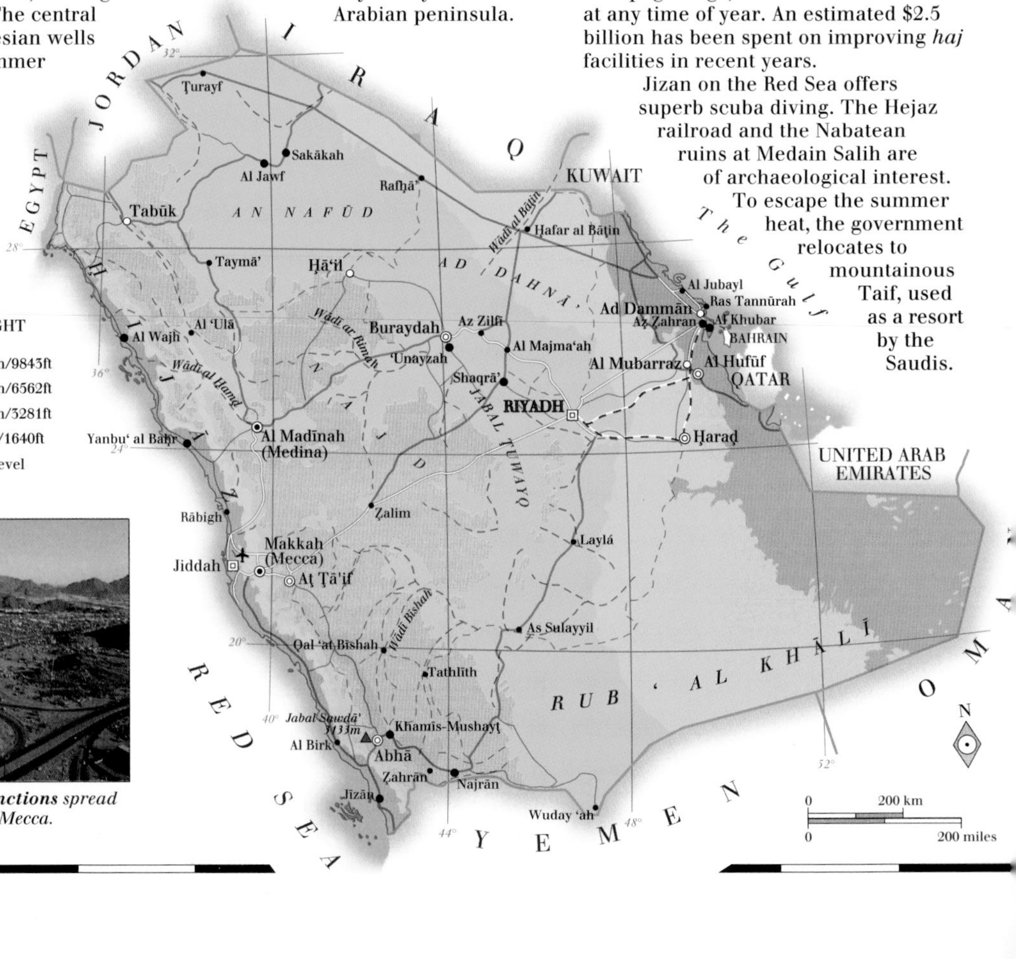
JORDAN
IRAQ
KUWAIT
EGYPT
Turayf
Sakākah
Al Jawf
Rafḩā'
Tabūk
AN NAFŪD
Ḩafar al Bāţin
Taymā'
Ḩā'il
AD DAHNĀ'
Al Jubayl
Ras Tannūrah
Ad Dammām
Aẕ Ẓahran
Al Khubar
BAHRAIN
Al 'Ulā
Al Wajh
Buraydah
Az Zilfī
Al Majma'ah
'Unayzah
Shaqrā'
Al Mubarraz
Al Hufūf
QATAR
RIYADH
Yanbu' al Baḩr
Al Madīnah (Medina)
Ḩaraḑ
UNITED ARAB EMIRATES
Rābigh
Ẓalim
Laylá
Makkah (Mecca)
Jiddah
Aţ Ţā'if
As Sulayyil
Qal'at Bīshah
Tathlīth
RUB' AL KHĀLĪ
OMAN
RED SEA
Jabal Sawdā' 3133m
Khamīs-Mushayţ
Al Birk
Abhā
Ẓahrān
Najrān
Jīzān
Wuday 'ah
YEMEN
0
200 km
200 miles
N

Network of modern road junctions spread out across the landscape near Mecca.

PEOPLE

Pop. density low

Arabic

10/km² (27/mi²)

THE URBAN/RURAL POPULATION SPLIT

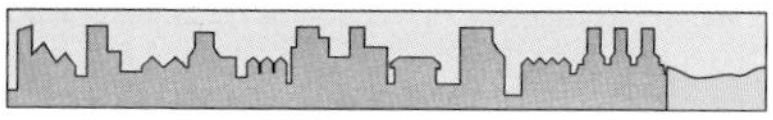
87%
13%

RELIGIOUS PERSUASION

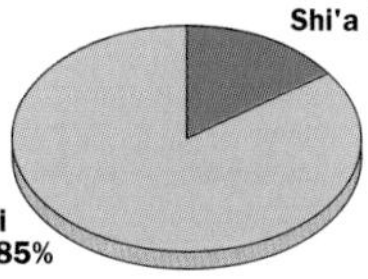
Shi'a Muslim 15%
Sunni Muslim 85%

ETHNIC MAKEUP

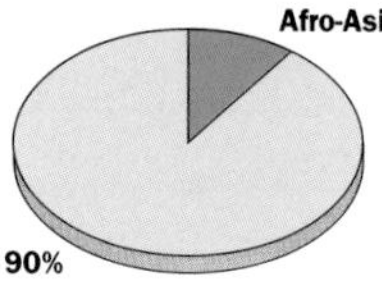
Afro-Asian 10%
Arab 90%

The Saudis, who take their name from the ruling al-Sa'ud family, were united by conquest between 1902 and 1932 by King Abd al-Aziz al-Sa'ud. The vast majority are Sunni Muslims who follow a puritanical Wahhabi interpretation of Islam and embrace *sharia* (Islamic law). The politically dominant Nejdi tribes from the central plateau around Riyadh are Bedouin in origin. The Hejazi tribes, from the south and west, have a more cosmopolitan, mercantile background, but are largely displaced from politics. In the eastern Al-Hasa province there is a Shi'a minority of some 300,000, many of whom work in the oil fields. Women have to wear the veil, cannot hold a driving license, have little role in public life, and are effectively barred from the workplace except as teachers and nurses. In 2000, however, Saudi Arabia decided to sign the UN convention on women's rights – provided it did not contradict *sharia* – and from 2001 issued women with identity cards.

POPULATION AGE BREAKDOWN

Female	Age	Male
	80+	
Data	60–79	Data
Unavailable	40–59	Unavailable
	20–39	
	0–19	

% of population by age group

POLITICS

No legislative elections

Not applicable

H.M. King Fahd ibn Abd al-Aziz

LEGISLATIVE OR ADVISORY BODIES

Consultative Council 120 seats

Saudi Arabia is an absolute monarchy. The king rules with the assistance of an appointed Council of Ministers and the Consultative Council

Saudi Arabia is an absolute monarchy. Since 1993 a Consultative Council (Majlis al-Shoura) has been appointed by the king.

PROFILE

The royal family, the House of Sa'ud, rules by carefully manipulating appointments in all sectors of government. Frequent changes of personnel within the armed forces ensure that officers do not build personal followings. All influential cabinet portfolios, apart from those of oil and religious affairs, are held by members of the royal family.

Absolutist rule means that domestic politics are virtually nonexistent. The regime retains feudal elements: at weekly *majalis*, or councils, citizens can present petitions or grievances to leading royals. Large cash sums are often dispensed at these meetings.

The legitimacy of the regime is built on its adherence to Islamic values, and the backing of the *ulema* (scholars). It is the emphasis on Islam that most colors Saudi life. The 5000-strong *mutawa* (religious police) enforce the five-times-a-day call to prayer, when businesses must close. During Ramadan the *mutawa* are especially active.

MAIN POLITICAL ISSUES

Questioning the ruling family
Following the 1991 Gulf War, a civil rights campaign emerged to challenge the authority of the ruling family, demanding closer adherence to Islamic values. The movement objected to the presence of US troops on Saudi territory and the consequent exposure to "corrupt" Western culture. The al-Sa'uds swiftly quashed the protest but exiled opponents have continued their activities using faxes and e-mail. The most vociferous denunciations of the royal family have come from terrorist mastermind Osama bin Laden, formerly a member of the inner circle, operating from bases abroad.

The succession issue
The question of succession and the possibility of a future power struggle, rooted in rivalries endemic to the House of Sa'ud, emerged in 1996, when King Fahd suffered a stroke. The management of day-to-day affairs passed briefly to his half-brother, Crown Prince Abdullah, who remains in effective, if no longer formal, control.

WORLD AFFAIRS

Joined UN in 1945

AL | Damasc | GCC | OIC | OPEC

Saudi Arabia's strategic importance is derived from its oil reserves and the presence of the holy sites of Mecca and Medina. Relations with the US, though close, have been frayed by the recent campaigns in Afghanistan and Iraq. After Iraq's invasion of Kuwait in 1990, the kingdom helped to lead the Arab coalition against Iraq, sheltering the Kuwaiti royal family, providing military bases to the Western allies, and supplying more troops than any other Arab state. The continued presence of foreign forces angers Saudi Islamist militants. Most of those who carried out the September 11, 2001, attacks on the US were Saudis, as is al-Qaida leader Osama bin Laden. The US pledged to withdraw troops after the successful invasion of Iraq, but attacks continued, with prominent suicide bombings of Westerners in Riyadh in May 2003.

A pact signed with Yemen in 2000 ended a simmering border dispute. In 2002 Crown Prince Abdullah's new peace plan for Israel/Palestine won praise from Arabs and the West – and hinted at a major change in Saudi foreign policy.

AID

Donor

$490m (donations)

Up 66% in 2001

Generous loans and grants from the Saudi Fund for Development are made to other Arab and developing countries, mainly for infrastructure projects. Saudi Arabia promotes Islam through charitable foundations, especially in Africa, Asia, and the former Soviet Union. The royal purse also supports scientific and medical research. Since the liberation of Kuwait in 1991, Saudi Arabia has given large sums to countries that supported the US-led alliance, notably Egypt, Syria, Morocco, and Turkey. In addition, the Saudi government substantially reimbursed the US and the UK for the cost of their expeditionary forces, as well as favoring companies from the allied countries for reconstruction contracts.

***King Fahd ibn Abd al-Aziz** acceded to the Saudi throne in 1982.*

***Crown Prince Abdullah**, effectively in control of the country.*

S

CHRONOLOGY

The unification of Saudi Arabia under King Abd al-Aziz (ibn Sa'ud) was achieved in 1932. The kingdom remains the only country in the world which is named after its royal family.

- **1937** Oil reserves discovered near Riyadh.
- **1939** Ceremonial start of oil production at Az Zahran.
- **1953** King Sa'ud succeeds on the death of his father Abd al-Aziz.
- **1964** King Sa'ud abdicates in favor of his brother Faisal.
- **1973** Saudi Arabia imposes oil embargo on Western supporters of Israel.
- **1975** King Faisal assassinated by a deranged nephew; succeeded by his brother Khalid.
- **1979** Muslim fundamentalists led by Juhaiman ibn Seif al-Otaibi seize Grand Mosque in Mecca, proclaim a *mahdi* (savior) on first day of Islamic year 1400.
- **1981** Formation of GCC, with its secretariat in Riyadh.
- **1982** King Fahd succeeds on the death of his brother King Khalid. Promises to create consultative assembly.
- **1986** Opening of King Fahd Causeway to Bahrain. Shaikh Yamani sacked as oil minister.
- **1987** Diplomatic relations with Iran deteriorate after 402 people die in riots involving Islamic fundamentalists at Mecca during the *haj* (pilgrimage).
- **1989** Saudi Arabia signs nonaggression pact with Iraq. Saudi Arabia brokers political settlement to Lebanese civil war.
- **1990** Kuwaiti royal family seeks sanctuary in Taif after Iraqi invasion. Many allegedly pro-Iraqi Jordanians and Yemenis expelled.
- **1990–1991** US, UK, French, Egyptian, and Syrian forces assemble in Saudi Arabia for Operation Desert Storm. Public executions are halted.
- **1991** Iraqis seize border town of Al Khafji, but are repulsed by Saudi, US, and Qatari forces.
- **1993** King Fahd appoints Consultative Council (Majlis al-Shoura).
- **1996** King Fahd briefly relinquishes control to Crown Prince Abdullah. Bomb attack at US military complex in Az Zahran kills 19 US citizens.
- **1997, 2001** Consultative Council expanded, first to 90 then to 120 members.
- **2002** Crown Prince Abdullah unveils Middle East peace plan; endorsed by AL summit in Beirut.

DEFENSE

No compulsory military service

$24.3bn

Up 10% in 2001

Saudi Arabia's substantial military contribution to the 1991 Gulf War, at a cost of $55 billion, enhanced its image as a major regional power. Military equipment is purchased mostly from the US, the UK, and France. Weapons systems are advanced and include Patriot missiles and AWACS early warning radar. However, skilled foreign personnel operate many of these: 1000 US air force troops are employed to keep AWACS flying.

The air force is the elite branch of the military. It had one brief period of politicization in 1969 when officers attempted a coup. The paramilitary National Guard is drawn from tribal supporters of the al-Sa'ud regime. Its commander-in-chief is the crown prince rather than the defense minister.

SAUDI ARABIAN ARMED FORCES

1055 main battle tanks (315 M-1A2 Abrams, 290 AMX-30, 450 M60A3)	75,000 personnel
4 frigates, 4 corvettes, and 26 patrol boats	15,500 personnel
294 combat aircraft (29 F-5, 158 F-15, 85 Tornado IDS, 22 Tornado ADV)	16,000 personnel
None	

ECONOMICS

Inflation 3.7% p.a. (1990–2001)

$181bn

3.7502 Saudi riyals (3.7504)

SCORE CARD

- World GNP Ranking....23rd
- GNP per Capita....$8460
- Balance of Payments....$14.5bn
- Inflation....–0.5%
- Unemployment....6%

EXPORTS

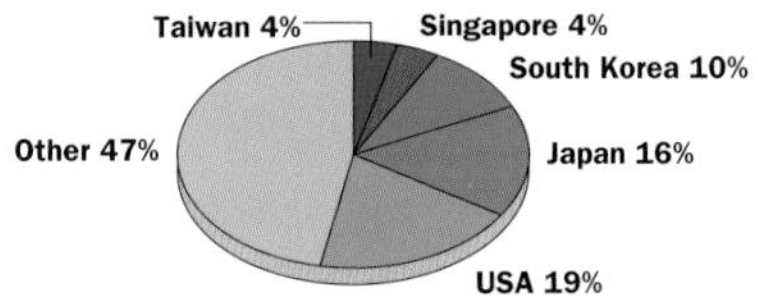
Taiwan 4%
Singapore 4%
South Korea 10%
Other 47%
Japan 16%
USA 19%

IMPORTS

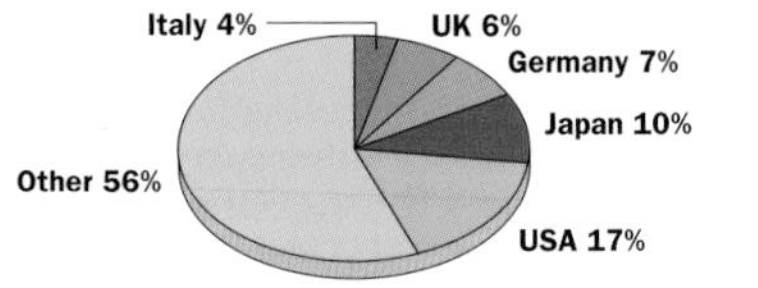
Italy 4%
UK 6%
Germany 7%
Japan 10%
Other 56%
USA 17%

Strengths
Vast oil and gas reserves. World-class associated industries. Accumulated surpluses and steady current income. Large earnings from two million pilgrims to Mecca annually.

Weaknesses
Lack of indigenous skilled workers. Heavily subsidized food production. Most consumer items and industrial raw materials imported. High youth unemployment. Large national debt. National wealth concentrated with royal family. Fears of political instability.

Profile
Great efforts have been made to reduce dependence on oil exports and to provide employment for young Saudis as opposed to foreign workers. Nonetheless, the country remains dependent on both. Saudi Arabia aims to control oil prices through OPEC in an effort to buoy up the industrialized countries while also undermining the drive to develop alternative energy. Since 2000, approved foreigners have been allowed complete ownership of Saudi businesses and rights to property. Large sums have been spent on creating an infrastructure to provide the basis for a manufacturing economy. A drive for privatization was announced in 2002.

ECONOMIC PERFORMANCE INDICATOR

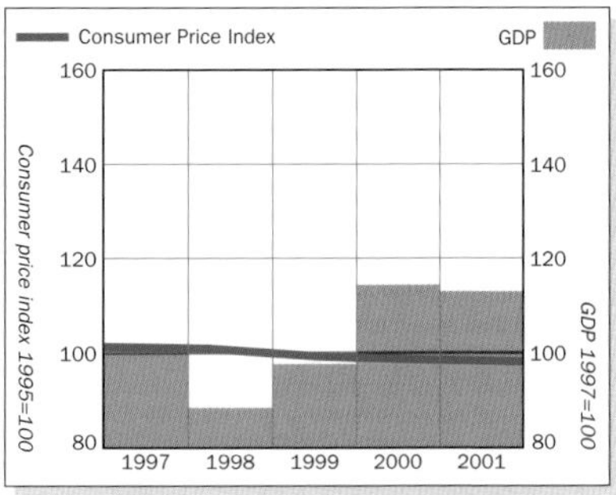
Consumer Price Index
GDP
160
140
120
100
80
Consumer price index 1995=100
GDP 1997=100
1997
1998
1999
2000
2001

SAUDI ARABIA : MAJOR BUSINESSES

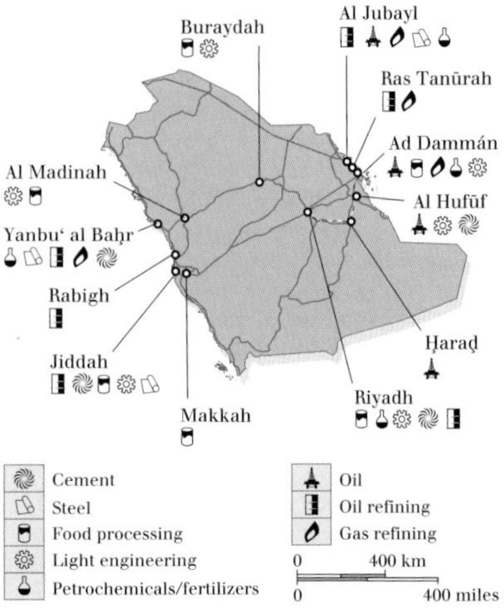
Buraydah
Al Jubayl
Ras Tanūrah
Ad Dammán
Al Hufūf
Al Madinah
Yanbu' al Bahr
Rabigh
Jiddah
Makkah
Riyadh
Harad
Cement
Steel
Food processing
Light engineering
Petrochemicals/fertilizers
Oil
Oil refining
Gas refining
0
400 km
0
400 miles

RESOURCES

Electric power 22.9m kW

55,654 tonnes

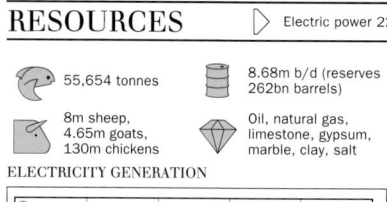

8.68m b/d (reserves 262bn barrels)

8m sheep, 4.65m goats, 130m chickens

Oil, natural gas, limestone, gypsum, marble, clay, salt

ELECTRICITY GENERATION

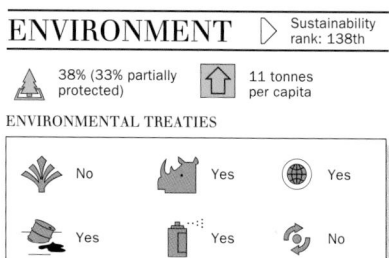

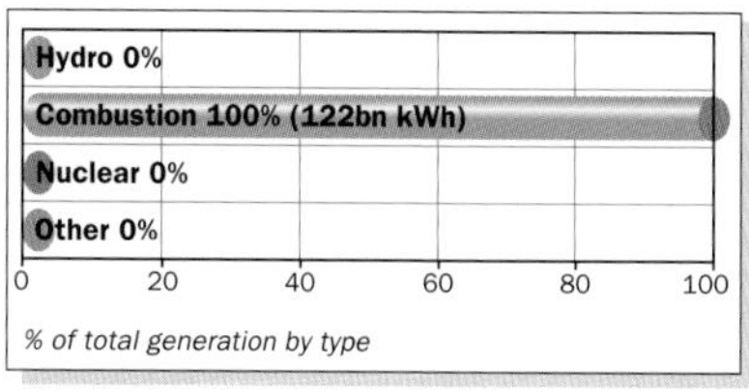
Hydro 0%
Combustion 100% (122bn kWh)
Nuclear 0%
Other 0%
0
20
40
60
80
100
% of total generation by type

SAUDI ARABIA : LAND USE

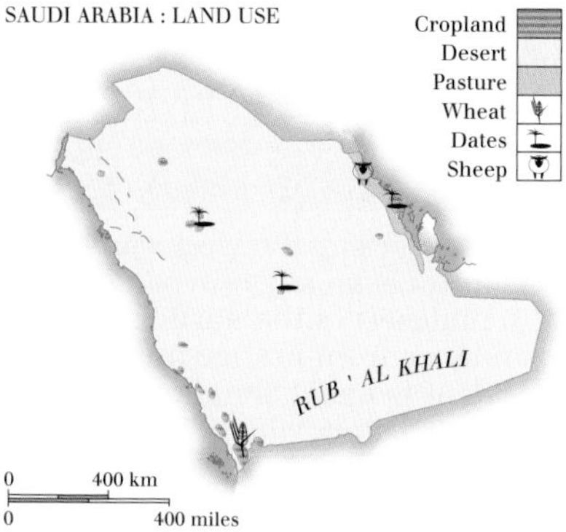
Cropland
Desert
Pasture
Wheat
Dates
Sheep
RUB ' AL KHALI
0
400 km
0
400 miles

With the world's biggest oil and sizable gas reserves, Saudi Arabia plays a key role in the global economy. Attempts at diversification have not altered heavy dependency on the oil markets.

ENVIRONMENT

Sustainability rank: 138th

38% (33% partially protected)

11 tonnes per capita

ENVIRONMENTAL TREATIES

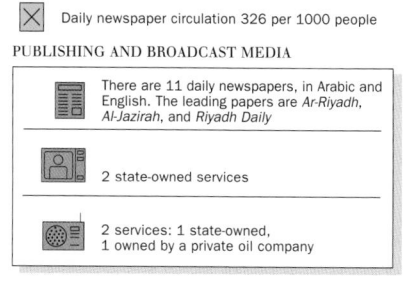

No | Yes | Yes

Yes | Yes | No

Pollution in the Gulf and Red Sea has threatened some wildlife and their habitats, as have hunters using high-velocity rifles and off-road vehicles. The government has taken steps to confine manufacturing to industrial estates. Environmental legislation is, nevertheless, poorly developed, though planning controls apply in the major cities.

MEDIA

TV ownership high

Daily newspaper circulation 326 per 1000 people

PUBLISHING AND BROADCAST MEDIA

There are 11 daily newspapers, in Arabic and English. The leading papers are *Ar-Riyadh*, *Al-Jazirah*, and *Riyadh Daily*

2 state-owned services

2 services: 1 state-owned, 1 owned by a private oil company

The government imposes total press censorship and insists on strict morality. In 1994, private citizens were banned from owning satellite dishes, but the authorities turn a blind eye to their use. No allowance is made for Arab satellite broadcasts, which have been criticized for covering anti-Islamic views. The international *Sharq Al Awsat* is a leading Arabic daily. In 2001 the government announced strict rules regarding references to the state and religion on the Internet.

CRIME

Death penalty in use

23,720 prisoners

Up sharply in 1999–2000

CRIME RATES

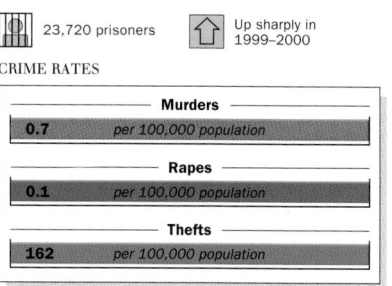

Murders
0.7 per 100,000 population

Rapes
0.1 per 100,000 population

Thefts
162 per 100,000 population

Strict Islamic punishments – stoning, amputation, and beheading – are enforced. Criticism for human rights abuses has increased, with an Amnesty International campaign in 2000.

EDUCATION

School leaving age: 11

77%

404,094 students

THE EDUCATION SYSTEM

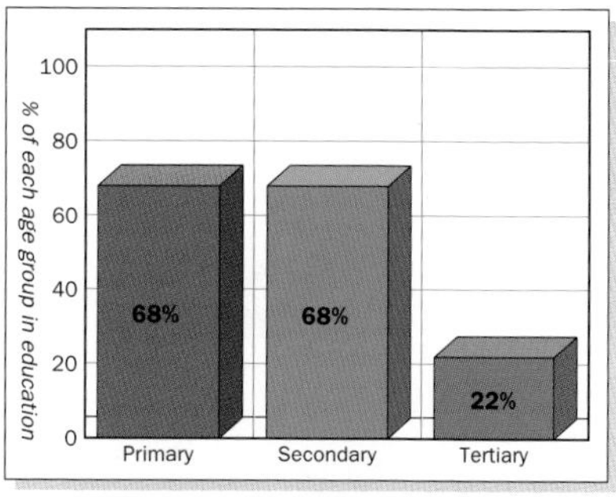
100
80
60
40
20
0
% of each age group in education
68%
68%
22%
Primary
Secondary
Tertiary

The growing number of Western-educated Saudis has intensified pressure for social and political change. In the 1950s, the religious establishment was persuaded to give women equal opportunities in education. Analysts have criticized universities for turning out many graduates in Islamic theology, but not enough engineers and technocrats; a high percentage of graduates struggle to find work.

HEALTH

Welfare state health benefits

1 per 654 people

Diarrheal, respiratory, heart, metabolic, and parasitic diseases

Infant mortality has dropped and endemic disease has been nearly eradicted. Health care outside major centers such as Riyadh and Jiddah still remains relatively undeveloped, given Saudi Arabia's huge economic resources. However, large sums have been spent on employing Western expertise. Many Saudis are still sent overseas by the government for treatment, especially for transplant operations, which pose some ethical problems for religious leaders. The private sector has also been encouraged.

SPENDING

GDP/cap. increase

CONSUMPTION AND SPENDING

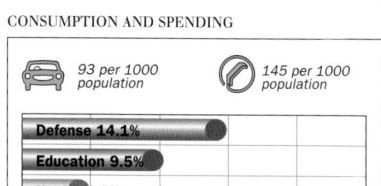

93 per 1000 population

145 per 1000 population

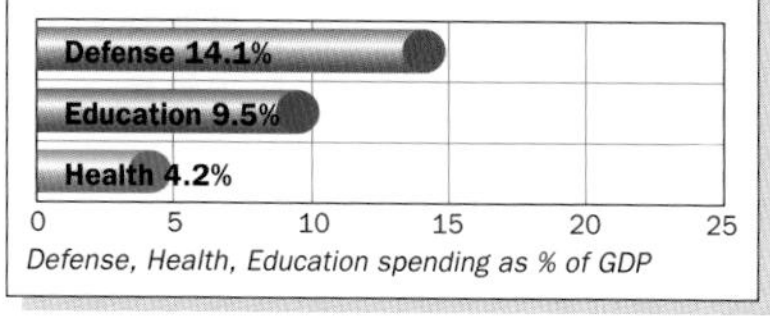
Defense 14.1%
Education 9.5%
Health 4.2%
0
5
10
15
20
25
Defense, Health, Education spending as % of GDP

Members of the Saudi elite are among the most wealthy people in the world. Non-Saudi citizens, especially guest workers from the Indian subcontinent and the Philippines, are much poorer. The al-Sa'uds have used their wealth to create a cradle-to-grave welfare system. Ownership of telephones, TVs, VCRs, and other consumer goods is high. The distribution of wealth is carefully controlled by the royal family through the *majlis* system. There is no stock market, though shares in public companies are traded privately. Many Saudis refuse for religious reasons to accept interest on deposits with banks, but Islamic banks offer profit-sharing investment schemes as an alternative.

WORLD RANKING

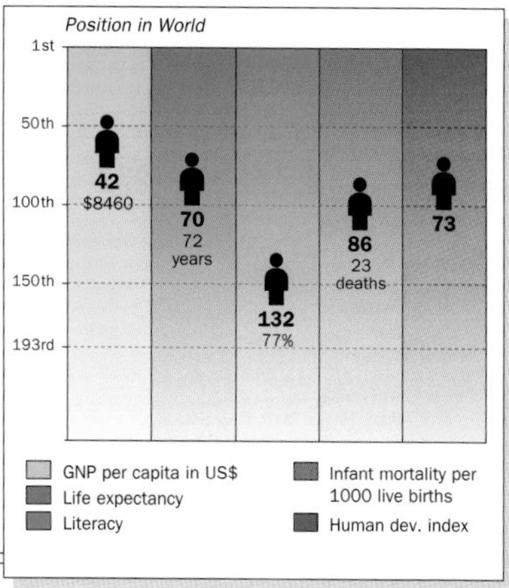
Position in World
1st
50th
100th
150th
193rd
42
$8460
70
72
years
132
77%
86
23
deaths
73
GNP per capita in US$
Life expectancy
Literacy
Infant mortality per 1000 live births
Human dev. index

S

SENEGAL

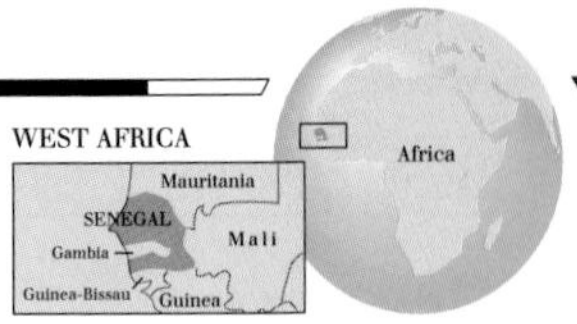
WEST AFRICA
Africa
Mauritania
SENEGAL
Gambia
Mali
Guinea-Bissau
Guinea

OFFICIAL NAME: Republic of Senegal **CAPITAL:** Dakar
POPULATION: 9.9 million **CURRENCY:** CFA franc **OFFICIAL LANGUAGE:** French

1960 | 1960 | April 4 | SN | 0 | +221 | .sn

SENEGAL'S CAPITAL, Dakar, lies on the westernmost cape of Africa. The country is mostly low-lying, with open savanna and semidesert in the north and thicker savanna in the south. After independence from France in 1960, Senegal was ruled until 1981 by President Léopold Senghor. He was succeeded by his prime minister, Abdou Diouf, who held power for almost 20 years until his election defeat in 2000.

CLIMATE

Steppe/tropical

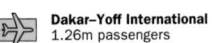

WEATHER CHART FOR DAKAR

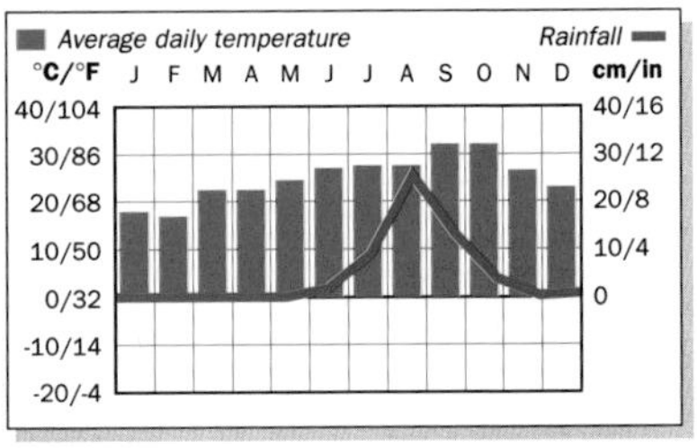
Average daily temperature
Rainfall
°C/°F
J F M A M J J A S O N D
cm/in
40/104
30/86
20/68
10/50
0/32
-10/14
-20/4
40/16
30/12
20/8
10/4
0

The coastal regions, which project into the path of the northern trade winds, are remarkably cool given their latitude.

TRANSPORTATION

Drive on right

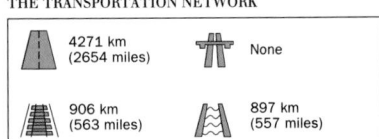

Dakar–Yoff International 1.26m passengers

188 ships 48,000 grt

THE TRANSPORTATION NETWORK

4271 km (2654 miles)

None

906 km (563 miles)

897 km (557 miles)

Dakar is a major west African port. The rail link to Mali was built in the 1920s. The 2002 *Joola* ferry disaster highlighted the overloading of the navy-run service between Ziguinchor and Dakar.

TOURISM

Visitors : Population 1:25

389,000 visitors

Up 5% in 2000

MAIN TOURIST ARRIVALS

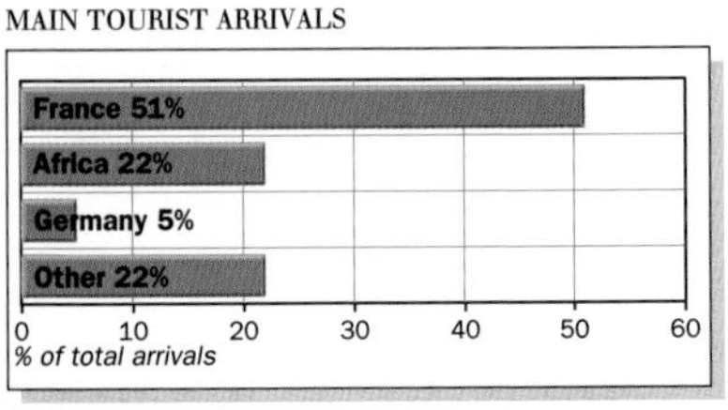
France 51%
Africa 22%
Germany 5%
Other 22%
0
10
20
30
40
50
60
% of total arrivals

In addition to French package tours to coastal resorts, tours for African-Americans to Gorée, a former slave island, are increasingly popular.

PEOPLE

Pop. density medium

Wolof, Fulani, Serer, Diola, Malinke, Soninke, Arabic, French

51/km² (133/mi²)

THE URBAN/RURAL POPULATION SPLIT

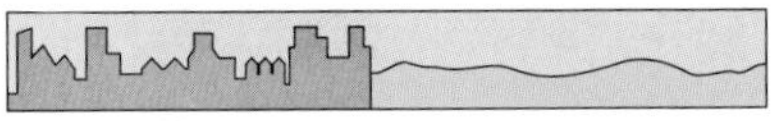
48%
52%

RELIGIOUS PERSUASION

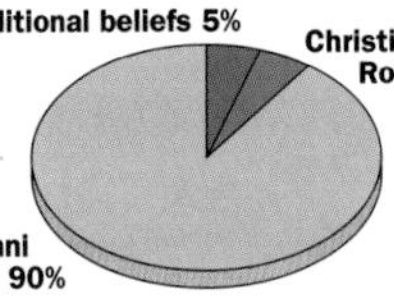
Traditional beliefs 5%
Christian (mainly Roman Catholic) 5%
Sunni Muslim 90%

National identity is fairly well developed, and intermarriage has reduced ethnic tensions. Groups can still be identified regionally, however. Dakar is a Wolof area, the Senegal River is dominated by the Toucouleur, the Malinke mostly live in the east, and the Diola (Jola) in Casamance, where the feeling of the Diola that they are excluded from politics has led to a long-running rebellion. A large Senegalese diaspora has increased global awareness of the country's culture, particularly its music. The 2001 constitution gave women property rights for the first time.

POLITICS

Multiparty elections

2001/2006

President Abdoulaye Wade

AT THE LAST ELECTION

National Assembly 120 seats

8% PS
2% AJ–PADS
74% SC
9% AFP
3% URD
4% Others

SC = Sopi (Change) coalition (led by the Senegalese Democratic Party – **PDS**) **AFP** = Alliance of Progressive Forces **PS** = Senegalese Socialist Party **URD** = Union for Democratic Renewal **AJ–PADS** = And Jëf – African Party for Democracy and Socialism

Senegal has been a multiparty democracy since 1981, when, under the then new president Abdou Diouf, the constitution was amended to allow more than four political parties. However, the PS held power from the 1950s until 2000, and its influence has been pervasive. Presidential elections in 2000 marked a political watershed. Diouf was defeated by Abdoulaye Wade of the liberal democratic PDS, the dominant party in the "Sopi" (Change) coalition which went on to win a landslide victory in the 2001 legislative elections.

A new constitution, approved in 2001 by referendum, abolished the Senate and restricts the president to two terms.

WORLD AFFAIRS

Joined UN in 1960

CILSS | ECOWAS | FZ | OIC | OMVG

Maintaining good relations with France, Senegal's main ally and aid donor, is the major foreign affairs concern. Relations with neighboring Gambia, Mauritania, and Guinea-Bissau continue to be a preoccupation.

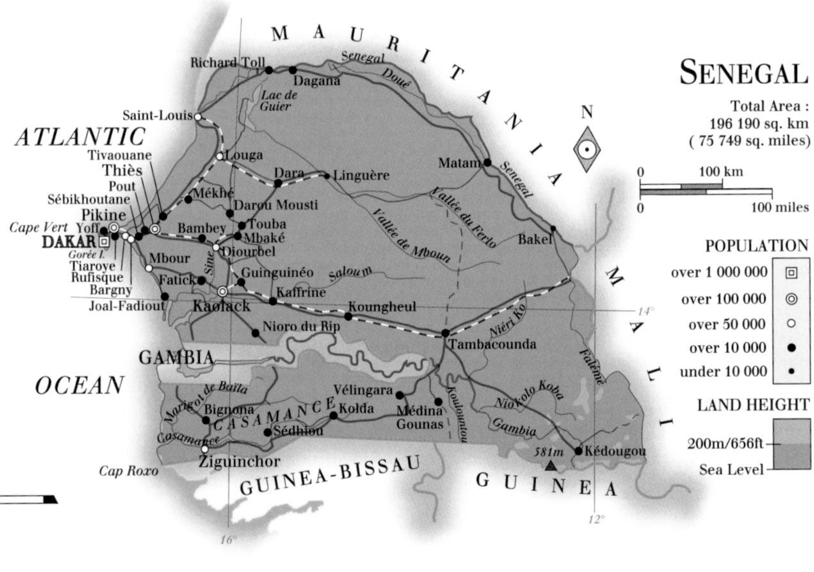
MAURITANIA
MALI
GAMBIA
GUINEA-BISSAU
GUINEA
ATLANTIC
OCEAN
SENEGAL
Total Area : 196 190 sq. km (75 749 sq. miles)
100 km
100 miles
POPULATION
over 1 000 000
over 100 000
over 50 000
over 10 000
under 10 000
LAND HEIGHT
200m/656ft
Sea Level
Richard Toll
Dagana
Lac de Guier
Saint-Louis
Louga
Dara
Linguère
Matam
Bakel
Tivaouane
Thiès
Pout
Sébikhoutane
Pikine
Cape Vert
Yoff
DAKAR
Gorée I.
Tiaroye
Rufisque
Bargny
Joal-Fadiout
Mékhé
Darou Mousti
Bambey
Touba
Mbaké
Diourbel
Mbour
Fatick
Guinguinéo
Kaffrine
Kaolack
Koungheul
Nioro du Rip
Tambacounda
Vélingara
Kolda
Médina Gounas
Bignona
Sédhiou
CASAMANCE
Ziguinchor
Cap Roxo
Kédougou
581m
Senegal
Saloum
Vallée du Ferlo
Vallée de Mboun
Niokolo Koba
Gambia
Falémé
Sine
Koulountou
Niéri Ko
Marigot de Baila
Casamance
Doué
14°
12°
16°
N

AID

Recipient

$419m (receipts) | Down 1% in 2001

Senegal is one of the highest recipients of aid per capita in Africa, mostly from France, the World Bank, and Japan. Aid is used to import 400,000 tonnes of rice annually, but also helps finance a sizable civil service, now being cut back. The IMF approved a three-year, $33 million poverty reduction and growth facility program in April 2003 to support economic reform.

The mosque in Touba, religious capital of the Muslim Mouride sect, which was founded in 1887 in Senegal's groundnut-growing district.

CHRONOLOGY

France colonized Senegal, a major entrepôt from the 15th century, in 1890. Dakar was the capital of French West Africa.

- **1885** Gambia split off from Senegal.
- **1960** Independence under Senghor.
- **1966–1976** One-party state.
- **1981** Full multipartyism restored.
- **2000** Presidency won by Abdoulaye Wade in first ever defeat for PS.
- **2001** New constitution.
- **2002** 1800 die in ferry disaster.

DEFENSE

Compulsory military service

$61m | Down 2% in 2001

France maintains an important naval base at Dakar. The armed forces total 9400, plus a paramilitary force of 5800, but the military has never intervened in politics. Senegalese troops took part in Operation Desert Storm in 1991, and intervened in conflicts in Liberia, Rwanda, and the Central African Republic. They also helped to quell revolts in Gambia and Guinea-Bissau.

ECONOMICS

Inflation 4.2% p.a. (1990–2001)

$4.74bn | 571.2 CFA francs (664.2)

SCORE CARD

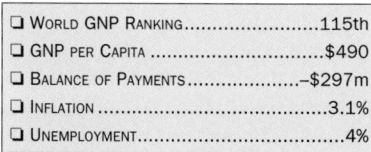

World GNP Ranking	115th
GNP per Capita	$490
Balance of Payments	–$297m
Inflation	3.1%
Unemployment	4%

Strengths

Good infrastructure. Relatively strong industrial sector. Revenue from sale of fishing rights. Dakar port an important west African entrepôt. Tourism potential.

Weaknesses

Few natural resources exploited, other than groundnuts, phosphates, and fish. Access to oil potential of Casamance region hampered by rebellion and poor transportation links.

EXPORTS

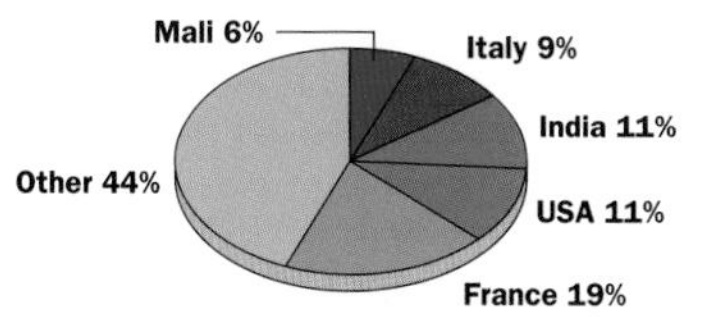
Mali 6%
Italy 9%
India 11%
USA 11%
France 19%
Other 44%

IMPORTS

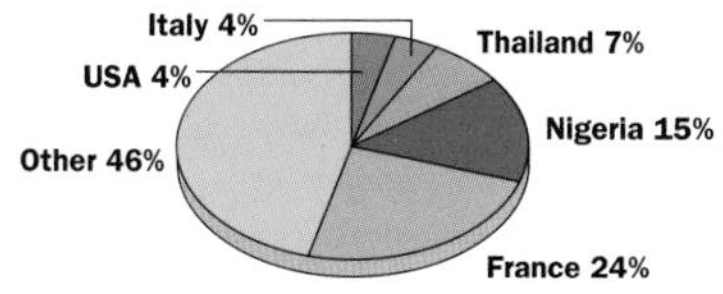
Italy 4%
USA 4%
Thailand 7%
Nigeria 15%
France 24%
Other 46%

EDUCATION

School leaving age: 12

38% | 29,303 students

Illiteracy is Senegal's major educational challenge. There are universities at Dakar and St.-Louis.

HEALTH

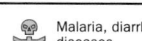

No welfare state health benefits

1 per 10,000 people | Malaria, diarrheal diseases

The state health system is rudimentary. A successful education campaign helps to contain the incidence of HIV/AIDS.

SPENDING

GDP/cap. increase

CONSUMPTION AND SPENDING

10 per 1000 population | 25 per 1000 population

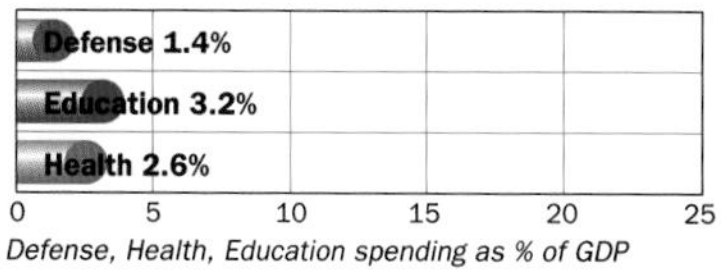
Defense 1.4%
Education 3.2%
Health 2.6%
0
5
10
15
20
25
Defense, Health, Education spending as % of GDP

Wealth disparities are considerable in Senegal, and poverty is widespread. Members of the former ruling PS are the wealthiest group.

RESOURCES

Electric power 235,000 kW

402,202 tonnes | Not an oil producer; refines 17,600 b/d

4.9m sheep, 4m goats, 45m chickens | Phosphates, bauxite, salt, natural gas, oil, marble, iron, copper

Senegal's electricity capacity is largely dependent on imported fuel; cheaper supplies are expected to become available soon from the Manantali Dam in Mali. Initial explorations suggest that oil reserves may exist off Casamance.

MEDIA

TV ownership medium

Daily newspaper circulation 5 per 1000 people

PUBLISHING AND BROADCAST MEDIA

There are 16 daily newspapers, including *Le Soleil*, *Wal Fadjiri*, and *Sud Quotidien*

3 services: 1 state-owned, 2 independent | 8 services: 1 state-owned, 7 independent

The independent media flourished with multipartyism. Senegal had the first satirical journal in Africa with the founding of *Le Politicien* in 1978.

ENVIRONMENT

Sustainability rank: 81st

12% (6% partially protected) | 0.4 tonnes per capita

Senegal, under pressure from neighboring Mauritania, abandoned plans to build a controversial dam on the Senegal River in 2000. The scheme caused concern that traditional farming practices, which rely on seasonal floods, might be disrupted.

CRIME

Death penalty not used in practice

5360 prisoners | Up 21% in 2000–2001

Crime rates are low in rural areas of Senegal, but Dakar and its surrounding shanty towns have become notorious for gang-related crime.

WORLD RANKING

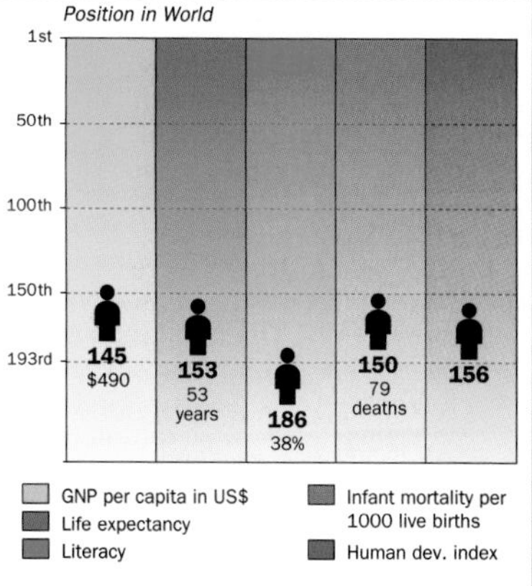
Position in World
1st
50th
100th
150th
193rd
145
$490
153
53 years
186
38%
150
79 deaths
156
GNP per capita in US$
Life expectancy
Literacy
Infant mortality per 1000 live births
Human dev. index

S

Serbia & Montenegro

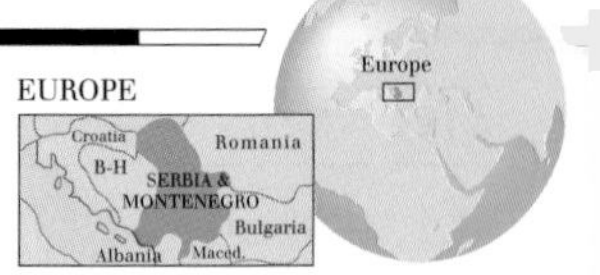
EUROPE
Europe
Croatia
B-H
Romania
SERBIA & MONTENEGRO
Bulgaria
Albania
Maced.

Official Name: Serbia and Montenegro **Capital:** Belgrade **Population:** 10.5 million
Currency: Dinar (Serbia); euro (Montenegro) **Official Language:** Serbo-Croat

1992
1992
Nov 29
YU
+1
+381
.yu

ADOPTING A NEW CONSTITUTION in 2003, Serbia and Montenegro redefined their relationship after their emergence from the wreckage of Yugoslavia. Aid is vital to the recovery of the economy after years of isolation. Serbia, forming the bulk of the country, has a troubled history as a would-be regional power. The machinations of former leader Slobodan Milosevic hastened the end of the former Yugoslavia and precipitated bloody conflicts in 1991–1995 and 1999. Montenegro, the "black mountain" republic, has few resources save for its access to the Adriatic, but is keen to pursue its dream of independence.

CLIMATE

Continental

WEATHER CHART FOR BELGRADE

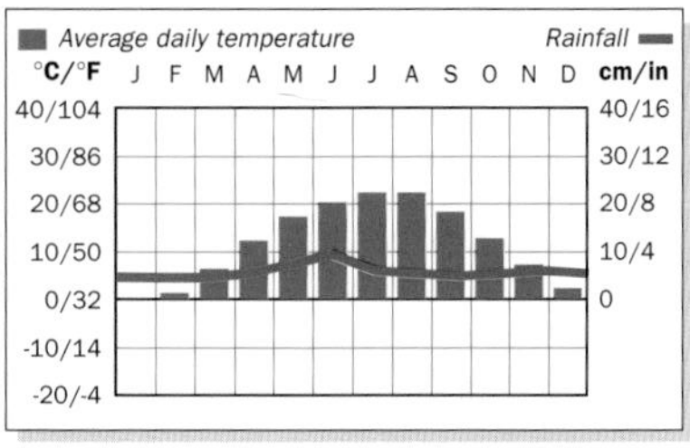
Average daily temperature
Rainfall
°C/°F J F M A M J J A S O N D cm/in
40/104
30/86
20/68
10/50
0/32
-10/14
-20/-4
40/16
30/12
20/8
10/4
0

There are three climate zones. The northern plains are characteristically continental: rainy springs, warm summers, and cold winters. While the southern highlands have colder winters with heavy snowfalls, the Adriatic coast boasts hot summers and milder winters.

TRANSPORTATION

Drive on right

Surcin, Belgrade
1.63m passengers

7 ships
3500 grt

THE TRANSPORTATION NETWORK

28,822 km (17,909 miles)

560 km (348 miles)

4058 km (2522 miles)

587 km (365 miles)

About one-third of railroads are electrified. The rail link to Greece via Macedonia is one of Serbia's main trading routes, and lines through Serbia remain the best link between Budapest and Sofia. For internal travel, trains are cheaper, but slower, than buses. Several daily flights link Belgrade with the airports in Montenegro.

Bridges and railroads were specifically targeted during the NATO bombing in 1999. The bombing of bridges over the Danube at Novi Sad closed the river as a major regional trading artery; with much international assistance it was finally cleared of debris in 2003, but traffic is unlikely to return to former levels.

***The country's stunning scenery** is a potential draw for tourists. Before the 1990s it attracted millions every year.*

TOURISM

Visitors : Population 1:30

351,000 visitors

Up 131% in 2000–2001

MAIN TOURIST ARRIVALS

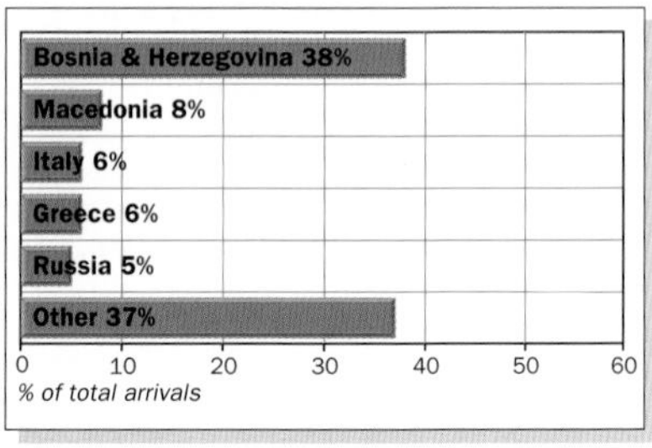
Bosnia & Herzegovina 38%
Macedonia 8%
Italy 6%
Greece 6%
Russia 5%
Other 37%
0 10 20 30 40 50 60
% of total arrivals

Instability, the impact of UN sanctions, and the Kosovo conflict meant that foreign tourism ceased in the 1990s. Serbia has never been a center for tourism, whereas the Montenegrin coast has renowned beaches. In the 1990s they were monopolized by Serbians, particularly by political and criminal elements of the Serbian elite. Hyperinflation and recession kept the average vacationer away.

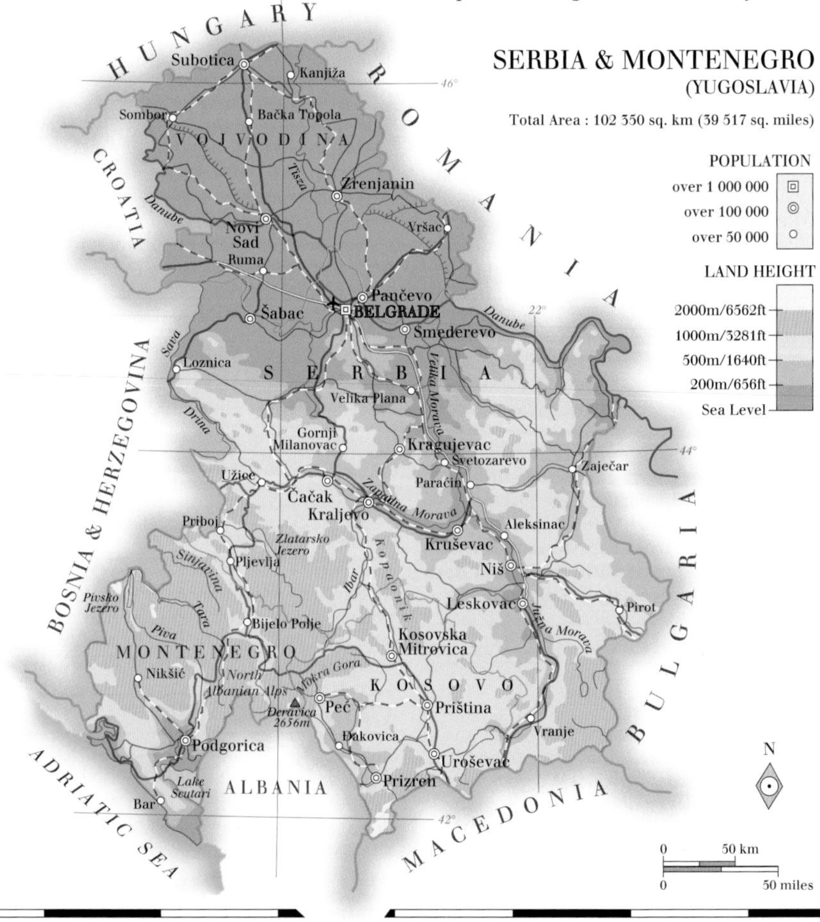
SERBIA & MONTENEGRO
(YUGOSLAVIA)
Total Area : 102 350 sq. km (39 517 sq. miles)
POPULATION
over 1 000 000
over 100 000
over 50 000
LAND HEIGHT
2000m/6562ft
1000m/3281ft
500m/1640ft
200m/656ft
Sea Level
HUNGARY
ROMANIA
CROATIA
BOSNIA & HERZEGOVINA
BULGARIA
MACEDONIA
ALBANIA
ADRIATIC SEA
VOJVODINA
SERBIA
MONTENEGRO
KOSOVO
Subotica
Kanjiža
Sombor
Bačka Topola
Zrenjanin
Novi Sad
Ruma
Vršac
Pančevo
BELGRADE
Šabac
Smederevo
Loznica
Velika Plana
Gornji Milanovac
Kragujevac
Svetozarevo
Zaječar
Paraćin
Užice
Čačak
Kraljevo
Aleksinac
Kruševac
Priboj
Pljevlja
Niš
Leskovac
Pirot
Bijelo Polje
Kosovska Mitrovica
Nikšić
Peć
Priština
Đakovica
Vranje
Podgorica
Uroševac
Prizren
Bar
Danube
Tisza
Sava
Drina
Velika Morava
Zapadna Morava
Južna Morava
Ibar
Tara
Piva
Lim
Sinjavina
Zlatarsko Jezero
Pivsko Jezero
Kopaonik
North Albanian Alps
Mokra Gora
Deravica 2656m
Lake Scutari
N
0 50 km
0 50 miles

PEOPLE

Pop. density medium

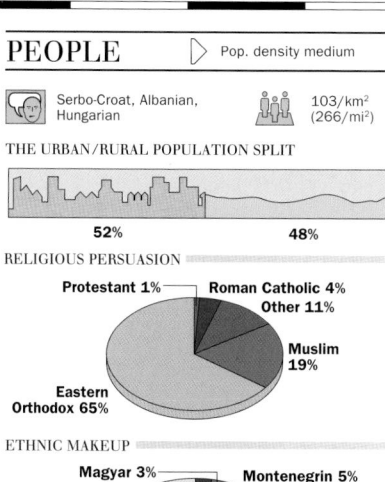

Serbo-Croat, Albanian, Hungarian

103/km² (266/mi²)

THE URBAN/RURAL POPULATION SPLIT

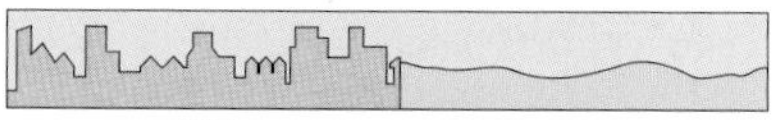
52%
48%

RELIGIOUS PERSUASION

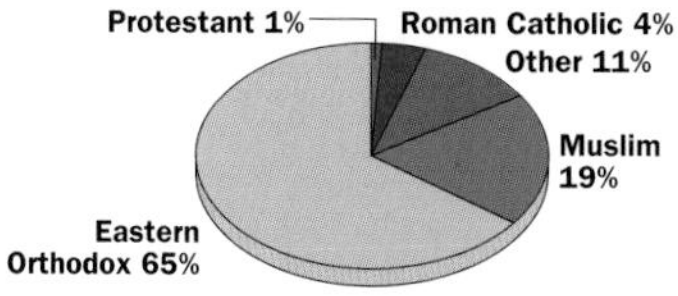
Protestant 1%
Roman Catholic 4%
Other 11%
Muslim 19%
Eastern Orthodox 65%

ETHNIC MAKEUP

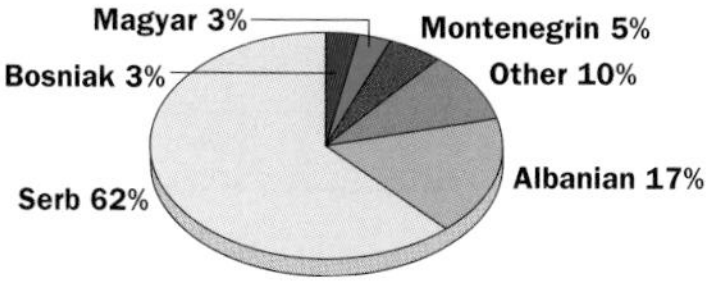
Magyar 3%
Montenegrin 5%
Bosniak 3%
Other 10%
Albanian 17%
Serb 62%

Society was severely shaken by the decade of conflict which followed the collapse of Socialist Yugoslavia. The wars were fueled by ethnic divisions. While the Serbs and Montenegrins share a language and a common religion (Orthodox Christianity), the mostly Muslim Kosovan Albanians have a different culture and heritage. Attempts by Milosevic to suppress Kosovan calls for autonomy directly prompted the 1999 NATO bombing; large migrations of refugees occurred. Albanian nationalism there has alienated the province's minority Serb population.

The Magyar (Hungarian) minority, mainly Roman Catholic, is concentrated in the relatively prosperous northern province of Vojvodina. Limited autonomy was restored in 2002, after economically motivated pressure from within the region. The Muslim Bosniak population has renewed calls for autonomy for their communities in the Sandzak region (shared by Serbia and Montenegro).

POPULATION AGE BREAKDOWN

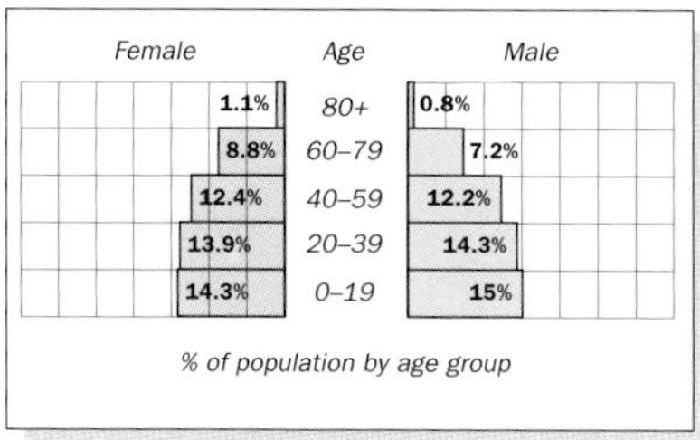
Female
Age
Male
1.1%
80+
0.8%
8.8%
60–79
7.2%
12.4%
40–59
12.2%
13.9%
20–39
14.3%
14.3%
0–19
15%
% of population by age group

POLITICS

Multiparty elections

2003/2005

President Svetozar Marovic

AT THE LAST ELECTION

Assembly of Serbia and Montenegro 126 seats

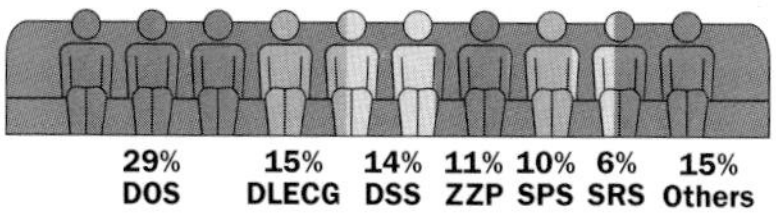
29% DOS
15% DLECG
14% DSS
11% ZZP
10% SPS
6% SRS
15% Others

DOS = Democratic Opposition of Serbia **DLECG** = Democratic List for European Montenegro (led by the Democratic Party of Socialists–**DPS**) **DSS** = Democratic Party of Serbia **ZZP** = Together for Changes (led by the Socialist People's Party–**SNP**) **SPS** = Socialist Party of Serbia **SRS** = Serbian Radical Party

Serbia and Montenegro agreed to a new confederal union in 2003. The separate republican governments maintain real power with control over domestic policy, while a small confederal authority governs overall foreign affairs and defense. Both republics will have the option for independence in 2006.

Profile

The overthrow in 2000 of Serbian nationalist Slobodan Milosevic marked the transition to full democracy. The DOS headed by Zoran Djindjic was swept to power in Serbia and Vojislav Kostunica elected federal president. The promising start was soon marred, however, as relations between the two men soured, particularly over the prosecution of Serbian "war criminals." The Montenegrin government, headed by Milo Djukanovic of the DPS, meanwhile sought to distance itself from Serbia as much as possible. The public remains disillusioned by high-level corruption and the nonappearance of the promised economic recovery.

In Serbia, Djindjic's assassination in 2003 prompted an immediate purge of the Serbian authorities, under Djindjic's replacement Zoran Zivkovic, aimed at removing links to the Milosevic-era security forces held responsible.

Main Political Issues

Kosovo

The withdrawal from Kosovo of the Yugoslav (effectively Serbian) army ended the NATO bombing of Serbia in 1999, and the region came under UN administration. A separate Kosovo assembly was elected in 2001. The ethnic Albanian majority awaits a promised referendum on its future. Local Serbs took part in regional elections, but are wary of Albanian calls for independence.

Milo Djukanovic *hopes to lead Montenegro to independence.*

Slobodan Milosevic, *disgraced former president charged with war crimes.*

WORLD AFFAIRS

Joined UN in 1945

CEI | IAEA | CE | IMF | OSCE

In 1995, mutual recognition among the countries which had constituted the Socialist Federal Republic of Yugoslavia paved the way for the normalization of relations.

The pariah status of the Milosevic regime in the late 1990s was underlined by his indictment by the International Criminal Tribunal for the former Yugoslavia (ICTY) in 1999 and the military action by NATO forces over "ethnic cleansing" in Kosovo. Russia, long an ally of Serbia, shares its Orthodox Christianity and its Slavic ethnicity, and strongly opposed the NATO military action, but backed the settlement proposals required to end it. The inauguration in 2000 of the Kostunica government was welcomed enthusiastically by the West and Russia. The new regime was quickly invited to take the vacant seat in the UN. Its agreement to cooperate with the ICTY has reopened aid channels.

AID

Recipient

$1.31bn (receipts)

Up 15% in 2001

Milosevic's removal was an explicit condition of large-scale Western aid, urgently needed to rebuild the damaged economy. The country rejoined the World Bank in May 2001 and received pledges of $1.3 billion in aid immediately on the extradition of Milosevic.

CHRONOLOGY

The Serbs were defeated by the Turks at the Battle of Kosovo in 1389. Parts of the region were later ruled by the Austro-Hungarian Empire.

- **1878** Independence gained by Serbia and Montenegro at Congress of Berlin.
- **1918** Joint Kingdom of Serbs, Croats, and Slovenes created.
- **1929** King Alexander of Serbia assumes absolute powers over state, which changes name to Yugoslavia.
- **1941** Germans launch surprise attack. Rival resistance groups: Chetniks (Serb royalist) and Partisans (communist, under Tito).
- **1945** Federal People's Republic of Yugoslavia founded with Tito as prime minister (and president from 1953).
- **1948** Tito breaks with Stalin.
- **1951** Farmers permitted to sell produce on free market.
- **1955** Yugoslav–Soviet détente.

S

CHRONOLOGY *continued*

- **1963** Third postwar constitution adopts name Socialist Federal Republic of Yugoslavia (SFRY).
- **1973** Economic cooperation agreement with West Germany. Noninterference accord with USSR.
- **1974** New constitution decentralizes government. Vojvodina and Kosovo given greater autonomy.
- **1980** Tito dies. Succeeded by collective presidency.
- **1981** Unrest among Kosovo Albanians; state of emergency.
- **1985** Serbian intellectuals publish memorandum listing Serb grievances within Yugoslavia.
- **1986** Slobodan Milosevic becomes leader of Communist (later Socialist) Party of Serbia.
- **1987** Wage freeze to combat inflation. Banking system crisis.
- **1988** Belgrade protests against economic austerity. Government brought down over budget failure.
- **1989** 600th anniversary of Battle of Kosovo. Kosovo Albanians protest against Serb police unit; crackdown ends Kosovo's autonomy. Milosevic elected president of Serbia.
- **1990** SPS wins elections in Serbia. Communists win presidency and dominate Montenegro elections.
- **1992** EU recognizes breakaway republics of Croatia, Slovenia, and Bosnia and Herzegovina. Bosnian war begins. UN sanctions imposed. Ibrahim Rugova elected president of self-declared republic of Kosovo. Milosevic reelected president of Serbia, but SPS loses majority.
- **1995** Bosnian peace accord.
- **1996** UN sanctions formally lifted.
- **1997** Concessions after big protests, acknowledging malpractice in municipal elections. Milosevic becomes federal president.
- **1998** Conflict in Kosovo escalates.
- **1999** March, "ethnic cleansing" in Kosovo precipitates mass exodus. NATO aerial bombing. June, withdrawal of Serbian forces and police from Kosovo, and entry of international force, KFOR.
- **2000** Milosevic refuses to accept defeat in presidential election. Opposition candidate Vojislav Kostunica swept to power. DOS dominates elections to Serbian parliament.
- **2001** Arrest of Milosevic, who is subsequently extradited to face war crimes tribunal in The Hague.
- **2002** Low turnouts invalidate republican presidential elections.
- **2003** February, new state of Serbia and Montenegro. March, Serbian Prime Minister Zoran Djindjic shot dead. Svetozar Marovic elected federal president.

S

DEFENSE

Compulsory military service

$609m

Down 67% in 2001

SERBIA & MONTENEGRO ARMED FORCES

1016 main battle tanks (721 T-55, 230 M-84, 65 T-72)	60,000 personnel
4 submarines, 3 frigates, and 31 patrol boats	3500 personnel
103 combat aircraft (MiG-21, MiG-29, Orao 1, Orao 2, Super Galeb G-4)	11,000 personnel
None	

Military capability was specifically targeted for "degrading" by the NATO air strikes in 1999. However, the impact on antiaircraft defenses, heavy weaponry, logistics capacity, and infrastructure was less severe than had first been claimed.

The Serbian military had played a major role in the conflicts in the former Yugoslavia in the early 1990s. Traditionally the center of Yugoslav armaments manufacture, Serbia was able to arm itself – though the need to create money to pay for domestically produced weapons was a major factor in the crippling hyperinflation of that era.

In 2002 the country made its first (modest) contribution to a UN peacekeeping force, in East Timor.

ECONOMICS

Not available

$9.89bn

56.48 dinars (61.51); 0.871 euros (1.013)

SCORE CARD

WORLD GNP RANKING	86th
GNP PER CAPITA	$930
BALANCE OF PAYMENTS	–$596m
INFLATION	40%
UNEMPLOYMENT	30%

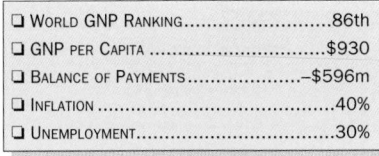

EXPORTS

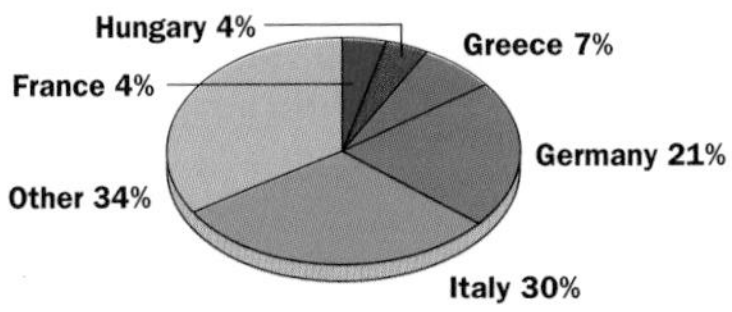
Hungary 4%
Greece 7%
France 4%
Germany 21%
Other 34%
Italy 30%

IMPORTS

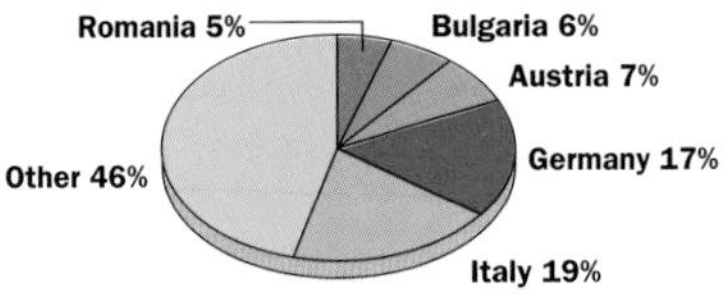
Romania 5%
Bulgaria 6%
Austria 7%
Germany 17%
Other 46%
Italy 19%

STRENGTHS
Return of international aid and investment in 2000–2001. Economic potential of Danube.

WEAKNESSES
Severe damage caused by sanctions and 1999 bombings. Low hard-currency reserves. Outflow of skilled professionals.

PROFILE
The living standards in the former Yugoslavia were among the most advanced of the socialist countries. It has now all but collapsed, although as much as 50% of all activity goes on within the resilient informal sector. The conflicts in the 1990s effectively stalled much-needed economic reform. Sanctions, maintained until 1996 and reimposed more fully in 1999, stifled trade and decimated both the emerging private and the state sectors. Hyperinflation had already pushed the economy to virtual collapse. NATO bombing in 1999 caused extensive damage to infrastructure; the EBRD estimated reconstruction costs at $20 billion over three years. Sanctions were lifted shortly after Milosevic's downfall, and investment prospects were boosted by his extradition and the agreement to cooperate with the ICTY.

ECONOMIC PERFORMANCE INDICATOR

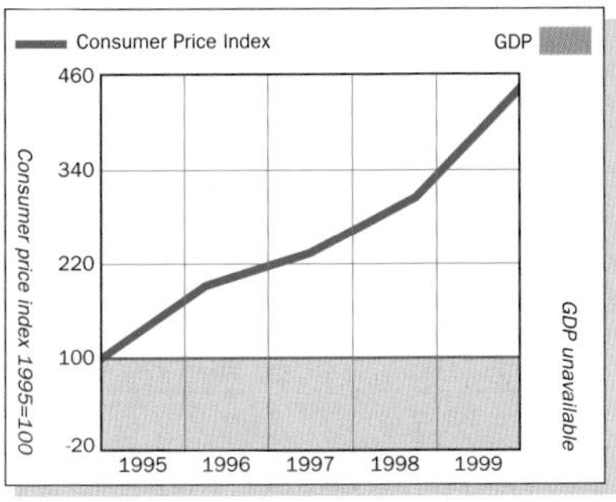
Consumer Price Index
GDP
460
340
220
100
-20
Consumer price index 1995=100
GDP unavailable
1995
1996
1997
1998
1999

SERBIA & MONTENEGRO : MAJOR BUSINESSES

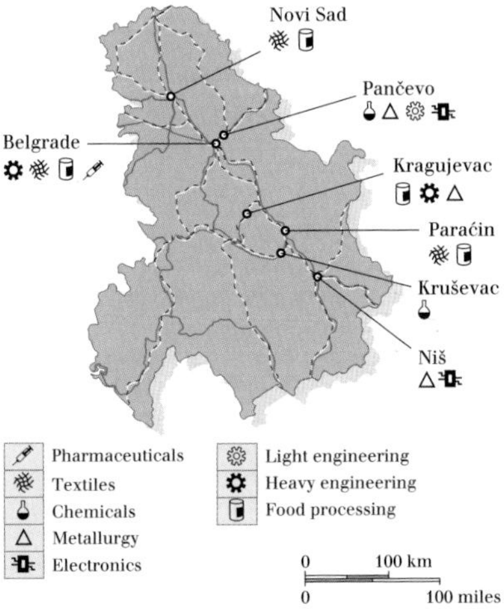
Novi Sad
Pančevo
Belgrade
Kragujevac
Paraćin
Kruševac
Niš
Pharmaceuticals
Textiles
Chemicals
Metallurgy
Electronics
Light engineering
Heavy engineering
Food processing
0 100 km
0 100 miles

RESOURCES

Electric power 11.8m kW

3939 tonnes

20,652 b/d (reserves 83m barrels)

3.61m pigs, 1.69m sheep, 1.36m cattle, 21.1m chickens

Coal, bauxite, iron, lead, copper, zinc

ELECTRICITY GENERATION

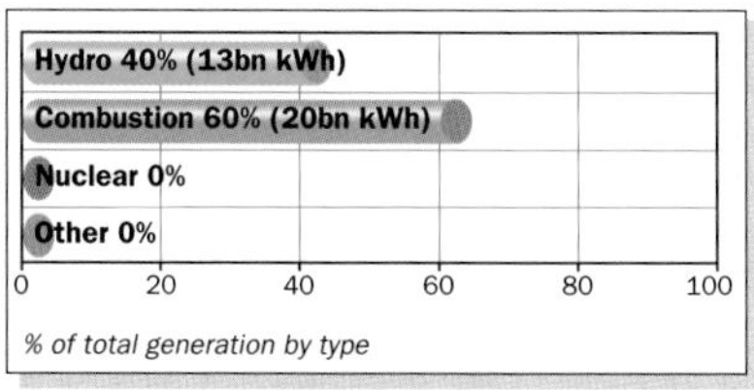
Hydro 40% (13bn kWh)
Combustion 60% (20bn kWh)
Nuclear 0%
Other 0%
0
20
40
60
80
100
% of total generation by type

The country is self-sufficient in coal and electricity production. Vojvodina's oil industry could cater for one-third of total demand, but was badly hit by NATO bombing in March–June 1999.

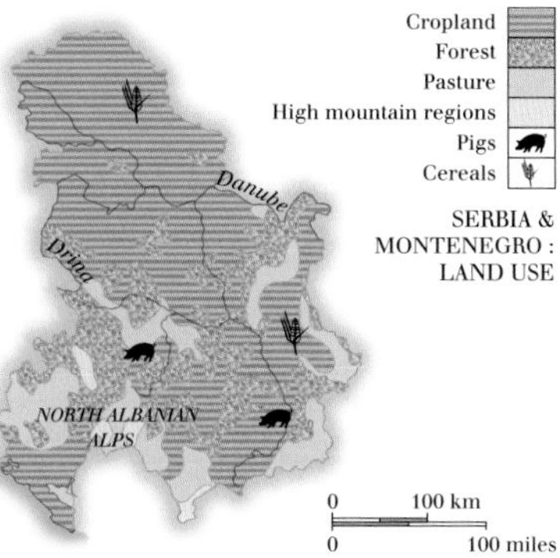
Cropland
Forest
Pasture
High mountain regions
Pigs
Cereals
Danube
Drina
NORTH ALBANIAN ALPS
0
100 km
0
100 miles

SERBIA & MONTENEGRO: LAND USE

ENVIRONMENT

Not available

3% (2% partially protected)

3.7 tonnes per capita

ENVIRONMENTAL TREATIES

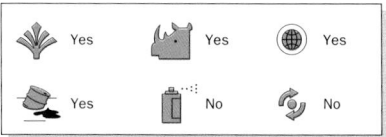

Yes	Yes	Yes
Yes	No	No

Ecological awareness peaked in the late 1980s, when the Ecological Forum was active. NATO bombing of Serbia in 1999 caused extensive pollution of the Danube and raised fears of contamination from dioxins. Depleted uranium from NATO munitions has also aroused serious concerns both in Serbia proper and in Kosovo.

CRIME

No death penalty

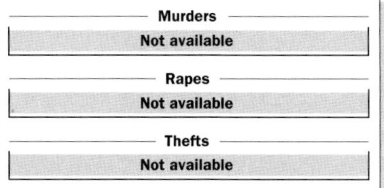

7000 prisoners

High crime levels

CRIME RATES

Murders	Not available
Rapes	Not available
Thefts	Not available

Organized crime was rife under Milosevic. The elite "red beret" police were implicated in the assassination of Serbian Prime Minister Zoran Djindjic in 2003. There has been full cooperation with the ICTY since 2001, and domestic war crimes trials began in Serbia in 2002.

MEDIA

TV ownership high

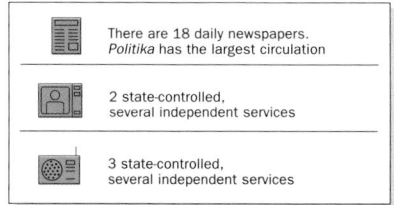

Daily newspaper circulation 107 per 1000 people

PUBLISHING AND BROADCAST MEDIA

There are 18 daily newspapers. *Politika* has the largest circulation

2 state-controlled, several independent services

3 state-controlled, several independent services

The state broadcasting center was a prime target in the October 2000 popular uprising against the Milosevic regime; it had used the broadcast media to control public opinion, while the press was held in check by government control of newsprint. Many journalists supported the opposition. The B92 radio station, when not forced off air, was a beacon of independent reporting. Free media have flourished under the post-Milosevic authorities.

EDUCATION

School leaving age: 14

98%

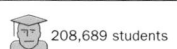

208,689 students

THE EDUCATION SYSTEM

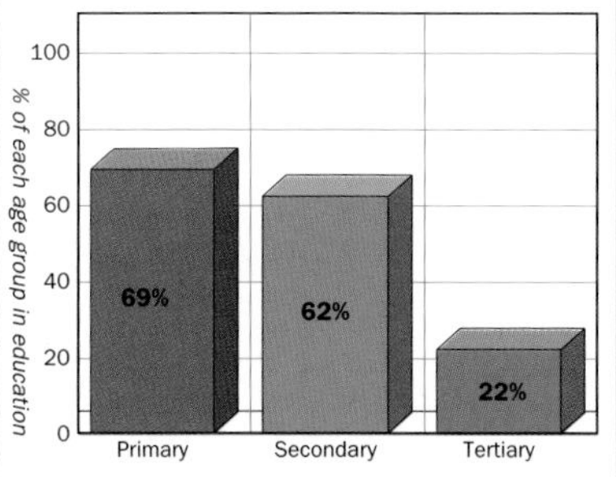
100
80
60
40
20
0
% of each age group in education
69%
62%
22%
Primary
Secondary
Tertiary

Schooling was totally disrupted by the Kosovo conflict in 1999, leaving the education system in crisis; the wealthy go abroad for their education. Literacy rates in Kosovo, where ethnic Albanian schools were closed in 1990, were low even before the conflict. Rebuilding the basic education system is key to reconstruction and reconciliation.

HEALTH

Welfare state health benefits

1 per 500 people

Heart diseases, cancers, cerebrovascular and respiratory diseases

Isolation from former trading partners has affected the quality of the health service, despite the exemption of medicines and medical supplies from sanctions. Social insurance is obligatory for those in employment, but medicines are scarce and costly, and death rates among infants and the elderly have risen dramatically. Health problems can be aggravated by bitingly cold winters.

SPENDING

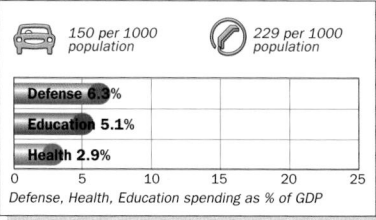

GDP/cap. increase

CONSUMPTION AND SPENDING

150 per 1000 population

229 per 1000 population

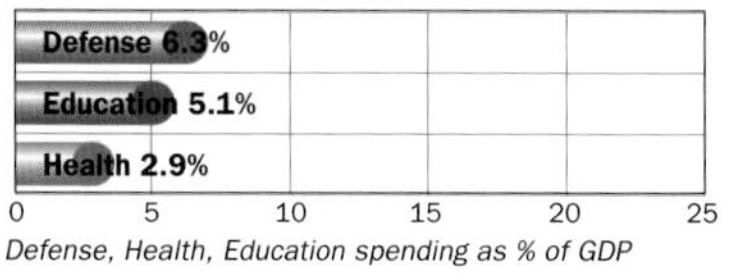
Defense 6.3%
Education 5.1%
Health 2.9%
0
5
10
15
20
25
Defense, Health, Education spending as % of GDP

The country as a whole was seriously impoverished by sanctions; real incomes fell dramatically, yet food prices remained higher than in much of western Europe. Bank collapses in 1992 and continuing hyperinflation in 1992–1994 wiped out dinar savings. One business that did expand was the illegal import of sanctions-busting goods for the few who could afford them – black marketeers and those close to Milosevic.

The lifting of sanctions in 1995–1996 had hardly begun to be reflected in improvements in living conditions when the Kosovo conflict brought further dislocation and hardship in 1999. Even before it erupted, an estimated two-thirds of the population were living below subsistence level. Apart from the desperate situation of refugees and internally displaced families, unsupported pensioners fare worst.

S

WORLD RANKING

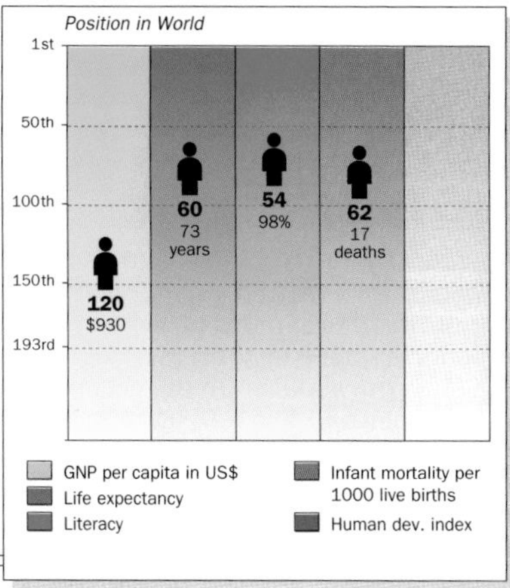
Position in World
1st
50th
100th
150th
193rd
120
$930
60
73 years
54
98%
62
17 deaths
GNP per capita in US$
Life expectancy
Literacy
Infant mortality per 1000 live births
Human dev. index

SEYCHELLES

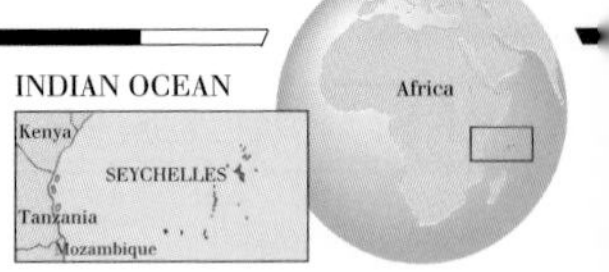
INDIAN OCEAN
Kenya
SEYCHELLES
Tanzania
Mozambique
Africa

OFFICIAL NAME: Republic of Seychelles **CAPITAL:** Victoria **POPULATION:** 80,098
CURRENCY: Seychelles rupee **OFFICIAL LANGUAGES:** French Creole, English, and French

1976 | 1976 | June 18 | SY | +4 | +248 | .sc

THE 115 ISLANDS of the Seychelles, lying in the Indian Ocean, support unique flora and fauna, including the giant tortoise and the world's largest seed, the *coco-de-mer*. Formerly a UK colony and then under one-party rule for 14 years, the Seychelles became a multiparty democracy in 1993. The economy relies on tourism.

CLIMATE

Tropical oceanic

WEATHER CHART FOR VICTORIA

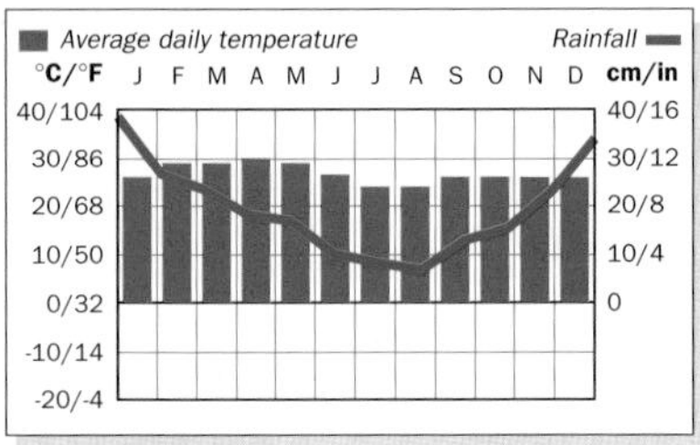
Average daily temperature
Rainfall
°C/°F J F M A M J J A S O N D cm/in
40/104 30/86 20/68 10/50 0/32 -10/14 -20/-4
40/16 30/12 20/8 10/4 0

The islands have a tropical oceanic climate, with only small temperature variations throughout the year.

TRANSPORTATION

Drive on left

Pointe Larue International, Mahé
155,000 passengers

25 ships
33,971 grt

THE TRANSPORTATION NETWORK

176 km (109 miles) | None
None | None

There are airstrips on the larger islands. Buses and roads are being renewed. Victoria's deep-sea harbor is one of the best run in the region.

TOURISM

Visitors : Population 1.6:1

130,000 visitors

Up 4% in 2000

MAIN TOURIST ARRIVALS

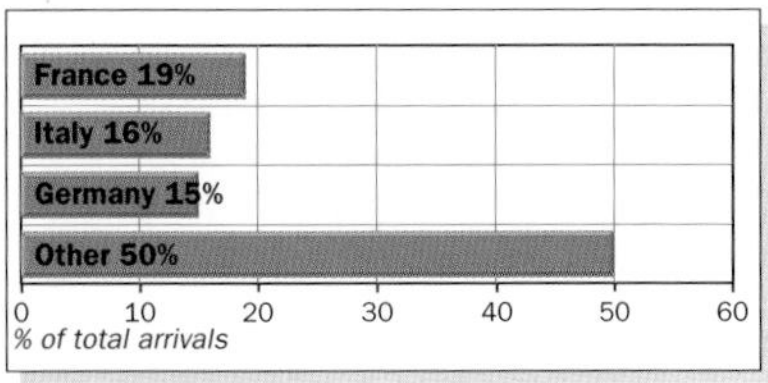
France 19%
Italy 16%
Germany 15%
Other 50%
0 10 20 30 40 50 60
% of total arrivals

Since the international airport was opened at Mahé in 1971, tourism has become the mainstay of the economy, and employs 30% of the workforce. New hotels must comply with laws to protect the islands' beauty and unique wildlife. There is substantial foreign investment.

PEOPLE

Pop. density high

French Creole, English, French

297/km² (770/mi²)

THE URBAN/RURAL POPULATION SPLIT

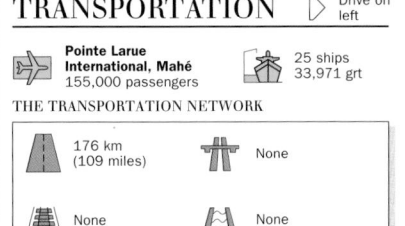

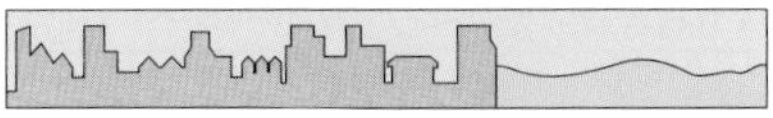
65%
35%

RELIGIOUS PERSUASION

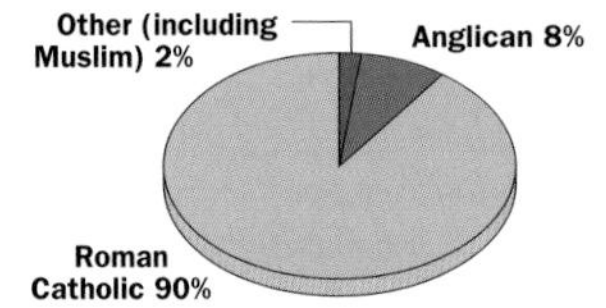
Other (including Muslim) 2%
Anglican 8%
Roman Catholic 90%

The Seychelles islands were uninhabited before French settlers arrived in the 1770s. Today, the population is markedly homogeneous as a result of intermarriage between different ethnic groups. The Creoles are descendants of Africans who were settled on the islands by British administrators and French settlers. There are small Chinese and Indian minorities.

Almost 90% of Seychellois live on Mahé. Population growth has been very low, as about 1000 people emigrate every year. It is conceivable that the transition to democracy could reverse this trend.

POLITICS

Multiparty elections

2002/2007

President France Albert René

AT THE LAST ELECTION

National Assembly 34 seats

68% SPPF | 32% SNP

SPPF = Seychelles People's Progressive Front
SNP = Seychelles National Party

Multiparty elections were held in 1993 after 14 years of one-party socialist rule. President France Albert René has ruled since seizing power soon after independence. Opposition divisions in the 1993 elections allowed him to retain the presidency. His SPPF kept its majority in the 1998 poll, abandoned its leftist ideology, and adopted a plan to develop the Seychelles as an International Trading Zone, with free-port facilities and new industry. René had to beat off a strong presidential challenge in 2001, and the 2002 legislative elections saw a leap in support for the opposition SNP.

WORLD AFFAIRS

Joined UN in 1976

OIF | Comm | COI | NAM | AU

The Seychelles is nonaligned, but is courted by world powers because of its strategic location. It has refused to join the Commonwealth and claims the UK-ruled Chagos Islands. It has trade accords with Indian Ocean states.

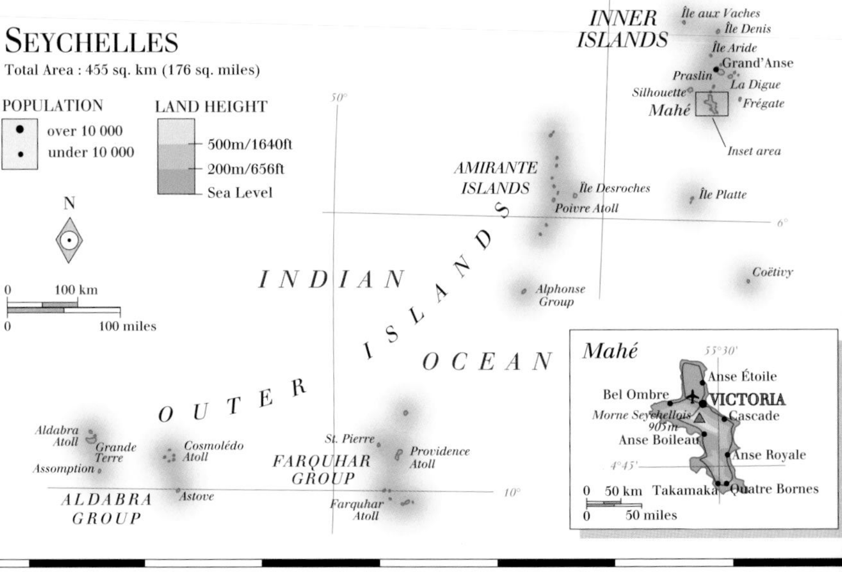
SEYCHELLES
Total Area : 455 sq. km (176 sq. miles)
POPULATION
over 10 000
under 10 000
LAND HEIGHT
500m/1640ft
200m/656ft
Sea Level
N
0 100 km
0 100 miles
INNER ISLANDS
Île aux Vaches
Île Denis
Île Aride
Grand'Anse
Praslin
La Digue
Silhouette
Mahé
Frégate
Inset area
AMIRANTE ISLANDS
Île Desroches
Poivre Atoll
Île Platte
INDIAN
OCEAN
OUTER ISLANDS
Alphonse Group
Coëtivy
Aldabra Atoll
Grande Terre
Assomption
Cosmolédo Atoll
Astove
ALDABRA GROUP
St. Pierre
FARQUHAR GROUP
Providence Atoll
Farquhar Atoll
Mahé
Anse Étoile
Bel Ombre
VICTORIA
Morne Seychellois 905m
Cascade
Anse Boileau
Anse Royale
Takamaka
Quatre Bornes
0 50 km
0 50 miles

S

AID

Recipient

$14m (receipts) — Down 22% in 2001

Multilateral agencies, notably the EU and the Arab Development Fund, support a range of development projects. Recent aid has focused on protecting the environment, transportation links, and rehabilitating Victoria Market. Bilateral aid comes from Japan, France, and other Western donors.

DEFENSE

No compulsory military service

$11m — No change in 2001

The Seychelles has a 200-strong army, and a paramilitary guard. The latter includes the coastguard, which is made up of air and sea forces. The army, set up in 1977, was initially trained by Tanzania, and Tanzanian troops were brought in for three years after a coup attempt in 1981. North Korea provided advisers until 1989.

ECONOMICS

Inflation 3.9% p.a. (1990–2001)

$538m — 5.618 Seychelles rupees (5.618)

SCORE CARD

- ❑ World GNP Ranking........169th
- ❑ GNP per Capita........$6530
- ❑ Balance of Payments........–$114m
- ❑ Inflation........6%
- ❑ Unemployment........9%

Strengths
Tourism. Fish exports, especially shrimp and tuna. Profitable reexport trade. International Trading Zone attracting foreign industrial interest. Copra, cinnamon, tea.

Weaknesses
Growing deficits in early 1990s, caused by drop in tourism, spending on hosting 1993 Indian Ocean Games, and cost of four elections. High debt-servicing costs. Need for food imports, especially for tourist industry. Copra production declining. Reliance on expatriate labor. Foreign exchange shortage. Corruption.

EXPORTS

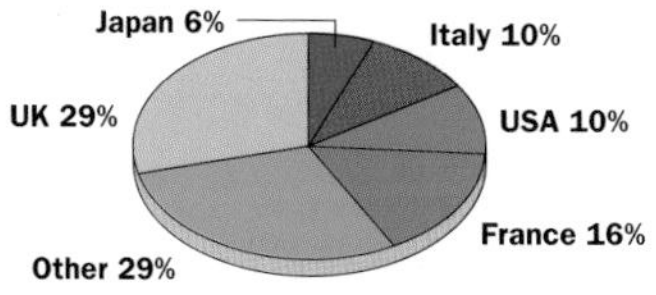
Japan 6%
Italy 10%
UK 29%
USA 10%
France 16%
Other 29%

IMPORTS

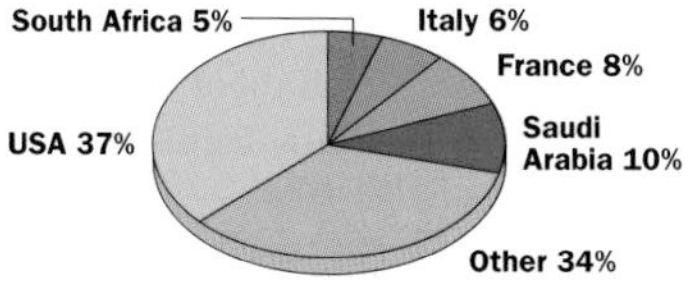
South Africa 5%
Italy 6%
France 8%
USA 37%
Saudi Arabia 10%
Other 34%

One of the Inner Islands, which are home to most of the population. Unlike any other mid-ocean islands, all but two are granitic.

RESOURCES

Electric power 28,000 kW

40,608 tonnes — Not an oil producer

18,500 pigs, 5150 goats, 540,000 chickens — Phosphates (guano), salt, granite, natural gas

Mineral resources are very limited. All fuel is imported; only three islands have electricity. Offshore discoveries of natural gas have spurred a search for oil. Natural habitat and the free trade environment are great assets.

ENVIRONMENT

Not available

111% partially protected (including marine areas) — 2.8 tonnes per capita

The Seychelles has been praised for its commitment to conservation. It has two natural World Heritage sites, and helped promote the idea of whale sanctuaries.

MEDIA

TV ownership medium

Daily newspaper circulation 46 per 1000 people

PUBLISHING AND BROADCAST MEDIA

There is 1 daily newspaper, the government-owned *Seychelles Nation*

2 independent services — 3 independent services

The state broadcasting company has been reorganized and is now ostensibly free of government control. Privately owned periodicals are now permitted.

CRIME

No death penalty

157 prisoners — Up slightly in 2000–2002

Violent crime is rare in the Seychelles. The main concern is the increasing rate of petty theft.

EDUCATION

School leaving age: 15

88% — 1682 students

The 1995–2008 Educational and Training Plan places special emphasis on increasing levels of female enrollment. National Youth Service is mandatory for entry to higher education.

CHRONOLOGY

The French claimed the islands in 1756. Franco-British rivalry for control ended when France ceded them to Britain in 1815.

- ❑ **1952** Political parties formed, led by F. A. René (proindependence) and James Mancham (pro-UK rule).
- ❑ **1965** UK returns Desroches, Aldabra, and Farquhar islands, which are leased to US until 1976.
- ❑ **1976** Independence. Coalition: Mancham president, René premier.
- ❑ **1977** René takes over in coup.
- ❑ **1979** One-party socialist state.
- ❑ **1979–1987** Several coup attempts.
- ❑ **1993** Democratic elections.
- ❑ **2001** René reelected in early presidential elections.
- ❑ **2002** Opposition gain in elections.

HEALTH

Welfare state health benefits

1 per 758 people — Heart and cerebrovascular diseases, cancers

State health care is free but provision is sparse, especially on remote islands. Private medicine is allowed under new social legislation.

SPENDING

GDP/cap. increase

CONSUMPTION AND SPENDING

94 per 1000 population — *261 per 1000 population*

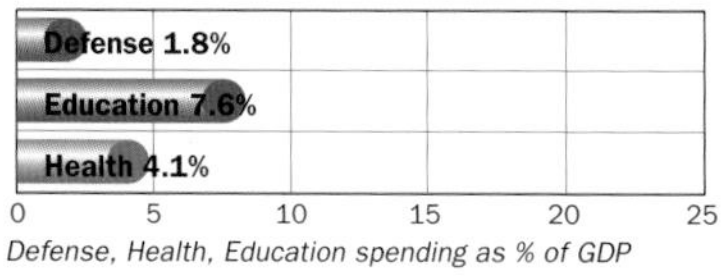
Defense 1.8%
Education 7.6%
Health 4.1%
0
5
10
15
20
25

Defense, Health, Education spending as % of GDP

Living standards are the highest among AU states. There are no slums in the Seychelles, and the state welfare system caters for all.

WORLD RANKING

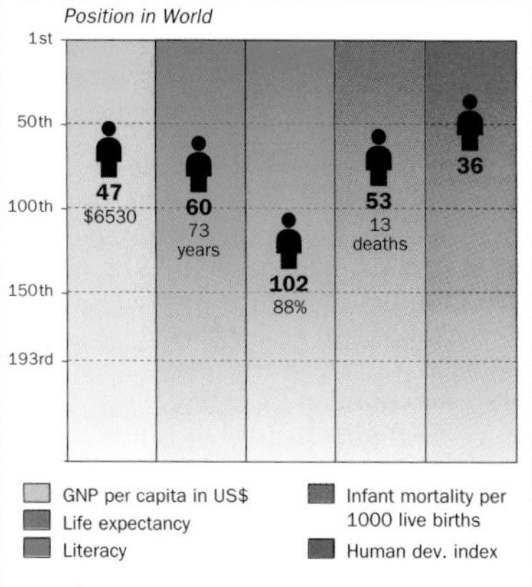
Position in World
1st
50th
100th
150th
193rd
47
$6530
60
73 years
102
88%
53
13 deaths
36
GNP per capita in US$
Life expectancy
Literacy
Infant mortality per 1000 live births
Human dev. index

S

SIERRA LEONE

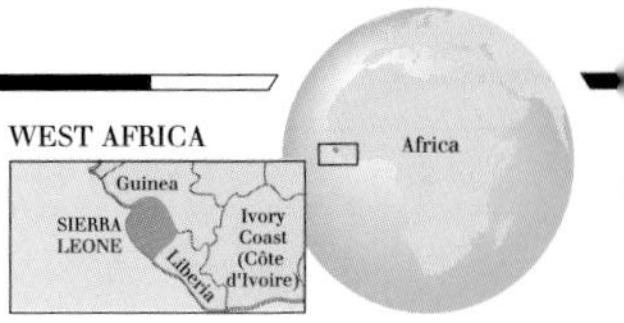
WEST AFRICA
Guinea
SIERRA LEONE
Liberia
Ivory Coast (Côte d'Ivoire)
Africa

OFFICIAL NAME: Republic of Sierra Leone **CAPITAL:** Freetown
POPULATION: 4.8 million **CURRENCY:** Leone **OFFICIAL LANGUAGE:** English

1961 | 1961 | April 27 | WAL | 0 | +232 | .sl

THE WEST AFRICAN state of Sierra Leone was founded by the British in 1787 for Africans freed from slavery. The terrain rises from coastal lowlands to mountains in the northeast. A democratic government took office in 1996 against a background of bloody rebellion. Sierra Leone soon plunged back into a savage civil war. Though a 1999 peace agreement was short-lived, an ECOWAS-brokered accord signed in late 2000 seems to be holding.

CLIMATE

Tropical equatorial/ monsoon

WEATHER CHART FOR FREETOWN

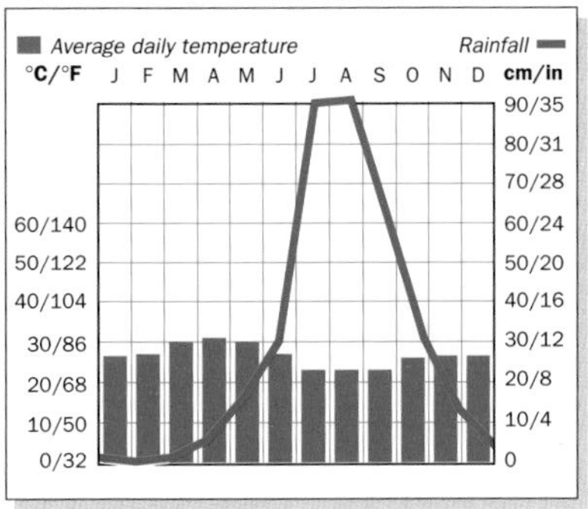
Average daily temperature
Rainfall
°C/°F J F M A M J J A S O N D cm/in
90/35
80/31
70/28
60/140 60/24
50/122 50/20
40/104 40/16
30/86 30/12
20/68 20/8
10/50 10/4
0/32 0

Coastal rainfall can be as high as 500 cm (197 in) a year, making Sierra Leone one of the wettest places in coastal west Africa. Humidity is consistently high – about 80% – during the rainy season. The dusty, northeasterly *harmattan* wind often blows during the hotter dry season from November to April. The northeastern savannas are drier, with 190–250 cm (75–98 in) of rain, and are one of the hottest areas.

TRANSPORTATION

Drive on right

Lungi International, Freetown 84,547 passengers

41 ships 13,148 grt

THE TRANSPORTATION NETWORK

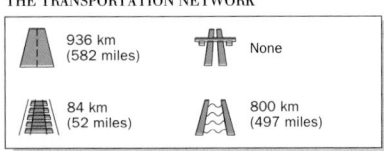

936 km (582 miles)

None

84 km (52 miles)

800 km (497 miles)

Little progress has been made in improving Sierra Leone's road system. The 300-km (190-mile) narrow-gauge railroad was abandoned in 1971 as uneconomic, though 84 km (52 miles) of track still run to the closed iron ore mines at Marampa. Having failed in 1987, Sierra Leone's national airline resumed flights in 1991. A limited ferry service across the estuary is the only link between Freetown and the airport at Lungi.

TOURISM

Visitors : Population 1:200

24,000 visitors

Up 140% in 2001

MAIN TOURIST ARRIVALS

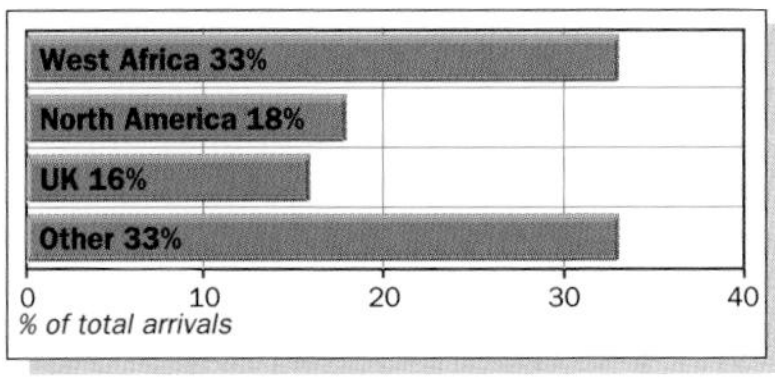
West Africa 33%
North America 18%
UK 16%
Other 33%
0 10 20 30 40
% of total arrivals

Sierra Leone has never attracted many tourists, apart from occasional cruise ship calls. Years of civil war have prevented the development of tourism. Among the chief potential attractions are the beaches along the Freetown peninsula, at present virtually undeveloped.

SIERRA LEONE

Total Area : 71 740 sq. km (27 698 sq. miles)

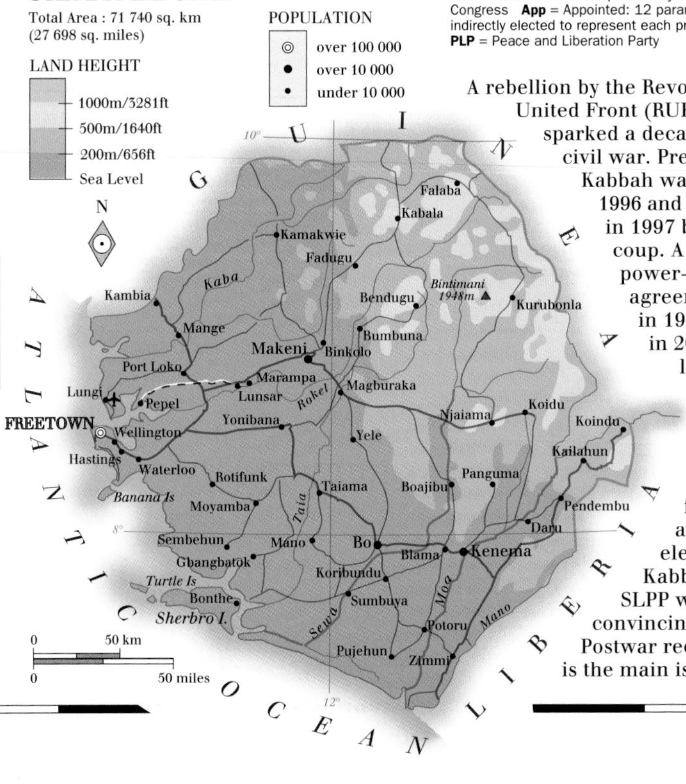
LAND HEIGHT
1000m/3281ft
500m/1640ft
200m/656ft
Sea Level
POPULATION
over 100 000
over 10 000
under 10 000
N
0 50 km
0 50 miles
GUINEA
ATLANTIC OCEAN
LIBERIA
Falaba
Kabala
Kamakwie
Fadugu
Kaba
Kambia
Bintimani 1948m
Bendugu
Kurubonla
Mange
Bumbuna
Makeni
Binkolo
Port Loko
Marampa
Lunsar
Rokel
Magburaka
Lungi
Pepel
FREETOWN
Wellington
Yonibana
Njaiama
Koidu
Koindu
Yele
Hastings
Waterloo
Kailahun
Rotifunk
Panguma
Banana Is
Taiama
Boajibu
Moyamba
Taia
Pendembu
Daru
Sembehun
Mano
Bo
Blama
Kenema
Gbangbatok
Koribundu
Turtle Is
Moa
Bonthe
Sherbro I.
Sumbuya
Sewa
Potoru
Mano
Pujehun
Zimmi
10°
8°
12°

PEOPLE

Pop. density medium

Mende, Temne, Krio, English

67/km² (174/mi²)

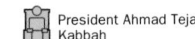

THE URBAN/RURAL POPULATION SPLIT

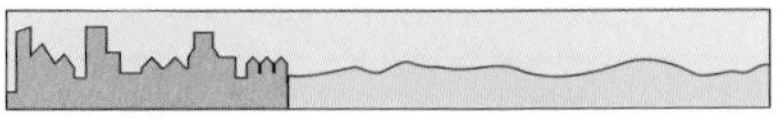
37%
63%

ETHNIC MAKEUP

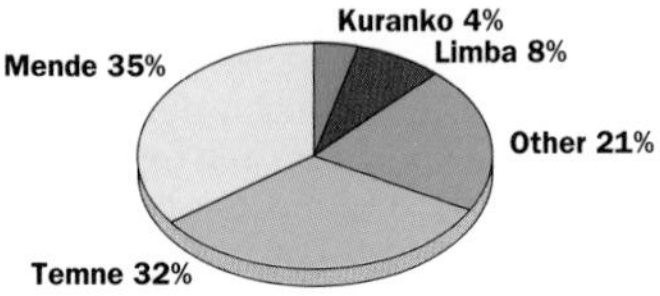
Kuranko 4%
Mende 35%
Limba 8%
Other 21%
Temne 32%

Freetown was founded as a settlement for people freed from slavery. There is a strongly anglicized Creole culture in the capital compared with the underdeveloped and rural interior. An estimated two million people were displaced by the civil war.

POLITICS

Multiparty elections

2002/2007

President Ahmad Tejan Kabbah

AT THE LAST ELECTION

Parliament 124 seats

67% SLPP
22% APC
10% App
1% PLP

SLPP = Sierra Leone People's Party **APC** = All People's Congress **App** = Appointed: 12 paramount chiefs are indirectly elected to represent each province
PLP = Peace and Liberation Party

A rebellion by the Revolutionary United Front (RUF) in 1991 sparked a decade of savage civil war. President Ahmad Kabbah was elected in 1996 and briefly ousted in 1997 by a military coup. A peace and power-sharing agreement, signed in 1999, collapsed in 2000, but a large UN and British force secured a new ceasefire later that year. The RUF failed to gain a single seat in elections in 2002, Kabbah and his SLPP winning a convincing victory. Postwar reconstruction is the main issue.

S

WORLD AFFAIRS

Joined UN in 1961

Comm | ECOWAS | MRU | AU | OIC

UN peacekeepers and British forces turned the tide in the civil war. There are tensions with war-torn Liberia.

AID

Recipient

$334m (receipts) | Up 84% in 2001

The IMF and the World Bank agreed in 2002 to drop 80% of Sierra Leone's debt in return for key reforms. Aid funds efforts to cope with the humanitarian needs of refugees from Liberia, internal migrants displaced by the civil war, and the near-collapse of public services.

DEFENSE

No compulsory military service

$12m | Up 20% in 2001

The UK has been retraining the army since 2000 and has established a new police force. Both sides in the civil war exploited child fighters.

ECONOMICS

Inflation 29% p.a. (1990–2001)

$693m | 2370 leones (2035)

SCORE CARD

❑ WORLD GNP RANKING	160th
❑ GNP PER CAPITA	$140
❑ BALANCE OF PAYMENTS	–$127m
❑ INFLATION	2.1%
❑ UNEMPLOYMENT	Widespread

STRENGTHS

Diamonds, though much of the output smuggled. Freetown port. Some bauxite and rutile production. Palm products.

WEAKNESSES

Legacy of war: disruption to diamond trade, agriculture, and mining sector. Traumatized and untrained youth population. Institutional corruption. Refugees and internally displaced population.

EXPORTS

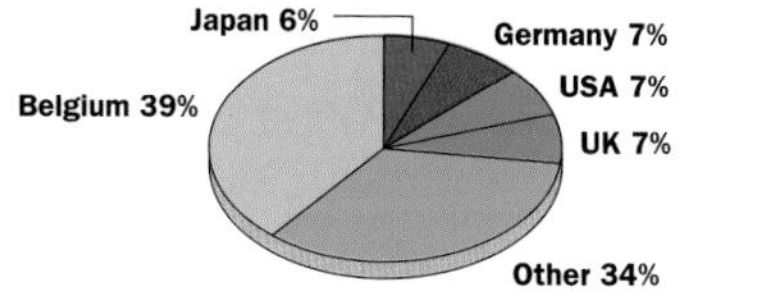
Japan 6%
Germany 7%
USA 7%
UK 7%
Belgium 39%
Other 34%

IMPORTS

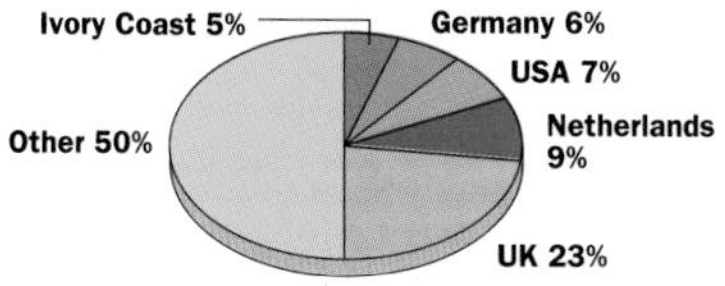
Ivory Coast 5%
Germany 6%
USA 7%
Netherlands 9%
Other 50%
UK 23%

RESOURCES

Electric power 130,000 kW

74,760 tonnes | Not an oil producer; refines 4400 b/d

400,000 cattle, 370,000 sheep, 7m chickens | Diamonds, rutile, bauxite, gold, titanium

Exploiting the large diamond deposits need fresh investment as areas currently being mined become exhausted. The southeast is the most fertile region.

ENVIRONMENT

Sustainability rank: 134th

2% partially protected | 0.1 tonnes per capita

Population pressures and the neglect resulting from years of civil war have depleted the land's productivity.

MEDIA

TV ownership low

Daily newspaper circulation 4 per 1000 people

PUBLISHING AND BROADCAST MEDIA

There is 1 daily newspaper, the *Daily Mail*, published by the government

1 state-controlled service | 1 state-controlled service

A broad range of periodicals is available. The government has promised press freedom, but the Internet is heavily censored.

CRIME

Death penalty in use

Sierra Leone does not publish prison figures | Crime is rising

The civil war resulted in savage atrocities and the mass looting of resources. As a consequence, the UN has initiated the setting up of a war crimes tribunal. International restrictions were imposed on trade in diamonds from war-torn areas, but illegal diamond mining and smuggling remain lucrative crimes.

EDUCATION

Schooling is not compulsory

36% | 8795 students

Freetown has a long tradition of education, and its university, Fourahbay College, became affiliated with Durham University in the UK in 1876. In recent times, its students have often been active in political dissent. Educational provision has inevitably deteriorated over the past decade.

HEALTH

No welfare state health benefits

1 per 11,111 people | Communicable diseases, malaria, malnutrition

Only traditional care is available outside the capital. WHO has ranked Sierra Leone's health care bottom in the world in terms of attainment and efficiency.

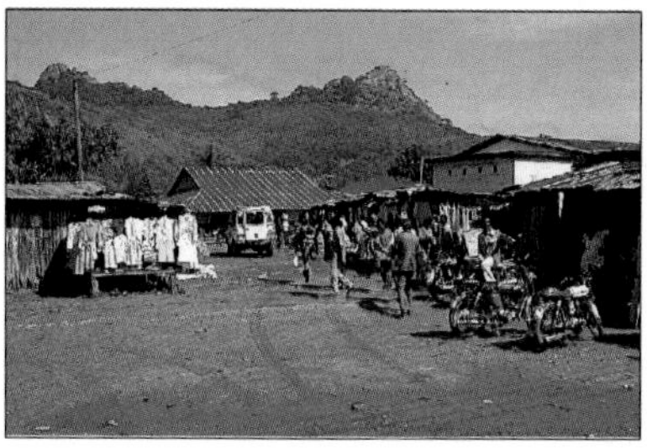

The main street, Kabala. *Sierra Leone is consistently at the bottom of the UN's human development index.*

CHRONOLOGY

Freetown was founded in 1787 and became a British colony in 1808; the interior was annexed in 1896.

- ❑ **1961** Independence.
- ❑ **1978** Single-party republic.
- ❑ **1991** RUF rebellion starts.
- ❑ **1996** Civilian rule restored after 1992 army coup; Kabbah president.
- ❑ **1997** Coup ousts Kabbah for a year.
- ❑ **1999–2000** Power-sharing attempt.
- ❑ **2001** RUF ends insurgency.
- ❑ **2002** Government and UN agree to set up war crimes court. Kabbah and SLPP reelected.

SPENDING

GDP/cap. decrease

CONSUMPTION AND SPENDING

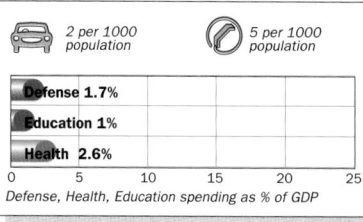

2 per 1000 population | *5 per 1000 population*

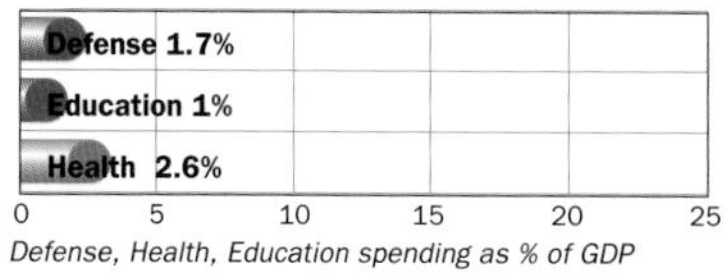
Defense 1.7%
Education 1%
Health 2.6%
0
5
10
15
20
25

Defense, Health, Education spending as % of GDP

In terms of quality of life, the UN has repeatedly ranked Sierra Leoneans as the world's poorest people. Any wealth is associated with political power.

WORLD RANKING

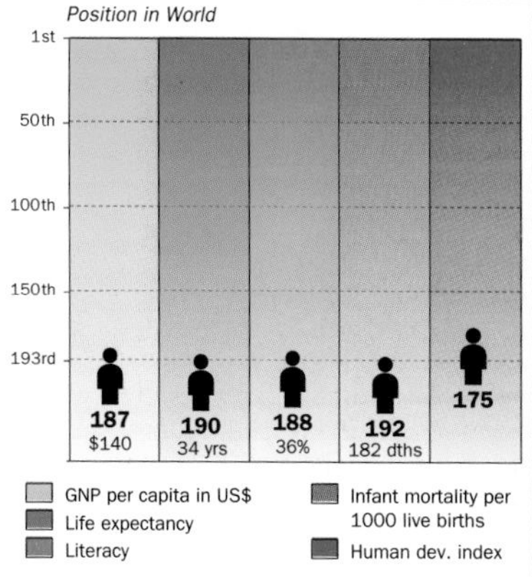
Position in World
1st
50th
100th
150th
193rd
187
$140
190
34 yrs
188
36%
192
182 dths
175
GNP per capita in US$
Life expectancy
Literacy
Infant mortality per 1000 live births
Human dev. index

S

SINGAPORE

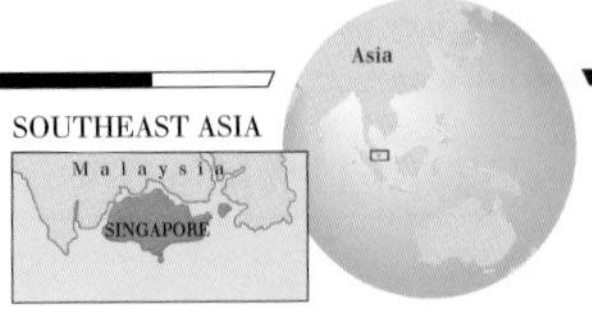
Asia
SOUTHEAST ASIA
Malaysia
SINGAPORE

OFFICIAL NAME: Republic of Singapore **CAPITAL:** Singapore **POPULATION:** 4.2 million
CURRENCY: Singapore dollar **OFFICIAL LANGUAGES:** Malay, English, Mandarin, and Tamil

1965 | 1965 | Aug 9 | SGP | +8 | +65 | .sg

AN ISLAND STATE now linked to the southernmost tip of the Malay Peninsula by a causeway, Singapore ("lion city") was largely uninhabited until the 19th century. In 1819, an official of the British East India Company, Sir Stamford Raffles, recognized the island's strategic position on key trade routes, and established a trading settlement. Today, Singapore remains one of the most important entrepôts in Asia.

CLIMATE

Tropical equatorial

WEATHER CHART FOR SINGAPORE

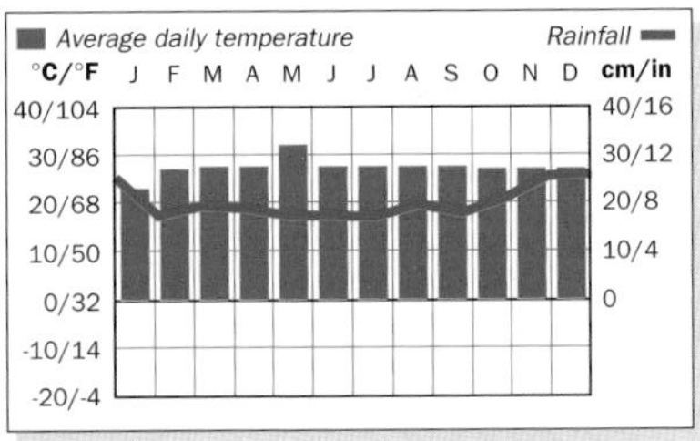
Average daily temperature
Rainfall
°C/°F J F M A M J J A S O N D cm/in
40/104 40/16
30/86 30/12
20/68 20/8
10/50 10/4
0/32 0
-10/14
-20/-4

The only variations in the hot, wet, and humid climate are the airless months of September and March, when the trade winds change direction.

TRANSPORTATION

Drive on left

Changi International 29m passengers

1729 ships 21m grt

THE TRANSPORTATION NETWORK

3066 km (1905 miles)

150 km (93 miles)

39 km (24 miles)

None

The Mass Rapid Transit System (subway), completed in 1991, is among the world's most efficient. Space for new roads has run out and monthly auctions are held to sell certificates entitling people to buy from a quota of new cars. The massive port at Pasir Panjang is being expanded on reclaimed land.

The financial center. *More than a quarter of Singapore's GDP is generated by financial and business services.*

TOURISM

Visitors : Population 1.6:1

6.73m visitors

Down 3% in 2001

MAIN TOURIST ARRIVALS

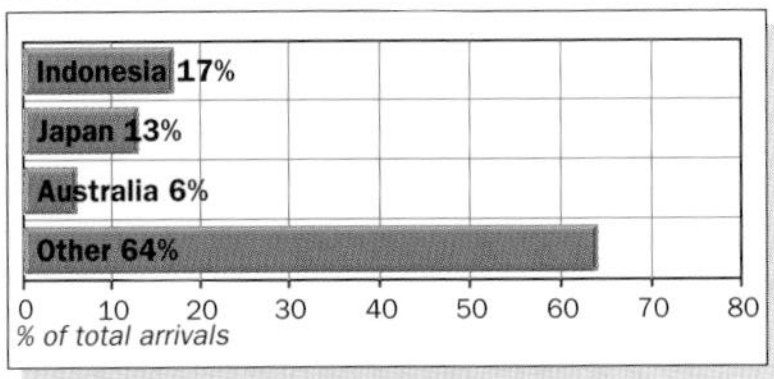
Indonesia 17%
Japan 13%
Australia 6%
Other 64%
0 10 20 30 40 50 60 70 80
% of total arrivals

The buildings of Chinatown, recognized as a picturesque tourist asset, are being restored. A Singaporean consortium was involved in developing a resort on Indonesia's Bintan island, some 45 km (28 miles) across the Strait of Singapore.

PEOPLE

Pop. density high

Mandarin, Malay, Tamil, English

6885/km² (17,797/mi²)

THE URBAN/RURAL POPULATION SPLIT

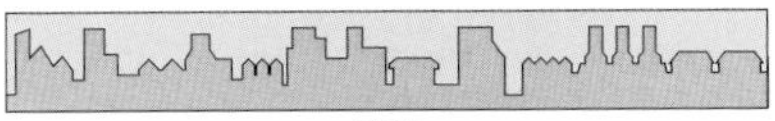
100%

ETHNIC MAKEUP

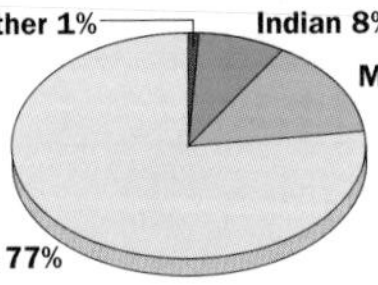
Other 1%
Indian 8%
Malay 14%
Chinese 77%

Singapore is dominated by the Chinese – the old-established English-speaking Straits Chinese and newer Mandarin speakers – who make up almost 80% of the community. Indigenous Malays are generally the poorest group, but today there is little overt ethnic tension. There is also a significant foreign workforce in Singapore.

Long-term plans to stabilize the population structure included the announcement in mid-2000 of cash bonuses for families with more than one child. Society is highly regulated and government campaigns to improve public behavior are frequent.

POLITICS

Multiparty elections

2001/2006

President S. R. Nathan

AT THE LAST ELECTION

Parliament 94 seats

1% SPP
1% WP
87% PAP
10% Nom
1% NC

PAP = People's Action Party **Nom** = Nominated
SPP = Singapore People's Party **NC** = Nonconstituency member **WP** = Workers' Party

In addition to the 84 elected members, up to six "nonconstituency" members may be nominated from the losers with the most votes and nine members may be nominated to ensure a wider representation in Parliament

Singapore is a multiparty democracy, though the ruling PAP effectively controls all parts of the political process and much of the economy. There are plans to create a national ideology ("shared values") based on Confucian traditions. In 1993, Ong Teng Cheong became the first president to be directly elected. The veteran politician, Lee Kuan Yew, prime minister for more than 30 years until his resignation in 1990, still exercises influence.

The PAP retains its grip on power, having given Singapore one of the highest living standards in the world, based on a free-market economy. The first antigovernment rally was permitted in 2001, but the PAP was sure of reelection in November even before the ballot, since fewer than half of the seats were contested. To improve parliamentary debate, the PAP formed an internal opposition faction.

WORLD AFFAIRS

Joined UN in 1965

APEC | ASEAN | Comm | NAM | WTO

Singapore has established diplomatic relations with China, while continuing to maintain close economic ties with Taiwan. It became the beneficiary in 2001 of Japan's first free trade agreement.

AID

Recipient

US$1m (receipts)

Little change in 2001

Aid is not an important issue in Singapore. Japan is the most important bilateral donor.

DEFENSE

Compulsory military service

US$4.28bn

Down 1% in 2001

Despite Singapore's small size, its armed forces have a total strength of over 60,000.

S

ECONOMICS

Inflation 0.9% p.a. (1990–2001)

US$88.8bn

1.761 Singapore dollars (1.7668)

SCORE CARD

- World GNP Ranking..........................38th
- GNP per Capita......................US$21,500
- Balance of Payments..............US$17.9bn
- Inflation..1%
- Unemployment..................................3%

EXPORTS

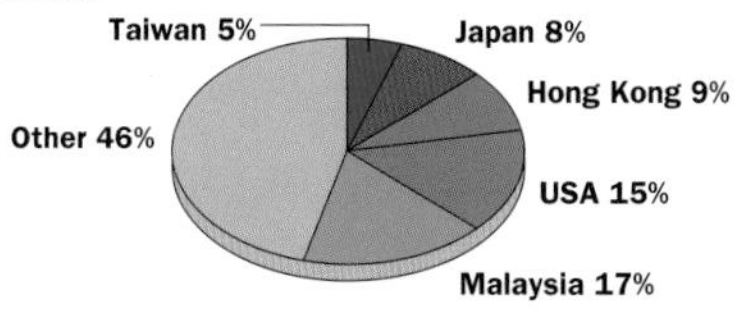

Taiwan 5%
Japan 8%
Hong Kong 9%
Other 46%
USA 15%
Malaysia 17%

IMPORTS

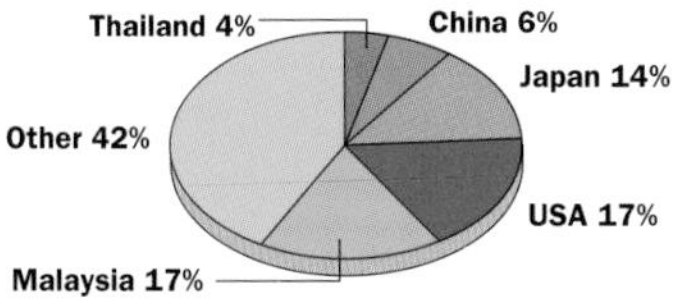

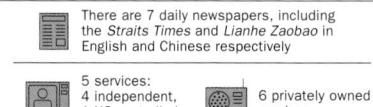

Thailand 4%
China 6%
Japan 14%
Other 42%
USA 17%
Malaysia 17%

Strengths
Massive accumulated wealth is derived from success as an entrepôt and as a center of high-tech industries. Singapore is a major producer of computer disk drives. Huge state enterprises, such as TAMESEK, with over 450 companies, have proved highly flexible in responding to market conditions. World leader in new biotechnologies.

Weaknesses
Dependence on Malaysia for water. Almost all food and energy imported. Skills shortages, notably in engineering. Fluctuations in world electronics market caused recession in 2001. Lack of land.

RESOURCES

Electric power 5.7m kW

10,483 tonnes

Not an oil producer; refines 854,000 b/d

600,000 ducks, 190,000 pigs, 2m chickens

None

Singapore has no strategic resources and has to import almost all the energy and food it needs. Its main resources, on which its wealth as a center of commerce has been built, are its strategic position and its people.

ENVIRONMENT

Not available

5% partially protected

13.9 tonnes per capita

There is a small green belt around the causeway. The streets are largely litter-free – due to instant heavy fines. Chewing gum is now available on prescription after a ten-year outright ban was lifted in 2002.

MEDIA

TV ownership high

Daily newspaper circulation 298 per 1000 people

PUBLISHING AND BROADCAST MEDIA

There are 7 daily newspapers, including the *Straits Times* and *Lianhe Zaobao* in English and Chinese respectively

5 services: 4 independent, 1 US-controlled

6 privately owned services

The government is very sensitive to any criticism. However, it has declared its intention partially to liberalize the local media, as a part of "constructive competition." Foreigners may not own newspapers or broadcasting stations.

CRIME

Death penalty in use

14,704 prisoners

Down 10% in 2000–2001

Crime is limited and punishment can be severe, but incidents of violent crime are rising. The main concern is intellectual piracy.

CHRONOLOGY

In 1819, Sir Stamford Raffles set up a trading post in the village of Singapore; by 1826 it was Britain's colonial center in southeast Asia.

- **1963** Included in Malay federation.
- **1965** Independence.
- **1990** Lee Kuan Yew resigns as prime minister.
- **1993** Ong Teng Cheong first directly elected president.
- **2001** PAP, in power since independence, wins elections.

EDUCATION

Schooling is not compulsory

93%

124,180 students

Schooling is not compulsory, but attendance is high. Education is seen as the key to a good salary, especially among the Chinese community.

HEALTH

Welfare state health benefits

1 per 741 people

Cancers, respiratory, heart, and cerebro-vascular diseases

Singapore has an efficient modern health system. There are incentives to ensure the continuation of the extended family, so that the elderly are cared for at home.

SPENDING

GDP/cap. increase

CONSUMPTION AND SPENDING

98 per 1000 population

471 per 1000 population

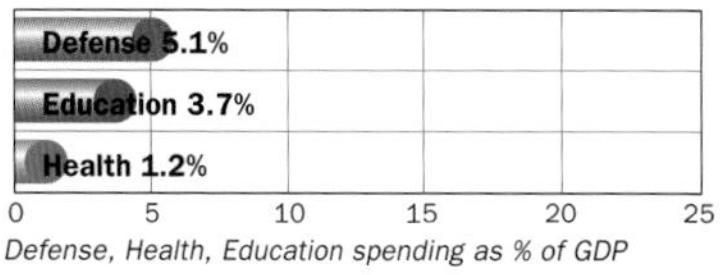

Defense 5.1%
Education 3.7%
Health 1.2%
0
5
10
15
20
25
Defense, Health, Education spending as % of GDP

The 2001 "Singapore Share" scheme promises to give Singaporeans a share in the country's economy.

WORLD RANKING

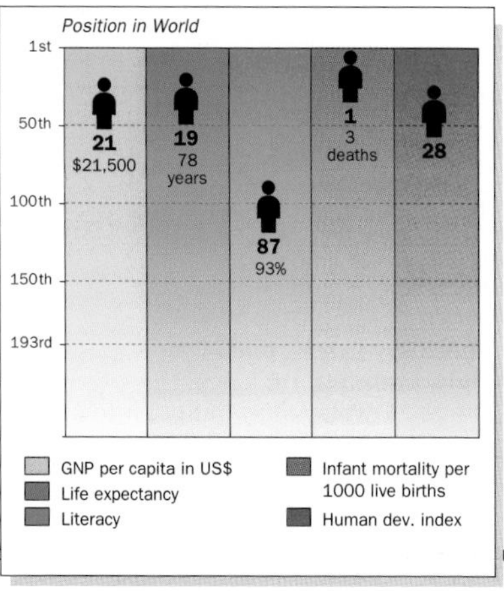

Position in World
1st
50th
100th
150th
193rd
21
$21,500
19
78 years
87
93%
1
3 deaths
28
GNP per capita in US$
Life expectancy
Literacy
Infant mortality per 1000 live births
Human dev. index

SINGAPORE

Total Area : 693 sq. km (267 sq. miles)

MALAYSIA
Johore Strait
Causeway
Sembawang
Sarimbun Res.
Lim Chu Kang
Murai Res.
Kranji Res.
Seletar Res.
Sungai Seletar Res.
Punggol
Pulau Ubin
Pulau Tekong Kechil
Pulau Tekong Res.
Pulau Tekong
Serangoon Harbour
Serangoon
Changi
Changi International Airport
Bukit Panjang
Bukit Panjang
Bukit Timah 163m
Upper Peirce Res.
MacRitchie Res.
Kallang
Bedok Res.
Poyan Res.
Choa Chu Kang
Tengeh Res.
Jurong
Jurong Lake
Jurong Town
Bukit Timah
Jurong Industrial Estate
Pandan Res.
Queenstown
City
Katong
Pulau Pesek
Pulau Pesek Kechil
Pulau Ayer Chawan
Pulau Sakra
Pulau Merlimau
Pulau Seraya
Pulau Retan Laut
Pasir Panjang
Telok Blangah
Singapore
Keppel Harbour
Pulau Ayer Merbau
Pulau Brani
Sentosa
Selat Pandan
Pulau Busing
Pulau Bukum
Pulau Hantu
Pulau Sudong
Pulau Pawai
Pulau Semakau
Pulau Tembakul
Pulau Sakijang Pelepah
Pulau Sakijang Bendera
Pulau Sebarok
Pulau Senang
Strait of Singapore
Johore Strait
SOUTH CHINA SEA
1°20'
103°40'
103°50'
104°
0 5 km
0 5 miles
N
Urban Areas
Open Areas
Nature Reserve

S

SLOVAKIA

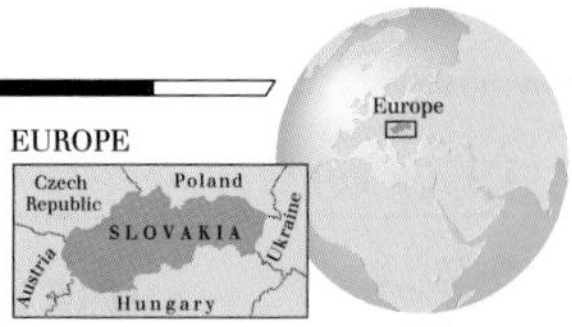
EUROPE
Europe
Czech Republic
Poland
SLOVAKIA
Ukraine
Austria
Hungary

OFFICAL NAME: Slovak Republic **CAPITAL:** Bratislava
POPULATION: 5.4 million **CURRENCY:** Slovak koruna **OFFICAL LANGUAGE:** Slovak

1993 | 1993 | Oct 1 | SK | +1 | +421 | .sk

DOMINATED FOR 900 YEARS by neighboring Hungary, Slovakia spent much of the 20th century as the less developed half of communist Czechoslovakia. An independent democracy since 1993, Slovakia has struggled to create a modern market-led economy, but is now among the ten countries set to join the EU in its next wave of expansion in 2004.

Levoča, in northeastern Slovakia, dates from the 13th century and still retains its medieval street plan and town walls.

CLIMATE

Continental

WEATHER CHART FOR BRATISLAVA

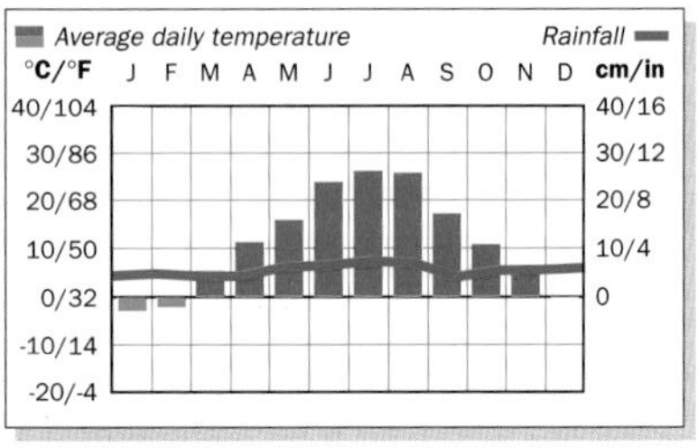
Average daily temperature
Rainfall
°C/°F
J F M A M J J A S O N D
cm/in
40/104
30/86
20/68
10/50
0/32
-10/14
-20/4
40/16
30/12
20/8
10/4
0

Slovakia has a continental climate. Snowfalls are heavy in winter, while summers are moderately warm.

TRANSPORTATION

Drive on right

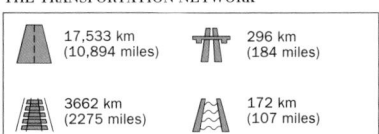

Milan Rastislav Stefanik, Bratislava 303,971 passengers

Has no fleet

THE TRANSPORTATION NETWORK

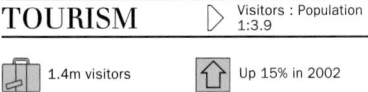

17,533 km (10,894 miles)

296 km (184 miles)

3662 km (2275 miles)

172 km (107 miles)

The River Danube is a vital artery. Trains are cheap and efficient. Buses and trams are the mainstay of urban transport.

TOURISM

Visitors : Population 1:3.9

1.4m visitors

Up 15% in 2002

MAIN TOURIST ARRIVALS

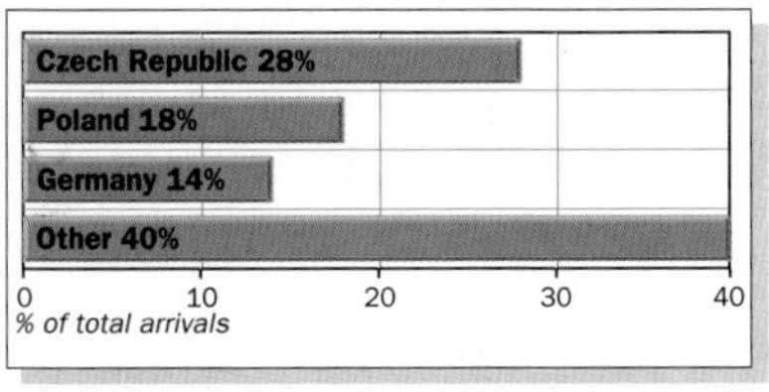
Czech Republic 28%
Poland 18%
Germany 14%
Other 40%
0
10
20
30
40
% of total arrivals

The High Tatras, one of the smallest high-mountain ranges in the world, and the Vrátna valley in the Little Tatras draw hikers and skiers. Tourists also visit Bratislava's castle and old city, and the many thermal-spring health spas.

PEOPLE

Pop. density medium

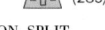

Slovak, Hungarian, Czech

110/km² (285/mi²)

THE URBAN/RURAL POPULATION SPLIT

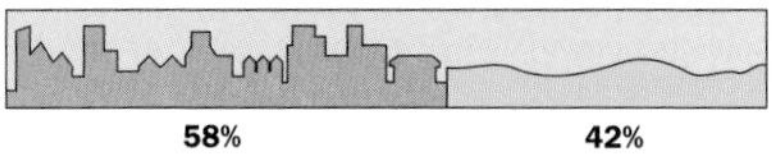
58%
42%

RELIGIOUS PERSUASION

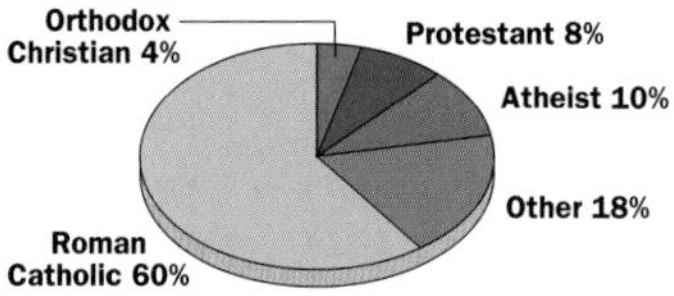
Orthodox Christian 4%
Protestant 8%
Atheist 10%
Other 18%
Roman Catholic 60%

Slovaks dominate society, but 11% of the population is Magyar, and there is a significant Roma minority which faces discrimination. The Magyar community, backed by Hungary, seeks protection for its language and culture. Tensions lessened in 1998 when its main political voice, the Hungarian Coalition Pary, joined Dzurinda's government. There were 300,000 Slovaks living in Czech lands in 1993. Dual citizenship is now permitted.

POLITICS

Multiparty elections

2002/2006

President Rudolf Schuster

AT THE LAST ELECTION

National Council of the Slovak Republic 150 seats

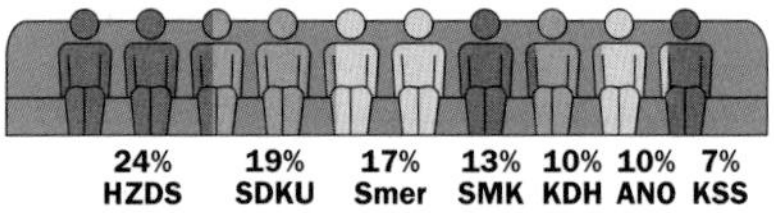
24% HZDS
19% SDKU
17% Smer
13% SMK
10% KDH
10% ANO
7% KSS

HZDS = Movement for a Democratic Slovakia
SDKU = Slovak Democratic and Christian Union
Smer = Direction **SMK** = Hungarian Coalition Party
KDH = Christian Democratic Movement **ANO** = New Civic Alliance **KSS** = Slovak Communist Party

The political ambitions of Slovak leader Vladimir Meciar were a major factor in the separation of the two halves of the former Czechoslovakia in 1993. The populist Meciar dominated Slovak politics until 1998, but clashed repeatedly with President Michal Kovac, both of them members of the HZDS.

Though the HZDS has remained the largest party in the National Council, it has been unable to form a government since elections in 1998. Instead Mikulas Dzurinda of the Democratic Coalition (now the SDKU) has led a broad center-right coalition. Meciar was again frustrated in 1999 when he lost the first direct presidential election to the pro-Western Rudolf Schuster.

The SDKU formed a new four-party coalition after the 2002 election, despite a strong showing again by the HZDS and by the new populist Smer party.

WORLD AFFAIRS

Joined UN in 1993

CE | CEFTA | OECD | EAPC | OSCE

Slovakia adopted a distinctly pro-Russian stance under Meciar. Since his defeat in 1998 it has turned to the West. It joined the OECD in 2000, and expects membership of both the EU and NATO in 2004.

AID

Recipient

$164m (receipts)

Up 45% in 2001

Foreign aid fell after the mid-1990s, but EU programs are now in place in preparation for EU membership.

DEFENSE

Compulsory military service

$386m

Up 13% in 2001

The Slovak armed forces include some 13,600 conscripts at any one time. Prime Minister Dzurinda, in office since late 1998, reversed Meciar's pro-Russian defense policies.

RESOURCES

Electric power 7.8m kW

3142 tonnes

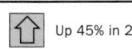

1323 b/d (reserves 7.2m barrels)

1.55m pigs, 607,835 cattle, 15m chickens

Coal, lignite, gas, oil, antimony, copper, iron, mercury, zinc

Slovakia's two nuclear plants, Mochovce and Jaslovske Bohunice, generated almost 60% of electricity in 2001.

S

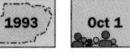

SLOVAKIA

Total Area : 48 845 sq. km
(18 859 sq. miles)

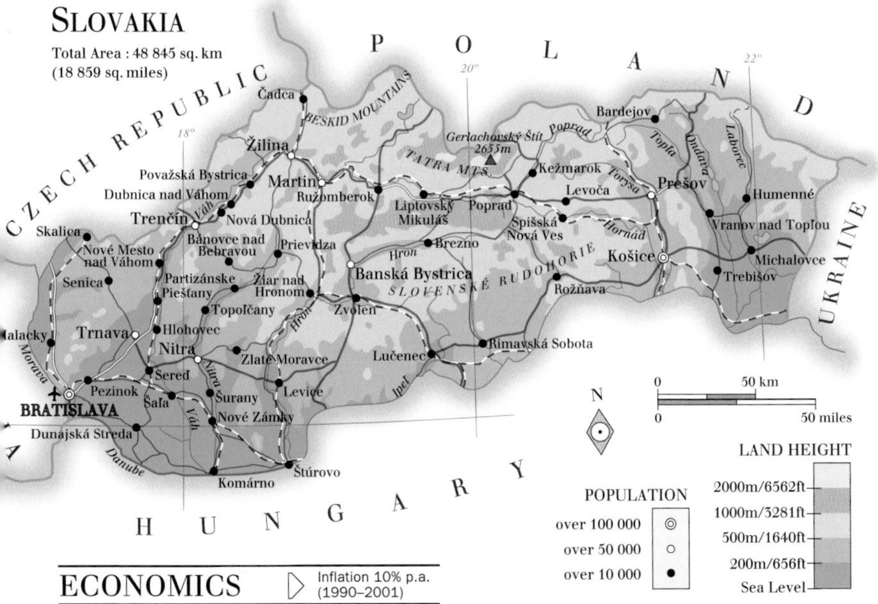
POLAND
CZECH REPUBLIC
UKRAINE
HUNGARY
Čadca
Žilina
Považská Bystrica
Dubnica nad Váhom
Trenčín
Skalica
Nové Mesto nad Váhom
Senica
Partizánske
Piešťany
Bánovce nad Bebravou
Nová Dubnica
Martin
Ružomberok
Prievidza
Žiar nad Hronom
Topoľčany
Hlohovec
Trnava
Nitra
Sered
Pezinok
Šaľa
BRATISLAVA
Dunajská Streda
Šurany
Nové Zámky
Levice
Komárno
Štúrovo
Zlaté Moravce
Zvolen
Banská Bystrica
Brezno
Liptovský Mikuláš
Poprad
Spišská Nová Ves
Kežmarok
Levoča
Gerlachovský Štít 2655m
TATRA MTS
BESKID MOUNTAINS
SLOVENSKÉ RUDOHORIE
Bardejov
Prešov
Humenné
Vranov nad Topľou
Michalovce
Trebišov
Košice
Rožňava
Rimavská Sobota
Lučenec
Danube
Váh
Hron
Morava
Hornád
Poprad
Topľa
Ondava
Laborec
Torysa
Ipeľ
Nitra
N
0 50 km
0 50 miles
POPULATION
over 100 000
over 50 000
over 10 000
LAND HEIGHT
2000m/6562ft
1000m/3281ft
500m/1640ft
200m/656ft
Sea Level

ECONOMICS

Inflation 10% p.a. (1990–2001)

$20.3bn

36.21 Slovak koruny (44.55)

SCORE CARD

- ❑ WORLD GNP RANKING........................60th
- ❑ GNP PER CAPITA..........................$3760
- ❑ BALANCE OF PAYMENTS..................–$694m
- ❑ INFLATION.......................................7.3%
- ❑ UNEMPLOYMENT................................19%

STRENGTHS

Expansion of manufacturing, especially in Bratislava and surrounding area. Increase in foreign investment and relative success of privatization program. Growth in exports to EU and promise of stability through membership. Potential for tourism, particularly skiing in the Tatra Mountains.

WEAKNESSES

High foreign indebtedness. Growing unemployment. Dependence on foreign trade makes the economy vulnerable to global recession. Heavy industry struggles with poor productivity. Much poorer eastern region. Collapse of "pyramid" investor schemes in 2002.

EXPORTS

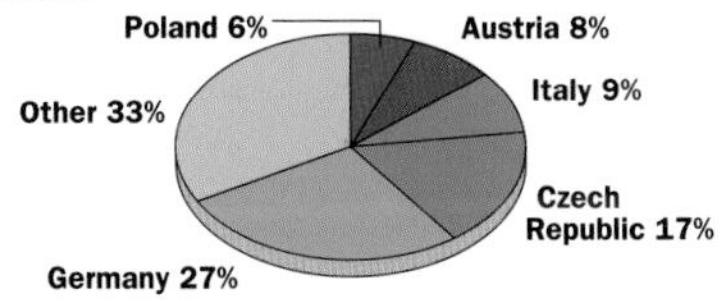
Poland 6%
Austria 8%
Italy 9%
Czech Republic 17%
Germany 27%
Other 33%

IMPORTS

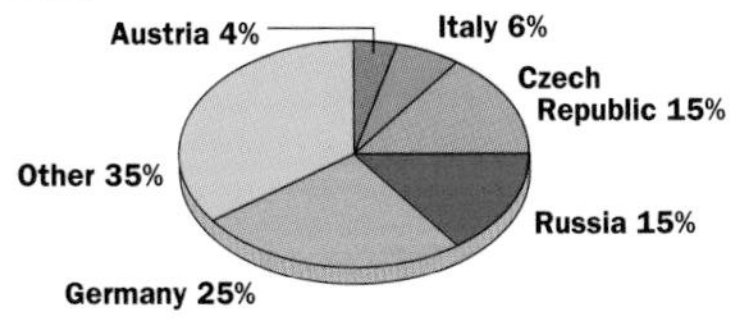
Austria 4%
Italy 6%
Czech Republic 15%
Russia 15%
Germany 25%
Other 35%

ENVIRONMENT

Sustainability rank: 14th

76% (61% partially protected)

7.7 tonnes per capita

The Gabcikovo Dam and the Bohunice nuclear reactors, now scheduled for partial closure, have provoked criticism.

MEDIA

TV ownership high

Daily newspaper circulation 131 per 1000 people

PUBLISHING AND BROADCAST MEDIA

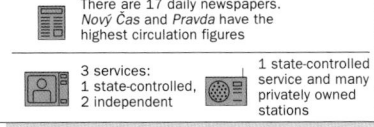

There are 17 daily newspapers. *Nový Čas* and *Pravda* have the highest circulation figures

3 services: 1 state-controlled, 2 independent

1 state-controlled service and many privately owned stations

The state news agency TASR, accused of lacking objectivity and depending on government funding, resisted the emergence of independent rival SITA.

CRIME

No death penalty

7509 prisoners

Down 3% in 1999–2001

Organized crime has increased rapidly in recent years, as has "white collar crime" such as business fraud. A new law to control money laundering took effect in 2001. A former economics minister accused of embezzlement was murdered in 1999.

EDUCATION

School leaving age: 15

99%

143,909 students

Schooling now draws on pre-1939 Slovak traditions but it is not adequately resourced, especially in rural areas. There is a modern university in Bratislava.

CHRONOLOGY

Once part of the Austro-Hungarian Empire, Slovakia and the Czech Lands formed the Republic of Czechoslovakia in 1918.

- ❑ **1939–1945** Separate Slovak state under pro-Nazi Jozef Tiso.
- ❑ **1945** Czechoslovak state restored.
- ❑ **1947** Communists seize power.
- ❑ **1968** "Prague Spring" ended by Warsaw pact invasion.
- ❑ **1989** "Velvet Revolution."
- ❑ **1993** 1st January, separate Slovak and Czech states established.
- ❑ **1994** HZDS election victory.
- ❑ **1998** Broad-based coalition under Dzurinda wins general election.
- ❑ **1999** Rudolf Schuster defeats Meciar in direct presidential poll.
- ❑ **2002** Dzurinda coalition reelected. EU approves membership for 2004.

HEALTH

Welfare state health benefits

1 per 311 people

Heart diseases, cancers, cerebro-vascular disease

Rising demand and costs are straining the health service severely. Restoring viability is now a government priority.

SPENDING

GDP/cap. increase

CONSUMPTION AND SPENDING

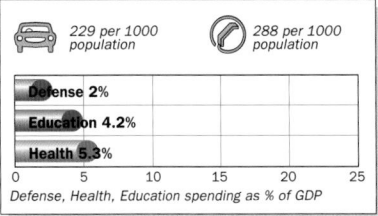

229 per 1000 population

288 per 1000 population

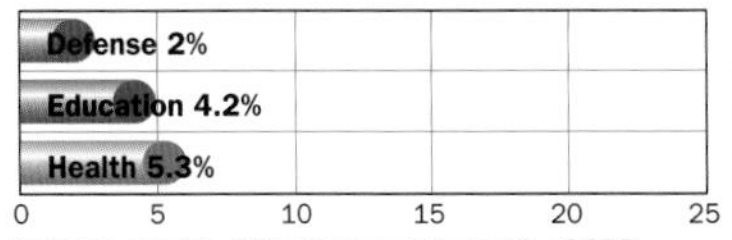
Defense 2%
Education 4.2%
Health 5.3%
0
5
10
15
20
25

Defense, Health, Education spending as % of GDP

A new elite is increasing demand for Western goods. Rural workers, Roma, and those living in the east are the poorest.

WORLD RANKING

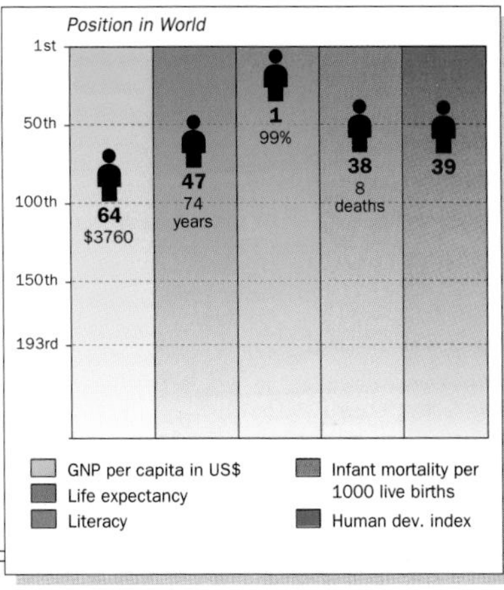
Position in World
1st
50th
100th
150th
193rd
64
$3760
47
74 years
1
99%
38
8 deaths
39
GNP per capita in US$
Life expectancy
Literacy
Infant mortality per 1000 live births
Human dev. index

S

SLOVENIA

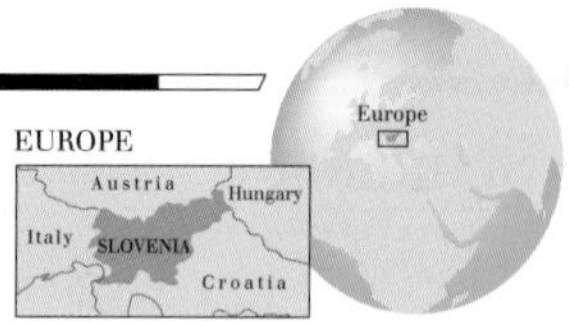
EUROPE
Europe
Austria
Hungary
Italy
SLOVENIA
Croatia

OFFICIAL NAME: Republic of Slovenia **CAPITAL:** Ljubljana
POPULATION: 1.96 million **CURRENCY:** Tolar **OFFICIAL LANGUAGE:** Slovene

1991 | 1991 | June 25 | SLO | +1 | +386 | .si

OF ALL THE FORMER Yugoslav republics, Slovenia has the closest links with western Europe. Located at the northeastern end of the Adriatic Sea, this small, Alpine country controls some of Europe's major transit routes. Slovenia's transition to independence in 1991 avoided the violence of the breakup of Yugoslavia. The most prosperous of the former communist European states, it is the only former Yugoslav republic to be invited to join the EU in 2004.

CLIMATE

Continental/ Mediterranean

WEATHER CHART FOR LJUBLJANA

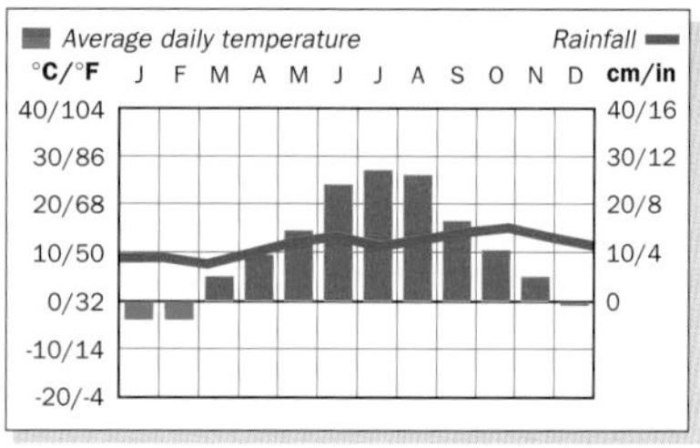
Average daily temperature
Rainfall
°C/°F J F M A M J J A S O N D cm/in
40/104
30/86
20/68
10/50
0/32
-10/14
-20/-4
40/16
30/12
20/8
10/4
0

Slovenia's interior has a continental climate. Its small coastal region has a mild Mediterranean climate.

TRANSPORTATION

Drive on right

Brnik International, Ljubljana 866,203 passengers

10 ships 1891 grt

THE TRANSPORTATION NETWORK

17,745 km (11,026 miles)

435 km (270 miles)

1201 km (746 miles)

None

Slovenia is strategically situated at some of Europe's major crossroads. In addition, its Adriatic ports provide Austria with its main maritime outlet.

TOURISM

Visitors : Population 1:1.5

1.3m visitors

Up 7% in 2002

MAIN TOURIST ARRIVALS

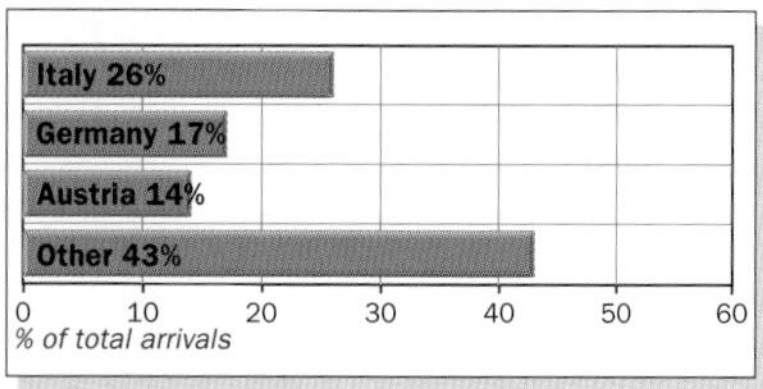
Italy 26%
Germany 17%
Austria 14%
Other 43%
0 10 20 30 40 50 60
% of total arrivals

A revival in tourism has been helped by Slovenia's political stability. Particular attractions include skiing in the Julian Alps, picturesque Ljubljana, and the wine-growing region around Ptuj.

PEOPLE

Pop. density medium

Slovene, Serbo-Croat

97/km² (251/mi²)

THE URBAN/RURAL POPULATION SPLIT

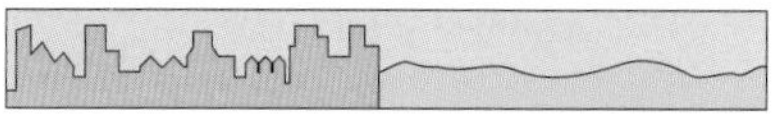
49%
51%

ETHNIC MAKEUP

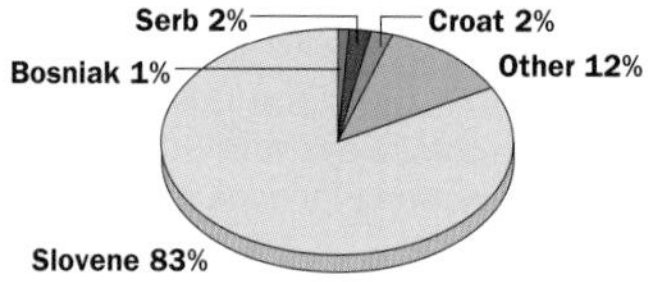
Serb 2%
Croat 2%
Bosniak 1%
Other 12%
Slovene 83%

Slovenes are ethnically very similar to the neighboring Croats and, like them, are predominantly Roman Catholic. However, Slovenia's long historical association with western Europe, and particularly with Austria, created a distinct Slovene identity, enabling a smooth transition to independence in 1991. The major non-Slavic minorities are small communities of Hungarians in the east and Italians in the southwestern Istrian region; tensions are few.

Women are not heavily disadvantaged in Slovenian society.

POLITICS

Multiparty elections

L. House 2000/2004
U. House 2002/2007

President Janez Drnovsek

AT THE LAST ELECTION

National Assembly 90 seats

12% ZLSD
9% NSi
13% Others
38% LDS
16% SDS
10% SLS/SKD
2% MR

LDS = Liberal Democracy of Slovenia
SDS = Social Democratic Party of Slovenia
ZLSD = United List of Social Democrats
SLS/SKD = Slovene People's Party/Christian Democrats of Slovenia **NSi** = New Slovenia – Christian People's Party
MR = Two seats are reserved for Italian and Hungarian minority representatives

National Council 40 seats

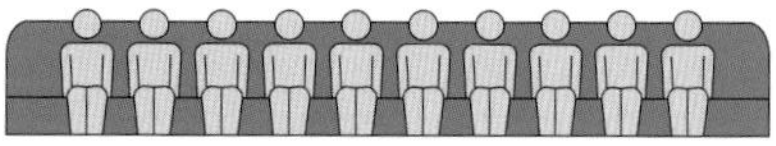

22 members of the National Council, which has an advisory role, are indirectly elected, and 18 are chosen by an electoral college to represent various interests

Slovenia has been strikingly stable since independence. Milan Kucan was elected president in 1990 and 1997, and Janez Drnovsek, leader of the center-left LDS, was prime minister almost continuously from 1992 until he was elected to replace Kucan in December 2002. Andrej Bajuk was briefly prime minister in 2000, but left his SLS party after a failed attempt at electoral reform, and soon lost office. Finance Minister Anton Rop was appointed prime minister in place of Drnovsek. Fragmented party politics makes coalition governments essential.

A smooth integration into the Western international community is the main political issue, while reform of the pension system in light of the aging population is also of concern.

SLOVENIA

Total Area : 20 253 sq. km (7820 sq. miles)

AUSTRIA
HUNGARY
ITALY
CROATIA
Murska Sobota
Maribor
Mura
Drava
Ptuj
Ravne na Koroškem
Jesenice
Tržič
Bovec
Soča
Triglav 2863m
Julian Alps
Tolmin
Kranj
Velenje
Kamnik
Celje
Rogaška Slatina
Trbovlje
LJUBLJANA
Sava
Idrija
Nova Gorica
Krško
Brežice
Trebnje
Postojna
Novo Mesto
Sežana
Ribnica
Gulf of Trieste
Gulf of Venice
Kočevje
ADRIATIC SEA
Koper
Piran
Ilirska Bistrica
Kolpa
Črnomelj
14°
16°
46°
N
0 25 km
0 25 miles
POPULATION
over 100 000
over 50 000
over 10 000
under 10 000
LAND HEIGHT
1000m/3281ft
500m/1640ft
200m/656ft
Sea Level

WORLD AFFAIRS

Joined UN in 1992

CE | EAPC | OSCE | PfP | CEFTA

Slovenia is the only former Yugoslav state to be included in the next round of enlargement of both the EU and NATO, due in 2004.

AID

Recipient

$126m (receipts) — Up 107% in 2001

Aid, overwhelmingly from the EU, mainly focuses on improving economic infrastructure and education, in preparation for EU membership.

DEFENSE

Phasing out conscription

$277m — Up 1% in 2001

Troops staved off Yugoslav forces after secession in 1991. It was announced in 2002 that military conscription would be phased out by 2004.

ECONOMICS

Inflation 18% p.a. (1993–2001)

$19.4bn — 203.7 tolars (227.1)

SCORE CARD

- ❑ WORLD GNP RANKING........................65th
- ❑ GNP PER CAPITA $9760
- ❑ BALANCE OF PAYMENTS......................–$66m
- ❑ INFLATION 9.4%
- ❑ UNEMPLOYMENT 7%

EXPORTS

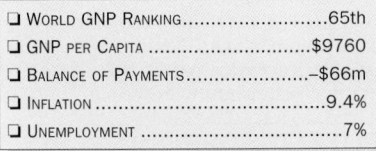

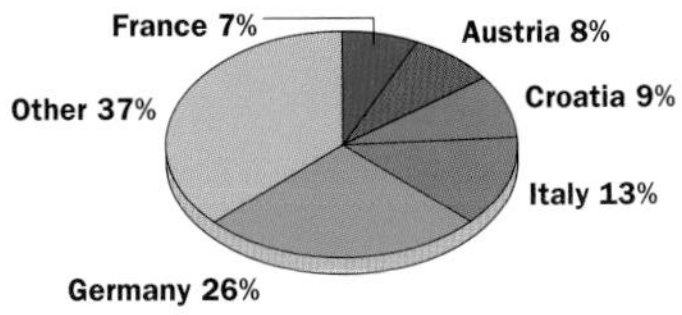
France 7%
Austria 8%
Croatia 9%
Other 37%
Italy 13%
Germany 26%

IMPORTS

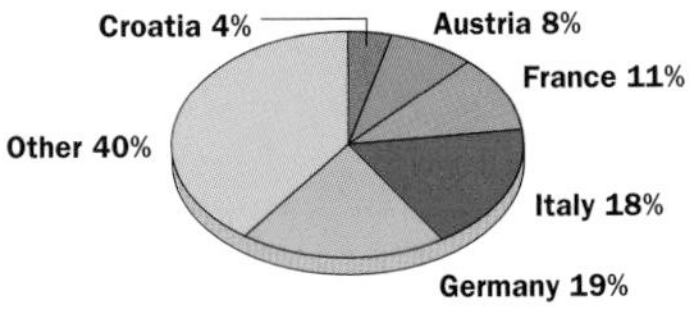
Croatia 4%
Austria 8%
France 11%
Other 40%
Italy 18%
Germany 19%

STRENGTHS

Stability. Competitive manufacturing industry. Healthy exports. Prospects of increased trade from EU membership. Revoz car plant: produces Renault Clios. Competitive port at Koper. Free trade pact with Bosnia from 2001. Least indebted of central and eastern European states.

WEAKNESSES

Foreign investment slow to take off despite market reforms. Sluggish privatization, particularly of banking sector. Unemployment high, but falling.

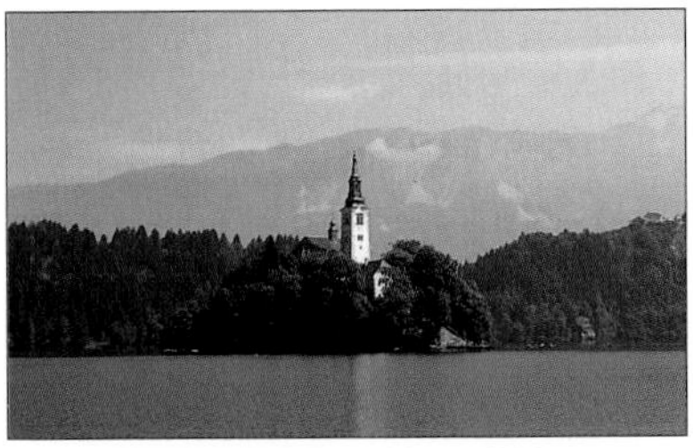

Lake Bled in the Julian Alps, *which lie astride the Slovenian–Italian border. The lake is a popular tourist destination.*

RESOURCES

Electric power 2.6m kW

3040 tonnes — 20 b/d

599,895 pigs, 477,075 cattle, 4.4m chickens — Coal, lignite, lead, zinc, uranium, silver, mercury, oil

Slovenia has come under pressure from Austria to close the nuclear plant at Krško, which provides one-third of Slovenia's power. There are deposits of brown coal and lignite, but they are difficult to extract and of poor quality.

ENVIRONMENT

Sustainability rank: 23rd

6% (2% partially protected) — 7.3 tonnes per capita

Protecting the country's alpine ecology is a priority. Pollution comes mainly from smelting, the chemicals industry, and burning brown coal and lignite.

MEDIA

TV ownership high

Daily newspaper circulation 169 per 1000 people

PUBLISHING AND BROADCAST MEDIA

There are 4 daily newspapers. *Dnevnik* is independently owned

4 services: 1 state-controlled, 3 independent — 4 services and many regional stations

A free and critical press has developed. State broadcasters have a new ethical code, protecting journalists' sources. POP TV is a commercial success.

CRIME

No death penalty

1120 prisoners — Up 10% in 2000

Slovenia's prison population is proportionately among the lowest in Europe. Smuggling people into western Europe is overtaking narcotics smuggling as the focus of organized crime.

EDUCATION

School leaving age: 14

99% — 91,494 students

Primary schooling now begins at the age of six, lowered from seven. Preschooling is available. Ljubljana and Maribor have universities.

CHRONOLOGY

Slovenia was part of the Austro-Hungarian Empire until 1918, when it joined the Kingdom of Serbs, Croats, and Slovenes (Yugoslavia).

- ❑ **1949** Tito's break with Moscow.
- ❑ **1989** Parliament confirms right to secede. Calls multiparty elections.
- ❑ **1990** Control over army asserted, referendum approves secession.
- ❑ **1991** Independence declared; first republic to secede. Yugoslav federal army repelled.
- ❑ **1992** First multiparty elections. Milan Kucan president, Janez Drnovsek prime minister.
- ❑ **1993** Joins IMF and World Bank.
- ❑ **2002** Drnovsek elected president; Anton Rop prime minister.
- ❑ **2003** EU membership for 2004 approved by referendum.

HEALTH

Welfare state health benefits

1 per 465 people — Cancers, heart, cerebrovascular, and respiratory diseases

National health care in Slovenia uses health centers and outpatient clinics to increase accessibility for patients.

SPENDING

GDP/cap. increase

CONSUMPTION AND SPENDING

426 per 1000 population — *401 per 1000 population*

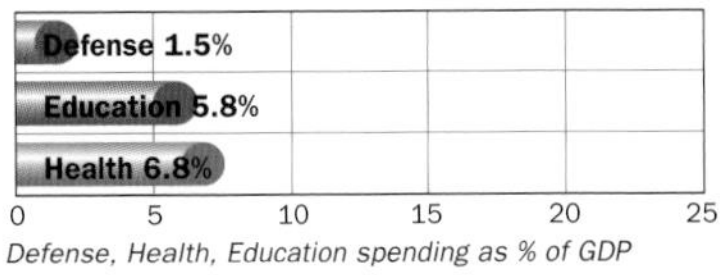
Defense 1.5%
Education 5.8%
Health 6.8%
0
5
10
15
20
25

Defense, Health, Education spending as % of GDP

Slovenia has the highest standard of living of all the central and eastern European states of the former Soviet bloc.

WORLD RANKING

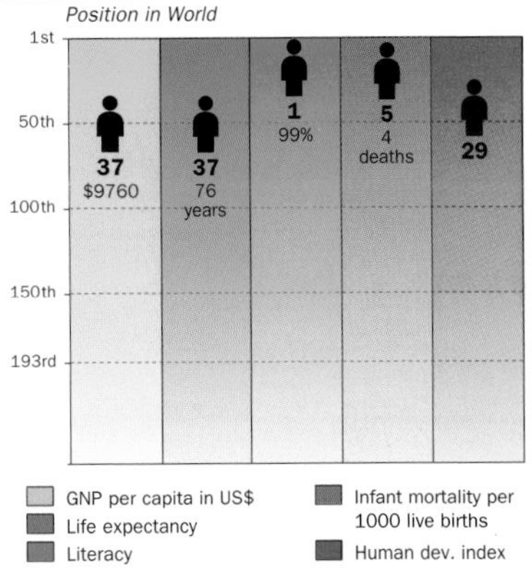
Position in World
1st
50th
100th
150th
193rd
37
$9760
37
76
years
1
99%
5
4
deaths
29
GNP per capita in US$
Life expectancy
Literacy
Infant mortality per 1000 live births
Human dev. index

S

SOLOMON ISLANDS

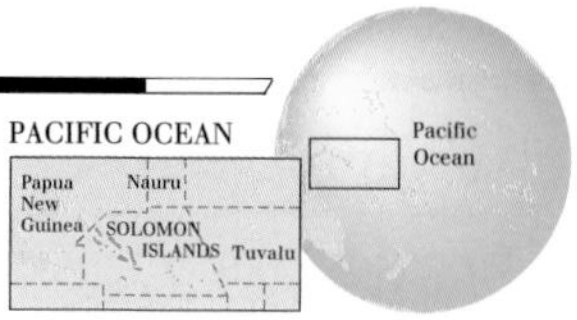
PACIFIC OCEAN
Papua New Guinea
Nauru
SOLOMON ISLANDS
Tuvalu
Pacific Ocean

OFFICIAL NAME: Solomon Islands **CAPITAL:** Honiara
POPULATION: 479,000 **CURRENCY:** Solomon Islands dollar **OFFICIAL LANGUAGE:** English

1978 | 1978 | July 7 | SLB | +11 | +677 | .sb

SCATTERED OVER 645,000 sq. km (250,000 sq. miles), the Solomons archipelago has several hundred islands, but most people live on the six largest – Guadalcanal, Malaita, New Georgia, Makira, Santa Isabel, and Choiseul. The Solomons have been settled since at least 1000 BCE; the Spanish arrived in 1568. Since 1998 ethnic conflict between rival islanders has destabilized the country. Most of the Solomons are coral reefs. Just 1% of the land area is cultivable.

CLIMATE

Tropical equatorial

WEATHER CHART FOR HONIARA

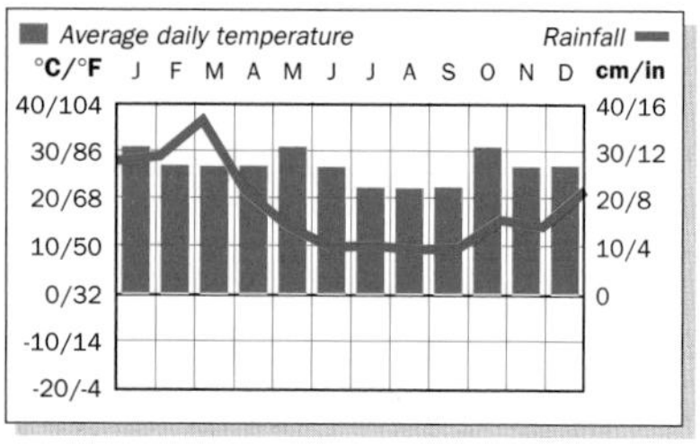
Average daily temperature
Rainfall
°C/°F
J F M A M J J A S O N D
cm/in
40/104
30/86
20/68
10/50
0/32
-10/14
-20/-4
40/16
30/12
20/8
10/4
0

There is little temperature variation in the humid climate, but ferocious cyclones can occur in the rainy season.

TRANSPORTATION

Drive on left

Henderson, Honiara 22,000 passengers | 28 ships 8400 grt

THE TRANSPORTATION NETWORK

34 km (21 miles) | None
None | None

International flights from the principal airport, 13 km (8 miles) outside Honiara, were resumed in late 2000 after the ending of open hostilities.

***Unloading seed coconuts** near Munda on New Georgia in the Solomons' northern chain of islands. Coconuts are by far the largest and most commercially important crop.*

TOURISM

Visitors : Population 1:23

21,000 visitors | Down in 2000

MAIN TOURIST ARRIVALS

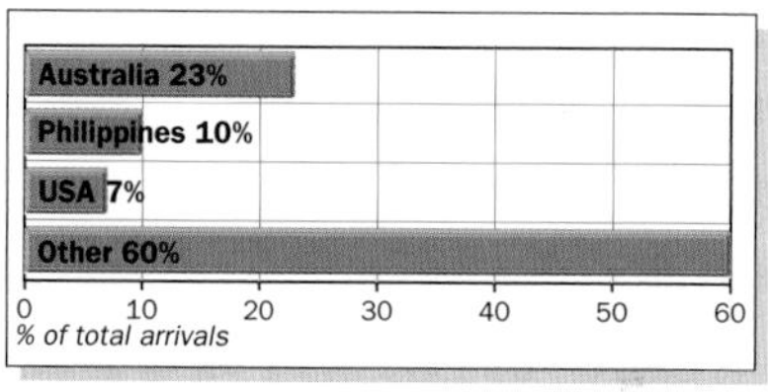
Australia 23%
Philippines 10%
USA 7%
Other 60%
0
10
20
30
40
50
60
% of total arrivals

The importance of Guadalcanal during World War II and the tranquility of the outer islands used to attract tourists. However, ethnic conflict all but destroyed tourism in 1998 and again when fighting intensified in 2000. Lack of funding hampers recovery.

PEOPLE

Pop. density low

English, Pidgin English, Melanesian Pidgin | 17/km² (44/mi²)

THE URBAN/RURAL POPULATION SPLIT

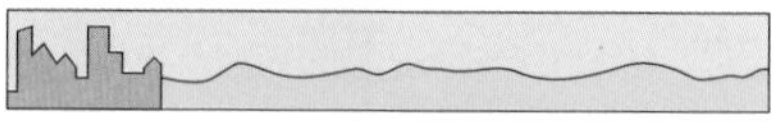
20%
80%

RELIGIOUS PERSUASION

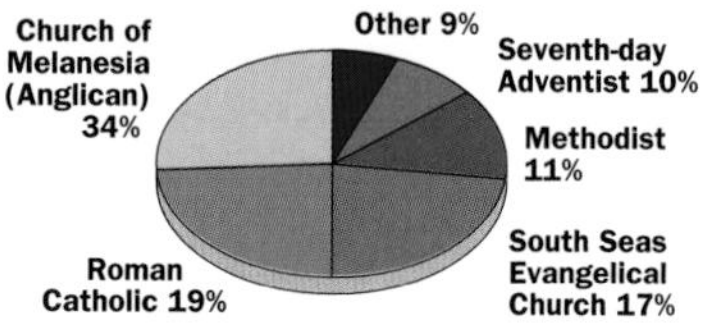
Church of Melanesia (Anglican) 34%
Other 9%
Seventh-day Adventist 10%
Methodist 11%
South Seas Evangelical Church 17%
Roman Catholic 19%

Almost all Solomon Islanders are Melanesian; relations between islands are tense. During the 1998–2000 conflict, 20,000 Malaitans were forced from their homes on Guadalcanal by native (Isatabu) militias. Authorities in outlying islands have pressed for greater autonomy. There are small communities of Micronesians who are descended from I-Kiribati temporarily relocated in 1957. More than 50 dialects are spoken. Though the islanders are nominally Christian, animist beliefs are widespread.

POLITICS

Multiparty elections

2001/2005 | H.M. Queen Elizabeth II

AT THE LAST ELECTION

National Parliament 50 seats

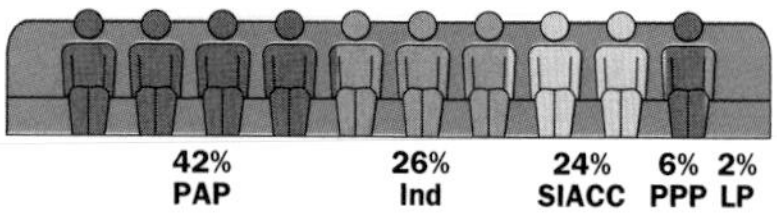
42% PAP
26% Ind
24% SIACC
6% PPP
2% LP

PAP = People's Alliance Party **Ind** = Independents
SIACC = Solomon Islands Alliance for Change Coalition
PPP = People's Progressive Party **LP** = Labour Party

Prominent "big men" still play a significant role in politics. The civil conflict on Guadalcanal briefly ousted the government in 2000. A semblance of stability was then restored, a new devolved "state system" promising greater regional autonomy. Aid funds were quickly outstripped by claims for "compensation" arising from the conflict, and the government is frequently close to bankruptcy. Maintaining security remains a serious concern for Prime Minister Allan Kamakeza and his PAP government, elected in 2001. Large areas of the country are in effect run by militias.

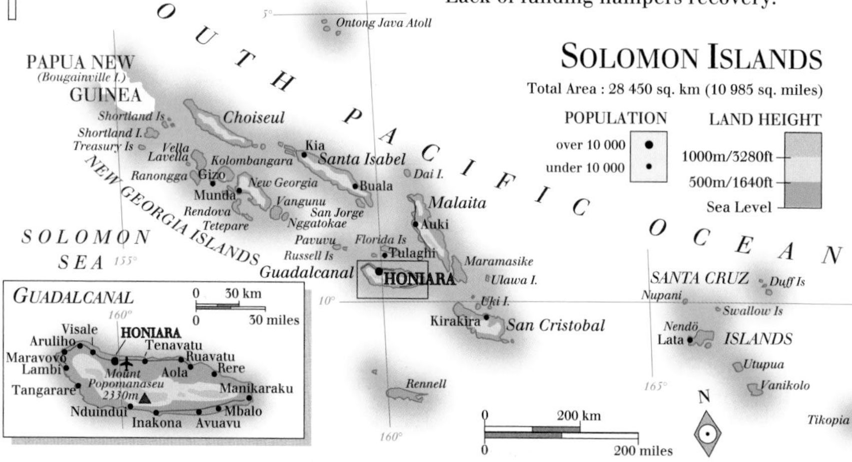
SOLOMON ISLANDS
Total Area : 28 450 sq. km (10 985 sq. miles)
POPULATION
over 10 000
under 10 000
LAND HEIGHT
1000m/3280ft
500m/1640ft
Sea Level
SOUTH PACIFIC OCEAN
SOLOMON SEA
PAPUA NEW GUINEA
(Bougainville I.)
Ontong Java Atoll
Shortland Is
Shortland I.
Treasury Is
Choiseul
Vella Lavella
Kolombangara
Ranongga
Gizo
Munda
New Georgia
Rendova
Vangunu
Tetepare
NEW GEORGIA ISLANDS
Kia
Santa Isabel
Buala
San Jorge
Nggatokae
Dai I.
Malaita
Auki
Pavuvu
Russell Is
Florida Is
Tulaghi
Guadalcanal
HONIARA
Maramasike
Ulawa I.
Uki I.
Kirakira
San Cristobal
Rennell
SANTA CRUZ ISLANDS
Nupani
Duff Is
Swallow Is
Nendö
Lata
Utupua
Vanikolo
Anuta
Fatutaka
Tikopia
GUADALCANAL
Visale
HONIARA
Tenavatu
Aruliho
Maravovo
Lambi
Tangarare
Aola
Ruavatu
Rere
Mount Popomanaseu 2330m
Manikaraku
Nduindui
Mbalo
Inakona
Avuavu
0 30 km
0 30 miles
0 200 km
0 200 miles
N

WORLD AFFAIRS

Joined UN in 1978

ACP | Comm | IBRD | PC | PIF

The intensification of violence in 2000 caused great concern around the Pacific, and heightened international mediation efforts, in which Australia in particular was involved. The Solomons government is increasingly eager to secure direct intervention in order to restore law and order. In 2003, Australia agreed to lead a regional peacekeeping force.

AID

Recipient

US$59m (receipts) | Down 13% in 2001

Aid has focused very specifically on restoring stability and rebuilding infrastructure after two years of brutal conflict. Regional powers Australia, New Zealand, and Taiwan are key in aiding recovery. Improved relations with Papua New Guinea brought aid of US$23 million between 1998 and 2001.

DEFENSE

No compulsory military service

Australia responsible for defense | Not applicable

The government's Peace Plan 2000 includes the creation of a panethnic security force. Under the Townsville peace accord, signed in October 2000, security was overseen by unarmed peacekeepers from neighboring Pacific states. The rival militias are effectively in control on Guadalcanal and Malaita.

ECONOMICS

Inflation 8.2% p.a. (1990–2001)

US$253m | 7.521 Solomon Islands dollars (7.102)

SCORE CARD

- WORLD GNP RANKING........................180th
- GNP PER CAPITA ....US$590
- BALANCE OF PAYMENTS ....US$21m
- INFLATION 7.9%
- UNEMPLOYMENT...........Some underemployment

EXPORTS

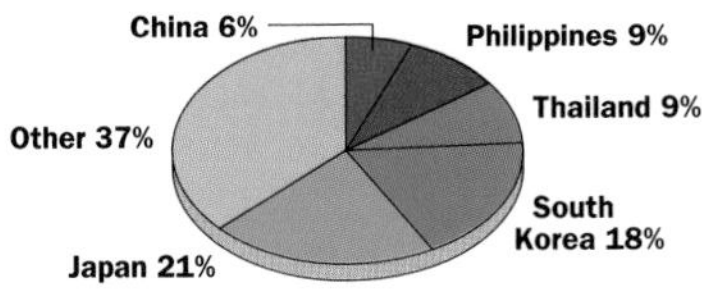
China 6%
Philippines 9%
Thailand 9%
South Korea 18%
Japan 21%
Other 37%

IMPORTS

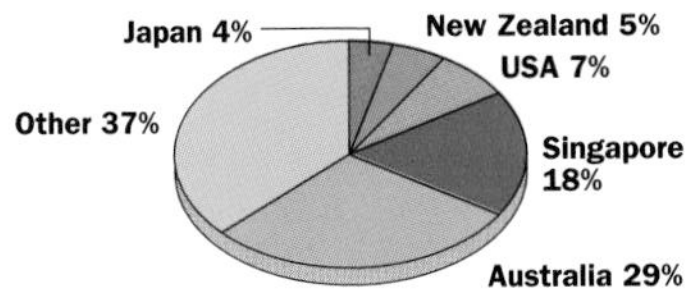
Japan 4%
New Zealand 5%
USA 7%
Singapore 18%
Australia 29%
Other 37%

STRENGTHS

Good mineral and agricultural resources. Influx of international aid.

WEAKNESSES

Economy near collapse after ethnic conflict. Destruction of infrastructure. Key gold mine shut by militias. Grossly inflated compensation claims from conflict. Revenue from copra, gold, fish, and palm oil dried up. Lack of social stability deters investment.

RESOURCES

Electric power 12,000 kW

23,458 tonnes | Not an oil producer

68,000 pigs, 13,000 cattle, 220,000 chickens | Gold, copper, bauxite, lead, zinc, silver, cobalt, phosphates

Bauxite deposits have been discovered on Rennell Island, and there are traces of gold and copper on Guadalcanal.

The bankrupted government was unable to pay for the electricity supply to Honiara in 2003.

ENVIRONMENT

Not available

0.3% partially protected | 0.4 tonnes per capita

The environmental movement is strong. Depletion of forest and marine resources are a major concern. In 1998 a sustainable forest-harvesting policy was introduced, but the need to restore the economy puts pressure on environmentally sensitive areas.

MEDIA

TV ownership low

Daily newspaper circulation 16 per 1000 people

PUBLISHING AND BROADCAST MEDIA

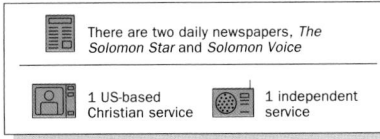

There are two daily newspapers, *The Solomon Star* and *Solomon Voice*

1 US-based Christian service | 1 independent service

Australia has donated technical equipment to the national broadcaster and has sponsored peace programs.

CRIME

No death penalty

134 prisoners | Crime is rising

Under the armed militias, extortion and gang-related violence have flourished, notably on Guadalcanal and Malaita.

CHRONOLOGY

Settled since before 1000 BCE by Melanesian peoples, the Solomons became a British colony in 1893.

- **1942–1943** Japanese occupation.
- **1978** Independence from UK.
- **1983** Diplomatic relations with Taiwan established.
- **1998–2000** Civil conflict between Guadalcanal and Malaita islanders.
- **2003** International peacekeeping force arrives.

EDUCATION

School leaving age: 14

77% | Not available

Education is modeled on the British system. Tertiary students go to the University of the South Pacific in Fiji.

HEALTH

Welfare state health benefits

1 per 7692 people | Not available

The main hospital has seriously reduced services; local patients are now expected to provide their own food. Gang violence has spread to hospital wards.

SPENDING

GDP/cap. decrease

CONSUMPTION AND SPENDING

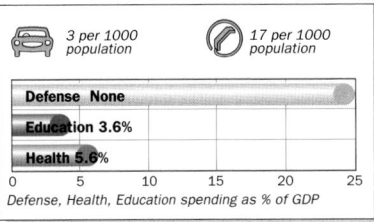

3 per 1000 population | *17 per 1000 population*

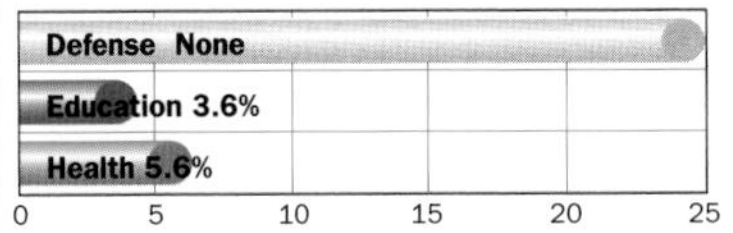
Defense None
Education 3.6%
Health 5.6%
0
5
10
15
20
25

Defense, Health, Education spending as % of GDP

Solomon Islanders in government jobs are the wealthiest group. Inhabitants of the outlying islands are extremely poor.

WORLD RANKING

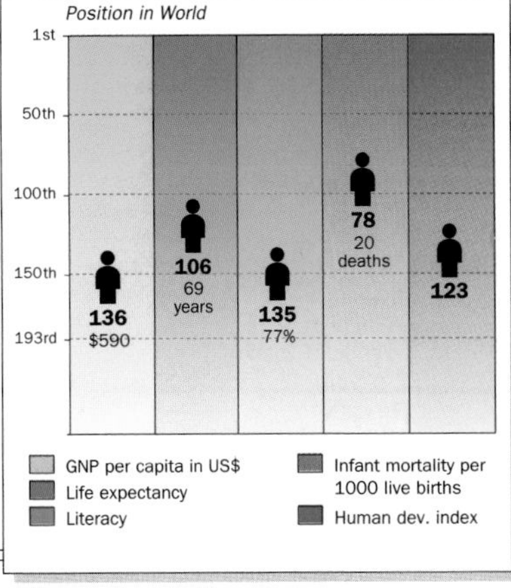
Position in World
1st
50th
100th
150th
193rd
136
$590
106
69 years
135
77%
78
20 deaths
123
GNP per capita in US$
Life expectancy
Literacy
Infant mortality per 1000 live births
Human dev. index

S

SOMALIA

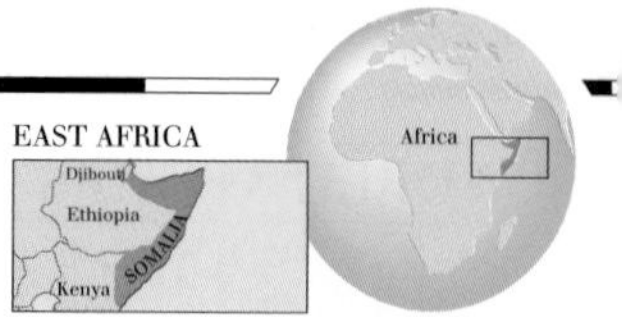
EAST AFRICA
Africa
Djibouti
Ethiopia
Kenya
SOMALIA

OFFICIAL NAME: Somalia **CAPITAL:** Mogadishu **POPULATION:** 9.6 million
CURRENCY: Somali shilling **OFFICIAL LANGUAGES:** Somali and Arabic

1960 | 1960 | Oct 21 | SO | +3 | +252 | .so

OCCUPYING THE HORN of Africa, Italian Somaliland and British Somaliland joined in 1960 to form an independent Somalia. Except in the more fertile south, the land is semiarid. Years of clan-based civil war have resulted in the collapse of central government, the frustration of US and UN intervention initiatives aimed at easing a huge refugee crisis, and mass starvation.

CLIMATE

Hot desert/steppe

WEATHER CHART FOR MOGADISHU

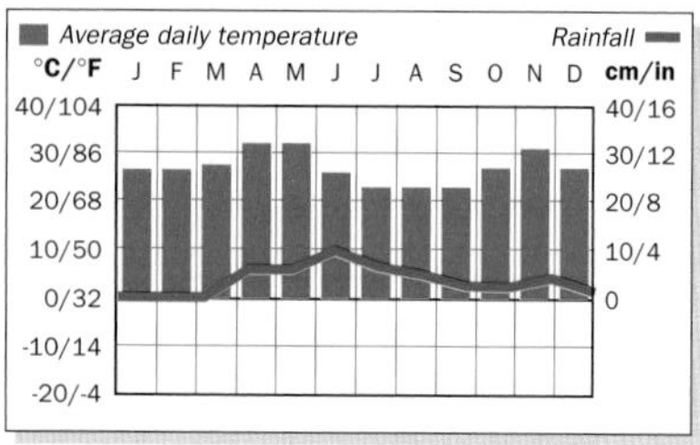
Average daily temperature
Rainfall
°C/°F
J F M A M J J A S O N D
cm/in
40/104
30/86
20/68
10/50
0/32
-10/14
-20/-4
40/16
30/12
20/8
10/4
0

Somalia is very dry. The northern coast is very hot and humid, the eastern less so. The interior has some of the world's highest mean yearly temperatures.

TRANSPORTATION

Drive on left

Mogadishu International

22 ships
11,400 grt

THE TRANSPORTATION NETWORK

2608 km (1621 miles)	None
None	None

About 50% of Somalis are nomads for whom the camel is the principal means of transportation. In 1990, the IDA agreed to repair the road network, but work on the seven-year project has not yet begun.

TOURISM

Visitors : Population 1:960

10,000 visitors

No change from year to year

MAIN TOURIST ARRIVALS

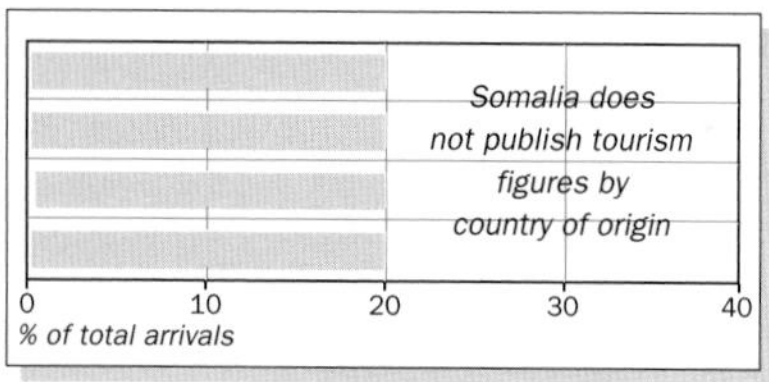
Somalia does not publish tourism figures by country of origin
0
10
20
30
40
% of total arrivals

Aid workers and foreign journalists are the only visitors. Land mines are a major hazard.

Baydhabo market. *Subsistence farming supports most people, despite chaos created by the fighting.*

PEOPLE

Pop. density low

Somali, Arabic, English, Italian

15/km² (40/mi²)

THE URBAN/RURAL POPULATION SPLIT

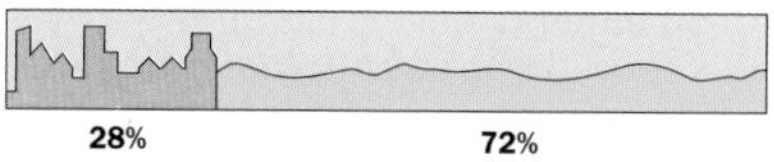
28%
72%

RELIGIOUS PERSUASION

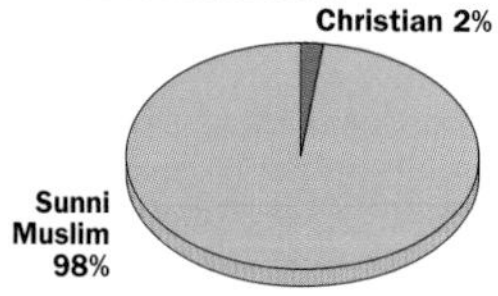
Christian 2%
Sunni Muslim 98%

The clan system is fundamental to Somalia. Shifting allegiances characterize its structure – a tendency stifled by Siad Barre's dictatorship but revived after his fall in 1991. His undermining of the traditional brokers of justice, the elders, contributed to the power vacuum that resulted in civil war, and his persecution of the Issaqs led to Somaliland's declaration of secession in 1991. However, the entire population is ethnic Somali, and national identity remains strong, shown by the widespread opposition to the UN's peacekeeping force.

POLITICS

No legislative elections

1984/Uncertain

No internationally recognized head of state

AT THE LAST ELECTION

National Assembly (suspended)

There has been no prospect of organizing new elections since the overthrow of Siad Barre. A transitional assembly was formed in 2000 on a nonparty basis.

Somalia has remained in anarchy since the former dictator President Siad Barre fled in 1991. The unified state dissolved amid conflict in the south and separatism in the north. Throughout the 1990s rival warlords, including the powerful Gen. Aideed, vied for power, undermining a US-led peacekeeping force in 1992.

A conference of businessmen and influential figures, held in neighboring Djibouti in 2000, established a transitional assembly and appointed former Barre minister Abdulkassim Salat Hassan as president. The new government, though warmly received in Mogadishu, was not backed by most of the warlords or by the northern self-declared authorities in "Somaliland" and "Puntland." It effectively became one faction among many. Greater support was given in 2003 to a new initiative, backed by Kenya, to create a national authority to govern until 2007.

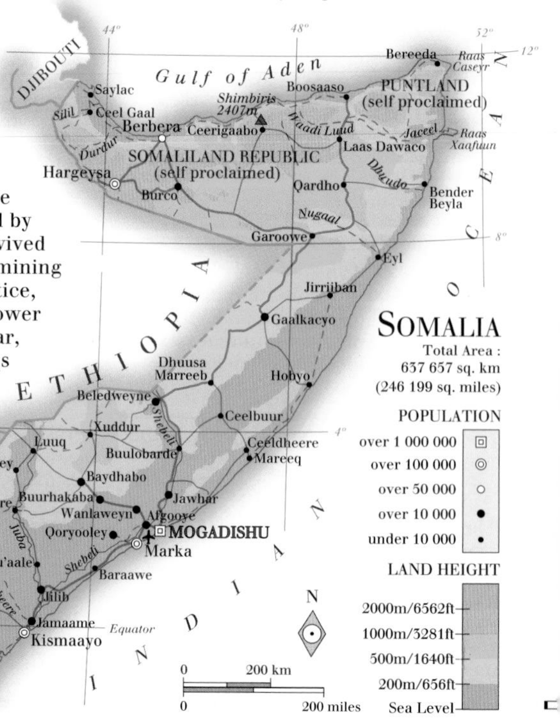
DJIBOUTI
Gulf of Aden
Saylac
Ceel Gaal
Berbera
Shimbiris 2407m
Ceerigaabo
Boosaaso
Bereeda
Raas Caseyr
PUNTLAND (self proclaimed)
Laas Dawaco
Raas Xaafuun
SOMALILAND REPUBLIC (self proclaimed)
Hargeysa
Burco
Qardho
Bender Beyla
Garoowe
Eyl
Jirriiban
Gaalkacyo
Hobyo
Dhuusa Marreeb
Beledweyne
Xuddur
Ceelbuur
Ceeldheere
Mareeg
Luuq
Buulobarde
Garbahaarrey
Baydhabo
Baardheere
Buurhakaba
Jawhar
Wanlaweyn
Afgooye
MOGADISHU
Qoryooley
Marka
Bu'aale
Baraawe
Jilib
Jamaame
Kismaayo
Equator
ETHIOPIA
KENYA
INDIAN OCEAN
SOMALIA
Total Area : 637 657 sq. km (246 199 sq. miles)
POPULATION
over 1 000 000
over 100 000
over 50 000
over 10 000
under 10 000
LAND HEIGHT
2000m/6562ft
1000m/3281ft
500m/1640ft
200m/656ft
Sea Level
0 200 km
0 200 miles

WORLD AFFAIRS

Joined UN in 1960

AL | IGAD | NAM | AU | OIC

After a UN force withdrew in 1995, the international community appeared to have abandoned Somalia until it gave support to the transitional assembly from 2000. Relations with Ethiopia are particularly tense; the government accuses Addis Ababa of sending troops to assist opposition warlords. The US belief in the existence in Somalia of terrorist training camps has eroded relations since September 11, 2001.

AID

Recipient

$149m (receipts)

Up 43% in 2001

Mass starvation among the Somali population in 1991 finally prompted the UN to launch a large-scale humanitarian aid effort. In this the UN was largely effective, averting widescale starvation and restoring food security.

DEFENSE

No compulsory military service

$39m

Down 2% in 2001

Former soldiers have been urged to reenlist, while efforts to demobilize the estimated 75,000 militia began in 2000.

ECONOMICS

Not available

$1.21bn

2620 Somali shillings (2620)

SCORE CARD

- ❑ WORLD GNP RANKING........................151st
- ❑ GNP PER CAPITA $120
- ❑ BALANCE OF PAYMENTS....................–$157m
- ❑ INFLATION................................Over 100%
- ❑ UNEMPLOYMENT..........Widespread underemployment

STRENGTHS

Very few. Export of livestock to Arabian peninsula resumed in the north. Inflow of money from Somalis abroad. Growing market in stolen food aid.

WEAKNESSES

Every commodity, except arms, in extremely short supply. Little economic potential in the south. Livestock destroyed by drought. Banditry, extortion, and kidnapping hamper aid agencies.

EXPORTS

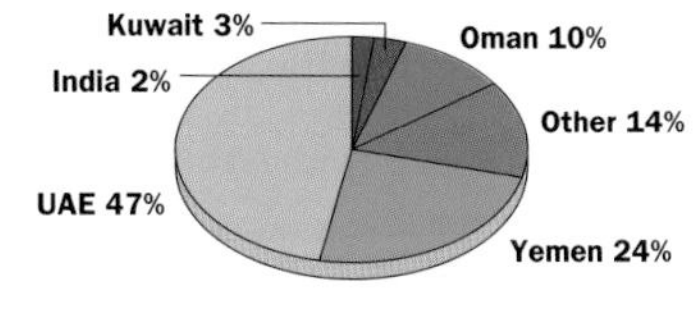
Kuwait 3%
Oman 10%
India 2%
Other 14%
UAE 47%
Yemen 24%

IMPORTS

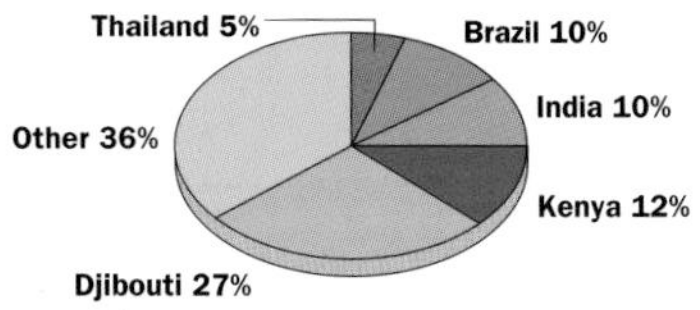
Thailand 5%
Brazil 10%
India 10%
Other 36%
Kenya 12%
Djibouti 27%

RESOURCES

Electric power 79,000 kW

20,200 tonnes

Not an oil producer

13.1m sheep, 12.7m goats, 6.2m camels

Salt, tin, zinc, copper, gypsum, manganese, uranium, iron

Commercially exploitable minerals remain untapped. An oil exploration agreement was signed with a French oil group in 2001.

ENVIRONMENT

Sustainability rank: 132nd

0.8% partially protected

0.003 tonnes per capita

Human deprivation and starvation caused by the effects of drought and war on land and livestock outweigh all ecological considerations.

MEDIA

TV ownership low

Daily newspaper circulation 1 per 1000 people

PUBLISHING AND BROADCAST MEDIA

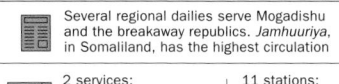

Several regional dailies serve Mogadishu and the breakaway republics. *Jamhuuriya*, in Somaliland, has the highest circulation

2 services: limited to the Mogadishu area

11 stations: mostly political or religious

Mogadishu has a number of faction-run radio stations. Somali Television Network, an independent multichannel, multilingual service, began broadcasting in 1999. Independent newspapers also serve the self-proclaimed areas.

CRIME

Death penalty in use

Somalia does not publish prison figures

Widespread breakdown of law and order since 1991

Armed clan factions (some, in remoter regions, engaged in family feuds rather than the war) and bandits rule large areas. In Mogadishu a "national" police force has been established, and possession of firearms outlawed. *Sharia* (Islamic law), now the de facto system, is run in a makeshift fashion by elders.

EDUCATION

School leaving age: 14

24%

10,400 students

The system collapsed during the civil war. There were reports of improvised open-air schools starting up again in urban areas in 1993. Somali has been a written language only since 1972.

CHRONOLOGY

The lands of the Somalis became British and Italian colonies in the 1880s. Most were unified as Somalia at independence in 1960.

- ❑ **1964–1987** Conflict with Ethiopia over Somali-inhabited Ogaden.
- ❑ **1969** Gen. Siad Barre takes power.
- ❑ **1991** Siad Barre ousted. Civil war and clan chaos. Mass starvation. Somaliland declares secession.
- ❑ **1992** Abortive US intervention.
- ❑ **1995** UN force withdrawn.
- ❑ **1997** Accord signed by 26 clans.
- ❑ **2000** National reconciliation conference appoints government; warlords dispute its authority.
- ❑ **2001** Somali Reconciliation and Restoration Council set up in south.
- ❑ **2003** Plans for new national authority.

HEALTH

No welfare state health benefits

1 per 20,000 people

Diarrheal, communicable, and parasitic diseases

The state-run system has collapsed entirely. A few very rudimentary facilities are run by foreign workers.

SPENDING

GDP/cap. decrease

CONSUMPTION AND SPENDING

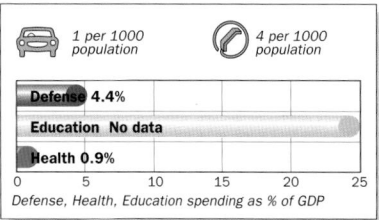

1 per 1000 population

4 per 1000 population

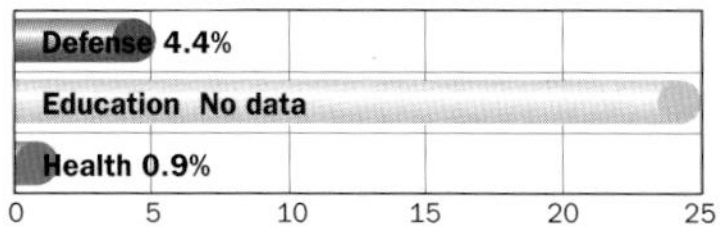
Defense 4.4%
Education No data
Health 0.9%
0
5
10
15
20
25

Defense, Health, Education spending as % of GDP

Bandits and warlords have gained rich pickings. Money sent by relatives living overseas is the main income for some people.

WORLD RANKING

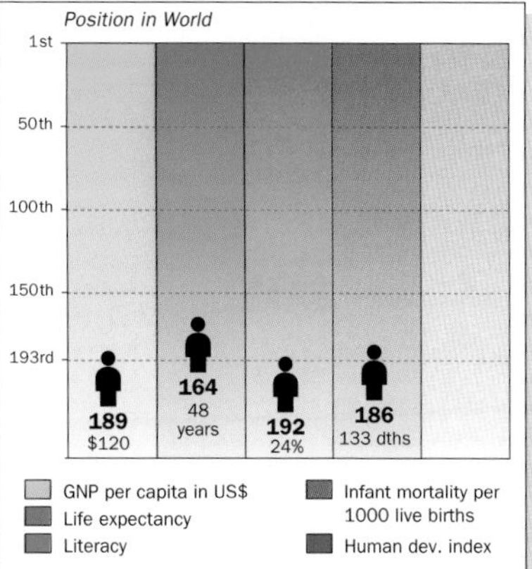
Position in World
1st
50th
100th
150th
193rd
189
$120
164
48 years
192
24%
186
133 dths
GNP per capita in US$
Life expectancy
Literacy
Infant mortality per 1000 live births
Human dev. index

S

SOUTH AFRICA

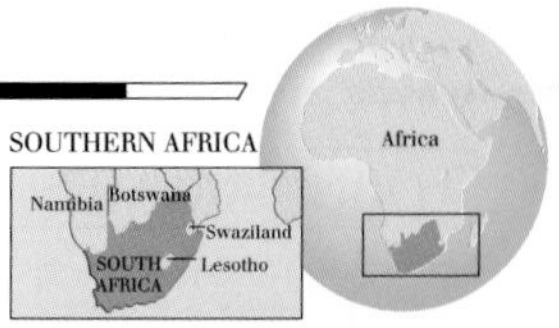
SOUTHERN AFRICA
Namibia
Botswana
Swaziland
SOUTH AFRICA
Lesotho
Africa

OFFICIAL NAME: Republic of South Africa **CAPITALS:** Pretoria; Cape Town; Bloemfontein
POPULATION: 44.8 million **CURRENCY:** Rand **OFFICIAL LANGUAGES:** Afrikaans, English, and 9 African languages

1934 | 1994 | April 27 | ZA | +2 | +27 | .za

RICH IN NATURAL RESOURCES, South Africa comprises a central plateau, or *veld*, bordered to the south and east by the Drakensberg Mountains. After eight decades of white minority rule, with racial segregation under the apartheid policy since 1948, from 1990 South Africa underwent a social and political revolution. The first multiracial elections were held in 1994 and the African National Congress (ANC), under Nelson Mandela and his successor Thabo Mbeki, has been the leading political movement ever since. Poverty and the spread of crime and HIV/AIDS are major problems.

Nelson Mandela, *who became president of South Africa in April 1994.*

Thabo Mbeki, *elected president in 1999 to succeed Mandela.*

CLIMATE

Desert/subtropical/ Mediterranean

WEATHER CHART FOR PRETORIA

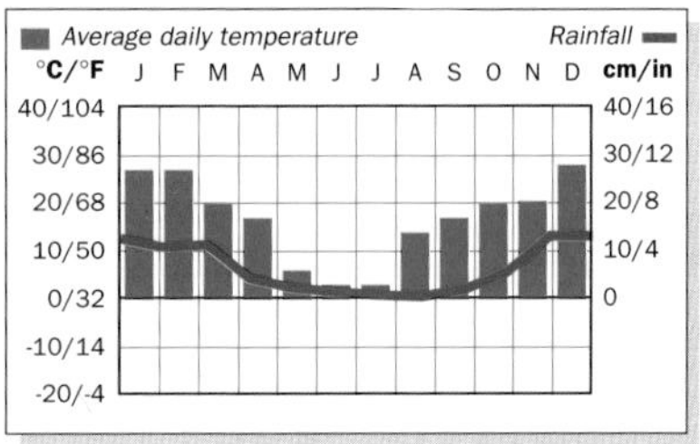
Average daily temperature
Rainfall
°C/°F
J F M A M J J A S O N D
cm/in
40/104
30/86
20/68
10/50
0/32
-10/14
-20/-4
40/16
30/12
20/8
10/4
0

Despite the moderating effects of oceans on three sides, the warm temperate climate is dry; 65% of the country has less than 50 cm (20 in) of rain a year. Drought is a periodic hazard.

TRANSPORTATION

Drive on left

Jan Smuts International, Johannesburg 12.7m passengers

197 ships 381,900 grt

THE TRANSPORTATION NETWORK

63,027 km (39,163 miles)

2032 km (1263 miles)

22,657 km (14,078 miles)

None

Priorities include expanding port capacity and cross-border rail networks. Public transportation is limited and expensive, but there is an extensive informal network of minibuses and taxis.

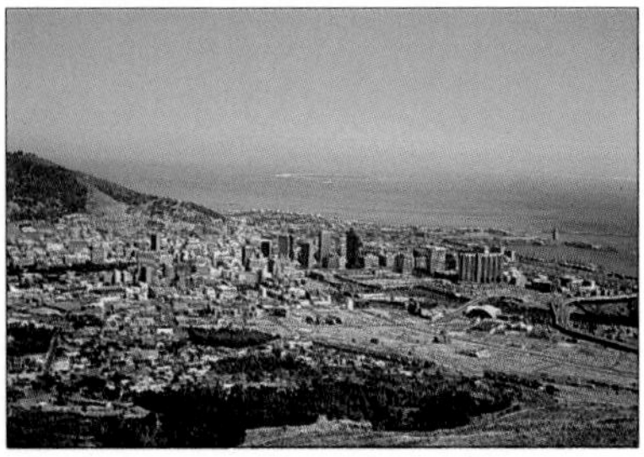

Cape Town, *set on a peninsula ending at the Cape of Good Hope, where the Indian and Atlantic Oceans meet.*

TOURISM

Visitors : Population 1:6.8

6.55m visitors

Up 11% in 2002

MAIN TOURIST ARRIVALS

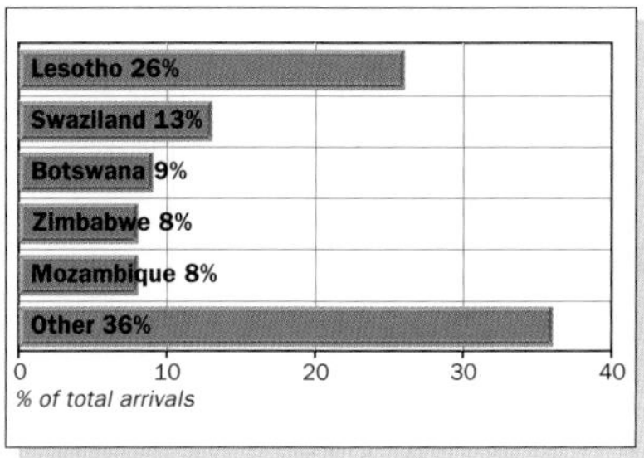
Lesotho 26%
Swaziland 13%
Botswana 9%
Zimbabwe 8%
Mozambique 8%
Other 36%
0
10
20
30
40
% of total arrivals

South Africa has huge tourist potential, with attractions ranging from beaches to mountains, from prizewinning vineyards to world-renowned wildlife reserves. The enormous Kruger National Park boasts 137 mammal species and 450 bird species. Visitor numbers increased throughout the 1990s, but tourism is still recovering from the country's isolation during the apartheid era. Today, the key constraint on growth is rising crime. Studies suggest that by 2005 tourism could create an additional 450,000 jobs and contribute 10% toward GDP (compared with 4% in 1995).

PEOPLE

Pop. density low

English, isiZulu, isiXhosa, Afrikaans, Sepedi, Setswana, Sesotho, Xitsonga, siSwati, Tshivenda, isiNdebele

37/km² (95/mi²)

THE URBAN/RURAL POPULATION SPLIT

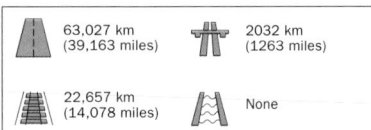

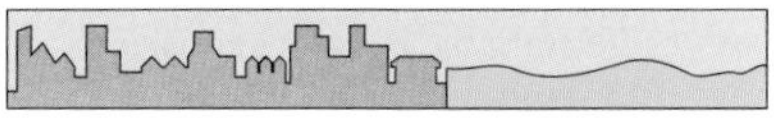

58% 42%

RELIGIOUS PERSUASION

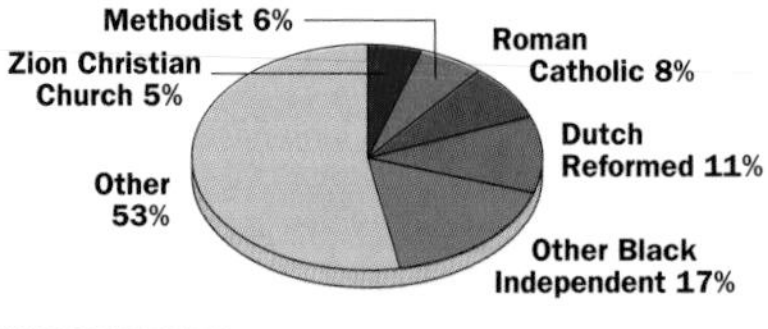
Methodist 6%
Zion Christian Church 5%
Roman Catholic 8%
Dutch Reformed 11%
Other 53%
Other Black Independent 17%

ETHNIC MAKEUP

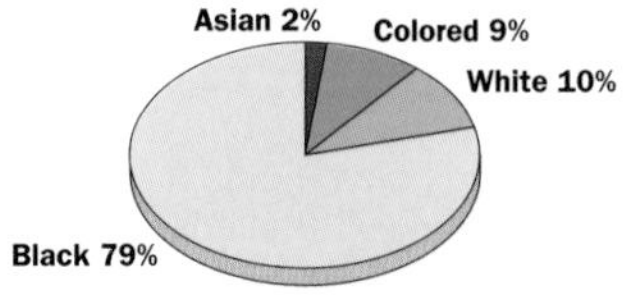
Asian 2%
Colored 9%
White 10%
Black 79%

Under apartheid, people were divided into racial categories: Whites (Afrikaners and English-speakers), with the most privileges, and three black groups – Coloreds (people whose descent was deemed mixed), Asians (mainly Indians), and Africans, by far the largest single group. While blacks now dominate politics, whites still control the economy.

The extended family has been undermined by the need for men to migrate to towns for work. While this was once enforced by the state, it remains as an economic necessity. A small black middle class has developed, but most blacks are underemployed. There is considerable resentment over wealth disparities in the many townships.

The expected postapartheid ethnic conflict failed to materialize. Race-based movements such as Inkatha have not made a national impact. An area of the Kalahari Desert was returned to a Khomani San tribe in 1999.

The constitution enshrines equality of the sexes; many women are now prominent in public life. South Africa has led the way in Africa in providing homosexuals with legal rights.

POPULATION AGE BREAKDOWN

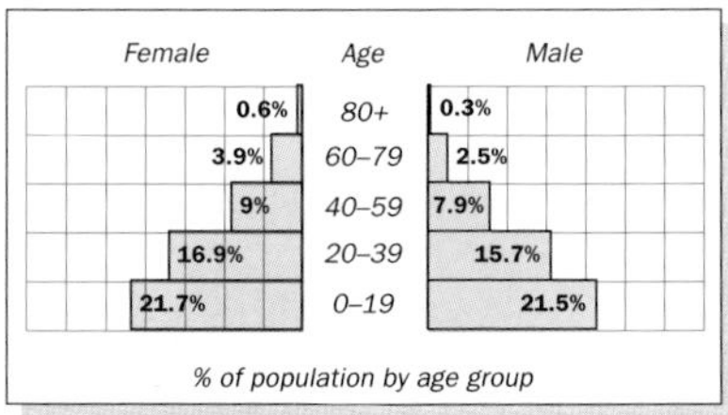
Female
Age
Male
0.6%
80+
0.3%
3.9%
60–79
2.5%
9%
40–59
7.9%
16.9%
20–39
15.7%
21.7%
0–19
21.5%
% of population by age group

S

POLITICS

Multiparty elections

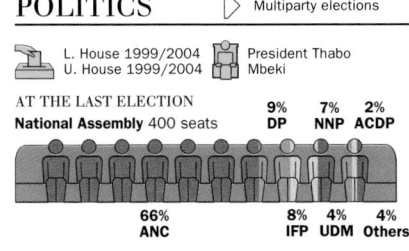

L. House 1999/2004
U. House 1999/2004

President Thabo Mbeki

AT THE LAST ELECTION

National Assembly 400 seats

9% DP
7% NNP
2% ACDP
66% ANC
8% IFP
4% UDM
4% Others

ANC = African National Congress **DP** = Democratic Party **IFP** = Inkatha Freedom Party **NNP** = New National Party **UDM** = United Democratic Movement **ACDP** = African Christian Democratic Party

National Council of Provinces 90 seats

10 members are elected to the National Council of Provinces by each of the nine provincial legislatures

South Africa became a multiracial democracy following elections in 1994.

Profile

The 1994 elections ended 45 years of apartheid and saw political power transferred to the ANC and to veteran ANC activist Nelson Mandela as president. In 1999 the party increased its majority, while Thabo Mbeki succeeded as president. Its dominance has enabled the introduction of reform but has stifled debate. It won the support of the former white-rule NNP in 2001 and in 2003 gained a two-thirds majority in the National Assembly through parliamentary defections.

Main Political Issues

Truth and reconciliation

The creation of the Truth and Reconciliation Commission (TRC) in 1996 to investigate and air the horrors of apartheid was a truly innovative step and one since replicated in other countries emerging from conflict. Two years of painful and often controversial hearings culminated in a final report in 1998. Initial praise has been modified by allegations of corruption. In 2003 the government agreed to pay $3800 to each victim of apartheid – a figure welcomed by some but derided by many as too little.

Coping with AIDS

South Africa is home to more than five million of the world's 40 million AIDS sufferers. The cost to the economy of health care, as well as coping with losses in the workforce, is debilitating and set to rise. The provision of treatments has been held up by controversy over international patents for drugs and even by President Mbeki's unorthodox stance on the nature of the infection itself. Public ignorance permeates national attitudes.

WORLD AFFAIRS

Joined UN in 1945

Comm | WTO | G24 | AU | SADC

After several decades of political isolation and economic sanctions, South Africa has been welcomed back into the international fold, and has rejoined the Commonwealth and the UN. It is a key member of the SADC and leads continental opinion on regional issues; it was in Durban that the AU was founded in 2002. Former president Mandela often intervened to help resolve foreign conflicts, and continues to act as a regional mediator, most notably in Burundi. He prompted some criticism from the West for his relations with apartheid-era supporters Libya and Cuba. His successor, Thabo Mbeki, has pushed forward the peace process in the Democratic Republic of the Congo, but has been criticized internationally for supporting Robert Mugabe's regime in neighboring Zimbabwe, and for his controversial opinions about HIV and AIDS.

South Africa

Total Area : 1 219 912 sq. km (471 008 sq. miles)

0 200 km
0 200 miles
N
ZIMBABWE
BOTSWANA
NAMIBIA
MOZAMBIQUE
SWAZILAND
LESOTHO
ATLANTIC OCEAN
INDIAN OCEAN
KALAHARI DESERT
LIMPOPO (NORTHERN)
NORTH WEST
GAUTENG
MPUMALANGA
FREE STATE
KWA ZULU NATAL
NORTHERN CAPE
NORTHERN KAROO
EASTERN CAPE
WESTERN CAPE
GREAT KAROO
DRAKENSBERG
LEBOMBO MOUNTAINS
Kruger National Park
Musina (Messina)
Louis Trichardt
Polokwane (Pietersburg)
Phalaborwa
Mokopane (Potgieterus)
Modimolle (Nylstroom)
Rustenburg
Johannesburg
PRETORIA
Mmabatho
Krugersdorp
Roodepoort-Maraisburg
Lichtenburg
Carletonville
Soweto
Benoni
Springs
Boksburg
Germiston
Middelburg
Witbank
Nelspruit
Ermelo
Potchefstroom
Klerksdorp
Vryburg
Vereeniging
Vaal
Sasolburg
Vanderbijlpark
Schweizer Reneke
Piet Retief
Kroonstad
Volksrust
Vryheid
Odendaalsrus
Welkom
Virginia
Bethlehem
Dundee
Harrismith
Lake St Lucia
Richard's Bay
Upington
Kaap Plato
Kimberley
Vaal
Orange
BLOEMFONTEIN
Estcourt
Giants Castle 3312m
Pietermaritzburg
Pinetown
Durban
Prieska
Grootvloer
Molopo
Caledon
De Aar
Colesberg
Aliwal North
Kokstad
Margate
Umtata
Middelburg
Queenstown
Beaufort West
Graaff-Reinet
Cradock
St Helena Bay
Great Fis
Mdantsane
East London
Paarl
Worcester
CAPE TOWN
Bellville
Uitenhage
George
Port Alfred
Port Elizabeth
Swellendam
Mosselbaai
Cape of Good Hope
24°
28°
32°
20°
Prince Edward Is
Prince Edward I.
Marion I.
Swart Peak 1230m
Cape Hooker
0 5 km
0 5 miles
37°30′
38°
47°
POPULATION
over 1 000 000
over 500 000
over 100 000
over 50 000
over 10 000
LAND HEIGHT
2000m/6562ft
1000m/3281ft
500m/1640ft
Sea Level

SOUTH AFRICA'S THREE CAPITALS

Pretoria - *administrative*
Cape Town - *legislative*
Bloemfontein - *judicial*

S

AID

Recipient

$428m (receipts) | Down 12% in 2001

Apartheid-era South Africa was denied aid, particularly from the World Bank and the IMF. It now seeks financial assistance for massive reconstruction programs. As part of Nepad – Africa's "Marshall Plan" launched in 2002 – President Mbeki stressed the importance of ending reliance on foreign aid.

CHRONOLOGY

Until 1652, what is now South Africa was peopled by Bantu-speaking groups and San nomads. Then Dutch settlers arrived. British colonizers followed in the 18th century.

- **1910** Union of South Africa set up as British dominion; white monopoly of power formalized.
- **1912** ANC formed.
- **1934** Independence.
- **1948** National Party (NP, now NNP) takes power; apartheid segregationist policy introduced.
- **1958–1966** Hendrik Verwoerd prime minister. "Grand Apartheid" policy implemented.
- **1959** Pan-Africanist Congress (PAC) formed.
- **1960** Sharpeville massacre. ANC, PAC banned.
- **1961** South Africa becomes republic; leaves Commonwealth.
- **1964** Senior ANC leader Nelson Mandela jailed.
- **1976** Soweto uprisings by black students; hundreds killed.
- **1978** P. W. Botha in office.
- **1984** New constitution: Indians and Coloreds get some representation. Growing black opposition.
- **1985** State of emergency. Sanctions.
- **1989** F. W. De Klerk replaces Botha as president.
- **1990** De Klerk legalizes ANC and PAC; frees Nelson Mandela.
- **1990–1993** International sanctions gradually withdrawn.
- **1991** Convention for a Democratic South Africa (CODESA) starts work.
- **1993** Mandela and De Klerk win Nobel Peace Prize.
- **1994** Multiracial elections won by ANC; Mandela president.
- **1996** TRC begins work.
- **1997** New constitution takes effect.
- **1998** TRC report condemns both apartheid crimes and ANC excesses.
- **1999** ANC election victory; Thabo Mbeki succeeds Mandela.
- **2000** Opposition alliance wins nearly 25% of votes in local elections.
- **2001–2002** Rand goes from record low to record high.
- **2002** World summit on sustainable development held in Johannesburg.

DEFENSE

No compulsory military service

$1.83bn | Down 9% in 2001

SOUTH AFRICAN ARMED FORCES

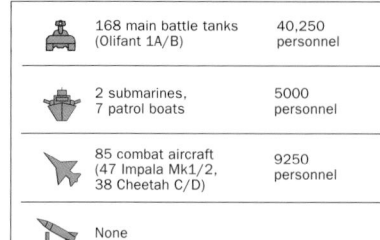

168 main battle tanks (Olifant 1A/B)	40,250 personnel
2 submarines, 7 patrol boats	5000 personnel
85 combat aircraft (47 Impala Mk1/2, 38 Cheetah C/D)	9250 personnel
None	

The creation by postapartheid South Africa of a truly national defense force seems almost miraculous, as it fuses together once bitter enemies: soldiers from the old white-run army, and guerrillas from the liberation groups.

However, doubts have been raised over the army's ability to operate effectively. A freeze on recruitment since 1994 has raised the average age of troops and created a glut of higher-ranking officers, while the incidence of AIDS is increasing. A large arms procurement program, announced in late 1998, failed to overcome the effects of previous swingeing cuts in spending. Few tanks are operational and the air force tends to run out of fuel toward the end of each financial year.

A major arms industry is the legacy of years of sanctions.

ECONOMICS

Inflation 9.3% p.a. (1990–2001)

$122bn | 7.51 rand (10.31)

SCORE CARD

- World GNP Ranking 30th
- GNP per Capita $2820
- Balance of Payments .... –$166m
- Inflation 5.7%
- Unemployment 30%

EXPORTS

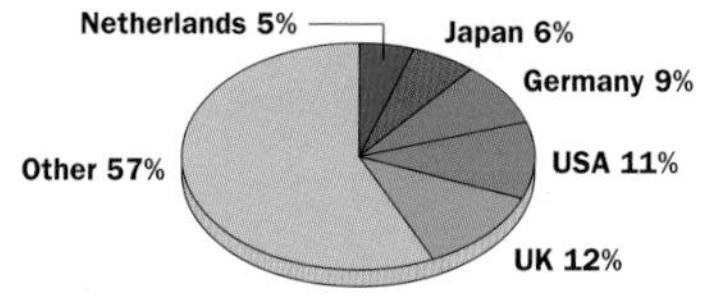
Netherlands 5%
Japan 6%
Germany 9%
USA 11%
UK 12%
Other 57%

IMPORTS

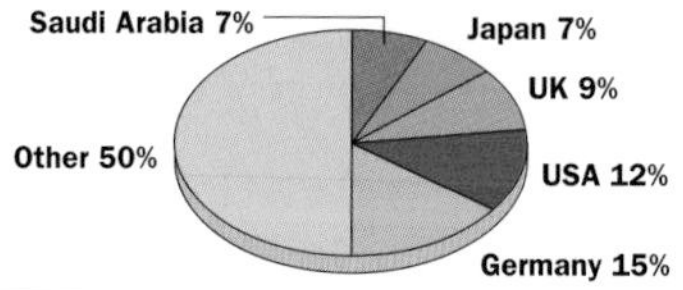
Saudi Arabia 7%
Japan 7%
UK 9%
USA 12%
Germany 15%
Other 50%

ECONOMIC PERFORMANCE INDICATOR

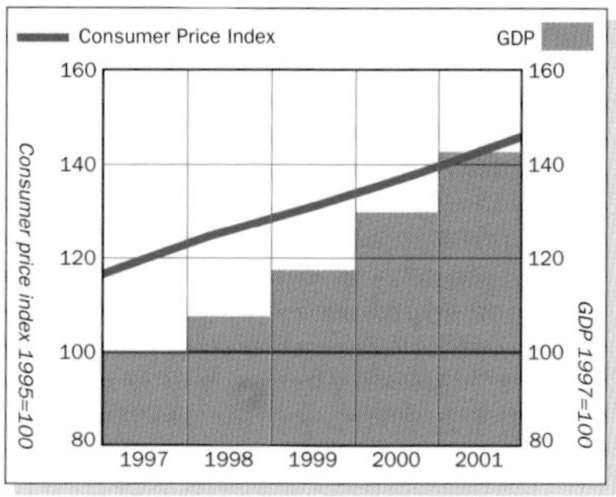
Consumer Price Index
GDP
160
140
120
100
80
Consumer price index 1995=100
GDP 1997=100
1997
1998
1999
2000
2001

Strengths

Africa's largest and most developed economy; highly diversified with modern infrastructure. Strong financial sector for mobilizing investment. Growing manufacturing sector. Varied resource base.

Weaknesses

Security fears deter investment. Growth too low to overcome deprivation among blacks; black unemployment growing by 2.5% a year. Cost of AIDS treatments. Emigration of skilled workers. Population boom. Falling gold price undermines many sectors.

Profile

South Africa has a large and diverse private sector, much of it controlled by multinationals. Privatizations have gone some way to reverse the strong state-control necessitated by apartheid-era sanctions. The ANC cooperates with big business in an effort to revivify the economy and develop the townships, but a report in 2003 showed that wealth disparities between the wealthy white elite and the majority black community are widening.

SOUTH AFRICA : MAJOR BUSINESSES

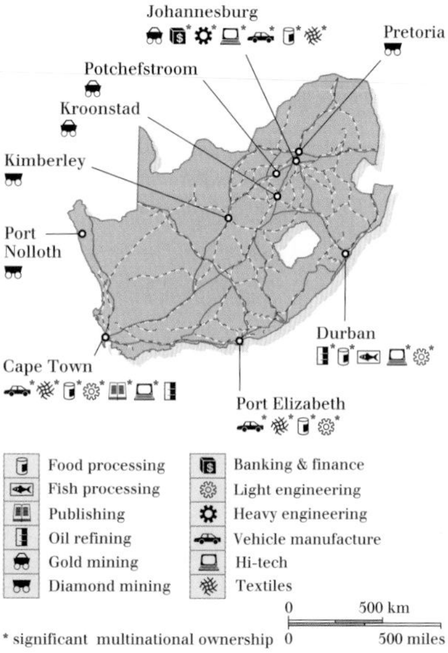
Johannesburg
Pretoria
Potchefstroom
Kroonstad
Kimberley
Port Nolloth
Durban
Cape Town
Port Elizabeth
Food processing
Fish processing
Publishing
Oil refining
Gold mining
Diamond mining
Banking & finance
Light engineering
Heavy engineering
Vehicle manufacture
Hi-tech
Textiles
0
500 km
500 miles
* significant multinational ownership

RESOURCES

Electric power 36.3m kW

647,763 tonnes

152,761 b/d (reserves 56m barrels)

29.1m sheep, 13.7m cattle, 119m chickens

Gold, coal, vanadium, vermiciline, diamonds, chromium, manganese, uranium, nickel

ELECTRICITY GENERATION

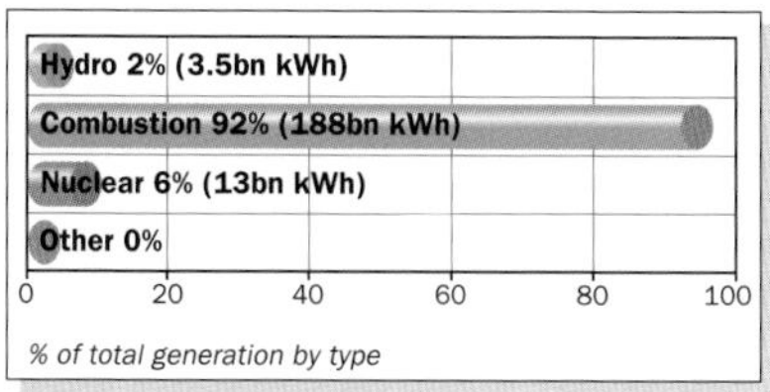
Hydro 2% (3.5bn kWh)
Combustion 92% (188bn kWh)
Nuclear 6% (13bn kWh)
Other 0%
0
20
40
60
80
100
% of total generation by type

South Africa has some of the continent's richest natural resources, in particular minerals. Its dominance of the world market in gold and diamonds helped it survive sanctions during apartheid. The falling price of gold in 2000 meant that for the first time sales of platinum group metals outstripped those of gold. South Africa is the largest single producer of manganese, chrome ore, vanadium, and vermiciline. It also produces uranium and nickel.

With little oil, South Africa pioneered the transformation of coal into oil, and otherwise uses its huge coal reserves to generate electricity. Almost 15 million black South Africans are without electricity, and nongrid options are being considered, including developing solar energy.

SOUTH AFRICA : LAND USE

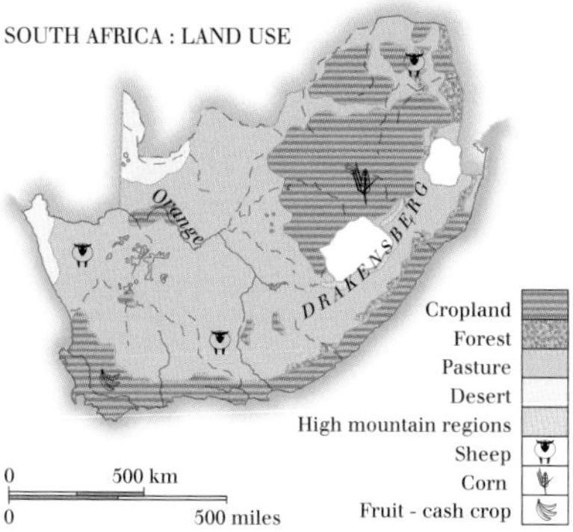
Orange
DRAKENSBERG
Cropland
Forest
Pasture
Desert
High mountain regions
Sheep
Corn
Fruit - cash crop
0
500 km
0
500 miles

ENVIRONMENT

Sustainability rank: 77th

6% (2% partially protected)

7.7 tonnes per capita

ENVIRONMENTAL TREATIES

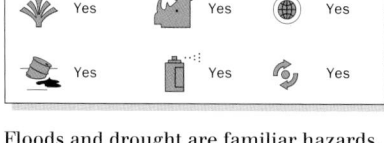

Yes | Yes | Yes

Yes | Yes | Yes

Floods and drought are familiar hazards. The world's largest game park, straddling the borders with Zimbabwe and Mozambique, was opened in 2002. The littering of flimsy plastic bags was so severe that they were banned in 2003.

MEDIA

TV ownership medium

Daily newspaper circulation 29 per 1000 people

PUBLISHING AND BROADCAST MEDIA

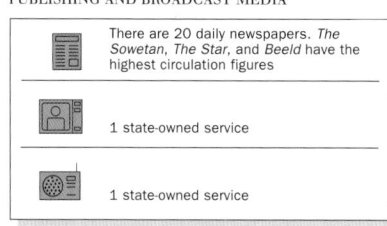

There are 20 daily newspapers. *The Sowetan, The Star*, and *Beeld* have the highest circulation figures

1 state-owned service

1 state-owned service

A drive to combat racial stereotyping in the media was launched following a report on the subject to the Human Rights Commission in early 2000.

CRIME

No death penalty

176,893 prisoners

Up 14% in 2000–2001

CRIME RATES

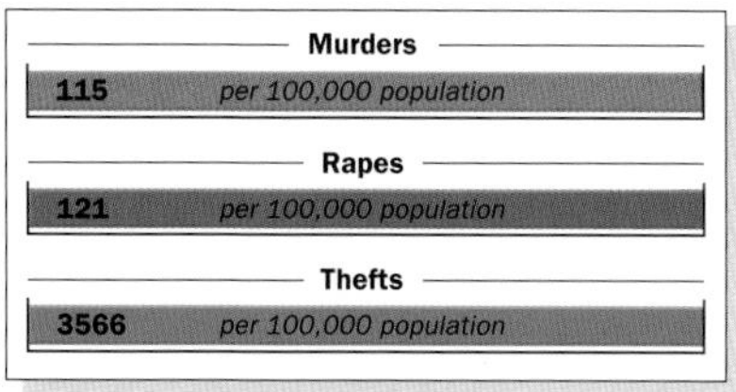
Murders
115
per 100,000 population
Rapes
121
per 100,000 population
Thefts
3566
per 100,000 population

South Africa is a dangerous country, and crime rates are rising: murders occur with extreme frequency, and rape, armed robberies, and muggings are rife. Vigilantism is a huge problem in the Cape. The death penalty was abolished in 1997. The government introduced new gun laws in 2000.

EDUCATION

School leaving age: 15

86%

644,763 students

THE EDUCATION SYSTEM

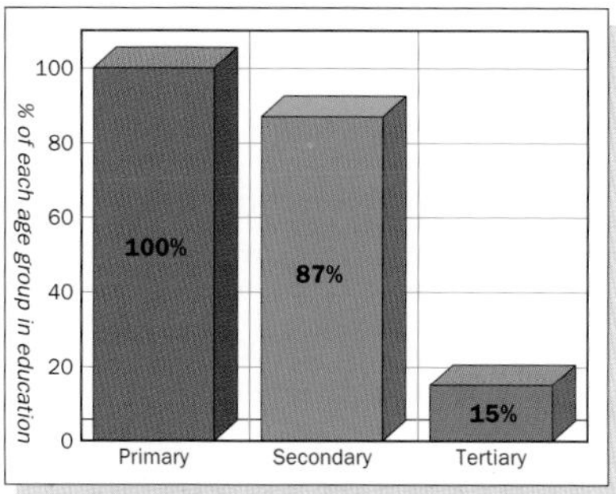
100
80
60
40
20
0
% of each age group in education
100%
87%
15%
Primary
Secondary
Tertiary

Education reform is a central task of the postapartheid government. Progress has been made in improving national literacy, and access to education has been widened through the Tirisano (working together) education program, launched in 2000. Long-established universities continue to be white-dominated.

HEALTH

Welfare state health benefits

1 per 226 people

Accidents, violence, AIDS, infectious and respiratory diseases

Health services were desegregated formally in 1990, but equal access to care is still a distant goal. Statistics on medical provision hide a strong bias toward whites and urban areas, where 80% of doctors work; 20% of children in rural areas die before the age of five, which is a rate considerably higher than the sub-Saharan average. South Africa has five million AIDS sufferers, more than any other country. The government has won the right to buy cheaper generic drugs for AIDS sufferers and has increased spending, but has balked at the potential cost of widespread provision.

SPENDING

GDP/cap. increase

CONSUMPTION AND SPENDING

94 per 1000 population

112 per 1000 population

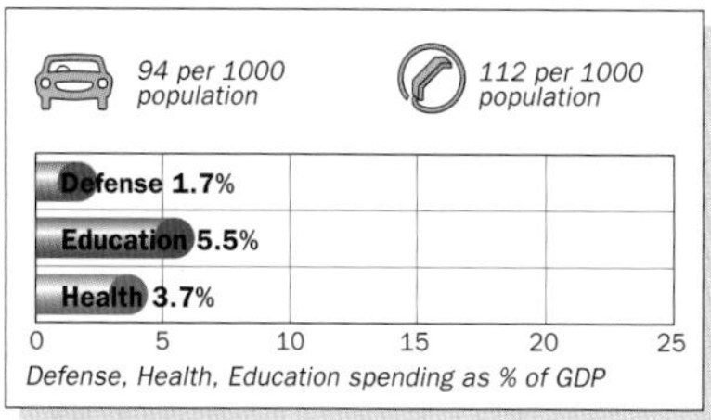
Defense 1.7%
Education 5.5%
Health 3.7%
0
5
10
15
20
25
Defense, Health, Education spending as % of GDP

Wealth disparities are marked and widening. At the top, the white elite enjoys living standards similar to those of Californians. In contrast, living conditions for the poorest group, the majority black community, are among Africa's lowest. More than 40% of black adults are unemployed. In between are the mixed race and Asian communities, who enjoyed more privileges under apartheid's strict racial hierarchy. However, a small black middle class is growing slowly, with some black-owned firms doing well on the stock market. In 2003, the government offered $3800 each to victims of apartheid.

S

WORLD RANKING

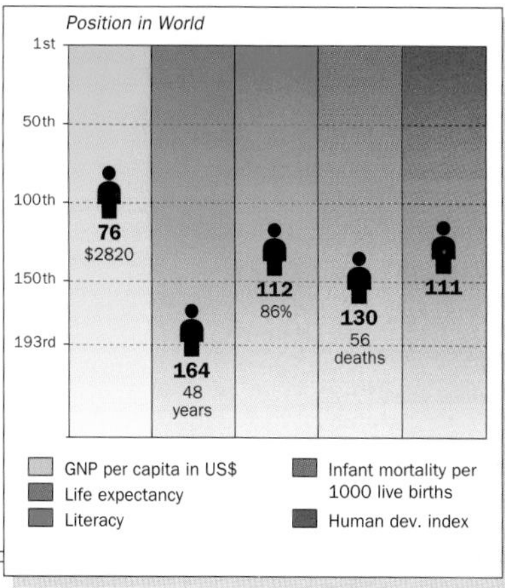
Position in World
1st
50th
100th
150th
193rd
76
$2820
164
48
years
112
86%
130
56
deaths
111
GNP per capita in US$
Life expectancy
Literacy
Infant mortality per 1000 live births
Human dev. index

Spain

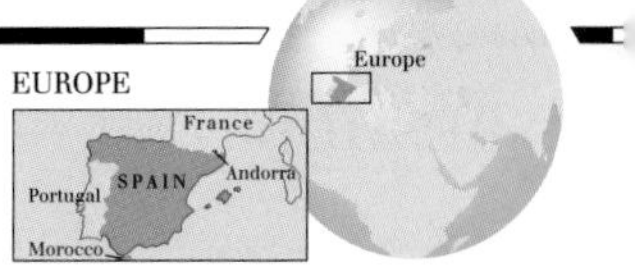
EUROPE
Europe
France
SPAIN
Andorra
Portugal
Morocco

Official Name: Kingdom of Spain **Capital:** Madrid **Population:** 39.9 million
Currency: Euro **Official Languages:** Spanish, Galician, Basque, and Catalan

1492 | 1713 | Oct 12 | E | +1 | +34 | .es

OCCUPYING THE MAJOR PART of the Iberian peninsula in southwest Europe, Spain has both an Atlantic and a Mediterranean coast, and is dominated by a central plateau. After the death of Gen. Franco in 1975, the country managed a rapid and relatively peaceful transition to democracy under the supervision of King Juan Carlos I. Since EU membership in 1986, there has been an increasing devolution of power to the regions. For just over 13 years from 1982, Spain had a center-left government, but the right-of-center Popular Party has dominated since 1996.

***Alcaudete, Jaén Province,** in the Andalusian mountains between the Guadalquivir River and Granada. The ruined castle is Moorish.*

CLIMATE

Mediterranean/maritime/mountain

WEATHER CHART FOR MADRID

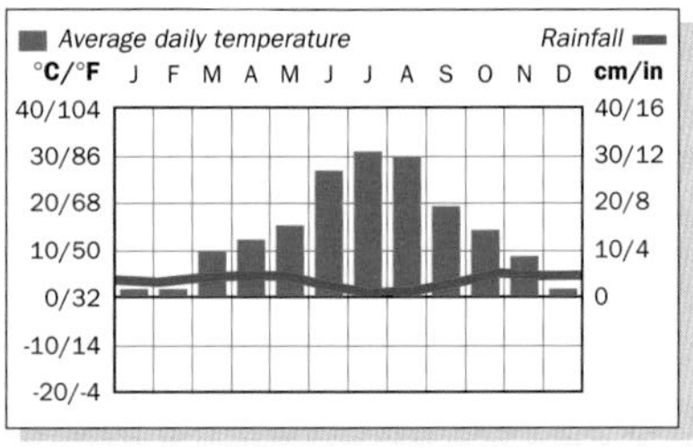
Average daily temperature
Rainfall
°C/°F
J F M A M J J A S O N D
cm/in
40/104
30/86
20/68
10/50
0/32
-10/14
-20/-4
40/16
30/12
20/8
10/4
0

The central plateau, or *meseta*, endures an extreme climate. Coastal areas are milder, and are wetter in the north than in the south.

TRANSPORTATION

Drive on right

Barajas, Madrid 33.9m passengers

1545 ships 2.15m grt

THE TRANSPORTATION NETWORK

343,389 km (213,372 miles)

9063 km (5631 miles)

13,868 km (8617 miles)

1045 km (649 miles)

The AVE high-speed train links Madrid and Seville; more routes are planned. The state-run rail company RENFE is to be privatized gradually.

PEOPLE

Pop. density medium

Spanish, Catalan, Galician, Basque

80/km² (207/mi²)

THE URBAN/RURAL POPULATION SPLIT

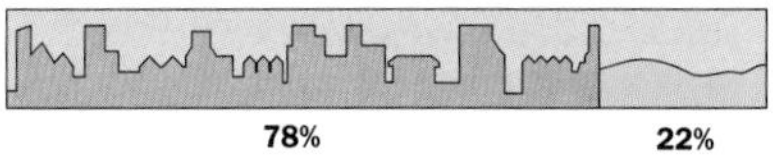
78%
22%

RELIGIOUS PERSUASION

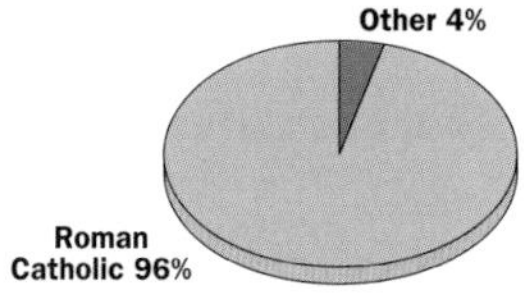
Other 4%
Roman Catholic 96%

ETHNIC MAKEUP

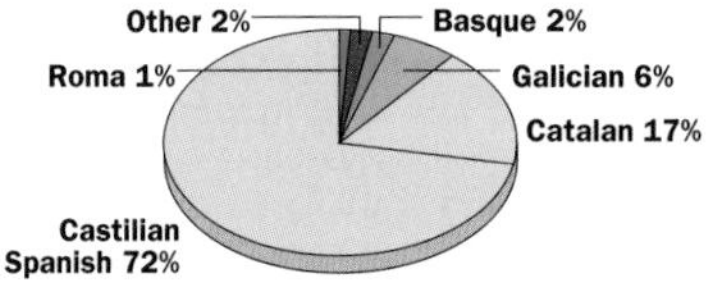
Other 2%
Basque 2%
Roma 1%
Galician 6%
Catalan 17%
Castilian Spanish 72%

POPULATION AGE BREAKDOWN

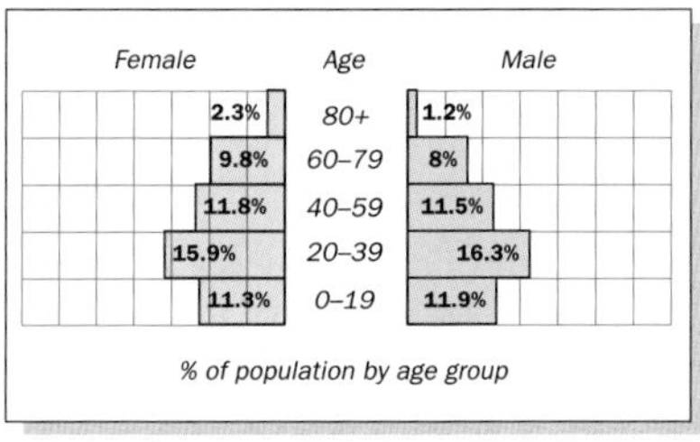
Female
Age
Male
2.3%
80+
1.2%
9.8%
60–79
8%
11.8%
40–59
11.5%
15.9%
20–39
16.3%
11.3%
0–19
11.9%
% of population by age group

A vigorous regionalism, suppressed under Franco, now flourishes. Catalonia is an example, with Barcelona its vibrant capital. In the Basque region, the ETA separatists who fight for independence by waging a high-profile terror campaign remain in a minority.

Spain today has one of the lowest birthrates in Europe, just half that of 1975. The influence of the Roman Catholic Church on personal behavior has declined, and attitudes to sexuality are now relaxed. Nonetheless, the divorce rate is very low, and family ties remain strong; men often live at home until their late 20s.

Migration from rural regions to the coast since the 1970s has been associated with the arrival of immigrants from Latin America and north Africa. A rise in racial tensions and racism has resulted. The relaxing in 2003 of immigration rules for second-generation Spanish emigrants was expected to draw over a million people, especially from Latin America.

Spanish women are increasingly emancipated and more influential in public life, making up over 25% of the deputies and senators in the Spanish parliament, and heading 30% of businesses.

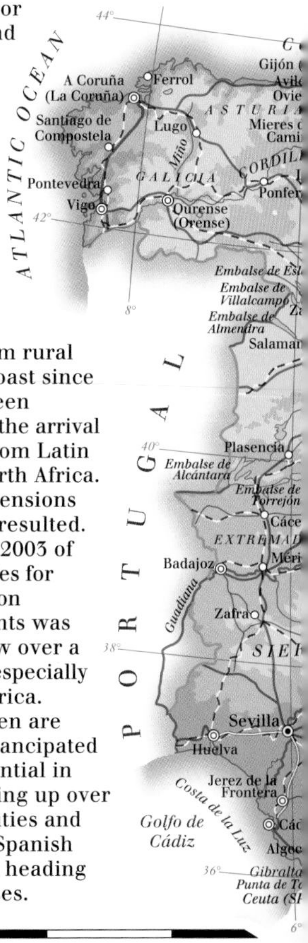
ATLANTIC OCEAN
A Coruña (La Coruña)
Ferrol
Santiago de Compostela
Lugo
Pontevedra
Vigo
GALICIA
Ourense (Orense)
PORTUGAL
Plasencia
Badajoz
Zafra
Sevilla
Huelva
Jerez de la Frontera
Golfo de Cádiz
Costa de la Luz

TOURISM

Visitors : Population 1.3:1

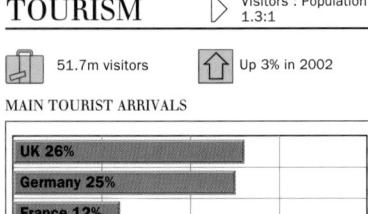

51.7m visitors

Up 3% in 2002

MAIN TOURIST ARRIVALS

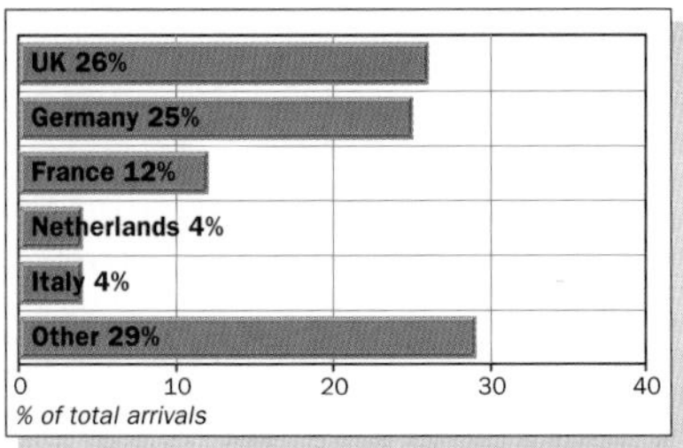
UK 26%
Germany 25%
France 12%
Netherlands 4%
Italy 4%
Other 29%
0
10
20
30
40
% of total arrivals

Tourism earnings in 2001 topped $33 billion. Long dominant in the vacation-package sector, Spain has recently adopted marketing strategies to boost additional cultural, historical, and environmental tourism. Several areas began levying an environmental tax on tourist arrivals in 2001. The cut-price package industry has benefited from political turbulence in potential competitor countries in the Mediterranean. The four Balearic Islands attract large numbers of visitors.

S

POLITICS

Multiparty elections

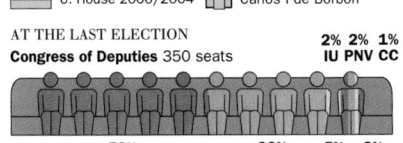

L. House 2000/2004
U. House 2000/2004

H.R.H. King Juan Carlos I de Borbón

AT THE LAST ELECTION

Congress of Deputies 350 seats

2% IU
2% PNV
1% CC
52% PP
36% PSOE
5% CiU
2% Others

PP = Popular Party **PSOE** = Spanish Socialist Workers' Party **CiU** = Convergence and Union **IU** = United Left **PNV** = Basque Nationalist Party **CC** = Canary Islands Coalition **App** = Appointed

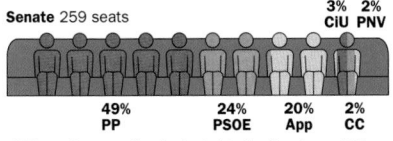

Senate 259 seats

3% CiU
2% PNV
49% PP
24% PSOE
20% App
2% CC

208 members are directly elected to the Senate, and 51 appointed by autonomous communities

Since 1978, Spain has been a semifederal multiparty parliamentary monarchy. Each region has a legislative assembly.

PROFILE

The PSOE's long period in power blurred the boundaries between party and state. The Cortes (parliament) failed to check executive power, and political disputes were often left to the judiciary, while corruption undermined voters' faith in Spain's political system. The PP government, led from 1996 by José María Aznar, benefited from being seen as a fresh start. Its relative success in running the economy helped it win a second term in 2000, despite a pact between the PSOE and the United Left. Ideological issues no longer sharply divide the main parties.

MAIN POLITICAL ISSUES

Increasing regionalism

Spain's 17 autonomous regions all vie for greater funds or independence from Madrid. Many have bypassed central government to borrow funds on the international money markets, and have come close to breaching their legal debt limits. In 1996 the PP government approved a fresh model of financing for the regions which gave them new powers for raising tax revenue. The Basque separatist movement ETA has, with intermittent cease-fire announcements, waged a protracted violent struggle for independence, prompting large-scale demonstrations against violence. Its political wing, Batasuna, was banned in 2003. The Basque country, Catalonia, and Galicia each use their own language alongside Castilian Spanish.

Clean government

Initially the PP government suffered less from the corruption scandals which had dogged the last years of its PSOE predecessor, but in 2001 its reputation was tarnished by the alleged involvement of several PP members in corruption cases, including the collapse of the Gescartera stockbroking house.

King Juan Carlos, who became head of state on the death of Franco in 1975.

José María Aznar, of the PP, was appointed prime minister in 1996.

WORLD AFFAIRS

Joined UN in 1955

CE | NATO | OECD | OSCE | EU

Relations with Morocco, strained over illegal immigrants, are jeopardized over sovereignty of rocky Mediterranean islets and the exclaves of Ceuta and Melilla. There is a long-standing disagreement with the UK over the status of Gibraltar. Recently, Spain and the UK have been willing to negotiate, but the colony itself opposes any change. The government's close alliance with the US and the UK over the 2003 war in Iraq ran contrary to public opinion. Elsewhere, Spain has sponsored an Ibero-American Community of Nations (a Hispanic Commonwealth). Spain's first contribution to a UN peacekeeping force was for operations in the Balkans.

SPAIN
Total Area : 504 782 sq. km (194 896 sq. miles)
POPULATION
over 1 000 000
over 500 000
over 100 000
over 50 000
over 10 000
LAND HEIGHT
3000m/9843ft
2000m/6562ft
1000m/3281ft
500m/1640ft
Sea Level
0 100 km
0 100 miles
FRANCE
ANDORRA
PYRENEES
MEDITERRANEAN SEA
Islas Baleares
Golfo de Valencia
Menorca
Mallorca
Eivissa
Formentera
Palma
Barcelona
Zaragoza
Valencia
Bilbao
Santander
Irún
Donostia-San Sebastian
Pamplona (Iruña)
Vitoria
Logroño
Burgos
Huesca
Lleida
Tarragona
Reus
Sabadell
Terrassa
Mataró
Badalona
Girona (Gerona)
Figueres
Tortosa
Teruel
Cuenca
Castellón de la Plana
Paterna
Gandia
Benidorm
Alicante
Elche
Elda
Cieza
Murcia
Cartagena
Lorca
Almería
Granada
Jaén
Linares
Málaga
Motril
Albacete
Soria
Segovia
Getafe
Alcalá de Henares
Melilla (SPAIN)
MOROCCO
Islas Canarias
La Palma
Santa Cruz de Tenerife
La Laguna
Gomera
Tenerife
Hierro
Gran Canaria
Las Palmas
Lanzarote
Fuerteventura

CHRONOLOGY

United under Ferdinand and Isabella in 1492, Spain became a dominant force. A long period of economic and political decline followed, however, and by the mid-19th century, Spain lagged behind many other European countries in stability and prosperity.

- **1874** Constitutional monarchy restored under Alfonso XII.
- **1879** PSOE founded.
- **1881** Trade unions legalized.
- **1885** Death of Alfonso XII.
- **1898** Defeat in war with US results in loss of Cuba, Puerto Rico, and the Philippines.
- **1914–1918** Spain neutral in World War I.
- **1921** Spanish army routed by Berbers in Spanish Morocco.
- **1923** Coup by Gen. Primo de Rivera accepted by King Alfonso XIII. Military dictatorship.
- **1930** Primo de Rivera dismissed by monarchy.
- **1931** Second Republic proclaimed. Alfonso XIII flees Spain.
- **1933** Center-right coalition wins general election.

S

CHRONOLOGY *continued*

- **1934** Asturias uprising quashed by army. Failure of attempt to form Catalan state.
- **1936** Popular Front wins elections. Right-wing military uprising against Republic. Gen. Francisco Franco subsequently appointed leader.
- **1939** Franco wins civil war which claims 300,000 lives.
- **1940** Franco meets Hitler, but does not enter World War II.
- **1946** UN condemns Franco regime.
- **1948** Spain excluded from the Marshall Plan.
- **1950** UN lifts veto.
- **1953** Concordat with Vatican. Spain grants US military bases.
- **1955** Spain joins UN.
- **1959** Stabilization Plan is basis for 1960s rapid economic growth.
- **1962** Franco government applies for eventual membership of EEC.
- **1969** Franco names Juan Carlos, grandson of Alfonso XIII, his successor.
- **1970** Spain signs preferential trade agreement with EEC.
- **1973** Basque separatists assassinate prime minister Luis Carrero Blanco; replaced by Carlos Arias Navarro.
- **1975** Death of Franco. Proclamation of King Juan Carlos I.
- **1976** King appoints Adolfo Suárez as prime minister.
- **1977** First democratic elections since 1936 won by Suárez's Democratic Center Union.
- **1978** New constitution declares Spain a parliamentary monarchy.
- **1981** Leopoldo Calvo Sotelo replaces Suárez. King foils military coup. Calvo takes Spain into NATO.
- **1982** Felipe González wins landslide victory for PSOE.
- **1986** Joins European Communities. González wins referendum on keeping Spain in NATO.
- **1992** Olympic Games held in Barcelona, Expo '92 in Seville.
- **1996** PSOE loses election; José María Aznar of PP prime minister.
- **1998** Former PSOE minister found guilty of involvement in Basque kidnappings. September, ETA cease-fire; holds until December 1999.
- **2000** Aznar and PP win elections.
- **2002** Euro adopted. Sunken oil tanker *Prestige* pollutes Galicia.

AID

Donor

$1.74bn (donations)

Up 45% in 2001

Spain has taken steps to increase grant aid after criticism that Spanish aid was of poor quality and tied to the acquisition of goods and services. Aid in 2001 represented 0.3% of GNP.

DEFENSE

No compulsory military service

$6.94bn

Down 2% in 2001

A substantial, largely state-owned, and commercially nonviable defense industry is subsidized for strategic reasons. Full integration of NATO military structures was approved in 1997. Government spending on defense has fallen in recent years, and is below the NATO average. National service has been abolished; the last conscripts worked out their terms of duty in the course of 2002.

SPANISH ARMED FORCES

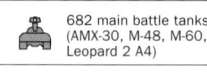

682 main battle tanks (AMX-30, M-48, M-60, Leopard 2 A4)	118,800 personnel
8 submarines, 1 carrier, 15 frigates, 37 patrol boats	26,950 personnel
198 combat aircraft (F-5B, EF/A-18 A/B, RF-4C, Mirage F-1CF/BE/EE)	22,750 personnel
None	

ECONOMICS

Inflation 3.9% p.a. (1990–2001)

$588bn

0.871 euros (1.013)

SCORE CARD

- World GNP Ranking 9th
- GNP per Capita $14,300
- Balance of Payments .... –$15.1bn
- Inflation 3.6%
- Unemployment 11%

EXPORTS

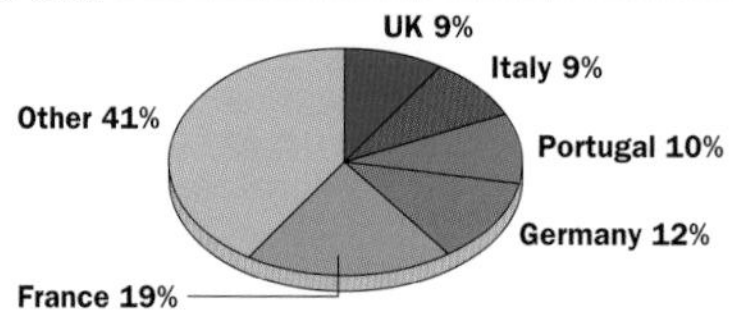
UK 9%
Italy 9%
Portugal 10%
Germany 12%
France 19%
Other 41%

IMPORTS

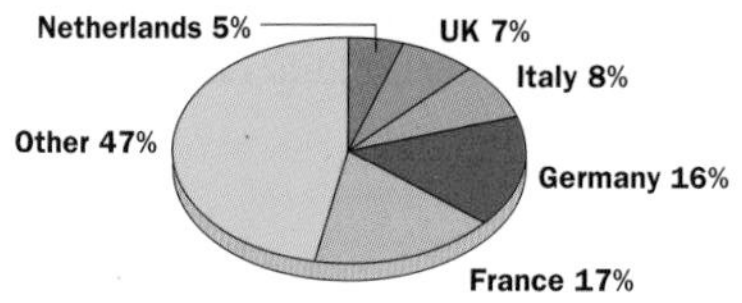
Netherlands 5%
UK 7%
Italy 8%
Germany 16%
France 17%
Other 47%

Strengths

One of the fastest-growing OECD economies. Well-qualified labor force with relatively low labor costs. Privatization has introduced greater competition into gas, oil-refining, electricity, and telecommunications sectors.

Weaknesses

Foreign penetration of economy, few homegrown multinationals. Low investment in research and development, concentration in declining industries, and low productivity – notably in agriculture. Persistent high unemployment. Recent major investments in Latin American market undermined by Argentine crisis.

Profile

Real convergence with the major European economies first became a realistic objective in the late 1980s, as Spain posted the highest investment-led output growth in the OECD.

ECONOMIC PERFORMANCE INDICATOR

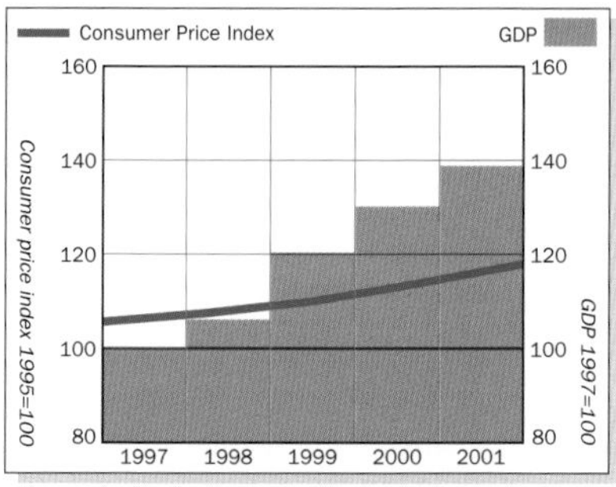
Consumer Price Index
GDP
160
140
120
100
80
1997
1998
1999
2000
2001
Consumer price index 1995=100
GDP 1997=100

By 1991, GDP per capita stood at almost 80% of the EU average. Recession in the early 1990s was turned around in mid-decade, and growth averaged 4% over 1997–2000, with public debt brought below 60% of GDP by 2001. The economy slowed markedly through 2001, and the annualized growth rate dropped to around 2%.

Spain succeeded in meeting the economic convergence criteria necessary for European economic and monetary union and was among the 12 EU countries to adopt the euro fully in January 2002.

SPAIN : MAJOR BUSINESSES

La Coruña
Bilbao
Zaragoza
Barcelona
Vigo
Madrid
Huelva
Valencia
Sevilla
Málaga
Cartagena
Textiles
Agribusiness
Chemicals
Shipbuilding
Vehicle manufacture
Heavy engineering
Light engineering
Fish processing
0 200 km
0 200 miles
* significant multinational ownership

RESOURCES

Electric power 50.9m kW

1.29m tonnes

5995 b/d (reserves 6.6m barrels)

24.3m sheep, 23.9m pigs, 128m chickens

Coal, oil, iron, uranium, mercury, fluorite, gypsum

ELECTRICITY GENERATION

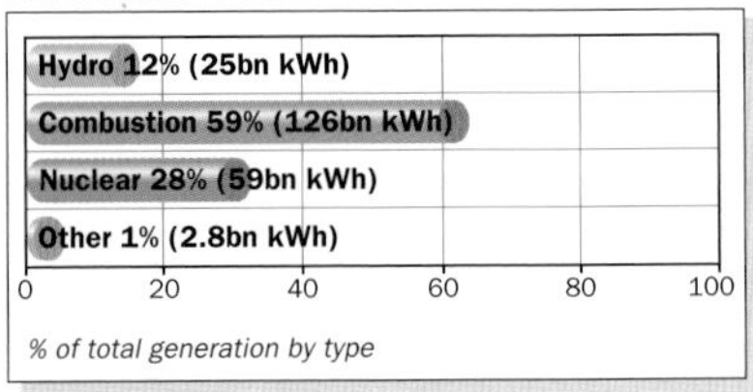
Hydro 12% (25bn kWh)
Combustion 59% (126bn kWh)
Nuclear 28% (59bn kWh)
Other 1% (2.8bn kWh)
0
20
40
60
80
100
% of total generation by type

Spain lacks natural resources, especially water, and is heavily dependent on imported oil and gas. Coal, mined mainly to generate industry, is a declining but still subsidized sector, concentrated in the Asturias region. Spain has one of the world's largest fishing fleets, but EU restrictions have forced cuts in catches since the 1990s.

SPAIN : LAND USE

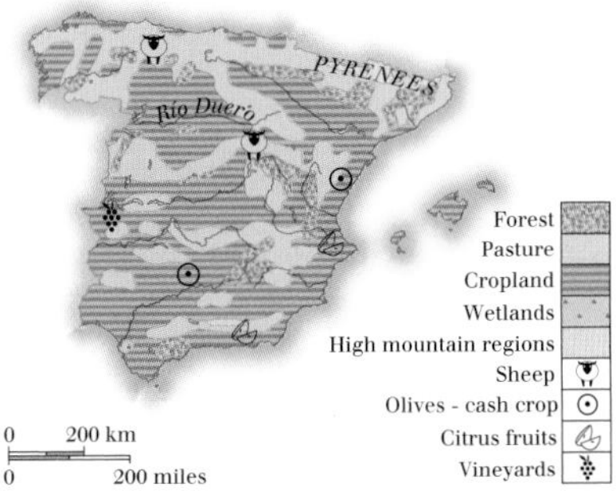
PYRENEES
Río Duero
Forest
Pasture
Cropland
Wetlands
High mountain regions
Sheep
Olives - cash crop
Citrus fruits
Vineyards
0 200 km
0 200 miles

ENVIRONMENT

Sustainability rank: 44th

9% (8% partially protected)

7.5 tonnes per capita

ENVIRONMENTAL TREATIES

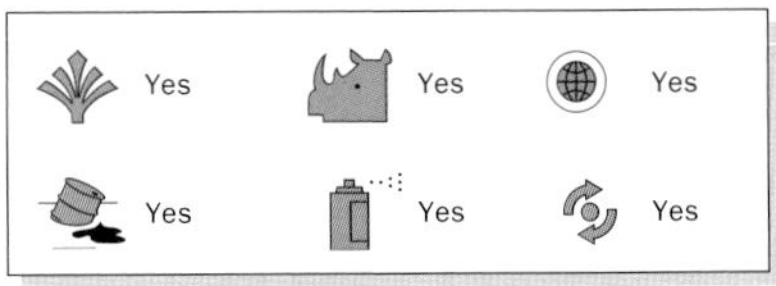
Yes
Yes
Yes
Yes
Yes
Yes

Public awareness of environmental matters is increasing. Renewable energy, though still tiny in extent, is becoming more visible, particularly with the growth of wind farms. The benefits of a national tree-planting scheme to reduce soil erosion have been offset by increasingly frequent intentional forest fires. More land has national park status than in any other country in Europe. While dams and canals are necessary to counter desertification in the south, environmentalists oppose their construction. A project to bring water from the Ebro River to the parched south is causing controversy. Oil from the *Prestige* oil tanker which sank off Galicia in 2002 caused extensive pollution.

MEDIA

TV ownership high

Daily newspaper circulation 100 per 1000 people

PUBLISHING AND BROADCAST MEDIA

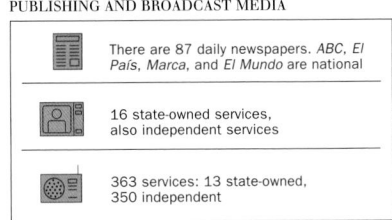

There are 87 daily newspapers. *ABC*, *El País*, *Marca*, and *El Mundo* are national

16 state-owned services, also independent services

363 services: 13 state-owned, 350 independent

Despite the large number of daily newspapers, readership is among the lowest in Europe. Both public and private TV services are popular. Radio is of a generally high standard.

CRIME

No death penalty

50,656 prisoners

Down 47% in 2000–2001

CRIME RATES

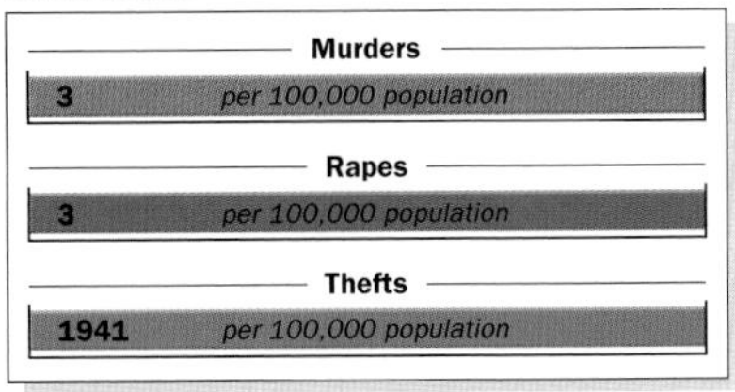
Murders
3 per 100,000 population
Rapes
3 per 100,000 population
Thefts
1941 per 100,000 population

Spain is a major crossroads in the world narcotics trade, and drugs-related crime is rising. Illegal immigration has soared, with authorities in the south unable to cope with the influx.

EDUCATION

School leaving age: 16

98%

1.83m students

THE EDUCATION SYSTEM

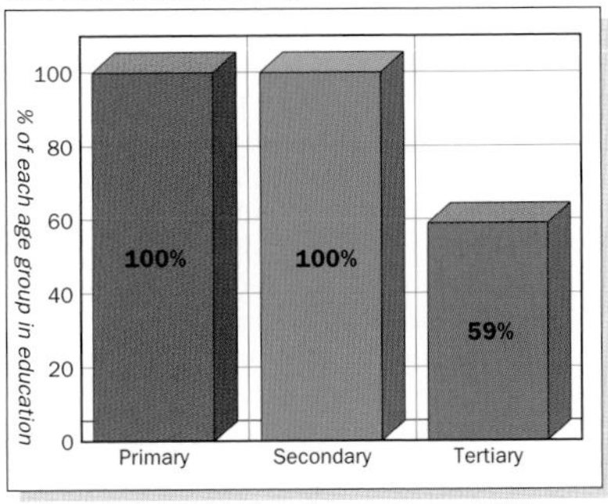
100
80
60
40
20
0
% of each age group in education
100%
100%
59%
Primary
Secondary
Tertiary

The school leaving age has risen since 1990 from 14 to 16. The latest secondary education reforms, announced in 2000, offer a number of additional subjects, improvements in mathematics, philosophy, and languages, and increasing attention to information technology. Autonomous regions regulate by decree the teaching of languages other than Castilian Spanish, such as Basque or Catalan.

HEALTH

Welfare state health benefits

1 per 229 people

Cancers, heart, cerebrovascular, and respiratory diseases

Public health care is of high quality and readily available. Public hospitals, though widely considered to be superior, are outnumbered by private ones. In spite of very high tobacco and alcohol consumption, Spain has a healthy population, possibly due to its Mediterranean diet. The incidence of AIDS has risen alarmingly, however, to become one of the highest in western Europe.

SPENDING

GDP/cap. increase

CONSUMPTION AND SPENDING

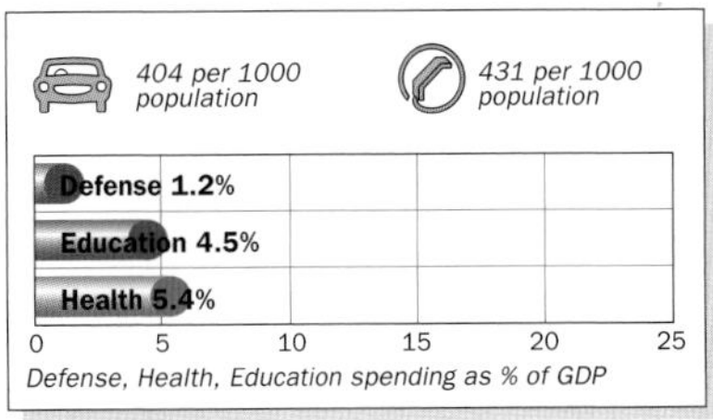
404 per 1000 population
431 per 1000 population
Defense 1.2%
Education 4.5%
Health 5.4%
0
5
10
15
20
25
Defense, Health, Education spending as % of GDP

In the late 1980s, it became fashionable in Spain to compete openly, make money, and acquire consumer goods. Rapid economic growth at this time greatly enriched the professional and managerial classes. The latter became the best-paid, in real terms, in Europe, and Spain quickly became an important market for luxury cars and yachts. In the early 1990s this ostentatious affluence waned in the face of recession and an unemployment rate which soared to become one of the highest in Europe. The boom of 1997–2000 boosted the number of jobs, but also gave rise to anxiety over inflation. By 2001 this boom too had subsided, and there was less financial security, with about one-third of employees on only temporary contracts.

WORLD RANKING

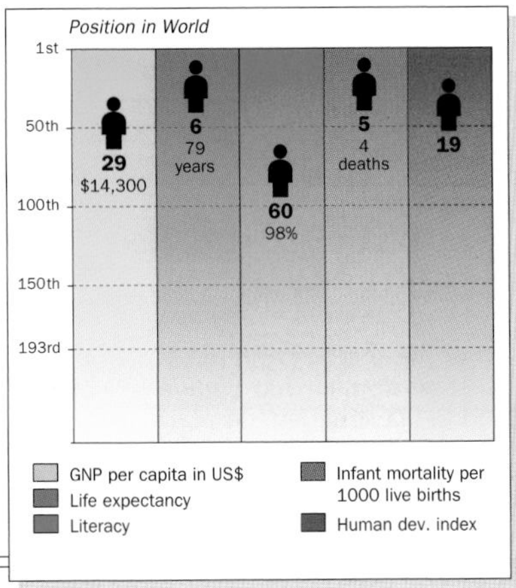
Position in World
1st
50th
100th
150th
193rd
29
$14,300
6
79 years
60
98%
5
4 deaths
19
GNP per capita in US$
Life expectancy
Literacy
Infant mortality per 1000 live births
Human dev. index

Sri Lanka

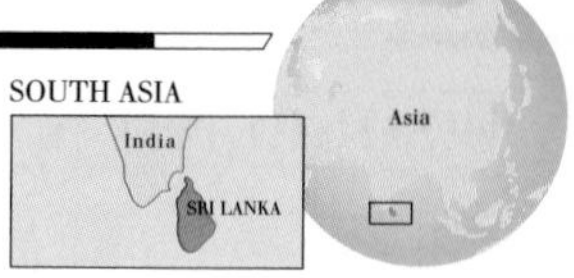
SOUTH ASIA
India
SRI LANKA
Asia

Official Name: Democratic Socialist Republic of Sri Lanka **Capital:** Colombo
Population: 19.3 million **Currency:** Sri Lanka rupee **Official Languages:** Sinhala, Tamil, and English

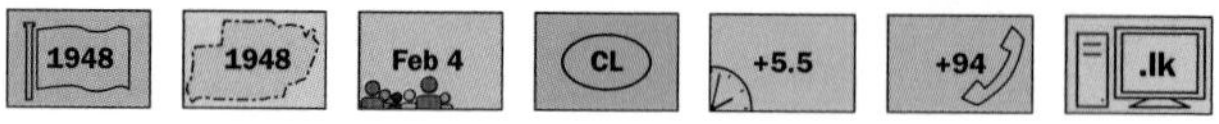
1948
1948
Feb 4
CL
+5.5
+94
.lk

THE TEARDROP-SHAPED island of Sri Lanka is separated from India by the Palk Strait. Rugged central uplands give way to fertile plains in the north. The majority Sinhalese, an Indo-Aryan people originating in northern India, have a Buddhism-based identity. Independent since 1948, Sri Lanka suffered from 1983 from a protracted civil war involving the attempted secession of the minority (and mainly Hindu) Tamils in the north and east.

CLIMATE

Tropical monsoon/equatorial

WEATHER CHART FOR COLOMBO

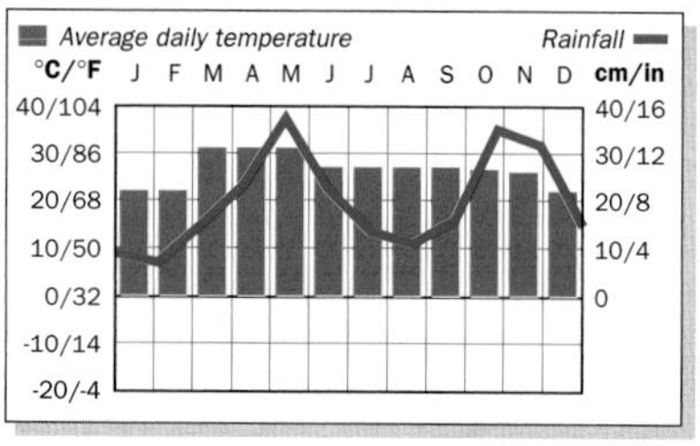
Average daily temperature
Rainfall
°C/°F
J F M A M J J A S O N D
cm/in
40/104
30/86
20/68
10/50
0/32
-10/14
-20/-4
40/16
30/12
20/8
10/4
0

The climate is tropical, with afternoon breezes on the coast and cooler air in the highlands. The northeast is driest.

TRANSPORTATION

Drive on left

Bandaranaike, Katunayake 2.77m passengers

69 ships 153,700 grt

THE TRANSPORTATION NETWORK

10,721 km (6662 miles)

None

1463 km (909 miles)

430 km (267 miles)

Main roads are crowded and slow. Routes to the Tamil-dominated north and east have been reopened.

TOURISM

Visitors : Population 1:49

393,000 visitors

Up 17% in 2002

MAIN TOURIST ARRIVALS

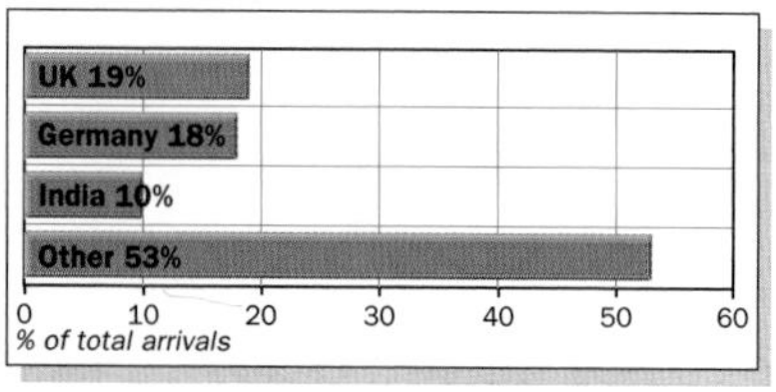
UK 19%
Germany 18%
India 10%
Other 53%
0
10
20
30
40
50
60
% of total arrivals

Stunning scenery and the Buddhist cultural heritage have made Sri Lanka a popular destination, despite years of civil war. High-profile attacks in Colombo did damage the industry, but peace has paved the way for a recovery.

PEOPLE

Pop. density high

Sinhala, Tamil, Sinhalese-Tamil, English

298/km² (772/mi²)

THE URBAN/RURAL POPULATION SPLIT

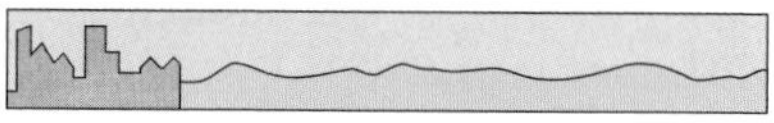
23%
77%

ETHNIC MAKEUP

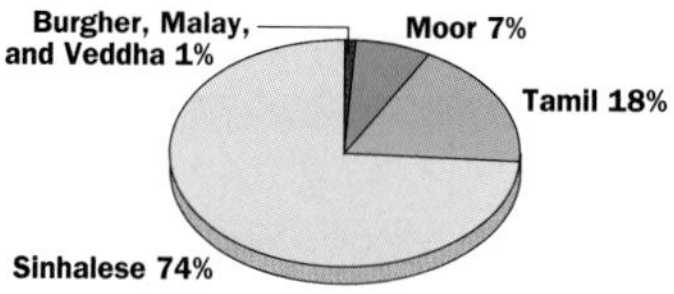
Burgher, Malay, and Veddha 1%
Moor 7%
Tamil 18%
Sinhalese 74%

Ethnic tensions focus on the 19-year conflict between the minority, Hindu, Tamils and majority, Buddhist, Sinhalese. Favored by the British colonial administration, the Tamils were subject to attempts by the Sinhalese to redress the balance after independence. The Tamil Tigers seek a Tamil homeland in the north. A tentative peace was reached in 2002 and talks continued through 2003.

The Moors are the Muslim descendants of Arab traders. A few indigenous forest-dwelling Veddhas survive in the remote east of the island.

POLITICS

Multiparty elections

2001/2007

President Chandrika Bandaranaike Kumaratunga

AT THE LAST ELECTION

Parliament 225 seats
7% 1%
TULF EPDP
48% UNP
34% PA
7% JVP
2% SLMC
1% DPLF

UNP = United National Party **PA** = People's Alliance, dominated by the Sri Lanka Freedom Party – **SLFP**
JVP = People's Liberation Front **TULF** = Tamil United Liberation Front **SLMC** = Sri Lanka Muslim Congress
EPDP = Eelam People's Democratic Party
DPLF = Democratic People's Liberation Front

Politics has been indelibly colored by the 19-year civil war, which has claimed more than 50,000 lives. Breakthrough came in 2001 when the ruling left-wing PA was soundly beaten in elections by the right-of-center UNP. Under Prime Minister Ranil Wickremasinghe, the UNP sought to bring a swift end to the conflict. A permanent cease-fire was agreed in 2002, and the separatist Liberation Tigers of Tamil Eelam (LTTE or Tamil Tigers) have since agreed in principle to settle for autonomy within Sri Lanka. The conservative Buddhist clergy remain influential, helping to preserve Sinhalese nationalism, and opposing compromise with the Tamils.

Sri Lanka

Total Area : 65 610 sq. km (25 332 sq. miles)

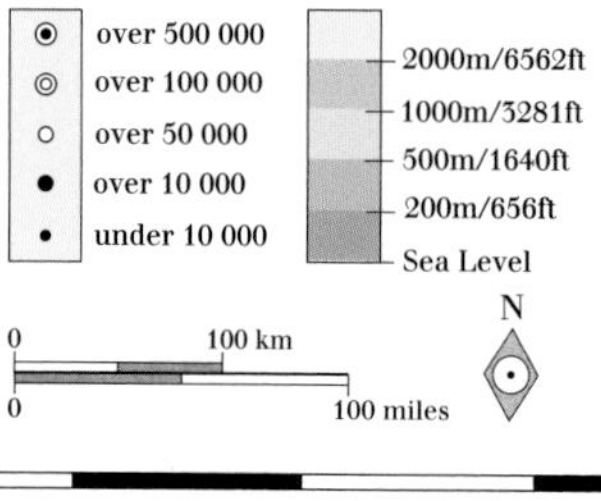
POPULATION
over 500 000
over 100 000
over 50 000
over 10 000
under 10 000
LAND HEIGHT
2000m/6562ft
1000m/3281ft
500m/1640ft
200m/656ft
Sea Level
0
100 km
0
100 miles
N

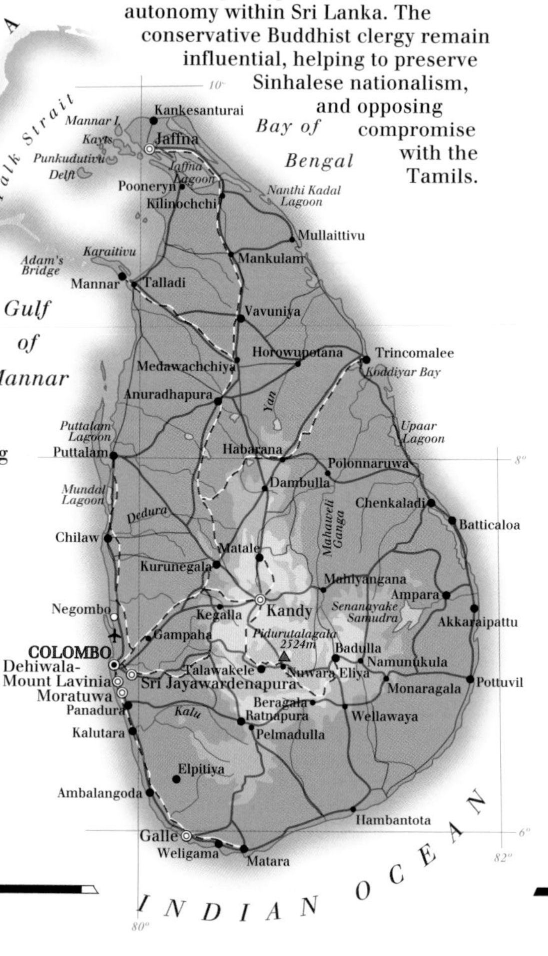
INDIA
Palk Strait
Mannar I.
Kayts
Punkudutivu
Delft
Kankesanturai
Jaffna
Jaffna Lagoon
Pooneryn
Kilinochchi
Bay of Bengal
Nanthi Kadal Lagoon
Mullaittivu
Adam's Bridge
Karaitivu
Mannar
Talladi
Mankulam
Gulf of Mannar
Vavuniya
Horowupotana
Trincomalee
Koddiyar Bay
Medawachchiya
Anuradhapura
Yan
Puttalam Lagoon
Puttalam
Upaar Lagoon
Habarana
Polonnaruwa
Dambulla
Mundal Lagoon
Dedura
Mahaweli Ganga
Chenkaladi
Batticaloa
Chilaw
Matale
Kurunegala
Mahiyangana
Ampara
Negombo
Kegalla
Kandy
Senanayake Samudra
Akkaraipattu
Gampaha
Pidurutalagala 2524m
COLOMBO
Dehiwala-Mount Lavinia
Moratuwa
Talawakele
Badulla
Namunukula
Sri Jayawardenapura
Nuwara Eliya
Monaragala
Pottuvil
Panadura
Beragala
Ratnapura
Kalu
Kalutara
Pelmadulla
Wellawaya
Elpitiya
Ambalangoda
Hambantota
Galle
Weligama
Matara
INDIAN OCEAN
10°
8°
6°
80°
82°

WORLD AFFAIRS

Joined UN in 1955

Comm | G24 | NAM | SAARC | WTO

Relations with India are paramount. However, India's role as peacemaker under the 1987 Indo-Sri Lankan accords was fiercely resisted by the Tamil Tigers, and India was forced to withdraw its peacekeeping troops. In recent years Norway has taken on the role of mediator in the conflict.

AID

Recipient

$330m (receipts)

Up 20% in 2001

International donors offered a four-year $4.5 billion aid package in 2003 in return for progress in the peace process.

DEFENSE

No compulsory military service

$786m

Down 11% in 2001

Recent drives to recruit 5000 more soldiers have shown a marked shift in policy, from simply enlarging the army to modernizing it.

ECONOMICS

Inflation 9.1% p.a. (1990–2001)

$16.4bn

97.16 Sri Lanka rupees (96.13)

SCORE CARD

- World GNP Ranking........73rd
- GNP per Capita........$880
- Balance of Payments........–$265m
- Inflation........14.2%
- Unemployment........9%

STRENGTHS

World's largest tea exporter. Foreign investment attracted by privatization, despite left-wing stance of President Kumaratunga.

WEAKNESSES

Civil war has severely drained government funds, and lingering tensions continue to deter investors and many tourists. High unemployment.

EXPORTS

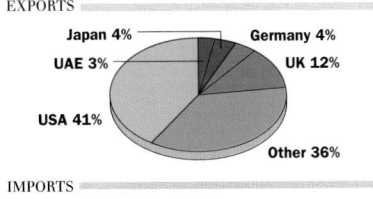

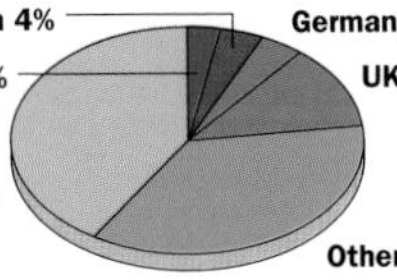
Japan 4%
Germany 4%
UAE 3%
UK 12%
USA 41%
Other 36%

IMPORTS

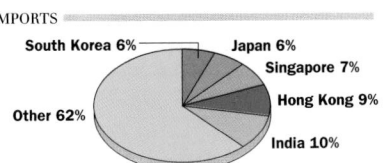

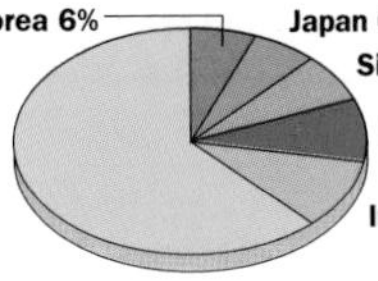
South Korea 6%
Japan 6%
Singapore 7%
Hong Kong 9%
Other 62%
India 10%

Adam's Peak in mountainous central Sri Lanka is a famous religious site with a Buddhist shrine at the summit.

RESOURCES

Electric power 1.8m kW

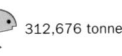

312,676 tonnes

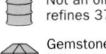

Not an oil producer; refines 37,000 b/d

1.57m cattle, 661,200 buffaloes, 10.7m chickens

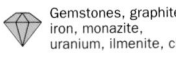

Gemstones, graphite, iron, monazite, uranium, ilmenite, clay

Sri Lanka has to import all its oil. Hydropower supplies around half of electricity; droughts are frequent and supplies can be erratic. Sri Lanka is keen to diversify power sources and is turning to coal-powered generation.

ENVIRONMENT

Sustainability rank: 55th

14% (5% partially protected)

0.5 tonnes per capita

Sri Lanka has successfully promoted national parks. Their development is opposed by the Veddha people, who have traditionally occupied such land.

MEDIA

TV ownership medium

Daily newspaper circulation 29 per 1000 people

PUBLISHING AND BROADCAST MEDIA

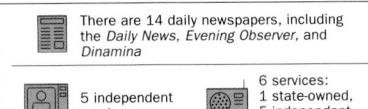

There are 14 daily newspapers, including the *Daily News, Evening Observer,* and *Dinamina*

5 independent services

6 services: 1 state-owned, 5 independent

In 2002, the government permitted Tamil Tigers openly to broadcast from their previously clandestine Voice of Tigers radio station in the north.

CRIME

Death penalty not used in practice

19,085 prisoners

Crime is rising

Extrajudicial killings and other human rights abuses increased the toll of deaths and disappearances during the civil war. New laws are being introduced to combat sex tourism.

EDUCATION

School leaving age: 13

92%

86,931 students

The ADB approved a $50 million loan in 2000 to modernize and expand the secondary education system.

CHRONOLOGY

Tamils and Sinhalese have inhabited Sri Lanka since before the 6th century. Named Ceylon by the British, it became independent in 1948.

- **1956** SLFP wins election, promotes Sinhalese language.
- **1972** Renamed Sri Lanka.
- **1983** Tamil Tigers begin civil war.
- **1993** President Premadasa killed.
- **1994** Left-wing PA wins election; Chandrika Kumaratunga president.
- **1995–1996** Collapse of peace talks.
- **1999** Kumaratunga reelected.
- **2000** Sirimavo Bandaranaike, world's first woman prime minister, dies.
- **2001** UNP wins early elections.
- **2002** Comprehensive cease-fire promises end to civil war.
- **2003** Over 200 die in worst flooding for 50 years.

HEALTH

Welfare state health benefits

1 per 2439 people

Heart attacks, cancers, pneumonia, strokes

Years of high spending on health have resulted in an accessible, fee-free system. Ayurvedic medicine is popular.

SPENDING

GDP/cap. increase

CONSUMPTION AND SPENDING

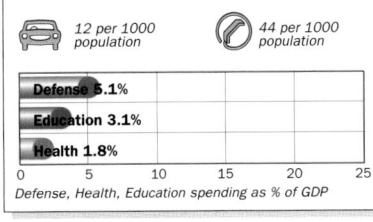

12 per 1000 population

44 per 1000 population

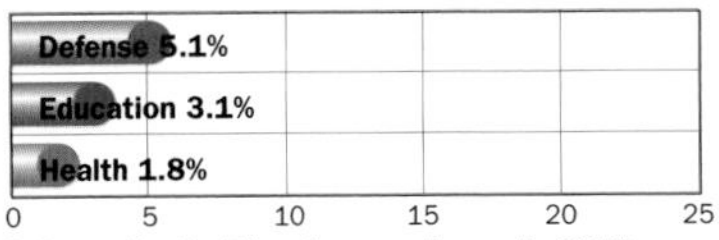
Defense 5.1%
Education 3.1%
Health 1.8%
0
5
10
15
20
25

Defense, Health, Education spending as % of GDP

Economic growth has created a new class of wealthy Sinhalese. Tamil tea workers are the poorest group.

WORLD RANKING

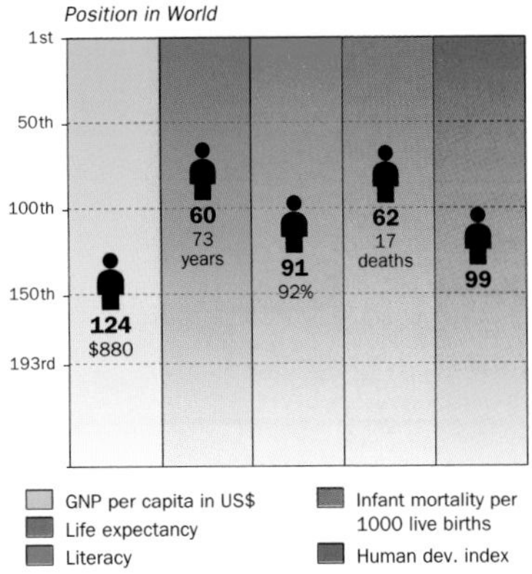
Position in World
1st
50th
100th
150th
193rd
124
$880
60
73 years
91
92%
62
17 deaths
99
GNP per capita in US$
Life expectancy
Literacy
Infant mortality per 1000 live births
Human dev. index

S

SUDAN

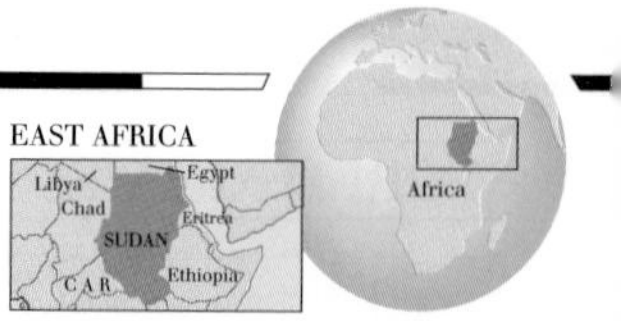
EAST AFRICA
Libya
Egypt
Chad
Eritrea
SUDAN
C.A.R.
Ethiopia
Africa

OFFICIAL NAME: Republic of Sudan **CAPITAL:** Khartoum **POPULATION:** 32.6 million
CURRENCY: Sudanese pound or dinar **OFFICIAL LANGUAGE:** Arabic

1956 | 1956 | Jan 1 | SUD | +2 | +249 | .sd

BORDERED ON THE EAST by the Red Sea, Sudan is the largest country in Africa. Its landscape changes from desert in the north to lush tropical in the south, with grassy plains and swamps in the center. Since independence from British and Egyptian rule in 1956, tensions between the Arab north and African south have led to two civil wars. The second of these conflicts remains unresolved. In 1989, an army coup installed a military Islamic fundamentalist regime.

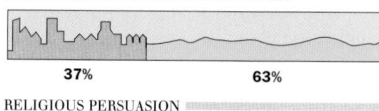

Camel caravan in the dry north. *Periodic drought coupled with war disruption mean that Sudan requires large amounts of food aid.*

CLIMATE

Hot desert/steppe/tropical

WEATHER CHART FOR KHARTOUM

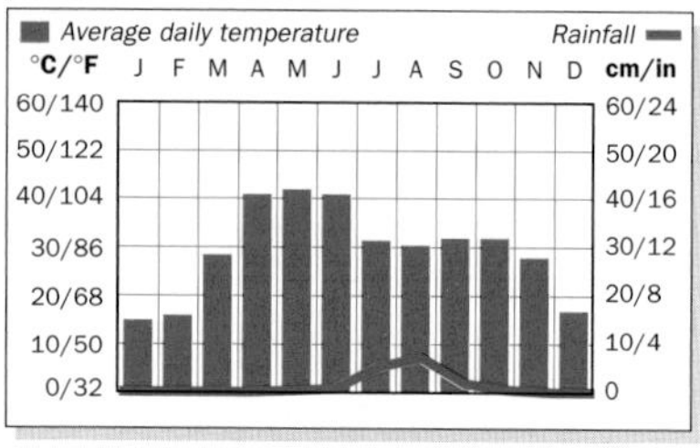
Average daily temperature
Rainfall
°C/°F
J F M A M J J A S O N D
cm/in
60/140
50/122
40/104
30/86
20/68
10/50
0/32
60/24
50/20
40/16
30/12
20/8
10/4
0

Sudan's northern half is hot arid desert with constant dry winds. The rest has a rainy season varying from two months in the center to eight in the south.

TRANSPORTATION

Drive on right

Khartoum International

18 ships 42,978 grt

THE TRANSPORTATION NETWORK

4320 km (2684 miles)

None

4599 km (2858 miles)

5310 km (3299 miles)

The Port Sudan–Khartoum railroad and road are Sudan's most important links. There are few other roads, but Iran is financing a north–south highway. Civil war has interrupted all Nile shipping.

TOURISM

Visitors : Population 1:652

50,000 visitors

Little change in 2001

MAIN TOURIST ARRIVALS

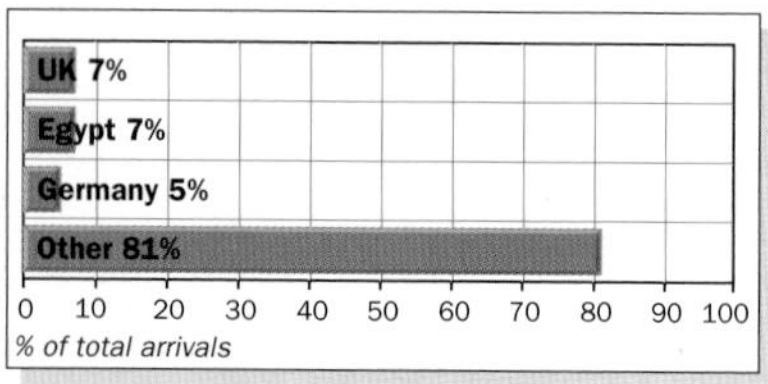
UK 7%
Egypt 7%
Germany 5%
Other 81%
0 10 20 30 40 50 60 70 80 90 100
% of total arrivals

The civil war means that Sudan has very few tourists. Visitors are mostly aid workers or on business.

PEOPLE

Pop. density low

Arabic, Dinka, Nuer, Nubian, Beja, Zande, Bari, Fur, Shilluk, Lotuko

13/km² (34/mi²)

THE URBAN/RURAL POPULATION SPLIT

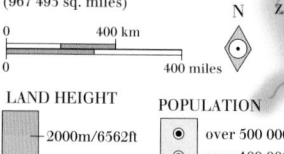

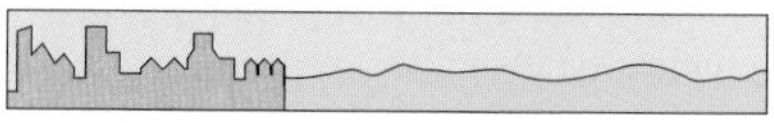
37%
63%

RELIGIOUS PERSUASION

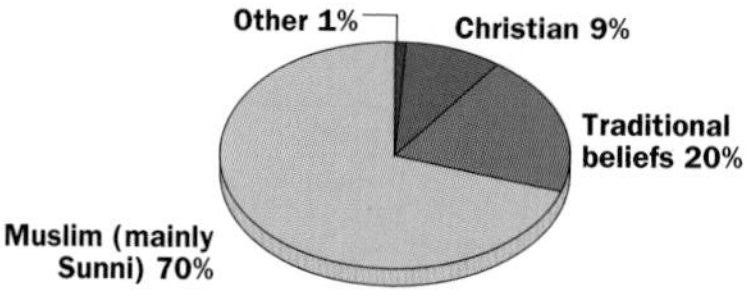
Other 1%
Christian 9%
Traditional beliefs 20%
Muslim (mainly Sunni) 70%

Sudan has a large number of ethnic and linguistic groups. About two million Sudanese are nomads. The major social division, however, is between the Arabized Muslims in the north and the mostly African, largely animist or Christian population in the south. Attempts to impose Arab and Islamic values throughout Sudan have been the root cause of the civil war that has ravaged the south since 1983. There are some non-Arab groups in the north and in the densely populated Darfur region. Women not wearing Islamic dress can suffer harassment or even public flogging. In 2002 the UN reported that thousands of people have been abducted into slavery within Sudan over the last 20 years.

POLITICS

Multiparty elections

2000/2004

President Omar Hassan Ahmad al-Bashir

AT THE LAST ELECTION

National Assembly 400 seats

89% NC
10% Vac
1% Ind

NC = National Congress supporters **Vac** = Vacant
Ind = Independents

Elections in 2000, boycotted by the opposition, returned Gen. Omar al-Bashir and his NC bloc to power. "Political associations" have been allowed since 1999, and pre-1989 parties were unbanned in 2002. An end may be in sight to two decades of war between Muslim north and Christian south, after lengthy peace talks were held with the southern Sudan People's Liberation Army (SPLA). Some question the extent to which all groups have been incorporated into the peace process. A key issue is how to divide the country's oil wealth.

SUDAN

Total Area : 2 505 810 sq. km (967 493 sq. miles)

0 400 km
0 400 miles

LAND HEIGHT

2000m/6562ft
1000m/3281ft
500m/1640ft
200m/656ft
Sea Level

POPULATION

over 500 000
over 100 000
over 50 000
over 10 000
under 10 000

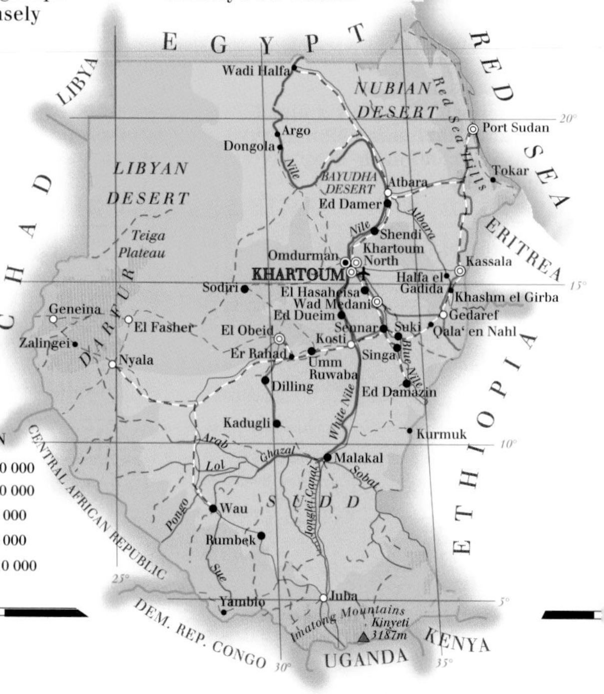
EGYPT
LIBYA
RED SEA
Wadi Halfa
NUBIAN DESERT
Port Sudan
Argo
Dongola
Tokar
LIBYAN DESERT
BAYUDHA DESERT
Atbara
Ed Damer
CHAD
ERITREA
Teiga Plateau
Shendi
Khartoum North
Omdurman
KHARTOUM
Kassala
Sodiri
El Hasaheisa
Halfa el Gadida
Khashm el Girba
Wad Medani
Geneina
El Fasher
Ed Dueim
Gedaref
DARFUR
El Obeid
Sennar
Suki
Qala' en Nahl
Zalingei
Kosti
Nyala
Er Rahad
Umm Ruwaba
Singa
Dilling
Ed Damazin
Kadugli
Kurmuk
ETHIOPIA
Malakal
CENTRAL AFRICAN REPUBLIC
Wau
SUDD
Rumbek
Yambio
Juba
Imatong Mountains
Kinyeti 3187m
DEM. REP. CONGO
UGANDA
KENYA
N

WORLD AFFAIRS

Joined UN in 1956

AL | OIC | COMESA | IGAD | AU

Suspicion that Sudan sponsors terrorism has led to its increasing international isolation. Only Iran, Yemen, and Libya maintain friendly ties, though relations with Uganda have recently improved.

AID

Recipient

$172m (receipts) | Down 24% in 2001

Aid comes predominantly from the EU and individual Western countries, most being spent on emergency food supplies.

DEFENSE

Compulsory military service

$588m | Up 1% in 2001

The NC controls the military and police and has its own paramilitary militia. Sudan's 112,500-strong army was for many years engaged in fighting the two southern factions – the SPLA and the Sudan People's Democratic Front.

ECONOMICS

Inflation 58% p.a. (1990–2001)

$10.7bn | 258.7 Sudanese dinars (258.7)

SCORE CARD

- ❑ WORLD GNP RANKING..........83rd
- ❑ GNP PER CAPITA..........$340
- ❑ BALANCE OF PAYMENTS..........–$618m
- ❑ INFLATION..........6.4%
- ❑ UNEMPLOYMENT..........4%

STRENGTHS
Oil, gas, cotton, gum arabic, sesame, sugar. Some gold mining.

WEAKNESSES
Low industrialization. Lack of foreign exchange for importing energy and spare parts for industry. Drought. Little transportation infrastructure. Huge distances between towns. Civil war delayed exploitation of oil reserves. Alienation of Arab donors and investors.

EXPORTS

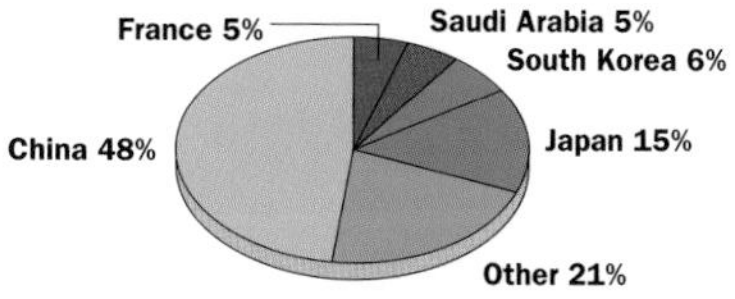
France 5%
Saudi Arabia 5%
South Korea 6%
China 48%
Japan 15%
Other 21%

IMPORTS

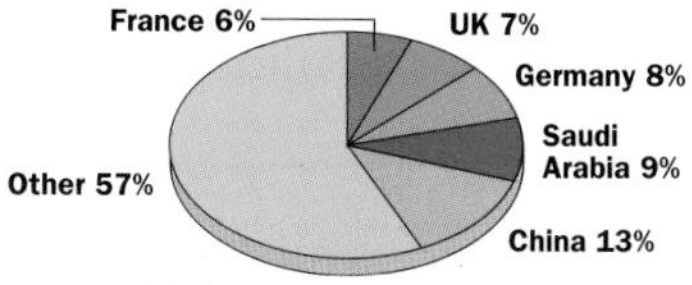
France 6%
UK 7%
Germany 8%
Other 57%
Saudi Arabia 9%
China 13%

RESOURCES

Electric power 695,000 kW

51,000 tonnes | 233,000 b/d (reserves 600m barrels)

47m sheep, 40m goats, 38.3m cattle, 37.5m chickens | Oil, gas, gold, copper, gypsum, marble, mica, silver, chromium, zinc

Large oil and gas reserves were found in the south in the 1980s; oil exports started in 1999. The half-thermal, half-hydroelectric generating capacity is insufficient, and weeklong power cuts are frequent. Gold mining has the potential for expansion.

ENVIRONMENT

Sustainability rank: 102nd

5% (2% partially protected) | 0.09 tonnes per capita

The Jonglei canal project, halted by rebel attacks when only 70% complete, could still devastate the Sudd, the world's largest swamp and a rich wetland habitat, fed by the White Nile.

MEDIA

TV ownership high

Daily newspaper circulation 26 per 1000 people

PUBLISHING AND BROADCAST MEDIA

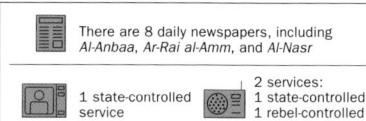

There are 8 daily newspapers, including *Al-Anbaa*, *Ar-Rai al-Amm*, and *Al-Nasr*

1 state-controlled service | 2 services: 1 state-controlled, 1 rebel-controlled

President Bashir promised in 2003 to lift restrictions on the media as part of peace negotiations.

CRIME

Death penalty in use

32,000 prisoners | Crime is rising

Antigovernment dissent is often suppressed by violence, and torture by the security forces is widespread. The UN has condemned Sudan's poor human rights record.

EDUCATION

School leaving age: 14

59% | 200,538 students

In 1991, measures were introduced to Islamize education. Primary school children must have two years of Islamic religious instruction, and men wishing to enter university must first serve for a year in the People's Militia.

HEALTH

Welfare state health benefits

1 per 6250 people | Infectious and parasitic diseases, malnutrition

Health service standards in rural areas are basic. The civil war has led to an increase in communicable diseases. The parasitic infection leishmaniasis is prevalent.

CHRONOLOGY

Northern Sudan was taken by Egypt in 1821, the south by Britain in 1877.

- ❑ **1882** British invade Egypt.
- ❑ **1883** Muslim revolt in Sudan led by Muhammad Ahmed, the Mahdi.
- ❑ **1898** Mahdists defeated. Anglo-Egyptian condominium set up.
- ❑ **1954** Becomes self-governing.
- ❑ **1955** Rebellion in south starts 17 years of civil war.
- ❑ **1956** Independence as republic.
- ❑ **1958–1964** Military rule.
- ❑ **1965** Civilian revolution, elections.
- ❑ **1969** Coup led by Col. Jaafar Nimeiri.
- ❑ **1972** South gets limited autonomy.
- ❑ **1973** Socialist Union sole party.
- ❑ **1983** Southern rebellion resumes. *Sharia* (Islamic law) imposed.
- ❑ **1984** Devastating drought.
- ❑ **1986** Army coup.
- ❑ **1989** Gen. Bashir takes over.
- ❑ **1991** *Sharia* penal code instituted. Pro-Iraq stance in Gulf War.
- ❑ **2000** Bashir ousts fundamentalist Turabi from leadership of NC.
- ❑ **2002** SPLA signs cease-fire. Fighting between rival factions over southern oil reserves escalates.

SPENDING

GDP/cap. increase

CONSUMPTION AND SPENDING

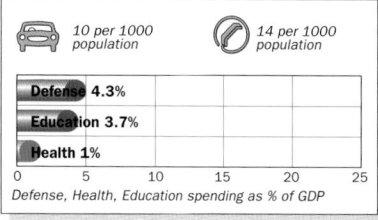

10 per 1000 population | *14 per 1000 population*

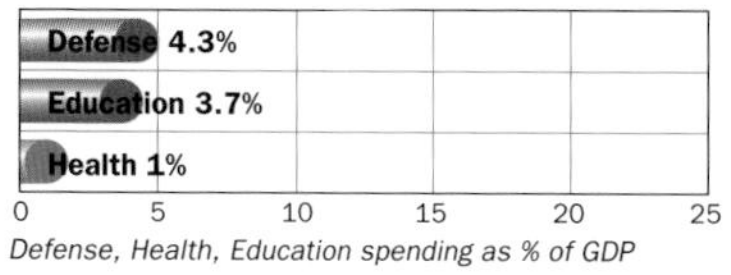
Defense 4.3%
Education 3.7%
Health 1%
0
5
10
15
20
25
Defense, Health, Education spending as % of GDP

There are large disparities between rich and poor. Wealth is limited to the NC and southern rebel elites. Most of the population struggles to survive.

WORLD RANKING

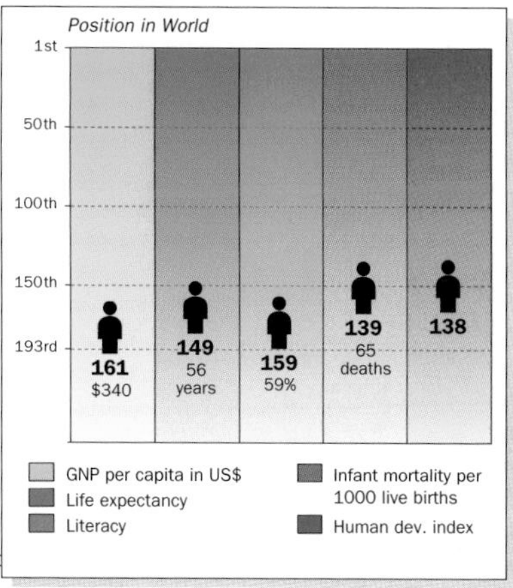
Position in World
1st
50th
100th
150th
193rd
161
$340
149
56
years
159
59%
139
65
deaths
138
GNP per capita in US$
Life expectancy
Literacy
Infant mortality per 1000 live births
Human dev. index

S

SURINAME

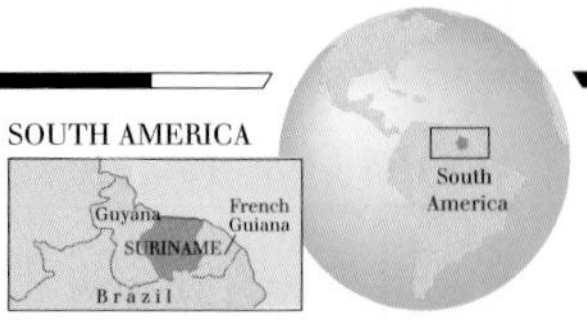
SOUTH AMERICA
Guyana
French Guiana
SURINAME
Brazil
South America

OFFICIAL NAME: Republic of Suriname **CAPITAL:** Paramaribo
POPULATION: 421,000 **CURRENCY:** Suriname guilder or florin **OFFICIAL LANGUAGE:** Dutch

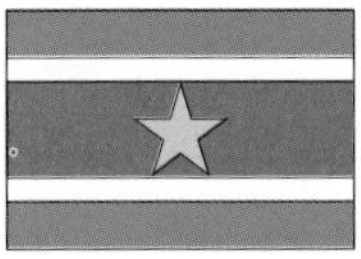

1975 | 1975 | Nov 25 | SME | -3 | +597 | .sr

Congested street in Paramaribo. It boasts 18th- and 19th-century Dutch architecture. The large mosque is next to a Jewish synagogue.

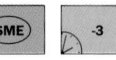

BOUNDED EAST AND WEST by rivers, Suriname sits on the north coast of South America in the center of the "Guyana Plateau." The interior is rainforested highlands; most people live near the coast. In 1975, after over 300 years of Dutch rule, Suriname became independent. The Netherlands is still its main aid supplier, and is home to one-third of Surinamese. Multiparty democracy was restored in 1991, after almost 11 years of military rule.

CLIMATE

Tropical equatorial

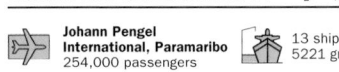

WEATHER CHART FOR PARAMARIBO

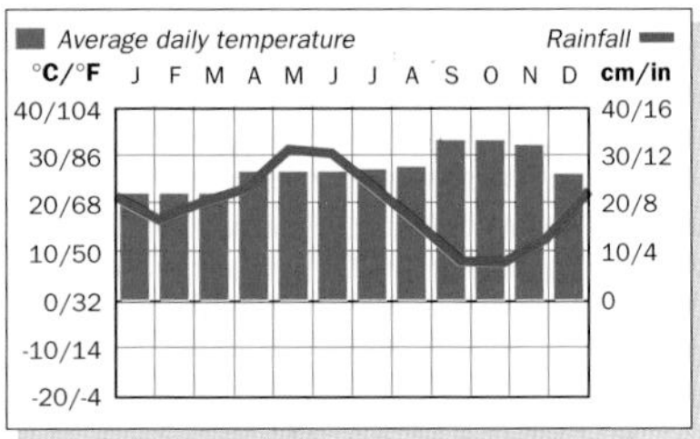
Average daily temperature
Rainfall
°C/°F J F M A M J J A S O N D cm/in
40/104 40/16
30/86 30/12
20/68 20/8
10/50 10/4
0/32 0
-10/14
-20/-4

Suriname's tropical climate is cooled by the trade winds. Annual rainfall varies from 150 to 300 cm (60 to 120 in) between coast and interior.

TRANSPORTATION

Drive on left

Johann Pengel International, Paramaribo 254,000 passengers

13 ships 5221 grt

THE TRANSPORTATION NETWORK

1178 km (732 miles)	None
166 km (103 miles)	1200 km (746 miles)

Rivers provide the main north–south links, and the interior relies on water or air transportation. The road network runs east–west and focuses on the coast and its immediate hinterland.

TOURISM

Visitors : Population 1:7.4

57,000 visitors

Up 4% in 1999

MAIN TOURIST ARRIVALS

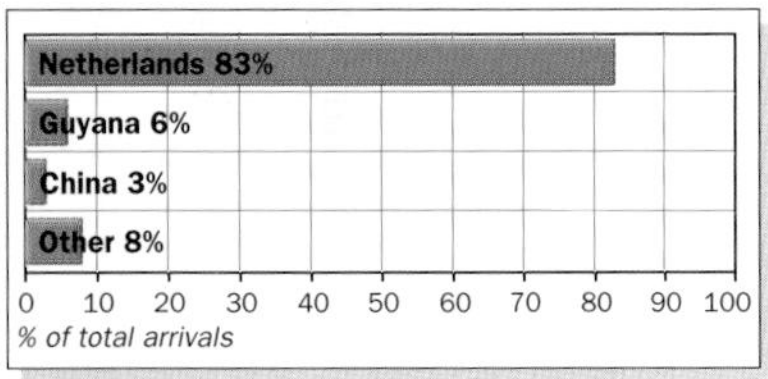
Netherlands 83%
Guyana 6%
China 3%
Other 8%
0 10 20 30 40 50 60 70 80 90 100
% of total arrivals

Tourism is undeveloped. Travelers outside Paramaribo are advised to carry their own hammock and food.

PEOPLE

Pop. density low

Sranan, Dutch, Javanese, Sarnami Hindi, Saramaccan, Chinese, Carib

3/km² (7/mi²)

THE URBAN/RURAL POPULATION SPLIT

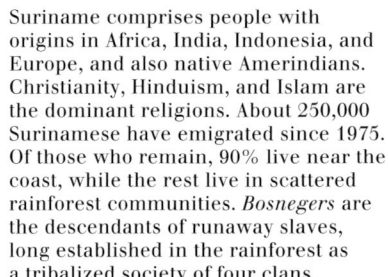

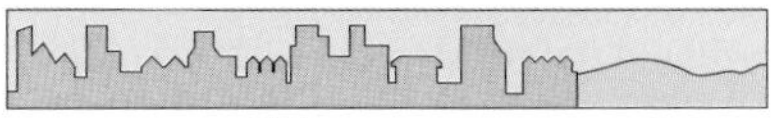
75%
25%

ETHNIC MAKEUP

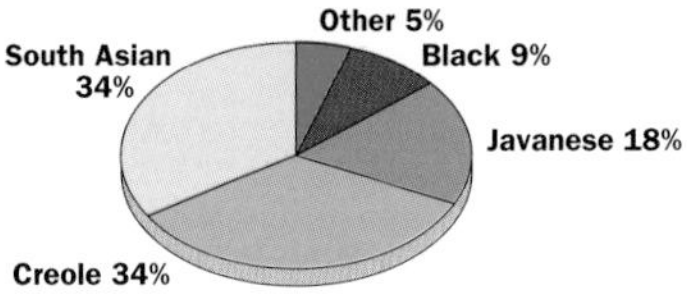
Other 5%
South Asian 34%
Black 9%
Javanese 18%
Creole 34%

Suriname comprises people with origins in Africa, India, Indonesia, and Europe, and also native Amerindians. Christianity, Hinduism, and Islam are the dominant religions. About 250,000 Surinamese have emigrated since 1975. Of those who remain, 90% live near the coast, while the rest live in scattered rainforest communities. *Bosnegers* are the descendants of runaway slaves, long established in the rainforest as a tribalized society of four clans.

POLITICS

Multiparty elections

2000/2005

President Ronald Venetiaan

AT THE LAST ELECTION

National Assembly 51 seats

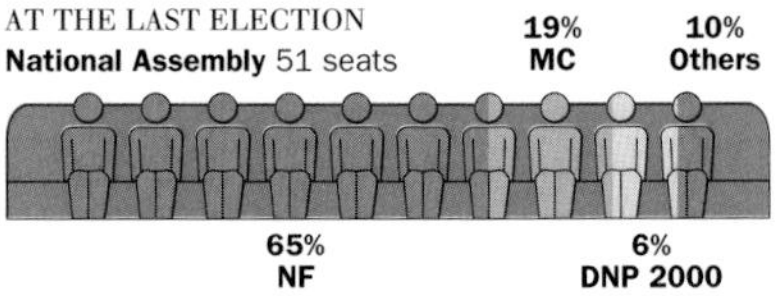
19% MC
10% Others
65% NF
6% DNP 2000

NF = New Front for Democracy and Development (includes the Suriname National Party, the Progressive Reform Party, the Suriname Labor Party, and Pertjajah Luhur)
MC = Millennium Combination (includes the National Democratic Party (**NDP**), the Democratic Alternative, and the Party for Unity and Harmony)
DNP 2000 = Democratic National Platform 2000

A coalition government representing Creoles, South Asians, and Javanese took power under Ronald Venetiaan in 1991. Five years later it was defeated by the NDP, controlled by Desi Bouterse, the military dictator from 1980 to 1988, and behind the 1990 coup which ended Suriname's first attempt at a return to democracy. Between 1996 and 2000 President Jules Wijdenbosch of the NDP withstood the efforts of opponents in the National Assembly to replace him. In the 2000 legislative elections, however, the NDP was massively defeated by the opposition NF. The new Assembly went on to elect NF leader Venetiaan as president.

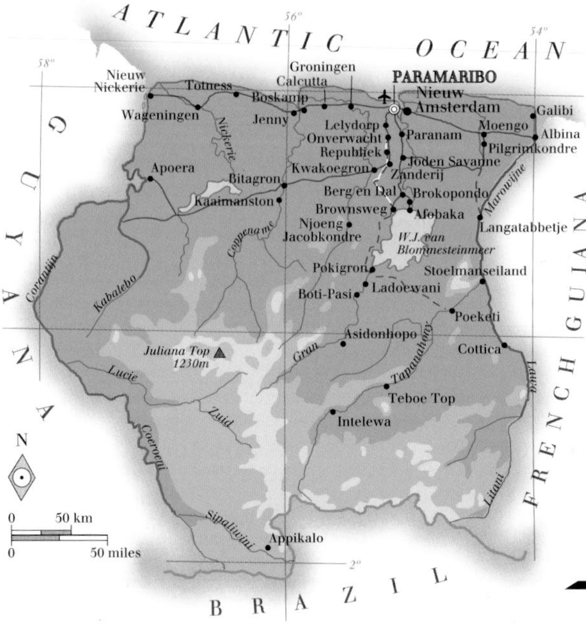
ATLANTIC OCEAN
GUYANA
FRENCH GUIANA
BRAZIL
PARAMARIBO
Nieuw Nickerie
Totness
Groningen
Calcutta
Boskamp
Jenny
Wageningen
Nieuw Amsterdam
Galibi
Moengo
Albina
Pilgrimkondre
Lelydorp
Onverwacht
Republiek
Paranam
Kwakoegron
Jodensavanne
Zanderij
Apoera
Bitagron
Berg en Dal
Brokopondo
Kaaimanston
Brownsweg
Afobaka
Njoeng Jacobkondre
W.J. van Blommesteinmeer
Langatabbetje
Pokigron
Stoelmanseiland
Boti-Pasi
Ladoewani
Poeketi
Asidonhopo
Cottica
Juliana Top 1230m
Teboe Top
Intelewa
Appikalo
Nickerie
Coppename
Corantijn
Kabalebo
Lucie
Coeroeni
Zuid
Gran
Tapanahony
Marowijne
Lawa
Litani
Sipaliwini
N
0 50 km
0 50 miles

SURINAME

Total Area : 163 270 sq. km (63 039 sq. miles)

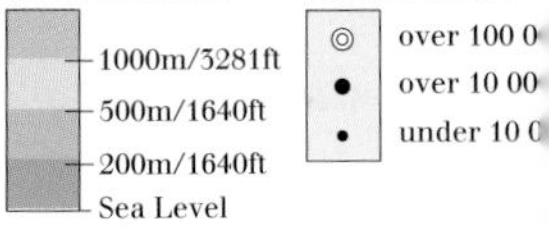
LAND HEIGHT
1000m/3281ft
500m/1640ft
200m/1640ft
Sea Level
POPULATION
over 100 0
over 10 00
under 10 0

WORLD AFFAIRS

Joined UN in 1975

ACS | AmCC | Caricom | OAS | OIC

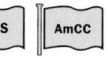

Relations with the Netherlands and the US, the key aid and trading partners, have been weakened over charges of official connivance in narcotics trafficking. Suriname claims the southeastern corner of Guyana in a border dispute. Relations were damaged further when Suriname took action against oil prospectors in 2000.

AID

Recipient

$23m (receipts) — Down 32% in 2001

The Netherlands is the largest donor, but it has on occasion suspended aid amid deteriorating relations. The IDB and European Investment Bank have granted loans for agricultural and industrial development.

DEFENSE

No compulsory military service

$24m — Up 14% in 2001

The army was politically dominant in the 1980s under Lt. Col. Desi Bouterse. A six-year war with *Bosneger* rebels ended in 1992. Aid and training have been provided in recent years by both the US and China.

ECONOMICS

Inflation 83% p.a. (1990–2001)

$761m — 2515 Suriname guilders (2179)

SCORE CARD

❑ World GNP Ranking	158th
❑ GNP per Capita	$1810
❑ Balance of Payments	$32m
❑ Inflation	36.2%
❑ Unemployment	11%

Strengths

Bauxite. Gold. Timber potential. Oil. Agricultural exports: rice, bananas, citrus fruits. Shrimp exports.

Weaknesses

Chronic economic mismanagement, leading to low, or even negative, growth, a weak currency, and failure to restore suspended Dutch aid. High inflation. High-cost, inefficient public sector. Net food importer.

EXPORTS

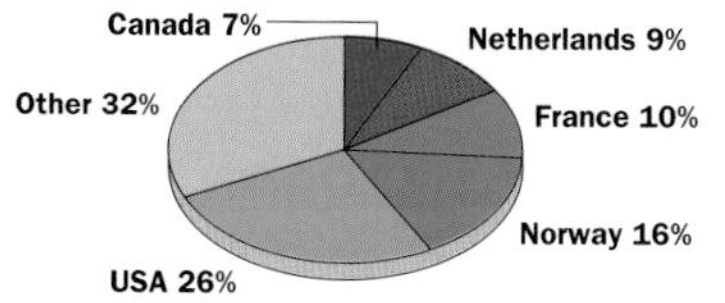
Canada 7%
Netherlands 9%
Other 32%
France 10%
Norway 16%
USA 26%

IMPORTS

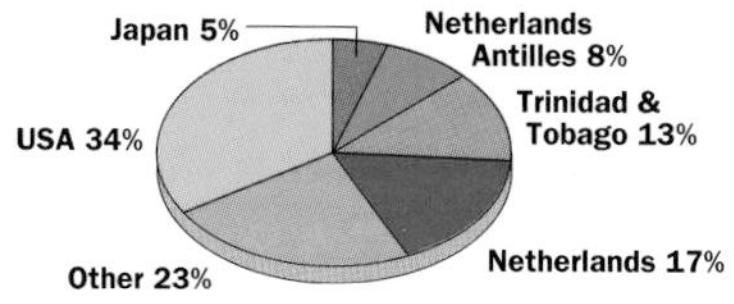
Japan 5%
Netherlands Antilles 8%
Trinidad & Tobago 13%
USA 34%
Netherlands 17%
Other 23%

RESOURCES

Electric power 425,000 kW

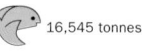

16,545 tonnes — 4972 b/d (reserves 87m barrels)

136,000 cattle, 66,000 ducks, 3.7m chickens — Bauxite, iron, gold, manganese, copper, nickel, platinum, oil

Suriname is a major exporter of aluminum and bauxite, but the minerals sector is affected by poor world prices, as is raw gold production. Oil consumption is almost double the level of oil production. Exploitation of the rainforests has begun. Rice and fruit are Suriname's key agricultural products.

ENVIRONMENT

Not available

10% partially protected — 5.1 tonnes per capita

In 1998 the government declared some 16,000 sq. km (6150 sq. miles) of rainforest – almost 10% of the country – to be a natural reserve barred to logging, but its exploitation for economic gain is still of real concern to environmentalists.

MEDIA

TV ownership medium

Daily newspaper circulation 68 per 1000 people

PUBLISHING AND BROADCAST MEDIA

There are 2 daily newspapers, *De Ware Tijd* and *De West*

2 state-owned services — 10 services: 1 state-owned, 9 independent

There are radio broadcasts in a number of languages. Dutch is used by the daily newspapers and for most TV programs.

CRIME

Death penalty not used in practice

1933 prisoners — Relatively high crime levels

Human rights abuses associated with the former military regime have largely ended. Rival armed factions remain in some regions in the interior. Narcotics trafficking and money laundering are a problem, as is urban street crime.

EDUCATION

School leaving age: 12

94% — 3000 students

Education is free and includes adult literacy programs. There is a long tradition of higher education, but most graduates now live in the Netherlands.

CHRONOLOGY

Dutch rule began in 1667, after an Anglo-Dutch treaty whose terms included Britain ceding its colony in Suriname to the Dutch but gaining Nieuw Amsterdam (New York).

- ❑ **1975** Independence.
- ❑ **1980** Coup. Rule by Lt. Col. Desi Bouterse.
- ❑ **1982** Opponents executed. Dutch suspend aid for six years.
- ❑ **1986–1992** War with *Bosneger* rebels.
- ❑ **1988–1991** Elections, coup, and new elections. Ronald Venetiaan elected president.
- ❑ **1992** Bouterse quits as army head.
- ❑ **1996** Pro-Bouterse NDP wins polls.
- ❑ **2000** NF defeats NDP. Venetiaan again elected president.

HEALTH

Welfare state health benefits

1 per 2222 people — Heart attacks, cancers, malaria, malnutrition, tuberculosis

Urban medical facilities in Suriname are relatively good; Paramaribo has several hospitals. However, provision in the interior is basic.

SPENDING

GDP/cap. increase

CONSUMPTION AND SPENDING

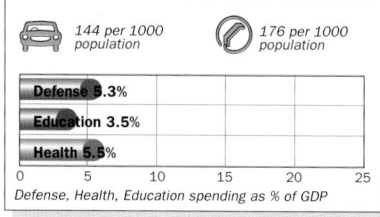

144 per 1000 population — *176 per 1000 population*

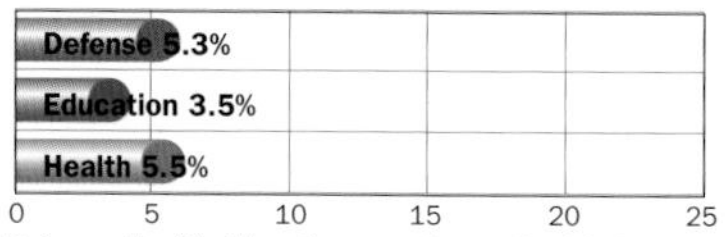
Defense 5.3%
Education 3.5%
Health 5.5%
0
5
10
15
20
25

Defense, Health, Education spending as % of GDP

Living standards have fallen since 1982, due to the effects of civil war and to aid and loan suspension. Urban Creoles dominate the rich elite. Amerindians and *Bosnegers* are the poorest groups.

WORLD RANKING

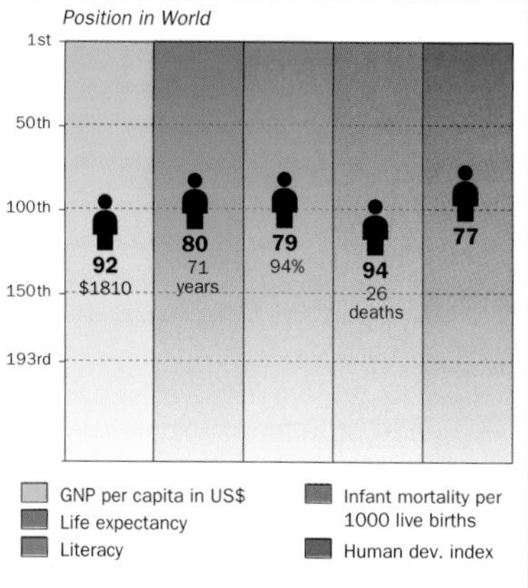
Position in World
1st
50th
100th
150th
193rd
92
$1810
80
71
years
79
94%
94
26
deaths
77
GNP per capita in US$
Life expectancy
Literacy
Infant mortality per 1000 live births
Human dev. index

S

SWAZILAND

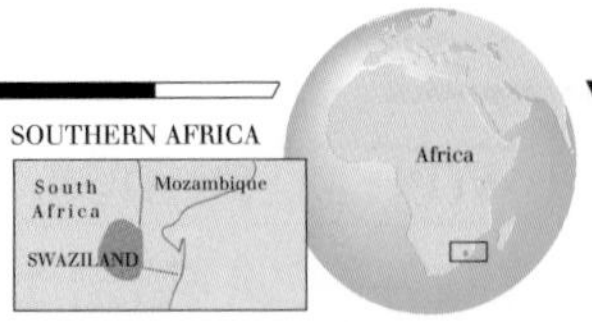
SOUTHERN AFRICA
South Africa
Mozambique
SWAZILAND
Africa

OFFICIAL NAME: Kingdom of Swaziland **CAPITAL:** Mbabane
POPULATION: 948,000 **CURRENCY:** Lilangeni **OFFICIAL LANGUAGES:** English and siSwati

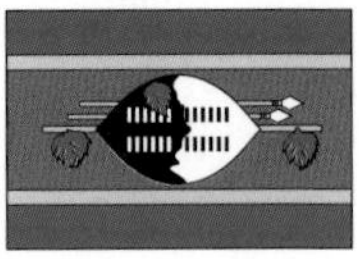

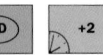

1968 | 1968 | Sept 6 | SD | +2 | +268 | .sz

THE TINY SOUTHERN African kingdom of Swaziland, bordered on three sides by South Africa and to the east by Mozambique, comprises mainly upland plateaus and mountains. Governed by a strong hereditary monarchy, Swaziland is a country in which tradition is being challenged by demands for modern multiparty government. King Mswati III, crowned in 1986, has overhauled the electoral process but is unwilling to legalize party politics.

CLIMATE

Subtropical

WEATHER CHART FOR MBABANE

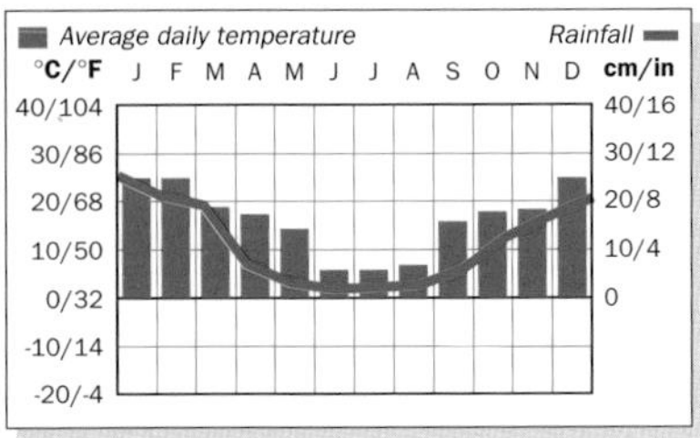
Average daily temperature
Rainfall
°C/°F J F M A M J J A S O N D cm/in
40/104 30/86 20/68 10/50 0/32 -10/14 -20/-4
40/16 30/12 20/8 10/4 0

Swaziland is temperate. Temperatures rise and rainfall declines as the land descends eastward, from high to low *veld*. The low *veld* is prone to drought.

TRANSPORTATION

Drive on left

Matsapha, Manzini 93,000 passengers

Has no fleet

THE TRANSPORTATION NETWORK

1064 km (661 miles)	None
297 km (185 miles)	None

A sharp rise in road traffic has necessitated road improvements. The railroad, running to Mozambique and South Africa, mainly carries freight.

TOURISM

Visitors : Population 1:3.4

281,000 visitors

Down 12% in 1999–2000

MAIN TOURIST ARRIVALS

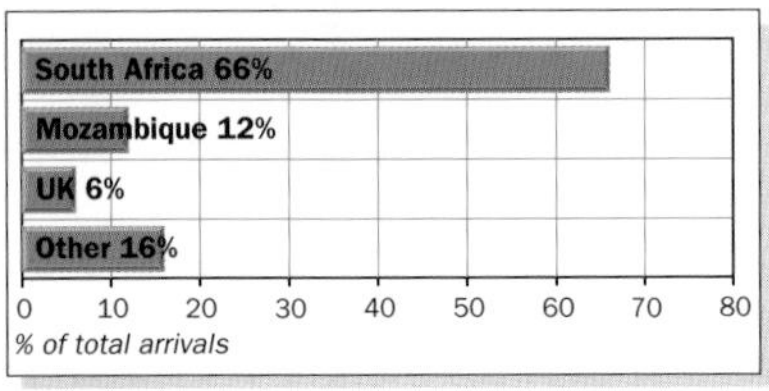
South Africa 66%
Mozambique 12%
UK 6%
Other 16%
0 10 20 30 40 50 60 70 80
% of total arrivals

Swaziland's attractions are its game reserves, mountain scenery, and, particularly for the numerous South African tourists, its casinos.

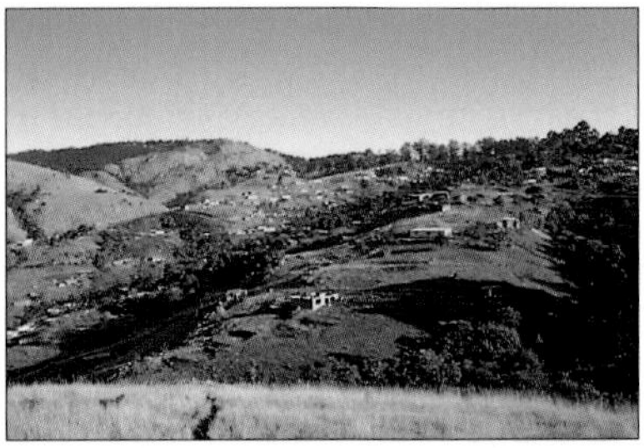

The outskirts of Mbabane. *It lies on the high veldt, where traditional cattle farming has become more difficult owing to overgrazing.*

PEOPLE

Pop. density medium

English, siSwati, isiZulu, Xitsonga

55/km² (143/mi²)

THE URBAN/RURAL POPULATION SPLIT

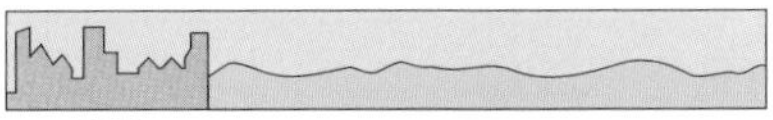
27%
73%

RELIGIOUS PERSUASION

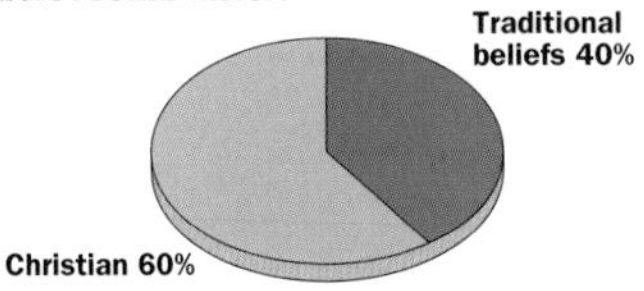
Traditional beliefs 40%
Christian 60%

Over 95% of the population belong to the Swazi ethnic group, making Swaziland one of Africa's most homogeneous states. It is also very conservative, but is now facing pressure from urban-based modernizers. The powerful monarchy dominates politics. Ancient traditions, such as *incwala*, the rainy season's annual movable feast, remain popular. Society is patriarchal and focused around the clan. Chiefs own much "national land," and wield authority through local consultations, or *tindkhundla*. Polygamy is tolerated. Women are openly discriminated against, even though the Queen Mother, the "Great She Elephant," ruled as regent during the mid-1980s. In an effort to combat the spread of AIDS, the king encourages chastity.

POLITICS

Nonparty elections

L. House 1998/2003
U. House 1998/2003

H.M. King Mswati III

AT THE LAST ELECTION

House of Assembly 65 seats

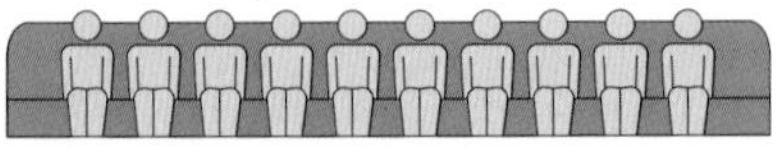

There are no political parties. Ten members of the House of Assembly are appointed by the king

Senate 30 seats

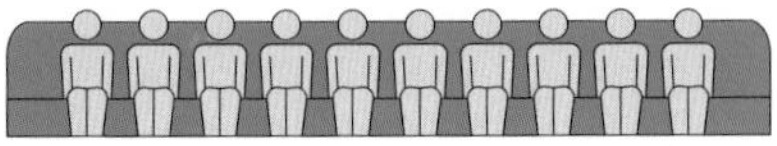

Twenty members of the Senate are appointed by the king and ten elected by the House of Assembly

King Mswati III, one of the world's last absolute monarchs, dominates politics. Political parties are banned, but opposition, led by the trade union movement, is vocal. Particular points of contention are the suppression of parties, nepotism favoring the ruling Dlamini clan, and even the king's personal life. After mounting pressure from 2000, a new constitution was issued in 2003 guaranteeing human rights but maintaining the ban on parties.

SWAZILAND

Total Area : 17 363 sq. km (6704 sq. miles)

POPULATION
over 50 000
over 10 000
under 10 000
LAND HEIGHT
1000m/3281ft
500m/1640ft
200m/656ft
Sea Level
N
0 25 km
0 25 miles
Emlembe 1862m
Bulembu
Rocklands
Kuthuleni
Piggs Peak
Komati
Bordergate
Lomahasha
Tshaneni
Mhlume
Madlangampisi
Mbuluzi
Mnjoli Dam
Simunye
Mhlumeni
Motjane
MBABANE
Ezulwini
Mhlambanyatsi
Nkanini
Manzini
Matsapha
Nkundla
Bhunya
Lonhlupheko
Ngogolo
Siteki
LEBOMBO MOUNTAINS
Sidvokodvo
Siphofaneni
Mankayane
Ngwempisi
Mayaluka
Big Bend
Sicunusa
Sitobela
Mkhondvo
Usutu
Gege
Salem
Hlathikulu
Maloma
Nsoko
Mbulungwane
Lukhalweni
Mahamba
Nhlangano
Ngwavuma
Mhlosheni
Salitje
Lavumisa
Jozini Dam
INKANGALA
MOZAMBIQUE
SOUTH AFRICA

S

WORLD AFFAIRS

Joined UN in 1968

ACP | Comm | NAM | AU | SADC

Swaziland's membership of the SACU reinforces its traditional dependence on its giant neighbor, South Africa. Having welcomed the election of an ANC-led government there, King Mswati has objected to its support for Swazi prodemocracy campaigners. Peace in Mozambique has meant the return there of 134,000 refugees.

AID

Recipient

$29m (receipts)

Up 123% in 2001

Aid helps the balance of payments, and funds the development of the Matsapha industrial estate, roads, and social projects. Donors include Germany, Japan, the UK, and the ADB. EU aid mainly targets "microprojects," such as schools, and supports constitutional reform.

DEFENSE

No compulsory military service

$23m

Up 15% in 2000

The Swaziland Defense Force numbers just 3000 troops. Though it does not play an overt political role, its loyalty is to the monarch and the status quo.

ECONOMICS

Inflation 12% p.a. (1990–2001)

$1.39bn

7.51 emalangeni (10.31)

SCORE CARD

- World GNP Ranking....147th
- GNP per Capita....$1300
- Balance of Payments....–$53m
- Inflation....5.9%
- Unemployment....22%

Strengths

Economy quite diversified and buoyant. Manufacturing. Investment rules attractive. Sugar. Wood pulp. Debt service low. Renewed regional stability has reduced risk to exports.

Weaknesses

Sugar vulnerable to price fluctuations. Dependence on South Africa for jobs, revenue, investment, electricity, and imported goods. Small plots of land and lack of land title hinder farm modernization. High population growth: increase in dependent children. AIDS: loss of workforce, cost of medical care.

EXPORTS

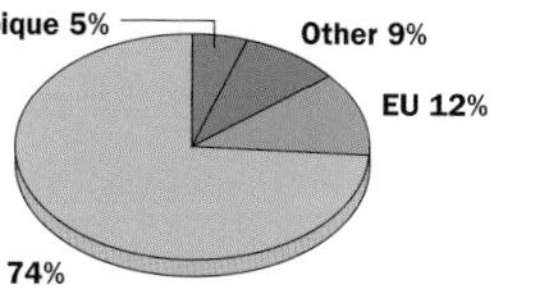
Mozambique 5%
Other 9%
EU 12%
South Africa 74%

IMPORTS

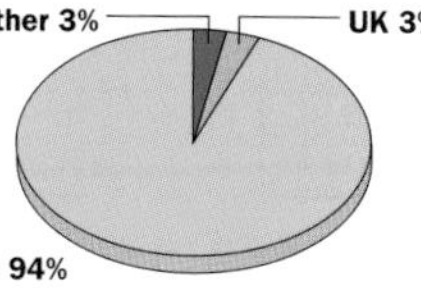
Other 3%
UK 3%
South Africa 94%

RESOURCES

Electric power: Included in South African total

139 tonnes

Included in South African total

615,000 cattle, 422,000 goats, 3.2m chickens

Coal, diamonds, gold, asbestos, cassiterite, iron, tin

Swaziland's main exports are sugarcane, wood pulp, and coal. Asbestos mining ceased in 2000. The development of hydroelectric power plants has cut energy imports from South Africa.

ENVIRONMENT

Not available

4% partially protected

0.4 tonnes per capita

In 1998 Swaziland, Mozambique, and South Africa began an ecological project on the world's largest wetlands – the foothills of the Lebombo Mountains.

MEDIA

TV ownership medium

Daily newspaper circulation 26 per 1000 people

PUBLISHING AND BROADCAST MEDIA

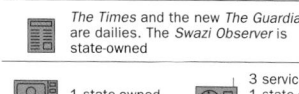

The Times and the new *The Guardian* are dailies. The *Swazi Observer* is state-owned

1 state-owned service

3 services: 1 state-owned, 2 independent

Laws on press freedoms have come under pressure, notably over the state-owned *Swazi Observer*, which was banned for a period in 2001.

CRIME

Death penalty in use

3400 prisoners

Up 28% in 2000

The crime rate is low. The numbers of illegal weapons brought in by refugees have boosted armed crime.

EDUCATION

School leaving age: 12

80%

4762 students

Parents must pay fees at all levels. Even so, primary enrollment (six- to 12-year-olds) is almost 100%. Drop-out rates at secondary level are high.

CHRONOLOGY

Swaziland became a British protectorate in 1903.

- **1968** Independence.
- **1973** King bans political activity, repeals constitution.
- **1978** New constitution confirms king's executive, legislative control.
- **1982** King Sobhuza dies. Queen Mother becomes regent for Prince Makhosetive. Power struggle between modernists and traditionalists in royal Dlamini clan.
- **1986** Makhosetive crowned King Mswati III at the age of 18.
- **1992** Limited electoral reforms; parties still banned.
- **1993** Elections under new system.
- **2000** Mass prodemocracy protests.
- **2003** New constitution offers human rights but parties still banned.

HEALTH

No welfare state health benefits

1 per 6667 people

Diarrheal and respiratory diseases, AIDS

Health facilities are rudimentary. Over a third of the population aged 15 to 49 is thought to have HIV/AIDS.

SPENDING

GDP/cap. increase

CONSUMPTION AND SPENDING

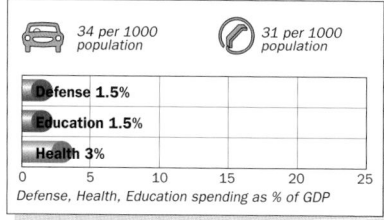

34 per 1000 population

31 per 1000 population

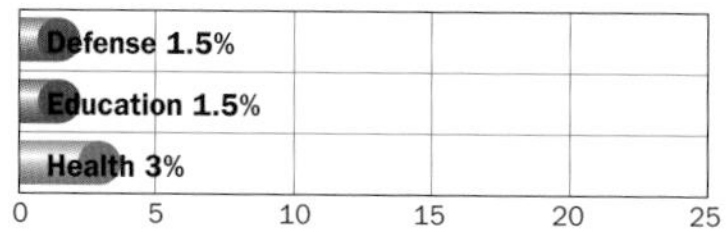
Defense 1.5%
Education 1.5%
Health 3%
0
5
10
15
20
25

Defense, Health, Education spending as % of GDP

About two-thirds of Swazis live below the poverty line. The royal Dlamini clan enjoys Western luxuries and travel.

WORLD RANKING

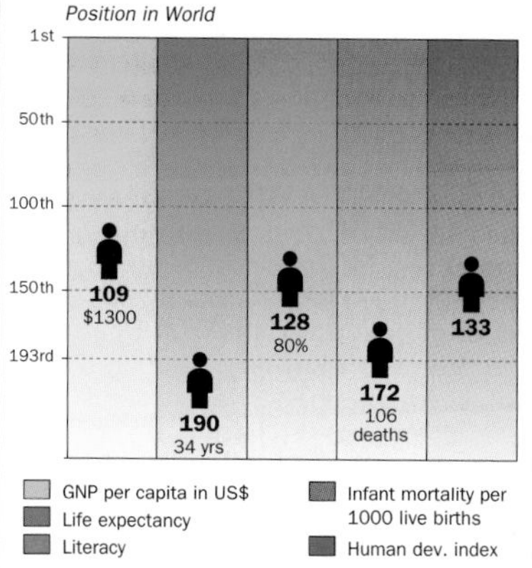
Position in World
1st
50th
100th
150th
193rd
109
$1300
190
34 yrs
128
80%
172
106 deaths
133
GNP per capita in US$
Life expectancy
Literacy
Infant mortality per 1000 live births
Human dev. index

S

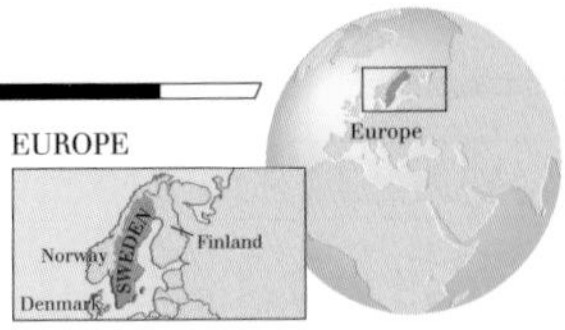
EUROPE
Europe
Norway
SWEDEN
Finland
Denmark

SWEDEN

OFFICIAL NAME: Kingdom of Sweden **CAPITAL:** Stockholm
POPULATION: 8.8 million **CURRENCY:** Swedish krona **OFFICIAL LANGUAGE:** Swedish

1523 | 1921 | June 6 | S | +1 | +46 | .se

SITUATED ON THE SCANDINAVIAN peninsula with Norway to its west, Sweden is a densely forested country with numerous lakes. The north of Sweden falls within the Arctic Circle; much of the south is fertile and widely cultivated. Sweden has one of the most extensive welfare systems in the world, and is among the world's leading proponents of equal rights for women. It is home to global companies including high-tech firm Ericsson, and notable car manufacturers Volvo and Saab. Unlike neighboring Norway, it is an EU member, having joined in 1995.

CLIMATE

Subarctic/continental

WEATHER CHART FOR STOCKHOLM

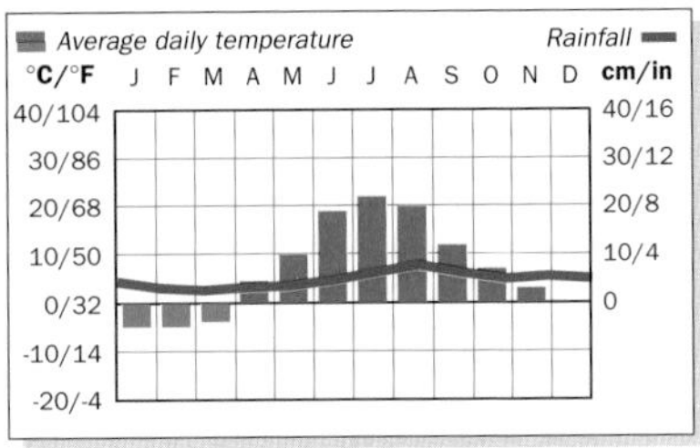
Average daily temperature
Rainfall
°C/°F
J F M A M J J A S O N D
cm/in
40/104
30/86
20/68
10/50
0/32
-10/14
-20/-4
40/16
30/12
20/8
10/4
0

Sweden has a largely continental climate. The Baltic Sea often freezes in winter, making the east coast much colder than western regions. Summers are mild everywhere, with temperatures varying surprisingly little between northern and southern regions.

TRANSPORTATION

Drive on right

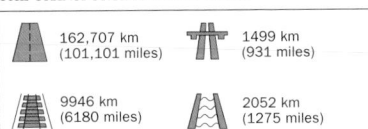

Arlanda, Stockholm 16.5m passengers | 578 ships 2.96m grt

THE TRANSPORTATION NETWORK

162,707 km (101,101 miles) | 1499 km (931 miles)

9946 km (6180 miles) | 2052 km (1275 miles)

Maintaining and improving transportation links are of prime concern in what is Europe's fifth-largest country. Swedish governments have traditionally spent large sums on infrastructure, as a way of boosting the economy as a whole.

The 16-km (10-mile) Øresund road and rail link by bridge and tunnel connecting Malmö with Copenhagen opened in 2000, providing Sweden with better communications with Denmark and the rest of Europe. A new rail link between Arlanda airport and Stockholm is also planned. By law, cars must travel with their headlights on at all times, and there are very strict laws against drink-driving.

TOURISM

Visitors : Population 1:1.2

7.49m visitors | Up 5% in 2002

MAIN TOURIST ARRIVALS

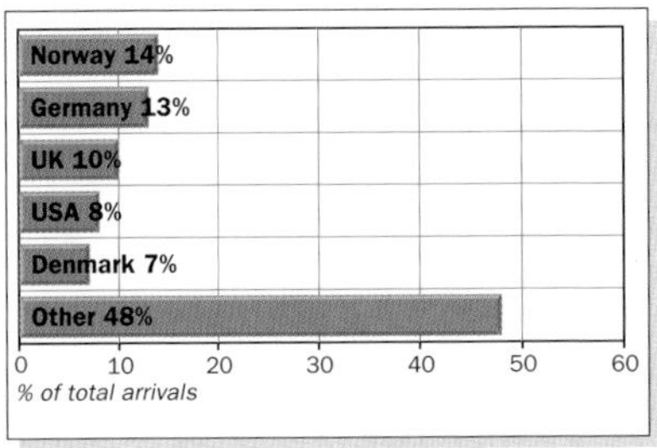
Norway 14%
Germany 13%
UK 10%
USA 8%
Denmark 7%
Other 48%
0 10 20 30 40 50 60
% of total arrivals

Sweden expanded rapidly as a tourist destination in the 1970s and 1980s. Stockholm is renowned for the beauty of its setting, its Old Town, and the *Vasa*, a magnificent 17th-century warship raised from the harbor bed in the 1960s.

Sweden has fewer lakes than Finland, and lacks Norway's dramatic scenery, but it has many natural attractions. The mountains of the "Midnight Sun" lie north of the Arctic Circle, while the southern coast has many white sandy beaches. The vast tracts of deserted landscape and the simple country communal living also attract visitors, but the cost of travel to Sweden means that Norwegians and Germans top the list of visitors.

A crofter's holding in Dalarna, *central Sweden, an area which is still mainly forested. The timber and paper industries play a major role in Sweden's economy.*

PEOPLE

Pop. density low

Swedish, Finnish, Sami | 21/km² (55/mi²)

THE URBAN/RURAL POPULATION SPLIT

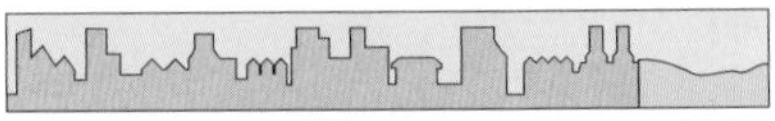
83%
17%

RELIGIOUS PERSUASION

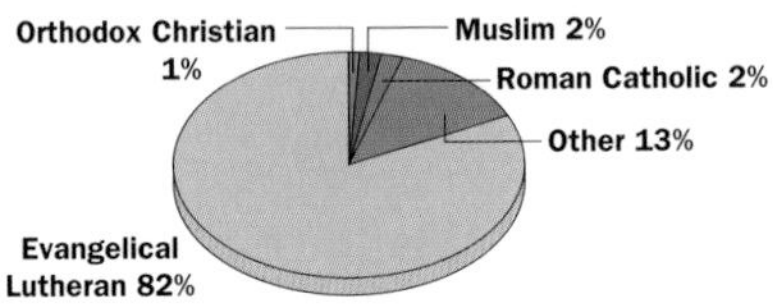
Orthodox Christian 1%
Muslim 2%
Roman Catholic 2%
Other 13%
Evangelical Lutheran 82%

ETHNIC MAKEUP

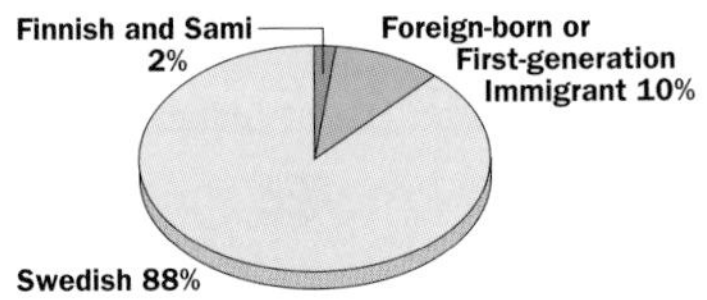
Finnish and Sami 2%
Foreign-born or First-generation Immigrant 10%
Swedish 88%

The nuclear family forms the basis of society. The birthrate is low with, on average, fewer than two children per family. Cohabitation is common, and the marriage rate is declining.

Swedish society has an egalitarian tradition. The role of the state is seen as providing conditions allowing each person to gain economic independence through employment. The welfare system is one of the most extensive in the world. However, in the early 1990s, recession reduced benefits; mothers in particular face problems with the closure of child-care facilities. Women make up nearly half the workforce. Over 45% of MPs are women, the highest percentage in the world. In 1999 the Swedish cabinet became the first in the world to have a majority of women ministers.

Sweden has generous asylum laws, and foreign-born or first-generation immigrants comprise about 10% of the population. A 15,000-strong minority of Sami live in northern Sweden. Their traditional way of life is protected.

The Evangelical Lutheran Church was disestablished in 2000.

POPULATION AGE BREAKDOWN

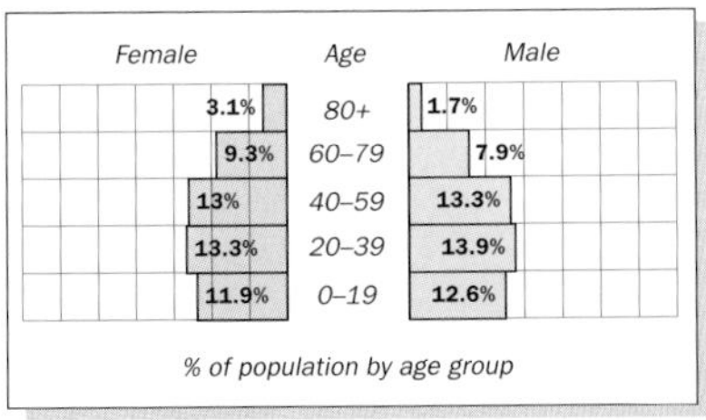
Female
Age
Male
3.1%
80+
1.7%
9.3%
60–79
7.9%
13%
40–59
13.3%
13.3%
20–39
13.9%
11.9%
0–19
12.6%
% of population by age group

S

POLITICS

Multiparty elections

2002/2006

H.M. King Carl XVI Gustaf

AT THE LAST ELECTION

Parliament (Riksdag) 349 seats

41%	16%	14%	9%	9%	6%	5%
SAP	M	FP	Kd	VP	CP	MpG

SAP = Social Democratic Labor Party **M** = Moderate Party
FP = Liberal Party **Kd** = Christian Democratic Party
VP = Left Party **CP** = Center Party **MpG** = Green Party

Sweden is a constitutional monarchy with an elected parliament under the leadership of the prime minister.

PROFILE

Politics has traditionally been split between the SAP and trade unions on the left, and a host of moderate center and right-wing parties. Since the 1930s, the SAP has governed every term, except in 1976–1982 and 1991–1994. A shift to the right in 1991 was reversed in the 1994 elections. Ingvar Carlsson, SAP leader, formed a minority government but resigned in 1996 and was replaced by Göran Persson. The SAP lost ground in elections in 1998, increasing its dependence on Left Party and Green support. A further shift in the 2002 elections left the Greens holding the balance of power.

MAIN POLITICAL ISSUES

EU membership
Sweden joined the EU in 1995. Like the UK and Denmark it opted out of introducing the euro, but is due to hold a referendum on the issue in September 2003. It supports expansion of the EU.

The high cost of the welfare state
The cost of the welfare system contributed to enormous budget deficits in the late 1980s and early 1990s. While this has been brought under control, and unemployment has been reduced, the growing number of pensioners means that social security pressures remain.

Carl XVI Gustaf, ascended the throne in 1973. His role is purely ceremonial.

Göran Persson of the SAP became prime minister in 1996.

SWEDEN

Total Area : 449 964 sq. km (173 731 sq. miles)

POPULATION
- over 1 000 000
- over 100 000
- over 50 000
- over 10 000

LAND HEIGHT
- 1000m/3281ft
- 500m/1640ft
- 200m/656ft
- Sea Level

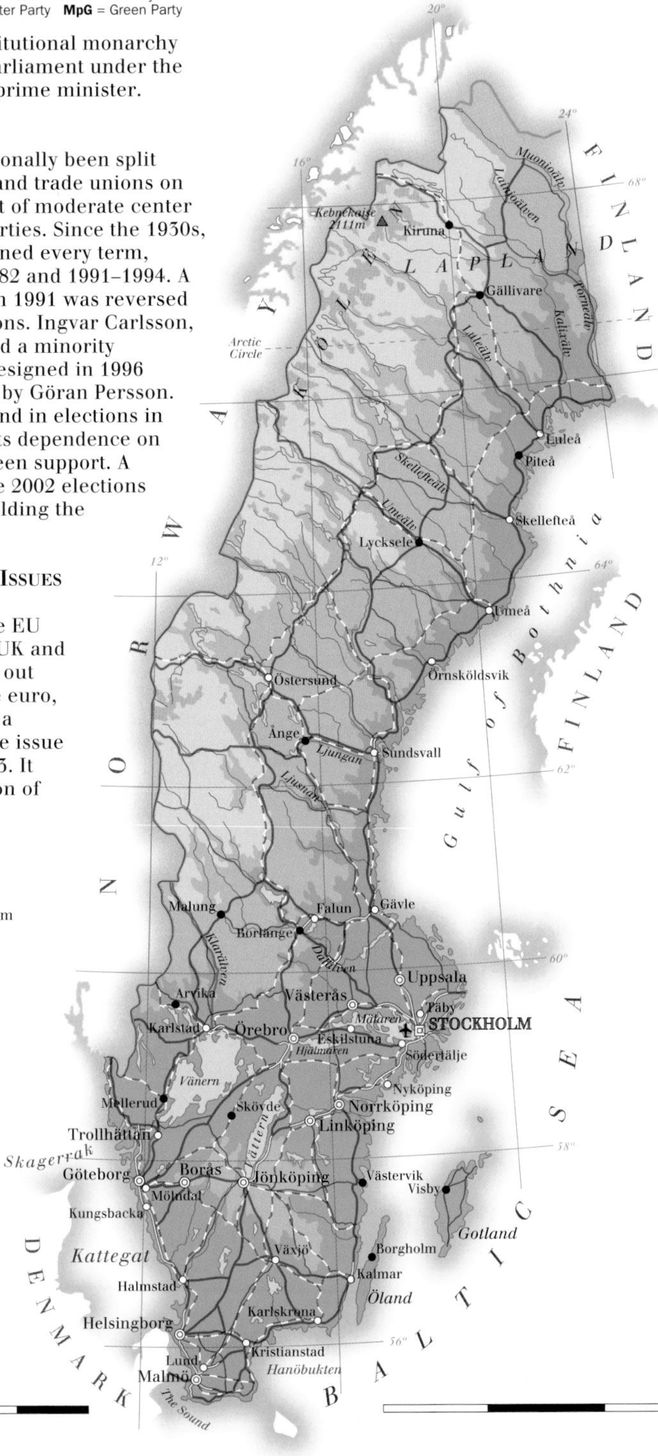
N
0 100 km
0 100 miles
NORWAY
FINLAND
LAPLAND
KÖLEN
Kebnekaise 2111m
Kiruna
Gällivare
Arctic Circle
Muonioälv
Lainioälven
Torneälv
Kalixälv
Luleälv
Luleå
Piteå
Skellefteälv
Skellefteå
Umeälv
Lycksele
Umeå
Gulf of Bothnia
Örnsköldsvik
Östersund
Ånge
Ljungan
Sundsvall
Ljusnan
Malung
Falun
Gävle
Borlänge
Klarälven
Dalälven
Uppsala
Arvika
Västerås
Täby
STOCKHOLM
Karlstad
Örebro
Mälaren
Eskilstuna
Hjälmaren
Södertälje
Vänern
Nyköping
Mellerud
Skövde
Norrköping
Trollhättan
Linköping
Vättern
Skagerrak
Göteborg
Borås
Jönköping
Västervik
Visby
Mölndal
Kungsbacka
Gotland
Kattegat
Växjö
Borgholm
Halmstad
Kalmar
Öland
Karlskrona
Helsingborg
Kristianstad
Hanöbukten
Lund
Malmö
The Sound
DENMARK
BALTIC SEA
12°
16°
20°
24°
56°
58°
60°
62°
64°
66°
68°

WORLD AFFAIRS

Joined UN in 1946

EU | CE | NC | OECD | OSCE

Sweden's main recent foreign policy concern has been its adjustment to membership of the EU, which it joined in 1995. In 1998 it voted to join the Schengen passport-free zone, but has not adopted the euro. In the 1980s, Sweden was a vociferous critic of the antagonistic policy pursued by the US toward the USSR. Since the collapse of the Soviet Union, and more recently the September 11, 2001, attack on the US, it has altered its traditionally neutral stance. Sweden has WEU observer status, and participates in NATO exercises and several UN peacekeeping operations.

AID

Donor

$1.67bn (donations)

Down 7% in 2001

Sweden is one of the few countries to exceed the UN target of 0.7% of GNP in development aid, and has declared its intention to increase its allocation.

CHRONOLOGY

Sweden's history has been closely linked to the control of the Baltic Sea and its highly profitable trade routes. Under the house of Vasa, Sweden became a major power, controlling much of the Baltic region. By the 18th century, however, Sweden's position had been eroded by its regional rivals, particularly Russia.

- **1814–1815** Congress of Vienna. Sweden cedes territory to Russia and Denmark. Prolonged period of peace begins.
- **1865–1866** Riksdag (parliament) reformed into a bicameral structure.
- **1905** Norway gains independence from Sweden.
- **1911** First Liberal government comes to power.
- **1914** Government resigns over defense policy.

S

CHRONOLOGY *continued*

- **1914–1917** Sweden remains neutral during WWI but supplies Germany. Allied blockade.
- **1917** Food shortages. Conservative government falls. Nils Edén forms a Liberal government: limits exports contributing to German war effort.
- **1919** Universal adult suffrage.
- **1921** Finland gains Åland Islands as retribution for Sweden's war role.
- **1932** Severe recession. Social Democrat government under Per Albin Hansson elected.
- **1939–1945** Sweden neutral. Grants transit rights to German forces.
- **1945–1976** Continuing Social Democratic rule under Tage Erlander establishes Sweden as world's most advanced welfare state, and one of the most affluent.
- **1950** Gustav VI Adolf becomes king.
- **1953** Joins Nordic Council.
- **1959** Founder member of EFTA.
- **1969** Erlander succeeded by Olof Palme as prime minister.
- **1973** Carl XVI Gustaf on throne.
- **1975** Major constitutional reform. Riksdag (parliament) becomes unicameral with a three-year term. Role of monarchy reduced to ceremonial functions.
- **1976** SAP loses power. Nonsocialist coalition led by Thorbjörn Fälldin in government.
- **1978** Fälldin resigns over issue of nuclear power. Ola Ullsten prime minister.
- **1979** Fälldin prime minister again.
- **1982** Elections. SAP forms minority government. Palme returns as prime minister.
- **1986** Palme shot dead. His deputy, Ingvar Carlsson, succeeds him. Police fail to find killer.
- **1990** Carlsson introduces moderate austerity package, cuts government spending, raises indirect taxes.
- **1991** Sweden applies to join EU. SAP wins election but is unable to form government; Carlsson resigns. Moderate Party leader Carl Bildt forms coalition of nonsocialist parties amid serious recession.
- **1992** Austerity measures succeed in reducing inflation but SAP refuses to support further spending cuts.
- **1994** EU membership terms agreed. Elections: SAP returns to power. Referendum favors joining EU.
- **1995** Joins EU.
- **1996** Carlsson resigns; replaced by Göran Persson.
- **1998** Persson remains in office, despite SAP losses in elections; dependent on Left and Greens for parliamentary majority.
- **2001** Defense reform program.
- **2002** Elections: SAP still largest party but lacking majority.

DEFENSE

Compulsory military service

$3.9bn

Down 15% in 2001

SWEDISH ARMED FORCES

Army	280 main battle tanks (160 Strv-121, 120 Strv-122)	19,100 personnel
Navy	7 submarines and 45 patrol boats	7100 personnel
Air force	203 combat aircraft (18 Saab AJSH-37/AJSF-37, 116 Saab JAS-39, 57 Saab JA-37)	7700 personnel
Missiles	None	

Sweden's sophisticated and powerful military force is supplied with weaponry manufactured by its advanced home defense industry, including Saab fighter jets and Bofors antiaircraft guns. However, with the ending of the Cold War, strategic priorities have changed. Sweden feels less bound to maintain its neutral stance: it has participated in NATO's Partnership for Peace program since 1994 and has WEU observer status. In 1999 spending cuts were announced, foreshadowing halving the size of the armed forces, because of the reduced military threat in the Scandinavian and Baltic region. A ten-year reform program began in 2001, offering personnel regular office hours and canceling large-scale exercises.

ECONOMICS

Inflation 2% p.a. (1990–2001)

$226bn

8.005 Swedish kronor (9.191)

SCORE CARD

World GNP Ranking	21st
GNP per Capita	$25,400
Balance of Payments	$6.7bn
Inflation	2.4%
Unemployment	4%

EXPORTS

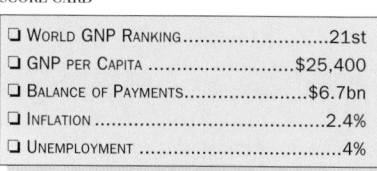

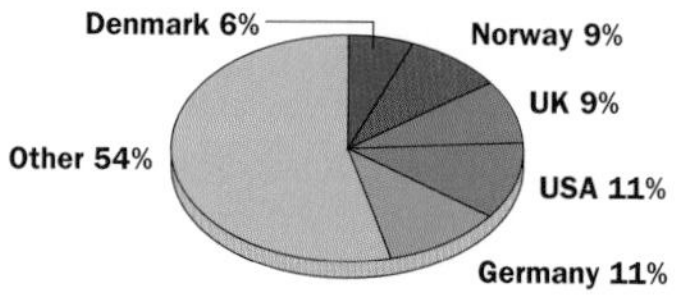
Denmark 6%
Norway 9%
UK 9%
USA 11%
Germany 11%
Other 54%

IMPORTS

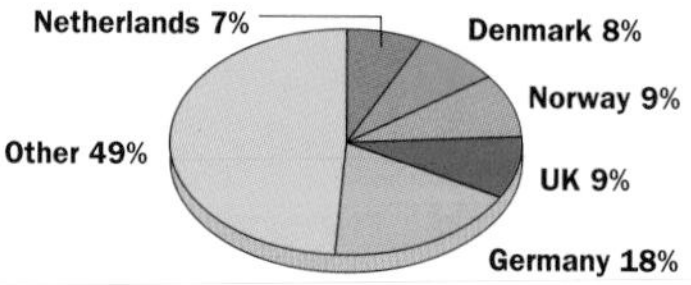
Netherlands 7%
Denmark 8%
Norway 9%
UK 9%
Germany 18%
Other 49%

ECONOMIC PERFORMANCE INDICATOR

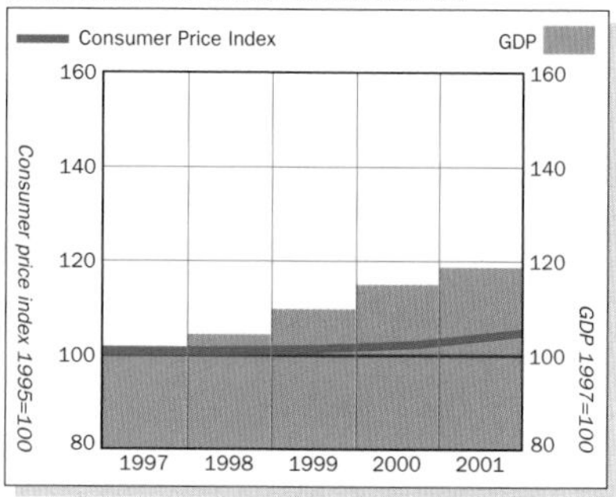
Consumer Price Index
GDP
160
140
120
100
80
Consumer price index 1995=100
GDP 1997=100
1997
1998
1999
2000
2001

Strengths

Companies of global importance, including Saab, Volvo, Electrolux and SKF, the world's biggest roller bearing manufacturer. Highly developed and constantly updated infrastructure. Sophisticated technology. Skilled labor force virtually bilingual in English.

Weaknesses

Labor costs remain uncompetitive. One of the highest rates of taxation in the OECD, accounting for almost 35% of GDP. Peripheral location, raising costs for producers and exporters. Major losses by Ericsson, giant telecoms company.

Profile

The state plays a significant role in the economy, particularly the services sector and infrastructure. Sweden's industrial giants have mostly been private-sector companies. Though the early 1990s saw a shift in economic policy to favor business, greater growth did not follow, and unemployment and welfare costs drove up the budget deficit to one of the OECD's highest in 1994. Growth has now been resumed, unemployment halved, and the deficit cut back, but inflation has started to rise. The world downturn in 2001 brought the krona under pressure. Sweden opted not to adopt the euro from 1999, but the ruling SAP adopted a pro-euro stance in 2000; the issue will be decided by referendum in 2003.

SWEDEN : MAJOR BUSINESSES

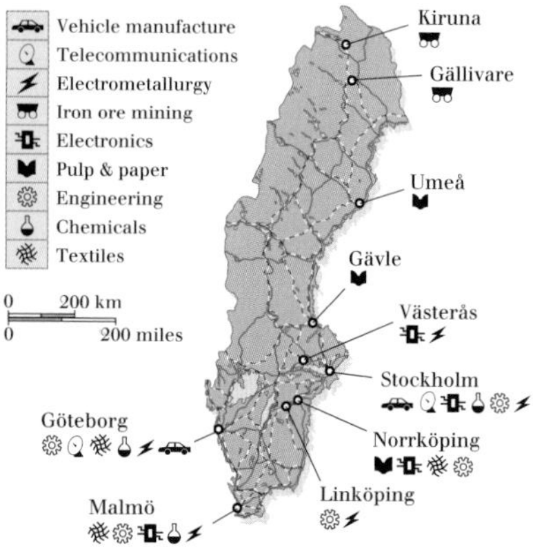
Vehicle manufacture
Telecommunications
Electrometallurgy
Iron ore mining
Electronics
Pulp & paper
Engineering
Chemicals
Textiles
0 200 km
0 200 miles
Kiruna
Gällivare
Umeå
Gävle
Västerås
Stockholm
Norrköping
Linköping
Göteborg
Malmö

S

RESOURCES

Electric power 34.5m kW

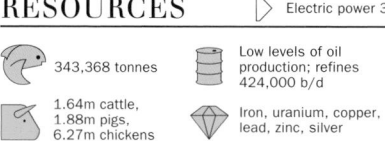

343,368 tonnes

Low levels of oil production; refines 424,000 b/d

1.64m cattle, 1.88m pigs, 6.27m chickens

Iron, uranium, copper, lead, zinc, silver

ELECTRICITY GENERATION

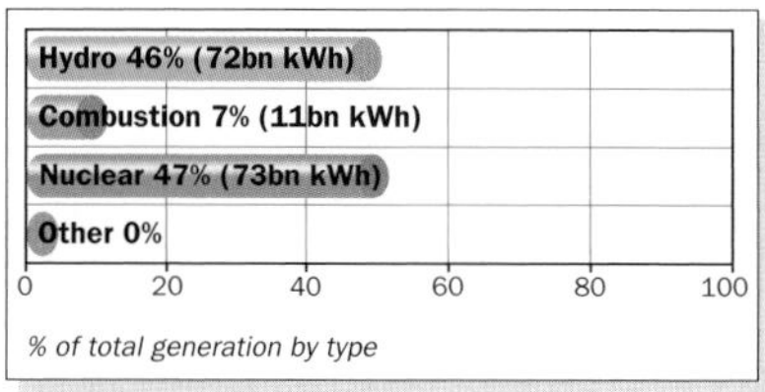

Hydro 46% (72bn kWh)
Combustion 7% (11bn kWh)
Nuclear 47% (73bn kWh)
Other 0%
0
20
40
60
80
100
% of total generation by type

Sweden is rich in minerals, including iron, copper, and silver. While mining and quarrying account for only 0.3% of GDP, they underpin other industrial sectors. In a referendum in 1980 Sweden decided, on environmental grounds, to abandon nuclear power by 2010. However, problems in securing sufficient new energy supplies and in cutting consumption meant that, by mid-2003, only one of the 12 nuclear reactors had been closed down and nuclear power still accounted for nearly half of electricity generation.

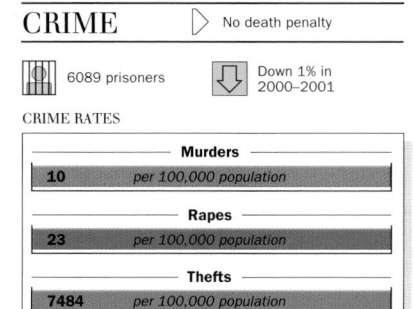

SWEDEN : LAND USE

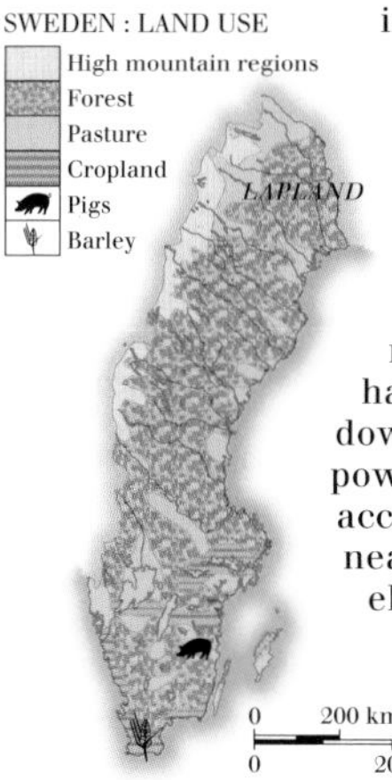

High mountain regions
Forest
Pasture
Cropland
Pigs
Barley
LAPLAND
0
200 km
0
200 miles

ENVIRONMENT

Sustainability rank: 3rd

13% (4% partially protected)

6.3 tonnes per capita

ENVIRONMENTAL TREATIES

Yes	Yes	Yes
Yes	Yes	Yes

Since Sweden's pioneering Environment Protection Act in 1969, it has invested heavily in environmental protection measures. It blames acid rain damage to forests and lakes on airborne sulfur dioxide from factories in western Europe. Swedish nuclear reactors are said to be very safe, with filtered venting systems designed to retain 90% of all radioactivity released if there were a core meltdown. Nonetheless, all reactors are due to be phased out.

MEDIA

TV ownership high

Daily newspaper circulation 410 per 1000 people

PUBLISHING AND BROADCAST MEDIA

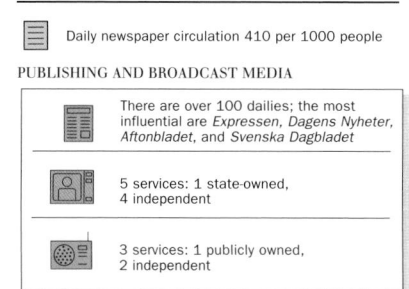

There are over 100 dailies; the most influential are *Expressen, Dagens Nyheter, Aftonbladet*, and *Svenska Dagbladet*

5 services: 1 state-owned, 4 independent

3 services: 1 publicly owned, 2 independent

Press freedom is strongly entrenched, though radical views are rarely expressed. The influence of the major daily newspapers is largely confined to Stockholm: the provinces have their own strong press.

Two-thirds of the population have cable or satellite TV.

CRIME

No death penalty

6089 prisoners

Down 1% in 2000–2001

CRIME RATES

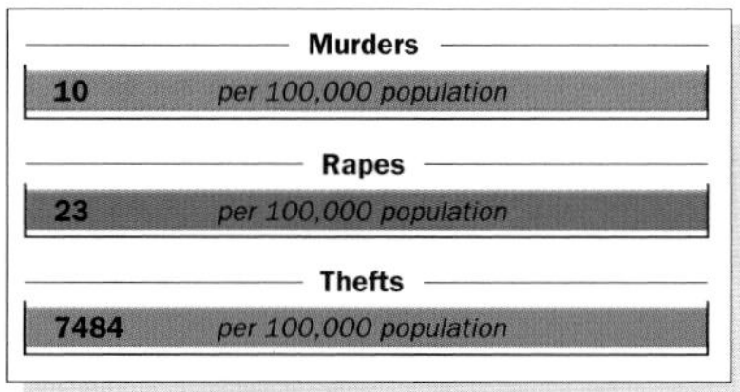

Murders
10 per 100,000 population
Rapes
23 per 100,000 population
Thefts
7484 per 100,000 population

Crime rates in Sweden are the worst in Scandinavia, and the high reporting rate puts them above the European average. Assault, rape, and theft are growing problems, especially in the cities.

EDUCATION

School leaving age: 16

99%

358,020 students

THE EDUCATION SYSTEM

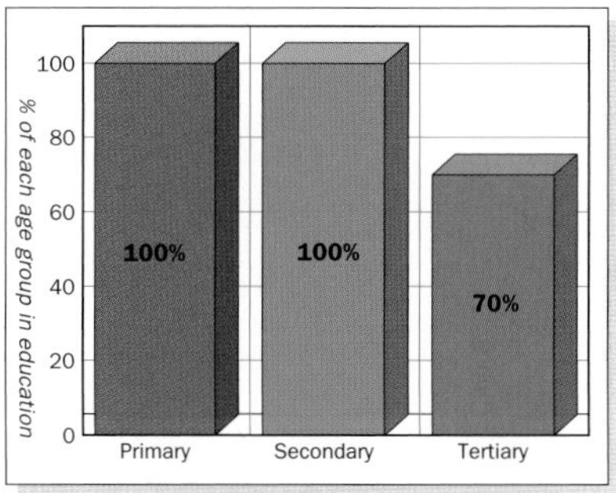

100
80
60
40
20
0
% of each age group in education
100%
100%
70%
Primary
Secondary
Tertiary

Education spending (public and private) is among the OECD's highest as a percentage of GDP.

Coeducational comprehensive schools are the norm. The higher education system is freely available to most of the population, and many adults return to college to do further courses.

HEALTH

Welfare state health benefits

1 per 322 people

Cancers, heart, cerebrovascular, and pulmonary diseases

Sweden's health care system is comprehensive and of a universally high standard. Spending fell by an average of 2% in real terms in the 1990s, but the trend is now being reversed. Savings have been made by increasing outpatient care, reducing the number of hospital beds, and cutting jobs. Since 1994 individuals have had the right to choose their own doctor, while doctors and specialists can now set up private practices. In 1999 the government agreed to compensate more than 60,000 people subjected to enforced sterilization in 1935–1975.

SPENDING

GDP/cap. increase

CONSUMPTION AND SPENDING

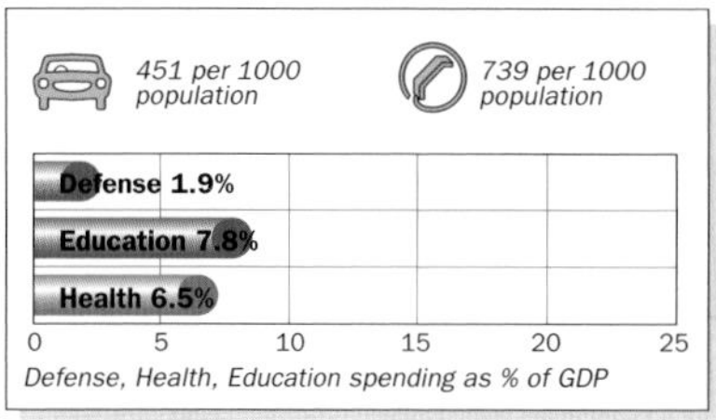

451 per 1000 population
739 per 1000 population
Defense 1.9%
Education 7.8%
Health 6.5%
0
5
10
15
20
25
Defense, Health, Education spending as % of GDP

Sweden has small income differentials, and Swedish executives are paid less than some of their European counterparts. Compared with other European states or the US, social competition and a sense of hierarchy are limited. Despite some cuts in services, the welfare system still rates highly in Europe.

Swedes are keen overseas property buyers, particularly of villas in Italy and France. Net overseas per capita investment remains among the highest in the world and about two-thirds of households own shares. PC ownership is high, and over 60% of Swedes had Internet access by 2002.

S

WORLD RANKING

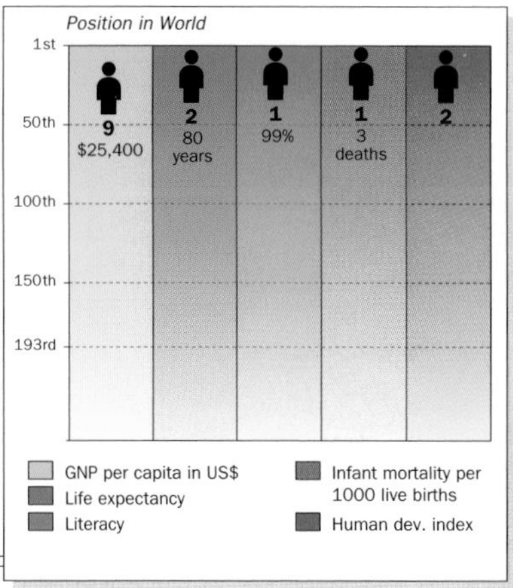

Position in World
1st
50th
100th
150th
193rd
9
$25,400
2
80 years
1
99%
1
3 deaths
2
GNP per capita in US$
Life expectancy
Literacy
Infant mortality per 1000 live births
Human dev. index

SWITZERLAND

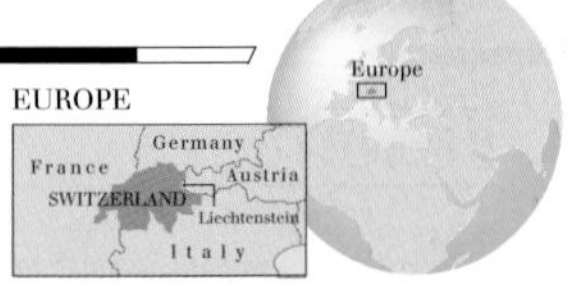
EUROPE
Europe
Germany
France
SWITZERLAND
Austria
Liechtenstein
Italy

OFFICIAL NAME: Swiss Confederation **CAPITAL:** Bern
POPULATION: 7.2 million **CURRENCY:** Swiss franc **OFFICIAL LANGUAGES:** French, German, and Italian

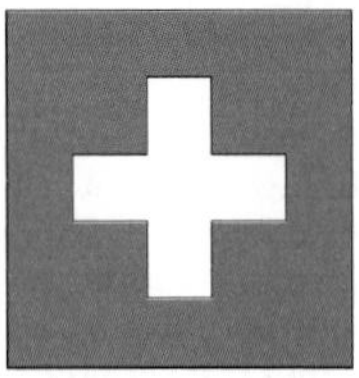

1291 | 1857 | Aug 1 | CH | +1 | +41 | .ch

SWITZERLAND LIES at the center of western Europe geographically, but outside it politically. Sometimes called Europe's water tower, it is the source of all four of the region's major river systems: the Po, the Rhône, the Rhine, and the Inn–Danube. Switzerland has built one of the world's most prosperous economies, aided by the fact that it has retained its neutral status through every major European conflict since 1815. The process of European integration has been the latest and strongest challenge to Swiss neutralism, but it remains outside the EU.

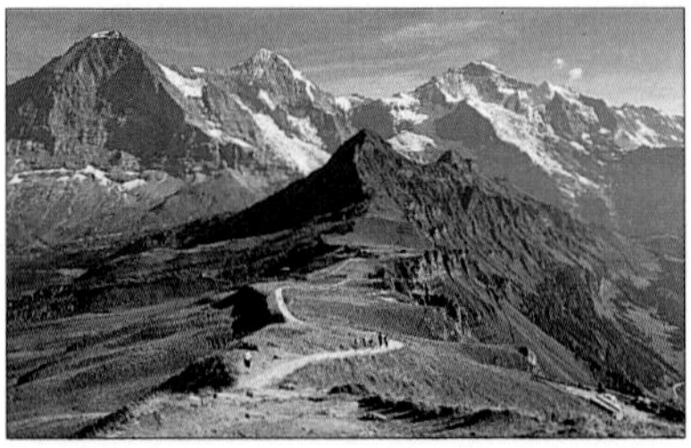

The Eiger in the Berner Oberland. *In 1994, a referendum voted to ban all truck transit traffic from the Swiss Alps from 2004.*

CLIMATE

Mountain/continental

WEATHER CHART FOR BERN

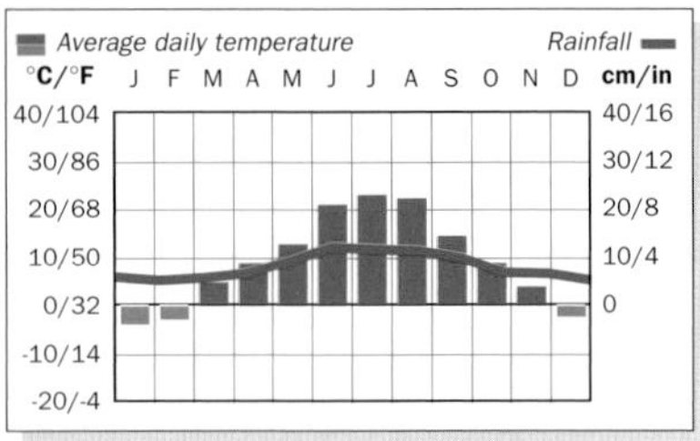
Average daily temperature
Rainfall
°C/°F
J F M A M J J A S O N D
cm/in
40/104
30/86
20/68
10/50
0/32
-10/14
-20/-4
40/16
30/12
20/8
10/4
0

Temperature and weather fluctuate enormously, not only seasonally but because of the huge variations in altitude and the country's location in central Europe. On the plateau north of the Alps, where most of the population lives, summers are warm and winters dry, cool, and often foggy. South of the Alps, it is warmer and sunnier. Strong southerly winds, or *föhn*, can bring summerlike weather even in winter. Avalanches have been a problem in recent years.

TRANSPORTATION

Drive on right

Kloten, Zürich
17.8m passengers

24 ships
502,000 grt

THE TRANSPORTATION NETWORK

71,059 km (44,154 miles)	1270 km (789 miles)
3216 km (1998 miles)	1214 km (754 miles)

Switzerland is a major freight transit route. Pollution and safety are major concerns: 11 people died in a fire in 2001 in the Gotthard road tunnel. The NEAT project, begun in 1996, will provide a high-speed rail link between Basel and Milan, whose trains will carry trucks. Swissair, bankrupt in 2001, has been replaced by a new airline, "Swiss."

TOURISM

Visitors : Population 1.4:1

9.97m visitors

Down 8% in 2002

MAIN TOURIST ARRIVALS

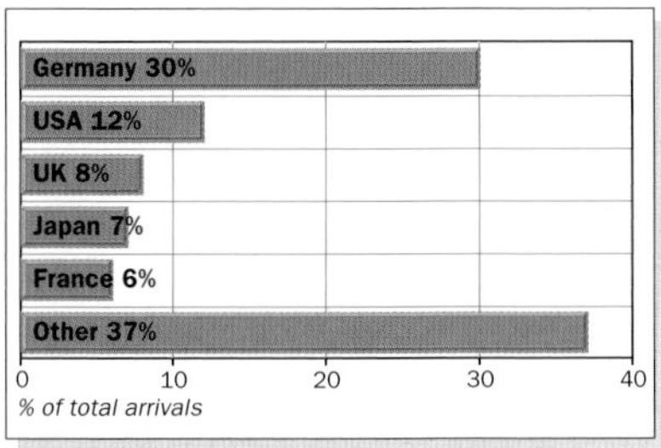
Germany 30%
USA 12%
UK 8%
Japan 7%
France 6%
Other 37%
0
10
20
30
40
% of total arrivals

Tourism is Switzerland's third-largest industry. About 350,000 Swiss earn their living from it, and it accounts for around 3% of GDP. The Alps are the main attraction, drawing winter and summer tourists from around the world, and Chillon Castle on Lake Geneva continues to be the country's most popular tourist site. In recent years, warmer winters have shortened the skiing season. "Suicide tourism," as a recent development has been termed, has seen terminally ill people taking advantage of less stringent Swiss laws on euthanasia.

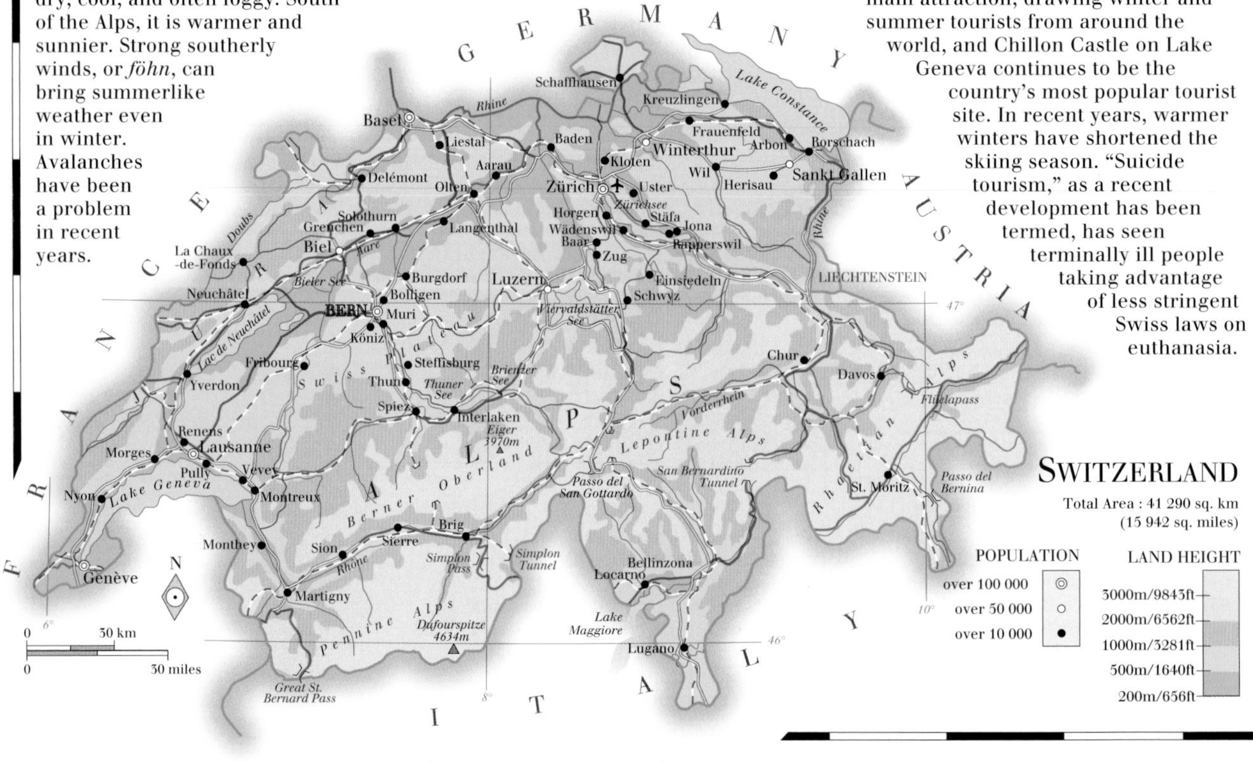
GERMANY
FRANCE
AUSTRIA
ITALY
LIECHTENSTEIN
Schaffhausen
Basel
Rhine
Liestal
Kreuzlingen
Lake Constance
Frauenfeld
Winterthur
Arbon
Rorschach
Baden
Aarau
Delémont
Kloten
Wil
Sankt Gallen
Herisau
Olten
Zürich
Uster
Zürichsee
Horgen
Stäfa
Wädenswil
Jona
Rapperswil
Baar
Zug
Solothurn
Grenchen
Langenthal
Biel
Aare
La Chaux-de-Fonds
Doubs
Burgdorf
Luzern
Bieler See
Einsiedeln
Neuchâtel
Bolligen
Schwyz
BERN
Muri
Vierwaldstätter See
Köniz
Lac de Neuchâtel
Fribourg
Steffisburg
Brienzer See
Chur
Yverdon
Swiss Plateau
Thun
Thuner See
Davos
Spiez
Interlaken
Eiger 3970m
Vorderrhein
Flüelapass
Renens
Lausanne
Berner Oberland
Lepontine Alps
Morges
Pully
Vevey
Passo del San Gottardo
San Bernardino Tunnel
Rhaetian Alps
St. Moritz
Passo del Bernina
Nyon
Lake Geneva
Montreux
Jura
Brig
Sierre
Monthey
Sion
Rhône
Simplon Pass
Simplon Tunnel
Bellinzona
Locarno
Genève
Martigny
Pennine Alps
Dufourspitze 4634m
Lake Maggiore
Lugano
Great St. Bernard Pass
N
0 30 km
0 30 miles
47°
46°
6°
8°
10°
SWITZERLAND
Total Area : 41 290 sq. km (15 942 sq. miles)
POPULATION
over 100 000
over 50 000
over 10 000
LAND HEIGHT
3000m/9843ft
2000m/6562ft
1000m/3281ft
500m/1640ft
200m/656ft

PEOPLE

Pop. density medium

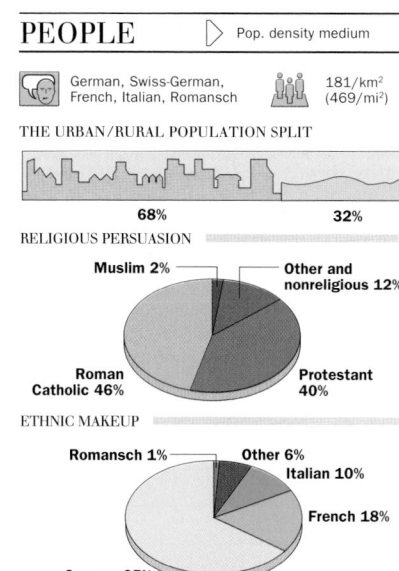

German, Swiss-German, French, Italian, Romansch

181/km² (469/mi²)

THE URBAN/RURAL POPULATION SPLIT

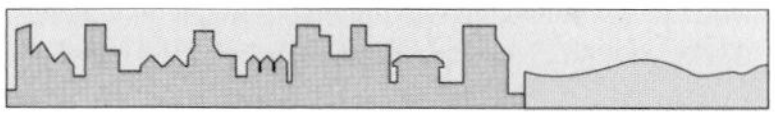
68%
32%

RELIGIOUS PERSUASION

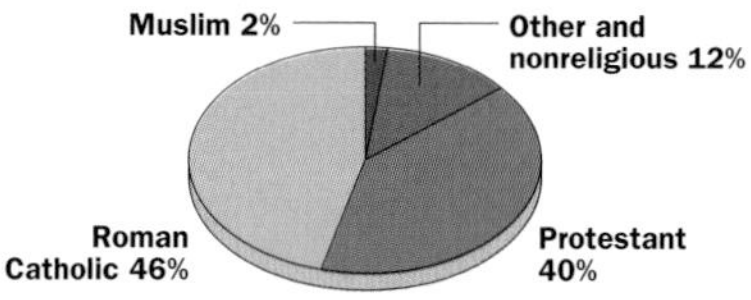
Muslim 2%
Other and nonreligious 12%
Roman Catholic 46%
Protestant 40%

ETHNIC MAKEUP

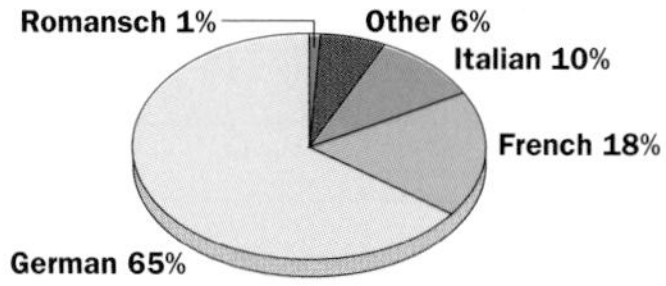
Romansch 1%
Other 6%
Italian 10%
French 18%
German 65%

The Swiss comprise distinct German-Swiss, French-Swiss, and Italian-Swiss linguistic groups. About 40,000 people in the eastern canton of Grisons speak Romansch. The German-Swiss, in the majority, are a tightly knit community, with a dialect that is impenetrable to most outsiders. In recent years, the three groups have grown further apart. The French-Swiss, in favor of joining the EU, are opposed by the German-Swiss. In Italian-speaking Ticino, a political party has emerged to champion Italian-Swiss interests. Despite tensions between Swiss and immigrant workers, referenda proposing strict limits on numbers of foreigners and the restriction of asylum were heavily defeated in 2000 and 2002 respectively.

Society retains strong conservative elements. Two half-cantons granted women the vote at regional level only in 1989 and 1990. The marriage rate is high and the divorce rate lower than the European average.

POPULATION AGE BREAKDOWN

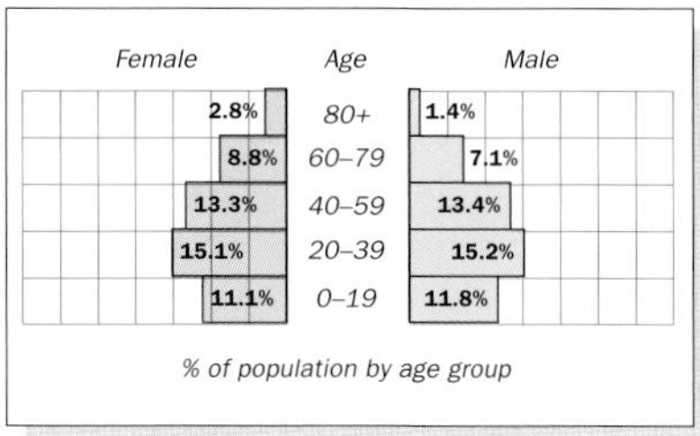
Female
Age
Male
2.8%
80+
1.4%
8.8%
60–79
7.1%
13.3%
40–59
13.4%
15.1%
20–39
15.2%
11.1%
0–19
11.8%
% of population by age group

WORLD AFFAIRS

Joined UN in 2002

CE G10 EFTA OSCE PfP

The basis of Swiss foreign policy remains its neutrality. Geneva is a center for many international organizations, including the ICRC and the European headquarters of the UN (though Switzerland only voted to join the UN in 2002). The city has often hosted diplomatic negotiations: those for the START nuclear reduction treaties and peace talks for the former Yugoslavia took place there.

A member of EFTA, Switzerland has so far not joined the process of closer European integration. In 1992 voters rejected EEA membership, widely seen as the first step toward EU membership. Many advocates of joining the EU believe that the economy will suffer without closer integration. Opponents argue that Switzerland's seeming isolation will enhance its role as an international tax haven. In 2001 a proposal to apply for EU membership was overwhelmingly rejected, though a series of bilateral cooperation agreements with the EU entered into force in 2002.

POLITICS

Multiparty elections

L. House 1999/2003
U. House 1999/2003

President Pascal Couchepin

AT THE LAST ELECTION

National Council 200 seats

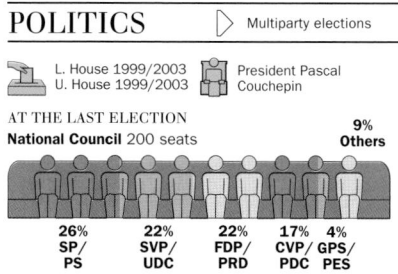

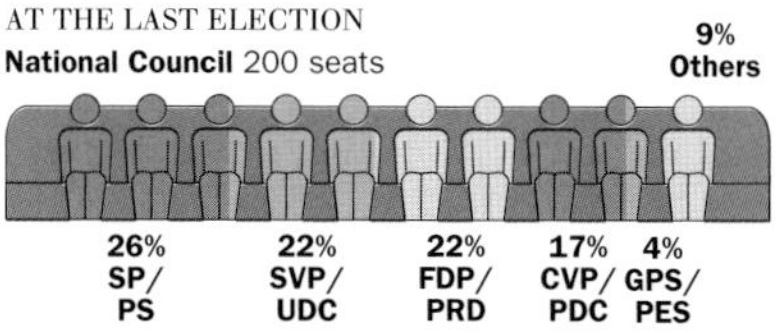
9% Others
26% SP/ PS
22% SVP/ UDC
22% FDP/ PRD
17% CVP/ PDC
4% GPS/ PES

SP/PS = Social Democratic Party **SVP/UDC** = Swiss People's Party **FDP/PRD** = Radical Democratic Party **CVP/PDC** = Christian Democratic People's Party **GPS/PES** = Green Party of Switzerland

Council of States 46 seats

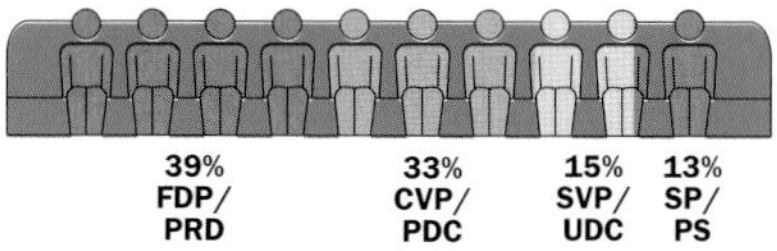
39% FDP/ PRD
33% CVP/ PDC
15% SVP/ UDC
13% SP/ PS

Switzerland is a federal democratic republic with 26 autonomous cantons. The presidency rotates every year.

PROFILE

The same four-party coalition has been in power in Switzerland since 1959. Domestic and foreign policies have changed little. Politics has recently become more contentious, however, with voting patterns becoming more polarized. Divisive issues are those of narcotics and of membership of the EU. Both right-wing and green minority parties have recently gained more seats in parliament. The right-wing SVP/UDC in particular capitalized on growing hostility to immigration to perform strongly in the 1999 elections.

Switzerland's political system is unique in Europe, in that taking important decisions depends on the results of referenda. A petition of more than 100,000 signatures can force a referendum on any issue.

MAIN POLITICAL ISSUES

European integration

Almost all politicians and business leaders favor joining the EU, or at least the European Economic Area (EEA), but voters remain sharply divided. The Swiss fear that their decentralized style of government would be lost within the EU. There are also worries that in a barrier-free Europe, Switzerland's high standards of living would fall because of a large influx of immigrants.

Switzerland and World War II

In 2002 the Bergier report criticized Swiss refusal to admit many Jewish refugees during World War II, but found that the banking system was not built on the assets of Holocaust victims. In 1998 the two largest Swiss banks had agreed to pay $1.25 billion to 31,500 victims and their families in return for agreement that there would be no future claims against Swiss banks or the government. A government Fund for Needy Holocaust Victims was wound up in 2002 after paying $179 million to 309,000 survivors.

Pascal Couchepin *of the FDP/PRD, who held the one-year presidency in 2003.*

Ruth Metzler-Arnold *of the CVP/PDC, vice president in 2003.*

CHRONOLOGY

The autonomy of the Swiss cantons was curtailed by the Habsburgs in the 11th century. In 1291, the three cantons of Unterwalden, Schwyz, and Uri set up the Perpetual League to pursue Swiss liberty. Joined by other cantons, they succeeded in 1499 in gaining virtual independence. The Habsburgs retained a titular role.

- ❑ **1648** Peace of Westphalia ending Thirty Years' War, in which Switzerland played no active part, recognizes full Swiss independence.
- ❑ **1798** Invaded by French.
- ❑ **1815** Congress of Vienna after Napoléon's defeat confirms Swiss independence and establishes its neutrality. Geneva and Valais join Swiss Confederation.

S

CHRONOLOGY *continued*

- **1848** New constitution after brief civil war (1847) – central government given more powers, but cantons' powers guaranteed.
- **1857** Neuchâtel joins confederation.
- **1863** Henri Dunant founds ICRC in Geneva.
- **1874** Referendum established as important decision-making tool.
- **1914–1918** Plays humanitarian role in World War I.
- **1919** Proportional representation ensures future political stability.
- **1920** Joins League of Nations.
- **1939–1945** Neutral in World War II.
- **1945** Refuses to join UN.
- **1959** Founder member of EFTA. Present four-party coalition comes to power, taking over FDP/PRD dominance of government.
- **1967** Right-wing groups make electoral gains, campaigning to restrict entry of foreign workers.
- **1971** Most women granted right to vote in federal elections.
- **1984** Parliament approves application for UN membership. Elisabeth Kopp is first woman minister (justice portfolio).
- **1986** Referendum opposes joining UN. Immigrant numbers restricted.
- **1988** Kopp resigns over allegedly violating secrecy of information laws.
- **1990** Kopp acquitted. Case revealed public prosecutor's office held secret files on 200,000 people. Violent protests. State security laws amended.
- **1991** Large increase in attacks on asylum-seekers' hostels.
- **1992** Joins IMF and World Bank. Referendum vetoes joining EEA.
- **1994** Referendum approves new antiracism law and tighter laws against narcotics traffickers and illegal immigrants.
- **1998** $1.25 billion compensation for Holocaust victims whose funds were deposited in Swiss banks.
- **1999** Ruth Dreifuss first woman president.
- **2002** Third referendum on joining UN gives approval. Legalization of abortions as currently carried out also approved by referendum.

AID

Donor

$908m (donations) — Up 2% in 2001

With total disbursements amounting to 0.34% of GNP in 2001, Switzerland ranks above the (OECD) average of 0.22% as an aid donor, though the level of assistance remains below its target of 0.4% of GNP, set in 1994. Good governance and promoting investment are current priorities.

DEFENSE

Compulsory military service

$2.84bn — Down 3% in 2001

SWISS ARMED FORCES

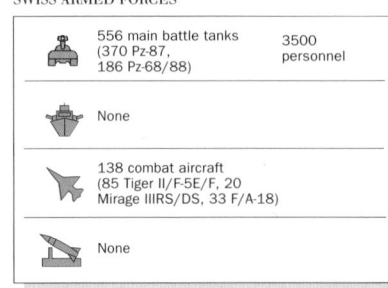

556 main battle tanks (370 Pz-87, 186 Pz-68/88)	3500 personnel
None	
138 combat aircraft (85 Tiger II/F-5E/F, 20 Mirage IIIRS/DS, 33 F/A-18)	
None	

The army is, in one sense, among the largest in Europe. It has an air wing and is organized so that almost 400,000 conscripts can be called up and armed in a few hours; it still uses skis, bicycles, and horses to protect the Alps. Bridges and tunnels are mined in accordance with a defense strategy drafted in the early 1900s. Military service and further training at intervals are compulsory for males up to the age of 50.

Force numbers are being cut in response to the end of the Cold War. In 1995, legislation allowing civilian service in place of military service was passed. Voters approved in 2001 a referendum proposal allowing Swiss soldiers to bear arms when on international peacekeeping operations.

ECONOMICS

Inflation 1.2% p.a. (1990–2001)

$277bn — 1.355 Swiss francs (1.488)

SCORE CARD

World GNP Ranking	17th
GNP per Capita	$38,330
Balance of Payments	$22.6bn
Inflation	1%
Unemployment	2%

EXPORTS

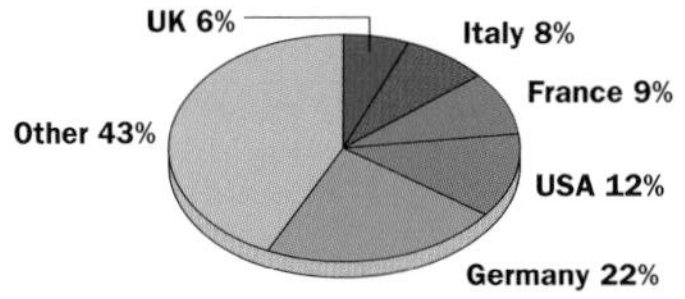
UK 6%
Italy 8%
France 9%
USA 12%
Germany 22%
Other 43%

IMPORTS

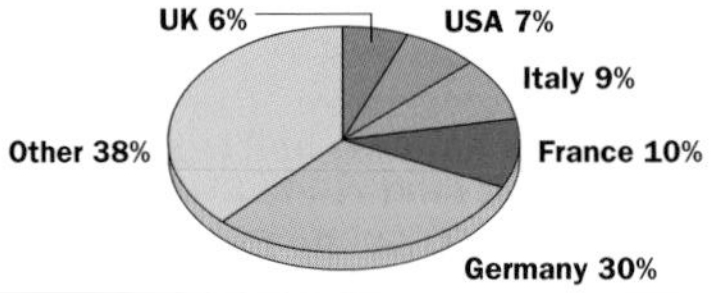
UK 6%
USA 7%
Italy 9%
France 10%
Germany 30%
Other 38%

ECONOMIC PERFORMANCE INDICATOR

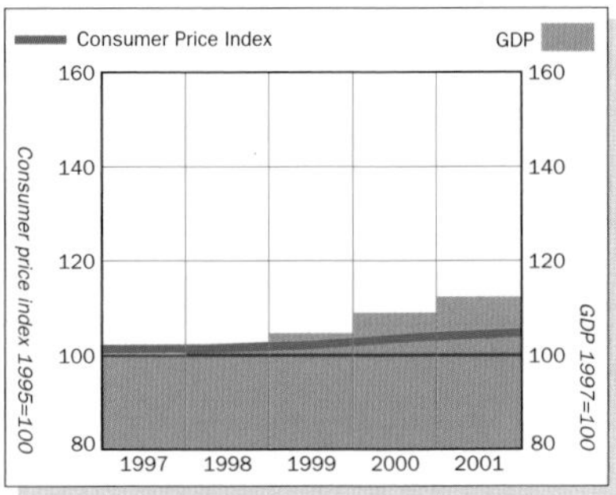
Consumer Price Index
GDP
160
140
120
100
80
1997
1998
1999
2000
2001
Consumer price index 1995=100
GDP 1997=100

Strengths
Highly skilled workforce. Reliable service provider. Major machine tool and precision engineering industries. Powerful chemical, pharmaceutical, and banking multinationals. Banking secrecy laws attract foreign capital; banking sector contributes 9% of GNP. Ability to innovate to capture mass markets, typified by Swatch watch and Swatch-designed Smart car.

Weaknesses
Protected cartels result in many overpriced goods. Highly subsidized agricultural sector.

Profile
The economy is widely diversified. There are several large multinational enterprises and a large banking sector managing around one-third of the world's offshore private wealth. There was limited growth during the 1990s, and an economic downturn since 2001 has resulted in job losses in such sectors as banking and civil aviation. There is pressure to cater for the needs of an aging population, and in 2003 plans were announced to raise the retirement age from 65 to 67.

SWITZERLAND : MAJOR BUSINESSES

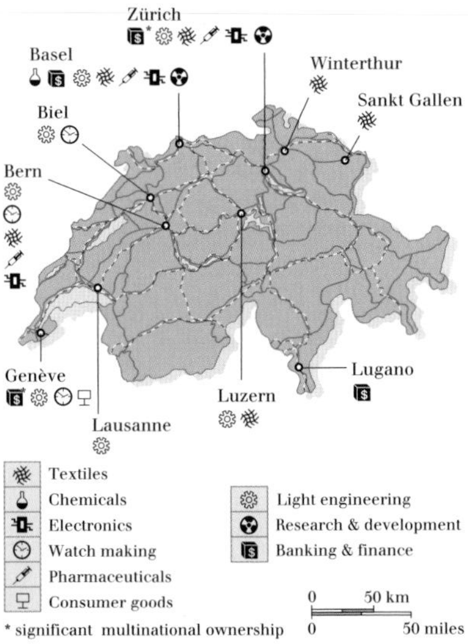
Zürich
Basel
Winterthur
Sankt Gallen
Biel
Bern
Genève
Lugano
Luzern
Lausanne
Textiles
Chemicals
Electronics
Watch making
Pharmaceuticals
Consumer goods
Light engineering
Research & development
Banking & finance
0 50 km
0 50 miles
* significant multinational ownership

RESOURCES

Electric power 16.6m kW

2759 tonnes

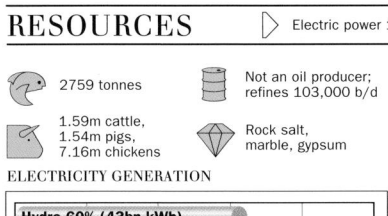

Not an oil producer; refines 103,000 b/d

1.59m cattle, 1.54m pigs, 7.16m chickens

Rock salt, marble, gypsum

ELECTRICITY GENERATION

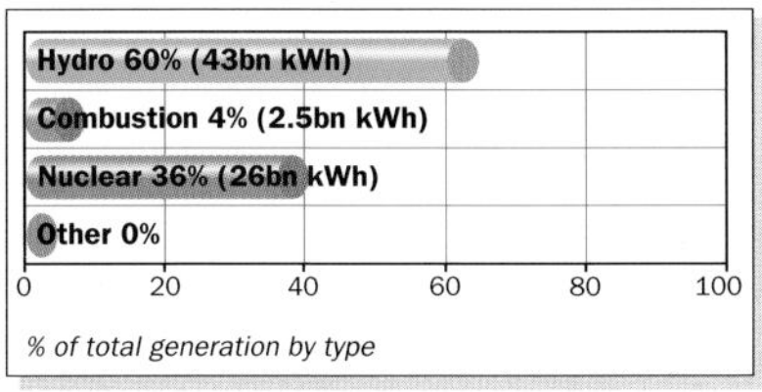
Hydro 60% (43bn kWh)
Combustion 4% (2.5bn kWh)
Nuclear 36% (26bn kWh)
Other 0%
0
20
40
60
80
100
% of total generation by type

Switzerland is poor in natural resources, having no valuable minerals in commercially exploitable quantities. Over half of its electricity comes from hydropower, while five nuclear plants supply most of the rest, so that spending on imported oil and coal is kept to a minimum – they account for less than 4% of the total import bill. Large-scale antinuclear power demonstrations in the 1980s led to the cancellation of plans for a new nuclear power plant, but a referendum approved continued use of existing plants.

SWITZERLAND : LAND USE

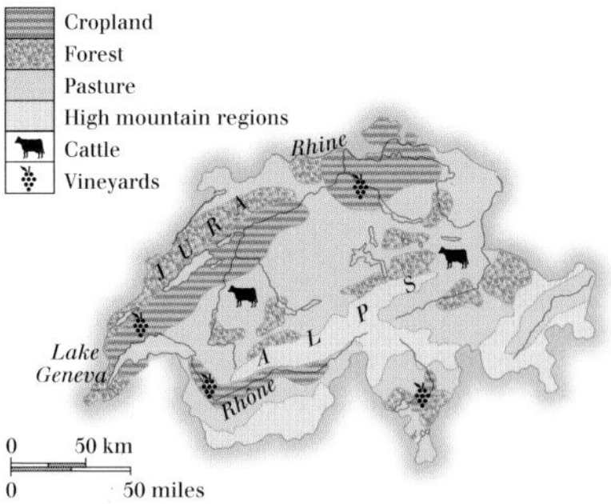
Cropland
Forest
Pasture
High mountain regions
Cattle
Vineyards
Rhine
JURA
ALPS
Lake Geneva
Rhône
0 50 km
0 50 miles

ENVIRONMENT

Sustainability rank: 5th

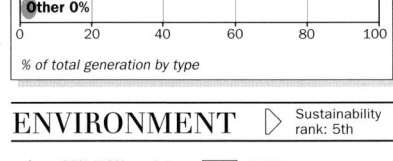

30% (18% partially protected)

6.1 tonnes per capita

ENVIRONMENTAL TREATIES

Yes Yes Yes
Yes Yes No

The Swiss are among the most environmentally conscious people in the world and are willing to back their convictions with money. The Basel–Milan link, designed to carry trucks by rail through a tunnel instead of having them cross the Alps by road, was approved by referendum, despite the estimated $13.3bn cost. The planners' aim is a total ban on carrying freight by road through Switzerland by 2004; this may not be necessary if major time savings make the tunnel sufficiently attractive. The Swiss are keen recyclers and taxation is used to encourage this.

MEDIA

TV ownership high

Daily newspaper circulation 376 per 1000 people

PUBLISHING AND BROADCAST MEDIA

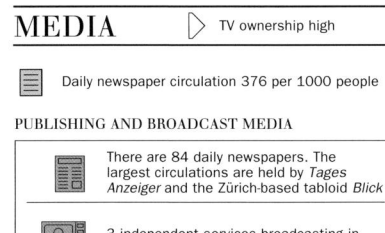

There are 84 daily newspapers. The largest circulations are held by *Tages Anzeiger* and the Zürich-based tabloid *Blick*

3 independent services broadcasting in German, Romansch, French, and Italian

3 independent services broadcasting in German, Romansch, French, and Italian

The Swiss media are organized broadly along regional lines, and reflect the country's linguistic divisions. The German-, Romansch-, French-, and Italian-language TV and radio stations tend to focus on the interests of their specific communities. German, Italian, and French satellite TV is widely available. Few newspapers are distributed throughout the country. *Tribune de Genève* and *Neue Zürcher Zeitung* are exceptions.

CRIME

No death penalty

4985 prisoners

Down 38% in 2000–2001

CRIME RATES

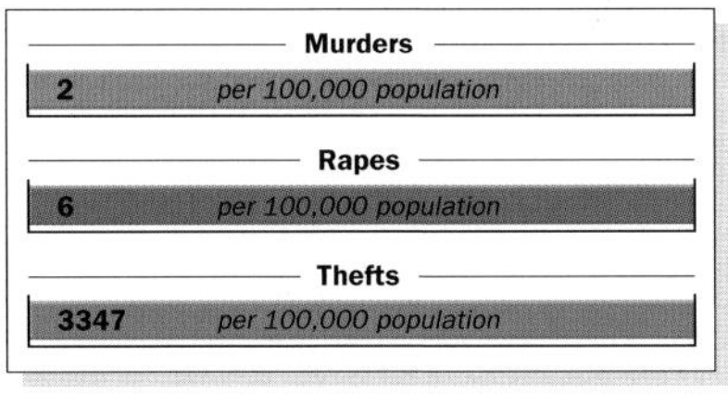
Murders
2 per 100,000 population
Rapes
6 per 100,000 population
Thefts
3347 per 100,000 population

Crime rates are low by international standards. Muggings and burglaries are on the increase and are often related to narcotics. More cases of banking secrecy laws attracting laundered funds are coming to light.

EDUCATION

School leaving age: 16

99%

163,373 students

THE EDUCATION SYSTEM

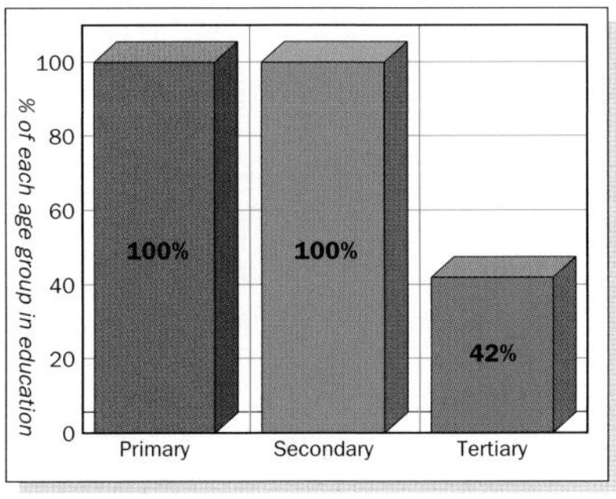
100
80
60
40
20
0
% of each age group in education
100%
100%
42%
Primary
Secondary
Tertiary

State spending on education is high. Primary and secondary education are controlled by the cantons, so that there are 26 different systems in operation. In some German-speaking cantons, including Zürich, children begin learning English before French or Italian.

Revelations of poor literacy levels among Swiss schoolchildren prompted an action plan, unveiled in mid-2003, which proposed lowering the school entry age from seven to five and providing extra help to foreign children.

HEALTH

Welfare state health benefits

1 per 298 people

Heart diseases, cancers, cerebrovascular and respiratory diseases

The health system is among the most efficient and pioneering in the world, and is ranked by WHO second, after Japan, for attainment. High health costs are covered by compulsory insurance schemes.

SPENDING

GDP/cap. increase

CONSUMPTION AND SPENDING

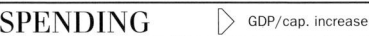

494 per 1000 population

746 per 1000 population

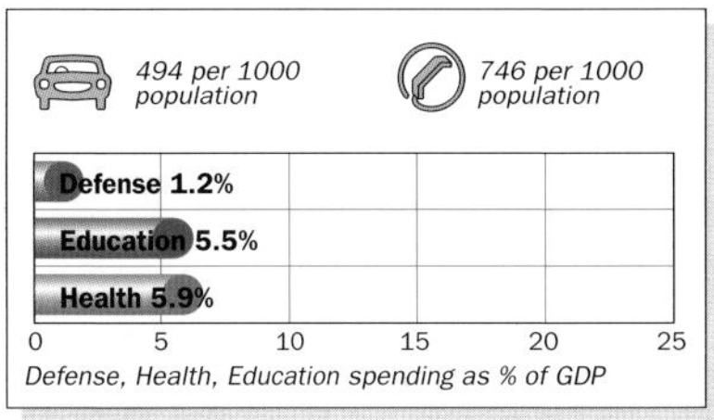
Defense 1.2%
Education 5.5%
Health 5.9%
0
5
10
15
20
25
Defense, Health, Education spending as % of GDP

Immigrant workers do most low-paid and menial jobs. Wages in office jobs are relatively high, though the cost of living is also well above the European average. Many workers choose to live in France and commute across the border. The property market is highly regulated.

WORLD RANKING

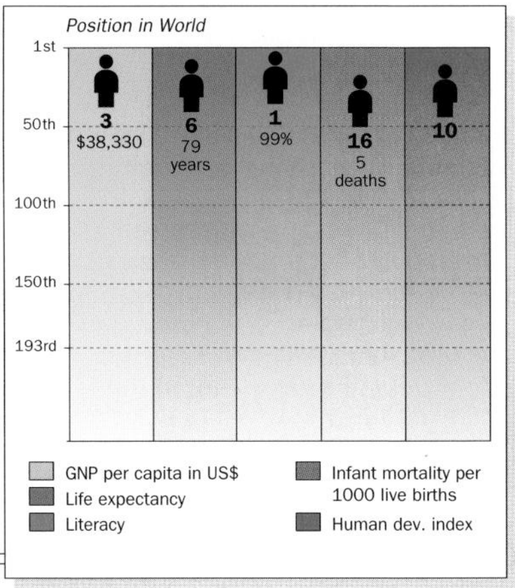
Position in World
1st
50th
100th
150th
193rd
3
$38,330
6
79 years
1
99%
16
5 deaths
10
GNP per capita in US$
Life expectancy
Literacy
Infant mortality per 1000 live births
Human dev. index

S

SYRIA

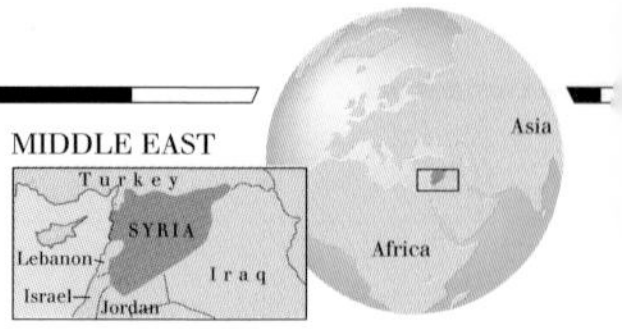
MIDDLE EAST
Turkey
SYRIA
Lebanon
Israel
Jordan
Iraq
Asia
Africa

OFFICIAL NAME: Syrian Arab Republic **CAPITAL:** Damascus
POPULATION: 17 million **CURRENCY:** Syrian pound **OFFICIAL LANGUAGE:** Arabic

1941 | 1967 | April 17 | SYR | +2 | +963 | .sy

SYRIA IS REGARDED by many of its people as an artificial creation of French-mandated rule, which lasted from 1920 to independence. They identify instead with a Greater Syria, a successor to the medieval Ummayad caliphate encompassing Lebanon, Jordan, and Palestine. Since independence, Syria's foreign relations have been turbulent, but the authoritarian Ba'athist regime of Hafez al-Assad (1970–2000) brought a measure of internal stability.

CLIMATE

Steppe/hot desert/ Mediterranean

WEATHER CHART FOR DAMASCUS

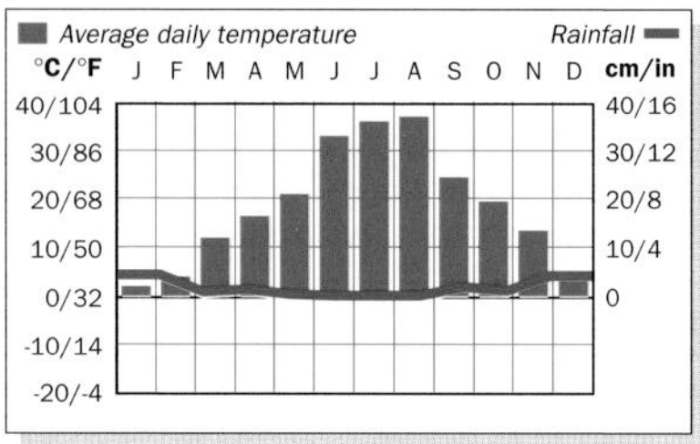
Average daily temperature
Rainfall
°C/°F
J F M A M J J A S O N D
cm/in
40/104
30/86
20/68
10/50
0/32
-10/14
-20/-4
40/16
30/12
20/8
10/4
0

The coastal climate is Mediterranean, with mild, wet winters and dry, hot summers. Most of the country gets fewer than 25 cm (10 in) of rainfall a year. Away from the coast, rainfall is very unpredictable and the country becomes increasingly arid, with some desert areas. In the mountains, snow is common in winter.

TRANSPORTATION

Drive on right

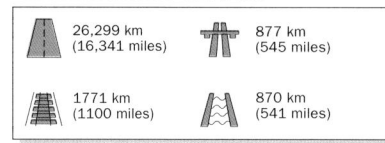

Damascus International 1.5m passengers

215 ships 498,200 grt

THE TRANSPORTATION NETWORK

26,299 km (16,341 miles)

877 km (545 miles)

1771 km (1100 miles)

870 km (541 miles)

The road network is unreliable in rural areas, especially during the winter after rain. Bus services operate to most towns from Damascus and Aleppo. Roads are integrated with the railroads, which carry over four million passengers a year and are vital to freight transportation. The rail link from Aleppo to Mosul, in Iraq, reopened in mid-2000. Damascus is the main international airport and Latakia the main port.

TOURISM

Visitors : Population 1:13

1.32m visitors

Down 7% in 2001

MAIN TOURIST ARRIVALS

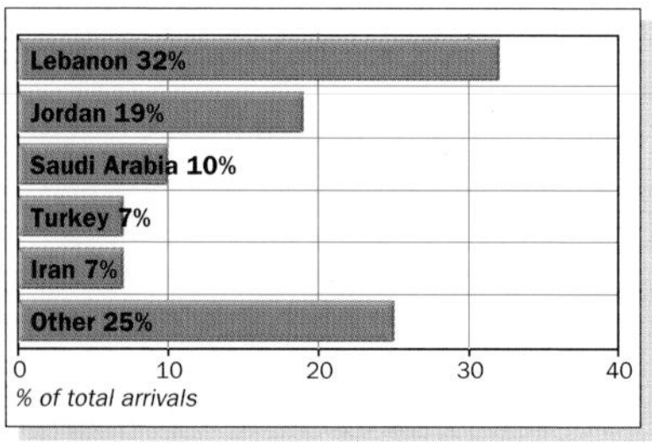
Lebanon 32%
Jordan 19%
Saudi Arabia 10%
Turkey 7%
Iran 7%
Other 25%
0
10
20
30
40
% of total arrivals

Years of political turbulence, allegations of human rights abuses committed under Hafez al-Assad's regime, and strict, complex travel regulations retarded the development of tourism. However, just before the 1990–1991 Gulf War, Syria began to compete with other Middle Eastern states as a tourist destination. Modern hotels were built in most cities and facilities improved to cater for growing numbers of Western visitors. Following the September 11, 2001, attacks on the US and the 2003 invasion of Iraq tourist numbers dropped sharply. Syria's main attractions are its antiquities, such as the ruined desert city of Palmyra; and historic cities, with their souks, baths, and mosques – Damascus, said to be the oldest inhabited city in the world, and Aleppo, with its citadel. Syria has a wealth of castles dating back to the Crusades and sites associated with the advent of Islam. In addition, there are as many as 3500 as yet unexcavated archaeological sites. Syria's coastline on the Mediterranean has fine beaches, and there are mountain resorts in Latakia.

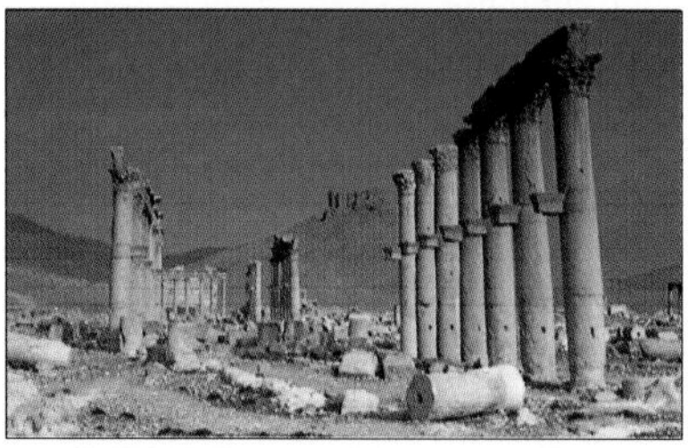

The ancient city of Palmyra, in Syria's central region, was once the capital of the kingdom of Queen Zenobia.

PEOPLE

Pop. density medium

Arabic, French, Kurdish, Armenian, Circassian, Turkic languages, Assyrian, Aramaic

92/km² (239/mi²)

THE URBAN/RURAL POPULATION SPLIT

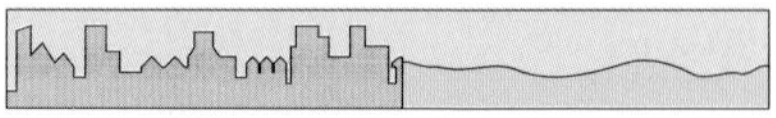
52%
48%

RELIGIOUS PERSUASION

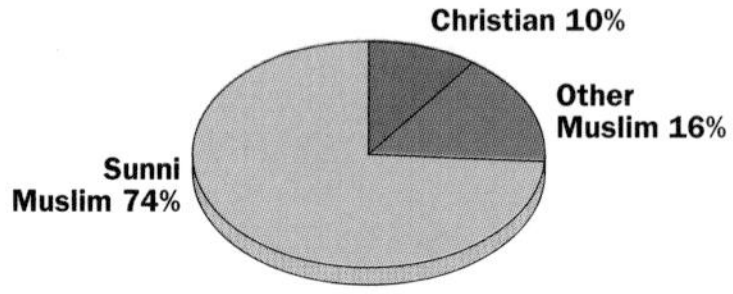
Christian 10%
Other Muslim 16%
Sunni Muslim 74%

ETHNIC MAKEUP

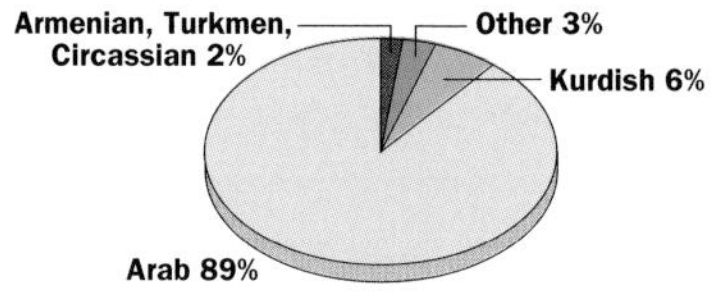
Armenian, Turkmen, Circassian 2%
Other 3%
Kurdish 6%
Arab 89%

Most Syrians live in the west, where the largest cities are sited. About 90% are Muslim. They include the politically dominant Alawis, a heterodox offshoot of Shi'a, comprising 12% of the population, based in Latakia and Tartous provinces. There is also a sizable Christian minority; there are three villages where Aramaic is spoken. In the west and north a mosaic of groups includes Kurds, Turkic-speakers, and Armenians, this last group based in cities. Damascus, Al Qamishli, and Aleppo have small Jewish communities. In addition, some 300,000 Palestinian refugees have settled in Syria. Minorities were initially attracted to the ruling Ba'ath Party because of its emphasis on the state over sectarian interests. However, disputes between factions led to the Alawis taking control, creating resentment among the Sunni Muslim majority.

The emancipation of women, promoted initially in the late 1960s, was carried forward under President Hafez al-Assad, whose first woman cabinet minister was appointed in 1976.

POPULATION AGE BREAKDOWN

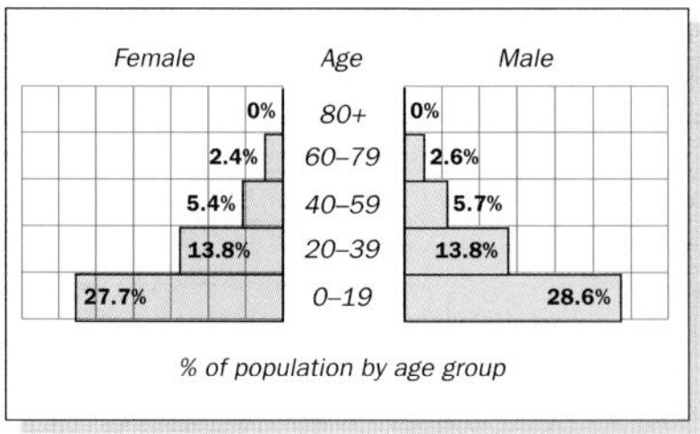
Female
Age
Male
0%
80+
0%
2.4%
60–79
2.6%
5.4%
40–59
5.7%
13.8%
20–39
13.8%
27.7%
0–19
28.6%
% of population by age group

S

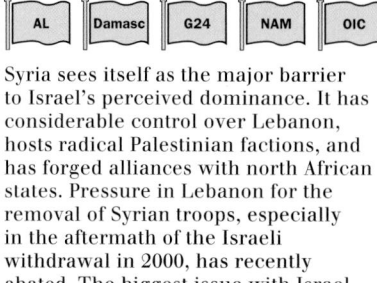

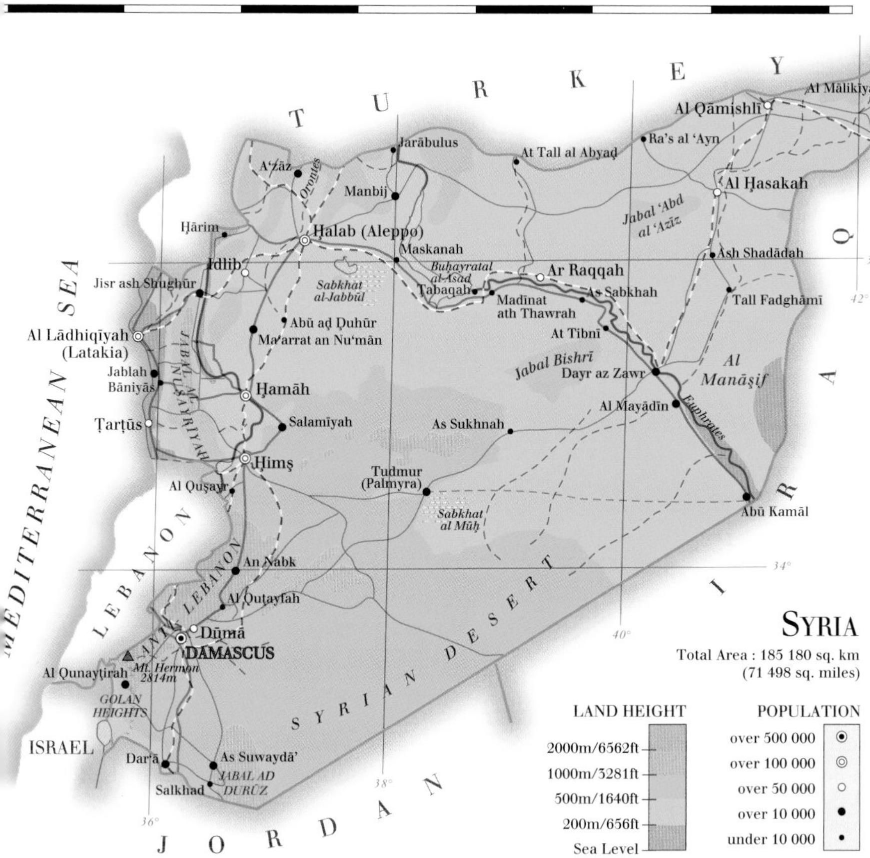
TURKEY
IRAQ
JORDAN
LEBANON
ISRAEL
MEDITERRANEAN SEA
SYRIAN DESERT
Jarābulus
At Tall al Abyaḑ
Ra's al 'Ayn
Al Qāmishlī
Al Mālikīyah
A'zāz
Manbij
Orontes
Ḩārim
Halab (Aleppo)
Maskanah
Idlib
Jisr ash Shughūr
Sabkhat al-Jabbūl
Buhayratal al-Asad
Ţabaqah
Madīnat ath Thawrah
Ar Raqqah
As Sabkhah
Jabal 'Abd al 'Azīz
Al Hasakah
Ash Shadādah
Tall Fadghāmī
Abū aḑ Ḑuhūr
Ma'arrat an Nu'mān
Al Lādhiqīyah (Latakia)
Jablah
Bāniyās
JABAL AN NUŞAYRĪYAH
Ḩamāh
Salamīyah
Ţarţūs
Ḩimş
Al Quşayr
At Tibnī
Jabal Bishrī
Dayr az Zawr
Al Manāşif
Al Mayādīn
Euphrates
As Sukhnah
Tudmur (Palmyra)
Sabkhat al Mūḩ
Abū Kamāl
An Nabk
ANTI-LEBANON
Al Quţayfah
Dūmā
DAMASCUS
Mt. Hermon 2814m
Al Qunayţirah
GOLAN HEIGHTS
Dar'ā
As Suwaydā'
JABAL AD DURŪZ
Salkhad
N
0 100 km
0 100 miles
36°
34°
38°
40°
42°
SYRIA
Total Area : 185 180 sq. km (71 498 sq. miles)
LAND HEIGHT
2000m/6562ft
1000m/3281ft
500m/1640ft
200m/656ft
Sea Level
POPULATION
over 500 000
over 100 000
over 50 000
over 10 000
under 10 000

WORLD AFFAIRS

Joined UN in 1945

AL | Damasc | G24 | NAM | OIC

Syria sees itself as the major barrier to Israel's perceived dominance. It has considerable control over Lebanon, hosts radical Palestinian factions, and has forged alliances with north African states. Pressure in Lebanon for the removal of Syrian troops, especially in the aftermath of the Israeli withdrawal in 2000, has recently abated. The biggest issue with Israel remains the strategically vital Golan Heights, seized by Israel during the Six-Day War in 1967. Peace negotiations foundered when Ariel Sharon came to power in Israel in 2001.

Tensions persist with Turkey over attitudes to Israel and to Turkish Kurdish guerrillas, access to water, and Syria's desire for the return of its former coastal Alexandretta Province.

Syria, alone among Arab states, backed Iran in the 1980s Iran–Iraq War. Hafez al-Assad joined the US-led allies in the 1991 Gulf War, legitimizing the action in Arab eyes. In 2000, however, Syria sent humanitarian aid to Iraq, in defiance of the UN blockade. The US has since accused it of supporting international terrorists and of aiding the ousted regime of Saddam Hussein during the 2003 invasion of Iraq. Traditionally, Syria enjoys better ties with Europe than with the US.

AID

Recipient

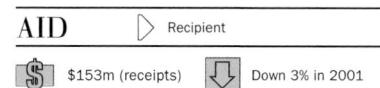

$153m (receipts) | Down 3% in 2001

Syria has historically received little aid owing to its human rights record and self-sufficiency in oil. In 1997, the Syrian government settled its debt of $526 million to the World Bank. Japan and Germany are the main bilateral aid donors; assistance also comes from the UN, France, Italy, and the EU.

Hafez al-Assad *ruled for three decades until his death in 2000.*

Bashar al-Assad *succeeded his father as president.*

POLITICS

No multiparty elections

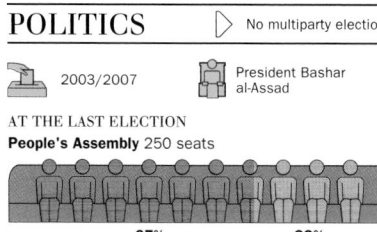

2003/2007 | President Bashar al-Assad

AT THE LAST ELECTION

People's Assembly 250 seats

67% **Ba'ath Party** | **33%** **Other Ba'ath**

Ba'ath Party = Members of the National Progressive Front (allies of the Ba'ath Party) **Other Ba'ath** = Parties allied to the Ba'ath Party

Syria is in effect a single-party state. Its leader from 1970 to 2000 was Hafez al-Assad, a lifelong Ba'ath Party militant. His personal dominance ensured the succession of his son Bashar after his death in June 2000.

Profile

The Ba'athist military swept to power in 1963 with a vision of uniting all Arab nations under a single Syrian-dominated socialist system. The coup ended the power of city elites and promoted citizens from rural areas.

Assad consolidated the Ba'ath Party as the major political force. Unrest among Islamist militants was crushed, notably in the army-led massacre at Hamah in 1982. Assad focused on foreign affairs, bidding to make Syria a major power, but plans to unite with fellow Ba'athist Iraq ended in 1981 amid mutual recriminations.

Main Political Issues

Human rights

Martial law has not been rescinded since 1963, but the regime has improved its human rights record in recent years. Political prisoners are released under frequent amnesties, and in 1994 all Jews were granted visas to travel abroad.

Political pluralism

Assad dominated politics for 30 years. His military-backed regime, drawn mainly from his own Alawi minority grouping, kept a tight hold on power, though in his last decade Sunnis gained high political posts. Despite international pressure Assad never permitted genuine multipartyism. Shortly before Assad's death, the modernizing Mohammed Miro replaced long-serving prime minister Mahmoud az-Zoubi, who was forced from office. Assad's death was followed immediately by his son's appointment to the party leadership, which was approved overwhelmingly by referendum. Initial tentative reforms – such as the spread of "discussion clubs" and the release of some jailed dissidents – were later curtailed and crackdowns occurred once again.

S

CHRONOLOGY

Under French mandate from 1920, Syria declared independence in 1941, and achieved full autonomy in 1946. From 1958 to 1961 Syria merged with Egypt to form the United Arab Republic.

- ❏ **1963** Ba'athist military junta seizes power. Maj. Gen. Amin al-Hafez president.
- ❏ **1966** Hafez ousted by military coup supported by radical Ba'ath Party members.
- ❏ **1967** Israel overruns Syrian positions above Lake Tiberias, seizes Golan Heights, and occupies Quneitra. Syria boycotts Arab summit and rejects compromise with Israel.
- ❏ **1970** Hafez al-Assad seizes power in "corrective coup."
- ❏ **1971–1999** Assad elected president; reelected four times.
- ❏ **1973** New constitution confirms dominance of Ba'ath Party. War launched with Egypt against Israel to regain territory lost in 1967. More territory temporarily lost to Israel.
- ❏ **1976** With peacekeeping mandate from Arab League, Syria intervenes to quell fighting in Lebanon.
- ❏ **1977** Relations broken off with Egypt after Egyptian president Sadat's visit to Jerusalem.
- ❏ **1978** National charter signed with Iraq for union.
- ❏ **1980** Membership of Muslim Brotherhood made capital offense. Treaty of Friendship with USSR.
- ❏ **1981** Israel formally annexes Golan Heights. Charter with Iraq collapses.
- ❏ **1982** Islamic extremist uprising in Hamah crushed. Israel invades Lebanon; Syrian missiles in Bekaa Valley destroyed.
- ❏ **1985** US claims Syrian links to Rome and Vienna airport bombings.
- ❏ **1986** Alleged Syrian complicity in planting of bomb on Israeli airliner in London. EU states, except Greece, impose sanctions and arms embargo.
- ❏ **1989** Diplomatic relations reestablished with Egypt.
- ❏ **1990–1991** Syrian forces crush renegade Gen. Aoun in Beirut. Steers Taif Accords over Lebanon.
- ❏ **1991** Troops take part in Operation Desert Storm. Damascus Declaration aid and defense pact signed with Egypt, Saudi Arabia, Kuwait, UAE, Qatar, Bahrain, and Oman.
- ❏ **1995** Inconclusive talks with Israel.
- ❏ **2000** Forced resignation after 13 years and subsequent suicide of prime minister, Mahmoud az-Zoubi. Death of Hafez al-Assad; succession of son Bashar.
- ❏ **2001** Israel bombs Syrian radar base in Lebanon.

DEFENSE

Compulsory military service

$1.88bn

Up 27% in 2001

Syria sees its extensive military capability as a significant deterrent to Israel's territorial expansion. It has fought four wars against Israel since 1948, and is the Arab world's strongest military power after Egypt. Most of its military equipment was obtained from the former Soviet Union. Defence spending as a percentage of DGP is among the highest in the world.

Throughout 2000, increasing numbers of Lebanese protested against the continuing presence of Syrian troops on their soil – in apparent contravention of the 1989 Taif Accords – and in 2001, Syrian troops were withdrawn from Beirut. In May 2002 a US State Department official accused Syria of harboring weapons of mass destruction.

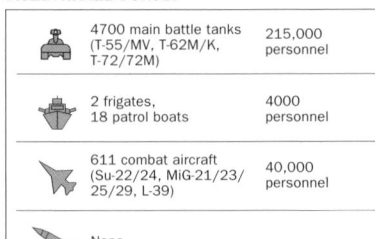

SYRIAN ARMED FORCES

4700 main battle tanks (T-55/MV, T-62M/K, T-72/72M)	215,000 personnel
2 frigates, 18 patrol boats	4000 personnel
611 combat aircraft (Su-22/24, MiG-21/23/25/29, L-39)	40,000 personnel
None	

ECONOMICS

Inflation 7.4% p.a. (1990–2001)

$17.3bn

46 Syrian pounds (51.4)

SCORE CARD

❏ World GNP Ranking	72nd
❏ GNP per Capita	$1040
❏ Balance of Payments	$1.06bn
❏ Inflation	0.3%
❏ Unemployment	20%

EXPORTS

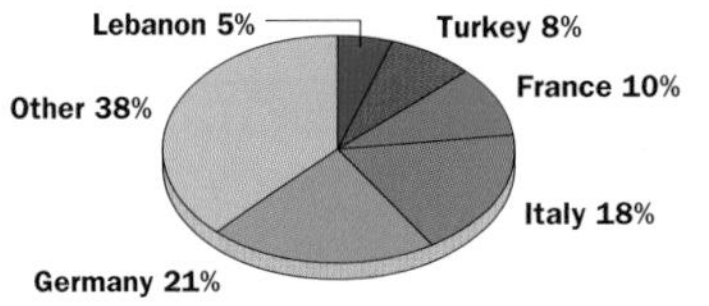
Lebanon 5%
Turkey 8%
France 10%
Italy 18%
Germany 21%
Other 38%

IMPORTS

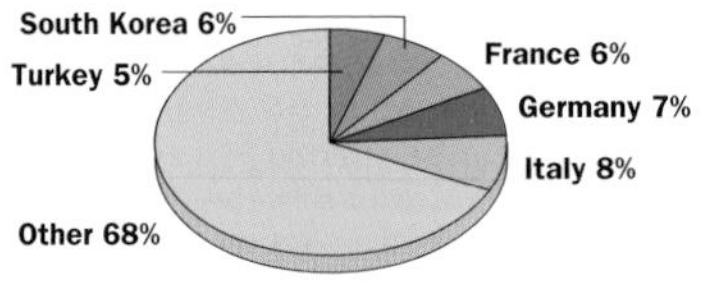
South Korea 6%
Turkey 5%
France 6%
Germany 7%
Italy 8%
Other 68%

ECONOMIC PERFORMANCE INDICATOR

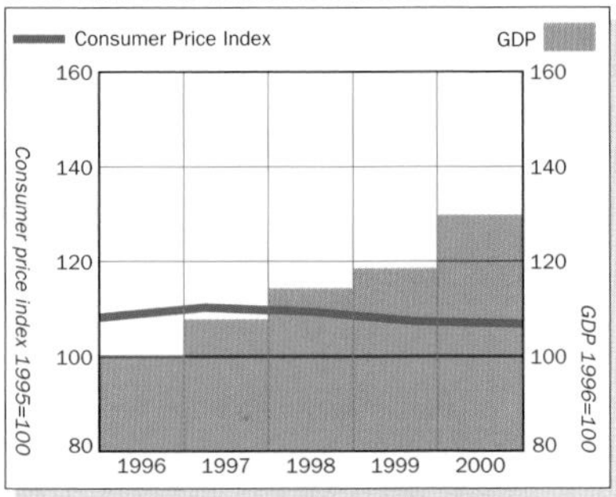
Consumer Price Index
GDP
160
140
120
100
80
Consumer price index 1995=100
GDP 1996=100
1996
1997
1998
1999
2000

Strengths

Exporter of crude oil – production increasing as a result of new oil strikes. Manufacturing base has grown. Thriving agricultural sector. Low inflation.

Weaknesses

High defense spending a major drain. Corruption. Domination of inefficient state-run companies. Lack of foreign investment. High population growth and unemployment. Vulnerable water supply. Slow implementation of reforms.

Profile

Billions of dollars flowed into the economy from the West and the Gulf states after the 1991 Gulf War. This cash injection, along with increased oil revenue, led to rapid growth. Diversion of water from the Euphrates toward fertile plains, rather than poorer land, led to a rise in agricultural output. However, long-term economic prospects remain uncertain. The public sector employs 20% of the workforce, and state controls inhibit private enterprise and investment, and have created a booming black market. Businessmen often channel funds through the freer Lebanese economy. An economic reform package in 2000 created a stock exchange and permitted private banks. Holding foreign currency has been allowed since late 2002.

SYRIA : MAJOR BUSINESSES

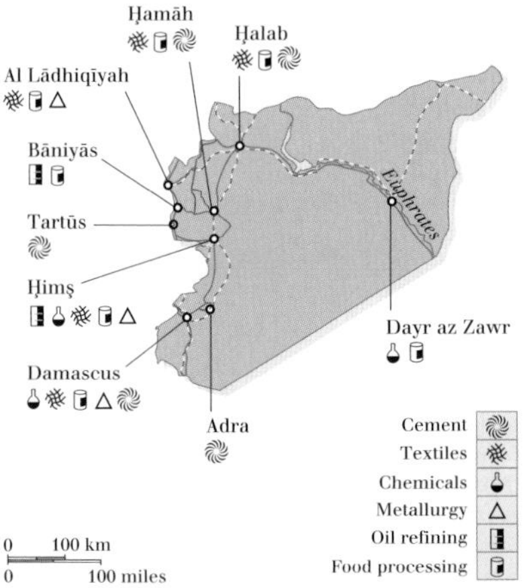
Ḥamāh
Ḥalab
Al Lādhiqīyah
Bāniyās
Tartūs
Ḥimṣ
Damascus
Adra
Dayr az Zawr
Euphrates
Cement
Textiles
Chemicals
Metallurgy
Oil refining
Food processing
0 100 km
0 100 miles

RESOURCES

Electric power 4.9m kW

13,369 tonnes

576,000 b/d (reserves 2.5bn barrels)

13.5m sheep, 931,886 goats, 28.6m chickens

Phosphates, oil, natural gas, iron

ELECTRICITY GENERATION

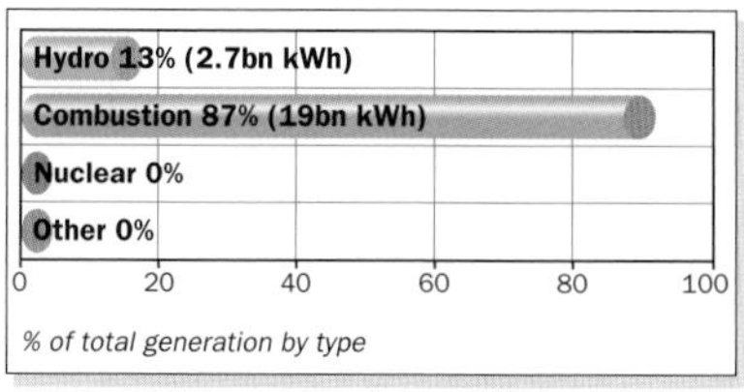
Hydro 13% (2.7bn kWh)
Combustion 87% (19bn kWh)
Nuclear 0%
Other 0%
0 20 40 60 80 100
% of total generation by type

Syria has reversed a trend of declining oil production in the late 1990s through intensifying oil and natural gas exploration efforts, and effecting a switch from oil- to natural-gas-fired electric power plants. Hydroelectric power is providing a growing share of electricity-generating capacity; known exploitable potential hydroelectric energy is 4500 MW. Manufacturing is largely limited to oil-derived industries, textiles, and food products. Cotton is the main cash crop; fruit and vegetables are also grown. Livestock, especially sheep and goats, support the rural economy.

SYRIA : LAND USE

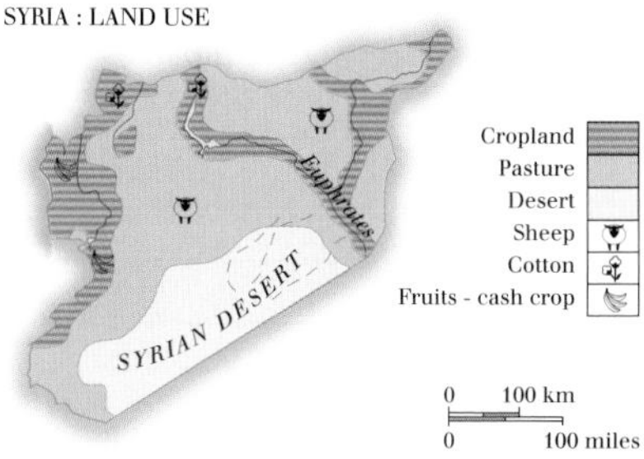
Euphrates
SYRIAN DESERT
Cropland
Pasture
Desert
Sheep
Cotton
Fruits - cash crop
0 100 km
0 100 miles

ENVIRONMENT

Sustainability rank: 107th

None

3.3 tonnes per capita

ENVIRONMENTAL TREATIES

Yes · Yes · Yes

Yes · Yes · No

The Assad regime's most expensive and controversial environmental project has been the Euphrates Dam, power plant, and irrigation network at Tabaqah. The dam's vast man-made reservoir, Buhayratal al-Assad, engulfed some 300 villages and destroyed 25,000 hectares (62,000 acres) of fertile farmland. A giant cement factory at Tartus, built by former East Germany in the mid-1970s, has increased pollution along a stretch of Syria's Mediterranean coastline. However, the interior of the country remains relatively unspoilt.

MEDIA

TV ownership medium

Daily newspaper circulation 20 per 1000 people

Information became freer after Jordanian papers were again allowed into Syria in 1999, and with the advent of satellite TV. Bashar al-Assad encourages Internet use, albeit highly regulated, and in 2001 he allowed independent publications, including *Ad-domari*, the first satirical journal in 38 years.

PUBLISHING AND BROADCAST MEDIA

There are 10 daily newspapers, including *Al-Ba'ath*, *Ath-Thawra*, and *Tishrin*

1 state-controlled service

1 state-controlled service; independent music stations were permitted from 2002

CRIME

Death penalty in use

14,000 prisoners

Up sharply in 1995–1999

CRIME RATES

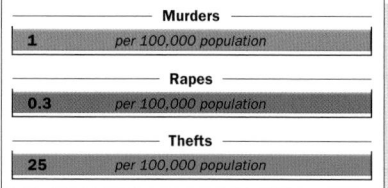

Crime	Rate
Murders	1 per 100,000 population
Rapes	0.3 per 100,000 population
Thefts	25 per 100,000 population

Most politicians imprisoned by President Hafez al-Assad in the 1970s have been released. In 1997 Syria was removed from the US government's list of major narcotics-distributing countries, following a joint eradication program with Lebanon. There are continued reports of torture in custody.

EDUCATION

School leaving age: 11

75%

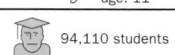

94,110 students

THE EDUCATION SYSTEM

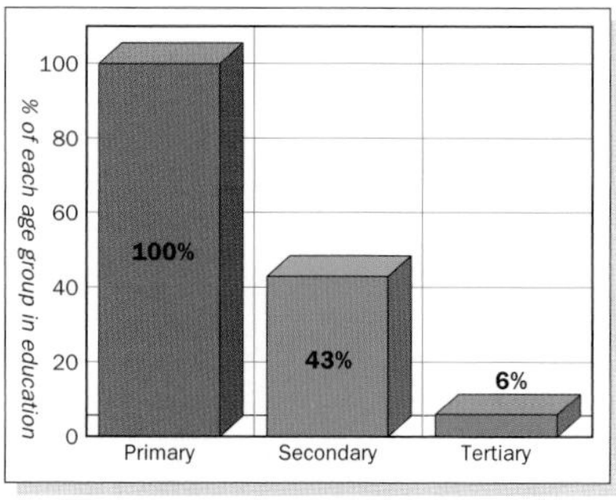
100 80 60 40 20 0
% of each age group in education
100%
43%
6%
Primary
Secondary
Tertiary

A modern and universally accessible system of education remains an important objective. Free and compulsory primary education for all was a priority of the Ba'ath Party when it came to power. Coeducation began in the cities and spread to rural areas under the Assad regime.There are seven state universities, notably at Damascus, Aleppo, Tishrin, and Homs. Private universities were allowed from 2001. Education ranks second, though is far behind defense, in government expenditure. UK and US politicians protest at incitement to racism in Syrian school textbooks.

HEALTH

Welfare state health benefits

1 per 704 people

Heart, respiratory, digestive, infectious, and parasitic diseases

An adequate system of primary health care has been set up since the Ba'ath Party came to power. Treatment is free for those unable to pay. However, hospitals often lack modern equipment and medical services are in need of further investment. Rural areas in particular need assistance to combat the spread of heart, respiratory, and infectious diseases.

SPENDING

GDP/cap. increase

CONSUMPTION AND SPENDING

9 per 1000 population

103 per 1000 population

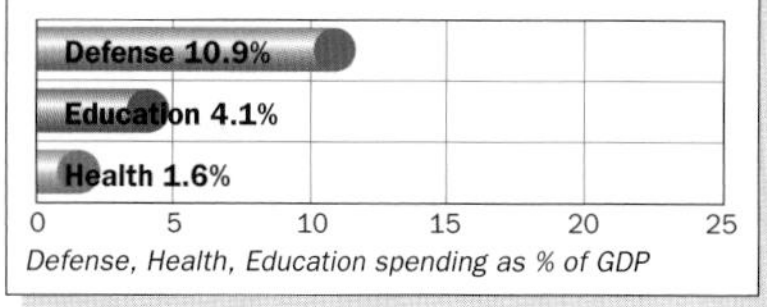
Defense 10.9%
Education 4.1%
Health 1.6%
0 5 10 15 20 25
Defense, Health, Education spending as % of GDP

Syria is far from the equitable society that early Ba'ath Party thinkers envisioned. The gulf between Syria's rich and poor is widening. The political elite, many of whom live in the West Malki suburb of Damascus, is more numerous and richer than ever before. Palestinian refugees and the urban unemployed make up the poorest groups.

WORLD RANKING

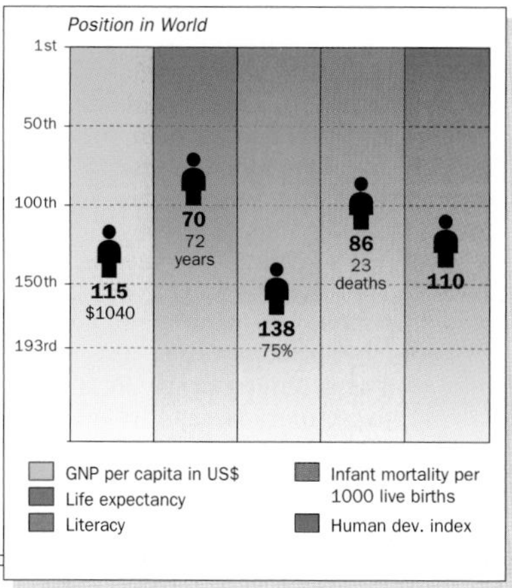
Position in World
1st
50th
100th
150th
193rd
115
$1040
70
72
years
138
75%
86
23
deaths
110
GNP per capita in US$
Life expectancy
Literacy
Infant mortality per 1000 live births
Human dev. index

S

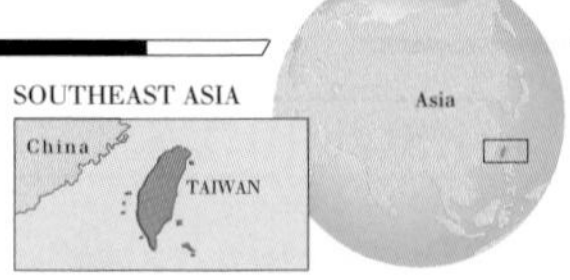
SOUTHEAST ASIA
China
TAIWAN
Asia

TAIWAN

OFFICIAL NAME: Republic of China (ROC) **CAPITAL:** Taipei
POPULATION: 22.5 million **CURRENCY:** Taiwan dollar **OFFICIAL LANGUAGE:** Mandarin Chinese

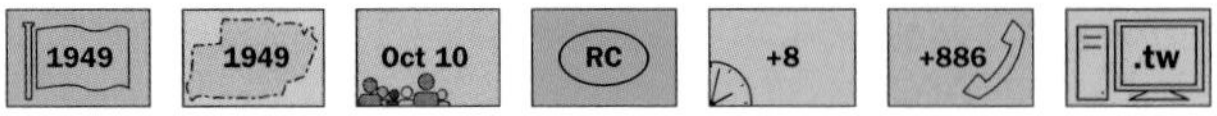
1949
1949
Oct 10
RC
+8
+886
.tw

THE ISLAND OF TAIWAN, formerly known as Formosa, lies off the southeast coast of mainland China. Mountains running north to south cover two-thirds of the island. The lowlands are highly fertile, planted mostly with rice, and densely populated. In 1949, when the Chinese Communists ousted Chiang Kai-shek's nationalist Kuomintang (KMT) from power on the mainland, he established the Republic of China government on the island. De facto military rule has been democratized progressively since 1986. Mainland China still considers Taiwan to be a renegade province, and only a few countries now give official recognition to the regime on the island.

Wen Wu Temple, *on the shores of Sun Moon Lake in the mountains of central Taiwan – a region famous for its many temples. Nearly the whole population is Buddhist.*

CLIMATE

Tropical monsoon

WEATHER CHART FOR TAIPEI

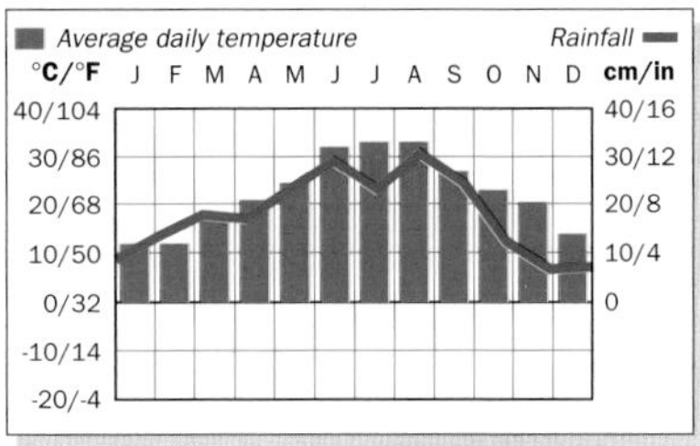
Average daily temperature
Rainfall
°C/°F
J F M A M J J A S O N D
cm/in
40/104
30/86
20/68
10/50
0/32
-10/14
-20/-4
40/16
30/12
20/8
10/4
0

Taiwan has a tropical monsoon climate similar to that of the southern Chinese mainland. Typhoons from the South China Sea between June and September bring the heaviest rains.

TRANSPORTATION

Drive on right

Chiang Kai-shek International, Taoyuan 19.2m passengers

656 ships 4.62m grt

THE TRANSPORTATION NETWORK

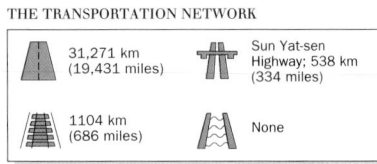

31,271 km (19,431 miles)

Sun Yat-sen Highway; 538 km (334 miles)

1104 km (686 miles)

None

A railroad encircles the island, and a US$16 billion high-speed rail link along the west coast, linking Taipei to Kaohsiung, is under construction with the help of the Japanese Shinkansen Corporation; it is due for completion in 2005. Car ownership has risen dramatically in the last 30 years. The bicycle is not as popular as in mainland China, but Taiwan is the world's biggest bicycle producer, exporting mostly to Europe and the US.

Access to mainland China has increased as relations slowly improve. By boat, passengers have to travel from the tiny offshore islands of Matsu and Quemoy. The number of visitors is limited both ways by yearly quotas.

TOURISM

Visitors : Population 1:8.3

2.73m visitors

Up 4% in 2002

MAIN TOURIST ARRIVALS

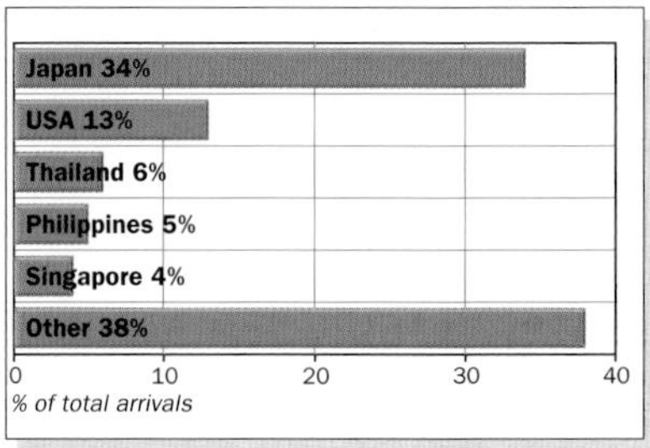
Japan 34%
USA 13%
Thailand 6%
Philippines 5%
Singapore 4%
Other 38%
0
10
20
30
40
% of total arrivals

Taiwan is not a major tourist destination, and it has only recently begun promoting itself in the US and Japan. Restrictions on Chinese tourists are being eased. Successive Six-Year Plans focus on upgrading hotels and improving tourist facilities at international airports. The major attraction is the Palace Museum in Taipei, which includes the massive treasure looted by the nationalists from Beijing. Only 5% can be shown at any one time. Sex tourism is an important business in Taipei. Sex establishments often masquerade as barbershops.

PEOPLE

Pop. density high

Amoy Chinese, Mandarin Chinese, Hakka Chinese

699/km² (1810/mi²)

THE URBAN/RURAL POPULATION SPLIT

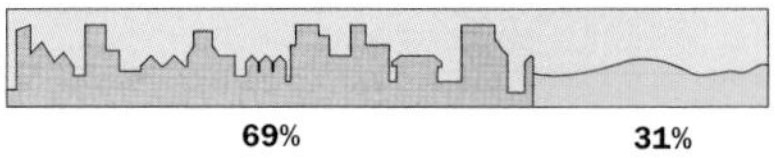
69%
31%

RELIGIOUS PERSUASION

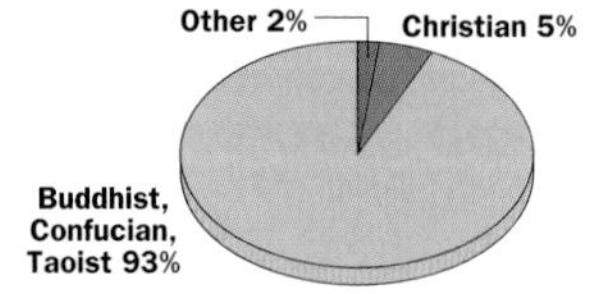
Other 2%
Christian 5%
Buddhist, Confucian, Taoist 93%

ETHNIC MAKEUP

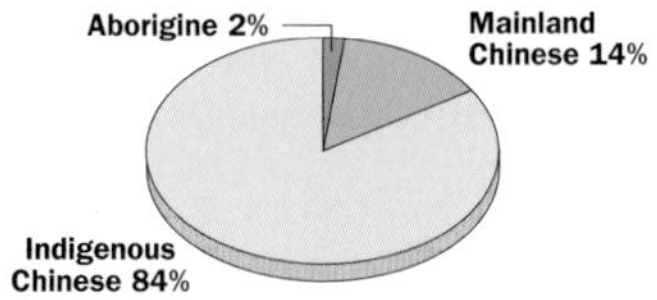
Aborigine 2%
Mainland Chinese 14%
Indigenous Chinese 84%

Most Taiwanese are Han Chinese, descendants of the 1644 migration of the Ming dynasty from mainland China. The 100,000 nationalists who arrived in 1949 established themselves as a ruling class and monopolized the most prestigious jobs in the civil service. This caused resentment among the local inhabitants, but as the generation elected on the mainland in 1947 has passed on, so local Taiwanese have entered the political process.

There is little ethnic tension in Taiwan, though the indigenous minorities who live in the eastern hills suffer considerable discrimination.

As in the rest of southeast Asia, the extended family is still important and provides a social security net for the elderly. However, the trend is toward European-style nuclear families. Housing shortages are a major issue.

Women are not well represented in the political process, but are prominent in business and the civil service.

POPULATION AGE BREAKDOWN

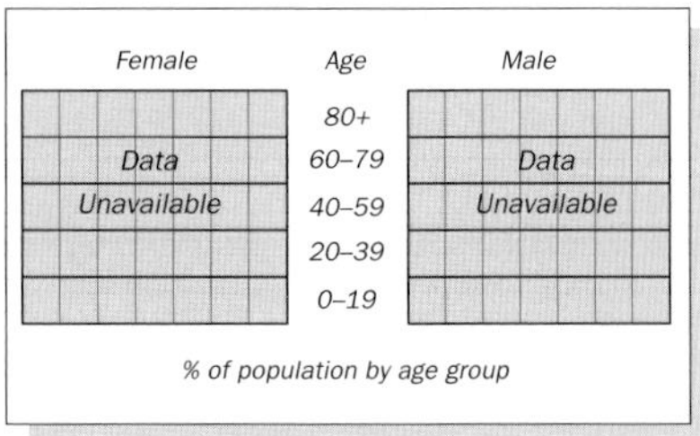
Female
Age
Male
80+
60-79
40-59
20-39
0-19
Data Unavailable
Data Unavailable
% of population by age group

POLITICS

Multiparty elections

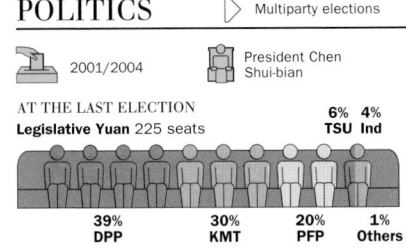

2001/2004 — President Chen Shui-bian

AT THE LAST ELECTION
Legislative Yuan 225 seats

39% DPP
30% KMT
20% PFP
1% Others
6% TSU
4% Ind

DPP = Democratic Progressive Party **KMT** = National Party of China (Kuomintang) **PFP** = People First Party **TSU** = Taiwan Solidarity Union **Ind** = Independents

Taiwan has been a multiparty democracy since 1986, though electoral domination by the KMT only ended in 2000. The government is headed by the president, who is answerable to the National Assembly, a body which is convened only when matters of constitutional significance arise.

PROFILE

For nearly four decades from the establishment of the Republic of China government on Taiwan in 1949, Chiang Kai-shek's KMT monopolized political power and ruled by strict martial law. In 1986, Gen. Chiang Ching-kuo, Chiang Kai-shek's son and successor, decided to open the way for more democracy. Later that year the first free multiparty elections were held. In March 1996 Lee Teng-hui became the country's first directly elected president.

Though the KMT retained power in the 1998 legislative elections, winning an absolute majority of seats, its 50-year political monopoly came to an end with the 2000 presidential elections. The KMT candidate came a poor third, and Chen Shui-bian of the proindependence DPP took office. The KMT went on to lose support in the 2001 legislative elections, when the DPP became the largest party in the Yuan, though it did not achieve a majority.

Chiang Kai-shek, who established the ROC in Taiwan in 1949.

Chen Shui-bian, the first non-KMT president since 1949.

MAIN POLITICAL ISSUES

Relations with China

The DPP has advocated independence from China, despite Chinese threats of military action. Adopting a more prudent stance after his election victory, President Chen promised to make no independence declaration during his term of office. The KMT, officially committed to eventual reunification with China, now favors a more flexible arrangement that presupposes the recognition of a separate Taiwanese national identity.

Political stability

The eclipse of the KMT in elections in 2000 ended over 50 years of enforced stability. Taiwanese politics has had to come to terms with the idea of consensus politics, since the victory of Chen and the DPP was based as much on the divisions of the right as on the strength of their own popularity. Opponents warned of a return to autocracy when he took over as chairman of the DPP in 2002.

TAIWAN

Total Area : 35 980 sq. km (13 892 sq. miles)

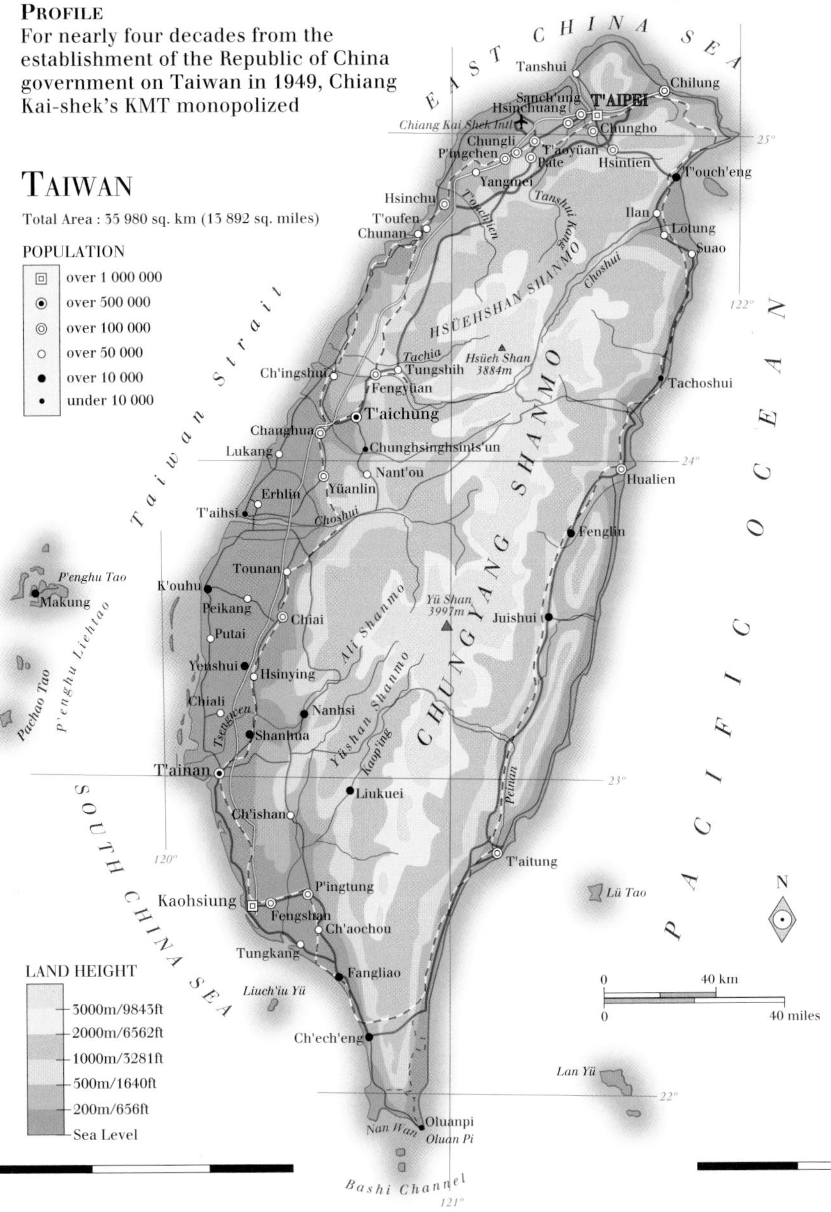
POPULATION
over 1 000 000
over 500 000
over 100 000
over 50 000
over 10 000
under 10 000
LAND HEIGHT
3000m/9843ft
2000m/6562ft
1000m/3281ft
500m/1640ft
200m/656ft
Sea Level
EAST CHINA SEA
PACIFIC OCEAN
SOUTH CHINA SEA
Taiwan Strait
Bashi Channel
T'AIPEI
Tanshui
Chilung
T'aichung
Kaohsiung
T'ainan
Hsinchu
Chunan
Changhua
Lukang
Chiai
Hualien
Fenglin
Juishui
T'aitung
Tachoshui
Suao
Ilan
Lotung
P'ingtung
Fengshan
Ch'aochou
Tungkang
Fangliao
Ch'ech'eng
Oluanpi
Nan Wan
Oluan Pi
Liuch'iu Yü
Lan Yü
Lü Tao
P'enghu Tao
Makung
Pachao Tao
Yü Shan 3997m
Hsüeh Shan 3884m
HSÜEHSHAN SHANMO
CHUNGYANG SHANMO
Ali Shanmo
Yüshan Shanmo
Chiang Kai Shek Intl
Ch'ingshui
Fengyüan
Tungshih
Chunghsinghsints'un
Nant'ou
Yüanlin
Erhlin
T'aihsi
Tounan
K'ouhu
Peikang
Putai
Yenshui
Hsinying
Chiali
Nanhsi
Shanhua
Ch'ishan
Liukuei
T'ouch'eng
Hsintien
Chungho
Yangmei
T'aoyüan
Chungli
0 40 km
0 40 miles
N

WORLD AFFAIRS

Not a UN member

APEC | ADB | WTO

Relations with China dominate. Reunification has long been the ultimate goal, though the idea of pursuing de facto independence has gained strength among younger Taiwanese; China insists on the "one country, two systems" approach pioneered in Hong Kong. Mention of Taiwanese statehood provokes a fierce reaction from Beijing, and military posturing on both sides is common. Both countries are acutely aware of their economic interdependence; Taiwan is a major foreign investor in China. Physical and economic links have been developed in recent years amid the rhetoric.

Taiwan lost its place at the UN to China in 1971. It is forced to conduct overseas relations via trade delegations. Aid plays a vital role in securing smaller states' support. There are strong bilateral ties with the US and Japan, and the US unofficially guarantees Taiwan's security.

AID

Donor

US$500m (donations) | Up in 2001

Taiwan has a large aid fund devoted to those states which have granted it diplomatic recognition. These include Pacific islands and countries in Africa, the Caribbean, and Central America. In return, aid recipients promote Taiwan's interests in the UN. In 1998 Taiwan donated more than US$2 million to seven Central American supporters, including Panama, to promote literacy.

CHRONOLOGY

Following the 1949 communist revolution in China, Gen. Chiang Kai-shek's nationalist KMT party sought refuge in the island province of Taiwan. The KMT saw the revolution as illegal and itself as the sole rightful Chinese government.

- **1971** People's Republic of China replaces Taiwan at UN, including on UN Security Council.
- **1973** Taipei's KMT regime rejects Beijing's offer of secret talks on reunification of China.
- **1975** President Chiang Kai-shek dies. His son Gen. Chiang Ching-kuo becomes KMT leader. Yen Chia-kan succeeds as president.
- **1978** Chiang Ching-kuo elected president.
- **1979** US severs relations with Taiwan and formally recognizes People's Republic of China.
- **1984** President Chiang reelected.
- **1986** Political reforms: KMT allows multiparty democracy, ends martial law, and permits visits to Chinese mainland for "humanitarian" purposes for first time in 38 years. From 1988, mainland Chinese are allowed to visit Taiwan on same basis.
- **1988** Lee Teng-hui president.
- **1990** KMT formally ends state of war with People's Republic of China.
- **1991** DPP draft constitution for an independent Taiwan opposed by ruling KMT and Beijing. KMT reelected with large majority.
- **1995–1996** Legislative elections. KMT majority reduced.
- **1996** Lee Teng-hui wins first direct presidential elections.
- **1998** KMT secures absolute majority in elections to Legislative Yuan.
- **1999** Chinese threats over reference to "separate states" status. Thousands die in earthquake.
- **2000** Chen Shui-bian of DPP wins presidency; ends KMT dominance.
- **2001** Elections: DPP largest single party. Taiwan admitted to WTO.

DEFENSE

Compulsory military service

US$10.4bn | Down 41% in 2001

China remains the main defense threat, given the recurring tensions over the issue of independence or reunification. Taiwan has the sixth-largest navy in the world and a sizable army, in order to face a possible Chinese invasion: there are over 1.5 million reservists, and military service lasts for two years. Worries about US loyalty have resulted in the purchase of French Mirage fighters in addition to US F-16s.

TAIWANESE ARMED FORCES

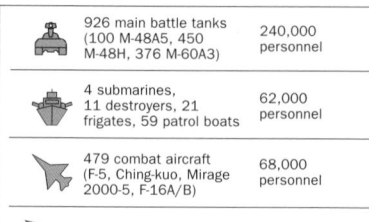

926 main battle tanks (100 M-48A5, 450 M-48H, 376 M-60A3)	240,000 personnel
4 submarines, 11 destroyers, 21 frigates, 59 patrol boats	62,000 personnel
479 combat aircraft (F-5, Ching-kuo, Mirage 2000-5, F-16A/B)	68,000 personnel
None	

ECONOMICS

Inflation 5% p.a. (1985–1996)

US$283bn | 34.61 Taiwan dollars (33.41)

SCORE CARD

❑ World GNP Ranking	16th
❑ GNP per Capita	US$13,450
❑ Balance of Payments	US$18.9bn
❑ Inflation	0.5%
❑ Unemployment	3%

EXPORTS

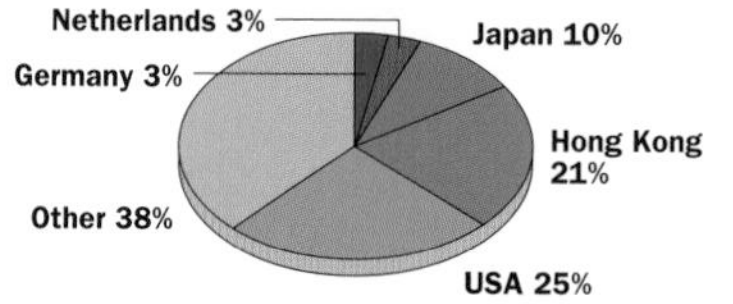

Netherlands 3%
Japan 10%
Germany 3%
Hong Kong 21%
Other 38%
USA 25%

IMPORTS

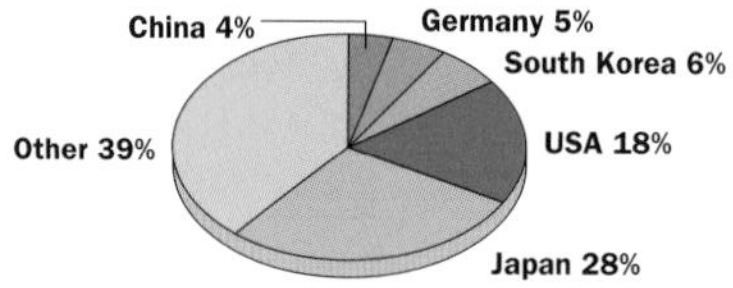

China 4%
Germany 5%
South Korea 6%
Other 39%
USA 18%
Japan 28%

Strengths

Highly educated and ambitious workforce, many US-trained and educated, with an inside knowledge of the US market. Manufacturing economy based on small companies which have proved extremely adaptable to changing market conditions. Track record of capturing major markets. Successively the world's biggest TV, watch, PC, and track shoe manufacturer. Economy in strong surplus, allowing it to invest in other southeast Asian economies.

Weaknesses

Small economic units lack the muscle of Western multinationals, and are unable to follow predatory pricing policies. Weak research and development: economy has no tradition of generating new products or creating new markets. Unresponsive banking system.

Profile

Taiwan's economy has proved resilient. Double-digit growth ended with the Asian financial crisis of 1997–1998, but

ECONOMIC PERFORMANCE INDICATOR

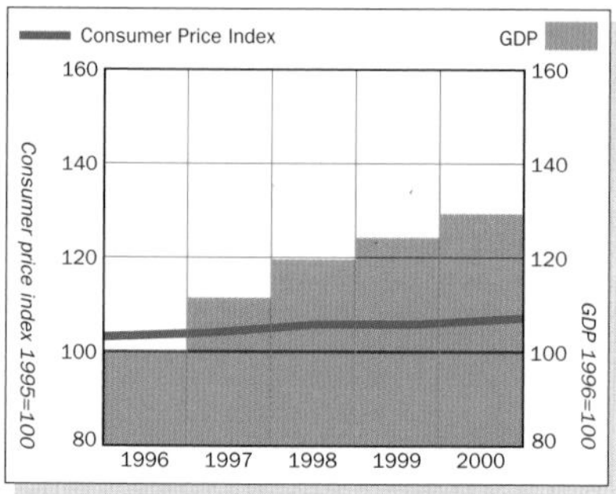

Consumer Price Index
GDP
160
140
120
100
80
Consumer price index 1995=100
GDP 1996=100
1996
1997
1998
1999
2000

Taiwan emerged relatively unscathed, and global downturn caused only a brief recession in 2001. Competition from underdeveloped countries with low production costs is dictating a difficult transition toward service industries. This will entail moving from labor-intensive to capital- and technology-intensive industries. Comprehensive Six-Year Plans reflect a strong element of state direction. Heavy investment abroad includes over 60% of inward investment into China since 1990. Taiwan was admitted to the WTO, along with China, in 2001.

TAIWAN : MAJOR BUSINESSES

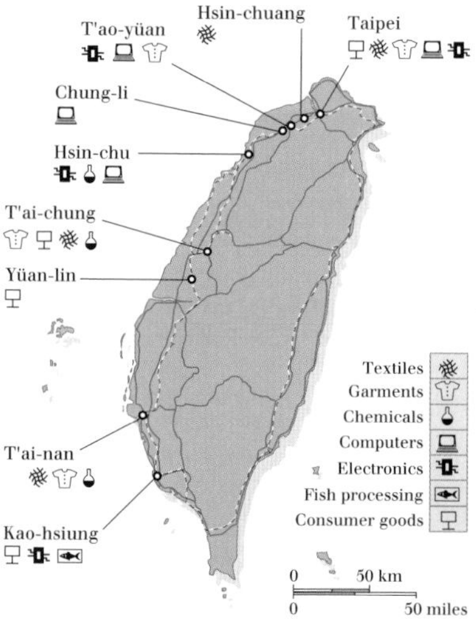

T'ao-yüan
Hsin-chuang
Taipei
Chung-li
Hsin-chu
T'ai-chung
Yüan-lin
T'ai-nan
Kao-hsiung
Textiles
Garments
Chemicals
Computers
Electronics
Fish processing
Consumer goods
0
50 km
0
50 miles

RESOURCES

Not available

1.29m tonnes

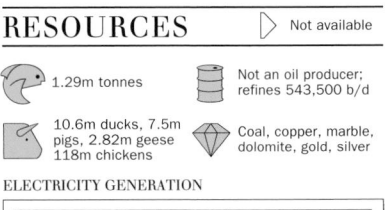

Not an oil producer; refines 543,500 b/d

10.6m ducks, 7.5m pigs, 2.82m geese 118m chickens

Coal, copper, marble, dolomite, gold, silver

ELECTRICITY GENERATION

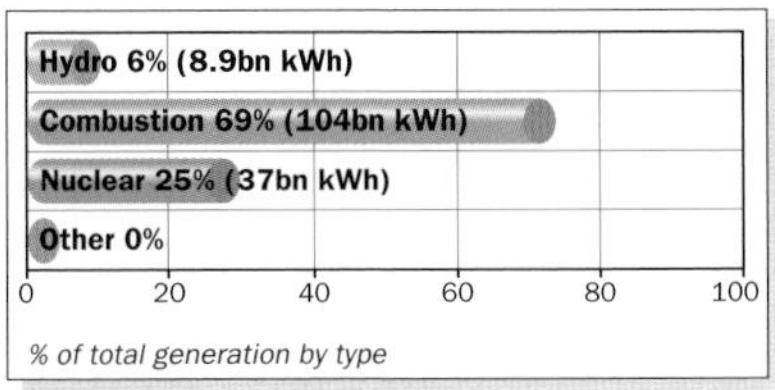
Hydro 6% (8.9bn kWh)
Combustion 69% (104bn kWh)
Nuclear 25% (37bn kWh)
Other 0%
0
20
40
60
80
100
% of total generation by type

Taiwan has few strategic resources and its minerals industry is not a major foreign exchange earner. Oil is imported. Taiwan is a major buyer of South African uranium, but proposals to increase reliance on nuclear power have met strong opposition on safety and waste disposal grounds. However, hydroelectric power has been largely exploited already, and combustion is also a controversial option.

Fishing is highly successful, and Taiwan is a major supplier to the huge Japanese market. The fleet is often accused of plundering Atlantic stocks.

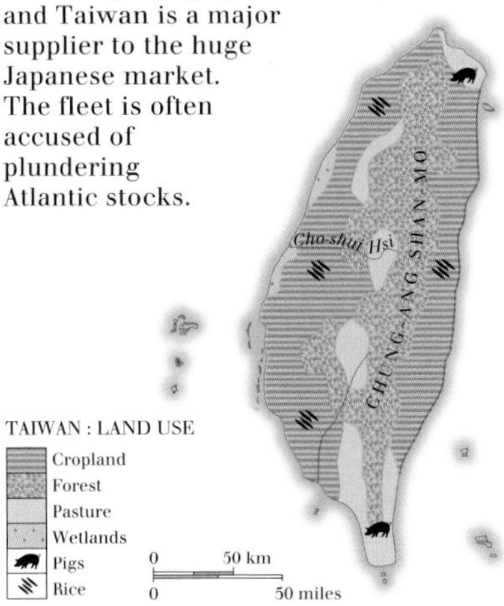
Cho-shui Hsi
CHUNG-YANG SHAN-MO
TAIWAN : LAND USE
Cropland
Forest
Pasture
Wetlands
Pigs
Rice
0
50 km
0
50 miles

ENVIRONMENT

Not available

11%

9.8 tonnes per capita

ENVIRONMENTAL TREATIES

No	No	No
No	No	No

The dash for growth meant the absence of city planning or pollution laws. There is growing opposition to a fourth nuclear power plant, set for completion in 2006, and concern over coal-fired thermal power. Taiwan's fishing industry has been criticized for using longline techniques which trap dolphins, and for plundering other countries' fishing grounds without regard to stock levels.

MEDIA

TV ownership medium

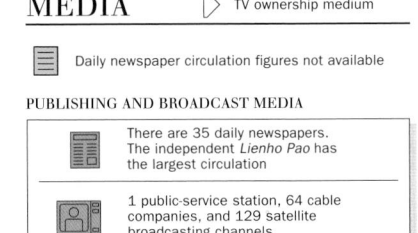

Daily newspaper circulation figures not available

PUBLISHING AND BROADCAST MEDIA

There are 35 daily newspapers. The independent *Lienho Pao* has the largest circulation

1 public-service station, 64 cable companies, and 129 satellite broadcasting channels

110 independent corporations

The rigid state control which used to exist over the media has been relaxed. Opposition parties now have access to the state media. Before the 1990s, print with simplified Chinese characters was banned, thus excluding all publications from the mainland. Taiwan has a large domestic TV and film industry.

CRIME

Death penalty in use

56,225 prisoners

Little change from year to year

CRIME RATES

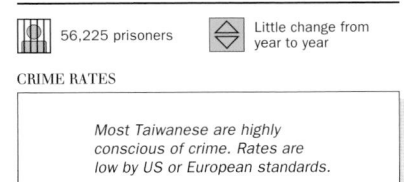

Most Taiwanese are highly conscious of crime. Rates are low by US or European standards.

Since the end of martial law in 1986, most political prisoners have been released. Taiwan does not suffer from organized crime to the extent found in Hong Kong or Japan. Multimedia pirating is a major problem.

EDUCATION

School leaving age: 15

96%

1.09m students

THE EDUCATION SYSTEM

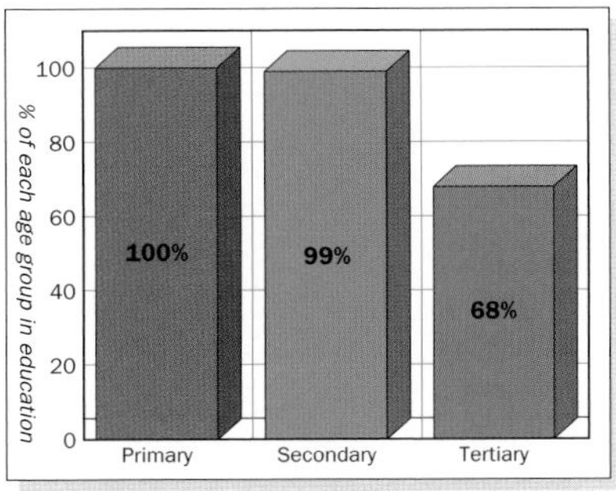
100
80
60
40
20
0
% of each age group in education
100%
99%
68%
Primary
Secondary
Tertiary

Since 2000, government funding has given less priority to higher education and more to reforming and improving the antiquated school system, which is rigid and heavily exam-oriented. Free schooling is available from the age of six to 15 and there are also a number of private schools.

Enrollment levels at tertiary and vocational institutions are among the highest in the world.

HEALTH

No welfare state health benefits

1 per 714 people

Cerebrovascular and heart diseases, hypertension

Most health provision in Taiwan is in the private sector. Taiwanese take out elaborate health insurance schemes and it is essential to prove cover before treatment is provided. Health facilities are on a par with the best in the world, and the Taiwanese enjoy a high life expectancy, similar to that in the US. The incidence of AIDS is low, but the rate of new infections is increasing. The 2003 outbreak of acute pneumonia (SARS) affected over 350 Taiwanese, killing more than 50 people.

SPENDING

GDP/cap. increase

CONSUMPTION AND SPENDING

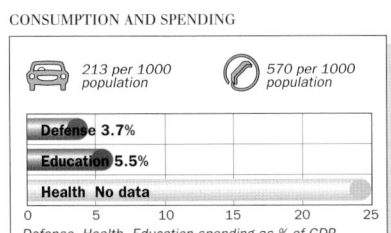

213 per 1000 population

570 per 1000 population

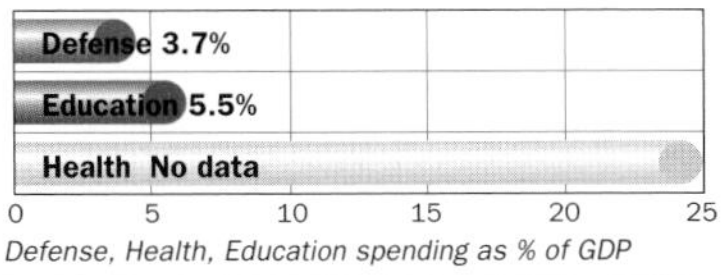
Defense 3.7%
Education 5.5%
Health No data
0
5
10
15
20
25
Defense, Health, Education spending as % of GDP

Export-led growth over a long period enabled Taiwan to build up large cash reserves. The Taiwanese people share much of the benefit of this success, and average living standards are among the highest in Asia. Inequalities of income distribution are comparatively small, and a high degree of social cohesion has been achieved. In part, this is the result of the land reforms of the 1950s, which gave agricultural workers control of the land while compensating landowners and encouraging them to set up in business in the cities. Today, the great majority of Taiwanese would describe themselves as middle class. Consumer goods are widely available, and conspicuous consumption is celebrated.

WORLD RANKING

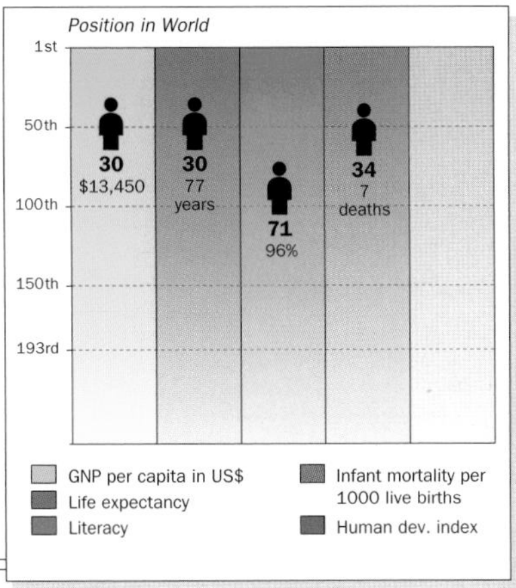
Position in World
1st
50th
100th
150th
193rd
30
$13,450
30
77
years
71
96%
34
7
deaths
GNP per capita in US$
Life expectancy
Literacy
Infant mortality per 1000 live births
Human dev. index

T

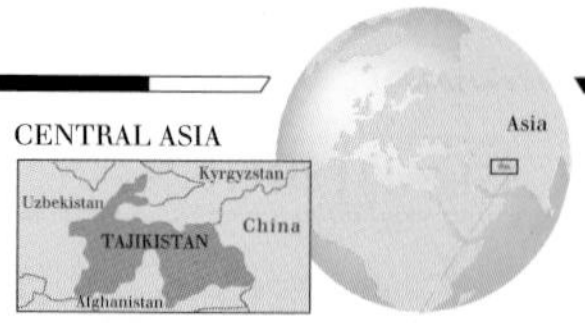
CENTRAL ASIA
Asia
Kyrgyzstan
Uzbekistan
China
TAJIKISTAN
Afghanistan

TAJIKISTAN

OFFICIAL NAME: Republic of Tajikistan **CAPITAL:** Dushanbe
POPULATION: 6.2 million **CURRENCY:** Somoni **OFFICIAL LANGUAGE:** Tajik

1991 | 1991 | Sept 9 | TJ | +5 | +992 | .tj

TAJIKISTAN LIES ON the western slopes of the Pamirs in central Asia. Language and traditions are similar to those of Iran rather than those of its northern Turkic neighbors. Tajikistan decided on independence only when neighboring Soviet republics declared theirs in late 1991. Fighting between communist government forces and Islamist rebels, which erupted shortly afterward, has been contained since 1997 by a fragile peace agreement.

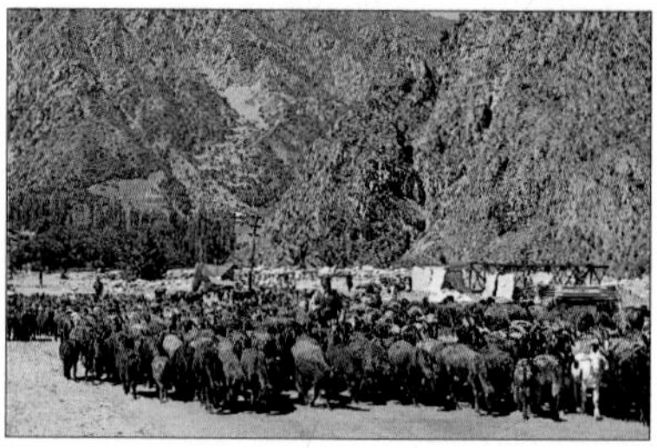

A herd of goats in the Varzob Gorge, north of Dushanbe. Livestock drives the rural economy.

CLIMATE

Mountain

WEATHER CHART FOR DUSHANBE

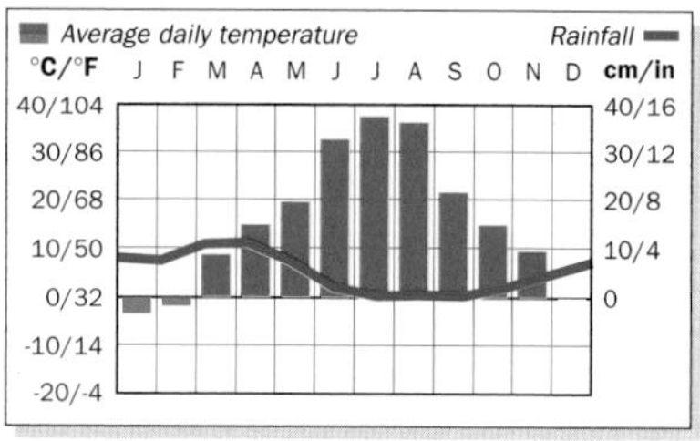
Average daily temperature
Rainfall
°C/°F
J F M A M J J A S O N D
cm/in
40/104
30/86
20/68
10/50
0/32
-10/14
-20/4
40/16
30/12
20/8
10/4
0

Rainfall is low in the valleys. Winter temperatures can fall below –45°C (–49°F) in mountainous areas.

TRANSPORTATION

Drive on right

Dushanbe International

Has no fleet

THE TRANSPORTATION NETWORK

11,330 km (7040 miles)	None
547 km (340 miles)	200 km (124 miles)

Tajikistan has good cross-border roads and well-maintained airfields, the result of its use by Soviet and US forces during conflicts in neighboring Afghanistan. The best way to reach the mountainous interior is by air.

TOURISM

Visitors : Population 1:1550

4000 visitors

Down 99% in 1999–2001

MAIN TOURIST ARRIVALS

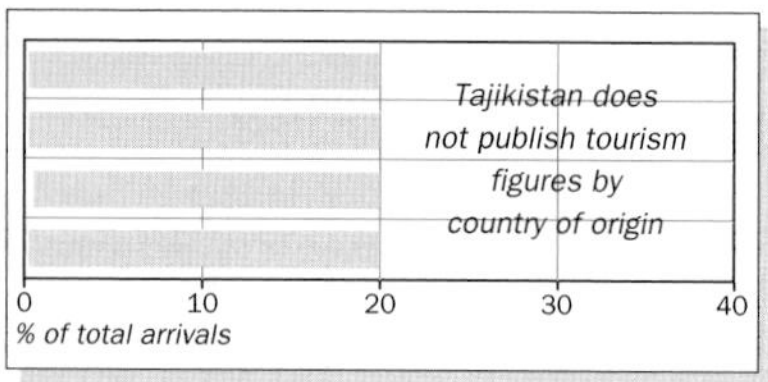
Tajikistan does not publish tourism figures by country of origin
0
10
20
30
40
% of total arrivals

Tourism is virtually nonexistent, and poverty and lack of security make it unlikely that it will be developed soon.

PEOPLE

Pop. density low

Tajik, Russian

43/km² (112/mi²)

THE URBAN/RURAL POPULATION SPLIT

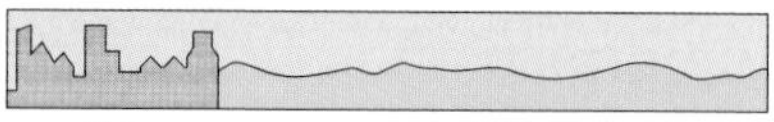
28%
72%

RELIGIOUS PERSUASION

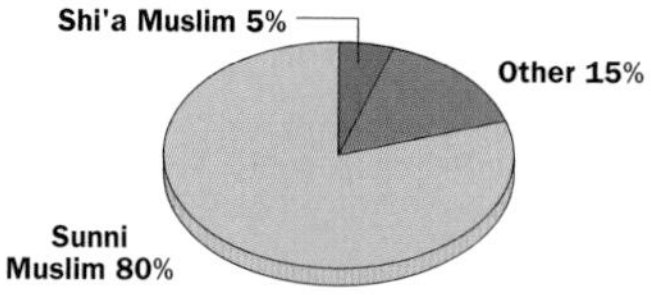
Shi'a Muslim 5%
Other 15%
Sunni Muslim 80%

Unlike the other former Soviet -stans, Tajikistan is dominated by a people of Persian (Iranian), rather than Turkic, origin; ethnic Tajiks make up around 65% of the population. The main ethnic conflict is with the Turkic Uzbeks. As in neighboring Uzbekistan, Russians are discriminated against, and their population has thinned from 400,000 in 1989 to under 200,000. By 1990, the 35,000-strong German minority had left. The struggle between Dushanbe-based communists and the Islamist militants in the central and eastern regions sent more than 50,000 refugees into Afghanistan.

POLITICS

Multiparty elections

L. House 2000/2005
U. House 2000/2005

President Imomali Rakhmanov

AT THE LAST ELECTION

Assembly of Representatives 63 seats

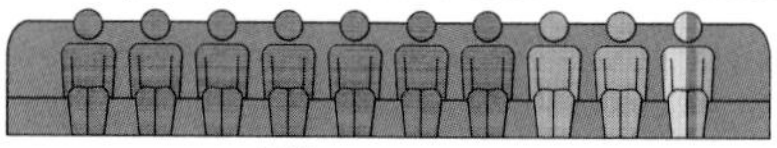
3% IRP
3% Others
71% PDPT
21% CPT
2% Vacant

PDPT = People's Democratic Party of Tajikistan and allies
CPT = Communist Party of Tajikistan
IRP = Islamic Revival Party

National Assembly 33 seats

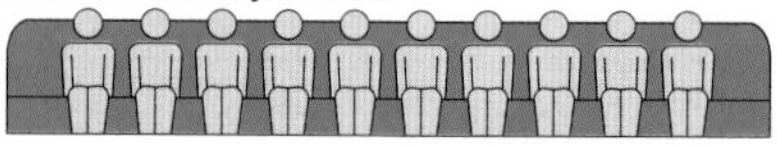

Five deputies are elected by each regional assembly, and a further eight deputies are appointed by the president

Peace has consolidated the regime of former communists led by President Rakhmanov. Under a 1997 peace accord the Islamist United Tajik Opposition (UTO) joined the government in 1998. The pro-Rakhmanov PDPT headed polls in 2000, claiming some support from former UTO members. Rakhmanov has been accused by human rights groups of using the international "war on terrorism" to crack down on political opponents. In 2003 a referendum endorsed two possible further terms for Rakhmanov.

TAJIKISTAN

Total Area : 143 100 sq. km (55 251 sq. miles)

POPULATION

- over 500 000
- over 100 000
- over 50 000
- over 10 000
- under 10 000

LAND HEIGHT

- 4000m/13 124ft
- 3000m/9843ft
- 2000m/6562ft
- 1000m/3281ft
- 500m/1640ft
- 200m/656ft

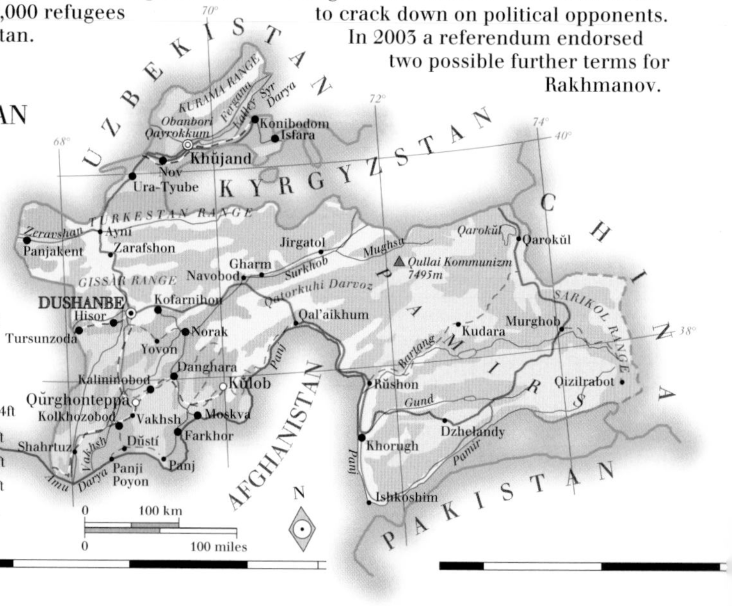
UZBEKISTAN
KYRGYZSTAN
CHINA
AFGHANISTAN
PAKISTAN
KURAMA RANGE
Fergana Valley
Syr Darya
Obanbori Qayrokkum
Konibodom
Isfara
Khujand
Nov
Ura-Tyube
TURKESTAN RANGE
Zeravshan
Ayni
Panjakent
Zarafshon
GISSAR RANGE
Jirgatol
Gharm
Navobod
Surkhob
Mughsu
Qarokŭl
Qullai Kommunizm 7495m
Qatorkuhi Darvoz
DUSHANBE
Hisor
Kofarnihon
Tursunzoda
Qal'aikhum
Norak
Yovon
Danghara
Kŭlob
Kalininobod
Qŭrghonteppa
Kolkhozobod
Vakhsh
Moskva
Farkhor
Dŭstí
Shahrtuz
Panji Poyon
Panj
Amu Darya
Vakhsh
Panj
PAMIRS
SARIKOL RANGE
Murghob
Kudara
Bartang
Rŭshon
Qizilrabot
Gund
Dzhelandy
Pamir
Khorugh
Ishkoshim
N
0 100 km
0 100 miles

WORLD AFFAIRS

Joined UN in 1992

CIS SCO PfP OIC OSCE

Tajikistan remains heavily dependent on Russia, particularly for economic and military assistance. The introduction of its own currency in 1995 enabled Tajikistan to wrest economic control from Russia. A joint operation with Uzbekistan and Kyrgyzstan was launched in 2000 to combat the Islamic Movement of Uzbekistan, based in northern Tajikistan. Tajik airfields were crucial during the US-led action in Afghanistan in 2001, and in 2002 Tajikistan became the last of the former Soviet Union countries to join NATO's Partnership for Peace program.

AID

Recipient

$159m (receipts) — Up 12% in 2001

The US, IMF, World Bank, and EU are the main donors. Aid worth $900 million over three years was pledged in 2003.

DEFENSE

Compulsory military service

$127m — Down 2% in 2001

The presence of some 20,000 international (mostly Russian) peacekeepers bolsters security along the border with Afghanistan. The Tajik army numbers only around 6000. The civil war left almost 20,000 land mines across the country.

ECONOMICS

Inflation 202% p.a. (1990–2001)

$1.1bn — 2.7804 somoni (2.7803)

SCORE CARD

❑ World GNP Ranking	152nd
❑ GNP per Capita	$180
❑ Balance of Payments	–$74m
❑ Inflation	33%
❑ Unemployment	6%

Strengths

Few. Uranium. Considerable potential of hydroelectric power. Carpet making. International donors' favorable attitude.

Weaknesses

Formal economy precarious; dependence on barter economy. No central planning. Little diversification in agriculture; only 6% of land is arable. Exodus of skilled Russians. High levels of inflation and poverty. Production in all sectors in decline.

EXPORTS

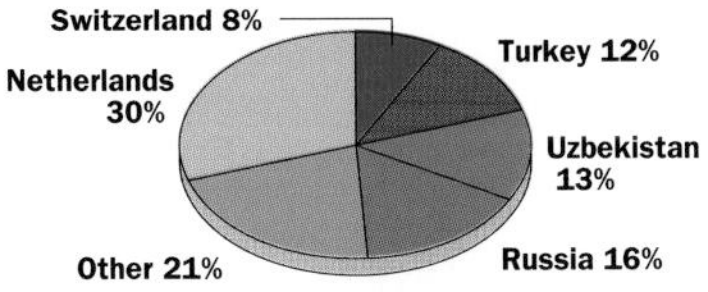
Switzerland 8%
Turkey 12%
Netherlands 30%
Uzbekistan 13%
Other 21%
Russia 16%

IMPORTS

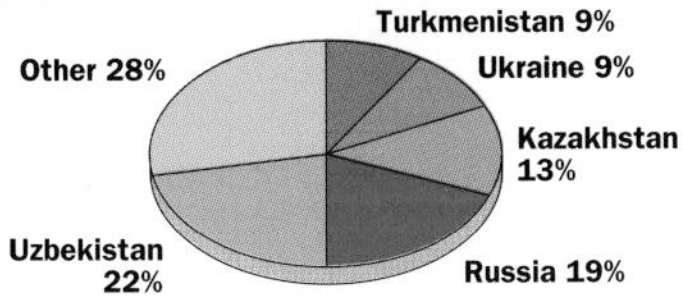
Turkmenistan 9%
Other 28%
Ukraine 9%
Kazakhstan 13%
Uzbekistan 22%
Russia 19%

RESOURCES

Electric power 4.4m kW

145 tonnes — 381 b/d (reserves 15m barrels)

1.49m sheep, 1.09m cattle, 1.32m chickens — Uranium, gold, iron, coal, lead, mercury, tin

Tajikistan has one key resource – uranium – which accounted for 30% of the USSR's total production before 1990. The end of the nuclear arms race has reduced its value, however. Most of Tajikistan is bare mountain, and just 6% of the land can be used for agriculture. Industry is concentrated in the Fergana Valley, close to the Uzbek border.

ENVIRONMENT

Sustainability rank: 110th

4% (3.5% partially protected) — 0.8 tonnes per capita

Landslides, particularly on the lower slopes of the Pamirs, are a serious problem. They are caused as much by the natural geography and by earthquakes as by human activity.

MEDIA

TV ownership high

Daily newspaper circulation 20 per 1000 people

PUBLISHING AND BROADCAST MEDIA

Weekly newspapers dominate. *Kurer Tajikistana* and the Russian-language *Biznes i Politika* have the highest circulation

5 services: 1 state-controlled, 4 independent — 3 state-controlled services

The underdeveloped media are prone to self-censorship and progovernment reporting. Foreign broadcasts may not be retransmitted.

CRIME

Death penalty in use

11,000 prisoners — Crime has been rising dramatically

Only remote areas escape the violence perpetrated by armed gangs. Narcotics smuggling along the border with Afghanistan continues to increase.

EDUCATION

School leaving age: 16

99% — 78,540 students

Russian was again made compulsory in 2003. The university at Dushanbe has lost many of its Russian academics.

CHRONOLOGY

In the 19th century, Tajikistan was a collection of semi-independent principalities, some under Russian control, others under the influence of the Emirate of Bukhara.

- ❑ **1925** Soviets take over Tajikistan.
- ❑ **1940** Cyrillic script introduced.
- ❑ **1989** Tajik becomes official language.
- ❑ **1991** Independence from Moscow.
- ❑ **1992** Islamists capture Dushanbe. Imomali Rakhmanov president.
- ❑ **1995** Tajik rouble introduced; replaced by somoni in 2000.
- ❑ **1997–1998** Peace accord with rebels; UTO joins government.
- ❑ **2000** Pro-Rakhmanov PDPT wins legislative elections.

HEALTH

Welfare state health benefits

1 per 483 people — Heart, respiratory, and infectious diseases, atherosclerosis

Theoretically health provision is free of charge; however, massive underfunding means that patients invariably have to pay to get treatment.

SPENDING

GDP/cap. decrease

CONSUMPTION AND SPENDING

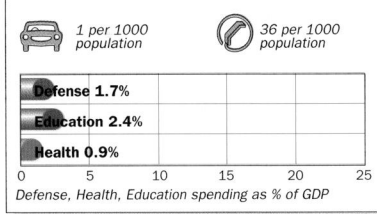

1 per 1000 population — *36 per 1000 population*

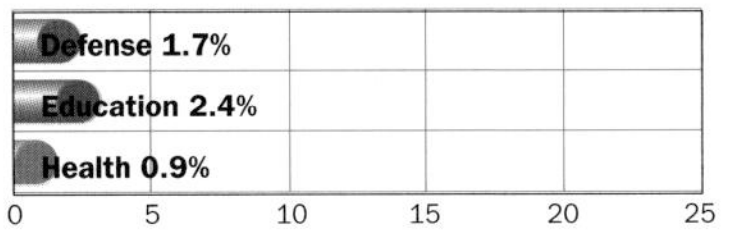
Defense 1.7%
Education 2.4%
Health 0.9%
0
5
10
15
20
25

Defense, Health, Education spending as % of GDP

Over half of the population of Tajikistan live below the UN poverty line; the war against the Islamist rebels worsened conditions. The former communist bureaucrats continue to be the wealthiest group.

WORLD RANKING

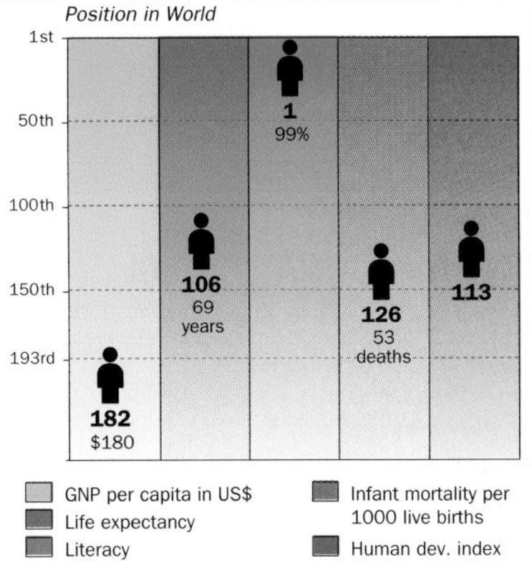
Position in World
1st
50th
100th
150th
193rd
182
$180
106
69
years
1
99%
126
53
deaths
113
GNP per capita in US$
Life expectancy
Literacy
Infant mortality per 1000 live births
Human dev. index

T

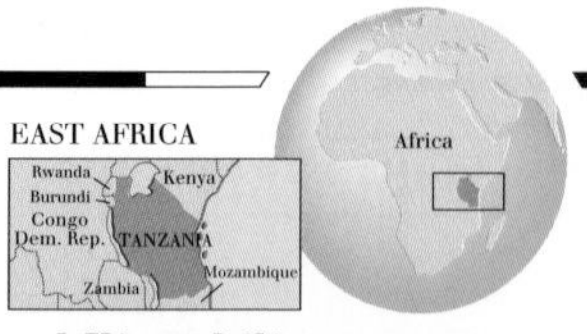

EAST AFRICA
Rwanda
Burundi
Congo
Dem. Rep.
Kenya
TANZANIA
Mozambique
Zambia
Africa

TANZANIA

OFFICIAL NAME: United Republic of Tanzania **CAPITAL:** Dodoma
POPULATION: 36.8 million **CURRENCY:** Tanzanian shilling **OFFICIAL LANGUAGES:** English and Kiswahili

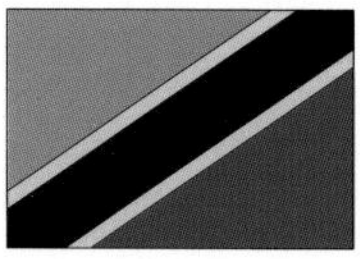

1964 | 1964 | April 26 | EAT | +3 | +255 | .tz

TANZANIA LIES BETWEEN Kenya and Mozambique on the east African coast. Formed by the union of Tanganyika and the Zanzibar islands, Tanzania comprises a coastal lowland, volcanic highlands, and the Great Rift Valley. It includes Mount Kilimanjaro, Africa's highest peak. Tanzania was led by the socialist Julius Nyerere from 1962 until 1985. His Revolutionary Party of Tanzania (CCM) has won multiparty elections held in 1995 and 2000.

Arusha National Park. *Lying within the Ngurdoto volcanic crater, the park has herds of buffalo, rhino, elephant, and giraffe.*

CLIMATE

Tropical/mountain

WEATHER CHART FOR DODOMA

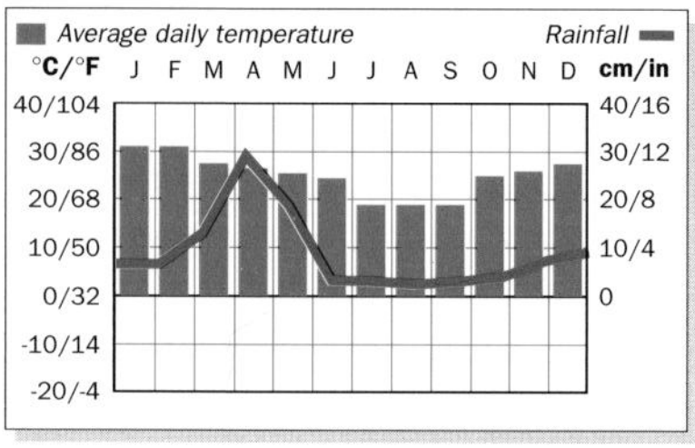

Average daily temperature
Rainfall
°C/°F
J F M A M J J A S O N D
cm/in
40/104
30/86
20/68
10/50
0/32
-10/14
-20/-4
40/16
30/12
20/8
10/4
0

The coast and Zanzibar are tropical. The central plateau is semiarid and the highlands are semitemperate.

TRANSPORTATION

Drive on left

Dar es Salaam International 703,483 passengers

57 ships 37,600 grt

THE TRANSPORTATION NETWORK

4250 km (2641 miles)

None

4582 km (2847 miles)

Lakes Tanganyika, Victoria, and Nyasa are navigable

The roads, railroads, and ports are being upgraded, notably by an $870 million program to improve 70% of Tanzania's trunk roads.

TOURISM

Visitors : Population 1:73

501,000 visitors

Up 9% in 2001

MAIN TOURIST ARRIVALS

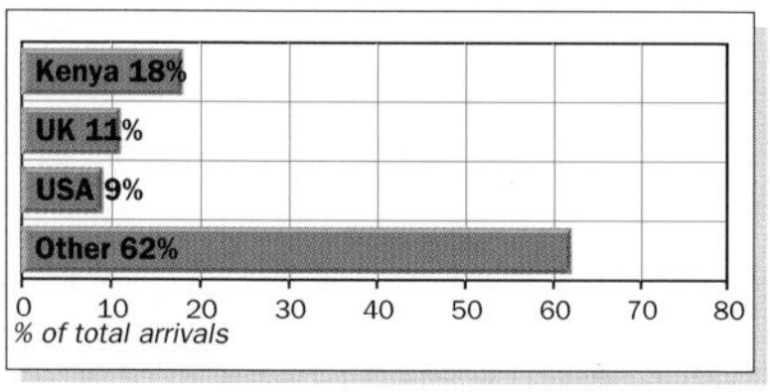

Kenya 18%
UK 11%
USA 9%
Other 62%
0 10 20 30 40 50 60 70 80
% of total arrivals

One-third of Tanzania is national park or game reserve. The Ngorongoro Crater and the Serengeti Plain are top attractions. Tourist numbers increased dramatically in the 1990s.

PEOPLE

Pop. density low

Kiswahili, Sukuma, Chagga, Nyamwezi, Hehe, Makonde, Yao, Sandawe, English

42/km² (108/mi²)

THE URBAN/RURAL POPULATION SPLIT

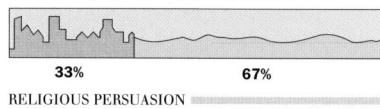

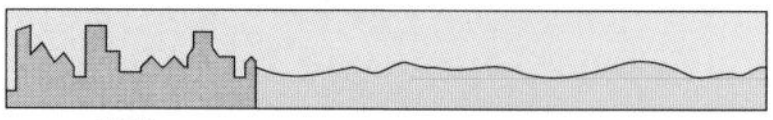

33%
67%

RELIGIOUS PERSUASION

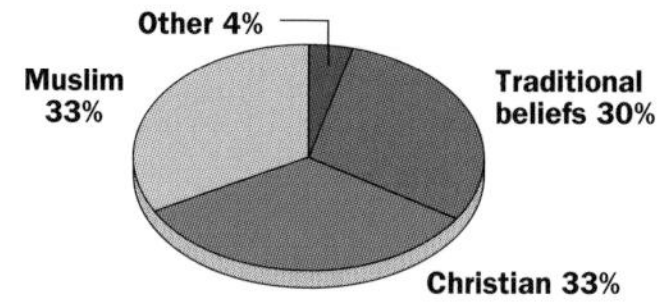

Other 4%
Muslim 33%
Traditional beliefs 30%
Christian 33%

For many Tanzanians the family is the focus of traditional rural life. About 99% belong to one of 120 small ethnic Bantu groups. The remainder comprise Arab, Asian, and European minorities. The use of Kiswahili as a *lingua franca* has helped make ethnic rivalries almost nonexistent.

POLITICS

Multiparty elections

2000/2005

President Benjamin Mkapa

AT THE LAST ELECTION

National Assembly 296 seats

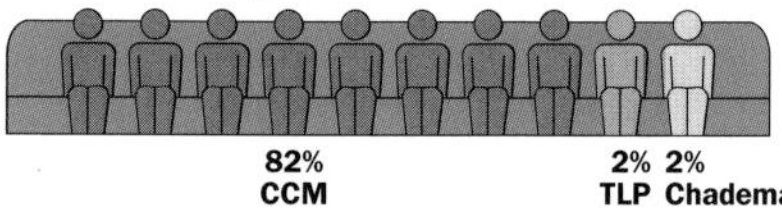

7% CUF
7% Others
82% CCM
2% TLP
2% Chadema

CCM = Revolutionary Party of Tanzania **CUF** = Civic United Front **TLP** = Tanzania Labor Party **Chadema** = Party for Democracy and Progress
Others include five members chosen by the Zanzibar House of Representatives, ten appointed by the president, and the attorney general who has a seat ex officio

Julius Nyerere was the dominant force in Tanzanian politics for over two decades. He founded the ruling party, the CCM, and his philosophy of African socialism guided Tanzania's development. Ali Hassan Mwinyi succeeded Nyerere as president in 1985, introducing a transition to multiparty democracy. Mwinyi stood down in 1995, and Benjamin Mkapa was elected president. Separatism in Zanzibar is a key issue; there were violent protests in 2001, and disaffection continues.

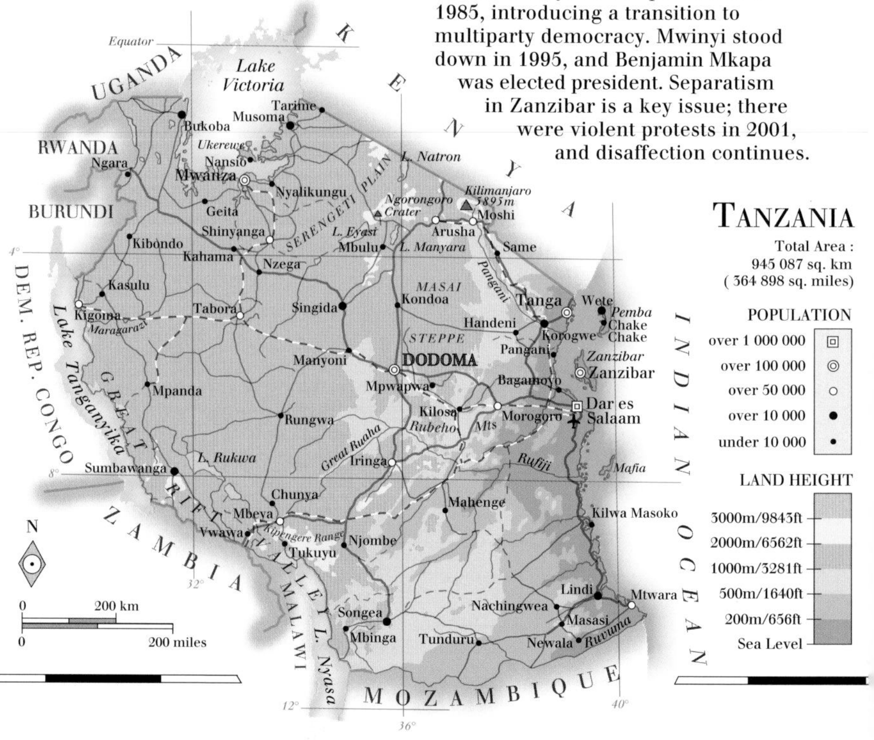

KENYA
UGANDA
RWANDA
BURUNDI
DEM. REP. CONGO
ZAMBIA
MALAWI
MOZAMBIQUE
INDIAN OCEAN
Equator
Lake Victoria
Bukoba
Musoma
Tarime
Ukerewe
Nansio
Mwanza
Ngara
L. Natron
Nyalikungu
SERENGETI PLAIN
Ngorongoro Crater
Kilimanjaro 5895m
Moshi
Arusha
Geita
Shinyanga
L. Eyasi
Mbulu
L. Manyara
Same
Kibondo
Kahama
Nzega
Pangani
Kasulu
MASAI STEPPE
Kondoa
Tanga
Wete
Pemba
Chake Chake
Kigoma
Maragarazi
Tabora
Singida
Handeni
Korogwe
Pangani
Zanzibar
Zanzibar
Manyoni
DODOMA
Bagamoyo
Mpwapwa
Dar es Salaam
Lake Tanganyika
Mpanda
Kilosa
Rubeho Mts
Morogoro
Rungwa
GREAT RIFT VALLEY
Great Ruaha
Rufiji
Mafia
Sumbawanga
L. Rukwa
Iringa
Chunya
Mahenge
Mbeya
Vwawa
Kipengere Range
Njombe
Tukuyu
Kilwa Masoko
Lindi
Mtwara
Nachingwea
Masasi
Songea
Mbinga
Tunduru
Newala
Ruvuma
L. Nyasa
N
0 200 km
0 200 miles
4°
8°
12°
32°
36°
40°
TANZANIA
Total Area : 945 087 sq. km (364 898 sq. miles)
POPULATION
over 1 000 000
over 100 000
over 50 000
over 10 000
under 10 000
LAND HEIGHT
3000m/9843ft
2000m/6562ft
1000m/3281ft
500m/1640ft
200m/656ft
Sea Level

T

WORLD AFFAIRS

Joined UN in 1961

Comm | ACP | EAC | AU | SADC

The instability of Tanzania's central African neighbors is a concern. Over half a million Rwandan and Burundian refugees arrived in the 1990s. By 2001, official numbers were almost unchanged; unofficial estimates added at least 300,000. Improved relations with Uganda and Kenya led to the rebirth in 2001 of the East African Community.

AID

Recipient

$1.23bn (receipts) — Up 18% in 2001

Tanzania is heavily dependent on aid to help offset a severe balance-of-payments deficit. Japan, the UK, and the World Bank are the major donors. Most aid is now linked to an IMF-backed economic reform program. In 2001 $3 billion of debt was canceled.

DEFENSE

Compulsory military service

$140m — Down 3% in 2001

Defense accounts for 3.5% of budget spending. The armed forces are closely linked with the ruling CCM. There is an 80,000-strong citizens' reserve force.

ECONOMICS

Inflation 20% p.a. (1990–2001)

$9.41bn — 1039 Tanzanian shillings (939)

SCORE CARD

- ❑ WORLD GNP RANKING..........................88th
- ❑ GNP PER CAPITA...............................$270
- ❑ BALANCE OF PAYMENTS....................–$738m
- ❑ INFLATION...5.1%
- ❑ UNEMPLOYMENT.........................Not available

STRENGTHS
Coffee, cotton, sisal, tea, cashew nuts. Zanzibar a major producer of cloves. Diamonds, gold. State commitment to effective reforms. Expansion in nontraditional exports. Rise in inward investment. Return to positive growth.

WEAKNESSES
Growth still too low to increase per capita income. Shortage of foreign exchange. Poor credit and equipment limit agricultural development.

EXPORTS

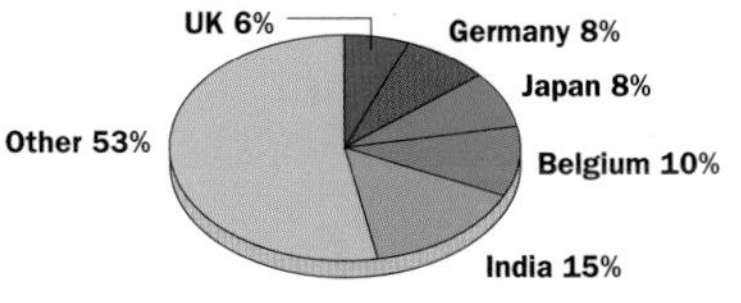
UK 6%
Germany 8%
Japan 8%
Belgium 10%
India 15%
Other 53%

IMPORTS

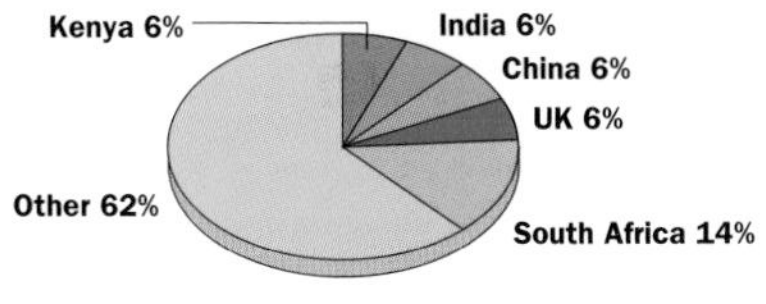
Kenya 6%
India 6%
China 6%
UK 6%
South Africa 14%
Other 62%

RESOURCES

Electric power 543,000 kW

332,989 tonnes — Not an oil producer; refines 12,000 b/d

17.7m cattle, 11.6m goats, 3.55m sheep, 29m chickens — Natural gas, oil, iron, diamonds, gold, salt, phosphates, coal

Agriculture accounts for almost half of GDP and 80% of employment and exports. Forests cover 50% of Tanzania. Wood and charcoal meet over 90% of energy demand. Hydropower provides 84% of electricity and is being expanded. Oil imports take 40% of export earnings, but offshore gas at Songo Songo is being exploited; oil has been discovered off Pemba Island. The opening of a gold mine near Mwanza makes Tanzania Africa's fourth-largest gold producer.

ENVIRONMENT

Sustainability rank: 80th

30% (24% partially protected) — 0.07 tonnes per capita

The demand for fuelwood is a threat to forests. Tourism's demands have to be carefully balanced with those of fragile wildlife environments such as the Ngorongoro Crater and the Serengeti.

MEDIA

TV ownership low

Daily newspaper circulation 4 per 1000 people

PUBLISHING AND BROADCAST MEDIA

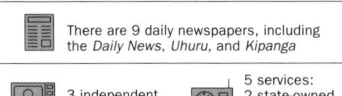

There are 9 daily newspapers, including the *Daily News*, *Uhuru*, and *Kipanga*

3 independent services — 5 services: 2 state-owned, 3 independent

The press has grown rapidly since the mid-1990s, with several independent papers. There is no national TV station.

CRIME

Death penalty in use

44,063 prisoners — Down 4% in 2000

Crime levels are low, though theft in Dar es Salaam has risen. Tanzania's human rights record is good.

EDUCATION

School leaving age: 14

76% — 21,960 students

Primary education, which begins at seven and lasts for seven years, is free; secondary students pay fees. Enrollment is 63% at primary level, but only 6% for secondary education.

CHRONOLOGY

The mainland became the German colony of Tanganyika in 1884. The Sultanate of Zanzibar became a British protectorate in 1890.

- ❑ **1918** Tanganyika under British mandate after World War I.
- ❑ **1961** Tanganyika independent.
- ❑ **1962** Nyerere becomes president.
- ❑ **1963** Zanzibar independent.
- ❑ **1964** Zanzibar signs union with Tanganyika to form Tanzania.
- ❑ **1985** President Mwinyi begins relaxation of socialist policies.
- ❑ **1992** Political parties allowed.
- ❑ **1995** Multiparty elections. Benjamin Mkapa becomes president.
- ❑ **1999** Death of Nyerere.
- ❑ **2000** Mkapa reelected.
- ❑ **2001** Increasing unrest among Zanzibar separatists.

HEALTH

Welfare state health benefits

1 per 25,000 people — Diarrheal and respiratory diseases, malaria

An immunization program for under-twos was introduced in 2001. There is a national campaign against HIV/AIDS, which affects 7.8% of adults.

SPENDING

GDP/cap. increase

CONSUMPTION AND SPENDING

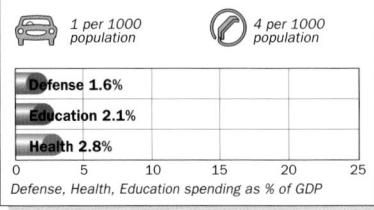

1 per 1000 population — *4 per 1000 population*

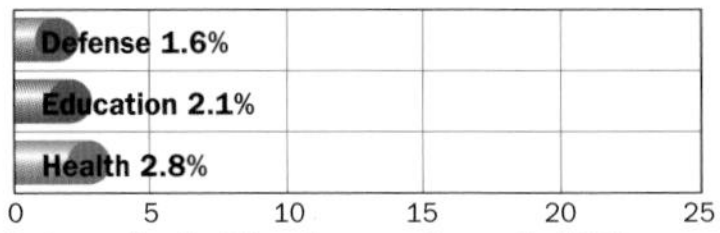
Defense 1.6%
Education 2.1%
Health 2.8%
0
5
10
15
20
25

Defense, Health, Education spending as % of GDP

The majority of Tanzanians are subsistence farmers. The small wealthy elite is composed mainly of Asian and Arab business families.

WORLD RANKING

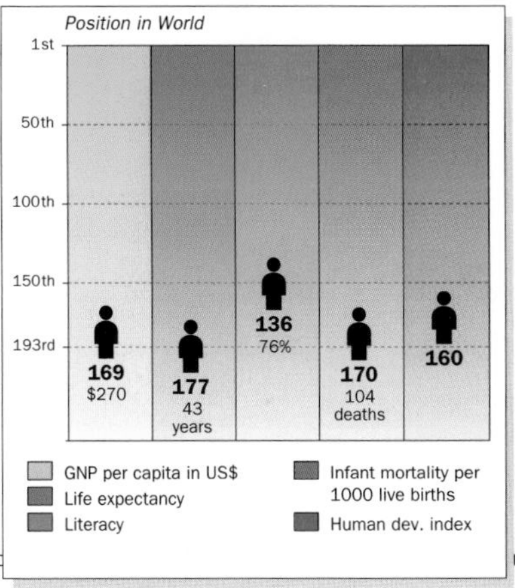
Position in World
1st
50th
100th
150th
193rd
169
$270
177
43
years
136
76%
170
104
deaths
160
GNP per capita in US$
Life expectancy
Literacy
Infant mortality per 1000 live births
Human dev. index

T

THAILAND

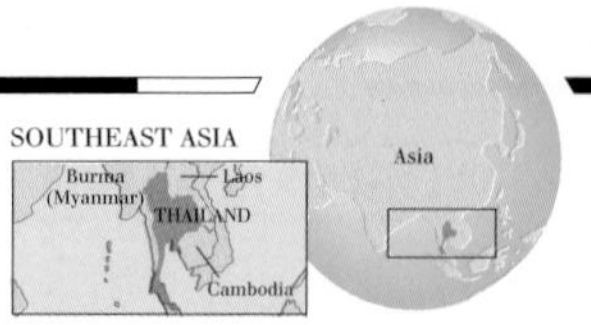
SOUTHEAST ASIA
Burma (Myanmar)
Laos
THAILAND
Cambodia
Asia

OFFICIAL NAME: Kingdom of Thailand **CAPITAL:** Bangkok
POPULATION: 64.3 million **CURRENCY:** Baht **OFFICIAL LANGUAGE:** Thai

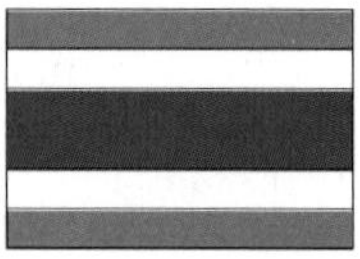

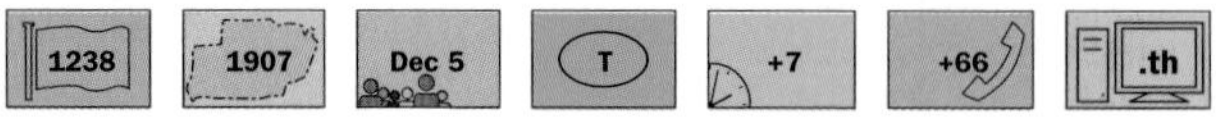
1238
1907
Dec 5
T
+7
+66
.th

THAILAND LIES IN THE HEART of southeast Asia. The north, the border with Burma, and the long Isthmus of Kra between the Andaman Sea and the Gulf of Thailand are mountainous. The central plain is the most fertile and densely populated area, while the low northeastern plateau is the poorest region. Thailand has been an independent kingdom for most of its history, and since 1932 a constitutional monarchy, though with frequent periods of military government. Continuing rapid industrialization results in massive congestion in Bangkok and a serious depletion of natural resources.

CLIMATE

Tropical equatorial/ monsoon

WEATHER CHART FOR BANGKOK

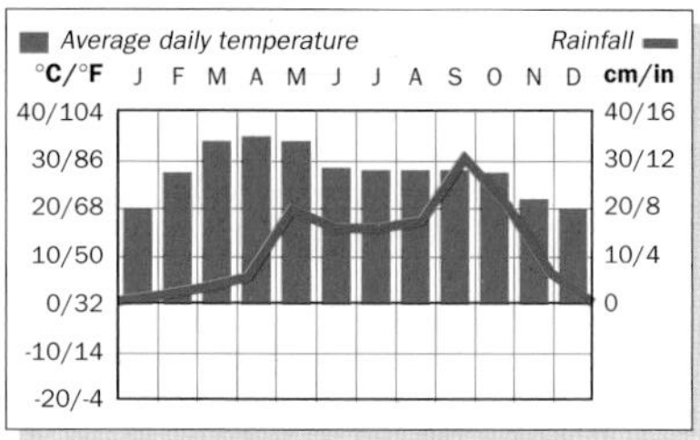
Average daily temperature
Rainfall
°C/°F
J F M A M J J A S O N D
cm/in
40/104
30/86
20/68
10/50
0/32
-10/14
-20/-4
40/16
30/12
20/8
10/4
0

Thailand's tropical monsoon climate has three seasons – a hot sultry period, rains from May to October, and a dry, cooler season from November to March.

TRANSPORTATION

Drive on left

Bangkok International
32.2m passengers

568 ships
1.77m grt

THE TRANSPORTATION NETWORK

62,985 km (39,137 miles)

None

4071 km (2530 miles)

4000 km (2485 miles)

Bangkok suffers from huge traffic jams. Its first mass transit system became operational in 1999; as well as the elevated railroad, subway lines are planned. A road corridor through Laos into Vietnam was agreed in 2001.

Island in the Andaman Sea. *Overdevelopment at Thailand's best-known resorts is pushing tourism into new, remoter locations.*

TOURISM

Visitors : Population 1:5.9

10.9m visitors

Up 7% in 2002

MAIN TOURIST ARRIVALS

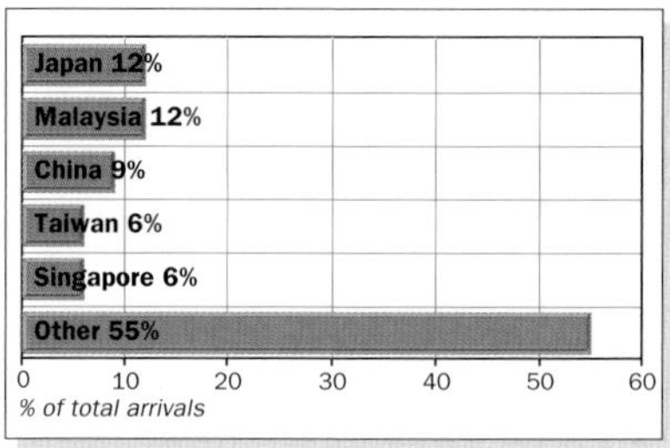
Japan 12%
Malaysia 12%
China 9%
Taiwan 6%
Singapore 6%
Other 55%
0 10 20 30 40 50 60
% of total arrivals

Tourism is an important contributor to the Thai economy. Tourist numbers fell in the early 1990s as a result of both the worldwide recession and local overdevelopment during the 1980s boom. Though the number of arrivals has since recovered, visitors are tending to seek the less-developed resorts. Bangkok's hotel occupancy rates continue to fall as yet more hotels are built. Pattaya beach resort, opposite Phetchaburi has seen such uncontrolled development that sea pollution is now a serious problem, while opposition to the intrusion of large numbers of tourists is growing among northern hill tribes.

Though prostitution is illegal, Bangkok and Pattaya are centers for sex tourism, which thrives despite the state's embarrassment at its effect on Thailand's image. Japanese and German men are among the main clients, while Burmese girls are increasingly recruited as prostitutes. Child prostitution is also a major problem.

There has been a boom in golf tourism, especially among the Japanese. The large number of new golf courses have made Thailand one of the largest golf destinations in Asia. The vast amounts of water needed to maintain the courses is aggravating Thailand's serious water shortage.

PEOPLE

Pop. density medium

Thai, Chinese, Malay, Khmer, Mon, Karen, Miao

126/km² (326/mi²)

THE URBAN/RURAL POPULATION SPLIT

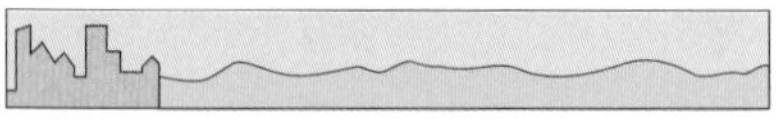
20%
80%

RELIGIOUS PERSUASION

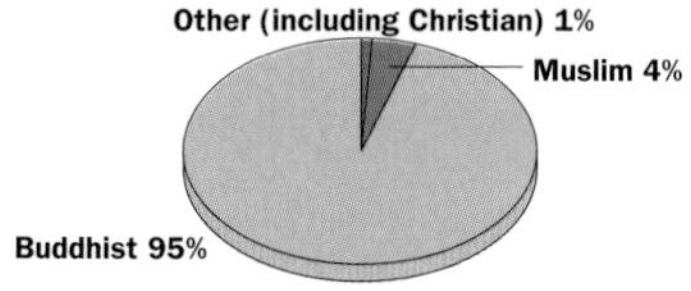
Other (including Christian) 1%
Muslim 4%
Buddhist 95%

ETHNIC MAKEUP

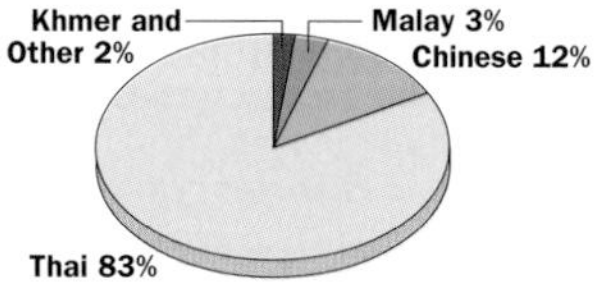
Khmer and Other 2%
Malay 3%
Chinese 12%
Thai 83%

There is little ethnic tension in Thailand, and Buddhism is a great binding force. The majority of Thais follow Theravada Buddhism, though the reformist Asoke Santi Buddhist sect, which advocates a new moral austerity, is gaining influence. Its principles have been championed by political parties in a bid to clean up politics.

The far north and northeast hills are home to about 600,000 tribespeople with their own languages, and to permanently settled refugees from Laos, mostly of the Hmong tribal group.

The large Chinese community is the most assimilated in southeast Asia. Sino-Thais are particularly dominant in agricultural marketing. Most of the one million Muslim Malays live in southern Thailand, close to Malaysia. They feel stronger affinity with Muslims in Malaysia than with Thai culture, and this has given rise to a secessionist movement and a low-level bombing campaign in 2002.

Women are important in business, but their involvement in national politics is limited.

POPULATION AGE BREAKDOWN

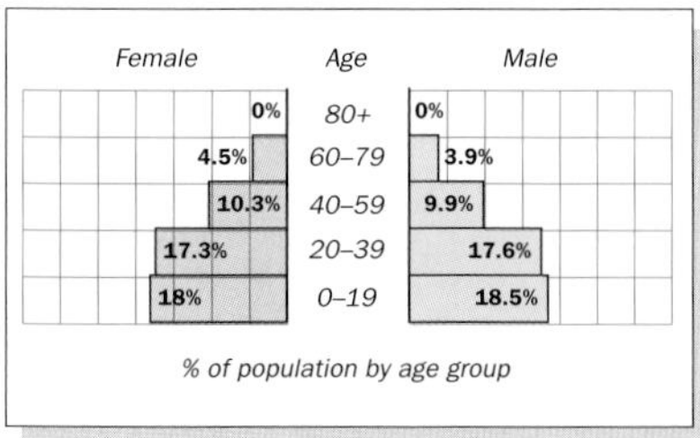
Female
Age
Male
0% 80+ 0%
4.5% 60–79 3.9%
10.3% 40–59 9.9%
17.3% 20–39 17.6%
18% 0–19 18.5%
% of population by age group

T

POLITICS

Multiparty elections

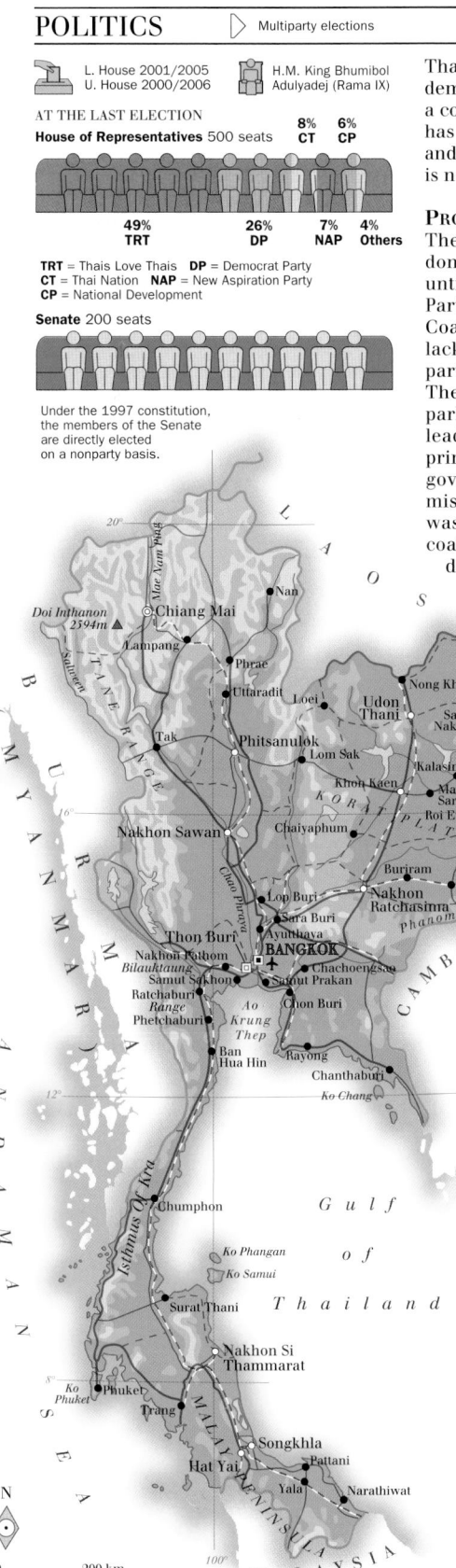

L. House 2001/2005
U. House 2000/2006

H.M. King Bhumibol Adulyadej (Rama IX)

AT THE LAST ELECTION

House of Representatives 500 seats

8% CT
6% CP
49% TRT
26% DP
7% NAP
4% Others

TRT = Thais Love Thais **DP** = Democrat Party
CT = Thai Nation **NAP** = New Aspiration Party
CP = National Development

Senate 200 seats

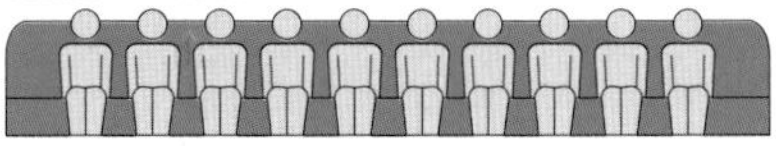

Under the 1997 constitution, the members of the Senate are directly elected on a nonparty basis.

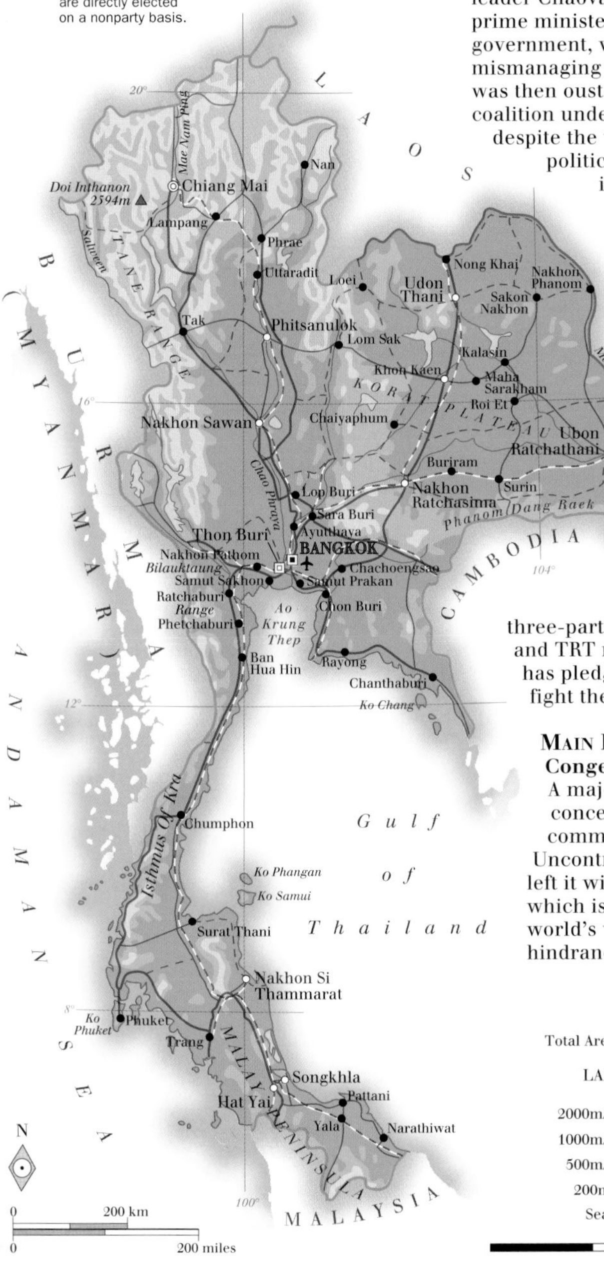
LAOS
BURMA (MYANMAR)
ANDAMAN SEA
CAMBODIA
MALAYSIA
Gulf of Thailand
Doi Inthanon 2594m
Chiang Mai
Lampang
Nan
Phrae
Uttaradit
Loei
Udon Thani
Nong Khai
Nakhon Phanom
Sakon Nakhon
Tak
Phitsanulok
Lom Sak
Kalasin
Khon Kaen
Maha Sarakham
Roi Et
Ubon Ratchathani
Nakhon Sawan
Chaiyaphum
Buriram
Surin
Nakhon Ratchasima
Lop Buri
Sara Buri
Ayutthaya
BANGKOK
Thon Buri
Nakhon Pathom
Samut Sakhon
Samut Prakan
Chachoengsao
Chon Buri
Ratchaburi
Phetchaburi
Rayong
Chanthaburi
Ko Chang
Ban Hua Hin
Ao Krung Thep
Chumphon
Ko Phangan
Ko Samui
Surat Thani
Nakhon Si Thammarat
Ko Phuket
Phuket
Trang
Songkhla
Hat Yai
Pattani
Yala
Narathiwat
Mae Nam Ping
Salween
TANEN RANGE
Bilauktaung Range
KORAT PLATEAU
Mekong
Chao Phraya
Phanom Dang Raek
Isthmus of Kra
MALAY PENINSULA
20°
16°
12°
8°
100°
104°
N
0 200 km
0 200 miles

Thailand is a multiparty parliamentary democracy. Despite his position as a constitutional monarch, the king has immense personal prestige, and criticism of the monarchy is not tolerated.

PROFILE

The Thai political process, which was dominated by the military for decades until the 1990s, is highly personalized. Parties seldom have strong ideologies. Coalitions are often unstable, while the lack of coordination between coalition partners has been a recurring problem. The NAP was the largest party in the parliament elected in 1996, but its leader Chaovalit Yongchaiyuth was prime minister for only a year. His government, which was blamed for mismanaging an economic crisis, was then ousted in favor of another coalition under the DP, which, despite the volatility of coalition politics, succeeded in staying in office for four years. However, in the 2001 elections the new populist TRT triumphed, winning just short of a majority of seats. TRT leader Thaksin Shinawatra, the country's richest man and a former deputy prime minister, formed a three-party government. The NAP and TRT merged in 2002. Thaksin has pledged to tackle poverty and fight the narcotics trade.

MAIN POLITICAL ISSUES

Congestion in Bangkok

A major issue is the concentration of industry and commerce in the Bangkok area. Uncontrolled development has left it with traffic congestion which is not only among the world's worst but is also a serious hindrance to economic activity. In December 1999 the first stage of a mass transit system – an elevated railroad – was formally opened. Since 1993, the government has offered incentives for relocating industry to the provinces. This is also intended to help distribute wealth more evenly – up to 60% of GDP is generated in the Bangkok area.

Narcotics smuggling

The flow of narcotics through Thailand is of serious concern. It badly damages international relations, takes money out of the legitimate economy, and has led to a rise in violent crime. In the south of the country narcotics smugglers have even targeted the police directly.

Prime Minister Thaksin launched a concerted campaign against narcotics in February 2003, noting that some 700 government officials were in some way connected to the trade. By the end of March almost 2000 people had been killed during police raids, 42,000 had been arrested, and $12 million worth of assets had been seized.

THAILAND

Total Area : 514 000 sq. km (198 455 sq. miles)

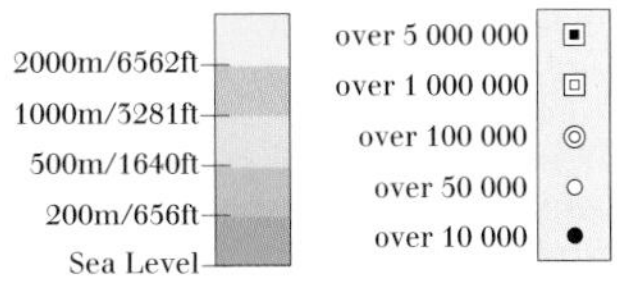
LAND HEIGHT
2000m/6562ft
1000m/3281ft
500m/1640ft
200m/656ft
Sea Level
POPULATION
over 5 000 000
over 1 000 000
over 100 000
over 50 000
over 10 000

King Bhumibol. On the throne since 1946, he is the world's longest-serving ruler.

Thaksin Shinawatra, a controversial billionaire, elected premier in 2001.

WORLD AFFAIRS

Joined UN in 1946

APEC | ASEAN | Mekong River | NAM | WTO

Thailand has friendly relations with China. However, relations with neighboring Burma have been strained over Burma's alleged support for Thai ethnic guerrillas operating along the Thai–Burmese border. Many Thai logging companies, often run by the military, have been active in Burma since Thailand's 1988 logging ban at home. Relations with Vietnam are now cordial, though Thailand had been opposed to the Vietnamese regime in Cambodia in the 1980s.

Thailand, Indonesia, and Malaysia have liberalized trade to promote development in each country in regions which are distant from their respective capitals.

Thailand maintains close relations with the US, despite some tension over intellectual property rights and minor trade issues, but no longer has any US military bases on its territory.

T

AID

Recipient

$281m (receipts) | Down 56% in 2001

Japan and Germany are the largest aid donors. Thailand has imposed a ceiling on foreign borrowing to keep its debt stable.

CHRONOLOGY

Thailand emerged as a kingdom in the 13th century, and by the late 17th century its then capital, Ayutthya, was the largest city in southeast Asia. In 1782, the present Chakri dynasty and a new capital, Bangkok, were founded.

- **1855** King Mongut signs Bowring trade treaty with British – Thailand never colonized by Europeans.
- **1868–1910** King Chulalongkorn westernizes Thailand.
- **1907** Thailand cedes western Khmer (Cambodia) to France.
- **1925** King Prajadhipok begins absolute rule.
- **1932** Bloodless military–civilian coup. Constitutional monarchy.
- **1933** Military takes control.
- **1941** Japanese invade. Government collaborates.
- **1944** Pro-Japanese prime minister and prewar military dictator Phibun voted out of office.
- **1945** Exiled King Ananda returns.
- **1946** Ananda assassinated. King Bhumibol accedes.
- **1947** Military coup. Phibun back.
- **1957** Military coup. Constitution abolished.
- **1965** Thailand allows US to use Thai bases in Vietnam War.
- **1969** New constitution endorses elected parliament.
- **1971** Army suspends constitution.
- **1973–1976** Student riots lead to interlude of democracy.
- **1976** Military takeover.
- **1980–1988** Gen. Prem Tinsulanond prime minister. Partial democracy.
- **1988** Elections. Gen. Chatichai Choonhaven, right-wing CT leader, named prime minister.
- **1991** Military coup. Civilian Anand Panyarachun caretaker premier.
- **1992** Elections. Gen. Suchinda named premier. Demonstrations. King forces Suchinda to step down and reinstalls Anand. Moderates win new elections.
- **1995** CT wins general election.
- **1996** Early elections; Chaovalit Yongchaiyuth of NAP becomes prime minister.
- **1997** Financial and economic crisis; Chaovalit government falls; DP's Chuan Leekpai prime minister.
- **2001** TRT, led by Thaksin Shinawatra, wins elections.

DEFENSE

No compulsory military service

$1.83bn | Down 24% in 2001

THAI ARMED FORCES

333 main battle tanks (50 PRC Type-69, 105 M-48A5, 178 M-60)	190,000 personnel
1 carrier, 12 frigates, and 88 patrol boats	68,000 personnel
194 combat aircraft (13 F-5A/B, 50 F-16A/B, 36 F-5E/F)	48,000 personnel
None	

The military either ruled Thailand, or played a prominent role in politics, for over half a century from 1932. In 1996, its role in the appointed Senate – hitherto a military stronghold – was reduced. Retired military figures are, however, prominent in the major political parties.

Since 1986, defense spending has tended to focus on the navy and air force. Naval vessels have been bought from China, Germany, and Spain, and aircraft from the UK, the US, and Russia.

Thailand's main defense concerns are border disputes with Cambodia, Burma, and Laos; the Muslim secessionist movement in the south; and piracy and fishing disputes in the South China Sea.

ECONOMICS

Inflation 3.9% p.a. (1990–2001)

$118bn | 42.04 baht (41.53)

SCORE CARD

World GNP Ranking	32nd
GNP per Capita	$1940
Balance of Payments	$6.23bn
Inflation	1.7%
Unemployment	4%

EXPORTS

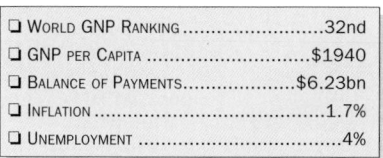

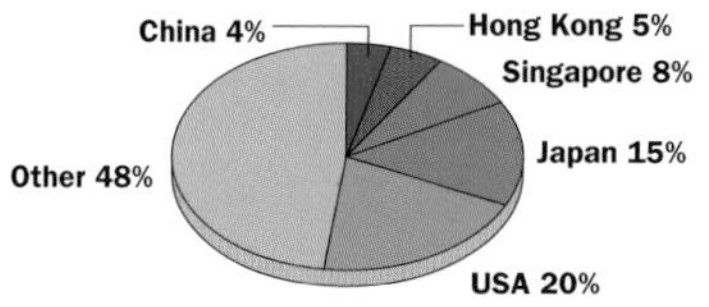
China 4%
Hong Kong 5%
Singapore 8%
Japan 15%
USA 20%
Other 48%

IMPORTS

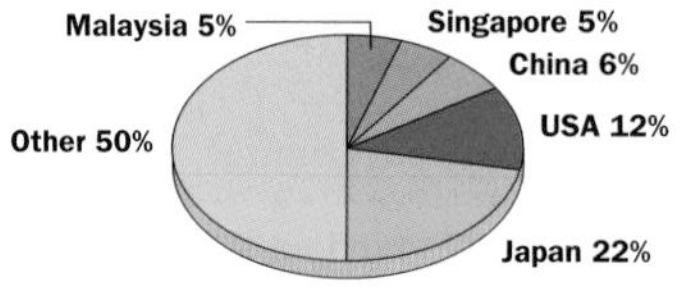
Malaysia 5%
Singapore 5%
China 6%
USA 12%
Japan 22%
Other 50%

ECONOMIC PERFORMANCE INDICATOR

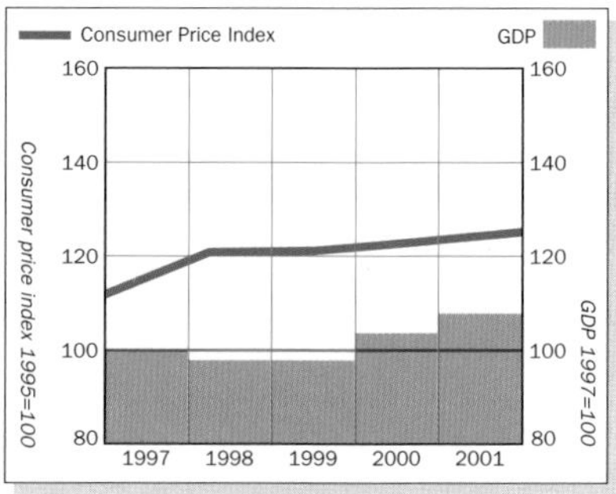
Consumer Price Index
GDP
160
140
120
100
80
Consumer price index 1995=100
GDP 1997=100
1997
1998
1999
2000
2001

Strengths

Success of export-based and import-substituting manufacturing. Rapid economic growth. Natural gas. Tourism. Major world exporter of rice and rubber.

Weaknesses

Concentration of economic activity in congested Bangkok area. Inadequate water storage facilities. Rapid growth of foreign debt. Low-profit farming.

Profile

Until the late 1990s, the economy grew at over 9% a year for a decade, driven by a rise in manufacturing and huge overseas investments, especially from Japan. However, as domestic wages rose, Thailand faced stiff competition from China and Vietnam. Thailand also lacked a skilled labor force to develop high-tech production, though it is a big producer of electronics goods.

In 1997 mounting foreign debt and the sharp depreciation of the baht made necessary an IMF-led rescue package. Massive retrenchment and stringent austerity measures followed. By 2000 the IMF had ended its direct involvement and was optimistic for future expansion. GDP grew by 4.4% in 2001, and Thailand's foreign debt rating was upgraded to "positive" in 2002.

THAILAND : MAJOR BUSINESSES

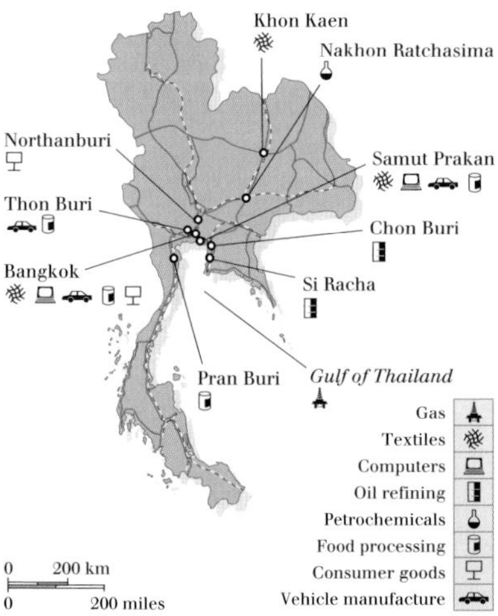
Khon Kaen
Nakhon Ratchasima
Northanburi
Samut Prakan
Thon Buri
Chon Buri
Bangkok
Si Racha
Pran Buri
Gulf of Thailand
Gas
Textiles
Computers
Oil refining
Petrochemicals
Food processing
Consumer goods
Vehicle manufacture
0 200 km
0 200 miles

T

RESOURCES

Electric power 23.6m kW

3.63m tonnes

197,000 b/d (reserves 600m barrels)

28.4m ducks, 6.69m pigs, 121m chickens

Tin, lignite, gas, gems, oil, tungsten, lead, zinc, antimony, gold, copper

ELECTRICITY GENERATION

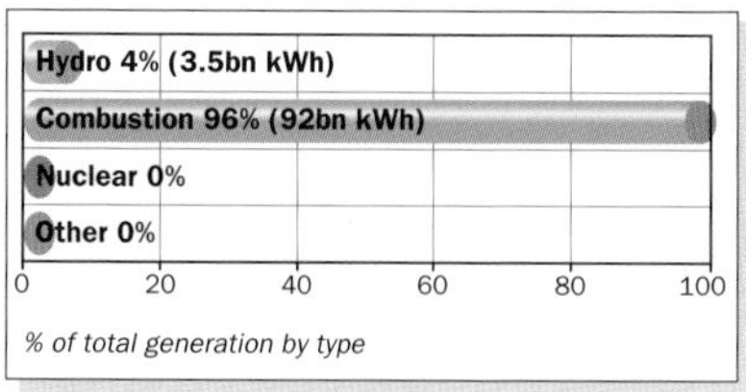
Hydro 4% (3.5bn kWh)
Combustion 96% (92bn kWh)
Nuclear 0%
Other 0%
0
20
40
60
80
100
% of total generation by type

Thailand has minimal crude oil and has rejected the nuclear option in favor of speeding up development of its large natural gas fields. It also has significant lignite deposits for power generation. World demand for Thailand's tin has declined, but recent gold and copper finds offer new potential. Thailand has valuable gemstone deposits. It is the world's largest producer of shrimp.

THAILAND : LAND USE

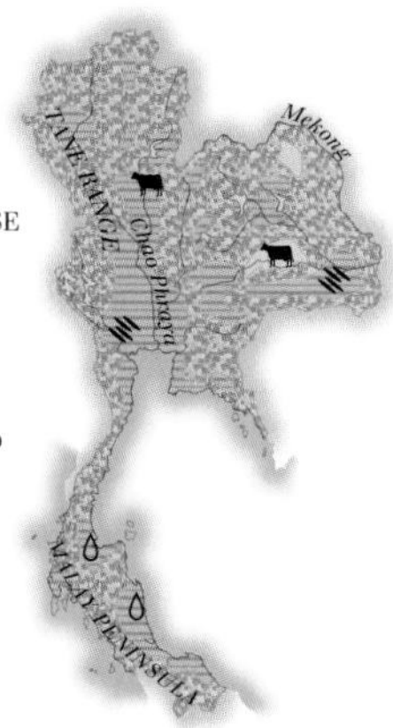
Cropland
Forest
Pasture
Cattle
Rubber - cash crop
Rice
Mekong
TANEN RANGE
Chao Phraya
MALAY PENINSULA
0 200 km
0 200 miles

ENVIRONMENT

Sustainability rank: 54th

14% (5% partially protected)

3.3 tonnes per capita

ENVIRONMENTAL TREATIES

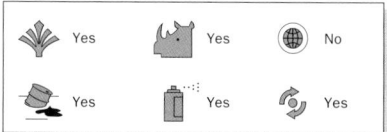

Yes	Yes	No
Yes	Yes	Yes

Deforestation, especially of the watersheds in the north, has led to the increasing severity of both floods and droughts. Particularly serious flooding in the south resulted in a total logging ban in 1988. Illegal logging continues, however. Reafforestation projects are often criticized for using quick-growing species. Intensive inland prawn farming leaves a legacy of salination. Mass tourism brings pollution problems to resorts, while backpackers lead the way in exposing remoter locations.

MEDIA

TV ownership high

Daily newspaper circulation 64 per 1000 people

PUBLISHING AND BROADCAST MEDIA

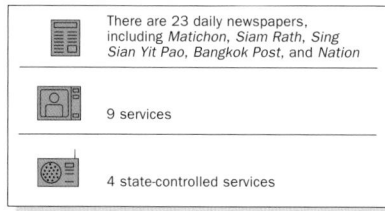

There are 23 daily newspapers, including *Matichon, Siam Rath, Sing Sian Yit Pao, Bangkok Post*, and *Nation*

9 services

4 state-controlled services

The media enjoy free political reporting but may be censored on military, royal, and other sensitive matters. Two TV services are run by the military. Most radio stations are in or near Bangkok.

CRIME

Death penalty in use

217,697 prisoners

Down 12% in 1996–2000

CRIME RATES

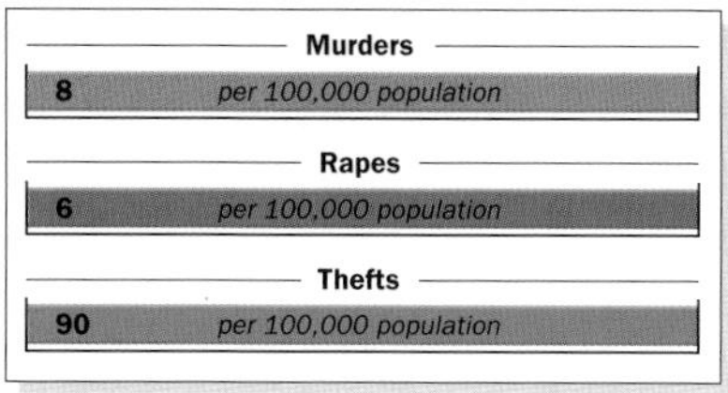
Murders
8 per 100,000 population
Rapes
6 per 100,000 population
Thefts
90 per 100,000 population

Political imprisonment is now extremely rare. There is some police involvement in crime, including extrajudicial killings and ill-treatment of prisoners in detention. The king has inspired an opium-substitution crop program. In the south, drug addiction is a major problem and crime is rising. Almost 2000 people were killed during a crackdown on narcotics in 2003.

EDUCATION

School leaving age: 14

96%

2.1m students

THE EDUCATION SYSTEM

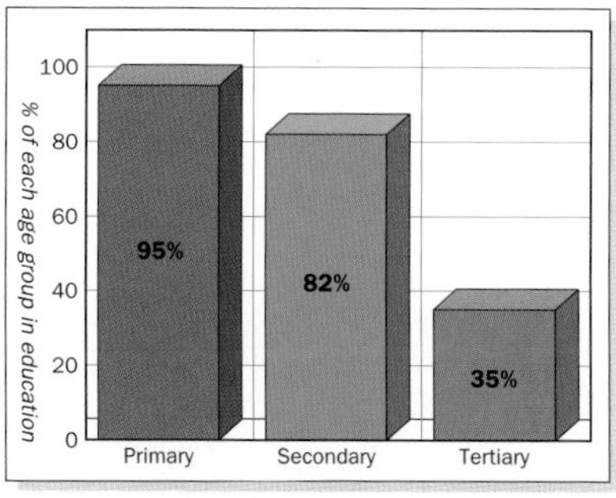
100
80
60
40
20
0
% of each age group in education
95%
82%
35%
Primary
Secondary
Tertiary

A poorly developed education system has led to a shortage of skills needed for the expansion of high-tech industries. The Education for All program aims to rectify this situation, and also to improve the standard of adult literacy.

HEALTH

Welfare state health benefits

1 per 4167 people

Heart diseases, gastroenteritis

High-quality health care is heavily concentrated in Bangkok. Most of the rural population has access to primary health care, and a new scheme to provide care for the poor for just $1 per person was launched in 2001. Trained personnel are aided by village health volunteers, monks, teachers, and traditional healers.

However, estimates suggest that only 30% of users can afford to pay. The poorest people can apply annually for a certificate entitling them to free health care.

High-profile family planning programs are slowing population growth. An effective AIDS prevention campaign has helped reduce the number of new infections, though the government has been in conflict with international drug companies over its right to produce cheaper generic drugs for AIDS sufferers. Prostitutes have benefited from an extensive sex education program.

SPENDING

GDP/cap. increase

CONSUMPTION AND SPENDING

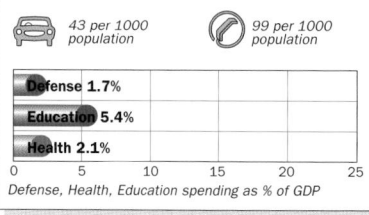

43 per 1000 population

99 per 1000 population

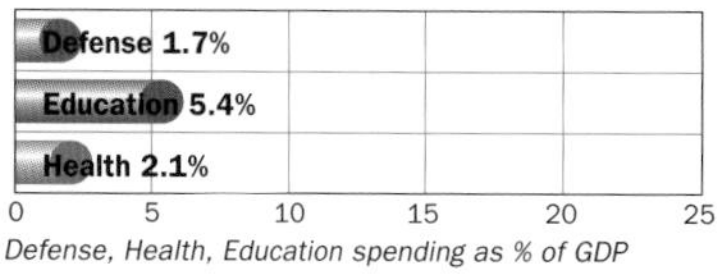
Defense 1.7%
Education 5.4%
Health 2.1%
0
5
10
15
20
25
Defense, Health, Education spending as % of GDP

The government is trying to distribute to the provinces the people and wealth currently concentrated to a very great extent in Bangkok. The northeast in particular is very poor. The gap between rich and poor is greater in Thailand than in other industrializing southeast Asian states.

WORLD RANKING

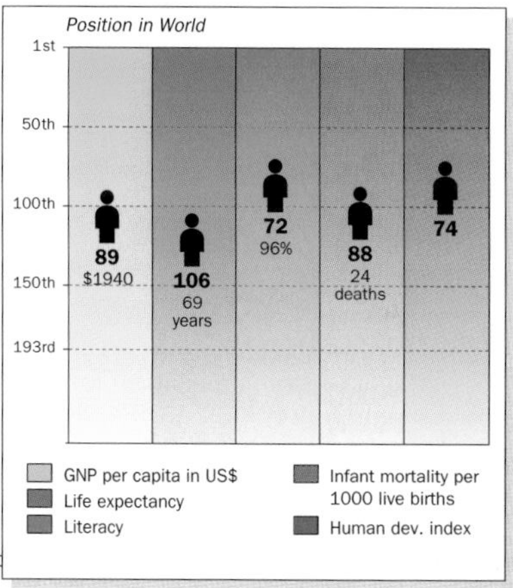
Position in World
1st
50th
100th
150th
193rd
89
$1940
106
69
years
72
96%
88
24
deaths
74
GNP per capita in US$
Life expectancy
Literacy
Infant mortality per 1000 live births
Human dev. index

T

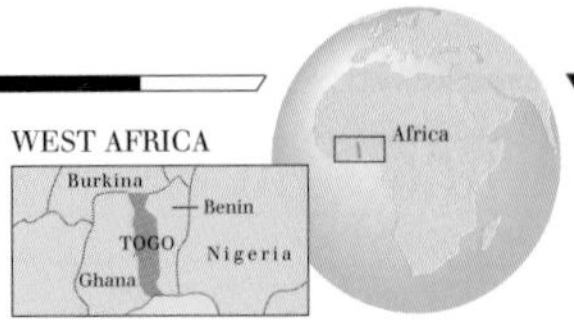
WEST AFRICA
Burkina
Benin
TOGO
Ghana
Nigeria
Africa

Togo

OFFICIAL NAME: Republic of Togo **CAPITAL:** Lomé **POPULATION:** 4.8 million
CURRENCY: CFA franc **OFFICIAL LANGUAGE:** French

1960 | 1960 | April 27 | TG | 0 | +228 | .tg

TOGO IS SANDWICHED between Ghana and Benin in west Africa. A central forested region is bounded by savanna lands to the north and south. The port of Lomé is an important entrepôt for west African trade. Togo's president, Gen. Gnassingbé Eyadéma, has been in power since 1967.

CLIMATE

Tropical equatorial/ wet and dry

WEATHER CHART FOR LOMÉ

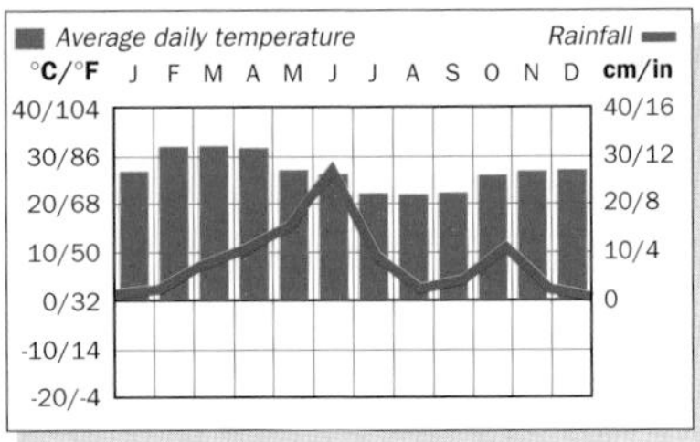
Average daily temperature
Rainfall
°C/°F
J F M A M J J A S O N D
cm/in
40/104
30/86
20/68
10/50
0/32
-10/14
-20/-4
40/16
30/12
20/8
10/4
0

Togo has a typical Gulf of Guinea climate – very hot and humid on the coast, and drier inland.

TRANSPORTATION

Drive on right

Tokoin, Lomé
200,246 passengers

1 ship
4212 grt

THE TRANSPORTATION NETWORK

2376 km (1476 miles)	None
525 km (326 miles)	50 km (31 miles)

Improving the already good road network and Lomé's port facilities are priorities, given Togo's role as an entrepôt. Air and rail links to the interior, however, are limited.

TOURISM

Visitors : Population 1:84

57,000 visitors

Down 5% in 2001

MAIN TOURIST ARRIVALS

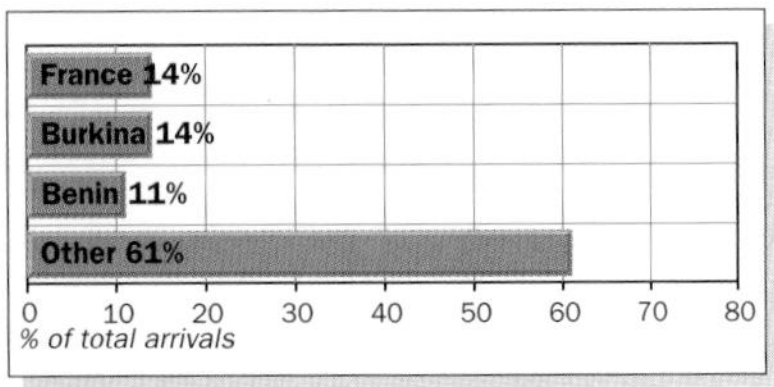
France 14%
Burkina 14%
Benin 11%
Other 61%
0 10 20 30 40 50 60 70 80
% of total arrivals

There is some package tourism, mainly French and German, to coastal tourist villages and hotels built during the expansion program of the 1980s. Tourists have been deterred by the political uncertainty since 1990.

PEOPLE

Pop. density medium

Ewe, Kabye, Gurma, French

88/km² (229/mi²)

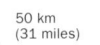

THE URBAN/RURAL POPULATION SPLIT

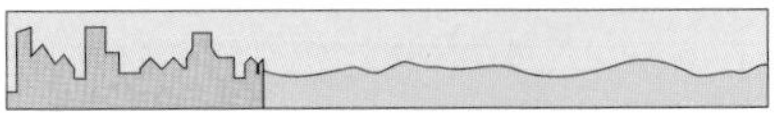
34%
66%

RELIGIOUS PERSUASION

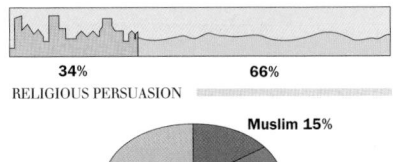

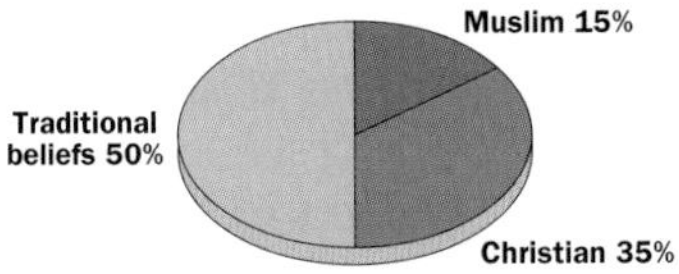
Muslim 15%
Traditional beliefs 50%
Christian 35%

A bitter divide has existed between north and south since before independence. Most southern resentment is directed toward a northern minority, the Kabye people from the Kabye plateau, because of their domination of the military. The Kabye and other northerners in turn resent their own underdevelopment in contrast to the high development, especially educationally, of all southerners. The dominant southern group is the Ewe, who make up more than 40% of the total population.

As elsewhere in Africa, the extended family is important and tribalism and nepotism are key factors in everyday life. Some Togolese ethnic groups, such as the Mina, have matriarchal societies. The "Nana Benz," the market-women of Lomé, control the retail trade and have considerable private money. Politics, however, remains a male preserve.

***Kabye cultivation near Kara,** in northern Togo. The main food crops grown are cassava, yams, and maize.*

POLITICS

Multiparty elections

2002/2007

President Gnassingbé Eyadéma

AT THE LAST ELECTION

National Assembly 81 seats

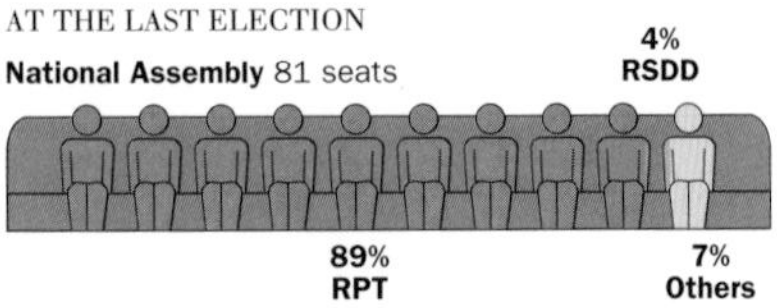
4%
RSDD
89%
RPT
7%
Others

RPT = Rally of the Togolese People
RSDD = Rally for Democracy and Development

Politics has been dominated for over three decades by Gen. Gnassingbé Eyadéma, in power since 1967 and Africa's longest-serving leader.

A democracy movement has been gathering momentum since 1990. Multiparty presidential elections held in 1993 were won by Eyadéma, some opposition candidates boycotting the poll. Eyadéma claimed victory again in presidential elections in 1998, amid accusations of malpractice and of the killing of hundreds of opposition supporters immediately afterward in the runup to the 1999 Assembly election. (Serious human rights violations were later confirmed in a UN/OAU report.) During subsequent negotiations, the opposition accepted the election results, Eyadéma stated that he would not stand for reelection in 2003, and an accord provided for a new independent electoral body and a political code of conduct. Eyadéma's RPT retained its huge majority in 2002 after the main opposition parties boycotted the repeatedly postponed poll. In December the constitution was amended, paving the way for Eyadéma's third-term victory in June 2003.

WORLD AFFAIRS

Joined UN in 1960

OIC | ECOWAS | FZ | AU | UEMOA

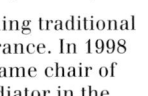

The priority is maintaining traditional links, especially with France. In 1998 President Eyadéma became chair of ECOWAS, acting as mediator in the Guinea-Bissau conflict and hosting talks on Sierra Leone. Regional relations are very good.

AID

Recipient

$47m (receipts)

Down 33% in 2001

Development projects and the health of the economy overall have suffered as a result of aid suspensions in the 1990s by donors including the US and the EU.

T

TOGO

Total Area : 56 785 sq. km (21 924 sq. miles)

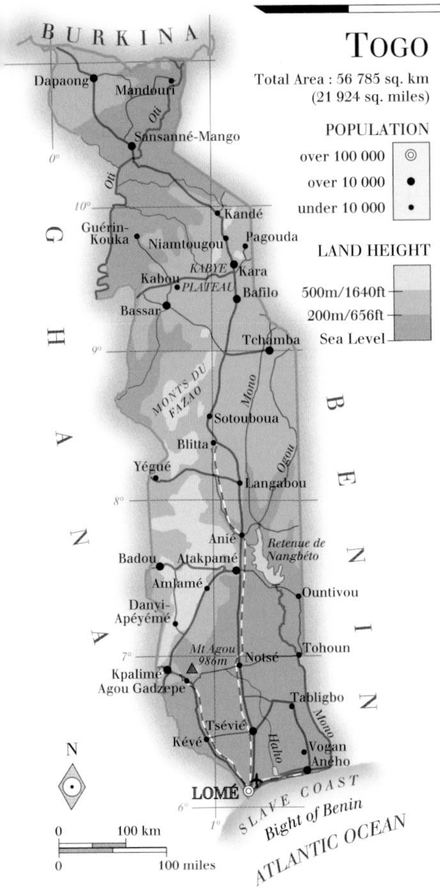
BURKINA
Dapaong
Mandouri
Oti
Sansanné-Mango
Guérin-Kouka
Niamtougou
Kandé
Pagouda
KABYE
PLATEAU
Kara
Kabou
Bafilo
Bassar
Tchamba
MONTS DU FAZAO
Mono
Sotouboua
Blitta
Yégué
Ogou
Langabou
Anié
Retenue de Nangbéto
Badou
Atakpamé
Amlamé
Danyi-Apéyémé
Ountivou
Mt Agou 986m
Notsé
Tohoun
Kpalimé
Agou Gadzepe
Tabligbo
Tsévié
Haho
Kévé
Vogan
Aneho
LOMÉ
SLAVE COAST
Bight of Benin
ATLANTIC OCEAN
GHANA
BENIN
N
0
100 km
100 miles
POPULATION
over 100 000
over 10 000
under 10 000
LAND HEIGHT
500m/1640ft
200m/656ft
Sea Level

DEFENSE

Compulsory military service

$31m

No change in 2001

The military has an important role in Togo, and spending on defense is quite high. The army's senior ranks are dominated by loyalists from President Eyadéma's northern Kabye tribe. France guarantees Togo's security through a defense accord, and supplies most military equipment and training.

RESOURCES

Electric power 38,000 kW

22,379 tonnes

Not an oil producer

1.7m sheep, 1.46m goats, 300,000 pigs, 8.5m chickens

Phosphates, iron, chromite, bauxite, marble, dolomite

Phosphates are Togo's most important resource. Offshore oil and gas deposits were found in 1999. The Nangbeto Dam, opened in 1988, has reduced dependence on Ghana for energy. Coffee, cocoa, and cotton are important cash crops.

ENVIRONMENT

Sustainability rank: 105th

8% (1% partially protected)

0.3 tonnes per capita

Ecologists have been critical of the transformation of nature reserves into hunting grounds for the military elite. Other problems include coastal erosion around Aneho and desertification.

MEDIA

TV ownership low

Daily newspaper circulation 2 per 1000 people

PUBLISHING AND BROADCAST MEDIA

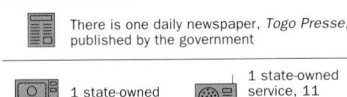

There is one daily newspaper, *Togo Presse*, published by the government

1 state-owned service

1 state-owned service, 11 private stations

Opposition papers now challenge the government daily *Togo-Presse*, despite some official harassment.

CRIME

Death penalty not used in practice

2043 prisoners

Crime is rising

Togo is normally relatively peaceable, but urban crime generally increased during the 1990s, particularly during periods of political unrest in the capital.

CHRONOLOGY

After colonization by Germany in 1894, Togoland was divided between France and the UK in 1922.

- ❑ **1960** French sector independent as Togo (UK part joined to Ghana).
- ❑ **1967** Eyadéma takes power.
- ❑ **1991–1992** General strike; repression.
- ❑ **1993** Eyadéma elected president.
- ❑ **1998, 1999** Disputed elections.
- ❑ **2002, 2003** RPT, Eyadéma reelected.

EDUCATION

School leaving age: 15

58%

15,171 students

Schooling is based on the French model. Unpaid grants provoked unrest at the University of Lomé in 2001.

HEALTH

No welfare state health benefits

1 per 12,500 people

Malaria, diarrheal, infectious, and parasitic diseases

Health care suffers from a lack of resources and funding. Around 6% of adults were HIV positive by 2000.

SPENDING

GDP/cap. increase

CONSUMPTION AND SPENDING

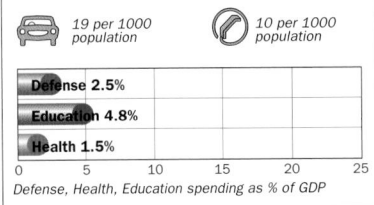

19 per 1000 population

10 per 1000 population

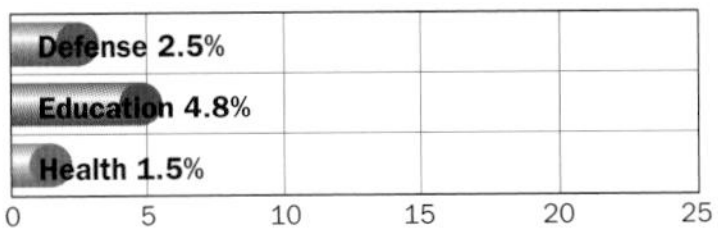
Defense 2.5%
Education 4.8%
Health 1.5%
0
5
10
15
20
25

Defense, Health, Education spending as % of GDP

Considerable wealth disparities exist between those who work the land and the country's political and business classes. However, the urban class was hit by an economic downturn in the late 1990s.

ECONOMICS

Inflation 6.6% p.a. (1990–2001)

$1.28bn

571.2 CFA francs (664.2)

SCORE CARD

- ❑ WORLD GNP RANKING........149th
- ❑ GNP PER CAPITA........$270
- ❑ BALANCE OF PAYMENTS........–$106m
- ❑ INFLATION........5.4%
- ❑ UNEMPLOYMENT........Not available

STRENGTHS

Efficient civil service. Ideal location for role as entrepôt, based on Lomé port. Resourceful entrepreneurs, notably market-women. Proceeds of widespread smuggling. Phosphate deposits have the world's highest mineral content. Self-sufficient in basic foodstuffs.

EXPORTS

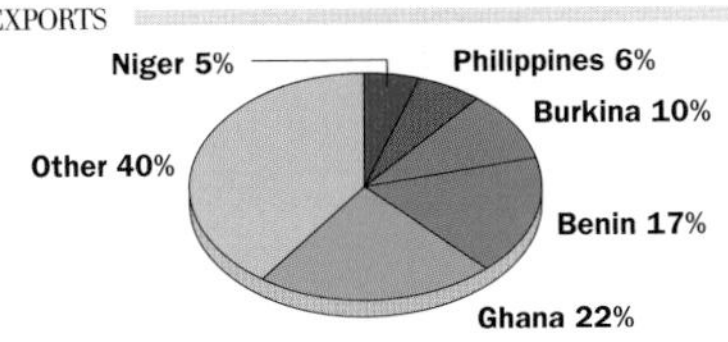
Niger 5%
Philippines 6%
Burkina 10%
Other 40%
Benin 17%
Ghana 22%

IMPORTS

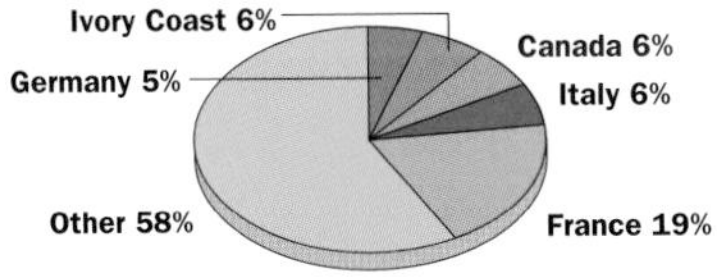
Ivory Coast 6%
Canada 6%
Germany 5%
Italy 6%
Other 58%
France 19%

WEAKNESSES

Political pariah status led to aid reductions in the 1990s. Low world prices for phosphates. Hydropower generation is vulnerable to drought.

WORLD RANKING

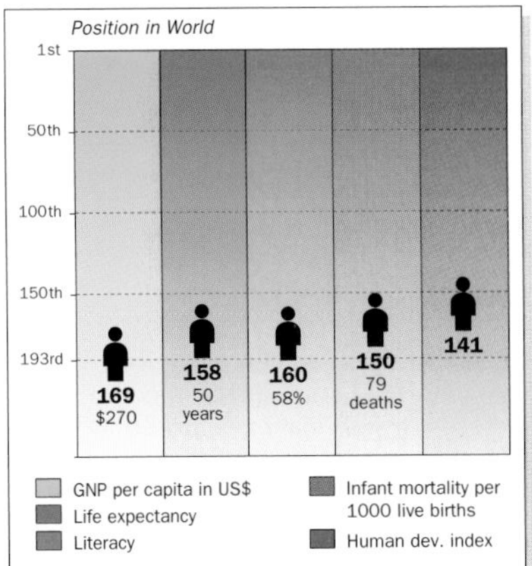
Position in World
1st
50th
100th
150th
193rd
169
$270
158
50
years
160
58%
150
79
deaths
141
GNP per capita in US$
Life expectancy
Literacy
Infant mortality per 1000 live births
Human dev. index

T

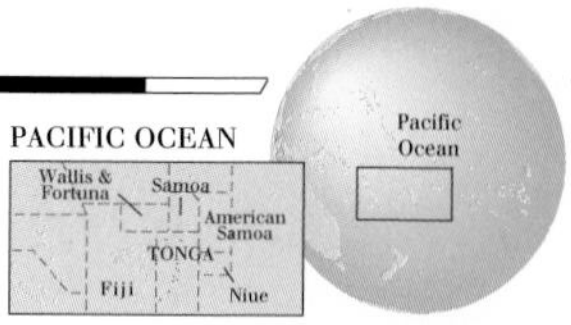
PACIFIC OCEAN
Wallis & Fortuna
Samoa
American Samoa
TONGA
Fiji
Niue
Pacific Ocean

TONGA

OFFICIAL NAME: Kingdom of Tonga **CAPITAL:** Nuku'alofa **POPULATION:** 106,137
CURRENCY: Pa'anga (Tongan dollar) **OFFICIAL LANGUAGES:** English and Tongan

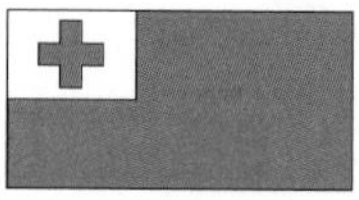

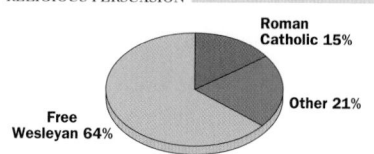

1970 | 1970 | June 4 | TO | +12 | +676 | .to

LOCATED IN THE SOUTH PACIFIC 1600 km (1000 miles) northeast of New Zealand, Tonga is an archipelago of 170 islands. These are divided into three main groups, Vava'u, Ha'apai, and Tongatapu. Tonga's easterly islands are generally low and fertile. Those in the west are higher and volcanic in origin. Tonga's economy is based on agriculture, especially coconut, cassava, and passion fruit production. Politics is effectively controlled by the king.

CLIMATE

Tropical oceanic

WEATHER CHART FOR NUKU'ALOFA

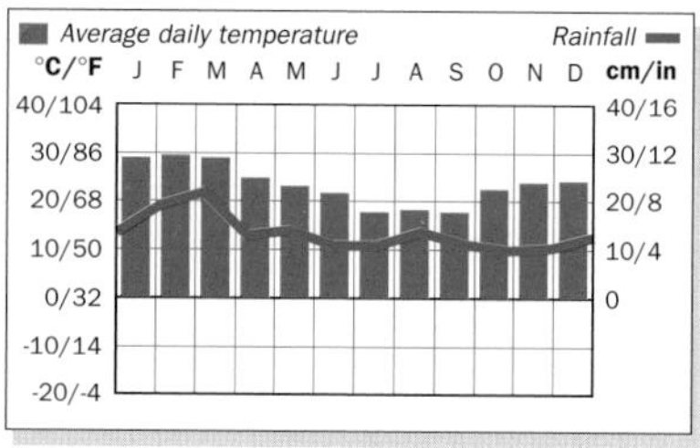
Average daily temperature
Rainfall
°C/°F
J F M A M J J A S O N D
cm/in
40/104
30/86
20/68
10/50
0/32
-10/14
-20/-4
40/16
30/12
20/8
10/4
0

Tonga has a tropical oceanic climate, with year-round temperatures ranging between 17°C (63°F) and 30°C (86°F).

TRANSPORTATION

Drive on left

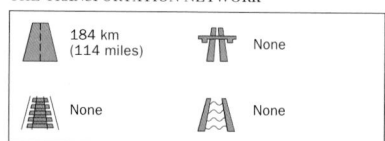

Fua'amotu International, Tongatabu
67,000 passengers

165 ships
337,600 grt

THE TRANSPORTATION NETWORK

184 km (114 miles) | None
None | None

Improvements at Fua'amotu Airport have led to an increase in flights to and from Tonga.

TOURISM

Visitors : Population 1:3

35,000 visitors

Up 13% in 2000

MAIN TOURIST ARRIVALS

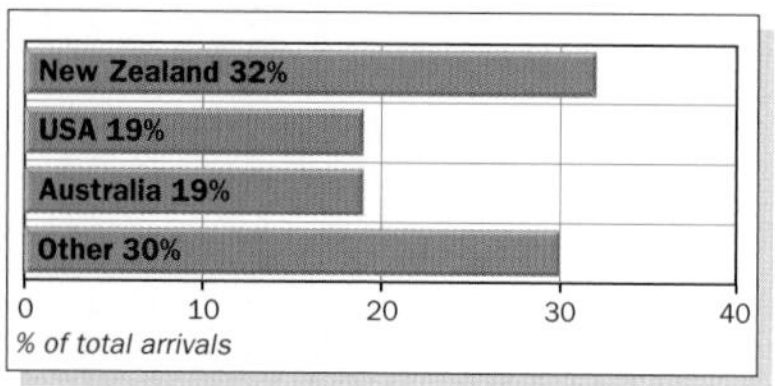
New Zealand 32%
USA 19%
Australia 19%
Other 30%
0
10
20
30
40
% of total arrivals

Tonga's main attractions are its tropical beaches. Flagging tourism has been boosted by political insecurity in the Solomon Islands and Fiji. Fears have been expressed that too many visitors may erode traditional Tongan culture.

Mountainous scenery *typical of the westerly islands. Tonga's 170 islands are scattered over a wide expanse of the South Pacific. Only 45 are inhabited.*

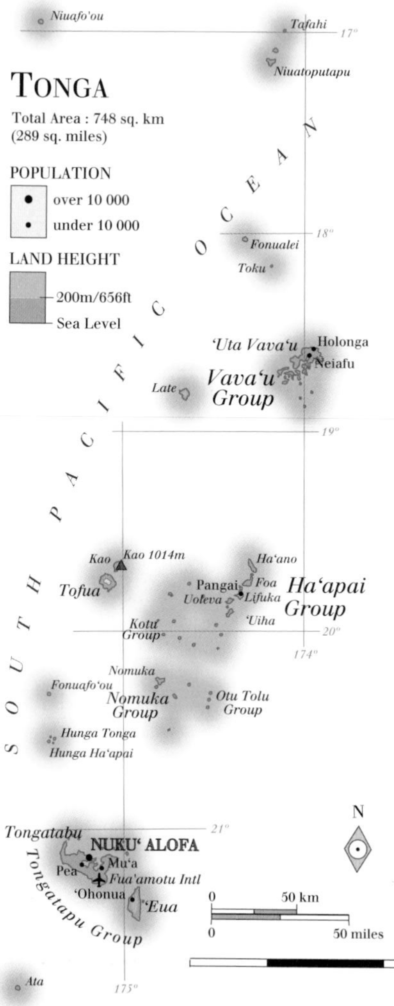
TONGA
Total Area : 748 sq. km (289 sq. miles)
POPULATION
over 10 000
under 10 000
LAND HEIGHT
200m/656ft
Sea Level
Niuafo'ou
Tafahi
Niuatoputapu
SOUTH PACIFIC OCEAN
Fonualei
Toku
'Uta Vava'u
Holonga
Neiafu
Late
Vava'u Group
Kao
Kao 1014m
Tofua
Ha'ano
Pangai
Foa
Uoleva
Lifuka
Ha'apai Group
'Uiha
Kotu Group
Nomuka
Fonuafo'ou
Nomuka Group
Otu Tolu Group
Hunga Tonga
Hunga Ha'apai
Tongatabu
NUKU' ALOFA
Mu'a
Pea
Fua'amotu Intl
'Ohonua
'Eua
Tongatapu Group
Ata
N
0
50 km
50 miles
17°
18°
19°
20°
21°
174°
175°

PEOPLE

Pop. density medium

English, Tongan

147/km² (382/mi²)

THE URBAN/RURAL POPULATION SPLIT

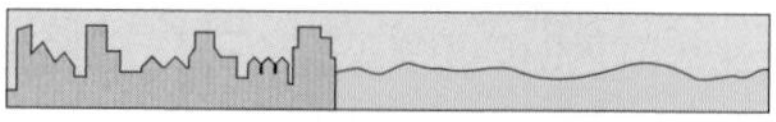
43%
57%

RELIGIOUS PERSUASION

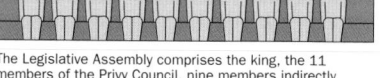

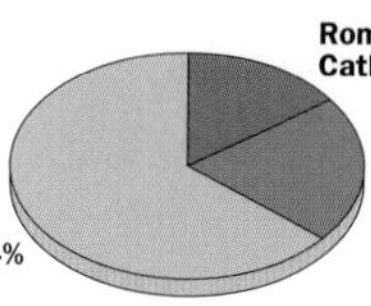
Roman Catholic 15%
Other 21%
Free Wesleyan 64%

Tonga has strong ethnic ties with eastern Fiji, and there has traditionally been considerable movement between the two states. Tongans see themselves as unique among Pacific islanders, retaining their monarchy and never having been fully colonized. Respect for traditional institutions and values remains high. Tongans are strong churchgoers; churches often fund education. A new generation of Western-educated Tongans queries some traditional attitudes. Apparent ethnic tensions and a drive to improve native employment prompted the government to ban unskilled immigrants in 2001.

POLITICS

Nonparty elections

2002/2005

H.M. King Taufa'ahau Tupou IV

AT THE LAST ELECTION

Legislative Assembly 30 seats

The Legislative Assembly comprises the king, the 11 members of the Privy Council, nine members indirectly elected by nobles, and nine directly elected members. There are no political parties: of those elected in 2002, seven were part of the Human Rights and Democracy Movement.

The main power brokers in Tongan politics are the king, the noble establishment, and the landowners. King Taufa'ahau, on the throne since 1965, frequently exercises kingly powers. His resistance to growing calls for democracy was typified in 2000 by his appointing his conservative third son, Prince 'Ulukalala Lavaka Ata, as premier for life, overlooking his reformist eldest son. There is an increasingly vocal opposition which was roused to anger in 2003 when the king, in an effort to silence permanently the independent *Taimi 'o Tonga* newspaper, demanded a revision of the constitution to prevent the courts from questioning his decrees.

T

WORLD AFFAIRS

Joined UN in 1999

ACP | Comm | PC | PIF | ADB

In 1998 Tonga broke off ties with Taiwan and instead forged links with China. The discovery of arms bound for Palestine aboard a Tongan-registered vessel in 2002 raised international concern over the security of its flag-of-convenience registration system.

AID

Recipient

$20m (receipts)

Up 5% in 2001

Aid finances major infrastructure projects; Japan, Australia, and New Zealand are primary donors. After losing aid in 1997, Tonga fought to reclaim its Least Developed Country status, which guarantees funds.

DEFENSE

No compulsory military service

$2m (estimate)

No significant change

Tonga has a small defense force, which includes both regulars and reserves. Tongan police assisted in security efforts in the Solomon Islands in 2000.

ECONOMICS

Inflation 2.2% p.a. (1990–2001)

$154m

1.491 pa'anga (1.781)

SCORE CARD

❑ World GNP Ranking	186th
❑ GNP per Capita	$1530
❑ Balance of Payments	Zero
❑ Inflation	8.3%
❑ Unemployment	13%

Strengths

Agriculture: contributes largest percentage of GDP. Tourism main source of hard currency earnings.

Weaknesses

Off main shipping routes. Aid-dependent. Importer of food. High youth unemployment. Corruption scandal in royal court in 2001.

EXPORTS

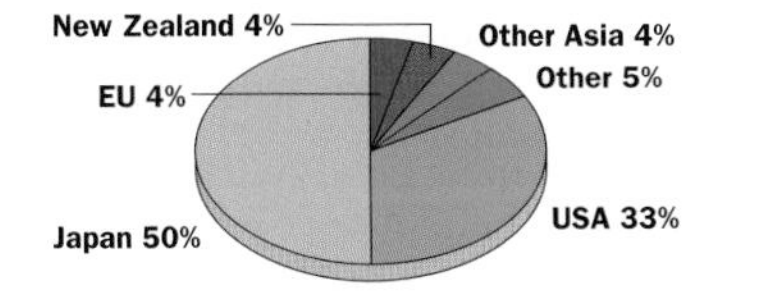
New Zealand 4%
Other Asia 4%
Other 5%
EU 4%
Japan 50%
USA 33%

IMPORTS

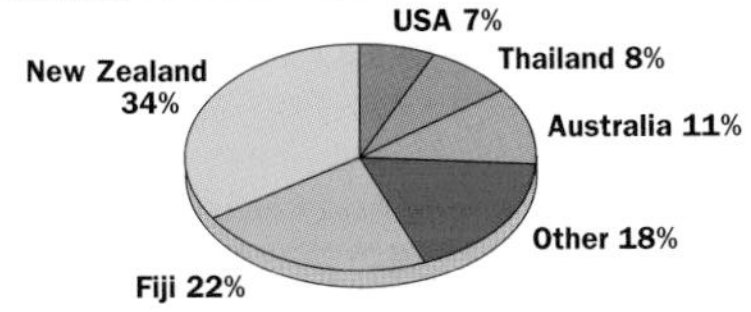
USA 7%
Thailand 8%
New Zealand 34%
Australia 11%
Other 18%
Fiji 22%

RESOURCES

Electric power 8000 kW

3531 tonnes

Not an oil producer

80,853 pigs, 12,500 goats, 300,000 chickens

None

Tonga has no strategic or mineral resources. Electricity is entirely generated from imported fuel. Recent exploration has failed to identify any oil reserves. Tongan waters contain large numbers of tuna.

ENVIRONMENT

Not available

5% (4.6% partially protected)

1.2 tonnes per capita

Many beaches in populated areas are affected by sand quarrying, and giant clams are under threat. Coral reefs are often poisoned and damaged in the search for fish. An increase in tourism could further disrupt the ecosystem.

MEDIA

TV ownership low

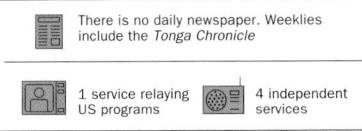

Daily newspaper circulation 72 per 1000 people

PUBLISHING AND BROADCAST MEDIA

There is no daily newspaper. Weeklies include the *Tonga Chronicle*

1 service relaying US programs

4 independent services

In 2003, the government banned the *Taimi 'o Tonga*, the country's only independent newspaper, raising concerns over freedom of speech.

CRIME

Death penalty not used in practice

113 prisoners

Crime is risng

Offenses such as breaking and entering have increased among young Tongans, along with unemployment. The practice of stranding young offenders on an uninhabited island has been questioned in parliament.

EDUCATION

School leaving age: 14

99%

364 students

Plans for a new national university were approved in 2000 following violence in Fiji, where Tongan students attend the University of the South Pacific. Scholarship schemes enable students to go abroad for higher education.

HEALTH

No welfare state health benefits

1 per 2273 people

Cerebrovascular, heart, and diarrheal diseases

Tonga has some modern health care facilities. However, patients have to be flown out to Australia or New Zealand for sophisticated surgery.

CHRONOLOGY

Originally discovered by the Polynesians, Tonga was visited by the Dutch in the 17th century and Capt. Cook in the 18th century. In the latter half of the 19th century, during the reign of King George Tupou I, the islands became a unified state after a period of civil war.

- ❑ **1875** First constitution established.
- ❑ **1900** Concern over German ambitions in region; Treaty of Friendship and Protection with UK.
- ❑ **1918–1965** Reign of Queen Salote Tupou III.
- ❑ **1958** Greater autonomy from UK enshrined in Friendship Treaty.
- ❑ **1965** King Taufa'ahau Tupou IV accedes on his mother's death.
- ❑ **1970** Full independence within British Commonwealth.
- ❑ **1988** Treaty allows US nuclear warships right of transit.
- ❑ **2000** King appoints third son as prime minister.
- ❑ **2001** Court jester steals US$20 million of state funds.
- ❑ **2002** Election sees strong showing by prodemocracy candidates, as in 1996 and 1999.

SPENDING

GDP/cap. increase

CONSUMPTION AND SPENDING

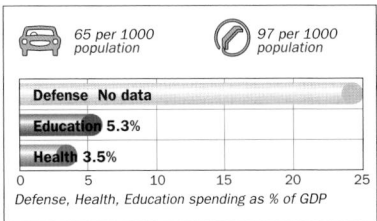

65 per 1000 population

97 per 1000 population

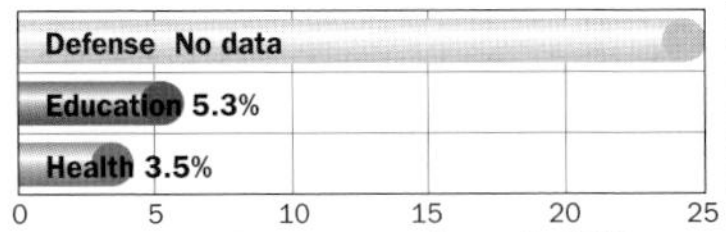
Defense No data
Education 5.3%
Health 3.5%
0
5
10
15
20
25

Defense, Health, Education spending as % of GDP

Tongans indulge in few ostentatious displays of wealth. The well-off provide financial support for relatives.

WORLD RANKING

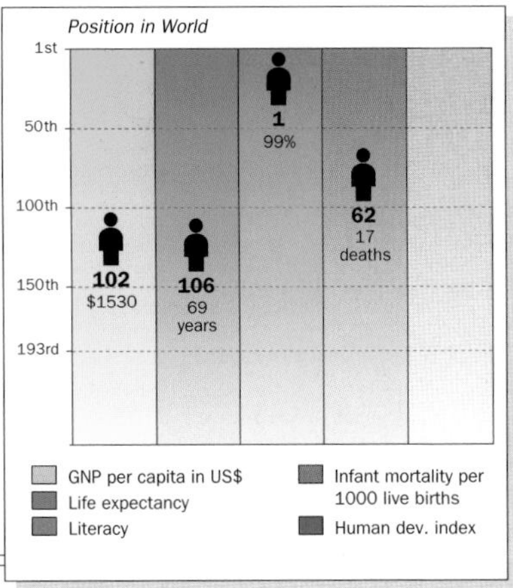
Position in World
1st
50th
100th
150th
193rd
102
$1530
106
69
years
1
99%
62
17
deaths
GNP per capita in US$
Life expectancy
Literacy
Infant mortality per 1000 live births
Human dev. index

T

TRINIDAD & TOBAGO

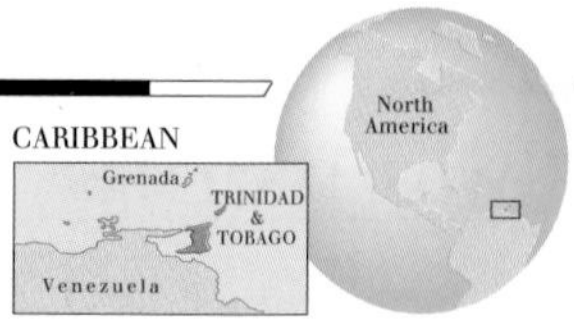
CARIBBEAN
Grenada
TRINIDAD & TOBAGO
Venezuela
North America

OFFICIAL NAME: Republic of Trinidad and Tobago **CAPITAL:** Port-of-Spain
POPULATION: 1.3 million **CURRENCY:** Trinidad and Tobago dollar **OFFICIAL LANGUAGE:** English

1962 | 1962 | Aug 31 | TT | -4 | +1868 | .tt

THE TWO ISLANDS OF Trinidad and Tobago are the most southerly of the Caribbean Windward Islands and lie just 15 km (9 miles) off the Venezuelan coast. They gained joint independence from Britain in 1962, and Tobago was given internal autonomy in 1987. The spectacular mountain ranges and large swamps are rich in tropical flora and fauna. Pitch Lake in Trinidad is the world's largest natural reservoir of asphalt.

CLIMATE

Tropical oceanic

WEATHER CHART FOR PORT-OF-SPAIN

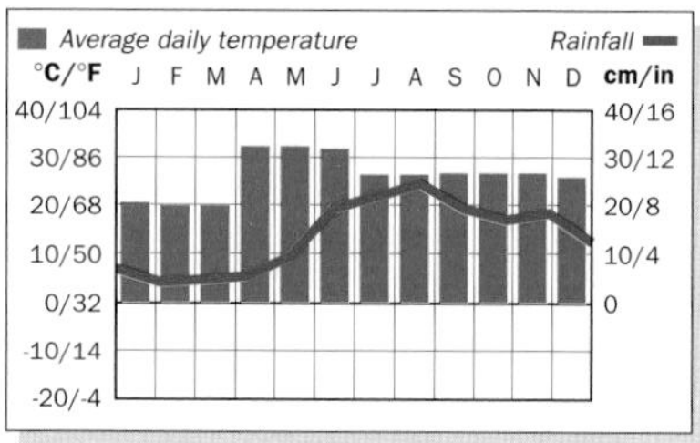
Average daily temperature
Rainfall
°C/°F J F M A M J J A S O N D cm/in
40/104
30/86
20/68
10/50
0/32
-10/14
-20/-4
40/16
30/12
20/8
10/4
0

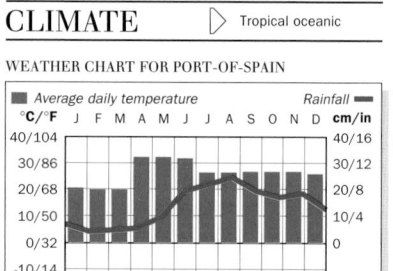

The islands are a little warmer than others in the Caribbean and escape the hurricanes, which pass by to the north.

TRANSPORTATION

Drive on left

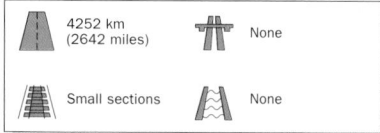

Piarco International, Port-of-Spain 1.92m passengers

67 ships 26,600 grt

THE TRANSPORTATION NETWORK

4252 km (2642 miles) | None
Small sections | None

The road network is well developed; there are taxis or minibuses for set routes. National carrier BWIA and Air Caribbean operate Trinidad–Tobago flights. BWIA also flies to the US.

TOURISM

Visitors : Population 1:3.4

379,000 visitors

Down 1% in 2002

MAIN TOURIST ARRIVALS

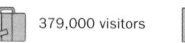

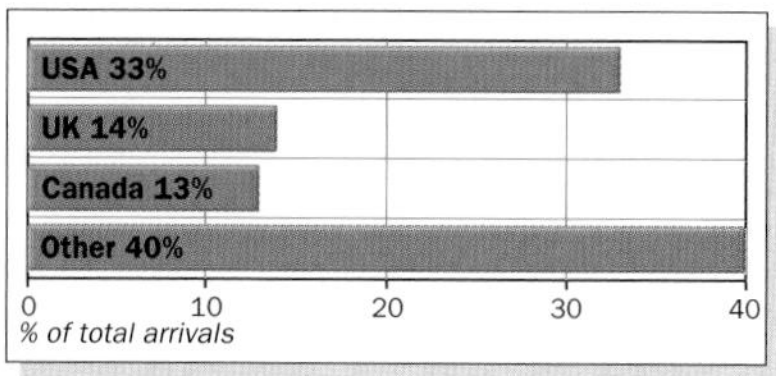
USA 33%
UK 14%
Canada 13%
Other 40%
0
10
20
30
40
% of total arrivals

Oil revenue meant that Trinidad was one of the last Caribbean states to develop tourism. Most is centered on Tobago (said to be the model for the island in *Robinson Crusoe*), famous for its huge variety of South American wildlife, including 210 species of tropical bird.

TRINIDAD & TOBAGO

Total Area : 5128 sq. km (1980 sq. miles)

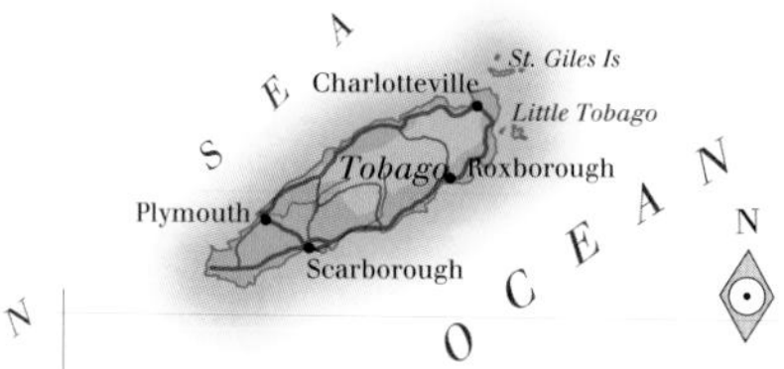
St. Giles Is
Charlotteville
Little Tobago
Tobago
Roxborough
Plymouth
Scarborough
SEA
ATLANTIC OCEAN
N

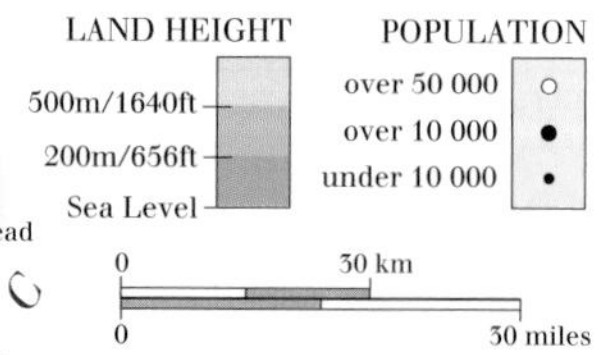
LAND HEIGHT
500m/1640ft
200m/656ft
Sea Level
POPULATION
over 50 000
over 10 000
under 10 000
0
30 km
0
30 miles

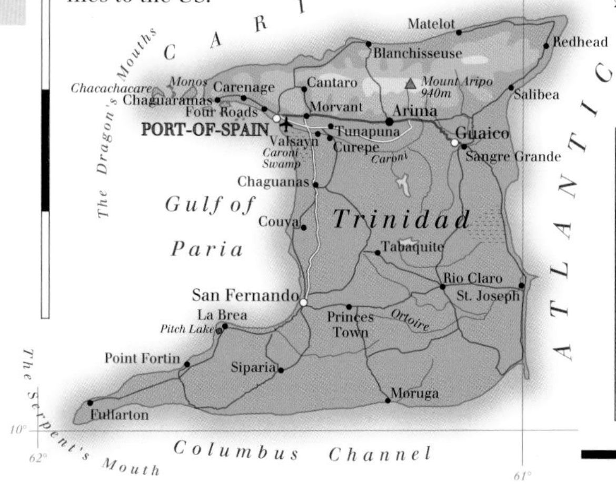
CARIBBEAN
Matelot
Redhead
Blanchisseuse
The Dragon's Mouths
Chacachacare
Monos
Chaguaramas
Carenage
Four Roads
Cantaro
Mount Aripo 940m
Salibea
Morvant
Arima
PORT-OF-SPAIN
Tunapuna
Valsayn
Curepe
Caroni Swamp
Caroni
Guaico
Sangre Grande
Chaguanas
Gulf of Paria
Couva
Trinidad
Tabaquite
Rio Claro
St. Joseph
San Fernando
La Brea
Pitch Lake
Princes Town
Ortoire
Point Fortin
Siparia
Moruga
Fullarton
The Serpent's Mouth
Columbus Channel
10°
62°
61°
11°

Tobago's white sand beaches, verdant landscape, and natural anchorages have enabled it to develop a thriving tourist industry.

PEOPLE

Pop. density high

English Creole, English, Hindi, French, Spanish

253/km² (656/mi²)

THE URBAN/RURAL POPULATION SPLIT

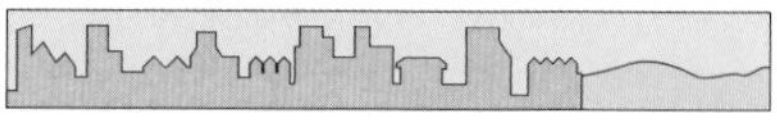
75%
25%

ETHNIC MAKEUP

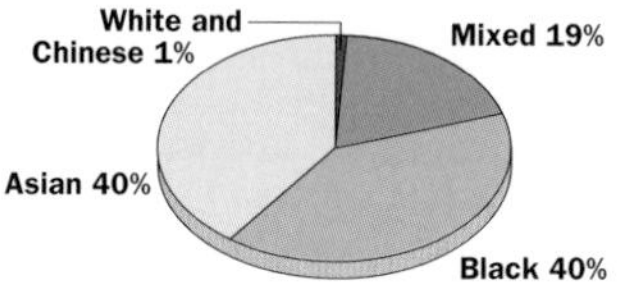
White and Chinese 1%
Mixed 19%
Asian 40%
Black 40%

Trinidad's south Asian community is the largest in the Caribbean and holds on to its Muslim and Hindu inheritance. Ethnic tensions with the predominantly Christian black Trinidadians continue to exist but are muted. Blacks form the majority on Tobago.

POLITICS

Multiparty elections

L. House 2002/2007
U. House 2002/2007

President Maxwell Richards

AT THE LAST ELECTION

House of Representatives 36 seats

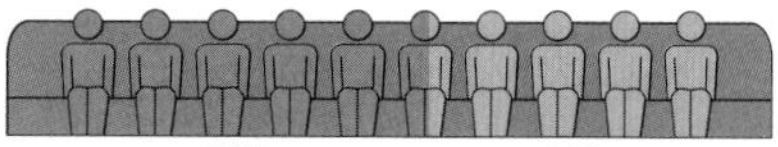
56% PNM
44% UNC

PNM = People's National Movement
UNC = United National Congress

Senate 31 seats

Senators are appointed by the president, including 16 nominated by the prime minister and six by the leader of the opposition

Politics is mainly polarized by race. The increasingly right-wing, and largely black-based, PNM dominated politics from independence in 1962 to the 1990s, leading to political fragmentation and an attempted coup by Muslim extremists in 1990. The UNC's Basdeo Panday, the first ethnic Asian prime minister, was elected in 1995. In elections six years later, the UNC's outright majority was reduced to a tie with the PNM. The political stalemate led to new elections being called in 2002, which were decisively won by the PNM, with Patrick Manning remaining in office as prime minister.

T

WORLD AFFAIRS

Joined UN in 1962

ACS | Caricom | Comm | NAM | OAS

Foreign policy aims for maximum economic advantage from the booming oil and gas industry and rapidly growing industrial and financial sectors. There are close economic ties with the US and good relations with the EU. Trinidad is strongly in favor of regional integration. Sea border disputes with Venezuela relate to fishing and marine oil rights.

AID

Recipient

No net receipts

Loan repayments exceeded aid received in 2001

Aid is modest: China provided an interest-free loan of US$20 million in 2000 to help small businesses.

DEFENSE

No compulsory military service

US$67m

Up 8% in 2001

Defense forces comprise a land army and a coast guard (with air wing), used to patrol fishing grounds.

ECONOMICS

Inflation 5.4% p.a. (1990–2001)

US$7.81bn

6.14 Trinidad and Tobago dollars (6.087)

SCORE CARD

❑ WORLD GNP RANKING	96th
❑ GNP PER CAPITA	US$5960
❑ BALANCE OF PAYMENTS	–US$644m
❑ INFLATION	5.6%
❑ UNEMPLOYMENT	13%

STRENGTHS

Oil, which accounts for 70% of export earnings. Gas increasingly exploited to support new industries. Methanol, ammonia, iron, and steel exports. Tourism, especially on Tobago. Strong commercial and financial sectors.

WEAKNESSES

High dependence on oil and gas. Failing sugar industry and persistent pockets of unemployment.

EXPORTS

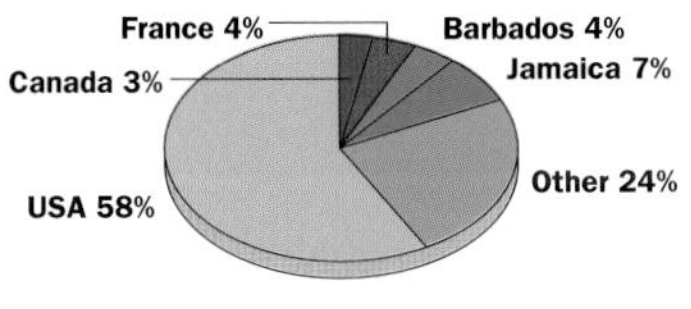
France 4%
Barbados 4%
Canada 3%
Jamaica 7%
Other 24%
USA 58%

IMPORTS

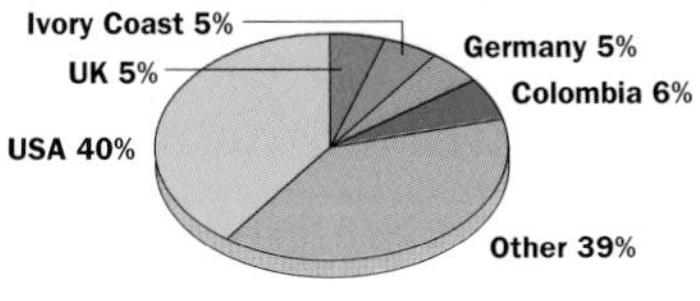
Ivory Coast 5%
UK 5%
Germany 5%
Colombia 6%
USA 40%
Other 39%

RESOURCES

Electric power 1.3m kW

9683 tonnes

155,000 b/d (reserves 700m barrels)

64,000 pigs, 60,500 goats, 25m chickens

Oil, natural gas, asphalt, iron

Oil and gas are major resources. Big offshore gas and oil finds in 1998 included the country's largest discovery of crude oil in 25 years.

ENVIRONMENT

Sustainability rank: 121st

6% (4% partially protected)

19.5 tonnes per capita

Spillages from oil tankers threaten coastal conservation areas such as the Caroni Swamp, with its many species of butterflies. Forest fires due to periodic drought, and traffic-related pollution and congestion are serious concerns.

MEDIA

TV ownership high

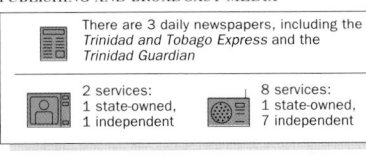

Daily newspaper circulation 123 per 1000 people

PUBLISHING AND BROADCAST MEDIA

There are 3 daily newspapers, including the *Trinidad and Tobago Express* and the *Trinidad Guardian*

2 services: 1 state-owned, 1 independent

8 services: 1 state-owned, 7 independent

Television schedules are dominated by US programs, while around carnival time radio stations play little but calypso.

CRIME

Death penalty in use

4794 prisoners

Up 3% in 1999–2001

Narcotics-related crime increases the murder rate. The country was party to the decision taken in 2001 to replace the authority of the UK's Privy Council with a Caribbean Court of Justice.

EDUCATION

School leaving age: 11

98%

8614 students

Education is based on the former British system. Most students go on to the University of the West Indies; Trinidad hosts the St. Augustine campus. Wealthy Trinidadians, however, go to universities in the US.

HEALTH

Welfare state health benefits

1 per 1266 people

Heart disease, cancers, diabetes, accidents, violence

Oil wealth has given Trinidad a better public health service than most Caribbean states and more private clinics, mainly serving the expatriate community. However, treatment delays are a problem. The spread of HIV/AIDS is of particular concern on Tobago.

CHRONOLOGY

Britain seized Trinidad from Spain in 1797 and Tobago from France in 1802. They were unified in 1888.

- ❑ **1956** Eric Williams founds PNM and wins general election, mainly with support from blacks.
- ❑ **1958–1961** Member of West Indian Federation.
- ❑ **1962** Independence.
- ❑ **1970** Black Power demonstrations.
- ❑ **1980** Tobago gets own House of Assembly; internal autonomy 1987.
- ❑ **1990–1991** Premier taken hostage in failed fundamentalist coup. PNM returned to power.
- ❑ **1995** UNC's Basdeo Panday is first ethnic Asian prime minister.
- ❑ **1998–1999** Trinidad withdraws from international human rights bodies over death sentences.
- ❑ **2001** Elections result in tie.
- ❑ **2002** PNM wins fresh elections.

SPENDING

GDP/cap. increase

CONSUMPTION AND SPENDING

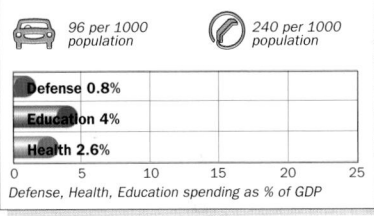

96 per 1000 population

240 per 1000 population

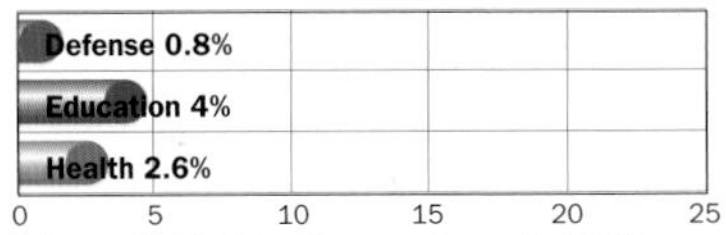
Defense 0.8%
Education 4%
Health 2.6%
0
5
10
15
20
25

Defense, Health, Education spending as % of GDP

In Trinidad wealth disparities between the affluent oil-rich business elite, many of whom are expatriate, and farm laborers are particularly marked. Service workers in Tobago's high-value tourism sector are poorly paid. Rural poverty in the interior, particularly among south Asian Trinidadian farmers, is a serious problem.

WORLD RANKING

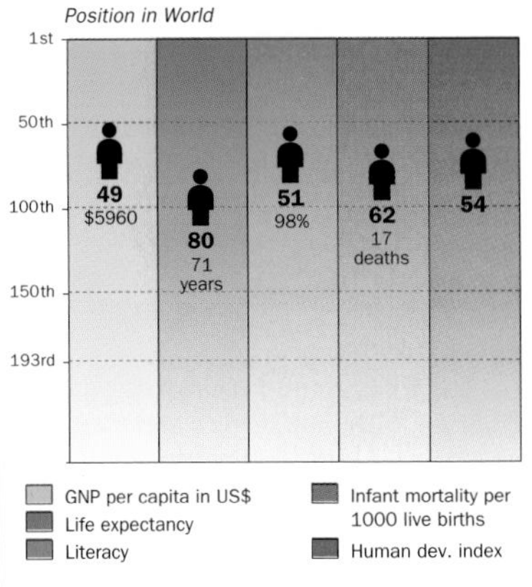
Position in World
1st
50th
100th
150th
193rd
49
$5960
80
71
years
51
98%
62
17
deaths
54
GNP per capita in US$
Life expectancy
Literacy
Infant mortality per 1000 live births
Human dev. index

T

TUNISIA

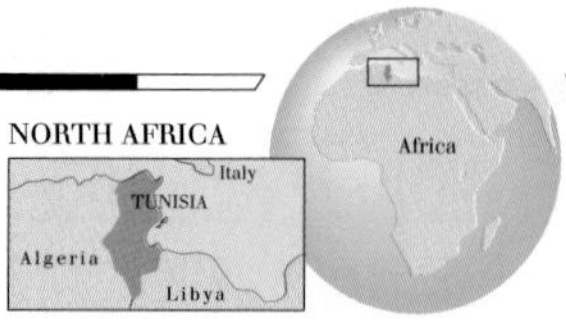
NORTH AFRICA
Italy
TUNISIA
Algeria
Libya
Africa

OFFICIAL NAME: Republic of Tunisia **CAPITAL:** Tunis
POPULATION: 9.7 million **CURRENCY:** Tunisian dinar **OFFICIAL LANGUAGE:** Arabic

1956 | 1956 | March 20 | TN | +1 | +216 | .tn

NORTH AFRICA'S SMALLEST country, Tunisia lies sandwiched between Libya and Algeria. The populous north is mountainous and fertile in places and has a long Mediterranean coastline. The south is largely desert. Habib Bourguiba ruled the country from independence in 1956 until a bloodless coup in 1987. Under President Ben Ali, the government has slowly moved toward multiparty democracy, but is challenged by Islamic fundamentalists. Closer ties with the EU, whose members include Tunisia's main trading partners, were strengthened through the first Euro-Mediterranean conference held in 1995. Manufacturing and tourism are expanding.

CLIMATE

Mediterranean/ hot desert

WEATHER CHART FOR TUNIS

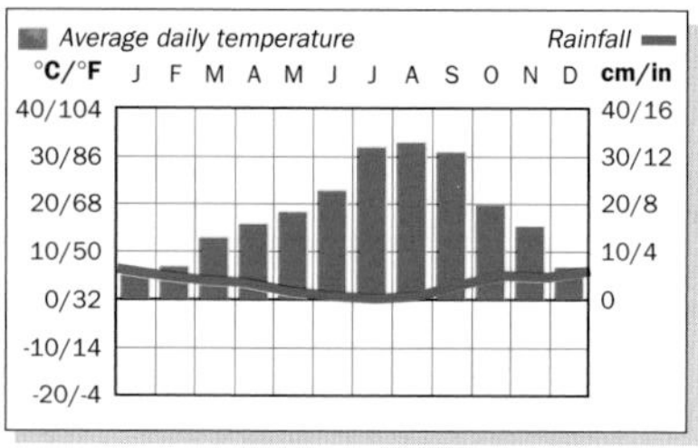
Average daily temperature
Rainfall
°C/°F J F M A M J J A S O N D cm/in
40/104
30/86
20/68
10/50
0/32
-10/14
-20/-4
40/16
30/12
20/8
10/4
0

Tunisia is hot in summer. The north is often wet and windy in winter. The far south is arid. The spring brings the dry, dusty *chili* wind from the Sahara.

TRANSPORTATION

Drive on right

Carthage, Tunis 3.21m passengers

77 ships 202,700 grt

THE TRANSPORTATION NETWORK

18,226 km (11,325 miles)

Highway from Tunis to Carthage airport

2142 km (1331 miles)

None

Tunisia has six international airports. A highway from Tunis to Carthage airport opened in 1993. Tunis has both a modern light metro system and a suburban railroad line. The southern third of the country has few roads.

TOURISM

Visitors : Population 1:1.9

5.06m visitors

Down 6% in 2002

MAIN TOURIST ARRIVALS

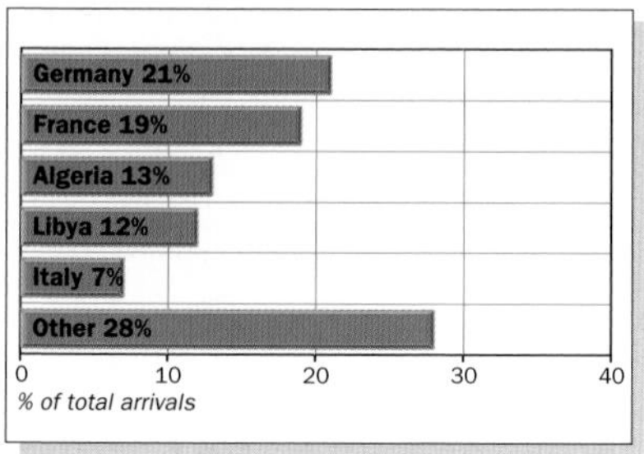
Germany 21%
France 19%
Algeria 13%
Libya 12%
Italy 7%
Other 28%
0
10
20
30
40
% of total arrivals

Tourists have flocked to Tunisia since the 1960s, attracted by its winter sunshine, beaches, desert, and archaeological remains. One of the Mediterranean's cheapest package destinations, Tunisia attracts almost three million European visitors a year, though some tourists are deterred by the fear of attacks by Islamists. In 2002, 14 German tourists were killed by a suicide bombing on the island of Jerba.

Tourism employs more than 200,000 people and is a focus of investment. However, concern about its environmental impact is growing.

PEOPLE

Pop. density medium

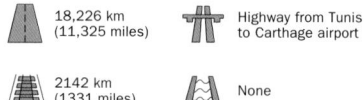

Arabic, French

62/km² (162/mi²)

THE URBAN/RURAL POPULATION SPLIT

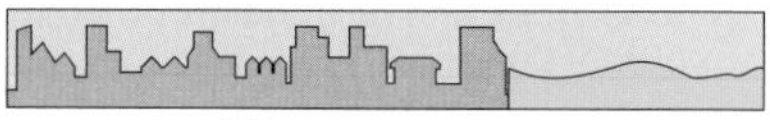
66%
34%

RELIGIOUS PERSUASION

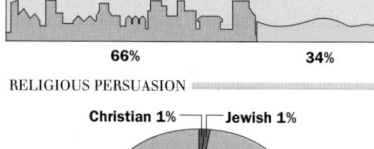

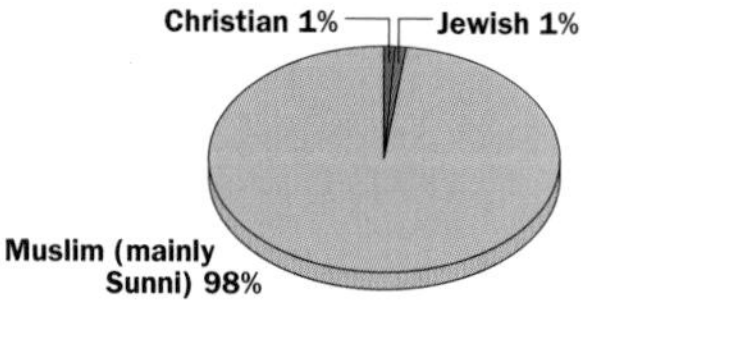
Christian 1%
Jewish 1%
Muslim (mainly Sunni) 98%

ETHNIC MAKEUP

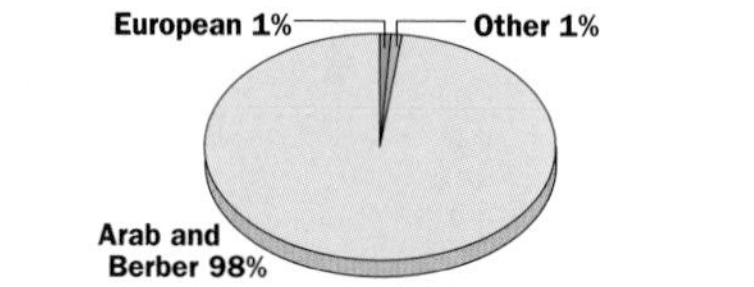
European 1%
Other 1%
Arab and Berber 98%

The population is almost entirely Muslim, of Arab and Berber descent, although there are Jewish and Christian minorities. Many Tunisians still live in extended family groups, in which three or four generations are represented.

Tunisia has traditionally been one of the most liberal Arab states. The 1956 Personal Statutes Code of President Bourguiba gave women fuller rights than in any other Arab country. Further legislation has since given women the right to custody of children in divorce cases, made family violence against women punishable by law, and helped divorced women to get alimony. Family planning and contraception were made freely available in the 1960s. Tunisia's population growth rate has halved since the 1980s. Women make up 31% of the total workforce and 35% of the industrial workforce. Company ownership by women is steadily increasing; politics, however, remains an exclusively male preserve.

These freedoms are threatened by the growth in recent years of Islamic fundamentalism, which also worries the mainly French-speaking political and business elite who wish to strengthen links with Europe.

The Ben Ali regime has been criticized for its actions against Islamist activists. Despite continuing condemnation of its human rights record, the government's efforts to foster democracy were praised in 2002 when it received the "Mediterranean Award," given by European human rights leagues.

POPULATION AGE BREAKDOWN

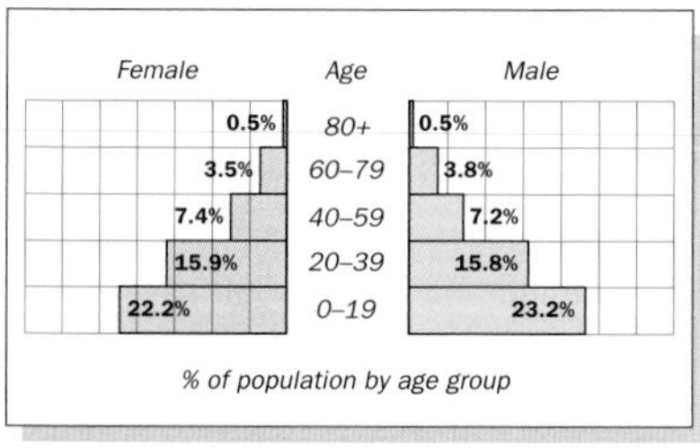
Female
Age
Male
0.5% 80+ 0.5%
3.5% 60–79 3.8%
7.4% 40–59 7.2%
15.9% 20–39 15.8%
22.2% 0–19 23.2%
% of population by age group

Roman remains *in the western Tozeur region. Diverse archaeological remains can be found throughout Tunisia.*

T

POLITICS

Multiparty elections

1999/2004

President Zine al-Abidine Ben Ali

AT THE LAST ELECTION

Chamber of Deputies 182 seats

4% PUP
3% MR
81% RCD
7% MDS
4% UDU
1% SLP

RCD = Constitutional Democratic Rally **MDS** = Movement of Social Democrats **PUP** = Popular Unity Party **UDU** = Unionist Democratic Union **MR** = Movement for Renewal **SLP** = Social Liberal Party

***President Ben Ali** became head of state in 1987.*

***Mohammed Ghannouchi,** prime minister since 1999.*

Formally a multiparty democracy since 1988, Tunisia is still dominated by the RCD and President Ben Ali.

PROFILE

President Ben Ali has made some effort to liberalize the political system. The life presidency has been abolished, and a proliferation of political parties encouraged. A number of parliamentary seats are allocated to opposition parties in proportion to the number of votes won. Nevertheless, the RCD won overwhelmingly in the 1994 and 1999 elections. Since 1994 there has been evidence of a renewed crackdown against the opposition. Measures to promote human rights and further democratization were overshadowed in 2002 when a referendum on constitutional change gave Ben Ali a mandate to stand for a further two terms.

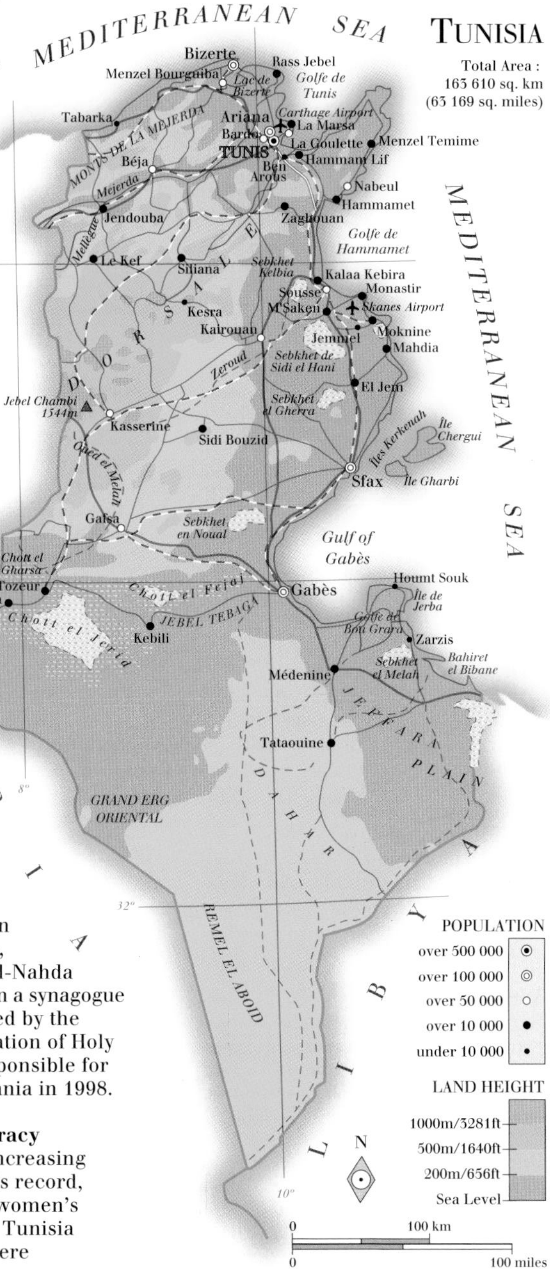
MEDITERRANEAN SEA
TUNISIA
Total Area :
163 610 sq. km
(63 169 sq. miles)
Bizerte
Menzel Bourguiba
Rass Jebel
Lac de Bizerte
Golfe de Tunis
Tabarka
Ariana
Carthage Airport
La Marsa
Bardo
TUNIS
La Goulette
Menzel Temime
Hammam Lif
Ben Arous
Béja
MONTS DE LA MEJERDA
Mejerda
Nabeul
Hammamet
Jendouba
Zaghouan
Golfe de Hammamet
Mellègue
Le Kef
Siliana
Sebkhet Kelbia
Kalaa Kebira
Sousse
Monastir
M'Saken
Skanes Airport
Kesra
Kairouan
Jemmel
Moknine
Mahdia
DORSALE
Zeroud
Sebkhet de Sidi el Hani
El Jem
Jebel Chambi 1544m
Kasserine
Sebkhet el Gherra
Îles Kerkenah
Île Chergui
Sidi Bouzid
Oued el Melah
Sfax
Île Gharbi
MEDITERRANEAN SEA
Sebkhet en Noual
Gafsa
Gulf of Gabès
Chott el Gharsa
Tozeur
Nefta
Chott el Fejaj
Gabès
Houmt Souk
Île de Jerba
JEBEL TEBAGA
Chott el Jerid
Kebili
Golfe de Bou Grara
Zarzis
Sebkhet el Melah
Bahiret el Bibane
Médenine
JEFFARA PLAIN
Tataouine
DAHAR
GRAND ERG ORIENTAL
REMEL EL ABOID
ALGERIA
LIBYA
POPULATION
over 500 000
over 100 000
over 50 000
over 10 000
under 10 000
LAND HEIGHT
1000m/3281ft
500m/1640ft
200m/656ft
Sea Level
N
0
100 km
0
100 miles

MAIN POLITICAL ISSUES

Fundamentalism

The RCD has clamped down on Islamic fundamentalists, particularly the outlawed al-Nahda (Renewal Party). An attack on a synagogue in Jerba in 2002 was claimed by the Islamic Army for the Liberation of Holy Places, the same group responsible for attacks in Kenya and Tanzania in 1998.

Human rights and democracy

The RCD has been under increasing attack over its human rights record, despite its commitment to women's rights. The activities of the Tunisia League of Human Rights were suspended in 2001.

WORLD AFFAIRS

Joined UN in 1956

AL | AMU | OIF | NAM | OIC

A foreign policy priority is to strengthen contacts with the West, which have generally been good because of Tunisia's liberal economic and social policies. Attention is focused on the EU, Tunisia's main export market. A Euro-Mediterranean agreement signed in 1998 commits Tunisia and the EU to creating a free trade area by 2010 alongside closer political ties.

Tunis was host to the Palestine Liberation Organization after it was expelled from Lebanon. Relations with some Arab states, particularly Kuwait and Saudi Arabia, were soured by Tunisia's support for Iraq in the 1991 Gulf War. The government regards the political impact of Islamic fundamentalism in neighboring Algeria with concern. Relations with Libya are improving, helped by the fact that Tunisia turned a blind eye to sanctions busters operating through its territory.

CHRONOLOGY

Tunisia has been home to the Zenata Berbers since earliest times and its history is linked to the rise and fall of the Mediterranean-centered empires. Carthage (near present-day Tunis), founded by the Phoenicians in the 9th century BCE, became the hub of a 1000-year trading empire which linked European and African trading networks. Tunisia was then ruled by the Romans, Byzantines, Egyptians, Ottomans, and, finally, the French.

- ❑ **1883** La Marsa Treaty makes Tunisia a French protectorate, ending its semi-independence. Bey of Tunis remains monarch.
- ❑ **1900** Influx of French and Italians.
- ❑ **1920** Destour (Constitution) Party formed; calls for self-government.
- ❑ **1935** Habib Bourguiba forms Neo-Destour (New Constitution) Party.
- ❑ **1943** Defeat of Axis powers by British troops restores French rule.
- ❑ **1955** Internal autonomy. Bourguiba returns from exile.
- ❑ **1956** Independence. Bourguiba elected prime minister. Personal Statutes Code gives rights to women. Family planning introduced.
- ❑ **1957** Bey is deposed. Tunisia becomes republic with Bourguiba as first president.
- ❑ **1964** Neo-Destour made sole legal party; renamed Destour Socialist Party (PSD). Moderate socialist economic program is introduced.
- ❑ **1969** Agricultural collectivization program, begun 1964, abandoned. ➪

T

CHRONOLOGY *continued*

- **1974** Bourguiba elected president-for-life by National Assembly.
- **1974–1976** Hundreds imprisoned for belonging to "illegal organizations."
- **1978** Trade union movement, UGTT, holds 24-hour general strike; more than 50 killed in clashes. UGTT leadership replaced with PSD loyalists.
- **1980** New prime minister Muhammed Mazli ushers in greater political tolerance.
- **1981** Elections. Opposition groups allege electoral malpractice.
- **1984** Widespread riots after food price increases.
- **1986** Gen. Zine al-Abidine Ben Ali becomes interior minister. Four Islamic fundamentalists sentenced to death.
- **1987** Fundamentalist leader Rachid Ghannouchi arrested. Ben Ali becomes prime minister; takes over presidency after doctors certify Bourguiba senile. PSD renamed RCD.
- **1988** Most political prisoners released. Constitutional reforms introduce multiparty system and abolish life presidency. Two opposition parties legalized.
- **1989** Elections: RCD wins all seats, Ben Ali president. Fundamentalists take 13% of vote.
- **1990** Tunisia backs Iraq over invasion of Kuwait. Clampdown on fundamentalists intensifies.
- **1991** Abortive coup blamed on al-Nahda; over 500 arrests.
- **1993** Multiparty agreement on electoral reform.
- **1994** Presidential and legislative elections. Ben Ali, sole candidate, is reelected.
- **1996** MDS leader Mohammed Moada imprisoned.
- **1999** Ben Ali and RCD win elections.
- **2002** Referendum allows Ben Ali to stand for office after 2004. Suicide bomb attack in Jerba kills 14 German tourists.

AID

Recipient

$378m (receipts) — Up 70% in 2001

The EU and France are the two major international donors, providing over half of all bilateral aid. Japan, Germany, Italy, Spain, and Belgium are other important sources of assistance. As a result of strong economic growth, the ratios of external debt to GNP and of debt service to exports receipts have improved markedly since the early 1990s; Tunisia's total external debt is now estimated at just over half of GNP.

DEFENSE

Compulsory military service

$377m — Up 6% in 2001

Despite its small size – 35,000 troops, of which around two-thirds are conscripts – the military is a major political force. Its weaponry comes mainly from the US, and officer training is carried out in the US and France, as well as in Tunisia. Border security with Algeria was tightened in 1995 after Algerian Islamists attacked Tunisian border guards in protest against Tunisian support for Algerian security forces.

TUNISIAN ARMED FORCES

84 main battle tanks (54 M-60A3, 30 M-60A1)	27,000 personnel
19 patrol boats	4500 personnel
29 combat aircraft (12 F-5E/F, 12 L-59, 5 MB-326K/L)	3500 personnel
None	

ECONOMICS

Inflation 4.3% p.a. (1990–2001)

$20bn — 1.275 Tunisian dinars (1.38)

SCORE CARD

World GNP Ranking	62nd
GNP per Capita	$2070
Balance of Payments	–$910m
Inflation	1.9%
Unemployment	16%

EXPORTS

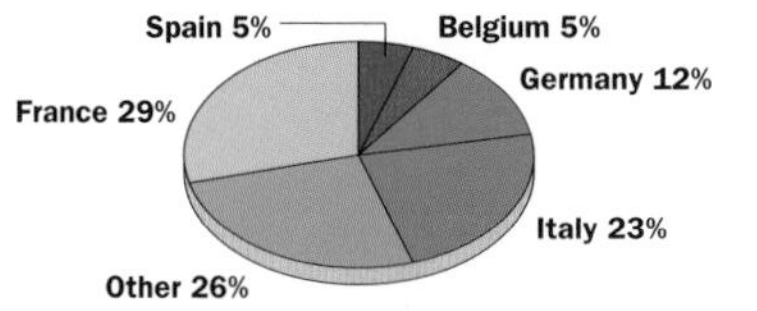
Spain 5%
Belgium 5%
Germany 12%
France 29%
Italy 23%
Other 26%

IMPORTS

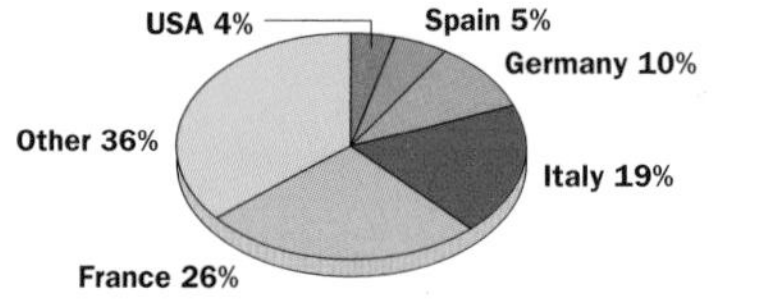
USA 4%
Spain 5%
Germany 10%
Other 36%
Italy 19%
France 26%

Strengths

Well-diversified economy, despite limited resources. Tourism. Oil and gas exports, also agricultural exports: olive oil, olives, citrus fruit, dates. Expanding manufacturing sector, average annual increase was 5.4% in 1990–1998; important sectors are textiles, construction materials, machinery, chemicals. European investment. Ranked as most competitive economy in Africa in World Economic Forum's 2000–2001 report.

Weaknesses

Dependence on growth of drought-prone agricultural sector. Growing domestic energy demand on oil and gas resources: net energy importer. High unemployment.

Profile

Since it began a process of structural adjustment in 1988, supported by the IMF and the World Bank, Tunisia has become an increasingly open, market-oriented economy. Real GDP growth has averaged 5% since 1987, rising to 6% in 2001. Annual inflation remained stable in 2000, despite higher food and energy prices. Prices have been freed, most state companies privatized, and import barriers reduced.

The balance of payments relies on fluctuating tourism receipts to offset a trade deficit. The government must also balance growth with better social provisions. The member states of the EU are Tunisia's main trading partners, accounting for well over 70% of its imports and nearly 80% of its exports; trade has increased significantly since 1999.

ECONOMIC PERFORMANCE INDICATOR

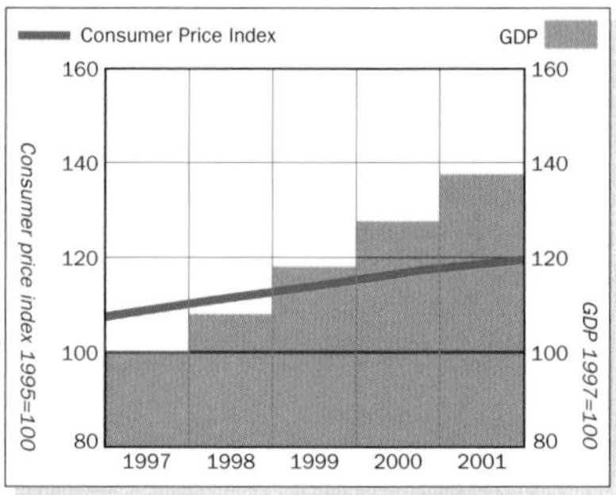
Consumer Price Index
GDP
160
140
120
100
80
1997
1998
1999
2000
2001
Consumer price index 1995=100
GDP 1997=100

TUNISIA : MAJOR BUSINESSES

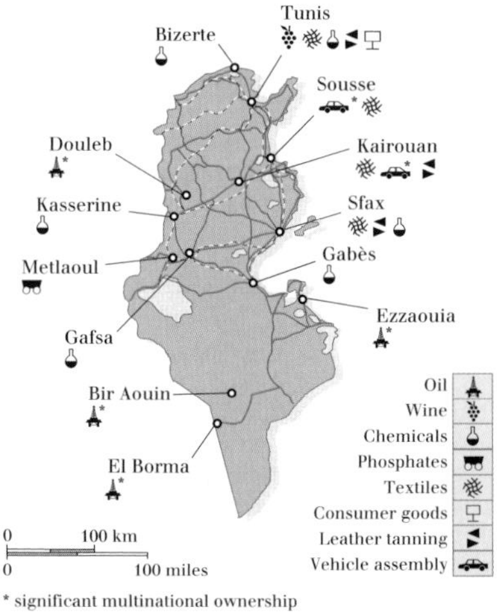
Tunis
Bizerte
Sousse
Douleb
Kairouan
Kasserine
Sfax
Metlaoui
Gabès
Ezzaouia
Gafsa
Bir Aouin
El Borma
Oil
Wine
Chemicals
Phosphates
Textiles
Consumer goods
Leather tanning
Vehicle assembly
0
100 km
0
100 miles
* significant multinational ownership

RESOURCES

Electric power 2.3m kW

97,103 tonnes

76,000 b/d (reserves 300m barrels)

6.85m sheep, 2.9m turkeys, 70m chickens

Phosphates, iron, zinc, lead, salt, oil, gas

ELECTRICITY GENERATION

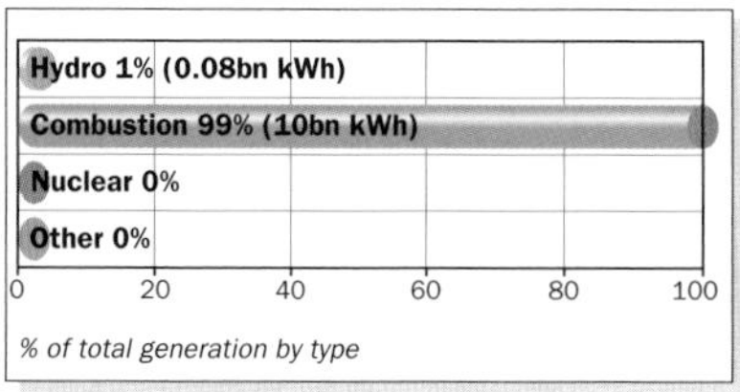
Hydro 1% (0.08bn kWh)
Combustion 99% (10bn kWh)
Nuclear 0%
Other 0%
0 20 40 60 80 100
% of total generation by type

Tunisia is a leading producer of phosphates for fertilizers, mainly from mines near Gafsa. Oil and gas are important exports, but growing domestic energy demands mean that Tunisia is now a net energy importer. Power plants are mainly gas- and oil-fired, with some hydropower.

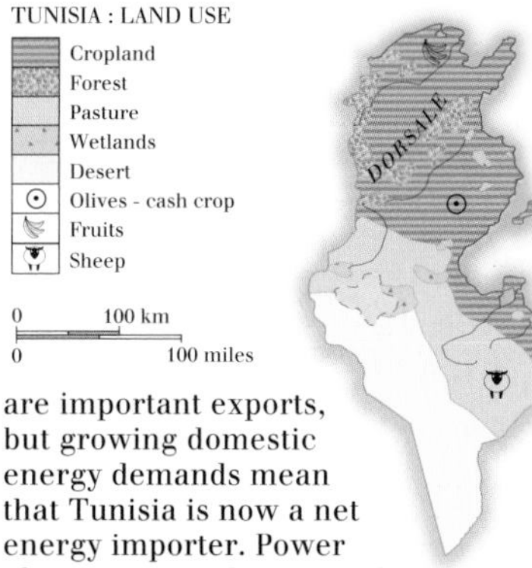
TUNISIA : LAND USE
Cropland
Forest
Pasture
Wetlands
Desert
Olives - cash crop
Fruits
Sheep
0 100 km
0 100 miles
DORSALE

ENVIRONMENT

Sustainability rank: 61st

0.3%

1.9 tonnes per capita

ENVIRONMENTAL TREATIES

Yes Yes Yes

Yes Yes Yes

Desertification is a serious problem in the largely arid central and southern regions. However, the dominant environmental issue is the rapid expansion of tourism since the 1980s. Large, insensitively designed hotel and resort developments, which do not fit in with the local architecture, are spoiling coastal areas such as the island of Jerba and Hammamet (though building height restrictions are applied here). Tourism is also making an impact on the fragile desert ecology of the south.

MEDIA

TV ownership medium

Daily newspaper circulation 23 per 1000 people

PUBLISHING AND BROADCAST MEDIA

There are 8 daily newspapers, including *al-Amal*, *La Presse de Tunisie*, and *As-Sabah*

2 state-owned services

1 state-owned service

Reforms since the late 1980s have in theory increased press freedom in Tunisia, traditionally considered a source of liberal ideas in the Arab world. In practice, government restrictions remain. The foreign press is also occasionally banned. Only the arrival of satellite TV from Europe has enabled people to receive a wide range of programs. The Internet is heavily censored.

CRIME

Death penalty in use

23,165 prisoners

Down 8% in 2000–2002

CRIME RATES

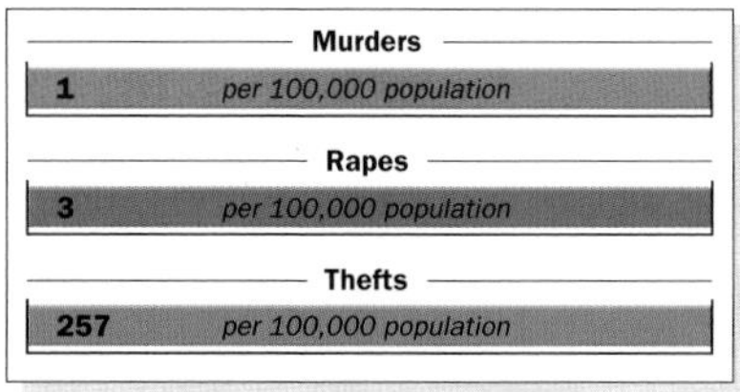
Murders
1 per 100,000 population
Rapes
3 per 100,000 population
Thefts
257 per 100,000 population

Street crime is unusual. However, Tunisia's poor human rights record has prompted criticism of its maltreatment of political and other detainees. Arbitrary arrests and torture while in police custody, especially of suspected Islamist activists, are routine.

EDUCATION

School leaving age: 16

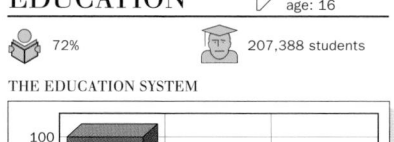

72%

207,388 students

THE EDUCATION SYSTEM

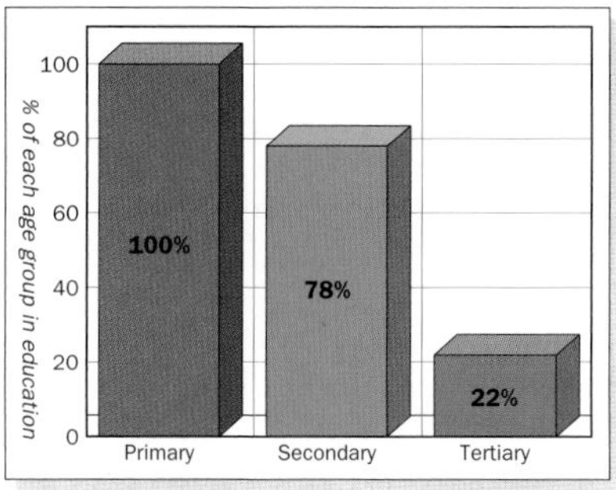
100
80
60
40
20
0
% of each age group in education
100%
78%
22%
Primary
Secondary
Tertiary

Education is compulsory for nine years from the age of six, with secondary education beginning at 12. Arabic is the first language in schools, but French is also taught, and is used almost exclusively in higher education. There are eight universities (one is private); student enrollment has doubled since 1995.

HEALTH

Welfare state health benefits

1 per 1429 people

Heart and cerebrovascular diseases

Well-developed family-planning facilities have almost halved Tunisia's birthrate over the past 30 years. The population growth rate has dropped from 3.2% to 1.1% – the lowest in the region. The mortality rate has been halved, to five per 1000 population, reflecting the extension of free medical services to over 70% of the population. While services lack sophistication, an umbrella of primary care facilities covers all but the most isolated rural communities. Regional committees organize care for the old, needy, and orphaned.

SPENDING

GDP/cap. increase

CONSUMPTION AND SPENDING

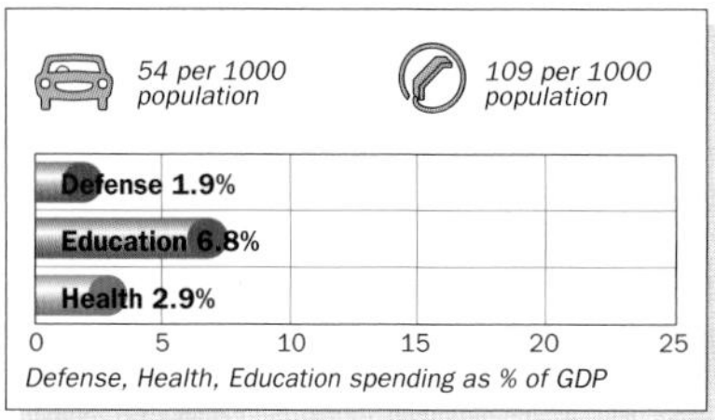
54 per 1000 population
109 per 1000 population
Defense 1.9%
Education 6.8%
Health 2.9%
0 5 10 15 20 25
Defense, Health, Education spending as % of GDP

Around 10% of Tunisians are estimated to live below the UN poverty line. The poorest in the community tend to live in the urban shanty towns, or *bidonvilles*. The Western-oriented elite has links with government or business.

Social security benefits cover sickness, old age, disability, and maternity, but not unemployment. The government is concerned that the lack of jobs is encouraging the spread of Islamic fundamentalism; economic growth is its medium-term solution to the problem. Special projects are being set up in the most deprived urban areas to offset the worst effects of poverty.

WORLD RANKING

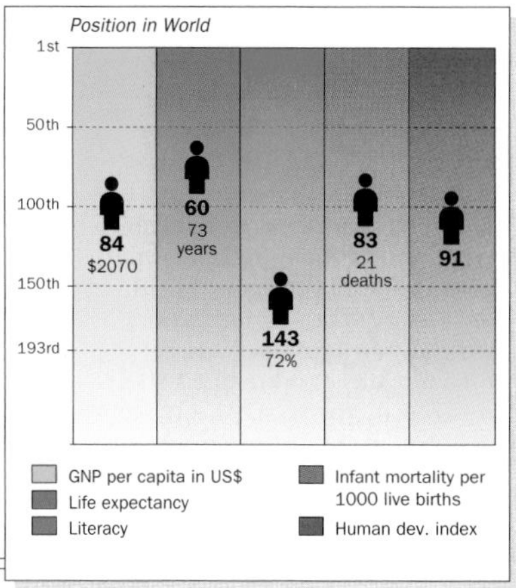
Position in World
1st
50th
100th
150th
193rd
84
$2070
60
73 years
143
72%
83
21 deaths
91
GNP per capita in US$
Life expectancy
Literacy
Infant mortality per 1000 live births
Human dev. index

T

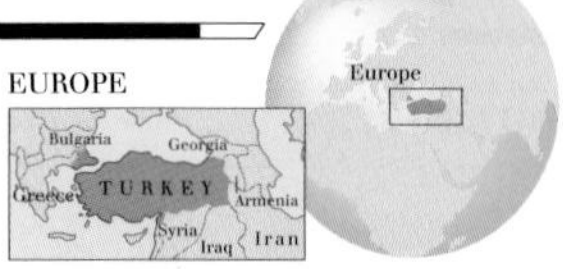
EUROPE
Europe
Bulgaria
Georgia
Greece
TURKEY
Armenia
Syria
Iraq
Iran

TURKEY

OFFICIAL NAME: Republic of Turkey **CAPITAL:** Ankara
POPULATION: 68.6 million **CURRENCY:** Turkish lira **OFFICIAL LANGUAGE:** Turkish

1923 | 1939 | Oct 29 | TR | +2 | +90 | .tr

THOUGH ITS TERRITORY lies mainly in western Asia, Turkey also includes the region of Eastern Thrace in Europe. It thus controls the entrance to the Black Sea, which is straddled by Turkey's largest city, Istanbul. Most Turks live in the western half of the country. The eastern and southeastern reaches of the Anatolia Plateau are Kurdish regions. Turkey's location gives it great strategic influence in the Black Sea, the Mediterranean, and the Middle East. Turkey lies on a major earthquake fault line, so that many towns are vulnerable to earthquakes such as that which devastated Izmit in 1999.

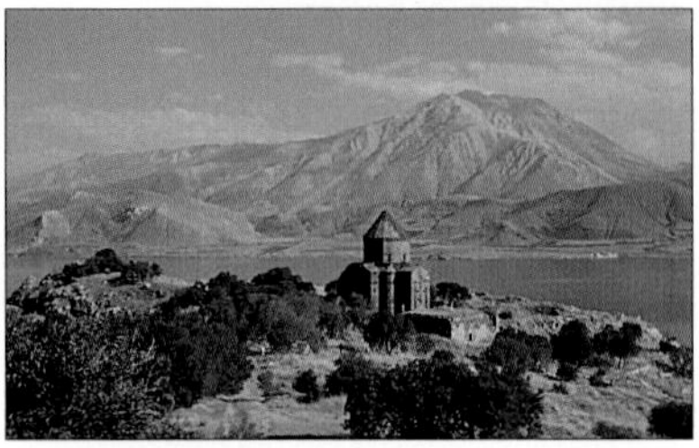

The Church of the Holy Cross, *on Akdamar Island in Lake Van, was built in the 10th century when Christianity was dominant in the region.*

CLIMATE

Mountain/ Mediterranean

WEATHER CHART FOR ANKARA

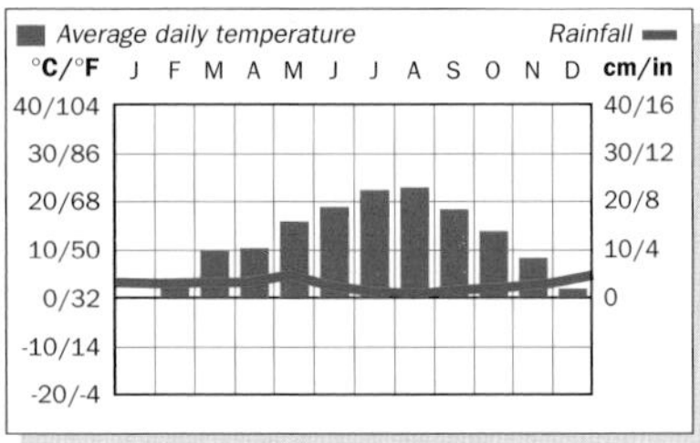
Average daily temperature
Rainfall
°C/°F J F M A M J J A S O N D cm/in
40/104 40/16
30/86 30/12
20/68 20/8
10/50 10/4
0/32 0
-10/14
-20/-4

Coastal regions have a Mediterranean climate. The interior has cold, snowy winters and hot, dry summers.

TRANSPORTATION

Drive on right

Atatürk International, Istanbul 13.4m passengers

1146 ships 5.9m grt

THE TRANSPORTATION NETWORK

106,976 km (66,472 miles)	1773 km (1102 miles)
8671 km (5388 miles)	1200 km (746 miles)

Recent rail projects include a high-speed link between Istanbul and Ankara, a line linking Turkey and Georgia, and a light rail system in Istanbul. An extensive network of ports and harbors includes Istanbul and Izmir.

PEOPLE

Pop. density medium

Turkish, Kurdish, Arabic, Circassian, Armenian, Greek, Georgian, Ladino

89/km² (231/mi²)

THE URBAN/RURAL POPULATION SPLIT

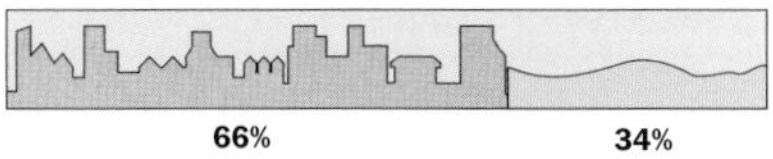
66%
34%

RELIGIOUS PERSUASION

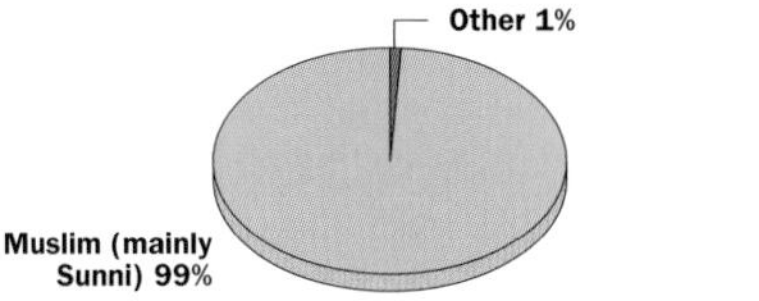
Other 1%
Muslim (mainly Sunni) 99%

ETHNIC MAKEUP

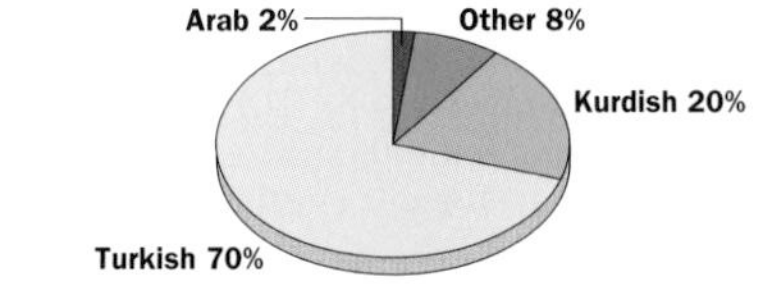
Arab 2%
Other 8%
Kurdish 20%
Turkish 70%

The Turks are racially diverse. Many are the descendants of refugees, often from the Balkans, but a strong sense of national identity is rooted in a shared language and religion. Most are Sunni Muslim, though a Shi'a community, including the heterodox Alawite sect, is growing fast. The largest minority are the Kurds, and there are some 500,000 Arabic speakers. While women have equal rights in law, men dominate political and even family life. In 2002 women gained the right to an equal portion in the case of divorce.

With population growth at 2%, Turkey is projected to have a larger population than any EU country by 2020.

POPULATION AGE BREAKDOWN

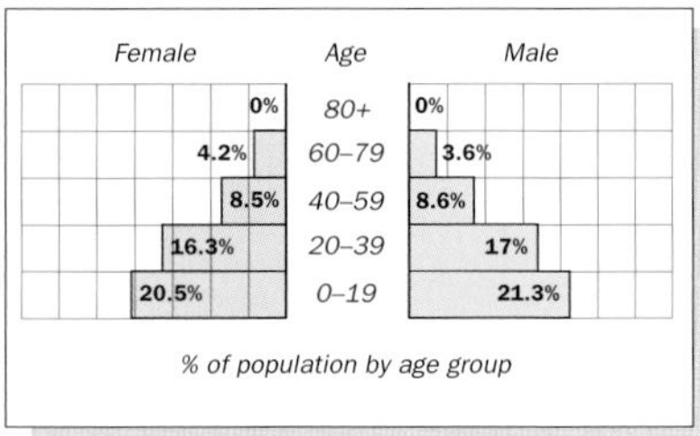
Female
Age
Male
0% 80+ 0%
4.2% 60–79 3.6%
8.5% 40–59 8.6%
16.3% 20–39 17%
20.5% 0–19 21.3%
% of population by age group

BULGARIA
B
Edirne
Kırklareli
İstanbul Boğazi
GREECE
Tekirdağ
Kâğıthane
İstanbul
Zong
Marmara Denizi
Yalova
İzmit
Adapazarı
Bolu
Bandırma
Dardenelles
Çanakkale
Bursa
Bilecik
Sakarya
Balıkesir
Eskişehir
Kütahya
AEGEAN SEA
Manisa
Akhisar
İzmir
Afyon
Uşak
Turgutlu
Aydın
Nazilli
Söke
Büyükmenderes
Denizli
Isparta
Burdur
Milas
Bodrum
Muğla
Antalya
Marmaris
Fethiye
Finike
Kaş
Antalya Körfezi
MEDITERRANE
40°
36°
28°

TOURISM

Visitors : Population 1:5.4

12.8m visitors

Up 19% in 2002

Visitors are attracted by fine beaches, classical sites such as Ephesus and Troy, and archaeological remains from the prehistoric to the Ottoman periods. Attacks on foreigners by Kurdish militants in 1994 hit the tourist trade, but business then recovered, and in 2000 tourists spent $7.6 billion. Visitor numbers dropped after the September 2001 attacks on the US, but bounced back in 2002.

MAIN TOURIST ARRIVALS

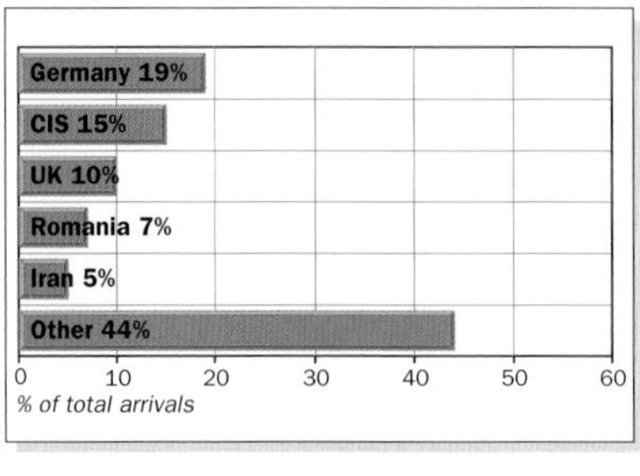
Germany 19%
CIS 15%
UK 10%
Romania 7%
Iran 5%
Other 44%
0 10 20 30 40 50 60
% of total arrivals

T

POLITICS

Multiparty elections

2002/2007

President Ahmet Necdet Sezer

AT THE LAST ELECTION

Turkish Grand National Assembly 550 seats

66%
AK
32%
CHP
2%
Ind

AK = Justice and Development Party
CHP = Republican People's Party **Ind** = Independents

Turkey is a multiparty republic. The president, who serves a seven-year term, appoints the prime minister.

Profile

The main ideological division in politics is Islamic–secular. In 2002 the powers of the National Security Council were restricted and its membership altered to give civilian dominance.

From 2000 on, the coalition government of Bulent Ecevit clashed with independent president Ahmet Necdet Sezer, and Ecevit's own ill health caused a political crisis in 2002. Fresh elections in November produced a stunning victory for the Islamist-dominated AK, while Ecevit's own party, and many others, failed even to gain representation in the legislature. AK leader Recep Tayyip Erdogan, banned from the 2002 election for previous militant remarks, succeeded his deputy as prime minister in March 2003.

Main Political Issues

Islamic fundamentalism

The popularity of Islamist parties has challenged Turkey's cherished identity as a secular state. In 1995 the Welfare Party (RP) became the largest party, forming the government in 1996. Ousted by the army in mid-1997, it was banned in 1998. Many of its members took refuge in its successor, the Virtue Party, which in turn was banned in 2001. The successor AK scored a comprehensive victory in 2002. It has asserted that it does not wish to impose a theocracy, but the army remains wary.

Kurdish separatism

From 1984 a bitter civil war was fought in southeast Turkey, killing thousands of people over the next two decades. In 1999 Abdullah Ocalan, leader of the secessionist Kurdistan Workers' Party (PKK),was sentenced to death, his sentence commuted in 2002 to life imprisonment. Meanwhile, the PKK disbanded and regrouped as a political organization committed to seeking equal rights for Kurds within Turkey (KADEK), under Ocalan's leadership. EU pressure has led to constitutional amendments lifting the harsh ban on broadcasting and education in Kurdish.

Human rights

Turkey's human rights record has been criticized internationally, especially for its curtailment of civil liberties, illegal executions, and the treatment of Kurds. Recent reforms have sought to meet EU standards. Civil liberties have been improved since 1995, and 2002 saw the banning of executions except in times of war, and the lifting of the last states of emergency in the southeast.

Recep Tayyip Erdogan, *AK leader and prime minister since 2003.*

Ahmet Necdet Sezer, *an independent, elected president in 2000.*

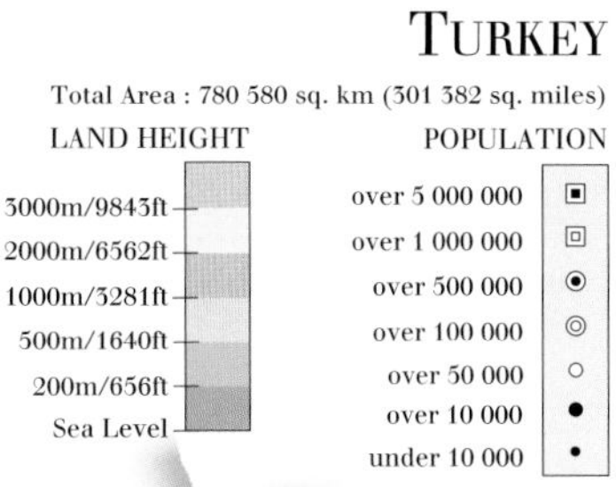
TURKEY
Total Area : 780 580 sq. km (301 382 sq. miles)
LAND HEIGHT
3000m/9843ft
2000m/6562ft
1000m/3281ft
500m/1640ft
200m/656ft
Sea Level
POPULATION
over 5 000 000
over 1 000 000
over 500 000
over 100 000
over 50 000
over 10 000
under 10 000

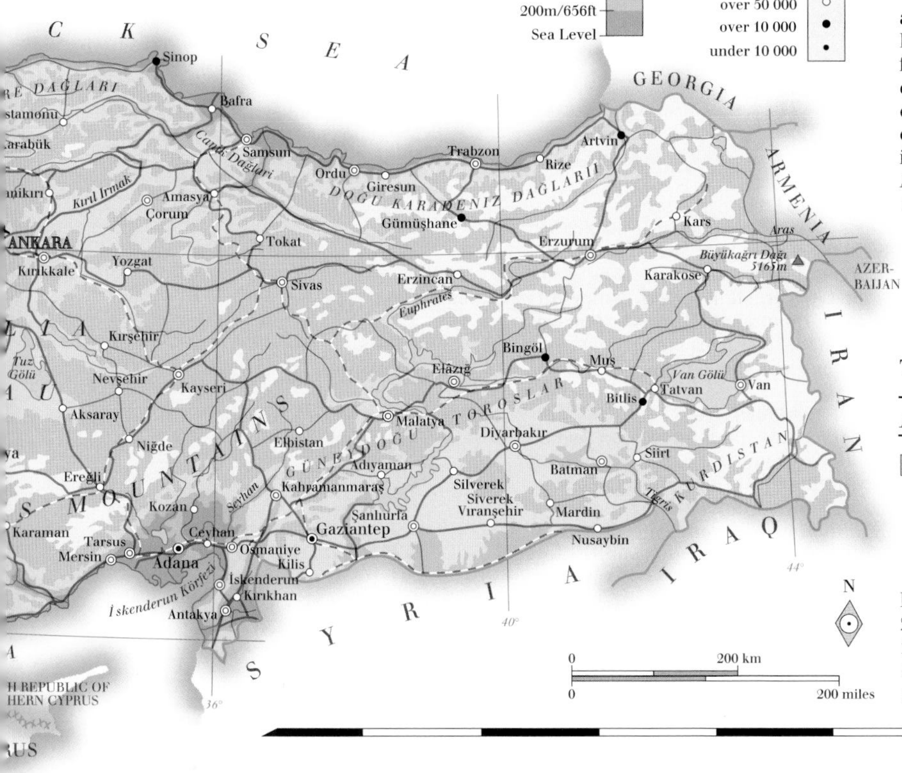
Sinop
Bafra
Samsun
Trabzon
Rize
Artvin
Ordu
Giresun
Amasya
Çorum
Gümüşhane
Kars
ANKARA
Tokat
Erzurum
Kırıkkale
Yozgat
Sivas
Erzincan
Karakose
GEORGIA
ARMENIA
AZER-BAIJAN
IRAN
Kırşehir
Nevşehir
Kayseri
Bingöl
Muş
Elâzığ
Van Gölü
Tatvan
Van
Bitlis
Aksaray
Malatya
Niğde
Elbistan
Diyarbakır
Siirt
Batman
Adıyaman
Kahramanmaraş
Ereğli
Silverek
Siverek
Viranşehir
Şanlıurfa
Mardin
Kozan
Karaman
Tarsus
Mersin
Adana
Ceyhan
Gaziantep
Nusaybin
Osmaniye
Kilis
İskenderun
Kırıkhan
Antakya
Euphrates
Tigris
Aras
Büyükağrı Dağı 5165m
Kızıl Irmak
Seyhan
SYRIA
IRAQ
Karadeniz Dağları
Taurus Mountains
200 km
200 miles

WORLD AFFAIRS

Joined UN in 1945

CE | NATO | OECD | OIC | OSCE

Turkey has strategic significance as the only Muslim member of NATO. Its support for the US during the 1991 Gulf War was not reiterated with such vigor in 2003, when it refused passage to US troops for the invasion of Iraq. The presence of an autonomous Kurdish region in north Iraq is of great concern.

Turkey retains close ties to Israel and the more moderate Muslim states. It has developed links with many former communist states, and especially with the Turkic-speaking central Asian countries. It is a member of the BSEC, sent arms to Uzbekistan in 2000, and has mediated between Armenia and Azerbaijan. In 2002 it held the leadership of the peacekeeping force in Afghanistan.

The quest to join the EU, though aided by recently improving relations with Greece, is impeded by EU concerns over human rights abuses and by the Turkish-backed partition of Cyprus.

AID

Recipient

$167m (receipts)

Down 49% in 2001

Turkey is a net recipient of aid (especially from the 1991 Gulf War allies), despite US suspension of aid in 1994 in protest at the treatment of Kurds. The acute economic crisis in 2000–2001 prompted a $10 billion loan from the IMF. Greece, a traditional adversary, offered humanitarian aid after the 1999 Izmit earthquake.

T

CHRONOLOGY

Following the collapse of the Ottoman Empire and Turkey's defeat in World War I, nationalist Mustafa Kemal Atatürk deposed the ruling sultan in 1922, declaring Turkey a republic in 1923.

- ❑ **1924** Religious courts abolished.
- ❑ **1928** Islam no longer state religion.
- ❑ **1934** Women given the vote.
- ❑ **1938** President Atatürk dies. Succeeded by Ismet Inönü.
- ❑ **1945** Turkey declares war on Germany. Joins UN.
- ❑ **1952** Joins CE and NATO.
- ❑ **1960** Military coup; National Assembly suspended.
- ❑ **1961** New constitution.
- ❑ **1963** Association agreement with European Economic Community.
- ❑ **1974** Invades northern Cyprus.
- ❑ **1980** Military coup; martial law.
- ❑ **1982** New constitution.
- ❑ **1983** Election won by Turgut Özal's Motherland Party (ANAP).
- ❑ **1984** Turkey recognizes "Turkish Republic of Northern Cyprus." Kurdish separatist PKK launches guerrilla war in southeast Turkey.
- ❑ **1990** US-led coalition launches air strikes on Iraq from Turkish bases.
- ❑ **1991** True Path Party (DYP) wins elections. Süleyman Demirel premier.
- ❑ **1992** Joins Black Sea alliance.
- ❑ **1993** Demirel elected president. Tansu Çiller DYP leader, heads coalition.
- ❑ **1995** Major anti-Kurdish offensive. Voting age lowered to 18. Çiller coalition collapses. Pro-Islamic RP wins election, but center-right DYP–ANAP coalition takes office. Customs union with EU.
- ❑ **1996–1997** RP leader Necmettin Erbakan heads first pro-Islamic government since 1923.
- ❑ **1997** Mesut Yilmaz reappointed to head minority ANAP government.
- ❑ **1998** RP banned. Yilmaz resigns, replaced by Bulent Ecevit of Democratic Left Party.
- ❑ **1999** Ecevit heads coalition after elections. Kurdish leader Abdullah Ocalan sentenced to death. Izmit earthquake kills 14,000.
- ❑ **2000** Demirel denied second term: Ahmet Necdet Sezer president.
- ❑ **2001** Acute financial crisis. Hunger strikes in high-security prisons. Virtue Party banned.
- ❑ **2002** Constitutional prodemocracy and human rights amendments, with goal of EU membership. April, PKK replaced by Kurdistan Freedom and Democracy Congress. November, early elections won by Islamist AK.
- ❑ **2003** Recep Tayyip Erdogan becomes prime minister after by-election.

DEFENSE

▷ Compulsory military service

$7.22bn

Down 28% in 2001

TURKISH ARMED FORCES

4205 main battle tanks (2876 M-48, 932 M-60, 397 Leopard)	402,000 personnel
13 submarines, 19 frigates, and 49 patrol boats	52,750 personnel
485 combat aircraft (224 F-16C/D, 87 F/NF-5A/B, 174 F-4E)	60,100 personnel
None	

Turkey's armed forces are the second-largest in NATO, which it joined in 1952. Turkey is a sizable military power, and it spends a higher percentage of GDP on defense than any other NATO country. NATO membership gives Turkey easy access to Western arms suppliers, though campaigners oppose sales to Turkey on human rights grounds. Israel is an important source for arms. Regular offensives against Kurdish separatists in northern Iraq and in Turkey's own southeastern provinces have involved over 50,000 troops and repeated incursions into Iraqi territory.

The great majority of Turkey's armed forces personnel are conscripts: 18 months' service is compulsory for all males when they reach the age of 20.

ECONOMICS

▷ Inflation 74% p.a. (1990–2001)

$167bn

1.418m Turkish lira (1.586m)

SCORE CARD

- ❑ World GNP Ranking 24th
- ❑ GNP per Capita $2530
- ❑ Balance of Payments $3.4bn
- ❑ Inflation 54.4%
- ❑ Unemployment 9%

EXPORTS

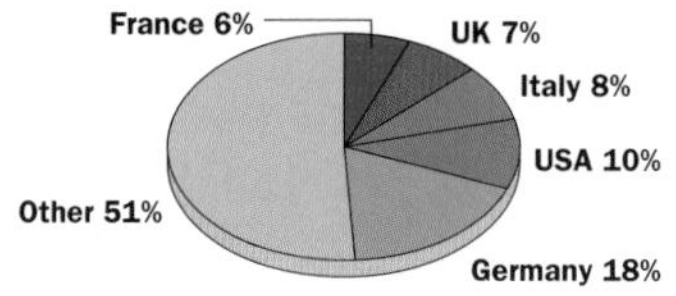
France 6%
UK 7%
Italy 8%
USA 10%
Germany 18%
Other 51%

IMPORTS

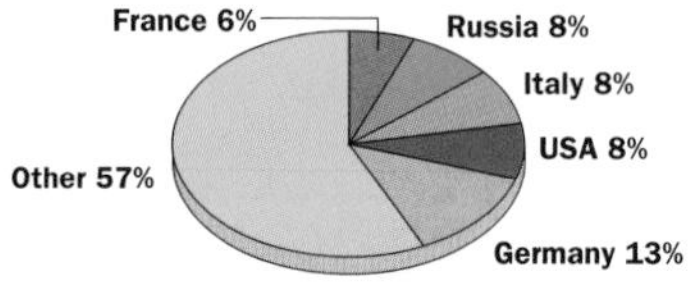
France 6%
Russia 8%
Italy 8%
USA 8%
Germany 13%
Other 57%

ECONOMIC PERFORMANCE INDICATOR

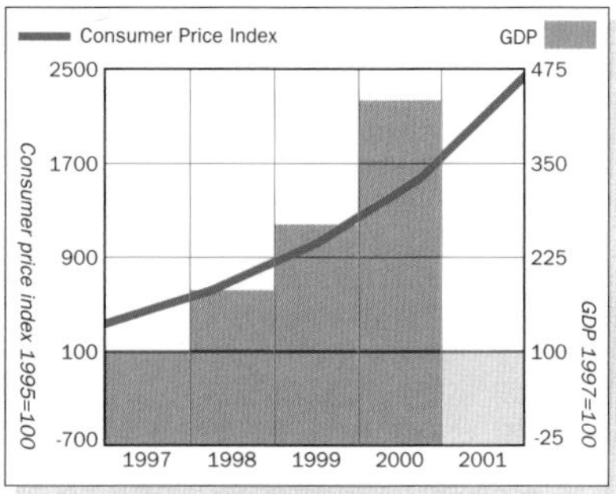
Consumer Price Index
GDP
2500
1700
900
100
-700
475
350
225
100
-25
1997
1998
1999
2000
2001
Consumer price index 1995=100
GDP 1997=100

Strengths

Liberalized economy: strong growth in the 1990s. Near self-sufficiency in agriculture. Textiles, manufacturing, and construction sectors competitive in world markets. Tourism industry. Dynamic private sector economy. Skilled labor force. Customs union with EU.

Weaknesses

Persistently high inflation. Unsound public finances. Large government bureaucracy. Uneven privatization program. Ailing banking sector. Influence of organized crime. High cost of military action against Kurds.

Profile

Turkey has one of the oldest and most advanced of the emerging market economies. In the 1990s it grew strongly, but continued to suffer from high inflation. Despite structural reforms the economy reached crisis point in early 2001, with a collapse of the banking system and the loss of over 500,000 jobs. This was compounded by the effect of the September 11 attack on the US. Three IMF rescue packages were agreed in the course of the year in return for the privatization of debt-laden state companies and banking reform, and growth returned in 2002.

TURKEY : MAJOR BUSINESSES

Istanbul
Ankara
Bursa
İzmit
Kırıkkale
Erzurum
Sivas
İsparta
Adana
Diyarbakır
İzmir
Mersin
Cement
Textiles
Chemicals
Electronics
Oil refining
Iron & steel
Food processing
Vehicle manufacture
0 200 km
0 200 miles
* significant multinational ownership

RESOURCES

Electric power 25.1m kW

582,376 tonnes

58,967 b/d (reserves 258m barrels)

27m sheep, 10.5m cattle, 7.02m goats, 218m chickens

Chromium, oil, copper, borax, coal, gas, bauxite, iron

ELECTRICITY GENERATION

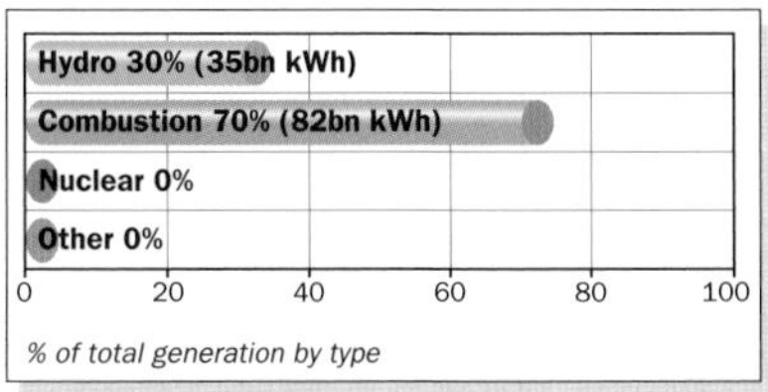
Hydro 30% (35bn kWh)
Combustion 70% (82bn kWh)
Nuclear 0%
Other 0%
0
20
40
60
80
100
% of total generation by type

Under the controversial Southeastern Anatolian Project (GAP) launched in the mid-1980s, Turkey is building 22 dams on the Tigris and Euphrates rivers. In 1999 controversy focused on the Ilisu Dam on the Tigris, which would flood a large number of towns and villages, and in 2001 on the Birecik Dam on the Euphrates, which has engulfed the ancient Roman town of Zeugma. Turkey produces oil around Raman, on the Tigris. Eastern provinces are rich in minerals, such as chromium, of which Turkey is a leading producer.

TURKEY : LAND USE

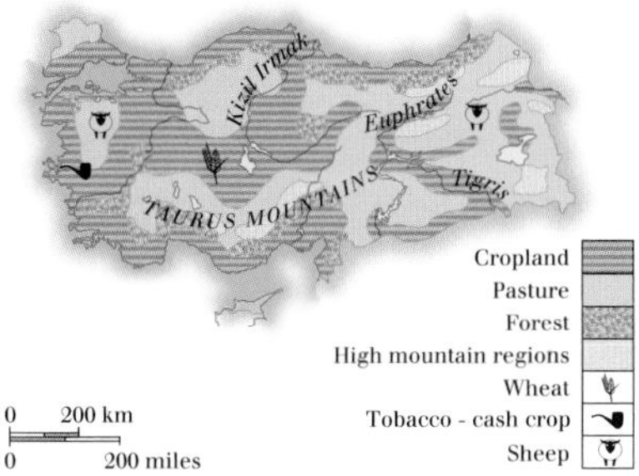
Kizil Irmak
Euphrates
Tigris
TAURUS MOUNTAINS
Cropland
Pasture
Forest
High mountain regions
Wheat
Tobacco - cash crop
Sheep
0 200 km
0 200 miles

ENVIRONMENT

Sustainability rank: 62nd

2% (1% partially protected)

3 tonnes per capita

ENVIRONMENTAL TREATIES

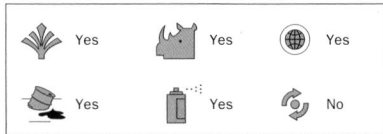

Yes Yes Yes

Yes Yes No

Turkey's program of dam-building on the Tigris and Euphrates has met with condemnation, particularly from Syria and Iraq, whose rivers will suffer reduced flow rates. Plans for the Ilisu Dam were shelved in 2001. Concern has also been expressed at proposals to build a nuclear power plant. There has been uncontrolled tourist development along the western coast.

CRIME

Death penalty not used in practice

61,336 prisoners

Up 4% in 2000–2002

CRIME RATES

Murders

4 *per 100,000 population*

Rapes

2 *per 100,000 population*

Thefts

217 *per 100,000 population*

The routine use of torture and rape by the police and the deaths of prisoners in custody cause concern among human rights groups worldwide. In 2002 the imposition of the death penalty was limited to "times of war" and terrorism.

HEALTH

Welfare state health benefits

1 per 787 people

Cerebrovascular, heart, respiratory, and digestive diseases

Turkey possesses an adequate national system of primary health care. By Western standards, however, hospitals are underequipped. There are fewer doctors per head than in any European country.

SPENDING

GDP/cap. increase

CONSUMPTION AND SPENDING

68 per 1000 population

285 per 1000 population

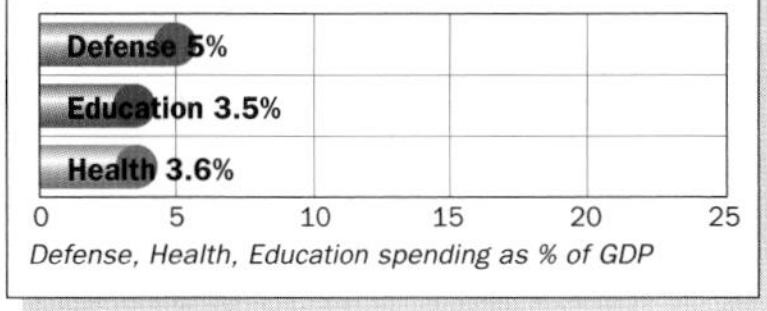
Defense 5%
Education 3.5%
Health 3.6%
0
5
10
15
20
25
Defense, Health, Education spending as % of GDP

The economic expansion of the 1980s has created a new class of wealthy entrepreneurs. Urban/rural differences remain pronounced. High inflation in the 1990s eroded earnings of those on fixed incomes, and income inequality has grown. Many Turks take jobs as *Gastarbeiter* (guest workers) in Germany and the Netherlands.

MEDIA

TV ownership high

Daily newspaper circulation 64 per 1000 people

PUBLISHING AND BROADCAST MEDIA

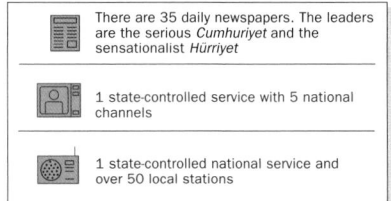

There are 35 daily newspapers. The leaders are the serious *Cumhuriyet* and the sensationalist *Hürriyet*

1 state-controlled service with 5 national channels

1 state-controlled national service and over 50 local stations

The Turkish press is diverse, vigorous, and largely privately owned. Almost all Istanbul newspapers are also printed in Ankara and Izmir on the same day.

Foreign satellite or cable broadcasts are available, as well as the five national channels of the state Turkish Radio and Television Corporation. Censorship laws have been amended to ease restrictions on non-Turkish-language broadcasting, and, after pressure from the EU, 30 minutes a day of Kurdish programming was allowed from 2002.

A particularly high number of journalists are imprisoned, and state control over Internet content was even increased in 2002.

EDUCATION

School leaving age: 14

86%

1.02m students

THE EDUCATION SYSTEM

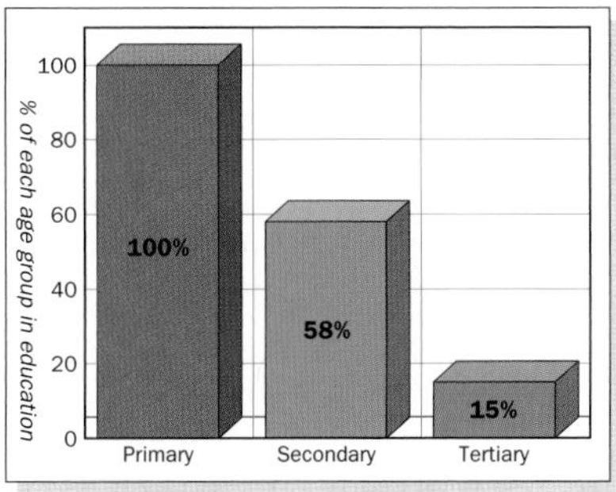
100
80
60
40
20
0
% of each age group in education
100%
58%
15%
Primary
Secondary
Tertiary

After 1923, educational establishments were nationalized. In 1928, a Turkish alphabet with Latin characters was introduced.

In 1997, compulsory education was extended from five to eight years, raising the age for entry into Islamic schools from 11 to 14, in a move seen as designed to reduce attendance at such schools. State schools are coeducational and free. Engineering is usually the strongest faculty in Turkey's many universities.

WORLD RANKING

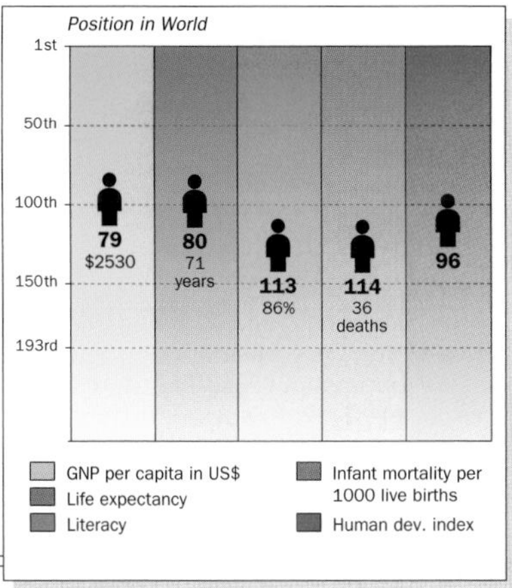
Position in World
1st
50th
100th
150th
193rd
79
$2530
80
71
years
113
86%
114
36
deaths
96
GNP per capita in US$
Life expectancy
Literacy
Infant mortality per 1000 live births
Human dev. index

T

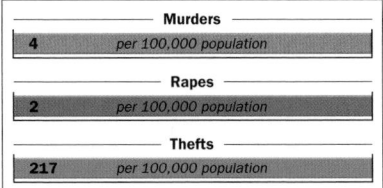

Turkmenistan

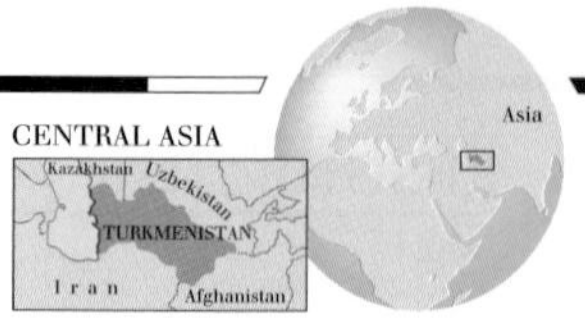
CENTRAL ASIA
Kazakhstan
Uzbekistan
TURKMENISTAN
Iran
Afghanistan
Asia

Official Name: Turkmenistan **Capital:** Ashgabat
Population: 4.9 million **Currency:** Manat **Official Language:** Turkmen

1991 | 1991 | Oct 27 | TM | +5 | +993 | .tm

ONCE THE POOREST of the former Soviet republics, Turkmenistan has adjusted better than most to independence, exploiting the market value of its abundant natural gas supplies. A largely Sunni Muslim country, Turkmenistan is part of the former Turkestan, the last expanse of central Asia incorporated into czarist Russia. Much of life is still based on tribal relationships. Turkmenistan is isolated – telephones are rare and other communications limited.

CLIMATE

Desert/steppe

WEATHER CHART FOR ASHGABAT

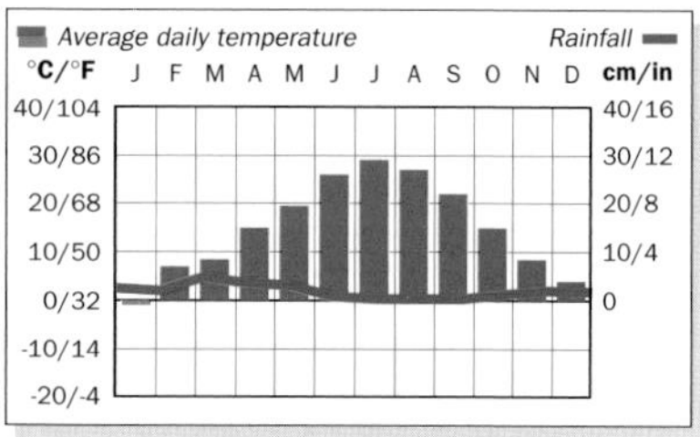
Average daily temperature
Rainfall
°C/°F
J F M A M J J A S O N D
cm/in
40/104
30/86
20/68
10/50
0/32
-10/14
-20/4
40/16
30/12
20/8
10/4
0

Most of Turkmenistan is arid desert, so that only 2% of the total land area is suitable for agriculture.

TRANSPORTATION

Drive on right

Turkmenistan International, Ashgabat

41 ships
45,700 grt

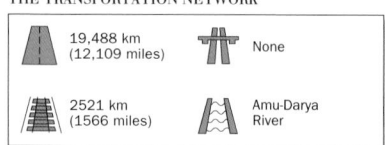

THE TRANSPORTATION NETWORK

19,488 km (12,109 miles)	None
2521 km (1566 miles)	Amu-Darya River

Trains are cramped and chaotic, and buses unreliable. The border with Iran is officially closed to "foreigners."

TOURISM

Visitors : Population 1:16

300,000 visitors

Up 26% in 1998

MAIN TOURIST ARRIVALS

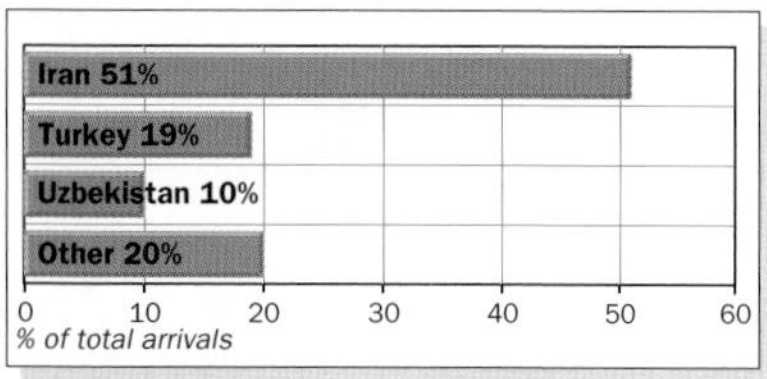
Iran 51%
Turkey 19%
Uzbekistan 10%
Other 20%
0
10
20
30
40
50
60
% of total arrivals

Most visitors are businessmen attracted by Turkmenistan's stability under President Niyazov. Turkmenistan may become a popular tourist destination in future; traditional Turkmen Muslim monuments are slowly being restored.

Karakum Canal zone: salt flats and the Kopetdag Mountains. The Karakumy Desert forms a large part of Turkmenistan's interior.

PEOPLE

Pop. density low

Turkmen, Uzbek, Russian

10/km² (26/mi²)

THE URBAN/RURAL POPULATION SPLIT

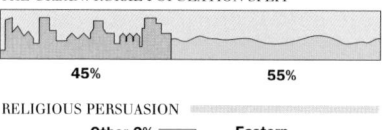

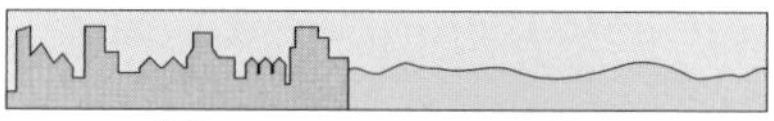
45%
55%

RELIGIOUS PERSUASION

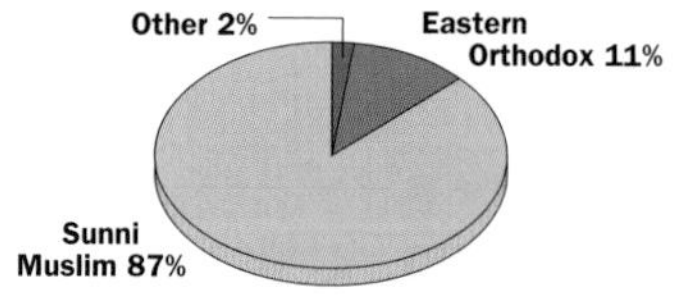
Other 2%
Eastern Orthodox 11%
Sunni Muslim 87%

Before czarist Russia annexed Turkmenistan in 1884, the Turkmen were a largely nomadic tribal people. The tribal unit remains strong – the largest tribes are the Tekke in the center, the Ersary on the eastern Afghan border, and the Yomud in the west. Tribal conflicts, rather than tensions with the two main minorities – Russian and Uzbek – are a source of strife. Paradoxically, this has meant that since 1991 nationalism has been less virulent than in other former Soviet republics. Since 1989, Turkmenistan has been rehabilitating its traditional language and culture, as well as reassessing its history. Islam is again central, though few perform the *haj* (pilgrimage) to Mecca and many continue to maintain a cult of ancestors. Russian is widely spoken and remains an important language.

POLITICS

No multiparty elections

L. House 1999/2004
U. House 2003/2008

President Saparmurad Niyazov

AT THE LAST ELECTION

Parliament 50 seats

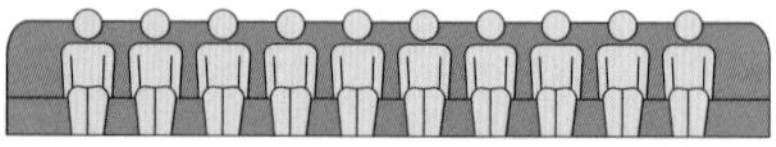

In elections to the Parliament in 1999 all of the seats were won by supporters of the ruling Democratic Party of Turkmenistan (**DPT**) – the only registered party.

People's Council 125 seats

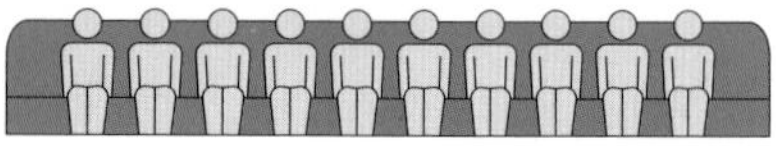

The People's Council has 65 directly elected members, the 50 members of the Parliament, ten appointed regional members and a varying number of ex-officio members.

Officially, Turkmenistan became a multiparty democracy at independence, but President Saparmurad Niyazov has banned the formation of new parties. As in some other ex-Soviet states, former communists, regrouped as the DPT, still dominate the political process, harboring the traditional communist suspicion of Islamic fundamentalism. A main political concern is to prevent the social and nationalistic conflicts that have blighted other CIS republics.

President Niyazov has encouraged an elaborate personality cult, adopting the title of Turkmenbashi (father of all Turkmen), and there are golden statues of him throughout Ashgabat. His spiritual guide to living, *Ruhnama*, has been adopted as a national code, and he has announced his intention to change the official names of the months of the year to commemorate the country's heroes and most potent national symbols.

WORLD AFFAIRS

Joined UN in 1992

CIS | ECO | EAPC | OIC | OSCE

Key relations are with Iran and Turkey. It needs investment from both countries, but is wary of Islamic fundamentalism. President Niyazov opposes economic union with the CIS and political union among Turkic-speaking states. Relations with Russia were soured in 2003 by the ending of dual citizenship for ethnic Russians.

AID

Recipient

$72m (receipts)

Up 125% in 2001

The World Bank has halted new loans in the light of Turkmenistan's failure to report its external debt.

T

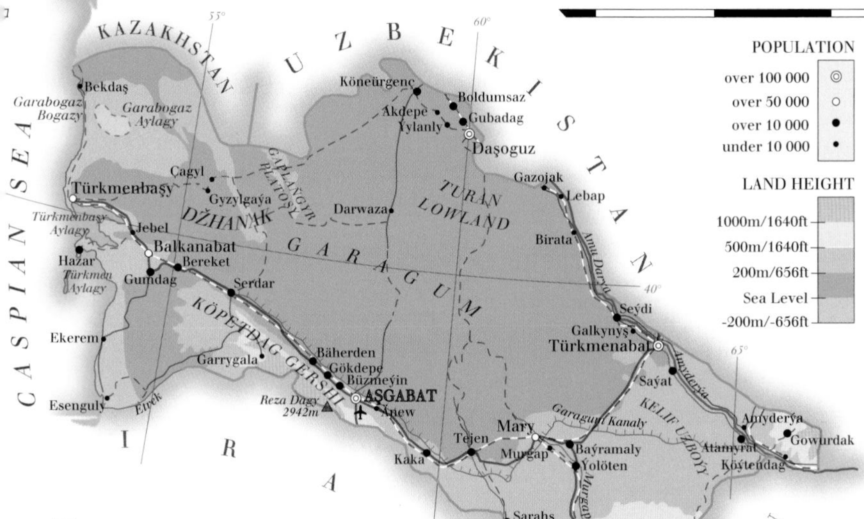
KAZAKHSTAN
UZBEKISTAN
CASPIAN SEA
IRAN
AFGHANISTAN
POPULATION
over 100 000
over 50 000
over 10 000
under 10 000
LAND HEIGHT
1000m/1640ft
500m/1640ft
200m/656ft
Sea Level
-200m/-656ft
Bekdaş
Garabogaz Bogazy
Garabogaz Aylagy
Köneürgenç
Boldumsaz
Akdepe
Gubadag
Ylanly
Daşoguz
Çagyl
Türkmenbaşy
Gyzylgaya
DŽHANAK
Darwaza
TURAN LOWLAND
Gazojak
Lebap
Birata
Jebel
Balkanabat
Bereket
Hazar
Gumdag
Serdar
GARAGUM
Seýdi
Galkynyş
Türkmenabat
Ekerem
Bäherden
Gökdepe
Büzmeýin
Garrygala
KÖPETDAG GERŞI
Reza Dagy 2942m
AŞGABAT
Änew
Esenguly
Sayat
Garagum Kanaly
Amyderýa
Gowurdak
Mary
Tejen
Kaka
Murgap
Baýramaly
Ýolöten
Atamyrat
Köýtendag
KELIF UZBOY
Sarahs
Sandykgaçy
GARABIL BELENTLIGI
Tagtabazar
Galaýmor
Serhetabat
BATHYZ
N
0 200 km
0 200 miles

TURKMENISTAN

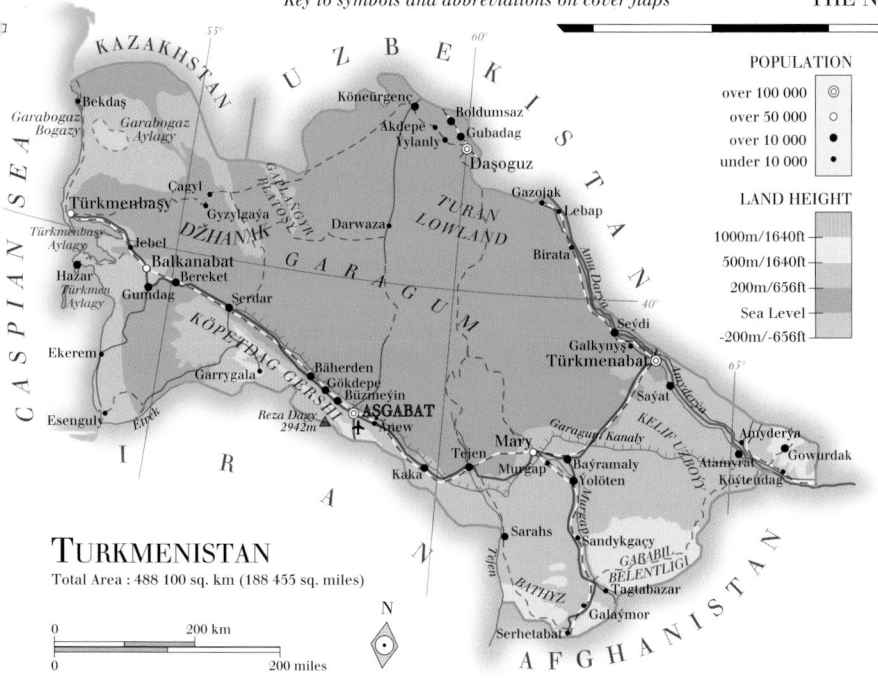

Total Area : 488 100 sq. km (188 455 sq. miles)

CHRONOLOGY

The nomadic peoples of western Turkestan came under Russian imperial control from the 1850s.

- ❑ **1924** Creation of Turkmenistan.
- ❑ **1991** Independence from USSR. Niyazov retains power, becoming president.
- ❑ **1994** Former communists win first elections.
- ❑ **1999** Niyazov's term extended indefinitely by parliament.

DEFENSE

Compulsory military sevice

$222m

Down 23% in 2001

Turkmenistan relies on Russia for defense. Pilots are trained in Pakistan.

ECONOMICS

Inflation 328% p.a. (1990–2001)

$5.14bn

5200.7 manats (5200.3)

SCORE CARD

- ❑ World GNP Ranking........................113th
- ❑ GNP per Capita $950
- ❑ Balance of Payments.....................–$74m
- ❑ Inflation 10%
- ❑ Unemployment 2%

Strengths

Cotton and gas. Decision to abolish collective farms gradually encouraging private initiative and enterprise.

Weaknesses

Cotton monoculture has forced rising food imports. Thriving black market threatens value of manat.

EXPORTS

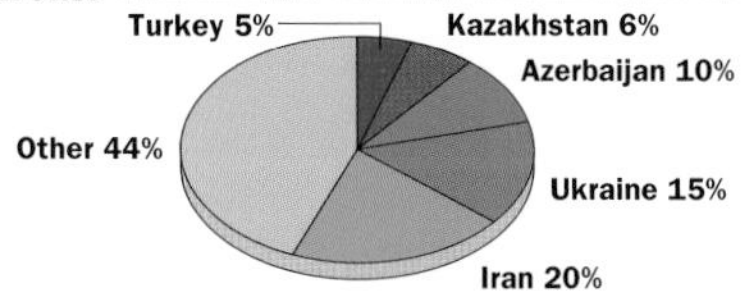
Turkey 5%
Kazakhstan 6%
Azerbaijan 10%
Other 44%
Ukraine 15%
Iran 20%

IMPORTS

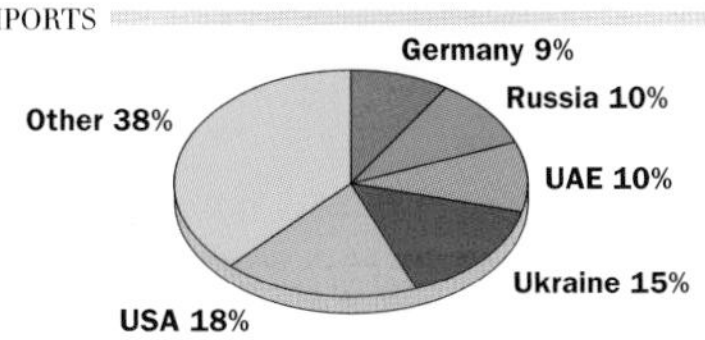
Germany 9%
Russia 10%
Other 38%
UAE 10%
Ukraine 15%
USA 18%

RESOURCES

Electric power 3.9m kW

12,775 tonnes

182,000 b/d (reserves 500m barrels)

6m sheep, 860,000 cattle, 4.8m chickens

Oil, natural gas, potassium, sulfur, sodium sulfate

Under a ten-year program, Turkmenistan aims to raise its oil production to nearly one million barrels per day by 2010.

ENVIRONMENT

Sustainability rank: 131st

4% (2% partially protected)

7.1 tonnes per capita

The building of the Karakum Canal has reduced the flow of water to the Aral Sea by 35%. Plans were announced in 2000 for the construction of a large artificial lake in the Karakumy Desert.

MEDIA

TV ownership medium

Daily newspaper circulation 7 per 1000 people

PUBLISHING AND BROADCAST MEDIA

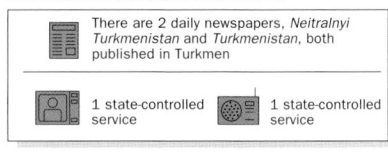

There are 2 daily newspapers, *Neitralnyi Turkmenistan* and *Turkmenistan*, both published in Turkmen

1 state-controlled service

1 state-controlled service

Iranian and Afghan radio stations, beaming in Islamic programs, are popular. TV is only available in cities.

CRIME

No death penalty

22,000 prisoners

Increasing levels of theft

Levels of crime are generally low. The death penalty was finally abolished in December 1999.

EDUCATION

School leaving age: 17

98%

76,000 students

University students must know the life and works of President Niyazov. They now have to work for two years after their first two years of study.

HEALTH

Welfare state health benefits

1 per 333 people

Heart, respiratory, pulmonary, and infectious diseases

Spending is now high for the region, but Turkmenistan's health indicators remain among the worst.

SPENDING

GDP/cap. decrease

CONSUMPTION AND SPENDING

No data

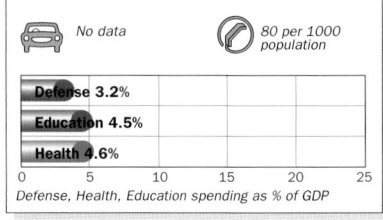

80 per 1000 population

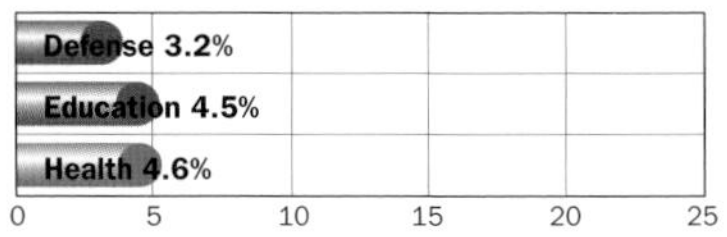
Defense 3.2%
Education 4.5%
Health 4.6%
0
5
10
15
20
25

Defense, Health, Education spending as % of GDP

The wealthiest group is connected to the government. Transition to a liberal economy has attracted high spending.

WORLD RANKING

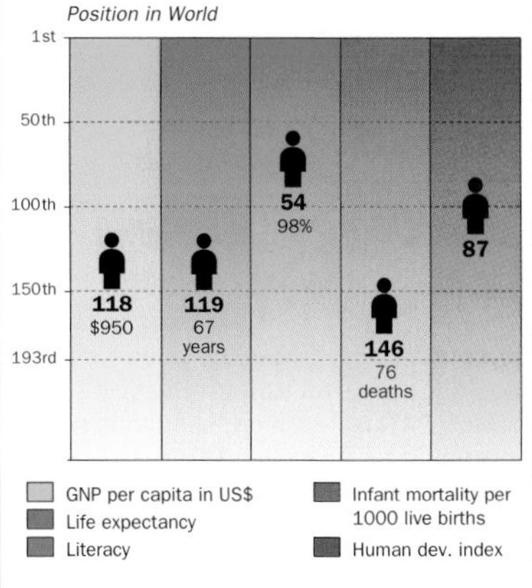
Position in World
1st
50th
100th
150th
193rd
118
$950
119
67 years
54
98%
146
76 deaths
87
GNP per capita in US$
Life expectancy
Literacy
Infant mortality per 1000 live births
Human dev. index

T

TUVALU

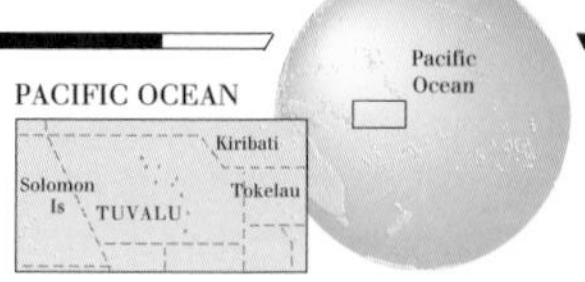
PACIFIC OCEAN
Pacific Ocean
Kiribati
Solomon Is
TUVALU
Tokelau

OFFICIAL NAME: Tuvalu **CAPITAL:** Fongafale, on Funafuti Atoll **POPULATION:** 11,146
CURRENCIES: Australian dollar and Tuvaluan dollar **OFFICIAL LANGUAGE:** English

1978
1978
Oct 1
TUV
+12
+688
.tv

ONE OF THE WORLD'S smallest, most isolated states, Tuvalu lies around 2000 km (1250 miles) north of Fiji in the Pacific. A chain of nine coral atolls, it has a land area of just 26 sq. km (10 sq. miles). As the Ellice Islands, it was linked to the Gilbert Islands (now Kiribati) as a British colony until independence in 1978. Politically and socially conservative, Tuvaluans live by subsistence farming and fishing.

CLIMATE

Tropical oceanic

WEATHER CHART FOR FONGAFALE

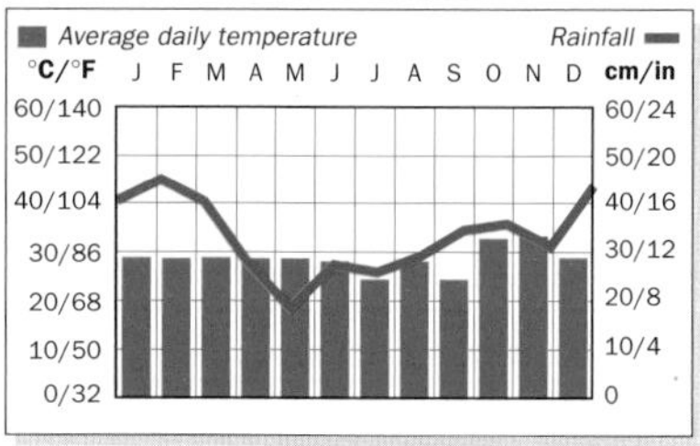
Average daily temperature
Rainfall
°C/°F
J F M A M J J A S O N D
cm/in
60/140
50/122
40/104
30/86
20/68
10/50
0/32
60/24
50/20
40/16
30/12
20/8
10/4
0

The climate is pleasantly warm, though average humidity exceeds 90%. The mean annual temperature is 29°C (84°F). The October–March hurricane season brings many violent storms.

TRANSPORTATION

Drive on right

There is an airstrip on Funafuti atoll

36,000 grt

THE TRANSPORTATION NETWORK

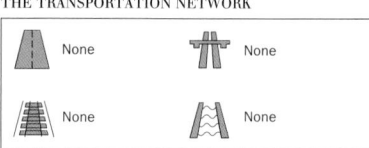

None

None

None

None

A ferry links the atolls. There are air links with Kiribati and Fiji. Funafuti and Nukufetau have deepwater berths.

TOURISM

Visitors : Population 1:11

1000 visitors

No change in 2000

MAIN TOURIST ARRIVALS

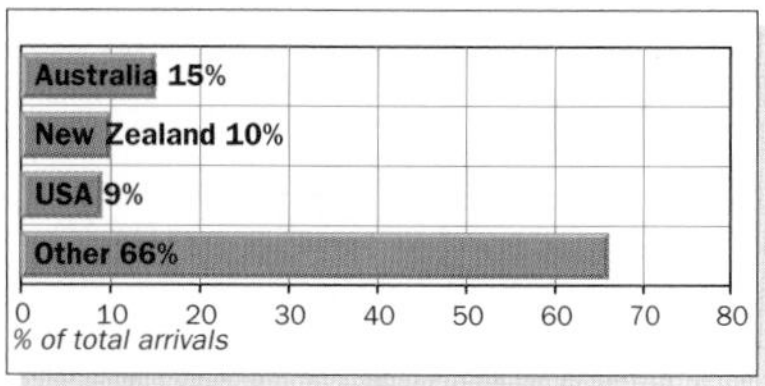
Australia 15%
New Zealand 10%
USA 9%
Other 66%
0 10 20 30 40 50 60 70 80
% of total arrivals

Unspoiled and lapped by some of the world's warmest waters, the remote islands of Tuvalu have surprisingly few visitors. The islands' only paved airstrip and sole hotel are to be found on Funafuti.

PEOPLE

Pop. density high

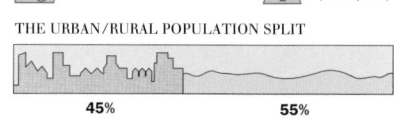

Tuvaluan, Kiribati, English

429/km² (1115/mi²)

THE URBAN/RURAL POPULATION SPLIT

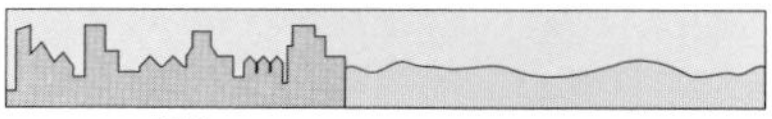
45%
55%

RELIGIOUS PERSUASION

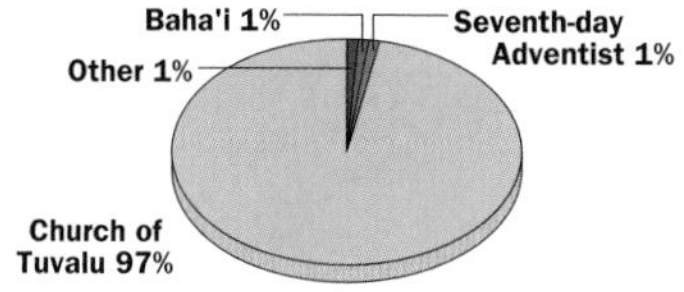
Baha'i 1%
Seventh-day Adventist 1%
Other 1%
Church of Tuvalu 97%

Around 95% of Tuvaluans are ethnically Polynesian. Their ancestors came from Tonga and Samoa 2000 years ago. Nui Atoll has Micronesian influences. There is an I-Kiribati community on Funafuti; many Tuvaluans who worked in Kiribati took local wives. Over 40% of the population now live on Funafuti, pushing its population density to almost 1600 per sq. km (4000 per sq. mile). Life is still communal, traditional, and hard. Droughts are common and fresh water is precious. Around two-thirds of people depend on subsistence farming, digging special pits out of the coral to grow most of the islands' limited range of crops. Fishing is also important, and Tuvaluans have a reputation as excellent sailors. About 2000 Tuvaluans work overseas, some in Nauru's phosphate mines, others as merchant seamen.

Tuvalu's soil is porous, but sufficiently fertile to support coconut palms, pandanus, and salt-tolerant plants. Fresh water supply is limited.

POLITICS

Nonparty elections

2002/2006

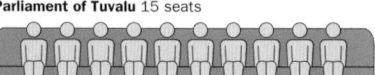

H.M. Queen Elizabeth II

AT THE LAST ELECTION

Parliament of Tuvalu 15 seats

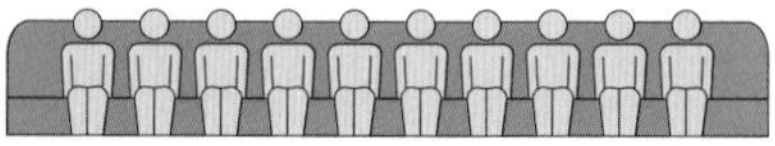

There are no political parties. All members are independent candidates

The 15 MPs, elected every four years, are independents who form loose political associations. The prime minister, an MP elected by parliament, works with a cabinet of up to four other MPs. Day-to-day administration lies in the hands of an elected council on each of Tuvalu's islands. From independence until 1998 politics was dominated by Tomasi Puapua (now governor-general) and Bikenibeu Paeniu. Parliamentary defections are common, and brought down the short-lived government of Prime Minister Faimalaga Luka in 2001. Saufatu Sopoanga was appointed prime minister after elections in 2002.

WORLD AFFAIRS

Joined UN in 2000

ACP Comm PC PIF ADB

Tuvalu was admitted as a full member of both the UN and the Commonwealth in 2000 in recognition of its regional importance. Agreements exist with Taiwan, South Korea, and the US, whose vessels may exploit Tuvalu's fish-rich territorial waters. Calls for cutting constitutional ties to the British monarchy have been revived by Prime Minister Saufatu Sopoanga.

AID

Recipient

US$10m (receipts)

Up 150% in 2001

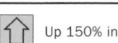

Tuvalu has a visible trade deficit, and aid is crucial. Most importantly, in 1987 a trust fund was set up, with US$29 million in grants from Australia, New Zealand, and the UK. While support from the UK has shrunk, aid from Taiwan and Japan grows. Tuvalu plans to reduce its reliance on aid through public-sector reform and privatization.

DEFENSE

No compulsory military service

There are no armed forces

Not applicable

Tuvalu has no military. Internal security is the responsibility of the small police force.

T

ECONOMICS

Not available

US$21m

1.491 Australian dollars (1.781)

SCORE CARD

- ❑ WORLD GNP RANKING 192nd
- ❑ GNP PER CAPITA ....US$1930
- ❑ BALANCE OF PAYMENTS ....Not available
- ❑ INFLATION 5%
- ❑ UNEMPLOYMENT ....Low

STRENGTHS
Sustainable subsistence economy. EEZ: source of jobs and income. Income from trust fund and multi-million-dollar Internet deal for use of ".tv" suffix.

WEAKNESSES
World's smallest economy. Physical isolation. Few exports: copra, stamps, garments. Dependence on imports and aid. Poor-quality soil. Remittances from overseas workers falling as Nauru's phosphate reserves run out.

EXPORTS

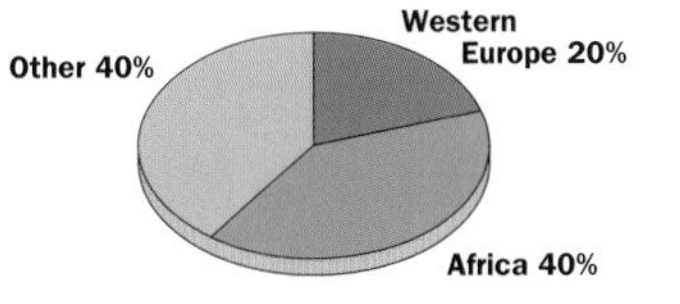
Other 40%
Western Europe 20%
Africa 40%

IMPORTS

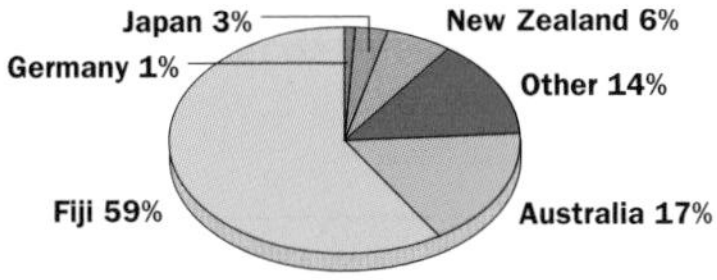
Japan 3%
Germany 1%
New Zealand 6%
Other 14%
Fiji 59%
Australia 17%

RESOURCES

Not available

400 tonnes

Not an oil producer

13,200 pigs, 10,000 ducks, 40,000 chickens

None

Tuvalu's resource potential lies in the waters of its 8.3 million sq. km (3.2 million sq. mile) EEZ. Its rich fish stocks are exploited mainly by foreign boats in return for licensing fees. The salination of soil is increasing, leaving less and less cultivable land. Solar energy is reducing dependence on gasoline for power generation. Fuel accounts for about 14% of import costs. Tuvalu has leased its ".tv" Internet suffix to a Californian media company for US$50 million over 12 years, plus 20% of profits.

TUVALU

Total Area : 26 sq. km (10 sq. miles)

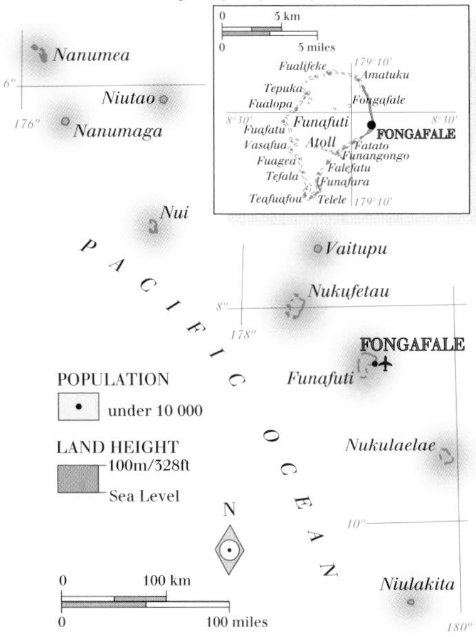
Nanumea
Niutao
Nanumaga
Nui
Vaitupu
Nukufetau
FONGAFALE
Funafuti
Nukulaelae
Niulakita
PACIFIC OCEAN
Fualifeke
Amatuku
Tepuka
Fualopa
Fongafale
Fuafatu
Funafuti Atoll
Vasafua
Fuagea
Tefala
Fatato
Funangongo
Falefatu
Funafara
Teafuafou
Telele
5 km
5 miles
POPULATION
under 10 000
LAND HEIGHT
100m/328ft
Sea Level
N
0
100 km
100 miles

ENVIRONMENT

Not available

132% partially protected (including marine areas)

0.5 tonnes per capita

Efforts to protect the environmentally fragile atolls include reafforestation and solar energy projects. On Funafuti, population pressure is leading to overfishing in the atoll lagoon. The "greenhouse effect" is a major concern, since climate changes attributed to it are blamed for a steep rise in cyclone frequency. Any rise in sea levels induced by global warming would quickly submerge the low-lying atolls.

MEDIA

TV ownership low

There are no daily newspapers

PUBLISHING AND BROADCAST MEDIA

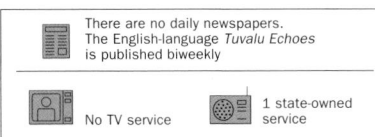

There are no daily newspapers. The English-language *Tuvalu Echoes* is published biweekly

No TV service

1 state-owned service

Tuvalu Echoes and its Tuvaluan version, *Sikuleo o Tuvalu*, are published by the government.

CRIME

No death penalty

6 prisoners

Little change from year to year

Crime is minimal and the result mainly of alcohol-related violence, particularly at the weekend.

EDUCATION

School leaving age: 14

98%

Not available

Each island has a primary school. A secondary school and a marine training school are based on Funafuti. Students who attend the University of the South Pacific in Fiji are state-funded.

CHRONOLOGY

The former Ellice Islands, together with the Gilbert Islands, were annexed by the UK in 1892.

- ❑ **1974** Ellice Islanders vote to separate from Gilbertese.
- ❑ **1978** Independence as Tuvalu.
- ❑ **1987** Tuvalu Trust Fund set up.
- ❑ **1998** Internet deal for ".tv" suffix.
- ❑ **2000** Joins UN as 189th member. Full member of Commonwealth.
- ❑ **2002** Saufatu Sopoanga appointed prime minister.

HEALTH

No welfare state health benefits

1 per 3333 people

Malaria, diarrheal, infectious and parasitic diseases

Concerted efforts since independence to improve health care facilities and programs have cut the incidence of communicable diseases. Serious cases of illness or injury are referred to better-equipped hospitals in Australia or New Zealand.

SPENDING

GDP/cap. increase

CONSUMPTION AND SPENDING

No data

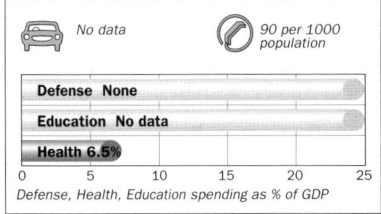

90 per 1000 population

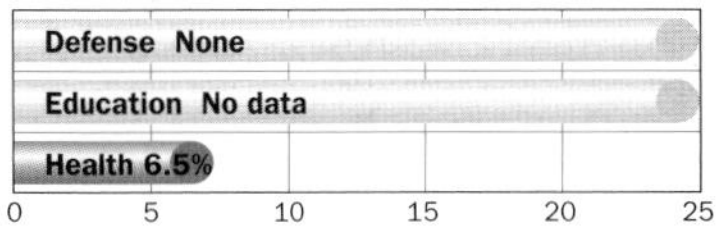
Defense None
Education No data
Health 6.5%
0
5
10
15
20
25

Defense, Health, Education spending as % of GDP

Though living standards are very low, traditional social support systems mean that extreme poverty is rare. Most people rely on subsistence agriculture and fishing, supplemented by remittances from expatriate Tuvaluans.

WORLD RANKING

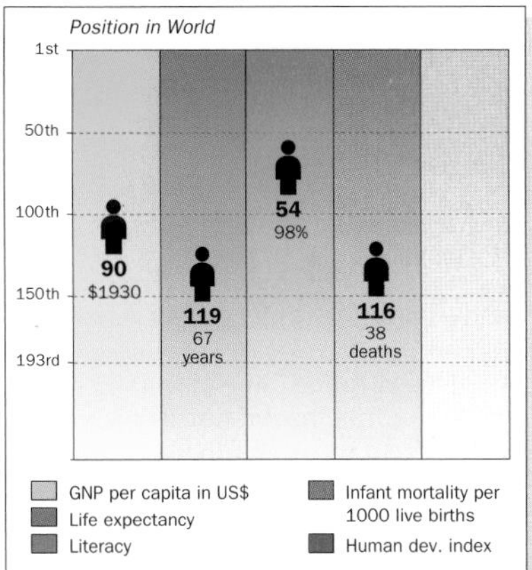
Position in World
1st
50th
100th
150th
193rd
90
$1930
119
67
years
54
98%
116
38
deaths
GNP per capita in US$
Life expectancy
Literacy
Infant mortality per 1000 live births
Human dev. index

T

UGANDA

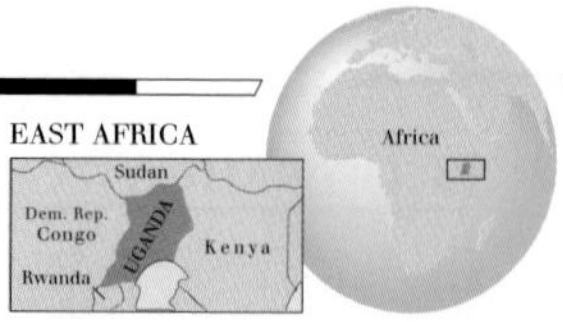
EAST AFRICA
Sudan
Dem. Rep. Congo
UGANDA
Kenya
Rwanda
Africa

OFFICIAL NAME: Republic of Uganda **CAPITAL:** Kampala **POPULATION:** 24.8 million
CURRENCY: New Uganda shilling **OFFICIAL LANGUAGE:** English

1962 | 1962 | Oct 9 | EAU | +3 | +256 | .ug

AN EAST AFRICAN COUNTRY of fertile upland plateaus and mountains, Uganda has outlets to the sea through Kenya and Tanzania. Its history from independence in 1962 until 1986 was one of ethnic strife. Since 1986, under President Museveni, peace has been restored and steps have been taken to rebuild the economy and democracy.

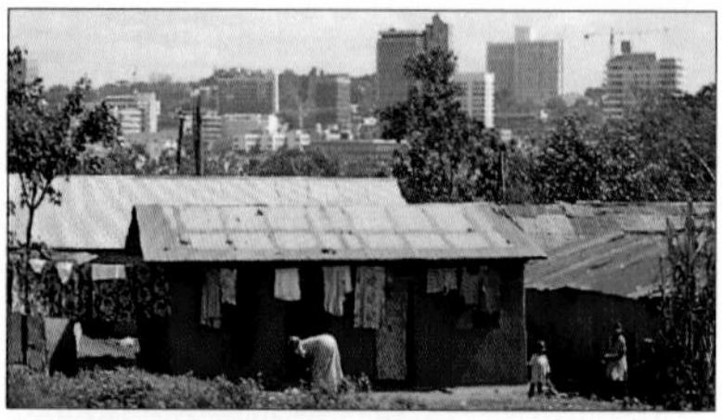

Kampala, Uganda's capital. *Only a tiny proportion of the city's households are supplied with running water*

CLIMATE

Tropical wet and dry

WEATHER CHART FOR KAMPALA

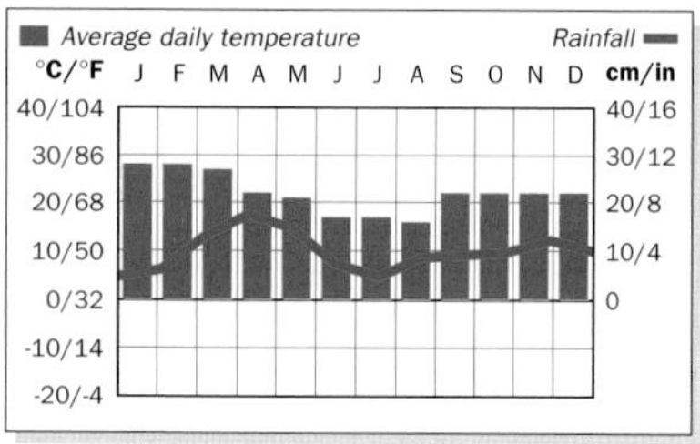
Average daily temperature
Rainfall
°C/°F
J F M A M J J A S O N D
cm/in
40/104
30/86
20/68
10/50
0/32
-10/14
-20/-4
40/16
30/12
20/8
10/4
0

Altitude and the influence of Lake Victoria moderate Uganda's climate. March–May is the wettest period.

TRANSPORTATION

Drive on left

Entebbe International 422,701 passengers

2 ships 5900 dwt

THE TRANSPORTATION NETWORK

1800 km (1118 miles)

None

261 km (162 miles)

Lake Victoria and other lakes are navigable

The government is rebuilding the transportation infrastructure with the help of international aid.

TOURISM

Visitors : Population 1:121

205,000 visitors

Up 36% in 2001

MAIN TOURIST ARRIVALS

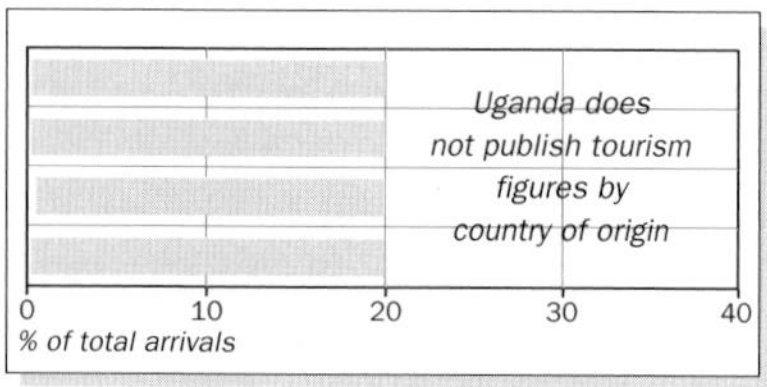
Uganda does not publish tourism figures by country of origin
0
10
20
30
40
% of total arrivals

Major attractions are Uganda's lakes and mountains, notably the rugged Ruwenzori range – the Mountains of the Moon. The brutal murder of eight foreign tourists by Rwandan fighters at the Bwindi national park in 1999 was a severe setback for Uganda's recovery as a tourist destination.

PEOPLE

Pop. density medium

Luganda, Nkole, Chiga, Lango, Acholi, Teso, Lugbara, English

124/km² (322/mi²)

THE URBAN/RURAL POPULATION SPLIT

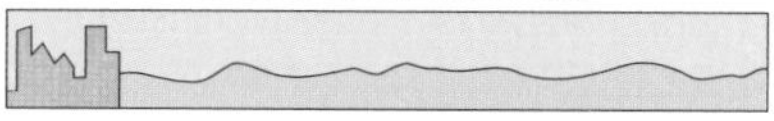
15%
85%

RELIGIOUS PERSUASION

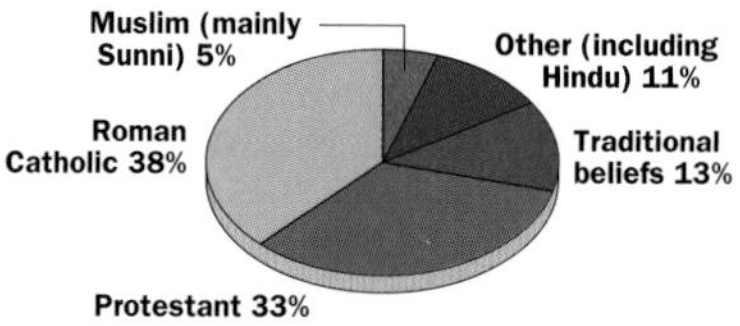
Muslim (mainly Sunni) 5%
Other (including Hindu) 11%
Traditional beliefs 13%
Roman Catholic 38%
Protestant 33%

The predominantly rural population comprises 13 main ethnic groups. Traditional animosities were manipulated by ex-rulers Amin and Obote. Since 1986 President Museveni has worked hard for reconciliation, but a noticeable north–south divide persists, with development focused on the south. Uganda now has one of the best human rights records in Africa.

POLITICS

Nonparty elections

2001/2006

President Yoweri Kaguta Museveni

AT THE LAST ELECTION

Parliament 276 members

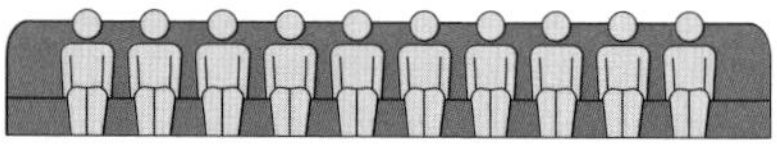

Elections to the Parliament took place on a "no-party" basis in June 2001

Since 1986, President Museveni has run a "no-party democracy," with political parties represented in a broadly based government, but banned from campaigning. Continuing to overcome ethnic tension is the main issue after its catastrophic effects in the 1970s and 1980s, when rebel insurgencies in the north and west led to the deaths, kidnapping, and displacement of tens of thousands of people, and destroyed the economy. In 2001, Museveni won another term in office, taking 69% of the vote, and in the legislative elections his supporters maintained a clear majority. Despite the endorsement of the "no-party" system in a referendum in 2000, in 2003 the government mooted a return to multipartyism.

UGANDA

Total Area : 236 040 sq. km (91 135 sq. miles)

SUDAN
KENYA
DEM. REP. CONGO
TANZANIA
RWANDA
Moyo
Yumbe
Arua
Atiak
Rhino Camp
Gulu
Kitgum
Kaabong
Loyoro
Kotido
Moroto
Pakwach
Lira
Amudat
Lake Albert
Butiaba
Hoima
Masindi
Lake Kwania
Kaberamaido
Lake Kyoga
Soroti
Lake Bisina
Kapchorwa
Mt Elgon 4321m
Mbale
Nakasongola
Kaliro
Tororo
Iganga
Jinja
Owen Falls Dam
Bombo
Mubende
Kabarole
Margherita Peak 5110m
Kasese
Equator
Lake George
Lake Edward
Katonga
Ntusi
Mpigi
KAMPALA
Entebbe
Buvuma I.
Kome I.
Masaka
Bukakata
Bukasa I.
Bugala I.
Sese Islands
Mbarara
Rukungiri
Kagera
Kisoro
Kabale
Lake Victoria
Albert Nile
Achwa
Pager
Victoria Nile
Ruwenzori

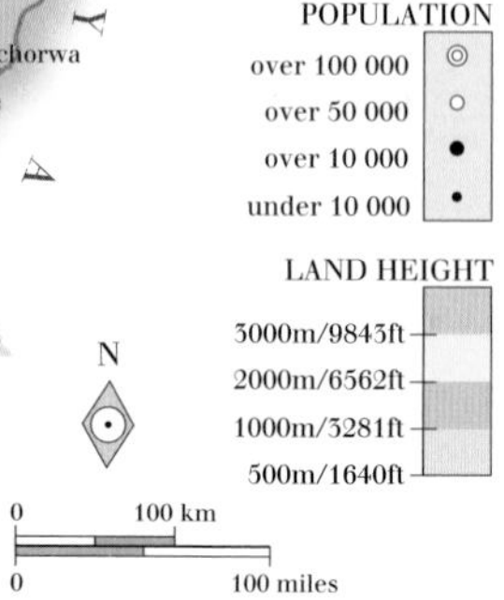
POPULATION
over 100 000
over 50 000
over 10 000
under 10 000
LAND HEIGHT
3000m/9843ft
2000m/6562ft
1000m/3281ft
500m/1640ft
N
0 100 km
0 100 miles

U

WORLD AFFAIRS

Joined UN in 1962

Comm | COMESA | IGAD | EAC | OIC

Conflicts in Sudan, the DRC (where Uganda was one of the protagonists), and Rwanda have caused a large influx of refugees into Uganda. Relations with Sudan have improved since 1999: each has dropped support for cross-border rebels and Sudan has allowed Ugandan forces to pursue Lord's Resistance Army (LRA) fighters into its territory.

AID

Recipient

$783m (receipts)

Down 4% in 2001

Aid, mainly from the World Bank and the UK, has risen, its donors encouraged by Uganda's adoption of economic liberalization and private-sector investment policies. Aid has focused on balance-of-payments support, the rehabilitation of the key transportation sector, and the fight against AIDS.

CHRONOLOGY

Uganda's ancient kingdoms were ruled under a British protectorate from 1893 until independence in 1962.

- **1962–1971** Milton Obote in power.
- **1971–1986** Ethnic strife, economic collapse under Idi Amin and Obote.
- **1986** President Museveni in power.
- **1996** Museveni wins first presidential elections.
- **2000** Referendum endorses "no-party" system.

DEFENSE

No compulsory military service

$126m

Down 7% in 2001

The pre-1986 army was responsible for many atrocities under Amin's rule. In the 1990s, Uganda was preoccupied with conflicts in neighboring countries, particularly the DRC, where it supported antigovernment rebels. The army has also been deployed to suppress internal rebellions, notably that of the Lord's Resistance Army.

ECONOMICS

Inflation 11% p.a. (1990–2001)

$5.93bn

2001 new Uganda shillings (1796)

SCORE CARD

World GNP Ranking	106th
GNP per Capita	$260
Balance of Payments	–$369m
Inflation	2%
Unemployment	Widespread

Strengths

Agriculture. Coffee brings in 93% of export earnings. Potential for more export crops. Road system is being repaired. Proinvestment policies.

Weaknesses

Lack of skilled workforce. Regional instability affects confidence. Unsustainable foreign debt. World coffee price fluctuations.

EXPORTS

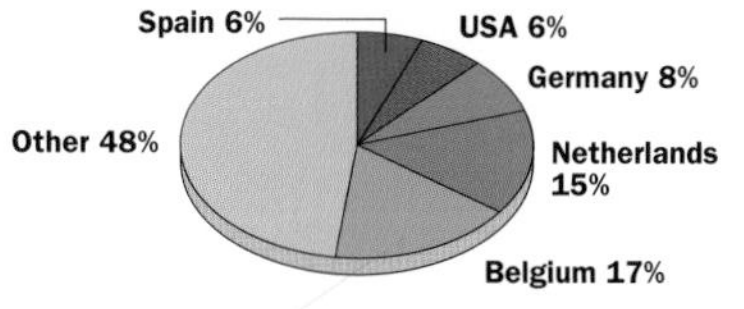
Spain 6%
USA 6%
Germany 8%
Netherlands 15%
Belgium 17%
Other 48%

IMPORTS

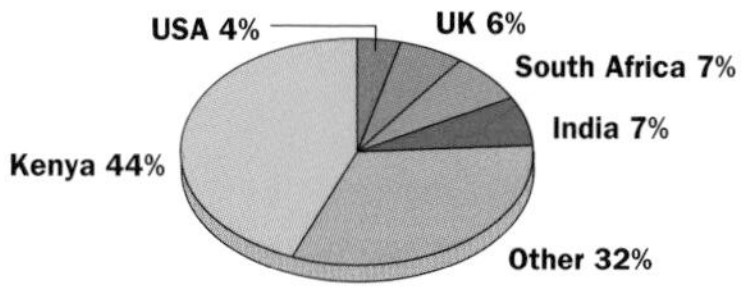
USA 4%
UK 6%
South Africa 7%
India 7%
Other 32%
Kenya 44%

RESOURCES

Electric power 194,000 kW

356,032 tonnes

Not an oil producer

6.6m goats, 5.9m cattle, 1.55m pigs, 25.5m chickens

Copper, cobalt, tin, apatite, magnetite, tungsten, gold

Mineral resources are varied but barely exploited. Uganda has sizable copper deposits; the mines, closed under Obote, are now being reopened. Gold and cobalt mining are also due to resume and oil exploration is under way. Hydroelectric output is being expanded, notably at Owen Falls, with the aim of replacing 50% of oil imports.

ENVIRONMENT

Sustainability rank: 76th

25% (17% partially protected)

0.06 tonnes per capita

Uganda's priority is economic reconstruction, but ecological issues are not ignored. The construction of a huge hydroelectric power plant at the Kabalega (Murchison) Falls, above Lake Albert, was canceled following widespread environmental objections.

MEDIA

TV ownership low

Daily newspaper circulation 2 per 1000 people

PUBLISHING AND BROADCAST MEDIA

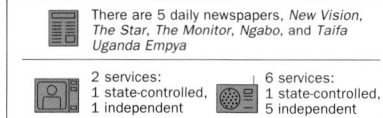

There are 5 daily newspapers, *New Vision, The Star, The Monitor, Ngabo,* and *Taifa Uganda Empya*

2 services: 1 state-controlled, 1 independent

6 services: 1 state-controlled, 5 independent

The 13 daily and weekly papers cover the political and religious spectrum; eight are published in English. Only *New Vision* is government-controlled.

CRIME

Death penalty in use

21,900 prisoners

Down 41% in 2000–2002

Crime levels are low, though theft is a growing problem in Kampala. In 2000, the remains were discovered of 780 followers of the cult of the Restoration of the Ten Commandments of God.

EDUCATION

Schooling is not compulsory

68%

63,165 students

All schools charge fees. Only 11% of pupils go on to secondary school and just 3% to tertiary education.

HEALTH

Welfare state health benefits

1 per 20,000 people

Malaria, respiratory, and diarrheal diseases, measles

A successful education and prevention campaign has reduced the prevalence of HIV/AIDS to about 5% of adults, from a peak of 14% in the early 1990s.

SPENDING

GDP/cap. increase

CONSUMPTION AND SPENDING

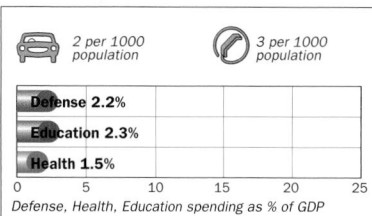

2 per 1000 population

3 per 1000 population

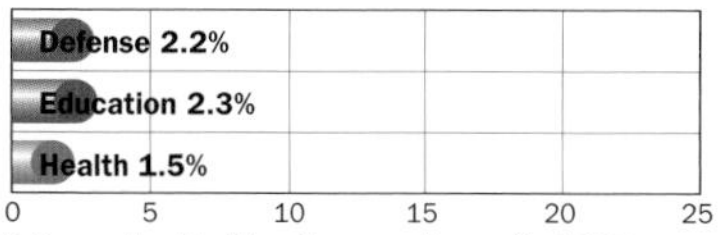
Defense 2.2%
Education 2.3%
Health 1.5%
0
5
10
15
20
25

Defense, Health, Education spending as % of GDP

Uganda has a small but growing middle class. Those close to the government form the wealthiest group. Some 96% of the population live below the poverty line.

WORLD RANKING

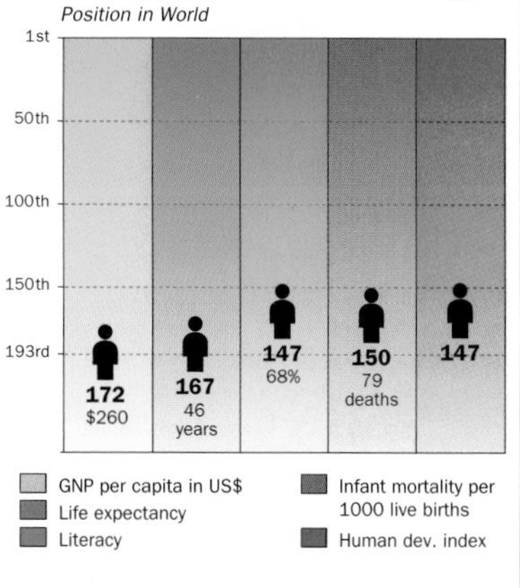
Position in World
1st
50th
100th
150th
193rd
172
$260
167
46 years
147
68%
150
79 deaths
147
GNP per capita in US$
Life expectancy
Literacy
Infant mortality per 1000 live births
Human dev. index

U

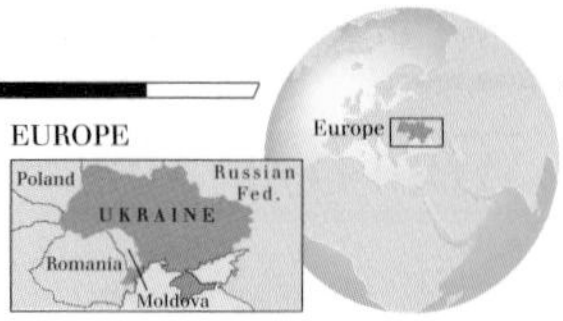
EUROPE
Europe
Poland
Russian Fed.
UKRAINE
Romania
Moldova

UKRAINE

OFFICIAL NAME: Ukraine **CAPITAL:** Kiev
POPULATION: 48.7 million **CURRENCY:** Hryvna **OFFICIAL LANGUAGE:** Ukrainian

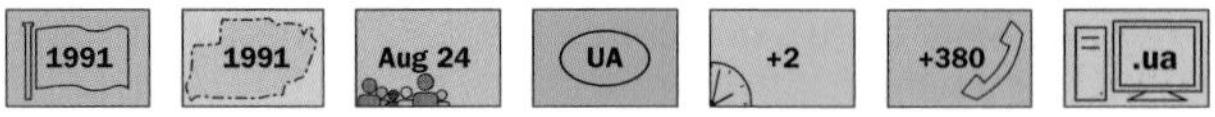
1991
1991
Aug 24
UA
+2
+380
.ua

View toward the Cathedral of the Assumption in Kharkiv. Many Ukrainian cities are equipped with elaborate trolley networks.

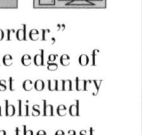

ITS NAME TRANSLATED literally as "on the border," Ukraine was long considered merely to be the edge of the Russian Empire. It is now the second-largest country in Europe, after Russia. An independent Ukrainian state was established in 1918, but was overrun the following year by Russian forces from the east and Polish forces from the west. In 1991, Ukraine again became independent. The country is divided between the nationally conscious and Ukrainian-speaking west (including areas which were part of Poland until World War II) and the east, which has a large ethnic Russian population.

CLIMATE

Continental/steppe/Mediterranean

WEATHER CHART FOR KIEV

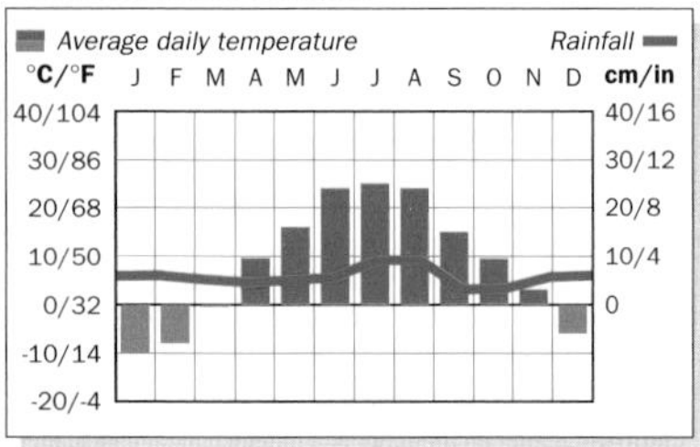
Average daily temperature
Rainfall
°C/°F
J F M A M J J A S O N D
cm/in
40/104
30/86
20/68
10/50
0/32
-10/14
-20/-4
40/16
30/12
20/8
10/4
0

Ukraine has a continental climate, with the exception of the southern coast of Crimea, which has a Mediterranean climate. There are four distinct seasons.

TRANSPORTATION

Drive on right

Boryspiel International, Kiev
1.81m passengers

838 ships
1.41m grt

THE TRANSPORTATION NETWORK

170,139 km (105,719 miles)	1770 km (1100 miles)
22,302 km (13,858 miles)	4499 km (2796 miles)

There are Soviet-style subways and trolley networks in the major cities. The rail system and the main highway linking Kiev and Lviv are being upgraded. Part of a former submarine port at Sevastopol has been opened to commercial shipping.

TOURISM

Visitors : Population 1:8.4

5.79m visitors

Up 37% in 2000–2001

MAIN TOURIST ARRIVALS

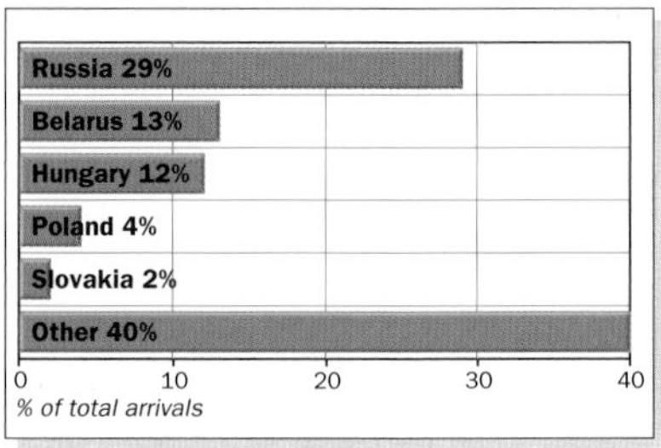
Russia 29%
Belarus 13%
Hungary 12%
Poland 4%
Slovakia 2%
Other 40%
0
10
20
30
40
% of total arrivals

Among potential tourist attractions are the resorts along the warm south coast, notably in Crimea, and the Carpathian Mountains. A highly regulated system of managing tourism has been maintained, and bureaucratic hurdles have held up the development of Western-style hotels.

BELARUS
RUSSIAN FEDERATION
POLAND
SLOVAKIA
HUNGARY
ROMANIA
MOLDOVA
BLACK SEA
Sea of Azov
Gulf of Taganrog
PRIPET MARSHES
PRYDNIPROVS'KA NYZOVYNA
PRYDNIPROVS'KA VYSOCHYNA
PODIL'S'KA VYSOCHYNA
PRYCHORNOMORS'KA NYZOVYNA
PRYAZOVS'KA VYSOCHYNA
CARPATHIAN MOUNTAINS
KRYM (CRIMEA)
Hoverla 2061m
Kiev
Kharkiv
Dnipropetrovs'k
Donets'k
Odesa
Zaporizhzhya
L'viv
Kryvyy Rih
Mykolayiv
Mariupol'
Luhans'k
Sevastopol'
Simferopol'
Kherson
Poltava
Chernihiv
Cherkasy
Sumy
Zhytomyr
Kirovohrad
Vinnytsya
Chernivtsi
Rivne
Ternopil'
Luts'k
Uzhhorod
Mukacheve
Kovel'
Chornobyl'
Shostka
Konotop
Nezhyn
Korosten'
Fastiv
Bila Tserkva
Lubny
Kremenchuk
Smila
Uman'
Oleksandriya
Dniprodzerzhyns'k
Pavlohrad
Slov"yans'k
Kup"yans'k
Horlivka
Alchevs'k
Yenakiyeve
Krasnyy Luch
Makiyivka
Nikopol'
Melitopol'
Berdyans'k
Nova Kakhovka
Yevpatoriya
Yalta
Kerch
Kam"yanets'-Podil's'kyy
Ivano-Frankivs'k
Khmel'nyts'kyy
Kyyivs'ke Vdskh.
Kanivs'ke Vdskh.
Kremenchuts'ke Vdskh.
Dniprodzerzhyns'ke Vdskh.
Kakhovs'ke Vdskh.
Ozero Lenina
Dnistrovs'kyy Lyman
Ozero Yalpuh
Karkinits'ka Zatoka
Zatoka Syvash
Desna
Bug
Dniester
Prut
Dnieper
Donets
Vorskla
Pivdennyy Bug
Danube
52°
48°
24°
28°
32°
36°
40°
UKRAINE
Total Area :
603 700 sq. km (233 089 sq. miles)
POPULATION
over 1 000 000
over 500 000
over 100 000
over 50 000
over 10 000
LAND HEIGHT
2000m/6562ft
1000m/3281ft
500m/1640ft
200m/656ft
Sea Level
0
100 km
0
100 miles
N

U

PEOPLE

Pop. density medium

Ukrainian, Russian, Tatar

81/km² (209/mi²)

THE URBAN/RURAL POPULATION SPLIT

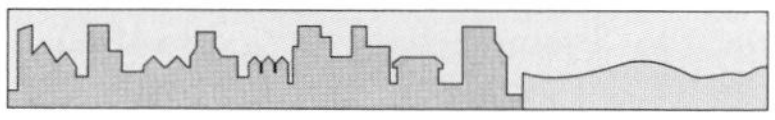

68%
32%

RELIGIOUS PERSUASION

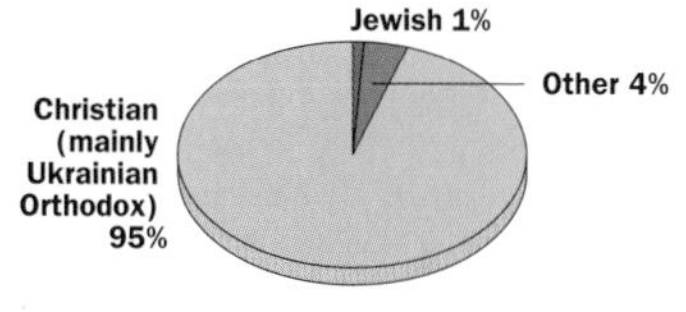

Jewish 1%
Other 4%
Christian (mainly Ukrainian Orthodox) 95%

ETHNIC MAKEUP

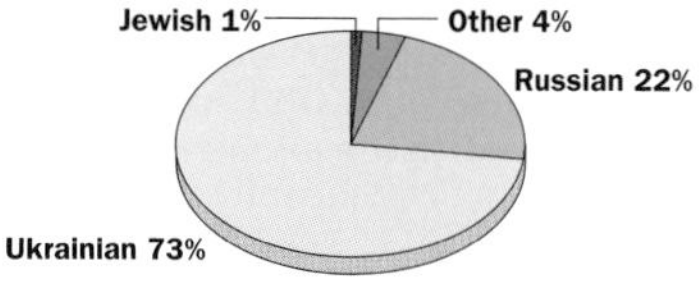

Jewish 1%
Other 4%
Russian 22%
Ukrainian 73%

In the cities and countryside of western Ukraine, Ukrainians make up the vast majority of the population. However, in several of the large cities of the east and south, ethnic Russians form a majority and Russian is spoken by 60% of Ukrainians, a legacy of 19th-century industrialization and of more recent migration in the Soviet era. At independence in 1991, most Russians accepted Ukrainian sovereignty, though tensions remain.

The central government is wary of separatist tendencies in Crimea, however, where Russians make up two-thirds of the population. The Crimea's other main minority, besides ethnic Ukrainians, is the Turkic-speaking Tatar people. Deported en masse to the eastern USSR in 1944 under Stalin, the Tatars have been returning to Crimea since 1990 and now make up 12% of its population. There is a Romanian-speaking minority in the southern Odessa region.

POPULATION AGE BREAKDOWN

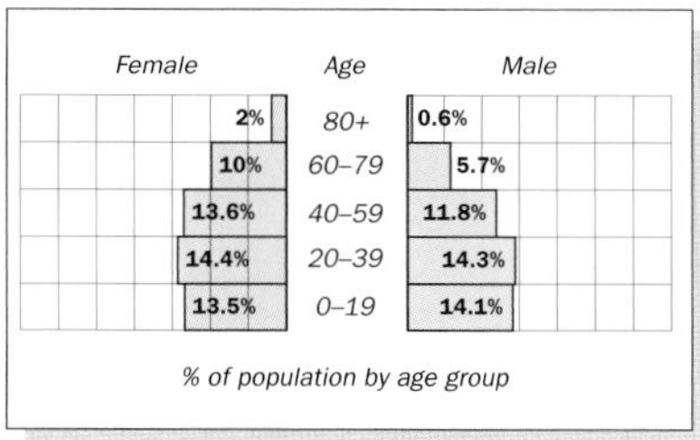

Female
Age
Male
2%
80+
0.6%
10%
60–79
5.7%
13.6%
40–59
11.8%
14.4%
20–39
14.3%
13.5%
0–19
14.1%
% of population by age group

POLITICS

Multiparty elections

2002/2006

President Leonid Kuchma

AT THE LAST ELECTION

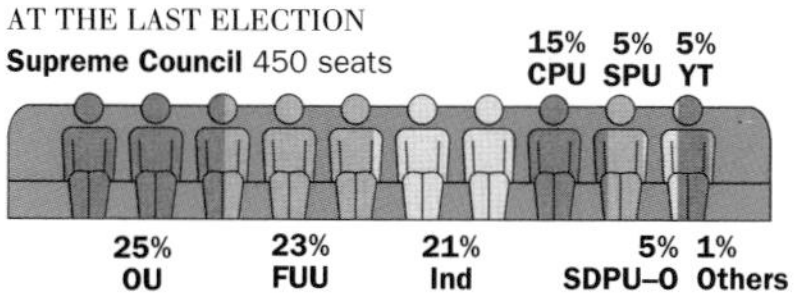

Supreme Council 450 seats
15% CPU
5% SPU
5% YT
25% OU
23% FUU
21% Ind
5% SDPU–O
1% Others

OU = Our Ukraine (Viktor Yushchenko bloc)
FUU = For United Ukraine **Ind** = Independents
CPU = Communist Party **SPU** = Socialist Party of Ukraine
SDPU–O = United Social-Democratic Party of Ukraine
YT = Yulia Timoshenko Election Bloc

Ukraine introduced a multiparty system in 1991.

PROFILE

Ex-premier Leonid Kuchma, who had defeated Ukrainian nationalist Leonid Kravchuk in the 1994 presidential elections, gained increased powers under constitutional changes in 1996. Multiparty legislative elections were first held in 1994, and the strong position of the communists and allied pro-Kuchma groups was confirmed four years later. Kuchma's own reelection in 1999 was fiercely contested, however, his opponents claiming fraud and violent confrontations taking place in parliament and on the streets. The boost which Kuchma gained in early 2000 from a referendum backing electoral changes, and Western enthusiasm for his new proreform government, was dissipated by a scandal linking him with the murder of a journalist later that year, and the uncovering of massive financial frauds. The ranks of his opponents included growing numbers of discarded former ministers, and the pro-Kuchma For United Ukraine was pushed into second place by the opposition Our Ukraine bloc in legislative elections in 2002.

MAIN POLITICAL ISSUE
Presidential integrity

Thousands of protestors gather regularly across Ukraine calling for President Kuchma's resignation, offering a litany of accusations.

The principal accusation is that he personally authorized the murder of outspoken Internet journalist Georgy Gongadze in 2000. Though the case was officially "solved" in 2001, the prosecutor-general announced in 2003 that it had been a politically motivated killing, and many believe that responsibility lies at least as high as the interior ministry.

Kuchma is also heavily criticized for the sale in 2000 of a Kolchuga early warning system to Iraq, in breach of international sanctions then in place, and for corruption in general.

He has failed notably to appease his opponents, despite offering in 2003 to water down the constitutional powers of the presidency, which he had himself increased and had approved by a dubious referendum in 2000.

Leonid Kuchma, who became president in 1994.

Viktor Yushchenko, prime minister in 1999–2001, now leads the opposition.

WORLD AFFAIRS

Joined UN in 1945

BSEC | CE | CIS | IAEA | OSCE

Over time the unqualified backing given to Ukraine by the West since its independence from the Soviet Union has been eroded by the West's relations with Russia and by distrust of President Kuchma. Conversely, Ukraine's ties with Russia, initially seen as a potential aggressor, have been strengthened under Kuchma. Though Ukraine signed a trade agreement with the EU in 1995 and was admitted to the Council of Europe in the same year, it has been increasingly censured for the slow pace of reform and for authoritarianism.

Despite an ongoing territorial dispute with Romania over the potentially oil-rich Serpents' Island, a friendship and cooperation treaty was signed in 1997.

In 2002 the US led international outrage over revelations that Ukraine had supplied the pariah regime of Saddam Hussein in Iraq with an early warning radar system two years previously.

CHRONOLOGY

In 1240, Kiev was conquered by the Mongols. The Ukrainian Cossacks later came under the domination of Lithuania, Poland, and Russia.

- **1918** Independent Ukrainian state after collapse of Russian and Austro-Hungarian empires.
- **1920** After two years of civil war, Ukrainian Soviet Socialist Republic (SSR) established.
- **1921** Treaty of Riga ends Soviet–Polish war: western Ukraine lost.
- **1922** USSR formed, Ukrainian SSR a founding member.
- **1922–1930** Cultural revival under Lenin's "Ukrainianization" policy to pacify national sentiment.
- **1932–1933** "Ukrainianization" policy reversed. Stalin uses famine to eliminate Ukraine as source of opposition; seven million die.

U

CHRONOLOGY *continued*

- **1939** Soviet Union invades Poland and incorporates its ethnic Ukrainian territories into the Ukrainian SSR.
- **1941** Germany invades USSR. 7.5 million Ukrainians die by 1945.
- **1942** Nationalists form Ukrainian Insurgent Army, which wages war against both Germans and Soviets.
- **1954** Crimea ceded to Ukrainian SSR.
- **1972** Widespread arrests of intellectuals and dissidents by Soviet state. Vladimir Shcherbitsky, a Brezhnevite, replaces moderate reformer Petr Shelest as head of Communist Party of Ukraine (CPU).
- **1986** World's worst nuclear disaster at Chernobyl power plant.
- **1989** First major coalminers' strike in Donbass. Pro-Gorbachev Volodymyr Ivashko heads CPU.
- **1990** Ukrainian parliament declares Ukrainian SSR a sovereign state. Leonid Kravchuk replaces Ivashko.
- **1991** Full independence declared, conditional on approval by referendum, supported by 90% of voters. CPU banned. Crimea becomes an autonomous republic within Ukrainian SSR.
- **1993** Major strike in Donbass results in costly settlement, which exacerbates budget deficit and stimulates hyperinflation. CPU reestablished at Donetsk congress.
- **1994** Crimea elects Yuri Meshkov as its first president. Leonid Kuchma defeats Kravchuk to become first democratically elected president of Ukraine.
- **1996** Hryvna replaces karbovanets as national currency. New constitution comes into force.
- **1997** Friendship treaty signed with Russia. Accord on Black Sea fleet.
- **1998** Ten-year cooperation agreement with Russia. CPU wins largest number of seats in election.
- **1999** Reelection of Kuchma. Opposition claims of fraud. Kuchma appoints proreform government.
- **2000** Chernobyl site closed.
- **2001** Kuchma linked with murder of journalist. Reformist premier Viktor Yushchenko replaced after parliamentary defeat.
- **2002** Opposition parties make large gains in legislative elections.

AID

Recipient

$519m (receipts) | Down 4% in 2001

In the 1990s US assistance was the world's fourth-largest aid program, and EU assistance totaled $3.5 billion. Aid was held up from 2002 over Ukraine's alleged dealings with Iraq.

DEFENSE

Phasing out conscription

$4.9bn | Down 4% in 2001

UKRAINIAN ARMED FORCES

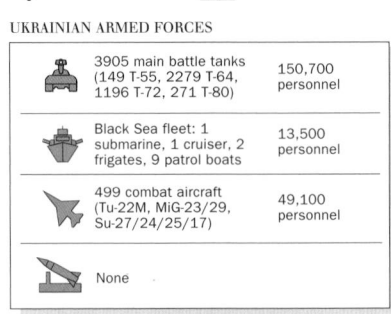

3905 main battle tanks (149 T-55, 2279 T-64, 1196 T-72, 271 T-80)	150,700 personnel
Black Sea fleet: 1 submarine, 1 cruiser, 2 frigates, 9 patrol boats	13,500 personnel
499 combat aircraft (Tu-22M, MiG-23/29, Su-27/24/25/17)	49,100 personnel
None	

Ukraine was a center for arms manufacture under the old Soviet system, and now has a major weapons export trade. A member of the CIS, Ukraine finally resolved in 1997 its long-smoldering dispute with Russia over control of the Black Sea fleet, with agreement on its division and a 20-year Russian lease on port facilities in Sevastopol. Meanwhile, the Ukrainian parliament had ratified the START-I nuclear disarmament treaty, and Ukraine's nuclear warheads were transferred to Russia under a trilateral weapons dismantling accord also involving substantial US aid.

In 2000 it was decided that compulsory military service, which lasts 18 months, should be ended by 2015. The armed forces have been slimmed down, with further cuts planned to result in a total strength of 285,000 (including paramilitary forces) by 2005.

Ukraine joined NATO's Partnership for Peace program in 1995, signed a security pact with the alliance in 1997, and applied in 2002 for full NATO membership.

ECONOMICS

Inflation 221% p.a. (1990–2001)

$35.2bn | 5.333 hryvnas (5.328)

SCORE CARD

- WORLD GNP RANKING....................56th
- GNP PER CAPITA....................$720
- BALANCE OF PAYMENTS....................$1.4bn
- INFLATION....................12%
- UNEMPLOYMENT....................12%

EXPORTS

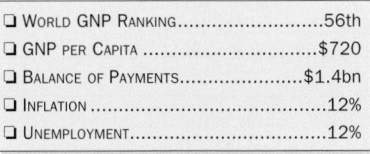

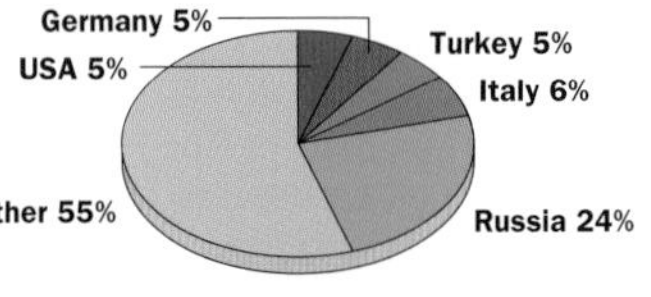
Germany 5%
USA 5%
Turkey 5%
Italy 6%
Other 55%
Russia 24%

IMPORTS

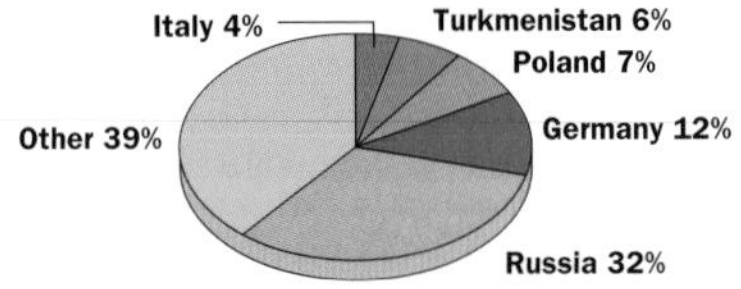
Italy 4%
Turkmenistan 6%
Poland 7%
Other 39%
Germany 12%
Russia 32%

STRENGTHS

Well-educated workforce. Potential for grain and food export. Mineral reserves. Strategic position near the EU. Technological potential, especially in aerospace and computers.

WEAKNESSES

Failure to reform centrally planned economy. Low foreign investment. Weak currency. Huge debt. Antireform political elites. Inefficient, subsidized manufacturing industries. Corruption.

PROFILE

Real growth was recorded at last in 2000, the economy having contracted by over half over ten years. Privatization of large enterprises has barely begun, and bureaucracy stifles private enterprise and investment. Lack of land reform holds back agriculture in the "bread basket" of Europe. Controversial legislation passed in 2001 paved the way for the sale of farmland after 2004.

ECONOMIC PERFORMANCE INDICATOR

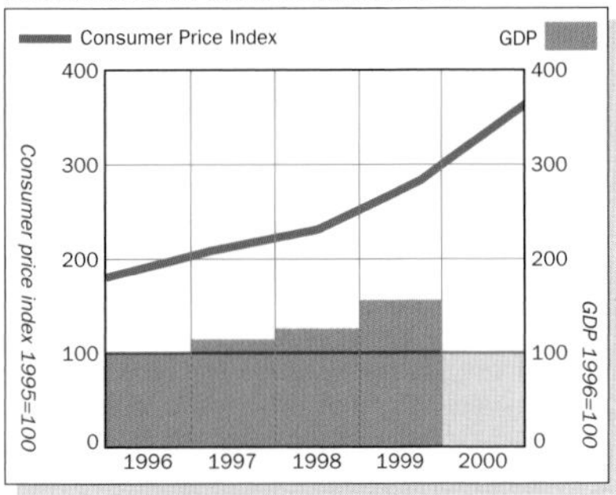
Consumer Price Index
GDP
400
300
200
100
0
Consumer price index 1995=100
GDP 1996=100
1996
1997
1998
1999
2000

UKRAINE : MAJOR BUSINESSES

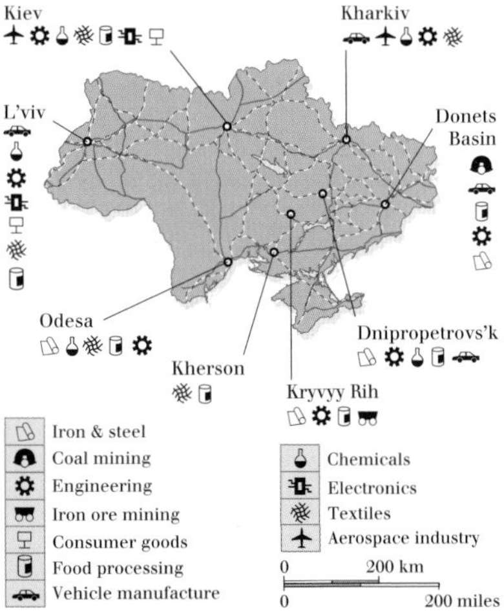
Kiev
Kharkiv
L'viv
Donets Basin
Odesa
Dnipropetrovs'k
Kherson
Kryvyy Rih
Iron & steel
Coal mining
Engineering
Iron ore mining
Consumer goods
Food processing
Vehicle manufacture
Chemicals
Electronics
Textiles
Aerospace industry
0 200 km
0 200 miles

U

RESOURCES

Electric power 53.9m kW

423,693 tonnes

76,190 b/d (reserves 1.6bn barrels)

20m ducks, 8.37m pigs, 9.42m cattle, 146m chickens

Coal, iron, oil, natural gas, manganese, lignite, peat, mercury

ELECTRICITY GENERATION

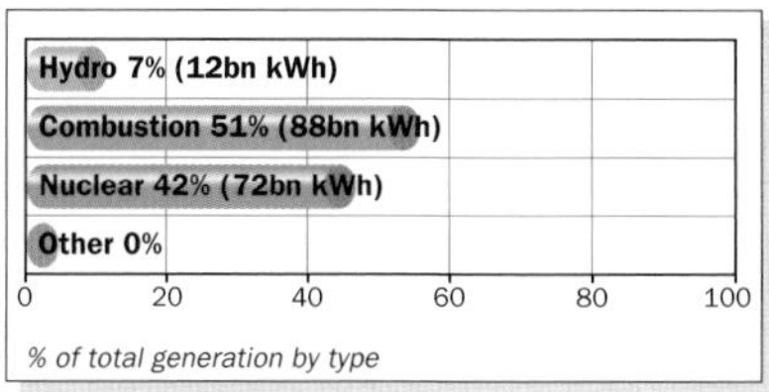
Hydro 7% (12bn kWh)
Combustion 51% (88bn kWh)
Nuclear 42% (72bn kWh)
Other 0%
0
20
40
60
80
100
% of total generation by type

Ukraine imports 90% of its oil and 80% of its gas, mostly from Russia. Some gas is in lieu of transit fees for pipelines carrying Russian gas, but it often misses payments for imports. Yet Ukraine has oil and gas reserves of its own. Coal is mined, in poor safety conditions, in the Donbass–Donetsk region. Just under half of electricity is nuclear-generated.

Ukraine has 5% of global mineral reserves, including the largest titanium reserves, the third-largest deposits of iron ore, and 30% of global manganese ore. There are also mercury, uranium, nickel, and some gold. In 2000, Ukraine exported $6 billion-worth of metal products, which accounted for 63% of the country's export earnings. The steel industry has begun to grow again after several years of decline.

UKRAINE : LAND USE

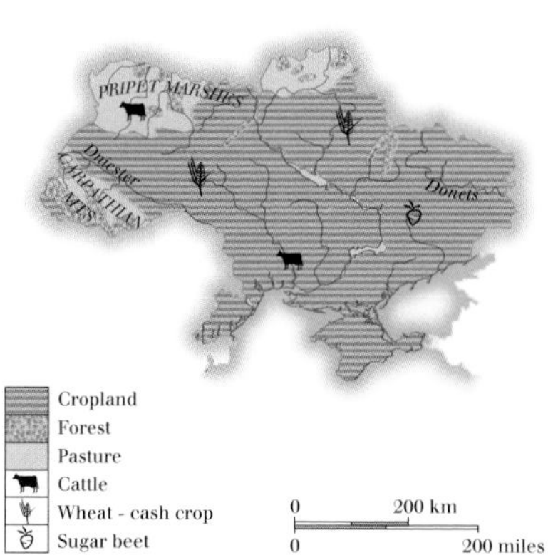
PRIPET MARSHES
Dniester
CARPATHIAN MTS
Donets
Cropland
Forest
Pasture
Cattle
Wheat - cash crop
Sugar beet
0
200 km
0
200 miles

ENVIRONMENT

Sustainability rank: 136th

4% (0.3% partially protected)

7.5 tonnes per capita

ENVIRONMENTAL TREATIES

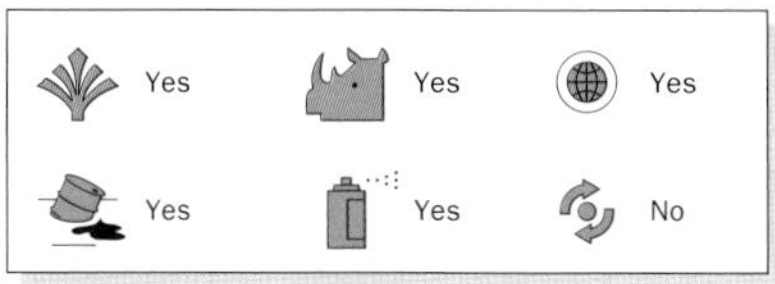
Yes
Yes
Yes
Yes
Yes
No

As a result of the Chernobyl nuclear disaster in 1986 – the world's worst nuclear accident – over three million Ukrainians live in dangerously radioactive areas and 12% of arable land is contaminated. The last working reactor at Chernobyl closed at the end of 2000, under agreements in which Western countries provided large-scale financial assistance. However, nuclear production continues elsewhere because of the cost of Russian oil and gas imports. Coal-fired power plants are old-fashioned, highly polluting, and inefficient. Industrial pollution is widespread, especially from steel and chemical works in the Donbass region, contributing to the acute problem of low air quality in eight major cities.

MEDIA

TV ownership high

Daily newspaper circulation 175 per 1000 people

PUBLISHING AND BROADCAST MEDIA

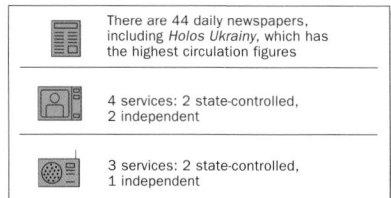

There are 44 daily newspapers, including *Holos Ukrainy*, which has the highest circulation figures

4 services: 2 state-controlled, 2 independent

3 services: 2 state-controlled, 1 independent

Mass-circulation newspapers are mainly in Russian. TV stations reflect regional differences. Journalists fear repression and extrajudicial violence.

CRIME

No death penalty

198,885 prisoners

Down 16% in 2000–2002

CRIME RATES

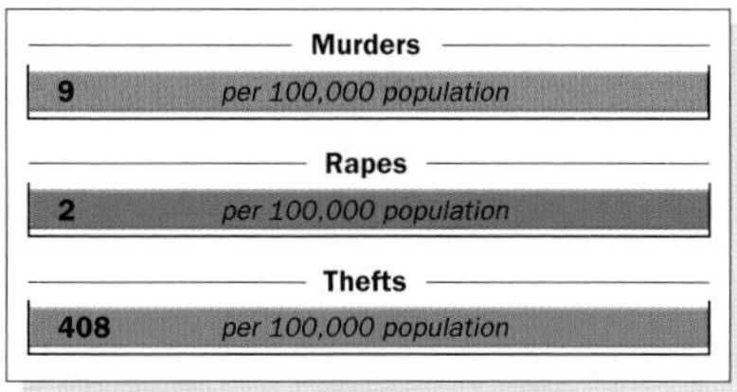
Murders
9 per 100,000 population
Rapes
2 per 100,000 population
Thefts
408 per 100,000 population

Street crime, robberies, violence, and carjackings have increased sharply. Ukraine is a major source of people-trafficking to the West. Corruption is rampant across the economy. Political killings make headlines, as did the murder in 2000 of journalist Georgy Gongadze. The death penalty was abolished in 2000.

EDUCATION

School leaving age: 15

99%

1.58m students

THE EDUCATION SYSTEM

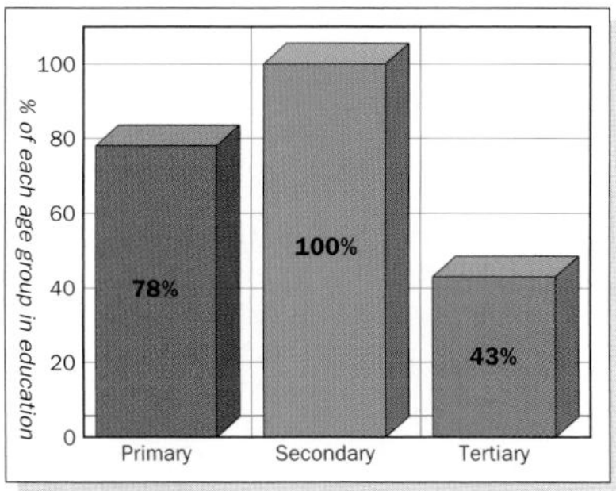
100
80
60
40
20
0
% of each age group in education
78%
100%
43%
Primary
Secondary
Tertiary

Using Ukrainian in schools is the main element in the drive to promote the once-banned language. Some schools in the west no longer teach Russian. Most university teaching is in Russian in eastern regions, and in Ukrainian in those in the west.

HEALTH

Welfare state health benefits

1 per 334 people

Cerebrovascular and heart diseases, cancers, accidents

Health care, supposedly free to all, has declined significantly in the post-Soviet period. A $2 million UN program provides treatment and preventive care for the 350,000 people who dealt with the Chernobyl disaster. By 2001, 1% of the population was HIV positive.

SPENDING

GDP/cap. decrease

CONSUMPTION AND SPENDING

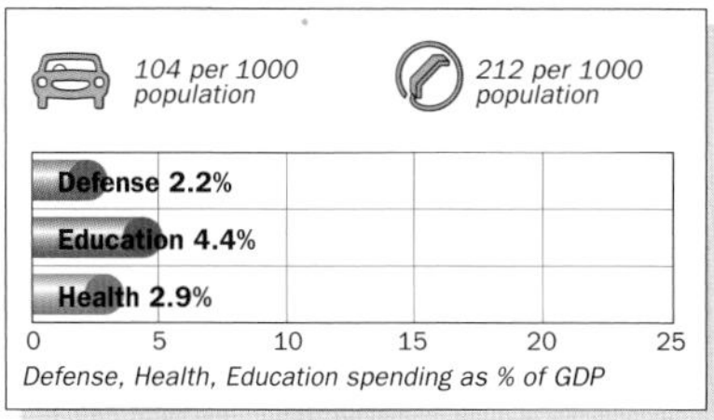
104 per 1000 population
212 per 1000 population
Defense 2.2%
Education 4.4%
Health 2.9%
0
5
10
15
20
25
Defense, Health, Education spending as % of GDP

Just under half the population live below the UN poverty line. Wage arrears – and massive hidden unemployment – are major problems.

WORLD RANKING

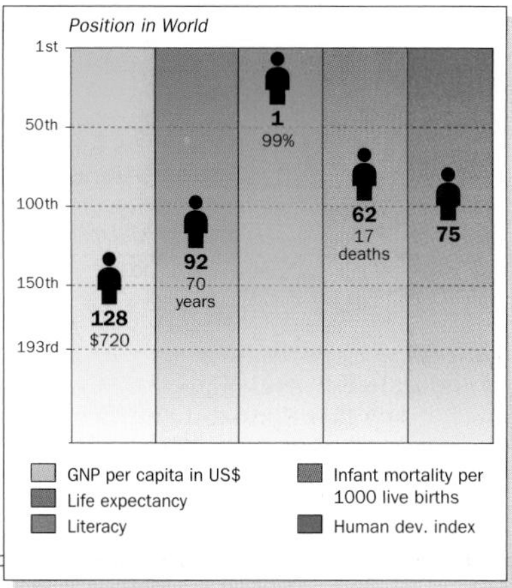
Position in World
1st
50th
100th
150th
193rd
128
$720
92
70 years
1
99%
62
17 deaths
75
GNP per capita in US$
Life expectancy
Literacy
Infant mortality per 1000 live births
Human dev. index

U

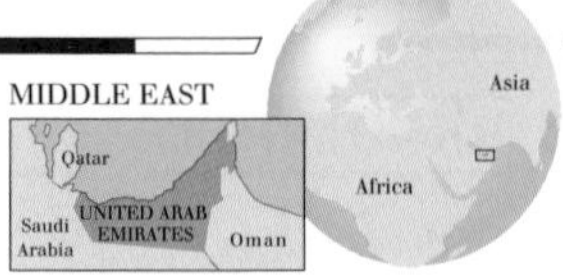
MIDDLE EAST
Asia
Africa
Qatar
Saudi Arabia
UNITED ARAB EMIRATES
Oman

UNITED ARAB EMIRATES

OFFICIAL NAME: United Arab Emirates **CAPITAL:** Abu Dhabi
POPULATION: 2.7 million **CURRENCY:** UAE dirham **OFFICIAL LANGUAGE:** Arabic

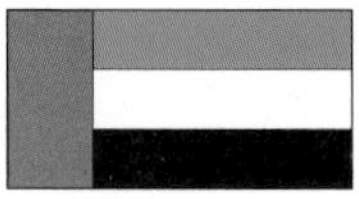

1971
1972
Dec 2
UAE
+4
+971
.ae

THE UNITED ARAB EMIRATES (UAE), created in 1971, is the Arab world's only working federation. Six of its seven emirates cluster around the northeastern corner of the country, while Abu Dhabi has a larger hinterland of semiarid desert relieved by occasional oases. The cities, watered by extensive irrigation systems, have lavish greenery. Prosperity once relied on pearls, but the UAE is now a sizable gas and oil exporter, and has a growing services sector.

CLIMATE

Hot desert

WEATHER CHART FOR ABU DHABI

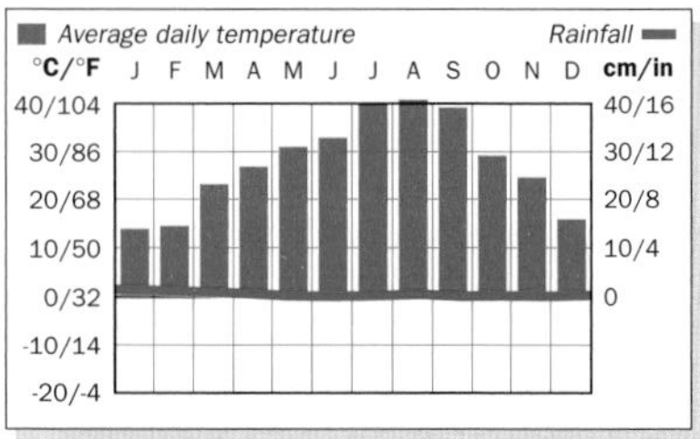
Average daily temperature
Rainfall
°C/°F J F M A M J J A S O N D cm/in
40/104
30/86
20/68
10/50
0/32
-10/14
-20/-4
40/16
30/12
20/8
10/4
0

Though rainfall is minimal, summers are humid. Sand-laden *shamal* winds often blow in winter and spring.

TRANSPORTATION

Drive on right

Dubai International
16m passengers

341 ships
746,400 grt

THE TRANSPORTATION NETWORK

4835 km
(3004 miles)

None

None

None

The roads are good. Five of the seven emirates have international airports, of which the busiest is Dubai International.

TOURISM

Visitors : Population
1.4:1

3.91m visitors

Up 15% in 2000

MAIN TOURIST ARRIVALS

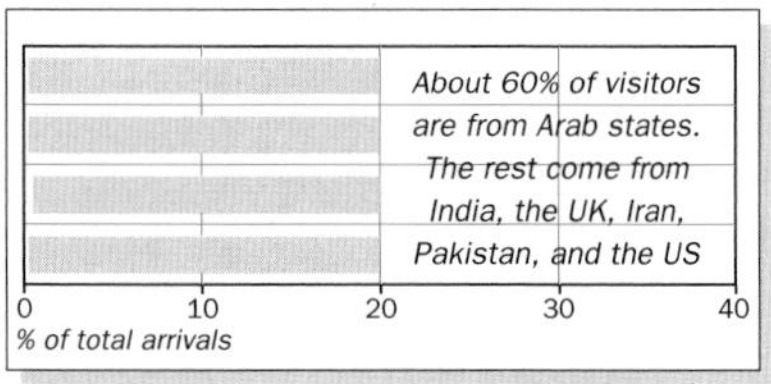
About 60% of visitors are from Arab states. The rest come from India, the UK, Iran, Pakistan, and the US
0
10
20
30
40
% of total arrivals

Until the mid-1980s, tourism was minimal. Led by Dubai, the UAE has now launched initiatives to attract Western visitors during the winter for sunshine, heritage, water sports, desert safaris, and duty-free shopping.

PEOPLE

Pop. density low

Arabic, Farsi, Indian and Pakistani languages, English

32/km²
(84/mi²)

THE URBAN/RURAL POPULATION SPLIT

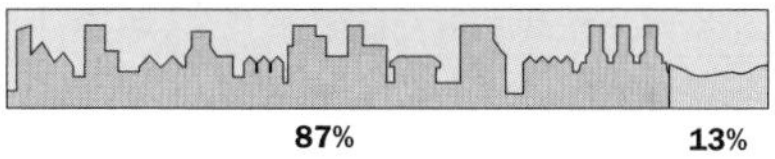
87%
13%

ETHNIC MAKEUP

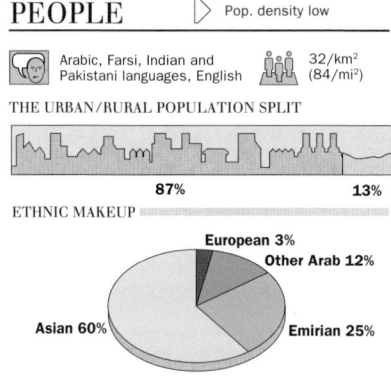

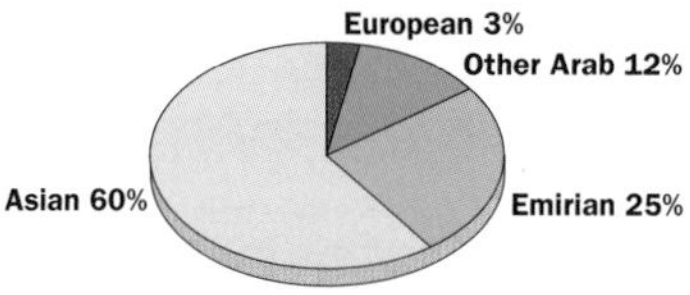
European 3%
Other Arab 12%
Asian 60%
Emirian 25%

UAE nationals are largely city dwellers, with Abu Dhabi and Dubai the main centers. They are greatly outnumbered by expatriates who arrived in the 1970s during the oil boom, and the Western expatriate community is permitted a virtually unrestricted lifestyle. Most UAE nationals are conservative Sunni Muslims of Bedouin descent, though there is a Shi'a community in Dubai with links to Iran. Islamic fundamentalism is a growing force among the young.

Poverty is rare in the UAE, where the government remains the biggest employer. Women in theory enjoy equal rights with men. A Presidential Marriage Fund discourages UAE men from taking foreign wives.

POLITICS

No legislative elections

Not applicable

President Shaikh Zayed bin Sultan al-Nahyan

LEGISLATIVE OR ADVISORY BODIES

Federal National Council 40 seats

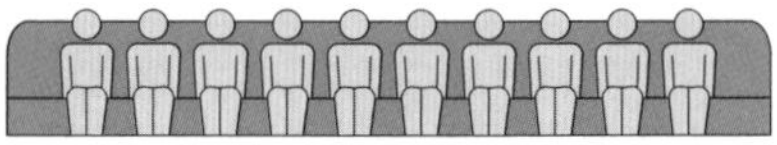

There are no political parties. The method of appointment of members of the Federal National Council is determined individually by each of the seven members of the federation.

The UAE's seven emirates – Abu Dhabi, Dubai, Sharjah, Ras al Khaimah, Ajman, Umm al Qaiwain, and Fujairah – are dominated by their ruling families. The main personalities are the ruler of Abu Dhabi, Shaikh Zayed, who holds the UAE presidency, and the four al-Maktoum brothers who control Dubai. The eldest, Shaikh Maktoum al-Maktoum, is ruler of Dubai as well as vice president and prime minister of the UAE.

President Zayed has relaunched the advisory Federal National Council in response to criticism of the lack of democracy. The growth of Islamic fundamentalism is also a concern. The freedoms granted to Westerners have aroused some anger but, for economic reasons, they are unlikely to be withdrawn.

UNITED ARAB EMIRATES

Total Area : 82 880 sq. km (32 000 sq. miles)

POPULATION
- over 100 000
- under 10 000

LAND HEIGHT
- 1000m/3281ft
- 500m/1640ft
- Sea Level

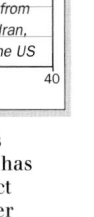

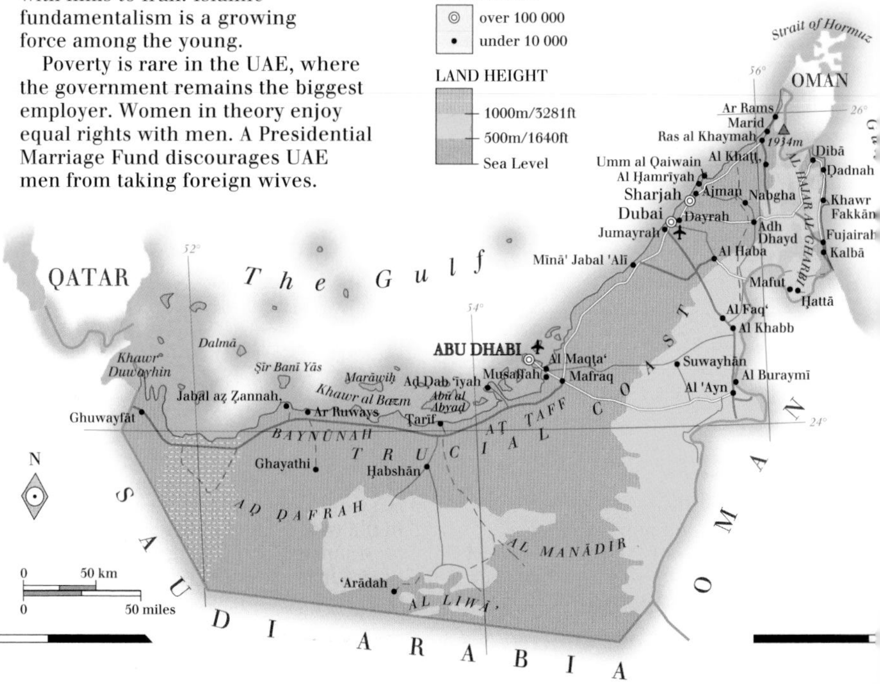
Strait of Hormuz
OMAN
Ar Rams
Marid
Ras al Khaymah
1934m
Dibā
Dadnah
Umm al Qaiwain
Al Khatt
Al Ḩamrīyah
Sharjah
Ajman
Nabgha
Khawr Fakkān
Dubai
Dayrah
Jumayrah
Adh Dhayd
Fujairah
Kalbā
Al Haba
Mīnā' Jabal 'Alī
QATAR
The Gulf
Mafut
Ḩattā
Al Faq'
Al Khabb
Dalmā
ABU DHABI
Al Maqta'
Khawr Duwayhin
Ṣīr Banī Yās
Marāwiḩ
Ad Dab 'iyah
Musaffah
Mafraq
Suwayhān
Al Buraymī
Al 'Ayn
Jabal az Zannah
Khawr al Bazm
Abū al Abyaḑ
Ar Ruways
Ghuwayfāt
Tarif
TRUCIAL COAST
BAYNŪNAH
Ghayathi
Ḩabshān
AD DAFRAH
AL MANĀDIR
'Arādah
AL LIWĀ
SAUDI ARABIA
OMAN
N
0 50 km
0 50 miles

WORLD AFFAIRS

Joined UN in 1971

AL | OIC | GCC | OAPEC | OPEC

The UAE is well known as a moderate Arab state. It maintains close links with the West, especially the UK and the US.

In 1992, conflict flared when Iran seized control of three disputed islands: negotiations continue. The UAE angered the Arab League in 2003 when it urged Iraqi president Saddam Hussein to resign to avoid war.

AID

Donor

$127m (donations) — Down 15% in 2001

Once a generous donor to developing countries, the UAE's contributions have fluctuated with energy prices.

DEFENSE

No compulsory military sevice

$3.07bn — Up 2% in 2001

The training of UAE forces is limited, and personnel are mainly drawn from other Arab states and the Indian subcontinent. US air bases in the UAE supply refueling craft and have been used consistently in regional conflicts, including the 2001 war in Afghanistan and the 2003 invasion of Iraq. The countries of the GCC signed their first defense pact in 2000.

ECONOMICS

Inflation 2.3% p.a. (1990–1999)

$49.2bn — 3.673 UAE dirhams (3.673)

SCORE CARD

❑ World GNP Ranking	49th
❑ GNP per Capita	$18,060
❑ Balance of Payments	$24.6bn
❑ Inflation	4.5%
❑ Unemployment	None

Strengths

Oil and gas reserves. Development of service industries and manufacturing sector. Improving education system. Regional tax-free base for e-commerce.

Weaknesses

Lack of skilled manpower. Most raw materials and foodstuffs imported. Water resources scarce and concentrated in Abu Dhabi.

EXPORTS

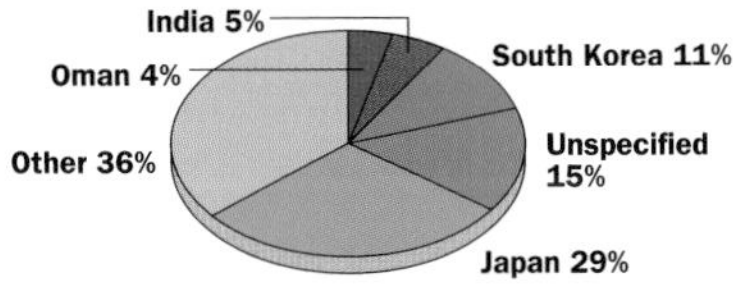
India 5%
Oman 4%
South Korea 11%
Other 36%
Unspecified 15%
Japan 29%

IMPORTS

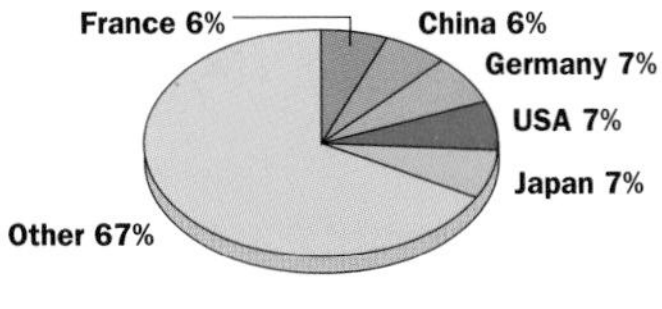
France 6%
China 6%
Germany 7%
USA 7%
Japan 7%
Other 67%

RESOURCES

Electric power 5.8m kW

105,456 tonnes — 2.27m b/d (reserves 97.8bn barrels)

1.3m goats, 510,000 sheep, 17m chickens — Oil, natural gas

The UAE is a major exporter of crude oil and natural gas. Oil production accounts for a great part of export revenue. Mina Jabal Ali in Dubai is the world's largest man-made port and has attracted companies from more than 50 countries. Saadiyat Island off Abu Dhabi is being developed as a financial resort.

ENVIRONMENT

Sustainability rank: 141st

None — 31.9 tonnes per capita

Despite the harsh desert climate, there is a rich variety of plants and animals. Shaikh Zayed champions conservation parks to avert the threat from hunting.

MEDIA

TV ownership high

Daily newspaper circulation 156 per 1000 people

PUBLISHING AND BROADCAST MEDIA

There are 7 daily newspapers. The leading Arabic newspaper is *Al-Ittihad*. *Emirates News* is its English-language counterpart

4 state-owned services — 7 state-owned services

Satellite TV is unrestricted. Dubai Media City, opened in 2001, promotes greater press freedom.

CRIME

Death penalty in use

6000 prisoners — Up 2% in 2000

Street crime and muggings are rare. Dubai is reputed to be a transit point for the smuggling of narcotics and caviar.

***An oasis village**, inland from Fujairah, now accessible by means of a well-developed network of new roads.*

CHRONOLOGY

The UAE was influenced by the Portuguese and the Ottomans, but the British became dominant in the 19th century.

- ❑ **1971** The UK withdraws as protecting power and UAE federation is formed.
- ❑ **1991** UAE offers bases to Western forces after Kuwait is invaded.
- ❑ **2000** GCC defense pact signed.

EDUCATION

School leaving age: 11

77% — 21,000 students

UAE citizens enjoy completely free education. Zayed University was set up in three emirates in 1998.

HEALTH

Welfare state health benefits

1 per 565 people — Circulatory and respiratory diseases, cancers

A high-quality system of primary health care is in place for all UAE citizens, with hospitals able to carry out most operations.

SPENDING

GDP/cap. increase

CONSUMPTION AND SPENDING

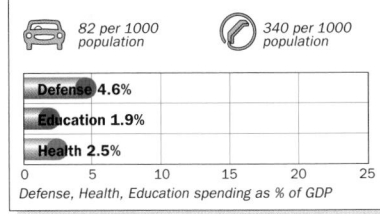

82 per 1000 population — *340 per 1000 population*

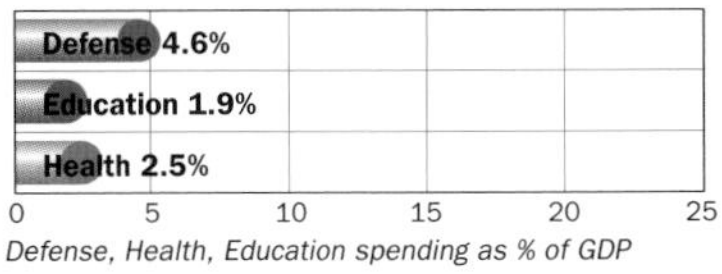
Defense 4.6%
Education 1.9%
Health 2.5%
0 5 10 15 20 25
Defense, Health, Education spending as % of GDP

UAE nationals enjoy one of the highest per capita incomes in the Arab world. There is no income tax, and oil revenues subsidize public services. Entrepreneurship is encouraged.

WORLD RANKING

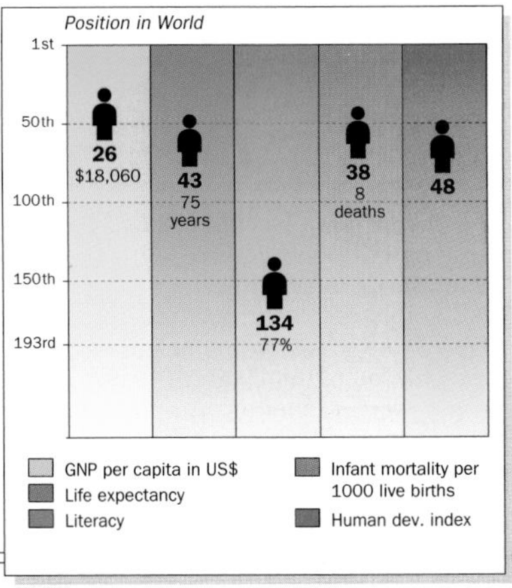
Position in World
1st
50th
100th
150th
193rd
26
$18,060
43
75 years
134
77%
38
8 deaths
48
GNP per capita in US$
Life expectancy
Literacy
Infant mortality per 1000 live births
Human dev. index

U

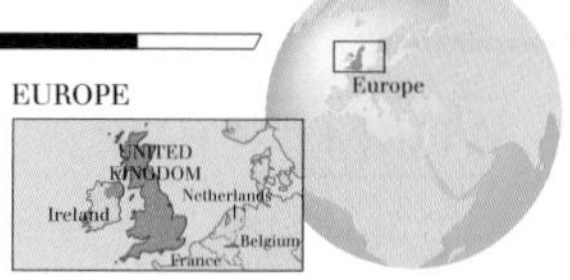
EUROPE
Europe
UNITED KINGDOM
Ireland
Netherlands
Belgium
France

UNITED KINGDOM

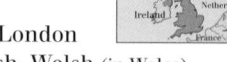

OFFICIAL NAME: United Kingdom of Great Britain and Northern Ireland **CAPITAL:** London
POPULATION: 58.8 million **CURRENCY:** Pound sterling **OFFICIAL LANGUAGES:** English, Welsh (in Wales)

1707 | 1922 | None | GB | 0 | +44 | .uk

LYING IN NORTHWESTERN Europe, the United Kingdom (UK) occupies the major portion of the British Isles. It includes the countries of England, Scotland, and Wales, the constitutionally distinct region of Northern Ireland, and several outlying islands. Its only land border is with the Irish republic. The UK is separated from the European mainland by the English Channel and the North Sea. To the west lies the Atlantic Ocean. The most densely populated region is the southeast, while Scotland is the wildest region, with the Highlands less populated today than in the 18th century. The UK joined the European Communities (EC – later the EU) in 1973, and most of its trade is now with its European partners. Leadership of the Commonwealth and membership of the UN Security Council give the UK a prominent role in international politics.

CLIMATE

Maritime

WEATHER CHART FOR LONDON

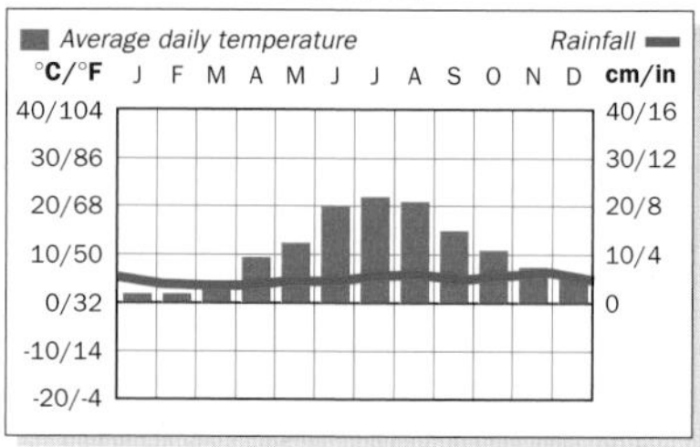
Average daily temperature
Rainfall
°C/°F J F M A M J J A S O N D cm/in
40/104
30/86
20/68
10/50
0/32
-10/14
-20/-4
40/16
30/12
20/8
10/4
0

The UK has a generally mild, temperate, and highly changeable climate. Rain, regarded as synonymous with Britain's weather, is fairly well distributed throughout the year, but recently unusually long dry or wet spells have caused water shortages in some areas, and flooding in others. The west is generally wetter than the east, and the south warmer than the north.

TRANSPORTATION

Drive on left

Heathrow, London 63.3m passengers

1462 ships 6.03m grt

THE TRANSPORTATION NETWORK

371,603 km (230,903 miles)

3453 km (2146 miles)

16,406 km (10,194 miles)

5700 km (3542 miles)

The government has not fulfilled its 1997 campaign promise of a more integrated policy, faced with congestion, pollution, and motorists' resentment of high fuel taxes. The rail system, after the rushed privatization of the 1990s, suffers from underinvestment, maintenance problems, and fragmented services. Central London introduced a "congestion charge" for road use in 2003.

TOURISM

Visitors : Population 1:2.5

23.9m visitors

Up 5% in 2002

MAIN TOURIST ARRIVALS

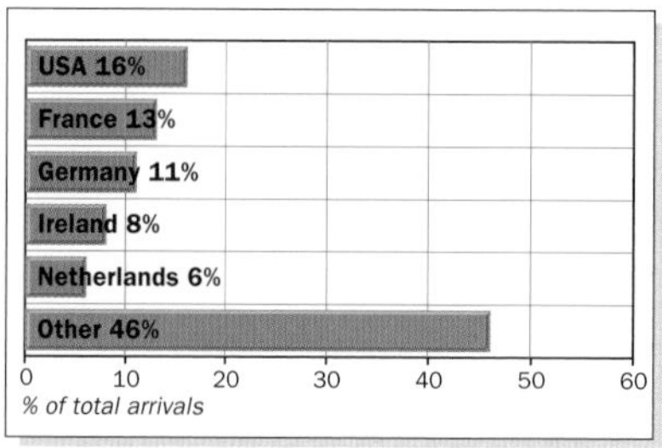
USA 16%
France 13%
Germany 11%
Ireland 8%
Netherlands 6%
Other 46%
0 10 20 30 40 50 60
% of total arrivals

The UK ranks sixth in the world as a tourist destination. Tourism is among its most important industries and is a growing source of employment. Heritage is the principal selling point, North Americans, French, and Germans are the main visitors, and London, with its art galleries, theaters, and historic buildings, remains the major destination. Visitors also head for the Roman splendors of Bath, Shakespeare's Stratford-upon-Avon, the medieval buildings of Oxford, Cambridge, and York, and Scotland, where the Highlands are a particular attraction.

Oxford, *home to the oldest university in the UK. Teaching began in 1096; the first college was founded in 1249. One of the city's finest buildings is the 17th-century semi-oval Sheldonian Theatre.*

PEOPLE

Pop. density high

English, Welsh, Scottish Gaelic, Irish Gaelic

243/km² (630/mi²)

THE URBAN/RURAL POPULATION SPLIT

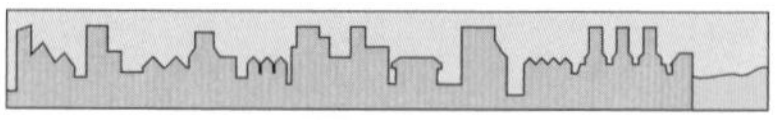
90%
10%

RELIGIOUS PERSUASION

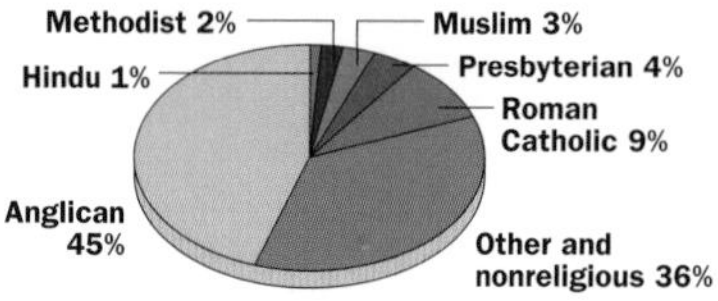
Methodist 2%
Muslim 3%
Hindu 1%
Presbyterian 4%
Roman Catholic 9%
Anglican 45%
Other and nonreligious 36%

ETHNIC MAKEUP

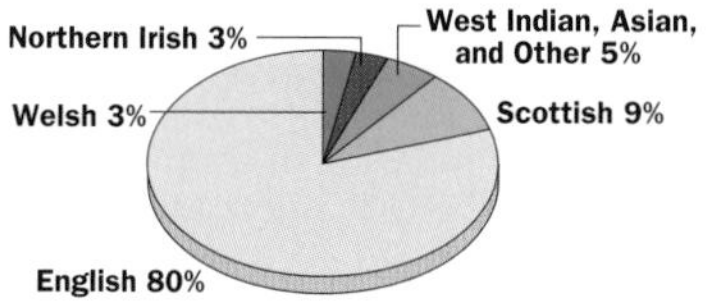
Northern Irish 3%
West Indian, Asian, and Other 5%
Welsh 3%
Scottish 9%
English 80%

The Scottish and Welsh nations remain recognizably distinct, despite forming part of a unified state. Scotland retains its own legal and educational systems, and recent steps in devolution have given both countries greater autonomy.

Britain's ethnic minorities account for 5% of the total population; over 50% of their members were born in Britain. Ethnic minority communities are generally concentrated in the inner cities, where they face problems of deprivation and social stress, and may also suffer from isolation, particularly women. Though there is not much support for overtly racist politics, multiethnic recruitment has made little progress in key areas such as policing, and prejudices persist. The level of institutionalized racism was criticized by the UN in 2000.

Two-fifths of all births occur outside marriage, compared with 12% in 1980, but most of these are to cohabiting couples. Single-parent households account for one-fifth of all families with children under 18.

POPULATION AGE BREAKDOWN

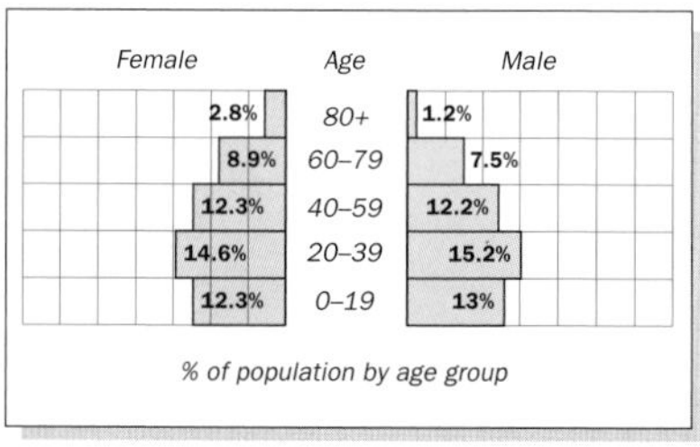
Female
Age
Male
2.8% 80+ 1.2%
8.9% 60–79 7.5%
12.3% 40–59 12.2%
14.6% 20–39 15.2%
12.3% 0–19 13%
% of population by age group

U

Black Mount, Rannoch Moor, *in the Scottish Highlands. The Highlands are one of the UK's wildest regions.*

CHRONOLOGY

Great Britain began the 20th century as one of the world's most advanced economies, backed by a massive trading empire.

- ❑ **1906** Reformist Liberal government.
- ❑ **1914** World War I begins.
- ❑ **1918** Armistice signals end of war. Cost to Britain: 750,000 dead.
- ❑ **1922** Irish Free State given dominion status.
- ❑ **1926** General Strike.
- ❑ **1929** World stock market crash. Widespread unemployment.
- ❑ **1931** UK leaves gold standard and devalues pound.
- ❑ **1936** Edward VIII abdicates over marriage to Wallis Simpson.
- ❑ **1938** Prime Minister Neville Chamberlain meets Hitler in Munich over Czech crisis, says threat of war with Germany averted.
- ❑ **1939** Germany invades Poland. UK declares war on Germany.
- ❑ **1940** Winston Churchill prime minister. Battle of Britain.
- ❑ **1944** 6th June, D-Day invasion of German-occupied France.
- ❑ **1945** End of World War II, costing 330,000 British lives. Labour government elected on social welfare platform.
- ❑ **1946** Nationalization of Bank of England, railroads, coal, utilities.
- ❑ **1947** Indian independence.

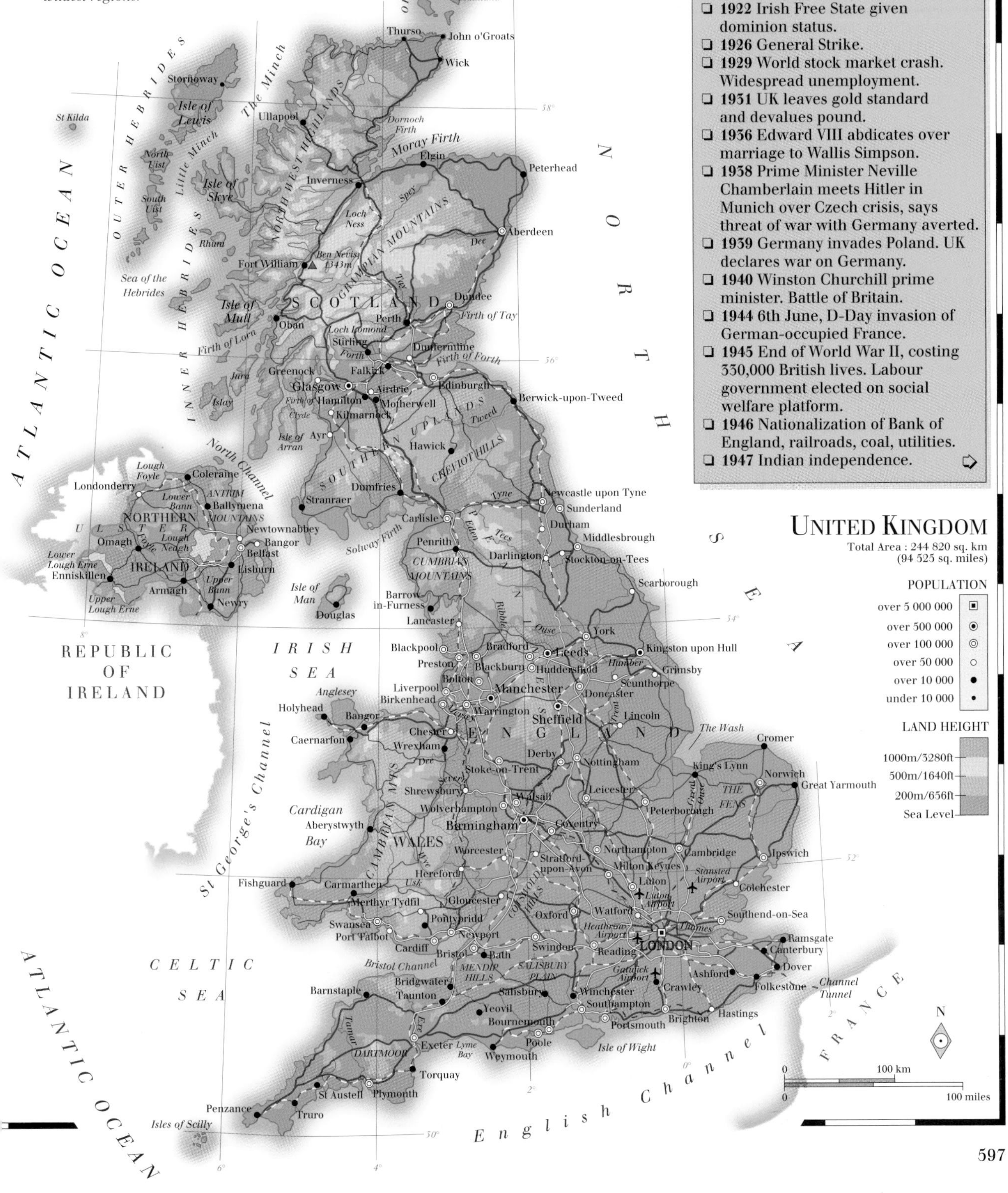
UNITED KINGDOM
Total Area : 244 820 sq. km
(94 525 sq. miles)
POPULATION
over 5 000 000
over 500 000
over 100 000
over 50 000
over 10 000
under 10 000
LAND HEIGHT
1000m/3280ft
500m/1640ft
200m/656ft
Sea Level
0
100 km
0
100 miles
N
ATLANTIC OCEAN
NORTH SEA
IRISH SEA
CELTIC SEA
English Channel
REPUBLIC OF IRELAND
FRANCE
SCOTLAND
ENGLAND
WALES
NORTHERN IRELAND
ULSTER
SHETLAND ISLANDS
ORKNEY ISLANDS
OUTER HEBRIDES
INNER HEBRIDES
Mainland
Lerwick
Fair I.
Kirkwall
Thurso
John o'Groats
Wick
Stornoway
Isle of Lewis
St Kilda
North Uist
South Uist
Isle of Skye
Rhum
Ullapool
The Minch
Little Minch
NORTH WEST HIGHLANDS
Dornoch Firth
Moray Firth
Elgin
Peterhead
Inverness
Loch Ness
Spey
GRAMPIAN MOUNTAINS
Aberdeen
Dee
Ben Nevis 1343m
Fort William
Sea of the Hebrides
Isle of Mull
Oban
Tay
Dundee
Firth of Tay
Perth
Loch Lomond
Stirling
Forth
Firth of Lorn
Dunfermline
Firth of Forth
Jura
Islay
Greenock
Glasgow
Falkirk
Airdrie
Edinburgh
Hamilton
Motherwell
Firth of Clyde
Kilmarnock
Berwick-upon-Tweed
Tweed
SOUTHERN UPLANDS
Isle of Arran
Ayr
Hawick
CHEVIOT HILLS
North Channel
Lough Foyle
Coleraine
Londonderry
Lower Bann
ANTRIM MOUNTAINS
Ballymena
Newtownabbey
Bangor
Belfast
Lough Neagh
Omagh
Lisburn
Lower Lough Erne
Enniskillen
Armagh
Upper Bann
Newry
Upper Lough Erne
Dumfries
Stranraer
Carlisle
Tyne
Newcastle upon Tyne
Sunderland
Durham
Solway Firth
Eden
Tees
Middlesbrough
Penrith
Darlington
Stockton-on-Tees
CUMBRIAN MOUNTAINS
PENNINES
Scarborough
Isle of Man
Douglas
Barrow-in-Furness
Lancaster
Ribble
Ouse
York
Kingston upon Hull
Humber
Grimsby
Blackpool
Bradford
Leeds
Preston
Blackburn
Huddersfield
Scunthorpe
Bolton
Liverpool
Birkenhead
Manchester
Doncaster
Anglesey
Holyhead
Bangor
Warrington
Sheffield
Trent
Lincoln
The Wash
Cromer
Caernarfon
Chester
Wrexham
Dee
Derby
Nottingham
King's Lynn
Norwich
Great Yarmouth
Stoke-on-Trent
Severn
Shrewsbury
Leicester
THE FENS
Great Ouse
Wolverhampton
Walsall
Peterborough
Cardigan Bay
Aberystwyth
Birmingham
Coventry
CAMBRIAN MTS
Wye
Worcester
Northampton
Cambridge
Ipswich
Stratford-upon-Avon
Milton Keynes
St George's Channel
Fishguard
Carmarthen
Usk
Hereford
Luton
Stansted Airport
Colchester
COTSWOLD HILLS
Luton Airport
Merthyr Tydfil
Gloucester
Southend-on-Sea
Pontypridd
Oxford
Watford
Swansea
Port Talbot
Newport
Heathrow Airport
Thames
LONDON
Ramsgate
Canterbury
Cardiff
Bristol
Bath
Swindon
Reading
Dover
Bristol Channel
MENDIP HILLS
SALISBURY PLAIN
Gatwick Airport
Ashford
Barnstaple
Bridgwater
Taunton
Salisbury
Winchester
Crawley
Folkestone
Channel Tunnel
Southampton
Yeovil
Hastings
Tamar
Exe
Bournemouth
Portsmouth
Brighton
Exeter
Lyme Bay
Poole
Isle of Wight
DARTMOOR
Weymouth
Torquay
St Austell
Plymouth
Penzance
Truro
Isles of Scilly

U

CHRONOLOGY *continued*

- **1948** NHS established.
- **1949** Founder member of NATO.
- **1956** Suez crisis: UK intervenes in Canal Zone, withdraws under US pressure.
- **1957** US nuclear missiles accepted on UK soil.
- **1961** UK application to join the EEC rejected by French president Charles de Gaulle.
- **1968** Abortion and homosexuality are legalized.
- **1969** British troops sent into Northern Ireland.
- **1973** Joins EEC under Conservative Edward Heath. Oil crisis. Industry on three-day week following strikes by power workers and miners.
- **1974** Labour government, under Harold Wilson, concedes miners' demands. High inflation.
- **1975** Referendum ratifies EC membership. First North Sea oil pipeline in operation.
- **1979–1997** Conservative rule, until 1990 under Margaret Thatcher.
- **1980** Anti-US Cruise missile protests. Rising unemployment. Inner-city riots.
- **1981** Privatization program begun.
- **1982** Argentina invades Falklands. Islands retaken by UK task force.
- **1983** Tax-cutting policies.
- **1986** Financial services market deregularized ("Big Bang").
- **1990** John Major replaces Thatcher.
- **1991** UK in Gulf War.
- **1992** Conservatives win fourth term.
- **1996** Dunblane primary school massacre; tightening of gun control laws. Health crisis linking "mad cow" disease (BSE) with fatal variant Creutzfeldt-Jakob disease (vCJD).
- **1997** Landslide election victory for Labour under Tony Blair. Diana, Princess of Wales, killed in car crash in Paris. Scottish and Welsh referenda approve creation of own assemblies.
- **1998–1999** Good Friday agreement on political settlement in Northern Ireland, endorsed by referendum but held up by disputes over decommissioning weapons.
- **1999** Involvement in NATO air war with Yugoslavia over Kosovo crisis. Scottish Parliament and Welsh Assembly elected, inaugurated. Devolution to power-sharing executive in Northern Ireland.
- **2001** Foot-and-mouth epidemic and mass livestock culling. June, Labour reelected by huge majority. October, military participation in US-led "war on terrorism" in Afghanistan.
- **2002** 50th anniversary of accession to throne of Queen Elizabeth II.
- **2003** UK troops invade Iraq alongside US forces.

U

POLITICS

Multiparty elections

L. House 2001/2006

H.M. Queen Elizabeth II

AT THE LAST ELECTION

House of Commons 659 seats

1% 1%
UU Others
63% Lab
25% Con
8% LD
1% SNP
1% PC

Lab = Labour Party **Con** = Conservative and Unionist Party **LD** = Liberal Democrats **UU** = Ulster Unionist parties – (official) Ulster Unionist Party, Democratic Unionist Party, UK Unionist **SNP** = Scottish National Party **PC** = Plaid Cymru

House of Lords 679 seats

The House of Lords is an unelected body of just under 100 hereditary peers, 26 spiritual peers (bishops), and over 500 life peers (including lords of appeal – judges), appointed by the monarch

The UK is a multiparty democracy. The monarch's power is largely ceremonial.

Profile

Tony Blair's "New Labour" government, occupying the political center, won power in 1997 after almost 18 years of Conservative rule, and retained a massive majority in the June 2001 election. In opposition, the Conservatives have so far failed to build a credible challenge around opposition to the euro and pledges to reduce taxes.

Main Political Issues

Europe

No date has been set for implementing Labour plans for a referendum on joining the euro single currency. Opinion polls show little public support, and the Conservatives, in opposition, have become increasingly "eurosceptic," considering that membership of the EU erodes national sovereignty.

Constitutional change

Major changes were made to the UK's system of government in the late 1990s. A separate Scottish Parliament, with substantial devolved powers, was elected in 1999, as was a new Welsh Assembly. The House of Lords was considerably changed by the abolition of voting rights for nearly all hereditary peers, pending its complete overhaul; there is as yet no agreement on the form it should take. London gained greater autonomy in 2000 with the election of its own assembly and mayor.

In Northern Ireland, the 1998 Good Friday agreement brought unionists and Irish republicans into a power-sharing government. Tensions between the Unionists and the republican Sinn Fein party has caused the joint executive formed in 1999 to be suspended and direct rule reimposed.

Queen Elizabeth II, *head of state since 1952 and head of the Commonwealth.*

Tony Blair, *prime minister since 1997, and leader of the Labour Party.*

Chancellor of the Exchequer Gordon Brown, *known as the "Iron Chancellor."*

Baroness Thatcher, *the country's only female prime minister (1979–1990).*

The economy

Fundamental alternatives on running the economy are no longer argued within mainstream politics. Labour has ceased believing in renationalizing privatized industries, and is wary of increasing taxes. Its belief in using private finance and management within publicly owned services, such as health and education, has alienated some traditional Labour supporters, and the financial benefits of this policy are questioned by others. The concept of elite "foundation hospitals," with substantial financial independence from the National Health Service, is especially controversial.

The war on Iraq

The prospect of participation in the US-led invasion of Iraq in 2003 without an explicit UN mandate aroused strong public opposition and huge public demonstrations. The failure to find weapons of mass destruction in Iraq following the invasion undermined Blair's main justification for the war.

London's City Hall, *designed by the world famous architect Sir Norman Foster. It has been home to the London Assembly since 2002.*

WORLD AFFAIRS

Joined UN in 1945

Comm | EU | G8 | NATO | OECD

In 2002 Prime Minister Blair claimed that the UK, if no longer a "great power," could still play a "pivotal role" in world affairs. It holds a permanent seat on the UN Security Council, and being the official head of the Commonwealth offers a means of maintaining diplomatic and economic links with the UK's former possessions.

The UK joined the EEC late, and resists the concept of full integration. While committed in principle to joining the euro, the government has as yet set no timetable for doing so.

Cherishing the UK–US "special relationship," the New Labour government was a fervent supporter of the US invasion of Iraq in 2003.

AID

Donor

$4.58bn (donations)

Up 2% in 2001

UK foreign aid fell between 1980 and 1997 to below the European average, and well below the nominal target of 0.7% of GNP for industrialized countries. After 1997 the government moved to end the decline, though the figure in 2001 was only 0.32% of GNP. More significant was its concentration on the poorest countries and on partnership with NGOs, building on a change of emphasis already introduced in 1996, when 85% of bilateral aid was directed at 20 states in sub-Saharan Africa and south Asia. The "trade for aid" provision, by which much of the aid budget was tied to contracts for British firms, has been abolished. The aid program's aims include encouraging good government, widening opportunities for women, and protecting the environment.

DEFENSE

No compulsory military service

$34.7bn

Up in 2002

UK ARMED FORCES

594 main battle tanks (386 Challenger 2, 205 Challenger, 3 Chieftain)	114,800 personnel
16 submarines, 3 carriers, 11 destroyers, 21 frigates, and 20 patrol boats	42,350 personnel
468 combat aircraft (301 Tornado, 66 Jaguar, 82 Harrier)	53,300 personnel
58 SLBM in 4 SSBN	

Despite significant post-Cold War cuts in army and navy personnel and equipment orders, defense spending is high and has risen in recent years, focusing on developing rapid reaction capabilities. The UK's independent nuclear deterrent has been scaled down. UK forces were prominent in peacekeeping in the Balkans and Sierra Leone and have been engaged in full conflicts over Kosovo in 1999 and in Iraq in 2003. Troops remain stationed in Northern Ireland; it was revealed in 2003 that army agents had colluded in terrorist activity while gathering intelligence there.

The UK is a leading arms exporter. Major buyers include Middle East and southeast Asian countries.

ECONOMICS

Inflation 2.8% p.a. (1990–2001)

$1477bn

0.606 pounds sterling (0.6561)

SCORE CARD

❑ WORLD GNP RANKING	4th
❑ GNP PER CAPITA	$25,120
❑ BALANCE OF PAYMENTS	–$29.4bn
❑ INFLATION	1.8%
❑ UNEMPLOYMENT	5%

EXPORTS

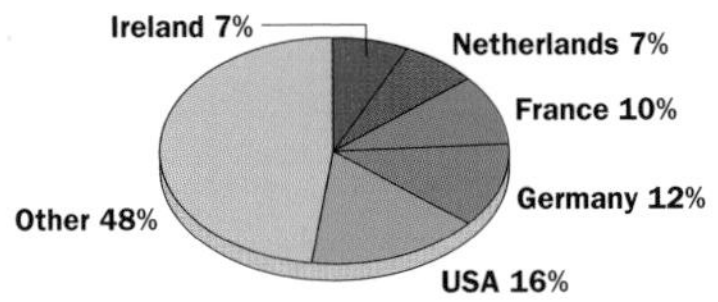
Ireland 7%
Netherlands 7%
France 10%
Germany 12%
USA 16%
Other 48%

IMPORTS

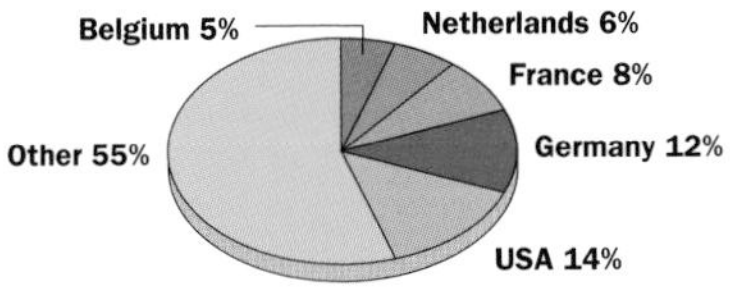
Belgium 5%
Netherlands 6%
France 8%
Germany 12%
USA 14%
Other 55%

STRENGTHS

World leader in financial services. Important pharmaceutical and defense industries. Strong multinationals. Precision engineering and high-tech industries, including telecommunications and biotechnology. Innovative in computer software development. Flexible working practices. Success in controlling inflationary tendencies. Low unemployment.

WEAKNESSES

Decline of manufacturing sector since 1970s. Need to plan for eventual end of North Sea oil and gas. Quick-return mentality behind many investment decisions. Nonparticipation in euro threatens former status as EU's largest recipient of inward investment; has prompted closure of UK factories.

PROFILE

Manufacturing has been in long-term decline, while sectors such as financial services have expanded rapidly. After sharp recession in 1991, revival was sluggish, but by the late 1990s growth in the UK was faster than that of its European competitors. The rural economy was hit hard by a foot-and-mouth epidemic in 2001, while the wider economy suffered in 2001–2003 after the US economic downturn and the collapse of the Internet "dotcom" boom. Interest rates were cut to try to boost domestic spending, while the government in 2002 massively increased its own spending on education, health, and defense. The government ruled in 2003 that the UK was not yet ready to join the eurozone, making entry unlikely before the next election.

ECONOMIC PERFORMANCE INDICATOR

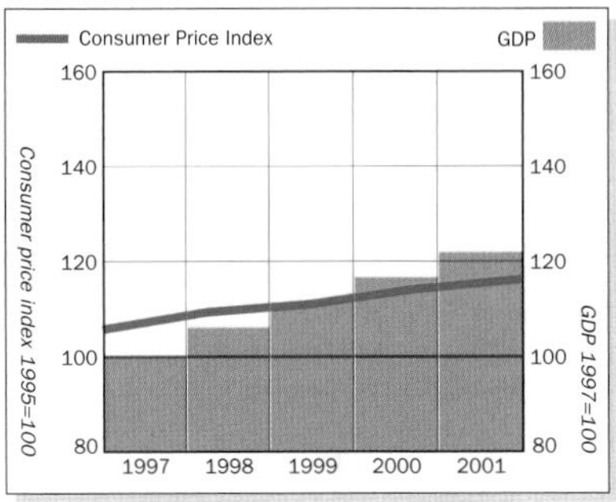
Consumer Price Index
GDP
Consumer price index 1995=100
GDP 1997=100
160
140
120
100
80
1997
1998
1999
2000
2001

UNITED KINGDOM : MAJOR BUSINESSES

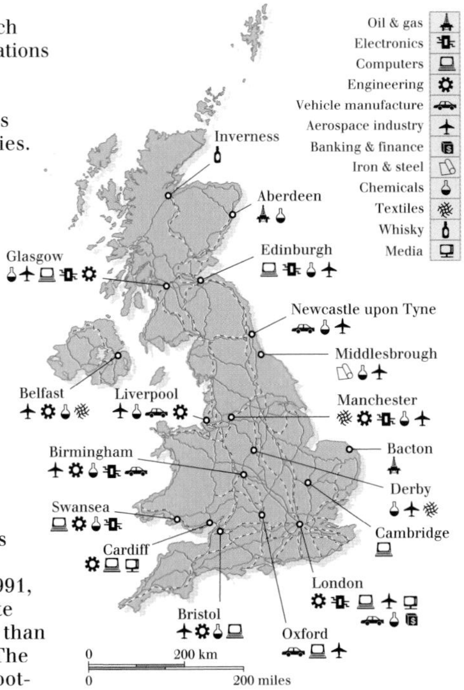
Oil & gas
Electronics
Computers
Engineering
Vehicle manufacture
Aerospace industry
Banking & finance
Iron & steel
Chemicals
Textiles
Whisky
Media
Inverness
Aberdeen
Glasgow
Edinburgh
Newcastle upon Tyne
Middlesbrough
Belfast
Liverpool
Manchester
Birmingham
Bacton
Derby
Swansea
Cambridge
Cardiff
London
Bristol
Oxford
0
200 km
0
200 miles

RESOURCES

Electric power 75.9m kW

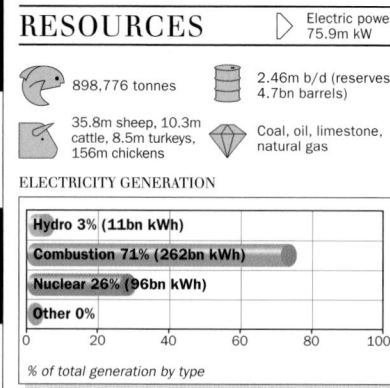

898,776 tonnes

2.46m b/d (reserves 4.7bn barrels)

35.8m sheep, 10.3m cattle, 8.5m turkeys, 156m chickens

Coal, oil, limestone, natural gas

ELECTRICITY GENERATION

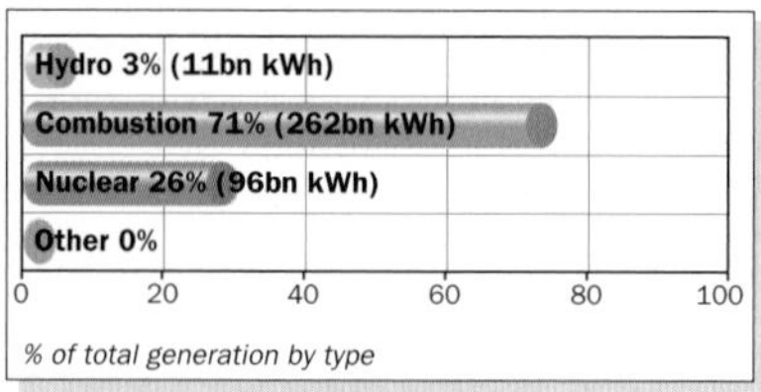
Hydro 3% (11bn kWh)
Combustion 71% (262bn kWh)
Nuclear 26% (96bn kWh)
Other 0%
0
20
40
60
80
100
% of total generation by type

The UK has the largest energy resources of any EU state, with substantial oil and gas reserves offshore on the continental shelf in the North Sea, and fresh fields in the north Atlantic. Drilled under difficult conditions, North Sea oil is of a high grade. Revenues from taxes on oil companies have been a major contributor to government finances, averaging around $12 billion a year.

Sizable coal reserves are economically unexploitable. Privatization of the electricity industry, and pressure to cut pollution, encouraged the switch from coal- to gas-fired power plants, prompting emergency government measures in the late 1990s and efforts to boost the role of "cleaner coal" technology. The UK is also developing tidal and wind power.

The UK produces few other minerals in significant quantities. Cornwall's last tin mines teeter between closure and rescue. Some very small-scale gold mining survives in Wales and Scotland.

UNITED KINGDOM : LAND USE

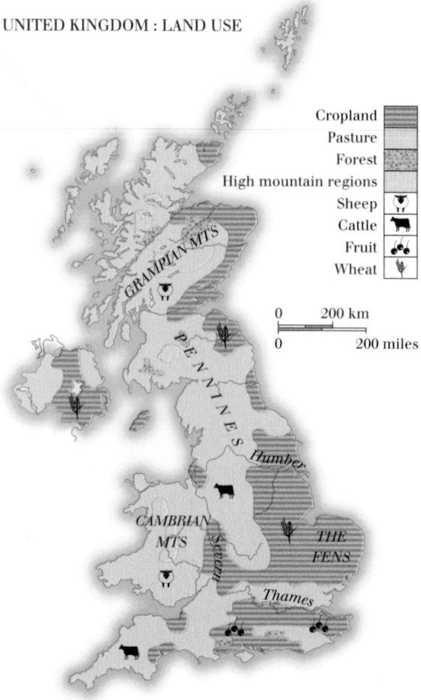
Cropland
Pasture
Forest
High mountain regions
Sheep
Cattle
Fruit
Wheat
0 200 km
0 200 miles
GRAMPIAN MTS
PENNINES
Humber
CAMBRIAN MTS
Severn
THE FENS
Thames

ENVIRONMENT

Sustainability rank: 91st

23% (20% partially protected)

9.2 tonnes per capita

ENVIRONMENTAL TREATIES

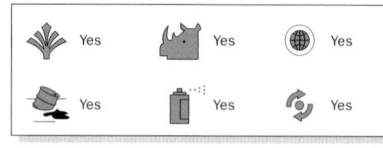

Yes	Yes	Yes
Yes	Yes	Yes

Apart from destruction of rural environments by road building and sprawling development, the most important issues are health-related. Urban air pollution from traffic is a major focus, as are nuclear safety issues. Food scares have gripped the public since BSE ("mad cow" disease) was linked in the mid-1990s with human deaths. Opposition to genetically modified (GM) foods is widespread, and GM crop trials have been disrupted for fear that modified genes could contaminate other species.

MEDIA

TV ownership high

Daily newspaper circulation 329 per 1000 people

PUBLISHING AND BROADCAST MEDIA

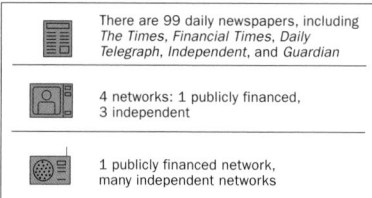

There are 99 daily newspapers, including *The Times, Financial Times, Daily Telegraph, Independent,* and *Guardian*

4 networks: 1 publicly financed, 3 independent

1 publicly financed network, many independent networks

Newspapers are owned mostly by large media corporations. Many publish Internet editions. Criticized for invasions of privacy, the press presents self-regulation as preferable to legislation. Publication deemed contrary to "national interests" may be banned. Satellite TV and digital terrestrial broadcasting have increased competition with the BBC. The BBC's World Service, despite cutbacks, remains an influential news source internationally.

***The Welsh coal industry** has virtually disappeared. Wales now has the highest percentage of small business start-ups, relative to the population, of any part of the UK.*

CRIME

No death penalty

80,144 prisoners

Down 4% in 1999–2001

CRIME RATES

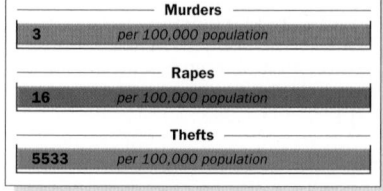

Murders	
3	*per 100,000 population*
Rapes	
16	*per 100,000 population*
Thefts	
5533	*per 100,000 population*

Violent crime and domestic abuse are growing problems. Inner-city violence is partly fueled by narcotics dependency and trafficking. The government has maintained a "tough on crime" stance, but sentencing policies place the penal system under serious strain. Marijuana is increasingly tolerated in order to focus on "harder" narcotics. "Antiterrorism" laws gave police extra powers in 2001. Public fear of pedophilia fueled a reform of outdated sex laws in 2002.

EDUCATION

School leaving age: 16

99%

2.07m students

THE EDUCATION SYSTEM

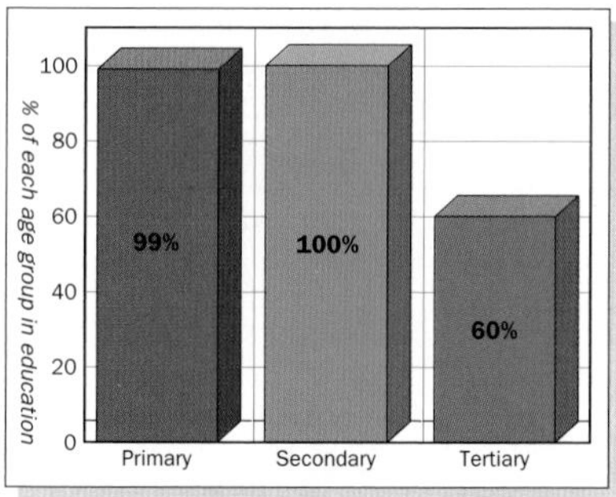
100
80
60
40
20
0
% of each age group in education
99%
100%
60%
Primary
Secondary
Tertiary

The state system is used by 94% of children. Fee-paying private schools include the traditional elite institutions confusingly known as public schools. There is now a new enthusiasm in government for "faith-based" schools.

From the 1960s onward, a two-tier state school system based on academic selection at age 11 was to a great extent replaced by mixed ability comprehensive schools. The 1988 education reforms introduced a national curriculum and weakened the role of local education authorities. The Labour government has focused on testing, assessing teaching standards, and tackling "failing" schools. Public spending targets in 2002 promised significantly increased education expenditure within four years, to 5.6% of GDP.

More colleges were given university status in the 1990s, but established centers, particularly Oxford and Cambridge, continue to be the most prestigious and best resourced.

REPRESENTATION AND DEVOLUTION

THE 1801 ACT OF UNION unified Great Britain – England, Wales, and Scotland – and Ireland. The principality of Wales had been joined with England in 1536. The English and Scottish crowns had been united in 1603 (James VI of Scotland becoming James I of England), and the 1707 Act of Union united their parliaments. The present full title of the UK – the United Kingdom of Great Britain and Northern Ireland – dates from 1922, when the Irish Free State was created.

The rise of Welsh and particularly Scottish nationalism prompted demands for more devolved government. New Labour fulfilled its 1997 campaign promise by creating new assemblies in Northern Ireland, Scotland, and Wales. Regional government in England remains embryonic, but in 2003 referenda on elected assemblies in three northern regions were promised.

SCOTLAND
Glasgow
Edinburgh
Newcastle upon Tyne
NORTHERN IRELAND
Belfast
Leeds
Liverpool
Manchester
ENGLAND
Birmingham
WALES
Cardiff
Bristol
LONDON

NORTHERN IRELAND

In Northern Ireland (pop. 1.65 million, area 14,120 sq. km/5450 sq. miles, capital Belfast) the majority Protestant community dominated a "home rule" parliament at Stormont throughout its 50-year existence, until 1972. After that the troubled province was mainly under direct rule from London, interspersed with attempts to create power-sharing institutions, until the 1998 Good Friday agreement. This created a 108-member Northern Ireland Assembly, elected that June by proportional representation, and a 12-member power-sharing executive. However, implementation of the agreement has repeatedly been held up by disputes, mainly about disarming rival Irish republican and unionist "loyalist" paramilitaries.

***The Scottish Parliament's** temporary home, pending completion of its controversial and expensive new building.*

SCOTLAND AND WALES

The Scottish National Party's electoral breakthrough in 1974 was fueled by the perception that independence could be viable, if Scotland controlled the oil wealth of the North Sea. The UK government offered devolution to both Scotland and Wales, but referenda in 1979 resulted in a too-small majority in Scotland and a "no" vote in Wales. The devolution proposals of 1997, on the other hand, won endorsement both in Scotland and (narrowly) in Wales.

Scotland (pop. 5.13 million, area 78,742 sq. km/30,394 sq. miles, capital Edinburgh) now has a Scottish Parliament of 129 MSPs, elected in 1999. The Scottish Executive, consisting of a first minister and an 11-member cabinet, is responsible to the parliament, whose powers notably cover education and changing tax rates to generate revenue for Scottish expenditure. One of its first distinctive initiatives was to reject the imposition of university tuition fees, so controversial elsewhere in the UK.

In Wales (pop. 2.9 million, area 20,761 sq. km/8041 sq. miles, capital Cardiff), a 60-member Welsh Assembly was also elected in 1999. It has fewer powers, not including tax-raising, exercised by an eight-member administration also headed by a first minister.

***The extensive upland areas** of both Scotland and Wales are used extensively for sheep farming and forestry.*

HEALTH

Welfare state health benefits

1 per 610 people

Cancers, heart, cerebrovascular, and respiratory diseases

The National Health Service (NHS) offers universal free health care, but financial pressures have led to shortages, hospital closures, and charges in some sectors. In response, the government in 2002 announced record levels of investment in the health service over a five-year period, aiming to match the European average on health spending (8% of GDP) by 2004. Recent crises have focused on food safety, from *E. coli* outbreaks to fatal brain disease attributed to eating beef from cattle with "mad cow" disease.

SPENDING

GDP/cap. increase

CONSUMPTION AND SPENDING

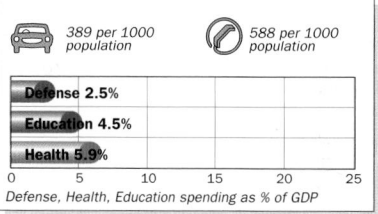

389 per 1000 population

588 per 1000 population

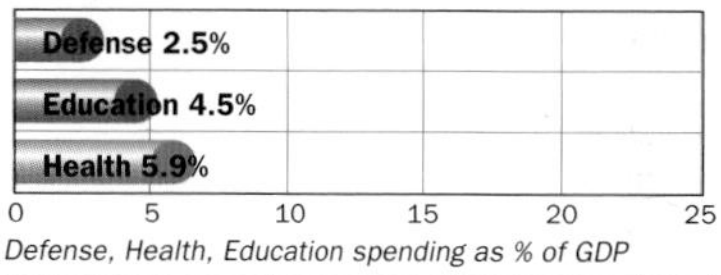
Defense 2.5%
Education 4.5%
Health 5.9%
0
5
10
15
20
25
Defense, Health, Education spending as % of GDP

Income inequality is greater than in 1884, when records began. In 2002 13.4% were living below the UN's "poverty" line – half of average income – with rates higher among some ethnic minorities. Average wages for manufacturing workers in 2001 were $29,000 a year, only 4% of the average received by chief executives in large companies. Under Conservative governments in the 1980s and early 1990s, taxation for higher earners was cut, whereas the value of state benefits and pensions fell. Since the mid-1990s, economic growth has helped to bring unemployment down. Labour's 1997 election promises precluded raising income tax. This limited any scope for redistributive action, leaving antipoverty strategies dependent on better targeting of welfare benefits.

WORLD RANKING

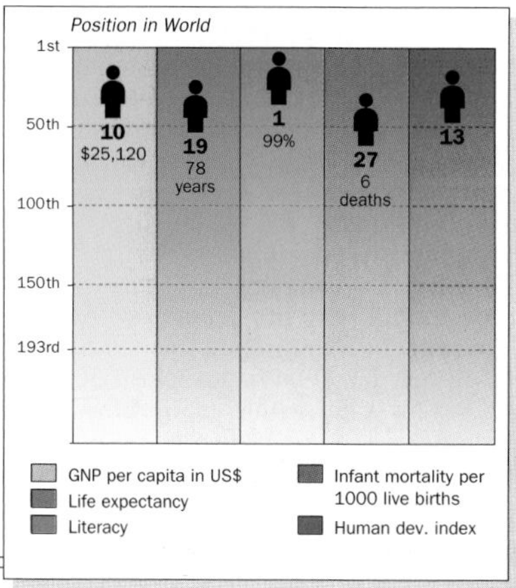
Position in World
1st
50th
100th
150th
193rd
10
$25,120
19
78 years
1
99%
27
6 deaths
13
GNP per capita in US$
Life expectancy
Literacy
Infant mortality per 1000 live births
Human dev. index

U

UNITED STATES

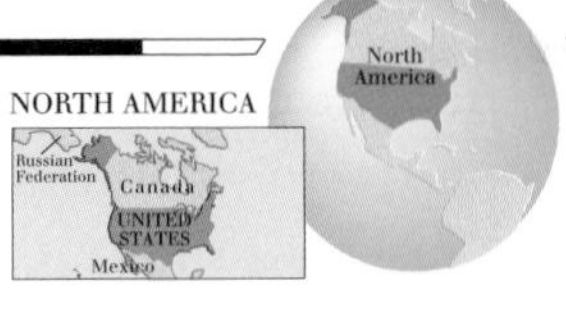
North America
NORTH AMERICA
Russian Federation
Canada
UNITED STATES
Mexico

OFFICIAL NAME: United States of America **CAPITAL:** Washington D.C.
POPULATION: 289 million **CURRENCY:** US dollar **OFFICIAL LANGUAGE:** English

1776
1959
July 4
USA
-5 to -11
+1
n/a

THE WORLD'S THIRD-LARGEST country, the United States is neither overpopulated (like China) nor in the main subject to extremes of climate (like much of Russia and Canada). Its main landmass, bounded by Canada and Mexico, contains 48 of its 50 states. The two others, Alaska at the northwest tip of the Americas and Hawaii in the Pacific, became states in 1959. The US was not built on ethnic identity but on a concept of nationhood intimately bound up with the 18th-century founding fathers' ideas of democracy and liberty – still powerful touchstones in both a political and an economic sense. Since the breakup of the Soviet Union, the US holds a unique position – but arouses extreme hatreds – as the sole global superpower.

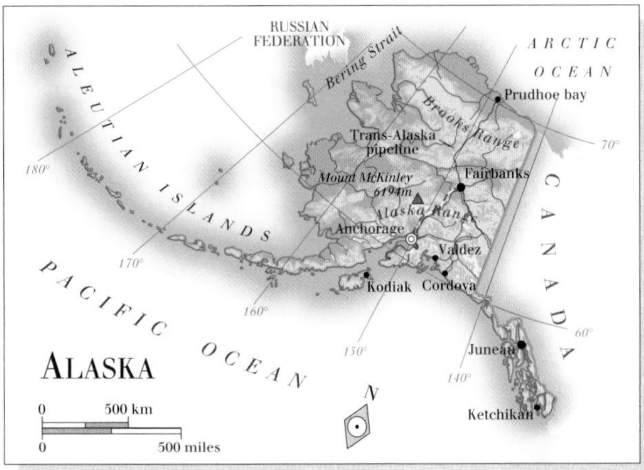
RUSSIAN FEDERATION
Bering Strait
ARCTIC OCEAN
Prudhoe bay
Brooks Range
Trans-Alaska pipeline
ALEUTIAN ISLANDS
Mount McKinley 6194m
Fairbanks
Alaska Range
Anchorage
Valdez
CANADA
Kodiak
Cordova
PACIFIC OCEAN
Juneau
Ketchikan
ALASKA
0 500 km
0 500 miles

CLIMATE

Continental/subtropical/mountain/desert/maritime

WEATHER CHART FOR WASHINGTON D.C.

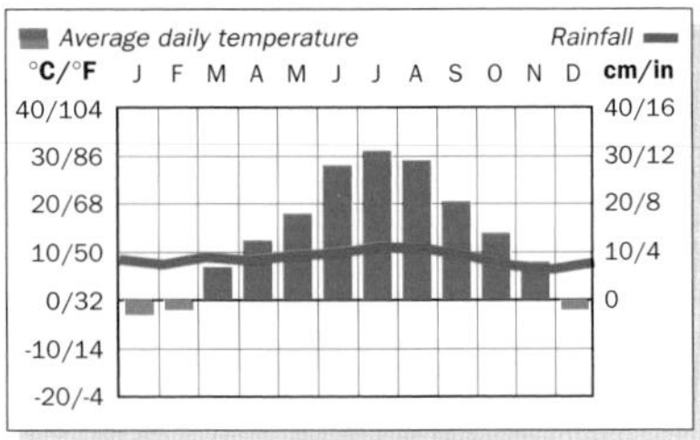
Average daily temperature
Rainfall
°C/°F J F M A M J J A S O N D cm/in
40/104 40/16
30/86 30/12
20/68 20/8
10/50 10/4
0/32 0
-10/14
-20/-4

Spanning a continent and extending far into the Pacific Ocean, the US displays a wide range of climatic conditions. Mean annual temperatures range from 29°C (84°F) in Florida to –13°C (9°F) in Alaska. Except for New England, Alaska, and the Pacific northwest, summer temperatures are higher than in Europe. Southern summers are humid; in the southwest they are dry. Winters are particularly severe in the western mountains and plains and in the Midwest – where the Great Lakes can freeze. The northeast can have heavy snow from November to April. The weather is frequently dramatic, with tornadoes, cyclones, thunderstorms, hurricanes, floods, and droughts. Since 1990, weather-related damage has risen, a trend linked with global climate change.

PACIFIC OCEAN
Seattle
Tacoma
Olympia
WASHINGTON
Spokane
Portland
Salem
Corvallis
Eugene
Columbia
Lewiston
Missoula
Great Falls
Helena
OREGON
IDAHO
Snake
Medford
Nampa
Boise
Idaho Falls
Pocatello
Twin Falls
Great Salt Lake
Ogden
COAST RANGES
CASCADE RANGE
ROCKY MOUNTAINS
Reno
Sacramento
Carson City
GREAT BASIN
Salt Lake City
Orem
Provo
Oakland
San Francisco
NEVADA
UTAH
SIERRA NEVADA
Mount Whitney 4418m
Grand Junction
Lake Powell
Las Vegas
CALIFORNIA
Lake Mead
Grand Canyon
Los Angeles
Colorado
ARIZONA
San Diego
Phoenix
Albuquerque
Tucson
Las Cruces
El Paso
MEXICO

The Chippendale Block, New York, a notable example of postmodern architecture by the influential US architect Philip Johnson.

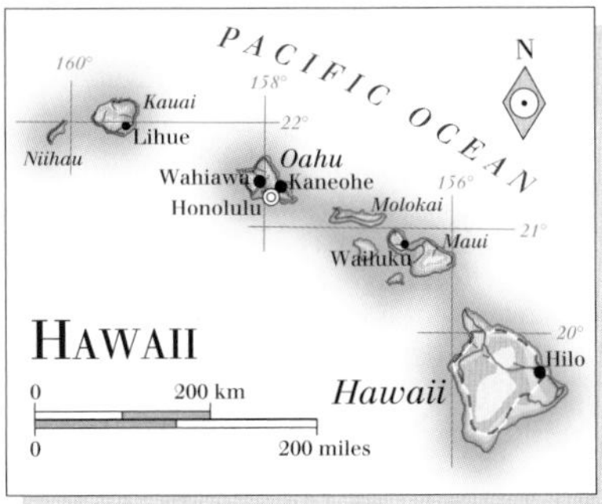
PACIFIC OCEAN
Kauai
Lihue
Niihau
Oahu
Wahiawa
Kaneohe
Honolulu
Molokai
Maui
Wailuku
Hilo
HAWAII
Hawaii
0 200 km
0 200 miles

U

TRANSPORTATION

Drive on right

Atlanta, Georgia 76.9m passengers

443 ships 15m dwt

THE TRANSPORTATION NETWORK

5.73m km (3.56m miles)	74,782 km (46,467 miles)
230,674 km (143,334 miles)	41,009 km (25,482 miles)

The Mississippi–Missouri river system provided the first transportation network in the US. Today, the US has the world's cheapest, most extensive internal air network and a good system of interstate highways. Railroads, comparatively neglected for years, mainly carry freight, though modern high-speed trains are starting to attract passengers back. Americans have been wedded to the car since Henry Ford began mass production in 1908. By 1919 there were nine million cars in the US. Today the total tops 210 million, including pickups and the ubiquitous "sports utes" (SUVs). Americans make more than half of the world's car journeys. Cheap gasoline underpinned the rise of the car, but problems of congestion and pollution, and the environmental costs of ever more oil production, mean that its role in society needs reviewing.

Malls, a typical feature of the suburban landscape, are losing popularity to speedier online shopping.

UNITED STATES
Total Area : 9 626 091 sq. km
(3 717 792 sq. miles)
POPULATION
over 5 000 000
over 1 000 000
over 500 000
over 100 000
over 50 000
over 10 000
under 10 000
LAND HEIGHT
3000m/9843ft
2000m/6562ft
1000m/3281ft
500m/1640ft
200m/656ft
Sea Level
ATLANTIC OCEAN
GULF OF MEXICO
BAHAMAS
Lake Superior
Lake Michigan
Lake Huron
L. Ontario
L. Erie
L. Okeechobee
St Lawrence
NORTH DAKOTA
SOUTH DAKOTA
NEBRASKA
KANSAS
OKLAHOMA
TEXAS
MINNESOTA
IOWA
MISSOURI
ARKANSAS
LOUISIANA
WISCONSIN
ILLINOIS
MICHIGAN
INDIANA
OHIO
KENTUCKY
TENNESSEE
MISSISSIPPI
ALABAMA
GEORGIA
FLORIDA
SOUTH CAROLINA
NORTH CAROLINA
VIRGINIA
WEST VIRGINIA
PENNSYLVANIA
NEW YORK
NEW JERSEY
MARYLAND
DEL.
CONN.
RHODE I.
MASS.
VERM.
NEW HAMP.
MAINE
APPALACHIAN MTS
WASHINGTON DC
Minot
Grand Forks
Bismarck
Fargo
Duluth
Aberdeen
Pierre
Rapid City
Minneapolis
St Paul
Rochester
Sioux Falls
Sioux City
Omaha
Lincoln
Grand Island
Des Moines
Cedar Rapids
Topeka
Kansas City
Jefferson City
Wichita
Tulsa
Oklahoma City
Norman
Lawton
Springfield
Fayetteville
Fort Smith
Little Rock
Hot Springs
Pine Bluff
Dallas
Fort Worth
Shreveport
Austin
Houston
San Antonio
Green Bay
Milwaukee
Madison
Racine
Rockford
Chicago
Davenport
Peoria
Gary
South Bend
Fort Wayne
Indianapolis
St Louis
Evansville
Louisville
Cincinnati
Dayton
Columbus
Toledo
Detroit
Ann Arbor
Lansing
Grand Rapids
Flint
Cleveland
Akron
Pittsburgh
Huntington
Charleston
Frankfort
Lexington
Knoxville
Nashville
Memphis
Huntsville
Chattanooga
Birmingham
Tuscaloosa
Greenville
Jackson
Meridian
Hattiesburg
Montgomery
Mobile
Biloxi
Baton Rouge
New Orleans
Atlanta
Macon
Savannah
Tallahassee
Jacksonville
Tampa
St Petersburg
Fort Lauderdale
Miami
Spartanburg
Charlotte
Winston-Salem
Greensboro
Raleigh
Richmond
Newport News
Norfolk
Annapolis
Baltimore
Dover
Wilmington
Philadelphia
Trenton
Harrisburg
Allentown
New York
JFK
New Haven
Hartford
Providence
Worcester
Springfield
Boston
Lowell
Manchester
Concord
Portland
Lewiston
Augusta
Bangor
Burlington
Montpelier
Albany
Syracuse
Rochester
Buffalo
Erie
Cheyenne
Ohio
Missouri
Mississippi
Red
Arkansas
Canadian
N. Platte
Pecos
Colorado
Rio Grande
Hudson
0 400 km
0 400 miles

TOURISM

Visitors : Population 1:6.9

41.9m visitors

Down 7% in 2002

MAIN TOURIST ARRIVALS

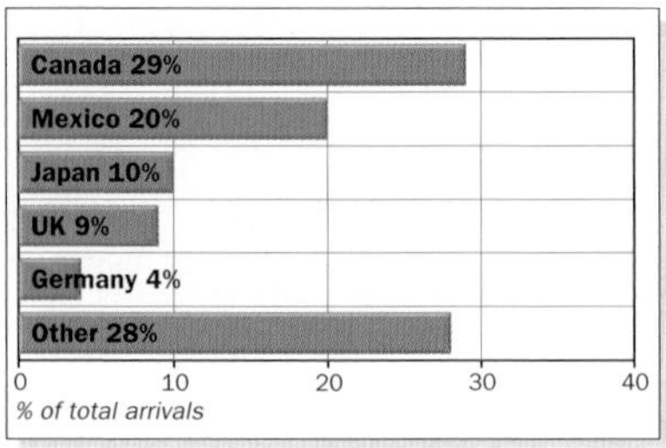
Canada 29%
Mexico 20%
Japan 10%
UK 9%
Germany 4%
Other 28%
0
10
20
30
40
% of total arrivals

The US as a destination for international tourism benefited greatly from the deregulation of air fares. Domestic tourism expanded just as rapidly, along with the rise in real incomes. The impact of the September 11, 2001, attacks was complex. While confidence in air travel took time to be rebuilt, the fact that US tourists put safety first meant that over 80% vacationed within the US in 2002. All the states have their attractions, and most court tourists. Top tourist destinations include Florida's Disney World and Disneyland in California, Niagara Falls, Las Vegas, New York, San Francisco, Los Angeles and Hollywood, the Grand Canyon, Death Valley, New Orleans, Atlantic City, and Washington D.C.

Tourism's rapid expansion has also brought some problems. The parks and sites run by the National Parks Service (NPS) have been particular casualties; visitor numbers rocketed in the three decades after 1970. To try and reduce pressure on the most popular areas, there has been a significant expansion in the area of protected land under NPS management since the mid-1970s. Even so, Yellowstone Park has a continuing traffic management crisis, bumper-to-bumper cars plague other high-profile attractions, and those wanting to take a raft ride down the Grand Canyon are likely to spend many months on a waiting list.

PEOPLE

Pop. density low

English, Spanish, German, Arabic, Polish, Korean, Chinese, Armenian, French, Italian, Amerindian languages

31/km² (82/mi²)

THE URBAN/RURAL POPULATION SPLIT

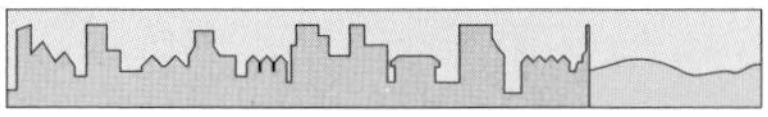
77%
23%

RELIGIOUS PERSUASION

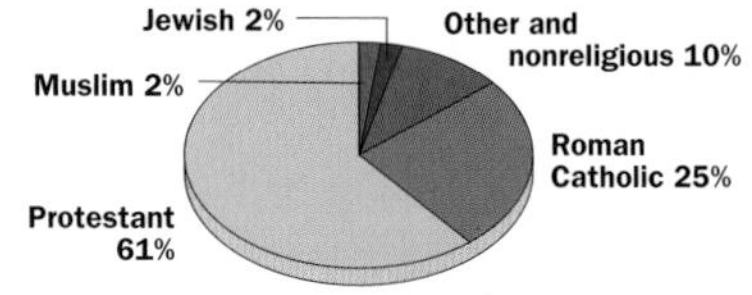
Jewish 2%
Other and nonreligious 10%
Muslim 2%
Roman Catholic 25%
Protestant 61%

ETHNIC MAKEUP

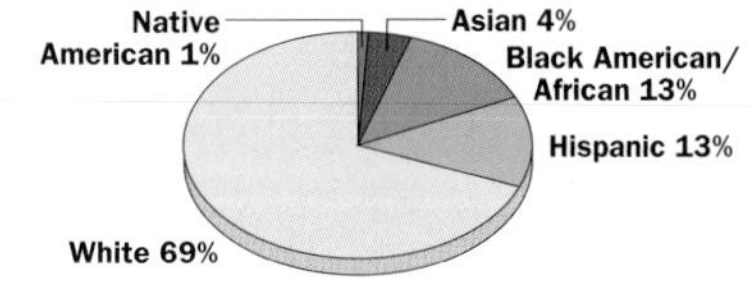
Native American 1%
Asian 4%
Black American/ African 13%
Hispanic 13%
White 69%

The demographic, economic, and cultural dominance of the white community is firmly entrenched after almost 400 years of settlement. However, the balance of ethnicity is rapidly shifting. An immigration boom peaked in the early 1990s, with many new arrivals from Latin America and Asia. The birthrate is particularly high in the Hispanic community, now the largest single minority in the US. The Census Bureau projects that in the year 2050 almost 25% of the population will be Hispanic, 14% black, and 9% Asians and Pacific islanders.

More than two-thirds of the Hispanic, or Latino, population originated in Mexico, and thousands of Mexicans risk their lives crossing the border every year. Despite its growing size, the Hispanic community still struggles to compete politically and economically with the better established, and more politically sensitive, black population.

Within the black community, their ancestors infamously brought to the New World as slaves, an African-American business leadership class has grown up, but only two black people – media moguls Oprah Winfrey and Robert L. Johnson – make the list of the 400 richest Americans.

The country's original inhabitants, the Native Americans, or Amerindians, were dispossessed in the 19th century and now make up little more than 1% of the population. Some of the worst poverty and deprivation in the US can be found in their reservations.

The separation of state and religion is guaranteed by the constitution, but Christian values dominate. The evangelical churches, particularly well established in the south, forcefully oppose abortion, the teaching of evolution, and the social acceptance of homosexuality.

POPULATION AGE BREAKDOWN

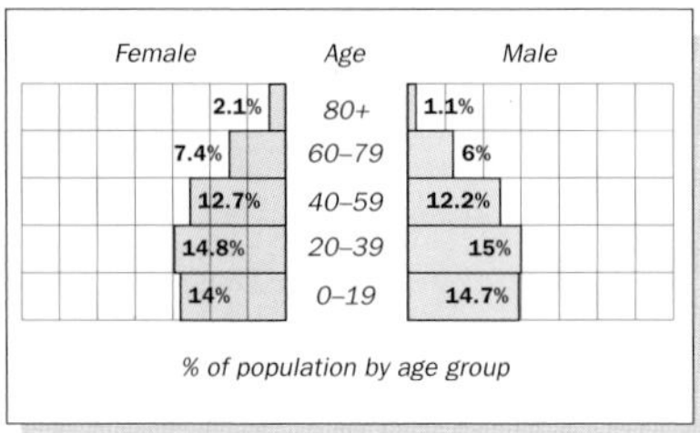
Female
Age
Male
2.1%
80+
1.1%
7.4%
60–79
6%
12.7%
40–59
12.2%
14.8%
20–39
15%
14%
0–19
14.7%
% of population by age group

POLITICS

Multiparty elections

L. House 2002/2004
U. House 2002/2004

President George W. Bush

AT THE LAST ELECTION

House of Representatives 435 seats

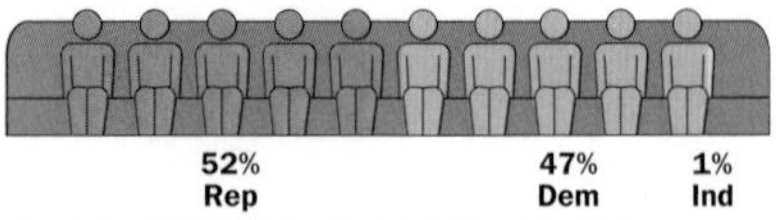
52%
Rep
47%
Dem
1%
Ind

Rep = Republican Party **Dem** = Democratic Party
Ind = Independents

Senate 100 seats

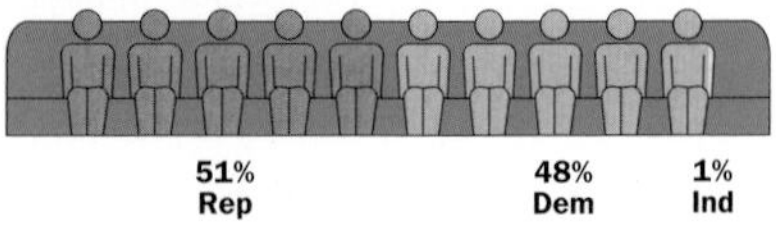
51%
Rep
48%
Dem
1%
Ind

Presidential elections take place every four years, House elections every two years. One-third of the senators are elected every two years for six-year terms.

The US is a democracy with a federal system of government. Many issues are dealt with by the 50 individual states. Each state sends two senators and a varying number of representatives (according to population size) to Congress.

Profile

US politics is dominated by two main parties. With few major differences between them, the right-wing Republicans and the right-of-center Democrats regularly trade position in control of the White House and Congress. Presidential elections are based largely on personalities, with televised debates, inaugurated in the 1960s, playing a significant role. Election campaigns are long-winded and increasingly expensive affairs.

Despite a "big business" affiliation, controversial policies (notably on energy), and divided popular opinion when he was first elected in 2000, Republican president George W. Bush gained overwhelming popular support in September 2001, when a wave of patriotic emotion rallied the nation behind him and his declaration of a "war on terrorism," after the attack on the World Trade Center and the Pentagon. His predecessors, whether Democrat or Republican, had struggled to get major initiatives enacted by a hostile Congress, but in midterm elections in 2002 Republicans gained

George W. Bush, *took office in 2001 after a controversial presidential election.*

Gen. Colin Powell, *who became the first African-American Secretary of State.*

U

POLITICS *continued*

firm control of the House and the Senate, giving Bush a complete congressional majority.

MAIN POLITICAL ISSUES

The limits of government

The US has a strong tradition of resisting the extension of government powers. The vigorous defense of constitutional liberties and the rights of citizens, such as freedom of speech or the right to bear arms, is sometimes taken to lengths which appear extreme to other societies. States resist the arrogation of powers by the federal authorities. In areas such as health care and education, conservatives oppose as interference what others see as the proper concern of government with social welfare. "Big government" is also denounced in the economic sphere. Opponents of environmental controls, for example, portray them as an obstruction of free enterprise and wealth creation.

The prestige of the presidency

When George W. Bush took office in January 2001, the presidency faced a number of challenges. First among them was the question of the legitimacy of his victory, given the contentious manner of his election, with fewer votes nationwide than his Democrat rival Al Gore and controversy over the conduct of polling in Florida. Bush himself was initially derided by opponents as an intellectual lightweight, prone to verbal gaffes and with an embarrassing lack of current affairs knowledge. The events of September 11, 2001, served to bolster Bush's presidency. The man himself rose in public esteem to appear unassailable within his first year in office. His simple messages of belief in "the American way" rallied a nation shocked by the implications of the terrorist attacks. This translated into electoral success in 2002 when, for the first time in 50 years, the party of the incumbent president made gains in the midterm elections.

Despite these successes, and the lack of an obvious challenger for the 2004 presidential race, Bush faces considerable criticism, not least for the state of the economy; the budget slipped into its first deficit in five years in 2002 and broke records when the deficit passed $300 billion dollars in 2003.

Hillary Clinton, senator for New York and wife of former president Bill Clinton.

Alan Greenspan, chairman of the Federal Reserve since 1987.

Energy and the environment

Bush advocated some controversial energy policies in 2001, amid a pressing crisis over electricity shortages in California. Conservation activists were appalled by plans to allow further oil exploration in Alaska, and the Senate excised funding for the search from the 2004 budget. The expansion of nuclear power was also revived under the energy plan, while the US, alone, chose to repudiate the international Kyoto agreement on cutting carbon dioxide emissions. To offset criticism, Bush has earmarked $1.2 billion for research into hydrogen fuel cells.

Crime, race, and poverty

Efforts to regenerate depressed urban areas have relied on new economic opportunities and programs that empower the poor (such as self-management of public housing projects). Rates of criminality and the number of victims are higher in the black community than in any other. Tough anticrime policies in cities such as New York have had a real impact in reducing the level of violence, but have also been accused of unfairly targeting minority ethnic groups; there remains the prospect of a permanently disaffected urban underclass.

The Mittens, Monument Valley, Arizona. *These striking natural rock formations are created by erosion of red sandstone. The valley is in the Navajo National Monument.*

WORLD AFFAIRS

Joined UN in 1945

G8 | NATO | NAFTA | OAS | OECD

Isolated by two great oceans, the US has been able for much of its history to choose the extent of its participation in world affairs. Only reluctantly drawn into the two world wars, after 1945 it swapped isolationism for involvement. The US took its seat on the Security Council of the new UN, based in New York, and helped to set up NATO. For the US the Cold War was most immediate – and costly – in the Korean and Vietnam wars. The death toll and shock of defeat in Vietnam in the 1970s kept the US out of direct military involvement overseas for over a decade. Instead, it focused on diplomacy, and on supporting the opponents of left-wing regimes in developing countries, including Nicaragua, Cuba, and Angola.

Since the collapse of the Eastern bloc after 1989 the US has had to redetermine the scope of its foreign responsibilities as the only remaining superpower. Until 2001 policy remained cautious. It had led the intervention in the 1991 Gulf War, but a fiasco in Somalia and a lack of clear objectives in Bosnia & Herzegovina and Haiti showed its uncertainty about a role as world policeman. The September 11, 2001, terrorist attacks provoked the Bush regime into reclaiming the international initiative. He is inspired in part by the right-wing doctrine of the "new American century," which advocates making use of unrivaled US power to shape world affairs to the country's benefit.

The first act under this new approach was the declaration of the "war on terrorism," which seeks to build a global, US-led consensus in the fight against nonstate combatants. The "successful" war in Afghanistan in late 2001 raised concerns in the Islamic world that Muslims were being unfairly targeted. Bush went on to increase tensions in February 2002 by declaring Iran, Iraq, and North Korea to be an "axis of evil" states which sponsored terrorists.

Threats against Iraq culminated in the 2003 invasion. France and Germany led world opinion against the war, and were later dubbed "old Europe" for their efforts by Defense Secretary Donald Rumsfeld. Even Russia, which had been welcomed into the heart of NATO decision-making in 2002, expressed strong disapproval. Many saw the war as an attempt to settle old scores and to seize the riches of Iraq's vast oil reserves. The US made it clear that its relations with the UN and with Europe would not stand in the way of realizing its foreign policy aims.

As a result, global opinion of the US has grown increasingly negative, potentially fueling the ranks of anti-US terrorist groups. This ideological opposition is backed by a popular grassroots movement in the developed world which identifies US military and economic hegemony, as well as its dominant culture, with the perceived evils of globalization.

THE IMPACT OF 9/11 AND THE "WAR ON TERRORISM"

AT 08:48 LOCAL TIME on "9/11" – September 11 – 2001, a hijacked American Airlines plane flew into the North Tower of the World Trade Center (WTC) in New York. The world's most devastating terrorist attack had begun. By 10:29 that morning three more hijacked planes had been crashed – one into the WTC's South Tower, another into the Pentagon military headquarters in Washington D.C. and one in rural Pennsylvania after passengers overpowered the hijackers. Around 3000 people died. The finger of blame was immediately pointed at Islamist terrorists of the extremist al-Qaida network, led by Osama bin Laden. The impact of the attacks, which were caught on camera and broadcast live around the world, was profound, both at home and abroad.

"War on terrorism"

Seen as a second Pearl Harbor, the 9/11 attacks incited the US administration to strike back with a "war on terrorism." The first round, a massive assault on the *taliban* regime in Afghanistan, which was sheltering bin Laden, began in October 2001. The "war" was strongly condemned by the Islamic world, which felt that it had been unduly targeted.

Those taken prisoner while fighting against the US and its allies in Afghanistan were transported to the US base at Guantánamo Bay in Cuba. Held there at the Camp Delta facility (formerly Camp X-Ray), they await trial in the US. Classifying them as "illegal combatants," the US has avoided the application of Geneva Convention III on the treatment of prisoners of war.

From Afghanistan the US turned its attention to Iraq, as well as supplying military aid to countries battling their own – usually Islamist – terrorists. Citing ill-defined links between al-Qaida and the Ba'ath Arab socialist regime of Saddam Hussein, and the

***Responses to the destruction** of the WTC have varied from vociferous patriotism to a fervent desire for peace.*

***The "Tribute in Light"** marked the site of the fallen WTC in 2002. Berlin-based architect Daniel Libeskind has been chosen to produce new buildings incorporating both commerce and commemoration.*

fear that Iraq had not destroyed its arsenal of weapons of mass destruction (WMD), the US led a Coalition of forces into Iraq in March 2003, toppling the regime in early April. The invasion was widely criticized abroad, while the subsequent lengthy and bloody process of reconstructing Iraq in the face of significant local hostility has prompted growing criticism from within the US. Of particular concern is the dubious nature of some of the "evidence" used to justify action against the Iraqi regime. The government has countered that acting on "murky intelligence" could have prevented the 9/11 attacks themselves, and was therefore entirely appropriate to prevent future atrocities.

Homeland security

The domestic effect of the 9/11 attacks has been to put the entire country on a near-permanent state of alert. There are frequent warnings of imminent terrorist attacks. In the immediate aftermath of 9/11 the Bush administration announced a new cabinet-level position to cover "homeland security." A full department was created the following year, on November 25, 2002, with Tom Ridge as its first secretary. It combines 22 previously disparate agencies, including the coast guard and border patrols, in an effort to coordinate the response to future attacks. It has the assistance of a reformed Central Intelligence Agency (CIA) which has been reoriented to pay special attention to international terrorism after being criticized for not preventing the 2001 atrocity.

Security at airports has obviously been heightened, but of more concern to human rights campaigners is the increased scrutiny applied to visitors arriving from Muslim countries. Men arriving from Iran, Iraq, Libya, Pakistan, Saudi Arabia, Sudan, Syria, or Yemen are now officially registered, photographed, and fingerprinted. There has also been a crackdown on immigrants from the Middle East and north Africa, hundreds having been detained after complying with new rules demanding their registration under antiterrorist legislation.

Culturally, there has been an increase in public patriotism, as well as acts of protest and defiance: public figures have been vilified for expressing disapproval of the government. Campaigns by celebrities against the "war" have been muted and bounded by caveats asserting patriotism alongside a desire for the respect of human rights.

Winning the war

Immediately the "war" began it was pointed out that little has been done to address the motivation of the 9/11 attackers – whose actions, as proclaimed by bin Laden, were directed at US cultural hegemony and in particular its historic support for Israel in its conflict with the Palestinians. A US "roadmap" for peace in the Middle East published in 2003 was seen as an attempt to address the Palestinian issue, but rapidly fell behind schedule and did not prevent atrocities in Israel and the West Bank. As for the burgeoning anti-US sentiment among the poorer Muslim societies of the region, it has been pointed out that unilateral invasions of sovereign states and the vilification of Arab leaders will likely swell the ranks of anti-US groups. This speculation has been borne out by the death toll of Coalition forces in Iraq, at the hands of "resistance" fighters and lone gunmen alike, since the invasion. Few now share the apparent initial confidence of those in the US administration who suggested that the "war on terrorism" could have a swift or indeed decisive end.

***Suspected terrorists and taliban fighters** from the 2001 war in Afghanistan have been imprisoned in harsh conditions at the US base at Guantánamo Bay in Cuba.*

AID

Donor

$11.4bn (donations)

Up 15% in 2001

The US gives only 0.1% of GNP in foreign aid, and aid allocations are often stalled in Congress. Russia, Egypt, and Israel are the major recipients. The US is keen to further its strategic aims with some high-profile pledges, including a $15 billion AIDS campaign and $5 billion to tackle poverty.

DEFENSE

No compulsory military service

$322bn

Up 6% in 2001

US ARMED FORCES

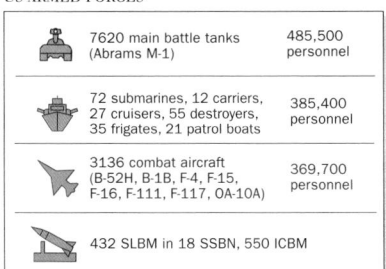

7620 main battle tanks (Abrams M-1)	485,500 personnel
72 submarines, 12 carriers, 27 cruisers, 55 destroyers, 35 frigates, 21 patrol boats	385,400 personnel
3136 combat aircraft (B-52H, B-1B, F-4, F-15, F-16, F-111, F-117, OA-10A)	369,700 personnel
432 SLBM in 18 SSBN, 550 ICBM	

Even before the 9/11 attacks, emphasis in defense policy had been shifting away from strategic nuclear deterrence and large warships to "smart" missile systems and "long-range power projection," with rapid intervention capabilities built around air power. Despite setbacks in early tests, the first "interceptor" missiles of the national missile defense "shield" system are due to be in place by 2004.

The enormous US military–industrial complex dates only from the close of World War II. In the 1990s, the end of the Cold War and the need to cut the budget deficit combined to slash defense funds to their lowest level in real terms since 1945. Nuclear weapons tests were superseded by computerized "virtual" tests after the creation of the powerful ASCI White computer.

However, the Bush administration has steadily increased defense spending. The 2002/2003 budget was up by 11% on the previous year to $350 billion, amounting to more than the combined defense budgets of the world's next nine largest military spenders. The government has also hinted that it is considering developing small and "precision" nuclear weapons as part of its expanding arsenal.

Fearing that its troops could be prosecuted for political reasons, the US opposed the establishment of the International Criminal Court. This stance threatens to undermine overseas peacekeeping missions, and has led to cuts in military aid to countries which have not agreed to protect US soldiers from prosecution.

ECONOMICS

Inflation 2% p.a. (1990–2001)

$9781bn

Currency is US dollar

SCORE CARD

❑ World GNP Ranking	1st
❑ GNP per Capita	$34,280
❑ Balance of Payments	–$417bn
❑ Inflation	2.8%
❑ Unemployment	6%

EXPORTS

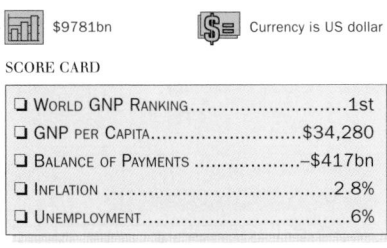

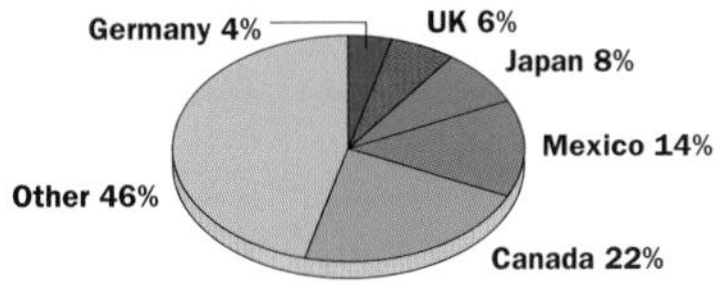
Germany 4%
UK 6%
Japan 8%
Mexico 14%
Canada 22%
Other 46%

IMPORTS

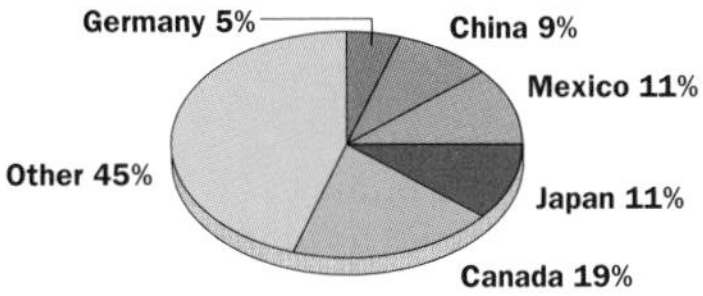
Germany 5%
China 9%
Mexico 11%
Japan 11%
Canada 19%
Other 45%

ECONOMIC PERFORMANCE INDICATOR

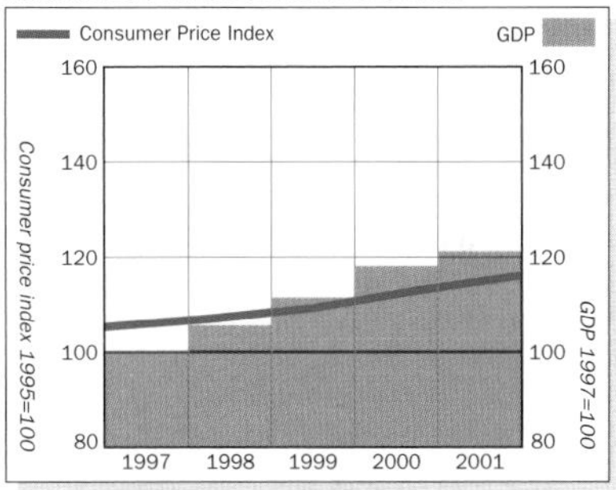
Consumer Price Index
GDP
160
140
120
100
80
1997
1998
1999
2000
2001
Consumer price index 1995=100
GDP 1997=100

STRENGTHS

World's largest economy. Wealth of natural resources: energy, raw materials, and food. Strong high-tech base; world-leading research and development. Global leader in computer software. World-class multinationals. Sophisticated service sector; advanced and competitive manufacturing industry. Entrepreneurial business ethic. High-quality postgraduate education, especially in high-tech business. Global dominance of US culture major boost to US manufacturers. Subsidized crops and favorable tariffs for domestic industries.

WEAKNESSES

Dramatic fall in manufacturing employment as jobs lost to lower-wage economies. Competition from Asia and EU in leading-edge technologies. Volatile market values driven by speculation. Weak business regulation and short-termism. Recent major corporate collapses. Increase in imports despite relatively weak dollar: competition from euro as global currency. Major budget deficit.

PROFILE

In 2001 a record nine-year boom came to an end. The downturn greatly affected big business. The collapse of WorldCom in 2002, the largest ever bankruptcy, threatened confidence in business values, while media-giant AOL Time Warner posted historic losses of $98.7 billion for 2002. Unemployment has increased as companies tighten their budgets, passing a nine-year high of 6.4% in June 2003.

Recovery efforts have focused on promoting consumer spending, and President Bush has pushed for a $2000 billion dollar package of tax cuts – though, in the event, the cuts were greatly watered down by Congress. Interest rates have been systematically cut and reached just 1% in June 2003, a 45-year low. However, government spending has increased, notably on defense: the war on Iraq in 2003 cost $48 billion. The budget and trade accounts have both fallen into record deficits.

UNITED STATES : MAJOR BUSINESSES

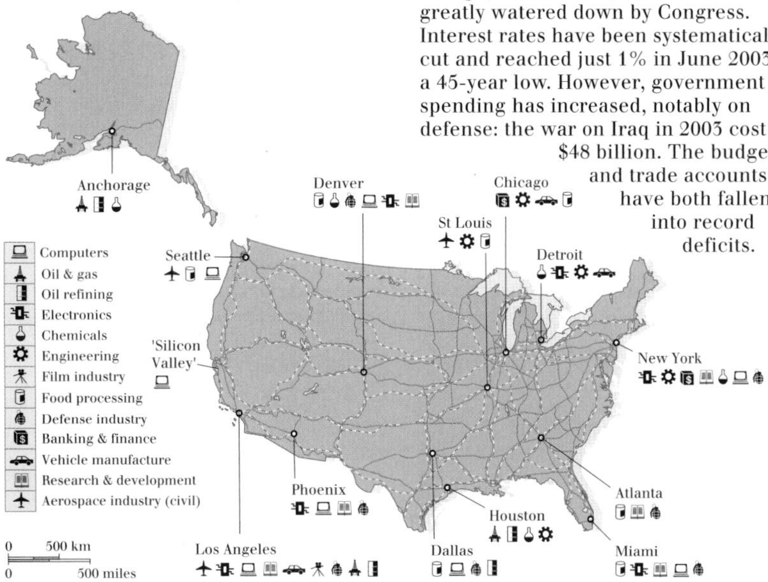
Anchorage
Denver
Chicago
St Louis
Seattle
Detroit
'Silicon Valley'
New York
Phoenix
Atlanta
Houston
Los Angeles
Dallas
Miami
Computers
Oil & gas
Oil refining
Electronics
Chemicals
Engineering
Film industry
Food processing
Defense industry
Banking & finance
Vehicle manufacture
Research & development
Aerospace industry (civil)
0 500 km
0 500 miles

U

CHRONOLOGY

The original 13 colonies, first established by British settlers on the eastern seaboard in the 17th century, joined to wage a war for independence (1775–1781), which Britain recognized in 1783. The 1776 Declaration of Independence was followed by the writing of the world's first constitution. A century of westward expansion began. Following the victory of the northern states in the 1861–1865 Civil War, slavery was ended throughout the US, but Native Americans were dispossessed of their land in a series of conflicts.

- **1917** US enters World War I.
- **1929** New York stock market collapse; economic depression.
- **1941** Japanese attack on Pearl Harbor; US enters World War II.
- **1950–1953** Korean War.
- **1950–1954** Senator Joe McCarthy investigates supposed communist sympathizers in witch hunt.
- **1954** Supreme Court rules racial segregation in schools to be unconstitutional. Blacks, seeking constitutional rights, start campaign of civil disobedience.
- **1959** Alaska, Hawaii become states.
- **1961** John F. Kennedy president. Promises aid to South Vietnam. US-backed invasion of Cuba defeated at Bay of Pigs.
- **1962** Soviet missile bases found on Cuba; resulting threat of nuclear war narrowly averted.
- **1963** Kennedy assassinated. Lyndon Baines Johnson president.
- **1964** US involvement in Vietnam stepped up. Civil Rights Act gives blacks constitutional equality.
- **1968** Martin Luther King is assassinated.
- **1969** Republican Richard Nixon takes office as president. Growing public opposition to Vietnam War.
- **1972** Nixon reelected. Makes historic visit to China.
- **1973** Withdrawal of US troops from Vietnam; 58,000 US troops dead by end of war.
- **1974** August, Nixon resigns following Watergate scandal over break-in to Democrat headquarters. Gerald Ford president.
- **1976** Democrat Jimmy Carter elected president.
- **1979** Seizure of US hostages in Iran.
- **1980** Ronald Reagan wins elections for Republicans. Adopts tough anticommunist foreign policy.
- **1983** Military invasion of Grenada.
- **1985** Air strikes against Libyan cities. Relations with USSR improve; first of three summits held.
- **1986** Iran–Contra affair revealed. ▷

RESOURCES

Electric power 794m kW

5.17m tonnes

7.7m b/d (reserves 30.4bn barrels)

96.7m cattle, 88m turkeys, 59.1m pigs, 1.94bn chickens

Phosphates, gypsum, oil, coal, sulfur, lead, zinc, copper, gold

ELECTRICITY GENERATION

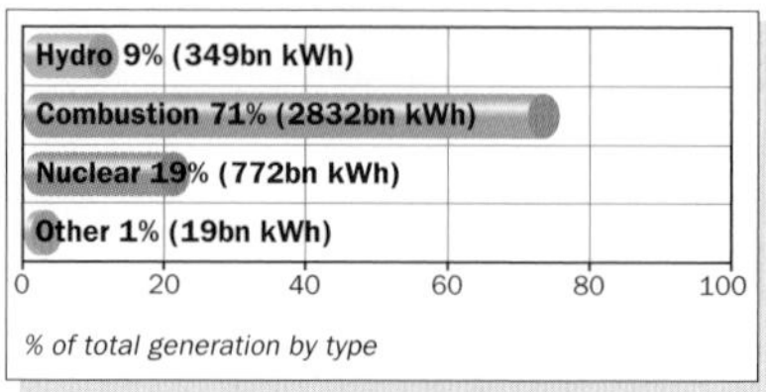

Hydro 9% (349bn kWh)
Combustion 71% (2832bn kWh)
Nuclear 19% (772bn kWh)
Other 1% (19bn kWh)
0 20 40 60 80 100
% of total generation by type

The US has an abundance of natural resources, including oil. The 2001 energy plan aimed to step up oil exploration and output, reducing the need for imports. There are massive deposits of coal in the western states – where almost all mining is open-cast – and substantial mineral deposits in the mountains and intramontane basins.

BROOKS RANGE
ALASKA RANGE

Environmental concerns halted the development of nuclear power after the 1979 accident at Three Mile Island, but expansion is now being considered.

The timber industry, forced to retreat by conservationists in the Pacific northwest, especially Washington State, has moved to the south, where great stands of pine are harvested as if they were fields of wheat. The US has harnessed hydroelectric power in the past; today, imports of hydropower from Canada are commonplace.

In comparison with western Europe, the US is not intensively farmed. The huge size of farms in the Midwest and west has allowed both arable and livestock farming to be based on a low-input for low-output model.

UNITED STATES : LAND USE

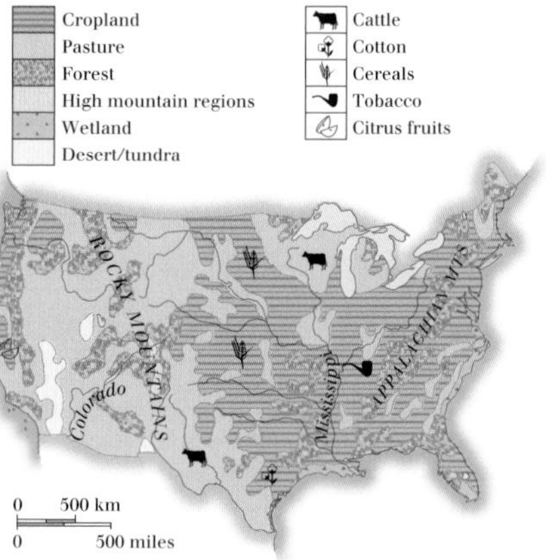

Cropland
Pasture
Forest
High mountain regions
Wetland
Desert/tundra
Cattle
Cotton
Cereals
Tobacco
Citrus fruits
ROCKY MOUNTAINS
APPALACHIAN MTS
Mississippi
Colorado
0 500 km
0 500 miles

ENVIRONMENT

Sustainability rank: 45th

26% (14% partially protected)

20.5 tonnes per capita

ENVIRONMENTAL TREATIES

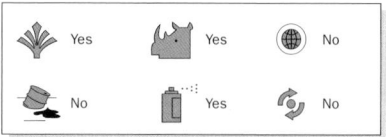

Yes	Yes	No
No	Yes	No

The US lags far behind other Western countries on environmental issues. The international commitment made at the 1997 Kyoto conference on cutting carbon dioxide emissions was scrapped by President Bush in 2001. The Rockies are a battleground between those who want to maintain their beauty, and those who advocate "wise use" – in practice this often means giving ranchers and miners free rein. In 2002, Congress approved plans to dump nuclear waste in Mt. Yucca, Nevada. Similar issues surround the arguments over extending oil drilling in the Alaskan wilderness. The US is leading the field in genetically modified (GM) food. Huge acreages have been planted with GM cereals, and by 2001 over 60% of soybean production was GM. A consumer backlash, especially in Europe, has worried many farmers.

MEDIA

TV ownership high

Daily newspaper circulation 201 per 1000 people

PUBLISHING AND BROADCAST MEDIA

There are 1480 daily newspapers, including the *New York Times*, the *Washington Post*, and the *Wall Street Journal*

10 major independent networks, 1145 commercial stations

7 major networks, 12,932 licensed commercial stations

Mass media as a phenomenon was born in the US. No other society has ever had anything quite like US network TV, or moved so easily into the world of multichannel TV; homes with 50 or more channels are commonplace. The Internet, the most recent in the series of nationwide communication revolutions, is now used regularly by the majority of the population. Newspapers, mostly local rather than national, tend to have very low cover prices, and gain most of their revenue from advertising. They are under increasing threat from cable TV and other outlets. Companies exploring multimedia and ways of providing online news and services are still trying to recover from the crash in their stock values in 2000.

U

CHRONOLOGY *continued*

- **1987** Intermediate Nuclear Forces Treaty signed by US and USSR.
- **1988** Republican George Bush Sr. wins presidency.
- **1989** US overthrows Panama's Gen. Noriega, then arrests him on narcotics charges.
- **1991** January–February, Gulf War against Iraq. US and USSR sign START arms reduction treaty.
- **1992** Black youths riot in Los Angeles and other cities. Bush–Yeltsin summit agrees further arms reductions. Democrat Bill Clinton defeats Bush in presidential election.
- **1994** Midterm elections: Republican majorities in both houses of Congress.
- **1995** Oklahoma bombing by Timothy McVeigh: over 160 die.
- **1998** Scandal over Clinton's affair with White House intern leads to impeachment proceedings. August, bombing of US embassies in Kenya and Tanzania; revenge air strikes on Sudan and Afghanistan. December, air strikes against Iraq.
- **1999** February, Clinton acquitted in Senate impeachment trial. April, Columbine High School shootings by two students. March–June, NATO involvement to end Kosovo conflict, bombardment of Yugoslavia.
- **2000** Democrat Al Gore concedes tightest presidential election ever to Republican George W. Bush.
- **2001** January, President Bush takes office. September 11, world's worst terrorist attack kills thousands as hijacked planes destroy World Trade Center, damage Pentagon. October, US-led military action in "war on terrorism" begins with intensive aerial bombing campaign in Afghanistan. December, accounting scandal at Enron.
- **2002** July, WorldCom bankruptcy is biggest ever corporate collapse.
- **2003** Bush launches war on Iraq, despite lack of UN backing.

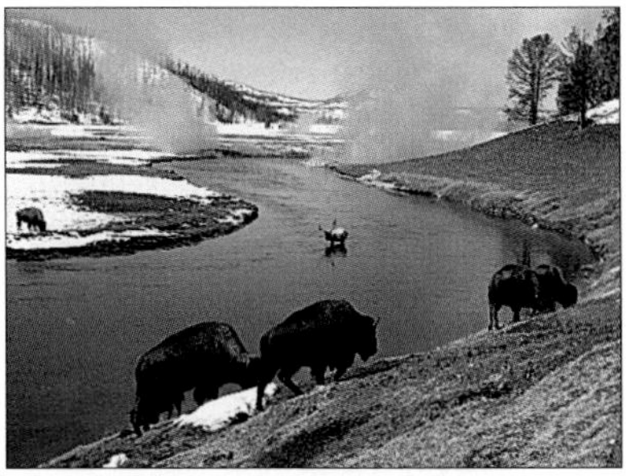

Bison in Yellowstone National Park. *The park's ecosystem is under severe strain due to the number of visitors it attracts.*

CRIME

Death penalty in use

2.02m prisoners

Down 18% in 1997–2001

CRIME RATES

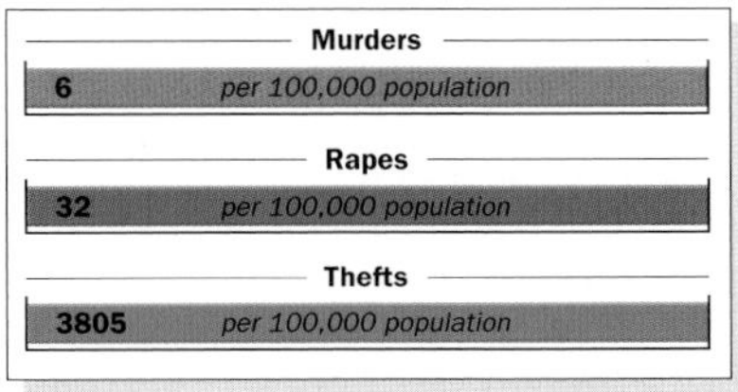
Murders
6 per 100,000 population
Rapes
32 per 100,000 population
Thefts
3805 per 100,000 population

Violent crime – especially murder – is much more common than in other developed countries, even in relatively well-off areas. However, the murder rate has fallen, and by 2001 was at its lowest for over 30 years. Mass shootings have made gun control a major issue, but a powerful lobby opposes restrictions, basing its arguments on the constitution and the defense of individual liberties.

Imprisonment for narcotics crimes in the US is much more widespread than in most Western countries. Capital punishment has increased since the 1980s, especially in the south. Texas carries out most executions. There are around two million people in prison in the US, almost a quarter of the world total.

EDUCATION

School leaving age: 17

99%

13.6m students

THE EDUCATION SYSTEM

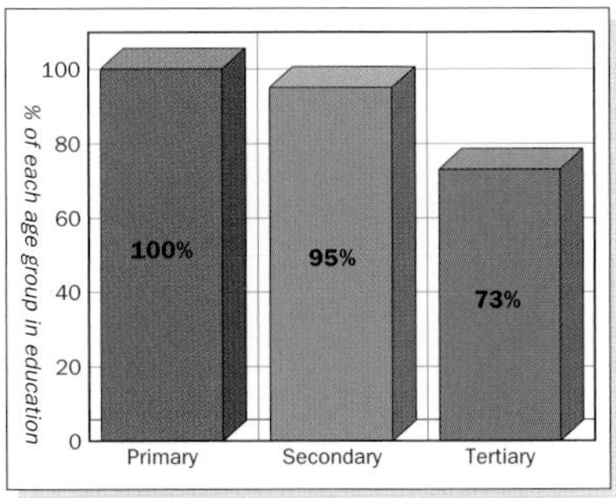
100
80
60
40
20
0
% of each age group in education
100%
95%
73%
Primary
Secondary
Tertiary

Education in the US is primarily the responsibility of the state governments.

Recent reports critical of standards in US high schools cite problems of discipline, poor structural maintenance, and lack of resources in many areas as driving people away from the public education sector. Private education at secondary level continues to develop rapidly. While the number of Roman Catholic private schools has shrunk, more nondenominational fee-paying schools have been founded.

Three out of every four high school students now go on to some form of tertiary college. The leading US universities are internationally recognized as being of world class.

HEALTH

Limited welfare state health benefits

1 per 362 people

Cancers, heart, cerebrovascular, and respiratory diseases

US researchers lead in pioneering new treatments. Sophisticated techniques are available to those with insurance (which they typically receive from their employer); the Texas Medical Center has a budget equivalent to that of some small countries. On the other hand, costs have skyrocketed, and facilities for those dependent on state medical care are woefully underfunded. Infant mortality rates in some areas are at levels more commonly found in developing countries. Around 30% of the population is clinically obese, and one in every two adults is overweight. Notable health campaigns have focused on smoking, which is now banned in public places in many major cities. Abortion is a highly sensitive issue and many Republicans would like to challenge its legality.

SPENDING

GDP/cap. increase

CONSUMPTION AND SPENDING

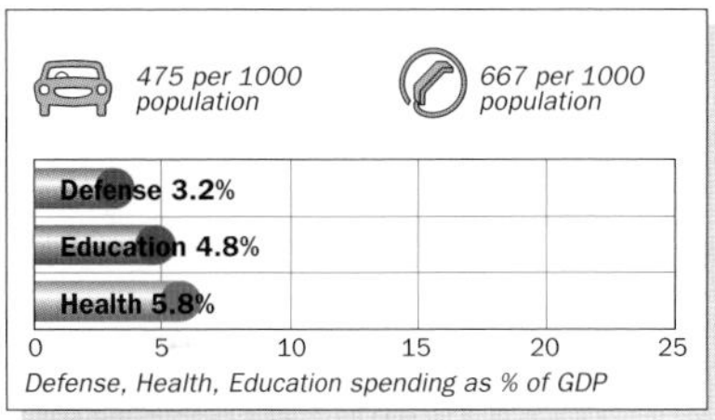
475 per 1000 population
667 per 1000 population
Defense 3.2%
Education 4.8%
Health 5.8%
0
5
10
15
20
25
Defense, Health, Education spending as % of GDP

Between 1945 and 1973, most Americans got richer. Since then, however, living standards have gone on rising only among those who finish high school. This "education effect" has led to noticeable class divisions, despite the long economic boom of the 1990s. The top 20% had average household incomes of $137,500 by 2000, whereas the incomes of the poorest 20% averaged only $13,000 – and were lower in real terms than in 1980.

WORLD RANKING

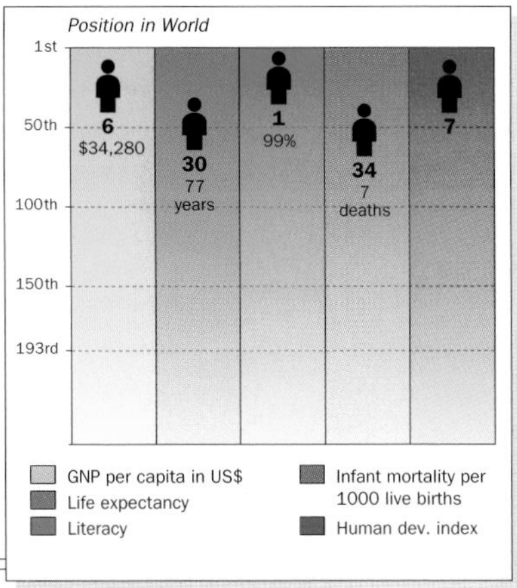
Position in World
1st
50th
100th
150th
193rd
6
$34,280
30
77
years
1
99%
34
7
deaths
7
GNP per capita in US$
Life expectancy
Literacy
Infant mortality per 1000 live births
Human dev. index

U

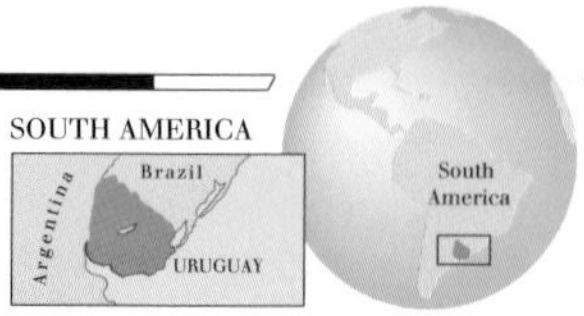
SOUTH AMERICA
Brazil
Argentina
URUGUAY
South America

URUGUAY

OFFICIAL NAME: Eastern Republic of Uruguay **CAPITAL:** Montevideo
POPULATION: 3.4 million **CURRENCY:** Uruguayan peso **OFFICIAL LANGUAGE:** Spanish

1828 | 1828 | Aug 25 | ROU | -3 | +598 | .uy

URUGUAY IS SITUATED IN the southeast of South America, sandwiched between its larger neighbors Brazil and Argentina. Its capital, Montevideo, is an Atlantic port on the River Plate, lying on the opposite bank to the Argentine capital Buenos Aires. Uruguay became independent in 1828, after nearly 150 years of Spanish and Portuguese control. Decades of liberal government ended in 1973 with a military coup that was to result in 12 years of dictatorship, during which 400,000 people emigrated. Most have since returned. Almost the entire low-lying landscape is devoted to the rearing of livestock, especially cattle and sheep. Uruguay is a leading wool exporter, but in recent years modern service industries have become increasingly important.

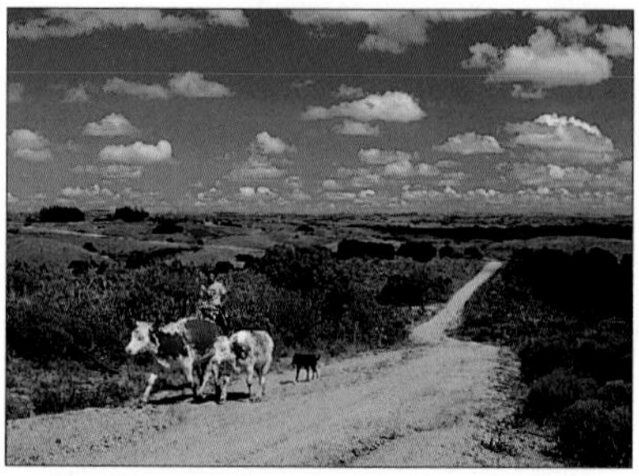

Uruguayan grasslands. *Rich pasture covers three-quarters of the country, ideal for cattle and sheep. Animals and animal products account for about a third of export earnings.*

CLIMATE

Subtropical

WEATHER CHART FOR MONTEVIDEO

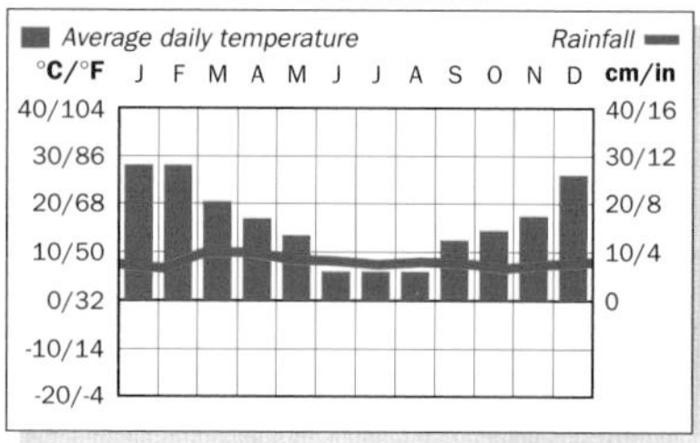
Average daily temperature
Rainfall
°C/°F
J F M A M J J A S O N D
cm/in
40/104
30/86
20/68
10/50
0/32
-10/14
-20/-4
40/16
30/12
20/8
10/4
0

Uruguay has one of the most benign climates in the world. It is uniformly temperate over the whole country. Winters are mild, frost is rare, and it never snows. Summers are generally cool for these latitudes and rarely tropically hot. The moderate rainfall tends to fall in heavy showers, leaving most days sunny.

TRANSPORTATION

Drive on right

Carrasco, Montevideo 1.17m passengers

90 ships 72,800 grt

THE TRANSPORTATION NETWORK

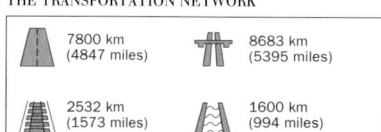

7800 km (4847 miles)

8683 km (5395 miles)

2532 km (1573 miles)

1600 km (994 miles)

The government has sold off its share in the national bus industry – there are extensive internal and international coach and bus services – and has closed down all passenger railroad services. In 1998 the Chamber of Senators gave the go-ahead for a $1 billion, 45-km (30-mile) road bridge across the River Plate from Colonia to Buenos Aires. Raising international finance for the project will be difficult.

TOURISM

Visitors : Population 1:1.8

1.89m visitors

Down 4% in 2001

MAIN TOURIST ARRIVALS

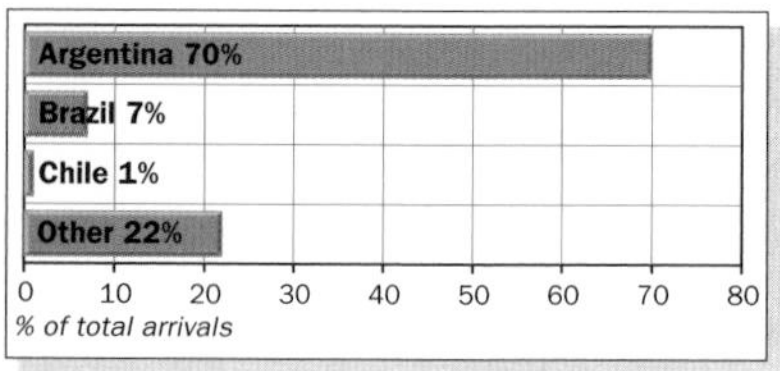
Argentina 70%
Brazil 7%
Chile 1%
Other 22%
0 10 20 30 40 50 60 70 80
% of total arrivals

Sandy beaches near the River Plate estuary are a major attraction. The old Spanish fortifications of Montevideo have been destroyed, but the city retains a colonial atmosphere. Punta del Este, 138 km (86 miles) east of the capital, is the main beach resort. Argentinians account for the majority of visitors.

PEOPLE

Pop. density low

Spanish

19/km² (50/mi²)

THE URBAN/RURAL POPULATION SPLIT

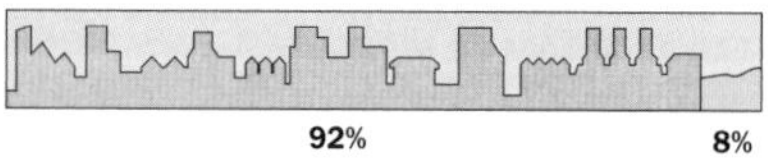
92%
8%

RELIGIOUS PERSUASION

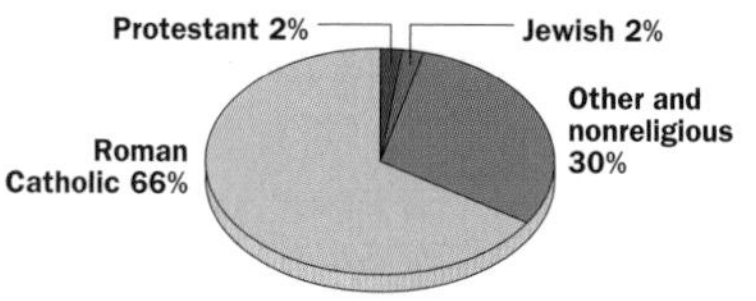
Protestant 2%
Jewish 2%
Other and nonreligious 30%
Roman Catholic 66%

ETHNIC MAKEUP

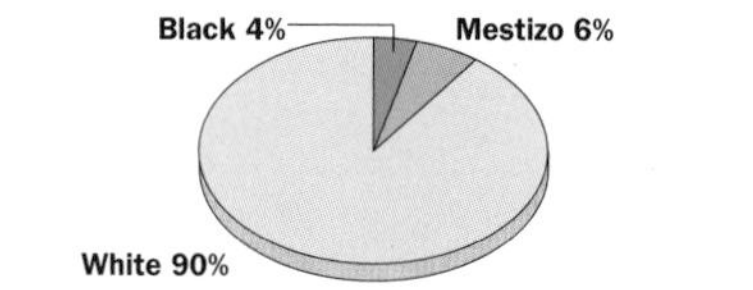
Black 4%
Mestizo 6%
White 90%

Most Uruguayans are second- or third-generation European, mainly of Spanish or Italian descent. There are also some *mestizos* (of mixed blood) and a small minority of people descended from Africans or immigrants from Brazil, who live near the Brazilian border or in or around Montevideo. All indigenous Amerindian groups became integrated in the *mestizo* population by the mid-19th century. More recent immigrants include Jews, Armenians, and Lebanese. Historically, ethnic tensions have been few. The birthrate is low for Latin America.

The considerable prosperity derived from cattle ranching allowed Uruguay to become a welfare state long before any other Latin American country. In spite of Uruguay's serious economic decline since the end of the 1950s, there is still a sizable, if less prosperous, middle class. A clear sign of the country's economic and social deterioration during the years of military dictatorship was the unprecedented growth of shanty towns around Montevideo.

Uruguay is largely a Roman Catholic country, but it is liberal in its attitude to religion, and all forms are tolerated. Divorce is legal. Women, who gained the vote in 1932, are regarded as equal to men.

POPULATION AGE BREAKDOWN

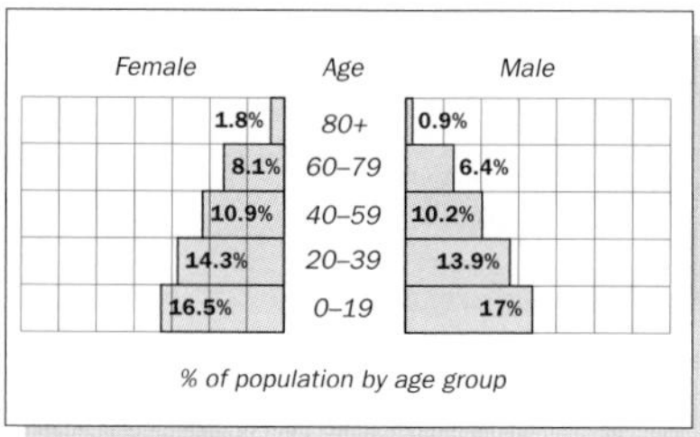
Female
Age
Male
1.8% 80+ 0.9%
8.1% 60–79 6.4%
10.9% 40–59 10.2%
14.3% 20–39 13.9%
16.5% 0–19 17%
% of population by age group

URUGUAY

Total Area : 176 220 sq. km (68 039 sq. miles)

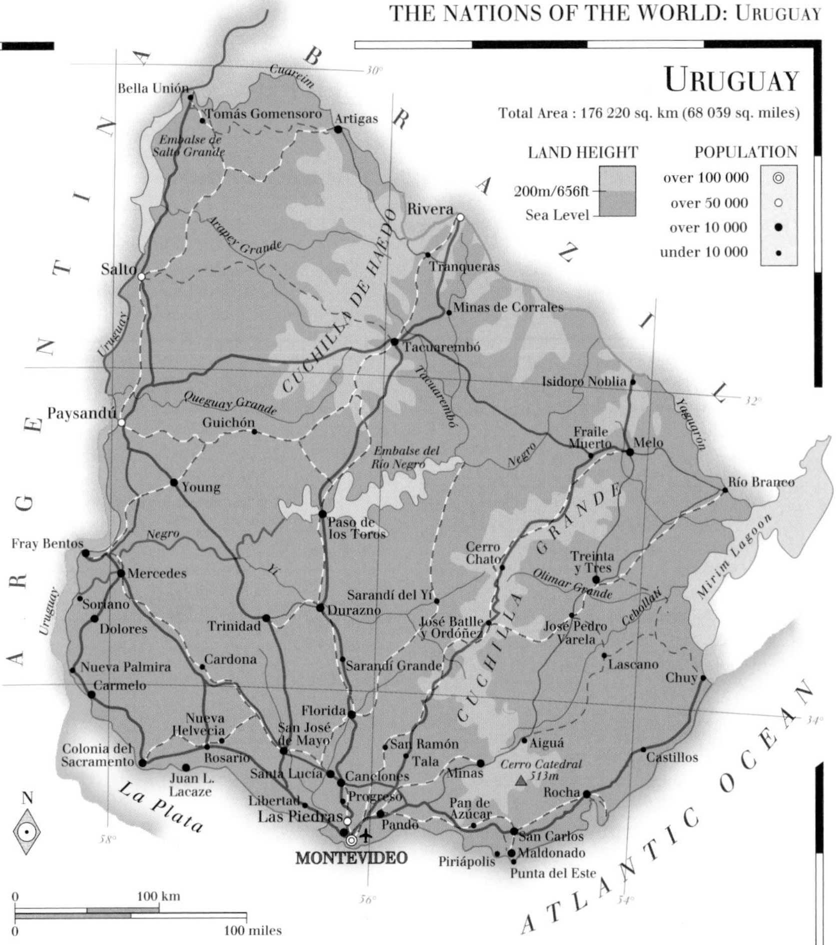
LAND HEIGHT
200m/656ft
Sea Level
POPULATION
over 100 000
over 50 000
over 10 000
under 10 000
ARGENTINA
BRAZIL
ATLANTIC OCEAN
La Plata
Bella Unión
Tomás Gomensoro
Artigas
Cuareim
Embalse de Salto Grande
Rivera
Arapey Grande
Salto
Tranqueras
Minas de Corrales
CUCHILLA DE HAEDO
Uruguay
Tacuarembó
Isidoro Noblia
Yaguarón
Paysandú
Queguay Grande
Guichón
Embalse del Río Negro
Negro
Fraile Muerto
Melo
Río Branco
Young
Paso de los Toros
Mirim Lagoon
CUCHILLA GRANDE
Fray Bentos
Cerro Chato
Treinta y Tres
Olimar Grande
Mercedes
Yí
Sarandí del Yí
Soriano
Durazno
José Batlle y Ordóñez
José Pedro Varela
Cebollatí
Dolores
Trinidad
Cardona
Lascano
Nueva Palmira
Sarandí Grande
Chuy
Carmelo
Florida
Nueva Helvecia
San José de Mayo
Colonia del Sacramento
Rosario
San Ramón
Aiguá
Tala
Castillos
Juan L. Lacaze
Santa Lucía
Canelones
Minas
Cerro Catedral 513m
Rocha
Libertad
Progreso
Pan de Azúcar
Las Piedras
Pando
San Carlos
MONTEVIDEO
Piriápolis
Maldonado
Punta del Este
N
0
100 km
100 miles

POLITICS

Multiparty elections

L. House 1999/2004
U. House 1999/2004

President Jorge Batlle Ibáñez

AT THE LAST ELECTION

Chamber of Representatives 99 seats

41% EPFA	33% PC	22% PN	4% NE

EPFA = Progressive Broad Front **PC** = Colorado Party (Colorados) **PN** = National Party (Blancos) **NE** = New Space **Res** = Reserved for the vice president

Chamber of Senators 31 seats

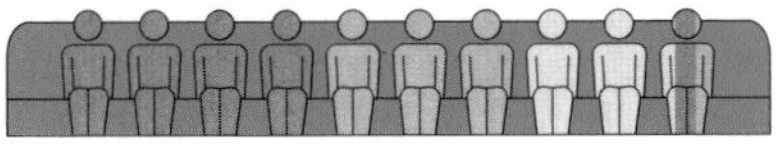

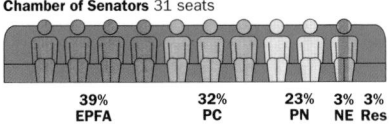

39% EPFA	32% PC	23% PN	3% NE	3% Res

Uruguay is a presidential multiparty democracy.

PROFILE

The elections of 1984 marked a return to democracy. Since then the main Colorado (PC) and Blanco (PN) parties have monopolized power, either alone or in coalitions, despite being traditional opponents. The left-wing EPFA has been the effective opposition, frequently in alliance with trade unions fighting austerity measures and reform of the social security system. Despite the crowded electoral calendar in 1999, and infighting among Blanco factions, there was broad consensus on the need for continuing economic reform. In the 1999 elections, Colorado candidate Jorge Batlle won the presidency in the face of an unusually strong left-wing challenge.

MAIN POLITICAL ISSUES

Government credibility

Batlle was seriously weakened by the early departure of junior coalition Blancos from his cabinet in 2002. With elections due in 2004, the Blancos were seen to be distancing themselves from Batlle's harsh austerity program, already affecting the Colorados' popularity.

Economic malaise

The economy entered its fifth year of recession in 2003. Government forecasts of a 2% contraction for the year were far below what independent economists predicted.

Luis Alberto Lacalle Herrera, *president in 1990–1995.*

Jorge Batlle Ibáñez, *who took office as president in 2000.*

WORLD AFFAIRS

Joined UN in 1945

Geplac | Mercsr | IBRD | OAS | RG

Regional integration is a major focus, but President Batlle's determination to clinch a bilateral trade deal with the US caused a row with the Brazilian government, which said that it contravened the official policy of Mercosur to negotiate trade agreements as a bloc. Argentina also took exception to plans to impose protective tariffs to cushion Uruguayan industry from the effects of Argentine devaluation. Such difficulties complicated diplomatic moves to strengthen Mercosur as a negotiating bloc in upcoming talks to establish a Free Trade Area of the Americas (FTAA).

Uruguay and the US have agreed a legal assistance treaty to allow easier access to bank accounts of those suspected of laundering the proceeds from narcotics trafficking.

AID

Recipient

$15m (receipts) — Down 12% in 2001

Uruguay received an IMF standby loan of $1.5 billion for 2002–2003, but aid remains otherwise modest.

CHRONOLOGY

The Spaniards were the first to colonize the area north of the River Plate. In 1680, the Portuguese also founded a colony there, at Colonia del Sacramento, so starting 150 years of rivalry between the colonial powers for control of the territory.

- **1726** Spaniards found Montevideo. By 1800, whole country is divided into large cattle ranches.
- **1808** Montevideo declares independence from Buenos Aires.
- **1811** Patriotic rancher and local caudillo, José Gervasio Artigas, fends off Brazilian attack.
- **1812–1820** Uruguayans, known as Orientales ("Easterners," from the eastern side of the River Plate), fight wars against Argentinian and Brazilian invaders. Brazil finally takes Montevideo.
- **1827** Gen. Lavalleja defeats Brazilians with Argentine help.
- **1828** Seeing trade benefits that an independent Uruguay would bring as a buffer state between Argentina and Brazil, Britain mediates and secures Uruguayan independence.
- **1836** Start of large-scale European immigration.

U

CHRONOLOGY *continued*

- **1838–1865** La Guerra Grande civil war between Blancos (Whites, future conservative party) and Colorados (Reds, future liberals).
- **1865–1870** President Venancio Flores of Colorados takes Uruguay into War of Triple Alliance against Paraguay.
- **1872** Peace under military rule. Blancos strong in country, Colorados in cities.
- **1890s** Violent strikes by immigrant trade unionists against landed elite enriched by massive European investment in ranching.
- **1903–1907** Reformist Colorado, José Batlle y Ordóñez, president.
- **1911–1915** Batlle serves second term in office. Batllismo creates the only welfare state in Latin America with pensions, social security, and free education and health service; also nationalizations, disestablishment of Church, abolition of death penalty.
- **1933** Military coup. Opposition groups excluded from politics.
- **1939–1945** Neutral in World War II.
- **1942** President Alfredo Baldomir dismisses government and tries to bring back proper representation.
- **1951** New constitution replaces president with nine-member council. Decade of great prosperity follows until world agricultural prices plummet. Sharp drop in foreign investment.
- **1958** Blancos win elections for first time in 93 years.
- **1962** Tupamaros urban guerrillas founded. Its guerrilla campaign lasts until 1973.
- **1966** Presidency reinstated. Colorados back in power.
- **1967** Jorge Pacheco president. Tries to stifle opposition to tough anti-inflation policies.
- **1973** Military coup. Promises to encourage foreign investment counteracted by denial of political freedom and brutal repression of the left; 400,000 emigrate.
- **1984–1985** Military step down. Elections. Julio Sanguinetti (Colorado) president.
- **1986** Those guilty of human rights abuse granted amnesty.
- **1989** Referendum endorses amnesty in interests of stability. Elections won by Luis Alberto Lacalle Herrera and Blancos.
- **1994–1995** Sanguinetti reelected, forms coalition government. Mercosur membership.
- **1999** October, presidential election won by Colorado Jorge Batlle.
- **2002** Uruguay loses investment grade status due to impact of Argentine crisis.

U

DEFENSE

No compulsory military service

$352m

Down 7% in 2001

The military withdrew from power in 1985 and has since respected civilian rule. "Lodges" operate within the army to promote officers' interests and have displayed opposition to the government's replacements and promotions within the military hierarchy. A 1986 law virtually blocked investigations into killings, torture, and "disappearances" during the dictatorship, but there is still pressure to bring guilty officers to justice. A presidential decree in 1997 granted amnesty to officers punished for political offenses under military rule.

URUGUAYAN ARMED FORCES

15 main battle tanks (T-55)	15,200 personnel
3 frigates, 8 patrol boats	5700 personnel
28 combat aircraft (10 A37B, 5 IA-58B)	3000 personnel
None	

The defense budget is modest; recent purchases have come from Israel and the Czech Republic.

ECONOMICS

Inflation 28% p.a. (1990–2001)

$19.2bn

26.82 Uruguayan pesos (18.73)

SCORE CARD

World GNP Ranking	66th
GNP per Capita	$5710
Balance of Payments	–$513m
Inflation	4.4%
Unemployment	14%

EXPORTS

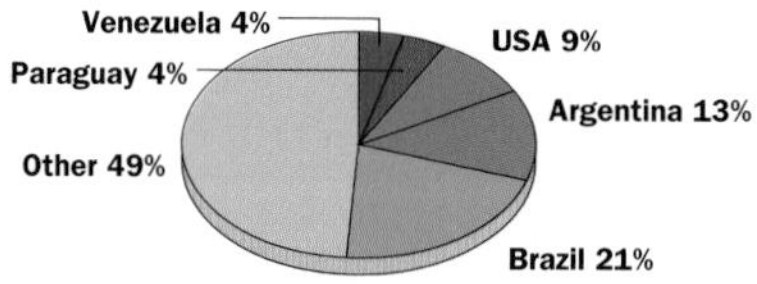
Venezuela 4%
USA 9%
Paraguay 4%
Argentina 13%
Other 49%
Brazil 21%

IMPORTS

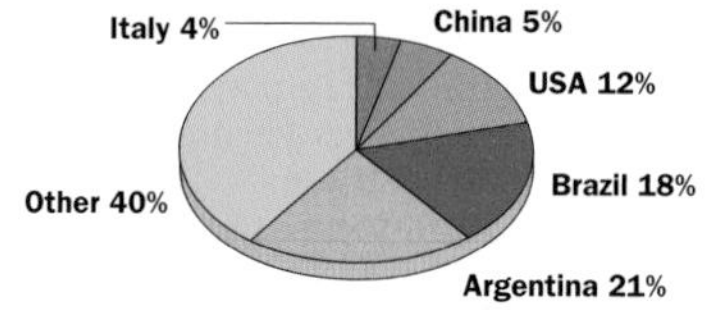
Italy 4%
China 5%
USA 12%
Other 40%
Brazil 18%
Argentina 21%

Strengths

Fertile grasslands. Major wool exporter. Beef-meat products. Fishing. Competitive exchange rate.

Weaknesses

Few natural resources. Dependence on Brazilian and Argentine markets. Modest industry. Large public sector deficit. Prolonged economic recession. Troubled banking sector.

Profile

Three-quarters of Uruguay, which is traditionally an agricultural economy, is rich pasture, supporting livestock. Much of the rest is given over to crops. Farming, which formerly brought great wealth, still employs about 15% of the labor force, accounting for some 19% of GDP. Livestock and animal products, especially meat and wool, bring in over one-third of export earnings.

ECONOMIC PERFORMANCE INDICATOR

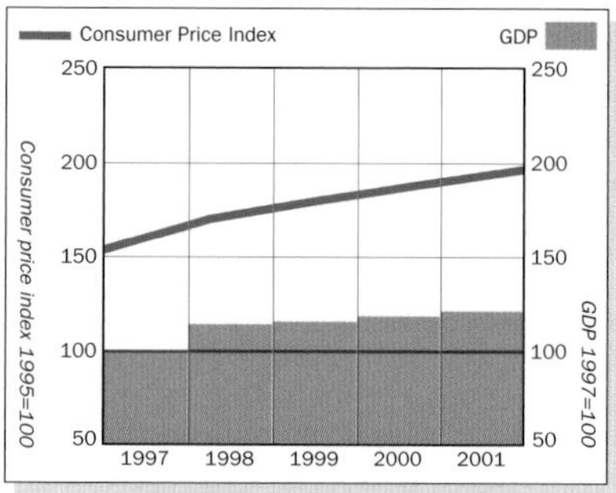
Consumer Price Index
GDP
250
200
150
100
50
Consumer price index 1995=100
GDP 1997=100
1997
1998
1999
2000
2001

Manufacturing, accounting for some 18% of GDP, is farm-based. Tourism is increasingly important. Most economic activity – and half the population – is concentrated in Montevideo. A shrinking economy has made it difficult to achieve GDP and fiscal targets agreed with the IMF. Unions resist spending cuts, and, with public opinion hostile to major privatizations, there has been little progress in necessary structural reforms.

URUGUAY : MAJOR BUSINESSES

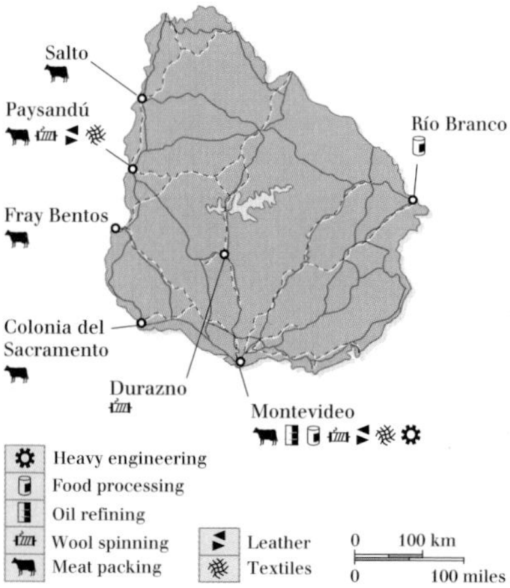
Salto
Paysandú
Río Branco
Fray Bentos
Colonia del Sacramento
Durazno
Montevideo
Heavy engineering
Food processing
Oil refining
Wool spinning
Meat packing
Leather
Textiles
0 100 km
0 100 miles

RESOURCES

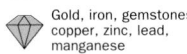

Electric power 2.2m kW

116,673 tonnes

Not an oil producer; refines 31,500 b/d

11.7m cattle, 11.2m sheep, 13.2m chickens

Gold, iron, gemstones, copper, zinc, lead, manganese

Most of Uruguay is farmland, much of it given over to cattle and sheep. Rice is the country's only other significant export. There are no known oil or natural gas resources; most electricity is imported. Considerable potential is believed to exist for the mining sector, but only small quantities of building materials and jewelry-quality agate and amethysts are so far extracted. The mining of gold deposits is currently being developed and exploration continues.

ELECTRICITY GENERATION

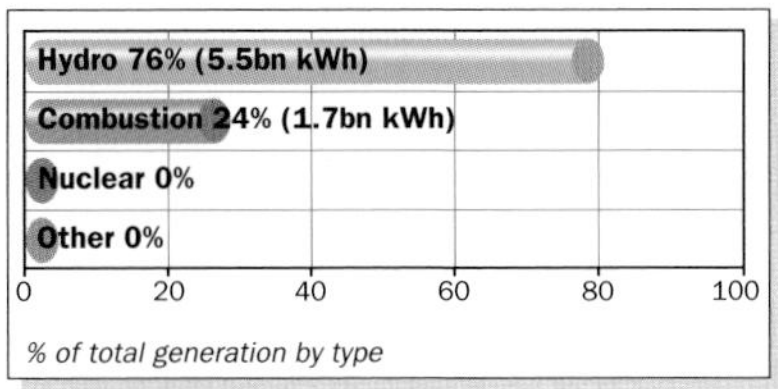
Hydro 76% (5.5bn kWh)
Combustion 24% (1.7bn kWh)
Nuclear 0%
Other 0%
0
20
40
60
80
100
% of total generation by type

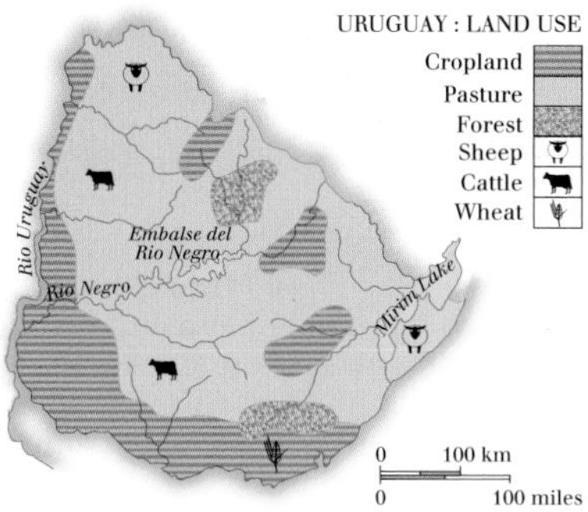
URUGUAY : LAND USE
Cropland
Pasture
Forest
Sheep
Cattle
Wheat
Río Uruguay
Embalse del Río Negro
Río Negro
Mirim Lake
0 100 km
0 100 miles

ENVIRONMENT

Sustainability rank: 6th

0.3% (0.2% partially protected)

2 tonnes per capita

ENVIRONMENTAL TREATIES

Yes	Yes	Yes
Yes	Yes	Yes

Pollution of the main Uruguay and Plate Rivers is a concern, as is traffic density in Montevideo.

MEDIA

TV ownership high

Daily newspaper circulation 293 per 1000 people

PUBLISHING AND BROADCAST MEDIA

There are 16 daily newspapers, including *El País*, *El Diario*, and *La Mañana*

4 services: 1 state-owned, 3 independent

6 services: 1 state-owned, 5 independent

The press is relatively free. *El País* supports the Blancos (PN), while *La Mañana* backs the Colorados (PC).

CRIME

No death penalty

4012 prisoners

Up 15% in 2000

CRIME RATES

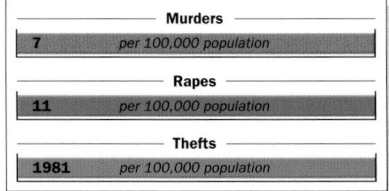

Crime	Rate
Murders	7 per 100,000 population
Rapes	11 per 100,000 population
Thefts	1981 per 100,000 population

Levels of violent crime are generally low in comparison with neighboring Brazil and Argentina. However, rises in street violence and organized crime are of growing concern.

EDUCATION

School leaving age: 15

98%

97,541 students

THE EDUCATION SYSTEM

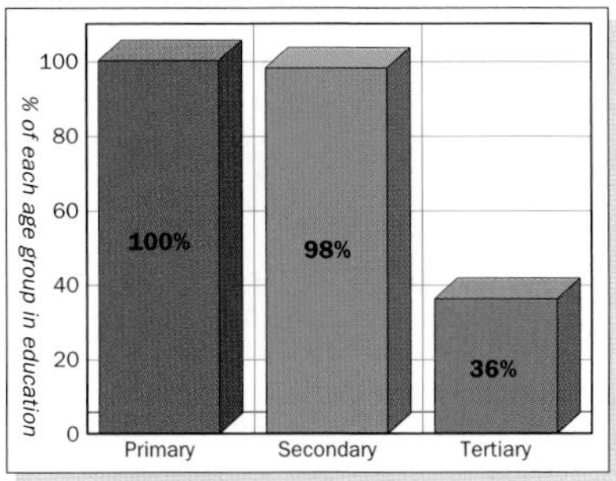
100
80
60
40
20
0
% of each age group in education
100%
98%
36%
Primary
Secondary
Tertiary

Education, inspired by the French *lycée* system, is state-funded for 12 years up to secondary level and is compulsory for all children for nine years from the age of six. Both state and private schools follow the same curriculum; private schools are monitored by the government. Facilities are rudimentary in rural areas. Uruguay has two state-funded universities. The children of wealthy Uruguayans tend to complete their studies in the US. Resistance to tax increases and pressure to reduce the fiscal deficit have both placed serious constraints on education spending. Secondary school students continue to stage protests against the resulting effects on the system.

HEALTH

Welfare state health benefits

1 per 267 people

Cancers, heart and cerebrovascular diseases

Most Uruguayans have easy access to health services. Average life expectancy is high. The health system faces a challenge, however, with a large number of people unable to afford health insurance. Despite opposition, the government has privatized some of the state medical establishments.

Health spending has in recent years been a victim of the budget cuts and social welfare reforms aimed at controlling the fiscal deficit.

SPENDING

GDP/cap. increase

CONSUMPTION AND SPENDING

158 per 1000 population

283 per 1000 population

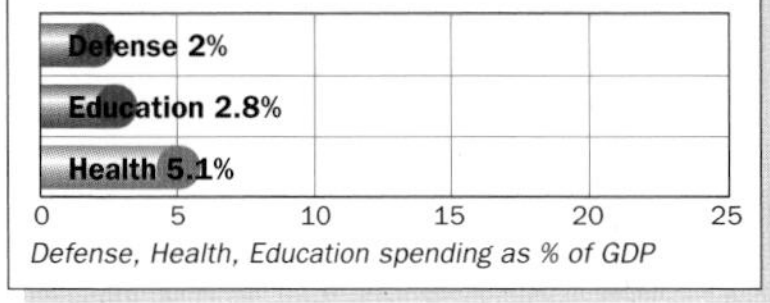
Defense 2%
Education 2.8%
Health 5.1%
0
5
10
15
20
25
Defense, Health, Education spending as % of GDP

Uruguay possesses the social mobility which is typical of countries created through decades of large-scale immigration, and many professionals come from modest backgrounds. A 1999 report by the IDB exempted Uruguay from the regional trend of serious income inequality.

The wealthy members of society either tend to be landowners or are employed in the financial sector. They have traditionally looked toward Europe, rather than the US, for luxury goods.

The most deprived sections of Uruguayan society are the urban poor of Montevideo, a large proportion of whom are of mixed African and European descent, and the rural poor, who own little or no land.

WORLD RANKING

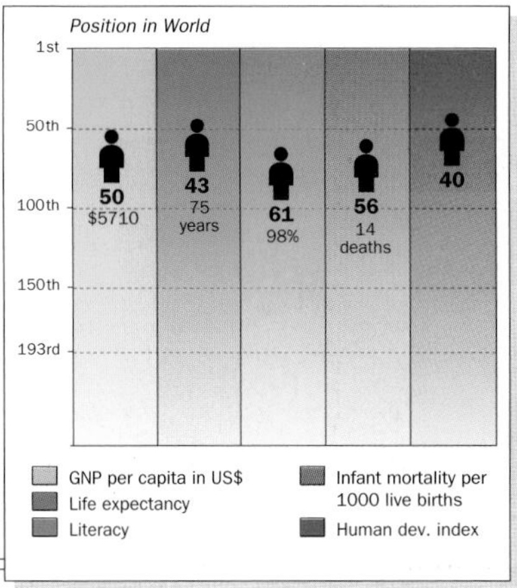
Position in World
1st
50th
100th
150th
193rd
50
$5710
43
75
years
61
98%
56
14
deaths
40
GNP per capita in US$
Life expectancy
Literacy
Infant mortality per 1000 live births
Human dev. index

U

CENTRAL ASIA
Asia
Kazakhstan
Kyrgyzstan
UZBEKISTAN
Turkmenistan
Tajikistan
Afghanistan

UZBEKISTAN

OFFICIAL NAME: Republic of Uzbekistan **CAPITAL:** Tashkent
POPULATION: 25.6 million **CURRENCY:** Som **OFFICIAL LANGUAGE:** Uzbek

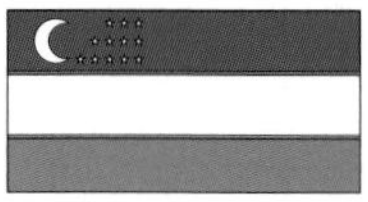

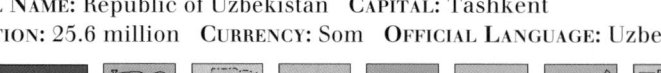

1991 | 1991 | Sept 1 | UZ | +5 to +6 | +998 | .uz

SHARING WHAT IS LEFT of the Aral sea with Kazakhstan, its northern neighbor, Uzbekistan contains the ancient cities of Samarqand, Bukhara (Bukhoro), Khiva, and Tashkent. It is the most populous central Asian republic and has considerable natural resources. The dictatorship of President Karimov has prevented the spread of Islamic fundamentalism.

CLIMATE

Desert/mountain

WEATHER CHART FOR TASHKENT

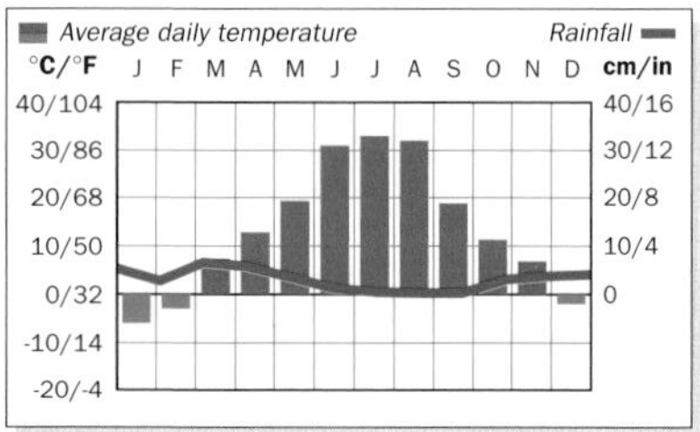
Average daily temperature
Rainfall
°C/°F
J F M A M J J A S O N D
cm/in
40/104
30/86
20/68
10/50
0/32
-10/14
-20/-4
40/16
30/12
20/8
10/4
0

Uzbekistan has a harsh continental climate. Summers can be extremely hot and dry. Large areas of the country are desert.

TRANSPORTATION

Drive on right

Tashkent International 1.72m passengers

Has no fleet

THE TRANSPORTATION NETWORK

71,237 km (44,265 miles)	None
3645 km (2265 miles)	1100 km (684 miles)

Uzbekistan has a well-developed transportation system. An extensive network of buses serves country areas, while good Soviet-style systems of trolley buses and trams operate in the major cities. Tashkent's subway system was the first in central Asia. Road and rail networks have deteriorated since 1991, however, and are concentrated in the south and east.

TOURISM

Visitors : Population 1:94

272,000 visitors

Up 196% 1995–1998

MAIN TOURIST ARRIVALS

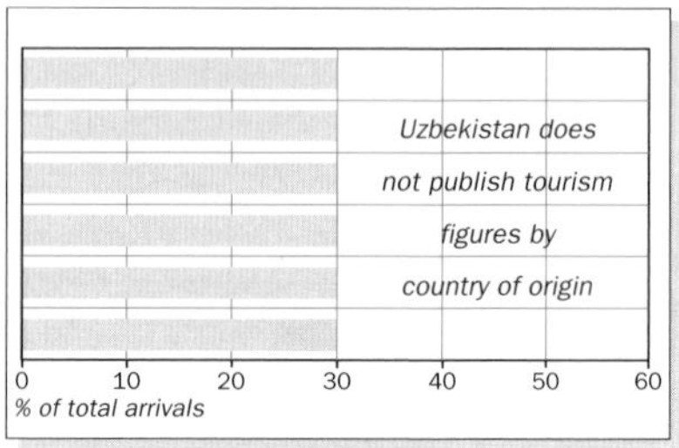
Uzbekistan does
not publish tourism
figures by
country of origin
0
10
20
30
40
50
60
% of total arrivals

Uzbekistan has considerable tourist potential. Bukhara, once a trading center on the silk route, is famous worldwide for its architecture and carpet-making. It has great religious significance for Muslims, who are encouraged to make at least one pilgrimage to its holy shrines. Bukhara's Kalyan Mosque is famous for its minaret built of unbaked bricks. The city of Samarqand was expanded in the 14th century by Timur, and contains the monumental gateway of the Shir Dar Madrasa, one of the most beautiful buildings in the Islamic world.

UZBEKISTAN
Total Area : 447 400 sq. km
(172 741 sq. miles)
LAND HEIGHT
3000m/9843ft
2000m/6562ft
1000m/3281ft
500m/1640ft
200m/656ft
Sea Level
POPULATION
over 1 000 000
over 100 000
over 50 000
over 10 000
KAZAKHSTAN
ARAL SEA
USTYURT PLATEAU
Mo'ynoq
Chimboy
Taxtako'pir
Qo'ng'irot
Amu Darya
Nukus
Xo'jayli
Taxiatosh
TURAN LOWLAND
KYZYL KUM
Uchquduq
Zarafshon
Urganch
Xiwa
To'rtko'l
TURKMENISTAN
Aydarko'l Ko'li
Nurota
NUROTA TIZMASI
Navoiy
G'ijduvon
Gazli
Buxoro
Kogon
Qorako'l
Oqtosh
Kattaqo'rg'on
Bulung'ur
Samarqand
Urgut
Kitob
Shahrisabz
Koson
Qarshi
GISSAR RANGE
Denov
Boysun
Jarqo'rg'on
Termiz
AFGHANISTAN
TAJIKISTAN
Jizzax
Sirdaryo
Guliston
Yangiyer
Bekobod
Syr Darya
TASHKENT
Yangiyo'l
Chirchiq
G'azalkent
CHATKAL RANGE
Angren
Olmaliq
Chust
Namangan
Andijon
Shahrixon
Asaka
Qo'qon
Marg'ilon
Farg'ona
Gora Manas 4488m
KYRGYZSTAN
N
0 100 km
0 100 miles

Mosque in Samarqand. *The city remained an Islamic stronghold, despite communist attempts at suppression, when Uzbekistan formed part of the Soviet Union.*

PEOPLE

Pop. density medium

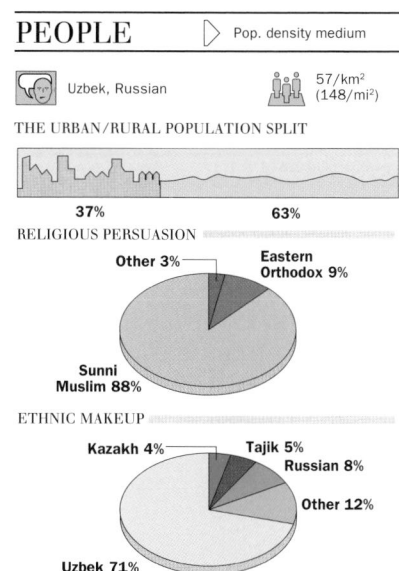

Uzbek, Russian

57/km² (148/mi²)

THE URBAN/RURAL POPULATION SPLIT

37%
63%

RELIGIOUS PERSUASION

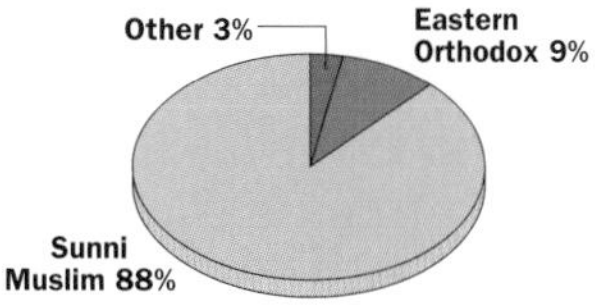
Other 3%
Eastern Orthodox 9%
Sunni Muslim 88%

ETHNIC MAKEUP

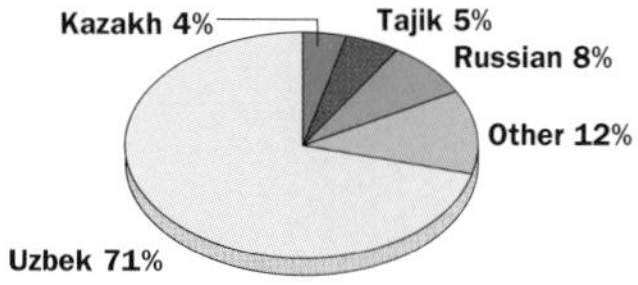
Kazakh 4%
Tajik 5%
Russian 8%
Other 12%
Uzbek 71%

Among the former Soviet republics, Uzbekistan has a relatively complex makeup. In addition to the Uzbeks, Russians, Tajiks, and Kazakhs, there are small minorities of Tatars and Karakalpaks. The proportion of Russians has been declining since the 1970s, when net emigration of Russians began. Tensions among ethnic groups have the potential to create regional and racial conflict. The authoritarian nature of the Karimov leadership has so far prevented these antagonisms from becoming violent. Incidents such as the 1989 and 1990 clashes between Meskhetians and Uzbeks are rare. The removal of the dominance of the Communist Party has meant that Uzbek society has reverted to traditional social patterns based on family, religion, clan, and region, rather than on membership of the party. Independence has done little to alter the minor role of women in politics. Arranged marriages are still the custom in the countryside.

POPULATION AGE BREAKDOWN

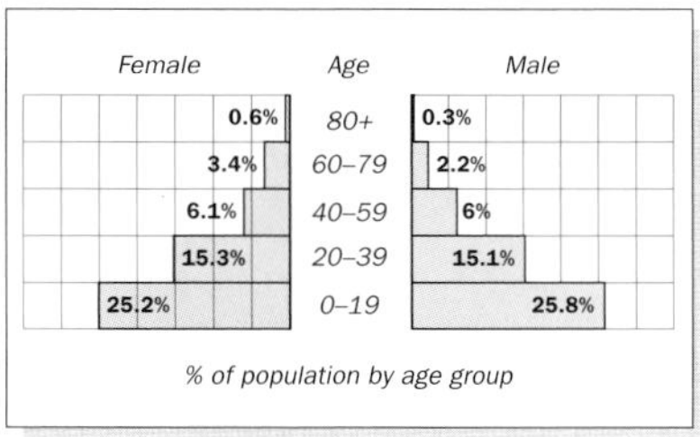
Female
Age
Male
0.6%
80+
0.3%
3.4%
60–79
2.2%
6.1%
40–59
6%
15.3%
20–39
15.1%
25.2%
0–19
25.8%
% of population by age group

POLITICS

Multiparty elections

1999/2004

President Islam Karimov

AT THE LAST ELECTION

Supreme Council 250 seats

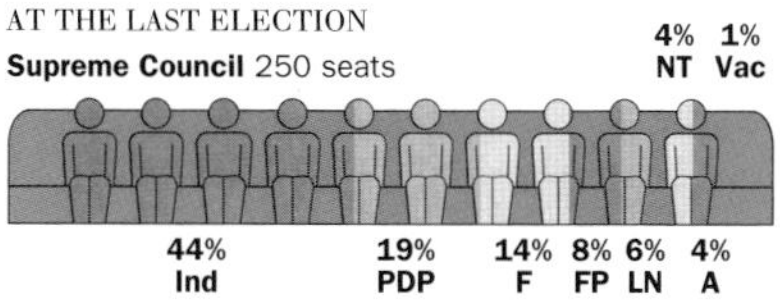
4% NT
1% Vac
44% Ind
19% PDP
14% F
8% FP
6% LN
4% A

Ind = Independents **PDP** = People's Democratic Party
F = Fidorkorlar **FP** = Fatherland Progress Party
LN = Local nominees **A** = Adolat
NT = National Renaissance **Vac** = Vacant

Uzbekistan is effectively run by a presidential dictatorship. In 2002 a referendum approved the creation of a second legislative chamber and lengthened the presidential term.

PROFILE

President Islam Karimov's former communist PDP has not been willing to devolve or share power. The 1992 constitution appeared to endorse multipartyism, but Karimov took advantage of his enhanced powers to ban several opposition parties, including the nationalist Birlik (Unity) and the Islamic Renaissance Party. Erk (Will), the only legal opposition party, was proscribed in 1993, and in 1995, a group of its activists received stiff sentences for political subversion. Opposition is now entirely underground. The intimidation and arbitrary imprisonment of dissidents are common, and have increased since bomb attacks in Tashkent in 1999. Karimov has kept the support of the Russian minority by avoiding nationalist rhetoric.

MAIN POLITICAL ISSUES

Islamic fundamentalism

Civil war in Tajikistan and the rise of the *taliban* in Afghanistan raised fears of Islamic fundamentalism. A joint operation with Kyrgyzstan and Tajikistan against the pan-regional Islamic Movement of Uzbekistan (IMU) took place in 2000, as cross-border attacks rose. IMU leader Juma Namangani was reported killed alongside *taliban* fighters in Afghanistan in late 2001. A clampdown against the Hizb-ut Tahrir group continues.

Regionalism

The high birthrate puts pressure on limited agricultural resources. Migration from poorer areas has led to calls for secession from some regions. In the densely populated eastern Fergana Valley there have been a number of violent incidents.

Islam Karimov, *first elected president in 1990 and Uzbekistan's sole leader since independence.*

WORLD AFFAIRS

Joined UN in 1992

CIS SCO OIC NAM OSCE

Unlike neighboring Turkmenistan, Kyrgyzstan, and Tajikistan, Uzbekistan has the resources to allow it to follow a relatively independent foreign policy. The Karimov leadership has used this to promote Uzbekistan as the leading central Asian state, a role for which it vies with Kazakhstan. It is a member of the Georgia–Ukraine–Uzbekistan–Azerbaijan–Moldova (GUUAM) group of ex-Soviet states, signifying a wish to maintain a certain distance in relations with Russia, though it suspended its membership for a year in 2002. It has border disputes with its immediate neighbors, in particular over the laying of land mines on its borders with Tajikistan and Kyrgyzstan to prevent terrorist incursions.

Ties with the US were strengthened when Uzbekistan played host to US forces during the war in Afghanistan in 2001. Relations with Turkey are also developing. While Western companies have difficulty in sealing contracts in Uzbekistan, Turkish companies have been commissioned to build vital installations such as those for telecommunications.

CHRONOLOGY

Once part of the great Mongol Empire, present-day Uzbekistan was incorporated into the Russian Empire between 1865 and 1876. Russification of the area was superficial, and it was not until Soviet rule that significant Russian immigration occurred. A further influx of Russians occurred during Stalin's program of forced collectivization.

- **1917** Soviet power established in Tashkent.
- **1918** Turkestan Autonomous Soviet Socialist Republic (ASSR), incorporating present-day Uzbekistan, proclaimed.
- **1923–1941** Alphabet changes, from Arabic to Latin to Iranized Tashkent, finally to Cyrillic.
- **1924** Basmachi rebels who resisted Soviet rule crushed. Uzbek SSR founded (which, until 1929, included the Tajik ASSR).
- **1925** Anti-Islamic campaign bans schools and closes mosques.
- **1936** Karakalpak ASSR (formerly part of the Russian Soviet Federative Socialist Republic) incorporated into the Uzbek SSR.
- **1937** Uzbek communist leadership is purged by Stalin.

U

CHRONOLOGY *continued*

- **1941–1945** Industrial boom.
- **1959** Sharaf Rashidov becomes first secretary of Communist Party of Uzbekistan (CPUz). Retains position until 1983.
- **1966** Tashkent razed by earthquake. Rebuilding brings in large number of Russian and other non-Uzbek migrants.
- **1982–1983** Yuri Andropov becomes leader in Moscow. His anticorruption purge results in emergence of a new generation of central Asian officials.
- **1989** First noncommunist political movement, Birlik (Unity), formed but not officially registered. June, clashes erupt between Meskhetians and indigenous Uzbek population of Fergana Valley, resulting in more than 100 deaths. October, Birlik campaign leads to Uzbek being declared official language.
- **1990** Islam Karimov becomes executive president of the new Uzbek Supreme Soviet. Further interethnic fighting in Fergana Valley; 320 killed.
- **1991** August, independence is proclaimed and Republic of Uzbekistan is adopted as official name. October, Uzbekistan signs treaty establishing economic community with seven other former Soviet republics. November, CPUz restructured as the People's Democratic Party of Uzbekistan (PDP); Karimov remains its leader. December, Karimov confirmed in post of president. Uzbekistan joins the CIS.
- **1992** Price liberalization provokes student riots in Tashkent. New post-Soviet constitution adopted along Western democratic lines. All religious parties banned. September, Uzbekistan sends troops to Tajikistan to suppress violence and strengthen border controls.
- **1993** Growing harassment of opposition political parties, Erk (Will) and Birlik.
- **1994** Introduction of som.
- **1995** January, Karimov's PDP wins legislative elections. March, referendum extends Karimov's presidential term until 2000. December, Utkur Sultanov replaces Abdulashim Mutalov as prime minister.
- **1999** Bomb attacks by Islamist terrorists lead to crackdown and arrests of hundreds of opposition activists. Legislative elections.
- **2000** Karimov reelected.
- **2002** Referendum extends president's term to seven years.

U

AID

Recipient

$153m (receipts) — Down 18% in 2001

Uzbekistan's lack of commitment to economic stabilization and record of human rights violations have generally deterred bilateral aid donors. Japan is now the largest donor, followed by the US, Germany, the EU, and France. The Asian Development Bank provides some special funds.

DEFENSE

Compulsory military service

$1.76bn — Up 1% in 2001

Uzbekistan has a standing army of around 40,000 personnel, mainly conscripts, as well as over 17,000 internal security troops and a 1000-strong National Guard. The military is being restructured, with a view to full professionalization of the armed forces.

A policy of mining the land borders with Kyrgyzstan and Uzbekistan to thwart incursions by Islamist militants has drawn international criticism.

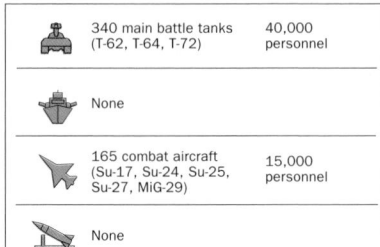

UZBEK ARMED FORCES

340 main battle tanks (T-62, T-64, T-72)	40,000 personnel
None	
165 combat aircraft (Su-17, Su-24, Su-25, Su-27, MiG-29)	15,000 personnel
None	

ECONOMICS

Inflation 211% p.a. (1990–2001)

$13.8bn — 974 som (750.05)

SCORE CARD

World GNP Ranking	78th
GNP per Capita	$550
Balance of Payments	–$113m
Inflation	23%
Unemployment	10%

EXPORTS

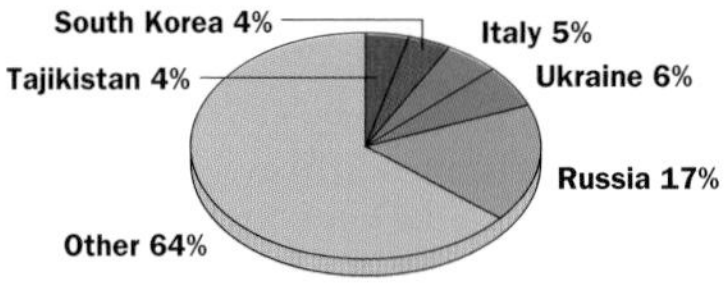
South Korea 4%
Italy 5%
Tajikistan 4%
Ukraine 6%
Russia 17%
Other 64%

IMPORTS

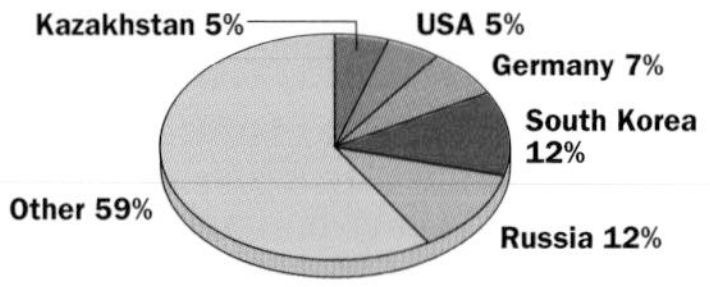
Kazakhstan 5%
USA 5%
Germany 7%
South Korea 12%
Other 59%
Russia 12%

ECONOMIC PERFORMANCE INDICATOR

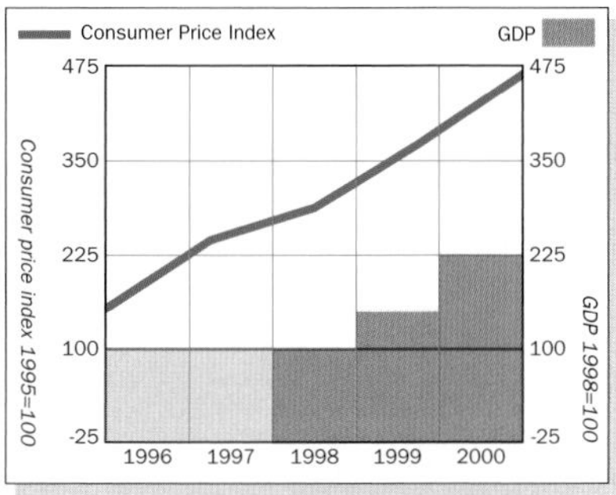
Consumer Price Index
GDP
475
350
225
100
-25
Consumer price index 1995=100
GDP 1998=100
1996
1997
1998
1999
2000

Strengths

Gold. Well-developed cotton market. Considerable unexploited deposits of oil and natural gas. Current production of natural gas makes significant contribution to electricity generation. Manufacturing tradition includes agricultural machinery and central Asia's first aviation factory.

Weaknesses

Dependent on grain imports, as domestic production meets only 25% of needs. Very limited economic reform. High inflation. Environmentally damaging irrigation scheme for cotton production.

Profile

With the exception of Tashkent, which became an industrial area during World War II, Uzbekistan's economy is predominantly agricultural. Promarket reforms have been slow, despite fresh assistance from the World Bank to increase the efficiency of privatized companies. The gold sector has attracted investment from US companies. Energy resources are still to be fully exploited. The som was devalued by 50% in 2001.

UZBEKISTAN : MAJOR BUSINESSES

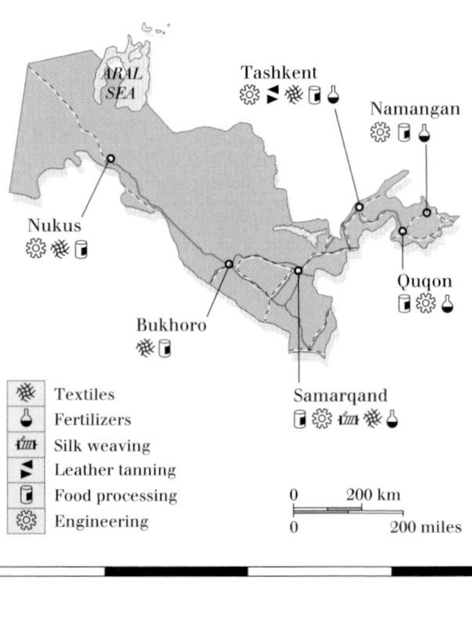
ARAL SEA
Tashkent
Namangan
Nukus
Quqon
Bukhoro
Samarqand
Textiles
Fertilizers
Silk weaving
Leather tanning
Food processing
Engineering
0 200 km
0 200 miles

RESOURCES

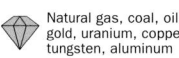

Electric power 11.7m kW

8529 tonnes

171,000 b/d (reserves 600m barrels)

8.22m sheep, 5.4m cattle, 14.5m chickens

Natural gas, coal, oil, gold, uranium, copper, tungsten, aluminum

ELECTRICITY GENERATION

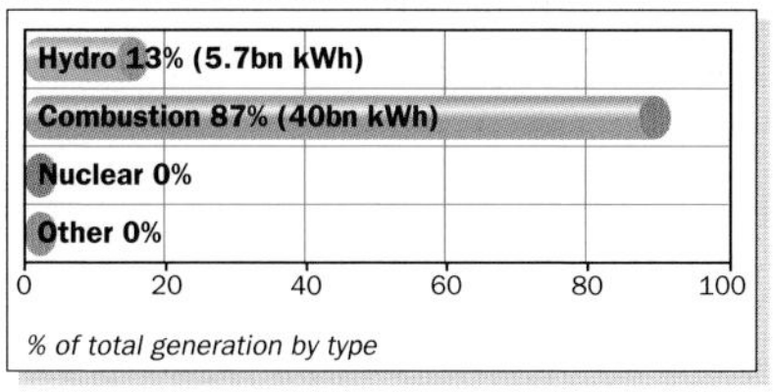
Hydro 13% (5.7bn kWh)
Combustion 87% (40bn kWh)
Nuclear 0%
Other 0%
0
20
40
60
80
100
% of total generation by type

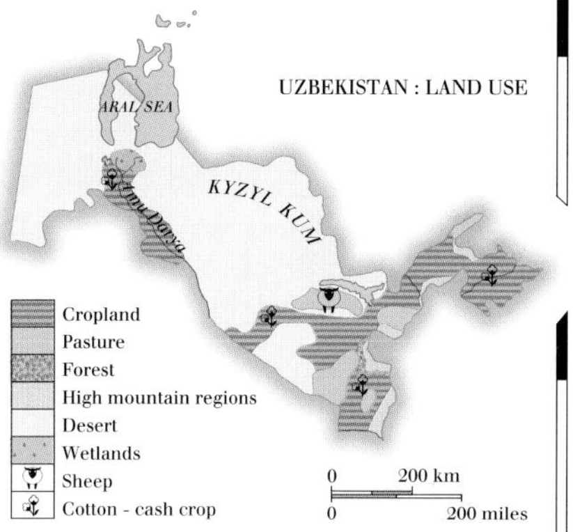
ARAL SEA
KYZYL KUM
UZBEKISTAN : LAND USE
Cropland
Pasture
Forest
High mountain regions
Desert
Wetlands
Sheep
Cotton - cash crop
0
200 km
0
200 miles

Uzbekistan has one of the world's largest gold mines, at Murantau in the Kyzyl Kum Desert, and also large deposits of natural gas, oil, coal, and uranium. An important oil field was discovered in 1992 in the Namangan region and production will rise with further investment. Most gas produced is currently used domestically, but it could also become a strong export.

Cotton is the main focus of agriculture: Uzbekistan is the world's fourth-largest producer. A decision after independence to diversify was reversed when the value of cotton as a commodity on the world market became clear. Fruit, silk cocoons, and vegetables for Russian markets are also of rising importance.

ENVIRONMENT

Sustainability rank: 118th

2%

4.8 tonnes per capita

ENVIRONMENTAL TREATIES

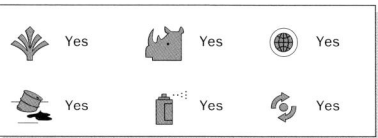

Yes	Yes	Yes
Yes	Yes	Yes

The irrigation schemes required to sustain the cotton industry have wreaked considerable environmental damage. Soil salination is now a major problem. The Aral Sea has also been seriously depleted. From 61,836 sq. km (23,875 sq. miles) in 1974, it had shrunk to less than half that area by 1997. In 1998 the World Bank approved more than $11 million to save the Aral Sea region. The indiscriminate use of fertilizers and pesticides to increase production has polluted many rivers.

MEDIA

TV ownership high

Daily newspaper circulation 3 per 1000 people

PUBLISHING AND BROADCAST MEDIA

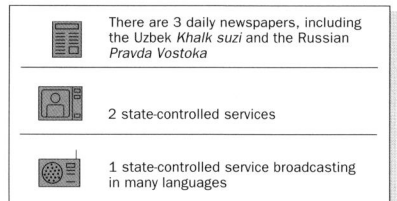

There are 3 daily newspapers, including the Uzbek *Khalk suzi* and the Russian *Pravda Vostoka*

2 state-controlled services

1 state-controlled service broadcasting in many languages

Uzbekistan's restrictions on independent publications are designed to encourage the promotion of the personality cult and policies of Karimov, and manifest themselves both in overt censorship and self-censorship by media outlets. Independent journalists face harassment. The expression of Islamist and nationalist opinion is forbidden.

CRIME

Death penalty in use

65,000 prisoners

Down 2% in 2000–2002

CRIME RATES

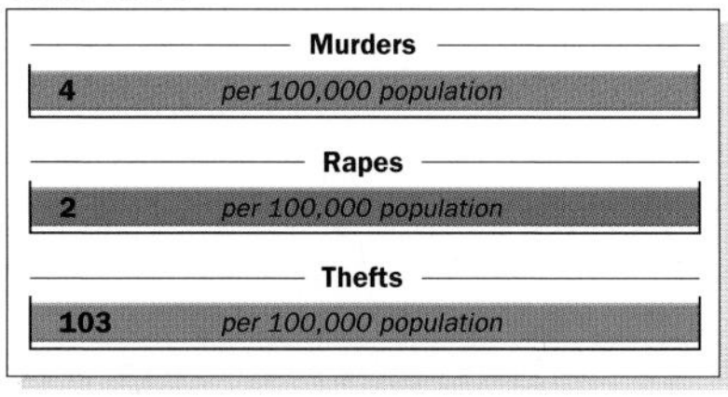
Murders
4
per 100,000 population
Rapes
2
per 100,000 population
Thefts
103
per 100,000 population

Crime rose in the 1990s as living standards declined. In 2001 the number of crimes carrying the death penalty was reduced to four. Unofficial Islamic courts in the Fergana Valley are a sign of opposition to the government.

EDUCATION

School leaving age: 18

99%

638,200 students

THE EDUCATION SYSTEM

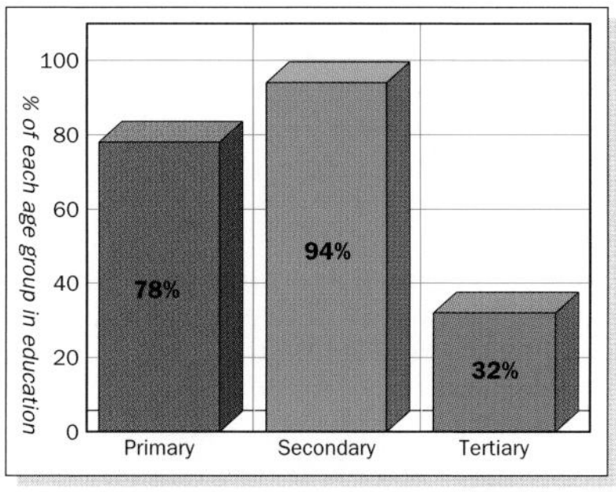
100
80
60
40
20
0
% of each age group in education
78%
94%
32%
Primary
Secondary
Tertiary

The state system still follows the Soviet model, though some instruction is in Uzbek. In the late 1980s, there were a few ethnic Tajik schools and a university in Samarqand. These were closed down in 1992 as relations deteriorated between Uzbekistan and Tajikistan. The rise in Islamic consciousness has led to a growing number of *madaris* – schools attached to mosques. In 1999 the establishment of Tashkent Islamic University was agreed.

HEALTH

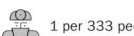

Welfare state health benefits

1 per 333 people

Heart, respiratory, and cerebrovascular diseases, cancers

The health service has been in decline since the dissolution of the USSR. Some rural areas are not served at all. In 1998 a $69.7 million project to improve health services was announced, with the World Bank providing a loan of some $30 million. Serious respiratory diseases among cotton growers are increasing.

SPENDING

GDP/cap. increase

CONSUMPTION AND SPENDING

No data

66 per 1000 population

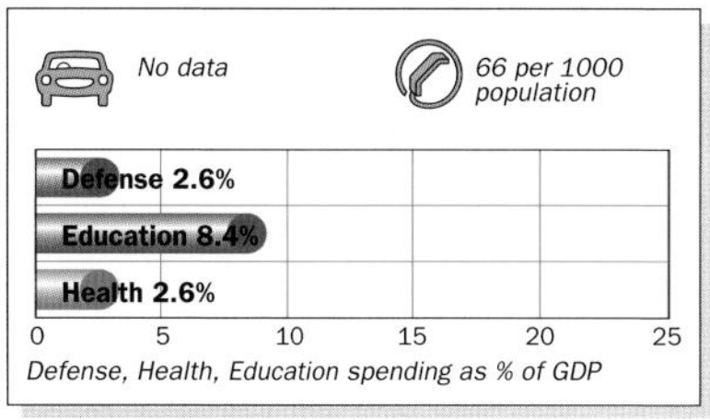
Defense 2.6%
Education 8.4%
Health 2.6%
0
5
10
15
20
25
Defense, Health, Education spending as % of GDP

Former communists are still the wealthiest group, since they retain control of the economy. Many rural poor live below the poverty line.

WORLD RANKING

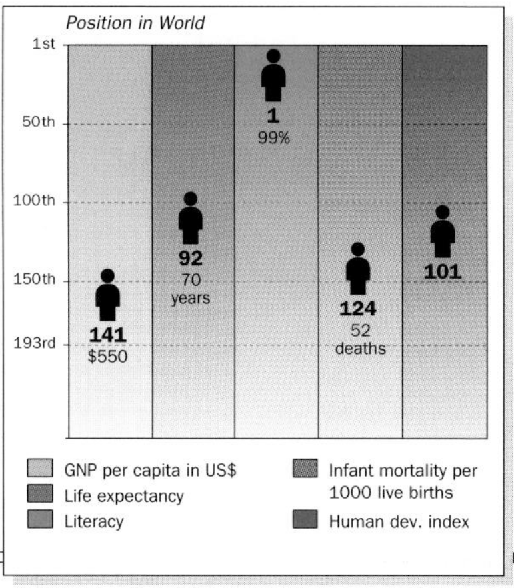
Position in World
1st
50th
100th
150th
193rd
141
$550
92
70
years
1
99%
124
52
deaths
101
GNP per capita in US$
Life expectancy
Literacy
Infant mortality per 1000 live births
Human dev. index

U

VANUATU

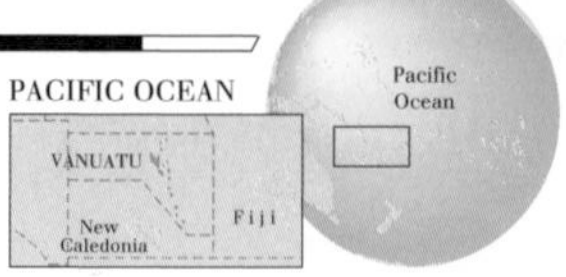
PACIFIC OCEAN
VANUATU
New Caledonia
Fiji
Pacific Ocean

OFFICIAL NAME: Republic of Vanuatu **CAPITAL:** Port Vila
POPULATION: 207,000 **CURRENCY:** Vatu **OFFICIAL LANGUAGES:** Bislama, English, and French

1980 | 1980 | July 30 | VU | +11 | +678 | .vu

THE ARCHIPELAGO OF Vanuatu stretches over 1300 km (800 miles) in the South Pacific. Mountainous and volcanic in origin, only 12 of the 82 islands are a significant size – Espiritu Santo and Malekula are the largest. Formerly known as the New Hebrides – ruled jointly by France and Britain from 1906 – Vanuatu became independent in 1980. Politics since then has been democratic but volatile.

CLIMATE

Tropical oceanic

WEATHER CHART FOR PORT VILA

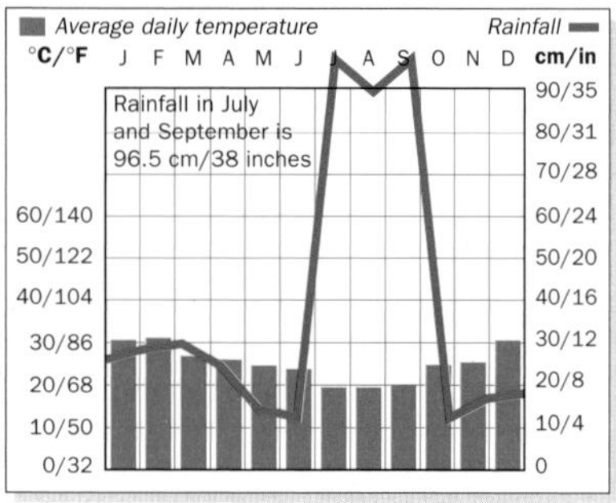
Average daily temperature
Rainfall
°C/°F
J F M A M J J A S O N D
cm/in
Rainfall in July and September is 96.5 cm/38 inches
90/35
80/31
70/28
60/140
60/24
50/122
50/20
40/104
40/16
30/86
30/12
20/68
20/8
10/50
10/4
0/32
0

The climate is tropical and hot. Rainfall and temperatures decrease north to south. Cyclones occur November–April.

TRANSPORTATION

Drive on right

Bauerfield, Port Vila

316 ships 1.5m grt

THE TRANSPORTATION NETWORK

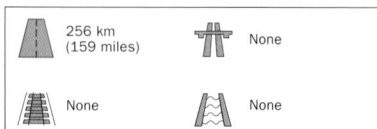

256 km (159 miles)

None

None

None

Road quality is generally poor, with routes on some remote islands impassable in the wet season.

TOURISM

Visitors : Population 1:3.6

57,000 visitors

Up 14% in 2000

MAIN TOURIST ARRIVALS

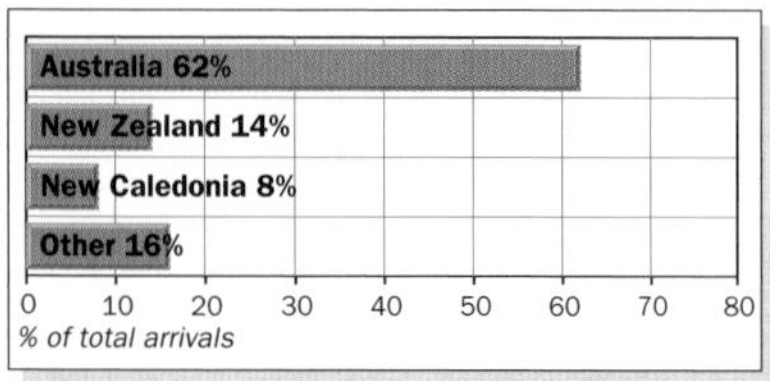
Australia 62%
New Zealand 14%
New Caledonia 8%
Other 16%
0
10
20
30
40
50
60
70
80
% of total arrivals

Tourism in Vanuatu is facing stiff competition from cheaper regional rivals. Organized tours include sea fishing, sailing, kayaking, and diving.

PEOPLE

Pop. density low

Bislama (Melanesian pidgin), English, French

17/km² (44/mi²)

THE URBAN/RURAL POPULATION SPLIT

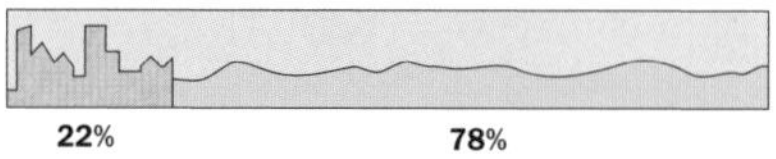
22%
78%

RELIGIOUS PERSUASION

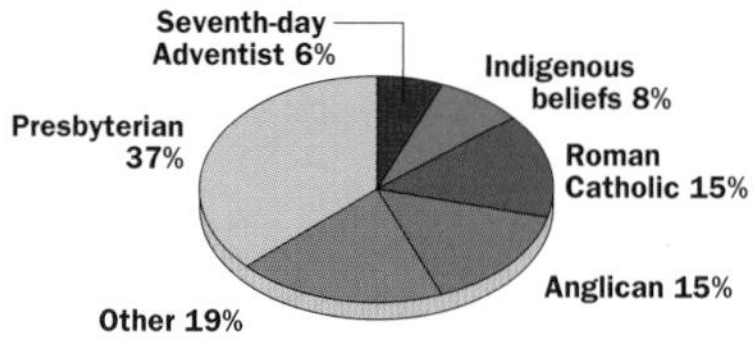
Seventh-day Adventist 6%
Indigenous beliefs 8%
Presbyterian 37%
Roman Catholic 15%
Anglican 15%
Other 19%

Indigenous Melanesians – ni-Vanuatu – comprise 94% of the population. Of Vanuatu's 82 islands, 67 are inhabited, but 80% of people live on 12 main islands. The population is becoming more urbanized and one in eight ni-Vanuatu now lives in Port Vila. However, 75% of the population still live by subsistence agriculture.

Vanuatu is home to some of the Pacific's most traditional peoples, and local social and religious customs are strong. With 105 indigenous languages, Vanuatu boasts the world's highest per capita density of languages. Bislama pidgin is the lingua franca.

Women have lower social status than men, and bride price is still commonly paid. Many educated women refuse to marry because of loss of property rights. To boost equality, primary schools are encouraged to take girls.

Vanuatu's unspoiled beaches are one of the reasons for the upsurge in the tourist industry.

POLITICS

Multiparty elections

2002/2006

President Fr. John Bani

AT THE LAST ELECTION
Parliament 52 seats

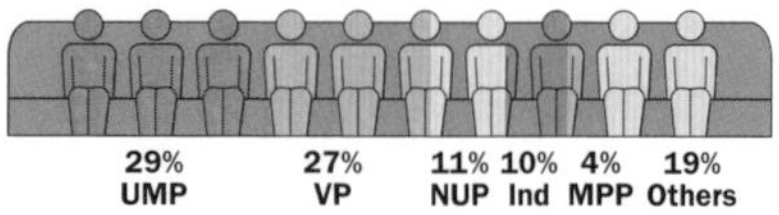
29% UMP
27% VP
11% NUP
10% Ind
4% MPP
19% Others

UMP = Union of Moderate Parties **VP** = Vanua'aku Pati
NUP = National United Party **Ind** = Independents
MPP = Melanesian Progressive Party

Ni-Vanuatu politics is best described as anarchic. Political allegiances are swiftly changed and governments frequently toppled. Independence leader Fr. Walter Lini remained a powerful political figure despite being ousted as VP leader and premier in 1991. He went on to lead the NUP until his death in 1999.

Power has shifted between shaky coalitions headed by either the VP (1980–1991) or the UMP (1991–2001). A grand coalition between the two parties was forged in 2001 under Edward Natapei of the VP. Though the UMP gained a marginal victory in the 2002 polls, Natapei continued as prime minister. His government was strengthened with the addition to the coalition of the NUP in 2003. Political corruption is a major issue and has fueled tensions.

WORLD AFFAIRS

Joined UN in 1981

OIF | Comm | NAM | PC | PIF

Political instability prompted France to recognize independence only reluctantly in 1980. The UK, on the other hand, did not share its partner's hesitation. The anti-French VP government of the day accused France of supporting an abortive bid for independence by Espiritu Santo that year. Vanuatu was the first South Pacific state to gain full membership of the Non-Aligned Movement. In 2002–2003 it was forced by the OECD to improve financial transparency.

AID

Recipient

$32m (receipts)

Down 30% in 2001

Vanuatu is heavily dependent on aid. Leading donors include Australia, France, the ADB, the EU, Japan, and New Zealand. Vanuatu is classed by the UN as a Least Developed Country (LDC), and as such receives guaranteed aid support.

V

DEFENSE

No compulsory military service

There is no army

Not applicable

There is no army. A small paramilitary force receives training from the US. Papua New Guinean troops helped to end the 1980 secessionist movement on Espiritu Santo.

ECONOMICS

Inflation 2.9% p.a. (1990–2001)

$212m

120.5 vatu (134.9)

SCORE CARD

❑ WORLD GNP RANKING	183rd
❑ GNP PER CAPITA	$1050
❑ BALANCE OF PAYMENTS	–$3m
❑ INFLATION	3.7%
❑ UNEMPLOYMENT	Low

STRENGTHS

Expanding services sector, including tourism. Major economic reforms instituted, including introduction of value-added tax and resizing public service in return for assistance from ADB. Large fishing potential.

WEAKNESSES

Large trade and budget deficits. Rate of growth stagnating: contracted in 1999 and 2001. Offshore banking stopped after international pressure. Dependence on agricultural sector, vulnerable to adverse weather and fluctuating market prices.

EXPORTS

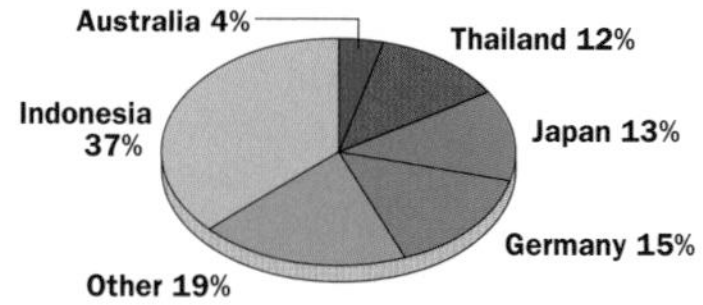
Australia 4%
Thailand 12%
Indonesia 37%
Japan 13%
Germany 15%
Other 19%

IMPORTS

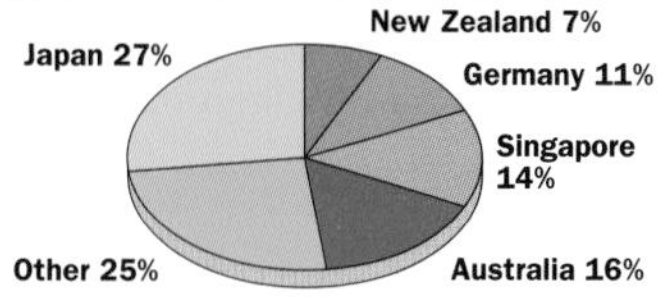
New Zealand 7%
Japan 27%
Germany 11%
Singapore 14%
Other 25%
Australia 16%

RESOURCES

Electric power 12,000 kW

73,490 tonnes

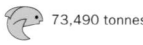

Not an oil producer

151,000 cattle, 62,000 pigs, 340,000 chickens

None

Vanuatu's main resources are its arable land – only partly utilized – and its forests and waters. These could be exploited by the tourist, timber, and fishing industries. New export crops are being explored to offset declining copra and cocoa exports. Beef is of growing importance. Nuclear power development was banned under 1983 legislation.

VANUATU

Total Area : 12 200 sq. km (4710 sq. miles)

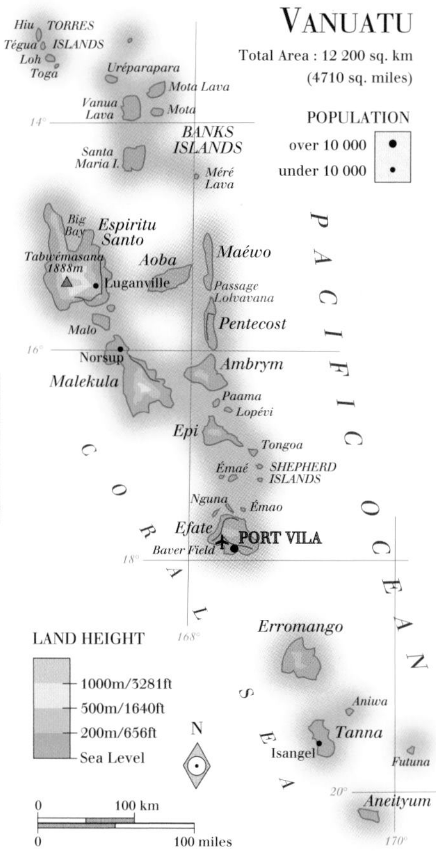
TORRES ISLANDS
Hiu
Tégua
Loh
Toga
Uréparapara
Mota Lava
Vanua Lava
Mota
BANKS ISLANDS
Santa Maria I.
Méré Lava
POPULATION
over 10 000
under 10 000
Big Bay
Espiritu Santo
Tabwémasana 1888m
Aoba
Maéwo
Luganville
Passage Lolvavana
Pentecost
Malo
Norsup
Malekula
Ambrym
Paama
Lopévi
Epi
Tongoa
Émaé
SHEPHERD ISLANDS
Nguna
Émao
Efate
PORT VILA
Baver Field
PACIFIC OCEAN
CORAL SEA
Erromango
Aniwa
Tanna
Isangel
Futuna
Aneityum
LAND HEIGHT
1000m/3281ft
500m/1640ft
200m/656ft
Sea Level
N
0
100 km
100 miles

ENVIRONMENT

Not available

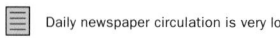

0.2% partially protected

0.4 tonnes per capita

Logging is increasing, but most of the rainforest remains intact, and roundwood exports are banned.

Population growth is high, at nearly 3% a year, but is falling. A majority of the population does not have access to a potable and reliable water supply.

MEDIA

TV ownership low

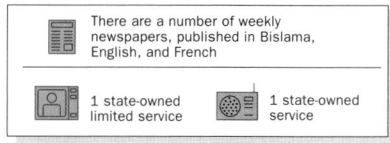

Daily newspaper circulation is very low

PUBLISHING AND BROADCAST MEDIA

There are a number of weekly newspapers, published in Bislama, English, and French

1 state-owned limited service

1 state-owned service

The *Vanuatu Weekly* appears in each official language. Television Blong Vanuatu broadcasts four hours a day.

CRIME

No death penalty

46 prisoners

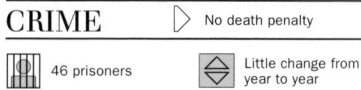

Little change from year to year

The Australian aid agency AusAID is funding a $1.4 million reform program for the Vanuatu police service.

CHRONOLOGY

In 1906, Britain and France set up the New Hebrides under joint rule.

- ❑ **1980** Independence; Walter Lini prime minister (until 1991). Secession bid by Espiritu Santo.
- ❑ **1999** Tidal wave. Death of Lini.
- ❑ **2001** Edward Natapei prime minister.
- ❑ **2002** Vanuatu's first ever hailstorm hits Tanna.
- ❑ **2003** Reforms take Vanuatu off blacklist of tax havens.

EDUCATION

Schooling is not compulsory

64%

52 students

The abolition of fees has helped to boost primary enrollment. Illiteracy is a major concern.

HEALTH

Welfare state health benefits

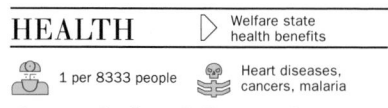

1 per 8333 people

Heart diseases, cancers, malaria

A network of rural clinics and village health workers has helped to improve health levels. Nominal fees are charged.

SPENDING

GDP/cap. decrease

CONSUMPTION AND SPENDING

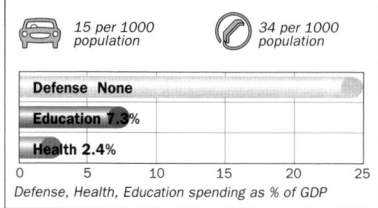

15 per 1000 population

34 per 1000 population

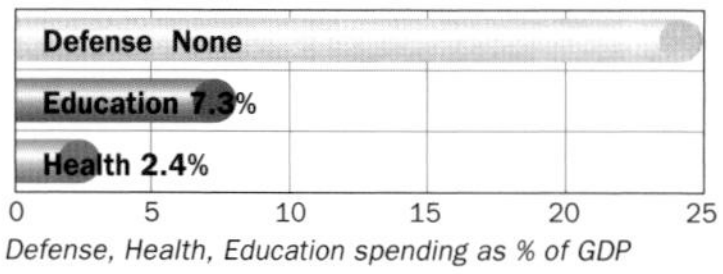
Defense None
Education 7.3%
Health 2.4%
0
5
10
15
20
25

Defense, Health, Education spending as % of GDP

The dominance of subsistence farming and small-scale cash cropping has helped to prevent extreme poverty. Most of the rich are not ni-Vanuatu.

WORLD RANKING

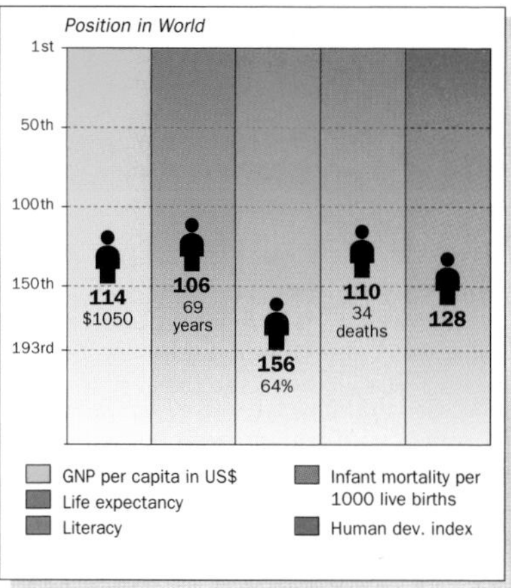
Position in World
1st
50th
100th
150th
193rd
114
$1050
106
69 years
156
64%
110
34 deaths
128
GNP per capita in US$
Life expectancy
Literacy
Infant mortality per 1000 live births
Human dev. index

V

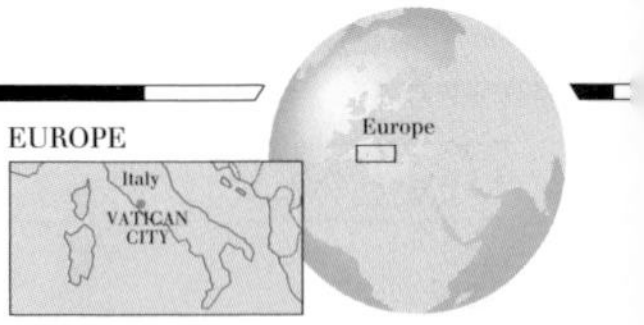
EUROPE
Europe
Italy
VATICAN CITY

VATICAN CITY

OFFICIAL NAME: State of the Vatican City **CAPITAL:** Vatican City
POPULATION: 900 **CURRENCY:** Euro **OFFICIAL LANGUAGES:** Italian and Latin

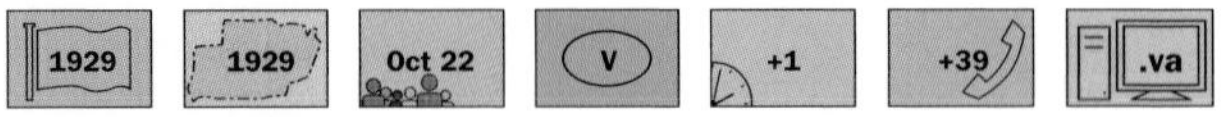
1929
1929
Oct 22
V
+1
+39
.va

THE VATICAN CITY, which lies in central Rome, is the world's smallest independent state. It includes ten other buildings in Rome and also the pope's summer residence at Castel Gandolfo. As the Holy See it is the seat of the Roman Catholic Church, deriving its income from investments and voluntary contributions known as Peter's Pence.

The buildings and gardens of the Vatican City. St. Peter's Basilica was built from 1506–1626 on the traditional site of St. Peter's tomb.

CLIMATE

Mediterranean

WEATHER CHART FOR THE VATICAN CITY

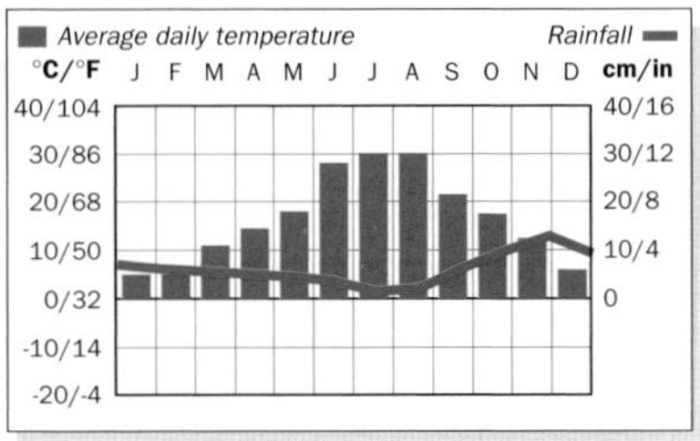
Average daily temperature
Rainfall
°C/°F
J F M A M J J A S O N D
cm/in
40/104
30/86
20/68
10/50
0/32
-10/14
-20/-4
40/16
30/12
20/8
10/4
0

Summers are hot; winters are mild. November is particularly rainy.

TRANSPORTATION

Drive on right

Heliport for official visitors

Has no fleet

THE TRANSPORTATION NETWORK

None

None

1 km (0.6 miles)

None

The railroad is used only for carrying freight. Official visitors are transferred from Rome airport by helicopter.

TOURISM

Not available

The Vatican museums can accommodate 20,000 visitors daily

Little change from year to year

MAIN TOURIST ARRIVALS

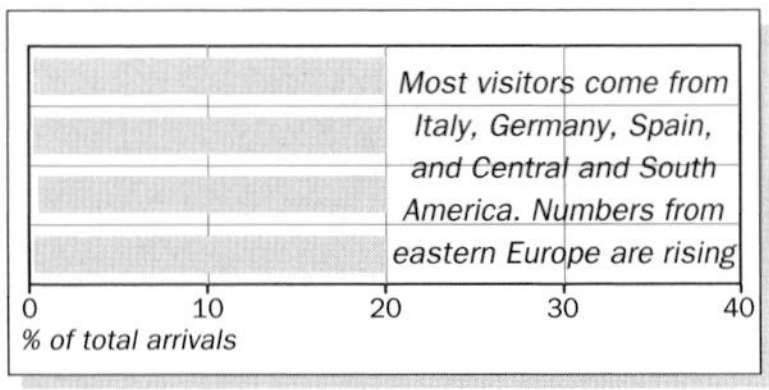
Most visitors come from Italy, Germany, Spain, and Central and South America. Numbers from eastern Europe are rising
0
10
20
30
40
% of total arrivals

Almost all tourists who visit Rome go to the Vatican, while others come as pilgrims. Up to 100,000 hear the pope's annual Easter Message in St. Peter's Square. The Vatican's art collections are among the greatest in the world. Years of restoration work on the Sistine Chapel frescoes were completed in 1999.

PEOPLE

Pop. density high

Italian, Latin

2045/km² (5294/mi²)

THE URBAN/RURAL POPULATION SPLIT

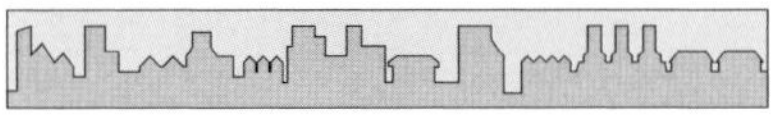

100%

RELIGIOUS PERSUASION

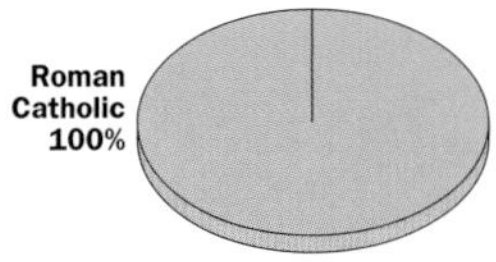
Roman Catholic 100%

The Vatican has about 900 citizens, including over 100 lay persons. Several hundred more lay staff are employed in the city-state. Citizenship can be acquired through stable residence and holding an office or job within the City. A citizen's family can gain residence only by authorization.

The pope is the spiritual leader of around 17% of the world's population. The countries with the largest number of Roman Catholics are Brazil, Mexico, Italy, the US, and the Philippines.

POLITICS

No legislative elections

On death of reigning pope

His Holiness Pope John Paul II

LEGISLATIVE OR ADVISORY BODIES

Sacred College of Cardinals 120 seats

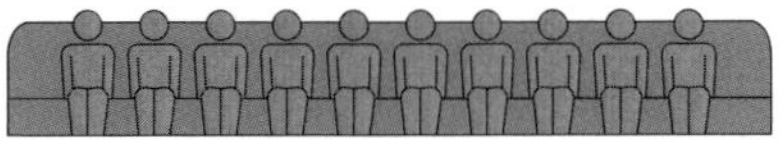

Cardinals under the age of 80 are eligible to elect a new pope. There are no political parties.

The Vatican City operates in the manner of an elected monarchy, as the reigning pope has supreme executive, legislative, and judicial powers, and holds office for life. He is elected by the College of Cardinals, who vote until one candidate for the position of Supreme Pontiff achieves a two-thirds majority.

The administration of the Vatican City State, of which the pope is temporal head, is conducted by the Pontifical Commission. The Holy See, which is the governing body of the Roman Catholic Church worldwide and of which the pope is spiritual head, is governed by the Roman Curia, the Church's administrative network. It is the Holy See that maintains diplomatic relations abroad. Pope John Paul II, elected in 1978, was the first non-Italian pope since 1523. Now in his 80s, he continues to fulfill his duties despite suffering from Parkinson's disease and arthritis.

VATICAN CITY

Total Area : 0.44 sq. km (0.17 sq. miles)

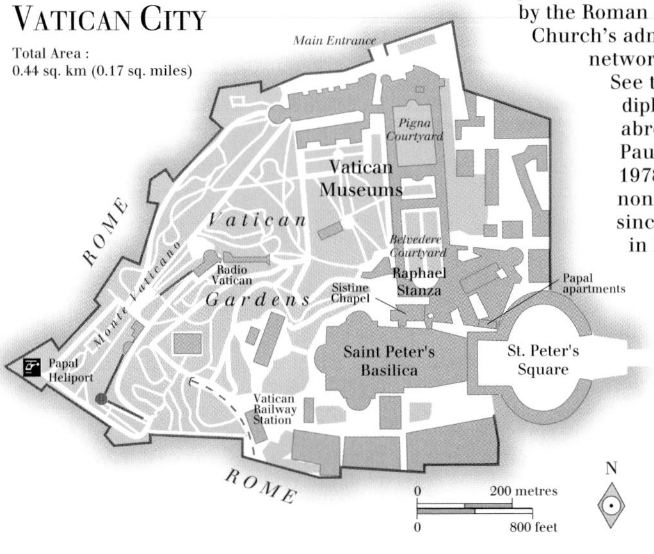
Main Entrance
Pigna Courtyard
Vatican Museums
Vatican
Gardens
ROME
Monte Vaticano
Belvedere Courtyard
Radio Vatican
Sistine Chapel
Raphael Stanza
Papal apartments
Saint Peter's Basilica
St. Peter's Square
Papal Heliport
Vatican Railway Station
ROME
0
200 metres
0
800 feet
N

V

WORLD AFFAIRS

Not a UN member

OSCE | IAEA

The Vatican is neutral, with observer status in many international organizations, but papal opinion greatly influences the world's one billion Catholics. In 2003 John Paul II was vital in building support in his native Poland for its membership of the EU.

The present pope has traveled more extensively than any other, completing his 100th foreign visit (to Croatia) in 2003. Trips are used to promote political as well as religious dialogue. In 2000 the pope made an unprecedented apology for 2000 years of anti-Judaism and in 2001 he became the first pope to enter (and pray in) a mosque and the first to visit Orthodox Christian Greece.

AID

Donor

Undisclosed

Undisclosed

Aid is donated through the pope's charities (such as the Holy Childhood Association, which distributes around $15 million a year to children's causes), through funds donated for use at the pope's discretion, and through religious orders acting under papal charter.

DEFENSE

No compulsory military service

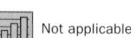

Ceremonial Swiss Guard only

Not applicable

The Vatican is strictly neutral territory. Under the 1954 Hague Convention, it is recognized as "a moral, artistic, and cultural patrimony worthy of being respected as a treasure for all mankind."

ECONOMICS

Not applicable

Not applicable

0.871 euros (1.013)

SCORE CARD

- ❑ WORLD GNP RANKING ....*The Vatican*
- ❑ GNP PER CAPITA......................*does not have*
- ❑ BALANCE OF PAYMENTS...................*a national*
- ❑ INFLATION ....*economy in the*
- ❑ UNEMPLOYMENT..........................*usual sense*

STRENGTHS

Istituto per le Opere di Religione has assets of $3–4 billion. Interest on investments. Voluntary contributions from Catholics worldwide (Peter's Pence). Gold reserves in Fort Knox, US. Stamp and coin issues. Receipts from tourists.

WEAKNESSES

Losses incurred by Radio Vaticana and *L'Osservatore Romano*. Cost of foreign papal visits, buildings maintenance, and diplomatic missions. Total lack of natural resources of any kind.

EXPORTS/IMPORTS

The Vatican produces no goods for export. All commodities are imported, mainly from Italy.

RESOURCES

Electric power: None

None

Not an oil producer

None

None

The Vatican imports all its energy. It has no farmland; its area is restricted to buildings and their formal gardens.

ENVIRONMENT

Not available

None

Not available

The Vatican is increasingly concerned about the need to balance development and conservation. In 1993, the pope urged a gathering of scientists to press colleagues worldwide to inform people on the need to protect the environment.

MEDIA

TV ownership medium

Daily newspaper circulation figures not available

PUBLISHING AND BROADCAST MEDIA

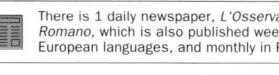

There is 1 daily newspaper, *L'Osservatore Romano*, which is also published weekly in 6 European languages, and monthly in Polish

1 state-owned service

1 state-owned service

Radio Vaticana's longwave broadcasts are continuing after a brief suspension caused by concern over radiation.

CRIME

No death penalty

There are no prisons in the Vatican City

Minimal crime levels

The reputation of the 105-strong Swiss Guard was shaken in 1998, when a young guard shot dead his commandant and the latter's wife and then committed suicide. Three Vatican Bank officials were earlier alleged to have been involved in the Banco Ambrosiano affair.

EDUCATION

Not applicable

99%

9389 students

The university, founded by Gregory XIII, is renowned for its theological and philosophical learning. There are more than 110,000 primary and secondary Catholic schools around the world.

CHRONOLOGY

The Vatican is located in Rome because tradition held that St. Peter was buried on the site of the Church of Constantine, which was pulled down in the Renaissance to make way for the building of St. Peter's Basilica. The Vatican has been the pope's usual residence since 1417, when the pontiffs returned from Avignon in France at the end of the 39 years of Great Schism.

- ❑ **1870** Italy annexes Papal States.
- ❑ **1929** Lateran Treaty – Fascist Italy accepts Vatican City as independent state.
- ❑ **1978** Cardinal Karol Wojtyla pope.
- ❑ **1981–1982** Attempts on pope's life.
- ❑ **1984** Catholicism disestablished as Italian state religion.
- ❑ **1985** Catholic Catechism revised for first time since 1566.
- ❑ **1994–1995** Opposition to abortion and contraception reiterated at UN conferences in Cairo and Beijing.
- ❑ **1998** Statement repenting Catholic passivity during Nazi Holocaust.
- ❑ **2000** Jubilee Year. Papal apology for Catholic violence and oppression over two millennia.
- ❑ **2001** John Paul II becomes first pope to enter a mosque.

HEALTH

Welfare state health benefits

Pope's own doctor is in permanent residence at Vatican

Heart and cardiovascular diseases, cancers

Pope John Paul II's strong opposition to abortion and contraception has prompted criticism from around the world, and from within the Church.

SPENDING

Not applicable

CONSUMPTION AND SPENDING

No data

No data

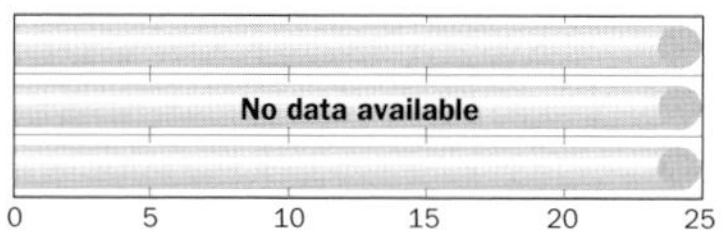
No data available
0
5
10
15
20
25
Defense, Health, Education spending as % of GDP

The wealth of the Vatican is primarily that of the Catholic Church. Its art treasures may not be sold. It is not known how much personal wealth its citizens have.

WORLD RANKING

The pope and his Vatican staff enjoy one of the highest standards of living in the world

V

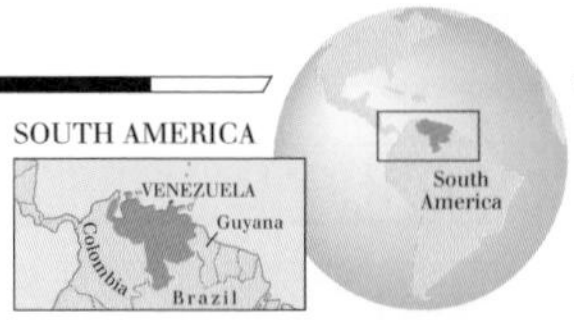
SOUTH AMERICA
VENEZUELA
Guyana
Colombia
Brazil
South America

VENEZUELA

OFFICIAL NAME: Bolivarian Republic of Venezuela **CAPITAL:** Caracas
POPULATION: 25.1 million **CURRENCY:** Bolívar **OFFICIAL LANGUAGE:** Spanish

1830 | 1830 | July 5 | YV | -4 | +58 | .ve

LOCATED IN THE NORTH of South America, with a long Caribbean coastline, Venezuela has a vast central plain drained by the Orinoco, while the Guiana Highlands dominate the southwest of the country. A Spanish colony until 1811, Venezuela was lauded as Latin America's most stable democracy until its recent political upheavals. Though the country has some of the largest known oil deposits outside the Middle East, much of Venezuela's population still lives in shanty-town squalor.

***President Hugo Chávez** changed the name of the country as part of his Bolivarian Revolution.*

CLIMATE

Tropical wet and dry/ equatorial

WEATHER CHART FOR CARACAS

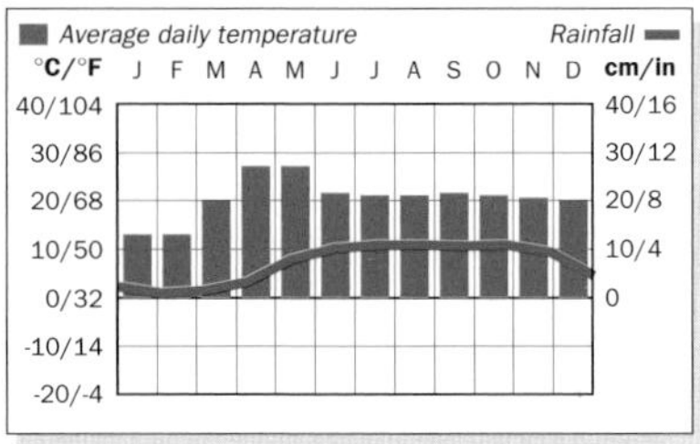
Average daily temperature
Rainfall
°C/°F
J F M A M J J A S O N D
cm/in
40/104
30/86
20/68
10/50
0/32
-10/14
-20/-4
40/16
30/12
20/8
10/4
0

The hot Maracaibo coast is surprisingly dry; the Orinoco Llanos are alternately parched or flooded. Uplands are cold.

TRANSPORTATION

Drive on right

Simón Bolívar International, Caracas 6.69m passengers

268 ships 872,200 grt

THE TRANSPORTATION NETWORK

32,308 km (20,075 miles)	2690 km (1671 miles)
336 km (209 miles)	7100 km (4412 miles)

Massive road building programs from the 1960s onward have benefited the oil and aluminum industries. Because of the limited railroad system, buses are the main form of transportation throughout most of the country. The French-designed subway in Caracas was completed in 1995.

***The Orinoco.** The huge Llanos ("plains") are grazed by five million cattle, which are herded close to the river in the dry season.*

TOURISM

Visitors : Population 1:54

469,000 visitors

Down 20% in 2000

MAIN TOURIST ARRIVALS

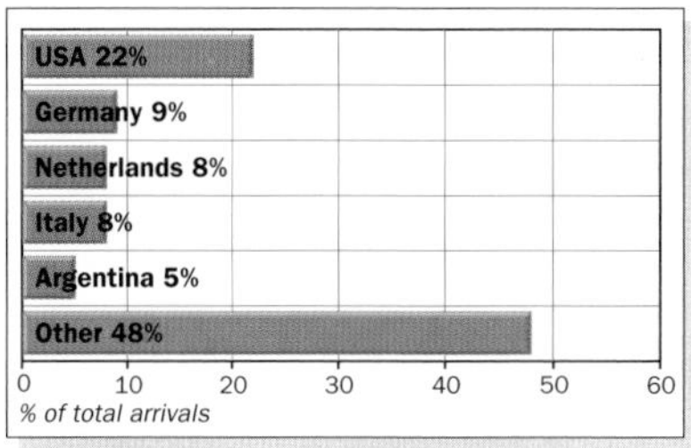
USA 22%
Germany 9%
Netherlands 8%
Italy 8%
Argentina 5%
Other 48%
0
10
20
30
40
50
60
% of total arrivals

Tourism is still a relatively minor industry in Venezuela, but one with enormous potential. Venezuela has many beaches that are the equal of any Caribbean island's, and a fascinating jungle interior which is a target for more adventurous tourists. For many years, the high value of the bolívar made Venezuela an expensive destination, but, after recent devaluations, it has become one of the cheapest in the Caribbean. Privatizing state-run hotels was part of a drive to attract foreign investment.

PEOPLE

Pop. density low

Spanish, Amerindian languages

28/km² (74/mi²)

THE URBAN/RURAL POPULATION SPLIT

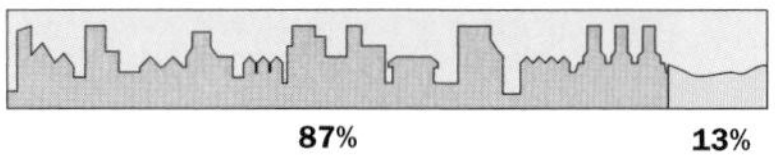
87%
13%

RELIGIOUS PERSUASION

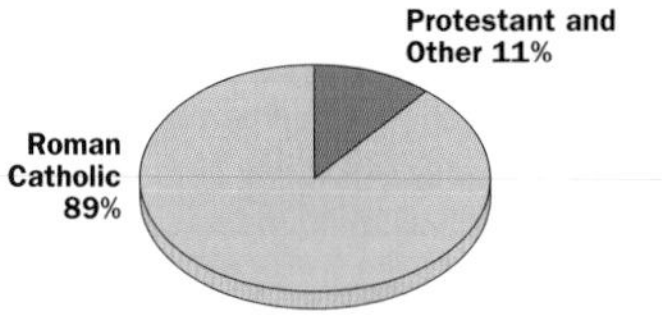
Protestant and Other 11%
Roman Catholic 89%

ETHNIC MAKEUP

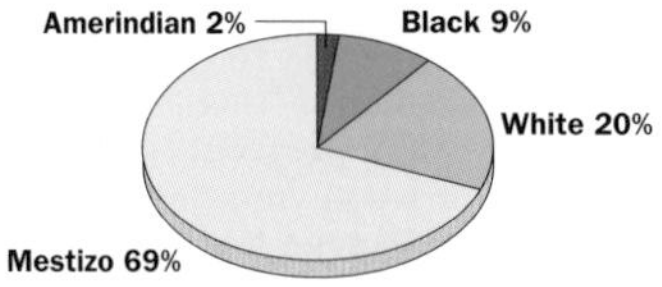
Amerindian 2%
Black 9%
White 20%
Mestizo 69%

Venezuela is one of the most highly urbanized societies in Latin America, with most of its population living in cities, mainly in the north. A historic "melting pot," it has experienced large-scale immigration from Italy, Portugal, Spain, and all over Latin America. There remains little of the white Hispanic aristocracy that survives in Colombia and Ecuador. The small number of native Amerindians, such as the Yanomami and Pemón, live in remote regions now threatened by illegal settlers. Most of the black population, who are descended from Africans brought over to work in the cacao industry in the 19th century, live along the Caribbean coast.

Oil wealth has brought comparative prosperity, but life in the *barrios* (shanty towns) which sprawl over the hillsides around Caracas is one of extreme poverty. Discontent peaked in the food riots of 1989 and 1991, leaving hundreds dead, along with the country's reputation for being a model democracy. The oil boom accelerated change for women, who today are to be found in all the professions. Politics, however, remains a largely masculine preserve. Oil wealth has also brought a measure of Americanization – boxing and baseball are among the most popular sports.

POPULATION AGE BREAKDOWN

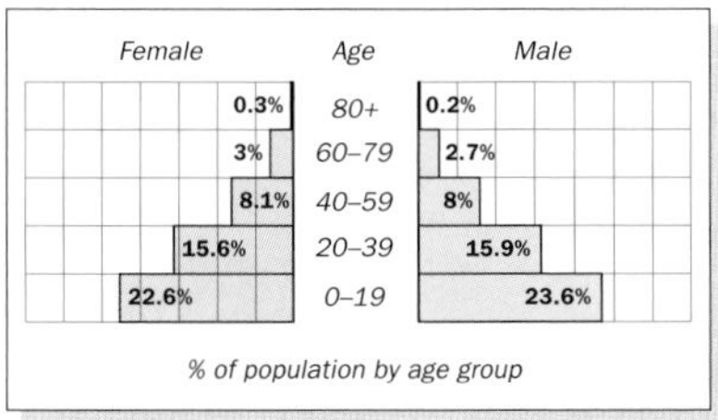
Female
Age
Male
0.3%
80+
0.2%
3%
60–79
2.7%
8.1%
40–59
8%
15.6%
20–39
15.9%
22.6%
0–19
23.6%
% of population by age group

V

Key to symbols and abbreviations on cover flaps

VENEZUELA

Total Area : 912 050 sq. km (352 143 sq. miles)

POPULATION

- over 1 000 000
- over 500 000
- over 100 000
- over 50 000
- over 10 000

LAND HEIGHT

- 3000m/9843ft
- 2000m/6562ft
- 1000m/3281ft
- 500m/1640ft
- Sea Level

Projected Railway

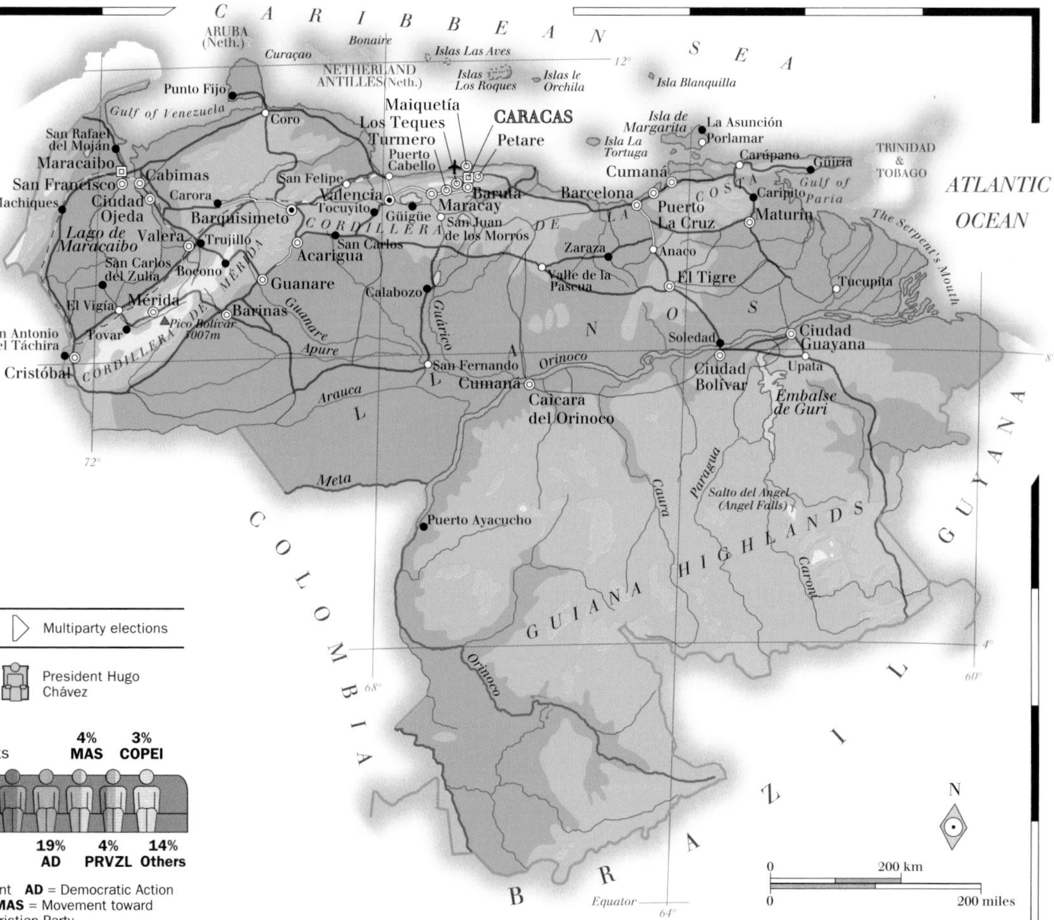
CARIBBEAN SEA
ARUBA (Neth.)
Curaçao
Bonaire
NETHERLAND ANTILLES (Neth.)
Islas Las Aves
Islas Los Roques
Islas le Orchila
Isla Blanquilla
Punto Fijo
Coro
Gulf of Venezuela
San Rafael del Moján
Maracaibo
San Francisco
Cabimas
Machiques
Ciudad Ojeda
Carora
Lago de Maracaibo
Valera
Trujillo
Barquisimeto
San Felipe
Valencia
Tocuyito
Puerto Cabello
Maiquetía
Los Teques
Turmero
CARACAS
Petare
Güigüe
Maracay
Baruta
San Juan de los Morros
CORDILLERA DE LA COSTA
Barcelona
Puerto La Cruz
Cumaná
Isla de Margarita
La Asunción
Porlamar
Isla La Tortuga
Carúpano
Güiria
Caripito
Gulf of Paria
Maturín
TRINIDAD & TOBAGO
ATLANTIC OCEAN
The Serpent's Mouth
Tucupita
San Carlos del Zulia
Boconó
Acarigua
San Carlos
Guanare
El Vigía
Mérida
Pico Bolívar 5007m
Tovar
Barinas
San Antonio del Táchira
San Cristóbal
CORDILLERA DE MÉRIDA
Calabozo
Guárico
Apure
Zaraza
Anaco
Valle de la Pascua
El Tigre
LLANOS
Soledad
Ciudad Guayana
Upata
Ciudad Bolívar
Embalse de Guri
San Fernando
Cumaná
Orinoco
Caicara del Orinoco
Arauca
Meta
Puerto Ayacucho
Caura
Paragua
Salto del Ángel (Angel Falls)
Caroní
GUIANA HIGHLANDS
GUYANA
COLOMBIA
BRAZIL
Equator
0 200 km
0 200 miles
N

POLITICS

Multiparty elections

2000/2005

President Hugo Chávez

AT THE LAST ELECTION

National Assembly 165 seats

Party	Share
MVR	56%
AD	19%
PRVZL	4%
MAS	4%
COPEI	3%
Others	14%

MVR = Fifth Republic Movement **AD** = Democratic Action **PRVZL** = Project Venezuela **MAS** = Movement toward Socialism **COPEI** = Social Christian Party
The Patriotic Front (**PP**) comprises the MVR, the MAS, and some smaller parties

Venezuela is a multiparty democracy.

Profile

Hugo Chávez led a coup attempt in 1992, against a backdrop of corruption, poverty, austerity, and riots in Caracas. His election as president in 1998 broke the traditional parties' stranglehold on power and raised expectations among the poor.

He embarked on root and branch reform of the political and judicial systems, and enacted a new "Bolivarian" constitution. With his mandate renewed in 2000, his command-style running of the country fomented political opposition and deterred investment. A one-day military coup in April 2002 failed when officers changed tack following mass protests and the largely unfavorable international response. Restored to office, Chávez mollified rather than punished opponents, but was unable to prevent protests from spiraling later that year into a prolonged general strike which paralyzed the country.

Main Political Issues

Political stability

The general strike petered out in early 2003, leaving a future referendum as the opposition's best chance of toppling Chávez. More unrest was forecast as his administration prepared to fight to the last.

Oil policy

Support of oil prices and quotas within OPEC remain central, despite Chávez's desire to use oil revenue to build a broader economy. The nine-week 2002–2003 general strike crippled the industry to the tune of billions of US dollars and forced the import of oil from Brazil.

WORLD AFFAIRS

Joined UN in 1945

ACS | AP | OAS | OPEC | RG

A traditionally pro-US orientation was challenged by Chávez, with his personal friendship with Cuba's Fidel Castro, visits to Libya and Iraq, and opposition to "Plan Colombia." The Bush administration acknowledged the new interim government during the April 2002 military coup, but denied helping to install it, though the main coup participants had made very public visits to the US State Department in preceding months. The OAS announced opposition to the coup, as did all of Venezuela's neighbors. Better regional economic integration with the Caribbean and Central and South America are important.

CHRONOLOGY

Venezuela was the first of the Spanish imperial colonies to repudiate Madrid's authority under the guidance of the revolutionary, Simón Bolívar, in 1811.

- **1821** Battle of Carabobo finally overthrows Spanish rule and leads to consolidation of independence within Gran Colombia (Venezuela, Colombia, and Ecuador).
- **1830** Gran Colombia collapses. José Antonio Páez rules Venezuela; coffee planters effectively in control.
- **1870** Guzmán Blanco in power. Rail system constructed.
- **1908** Gen. Juan Vicente Gómez dictator; oil industry developed.
- **1935** Gómez falls from power. Increasing mass participation in political process.
- **1945** Military coup. Rómulo Betancourt of AD takes power as leader of a civilian–military junta.
- **1948** AD wins elections, with novelist Rómulo Gallegos as presidential candidate. Military coup. Marcos Pérez Jiménez forms government, with US and military backing.

V

CHRONOLOGY *continued*

- **1958** General strike. Adm. Larrázabal leads military coup. Free elections. Betancourt, newly returned from exile, wins presidential election for AD. Anticommunist campaign mounted. A few state welfare programs introduced.
- **1960** Movement of the Revolutionary Left (MIR) splits from AD, begins antigovernment activities.
- **1961** Founder member of OPEC.
- **1962** Communist-backed guerrilla warfare attempts repetition of Cuban revolution in Venezuela; fails to gain popular support.
- **1963** Raúl Leoni (AD) elected president – first democratic transference of power. Antiguerrilla campaign continues.
- **1966** Unsuccessful coup attempt by supporters of former president, Pérez Jiménez.
- **1969** Rafael Caldera Rodríguez of COPEI becomes president. Continues Leoni policies.
- **1973** Oil and steel industries nationalized. World oil crisis. Venezuelan currency peaks in value against the US dollar.
- **1978** Elections won by COPEI's Luis Herrera Campíns. Disastrous economic programs.
- **1983** AD election victory under Jaime Lusinchi. Fall in world oil prices leads to unrest and cuts in state welfare.
- **1988** Carlos Andrés Pérez of AD wins presidency.
- **1989** Caracas food riots; 1500 dead.
- **1992** Attempted coup, led by Col. Hugo Chávez.
- **1993–1995** Andrés Pérez ousted for corruption; Caldera Rodríguez reelected. More social unrest.
- **1998–2000** Chávez and PP defeat COPEI-led coalition in elections; embark on radical political reform. New controversial Constituent Assembly approves new constitution, later endorsed by referendum. Chávez mandate confirmed by presidential elections. New unicameral National Assembly.
- **2002** April, Chávez ousted in military coup. Reinstalled a day later, after foreign and domestic protests. December, mass strike cripples economy (ends early 2003).

V

AID

Recipient

$45m (receipts)

Down 42% in 2001

The IDB provided loans totaling $52.5 million in 2002 for the promotion of child care and agricultural technology.

DEFENSE

Compulsory military service

$1.9bn

Up 36% in 2001

Chávez had led officers opposed to austerity and corruption in a 1992 coup attempt. Military leaders claimed in April 2002 that civil unrest forced them to oust him, and they backed interim president Pedro Carmona, who dissolved the National Assembly and Supreme Court by decree. After widespread protests middle-ranking officers got cold feet and rapidly reinstalled Chávez.

VENEZUELAN ARMED FORCES

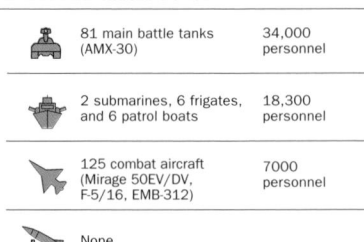

Army	81 main battle tanks (AMX-30)	34,000 personnel
Navy	2 submarines, 6 frigates, and 6 patrol boats	18,300 personnel
Air force	125 combat aircraft (Mirage 50EV/DV, F-5/16, EMB-312)	7000 personnel
Missiles	None	

ECONOMICS

Inflation 43% p.a. (1990–2001)

$117bn

1598 bolívares (1346)

SCORE CARD

World GNP Ranking	33rd
GNP per Capita	$4760
Balance of Payments	$4.36bn
Inflation	12.5%
Unemployment	16%

EXPORTS

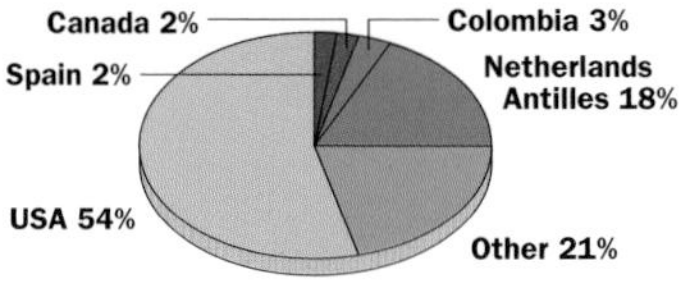

Canada 2%
Colombia 3%
Spain 2%
Netherlands Antilles 18%
USA 54%
Other 21%

IMPORTS

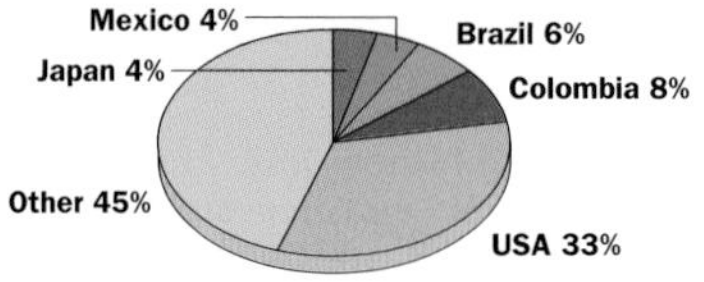

Mexico 4%
Brazil 6%
Japan 4%
Colombia 8%
Other 45%
USA 33%

Strengths

Large proven oil deposits. Massive reserves of coal, bauxite, iron, and gold; successful development of new bitumen fuel which has attracted considerable foreign investment. Telecommunications, banking, iron, and steel also attract foreign capital. Producer of high-grade aluminum. Labor market becoming more flexible.

Weaknesses

Political instability. Huge, cumbersome state sector; despite some privatization, large areas still overmanned, inefficient, and subject to widespread corruption. Poor public services which, despite Venezuela's wealth during the oil-boom years, have been badly maintained. Fluctuations in world oil prices. Major infrastructure renewal is now long overdue. Widespread tax evasion.

Profile

Government finances have habitually been in crisis due to a culture

ECONOMIC PERFORMANCE INDICATOR

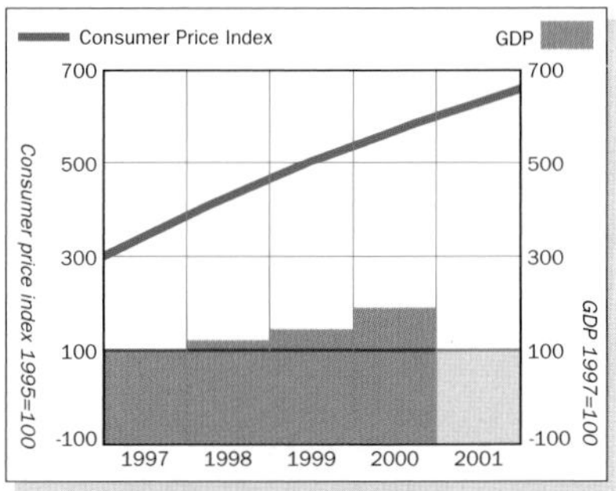

Consumer Price Index
GDP
700
500
300
100
-100
Consumer price index 1995=100
GDP 1997=100
1997
1998
1999
2000
2001

of nonaccountability and patronage in state-owned industries and government bureaucracies. Privatizations and government cuts have failed to solve the problem. Promises by President Chávez to deal with excesses and diversify the economy, by promoting domestic processing industries over crude oil exports, have received a mixed response from investors, who favor more market-oriented reforms. A general strike in late 2002–early 2003 crippled the economy, especially the oil industry. The bolívar was pegged to the US dollar on favorable terms in 2003, but without marked economic improvement this link looked unsustainable.

VENEZUELA : MAJOR BUSINESSES

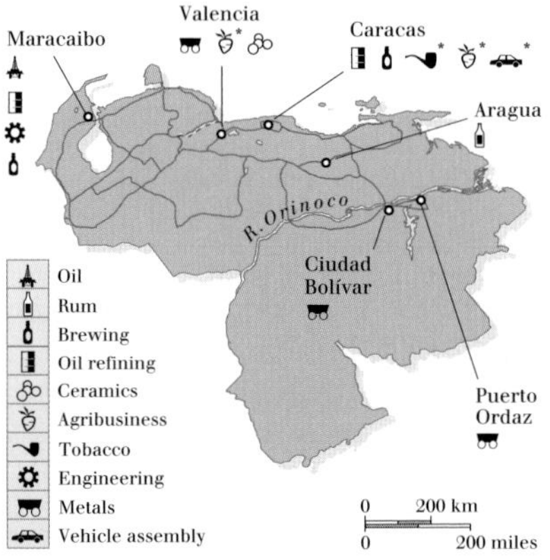

Maracaibo
Valencia
Caracas
Aragua
R. Orinoco
Ciudad Bolívar
Puerto Ordaz
Oil
Rum
Brewing
Oil refining
Ceramics
Agribusiness
Tobacco
Engineering
Metals
Vehicle assembly
0 200 km
0 200 miles

* significant multinational ownership

RESOURCES

Electric power 21.6m kW

403,925 tonnes

2.94m b/d (reserves 77.8bn barrels)

14.5m cattle, 5.65m pigs, 4m goats, 115m chickens

Oil, bauxite, iron, natural gas, coal, gold, diamonds, aluminum

ELECTRICITY GENERATION

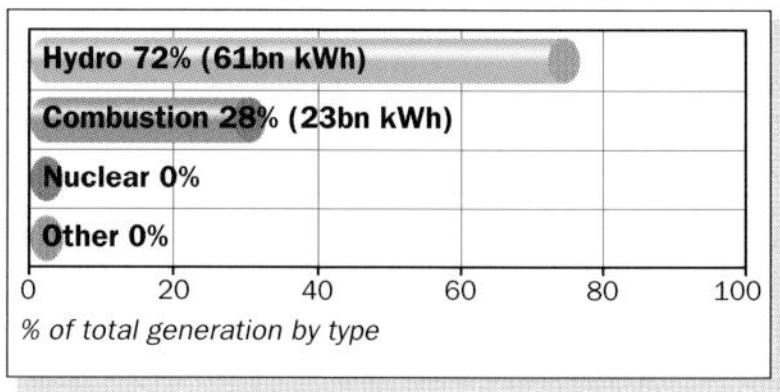
Hydro 72% (61bn kWh)
Combustion 28% (23bn kWh)
Nuclear 0%
Other 0%
0 20 40 60 80 100
% of total generation by type

Venezuela has a remarkable diversity of resources. It has the world's sixth-largest proven oil reserves, vast quantities of coal, iron ore, bauxite, and gold, and cheap hydroelectric power. Huge investment programs are currently under way to raise production in all these sectors as well as in oil-refining capacity. However, the Chávez government wants to cut the investment budget of the state oil company, PDVSA, reduce its output, and increase its contributions to the exchequer. Such uncertainty has deterred private investors. Venezuela has begun exploitation of Orimulsion, a new bitumen-based fuel from the Orinoco; commercially exploitable reserves are estimated at 270 billion barrels. Venezuela's aim to be the world's largest aluminum producer is threatened after difficulties associated with privatizing the sector.

VENEZUELA : LAND USE

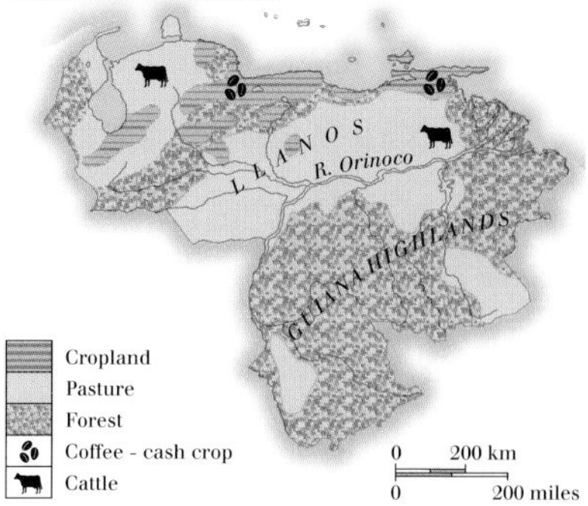
LLANOS
R. Orinoco
GUIANA HIGHLANDS
Cropland
Pasture
Forest
Coffee - cash crop
Cattle
0 200 km
0 200 miles

ENVIRONMENT

Sustainability rank: 48th

64% (40% partially protected)

5.3 tonnes per capita

ENVIRONMENTAL TREATIES

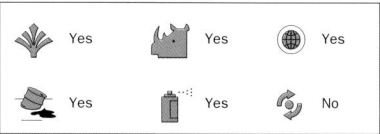

Yes	Yes	Yes
Yes	Yes	No

Flooding and mudflows, exacerbated by overdevelopment of the coastal strip, caused thousands of deaths in late 1999.

SPENDING

GDP/cap. increase

CONSUMPTION AND SPENDING

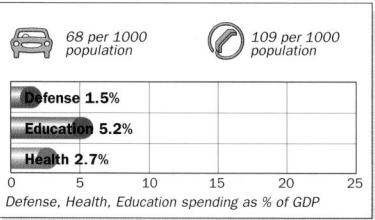

68 per 1000 population

109 per 1000 population

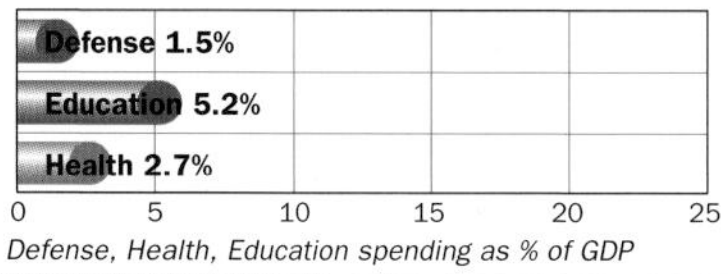
Defense 1.5%
Education 5.2%
Health 2.7%
0 5 10 15 20 25
Defense, Health, Education spending as % of GDP

EDUCATION

School leaving age: 12

93%

550,783 students

THE EDUCATION SYSTEM

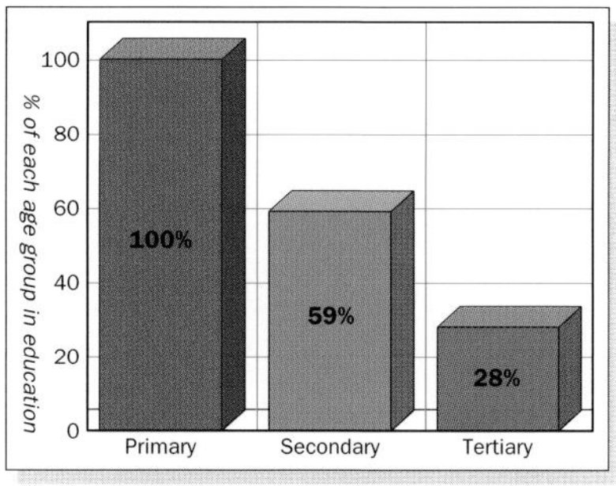
% of each age group in education
100
80
60
40
20
0
100%
59%
28%
Primary
Secondary
Tertiary

An extra $1 billion in social spending approved in 2000 includes raising entitlement in the state sector. Education is characterized by teacher shortages and a high drop-out rate; the quality of education at state universities is low. The private sector is growing.

The oil boom years of the 1970s largely benefited those already rich, and middle-income consumers did well out of state-sponsored improvements in health and education and subsidized goods, largely at the expense of the poor.

The collapse of world oil prices, economic austerity measures, high inflation, and the devaluation of the bolívar in the 1980s and 1990s have squeezed the middle class and in addition seriously eroded the living standards of working-class households. In 2001, more than 20% of people were living in extreme poverty, according to official figures. An estimated 16% of the labor force were unemployed in 2002, and many of those who were working were in the informal sector.

MEDIA

TV ownership medium

Daily newspaper circulation 206 per 1000 people

PUBLISHING AND BROADCAST MEDIA

There are 86 daily newspapers. *El Universal* and *El Nacional* are the most prominent

9 services: 2 state-owned, 7 private

1 state-owned service, 500 independent stations

In 2003 President Chávez threatened to revoke private TV broadcasters' licenses, accusing stations of supporting the crippling two-month general strike.

CRIME

No death penalty

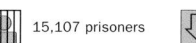

15,107 prisoners

Down 20% in 1997–2000

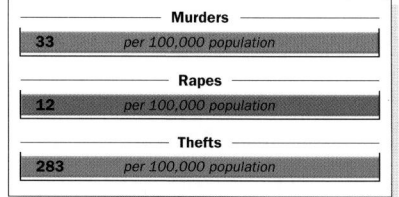

CRIME RATES

Murders

33 *per 100,000 population*

Rapes

12 *per 100,000 population*

Thefts

283 *per 100,000 population*

Urban robberies and violence involving young delinquents are major problems, as is narcotics-related crime. Cattle smuggling to Colombia is rife.

HEALTH

Welfare state health benefits

1 per 493 people

Cerebrovascular and heart diseases, cancers, violence, accidents

The health service suffered along with other public services from poor management in the 1970s and severe cuts in the 1980s and 1990s. Most health care is concentrated in the towns, and people from indigenous communities often have to travel long distances to receive treatment. Medicines, which have to be paid for, are expensive, and preventable diseases are recurring. Hospitals need modernization.

An additional $1 billion in social spending approved in 2000 includes spending on health.

WORLD RANKING

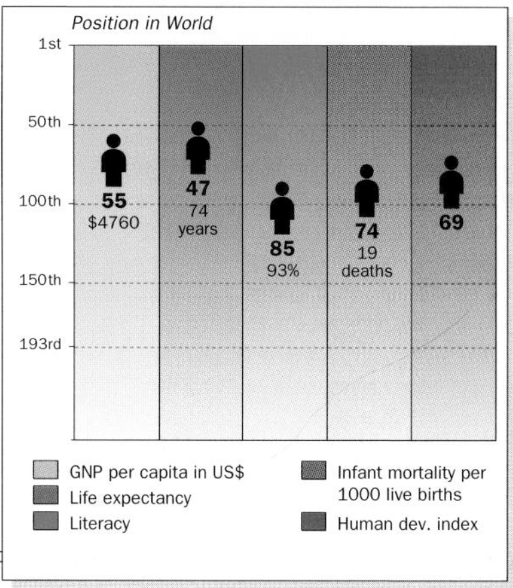
Position in World
1st
50th
100th
150th
193rd
55
$4760
47
74 years
85
93%
74
19 deaths
69
GNP per capita in US$
Life expectancy
Literacy
Infant mortality per 1000 live births
Human dev. index

V

VIETNAM

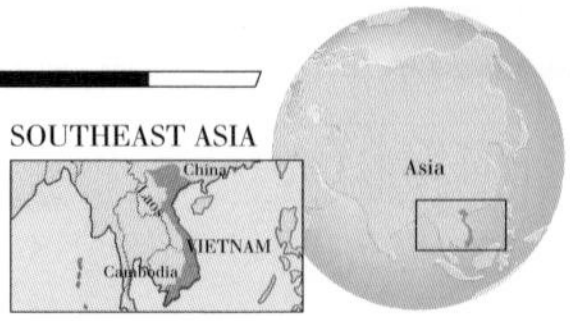
SOUTHEAST ASIA
China
VIETNAM
Cambodia
Asia

OFFICIAL NAME: Socialist Republic of Vietnam **CAPITAL:** Hanoi
POPULATION: 80.2 million **CURRENCY:** Dông **OFFICIAL LANGUAGE:** Vietnamese

1976 | 1976 | Sept 2 | VN | +7 | +84 | .vn

VIETNAM LIES ON the eastern side of the Indochinese peninsula. Over half the country is dominated by the heavily forested mountain range, the Chaîne Annamitique. The most populated areas, which are also the most intensively cultivated, are along the Red and Mekong Rivers. Partitioned after World War II, Vietnam was not reunited until 1976, a few months after the communist north finally defeated the southern regime and its US allies in the Vietnam War. Vietnam is now a single-party state ruled by the Communist Party. Since 1986, the regime has pursued a liberal economic policy known as *doi moi* (renovation).

CLIMATE

Tropical monsoon

WEATHER CHART FOR HANOI

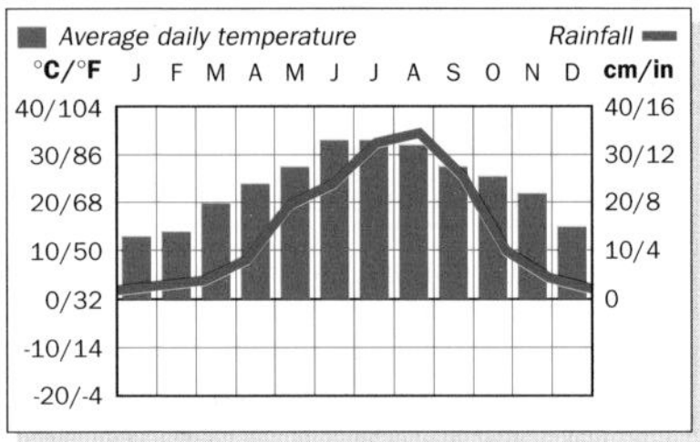
Average daily temperature
Rainfall
°C/°F
J F M A M J J A S O N D
cm/in
40/104
30/86
20/68
10/50
0/32
-10/14
-20/-4
40/16
30/12
20/8
10/4
0

Vietnam's geography means that there are sharp local contrasts in the climate. The north has cool winters, while the south is tropical, with even temperatures all year round. The central provinces are affected by typhoons. The northern Red River delta is subject to drought, while the Mekong delta in the south suffers heavy flooding.

TRANSPORTATION

Drive on right

Tan Son Naht Intl, Ho Chi Minh City
5.35m passengers

700 ships
1.07m grt

THE TRANSPORTATION NETWORK

23,418 km (14,551 miles)

430 km (267 miles)

2632 km (1636 miles)

17,702 km (10,999 miles)

Rebuilding infrastructure is still a priority. The flagship project, the four-lane Ho Chi Minh Highway linking Hanoi and the south, has had its target completion date put back until after 2005. A major port development plan is under way. Trains travel slowly, with an average speed of around 15 km/h (9 mph), and Hanoi to Ho Chi Minh City takes three days. The bus network is extensive but journeys are also time-consuming. Taxis and cycles provide cheap local transportation. Hanoi has plans for an elevated metro line.

TOURISM

Visitors : Population 1:58

1.38m visitors

Up 14% in 2000

MAIN TOURIST ARRIVALS

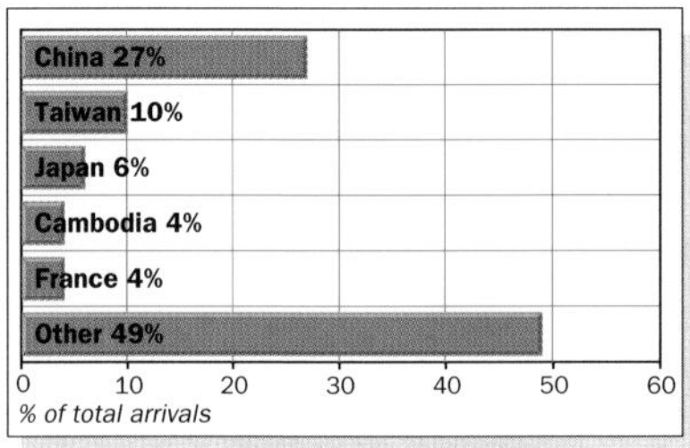
China 27%
Taiwan 10%
Japan 6%
Cambodia 4%
France 4%
Other 49%
0
10
20
30
40
50
60
% of total arrivals

Until the government opened the way to large-scale tourism in the 1990s, Russians, eastern Europeans, and backpackers from the West made up the bulk of visitors. Other travelers were either on business, or overseas Vietnamese, *Viet Kie*, who were visiting relatives.

Under a "master plan" adopted in 1995, massive investment was channeled into hotels, with an official target of three million tourists a year by 2000. However, arrivals failed to reach even half that figure. Poor transportation infrastructure remains a problem. Vietnam's appeal lies in its unspoiled Asian way of life and in the areas of spectacular natural beauty such as Ha Long Bay on the Red River delta.

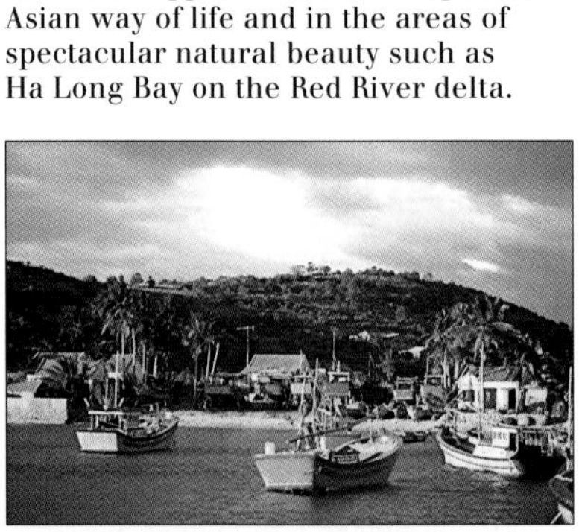

Boats moored near Nha Trang. *With 3444 km (2140 miles) of coastline, use of the sea, for transportation and fishing, is vital to Vietnam.*

PEOPLE

Pop. density high

Vietnamese, Chinese, Thai, Khmer, Muong, Nung, Miao, Yao, Jarai

246/km² (638/mi²)

THE URBAN/RURAL POPULATION SPLIT

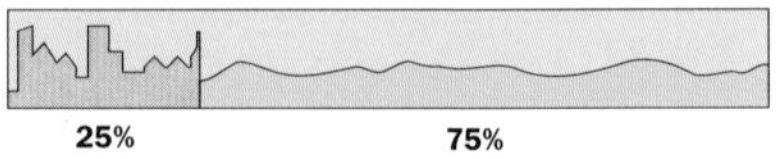
25%
75%

RELIGIOUS PERSUASION

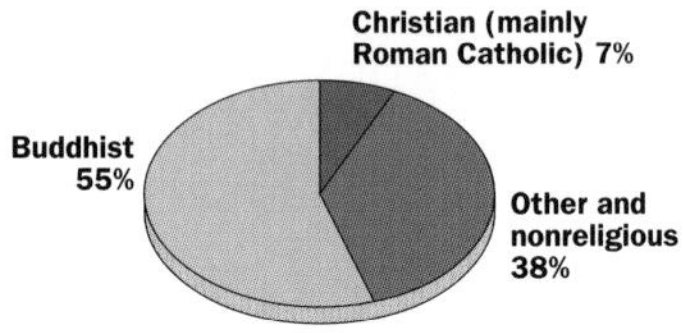
Christian (mainly Roman Catholic) 7%
Buddhist 55%
Other and nonreligious 38%

ETHNIC MAKEUP

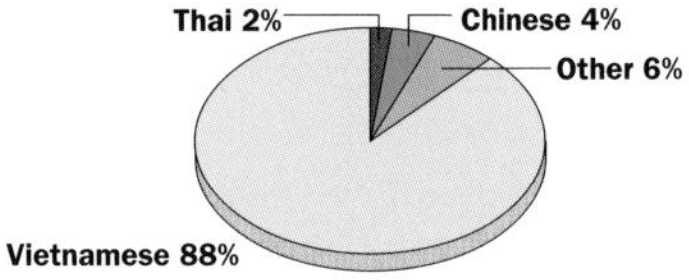
Thai 2%
Chinese 4%
Other 6%
Vietnamese 88%

Family life is strong and is based on kinship groups within village clans. A pronounced north–south cultural split remains evident in the cities. Chinese are the largest minority group. When the victorious communists reunited north and south Vietnam in 1976, they viewed the Saigon Chinese (in what was renamed Ho Chi Minh City), with their Taiwanese links, as a corrupt bourgeoisie. The northern Mountain Chinese were also suspect as a possible fifth column for China's ambitions in Vietnam. Various other mountain minorities (*montagnards*), with a history of collaboration with the French and Americans, were also sidelined by the regime in Hanoi. *Montagnard* resentment over the resettling of lowlanders in mountain regions sparked violent protests in early 2001.

War deaths cause older generations of women to outnumber men. Women form a high proportion of the laborforce, and are starting to gain greater political prominence, most notably Vice President Nguyen Thi Binh. Female conscription was reinstated in 2001.

POPULATION AGE BREAKDOWN

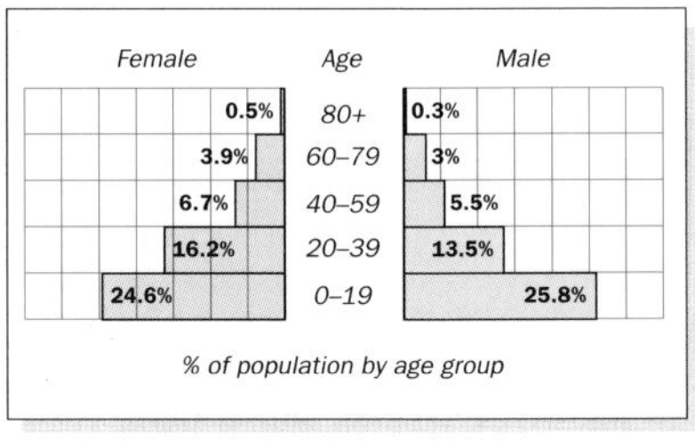
Female
Age
Male
0.5%
80+
0.3%
3.9%
60–79
3%
6.7%
40–59
5.5%
16.2%
20–39
13.5%
24.6%
0–19
25.8%
% of population by age group

Tran Duc Luong, *elected president in 1997.*

Nong Duc Manh, *powerful general secretary of the CPV.*

POLITICS

No multiparty elections

2002/2007

President Tran Duc Luong

AT THE LAST ELECTION

National Assembly 500 seats

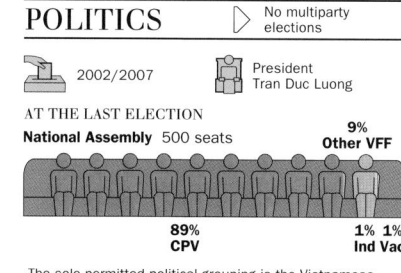

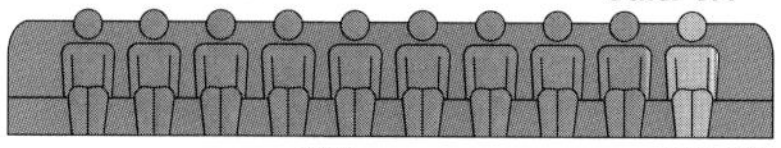
9%
Other VFF
89%
CPV
1% 1%
Ind Vac

The sole permitted political grouping is the Vietnamese Fatherland Front (**VFF**), which is dominated by the Communist Party of Vietnam (**CPV**)
Ind = Independents **Vac** = Vacant

Vietnam is effectively a single-party communist state.

PROFILE

A traditional communist system is still in place, with a powerful politburo elected by the party central committee. The CPV general secretary wields much power, alongside the prime minister and president. Changes in senior posts in 1997 left reformers such as new prime minister Phan Van Khai still outnumbered by conservatives. The 2001 party congress balanced the theme of greater democracy with a renewed commitment to socialism.

MAIN POLITICAL ISSUES

Economic reform

Vietnam is attempting to move to a market economy without political liberalization. Economic reformer Nong Duc Manh became party leader in 2001, but real concern remains that "individualism" will be encouraged, stability undermined, and the party's monopoly of power weakened by the opening to competition of collective farming and state enterprises.

Corruption

An investigation into crime boss Nam Cam (sentenced to death in 2003) revealed worrying levels of official collusion with organized crime.

VIETNAM
Total Area : 329 560 sq. km (127 243 sq. miles)
POPULATION
over 1 000 000
over 500 000
over 100 000
over 50 000
over 10 000
under 10 000
LAND HEIGHT
2000m/6562ft
1000m/3281ft
500m/1640ft
200m/656ft
Sea Level
100 km
100 miles
C H I N A
L A O S
C A M B O D I A
S O U T H C H I N A S E A
Gulf of Tongking
Gulf of Thailand
HANOI
Hai Phong
Ho Chi Minh
Da Năng
Huê
Vinh
Thanh Hoa
Nam Đinh
Quang Ngai
Qui Nhơn
Nha Trang
Cam Ranh
Đa Lat
Buôn Ma Thuôt
Vung Tau
Cân Thơ
Ca Mau
Điên Biên
Lai Châu
Lao Cai
Ha Giang
Cao Băng
Lang Sơn
Mekong Delta
Côn Đao

WORLD AFFAIRS

Joined UN in 1977

ASEAN | CP | OIF | Mekong River | NAM

Economic liberalization has improved relations with the US, with lifting of the aid and trade embargo in 1993, full diplomatic relations in 1995, and a landmark bilateral trade agreement in 2000, ahead of a visit by US president Bill Clinton that November.

Vietnam joined ASEAN in 1995, in the wake of the settlement of the Cambodia issue. Trade and economic cooperation links with Japan have been strengthened. Tension with China was reduced by an agreement in 1999 over their mutual land border, though competing claims to the Spratly Islands remain a source of friction.

AID

Recipient

$1.44bn (receipts)

Down 16% in 2001

Vietnam's invasion of Cambodia in 1978 halted all aid from China, Japan, and the West (except for Scandinavian countries), leaving it mostly dependent on the USSR. Western donors resumed assistance in the early 1990s. Their aid rapidly became the main source of capital for improving infrastructure, though foreign investment fell away significantly in the late 1990s.

CHRONOLOGY

From 1825, the brutal persecution of the Catholic community, originally converted by French priests in the 17th century, gave France the excuse to colonize Cochin-China, Annam, and Tonkin, and then merge them with Laos and Cambodia.

- ❑ **1920** *Quoc ngu* (Roman script) replaces Chinese script.
- ❑ **1930** Ho Chi Minh founds Indo-China Communist Party.
- ❑ **1940** Japanese invasion.
- ❑ **1941** Viet Minh resistance founded in exile in China.
- ❑ **1945** Viet Minh take Saigon and Hanoi. Emperor abdicates. Republic proclaimed with Ho Chi Minh as president.
- ❑ **1946** French reenter. First Indochina war.
- ❑ **1954** French defeated at Dien Bien Phu. Vietnam divided at 17°N. USSR supports North; US arms South.
- ❑ **1960** Groups opposed to southern regime unite as Viet Cong.
- ❑ **1964** US Congress approves war.
- ❑ **1965** Gen. Nguyen Van Thieu takes over military government of South. First US combat troops arrive.
- ❑ **1965–1968** Operation Rolling Thunder – intense bombing

➪

CHRONOLOGY *continued*

of North by South and US.

- **1967** Antiwar protests start in US and elsewhere.
- **1968** Tet (New Year) Offensive – 105 towns attacked simultaneously in South with infiltrated arms. Viet Cong suffer serious losses. Peace talks begin. US eases bombing and starts withdrawing troops.
- **1969** Ho Chi Minh dies. Succeeded by Le Duan. War intensifies in spite of talks.
- **1972** 11-day Christmas Campaign is heaviest US bombing of war.
- **1973** Paris Peace Agreements signed, but fighting continues.
- **1975** Fall of Saigon to combined forces of North and Provisional Revolutionary (Viet Cong) Government of South. One million flee after end of war.
- **1976** Vietnam united as Socialist Republic of Vietnam. Saigon renamed Ho Chi Minh City.
- **1978** Invasion of Cambodia to oust Pol Pot regime (by January 1979).
- **1979** Nine-Day War with China. Chinese troops pushed back after destroying everything for 40 km (25 miles) inside Vietnam. "Boat people" crisis. At UN conference, Vietnam agrees to allow legal emigration, but exodus continues.
- **1986** Death of Le Duan. Nguyen Van Linh, new Communist Party general secretary, initiates liberal economic policy of *doi moi* (renovation).
- **1987** Fighting in Thailand as Vietnam pursues Kampuchean resistance fighters across border.
- **1989** Troops leave Cambodia.
- **1991** Open anticommunist dissent made a criminal offense.
- **1992** Revised constitution allows foreign investment, but essential role of Communist Party is unchanged.
- **1994** US lifts its 30-year trade embargo.
- **1995** US–Vietnamese relations normalized. Vietnam joins ASEAN.
- **1997** Tran Duc Luong elected president, Phan Van Khai prime minister, by National Assembly.
- **1998** Asian financial crisis dampens economic boom.
- **1999** Signing of border treaty with China.
- **2000** Worst flooding along Mekong for 40 years. November, Bill Clinton becomes first US president to visit Vietnam since the war.
- **2001** March, visit by Russian president Vladimir Putin. April, ninth party congress. Nong Duc Manh becomes general secretary.
- **2003** An outbreak of acute pnuemonia (SARS) is contained.

DEFENSE

Compulsory military service

$2.35bn

Up 2% in 2001

Vietnam has large and well-equipped armed forces, notably the world's seventh-largest army. Military service is compulsory, and conscripts serve a two-year term. The army's role in preserving both stability and socialism was reaffirmed in 2001. Increased defense spending on the navy reflects tensions in the South China Sea, where there are disputed claims to the Spratly and Paracel Islands.

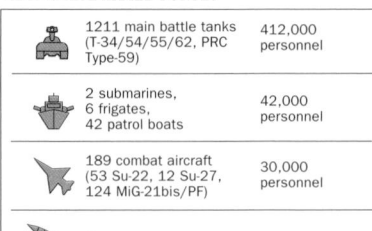

VIETNAMESE ARMED FORCES

1211 main battle tanks (T-34/54/55/62, PRC Type-59)	412,000 personnel
2 submarines, 6 frigates, 42 patrol boats	42,000 personnel
189 combat aircraft (53 Su-22, 12 Su-27, 124 MiG-21bis/PF)	30,000 personnel
None	

ECONOMICS

Inflation 14% p.a. (1990–2001)

$32.8bn

15,497 dông (15,273)

SCORE CARD

World GNP Ranking	58th
GNP per Capita	$410
Balance of Payments	$682m
Inflation	–0.4%
Unemployment	25%

EXPORTS

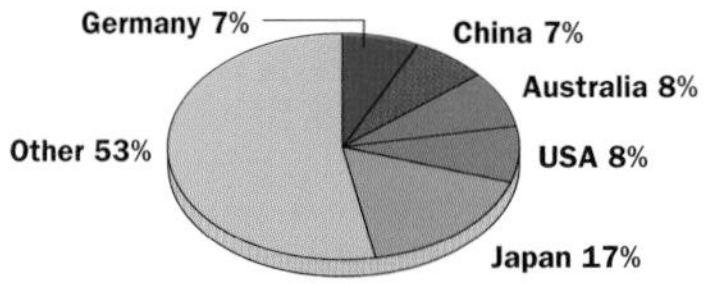
Germany 7%
China 7%
Australia 8%
USA 8%
Japan 17%
Other 53%

IMPORTS

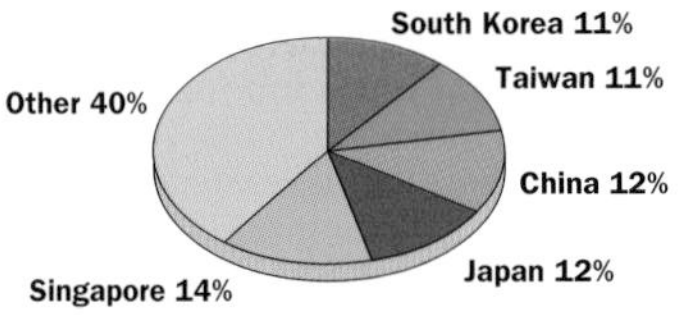
South Korea 11%
Taiwan 11%
China 12%
Japan 12%
Singapore 14%
Other 40%

Strengths

Diverse resource base; unexploited gas reserves. Young, literate, low-cost labor force. Strong light industrial and handicraft export industries.

Weaknesses

Weak economic institutions. Weight of bureaucracy. Heavy dependence on aid for reconstruction. Enduring suspicion of entrepreneurial southern attitudes and "individualism." Corruption.

Profile

The encouragement of private enterprise began in 1988. Touted in the mid-1990s as the next Asian "tiger," Vietnam has aimed at more moderate growth since the crisis of 1997–1998. Annual GDP increases, over 5% again by 2000, are impressive. Inflation, once a huge problem, was held down in the 1990s, and is now under firm control. Increased rice production has boosted incomes, and domestic demand helped the post-1998 upswing. The government has promised massive investment in agriculture, but plans to cut back coffee production as world prices have fallen.

Attracting foreign investment through reform is essential; government policies regarding state-owned enterprises promise more scope for joint ventures, and new laws on trade-licensing and investment were passed in 2000. Also that year the country's first stock exchange opened. The government has set a target of doubling GDP in the next decade. The potential certainly exists, based on an educated and highly motivated young labor force and on mineral resources, located mostly in the north.

ECONOMIC PERFORMANCE INDICATOR

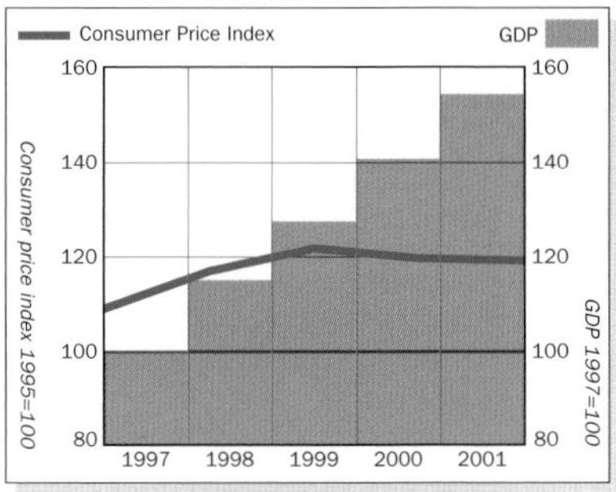
Consumer Price Index
GDP
Consumer price index 1995=100
GDP 1997=100
160
140
120
100
80
1997
1998
1999
2000
2001

VIETNAM : MAJOR BUSINESSES

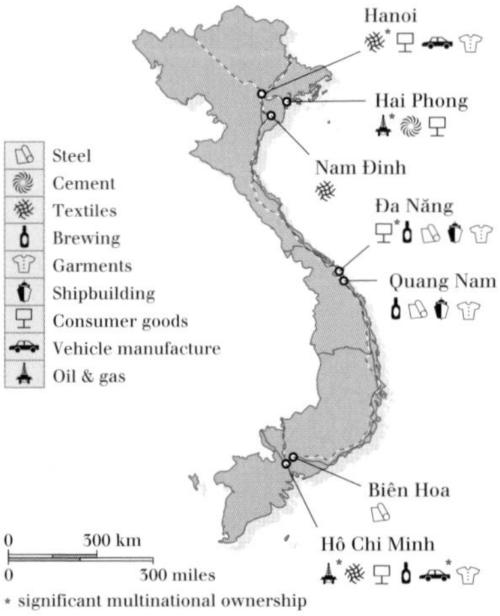
Hanoi
Hai Phong
Nam Đinh
Đa Năng
Quang Nam
Biên Hoa
Hô Chi Minh
Steel
Cement
Textiles
Brewing
Garments
Shipbuilding
Consumer goods
Vehicle manufacture
Oil & gas
0 300 km
0 300 miles
* significant multinational ownership

V

RESOURCES

Electric power 5m kW

1.95m tonnes

354,000 b/d (reserves 600m barrels)

23.2m pigs, 4.06m cattle, 60m ducks, 163m chickens

Coal, oil, tin, zinc, iron, antimony, gas, apatite, salt, bauxite

ELECTRICITY GENERATION

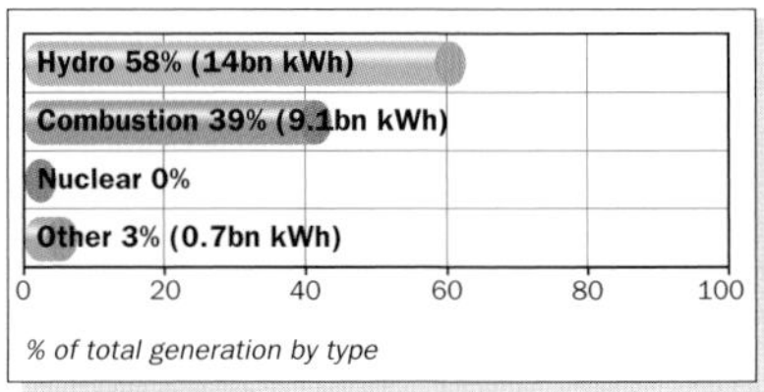
Hydro 58% (14bn kWh)
Combustion 39% (9.1bn kWh)
Nuclear 0%
Other 3% (0.7bn kWh)
0
20
40
60
80
100
% of total generation by type

Vietnam is now the world's second-largest coffee producer and is the third-largest exporter of rice – to the detriment of domestic stocks.

Oil production, small by world standards, is sufficient to make it Vietnam's biggest export earner. The Oil and Gas Corporation of Vietnam (PetroVietnam) is involved in joint ventures with international oil firms. Vietnam has unexploited gas reserves in the South China Sea; gas from the only producing field has to be flared off.

Timber exports have been banned since 1997 to preserve forests. Northern Vietnam has a surplus of electricity, mainly from hydroelectric schemes.

ENVIRONMENT

Sustainability rank: 94th

4% (2% partially protected)

0.6 tonnes per capita

ENVIRONMENTAL TREATIES

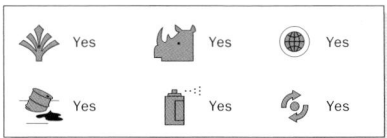

Yes · Yes · Yes

Yes · Yes · Yes

In the Vietnam War, seven million tonnes of bombs were dropped, and the defoliant chemical Agent Orange was sprayed over vast areas; a "census" of the continuing health impact was announced in 1999. Half of Vietnam's forests were seriously damaged and some 5% destroyed. Deforestation continued into the 1990s due to logging and expansion of coffee-growing, causing soil erosion and flooding. Floods along the Mekong in 2000 were the worst for 40 years.

MEDIA

TV ownership medium

Daily newspaper circulation 4 per 1000 people

PUBLISHING AND BROADCAST MEDIA

There are 7 daily newspapers, including *Nhan Dan, Quan Doi Nhan Dan, Hanoi Moi,* and *Sai Gon Giai Phong*

1 state-owned service with 53 provincial stations

1 state-owned service with more than 6000 local stations

The media are tightly regulated. TV is the dominant medium. All editors have to be Party members, but criticism of the authorities is still possible. Even *Nhan Dan*, the CPV newspaper, has been known to expose laxity in the judiciary system, especially in the judiciary. However, in 2002 the authorities sought out and destroyed books by proscribed authors.

CRIME

Death penalty in use

55,000 prisoners

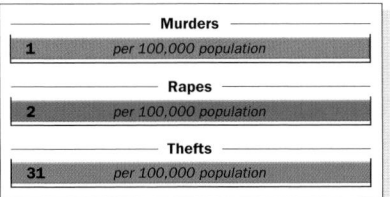

Up 13% in 2000

CRIME RATES

Murders

1 per 100,000 population

Rapes

2 per 100,000 population

Thefts

31 per 100,000 population

The judicial system is based on the Soviet model. The education camps established after liberation have now closed, but religious and political dissidents are still held without trial.

Corruption has risen sharply since economic liberalization, as has the illegal drift of young people to urban areas, where they are blamed for increasing petty crime and "social evils" such as begging, prostitution, and drug-taking. Theft from foreigners is a problem in major cities.

EDUCATION

School leaving age: 10

93%

749,914 students

THE EDUCATION SYSTEM

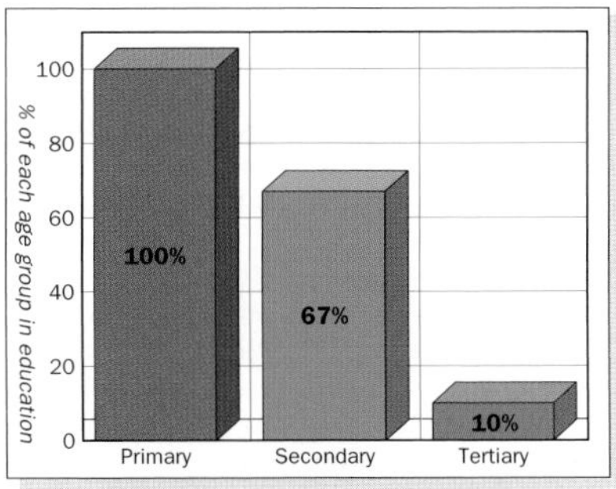
100
80
60
40
20
0
% of each age group in education
100%
67%
10%
Primary
Secondary
Tertiary

Private sponsorship helps fund education. Vietnamese universities have a strong liberal arts tradition. Social pressure to obtain a degree leads to high levels of cheating among university applicants.

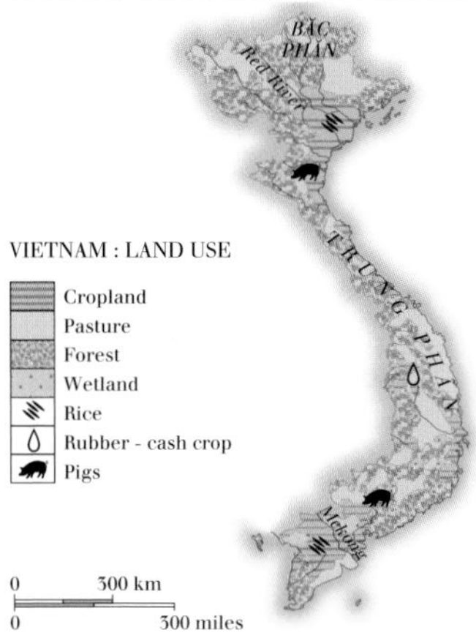
BAC PHAN
Red River
TRUNG PHAN
Mekong
VIETNAM : LAND USE
Cropland
Pasture
Forest
Wetland
Rice
Rubber - cash crop
Pigs
0
300 km
0
300 miles

HEALTH

Welfare state health benefits

1 per 1923 people

Heart disease, cancers, malaria

Vietnam's medical achievements include developing a vaccine for hepatitis B, and extracting an antimalarial drug, artemisinin, from the indigenous thanh hao tree. An extensive campaign is under way to combat the spread of AIDS.

SPENDING

GDP/cap. increase

CONSUMPTION AND SPENDING

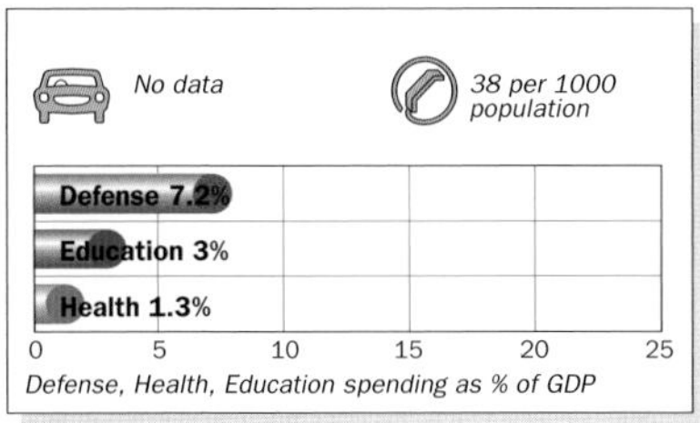
No data
38 per 1000 population
Defense 7.2%
Education 3%
Health 1.3%
0
5
10
15
20
25
Defense, Health, Education spending as % of GDP

Ostentatious consumerism is rising despite official disapproval, but is beyond most people's reach. Wealth disparities are growing, with rural areas falling deep into poverty.

WORLD RANKING

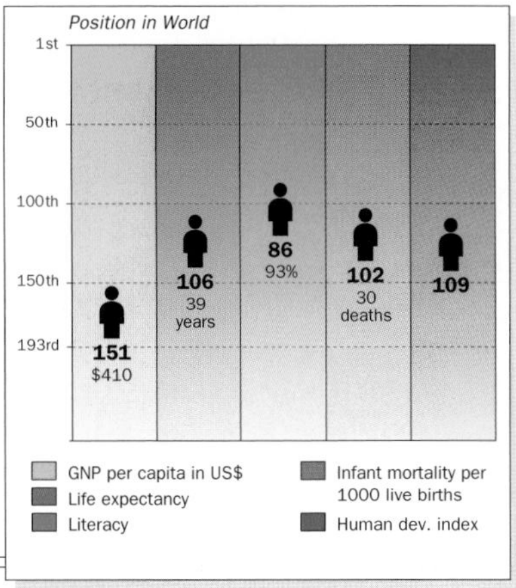
Position in World
1st
50th
100th
150th
193rd
151
$410
106
39 years
86
93%
102
30 deaths
109
GNP per capita in US$
Life expectancy
Literacy
Infant mortality per 1000 live births
Human dev. index

V

YEMEN

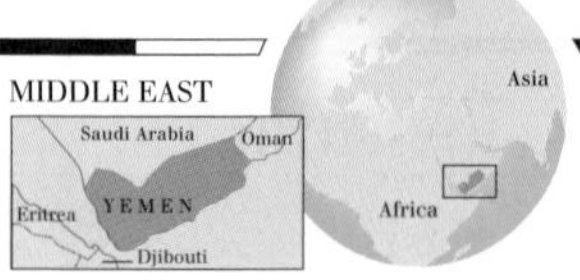
MIDDLE EAST
Saudi Arabia
Oman
Eritrea
YEMEN
Djibouti
Asia
Africa

OFFICIAL NAME: Republic of Yemen **CAPITAL:** Sana
POPULATION: 19.9 million **CURRENCY:** Yemeni rial **OFFICIAL LANGUAGE:** Arabic

1990 | 1990 | May 22 | ADN | +3 | +967 | .ye

YEMEN IS LOCATED in southern Arabia. The west is mountainous, with a fertile strip along the Red Sea. The center and south are largely arid mountains and desert. Until 1990 Yemen was two countries, the Yemen Arab Republic (YAR) in the west and the People's Democratic Republic of Yemen (PDRY) in the south. The YAR was run by successive military regimes; the poorer PDRY was the Arab world's only Marxist state. Postunification conflict between the two ruling hierarchies, nominally in coalition, led to a two-month civil war in 1994, the ousting of the former Marxists, and a new constitution.

CLIMATE

Hot desert/mountain

WEATHER CHART FOR SANA

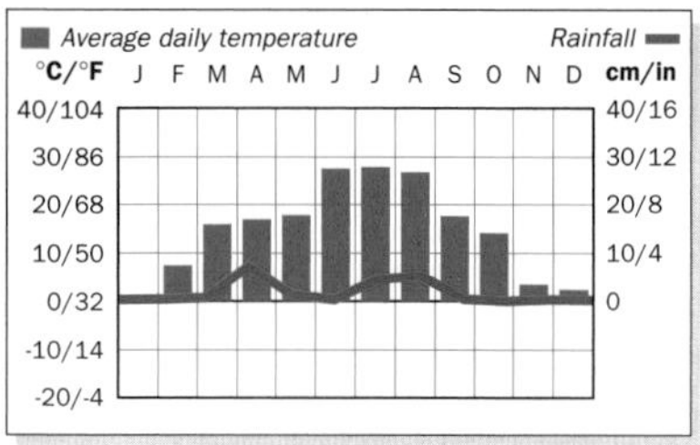
Average daily temperature
Rainfall
°C/°F
J F M A M J J A S O N D
cm/in
40/104
30/86
20/68
10/50
0/32
-10/14
-20/-4
40/16
30/12
20/8
10/4
0

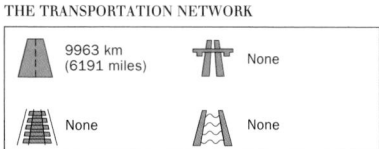

The desert climate is modified by altitude, which affects temperatures by as much as 12°C (22°F). Rainfall increases in northwest and central Yemen.

TRANSPORTATION

Drive on right

Sana International 997,990 passengers

44 ships 73,800 grt

THE TRANSPORTATION NETWORK

9963 km (6191 miles)

None

None

None

Aden's history as a port stretches back 3000 years. Adequate roads link the main cities, but many rural areas are inaccessible. International airlines, including the modern fleet of Yemenia, serve Sana and Aden.

***Hilltop village** in northern Yemen, showing traditionally decorated, multistory houses built from unbaked mud bricks.*

TOURISM

Visitors : Population 1:262

76,000 visitors

Up 4% in 2001

MAIN TOURIST ARRIVALS

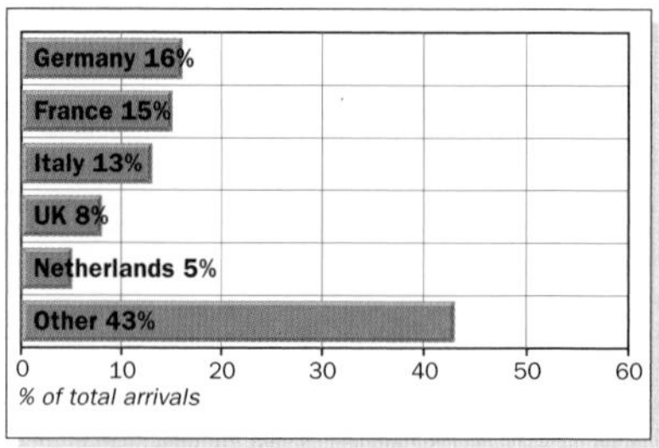
Germany 16%
France 15%
Italy 13%
UK 8%
Netherlands 5%
Other 43%
0
10
20
30
40
50
60
% of total arrivals

The home of the legendary Queen of Sheba, Yemen attracts tourists interested in Arab society, architecture, archaeology, and historical remains. The Romans called Yemen *Arabia Felix* because of its fertile farmlands and dominance in the frankincense trade. Yemen was the second country, after Saudi Arabia, to convert to Islam.

Southern Yemen has been open to Western visitors only since 1990. Its run-down infrastructure and lack of hotels, especially on the coast, have hindered tourism. Sana, a walled medieval city, is the more interesting center for tourists. It has impressive architecture, particularly tall stone and mud-brick Arab houses, and the palaces of the former imamate. Over 100 km (60 miles) from the capital, the Marib Dam, built in ancient times, is another major attraction.

German and French tourists were the first to travel to northwest Yemen during the 1980s. Hopes of a major rise in tourism following the end of the 1994 civil war were dashed in 1998 after tribesmen kidnapped and killed four tourists.

Tourists are subject to a ban on the consumption of alcohol, except in five-star hotels. Whisky and beer are available on the black market, which operates out of Djibouti.

PEOPLE

Pop. density low

Arabic

35/km² (92/mi²)

THE URBAN/RURAL POPULATION SPLIT

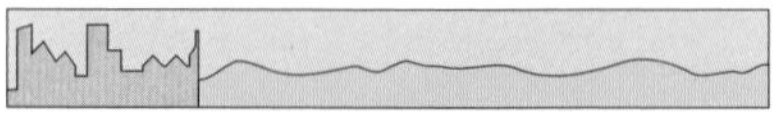
25%
75%

RELIGIOUS PERSUASION

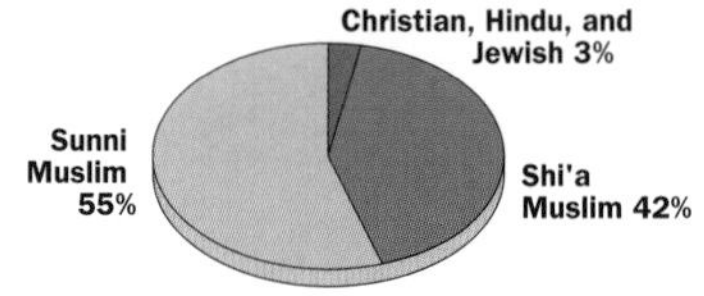
Christian, Hindu, and Jewish 3%
Sunni Muslim 55%
Shi'a Muslim 42%

ETHNIC MAKEUP

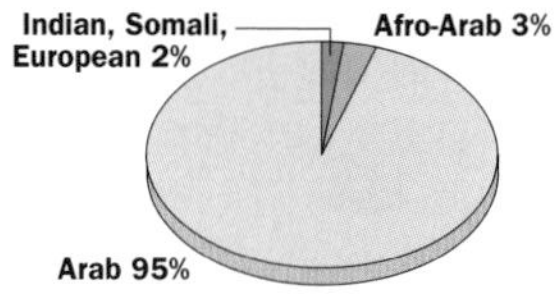
Indian, Somali, European 2%
Afro-Arab 3%
Arab 95%

Yemenis are almost entirely of Arab and Bedouin descent, though there is a small, dwindling, Jewish minority and people of mixed African and Arab descent along the south coast. The majority are Sunni Muslims, of the Shafi sect. However, Zaydi Shi'a are strong in the north, where many people have close family in Saudi Arabia. Many Yemenis consider Saudi Arabia's Asir province to be part of Yemen.

Over a million Yemenis went to work in neighboring states during the 1970s oil boom, but most were forced to return in 1990 due to Yemen's support for Iraq's invasion of Kuwait.

Tensions, which in 1994 led to civil war, continue to exist between the south, led by cosmopolitan Aden, and the more conservative west.

In rural areas and in the western highlands, semifeudal tribal chiefs hold sway, Islamic orthodoxy is strong, and most women wear the veil. In the south, however, women still claim the educational, professional, and social freedoms they had under the Marxist regime, especially in urban areas.

POPULATION AGE BREAKDOWN

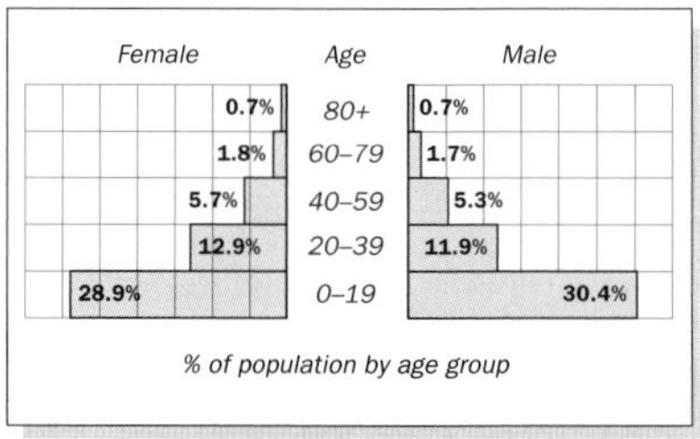
Female
Age
Male
0.7%
80+
0.7%
1.8%
60–79
1.7%
5.7%
40–59
5.3%
12.9%
20–39
11.9%
28.9%
0–19
30.4%
% of population by age group

Y

YEMEN

Total Area : 527 970 sq. km
(203 849 sq. miles)

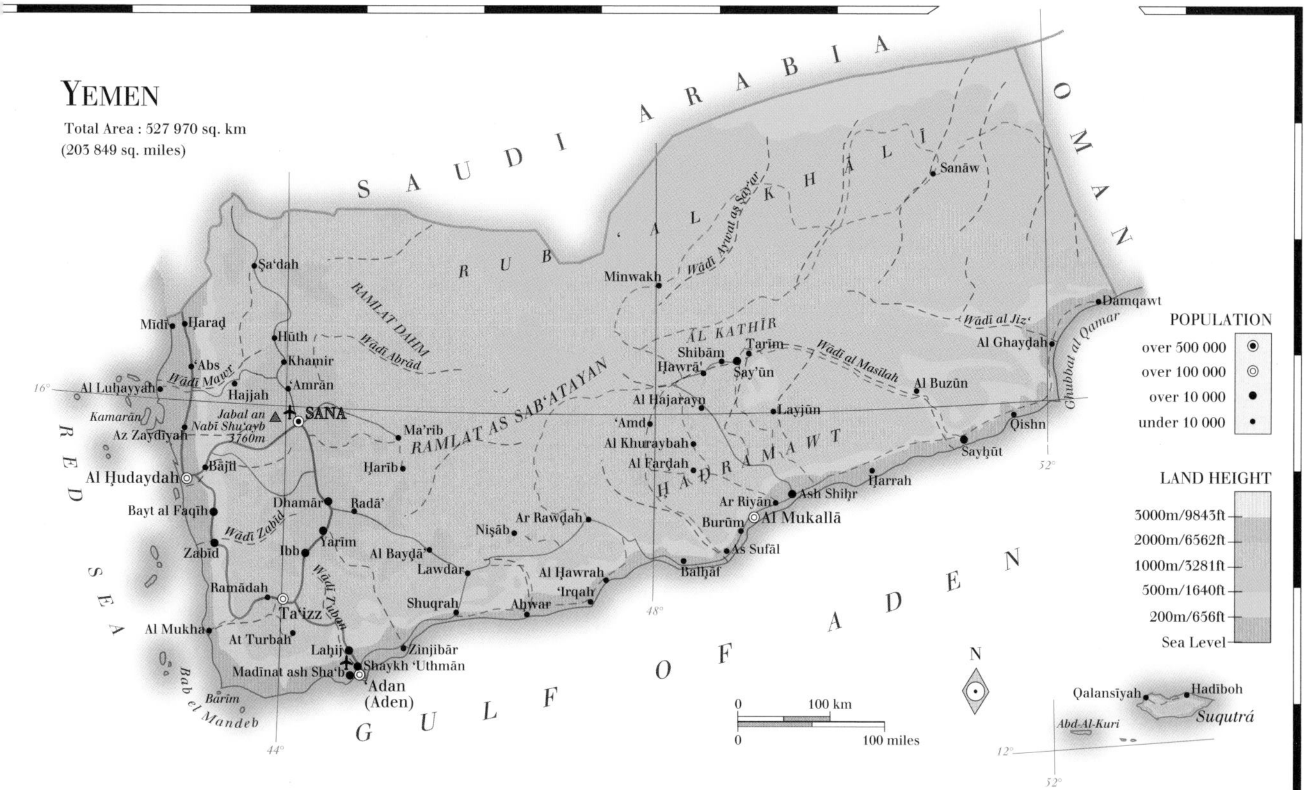
SAUDI ARABIA
OMAN
RUB' AL KHALI
RAMLAT DAHM
RAMLAT AS SAB'ATAYAN
AL KATHĪR
HADRAMAWT
RED SEA
GULF OF ADEN
Bab el Mandeb
Ghubbat al Qamar
Wādī Abrād
Wādī Aywat as Say'ar
Wādī al Masīlah
Wādī al Jiz'
Wādī Mawr
Wādī Zabīd
Wādī Tuban
Jabal an Nabī Shu'ayb 3760m
SANA
Sa'dah
Midī
Harad
Hūth
Khamir
'Abs
'Amrān
Hajjah
Al Luhayyah
Kamarān
Az Zaydīyah
Bājil
Al Hudaydah
Bayt al Faqīh
Zabīd
Dhamār
Radā'
Yarīm
Ibb
Ramādah
Ta'izz
Al Mukhā
At Turbah
Lahij
Madīnat ash Sha'b
Shaykh 'Uthmān
'Adan (Aden)
Zinjibār
Barīm
Ma'rib
Harīb
Al Baydā'
Lawdar
Shuqrah
Nişāb
Ar Rawdah
Al Hawrah
'Irqah
Ahwar
Minwakh
Shibām
Tarīm
Hawrā'
Say'ūn
Al Hajarayn
'Amd
Al Khuraybah
Al Fardah
Layjūn
Ar Riyān
Ash Shihr
Burūm
Al Mukallā
As Sufāl
Balhāf
Harrah
Sayhūt
Qishn
Al Buzūn
Al Ghaydah
Damqawt
Sanāw
Qalansīyah
Hadīboh
Abd-Al-Kuri
Suqutrá
POPULATION
over 500 000
over 100 000
over 10 000
under 10 000
LAND HEIGHT
3000m/9843ft
2000m/6562ft
1000m/3281ft
500m/1640ft
200m/656ft
Sea Level
0 100 km
0 100 miles

POLITICS

Multiparty elections

2003/2009

President Ali Abdullah Saleh

AT THE LAST ELECTION

House of Representatives 301 seats

1% Ind
1% Ba'ath
79% GPC
15% al-Islah
3% YSP
1% NUPO

GPC = General People's Congress **al-Islah** = Yemeni Alliance for Reform **YSP** = Yemen Socialist Party **Ind** = Independents **NUPO** = Nasserite Unionist Popular Organization **Ba'ath** = Arab Socialist Ba'ath Party

Yemen is a multiparty, presidential democracy.

PROFILE

The merger of the YAR and the PDRY in 1990 united Yemenis under one ruler for the first time since 1735; free elections were held in 1993. President Ali Saleh initially maintained unity. Then, in 1994, a bloody civil war erupted, fueling a secessionist movement in the south. By mid-1994, the southerners were crushed. In 1999 Saleh won the region's first democratic presidential election. His GPC increased its absolute majority in 2003, despite the participation in the poll of the former southern-ruling YSP – it had boycotted the 1997 election. The government still faces anger at the levels of poverty in an oil-rich country, and relies on familial ties to the military to maintain power. The Islamist al-Islah party, formerly a junior partner of the GPC, now forms the chief opposition.

MAIN POLITICAL ISSUES

Relations with Saudi Arabia

Relations have long been strained – over oil exploration rights, Yemeni claims on Asir, and accusations that Riyadh funds insurgent tribesmen. The two sides clashed violently in 1998 over 1600 km (1000 miles) of disputed border, despite a 1995 memorandum of understanding. In early 2001, both sides withdrew border troops under a pact reached the previous June.

Instability

For a decade, stability has been threatened by the border dispute with Saudi Arabia, growing tribal insurgency, and rising popular discontent with Saleh's government. Since 1992, tribesmen have kidnapped more than 100 foreigners, including diplomats and tourists.

Ali Abdullah Saleh, *former YAR president, now leader of the unified Yemen.*

Shaikh Abdullah al-Ahmar, *leader of the opposition al-Islah.*

CHRONOLOGY

From the 9th century, the Zaydi dynasty ruled Yemen until their defeat by the Ottoman Turks in 1517. The Turks were expelled by the Zaydi imams in 1636.

- **1839** Britain occupies Aden.
- **1918** Western Yemen independent.
- **1937** Aden made a crown colony, hinterland a protectorate.
- **1962** Army coup in west. Imam deposed, Yemen Arab Republic (YAR) declared. Civil war.
- **1963** Aden and protectorate united to form Federation of South Arabia.
- **1967** South Arabia independent as People's Republic of South Yemen. British troops leave Aden.
- **1970** South Yemen renamed People's Democratic Republic of Yemen (PDRY). Republican victory in YAR civil war.
- **1972** War between YAR and PDRY ends in peace settlement.
- **1974** Army coup in YAR.
- **1978** Lt. Col. Ali Saleh YAR president. Coup in PDRY: radical Abdalfattah Ismail in power.
- **1979** PDRY signs 20-year treaty with USSR.
- **1980** Ismail replaced by moderate Ali Muhammed.
- **1982** PDRY peace treaty with Oman. Major earthquake kills 3000.
- **1984** YAR signs 20-year cooperation treaty with USSR.

CHRONOLOGY *continued*

- ❑ **1986** Coup attempt in PDRY leads to civil war. Rebels take control of Aden. New PDRY president meets YAR counterpart.
- ❑ **1987** Oil production starts in YAR.
- ❑ **1988** YAR holds elections for consultative council; Muslim Brotherhood gains influence.
- ❑ **1989** Speeding-up of unification process. PDRY publishes a program of free-market reforms. YAR and PDRY sign unification agreement. Constitution of unified Yemen published.
- ❑ **1990** Restrictions on travel between YAR and PDRY lifted. Ali Saleh becomes president of Republic of Yemen. May, formal unification. Pro-Islamic groups oppose secular constitution.
- ❑ **1991** Yemeni guest workers expelled by Saudi Arabia in retaliation for Yemen's position over Iraqi invasion of Kuwait. Arab states boycott independence celebrations.
- ❑ **1992** Assassinations, food riots, and political unrest delay elections.
- ❑ **1994** Southern secessionists defeated in civil war. Amended constitution adopted.
- ❑ **1997** Saleh's GPC wins absolute majority in general election.
- ❑ **1998–1999** Violent border dispute with Saudi Arabia. Kidnapping of tourists, four killed; three members of Islamic Army of Aden (IAA) sentenced to death.
- ❑ **1999** Saleh reelected.
- ❑ **2000** Yemen agrees border with Saudi Arabia after 66-year dispute. October, terror attacks on US naval vessel and UK embassy.
- ❑ **2001** Referendum approves extension of presidential term to seven years.
- ❑ **2002** Government targets suspected al-Qaida allies in tribal areas, expels 100 foreign "scholars."

WORLD AFFAIRS

Joined UN in 1947/1967

AL | AMF | IBRD | NAM | OIC

Isolated since its support for Iraq during the 1991 Gulf War, Yemen now actively supports the US, and US agents operate on its soil in an attempt to tackle heavily armed Islamist terrorists known to be based there.

AID

Recipient

$426m (receipts) | Up 61% in 2001

International donors pledged $2.3 billion in 2002 to fund the government's antipoverty programs. The World Bank is the largest donor.

DEFENSE

Compulsory military service

$531m | Up 6% in 2001

Following unification in 1990, mutual suspicion hampered the integration of the two separate defense forces. Sporadic, bitter clashes have taken place.

The main domestic security concern is insurgent tribesmen and, internationally, anti-Western terrorist activity such as the sinking of USS *Cole* off Aden in late 2000. US military aid has increased accordingly.

YEMENI ARMED FORCES

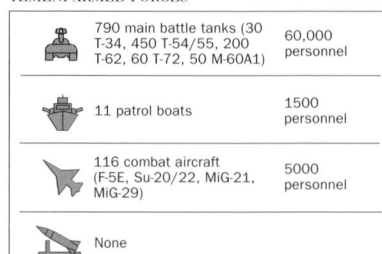

790 main battle tanks (30 T-34, 450 T-54/55, 200 T-62, 60 T-72, 50 M-60A1)	60,000 personnel
11 patrol boats	1500 personnel
116 combat aircraft (F-5E, Su-20/22, MiG-21, MiG-29)	5000 personnel
None	

ECONOMICS

Inflation 21% p.a. (1990–2001)

$8.18bn | 178 Yemeni rials (174.3)

SCORE CARD

❑ World GNP Ranking	93rd
❑ GNP per Capita	$450
❑ Balance of Payments	$1.11bn
❑ Inflation	10%
❑ Unemployment	30%

EXPORTS

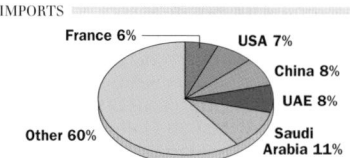

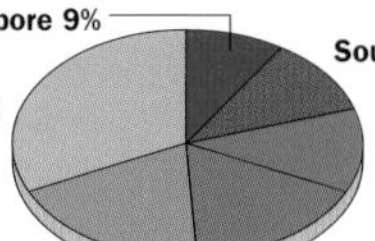
Singapore 9%
South Korea 11%
Other 32%
China 12%
India 19%
Thailand 17%

IMPORTS

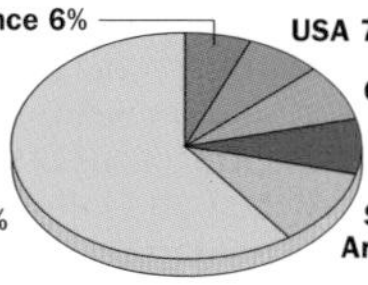
France 6%
USA 7%
China 8%
UAE 8%
Other 60%
Saudi Arabia 11%

Strengths

Rising oil production. Salt mining. Deposits of copper, gold, lead, zinc, and molybdenum. Industries include oil refining, chemicals, foodstuffs, cement, leather. Improving private sector.

Weaknesses

Political instability deters foreign investment. Damage caused by civil war. Well-organized black market undermines tax base. Subsistence agriculture. High population growth, leading to unemployment. Lack of central control, poor integration, and patronage politics hamper economic revival.

Profile

Unification in 1990 aimed to transform the economy, particularly through the exploitation of large oil and gas reserves, discovered in 1984; exports of oil began in 1987. Industrial investment around Aden was planned. These policies were severely affected by the 1990–1991 Gulf War. In addition, the expulsion of over one million Yemeni guest workers from Saudi Arabia imposed a huge burden on the economy, boosting unemployment and ending the flow of workers' remittances.

The 1994 civil war seriously damaged oil refineries, water systems, and communications centers. Economic crisis forced the government to reduce expenditure and subsidies on certain staple foods. This provoked widespread civil unrest – there were particularly violent demonstrations in 1998. Many farmers switched from food crops, such as wheat, to growing the more profitable narcotic plant *qat*, forcing Yemen to import food supplies. Strong oil prices in recent years and IMF-backed "streamlining" have encouraged susbstantial foreign debt relief.

ECONOMIC PERFORMANCE INDICATOR

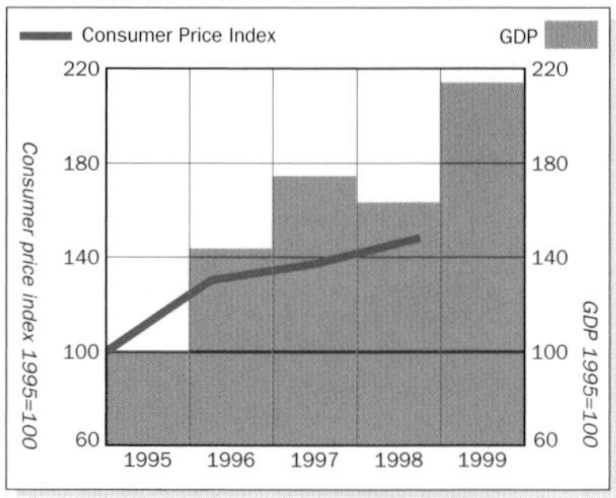
Consumer Price Index
GDP
220
180
140
100
60
Consumer price index 1995=100
GDP 1995=100
1995
1996
1997
1998
1999

YEMEN : MAJOR BUSINESSES

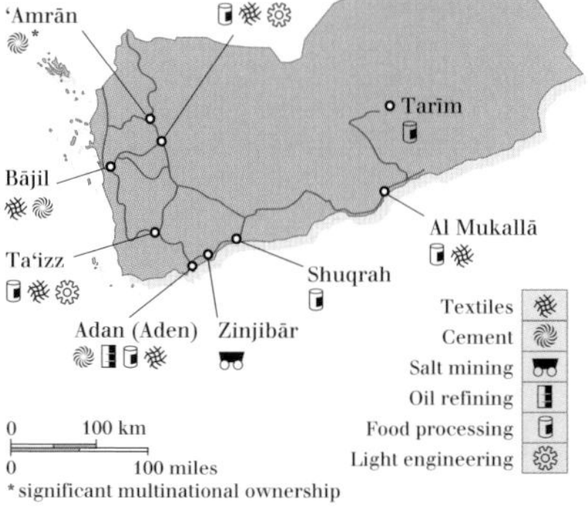
Sana
'Amrān
Tarīm
Bājil
Al Mukallā
Ta'izz
Shuqrah
Adan (Aden)
Zinjibār
Textiles
Cement
Salt mining
Oil refining
Food processing
Light engineering
0 100 km
0 100 miles
* significant multinational ownership

Y

RESOURCES

Electric power 810,000 kW

114,751 tonnes

473,000 b/d (reserves 4bn barrels)

5.03m sheep, 4.45m goats, 34.8m chickens

Oil, natural gas, salt, copper, gold, lead, zinc, molybdenum

ELECTRICITY GENERATION

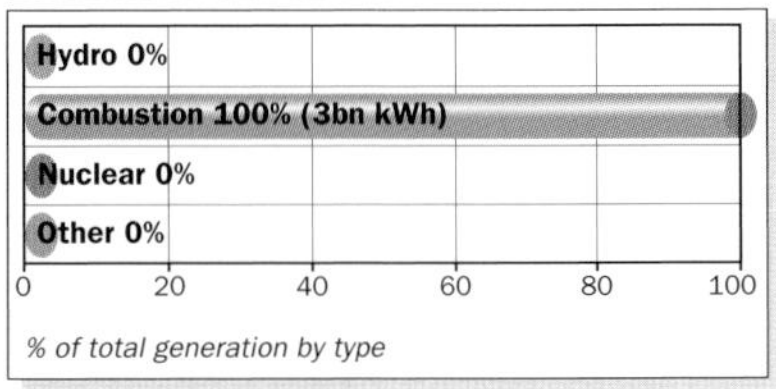
Hydro 0%
Combustion 100% (3bn kWh)
Nuclear 0%
Other 0%
0
20
40
60
80
100
% of total generation by type

Oil reserves are considerable, though initial estimates were exaggerated. The 2000 border agreement with Saudi Arabia promises better Yemeni access to oil fields. Salt is the only other mineral to be commercially exploited, and its production continues to grow steadily.

The agricultural sector employs just under half the working population. Cotton is a cash crop. Livestock and livestock products, including dairy produce and hides, are mainstays of the north. Yemen's rich fishing grounds in the Arabian Sea now provide a major source of earnings, despite poor equipment. Ambitious plans for an Aden free port, first revealed in 1994, have yet to be realized.

Yemen's population growth, averaging around 4% a year and among the highest in the world, is putting severe strain on the country's natural resources, especially water.

YEMEN : LAND USE

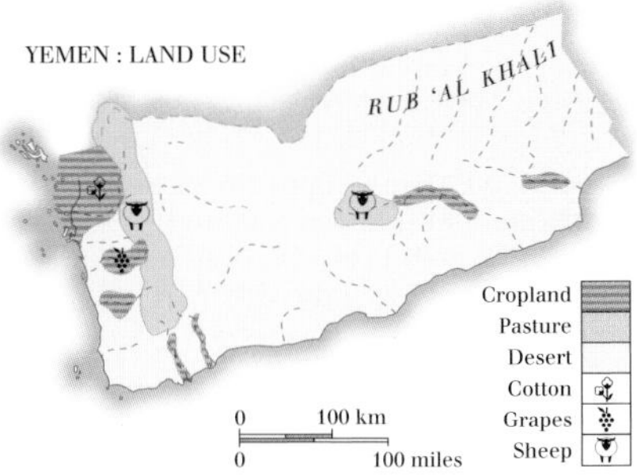
RUB 'AL KHALI
Cropland
Pasture
Desert
Cotton
Grapes
Sheep
0
100 km
0
100 miles

ENVIRONMENT

Not available

None

1 tonne per capita

ENVIRONMENTAL TREATIES

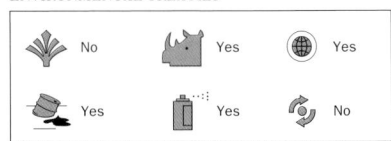

No	Yes	Yes
Yes	Yes	No

Large areas remain untouched by development, preserving habitats for rare birds. Problems include water scarcity, overgrazing, and soil erosion.

MEDIA

TV ownership low

Daily newspaper circulation 15 per 1000 people

PUBLISHING AND BROADCAST MEDIA

There are 4 daily newspapers, including *Ath-Thawra* and *Al-Jumhuriyah*, which have the largest circulations

1 state-controlled service

1 state-controlled service

Yemen has a distinguished tradition of intellectual debate, and legislation embodies freedom of the press, but in practice this remains poorly developed. The government keeps tight control of the media and vets the entry of foreign journalists. TV and radio are state-controlled and have a limited range around the principal cities. Satellite TV is not generally available. Ownership of radio and TV receivers is low; only a tiny minority own a television set.

CRIME

Death penalty in use

14,000 prisoners

Up 6% in 1997–1999

CRIME RATES

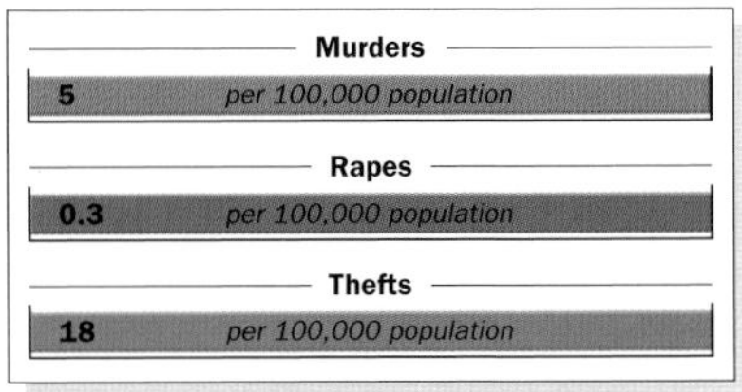
Murders
5
per 100,000 population
Rapes
0.3
per 100,000 population
Thefts
18
per 100,000 population

Political assassinations continue to threaten stability. There is little formal law enforcement outside the main cities; foreign companies risk kidnappings and theft by Bedouin raiders. There is a proliferation of illicit weapons: the number of firearms has been estimated at 60 million – three times the population size. Some blame lawlessness on the narcotic, *qat*.

EDUCATION

School leaving age: 14

48%

164,166 students

THE EDUCATION SYSTEM

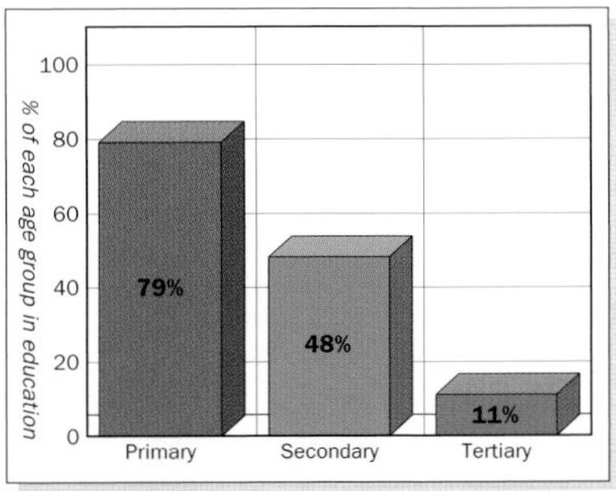
100
80
60
40
20
0
% of each age group in education
79%
48%
11%
Primary
Secondary
Tertiary

Some 80% of the population have had no formal classroom education. Schooling barely extends into the rural areas. Illiteracy is especially high among women: 75% cannot read or write. Only 13% of students at Yemen's two universities – Sana and Aden – are female. Yemen also has some technical colleges. The government's unpopular economic policies have encouraged student activism.

HEALTH

No welfare state health benefits

1 per 4545 people

Diarrheal diseases, tuberculosis, malaria, bilharzia

The major cities have an adequate primary health care system. A new 300-bed hospital in Sana is due to be completed in 2004. Rural areas are less well served. Health services are under threat from tribal gangs. In 2002 the World Bank approved a $27 million credit for a Health Reform Support Project to increase health provisions in poor communities.

SPENDING

GDP/cap. increase

CONSUMPTION AND SPENDING

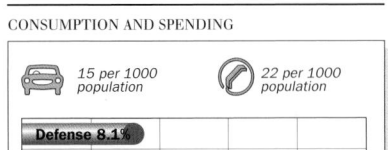

15 per 1000 population

22 per 1000 population

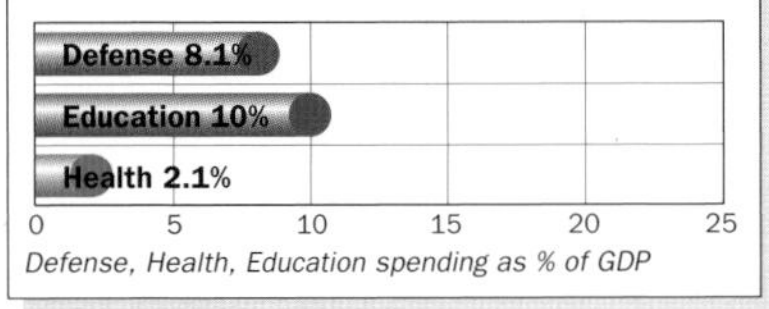
Defense 8.1%
Education 10%
Health 2.1%
0
5
10
15
20
25
Defense, Health, Education spending as % of GDP

Most Yemenis suffered a fall in living standards after Saudi Arabia expelled its Yemeni workers. A lack of jobs in other Gulf states has fueled unemployment, estimated at around 30%. Except for a small elite, the ownership of consumer goods is low.

WORLD RANKING

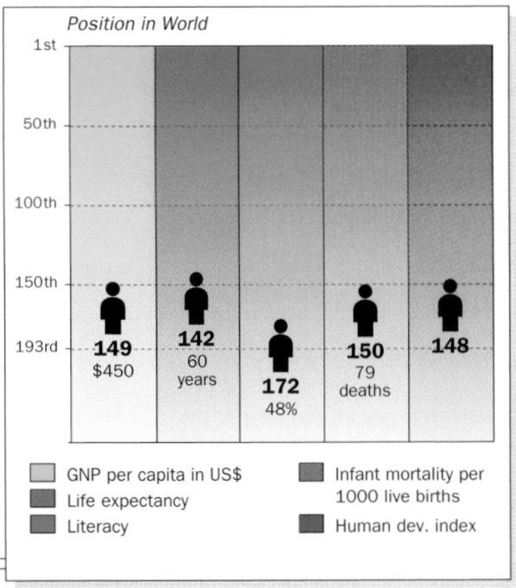
Position in World
1st
50th
100th
150th
193rd
149
$450
142
60
years
172
48%
150
79
deaths
148
GNP per capita in US$
Life expectancy
Literacy
Infant mortality per 1000 live births
Human dev. index

Y

ZAMBIA

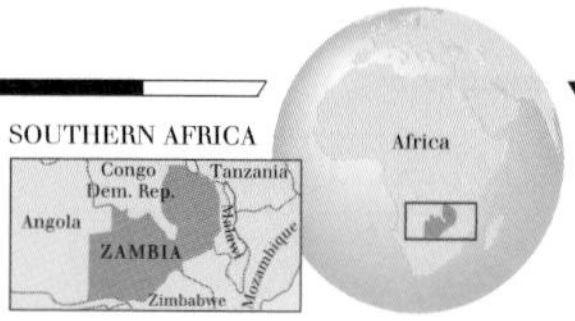
SOUTHERN AFRICA
Africa
Congo
Dem. Rep.
Tanzania
Angola
ZAMBIA
Malawi
Mozambique
Zimbabwe

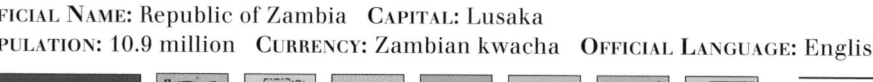

OFFICIAL NAME: Republic of Zambia **CAPITAL:** Lusaka
POPULATION: 10.9 million **CURRENCY:** Zambian kwacha **OFFICIAL LANGUAGE:** English

1964 | 1964 | Oct 24 | Z | +2 | +260 | .zm

LYING IN THE HEART of southern Africa, Zambia is a country of upland plateaus, bordered to the south by the Zambezi River. Its economic fortunes are tied to the copper industry. Falling copper prices in the late 1970s, and then the growing inaccessibility of remaining reserves, have led to a severe decline in the economy. In 1991, Zambia achieved a peaceful transition from single-party rule to multiparty democracy.

CLIMATE

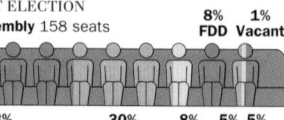

Tropical wet and dry

WEATHER CHART FOR LUSAKA

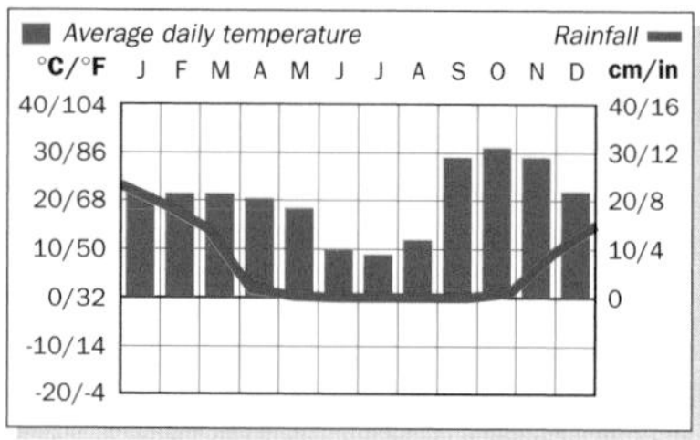
Average daily temperature
Rainfall
°C/°F J F M A M J J A S O N D cm/in
40/104
30/86
20/68
10/50
0/32
-10/14
-20/-4
40/16
30/12
20/8
10/4
0

Zambia has a tropical climate, with rains from November to April. The southwest is prone to drought.

TRANSPORTATION

Drive on left

Lusaka International
392,289 passengers

Has no fleet

THE TRANSPORTATION NETWORK

39,700 km (24,668 miles)

60 km (37 miles)

1273 km (791 miles)

2250 km (1398 miles)

The poor rail and road networks, in need of urgent rehabilitation, could sabotage economic recovery. Zambian Airways was liquidated in 1994, and private airlines are now in operation.

TOURISM

Visitors : Population 1:19

574,000 visitors

Up 26% in 2000

MAIN TOURIST ARRIVALS

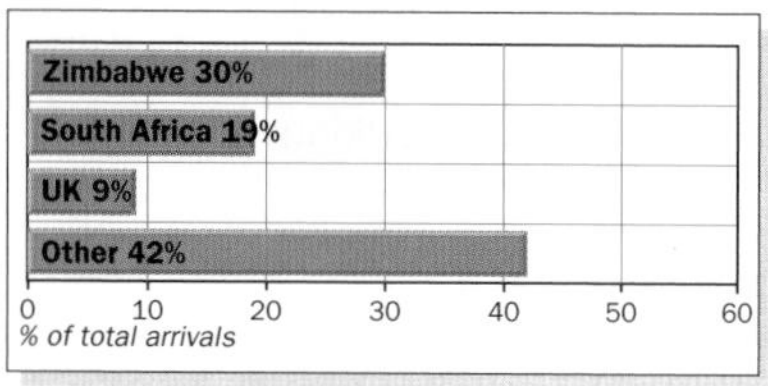
Zimbabwe 30%
South Africa 19%
UK 9%
Other 42%
0 10 20 30 40 50 60
% of total arrivals

Wildlife, the Victoria Falls, and white-water rafting are major attractions. Recent increases in tourism have been at the expense of neighboring Zimbabwe.

PEOPLE

Pop. density low

Bemba, Nyanja, Tonga, Kaonde, Lunda, Luvale, Lozi, English

15/km² (38/mi²)

THE URBAN/RURAL POPULATION SPLIT

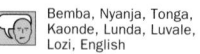

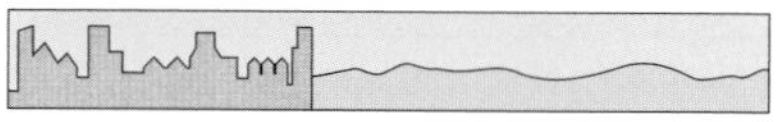
40%
60%

RELIGIOUS PERSUASION

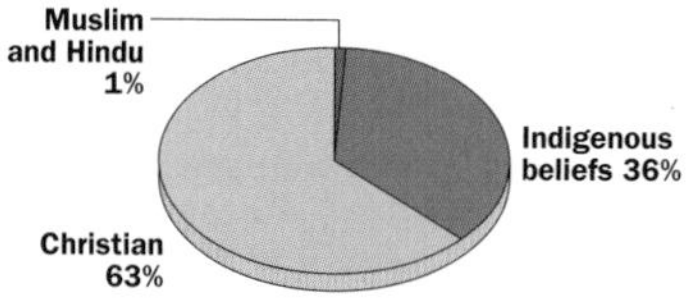
Muslim and Hindu 1%
Indigenous beliefs 36%
Christian 63%

Though ethnically heterogeneous, with more than 70 different groups, Zambia has been less affected by ethnic tension than many African states. The largest group, about 34% of the population, is the Bemba, who live in the northeast and also predominate in the central Copperbelt. Other major groups are the southern Tonga, the eastern Nyanja, and the Lozi in the west. There are also thousands of refugees, mainly from Angola.

Zambia's main urban area is the Copperbelt, where many third- and fourth-generation town dwellers live. Some half a million children are employed there in hazardous conditions. The rural population lives mainly by subsistence farming.

A National Gender Policy was issued in October 2000 to redress inequalities between the sexes.

Musi-o-Tunya (The Smoke That Thunders), known in English as Victoria Falls. Spray from the falls can be seen 30 km (20 miles) away.

POLITICS

Multiparty elections

2001/2006

President Levy Mwanawasa

AT THE LAST ELECTION
National Assembly 158 seats

8% FDD
1% Vacant
43% MMD
30% UPND
8% UNIP
5% App
5% Others

MMD = Movement for Multiparty Democracy **UPND** = United Party for National Development **UNIP** = United National Independence Party **FDD** = Forum for Democracy and Development **App** = Appointed

Up to eight members are appointed by the president, and the speaker is also a member

Frederick Chiluba and the MMD defeated long-term president Kenneth Kaunda and the UNIP in 1991. Despite painful reforms Chiluba was eventually accused of the same failings as Kaunda: a struggling economy and authoritarian rule. In 2001 he purged the MMD of critics, prompting the formation of new opposition parties, and made way for his chosen successor, Levy Mwanawasa, to win disputed elections. Mwanawasa condemned Chiluba's corruption, but he too soon faced the usual criticisms. He angered opposition parties by creating without their official consent a cross-party "national unity" government in 2003. He has questioned privatization policies, jeopardizing aid flows.

WORLD AFFAIRS

Joined UN in 1964

Comm | ACP | NAM | AU | SADC

Zambia led Africa's opposition to apartheid South Africa and now enjoys close links with Pretoria. It also has a significant role as a mediator in neighboring conflicts.

AID

Recipient

$374m (receipts)

Up in 2002

Regional drought in 2002 dramatically increased the need for aid. Donors pledged $1.3 billion, returning aid to the yearly levels seen before a freeze in 1997 prompted by state corruption. The government has rejected food aid in genetically modified form.

DEFENSE

No compulsory military service

$27m

Down 7% in 2001

Despite the relatively small budget, the 21,600-strong armed forces are well equipped. Security along the Angolan border is a main concern.

ECONOMICS

Inflation 48% p.a. (1990–2001)

$3.33bn

4768 Zambian kwacha (4468)

SCORE CARD

- ❑ World GNP Ranking........................128th
- ❑ GNP per Capita $320
- ❑ Balance of Payments....................–$584m
- ❑ Inflation 21.5%
- ❑ Unemployment...................................50%

STRENGTHS

Potential food self-sufficiency. Boom in new export crops such as cotton and flowers. Minerals, notably copper, cobalt, and coal. Market-oriented reforms and privatization attracting foreign private investors. Copper industry finally privatized in 2003. Strategic location. Reduced customs duties.

WEAKNESSES

Falling value of copper, which still accounts for around half of export earnings. Domestic reserves declining. Shortage of finance for restructuring. High inflation, negative growth, serious droughts. Arable land underused. Delays in privatization programs.

EXPORTS

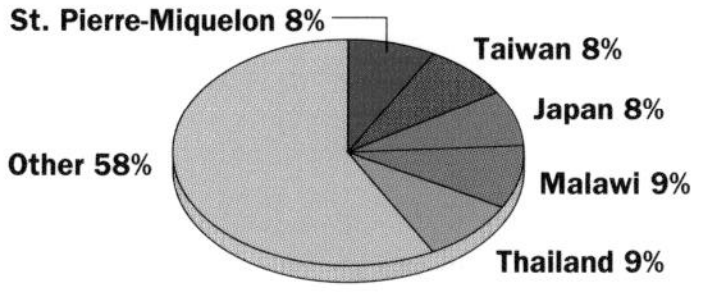

St. Pierre-Miquelon 8%
Taiwan 8%
Japan 8%
Malawi 9%
Thailand 9%
Other 58%

IMPORTS

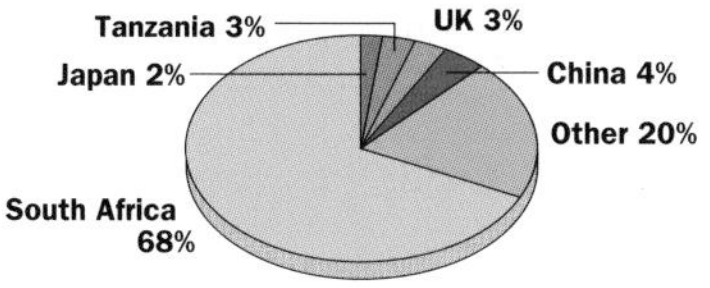

Tanzania 3%
UK 3%
Japan 2%
China 4%
Other 20%
South Africa 68%

RESOURCES

Electric power 2.3m kW

70,911 tonnes

Not an oil producer; refines 4600 b/d

2.6m cattle, 1.27m goats, 30m chickens

Copper, cobalt, coal, zinc, lead, gold, emeralds, amethysts

Copper production is continuing to decline; levels are now below 30% of 1969's peak production. Zambia has rich hydropower potential.

ENVIRONMENT

Sustainability rank: 69th

61% (22% partially protected)

0.2 tonnes per capita

Drought is a recurrent hazard. Rhinos are almost extinct as a result of poaching. Revenues from legal hunting are being channeled into villages to encourage support for conservation.

MEDIA

TV ownership medium

Daily newspaper circulation 12 per 1000 people

PUBLISHING AND BROADCAST MEDIA

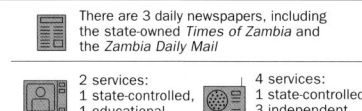

There are 3 daily newspapers, including the state-owned *Times of Zambia* and the *Zambia Daily Mail*

2 services: 1 state-controlled, 1 educational

4 services: 1 state-controlled, 3 independent

Broadcasting is dominated by the government. Opposition journalists have been accused of treason.

CRIME

Death penalty in use

13,173 prisoners

Crime is rising

Cases of violent crime, burglary, and rape are rising rapidly. In 1998 Zambia promised to overhaul its prison and police services.

CHRONOLOGY

Northern Rhodesia was developed by Britain solely for its copper. The UNIP, led by Kenneth Kaunda, took power at Zambian independence in 1964.

- ❑ **1972** UNIP one-party government.
- ❑ **1982–1991** Austerity measures and corruption: pressure for democracy.
- ❑ **1991** MMD government elected; Frederick Chiluba defeats Kaunda.
- ❑ **1996** Controversial elections.
- ❑ **2002** Levy Mwanawasa president.

EDUCATION

School leaving age: 13

79%

24,553 students

Primary education is compulsory. Fees for secondary students have affected the already very low attendance rate.

HEALTH

Welfare state health benefits

1 per 14,286 people

Respiratory infections, diarrheal diseases, AIDS, malaria

HIV prevention programs are reducing infection rates in Lusaka. However, over 25% of town dwellers are HIV-positive.

SPENDING

GDP/cap. increase

CONSUMPTION AND SPENDING

17 per 1000 population

8 per 1000 population

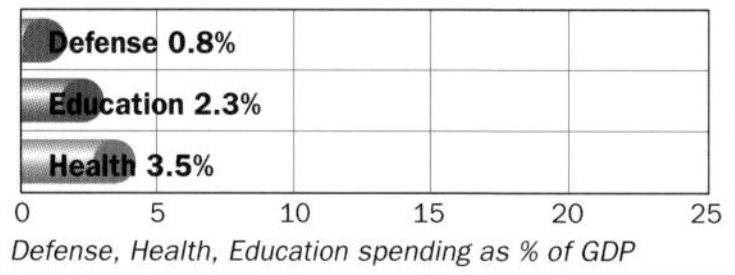

Defense 0.8%
Education 2.3%
Health 3.5%
0
5
10
15
20
25
Defense, Health, Education spending as % of GDP

Standards of living for most Zambians are now lower in real terms than at independence in 1964. Many people lack basic nutrition.

WORLD RANKING

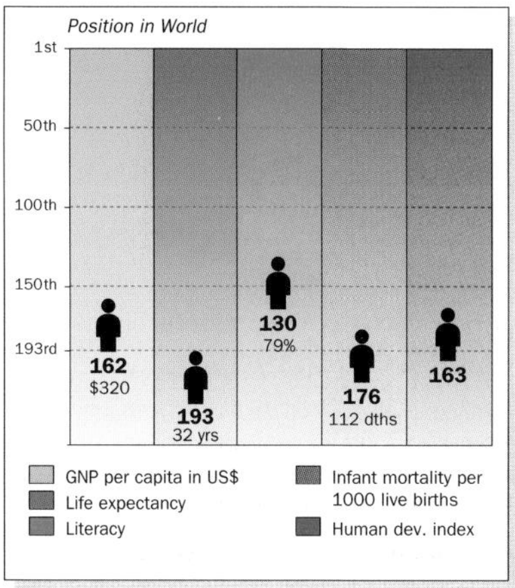

Position in World
1st
50th
100th
150th
193rd
162
$320
193
32 yrs
130
79%
176
112 dths
163
GNP per capita in US$
Life expectancy
Literacy
Infant mortality per 1000 live births
Human dev. index

ZAMBIA

Total Area : 752 614 sq. km (290 584 sq. miles)

POPULATION

- ◉ over 500 000
- ◎ over 100 000
- ○ over 50 000
- ● over 10 000
- • under 10 000

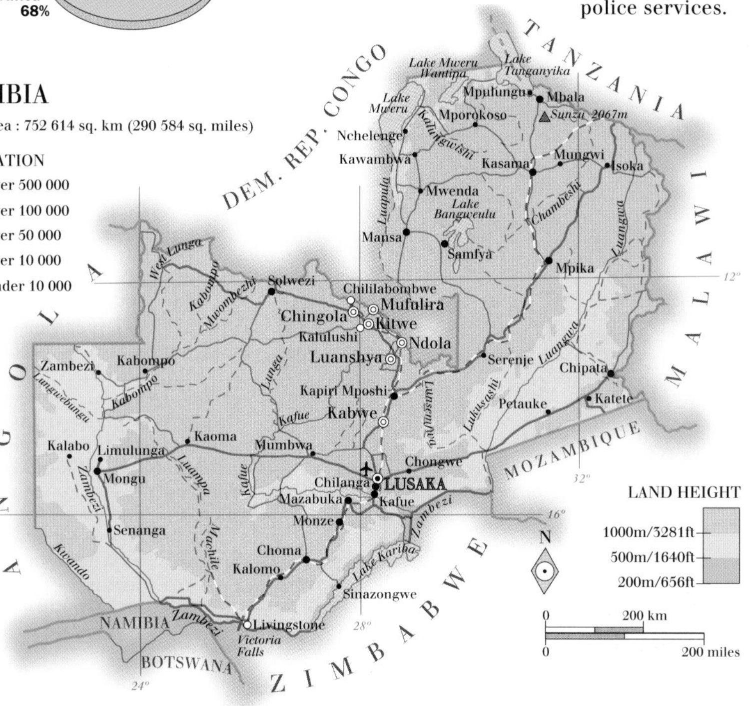

TANZANIA
DEM. REP. CONGO
ANGOLA
MALAWI
MOZAMBIQUE
ZIMBABWE
NAMIBIA
BOTSWANA
Lake Mweru Wantipa
Lake Tanganyika
Lake Mweru
Mpulungu
Mbala
Sunzu 2067m
Mporokoso
Nchelenge
Kawambwa
Kasama
Mungwi
Isoka
Mwenda
Lake Bangweulu
Mansa
Samfya
Mpika
Solwezi
Chililabombwe
Mufulira
Chingola
Kitwe
Kalulushi
Ndola
Luanshya
Serenje
Chipata
Katete
Petauke
Kapiri Mposhi
Kabwe
Zambezi
Kabompo
Kaoma
Kalabo
Limulunga
Mongu
Mumbwa
Chongwe
Chilanga
LUSAKA
Mazabuka
Kafue
Monze
Senanga
Choma
Kalomo
Sinazongwe
Livingstone
Victoria Falls
Lake Kariba
LAND HEIGHT
1000m/3281ft
500m/1640ft
200m/656ft
0
200 km
200 miles

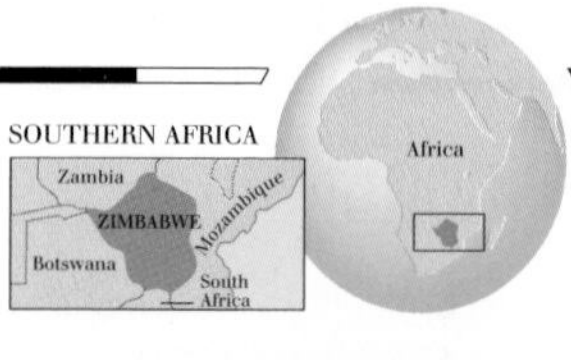
SOUTHERN AFRICA
Zambia
ZIMBABWE
Mozambique
Botswana
South Africa
Africa

ZIMBABWE

OFFICIAL NAME: Republic of Zimbabwe **CAPITAL:** Harare
POPULATION: 13.1 million **CURRENCY:** Zimbabwe dollar **OFFICIAL LANGUAGE:** English

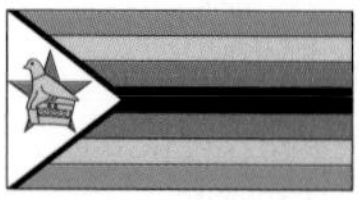

1980 | 1980 | April 18 | ZW | +2 | +263 | .zw

ZIMBABWE IS SITUATED in southern Africa. Its upland center is crisscrossed by rivers flowing into Lake Kariba and the Zambezi River, on which lies the region's most spectacular natural feature, the Victoria Falls (Musi-o-Tunya). Attempts to preserve white rule in the former British colony led to a long guerrilla war before independence in 1980. Robert Mugabe, the country's leader since then and its president since 1987, has become increasingly authoritarian and divisive. Violent seizure of white-owned farmland and severe drought have contributed to virtual economic collapse.

The Kariba Dam, which has created the vast Lake Kariba on the Zambezi River, lies on Zimbabwe's northwest border with Zambia.

CLIMATE

Tropical wet and dry/steppe

WEATHER CHART FOR HARARE

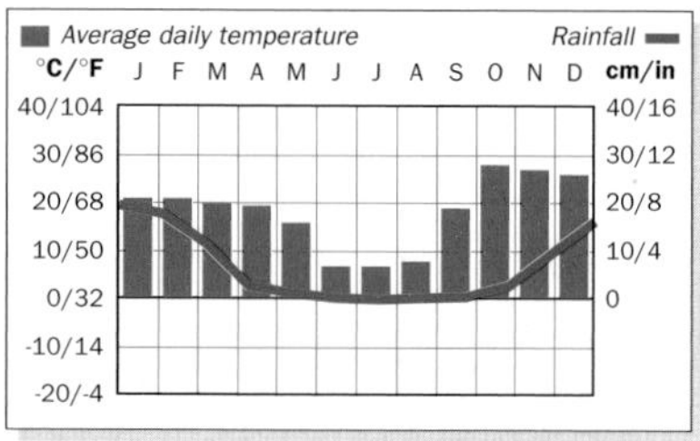
Average daily temperature
Rainfall
°C/°F
J F M A M J J A S O N D
cm/in
40/104
30/86
20/68
10/50
0/32
-10/14
-20/-4
40/16
30/12
20/8
10/4
0

Because of its altitude, Zimbabwe is comparatively temperate for a country in the tropics; humidity is also low. The rainy season occurs between November and March but, with the exception of the eastern highlands, rainfall is erratic and drought is common. Annual rainfall ranges from 140 cm (55 in) in the eastern highlands to 40 cm (16 in) in the Limpopo valley.

TRANSPORTATION

Drive on left

Harare International
636,129 passengers

Has no fleet

THE TRANSPORTATION NETWORK

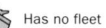

8692 km (5401 miles)		None	
3077 km (1912 miles)		Lake Kariba and the Mazowe River	

The number of international air links has been increased. Zimbabwe's rail network, among the densest in sub-Saharan Africa, requires modernizing.

TOURISM

Visitors : Population 1:7

1.87m visitors

Down 11% in 2000

MAIN TOURIST ARRIVALS

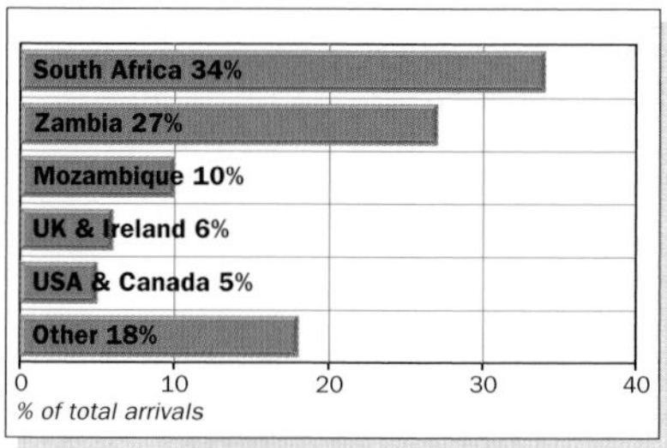
South Africa 34%
Zambia 27%
Mozambique 10%
UK & Ireland 6%
USA & Canada 5%
Other 18%
0
10
20
30
40
% of total arrivals

Zimbabwe's principal attractions are the Victoria Falls, the Kariba Dam, numerous national parks, the Great Zimbabwe ruins near Masvingo, and World's View in the Matopo Hills. Invasions led by "war veterans" of large commercial farms, the violence in the run-up to the parliamentary elections in 2000, and the ensuing violent suppression of domestic political opposition put Zimbabwe on the list of unsafe destinations for many visitors. Fuel and foreign currency shortages have further undermined the tourism sector.

In addition to these factors, Zimbabwe is wary that mass-market tourism might seriously damage the environment. However, the lure of foreign exchange has encouraged the development of conference facilities in Harare and vacation complexes, such as Elephant Hills, around Victoria Falls. State law requires that there be 30% local ownership of tourist ventures.

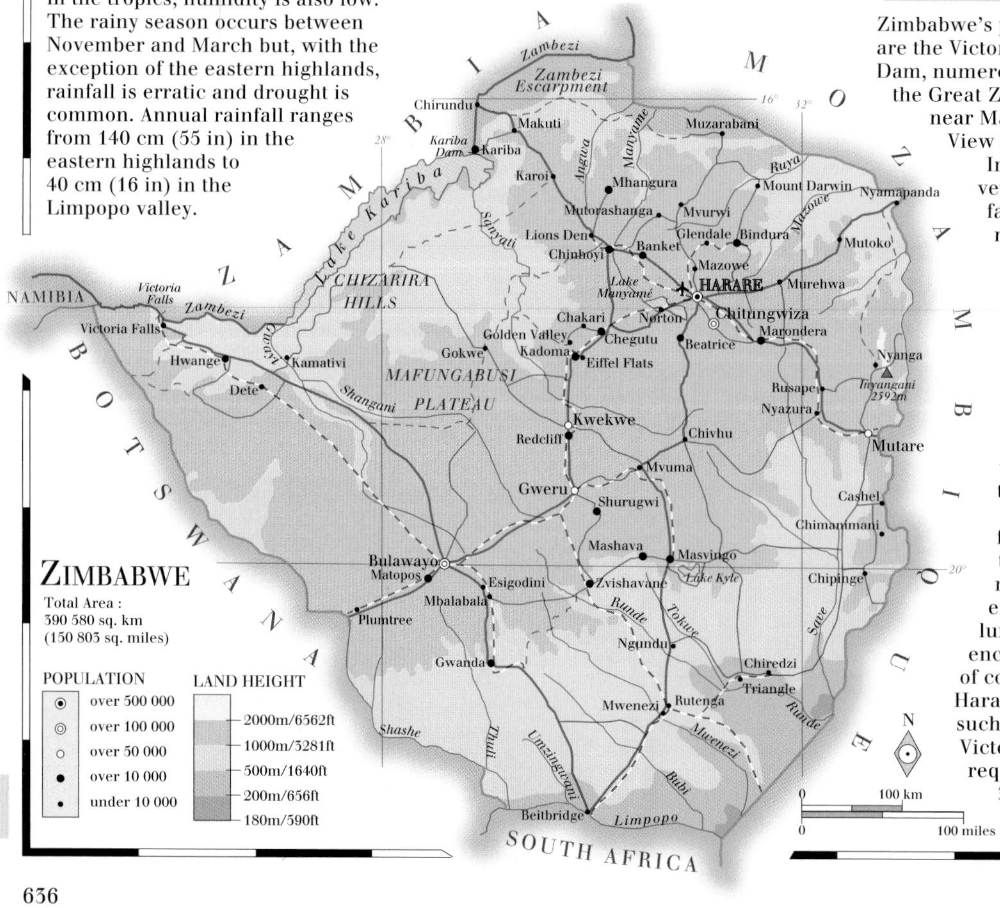
ZAMBIA
MOZAMBIQUE
BOTSWANA
NAMIBIA
SOUTH AFRICA
Zambezi
Zambezi Escarpment
Chirundu
Makuti
Kariba Dam
Kariba
Karoi
Lake Kariba
Muzarabani
Mhangura
Mount Darwin
Nyamapanda
Mutorashanga
Mvurwi
Glendale
Bindura
Lions Den
Chinhoyi
Banket
Mutoko
Mazowe
HARARE
Murehwa
Lake Manyame
Chitungwiza
Norton
Marondera
Chakari
Golden Valley
Chegutu
Beatrice
Kadoma
Eiffel Flats
Gokwe
Victoria Falls
Hwange
Kamativi
Dete
CHIZARIRA HILLS
MAFUNGABUSI PLATEAU
Shangani
Nyanga
Inyangani 2592m
Rusape
Nyazura
Kwekwe
Redcliff
Chivhu
Mutare
Mvuma
Gweru
Shurugwi
Cashel
Chimanimani
Mashava
Masvingo
Lake Kyle
Chipinge
Bulawayo
Matopos
Esigodini
Zvishavane
Mbalabala
Plumtree
Ngundu
Gwanda
Chiredzi
Triangle
Mwenezi
Rutenga
Beitbridge
Limpopo
Shashe
Thuli
Umzingwani
Bubi
Mwenezi
Runde
Tokwe
Save
Ruya
Mazowe
Manyame
Angwa
Sanyati
Gwai
ZIMBABWE
Total Area : 390 580 sq. km (150 803 sq. miles)
POPULATION
over 500 000
over 100 000
over 50 000
over 10 000
under 10 000
LAND HEIGHT
2000m/6562ft
1000m/3281ft
500m/1640ft
200m/656ft
180m/590ft
N
100 km
100 miles

Z

PEOPLE

Pop. density low

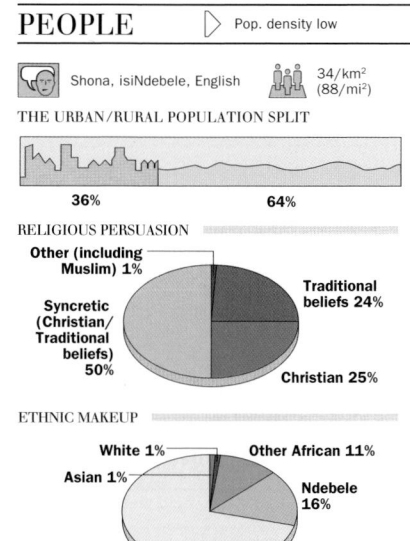

Shona, isiNdebele, English

34/km² (88/mi²)

THE URBAN/RURAL POPULATION SPLIT

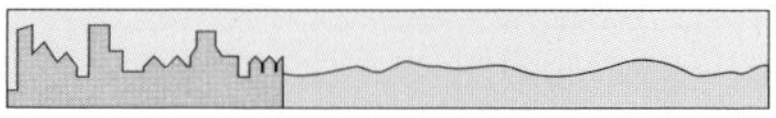
36%
64%

RELIGIOUS PERSUASION

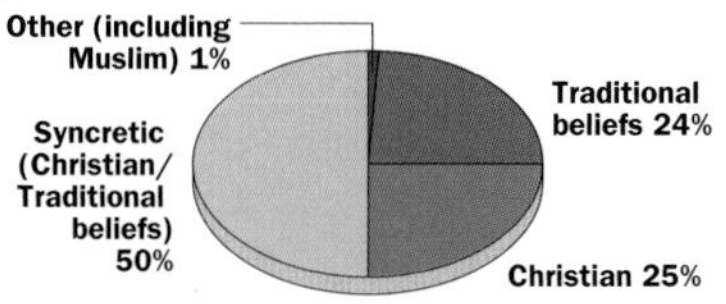
Other (including Muslim) 1%
Traditional beliefs 24%
Syncretic (Christian/ Traditional beliefs) 50%
Christian 25%

ETHNIC MAKEUP

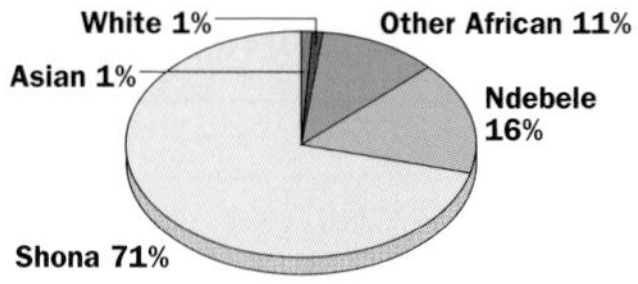
White 1%
Other African 11%
Asian 1%
Ndebele 16%
Shona 71%

There are two main ethnic groups, the majority Shona in the north and the Ndebele in the south. Europeans and Asians comprise 2% of the population.

Ethnic tensions plagued the 1980s. In 1983 alone 1500 Ndebele were massacred by the army as the ruling, Shona-dominated, ZANU–PF attempted to suppress the predominantly Ndebele Zimbabwe African People's Union (PF–ZAPU). A Unity Accord in 1987 eased the conflict, and ZAPU leader Joshua Nkomo was appointed vice president in 1990.

As a legacy of colonial rule, whites remain generally far more affluent than blacks, an imbalance partly redressed by policies to improve black education and increase employment. Redistribution of land, previously slow and dogged by accusations of corruption, was stepped up in 2000. A movement to seize white-owned farms has been backed by the government, and discrimination against whites officially endorsed. Tensions have increased massively.

POPULATION AGE BREAKDOWN

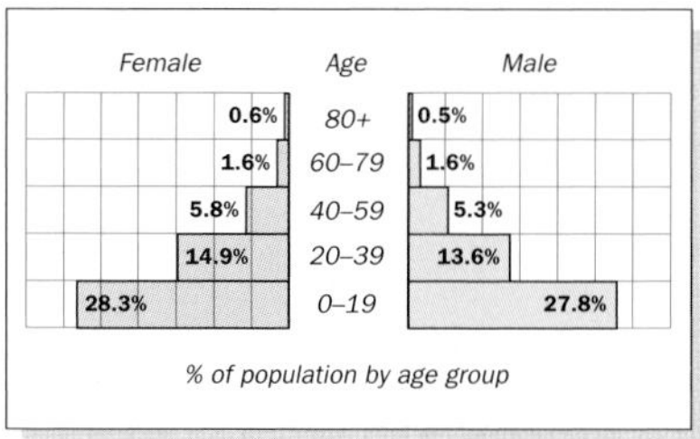
Female
Age
Male
0.6%
80+
0.5%
1.6%
60–79
1.6%
5.8%
40–59
5.3%
14.9%
20–39
13.6%
28.3%
0–19
27.8%
% of population by age group

Families are large, and almost half the population is under 15. Zimbabwean society is traditionally patriarchal. In 1999 a Supreme Court ruling provoked protest by according only "junior male" status to black women, especially those marrying under traditional law.

POLITICS

Multiparty elections

2000/2005

President Robert Gabriel Mugabe

AT THE LAST ELECTION

Parliament 150 seats

1% ZANU–Ndonga
41% ZANU–PF
38% MDC
20% App

ZANU–PF = Zimbabwe African National Union–Patriotic Front **MDC** = Movement for Democratic Change **App** = Appointed **ZANU–Ndonga** = Zimbabwe African National Union – Ndonga

30 seats are set aside for presidential appointments and traditional chiefs

80% of MPs are elected. The president is directly elected every six years.

Profile

After leading Zimbabwe to independence as a democracy and winning an internal dispute with the Zimbabwe African People's Union (ZAPU), Robert Mugabe's ZANU–PF has since dominated politics. However, its status has been questioned as support for the opposition MDC has grown since its formation in 1999. Despite widespread preelection intimidation, the MDC won a convincing share of votes, particularly in Harare and Bulawayo, in 2000, and its members have since been victimized by government thugs. MDC leader Morgan Tsvangirai was charged with treason in 2002 and has been repeatedly arrested for organizing strikes. There are increasingly frequent reports of division within ZANU–PF.

Main Political Issues

The rule of President Mugabe

Mugabe, hitherto prime minister, was elected president unopposed in 1987. He dropped attempts to create a one-party socialist state in 1991. His position has become increasingly precarious as ZANU–PF has lost support in the face of economic collapse and a reinvigorated opposition led by the MDC. He has resorted to authoritarian and violent policies to stay in power. The circumstances of his reelection in 2002 drew widespread criticism.

Land redistribution

Though most agree that the distribution of farmland unfairly favored the white minority, the speed and method of belated land redistribution has provoked protest. White-owned farms have been confiscated without compensation and violently occupied by self-styled "war veterans" who have government blessing. The policy has led to a huge drop in grain production.

Robert Mugabe, *elected prime minister in 1980 and president in 1987.*

Morgan Tsvangirai, *leader of the opposition MDC.*

AID

Recipient

US$159m (receipts)

Down 11% in 2001

Bilateral aid fell by a third between 1994 and 1996, after donors including the UK, Denmark, the US, France, and Germany learned that aid intended for small farmers and indigenous enterprises was siphoned off to large industrial projects. In 1998 the IMF approved US$175 million in standby credit. However, political violence since 2000 has prompted most international aid donors to suspend financial support. Struggling under massive food shortages, Zimbabwe agreed in 2002 to accept genetically modified food aid.

WORLD AFFAIRS

Joined UN in 1980

WTO G15 NAM AU SADC

Zimbabwe is an active member of the SADC and the Preferential Trade Area for East and South Africa. Relations with postapartheid South Africa are particularly strong. Zimbabwean troops were active in the DRC from 1998 to 2002. This strong involvement in African affairs and Mugabe's own role as an anticolonial champion have led to regional support for the confrontational policy against white commercial farmers. However, his increasingly antidemocratic stance has brought near-total isolation from the wider international community. The EU, the US, and the UK have been vociferous in their condemnation of Mugabe's regime, and sanctions and aid suspensions have contributed to the perilous state of the economy. In 2002 South Africa and Nigeria were party to the decision to suspend Zimbabwe from the Commonwealth, in a rare display of African displeasure at Mugabe's "unfree and unfair" reelection.

CHRONOLOGY

In 1953, the British colony of Southern Rhodesia became part of the Federation of Rhodesia and Nyasaland with Northern Rhodesia (now Zambia) and Nyasaland (now Malawi).

- ❑ **1961** Joshua Nkomo forms ZAPU.
- ❑ **1962** ZAPU banned. Segregationist Rhodesian Front (RF) wins polls.
- ❑ **1963** African nationalists in Northern Rhodesia and Nyasaland demand dissolution of Federation. ZANU, offshoot of ZAPU, formed by Rev. Sithole and Robert Mugabe.
- ❑ **1964** New RF prime minister Ian Smith rejects British demands for majority rule. ZANU banned.
- ❑ **1965** May, RF reelected. November, state of emergency declared (renewed until 1990). Smith's unilateral declaration of independence. UK imposes economic sanctions. ANC, ZANU, and ZAPU begin guerrilla war.
- ❑ **1974** RF regime agrees cease-fire terms with African nationalists.
- ❑ **1976** ZANU and ZAPU unite as Patriotic Front (PF).
- ❑ **1977** PF backed by "frontline" African states: Mozambique, Tanzania, Botswana, and Zambia.
- ❑ **1979** Lancaster House talks produce agreement on constitution.
- ❑ **1980** Independence as Zimbabwe. Following violent election campaign, Mugabe becomes prime minister of ZANU–PF/ PF–ZAPU coalition. Relations severed with South Africa.
- ❑ **1983–1984** Unrest in Matabeleland, PF–ZAPU's power base.
- ❑ **1985** Elections return ZANU–PF, with manifesto to create one-party state. Many PF–ZAPU members arrested.
- ❑ **1987** Provision for white seats in parliament abolished. ZANU–PF and PF–ZAPU sign unity agreement (merge in 1989). Mugabe elected president.
- ❑ **1990** Elections won by ZANU–PF. Mugabe reelected president.
- ❑ **1991** Mugabe abandons plan for one-party state. Severe drought.
- ❑ **1999** Death of Vice President Nkomo. Opposition forms MDC.
- ❑ **2000** Government loses referendum on new constitution. Expropriations of white-owned farmland by squatters. Strong MDC performance in polls. ZANU–PF accused of using intimidation to retain majority.
- ❑ **2002** Mugabe reelected in flawed poll. Commonwealth membership suspended. Government deadline for white farmers to leave land. Threat of mass starvation and economic collapse.

DEFENSE

No compulsory military service

US$267m

Down 3% in 2001

Nationalist guerrillas were the heroes of independence in 1980. By the late 1990s, however, resentment grew when ex-combatants demanded enormous pensions.

Though formally nonaligned, Zimbabwe supported the Mozambican regime against Renamo guerrillas and backed the US-led operation in Somalia in 1992–1995. The withdrawal of troops from the Democratic Republic of the Congo (DRC), dispatched there in 1998 to help President Laurent Kabila fight rebels, began in April 2001, following the Lusaka peace accord. Troops remained in the DRC for many months after the withdrawal was officially completed in 2002.

Zimbabwe has in the past received military aid and training from the UK and South Korea.

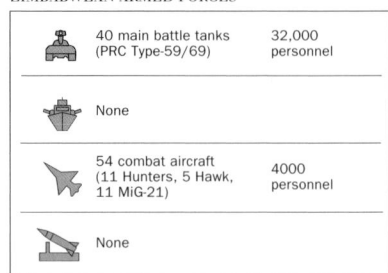

ZIMBABWEAN ARMED FORCES

40 main battle tanks (PRC Type-59/69)	32,000 personnel
None	
54 combat aircraft (11 Hunters, 5 Hawk, 11 MiG-21)	4000 personnel
None	

ECONOMICS

Inflation 28% p.a. (1990–2001)

US$6.16bn

824 Zimbabwe dollars (55.5)

SCORE CARD

❑ World GNP Ranking	104th
❑ GNP per Capita	US$480
❑ Balance of Payments	–US$425m
❑ Inflation	76.7%
❑ Unemployment	50%

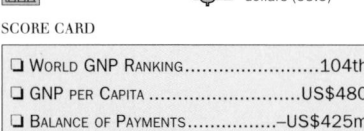

EXPORTS

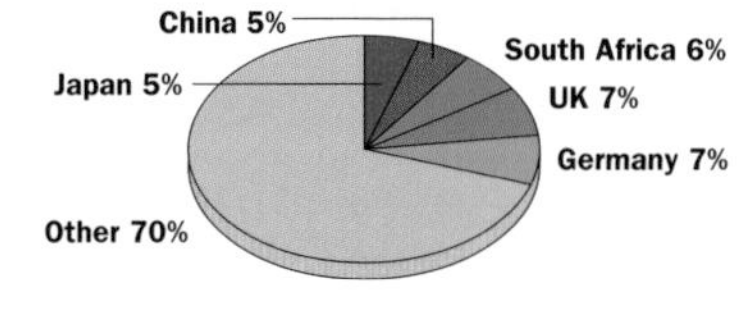
China 5%
South Africa 6%
Japan 5%
UK 7%
Germany 7%
Other 70%

IMPORTS

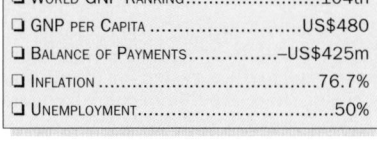

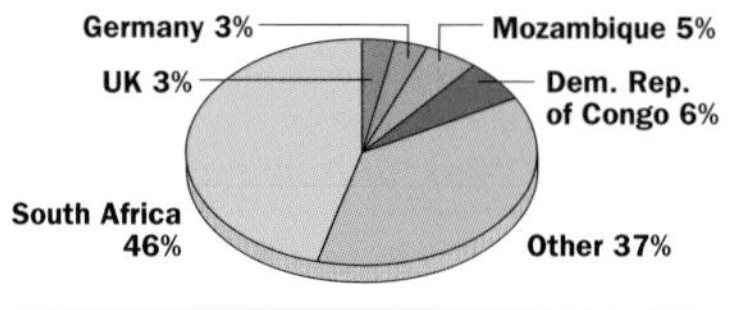
Germany 3%
Mozambique 5%
UK 3%
Dem. Rep. of Congo 6%
South Africa 46%
Other 37%

Strengths

Sound infrastructure. Broad-based economy. Virtual self-sufficiency in energy. Gold, coal, horticulture, tobacco. Tourist potential. Good education system.

Weaknesses

Agricultural and hydroelectric output affected by drought. Large budget deficits, unemployment, and inflation. Labor unrest, bank collapses, food price riots. Currency value halved in 1998; devalued again in 2000. Cheap imports damage local industries. Political violence since 2000 has scared off investors. Massive food shortages; risk of famine. Shortages of fuel and cash.

Profile

In 1991 a more market-oriented economy superseded the socialist policies of the 1980s, which increased unemployment and inflation. Prospects for the mining industry appear particularly bleak: privatization of state copper interests was repeatedly delayed, while collapsing mineral prices forced the closure of diamond, gold, platinum, and chromium mines. The cost of living and inflation (now in triple figures) have soared amid economic chaos. Prices for basic provisions were fixed in 2001.

ECONOMIC PERFORMANCE INDICATOR

Consumer Price Index
GDP
850
600
350
100
-150
Consumer price index 1995=100
GDP 1997=100
1997
1998
1999
2000
2001

ZIMBABWE : MAJOR BUSINESSES

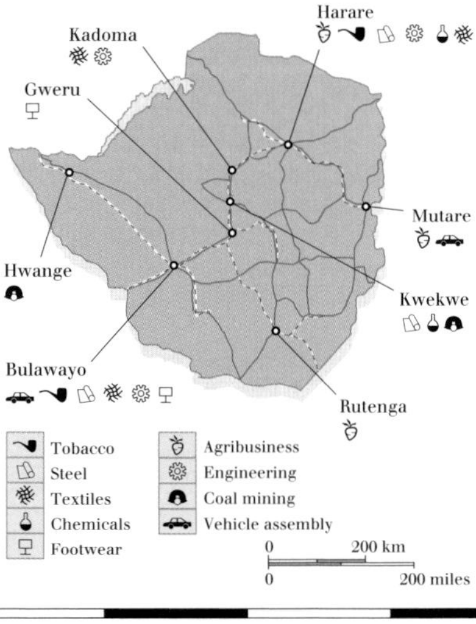
Harare
Kadoma
Gweru
Mutare
Hwange
Kwekwe
Bulawayo
Rutenga
Tobacco
Steel
Textiles
Chemicals
Footwear
Agribusiness
Engineering
Coal mining
Vehicle assembly
0
200 km
0
200 miles

Z

RESOURCES

Electric power 2m kW

13,299 tonnes

Not an oil producer

5.75m cattle, 2.97m goats, 22m chickens

Gold, coal, asbestos, nickel, copper, silver, iron, emeralds, lithium, diamonds

ELECTRICITY GENERATION

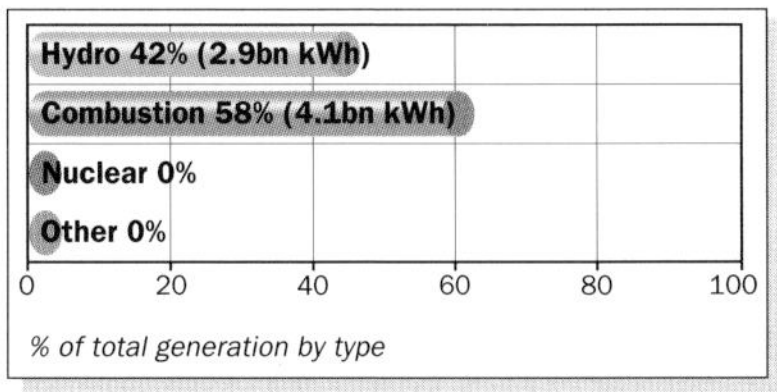
Hydro 42% (2.9bn kWh)
Combustion 58% (4.1bn kWh)
Nuclear 0%
Other 0%
0
20
40
60
80
100
% of total generation by type

Over 40% of Zimbabwe's electricity needs are met by hydropower, notably from the Kariba Dam, jointly owned with Zambia. The state power company is seeking to maximize capacity. In 1991, the government agreed to build an extension facility at Kariba South, and with Zambia a joint HEP plant at Bartoka Gorge. An oil pipeline from Beira, Mozambique, to Mutare has been extended to Harare. Coal production declined by 17% at Hwange in 2000, but Malaysian investments there are set to exploit large deposits.

ZIMBABWE : LAND USE

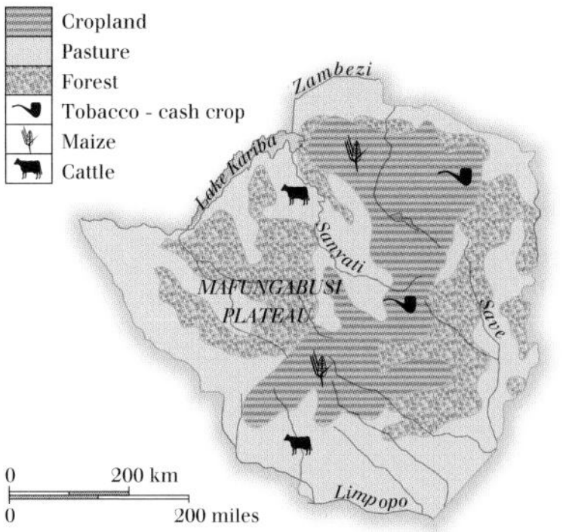
Cropland
Pasture
Forest
Tobacco - cash crop
Maize
Cattle
Zambezi
Lake Kariba
Sanyati
MAFUNGABUSI PLATEAU
Save
Limpopo
0
200 km
0
200 miles

ENVIRONMENT

Sustainability rank: 46th

13% (6% partially protected)

1.4 tonnes per capita

ENVIRONMENTAL TREATIES

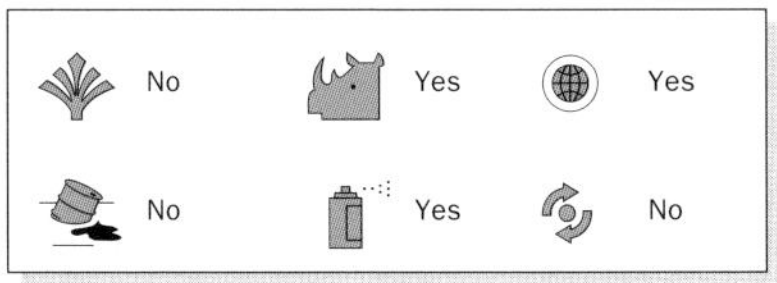
No
Yes
Yes
No
Yes
No

The 1991–1992 drought left half the population in need of drought relief, and used up 20% of public spending.

In communal areas, the land is suffering from overpopulation and overstocking. Deforestation, soil erosion, and deterioration of wildlife and water resources are widespread.

Measures have been taken to protect the black rhinoceros, including moving animals to safer areas and combating poaching – patrols have killed 150 poachers since 1986. The government also supports a scheme for dehorning rhinos – the horn is the poachers' main target. In 1997 Zimbabwe led the move at the Convention on International Trade in Endangered Species to allow a limited resumption of international trade in ivory. An increase in ivory poaching since 1999 has led to calls for more protection for elephants.

MEDIA

TV ownership low

Daily newspaper circulation 18 per 1000 people

PUBLISHING AND BROADCAST MEDIA

There are 3 daily newspapers, the state-controlled *Herald* and *Chronicle*, and the privately run *Daily News*

1 state-controlled service

1 state-controlled service

The state has a controlling interest in the *Herald* newspaper. Persecution of journalists has increased since a 2002 press law – though the law was challenged in court in 2003.

CRIME

Death penalty in use

21,000 prisoners

Up 17% in 2000–2001

CRIME RATES

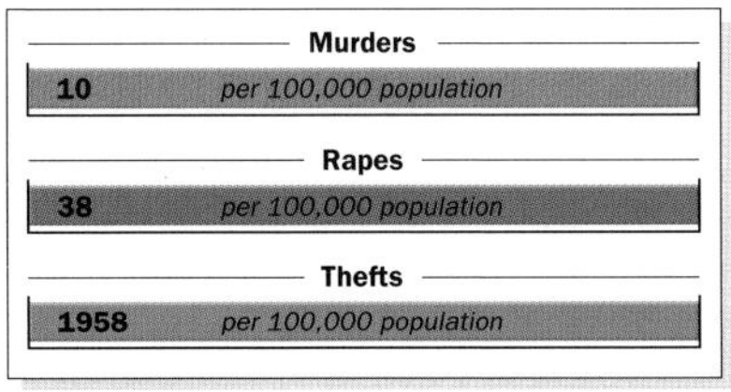
Murders
10
per 100,000 population
Rapes
38
per 100,000 population
Thefts
1958
per 100,000 population

Murder and narcotics-related offenses are rife in urban areas. The illegal occupation of white-owned farms, supported by the government, and electoral violence have led to many deaths. The secret service and the army have been criticized for human rights abuses.

EDUCATION

School leaving age: 12

89%

48,894 students

THE EDUCATION SYSTEM

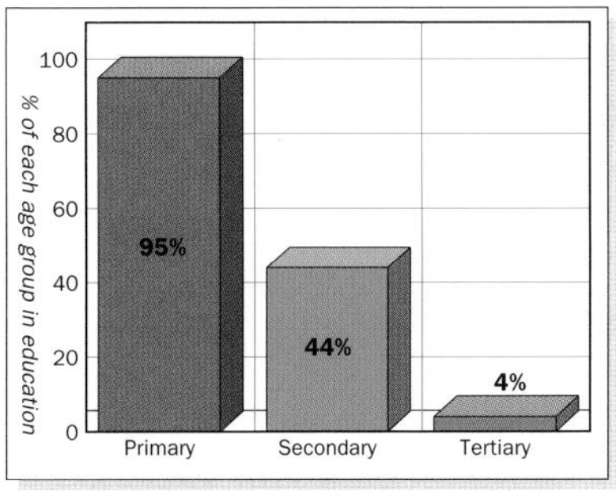
100
80
60
40
20
0
% of each age group in education
95%
44%
4%
Primary
Secondary
Tertiary

Improving education has been one of ZANU–PF's great successes. In barely ten years, primary school attendance rose from 820,000 to some 2.3 million. Education is compulsory and instruction is in English. Fees were introduced after 1992. There are two state-run universities, at Harare and Bulawayo; the government encourages vocational training to create a workforce with skills in agriculture, medicine, and engineering.

HEALTH

Welfare state health benefits

1 per 7143 people

AIDS, tuberculosis, accidents, malaria, heart disease, cancers

The largest threat to health is AIDS. It has dramatically reduced average life expectancy, created around a million orphans, and kills 3000 people a week. A belated AIDS program, offering generic drugs, is now in place. Malaria and tuberculosis account for many other deaths. The beleaguered health system is free for the poor.

SPENDING

GDP/cap. increase

CONSUMPTION AND SPENDING

29 per 1000 population

19 per 1000 population

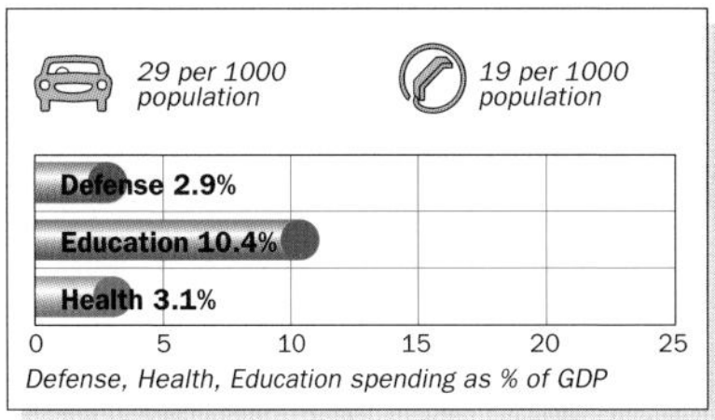
Defense 2.9%
Education 10.4%
Health 3.1%
0
5
10
15
20
25
Defense, Health, Education spending as % of GDP

Socialist policies in the 1980s lessened the gap between blacks and whites. But currency depreciation and inflation have since greatly reduced real wages.

WORLD RANKING

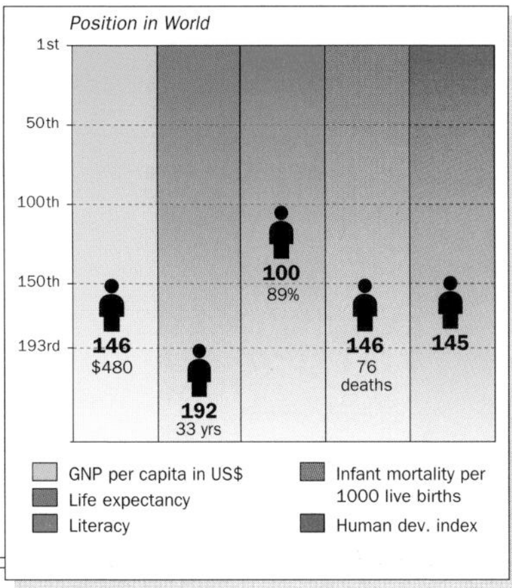
Position in World
1st
50th
100th
150th
193rd
146
$480
192
33 yrs
100
89%
146
76
deaths
145
GNP per capita in US$
Life expectancy
Literacy
Infant mortality per 1000 live births
Human dev. index

Z

Overseas Territories & Dependencies

DESPITE THE RAPID process of decolonization since 1945 (pages 52–55), roughly seven million people around the world still live in nonsovereign territories under the protection of the UK, the US, France, Netherlands, Denmark, Norway, Australia, or New Zealand. These remnants of former colonial empires may have persisted for economic, strategic, or political reasons. Hong Kong and Macao reverted to Chinese control in the late 1990s. Others await political developments, such as referenda, which will determine their future status. Finally, there is a large group of territories that are considered too small, remote, or weak to be able to survive as independent states.

Svalbard (to Norway)
BARENTS SEA
Jan Mayen (to Norway)
Faeroe Islands (to Denmark)
NORWAY
BALTIC SEA
NORTH SEA
Isle of Man (to UK)
UNITED KINGDOM
DENMARK
NETHERLANDS
Channel Islands: Guernsey and Jersey (to UK)
FRANCE
EUROPE
ASIA
SEA OF JAPAN
Gibraltar (to UK)
MEDITERRANEAN SEA
YELLOW SEA
EAST CHINA SEA
AFRICA
ARABIAN SEA
Paracel Islands (Disputed)
SOUTH CHINA SEA
Northern Mariana Islands (to US)
Guam (to US)
Spratly Islands (Disputed)
British Indian Ocean Territory (to UK)
Cocos (Keeling) Islands (to Australia)
JAVA SEA
ARAFURA SEA
Ascension (Administered by St Helena)
Mayotte (to France)
Christmas Island (to Australia)
Ashmore & Cartier Islands (to Australia)
St Helena (to UK)
ATLANTIC OCEAN
Réunion (to France)
Europa (Administered by Réunion)
Bassas da India (Administered by Réunion)
INDIAN OCEAN
AUSTRALIA
Tristan da Cunha (Administered by St Helena)
Gough Island (Administered by St Helena)
Amsterdam Island
St. Paul Island
French Southern & Antarctic Territories (France)
Crozet Islands
Kerguelen
Heard & McDonald Islands (to Australia)
Bouvet Island (to Norway)

United Kingdom

THE UK STILL HAS THE LARGEST number of overseas territories in the world. What were previously known as Crown colonies and dependent territories are now British overseas territories. Residents are full British citizens. Most territories sustain a large degree of local autonomy, and if they express a consitutional desire for independence then they may have it, as long as they can form a viable independent country. The Isle of Man and the Channel Islands retain their special connection as Crown dependencies, neither a part of the UK nor colonies.

French Southern and Antarctic territories are not included in the following section. Any territories which involve an Antarctic claim are not shown.

New Zealand

NEW ZEALAND'S GOVERNMENT has no desire to retain any overseas territories. However, the economic weakness of its dependent territory Tokelau and its freely associated states, Niue and the Cook Islands, has forced New Zealand to remain responsible for their foreign policy and defense.

UNITED STATES OF AMERICA

THE OVERSEAS TERRITORIES OF THE US have been seen as strategically useful, if expensive, parts of its backyard. The US has, in most cases, given the local population a say in deciding its own status. Thus, full sovereignty has been granted to three successor states of the former US-administered UN Trust Territory of the Pacific Islands. A US commonwealth territory, such as Puerto Rico, has a greater level of independence than that of a US unincorporated or external territory.

OVERSEAS TERRITORIES AND DEPENDENCIES
Australia
New Zealand
United Kingdom
United States
France
Denmark
Netherlands
Norway
Disputed
ARCTIC OCEAN
BEAUFORT SEA
BERING SEA
NORTH AMERICA
Greenland (to Denmark)
ATLANTIC OCEAN
St Pierre & Miquelon (to France)
UNITED STATES OF AMERICA
Bermuda (to UK)
Turks & Caicos Islands (to UK)
Puerto Rico (to US)
British Virgin Islands (to UK)
Anguilla (to UK)
Virgin Islands (to US)
Guadeloupe (to France)
CARIBBEAN SEA
Netherlands Antilles (to Neth.)
Montserrat (to UK)
Aruba (to Neth.)
Martinique (to France)
Midway Islands (to US)
Gulf of Mexico
Wake Island (to US)
Cayman Islands (to UK)
Navassa Island (to US)
CARIBBEAN SEA
Johnston Atoll (to US)
PACIFIC OCEAN
Clipperton Island (Administered by French Polynesia)
Kingman Reef (to US)
Palmyra Atoll (to US)
French Guiana (to France)
Baker & Howland Islands (to US)
Jarvis Island (to US)
Tokelau (to NZ)
Wallis & Futuna (to France)
Cook Islands (to NZ)
SOUTH AMERICA
American Samoa (to US)
French Polynesia (to France)
Niue (to NZ)
Pitcairn Islands (to UK)
New Caledonia (to France)
Norfolk Island (to Australia)
NEW ZEALAND
Falkland Islands (to UK)
South Georgia and South Sandwich Islands (to UK)

FRANCE

FRENCH *TERRITOIRES D'OUTRE-MER* are considered an indivisible part of the French Republic. As a result, France has developed economic ties, and stressed the advantage of interdependence over independence, with its overseas territories. A distinct hierarchy has been developed. Overseas *départements*, officially part of France, have their own governments. Territorial *collectivités* are administered by a French-appointed commissioner and a locally elected council, while overseas *territoires* have varying degrees of autonomy.

American Samoa

STATUS: Unincorporated territory of the US **CLAIMED:** 1900
CAPITAL: Pago Pago **POP.:** 68,688 **DENSITY:** 352/km² (916/mi²)

COMPRISING THE EASTERN half of the Samoan islands, American Samoa sits on the edge of Polynesia in the South Pacific Ocean. Though Christianity, introduced in the 19th century, has taken a very firm hold – Samoa is known as the "Bible Belt" of the Pacific – the traditional and conservative *fa'a Samoa* (Samoan way of life) continues to dominate the islands' culture. At its base is the extended family, the *aiga*, while traditional chiefs, or *matai*, retain their central role in government. Samoa came under the control of the US in 1900, and life there remained largely unchanged until a US-led drive for modernization in the 1960s. Along with better health care and industrial development, *fa'a Amerika* also meant unemployment, pollution, and rising petty crime fueled by alcohol. Tuna processed by Pago Pago's canneries represent 93% of American Samoa's exports. Efforts to diversify include the development of other light industries and tourism.

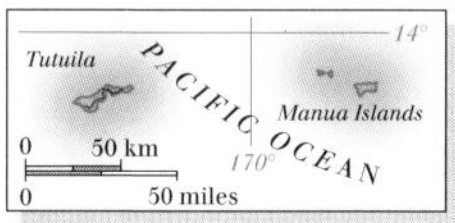
Tutuila
PACIFIC OCEAN
Manua Islands
14°
170°
0 50 km
0 50 miles

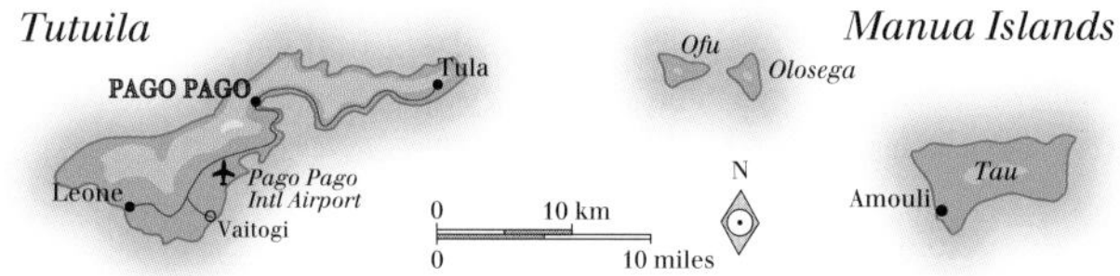
Tutuila
PAGO PAGO
Tula
Leone
Pago Pago Intl Airport
Vaitogi
0 10 km
0 10 miles
N
Ofu
Olosega
Manua Islands
Amouli
Tau

Anguilla

STATUS: British overseas territory **CLAIMED:** 1650
CAPITAL: The Valley **POP.:** 12,446 **DENSITY:** 130/km² (336/mi²)

LYING IN THE CENTER of the Leeward Islands, in the Caribbean, Anguilla has a subtropical climate, the heat and humidity being tempered by trade winds. Lumped by the UK into a joint colonial administration with St. Kitts and Nevis, Anguillans took up arms to protect their dependent status in 1967 when St. Kitts and Nevis were awarded internal self-government. Lacking any major industry, Anguilla relied on the economic stability that came with being an overseas territory. In the 1980s the island's government resolved to introduce a tourist industry and targeted the luxury end of the market. Tourism is now Anguilla's main source of income. Almost 50,000 tourists, around 60% from the US, take their vacations in Anguilla every year.

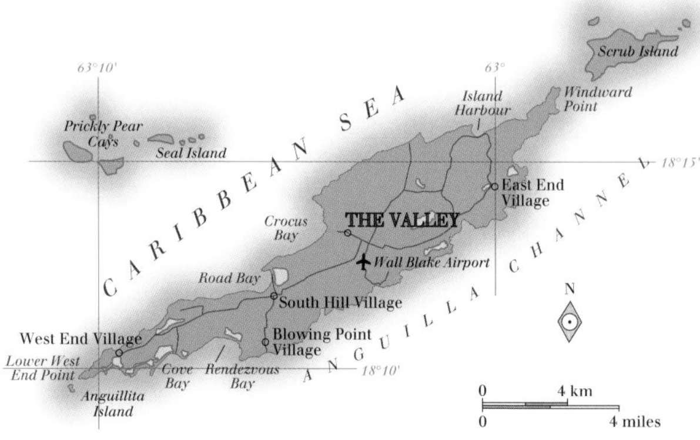
Scrub Island
63°10'
63°
Island Harbour
Windward Point
Prickly Pear Cays
Seal Island
CARIBBEAN SEA
18°15'
East End Village
THE VALLEY
Crocus Bay
Wall Blake Airport
Road Bay
South Hill Village
West End Village
Blowing Point Village
ANGUILLA CHANNEL
Lower West End Point
Cove Bay
Rendezvous Bay
18°10'
Anguillita Island
N
0 4 km
0 4 miles

Aruba

STATUS: Autonomous part of the Netherlands **CLAIMED:** 1643
CAPITAL: Oranjestad **POP.:** 70,441 **DENSITY:** 365/km² (939/mi²)

THE MOST DEVELOPED island among the Dutch Caribbean territories, Aruba lies 25 km (15 miles) off the coast of Venezuela. Its tropical climate is moderated by constant trade winds sweeping in from the Atlantic. Formerly the richest island in the Netherlands Antilles, Aruba became a separate dependency of the Netherlands in 1986. Transition to full independence, expected in 1996, was halted in 1994 after an agreement was reached between the governments of the Netherlands, Aruba, and the Netherlands Antilles. The Netherlands voiced concern over the island's security and the danger of its becoming a base for narcotics trafficking, and the Aruban government questioned the desirability of full independence, citing high unemployment and economic instability.

Since 1986, the economy of Aruba, formerly dependent on oil refining, has diversified. Tourism and offshore finance have become the most important sectors of the economy, and there are now more than 700,000 visitors annually; over 60% of them come from the US. However, the rapid expansion of tourism has put considerable strain on Aruba's infrastructure, and some attempt has been made to restrict the number of visitors. At the same time facilities have been improved to encourage the growth of a data-processing industry.

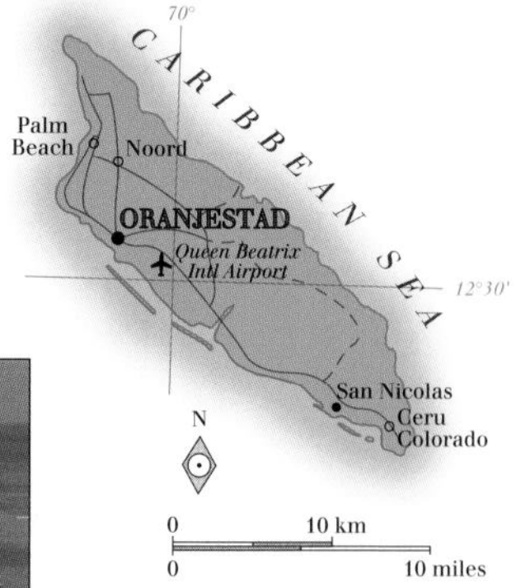
70°
CARIBBEAN SEA
Palm Beach
Noord
ORANJESTAD
Queen Beatrix Intl Airport
12°30'
San Nicolas
Seru Colorado
N
0 10 km
0 10 miles

***Palm Beach, Aruba,** also known as the Turquoise Coast, lies on the western side of the island. The beach stretches for 10 km (6 miles) and is the site of a low-rise beach resort.*

***Oranjestad,** Aruba's capital, contains many Dutch colonial-style buildings. Though first claimed by the Spanish in 1499, Aruba was colonized by the Dutch in the 17th century.*

Aruba's cooperation with the US in the region includes support for its actions against narcotics trafficking from South America, and since the closure of the US base in Panama in 1999, US aircraft have used bases on the island to launch reconnaissance flights. Those who oppose this cooperation fear that it could drag Aruba unnecessarily into the civil conflict in Colombia.

LAND HEIGHT: above Sea Level; 200m/656ft; 500m/1640ft; 1000m/3281ft; 1500m/4572ft; above 2000m/6562ft

BERMUDA

STATUS: British overseas territory **CLAIMED:** 1612
CAPITAL: Hamilton **POP.:** 63,960 **DENSITY:** 1207/km² (3198/mi²)

SITUATED MORE THAN 1000 km (650 miles) off the coast of the US, Bermuda consists of a chain of more than 150 coral islands. The Gulf Stream, flowing between Bermuda and the eastern seaboard of the US, keeps the climate mild and humid. Bermuda is racially mixed; some 60% of the population are of mostly European extraction. Racial tension has lessened since the 1960s and 1970s. A more representative electoral system was established after a Royal Commission visited Bermuda in 1978.

For 30 years after the first general election, held in 1968, Bermuda was ruled by the conservative United Bermuda Party (UBP). Its veteran leader, Sir John Swan, resigned as prime minister and party leader in 1995, when a referendum decisively rejected his campaign for independence from the UK. In a general election in 1998 the UBP was heavily defeated by the Progressive Labour Party, which pledged to suppress its proindependence aspirations while in government. Major issues are the social and economic challenges posed by the withdrawal in 1995 of both the US naval base and the British military base, environmental issues, and narcotics trafficking. Bermuda is overwhelmingly a service economy. Lilies are grown for export, but few other agricultural products are grown in sufficient quantity, and the islands are heavily dependent on food imports.

Tourist figures have been falling steadily, but tourism is still a significant industry, most visitors coming from the US. However, financial services have become the most important sector of the economy, helping to maintain one of the highest per capita incomes in the world. The government has attempted to head off international criticism of its financial environment through a series of reforms. Bermuda also operates one of the world's largest flag-of-convenience shipping fleets.

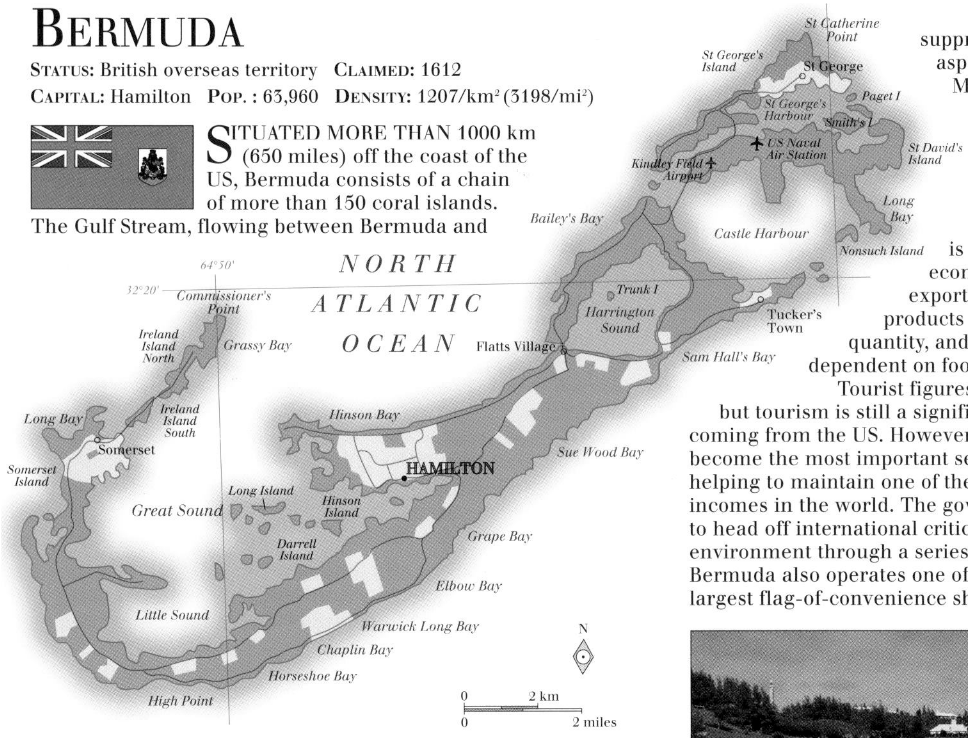
St Catherine Point
St George's Island
St George
Paget I
St George's Harbour
Smith's I
US Naval Air Station
St David's Island
Kindley Field Airport
Long Bay
Bailey's Bay
Castle Harbour
Nonsuch Island
64°50'
32°20'
NORTH ATLANTIC OCEAN
Commissioner's Point
Trunk I
Harrington Sound
Tucker's Town
Ireland Island North
Grassy Bay
Flatts Village
Sam Hall's Bay
Long Bay
Ireland Island South
Hinson Bay
Somerset
Sue Wood Bay
Somerset Island
HAMILTON
Long Island
Hinson Island
Great Sound
Grape Bay
Darrell Island
Elbow Bay
Little Sound
Warwick Long Bay
Chaplin Bay
Horseshoe Bay
High Point
N
0 2 km
0 2 miles

***Bermuda** has one of the highest densities of golf courses in the world. Nine courses have now been developed.*

BRITISH INDIAN OCEAN TERRITORY

STATUS: British overseas territory **CLAIMED:** 1814
CAPITAL: Diego Garcia **POP.:** 3500 **DENSITY:** 58/km² (152/mi²)

THE BRITISH Indian Ocean Territory, or Chagos Islands, lies in the middle of the Indian Ocean. The coral atolls are uninhabited, except for the UK–US military base on Diego Garcia, and the UK has undertaken to cede the islands to Mauritius when they are no longer required. In 2000 the Ilois people, evicted by the UK from the islands in 1968, won the right in the UK High Court to return, but face strong resistance from the US.

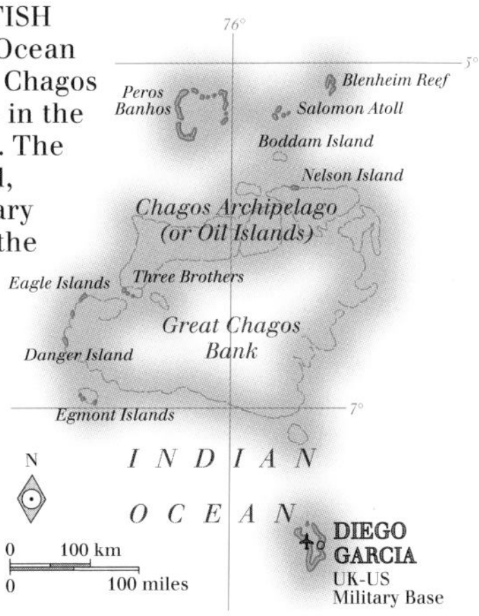
76°
5°
Peros Banhos
Blenheim Reef
Salomon Atoll
Boddam Island
Nelson Island
Chagos Archipelago (or Oil Islands)
Eagle Islands
Three Brothers
Great Chagos Bank
Danger Island
Egmont Islands
7°
INDIAN OCEAN
N
DIEGO GARCIA
UK-US Military Base
0 100 km
0 100 miles

BRITISH VIRGIN ISLANDS

STATUS: British overseas territory **CLAIMED:** 1672
CAPITAL: Road Town **POP.:** 21,272 **DENSITY:** 139/km² (361/mi²)

AN ARCHIPELAGO of 60 Caribbean islands, 15 of them inhabited, the British Virgin Islands lie at the northwestern end of the Leeward Islands chain. Tourism, now a major economic activity, is suited to the tropical climate, but there is concern about its effect on the environment. There are also fears that traditional place-names are being altered to be more tourist-friendly. The offshore finance sector is important, and has been more tightly regulated since 1990, following scandals involving foreign firms registered in the territory.

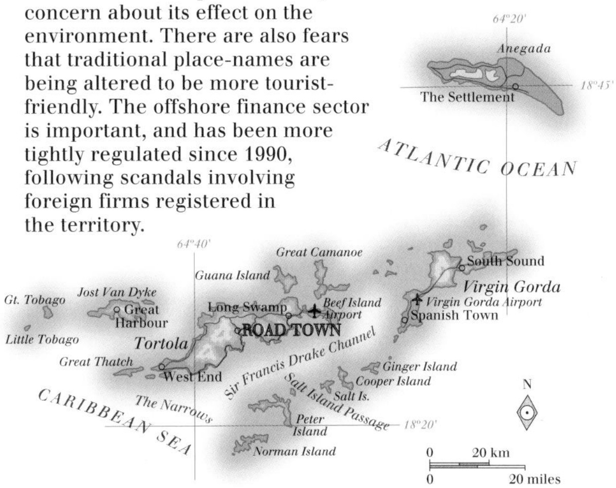
64°20'
Anegada
18°45'
The Settlement
ATLANTIC OCEAN
64°40'
Great Camanoe
South Sound
Guana Island
Virgin Gorda
Gt. Tobago
Jost Van Dyke
Great Harbour
Long Swamp
Beef Island Airport
Virgin Gorda Airport
Spanish Town
ROAD TOWN
Little Tobago
Tortola
Sir Francis Drake Channel
Great Thatch
West End
Ginger Island
Cooper Island
Salt Island Passage
Salt Is.
The Narrows
CARIBBEAN SEA
Peter Island
18°20'
Norman Island
N
0 20 km
0 20 miles

CAYMAN ISLANDS

STATUS: British overseas territory **CLAIMED:** 1670
CAPITAL: George Town **POP.:** 36,273 **DENSITY:** 140/km² (363/mi²)

THE LARGEST OF BRITAIN'S territories in the Caribbean, the Cayman Islands lie 225 km (140 miles) west of Jamaica and south of Cuba. The abundance of exotic wildlife, especially marine life, is a powerful draw for tourists. Grand Cayman is credited as the home of modern scuba diving, the first ever specialist shop opening there in 1957. The islanders have rejected greater autonomy, persuaded that their economic stability is linked to their status as an overseas territory. Thanks to the absence of tax and foreign-exchange controls, the islands form one of the world's largest offshore financial centers, but tourism continues to underpin the economy.

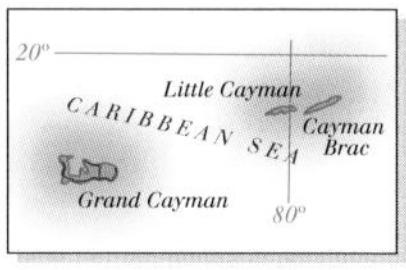
20°
Little Cayman
CARIBBEAN SEA
Cayman Brac
Grand Cayman
80°

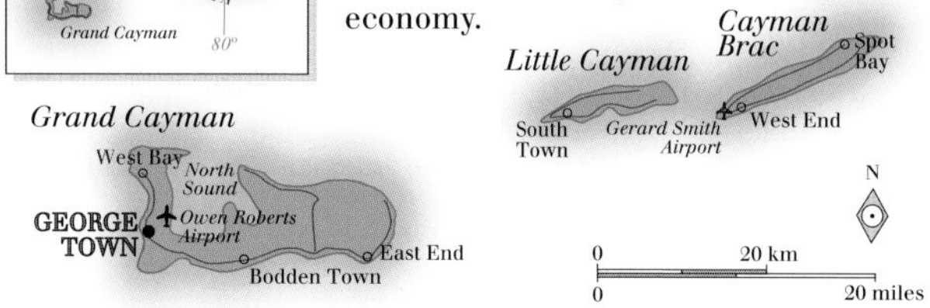
Little Cayman
Cayman Brac
Spot Bay
South Town
Gerard Smith Airport
West End
Grand Cayman
West Bay
North Sound
GEORGE TOWN
Owen Roberts Airport
Bodden Town
East End
N
0 20 km
0 20 miles

CHRISTMAS ISLAND

STATUS: Australian external territory **CLAIMED:** 1958
CAPITAL: Flying Fish Cove **POP.:** 474 **DENSITY:** 4/km² (9/mi²)

SO NAMED because it was sighted on Christmas Day in 1643, Christmas Island lies in the Indian Ocean, 380 km (240 miles) south of Java. Its population is mostly Malay and Chinese, descended from laborers imported to mine rich phosphate deposits. A national park covers some 70% of the island. In 2001 Australia agreed with Russia to begin construction of a major rocket-launching site on the island.

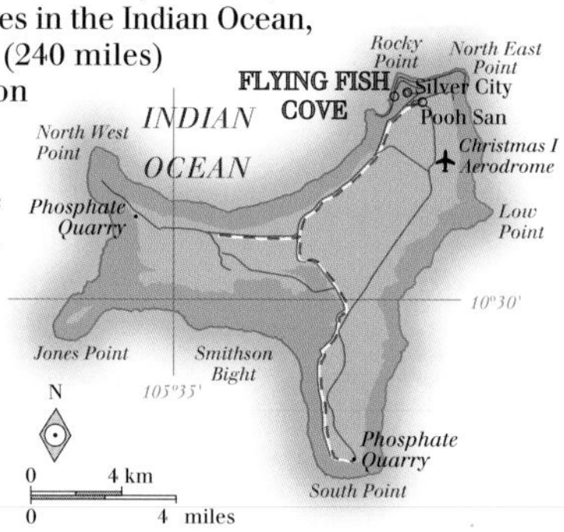
Rocky Point
North East Point
FLYING FISH COVE
Silver City
Poon San
INDIAN OCEAN
North West Point
Christmas I Aerodrome
Phosphate Quarry
Low Point
10°30'
Jones Point
Smithson Bight
105°35'
N
Phosphate Quarry
South Point
0 4 km
0 4 miles

COCOS (KEELING) ISLANDS

STATUS: Australian external territory **CLAIMED:** 1955
CAPITAL: West Island **POP.:** 632 **DENSITY:** 45/km² (126/mi²)

IN ALL, 27 coral atolls make up the Cocos (Keeling) Islands. Situated in the Indian Ocean, roughly halfway between Australia and Sri Lanka, they have been part of the Northern Territory electoral district since 1992. The inhabited islands are the European-dominated West Island and Home Island, which has a mainly Cocos Malay community. Coconuts are the sole cash crop.

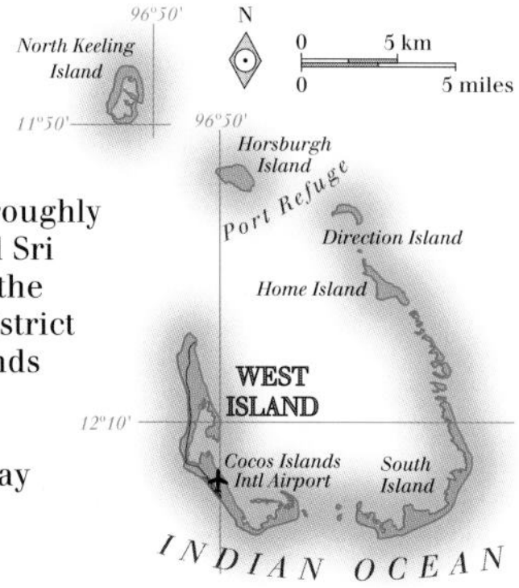
96°50'
North Keeling Island
N
0 5 km
0 5 miles
11°50'
96°50'
Horsburgh Island
Port Refuge
Direction Island
Home Island
WEST ISLAND
12°10'
Cocos Islands Intl Airport
South Island
INDIAN OCEAN

COOK ISLANDS

STATUS: Territory in free association with New Zealand **CLAIMED:** 1901
CAPITAL: Avarua **POP.:** 20,811 **DENSITY:** 88/km² (226/mi²)

LYING IN THE MIDDLE of the South Pacific 3000 km (1900 miles) from New Zealand, the Cook Islands are a combination of 24 coral atolls and volcanic islands. Achieving self-government in 1965, they have adopted a diversified economy focusing primarily on tourism and banking, but with significant trade in giant clams and pearls.

Depopulation is of serious concern, as over 40,000 of the indigenous Maori population have migrated, seeing greater opportunities beyond the islands, and now live in New Zealand and Australia. This outflow of labor poses a major problem for the islands' future development, though remittances to relatives form an important source of income.

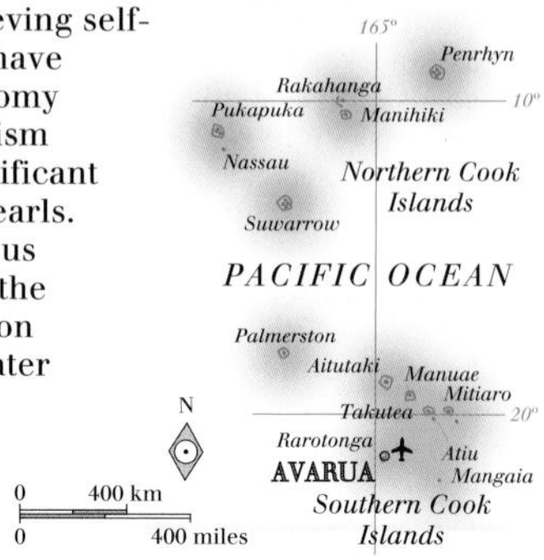
165°
Penrhyn
Rakahanga
Pukapuka
Manihiki
10°
Nassau
Northern Cook Islands
Suwarrow
PACIFIC OCEAN
Palmerston
Aitutaki
Manuae
Mitiaro
Takutea
20°
N
Rarotonga
AVARUA
Atiu
Mangaia
Southern Cook Islands
0 400 km
0 400 miles

The government of the Cook Islands, headed since 2002 by centrist Prime Minister Robert Woonton, is advised by a traditional council known as the House of Ariki. It is seeking a program of political reform, including devolving administration to the outer islands and cutting back an expensive bureaucracy.

FAEROE ISLANDS

STATUS: Self-governing territory of Denmark **CLAIMED:** 1380
CAPITAL: Tórshavn **POP.:** 46,011 **DENSITY:** 33/km² (85/mi²)

MIDWAY BETWEEN Scotland and Iceland in the north Atlantic, the Faeroe Islands have a moderate climate for their latitude – a result of the warm Gulf Stream current. Home rule since 1948 has given the Faeroese a strong sense of national identity – they voted against joining the European Communities with Denmark in 1973, but now have favorable terms of trade with most EU members. Fishing is the dominant industry, providing over 90% of exports. In the face of international criticism, the Faeroese have continued their traditional cull of pilot whales and bottle-nosed dolphins. Sheep farming is important, and there is a small textile industry which exports traditional woolens and puffin and eider-duck feathers.

Denmark's moves toward ever closer European integration have strengthened calls in the Faeroes for full independence. Negotiations to establish a "sovereign nation" under the Danish monarchy began in 1998. However, the Danish government's threat in 2001 to suspend subsidies to the islands quashed calls for a referendum.

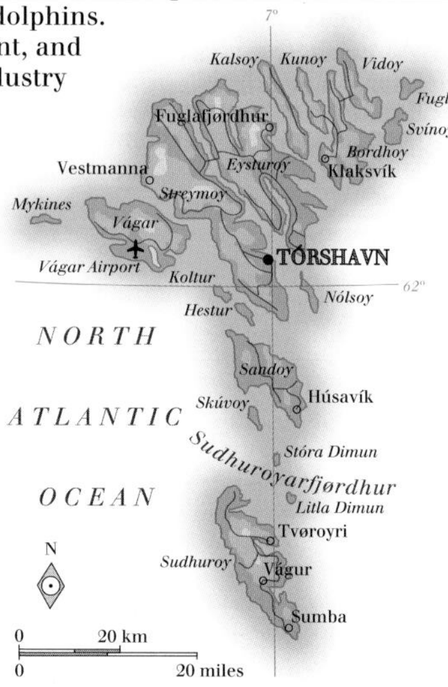
7°
Kalsoy
Kunoy
Vidoy
Fugloy
Svínoy
Fuglafjordhur
Bordhoy
Vestmanna
Eysturoy
Klaksvík
Mykines
Streymoy
Vágar
TÓRSHAVN
Vágar Airport
Koltur
Nólsoy
62°
Hestur
NORTH
Sandoy
ATLANTIC
Skúvoy
Húsavík
Sudhuroyarfjørdhur
Stóra Dimun
Litla Dimun
OCEAN
Tvøroyri
N
Sudhuroy
Vágur
Sumba
0 20 km
0 20 miles

LAND HEIGHT above Sea Level 200m/656ft 500m/1640ft 1000m/3281ft 1500m/4572ft above 2000m/6562ft

FALKLAND ISLANDS

STATUS: British overseas territory **CLAIMED:** 1832
CAPITAL: Port Stanley **POP.:** 2967 **DENSITY:** 0.24/km² (0.63/mi²)

SITUATED IN THE South Atlantic Ocean, over 12,000 km (7440 miles) from the UK, the Falkland Islands are influenced by the cold Antarctic current. The main islands of East and West Falkland and the hundreds of outlying islands have a cool, temperate climate with frequent strong winds.

The islands gained international attention with the Argentine invasion, and subsequent British recapture, in 1982. Since then, the UK government has invested heavily in a "Fortress Falklands" policy. A new runway and a military base to house an enlarged garrison were built at Mount Pleasant. The islanders, for their part, are determined to maintain the political status quo, but in 1999 improving relations led to the restoration of scheduled air connections with Argentina. Since the Falklands War, the economy of the islands has prospered. Falklanders invested heavily in schools, roads, and tourism in a fresh drive for a strong identity. By 1987, the Falklands had become financially solvent through the sale of fishing licenses. Though sales by Argentina of cheaper, less restrictive licenses caused a fall in fishing revenues, fishing (mostly of squid) is still the major source of income and employment. Depressed wool prices caused a slump in the fortunes of the sheep-farming industry. The UK and Argentina reached agreement in 1995 on oil exploration, and the discovery of oil reserves in the Falklands' territorial waters is revolutionizing prospects for the economy. Tourist numbers, including birdwatchers, photographers, and military historians, are increasing rapidly.

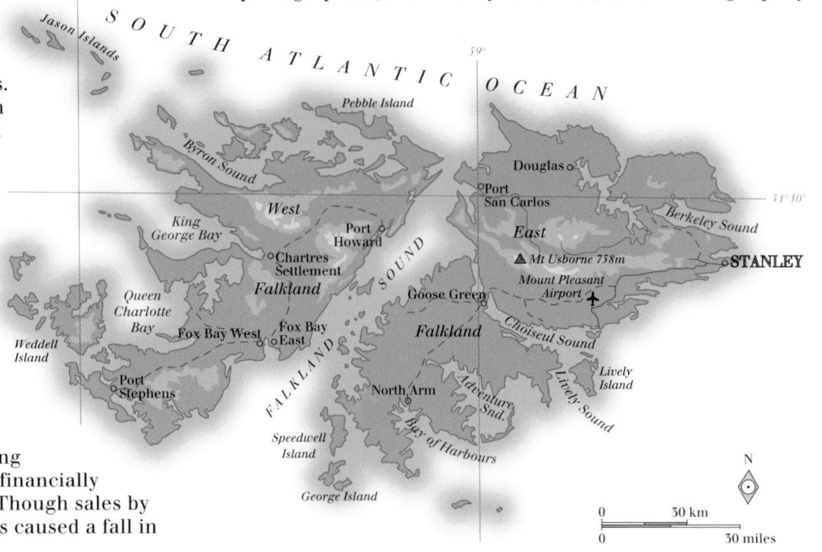
SOUTH ATLANTIC OCEAN
Jason Islands
Pebble Island
Byron Sound
Douglas
Port San Carlos
West
King George Bay
Port Howard
East
Berkeley Sound
Chartres Settlement
Falkland
Mt Usborne 758m
STANLEY
Mount Pleasant Airport
Queen Charlotte Bay
FALKLAND SOUND
Goose Green
Fox Bay West
Fox Bay East
Falkland
Choiseul Sound
Weddell Island
Port Stephens
North Arm
Adventure Snd.
Lively Island
Lively Sound
Speedwell Island
Bay of Harbours
George Island
N
0 30 km
0 30 miles

FRENCH GUIANA

STATUS: French overseas department **CLAIMED:** 1817
CAPITAL: Cayenne **POP.:** 182,333 **DENSITY:** 2/km² (5/mi²)

SANDWICHED BETWEEN Brazil and Suriname, French Guiana is the only remaining colony in South America. A belt of coastal marsh, and an interior of equatorial jungle, combine in a location which was, for years, notorious for the offshore penal colony, Devil's Island. The rainforest, which covers 90% of the territory, is particularly rich in flora and fauna. It harbors over 400,000 species, including more different species of bird than in the whole of Europe.

Concentrated near the coast, the population is ethnically mixed. While 40% are creoles, there are over 20,000 Amerindians and a village of 1000 Hmong who fled civil war in Laos in the 1980s.

Kourou *was selected for the launch of the ESA's Ariane rockets because of its equatorial site. The town has grown from 800 to 23,000 people.*

A campaign for greater autonomy in the late 1970s and early 1980s led to limited devolution of power to a regional council. The grip on local power by the Guianese Socialist Party (PSG) has been undermined since 1993 by a more unified opposition, but it is still the largest party in the regional council.

During the 1990s the people have become increasingly vocal in their condemnation of the French government's perceived indifference to their country's problems, and there were riots in 1996 and 1997 over the education system. The PSG has accordingly campaigned for greater autonomy. As an overseas *département* of metropolitan France, French Guiana is also a region of the EU, but it is heavily dependent on France itself for aid, food, and manufactured goods. It has a number of valuable natural resources, including gold, fishing, and forestry, and also has potential for increased tourism, but these are yet to be fully exploited because of a lack of skilled labor and investment and an underdeveloped infrastructure. The Guiana Space Center, which is situated on the coast at Kourou, has been operational since 1964. From there the Ariane rockets of the European Space Agency (ESA) are launched.

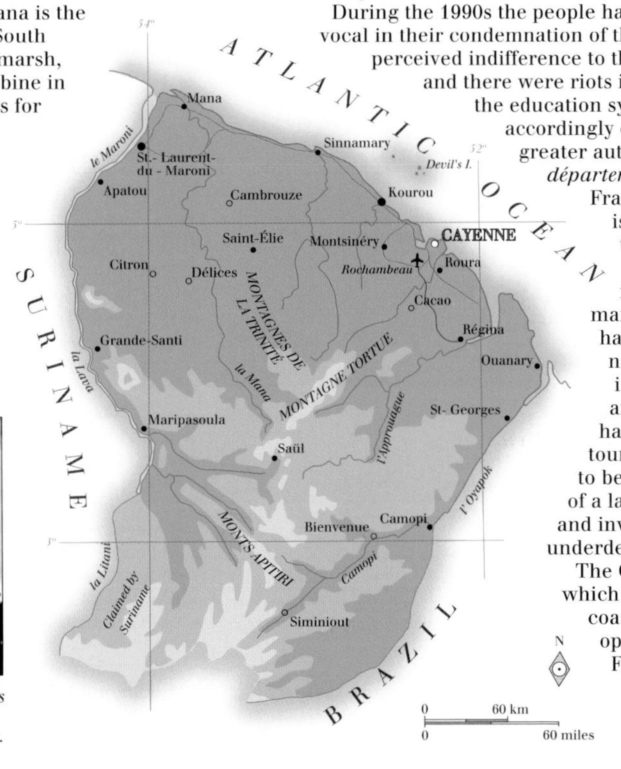
ATLANTIC OCEAN
Mana
le Maroni
St.-Laurent-du-Maroni
Sinnamary
Devil's I.
Apatou
Cambrouze
Kourou
Saint-Élie
Montsinéry
CAYENNE
Citron
Délices
Rochambeau
Roura
Cacao
MONTAGNES DE LA TRINITÉ
Régina
Grande-Santi
MONTAGNE TORTUE
Ouanary
la Lawa
la Mana
L'Approuague
St- Georges
SURINAME
Maripasoula
Saül
l'Oyapok
MONTS APTIRI
Bienvenue
Camopi
la Litani
Claimed by Suriname
Camopi
Siminiout
BRAZIL
N
0 60 km
0 60 miles

POPULATION ○ under 5000 ● under 10 000 ● over 10 000 ○ over 50 000 ◎ over 100 000 ▢ Urban areas AIRPORTS ✈ International ✈ Local

French Polynesia

Status: French overseas territory **Claimed:** 1843
Capital: Papeete **Pop.:** 245,405 **Density:** 70/km² (181/mi²)

A SCATTER OF 130 South Pacific islands and coral atolls over an area the size of Europe combine to form French Polynesia. The average temperature varies during the year between 20°C (68°F) and 29°C (84°F), with rainfall of over 150 cm (58 in). Nearly 75% of the population live on Tahiti, the main island. The French administration has developed the islands with little regard for local wishes, and the 70% West Polynesian (Mahoi) majority have seen their simple, self-sufficient economy transformed into one dependent on the French military and tourism. Nuclear testing on Mururoa Atoll created many jobs, but there was growing opposition, and a final series of tests, held in 1995-1996 despite widespread international protests, provoked local demonstrations and riots in Papeete.

The Polynesian majority has called increasingly for more autonomy, reduced tourism, and the rebuilding of indigenous trade. Future hopes rest largely on new tuna-fishing ventures.

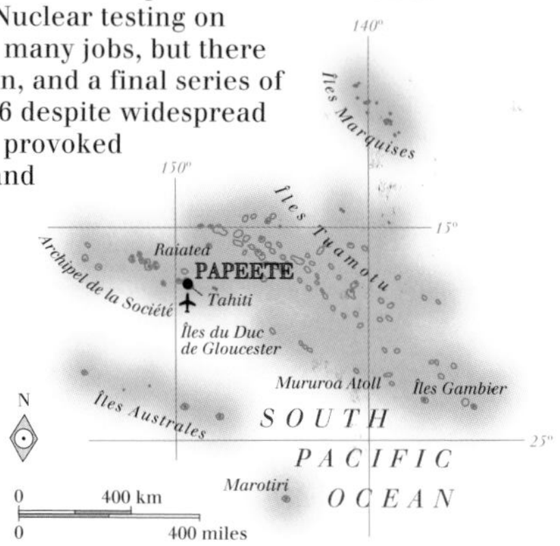
140°
Îles Marquises
150°
Îles Tuamotu
15°
Archipel de la Société
Raiatea
PAPEETE
Tahiti
Îles du Duc de Gloucester
Mururoa Atoll
Îles Gambier
Îles Australes
SOUTH PACIFIC OCEAN
25°
Marotiri
N
0 400 km
0 400 miles

Gibraltar

Status: British overseas territory **Claimed:** 1713
Capital: Gibraltar **Pop.:** 27,714 **Density:** 3959/km² (9238/mi²)

GUARDING THE western entrance to the Mediterranean, Gibraltar has survived on military and marine revenues. However, as Britain has cut defense spending, so its military presence on the Rock has declined. In response Gibraltarians have developed a vigorous offshore banking industry. Strict antismuggling legislation, in force since 1995, has curbed extensive smuggling from north Africa into Spain. Gibraltar's relationship with Britain and Spain remains contentious. The two governments' talks on the territory's status have prompted mass protests from the colony's inhabitants, who have felt sidelined in the discussions, and an unofficial referendum in 2002 rejected joint sovereignty.

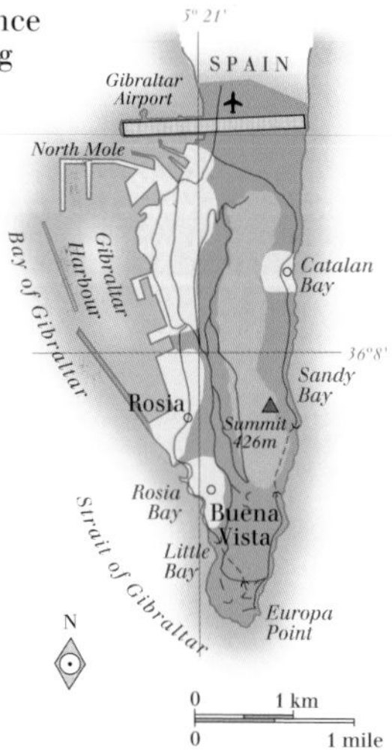
5° 21'
SPAIN
Gibraltar Airport
North Mole
Gibraltar Harbour
Bay of Gibraltar
Catalan Bay
36°8'
Sandy Bay
Rosia
Summit 426m
Rosia Bay
Buena Vista
Little Bay
Strait of Gibraltar
Europa Point
N
0 1 km
0 1 mile

The Rock of Gibraltar. The British excavated 143 caves, and built 50 km (30 miles) of roads and as many km of tunnels, for defensive purposes.

Greenland

Status: Self-governing territory of Denmark **Claimed:** 1380
Capital: Nuuk **Pop.:** 56,376 **Density:** 0.03/km² (0.07/mi²)

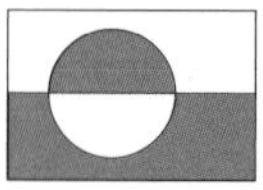

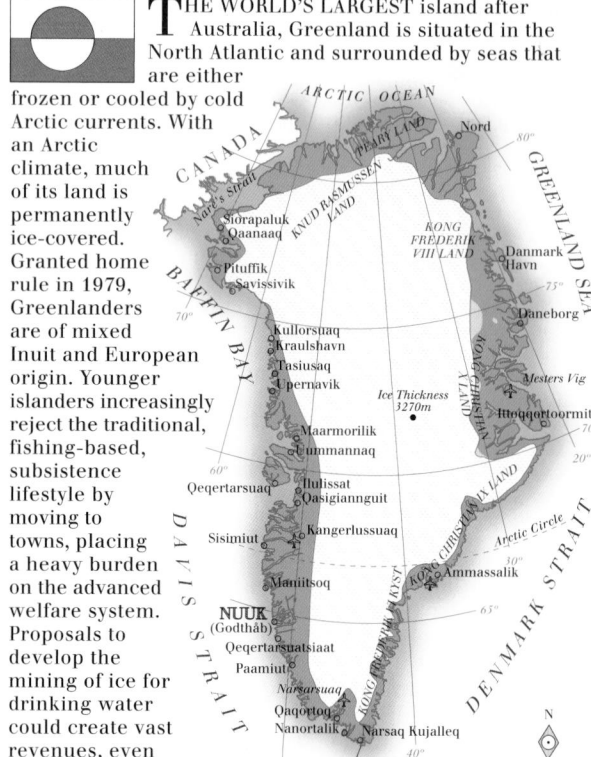

THE WORLD'S LARGEST island after Australia, Greenland is situated in the North Atlantic and surrounded by seas that are either frozen or cooled by cold Arctic currents. With an Arctic climate, much of its land is permanently ice-covered. Granted home rule in 1979, Greenlanders are of mixed Inuit and European origin. Younger islanders increasingly reject the traditional, fishing-based, subsistence lifestyle by moving to towns, placing a heavy burden on the advanced welfare system. Proposals to develop the mining of ice for drinking water could create vast revenues, even raising the possibility of economic independence.

ARCTIC OCEAN
PEARY LAND
Nord
80°
CANADA
Nares Strait
KNUD RASMUSSEN LAND
GREENLAND SEA
Siorapaluk
Qaanaaq
KONG FREDERIK VIII LAND
Danmark Havn
Pituffik
Savissivik
BAFFIN BAY
75°
70°
Daneborg
Kullorsuaq
Kraulshavn
Tasiusaq
Upernavik
KONG CHRISTIAN X LAND
Mesters Vig
Ice Thickness 3270m
Ittoqqortoormiit
Maarmorilik
Uummannaq
70°
20°
60°
Qeqertarsuaq
Ilulissat
Qasigiannguit
KONG CHRISTIAN IX LAND
DAVIS STRAIT
Sisimiut
Kangerlussuaq
Arctic Circle
30°
Ammassalik
DENMARK STRAIT
Maniitsoq
65°
NUUK (Godthåb)
KONG FREDERIK VI KYST
Qeqertarsuatsiaat
Paamiut
Narsarsuaq
Qaqortoq
Nanortalik
Narsaq
Kujalleq
40°
50°
Nunap Isua (Kap Farvel)
N
0 400 km
0 400 miles

Guadeloupe

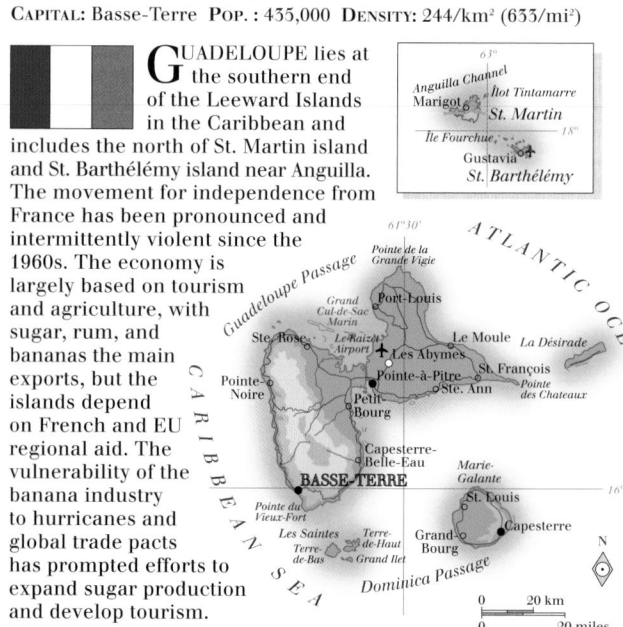

Status: French overseas department **Claimed:** 1635
Capital: Basse-Terre **Pop.:** 435,000 **Density:** 244/km² (633/mi²)

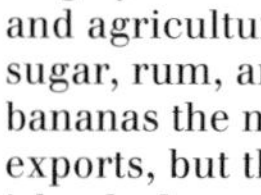

GUADELOUPE lies at the southern end of the Leeward Islands in the Caribbean and includes the north of St. Martin island and St. Barthélémy island near Anguilla. The movement for independence from France has been pronounced and intermittently violent since the 1960s. The economy is largely based on tourism and agriculture, with sugar, rum, and bananas the main exports, but the islands depend on French and EU regional aid. The vulnerability of the banana industry to hurricanes and global trade pacts has prompted efforts to expand sugar production and develop tourism.

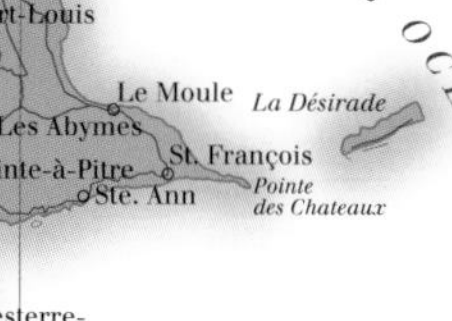
63°
Anguilla Channel
Marigot
Îlot Tintamarre
St. Martin
18°
Île Fourchue
Gustavia
St. Barthélémy

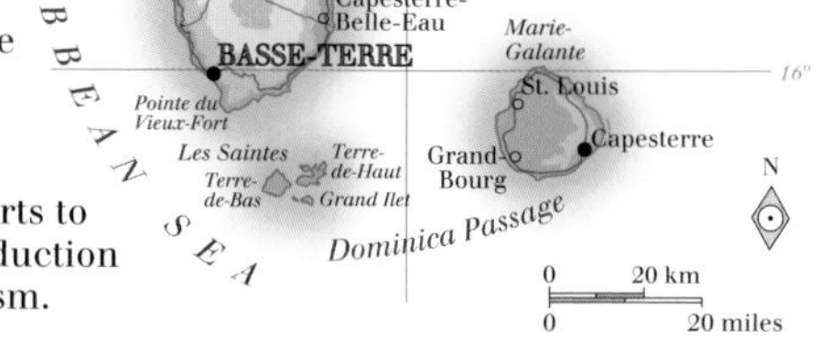
61°30'
ATLANTIC OCEAN
Pointe de la Grande Vigie
Guadeloupe Passage
Grand Cul-de-Sac Marin
Port-Louis
Ste. Rose
Le Raizet Airport
Le Moule
La Désirade
Les Abymes
St. François
Pointe-à-Pitre
Ste. Ann
Pointe des Chateaux
Pointe-Noire
Petit Bourg
CARIBBEAN SEA
Capesterre-Belle-Eau
Marie-Galante
BASSE-TERRE
16°
St. Louis
Pointe du Vieux-Fort
Capesterre
Les Saintes
Terre-de-Haut
Terre-de-Bas
Grand Ilet
Grand-Bourg
Dominica Passage
N
0 20 km
0 20 miles

GUAM

STATUS: Unincorporated territory of the US **CLAIMED:** 1898
CAPITAL: Hagåtña **POP.:** 162,000 **DENSITY:** 295/km² (764/mi²)

THE VOLCANIC island of Guam lies at the southern end of the Mariana archipelago in the Pacific. Its tropical climate has encouraged tourism, though it lies in a region where typhoons are common. Guam's indigenous Chamorro people, who comprise around 40% of the population, dominate the island's political and social life. They are famous for a set of facial expressions, called "eyebrow," which virtually constitutes a language of its own. Though English is the official language, Chamorro is commonly spoken, and in 1998 the spelling of the capital was changed from Agaña to the Chamorran Hagåtña. The US military base, covering one-third of the island, has made Guam strategically important to the US. Military spending and tourism revenues have failed to benefit all islanders, and 23% live below the poverty line. The influx of US culture has also threatened to upset Guam's social stability. Greater independence has been an issue since the early 1980s, with a series of referenda since 1982. A draft Commonwealth Act was rejected by the US Congress after nearly 15 years of deliberation.

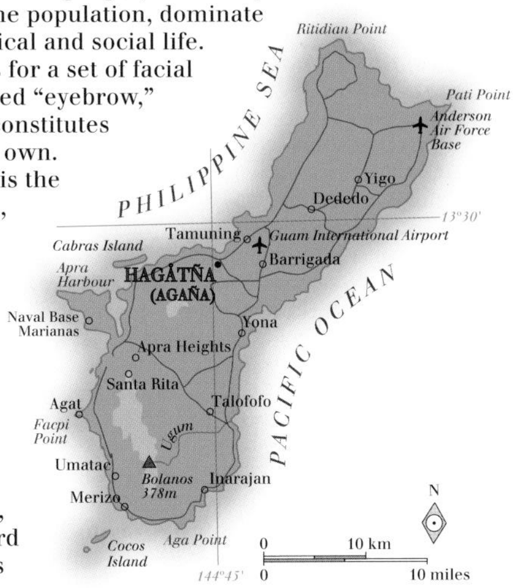

Ritidian Point
PHILIPPINE SEA
Pati Point
Anderson Air Force Base
Yigo
Dededo
13°30'
Tamuning
Guam International Airport
Cabras Island
Apra Harbour
HAGÅTÑA (AGAÑA)
Barrigada
Naval Base Marianas
Yona
Apra Heights
PACIFIC OCEAN
Santa Rita
Agat
Talofofo
Facpi Point
Ugum
Umatac
Bolanos 378m
Inarajan
Merizo
Cocos Island
Aga Point
144°45'
N
0 10 km
0 10 miles

A World War II Japanese anti-aircraft gun emplacement, *Agat Bay. Guam's history as a battle-ground during the Pacific War helps to attract tourists.*

GUERNSEY

STATUS: British Crown dependency **CLAIMED:** 1066
CAPITAL: St. Peter Port **POP.:** 64,587 **DENSITY:** 994/km² (2583/mi²)

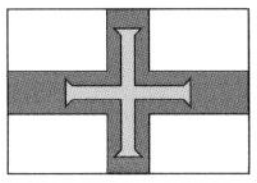

LYING 47 KM (29 miles) off the coast of France, Guernsey and its dependencies form the northwestern part of the Channel Islands, historically part of the Duchy of Normandy. English is the language most commonly used, but the Norman patois is spoken in some villages, and some formal business of the legislature is conducted in French. Travel to France is easier than to the UK: Alderney is only 13 km (8 miles) from the French mainland. Residents on the smaller islands have no need for cars, and life continues in an unhurried manner that has changed little through the centuries. The islanders guard this lifestyle with strict residence laws. Guernsey's mild climate has encouraged the development of tourism and market gardening as major industries. Tomatoes and flowers are produced mainly for the UK market. The low tax system, independent of the UK, has led to a substantial and profitable financial services industry. Many international banks have Guernsey subsidiaries.

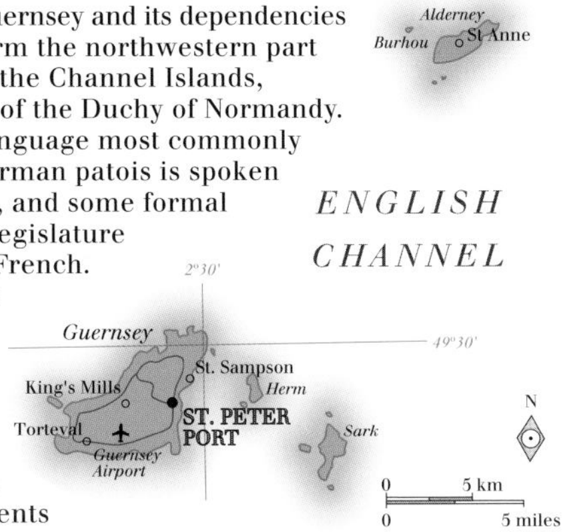

Alderney
Burhou
St Anne
ENGLISH CHANNEL
2°30'
Guernsey
49°30'
King's Mills
St. Sampson
Herm
Torteval
ST. PETER PORT
Sark
Guernsey Airport
N
0 5 km
0 5 miles

ISLE OF MAN

STATUS: British Crown dependency **CLAIMED:** 1765
CAPITAL: Douglas **POP.:** 73,873 **DENSITY:** 129/km² (334/mi²)

LYING HALFWAY BETWEEN England and Northern Ireland in the Irish Sea, the Isle of Man has been inhabited for centuries by the Celtic Manx people. Established by the Vikings in the 9th century, the Manx parliament, the Tynwold, has autonomy from the UK in a number of matters, including taxation, and the death penalty was only officially abolished in 1993. The islanders have used this independence to establish a thriving financial and business sector, which has aided employment as the traditional industries of agriculture and fishing decline. There is still a shellfish industry, specializing in scallops. Tourism is also important: there are around 300,000 visitors each year. Publicity has been increased by the growing number of films being made on the island. Manx culture received a boost in 1993, when the local language, in danger of dying out, began to be taught in the island's schools once more. The Calf of Man, a small uninhabited island, is administered as a nature reserve.

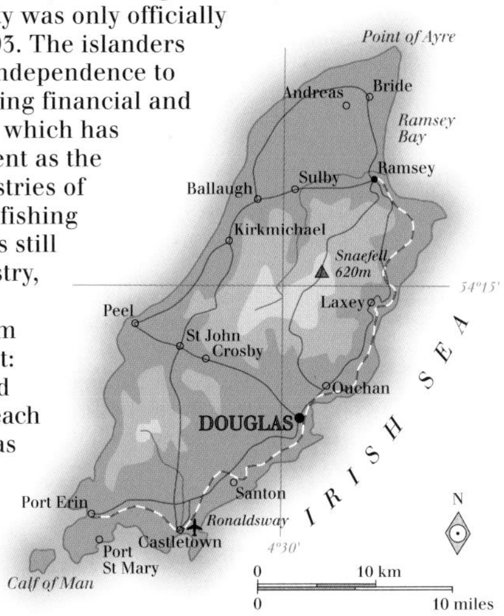

Point of Ayre
Andreas
Bride
Ramsey Bay
Ramsey
Ballaugh
Sulby
Kirkmichael
Snaefell 620m
54°15'
Laxey
Peel
St John
Crosby
IRISH SEA
Onchan
DOUGLAS
Santon
Port Erin
Ronaldsway
Castletown
Port St Mary
4°30'
Calf of Man
N
0 10 km
0 10 miles

The annual TT motorbike race *on the Isle of Man. Thousands of people come to watch the island's famous Touring Trophy race.*

Jersey

Status: British Crown dependency **Claimed:** 1066
Capital: St. Helier **Pop.:** 89,775 **Density:** 774/km² (1995/mi²)

THE BAILIWICK OF JERSEY, the largest of the Channel Islands, lies some 22 km (14 miles) from the coast of Normandy in France. The official language (since 1960) is English, but French is still used in the courts. The island has a mild climate owing to the Gulf Stream, fine beaches, and more sunshine than anywhere else in the British Isles. Jersey has its own legislative and taxation systems which are a blend of the French and British versions. The Jersey States Assembly is one of the oldest legislative bodies in the world. Members stand as independents, rather than for political parties. It is considered a "Peculiar" of the UK monarchy, and has the right to reject "unacceptable" UK laws.

Historically, agriculture has been Jersey's most important industry, with dairy cows its most famous export, closely followed by early-harvested potatoes, tomatoes, and flowers. By the end of the 20th century, however, farming had been eclipsed by the rise of offshore finance and tourism. The growth of these sectors, and rigid controls on the rights of residence, have ensured high living standards for most of the inhabitants. Jersey is also host to a large Portuguese community which works in the island's tourist industry.

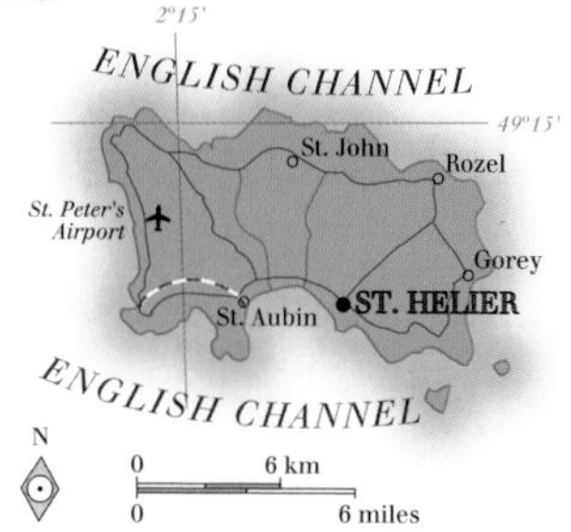
2°15'
ENGLISH CHANNEL
49°15'
St. John
Rozel
St. Peter's Airport
Gorey
St. Aubin
ST. HELIER
ENGLISH CHANNEL
N
0 6 km
0 6 miles

Johnston Atoll

Status: Unincorporated territory of the US **Claimed:** 1858
Capital: *Not applicable* **Pop.:** *Not applicable*

JOHNSTON ATOLL LIES 1150 km (714 miles) southwest of Hawaii. The atoll consists of a coral reef, two highly modified natural islands, Johnston and Sand, and two completely man-made islands, Akau (North) and Hikina (East). The islands, which were used by the US for nuclear weapons tests, were seriously contaminated with plutonium in 1962, when a nuclear missile exploded during testing. Regular tests began in 1971, and until 2000 the islands were also used for the storage of nuclear material and the destruction of chemical and biological weapons, including sarin nerve gas and the defoliant Agent Orange. Cleanup operations began in 2000. The only inhabitants left are US government personnel and civilian contractors who maintain the plant. The islands have also been designated by the US as a wildlife refuge: a breeding place for seabirds and green turtles. The US army intends to evacuate the base entirely by 2004.

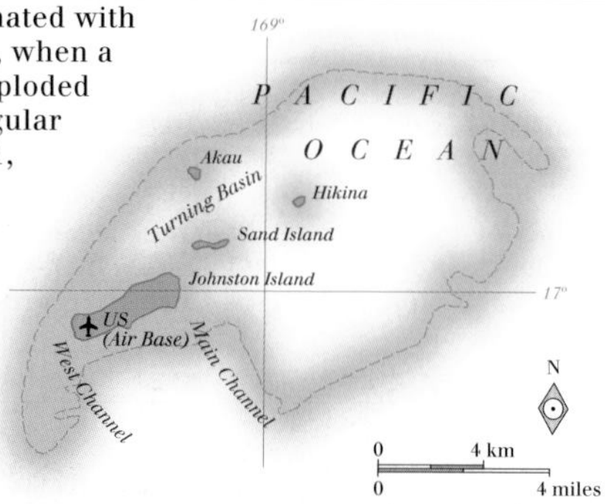
169°
PACIFIC OCEAN
Akau
Turning Basin
Hikina
Sand Island
Johnston Island
17°
US (Air Base)
West Channel
Main Channel
N
0 4 km
0 4 miles

Martinique

Status: French overseas department **Claimed:** 1635
Capital: Fort-de-France **Pop.:** 388,000 **Density:** 344/km² (890/mi²)

CHRISTOPHER COLUMBUS described Martinique as "the most beautiful country in the world." It lies in the middle of the Caribbean Windward Islands but has retained remarkably close links both culturally and economically to mainland France. The island is dominated by the Montagne Pelée volcano, which violently erupted and engulfed the old capital, St. Pierre, in 1902. Situated in the Caribbean's hurricane belt, Martinique suffers an average of one natural disaster every five years.

Its long association with France and its status as an overseas *département* have left Martinique with a distinctly French feel; nonetheless nearly 90% of the population are of African or mixed ethnicity, and this influence has created a vibrant Caribbean tradition, particularly in music. Some of Martinique's more famous children include Joséphine Bonaparte (Napoléon's first wife) and Frantz Fanon, the black revolutionary who influenced anticolonial movements in the 20th century.

Economic power remains in the hands of the *Bekes* (descendants of white colonial settlers), who own most of the agricultural land. This situation has led in the past to outbreaks of violence and calls for greater autonomy. However, high living standards depend on French subsidies and a French-style social welfare system. The traditionally agricultural economy, based on the cultivation of sugarcane and bananas, has been forced to diversify as EU subsidy cuts come into effect, and high-class tourism is now the biggest source of income and the largest provider of employment. Almost 80% of the half-million annual visitors come from France. Since the late 1980s unemployment and emigration have been high, with the result that over 30% of Martiniquais nationals are resident in metropolitan France.

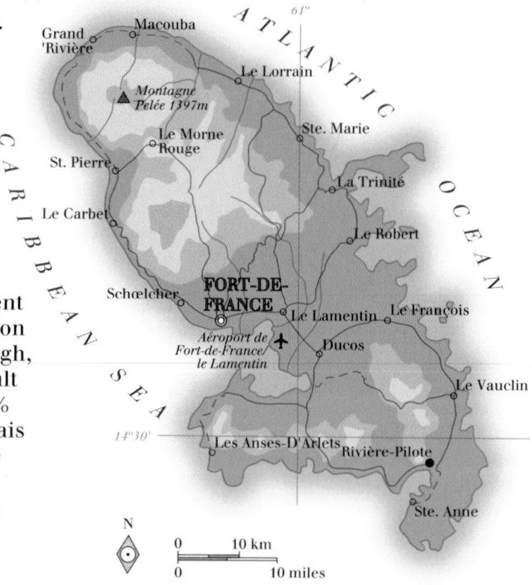
61°
ATLANTIC OCEAN
Grand 'Rivière
Macouba
Le Lorrain
Montagne Pelée 1397m
Ste. Marie
Le Morne Rouge
St. Pierre
La Trinité
Le Carbet
Le Robert
CARIBBEAN SEA
Schœlcher
FORT-DE-FRANCE
Le Lamentin
Le François
Aéroport de Fort-de-France/le Lamentin
Ducos
Le Vauclin
14°30'
Les Anses-D'Arlets
Rivière-Pilote
Ste. Anne
N
0 10 km
0 10 miles

Martinique. *Tourists are attracted to the island's beaches, its mountainous interior, and the historic towns of Fort-de-France and Saint Pierre.*

LAND HEIGHT: above Sea Level | 200m/656ft | 500m/1640ft | 1000m/3281ft | 1500m/4572ft | above 2000m/6562ft

MAYOTTE

STATUS: French territorial collectivity **CLAIMED:** 1843
CAPITAL: Mamoudzou **POP.:** 170,879 **DENSITY:** 457/km² (1187/mi²)

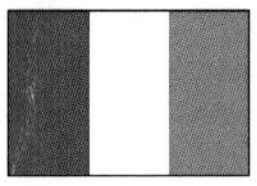

PART OF THE COMOROS archipelago, Mayotte lies about 8000 km (5000 miles) from France, between Madagascar and the east African coast. It was the only island in the archipelago to vote against independence from France in a 1974 referendum. The other islands declared unilateral independence in 1975 and laid claim to Mayotte. Despite widespread poverty, endemic unemployment, and a cost of living twice that of France, the Mahorais voted again in 1976 to maintain the link. The main political movement has since unsuccessfully demanded that Mayotte be given the status of a French *département*, hoping that this would bring more aid to develop their largely agricultural economy. France opposes this idea because of the costs involved, but did grant the island *département*-style autonomy in 2000. The economy is still largely agricultural, producing crops both for internal consumption and for export. However, large quantities of foodstuffs are also imported. France has invested in an airport and port, but tourism has been slow to develop. Nevertheless, the relative prosperity of Mayotte has encouraged separatist movements on the two other small Comoros islands to seek closer relations with France.

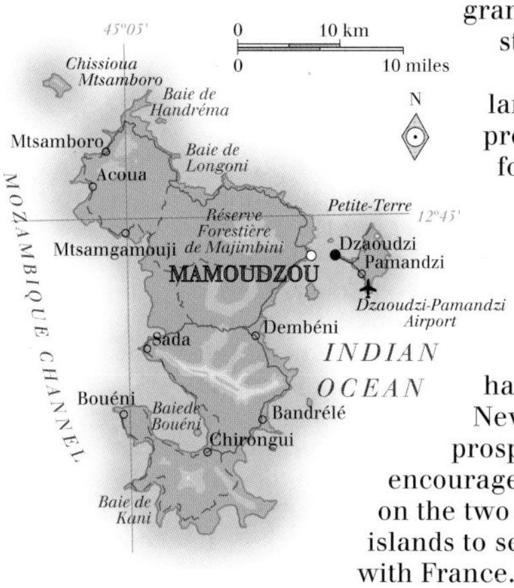

45°05'
0
10 km
10 miles
N
Chissioua Mtsamboro
Baie de Handréma
Mtsamboro
Acoua
Baie de Longoni
MOZAMBIQUE CHANNEL
Réserve Forestière de Majimbini
Petite-Terre
12°45'
Mtsamgamouji
Dzaoudzi
Pamandzi
MAMOUDZOU
Dzaoudzi-Pamandzi Airport
Sada
Dembéni
INDIAN OCEAN
Bouéni
Baie de Bouéni
Bandrélé
Chirongui
Baie de Kani

MIDWAY ISLANDS

STATUS: Unincorporated territory of the US **CLAIMED:** 1867
CAPITAL: *Not applicable* **POP.:** *Not applicable*

NAMED BECAUSE of its position between California and Japan, Midway is a coral atoll at the western end of the Hawaiian islands; there have been moves to make it part of Hawaii. The site of a major World War II battle, the atoll comprises two large islands, totaling over 4 sq. km (1.5 sq. miles), and several smaller ones. It functions as a naval air base and wildlife refuge. The population is limited to military personnel and civilian contractors, but some tourism is permitted, mainly connected with the wildlife.

MONTSERRAT

STATUS: British overseas territory **CLAIMED:** 1632
CAPITAL: Plymouth **POP.:** 8437 **DENSITY:** 83/km² (216/mi²)

MONTSERRAT IS ONE of the Leeward Islands chain in the eastern Caribbean. It has been devastated by volcanic eruptions which began in 1995 and culminated in massive explosions of the Soufrière Hills volcano in 1997 and 1998. As a result, the southern two-thirds of the island, where Plymouth and Blackburne airport are located, have become uninhabitable and it is illegal to enter the volcano "exclusion zone." Some two-thirds of the population left for neighboring islands or the UK in 1997. Calls for independence, based on a tourist boom in the 1980s, have been largely dropped, as the island is now dependent on UK aid. The disaster soured relations, setting off a bitter dispute over the cost of resettlement and reconstruction. A new capital, tentatively named Port Diana, is planned for the "safe" northern coast. The tourism industry is struggling to rebuild itself, but is hindered by the fact that both the airport and the seaport were closed by the eruption. Montserrat can now only be reached via neighboring Antigua.

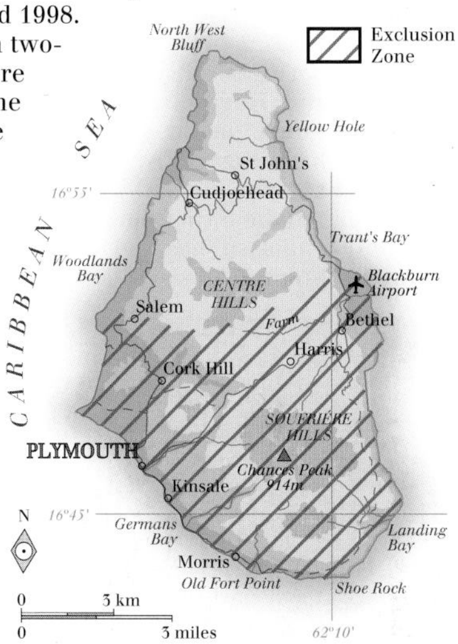

Exclusion Zone
North West Bluff
Yellow Hole
CARIBBEAN SEA
St John's
16°55'
Cudjoehead
Trant's Bay
Woodlands Bay
Blackburn Airport
CENTRE HILLS
Salem
Farm
Bethel
Harris
Cork Hill
SOUFRIÈRE HILLS
PLYMOUTH
Chances Peak 914m
Kinsale
N
16°45'
Germans Bay
Landing Bay
Morris
Old Fort Point
Shoe Rock
0
3 km
3 miles
62°10'

NETHERLANDS ANTILLES

STATUS: Autonomous part of the Netherlands **CLAIMED:** 1816
CAPITAL: Willemstad **POP.:** 219,000 **DENSITY:** 274/km² (709/mi²)

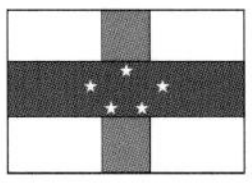

THE NETHERLANDS Antilles are composed of two Caribbean island groups. Curaçao – the richest and wealthiest island – and Bonaire lie just off the Venezuelan coast, while Saba, St. Eustatius, and Sint Maarten – whose northern half is part of Guadeloupe – lie 800 km (500 miles) to the north. Financial scandals, political instability, and the issue of the federation's future, among other things, have strained relations with the Dutch government, the major aid provider. Refining petroleum using oil from Venezuela is the islands' principal industrial activity.

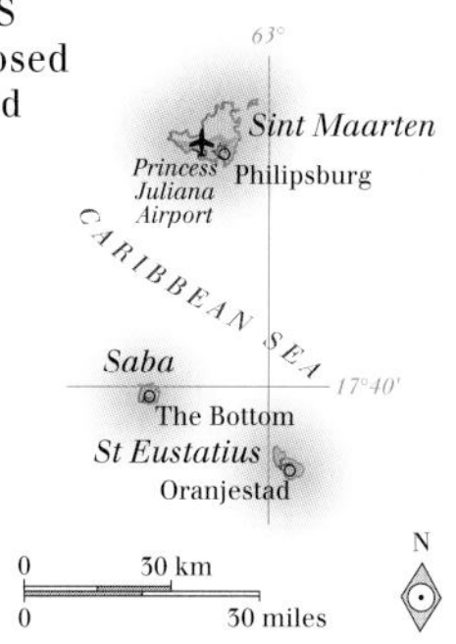

63°
Sint Maarten
Princess Juliana Airport
Philipsburg
CARIBBEAN SEA
Saba
17°40'
The Bottom
St Eustatius
Oranjestad
0
30 km
30 miles
N

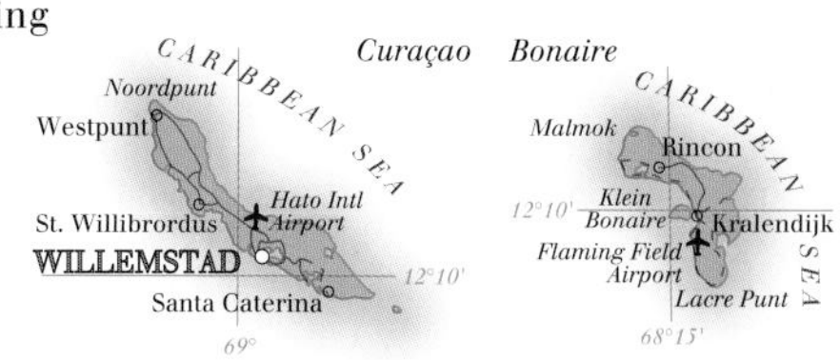

Curaçao
Bonaire
CARIBBEAN SEA
Noordpunt
Westpunt
Hato Intl Airport
St. Willibrordus
WILLEMSTAD
12°10'
Santa Caterina
69°
Malmok
Rincon
Klein Bonaire
Kralendijk
Flaming Field Airport
Lacre Punt
68°15'

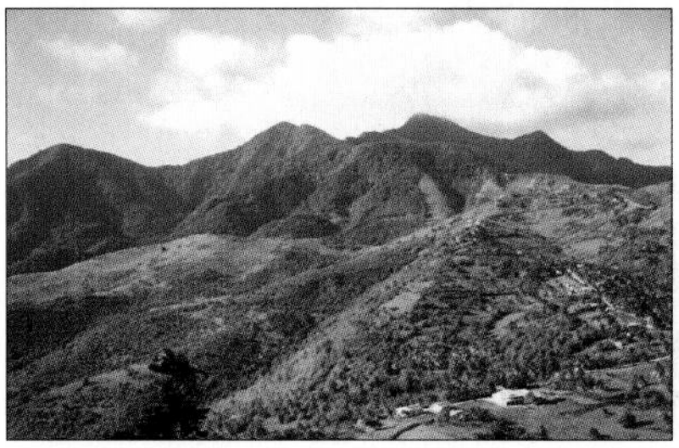

Montserrat. *Known as the Caribbean's "emerald isle" because of its luxuriant flora and Irish heritage.*

POPULATION ○ under 5000 ● under 10 000 ● over 10 000 ○ over 50 000 ◎ over 100 000 ▢ Urban areas AIRPORTS ✈ International ✈ Local

NEW CALEDONIA

STATUS: French overseas territory **CLAIMED:** 1853
CAPITAL: Nouméa **POP.:** 224,000 **DENSITY:** 12/km² (30/mi²)

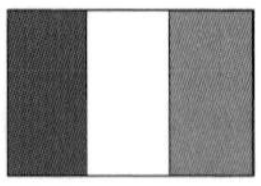

NEW CALEDONIA, or, as it is known to the indigenous Kanaks, Kanaky, is an island group 400 km (250 miles) west of Vanuatu and 1350 km (840 miles) off the coast of eastern Australia. Tension over socioeconomic inequalities and independence between the Melanesian Kanaks, who form over half of the population, and the influential expatriate *Caldoches*, resulted in a long history of political violence. Under the 1988 Matignon Accord, France imposed a year of direct rule as the prelude to a new constitutional structure which attempted to address Kanak grievances by providing greater provincial autonomy. Though some racial violence continued after 1988, it has not again reached the same level. The Nouméa accord, signed in 1998, set out a 15-year program for gradual autonomy which would end in a vote on self-determination.

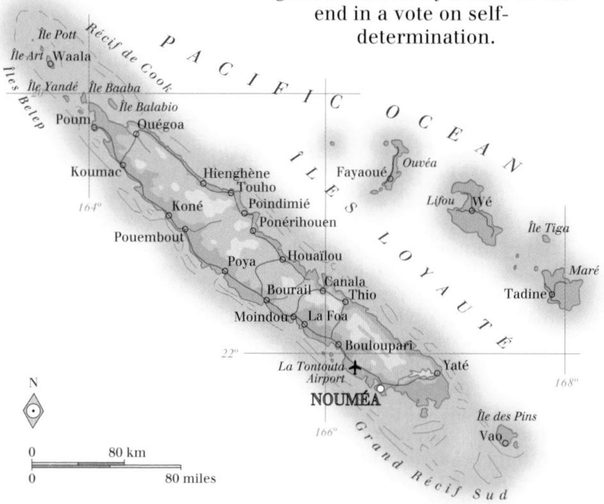
PACIFIC OCEAN
ÎLES LOYAUTÉ
Récif de Cook
Îles Belep
Île Pott
Île Art
Waala
Île Yandé
Île Baaba
Île Balabio
Poum
Ouégoa
Koumac
Hienghène
Touho
Poindimié
Ponérihouen
Koné
Pouembout
Poya
Houaïlou
Canala
Thio
Bourail
Moindou
La Foa
Boulouparí
Yaté
La Tontouta Airport
NOUMÉA
Île des Pins
Vao
Grand Récif Sud
Fayaoué
Ouvéa
Lifou
Wé
Île Tiga
Maré
Tadine
164°
166°
168°
22°
N
0 80 km
0 80 miles

Nickel mining is the territory's most valuable export industry, generating around 80% of export income. New Caledonia has about 25% of world reserves, and is the fourth-largest producer in the world, but the industry employs relatively few people, and is vulnerable to fluctuations in the world price. It was seriously affected by the Asian financial crisis of 1997–1998, but recovered on the back of high world prices in 2000. Tourism and agriculture are bigger employers, though less than 1% of total land area is cultivated. Corn, yams, sweet potatoes, and coconuts have traditionally been the main crops, and since the 1990s melons have been exported to Japan in large quantities. Fishing is important, the main catches being tuna and shrimp, most of which are also exported to Japan. A project for farming giant clams started in 1996. Unemployment nevertheless remains high among young Kanaks.

A nickel mine, *New Caledonia. The importance of the nickel industry to the territory's economy has made the control of reserves a dominant issue in politics, and in negotiations over the island's independence from France.*

NIUE

STATUS: Territory in free association with New Zealand **CLAIMED:** 1901
CAPITAL: Alofi **POP.:** 2134 **DENSITY:** 8/km² (21/mi²)

THE WORLD'S LARGEST coral island, Niue lies 2400 km (1500 miles) northeast of New Zealand. Tropical fruits form part of the subsistence economy, while tourism and the sale of postage stamps provide foreign currency. The island's financial services have recently received warnings from international monitors. Mass emigration has seen the Niuean community in New Zealand grow to over 20,000. In an effort to stem the tide, New Zealand has invested heavily in the Niuean economy. Despite this boost, growth is slow.

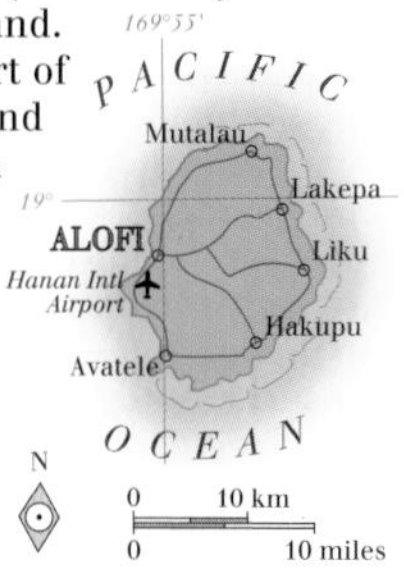
PACIFIC OCEAN
169°55'
19°
Mutalau
Lakepa
Liku
ALOFI
Hanan Intl Airport
Hakupu
Avatele
N
0 10 km
0 10 miles

NORFOLK ISLAND

STATUS: Australian external territory **CLAIMED:** 1774
CAPITAL: Kingston **POP.:** 1866 **DENSITY:** 53/km² (144/mi²)

INHABITED by Australian migrants and descendants of the mutineers of HMS *Bounty*, Norfolk Island lies 1400 km (869 miles) east of Australia. Islanders speak a hybrid language, mixing Westcountry English, Gaelic, and ancient Tahitian. They enjoy substantial autonomy, and in 1991 rejected a plan to become part of the Australian federal state. Tourists, attracted by the climate and unique flora, have brought islanders a relatively high standard of living.

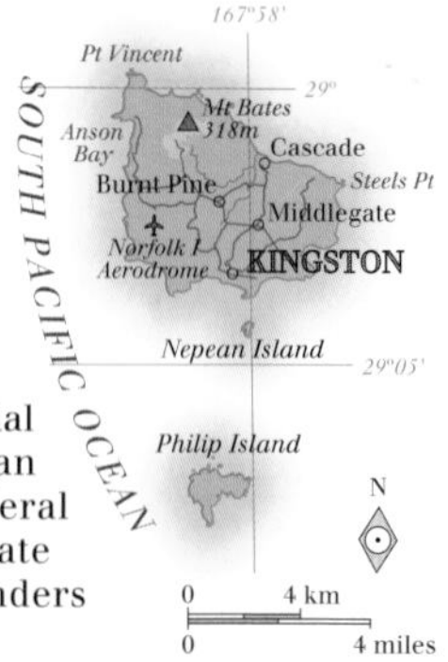
SOUTH PACIFIC OCEAN
167°58'
29°
29°05'
Pt Vincent
Anson Bay
Mt Bates 318m
Cascade
Steels Pt
Burnt Pine
Middlegate
Norfolk I. Aerodrome
KINGSTON
Nepean Island
Philip Island
N
0 4 km
0 4 miles

NORTHERN MARIANA IS.

STATUS: Commonwealth territory of the US **CLAIMED:** 1947
CAPITAL: Saipan **POP.:** 77,311 **DENSITY:** 169/km² (439/mi²)

A FORMER UN trust territory, the Northern Marianas preferred in 1987 to retain links with the US rather than opt for independence. However, local politicians have questioned their current status. US aid fueled a boom during the 1980s, but it depended on immigrant workers who by the early 1990s outnumbered the local Chamorro population. In addition, tourism has speeded the decline of the traditional subsistence economy.

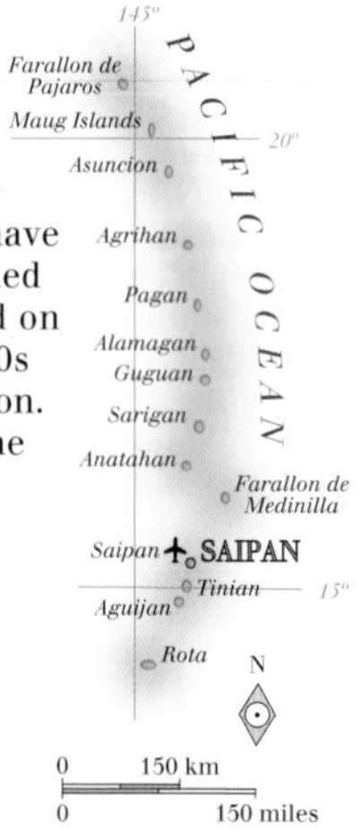
PACIFIC OCEAN
145°
20°
15°
Farallon de Pajaros
Maug Islands
Asuncion
Agrihan
Pagan
Alamagan
Guguan
Sarigan
Anatahan
Farallon de Medinilla
Saipan
SAIPAN
Tinian
Aguijan
Rota
N
0 150 km
0 150 miles

Rota, Northern Marianas. *The limestone outcrop of Wedding Cake Mountain overlooks the small village of Songsong.*

LAND HEIGHT: above Sea Level | 200m/656ft | 500m/1640ft | 1000m/3281ft | 1500m/4572ft | above 2000m/6562ft

PARACEL ISLANDS

STATUS: *Disputed* **CLAIMED:** *Not applicable*
CAPITAL: *Not applicable* **POPULATION:** *Unknown*

OCCUPIED BY CHINESE FORCES (who call them the Xisha Islands), but also claimed by Taiwan and Vietnam, the Paracel Islands are a small collection of coral atolls situated some 325 km (200 miles) east of Vietnam, in the South China Sea. Subject to frequent typhoons and with a tropical climate, the Paracels are at the center of a regional dispute over the vast reserves of oil and natural gas which are believed to lie beneath their territorial waters. China has built port facilities and an airport on Woody Island to support its claim.

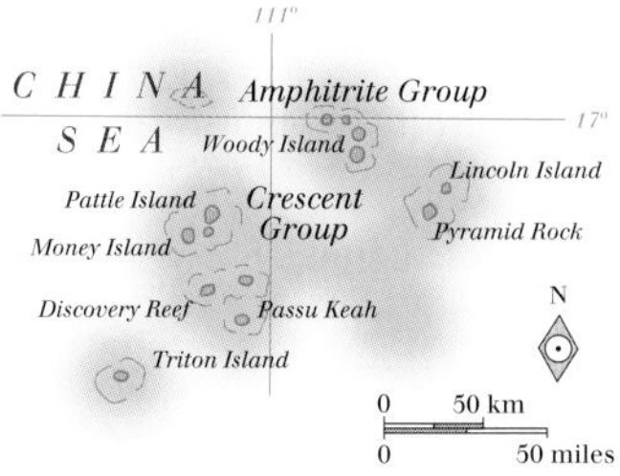
111°
C H I N A
S E A
Amphitrite Group
Woody Island
17°
Lincoln Island
Pattle Island
Crescent Group
Money Island
Pyramid Rock
Discovery Reef
Passu Keah
Triton Island
N
0 50 km
0 50 miles

PITCAIRN ISLANDS

STATUS: British overseas territory **CLAIMED:** 1887
CAPITAL: Adamstown **POP.:** 47 **DENSITY:** 1.3/km² (3/mi²)

A GROUP OF volcanic South Pacific islands, Pitcairn is Britain's most isolated dependency. Pitcairn Island was the last refuge for the 18th-century mutineers from HMS *Bounty*. The economy operates by barter, fishing, and subsistence farming, and is reliant on regular airdrops from New Zealand and periodic visits by supply vessels. Postage stamp sales provide foreign currency earnings. In 2003, nine Pitcairners were charged with sexual assault.

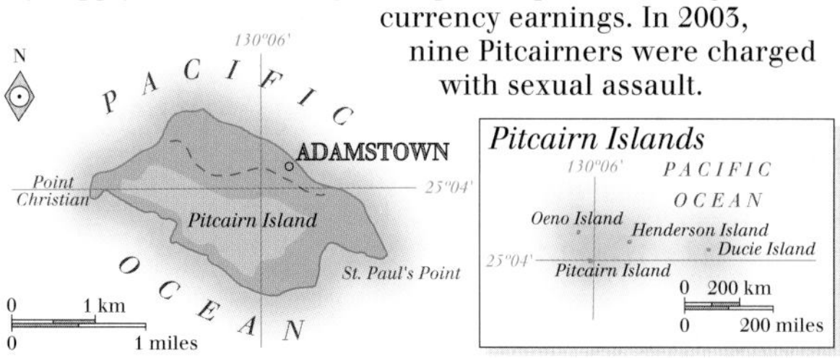
130°06'
P A C I F I C
O C E A N
N
ADAMSTOWN
Point Christian
25°04'
Pitcairn Island
St. Paul's Point
0 1 km
0 1 miles
Pitcairn Islands
130°06'
PACIFIC
OCEAN
Oeno Island
Henderson Island
Ducie Island
25°04'
Pitcairn Island
0 200 km
0 200 miles

PUERTO RICO

STATUS: Commonwealth territory of the US **CLAIMED:** 1898
CAPITAL: San Juan **POP.:** 4 million **DENSITY:** 442/km² (1144/mi²)

PUERTO RICO, a US territory since its invasion in 1898, is by far the most populous nonindependent territory. It is the easternmost of the Greater Antilles chain in the Caribbean. The population density, highest around San Juan, is comparable with the Netherlands and is higher than in any US state. The tropical climate attracts growing numbers of tourists, 85% from the US, and there have been major efforts to expand hotel and resort facilities.

Puerto Rico was granted its current commonwealth status in 1952, four years after an abortive proindependence uprising. The inhabitants have US citizenship but only limited self-government. In three plebiscites, in 1967, 1993, and 1998, the islanders endorsed continued commonwealth status rather than opting for either US statehood or independence. The most recent of these votes was extremely close, but the pro-statehood governor who called the 1993 and 1998 votes, Pedro Rossello, was replaced by the anti-statehood Sila Calderón – the first female governor of Puerto Rico – in 2001.

Though thousands of the mostly Spanish-speaking Puerto Ricans have migrated to the US mainland in search of higher wages, the islanders have one of the highest living standards in the region. Tax relief, cheap labor, and the island's role as an export-processing zone, mainly for the US market, attracted many businesses. Clothing, electronics, petrochemical, and pharmaceutical industries traditionally dominated, but the decision to phase out tax exemptions for companies reinvesting in the island caused a slump in 1996, and more emphasis is now being placed on the service sector. New industries include health care and clinical testing, biotechnology, and other knowledge-based areas.

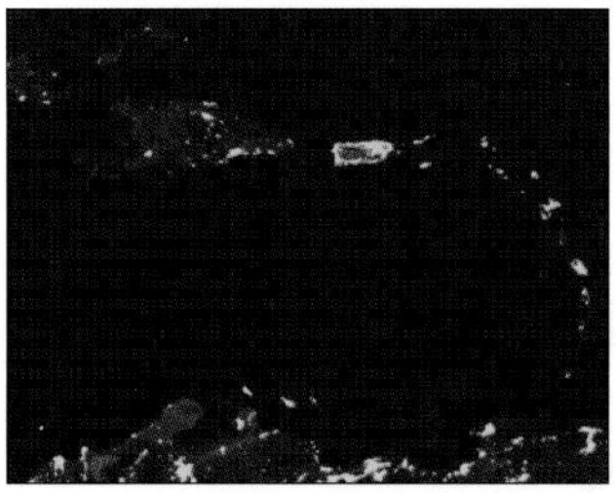

***At night,** the bright lights of Puerto Rico's well-developed roads, settlements, and busy ports are in sharp contrast to the rest of the Caribbean – notably the dark outline of Haiti, just to the west.*

Governor Calderón spearheaded the campaign to stop the US navy from using the populated eastern island of Vieques for bombing practice. In 2000 an invasion of the bombing range by protesters led to some high-profile arrests, including that of Robert Kennedy Jr. A year later newly elected US president George W. Bush announced that the navy would not use the island after 2003.

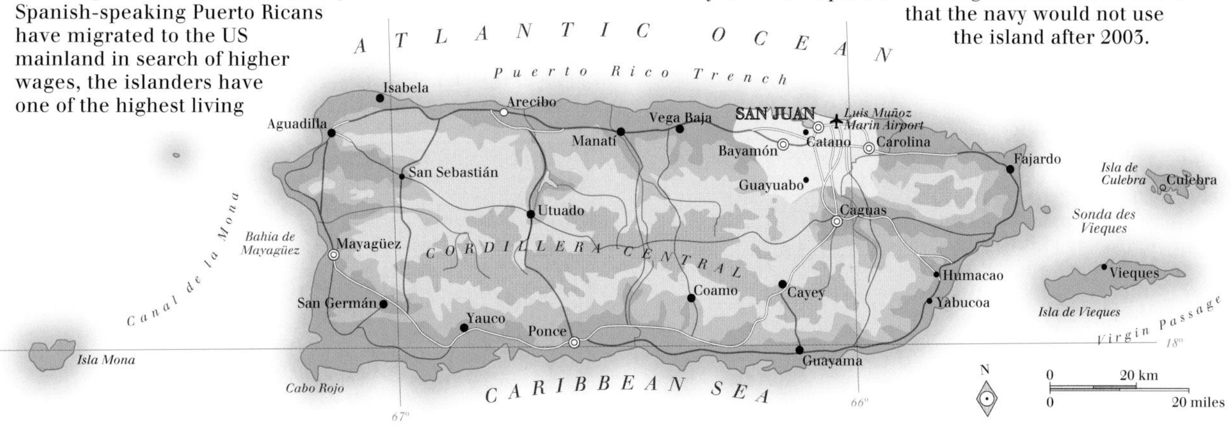
A T L A N T I C O C E A N
Puerto Rico Trench
Isabela
Arecibo
Aguadilla
Vega Baja
SAN JUAN
Luis Muñoz Marín Airport
Manatí
Bayamón
Cataño
Carolina
Fajardo
San Sebastián
Guayuabo
Isla de Culebra
Culebra
Utuado
Caguas
Sonda des Vieques
Bahía de Mayagüez
Mayagüez
CORDILLERA CENTRAL
Humacao
Vieques
Canal de la Mona
Coamo
Cayey
San Germán
Yabucoa
Isla de Vieques
Yauco
Ponce
Virgin Passage
18°
Isla Mona
Guayama
Cabo Rojo
CARIBBEAN SEA
67°
66°
N
0 20 km
0 20 miles

POPULATION ○ under 5000 • under 10 000 ● over 10 000 ○ over 50 000 ◎ over 100 000 ▢ Urban areas AIRPORTS ✈ International ✈ Local

Réunion

Status: French overseas department **Claimed:** 1638
Capital: Saint-Denis **Pop.:** 742,000 **Density:** 295/km² (765/mi²)

The large volcanic island of Réunion, 800 km (500 miles) east of Madagascar, provides France with an important strategic presence – and a large military base – in the Indian Ocean. Its mountainous interior has forced the majority of the population to live along the coast. Tensions still exist between the very poor black community and the wealthy Indian and European groups, though the violence of 1991 has not been repeated. Despite the introduction of measures applicable to all French overseas *départements*, intended to improve social and economic standards, unemployment remains high and the cost of living very expensive. Réunion's main crop is sugarcane, though Cyclone Dina devastated production in 2002.

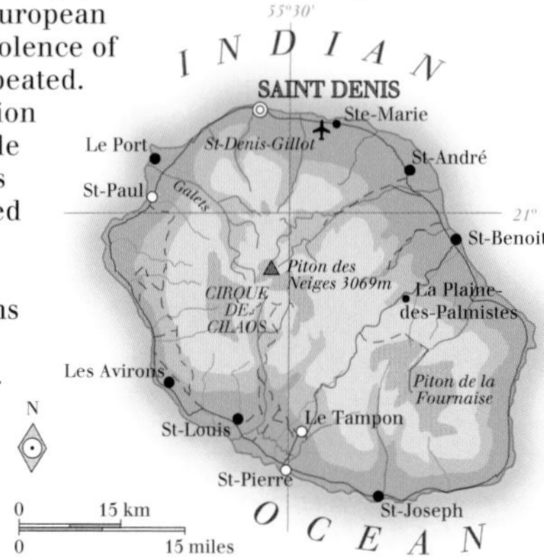
INDIAN
OCEAN
SAINT DENIS
Ste-Marie
St-Denis-Gillot
Le Port
St-André
St-Paul
Galets
St-Benoit
Piton des Neiges 3069m
CIRQUE DE CILAOS
La Plaine-des-Palmistes
Les Avirons
Piton de la Fournaise
St-Louis
Le Tampon
St-Pierre
St-Joseph
N
0 15 km
0 15 miles

St. Pierre & Miquelon

Status: French territorial collectivity **Claimed:** 1604
Capital: St. Pierre **Pop.:** 6954 **Density:** 29/km² (75/mi²)

St. Pierre & Miquelon is a group of barren islands lying just off the south coast of Newfoundland, Canada. The islands are surrounded by some of the world's richest fishing grounds. Their inhabitants have traditionally earned a living from fishing, and from servicing foreign trawler fleets off the coast. A long-running and sometimes bitter dispute between Canada and France over fishing and mineral rights was settled in 1992. The ruling, which was generally deemed to be in Canada's favor, has led the French authorities to diversify the economy by developing port facilities and encouraging tourism.

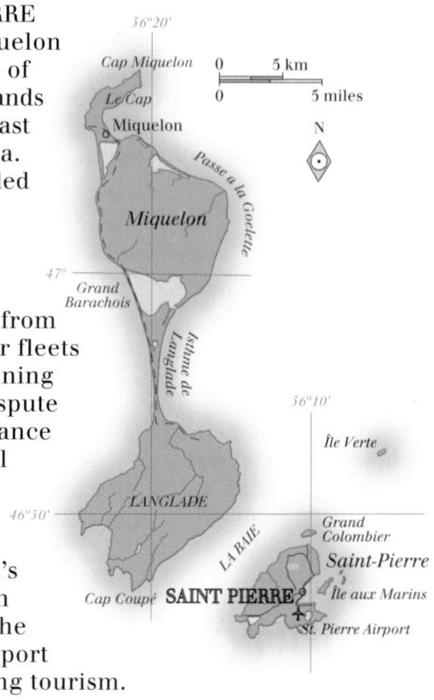
Cap Miquelon
Le Cap
Miquelon
Passe a la Goelette
Miquelon
Grand Barachois
Isthme de Langlade
Île Verte
LANGLADE
LA BAIE
Grand Colombier
Saint-Pierre
Cap Coupé
SAINT PIERRE
Île aux Marins
St. Pierre Airport
N
0 5 km
0 5 miles

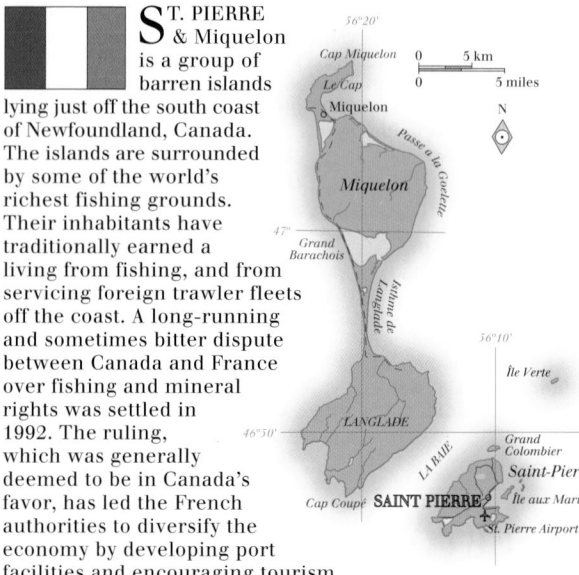

St. Helena & Dependencies

Status: British overseas territory **Claimed:** 1673
Capital: Jamestown **Pop.:** 7317 **Density:** 60/km² (156/mi²)

Together, the islands of St. Helena, Tristan da Cunha, and Ascension form Britain's main dependency in the south Atlantic. St. Helena is famed for being the final place of exile for Napoléon. Its main economic activities – fishing, livestock farming, and the sale of handicrafts – are unable to support the population; as a result, underemployment on the island is a major problem. Many "Saints" have been forced to seek work on Ascension, which has no resident population and is operated as a military base and communications center, though civilian flights have been permitted since 1998. Tristan da Cunha, a volcanic island 2000 km (1240 miles) south of St. Helena, is inhabited by a small, closely knit farming community. It was badly hit by severe winter storms in 2001. The 2002 British Overseas Territories Act granted all overseas citizens full British citizenship, assuaging a source of local resentment.

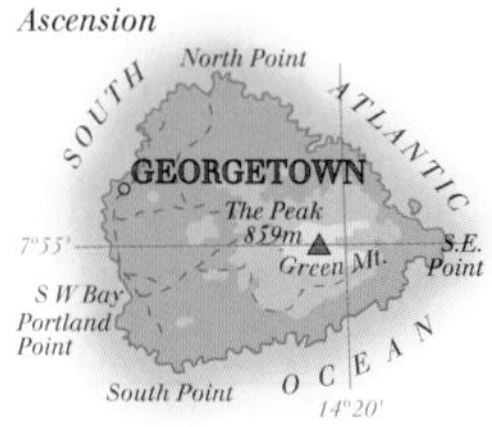
Ascension
North Point
SOUTH ATLANTIC OCEAN
GEORGETOWN
The Peak 859m
Green Mt.
S.E. Point
S W Bay
Portland Point
South Point

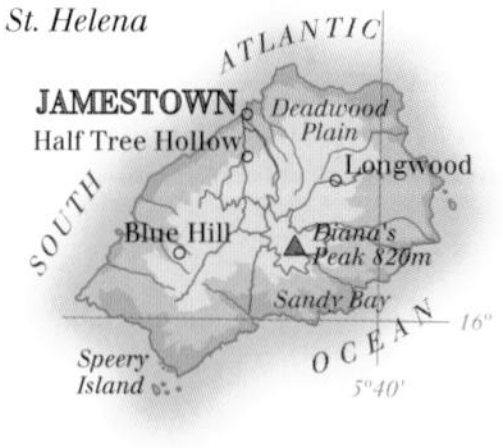
St. Helena
SOUTH ATLANTIC OCEAN
JAMESTOWN
Half Tree Hollow
Deadwood Plain
Longwood
Blue Hill
Diana's Peak 820m
Sandy Bay
Speery Island

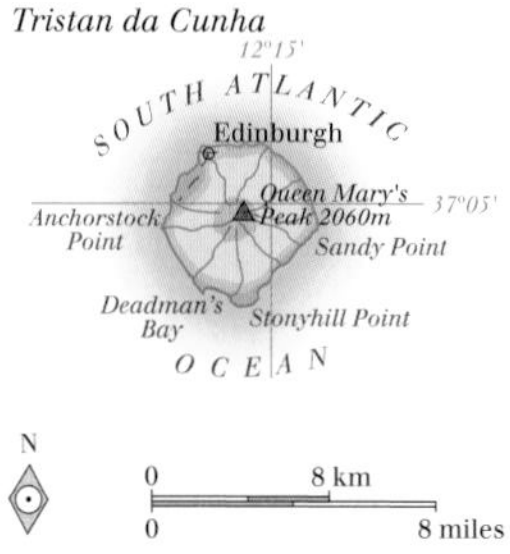
Tristan da Cunha
SOUTH ATLANTIC OCEAN
Edinburgh
Queen Mary's Peak 2060m
Anchorstock Point
Sandy Point
Deadman's Bay
Stonyhill Point
N
0 8 km
0 8 miles

Spratly Islands

Status: *Disputed* **Claimed:** *Not applicable*
Capital: *Not applicable* **Population:** *Unknown*

Scattered across a large area of the South China Sea, the reefs, islands, and atolls that make up the Spratly Islands have become one of South Asia's most serious security issues. Strategically, the islands lie in one of the world's busiest shipping areas. In addition, surveys suggest that some of the largest oil and gas reserves yet found lie in the Spratlys' territorial waters. Claimed, all or in part, by China, Taiwan, Vietnam, Brunei, Malaysia, and the Philippines, more than 40 of the larger islands now have garrisons from some of the claimant states. A code of conduct allowing freedom of navigation was agreed in 2002.

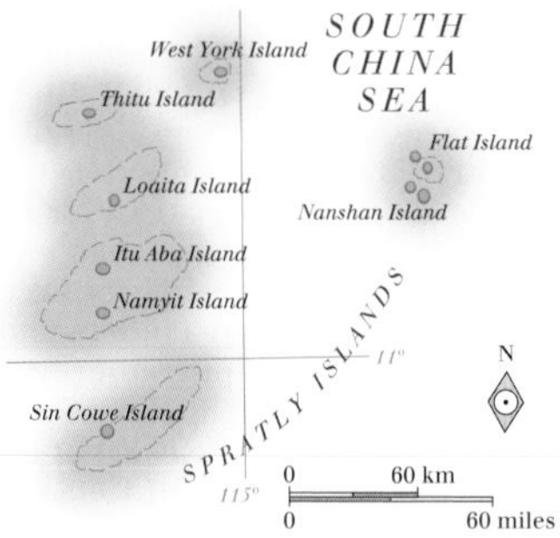
SOUTH CHINA SEA
West York Island
Thitu Island
Flat Island
Loaita Island
Nanshan Island
Itu Aba Island
Namyit Island
SPRATLY ISLANDS
Sin Cowe Island
N
0 60 km
0 60 miles

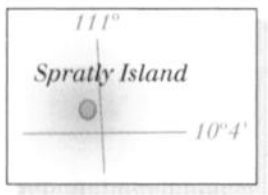
Spratly Island

The isolated Chinese occupying force on one of the Spratly Islands.

LAND HEIGHT: above Sea Level | 200m/656ft | 500m/1640ft | 1000m/3281ft | 1500m/4572ft | above 2000m/6562ft

SVALBARD

STATUS: Norwegian dependency **CLAIMED:** 1920

CAPITAL: Longyearbyen **POP.:** 2868 **DENSITY:** 0.05/km² (0.12/mi²)

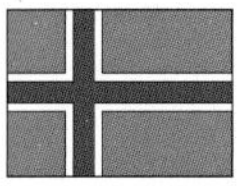

MORE THAN 150 ice-covered Arctic islands 650 km (400 miles) north of Norway make up Svalbard. In accordance with the Spitsbergen Treaty of 1920, nationals of the treaty powers have equal rights to exploit the coal deposits, subject to regulation by Norway. The only companies still mining are Norwegian and Russian. There has been conflict with Iceland over fishing rights. Over half of the area of the islands is designated as environmentally protected.

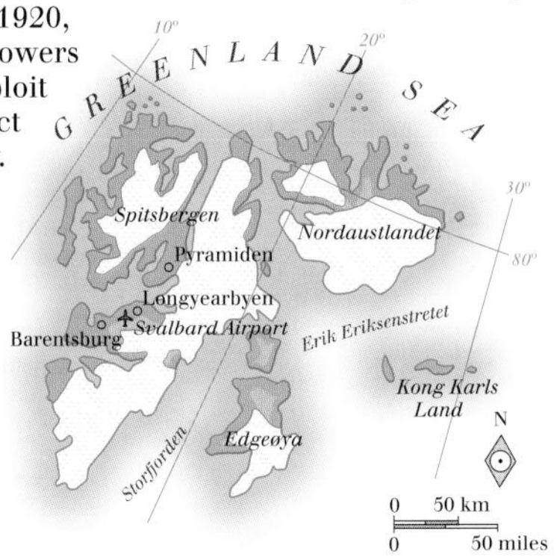
GREENLAND SEA
Spitsbergen
Pyramiden
Nordaustlandet
Longyearbyen
Barentsburg
Svalbard Airport
Erik Eriksenstretet
Kong Karls Land
Storfjorden
Edgeøya
N
0 50 km
0 50 miles

VIRGIN ISLANDS (US)

STATUS: Unincorporated territory of the US **CLAIMED:** 1917

CAPITAL: Charlotte Amalie **POP.:** 123,498 **DENS.:** 356/km² (922/mi²)

THE US VIRGIN ISLANDS are a collection of 53 volcanic islands, just to the east of Puerto Rico. Most of the population – a mix of African and European ethnic groups – live on the main islands of St. John, St. Thomas, and St. Croix. Tourism is the principal activity, though St. Croix has also used federal aid to develop industry. It has one of the world's largest oil refineries.

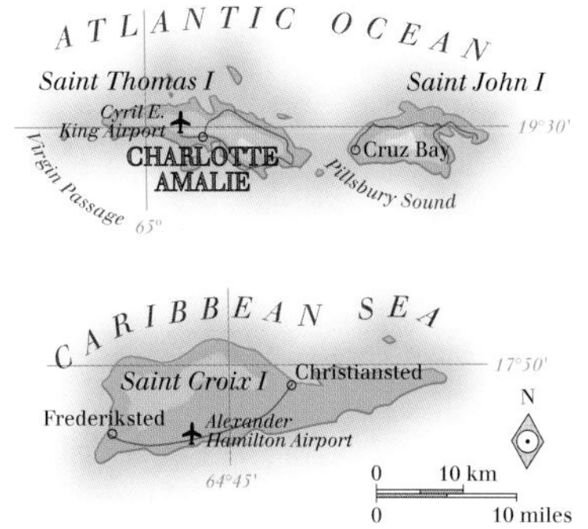
ATLANTIC OCEAN
Saint Thomas I
Saint John I
Cyril E. King Airport
CHARLOTTE AMALIE
Cruz Bay
Virgin Passage
Pillsbury Sound
CARIBBEAN SEA
Saint Croix I
Christiansted
Frederiksted
Alexander Hamilton Airport
N
0 10 km
0 10 miles

St. Thomas, US Virgin Islands, is a major stop-off for Caribbean cruise ships. Tourists are attracted by the island's duty-free shopping.

TOKELAU

STATUS: New Zealand dependent territory **CLAIMED:** 1926

CAPITAL: *Not applicable* **POP.:** 1431 **DENSITY:** 143/km² (358/mi²)

A 1989 UN REPORT states that in the 21st century these islands in the South Pacific will disappear under the sea, unless action is taken to stop global warming. The economy depends on a tuna cannery and the sale of fishing licenses, postage stamps, and coins; a catamaran link between the atolls has increased tourist potential. Tokelau's small size and economic fragility make independence unlikely, but in 1996 it gained the right to enact its own internal legislation, and since 2001 the local authorities have had full control of the islands' public services. More than 6000 Tokelauans live in New Zealand.

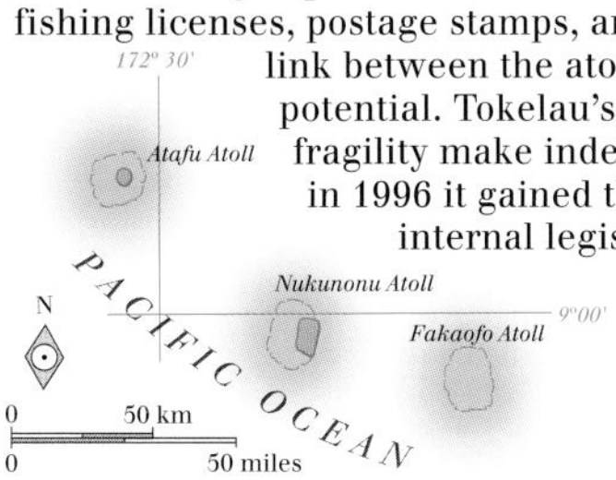
Atafu Atoll
Nukunonu Atoll
Fakaofo Atoll
PACIFIC OCEAN
N
0 50 km
0 50 miles

WAKE ISLAND

STATUS: Unincorporated territory of the US **CLAIMED:** 1898

CAPITAL: *Not applicable* **POP.:** *Not applicable*

WAKE ISLAND, in fact three islands that form the rim of an extinct volcano, has a US air base, whose airstrip can be used in emergencies by trans-Pacific flights. After widespread condemnation a 1998 proposal to store nuclear waste there was dropped. It is claimed by the Marshall Islands.

TURKS & CAICOS ISLANDS

STATUS: British overseas territory **CLAIMED:** 1766

CAPITAL: Cockburn Town **POP.:** 18,738 **DENSITY:** 44/km² (113/mi²)

SITUATED 40 km (25 miles) south of the Bahamas, the Turks and Caicos Islands is a group of 30 low-lying islands, eight of which are inhabited. A traditional salt-based economy was exhausted in 1964, leading to two decades of stagnation. Since the 1980s, however, tourism and offshore banking have led a dramatic turnaround in the islands' fortunes.

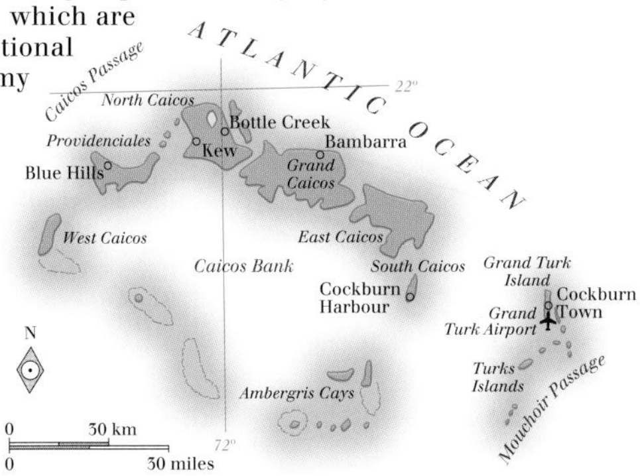
ATLANTIC OCEAN
Caicos Passage
North Caicos
Bottle Creek
Bambarra
Providenciales
Kew
Blue Hills
Grand Caicos
West Caicos
East Caicos
Caicos Bank
South Caicos
Grand Turk Island
Cockburn Harbour
Cockburn Town
Grand Turk Airport
Turks Islands
Ambergris Cays
Mouchoir Passage
N
0 30 km
0 30 miles

WALLIS & FUTUNA

STATUS: French overseas territory **CLAIMED:** 1842

CAPITAL: Matá'Utu **POP.:** 15,585 **DENSITY:** 57/km² (147/mi²)

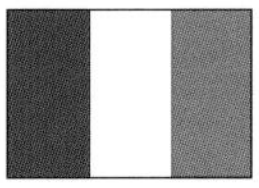

UNLIKE THOSE OF France's other South Pacific overseas territories, the inhabitants of Wallis and Futuna have little desire for greater autonomy. The islands' subsistence economy produces a variety of tropical crops, while expatriate remittances and the sale of licenses to Japanese and South Korean fishing fleets provide foreign exchange. Deforestation, leading to soil erosion, is of great concern.

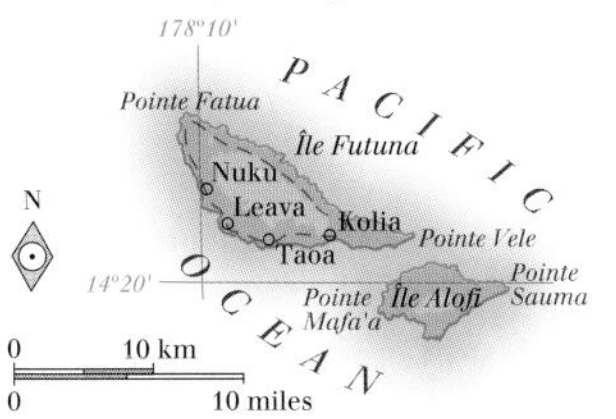
PACIFIC OCEAN
Pointe Fatua
Île Futuna
Nuku
Leava
Kolia
Taoa
Pointe Vele
Pointe Sauma
Pointe Mafa'a
Île Alofi
N
0 10 km
0 10 miles

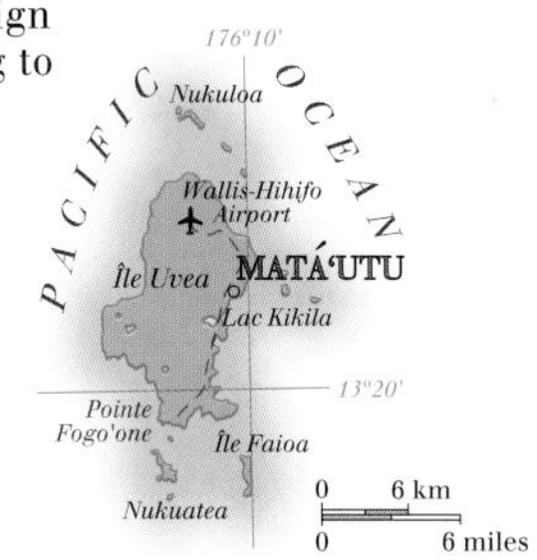
PACIFIC OCEAN
Nukuloa
Wallis-Hihifo Airport
Île Uvea
MATÁ'UTU
Lac Kikila
Pointe Fogo'one
Île Faioa
Nukuatea
0 6 km
0 6 miles

GLOSSARY OF GEOGRAPHICAL TERMS

THE GLOSSARY FOLLOWING lists all geographical terms occurring on the maps and in main-entry names in the Index~Gazetteer. These terms may precede, follow, or be run together with the proper element of the name; where they precede it the term is reversed for indexing purposes – thus Poluostrov Yamal is indexed as Yamal, Poluostrov.

KEY
Geographical term *Language*, Term

A
Å *Danish, Norwegian*, River
Alpen *German*, Alps
Altiplanicie *Spanish*, Plateau
Älv(en) *Swedish*, River
Anse *French*, Bay
Archipiélago *Spanish*, Archipelago
Arcipelago *Italian*, Archipelago
Arquipélago *Portuguese*, Archipelago
Aukštuma *Lithuanian*, Upland

B
Bahía *Spanish*, Bay
Baía *Portuguese*, Bay
Baḩr *Arabic*, River
Baie *French*, Bay
Bandao *Chinese*, Peninsula
Banjaran *Malay*, Mountain range
Batang *Malay*, Stream
-berg *Afrikaans, Norwegian*, Mountain
Birket *Arabic* , Lake
Boğazı *Turkish*, Lake
Bucht *German*, Bay
Bugten *Danish*, Bay
Buḩayrat *Arabic*, Lake, reservoir
Buḩeirat *Arabic*, Lake
Bukit *Malay*, Mountain
-bukta *Norwegian*, Bay
bukten *Swedish*, Bay
Burnu *Turkish*, Cape, point
Buuraha *Somali*, Mountains

C
Cabo *Portuguese*, Cape
Cap *French*, Cape
Cascada *Portuguese*, Waterfall
Cerro *Spanish*, Mountain
Chaîne *French*, Mountain range
Chau *Cantonese*, Island
Chāy *Turkish*, River
Chhâk *Cambodian*, Bay
Chhu *Tibetan*, River
-chŏsuji *Korean*, Reservoir
Chott *Arabic*, Salt lake, depression
Ch'ün-tao *Chinese*, Island group
Chuôr Phnum *Cambodian*, Mountains
Cordillera *Spanish*, Mountain range
Costa *Spanish*, Coast
Côte *French*, Coast
Cuchilla *Spanish*, Mountains

D
Dağı *Azerbaijani, Turkish*, Mountain
Dağları *Azerbaijani, Turkish*, Mountains
-dake *Japanese*, Peak
Danau *Indonesian*, Lake
Đao *Vietnamese*, Island
Daryā *Persian*, River
Daryācheh *Persian*, Lake
Dasht *Persian*, Plain, desert
Dawḩat *Arabic*, Bay
Dere *Turkish*, Stream
Dili *Azerbaijani*, Spit
-do *Korean*, Island
Dooxo *Somali*, Valley
Düzü *Azerbaijani*, Steppe
-dwīp *Bengali*, Island

E
Embalse *Spanish*, Reservoir
Erg *Arabic*, Dunes
Estany *Catalan*, Lake
Estrecho *Spanish*, Strait
-ey *Icelandic*, Island
Ezero *Bulgarian, Macedonian*, Lake

F
Fjord *Danish*, Fjord
-fjorden *Norwegian*, Fjord
-fjørdhur *Faeroese*, Fjord
Fleuve *French*, River
Fliegu *Maltese*, Channel
-fljór *Icelandic*, River

G
-gang *Korean*, River
Ganga *Nepali, Sinhala*, River
Gaoyuan *Chinese*, Plateau
-gawa *Japanese*, River
Gebel *Arabic*, Mountain
-gebirge *German*, Mountains
Ghubbat *Arabic*, Bay
Gjiri *Albanian*, Bay
Gol *Mongolian*, River
Golfe *French*, Gulf
Golfo *Italian, Spanish*, Gulf
Gora *Russian, Serbian*, Mountain
Gory *Russian*, Mountains
Guba *Russian*, Bay
Gunung *Malay*, Mountain

H
Ḩadd *Arabic*, Spit
-haehyŏp *Korean*, Strait
Haff *German*, Lagoon
Hai *Chinese*, Sea, bay
Ḩammādat *Arabic*, Plateau
Hāmūn *Persian*, Lake
Hawr *Arabic*, Lake
Hāyk' *Amharic*, Lake
He *Chinese*, River
Helodrano *Malagasy*, Bay
-hegység *Hungarian*, Mountain range
Hka *Burmese*, River
-ho *Korean*, Lake
Hô *Korean*, Reservoir
Ḫolot *Hebrew*, Dunes
Hora *Belarussian*, Mountain
Hrada *Belarussian*, Mountains, ridge
Hsi *Chinese*, River
Hu *Chinese*, Lake

I
Île(s) *French*, Island(s)
Ilha(s) *Portuguese*, Island(s)
Ilhéu(s) *Portuguese*, Islet(s)
Irmak *Turkish*, River
Isla(s) *Spanish*, Island(s)
Isola (Isole) *Italian*, Island(s)

J
Jabal *Arabic*, Mountain
Jāl *Arabic*, Ridge
-järvi *Finnish*, Lake
Jazīrat *Arabic*, Island
Jazīreh *Persian*, Island
Jebel *Arabic*, Mountain
Jezero *Serbo-Croat*, Lake
Jiang *Chinese*, River
-joki *Finnish*, River
-jökull *Icelandic*, Glacier
Juzur *Arabic*, Islands

K
Kaikyō *Japanese*, Strait
-kaise *Lappish*, Mountain
Kali *Nepali*, River
Kalnas *Lithuanian*, Mountain
Kalns *Latvian*, Mountain
Kang *Chinese*, Harbor
Kangri *Tibetan*, Mountain(s)
Kaôh *Cambodian*, Island
Kapp *Norwegian*, Cape
Kavīr *Persian*, Desert
K'edi *Georgian*, Mountain range
Kediet *Arabic*, Mountain
Kepulauan *Indonesian, Malay*, Island group
Khalîg, Khalīj *Arabic*, Gulf
Khawr *Arabic*, Inlet
Khola *Nepali*, River
Khrebet *Russian*, Mountain range
Ko *Thai*, Island
Kolpos *Greek*, Bay
-kopf *German*, Peak
Körfäzi *Azerbaijani*, Bay
Körfezi *Turkish*, Bay
Kõrgustik *Estonian*, Upland
Koshi *Nepali*, River
Kowtal *Persian*, Pass
Kūh(hā) *Persian*, Mountain(s)
-kundo *Korean*, Island group
-kysten *Norwegian*, Coast
Kyun *Burmese*, Island

L
Laaq *Somali*, Watercourse
Lac *French*, Lake
Lacul *Romanian*, Lake
Lago *Italian, Portuguese, Spanish*, Lake
Laguna *Spanish*, Lagoon, Lake
Laht *Estonian*, Bay
Laut *Indonesian*, Sea
Lembalemba *Malagasy*, Plateau
Lerr *Armenian*, Mountain
Lerrnashghtʻa *Armenian*, Mountain range
Les *Czech*, Forest
Lich *Armenian*, Lake
Liqeni *Albanian*, Lake
Lumi *Albanian*, River
Lyman *Ukrainian*, EstuaryLake

M
Mae Nam *Thai*, River
-mägi *Estonian*, Hill
Maja *Albanian*, Mountain
-man *Korean*, Bay
Marios *Lithuanian*, Lake
-meer *Dutch*, Lake
Melkosopochnik *Russian*, Plain
-meri *Estonian*, Sea
Mifraẕ *Hebrew*, Bay
Monkhafad *Arabic*, Depression
Mont(s) *French*, Mountain(s)
Monte *Italian, Portuguese*, Mountain
More *Russian*, Sea
Mörön *Mongolian*, River

N
Nagor'ye *Russian*, Upland
Naḩal *Hebrew*, River
Nahr *Arabic*, River
Nam *Laotian*, River
Nehri *Turkish*, River
Nevado *Spanish*, Mountain (snow-capped)
Nisoi *Greek*, Islands
Nizmennost' *Russian*, Lowland, plain
Nosy *Malagasy*, Island
Nur *Mongolian*, Lake
Nuruu *Mongolian*, Mountains
Nuur *Mongolian*, Lake
Nyzovyna *Ukrainian*, Lowland, plain

O
Ostrov(a) *Russian*, Island(s)
Oued *Arabic*, Watercourse
-oy *Faeroese*, Island
-øy(a) *Norwegian*, Island
Oya *Sinhala*, River
Ozero *Russian, Ukrainian*, Lake

P
Passo *Italian*, Pass
Pegunungan *Indonesian, Malay*, Mountain range
Pelagos *Greek*, Sea
Penisola *Italian*, Peninsula
Peski *Russian*, Sands
Phanom *Thai*, Mountain
Phou *Laotian*, Mountain
Pi *Chinese*, Point
Pic *Catalan*, Peak
Pico *Portuguese, Spanish*, Peak
Pik *Russian*, Peak
Planalto *Portuguese*, Plateau
Planina, Planini *Bulgarian, Macedonian, Serbo-Croat*, Mountain range
Ploskogor'ye *Russian*, Upland
Poluostrov *Russian*, Peninsula
Potamos *Greek*, River
Proliv *Russian*, Strait
Pulau *Indonesian, Malay*, Island
Pulu *Malay*, Island
Punta *Portuguese, Spanish*, Point

Q
Qā' *Arabic*, Depression
Qolleh *Persian*, Mountain

R
Raas *Somali*, Cape
-rags *Latvian*, Cape
Ramlat *Arabic*, Sands
Ra's *Arabic*, Cape, point, headland
Ravnina *Bulgarian, Russian*, Plain
Récif *French*, Reef
Represa (Rep.) *Spanish, Portuguese*, Reservoir
-rettō *Japanese*, Island chain
Riacho *Spanish*, Stream
Riban' *Malagasy*, Mountains
Rio *Portuguese*, River
Río *Spanish*, River
Riu *Catalan*, River
Rivier *Dutch*, River
Rivière *French*, River
Rowd *Pashtu*, River
Rūd *Persian*, River
Rudohorie *Slovak*, Mountains
Ruisseau *French*, Stream

S

Sabkhat *Arabic,* Salt marsh
Ṣaḥrā' *Arabic,* Desert
Samudra *Sinhala,* Reservoir
-san *Japanese, Korean,* Mountain
-sanchi *Japanese,* Mountains
-sanmaek *Korean,*
Sarīr *Arabic,* Desert
Sebkha, Sebkhet *Arabic,* Salt marsh, depression
See *German,* Lake
Selat *Indonesian,* Strait
-selkä *Finnish,* Ridge
Selseleh *Persian,* Mountain range
Serra *Portuguese,* Mountain
Serranía *Spanish,* Mountain
Sha'īb *Arabic,* Watercourse
Shamo *Chinese,* Desert
Shan *Chinese,* Mountain(s)
Shan-mo *Chinese,* Mountain range
Shaṭṭ *Arabic,* Distributary
-shima *Japanese,* Island
Shiqqat *Arabic,* Depression
Shui-tao *Chinese,* Channel
Sierra *Spanish,* Mountains
Sơn *Vietnamese,* Mountain
Sông *Vietnamese,* River
-spitze *German,* Peak
Štít *Slovak,* Peak
Stoeng *Cambodian,* River
Stretto *Italian,* Strait
Su Anbarı *Azerbaijani,* Reservoir
Sungai *Indonesian, Malay,* River
Suu *Turkish,* River

T

Tal *Mongolian,* Plain
Tandavan' *Malagasy,* Mountain range
Tangorombohitr' *Malagasy,* Mountain massif
Tao *Chinese,* Island
Tassili *Berber,* Plateau, mountain
Tau *Russian,* Mountain(s)
Taungdan *Burmese,* Mountain range
Teluk *Indonesian, Malay,* Bay
Terara *Amharic,* Mountain
Tog *Somali,* Valley
Tônlé *Cambodian,* Lake
Top *Dutch,* Peak
-tunturi *Finnish,* Mountain
Tur'at *Arabic,* Channel

V

Väin *Estonian,* Strait
-vatn *Icelandic,* Lake
-vesi *Finnish,* Lake
Vinh *Vietnamese,* Bay
Vodokhranilishche (Vdkhr.) *Russian,* Reservoir
Vodoskhovyshche (Vdskh.) *Ukrainian,* Reservoir
Volcán *Spanish,* Volcano
Vozvyshennost' *Russian,* Upland, plateau
Vrh *Macedonian,* Peak
Vysochyna *Ukrainian,* Upland
Vysočina *Czech,* Upland

W

Waadi *Somali,* Watercourse
Wādī *Arabic,* Watercourse
Wāḥat, Wâhat *Arabic,* Oasis
Wald *German,* Forest
Wan *Chinese,* Bay
Wyżyna *Polish,* Upland

X

Xé *Laotian,* River

Y

Yarımadası *Azerbaijani,* Peninsula
Yazovir *Bulgarian,* Reservoir
Yoma *Burmese,* Mountains
Yü *Chinese,* Island

Z

Zaliv *Bulgarian, Russian,* Bay
Zatoka *Ukrainian,* Bay
Zemlya *Russian,* Bay

GLOSSARY OF ABBREVIATIONS

THIS GLOSSARY provides a comprehensive guide to the abbreviations used.

A

abbrev. abbreviated
ABM antiballistic missile(s)
Adm. Admiral
AIDS acquired immunodeficiency syndrome
Amh. Amharic
ANC African National Congress
APC armored personnel carrier(s)
approx. approximately
ASSR Autonomous Soviet Socialist Republic

B

BBC British Broadcasting Corporation
BCE Before Common Era
b/d barrels per day
B-H Bosnia and Herzegovina
bn billion (1000 million)
Brig. Brigadier
BSE bovine spongiform encephalopathy

C

C central
c. circa
C. Cape
°C degrees (Centigrade)
cap. capita
Capt. Captain
CAR Central African Republic
CD compact disc
CE Common Era
CIA Central Intelligence Agency
cm centimeter(s)
Cmdr. Commander
CNN Cable News Network
Co. Company
Col. Colonel
Czech Rep. Czech Republic

D E

D.C. District of Columbia
Dens density
dept. department
dths deaths
dev. development
Dr. Doctor
DRC Democratic Republic of the Congo
dwt dead weight tonnage
E east
EC$ Eastern Caribbean dollar(s)
EEC/EC European Community
EEZ Exclusive Economic Zone
ECU European Currency Unit
EMS European Monetary System
est. estimated

F G

°F degrees (Fahrenheit)
Flt. Lt. Flight Lieutenant
Fr. Father
Fr. French/France
ft foot/feet
FYRM Former Yugoslav Republic of Macedonia
GATT General Agreement on Tariffs and Trade
GDP Gross Domestic Product (the total value of goods and services produced by a country excluding income from foreign countries)
Gen. General
Geplac Geplacea
GNP Gross National Product (the total value of goods and services produced by a country)
grt gross tonnage

H I

HEP hydroelectric power
HH His/Her Highness
HIPC heavily indebted poor country(ies)
hist. historical
HIV human immunodeficiency virus
H.M. His/Her Majesty
HMS His/Her Majesty's ship
H.R.H His/Her Royal Highness
H.S.H His/Her Serene Highness
I. Island
ICBM intercontinental ballistic missile(s)
in inch(es)
Intl International
IRBM intermediate-range ballistic missile(s)
Is Islands

J K L

kg kilogram(s)
km kilometer(s)
km² square kilometer (singular)
kW kilowatt(s)
kWh kilowatt hour(s)
CE Common Era
L. lower
Ltd. Limited
Lt. Lieutenant
Lux. Luxembourg

M N

m million/meter(s)
Maced. Macedonia
Maj. Major
MBA Master of Business Administration
CE Common Era
Mercsr Mercosur
mi² square mile(s)
mm millimeter(s)
Mon. Montenegro
MP Member of Parliament
MSP Member of Scottish Parliament
Mt. Mountain/Mount
Mts Mountains
MW megawatt(s)
N north
NASA National Aeronautics and Space Administration
Nepad New Partnership for Africa's Development
Neth. Netherlands
NGO Nongovernmental Organization
NIC Newly Industrialized Country
NPT Non-Proliferation Treaty
NZ New Zealand

P Q R

p.a. per annum
PLO Palestine Liberation Organization
PNG Papua New Guinea
pop. population
Rep. Republic
Res. Reservoir
Rev. Reverend
Russian Fed. Russian Federation

S

S south
S. & Mon. Serbia & Montenegro
SARS server acute respiratory syndrome
Serb. Serbia
SLBM submarine-launched ballistic missile(s)
sq. square
SSBN nuclear-fuelled ballistic-missile submarine(s)
SSR Soviet Socialist Republic
St. Saint
START Strategic Arms Reduction Treaty
Switz. Switzerland

T U

TGV *train à grande vitesse*
TV television
UAE United Arab Emirates
UK United Kingdom
UN United Nations
US/USA United States of America
USS United States ship
USSR Union of Soviet Socialist Republics
U. upper
Uzb. Uzbek

V W

VCR video cassette recorder
W west

THE MAPS

The maps in the Nations of the World section of this book have used the most up-to-date reference sources available to provide local name forms and spellings, that is to say those used within the country. In an age when international travel, on holiday or on business, is commonplace, this criterion seems the most appropriate. English conventional forms have been used for all international features and for all capital cities. English conventional forms also appear on all the maps in the World Factfile.

ACKNOWLEDGMENTS

DORLING KINDERSLEY would like to express their thanks to the following individuals, companies and institutions for their help in preparing this atlas:

ADDITIONAL CARTOGRAPHY

Advanced Illustration (Congleton, UK)
Andrew Bright
Cosmographics (Watford, UK)
Malcolm Porter
Swanston Publishing (Derby, UK)
Andrew Thompson

DESIGN

Boyd Annison, Icon Solutions (Chesham, UK) *for Macintosh consultancy and chart templates*
Bruno Maag, Dalton Maag (London, UK) *for font consultancy and production*

RESEARCH AND REFERENCE

Dr D Alkhateeb, Organization of Petroleum Exporting Countries (OPEC, Vienna, Austria)
Amnesty International (London, UK)
Caroline Blunden
CNN International (New York, USA)
DATAQUEST EUROPE SA (PARIS, FRANCE)
CSL Davies
Department of Trade and Industry Export Market Information Centre (London, UK)
The Flag Institute (Chester, UK)
Foreign and Commonwealth Office (London, UK)
Alexander Fyges-Walker
Christel Heideloff, Institute of Shipping Economics and Logistics (Bremen, Germany)
International Bank for Reconstruction and Development (World Bank, Washington, DC, USA)
International Committee of the Red Cross (ICRC, Geneva, Switzerland)
International Civil Aviation Organization (ICAO, Montreal, Canada)
International Criminal Police Organization (INTERPOL, Lyon, France)
International Institute for Strategic Studies, for information from *The Military Balance* (London, UK)
International Boundaries Research Unit, University of Durham
Institute of Latin American Studies, University of London (London, UK)
Intermediate Technology Development Group (Rugby, UK)
Chris Joseph, United States Travel and Tourism Administration (USTTA, London, UK)
Latin American Bureau (London, UK)
Patrick Mahaffey, Ohio European Office (Brussels, Belgium)
Peter Mansfield
Robert Minton-Taylor
National Meteorological Library and Archive (Bracknell, UK)
Oil and Gas Journal (Houston, Texas)
Organization for Economic Cooperation and Development (OECD, Paris, France)
Penal Reform International (London, UK)
Matt Ridley
Screen Digest (London, UK)
William Smith, Chicago Sun-Times (Chicago, USA)
Tourism Concern (London, UK)
United Nations Crime Prevention and Criminal Justice Branch (UNCPC, Vienna, Austria)
United Nations Development Programme (UNDP, New York, USA)
United Nations Environment Programme (UNEP, Nairobi, Kenya)
United Nations Food and Agriculture Organization (UNFAO, Rome, Italy)
United Nations International Labour Organization (UNILO, Geneva, Switzerland)
United Nations Population Fund (UNFPA, New York, USA)
Westminster Reference Library (London, UK)
World Conservation Monitoring Centre (Cambridge, UK)
World Health Organization (WHO, Geneva, Switzerland)
World Tourism Organization (Madrid, Spain)

The many embassies, High Commissions, airports, national information and tourist offices in London and around the world.

PICTURE CREDITS

t=top, b=below, a=above, l=left, r=right, c=center

Agence France Presse: 300crb, 332tr, 337tc, 445cr; Victor Drachev 123bcr; Vassil Donev 153bcr; Gonzalo Espinoza 137cr; Eric Feferberg 188br; Francois Guillot 256crb; Martyn Hayhow 256bcr; Doug Kanter 601tr; Attila Kisbenedek 293br; John MacDougall 77tr; Shah Marai 78br; Tatiana Munoz 195tcr; Keld Navntoft 219tcr; Inacio Rosa 475bcr; Dibyangshu Sarkar 303tc; Bernd Settnik 269br; Sergei Supinsky 587tr; Weda 229tc; Greg Wood 337bl; **Alamy:** Bryan & Cherry Alexander Photography 489bl; Jon Arnold Images 243tr; Popperfoto 245bcr; Springfield Photography 598br; Stock Connection Inc / Rob Crandall 291tc; **Ancient Art & Architecture Collection:** 44bcr; 45bl; 45cr; 47tc; G Tortoli 45tcb; **Arcaid:** P Mauss Esto 598bc; **Art Archive:** 44bl; 49bl; 49cr; 51tcl; **Aspect Picture Library:** 202tr; Brian Seed 418c; D Bayes 370bl; Fiona Nichols 304tr; **Associated Press AP:** AFP 415bcr; Aaron Favila 467crl; Humberto Pradera/Agencia Estado 149cb; Bullit Marquez 191bl; Jan Bauer 271cb; **Bridgeman Art Library, London/New York:** Hermitage, St Petersburg 46bc; Lauros - Giraudon / Château de Malmaison 48bcr; National Maritime Museum, London 47br; Private Collection 48bcl; **D Donne Bryant Stock Picture Agency:** 461tc; Byron Augustin 436tr; **Dale Buckton:** 594br; **Camera Press:** A Pucciano 95cr; F Goodman 649bca; H Andrews 627bcr; S Smith 245bcl; T Charlier 607bl; **The Canadian Alliance:** 172crb; **Nick Carroll:** 647tr; **The J Allan Cash Photolibrary:** 55tl; 106c; 116bc; 146br; 149tl; 168tr; 171tr; 241tr; 308tr; 320br, 339cr; 342bl; 383tc; 386c; 438bc; 440tr; 451bc; 474tr; 566bc; **CDA:** 429tcr; **Bruce Coleman Ltd:** 498bl; B&C Calhoun 174bc; Dr MP Kahl 94tr; F Prenzel 104tc; Gerald Cubitt 88tr; Gerald Cubitt 244bc; Gordon Langsbury 262bc; J Fry 511tc; J Jurka 542bc; K. Maj 470c; Kim Taylor 515tr; L Lee Rue 91tl; LC Marigo 281tc; M Berge 396tr; MPL Fogden 462ca; O Langrand 370tr; P Davey 214bc; S Prato 274bc; **Colorific:** J Polleross / M Kreiner 54cl; M Rogers 536tr; Sandro Tucci 159bl; **Comstock:** 194bc, 24tl, 535tc; Tor Eigeland 399tc; **Corbis:** AFP 387bcl; 233bcr, 555tcr; Bob Krist 642br; Francoise de Mulder 141bc; Jack Fields 648bl, 650bl; Brooks Kraft 471tr; Miki Kratsman 486br; Franz-Marc Frei 261cb; Christopher J Morris 172cbr; Alan Schein Photography 606br; Nick Wheeler 175tc, 647br; Peter Wilson 327cb; Joseph Sohm 603bl; **Corbis Sygma:** Vernier Jean Bernar 195tr; David Brauchli 513bcl; Shandiz Mohsen 309tcl; **James Davis Travel Photography:** 144bl; 145tl; 218c; 250bc; 330bc; 379tl; 390tr; 401tc; 411tl; 428bc; 432bc; 493tc; 494bl; 496bl; 502tr; 550bc; 558tr; 586tr; 626bl; 643cr; Prisma 86cla; Prisma / Schwarz 226tr; S Begawan 151tl; S Thingeyjar 297tc; World View - Fototheek Amsterdam 177tc; **Mary Evans Picture Library:** 47bl, 47trb; **Chris Fairclough Colour Library:** 51cr; 375tl; 572br; **Government House Canberra:** 102cbr; **Robert Harding Picture Library:** 76tr; 180c; 225tl; 273tc; 282bl; 293tr; 312tr; 336bl; 358bc; 449tc; 466tr; 480tr; 484tr; 501tc; 513tc; A Woolfitt 114bc; C Martin 266bc; C Rennie 580ca; D Hughes 259bc; Explorer 377tc; Explorer / Roy 110tr; F Dubes 148bl; Frerck / Odyssey 402tr; G Hellier 217tr; G Hellier 518tr; G Roli 444tr; Gascoine 610bl; P Craven 254tr; Photri 222ca; R Rainford 593tl; Rosehaven Management Ltd 653cr; Sassoon 134cb; Sassoon 264cl; **Paul Harris Photography:** Paul Harris Photography 491bl; **Hulton Getty:** 50bcr; 51br; 53br; **Robert Hunt Library:** 53tc; **Hutchison Library:** 136bl; 369tc; 596bc; 636tr; Andrew Hill 634bc; Bernard Gérard 261bc; Christine Pemberton 210tr; J Henderson 286ca; JG Fuller 650bcr; L Taylor 484bl; M Macintyre 568ca; Robert Francis 560tr; Trevor Page 524ca; **Image Bank:** 394bl; A Rippy 186tr; G Jung 576tr; GA Rossi 646bl; M Beebe 209cl; ME Newman 324tr; P Trummer 232tr; T Madison 187br; **Images Colour Library:** 426bl; **Image Select:** Ann Ronan 42bc; **Impact Photos:** A le Garsmeur 412ca; Alain leGarsmeur 175bl; Ben Edwards 450tr; C Penn 584tr; G-J Norman 356tr; J Arthur 526tcr; Mark Henley 188tr; Robin Lubbock 236tr; Ben Edwards 303bl; **David King Collection:** 55tcb **Magnum:** H Cartier-Bresson 53tcb; **Panos Pictures:** B Tobiasson 329bc; Chris Stowers 333bl; D Hulcher 360tr; Jeremy Hartley 156bc; Marc French 289tc; Morris Carpenter 365bc; Neil Cooper 130tr; R Giling 538tr; S Sprague 160tr; Sean Sprague 136c; Penny Tweedie 105tc; Michael Harvey 149cl; John Miles 190tr;.JC Tordai 320cl; 597cb; 602bl; **Pa Photos:** AFP 419cbl; EPA 146tr, 188bcr, 353bcr, 551cr, 631bcr; **Popperfoto:** 51trb; 52br; 55bl; AFP / Armand 54br; David Mercado / Reuters 137crl; Will Burgess / Reuters 105bl; Reuters 271cl; Jeremy Piper / Reuters 102bcr; John Cobb / EPA 275tr; Reuters 345tr; Official U.S. Air Force Photo 55cr; **Popperfoto / Reuters**: Peter Andrews 637cr; Simon Baker 433tlb; Denis Balibouse 203cl; Russell Boyce 594cra; Bogdan Cristel 481cr; Dimitar Dilkoff 153bcl; Larry Downing 601bl; Marcus Gyger 107bcl; Mohamed Hammi 573tcr; Hyungwon Kang 601bcr; Sergei Karpukhin 487bcl; Kamal Kishore 300cbr; Francois Lenoir 127bcr; Havakuk Levison 318bcr; David Loh 623tcl; Alexander Natruskin 487bl; Patrick de Noirmont 159bcl; Enny Nuraheni 305bcr; Pilar Olivares 463tcl; Hrvoje Polan 293bcr; Romero Ranoco 467cr; Molly Riley 268bcr; Oswaldo Rivas 555tr; Henry Romero 403bcl; Jayanta Shaw 623tl; Ruben Sprich 547cr; STR 451tr, 577car; 293bcl, 577trb, 607bcl; Eriko Sugita 334cbr; Sukree Sukplang 563tr; Susumu Takahashi 334cbl; Martin Thomas 182tr; Pierre Virot 476bcl; Haydn West 594tcr; Kimberly White 618tcr; Darren Whiteside 165tcr; Rick Wilking 600bcr, 600br; **Reuters:** 123bcl, tcr; 507br; **Rex Features:** 116tcbr; 172bcr; 256cb; 275tcr; 341bcl; 481cbr; 486bcr; 516bl; 526tr; 543tcl; 587tcr; 594tr; 594trb; 606bl; 611bc; 627bcl; Action Press 415bcl; ArgenPress 95crb; Giuseppe Aresu 324cbr; Gustafsson 251tr; J Sutton Hibbert 597ct; Paul Browncr; David Hartley 219tr; ISOPress 581car; F Stevens 211bcl; Farnood 309tcr; Ken McKay 531tr; Ron Sachs 631bcl; Sipa-Press 77tcr; Sipa-Press 95cbr; Sipa-Press 83bcl; Sipa-Press 127bcl; Sipa-Press 188bcr; Sipa-Press 318br; Sipa-Press 429tcl; Sipa-Press 445c; Sipa-Press 563tcr; Sipa-Press 645bl; Tony Kyriacou 353bcl; Paul Marnef 471tcr; Torregano 419cl; **Sistani.org:** 313c; **Harry Smith Collection:** 46clb; **South American Pictures:** Jevan Berrange 206br; P Dixon 456tr; T Morrison 606tr; **Sovfoto/Eastfoto:** 652br; **Frank Spooner Pictures:** 53bl; 83bl; 324bc;345tcr; 543tr; A Denize 371tcr; Alain Morvan / Gamma 547c; Alexis Duclos 182tcr; C Poulet 647cr; Tim Crosby / Gamma - Liaison 602ct; Gamma / B Iverson 233bcl; Gamma / F Apesteguy 507bcr; Gamma / Iliona - Figaro Magazine 113tc; Gamma / K Al Arab 573tcl; Gamma / L Chaperon 268cbr; Gamma / N Jallot 408tr; Gamma / Najer 387bcr; Gamma / Xinhua 188bcl; Georges Merillon 441bcl; KJ Eddy 107bcl; Liason / Peterson 441bcr; Liason / Markel 637c; N Sagansky 203cr; P Perrin 313cr; Patrick Piel 268bra; Reglain 165tr; Victoria Brynner 451tcr; **Tony Stone Images:** 179bc; 198tr; 354bl; 444br; A Cassidy 302br; Alan Kearney 182bc; Alan Smith 362c; C Waite 592bc; D Armand 172tr; D Hanson 562bl; D Schultz 50bl; Dennis Stone 344tr; G Allison 605bl; H Kurihara 270bc; J Pragen 616tr; Joe Cornish 317bc; Marcus Brooke 158tr; O Benn 93tc; 279tr; P Chesley 406ca; Penny Tweedie 384bc; R Evans 152tr; R. Everts 415tr; R Smith 102tr; R Smith 231tl; S Egan 530tr; S Egan 546tr; Steven Rothfeld 393tc; **Sygma:** Valdev 350ca; R Reuter 502bl; **Telegraph Colour Library:** 100tr; Ford Motor Company Ltd 52clb; **Topham Picturepoint:** 133tc; 238tr; 320br; 327cl; 371tr; 433cal; 478bc; 487tr; 504bc; 642c; Keystone 324cbl; **Trip:** 506bl; G Spenceley 380tr; T Goodman 285tc; V Shuba 122c; V Sidoropolev 340tr; **World Pictures:** 83cla; 322bl; 422ca; 554tr; **Zefa Picture Library**: 80bc; 120bl; 200ca; 526bl; 570bc; 618bl; Everts 630ca; F Lanting 142tr; Streichan 268bl.